LE LOGICIEL = SOFTWARE
EPLURER = DEBUG
À LA PAGE = UP-TO-DATE
LES JAMBIÈRES = L
LES GÉNÉRIQUE
LE DÉCOLLAGE
L'EMBOUTEILLA

Are you a student reading ... or contemporary novels? Do you enjoy French films? Are you a business person studying newspapers, magazines, or technical publications filled with slang, jargon, and mysterious abbreviations? Or are you a tourist taking in the sights and doing some shopping?

If you want to pronounce French correctly, know precisely what a word means and exactly how to use it, have rapid, easy reference to an extensive French and English vocabulary, *Kettridge* is the only bilingual French and English dictionary for you.

STANLEY AND ELEANOR HOCHMAN are professional editors, writers, and translators. Among their French translations, done both separately and as a team, are works ranging from such nineteenth-century classics as Zola's *Germinal* and the one-act plays of Jules Renard to books of contemporary interest in the fields of political science, film criticism, Latin American history, and science fiction. They have graduate degrees from Columbia University and have done postgraduate study at the Sorbonne and the University of Florence.

SIGNET Reference Books

(0451)

☐ **A DICTIONARY OF DIFFICULT WORDS by Robert H. Hill.** The essential companion to every abridged dictionary complete with 15,000 entries on business, technology, culture, medicine, science, acronyms, and foreign words. (118030—$3.95)

☐ **THE NEW HORIZON LADDER DICTIONARY OF THE ENGLISH LANGUAGE by John Robert Shaw with Janet Shaw.** Prepared for the vocabulary needs of young readers, it is based on 5000 of the most frequently used words in written English. Unusual features include full sentence examples, a simple pronunciation system, large type, and across the page printing for easier reading. (124219—$2.95)

☐ **THE NEW AMERICAN WEBSTER HANDY COLLEGE DICTIONARY.** Over 100,000 definitions in this comprehensive dictionary which includes illustrations, abbreviations, geographical names and colloquialisms. (125371—$2.50)*

☐ **THE NEW AMERICAN ROGET'S COLLEGE THESAURUS in Dictionary Form.** Revised edition. Synonyms and antonyms in an alphabetical listing. Easy to use. A must for every library. (125398—$2.95)*

*Prices slightly higher in Canada

Buy them at your local bookstore or use this convenient coupon for ordering.

NEW AMERICAN LIBRARY
P.O. Box 999, Bergenfield, New Jersey 07621

Please send me the books I have checked above. I am enclosing $_____
(please add $1.00 to this order to cover postage and handling). Send check or money order—no cash or C.O.D.'s. Prices and numbers are subject to change without notice.

Name_____

Address_____

City _____ State _____ Zip Code _____

Allow 4-6 weeks for delivery.
This offer is subject to withdrawal without notice.

KETTRIDGE'S FRENCH–ENGLISH ENGLISH–FRENCH DICTIONARY

NEW REVISED EDITION

Edited, revised, and updated by
Stanley and Eleanor Hochman

HAMTRAMCK PUBLIC LIBRARY
ALBERT J. ZAK MEMORIAL

OCT   1990

DISCARDED

A SIGNET BOOK

NEW AMERICAN LIBRARY

NAL BOOKS ARE AVAILABLE AT QUANTITY DISCOUNTS
WHEN USED TO PROMOTE PRODUCTS OR SERVICES.
FOR INFORMATION PLEASE WRITE TO PREMIUM MARKETING DIVISION,
NEW AMERICAN LIBRARY, 1633 BROADWAY,
NEW YORK, NEW YORK 10019.

Copyright © 1968, 1984 by New American Library

All rights reserved

Library of Congress Catalog Card Number: 83-63045

SIGNET TRADEMARK REG. U.S. PAT. OFF. AND FOREIGN COUNTRIES
REGISTERED TRADEMARK—MARCA REGISTRADA
HECHO EN CHICAGO, U.S.A.

SIGNET, SIGNET CLASSIC, MENTOR, PLUME, MERIDIAN
and NAL BOOKS are published by
New American Library,
1633 Broadway, New York, New York 10019

First Signet Printing, November, 1968
Tenth Signet Printing (First Printing, Revised Edition), July, 1984

10 11 12 13 14 15 16 17 18

PRINTED IN THE UNITED STATES OF AMERICA

CONTENTS

KEY TO INTERNATIONAL PHONETIC TRANSCRIPTION

VOWELS

a papa, femme, roi (papa, fam, rwa)

ɑ passer, bâiller, bas, (pɑse, bɑje, bɑ)

ɑ̃ rampant, encan, temps (rɑ̃pɑ̃, ɑ̃kɑ̃, tɑ̃)

e récréer, fée, chez (rekree, fe, ʃe)

ə de, que, recevoir (də, kə, rəsəvwaːr)

ɛ frais, près, rets, bel (frɛ, prɛ, rɛ, bɛl)

ɛ̃ bien, bain, vin, oint (bjɛ̃, bɛ̃, vɛ̃, wɛ̃)

i civilité, nihiliste, y (sivilite, niilist, i)

o gros, tôt, peau, aux (gro, to, po, o)

ɔ colonne, opossum (kɔlɔn, ɔpɔsœm)

ɔ̃ componction, mont (kɔ̃pɔ̃ksjɔ̃, mɔ̃)

œ œuf, cueillir, seul (œf, kœjiːr, sœl)

œ̃ un, parfum, défunt (œ̃, parfœ̃, defœ̃)

ø bleu, creux, vœu (blø, krø, vø)

u trou, goût, courroux (tru, gu, kuru)

y vu, une, murmurer (vy, yn, myrmyre)

ː indicates that the sound represented by the preceding symbol is long; thus:

aː car, bail, soir (kaːr, baːj, swaːr)

ɑː passe, âme, paille (pɑːs, ɑːm, pɑːj)

ɑ̃ː ambre, antre, centre (ɑ̃ːbr, ɑ̃ːtr, sɑ̃ːtr)

ɛː faire, ère, guerre (fɛːr, ɛːr, gɛːr)

ɛ̃ː sainte, linge, peintre (sɛ̃ːt, lɛ̃ːʒ, pɛ̃ːtr)

iː fille, lyre, abîme (fiːj, liːr, abiːm)

oː dôme, rose, haute (doːm, roːz, oːt)

ɔː fort, bord, corps (fɔːr, bɔːr, kɔːr)

ɔ̃ː fondre, pompe, onze (fɔ̃ːdr, pɔ̃ːp, ɔ̃ːz)

œː œil, deuil, beurre (œːj, dœːj, bœːr)

œ̃ː humble, défunte (œ̃ːbl, defœ̃ːt)

øː creuse, aqueuse (krøːz, akøːz)

uː tour, cours, bourre (tuːr, kuːr, buːr)

yː murmure, usure (myrmyːr, yzyːr)

CONSONANTS

g gangue, gué, exil (gɑ̃ːg, ge, egzil)

j fiancé fouille, ayant (fjɑ̃se, fuːj, ɛjɑ̃)

ɲ cognac, baigner (kɔɲak, bɛɲe)

ʃ chat, chiche, hache (ʃa, ʃiʃ, aʃ)

ʒ je, juge, géologie (ʒə, ʒyːʒ, ʒeɔlɔʒi)

ɥ cuir, huile, fruit (kɥiːr, ɥil, frɥi)

The following consonants have their usual values:

b	bonbon, bimbelot (bɔ̃bɔ̃, bɛ̃blo)	n	nonne, inanition (nɔn, in-anisjɔ̃)
d	dedans, demande (dədɑ̃, də-mɑ̃ːd)	p	papier, obscur (papje, ɔpskyːr)
f	fifre, graphique (fifr, grafik)	r	rare, bizarrerie (raːr, bizarri)
h	=h aspirated about as in English (chiefly French interjections)	s	si, ceci, stoïcisme (si, səsi, stɔisism)
		t	quantité, théâtre (kɑ̃tite, teaːtr)
k	kaki, caquet, extra (kaki, kakɛ, ɛkstra)	v	vive, verve, wagon (viːv, vɛrv, vagɔ̃)
l	lilas, parallèle (lila, paralɛl)	w	ouest, gloire, allouer (wɛst, glwaːr, alwe)
m	momie, minimum (momi, minimɔm)	z	zigzag, magasin (zigzag, mag-azɛ̃)

The sounds of the symbols to be learned can only be acquired by hearing them spoken, just as colors must be seen to be appreciated.

NOTE

The author considers himself fortunate in having at his disposal the International Phonetic System, and if the reader will take the trouble to learn it, he will, the author feels sure, hold himself equally blessed.

Gone forever for all practical purposes are the fantastic "imitated" pronunciations. Every language has certain sounds which are peculiar to itself and have no equivalents in another. For this reason, imitated pronunciations, although capable of transcribing French into French phonetically, English into English, and so on, are inherently incapable of transliterating one language into another, and are responsible in large measure for many people's bad pronunciation of foreign languages.

Pronunciation of French is very difficult for the foreigner. Exceptions to rule, silent letters, and other peculiarities abound. Therefore, every time he refers to a word in the French vocabulary, the English reader is advised to compare, and correct if necessary, his notion of how it should be pronounced.

ARRANGEMENT

As far as is reasonably possible, set or inseparable word groups are entered under the first word of the group.

ABBREVIATIONS USED IN THIS DICTIONARY

†

ADVERBS

Most French adverbs of manner are formed by adding -ment to the feminine singular of the adjective, corresponding to the English suffix -ly (-le being changed into -ly, -ic into -ically, and -y into -ily); thus,

naturel (natyrɛl)	**correct** (kɔrɛkt)	**relatif** (rəlatif)
naturelle (rɛl)	**correcte** (rɛkt)	**relative** (tiːv)
naturellement (rɛlmã)	**correctement** (təmã)*	**relativement** (tivmã‡)
natural; naturally	correct; correctly	relative; relatively

So also with adjectives ending in **e** of identical form in both genders; as,

énergique (enɛrʒik); **énergiquement** (ʒikmã), energetic; energetically.
admirable (admirabl); **admirablement** (bləmã*), admirable; admirably.
ordinaire (ɔrdinɛːr); **ordinairement** (nɛrmã‡), ordinary; ordinarily.

Adjectives whose masculine form ends in -**ai** (as **vrai**), -**é** (as **modéré**), -**i** (as **hardi**), and -**u** (as **absolu**), add the suffix -**ment** to the masculine form; thus,
modéré (mɔdere)   **modérée** (re)   **modérément** (remã)
          moderate;   moderately

In order to economize space (most adverbs of manner being long words), French and English adverbs ending regularly as above, and with no appreciable change of meaning †, are not given in the dictionary. Instead, the adjectives are marked † (e.g, **naturel, le**†, **modéré**†, e), in reference hereto. Adverbs not formed according to these rules, particularly those presenting peculiarity or difficulty, are given in the ordinary way.

* Note:—When two pronounced consonants immediately precede the ending -**ement**, the e of **ement** is pronounced (ə). Otherwise it is silent.
‡ Note that the vowel sound is short here, rəlatiːv, tivmã; ɔrdinɛːr, nɛrmã.

It may be observed that most ordinary English adverbs of manner for which no French form ending in -**ment** exists can be translated by *d'une manière*, plus the corresponding feminine adjective, as **satisfactorily**, *d'une manière satisfaisante*.

The swing dash (~) signifies repetition in the singular of a leading vocabulary word (word printed in **times roman type**). Followed by *s* (~*s*), it signifies the like repetition in the plural.

The paragraph (¶) also signifies repetition of a leading vocabulary word, but indicates the commencement of a different part of speech. This symbol is used to make the point of transition conspicuous.

An initial letter followed by a period signifies repetition of a translation.

[Brackets] enclose words, or parts of words, which can be used or omitted at will.

SUBJECT INDICATIONS

Avn.	Aviation	*Mach.*	Machinery; Machine
Agric.	Agriculture	*Math.*	Mathematics
Anat.	Anatomy	*Meas.*	Measurement;
Arch.	Architecture		Measure
Arith.	Arithmetic	*Mech.*	Mechanics
Artil.	Artillery	*Med.*	Medicine; Medical
Astr.	Astronomy	*Metall.*	Metallurgy
Bil.	Billiards	*Meteor.*	Meteorology
Biol.	Biology	*Mil.*	Military
Bkkpg.	Bookkeeping	*Min.*	Mining
Boat.	Boating	*Miner.*	Mineralogy
Bookb.	Bookbinding	*Mol.*	Mollusc
Bot.	Botany	*Motor.*	Motoring; Motor car
Box.	Boxing	*Mus.*	Music
Build.	Building	*Myth.*	Mythology
Carp.	Carpentry	*Nat. Hist.*	Natural History
Chem.	Chemistry	*Naut.*	Nautical
Com.	Commerce	*Nav.*	Navy; Naval
Conch.	Conchology, Shell-	*Need.*	Needlework
	fish, Shells	*Opt.*	Optics
Cook.	Cookery	*Path.*	Pathology
Crust.	Crustacea(n)	*Phar.*	Pharmacy
Cust.	Customs	*Philos.*	Philosophy
Danc.	Dancing	*Phot.*	Photography
Eccl.	Ecclesiastical	*Phys.*	Physics
Elec.	Electricity; Electric	*Phys. Geog.*	Physical Geography
Emb.	Embroidery	*Poet.*	Poetry; Poetic
Engin.	Engineering	*Pol.*	Politics
Fenc.	Fencing	*Post*	Post Office; Postal
Fin.	Finance	*Pros.*	Prosody
Fish.	Fishing	*Radio*	Wireless
Foot.	Football	*Relig.*	Religion
Geog.	Geography	*Rhet.*	Rhetoric
Geol.	Geology	*Rly.*	Railway(s)
Geom.	Geometry	*Sch.*	School
Gram.	Grammar	*Ship.*	Shipping
Gym.	Gymnastics	*Shipbldg.*	Shipbuilding
Her.	Heraldry	*Stk Ex.*	Stock Exchange
Hist.	History; Historical	*Surg.*	Surgery
Horol.	Horology, Clocks	*Surv.*	Surveying
	& Watches	*Swim.*	Swimming
Hort.	Horticulture	*Teleg.*	Telegraphy
Hunt.	Hunting	*Teleph.*	Telephony
Hyd.	Hydraulics	*Ten.*	Tennis
Inc. Tax	Income Tax	*Theat.*	Theater; Theatrical
Insce.	Insurance	*Theol.*	Theology
Join.	Joinery	*Typ.*	Typography;
Jump.	Jumping		Printing
Knit.	Knitting	*Univ.*	University
Lit.	Liturgy	*Vet.*	Veterinary
Log.	Logic	*Zool.*	Zoology

a	adjective
abb	abbreviation
abs	absolutely, i.e, (verb) used without its object
ad	adverb or adverbial phrase (see also †ADVERBS, page viii)
a.f	adjective feminine only, i.e, not masculine also
a.m	adjective masculine only, i.e, not feminine also
art	article
att	attributively, i.e, (noun) used as adjective
aux	auxiliary (verb)
c	conjunction or conjunctive phrase
Cf.	Compare
col	collectively, collective noun
comps	compounds; in combination
e.g	for example
Eng.	England; English
&	and, et (The sign & is used in the dictionary only to save space)
etc.	et cetera
f	feminine. In the French-English section, *f* = noun feminine
fig.	figuratively
f.pl.	feminine plural. In the French-English section, *f.pl* = noun feminine plural
Fr.	France; French
f.s	feminine singular. In the French-English section, *f.s* = noun feminine singular
i	interjection
i.e	that is to say
imp	impersonal
inv	invariable
ir	irregular (verb)
lit.	literally
m	masculine. In the French-English section, *m* = noun masculine
m.f	masculine & feminine (noun)
m.pl	masculine plural. In the French-English section, *m.pl* = noun masculine plural
m.s	masculine singular. In the French-English section, *m.s* = noun masculine singular
n	noun. In the French-English section, *n* = noun masculine & feminine (of persons)
neg.	negative; (used) negatively
oft.	often
opp.	opposed to
p.a	participial adjective
pers.	person(s)
pl	plural
pn	pronoun
p.p	participle past
p.pr	participle present
pr	preposition or prepositional phrase
s	singular
v.i	verb intransitive
v.i. & t	verb intransitive & verb transitive
v.pr.	verb pronominal
v.t	verb transitive
v.t. & i	verb transitive & verb intransitive

FRENCH-ENGLISH
DICTIONARY

FRENCH-ENGLISH DICTIONARY

A

a *see* **avoir.**

à (a) (à le *is contracted into* **au,** à les *into* **aux**) *pr,* to; at; in; within; into; on; by; with; for; of; after; from; under; according to; between; till, until; and. *When coupled with noun, often rendered in English by noun used attributively, as, canne à sucre,* sugar cane. *un homme ~ craindre,* a man to be feared *or* to fear. *~ prendre après les repas,* to be taken after meals. *~ ne pas confondre avec . . .,* not to be confused with . . . *de 2 ~ 3 fois par jour,* 2 or 3 times a day.

abaissement (abɛsmɑ̃) *m,* lowering; sinking; fall; humiliation. **abaisser** (se) *v.t,* to lower, let down; humble, abase. **s'~,** to subside; sink; humble oneself.

abandon (abɑ̃dɔ̃) *m,* abandonment, dereliction, desertion; unconstraint. *à l'~,* in confusion, at random, anyhow; derelict. **abandonnement** (dɔnmɑ̃) *m,* profligacy. **abandonner** (ne) *v.t,* to abandon, leave, desert, forsake; give up, relinquish, surrender; concede. **s'~ à,** to give way to, indulge in.

abaque (abak) *m,* abacus; diagram.

abasourdir (abazurdi;r) *v.t,* to dumbfound, stun.

abâtardir (s') (abɑtardi;r) *v.pr,* to degenerate.

abat-jour (abaʒu;r) *m,* shade, lampshade. **abats** (ba) *m.pl.* Same as *abattis.* **abat-son** (abasɔ̃) *m,* louvers. **abattage** (bata;ʒ) *m,* felling; slaughtering. **abattant** (tɑ̃) *m,* flap. **abattement** (tmɑ̃) *m,* prostration, depression, dejection, despondency; deductions (*for dependents, Inc. Tax*). **abatteur** (tœ;r) *m,* feller; slaughterman. **abattis** (ti) *m,* demolitions; fell; kill; giblets. **abattoir** (twa;r) *m,* slaughterhouse, abattoir. **abattre** (tr) *v.t.ir,* to knock down; bring down; cut down; lay; fell; slaughter, kill; mine; deject. **s'~,** to fall down; become depressed; subside. **abattu, e** (ty) *a,* depressed, low-spirited, downcast. **abat-vent** (abavɑ̃) *m,* windshield. **abat-voix** (abavwa) *m,* sounding board.

abbaye (abɛi) *f,* abbey. **abbé** (be) *m,* abbot; priest. **abbesse** (bɛs) *f,* abbess.

abcès (apsɛ) *m,* abscess, gathering. *~ aux gencives,* gumboil.

abdication (abdikasjɔ̃) *f,* abdication. **abdiquer** (ke) *v.t. & abs,* to abdicate; surrender, waive.

abdomen (abdɔmɛn) *m,* abdomen.

abeille (abɛ;j) *f,* bee. *~ ouvrière,* worker b.

aberration (abɛrasjɔ̃) *f,* aberration.

abêtir (abɛti;r) *v.t,* to make dull.

abhorrer (abɔre) *v.t,* to abhor, loathe, detest.

abîme (abi;m) *m,* abyss, gulf, chasm. **abîmer** (bime) *v.t,* to swallow up; ruin, spoil. **s'~,** to bury (*or* immerse) oneself, welter; get spoiled.

abject, e (abʒɛkt) *a,* abject, mean. **abjection** (sjɔ̃) *f,* abjectness, etc.

abjurer (abʒyre) *v.t,* to abjure, forswear, renounce.

ablatif (ablatif) *m,* ablative [case].

abnégation (abnegasjɔ̃) *f,* abnegation, self-denial.

aboiement (abwamɑ̃) *m,* bark[ing], bay[ing]. **aux abois** (bwa), at bay; hard pressed, at one's wit's end.

abolir (abɔli;r) *v.t,* to abolish. **abolition** (lisjɔ̃) *f,* abolition; repeal. **abolitioniste** (lisjɔnist) *m,* freetrader.

abominable† (abɔminabl) *a,* abominable, nefarious. **abomination** (sjɔ̃) *f,* abomination. **abominer** (ne) *v.t,* to abominate.

abondance (abɔ̃dɑ̃;s) *f,* abundance, plenty, galore; fullness. *parler d'~,* to speak extempore. **abondant, e** (dɑ̃, ɑ̃;t) *a,* abundant,

plentiful, plenteous. profuse.
abondamment (damã) *ad*, abundantly, etc. **abonder** (de) *v.i*, to abound. ~ *dans le sens de*, to quite agree with, chime in with.
abonné, e (abɔne) *n*, subscriber; commuter; consumer (*gas, elec.*). **abonnement** (nmã) *m*, subscription, season ticket; commutation ticket. **abonner** (ne) *v.t*, to subscribe for. s'~, to subscribe.
abonnir (abɔniːr) *v.t*, to improve.
abord (abɔːr) *m*, landing; approach, access. [*tout*] d'~, *au premier* ~, *de prime* ~, at first, first of all, to begin with. **abordable** (bɔrdabl) *a*, accessible, approachable. **abordage** (daːʒ) *m*, landing; collision, fouling. **aborder** (de) *v.i. & t*, to land; approach; broach; board; collide with, foul.
aborigène (abɔriʒɛːn) *a. & m*, aboriginal; (*m.pl.*) aborigines.
abortif, ive (abɔrtif, iːv) *a*, abortive (*of premature birth*).
aboucher (abuʃe) *v.t*, to bring together; join up.
aboutir (abutiːr) *v.i*, to end, lead; eventuate, materialize; come to a head, culminate.
aboutissement (abutismã) *m*, result, issue, outcome, effect.
aboyer (abwaje) *v.i*, to bark, bay; be in full cry; cry out. **aboyeur** (jœːr) *m*, barker (*circus, etc.*).
abrégé (abreʒe) *m*, abridgement, epitome, abstract, summary. *en* ~, shortly, briefly; abbreviated. **abréger** (ʒe) *v.t*, to abridge, epitomize; abbreviate.
abreuver (abrœve) *v.t*, to water; season; soak, steep, drench; prime (*pump*). s'~, to drink, soak, fill oneself, wallow, bathe. **abreuvoir** (vwaːr) *m*, watering place, horse pond, drinking trough.
abréviation (abrevjasjɔ̃) *f*, abbreviation; contraction.
abri (abri) *m*, shelter, cover, dug-out; cab (*locomotive*). *à l'* ~ *de*, under cover of, sheltered from. ~ *blindé*, bombshelter.
abricot (abriko) *m*, apricot; vagina (*obscene*). **abricotier** (kɔtje) *m*, apricot tree.

abriter (abrite) *v.t*, to shelter, shield, screen.
abrivent (abrivã) *m*, shelter, hut; matting, screen.
abrogation (abrɔgasjɔ̃) *f*, abrogation, repeal. **abroger** (ʒe) *v.t*, to abrogate.
abrupt, e (abrypt) *a*, abrupt, sheer.
abruti, e (abryti) *p.a*, brutish, besotted, sottish; stupefied (*alcohol, fatigue*). ¶ *m*, beast (*pers.*). **abrutir** (tiːr) *v.t*, to brutalize, besot. **abrutissement** (tismã) *m*, brutishness.
absence (apsãːs) *f*, absence. ~ [*d'esprit*], absence of mind. **absent, e** (sã, ãːt) *a*, absent, away [from home], out, not at home. ~ *par congé*, away on holiday. ¶ *m*, absentee. s'**absenter** (sãte) *v.pr*, to absent oneself, keep away.
abside (apsid) *f*, apse.
absinthe (apsɛ̃ːt) *f*, wormwood; absinth.
absolu†, e (apsɔly) *a*, absolute; hard & fast; positive; peremptory.
absolution (apsɔlysjɔ̃) *f*, absolution; acquittal.
absorbant, e (apsɔrbã, ãːt) *a*, absorbent, bibulous; absorbing, engrossing. **absorber** (be) *v.t. & abs*, to absorb, drink in, imbibe; engross. **absorption** (psjɔ̃) *f*, absorption.
absoudre (apsudr) *v.t.ir*, to absolve.
abstème (apstɛːm) *a*, abstemious. ¶ *n*, abstainer. s'**abstenir** (stəniːr) *v.pr*, to abstain, refrain, forbear. **abstention** (stãsjɔ̃) *f*, abstention. **abstinence** (stinãːs) *f*, abstinence, temperance.
abstinent (apstinã) *m*, teetotaller.
abstraction (apstraksjɔ̃) *f*, abstraction. ~ *faite de*, apart from, setting aside. **abstraire** (strɛːr) *v.t.ir*, to abstract. **abstrait, e** (strɛ, ɛːt) *a*, abstract. l'**abstrait**, *m*, the abstract (opp. *concrete*).
abstrus, e (apstry, yːz) *a*, abstruse, recondite.
absurde† (apsyrd) *a*, absurd, preposterous. l'**absurde**, *m*, the absurd, an absurdity. **absurdité** (dite) *f*, absurdity, nonsense.

abus (aby) *m*, abuse, misuse; breach. **abuser** (ze) *v.t*, to deceive, delude, mislead, misguide. ~ *de*, to abuse, misuse, trespass on. **s'~**, to delude oneself. **abusif, ive†** (zif, i;v) *a*, abusive, improper.

abysse (abis) *m*, abyss.

Abyssinie (l') (abisini) *f*, Abyssinia. **abyssinien, ne** (njɛ̃, ɛn) *a.* & *A~*, *n*, ou **abyssin, e** (sɛ̃, in) *a.* & *A~*, *n*, Abyssinian.

acabit (akabi) *m*, stamp, sort, nature. *de même ~*, of the same sort or type.

acacia (akasja) *m*, acacia.

académicien, ne (akademisjɛ̃, ɛn) *n*, academician. **académie** (mi) *f*, academy, college; academy figure. **académique** (mik) *a*, academic(al).

acagnarder (akaɲarde) *v.t*, to make lazy.

acajou (akaʒu) *m*, mahogany. *~des Antilles*, Spanish mahogany.

acare (aka;r) *m*, mite, tick.

acariâtre (akarja;tr) *a*, peevish, sour[-tempered].

accablant (akɑblɑ̃) *a*, crushing, overwhelming.

accablement (akɑbləmɑ̃) *m*, despondency, dejection; prostration; great pressure (*of business*). **accabler** (ble) *v.t*, to overwhelm, crush, overcome.

accalmie (akalmi) *f*, lull.

accaparer (akapare) *v.t*, to corner, buy up, monopolize. **accapareur, euse** (rœ;r, ɸ;z) *n*, monopolist.

accéder à (aksede), to accede to, consent to; reach.

accélérateur (akseleratœ;r) *m*, accelerator. **accélérer** (re) *v.t*, to accelerate, quicken. *pas accéléré*, on the double, quick march.

accent (aksɑ̃) *m*, accent; stress; tone, pronunciation; (*pl.*) strains. **accentuer** (tɥe) *v.t*, to accent, accentuate, emphasize, stress. **s'~**, to become more noticeable, grow stronger, increase.

acceptable (akseptabl) *a*, acceptable. **acceptation** (sjɔ̃) *f*, acceptance. **accepter** (te) *v.t. abs*, to accept, undertake. **accepteur** (tœ;r) *m*, acceptor. **acception** (psjɔ̃) *f*, re-spect, acceptation (*of a word*).

accès (aksɛ) *m*, access, approach; fit, attack, flush. ~ *direct*, direct access (*computers*). ~ *séquentiel*, serial access (*computers*). **accessible** (sɛsibl) *a*, accessible, approachable.

accession (aksɛsjɔ̃) *f*, accession; consent.

accessoire† (aksɛswa;r) *a*, accessory. ¶ *m*, accessory, adjunct; (*pl.*) fittings, furniture; properties (*Theat.*). **accessoiriste** (ist) *n*, property manager (*Theat.*). ~ *de plateau*, property manager (*cinema*).

accident (aksidɑ̃) *m*, accident; smash; unevenness; hazard (*Golf*); accidental (*Mus.*). **accidenté, e** (te) *a*, hilly, broken; checkered, eventful. **accidentel, le†** (tɛl) *a*, accidental, casual.

acclamation (aklamasjɔ̃) *f*, acclamation, cheering. **acclamer** (me) *v.t*, to acclaim, hail, cheer.

acclimatation (aklimatasjɔ̃) *f*, acclimatization. *jardin d'~*, zoo. **acclimater** (te) *v.t*, to acclimatize. **s'~**, to become accustomed to.

accointance (akwɛ̃tɑ̃;s) *f. oft. pl*, intimacy; dealings.

accolade (akɔlad) *f*, embrace, hug; brace, bracket (*Typ.*). **accoler** (le) *v.t*, to brace, bracket.

accommodation (akɔmɔdasjɔ̃) *f*, accommodation. **accommodement** (dmɑ̃) *m*, compromise, arrangement, settlement, terms. **accommoder** (de) *v.t*, to suit; please; reconcile; adapt; prepare (*food*); arrange, settle. **s'~à**, to adapt oneself to. **s'~ de**, to put up with.

accompagnateur trice (akɔ̃paɲatœ;r, tris) *n*, accompan[y]ist. **accompagnement** (ɲmɑ̃) *m*, accompaniment; concomitant. **accompagner** (ɲe) *v.t*, to accompany, attend, escort.

accompli, e (akɔ̃pli) *a*, accomplished, thorough. **accomplir** (pli;r) *v.t*, to accomplish, achieve, perform, carry out. **s'~**, to happen. **accomplissement** (plismɑ̃) *m*, accomplishment, etc.

accord (akɔ;r) *m*, accord, agreement; harmony, concord; consent; chord (*Mus.*); tune; (*pl.*) betrothal. *d'~*, agreed, granted; in tune. *d'un commun ~*, with one accord. **accordage** (kɔrdaːʒ) *m*, tuning. **accordailles** (daːj) *f.pl*, betrothal. **accordéon** (deɔ̃) *m*, accordion. **accorder** (de) *v.t*, to accord, grant, bestow, allow; afford; spare; reconcile; tune; attune. *s'~*, to agree; accord; tune [up]. accordeur (dœːr) *m*, tuner.

accort, e (akɔːr, ɔrt) *a*, amiable, pleasing.

accostage (akɔstaːʒ) *m*, docking (*ships, spaceships*). **accoster** (kɔste) *v.t*, to accost; come alongside.

accotement (akɔtmɑ̃) *m*, side path, greensward, verge. **accoter** (te) *v.t*, to hold up; lean, rest. **accotoir** (twaːr) *m*, rest, arm.

accouchement (akuʃmɑ̃) *m*, confinement, lying-in, childbirth. **accoucher** (ʃe) *v.i*, to be confined, give birth, deliver, bring forth; speak out. **accoucheur** (ʃœːr) *m*, maternity doctor. **accoucheuse** (jøːz) *f*, midwife.

accouder (s') (akude) *v.pr*, to rest (*or* lean) on one's elbow(s). **accoudoir** (dwaːr) *m*, arm; rail.

accouple (akupl) *f*, leash. **accoupler** (ple) *v.t*, to couple, connect, yoke; pair, mate.

accourcie (akursi) *f*, shortcut. **accourcir** (siːr) *v.t*, to shorten.

accourir (akuriːr) *v.i.ir*, to run [up], rush.

accoutrement (akutrəmɑ̃) *m*, trappings, garb, rig. **accoutrer** (tre) *v.t*, to rig out.

accoutumance (akutymɑ̃ːs) *f*, habit, use. **accoutumer** (me) *v.t*, to accustom, inure.

accréditer (akredite) *v.t*, to accredit, open a credit for. *s'~*, to gain credence.

accroc (akro) *m*, rent, tear; snag, hitch; stain.

accroche-cœur (akroʃkœːr) *m*, lovelock, kiss-curl. **accrocher** (ʃe) *v.t*, to hook; grapple; hang [up]; run against; catch. *s'~*, to hang on.

accroire (akrwaːr) *v.t: faire ~ à*, to cause to believe. *en faire ~ à*, to impose [up]on. *s'en faire ~*, to be conceited.

accroître (akrwaːtr) *v.t. & i. ir*, to increase, grow, accrue. **accroissement** (krwasmɑ̃) *m*, increase, etc.

accroupir (s') (akrupiːr) *v.pr*, to squat, crouch, cower.

accueil (akœːj) *m*, reception, welcome; honor (*bill*). **accueillir** (kœjiːr) *v.t.ir*, to receive, welcome, greet; entertain; honor, meet (*bill*).

accul (akyl) *m*, cove, creek; lair. **acculer** (akyle) *v.t*, to [drive into a] corner. *s'~*, to stand at bay; jib. *s'~ contre*, to set one's back against.

accumulateur (akymylatœːr) *m*, accumulator, [storage] battery. **accumulation** (sjɔ̃) *f*, accumulation. **accumuler** (le) *v.t. & abs. & s'~*, to accumulate; gather.

accusateur, trice (akyzatœːr, tris) *n*, accuser. ¶ *a*, accusing. **accusatif** (tif) *m*, accusative [case]. **accusation** (sjɔ̃) *f*, accusation, charge; indictment. **accusé, e** (ze) *n*, accused, prisoner at the bar. **accusé de réception**, *m*, acknowledgment. **accuser** (ze) *v.t*, to accuse, charge; indict; impeach; blame; show, betray; bring out; complain of (*medically*). *~ réception de*, to acknowledge receipt of. *s'~ de*, to avow, acknowledge, confess. *s'~ soi-même*, to plead guilty.

acerbe (asɛrb) *a*, sour, sharp, harsh.

acéré, e (asere) *a*, steeled, sharp, keen, cutting. **acérer** (re) *v.t*, to steel.

acétique (asetik) *a*, acetic.

achalandage (aʃalɑ̃daːʒ) *m*, bringing custom; custom, connection, patronage. **achalandé, e** (de) *p.a*, patronized. **achalander** (de) *v.t*, to bring custom; commercialize. *s'~*, to get custom.

acharné, e (aʃarne) *a*, rabid, furious, fierce, desperate, relentless, ruthless; obstinate, bitter, inveterate, confirmed; intense, eager; fleshed. **acharnement** (nəmɑ̃) *m*, rabidness, etc. **acharner** (ne) *v.t*, to set on, set against; flesh. *s'~*, to attack furiously; be set,

achat (aʃa) *m*, purchase, buying.

acheminement (aʃminmã) *m*, way; progress; forwarding; routing; step. **acheminer** (ne) *v.t*, to direct; expedite; forward, dispatch, route. **s'~**, to proceed.

acheter (aʃte) *v.t*, to buy, purchase. **acheteur, euse** (tœːr, øːz) *n*, buyer, purchaser.

achevé, e (aʃve) *a*, accomplished, perfect, thorough, out & out, arrant. **achèvement** (ʃɛvmã) *m*, finishing, completion. **achever** (ʃve) *v.t*, to finish, perfect, end. *achevez donc!* out with it!

achopper (aʃɔpe) *v.i*. & **s'~**, to stumble.

achromatique (akrɔmatik) *a*, achromatic.

acide (asid) *a*, acid, sour, sharp, tart. ¶ *m*, acid. **acidité** (dite) *f*, acidity, etc. **aciduler** (dyle) *v.t*, to acidulate.

acier (asje) *m*, steel. ~ *sur sole*, open hearth s.; ~ *Thomas*, basic Bessemer s.; ~ *trempé et revenu*, tempered s. **aciérer** (sjere) *v.t*, to steel, caseharden. **aciérie** (ri) *f*, steel works.

acné (akne) *f*, acne.

acolyte (akɔlit) *m*, acolyte.

acompte (akɔ̃ːt) *m*, installment; cover, margin. ~ *de dividende*, interim dividend. ~ *de préférence*, option money (*on a property*).

aconit (akɔnit) *m*, aconite, monk's-hood, wolfsbane.

acoquinant, e (akɔkinã, ãːt) *a*, enticing. **s'acoquiner à, auprès** (ne), to get fond of, become attached to.

Açores (les) (asɔːr) *f.pl*, the Azores.

à-coup (aku) *m*, jerk, shock; (*pl.*) backlash (*gears*).

acoustique (akustik) *a*, acoustic. ¶ *f*, acoustics.

acquéreur (akerœːr) *m*, purchaser, buyer. **acquérir** (riːr) *v.t.ir*, to acquire, get, win, purchase; (*abs.*) to improve. **s'~**, to accrue.

acquêts (akɛ) *m.pl*, acquisition; windfall.

acquiescement (akjɛsmã) *m*, acquiescence. **acquiescer (se)** *v.i*, to acquiesce.

acquis, e (aki, iːz) *p.a*, acquired; earned; devoted; vested (*rights*). ¶ *m. s. & pl*, acquirements, attainments, experience. **acquisition** (kizisjɔ̃) *f*, acquisition, purchase; haul.

acquit (aki) *m*, receipt, discharge. [*pour*] ~, received [with thanks], paid. *à l'~ de*, on behalf of, on account of. **acquit-à-caution** (kitakosjɔ̃) *m*, bond note, transhipment bond. **acquitté, e** (te) *a*, duty-paid (*Cust.*).*à l'acquitté*, *ad*, duty paid, ex bond. **acquittement** (tmã) *m*, discharge, acquittal. **acquitter** (te) *v.t*, to acquit, discharge; receipt (*bill*). **s'~**, to acquit oneself, perform; be quits, catch up (*games*).

âcre (ɑːkr) *a*, acrid, tart, sour, sharp, pungent. **âcreté** (ɑkrəte) *f*, acridity, etc.

acrimonie (akrimɔni) *f*, acrimony. **acrimonieux, euse** (njø, øːz) *a*, acrimonious.

acrobate (akrɔbat) *n*, acrobat, tumbler. **acrobatie** (si) *f*, acrobatics; stunt. **acrobatique** (tik) *a*, acrobatic.

acrostiche (akrɔstiʃ) *m. & a*, acrostic.

acte (akt) *m*, act, action; deed, indenture, instrument, document, agreement, contract; bond; certificate; licence; (*pl.*) transactions (*of a society*). ~ *d'accusation*, indictment. ~ *de dernière volonté*, last will & testament. ~ *de naissance, de mariage, de décès*, certificate of birth, of marriage, of death. ~ *dommageable*, tort (*law*). ~ *sous seing privé* (sɛ̃), simple contract. [*pièce en un*] ~, one-act play. *prendre* ~ *de*, to take note of. **acteur, trice** (tœːr, tris) *n*, actor, actress, player. ~ *à transformations*, quick-change artist. ~ *de composition*, character actor.

acter (akte) *v.i*, to take action.

actif, ive (aktif, iːv) *a*, active, brisk; busy. ¶ *m*, active voice; assets.

action (aksjɔ̃) *f*, action, act, deed;

effect, agency; share, (*pl.*) stock. ~*s au porteur*, bearer shares, b. stock. ~[*s*] *de grâce*, thanksgiving. ~*s de priorité*, ~*s privilégiées*, preference shares, preferred stock. ~*s nominatives*, registered shares, r. stock. ~*s gratuites*, bonus shares. ~*s* [*entièrement*] *libérées*, fully paid shares. ~*s non libérées*, partly paid shares. *par* ~*s*, joint-stock (*att.*). **actionnaire** (ɔnɛːr) *n*, shareholder, stockholder. **actionnariat** (ɔnarja) *f*, employee shareholding.

actionner (aksjɔne) *v.t*, to drive, actuate, run, work; bring an action against, sue.

activement (aktivmɑ̃) *ad*, actively, briskly. **activer** (ve) *v.t*, to quicken, urge, press, rouse, stir up, speed up, hurry. **activité** (vite) *f*, activity, briskness. *en* ~ [*de service*], on active service. *en pleine* ~, in full operation, in full swing.

actuaire (aktɥɛːr) *m*, actuary.

actualité (aktɥalite) *f*, actuality, present state; (*pl.*) passing (*or* current) events, questions of the hour; news (*movies*). ~*s de la mode*, present-day fashions. **actuel, le** (tɥɛl) *a*, present, for the time being. **actuellement** (lmɑ̃) *ad*, now, at present.

acuité (akɥite) *f*, sharpness, acuteness, keenness; shrillness.

adage (adaːʒ) *m*, adage, saying, saw. ~ *de droit*, legal maxim.

adaptation (adaptasjɔ̃) *m*, adaptation, adjustment. ~ *à l'usager*, customization.

adapter (adapte) *v.t*, to adapt, fit, suit. **adapteur** (tœːr) *m*, adapter (*Phot.*).

addition (adisjɔ̃) *f*, addition, cast, tot; bill (*at restaurant*). **additionnel, le** (ɔnɛl) *a*, additional. **additionner** (ne) *v.t*, to add [up], cast, tot up.

adénoïde (adenɔid) *a*, adenoid.

adepte (adɛpt) *n*, adept.

adhérence (aderɑ̃ːs) *f*, adherence, adhesion. **adhérent, e** (rɑ̃, ɑ̃ːt) *n*, adherent, supporter, member. **adhérer** (re) *v.i*, to adhere, cohere, stick. **adhésion** (zjɔ̃) *f*,

adhesion, adhesiveness; membership.

adieu (adjø) *i. & m*, good-bye, farewell, adieu; parting.

adipeux, euse (adipø, øːz) *a*, adipose, fatty.

adjacent, e (adʒasɑ̃, ɑ̃ːt) *a*, adjacent, adjoining.

adjectif (adʒɛktif) *a.m*, adjectival. ¶ *m*, adjective. ~ *attribut*, predicative a. ~ *épithète*, attributive a. ~ *verbal*, participial a. (*present*). **adjectivement** (tivmɑ̃) *ad*, adjectivally, attributively.

adjoindre (adʒwɛ̃ːdr) *v.t.ir*, to join, associate. **adjoint, e** (ʒwɛ̃, ɛ̃ːt) *a. & n*, assistant.

adjudant (adʒydɑ̃) *m*, sergeant major. ~ *major*, adjutant.

adjudicataire (adʒydikatɛːr) *n*, purchaser; contractor. **adjudication** (sjɔ̃) *f*, adjudication; award of contract; auction. **adjuger** (ʒe) *v.t*, to adjudge, adjudicate; award; award the contract for; knock down.

adjurer (adʒyre) *v.t*, to adjure, beseech.

admettre (admɛtr) *v.t.ir*, to admit, allow, grant; pass (*at exam*).

administrateur, trice (administratœːr, tris) *n*, director; administrator, trix. ~ *délégué*, ~ *directeur*, managing director. **administration** (sjɔ̃) *f*, administration, management, direction; board, directorate; authorities. ~ *publique*, civil service. *conseil d'*~, board of directors. **administrer** (tre) *v.t*, to administer, manage, direct.

admirable† (admirabl) *a*, admirable, wonderful, capital. **admirateur, trice** (tœːr, tris) *n*, admirer. **admiration** (sjɔ̃) *f*, admiration, wonder. **admirer** (re) *v.t*, to admire, wonder at.

admis (admi) *a*, admitted; accepted; conventional.

admissible (admisibl) *a*, admissible. **admission** (sjɔ̃) *f*, admission, admittance; intake; entrance.

admonester (admɔnɛste) *v.t*, to admonish, reprimand. **admonestation** (tasjɔ̃) *f*, **admonition** (nisjɔ̃) *f*, admonition, etc.

adolescence (adɔlɛsɑ̃:s) *f*, adolescence, youth. **adolescent, e** (sɑ̃, ɑ̃:t) *a*, adolescent. ¶ *n*, adolescent, youth, girl.

adonner (s') (adɔne) *v. pr*, to give (*or* apply) oneself, addict oneself, take.

adopter (adɔpte) *v.t*, to adopt, carry, pass, confirm. **adoptif, ive** (tif, i:v) *a*, adoptive, adopted. **adoption** (sjɔ̃) *f*, adoption, etc.

adorable (adɔrabl) *a*, adorable, charming, lovely, delightful. **adorateur, trice** (tœ:r, tris) *n*, adorer, worshiper, votary. **adoration** (sjɔ̃) *f*, adoration, worship. **adorer** (re) *v.t*, to adore, worship.

adosser (adose) *v.t*, to back, lean. **s'~**, to lean one's back against.

adoucir (adusi:r) *v.t*, to sweeten; soften; smooth, temper, subdue, allay, alleviate, soothe, ease, appease, assuage, mollify, qualify.

adresse (adrɛs) *f*, address, direction; skill, dexterity, craft, deftness; shrewdness; handiness; clever move. **adresser** (se) *v.t*, to address, direct, send. **s'~ à**, to address, apply to; inquire of; cater for.

Adriatique (adriatik) *a. & f*, Adriatic.

adroit, e† (adrwa, at) *a*, adroit, dext[e]rous, deft, handy, skillful, clever, neat; shrewd.

adulateur, trice (adylatœ:r, tris) *a*, adulatory. **adulation** (sjɔ̃) *f*, adulation. **aduler** (le) *v.t*, to adulate.

adulte (adylt) *a. & n*, adult, grown-up.

adultère (adyltɛ:r) *n*, adulterer, ess; (*m.*) adultery. ¶ *a*, adulterous.

advenir (advəni:r) *v.i.ir*, to happen, occur, befall, come to pass. *advienne que pourra*, come what may, whate'er betide.

adverbe (advɛrb) *m*, adverb. ~ *de quantité*, a. of number. **adverbial, e†** (bjal) *a*, adverbial.

adversaire (advɛrsɛ:r) *m*, adversary, opponent, foe. **adverse** (vɛrs) *a*, adverse, opposing. **adversité** (site) *f*, adversity, misfortune.

aérage (aera:ʒ) *m*, **aération** (rasjɔ̃) *f*, ventilation, airing; draft; aeration. **aérer** (re) *v.t*, to ventilate, air; aerate.

aérien, ne (aerjɛ̃, ɛn) *a*, aerial, airy, air (*att.*); overhead.

aérodrome (aerɔdro:m) *m*, airport, aviation ground.

aérodynamique (aerɔdinamik) *a*, aerodynamic; streamlined. ¶ *f*, aerodynamics. **aérodynamisme** (mism) *m*, streamlining.

aérogare (aerɔga:r) *f*, air terminal.

aéroglisseur (aerɔglisœ:r) *m*, hovercraft.

aérolithe (aerɔlit) *m*, aerolite, meteorite.

aéronaute (aerɔno:t) *n*, aeronaut. **aéronautique** (notik) *a*, aeronautic(al),. air (*att.*). ¶ *f*, aeronautics.

aéronef (aerɔnɛf) *m*, aircraft.

aéroplane (aerɔplan) *m*, [air]-plane.

aéroport (aerɔpɔ:r) *m*, airport.

aérospatial (aerɔspajal) *a*, aerospatial.

aérostat (aerɔsta) *m*, lighter than air machine; balloon. **aérostation** (sjɔ̃) *f*, lighter than air aviation *or* branch (*army*); ballooning. **aérostier** (tje) *m*, balloonist.

affabilité (afabilite) *f*, affability. **affable** (bl) *a*, affable.

affacturage (afaktyraʒ) *m*, factoring (*Fin.*).

affadir (afadi:r) *v.t*, to sicken; make insipid, flatten. **affadissement** (dismɑ̃) *m*, loss of flavor; nauseousness.

affaiblir (afɛbli:r) *v.t*, to weaken, enfeeble; reduce (*Phot.*). **affaiblissement** (blismɑ̃) *m*, weakening, diminution, fading.

affaire (afɛ:r) *f*, affair, matter, case, thing, job, proposition, business, piece of business, concern; transaction, dealing, bargain; lawsuit; re (*law*); engagement (*Mil.*). ~*s par correspondance*, mail order business. ~ *roulante*, going concern. *ce malade est hors d'*~, this patient is out of danger. *son* ~ *est faite*, he's done for. **affairé, e** (fɛre) *a*, busy. ¶ *n*, busy man, woman.

affaissement (afɛsmɑ̃) *m*, subsidence, sinking; collapse. **affaisser** (se) *v.t*, to cause to subside; weigh down. s'~, to subside, sink, collapse.

affaler (afale) *v.t*, to haul down. affale! lower away! s'affaler, to sink, drop, down.

affamé, e (afame) *a*, famished, hungry, starving, craving. ¶ *n*, starveling. **affamer** (me) *v.t*, to famish, starve.

affecté, e (afɛkte) *a*, affected; prim. **affecter** (te) *v.t*, to assign, design, charge, apply, set aside; aspire to; assume; affect; move. **affectation** (tasjɔ̃) *f*, assignment (*Mil.*); affectation; appropriation.

affection (afɛksjɔ̃) *f*, affection, liking; complaint (*Med.*). **affectionné, e** (ɔne) *a*, **affectueux, euse†** (tɥø, ø:z) *a*, affectionate, fond, loving. **affectionner** (ɔne) *v.t*, to be fond of, like.

afférent (afɛrɑ̃) *a*, relating, pertaining, to.

affermer (afɛrme) *v.t*, to lease, let out, farm [out], rent.

affermir (afɛrmi:r) *v.t*, to strengthen.

affété, e (afete) *a*, affected, mincing. **afféterie** (tri) *f*, affectation.

affiche (afiʃ) *f*, poster, bill, placard; sign. ~ *lumineuse*, electric sign. **afficher** (ʃe) *v.t*, to post, bill, placard, stick (*bills*); proclaim, advertise, show up. s'~, to show off. **afficheur** (ʃœ:r) *m*, billposter, billsticker.

affilé, e (afile) *a*, sharp (*tongue*). d'affilée, *ad*, at a stretch. **affiler** (le) *v.t*, to sharpen (*tools*).

affilier (afilje) *v.t*, to affiliate.

affiloir (afilwa:r) *m*, steel; strop.

affinage (afina3) *m*, refining. **affiner** (ne) *v.t*, to refine. **affinerie** (nri) *f*, refinery. **affineur** (nœ:r) *m*, refiner.

affinité (afinite) *f*, affinity.

affiquets (afikɛ) *m.pl*, getup, finery.

affirmatif, ive† (afirmatif, i:v) *a. & f*, affirmative. **affirmation** (sjɔ̃) *f*, affirmation. **affirmer** (me) *v.t*, to affirm, assert, aver, vouch.

affixe (afiks) *m*, affix.

affleurement (aflœrmɑ̃) *m*, leveling; outcrop (*Geol.*). **affleurer** (re) *v.t*, to level, flush; (*v.i.*) to crop out.

affliction (afliksjɔ̃) *f*, affliction. **affliger** (3e) *v.t*, to afflict, distress, grieve; mortify; curse.

affluence (aflyɑ̃:s) *f*, affluence; crowd; flow, flood; concourse. **affluent** (ɑ̃) *m*, tributary, affluent, feeder. **affluer** (e) *v.i*, to flow; run; abound, flock.

affolement (afɔlmɑ̃) *m*, panic; distraction. **affoler** (afɔle) *v.t*, to infatuate; madden; distract.

affouiller (afuje) *v.t*, to undermine, wash away.

affourché, e (afurʃe) *a*, astride, astraddle.

affranchi, e (afrɑ̃ʃi) *n*, emancipated slave. **affranchir** (ʃi:r) *v.t*, to [set] free, liberate; relieve; prepay, stamp (*Post*). **affranchissement** (ʃismɑ̃) *m*, emancipation, enfranchisement; prepayment.

affres (afr) *f.pl*, pangs, throes.

affrètement (afrɛtmɑ̃) *m*, freighting, chartering. **affréter** (frete) *v.t*, to charter. **affréteur** (tœ:r) *m*, charterer.

affreux, euse† (afrø, ø:z) *a*, frightful, fearful, ghastly. ¶ *m*, dangerous person, mercenary (*soldier*).

affriander (afriɑ̃de) *& affrioler* (ɔle) *v.t*, to allure, tempt; make attractive.

affront (afrɔ̃) *m*, affront; slight, cut.

affronter (afrɔ̃te) *v.t*, to front, confront, face, brave.

affubler (afyble) *v.t*, to dress up.

affût (afy) *m*, hiding place; stand; [gun] carriage. à l'~, on the watch, on the lookout.

affûter (afyte) *v.t*, to sharpen, grind.

afghan, e (afgɑ̃, an) *a. & A~, n*, Afghan.

afin de (afɛ̃) *pr*, in order to, so as to, to. **afin que**, *c*, in order that, so that, that.

africain, e (afrikɛ̃, ɛn) *a. & A~, n*, African. **l'Afrique** (frik) *f*, Africa.

agacer (agase) *v.t*, to set on edge, irritate, annoy; provoke, excite.

agacement (smɑ̃) *m*, setting on edge, etc. **agacerie** (sri) *f*, provocation.

agate (agat) *f*, agate.

âge (ɑ:ʒ) *m*, age. *l'~ de raison*, years of discretion. *l'~ ingrat*, the awkward age. *l'~ viril*, man's estate. *troisième ~*, the "golden years"; senior citizens. *d'un certain ~*, no longer young. *quel ~ a-t-il?* how old is he? *il n'est pas en ~*, he is not of (*or* is under) age. *âgé, e* (aʒe) *a*, aged, old. *~ de 20 ans*, 20 years old.

agence (aʒɑ̃:s) *f*, agency, bureau. *~ d'information*, news agency. *~ de presse*, wire service, news agency. *~ de renseignements*, mercantile office, m. agency. *~ immobilière*, real estate agency.

agencé, e (aʒɑ̃se) *p.p*, dressed, got up. **agencement** (smɑ̃) *m*, arrangement; fittings & fixtures. **agencer** (se) *v.t*, to arrange, fit [up].

agenda (aʒɛ̃da) *m*, diary; agenda; memorandum book.

agenouiller [(s')] (aʒnuje) *v.pr*, to kneel [down]. **agenouilloir** (jwa:r) *m*, hassock.

agent (aʒɑ̃) *m*, agent; broker; officer; medium. *~ comptable*, accountant. *~ de change*, stockbroker (*nominated by the government*). *~ de la douane*, customs officer. *~ de liaison*, liaison officer. *~ [de police]*, policeman. *~ de police des côtes à terre*, coastguard. *~ de recouvrements*, debt collector, dun. *~ du service sanitaire*, health officer. *~ en douane*, customs agent. *~ maritime*, shipping agent. *~s s'abstenir*, no agents.

aggloméré (aglɔmere) *m*, briquet[te], compressed fuel; conglomerate. **agglomérer** (re) *v.t*, to agglomerate. .

agglutiner (aglytine) *v.t*, to agglutinate.

aggraver (agrave) *v.t*, to aggravate; increase.

agile† (aʒil) *a*, agile, nimble, lithe, active. **agilité** (lite) *f*, agility, etc.

agio (aʒjo) *m*, exchange [premium]; agio; discount charges.

agiotage (ʒjɔta:ʒ) *m*, gambling, jobbery, rigging; exchange business. **agioter** (te) *v.i*, to speculate, gamble. **agioteur** (tœ:r) *m*, speculator, gambler.

agir (aʒi:r) *v.i*, to act, operate, work, do; proceed (*law*). *s'~*, *v.imp*, to be the matter, be in question. **agissant, e** (ʒisɑ̃, ɑ̃:t) *a*, active. **agissements** (smɑ̃) *m. pl*, goings-on, doings (*underhand*).

agitateur (aʒitatœ:r) *m*, agitator (*Pol.*); stirrer (*rod*). **agiter** (te) *v.t*, to agitate, perturb, shake, stir; wag; wave; debate, discuss, *nuit agitée* restless night. *mer agitée*, rough sea. **agitation** (tasjɔ̃) *f*, agitation; unrest

agneau (aɲo) *m*, lamb. *~femelle*, ewe lamb. **agneler** (nəle) *v.i*, to lamb, yean. **agnelet** (lɛ) *m*, lambkin.

agonie (agɔni) *f*, [death] agony, death struggle. *à l'~*, dying. **agonir** (ni:r) *v.t*, to load (*with abuse*). **agonisant, e** (nizɑ̃, ɑ̃:t) *a*, dying. **agoniser** (ze) *v.i*, to be dying.

agrafe (agraf) *f*, hook, clasp, fastener, snap, staple, cramp. *~ & porte*, hook & eye. **agrafer** (fe) *v.t*, to hook, etc; do up (*dress*); grab, nab. **agrafeuse** (fø:z) *f*, stapler.

agraire (agrɛ:r) *a*, agrarian, land (*att.*).

agrandir (agrɑ̃di:r) *v.t*, to enlarge. **agrandisseur** (disœ:r) *m*, enlarger (*Phot.*).

agréable† (agreabl) *a. & m*, agreeable, pleasant, nice, congenial; acceptable, palatable.

agréé (agree) *m*, lawyer (at *tribunal de commerce*). **agréer** (gree) *v.t*, to accept, approve, agree; (*v.i*) to please, suit. *agréez, monsieur, mes salutations empressées*, yours faithfully.

agrégation (agregasjɔ̃) *f*, admission; aggregation. **agréger** (ʒe) *v.t*, to admit (*as member*).

agrément (agremɑ̃) *m*, consent, approval; agreeableness, pleasantness, amenity; pleasure, charm; trimming (*dress*). (*pl.*) amenities (*housing*). **agrémenter**

(te) *v.t*, to adorn, ornament, trim.

agrès (agrɛ) *m.pl*, tackle, gear, rigging.

agresseur (agrɛsœːr) *m*, aggressor. **agressif, ive** (sif, iːv) *a*, aggressive. **agression** (sjɔ̃) *f*, aggression.

agreste (agrɛst) *a*, rustic; uncouth.

agricole (agrikɔl) *a*, agricultural. **agriculteur** (kyltœːr) *m*, agricultur[al]ist, farmer. **agriculture** (tyːr) *f*, agriculture, farming, husbandry.

agriffer (s') (agrife) *v.pr*, to claw, cling, lay hold.

agripper (agripe) *v.t*, to lay hold of, clutch, grab, grip.

agronome (agrɔnɔm) *m*, agronomist. **agronomie** (mi) *f*, agronomy, husbandry.

aguerrir (ageriːr) *v.t*, to harden to war; inure, season.

aguets (être aux) (agɛ), to be on the watch *or* lookout.

aguicher (agiʃe) *v.t*, to excite, tease (*intellectually, sexually*); give the eye to.

aheurtement (aœrtəmɑ̃) *m*, obsession. **s'aheurter** (te) *v.pr.*, to cling, be obsessed, be bent.

ahurir (ayriːr) *v.t*, to flurry, fluster, bewilder, daze.

aide (ɛːd) *f*, aid, help, assistance. *à l'~!* help! ¶ *n*, assistant, helper, mate. *~ de camp*, *m*, aide-de-camp. **aider** (ɛde) *v.t*, to aid, help, assist. *s'~ de*, to make use of.

aide-mémoire (ɛdmemwaːr) *m*, handbook, manual; aide-mémoire (*diplomatic*).

aïe (aːj) *i*, ow!, ouch!

aïeul, e (ajœl) *n*, grandfather, -mother. **aïeux** (ajø) *m.pl*, forefathers.

aigle (ɛgl) *m*, eagle (*male bird*); genius, mastermind; (*f.*) eagle (*hen bird & standard*). **aiglon, ne** (glɔ̃, ɔn) *n*, eaglet.

aigre† (ɛːgr) *a*, sour, tart; bitter; sharp; churlish; shrill. ¶ *m*, sourness, etc; chill (*in the air*). **~-doux, ce** (ɛgrədu, us) *a*, bittersweet, sub-acid. **aigrefin** (fɛ̃) *m*, sharper; haddock. **aigrelet, te** (lɛ, ɛt) *a*, sourish, tart. **aigret, te** (grɛ, ɛt) *a*, sourish, tartish.

aigrette (ɛgrɛt) *f*, aigrette, egret, plume. **aigretté, e** (te), *a*, tufted, crested.

aigreur (ɛgrœːr) *f*, sourness, acerbity. **aigrir** (griːr) *v.t*, to sour, embitter.

aigu, ë (egy) *a*, acute, sharp, pointed; shrill. ¶ *m*, upper register (*Mus.*).

aigue-marine (ɛgmarin) *f*, aquamarine.

aiguière (ɛgjɛːr) *f*, ewer.

aiguillade (egɥijad) *f*, goad.

aiguille (egɥiːj) *f*, needle; hand, pointer; switch (*Rly.*). *~ à coudre*, sewing needle. *~ à passer*, bodkin. *~ à repriser*, darning needle. *~ à tricoter*, knitting n., k. pin. *~ de glace*, icicle. **aiguillée** (gɥije) *f*, needleful. **aiguiller** (egɥije) *v.t*, to shunt; switch (*Rly.*).

aiguillon (egɥijɔ̃) *m*, goad; sting; prickle; spur, stimulus, incentive. **aiguillonner** (jɔne) *v.t*, to goad, spur on, stimulate.

aiguiser (egɥize) *v.t*, to sharpen, grind, whet; stimulate.

ail (aːj) *m*, garlic. *gousse d'~*, garlic clove. **ailloli** (ajɔli), *m*, garlic mayonnaise.

aile (ɛl) *f*, wing; aisle; flange; blade, vane; fender. **ailé, e** (le) *a*, winged. **aileron** (lrɔ̃) *m*, pinion; fin; paddle board; aileron.

ailleurs (ajœːr) *ad*, elsewhere, somewhere else. *par ~*, incidentally. *d'~*, *ad*, besides, moreover.

aimable† (ɛmabl) *a*, amiable, pleasant; kind; lovable. **aimant, e** (mɑ̃, ɑ̃ːt) *a*, loving, affectionate.

aimant (ɛmɑ̃) *m*, magnet. **aimanter** (te) *v.t*, to magnetize.

aimer (ɛme) *v.t. & abs*, to love; be fond of; like.

aine (ɛn) *f*, groin (*Anat.*).

aîné, e (ɛne) *a. & n*, elder; eldest; senior. **aînesse** (nɛs) *f*, seniority.

ainsi (ɛ̃si) *ad*, so, thus. *~soit-il*, so be it. *~ que*, *c*, [just] as; as also.

air (ɛːr) *m*, air; look, likeness; manner; way; mien; aria; tune, song. *en l'~*, in the air, airy (*schemes*); idle (*tales*); groundless (*fears*); empty (*threats*). *de plein ~*, outdoor (*as games*). en plein ~, in the open air, alfresco.

airain (ɛrɛ̃) (*Poet.*) *m*, bronze, brass.

aire (ɛːr) *f*, area, floor; eyrie; threshing floor. ~ de lancement, launching pad. ~ de vent, point of the compass.

airelle (ɛrel) *f*, blueberry, huckleberry.

aisance (ɛzɑ̃ːs) *f*, ease; freedom; affluence, sufficiency, competence. **aise** (ɛːz) *a*, glad, pleased. ¶ *f*, ease, comfort; joy, pleasure; (*pl.*) creature comforts. **aisé, e** (ɛze) *a*, easy; comfortable; well-off, affluent. **aisément** (mɑ̃) *ad*, easily; comfortably; readily.

aisselle (ɛsɛl) *f*, armpit.

ajonc (aʒɔ̃) *m*, furze, gorse, whin.

ajouré, e (aʒure) *a*, perforated, pierced; open-work (*att.*).

ajourner (aʒurne) *v.t*, to adjourn, postpone, put off; subpoena; defer (*draft*).

ajouté (aʒute) *m*, rider, addition. **ajouter** (te) *v.t*, to add; implement.

ajustage (aʒystaːʒ) *m*, fitting, setting up. **ajustement** (təmɑ̃) *m*, adjustment; arrangement, settlement. **ajuster** (te) *v.t*, to adjust, fit [up]; lay out; deck out, array; set straight; aim at (*with gun*). s'~, to tidy oneself up. **ajusteur** (tœːr) *m*, fitter, artificer.

ajutage (aʒytaːʒ) *m*, nozzle, jet.

alambic (alɑ̃bik) *m*, still. **alambiquer** (ke) *v.t*, to puzzle; spin out, wiredraw (*fig.*).

alanguir (alɑ̃giːr) *v.t*, to make languid.

alarmant, e (alarmɑ̃, ɑ̃ːt) *a*, alarming. **alarme** (larm) *f*, alarm. **alarmer** (me) *v.t*, to alarm; startle.

albâtre (albɑːtr) *m*, alabaster.

alcali (alkali) *m*, alkali. **alcalin, e** (lɛ̃, in) *a*, alkaline.

alchimie (alʃimi) *f*, alchemy. **alchimiste** (mist) *m*, alchemist.

alcool (alkɔl) *m*, alcohol, spirit[s]. ~ ammon aromatique, sal volatile. ~ dénaturé, ~ à brûler, methylated spirit. **alcoolique** (kɔlik) *a. & n*, alcoholic.

alcootest (alkɔtɛst) *m*, breathalyzer test.

alcôve (alkoːv) *f*, alcove, recess. ~ de dortoir, cubicle.

alcyonien (alsjɔnjɛ̃) *a.m*, halcyon.

aléa (alea) *m*, chance. **aléatoire** (twaːr) *a*, uncertain, contingent, aleatory.

alène (alɛːn) *f*, awl.

alentour (alɑ̃tuːr) *ad*, around, round about. d'~, surrounding. ~s, *m.pl*, surroundings.

alerte (alɛrt) *a*, alert, wide-awake. ¶ *i*, up! look out! ¶ *f*, alarm, alert.

aléser (aleze) *v.t*, to ream, broach, bore [out]. **alésage** (zaːʒ) *m*, reaming, etc; bore. **alésoir** (zwaːr) *m*, reamer, broach.

alevin (alvɛ̃) *m*, fry, young fish.

Alexandrie (alɛksɑ̃dri) *f*, Alexandria. **alexandrin, e** (drɛ̃, in) *a*, Alexandrian; Alexandrine.

alfa (alfa) *m*, alfa [grass], esparto [grass].

algarade (algarad) *f*, storm of abuse, blowing up.

algèbre (alʒɛbr) *m*, algebra; Greek (*fig.*).

Alger (alʒɛ) *m*, Algiers. **l'Algérie** (ʒeri) *f*, Algeria. **algérien, ne** (rjɛ̃, ɛn) *a. & A~, n*, Algerian.

algue (alg) *f*, seaweed, alga.

alibi (alibi) *m*, alibi.

aliboron (alibɔrɔ̃) *m: un maître* ~, an ass, a blockhead.

aliéné, e (aljene) *n*, mental patient, lunatic. **aliénation d'esprit, ~ mentale** (nasjɔ̃), insanity, lunacy, madness. **aliéner** (ne) *v.t*, to alienate, estrange; derange, unhinge (*mind*); transfer (*property*).

aligner (aliɲe) *v.t*, to align, range; finish off (*phrases*). **alignement** (ɲmɑ̃) *m*, alignment, etc; building line.

aliment (alimɑ̃) *m*, food; nutriment; fuel (*fig.*); (*pl.*) sustenance; (*pl.*) cud. **alimentaire** (tɛːr) *a*, alimentary, feeding, feed, food (*att.*). **alimentation** (tasjɔ̃) *f*, feeding; feed. **alimenter** (te) *v.t*, to feed, supply.

alinéa (alinea) *m*, [fresh] paragraph, new par[agraph]; subsection.

alité, e (alite) *a*, laid up, bedridden. **aliter** (te) *v.t*, to keep in bed.

alizé (alize) *a*, trade (*wind*).

allaiter (alɛte) *v.t*, to suckle, nurse.

allant, e (alɑ̃, ɑ̃ːt) *a*, active. ¶ *m*, activity; go; initiative. ~*s* & *venants*, passersby, comers & goers.

allécher (aleʃe) *v.t*, to allure, entice.

allée (ale) *f*, walk, lane, path; drive; passage. ~ *en berceau*, covered walk. ~*s* & *venues*, coming & going, running about.

allégation (alegasjɔ̃) *f*, allegation.

allège (alɛːʒ) *f*, lighter, barge, craft. **alléger** (leʒe) *v.t*, to lighten; thin; alleviate. **allégement** (leʒmɑ̃) *m*, lightening, etc.

allégorie (allegɔri) *f*, allegory. **allégorique†** (rik) *a*, allegoric(al).

allègre (allɛːgr) *a*, lively, cheerful, brisk. **allégresse** (allegrɛs), *f*, joy[fulness], cheerfulness.

alléguer (alege) *v.t*, to allege, adduce; plead, urge; quote, cite.

Alléluia (allelɥija) *m*, hallelujah.

Allemagne (l') (almaɲ) *f*, Germany. **allemand, e** (mɑ̃, ɑ̃ːd) *a*. & A~, *n*, German. **l'allemand**, *m*, German (*language*).

aller (ale) *m*, going, outward journey. ~ & *retour*, roundtrip ticket. *l'*~ & *le venir*, the come-&-go. ~ *à la dérive*, to drift. ¶ *v.i.ir*, to go; run; be (*well, ill, etc.*); get; do; fare; fit, suit. ~ *à bicyclette*, to cycle. ~ *à cheval*, to ride. ~ *en auto*, ~ *en voiture*, to drive. **s'en** ~, to go [away], be off.

alliage (aljaːʒ) *m*, alloy. **alliance** (jɑ̃ːs) *f*, alliance, union; match; intermarriage; wedding ring. *cousin, par* ~, cousin by marriage. **allié, e** (je) *n*, ally; relation [by marriage]. **allier** (je) *v.t*, to ally, unite; match; alloy. **s'**~, to unite; marry; intermarry.

alligator (aligatɔːr) *m*, alligator.

allô (alo) (*Teleph.*) *i*, hello!

allocation (allɔkasjɔ̃) *f*, allocation, allowance.

allocution (allɔkysjɔ̃) *f*, speech, address.

allonge (alɔ̃ːʒ) *f*, lengthening

piece; rider (*to bill of exchange*). **allonger** (lɔ̃ʒe) *v.t*, to lengthen, elongate; eke out; stretch [out]; deal (*blow*).

allotissement (alɔtismɑ̃) *m*, apportionment, allotment; grouping into lots.

allouer (alwe) *v.t*, to allocate, allow, grant.

allumage (alymaːʒ) *m*, lighting, ignition. *couper l'*~, to switch off the ignition. **allumer** (me) *v.t*, to light, ignite; kindle; fire, stir up. ~ *la lumière*, ~ *l'électricité*, to switch (*or* turn) on the light. **allumette** (mɛt) *f*, match. ~ *bougie*, wax vesta. ~*s de sûreté*, safety matches. ~*s en carnet*, book matches. **allumeur** (mœːr) *m*, lighter. **allumeuse** (møːz) *f*, flirt.

allure (alyːr) *f*, walk, gait, pace; demeanor, carriage; trim; way. *à toute* ~, at top speed. *d'* ~ *louche*, suspicious-looking.

allusion (allyzjɔ̃) *f*, allusion; hint, innuendo.

almanach (almana) *m*; *in liaison*, -nak) *m*, almanac.

aloès (alɔɛs) *m*, aloe. [*suc d'*] ~, aloes.

aloi (alwa) *m*, standard, quality; legal tender. *de bon* ~, genuine.

alors (alɔːr) *ad*, then. ~ *que*, *a*, when.

alouette (alwɛt) *f*, lark. ~ *des champs*, skylark.

alourdir (alurdiːr) *v.t*, to make heavy.

aloyau (alwajo) *m*, sirloin (*beef*).

alpaga (alpaga) *m*, alpaca.

Alpes (les) (alp) *f.pl*, the Alps. **alpestre** (pɛstr) *a*, Alpine.

alpha (alfa) *m*, alpha. **alphabet** (bɛ) *m*, alphabet; A B C, primer. **alphabétique†** (betik) *a*, alphabetical.

alphabétisation (alfabetizasjɔ̃) *f*, instruction of nation or group (*not individual*) in literacy.

alpin, e (alpɛ̃, in) *a*, Alpine. **l'alpinisme** (pinism) *m*, mountaineering. **alpiniste** (nist) *n*, Alpinist, mountaineer.

Alsace (l') (alzas) *f*, Alsace. **alsacien, ne** (sjɛ̃, ɛn) *a*. & A~, *n*, Alsatian.

altérant, e (alterɑ̃, ɑ̃ːt) *a*, thirst-creating.

altération (alterasjɔ̃) *f*, alteration, change; adulteration; faltering voice; heavy thirst.

altercation (altɛrkasjɔ̃) *f*, altercation.

altérer (altere) *v.t*, to change; debase, adulterate; garble; weather (*Geol.*); make thirsty. *altéré de sang*, bloodthirsty.

alternatif, ive† (altɛrnatif, i;v) *a*, alternative; alternate; alternating. ¶ *f*, alternative; option. **alterner** (ne) *v.i. & t*, to alternate.

altesse (altɛs) *f*, highness (*title*).

altier, ère (altje, ɛ;r) *a*, haughty, lofty, lordly.

altitude (altityd) *f*, altitude, height, elevation.

alto (alto) *m*, alto; tenor violin, viola; alto saxhorn.

altruiste (altryist) *n*, altruist. ¶ *a*, altruistic.

aluminium (alyminjɔm) *m*, aluminum.

alun (alœ̃) *m*, alum.

alunir (alyni;r) *v.i*, to land on the moon.

alvéole (alveɔl) *m*, cell; socket (*tooth*).

amabilité (amabilite) *f*, amiability, kindness.

amadou (amadu) *m*, tinder, touchwood. **amadouer** (dwe) *v.t*, to coax, wheedle, cajole.

amaigrir (amɛgri;r) *v.t*, to [make] thin, emaciate.

amalgame (amalgam) *m*, amalgam; mixture. **amalgamer** (me) *v.t*, to amalgamate.

amande (amɑ̃;d) *f*, almond. **amandier** (mɑ̃dje) *m*, almond [tree].

amant (amɑ̃) *m*, paramour; lover.

amariner (amarine) *v.t*, to make a sailor of; man (*prize ship*).

amarrage (amara;ʒ) *m*, mooring; docking (*spacecraft*).

amarre (ama;r) *f*, [mooring] rope, fast, line; hawser. **amarrer** (mare) *v.t*, to make fast, moor; lash, seize; berth; belay.

amas (amɑ) *m*, heap, pile, mass, collection; drift (*snow*); hoard. **amasser** (se) *v.t*, to amass, heap [up], pile up, lay up, hoard.

amateur (amatœ;r) *m*, lover (*devotee*); amateur; fancier. *il est*

[*grand*] ~ *de* . . ., he is [very] fond of . . . (*e.g, art, collecting, gardening*); . . . is his hobby.

amazone (amazo;n) *f*, Amazon; horsewoman. [*habit d'*]~, riding habit. l'**A~**, *m*, **le fleuve des A~s**, the Amazon (*river*).

ambages (ãba;ʒ) *f.pl*, circumlocution. *sans* ~, candidly.

ambassade (ãbasad) *f*, embassy; errand. **ambassadeur, drice** (dœ;r, dris) *n*, ambassador, dress; messenger. *l'*~ *de France*, the French ambassador.

ambiance (ãbjã;s) *f*, environment. **ambiant, e** (ã, ã;t) *a*, surrounding, ambient.

ambigu†, **ë** (ãbigy) *a*, ambiguous. ¶ *m*, mixture. **ambiguïté** (gɥite) *f*, ambiguity.

ambitieux, euse† (ãbisjø, ø;z) *a*, ambitious. **ambition** (sjɔ̃) *f*, ambition. **ambitionner** (ɔne) *v.t*, to be eager for, aspire to.

ambre (ã;br) *m*, amber. ~ *gris*, ambergris.

ambroisie (ãbrwazi) *f*, ambrosia.

ambulance (ãbylã;s) *f*, ambulance. **ambulant, e** (lã, ã;t) *a*, itinerant, strolling; traveling.

âme (ɑ;m) *f*, soul, mind, spirit, ghost, life, heart; mainstay; soundpost; core; web; bore (*gun*); motto. *dans l'*~, at heart. ~ *damnée*, [mere] tool (*pers.*).

améliorer (ameljɔre) *v.t, & s'*~, to ameliorate, better, improve, mend; appreciate.

aménager (amenaʒe) *v.t*, to lay out, fit; harness (*waterfall*); reclaim (*submerged land*). **aménagement** (ʒmã) *m*, layout; accommodation, appointments. **aménageur** (aʒœr) *m*, urban planner.

amende (amã;d) *f*, fine. ~ *honorable*, apology.

amender (amãde) *v.t*, to amend; improve.

amène (amɛ;n) *a*, pleasing, agreeable.

amener (amne) *v.t*, to bring, lead; lead up to; haul down; strike (*colors*). *amené de loin*, farfetched. *s'*~, to arrive, turn up.

aménité (amenite) *f*, amenity, graciousness.

amenuiser (amənqize) *v.t*, to thin.

amer, ère† (amɛːr) *a*, bitter; briny. ¶ *m*, bitter, bitterness; (*pl*.) bitters; gall; sea mark, landmark (*Naut*.).

américain, e (amerikɛ̃, ɛn) *a*. & A~, *n*, American. *avoir l'œil* ~, to keep a sharp lookout. *idiotisme* ~, Americanism. **l'Amérique** (rik) *f*, America.

Amerlo, Amerloque (amɛrlo, lɔk) *m*, an American (*slang*).

amerrir (ameriːr) *v.i*, to alight [on the water] (*seaplane*).

amertume (amɛrtym) *f*, bitterness.

ameublement (amœbləmɑ̃) *m*, [suite of] furniture.

ameuter (amøte) *v.t*, to train in a pack (*dogs*); stir up (*mob*). s'~, to assemble.

ami, e (ami) *a*, friendly; kindly. ¶ *n*, friend; lover. ~ *de cœur*, bosom friend. *amis & parents*, kith & kin; *petite* ~*e*, mistress. **amiable**† (mjabl) *a*, **amical, e**† (mikal) *a*, amicable, friendly, kind. *amiable compositeur*, arbitrator (*law*). *à l'amiable*, amicably; by private treaty (*sale*).

amidon (amidɔ̃) *m*, starch. **amidonner** (dɔne) *v.t*, to starch.

amincir (amɛ̃siːr) *v.t*, to thin.

amiral (amiral) *m*, admiral; flagship. ~ *commandant d'escadre*, admiral of the fleet.

amirauté (rote) *f*, admiralty; admiralship.

amitié (amitje) *f*, friendship, kindness, love, liking; (*pl*.) kind regards.

ammoniaque (amɔnjak) *f*, ammonia.

amnistie (amnisti) *f*, amnesty, oblivion.

amodiation (amɔdjasjɔ̃) *f*, leasing (*land, fishing, mining rights*). **amodier**, (ɔdje) *v.t*, to farm out, lease, sublease.

amoindrir (amwɛ̃driːr) *v.t*, to lessen, decrease.

amollir (amɔliːr) *v.t*, to soften, mollify; enervate.

amonceler (amɔ̃sle) *v.t*, to heap [up], pile up, drift.

amont (amɔ̃) *m*, headwaters; upper part. **en** ~, *ad*, upstream, up. **en** ~ **de**, *pr*, above, up.

amorçage (amɔrsaːʒ) *m*, priming; starting (*Elec*.); baiting (*fish*).

amorce (amɔrs) *f*, bait; allurement; [percussion] cap; priming; beginning, start; leader (*tape, etc*.). **amorcer** (se) *v.t*, to bait, etc.; energize (*Elec*.). ~ *un arc*, to strike an arc.

amorphe (amɔrf) *a*, amorphous.

amortir (amɔrtiːr) *v.t*, to deaden, damp; redeem, amortize, sink, pay off; write off, depreciate. **amortisseur** (tisœːr) *m*, shock absorber (*motor*); damper (*Radio*).

amour (amuːr) *m*, love; passion; idol; (*pl*.) love affairs, amours. ~ *intéressé*, cupboard love. ~ *vache*, brutal lovemaking. *mal d'*~, lovesickness. *pour l'*~ *de*, for the sake (*or* love) of. **amouracher** (muraʃe) *v.t*, to enamor. **amoureux, euse**† (rø, øːz) *a*, in love, enamored; loving, amorous; tender, soft. ¶ *n*, lover, sweetheart. **amour-propre** (amurprɔpr) *m*, self-respect, pride; self-esteem.

amovible (amɔvibl) *a*, removable, detachable.

ampère (ɑ̃pɛːr) *m*, ampere.

amphibie (ɑ̃fibi) *a*, amphibious. ¶ *m*, amphibian.

amphithéâtre (ɑ̃fiteɑːtr) *m*, amphitheater.

ample† (ɑ̃ːpl) *a*, ample, full; wide. **ampleur** (ɑ̃plœːr) *f*, ampleness, etc. **ampliation** (pliasjɔ̃) *f*, duplicate, office copy. *pour* ~, [certified] a true copy. **amplificateur** (fikatœːr) *m*, enlarger (*Phot*.); amplifier (*Radio*). **amplifier** (fje) *v.t*, to amplify. **amplitude** (tyd) *f*, amplitude.

ampoule (ɑ̃pul) *f*, phial; blister; bulb (*elec. lamp, thermometer*). **ampoulé, e** (le) *a*, inflated, bombastic, high-flown.

amputer (ɑ̃pyte) *v.t*, to amputate, cut off.

amulette (amylɛt) *f*, amulet, charm.

amure (amyːr) *f*, tack (*sail*).

amuse-gueule (amyːzgœl) *m*, tidbit, cocktail snack.

amuser (amyze) *v.t*, to amuse, entertain; beguile, fool, trifle with. **s'~**, to amuse (*or* enjoy) oneself; dally, loiter. **amuse-ment** (zmɑ̃) *m*, amusement, etc. **amusette** (zɛt) *f*, plaything.

amygdale (amigdal) *f*, tonsil. **amygdalite** (lit) *f*, tonsillitis.

an (ɑ̃) *m*, year. *il a 10 ~s*, he is 10 years old. *le jour de l'~*, New Year's day.

anachorète (anakɔrɛt) *m*, anchoret, anchorite.

anachronisme (anakrɔnism) *m*, anachronism.

analogie (analɔ́ʒi) *f*, analogy. **analogue** (lɔg) *a*, analogous, like.

analyse (anali:z) *f*, analysis. ~ *grammaticale*, parsing. **analyser** (lize) *v.t*, to analyze; parse. **ana-lyseur** (lizœ:r) *m*, analyzer; scan-ner (*TV*). **analyste** (list) *m*, ana-lyst. **analytique†** (tik) *a*, ana-lytic(al).

ananas (anana) *m*, pineapple.

anarchie (anarʃi) *f*, anarchy. **an-archique†** (ʃik) *a*, anarchic(al). **anarchiste** (ʃist) *n. & a*, anarchist.

Anastasie (anastazi) *f*, censor-ship (*slang*).

anatomie (anatɔmi) *f*, anatomy. **anatomique†** (mik) *a*, anatomi-cal.

ancestral, e (ɑ̃sɛstral) *a*, ances-tral. **ancêtre** (sɛ:tr) *m*, ancestor.

anche (ɑ̃:ʃ) *f*, reed (*Mus.*).

anchois (ɑ̃ʃwa) *m*, anchovy.

ancien, ne (ɑ̃sjɛ̃, ɛn) *a*, ancient, old; of long standing; former; bygone; quondam; late, ex-; senior. *ancien combattant*, ex-service man. ¶ *m*, ancient; elder (*Eccl.*). **anciennement** (ɛnmɑ̃) *ad*, anciently, of old, formerly. **ancienneté** (nte) *f*, ancientness, antiquity; seniority. *de toute ~*, from time immemorial.

ancolie (ɑ̃kɔli) *f*, columbine (*Bot.*)

ancrage (ɑ̃kra:ʒ) *m*, anchorage; anchoring.

ancre (ɑ̃:kr) *f*, anchor. ~ *à jet*, kedge [a.]. ~ *de veille* (*Naut.*) & ~ *de salut* (*fig.*), sheet anchor. **ancrer** (ɑ̃kre) (*Build.*) *v.t*, to anchor, fix.

andain (ɑ̃dɛ̃) *m*, swath, wind row.

andouille (ɑ̃du:j) *f*, chitterlings (*sausage*); fool, boob. ~ *de cal-cif*, penis (*obscene*).

andouiller (ɑ̃duje) *m*, tine, ant-ler.

âne (ɑ:n) *m*, ass, jackass, donkey; dunce, dolt.

anéantir (aneɑ̃ti:r) *v.t*, to an-nihilate, crush; prostrate. **s'~**, to humble oneself.

anecdote (anɛgdɔt) *f*, anecdote.

anémie (anemi) *f*, anemia. **anémi-que** (mik) *a*, anemic.

ânerie (ɑnri) *f*, gross stupidity.

anéroïde (aneroid) *a*, aneroid.

ânesse (anɛs) *f*, [she] ass, jenny.

anesthésie (anɛstezi) *f*, anes-thesia. ~ *à la reine*, twilight sleep. **anesthésique** (zik) *a. & m*, anesthetic.

anfractueux, euse (ɑ̃fraktɥǿ, ǿ:z) *a*, winding; craggy.

ange (ɑ̃:ʒ) *m*, angel. ~ *déchu*, fallen a. *être aux ~s*, to be in raptures. **angélique†** (ɑ̃ʒelik) *a*, angelic(al). ¶ *f*, angelica. **An-gélus** (ly:s) *m*, angelus [bell].

angine (ɑ̃ʒin) *f*, angina, quinsy. ~ *de poitrine*, angina pectoris.

anglais, e (ɑ̃glɛ, ɛ:z) *a*, English; British; imperial. **A~**, *n*, English-man, -woman, Briton. *l'anglais*, *m*, English (*language*). *avoir ses ~, les ~ sont débarqués*, to be menstruating (*slang*).

angle (ɑ̃:gl) *m*, angle, corner.

Angleterre (l') (ɑ̃glətɛ:r) *f*, Eng-land. **anglicisme** (glisism) *m*, An-glicism. **anglomanie** (glɔmani) *f*, Anglomania. **les îles Anglo-Nor-mandes**, the Channel Islands. **anglophile** (fil) *a. & n*, Anglo-phile, pro-British. **anglophobe** (fɔb) *a. & n*, Anglophobe, anti-British. **anglo-saxon, ne** (saksɔ̃, ɔn) *a. & A~-S~**, *n*, Anglo-Saxon.

angoisse (ɑ̃gwas) *f*, anguish, pang. **angoisser (se)** *v.t*, to distress, pain. *poire d'~*, choke pear.

angora (ɑ̃gɔra) *m*, Persian [cat].

anguillade (ɑ̃gijad) *f*, lash, cut. **anguille** (ɑ̃gi:j) *f*, eel. ~ *de cale-çon*, penis (*obscene*). ~ *de mer*, conger [eel]. *quelque ~ sous roche* (*fig.*), something in the wind.

angulaire (ɑ̃gylɛ:r) *a*, angular, corner (*att.*). *pierre ~*, corner-stone.

anicroche (anikrɔʃ) *f*, hitch, snag.

ânier, ère (ɑnje, ɛːr) *n*, donkey driver.

animal, e (animal) *a*, animal. ¶ *m*, animal, dumb animal, beast, brute; creature.

animateur, trice (animatœːr, tris) *n*, animator, moving spirit; disk jockey (*Radio*); host, emcee (*TV, Radio*); cartoonist (*cinema*). **animation** (sjɔ̃) *f*, animation, liveliness, bustle, life. **animé, e** (me) *a*, animate; animated, lively, buoyant, spirited, brisk, bustling, agog, astir; instinct. **animer** (me) *v.t*, to animate, quicken, brighten, enliven, inspirit; actuate, impel.

animosité (animozite) *f*, animosity, animus, spite.

anis (ani) *m*, anise. [*graine d'*]~, aniseed.

ankylose (ɑ̃kiloːz) *f*, anchylosis; cramp. **ankyloser** (lose) *v.t*, to stiffen.

annales (anal) *f.pl*, annals.

anneau (ano) *m*, ring; coil (*snake*); ringlet; link.

année (ane) *f*, year, twelvemonth. ~ *à millésime*, vintage year.

annexe (anɛks) *f*, annex; dependency (*country*); schedule; enclosure; tender (*boat*). *lettre* ~, covering letter. **annexer** (kse) *v.t*, to annex, attach. **annexion** (ksjɔ̃) *f*, annexation.

annihiler (aniile) *v.t*, to annihilate; annul.

anniversaire (anivɛrsɛːr) *a & m*, anniversary. *l'*~ *de ma naissance*, my birthday.

annonce (anɔ̃ːs) *f*, announcement, advertisement; bans. ~-*article, f*, puff paragraph. ~ *de fantaisie*, ~ *courante*, display advertisement. *petite annonce*, classified ad. **annoncer** (nɔ̃se) *v.t*, to announce, advertise, proclaim, herald; give out; betoken, foreshadow; inform; state; show in, usher in; preach; foretell. *ça s'annonce bien*, that's promising. **annonceur** (sœːr) *m*, advertiser; announcer. **l'Annonciation** (sjasjɔ̃) *f*, the Annunciation, Lady Day.

annoter (anɔte) *v.t*, to annotate.

annuaire (anɥɛːr) *m*, annual, year book, directory (*telephone*); list (*Army, Navy, etc.*). **annuel,**

le† (nɥɛl) *a*, annual, yearly. **annuité** (nɥite) *f*, annuity.

annulaire (anylɛːr) *a*, annular. [*doigt*] ~, *m*, ring finger, third f.

annulation (anylasjɔ̃) *f*, annulment; cancellation.

annuler (anyle) *v.t*, to annul, nullify, quash, cancel; contra.

anoblir (anɔbliːr) *v.t*, to ennoble.

anode (anɔd) *f*, anode.

anodin, e (anɔdɛ̃, in) *a*, anodyne, soothing; harmless, mild, tame. ¶ *m*, anodyne.

anomal, e (anɔmal) *a*, anomalous. **anomalie** (li) *f*, anomaly.

ânon (ɑnɔ̃) *m*, young ass, foal. **ânonner** (nɔne) *v.i*, to falter, hem & haw.

anonyme (anɔnim) *a*, anonymous; unnamed.

anormal, e (anɔrmal) *a*, abnormal.

anse (ɑ̃ːs) *f*, handle; bow; cove. *faire le pot à deux* ~*s*, to set one's arms akimbo.

anspect (ɑ̃spɛk) *m*, handspike.

antagonisme (ɑ̃tagɔnism) *m*, antagonism. **antagoniste** (nist) *m*, antagonist, opponent.

antan (ɑ̃tɑ̃) *m*, yesteryear.

antarctique (ɑ̃tar[k]tik) *a*, antarctic.

antécédent, e (ɑ̃tesedɑ̃, ɑ̃ːt) *a. & m*, antecedent.

antédiluvien, ne (ɑ̃tedilyvjɛ̃, ɛn) *a*, antediluvian.

antenne (ɑ̃tɛn) *f*, antenna, feeler, horn; aerial (*Radio*); branch line (*Rly.*). ~ *d'appartement*, indoor aerial. *droit à l'*~, right to broadcast time.

antérieur, e† (ɑ̃terjœːr) *a*, anterior, prior, previous. **antériorité** (rjɔrite) *f*, priority.

anthère (ɑ̃tɛːr) *f*, anther.

anthologie (ɑ̃tɔlɔʒi) *f*, anthology.

anthracite (ɑ̃trasit) *m*, anthracite.

anthrax (ɑ̃traks) *m*, carbuncle. (*Med.*)

anthropophage (ɑ̃trɔpɔfaːʒ) *a. & m*, cannibal.

anti-aérien, ne (ɑ̃tiaerjɛ̃, ɛn) *a*, antiaircraft.

antialcoolique (ɑ̃tialkɔɔlik) *a*, teetotal.

anti-aveuglant (ɑ̃tiavœglɑ̃) *a*, antiglare, antidazzle.

antichambre (ãtiʃãːbr) *f*, ante-chamber, anteroom. *faire~chez,* to dance attendance on.

antichar (ãtiʃaːr) *m*, antitank weapon.

anticipation (ãtisipasjɔ̃) *f*, anticipation, advance. **anticiper** (pe) *v.t*, to anticipate, forestall. ~ *sur,* to encroach on.

antidater (ãtidate) *v.t*, to ante-date.

antidérapant, e (ãtiderapã, ãːt) *a*, nonskid.

antidote (ãtidɔt) *m*, antidote.

antienne (ãtjɛn) *f*, anthem.

antigel (ãtiʒel) *m*, antifreeze.

Antilles (les) (ãtiːj) *f.pl*, the West Indies, the Antilles. *la mer des ~,* the Caribbean sea.

antilope (ãtilɔp) *f*, antelope.

antimoine (ãtimwan) *m*, anti-mony.

antipathie (ãtipati) *f*, antipathy, dislike. **antipathique** (tik) *a*, antipathetic.

antipatriotique (ãtipatriɔtik) *a*, unpatriotic.

antipodes (ãtipɔd) *m.pl*, antipodes.

antiquailles (ãtikaːj) *f.pl*, worthless antiques. **antiquaire** (kɛːr) *n*, antiquary, -rian. **antique** (tik) *a*, ancient, antique. ¶ *m*, antique *(style); (f.)* antique *(relic).* *magasin d'~s,* antique shop. **antiquité** (kite) *f*, antiquity.

antiseptique (ãtisɛptik) *a. & m*, antiseptic; preservative *(for perishable foodstuffs).*

antithèse (ãtiteːz) *f*, antithesis.

antivol (ãtivɔl) *m*, ignition lock; theft-proof device *(bicycle, etc.).*

antre (ãːtr) *m*, cave, den, lair.

anus (anyːs) *m*, anus.

Anvers (ãvɛːr, -vɛrs) *m*, Antwerp. **anversois, e** (vɛrswa, aːz) *a*, of Antwerp.

anxiété (ãksjete) *f*, anxiety. **anxieux, euse** (ksjø, øːz) *a*, anxious.

aorte (aɔrt) *f*, aorta.

août (u) *m*, August. **aoûtien, ne** (jɛ̃, jɛn) *n*, person who vacations in August.

apache (apaʃ) *m*, Apache, desperado; hooligan, rough.

apaiser (apɛze) *v.t*, to appease, allay, assuage, quiet, quell, quench. **s'~,** to abate.

aparté (aparte) *m*, aside, stage whisper.

apathie (apati) *f*, apathy, **apathique** (tik) *a*, apathetic, lacka-daisical.

apatride (apatrid) *m*, stateless person.

apercevoir (apɛrsəvwaːr) *v.t*, to perceive, see, espy. **s'~,** to perceive, find. **apercu** (sy) *m*, out-line, summary; rough estimate; insight.

apéritif (aperitif) *m*, appetizer.

à-peu-près (apøprɛ) *m*, approximation, rough estimate.

aphone (afɔn) *a*, voiceless, aphonic.

aphorisme (afɔrism) *m*, aphorism.

apiculture (apikyltyːr) *f*, bee-keeping.

apitoyer (apitwaje) *v.t*, to move to pity.

aplanir (aplaniːr) *v.t*, to level; smooth.

aplatir (aplatiːr) *v.t*, to flat[ten]; squash; smooth; plane. **aplatisse-ment** (tismã) *m*, flatt[en]ing; flat-ness.

aplomb (aplɔ̃) *m*, perpendicular-ity, plumb; self-possession. **d'~,** plumb, upright.

Apocalypse (apɔkalips) *f*, Revelation, Apocalypse.

apogée (apɔʒe) *m*, apogee; height; zenith, acme, high-water mark *(fig.).*

apologétique (apɔlɔʒetik) *a*, apologetic. **apologie** (ʒi) *f*, apologia, justification.

apoplectique (apɔplɛktik) *a. & m*, apoplectic. **apoplexie** (ksi) *f*, apoplexy.

apostasie (apɔstazi) *f*, apostasy, defection. **apostat** (ta) *m. & att*, apostate.

aposter (apɔste) *v.t*, to station, post, set.

apostille (apɔstiːj) *f*, marginal note, side note; recommendation. **apostiller** (tije) *v.t*, to make a note on.

apostolat (apɔstɔla) *m*, aposto-late, apostleship. **apostolique†** (lik) *a*, apostolic(al).

apostrophe (apɔstrɔf) *f*, apos-trophe; reproach. **apostropher**

(fe) *v.t*, to apostrophize; upbraid.

apothéose (apɔteo:z) *f*, apotheosis.

apôtre (apo:tr) *m*, apostle. *bon ~*, hypocrite.

apparaître (aparɛ:tr) *v.i.ir*, to appear.

apparat (apara) *m*, state, show, pomp.

appareil (aparɛ:j) *m*, array; apparatus, appliance, plant, gear, tackle, rig; telephone; attachment (*to machine*); dressing (*on wound*); camera. *~ dentaire*, dental brace. *~ reflex*, reflex camera. *~ à sous*, coin-operated or slot machine. **appareillage** (ja:ʒ) *m*, installation; equipment; preparation; accessories; matching (colors, etc.); getting under weigh (*Naut.*). **appareiller** (rɛje) *v.t. & i*, to match, pair, mate; fit; get under weigh. **appareilleur** (jœ:r) *m*, fitter.

apparemment (aparamɑ̃) *ad*, apparently. **apparence** (rɑ̃:s) *f*, appearance, look; guise; likelihood. **apparent, e** (rɑ̃, ɑ̃:t) *a*, apparent, seeming.

apparenté, e (apparɑ̃te) *a*, related, akin, connected. **apparenter** (te) *v.t*, to connect, ally. **s'~**, to marry (*à =* into); blend.

apparier (aparje) *v.t*, to match, pair.

appariteur (aparitœ:r) *m*, usher; beadle.

apparition (aparisjɔ̃) *f*, appearance, advent; apparition.

appartement (apartəmɑ̃) *m*, [suite of] rooms, apartment.

appartenir (apartəni:r) *v.i.ir*, to belong, [ap]pertain, concern. **s'~**, to be one's own master *or* mistress.

appas (apɑ) *m.pl*, attractions, charms. **appât** (pɑ) *m*, bait, allurement; lure, draw. **appâter** (te) *v.t*, to bait; allure; cram (*poultry*).

appauvrir (apovri:r) *v.t*, to impoverish, beggar; thin (*wine*).

appeau (apo) *m*, bird call.

appel (apɛl) *m*, call, calling [up]; appeal; invitation; muster; challenge. *~ telephonique*, phone

call. *~ de fonds*, call. *~[nominal]*, roll call, muster, call over. *en ~ à*, to appeal to. **appelant** (plɑ̃) *m*, decoy bird. **appeler** (ple) *v.t. & i*, to call; term; appeal; invite; challenge. **s'~**, to be called. *je m'appelle Adam*, my name is Adam.

appendice (apɛ̃dis) *m*, appendage, appendix. **appendicite** (sit) *f*, appendicitis.

appendre (apɑ̃:dr) *v.t*, to hang up.

appentis (apɑ̃ti) *m*, lean-to, penthouse; outhouse.

appesantir (apəzɑ̃ti:r) *v.t*, to make heavy, dull, weigh down.

appéter (appete) *v.t*, to crave for, long for.

appétissant, e (apetisɑ̃, ɑ̃:t) *a*, appetizing, tempting. **appétit** (ti) *m*, appetite; desire, lust.

applaudir (aplodi:r) *v.t. & i*, to applaud, cheer. *~ à*, to commend. **s'~ de**, to congratulate oneself on. **applaudissement** (dismɑ̃) *m. oft. pl*, applause, cheer, plaudit.

application (aplikasjɔ̃) *f*, application; infliction; diligence. [*dentelle d'*]~, appliqué lace. **applique** (plik) *f*, appliqué [work] (*metal*); sconce, bracket. **appliqué, e** (ke) *p.a*, applied; close, studious. **appliquer** (ke) *v.t*, to apply, put, lay on; give charge; inflict. **s'~ à**, to apply oneself to.

appoint (apwɛ̃) *m*, addition; small coin, [small] change, odd money; help. **appointements** (tmɑ̃) *m.pl*, salary. **appointer** (te) *v.t*, to put on a salary basis (*in p.p*, salaried); point; sew up, stitch together.

appontement (apɔ̃tmɑ̃) *m*, wharf.

apport (apɔ:r) *m*, bringing; transfer, assignment; capital brought in; assets transferred *or* taken over; contribution; collection (*of goods by Rly. Co.*); drift (*Geol.*). *valeurs d'~*, vendor's assets. **apporter** (porte) *v.t*, to bring, fetch; transfer, assign; give; waft. **apportel** fetch it! (*to dog*). **apporteur** (tœ:r) *m*, vendor.

apposer (apoze) *v.t*, to affix, put,

append, set. **apposition** (zisjɔ̃) *f*, affixture, etc; apposition. **en ~** (*Gram.*), in apposition; attributively.

appréciable (apresjabl) *a*, appreciable; measurable. **appréciation** (sjɔ̃) *f*, valuation, estimate; appreciation. **apprécier** (sje) *v.t*, to value; estimate; esteem.

appréhender (apreɑ̃de) *v.t*, to apprehend; arrest. **appréhension** (sjɔ̃) *f*, apprehension; arrest.

apprendre (aprɑ̃:dr) *v.t. & abs. ir*, to learn, hear, understand; teach; inform, tell. *mal appris*, ill-bred.

apprenti, e (aprɑ̃ti) *n*, apprentice; learner; novice, tyro. **apprentissage** (sa:ʒ) *m*, apprenticeship; articles. *mettre en ~*, to apprentice.

apprêt (apre) *m*, dressing; affectation; editing (*computers*); (*pl.*) preparations. **apprêté, e** (te) *a*, affected. **apprêter** (te) *v.t*, to prepare, dress prime.

apprivoiser (aprivwaze) *v.t*, to tame. **s' ~**, to grow tame; become sociable.

approbation (aprɔbasjɔ̃) *f*, approbation, approval, confirmation.

approchant, e (aprɔʃɑ̃, ɑ̃:t) *a*, approximating, like. **approche** (prɔʃ) *f*, approach. **approcher** (ʃe) *v.t. & i*, to approach, draw near; resemble, border on.

approfondi, e (aprɔfɔ̃di) *p.a*, thorough, exhaustive. **approfondir** (di:r) *v.t*, to deepen; dive into.

approprier (aprɔprie) *v.t*, to adapt, suit. **s' ~**, to appropriate.

approuver (apruve) *v.t*, to approve, countenance, confirm, pass.

approvisionner (aprɔvizjɔne) *v.t*, to supply, store, stock, provision. **s' ~ de**, to lay in [a stock of]. **approvisionnement** (nmɑ̃) *m*, supplying, etc; supply, etc.

approximatif, ive† (aprɔksimatif, i:v) *a*, approximate, rough. **approximation** (sjɔ̃) *f*, approximation.

appui (apɥi) *m*, support, rest; fulcrum; stress (*Gram.*); windowsill. *à hauteur d'~*, elbow-high, breast-high. **~-bras**, armrest. **~-**

tête, headrest. **~-main**, maulstick. **appuyer** (pɥije) *v.t. & i*, to support; back; second; hold up; lean, rest; bear; press; lay stress. **s'~**, to rest, lean; rely, depend.

âpre† (ɑ:pr) *a*, rough, harsh; sharp; ruthless; greedy, grasping.

après (apre) *pr*, after. *ap. J.-C.*, *A.D.* ¶ *ad*, after[wards]. **~ que**, *c*, after, when. **d'~**, *pr*, according to, after, from. **~ coup**, *ad*, too late, after the event, a day after the fair. **~-demain**, *ad. & m*, the day after tomorrow. **d'~-guerre**, *a*, postwar. **~-midi**, *m*, afternoon. *de l'~-midi*, post meridiem, p.m.

âpreté (aprəte) *f*, roughness, etc, as *âpre*; asperity.

à-propos (aprɔpo) *m*, aptness; opportuneness.

apte (apt) *a*, fit[ted], competent, qualified; apt. **aptitude** (tityd) *f*, aptitude, aptness, etc; faculty, flair.

apurer (apyre) *v.t*, to agree, reconcile; wipe off (*debt, etc.*); audit; get discharged, get canceled.

aquafortiste (akwafɔrtist) *m*, etcher.

aquaplane (akwaplan) *m*, surfboard.

aquarelle (akwarɛl) *f*, watercolor.

aquarium (akwarjɔm) *m*, aquarium.

aquatique (akwatik) *a*, aquatic, water (*att.*).

aqueduc (akdyk) *m*, aqueduct.

aqueux, euse (akø, ø:z) *a*, aqueous, watery.

à quia (kɥia), nonplussed.

aquilin (akilɛ̃) *a.m*, aquiline, hook[ed], Roman (*nose*).

ara (ara) *m*, macaw, ara.

arabe (arab) *a*, Arab; Arabian; Arabic. ¶ *m*, Arabic (*language*). **A~**, *n*, Arab[ian] (*pers.*). **arabesque** (bɛsk) *f*, arabesque, l'**Arabie** (bi) *f*, Arabia. **Arabique** (bik) *a*, Arabian (*gulf*).

arable (arabl) *a*, arable, tillable.

arachide (araʃid) *f*, groundnut, peanut, monkey nut.

araignée (arɛɲe) *f*, spider.

aratoire (aratwa:r) *a*, agricultural, farming.

arbitrage (arbitra:ӡ) *m*, arbitration; arbitrament; arbitrage. **arbitrairet** (trɛ:r) *a*, arbitrary; high-handed. **arbitre** (tr) *m*, arbitrator, arbiter; referee, umpire. *libre* ~, freewill. ~ *de lignes*, linesman (*Ten.*). **arbitrer** (tre) *v.t*, to arbitrate; arrange; referee, umpire.

arborer (arbɔre) *v.t*, to raise, hoist, set up; flaunt.

arbre (arbr) *m*, tree; shaft, axle, spindle, mandrel, -il, arbor. ~ *de haute futaie*, timber tree. ~ *de plein vent*, standard. ~ *en espalier*, wall tree. ~ *moteur*, ~ *de couche*, driving shaft. ~ *toujours vert*, evergreen. **arbrisseau** (briso) *m*, shrub.

arbuste (arbyst) *m*, bush.

arc ark) *m*, bow; arc; arch. **arcade** (kad) *f*, archway; arch; (*pl.*) arcade.

arc-boutant (arkbutɑ̃) *m*, [flying] buttress; raking shore; strut, spur, brac. **arc-bouter** (te) *v.t*, to buttress.

arceau (arso) *m*, arch; hoop; cradle (*Surg.*).

arc-en-ciel (arkɑ̃sjɛl) *m*, rainbow.

archaïque (arkaik) *a*, archaic.

archange (arkɑ̃ӡ) *m*, archangel.

arche (arʃ) *f*, arch; ark. *l'~ d'alliance*, the Ark of the Covenant. *l'~ de Noé* (nɔe), Noah's ark.

archéologie (arkeɔlɔӡi) *f*, archaeology. **archéologique** (ӡik) *a*, archaeologic(al). **archéologue** (lɔg) *m*, archaeologist.

archer (arʃe) *m*, archer, bowman. **archet** (ʃɛ) *m*, bow, fiddlestick.

archevêché (arʃəveʃe) *m*, archbishopric; palace. **archevêque** (vɛ:k) *m*, archbishop.

archidiacre (arʃidjakr) *m*, archdeacon.

archipel (arʃipɛl) *m*, archipelago.

architecte (arʃitɛkt) *m*, architect. **architectural, e** (tyral) *a*, architectural. **architecture** (ty:r) *f*, architecture.

archives (arʃi:v) *f.pl*, archives, records.

arçon (arsɔ̃) *m*, saddle bow; bow.

arctique (arktik) *a*, arctic.

ardent, e (ardɑ̃, ɑ̃:t) *a*, burning, hot, fiery, raging, blazing, live; ardent, keen, fervent, fervid, eager, earnest, spirited; passionate. **ardemment** (damɑ̃) *ad*, ardently, etc. **ardeur** (dœ:r) *f*, ardor, heat, etc; zest. ~ *d'estomac*, heartburn.

ardoise (ardwa:z) *f*, slate. **ardoisé, e** (dwaze) *a*, s.-colored. **ardoisière** (zjɛ:r) *f*, s. quarry.

ardu, e (ardy) *a*, steep; arduous, hard, uphill.

are (a:r) *m*, are = 100 square meters *or* 119.60 sq. yards.

arène (arɛn) *f*, arena, lists, ring; cockpit; sand (*Poet.*).

arête (arɛt) *f*, [fish]bone; ridge, edge, arris; arête; groin, hip (*Arch.*); awn, beard (*Bot.*). ~ *vive*, sharp edge.

argent (arӡɑ̃) *m*, silver; money; cash. ~ *comptant*, ready money, spot cash. ~ *doré*, silver-gilt. *un* ~ *fou*, a mint of money. ~ *liquide*, ready money. ~ *mignon*, small savings (*to spend on pleasure*). ~*sec*, hard cash. ~ *sur table*, cash down. **argenter** (te) *v.t*, to silver[-plate], [electro]plate. **argenterie** (tri) *f*, silver, [s.] plate. **argentin, e** (tɛ̃, in) *a*, argentine, silvery, silvern. ¶ *a. & A~, n*, Argentine (*Geog.*). **l'Argentine, *f***, the Argentina.

argile (arӡil) *f*, clay. ~ *réfractaire*, fire clay. **argileux, euse** (lø, ø:z) *a*, clayey, argillaceous.

argot (argo) *m*, slang.

arguer (argчe) *v.t*, to infer, deduce. **argument** (gymɑ̃) *m*, argument; synopsis. **argumenter** (te) *v.t*, to argue.

argutie (argysi) *f*, quibble, cavil, hairsplitting.

aria (arja) *m*, bother, ado, to-do.

aride (arid) *a*, arid, dry, barren. **aridité** (dite) *f*, aridity, etc.

aristocrate (aristɔkrat) *n*, aristocrat. ¶ *att. &* **aristocratiquet** (tik) *a*, aristocratic(al). **aristocratie** (si) *f*, aristocracy.

arithméticien, ne (aritmetisjɛ̃, ɛn) *n*, arithmetician. **arithmétiquet** (tik) *a*, arithmetical. ¶ *f*, arithmetic.

arlequin (arləkɛ̃) *m*, harlequin;

turncoat (*pers.*); scraps, leavings, leftovers, orts, hash. **arlequinade** (kinad) *f*, harlequinade.

armateur (armatœːr) *m*, [ship]-owner, [registered] manager (*ship's*).

armature (armatyːr) *f*, trussing; bracing; fastening; strap; reinforcement; armor, sheathing, plating; gear (*pump*); armature (*Phys.*); key signature (*Mus.*); framework (*fig.*).

arme (arm) *f*, arm, weapon; (*pl.*) arms (*Mil.*); branch of the service; [coat of] arms, [armorial] bearings. ~ *à feu*, firearm. ~ [*à feu*] *portative*, small arm. ~ *blanche*, side arm; cold steel. *sans* ~*s*, unarmed. *faire* (*ou tirer*) *des* ~*s*, to fence. *faire ses premières* ~*s*, to participate in one's first battle; make one's debut.

armée (arme) *f*, army, force[s]; host. ~ *active*, regular army. *A*~ *du Salut*, Salvation Army. *zone des* ~*s*, theater of operations.

armeline (arməlin) *f*, ermine (*fur*).

armement (arməmɑ̃) *m*, arming; armament; fitting out, equipment; manning; shipping; ship-owners.

Arménie (l') (armeni) *f*, Armenia. **arménien, ne** (njɛ̃, ɛn) *a*. & *A*~, *n*, Armenian.

armer (arme) *v.t*, to arm; fit out, equip; man; commission (*ship*); truss, brace; reinforce, armor, sheathe; set (*Phot. shutter*); cock (*gun*), sign (*clef*); dub (*knight*); (*v.i.*) to arm.

armoire (armwaːr) *f*, cupboard, cabinet, wardrobe. ~ *à pharmacie*, medicine cabinet. ~ *vitrée*, display cabinet, china cabinet.

armoiries (armwari) *f.pl*, [coat of] arms, [armorial] bearings. **armorial, e** (mɔrjal) *a*. & *m*, armorial. **armorier** (rje) *v.t*, to [em]blazon.

armure (armyːr) *f*, armor, sheathing; armature (*Phys.*). ~ *complète*, suit of armor. **armurier** (myrje) *m*, gunsmith; armorer.

arnaque (arnak) *f*, swindle, trickery, sting. **arnaquer** (ke) *v.t*, to swindle.

arnica (arnika) *f*, arnica.

aromatique (arɔmatik) *a*, aromatic. **arôme** (roːm) *m*, aroma.

arpège (arpɛːʒ) *m*, arpeggio.

arpent (arpɑ̃) *m*, acre.

arpentage (arpɑ̃taːʒ) *m*, land measuring, surveying. **arpenter** (te) *v.t*, to measure, survey; pace, tramp. **arpenteur** (tœːr) *m*, [land] surveyor.

arquer (arke) *v.t*. & *i*. & *s'*~, to arch, curve, bend.

arrache-clou (araʃklu) *m*, nail extractor. **d'arrache-pied**, *ad*, without intermission; on end, at a stretch. **arracher** (ʃe) *v.t*, to pluck, pull, tear, draw; drag; uproot, dig up; extract; wring; snatch; squeeze, extort, screw out. **arracheur, euse** (ʃœːr, øːz) *n*, drawer, puller; (*f.*) grubber.

arraisonner (arɛzɔne) *v.t*, to visit. (*Cust.*).

arrangeant, e (arɑ̃ʒɑ̃, ɑ̃ːt) *a*, accommodating, obliging. **arrangement** (ʒmɑ̃) *m*, arrangement; settlement. **arranger** (ʒe) *v.t*, to arrange; settle (lawsuit). *s'*~, to agree, come to terms; settle down; get on, manage. *arrangez-vous!* do the best you can! do as you like!

arrenter (arɑ̃te) *v.t*, to lease.

arrérager (areraʒe) *v.i*, to get (*or* fall) into arrear[s]. **arrérages** (raːʒ) *m.pl*, interest (*on Government stocks or the like*); rent, pension, or the like, accrued & due.

arrestation (arɛstasjɔ̃) *f*, arrest, custody. **arrêt** (rɛ) *m*, stoppage; stop; arrest; seizure, detention; standstill; catch; tackle (*Foot.*); judgment, sentence; decree. ~ *en cours de route*, break of journey. ~ *facultatif*, cars stop here if requested. ~ *fixe*, all cars stop here. *aux* ~*s*, under arrest (*Mil.*); kept in (*Sch.*). ~ *d'urgence*, emergency shutdown, scram (*atomic physics*). ~ *sur l'image*, freeze frame (*cinema*). *chien d'* ~, setter, pointer. *prononcer un* ~, to pass sentence. **arrêté, e** (te) *p.a*, decided, settled, preconcerted. ¶ *m*, order, decree; making up, closing, ruling off, rest

(*Bkkpg.*). **arrêter** (te) *v.t. & i*, to stop; arrest; seize, detain; fix; retain, engage; conclude; make up, close, rule off (*Bkkpg.*); fasten off (*Need.*); agree upon; decide on; (*v.t. & abs.*) point, set (*dog*). s'~, to stop, stay, call; draw up (*car*).

arrhes (aːr) *f.pl*, deposit, earnest [money].

arrière (arjɛːr) *m*, back [part]; back (*Foot.*); rear; tail; stern. **en ~**, behind; behind-hand; back, at the back, in the rear; astern; with one's back to the engine. *Note: arrière in comps is pronounced* arjɛr, *thus*, ~-**bouche** (arjɛrbuʃ) *f*, fauces. ~-**garde**, *f*, rear guard. **arrière-grand-mère**, *f*, **arrière-grand-père**, *m*, great-grandmother, -father. ~-**main**, *m*, backhand (*Ten.*). ~-**neveu**, *m*, ~-**nièce**, *f*, grandnephew, -niece. ~-**pensée**, *f*, ulterior motive, mental reservation. ~-**petite-fille**, *f*, great-granddaughter. ~-**petit-fils**, *m*, g.-grandson. ~-**petits-enfants**, *m.pl*, g.-grandchildren. ~-**plan**, *m*, background. ~-**point**, *m*, backstitch (*Need.*). ~-**port**, *m*, inner harbor. **arriéré, e** (rjere) *a*, overdue, in arrear[s]; outstanding, owing; behindhand; backward (*child*); old-fashioned. ¶ *m*, arrears. **arriérer** (re) *v.t*, to put off, defer, hold over. s'~, to fall behind; get into arrears.

arrimer (arime) *v.t*, to stow, trim. **arrimeur** (mœːr) *m*, stower, trimmer; stevedore.

arrivage (arivaːʒ) *m*, arrival. **arrivée** (ve) *f*, arrival, coming; finish[ing] (*sport*), [winning] post; home (*running*); inlet. **à l'~ & d'~**, incoming; at the finish, finishing. **arriver** (ve) *v.i*, to arrive, come; get; finish; happen, come about, c. to pass, occur, befall; be due (*train*); succeed. ~ **à égalité**, to tie (*sport*). *arrive que pourra*, come what may. **en ~ à**, to come to, be reduced to. **arriviste** (arivist) *m.f*, pusher, social climber.

arrogamment (arɔgamɑ̃) *ad*, arrogantly. **arrogance** (gɑ̃ːs) *f*, arrogance, assumption. **arrogant, e** (gɑ̃, ɑ̃ːt) *a*, arrogant, overbearing. **s'arroger** (ɔʒe)

v.pr, to arrogate [to oneself]; assume.

arroi (arwa) *m*, plight, pickle.

arrondir (arɔ̃diːr) *v.t*, to round [off]. **arrondissement** (dismɑ̃) *m*, rounding; ward, district.

arroser (aroze) *v.t*, to water, [be]sprinkle, bedew, wet; baste; stand treat. *ça s'arrose*, that calls for a drink. **arrosoir** (zwaːr) *m*, watering can.

arsenal (arsənal) *m*, arsenal. ~ **maritime**, naval dockyard.

art (aːr) *m*, art, skill; artfulness; artifice. ~**s d'agrément**, accomplishments. *septième* ~, cinema. *huitième* ~, television.

artère (artɛːr) *f*, artery; thoroughfare; feeder (*Elec.*). **artériel, le** (terjel) *a*, arterial.

artésien, ne (artezjɛ̃, ɛn) *a*, Artesian.

arthrite (artrit) *f*, arthritis.

artichaut (artiʃo) *m*, artichoke; spikes.

article (artikl) *m*, article, subject, matter; section, clause, item, entry; requisite, material, commodity; (*pl.*) wares. ~ **à côté**, side line. ~ **de fond**, leading article, leader. ~ **de tête**, lead story (*newspaper*). ~[s] **de Paris**, artistic novelties, fancy goods. ~**s dépareillés**, oddments.

articulation (artikylasjɔ̃) *f*, articulation, joint; deployment; knuckle; utterance. **articuler** (le) *v.t. & i. & s'~*, to articulate, joint; link; utter.

artifice (artifis) *m*, artifice, artfulness; craft; contrivance; art. ~**s de théâtre**, stage effects. **artificiel, le†** (sjel) *a*, artificial. **artificier** (sje) *m*, pyrotechnist. **artificieux, euse†** (sjø, øːz) *a*, artful, cunning, crafty.

artillerie (artijri) *f*, artillery, ordnance; gunnery. ~ **de place**, garrison artillery. **artilleur** (jœːr) *m*, artilleryman, gunner.

artimon (artimɔ̃) *m*, mizzen mast; m. sail.

artisan, e (artizɑ̃, an) *n*, artisan; craftsman; operative; (*fig.*) author, originator, artificer, architect. ~ **en bois**, woodworker.

artison (artizɔ̃) *m*, wood worm;

clothes moth. **artisonné, e** (zɔne)
a, worm-eaten; moth-eaten.

artiste (artist) *n*, artist; artiste,
performer. **artiste†** & **artistique**
(tik) *a*, artistic.

aryen, ne (arjɛ̃, ɛn) *a*, Aryan.

as (ɑːs) *m*, ace. ~ *de l'aviation*,
flying ace. ~ *de pique*, ace of
spades (*Cards*); rump, parson's
nose (*fowl*).

asbeste (azbɛst) *m*, asbestos.

ascendance (asɑ̃dɑ̃ːs) *f*, ancestry.

ascendant, e (asɑ̃dɑ̃, ɑ̃ːt) *a*, ascending, upward. ¶ *m*, ascendant, -ent; ascendancy, -ency;
(*pl.*) ancestry. **ascenseur** (sœːr)
m, elevator. **ascension** (sjɔ̃) *f*,
ascent, climb, rising, ascension.
l'A~, Ascension day. **ascensionniste** (ɔnist) *n*, climber, mountaineer.

ascète (asɛt) *n*. & **ascétique**
(setik) *a*, ascetic.

asiatique (azjatik) *a*. & A~, *n*,
Asiatic. **l'Asie** (zi) *f*, Asia. *l'~
Mineure*, Asia Minor.

asile (azil) *m*, asylum, shelter;
home; haven, sanctuary. ~ *d'a-
liénés*, mental institution.

aspect (aspɛ) *m*, aspect, sight, appearance, look, bearing; complexion.

asperge (aspɛrʒ) *f*, asparagus.

asperger (aspɛrʒe) *v.t*, to [be]-
sprinkle, asperse.

aspérité (asperite) *f*, asperity,
roughness.

aspersion (aspɛrsjɔ̃) *f*, aspersion,
sprinkling.

asphalte (asfalt) *m*, asphalt.

asphyxie (asfiksi) *f*, asphyxia,
suffocation, gassing. **asphyxier**
(sje) *v.t*, to asphyxiate, etc.

aspic (aspik) *m*, asp; slanderer,
backbiter; aspic.

aspirail (aspiraj) *m*, air hole,
vent, flue.

aspirant, e (aspirɑ̃, ɑ̃ːt) *n*, aspirant, suitor; candidate. ~ [*de
marine*], midshipman. **aspirateur
[de poussières]** (ratœːr) *m*, vacuum cleaner. **aspiration** (sjɔ̃) *f*,
aspiration; inspiration; yearning.
aspirer (re) *v.t*, to inspire, inhale,
exhaust, suck, draw; aspirate;
(*v.i.*) to aspire.

aspirine (aspirin) *f*, aspirin.

assagir (asaʒiːr) *v.t*, to make
wiser; sober; steady.

assaillant (asajɑ̃) *m*, assailant.
assaillir (jiːr) *v.t.ir*, to assail,
assault.

assainir (asɛniːr) *v.t*, to cleanse,
sanitate.

assaisonnement (asɛzɔnmɑ̃) *m*,
seasoning, flavoring; dressing
(*salad*); condiment, relish. **assaisonner** (ne) *v.t*, to season, etc.
leaven (*fig.*).

assassin, e (asasɛ̃, in) *n*, assassin,
murderer, ess. *à l'~!* murder!
¶ *a*, bewitching, killing (*looks,
eyes*). **assassinat** (sina) *m*, assas-
sination, murder. **assassiner** (ne)
v.t, to assassinate, murder, kill;
tire to death, bore, plague.

assaut (aso) *m*, assault, storming,
onset, onslaught; match, bout.
~ *d'armes*, assault of (*or* at)
arms, fencing match. ~ *de démonstration*, sparring match.

assèchement (asɛʃmɑ̃) *m*, drainage; drying. **assécher** (seʃe) *v.t.
& i*, to drain, dry.

assemblage (asɑ̃blaːʒ) *m*, assemblage, congregation; joint
(*in wood, metal, etc.*). **assemblée** (ble) *f*, meeting, assembly,
conclave, congregation; meet
(*Hunt.*). **assembler** (ble), *v.t*, to
assemble, collect, gather, summon; join. **s'~**, to meet, assemble, congregate, flock.

assener (asəne) *v.t*, to strike,
deal (*blow*).

assentiment (asɑ̃timɑ̃) *m*, assent.

asseoir (aswaːr) *v.t.ir*, to seat, set,
bed, base, fix, secure, establish;
pitch (*camp, tent*). **s'~**, to sit
[down].

assermenter (asɛrmɑ̃te) *v.t*, to
swear in.

assertion (asɛrsjɔ̃) *f*, assertion.

asservir (asɛrviːr) *v.t*, to enslave.

assez (ase) *ad*, enough, rather,
pretty, fairly.

assidu, e (asidy) *a*, assiduous,
sedulous, industrious; regular.
assiduité (dµite) *f*, assiduity, etc.
assidûment (dymɑ̃), *ad*, assidu-
ously, etc.

assiégeant (asjeʒɑ̃) *m*, besieger.
assiéger (ʒe) *v.t*, to besiege, be-

leaguer, beset, crowd round, throng; dun.

assiette (asjɛt) *f*, plate; seat; seating, bed, base, foundation; basis; set, firmness, steadiness, stability, security; trim (*ship*). **assiettée** (te) *f*, plateful.

assignation (asiɲasjɔ̃) *f*, assignation; assignment; charge; summons; writ; subpoena. **assigner** (ɲe) *v.t*, to assign; charge; summon; cite; subpoena.

assimiler (asimile) *v.t*, to assimilate, liken, compare.

assis (asi) *p.a*, seated, sitting; established.

assise (asi:z) *f*, bed, foundation; course (*Build.*); (*pl.*) assize[s] (*law*).

assistance (asistã:s) *f*, assistance, aid, help; attendance, audience. ~ *judiciaire*, legal aid. ~ *privée*, private charity. ~ *publique*, public assistance *or* relief. ~ *sociale*, social welfare work. **assistant, e** (tã, ã:t) *n*, assistant; bystander, onlooker. **assister** (te) *v.t*, to assist, aid, help. ~ *à*, to attend, be present at, witness.

association (asɔsjasjɔ̃) *f*, association; society; g[u]ild; partnership. **associé, e** (sje) *n*, associate, member, partner. **associer** (sje) *v.t*, to associate; take into partnership. s'~ *avec*, to go into partnership; join with; sympathize with.

assoiffé (aswafe) *a*, thirsty.

assolement (asɔlmã) *m*, rotation (*crops*).

assombrir (asɔ̃bri:r) *v.t*, to darken, gloom, cloud.

assommant, e (asɔmã, ã:t) *a*, killing, oppressive, overwhelming, tiresome, wearisome, boring. **assommer** (me) *v.t*, to knock down, fell, strike dead; beat, thrash, nearly kill; overwhelm, weary to death, bore. **assommoir** (mwa:r) *m*, bludgeon, life preserver, lethal weapon; pole-axe; deadfall; dram shop.

assomption (asɔ̃psjɔ̃) *f*, Assumption (*Eccl.*).

assortiment (asɔrtimã) *m*, assortment; set; blend; match. **assortir** (ti:r) *v.t. & i*, to assort, supply; stock; blend; match; suit.

assortissant, e (tisã, ã:t) *a*, suitable, becoming.

assoupir (asupi:r) *v.t*, to make drowsy, send to sleep, lull, deaden; hush up. s'~, to doze; die down. **assoupissant, e** (pisã, ã:t) *a*, dull, humdrum. **assoupissement** (pismã) *m*, drowsiness; lethargy.

assouplir (asupli:r) *v.t*, to make supple; make tractable; soften.

assourdir (asurdi:r) *v.t*, to deafen, muffle; tone down.

assouvir (asuvi:r) *v.t*, to satiate, glut.

assujettir (asyʒɛti:r) *v.t*, to subject, subdue; bind, tie down; fix, fasten.

assumer (asyme) *v.t*, to assume.

assurance (asyrã:s) *f*, assurance; confidence; security, pledge; insurance. ~ *contre les accidents du travail*, workmen's compensation i. ~ *maritime*, marine i., sea i. ~*s sociales*, social security. ~ *sur la vie*, life i. **assuré†**, e (re) *a*, assured, sure, safe; confident, bold. *mal* ~, insecure, unsafe. ¶ (*pers.*) *n*, insured, assured. **assurer** (re) *v.t*, to assure, ensure, insure, secure, guarantee; make fast, steady, set, strengthen; affirm; confirm. s'~, to make sure; trust; insure (*Insce.*). **assureur** (rœ:r) *m*, insurer, underwriter.

Assyrie (l') (asiri) *f*, Assyria. **assyrien, ne** (rjẽ, ɛn) *a. & A~, n*, Assyrian.

aster (astɛ:r) *m*, aster.

astérisque (asterisk) *m*, asterisk, star.

astéroïde (asterɔid) *m*, asteroid.

asthmatique (asmatik) *a. & n*, asthmatic. **asthme** (asm) *m*, asthma.

asticot (astiko) *m*, gentle, maggot.

asticoter (astikɔte) *v.t*, to tease.

astigmate (astiɡmat) *a*, astigmatic.

astiquer (astike) *v.t*, to polish.

astre (astr) *m*, star, luminary.

astreindre (astrẽ:dr) *v.t.ir*, to bind, tie down, compel. **astreinte** (trɛ:t) *f*, penalty.

astringent, e (astrẽʒã, ã:t) *a. & m*, astringent.

astrologie (astrɔlɔʒi) *f*, astrology. **astrologue** (lɔg) *m*, astrologer.

astronaute (astrono:t) *m*, astronaut.

astronef (astrɔnɛf) *m*, spacecraft, spaceship.

astronome (astronɔm) *m*, astronomer. **astronomie** (mi) *f*, astronomy. **astronomique**† (mik) *a*, astronomic(al).

astuce (astys) *f*, astuteness, artfulness, craftiness, guile. **astucieux, euse**† (sjø, ø:z) *a*, astute, etc.

atelier (atəlje) *m*, [work]shop, mill, house, workroom, studio; staff; students.

atermoiement (atɛrmwamɑ̃) *m*, delay, procrastination, evasion. **atermoyer** (je) *v.i*, to procrastinate.

athée (ate) *m*, atheist. ¶ *a*, atheistic. **athéisme** (teism) *m*, atheism. **Athènes** (atɛn) *f*, Athens. **athénien, ne** (tenje, ɛn) *a*. & **A~**, *n*, Athenian.

athlète (atlɛt) *m*, athlete. **athlétique** (letik) *a*, athletic. **athlétisme** (letism) *m*, athletics.

atlantique (atlɑ̃tik) *a*, Atlantic. **l'[océan]** A~, *m*, the A. [ocean]. **atlantiste** (tist) *m*, person favoring inclusion of France in NATO.

atlas (atlɑ:s) *m*, atlas; [book of] plates.

atmosphère (atmɔsfɛ:r) *f*, atmosphere; medium (*ether*). **atmosphérique** (ferik) *a*, atmospheric(al), air (*att.*).

atome (ato:m) *m*, atom; mote. **atomique** (tɔmik) *a*, atomic(al). **atomiser** (tɔmize) *v.t*, to atomize, pulverize.

atone (ato:ne) *a*, atonic, toneless, lackluster, dull; unstressed (*Gram.*).

atours (atu:r) *m.pl*, finery.

atout (atu) *m*, trump [card], trumps.

âtre (ɑ:tr) *m*, hearth, fireplace.

atroce† (atrɔs) *a*, atrocious, heinous, outrageous; excruciating. **atrocité** (site) *f*, atrocity, etc.

atrophie (atrɔfi) *f*, atrophy, wasting away.

attabler (s') (atable) *v.pr*, to sit down [to table].

attachant, e (ataʃɑ̃, ɑ̃:t) *a*, interesting; engaging, winning. **attache** (taʃ) *f*, tie, fastening, leash, binder, bond, band, clip, paper fastener; attachment. **attaché** (ʃe) *m*, attaché. **attachement** (ʃmɑ̃) *m*, attachment; fondness; devotion. **attacher** (ʃe) *v.t*, to attach, tie, fasten, bind; rivet (*attention*). **s'~**, to fasten, devote oneself, cling, stick.

attaque (atak) *f*, attack, onset, onslaught, raid; fit, stroke, seizure, **attaquer** (ke) *v.t*, to attack, set on, assault; spur on; impugn. ~ *en justice*, to bring an action against. **s'~à**, to attack; tackle, grapple with.

attardé (atarde) *a*, belated; backward, old-fashioned. **attarder** (s') (atarde) *v.pr*, to loiter, linger.

atteindre (atɛ̃:dr) *v.t.ir*, to reach, attain; strike; hit; overtake, catch [up]; affect. **atteinte** (tɛ:t) *f*, reach, etc.; blow, stroke, cut; reflection, slur.

attelage (atla:ʒ) *m*, harnessing; coupling; team. **atteler** (tle) *v.t*, to harness, yoke, attach, couple. **attelle** (atɛl) *f*, splint; (*pl.*) hames.

attenant, e [à] (atnɑ̃, ɑ̃:t) *a*, adjoining.

attendant (en) (atɑ̃dɑ̃) *ad*, meanwhile, in the mean time. ¶ *pr*, pending. **en attendant que,** *c*, till, until. **attendre** (tɑ̃:dr) *v.t*. & *i*, to wait for, wait, stay, expect, await, bide, look forward to. **s'~** à, to expect, look for; rely on.

attendrir (atɑ̃dri:r) *v.t*, to soften, move, melt, affect. **s'~**, to be moved.

attendu (atɑ̃dy) *pr*, considering. ~ *que*, *c*, seeing that, whereas.

attentat (atɑ̃ta) *m*, (criminal) attempt, assault, outrage. **attentatoire** (twa:r) *a*, prejudicial.

attente (atɑ̃:t) *f*, waiting, expectation.

attenter à (atɑ̃te), to make an attempt on.

attentif, ive† (atɑ̃tif, i:v) *a*, attentive, careful, mindful. **attention** (sjɔ̃) *f*, attention; notice; care[fulness], heed; kindness. *faire* ~, to pay attention, mind.

atténuer (atenɥe) *v.t*, to attenuate, weaken; minimize; extenuate.

atterrer (atɛre) *v.t*, to overwhelm, dumbfound.

atterrir (atɛri:r) *v.i*, to land, alight. **atterrissage** (risa:ʒ) *m*, landing (*plane, spacecraft*); making land (*ship*). ~ *plané*, glide landing.

attestation (atɛstasjɔ̃) *f*, attestation; certificate, testimonial. **attester** (te) *v.t*, to attest, testify, vouch, certify, witness.

attiédir (atjedi:r) *v.t*, to cool; warm; make lukewarm.

attifer (atife) *v.t*, to dress up.

attique (atik) *a*, Attic.

attirail (atira:j) *m*, appliances, apparatus, implements, habiliment; string; baggage, paraphernalia; show, pomp.

attirance (atirɑ̃:s) *f*, attraction. **attirer** (re) *v.t*, to attract, draw; lure; win. **s'~**, to incur, win.

attiser (atize) *v.t*, to stir, poke; fan (*fig.*).

attitré, e (atitre) *a*, accredited, recognized; by appointment.

attitude (atityd) *f*, attitude, posture.

attouchement (atuʃmɑ̃) *m*, touching, contact.

attractif, ive (atraktif, i:v) *a*, attractive (*Phys.*). **attraction** (ksjɔ̃) *f*, attraction; draw; loadstone; (*pl.*) varieties (*Theat.*); (*pl.*) cabaret [show].

attrait (atrɛ) *m*, attraction; draw; appeal; inclination, bent; (*pl.*) charms; amenities (*housing*).

attrape (atrap) *f*, trap, catch, hoax. ~*-nigaud, m*, booby trap. ~*-plats*, potholder. **attraper** (pe) *v.t*, to [en]trap, [en]snare, catch, take in, hoax; draw (*in lottery*); hit; tell off, scold (*slang*); hit off. **s'~**, to get caught.

attrayant, e (atrɛjɑ̃, ɑ̃:t) *a*, attractive, engaging, winning.

attribuer (atribɥe) *v.t*, to attribute, ascribe; predicate; father; allot. **attribuable** (abl) *a*, attributable, etc. **attribut** (by) *m*, attribute; predicate. **attributaire** (tɛ:r) *n*, allottee. **attribution** (sjɔ̃) *f*, attribution; allotment. *les ~s*, powers, duties.

attrister (atriste) *v.t*, to sadden.

attrition (atrisjɔ̃) *f*, attrition, abrasion.

attroupement (atrupmɑ̃) *m*, unlawful assembly; mob; riot.

aubade (obad) *f*, aubade; catcalling.

aubaine (obɛn) *f*, windfall, godsend.

aube (o:b) *f*, dawn; alb; blade, vane, paddle, float.

aubépine (obepin) *f*, hawthorn.

auberge (obɛrʒ) *f*, inn; hostel. ~ *de jeunesse*, youth hostel. *vous n'êtes pas encore sorti de l'~*, you're still in trouble. **aubergiste** (ʒist) *n*, innkeeper, landlord, -lady.

aubergine (obɛrʒin) *f*, eggplant.

aubier (obje) *m*, sapwood.

aucun, e (okœ̃, yn) *a. & pn*, any; anyone; (*neg.*) no, none; no one. **aucunement** (kynmɑ̃) *ad*, in any way; (*neg.*) not at all, by no means, nowise.

audace (odas) *f*, audacity, boldness, daring. *payer d'~*, to face the music. **audacieux, euse†** (sjø, ø:z) *a*, audacious, etc.

au-delà, au-dessous *see* **delà, dessous**.

au-devant (odvɑ̃) *ad*, forward, ahead. *aller ~ de*, to go to meet.

audience (odjɑ̃:s) *f*, audience, hearing; court. **auditeur, trice** (ditœ:r, tris) *n*, hearer, listener, auditor; prosecutor. **audition** (sjɔ̃) *f*, hearing, audition; concert; recital. **auditoire** (twa:r) *m*, audience; auditorium; congregation.

auge (o:ʒ) *f*, **auget** (oʒɛ) *m*, trough, bucket. **augée** (oʒe) *f*, troughful, bucketful.

augmenter (ɔgmɑ̃te) *v.t. & i*, to increase, augment, enlarge, enhance; supplement. **augmentation** (tasjɔ̃) *f*, increase; raise (*in salary*).

augure (ogy:r) *m*, augury, omen; prophet, augur. **augurer** (gyre) *v.t*, to augur, make.

auguste (ogyst) *a*, august.

aujourd'hui (oʒurdɥi) *ad. & m*, today. *d'~ en huit, en quinze*, a week from today, fortnight.

aumône & l'aumône (omo:n) *f*, alms, charity. **aumônier** (monje) *m*, chaplain.

une (o:n) *m*, alder.

auparavant (oparavɑ̃), *ad*, before[hand].

auprès (oprɛ) *ad*, near, close [by], [near] at hand. **~ de**, *pr*, near, close to *or* by, by; [attached] to; with; in.

auquel *see* **lequel**.

auréole (ɔreɔl) *f*, aureole, halo; halation (*Phot.*).

auriculaire (ɔrikylɛ:r) *a*, auricular, ear (*att.*). **[doigt] ~**, *m*, little (*or* fourth) finger.

aurifère (ɔrifɛ:r) *a*, auriferous, gold (*att.*).

aurore (ɔrɔ:r) *f*, dawn, daybreak, morn; aurora. **~ boréale**, aurora borealis, northern lights.

ausculter (ɔskylte) *v.t*, to sound (*Med.*).

auspice (ɔspis) *m*, auspice, omen.

aussi (osi) *ad*, also, too, likewise; so; as. **¶ c**, therefore, consequently, so. **~ bien**, besides, moreover. **~ bien que**, *c*, as well as. **aussitôt** (to) *ad*, directly, at once. **~ dit**, **~ fait**, no sooner said than done. **~ que**, *c*, as soon as.

austère† (ostɛ:r) *a*, austere, stern. **austérité** (terite) *f*, austerity, etc.

austral, e (ostral) *a*, austral, southern. **l'Australasie** (lazi) *f*, Australasia. **l'Australie** (li), Australia. **australien, ne** (ljɛ̃, ɛn) *a. & A~*, *n*, Australian.

autan (otɑ̃) (*Poet.*) *m*, storm, blast.

autant (otɑ̃), *ad*, as (*or* so) much, as many, as far; as well, as good, as often. **~ que**, as much as, as far as. **d'~ que**, *c*, especially as.

autel (otɛl) *m*, altar.

auteur (otœ:r) *m*, author; writer; composer; originator; founder (*race*); progenitor; perpetrator (*crime*); party at fault (*accident*); inventor; designer; informant; doer. *les ~s de nos jours*, our progenitors. **~ dramatique**, playwright.

authentique† (otɑ̃tik) *a*, authentic, genuine. **authenticité** (site) *f*, authenticity, etc.

auto (otɔ, oto) *préfixe*, auto, self-, *e.g*, *papier ~-vireur*, self-toning paper (*Phot.*).

auto (ɔto, oto)*f*, auto, car.

autobiographie (otɔbiɔgrafi) *f*, autobiography.

autobus (otɔby:s) *m*, bus.

autocar (otɔka:r) *m*, interurban bus.

auto-caravane (otɔkaravan) *f*, camper, mobile home.

autochenille (otoʃni:j) *f*, caterpillar tractor.

autocrate, trice (otɔkrat, tris) *n*, autocrat. **autocratie** (si) *f*, autocracy. **autocratique** (tik) *a*, autocratic(al).

autocuisseur (otɔkɥizœ:r) *m*, pressure cooker.

autodidacte (otɔdidakt) *a*, self-taught.

autogène (otɔʒɛ:n) *a*, autogenous.

autogestion (otɔʒɛstjɔ̃) *f*, management of a firm by its employees.

autographe (otɔgraf) *m. & a*, autograph.

automate (otɔmat) *m*, automaton. **automatique†** (tik) *a*, automatic(al), self-acting.

automnal, e (otɔmnal) *a*, autumnal. **automne** (tɔn) *m*, autumn, fall.

automobile (o- *ou* ɔtɔmɔbil) *a*, self-propelling, motor (*att.*). **¶ f**, automobile. **automobilisme** (lism) *m*, motoring. **automobiliste** (list) *n*, motorist.

automotrice (otɔmɔtris) *f*, railcar, self-propelling railway car.

autonome (otɔnɔm) *a*, autonomous, self-governing; off line (*computers*). **autonomie** (mi) *f*, autonomy, self-government.

autopsie (otɔpsi) *f*, postmortem, autopsy.

autorisation (otɔrizasjɔ̃) *f*, authorization, leave; warrant. **autoriser** (ze) *v.t*, to authorize, empower, allow. **autoritaire** (tɛ:r) *a*, authoritative. **autorité** (te) *f*, authority; power. *faire ~*, to be regarded as an authority.

autoroute (otorut) *f*, express highway.

auto-stop (otɔstɔp) *m*, hitchhiking. **auto-stoppeur, euse** (pœ:r, ø:z) *n*, hitchhiker.

autour (otu:r) *m*, goshawk.

autour (otu:r) *ad.* & **autour de**, *pr*, round, around, about.

autre (o:tr) *a* & *pn*, other; another; next (*world*); else. *un ~ soi-même*, one's second self. *~ part*, elsewhere. *à d'~s!* nonsense! **autrefois** (otrəfwa) *ad*, formerly; once [upon a time]. **d'~**, of old, of yore; bygone. **autrement** (otrəmɑ̃) *ad*, otherwise; differently; [or] else.

Autriche (l') (otriʃ) *f*, Austria. **autrichien, ne** (ʃjɛ̃, ɛn) *a.* & A~, *n*, Austrian.

autruche (otryʃ) *f*, ostrich.

autrui (otrɥi) *pn*, others, other people.

auvent (ovɑ̃) *m*, penthouse; weatherboard; porch roof; hood.

auxiliaire (oksiljɛ:r) *a.* & *m*; auxiliary.

avachi, e (avaʃi) *a*, flabby, baggy; out of shape.

aval (aval) *m*, lower part; tail; guarantee, backing; endorsement. **en ~**, *ad*, downstream, down. **en ~ de**, *pr*, down, below.

avalanche (avalɑ̃:ʃ) *f*, avalanche; shower (*fig.*).

avaler (avale) *v.t*, to swallow, devour; stomach; lower; (*v.i.*) to go downstream.

avaliser (avalize) *v.t*, to guarantee, back.

à-valoir (avalwa:r) *m.inv*, advance payment.

avaloire (avalwa:r) *f*, gullet, throat.

avance (avɑ̃:s) *f*, advance, start; lead; projection; fast (*on clock*). **à l'~, d'~, en ~, par ~**, *ad*, in advance, beforehand. **avancé, e** (vɑ̃se) *p.a*, advance[d]; projecting; late (*hour, etc.*); high (*meat*). **avancer** (se) *v.t*, to advance, put forward, push, hasten; help; promote, further; set ahead (*clock*); (*v.i.*) to advance; project, jut out; gain (*of clock*). **avancement** (smɑ̃) *m*, advancement; feed (*Mach.*). *recevoir de l'~*, to be promoted.

avanie (avani) *f*, affront, insult.

avant (avɑ̃) *pr*, before; till, until. *av. J.C.*, B.C. *avant terme*, premature(ly) (*childbirth*). *~ [que] de*, *pr*, *~ que*, *c*, before. ¶ *ad*,

forward, before, far, deep[ly] *de l'~* à *l'arrière*, fore & aft (*Naut.*). **en ~**, *ad*, forward, on onward[s], ahead, before. **en ~ forward!** go ahead! on! *en ~, marche!* quick march! ¶ *m*, front, forepart; fore; head, bow (*Naut.*); steerage; forward (*Foot.*). *~ [du] centre*, center forward. **~-bras**, *m*, forearm. **~-coureur**, *m*, forerunner, harbinger, herald; (*att.*) premonitory. **~-dernier, ère**, *a.* & *n*, last but one. **~-garde**, *f*, van[guard]. **~-goût**, *m*, foretaste, earnest. **d'~-guerre**, *a*, prewar. **~-hier**, *ad.* & *m*, the day before yesterday. **~-hier soir**, the night before last. **~-main**, *m*, forehand (*Ten.*). **~-port**, *m*, outer harbor. **~-poste**, *m*, outpost. **~-première**, *f*, dress rehearsal; private view (*art*). **~-projet**, *m*, rough draft. **~-pos**, *m*, foreword, preface. **~-scène**, *f*, proscenium; stage box. **~-toit**, *m*, eaves. *l'~-veille*, *f*, two days before.

avantage (avɑ̃ta:ʒ) *m*, advantage, benefit; odds; leverage; upper hand, pull. *~ [de jeu]*, [ad]vantage [game] (*Ten.*). **avantager** (taʒe) *v.t*, to benefit, favor, endow. **avantageux, euse†** (ʒø, ø:z) *a*, advantageous, good, beneficial.

avare† (ava:r) *a*, avaricious; miserly, sparing, chary. ¶ *n*, miser, screw. **avarice** (varis) *f*, avarice. **avaricieux, euse** (sjø, ø:z) *a*, avaricious.

avarie (avari) *f*, damage; average (*Marine Law*). **avarier** (rje) *v.t*, to damage. **s'~**, to deteriorate, go bad (*meat, etc.*).

avec (avɛk) *pr*, with. **d'~**, from.

aveline (avlin) *f*, filbert, cob[nut]. **avelinier** (nje) *m*, filbert [tree].

avenant (avnɑ̃) *m*, endorsement (*Insce.*). **à l'~ de**, *pr*, in keeping with.

avenant, e (avnɑ̃, ɑ̃:t) *a*, prepossessing, comely. *à l'~*, in keeping, accordingly. ¶ *m*, codicil, rider (*contract, treaty, etc.*).

avènement (avɛnmɑ̃) *m*, accession; advent, coming (*of Christ*).

avenir (avni:r) *m*, future, pros-

pect, outlook; promise. **à l'~,
ad,** in future, hereafter; henceforth.

avent (l') (avā) *m,* advent (*Eccl.*).

aventure (avãty:r) *f,* [ad]venture. *dire la bonne* **~,** to tell fortunes. **à l'~,** **ad,** haphazard, at random. **d'~, par ~,** by chance, perchance. **aventurer** (ty1e) *v.t,* to [ad]venture. **aventureux, euse** (rø, ø:z) *a,* [ad]venturous. **aventurier, ère** (rje, ɛ:r) *n,* adventurer, ess.

avenu (avny) *a,* in modern French used exclusively in phrase **nul et non ~,** null and void.

avenue (avny) *f,* avenue; drive.

avéré, e (avere) *p.a,* established, proved. **avérer** (avere) *v.t,* to establish; authenticate.

avers (avɛ:r) *m,* obverse (*coin*).

averse (avɛrs) *f,* shower.

aversion (avɛrsjɔ̃) *f,* aversion, dislike.

avertir (avɛrti:r) *v.t,* to notify, [fore]warn, caution. **avertissement** (tismã) *m,* notification; warning; demand note (*taxes*). **avertisseur** (sœ:r) *m,* call boy; alarm; hooter; horn. **~ d'incendie,** fire alarm.

aveu (avø) *m,* avowal, admission, confession; consent.

aveugle (avœ:gl) *a,* blind. ¶ *n,* blind man, woman. *les* **~s,** *m.pl,* the blind. **aveuglement** (glemã) *m,* blindness (*fig.*). **aveuglément** (glemã) *ad,* blindly. **aveugler** (gle) *v.t,* to blind; stop (*leak*). **à l'aveuglette** (glɛt), blindly.

aviateur, trice (avjatœr, tris) *a,* flying, flight (*att.*). ¶ *n,* aviator, flier. **aviation** (sjɔ̃) *f,* aviation, flying.

aviculture (avikylty:r) *f,* aviculture; poultry farming.

avide† (avid) *a,* greedy, grasping, eager, athirst, avid. **avidité** (dite) *f,* avidity, greed[iness].

avilir (avili:r) *v.t,* to degrade, debase; depreciate.

aviné, e (avine) *a,* intoxicated; smelling of drink; tipsy (*walk*).

avion (avjɔ̃) *m,* airplane. **~ à réaction,** jet. **par ~,** by airmail.

aviron (avirɔ̃) *m,* oar. **~ de**

couple, scull. **~ de pointe,** single oar (opp. *scull*). **l'~,** rowing.

avis (avi) *m,* opinion; mind; [way of] thinking; judgment; advice; notice, intimation. *jusqu'à nouvel* **~,** until further notice. **avisé, e** (ze) *a,* prudent, circumspect, canny. **aviser** (ze) *v.t,* to advise, notify, warn; espy. *s'~* **de,** to bethink oneself of, dare to. **aviso** (zo) *m,* dispatch boat.

aviver (avive) *v.t,* to revive, brighten; sharpen (*tool*).

avocasserie (avɔkasri) *f,* pettifoggery. **avocat, e** (ka, kat) *n,* counsel, lawyer; advocate. **~ général,** attorney general.

avoine (avwan) *f,* oats.

avoir (avwa:r) *m,* possessions, property, holding(s); credit[or]. Cr (*Bkkpg.*). *tout son* **~,** one's all. ¶ *v.t.ir,* to have; hold, keep; get; be; measure; have on; be the matter with, ail. *en* **~,** to have some or any. *il y a,* there is, there are; it is; ago; for. *il y en a,* there is (are) some. *il n'y en a plus,* there is none left. *se faire* **~,** to be taken in.

avoisinant, e (avwazinã, ã:t) *a,* neighboring, bordering on. **avoisiner** (ne) *v.t,* to border on.

avortement (avɔrtemã) *m,* abortion; miscarriage (*fig.*). **avorter** (te) *v.i,* to abort; miscarry. **avorton** (tɔ̃) *m,* abortion (*creature*).

avoué, e (avwe) *p.a,* acknowledged; ostensible. ¶ *m,* lawyer. **avouer** (we) *v.t,* to avow, confess; acknowledge, own. *s'~ coupable,* to plead guilty.

avril (avril) *m,* April. *donner un poisson d'* **~ à,** to make an April fool of.

axe (aks) *m,* axis; spindle; axle. **~ de manivelle,** crankshaft.

axiome (aksjo:m) *m,* axiom.

ayant cause (ɛjã) *m,* assign. **ayant droit,** *m,* party [entitled].

azalée (azale) *f,* azalea.

azimut (azimyt) *m,* azimuth. *prendre un* **~,** to take a bearing. *direction tous les* **~s,** facing all directions.

azotate (azɔtat) *m,* nitrate. **azote** (zɔt) *m,* nitrogen. **azoteux, euse**

(tø, ɸːz) *a*, nitrous. **azotique** (tik) *a*, nitric.

azur (azyːr) *m*, azure. **azuré, e** (zyre) *a*, azure.

azyme (azim) *a*, unleavened.

B

baba (baba) *a.inv*, dumbfounded. ¶ *m*, rum-soaked cake.

babeurre (babœːr) *m*, butter-milk; churn dash[er].

babil (babi) *m*, chatter, tattle, prattle, babble. **babillard, e** (bi-jaːr, ard) *n*, chatterbox. **babiller** (je) *v.i*, to chatter, etc.

babine (babin) *f*, lip, chap, chop.

babiole (babjɔl) *f*, toy, play-thing; trifle, bauble, gewgaw.

bâbord (babɔːr) *m*, port [side] (*Naut.*).

babouches (babuʃ) *f.pl*, mules (*slippers*).

babouin (babwɛ̃) *m*, baboon. *petit* ~, *petite babouine* (win), young monkey (*child*).

babylonien, ne (babilɔnjɛ̃, ɛn) *a*, Babylonian.

bac (bak) *m*, ferry[boat]; vat, trough. ~ *aérien*, air ferry. ~ *d'éléments*, cell jar (*Elec.*). ~ *de batterie*, battery case. ~ *trans-bordeur*, train ferry.

baccalauréat (bakalɔrea) *m*, bachelor's degree.

bacchanal (bakanal) *m*, row; orgy. **bacchanales** (nal) *f.pl*, Bacchanalia.

bâche (baːʃ) *f*, sheet; cloth; tilt; tank; forcing frame. ~ *goudron-née*, tarpaulin.

bachelier, ère (baʃəlje, ɛːr) *n*, bachelor (*science*).

bachique (baʃik) *a*, Bacchic; drinking (*song*).

bachot (baʃo) *m*, wherry; punt; bachelor's degree.

bacille (basil) *m*, bacillus.

bâcler (baklə) *v.t*, to bar, bolt; scamp.

bactéries (bakteri) *f.pl*, bacteria.

badaud, e (bado, oːd) *n*, saun-terer, idler, gaper.

badigeon (badiʒɔ̃) *m*, distemper; whitewash (*paint*).

badin, e (badɛ̃, in) *a*, playful, jocose. ¶ *n*, wag. **badine** (din) *f*, switch, cane; (*pl.*) tongs. ba-

diner (ne) *v.i*, to jest, poke fun, banter, play, toy; flutter.

bafouer (bafwe) *v.t*, to scoff at.

bafouiller (bafuje) *v.t*, to stam-mer; talk foolishness.

bâfrer (bafre) *v.i*, to guzzle, gor-mandize.

bagage (bagaːʒ) *m. oft. pl*, lug-gage, baggage.

bagarre (bagaːr) *f*, fray, brawl, broil, scuffle.

bagatelle (bagatɛl) *f*, trifle, baga-telle.

bagne (baɲ) *m*, convict prison.

bagnole (baɲɔl) *f*, cart; automo-bile.

bagou (bagu) *m*, gift of gab.

bague (bag) *f*, ring; collar; bush (*Mach.*).

baguenauder (bagnode) *v.i*, to trifle, fiddle, peddle, fool about.

baguer (bage) *v.t*, to tack, baste (*Need.*).

bagues sauves (bag soːv), safe & sound, without a scratch.

baguette (bagɛt) *f*, rod, stick, wand; loaf of bread; ramrod; bead (*Arch., etc.*). ~*s à jour*, open clocks *or* clox (*stockings*). ~ *divinatoire* (divinatwaːr), dowsing rod, divining rod.

bahut (bay) *m*, chest, trunk.

bai, e (bɛ) *a. & m*, bay (*horse*).

baie (bɛ) *f*, bay (*Geog.*); berry (*Bot.*); opening (*in wall*). ~ *de porte*, doorway.

baignade (bɛɲad) *f*, bathing; dip; bathing place. **baigner** (ɲe) *v.t. & i. se* ~, to bathe, dip; wash; steep; suffuse; welter. **baigneur, euse** (ɲœːr, øːz) *n*, bather; bath-man, bath attendant. **baignoire** (ɲwaːr) *f*, bath (*tub*); box (*Theat.*).

bail (baːj) *m*, lease.

bâiller (baje) *v.i*, to yawn, gape; be ajar.

bailleur, eresse (bajœːr, jrɛs) *n*, lessor. *bailleur de fonds*, money lender; silent partner; fi-nancial backer.

bâillon (bajɔ̃) *m*, gag. **bâillonner** (jone) *v.t*, to gag.

bain (bɛ̃) *m*, bath; (*pl. & s.*) bath-ing; (*pl.*) watering place, spa. ~ *de développement*, ~ *révélateur*, developing bath (*Phot.*). ~ *douche*, shower bath. ~ *de siège*, sitz b., hip b. ~ *de soleil*, sun-bath. ~*s de soleil*, sunbathing. ~ *de virage-fixage*, fixing & toning bath (*Phot.*). ~*-marie* (mari) *m*, water bath; double boiler; boiler (*in range*). ~ *mixte*, mixed bath-ing.

baionnette (bajɔnɛt) *f*, bayonet.

baisemain (bɛzmɛ̃) *m*, kissing [of] hands. **baiser** (ze) *m*, kiss. ¶ *v.t*, to kiss. *Note*: (*slang*) to have sexual intercourse. I kissed my sister, is in French *j'ai em-brassé ma sœur*. **baisoter** (zɔte) *v.t*, to smother with kisses, kiss & cuddle.

baisse (bɛs) *f*, fall, drop. **baisser** (se) *v.t. & i*, to lower, let down, put down; drop; cast down; fall; sink. se ~, to stoop, bend. **bais-sier** (sje) (*Stk Ex.*) *m*, bear, short.

baisure (bezyːr) *f*, kissing crust.

bajoue (baʒu) *f*, chop, chap.

bal (bal) *m*, ball, dance; d. hall. ~ *costumé*, ~ *travesti*, fancy dress ball. ~ *masqué*, masked ball. ~ *par souscription*, subscription dance.

balader (balade) *v.i*, to stroll; take a walk. *envoyer* ~, to get rid of (*person or thing*). **baladeur** (dœːr) *m*, stroller, saunterer; selector rod (*auto*); portable radio or cas-sette player with headphone. **bal-adeuse** (døːz) *f*, trailer; handcart; portable lamp.

baladin, e (baladɛ̃, in) *n*, mountebank, clown; buffoon.

balafre (balafr) *f*, gash, slash; scar. **balafrer** (fre) *v.t*, to gash, etc.

balai (balɛ) *m*, broom; brush; windshield wiper. ~ *d'âtre*, hearth brush. ~ *de bouleau*, birch broom, besom. ~ *de tapis*, carpet broom. ~ *garde-robe*, lavatory brush. ~ *mécanique pour tapis*, carpet sweeper.

balance (balɑ̃ːs) *f*, balance; poise; scale; [pair of] scales; suspense. ~ *de vérification*, ~ *d'ordre*, trial balance (*Bkkpg.*). *faire pencher la* ~, to turn the scale. **balancer** (lɑ̃se) *v.t. & i*, to balance, poise, weigh, offset; swing, sway, rock; hold in suspense, be in suspense, waver, halt; dismiss, fire; throw

away. se ~, to swing, sway, rock; seesaw; hover. **balancement** (smɑ̃) *m*, balancing. **balancier** (sje) *m*, balancing pole (*tight rope*); beam, bob (*Mach.*); fly press; balance wheel (*Horol.*); pendulum (*Horol.*); scale maker. ~ *monétaire*, coining press. **ba-lançoire** (swaːr) *f*, seesaw; swing (*child's*); twaddle.

balayage (balɛjaːʒ) *m*, sweeping; picture scanning (*TV*). **balayer** (je) *v.t*, to sweep [out, up]; scav-enge. **balayette** (jɛt) *f*, whisk [brush, broom], flick; penis (*ob-scene*). **balayeur, euse** (jœːr, øːz) *n*, sweeper, scavenger. **balayeuse**, *f*, street sweeper (*Mach.*). ~ *mécanique pour tapis*, carpet sweeper. **balayures** (jyːr) *f.pl*, sweepings.

balbutier (balbysje) *v.t. & i*, to stammer, mumble.

balcon (balkɔ̃) *m*, balcony. [*pre-mier*] ~, dress circle; woman's breasts (*slang*).

baldaquin (baldakɛ̃) *m*, canopy; tester.

baleine (balɛn) *f*, whale; whale-bone; steel (*corset*); rib (*um-brella*). **baleineau** (no) *m*, whale calf. **baleinier** (nje) *m*, whaler (*ship*). **baleinière** (njeːr) *f*, whale-boat.

balise (baliːz) *f*, beacon; sea mark; tow path. **baliser** (lize) *v.t*, to beacon; buoy.

baliverne (balivɛrn) *f. oft. pl*, twaddle.

Balkans (les) (balkɑ̃) *m.pl*, the Balkans. **balkanique** (kanik) *a*, Balkan.

ballade (balad) *f*, ballad (*po-em*).

ballant, e (balɑ̃, ɑ̃ːt) *a*, swing-ing, dangling.

ballast (balast) *m*, ballast (*road*, *Rly*).

balle (bal) *f*, ball; franc (*slang*); bullet, shot; bale; pack; husk, chaff; glume; fore! (*Golf*). ~ *à la volée*, trap ball. ~ *au but*, ~ *mise*, hit.

ballerine (balrin) *f*, ballet girl. **ballet** (lɛ) *m*, ballet (*Theat.*).

balloches (balɔʃ) *m.pl*, balls, tes-ticles (*obscene*).

ballon (balɔ̃) *m*, balloon; ball;

flask, bulb (*Chem.*). ~ *au panier*, basketball. ~ *d'enfant*, toy balloon. ~ *d'essai*, pilot balloon; feeler (*fig.*). ~ *de boxe*, punching bag. ~ [*de football*], [foot]ball. **balloné, e** (lɔne) *p.a*, distended; **ballooned** (*dress*). **ballonner** (ne) *v.t*, to distend (*stomach*).

ballot (balo) *m*, bale; pack; pack (*Mil.*). **ballotter** (lɔte) *v.t. & i*, to toss, shake, rattle; bob; send from pillar to post; bandy [about].

balnéaire (balnɛːr) *a*, bathing, watering (*place*), seaside (*resort*).

balourd, e (baluːr, urd) *n*, lumpish person, hulking fellow. **balourdise** (lurdiːz) *f*, stupidity; blunder.

balsamier (balzamje) *m*, balsam [tree]. **balsamine** (min) *f*, garden balsam (*plant*). **balsamique** (mik) *a*, balsamic; balmy.

Baltique (la) [mer] (baltik), the Baltic sea [sea].

balustrade (balystrad) *f*, balustrade; railing. **balustre** (tr) *m*, baluster, banister; railing.

bambin, e (bɑ̃bɛ̃, in) *n*, kid, youngster.

bamboche (bɑ̃bɔʃ) *f*, spree.

bambou (bɑ̃bu) *m*, bamboo.

ban (bɑ̃) *m*, ban. ~*s de mariage*, banns. *mettre aux* ~*s*, to outlaw, banish. *en rupture de* ~, to have broken parole, be on a spree. *le* ~ *et l'arrière* ~, everybody; both regulars and reserves (*Mil.*).

banal, e (banal) *a*, banal, common[place], trite, hackneyed, humdrum. *voiture banalisée*, unmarked car (*police*). **banaliser** (lize) *v.t*, to vulgarize.

banane (banan) *f*, banana. **bananier** (nje) *m*, banana [plant, tree].

banc (bɑ̃) *m*, bench, form, seat, settle; box (*jury*); bank, bed, reef; shoal (*sand, fish*); school (*fish*); floe (*ice*). ~ *à coulisses*, sliding seat (*rowboat*). ~ [*d'église*], pew, ~ *des prévenus*, dock. *sur les* ~*s*, at school (*fig.*).

bancal, e (bɑ̃kal) *a*, bandy[-legged]; rickety.

bandage (bɑ̃daː3) *m*, bandage; tire; stretching. ~ [*herniaire*] (ɛrnjeːr), truss. **bande** (bɑ̃ːd) *f*,

band, strip, slip, tape, belt, strap, bandage; streak; wrapper; heel, list (*Naut.*); cushion (*Bil.*); blurb; troop, company, pack, gang, crew, party, set; ring; flock, flight. ~ *civile*, citizens' band (*CB Radio*). ~ *dessinée*, comic strip. ~ *molletière*, puttee. ~ *noire*, terrorist band. ~ *sonore*, sound track. ~-*amorce*, leader (*film, tape*). ~-*annonce*, trailer (*cinema*). ~-*video*, video tape. **bandeau** (bɑ̃do) *m*, headband, bandeau; bandage (*over eyes*); veil (*fig.*), **bander** (de) *v.t*, to bandage, bind, tie up; stretch, tense, bend, key up, brace; tire (*wheels*). ~ [*les yeux à, de*], to blindfold; hoodwink. *v.i*, to have an erection (*obscene*); strain; touch cushion (*billiards*).

banderole (bɑ̃drɔl) *f*, banderol[e], streamer.

bandit (bɑ̃di) *m*, bandit, robber; ruffian.

bandoulière (bɑ̃duljɛːr) *f*, bandolier, shoulder strap. *en* ~, slung [over shoulder].

banlieue (bɑ̃ljø) *f*, suburbs, outskirts. *de* ~, suburban.

banne (ban) *f*, sheet; tilt; awning; blind (*shop*); hamper.

bannière (banjɛːr) *f*, banner.

bannir (baniːr) *v.t*, to banish; expel.

banque (bɑ̃ːk) *f*, bank; banking; workbench. ~ *de données*, data bank. *carnet, livret, de* ~, passbook. *faire sauter la* ~, to break the bank.

banqueroute (bɑ̃krut) *f*, bankruptcy. *faire* ~, to go bankrupt. **banqueroutier, ère** (tje, ɛːr) *n*, bankrupt.

banquet (bɑ̃kɛ) *m*, banquet.

banquette (bɑ̃kɛt) *f*, bench, seat; bunker (*golf*).

banquier (bɑ̃kje) *m*, banker; broker. ~ *en valeurs*, stockbroker. ¶ *a*, banking.

banquise (bɑ̃kiːz) *f*, ice floe.

banquiste (bɑ̃kist) *m*, humbug, charlatan.

baptême (batɛːm) *m*, baptism, christening. ~ *du tropique*, ~ *de la ligne*, crossing the line ducking. **baptiser** (tize) *v.t*, to baptize, christen; bless (*bell,* *etc.*); nickname, dub; water, dilute. **baptismal, e** (tismal) *a*, baptismal. **baptistère** (tɛːr) *m*, baptistry.

baquet (bakɛ) *m*, bucket, tub, trough. **~-baignoire,** *m*, bathtub.

bar (baːr) *m*, bar (*drinking*); bass (*fish*).

baragouin (baragwɛ̃) *m*, gibberish, jargon, lingo. **baragouiner** (gwine) *v.i. & t*, to gibber; jabber.

baraque (barak) *f*, hut; booth; hovel.

baraterie (baratri) *f*, barratry.

baratin (baratɛ̃) *m*, patter, sweet talk, line. **baratiner** (tine) *v.i. & t*, to sweet-talk, spin a yarn.

baratte (barat) *f*, churn. **baratter** (te) *v.t*, to churn.

Barbade (la) (barbad), Barbado[e]s.

barbare (barbaːr) *a*, barbaric; barbarian; barbarous. ¶ *m*, barbarian. **barbarie** (bari) *f*, barbarism; barbarity. **barbarisme** (rism) *m*, barbarism (*Gram.*).

barbe (barb) *f*, beard; shaving; shave; barb (*feather*); awn; whiskers (*cat*); wattle; (*pl.*) burr; mold (*fungi*). *B~-Bleue,* m, Bluebeard. *~ de bouc,* goatee. *la ~!,* enough! *vivre dans sa ~,* to laugh up one's sleeve. *se faire faire la ~,* to get shaved. **barbelé, e** (bəle) *a*, barbed, spiked. **barbiche** (biʃ) *f*, goatee. **barbier** (bje) *m*, barber. **barbifier** (fje) *v.t*, to shave. **barbon** (bɔ̃) *m*, [old] fog[e]y. **barbouse** (buz) *m*, bearded man; secret agent (*slang*).

barboter (barbɔte) *v.i*, to dabble, paddle, splash about; flounder; wade; mumble. **barbotage** (taːʒ) *m*, dabbling, etc; mash (*for cattle*). **barboteur** (tœːr) *m*, paddler; mudlark; muddler, flounderer; duck (*tame*). **barboteuse** (tɵːz) *f*, rompers.

barbouiller (barbuje) *v.t*, to daub, [be]smear; blur; scribble; bungle; mumble.

barbu, e (barby) *a*, bearded. ¶ *f*, brill.

Barcelone (barsələn) *f*, Barcelona.

bardane (bardan) *f*, burdock, bur[r].

barde (bard) *m*, bard, poet; (*f.*) packsaddle; slice of bacon.

bardot (bardo) *m*, hinny.

barême (barɛːm) *m*, ready reckoner; scale; graph.

barguigner (barɡiɲe) *v.t*, to shilly-shally, haggle.

baril (bari) *m*, barrel, cask. **barillet** (rijɛ) m, keg; cylinder, barrel, drum.

bariolage (barjɔlaːʒ) *m*, medley, motley. **bariolé (le)** *p.a*, motley, particolored, pied.

barnum (barnɔm) *m*, showman.

baromètre (barɔmɛtr) *m*, barometer, glass. **barométrique** (metrik) *a*, barometric(al).

baron, ne (barɔ̃, ɔn) *n*, baron, ess.

baroque (barɔk) *a*, odd, queer, quaint.

barque (bark) *f*, boat, smack, bark.

barrage (baraːʒ) *m*, barrier; dam; weir; barrage; closing (*street*); playing off (*tie*). **barre** (baːr) *f*, bar, rod, rail; stroke; stripe; cross (*on letter* t); helm, tiller, wheel (*Naut.*). *~ à sphères,* barbell. *~ de commande,* control rod (*nuclear reactor*). *~ d'eau,* [tidal] bore. *~ de dopage,* booster rod (*nuclear reactor*). *~ de flot,* tidal wave. *~ de pilotage,* regulating rod (*nuclear reactor*). *~ de plage,* surf. *~ fixe,* horizontal bar. [*jeu de*] *~s,* prisoner's base. **barreau** (baro) *m*, bar (*lit. & law*); rung. **barrer** (re) *v.t*, to bar, rail, fence off; close; dam; cross out, strike out, blue-pencil. *~ un chèque,* to mark a check "for deposit only." **barrette** (rɛt) *f*, (small) bar; bar brooch; biretta; cardinal's cap. **barreur** (rœːr) *m*, man at the wheel; helmsman; coxswain.

barricade (barikad) *f*, barricade. **barricader (de)** *v.t*, to barricade.

barrière (barjɛːr) *f*, barrier, fence; bar; gate; toll gate; starting post; lists (*Hist.*).

barrique (barik) *f*, cask, hogshead.

barrir (bariːr) *v.i*, to trumpet (*elephant*).

baryton (baritɔ̃) *m*, baritone; b. saxhorn.

bas, se (bɑ, ɑːs) *a*, low, lower, nether, down; shallow; cloudy; mean, vile, base, degrading; vulgar; cheap. *bas âge*, infancy. *avoir la vue basse*, to be short-sighted. *faire main basse sur*, to lay violent hands on. bas, *ad*, low, low down, down; off. ¶ *m*, bottom, foot; lower notes (*Mus.*); stocking; (*pl.*) hose. à ~, *ad*, down [with] . . . ! *bas les mains!* hands off! en ~, *ad*, at the bottom; below; down; downward; downstairs.

basalte (bazalt) *m*, basalt.

basane (bazan) *f*, sheepskin, roan, basan, basil. **basané, e** (ne) *a*, tanned, tawny, swarthy, sunburnt.

bas-bleu (bɑblø) *m*, bluestocking.

bas-côté (bɑkote) *m*, aisle.

bascule (baskyl) *f*, balanced lever; rocker; seesaw. [*balance à* ~, weighing machine, scale[s]. ~ *romaine*, platform scales. à ~, flip-flop (*computers*). **basculer** (le) *v.i*, to seesaw, swing, rock, tip [up], tilt. *faire* ~, to dip (*auto headlights*).

base (bɑːz) *f*, base, bottom, foot; basis, groundwork; group of militants in a political party or union. ~ *de lancement*, launching base, range (*missiles, spacecraft*). *jeter les* ~*s*, to lay foundations.

bas-fond (bɑfɔ̃) *m*, lowland, flat, bottom; shallows (*Naut.*). ~*s de la société*, underworld.

basilic (bazilik) *m*, [sweet] basil; basilisk.

basilique (bazilik) *f*, basilica.

basique (bɑzik) *a*, basic, basal.

basque (bask) *f*, skirt, tail.

bas-relief (barəljɛf) *m*, low relief, bas-relief.

basse (bɑːs) *f*, bass [voice, singer, string, tuba]; cello; reef, flat (*Naut.*).

basse-cour (baskuːr) *f*, farmyard, barnyard, poultry yard, stable yard.

bassement (bɑsmɑ̃) *ad*, meanly, basely. **bassesse** (sɛs) *f*, meanness, etc; humbleness (*birth*).

basset (basɛ) *m*, basset. ~ *allemand*, dachshund.

bassin (basɛ̃) *m*, basin, bowl, pan; scale (*pan*); [collection] plate; ornamental lake; dock; pelvis. ~ *à flot*, wet dock. ~ *à sec*, dry dock. ~ [*de garde-robe*], ~ *pour malade*, ~ *de lit*, bedpan. **bassine** (sin) *f*, pan, copper. **bassinet** (nɛ) *m*, buttercup. **bassinoire** (nwaːr) *f*, warming pan.

basson (bɑsɔ̃) *m*, bassoon.

bastonnade (bɑstɔnad) *f*, cudgeling.

bas-ventre (bɑvɑ̃ːtr) *m*, lower part of the abdomen.

bât (bɑ) *m*, packsaddle.

bataclan (bataklɑ̃) *m*, traps, hamper.

bataille (bataːj) *f*, battle, fight, fray. **batailler** (taje) *v.i*, to battle, fight; struggle; wrangle. **batailleur, euse** (jœːr, øːz) *a*, combative, pugnacious. **bataillon** (tajɔ̃) *m*, battalion, host; heap. ~ *de travailleurs*, labor battalion.

bâtard, e (bataːr, ard) *a. & n*, bastard, mongrel; loaf of bread. **bâtardise** (tardiːz) *f*, bastardy.

bateau (bato) *m*, boat, ship, vessel, smack. ~ *à rames*, row[ing] boat. ~ *à roues*, paddle b. ~ *à vapeur*, steamboat. ~ *à voiles*, sailing b. ~*citerne*, tanker. ~ *d'habitation*, houseboat. ~ *de passage*, ferryboat. ~ *de promenade*, row[ing] b. (*pleasure*). ~ *de sauvetage*, lifeboat. ~*-feu*, lightship. ~ *omnibus*, ~*-mouche*, water [omni]bus. ~*-porte*, *m*, caisson (*dock*). *mener quelqu'un en* ~, to trick someone. *monter un* ~ *à quelqu'un*, to pull a trick on someone. **batelage** (tlaːʒ) *m*, lighterage; acrobatic tricks. **batelée** (tle) *f*, boatload. **bateleur** (tlœːr) *m*, knock-about comedian. **batelier** (təlje) *m*, bargeman, bargee, lighterman. **batellerie** (tɛlri) *f*, inland navigation; small craft.

bâti (bati) *m*, tacking, basting (*Need.*); frame[work], casing. ~ [*d'assise*], bed plate. ~ *de forge*, smith's hearth.

batifoler (batifɔle) *v.i*, to romp, frolic, skylark; dally (*amorously*).

bâtiment (batimɑ̃) *m*, building; house; vessel, ship. ~ *de guerre*, man-of-war. **bâtir** (tiːr) *v.t. & abs*, to build; tack, baste (*Need.*). **bâtisse** (tis) *f*, masonry.

batiste (batist) *f*, cambric, batiste.

bâton (batɔ̃) *m*, stick; cudgel; tinglestick; staff; truncheon; balon; pole; perch; support (*fig.*). ~ *d'or*, wallflower. ~ *de rouge* [*pour les lèvres*], lipstick. *à* ~*s rompus*, by fits & starts, desultorily. **bâtonner** (tɔne) *v.t*, to beat; cudgel. **bâtonnet** (nɛ) *m*, [tip]cat; chopstick.

battage (bataːʒ) *m*, beating; threshing; churning. **battant** (tɑ̃) *m*, clapper (*bell*); leaf (*door*). ~ *neuf*, brand-new. *pluie battante*, pelting rain. **batte** (bat) *f*, beater. ~ *à beurre*, churn dash[er]. **battement** (tmɑ̃) *m*, beating, beat, etc, as *battre*. **batterie** (tri) *f*, fight, scuffle; battery; beat[ing]; set, utensils; percussion instruments; (*s. & pl.*) plan(s), tactics. ~ *de tambour*, roll of the drum. **batteur** (tœːr) *m*, beater; whisk. ~ *de pavé*, lounger, loafer. ~ *en grange*, thresher (*pers.*). **batteuse** (tøːz) *f*, threshing machine. **battoir** (twaːr) *m*, beater; battledore. **battre** (tr) *v.t. & i. ir*, to beat, strike, batter; scour (*country*); thrash; thresh; churn; hammer; ram; coin, mint; raise (*money*); fly (*national flag*); shell (*Mil.*); clap (*hands*); shuffle (*cards*); bang; flap; jar; throb, pulsate, pant; tick (*clock*). ~ *contre-vapeur*, to reverse steam. se ~, to fight. *se* ~ *les flancs*, to lash its tail. **battu, e** (ty) *p.a*, beaten. ¶ *f*, drive, battue, beat (*Hunt.*); tramp (*of horse*).

bau (bo) *m*, beam (*ship's timber*).

baudet (bodɛ) *m*, donkey.

baudrier (bodrie) *m*, cross belt.

baudruche (bodryʃ) *f*, goldbeater's skin.

baume (boːm) *m*, balsam, balm. **baumier** (bomje) *m*, balsam [tree].

bavarder (bavarde) *v.i*, to prate, blab; gossip.

bavarois, e (bavarwa, aːz) *a. & B~, n*, Bavarian.

bave (baːv) *f*, drivel; slobber; slime. **baver** (bave) *v.i*, to drivel; slobber. **bavette** (vɛt) *f*, bavoir (vwaːr) *m*, bib, feeder. **bavure** (vyːr) *f*, smear; burr; seam.

Bavière (la) (bavjɛːr), Bavaria.

bayer aux corneilles (baje), to stargaze, gape [at the moon].

bayette (bɛjɛt) *f*, baize.

bazar (bazaːr) *m*, bazaar, arcade (*of shops*); (*cheap*) stores.

béant, e (beɑ̃, ɑ̃ːt) *a*, gaping, yawning, open.

béat, e† (bea, at) *a*, sanctimonious; blissful; smug, self-satisfied. ¶ *n*, saint. **béatifier** (tifje) *v.t*, to beatify. **béatitude** (tyd) *f*, beatitude, blessedness, bliss.

beau, bel, belle (bo, bɛl) *a*, beautiful, fine, handsome, fair, pretty, comely, lovely, good, nice; graceful; fashionable, smart; bright; palmy (*days*). *le beau monde*, fashionable society. *avoir beau dire*, to speak in vain. *bel esprit*, [man of] wit; witling. *bel & bien*, *ad*, fairly; plainly. *à la belle étoile*, in the open [air]. **beau, m**, beautiful, beau, Adonis. *au* ~, *au* ~ *fixe*, at fair, at set fair (*barometer*). *faire le* ~, to beg (*dog*). *tout* ~!, careful!, hold it! **beaucoup** (ku) *ad. & m*, a great (*or* good) deal, a good (*or* great) many, very much; much, many, greatly. *de* ~, by far. **beau-fils**, *m*, stepson. **beau-frère**, *m*, brother-in-law. **beau-père**, *m*, father-in-law; stepfather.

beaupré (bopre) *m*, bowsprit.

beauté (bote) *f*, beauty, fairness, loveliness, comeliness; belle.

beaux-arts (bozaːr) *m.pl*, fine arts, art.

bébé (bebe) *m*, baby; [baby] doll. ~ *dormeur*, sleeping doll.

bec (bɛk) *m*, beak, bill; nose, nozzle, snout; jaw; spout; mouthpiece; mouth; lip, tip; burner, jet; nib; point; cutwater. ~ *de gaz*, gas burner; lamppost. *le* ~ *dans l'eau*, in a fix, mess.

bécarre (bekaːr) (*Mus.*) *m. & a*, natural, cancel.

bécasse (bekas) *f*, woodcock. **bécasseau** (so) *m*, sandpiper. **bécassine** (sin) *f*, snipe.

bec-de-cane (bɛkdəkan) *m*, slide bolt; lever handle; flat-nosed pliers.

bec-de-corbeau (bɛkdəkɔrbo) *m*, wire cutter.

bec-de-lièvre (bɛkdəljɛːvr) *m*, harelip.

bêche (bɛʃ) *f*, spade. **bêcher** (ʃe) *v.t*, to dig, spade.

becquetance (bɛktãːs) *f*, food, grub (*slang*).

becqueter (bɛkte) *v.t*, to peck, pick. se ~, to bill.

bedeau (bədo) *m*, beadle; verger.

beffroi (bɛfrwa) *m*, belfry; gantry.

bégayer (begɛje) *v.i. & t*, to stutter, stammer, lisp, falter. **bégaiement** (gɛmã) *m*, stuttering, etc.

bègue (bɛːg) *n*, stutterer, stammerer.

bégueule (begœl) *f*, prude. ¶ *a*, prudish, squeamish, straitlaced. **bégueulerie** (lri) *f*, prudery, etc.

beignet (bɛɲɛ) *m*, fritter (*Cook.*).

bêlement (bɛlmã) *m*, bleat[ing], baa[ing]. **bêler** (le) *v.i*, to bleat, baa.

belette (bəlɛt) *f*, weasel.

belge (bɛlʒ) *a. &* B~, *n*, Belgian. **la Belgique** (ʒik), Belgium.

bélier (belje) *m*, ram, tup; battering ram.

belladone (bɛladɔn) *f*, belladonna, deadly nightshade.

bellâtre (bɛlɑːtr) *a*, dandified, foppish.

belle (bɛl) *f*, beauty; deciding game, rubber. *la* B~ *au bois dormant*, the Sleeping Beauty. *la* B~ *& la Bête*, Beauty & the Beast. ~-de-jour, *f*, convolvulus. ~-fille, *f*, stepdaughter; daughter-in-law. **bellement** (lmã) *ad*, softly, gently. **belle-mère**, *f*, stepmother; mother-in-law. **belles-lettres**, *f.pl*, polite letters *or* literature. **belle-sœur**, *f*, sister-in-law.

belligérant, e (bɛliʒerã, ãːt) *a. & n*, belligerent. **belliqueux, euse** (bɛlikø, øːz) *a*, warlike, bellicose.

bellot, te (bɛlo, ɔt) *a*, pretty; dapper.

belvédère (bɛlvedɛːr) *m*, belvedere, lookout.

bémol (bemɔl) *m. & att*, flat (*Mus.*).

bénédicité (benedisite) *m*, grace, blessing (*before meals*). **bénédiction** (ksjɔ̃) *f*, consecration,

blessing; benedicñion. *que c'est une* ~, with a vengeance, & no mistake.

bénéfice (benefis) *m*, advantage, benefit; profit; living, benefice (*Eccl.*). **bénéficiaire** (sjeːr) *a*, [showing a] profit; in credit. ¶ *n*, beneficiary, payee. **bénéficier** (sje) *v.i*, to [make a] profit, benefit.

benêt (bənɛ) *a.m*, silly, simple, foolish. ¶ *m*, booby, simpleton, noodle.

bénévole† (benevɔl) *a*, kind; voluntary.

Bengale (le) (bɛgal), Bengal **bengali (li)** *a.inv. & (bird) m. &* B~ (*pers.*) *m*, Bengali.

béni, e (beni) *p.p*, blessed, blest. **bénin, igne†** (nɛ̃, iɲ) *a*, benign, benignant, kind; mild. **bénir** (niːr) *v.t*, to consecrate; bless; thank. **bénit, e** (ni, ite) *p.p*, consecrated, holy (*bread, water*). **bénitier** (tje) *m*, holy-water basin, stoup.

benjoin (bɛ̃ʒwɛ̃) *m*, benzoin, benjamin.

benne (bɛn) *f*, hamper, basket; bucket, kibble, tub (*Min.*).

benzine (bɛ̃zin) *f*, benzine.

benzol (bɛ̃zɔl) *m*, benzol, benzene.

béquille (bekiːj) *f*, crutch; crutch handle; crutch key; spud (*Agric.*).

bercail (bɛrkaːj) *m*, fold (*Relig.*).

berceau (bɛrso) *m*, cradle; cot; arbor, bower. **bercelonnette** (səlɔnɛt) *f*, bassinet, cot. **bercer** (se) *v.t*, to rock, dandle; lull; bring up; cherish. **berceuse** (søːz) *f*, rocker (*pers.*); rocking chair; lullaby.

béret [basque] (berɛ) *m*, beret.

bergamote (bɛrgamɔt) *f*, bergamot (*orange, pear*). **bergamotier** (tje) *m*, bergamot [tree] (*orange*).

berge (bɛrʒ) *f*, bank (*river, road*); year (*usually plural*).

berger (bɛrʒe) *m*, shepherd; swain. **bergère** (ʒɛːr) *f*, shepherdess, nymph; easy chair. **bergerie** (ʒəri) *f*, [sheep]fold, pen. **bergeronnette** (rɔnɛt) *f*, wagtail.

berline (bɛrlin) *f*, four-door sedan.

berlue (bɛrly) *f*, faulty vision. *avoir la ~*, to get it all wrong.

Bermudes (les) (bɛrmyd) *f.pl*, the Bermudas.

bernacle (bɛrnakl) *f*, barnacle (*Crust.*). **bernard-l'ermite** (narlɛrmit) *m*, hermit crab.

berne (bɛrn) *f*, banter. *en ~*, at half-mast (*flag*). **berner** (ne) *v.t*, to make fun of; chaff.

bernique (bɛrnik) *i*, nothing doing!

béryl (beril) *m*, beryl.

besace (bəzas) *f*, scrip, wallet (*beggar's*). *réduit à la ~*, reduced to beggary.

besicles (bəzikl) *f.pl*, eyeglasses.

besogne (bəzɔɲ) *f*, [piece of] work, task, job. *~ alimentaire*, potboiler. **besogneux, euse** (nø, ø:z) *a*, needy, impecunious. **besoin** (zwɛ̃) *m*, need; requirement; pinch; [referee in] case of need (*Com.*).

bestial, e† (bɛstjal) *a*, bestial; beastly; hoggish. **bestiaux** (tjo) *m.pl*, cattle. **bêta** (bɛta) *m*, blockhead, fool. **bétail** (beta:j) *m*, cattle. **bête** (bɛ:t) *f*, beast, animal; creature; fool. *~ à bon Dieu*, ladybird. *~ noire*, pet aversion. *~s fauves*, deer; wild beasts (*big felines*). *chercher la petite ~*, to look for trouble. ¶ †, *a*, stupid, foolish, silly. **bêtise** (beti:z) *f*, stupidity; nonsense.

béton (betɔ̃) *m*, concrete. *~ armé*, reinforced concrete.

bette (bɛt) *f*, white beet. **betterave** (tra:v) *f*, beetroot, beet. *~ à sucre*, sugar beet. *~ fourragère*, mangel[-wurzel].

beugler (bøgle) *v.i. & t*, to bellow, low, moo; bawl.

beurre (bœ:r) *m*, butter. *~ d'anchois*, anchovy paste. *un oeil au ~ noir*, a black eye. **beurrée** (bœre) *f*, slice of bread & butter. **beurrer** (re) *v.t*, to butter. **beurrier** (rje) *m*, butter dish.

bévue (bevy) *f*, blunder; howler.

biais (bjɛ) *m*, slant; skew; bias; bent; dodge, shift. **biaiser** (ze) *v.i*, to slant; dodge, shuffle, shift.

bibelot (biblo) *m*, curio, knick-knack.

biberon, ne (bibrɔ̃, ɔn) *n*, tippler; (*m.*) feeding bottle.

Bible (bibl) *f*, Bible. **bibliographie** (bliɔgrafi) *f*, bibliography. **bibliophile** (fil) *m*, bibliophile, book-lover. **bibliothécaire** (teke:r) *n*, librarian. **bibliothéconomie** (tekɔnɔmi) *f*, library science. **bibliothèque** (tɛk) *f*, library; bookcase; bookstall. *~ circulante*, circulating library. *~ de prêt*, lending l. *~ où les livres se consultent sur place & ~ d'ouvrages à consulter*, reference library. **biblique** (blik) *a*, biblical; Bible (*Society*). **biblorhapte** (blɔrapt) *m*, binder.

bic (bik) *m*, ballpoint pen.

biceps (bisɛps) *m*, biceps.

biche (biʃ) *f*, hind (*deer*).

bichon, ne (biʃɔ̃, ɔn) *n*, Maltese [dog, bitch], lap dog. **bichonner** (ʃɔne) *v.t*, to curl; titivate.

bicot (biko) *m*, kid (*goat*); Arab (*pejorative*).

bicoque (bikɔk) *f*, shanty.

bicycle (bisikl) *m*, bicycle. **bicyclette** (klɛt) *f*, [safety] bicycle, cycle. *~ de course*, racer. **bicycliste** (klist) *n*, [bi]cyclist.

bidasse (bidas) *m*, private (*soldier*).

bidet (bidɛ) *m*, nag, cob; bidet.

bidon (bidɔ̃) *m*, canteen, water bottle (*Mil.*); drum (*gasoline, etc.*), can. **bidonville** (vil) *m*, hooverville, shantytown.

bidule (bidyl) *m*, thing, gadget, thingamabob.

bief (bjɛf) *m*, race[way] (*mill*); pond (*canal*).

bielle (bjɛl) *f*, [connecting] rod; strut, brace.

bien (bjɛ̃) *ad*, well; right, proper; nicely, all right; clearly; fully; thoroughly; much; very; far; fast; fain; indeed; duly; really, quite. *~ de*, much, many. *~ que*, *c*, [al]though. ¶ *m*, good; weal; blessing; endowment; mercy; (*oft. pl.*) possessions, property, chattel, estate, substance. *~ immeubles*, real property. *~s mal acquis*, ill-gotten gains. *~s [transmissibles par voie de succession]*, hereditable.

bien-aimé, e ou **bienaimé,** ‹ (bjɛ̃nɛme) *a. & n*, [well-]beloved, darling.

bien-dire (bjɛ̃di:r) *m*, fine speaking. **bien-disant, e** (dizɑ̃, ɑ̃:t) *a*, well-spoken, fair-spoken.

bien-être (bjɛ̃nɛːtr) *m*, well-being; welfare.

bienfaisance (bjɛ̃fəzɑ̃ːs) *f*, beneficence; benevolence; bounteousness; charity, donations. **bienfaisant, e** (zɑ̃, ɑ̃ːt) *a*, beneficent, etc. **bienfait** (fɛ) *m*, kindness, benefaction, benefit, boon; mercy. **bienfaiteur, trice** (tœːr, tris) *n*, benefactor, tress.

bienheureux, euse (bjɛ̃nœrø, øːz) *a*, blessed; blissful.

biennal, e (bjɛnal) *a*, biennial.

bienséant, e (bjɛ̃seɑ̃, ɑ̃ːt), *a*, proper, becoming, decorous.

biens-fonds (bjɛ̃fɔ̃) *m.pl*, real estate.

bientôt (bjɛ̃to) *ad*, soon, shortly.

bienveillant, e (bjɛ̃vɛjɑ̃, ɑ̃ːt) *a*, kind[ly], friendly.

bienvenue (bjɛ̃vny) *f*, welcome; footing.

bière (bjɛːr) *f*, beer; coffin. ~ *au tonneau*, ~ *à la pompe*, draught beer. ~ *blonde*, pale ale. ~ *brune*, dark ale.

biffer (bife), *v.t*, to strike out, cross out, delete, rule out, cancel.

bifteck (biftɛk) *m*, [beef]steak.

bifurcation (bifyrkasjɔ̃) *f*, bifurcation, fork; junction.

bigame (bigam) *a*, bigamous. ¶ *n*, bigamist. **bigamie** (mi) *f*, bigamy.

bigarade (bigarad) *f*, Seville orange.

bigarré, e (bigare) *p.a*, variegated, particolored, pied, motley. **bigarrer** (re) *v.t*, to variegate, medley; [inter]lard.

bigorneau (bigɔrno) *m*, [peri]winkle (*Crust.*).

bigot, e (bigo, ɔt) *a*, bigoted. ¶ *n*, bigot. **bigoterie** (gɔtri) *f*, bigotry.

bigoudi (bigudi) *m*, hair curler.

bijou (biʒu) *m*, jewel, gem; darling. **bijouterie** (tri) *f*, jewelry. **bijoutier, ère** (tje, ɛːr) *n*, jeweler.

bilan (bilɑ̃) *m*, balance sheet; statement of affairs. *déposer son* ~, to file a petition in bankruptcy.

bilboquet (bilbɔkɛ) *m*, cup & ball.

bile (bil) *f*, bile. *se faire de la* ~, to get upset, worry. **bilieux, euse** (ljø, øːz) *a*, bilious.

billard (bijaːr) *m*, billiards. [*salle de*] ~, billiard room.

bille (biːj) *f*, ball; billiard ball; marble (*games*); sawlog; bar.

billet (bijɛ) *m*, note, bill; ticket. ~ *à ordre*, note of hand, promissory note. ~ *à prix réduit*, cheap ticket. ~ *d'aller & retour*, round-trip ticket. ~ *de banque*, bank note. ~ *de complaisance*, accommodation note. ~ *de faire-part*, wedding or funeral announcement. ~ *de faveur*, free pass, complimentary ticket. ~ *de quai*, platform ticket. ~ *de logement*, billet (*Mil.*). ~ *doux*, love letter. ~ *garde-place*, ~ *de location de place*, reserved seat ticket. ~ *global*, through ticket (*sea-land-sea*). ~ *perdant*, blank (*lottery*).

billevesée (bilvəze) *f*, nonsense.

billion (biljɔ̃) *m*, billion.

billon (bijɔ̃) *m*, ridge (*Agric.*); copper &/or nickel [coin].

billot (bijo) *m*, [chopping] block.

bimbelot (bɛ̃blo) *m*, fancy article. **bimbeloterie** (blɔtri) *f*, fancy goods.

bimensuel, le (bimɑ̃sɥɛl) *a*, semimonthly, twice monthly. **bimestriel, le** (mɛstriɛl) *a*, bimonthly, [in] alternate months.

binaire (binɛːr) *a*, binary. *chiffre* ~, binary digit (*computers*). *nombre* ~, binary number. *notation* ~, binary notation.

biner (bine) *v.t*, to hoe. **binette** (nɛt) *f*, hoe.

binocle (binɔkl) *m*, eyeglasses.

biographe (biɔgraf) *m*, biographer. **biographie** (fi) *f*, biography.

biologie (biɔlɔʒi) *f*, biology. **biologiste** (ʒist) *n*, **biologue** (lɔg) *m*, biologist.

bipasse (bipas) *m*, bypass, shunt.

bipède (bipɛd) *a*, biped[al]. ¶ *m*, biped.

biplan (biplɑ̃) *m*, biplane.

bique (bik) *f*, nanny [goat]. *vieille* ~, unpleasant old woman.

birman, e (birmɑ̃, an) *a*. & **B~**, *n*, Burmese. **la Birmanie** (mani), Burma.

bis, e (bi, iːz) *a*, brownish gray; brown (*bread*).

bis (bis) *ad*, bis, repeat (*Mus.*).

encore. ¶ *m*, encore. ¶ *a*, ▲, ½ (*house number*).

bisaïeul, e (bizajœl) *n*, great-grandfather, -mother.

bisannuel, le (bizanɥɛl) *a*, biennial.

bisbille (bizbi:j) *f*, squabble. *en* ~, at loggerheads.

biscornu, e (biskɔrny) *a*, misshapen; queer, odd.

biscotte (biskɔt) *f*, rusk. **biscuit** (kɥi) *m*, biscuit; zwieback. ~ *de Savoie*, sponge cake.

bise (bi:z) *f*, north wind, chilly blast of wind; kiss on the cheek. *se faire la* ~, to kiss each other on the cheek. *biser* (ze) *v.t*, to kiss.

biseau (bizo) *m*, bevel. **biseauter** (te) *v.t*, to bevel.

bismuth (bismyt) *m*, bismuth.

bison (bizɔ̃) *m*, bison.

bissac (bisak) *m*, wallet, bag.

bissection (bisɛksjɔ̃) *f*, bisection.

bisser (bise) *v.t*, to encore.

bissextile (bisɛkstil) *a*, leap (*year*).

bistourner (bisturne) *v.t*, to twist, wrench.

bit (bit) *m*, bit (*Min.*); bit (*computers, Math.*).

bite (bit) *f*, penis (*obscene*).

bitume (bitym) *m*, bitumen, pitch, asphalt. **bitumineux, euse** (minø, ø:z) *a*, bituminous; tarry.

bivalve (bivalv) *a. & m*, bivalve.

bivouac (bivwak) *m*, bivouac. **bivouaquer** (ke) *v.i*, to bivouac, camp out.

bizarre† (biza:r) *a*, odd, queer, peculiar, freakish, outlandish. **bizarrerie** (zarri) *f*, oddness, etc.

blackbouler (blakbule) *v.t*, to blackball.

blafard, e (blafa:r, ard) *a*, pale, pallid, wan; lurid.

blague (blag) *f*, [tobacco] pouch; gammon, bunkum, rubbish, humbug, blarney, chaff; bounce, brag. *sans* ~, you don't say. **blaguer** (blage) *v.i*, to joke; rib. **blagueur** (gœ:r) *m*, joker; humbug.

blaireau (blɛro) *m*, badger; shaving brush.

blâme (blɑ:m) *m*, blame, reprimand. **blâmer** (blame) *v.t*, to blame.

blanc, che (blɑ̃, ɑ̃:ʃ) *a*, white;

hoary; blank, clean; fair (*skin*). *le mont Blanc*, Mont Blanc. ~ *de lessive*, fresh from the wash. ¶ *m*, white (*color, man, etc.*); blank; margin (*book page*), chalk (*Bil.*); breast (*fowl*). ~ *de baleine*, spermaceti. ~ *de céruse*, white lead. ~ *de champignon*, mushroom spawn. ~ *de chaux*, whitewash. ~ *de craie*, whiting. ~ *de grand fond*, front margin. ~ *de petit fond*, back margin, (*pl. col.*) gutter. ~ *de pied*, bottom margin. ~ *de terre à pipe*, pipe clay. ~ *de tête*, top margin. *nuit blanche*, sleepless night.

blanc-bec (blɑ̃bɛk) *m*, callow youth.

blanchaille (blɑ̃ʃɑ:j) *f*, fry; whitebait.

blanchâtre (blɑ̃ʃɑ:tr) *a*, whitish. **blanche** (blɑ̃:ʃ) *f*, white (*woman, ball*); minim (*Mus.*). **blancheur** (blɑ̃ʃœ:r) *f*, whiteness. **blanchir** (ʃi:r) *v.t. & i*, to whiten; blanch; bleach; whitewash; wash; wash for; launder; clean up; scald. ~ *à la chaux*, to whitewash. **blanchisserie** (ʃisri) *f*, laundry. **blanchisseuse** (sø:z) *f*, washerwoman. ~ [*de fin*], [fine] laundress.

blanc-manger (blɑ̃mɑ̃ʒe) *m*, blancmange.

blanc-seing (blɑ̃sɛ̃) *m*, blank signature.

blaser (blɑze) *v.t*, to blunt, surfeit, pall on.

blason (blɑzɔ̃) *m*, coat of arms, armorial bearings; blazon[ry], heraldry. **blasonner** (zɔne) *v.t*, to [em]blazon; malign.

blasphémateur, trice (blasfematœ:r, tris) *n*, blasphemer. **blasphématoire** (twa:r) *a*, blasphemous. **blasphème** (fɛ:m) *m*, blasphemy; profanity. **blasphémer** (feme) *v.i. & t*, to blaspheme, curse.

blatte (blat) *f*, cockroach, black beetle.

blé (ble) *m*, wheat. [*champ de*] ~, wheatfield. ~ *à moudre*, grist. ~ *de Turquie*, Indian corn, maize. ~ *noir*, buckwheat.

bled (blɛd) *f*, inland country (*in North Africa*); burg, one-horse town. *quelle* ~, what a dump!

blême (blɛːm) *a*, pale, pallid, wan, ghastly. **blêmir** (blemiːr) *v.i*, to [turn] pale.

bléser (bleze) *v.i*, to lisp.

blesser (blɛse) *v.t*, to wound, hurt, injure, gall; grate upon (*ear*); shock, offend; pinch (*shoes*). ~ *à mort*, to injure fatally. ~ *quelqu'un au cœur*, to hurt someone's feelings. **blessure** (syːr) *f*, wound, etc.

blet, te (blɛ, ɛt) *a*, overripe, soft.

bleu, e (blø) *a*, blue; underdone (*meat*); ¶ *m*, blue; blue mark (*bruise*); blueprint; recruit (*Mil.*); ~ *de ciel*, ~ *céleste*, sky blue. ~ *marine*, navy b. *conte* ~, fairy tale. **bleuâtre** (ɑːtr) *a*, bluish. **bleuet** (ɛ) *m*, cornflower. **bleuir** (iːr) *v.t. & i*, to blue.

blindage (blɛ̃daː3) *m*, armor-plating; armor; sheeting; shield (*atomic physics*).

bloc (blɔk) *m*, block, lump; coalition (*Pol.*); guardroom. ~ *journalier*, block calendar.

blocage (blɔkaːʒ) , rubble[work]; clamping, as *bloquer;* locking (*screw, etc.*); price &/or wage freeze. **blocaille** (kɑːj) *f*, rubble[stone], ballast.

bloc-film (blɔkfilm) *m*, film pack.

blockhaus (blɔkoːs) *m*, blockhouse; conning tower.

bloc-mémorandum (blɔk-memɔrɑ̃dɔm) *m*, scribbling block. **bloc-notes** (nɔt) *m*. ou *bloc de correspondance*, (*writing*) pad. **bloc-sténo** (steno) *m*, shorthand notebook.

blocus (blɔkyːs) *m*, blocade.

blond, e (blɔ̃, ɔ̃ːd) *a*, fair, flaxen, blond, e; light. ¶ *n*, fair-haired person, blond, e. ¶ *m*, blond, e, flaxen (*color*). ~ *ardent*, auburn. ~ *cendré*, ash blonde. ~ *doré*, golden (*hair*). ~ *hasardé*, reddish (*hair*). ~ *platine*, platinum blonde. ~ *roux*, sandy (*hair*).

bloquer (blɔke) *v.t*, to clamp, lock; tie up; lump; blockade, block.

blottir (se) (blɔtiːr) *v.pr*, to squat, crouch, couch, cower; lie hid; cuddle up, nestle, snuggle, nuzzle, huddle.

blouse (bluːz) *f*, smock; blouse. ~[-*paletot*], *f*, overalls. **blouser** (bluze) *v.t*, to take in, dupe. **blouson** (zɔ̃) *m*, lumber-jacket. ~ *doré*, spoiled rich kid. ~ *noir*, black leather jacket, juvenile delinquent.

bluette (blyɛt) *f*, literary trifle.

bluter (blyte) *v.t*, to bolt, sift.

boa (bɔa) *m*, boa (*wrap*). ~ *constrictor* (kɔ̃striktɔːr), boa constrictor.

bobine (bɔbin) *f*, bobbin, drum, reel, spool; coil (*Elec.*). ~ *débitrice*, supply reel. ~ *d'enroulement*, take-up reel. **bobiner** (ne) *v.t*, to wind, coil.

bobo (bɔbo) *m*, slight injury; bump.

bocage (bɔkaː3) *m*, grove. **bocager, ère** (kaʒe, ɛːr) *a*, sylvan, wood (*nymph*).

bocal (bɔkal) *m*, bottle, jar; globe, fishbowl.

bocard (bɔkaːr) *m*, stamp [mill]. **bocarder** (karde) *v.t*, to mill, stamp (*ore*).

bock (bɔk) *m*, glass (*for, or of, beer*).

bœuf (bœf) *m*, ox, bullock; beef. ~ *salé*, corned beef.

bohème (bɔɛːm) *n. & a*, Bohemian (*n. & a.*), free & easy. *la* ~, Bohemia (*fig.*). **bohémien, ne** (emjɛ̃, ɛn) *n*, gypsy.

boire (bwaːr) *v.t. & i. ir*, to drink; absorb; imbibe; swallow; pocket (*insult*); drown. ~ *un coup*, to have a drink.

bois (bwa) *m*, wood; park; horns, antlers, head (*stag*); stock (*rifle, plane*); stuff (*one is made of*); (*pl.*) wood[-wind] (*Mus.*). ~ *à brûler*, ~ *de chauffage*, firewood. ~ *contreplaqué*, plywood. ~ [*de charpente*], timber, lumber. ~ *de lit*, bedstead. ~ *de placage*, veneer. ~ *de rose*, tulip wood. ~*de satin*, satin w. ~ *plaqué triplé*, 3-ply w. **boisage** (zaː3) *m*, timbering. **boisement** (zmɑ̃) *m*, afforestation. **boiser** (ze) *v.t*, to timber; wainscot; afforest. **boiserie** (zri) *f*, woodwork; wainscoting.

boisseau (bwaso) *m*, bushel.

boisson (bwasɔ̃) *f*, drink, beverage, liquor.

boîte (bwaːt) *f*, box, case, chest, caddy, canister; can; a place of work. ~ *noire*, black box (*airplane*). *une grosse* ~, important business firm. ~ [*à conserves*], [preserving] can. ~ *à musique*, music box. ~ *de nuit*, nightclub. ~ *de vitesses*, gear box. *mettre en* ~, to pull somebody's leg.

boiter (bwate) *v.i*, to limp, halt, hobble. **boiterie** (tri) *f*, lameness. **boiteux, euse** (tø, ø:z) *a*, lame; halting; rickety.

boitier (bwatje) *m*, box with divisions; case (*watch*).

bol (bɔl) *m*, bowl, basin; bolus. ~ *rince-doigts*, finger bowl.

bolduc (bɔldyk) *m*, ribbon for gift wrapping; red tape.

Bolivie (la) (bɔlivi), Bolivia. **bolivien, ne** (vjɛ̃, ɛn) *a*. & **B~**, *n*, Bolivian.

Bologne (bɔlɔɲ) *f*, Bologna.

bombance (bɔ̃bɑ̃:s) *f*, feasting, junketing.

bombardement (bɔ̃bardəmɑ̃) *m*, bombardment, shelling, bombing. **bombarder** (de) *v.t*, to bombard. ~ *quelqu'un à une place*, to pitchfork someone into an office. **bombe** (bɔ̃:b) *f*, bomb; ball (*signal*); bombshell (*fig.*). *faire la* ~, to paint the town red.

bomber (bɔ̃be) *v.t*. & *i*. & *se* ~, to bulge, swell, camber, belly; bend.

bon, ne (bɔ̃, ɔn) *a*, good; sound; kind; nice; fine; boon (*companion*); palatable; fit; right; proper; safe; fast (*color*). **bon**, *comps:* ~ *enfant*, good-natured. [*à*] ~ *marché*, *a*, cheap, *à* ~ *marché*, *ad*, cheap[ly]. ~ *sens* (sɑ̃), [common] sense, [right] senses. **bonne**, *comps: la* ~ *année*, a happy New Year. ~ *bouche*, tidbit. ~ *femme*, simple good-natured woman. ~ *fin*, meeting (*engagement, bills*), protection (*bills*). ~ *maman*, grandmama, granny. **bon**, stet (*Typ.*). **bon à tirer**, [for] press (*Typ.*). ¶ *m*, good; cream (*of story*); order, note; license; voucher; bond; draft; scrip; profit. (*un*) ~ *à rien*, *m*. & *a*, (a) good-for-nothing, (a) ne'er-do-well. ~ *d'ouverture*, inspection order (*Cust.*). ~ *de bord*, mate's receipt. ~ *d'échange*, voucher.

bonasse (bɔnas) *a*, good-hearted; easy-going; simple-minded.

bonbon (bɔ̃bɔ̃) *m*, candy; (*pl.*) confectionery. ~*s de chocolat*, chocolates. **bonbonnière** (bɔ̃bɔnjɛ:r) *f*, confectionery box, chocolate box; sweet bowl; pretty little place (*house*).

bond (bɔ̃) *m*, bound, bounce, spring; rebound; spurt.

bonde (bɔ̃:d) *f*, bung[hole]; bung, plug. **bonder** (bɔ̃de) *v.t*, to fill to the bung, cram.

bondir (bɔ̃di:r) *v.i*, to bound, etc, as *bond*.

bondon (bɔ̃dɔ̃) *m*, bung; bondon. **bondonner** (dɔne) *v.t*, to bung.

bonheur (bɔnœ:r) *m*, happiness, welfare; [good] luck; blessing. *le* ~ *du célibat*, single blessedness. *au petit* ~, haphazardly.

bonhomie (bɔnɔmi) *f*, good nature, geniality; credulity. **bonhomme** (nɔm) *m*, simple good-natured man. *le* ~ *Noël*, Santa Claus.

bonification (bɔnifikasjɔ̃) *f*, improvement; allowance. **bonifier** (fje) *v.t*, to improve; allow, credit.

boniment (bɔnimɑ̃) *m*, patter (*showman's*); claptrap.

bonjour (bɔ̃ʒu:r) *m*, good morning, good afternoon, good day.

bonne (bɔn) *f*, [maid]servant, servant[girl]; waitress. ~ *à tout faire*, general servant, maid-of-all-work. [*d'enfant*], nurse[maid].

bonnement (bɔnmɑ̃) *m*, candidly, plainly.

bonnet (bɔnɛ) *m*, cap, hat. ~ *de police*, forage cap. ~ *magique*, wishing cap. *gros* ~, bigwig.

bonneterie (bɔntri) *f*, hosiery.

bonneteur (bɔntœ:r) *m*, card-sharper.

bonnetier (bɔntje) *m*, hosier.

bonniche (bɔniʃ) *f*, maid, female domestic (*pejorative*).

bonsoir (bɔ̃swa:r) *m*, good evening, good night.

bonté (bɔ̃te) *f*, goodness, kindness.

bookmaker (bukmekɛ:r) *m*, bookmaker. ~ *marron*, welsher.

booléen, ne (bulɛ, ɛn) *a*, Boolean. *algèbre booléen*, Boolean algebra. *opérateur booléen*, Boolean connective. *opération booléenne*, Boolean operation.

boom (bum) *m*, boom (*Fin.*); party or dance for young people.

borax (boraks) *m*, borax.

bord (bɔːr) *m*, edge, border, brink, verge, fringe, rim, margin; brim; flap; edging, binding, hem; bank, side, shore, coast, strand; board, side (*ship*); tack (*Naut.*); ship. *à* ~, on board, aboard. *à grands* ~*s*, broad-brimmed (*hat*). *à pleins* ~*s*, brimful. *par-dessus* ~, overboard.

bordé (borde) *m*, braid; gimp; planking; plating (*ship*).

bordeaux (bordo) *m*, Bordeaux, claret.

bordée (borde) *f*, broadside; volley (*fig.*); board, tack (*ship*); watch (*Naut.*).

bordel (bordɛl) *m*, brothel; general disorder.

border (borde) *v.t*, to border, edge, hem, bind; flange; tuck in (*bed*); line; plate (*ship*); ship (*oars*); run along, fringe; curb.

bordereau (bordəro) *m*, memorandum, list, schedule, statement, slip, note, contract [note].

bordier (bordje) *a.m. & m*, lopsided (boat).

bordure (bordyːr) *f*, border, edge, edging, binding, hem, skirt, rim; curb; front (*sea, river*). ~ *de fleurs vivaces*, herbaceous border.

bore (boːr) *m*, boron (*Chem.*).

boréal, e (boreal) *a*, boreal, north[ern].

borgne (bɔrɲ) *a. & n*, one-eyed (person); blind; dark, dingy; frowsy; low, of ill fame. *rue* ~, blind alley, dead end.

borique (bɔrik) *a*, boric, boracic.

borne (bɔrn) *f*, bound[ary], landmark, post; spur; terminal (*Elec.*). ~ *kilométrique*, milestone. ~ *postale*, pillar box. *dépasser les* ~*s*, to go too far. **borner** (ne) *v.t*, to bound, confine, mark out; restrict; stint.

bornoyer (bɔrnwaje) *v.t*, to squint over (*an alignment*).

Bosphore (le) (bɔsfɔːr), the Bosphorus.

bosquet (bɔskɛ) *m*, grove, spinney, thicket, shrubbery.

bosse (bɔs) *f*, hunch, hump; bump; dent, dint, bruise; mound; painter

(*boat*). *avoir la* ~ *de*, to have a talent for. **bosseler** (sle) *v.t*, to [em]boss; dent, dint, bruise, batter. **bossoir** (swaːr) *m*, davit; cathead. **bossu, e** (sy) *a*, hunchbacked, humpbacked. ¶ *n*, hunchback, humpback. **bossuer** (sɥe) *v.t*, to dent, dint, bruise, batter.

bosser (bɔse) *v.i*, to work like a dog.

bot (bo) *a.m*, club (*foot*).

botanique (bɔtanik) *a*, botanic(al). ¶ *f*, botany. **botaniste** (nist) *m*, botanist.

botte (bɔt) *f*, bundle, bunch; truss; coil; clump; thrust, lunge, pass; [high] boot. ~*s à genouillère*, jackboots. ~*s à l'écuyère*, riding boots. ~*s à revers*, top boots. ~*s cuissardes* (kɥisard) thigh boots; waders. ~*s montant aux genoux*, Wellingtons. **botteler** (tle) *v.t*, to bundle, bunch; truss (*hay*). **botter** (te) *v.t*, to boot, fit, put boots on. **bottier** (tje) *m*, bootmaker. **bottine** (tin) *f*, [half] boot. ~*s d'escalade*, climbing boots.

bottin (bɔtɛ̃) *m*, directory; who's who.

bouc (buk) *m*, he-goat, billy g. ~ *émissaire*, scapegoat.

boucan (bukɑ̃) *m*, noise, racket, etc.

boucanier (bukanje) *m*, buccaneer.

boucaut (buko) *m*, cask, hogshead.

bouche (buʃ) *f*, mouth; muzzle (*gun*); nozzle; hydrant, plug, flue; living. ~ *à feu*, piece of ordnance. ~ *béante*, ~ *bée*, open-mouthed. ~ *close!* not a word! mum['s the word]! ~ *d'incendie*, fire hydrant. **bouchée** (ʃe) *f*, mouthful, bite; patty, pasty. **boucher** (ʃe) *v.t*, to stop, obstruct; shut; close; plug, seal; bung; stopper, cork. *se* ~ *le nez*, to hold one's nose. *bouché à l'émeri*, stoppered (*bottle*).

boucher (buʃe) *m*, butcher. **boucherie** (ʃri) *f*, butcher's shop; butchery; slaughter.

bouche-trou (buʃtru) *m*, stopgap.

bouchon (buʃɔ̃) *m*, stopper, cork; plug, cap, bung; wisp; bundle;

tavern; float. ~ *de vapeur*, air-lock. *goût de* ~, corky taste. **bouchonner** (ʃɔne) *v.t*, to bundle up, rub down (*horse*).

boucle (bukl) *f*, buckle, ring, shackle; loop; sweep; eye, bight; curl, lock, ringlet; handle. ~ *d'amarrage*, ringbolt. **boucler** (kle) *v.t, & i*, to buckle; ring (*bull, etc*.); curl; loop; bulge; lock up; put away; balance (*budget*). ~ *la boucle*, to loop the loop. **bouclier** (klie) *m*, shield, buckler; shield (*atomic physics*). ~ *thermique*, heat shield.

bouddhique (budik) *a*, buddhist. **bouddhiste** (dist) *m*, buddhist.

bouder (bude) *v.i*, to sulk; shirk.

boudin (budɛ̃) *m*, blood-sausage; corkscrew curl; saddlebag; flange. ~ *d'air*, inner tube.

boue (bu) *f*, mud, dirt, mire; slime, sludge, swarf.

bouée (bue) *f*, buoy. ~ *de sauvetage*, life b.

boueux, euse (buø, ø:z) *a*, muddy, dirty, miry, mud (*spring*). ¶ *m*, scavenger.

bouffe (buf) *a*, comic.

bouffée (bufe) *f*, puff, breath, fume, whiff, gust; fit. **bouffer** (fe) *v.i*, to puff, swell; rise; bulge; *v.t*, to puff out; eat greedily (*slang*). ~ *de la vache enragée*, to have a hard time, be very poor. *se* ~ *le nez*, to have a bitter argument. **bouffi, e** (fi) *a*, puffy, swollen, bloated; turgid, bombastic. **bouffir** (fi:r) *v.t*, to swell, bloat.

bouffon, ne (bufɔ̃, ɔn) *a*, comic(al), clownish, farcical. ¶ *m*, buffoon, jester, clown; laughing-stock, butt. **bouffonnerie** (fɔnri) *f*, buffoonery, foolery.

bouge (bu:ʒ) *m*, hole, hovel, den; bulge; bilge (*cask*).

bougeoir (buʒwa:r) *m*, candle-stick.

bouger (buʒe) *v.i*, to budge, move, stir.

bougie (buʒi) *f*, candle. ~ *d'allumage*, spark plug. ~ *de préchauffage*, glow plug (*diesel*). *une lampe de 60* ~*s*, a 60 candle-power lamp.

bougonner (bugɔne) *v.i*, to grumble, grouse.

bougran (bugrɑ̃) *m*, buckram.

bougre (bu:gr) *m*, fellow, guy.

bouillant, e (brijɑ̃, ɑ̃:t) *a*, boiling; fiery, hotheaded. **bouillie** (ji) *f*, pap; porridge, gruel; pulp; mush. **bouilleur** (jœ:r) *m*, brandy distiller. ~ *de cru*, legal home distiller. **bouillir** (ji:r) *v.i.ir*, to boil. *faire* ~, to boil. *v.t*, ~ *à demi*, to parboil. **bouilloire** (jwa:r) *f*, kettle. ~ *à sifflet*, singing k. **bouillon** (jɔ̃) *m*, bubble; gush, spirt, spurt; broth, soup, bouillon, cup of broth, tea (*beef, etc*.); slops (*liquid diet*); restaurant; blow[hole]; puff, returns (*newspaper*). **bouillonner** (jɔne) *v.i*, to bubble, boil, seethe. **bouillotte** (jɔt) *f*, kettle; foot warmer. ~ *à eau chaude*, hot-water bottle.

boujaron (buʒarɔ̃) *m*, tot (*of rum, etc*.).

boulanger, ère (bulɑ̃ʒe, ɛ:r) *n*, baker. **boulangerie** (ʒri) *f*, baking; bakery.

boule (bul) *f*, ball; bowling ball; head (*slang*). ~ *d'eau chaude*, hot-water bottle. ~ *de neige*, snowball; guelder rose. [*jeu de*] ~*s*, [game of] bowls.

Boule (bul) *m*, buhl[work].

bouleau (bulo) *m*, birch [tree]. ~ *blanc*, silver birch. [*verge de*] ~, birch [rod].

bouledogue (buldɔg) *m*, bulldog.

bouler (bule) *v.t*, to send rolling; swell; blunder.

boulet (bulɛ) *m*, cannon ball; ball. **boulette** (lɛt) *f*, pellet.

boulevard (bulva:r) *m*, boulevard, avenue; bulwark (*fig*.).

bouleverser (bulvɛrse) *v.t*, to convulse, wreck, upset, overthrow.

boulier (bulje) *m*, ball frame, abacus; scoring board, string (*Bil*.).

boulin (bulɛ̃) *m*, pigeonhole (*in dovecot*); putlog.

boulingrin (bulɛ̃grɛ̃) *m*, lawn, grass plot.

boulon (bulɔ̃) *m*, bolt, pin. **boulonner** (lɔne) *v.t*, to bolt.

boulot, te (bulo, ɔt) *a*, dumpy, squat, squab[by], stumpy. ¶ *m*, work. *métro*, ~, *dodo*, subway, work, sleep.

bouquet (bukɛ) *m*, bouquet, nosegay, posy, bunch, cluster, tuft, clump; aroma; crowning piece; climax; prawn. *c'est le* ~, that's the last straw. **bouquetière** (ktjɛːr) *f*, flower girl.

bouquetin (buktɛ̃) *m*, ibex.

bouquin (bukɛ̃) *m*, old he-goat; buck hare; buck rabbit; [old] book (*of little value*). **bouquineur** (kinœːr) *m*, book hunter; lover of old books. **bouquiniste** (nist) *m*, secondhand bookseller.

bourbe (burb) *f*, mud. **bourbeux, euse,** (bø, øːz) *a*, muddy. **bourbier** (bje) *m*, slough, quag[mire]; scrape, fix.

bourde (burd) *f*, fib; blunder. *débiter des* ~s, to fib. *donneur* (*ou conteur) de* ~s, fibber.

bourdon (burdɔ̃) *m*, pilgrim's staff; bumblebee; great bell; drone (*Mus.*); drone [bee]; out[, see copy] (*Typ.*). **bourdonner** (dɔne) *v.i. & t*, to hum, buzz, drone, boom, din, sing (*in ears*).

bourg (buːr) *m*, market town, borough. **bourgade** (burgad) *f*, small town, straggling village.

bourgeois, e (burʒwa, aːz) *a*, middle-class; homely; plain (*cooking, etc.*); private (*house*). *en bourgeois*, in plain clothes, in mufti. ¶ *n*, middle-class man, woman. **bourgeoisie** (ʒwazi) *f*, middle class[es]; bourgeoisie.

bourgeon (burʒɔ̃) *m*, bud; shoot; pimple. **bourgeonner** (ʒɔne) *v.i*, to bud, etc.

bourgogne *ou* **vin de B**~(burgɔɲ) *m*, burgundy.

bourlinguer (burlɛ̃ge) *v.i*, to wallow; strain (*Naut.*); rough it.

bourrade (burad) *f*, blow, thump.

bourrage (buraːʒ) *m*, stuffing, padding; cramming (*exam, etc.*); card or paper jam (*computers*). ~ *de crâne*, eyewash, tripe, foolish ideas.

bourrasque (burask) *f*, squall; gust; tantrum.

bourratif (buratif) *a*, filling (*food*).

bourre (buːr) *f*, hair, flock, waste, down, fluff, floss; padding, stuffing, wad.

bourreau (buro) *m*, executioner, headsman, hangman; tyrant; tormentor. ~ *d'argent*, spendthrift.

~ *des cœurs*, lady-killer. **bourreler** (rle) *v.t*, (*of conscience*) to torment, prick, sting. *avoir une conscience bourrelée de remords*, to be conscience-stricken.

bourrelet (burlɛ) *m*, cushion; pad; flange. **bourrelier** (rəlje) *m*, harness maker.

bourrer (bure) *v.t*, to stuff, pad; cram, choke; tamp, ram, pack, snap at; belabor, thrash.

bourriche (buriʃ) *f*, basket, frail.

bourrique (burik) *f*, she-ass, donkey.

bourru, e (bury) *a*, surly, churlish, crusty, grumpy, gruff; rough; downy. ¶ *m*, churl, bear, curmudgeon.

bourse (burs) *f*, purse, bag; pouch; scholarship; exhibition; stock exchange, market, house; session, business day, working day (*stock market*). ~ *à pasteur*, shepherd's-purse (*Bot.*). ~ [*des valeurs*], stock exchange ~ *de marchandises*, ~ *de commerce*, produce exchange, commercial sale rooms. **boursicoter** (sikɔte) *v.i*, to dabble on the stock exchange. **boursier, ère** (sje, ɛɪr) *n*, scholarship holder; speculator.

boursouflé, e (bursufle) *p.a*, inflated, turgid, bombastic. **boursoufler** (fle) *v.t. & se* ~, to swell, puff, bloat.

bousculade (buskylad) *f*, scrimmage, hustle, rush. **bousculer** (le) *v.t*, to upset; push about, jostle; hustle; ride out (*polo*).

bouse (buːz) *f*, dung (*cattle*).

bousillage (buzijaːʒ) *m*, cob, daub, mud; bungle, botch.

bousiller (buzije) *v.t*, to ruin; botch, bungle; smash. ~ *une voiture*, smash a car. *se faire* ~, to get killed.

boussole (busɔl) *f*, [magnetic] compass, dial; (*fig.*) head, wits; guide. ~ *marine*, mariner's compass. *perdre la* ~, to go mad.

boustifaille (bustifaːj) *f*, food, grub (*slang*). **boustifailler** (faje) *v.i*, to stuff oneself with food.

bout (bu) *m*, end; finish; extremity; tip; cap; bottom; bit, stump; ferrule; button. [*petit*] ~ *d'homme*, midget, chit, manikin. ~ *de lettre*,

line or two. ~ *de rôle*, small part
(*Theat.*). *au ~ de son rouleau*, at
the end of one's rope. *faire un ~
de toilette*, to tidy oneself up. ~
de vergue, yardarm. ~ *du sein*,
nipple, teat. *à ~ portant*, point-
blank. *être à ~*, to be exhausted.

boutade (butad) *f*, whim, crotchet, fancy, fit; sally (*wit*).
par ~s, in fits & starts.

boute-en-train (butãtrẽ) *m*,
life [& soul] (*of the party*).

boutefeu (butfø) (*fig.*) *m*, firebrand, mischief-maker.

bouteille (butɛːj) *f*, bottle, flask,
jar. ~ *thermos*, thermos. ~ *à
gaz*, gas cylinder.

bouteur (butœr) *m*, bulldozer. ~
biais, angledozer.

boutique (butik) *f*, shop, stall,
booth, stand; stock (*in shop*);
shady concern; concern. ~
franche, duty-free shop. **boutiquier**, **ère** (kje, ɛːr) *n*, shopkeeper, tradesman, -woman.

boutoir (butwaːr) *m*, snout (*boar*).

bouton (butɔ̃) *m*, bud; pimple; button; stud (*collar*); knob, handle.
~ *poussoir*, push button. ~ *à
pression*, snap fastener. ~ *d'or*,
buttercup. *~s de manchettes*,
cuff links. ~ *de manivelle*, crank
pin. ~ *de sonnette*, bell push. ~
du sein, nipple, teat. **boutonner**
(tɔne) *v.t*, button [up]; (*v.i.*) to
bud; break out in pimples. *se ~*,
to button oneself up. **boutonnière**
(njɛːr) *f*, buttonhole; cut, gash.

bouture (butyːr) *f*, slip, cutting
(*Hort.*).

bouverie (buvri) *f*, cattle pen,
ox stall. **bouvier**, **ère** (vje, ɛːr) *n*,
cowherd, herdsman. **bouvillon**
(vijɔ̃) *m*, steer.

bouvreuil (buvrœːj) *m*, bullfinch.

bovin, **e** (bɔvɛ̃, in) *a*, bovine, neat,
cattle (*att.*).

box (bɔks) *m*, box stall (*horse*); garage space.

boxe (bɔks) *f*, boxing. ~ *à poings
nus*, bare-fist boxing, knuckle
fighting. ~ *contre son ombre*,
shadowboxing. **boxer** (kse) *v.i.
& t*, to box, spar. **boxeur** (ksœːr)
m, boxer. ~ *professionnel*, prize-
fighter.

boyau (bwajo) *m*, gut; hose

(*pipe*); tubular [tire] (*bicycle*);
passageway. ~ *de tranchée*, communication trench.

bracelet (braslɛ) *m*, bracelet,
wristlet, strap, bangle. *~-montre*,
wristwatch.

braconner (brakɔne) *v.i*, to
poach. **braconnier** (nje) *m*,
poacher.

brader (brade) *v.t*, to sell merchandise cheaply. **braderie** (dri) *f*,
clearance sale; surplus sale.

braguette (bragɛt) *f*, fly (*trousers*).

brahmane (braman) *m*, brahmin.

brai (brɛ) *m*, pitch, tar.

brailler (braje) *v.i*, to bawl,
squall.

braiment (brɛmã) *m*, bray[ing].
braire (brɛːr) *v.i.ir*, to bray.

braise (brɛːz) *f*, embers; breeze;
cinders; money (*slang*). **braiser**
(breze) *v.t*, to braise. **braisière**
(zjɛːr) *f*, stew-pan.

bramer (brame) *v.i*, to bell, troat.

brancard (brãkaːr) *m*, stretcher;
shaft; wheelbarrow. **brancardier**
(kardje) *m*, stretcher-bearer.

branchage (brãʃaːʒ) *m*,
branches; horns. **branche** (brãːʃ)
f, branch; leg (*compass, tripod*);
prong, tooth, tine; shank; stick. ~
de tranchée, communication
trench. ~ *gourmande*, sucker
(*Hort.*). *vieille ~*, old fellow.
branchement (brãʃmã) *m*,
branch[ing]; branch pipe; branch,
tap (*Elec.*); lead (*Elec. service*);
turnout (*Rly.*). **brancher** (ʃe) *v.t*,
to branch; connect, plug in; (*v.i.*)
to perch. **branchette** (ʃet) *f*, twig.
branchies (ʃi) *f.pl*, gills (*fish*).

brande (brãːd) *f*, heather; heath,
moor[land].

brandiller (brãdije) *v.t*, to
swing, dangle.

brandir (brãdiːr) *v.t*, to brandish, flourish.

brandon (brãdɔ̃) *m*, [fire]brand,
spark (*from conflagration*).

branlant, **e** (brãlã, ãːt) *a*, shaky,
loose, rocking. **branle** (brãːl) *m*,
swing[ing]; jangle; impulse, impetus; (*fig.*) dance, running, lead,
example. en *~-bas* (brãlba), astir,
agog. **branler** (brãle) *v.t. & i*, to
swing, shake, wag[gle], be loose,

dance, bob. *se* ~, to masturbate.

braque (brak) *m*, hound; madcap. **braquer** (ke) *v.t*, to aim (*gun*); point (*telescope*); fix (*eyes*).

bras (brɑ) *m*, arm; flipper; (*pl.*) hands (*workmen*); handle (*oar, etc.*); brace (*Naut.*); (*pl.*) jaws (*of death*). **en** ~ **de chemise**, in shirt sleeves. ~ *de mer*, arm of sea, sound. ~ *dessus*, ~ *dessous*, arm in arm. **à** [*force de*] ~, [by] hand[-power], manual.

braser (brɑze) *v.t*, to braze, hardsolder.

brasero (brɑzero) *m*, brazier; fire basket. **brasier** (zje) *m*, bright fire; inferno. **brasiller** (zije) *v.t*, to broil; (*v.i.*) to sparkle.

brassage (brasa:ʒ) *m*, brewing; stirring.

brassard (brasa:r) *m*, armlet, brassard, badge, band.

brasse (bras) *f*, fathom (Fr. *brasse marine* = 1 meter 62; Eng. *fathom* = 6 feet); stroke (*distance covered at one swimming movement*); breaststroke.

brassée (brase) *f*, armful; stroke (*one swimming movement*).

brasser (brase) *v.t*, to brew, mash; stir; dispatch; brace (*Naut.*). **brasserie** (sri) *f*, brewery, restaurant. **brasseur** (sœ:r) *m*, brewer. ~ *d'affaires*, man with many irons in the fire; shady financier.

brassiage (brasja:ʒ) *m*, fathoming, sounding.

brassière (brasjɛ:r) *f*, vest (*baby's*); shoulder strap; (*pl.*) leading strings. ~ *de sauvetage*, life jacket, cork j.

brasure (brɑzy:r) *f*, brazing; braze (*joint*).

bravache (bravaʃ) *m*, blusterer, swaggerer, bully, hector. **bravade** (vad) *f*, bravado, bluster. **brave** (bra:v) *a*, brave, gallant, bold, stout; honest, good, worthy. ¶ *m*, brave man. *mon* ~, my good man. **bravement** (bravmɑ̃) *ad*, bravely, etc; ably. **braver** (ve) *v.t*, to brave, face; dare, defy. **bravo** (vo) *ad*, bravo! hurrah, -ray! well done! hear! hear! ¶ *m*, cheer. **bravoure** (vu:r) *f*, bravery, gallantry.

brayer (brɛje) *m*, truss (*Surg.*).

break (brɛk) *m*, break, brake; station wagon.

brebis (brɔbi) *f*, ewe, sheep. ~ *galeuse*, plague, nuisance (*pers.*); black sheep (*fig.*).

brèche (brɛʃ) *f*, breach, gap; nick.

bredouille (brɔdu:j) *a*, emptyhanded. **bredouiller** (duje) *v.i*, to stammer, mumble.

bref, ève (brɛf, ɛ:v) *a*, brief; curt. [*syllabe*] *brève*, *f*, short [syllable]. **bref**, *ad*, briefly, in short, in fine.

breloque (brɔlɔk) *f*, charm (*seal, etc.*). *battre la* ~, to sound the all-clear; be nutty (*pers.*).

brème (brɛm) *f*, bream (*fish*); identity or playing card (*slang*). *taper les* ~*s*, to play cards.

Brême (brɛ:m) *f*, Bremen.

Brésil (le) (brezil), Brazil. **brésilien, ne** (ljɛ̃, ɛn) *a. & B~*, *n*, Brazilian.

Bretagne (la) (brɔtaɲ), Brittany.

bretelle (brɔtɛl) *f*, brace, suspender, sling; (*pl.*) suspenders, (*men's*); shoulder straps (*women's*).

breuil (brœ:j) *m*, covert (*game*).

breuvage (brœva:ʒ) *m*, beverage, drink; draught.

brevet (brɔvɛ) *m*, diploma, certificate; patent, license. indentures (*apprenticeship*). **breveter** (vte) *v.t*, to patent; license.

bréviaire (brevjɛ:r) *m*, breviary; favorite author (*book*).

bribes (brib) *f.pl*, scraps, leavings; odds & ends; excerpts; snatches.

bric, *ad* : *de* ~ *& de broc* (brik, brɔk), here a little & there a little. **bric-à-brac** (kabrak) *m*, bric-à-brac.

brick (brik) *m*, brig (*Naut.*).

bricole (brikɔl) *f*, breast strap; (*pl.*) odd jobs. **bricoler** (le) *v.i*, to do odd jobs (repairs, etc.). **bricoleur** (lœ:r) *m*, do-it-yourselfer.

bride (brid) *f*, bridle; rein[s]; curb, check; clamp, cramp; flange; treble (*crochet*). *à toute* ~, *à* ~ *abattue*, at full speed. **brider** (de) *v.t. & i*, to bridle; check, curb; bind; pinch, be

tight; clamp. *des yeux bridés,*
slit (or almond) eyes.
bridge (bridʒ) *m,* bridge (*cards*).
~ *aux enchères,* auction b. ~
plafond, ~ *contrat,* contract b.
brièvement (briɛvmã) *ad,* briefly, shortly. **brièveté** (vte) *f,*
brevity.
brigade (brigad) *f,* brigade;
party, posse, gang. **brigadier**
(dje) *m,* colonel commandant;
bombardier; corporal (*cavalry*);
sergeant (*police*); bowman
(*boat*).
brigand (brigã) *m,* brigand,
highwayman, robber; scamp.
brigandage (da:ʒ) *m,* brigandage,
highway robbery.
brigue (brig) *f,* intrigue; faction.
briguer (ge) *v.i. & t,* to intrigue;
intrigue for; canvass, court,
aspire to.
brillamment (brijamã) *ad,* brill-
liantly, brightly. **brillant, e** (jã,
ã:t) *a,* brilliant, bright, shining,
glittering; blooming; splendid;
glossy (*phot. paper*). ¶ *m,* brill-
liant (*diamond*). **brillantine**
(jãtin) *f,* brilliantine. **briller** (je)
v.i, to shine, brighten; glitter,
glisten; glow.
brimade (brimad) *f,* practical
joke (*on newcomer*).
brimbale (brɛbal) *f,* pump
handle. **brimbaler** (le) *v.i,* to
dangle; wobble.
brimborion (brɛbɔrjɔ̃) *m,* knick-
knack, bauble.
brin (brɛ̃) *m,* blade; slip; sprig;
shoot; strand (*rope*); joint (*fishing rod*); bit. ~ *d'osier,* withe,
withy. *un beau ~ d'homme, de
fille,* a fine youth, girl. **brindille**
(di:j) *f,* sprig, twig.
brioche (briɔʃ) *f,* brioche; blunder; potbelly (*slang*).
brique (brik) *f,* brick; bar (*soap,
etc.*); 10,000 francs (*slang*). *bouffer des ~s,* to have nothing to eat.
briquet (brikɛ) *m,* lighter (*gasoline, etc.*); tinder box, [flint &]
steel.
briquetage (brikta:ʒ) *m,* brickwork. **briqueterie** (ktri) *f,* brick-
field. **briquetier** (ktje) *m,* brick-
maker. **briquette** (kɛt) *f,* briquet[te].
bris (bri) *m,* breaking; wreck-

[age]. **brisant** (zã) *m,* reef;
breakwater; breaker (*wave*);
(*pl.*) broken water.
brise (bri:z) *f,* breeze (*wind*).
brise-bise (brizbi:z) *m,* draft
protector; short curtain, brise-
bise. **brisées** (ze) *f.pl,* footsteps
(*fig.*). **brise-jet** (brizʒɛ) *m,* anti-
splash tap nozzle. **brise-lames**
(lam) *m,* breakwater. **brisement**
(zmã) *m,* breaking, etc, as *briser.*
~ *de cœur,* contrition (*Theol.*);
heartbreak. **briser** (ze) *v.t. & i,*
to break, smash, shatter, shiver,
dash; exhaust. *se* ~, to break;
come apart (*be detachable*),
fold [up]. **brise-tout** (ztu) *m,* destructive person. **briseur** (zœ:r)
m, breaker (*pers.*). **brisure** (zy:r)
f, break; wristband; neckband.
bristol (bristɔl) *m,* visiting or
business card.
britannique (britanik) *a,* British, Britannic. *les îles B~s,* the
British Isles.
broc (bro) *m,* jug, pitcher. ~ *de
toilette,* water jug, ewer.
brocanter (brɔkãte) *v.i,* to deal
in works of art, curios, bargains,
used goods.
brocard (brɔka:r) *m,* gibe, lampoon.
brocart (brɔka:r) *m,* brocade.
brochant sur le tout (brɔʃã),
to cap all. **broche** (brɔʃ) *f,* spit,
broach; knitting needle; spindle;
arbor; spike; pin, pintle; drift-
[pin]; brooch; (*pl.*) tusks (*wild
boar*). **brochée** (ʃe) *f,* spitful.
brocher (ʃe) *v.t,* to brocade;
stitch, sew (*books*); drift (*rivets*);
scamp (*work*). *un livre broché,*
a paperback book. **brochet** (ʃɛ)
m, pike, jack (*fish*). **brochette**
(ʃɛt) *f,* skewer. **brochure** (ʃy:r)
f, interwoven pattern (*fabrics*);
stitching, sewing; pamphlet,
booklet, brochure; paperback
binding.
brocoli (brɔkɔli) *m,* broccoli.
brodequin (brɔdkɛ̃) *m,* lace
boot; buskin; sock (*comedy*).
broder (brɔde) *v.t,* to embroider.
broderie (dri) *f,* embroidery. ~ ~
à fils couchés, couching. ~-*application,* appliqué (or applied)
work. **brodeur, euse** (dœ:r, ∅:z)
n, embroiderer, ess.

brome (bro:m) *m*, bromine. **bromure** (brɔmy:r) *m*, bromide.

broncher (brɔ̃ʃe) *v.i*, to stumble, trip; flinch, falter.

bronches (brɔ̃:ʃ) *f.pl*, bronchia. **bronchite** (brɔ̃ʃit) *f*, bronchitis.

bronze (brɔ̃:z) *m*, bronze. ~ [*industriel*] gun metal. **bronzer** (brɔ̃ze) *v.t*, to bronze; (*fig.*) steel, [case]harden; tan.

broquette (brɔkɛt) *f*, tack(s).

brosse (brɔs) *f*, brush. ~ *à barbe*, shaving b. ~ *à cheveux*, ~ *à tête*, hairbrush. ~ *à cirer*, shoe b. ~ *à dents*, toothbrush. ~ *à habits*, clothes b. ~ *à laver*, scrubbing b. ~ *à miettes* [*pour la table*], crumb b. ~ *rude, douce*, hard, soft, b. *cheveux en* ~, crew cut. **brossée** (se) *f*, brushing; beating, drubbing. **brosser** (se) *v.t*, to brush; scrub (*floor*); thrash, drub. ~ *un tableau*, to sketch in a situation (*verbally*). *se* ~ *la tête, les dents*, to brush one's hair, teeth. **brosserie** (sri) *f*, brush making; b. works. **brossier, ère** (sje, ɛ:r) *n*, brush maker.

brou (bru) *m*, husk (*walnut, almond*); juice (*of walnut husk*).

brouette (bruɛt) *f*, [wheel]-barrow.

brouhaha (bruaa) *m*, hubbub, din, pother.

brouillamini (brujamini) *m*, disorder, muddle.

brouillard (bruja:r) *m*, fog, mist, haze; rough book. **brouillasse** (jas) *f*, [Scotch] mist. **brouille** (bru:j) *f*, discord, misunderstanding. **brouiller** (bruje) *v.t*, to jumble, muddle, blur, embroil; shuffle (*cards*); scramble (*eggs*). se ~, to break up (*weather*); fall out; get confused, be at loggerheads. **brouilleur** (jœ:r) *m*, jammer (*Radio*), scrambler (*code*). **brouillon, ne** (jɔ̃, ɔn) *n*, muddler; (*m.*) [rough] draft; rough copy; scratch pad.

brouir (brui:r) *v.t*, to wither, blast, blight. **brouissure** (isy:r) *f*, blight.

broussailles (brusɑ:j) *f.pl*, brushwood, undergrowth, scrub. *en* ~, unkempt. **brousse** (brus) *f*, bush (*scrub*).

broussin (brusɛ̃) *m*, gnarl (*on tree*).

brout (bru) *m*, browse. **brouter** (te) *v.t. & abs*, to browse (on), nibble; chatter (*tool*). ~ *le cresson*, to perform cunnilingus (*obscene*).

broutilles (bruti:j) *f.pl*, twigs; trifles.

broyer (brwaje) *v.t*, to crush, grind, mill.

bruant (bryɑ̃) *m*, bunting (*bird*).

brucelles (brysɛl) *f.pl*, tweezers.

brugnon (bryɲɔ̃) *m*, nectarine.

bruine (bryin) *f*, drizzle, mizzle. **bruiner** (ne) *v.imp*, to drizzle, mizzle.

bruire (bryi:r) *v.i.ir*, to murmur, rustle, sough. **bruissement** (ismɑ̃) *m*, murmur, etc.

bruit (bryi) *m*, noise, row, racket, din, clatter, ado, fuss; rumor, report, news. ~ *de pas*, tramp. **bruiteur** (tœ:r) *m*, sound effects man.

brûlant, e (brylɑ̃, ɑ̃:t) *a*, burning, hot, scorching, broiling; afire. **brûle-gueule** (bryl) *m*, short tobacco pipe. **brûle-parfum**, *m*, incense burner. **à brûle-pourpoint** (purpwɛ̃) *ad*, point-blank, to one's face. **brûlé** (le) *m*, burning (*smell, taste*). **brûler** (le) *v.t. & i*, to burn, scorch, parch, sear; singe; nip; roast; mull (*wine*). *je me suis brûlé le bras*, I have burnt my arm. *se* ~ *la cervelle*, to blow one's brains out. ~ *un feu*, to go through a red light. **brûleur** (lœ:r) *m*, burner. **brûlure** (ly:r) *f*, burn; scald.

brume (brym) *f*, fog, mist, haze. **brumeux, euse** (mø, ø:z) *a*, foggy, wintry.

brun, e (brœ̃, yn) *a*, brown; dark, dusky. ¶ *m*, brown; (*f.*) dusk, gloaming. **brunâtre** (brynɑ:tr) *a*, brownish. **brunet** (nɛ) *m*, dark man, dark boy. **brunette** (nɛt) *f*, brunette. **brunir** (ni:r) *v.t*, to brown; tan; burnish. **brunissage** (nisa:ʒ) *m*, burnishing.

brusque† (brysk) *a*, blunt, bluff, brusque, offhand, curt, abrupt, gruff. **brusquer** (ke) *v.t*, to treat abruptly; precipitate, rush. ~ *l'aventure*, to chance it. **brusquerie** (kəri) *f*, bluntness, etc.

brut, e (bryt) *a*, raw, crude; uncut (*gem*); unmanufactured; unpolished; unsweetened (*wine*); rough; gross (*Com.*); inorganic; brute (*beast, force*). *art* ~, instinctive art. **brutal, e†** (tal) *a*, brutal; brutish, coarse, rough. ¶ *m*, brute, bully. **brutaliser** (lise) *v.t*, to maltreat; bully. **brutalité** (te) *f*, brutality, etc. **brute** (bryt) *f*, brute.

Bruxelles (brysɛl) *f*, Brussels.

bruyant, e (bryjɑ̃, ɑ̃:t) *a*, noisy, boisterous, rollicking, clamorous, loud, blatant; hoydenish. **bruyamment** (jamɑ̃) *ad*, noisily.

bruyère (bryjɛ:r) *f*, heather; heath, moor; brier, briar (*pipe wood*).

buanderie (byɑ̃dri) *f*, washhouse, laundry. **buandier, ère** (dje, ɛ:r) *n*, bleacher.

buccin (byksɛ̃) *m*, whelk (*Mol.*).

bûche (by:ʃ) *f*, log, billet; chump; Swiss roll; blockhead. ~ *de Noël*, yule log. *ramasser une* ~, to take a tumble. **bûcher** (byʃe) *m*, woodshed; pile, stack (*firewood*); pyre; stake (*for burning alive*). ¶ *v.t. & i*, to rough-hew, dress, trim; swot. **bûcheron** (ʃrɔ̃) *m*, woodman, lumberman. **bûchette** (ʃet) *f*, stick. **bûcheur, euse** (ʃœ:r, ø:z) *n*, plodder, brain worker.

bucolique (bykɔlik) *a. & f*, bucolic.

budget (bydʒɛ) *m*, budget; estimates (*parliamentary*).

buée (bɥe) *f*, steam, moisture; fumes.

buffet (byfɛ) *m*, cupboard; sideboard, buffet; refreshment bar *or* room; running buffet.

buffle (byfl) *m*, buffalo. [*peau de*] ~, buff [*leather*].

bugle (bygl) *m*, flügel horn; (*f*.) bugle (*Bot.*).

buire (bɥi:r) *f*, beaker, flagon, jug.

buis (bɥi) *m*, box [tree]; boxwood.

buisson (bɥisɔ̃) *m*, bush. **buissonneux, euse** (sɔnø, ø:z) *a*, bushy. *faire l'école buissonnière* (njɛ:r), to play hooky.

bulbe (bylb) *f*, bulb (*Bot.*); (*m*.) bulb (*Anat.*). **bulbeux, euse** (bø, ø:z) *a*, bulbous.

bulgare (bylga:r) *a. & B~, n*, Bulgarian. **la Bulgarie** (gari), Bulgaria.

bulle (byl) *f*, bubble; blister, bleb; bull (*Pope's*).

bulletin (byltɛ̃) *m*, paper, note, bulletin, letter; ticket; voucher; form; list; report. ~ *de la cote*, stock exchange daily official list. ~ *de vote*, ballot. ~ *météorologique*, weather forecast.

buraliste (byralist) *n, in France*, keeper of a state-owned tobacco shop (*bureau de tabac*), where also postage stamps are sold, & licenses are issued. *Also*, clerk, tax collector. **bureau** (ro) *m*, writing table; table, desk; bureau; office; counting house; agency; exchange; committee, executive. ~ *américain*, ~ *à rideau*, rolltop desk. ~ [*central téléphonique*], [telephone] exchange. ~ *d'esprit*, coterie of wits. ~ [*de location*], box office. ~ *de garantie*, government assay office. ~ *de placement*, employment agency, registry office. ~ *de police*, police station. ~ *de poste*, post office. ~ *de scrutin*, polling station. ~ *de tabac*, tobacconist's shop. ~ *des objets trouvés*, lost property office. ~ *des rebuts*, dead letter office. ~ *ministre*, pedestal desk, kneehole d. ~ *municipal de placement gratuit*, labor exchange. *à* ~[*s*] *ouvert*[*s*], on demand, on presentation. ~ *restant*, to be called for. *sur le* ~, (*matter*) under consideration. *le deuxième* ~ Intelligence Dept. (*Mil.*). **bureaucrate** (krat) *m*, bureaucrat. **bureaucratie** (si) *f*, bureaucracy.

burette (byrɛt) *f*, bottle (oil, vinegar); cruet (*Eccl.*). ~ [*à huile*], oil can; (*pl.*) testicles (*obscene*).

burin (byrɛ̃) *m*, graver; chisel. ~ [*à froid*], cold chisel. **buriner** (rine) *v.t*, to engrave; chisel, chip.

burlesque (byrlɛsk), *a. & m*, burlesque, farcical; comic(al).

buse (by:z) *f*, buzzard; air pipe; nozzle; blockhead.

buste (byst) *m*, bust.

but (by; *in liaison*, byt) *m*, butt, mark; target; goal; winning post; aim, object, end, intention, pur-

pose, point. ~ *de transformation*, converted goal. *de ~ en
blanc*, point-blank, bluntly. ~ *à
~*, even (*games*).
butée (byte) *f*, abutment (*bridge*);
shore (*prop*); thrust (*Mech.*);
stop. **buter** (te) *v.i. & t*, to butt;
stumble; shore. **se ~ à** (*fig.*), to
be bent on; be up against.
butin (bytɛ̃) *m*, booty, spoil, loot,
plunder. **butiner** (tine) *v.i. & t*,
to pillage, plunder, loot.
butoir (bytwaːr) *m*, stop; stop
blocks; buffer.
butor (bytɔːr) *m*, bittern; dolt.
butte (byt) *f*, mound, knoll, hillock; butts (*behind target*). **butter** (te) *v.t*, to ridge; earth, hill.
buvable (byvabl) *a*, drinkable;
acceptable. **buvard** (vaːr) *m*,
blotter, blotting pad *or* case. **buvette** (vɛt) *f*, refreshment bar *or*
room; pump room (*spa*). **buveur, euse** (vœːr, øːz) *n*, drinker.
~ *d'eau*, teetotaller. **buvoter**
(vɔte) *v.i*, to sip; tipple.

C

ça (sa) *pn*. Contraction of *cela*.
çà (sa) *ad*: ~ & *là*, here & there,
hither & thither, this way & that.
~ *va?*, how are you? is that all
right? ~ *va*, all right, okay. ~ *y
est*, that's all right, that does it.
ah! çà, *i*, now then! come now!
cabale (kabal) *f*, cabal; caucus.
cabaler (le) *v.i*, to plot, intrigue.
cabane (kaban) *f*, cabin, hut;
kennel; hutch. ~ *de bois*, log
cabin, 1. hut. **cabanon** (nɔ̃) *m*,
padded cell.
cabaret (kabarɛ) *m*, wine shop
or cellar; tavern, public house;
restaurant; set *or* service (*china,
liqueur, etc.*). **cabaretier, ère**
(bartje, ɛːr) *n*, innkeeper; publican.
cabas (kabɑ) *m*, frail; shopping
basket.
cabestan (kabɛstɑ̃) *m*, capstan;
winch.
cabillaud (kabijo) *m*, cod[fish].
cabine (kabin) *f*, cabin; box; cage;
car; telephone booth. ~ *de projection*, projection booth (*cinema*). *operateur de ~*, projection-
ist (*cinema*).

cabinet (kabinɛ) *m*, room, closet;
chambers; den; practice (*professional*); cabinet (*ministerial*);
collection (*curiosities*). ~*s* ou ~
[*d'aisances*], toilet. ~ *de consultation*, consulting room, surgery.
~ *de débarras*, lumber room. ~
de lecture, reading room, newsroom; lending library. ~ *de toilette*, dressing room, toilet. ~ *de
travail*, study. ~ *de verdure*, arbor, bower. ~ *noir*, darkroom
(*Phot.*). *vie de ~*, indoor life.
câble (kɑːbl) *m*, rope, cable, line,
wire, cord. **câbler** (kɑble) *v.t*, to
cable (*Teleg.*). **cabliste** (list) *m*,
cableman (*TV*).
caboche (kabɔʃ) *f*, pate, noddle,
head; hobnail. **cabochon** (ʃɔ̃) *m*,
cabochon; brass nail.
cabosser (kabɔse) *v.t*, to dent,
batter.
cabotage (kabɔtaːʒ) *m*, coasting;
coasting trade, home trade. **ca-
boter** (te) *v.i*, to coast. **caboteur**
(tœːr) *m*, coaster.
cabotin, e (kabɔtɛ̃, in) *n*, strolling player; ham actor; theatrical
person (*affected*).
caboulot (kabulo) *m*, dive, seamy
café.
cabrer (se) (kɑbre) *v.pr*, to rear;
jib (*fig.*), take offense. **cabri**
(kabri) *m*, kid (*goat*). **cabriole** (ɔl)
f, leap. **cabrioler** (le) *v.i*, to caper.
cabriolet (lɛ) *m*, gig, cabriolet;
handcuffs (*of cord*).
caca (kaka) *m*, excrement (*children's term*). ~ *d'oie*, gosling
green.
cabrer (se) (kɑbre) *v.pr*, to rear;
jib (*fig.*), take offense. **cabri**
(kabri) *m*, kid (*goat*). **cabriole** (ɔl)
f, leap. **cabrioler** (le) *v.i*, to caper. **cabriolet** (lɛ) *m*, gig, cabriolet; handcuffs (*of cord*).
cacahuète (kakawɛt) *f*, peanut.
cacao (kakao) *m*, cacao, cocoa.
cacaoyer (ɔje) *ou* **cacaotier** (ɔtje)
m, cacao [tree].
cacatoès (kakatɔɛs) *m*, cockatoo,
parakeet.
cachalot (kaʃalo) *m*, sperm
whale, cachalot.
cache (kaʃ) *f*, hiding place; mask
(*Phot.*). **~ampoule**, *m*, bulb
shade (*Elec.*). **~cache**, *m*, hide-

&-seek. **~-corset,** *m,* camisole, underbodice.

cachemire (kaʃmiːr) *m,* cashmere.

cache-nez (kaʃne) *m,* muffler, comforter, scarf. **cache-pot** (po) *m,* jardinière (*pot*). **cache-poussière** (pusjɛːr) *m,* dust coat. **cache-sex** (sɛks) *m,* bikini, G-string. **cacher** (ʃe) *v.t,* to hide, conceal, secrete; mask. ~ *son jeu,* to be underhanded. **cachet** (ʃɛ) *m,* seal, signet; cachet; ticket, voucher; stamp (*fig.*); fee, salary. **cacheter** (ʃte) *v.t,* to seal, do up. **cachette** (ʃɛt) *f,* hiding place. *en ~,* secretly, stealthily, covertly, on the sly. **cachot** (ʃo) *m,* dungeon, cell. **cachotter** (ʃɔte) *v.t,* to make a mystery of. **cachottier,** ère (tje, ɛːr) *n,* sly-boots; (*att.*) secretive.

cachou (kaʃu) *m,* cachou.

cacochyme (kakɔʃim) *a,* sensitive [to illness]; queer.

cacophonie (kakɔfɔni) *f,* cacophony.

cactus (kaktyːs) *m,* cactus.

cadastre (kadastr) *m,* cadastral survey; valuation list (*basis for taxes*). **cadastrer** (tre) *v.t,* to survey [& value]; enter (*in valuation list*).

cadavéreux, euse (kadaverø, øːz) *a,* cadaverous, corpselike. **cadavre** (daːvr) *m,* corpse; carcass; skeleton.

cadeau (kado) *m,* present, gift.

cadenas (kadna) *m,* padlock. **cadenasser** (dnase) *v.t,* to padlock; fasten.

cadence (kadãːs) *f,* cadence, rhythm, time, step; tune (*fig.*). *aller en ~,* to keep time.

cadet, te (kadɛ, ɛt) *a. & n,* younger (brother, sister); cadet, junior, minor; caddie (*golf*); least (*fig.*).

Cadix (kadiks) *m,* Cadiz.

cadrage (kadraʒ) *m,* framing (*cinema*).

cadran (kadrã) *m,* dial [plate], face [plate]. ~ [*solaire*], [sun] dial.

cadre (kaːdr) *m,* frame, framework; frame aerial; limits, scheme, scope, compass; upper echelon employee, administrator. *les ~s,* commissioned and non-commissioned officers (*Mil.*).

cadrer (kadre) *v.i,* to square, agree, tally, suit, fit, match; to frame (*cinema*). **cadreur** (rœr) *m,* cameraman (*cinema*).

caduc, uque (kadyk) *a,* broken, decrepit, declining, frail; lapsed, statute barred. **caducité** (dysite) *f,* dilapidated state; decrepitude, senile decay; lapsing, nullity.

cafard, e (kafaːr, ard) *n,* canter, hypocrite; tell-tale, sneak; (*m.*) cockroach, black beetle; desert madness. *avoir le ~,* to have the blues.

café (kafe) *m,* coffee; café. ~ *complet,* coffee, roll & butter. **caféier** (feje) *m,* coffee tree; c. planter. **cafetier, ère** (ftje, ɛːr) *n,* café keeper, caterer; (*f.*) coffeepot.

cage (kaːʒ) *f,* cage; case, housing; shaft (*lift*). ~ *à poulets,* chicken coop. ~ *d'escalier,* staircase, stairway.

cagnard, e (kaɲaːr, ard) *a,* lazy, slothful. ¶ *n,* lazybones. **cagnardise** (ɲardiːz) *f,* laziness, sloth.

cagneux, euse (kaɲø, øːz) *a,* knock-kneed; crooked (*legs*).

cagnotte (kaɲɔt) (*cards*) *f,* pool, kitty, pot.

cagot, e (kago, ɔt) *n,* hypocrite; (*att.*) sanctimonious.

cagoule (kagul) *f,* (monk's) hooded cloak; penitent's hood.

cahier (kaje) *m,* notebook. ~ *de dessin,* sketch book. ~ *des charges,* specification.

cahin-caha (kaɛ̃kaa) *ad,* so so, middling. *aller ~,* to jog on.

cahot (kao) *m,* jolt, bump; vicissitude. **cahoter** (ɔte) *v.t. & i,* to jolt, bump; toss about.

cahute (kayt) *f,* hovel; hut.

caïd (kaid) *m,* Arab chief; gang leader; expert.

caille (kaːj) *f,* quail.

caillé (kaje) *m,* **caillebotte** (kajbɔt) *f,* curd[s]. **cailler** (kaje) *v.t. & se ~,* to curd[le]; clot.

cailletage (kajtaːʒ) *m,* gossip. **caillette** (jɛt) *f,* gossip (*pers.*).

caillot (kajo) *m*, clot.

caillou (kaju) *m*, pebble; flint; stone; boulder (*Geol.*). **cailloux-teux, euse** (tø, ø:z) *a*, pebbly; stony, flinty. **cailloutis** (ti) *m*, pebblestone, roadstones.

Caire (le) (kɛ:r), Cairo.

caisse (kɛs) *f*, case, box; tub (*for shrub*); body (*vehicle*); drum; cash; cash box, cash register, till; coffer, chest; cashier's office *or* desk *or* counter, pay office; bank, treasury, fund, association. **en ~**, in (*or* on) hand, in the till. **~ à eau**, tank. **~ à médicaments**, medicine chest. **~ claire**, snare drum. **~ d'amortissement**, sinking fund. **~ de dépôts**, safe deposit (*institution*). **~ de retraites pour la vieillesse**, old-age pension fund. **~ doublée de fer-blanc**, tin-lined case. **~ enregistreuse**, **~ contrôleuse**, cash register. **~ d'épargne**, savings bank.

caissier, ère (kɛsje, ɛ:r) *n*, cashier; teller (*bank*). **~-comptable**, cashier & bookkeeper. **~ des titres**, securities clerk.

caisson (kɛsɔ̃) *m*, caisson, pontoon; bin, bunker, box, locker.

cajoler (kaʒɔle) *v.t*, to cajole, wheedle, coax. **cajolerie** (lri) *f*, cajolery, etc.

cake (kɛk) *m*, fruitcake (*other cake: "gateau"*).

cal (kal) *m*, callosity, callus.

calaison (kalɛzɔ̃) *f*, load draught (*ship*).

calamité (kalamite) *f*, calamity. **calamiteux, euse** (tø, ø:z) *a*, calamitous.

calandre (kalɑ̃:dr) *f*, calender; mangle; weevil. **calandrer** (lɑ̃dre) *v.t*, to calender; mangle.

calcaire (kalkɛ:r) *m*, limestone. ¶ *a*, calcareous, lime[stone] (*att.*)

calciner (kalsine) *v.t*, to calcine, burn.

calcium (kalsjɔm) *m*, calcium.

calcul (kalkyl) *m*, calculation, reckoning; arithmetic; sum; calculus, stone (*Med.*). **calculer** (le) *v.t. & abs*, to calculate, reckon; compute. **calculateur** (atœ:r) *m*,

calculator; computer (*small one for simple mathematical functions*). **~ electronique**, electronic computer. **~ numérique**, digital computer. **calculatrice** (atris) *f*, calculator (*desk size*).

cale (kal) *f*, hold (*of ship*); wedge, key, scotch. **~ [de construction]**, stocks, slip[s] (*Shipbldg.*). **~ de halage**, slipway. **~ sèche**, **~ de radoub**, dry dock.

calebasse (kalbas) *f*, calabash, gourd.

caleçon (kalsɔ̃) *m*, pants, drawers. **~ de bain**, swimming trunks.

calembour (kalɑ̃bu:r) *m*, pun. **faire des ~s**, to pun. **faiseur de ~s**, punster.

calembredaine (kalɑ̃brədɛn) *f*. *oft. pl*, nonsense, foolery.

calendes (kalɑ̃:d) *f.pl*, calends. **~ grecques** (*fig.*), doomsday. **calendrier** (lɑ̃drie) *m*, calendar.

calepin (kalpɛ̃) *m*, notebook; working drawing.

caler (kale) *v.t. & i*, to wedge, key; scotch; draw (*so much water—ship*); strike (*sail*); stall (*motor*). **~ [la voile]**, to give in, knuckle under. **être calé en**, to be well up in (*subject*). **calé** (le) *a*, well-informed; clever; difficult.

calfater (kalfate) *v.t*, to calk.

calfeutrage (kalføtra:ʒ) *m*, weatherstripping.

calfeutrer (kalføtre) *v.t*, to list (*door*). **se ~**, to make oneself cosy, shut oneself in.

calibre (kalibr) *m*, caliber, bore; standing (*fig.*); gauge; template, pattern, shape; calliper[s]. **calibrer** (bre) *v.t*, to gauge, calliper, calibrate.

calice (kalis) *m*, chalice, communion cup, cup; calyx.

calicot (kaliko) *m*, calico.

calife (kalif) *m*, caliph.

Californie (la) (kalifɔrni), California. **californien, ne** (njɛ̃, ɛn) *a. & C~*, *n*, Californian.

califourchon (à) (kalifurʃɔ̃) *ad*, astride, astraddle.

câlin, e (kɑlɛ̃, in) *a*, caressing, wheedling. ¶ *n*, pet, darling; wheedler. **câliner** (line) *v.t*, to fondle, pet, cuddle; wheedle. **câ-linerie** (nri) *f*, fondling; wheedling.

calleux, euse (kalø, ø:z) *a*, callous, horny.

calligraphie (kaligrafi) *f*, calligraphy, penmanship.

callosité (kalozite) *f*, callosity.

calmant (kalmã) *m*, sedative, soother.

calmar (kalma:r) *m*, calamary, squid.

calme (kalm) *a*, calm, quiet, still; composed, collected, cool. ¶ *m*, calm, calmness. ~ *plat*, dead calm. **calmer** (me) *v.t.* & *i.* & se ~, to calm; soothe, salve; subside, abate.

calomnie (kalɔmni) *f*, calumny, slander. **calomnier** (nje) *v.t*, to calumniate, slander. **calomnieux, euse** (njø, ø:z) *a*, calumnious, slanderous.

calorie (kalɔri) *f*, calorie. **calorifère** (rifɛ:r) *m*, heater. ~ *à feu continu*, slow-combustion stove. **calorique** (rik) (*Phys.*), *m*, caloric, heat.

calot (kalo) *m*, forage cap. **calotte** (lɔt) *f*, skull cap; cap; calotte; canopy (*heaven*); cuff (*blow*). **calotter** (te) *v.t*, to cuff.

calque (kalk) *m*, tracing; copy (*fig.*). **calquer** (ke) *v.t*, to trace; copy.

calus (kaly:s) *m*, callus, callosity.

Calvaire (kalvɛ:r) *m*, Calvary (*place*). **calvaire**, (*representation*); cross (*fig.*).

calvitie (kalvisi) *f*, baldness.

camarade (kamarad) *n*, comrade, fellow, mate, chum, companion. ~ *d'atelier*, fellow workman. ~ *d'école*, schoolfellow, schoolmate. ~ *de bord*, shipmate. ~ *de bouteille*, boon companion. ~ *de collège*, fellow student. ~ *de jeu*, playfellow, playmate. ~ *de lit*, ~ *de chambrée*, bedfellow, roommate. ~ *de malheur*, fellow sufferer. ~ *de plat*, messmate. ~ *de promotion*, class mate. **camaraderie** (dri) *f*, comradeship, fellowship, friendship.

camard, e (kama:r, ard) *a*, snub-nosed. *la camarde*, [grim] death (*fig.*).

cambouis (kãbwi) *m*, cart grease.

cambrer (kãbre) *v.t.* & se ~, to camber, arch, bend, curve.

cambriolage (kãbriola:ʒ) *m*, housebreaking, burglary. **cambrioler** (le) *v.t*, to burgle. **cambrioleur** (lœ:r) *m*, burglar, cracksman. ~ *chat*, cat burglar.

cambrure (kãbry:r) *f*, camber. ~*support*, *f*, arch support (*for foot in shoe*).

cambuse (kãby:z) *f*, steward's room (*ship*). **cambusier** (byzje) *m*, steward's mate; storekeeper (*Naut.*).

came (kam) *f*, cam, wiper, lifter; drugs (*heroin, etc.*).

camé, e (kame) *a*, drugged. ¶ *m*, drug addict, junkie.

camée (kame) *m*, cameo.

caméléon (kameleɔ̃) *m*, chameleon, trimmer, time server.

camélia (kamelja) *m*, camellia.

camelot (kamlo) *m*, hawker, street vender (*as newsboy*); handbill distributor. **camelote** (lɔt) *f*, rubbish, trash.

camera (kamera) *m*, movie camera.

camion (kamjɔ̃) *m*, wagon, truck; ~*-citerne*, *m*, tank truck. ~ *à benne basculante*, dump truck. **camionnage** (ɔna:ʒ) *m*, cartage. **camionnette** (nɛt) *f*, light truck, **camionneur** (nœr) *m*, truck driver, carter, carman; van horse, vanner.

camisole (kamizɔl) *f*, vest (*woman's*). ~ *de force*, straitjacket.

camomille (kamɔmi:j) *f*, camomile.

camouflage (kamufla:ʒ) *m*, camouflage. **camoufler** (fle) *v.t*, to disguise, camouflage.

camouflet (kamuflɛ) *m*, snub.

camp (kã) *m*, camp, field; side. ~ *de concentration* (civil), ~ *de prisonniers* (Mil.), internment camp. ~ *volant*, temporary camp; flying column.

campagnard, e (kãpaɲa:r, ard) *n*, countryman, -woman. **campagne** (paɲ) *f*, country, countryside, fields; field (*Mil.*); campaign; run; cruise (*Nav.*). *faire une bonne* ~, to have a good year (*business*).

campagnol (kɑ̃paɲɔl) *m*, vole.

campanile (kɑ̃panil) *m*, campanile, bell tower.

campanule (kɑ̃panyl) *f*, campanula, bell [flower]. ~ *à grandes fleurs*, Canterbury Bell.

campêche (kɑ̃pɛʃ) *m*, logwood.

campement (kɑ̃pmɑ̃) *m*, encampment; camping [out]. **camper** (pe) *v.i.* & *t*, to [en]camp; lodge, ensconce; put, clap, stick. ~ *là*, to leave in the lurch. ~ *un personnage*, to play a theatrical role (*well*).

camphre (kɑ̃ːfr) *m*, camphor. **camphrer** (kɑ̃fre) *v.t*, to camphorate.

campos (kɑ̃po) *m*, holiday.

camus, e (kamy, yːz) *a*, flat-nosed, snub-nosed; pug-nosed.

Canada (le) (kanada), Canada. **canadien, ne** (djɛ̃, ɛn) *a*. & C~, *n*, Canadian; sheepskin jacket.

canaille (kanɑːj) *f*, rabble, mob, riffraff, ragtag [& bobtail]; blackguard, scoundrel, rascal.

canal (kanal) *m*, canal, channel, duct, pipe, passage, race[way], ditch, sluice[way]. ~ *de dérivation*, leat. ~ *banalisé*, citizens' band (*CB radio*). ~ *maritime*, ship canal. **canalisation** (lizasjɔ̃) *f*, canalization, piping, pipeline; mains. **canaliser** (ze) *v.t*, to canalize, pipe; (*fig.*) concentrate, focus, centralize.

canapé (kanape) *m*, sofa, couch, lounge. ~-*divan*, chesterfield. ~-*lit*, sofa bed.

canard (kanaːr) *m*, duck, drake; canard, hoax; rag (*worthless newspaper*). *bâtiment* ~, pitching ship. **canarder** (narde) *v.t*, to snipe (*Mil.*); pepper (*with shot*); (*v.i.*) to pitch (*ship*). **canardière** (djɛːr) *f*, duck pond; decoy (*place*); fowling piece.

canari (kanari) *m*, canary (*bird*). **les [îles] Canaries**, *f.pl*, the Canary Islands, the Canaries.

cancan (kɑ̃kɑ̃) *m*, cancan (*dance*); tattle, scandal, backbiting.

cancer (kɑsɛːr) *m*, cancer (*Med.*),

le ~, crab (*Astr.*). **cancéreux, euse** (serø, øːz) *a*, cancerous.

cancre (kɑ̃ːkr) *m*, crab (*Crust.*); dunce, duffer.

cancrelat (kɑ̃krəla) *m*, cockroach.

candélabre (kɑ̃delɑːbr) *m*, candelabrum; multi-light fixture.

candeur (kɑ̃dœːr) *f*, guilelessness, ingenuousness.

candidat, e (kɑ̃dida, at) *n*, candidate; examinee. ~ *à la députation*, parliamentary candidate. **candidature** (tyːr) *f*, candidature. *poser sa* ~, to apply for a job; announce one's candidacy.

candide† (kɑ̃did) *a*, guileless, ingenuous.

candir (se) (kɑ̃diːr) *v.pr*, to candy. *fruits candis* (di), crystalized fruits. [**sucre**] **candi** (di), *m*, [sugar] candy.

cane (kan) *f*, duck (*female*). **caner** (ne) *v.i*, to run away, show the white feather. **caneton** (ntɔ̃) duckling (*male*). **canette** (nɛt) *f*, duckling (*female*); [spring-stoppered] bottle (*for, or of, beer*); bobbin.

canevas (kanva) *m*, canvas; sketch; groundwork, outline, skeleton.

caniche (kaniʃ) *n*. & *a*, poodle.

canicule (kanikyl) *f*, dog days.

canif (kanif) *m*, penknife.

canin, e (kanɛ̃, in) *a*, canine, dog (*att.*).

caniveau (kanivo) *m*, gutter, gully, kennel [stone]; conduit.

canne (kan) *f*, cane; stick; walking stick; singlestick. ~ *à épée*, sword stick. ~ *à lancer*, casting rod (*Fish.*). ~ *à mouche*, fly rod (*Fish.*). ~ *à pêche*, fishing rod. ~ *à sucre*, sugarcane. ~ *plombée*, loaded stick. ~-*siège*, sportsman's seat, stick s.

canneberge (kanbɛrʒ) *f*, cranberry.

canneler (kanle) *v.t*, to channel, flute, groove, corrugate, rifle. **cannelle** (kanɛl) *f*, cinnamon; butt cock. **cannelure** (kanlyːr) *f*, channel-[ling], etc. as *canneler*.

canner (kane) *v.t*, to cane (*chairs*).

cannibale (kanibal) *m*, cannibal, man-eater; savage (*fierce man*).

canoë (kanɔe) *m*, canoe.

canon (kanɔ̃) *m*, gun, cannon; cañon, canyon; barrel, pipe, tube; canon (*rule—Eccl.*). ~ *d'amarrage*, bollard. ~ *de campagne à tir rapide*, quick-firing field gun. *droit* ~, canon law. **canonicat** (nɔnika) *m*, canonicate, canonry; sinecure. **canoniser** (ze) *v.t*, to canonize. **canonnade** (nad) *f*, cannonade. **canonnage** (na:ʒ) *m*, gunnery. **canonner** (ne) *v.t*, to cannonade, bombard, shell. **canonnier** (nje) *m*, gunner. **canonnière** (njɛːr) *f*, gunboat; pop gun (*toy*).

canot (kano) *m*, boat; dinghy; cutter. ~ *à rames*, rowboat. ~ *de sauvetage*, lifeboat. **canotage** (nɔta:ʒ) *m*, boating, rowing. **canoter** (te) *v.i*, to boat, row. **canotier** (tje) *m*, rower, oarsman; boatman, waterman; boat keeper. [*chapeau*] ~, boater.

cantate (kɑ̃tat) *f*, cantata. **cantatrice** (tris) *f*, professional singer (*woman*), vocalist.

cantharide (kɑ̃tarid) *f*, Spanish fly.

cantine (kɑ̃tin) *f*, canteen. **cantinier, ère** (nje, ɛːr) *n*, canteen keeper.

cantique (kɑ̃tik) *m*, canticle, song, hymn.

canton (kɑ̃tɔ̃) *m*, canton, district. **cantonade** (tɔnad) *f*, wings (*Theat.*). **cantonnement** (nmɑ̃) *m*, cantonment, quarters; billets. ~ *de pêche*, stretch of fishing. **cantonner** (ne) *v.t*. & *i*, to canton, quarter, billet. *se* ~ *dans*, to withdraw to; keep oneself to. **cantonnier** (nje) *m*, roadman, road mender.

canular (kanyla:r) *m*, hoax, practical joke; tall tale.

canule (kanyl) *f*, nozzle; butt cock.

caoutchouc (kautʃu) *m*, rubber, elastic; [rubber] tire; waterproof, mackintosh; galosh, golosh, overshoe. ~ *durci*, vulcanite. **caoutchouter** (ʃute) *v.t*, to rubber[ize], waterproof; rubber-tire.

cap (kap) *m*, cape, headland, foreland; head. ~ *à pic*, bluff. *le* ~ *de Bonne-Espérance*, the Cape of Good Hope. *le* ~ *Vert*, Cape Verde. *mettre le* ~ *sur*, to head for.

capable (kapabl) *a*, capable; able, fit; efficient, qualified. **capacité** (site) *f*, capacity, capability, etc.

caparaçonner (kaparasɔne) *v.t*, to caparison.

cape (kap) *f*, hooded cape; hood; bowler [hat]. *rire sous* ~, to laugh up one's sleeve, chuckle. **capeline** (plin) *f*, hood.

capharnaüm (kafarnaɔm) *m*, jumble shop.

capillaire (kapillɛːr) *a*, capillary. ¶ *m*, maidenhair [fern].

capilotade (kapilɔtad) *f*, hash; pulp.

capitaine (kapitɛn) *m*, captain; master, skipper. ~ *au long cours*, deep-sea captain, master of foreign-going vessel. ~ *d'armement*, marine superintendent. ~ *d'entraînement*, coach. ~ *de corvette*, lieutenant commander (*Nav.*). ~ *de frégate*, commander (*Nav.*). ~ *de port*, harbor master. ~ *de vaisseau*, captain (*Nav.*). ~ *marchand*, captain of merchant ship, master mariner.

capital, e (kapital) *a*, capital, principal, main, essential; deadly (*sins*). ¶ *m. oft. pl*, principal, capital, capital sum; capital stock; money; assets. ~*-actions*, *m*, share capital. ~ *de roulement*, working c. ~ *engagé*, trading c. ~*-risque*, venture c. *le* ~ & *le travail*, Capital & Labor. *peine* ~, death penalty. ¶ *f*, capital (*town, letter*); metropolis. **capitaliser** (lize) *v.t*, to capitalize. **capitaliste** (list) *n*, capitalist.

capitan (kapitɑ̃) *m*, blusterer.

capitation (kapitasjɔ̃) *f*, poll tax.

capiteux, euse (kapitø, øːz) *a*, heady.

capitonner (kapitɔne) *v.t*, to upholster; quilt.

capituler (kapityle) *v.i*, to capitulate; compromise (*with conscience*).

capon, ne (kapɔ̃, ɔn) *n*, coward; sneak (*Sch.*).

caporal (kapɔral) *m*, corporal; caporal (*tobacco*).

capot (kapo) *m*, bonnet, hood, cover. *être* ~, to be defeated. *faire* ~, to capsize. **capote** (pɔt) *f*, greatcoat, overcoat (*Mil.*); hood, bonnet, cowl; top of convertible automobile. ~ *anglaise*, condom. ~ *pliante*, collapsible top (*auto*). **capoter** (te) *v.i*, to capsize, overturn.

câpre (kɑːpr) *f*, caper (*Bot.*).

caprice (kapris) *m*, caprice, whim, freak; [passing] fancy; vagary. **capricieux, euse,†** (sjø, øːz) *a*, capricious; temperamental; wayward.

capsule (kapsyl) *f*, capsule; seal (*bottle*); [percussion] cap.

capter (kapte) *v.t*, to catch, collect, save, recover; obtain by undue influence. *vouloir* ~, to make a bid for. ~ *les suffrages de*, win the votes of. **capteur** (tœːr) *m*, captor; sensor, gauge. ~ *de pression*, pressure gauge.

captieux, euse (kapsjø, øːz) *a*, captious.

captif, ive (kaptif, iːv) *a. & n*, captive. **captiver** (tive) *v.t*, to captivate. **captivité** (vite) *f*, captivity, bondage. **capture** (tyːr) *f*, capture. **capturer** (tyre) *v.t*, to capture, take; catch.

capuce (kapys), **capuchon** (ʃɔ̃) *m*, hood, cowl.

capucin, e (kapysɛ̃, in) *n*, Capuchin friar, nun; (*f.*) nasturtium. **capucinade** (sinad) *f*, dull discourse.

caque (kak) *f*, barrel, keg. **caquer** (ke) *v.t*, to cure (*herrings*); barrel.

caquet (kakɛ) *m*, cackle; chatter. **caqueter** (kte) *v.i*, to cackle; chatter.

car (kaːr) *c*, for, because. ¶ *m*, bus.

carabin (karabɛ̃) *m*, medical student; saw-bones. **carabine** (bin) *f*, carbine, rifle. **carabiné, e** (ne) *a*, strong, stiff.

caracole (karakɔl) *f*, caracole.

caractère (karaktɛːr) *m*, character; characteristic, property, nature; complexion; authority; temper; type, (*pl.*) print. *écrire en ~s d'imprimerie*, to write in block

letters. *jeu de* ~*s*, character set (*computers*). **caractériser** (terize) *v.t*, to characterize. **caractéristique** (ristik) *a*, characteristic. ¶ *f*, characteristic, feature.

carafe (karaf) *f*, water bottle, jug, decanter. **carafon** (fɔ̃) *m*, [small] decanter.

carambolage (karɑ̃bɔlaːʒ) · *m*, cannon (*Bil.*).

caramel (karamɛl) *m*, caramel.

carapace (karapas) *f*, carapace, shell.

carat (kara) *m*, carat; carat goods; year (*age*). *sot à vingt-quatre* (ou *à trente-six*) ~*s*, champion idiot, out & out fool.

caravane (karavan) *f*, caravan. **caravansérail** (vɑ̃seraːj) *m*, caravanserai.

carbonate (karbɔnat) *m*, carbonate. **carbone** (bɔn) *m*, carbon. **carbonifère** (nifɛːr) *a*, carboniferous, coal[-bearing]. **carbonique** (nik) *a*, carbonic. **carboniser** (ze) *v.t*, to carbonize, char. **carbonnade** (nad) *f*, grill[ed meat]. *à la* ~, grilled.

carburant (karbyrɑ̃) *m*, motor fuel.

carburateur (karbyratœːr) *m*, carburetor. **carbure** (byːr) *m*, carbide.

carcan (karkɑ̃) *m*, carcan (*Hist.*); yoke.

carcasse (karkas) *f*, carcass, carcase, body, skeleton, shell, frame[work]; shape (*hat, etc.*).

cardiaque (kardjak) *a*, cardiac. *crise* ~, heart attack. ¶ *n*, heart case (*pers.*).

cardinal, e (kardinal) *a*, cardinal. ¶ *m*, cardinal (*Eccl.*).

cardiogramme (kardjɔgram) *m*, cardiogram. **cardiograph** (graf) *m*, cardiographer; cardiogram. **cardiologue** (lɔg) *m*, cardiologist.

carême (karɛːm) *m*, lent.

carence (karɑ̃ːs) *f*, assets nil; insolvency.

carène (karɛn) *f*, bottom (*of ship*). **caréner** (rene) *v.t*, to careen.

caresse (karɛs) *f*, caress, endearment; blandishment. **caresser** (se) *v.t*, to caress; fondle; stroke; pat; cherish; flatter; indulge.

cargaison (kargεz5) *f*, cargo, lading.

cargo (kargo) *m*, cargo boat.

cari (kari) *m*, curry.

caricature (karikaty:r) *f*, caricature; cartoon; sight. **caricaturer** (tyre) *v.t*, to caricature. **caricaturiste** (rist) *n*, caricaturist, cartoonist.

carie (kari) *f*, caries, decay; rot. **carier** (rje) *v.t*, & se ~, to rot, decay.

carillon (karij5) *m*, chime[s]; carillon; peal; racket, row. **carillonner** (jone) *v.i.* & *t*, to chime, ring a peal; clatter; noise abroad. **carillonneur** (nœ:r) *m*, [bell] ringer.

carlin (karlɛ̃) *m*, pug [dog].

carlingue (karlɛ̃:g) *f*, ke[e]lson (*Naut.*); cockpit (*Avn.*).

carme (karm) *m*, Carmelite [friar]. **carmélite** (melit) *f*, Carmelite [nun].

carmin (karmɛ̃) *m*, carmine.

carnage (karna:ʒ) *m*, carnage, slaughter, bloodshed. **carnassier, ère** (nasje, ɛ:r) *a*, carnivorous. ¶ *m*, carnivore; (*f.*) game bag.

carnaval (karnaval) *m*, carnival.

carné, e (karne) *a*, flesh-colored; meaty (*food*); meat (*diet*).

carneau (karno) *m*, flue.

carnet (karnɛ) *m*, notebook, memorandum book; book. ~ *de bal*, dance program. ~ *de chèques*, checkbook. ~ *de compte*, ~ *de banque*, [bank] pass book. ~-*répertoire*, address book.

carnier (karnje) *m*, game bag. **carnivore** (nivɔ:r) *a*, carnivorous. ~s, *m.pl*, carnivora.

caroncule (kar5kyl) *f*, wattle (*turkey*).

carotte (karɔt) *f*, carrot; bore core; plug, twist (*tobacco*); trick. *des cheveux* ~, carroty hair, ginger hair.

caroube (karub) *f*, carob [bean], locust [bean].

Carpathes (les) (karpat) *m.pl*, the Carpathians.

carpe (karp) *f*, carp (*fish*). *m*, wrist.

carpette (karpɛt) *f*, bordered [& seamless] carpet; rug.

carquois (karkwa) *m*, quiver (*for arrows*).

carre (ka:r) *f*, cross section; corner.

carré, e (kɑre) *a*, square. ¶ *m*, square; bed, patch (*Hort.*); landing, floor. ~ *des officiers*, ward room; mess room. ~ *long*, rectangle, oblong. **carreau** (ro) *m*, tile; floor; squab, cushion; hassock; diamonds (*cards*); pane, square. **carrefour** (karfu:r) *m*, crossroads; intersection (*in city*). *de* ~, street (*musician*); gutter (*language*). **carrelage** (rla:ʒ) *m*, tile floor[ing]. ~ *en briques*, brick paving. **carrelet** (rlɛ) *m*, square ruler; square file; plaice. **carrément** (remɑ̃) *ad*, square[ly], outright, flat[ly], straightforwardly. **carrer** (re) *v.t*, to square. se ~, to strut, swagger; settle oneself.

carrier (kɑrje) *m*, quarryman. **carrière** (ɛ:r) *f*, career, course, scope, play, vent, head; walk of life; quarry, pit.

carriole (karjɔl) *f*, light cart.

carrosse (karɔs) *m*, coach. **carrosserie** (sri) *f*, coachbuilding; (*car*) body; bodywork. **carrossier** (sje) *m*, coachbuilder; motor body builder; coach horse.

carrousel (karuzɛl) *m*, tournament; merry-go-round; turntable, carousel (*air terminal baggage*).

carrure (kary:r) *f*, breadth of shoulders.

cartable (kartabl) *m*, satchel (*Sch.*).

carte (kart) *f*, card; ticket; map, chart. ~*s à jouer*, playing cards. ~ *blanche*, free hand, full discretionary power. ~ *céleste*, star map, map of the heavens. ~ *d'abonnement*, season ticket. ~ *d'adresse*, address card, business c. ~ *d'État-major*, ordnance [survey] map. ~ *de résultats*, scoring card (*golf*). ~ [*de visite*], [visiting] card. ~ *des vins*, wine list. ~ *du jour*, bill of fare, menu. ~ *en courbes de niveau*, contour map. ~ *grise*, registration (*auto*). ~ *orange*, monthly subway or bus pass. ~ *perforée*, punched card. ~ *postale illustrée*, picture postcard. ~ *vermeil*, senior citizen's reduction card.

cartel (kartɛl) *m*, challenge; cartel; coalition.

carter (kartɛːr) *m*, gear case.

cartilage (kartila:ʒ) *m*, cartilage, gristle.

cartographe (kartɔgraf) *m*, cartographer, map producer.

cartomancien, ne (kartɔmɑ̃sjɛ̃, ɛn) *n*, fortuneteller (*by cards*).

carton (kartɔ̃) *m*, cardboard, pasteboard, millboard; [cardboard] box *or* case, carton; mount (*Phot.*); cartoon; offcut (*Bookb.*); cancel (*Bookb.*). ~ *à chapeau*, hat box. ~ *de débarquement*, landing ticket. ~ *de dessins*, portfolio of drawings. ~ *de modiste*, bandbox. ~-*paille*, *m*, strawboard. ~-*pâte*, *m*, papier-mâché. **cartonné, e** (tɔne) *p.a*, in boards (*book*). **cartonnier** (nje) *m*, cardboard [box] maker; file case.

cartouche (kartuʃ) *f*, cartridge, round [of ammunition]; case (*firework*); (*m.*) cartouche. ~ *à balle*, ball cartridge. ~ *à blanc*, blank c. **cartoucherie** (ʃri) *f*, cartridge factory. **cartouchière** (ʃjɛːr) *f*, cartridge pouch.

carvi (karvi) *m*, caraway.

cas (kɑ) *m*, case, event, circumstance, instance; matter; cause (*law*). ~ *limite*, borderline case. *faire ~ de*, to think highly of.

casanier, ère (kazanje, ɛ:r) *a. & n*, stay-at-home.

casaque (kazak) *f*, jumper (*woman's*). *tourner ~*, to sell out (*Pol.*).

cascade (kaskad) *f*, cascade, waterfall, fall[s]; prank, spree; gag (*actor's*). **cascadeur** (œ:r) *m*, stuntman (*cinema*); trapeze artist; reveller. **cascatelle** (tɛl) *f*, cascade.

case (kɑːz) *f*, compartment, division, pigeon hole; square (*chessboard*); frame, space (*on printed form*); locker; bin; native hut, cabin.

casemate (kazmat) *f*, casemate.

caser (kɑze) *v.t*, *t*o put away; find a situation for, settle.

caserne (kazɛrn) *f*, barrack[s]. **caserner** (ne) *v.t*, to barrack.

casier (kazje) *m*, cabinet, nest of drawers, [set of] pigeon holes; bin; rack. ~ *judiciaire*, police records.

casino (kazino) *m*, casino.

Caspienne (la mer) (kaspjɛn), the Caspian sea.

casque (kask) *m*, helmet; headphones, earphones. ~ *blindé*, crash helmet. ~ *de soleil*, sun helmet. ~ *en moelle*, pith helmet. ~ *respiratoire*, smoke helmet, gas mask (*fire*). **casquette** (kɛt) *f*, (*man's or boy's*) [peak] cap.

cassant, e (kɑsɑ̃, ɑ̃:t) *a*, brittle, crisp, short, hard; blunt, curt. **cassation** (sasjɔ̃) *f*, cassation, quashing, reduction to the ranks. **casse** (kɑ:s) *f*, breakage, breakages; cassia; case (*Typ.*); ladle, scoop. ¶ (kɑs) *comps:* ~-*cou*, *m*, breakneck [place], death trap; dare-devil; roughrider; (*i.*) look out! mind! ~-*couilles*, *m*, ball-breaker (*obscene*). ~-*croûte*, *m*, snack; s. bar. ~-*noisettes*, *m*, nutcrackers; nuthatch. ~-*noix*, *m*, nutcrackers; nutcracker (*bird*). ~-*pieds*, *m*, bore (*person*). ~-*pierres*, *m*, stone breaker (*Mach.*). ~-*pipes*, *m*, war (*slang*). ~-*tête*, *m*, club, life preserver; puzzle, teaser. **casser** (kɑse) *v.t. & i*, to break, crack, snap; shatter; quash, set aside (*law*); cashier; reduce to the ranks. ~ *les prix*, to bring prices down. ~ *aux gages*, to pay off. *se ~ la tête*, to break one's head; puzzle (*or* rack) one's brains. *se ~*, to take off, leave (*slang*).

casserole (kasrɔl) *f*, saucepan, stewpan. ~ [*en terre cuite*], casserole.

cassette (kasɛt) *f*, casket, case; money box; privy purse; cassette (*magnetic tape*).

casseur (kasœ:r) *m*, breaker. ~ *d'assiettes*, brawler.

cassier (kasje) *m*, cassia tree.

cassine (kasin) *f*, country cottage.

cassis (kɑsis) *m*, black currant(s); b. c. bush; b. c. cordial; water bar (*across road*).

cassonade (kasɔnad) *f*, moist sugar, brown s.

cassure (kɑsy:r) *f*, break, crack, fracture.

castagnette (kastaɲɛt), *f*, castanet.

caste (kast) *f*, caste. *esprit de ~*, class consciousness.

castor (kastɔ:r) *m*, beaver. *~ du Canada*, musquash (*fur*).

castration (kastrasjɔ̃) *f*, castration; gelding.

casuel, le (kɑzɥɛl) *a*, casual; case (*ending—Gram*.). ¶ *m*, casual profits; perquisites.

casuistique (kɑzɥistik) *f*, casuistry.

cataclysme (kataklism) *m*, cataclysm, disaster.

catacombe (katakɔ̃:b) *f*, catacomb.

catafalque (katafalk) *m*, catafalque.

catalogue (katalɔg) *m*, catalog, list. *~ par ordre de matières*, subject catalog. *~ raisonné*, descriptive c. **cataloguer** (ge) *v.t*, to catalog, list.

cataplasme (kataplasm) *m*, poultice.

catapulte (katapylt) *f*, catapult (*Hist. & Avn.*).

cataracte (katarakt) *f*, cataract (*falls & Med.*); (*pl.*) sluice gates (*of heaven*).

catarrhe (kata:r) *m*, catarrh.

catastrophe (katastrɔf) *f*, catastrophe.

catch (katʃ) *m*, wrestling (*sport*). **catcheur** (ʃœ:r) *m*, wrestler.

catéchiser (kateʃize) *v.t*, to catechize; reason with, try to persuade. **catéchisme** (ʃism) *m*, catechism.

catégorie (kategɔri) *f*, category, class; predicament (*Log.*). **catégorique†** (rik) *a*, categorical; flat (*refusal*).

caténation (katenasjɔ̃) *f*, concatenation, series.

cathédrale (katedral) *f*, cathedral, minster.

cathode (katɔd) *f*, cathode.

catholicisme (katɔlisism) *m*, catholicism, Roman Catholicism. **catholique** (lik) *a*, catholic, Roman Catholic; orthodox. ¶ *n*, catholic, Roman Catholic.

catimini (en) (katimini) *ad*, stealthily, on the sly.

catin (katɛ̃) *f*, whore; slut (*slang*).

Caucase (le) (koka:z), the Caucasus. **caucasien, ne** (kazjɛ̃, ɛn) *a*. & **C~**, *n*, Caucasian.

cauchemar (koʃma:r) *m*, nightmare, incubus; bugbear.

caudataire (kodatɛ:r) *m*, train bearer; toady, toadeater, lickspittle.

cause (ko:z) *f*, cause, occasion, ground[s]; case, action (*law*); brief (*law*); consideration (*equivalent, law*). *~ célèbre*, famous case. *à ~ de*, on account of, because of, for; for the sake of, through. *en tout état de ~*, in any case. *& pour ~*, & for good reasons, & very properly. *sans ~*, briefless (*lawyer*). **causer** (koze) *v.t*, to cause, occasion.

causer (koze) *v.i*, to talk, converse, chat; talk of; sit out (*a dance*). *assez causé!* that'll do! **causerie** (zri) *f*, talk, chat, chit-chat; causerie. **causette** (zɛt) *f*, little chat. **causeur, euse** (zœ:r, ø:z) *n*, talker, conversation[al]ist; (*f.*) settee.

caustique (kostik) *a*, caustic, biting, cutting. ¶ *m*, caustic (*Phar.*).

cauteleux, euse (kotlø, ø:z) *a*, cunning, crafty.

cautère (kotɛ:r) *m*, cautery. **cautériser** (terize) *v.t*, to cauterize, sear.

caution (kosjɔ̃) *f*, surety, security, guarantee, -ty, guarantor, indemnity, bail. *se rendre ~ pour*, to go bail for. *sujet à ~*, unreliable. **cautionnement** (ɔnmɑ̃) *m*, security, indemnity, deposit, bail, surety (*or indemnity*) bond, qualification (*in shares*). **cautionner** (ne) *v.t*, to become security for, guarantee, bail; give security for, answer for.

cavalcade (kavalkad) *f*, cavalcade; pageant; ride.

cavalerie (kavalri) *f*, cavalry; horse (*troop*); stable (*horses*). **cavalier, ère†** (lje, ɛ:r) *a*, offhand, cavalier; free & easy; riding (*track*); bridle (*path*). ¶ *m*, horseman, rider, equestrian; trooper; gentleman, man; **cavalier**, escort; partner (*at dance*); knight (*chess*); [wire] staple. ¶ *f*, horsewoman, rider, equestrian.

cave (ka:v) *a*, hollow, sunk[en]. ¶ *f*, cellar, vault; pool (*cards*). ~ *à liqueurs*, liqueur case *or* set; tantalus. ~ *forte*, strong room. ¶ *m*, square (*person*); john (*prostitute's client*). **caveau** (kavo) *m*, [small] cellar; vault (*family grave*). **caver** (ve) *v.t*, to hollow, scoop out, [under]mine, wear away *or* hollow; put up (*money at cards*). **caverne** (vɛrn) *f*, cavern, cave; den. **caverneux, euse** (nø, ø:z) *a*, cavernous, hollow.

caviar (kavja:r) *m*, caviar[e].

cavité (kavite) *f*, cavity, hollow.

cawcher, ère (kauʃe, ɛ:r) *a*, kosher.

ce, cet, cette, *pl*. **ces** (sə, sɛt, sɛt, se) *a*, this; that; such [a]; (*pl.*) these; those; such. *cette rue-ci & non cette rue-là*, this street & not that street. *ce soir*, this evening, tonight. *cette nuit*, last night.

ce (sə), **c'** *ou* **ç'** *as in* c'est, ç'a été, *pn*, it; this, that; he, she; they; those. *c'est-à-dire* (*abb*. c.-à-d.) that is to say, i.e., viz. *ce que*, what, that which.

cébiste (sebist) *m*, one who uses CB radio.

ceci (səsi) *pn*, this.

cécité (sesite) *f*, blindness. ~ *des neiges*, snow b. ~ *pour les couleurs*, color b.

cédant, e (sedã, ã:t) *n*, transferor, assignor. **céder** (de) *v.t. & i. & abs*, to cede, yield, give up; give in, surrender, cave in; assign, transfer; dispose of, give way. [*le*] ~ *à*, to yield [the palm] to, be second to.

cédille (sedi:j) *f*, cedilla.

cédrat (sedra) *m*, citron.

cèdre (sɛ:dr) *m*, cedar. ~ *du Liban* (libã), c. of Lebanon.

cédule (sedyl) *f*, schedule (*Inc. Tax*).

ceindre (sɛ̃:dr) *v.t.ir*, to surround, [en]compass, [en]circle, gird[le], belt, wreathe. **ceinture** (sɛ̃ty:r) *f*, belt, girdle, sash, waistband; waist, middle; waist lock (*wrestling*); enclosure. ~ *cartouchière*, cartridge belt. ~ *de sauvetage*, life b. ~ *porte-jarretelles*, suspender b. ~ *de securité*, safety b. (*auto*). **ceinturer** (tyre) *v.t*, to grasp round the body. **ceinturon** (rɔ̃) *m*, belt (*sword*, *etc.*).

cela (səla) *pn*, that; it; so. *c'est* ~, that is it; that's right, just so.

célèbre (selebr) *a*, celebrated, famous, noted. **célébrer** (lebre) *v.t*, to celebrate; solemnize, hold (*funeral*); sing (*praises of*). **célébrité** (brite) *f*, celebrity.

celer (səle) *v.t*, to conceal, hide.

céleri (selri) *m*, celery.

célérité (selerite) *f*, celerity, swiftness, dispatch.

céleste (selɛst) *a*, celestial, heavenly; of the heavens (*map*), star (*map*); sky (*blue*).

célibat (seliba) *m*, celibacy, single life. **célibataire** (tɛ:r) *n*, bachelor, celibate, single man, woman.

cellérier (selerje) *m*, cellarer. **cellier** (lje) *m*, storeroom (*wines*).

cellulaire (selylɛ:r) *a*, cellular. *voiture* ~, police van. **cellule** (lyl) *f*, cell; light meter. **celluloïd** (lɔid) *m*, celluloid. **cellulose** (lo:z) *f*, cellulose.

Celte (sɛlt) *n*, Celt, Kelt. **celtique** (tik) *a. & m.* (*language*), Celtic, Keltic.

celui, celle, *pl*. **ceux, celles** (səlɥi, sɛl, sø, sɛl) *pn*, he, she, those; the one. *celui-ci, celle-ci*, this one, this, the latter. *celui-là, celle-là*, that one, that, the former.

cémenter (semãte) *v.t*, to cement (*metal*); caseharden.

cénacle (senakl) *m*, group, coterie (*especially literary*).

cendre (sã:dr) *f. oft. pl*, ash[es]; dust; embers. **cendré, e** (sã:dre) *a*, ash[-colored], ashen, ashy; gray (*brain matter*). ¶ *f*, cinders (*track*). **cendrier** (drie) *m*, ash pan; ash tray. ~ *sur pied*, smokers' stand.

Cendrillon (sãdrijɔ̃) *f*, Cinderella.

Cène (sɛ:n) *f*, Last Supper; Lord's supper.

cenelle (sənɛl) *f*, haw; holly berry.

cénotaphe (senɔtaf) *m*, cenotaph.

censé, e (sɑ̃se) *a*, deemed, reputed, supposed. censément
(mɑ̃) *ad*, supposedly, virtually.
censeur (sœːr) *m*, censor; critic;
auditor; vice principal (*college*);
examiner (*plays*). censure (syːr)
f, censorship; [vote of] censure;
[board of] censors. censurer
(syre) *v.t*, to censure, criticize,
find fault with, reprehend.

cent (sɑ̃) *a. & m*, hundred. centaine (tɛn) *f*, hundred [or so],
about a hundred.

centaure (sɑ̃tɔːr) *m*, centaur.

centenaire (sɑ̃tnɛːr) *n*, centenarian; (*m*.) centenary.

centième (sɑ̃tjɛm) *a. & m*, hun-
dredth.

centigrade (sɑ̃tigrad) *a*, centigrade. Water freezes 0° Cent. =
32 Fahr. Water boils 100° C.
= 212 F. *To convert* :—F. = ⅘
C. + 32 [thus, 100 C. × 9 = 900
÷ 5 = 180 + 32 = 212 F.]. C.
= ⅘ (F. − 32) [thus, 212 F.
− 32 = 180 × 5 = 900 ÷ 9 =
100 C.].

centigramme (sɑ̃tigram) *m*,
centigram = ¹⁄₁₀₀ gram *or* 0.154
grain.

centilitre (sɑ̃tilitr) *m*, centiliter
= ¹⁄₁₀₀ liter *or* 0.070 gill.

centime (sɑ̃tim) *m*, centime =
¹⁄₁₀₀ of franc.

centimètre (sɑ̃timɛtr) *m*, centimeter = ¹⁄₁₀₀ meter *or* 0.3937
inch; tape measure (divided into
cms, 1½ meters long). ~ carré,
square centimeter = 0.15500 sq.
inch. ~ cube, cubic centimeter
= 0.0610 cub. inch.

central, e (sɑ̃tral) *a*, central. ¶ *m*,
telephone exchange. centraliser
(lize) *v.t*, to centralize. centre
(sɑːtr) *m*, center, middle; hub
(*fig*.). ~ de direction, control
center. ~ de table, table center.
~ de villégiature, holiday resort.
centrer (sɑ̃tre) *v.t*, to center. centrifuge (trify:ʒ) *a*, centrifugal. centripète (pɛt) *a*, centripetal.

centuple (sɑ̃typl) *m*, centuple,
hundredfold.

cep (sɛp) *m*, stock (*vine*); (*pl*.)
stocks (*Hist*.). cépée (sepe) *f*,

head of shoots (*willow, etc.*).

cependant (səpɑ̃dɑ̃) *ad*, in the
mean time, meantime, mean-
while. ¶ *c*, yet, still, nevertheless,
though.

céramique (seramik) *f*, ceramics.

cerceau (sɛrso) *m*, hoop; cradle
(*Surg*.).

cercle (sɛrkl) *m*, circle; ring,
hoop, band; club (*of people*).
~ des fées, fairy ring. en ~s, in
the wood (*wine*). cercler (kle)
v.t, to hoop (*casks*).

cercueil (sɛrkœːj) *m*, coffin, shell;
cocktail made of beer, Picon, and
grenadine.

céréale (sereal) *a.f. & f*, cereal.

cérébral, e (serebral) *a*, cerebral,
brain (*att*.).

cérémonial (seremɔnjal) *m*, ceremonial. cérémonie (ni) *f*, ceremony, circumstance, fuss, ado.
visite de ~, formal visit. cérémonieux, euse† (njø, ø:z) *a*, ceremo-
nious, formal.

cerf (sɛːr & sɛrf) *m*, stag, hart,
deer.

cerfeuil (sɛrfœːj) *m*, chervil.

cerf-volant (sɛrvɔlɑ̃) *m*, stag
beetle; kite (*paper*).

cerisaie (sərizɛ) *f*, cherry orchard. cerise (riːz) *f*, cherry.
¶ *a. & m*, cherry-red; cerise. cerisier (rizje) *m*, cherry [tree].

cerne (sɛrn) *m*, ring (*tree, eyes,
moon*), circle. cerner (ne) *v.t*,
to surround, [en]circle, [en]com-
pass, ring, hem in; invest (*Mil*.);
shell (*nuts*); dig round (*tree*).
les yeux cernés, rings under the
eyes.

certain, e (sɛrtɛ̃, ɛn) *a*, certain;
sure; stated; some. le certain,
fixed (*rate of*) exchange. certainement (tɛnmɑ̃) *ad*, certainly,
of course, by all means. certes
(sɛrt) *ad*, most certainly, indeed.

certificat (sɛrtifika) *m*, certificate, scrip; testimonial, character. ~ d'action(s), stock certificate. certifier (fje) *v.t*, to certify;
witness.

certitude (sɛrtityd) *f*, certainty.

céruse (sery:z) *f*, ceruse, white
lead.

cerveau (sɛrvo) *m*, brain; brains,
intellect, mind, head. ~ brûlé,
madcap, hothead. ~ creux,

dreamer. **cervelle** (vɛl) *f*, brain[s], mind, head; pith (*palm tree*); (*s. & pl. Cook.*) brains. *rompre la ~ à quelqu'un*, to drive someone crazy.

cervelas (servəla) *m*, cervelat sausage.

Cervin (le mont) (sɛrvɛ̃), the Matterhorn.

cessation (sɛsasjɔ̃) *f*, cessation, discontinuance; suspension. **sans cesse** (sɛs), without cease, unceasingly. **cesser** (se) *v.i. & t*, to cease, leave off, break off, stop. *faire ~*, to put a stop to.

cessible (sɛsibl) *a*, transferable. **cession** (sjɔ̃) *f*, transfer, assignment. *~ d'intérêt*, farming out, leasing out, subleasing. **cession-bail** (baːj) *f*, lease-back. **cessionnaire** (ɔnɛːr) *n*, transferee.

Ceylan (selɑ̃) *m*, Ceylon.

chablis (ʃabli) *m*, windfall (*tree*); Chablis (*wine*).

chabot (ʃabo) *m*, chub (*fish*).

chacal (ʃakal) *m*, jackal.

chacun, e (ʃakœ̃, yn) *pn*, each, each one, every one. ¶ *m*, everybody, everyone, every one.

chafouin, e (ʃafwɛ̃, in) *a. & n*, sorry (fellow), poor (creature).

chagrin, e (ʃagrɛ̃, in) *a*, sorrowful, glum, moody, grieved, vexed, fretful. ¶ *m*, grief, sorrow, vexation, fret[fulness], chagrin; shagreen. *~ d'amour*, disappointment in love. **chagriner** (grine) *v.t*, to grieve, afflict; vex. **se ~**, to grieve, fret, repine.

chah (ʃa) *m*, shah.

chahut (ʃay) *m*, uproar; prank. **chahuter** (te) *v.t. & i*, to behave in an undisciplined manner; heckle. *vol chahuté*, rough flight (*Avn.*).

chaîne (ʃɛːn) *f*, chain; range (*hills*); channel (*TV*). (*pl.*) fetters, bonds; warp. *~ de mailles*, chain of stitches, casting off (*Knit.*). *faire une ~ de mailles*, to cast off. *travail à la ~*, assembly-line work. **chaînette** (ʃɛnɛt) *f*, chain (*small*). **chaînon** (nɔ̃) *m*, link. *~ manquant*, missing link.

chair (ʃɛːr) *f. sometimes pl*, flesh; meat; pulp (*of fruit*). *~ à pâté*, mincemeat. *~s baveuses*, proud flesh. *~ de poule*, gooseflesh (*fig.*). *cela fait venir la ~ de*

poule, it makes one's flesh creep.

chaire (ʃɛːr) *f*, pulpit; desk; throne (*bishop's*); chair, professorship; mastership; see.

chaise (ʃɛːz) *f*, chair, seat; stall (*choir*); hanger (*Mach.*). *~ à porteurs*, sedan [chair]. *~ de pont*, deck chair. *~ paillée*, rush-seat chair. *~ [percée]*, [night] commode.

chaland (ʃalɑ̃) *m*, barge, lighter, scow.

chaland, e (ʃalɑ̃, ɑ̃ːd) *n*, customer, patron.

chalandage (ʃalɑ̃daʒ) *m*, window shopping, browsing (*in stores*).

châle (ʃɑːl) *m*, shawl, wrap.

chalet (ʃalɛ) *m*, chalet, cottage. *~ de nécessité*, public convenience.

chaleur (ʃalœːr) *f*, heat, warmth, glow. **chaleureux, euse†** (lœrø, øːz) *a*, warm (*fig.*), cordial.

chaloupe (ʃalup) *f*, launch, longboat. *~ canonnière*, gunboat.

chalumeau (ʃalymo) *m*, blowpipe; reed; drinking straw; [shepherd's] pipe.

chalut (ʃaly) *m*, trawl [net]. **chalutier** (tje) *m*, trawler.

chamade (ʃamad) *f*, parley, chamade. *battre la ~*, to signal for a parley; be in a panic.

chamailler (se) (ʃamaje) *v.pr*, to bicker, wrangle, squabble, brawl.

chamarrer (ʃamare) *v.t*, to bedizen, bedeck; lard (*fig.*).

chambranle (ʃɑ̃brɑ̃ːl) *m*, frame (*door, window*).

chambre (ʃɑ̃ːbr) *f*, room, chamber, apartment, lodging; cabi (*ship's*); house; committee; court *~ à air*, inner tube (*tire*). *~ [à coucher]*, [bed]room. *~ à deux lits*, double[-bedded] room. *~ à un lit*, single r. *~ d'ami*, guest room, spare [bed]room. *~ d'enfants*, nursery. *~ d'explosion* combustion chamber (*motor*) *~ de chauffe*, stokehole; boiler room. *~ de compensation*, clearing house. *~ de [mise à] mort* death chamber. *C~ des communes, des pairs*, House of Commons, of Lords. *C~ des députés*

Chamber of Deputies. ~ *des valeurs*, strong room (*ship*). ~*s en enfilade*, suite of rooms. ~ *sur le derrière*, ~ *sur la cour*, back room. ~ *sur le devant*, ~ *sur la rue*, front r. ~ *syndicale des agents de change*, stock exchange committee. ~ **noire**, darkroom (*Phot.*); camera obscura. **chambrée** (ʃãbre) *f*, roomful; house (*audience*); barrack room. **chambrer** (bre) *v.t*, to confine, closet; chamber, hollow out; take the chill off (*wine*).

chameau (ʃamo) *m*, camel; rascal; brute; s.o.b (*slang*). **chamelier** (məlje) *m*, c. driver. **chamelle** (mɛl) *f*, she camel.

chamois (ʃamwa) *m*, chamois. [*peau de*] ~, wash leather, chamois [leather].

champ (ʃã) *m*, field, ground; scope, range; shot (*cinema*); edge. ~*s communs*, common [land]. ~ *d'aviation*, airfield. ~ *de courses*, racecourse. ~ *de manœuvres*, drill ground, parade g., ~ *de massacre*, shambles. ~ *de tir*, rifle range, shooting r. ~ *du repos*, churchyard. ~ *visuel*, field of vision. *hors* ~, off camera, screen. *dans le champ*, on screen, in (*sound*). *profondeur de* ~, depth of field (*cinema*). ~-*contre*-~, angle/reverse angle (*cinema*).

champagne *ou* **vin de C**~ (ʃãpaɲ) *m*, champagne. ~ *frappé* [*de glace*], iced c.

champêtre (ʃãpɛːtr) *a*, rural, country (*att.*), rustic, sylvan.

champignon (ʃãpiɲɔ̃) *m*, mushroom, wigstand. ~ [*vénéneux*], fungus, toadstool. **champignonnière** (ɲɔnjɛːr) *f*, mushroom bed.

champion (ʃãpjɔ̃) *m*, champion. **championnat** (ɔna) *m*, championship.

chance (ʃãːs) *f*, chance; luck.

chanceler (ʃãsle) *v.i*, to totter, reel, stagger; waver, falter.

chancelier (ʃãsəlje) *m*, chancellor. **chancelière** (ljɛːr) *f*, foot muff. **chancellerie** (sɛlri) *f*, chancellery.

chanceux, euse (ʃãsø, øːz) *a*, lucky; hazardous.

chancre (ʃãːkr) *m*, canker; ulcer.

chandail (ʃãdaːj) *m*, sweater (*dress*).

chandelier (ʃãdəlje) *m*, chandler; candlestick. **chandelle** (dɛl) *f*, candle; prop, post, shore; lob (*Ten.*). *je lui dois une fière* ~, I have reason to be grateful to him.

chanfrein (ʃãfrɛ̃) *m*, chamfer; forehead (*horse*).

change (ʃãːʒ) *m*, exchange (*Fin.*). *bureau de* ~, foreign exchange office. **changeant, e** (ʃãʒã, ã:t) *a*, changeable, variable; fitful; fickle; shot (*fabrics*). **changement** (ʒmã) *m*, change, alteration; turn (*tide*); shift (*wind*); amendment (*to document*). ~ *à vue*, transformation scene. ~ *de décor*[*ation*], scene shifting. ~ *de marche*, reversing; r. gear. ~ *de vitesse*, gear shift. ~ [*de voie*], switch points (*Rly.*). **changer** (ʒe) *v.t. & abs. & i*, to change, alter; turn; exchange; shift; amend. ~ *d'avis, de linge*, to change one's mind. on~'*s linen*. ~ *de pas*, to change step. **changeur** (ʒœːr) *m*, money changer.

chanoine (ʃanwan) *m*, canon (*Eccl.*).

chanson (ʃãsɔ̃) *f*, song, ballad, ditty; lay; story. ~ [*de bord*], [sea] chanty. ~ *de circonstance*, topical song. ~ *de route*, marching song. ~*s*, [~*s*]*l* nonsense! humbug! fiddlesticks! **chansonner** (sone) *v.t*, to lampoon. **chansonnette** (nɛt) *f*, ditty; comic song. **chansonnier, ère** (nje, ɛːr) *n*, song writer; (*m.*) song book; small revue-theater.

chant (ʃã) *m*, singing, song, lay, chant; melody; canto; warbling, crowing, chirp. ~ *d'allégresse*, carol. ~ *du coq*, cockcrow[ing]. ~ *du cygne*, swan song. ~ *funèbre*, ~ *de mort*, dirge, lament. *de* ~, edgeways, edgewise, on edge.

chantage (ʃãtaːʒ) *m*, blackmail. **chantant, e** (ʃãtã, ã:t) *a*, musical, tuneful; singsong.

chanteau (ʃãto) *m*, [c]hunk; cutting (*snip of cloth*).

chanter (ʃãte) *v.i. & t*, to sing, chant, play the air; warble, crow, chirp; talk [about]; say, cry. ~

toujours la même antienne, to be always harping on the same string. ~ *victoire sur,* to crow over. *faire ~ quelqu'un,* to blackmail someone. *si ça vous chante,* if that suits you. **chanterelle** (trɛl) *f,* highest string; call bird. **chanteur, euse** (tœːr, øːz) *n,* singer; vocalist; songster, songstress; *(att.)* song *(bird).*

chantier (ʃɑ̃tje) *m,* yard; floor *(foundry)*; shipyard; dockyard dunnage; gantry, scantling *(for cask).* *sur le ~,* work in hand.

chantonner (ʃɑ̃tɔne) *v.i,* to hum *(tune).*

chantourner (ʃɑ̃turne) *v.t,* to jig-saw.

chantre (ʃɑ̃ːtr) *m,* cantor; Bard.

chanvre (ʃɑ̃ːvr) *m,* hemp; hash *(drug).*

chaos (kao) *m,* chaos. **chaotique** (ɔtik) *a,* chaotic.

chaparder (ʃaparde) *v.t,* to steal, swipe; scrounge.

chape (ʃap) *f,* cope; chape; cover, cap, lid; shell; strap; bearings; coating, covering.

chapeau (ʃapo) *m,* hat, bonnet; cap, cover, hood. ~ *à cornes,* cocked hat. ~ *claque,* crush h., opera h. ~ *haut de forme, ~ de soie,* high hat, silk h. ~ *melon,* bowler [h.]. ~ *rabattu,* slouch h. ~ *souple,* felt h. ~ *bas,* hat in hand. ~x *bas!,* hats off. (In student circles, the cry "*chapeau!*" warns offender to remove his/her hat.)

chapechute (ʃapʃyt) *f,* godsend, windfall.

chapelain (ʃaplɛ̃) *m,* chaplain.

chapelet (ʃaplɛ) *m,* rosary; [string of] beads; string, rope.

chapelier (ʃapəlje) *m,* hatter. [**malle**] **chapelière** (ɛːr) *f,* Saratoga [trunk].

chapelle (ʃapɛl) *f,* chapel; meeting house; [church] plate; coterie, set. ~ *ardente,* mortuary chapel. ~ *de la Vierge,* Lady chapel. ~ *sépulcrale,* mortuary chapel. *petite ~,* artistic clique or coterie.

chapellerie (ʃapɛlri) *f,* hat trade; h. shop.

chapelure (ʃaplyːr) *f,* grated bread crumbs.

chaperon (ʃaprɔ̃) *m,* chaperon;

coping. **chaperonner** (prɔne) *v.t,* to chaperon; cope *(wall).*

chapiteau (ʃapito) *m,* capital *(Arch.)*; head, cap, top.

chapitre (ʃapitr) *m,* chapter *(book, canons)*; head[ing], item; subject, matter, point. **chapitrer** (tre) *v.t,* to lecture, reprimand.

chapon (ʃapɔ̃) *m,* capon.

chaque (ʃak) *a,* each, every; either.

char (ʃaːr) *m,* chariot; wagon. ~ *à bancs,* charabanc *(horse).* ~ *d'assaut,* tank *(Mil.).* ~ [*de deuil*], ~ *funèbre,* hearse.

charade (ʃarad) *f,* charade; conundrum.

charançon (ʃarɑ̃sɔ̃) *m,* weevil.

charbon [ʃarbɔ̃] *m,* coal[s]; charcoal; carbon; embers; carbuncle *(Med.)*; anthrax; blight *(Agric.).* ~ *à dessin,* charcoal [pencil]. *en ~,* burnt to a cinder *(meat). faire du ~,* to coal. *sur des ~s* [*ardents*], on tenterhooks. **charbonnage** (bɔnaːʒ) *m,* coal mining; *(pl.)* coal mines. **charbonner** (ne) *v.t,* to black *(face, etc.).* *se ~, v.pr. ou ~, v.i,* to char, carbonize; *(v.i.)* to smoke *(lamp).* **charbonnerie** (nri) *f,* coal yard. **charbonnier** (nje) *m,* charcoal burner; coal merchant; coalman; coal cellar; collier *(ship).*

charcuter (ʃarkyte) *v.t,* to hack, mangle *(in carving).* **charcuterie** (tri) *f,* pork butchery; [dressed] pork, pig meat. **charcutier, ère** (tje, ɛːr) *n,* pork butcher.

chardon (ʃardɔ̃) *m,* thistle; spikes. ~ *à bonnetier, ~ à foulon,* teasel. **chardonneret** (dɔnrɛ) *m,* goldfinch.

charge (ʃarʒ) *f,* load, burden; charge, encumbrance, onus; expense; stress; pressure; head [of water]; loading; shipment; cargo; trust, care, custody; cure *(of souls)*; duty, office; practice; membership, seat; instructions, directions; caricature; overacting; impersonation *(Theat.)*; joke. ~ *à la cueillette,* general cargo. *à* [*la*] ~ *de,* on condition that, provided that. *à la ~ de,* chargeable to, payable by, at the expense of; dependent on. *en ~,* live *(Elec.)*; load *(water line)*; [now] loading (*ship*). ~ *de pointe*, peak load (*computers*). ~ *utile*, payload. **chargé, e** (3e) *a*, loaded; full; live (*shell*); furred (*tongue*); overcast, heavy (*weather*); insured (*Post*). **chargé d'affaires**, *m*, chargé d'affaires. **chargement** (3ǝmɑ̃) *m*, loading, lading; charging, filling; shipping, shipment; cargo; consignment; insurance (*Post*); registered package. ~ *en plein jour*, daylight loading (*Phot.*). **charger** (3e) *v.t*, to load, lade, burden, charge, fill; stress; inflate (*account*); clog, saddle; lie heavy on; ship; instruct, order, direct; entrust; overact; overdo; overdraw; overcharge; caricature; [in]criminate; insure (*Post*). se ~ **de**, to undertake, take charge of, attend to. **chargeur** (3œ:r) *m*, charger, loader; shipper; stoker (*Mach.*).

chariot (ʃarjo) *m*, truck, wagon, wain, trolley, car; go-cart; carriage, carrier; dolly (*cinema*).

charitable† (ʃaritabl) *a*, charitable, benevolent. **charité** (te) *f*, charity; alms; dole.

charivari (ʃarivari) *m*, charivari, hubbub.

charlatan (ʃarlatɑ̃) *m*, charlatan, quack. **charlatanerie** (tanri) *f*, quackery.

charmant, e (ʃarmɑ̃, ɑ̃:t) *a*, charming, fascinating, delightful. **charme** (ʃarm) *m*, charm, spell; attraction, allurement; hornbeam, yoke elm. *sous le* ~, spellbound. **charmer** (me) *v.t*, to charm, delight, bewitch; beguile, while away. **charmeur, euse** (mœ:r, ø:z) *n*, charmer. **charmille** (mi:j) *f*, hedge or bower (*of hornbeam*).

charnel, le† (ʃarnɛl) *a*, carnal, sensual. **charnier** (nje) *m*, charnel house, ossuary.

charnière (ʃarnjɛ:r) *f*, hinge. *à* ~, *à* ~*s*, hinged.

charnu, e (ʃarny) *a*, fleshy, brawny. **charnure** (ny:r) *f*, flesh (*of pers.*). **charogne** (rɔɲ) *f*, carrion.

charpente (ʃarpɑ̃:t) *f*, frame[work]. ~ [*en bois*], timber work. ~ *en fer*, ironwork. ~ *métallique*, iron & steel construc-

tional work. **charpenter** (pɑ̃te) *v.t*, to carpenter, frame, put together. *bien charpenté*, well-knit, well-built, of sturdy build. **charpenterie** (tri) *f*, carpentry; (*ship's*) timber yard. **charpentier** (tje) *m*, carpenter. ~ *de vaisseau*, shipwright. ~ *en fer*, ironworker.

charpie (ʃarpi) *f*, lint; shreds.

charretée (ʃarte) *f*, cartload. charretier, ère (tje, ɛ:r) *n*, carter. **charrette** (rɛt) *f*, cart. ~ *anglaise*, dogcart, trap. **charrier** (rje) *v.t*, to cart, carry, convey; drift; make fun of. **charroi** (rwa) *m*, cartage. **charroyer** (rwaje) *v.t*, to cart. **charron** (rɔ̃) *m*, wheelwright.

charrue (ʃary) *f*, plow. ~ *multiple*, gang p.

charte (ʃart) *f*, charter; deed (*ancient*). ~**partie**, *f*, charter [party]. ~ *de grain*, grain charter.

chartreuse (ʃartrø:z) *f*, Carthusian monastery; lone cottage; chartreuse (*liqueur*). **chartreux** (trø) *m*, Carthusian [monk].

chas (ʃa) *m*, eye (*needle, etc.*).

chasse (ʃas) *f*, chase, hunt, hunting; shooting; shoot; pursuit; kill (*of game*); play, clearance (*Mech.*); set (*of saw teeth*); (*pl.*) squares (*bookbinding*). ~ *à courre* (ku:r), hunt[ing] (*riding to hounds*). ~ *à la grosse bête*, big-game hunting. ~ *au cerf à l'affût*, deer stalking. ~ *au lévrier*, coursing. ~ *aux oiseaux*, fowling. ~ *d'air*, blast (*or* rush) of air. ~ [*d'eau*], flush. ~ *gardée*, ~ *réservée*, [game] preserves. ~ *aux sorcières*, witch-hunt.

châsse (ʃɑ:s) *f*, reliquary, shrine; frame (*spectacles*); scales (*lancet*).

chassé (ʃase) *m*, chassé (*Danc.*).

chasse-mouches (ʃasmuʃ) *m*, fly whisk; fly net. **chasse-neige** (nɛ:3) *m*, snow squall; snowplow.

chasser (ʃase) *v.t. & abs. & i*, to drive, drive away or out or off or in; expel; chase; chevy, chivy; hound out; hunt; shoot; course; pursue; dismiss; dispel; drift; drag (*anchor*); chassé (*Danc.*). ~ *à l'affût*, to stalk. **chasseur, euse** (sœ:r, ø:z) *n*, hunter, huntress, huntsman; -catcher (*butter-*

flies, etc.); messenger, commissionaire, page[boy]; chaser (*Nav.*). fighter (*Avn.*).

chassieux, euse (ʃasjø, ø:z) *a*, gummy (*eyes*), blear-eyed.

châssis (ʃasi) *m*, frame; sash; chassis (*motor*); panel (*radio*); chase (*Typ.*); flat (*Theat.*); stretcher (*for painter's canvas*). ~ à fiches, casement, French sash.

chaste† (ʃast) *a*, chaste. **chasteté** (təte) *f*, chastity.

chasuble (ʃazybl) *f*, chasuble.

chat (ʃa) *m*, chatte (ʃat) *f*, cat, tom [cat], he-cat, she-cat, puss, pussy [cat]; female sex organ (*slang*). (*m.*) tag (*game*). le Chat botté, Puss in Boots. cambrioleur ~, cat burglar. ~ d'Espagne, tortoise-shell cat. ~ de Siam, Siamese c. ~ de gouttières, stray c. ~ persan, ~ angora, Persian c.

châtaigne (ʃatɛɲ) *f*, [sweet] chestnut. **châtaignier** (nje) *m*, chestnut [tree]. **châtain, e** (tɛ̃, ɛn) *a*, [chestnut-]brown (*hair*).

château (ʃato) *m*, castle; palace; manor [house], [country] seat, mansion, hall. ~ d'eau, water tower. ~ de cartes, house of cards. ~x en Espagne, castles in the air *or* in Spain. **châtelain** (tlɛ̃) *m*, lord of the manor, squire. **châtelaine** (tlɛn) *f*, lady of the manor; chatelaine, key chain.

chat-huant (ʃayɑ̃) *m*, tawny owl, brown o.

châtier (ʃatje) *v.t*, to chastise, castigate; chasten. **châtiment** (timɑ̃) *m*, chastisement, etc.

chatoiement (ʃatwamɑ̃) *m*, shimmer; sheen; play of light.

chaton (ʃatɔ̃) *m*, kitten; bezel; setting (*jewel*).

chatouiller (ʃatuje) *v.t*, to tickle; touch up. **chatouilleux, euse** (tujø, ø:z) *a*, ticklish; touchy; sensitive; punctilious.

chatoyant, e (ʃatwajɑ̃, ɑ̃:t) *a*, iridescent; shot (*fabrics*). **chatoyer** (je) *v.i*, to shimmer; sparkle.

châtrer (ʃatre) *v.t*, to castrate, geld; prune, thin.

chattemite (ʃatmit) *f*, unctuous hypocrite, Chadband.

chatteries (ʃatri) *f.pl*, blandishments; delicacies, dainties.

chaud, e† (ʃo, o:d) *a*, hot, warm. à chaud, [while] hot. pleurer à chaudes larmes, to cry bitterly. avoir chaud, to be warm (*of pers.*). faire ~, to be warm (*weather*).

chaudière (ʃodjɛ:r) *f*, boiler; copper. **chaudron** (drɔ̃) *m*, caldron, pot. [petite] **chaudronnerie** (drɔnri) *f*, coppersmith's [& brazier's] trade. [grosse] **chaudronnerie**, boiler-making *or* works. **chaudronnier** (nje) *m*, coppersmith, brazier; boiler maker. ~ ambulant, tinker.

chauffage (ʃofa:ʒ) *m*, heating, warming; stoking, firing. ~ central, central heating. **chauffard** (fa:r) *m*, reckless driver, etc. **chauffe** (ʃo:f) *f*, fire chamber; stoking, firing; heat, melt; heating. ~-bain (ʃof) *m*, water heater. ~-lit, *m*, warming pan. ~-pieds, *m*, foot warmer. ~-plats, *m*, chafing dish. **chauffer** (ʃofe) *v.t*, to heat, warm; air (*linen*); stoke, fire, fuel; push on with; urge on; cram (*exam*); (*v.i.*) to heat, get hot; run hot; get up steam. se ~, to warm oneself, bask. se ~ les pieds, to warm one's feet. **chaufferette** (frɛt) *f*, foot warmer. **chaufferie** (fri) *f*, chafery; stokehole; boiler room. **chauffeur** (fœ:r) *m*, stoker, fireman; driver (*auto*), chauffeur. ~-mécanicien, engineman. **chauffeuse** (fø:z) *f*, woman driver, fireside chair.

chaufour (ʃofu:r) *m*, lime kiln. **chanfournier** (furnje) *m*, lime burner.

chauler (ʃole) *v.t*, to lime.

chaume (ʃo:m) *m*, culm (*Bot.*); stubble; s. field; thatch; cottage (*fig.*). couvrir en ~, to thatch. **chaumière** (ʃomjɛ:r) *f*, [thatched] cottage.

chaussée (ʃose) *f*, bank; causeway, road[way].

chausse-pied (ʃospje) *m*, shoehorn. **chausser** (se) *v.t*, to put on (*shoes, stockings*); shoe, boot, make shoes for; suit, fit (*of footwear*); hill, earth up. se ~ d'une opinion, to get an

opinion into one's head. **chaus-
settes** (sɛt) *f.pl*, socks, half-hose.
chausson (ʃɔ̃) *m*, slipper (*list*);
shoe; bootee; bed sock; savate;
turnover (*Cook.*). **chaussure**
(sy:r) *f*, footwear; shoe. ~ [*montante*], boot. ~s de marche, de
ski, walking, ski, boots. ~s ver-
nies, patent leather shoes; dress
shoes.

chauve (ʃo;v) *a*, bald. ¶ *m*, bald-
head (*pers.*). ~-souris (ʃovsuri)
f, bat.

chauvinisme (ʃovinism) *m*,
chauvinism, jingoism.

chaux (ʃo) *f*, lime. ~ vive, quick-
lime.

chavirer (ʃavire) *v.i*, to capsize,
overturn, upset; fail. [faire] ~,
v.t, to capsize, etc; tip, dump,
shoot.

chef (ʃɛf) *m*, head, chief; chieftain;
commander, commanding officer;
general (*Mil.*); leader; principal;
master; superior; superintendent;
manager; foreman; head, heading; authority; right. ~ d'accusation, count of indictment. ~ d'a-
telier, shop foreman. ~ d'attaque, leader (*violin, chorus*). ~
d'émeute, ringleader. ~ d'équipe,
foreman. ~ d'orchestre, conductor. ~ de bataillon, major. ~ [de
cuisine], head cook, chef. ~ de
file, leader; file leader; fugleman;
leading ship. ~ de gare, station
master. ~ de maison, householder. ~ de musique, bandmas-
ter (*Mil.*). ~ de nage, stroke
(*oarsman*). ~ de pièce, gun captain. ~ de rayon, floorwalker. ~
de salle, headwaiter. ~ de théâtre, musical director. ~ du jury,
foreman of the jury. ~ du service
des ateliers, works manager. ~
éclaireur, scout master. de ce ~,
under this head[ing], hereunder.
de mon propre ~, on my own authority.

chef-d'œuvre (ʃɛdœ:vr) *m*, mas-
terpiece; mess.

chef-lieu (ʃɛfljø) *m*, capital (*department, county*), county seat;
headquarters, seat.

cheik (ʃɛk) *m*, sheikh.

chelem (ʃlɛm) *m*, slam (*cards*).

chemin (ʃəmɛ̃) *m*, way, road,
lane, path, track; headway. ~

d'escalier, stair carpet. ~ de fer,
railway, railroad. ~ de kalage,
tow[ing] path. ~ des écoliers,
longest way round, roundabout
way. ~ de la croix, stations of
the Cross. ~ de traverse, crossroad. ~ faisant, on the way.
faire son ~, to make one's way.
il n'y va pas par quatre ~s, he
doesn't beat about the bush.

chemineau (ʃəmino) *m*, tramp,
hobo.

cheminée (ʃəmine) *f*, chimney,
smoke stack, shaft, funnel; fireplace, chimney piece, mantelpiece; chimney pot; vent; chute,
shoot.

cheminer (ʃəmine) *v.i*, to tramp,
walk; trudge; move along, proceed; meander, creep.

cheminot (ʃəmino) *m*, railway-
man.

chemise (ʃəmi:z) *f*, shirt (*man's*);
chemise (*woman's*); jacket (*water, steam*); cover, lining, case,
wrapper. ~ de nuit, nightshirt
(*man's*); n. dress, n. gown (*woman's*). ~ de soirée, dress shirt.
~ de ville, tunic s. ~ [pour dos-
sier], folder. **chemiserie** (mizri)
f, shirt making, hosiery. **chemisier, ère** (zje, ɛ:r) *n*, shirt-
maker, hosier.

chenal (ʃənal) *m*, channel, race,
course; fairway; gutter.

chenapan (ʃnapɑ̃) *m*, scamp,
rogue.

chêne (ʃɛn) *m*, oak. ~-liège, *m*,
cork tree.

chéneau (ʃeno) *m*, gutter (*eaves*).

chenet (ʃənɛ) *m*, [fire]dog, andiron.

chènevis (ʃɛnvi) *m*, hemp seed.

chenil (ʃəni) *m*, kennel (*hounds*);
hovel.

chenille (ʃəni:j) *f*, caterpillar;
track.

chenu, e (ʃəny) *a*, snow-capped;
snow-clad; bare at the top (*trees*).

cheptel (ʃətɛl) *m*, livestock, cattle.

chèque (ʃɛk) *m*, check. ~ sans
provision, worthless c.

cher, ère† (ʃɛ:r) *a*, dear, high
[-priced], expensive, costly; precious, scarce (*time*). ma chère,
my dear. mon cher, my dear fellow. **cher,** *ad*, dearly; much.

chercher (ʃɛrʃe) *v.t*, to look for, try to find, search for, hunt for, seek; beg; pick (*quarrel*). *aller* ~, to go for, [go &] fetch, go to look for. *venir* ~, to come for, come & fetch, come to look for. **chercheur**, **euse** (ʃœːr, øːz) *n*, seeker, searcher, inquirer, investigator, research worker. ~ *d'aventures*, adventurer. ~*d'or*, gold digger. ¶ *att*, inquiring (*mind*, *etc*.)

chère (ʃɛːr) *f*, living, fare, cheer. *faire bonne* ~, to fare (*feed*) well. *faire maigre* ~, to fare badly.

chérir (ʃeriːr) *v.t*, to cherish, hold dear; cling to, hug (*as error*). *mon chéri, ma chérie*, my love, my darling, dearest.

cherté (ʃɛrte) *f*, dearness, costliness.

chérubin (ʃerybɛ̃) *m*, cherub.

chester (ʃɛstɛːr) *m, in France*, Cheddar *or* Cheshire cheese.

chétif, ive† (ʃetif, iːv) *a*, mean, miserable, sorry, paltry, puny, stunted, sickly, wretched.

cheval (ʃəval) *m*, horse. ~ *à bascule*, rocking h. ~ *côtier*, ~ *de renfort*, trace h. ~ *d'attelage*, carriage h. ~ *de bât*, packhorse, drudge. ~ *de bataille*, war horse, charger; pet argument. *chevaux de bois*, merry-go-round. ~ *de charrette*, cart h. ~ *de chasse*, hunter. ~ *de course*, racehorse. ~ *de louage*, hack. ~ *de race*, ~ *pur sang*, thoroughbred [horse]. ~ *de retour*, old offender, jail bird. ~ *de volée*, leader (*horse*). ~ [*vapeur*], horse power (Fr. h.p. = 75 kilogrammetres per second; Eng. h.p. = 550 foot pounds per sec.). *une [automobile de] 10 chevaux*, a 10 horse [power] car. *à* ~, on horseback. **chevalement** (ʃəvalmã) *m*, trestle shore; [pit-]headframe; derrick. **chevaler** (le) *v.t*, to shore. **chevaleresque** (ʃrɛsk) *a*, chivalrous, knightly. **chevalerie** (lri) *f*, knighthood, chivalry. ~ *errante*, knight errantry. **chevalet** (lɛ) *m*, horse, trestle; easel; rest (*Bil., etc*.); bridge (*violin, etc*.). **chevalier** (lje) *m*, knight, chevalier. ~ *d'industrie*, adventurer, swindler. **chevalière** (ljɛːr) *f*, signet ring. **chevalin, e** (lɛ̃, in)

a, equine, horsy; horse (*species*). **chevauchée** (voʃe) *f*, ride. **chevaucher** (ʃe) *v.i. & t*, to ride; straddle; span; overlap.

chevelu, e (ʃəvly) *a*, longhaired; hairy; bearded. **chevelure** (vlyːr) *f*, [head of] hair, locks; scalp (*trophy*); coma (*Bot. & comet*); foliage.

chevet (ʃəvɛ) *m*, bolster, pillow; bedhead; bedside.

cheveu (ʃəvø) *m*, (*a single human*) hair. *les* ~*x*, the hair. ~*x en brosse*, crewcut. *couper un* ~ *en quatre*, to split hairs.

cheville (ʃəviːj) *f*, pin, peg; treenail; bolt; pintle; spike; expletive (*in verse*). ~ [*du pied*], ankle. ~ *ouvrière*, king bolt, center pin; mainspring (*fig*.), master mind, prime mover. *se fouler la* ~, to sprain one's ankle. **cheviller** (vije) *v.t. & i*, to pin, peg, bolt; pad (*verses*).

chèvre (ʃɛːvr) *f*, goat (*in general*); she-goat, nanny [goat]; gin (*Mech*.); sawhorse; jack. ~ *carrossier*, carriage jack. ~ [*verticale*], derrick [crane]. **chevreau** (ʃəvro) *m*, kid; kid [leather]. **chèvrefeuille** (ʃɛvrəfœːj) *m*, honeysuckle, woodbine. **chevrette** (ʃəvrɛt) *f*, kid; she-goat; roe-doe; shrimp, prawn; trivet. **chevreuil** (vrœːj) *m*, roebuck; venison. **chevrier, ère** (vrie, ɛːr) *n*, goatherd. **chevron** (vrɔ̃) *m*, rafter; chevron; stripe (*long Mil. service*). **chevroter** (vrɔte) *v.i*, to bleat (*goat & fig*.); quaver, shake; kid. **chevrotin** (tɛ̃) *m*, fawn; musk deer; kid [leather]. **chevrotine** (tin) *f*, buckshot.

chez (ʃe) *pr*, at; at (*or* to) (*or* in) the house, etc, of; care of, c/o; of, stocked by; with; among, in. ~ *moi*, ~ *lui*, ~ *vous*, at home. *mon* ~*-moi*, my home. ~ *soi*, [*at*] home. *un* ~*-soi*, a home of one's own.

chialer (ʃjale) *v.i*, to weep; snivel; complain.

chiasse (ʃjas) *f*, speck (*fly*); cast (*worm*); scum, dross (*metal*).

chic (ʃik) *a*, stylish, chic, smart. ~ *type*, a good fellow. ¶ *m*, stylishness.

chicane (ʃikan) *f*, chicanery, quibble, pettifoggery, cavil, shuffle; baffle [plate]. **chicaner** (kane) *v.i,* to chicane; (*v.t.*) to cavil at, carp at; dispute every inch of (*ground*); hug (*wind, Naut.*). **chicanerie** (nri) *f,* chicanery, etc.

chiche† (ʃiʃ) *a,* stingy, mean, niggardly, chary, sparing. ¶ *pois* ~, *n,* chickpea. ¶ *int, chiche!,* I dare you! You're on!

chicorée (ʃikɔre) *f,* chicory.

chicot (ʃiko) *m,* stump, snag. **chicoter** (kɔte) *v.i,* to wrangle (*about trifles*).

chien, ne (ʃjɛ̃, ɛn) *n,* dog, bitch, hound; (*m.*) hammer, cock (*of gun*); dog, pawl, catch. ~ *couchant,* setter. *faire le* ~ *couchant,* to toady, cringe. ~ *courant,* ~ *de chasse,* hound. ~ *d'arrêt,* pointer. ~ *de berger,* sheep dog. ~ *de garde,* ~ *d'attache,* watch d. ~ *de luxe,* fancy d. ~ *de mer,* dog fish. ~ *de Saint-Bernard* (sɛ̃bɛrnaːr), St. Bernard dog. ~ *de salon,* lap d. ~*-loup,* Alsatian. ~ *savant,* performing dog. *entre chien & loup,* at dusk.

chiendent (ʃjɛ̃dɑ̃) *m,* couch [grass]; problem, difficulty.

chier (ʃje) *v.i,* to defecate (*obscene*). *faire* ~, to annoy, disturb. ~ *du poivre,* shake off the police.

chiffe (ʃif) *f,* rag. **chiffon** (fɔ̃) *m,* bit of stuff (*old or new*); rag, clout; scrap; fallal; chiffon; (*pl.*) dress, finery. **chiffonner** (fɔne) *v.t,* to [c]rumple; ruffle, annoy, vex, bother; (*v.i.*) to do needlework, use one's needle. **chiffonnier, ère** (nje, ɛːr) *n,* rag picker *or* merchant, rag [& bone] man; (*m.*) chiffonier.

chiffre (ʃifr) *m,* figure, number, numeral, cipher; amount; monogram; colophon. *un* [*seul*] ~, a digit (*0-9*). *en* ~*s connus,* in plain figures. ~ *d'affaires,* turnover. ~*-indice,* index number. **mot en chiffré** (fre), word in cipher. **chiffrer** (fre) *v.i,* to reckon, cipher; figure, appear; (*v.t.*) to number, figure, cipher. *se* ~, to figure out, work out, amount.

chignon (ʃiɲɔ̃) *m,* chignon.

Chili (le) (ʃili) Chile, -li. **chilien, ne** (ljɛ̃, ɛn) *a. &* C~, *n,* Chilean.

chimère (ʃimɛːr) *f,* chimera. **chimérique** (merik) *a,* chimerical; visionary, fanciful.

chimie (ʃimi) *f,* chemistry. **chimique**† (mik) *a,* chemical; actinic (*rays*). **chimiste** (mist) *n,* chemist (*scientist*).

chimpanzé (ʃɛ̃pɑ̃ze) *m,* chimpanzee.

Chine (la) (ʃin) China. **chinois, e** (nwa, aːz) *a. &* C~ (*pers.*), *n,* Chinese. **le chinois,** Chinese (*language*); penis (*obscene*); Maoist. **chinoiserie** (nwazri) *f,* Chinese curio; (*pl.*) red tape, complicated formalities.

chiner (ʃine) *v.i,* to shop flea markets or secondhand stores. ¶ *v.t,* to mock; to cadge.

chiourme (ʃjurm) *f,* galley slaves; gang of convicts.

chiper (ʃipe) *v.t,* to swipe, filch, pilfer.

chipie (ʃipi) *f,* ill-natured woman. **chipoter** (pɔte) *v.i,* to nibble; haggle.

chique (ʃik) *f,* quid, chew (*of tobacco*); jigger (*insect*).

chiqué (ʃike) *m,* pretense, sham, fuss.

chiquenaude (ʃiknoːd) *f,* fillip, flip, flick; snap of fingers.

chiquer (ʃike) *v.t. & i,* to chew (*tobacco*).

chirographaire (kirɔgrafɛːr) *a,* unsecured (*creditors, debts*); simple, naked (*debentures*).

chiromancie (kirɔmɑ̃si) *f,* palmistry, chiromancy. **chiromancien, ne** (sjɛ̃, ɛn) *n,* palmist, chiromancer.

chiropraxie, chiropractie (ʃirɔpraksi, prakti) *f,* chiropractic.

chirurgical, e (ʃiryrʒikal) *a,* surgical. **chirurgie** (ʒi) *f,* surgery. **chirurgien** (ʒjɛ̃) *m,* surgeon.

chiure (ʃjyːr) *f,* flyspeck.

chlorate (klɔrat) *m,* chlorate. **chlore** (klɔːr) *m,* chlorine. **chlorhydrique** (klɔridrik) *a,* hydrochloric, muriatic (*acid*). **chloroforme** (rɔfɔrm) *m,* chloroform. **chloroformer** (me) *v.t,* to chloroform. **chlorure** (ryːr) *m,* chloride. ~ *de chaux,* c. of lime.

choc (ʃɔk) *m,* shock, impact, brunt, onset, onslaught, clash;

chocolat (ʃɔkɔla) *m*, chocolate. ~ *au lait*, c. with milk; milk c. ~*s fourrés à la crème*, c. creams. ~ *lacté*, milk c. **chocolatier**, **ère** (latje ɛːr) *n*, c. manufacturer; c. seller; (*f.*) c. pot.

chœur (kœːr) *m*, choir, quire; chorus; chancel. *faire* ~ *au refrain*, to join in the chorus.

choir (ʃwaːr) *v.i.ir*, to fall.

choisi, e (ʃwazi) *a*, select, choice. **choisir** (ziːr) *v.t*, to choose, select, pick. **choix** (ʃwa) *m*, choice, selection; pick; option; quality. *au* ~, all at the same price.

choléra (kɔlera) *m*, cholera.

chômage (ʃomaːʒ) *m*, closing, idleness, standing [idle], shutting down, unemployment; demurrage (*Rly.*); lying up (*ship*). ~ *du dimanche*, Sunday closing. **chômer** (me) *v.i*, to close, lie idle; lie fallow; shut down, stop work, be out [of work]; be short; (*v.t.*) to keep (*une fête* = *a saint's day*). **chômeur, euse** (mœːr, øːz) *n*, unemployed person. *les chômeurs*, the unemployed.

chope (ʃɔp) *f*, glass (*for, or of, beer*). **chopine** (pin) *f*, pint (about ½ liter). **chopiner** (ne) *v.i*, to tipple.

chopper (ʃɔpe) *v.i*, to stumble; blunder.

choquant, e (ʃɔkɑ̃, ɑ̃ːt) *a*, shocking; offensive. **choquer** (ke) *v.t*, to shock, strike, clash with; clink, chink; offend.

choral, e (kɔral) *a*, choral. [*société*] *chorale*, *f*, choral society.

chorégraphie (kɔregrafi) *f*, choreography.

choriste (kɔrist) *n*, chorister; chorus singer (*opera*). **faire chorus** (ryːs), to [repeat in] chorus.

chose (ʃoːz) *f*, thing; matter; fact; chattel; property; compliment. *la* ~ *publique*, the common weal, the public welfare. ~ *qui va sans dire*, matter of course. *où en sont les* ~*s*? how do things stand?

chott (ʃɔt) *m*, salt lake (*N. Africa*).

chou (ʃu) *m*, cabbage; cream puff (*pastry*). ~ *de Bruxelles*, Brussels sprouts. ~ *de Milan* (milɑ̃),

savoy. ~*-fleur*, *m*, cauliflower. ~ *frisé*, kale. ~ *marin*, sea kale. ~*navet*, rutabaga. ~*-rave*, *m*, kohlrabi. **chou[chou]**, *m*, darling, ducky, honey. *le chouchou*, the pet.

choucas (ʃuka) *m*, jackdaw.

choucroute (ʃukrut) *f*, sauerkraut; dish of sauerkraut, sausages, ham hocks, etc.

chouette (ʃwɛt) *f*, owl. ¶ *a*. & *int*, great! ~ *alors!*, that's great! *c'est* ~*!*, it's great!

choyer (ʃwaje) *v.t*, to pamper, pet, coddle; cherish.

chrétien, ne (kretjɛ̃, ɛn) *a*. & *n*, Christian. **chrétiennement** (ɛnmɑ̃) *ad*, christianly. **chrétienté** (ête) *f*, Christendom. **le Christ** (krist), Christ. **christ**, *m*, crucifix. **christianiser** (tjanize) *v.t*, to christianize. **christianisme** (nism) *m*, Christianity.

chromate (krɔmat) *m*, chromate.

chromatique (krɔmatik) *a*, chromatic.

chrome (kroːm) *m*, chromium, chrome. **chromé e** (krome) *a*, chrome (*steel, leather*); chromium (*steel*); chromium-plated.

chronique (krɔnik) *a*, chronic. ¶ *f*, chronicle; gossip; intelligence, notes (*in newspaper*). **chroniqueur** (kœːr) *m*, chronicler; reporter (*news*).

chronographe (krɔnɔgraf) *m*, chronograph; stop-watch.

chronologie (krɔnɔlɔʒi) *f*, chronology. **chronologique†** (ʒik) *a*, chronological.

chronométrage (krɔnɔmetraːʒ) *m*, timing (*race*). **chronomètre** (metr) *m*, chronometer. **chronométrer** (metre) *v.i*, to time. **chronométreur** (trœːr) *m*, timekeeper (*Sport*). ~*-analyseur*, time-study analyst.

chrysalide (krizalid) *f*, chrysalis, pupa.

chrysanthème (krizɑ̃tɛːm) *m*, chrysanthemum.

chuchoter (ʃyʃɔte) *v.i*. & *t*, to whisper. **chuchoterie** (tri) *f*, whispering. **chuchoteur, euse** (tœːr, øːz) *n*, whisperer.

chuinter (ʃɥɛte) *v.i*, to hoot (*owl*).

chut (ʃyt, ʃt) *i*, hush!

chute (ʃyt) *f*, fall, drop; downfall, collapse, smash, crash; failure (*of a play*); spray (*flowers, Need.*). ~ [*d'eau*], [water]fall, falls. *la ~ des reins*, the small of the back. *la ~ du jour*, the close of day, nightfall, eventide.

chuter (ʃyte) *v.t*, to hiss (an *actor*).

Chypre (ʃipr) *f*, Cyprus.

ci (si) *ad*, here. ~*-après*, hereinafter, further on, below. ~*-contre*, opposite. ~*-dessous*, below, undermentioned, hereunder. ~*-dessus*, above[-mentioned]. ~*-devant*, formerly, late. ~*-gît*, here lies (*grave*). ~*-inclus, e & ci-joint, e*, enclosed, herewith, subjoined. ¶ *pn*, this.

cible (sibl) *f*, target; butt (*fig.*).

ciboire (sibwaːr) *m*, ciborium, pyx.

ciboule (sibul) *f*, spring onion, scallion. **ciboulette** (lɛt) *f*, chive.

cicatrice (sikatris) *f*, scar, mark. **cicatriser** (ze) *v.t. & se ~*, to scar; mark; heal, skin over.

cicerone (siseron) *m*, cicerone, guide.

cidre (siːdr) *m*, cider.

ciel (sjɛl) *m*, heaven, heavens, sky; air; climate, clime; tester, canopy; roof. *à ~ ouvert*, in the open air; open-cast, daylight (*Min.*).

cierge (sjɛrʒ) (*Eccl.*) *m*, [wax] candle, taper.

cigale (sigal) *f*, cicada, grasshopper.

cigare (sigaːr) *m*, cigar. ~ *de la Havane*, Havana c. **cigarette** (garɛt) *f*, cigarette.

cigogne (sigɔɲ) *f*, stork.

ciguë (sigy) *f*, hemlock.

cil (sil) *m*, eyelash; hair (*Bot.*). **ciller** (sije) *v.i*, to blink; move an eyelid.

cime (sim) *f*, top, summit, peak.

ciment (simã) *m*, cement. **cimenter** (te) *v.t*, to cement.

cimeterre (simtɛːr) *m*, scimitar.

cimetière (simtjɛːr) *m*, cemetery, burial ground, graveyard, churchyard.

cimier (simje) *m*, crest; haunch (*venison*); buttock (*beef*).

cinabre (sinaːbr) *m*, cinnabar.

cinéaste (sineast) *m*, filmmaker.

ciné-actualités (sineaktyalite) *f*, newsreel theater.

ciné-club (sineklœb) *m*, film society.

cinégramme (sinegram) *m*, kinescope (*TV*).

cinémathèque (sinematɛk) *f*, film library; museum offering film showings.

cinématographe (sinematɔgraf), **cinéma**, *abb*, *m*, movie theater; movies. ~ *d'essai*, art theater. ~ *d'exclusivité*, first-run theater. ~ *permanent*, continuous-show theater.

cinéphile (sinefil) *m. & f*, film enthusiast, fan.

cinéprojecteur (sineprɔʒɛktœːr) *m*, film projector.

cinéraire (sinerɛːr) *a*, cinerary. ¶ *f*, cineraria (*Bot.*).

ciné-roman (sinerɔmã) *m*, film serial; novelized & illustrated story of a film.

cinéscope (sineskɔp) *m*, kinescope (*TV*).

cinétique (sinetik) *a*, kinetic.

cingalais, e (sɛ̃galɛ, ɛːz) *a. & C~*, *n*, Cingalese.

cinglé (sɛ̃gle) *a*, nutty, crazy, etc.

cingler (sɛ̃gle) *v.t*, to lash, cut, whip; shingle (*Metall.*); to sail, scud.

cinq (sɛ̃[ːk; *before a consonant*, sɛ̃]) *a. & m*, five; fifth; cinq[ue]. **cinquantaine** (sɛ̃kãtɛn) *f*, fifty [or so]; golden wedding. **cinquante** (kãːt) *a. & m*, fifty. **cinquantenaire** (kãtnɛːr) *m*, fiftieth anniversary. **cinquantième** (tjɛm) *a. & n*, fiftieth. **cinquième†** (kjɛm) *a. & n*, fifth.

cintre (sɛ̃ːtr) *m*, arch, curve; center (*for arch*); clothes hanger. **cintrer** (sɛ̃tre) *v.t*, to arch, bend, curve.

cipaye (sipaːj) *m*, sepoy.

cirage (siraːʒ) *m*, waxing; polishing; shoe polish.

circoncire (sirkɔ̃siːr) *v.t.ir*, to circumcise.

circonférence (sirkɔ̃ferãːs) *f*, circumference, girth.

circonflexe (sirkɔ̃flɛks) *a. & m*, circumflex.

circonlocution (sirkɔlɔkysjɔ̃) f, circumlocution.

circonscription (sirkɔ̃skripsjɔ̃) f, circumscription; area. ~ *électorale*, constituency. **circonscrire** (skri:r) v.t.ir, to circumscribe; locate.

circonspect, e (sirkɔ̃spɛ[k], ɛkt) a, circumspect, cautious, wary, guarded.

circonstance (sirkɔ̃stɑ̃:s) f, circumstance, occasion; nonce. *de ~*, for the occasion. **circonstancié, e** (stɑ̃sje) p.a, circumstantial, detailed (*account*). **circonstancier** (sje) v.t, to detail.

circonvenir (sirkɔ̃vni:r) v.t.ir, to circumvent, outwit, overreach.

circonvoisin, e (sirkɔ̃vwazɛ̃, in) a, surrounding.

circuit (sirkɥi) m, circuit, round. *~ de paroles*, circumlocution.

circulaire† (sirkylɛ:r) a. & f, circular. **circulant, e** (lɑ̃, ɑ̃:t) a, circulating, floating. **circulation** (lasjɔ̃) f, circulation, running, traveling, working; traffic; currency; turnover, sales. **circuler** (le) v.i, to circulate, run, travel. **circulez!** move on! pass along!

cire (si:r) f, wax. *~ à cacheter*, sealing wax. **ciré** (sire) m, oilskin. **cirer** (re) v.t, to wax; polish (*shoes*). **cireur** (rœ:r) m, bootblack. **cireuse** (rø:z) f, floor polisher (*Mach.*). **cirier** (rje) m, wax chandler.

ciron (sirɔ̃) m, mite (*insect*).

cirque (sirk) m, circus; corrie.

cirrhose (siro:z) f, cirrhosis.

cirrus (sir[r]y:s) m, cirrus (*Meteor.*).

cisailler (sizaje) v.t, to shear, clip. **cisailles** (zɑ:j) f.pl, shears, shearing machine. **ciseau** (zo) m, chisel. *~ à déballer*, case opener. *~ à froid*, cold chisel. *~x*, pl, [pair of] scissors; shears, clippers. **ciseler** (zle) v.t, to chisel, chase. **ciselet** (zlɛ) m, graver. **ciselure** (zly:r) f, chiseling; chasing.

citadelle (sitadɛl) f, citadel; stronghold.

citadin, e (sitadɛ̃, in) n, townsman, citizen.

citation (sitasjɔ̃) f, citation, quotation; summons, subpoena. *~ à l'ordre de l'armée*, mention in dispatches.

cité (site) f, city., *~-dortoir*, bedroom community.

citer (site) v.t, to cite, quote; mention; instance; summon; summons; subpoena.

citérieur, e (siterjœ:r) a, hither (*Geog.*).

citerne (sitɛrn) f, tank, cistern.

cithare (sita:r) f, zither.

citoyen, ne (sitwajɛ̃, ɛn) n, citizen.

citrique (sitrik) a, citric. **citron** (trɔ̃) m, lemon; citron. *~ pressé*, lemon squash. **citronnade** (trɔnad) f, lemonade. **citronnier** (nje) m, lemon tree; citron tree.

citrouille (situ:j) f, pumpkin.

cive[tte] (siv[ɛt]) f, chive.

civet de lièvre (sivɛ) m, jugged hare.

civette (sivɛt) f, civet [cat].

civière (sivjɛ:r) f, handbarrow; stretcher, litter; bier.

civil, e† (sivil) a, civil; calendar (*month, year*). ¶ m, civilian; noncombatant. *en ~*, in plain clothes, in mufti. **civilisateur, trice** (lizatœ:r, tris) a, civilizing. **civilisation** (sjɔ̃) f, civilization. **civiliser** (ze) v.t, to civilize. **civilité** (te) f, civility; (*pl.*) compliments.

civique (sivik) a, civic.

clabauder (klabode) v.i, to babble (*of hound*); backbite.

claie (klɛ) f, hurdle; fence. *passer à la ~*, to screen.

clair, e† (klɛ:r) a, clear; bright; light; thin; plain, explicit. *sabre au clair*, with drawn sword. *tirer au clair*, v.t, to clear up. **clair**, ad, clearly, plainly; thinly. ¶ m, light; plain language (*Teleg.*). *~ de lune*, moonlight. **clairet** (klɛrɛ) a.m, pale (*wine, precious stone*).

claire-voie (klɛrvwa) f, grating. *à ~*, openwork, lattice (*att.*).

clairière (klɛrjɛ:r) f, glade; clearing; lane.

clair-obscur (klɛrɔpsky:r) m, chiaroscuro, light & shade.

clairon (klɛrɔ̃) *m*, bugle; bugler; clarion. **claironner** (rɔne) *v.t*, to noise abroad.

clairsemé, e (klɛrsəme) *a*, thinly sown; sparse, few & far between.

clairvoyance (klɛrvwajɑ̃:s) *f*, clear-sightedness, shrewdness.

clameur (klamœ:r) *f*, clamor, outcry.

clampin (klɑ̃pɛ̃) *m*, slowcoach.

clan (klɑ̃) *m*, clan, set.

clandestin, e† (klɑ̃dɛstɛ̃, in) *a*, clandestine, underhand.

clapet (klapɛ) *m*, clack [valve], flap.

clapier (klapje) *m*, rabbit burrow, r. hutch.

clapoter (klapɔte) *v.i*, to plash, swash. **clapoteux, euse** (tø, ø:z) *a*, choppy (*water*).

clapper (klape) *v.i*, to smack (*tongue*).

claque (klak) *f*, slap, smack; claque (*Theat.*). ¶ *m*, crush hat, opera hat.

claquedent (klakdɑ̃) *m*, starveling; brothel; gambling den.

claquemurer (klakmyre) *v.t*, to coop up, immure, closet.

claquer (klake) *v.i. & t*, to clap, clatter, slap, snap, crack, chatter, slam; die; go to pieces. **claquet** (kɛ) *m*, **claquette** (kɛt) *f*, **claquoir** (kwa:r) *m*, clapper. **claquettes**, *f.pl*, step dance, tap d.

clarifier (klarifje) *v.t*, to clarify, fine.

clarine (klarin) *f*, cowbell.

clarinette (klarinɛt) *f*, clarinet.

clarté (klarte) *f*, clearness; brightness; light.

classe (klɑ:s) *f*, class, order; rate; grade (*at school*); school; contingent (*of recruiting year*). ~ *moyenne*, middle class[es]. [*salle de*] ~, classroom. **classement** (klɑsmɑ̃) *m*, classing, classification; rating; filing; order, position (*running, etc.*). **classer** (se) *v.t*, to class, classify; sort, grade; file (*letters, etc.*); position; marshal. **classeur** (sœ:r) *m*, file; filing cabinet; stationery rack. **classification** (klasifikasjɔ̃) *f*, classification. **classique†** (sik) *a*, classic; classical; class, school

(*att.*); educational; standard. ¶ *m*, classic.

claudication (klodikasjɔ̃) *f*, lameness.

clause (klo:z) *f*, clause, term, provision, stipulation.

claustral, e (klostral) *a*, claustral, cloistral.

claveau (klavo) *m*, arch-stone, voussoir; sheep pox.

clavecin (klavsɛ̃) *m*, harpsichord.

clavelée (klavle) *f*, sheep pox.

clavette (klavɛt) *f*, key, cotter, pin. ~ *d'essieu*, axle pin, linchpin. ~ *fendue*, split pin.

clavicule (klavikyl) *f*, collar bone.

clavier (klavje) *m*, keyboard; manual; (*musical*) compass, range.

clayonnage (klɛjɔna:ʒ) *m*, wattling; mat[tress].

clef, *sometimes* **clé** (kle) *f*, key; clue (*puzzle*); wrench; plug, spigot; clef. ~ *à marteau*, screw hammer; adjustable wrench. ~ *anglaise*, monkey wrench. ~ *de contact*, (*allumage*), ignition key switch. ~ *d'ut*, C (*or* tenor) (*or* alto) clef. ~ *de fa*, F (*or* bass) c. ~ *de sol*, G (*or* treble) c. ~ *de voûte*, keystone. *sous* ~, locked up, under lock & key.

clématite (klematit) *f*, clematis.

clémence (klemɑ̃:s) *f*, clemency, mercy, leniency; mildness. **clément, e** (mɑ̃, ɑ̃:t) *a*, clement, etc.

clémentine (klemɑ̃tin) *f*, tangerine; clementine.

cleptomane (klɛptɔman) *n*, kleptomaniac. **cleptomanie** (ni) *f*, kleptomania.

clerc (klɛ:r) *m*, clerk (*Relig.*, law). *pas de* ~, false step, error. **clergé** (klɛrʒe) *m*, clergy; priesthood. **clérical, e** (klerikal) *a. & m*, clerical.

cliché (kliʃe) *m*, plate (*Typ.*); negative (*Phot.*); stock phrase, hackneyed p., tag. ~ *au trait*, linecut, line engraving. ~ *simili*, ~ *tramé*, half-tone engraving. **clicher** (ʃe) *v.t*, to stereotype.

client, e (kliɑ̃, ɑ̃:t) *n*, client, customer; patient. **clientèle** (ɑ̃tɛl) *f*, clientele, public, connection, custom; goodwill, practice.

cligner (kliɲe) v.i, to wink; blink; wince. **clignotant** (ɲɔtɑ̃) a, blinking. ¶ m, flashing traffic light. *les* ~*s*, direction signal-lights. **clignoter** (ɲɔte) v.i, to blink, twinkle; twitch.

climat (klima) m, climate. **climatérique** (materik) a, climacteric (*Med.*); climatic. **climatique** (tik) a, climatic. **climatiser** (tize) v.t, to air-condition.

clin d'œil (klɛ̃dœ:j) m, wink; twinkling of an eye, trice.

clinicien (klinisjɛ̃) m, clinician. **clinique** (nik) a, clinical. ¶ f, clinic; nursing home; surgery (*room*).

clinquant (klɛ̃kɑ̃) m, tinsel; foil; showiness.

clique (klik) f, clique, set, gang; drums & bugles (*Mil. band*).

cliquet (klikɛ) m, pawl, click, catch. ~ [*à canon*], engineer's ratchet brace. ~ [*simple*], ratchet. **cliqueter** (kte) v.i, to click, clank, clash, rattle, jingle. **cliquetis** (kti) m, click[ing], *etc.* **cliquettes** (kɛt) f.pl, bones, castanets.

clisser (klise) v.t, to wicker (*bot-*ˡ*es*).

clivage (kliva:ʒ) m, cleavage (*Miner.*); separation of social strata.

cloaque (klɔak) m, cesspool; sink (*fig.*).

clochard (klɔʃa:r) m, tramp, hobo.

cloche (klɔʃ) f, bell; bell glass; bell jar; dish cover; cloche. ~ *à fromage*, cheese cover. ~ *à plongeur*, diving bell.

clochement (klɔʃmɑ̃) m, hobble, limp.

cloche-pied (à) (klɔʃpje) ad, on one leg. *sauter à* ~, to hop.

clocher (klɔʃe) m, belfry. ~ [*pointu*], steeple. *de* ~ (*fig.*), parish (*att.*), parochial.

clocher (klɔʃe) v.i, to hobble, limp, halt, be lame. *il y a quelque chose qui cloche*, something's wrong.

clocheton (klɔʃtɔ̃) m, bell turret.

clochette (klɔʃɛt) f, hand bell; bell [flower]. ~ *d'hiver*, snowdrop.

cloison (klwazɔ̃) f, partition; bulkhead; septum. ~ *étanche*, watertight bulkhead. [émail] **cloisonné** (zɔne) m, cloisonné [enamel]. **cloisonner** (ne) v.t, to partition [off].

cloître (klwa:tr) m, cloister. **cloîtrer** (wɑtre) v.t, to cloister, immure.

clopin-clopant (klɔpɛ̃klɔpɑ̃) ad, hobbling along. **clopiner** (pine) v.i, to hobble.

cloporte (klɔpɔrt) m, wood louse.

cloque (klɔk) f, blister; rust (*Agric.*).

clore (klɔ:r) v.t. & i. ir, to close, shut; enclose; conclude. **clos** (klo) m, enclosure. **clôture** (kloty:r) f, enclosure, fence, fencing; screen (*choir*); closure; closing; conclusion (*sessions, sittings*). *cours de* ~, closing price. *date de* ~, closing date. ~ *à clairevoie*, paling.

clou (klu) m, nail; boil (*Med.*). *les* ~*s*, studded crossing (*pedestrian*). ~ *à crochet*, tenterhook. ~ *à dessin*, drawing pin. ~ *à deux pointes*, [wire] staple. ~ *de girofle*, clove. ~ *de la fête*, chief attraction, star turn. ~ *de Paris*, French nail, wire n. ~ *découpé*, cut n. *mettre au* ~, to pawn something. (*pl.*) crosswalk. **clouer** (klue) v.t, to nail [up, down]; pin; tie. ~ *la bouche à quelqu'un*, to shut someone up (*silence*). **clouter** (te) v.t, to stud. *passage clouté*, studded crossing (*pedestrian crossing*). **clouterie** (tri) f, nailmaking; n. works. **cloutier** (tje) m, nailmaker.

clovisse (klɔvis) f, cockle (*Mol.*).

clown (klun) m, clown. **clownerie** (nri) f, clownery.

club (klyb) m, club. ~ *de golf*, golf club (*people & stick*).

coaguler (koagyle) v.t, to coagulate.

coaliser (se) (koalize) v.pr, to combine. **coalition** (sjɔ̃) f, coalition; combine, ring.

coaltar (kɔlta:r) m, coal tar.

coasser (koase) v.i, to croak (*frog*).

coaxial (kɔaksjal) m, feeder cable.

cobalt (kɔbalt) m, cobalt.

cobaye (kɔba:j) m, guinea pig.

cobra (kɔbra) m, cobra.

cocaïne (kɔkain) *f*, cocaine.

cocarde (kɔkard) *f*, cockade, rosette.

cocasse (kɔkas) *a*, droll, comical.

coccinelle (kɔksinɛl) *f*, ladybird.

coche (kɔʃ) *f*, sow; notch, score. ¶ *m*, stagecoach.

cochenille (kɔʃniːj) *f*, cochineal.

cocher (kɔʃe) *m*, coachman, driver. ~ *de fiacre*, cabman.

cocher (kɔʃe) *v.t*, to notch, score.

cochet (kɔʃɛ) *m*, cockerel.

cochon (kɔʃɔ̃) *m*, hog, pig, porker, swine; dirty pig (*man*). ~ *d'Inde*, guinea pig. ~ *de lait*, sucking pig. **cochonnée** (ʃɔne) *f*, farrow, litter. **cochonner** (ne) *v.i*, to farrow, pig. **cochonnerie** (nri) *f*, filthiness, obscenity.

coco (kɔko) *m*, coco[nut].

coco (kɔko) *m*, cocotte (kɔt) *f*, darling.

cocon (kɔkɔ̃) *m*, cocoon.

cocorico (kɔkɔriko) *m*, cock-a-doodle-doo.

cocotier (kɔkɔtje) *m*, coco[nut] palm.

cocotte (kɔkɔt) *f*, stew pot; kept woman, loose w.; darling (*endearment*). ~-*minute* (minyt), pressure cooker.

code (kɔd) *m*, code; statute book; law; canons (*taste*). ~ *de la route*, highway code, road code, code of the road. *mettre en* ~, to dim (*auto lights*). Cf. *pharecode*.

codétenteur, trice (kɔdetɑ̃tœːr, tris) *n*, joint holder.

codex [pharmaceutique] (kɔdɛks) *m*, pharmacopoeia.

codicille (kɔdisil) *m*, codicil.

codifier (kɔdifje) *v.t*, to codify.

codirecteur, trice (kɔdirɛktœːr, tris) *n*, joint manager, ess.

coefficient (kɔefisjɑ̃) *m*, coefficient.

cœur (kœːr) *m*, heart; courage; feelings; core; height (*of summer*); depth (*of winter*); hearts (*cards*). *à* ~ *joie*, as much as you want. *de bon* ~, willingly, gladly.

coffre (kɔfr) *m*, chest, box, trunk, bin, locker, coffer; case. ~-*fort* (frəfɔːr) *m*, safe. **coffrer** (fre) *v.t*, to lock up (*pers.*). **coffret** (frɛ) *m*, casket, box, chest. ~ *à monnaie*, cash box. ~ *de pharmacie*, medicine chest.

cogérant, e (kɔʒerɑ̃, ɑ̃ːt) *n*, joint manager, ess.

cogestion (kɔʒɛstjɔ̃) *f*, joint management.

cognac (kɔɲak) *m*, cognac, brandy.

cognassier (kɔɲasje) *m*, quince [tree].

cognée de bûcheron (kɔɲe) *f*, felling axe. **cogner** (ɲe) *v.t. & i*, to drive in; knock, bump, thump.

cohabiter (koabite) *v.i*, to cohabit.

cohérence (kɔerɑ̃ːs) *f*, coherence. **cohérent, e** (rɑ̃, ɑ̃ːt) *a*, coherent, connected; cohesive. **cohésion** (zjɔ̃) *f*, cohesion.

cohorte (kɔɔrt) *f*, cohort.

cohue (koy) *f*, crowd, crush.

coi, te (kwa, at) *a*, still, quiet.

coiffe (kwaf) *f*, headdress; cap; lining (*hat*); nosecone. **coiffer** (fe) *v.t*, to hat; cap; fit, suit (*hat*); dress (*or do*) [the hair of]. *se* ~ *de* (*fig.*), to be infatuated with. **coiffeur, euse** (fœːr, øːz) *n*, hairdresser. ¶ *f*, dressing table. ~ *psyché*, cheval d. t. **coiffure** (fyːr) *f*, headdress, headgear; style of hairdressing. ~ *à la Ninon* (ninɔ̃), ~ *à la Jeanne d'Arc* (ʒɑ̃ndark) bob[bed hair]. ~ *de cotillon*, paper hat (*Danc.*).

coin (kwɛ̃) *m*, corner, angle; wedge, key, quoin; die; stamp; mark; plot, patch (*land*). ~ *du feu*, fireside, chimney corner. **coincer** (kwɛ̃se) *v.t*, to wedge, key; jam.

coïncidence (kɔɛ̃sidɑ̃ːs) *f*, coincidence. **coïncider** (de) *v.i*, to coincide.

coing (kwɛ̃) *m*, quince (*fruit*).

coïntéressé, e (kɔɛ̃terɛse) *n*, co-adventurer.

coke (kɔk) *m*, coke.

col (kɔl) *m*, collar; neck (*bottle*); pass, col, saddle. ~ *rabattu*, double collar, turndown c. (*attached*). ~ *souple*, soft c. ~ *tenant*, c. attached (*to shirt*). ~ *transformable*, two-way c. *faux* ~, [shirt] collar (*detached*). *faux* ~ *cassé*, wing c. *faux* ~ *montant*, *faux* ~ *droit*, high c., stand-up c.

faux ~ *rabattu*, double c., turn-down c. ~ *roulé*, turtleneck c.

col-blanc (kɔlblɑ̃) *m*, white-collar worker.

col-bleu (kɔlblø) *m*, blue-collar worker; bluejacket (*Nav.*).

coléoptère (kɔleɔptɛːr) *a*, coleopterous. ¶ *m*, coleopter[an], beetle.

colère (kɔlɛːr) *f*, anger, rage, passion, temper, fume. ~ *bleue*, towering rage. **colère & colérique** (lerik) *a*, quick-tempered, hasty, peppery, choleric.

colibri (kɔlibri) *m*, humming bird.

colifichet (kɔlifiʃɛ) *m*, knickknack; (*pl.*) frippery.

colimaçon (kɔlimasɔ̃) *m*, snail. *en* ~, spiral.

colin-maillard (kɔlɛ̃majaːr) *m*, blindman's buff.

colique (kɔlik) *f*, colic, gripes.

colis (kɔli) *m*, parcel, package; article [of luggage]. ~ *à livrer par exprès*, express parcel (*Post*). ~-*avion*, air p. ~ *contre remboursement*, cash on delivery p. *par* ~ *postal*, by parcel post.

collaborateur, trice (kɔlabɔratœːr, tris) *n*, collaborator, contributor. **collaborer** (re) *v.i*, to collaborate. ~ *à*, to contribute to, write for (*journal*).

collage (kɔlaːʒ) *m*, sticking, pasting; gluing; sizing; hanging (*paper*); fining (*wine*); free union of a couple; splicing (*film*). ~ *à sec*, drymounting (*Photo.*). **collant, e** (lɑ̃, ɑ̃ːt) *a*, sticky; tacky; tight, close-fitting. ¶ *m*, pantyhose.

collatéral, e (kɔlateral) *a*, collateral, side (*att.*).

collation (kɔlasjɔ̃) *f*, collation; light meal, snack. **collationner** (ɔne) *v.t*, to collate, compare, read over; repeat; (*v.i.*) to have a snack.

colle (kɔl) *f*, glue, paste; oral test (*exams*); detention (*Sch.*); difficult question. ~ [*de poisson*], isinglass; fish glue. ~ *forte*, glue.

collecte (kɔlɛkt) *f*, collection (*money*); collect. **collecteur** (tœːr) *m*, collector; main (*drain*). ~ *d'impôts*, tax collector. **collec-**

tif, ive† (tif, iːv) *a*, collective, joint. **collection** (sjɔ̃) *f*, collection; file (*newspapers*). **collectionner** (ɔne) *v.t*, to collect. **collectionneur, euse** (nœːr, øːz) *n*, collector.

collège (kɔlɛːʒ) *m*, college, high school. ~ *électoral*, electoral college. **collégial, e** (leʒjal) *a*, collegiate. **collégien, ne** (ʒjɛ̃, ɛn) *n*, collegian, schoolboy -girl.

collègue (kɔleg) *m*, colleague.

coller (kɔle) *v.t*, to stick; paste; glue; size; hang (*paper*); fine (*wine*); fix, fasten; cushion (*Bil.*); to fail (*exam*); (*v.i.*) to fit tightly, cling; to be punished (*Sch.*). *se* ~, to stick, cling, cleave.

collerette (kɔlrɛt) *f*, collaret[te]; flange.

collet (kɔlɛ) *m*, collar; collet; neck; scrag (*mutton*); scruff of the neck; flange. ~ *monté* (*fig.*), straitlaced; prim. **colleter** (lte) *v.t*, to collar, grapple with.

colleur (kɔlœːr) *m*, paperhanger; billposter, billsticker; examiner (*Sch.*).

colleuse (kɔløːz) *f*, splicer (*film*).

collier (kɔlje) *m*, necklace; collar; strap; ring. ~ *de misère*, drudgery.

colline (kɔlin) *f*, hill.

collision (kɔlizjɔ̃) *f*, collision, clash.

collocation (kɔlɔkasjɔ̃) *f*, settling the list of creditors; dividend (*to creditors*). *bordereau de* ~, list of creditors.

colloque (kɔlɔk) *m*, colloquy, conversation.

colloquer (kɔlɔke) *v.t*, to collocate; foist.

collusion (kɔlysjɔ̃) *f*, collusion.

colombe (kɔlɔ̃ːb) *f*, dove.

Colombie (la) (kɔlɔ̃bi), Columbia.

colombier (kɔlɔ̃bje) *m*, dovecote.

colon (kɔlɔ̃) *m*, colonist, settler.

colonel (kɔlɔnɛl) *m*, colonel.

colonial, e (kɔlɔnjal) *a*, colonial. **colonie** (ni) *f*, colony, settlement. *la* ~ *du Cap*, Cape Colony. **coloniser** (nize) *v.t*, to colonize.

colonnade (kɔlɔnad) *f*, colonnade. **colonne** (lɔn) *f*, column, pillar; post. ~ *vertébrale*, spinal column.

colophane (kɔlɔfan) *f*, resin (*violin*).

colorer (kɔlɔre) *v.t*, to color; stain (*glass*). **colorier** (rje) *v.t*, to color. **coloris** (ri) *m*, color[ing], hue.

colossal, e† (kɔlɔsal) *a*, colossal. **colosse** (lɔs) *m*, colossus; giant.

colporter (kɔlpɔrte) *v.t*, to hawk, peddle; spread (*news, gossip*). **colporteur** (tœːr) *m*, peddler.

coltineur (kɔltinœːr) *m*, porter (*dock*); heaver (*coal*).

colza (kɔlza) *m*, colza.

coma (kɔma) *m*, coma (*Med.*). **comateux, euse** (tø, øːz) *a*, comatose.

combat (kɔ̃ba) *m*, combat, fight, battle, action; war (*elements*); contest, bout, match. ~ *de boxe*, boxing match. ~ *de boxe professionel*, prize fight[ing]. ~ *de près*, infighting (*Box.*). hors de ~, disabled. **combativité** (tā) *f*, combativeness. **combattant** (tā) *m*, combatant, fighter. *ancien* ~, veteran. **combattre** (tr) *v.t. & i. ir*, to fight; oppose; combat; contend with; strive; vie.

combe (kɔ̃ːb) *f*, coomb, combe, dale.

combien (kɔ̃bjɛ̃) *ad*, how much; how many; how far; how. ~ *de fois?* how many times? how often? ~ *de temps?* how long?

combinaison (kɔ̃binɛzɔ̃) *f*, combination; plan, contrivance; scheme; lady's slip; overalls. **combine** (bin) *f*, trick, scheme (*generally not quite legal or moral*). **combiner** (ne) *v.t*, to combine; contrive, devise.

comble (kɔ̃ːbl) *a*, full, crowded. ¶ *m*, heaping; top, height, highest pitch; acme, summit, sum; last straw; roof. ~ *brisé*, mansard roof. *salle* ~, full house (*Theat.*). **combler** (kɔ̃ble) *v.t*, to heap, shower, fill, load, overwhelm; make up, make good.

combustible (kɔ̃bystibl) *a*, combustible; fuel (*att.*). ¶ *m*, fuel, firing. **combustion** (tjɔ̃) *f*, combustion; burning; conflagration, fire (*fig.*); burnup (*nuclear*).

Côme (le lac de) (koːm), Lake Como.

comédie (kɔmedi) *f*, comedy; theatricals; players; sham. **comédien, ne** (djɛ̃, ɛn) *n*, comedian, enne, actor, tress, player.

comestible (kɔmɛstibl) *a*, edible. ~**s**, *m.pl*, eatables, provisions.

comète (kɔmɛt) *f*, comet; head-band (*Bookb.*).

comice agricole (kɔmis) *m*, agricultural show, cattle show.

comique† (kɔmik) *a*, comic; comical; funny, ludicrous. ¶ *m*, comedy; c. writer; comic actor; funny part, joke. ~ *de la troupe* (*fig.*), funny man.

comité (kɔmite) *m*, committee. *en petit* ~, select group; insiders only.

commandant (kɔmɑ̃dɑ̃) *m*, commander, commanding officer; commandant; major (*Mil.*); commodore (*Naut.*); squadron leader (*Avn.*). **commande** (mɑ̃ːd) *f*, order; indent; driving; drive; driving gear; control. *de* ~, [arranged] to order; feigned. *sur* ~, (*made*) to order, commissioned. *bulletin de* ~, order form. *touche de* ~, command key (*computers*). **commandement** (mɑ̃dmɑ̃) *m*, command, order; commandment; behest; word of command. **commander** (de) *v.t. & i*, to command, order, bespeak; govern; demand; drive (*Mach.*).

commanditaire (kɔmɑ̃ditɛːr) *m*, silent partner; sponsor. **commandite** (dit) *f*, limited liability; finance, interest. **commandité** (te) *m*, acting partner. **commanditer** (te) *v.t*, to finance, take an interest in; sponsor.

comme (kɔm) *ad*, as, like, such as; how. ~ *ci,* ~ *ça*, so so, middling. ¶ *c*, as, since.

commémorer (kɔmemɔre) *v.t*, to commemorate.

commençant, e (kɔmɑ̃sɑ̃, ɑ̃ːt) *n*, beginner, tyro, learner. **commencement** (smɑ̃) *m*, beginning, start, commencement, inception, outset. **commencer** (se) *v.t. & i*, to begin, commence, start.

commensal, e (kɔmɑ̃sal) *n*, messmate, fellow boarder.

comment (kɔmɑ̃) *ad*, how; what! why! ~*!*, of all the nerve! how dare you! ~?, what? I don't understand. *et* ~!, and how!

commentaire (kɔmɑ̃tɛːr) *m*, commentary; comment. **commentateur** (tatœːr) *m*, narrator; annotator; news commentator (*TV*). **commenter** (te) *v.t*, or ~ sur, to comment on.

commérage (kɔmeraːʒ) *m*, gossip, tittle-tattle.

commerçant, e (kɔmɛrsɑ̃, ɑ̃:t) *a*, commercial, trading, business (*att.*). ¶ *n*, trader, merchant. **commerce** (mɛrs) *m*, commerce, trade, trading, business; traders; intercourse; dealings. ~ *de détail,* retail trade. *d'un ~ agréable,* easy to get on with. **commercer** (mɛrse) *v.i*, to trade, deal; hold intercourse. **commercial,** e† (sjal) *a*, commercial, business, trade, trading (*att.*); produce (*market*).

commère (kɔmɛːr) *f*, fellow sponsor; gossip; busybody; shrewd woman; leading lady (*revue*).

commettant (kɔmɛtɑ̃) *m*, principal (*law*); (*pl.*) constituents (*Pol.*). **commettre** (mɛtr) *v.t.ir*, to commit; perpetrate; appoint; entrust; compromise. **commis** (mi) *m*, clerk. ~ *aux vivres,* ship's steward. ~ *d'entreprise,* clerk of [the] works. ~ *de magasin,* shop assistant. ~ *voyageur,* traveling salesman. **commissaire** (sɛːr) *m*, commissioner; officer (*emigration*); steward (*fête, race meeting, etc.*); purser (*ship*); paymaster (*navy*); superintendent (*police*). ~ *des* (ou *aux*) *comptes,* auditor. ~ *priseur,* auctioneer. **commissariat** (sarja) *m*, the status or office (rooms) of a *commissaire*; thus, ~ *de police,* central police station. ~ *des comptes,* auditorship.

commission (kɔmisjɔ̃) *f*, commission; errand; committee. **commissionnaire** (ɔnɛːr) *m*, agent, commission agent, factor; messenger; porter. ~ *chargeur,* shipping agent. ~ *de transport[s],* forwarding a. ~ *en douane,* customs a. **commissionner** (ne) *v.t*, to commission.

commode (kɔmɔd) *f*, [chest of]

drawers. ¶ *a*, convenient, handy; commodious, pleasant; easy, easy-going. **commodément** (demɑ̃) *ad*, conveniently. **commodité** (dite) *f*, convenience; commodiousness; (*pl.*) toilet.

commotion (kɔmosjɔ̃) *f*, commotion, upheaval; shock; shell shock. ~ *au cerveau,* concussion of the brain.

commuer (kɔmɥe) *v.t*, to commute.

commun, e (kɔmœ̃, yn) *a*, common; usual; general; ordinary; commonplace; vulgar; average. *peu* ~, uncommon. ¶ *m*, generality, run. *en, hors du,* ~, in, out of the, common. **communal,** e (mynal) *a*, communal; parish (*att.*). ¶ *m*, common [land]. **communauté** (note) *f*, community; commonwealth; sisterhood. *la C~ d'Australie,* the Commonwealth of Australia. **commune** (myn) *f*, commune, parish (*civil*). **communément** (nemɑ̃) *ad*, commonly, generally.

communiant, e (kɔmynjɑ̃, ɑ̃:t) *n*, communicant.

communicatif, ive (kɔmynikatif, iːv) *a*, communicative. **communication** (sjɔ̃) *f*, communication; touch; intercourse; interchange; discovery; access (*of, to, documents*); call (*Teleph.*).

communier (kɔmynje) *v.i. & t*, to communicate (*Eccl.*). **communion** (njɔ̃) *f*, communion; sacrament; fellowship; persuasion, faith, denomination.

communiqué (kɔmynike) *m*, official statement (*to press*); communiqué. **communiquer** (ke) *v.t. & i*, to communicate; impart, convey; produce (*documents*).

communisme (kɔmynism) *m*, communism. **communiste** (nist) *n*, communist.

commutateur (kɔmytatœːr) *m*, switch; commutator. ~ *code,* dimmer (*auto*). **commutation** (sjɔ̃) *f*, commutation.

compacité (kɔ̃pasite) *f*, compactness, closeness. **compact,** e (pakt) *a*, compact, dense; concise, compendious.

compagne (kɔ̃paɲ) *f*, companion; mate; partner (*wife*). ~ *de voyage*, fellow passenger, f. traveler. **compagnie** (ɲi) *f*, company; companionship; bevy; covey. *de bonne* ~, well-bred, gentlemanly, ladylike. *de mauvaise* ~, ill-bred, ungentlemanly, unladylike. **& Cie** (e kɔ̃paɲi), **& Co.** **compagnon** (ɲɔ̃) *m*, companion; mate; journeyman. ~ *de malheur*, fellow sufferer. ~ *de voyage*, fellow passenger, f. traveler.

comparable (kɔ̃parabl) *a*, comparable. **comparaison** (rɛzɔ̃) *f*, comparison; simile.

comparaître (kɔ̃parɛːtr) *v.i.ir*, to appear (*law*).

comparatif, ive† (kɔ̃paratif, iːv) *a*, comparative. ¶ *m*, comparative (*Gram.*). **comparé,** e (re) *p.a*, comparative (*sciences*). **comparer** (re) *v.t*, to compare, liken.

comparse (kɔ̃pars) *n*, supernumerary (*Theat.*); (*m.*) cipher (*pers.*).

compartiment (kɔ̃partimɑ̃) *m*, compartment.

comparution (kɔ̃parysjɔ̃) *f*, appearance (*law*).

compas (kɔ̃pɑ) *m*, [pair of] compasses; compass. **compassé** (se) *a*, formal, stiff; regular. **compasser** (se) *v.t*, to measure.

compassion (kɔ̃pasjɔ̃) *f*, compassion. **compatible** (tibl) *a*, compatible, consistent. **compatir** (tiːr) *v.i*, to sympathize, bear. **compatissant,** e (tisɑ̃, ɑ̃ːt) *a*, compassionate.

compatriote (kɔ̃patriɔt) *n*, compatriot, [fellow] countryman, -woman.

compendieusement (kɔ̃pɑ̃djøzmɑ̃) *ad*, briefly. **compendium** (pɛ̃djɔm) *m*, compendium.

compensateur, trice (kɔ̃pɑ̃satœːr, tris) *a*, compensating; countervailing (*duty*). **compensation** (sjɔ̃) *f*, compensation; set off, offset; quid pro quo; making up (*Stk Ex.*); clearing (*banking*). **compenser** (se) *v.t*, to compensate, offset; make up; clear. ~ *les dépens*, to order each party to pay its own costs.

compère (kɔ̃pɛːr) *m*, fellow sponsor; fellow; crony; confederate; leading man (*revue*); compère. ~**-loriot,** *m*, sty (*eye*).

compétence (kɔ̃petɑ̃ːs) *f*, competence; jurisdiction; province. **compétent,** e (tɑ̃, ɑ̃ːt) *a*, competent.

compétiteur, trice (kɔ̃petitœːr, tris) *n*, competitor. **compétition** (sjɔ̃) *f*, competition.

compiler (kɔ̃pile) *v.t. & abs*, to compile.

complainte (kɔ̃plɛ̃ːt) *f*, ballad, lay.

complaire à (kɔ̃plɛːr) *v.ir*, to gratify, humor. **se complaire,** to take pleasure, [take] delight, fancy oneself, pat oneself on the back. **complaisamment** (plɛzamɑ̃) *ad*, complacently; obligingly. **complaisance** (zɑ̃ːs) *f*, complaisance; deference; kindness; willingness; complacence, -cy; accommodation (*Fin.*). **complaisant,** e (zɑ̃, ɑ̃ːt) *a*, obliging, willing; complaisant, accommodating; compliant; complacent. ¶ *n*, time server.

complément (kɔ̃plemɑ̃) *m*, complement. ~ *de poids*, makeweight. **complémentaire** (tɛːr) *a*, complementary, fuller.

complet, ète (kɔ̃plɛ, ɛt) *a*, complete, total, whole, full; unabridged; utter; wholemeal (*bread*). *wagon complet, charge complète*, truckload. *complet*, full house (*Theat.*) *c'est* ~*!*, that's the last straw. ¶ *m*, complement; suit [of clothes] (*man's*). *au* ~, complete, full. **complètement** (plɛtmɑ̃) *ad*, completely; quite; thoroughly. ¶ *m*, completion. **compléter** (plete) *v.t*, to complete.

complexe (kɔ̃plɛks) *a*, complex; many-sided; compound. ¶ *m*, complex. ~ *d'infériorité*, inferiority c. *être bourré de* ~*s*, to be extremely inhibited.

complexion (kɔ̃plɛksjɔ̃) *f*, constitution; disposition.

complexité (kɔ̃plɛksite) *f*, complexity.

complication (kɔ̃plikasjɔ̃) *f*, complication; intricacy.

complice (kɔ̃plis) *a*, accessory,

privy, a party (*de* = to). ¶ *n*, accomplice, confederate. **~ en** *adultère*, co-respondent. **complicité** (site) *f*, complicity.

complies (kɔpli) *f.pl*, complin[e] (*Eccl.*).

compliment (kɔplimɑ̃) *m*, compliment, congratulation; (*pl.*) kind regards. **complimenter** (te) *v.t*, to compliment. **complimenteur, euse** (tœːr, øːz) *a*, overcivil. ¶ *n*, flatterer.

compliquer (kɔplike) *v.t*, to complicate.

complot (kɔplo) *m*, plot. **comploter** (plɔte) *v.t*, to plot.

componction (kɔpɔ̃ksjɔ̃) *f*, compunction.

comporter (kɔpɔrte) *v.t*, to admit of; call for, require. **se ~**, to behave.

composant, e (kɔpozɑ̃, ɑ̃ːt) *a. & m*, component, constituent. **composé, e** (ze) *a*, compound, composite; composed, demure. *bien composée*, select (*company of people*). ¶ *m*, compound. **composer** (ze) *v.t. & i*, to compose; compound; settle; set (*Typ.*); dial (*Teleph.*). **se ~**, to be composed, consist. **compositeur, trice** (pozitœːr, tris) *n*, composer; compositor, [type] setter. **composition** (sjɔ̃) *f*, composition; settlement; [type] setting; essay; examination (*Sch.*); paper (*Sch.*). **composteur** (postœːr) *m*, composing stick; office printing outfit.

composter (kɔposte) *v.t*, to date or punch (*railway ticket, etc.*). *compostez vos billets*, have your tickets punched.

compote (kɔpɔt) *f*, compote, stewed fruit. **~ de pommes**, stewed apples. **en ~**, overdone (*meat*); to a jelly (*face injury*). **compotier** (tje) *m*, fruit bowl.

compréhensif, ive (kɔpreɑ̃sif, iːv) *a*, comprehensive. **compréhension** (sjɔ̃) *f*, comprehension, understanding. **comprendre** (prɑ̃ːdr) *v.t.ir*, to comprehend, understand, make out; comprise, include, cover. *y compris*, including. *non compris*, not including, exclusive of.

compresse (kɔprɛːs) *f*, compress

(*Med.*). **compresseur** (prɛsœːr) *m*, compressor. **compression** (sjɔ̃) *f*, compression; repression; cut (*in expenditure*). **comprimer** (prime) *v.t*, to compress; repress; restrain.

comprimé (kɔprime) *m*, pill, tablet; pack (*computers*).

compromettre (kɔprɔmɛtr) *v.t. & i. ir*, to compromise; impair. **se ~**, to compromise (*or* commit) oneself. **compromis** (mi) *m*, compromise; bond.

comptabilité (kɔtabilite) *f*, bookkeeping; accountancy; accounts. **comptable** (bl) *a*, accountable, responsible; book (*entry, value*); accounting *or* bookkeeping (*machine*). ¶ *n*, accountant, bookkeeper. **comptant** (tɑ̃) *m*, cash, prompt (*or* spot) cash, ready money. [*au*] **~**, in (*or* for) cash, cash down. **compte** (kɔːt) *m*, counting, count; reckoning; account. **~-gouttes** (kɔt-gut) *m*, dropper. **~-pas**, *m*, pedometer. **~ rendu**, report; review. **~ à rebours**, countdown. **~ rond**, round figures, r. numbers; even money. **à ~**, on account. *tout ~ fait*, all told. *se rendre ~ de*, to realize. **compter** (kɔte) *v.t. & i*, to count, reckon, number; rely, depend, calculate; intend, mean. **compteur** (tœːr) *m*, meter, counter; taximeter, clock; computer. **~ de bicyclette**, cyclometer. **~ de sport**, stopwatch, recorder. **~ de tours**, speed (*or* revolution) counter. **~ de vitesse**, speedometer. **comptoir** (twaːr) *m*, counter; bar; branch, agency; office.

compulser (kɔpylse) *v.t*, to go through, examine.

comte (kɔ̃ːt) *m*, count (*title*). **comté** (kɔte) *m*, county, shire. **comtesse** (tɛs) *f*, countess.

con (kɔ̃) *m*, cunt. **con, ne** (ɔn) *n*, imbecile. *le roi de* **~s**, the king of fools. **conard** (naːr) *m*, idiot, fool, etc. **conasse** (nas) *f*, stupid woman; slut. **connerie** (kɔnri) *f*, imbecility. *faire une* **~**, to do something foolish.

concasser (kɔkɑse) *v.t*, to pound, break, crush.

concave (kɔkaːv) *a*, concave. **concavité** (kavite) *f*, concavity.

concéder (kɔ̃sede) *v.t*, to concede, grant.

concentration (kɔ̃sɑ̃trasjɔ̃) *f*, concentration. **concentrer** (tre) *v.t*, to concentrate; center (*fig.*); repress. **concentrique** (trik) *a*, concentric.

concepteur (kɔ̃sɛptœːr) *m*, idea man. ~*-projecteur*, author of a project.

conception (kɔ̃sɛpsjɔ̃) *f*, conception.

concernant (kɔ̃sɛrnɑ̃) *pr*, concerning. **concerner** (ne) *v.t*, to concern, affect.

concert (kɔ̃sɛːr) *m*, concert; chorus (*fig.*). **concertant**, e (sɛrtɑ̃, ɑ̃ːt) *n*, concert performer. **concerter** (te) *v.t*, to concert, plan. **concerto** (sɛrto) *m*, concerto.

concession (kɔ̃sɛsjɔ̃) *f*, concession, grant, claim, license. **concessionnaire** (ɔnɛːr) *n*, concession[n]aire, grantor, claimholder.

concevable (kɔ̃s[ə]vabl) *a*, conceivable. **concevoir** (səvwaːr) *v.t. & abs*, to conceive; entertain; understand; word, couch.

concierge (kɔ̃sjɛrʒ) *n*, doorkeeper, [hall] porter, caretaker, housekeeper; keeper (*prison*).

concile (kɔ̃sil) *m*, council (*Eccl.*).

conciliabule (kɔ̃siljabyl) *m*, secret meeting; confabulation.

concilier (kɔ̃silje) *v.t*, to conciliate, reconcile; win.

concis, e (kɔ̃si, iːz) *a*, concise, terse, crisp, brief. **concision** (sizjɔ̃) *f*, conciseness, brevity.

concitoyen, ne (kɔ̃sitwajɛ̃, ɛn) *n*, fellow citizen.

concluant, e (kɔ̃klyɑ̃, ɑ̃ːt) *a*, conclusive. **conclure** (klyːr) *v.t. & i. ir*, to conclude, end; clinch; infer. **conclusion** (klyzjɔ̃) *f*, conclusion, inference; (*pl.*) pleas (*law*).

concombre (kɔ̃kɔ̃ːbr) *m*, cucumber.

concordance (kɔ̃kɔrdɑ̃ːs) *f*, agreement, reconciliation; concordance; concord. **concordat** (da) *m*, composition; concordat. **concorde** (kɔrd) *f*, concord, harmony. **concorder** (de) *v.i*, to agree, tally.

concourir (kɔ̃kuriːr) *v.i.ir*, to concur; compete; rank. **concours** (kuːr) *m*, concurrence; assistance, help; concourse; confluence; competition, contest; meeting; show; [competitive] examination; equality. ~ *orthographique*, spelling bee.

concret, ète (kɔ̃krɛ, ɛt) *a*, concrete. *le concret*, the concrete (opp. *abstract*).

conçu, *p.p*, concevoir.

concubine (kɔ̃kybin) *f*, concubine.

concupiscence (kɔ̃kypisɑ̃ːs) *f*, concupiscence.

concurrence (kɔ̃kyrɑ̃ːs) *f*, competition; equality [of rank]. *à* ~ *de*, amounting to. *jusqu'à* ~ *de*, up to, not exceeding. **concurrent, e** (rɑ̃, ɑ̃ːt) *a*, concurrent. ¶ *n*, competitor.

concussion (kɔ̃kysjɔ̃) *f*, misappropriation.

condamnation (kɔ̃dɑnasjɔ̃) *f*, condemnation; sentence; judgment; conviction. **condamné, e** (ne) *n*, convict. ~ *à mort*, condemned man, woman. **condamner** (ne) *v.t*, to condemn; doom; convict; sentence; mulct; give up (*patient*); block up (*door*); board up (*window*); batten down (*Naut.*).

condé (kɔ̃de) *m*, a tacit agreement with the police; a police detective.

condensateur (kɔ̃dɑ̃satœːr) *m*, condenser (*Phys., Elec., Opt.*). **condensation** (sjɔ̃) *f*, condensation. **condenser** (dɑ̃se) *v.t*, to condense; boil down; pack (*computers*). **condenseur** (sœːr) *m*, condenser (*steam*).

condescendance (kɔ̃desɑ̃dɑ̃ːs) *f*, condescension. **condescendre** (dr) *v.i*, to condescend; comply.

condiment (kɔ̃dimɑ̃) *m*, condiment.

condisciple (kɔ̃disipl) *m*, fellow student, schoolfellow.

condition (kɔ̃disjɔ̃) *f*, condition; (*pl.*) terms; position. ~*provisionnelle*, proviso. *à* ~, on approval. *en* ~, in (*domestic*) service. **conditionnel, le†** (ɔnɛl) *a*, conditional. **conditionner**(ne) *v.t*, to condition; make up.

condoléance (kɔ̃dɔleɑ̃ːs) *f*, condolence.

conducteur, trice (kɔ̃dyktœːr, tris) *n*, conductor, tress; driver; drover; guard (*Rly.*). ~ *des travaux*, foreman of job, factory foreman (*Build.*). ~ *principal*, main, lead (*Elec.*). **conduire** (dɥiːr) *v.t. & abs. ir*, to conduct, lead, guide, show; direct, manage, run; drive; steer; take, carry, convey; conduce. **se** ~, to behave. **conduit** (dɥi) *m*, pipe, conduit, duct. **conduite** (dɥit) *f*, conduct, behavior, bearing; management; lead; care; driving; pipe. ~ [*maîtresse*], main.

cône (koːn) *m*, cone; taper.

confection (kɔ̃fɛksjɔ̃) *f*, making up; ready-made clothes, *or* business; outfitting. **confectionner** (ɔne) *v.t*, to make up; concoct. **confectionneur, euse** (nœːr, øːz) *n*, clothier, outfitter.

confédération (kɔ̃federasjɔ̃) *f*, confederation, confederacy. **se confédérer** (re) *v.pr*, to confederate.

conférence (kɔ̃ferɑ̃ːs) *f*, conference; lecture; debating society. **conférencier, ère** (rɑ̃sje, ɛːr) *n*, lecturer. **conférer** (re) *v.i. & t*, to confer; bestow; compare.

confesse (kɔ̃fɛs) *f*, confession (*to priest*). **confesser** (se) *v.t*, to confess, own. **se** ~, to confess [one's sins]. **confesseur** (sœːr) *m*, confessor. **confession** (sjɔ̃) *f*, confession. **confessionnal** (ɔnal) *m*, confessional [box]. **confessionnel, le** (nɛl) *a*, confessional; denominational.

confiance (kɔ̃fjɑ̃ːs) *f*, confidence, trust, faith, reliance, dependence. **confiant, e** (ɑ̃, ɑ̃ːt) *a*, confident, sanguine, hopeful; confiding. **confidemment** (fidamɑ̃) *ad*, confidentially. **confidence** (dɑ̃ːs) *f*, confidence, secrecy. **confident, e** (dɑ̃, ɑ̃ːt) *n*, confidant, e. **confidentiel, le**† (sjɛl) *a*, confidential. **confier** (fje) *v.t*, to entrust, confide; trust, commit; vest. **se** ~, to confide, rely.

configuration (kɔ̃figyrasjɔ̃) *f*, configuration, lie, lay.

confiner (kɔ̃fine) *v.i*, to border;

(*v.t.*) to confine. **confins** (fɛ̃) *m.pl*, confines; ends.

confire (kɔ̃fiːr) *v.t.ir*, to preserve; pickle.

confirmer (kɔ̃firme) *v.t*, to confirm.

confiscation (kɔ̃fiskasjɔ̃) *f*, confiscation.

confiserie (kɔ̃fizri) *f*, confectionery; confectioner's shop. **confiseur, euse** (zœːr, øːz) *n*, confectioner.

confisquer (kɔ̃fiske) *v.t*, to confiscate; impound.

confiture (kɔ̃fityːr) *f. oft. pl*, preserve, jam. ~ *d'oranges*, [orange] marmalade.

conflagration (kɔ̃flagrasjɔ̃) *f*, conflagration.

conflit (kɔ̃fli) *m*, conflict, clash, strife.

confluent (kɔ̃flyɑ̃) *m*, confluence, meeting. **confluer** (flye) *v.i*, to join, meet.

confondre (kɔ̃fɔ̃ːdr) *v.t*, to confound; mingle; blend; confuse; mistake; discomfit; overwhelm.

conformation (kɔ̃fɔrmasjɔ̃) *f*, conformation. **conforme** (fɔrm) *a*, conformable; according; in harmony; agreeable. *pour copie* ~, [certified] a true copy. **conformé, e** (me) *p.a*, (*well, ill*) formed. **conformément** (mɑ̃) *ad*, conformably, according. **conformer** (me) *v.t. & se* ~, to conform. **conformité** (mite) *f*, conformity, compliance.

confort (kɔ̃fɔːr) *m*, comfort(s). **confortable**† (fɔrtabl) *a*, comfortable, snug.

confraternité (kɔ̃fratɛrnite) *f*, confraternity, brotherhood. **confrère** (frɛːr) *m*, colleague, confrere, brother; contemporary. **confrérie** (freri) *f*, brotherhood, sisterhood; confraternity.

confronter (kɔ̃frɔ̃te) *v.t*, to confront; compare.

confus, e (kɔ̃fy, yːz) *a*, confused; jumbled; indiscriminate; embarrassed. **confusément** (fyzemɑ̃) *ad*, confusedly; dimly. **confusion** (zjɔ̃) *f*, confusion; embarrassment.

congé (kɔ̃ʒe) *m*, leave; vacation; furlough; dismissal, discharge; notice [to quit]; permission; clearance (*ship*); cart note (*Cust.*); fillet (*Arch.*). donner ~, to fire (*employee*). **congédier** (dje) *v.t.* to dismiss, discharge; pay off.

congélation (kɔ̃ʒelasjɔ̃) *f*, congelation, freezing; frostbite. **congeler** (ʒle) *v.t.* & se ~, to congeal, freeze.

congénital, e (kɔ̃ʒenital) *a*, congenital.

congère (kɔ̃ʒɛːr) *f*, snowdrift. ~ de sable, sand drift.

congestion (kɔ̃ʒɛstjɔ̃) *f*, congestion. ~ cérébrale, pulmonaire, sanguine, c. of the brain, of the lungs, of the blood. **congestionner** (ɔne) *v.t*, to congest (*Med.*).

conglomérat (kɔ̃glɔmera) *m*, conglomerate.

congratulation (kɔ̃gratylasjɔ̃) *f*, congratulation. **congratuler** (le) *v.t*, to congratulate.

congre (kɔ̃ːgr) *m*, conger [eel].

congrégation (kɔ̃gregasjɔ̃) *f*, congregation (*Eccl.*).

congrès (kɔ̃grɛ) *m*, congress. **congressiste** (sist) *n*, member of the (*or* a) congress.

congru, e (kɔ̃gry) *a*, congruous, fitting. à la portion congrue, on short pay, on a meager income. **congrûment** (grymã) *ad*, congruously.

conifère (kɔnifɛːr) *a*, coniferous. ¶ *m*, conifer.

conique (kɔnik) *a*, conic(al); taper[ing].

conjectural, e† (kɔ̃ʒɛktyral) *a*, conjectural. **conjecture** (tyːr) *f*, conjecture, surmise, guess. **conjecturer** (tyre) *v.t*, to conjecture.

conjoindre (kɔ̃ʒwɛ̃ːdr) *v.t.ir*, to [con]join, unite. **conjoint, e†** (ʒwɛ̃, ɛ̃ːt) *a*, [con]joint. ¶ *n*, party to a (*or* the) marriage (*law*). **conjonction** (ʒɔ̃ksjɔ̃) *f*, conjunction, union. **conjoncture** (ʒɔ̃ktyːr) *f*, conjuncture.

conjugaison (kɔ̃ʒygɛzɔ̃) *f*, conjugation.

conjugal, e† (kɔ̃ʒygal) *a*, conjugal, connubial, matrimonial, marriage (*tie*), married (*life*).

conjuguer (kɔ̃ʒyge) *v.t*, to conjugate. machines conjuguées, twin engines.

conjuration (kɔ̃ʒyrasjɔ̃) *f*, con-

spiracy; conjuration. **conjuré** (re) *m*, conspirator. **conjurer** (re) *v.t.* & *i*, to conspire; conjure.

connaissance (kɔnɛsɑ̃ːs) *f*, knowledge; ken; acquaintance; consciousness, senses; cognizance; (*pl.*) learning, attainments, acquirements. avoir sa ~, to be conscious (*awake*). en ~ de cause, advisedly. figure de ~, familiar face. prendre ~ de, to take note of. sans ~, unconscious, insensible, senseless.

connaissement (kɔnɛsmã) *m*, bill of lading.

connaisseur, euse (kɔnɛsœːr, øːz) *n*, connoisseur, judge. **connaître** (nɛːtr) *v.t.* & *abs. ir*, to know, be acquainted with; be aware of; take cognizance. se ~ à (ou en), to be a [good] judge of. se faire ~ , to introduce oneself, make oneself known; become known.

connexe (kɔnɛks) *a*, connected, allied, like. & ~s, & the like. **connexion** (ksjɔ̃), **connexité** (ksite) *f*, connection.

connivence (kɔnivɑ̃ːs) *f*, connivance. être de ~ pour, to connive at.

connu (le) (kɔny), the known.

conque (kɔ̃ːk) *f*, conch.

conquis, *p.p*, conquérir.

conquérant, e (kɔ̃kerã, ɑ̃ːt) *n*, conqueror, ess. **conquérir** (riːr) *v.t.ir*, to conquer. **conquête** (kɛːt) *f*, conquest.

consacrer (kɔ̃sakre) *v.t*, to consecrate, hallow; dedicate; devote; appropriate, set apart; sanction. consacré (à la mémoire de), sacred. terme consacré, accepted term.

consanguinité (kɔ̃sɑ̃ginite) *f*, consanguinity, blood relationship.

conscience (kɔ̃sjɑ̃ːs) *f*, conscience; conscientiousness; consciousness. se faire ~ de, to be reluctant to. avoir ~ de, to be aware of. **consciencieux, euse†** (ɑ̃sjø, øːz) *a*, conscientious. **conscient, e** (sjɑ̃, ɑ̃ːt) *a*, conscious (*aware*); sentient (*being*).

conscription (kɔ̃skripsjɔ̃) *f*, conscription. **conscrit** (skri) *m*,

conscript, draftee; tyro; fresh-
man (*Sch.*).
consécration (kɔ̃sekrasjɔ̃) *f*,
consecration; dedication; sanction.
consécutif, ive† (kɔ̃sekytif, i:v)
a, consecutive.
conseil (kɔ̃sɛ:j) *m*, advice, counsel; board; council; counsel;
counsel (*pers. law*). ~ de prud'hommes, conciliation board. C~ des
ministres, C~ de Cabinet, cabinet council. ~ d'administration,
board [of directors]. ~ de guerre,
council of war; court martial.
conseiller (sɛje) *v.t*, to advise,
counsel. **conseiller, ère** (je, ɛ:r)
n, adviser, councilor. **conseilleur,
euse** (jœ:r, ø:z) *n*, officious adviser.
consentement (kɔ̃sɑ̃tmɑ̃) *m*,
consent; assent. **consentir** (ti:r)
v.i.ir, to consent, agree.
conséquemment (kɔ̃sekamɑ̃)
ad, consequently, accordingly.
~ à, consistently with. **conséquence** (kɑ̃:s) *f*, consequence;
outcome, sequel; inference. **conséquent, e** (kɑ̃, ɑ̃:t) *a*, consistent, rational; consequent. *par
conséquent*, consequently, accordingly, therefore.
conservateur, trice (kɔ̃sɛrva-
tœ:r, tris) *n*, conservator, keeper;
warden; ranger; curator, trix;
conservative (*Pol.*); registrar
(*mortgages*). **conservation** (sjɔ̃)
f, preservation; care; registry. ~
par le froid, cold storage. **conservatoire** (twa:r) *m*, school,
academy (*music, etc.*); museum.
conserve (sɛrv) *f*, preserve; (*pl.*)
canned food; (*pl.*) dark glasses;
consort (*Naut.*). ~s au vinaigre,
pickles. **conserver** (ve) *v.t. &
abs*, to preserve; pickle; conserve,
keep. ~ la composition, to keep
the type standing.
considérable† (kɔ̃siderabl) *a*,
considerable; eminent; large. **con-
sidérant** (rɑ̃) *m*, preamble. **considération** (rasjɔ̃) *f*, consideration; regard. **considérer** (re) *v.t*,
to consider; esteem; regard, deem.
consignataire (kɔ̃siɲatɛ:r) *m*,
trustee; consignee. **consignateur**
(tœ:r) *m*, consignor. **consignation**
(sjɔ̃) *f*, deposit; consignment. con-

signe (si:ɲ) *f*, orders (*to sentry*);
confinement to barracks; check-
room, baggage room; deposit
(*bottles, etc.*). **consigner** (ɲe) *v.t*,
to deposit; consign; record,
chronicle; confine [to barracks].
~ à la porte, to refuse admittance.
consistance (kɔ̃sistɑ̃:s) *f*, con-
sistence, -cy; stability; credit,
standing. **consistant, e** (tɑ̃, ɑ̃:t)
a, firm, set. **consister** (te) *v.i*, to
consist. **consistoire** (twa:r) *m*,
consistory.
consolateur, trice (kɔ̃sɔlatœ:r,
tris) *n*, consoler, comforter. **consolation** (sjɔ̃) *f*, consolation,
comfort, solace, cheer. **console**
(sɔl) *f*, bracket; console; console
table. **consoler** (le) *v.t*, to console.
consolider (kɔ̃sɔlide) *v.t*, to consolidate, strengthen; unify, fund
(*debt*); exercise, take up (*option*). **consolidation** (dasjɔ̃) *f*,
consolidation.
consommateur (kɔ̃sɔmatœ:r) *m*,
consumer; customer (*at café*).
consommation (sjɔ̃) *f*, consumption, use; drink; consummation.
consommé, e (me) *a*, consummate. ¶ *m*, stock (*Cook.*); clear
soup. **consommer** (me) *v.t*, to
consume; use; drink, spend
(*money in café*); consummate.
consomption (sɔ̃psjɔ̃) *f*, consumption (*destruction & Med.*).
consonance (kɔ̃sɔnɑ̃:s) *f*, consonance. **consonant, e** (nɑ̃, ɑ̃:t)
a, consonant. **consonne** (sɔn) *f*,
consonant.
consorts (kɔ̃sɔ:r) *m.pl*, confed-
erates. **consortium** (sɔrsjɔm) *m*,
syndicate, consortium.
conspirateur, trice (kɔ̃spira-
tœ:r, tris) *n*, conspirator, plotter. **conspiration** (sjɔ̃) *f*, conspiracy, plot. **conspirer** (re) *v.i.
& t*, to conspire; plot; tend.
conspuer (kɔ̃spɥe) *v.t*, to con-
spue; hoot, boo, barrack. *con-
spuez-le!* down with him!
constamment (kɔ̃stamɑ̃) *ad*,
constantly. **constance** (stɑ̃:s) *f*,
constancy; steadfastness; persist-
ence, perseverance; patience.
avec ~, steadfastly. **constant, e**
(stɑ̃, ɑ̃:t) *a*, constant; steadfast;

enduring; obvious. ¶ *f,* constant.
constater (kɔ̃state) *v.t,* to ascertain; verify, prove, establish; declare; attest; evidence; record; note; show; mention; be of opinion. **constatation** (tasjɔ̃) *f,* ascertainment, etc.

constellation (kɔ̃stɛllasjɔ̃) *f,* constellation; galaxy (*fig.*). **constellé, e** (stɛlle) *a,* constellated; studded.

consternation (kɔ̃stɛrnasjɔ̃) *f,* consternation, dismay. **consterner** (ne) *v.t,* to dismay, stagger.

constipation (kɔ̃stipasjɔ̃) *f,* constipation, costiveness. **constiper** (pe) *v.t,* to constipate, bind.

constituant, e (kɔ̃stitɥɑ̃, ɑ̃:t) *a,* constituent, component. **constituer** (tɥe) *v.t,* to constitute; form, incorporate; settle; instruct; brief; appoint. *se ~ prisonnier,* to give oneself up [to the police]. **constitution** (tysjɔ̃) *f,* constitution; composition. *~ de dot,* marriage settlement. **constitutionnel, le†** (ɔnɛl) *a,* constitutional; temperamental.

constructeur (kɔ̃stryktœ:r) *m,* builder, maker, constructor. **construction** (sjɔ̃) *f,* construction; building; making; build; engineering; erection; structure. **construire** (strɥi:r) *v.t.ir,* to construct; build, erect; make; construe.

consul (kɔ̃syl) *m,* consul. *le C~ britannique,* the British c. *le ~ de France,* the French c. **consulaire** (lɛ:r) *a,* consular. **consulat** (la) *m,* consulate; consulship.

consultant, e (kɔ̃syltɑ̃, ɑ̃:t) *a,* consulting. **consultation** (tasjɔ̃) *f,* consultation; opinion (*legal*), advice. **consulter** (te) *v.t. & i,* to consult; refer to.

consumer (kɔ̃syme) *v.t,* to consume; waste, spend.

contact (kɔ̃takt) *m,* contact; touch; connection (*Elec.*).

contagieux, euse (kɔ̃taʒjø, ø:z) *a,* contagious, infectious, catching. **contagion** (ʒjɔ̃) *f,* contagion; contagiousness.

contamination (kɔ̃taminasjɔ̃) *f,* contamination. **contaminer** (ne) *v.t,* to contaminate.

conte (kɔ̃:t) *m,* story; tale, yarn; short story; fable. *~ de bonne femme, ~ de vieille, ~ à dormir debout,* nonsense. *~ de fées, ~ bleu,* fairy tale. *~ rimé,* nursery rhyme. *~s en l'air,* cock-&-bull story, moonshine.

contemplatif, ive (kɔ̃tɑ̃platif, i:v) *a,* contemplative. **contemplation** (sjɔ̃) *f,* contemplation; gazing. **contempler** (ple) *v.t,* to contemplate, view; gaze on; meditate upon.

contemporain, e (kɔ̃tɑ̃pɔrɛ̃, ɛn) *a,* contemporaneous, contemporary. ¶ *n,* contemporary.

contempteur, trice (kɔ̃tɑ̃ptœ:r, tris) *n,* scorner.

contenance (kɔ̃tnɑ̃:s) *f,* capacity, content; countenance, demeanor, bearing. *perdre ~,* to lose face. **contenant** (tnɑ̃) *m,* container. **contenir** (tni:r) *v.t.ir,* to contain, hold; accommodate; comprise; restrain, control.

conteneur (kɔ̃tnœr) *m,* container. **conteneurisation** (izasjɔ̃) *f,* containerization. **conteneuriser** (ize) *v.t,* to containerize.

content, e (kɔ̃tɑ̃, ɑ̃:t) *a,* content; contentedly; satisfied; pleased; glad. ¶ *m,* fill; heart's content. **contentement** (tɑ̃tmɑ̃) *m,* content[ment]; satisfaction. **contenter** (te) *v.t,* to content, satisfy, gratify.

contentieux, euse (kɔ̃tɑ̃sjø, ø:z) *a,* contentious, law (*att.*). ¶ *m,* law department or office; contentious business. **contention** (sjɔ̃) *f,* application, intentness.

contenu (kɔ̃tny) *m,* contents.

conter (kɔ̃te) *v.t,* to tell, relate.

contestable (kɔ̃tɛstabl) *a,* questionable, debatable, moot. **contestation** (sjɔ̃) *f,* dispute, contestation. **contestataire** (tatɛ:r) *a,* tending to challenge. ¶ *m,* challenger; social militant. **sans conteste** (tɛst), indisputably. **contester** (te) *v.t. & abs,* to contest, challenge, question, dispute.

conteur, euse (kɔ̃tœ:r, ø:z) *n,* narrator; storyteller.

contexte (kɔ̃tɛkst) *m,* context.

contexture (kɔ̃tɛksty:r) *f,* [con]texture.

contigu, ë (kɔ̃tigy) *a*, contiguous, adjoining. **contiguïté** (gɥite) *f*, contiguity.

continence (kɔ̃tinã:s) *f*, continence. **continent, e** (nã, ã:t) *a*, continent; modest.

continent (kɔ̃tinã) *m*, continent, mainland. *le c~*, the Continent (*Europe*). **continental, e** (tal) *a*, continental.

contingence (kɔ̃tẽʒã:s) *f*, contingency. **contingent, e** (ʒã, ã:t) *a*, contingent. ¶ *m*, contingent, share; quota. **contingentement** (ʒãtmã) *m*, curtailment. **contingenter** (te) *v.t*, to fix quotas for.

continu, e (kɔ̃tiny) *a*, continuous; direct (*Elec. current*). **continuation** (nɥasjɔ̃) *f*, continuation; continuance. **continuel, le†** (nɥel) *a*, continual, unceasing. **continuer** (nɥe) *v.t. & i*, to continue; carry on; go on; proceed; keep on. **continuité** (nɥite) *f*, continuity; ceaselessness. **continûment** (nymã) *ad*, continuously.

contondant, e (kɔ̃tɔ̃dã, ã:t) *a*, blunt (*instrument*).

contorsion (kɔ̃tɔrsjɔ̃) *f*, contortion; twist.

contour (kɔ̃tu:r) *m*, contour, outline. *~ de hanches, de poitrine*, hip, bust, measurement. **contourner** (turne) *v.t*, to contort, twist; encircle.

contractant, e (kɔ̃traktã, ã:t) *a*, contracting. ¶ *n*, contractant. **contracter** (te) *v.t. & abs*, to contract; enter into; take out, effect (*Insce. policy*). **contraction** (sjɔ̃) *f*, contraction, shrinkage. **contractuel, le** (tɥel) *a*, contractual.

contradiction (kɔ̃tradiksjɔ̃) *f*, contradiction; discrepancy. **contradictoire** (twa:r) *a*, contradictory; conflicting; after trial; check, control (*att.*), joint. *examen ~*, cross-examination.

contraindre (kɔ̃trɛ̃:dr) *v.t.ir*, to constrain, compel, force, coerce, drive; restrain. *~ par saisie de biens*, to distrain upon (*pers.*). **contrainte** (trɛ̃:t) *f*, constraint, compulsion.

contraire (kɔ̃trɛ:r) *a*, contrary, converse, opposed; unfavorable. ¶ *m*, contrary, reverse, converse, opposite. *au ~*, on the contrary.

contrairement (trɛrmã) *ad*, contrarily, contrary, counter.

contralto (kɔ̃tralto) *m*, contralto.

contrariant, e (kɔ̃trarjã, ã:t) *a*, trying, provoking. **contrarier** (rje) *v.t. & abs*, to thwart, interfere with, impede, cross; vex. **contrariété** (rjete) *f*, contrariety; annoyance, nuisance.

contraste (kɔ̃trast) *m*, contrast. **contraster** (te) *v.i. & t*, to contrast.

contrat (kɔ̃tra) *m*, contract; agreement; deed, indenture; articles; letter; bond. *dresser un ~*, to draw up a deed.

contravention (kɔ̃travãsjɔ̃) *f*, contravention; breach, infringement; offense; ticket or fine (*auto*). *dresser une ~ à* to summons (*legal*).

contre (kɔ̃:tr) *pr. & ad*, against; contrary to; to (*as* 3 to 1); by, close to; versus. *~ nature*, unnatural.

contre-allée (kɔ̃trale) *f*, side walk.

contre-amiral (kɔ̃tramiral) *m*, rear admiral.

contre-attaque (kɔ̃tratak) *f*, counterattack.

contre-avions (kɔtravjɔ̃) *a*, antiaircraft.

contrebalancer (kɔ̃trəbalãse) *v.t*, to counterbalance, counterpoise.

contrebande (kɔ̃trəbã:d) *f*, smuggling, contraband. *de ~* (*fig.*), counterfeit. **contrebandier, ère** (bãdje, ɛ:r) *n*, smuggler.

contrebas (en) (kɔ̃trəba) *ad*, below, lower down; downwards.

contrebasse (kɔ̃trəba:s) *f*, double bass, contrabass.

contrecarrer (kɔ̃trəkare) *v.t*, to thwart, cross; counteract.

contre-champ (kɔ̃trəʃã) *m*, reverse angle shot (*cinema, TV*).

contrecœur (à) (kɔ̃trəkœ:r) *ad*, reluctantly.

contrecoup (kɔ̃trəku) *m*, rebound; recoil; reaction.

contredanse (kɔ̃trədã:s) *f*, quadrille; ticket (*parking, traffic, etc.*).

contredire (kɔ̃trədi:r) *v.t. & abs. ir*, to contradict, gainsay.

se~, to contradict oneself; conflict. **sans contredit** (di), unquestionably.

contrée (kɔtre) *f,* country, region.

contre-écrou (kɔ̃trekru) *m,* locknut.

contre-expertise (kɔ̃trɛkspɛrtiːz) *f,* countervaluation.

contrefaçon (kɔ̃trəfasɔ̃) *f,* counterfeit; forgery; infringement; piracy; imitation. **~** *littéraire,* **~** *de librairie,* infringement of copyright. **contretacteur** (faktœːr) *m,* counterfeiter, etc. **contrefaire** (fɛːr) *v.t.ir,* to counterfeit; mimic, take off; pretend to be; disguise; deform. **contrefaiseur, euse** (fəzœːr, øːz) *n,* mimic.

contre-fiche (kɔ̃trəfiʃ) *f,* strut, brace; raking shore.

contre-fil (à) (kɔ̃trəfil) *ad,* against the grain.

contrefort (kɔ̃trəfɔːr) *m,* buttress; spur.

contre-haut (en) (kɔ̃trəo) *ad,* above, higher up; upwards.

contre-jour (kɔ̃trəʒuːr) *m,* unfavorable light; backlighting. *à* **~,** against the light; with one's back to the light.

contremaître (kɔ̃trəmɛːtr) *m,* foreman; first mate (*Naut.*).

contremander (kɔ̃trəmɑ̃de) *v.t,* to countermand; call off.

contremarque (kɔ̃trəmark) *f,* countermark; pass-out check (*Theat.*).

contrepartie (kɔ̃trəparti) *f,* counterpart; contra; contrary [opinion]; other side *or* party; another dealer; running stock (*against one's client*).

contrepasser (kɔ̃trəpase) *v.t,* to write back, reverse, contra; endorse back.

contre-pédaler (kɔ̃trəpedale) *v.i,* to back-pedal.

contre-petterie (kɔ̃trəpɛtri) *f,* Spoonerism.

contre-pied (kɔ̃trəpje) *m,* opposite (*course, view*).

contreplaqué (kɔ̃trəplake) *m,* plywood. **~** *en trois,* three-ply [wood].

contre-plongée (kɔ̃trəplɔ̃ʒe) *f,* low-angle shot (*cinema, TV*).

contrepoids (kɔ̃trəpwa) *m,* counterweight, counterpoise, counterbalance, balance weight.

contre-poil (à) (kɔ̃trəpwal), the wrong way.

contrepoint (kɔ̃trəpwɛ̃) *m,* counterpoint.

contre-pointe (kɔ̃trəpwɛ̃t) *f,* loose headstock, tailstock.

contrepoison (kɔ̃trəpwazɔ̃) *m,* antidote.

contre-porte (kɔ̃trəpɔrt) *f,* screen door.

contreseing (kɔ̃trəsɛ̃) *m,* counter signature.

contresens (kɔ̃trəsɑ̃ːs) *m,* misconstruction; mistranslation; misinterpretation; bull; wrong way *or* sense.

contresigner (kɔtrəsiɲe) *v.t,* to countersign.

contretemps (kɔ̃trətɑ̃) *m,* mishap, unfortunate occurrence, awkward incident, hitch. *à* **~,** inopportunely.

contre-torpilleur (kɔ̃trətɔrpijœːr) *m,* [torpedo-boat] destroyer.

contretype (kɔ̃trətip) *m,* duplicate (*film*). **~** *négatif,* internegative.

contrevenir à (kɔ̃trəvəniːr) *v.ir,* to contravene, infringe, transgress.

contrevent (kɔ̃trəvɑ̃) *m,* outside shutter.

contrevérité (kɔ̃trəverite) *f,* untruth.

contribuable (kɔ̃tribɥabl) *n,* taxpayer. **¶** *a,* taxable. **contribuer** (bɥe) *v.i,* to contribute; conduce. **contribution** (bysjɔ̃) *f,* contribution; tax; excise.

contrister (kɔ̃triste) *v.t,* to sadden, grieve.

contrit, e (kɔ̃tri, it) *a,* contrite. **contrition** (sjɔ̃) *f,* contrition.

contrôle (kɔ̃troːl) *m,* control; supervision; roster; hallmark; inspection; check; ticket office; box office. **~** *de présence,* timekeeping. **contrôler** (trole) *v.t,* to control; inspect; supervise; check; hallmark. **contrôleur** (lœːr) *m,* controller, comptroller; supervisor; examiner; ticket collector; inspector; checker; timekeeper; telltale (*Mach.*). ~ *des tours,* lap scorer.

contrordre (kɔ̃trɔrdr) *m,* counter instructions.

controuvé, e (kɔ̃truve) *p.p,* fabricated, invented.

controverse (kɔ̃trɔvɛrs) *f,* controversy. **controversé, e** (se) *p.p,* debated.

contumace (kɔ̃tymas) *f,* contumacy.

contus, e (kɔ̃ty, y:z) *a,* bruised. **contusion** (tyzjɔ̃) *f,* bruise, contusion. **contusionner** (ɔne) *v.t,* to bruise, contuse.

convaincant, e (kɔ̃vɛ̃kɑ̃, ɑ̃:t) *a,* convincing, cogent. **convaincre** (vɛ̃:kr) *v.t.ir,* to convince; convict.

convalescence (kɔ̃valesɑ̃:s) *f,* convalescence. **convalescent, e** (sɑ̃, ɑ̃:t) *a. & n,* convalescent.

convenable† (kɔ̃vnabl) *a,* proper, fit, [be]fitting, becoming, decorous; suitable, convenient; expedient. **convenance** (vnɑ̃:s) *f,* propriety, fitness, congruity; harmony; convenience; expedience, -cy. **convenir** (vni:r) *v.i.ir,* to agree; own; suit; befit; be expedient; become, do. *mot convenu,* code word. *rédiger en langage convenu,* to code. **convention** (vɑ̃sjɔ̃) *f,* covenant; agreement, contract; convention. **de ~ & conventionnel, le** (ɔnɛl) *a,* conventional.

converger (kɔ̃vɛrʒe) *v.i,* to converge.

convers, e (kɔ̃vɛ:r, ɛrs) *a,* lay (*brother, sister*). **converse,** *a.f. & f,* converse. conversation, talk; call (*Teleph.*).

conversation (kɔ̃vɛrsasjɔ̃) *f,* **converser** (se) *v.i,* to converse, talk, commune; wheel (*Mil.*).

conversion (sjɔ̃) *f,* conversion; change. **convertible** (tibl) *a,* convertible. **converti, e** (ti) *n,* convert. **convertir** (ti:r) *v.t,* to convert, change, turn. **se ~,** to become converted (*Relig.*). **convertissable** (tisabl) *a,* convertible (*Fin.*). **convertissement** (smɑ̃) *m,* conversion (*Fin.*). **convertisseur** (sœ:r) *m,* converter.

convexe (kɔ̃vɛks) *a,* convex. **convexité** (ite) *f,* convexity.

conviction ((kɔ̃viksjɔ̃) *f,* conviction.

convié, e (kɔ̃vje) *n,* guest. **convier** (vje) *v.t,* to invite; (*fig.*), urge. **convive** (vi:v) *n,* guest; table companion.

convocation (kɔ̃vɔkasjɔ̃) *f,* convocation, calling; notice [of meeting]; calling-up (*Mil.*).

convoi (kɔ̃vwa) *m,* convoy; train (*Rly.*); funeral [procession].

convoiter (kɔ̃vwate) *v.t,* to covet, lust after. **convoiteux, euse** (tø, (ø:z) *a,* covetous. **convoitise** (ti:z) *f,* covetousness; lust.

convoler (kɔ̃vɔle) *v.i. & abs,* to marry again. ~ *en secondes, en troisièmes, noces,* to marry a second, a third, time.

convoquer (kɔ̃vɔke) *v.t,* to convoke, call, summon, convene; call together.

convoyer (kɔ̃vwaje) *v.t,* to convoy; escort.

convulsif, ive† (kɔ̃vylsif, i:v) *a,* convulsive. **convulsion** (sjɔ̃) *f,* convulsion; upheaval.

coopératif, ive (kɔɔperatif, i:v) *a,* cooperative. [*société*] *coopérative,* cooperative society. **coopération** (sjɔ̃) *f,* cooperation. **coopérer** (re) *v.i,* to cooperate.

coordonné (kɔɔrdɔne) *a,* coordinated. **coordonnées** (kɔɔrdɔne) *f. pl,* coordinates. *donner ses ~,* to give one's name, address, & phone number.

coordonner (kɔɔrdɔne) *v.t,* to coordinate.

copain (kɔpɛ) *m,* buddy, pal.

copeau (kɔpo) *m,* shaving; chip.

Copenhague (kɔpenag) *f,* Copenhagen.

copie (kɔpi) *f,* copy; paper (*Sch.*). ~ *en clair,* hard copy, printout (*computers*). **copier** (pje) *v.t. & abs,* to copy; transcribe; imitate.

copieux, euse† (kɔpjø, ø:z) *a,* copious, full; hearty (*meal*).

copine (kɔpin) *f,* friend (*female*).

copiste (kɔpist) *n,* copyist; fraudulent copier of fashion designs presented by couturiers.

copropriétaire (koprɔprietɛ:r) *n,* joint owner.

copulation (kɔpylasjɔ̃) *f*, copulation.

coq (kɔk) *m*, cock, rooster; weathercock; bantam (*Box.*); cook (*ship's*). ~-à-l'âne, *m*, cock-&-bull story. ~ d'Inde, turkey-cock. ~ d bruyère, heathcock, blackcock, moor cock. ~ de combat, game c. ~ du village, cock of the walk. comme un ~ en pâte, sitting pretty. [~] faisan, cock pheasant.

coque (kɔk) *f*, shell; hull (*ship*); husk; pod; cocoon; cockle (*Mol.*); loop (*of ribbon, hair*). œuf à la ~, boiled egg.

coquelicot (kɔkliko) *m*, poppy.

coqueluche (kɔklyʃ) *f*, whooping cough; darling.

coquemar (kɔkma:r) *m*, kettle, pot.

coquerico (kɔkəriko) *m*, cock-a-doodle-doo.

coquet, te† (kɔkɛ, ɛt) *a*, coquettish, skittish; stylish, smart, natty, trim. ¶ *n*, flirt, coquette. **coqueter** (kte) *v.i*, to coquet, flirt.

coquetier (kɔktje) *m*, egg cup; egg merchant.

coquetterie (kɔkɛtri) *f*, coquetry; as coquet, te.

coquillage (kɔkija:ʒ) *m*, shellfish; shell, conch. **coquille** (ki:j) *f*, shell; bush (*Mach.*); misprint, literal [error]; demy (*paper*).

coquin, e (kɔkɛ̃, in) *n*, rogue, rascal, knave, scamp; (*f.*) hussy, jade, minx. **coquinerie** (kinri) *f*, knavery, roguery, rascality.

cor (kɔ:r) *m*, horn (*Mus.*); corn (on foot); antler, tine. ~ d'harmonie, French horn. à ~ & à cri, clamorously.

corail (kɔra:j) *m*, coral. **corailleur** (rajœ:r) *m*, coral fisher. **banc corallifère** (ralifɛ:r), coral reef.

Coran (kɔrɑ̃) *m*, Koran.

corbeau (kɔrbo) *m*, raven; crow; corbel.

corbeille (kɔrbɛ:j) *f*, basket; dress circle (*Theat.*). ~ à papiers, wastepaper b. ~ [de mariage], (bridegroom's) wedding presents.

corbillard (kɔrbija:r) *m*, hearse.

cordage (kɔrda:ʒ) *m*, rope; (pl.) cordage. **corde** (kɔrd) *f*, rope, cord, line; band; thread; string;

halter (hanging); chord. les ~s, the strings (orchestra). à~s, string[ed] (*Mus.*). ~ à boyau, catgut. ~ à linge, clothes line. ~ à piano, piano wire. ~ à sauter, skipping rope. ~ sensible, sensitive spot. **cordeau** (do) *m*, line, string; chalk-line (cord); fuse. **cordelette** (dəlɛt) *f*, cord, string. **cordelière** (ljɛ:r) *f*, girdle. **corder** (de) *v.t*, to twist; cord, rope. **corderie** (dri) *f*, rope works; r. making.

cordial, e† (kɔrdjal) *a*, cordial, hearty. ¶ *m*, cordial. **cordialité** (lite) *f*, cordiality, etc.

cordier (kɔrdje) *m*, rope maker; drifter (boat). **cordon** (dɔ̃) *m*, strand, twist; string; cord; lace (shoe); pull (bell); border; milled edge; row; cordon, ribbon. ~ sanitaire, quarantine line. **cordonner** (dɔne) *v.t*, to twist, twine. **cordonnerie** (nri) *f*, shoemaker's shop; boot & shoe trade. **cordonnet** (nɛ) *m*, braid, cord, twist; milled edge; overcast (*Emb.*). **cordonnier, ère** (nje, ɛ:r) *n*, boot & shoe repairer, shoemaker.

Corée (la) (kɔre), Korea. **coréen, ne** (reɛ̃, ɛn) *a. & C~, n*, Korean.

coriace (kɔrjas) *a*, leathery, tough.

corindon (kɔrɛ̃dɔ̃) *m*, corundum.

Corinthe (kɔrɛ̃:t) *f*, Corinth. **corinthien, ne** (rɛ̃tjɛ̃, ɛn) *a. & C~, n*, Corinthian.

cormoran (kɔrmɔrɑ̃) *m*, cormorant.

cornac (kɔrnak) *m*, mahout; keeper; guide.

cornaline (kɔrnalin) *f*, carnelian.

corne (kɔrn) *f*, horn; dog['s] ear; gaff (spar). ~ d'abondance, horn of plenty, cornucopia. ~ de cerf, deerhorn. **corné, e** (ne) *a*, horny. **corneille** (kɔrnɛ:j) *f*, crow; rook. bayer aux ~s, to rubberneck. **cornemuse** (kɔrnəmy:z) *f*, bagpipe[s].

corner (kɔrne) *v.i*, to sound a horn; hoot (auto); speak in ear trumpet; din; ring (ears); (v.t.) to trumpet, din; dog ear; turn down. **cornet** (nɛ) *m*, horn; cornet (cone). ~ [à dés], dice box. ~ à pistons, cornet (*Mus.*). ~

[acoustique], ear trumpet. ~ [avertisseur], horn (auto).

corniche (kɔrniʃ) f, cornice; ledge.

cornichon (kɔrniʃɔ̃) m, gherkin.

cornier, ère (kɔrnje, ɛːr) a, corner, angle (att.). ¶ f, angle iron.

Cornouailles (la) (kɔrnwɑːj), Cornwall.

cornu, e (kɔrny) a, horned; absurd. ¶ f, retort, still.

corollaire (kɔrɔlɛːr) m, corollary.

coron (kɔrɔ̃) m, (coal) miner's dwelling; mining village.

corporation (kɔrpɔrasjɔ̃) f, corporation, guild. **corporel, le†** (rɛl) a, corporeal; corporal, bodily. **corps** (kɔːr) m, body; substance; corps, brigade; bodice; barrel, cylinder; hull (ship). ~ 6, 8 ou ~ de 6, de 8, points, 6, 8, point [size] (Typ.). ~ à ~, hand to hand (fight); clinch (Box.). ~ composé, compound (Chem.). ~ de garde, guardhouse, guardroom. ~ de logis, ~ de bâtiment, main [portion of] building. ~ de métier, guild. ~ électoral, electorate, country. ~ & biens, crew & cargo, life & property. ~ [mort], [dead] body, corpse. ~ mort, dolphin, moorings (Naut.). à ~ perdu, recklessly. ~ simple, element (Chem.). prendre ~, to take shape.

corpulence (kɔrpylɑ̃ːs) f, stoutness, corpulence, -ency, portliness, burliness. **corpulent, e** (lɑ̃, ɑ̃t) a, corpulent.

corpuscule (kɔrpyskyl) m, corpuscle.

correct, e† (kɔrɛkt) a, correct. **correcteur, trice** (tœːr, tris) n, corrector. ~ d'imprimerie, proofreader. **correctif** (tif) m, corrective. **correction** (sjɔ̃) f, correction; correctness; propriety; punishment. ~ des épreuves, proofreading. **correctionnel, le†** (ɔ̃nɛl) a, correctional. tribune ~, police court.

corrélatif, ive (kɔrelatif, iːv) a, correlative.

correspondance (kɔrɛspɔ̃dɑ̃ːs) f, correspondence; letters; connection, transfer point, inter-

change. **correspondant, e** (dɑ̃, ɑ̃ːt) a, corresponding. ¶ n, correspondent; friend acting for parents (to pupil). **correspondre** (pɔ̃ːdr) v.i, to correspond; tally; communicate.

corridor (kɔridɔːr) m, corridor, passage.

corrigé (kɔriʒe) m, fair copy (Sch.); pony (book). **corriger** (ʒe) v.t, to correct; compensate for; chastise.

corroborer (kɔrɔbɔre) v.t, to corroborate.

corroder (kɔrɔde) v.t, to corrode.

corroi (kɔrwa) m, currying (leather); puddle (clay).

corrompre (kɔrɔ̃ːpr) v.t, to corrupt, taint, spoil; bribe.

corrosif, ive (kɔrozif, iːv) a. & m, corrosive. **corrosion** (zjɔ̃) f, corrosion.

corroyer (kɔrwaje) v.t, to curry (leather); puddle, pug; weld; trim, dress.

corruptible (kɔryptibl) a, corruptible. **corruption** (sjɔ̃) f, corruption; bribery.

corsage (kɔrsaːʒ) m, bust; bodice, corsage.

corsaire (kɔrsɛːr) m, corsair, privateer; shark (Fin.). pantalon ~, pedal pushers.

Corse (la) (kɔrs), Corsica. **corse**, a. & C~, n, Corsican.

corsé, e (kɔrse) p.a, full-bodied (wine); strong, forcible (language). **corser (se)** v.t, to fortify, strengthen. se~, to become serious.

corset (kɔrsɛ) m, corset, stays. **corseter** (səte) v.t, to corset. **corsetier, ère** (tje, ɛːr) n, corset maker.

cortège (kɔrtɛːʒ) m, retinue, train; procession; pageant.

corvée (kɔrve) f, statute (or forced) labor, corvée; fatigue (Mil.); drudgery.

cosmétique (kɔsmetik) a. & m, cosmetic.

cosmique (kɔsmik) a, cosmic.

cosmonaute (kɔsmɔnot) n, astronaut.

cosmopolite (kɔsmɔpolit) m. & a, cosmopolite; cosmopolitan.

cosse (kɔs) f, pod, cod, shell,

husk, hull; thimble, eye[let] (*Naut.*).

cosser (kɔse) *v.i*, to butt (*rams*).

cossu, e (kɔsy) *a*, well off; rich.

costard (kɔsta:r) *m*, man's business suit (*slang*).

costaud (kɔsto) *a*, hefty, sturdy. ¶ *m*, muscleman.

costume (kɔstym) *m*, costume, dress, garb; suit; frock. ~ *marin*, sailor suit. **costumer** (me) *v.t*, to dress (*in fancy dress*). **costumier, ère** (mje, ɛ:r) *n*, theatrical & fancy costumer; wardrobe keeper (*Theat.*).

cote (kɔt) *f*, quota, share, contribution; assessment, rating; quotation(s), price(s), rates, mark(s), marking, call, list; due dating (*bill*); character, class (*ship*); odds, betting; reading (*survey*). ~ *d'amour*, favoritism, backstairs influence. ~ *de la bourse*, stock exchange daily official list. ~ *des changes*, [foreign] exchange rates. ~ *mal taillée*, rough & ready settlement, compromise.

côte (ko:t) *f*, rib; slope; hill; [sea]-coast, shore, seaboard. *à* ~*s*, ribbed, corded. ~ *à* ~, side by side, alongside. *de la* ~ *de*, descended from. *faire* ~, to run ashore. *la* C~ *d'Azur*, the Riviera. *la* C~ *d'Ivoire*, the Ivory Coast. *la* C~ *de l'Or*, the Gold Coast.

côté (kote) *m*, side; way, direction; [broad]side (*Naut.*); beam ends (*Naut.*). ~ *du vent*, weather side. ~ *faible*, weak spot (*fig. of pers.*). ~ *sous le vent*, lee [side]. *à* ~, *ad*, near, to one side. *à* ~ *de*, *pr*, by the side of; next to; next door to; beside. **de**~, *ad*, sideways; sidelong; aside, apart, on one side, by. *de l'autre* ~, on the other side *or* hand; over the way.

coteau (kɔto) *m*, hill, hillside, slope.

côtelé, e (kotle) *a*, ribbed, corduroy.

côtelette (kotlɛt) *f*, chop, cutlet. ~ *de filet*, loin chop.

coter (kɔte) *v.t*, to letter; number; mark; page; assess, rate; quote;

class; rank. *croquis coté*, dimensioned sketch.

coterie (kɔtri) *f*, set, clique, circle.

cothurne (kɔtyrn) *m*, buskin, cothurnus.

côtier, ère (kotje, ɛ:r) *a*, coast[ing]; inshore. [*bateau*] *côtier*, coaster. [*cheval*] *côtier*, trace horse.

cotillon (kɔtijɔ̃) *m*, petticoat; cotillion.

cotisation (kɔtizasjɔ̃) *f*, quota, share, contribution; subscription; fee; assessment. **cotiser** (ze) *v.t*, to assess. **se** ~, to club together; subscribe.

coton (kɔtɔ̃) *m*, cotton; c wool; down, fluff. ~ *hydrophile*, *m*, absorbent cotton. ~-*poudre*, *m*, guncotton. *c'est* ~, it's difficult. *filer un mauvais* ~, to be in trouble (*health, financial*). **cotonnade** (tɔnad) *f*, cotton [cloth, goods]. **cotonneux, euse** (nø, ø:z) *a*, cottony; downy; fluffy; wooly. **cotonnier, ère** (nje, ɛ:r) *a*, cotton (*att.*). ¶ *m*, cotton plant.

côtoyer (kotwaje) *v.t. & abs*, to run along, hug (*shore*); skirt; coast; border upon.

cotre (kɔtr) *m*, cutter (*boat*). ~ *de la douane*, revenue cutter.

cotret (kɔtrɛ) *m*, fagot, stick.

cotte (kɔt) *f*, petticoat; overalls. ~ *de mailles*, coat of mail.

cou (ku) *m*, neck.

couard, e (kua:r, ard) *a*, coward-[ly]. ¶ *n*, coward. **couardise** (kuardi:z) *f*, cowardice.

couchant (kuʃɑ̃) *m*, setting; west; wane, decline. **couche** (kuʃ) *f*, bed, couch; hotbed; layer; stratum; seam; sheet; coat[ing]; course; lap[ping]; diaper; ring (*in tree*); (*pl.*) confinement, lying-in, childbed; delivery, birth. **coucher** (kuʃe) *m*, going to bed; setting (*sun, etc.*); night's lodging, board; bed[ding]. ~ *de soleil*, sunset. *au* ~ *du soleil*, at sunset, at sundown. ¶ *v.t*, to lay; lay down; put to bed; lay low; beat down, slope. ~ *en joue*, to aim (at). ~ *par écrit*, to commit to (*or* put in) (*or* set down in) writing. ¶ *v.i*, to lie, lie down; spend the night, sleep. **se** ~, to lie down, go to bed; couch; set, go down (*sun, moon*). **couchette** (ʃɛt) *f*, crib, cot; berth, bunk, couchette.

couci-couça (kusikusa), **couci-couci**, *ad*, so so, middling.

coucou (kuku) *m*, cuckoo; cowslip. [*pendule à*] ~, cuckoo clock.

coude (kud) *m*, elbow; bend; crank. *jouer des* ~*s*, to elbow one's way. *huile de* ~, elbow grease. **coudées franches** (kude) *f.pl*, elbowroom (*fig.*); scope.

cou-de-pied (kudpje) *m*, instep.

couder (kude) *v.t*, to bend, crank. **coudoyer** (dwaje) *v.t*, to elbow, jostle; run up against; come very near to.

coudre (kudr) *v.t. & abs. ir*, to sew; s. up; s. on; stitch; piece, tack (*fig.*).

coudrier (kudrie) *m*, hazel (*bush*).

couenne (kwan) *f*, rind (*bacon*); crackling (*pork*); mole (*Med.*).

couguar (kugwaːr) *m*, cougar, puma.

couille (kuj) *f*, testicle (*slang*). ~ *molle*, sissy, milksop. **couillon** (jɔ̃) *m*, idiot, fathead.

coulage (kulaːʒ) *m*, running; pouring, casting; leakage. **coulant**, e (lɑ̃, ɑ̃ːt) *a*, flowing, easy, liquid, running, loose; accommodating. ¶ *m*, runner (*Hort. & Mech.*); slide. **coulé** (le) *m*, slur (*Mus.*); follow [shot] (*Bil.*); casting. **coulée** (le) *f*, running; flow; cast[ing]; tapping; run (*animal track*); running hand. **couler** (le) *v.t*, to pour, tap, cast; strain; sink, slide; slur (*Mus.*); (*v.i.*) to flow, run; trickle; gutter; leak; glide, slide, slip. ~ *ou* ~ *à fond ou* ~ *à pic ou* ~ *bas*, to sink, founder, go down. *faire* ~, to spill, shed; slip, turn on water. *se* ~, to slide, slip.

couleur (kulœːr) *f*, color; coloring; paint; dye; complexion; suit (*cards*); (*pl.*) colors (*flag*). *sous* ~ *de*, under color of (*fig.*).

couleuvre (kulœːvr) *f*, snake; bitter pill (*fig.*). ~ *à collier*, common snake. *avaler une* ~, to swallow an insult.

coulis (kuli) *m*, grout[ing].

coulisse (kulis) *f*, slide; slideway; heading, hem (*for tape*); link (*Mach.*); link motion; side scene (*Theat.*); (*pl.*) slips, wings (*Theat.*); coulisse (*unofficial or free market on Paris Bourse*). *dans la* ~, behind the scenes. *à* ~, sliding. *regard en* ~, sidelong glance. **coulissier** (sje) *m*, coulissier (*broker on Paris coulisse market*).

couloir (kulwaːr) *m*, passage, corridor; lobby.

couloire (kulwaːr) *f*, strainer.

coup (ku) *m*, blow; stroke; hit; chop; coup; knock; thrust; poke; cut, slash; nip; prick; dig; whack; slap; stab; shock; clap, peal; flap; rap; wave, sweep; touch; shot; report; rush; beat; blast; gust; move (*chess, etc.*); knack; glass, drink; time, moment; try, go; pitch (*angler's*). ~ *au but*, hit. ~ *d'air*, rush of air; chill (*Med.*). ~ *d'amende*, penalty stroke (*golf*). ~ *d'assommoir*, knock-down blow (*fig.*). ~ *d'envoi*, kick-off (*Foot.*). ~ *d'épaule*, lift. ~ *d'épingle*, pin prick. ~ *d'éponge* (*fig.*), clean slate. ~ *d'essai*, first attempt, trial shot. ~*s d'essai*, practice (*Ten.*). ~ *d'œil*, glance, twinkling; look; judgment; view. ~ *d'ongle*, scratch. *à* ~*s de*, with (*blows from*). ~ *de balai*, sweep. ~ *de bec*, peck. ~ *de brosse*, brush. ~ *de chapeau*, salute, bow. ~ *de chiffon*, wipe, rub with a cloth. *à* ~*s de ciseaux*, with scissors & paste (*fig.*). ~ *de collier*, tug. ~ *de corne*, butt. ~ *de coude*, nudge. ~ *de dents*, bite. *traduire à* ~*s de dictionnaire*, to translate by looking up every other word in the dictionary. ~ *de feu*, shot. ~ *de filet*, cast; haul; catch. ~ *de fleuret*, pass (*Fenc.*). ~ *de force*, feat of strength. ~ *de foudre*, thunderbolt. ~ *de fouet*, lash; fillip. ~ *de froid*, cold snap; chill (*Med.*). ~ *de grâce*, finishing stroke, quietus. ~ *de griffe*, scratch. *à* ~*s de hache*, in a rough & ready fashion. ~ *de hasard*, fluke. ~ *de l'étrier*, stirrup cup. ~ *de lumière*, burst of light.

~ [de lunette], sight. ~ de main, surprise attack; swift bold stroke (action), lightning move; helping hand. ~ de marteau, knock (at the door). ~ de massue, stunning blow. un ~ de mer, a great wave, a heavy sea. ~ de patte, dig (fig.). ~ [de pied], kick. ~ de poing, punch; fisticuffs; knuckle-duster. ~ de sang, [apoplectic] stroke. ~ de sifflet, [blast of a] whistle. ~ de soleil, sunstroke. ~ de sonnette, ring [of a bell]. ~ de téléphone, ring [of the telephone]. ~ de tête, butt; rash act. ~ de théâtre, stage trick; sensation[al event]. ~ de tonnerre, thunderclap, peal of t. ~ de vent, squall, gust of wind; flurry; blast; gale. ~ déloyal, foul (Box.). ~s & blessures, assault & battery. ~ manqué, miss, failure. ~ monté, put-up job. ~ sur ~, one after another. à ~ sûr, assuredly. sur le~, at the time.

coupable (kupabl) a, guilty, culpable; sinful. ¶ n, culprit, offender.

coupage (kupaːʒ) m, blending (wines). **coupant, e** (pã, ãːt) a, cutting, sharp; edge[d]. ¶ m, [cutting] edge. **coupe** (kup) f, cutting; cutting out (clothes); cut; division; section; length (piece of a stuff); overarm stroke (swim.); cup, chalice, goblet, glass; bowl, dish; cup (sport); plate (turf). **coupé** (pe) m, brougham; coupé. **coupe-cigares,** m, cigar cutter. **coupe-circuit,** m, cut-out (Elec.). **coupe-gorge,** m, cutthroat place. **coupe-jarret,** m, cutthroat (pers.); **coupe-verre à molette,** m, wheel glass cutter. **coupé-lit,** m, sleeping compartment (Rly.). **coupelle** (pɛl) f, cupel. **coupeller** (le) v.t, to cupel. **coupe-papier,** m, paper knife. **couper** (pe) v.t. & abs, to cut; c. off; c. down; c. in (on road, etc.); c. out; chop off; intersect, cross; slice (ball); blend (wines); dilute, water; interrupt; switch off. se ~, to cut oneself; cut; contradict oneself; intersect. se faire ~ les cheveux, to have one's hair cut. **couperet** (prɛ) m, cleaver, chopper; knife.

couperose (kuproːz) f, copperas, vitriol; acne; blotched face.

coupeur, euse (kupœːr, øːz) n, cutter. ~ de bourses, pickpocket.

couple (kupl) f, couple, two; brace; yoke; leash. ¶ m, couple (pers.); pair; cell (Elec.); timber (ship). ~ [moteur], torque, couple. **coupler** (ple) v.t, to couple, connect. **couplet** (plɛ) m, verse; strap hinge.

coupole (kupɔl) f, cupola, dome.

coupon (kupɔ) m, remnant; short length; coupon; half (Rly. ticket), **coupure** (pyːr) f, cut; clipping (newspaper); denomination; power cut (Elec.).

cour (kuːr) f, court; [court]yard; courtship, suit. ~ de cassation, supreme court of appeal. ~ de l'église, churchyard. faire la ~ à, to court, woo, make love to.

courage (kuraːʒ) m, courage, fortitude, spirit, pluck, nerve. ~ arrosé, Dutch courage. ¶ i, courage! cheer up! **courageux, euse** (raʒø, øːz) a, courageous, game.

couramment (kuramã) ad, fluently; usually, commonly. **courant, e** (rã, ãːt) a, current; running; instant, present; run (measurement). ¶ m, current; stream; tide; course; current (or present) month. ~ alternatif, alternating current (Elec.). ~ continu, direct c. ~ d'affaires, turnover. ~ d'air, draft; blast. ~ de jusant, ebb tide. ~ de palan, tackle fall. fin ~, at end of the month. au ~, up-to-date. se mettre au ~ de, to become informed about. ~ de pointe, peak current. ~-jet, jet stream (Meteor.). ¶ f, diarrhea.

courbatu, e (kurbaty) a, tired out; stiff in the joints. **courbature** (tyːr) f, stiffness, tiredness.

courbe (kurb) a, curve[d]. ¶ f, curve, bend, sweep. ~ de niveau, contour line. **courber** (be) v.t. & i. & se ~, to bend, curve, bow. **courbette** (bɛt) f, curvet. faire des ~s, to curvet; bow & scrape. faire une ~, to duck. **courbure** (byːr) f, curvature, bend.

coureur, euse (kurœːr, øːz) n, runner; racer; wanderer, rover; gadabout; frequenter; rake. ~ cycliste, racing cyclist. ~ de bals,

dancing man. ~ *de spectacles,*
playgoer. ~ *de vitesse,* sprinter.

courge (kurʒ) *f,* pumpkin; gourd.
~ *à la moelle,* vegetable marrow.

courir (kuri:r) *v.i. & t. ir,* to run;
go; run about; hurry; slip (*or*
pass) away; race; sail; circulate,
go round; be in fashion; be rife;
accrue; tramp up & down; run
after; pursue; frequent; hunt;
course; hunt after; incur; go
through; travel. *le bruit court
que . . .,* it is reported that . . .,
there is a rumor abroad that . . .

courlis (kurli) **courlieu** (ljø) *m,*
curlew.

couronne (kurɔn) *f,* crown;
wreath; coronet; corona; circlet;
ring; tonsure. ~ [*mortuaire*],
wreath (*funeral*). **couronnement**
(nmɑ̃) *m,* coronation; crowning;
crowning piece; coping; taffrail.
couronner (ne) *v.t,* to crown;
wreathe; cap; cope; award a
prize to; reward; surround.

courrier (kurje) *m,* mail, post,
letters; courier, messenger; news,
intelligence; mail coach. **cour-
riériste** (rjerist) *m,* par writer.

courroie (kurwa) *f,* belt, band;
strap. ~*s* [*de transmission*], belt-
ing. ~ *de ventilateur,* fanbelt. ~
trapézoïdal, V-belt.

courroucer (kuruse) *v.t,* to incense, anger. **courroux** (ru) *m,*
wrath, anger, ire, rage.

cours (ku:r) *m,* course; flow; run;
stream; way; class (*Sch.*); currency; tender (*legal*); price, rate,
quotation; avenue. ~ *authentique & officiel,* stock exchange
daily official list. ~ *d'eau,* stream,
watercourse. ~ *de danse,* dancing class, school of dancing. **en**
~, current; present, instant; in
progress.

course (kurs) *f,* run; race; (*pl.*)
running, racing; outing, trip; errand; way; course; career; fare;
stroke, travel; privateering. **de** ~,
racing (*as cycle, ski*); race (*as
horse*); speed (*skates*). **en** ~, out
[on business]. ~ *aux armements,*
arms race. ~ *à pied,* foot race. ~
d'obstacles, steeplechase; obstacle race. ~ *de barrage,* runoff
(*from dead heat*). ~ *de chars,*

chariot race. ~ *de côte,* hill
climb. ~ *de demifond,* middle-
distance race. ~ *de fond,* long-
distance r.; distance swim. ~ *de
haies,* hurdle race. ~*s de lévriers,*
greyhound racing, dog r., dogs. ~
de (or *à*) *relais,* relay r. ~ *de taureaux,* bullfight. ~ *en sacs,* sack
race. ~ *nulle,* ~ *à égalité,* dead
heat. ~ *par équipes,* team race. ~
sur piste, track r., ~ *sur route,*
road race. ~*s sur route,* road racing. **coursier** (sje) *m,* charger
(*horse*), steed, courser.

court, e (ku:r, urt) *a,* short; limited. *à courtes vues,* short-sighted (*fig.*). *à court de,* short of;
out of stock of. **court,** *ad,* short.

court (kɔrt *ou* ku:r) *m,* court
(*Ten.*).

courtage (kurta:ʒ) *m,* broking,
brokerage; commission.

courtaud, e (kurto, o:d) *n,* thickset (*or* dumpy) person. **court-
auder** (tode) *v.t,* to crop the
tail of.

court-circuit (kursirkɥi) *m,*
short [circuit].

courte-botte (kurtəbɔt) *m,*
shrimp (*pers.*).

courtement (kurtəmɑ̃) *ad,*
shortly.

courtepointe (kurtəpwɛ̃:t) *f,*
[down] quilt.

courtier, ère (kurtje, ɛ:r) *n,*
broker.

courtisan (kurtizɑ̃, an) *a,* flattering, obsequious. ¶ *m,* courtier.
¶ *f,* courtesan. **courtiser** (ze)
v.t, to court; woo; fawn on. **courtois, e**† (twa, a:z) *a,* courteous;
courtly, urbane. **courtoisie** (twazi) *f,* courtesy, etc.

couseur, euse (kuzœ:r, ø:z), *n,*
sewer (*Need.*).

cousin, e (kuzɛ̃, in) *n,* cousin;
friend. ~ *germain, e,* first cousin. ~ *issu(e) de germain,* second
c. ¶ *m,* gnat, midge. **cousiner**
[ensemble] (zine) *v.i,* to get on
well [together].

coussin (kusɛ̃) *m,* cushion; hassock; bolster; pillow; pad. **coussinet** (sinɛ) *m,* [small] cushion;
pad; bearing, brass, bush; [screw-
ing] die; [rail] chair (*Rly.*).

cousu (kuzy) *a,* sewn. ~ *main,*

handsewn. *du ~ main,* a sure thing, no problem, easy.

coût (ku) *m,* cost. **coûtant** (tã) *a, au prix ~,* at cost price.

couteau (kuto) *m,* knife; cutter; knife edge. *~ à découper,* carving knife, [meat] carver. *~ à dessert,* cheese knife. *~ à virole, ~ à cran d'arrêt,* clasp k., jackknife. *à ~,* eating (*apples, etc.*). *à ~x tirés,* at daggers drawn (*fig.*). *le ~ à la gorge,* a pistol [held] at one's head (*fig.*). **coutelas** (tla) *m,* big kitchen knife. **coutelier, ère** (təlje, ɛ:r) *n,* cutler. **coutellerie** (tɛlri) *f,* cutlery; c. works or shop.

coûter (kute) *v.i,* to cost; (*abs.*) to cost money. *coûte que coûte,* at all costs. **coûteusement** (təzmã) *ad,* expensively. **coûteux, euse** (tø, ø:z) *a,* costly, expensive.

coutil (kuti) *m,* [canvas] tick[ing]; drill; duck.

coutume (kutym) *f,* custom, usage, habit, practice, wont. *de ~,* usual. **coutumier, ère** (mje, ɛ:r) *a,* accustomed, in the habit; customary; common, unwritten (*law*). *~ du fait,* in the habit of doing so.

couture (kuty:r) *f,* seam; sewing; needlework; scar; pock, pit. *~ [à la main],* plain sewing. *battre à plate ~,* to beat hollow (or soundly). **couturer** (tyre) *v.t,* to scar, seam (*with wounds*); pock, pit. **couturier** (rje) *m,* costum[i]er, mantlemaker. **couturière** (rjɛ:r) *f,* dressmaker; seamstress, needlewoman.

couvain (kuvɛ̃) *m,* nest of (*insects'*) eggs. **couvaison** (vɛzɔ̃) *f,* brooding time, sitting t. **couvée** (ve) *f,* brood, hatch, clutch; progeny.

couvent (kuvã) *m,* convent, monastery, nunnery; convent school.

couver (kuve) *v.t,* to sit on (*eggs*); hatch; incubate; (*abs.*) to brood, sit; mother (*fig.*); (*v.i.*) to smolder; brew. *~ des yeux,* to gaze at; gloat over. *mettre ~,* to set (*hen*).

couvercle (kuvɛrkl) *m,* cover, lid, cap, head.

couvert, e (kuvɛ:r, ɛrt) *p.a,* covered; clad; overgrown; wooded; shady; overcast; covert. ¶ *m,* table [things]; knife, fork, & spoon; spoon & fork; cover; shady retreat. *le ~,* shelter, lodging. *mettre, ôter, le ~,* to lay, clear, the table. *à ~,* under cover, sheltered; covered; packed (*consignment*). ¶ *f,* blanket; glaze (*on pottery*). **couverture** (vɛrty:r) *f,* covering; cover; margin; roofing; blanket; counterpane; rug (*traveling*); cloth (*horse*).

couveuse (kuvø:z) *f,* brood hen, sitting hen; incubator. **couvi** (vi) *a.m,* addle[d].

couvre-chef (kuvrəʃɛf) *m,* headgear. **couvre-engrenages** (vrãgrəna:ʒ) *m,* gearcase. **couvre-feu** (vrə) *m,* lights out (*Mil.*); curfew. **couvre-joint,** *m,* welt, butt strap. **couvre-lit,** *m,* bedspread. **couvre-livre,** *m,* jacket, dust cover (*book*). **couvre-pied,** *m,* down quilt. **couvre-théière,** *m,* tea cosy. **couvreur** (vrœ:r) *m,* slater; tiler; thatcher. **couvrir** (vri:r) *v.t.ir,* to cover; roof; load (*with praise, abuse*); drown (*sounds*). *se ~,* to cover oneself, wrap up; put one's hat on; become overcast.

crabe (krab) *m,* crab (*Crust.*).

crac (krak) *m,* crack, snap; (*i.*) before you could say Jack Robinson.

crachat (kraʃa) *m,* spit[tle], star (*decoration*). **crachement** (ʃmã) *m,* spitting. **cracher** (ʃe) *v.i,* to spit; spit out; splutter; splash (*tap*); spout; pay unwillingly, cough up. *tout craché,* to a tee. **crachoir** (ʃwa:r) *m,* spittoon. *tenir le ~,* to monopolize the conversation.

crack (krak) *m,* crack (*racehorse*). **Cracovie** (krakɔvi) *f,* Krakow. **crado** (krado) *a,* filthy (*slang*).

crack (krak) *m,* crack (*racehorse*).

Cracovie (krakɔvi) *f,* Krakow. **craie** (krɛ) *f,* chalk. **craindre** (krɛ̃:dr) *v.t. & abs. ir,* to fear, be afraid of, dread; cannot stand. *craint l'humidité, la* *chaleur,* to be kept dry, cool *or* in a dry, cool, place. **crainte** (krɛ̃:t) *f,* fear, dread, awe. **craintif, ive†** (krɛ̃tif, i:v) *a,* timid, timorous, fearful, afraid.

cramoisi, e (kramwazi) *a. & m,* crimson.

crampe (krɑ̃:p) *f,* cramp (*Med.*); staple. **crampon** (krɑ̃pɔ̃) *m,* cramp [iron], clamp, holdfast; fastener, catch; staple; [dog] spike; crampon, stud; bore (*pers.*). **cramponner** (pone) *v.t,* to cramp, clamp, fasten; pester. **se ~,** to cling, fasten.

cran (krɑ̃) *m,* notch, nick; peg (*fig.*); pluck, mettle. **~ d'arrêt,** safety catch.

crâne (krɑ:n) *m,* skull, cranium. ¶ †, *a,* plucky, jaunty. **crâner** (krɑne) *v.i,* to swagger; brazen it out.

crapaud (krapo) *m,* toad; low easy chair; baby grand; firecracker; flaw. *laid comme un ~,* [as] ugly as sin. **crapaudière** (djɛ:r) *f,* toad hole. **crapaudine** (din) *f,* toadstone; strainer, grating; plug hole; center casting.

crapoussin, e (krapusɛ̃, in) *n,* shrimp (*pers.*).

crapule (krapyl) *f,* debauchery; debauchee. **crapuleux, euse†** (lø, ø:z) *a,* debauched, lewd; filthy.

craque (krak) *f,* fib, cram.

craquelin (kraklɛ̃) *m,* cracknel. **craquelure** (krakly:r) *f,* crack(s) (*in enamel, etc.*). **craquer** (ke) *v.i,* to crack, crackle, crunch, creak. **craqueter** (kte) *v.i,* to crackle.

craqueur (krakœ:r) *m,* liar (*slang*), cracker (*oil production*).

crasse (kras) *a.f,* crass. ¶ *f,* dirt, filth, grime, squalor; scum, dross, slag, clinker; scale; gutter (*fig.*); sordidness. **crasseux, euse** (sø, ø:z) *a,* dirty, filthy, grimy, grubby, unwashed, foul, squalid.

cratère (kratɛ:r) *m,* crater.

cravache (kravaʃ) *f,* riding whip, horsewhip, crop. **cravacher** (ʃe) *v.t,* to flog; horsewhip.

cravan (kravɑ̃) *m,* barnacle (*on ship*).

cravate (kravat) *f,* [neck]tie; bow & tassels (*of color staff*). **~ de soirée,** dress bow.

crayeux, euse (krɛjø, ø:z) *a,* chalky. **crayon** (jɔ̃) *m,* pencil; sketch, outline. **~ à mine de plomb,** lead pencil. **~ pastel,** crayon. **crayonner** (jɔne) *v.t,* to pencil; sketch, outline.

créance (kreɑ̃:s) *f,* credence, belief, trust; credit; [book] debt; indebtedness; claim. **créancier, ère** (ɑ̃sje, ɛ:r) *n,* creditor. **~ hypothécaire,** mortgagee.

créateur, trice (kreatœ:r, tris) *n,* creator, tress, maker; founder, foundress; (*att.*) creative. **création** (sjɔ̃) *f,* creation; founding. **créature** (ty:r) *f,* creature.

crécelle (kresɛl) *f,* rattle (*toy, etc.*).

crécerelle (kresrɛl) *f,* kestrel.

crèche (krɛ:ʃ) *f,* crib, manger; day nursery, crèche.

crédence (kredɑ̃:s) *f,* sideboard; credence [table].

crédibilité (kredibilite) *f,* credibility. **crédit** (di) *m,* credit; trust; influence; repute; creditor; bank; (*pl.*) supplies (*parliamentary*). *au comptant ou à ~,* cash or terms (*sales*). *~ foncier,* loan, building society (*government controlled*). *~ municipal,* mortgage loan office & pawnshop. **créditer** (te) *v.t,* to credit. **créditeur** (tœ:r) *m. & att,* creditor.

credo (kredo) *m,* creed, credo; gospel (*fig.*). **crédule** (kredyl) *a,* credulous, gullible. **crédulité** (lite) *f,* credulity.

créer (kree) *v.t. & abs,* to create, make; establish, found; make out, write out (*check*).

crémaillère (kremajɛ:r) *f,* pothook; rack (*toothed*). *pendre la ~,* to give a housewarming.

crémation (kremasjɔ̃) *f,* cremation.

crème (krɛm) *f,* cream; custard. *~ chocolatée,* chocolate cream. *~ glacée,* ice cream, cream ice. **crémerie** (mri) *f,* dairy; creamery; tea shop. **crémeux, euse** (kremø, ø:z) *a,* creamy. **crémier, ère** (mje, ɛ:r) *n,* dairyman, -woman; (*m.*) cream jug.

Crémone (kremɔn) *f,* Cremona. **c~,** *f,* espagnolette.

créneau (kreno) *m,* battlement; loophole; gap (*in time schedule*);

parking space between two cars. *faire un ~*, to squeeze into a parking space. **créneler** (nle) *v.t.*, to crenellate, castellate, battlement, embattle; tooth, ratchet; mill (*coin*).

créole (kreɔl) *n. & a*, creole.

créosote (kreɔzɔt) *f*, creosote.

crêpe (krɛ:p) *m*, crape, crêpe; (*f.*) pancake. **crêper** (krɛpe) *v.t*, to crimp, crisp, frizz[le].

crépi (krepi) *m*, roughcast (*Build.*).

crépine (krepin) *f*, fringe; strainer, rose.

crépins (krepɛ̃) *m.pl*, grindery.

crépir (krepi:r) *v.t*, to roughcast; grain (*leather*).

crépiter (krepite) *v.i*, to crackle, patter (*rain*); crepitate.

crépu, e (krepy) *a*, woolly, fuzzy (*hair*).

crépuscule (krepyskyl) *m*, twilight, gloaming; decline.

crescendo (krɛsɛ̃do) *ad. & m*, crescendo.

cresson (krəsɔ̃) *m*, cress, watercress. **cressonnière** (sɔnjɛ:r) *f*, watercress bed.

Crésus (krezy:s) *m*, Croesus.

Crète (la) (krɛ:t), Crete.

crête (krɛ:t) *f*, comb; crest; ridge. *~-de-coq*, cockscomb (*Bot.*). **crêté, e** (krɛte) *a*, crested.

crétin, e (kretɛ̃, in) *n*, cretin; idiot; dunce.

cretonne (krətɔn) *f*, cretonne.

creuser (krøze) *v.t. & abs*, to dig; hollow; excavate; scoop; sink; deepen. *se ~*, to grow hollow; rise (*sea*). *~ la tête*, to rack one's brains. **creusage** (za:ʒ), **creusement** (zmɑ̃) *m*, digging.

creuset (krøzɛ) *m*, crucible, [melting] pot.

creux, euse (krø, ø:z) *a*, hollow, deep; sunken; shallow, empty. *heures creuses*, off-peak hours. *saison creuse*, slack season. ¶ *m*, hollow, cavity; hole; pit; trough (*wave*); space; hollowness; mold.

crevaison (krəvɛzɔ̃) *f*, death (*animals*); bursting; puncture (*tire*, *balloon*).

crevasse (krəvas) *f*, crevice, chink, crack, fissure, rift, crevasse; chap (*skin*). **crevasser** (se) *v.t*, to crack; chap.

crève-cœur (krɛvkœ:r) *m*, keen disappointment, wrench (*fig.*).

crever (krəve) *v.i. & t*, to burst; break; crack; split; puncture; put out (*eyes*); die. *à crevés* (ve), slashed, slit (*dress*).

crevette (krəvɛt) *f*: *~* [*grise*], shrimp. *~* [*rose*], prawn.

cri (kri) *m*, cry, snout; scream; shriek, screech; squeal; halloo; chirp; outcry; opinion. *~ de guerre*, war cry; slogan (*Pol.*). **criailler** (ɑje) *v.i*, to squeal; scold, nag. **criant, e** (ɑ̃, ɑ̃:t) *a*, crying, glaring. **criard, e** (a:r, ard) *a*, squealing, squalling, screaming, clamorous; blatant; pressing (*debts*).

crible (kribl) *m*, sieve, riddle, screen. **cribler** (ble) *v.t*, to sift, riddle, screen; honeycomb. **criblure** (bly:r) *f*, siftings, screenings.

cric (kri) *m*, [lifting] jack. *~ crac!* (krikkrak) crack! snap!

cricri (krikri) *m*, chirp; cricket (*insect*).

criée (krie) *f*, auction. **crier** (e) *v.i. & t*, to cry, shout; scream, shriek, screech; call out, clamor, protest; halloo; chirp; creak; keep telling. **crieur, euse** (œ:r, ø:z) *n*, crier; hawker. *~ de journaux*, newsboy.

crime (krim) *m*, crime; felony; offense; sin. *~ d'État*, treason. *~ de faux*, forgery. *~ passionnel* (pɑsjɔnɛl), love tragedy.

Crimée (la) (krime), the Crimea.

criminel, le† (kriminɛl) *a*, criminal; felonious; guilty. ¶ *n*, criminal; felon.

crin (krɛ̃) *m*, [horse]hair; (*vegetable*) fiber; (*pl.*) mane [& tail]. *à tous ~s*, out & out.

crincrin (krɛ̃krɛ̃) *m*, (*bad*) fiddle.

crinière (krinjɛ:r) *f*, mane; horsetail plume; abundant crop (*hair*).

crique (krik) *f*, creek, inlet (*sea*).

criquet (krikɛ) *m*, locust; cricket.

crise (kri:z) *f*, crisis; shortage, slump; attack, fit. *~ du logement*, housing problem.

crispation (krispasjɔ̃) *f*, shriveling; twitching; (*pl.*) fidgets. **crisper** (pe) *v.t*, to clench. **se ~**, to shrivel [up].

crisser (krise) *v.t. & i,* grate; squeak (*brakes*).

cristal (kristal) *m,* crystal; [crystal] glass. ~ *taillé,* cut [crystal] glass. *cristaux de soude,* [washing] soda. **cristallerie** (lri) *f,* crystal glass[ware] making *or* works. **cristallin** (lẽ, in) *a,* crystalline. ¶ *m,* crystalline lens (*eye*). **cristalliser** (lize) *v.t. & i. & se* ~, to crystallize. **cristallomancie** (talɔmãsi) *f,* crystal gazing.

critère (kritɛ:r), **critérium** (terjɔm) *m,* criterion, standard; eliminating test, preliminary trial.

critiquable (kritikabl) *a,* criticizable, open to criticism, exceptionable. **critique** (tik) *a,* critical, censorious; crucial; ticklish. ¶ *m,* critic; reviewer. ¶ *f,* criticism, critique; review; critics (*pers.*); censure, stricture. **critiquer** (ke) *v.t,* to criticize, censure.

croasser (krɔase) *v.i,* to caw, croak.

croc (kro) *m,* hook; boat hook; fang; tusk (*walrus, etc.*). **en** ~, curled, turned up (*moustache*). ¶ (krɔk) *i,* [s]crunch! ~**en-jambe** (krɔkã3ã:b) *m,* trip [up]; leg lock; dirty trick. **croche** (krɔʃ) *a,* crooked. ¶ *f,* quaver (*Mus.*). **crochet** (ʃɛ) *m,* hook; crook; crank tool; tenterhook; crochet (*Need.*); c. hook; picklock, skeleton key; sudden turn, swerve; detour; fang; [square] bracket; hook (*Box.*). ~ *à la fourche,* hairpin crochet. ~ *de suspension,* hanger, hook. **aux** ~*s de,* at the expense of. **crocheter** (ʃte) *v.t,* to pick, force the lock of. **crochu, e** (ʃy) *a,* hooked, crooked.

crocodile (krɔkɔdil) *m,* crocodile.

croire (krwa:r) *v.t. & abs. ir,* to believe; trust; think; take for.

croisade (krwazad) *f,* crusade. **croisé, e** (ze) *p.a,* crossed; cross; double-breasted (*coat*). *mots croisés,* crossword puzzle. ¶ *m,* crusader; twill. ¶ *f,* crossing; casement [window]. **croisement** (zmã) *m,* crossing; cross; cross-

breeding; frog (*Rly.*). **croiser** (ze) *v.t,* to cross; fold; pass; thwart; twill; (*v.i.*) to lap over; cruise. **se** ~, to intersect; fold (*one's arms*). **croiseur** (zœ:r) *m,* cruiser. ~ *cuirassé de combat,* battle c. **croisière** (zjɛ:r) *f,* cruise; cruising ground; cruising fleet. **croisillon** (zijõ) *m* cross [piece]; arm (*of cross*); bar (*window*).

croissance (krwasã:s) *f,* growth. **croissant, e** (sã, ã:t) *a,* growing, increasing. ¶ *m,* crescent; billhook; pruning hook; horseshoe roll. **croître** (krwa:tr) *v.i. ir,* to grow; increase; rise; draw out (*days*); wax (*moon*).

croix (krwa) *f,* cross; rood; dagger, obelisk (*Typ.*). ~ *de Malte,* Maltese cross. **la C~** *Rouge,* the Red Cross.

croquant, e (krɔkã, ã:t) *a,* crisp ¶ *m,* peasant, hick (*slang*).

croque-mitaine (krɔkmitɛn) *m,* bog[ey] [man]; bugbear **croque-mort,** *m,* undertaker's man.

croquer (krɔke) *v.i. & t,* to [s]crunch; munch; gobble up; sketch; croquet. **croquet** (kɛ) *m,* croquet (*game*). **croquette** (kɛt) *f,* croquette (*Cook.*). **croquis** (ki) *m,* sketch.

crosse (krɔs) *f,* crosier, crook; butt (*rifle*); crosshead (*piston*); crutch (*or* hook) stick; stick (*hockey*); club (*golf*); crosse (*lacrosse*). **la** ~ *canadienne,* lacrosse. **crossée** (se) *f,* drive (*golf*). **crosser** (se) *v.t,* to strike (*ball*); spurn.

crotte (krɔt) *f,* (*street*) mud, dirt; gutter (*fig.*); dung, droppings (*fig.*). **crotté, e** (te) *p.a,* muddy, dirty **crotter** (te) *v.t,* to dirty, bespatter. **crottin** (tɛ̃) *m,* dung (*horse*).

crouler (krule) *v.i,* to collapse sink; crumble.

croup (krup) *m,* croup (*Med.*)

croupe (krup) *f,* croup[e], crupper, rump; ridge (*hill*); hip (*roof*). **croupier** (pje) *m,* croupier (*gaming*). **croupière** (pjɛ:r) *f,* crupper (*harness*); sternfast **croupion** (pjõ) *m,* rump; parson's nose (*fowl*). **croupir** (pi:r) *v.i,* to wallow; stagnate. **crou**

pissant, e (pisā, ā:t) a, stagnant.
croustillant, e (krustijā, ā:t) a,
crisp, crusty, short. **croustille**
(ti:j) f, (bit of) crust (bread).
croustilleux, euse (tijø, ø:z) a,
spicy, smutty. **croûte** (krut) f,
crust; rind (cheese); scab; daub.
casser la ~, to have a snack.
vieille ~, a has-been (sports journalism). **croûton** (tō) m, crust[y]
end; sippet; [old] fogy.
croyable (krwajabl) a, credible,
believable; trustworthy. **croyance** (jā:s) f, belief; credit;
creed; faith; persuasion. **croyant,
e** (jā, ā:t) a, believing. ¶ n,
believer; (pl.) the faithful.
cru, p.p, **croire.**
crû, p.p, **croître.**
cru (kry) m, growth; vintage; invention.
cru, e (kry) a, raw, crude; garish, indigestible; hard (water);
blunt; tree, broad. à **cru,** next
the skin; bareback[ed] (riding).
cruauté (kryote) f, cruelty.
cruche (kryʃ) f, pitcher, jug; dolt,
dunce.
crucial, iaux (krysjal, jo) a,
cross-shaped (surg.); crucial (situation, argument, etc.).
crucifiement (krysifimā) m, crucifixion. **crucifier** (fje) v.t, to crucify. **crucifix** (fi) m, crucifix. **crucifixion** (fiksjɔ) f, crucifixion.
crudité (krydite) f, rawness, raw
food; crudity, crudeness; hardness (water); belching. les ~s,
raw vegetables (on a menu).
crue (kry) f, rising, flood, spate,
freshet; advance (glacier).
cruel, ɪeŧ (kryɛl) a, cruel; grievous; sore; bitter.
crûment (krymā) ad, crudely,
bluntly.
crustacé, e (krystase) a. & m,
crustacean.
crypte (kript) f, crypt; follicle.
cubage (kyba:3) m, cubic content; measurement; yardage.
cubain, e (kybɛ̃, ɛn) a. & C~,
n, Cuban.
cube (kyb) m, cube. ¶ a, cubic,
cube (root). **cuber** (be) v.t, to
cube; measure, gauge.
cubilot (kybilo) m, cupola [fur-
nace].

cubique (kybik) a, cubic(al);
cube (root). **cubisme** (bism) m,
cubism. **cubiste** (bist) n, cubist.
cueillette (kœjɛt) f, gathering,
picking; crop. **cueilleur, euse**
(jœ:r, ø:z) n, picker. **cueillir**
(ji:r) v.t.ir, to gather, pick, cull,
pluck; snatch (kiss); buttonhole
(pers.).
cuiller ou **cuillère** (kɥijɛ:r) f,
spoon; ladle; scoop; spoon [bait].
~ à café, ~ à moka, coffee spoon.
~ à dessert, ~ à entremets, dessert s. ~ à potage, soup ladle.
~ à ragoût, gravy spoon. ~ à
soupe, tablespoon. ~ à thé, tea-
spoon. **cuillerée** (jre) f, spoonful. ~ à bouche, tablespoonful.
cuir (kɥi:r) m, leather; hide, skin;
strop; incorrect liaison (in
speaking). ~ chevelu, scalp
(Anat.). ~ de porc, pigskin.
~ de vache, cowhide. ~ verni,
patent leather.
cuirasse (kɥiras) f, cuirass; armor [plating]; sheathing; saddle
(lathe). **cuirassé, e** (se) a, ar-
mored, ironclad; (fig.) steeled;
[case]hardened; proof. [navire]
cuirassé, battleship, ironclad.
cuirassier (sje) m, cuirassier.
cuire (kɥi:r) v.t. & i. ir, to cook;
roast; bake; burn; fire (bricks);
boil; ripen; smart. **cuisant, e**
(kɥizā, ā:t) a, smarting, burning;
biting (cold); bitter. **cuisine** (zin) f,
kitchen; galley, caboose; cook-
ery, cooking; food; machination.
cuisiner (ne) v.i, to cook; (v.t.) to
cook; (fig.) concoct, fudge; pump
(pers.). **cuisinette** (nɛt) f, kitchen-
ette. **cuisinier, ère** (nje, ɛ:r) n,
cook. ¶ m, cookery book. ¶ f,
cooker, cooking range; Dutch
oven.
cuisse (kɥis) f, thigh; leg (fowl).
cuisson (kɥisɔ̃) f, cooking; baking; burning, firing; smarting.
cuissot (kɥiso) m, haunch (venison).
cuistre (kɥistr) m, self-conceited
pedant; ill-mannered man.
cuit (kɥi) a, cooked; baked; done.
trop ~, overdone. ~ à point,
done to a turn. **cuite** (kɥit) f,
baking. prendre une ~, to get
drunk.

cuivre (kɥi:vr) *m*, copper; copperplate; copper bit (*soldering*). ~ [*jaune*], brass. ~ [*rouge*], copper. *les ~s*, the brass (*Mus.*). **cuivré, e** (kɥivre) *a*, copper-colored; metallic (*voice*); brassy; lurid. **cuivrer** (vre) *v.t*, to copper.

cul (ky) *m*, backside; tail (*cart*). **culasse** (las) *f*, breech (*gun*). *se chargeant par la* ~, breech-loading. **culbutage** (byta:ʒ) *m*, somersaulting; knocking over; dumping. **culbutant** (kylbytɑ̃) *m*, tumbler (*pigeon*). **culbute** (byt) *f*, somersault; tumble; fall. **culbuter** (te) *v.i. & t*, to tumble, topple over; tip, tilt, dump, shoot; overthrow; rout. **cul-de-jatte** (kydʒat) *m*, legless cripple. **cul-de-lampe** (kydlɑ̃:p) *m*, cul-de-lampe; tailpiece (*Typ.*). **cul-de-sac** (kydsak) *m*, blind alley, dead end. **culée** (kyle) *f*, abutment (*bridge*).

culinaire (kylinɛːr) *a*, culinary. **culminant, e** (kylminɑ̃, ɑ̃:t) *a*, culminating. **culminer** (ne) *v.i*, to culminate (*Astr.*).

culot (kylo) *m*, container (*lamp*); base; cap; plug; youngest; nerve. *avoir du* ~, to have a lot of nerve. **culotte** (lɔt) *f*, breeches; knee b——s; knickerbockers; knickers; rump (*beef*). ~ *courte*, shorts, trunks. ~ *de cheval*, riding breeches. ~ *de peau*, buckskins. ~ *pour le golf*, plus-fours. **culotté, e** (te) *p.p*, trousered. **culotter** (te) *v.t*, to put trousers on; season (*pipe*).

culpabilité (kylpabilite) *f*, culpability, guilt.

culte (kylt) *m*, worship; cult; creed. *le* ~ *des scientistes chrétiens*, Christian science.

cultivateur, trice (kyltivatœːr, tris) *n*, cultivator, grower, agricultur[al]ist, farmer, husbandman. **cultiver** (ve) *v.t*, to cultivate, grow; raise; farm, till. **culture** (tyːr) *f*, culture, cultivation, farming; (*pl.*) land [under cultivation]. ~ *maraîchère*, market gardening.

cumul (kymyl) *m*, plurality (*of offices*). **cumulatif, ive** (latif, iːv) *a*, cumulative. **cumulus** (lyːs) *m*, cumulus.

cunéiforme (kyneifɔrm) *a*, cuneiform.

cupide (kypid) *a*, covetous, grasping. **cupidité** (ite) *f*, greed.

Cupidon (kypidɔ̃) *m*, Cupid.

curable (kyrabl) *a*, curable.

curage (kyra:ʒ) *m*, cleansing; flushing.

curatelle (kyratɛl) *f*, guardianship, trusteeship. **curateur, trice** (tœːr, tris) *n*, guardian, trustee, administrator, trix.

curatif, ive (kyratif, iːv) *a. & m*, curative. **cure** (kyːr) *f*, cure; vicarship, rectorship; vicarage, rectory. **curé** (kyre) *m*, parish priest; vicar, rector.

cure-dent (kyrdɑ̃) *m*, toothpick. *venir en* ~, to be invited after dinner.

curée (kyre) *f*, quarry (*given to hounds*); scramble.

curer (kyre) *v.t*, to cleanse, clean; flush; pick (*teeth*). **curette** (kyrɛt) *f*, scraper, cleaner. **cureur** (rœːr) *m*, cleaner; sewerman.

curieux, euse† (kyrjø, øːz) *a*, curious; interested; odd; quaint; inquisitive, prying. ¶ *n*, curious (*or* inquisitive) person; sightseer; onlooker; bystander; (*m.*) curious part *or* thing; collector (*art, books*). **curiosité** (ozite) *f*, curiosity; quaintness; curio; (*pl.*) sights (*of a city*).

curseur (kyrsœːr) *m*, runner; slide[r] (*Mech.*); cursor (*computers*). **cursif, ive** (sif, iːv) *a*, cursive, running.

curviligne (kyrviliɲ) *a*, curvilinear.

cutané, e (kytane) *a*, cutaneous; skin (*att.*). **cuticule** (tikyl) *f*, cuticle.

cuve (kyːv) *f*, vat. ~-*matière*, mash tub. **cuvée** (kyve) *f*, vatful; vintage. **cuveler** (vle) *v.t*, to tub, case (*Min.*).

cuver (kyve) *v.i*, to ferment (*wine*). ~ *son vin*, to sleep off a drunk. **cuvette** (kyvɛt) *f*, washbasin; basin; dish; tray; bowl; cup, cistern (*barometer*). **cuvier** (vje) *m*, washtub.

cyanure (sjanyːr) *m*, cyanide.

cyclamen (siklamɛn) *m*, cyclamen.

cycle (sikl) *m*, cycle; cycle trade.

cyclisme (klism) *m*, cycling.
cycliste (klist) *n*, cyclist.
cyclomoteur (siklɔmɔtœr) *m*,
motorbike.
cyclone (siklon) *m*, cyclone.
cygne (siɲ) *m*, swan.
cylindre (silɛ̃;dr) *m*, cylinder;
roller; roll; barrel, drum. ~
compresseur à vapeur, steam-
roller. **cylindrer** (lɛ̃dre) *v.t*, to
roll; mangle; calender; round.
cylindrique (drik) *a*, cylindrical;
parallel (*drill shank*).
cymbales (sɛ̃bal) *f.pl*, cymbals.
cynique† (sinik) *a*, cynic, cyni-
cal. ¶ *m*, cynic. **cynisme** (nism)
m, cynicism.
cyprès (siprɛ) *m*, cypress.
cytise (siti;z) *m*, laburnum.

D

dac, d'ac (dak) *i*, ok, agreed (*short
for "d'accord"*).
dactylographe (daktilɔgraf) *n*,
typist. **dactylographie** (fi) *f*,
typewriting, typing.
dada (dada) *m*, gee-gee; hobby
horse; pet subject, fad.
dadais (dadɛ) *m*, booby, ninny.
dague (dag) *f*, dagger, dirk.
dahlia (dalja) *m*, dahlia.
daigner (dɛɲe) *v.i*, to deign to,
be pleased to, vouchsafe.
daim (dɛ̃) *m*, [fallow] deer, buck.
[*peau de*] ~, buckskin, doeskin.
daine (dɛn) *f*, doe.
dais (dɛ) *m*, canopy; hood (*car*).
dallage (dala;ʒ) *m*, flagging,
pavement. **dalle** (dal) *f*, flag-
[stone]; slab. **daller** (le) *v.t*, to
pave, flag.
dalmate (dalmat) *a*, Dalmatian.
la Dalmatie (si), Dalmatia.
dalot (dalo) *m*, scupper.
daltonisme (daltɔnism) *m*, col-
or-blindness.
dam (dã) *m*, injury, prejudice; displeasure. *peine du* ~, eternal
damnation.
damas (damɑ) *m*, damask; damson. **D~**, *m*, Damascus. **damasquiner** (maskine) *v.t*, to
damascene.
dame (dam) *f*, lady; dame; partner (*dance*); queen (*cards, chess*);

king (*checkers*); beetle, rammer.
la ~, Mrs. (*law*). *les* ~*s*, checkers (*game*). ~ *d'onze heures*,
star of Bethlehem. ~ *de compagnie*, lady companion. ~ [*de
nage*], rowlock. ~*jeanne* (ʒɑ;n),
f, demijohn. ¶ *i*, why! indeed!
well! **damer** (me) *v.t*, to crown
(*checkers*); queen (*chess*); tamp,
ram. **damier** (mje) *m*, checker-
board.
damnable† (dɑnabl) *a*, damnable. **damnation** (sjõ) *f*, damnation. **damné, e** (ne) *a. & n*,
damned. **damner** (ne) *v.t*, to
damn.
damoiseau (damwazo) *m*, galant.
dandiner (se) (dɑ̃dine) *v.pr*,
to waddle.
dandy (dɑ̃di) *m*, dandy.
Danemark (le) (danmark),
Denmark.
danger (dɑ̃ʒe) *m*, danger, jeopardy; fear. **dangereux, euse†**
(ʒrø, ø;z) *a*, dangerous.
danois, e (danwa, a;z) *a. &
(language) *m*, Danish. **D~**
(*pers*.) *n*, Dane.
dans (dã) *pr*, in; into; within; during; among; about; out of; with;
hence. ~ *les présentes*, herein
(*law*). ~ *œuvre*, inside, in the
clear (*Meas*.). ~ *le temps*, in ear-
lier days, formerly.
dansant, e (dɑ̃sɑ̃, ɑ̃;t) *a*, dancing; dance (*tea*). **danse** (dɑ̃;s)
f, dance; dancing. ~ *de Saint-
Guy* (gi), St. Vitus's dance. **D~
macabre, Dance of Death, Dance
Macabre. **danser** (dɑ̃se) *v.i. &
t, to dance. **danseur, euse** (sœ;r,
ø;z) *n*, dancer; partner; ballet
dancer. ~ *mondain, e*, ballroom
dancer.
dard (da;r) *m*, dart; sting (*insect's*); pistil; pace (*fish*). **darder** (darde) *v.t*, to dart, hurl,
fling, shoot; spear.
dare-dare (darda;r) *ad*, quickly
(*slang*).
dartre (dartr) *f*, herpes, skin disease.
date (dat) *f*, date (*time*). *de
longue* ~, of long standing. **dater**
(te) *v.t*, to date. *à* ~ *de*, from,
on & after.
datif (datif) *m*, dative [case].

datte (dat) *f*, date (*fruit*). **dat-tier** (tje) *m*, date palm.

dauber (dobe) *v.t*, to drub, thump; jeer at. ~ *sur*, to jeer at.

dauphin (dofɛ̃) *m*, dolphin (*Zool.*).

davantage (davɑ̃taːʒ) *ad*, more, further; longer.

davier (davje) *m*, forceps (*dentist's*); davit (*Naut.*).

de (də), **d'** (d) (**de le** *is contracted into* **du**, **de les** *into* **des**) *pr*, of; from; by; for; in; on; some; any; than; between; with; to. *When coupled with Fr. noun, often rendered in Eng. by noun used attributively, as, mine de charbon, coal mine.*

dé (de) *m*, thimble; die (*gaming & Mach.*); bearing (*Mach.*); tee (*golf*).

déambuler (deɑ̃byle) *v.i*, to stroll, saunter, walk up and down.

débâcle (debɑːkl) *f*, breaking up (*ice*); crash, collapse; landslide (*Pol.*). **débâcler** (bɑkle) *v.t*, to clear; (*v.i.*) to break up.

déballage (debalaːʒ) *m*, unpacking; show (*of wares*). **déballer** (le) *v.t*, to unpack.

débandade (debɑ̃dad) *f*, stampede, rout. *à la* ~, helter-skelter; anyhow. **débander** (de) *v.t*, to relax, unbend; unbandage; to disband (*Mil.*). **se** ~, to break ranks in disorder.

débaptiser (debatize) *v.t*, to change the name of, rename.

débarbouiller (debarbuje) *v.t*, to wash (*someone's*) face; extricate.

débarcadère (debarkadɛːr) *m*, landing [place *or* stage], wharf; platform (*Rly.*).

débarder (debarde) *v.t*, to unload. **débardeur** (dœːr) *m*, docker; longshoreman; sleeveless undershirt.

débarquer (debarke) *v.t. & i*, to land, disembark; detrain; discharge; get rid of; alight. **débarquement** (kəmɑ̃) *m*, landing, etc. *au* ~, ex ship, ex steamer (*sales*).

débarras (debarɑ) *m*, riddance; lumber room; storeroom. **dé-**barrasser (rase) *v.t*, to clear, rid, extricate, disburden, relieve. *se* ~ *de*, to get rid of, scrap.

débat (deba) *m*, discussion; debate; (*pl.*) proceedings; (*pl.*) trial, hearing; dispute. **débattre** (tr) *v.t.ir*, to debate, discuss, argue; arrange. **se** ~, to struggle; flounder; wriggle.

débauche (deboːʃ) *f*, debauch[ery]; carousal; riot (*fig.*); treat. ~ *de boisson*, drunken bout. **débauché, e** (boʃe) *n*, debauchee, rake. **débaucher** (ʃe) *v.t*, to debauch, corrupt; induce to strike; seduce from duty; lead astray; reduce the staff.

débecqueter *or* **débecter** (debɛkte) *v.t*, to disgust (*slang*).

débile† (debil) *a*, weakly; weak; feeble. **débilité** (lite) *f*, debility; weakness. **débiliter** (te) *v.t*, to debilitate, enfeeble.

débit (debi) *m*, sale (*retail*); market, demand; (*government*) license to sell; (*licensed*) shop; flow, discharge, yield, output, capacity, feed; delivery (*pump, speech*); cutting up, chopping; debit [side], debtor [side]. ~ *de tabac*, license to sell tobacco; tobacconist's shop. **débitant, e** (tɑ̃, ɑ̃ːt) *n*, dealer, retailer. ~ *de spiritueux*, licensed victualler. ~ *de tabac*, tobacconist. **débiter** (te) *v.t*, to retail, sell; discharge, yield; deliver, utter; spread (*news*); spin (*yarns*); cut up; saw; chop (*firewood*); debit. **débiteur, euse** (tœːr, øːz) *n*, utterer (*lies*); -monger (*news, scandal*); (*f.*) (*also* **débitrice**) (*In Fr. stores*) girl who conducts customers to cash desk to see that they pay. **débiteur, trice** (tœːr, tris) *n. & att*, debtor, debit (*att.*). ~ *hypothécaire*, mortgagor.

déblai (deblɛ) *m*, cut[ting], excavation; (*s. & pl.*) waste, rubbish, spoil.

déblaterer contre (deblatere), to abuse.

déblayer (deblɛje) *v.t*, to clear, c. out, c. away.

débloquer (deblɔke) *v.t*, to free, relieve, unblock, unlock; rave, speak incoherently.

déboire (debwa:r) *m*, (*nasty*) aftertaste; disappointment.

déboiser (debwaze) *v.t*, to deforest.

déboitement (debwatmᾶ) *m*, dislocation (*limb*). **déboiter** (te) *v.t*, to dislocate; disjoint.

débonder (debɔ̃de) *v.t*, to unstop; open the sluice gates of; open, relax (*Med.*). [se] ~, to burst forth, break out, escape.

débonnaire† (debɔne:r) *a*, meek; easy-going; accommodating.

débordement (debɔrdəmᾶ) *m*, overflow; outburst; excess, licentiousness. ~ *inférieure*, underflow (*computers*). **déborder** (de) *v.i*, to overflow, brim over, run over; slop [over]; break out; (*v.t.*) to overlap; outflank; untuck; trim the edges of; unship (*oars*). *être débordé*, to be overwhelmed (*by work or events*).

débotter (debɔte) *v.t*, to take (*someone's*) boots off. **se ~**, to take one's boots off. **au débotté** (te), immediately upon arrival.

débouché (debuʃe) *m*, opening, outlet, issue; waterway;. prospects; market sale. **déboucher** (ʃe) *v.t*, to open, unstop, uncork; (*v.i.*) to open, emerge, debouch; lead into.

déboucler (debukle) *v.t*, to unbuckle; uncurl.

débouler [dans] (debule) *v.i*, to tumble down (*as stairs*).

déboulonner (debulɔne) *v.t*, to unrivet; debunk.

débourber (deburbe) *v.t*, to clean out, cleanse; extricate.

débourrer (debure) *v.t*, to ream (*pipe*); unstop; break in (*horse*).

débours (debu:r) & **déboursé** (burse) *m, both mostly pl*, disbursement, out of pocket expense, outlay. **débourser** (se) *v.t*, to disburse, lay out, spend.

debout (dəbu) *ad*, on end, erect; standing; up; head (*wind*). *mourir ~*, to die in harness.

débouter (debute) *v.t*, to nonsuit, dismiss (*law*).

déboutonner (debutɔne) *v.t*, to unbutton. **se ~** (*fig.*), to open out, speak one's mind.

débraillé, e (debraje) (*fig.*) *a*, dissolute. **se débrailler** (je) *v.pr*, to unbutton oneself (*unbecomingly*).

débrayer (debreje) (*Mech.*) *v.t*, to throw out of gear, disconnect; let out the clutch (*auto*); go on strike.

débrider (debride) *v.t*, to unbridle. *sans ~*, without stopping.

débris (debri) *m.pl*, remains, debris, litter; scrap; wreck[age].

débrouillard, e (debruja:r, ard) *a*, resourceful. ¶ *n*, resourceful person.

débrouiller (debruje) *v.t*, to unravel, disentangle, clear up. **se ~**, to extricate oneself; manage.

débucher (debyʃe) *v.i*, to break cover.

débusquer (debyske) *v.t*, to dislodge, drive out; oust.

début (deby) *m*, beginning, opening, outset, outbreak, start; first appearance; f. work; coming out (*in society*). **débutant, e** (tᾶ, ᾶ:t) *n*, beginner; débutant, e. **débuter** (te) *v.i*, to begin, start, make one's first appearance; lead (*cards*).

deçà (dəsa) *ad*, on this side. ~, *delà* ou ~ & *delà*, here & there, to & fro. *en ~ de*, *pr*, on this side of.

décacheter (dekaʃte) *v.t*, to unseal, open.

décade (dekad) *f*, ten days; decad[e] (*books*).

décadence (dekadᾶ:s) *f*, decadence, decline, decay. **décadent, e** (dᾶ, ᾶ:t) *a*, decadent.

décaféiner (dekafeine) *v.t*, to decaffeinate.

décagone (dekagɔn) *m*, decagon.

décaisser (dekɛse) *v.t*, to unpack; withdraw (*money*).

décalage (dekala:ʒ) *m*, unwedging; staggering; gap, lag; setback (*fig*). **décaler** (kale) *v.t*, to unwedge; shift; stagger; readjust.

décalcomanie (dekalkɔmani) *f*, transfer (*for china & as a toy*); decal.

décalitre (dekalitr) *m*, decaliter = 10 liters *or* 2.200 gallons.

décalotter (dekalɔte) *v.t*, to uncap; remove the end of (*lemòn, egg, etc.*); circumcize.

décalque (dekalk) *m*, transfer (*Emb.*); tracing. **décalquer** (ke) *v.t*, to transfer, trace.

décamètre (dekamɛːtr) *m*, decameter = 10 meters *or* 10.936 yards. ~ *d'arpenteur*, measuring tape.

décamper (dekɑ̃pe) *v.i*, to decamp, make off.

décanat (dekana) *m*, deanery (*office*).

décanter (dekɑ̃te) *v.t*, to decant.

décaper (dekape) *v.t*, to scour.

décapiter (dekapite) *v.t*, to behead, decapitate.

décapotable (dekapɔtabl) *m*, convertible (*auto*).

décatir (dekatiːr) *v.t*, to sponge, steam (*fabrics*); take gloss off. se ~, to become worn, show one's age.

décéder (desede) *v.i*, to decease.

déceler (desle) *v.t*, to reveal, betray.

décembre (desɑ̃ːbr) *m*, December.

décemment (desamɑ̃) *ad*, decently. **décence** (sɑ̃ːs) *f*, decency, propriety.

décennal, e (desɛnal) *a*, decennial.

décennie (deseni) *f*, decade.

décent, e (desɑ̃, ɑ̃ːt) *a*, decent; proper.

décentraliser (desɑ̃tralize) *v.t*, to decentralize.

déception (desɛpsjɔ̃) *f*, disappointment.

décerner (desɛrne) *v.t*, to award.

décès (desɛ) *m*, death, decease, demise.

décevant, e (desvɑ̃, ɑ̃ːt) *a*, deceptive, misleading. **décevoir** (s[ə]vwaːr) *v.t*, to deceive; disappoint.

déchaîner (deʃɛne) *v.t*, to unchain, let loose. se ~, break loose; break out.

déchanter (deʃɑ̃te) *v.i*, to sing small, change one's tone.

décharge (deʃarʒ) *f*, discharge; unloading; outflow; outfall; volley; release; relief; composition (*to creditors*); waste heap. **décharger** (ʒe) *v.t. & abs*, to discharge; unload; empty; relieve, disburden, ease; deal (*blow*); come off (*ink*). **déchargeur** (ʒœːr) *m*, stevedore; lightning rod.

décharné, e (deʃarne) *p.a*, emaciated, gaunt, skinny, scraggy.

déchausser (deʃose) *v.t*, to take off (*someone's*) shoes; [lay] bare; dislodge.

dèche (dɛʃ) *f*, tightened straits, poverty, want. *être dans la* ~, to be down and out.

déchéance (deʃeɑ̃ːs) *f*, [down] fall; loss, forfeiture; lapse, expiration.

déchet (deʃɛ) *m. oft. pl*, waste, loss; scrap, refuse.

déchiffrer (deʃifre) *v.t.' & abs*, to decipher, decode, make out, read (*or* play) at sight.

déchiqueter (deʃikte) *v.t*, to slash; jag; shred.

déchirant, e (deʃirɑ̃, ɑ̃ːt) *a*, heartrending, harrowing. **déchirer** (re) *v.t*, to tear, rend, rip, lacerate; tear up; break up; harrow; split (*ears with noise*). **déchirure** (ryːr) *f*, tear, rent, rip.

déchoir (deʃwaːr) *v.i.ir*, to fall, decline. ~ *de*, to forfeit.

décibel (desibɛl) *m*, decibel (*Phys.*).

décidé, e (deside) *a*, decided; settled, determined. **décidément** (mɑ̃) *ad*, decidedly; definitely. **décider** (de) *v.t. & abs*, to decide, settle, resolve, determine; induce, persuade, prevail upon. se ~, to decide, make up one's mind.

décidu, e (desidy) *a*, deciduous.

décigramme (desigram) *m*, decigram = ¹⁄₁₀ gram *or* 1.543 grains.

décilitre (desilitr) *m*, deciliter = ¹⁄₁₀ liter *or* 0.176 pint.

décimal, e (desimal) *a. & f*, decimal.

décime (desim) *m*, 10 centimes; 10% surtax. **décimer** (me) *v.t*, to decimate.

décimètre (desimɛtr) *m*, decimeter = ¹⁄₁₀ meter *or* 3.937 inches; decimeter rule. *double* ~, 2-decimeter rule. ~ *carré*, square d. = 15.500 sq. ins. ~ *cube*, cubic d. = 61.024 cub. ins.

décisif, ive† (desizif, iːv) *a*, decisive; critical; positive. **décision** (zjɔ̃) *f*, decision; conclusion; resolution; ruling, award.

déclamateur (deklamatœːr) *m*, stump orator, spouter. **déclamation** (sjɔ̃) *f*, declamation, elocution; delivery; rant. **déclamer (me)** *v.t. & abs. & i,* to declaim; recite; spout, rant.

déclaration (deklarasjɔ̃) *f,* declaration; statement; return; proclamation; finding (*jury*). *~ sous serment,* affidavit. **déclarer (re)** *v.t,* to declare, state, report; proclaim; certify; disclose; find (*juries*). **se ~,** to declare oneself; show itself; break out.

déclassé, e (deklɑse) *n,* [social] outcast. **déclasser (se)** *v.t,* to degrade; transfer from one class to another.

déclencher (deklɑ̃ʃe) *v.t,* to trip, release; disengage (*Mech.*); launch (*attack*). **déclencheur** (ʃœːr) *m,* [shutter] release (*Phot.*).

déclic (deklik) *m,* trigger, catch, trip, release.

déclin (deklɛ̃) *m,* decline, wane. **déclinaison** (klinɛzɔ̃) *f,* declination; declension (*Gram.*). **décliner (ne)** *v.i. & t,* to decline; wane; give, state (*name, etc.*).

déclive (dekliːv) *a,* sloping. **déclivité** (klivite) *f,* declivity, slope.

décocher (dekɔʃe) *v.t,* to let off, let fly.

décoction (dekɔksjɔ̃) *f,* decoction.

décoiffer (dekwafe) *v.t,* to take off the hat of; uncork, crack (*a bottle*); disarrange (*hair*).

décollage (dekɔlaːʒ) *m,* unsticking, ungluing; liftoff (*missiles, spacecraft*). **décoller** (kɔle) *v.t,* to unglue, unstick; *v.i,* take off (*Avn.*); lift o. (*spacecraft*). **se ~,** to come unstuck, part.

décolleté, e (dekɔlte) *a,* low-necked; free, licentious. ¶ *m,* low-necked dress; court shoes.

décoloniser (dekɔlɔnize) *v.t,* to decolonize; liberate (*women, minorities, etc.*).

décolorer (dekɔlɔre) *v.t,* to discolor.

décombres (dekɔ̃ːbr) *m.pl,* demolitions, rubbish.

décommander (dekɔmɑ̃de) *v.t,* to countermand, cancel; call off; ask not to come.

décomposer (dekɔ̃poze) *v.t,* to decompose; distort.

décompte (dekɔ̃ːt) *m,* deduction;

working out; table, sheet. *éprouver du ~ dans,* to be disappointed in. **décompter** (kɔ̃te) *v.t. & abs,* to deduct; work out; suffer disappointment.

déconcerter (dekɔ̃sɛrte) *v.t,* to disconcert; upset.

déconfire (dekɔ̃fiːr) *v.t.ir,* to nonplus. **déconfiture** (fityːr) *f,* insolvency.

déconner (dekɔne) *v.i,* to talk nonsense, babble (*slang*).

déconseiller (dekɔ̃sɛje) *v.t,* to dissuade.

déconsidérer (dekɔ̃sidere) *v.t,* to discredit.

décontenancement (dekɔ̃tnɑ̃smɑ̃) *m,* surprise, shock (*at a movie, book, etc.*).

décontenancer (dekɔ̃tnɑ̃se) *v.t,* to abash.

décontracter (dekɔ̃trakte) *v.t,* to relax (*physically, mentally*). *un type décontracté,* a laid-back guy.

déconvenue (dekɔ̃vny) *f,* discomfiture.

décor (dekɔːr) *m,* decoration; set (*Theat.*); (*pl.*) scenery; (*pl.*) regalia (*freemasons'*). **décorateur** (kɔratœːr) *m,* decorator; scene painter, stage designer. **décoratif, ive** (tif, iːv) *a,* decorative. **décoration** (sjɔ̃) *f,* decoration; order, medal; scenery. **décorer (re)** *v.t,* to decorate; dignify.

décortiquer (dekɔrtike) *v.t,* to bark; peel.

décorum (dekɔrɔm) *m,* decorum; etiquette.

découcher (dekuʃe) *v.i,* to sleep out.

découdre (dekudr) *v.t.ir,* to unstitch; rip.

découler (dekule) *v.i,* to trickle, run down; proceed, issue.

découpage (dekupaːʒ) *m,* shooting script, continuity script. *~ technique,* final shooting script, shot list.

découper (dekupe) *v.t. & abs,* to carve (*meat*); cut up; cut out; fretsaw; punch [out]. **se ~,** to stand out. **découpeur, euse** (pœːr, øːz) *n,* carver (*pers.*).

découpler (dekuple) *v.t,* to slip, uncouple.

découpoir (dekupwaːr) *m,* [hollow] punch. **découpure** (py:r) *f*, cutting out; fretwork.

découragement (dekuraʒmã) *m*, discouragement, despondency. **décourager** (ʒe) *v.t*, to discourage, dishearten, depress, dispirit; daunt; deter. **se ~**, to lose heart, despond.

décousu, e (dekuzy) (*fig.*) *a*, loose, disconnected, disjointed, rambling, desultory. ¶ *m*, looseness.

découvert, e (dekuvɛːr, ɛrt) *a*, uncovered, bare, open; unprotected. **à découvert**, *ad*, uncovered, open; unpacked; unsecured (*loan*); overdrawn. **découvert**, *m*, overdraft; bear account, bears (*Stk Ex.*). **découverte**, *f*, discovery; find; detection; disclosure; background set (*cinema*). *aller à la ~*, to scout. **découvrir** (vriːr) *v.t.ir*, to uncover, bare, open; discover, detect; descry, espy; find; f. out. **se ~**, to expose oneself; take one's hat off; come to light.

décrasser (dekrase) *v.t*, to cleanse, clean, scour.

décréditer (dekredite) *v.t*, to discredit.

décrépit, e (dekrepi, it) *a*, decrepit. **décrépitude** (tyd) *f*, decrepitude, senile decay.

décret (dekrɛ) *m*, decree, fiat, ordinance, order, enactment. **décréter** (krete) *v.t*, to decree, enact, ordain.

décri (dekri) *m*, disrepute. **décrier** (krie) *v.t*, to decry, run down.

décrire (dekriːr) *v.t. & abs. ir*, to describe.

décrocher (dekrɔʃe) *v.t*, to unhook; take down.

décroître (dekrwaːtr) *v.i.ir*, to decrease, shorten, dwindle, wane.

décrotter (dekrɔte) *v.t*, to clean, brush, scrape. **décrotteur** (tœːr) *m*, bootblack (*pers.*). **décrottoir** (twaːr) *m*, scraper [mat].

décrue (dekry) *f*, fall (*river*); retreat (*glacier*). **déçu**, p.p, **décevoir**.

décuple (dekypl) *a. & m*, tenfold. **décupler** (ple) *v.t. & i*, to increase tenfold.

dédaigner (dedɛɲe) *v.t*, to disdain, scorn, despise. **dédaigneux,**

euse† (nø, øːz) *a*, disdainful, scornful, supercilious. **dédain** (dɛ̃) *m*, disdain, disregard, scorn.

dédale (dedal) *m*, maze, labyrinth.

dedans (dədɑ̃) *ad*, inside, in. *de ~*, from within. (*rire*) *ad*, inwardly. *en ~*, *pr*, within. ¶ *m*, inside, interior.

dédicace (dedikas) *f*, dedication; inscription. **dédier** (dje) *v.t*, to dedicate; devote; inscribe.

dédire (dediːr) *v.t.ir*, to gainsay. **se ~ de**, to retract, unsay. **dédit** (di) *m*, retractation; penalty, forfeit.

dédouaner (dedwane) *v.t*, to clear, take out of bond (*Cust.*).

dédommagement (dedɔmaʒmɑ̃) *m*, indemnity, compensation, damages. **dédommager** (ʒe) *v.t*, to compensate, recoup, indemnify.

dédoubler (deduble) *v.t*, to divide into two; duplicate (*train*); unline. *~ les rangs*, to form single file.

déductif, ive (dedyktif, iːv) *a*, deductive, inferential. **déduction** (ksjɔ̃) *f*, deduction; allowance, relief; inference. **déduire** (dɥiːr) *v.t.ir*, to deduct; deduce, infer.

déesse (deɛs) *f*, goddess.

défaillance (defajɑ̃ːs) *f*, swoon, fainting [fit]; lapse; failing; default; eclipse. **défaillant, e** (jɑ̃, ɑ̃ːt) *a*, failing; drooping; defaulting. ¶ *n*, defaulter. **défaillir** (jiːr) *v.i.ir*, to faint; fail; flinch; falter.

défaire (defɛːr) *v.t.ir*, to undo; take off; defeat, rout. **se ~**, to come undone. **se ~ de**, to get rid of; unload (*stocks*); make away with. **défait, e** (fɛ, ɛt) *a*, undone; defeated; drawn (*look*). **défaite**, *f*, defeat; shuffle, evasion.

défalcation (defalkasjɔ̃) *f*, deduction. **défalquer** (ke) *v.t*, to deduct.

défaut (defo) *m*, defect, fault, flaw, blemish; default, failure, want, lack, deficiency.

défaveur (defavœːr) *f*, disfavor. **défavorable†** (vɔrabl) *a*, unfavorable, inauspicious. **défavoriser** (ize) *v.t*, to disadvantage.

défectif, ive (defɛktif, iːv) *a*, defective. **défection** (sjɔ̃) f, defection. **défectueux, euse†** (tyø, ø:z) a, defective, faulty, deficient. **défectuosité** (tɥozite) f, defect, fault, flaw.

défendable (defɑ̃dabl) a, defensible. **défendeur, eresse** (dœ:r, drɛs) n, defendant; respondent (law). **défendre** (fɑ̃:dr) v.t, to defend; protect, shield; forbid, prohibit. **se ~**, to defend oneself; deny; excuse oneself; manage somehow; engage in prostitution. **défense** (fɑ̃:s) f, defense; (pl.) plea; protection; prohibition; tusk; fender (Naut.). **~ d'afficher**, post no bills. **~ d'entrer** [sans autorisation], no admittance [except on business], private. **~ d'entrer sous peine d'amende**, trespassers will be prosecuted. **~ de circuler sur l'herbe**, [please] keep off the grass. **~ de fumer**, no smoking. **~ de passer**, no thoroughfare. **~ de toucher**, [please] do not touch. **~ expresse** (ou absolue) de fumer, smoking strictly prohibited. **~ passive**, civil defense. **~ légitime**, self-defense. **défenseur** (fɑ̃sœ:r) m, defender; advocate; counsel for the defense. **défensif, ive** (sif, i:v) a. & f, defensive.

déféquer (defeke) v.t. & i, to defecate.

déférence (deferɑ̃:s) f, deference, respect. **déférent, e** (rɑ̃, ɑ̃:t) a, deferential. **déférer** (re) v.t, to confer, bestow; refer (to court); hand over (to justice); administer (oath); (v.i.) to defer (submit).

déferler (deferle) v.t, to unfurl; (v.i.) to break (waves).

déferrer (defere) v.t, to unshoe (horse); disconcert.

défi (defi) m, challenge; defiance. **défiance** (fjɑ̃:s) f, distrust, mistrust. **~ de soi-même**, diffidence. **défiant, e** (ɑ̃, ɑ̃:t) a, distrustful, mistrustful; wary.

déficit (defisi) m, deficit, deficiency, short[age], minus quantity. **déficitaire** (tɛ:r) a, debit (att.), showing a loss, adverse; short.

défier (defje) v.t, to challenge; brave; dare; defy; baffle. **se ~ de**,

to distrust, mistrust; beware of.

défigurer (defigyre) v.t, to disfigure; deface; distort.

défilé (defile) m, defile; march past; procession; parade. **défiler** (le) v.t, to unthread; (v.i.) to defile; file off; march past. **se ~** (fig.), to make off.

défini, e (defini) p.a, definite; finite (mood, Gram.). **définir** (ni:r) v.t, to define; describe; determine; decide. **définissable** (nisabl) a, definable. **définitif, ive†** (tif, i:v) a, definitive; absolute (decree); final; ultimate; standard (edition). **en définitive**, ad, finally, in short. **définition** (sjɔ̃) f, definition; decision.

déflation (deflasjɔ̃) f, deflation (Fin.).

défléchir (defleʃi:r) v.t, to deflect.

défleurir (deflœri:r) v.i, to shed its blossoms; (v.t.) to deflower, strip of flowers. **défloraison** (florɛzɔ̃) f, defloration (stripping). **défloration** (rasjɔ̃) f, defloration (ravishment). **déflorer** (re) v.t, to deflower (strip of flowers or ravish); take the freshness off (news).

défoncer (defɔ̃se) v.t, to stave [in]; break up.

déformer (deforme) v.t, to deform; distort; strain (Mech.).

défouler (defule) v.t, to eliminate complexes. **défoulement** (mɑ̃) m, liberation (from inhibitions).

défourner (defurne) v.t, to take out of the oven.

défraîchi, e (defrɛʃi) p.a, shopworn. **défraîchir** (ʃi:r) v.t. & se **~**, to fade.

défrayer (defrɛje) v.t, to defray; entertain; keep up (conversation).

défricher (defriʃe) v.t, to clear, grub, reclaim.

défriser (defrize) v.t, to uncurl; disconcert.

défroncer (defrɔ̃se) v.t, to iron out; smooth.

défroque (defrɔk) f, cast-off clothing. **défroquer** (ke) v.t, to unfrock.

défunt, e (defœ̃, œ̃:t) a. & n, deceased, defunct, departed, late (*a.*).

dégagé, e (degaʒe) *a*, free, easy, unconstrained; perky. **dégagement** (ʒmã) *m*, redemption; clearing; disengagement, evolution; exit. **dégager** (ʒe) *v.t*, to redeem; make out (*meaning*); relieve; extricate; free, disengage, give off, evolve, emit; clear; set off (*figure*).

dégaine (degɛ:n) *f*, awkwardness. **dégainer** (gɛne) *v.t. & abs*, to unsheathe, draw.

déganter (se) (degãte) *v.pr*, to take off one's gloves.

dégarnir (degarni:r) *v.t*, to strip, dismantle.

dégât (dega) *m. oft. pl*, damage, havoc.

dégauchir (degoʃi:r) *v.t*, to true, straighten.

dégel (deʒɛl) *m*, thaw. **dégeler** (ʒle) *v.t. & i. & se ~*, to thaw.

dégénérer (deʒenere) *v.i*, to degenerate. **dégénérescence** (resã:s) & **dégénération** (rasjɔ̃) *f*, degeneration, degeneracy.

dégingandé, e (deʒɛ̃gɑ̃de) *a*, ungainly, gawky.

dégivrer (deʒivre) *v.t*, to de-ice; defrost (*refrigerator*). **dégivreur** (rœ:r) *m*, de-icing device.

dégoiser (degwaze) *v.t*, to spout (*abuse*).

dégommer (degɔme) *v.t*, to ungum; oust.

dégonfler (degɔ̃fle) *v.t*, to deflate; relieve. **se ~**, to collapse; back down.

dégorger (degɔrʒe) *v.t*, to disgorge; unstop. [se] **~**, to discharge; overflow.

dégouliner (deguline) *v.i*, to trickle, drip.

dégourdi, e (degurdi) *p.a*, wide-awake, alive. **dégourdir** (di:r) *v.t*, to revive. **faire ~**, to take the chill off (*water*).

dégoût (degu) *m*, want of appetite; distaste, dislike, disrelish; disgust, loathing, aversion; disappointment. **dégoûtant, e** (tã, ã:t) *a*, disgusting, loathsome; disheartening. **dégoûter** (te) *v.t*, to make one sick of; disgust. *faire le dégoûté*, to be fastidious, be squeamish.

dégoutter (degute) *v.i. & abs*, to drip, trickle, dribble.

dégradateur (degradatœ:r) *m*, vignetter (*Phot.*). **dégradation** (sjɔ̃) *f*, degradation; defacement; dilapidation. **dégrader** (de) *v.t*, to degrade; deface; dilapidate; damage; shade [off], vignette.

dégrafer (degrafe) *v.t*, to unhook, unfasten.

dégraisser (degrɛse) *v.t*, to take off the grease (*or* fat) from; skim; scour.

dégras (degrɑ) *m*, dubbin[g].

degré (dəgre) *m*, degree; step, stair; grade; stage; pitch; extent.

dégrèvement (degrɛvmɑ̃) *m*, relief, reduction, cut (*taxes*). **dégrever** (grəve) *v.t*, to relieve; cancel; disencumber (*from mortgage*).

dégringolade (degrɛ̃gɔlad) *f*, tumble; collapse, slump. **dégringoler** (le) *v.t*, to rush down. **~ dans**, to tumble (*or* fall) down *or* into.

dégriser (degrize) *v.t*, to sober; disillusion.

dégrossir (degrosi:r) *v.t*, to rough down; rough-hew; sketch out; break in.

déguenillé, e (degnije) *a*, tattered, ragged.

dégueulasse (degœlas) *a*, disgusting (*food, person, etc.*). **dégueuler** (le) *v.i*, to vomit; spew out.

déguerpir (degɛrpi:r) *v.i*, to move out; pack off.

déguisement (degizmɑ̃) *m*, disguise; fancy dress. **déguiser** (ze) *v.t*, to disguise; conceal; change (*name*). **se ~**, to disguise oneself, masquerade.

dégustateur (degystatœ:r) *m*, taster. **dégustation** (sjɔ̃) *f*, tasting. **déguster** (te) *v.t*, to taste, sample.

déhanchement (deɑ̃ʃmɑ̃) *m*, waddle.

déharnacher (dearnaʃe) *v.t*, to unharness.

dehors (dəɔ:r) *ad*, out; outside; out of doors; in the offing. **¶ ~!** out! (*Box., etc.*). **de ~**, from without. **en ~**, *ad*, outside, outward; frank. **en ~ de**, *pr*, outside, without. **¶** *m*, outside, exterior; (*pl.*) outworks (*Mil.*); (*pl.*) grounds (*of mansion*); (*pl.*) appearances.

déifier (deifje) *v.t,* to deify. **dé- ité** (te) *f,* deity.

déjà (deʒa) *ad,* already; before.

déjection (deʒɛksjɔ̃) *f,* evacuation (*bowels*).

déjeter (deʒte) *v.t.* & se ~, to warp (*wood*); buckle.

déjeuner (deʒœne) *v.i,* to breakfast; lunch. ¶ *m,* breakfast set, b. service. *petit* ~, breakfast.

déjouer (deʒwe) *v.t,* to baffle, thwart, frustrate, foil, outwit, outmaneuver.

déjucher (deʒyʃe) (*fig.*) *v.i,* to come down; (*v.t.*) to bring down.

delà (dəla) *pr,* beyond. *au-~,* beyond; more. *au-~ de,* beyond; more. [*plus*] *en* ~, farther [off]. *par-~,* beyond. **l'au-~,** *m,* the beyond (*future life*).

délabré, e (delabre) *p.a,* dilapidated; brokendown; tumbledown; ramshackle, gimcrack. **dé- labrement** (brəmɑ̃) *m,* dilapidation; wreck. **délabrer** (bre) *v.t,* to dilapidate, shatter.

délacer (delase) *v.t,* to unlace.

délai (delɛ) *m,* time, extension [of time]; delay. ~ *de congé,* [term of] notice.

délaissement (delɛsmɑ̃) *m,* abandonment, desertion; destitution. **délaisser** (se) *v.t,* to forsake; abandon, desert; jilt.

délassement (delasmɑ̃) *m,* relaxation, recreation. **délasser** (se) *v.t.* & *abs,* to refresh, relax.

délateur, trice (delatœ:r, tris) *n,* informer.

délateur, trice (delatœ:r, tris) *n,* informer. **délation** (sjɔ̃) *f,* denunciation; squealing.

délaver (delave) *v.t,* to soak; dilute.

délayer (delɛje) *v.t,* to add water to, thin; spin out.

deleatur (deleaty:r) *m,* delete (*sign, Typ.*).

délecter (delɛkte) *v.t.* & se ~, to delight.

délégation (delegasjɔ̃) *f,* delegation, deputation. **délégué, e** (ge) *n,* delegate; deputy. **déléguer** (ge) *v.t,* to delegate, depute.

délester (delɛste) *v.t,* to unballast; relieve.

délétère (deletɛ:r) *a,* deleterious.

délibération (deliberasjɔ̃) *f,* deliberation, consideration, proceedings; transaction, business; decision, resolution. **délibéré†, e** (re) *a,* deliberate. **délibérer** (re) *v.i,* to deliberate, consult; (*v.t.*) to decide, resolve on. ~ *sur,* to consider, transact (*business at meeting*).

délicat, e† (delika, at) *a,* delicate; nice; refined; dainty, fastidious, squeamish; tender; ticklish, tricky. **délicatesse** (tɛs) *f,* delicacy.

délice (delis) *m,* delight, pleasure, luxury. ~*s, f.pl,* delight(s), pleasure(s), delectation. **délicieux, euse†** (sjø, ø:z) *a,* delicious; delightful; charming.

délictueux (deliktyø) *a,* unlawful, illegal, felonious.

délié, e (delje) *a,* thin, slender, slim; glib. ¶ *m,* thin stroke, up stroke. **délier** (lje) *v.t,* to untie; loose[n]; release.

délimiter (delimite) *v.t,* to delimit.

délinéation (delineasjɔ̃) *f,* delineation.

délinquant, e (delɛ̃kɑ̃, ɑ̃:t) *n,* delinquent, offender.

déliquescence (delikɥɛsɑ̃:s) *f,* deliquescence; corruption (*fig.*).

délirant, e (delirɑ̃, ɑ̃:t) *a,* delirious; frenzied. **délire** (li:r) *m,* delirium; frenzy. **délirer** (lire) *v.i,* to be delirious.

délit (deli) *m,* offense, misdemeanor. *en flagrant* ~, in the act.

délivrance (delivrɑ̃:s) *f,* deliverance; rescue; release; delivery; issue. **délivrer** (vre) *v.t,* to deliver; rescue; release; hand [over]; issue (*tickets*).

déloger (deloʒe) *v.i,* to [re]move; (*v.t.*) to turn out; dislodge.

déloyal, e† (delwajal) *a,* disloyal; unfair; dishonest. **déloyauté** (jote) *f,* disloyalty.

delta (dɛlta) *m,* delta.

déluge (dely:ʒ) *m,* deluge, flood; [down]pour.

déluré, e (delyre) *a,* wide-awake; knowing.

démagogue (demagɔg) *m*, demagogue.

démailler (demaje) *v.t*, to undo (*knitting*). se ~, to run (*stocking*).

demain (dəmɛ̃) *ad. & m*, tomorrow. ~ *matin*, tomorrow morning.

démancher (demɑ̃ʃe) *v.t*, to unhandle; dislocate.

demande (dəmɑ̃:d) *f*, request, desire; application; inquiry; demand; call; indent; claim; bid; instance; suit; proposal (*marriage*); question. ~ *d'emploi*, situation wanted. **demander** (mɑ̃de) *v.t*, to ask, a. for; request; charge; inquire; apply for; claim; want; bid [for]; beg; sue for. ~ *par voie d'annonces*, to advertise for. *on demande un . . .*, wanted a . . . se ~, to ask onself, wonder. **demandeur, euse** (dœ:r, ø:z) *n*, petitioner; applicant. **demandeur, eresse** (dœ:r, drɛs) *n*, plaintiff.

démangeaison (demɑ̃ʒɛzɔ̃) *f*, itch[ing]; urge; longing. **démanger** (ʒe) *v.i*, to itch; long. *le bras me démange*, my arm itches. *la langue lui démange*, he is itching (*or* longing) to speak.

démanteler (demɑ̃tle) *v.t*, to dismantle.

démantibuler (demɑ̃tibüle) *v.t*, to break to pieces.

démarcation (demarkasjɔ̃) *f*, demarcation.

démarche (demarʃ) *f*, gait, walk, bearing; step, measure. **démarcheur** (ʃœ:r) *m*, canvasser, runner, share pusher.

démarier (demarje) *v.t*, to unmarry; thin (*plants*).

démarquer (demarke) *v.t*, to mark down (*prices*); remove identification; plagiarize.

démarrage (demara:ʒ) *m*, unmooring; starting. ~ *à chaud, à froid*, warm start, cold start (*computers*). **démarrer** (re) *v.t*, to unmoor; (*v.i.*) to leave her moorings; cast off; start; stir. **démarreur** (œ:r) *m*, starter (*auto*).

démasquer (demaske) *v.t*, to unmask; uncover; show up.

démâter (demɑte) *v.t*, to dismast.

démêlé (demɛle) *m*, contention. **démêler** (le) *v.t*, to disentangle, unravel; comb out; quarrel about. *se ~ de*, to get out of. **démêloir** (lwa:r) *m*, rake comb.

démembrer (demɑ̃bre) *v.t*, to dismember.

déménagement (demenaʒmɑ̃) *m*, removal, moving. **déménager** (ʒe) *v.t. & abs*, to remove, move [out] (*house*); (*v.i.*) to be off; go off one's head. **déménageur** (ʒœ:r) *m*, removal contractor, [furniture] remover.

démence (demɑ̃:s) *f*, insanity, madness, dementia.

démener (se) (demne) *v.pr*, to throw oneself about; strive hard.

dément, e (demɑ̃, ɑ̃:t) *a. & n*, crazy, mad (*person*).

démenti (demɑ̃ti) *m*, denial, contradiction, lie; failure, disappointment. **démentir** (ti:r) *v.t.ir*, to give the lie to; contradict; belie.

démerder (se) (demɛrde) *v.i*, to manage somehow, figure something out; hurry up, get a move on (*slang*).

démérite (demerit) *m*, demerit, unworthiness. **démériter** (te) *v.i. & abs*, to deserve censure, offend.

démesuré†, e (dem[ə]zyre) *a*, inordinate; enormous, huge.

démettre (demɛtr) *v.t.ir*, to dislocate, put out of joint. se ~ de, to resign, retire.

demeurant (au) (dəmœrɑ̃), after all, in other respects. **demeure** (mœ:r) *f*, residence, dwelling, abode; delay. *à ~*, fixed, stationary, set. *en ~*, in arrears. **demeurer** (mœre) *v.i*, to reside, live, dwell; stay, remain, stop; lie.

demi, e (dəmi) *a*, half. demi, *ad*, half. ¶ *m*, half; halfback (*Foot.*); a beer (*ordered in a café*). à ~, *ad*, half, by halves.

demi (dəmi) *comps*: ~-*bas*, *m.pl*, half-hose. ~-*cercle*, *m*, semicircle. ~-*dieu*, *m*, demigod. ~-*finale*, *f*, semi-final. ~-*frère*, *m*, half-brother, stepbrother. ~-*gros*, *m*, small wholesale trade. *une* ~-*heure*, half an hour. ~-*jour*, *m*, half-light, twilight. ~-*lune*, *f*, crescent (*of buildings*). ~-*mot*, *m*, hint. **~-pensionnaire**, *n*, day boarder. **~-place**, *f*, half fare, half price. **~-relief**, *m*, mezzo-relievo. **~-sœur**, *f*, half-sister, stepsister. **en ~-solde**, on half pay (*Mil.*). **~-ton**, *m*, semitone. *à ~-voix*, in an undertone.

demie (dəmi) *f*, (a) half; half-hour; half past. *une heure & ~*, an hour & a half; half-past one.

démission (demisjɔ̃) *f*, resignation. **démissionner** (ɔne) *v.i*, to resign.

démobiliser (demɔbilize) *v.t*, to demobilize.

démocrate (demɔkrat) *m*, democrat. **démocratie** (si) *f*, democracy. **démocratique** (tik) *a*, democratic.

démodé, e (demɔde) *a*, old-fashioned; out of date.

demoiselle (dəmwazel) *f*, young lady; girl; single woman, maiden [lady], spinster; miss; damsel; dragon fly; beetle, rammer; rowlock. **~ de compagnie**, lady companion. **~ d'honneur**, bridesmaid.

démolir (demɔliːr) *v.t*, to demolish, break up; explode (*fig.*). **démolisseur** (lisœːr) *m*, breaker (*house, ship*); iconoclast. **démolition** (sjɔ̃) *f*, demolition; (*pl.*) demolitions.

démon (demɔ̃) *m*, demon, devil, fiend; demon; genius; imp. **~ familier**, familiar [spirit].

démonétiser (demɔnetize) *v.t*, to demonetize, call in; discredit.

démoniaque (demɔnjak) *a*, demoniac(al). ¶ *n*, demoniac.

démonstrateur (demɔ̃stratœːr) *m*, demonstrator. **démonstratif, ive** (tif, iːv) *a*, conclusive; demonstrative. **démonstration** (sjɔ̃) *f*, demonstration; proof. **~ par l'absurde**, reduction to absurdity, reductio ad absurdum.

démontable (demɔ̃tabl) *a*, sectional. **démonter** (te) *v.t*, to dismount; unhorse; throw; take to pieces; upset, nonplus.

démontrer (demɔ̃tre) *v.t*, to demonstrate, prove; show.

démoraliser (demɔralize) *v.t*, to demoralize

démordre (demɔrdr) *v.i*, to let go; desist.

démoscopie (demɔskɔpi) *f*, science of opinion-sounding of masses.

démunir (se) de (demyniːr), to part with.

démuseler (demyzle) *v.t*, to unmuzzle.

dénaturer (denatyre) *v.t*, to denature; pervert, render unnatural; distort; misrepresent.

dénébulateur (denebylatœːr) *m*, fog-dispersal device. **dénébulation** (lasjɔ̃) *f*, fog dispersal. **dénébuler** (le) *v.t*, to disperse fog.

dénégation (denegasjɔ̃) *f*, denial; disclaimer.

déni (deni) *m*, denial; refusal.

déniaiser (denjɛze) *v.t*, to sharpen (*wits*).

dénicher (denife) *v.t*, to take out of the nest; ferret out; (*v.i.*) to fly [away]. **dénicheur** (fœːr) *m*, birds'-nester; hunter (*curios*).

denier (dənje) *m*: **~ à Dieu**, earnest money; key money. **le ~ de la veuve**, the widow's mite. **le ~ de Saint-Pierre**, Peter's pence. **~s**, *pl*, money, funds.

dénier (denje) *v.t*, to deny; disclaim.

dénigrer (denigre) *v.t*, to disparage, run down, detract from.

dénombrement (denɔ̃brəmɑ̃) *m*, count; census.

dénominateur (denɔminatœːr) *m*, denominator. **dénommer** (me) *v.t*, to name, denominate.

dénoncer (denɔ̃se) *v.t*, to proclaim, declare; denounce, inform against. **dénonciation** (sjasjɔ̃) *f*, denunciation; information.

dénoter (denɔte) *v.t*, to denote, betoken.

dénouement (denumɑ̃) *m*, upshot; ending. **dénouer** (nwe) *v.t*, to untie, undo; loosen; unravel.

dénoyauter (denwajote) *v.t*, to pit (*fruit*).

denrée (dɑ̃re) *f*, oft. *pl*, commodity, produce. **~ alimentaire**, foodstuff.

dense (dɑ̃ːs) *a*, dense, close; thick. **densité** (dɑ̃site) *f*, density.

dent (dɑ̃) *f*, tooth; prong; cog; tusk; serration; [jagged] peak.

~s de dessous, de dessus, de devant, du fond, de lait, de sagesse, lower, upper, front, back, milk, wisdom, teeth. **dentaire** (tɛːr) a, dental (*Anat.*). **dental, e** (tal) a, dental (*Anat. & phonetics*). ¶ f, dental (*phonetics*). **denté, e** (te) a, toothed, cogged; dentate. ~ en scie, serrate. **denteler** (tle) v.t, to indent, notch, jag, serrate. **dentelle** (tɛl) f, lace; laced paper; tracery. ~ à l'aiguille, needle-made lace. ~ au point à l'aiguille, needle-point l. ~ aux fuseaux, pillow l. **dentelure** (tlyːr) f, indentation, serration. **dentier** (tje) m, set of (*artificial*) teeth, denture, [dental] plate. **dentifrice** (tifris) m, toothpaste; tooth powder. **dentiste** (tist) m, dentist; (*att.*) dental (*surgeon*). **dentition** (sjɔ̃) f, dentition, teething. **denture** (tyːr) f, set of (*natural*) teeth; teeth (*cogs*). ~ artificielle, denture, [dental] plate.

dénuder (denyde) v.t, to denude, bare, strip.

dénué, e (denɥe) a, devoid, destitute. **dénuement** (nymɑ̃) m, destitution, penury. **se dénuer de** (nɥe), to part with.

dépannage (depanaːʒ) m, auto repairs. **dépanner** (ne) v.t, to repair, help. **dépanneuse** (nøːz) f, tow truck.

dépaqueter (depakte) v.t, to unpack.

dépareillé, e (depareje) a, odd (*pair or set*). **dépareiller** (je) v.t, to break up (*a set*).

déparer (depare) v.t, to strip; spoil, mar; pick out the best.

déparler (deparle) v.i, with neg, to stop talking.

départ (depaːr) m, departure, sailing; start; parting (*Chem.*). faire le ~ entre, de, to discriminate between. ~ arrêté, standing start. ~ lancé, flying start. ~ usines, ex works, ex mill (*sales*).

départager (departaʒe) v.t, to decide between. ~ les voix, to give the casting vote.

département (departəmɑ̃) m, department; county; province, line. **départemental, e** (tal) a, departmental.

départir (departiːr) v.t.ir, to divide; part (*metals*); distribute, dispense, endow. **se ~**, to desist, swerve (*fig.*).

dépassement (depasmɑ̃) m, going beyond; excess.

dépasser (depase) v.t, to go beyond, go over, exceed, be above, top; turn (*a certain age*); pass, leave behind, overshoot, overreach; be longer; project beyond.

dépaver (depave) v.t, to unpave.

dépaysé, e (depeize) p.a, lost; among strangers; out of one's element. **dépayser** (ze) v.t, to remove from usual surroundings.

dépecer (depəse) v.t, to cut up; break up.

dépêche (depɛːʃ) f, dispatch; message; telegram. **dépêcher** (peʃe) v.t, to dispatch. **se ~**, to make haste, be quick, hurry up; look sharp.

dépeindre (depɛ̃ːdr) v.t.ir, to depict, portray, delineate, picture.

dépenaillé, e (depnaje) a, in rags; ill-dressed.

dépendance (depɑ̃dɑ̃ːs) f, dependence; subjection; dependency; outbuilding, outhouse; annex[e]. **dépendant, e** (dɑ̃, ɑ̃ːt) a, dependent. **dépendre** (pɑ̃ːdr) v.i, to depend, belong; be a dependency (*de* = of); to take down, to unhang.

dépens (depɑ̃) m.pl, expense; [law] costs. **dépense** (pɑ̃ːs) f, expense, charge, cost, expenditure; efflux; steward's room. ~ de bouche, living expenses. **dépenser** (pɑ̃se) v.t, to spend, expend. **dépensier, ère** (sje, ɛːr) a, extravagant, thriftless. ¶ n, spendthrift; bursar.

déperdition (depɛrdisjɔ̃) f, waste, loss.

dépérir (deperiːr) v.i, to dwindle, pine away, wither, decay.

dépêtrer (depɛtre) v.t, to extricate.

dépeupler (depœple) v.t, to depopulate; unstock.

déphasage (defazaːʒ) m, phase displacement (*Elec.*); lag (*cultural, social, etc.*). **déphasé** (ze) a, disoriented.

dépiler (depile) *v.t*, to depilate, pluck; unhair.

dépiquer (depike) *v.t*, to unquilt; transplant; thresh (*grain*); cheer up.

dépister (depiste) *v.t*, to track down, run to earth; throw off the scent, foil.

dépit (depi) *m*, spite, spleen, despite. **dépiter** (te) *v.t*, to vex; spite.

déplacé, e (deplase) *a*, out of place, ill-timed; uncalled for. **déplacement** (smɑ̃) *m*, displacement, removal, shift[ing]; traveling. **déplacer** (se) *v.t*, to displace; [re]move, shift.

déplaire (deplɛːr) *v.i.ir*, to be displeasing, offend. ~ à, to displease. se ~, to be unhappy; not to thrive. **déplaisant, e** (plɛzɑ̃, ɑ̃ːt) *a*, unpleasing, unpleasant. **déplaisir** (ziːr) *m*, displeasure.

déplanter (deplɑ̃te) *v.t*, to take up. **déplantoir** (twaːr) *m*, trowel (*Hort.*).

dépliant (depliɑ̃) *m*, folder. **déplier** (plie) *v.t*, to unfold.

déplisser (deplise) *v.t*, to unpleat, iron out.

déploiement (deplwamɑ̃) *m*, unfolding; deployment.

déplorable† (deplɔrabl) *a*, deplorable. **déplorer** (re) *v.t*, to deplore, bewail.

déployer (deplwaje) *v.t*, to unfold; unfurl; deploy; spread [out]; expand; display.

déplumer (deplyme) *v.t*, to pluck, deplume. se ~, to molt.

déplu, *p.p*, déplaire.

dépolir (depoliːr) *v.t*, to take the surface off. *verre dépoli*, ground glass, frosted glass.

dépolitisation (depolitizasjɔ̃) *f*, depoliticization. **dépolitiser** (tize) *v.t*, to depoliticize.

dépolluer (depolye) *v.t*, to cleanse, depollute.

déportements (depɔrtəmɑ̃) *m.pl*, misconduct.

déporter (depɔrte) *v.t*, to deport; transport (*convict*). se ~, to withdraw claims (*law*).

déposant, e (depozɑ̃, ɑ̃ːt) *n*, deponent; depositor, customer (*bank*). **dépose** (poːz) *f*, taking

up; t. down; t. off. **déposer** (poze) *v.t*, to lay down; l. aside; deposit, place, lodge, hand in; file, lay; depose; register (*trade mark*); prefer; take up, t. down, t. off. se ~, to settle. **dépositaire** (pozitɛːr) *n*, depositary; trustee; storer (*furniture warehouseman*). **déposition** (sjɔ̃) *f*, deposition; evidence.

déposséder (deposede) *v.t*, to dispossess, oust.

dépôt (depo) *m*, deposit; deposition; trust; handing in; filing; depot, store[house], warehouse, repository, depository; shed; yard; cells (*prison*); sediment. *en ~*, on sale [or return]; in bond.

dépoter (depɔte) *v.t*, to plant out; decant.

dépotoir (depɔtwaːr) *m*, refuse dump; refuse disposal plant.

dépouille (depuːj) *f*, slough (*serpent, worm*); skin (*wild beast*); spoil; remains (*mortal*). **dépouiller** (puje) *v.t*, to skin; cast (*skin*); strip, divest, despoil; go through; analyze; count (*votes*). se ~, to slough, cast its skin; shed its leaves.

dépourvoir (depurvwaːr) *v.t.ir*, to deprive. **dépourvu, e** (vy) *p.a*, destitute, bereft, devoid. *au dépourvu*, *ad*, unawares, napping.

dépravation (depravasjɔ̃) *f*, depravation; depravity. **dépraver** (ve) *v.t*, to deprave, vitiate.

dépréciation (depresjasjɔ̃) *f*, depreciation. **déprécier** (sje) *v.t*, to depreciate, underrate, undervalue, disparage.

déprédation (depredasjɔ̃) *f*, depredation.

déprendre (se) (deprɑ̃ːdr) *v.pr.ir*, to break away, part.

dépression (deprɛsjɔ̃) *f*, depression. ~ *nerveuse*, nervous breakdown. **déprimer** (prime) *v.t*, to depress; dispirit.

depuis (dəpɥi) *pr. & ad*, since, for, from. ~ *quand?* how long? *since when?* ~ *que, c*, since.

députation (depytasjɔ̃) *f*, deputation; membership (*parliament*). **député** (te) *m*, deputy; congressman; delegate. **députer** (te) *v.t*, to depute.

déraciné, e (derasine) (*pers.*) *n*, fish out of water. **déraciner** (ne) *v.t*, to uproot, eradicate.

déraidir (se) (derɛdiːr) (*fig.*) *v.pr*, to unbend, thaw.

dérailler (derɑje) *v.i*, to derail; go astray (*fig.*). **dérailleur** (rɑjœːr) *m*, bicycle gearshift; shifting track (*Rly.*).

déraison (derɛzɔ̃) *f*, unreason- [ableness]. **déraisonnable†** (zɔ- nabl) *a*, unreasonable, prepos- terous. **déraisonner** (ne) *v.i*, to talk nonsense.

dérangement (derɑ̃ʒmɑ̃) *m*, derangement; disturbance; fault. **déranger** (ʒe) *v.t*, to disarrange; disturb; upset; trouble; put out of order; derange, unsettle.

déraper (derape) *v.t. & i*, to trip (*anchor*); skid; side-slip.

déréaliser (derealize) *v.t*, to strip of psychological reality.

déréglé, e (deregle) *a*, out of order; lawless. **déréglement** (rɛgləmɑ̃) *m*, disordered state; irregularity; derangement; prof- ligacy. **dérégler** (regle) *v.t*, to put out of order; derange; disorder.

dérider (deride) *v.t*, to smooth, unwrinkle; cheer up.

dérision (derizjɔ̃) *f*, derision. **dé- risoire** (zwaːr) *a*, derisory, laugh- able.

dérivation (derivasjɔ̃) *f*, deriva- tion; deflection; loop [line]; flume; shunt (*Elec.*). **dérive** (riːv) *f*, leeway; drift; breakaway. **en ~, à la ~**, adrift **dérivé** (ve) *m*, derivative. **dériver** (ve) *v.t*, to divert; shunt (*Elec.*); unrivet; (*v.i.*) to be derived; spring, origi- nate; drift, drive (*Naut.*).

dernier, ère (dɛrnje, ɛːr) *a*, last; hindmost; latter; late; latest; fi- nal; closing; junior (*partner*); highest; utmost; extreme; dire; lowest, worst. *dernier cri*, latest [thing out]. *dernier jugement*, crack of doom. *dernières gale- ries*, gallery (*Theat.*) *dernière main*, finishing touches. **der- nièrement** (njɛrmɑ̃) *ad*, lately, latterly, not long ago.

dérobé, e (derɔbe) *a*, secret, hid-

den, concealed; spare (*time*). **à la dérobée**, *ad*, by stealth, on the sly. **dérober** (be) *v.t*, to steal, rob; snatch; conceal, hide. *se ~ à*, to shirk. *se ~ de*, to steal away from. *se ~ sous*, to give way under.

déroger (derɔʒe) *v.i*, to derogate.

dérouiller (deruje) *v.t*, to rub off the rust from; beat up, punish. *se ~*, to stretch (*muscles, legs*).

déroulement (derulmɑ̃) *m*, un- folding; development; passing. **dérouler** (rule) *v.t*, to unroll, un- fold; evolve.

déroute (derut) *f*, rout; ruin. *mettre en ~*, to rout. **dérouter** (te) *v.t*, to lead astray; baffle, nonplus.

derrière (dɛrjɛːr) *pr. & ad*, be- hind; aft; astern. ¶ *m*, back; rear; hinder part; tail (*cart*).

derviche (dɛrviʃ) *ou* **dervis** (vi) *m*, dervish.

des *see* **de**.

dès (dɛ) *pr*, from; since. *~ à présent*, from now onward. *~ lors*, ever since then; consequent- ly. *~ que, c*, as soon as.

désabonner (se) (dezabɔne) *v.pr*, to discontinue one's sub- scription *or* season ticket.

désabuser (dezabyze) *v.t*, to dis- abuse, undeceive.

désaccord (dezakɔːr) *m*, disagree- ment; discord (*Mus.*). **désaccor- der** (kɔrde) *v.t*, to put out of tune. *se ~*, to break their en- gagement (*marriage*).

désaccoupler (dezakuple) *v.t*, to uncouple.

désaccoutumer (dezakutyme) *v.t*, to break of the habit.

désaffection (dezafɛksjɔ̃) *f*, dis- affection.

désagréable† (dezagreabl) *a*, disagreeable, unpleasant. *~ au goût*, distasteful; unpalatable.

désagréger (dezagreʒe) *v.t*, to disintegrate, weather.

désagrément (dezagremɑ̃) *m*, source of annoyance; unpleasant- ness; vexation.

désajuster (dezaʒyste) *v.t*, to de- range; disarrange.

désaltérer (dezaltere) *v.t*, to quench (*someone's*) thirst.

désamorcer (dezamɔrse) *v.t*, to unprime.

désappointement (dezapwɛ̃tmã) *m*, disappointment. **désappointer** (te) *v.t*, to disappoint.

désapprendre (dezaprã:dr) *v.t. & abs. ir*, to forget; unlearn.

désapprobation (dezaprɔbasjɔ̃) *f*, disapprobation, disapproval. **désapprouver** (pruve) *v.t*, to disapprove [of], frown [up]on.

désarçonner (dezarsɔne) *v.t*, to unseat, unhorse, throw; silence, floor.

désarmement (dezarməmã) *m*, disarmament; laying up (*ship*). **désarmer** (me) *v.t. & i*, to disarm, unarm; uncock (*gun*); lay up.

désarroi (dezarwa) *m*, disarray, disorder.

désassembler (dezasãble) *v.t*, to take to pieces, disconnect, disjoint.

désastre (dezastr) *m*, disaster. **désastreux, euse** (trø, ø:z), *a*, disastrous.

désavantage (dezavãta:ʒ) *m*, disadvantage, drawback. **désavantager** (taʒe) *v.t*, to place at a disadvantage, handicap. **désavantageux, euse†** (ʒø, ø:z) *a*, disadvantageous.

désaveu (dezavø) *m*, disavowal, denial, disclaimer. **désavouer** (vwe) *v.t*, to disavow; disown; disclaim; disapprove.

desceller (desele) *v.t*, to unseal.

descendance (desãdã:s) *f*, descent, lineage; descendants. **descendant, e** (dã, ã:t) *a*, descending, downward; down (*train, etc.*); outgoing (*tide*). ¶ *n*, descendant; (*pl.*) progeny. **descendre** (sã:dr) *v.i. & t*, to descend, go down; alight, dismount, get down; stay, stop, put up (*at a hotel*); lower; drop; fall; sink; make a descent; kill (*slang*). ~ [à terre], to land. ~ *en vol plané*, to plane down. **descente** (sã:t) *f*, descent; fall; lowering; slope, incline; downpipe; raid (*of depositors on bank*). ~ *de bain*, bath mat. ~ *de justice*, domiciliary visit. ~ *de lit*, bedside rug.

description (dɛskripsjɔ̃) *f*, description; inventory.

désemparer (dezãpare) *v.t*, to disable (*ship*); quit, leave. *sans* ~, on the spot, there & then; without intermission, continuous(ly).

désemplir (dezãpli:r) *v.t*, to partly empty; (*v.i.*) to empty. *ne pas* ~, to be always full.

désenchanter (dezãʃãte) *v.t*, to disenchant; disillusion.

désencombrer (dezãkɔ̃bre) *v.t*, to disencumber, clear.

désenfiler (dezãfile) *v.t*, to unthread.

désenfler (dezãfle) *v.t*, to deflate; (*v.i.*) to go down (*swelling*).

désenivrer (dezãnivre) *v.t*, to sober. *il ne désenivre point*, he is never sober.

désennuyer (dezãnɥije) *v.t*, to divert, amuse.

désenrhumer (dezãryme) *v.t*, to cure of a cold. **désenrouer** (rwe) *v.t*, to cure of hoarseness.

déséquilibré, e (dezekilibre) *a*, unbalanced.

désert, e (dezɛːr, ɛrt) *a*, desert; deserted, empty, desolate. ¶ *m*, desert, wilderness. **déserter** (zerte) *v.t. & abs*, to desert, forsake. ~ *de*, to leave. **déserteur** (tœ:r) *m*, deserter. **désertion** (sjɔ̃) *f*, desertion. **désertique** (tik) *a*, desert.

désespérance (dezɛsperã:s) *f*, despair. **désespérant, e** (rã, ã:t) *a*, heartbreaking. **désespéré†, e** (re) *a*, desperate, hopeless. ¶ *n*, desperate man, woman, madman. **désespérer** (re) *v.i. & abs*, to despair; (*v.t.*) to drive to despair. **désespoir** (pwa:r) *m*, despair; desperation.

désétatiser (dezetatize) *v.t*, to return to the private sector.

déshabillé (dɛzabije) *m*, undress, dishabille; wrap; true colors (*fig.*). **déshabiller** (je) *v.t*, to undress, disrobe, strip; lay bare (*fig.*).

déshabituer (dezabitɥe) *v.t*, to break of the habit.

déshérence (dezerã:s) *f*, escheat.

déshériter (dezerite) *v.t*, to disinherit.

déshonnête† (dezɔnɛːt) *a*, indecent, immodest.

déshonneur (dezɔnœːr) *m*, dishonor, disgrace. **déshonorant, e** (norã, ãːt) *a*, dishonorable, discreditable. **déshonorer** (re) *v.t*, to dishonor, disgrace.

déshydrater (dezidrate) *v.t*, to dehydrate. **déshydrateur** (tœːr) *m*, dehydrator.

desiderata (deziderata) *m.pl*, desiderata, wants.

désigner (deziɲe) *v.t*, to designate; indicate, point out; describe; nominate; appoint. **désignation** (ɲasjɔ̃) *f*, designation.

désillusionner (dezilyzjɔne) *v.t*, to disillusion, undeceive.

désincorporer (dezɛ̃kɔrpore) *v.t*, to disincorporate, disembody.

désinence (dezinãːs) *f*, ending (*word*).

désinfectant (dezɛ̃fɛktã) *m*, disinfectant. **désinfecter** (te) *v.t*, to disinfect, deodorize. **désinfection** (sjɔ̃) *f*, disinfection.

désintégration (dezɛ̃tegrasjɔ̃) *f*, disintegration, breaking up; splitting (*atom*). **désintegrer** (gre) *v.t*, to crush, break up; split, smash (*atom*).

désintéressé, e (dezɛ̃terɛse) *a*, not implicated; disinterested; candid; unselfish. **désintéressement** (smã) *m*, disinterestedness; unselfishness. **désintéresser** (se) *v.t*, to buy out, satisfy, pay off. *se* ~ *de*, to take no further interest in.

désinviter (dezɛ̃vite) *v.t*, to ask not to come.

désinvolte (dezɛ̃vɔlt) *a*, easy. **désinvolture** (tyːr) *f*, unconstraint; free & easy manner.

désir (deziːr) *m*, desire, wish. **désirable** (zirabl) *a*, desirable. **désirer** (re) *v.t. & abs*, to desire, want, be desirous of, wish, w. for. **désireux, euse** (rø, øːz) *a*, desirous, wishful, anxious.

désistement (dezistəmã) *m*, waiver (*law*); withdrawal. se **désister de** (te), to waive; withdraw from; stand down from (*candidacy*).

désobéir (dezɔbeiːr) *v.i. & abs*, to disobey. ~ *à*, to disobey (*v.t.*). **désobéissance** (isãːs) *f*, disobedience. **désobéissant, e** (sã, ãːt) *a*, disobedient.

désobligeance (dezɔbliʒãːs) *f*, disobligingness, unkindness. **désobligeant, e** (ʒã, ãːt) *a*, disobliging, unkind, ungracious. **désobliger** (ʒe) *v.t*, to disoblige.

désobstruer (dezɔpstrye) *v.t*, to clear.

désoccupé, e (dezɔkype) *a*, unoccupied.

désœuvré, e (dezœvre) *a*, idle, at a loose end. ¶ *n*, idler. **désœuvrement** (vrəmã) *m*, idleness.

désolation (dezɔlasjɔ̃) *f*, desolation. **désolé, e** (le) *p.a*, desolate; disconsolate, forlorn, distressed, extremely sorry. **désoler** (le) *v.t*, to desolate, distress, grieve.

désopilant, e (dezɔpilã, ãːt) *a*, highly amusing.

désordonné, e (dezɔrdɔne) *a*, untidy; disorderly; inordinate. **désordre** (dr) *m*, disorder; disorderliness. ~*s*, riots.

désorganiser (dezɔrganize) *v.t*, to disorganize.

désorienter (dezɔrjãte) *v.t*, to disconcert, bewilder.

désormais (dezɔrmɛ) *ad*, henceforth; hereafter.

désosser (dezose) *v.t*, to bone; take apart (*mechanism, etc.*).

despote (dɛspɔt) *m*, despot. **despotique†** (tik) *a*, despotic. **despotisme** (tism) *m*, despotism.

desquels, desquelles, *see* lequel.

dessaisir (desɛziːr) *v.t*, to release; dispossess, deprive; unlash (*Naut.*).

dessaler (dɛsale) *v.t*, to unsalt; soak (*meat*); sharpen wits.

dessécher (deseʃe) *v.t*, to desiccate; dry up, drain; wither, parch. **dessèchement** (sɛʃmã) *m*, desiccation, etc.

dessein (dɛsɛ̃) *m*, design, plan, project; purpose. *à* ~, on purpose, designedly.

desseller (desɛle) *v.t*, to unsaddle.

desserrer (desɛre) *v.t*, to loosen, slack[en]; open.

dessert (desɛ:r) *m*, dessert (*dessert, cheese, fruit*).

desserte (desert) *f*, duties. **desservir** (vi:r) *v.t.ir*, to serve; minister to (*Eccl.*). ~ [*la table*], to clear the table.

dessiccation (dɛsikasjɔ̃) *f*, dessiccation.

dessiller (desije) *v.t*, to open (*eyes*) (*fig.*).

dessin (desɛ̃) *m*, drawing, sketching; design, pattern; sketch; cartoon; plan. ~ *à carreaux*, check [pattern]. ~ *à main levée*, freehand drawing. ~ *au trait*, outline d. ~ *industriel*, mechanical d. ~ *ombré*, shaded d. ~ *animé*, animated cartoon. **dessinateur, trice** (sinatœ:r, tris) *n*, sketcher; drawer; draftsman; cartoonist; designer. ~ *de jardins*, landscape gardener. **dessiner** (sine) *v.t*, to draw, sketch; design; show; outline. se ~, to stand out; show up; loom; take shape.

dessoûler (desule) *v.t*, to sober. *il ne dessoule jamais*, he is never sober.

dessous (dəsu) *ad. & pr*, under; under it, them; underneath; beneath, below. *au-~* (otsu) *ad*, under[neath], below. *au-~ de*, *pr*, below, under, beneath. *en ~*, *ad*, underneath; underhand; stealthily; sly. *là-~*, *ad*, under there, under that, underneath. *par-~*, *pr. & ad*, under[neath], beneath. ¶ *m*, under part, underside, bottom; face (*card*); wrong side (*fabric*); worst of it (*fig.*); (*pl.*) underclothing, underwear (*women's*). ~ *de plat*, table mat.

dessus (dəsy) *ad*, over, above; on, upon, [up]on it, them. *au-~* (otsy) *ad*, above [it], over it; upwards. *au-~ de*, *pr*, above, over; beyond. *en ~*, *ad*, on [the] top. *là-~*, *ad*, on that, thereon; thereupon. *par-~*, *pr. & ad*, over; into. *par-~ bord*, overboard. ¶ *m*, upper part; top; back (*hand*); treble (*Mus.*), soprano; right side (*fabric*); *prendre le ~*, to get the upper hand, mastery, whip hand; best of it. ~ *de coussin*, cushion cover. ~ *de fourneau*, top of grate. ~ *de plateau*, tray cloth. ~

de lit, bedspread. ~ *du panier*, pick of the basket.

destin (dɛstɛ̃) *m*, destiny, fate, lot, doom. **destinataire** (tinatɛ:r) *n*, consignee; receiver, recipient; addressee. *aux risques & périls du* ~, at owner's risk. **destination** (sjɔ̃) *f*, destination; purpose. *à* ~ *de*, [bound] for. **destinée** (ne) *f*, destiny, lot. **destiner** (ne) *v.t*, to destine, design, intend, mean; allot, assign; fate, doom.

destitué, e (dɛstitɥe) *p.a*, devoid, lacking. **destituer** (tɥe) *v.t*, to dismiss, remove, displace. **destitution** (tysjɔ̃) *f*, dismissal; removal.

destructeur, trice (destryktœ:r, tris) *a*, destructive. ¶ *n*, destroyer. **destructif, ive** (tif, i:v) *a*, destructive. **destruction** (sjɔ̃) *f*, destruction.

désuet, te (desɥe, ɛt) *a*, obsolete. ~ *calculée*, planned obsolescence. **désuétude** (sɥetyd) *f*, disuse.

désunion (dezynjɔ̃) *f*, disunion. **désunir** (ni:r) *v.t*, to disunite.

détachement (detaʃmɑ̃) *m*, detachment; detail (*men*). **détacher** (ʃe) *v.t*, to detach, untie, undo, unfasten; take off, t. down; detail (*Mil.*). se ~, to come away; break off; b. away; stand out.

détail (detaj) *m*, detail, particular; retail. **détaillant, e** (tajɑ̃, ɑ̃:t) *n*, retailer. **détailler** (je) *v.t*, to cut up; retail, peddle; detail.

détaler (detale) *v.i*, to make off, scamper away.

détaxer (detakse) *v.t*, to return (*or* remit) the duties (*or* charges) on; untax.

détecteur (detɛktœ:r) *m*, detector (*radio*). **détective** (ti:v) *m*, detective.

déteindre (detɛ̃:dr) *v.t. & i. tr*, to fade. ~ *sur*, to come off on (*dye*); influence.

dételer (detle) *v.t. & abs*, to unharness; unyoke; ease off, stop.

détendre (detɑ̃:dr) *v.t. & abs. & se* ~, to unbend, slack[en], relax, expand; take down.

détenir (detni:r) *v.t.ir*, to hold; detain.

détente (detɑ̃:t) *f*, relaxation; expansion; trigger.

détenteur, trice (detɑ̃tœːr, tris) *n*, holder (*pers.*). **détention** (sjɔ̃) *f*, holding; detention, detainment. **détenu, e** (tny) *n*, prisoner.

détergent (detɛrʒɑ̃) *a*, detergent (*Med.*). ¶ *m*, detergent, cleansing product.

détérioration (deterjɔrasjɔ̃) *f*, deterioration, impairment, damage, dilapidation. **se détériorer** (re) *v.pr*, to deteriorate.

détermination (detɛrminasjɔ̃) *f*, determination; resolution; resolve. **déterminé, e** (ne) *a*, determinate, definite; determined, resolute; keen; specific. **déterminer** (ne) *v.t*, to determine; fix; decide (upon); resolve; bring about. **se ~**, to resolve, make up one's mind.

déterrer (detɛre) *v.t*, to unearth, dug up; disinter, exhume.

détestable (detɛstabl) *a*, detestable. **détester** (te) *v.t*, to detest, hate.

détonation (detɔnasjɔ̃) *f*, detonation, report. **détoner** (ne) *v.i*, to detonate.

détonner (detɔne) *v.i*, to be (*or* sing) (*or* play) out of tune; sing flat; jar; be out of keeping; be out of one's element.

détordre (detɔrdr) *v.t*, to untwist. **détors, e** (tɔːr, ɔrs) *a*, untwisted. **détortiller** (tɔrtije) *v.t*, to untwist; disentangle.

détour (detuːr) *m*, winding; turn-[ing]; detour; dodge. *sans ~*, straightforwardly. **détourné, e** (turne) *a*, by (*road*); roundabout, circuitous, devious. **détourner** (ne) *v.t*, to divert, deflect, distract; turn aside, avert; deter; twist; dissuade; make away with, misappropriate, misapply, embezzle, peculate; abduct. **détournement** (nəmɑ̃) *m*, diversion, etc.

détracteur (detraktœːr) *m*, detractor.

détraquer (detrake) *v.t*, to derange.

détrempe (detrɑ̃ːp) *f*, distemper (*paint*); softening (*steel*). *peindre à la ~*, to distemper. **détremper** (trɑ̃pe) *v.t*, to soak, sodden, dilute; soften.

détresse (detrɛs) *f*, distress; straits.

détriment (detrimɑ̃) *m*, detriment, prejudice.

détritus (detrityːs) *m*, detritus, litter, rubbish.

détroit (detrwa) *m*, strait, straits; sound. *le ~ de Gibraltar, de Pas de Calais*, the Straits of Gibraltar, of Dover.

détromper (detrɔpe) *v.t*, to undeceive.

détrôner (detrone) *v.t*, to dethrone.

détrousser (detruse) *v.t*, to rob. **détrousseur** (sœːr) *m*, footpad.

détruire (detrɥiːr) *v.t. & abs.*, to demolish; destroy; ruin.

dette (dɛt) *f*, debt; indebtedness. *~ [active]*, assets. *~ [passive]*, liabilities.

deug *or* **D.E.U.G.** (dœg) *m*, diploma (*diplôme d'études universitaires générales*); similar to that of community or junior college.

deuil (dœːj) *m*, mourning; bereavement; mourners. *conduire le ~*, to be chief mourner. *~ de veuve*, widow's weeds.

Deutéronome (døteronom) *m*, Deuteronomy.

deux (dø; *in liaison* døz) *a*, two; second; a (*word, line*); a few (*steps*). *tous les ~ jours*, every other day. *~ jumeaux, elles jumelles*, twins. ¶ *m*, two; deuce (*cards, dice*). **deuxième†** (døzjɛm) *a. & n*, second. *~ de change*, second of exchange.

deux-points (døpwɛ̃) *m*, colon.

dévaler (devale) *v.i. & t*, to go down.

dévaliser (devalize) *v.t*, to rifle, strip, rob.

dévaluation (devalɥasjɔ̃) *f*, devaluation.

devancer (dəvɑ̃se) *v.t*, to get the start of; precede; forestall; outstrip, outdo, outrival. **devancier, ère** (sje, ɛːr) *n*, predecessor.

devant (dəvɑ̃) *ad*, before, in front, ahead. ¶ *pr*, before, in front of, ahead of. *aller au-de*, to go to meet; anticipate. *par~*, *ad. & pr*, in front, before; in the presence of. ¶ *m*, front; fore; frontage; (*pl.*) foreground;

devanture (d[ə]vãty:r) *f*, front (*store, etc.*); window (*store*).

dévastateur, trice (devasta-tœ:r, tris) *a*, devastator. **dévastation** (sjɔ̃) *f*, devastation. **dévaster** (te) *v.t*, to devastate.

déveine (devɛn) *f*, bad luck.

développateur (devlɔpatœ:r) *m*, developer (*proper*) (*Phot.*). **développement** (pmã) *m*, opening out; spread; growth; development; evolution (*Geom.*); gear (*bicycle*). **développer** (pe) *v.t*, to open out; unwrap; develop.

devenir (dəvni:r) *v.i.ir*, to become; grow; wax; go; get.

dévergondage (devɛrgɔ̃da:ʒ) *m*, licentiousness; extravagance (*fig.*). **dévergondé, e** (de) *a. & n*, licentious, shameless, profligate (person).

déverrouiller (devɛruje) *v.t*, to unbolt.

devers (dəvɛ:r): *par~, pr*, by, before.

dévers, e (devɛ:r, ɛrs) *a*, out of plumb, out of true. ¶ *m*, cant. **déverser** (vɛrse) *v.t*, to warp; incline; discharge; pour. **déversoir** (swa:r) *m*, weir.

dévêtir (se) (deveti:r) *v.pr.ir*, to strip, undress; leave off some of one's (*warm*) clothes.

déviation (devjasjɔ̃) *f*, deviation; deflection; detour. *~ de la colonne vertébrale*, curvature of the spine.

dévider (devide) *v.t*, to wind, reel; unwind. **dévidoir** (dwa:r) *m*, reel, spool.

dévier (devje) *v.i*, to deviate, swerve; curve (*spine*); (*v.t.*) to deflect, curve.

devin, ineresse (dəvɛ̃, vinrɛs) *n*, diviner, soothsayer. **deviner** (vine) *v.t, & abs*, to divine; guess. **devinette** (nɛt) *f*, riddle, conundrum.

devis (dəvi) *m*, chat, talk; estimate; specification; manifest (*stowage*).

dévisager (devizaʒe) *v.t*, to stare at.

devise (dəvi:z) *f*, device; motto. *~ [étrangère]*, [foreign] currency, [f.] bill, [f.] exchange. *~ publicitaire*, slogan.

deviser (dəvize) *v.i*, to chat.

dévisser (devise) *v.t*, to unscrew.

dévoiement (devwamã) *m*, looseness (*bowels*).

dévoiler (devwale) *v.t*, to unveil; reveal, disclose.

devoir (dəvwa:r) *m*, duty; exercise; (*pl.*) homework; (*pl.*) respects. ¶ *v.t. & abs. ir*, to owe. *Followed by infinitive*: should, ought; must, have to; am to.

dévolu, e (devɔly) *a*, devolved, vested.

dévorant, e (devɔrã, ã:t) *a*, ravenous; consuming; wasting; devouring. **dévorer** (re) *v.t*, to devour, lap up; swallow; stifle.

dévot, e† (devo, ɔt) *a*, devout, devotional; religious; sanctimonious. ¶ *n*, devout person; devotee. **dévotion** (vosjɔ̃) *f*, devotion, devoutness.

dévouement (devumã) *m*, devotion, self-sacrifice. **dévouer** (vwe) *v.t*, to dedicate; devote.

dévoyer (se) (devwaje) *v.pr*. (*Conjugated like envoyer, except Future* je dévoierai), to go astray (*fig.*).

dextérité (dɛksterite) *f*, dexterity, skill.

dextrine (dɛkstrin) *f*, dextrin.

diabète (djabɛt) *m*, diabetes.

diable (djɑ:bl) *m*, devil, deuce; dolly, truck. ¶ *i*, the devil! the deuce! the dickens! *au ~ vauvert*, a long way off, to hell and gone. **diablerie** (djablǝri) *f*, devilry, devilment. **diablesse** (blɛs) *f*, shedevil. **diablotin** (blɔtɛ̃) *m*, little devil, imp. **diabolique†** (bɔlik) *a*, diabolic(al), devilish, fiendish.

diabolo (djabɔlo) *m*, dolly, twin-wheel assembly (*automotive*).

diacre (djakr) *m*, deacon.

diacritique (djakritik) *a*, diacritical.

diadème (djadɛm) *m*, diadem.

diagnostic (djagnɔstik) *m*, diagnosis. **diagnostiquer** (ke) *v.t*, to diagnose.

diagonal, e† (djagɔnal) *a. & f*, diagonal.

diagramme (djagram) *m*, diagram, chart.

dialecte (djalɛkt) *m*, dialect.

dialectique (djalɛktik) *f*, dialectics.

dialogue (djalɔg) *m*, dialogue. **dialoguer** (ge) *v.i*, to converse; write in dialogue. **dialogiste** (gist) *m*, scriptwriter, screenwriter.

diamant (djamɑ̃) *m*, diamond.

diamétral, e† (djametral) *a*, diametric. **diamètre** (mɛtr) *m*, diameter.

diane (djan) *f*, reveille (*Mil.*).

diantre (djɑ̃:tr) *m*, the deuce.

diapason (djapazɔ̃) *m*, diapason, pitch; compass, range. ~ *à bouche*, pitch pipe. ~ *à branches*, tuning fork. ~ *normal*, concert pitch.

diaphane (djafan) *a*, diaphanous.

diaphragme (djafragm) *m*, diaphragm; stop.

diapositive (djapozitiv) *f*, color slide, transparency. (*sometimes* diapo (djapo) *f*.).

diaprer (djapre) *v.t*, to diaper, variegate. *étoffe diaprée*, diaper.

diarrhée (djare) *f*, diarrhea.

diatonique (djatɔnik) *a*, diatonic.

diatribe (djatrib) *f*, diatribe.

dictateur (diktatœ:r) *m*, dictator. **dictatorial,** e (tɔrjal) *a*, dictatorial. **dictature** (ty:r) *f*, dictatorship.

dictée (dikte) *f*, dictation. **dicter** (te) *v.t. & abs*, to dictate **diction** (sjɔ̃) *f*, diction, delivery. **dictionnaire** (ɔnɛ:r) *m*, dictionary. ~ *géographique*, gazetteer. **dicton** (tɔ̃) *m*, saying, dictum; saw, byword.

didactique (didaktik) *a*, didactic.

dièse (djɛ:z) *m*, sharp (*Mus.*).

diète (djet) *f*, diet. ~ *absolue*, starvation d. **mettre à la ~,** *v.t*, **faire ~,** *v.i*, to diet.

Dieu (djø) *m*, God; goodness! **d~,** god.

diffamation (difamasjɔ̃) *f*, defamation, libel, slander. **diffamatoire** (twa:r) & **diffamant,** e (mɑ̃, ɑ̃:t) *a*, defamatory, etc. **diffamer** (me) *v.t*, to defame, malign.

différé (difere) *a*, deferred; offline (*computers*). *émission en ~*, prerecorded broadcast.

différemment (diferamɑ̃) *ad*, differently. **différence** (rɑ̃:s) *f*, difference; odds. **différencier** (rɑ̃sje) *v.t*, to differentiate. **différend** (rɑ̃) *m*, difference, dispute. **différent,** e (rɑ̃, ɑ̃:t) *a*, different, various. **différentiel, le** (rɑ̃sjɛl) *a. & m*, differential. **différer** (re) *v.t. & abs*, to defer, delay, put off, postpone, hold over, tarry; (*v.i.*) to differ; be at variance.

difficile (difisil) *a*, difficult, hard; fastidious; trying. **difficilement** (lmɑ̃) *ad*, with difficulty. **difficulté** (kylte) *f*, difficulty; tiff. **difficultueux, euse** (tчø, ø:z) *a*, troublesome; fussy.

difforme (difɔrm) *a*, deformed, misshapen, unshapely. **difformité** (mite) *f*, deformity.

diffus, e (dify, y:z) *a*, diffused; diffuse; long-winded, wordy. **diffuser** (fyze) *v.t*, to diffuse; broadcast. **diffusion** (zjɔ̃) *f*, diffusion; broadcasting; long-windedness, wordiness.

digérer (diʒere) *v.t. & abs*, to digest; brook, stomach. *je ne digère pas la viande*, meat does not agree with me. **digestible** (ʒɛstibl) *a*, digestible. **digestif, ive** (tif, i:v) *a. & m*, digestive. **digestion** (tjɔ̃) *f*, digestion.

digicode (diʒikɔd) *m*, coded pushbutton system for controlling access to buildings, rooms, etc.

digital, e (diʒital) *a*, digital, finger (*att.*). ¶ *f*, foxglove; digitalis (*Phar.*).

digne (diɲ) *a*, worthy; deserving; dignified. **dignement** (ɲmɑ̃) *ad*, worthily, with dignity; adequately. **dignitaire** (ɲitɛ:r) *m*, dignitary. **dignité** (te) *f*, dignity; rank.

digression (digrɛsjɔ̃) *f*, digression.

digue (dig) *f*, dike, dam; sea wall; barrier (*fig.*).

dilapider (dilapide) *v.t*, to squander; misappropriate.

dilater (dilate) *v.t*, to dilate; expand; swell.

dilemme (dilɛm) *m*, dilemma.

dilettante (dilɛttɑ̃:t) *m*, dilettante, amateur.

diligemment (diliʒamɑ̃) *ad*,

diligently. **diligence** (ʒɑ̃ːs) f,
diligence; industry; despatch;
proceedings, suit (*law*); stage
coach. **diligent, e** (ʒɑ̃, ɑ̃ːt) a,
diligent; industrious; expeditious.

diluer (dilɥe) v.t, to dilute; water
(*stock, Fin.*).

diluvien, ne (dilyvjɛ̃, ɛn) a,
diluvial; torrential (*rain*).

dimanche (dimɑ̃ːʃ) m, Sunday,
sabbath. ~ *des Rameaux,* Palm
Sunday.

dîme (diːm) f, tithe.

dimension (dimɑ̃sjɔ̃) f, dimension, size, measurement; particularity, aspect.

diminuer (diminɥe) v.t. & i, to
diminish, decrease, reduce, abate,
lower; taper; get thin. *aller en
diminuant,* to taper. *entièrement
diminué,* fully fashioned (*stocking*). **diminutif, ive** (nytif, iːv)
a, diminutive (*Gram.*). ¶ m,
diminutive (*Gram.*); miniature.
diminution (sjɔ̃) f, diminution,
etc., as *diminuer.*

dinanderie (dinɑ̃dri) f, brass-
wares; kitchen utensils. **dinandier** (dje) m, brazier.

dînatoire (dinatwaːr) a, substantial (*lunch*).

dinde (dɛ̃ːd) f, turkey [hen];
goose (*fig.*). **dindon** (dɛ̃dɔ̃) m,
turkey [cock]; goose (*fig.*); dupe.
dindonneau (dɔno) m, turkey
poult.

dîner (dine) m, dinner. ¶ v.i, to
dine. **dînette** (nɛt) f, little dinner; doll's dinner party. **dîneur,
euse** (nœːr, øːz) n, diner.

dingue (dɛ̃ːg) a, loony, cracked
(*slang*). ¶ m, a loony, madcap,
nut (*person*).

diocésain, e (djɔsezɛ̃, ɛn) a, diocesan. **diocèse** (sɛːz) m, diocese.

dioptrie (djɔptri) f, diopter.

diphtérie (difteri) f, diphtheria.

diphtongue (diftɔ̃ːg) f, diphthong.

diplomate (diplɔmat) m, diplomat[ist]; (*att.*) diplomatic. **diplomatie** (si) f, diplomacy. **diplomatique** (tik) a, diplomatic.

diplôme (ploːm) m, diploma,
certificate. **diplômé, e** (plome)
a. & n, certified (teacher, etc.).

dire (diːr) m, saying, assertion;
allegation. ¶ v.t.ir, to say; tell;

speak; bid (*adieu, etc.*); mean.
~ *son fait à quelqu'un,* to give
someone a piece of one's mind.
dites donc! look here!

direct, e (dirɛkt) a, direct;
straight; through (*Rly.*); flat (*contradiction*). *un direct du droit, du
gauche,* a straight right, left
(*Box.*). *en* ~, live (*TV, etc.*); on-
line (*computers*). **directement**
(təmɑ̃) ad, directly, direct;
straight; due; through.

directeur, trice (dirɛktœːr, tris)
n, manager; principal, headmaster, headmistress; editor; director; warden; leader. [*arbitre*] ~
de combat, referee (*Box.*). ~ *de
conscience,* spiritual director. ~
*général des postes, télégraphes &
téléphones,* postmaster general.
~ *de production,* production
manager, associate producer (*cinema*). ~ *de salle,* movie theater
manager. **direction** (sjɔ̃) f, direction; strike (*lode*); way; management; manager's office; guidance;
lead[ership]; mastership; steering. **Directoire** (twaːr) m, Directory; Directoire. **dirigeable**
(riʒabl) a, dirigible. ¶ m, airship,
dirigible. **diriger** (ʒe) v.t, to direct; manage; steer; train (*gun*).
se ~, to make, steer (*vers =* for).
dirigisme (ʒism) m, planning;
state control. ~ *économique,*
planned economy.

discernement (disɛrnəmɑ̃) m,
discrimination; discernment. **discerner** (ne) v.t, to discern; distinguish; discriminate.

disciple (disipl) m, disciple, follower. **disciplinaire** (plineːr) a,
disciplinary. ¶ m, disciplinarian.
discipline (plin) f, discipline.
discipliner (ne) v.t, to discipline.

discontinuer (diskɔ̃tinɥe) v.t,
to discontinue.

disconvenance (diskɔ̃vnɑ̃ːs) f,
dissimilarity, disparity. **disconvenir** (vniːr) v.i.ir, to deny. ~
de, to gainsay.

discordance (diskɔrdɑ̃ːs) f, discordance, disagreement; lack of
harmony, difference. **discorde**
(kɔrd) f, discord, strife, contention.

discourir (diskuriːr) v.i. & abs.
ir, to discourse, descant. **discours**

(ku:r) *m*, talk; discourse, speech, oration, address. ~ *d'apparat*, set speech.

discourtois, e (diskurtwa, a:z) *a*, discourteous. **discourtoisie** (twazi) *f*, discourtesy.

discrédit (diskredi) *m*, discredit, disrepute. **discréditer** (te) *v.t*, to discredit.

discret, ète† (diskrɛ, ɛt) *a*, discreet; unobtrusive; unpretentious; discrete. **discrétion** (kresjɔ̃) *f*, discretion; secrecy. *à* ~, as much as you want.

discrimination (diskriminasjɔ̃) *f*, discrimination.

disculper (diskylpe) *v.t*, to exculpate.

discursif, ive (diskyrsif, i:v) *a*, discursive. **discussion** (kysjɔ̃) *f*, discussion; debate; question, dispute. **discutable** (tabl) *a*, debatable, arguable, moot. **discuter** (te) *v.t. & abs. & v.i*, to discuss, debate, argue; controvert; auction off to pay debts.

disert, e (dize:r, ɛrt) *a*, fluent.

disette (dizɛt) *f*, dearth, scarcity. ~ *d'argent*, penury. ~ *d'eau*, drought.

diseur, euse (dizœ:r, ø:z) *n*, talker. ~ *de bonne aventure*, fortune teller. ~ *de bons mots*, wit. ~ *de chansonnettes*, entertainer; humorist (*at concert*).

disgrâce (disgrɑ:s) *f*, disgrace, disfavor; misfortune. **disgracier** (grasje) *v.t*, to dismiss from favor, disgrace. **disgracieux, euse** (sjø, ø:z) *a*, uncouth, ungraceful.

disjoindre (disʒwɛ̃:dr) *v.t.ir*, to disjoin.

disjoncteur (dizʒɔ̃ktœ:r) *m*, switch, circuit-breaker.

dislocation (dislɔkasjɔ̃) *f*, dislocation; dismemberment; dispersal (*troops, convoy*).

disloquer (dislɔke) *v.t*, to dislocate, put out of joint; dismember; break up; dislodge. **dislocation** (kasjɔ̃) *f*, dislocation; breakaway.

dispache (dispaʃ) *f*, average adjustment (*Insce.*).

disparaître (disparɛ:tr) *v.i.ir*, to disappear, vanish.

disparate (disparat) *a*, disparate,

ill-assorted. ¶ *f*, incongruity. **disparité** (rite) *f*, disparity.

disparition (disparisjɔ̃) *f*, disappearance. **les disparus** (ry) *m.pl*, the missing (*soldiers*).

dispendieux, euse (dispɑ̃djø, ø:z) *a*, expensive, costly.

dispensaire (dispɑ̃sɛ:r) *m*, dispensary. **dispensateur, trice** (satœ:r, tris) *n*, dispenser. **dispense** (pɑ̃:s) *f*, dispensation; exemption. ~ *de bans*, marriage license. **dispenser** (pɑ̃se) *v.t*, to dispense, exempt, excuse, spare.

disperser (dispɛrse) *v.t*, to disperse, scatter. *ordre dispersé*, extended order (*Mil.*). **dispersion** (sjɔ̃) *f*, dispersion, dispersal.

disponibilité (dispɔnibilite) *f*, availability; (*pl.*) available funds, liquid assets. *en* ~, unattached (*Mil.*). **disponible** (bl) *a*, available, spare, disposable; liquid; on hand; unattached; in print.

dispos, e (dispo, o:z) *a*, fit, well, hearty; good (*humor*). **disposer** (poze) *v.t*, to dispose; arrange; lay out; incline; provide; draw (*bill*). **dispositif** (pozitif) *m*, purview (*law*); device, arrangement, contrivance, gear. ~ *à 3 vitesses*, 3-speed gear. ~ *de fortune*, ~ *de circonstance*, makeshift. ~*s de mines*, preparatory work (*Min.*). ~ *passe-vues*, slide changer. **disposition** (sjɔ̃) *f*, disposition, ordering, arrangement; lie; layout; tendency; tone; frame of mind; state; humor; aptitude, flair; disposal; provision (*of a law*); dispensation (*of Providence*); draft (*Fin.*).

disproportion (disprɔpɔrsjɔ̃) *f*, disproportion. **disproportionné, e** (ɔne) *a*, disproportionate.

disputailler (dispytaje) *v.i*, to wrangle, bicker. **dispute** (pyt) *f*, dispute; contest; contention. **disputer** (te) *v.i. & t*, to dispute; contend; vie; contest. *se* ~, to wrangle.

disqualifier (diskalifje) *v.t*, to disqualify (*sport*).

disquaire (diskɛ:r) *m*, phonograph record dealer. **disque** (disk) *m*, disk, disc, discus; wheel; phonograph record. ~ *de sta-*

tionnement, parking disk (*for use in a* zone bleue—*limited parking area*). **disquette** (ɛt) *f,* floppy disk, diskette (*computers*).

dissection (disɛksjɔ̃) *f,* dissection.

dissemblable (disɑ̃blabl) *a,* dissimilar. **dissemblance** (blɑ̃s) *f,* dissimilarity.

disséminer (disemine) *v.t,* to disseminate; scatter.

dissension (disɑ̃sjɔ̃) *f,* dissension.

dissentiment (disɑ̃timɑ̃) *m,* dissent, disagreement.

disséquer (diseke) *v.t,* to dissect.

dissertation (disɛrtasjɔ̃) *f,* dissertation, disquisition, essay.

dissidence (disidɑ̃s) *f,* dissidence, dissent. **dissident, e** (dɑ̃, ɑ̃ːt) *a,* dissentient; dissenting. ¶ *n,* dissentient; dissenter.

dissimilaire (disimilɛːr) *a,* dissimilar.

dissimulé, e (disimyle) *a,* secretive. **dissimuler** (le) *v.t. & abs,* to dissimulate; dissemble; conceal.

dissipateur, trice (disipatœːr, tris) *n. & a,* spendthrift. **dissipation** (sjɔ̃) *f,* dissipation; extravagance. **dissiper** (pe) *v.t,* to dissipate; dispel; disperse; scatter; fritter away.

dissocier (disɔsje) *v.t,* to dissociate.

dissolu, e (disɔly) *a,* dissolute, profligate. **dissolution** (sjɔ̃) *f,* dissolution; solution; dissoluteness. **dissolvant, e** (vɑ̃, ɑ̃ːt) *a. & m,* [dis]solvent.

dissonance (disɔnɑ̃ːs) *f,* dissonance; discord. **dissonant, e** (nɑ̃, ɑ̃ːt) *a,* dissonant, discordant.

dissoudre (disudr) *v.t.ir,* to dissolve.

dissuader (disɥade) *v.t,* to dissuade.

dissuasion (disɥazjɔ̃) *f,* dissuasion. *la force de ~,* dissuasive military power. *arme de ~,* military deterrent.

dissyllabe (disilab) *m,* disyllable.

dissymétrique (disimetrik) *a,* unsymmetrical.

distance (distɑ̃ːs) *f,* distance; range; way [off]. *garder ses ~s*

(*fig.*), to keep one's distance. *commande à ~,* remote control. **distancer** (tɑ̃se) *v.t,* to [out] distance. **distanciation** (tɑ̃sjasjɔ̃) *f,* alienation effect (*Theat.*). **distant, e** (tɑ̃, ɑ̃ːt) *a,* distant; aloof.

distendre (distɑ̃ːdr) *v.t,* to distend.

distillateur (distilatœːr) *m,* distiller. **distillation** (sjɔ̃) *f,* distillation; distillate. **distiller** (le) *v.t,* to distil; exude. **distillerie** (lri) *f,* distillery.

distinct, e† (distɛ̃ːkt) *a,* distinct; clear, plain. **distinctif, ive** (tɛ̃ktif, iːv) *a,* distinctive. **distinction** (sjɔ̃) *f,* distinction. **distingué, e** (tɛ̃ge) *a,* distinguished; refined; gentlemanly; ladylike. **distinguer** (ge) *v.t,* to distinguish; discriminate; make out; single out.

distique (distik) *m,* distich; couplet.

distorsion (distɔrsjɔ̃) *f,* distortion.

distraction (distraksjɔ̃) *f,* distraction; absence of mind; appropriation; severance; amusement, hobby. **distraire** (trɛːr) *v.t.ir,* to distract; appropriate; set aside; take away, t. off; amuse. **distrait, e†** (trɛ, ɛt) *a,* absentminded; listless, vacant.

distribuer (distribɥe) *v.t,* to distribute, give out; deal out; issue; deliver (*letters*); arrange; cast (*actors' parts*). **distributeur, trice** (bytœːr, tris) *n,* distributor; gasoline pump. *distributeur automatique,* automatic [delivery] machine, slot machine. **distribution** (sjɔ̃) *f,* distribution; issue; allotment; delivery (*post*); valve gear; arrangement, layout. *~ de prix,* prize giving; speech day. *~ des aumônes,* almsgiving. *~ [des rôles],* cast[ing] (*Theat.*). *~ par coulisse,* link motion.

district (distrikt) *m,* district, field.

dito (dito) (*abb.* d°) *ad,* ditto, do.

diurne (djyrn) *a,* diurnal.

diva (diva) *f,* prima donna, diva.

divagation (divagasjɔ̃) *f,* digression; wandering, rambling. **divaguer** (ge) *v.i,* to digress.

divan (divɑ̃) *m,* divan; settee.

divergence (divɛrʒɑ̃:s) *f*, divergence. **divergent**, e (ʒɑ̃, ɑ̃:t) *a*, divergent. **diverger** (ʒe) *v.i*, to diverge.

divers, e† (divɛːr, ɛrs) *a*, different, diverse; sundry, miscellaneous; various, many. **diversifier** (versifje) *v.t*, to diversify, vary. **diversion** (sjɔ̃) *f*, diversion. **diversité** (site) *f*, diversity, variety, difference. **divertir** (tiːr) *v.t*, to divert; amuse, entertain. *se ~ aux dépens de*, to make fun of, make merry over. **divertissement** (tismɑ̃) *m*, diversion; amusement, entertainment; divertissement.

divette (divɛt) *f*, variety actress.

dividende (dividɑ̃ːd) *m*, dividend.

divin, e† (divɛ̃, in) *a*, divine; godlike. **divination** (vinasjɔ̃) *f*, divination. **diviniser** (nize) *v.t*, to deify. **divinité** (te) *f*, divinity, godhead; deity.

diviser (divize) *v.t*, to divide; part. **diviseur** (zœːr) *m*, divisor. **division** (zjɔ̃) *f*, division; department; hyphen (*end of line*).

divorce (divɔrs) *m*, divorce. **divorcer** (se) *v.i*, to be divorced. *~ d'avec*, to divorce.

divulguer (divylge) *v.t*, to divulge, blab.

dix (*in liaison*, diz; *before consonant or 'h,'* di) *a*, ten. ¶ (dis) *m*, ten; 10th. **~-huit** (dizɥit; *bef. cons. or 'h,'* qi) *a. & m*, eighteen; 18th. **~-huitième** (tjɛm) *a. & n*, eighteenth. **dixième**† (dizjɛm) *a. & n*, tenth; tenth of a lottery ticket. **dix-neuf** (diznœf; *in liaison*, nœv; *bef. cons. or 'h,'* nœ) *a. & m*, nineteen; 19th. **dix-neuvième** (vjɛm) *a. & n*, nineteenth. **dix-sept** (disset; *bef. cons. or 'h,'* sɛ) *a. & m*, seventeen; 17th. **dix-septième** (tjɛm) *a. & n*, seventeenth.

dizain (dizɛ̃) *m*, ten-line stanza. **dizaine** (zɛn) *f*, ten [or so], about ten; ten; decade.

do (do) (*Mus.*) *m*, C.

docile† (dɔsil) *a*, docile, amenable, ductile. **docilité** (lite) *f*, docility.

dock (dɔk) *m*, dock; dock warehouse, warehouse, store. *~ fri-*

gorifique, cold store. **docker** (kɛːr) *m*, docker. .

docte† (dɔkt) *a*, learned. **docteur** (tœːr) *m*, doctor. **doctoral**, e† (tɔral) *a*, doctoral; pompous; grandiloquent. **doctorat** (ra) *m*, doctorate.

doctrinaire (dɔktrinɛːr) *m. & a*, doctrinaire. **doctrine** (trin) *f*, doctrine, tenet.

document (dɔkymɑ̃) *m*, document. *~s à l'appui*, supporting documents. **documentaire** (tɛːr) *a*, documentary. **documenter** (te) *v.t*, to document.

dodeliner (dɔdline) *v.t*, to rock, dandle. *~ de*, to wag (*head*).

dodo (dɔdo) *m*, bye-bye; cot.

dodu, e (dɔdy) *a*, plump, rotund.

dogmatique† (dɔgmatik) *a*, dogmatic. **dogmatiser** (ze) *v.i*, to dogmatize. **dogme** (dɔgm) *m*, dogma; tenet.

dogue (dɔg) *m*, watchdog; mastiff. bear (*fig., pers.*).

doigt (dwa) *m*, finger; digit; thimbleful, nip (*liquor*). *~ [de pied]*, toe. *à deux ~s de*, within an ace of. **doigté** (dwate) *m*, fingering (*Mus.*); diplomacy, tact. **doigter** (te) *v.i. & t*, to finger (*Mus.*). **doigtier** (tje) *m*, fingerstall.

doit (dwa) *m*, debit [side], debtor [side].

dol (dɔl) *m*, wilful misrepresentation.

doléance (dɔleɑ̃:s) *f*, complaint, grievance. **dolent**, e (lɑ̃, ɑ̃:t) *a*, doleful; painful; out of sorts.

dollar (dɔlaːr) *m*, dollar.

domaine (dɔmɛn) *m*, domain, demesne, estate; property; land; province.

dôme (doːm) *m*, dome; canopy.

domesticité (dɔmɛstisite) *f*, service; [staff of] servants, household; domesticity. **domestique** (tik) *a*, domestic, home. ¶ *n*, servant, domestic; man[servant]; maid[servant]. **domestiquer** (ke) *v.t*, to domesticate.

domicile (dɔmisil) *m*, residence, abode, house, premises, domicile. *franco à ~*, free delivery. **domicilier** (lje) *v.t*, to domicile.

dominant, e (dɔminɑ̃, ɑ̃:t) *a*, dominant, ruling; prevailing. ¶

f, dominant (*Mus.*). **dominateur, trice** (natœːr, tris) *n*, ruler; (*att.*) ruling; domineering. **domination** (sjɔ̃) *f*, domination; dominion; rule, sway. ~ *de la lie du peuple*, mob law. **dominer** (ne) *v.i. & t*, to dominate; overlook; tower above; rule; domineer.

dominicain, e (dɔminikɛ̃, ɛn) *n*, Dominican.

dominical, e (dɔminikal) *a*, dominical; Sunday (*rest*); Lord's (*prayer*).

domino (dɔmino) *m*, domino.

dommage (dɔmaːʒ) *m*, damage, injury, loss; pity (*regret*). ~**s-intérêts**, damages (*law*).

dompter (dɔ̃te) *v.t*, to tame; break in; subdue. **dompteur, euse** (tœːr, øːz) *n*, tamer.

don (dɔ̃) *m*, bestowal; gift; present; donation; dower; knack. **donataire** (dɔnatɛːr) *n*, donee. **donateur, trice** (tœːr, tris) *n*, donor. **donation** (sjɔ̃) *f*, donation, gift.

donc (dɔ̃; *in liaison or emphatically*, dɔ̃ːk) *c*, therefore, then, hence, so; to be sure.

dondon (dɔ̃dɔ̃) *f*, bouncing girl; plump woman.

donjon (dɔ̃ʒɔ̃) *m*, keep (*castle*).

donnant, e (dɔnɑ̃, ɑ̃ːt) *a*, generous. **donnant donnant**, *ad*, give & take, tit for tat. **donne** (dɔn) *f*, deal (*cards*). **donnée** (ne) *f*, datum; fundamental idea, motif. **donner** (ne) *v.t*, to give, bestow; impart, afford; tender; make; let; yield, give up; show; teach (*someone a lesson*); set (*task*); perform (*play*); deal (*cards*); (*v.i.*) to strike, hit; fall; run; sag. ~ *sur*, to face, front, look on, give on, overlook (*street, etc.*). ~ *dans le piège*, to fall into the trap. **donneur, euse** (nœːr, øːz) *n*, giver; donor; dealer (*cards*). ~ *d'ordre*, principal.

Don Quichotte (dɔ̃kiʃɔt) *m*, Quixote, champion (*of lost causes*).

dont (dɔ̃) *pn*, whose; of whom; of *or* from *or* by whom *or* which; whereof; as per.

donzelle (dɔ̃zɛl) *f*, wench.

doper (dɔpe) *v.t*, to dope; boost (*Elec.*); add power to.

dorade (dɔrad) *f*, dorado, dolphin; goldfish. **doré, e** (re) *a*, gilt, gilded; golden. ~ *sur tranche*, gilt-edged. **dorée, f**, [John] dory.

dorénavant (dɔrenavɑ̃) *ad*, henceforth.

dorer (dɔre) *v.t*, to gild; block (*Bookb.*); glaze (*pastry*). **doreur, euse** (rœːr, øːz) *n*, gilder; blocker.

dorique (dɔrik) *a. & m*, Doric.

dorloter (dɔrlɔte) *v.t*, to coddle; pamper.

dormant, e (dɔrmɑ̃, ɑ̃ːt) *a*, sleeping, dormant, still, standing, stagnant. ¶ *m*, casing, frame. **dormeur, euse** (mœːr, øːz) *n*, sleeper. ¶ *f*, lounge chair; stud earring; sleeping suit. **dormir** (miːr) *v.i.ir*, to sleep, be asleep; lie dormant. ~ *comme une souche*, to sleep like a log. **dormitif** (mitif) *m*, sleeping draft.

dorsal, e (dɔrsal) *a*, dorsal.

dortoir (dɔrtwaːr) *m*, dormitory.

dorure (dɔryːr) *f*, gilding; blocking (*Bookb.*); gilt; glazing (*pastry*).

dos (do) *m*, back; back, spine (*book*); bridge (*nose*). en ~ *d'âne*, hogbacked.

dose (doːz) *f*, dose, measure. **doser** (doze) *v.t*, to proportion, measure out, dose.

dossier (dosje) *m*, back; bundle (*papers*); dossier; brief (*law*); record.

dot (dɔt) *f*, dowry, dower, [marriage] portion. **dotal, e** (tal) *a*, dowral, dotal. **dotation** (sjɔ̃) *f*, endowment. **doter** (te) *v.t*, to dower, portion; endow.

douairière (dwɛrjɛːr) *f*, dowager.

douane (dwan) *f*, customs; custom house. **douanier, ère** (nje, ɛːr) *a*, customs (*att.*). ¶ *m*, customs officer.

doublage (dublaːʒ) *m*, doubling; lining; sheathing (*ship*). **double** (bl) *a*, double; twofold; dual; double-dealing. ~ *croche*, *f*, semiquaver. ~ *emploi*, *m*, duplication. *à* ~ *face*, double-faced. ~ *fond*, *m*, false bottom. ¶ *ad*, double; in duplicate. ¶ *m*, double; duplicate, counterpart. ~ *messieurs*, *dames, mixte*, men's, women's, mixed, doubles (*Ten.*). **double-ment** (bləmã) *ad*, doubly. ¶ *m*, doubling. **doubler** (ble) *v.t*, to double; understudy; overtake; line; sheathe; weather (*cape*); dub (*movies*); (*v.i.*) to double. *non doublé, e*, unlined. *doublé or*, rolled gold. **doublure** (bly:r) *f*, lining; understudy; stunt person (*cinema*).

douceâtre (dusɑ:tr) *a*, sweetish. **doucement** (smã) *ad*, gently; softly; sweetly; slowly; gingerly; quietly; peacefully; smoothly, easily; so-so; pretty well. **doucereux, euse** (srø, ø:z) *a*, mawkish, sickly; mealy-mouthed, smooth-tongued. **douceur** (sœ:r) *f*, sweetness; softness; gentleness; mildness; meekness; pleasure; (*pl.*) dainties, sweets; soft nothings.

douche (duʃ) *f*, shower (*bath*); douche. **doucher** (ʃe) *v.t*, to shower; douche.

doucine (dusin) *f*, ogee.

douer (dwe) *v.t*, to endow, endue, gift.

douille (du:j) *f*, socket, holder; case (*cartridge*).

douillet, te† (duje, ɛt) *a*, soft, downy; cosy.

douleur (dulœ:r) *f*, pain, ache; throe; sorrow, grief, woe. **douloureux, euse†** (lurø, ø:z) *a*, painful; sore; mournful, grievous, sad.

doute (dut) *m*, doubt, misgiving. **douter** (te) *v.i. & abs*, to doubt, question. *~ de*, to doubt, question (*v.t.*). *se ~ de*, to suspect. **douteux, euse†** (tø, ø:z) *a*, doubtful, dubious, questionable.

douve (du:v) *f*, stave (*cask*); ditch (*Agric.*); moat (*castle*); water jump (*turf*); water hazard (*golf*).

Douvres (du:vr) *m*, Dover.

doux, ouce (du, us) *a*, sweet; soft; dulcet; gentle; mild; meek; quiet (*horse*); smooth; easy; pleasant; fresh (*water*). *tout doux*, gently. *en douce*, on the q.t. *le doux*, the sweet (*opp*. the bitter).

douzaine (duzɛn) *f*, dozen. **douze** (du:z) *a. & m*, twelve;

12th. **douzième†** (duzjɛm) *a. & n*, twelfth.

doyen, ne (dwajɛ̃, ɛn) *n*, dean; doyen; senior. **doyenné** (jɛne) *m*, deanery.

drachme (drakm) *f*, drachma.

dragage (draga:ʒ) *m*, dredging; dragging; sweeping (*for mines*).

dragée (draʒe) *f*, sugar almond; pill; birdshot.

drageon (draʒɔ̃) *m*, sucker (*Bot., Hort.*).

dragon (dragɔ̃) *m*, dragon; dragoon; termagant, virago.

drague (drag) *f*, dredge[r]; drag; d. net; grains, draff. **draguer** (ge) *v.t*, to dredge, drag, sweep; to go looking for women; cruise for sexual partners. **dragueur** (gœ:r) *m*, dredger (*pers. & boat*). *~ de mines*, mine sweeper.

drain (drɛ̃) *m*, drain; d. pipe. **drainage** (drɛna:ʒ) *m*, drainage; drain (*demand*). **drainer** (ne) *v.t*, to drain.

dramatique† (dramatik) *a*, dramatic; operatic. **dramatiser** (ze) *v.t*, to dramatize. **dramatiste** (tist) *m*, **dramaturge** (tyrʒ) *n*, dramatist, playwright, dramaturge. **drame** (dram) *m*, drama; tragedy, sensational affair. *~ pleureur*, sob-stuff.

drap (dra) *m*, cloth; sheet; pickle (*fig.*). *~ mortuaire*, pall. *~ vert*, green baize. *être dans le beau ~s*, to be in a nasty situation. **drapeau** (po) *m*, flag, colors. **draper** (pe) *v.t*, to drape; pillory (*fig.*). **draperie** (pri) *f*, drapery; cloth trade; bunting. **drapier** (pje) *m*, draper, clothier, cloth merchant; cloth manufacturer.

drastique (drastik) *a*, drastic.

drawback (drobak) *m*, drawback (*Cust.*).

drêche (drɛʃ) *f*, grains, draff.

drelin-drelin (drəlɛ̃) tinkle! tinkle!

drenne (drɛn) *f*, missel thrush.

Dresde (drɛzd) *f*, Dresden.

dresser (drɛse) *v.t*, to erect, raise, set up, rear; prick up (*ears*); pitch (*tent*); set (*trap*); draw up, make out, prepare; make (*bed*, etc.); lay (*table*); trim; dish up; true, straighten, dress, face; train; drill; break in. **dresseur**

(sœːr) *m*, trainer (*animals*). **dressoir** (swaːr) *m*, sideboard.

drille (driːj) *m*, fellow. ¶ *f*, drill, brace; (*pl.*) rags (*for paper-making*).

drisse (dris) *f*, halyard.

drogman (drɔgmɑ̃) *m*, drago-man.

drogue (drɔg) *f*, drug; nostrum; trash; worthless person. **droguer** (ge) *v.t.* to physic; drug; (*v.i.*) to wait, cool one's heels. **dro-guerie** (gri) *f*, druggist's business; drugstore.

droguet (drɔgɛ) *m*, drugget.

droguiste (drɔgist) *m*, druggist (*wholesale*); drysalter.

droit, e (drwa, at) *a*, straight; up-right, erect, plumb; straightfor-ward, honest; right, right-hand[ed]; single-breasted. **droit**, *ad*, straight; s. on; due (*south, etc.*) **droit**, *m*, right; due, duty, fee; law; reason. ~*s d'adaptation au cinéma*, film rights. ~ *d'aînesse*, ~ *du sang*, birthright. ~ *d'auteur*, copyright; royalty. ~ *de cité*, citizenship. ~*s de douane*, customs duties. ~*s de reproduction dans les journaux & périodiques*, serial rights. ~ *de rétention*, lien. ~*s de succession*, inheritance taxes. ~ *de vendre*, li-cense to sell. *de* ~, de jure. *faire son* ~, to study law. **droite**, *f*, right hand, r. side; right. *à* ~, on (*or* to) the right. **droitement** (tmɑ̃), *ad*, uprightly, righteously. **droi-tier, ère** (tje, ɛːr) *n*, right-handed person *or* player; rightist (*Pol.*). **droiture** (tyːr) *f*, uprightness, straightforwardness, rectitude.

drolatique (drɔlatik) *a*, comic, humorous. **drôle†** (droːl) *a*, funny, humorous, droll; queer, odd. *un* ~ *de corps*, a queer fellow, an oddity. ¶ *m*, funny (*queer*) man; rascal. **drôlerie** (drolri) *f*, drollery, fun. **drôlesse** (lɛs) *f*, hussy.

dromadaire (drɔmadɛːr) *m*, dromedary.

drome (drɔm) *f*, raft.

dru, e (dry) *a*, thick; sturdy. **dru**, *ad*, thick[ly].

drugstore (drœgstɔr) *m*, store selling a variety of items (*books, cosmetics, records*) and often in-cluding a bar or restaurant. Not a "drugstore" in the American sense ("*pharmacie*").

druide (drɥid) *m*, Druid.

dryade (driad) *f*, dryad.

dû, due (dy) *p.p. & p.a*, due; owing; forward (*carriage*); proper. ¶ *m*, due (*right*).

dualité (dyalite) *f*, duality.

duc (dyk) *m*, duke. **ducal, e** (kal) *a*, ducal. **duché** (ʃe) *m*, duchy; dukedom. **duchesse** (ʃɛs) *f*, duchess.

ductile (dyktil) *a*, ductile.

duègne (dɥɛɲ) *f*, duenna.

duel (dɥel) *m*, duel. **duelliste** (list) *m*, duellist.

dûment (dymɑ̃) *ad*, duly, prop-erly.

dune (dyn) *f*, dune, sand hill, down.

dunette (dynɛt) *f*, poop; poop deck.

Dunkerque (dœ̃kɛrk) *m*, Dun-kirk.

duo (dyo) *m*, duet.

duodécimal, e (dyɔdesimal) *a*, duodecimal.

dupe (dyp) *f*, dupe, gull. **duper** (pe) *v.t*, to dupe, gull, take in, fool. **duperie** (pri) *f*, dupery, trickery, take-in. **dupeur, euse** (pœːr, øːz) *n*, trick[st]er.

duplicata (dyplikata) *m*, dupli-cate.

duplicité (dyplisite) *f*, duplicity; double dealing.

duquel *see* **lequel**.

dur, e (dyːr) *a*, hard; tough; hard-ened, inured; dire; harsh; hard-boiled (*egg*).

durable (dyrabl) *a*, durable, lasting, abiding.

durant (dyrɑ̃) *pr*, during, for.

durcir (dyrsiːr) *v.t. & i. & se* ~, to harden. **durcissement** (sismɑ̃) *m*, hardening.

dure (dyːr) *f*, bare ground.

durée (dyre) *f*, duration, length, life.

durement (dyrmɑ̃) *ad*, hard; harshly.

durer (dyre) *v.i. & abs*, to last; hang heavy (*time*); hold out, stand; live.

dureté (dyrte) *f*, hardness; toughness; harshness. ~ *d'oreille*, hardness of hearing.

durillon (dyrijɔ̃) *m*, callus, hard skin.

duvet (dyvɛ) *m*, down; nap. **duveté, e** (vte) *a*, downy, fluffy.

dynamique (dinamik) *a*, dynamic. ¶ *f*, dynamics.

dynamite (dinamit) *f*, dynamite.

dynamo (dinamo) *f*, dynamo. **~-électrique** (mɔ) *a*, dynamoelectric.

dynastie (dinasti) *f*, dynasty.

dysenterie (disɑ̃tri) *f*, dysentery.

dyspepsie (dispɛpsi) *f*, dyspepsia.

E

eau (o) *f*, water; rain. ~ *bénite de cour*, fair promises, empty words. ~ *de boudin* (odbudɛ̃), thin air, smoke (*fig.*). ~*de cale*, bilge water. ~*-de-vie* (odvi), brandy. ~ *douce*, fresh water. ~ *dentifrice*, mouthwash. ~*-forte*, aqua fortis; etching. ~ *minérale* [*artificielle*], mineral [water]. ~ *minérale* [*naturelle*], mineral w.; table w. *de la plus belle* ~, of the finest water (*gem*); of the deepest dye (*fig.*). *être en* ~, to be in a sweat. *faire* ~, to make water, leak. *faire de l'*~, to [take in] water.

eaux (o) *f.pl*, waters, water; fountains; watering place, spa; tide; wake (*ship*). *marcher dans les* ~ *de*, to follow in the wake of (*Naut. & fig.*). ~ *à marée*, tidal water. ~ *d'égout*, sew[er]age. ~ *ménagères*, slops. ~*-vannes*, waste water; sewage [water]. ~ *vives*, spring tide.

ébahir (ebaiːr) *v.t*, to dumbfound, amaze.

ébarber (ebarbe) *v.t*, to take the burr off; trim (*edges*); wipe (*joint*).

ébattre (s') (ebatr) *v.pr.ir.* ou **prendre ses ébats** (eba), to frolic, gambol; hop about.

ébaubi, e (ebobi) *a*, dumbfounded.

ébauche (eboːʃ) *f*, [rough] sketch, draft, outline. **ébaucher** (boʃe) *v.t*, to sketch [out], draft; rough out; rough down.

ébène (ebɛn) *f*, ebony. **ébénier** (benje) *m*, ebony [tree]. **ébéniste** (nist) *m*, cabinetmaker. **ébénisterie** (tri) *f*, cabinetmaking; cabinetwork.

éberluer (ebɛrlye) *v.t*, to amaze, astound; hoodwink.

éblouir (ebluiːr) *v.t. & abs*, to dazzle, glare.

ébonite (ebɔnit) *f*, ebonite, vulcanite.

éborgner (ebɔrɲe) *v.t*, to blind in one eye; disbud; shut out view from.

éboueur (ebuœːr) *m*, streetcleaner; scavenger.

ébouillanter (ebujɑ̃te) *v.t*, to plunge into boiling water; scald.

éboulement (ebulmɑ̃) *m*, falling in, caving in; fall, slip. **ébouler (le)** (le) *v.i*, to fall in, cave in, slip. **éboulis** (li) *m*, fall (*earth*).

ébourgeonner (eburʒɔne) *v.t*, to disbud.

ébouriffer (eburife) *v.t*, to dishevel, ruffle, tousle; stagger.

ébouter (ebute) *v.t*, to cut off the end of.

ébrancher (ebrɑ̃ʃe) *v.t*, to lop.

ébranlement (ebrɑ̃lmɑ̃) *m*, shaking; shock, concussion; tottering; jangle. **ébranler (le)** (le) *v.t*, to shake; jangle. *s'*~, to shake, totter; move off.

ébraser (ebraze) *v.t*, to splay.

ébrécher (ebreʃe) *v.t*, to chip, jag; break (*jaw*); make a hole in (*fortune*).

ébriété (ebriete) *f*, drunkenness.

ébrouer (s') (ebrue) *v.pr*, to sneeze (*animals*); snort.

ébruiter (ebrɥite) *v.t*, to noise abroad.

ébullition (ebylisjɔ̃) *f*, boiling, ebullition; turmoil; bubble.

écacher (ekaʃe) *v.t*, to crush; flatten.

écaille (ekɑːj) *f*, scale; flake; chip; shell. ~ [*de tortue*], tortoise shell. **écailler** (kɑje) *v.t*, to scale; open (*oysters*). *s'*~, to scale, flake; peel [off]. **écailler, ère** (je, ɛːr) *n*, oysterman, -woman. **écailleux, euse** (jø, øːz) *a*, scaly, flaky.

écale (ekal) *f*, shell; pod. **écaler (le)** *v.t*, to shell.

écarbouiller (ekarbuje) *v.t*, to crush, squash.

écarlate (ekarlat) *f. & a*, scarlet.

écarquiller (ekarkije) *v.t*, to open wide (*eyes*). ~ *les yeux*, to stare.

écart (ekaːr) *m*, variation, difference; error; digression; flight; straddling; strain (*Vet.*). *faire un* ~, to side-step; (*horse*) shy. *à l'*~, aside, on one side; aloof. *à l'*~ *de*, at some distance from. **écarté, e** (karte) *p.a*, out-of-the-way, remote, secluded, lonely. **écarté**, *m*, écarté (*cards*).

écarteler (ekartəle) *v.t*, to quarter.

écartement (ekartəmᾶ) *m*, spreading; distance apart; d. between; gauge (*Rly.*). ~ *des essieux*, wheelbase. **écarter** (te) *v.t*, to separate, spread, open; turn (*or* push) aside *or* out of the way; avert, ward off; divert; discard (*cards*). **s'**~, to stand aside; deviate; wander, stray, swerve.

Ecclésiaste (l') (ɛklezjast) *m*, Ecclesiastes. **ecclésiastique†** (tik) *a*, ecclesiastical, clerical. ¶ *m*, ecclesiastic, clergyman, cleric. **l'E**~, Ecclesiasticus.

écervelé, e (esɛrvəle) *a*, giddy, hare-brained. ¶ *n*, madcap.

échafaud (eʃafo) *m*, scaffold, stage. **échafaudage** (daː3) *m*, scaffolding; structure, fabric (*fig.*). **échafauder** (de) *v.i*, to erect a scaffold; (*v.t.*) to build up (*fig.*).

échalas (eʃalɑ) *m*, pole (*hop, etc.*); prop, stick. **échalasser** (se) *v.t*, to pole, prop.

échalier (eʃalje) *m*, stile; hurdle fence.

échalote (eʃalɔt) *f*, shallot, eschalot.

échancrer (eʃᾶkre) *v.t*, to cut away (*neck of garment*); notch, indent. *col très échancré*, very low neck. **échancrure** (kryːr) *f*, (*neck*) opening; notch; indentation.

échange (eʃᾶːʒ) *m*, exchange, barter; interchange. *quelques* ~*s*, practice (*Ten.*). **échanger** (ʃᾶʒe) *v.t*, to exchange; barter.

échanson (eʃᾶsɔ̃) *m*, cupbearer.

échantillon (eʃᾶtijɔ̃) *m*, sam-

ple; dimension, size, section; pattern (*of stuff, etc.*), specimen, taste. **échantillonner** (jɔne) *v.t*, to sample, cut off a pattern from; gauge; tram (*tapestry work*).

échappatoire (eʃapatwaːr) *f*, loophole; evasion. **échappé, e** (pe) *n*, runaway. ~ *de prison*, escaped prisoner. **échappée** (pe) *f*, prank; snatch; spell; turning space; headroom. ~ [*de vue*], vista; glimpse, peep. **échappement** (pmᾶ) *m*, exhaust, release (*steam*); escape, leak (*gas, etc.*); escapement (*Horol.*); turning space, headroom. **échapper** (pe) *v.i. & abs*, to escape, run away; slip; (*v.t.*) to escape. *l'*~ *belle*, to have a narrow escape. *laisser* ~, to overlook. **s'**~, to escape; leak; fly off; vanish; forget oneself.

écharde (eʃard) *f*, splinter, prickle.

écharpe (eʃarp) *f*, scarf; stole; sash; sling. *en* ~, scarfwise; aslant; in a sling. **écharper** (pe) *v.t*, to cut to pieces, hack; lynch.

échasse (eʃaːs) *f*, stilt; pole (*scaffold*). **échassier** (ʃasje) *m*, wader (*bird*).

échauder (eʃode) *v.t*, to scald. **s'**~, (*fig.*), to burn one's fingers.

échauffé, e (eʃofe) *n*, hothead (*pers.*). **échauffement** (fmᾶ) *m*, heating; overheating. **échauffer** (fe) *v.t*, to heat; overheat; warm; parboil (*fig.*); excite. **s'**~, to get warm *or* heated *or* overheated *or* excited. **échauffourée** (fure) *f*, affray, brush.

échéance (eʃeᾶːs) *f*, due date; date [payable]; maturity; tenor, term, currency; expiration. *à courte* ~, short-term loan. *venir à* ~, to fall due. *le cas échéant* (ʃeᾶ, in that case, should it so happen.

échec (eʃek) *m*, check, failure, repulse; (*pl.*) chess; chessmen. ¶ *i*, check! ~ *& mat*, checkmate. *faire quelqu'un* ~ *& mat*, to checkmate someone.

échelle (eʃɛl) *f*, ladder; scale. ~ *à coulisse*, extension ladder. ~ *de sauvetage*, fire escape. ~ *double*, [pair of] steps. ~ *mobile*, sliding scale. ~*s du Levant*, Levantine ports. *faire la courte* ~, to give a helping hand. **éche-**

lon (ʃlɔ̃) *m*, rung, round; step, stepping stone (*fig.*); echelon (*Mil.*). **échelonner** (ʃlɔne) *v.t*, to spread; echelon.

écheniller (eʃnije) *v.t*, to clear of caterpillars; remove undesirables (*things, people*); polish (*text, etc.*).

écheveau (eʃvo) *m*, skein, hank.

échevelé, e (eʃəvle) *a*, disheveled (*hair*).

échine (eʃin) *f*, spine, backbone; chine. **échinée** (ne) *f*, chine (*Cook.*). **échiner** (ne) *v.t*, to break (*someone's*) back; belabor. **s'~**, to break one's back; slave.

échiquier (eʃikje) *m*, chessboard; intricacies.

écho (eko) *m*, echo; (*pl.*) news items (*in paper*). **faire ~**, to echo (*v.i.*). **se faire l'~ de**, to echo (*v.t.*).

échoir (eʃwaːr) *v.i.ir*, to fall, devolve; fall due, mature; expire. *intérêts à ~*, accruing interest.

échoppe (eʃɔp) *f*, stall, booth.

échotier (ekɔtje) *m*, gossip columnist.

échouer (eʃwe) *v.i. & t. & s'~*, to strand, ground, beach; fail; miscarry, fall through. *échoué à sec*, high & dry (*Naut.*).

échu, e (eʃy) *p.a*, due, outstanding, owing; matured.

éclabousser (eklabuse) *v.t*, to splash, [be]spatter. **éclaboussure** (syːr) *f*, splash, spatter.

éclair (eklɛːr) *m*, flash [of light]; [flash of] lightning; flash; glint, gleam. *~ au chocolat*, chocolate éclair. *~[s] de chaleur*, heat lightning, summer l. *~ diffus, ~ en nappes*, sheet l. *~ ramifié*, forked l. **éclairage** (klɛraːʒ) *m*, lighting, illumination; light. *par projection*, flood lighting. **éclairant, e** (rɑ̃, ɑ̃ːt) *a*, lighting.

éclaircie (eklɛrsi) *f*, break, opening, rift; bright interval (*Meteor.*); clearing, glade; thinning out. **éclaircir** (siːr) *v.t*, to clear, c. up; brighten; thin, t. out; elucidate, enlighten.

éclairé, e (eklɛre) *p.p*, enlightened. **éclairer** (re) *v.t. & abs*, to light [up], lighten, illuminate, illumine; throw light upon; clear up; enlighten; reconnoiter (*Mil.*);

(*v.i.*) to shine; (*v.imp.*) to lighten (*emit lightning*). **éclaireur** (rœːr) *m*, scout; boy scout. **éclaireuse** (røːz) *f*, girl scout.

éclanche (eklɑ̃ːʃ) *f*, shoulder of mutton.

éclat (ekla) *m*, splinter; chip; fragment; burst, roar, shout; peal, clap; noise, scandal; shake (*timber*); brilliancy, radiancy, brightness; flash; glare; glamour. *faire un ~*, to make a stir. *rire aux ~s*, to laugh heartily. **éclatant, e** (tɑ̃, ɑ̃ːt) *a*, bright, brilliant, shining; piercing, shrill; splendid; striking, glaring, signal. **éclatement** (tmɑ̃) *m*, bursting, explosion. **éclater** (te) *v.i*, to burst, explode, blow up; fly; split; splinter; break out; burst out; shine, flash.

éclectique (eklɛktik) *a*, eclectic. **éclectisme** (tism) *m*, eclecticism.

éclipse (eklips) *f*, eclipse. **éclipser** (se) *v.t*, to eclipse; outshine, overshadow. **s'~**, to become eclipsed; vanish. **écliptique** (tik) *a. & f*, ecliptic.

éclisse (eklis) *f*, split-wood; splint (*Surg.*); fish[plate] (*Rly.*). **éclisser** (se) *v.t*, to fish[plate].

éclopé, e (eklɔpe) *a*, footsore, lame, crippled.

éclore (eklɔːr) *v.i.ir*, to hatch; open (*flower*); come to light. **éclosion** (klozjɔ̃) *f*, hatching; opening.

écluse (eklyːz) *f*, (*canal*) lock; lock gate; floodgate (*fig.*). **éclusée** (klyze) *f*, (*lock*) feed; locking, lockage. **écluser** (ze) *v.t*, to lock; shut off. **éclusier, ère** (zje, ɛːr) *n*, lock keeper.

écœurer (ekœre) *v.t*, to sicken, nauseate.

école (ekɔl) *f*, school, college; drill, training; blunder. *~ de peloton*, squad drill. *~ maternelle*, nursery school. *~ normale*, normal school, training college (*teachers*). *~ pratique*, technical school. *~ professionelle*, training center (*trade*). **écolier, ère** (lje, ɛːr) *n*, schoolboy, -girl, pupil, scholar; tyro.

écologie (ekɔlɔʒi) *f*, ecology. **écologique** (ʒik) *a*, ecological.

éconduire (ekɔ̃dɥiːr) *v.t.ir*, to show out; put off (*with excuse*).

économat (ekɔnɔma) *m*, stewardship; bursarship; bursar's office; store. **économe** (nɔm) *a*, economical, thrifty, sparing. ¶ *n*, steward; bursar; housekeeper. **économie** (mi) *f*, economy, thrift, saving; management; arrangement. ~ *de bouts de chandelle*, cheeseparing. ~ *domestique*, domestic economy, housekeeping. ~ *politique*, political economy. ~ *rurale*, husbandry. **économique†** (mik) *a*, economical; economic. **économiser** (ze) *v.t. & abs*, to economize, save. **économiste** (mist) *m*, economist.

écope (ekɔp) *f*, scoop, bailer. **écoper** (pe) *v.t*, to bail (*or* bale) [out]; (*v.i.*) to catch it (*suffer*).

écoperche (ekɔperʃ) *f*, scaffold pole.

écorce (ekɔrs) *f*, bark; peel, rind, skin; crust (*earth's*); surface (*fig.*). **écorcer** (se) *v.t*, to bark; peel.

écorcher (ekɔrʃe) *v.t*, to flay, skin; abrade, graze, scrape, gall, chafe; grate on (*ears*); fleece (*fig.*). **écorcheur, euse** (ʃœːr, øːz) *n*, shark, extortioner; (*m.*) knacker. **écorchure** (ʃyːr) *f*, abrasion, gall, graze, scrape.

écorner (ekɔrne) *v.t*, to break off a horn *or* corner; chip; dogear; curtail.

écornifler (ekɔrnifle) *v.t*, to cadge; sponge on.

écornure (ekɔrnyːr) *f*, chip.

écossais, e (ekɔse, ɛːz) *a*, Scotch, Scottish. É~, *n*, Scotchman, -woman, Scot. l'Écosse (kɔs) *f*, Scotland, North Britain. **écosser** (ekɔse) *v.t*, to shell, hull.

écot (eko) *m*, share; score; reckoning; lopped tree; stick, fagot.

écoulement (ekulmɑ̃) *m*, flow, outflow; drainage; discharge; gleet; passing; placing, sale. **écouler** (le) *v.t*, to place, sell. s'~, to flow out *or* away, run off; disperse; pass (*or* slip) away, elapse; sell.

écourter (ekurte) to cut short; crop, dock; curtail.

écoute (ekut) *f*, sheet (*Naut.*); listening post. **aux écoutes**, on the watch *or* lookout. **écouter**

(te) *v.t. & abs*, to listen to, listen, hearken; listen in; hear. ~ *aux portes*, to eavesdrop. s'~ *trop*, to coddle oneself. **écouteur, euse** (tœːr, øːz) *n*, listener. ~ *aux portes*, eavesdropper. ¶ *m*, receiver, earpiece (*Teleph.*). **écouteux** (tø) *a.m*, skittish (*horse*).

écoutille (ekutiːj) *f*, hatch[way].

écouvillon (ekuvijɔ̃) *m*, mop; sponge (*gun*); swab (*Med.*).

écrabouiller (ekrabuje) *v.t*, to crush, squash.

écran (ekrɑ̃) *m*, screen; filter (*Phot.*); shade. ~ *à pied*, fire screen. ~ *fumigène* (fymiʒɛn), smoke screen.

écrasé, e (ekraze) *p.a*, squat. **écraser** (ze) *v.t*, to crush; squash; run over; overwhelm. *en* ~, to sleep very soundly. s'~, to collapse, crumple up, crash.

écrémer (ekreme) *v.t*, to cream, skim.

écrevisse (ekrəvis) *f*, crayfish, crawfish (*river*).

écrier (s') (ekrie) *v.pr*, to exclaim, cry; c. out.

écrin (ekrɛ̃) *m*, case, jewel case, casket. ~ *manucure*, manicure set.

écrire (ekriːr) *v.t. & abs. ir*, to write; spell. ~ *à la machine*, to type. **écrit** (kri) *m*, writing; document. **écrit, e** (kri, it) *p.p*, written; w. on; statute (*law*). **écriteau** (to) *m*, bill, notice; n. board. **écriture** (tyːr) *f*, writing; handwriting. ~ *à la machine*, typewriting, typing. ~ *de pattes de mouche*, crabbed handwriting. l'Écriture [*sainte*] ou *les* [*saintes*] *Écritures*, [Holy] Scripture, the Scriptures, Holy Writ. **écrivailler** (vaje) *ou* **écrivasser** (vase) *v.i*, to scribble (*of author*). **écrivailleur, euse** (vajœːr, øːz) *ou* **écrivassier, ère** (vasje, ɛːr) *n*, scribbler, hack, penny-a-liner. **écrivain** (vɛ̃) *m*, writer, author.

écrou (ekru) *m*, nut; entry (*in prison register*). ~ *à dix pans*, octagonal nut. ~ *à oreilles* ~ *papillon*, wing n. ~ *à six pans*, hexagonal n. **écrouer** (ekrue) *v.t*, to enter (*in prison register*).

écroulement (ekrulmɑ̃) *m*, collapse. s'écrouler (le) *v.pr,* to collapse, give way.

écru, e (ekry) *a,* raw; unbleached.

écu (eky) *m,* shield; escutcheon; (*pl.*) money.

écueil (ekœij) *m,* reef, rock, shelf; pitfall; cause of downfall.

écuelle (ekyɛl) *f,* bowl; porringer. écuellée (le) *f,* bowlful.

éculer (ekyle) *v.t,* to wear down (*shoe*) at heel.

écume (ekym) *f,* foam; froth; lather; scum, dross, skimmings. ~ de mer, [sea] wrack; meerschaum. écumer (me) *v.i,* to foam, froth; (*v.t.*) to skim [off], scum; scour, rove (*seas*); pick up (*news*). écumeux, euse (mø, ǿːz) *a,* foamy, frothy. écumoire (mwaːr) *f,* skimmer.

écurer (ekyre) *v.t,* to scour, cleanse, clean out.

écureuil (ekyrœij) *m,* squirrel.

écurie (ekyri) *f,* stable, (*pl.*) mews; stud (*racing*).

écusson (ekysɔ̃) *m,* [e]scutcheon, shield, hatchment.

écuyer, ère (ekɥije, ɛːr) *n,* riding master; horseman, -woman; rider; equestrian; equerry; [e]squire (*Hist.*).

eczéma (egzema) *m,* eczema.

édelweiss (edɛlvajs *ou* -vɛs) *m,* edelweiss.

éden (edɛn) *m,* Eden (*fig.*). l'É~, [the Garden of] Eden.

édenté, e (edɑ̃te) *a,* toothless.

édicter (edikte) *v.t,* to decree, enact.

édicule (edikyl) *m,* kiosk, shelter; public convenience.

édification (edifikasjɔ̃) *f,* erection; edification. édifice (fis) *m,* edifice, building, structure. édifier (fje) *v.t,* to erect, build; b. up; edify; enlighten.

édile (edil) *m,* magistrate; aedile (*Hist.*). édilité (lite) *f,* magistrature.

Edimbourg (edɛ̃buːr) *m,* Edinburgh.

édit (edi) *m,* edict.

éditer (edite) *v.t,* to publish; edit. éditeur, trice (tœːr, tris) *n,* publisher; editor, tress. édition (sjɔ̃) *f,* edition; publishing. ~ à tirage restreint, limited edition.

édredon (edrədɔ̃) *m,* eiderdown.

éducateur, trice (edykatœːr, tris) *n,* educator. éducation (sjɔ̃) *f,* education; training; upbringing; rearing; nurture. sans ~, ill-bred. éduquer (ke) *v.t,* to bring up; train.

éfaufiler (efofile) *v.t,* to unravel.

effacé, e (efase) *p.a,* unobtrusive. effacer (se) *v.t,* to efface, obliterate, delete; erase, rub out, blot out, wipe out, expunge; outshine. s'~, to wear away; keep in the background; stand aside. effaçure (syːr) *f,* obliteration, deletion; erasure.

effarement (efarmɑ̃) *m,* fright. effarer (re) *v.t,* to scare, frighten. effaroucher (ruʃe) *v.t,* to startle, frighten away. s'~, to take fright.

effectif, ive† (efɛktif, iːv) *a,* effective; real; actual; in cash, in coin; paid up (*capital*). ¶ *m,* effective, strength, complement, force (*men*). effectuer (tɥe) *v.t,* to effect, carry out, make, execute.

efféminé, e (efemine) *a,* effeminate, womanish, unmanly, ladylike. ¶ *m,* effeminate [man]. efféminer (ne) *v.t,* to [make] effeminate.

effervescence (efɛrvɛsɑ̃ːs) *f,* effervescence, -ency; ferment (*fig.*), unrest. effervescent, e (sɑ̃, ɑ̃ːt) *a,* effervescent.

effet (efɛ) *m,* effect; action; purpose, avail; impression; screw, break, spin (*on ball*); negotiable instrument; bill [of exchange], bill or note, draft; (*pl.*) effects, goods, belongings, things; securities, stock[s & shares]. ~ à payer, à recevoir, bill payable, receivable. à ~, intended for effect. en ~, in fact, indeed.

effeuiller (efœje) *v.t,* to thin out, pluck (*leaves, petals, hopes*).

efficace† (efikas) *a,* efficacious; effectual; efficient; able; adequate. efficacité (site) *f,* efficacy; efficiency.

effigie (efiʒi) *f,* effigy.

effilé, e (efile) *a,* slender; slim; tapering, streamlined. ¶ *m,* fringe. effiler (le) *v.t,* to unravel. s'effilocher (lɔʃe) *v.pr,* to fray. effilure (lyːr) *f,* ravelings.

efflanqué, e (eflãke) *p.a*, emaciated; lank[y].

effleurer (eflœre) *v.t*, to touch, t on; graze; glance, skim; scratch.

effleurir (eflœriːr) *v.i. & s'~*, to effloresce. **efflorescence** (eflɔresãɪs) *f*, efflorescence.

effluve (eflyːv) *m*, effluvium.

effondrement (efɔdrəmã) *m*, fall; subsidence; collapse, downfall; slump. **effondrer** (dre) *v.t*, to break open, stave in. *s'~*, to fall in, cave in; collapse, slump. **effondrilles** (driːj) *f.pl*, grounds, sediment.

efforcer (s') (efɔrse) *v.pr. & abs*, to endeavor, strive, do one's utmost. **effort** (fɔːr) *m*, effort, exertion, endeavor; force; stress (*Mech.*); strain. *~ de traction*, pull.

effraction (efraksjɔ̃) *f*, housebreaking.

effraie (efrɛ) *f*, barn owl, screech owl.

effranger (efrãʒe) *v.t*, to fray.

effrayant, e (efrejã, ãɪt) *a*, dreadful, frightful. **effrayer** (je) *v.t*, to frighten, scare.

effréné, e (efrene) *a*, unbridled, unrestrained; frantic.

effriter (efrite) *v.t*, to exhaust. *s'~*, to crumble.

effroi (efrwɑ) *m*, fright, terror.

effronté, e (efrɔ̃te) *a*, shameless, brazen, impudent, barefaced. **effrontément** (mã) *ad*, shamelessly. **effronterie** (tri) *f*, effrontery.

effroyable† (efrwajabl) *a*, frightful; awful.

effusion (ɛfyzjɔ̃) *f*, effusion, outpouring; shedding; overflowing; effusiveness. *~ de sang*, bloodshed.

égal, e (egal) *a*, equal; even, level; equable; alike; [all] the same, all one. ¶ *n*, equal (*of pers.*). *à l'égal de*, like. **également** (lmã) *ad*, equally, alike. **égaler** (le) *v.t*, to equalize, make equal; equal; match. **égaliser** (lize) *v.t*, to equalize; level. **égalité** (te) *f*, equality; evens (*betting*); evenness; smoothness. *~ à rien*, love all (*Ten.*). *~ de points*, tie (*sport*). *~ de voix*, tie (*voting*). *à ~*, deuce (*40 all*) (*Ten.*).

égard (egaɪr) *m*, regard, consideration, respect; sake. *à l'~ de*, with regard (*or* respect) (*or* reference) to. *en ~ à*, considering.

égaré, e (egare) *a*, lost, stray[ed]; erring; wild (*eyes*). **égarer** (re) *v.t*, to mislead, misguide, lead astray; bewilder; mislay. *s'~*, to go astray, lose one's way; miscarry.

égayer (egɛje) *v.t*, to enliven, cheer [up], exhilarate. *s'~*, to make merry.

Égée (la mer) (eʒe), the Aegean sea.

égide (eʒid) *f*, aegis, wing.

églantier (eglãtje) *m*, wild (*or* dog) rose (*bush*). *~ odorant*, sweetbriar. **églantine** (tin) *f*, wild (*or* dog) rose (*flower*). *~ odorante*, sweetbriar, eglantine.

église (egliːz) *f*, church. *l'É~ anglicane* (ãglikan), the Church of England. *l'É~ d'État*, the established Church. *~ de monastère*, *~ abbatiale* (abasjal), minster.

égoïsme (egoism) *m*, egoism, selfishness. **égoïste†** (ist) *a*, egoistic(al), selfish. ¶ *n*, egoist.

égorger (egɔrʒe) *v.t*, to cut the throat of; butcher, slaughter; ruin.

égosiller (s') (egozije) *v.pr*, to shout (*or* sing) oneself hoarse.

égotisme (egotism) *m*, egotism. **égotiste** (tist) *a*, egotistic(al). ¶ *n*, egotist.

égout (egu) *m*, drainage (*surplus water*); drip[pings]; sewer, drain. **égoutier** (tje) *m*, sewerman. **égoutter** (te) *v.t. & i. & s'~*, to drain; drip. **égouttoir** (twaɪr) *m*, drainer, draining rack; plate rack. **égoutture** (tyɪr) *f*, drainings; drippings.

égratigner (egratiɲe) *v.t*, to scratch. **égratignure** (ɲyɪr) *f*, scratch.

égrener (egrəne) *v.t*, to pick off; shell; gin (*cotton*); tell (*beads*). *s'~*, to seed.

égrillard, e (egrijaɪr, ard) *a*, ribald.

Égypte (l') (eʒipt) *f*, Egypt. **égyptien, ne** (sjɛ̃, ɛn) *a. & É~*, *n*, Egyptian. **égyptologie** (tɔlɔʒi) *f*, Egyptology. **égyptologue** (lɔg) *m*, Egyptologist.

eh (e) *i*, [h]eh! ~ *bien!* now then! well!

éhonté, e (eõte) *a*, shameless, barefaced.

eider (edɛːr) *m*, eider [duck].

éjaculation (eʒakylasjɔ̃) *f*, ejaculation (*fluid*); fervent prayer. **éjaculer** (le) *v.t.* & *i*, to ejaculate (*fluid*).

éjecteur (eʒɛktœːr) *m*, ejector.

élaborer (elabɔre) *v.t*, to elaborate; work out, evolve.

élagage (elagaːʒ) *m*, lopping; pruning; prunings. **élaguer** (ge) *v.t*, to lop; prune.

élan (elɑ̃) *m*, bound, spring; dash, dart, rush, run[-up] (*Jump.*); [out]burst; impetus, momentum; flight; glow; elk, moose, eland. *avec ~*, running (*jump, dive*). *sans ~*, standing (*j., d.*). **élancé, e** (se) *a*, slender, slim. **élancements** (smɑ̃) *m.pl*, shooting pains, twinges; yearning (*soul*). **élancer** (se) *v.i*, to throb, shoot. *s'~*, to bound, spring, leap, dash, dart.

élargir (elarʒiːr) *v.t*, to enlarge; broaden; widen; let out; extend; release (*prisoner*).

élasticité (elastisite) *f*, elasticity, spring[iness], resilience. **élastique** (tik) *a*, elastic, spring[y]; resilient; bouyant. ¶ *m*, elastic.

Elbe(l'île d') (ɛlb) *f*, the Island of Elba. **l'Elbe**, *m*, the Elbe (*river*).

eldorado (ɛldɔrado) *m*, El Dorado.

électeur, trice (elɛktœːr, tris) *n*, elector, constituent. **élection** (sjɔ̃) *f*, election, polling. *~ de remplacement*, *~ partielle*, by-election. **électorat** (tɔra) *m*, franchise.

électricien (elɛktrisjɛ̃) *m*, electrician. **électricité** (site) *f*, electricity. **électrification** (fikasjɔ̃) *f*, electrification. **électrifier** (fje) *v.t*, to electrify. **électrique** (trik) *a*, electric(al). **électriser** (ze) *v.t*, to electrify, electrize; thrill. **électro-aimant** (trɔɛmɑ̃) *m*, electromagnet. **électrocuter** (kyte) *v.t*, to electrocute. **électrode** (trɔd) *f*, electrode. **électrolyse** (liːz) *f*, electrolysis. **électron** (trɔ̃) *m*,

electron. **électrotype** (tip) *m*, electrotype.

élégamment (elegamɑ̃) *ad*, elegantly, stylishly. **élégance** (gɑ̃ːs) *f*, elegance, stylishness. **élégant, e** (gɑ̃, ɑ̃ːt) *a*, elegant, stylish, fashionable. ¶ *n*, man, woman, of fashion.

élégie (eleʒi) *f*, elegy.

élément (elemɑ̃) *m*, element; (*pl.*) rudiments (*of a science, an art*); unit; cell (*Phys.*). **élémentaire** (tɛːr) *a*, elementary.

éléphant (elefɑ̃) *m*, elephant.

élevage (elvaːʒ) *m*, breeding, rearing, stock farming. **élévateur** (elevatœːr) *m*, elevator. **élévation** (sjɔ̃) *f*, elevation; raising; rise; eminence; height; loftiness; altitude. **élévatoire** (twaːr) *m*, elevator (*Surg.*). **élève** (elɛːv) *n*, pupil, student; rearing (*animal reared*). *~ de l'école navale*, naval cadet. ¶ *f*, breeding, rearing (*act*). **élevé, e** (elve) *p.a*, high; lofty; bred, brought up. **élever** (ve) *v.t*, to elevate, raise, lift; erect; bring up, rear, breed. *s'~*, to rise; arise. *s'~ à*, to reach, amount to. **éleveur** (lvœːr) *m*, grazier; breeder.

elfe (ɛlf) *m*, elf, brownie.

élider (elide) *v.t*, to elide.

éligible (eliʒibl) *a*, eligible.

élimer (elime) *v.t*, to wear threadbare.

éliminatoire (eliminatwaːr) *a.* & *f*, eliminating *or* trial (heat). **éliminer** (ne) *v.t*, to eliminate; weed out.

élingue (elɛ̃ːg) *f*, sling.

élire (eliːr) *v.t.ir*, to elect; return.

élision (elizjɔ̃) *f*, elision.

élite (elit) *f*, elite.

élixir (eliksiːr) *m*, elixir.

elle (ɛl) *pn*, she; her; it; herself. *~-même*, herself; itself. *~s*, *pl*, they; them. *~-mêmes*, themselves.

ellipse (elips) *f*, ellipse; ellipsis. **elliptique†** (tik) *a*, elliptic(al).

élocution (elɔkysjɔ̃) *f*, elocution.

éloge (elɔːʒ) *m*, eulogy, praise, encomium. **élogieux, euse†** (lɔʒjø, øːz) *a*, eulogistic.

éloigné, e (elwaɲe) *p.a*, distant, outlying, far [off *or* away], remote. **éloignement** (ɲmã) *m*, removal; estrangement; distance, remoteness; dislike. **éloigner** (ɲe) *v.t*, to remove; keep away; defer; estrange; disincline. **s'~**, to withdraw, go away; differ; swerve.

éloquemment (elɔkamã) *ad*, eloquently. **éloquence** (kã:s) *f*, eloquence, oratory. **éloquent, e** (kã, ã:t) *a*, eloquent.

Elseneur (ɛlsənœːr) *f*, Elsinore.

élu, e (ely) *n*, elected member. *les élus*, the elect (*Relig.*).

élucider (elyside) *v.t*, to elucidate.

élucubration (elykybrasjɔ̃) *f*, lucubration.

éluder (elyde) *v.t*, to elude, evade, shirk.

élyme (elim) *m*, lyme-grass.

élysée & (*Myth.*) É~ (elize) *m*, Elysium. *l'É~*, the Élysée, Paris residence of French president. **élyséen, ne** (zeɛ̃, ɛn) *a*, Elysian.

émacié, e (emasje) *a*, emaciated.

émail (emaːj) *m*, enamel; e. ware; glaze. **émaillage** (majaːʒ) *m*, enameling. **émailler** (je) *v.t*, to enamel; glaze; stud; intersperse.

émanation (emanasjɔ̃) *f*, emanation, efflux, effluence.

émanciper (emãsipe) *v.t*, to emancipate. **s'~**, to overstep the mark (*fig.*), forget oneself.

émaner (emane) *v.i*, to emanate, issue.

émarger (emarʒe) *v.t*, to sign [in the margin]; draw (*salary*); trim the margins of.

émasculer (emaskyle) *v.t*, to emasculate.

emballage (ãbalaːʒ) *m*, packing; spurt, burst (*speed*). **emballement** (lmã) *m*, bolting (*horse*); racing (*Mach.*); boom (*Stk Ex.*); excitement. **emballer** (le) *v.t*, to pack [up], wrap [up]; pack off, bundle off; carry away (*fig.*). **s'~**, to bolt; race; be carried away. **emballeur** (lœːr) *m*, packer.

embarcadère (ãbarkadɛːr) *m*, landing [place *or* stage]; wharf; platform (*Rly.*). **embarcation** (sjɔ̃) *f*, craft, boat, launch.

embardée (ãbarde) *f*, lurch,

[sudden] swerve; yaw. *faire une ~*, to yaw; swerve; catch a crab (*boating*).

embargo (ãbargo) *m*, embargo.

embarquement (ãbarkəmã) *m*, embarkation; shipment; entrainment. **embarquer** (ke) *v.t. & s'~*, to embark; ship; entrain; (*v.i.*) to ship water, ship a sea. *s'~ clandestinement*, to stow away.

embarras (ãbara) *m*, obstruction, block, jam; traffic jam; encumbrance; inconvenience; superfluity; airs (*affectation*); perplexity, fix, quandary, embarrassment; straits; difficulty, scrape. *~ de la langue*, impediment of speech, i. in one's s. *faire des ~*, to be fussy. **embarrassant, e** (sã, ã:t) *a*, cumbersome; awkward, embarrassing. **embarrasser** (se) *v.t*, to obstruct, block [up]; [en]cumber, hamper; be in the way of; entangle; embarrass, perplex, nonplus.

embâter (ãbate) *v.t*, to saddle.

embaucher (ãboʃe) *v.t*, to engage, take on (*workmen*). *bureau d'embauche*, hiring office. **embauchoir** (ʃwaːr) *m*, shoe tree.

embaumer (ãbome) *v.t*, to embalm; perfume, scent.

embéguiner (ãbegine) *v.t*, to muffle up; infatuate.

embellie (ãbɛli) *f*, lull. **embellir** (liːr) *v.t*, to embellish, beautify; improve; (*v.i.*) to grow more beautiful.

emberlificoter (ãbɛrlifikɔte) *v.t*, to entangle.

embesogné, e (ãbəzɔɲe) *a*, very busy.

embêtant, e (ãbɛtã) *a*, annoying, boring.

embêter (ãbɛte) *v.t*, to annoy; bore.

emblée (d') (ãble) *ad*, at the very outset, right away, straight off.

emblématique (ãblematik) *a*, emblematic(al). **emblème** (blɛːm) *m*, emblem; attribute.

embob[el]iner (ãbɔb[l]ine) *v.t*, to wheedle, coax.

emboîter (ãbwate) *v.t*, to fit

in[to], box, nest, house; socket.
embolie (ãbɔli) f, embolism.
embonpoint (ãbɔ̃pwɛ̃) m, stoutness, plumpness, flesh.
emboucher (ãbuʃe) v.t, to put to one's mouth; blow. *mal embouché*, foul-mouthed. **embouchoir** (ʃwaːr) m, mouthpiece; shoe tree. **embouchure** (ʃyɪr) f, mouthpiece; mouth.
embouer (ãbwe) v.t, to muddy.
embourber (ãburbe) v.t, to bog, mire; involve. **s'~**, to stick in the mud.
embourgeoiser (s') (ãburʒwaze) v.pr, to marry into (or mix with) the middle classes.
embout (ãbu) m, ferrule; capping.
embouteillage (ãbutejaːʒ) m, bottling (*wine, etc.*); bottling up (*harbor*); traffic jam. **embouteiller** (eje) v.t, to bottle; b. up; block.
embouter (ãbute) v.t, to ferrule, tip.
emboutir (ãbutiːr) v.t, to shape, stamp, press; ferrule.
embranchement (ãbrãʃmã) m, branching [off]; junction (*Rly.*). **~** *particulier*, private siding (*Rly.*). **embrancher** (ʃe) v.t, to branch off.
embrasement (ãbrazmã) m, conflagration, burning; illumination. **embraser** (ze) v.t, to [set on] fire; illuminate (*festively*).
embrassade (ãbrasad) f, embrace, hug. **embrasse** (bras) f, curtain holder. **embrassement** (smã) m, embrace. **embrasser** (se) v.t, to embrace; hug; kiss (Cf. *baiser*); take in; take up; espouse. *je vous embrasse* [*de tout cœur*], [with] [best] love (*letter*).
embrasure (ãbrazyɪr) f, recess; embrasure.
embrayer (ãbreje) v.t, to engage (*Mach.*), throw into gear. **embrayage** (jaːʒ) m, engaging; clutch.
embrever (ãbreve) v.t, to joggle.
embrigader (ãbrigade) v.t, to brigade; enroll.
embrocation (ãbrɔkasjɔ̃) f, embrocation.
embrocher (ãbrɔʃe) v.t, to spit; run through, impale.

embrouillamini (ãbrujamini) m, confusion. **embrouiller** (je) v.t, to ravel, tangle; embroil, muddle, confuse.
embroussaillé, e (ãbrusaje) a, brushy; bushy; matted.
embrumer (ãbryme) v.t, to fog, shroud, darken. **embrun** (brœ̃) m, spray, spindrift.
embryon (ãbriɔ̃) m, embryo. **embryonnaire** (ɔnɛɪr) a, embryonic.
embûche (ãbyʃ) f, trap. **embuscade** (byskad) f, ambush, ambuscade. *se tenir en ~*, to lie in wait. **embusqué** (ke) m, shirker. **embusquer** (ke) v.t, to place in ambush. **s'~**, to ambush, lie in wait; shirk.
émeraude (emroːd) f, emerald.
émerger (emɛrʒe) v.i, to emerge; loom; peep.
émeri (emri) m, emery.
émerillon (emrijɔ̃) m, merlin (*bird*); swivel. **émerillonné, e** (jɔne) a, bright, sparkling.
émérite (emerit) a, experienced; confirmed; emeritus.
émerveiller (emɛrveje) v.t, to astonish. **s'~**, to marvel.
émétique (emetik) a. & m, emetic.
émetteur (emetœːr) m, issuer; (*att.*) transmitter (*Teleg.*). **émettre** (tr) v.t.ir, to emit; utter; express; issue; broadcast; transmit.
émeute (emøːt) f, riot, disturbance, outbreak. **émeutier** (møtje) m, rioter.
émietter (emjɛte) v.t. & **s'~**, to crumble.
émigrant, e (emigrã, ãːt) n, emigrant. **émigration** (grasjɔ̃) f, emigration. **émigré, e** (gre) n, refugee; émigré (*Hist.*). **émigrer** (gre) v.i, to emigrate; migrate.
émincé, e (emɛ̃se) p.p, cut into thin slices. ¶ m, hash.
éminemment (eminamã) ad, eminently, highly. **éminence** (nãɪs) f, eminence; height; ball (*thumb*). *Son E~*, f, His Eminence (*cardinal*). **éminent, e** (nã, ãɪt) a, eminent; distinguished; prominent. **éminentissime** (nãtisim) a, most eminent.
émir (emiːr) m, emir; ameer; amir.

émissaire (emisɛːr) *m*, emissary.

émission (sjɔ̃) *f*, emission; issue; uttering; broadcasting, transmission. ~ *en différé*, prerecorded broadcast. ~ *en direct*, live broadcast.

emmagasiner (ɑ̃magazine) *v.t*, to store, s. up; warehouse.

emmailloter (ɑ̃majɔte) *v.t*, to swathe; bandage.

emmancher (ɑ̃mɑ̃ʃe) *v.t*, to handle; fix; set about. **emmanchure** (ʃyːr) *f*, armhole.

emmêler (ɑ̃mɛle) *v.t*, to [en]-tangle; muddle.

emménagement (ɑ̃menaʒmɑ̃) *m,.* moving in (*house*); accommodation, appointments (*ship*). **emménager** (ʒe) *v.t*, to install, settle;. move into; (*v.i.*) to move in.

emmener (ɑ̃mne) *v.t*, to take away.

emmerdant (ɑ̃mɛrdɑ̃) *a*, annoying, irritating. **emmerdement** (dmɑ̃) *m*, nuisance, irritation; problem; difficulty. **emmerder** (de) *v.t*, to annoy, irritate. s'~, to be bored.

emmiellé, e (ɑ̃mjɛle) *a*, honeyed.

emmitoufler (ɑ̃mitufle) *v.t*, to muffle up.

emmortaiser (ɑ̃mɔrtɛze) *v.t*, to mortise.

émoi (emwa) *m*, emotion, agitation,. flutter.

émollient, e (emɔljɑ̃, ɑ̃ːt) *a*. & *m*, emollient.

émoluments (emɔlymɑ̃) *m.pl*, emoluments.

émonder (emɔ̃de) *v.t*, to prune. **émondes** (mɔ̃d) *f.pl*, prunings.

émotion (emosjɔ̃) *f*, emotion; thrill;. excitement.

émoucher (emuʃe) *v.t*, to drive away the flies from.

émouchet (emuʃɛ) *m*, kestrel.

émouchette (emuʃɛt) *f*, fly net. **émouchoir** (ʃwaːr) *m*, fly whisk.

émoulu, e (emuly) *a: frais ~ de*, fresh from (*college*); well up in (*subject*).

émousser (emuse) *v.t*, to blunt, dull; remove the moss from.

émoustiller (emustije) *v.t*, to exhilarate.

émouvant (emuvɑ̃) *a*, moving, touching, thrilling.

émouvoir (emuvwaːr) *v.t.ir*, to move; stir [up], rouse.

empailler (ɑ̃paje) *v.t*, to cover (*or* pack) (*or* stuff) with straw; stuff (*dead animal*). **empailleur, euse** (jœːr, øːz) *n*, chair caner, taxidermist.

empanacher (ɑ̃panaʃe) *v.t*, to plume; adorn.

empaqueter (ɑ̃pakte) *v.t*, to pack [up]. s'~, to wrap [oneself] up.

emparer (s') de (ɑ̃pare) *v.pr*, to seize, take possession of; monopolize, engross.

empâter (ɑ̃pate) *v.t*, to paste; make sticky; fatten, force-feed (*poultry*); impaste.

empattement (ɑ̃patmɑ̃) *m*, footing (*Build.*); wheelbase; serif.

empaumer (ɑ̃pome) *v.t*, to strike (*ball*); manipulate (*pers.*).

empêché, e (ɑ̃peʃe) *p.p*, puzzled, at a loss. **empêchement** (ʃmɑ̃) *m*, hindrance, impediment, obstacle, bar; prevention. **empêcher** (ʃe) *v.t*, to prevent, hinder, impede; keep from; preclude. s'~, to forbear, refrain, help.

empeigne (ɑ̃pɛɲ) *f*, vamp, upper (*shoe*).

empereur (ɑ̃prœːr) *m*, emperor.

empesé, e (ɑ̃pəze) *a*, starchy, stiff. **empeser** (ze) *v.t*, to starch.

empester (ɑ̃peste) *v.t*, to infect; corrupt; (*abs.*) to stink.

empêtrer (ɑ̃pɛtre) *v.t*, to entangle, hamper; embarrass; involve.

emphase (ɑ̃fɑːs) *f*, bombast, pomposity, fustian; magniloquence; emphasis. **emphatique†** (fatik) *a*, bombastic, pompous; magniloquent; emphatic.

empiècement (ɑ̃pjɛsmɑ̃) *m*, yoke (*dress*).

empierrer (ɑ̃pjere) *v.t*, to pave, macadamize; fill with stones (*drainage ditch*).

empiètement (ɑ̃pjɛtmɑ̃) *m*, encroachment, trespass. **empiéter sur** (pjete), to encroach on; trespass on (*fig.*).

empiffrer (ɑ̃pifre) *v.t*, to stuff, gorge.

empiler (ăpile) *v.t*, to pile [up]; stack; herd together.

empire (ăpi:r) *m*, dominion, sway, hold; mastery; rule; empire. ~ *sur soi-même*, self-control.

empirer (ăpire) *v.t*, to make worse; (*v.i.*) to grow worse.

empirique (ăpirik) *a*, empiric(al), rule-of-thumb. ¶ *m*, empiric[ist]. **empiriquement** (kmã) *ad*, empirically, by rule of thumb. **empirisme** (rism) *m*, empiricism.

emplacement (ăplasmã) *m*, site, position, location.

emplâtre (ăplɑ:tr) *m*, plaster (*Phar.*); futile person. ~ *adhésif*, adhesive plaster.

emplette (ăplɛt) *f*, purchase, shopping; bargain.

emplir (ăpli:r) *v.t. & s'~*, to fill; (*v.i.*) to be swamped (*boat*).

emploi (ăplwa) *m*, employment; job; use; entry (*Bkkpg.*); part, line (*of actor*). plein ~, full employment. **employé, e** (je) *n*, employee; clerk. ~ *d'administration*, civil servant. ~ *du gaz*, gas man. **employer** (je) *v.t*, to employ; use. s'~, to occupy (*or* exert) (*or* busy) oneself. **employeur, euse** (jœːr, øːz) *n*, employer.

emplumé, e (ăplyme) *p.a*, feathered. **emplumer** (me) *v.t*, to feather; tar & feather.

empocher (ăpoʃe) *v.t*, to pocket.

empoignant, e (ăpwaɲɑ̃, ɑ̃:t) *a*, thrilling, poignant. **empoigner** (ɲe) *v.t*, to grasp; grip; clutch; grab; take to task, abuse; thrill.

empois (ăpwa) *m*, starch [paste].

empoisonnement (ăpwazɔnmɑ̃) *m*, poisoning. **empoisonner** (ne) *v.t*, to poison; infect; corrupt; (*abs.*) to be poisonous; stink. **empoisonneur, euse** (nœːr, øːz) *n*, poisoner; bad cook.

empoissonner (ăpwasɔne) *v.t*, to stock (*pond*) with fish.

emporté, e (ăpɔrte) *a*, hasty, quick-tempered, fiery, passionate. **emportement** (təmɑ̃) *m*, transport (*fig.*); outburst, fit of anger.

emporte-pièce (ăpɔrtəpjɛs) *m*, [hollow] punch. *à l'*~ (*fig.*), trenchant.

emporter (ăpɔrte) *v.t*, to carry (*or* take) (*or* sweep) (*or* wash) away (*or* off) (*or* out); (*Mil.*) carry (*place*). l'~ *sur*, to surpass, outdo; overrule; prevail over, preponderate over. s'~, to get angry, fire up; bolt (*horse*).

empoté, e (ăpote) *a*, clumsy. **empoter** (te) *v.t*, to pot.

empourprer (ăpurpre) *v.t*, to purple; crimson.

empreindre (ăprɛ̃:dr) *v.t.ir*, to imprint, impress, stamp. **empreinte** (prɛ̃:t) *f*, impress[ion], [im]print; stamp (*fig.*); mold (*Typ.*). ~ *de pas*, ~ *du pied*, footprint. ~ *digitale*, fingerprint. ~ *du doigt*, fingermark.

empressé, e (ăprese) *a*, eager, zealous; attentive. **empressement** (smã) *m*, eagerness, alacrity, readiness. **s'empresser** (se) *v.pr*, to hasten; be eager. ~ *auprès de*, to dance attendance on.

emprise (ăpri:z) *f*, hold, ascendancy.

emprisonnement (ăprizɔnmɑ̃) *m*, imprisonment. ~ *cellulaire*, separate cell system. **emprisonner** (ne) *v.t*, to imprison, confine.

emprunt (ăprœ̃) *m*, borrowing, loan; [making] use. ~ *de la Défense nationale*, war loan. *d'*~ (*fig.*), artificial, sham, assumed. **emprunté, e** (te) *p.a*, borrowed; assumed (*name*); awkward. **emprunter** (te) *v.t*, to borrow; assume (*name*); use, make use of. **emprunteur, euse** (tœːr, øːz) *n*, borrower.

empuantir (ăpɥɑ̃ti:r) *v.t*, to infect.

empyrée (ăpire) *m*, empyrean.

ému, *p.p*, émouvoir.

émulation (emylasjɔ̃) *f*, emulation. **émule** (myl) *n*, emulator, rival.

émulsion (emylsjɔ̃) *f*, emulsion.

en (ɑ̃) *pr*, in; into; within; on; to; at; with; in the; in a; like [a]; as [a]; by; while; of; under. ~ *voiture!* all aboard!

en (ɑ̃) *pn. & ad*, of it, its, of them, their, of him, of her; about it, about them, etc.; for (*or* by) (*or* with) (*or* from) it *or* them, etc.;

some, any. ~ *sus*, or *plus*, in addition. ~ *venir là*, to come (*sink*) to that point. *je n'*~ *ai pas*, I don't have any. *si le cœur vous* ~ *dit*, if you feel like doing it.

enamourer (s') (ănamure) *v.pr*, to fall in love.

énarque (enark) *m*, civil service administrator, student or graduate of the École Nationale d'Administration.

encadrement (ăkadramă) *m*, framing; officering (*Mil.*); frame; framework. ~ *de credit*, credit regulation.

encadrer (ăkadre) *v.t*, to frame; surround; incorporate; officer.

encager (ăkaʒe) *v.t*, to [en]cage.

encaisse (ăkes) *f*, cash [in hand]. ~ *métallique*, cash & bullion in hand. **encaisser** (se) *v.t*, to [en]case; cash; collect; put in the cash box; embank (*river, road*); put up with. *il ne peut pas l'*~, he can't stand him.

encan (ăkă) *m*, auction.

encanailler (s') (ăkanaje) *v.i*, to contract low habits.

encaquer (ăkake) *v.t*, to barrel. *encaqués comme des harengs*, packed like sardines (*people*).

encart (ăkaːr) *m*, insert (*Bookb.*). **encarter** (karte) *v.t*, to inset (*Bookb.*); insert (*Bookb.*); card; card index; register.

en-cas (ăka) *m*, something (*ready to eat*) in case of need; umbrella-sunshade.

encastrer (ăkastre) *v.t*, to house; embed.

encaustique (ăkostik) *a. & f*, encaustic. ~ *pour meubles*, furniture polish. **encaustiquer** (ke) *v.t*, to polish (*furniture*).

encaver (ăkave) *v.t*, to cellar.

enceindre (ăsɛ̃ːdr) *v.t.ir*, to enclose, gird, surround. **enceinte** (sɛ̃ːt) *a.f*, pregnant, with child, expectant. ¶ *f*, enclosure; precinct; ring (*Box.*); fencing; wall; hall. ~ *du pesage*, paddock (*turf*). ~ *de confinement*, containment (*reactor*).

encens (ăsă) *m*, incense. ~ *mâle*, frankincense. **encenser** (se) *v.t*, to [in]cense, burn i. to; flatter. **encensoir** (swaːr) *m*, censer.

encercler (ăsɛrkle) *v.t*, to hoop; encircle.

enchaînement (ăʃɛnmă) (*fig.*) *m*, chain, series, train. **enchaîner** (ne) *v.t*, to chain [up]; enchain, fetter, manacle; bind; link; enslave; enthrall.

enchantement (ăʃătmă) *m*, enchantment, magic, spell; glamour, witchery; delight. **enchanter** (te) *v.t*, to enchant, bewitch; delight, enrapture. **enchanteur, eresse** (tœːr, trɛːs) *n*, enchanter, tress; (*att.*) enchanting, bewitching.

enchâsser (ăʃase) *v.t*, to set, mount; enshrine; incorporate. **enchâssure** (syːr) *f*, setting.

enchère (ăʃɛːr) *f*, bid[ding]; auction, sale. **enchérir** (ʃeriːr) *v.t*, to raise the price of; (*v.i.*) to rise in price; bid. ~ *sur*, to outbid; outdo. **enchérisseur** (risœːr) *m*, bidder.

enchevêtrer (s') (ăʃvetre) *v.pr*, to get [en]tangled (*or* confused).

enchifrènement (ăʃifrɛnmă) *m*, cold in the head, snuffles.

enclave (ăklaːv) *f*, land-locked property (*law*); enclave (*international*); recess (*Build.*). **enclaver** (klave) *v.t*, to enclose, shut in, fit in.

enclin, e (ăklɛ̃, in) *a*, inclined, prone, minded, given.

enclore (ăkloːr) *v.t.ir*, to enclose, fence in. **enclos** (klo) *m*, enclosure; paddock.

enclouer (ăklue) *v.t*, to spike (*gun*). **enclouure** (kluyːr) (*fig.*) *f*, rub.

enclume (ăklym) *f*, anvil.

encoche (ăkɔʃ) *f*, notch, nick, slot. ~*s*, thumb index (*books*). **encocher** (ʃe) *v.t*, to notch.

encodage (ăkɔdaːʒ) *m*, encoding (*computer, etc.*). **encoder** (de) *v.t*, to encode. **encodeur** (dœːr) *m*, encoder (*computers*).

encoignure (ăkɔɲyːr) *f*, corner; corner cupboard.

encollage (ăkɔlaːʒ) *m*, sizing; size (*glue*). **encoller** (le) *v.t*, to size.

encolure (ăkɔlyːr) *f*, neck; neck measurement, [neck] size; look (*fig.*).

encombrant, e (ăkɔ̃brɑ̃, ɑ̃:t) *a*, bulky; cumbersome, in the way; embarrassing. **sans encombre** (kɔ̃:br), without hindrance. **encombrement** (kɔ̃brəmɑ̃) *m*, block, congestion, [over]crowding; glut[ting]; litter; space occupied, floor space; measurement (*Ship.*). **encombrer** (bre) *v.t*, to block, congest, overcrowd; glut, overstock; encumber, litter.

encontre (à l'~ de) (ăkɔ̃:tr), in opposition to. **aller à l'~ de**, to run counter to.

encorbellement (ăkɔrbɛlmɑ̃) *m*, cantilever.

encore (ăkɔ:r) *ad*, still; yet; again; also; moreover; too; more; else. ~ **un, une**, one more, another. ~ **un coup**, once again, once more. ~ **un peu**, a little more *or* longer. ~ **que**, *c*, although.

encourager (ăkuraʒe) *v.t*, to encourage, hearten; foster; promote; countenance, abet; halloo (*dogs*).

encourir (ăkuri:r) *v.t.ir*, to incur, run.

encrasser (ăkrase) *v.t*, to foul, dirty, grime; clog.

encre (ɑ̃:kr) *f*, ink. ~ **à marquer le linge**, marking i. ~ **de Chine**, Indian i. ~ **stylographique** (stilɔgrafik), fountain pen i. **encrer** (ăkre) *v.t*, to ink. **encrier** (krie) *m*, inkstand, inkpot. ~ **d'écolier**, inkwell.

encroûté, e (ăkrute) (*fig.*) *a*, crusted, fogyish.

enculer (ăkyle) *v.t*, to sodomize; get the better of (*obscene*).

encuver (ăkyve) *v.t*, to vat; put in the tub.

encyclique (ăsiklik) *a. & f*, encyclic(al).

encyclopédie (ăsiklɔpedi) *f*, [en]cyclopedia.

endémique (ădemik) *a*, endemic.

endenter (ădɑ̃te) *v.t*, to tooth, cog.

endetté, e (ădɛte) *p.a*, in debt. **endetter** (te) *v.t*, to involve in debt. **s'~**, to run into d.

endeuiller (ădœje) *v.t*, to put into mourning; make gloomy.

endêvé, e (ădɛve) *a*, exasperated. **endêver** (ve) *v.i*, to be furious.

endiablé, e (ădjable) *a*, (*as if*) possessed; wild, frenzied. **endiabler** (ble) *v.i*, to be furious.

endiguer (ădige) *v.t*, to dike; dam.

endimancher (s') (ădimɑ̃ʃe) *v.pr*, to put on one's Sunday best.

endive (ădi;v) *f*, chicory; endive.

endoctriner (ădɔktrine) *v.t*, to indoctrinate; coach.

endolorir (ădɔlɔri:r) *v.t*, to make ache.

endommager (ădɔmaʒe) *v.t*, to damage, injure.

endormant, e (ădɔrmɑ̃, ɑ̃:t) *a*, soporific; wearisome. **endormeur** (mœ:r) *m*, bore. **endormi, e** (mi) *p.a*, asleep; sleepy; drowsy. ¶ *n*, sleepyhead. **endormir** (mi:r) *v.t.ir*, to send to sleep; lull. **s'~**, to fall asleep, go to sleep.

endos[sement] (ădo[smɑ̃]) *m*, endorsement. **endosser** (se) *v.t*, to put on, don; take on, shoulder; endorse. **endosseur** (sœ:r) *m*, endorser.

endroit (ădrwa) *m*, place, spot, part; right side, face (*fabric*). **à l'~ de**, towards, regarding.

enduire (ădɥi:r) *v.t.ir*, to smear; coat; render. **enduit** (dɥi) *m*, coat[ing]; rendering.

endurance (ădyrɑ̃:s) *f*, endurance. **endurant, e** (rɑ̃, ɑ̃:t) *a*, patient. **rendre ~**, to harden. **endurcir** (si:r) *v.t. & s'~*, to harden. **endurcissement** (sismɑ̃) *m*, hardness, callousness, obduracy. **endurer** (re) *v.t*, to endure.

énergétique (enɛrʒetik) *f*, energetics (*Phys.*). **énergie** (ʒi) *f*, energy, power; emphasis; efficacy (*remedy*); backbone. **énergique†** (ʒik) *a*, energetic, powerful, strong; forcible, emphatic; strenuous.

énergumène (enɛrgymɛn) *m.f*, fanatic; ranter.

énerver (enɛrve) *v.t*, to enervate; exasperate.

enfance (ăfɑ̃:s) *f*, childhood; infancy; second childhood, dotage; A B C (*of an art*). **enfant** (fɑ̃) *n*, child; infant; boy; girl; fellow, lad. ~ **de chœur**, choir boy, chorister. **~s perdus**, forlorn hope (*Mil.*). ~ *prodige*, infant prodigy. ~ *prodigue*, prodigal son. ~ *trouvé*, foundling; stowaway. **enfantement** (tmᾶ) *m*, birth (*fig.*). **enfanter** (te) *v.t*, to give birth to (*fig.*). **enfantillage** (tija:ʒ) *m*, childishness, **enfantin, e** (tᾶ, in) *a*, infantile; childish; infant (*class*); nursery (*language*).

enfariner (ᾶfarine) *v.t*, to [cover with] flour.

enfer (ᾶfɛ:r) *m*, hell, inferno. *les* ~*s*, the nether regions, the underworld, Hades. *d'*~, infernal; blazing (*fire*).

enfermer (ᾶfɛrme) *v.t*, to shut up; lock up; enclose; impound; contain.

enferrer (ᾶfɛre) *v.t*, to run through (*with sword*). *s'*~, to become involved. *s'*~ *soi-même*, to give oneself away.

enfieller (ᾶfjɛle) *v.t*, to embitter, sour.

enfiévrer (ᾶfjevre) *v.t*, to make feverish.

enfilade (ᾶfilad) *f*, suite; series, string; row; enfilade. **enfiler** (le) *v.t*, to thread; string; run (*or* go) through; go along; enfilade, rake; draw in (*person to reckless gaming*).

enfin (ᾶfᾶ) *ad*, at last, lastly, after all; in short, in fine; in fact; come now!

enflammer (ᾶflame) *v.t*, to [set on] fire, ignite; inflame. *s'*~, to catch (*or* take) fire, ignite, fire up.

enfler (ᾶfle) *v.t. & i. & s'*~, to swell, inflate. **enflure** (fly:r) *f*, swelling, etc.

enfoncer (ᾶfᴐse) *v.t*, to drive [in]; sink, bury, immerse; break open, b. in; b. up; stave in; (*v.i. & abs.*) to sink. **enfoncement** (smᾶ) *m*, driving [in]; hollow, depression; recess; background. **enfonçure** (sy:r) *f*, hole; bottom (*cask*).

enfouir (ᾶfwi:r) *v.t*, to bury, hide.

enfourcher (ᾶfurʃe) *v.t*, to bestride; ride to death (*fig.*).

enfourner (ᾶfurne) *v.t*, to put in the oven.

enfreindre (ᾶfrɛ̃:dr) *v.t.ir*, to infringe, break.

enfuir (s') (ᾶfɥi:r) *v.pr*, to flee; escape; run away; elope; leak; fly; vanish.

enfumer (ᾶfyme) *v.t*, to smoke; s. out.

engageant, e (ᾶgaʒᾶ, ᾶ:t) *a*, engaging, winning; inviting. **engagement** (ʒmᾶ) *m*, engagement; booking; entry (*sporting event*); enlistment; signing on; commitment; liability, undertaking; pledging, pledge, pawning, hypothecation. **engager** (ʒe) *v.t*, to engage; book; enter; enlist; sign [on]; betroth; bind; plight; pledge, pawn; mortgage, hypothecate; invite, urge, induce; foul (*ropes*). **engagé**, *p.p*, on her beam ends; waterlogged (*boat*). **s'engager**, to undertake, covenant; enlist; enter; foul.

engainer (ᾶgɛne) *v.t*, to sheathe, case.

engeance (ᾶʒᾶ:s) *f*, brood, lot (*of despicable people*).

engelure (ᾶʒly:r) *f*, chilblain.

engendrer (ᾶʒᾶdre) *v.t*, to beget; sire; engender; breed; generate.

engerber (ᾶʒɛrbe) *v.t*, to sheaf, bind.

engin (ᾶʒᾶ) *m*, appliance, contrivance, gear, tackle; engine (*of war*); missile. ~ *spatiale*, spacecraft.

englober (ᾶglᴐbe) *v.t*, to include, embody.

engloutir (ᾶgluti:r) *v.t*, to swallow; s. up; bolt (*food*); engulf, swamp.

engluer (ᾶglye) *v.t*, to [bird] lime; ensnare; take in.

engoncé (ᾶgᴐse) *a*, stiff, awkward; bundled up; bound up in.

engorger (ᾶgᴐrʒe) *v.t*, to choke [up], stop up.

engouer (s') (ᾶgue) *v.pr*, to become infatuated.

engouffrer (ᾶgufre) *v.t*, to engulf, swallow up.

engourdir (ᾶgurdi:r) *v.t*, to [be] numb, dull. **engourdissement** (dismᾶ) *m*, numbness (*physical or mental*); sluggishness (*Com.*).

engrais (ᾶgrɛ) *m*, fattening food; manure. ~ *chimique*, fertilizer.

engraisser (se) *v.t*, to fatten; manure.

engranger (ãgrãʒe) *v.t*, to garner, get in.

engraver (ãgrave) *v.t*, to strand; (*v.i.*) to ground (*boat*).

engrenage (ãgrəna:ʒ) *m*, gear-[ing]; meshes, toils (*fig.*). **engrener** (ne) *v.t*, to [throw into] gear, mesh, engage; set going.

engrosser (ãgrose) *v.t*, to make pregnant.

engrossir (ãgrosi:r) *v.i*, to become pregnant.

engueulade (ãgœlad) *m*, bawling out, angry reproof. **engueuler** (le) *v.t*, to bawl out, scold. s'~ *avec*, to argue angrily with. *se faire* ~, to be bawled out.

engrumeler (ãgrymle) *v.t*, to clot, curdle.

enguirlander (ãgirlãde) *v.t*, to garland, wreathe; wheedle.

enhardir (ãardi:r) *v.t*, to embolden.

énigmatique† (enigmatik) *a*, enigmatic(al). **énigme** (nigm) *f*, riddle, conundrum, puzzle, enigma.

enivrer (ãnivre) *v.t*, to intoxicate, inebriate; elate.

enjambée (ãʒãbe) *f*, stride. **enjamber** (be) *v.t. & abs*, to stride [over or along]; (*v.i.*) to encroach, project.

enjeu (ãʒø) *m*, stake (*wager*).

enjoindre (ãʒwɛ̃:dr) *v.t.ir*, to enjoin.

enjôler (ãʒole) *v.t*, to wheedle, inveigle, bamboozle.

enjoliver (ãʒɔlive) *v.t*, to embellish; set off.

enjolivure (ãʒɔlivy:r) *m*, hubcap.

enjoué, e (ãʒwe) *a*, playful, jocular, vicacious. **enjouement** (ʒumã) *m*, playfulness.

enlacer (ãlase) *v.t*, to [en]lace; entwine; clasp, fold.

enlaidir (ãlɛdi:r) *v.t*, to make ugly; disfigure.

enlevage (ãlva:ʒ) *m*, spurt (*rowing*). **enlever** (lve) *v.t*, to lift, raise; carry (*or* take) (*or* clear) (*or* sweep) away (*or* off); remove, collect; kidnap; abduct, rape, buy up; take up (*shares*); snap up (*bargain*). *être enlevé par la mer ou par les lames*, to be washed overboard. *se faire* ~ *par*, to elope with. **enlèvement** (lɛvmã) *m*, lifting, etc.; elopement; kidnapping; storming (*military position*).

enliser (s') (ãlize) *v.pr*, to sink [into the sand *or* mud].

enluminer (ãlymine) *v.t*, to color, illuminate (*MS.*); flush, redden. **enluminure** (ny:r) *f*, coloring; illumination; high color.

ennemi, e (ɛnmi) *n*, enemy, foe. ¶ *a*, enemy, inimical, hostile; averse; clashing.

ennoblir (ãnobli:r) *v.t*, to ennoble, uplift, dignify.

ennui (ãnɥi) *m*, wearisomeness, tedium, boredom; bother, nuisance; worry, trouble. **ennuyer** (nɥije) *v.t*, to weary, tire, bore; annoy, worry. **ennuyeux, euse†** (jø, ø:z) *a*, tiresome, tedious, irksome; prosy.

énoncé (enõse) *m*, statement. **énoncer** (se) *v.t*, to state, enunciate, express, specify. **énonciation** (sjasjõ) *f*, stating, enunciation.

enorgueillir (ãnorgœji:r) *v.t*, to make proud, elate. s'~, to pride oneself.

énorme (enɔrm) *a*, enormous, huge; mountainous, tremendous; outrageous. **énormément** (memã) *ad*, enormously. **énormité** (mite) *f*, enormousness; enormity.

enquérir (s') (ãkeri:r) *v.pr.ir*, to inquire, ask. **enquête** (kɛ:t) *f*, inquiry, investigation; inquest.

enraciner (ãrasine) *v.t. & s'*~, to take root.

enragé, e (ãraʒe) *p.a*, mad; rabid; enraged, infuriated; raging; wild. ¶ *m*, madman, fiend (*fig.*). **enrageant, e** (ʒã, ã:t) *a*, maddening. **enrager** (ʒe) *v.i*, to fume. *faire* ~, to madden, infuriate.

enrayer (ãrɛje) *v.t*, to drag, skid, lock (*wheel*); spoke (*wheel*); brake; stop, check (*fig.*).

enrégimenter (ãreʒimãte) (*fig.*) *v.t*, to enroll.

enregistrer (ãrəʒistre) *v.t*, to register; file; score; record; book; chronicle. **enregistrement** (trəmã) *m*, registration; registry; recording. ~ *magnétophonique*, tape recording. ~ *fractionné*, rerecording, duoplay (*sound recording*). enregistreur (trœːr) *m*, recording instrument. ~ *de vol*, flight recorder.

enrhumer (ăryme) *v.t*, to give (*someone*) a cold. s'~, to catch [a] cold.

enrichi, e (ărɪʃi) *n*, one who has become rich. **enrichir** (ʃiːr) *v.t*, to enrich. s'~, to make money.

enrober (ărɔbe) *v.t*, to encase.

enrôler (ărole) *v.t*, to enroll, enlist.

enrouer (ărwe) *v.t*, to make hoarse *or* husky.

enrouler (ărule) *v.t*, to wind, coil, wrap, roll [up].

ensablement (ăsablemă) *m*, sandbank. **ensabler** (ble) *v.t*, to sand [up]; run aground.

ensacher (ăsaʃe) *v.t*, to bag, sack.

ensanglanter (ăsăglăte) *v.t*, to stain with blood.

enseigne (ăsɛɲ) *f*, sign; sign [board]; ensign. *à bonnes ~s*, on sure grounds; on good security. *à telles ~s que*, in proof of which. ~ *de vaisseau*, *m*, ensign (*Nav.*).

enseignement (ăsɛɲmă) *m*, teaching, tuition, training, education; (*pl.*) teachings, lessons. ~ *programmé*, programmed instruction. **enseigner** (ne) *v.t*, to show; tell of; teach, teach how.

ensellé, e (ăsele) *a*, saddlebacked.

ensemble (ăsăːbl) *ad*, together. ¶ *m*, whole; aggregate; general effect; unity, harmony. ~ *deux pièces*, two-piece set, ensemble; suit. ~ *de données*, data set (*computers*). ~ *spécialisé*, dedicated system (*computers*). *dans l'~*, on the whole. *vue d'~*, overall view.

ensemencer (ăsmăse) *v.t*, to sow (*land*).

enserrer (ăsɛre) *v.t*, to encompass, enclose; tie up (*fig.*); put under glass (*Hort.*).

ensevelir (ăsɛvliːr) *v.t*, to bury, entomb; plunge; shroud.

ensoleillé, e (ăsɔleje) *a*, sunny, sunlit. **ensoleiller** (je) *v.t*, to sun; light up, brighten.

ensommeillé, e (ăsɔmeje) *a*, sleepy, drowsy.

ensorceler (ăsɔrsele) *v.t*, to bewitch.

ensuite (ăsɥit) *ad*, afterwards, then, next. **s'ensuivre** (sɥiːvr) *v.pr.ir*, to follow, ensue.

entablement (ătablemă) *m*, entablature.

entacher (ătaʃe) *v.t*, to taint; vitiate.

entaille (ătaːj) *f*, notch, nick, groove, slot; gash, hack. **entailler** (taje) *v.t*, to notch.

entame (ătam) *f*, first cut, outside [cut]. **entamer** (me) *v.t*, to cut [into] (*slightly*); injure; penetrate; break into, broach; shake (*one's faith*); fathom; begin, open, initiate.

entasser (ătase) *v.t*, to heap up, pile up, stack, huddle.

ente (ăːt) (*Hort.*) *f*, graft; stock.

entendement (ătădmă) *m*, understanding; intelligence. **entendre** (tăːdr) *v.t. & abs*, to hear; listen to; understand; mean; require. *laisser ~*, to hint. ~ *à*, to consent to. s'~, to understand; u. each other; come to an understanding; get on; be subject to. **entendu**, e (tădy) *a*, capable, businesslike; versed; arranged; conceived. *bien entendu*, clearly understood; of course. *entendu!* agreed! okay! **entente** (tăːt) *f*, understanding. *mot*, *phrase*, *à double ~*, word, phrase, with a double meaning, double entendre.

enter (ăte) *v.t*, to [en]graft.

entériner (ăterine) *v.t*, to ratify, confirm; rubber-stamp.

entérique (ăterik) *a*, enteric.

enterrement (ătɛrmă) *m*, burial, interment; funeral. **enterrer** (re) *v.t*, to bury, inter; sink (*money, a fortune, en =* in); outlive.

en-tête (ătɛːt) *m*, head[ing] (*letter, bill, ledger*).

entêté, e (ătete) *p.a*, obstinate, headstrong, stubborn. **entêtement** (tmă) *m*, obstinacy. **entêter** (te) *v.t. & abs*, to make giddy; go to the head; infatuate. s'~, to be obstinate.

enthousiasme (ătuzjasm) *m*, enthusiasm; rapture. **enthousiasmer** (me) *v.t*, to enrapture, carry away. **s'~**, to go into raptures. **enthousiaste** (ast) *a*, enthusiastic, ¶ *n*, enthusiast.

enticher (ătiʃe) *v.t*, to taint; infatuate.

entier, ère (ătje, ɛɪr) *a*, entire, whole; full; the same, as it was; headstrong, self-willed. ¶ *m*, entirety. [*nombre*] ~, whole number, integer. *en* ~, entirely, in full, right through. **entièrement** (tjɛrmɑ̃) *ad*, entirely, wholly; fully; quite; clean (*shaven*).

entité (ătite) *f*, entity.

entoiler (ătwale) *v.t*, to mount [on calico *or* linen]; bind in cloth.

entomologie (ătɔmɔlɔʒi) *f*, entomology. **entomologiste** (ʒist) *m*, entomologist.

entonner (ătɔne) *v.t. & abs*, to intone, intonate; strike up (*tune*); barrel.

entonnoir (ătɔnwaɪr) *m*, funnel; hollow; shell hole; mine crater.

entorse (ătɔrs) *f*, sprain, strain, twist, wrench. **entortiller** (tije) *v.t*, to twist, [en]twine, wind, wrap; get round (*someone*).

entour (ătuɪr) *m: à l'*~, around, round about. ~**s**, *pl*, environs, outskirts, purlieus; associates; aspects. **entourage** (turaɪʒ) *m*, setting, surroundings; environment, associates. **entourer** (re) *v.t*, to surround, beset, hedge.

entournure (ăturnyɪr) *f*, armhole (*garment*). *être gêné aux* ~**s**, to be in a financial bind.

en-tout-cas (ătuka) *m*, umbrella-sunshade.

entracte (ătrakt) *m*, interval, entr'acte; interlude.

entraide (ătrɛɪd) *f*, helpfulness to each other. **s'entraider** (trede) *v.pr*, to help one another.

entrailles (ătraɪj) *f.pl*, entrails, bowels, inwards; compassion, heart.

entr'aimer (s') (ătrɛme) *v.pr*, to love one another.

entrain (ătrɛ̃) *m*, liveliness, spirit, go, gusto. **entraînant, e** (trɛnɑ̃, ɑ̃ɪt) *a*, inspiriting, stirring. **entraînement** (nmɑ̃) *m*, impulse;

force; enthusiasm; training (*sport*); sparring; coaching; pacemaking; feed (*Mach.*). **entraîner** (ne) *v.t*, to carry (*or* draw) (*or* wash) away *or* along; drift; involve, entail; lead; train; coach; pace. *s'~ à la boxe*, to spar. **entraîneur** (nœɪr) *m*, trainer; coach; pacemaker. **entraîneuse** (nøɪz) *f*, bargirl, shill.

entrait (ătrɛ) *m*, tie beam; tie rod.

entrant, e (ătrɑ̃, ɑ̃ɪt) *a*, ingoing; insinuating.

entrave (ătraɪv) *f*, fetter, shackle, trammel, clog, obstacle; hobble. **entraver** (trave) *v.t*, to fetter; impede, hinder, hamper.

entre (ăɪtr) *pr*, between; in, into; among[st]; of. ~ *deux*, *ad*, in between; middling. ~ *deux âges*, middle-aged. ~ *deux eaux*, under water.

entrebâillé, e (ătrəbaje) *a*, half-open, ajar. **entrebâilleur de fenêtre** (jœɪr) *m*, casement stay.

entrechat (ătrəʃa) *m*, entrechat; caper.

entrechoquer (ătrəʃɔke) *v.t*, to strike against each other. **s'~**, to clash, collide.

entrecôte (ătrəkoɪt) *f*, rib steak.

entrecouper (ătrəkupe) *v.t*, to intersect; break.

entrecroiser (s') (ătrəkrwaze) *v.pr*, to intersect; criss-cross.

entre-déchirer (s') (ătrədeʃire) *v.pr*, to tear one another to pieces.

entre-deux (ătrədø) *m*, space [between]; parting; trough (*sea*).

entrée (ătre) *f*, entrance, entry; ingress; admittance, admission; [admission] ticket; way in; access; entrée; beginning; mouth; inlet; gate. ~ *dans le monde*, birth; coming out (*in society*). *les* ~**s** *de faveur*, the free list (*Theat.*). ~ *de serrure*, keyhole. ~ *en douane*, clearance (*or* entry) inwards. ~ *en séance*, opening of the sitting. [*droit d'*]~, import duty. ~ *des artistes*, stage door; anus (*obscene*).

entrefaite (ătrəfɛt) *f: sur ces* ~**s**, in the midst of all this.

entrefilet (ătrəfilɛ) *m*, [short] paragraph (*newspaper*).

entregent (ãtrəʒã) *m*, tact; gumption.

entrelacer (ãtrəlase) *v.t*, to interlace, intertwine, interweave.

entrelardé, e (ãtrəlarde) *p.a*, streaky (*meat*). **entrelarder** (de) *v.t*, to lard; interlard.

entre-ligne (ãtrəliɲ) *m*, interlineation.

entremêler (ãtrəmɛle) *v.t*, to [inter]mix, intermingle; intersperse.

entremets (ãtrəmɛ) *m*, side dish; dessert (*dinner course*).

entremetteur, euse (ãtrəmɛtœːr, øːz) *n*, go-between. **s'entremettre** (tr) *v.pr.ir*, to intervene. **entremise** (miːz) *f*, intervention; agency, medium.

entrepont (ãtrəpɔ̃) *m*, betweendecks.

entreposer (ãtrəpoze) *v.t*, to warehouse, store; bond. **entreposeur** (zœːr) *m*, warehouse keeper; bonded storekeeper. **entrepositaire** (ziteːr) *n*, bonder. **entrepôt** (po) *m*, warehouse, store; emporium, mart. ~ *frigorifique*, cold storage. ~ [*légal*], ~ *de douane*, bond[ed warehouse]. *en* ~ ou *à l'*~ ou *en E.*, in bond[ed warehouse].

entreprenant, e (ãtrəprənã, ãːt) *a*, enterprising, pushing. **entreprendre** (prãːdr) *v.t.ir*, to undertake; contract for; tackle (*pers.*) ~ *sur*, to encroach on. **entrepreneur** (prənœːr) *m*, contractor. ~ *de monuments funéraires*, ~ *de pompes funèbres*, undertaker. ~ *de transports*, ~ *de roulage*, haulage contractor, carrier. **entreprise** (priːz) *f*, undertaking; enterprise; concern; business; contract; encroachment.

entrer (ãtre) *v.i*, to enter; come in; go in; walk in; march in; step in; get in; go; come. ~ *en déchargement*, to break bulk (*Ship.*). *X. entre* [*en scène*], enter X. (*Theat.*). ¶ *v.t*, to introduce. ~ *en fraude*, to smuggle in.

entresol (ãtrəsɔl) *m*, mezzanine [floor].

entrée-sortie (ãtresɔrti) *f*, inputoutput (*computers*).

entre-temps (ãtrətã) *ad*, meanwhile. ¶ *m*, interval.

entretenir (ãtrətniːr) *v.t.ir*, to maintain; keep in repair; keep up; support, keep; speak to, report to. *s'*~, to last; hold together; converse. *s'*~ *la main*, to keep one's hand in. **entretien** (tjɛ̃) *m*, maintenance; upkeep; support, keep; clothes, dress; talk; interview.

entretoile (ãtrətwal) *f*, lace insertion.

entretoise (ãtrətwaːz) *f*, brace, strut, cross-piece; stay-bolt.

entrevoir (ãtrəvwaːr) *v.t.ir*, to catch a glimpse of; see indistinctly; sense. *s'*~, to see each other, meet. **entrevue** (vy) *f*, interview.

entrouvrir (ãtruvriːr) *v.t.ir*, to half-open.

énumérer (enymere) *v.t*, to enumerate, rehearse; recite.

envahir (ãvaiːr) *v.t*, to invade, break into; overrun; flood; overgrow; encroach on, trench on. **envahissement** (ismã) *m*, invasion; inrush; encroachment. **envahisseur** (sœːr) *m*, invader.

envaser (s') (ãvaze) *v.pr*, to silt up; sink in the mud.

enveloppe (ãvlɔp) *f*, envelope; wrapper; cover[ing]; jacket[ing]; sheath[ing]; lagging; casing; exterior (*fig.*). ~ *à panneau*, ~ *à fenêtre*, window envelope. ~ *affranchie pour la réponse*, stamped addressed e. **envelopper** (vlɔpe) *v.t*, to envelop; wrap [up]; enfold; [en]shroud; cover; case; jacket; lag; involve.

envenimer (ãvnime) *v.t*, to poison; envenom, embitter.

envergure (ãvɛrgyːr) *f*, spread, span; wing spread, w. span; stretch; expanse; breadth.

envers (ãvɛːr) *m*, wrong side, back, reverse; seamy side. *à l'*~, inside out; topsy-turvy. ¶ *pr*, towards, to. ~ *& contre tous*, through thick & thin.

envi (à l') (ãvi), in emulation, vying.

envie (ãvi) *f*, envy; wish, desire, mind, longing, fancy; birthmark; agnail, hang-nail. **envier** (vje) *v.t*, to envy, begrudge. **envieux, euse** (vjø, ∅:z) *a*, envious.

environ (ãvirɔ̃) *ad*, about, thereabouts. **∼s,** *m.pl*, environs, outskirts, purlieus, neighborhood. **environner** (rɔne) *v.t*, to environ, surround; beset.

envisager (ãvizaʒe) *v.t*, to look in the face; look on; envisage; contemplate, view.

envoi (ãvwa) *m*, sending, forwarding, dispatch; sending in, s. out; remittance; consignment; parcel, package; article (*Post*). **∼ contre remboursement**, cash on delivery.

envol (ãvɔl) *m*, flight; taking off (*Avn.*). **envolée** (le) *f*, flight (*fig.*). **s'envoler** (le) *v.pr*, to fly [away]; take off (*Avn.*).

envoûter (ãvute) *v.t*, to bewitch.

envoyé, e (ãvwaje) *n*, envoy, messenger. **∼ spécial**, special correspondent. **envoyer** (je) *v.t*, to send, forward, dispatch; send in, s. out; remit; tender. **envoyeur, euse** (jœːr, ∅:z) *n*, sender.

éolien, ne (eɔljẽ, ɛn) *a*, Aeolian, wind (*att.*).

épagneul, e (epaɲœl) *n*, spaniel.

épais, e (epɛ, ɛːs) *a*, thick, dense. **∼ de**, thick (*Meas.*). **épais,** *ad*, thick[ly]. **¶** *m*, thickness. **épaisseur** (pɛsœːr) *f*, thickness; ply; thick; density. **épaissir** (siːr) *v.t*, to thicken. **∼,** *v.i. & s'∼*, to thicken; get stout.

épanchement (epɑ̃ʃmɑ̃) *m*, effusion, outpouring. **∼ de synovie** (sinɔvi), water on the knee. **épancher** (ʃe) *v.t*, to pour out; vent; open (*heart*). **s'∼**, to overflow.

épandre (epɑ̃ːdr) *v.t*, to spread; shed.

épanoui (epanwi) *a*, in full bloom; beaming, cheerful, etc.

épanouir (epanwiːr) *v.t. & s'∼*, to open, expand; brighten; blossom. **épanouissement** (wismɑ̃) *m*, blooming, beaming.

épargne (eparɲ) *f*, saving, economy, thrift. **la petite ∼**, the small investor. **épargner** (ɲe) *v.t*, to save [up], lay by, economize, husband; spare, grudge, stint.

éparpiller (eparpije) *v.t*, to scat-

ter; fritter away. **épars, e** (paɪr, ars) *a*, scattered, straggling.

épatant (epatã) *a*, fine, wonderful, terrific.

épaté, e (epate) *p.a*, amazed; with crippled foot; flat (*nose*). **épater** (te) *v.t*, to astonish.

épaulard (epolaːr) *m*, grampus, orc.

épaule (epoːl) *f*, shoulder. **épaulée** (pole) *f*, push with the shoulder. **épaulement** (lmã) *m*, shoulder (*Carp.*). **épauler** (le) *v.t*, to splay; shoulder; bring (*rifle*) to the shoulder; back up. **épaulette** (lɛt) *f*, yoke (*dress*); shoulder strap; epaulet[te].

épave (epaːv) *a*, stray[ed]. **¶** *f*, stray; derelict, wreck; (*pl.*) wreckage; jetsam; flotsam; lagan; remnant.

épée (epe) *f*, sword. **∼ de chevet**, fallback; ruling passion.

épeler (eple) *v.t*, to spell. **épellation** (pɛlasjɔ̃) *f*, spelling.

éperdu†, e (epɛrdy) *a*, distracted, desperate.

éperlan (epɛrlã) *m*, smelt (*fish*).

éperon (eprɔ̃) *m*, spur; buttress; ram (*battleship*). **éperonner** (prɔne) *v.t*, to spur; s. on.

épervier (epɛrvje) *m*, sparrow hawk; sweep net, cast net.

éphélide (efelid) *f*, freckle.

éphémère (efemɛːr) *a*, ephemeral, mushroom. **¶** *m*, ephemera, -ron, Mayfly. **éphéméride** (merid) *f*, ephemeris; block calendar.

épi (epi) *m*, ear (*grain*); cob (*corn*); spike (*flower*); spray (*jewels*).

épice (epis) *f*, spice. **épicé, e** (se) *a*, spicy. **épicer** (se) *v.t*, to spice. **épicerie** (sri) *f*, grocery; grocer's shop; spices. **épicier, ère** (sje, ɛːr) *n*, grocer.

épicurien, ne (epikyrjẽ, ɛn) *a. & m*, epicurean.

épidémie (epidemi) *f*, epidemic, outbreak (*disease*). **épidémique** (mik) *a*, epidemic.

épiderme (epidɛrm) *m*, epidermis. **avoir l'∼ sensible**, to be thin-skinned (*fig.*).

épier (epje) *v.t*, to spy [on], watch.

épieu (epjø) *m*, boar spear.

épiglotte (epiglɔt) *f*, epiglottis.

épigramme (epigram) *f*, epigram; skit.

épigraphe (epigraf) *f*, epigraph, quotation, motto (*prefixed to book or chapter*).

épilepsie (epilɛpsi) *f*, epilepsy. **épileptique** (tik) *a. & n*, epileptic.

épiler (epile) *v.t*, to depilate, pluck [out hairs].

épilogue (epilɔg) *m*, epilogue. **épiloguer** (ge) *v.i*, to find fault. **épilogueur, euse** (gœːr, øːz) *n*, faultfinder.

épinard (*Bot.*) *m. &* ~s (*Cook.*) *pl.* (epinaːr), spinach. ~s *en branches*, leaf s.

épine (epin) *f*, thorn [bush]; thorn; spine (*Bot.*). ~ *blanche*, hawthorn, whitethorn. ~ *noire*, blackthorn. ~ *dorsale*, spine, backbone. **épineux, euse** (nø, øːz) *a*, thorny, spiny, prickly; knotty. **épine-vinette** (vinɛt) *f*, barberry, berberry.

épingle (epɛ̃ːgl) *f*, pin. ~ *à friser*, hair curler. ~ *à linge*, clothespin. ~ *de sûreté*, ~ *de nourrice*, ~ *anglaise*, safety pin. ~s, pin money. *tiré à quatre* ~s, spic & span. **épingler** (pɛ̃gle) *v.t*, to pin.

épinoche (epinɔʃ) *f*, sticklevack.

Épiphanie (epifani) *f*, Epiphany.

épique (epik) *a*, epic.

épiscopal, e (episkɔpal) *a*, episcopal. **épiscopat** (pa) *m*, episcopate; episcopacy.

épisode (epizɔd) *m*, episode.

épisser (epise) *v.t*, to splice (*rope*). **épissoir** (swaːr) *m*, marline spike, marlinspike. **épissure** (syːr) *f*, splice.

épistolaire (epistɔlɛːr) *a*, epistolary. **épistolier, ère** (lje, ɛːr) *n*, letter writer (*pers.*).

épitaphe (epitaf) *f*, epitaph.

épithète (epitɛt) *f*, epithet.

épitomé (epitɔme) *m*, epitome.

épître (epiːtr) *f*, epistle; letter.

éploré, e (eplɔre) *a*, tearful, in tears, weeping.

éplucher (eplyʃe) *v.t*, to prepare, clean; peel, pare; preen, prink; sift (*fig.*), scan. s'~, to plume (*or* preen) (*or* prink) its feathers. **épluchures** (ʃyːr) *f.pl*, parings, peelings.

épointer (epwɛ̃te) *v.t*, to break the point of; point (*sharpen*).

éponge (epɔ̃ːʒ) *f*, sponge. **éponger** (pɔ̃ʒe) *v.t*, to sponge; mop; mop up; dab; blot.

épontille (epɔ̃tiːj) *f*, stanchion (*ship*).

épopée (epɔpe) *f*, epic, epopee, epos.

époque (epɔk) *f*, epoch; era, age; time, date, period.

époumoner (epumɔne) *v.t*, to puff.

épouse (epuːz) *f*, wife, spouse, consort. **épouser** (puze) *v.t*, to marry, wed; espouse. ~ [*la forme de*], to correspond (*or* conform) in shape to; adapt itself to, fit.

épousseter (epuste) *v.t*, to dust; rub down.

épouvantable† (epuvɑ̃tabl) *a*, frightful, fearful, dreadful. **épouvantail** (taːj) *m*, scarecrow; bugbear. **épouvante** (vɑ̃ːt) *f*, terror, fright. **épouvanter** (vɑ̃te) *v.t*, to terrify, frighten, scare.

époux (epu) *m*, husband, spouse, consort; (*pl.*) husband & wife, [married] couple.

épreindre (eprɛ̃ːdr) *v.t.ir*, to press [out], squeeze [out].

éprendre (s') (eprɑ̃ːdr) *v.pr.ir*, to be smitten, be enamored, be taken, fall in love. **épris** (**epri**) *a*, smitten; in love.

épreuve (eprœːv) *f*, test[ing]; trial; ordeal; proof (*Typ.*); heat (*sport*); event (*sport*). ~ *de force*, showdown. ~s *de tournage*, rushes (*TV, cinema*). ~ *d'imprimerie*, printer's proof. ~ *en placard*, galley proof. [~] *finale*, final [heat]. ~ *négative*, negative (*Phot.*). ~ *nulle*, dead heat. ~ [*positive*], print, positive (*Phot.*). *à l'*~ *de*, proof against. *à l'*~ *du feu, des intempéries, des maladresses*, fireproof, weather-p., fool-p. *à toute* ~, unflinching; trusty. **éprouver** (pruve) *v.t*, to test, prove, try; experience, meet with, sustain, undergo; suffer; feel. **éprouvette** (vɛt) *f*, test glass; t. tube; t. piece; probe (*Surg.*).

épris (epri) *a*, smitten, enamoured, infatuated.

épuisé, e (epuize) *p.a*, exhausted, spent; effete; out of print. **épuisement** (mɑ̃) *m*, *arrêt par* ~, burnout. **épuiser** (ze) *v.t*, to exhaust;

drain; empty. **épuisette** (zɛt) f, landing net; scoop, bailer.

épuration (epyrasjɔ̃) f, purification; refining. **épure** (py:r) f, working drawing; diagram. **épurer** (pyre) v.t, to purify; refine; weed out; debug (computers).

équarrir (ekari:r) v.t, to square; quarter, cut up (dead animal).

équateur (ekwatœ:r) m, equator. l'E~ (Geog.), Ecuador.

équation (ekwasjɔ̃) f, equation.

équatorial, e (ekwatɔrjal) a, equatorial. ¶ m, equatorial [telescope].

équerre (ekɛ:r) f, square (instrument & at right angles).

équestre (ekɛstr) a, equestrian.

équilibre (ekilibr) m, equilibrium; [equi]poise; balance; b. of power (Pol.). **équilibrer** (bre) v.t, to equilibrate, poise, balance, counterbalance.

équinoxe (ekinɔks) m, equinox. **équinoxial, e** (ksjal) a, equinoctial.

équipage (ekipa:ʒ) m, crew (ship); outfit, rig; set; train; equipage, turnout; plight. ~ de chasse, hunt. équipe (kip) f, train (of boats); shift, gang, corps, squad; crew (boat); team, side (sport). ~ de tournage, film unit. chef d'~, foreman. **équipée** (pe) f, escapade, lark. **équipement** (pmɑ̃) m, equipment; outfit. ~ de survie, survival kit. ~ de vie, life-support system. **équiper** (pe) v.t, to equip, fit out, rig [out].

équitable† (ekitabl) a, equitable, fair, just.

équitation (ekitasjɔ̃) f, riding, horsemanship.

équité (ekite) f, equity, fairness.

équivalent, e (ekivalɑ̃, ɑ̃:t) a. & m, equivalent. **équivaloir** (lwa:r) v.i.ir, to be equivalent; be tantamount.

équivoque (ekivɔk) a, equivocal; ambiguous, dubious, questionable. ¶ f, equivocation, ambiguity, prevarication. **équivoquer** (ke) v.i, to equivocate, prevaricate.

érable (erabl) m, maple. ~ madré, bird's-eye maple.

éradication (eradikasjɔ̃) f, eradication.

érafler (erɑfle) v.t, to scratch, graze. **éraflure** (fly:r) f, scratch.

éraillé, e (erɑje) p.a, frayed; husky, hoarse; bloodshot. **érailler** (je) v.t, to fray.

ère (ɛ:r) f, era, epoch.

Érèbe (l') (erɛb) m, Erebus.

érection (erɛksjɔ̃) f, erection; raising.

éreinter (erɛ̃te) v.t, to break the back of; tire out; lash (fig.), slate, pull to pieces.

ergol (ergɔl) m, propellant.

ergot (ergo) m, spur (bird); snug, lug; pin; ergot (Bot. & Med.). **ergoté, e** (gote) a, spurred (bird). **ergoter** (te) v.i, to cavil, quibble.

Érié (le lac) (erje), Lake Erie.

ériger (eriʒe) v.t, to erect, put up; raise, set up.

ermitage (ɛrmita:ʒ) m, hermitage. **ermite** (mit) m, hermit.

éroder (erɔde) v.t, to erode. **érosion** (zjɔ̃) f, erosion.

érotique (erɔtik) a, erotic; amatory. **érotisme** (tism) m, eroticism.

errant, e (ɛrɑ̃, ɑ̃:t) a, wandering; roving; stray; errant. **erratique** (ratik) a, erratic (Geol., Med., etc.).

erratum (ɛratɔm) m, erratum.

erre (ɛ:r) f, [head]way (Naut.); (pl.) track, spoor; (pl.) footsteps (fig.). **errements** (ɛrmɑ̃) m.pl, ways, methods. **errer** (ɛre) v.i, to wander, roam, rove, stroll, stray; err. **erreur** (rœ:r) f, error, mistake; fallacy. ~ de calcul, miscalculation. ~ de nom, misnomer. ~ de (ou sur la) personne, mistaken identity. ~ typographique, misprint. **erroné, e** (rɔne) a, erroneous, wrong, mistaken.

éructation (eryktasjɔ̃) f, eructation, belch[ing]. **éructer** (te) v.i, to eruct, belch.

érudit, e (erydi, it) a, erudite, scholarly, learned. ¶ m, scholar, learned man. **érudition** (disjɔ̃) f, erudition, learning, scholarship.

éruption (erypsjɔ̃) f, eruption; rash; blowout (well).

ès (ɛs) pr, of; in.

escabeau (ɛskabo) m. & **escabelle** (bɛl) f, stool.

escadre (ɛska:dr) f, squadron

(*Nav.*). **escadrille** (kadri:j) *f*, flotilla (*Nav.*); squadron (*air*). **escadron** (dr5) *m*, squadron (*cavalry*).

escalade (ɛskalad) *f*, scaling; escalation (*Mil.*). ~ *militaire & diplomatique*, military & diplomatic escalation. **escalader** (de) *v.t*, to scale, climb [over].

escale (ɛskal) *f*, call (*Ship.*); port of call. *faire* ~, to call.

escalier (ɛskalje) *m*, stair[s], staircase. ~ *d'honneur*, grand staircase. ~ *roulant*, escalator. ~ *tournant*, spiral (*or* winding) stairs.

escalope (ɛskalɔp) *f*, cutlet.

escamotage (ɛskamɔta:ʒ) *m*, juggling, conjuring. **escamoter** (te) *v.t*, to conjure away, spirit away; filch; (*abs.*) to juggle, conjure. **escamoteur** (tœ:r) *m*, juggler, conjuror, -er; pickpocket.

escampette (ɛskãpɛt) *f*: *prendre la poudre d'*~, to bolt, skedaddle.

escapade (kapad) *f*, escapade, prank, lark.

escarbille (ɛskarbi:j) *f*, [coal] cinder.

escarbot (ɛskarbo) *m*, dung beetle.

escargot (ɛskargo) *m*, (*edible*) snail.

escarmouche (ɛskarmuʃ) *f*, skirmish. **escarmoucher** (ʃe) *v.i*, to skirmish.

escarpe (ɛskarp) *f*, [e]scarp. ¶ *m*, cutthroat, desperado. **escarpé, e** (pe) *a*, precipitous, steep, bluff. **escarpement** (pəmã) *m*, steepness; escarpment; slope.

escarpin (ɛskarpɛ̃) *m*, pump (*dress shoe*).

escarpolette (ɛskarpɔlɛt) *f*, swing (*child's*).

escarre (ɛska:r) *f*, scab (*Med.*).

Escaut (l') (ɛsko) *m*, the Scheldt.

escient (ɛsjã) *m*, knowledge. *à bon* ~, knowingly, wittingly.

esclaffer (s') (ɛsklafe) *v.pr*, to burst out laughing.

esclandre (ɛsklã:dr) *m*, scandal, scene.

esclavage (ɛsklava:ʒ) *m*, slavery, bondage, thraldom. **esclave** (kla:v) *n*, slave, thrall.

escobarder (ɛskɔbarde) *v.i*, to shuffle.

escogriffe (ɛskɔgrif) *m*, gawk, lout.

escompte (ɛsk5:t) *m*, discount; discounting. **escompter** (k5te) *v.t*, to discount; cash (*a check for someone*); anticipate; bank on.

escorte (ɛskɔrt) *f*, escort; convoy. **escorter** (te) *v.t*, to escort; convoy.

escouade (ɛskwad) *f*, squad, gang.

escrime (ɛskrim) *f*, fencing, swordsmanship. **s'escrimer** (me) *v.pr*, to try hard.

escroc (ɛskro) *m*, swindler, sharper, crook. **escroquer** (krɔke) *v.t. & abs*, to swindle, swindle out of.

espace (ɛspas) *m*, space; room; (*f.*) space (*Typ.*). ~*s verts*, open or green spaces (*city planning*). ~ *lointain*, deep space. ~ *extra-atmosphérique*, outer space. **espacer** (se) *v.t.*, to space.

espadon (ɛspad5) *m*, swordfish.

espadrille (ɛspadri:j) *f*, canvas shoe with hempen sole.

Espagne (l') (ɛspaɲ) *f*, Spain. **espagnol, e** (l') (ɲɔl) *a. & (language) m*, Spanish. E~, *n*, Spaniard. **espagnolette** (lɛt) *f*, window hasp.

espalier (ɛspalje) *m*, espalier.

espar (ɛspa:r) *m*, spar (*Naut.*); handspike (*Mil.*).

espèce (ɛspɛs) *f*, kind, sort, species; case in point (*law*); (*pl.*) cash, coin, specie. *l'~ animale*, the brute creation. *l'~ humaine*, mankind. ~*s sonnantes*, hard cash.

espérance (ɛsperã:s) *f*, hope, expectation; (*pl.*) promise. **espérer** (re) *v.t. & abs*, to hope for, expect; trust; hope.

espiègle (ɛspjɛgl) *a*, roguish, mischievous, impish, elfish; arch. ¶ *n*, rogue (*playfully*). **espièglerie** (glɛri) *f*, roguishness, mischief, prank.

espion, ne (ɛspj5, ɔn) *n*, spy. **espionnage** (ɔna:ʒ) *m*, espionage, spying. **espionner** (ne) *v.t. & abs*, to spy upon, watch; spy.

esplanade (ɛsplanad) *f*, esplanade, parade.

espoir (ɛspwaːr) *m*, hope, expectation.

esprit (ɛspri) *m*, spirit; ghost; mind; nous; feeling; sense; head; wit; temper. *l'~ de caste*, class consciousness. *~ de corps*, esprit de corps; team spirit. *~ fort*, free thinker. *le Saint-Esprit* ou *l'Esprit-Saint*, the Holy Ghost, the Holy Spirit.

esquif (ɛskif) *m*, skiff.

esquille (ɛskiːj) *f*, splinter (*of bone*).

ésquimau (ɛskimo) *a*, Eskimo. ¶ *m*, Eskimo; child's snowsuit; chocolate ice-cream pop.

esquinter (ɛskɛ̃te) *v.t*, to exhaust, tire; kill (*slang*).

esquisse (ɛskis) *f*, sketch; outline. **esquisser (se)** *v.r*, to sketch.

esquive (ɛskiːv) *f*, slip (*Box.*), dodging. **esquiver** (kive) *v.t*, to avoid, evade; dodge, slip. s'~, to slip away.

essai (ɛsɛ) *m*, test[ing], trial; attempt; assay[ing]; essay. *coup d'~*, first try.

essaim (ɛsɛ̃) *m*, swarm (*bees*). **essaimer** (ɛseme) *v.i*, to swarm; branch out (*fig.*).

essanger (ɛsɑ̃ʒe) *v.t*, to soak (*dirty linen*).

essarter (ɛsarte) *v.t*, to clear; grub up.

essayage (ɛsɛjaːʒ) *m*, testing; fitting; trying on.

essayer (ɛsɛje) *v.t*, to try, essay, endeavor, attempt; try on (*clothes*); test, essay. *s'~ à*, to try one's hand (*or* skill) at. **essayeur, euse** (jœːr, øːz) *n*, essayer; fitter (*clothes*). **essayiste** (jist) *n*, essayist.

esse (ɛs) *f*, S; S hook; linchpin.

essence (ɛsɑ̃s) *f*, essence; spirit; gasoline; kind *or* species (*of tree* or *wood*). *~ de bergamote*, bergamot oil. *~ de roses*, otto of roses, attar [of roses]. *poste d'~*, filling station. **essentiel, le†** (sɑ̃sjɛl) *a*, essential, material. ¶ *m*, essential, main point.

esseulé, e (ɛsœle) *p.p*, lone[some].

essieu (ɛsjø) *m*, axle, axletree.

essor (ɛsɔːr) *m*, flight, soaring, wing; play; scope; progress, strides.

essorer (ɛsɔre) *v.t*, to dry; wring (*washing*). **essoreuse** (røːz) *f*, wringer.

essoriller (ɛsɔrije) *v.t*, to crop.

essouffler (ɛsufle) *v.t*, to blow, wind.

essuie-glace (ɛsɥi) *m*, windshield wiper. **essuie-main**, *m*, [hand] towel. **essuie-plume**, *m*, penwiper. **essuie-verres**, *m*, glass cloth. **essuyer** (sɥije) *v.t*, to wipe [up], dry; mop up; endure, go through; experience, meet with.

est (ɛst) *m*, east.

estacade (ɛstakad) *f*, wing dam; jetty; boom (*harbor*); coal stage.

estafette (ɛstafɛt) *f*, courier; dispatch rider.

estafilade (ɛstafilad) *f*, gash; rent.

estame (ɛstam) *f*, worsted (*fabric*).

estaminet (ɛstaminɛ) *m*, small café & bar.

estampe (ɛstɑ̃ːp) *f*, print, engraving; swage. **estamper** (tɑ̃pe) *v.t*, to stamp; emboss; swage; dropforge; rub (*inscription*).

estampille (ɛstɑ̃piːj) *f*, stamp; trademark. **estampiller** (pije) *v.t*, to stamp; mark.

esthétique (ɛstetik) *a*, aesthetic.

estimation (ɛstimasjɔ̃) *f*, estimate, valuation; dead reckoning (*Naut.*). **estime** (tim) *f*, esteem, estimation; dead reckoning (*Naut.*). **estimer** (me) *v.t*, to estimate; value; esteem; deem; reckon.

estival, e (ɛstival) *a*, summer (*att.*). **estiver** (ve) *v.t*, to summer (*cattle*).

estoc (ɛstɔk) *m*, point (*sword*); stock (*tree*). **estocade** (kad) *f*, thrust (*Fenc.*). **estocader** (de) *v.t*, to thrust.

estomac (ɛstɔma) *m*, stomach; pluck. **estomaquer** (make) *v.t*, to take (*someone's*) breath away; offend.

estompe (ɛstɔ̃ːp) *f*, stump (*art*). **estomper** (tɔ̃pe) *v.t*, to stump; tone down (*fig.*).

Estonie (l') (ɛstɔni) *f*, Estonia.

estouffade (ɛstufad) *f*, steaming (*Cook.*).

estrade (ɛstrad) *f*, platform, stage; dais.

estragon (ɛstragɔ̃) *m*, tarragon.

estropié, e (ɛstrɔpje) *n,* cripple. **estropier** (pje) *v.t,* to cripple, lame; maim; murder (*language*).

estuaire (ɛstɥɛːr) *m,* estuary, firth.

esturgeon (ɛstyrʒɔ̃) *m,* sturgeon.

et (e) *c.* (*abb. &*), and, and. ~ . . . ~ . . ., both . . . and . . . ~ *ainsi de suite,* and so on; and so forth. ~ *patati,* ~ *patata* (patati, ta), and so on, and so forth. ~*/ou,* and/or.

étable (etabl) *f,* (*cattle*) shed, house; sty. **établer** (ble) *v.t,* to stable, stall; sty.

établi (etabli) *m,* [work] bench, stand. **établir** (bliːr) *v.t,* to establish; set up; set (*a sail*); lay down; settle; draw [up], make out; strike (*balance*); prove; substantiate. **établissement** (blismã) *m,* establishment, etc; institution; capital expenditure.

étage (etaːʒ) *m,* floor, stor[e]y; stage, level; step; tier; rank, degree; measures (*Geol.*). **étager** (taʒe) *v.t,* to range; terrace; spread. **étagère** (ʒɛːr) *f,* [set of] shelves; whatnot; dresser. ~ *de cheminée,* mantelpiece.

étai (etɛ) *m,* shore, prop, post; stay.

étain (etɛ̃) *m,* tin; pewter. *feuille d'~,* tinfoil.

étal (etal) *m,* butcher's shop. **étalage** (laːʒ) *m,* (*shop*) window [show]; window dressing; show; display; stall. **étalagiste** (laʒist) *n,* frontsman; stall holder; window dresser.

étale (etal) *a.inv,* slack (*water*) (*Naut.*).

étaler (etale) *v.t,* to expose for sale; show; show off, flaunt, air; display; lay out; spread [out]; stem (*the tide*). **s'~,** to sprawl.

étalon (etalɔ̃) *m,* stallion, stud horse; standard (*of values*). **étalonner** (lɔne) *v.t,* to stamp (*weights, etc.*); rate; standardize.

étambot (etãbo) *m,* sternpost (*ship*).

étamer (etame) *v.t,* to tin; silver (*mirror*).

étamine (etamin) *f,* bolting cloth; filter cloth; stamen (*Bot.*). ~ *à pavillon,* bunting.

étamper (etãpe) *v.t,* to stamp, press; swage; drop-forge.

étanche (etãːʃ) *a,* tight; watertight; impervious. **étancher** (tãʃe) *v.t,* to staunch, stop; make watertight; dry; quench, slake.

étançon (etãsɔ̃) *m,* shore; stanchion. **étançonner** (sɔne) *v.t,* to shore [up].

étang (etã) *m,* pond, pool.

étape (etap) *f,* stage, stopping place.

état (eta) *m,* state; condition; frame (*of mind*); plight; repair; order; fettle, trim; status; position, posture; profession, occupation; statement, account, return, list; state (*stage of engraved or etched plate*). en [*bon*] ~ *de navigabilité,* seaworthy; airworthy. ~ *de siège,* state of siege. ~ *des malades,* sick list. ~ *civil,* legal or civil status. ~*-major,* general staff. *en* ~ *de,* fit for. *hors d'~,* useless. **État,** *m,* State government. *les* ~*s-Unis [d'Amérique],* the United States [of America]. **étatisme** (tism) *m,* State socialism, nationalism. **État-major** (maʒɔːr) *m,* staff (*Mil.*); [staff] headquarters; senior officers, executive.

étau (eto) *m,* vise (*tool*). ~*-limeur* (limœːr), shaping machine.

étayer (eteje) *v.t,* to shore [up]; prop, support.

et cætera (etsetera) *phrase & m.* (*abb. etc.*), et cetera, etc.

été (ete) *m,* summer; prime [of life]. ¶ *p.p,* être.

éteignoir (etɛɲwaːr) *m,* extinguisher (*light*); damper, wet blanket (*fig., pers.*). **éteindre** (tɛ̃ːdr) *v.t.ir,* to extinguish, put out; silence (*enemy's fire*); slake, slack; quench; pay off; soften. ~ *la lumière,* ~ *l'électricité,* to switch off (*or turn off*) the light. **s'~,** to go out (*light*); pass away; die [out]. **éteint, e** (tɛ̃, ɛːt) *p.a,* extinct; out; dull.

étendage (etãdaːʒ) *m,* hanging out (*washing*); spreading; clotheslines; lying at full length. **étendard** (daːr) *m,* standard, flag, colors. **étendoir** (dwaːr) *m,* clothesline; drying yard. **étendre** (tãːdr) *v.t,* to spread, extend;

expand; widen; stretch [out]; reach [out]; lay [out]; hang out; dilute. **s'~,** to extend; spread; stretch; reach; expatiate, enlarge. **étendu, e** (tãdy) *a,* extensive, wide, far-reaching; outspread; outstretched. **étendue** (dy) *f,* extent; area; compass; stretch, expanse, sweep, tract; reach; range; scope; length.

éternel, le† (etɛrnɛl) *a,* eternal, everlasting; never-ending. **éterniser** (nize) *v.t,* to eternalize; protract. **s'~,** to last (*or* stay) forever. **éternité** (te) *f,* eternity.

éternuement (etɛrnymã) *m,* sneezing; sneeze. **éternuer** (nɥe) *v.i,* to sneeze.

étêter (etɛte) *v.t,* to top, poll; take the head off.

éteule (etœl) *f,* stubble.

éther (etɛːr) *m,* ether. **éthéré, e** (tere) *a,* ethereal.

Éthiopie (l') (etjɔpi) *f,* Ethiopia. **éthiopien, ne** (pjɛ̃, ɛn) *a. & É~, n,* Ethiopian.

éthique (etik) *a,* ethical. ¶ *f,* ethics.

ethnie (ɛtni) *f,* ethnos, ethnic group.

ethnographie (ɛtnɔgrafi) *f,* ethnography. **ethnologie** (lɔʒi) *f,* ethnology. **ethnologique** (ʒik) *a,* ethnologic(al). **ethnologue** (lɔg) *m,* ethnologist.

éthyle (etil) *m,* ethyl.

étiage (etjaːʒ) *m,* low water; low-water mark (*river*).

étinceler (etɛ̃sle) *v.i,* to sparkle, glitter, glisten, flash. **étincelle** (sɛl) *f,* spark; sparkle, flash.

étioler (etjɔle) *v.t,* to etiolate, blanch. **s'~,** to droop, wilt.

étique (etik) *a,* emaciated, skinny.

étiqueter (etikte) *v.t,* to label; ticket. **étiquette** (kɛt) *f,* label; tally; ticket; etiquette. **~ volante,** tie-on label, tag label.

étirer (etire) *v.t,* to stretch, draw [out].

étoffe (etɔf) *f,* stuff; fabric; material; grit (*fig.*); establishment charges (*printer's*). **~ à carreaux, ~ en damier,** check [material]. **étoffé, e** (fe) *p.a,* stuffed; stocky. **étoffer** (fe) *v.t,* to use sufficient material in; stuff; fill out.

étoile (etwal) *f,* star; asterisk. **~ de mer,** starfish. **~ du matin, ~ matinière** (matinjɛːr), morning star. **~ tombante, ~ filante,** shooting s., falling s. *à la belle ~,* in the open. **étoilé, e** (le) *a,* starry; starli[ght]; starred.

étole (etɔl) *f,* stole.

étonnant, e (etɔnã, ãːt) *a,* astonishing, amazing, surprising; wonderful. **étonnamment** (namã) *ad,* astonishingly. **étonnement** (nmã) *m,* astonishment. **étonner** (ne) *v.t,* to astonish, amaze, surprise. **s'~,** to be astonished, wonder, marvel.

étouffant, e (etufã, ãːt) *a,* stifling, sultry; stuffy. **étouffée** (etufe) *f,* steaming (*Cook.*).

étouffer (etufe) *v.t. & i,* to choke, stifle; smother; quell; hush up. **étouffoir** (fwaːr) *m,* charcoal extinguisher; damper (*piano*).

étoupe (etup) *f,* tow, junk, oakum. **étouper** (pe) *v.t,* to caulk.

étoupille (etupiːj) *f,* friction tube; fuse.

étourderie (eturdəri) *f,* thoughtlessness. **étourdi, e** (di) *a,* thoughtless, heedless; flighty. ¶ *m,* scatterbrain. **à l'étourdie & étourdiment** (dimã) *ad,* thoughtlessly. **étourdir** (diːr) *v.t,* to stun; deafen; din; make dizzy; daze; deaden. **s'~,** to forget (*or* drown) one's troubles. **étourdissement** (dismã) *m,* dizziness, giddiness; stupefaction.

étourneau (eturno) *m,* starling (*bird*); foolish youth.

étrange† (etrãːʒ) *a,* strange, odd, queer; quaint. **étranger, ère** (trãʒe, ɛ) *a,* foreign; strange; unfamiliar; extraneous; alien, irrelevant. ¶ *n,* foreigner, alien; stranger. ¶ *m,* foreign parts. **à l'~,** *ad,* abroad. *de l'~,* from abroad. **étrangeté** (ʒte) *f,* strangeness, oddness; quaintness.

étranglement (etrãgləmã) *m,* strangulation. **étrangler** (gle) *v.t,* to strangle, throttle, choke; narrow; squeeze; strangulate; (*v.i.*) to choke.

étrave (etraːv) *f,* stem (*ship*).

être (ɛːtr) *m,* being; creature; thing; reality; stock (*tree*); (*pl.*)

arrangements or disposition of a building. ¶ *v.i.ir*, to be; belong; come; have. *y* ~, to get it, understand. *où en êtes-vous?*, how far have you got?

étrécir (etresi¡r) *v.t. & i. & s'~*, to narrow, shrink, contract.

étreindre (etrɛ̃¡dr) *v.t.ir*, to clasp, hug, grip; wring; bind. **étreinte** (trɛ̃t) *f*, grip, grasp; hug, embrace.

étrenne (etrɛn) *f*, first use; (*pl.*) New Year's gift, handsel; Christmas present. (*In Fr. presents are given on or about Jan. 1*). **étrenner** (trɛne) *v.t*, to be the first customer of; use (*or* wear) for the first time, handsel.

étrésillon (etrezijɔ̃) *m*, strut, brace; flying shore.

étrier (etrie) *m*, stirrup; U bolt; strap.

étrille (etri¡j) *f*, currycomb. **étriller** (trije) *v.t*, to curry; drub; fleece.

étriper (etripe) *v.t*, to gut.

étriqué, e (etrike) *a*, scant[y], narrow; cramped. **étriquer** (ke) *v.t*, to skimp.

étrivière (etrivjɛ¡r) *f*, stirrup leather; (*pl.*) thrashing.

étroit, e† (etrwa, at) *a*, narrow; limited; close; tight; strict. **étroitesse** (tɛs) *f*, narrowness, etc.

étude (etyd) *f*, study; preparation (*Sch.*); survey; (*lawyer's*) office; practice. **étudiant, e** (djã, ã¡t) *n*, student. **étudier** (dje) *v.t. & i*, to study; read; survey. **s'~**, to try hard, be careful.

étui (etɥi) *m*, case, box; cover.

étuve (ety¡v) *f*, drying stove; oven (*fig.*). ~ *humide*, steam room (*bath*). ~ *sèche*, hot room, sweating r. (*bath*). **étuvée** (tyve) *f*, steaming (*Cook.*). **étuver** (ve) *v.t*, to stove; stew; foment (*Med.*).

étymologie (etimɔlɔʒi) *f*, etymology. **étymologique†** (ʒik) *a*, etymologic(al).

eucalyptus (økalipty¡s) *m*, eucalyptus.

Eucharistie (økaristi) *f*, Eucharist, holy communion.

eugénie (øʒeni) *f*, eugenics. **eugénique** (nik) *a*, eugenic.

euh (ø) *i*, hem! hum! h'm!

eunuque (ønyk) *m*, eunuch.

euphémique (øfemik) *a*, euphemistic. **euphémisme** (mism) *m*, euphemism.

euphonie (øfɔni) *f*, euphony. **euphonique** (nik) *a*, euphonic, euphonious.

Euphrate (l') (øfrat) *m*, the Euphrates.

Europe (l') (ørɔp) *f*, Europe. **européen, ne** (peɛ̃, ɛn) *a. & E~*, *n*, European.

eux (ø) *pn.m.pl.* See **lui**.

évacuer (evakɥe) *v.t & abs*, to evacuate, void, clear out.

évader (s') (evade) *v.pr*, to escape, get away.

évaluation (evalɥasjɔ̃) *f*, valuation, estimate; casting off (*Typ.*). **évaluer** (lɥe) *v.t*, to value, estimate; cast off.

évanescent, e (evanɛsã, ã¡t) *a*, evanescent.

évangélique† (evãʒelik) *a*, evangelic(al). **évangéliste** (list) *m*, evangelist. **évangile & É~** (ʒil) *m*, gospel.

évanouir (s') (evanwi¡r) *v.pr*, to faint, swoon; vanish, fade away. **évanouissement** (wismã) *m*, fading (*radio, sound, etc.*); fainting fit.

évaporation (evaporasjɔ̃) *f*, evaporation. **évaporé, e** (re) *n*, feather-brained creature. **évaporer** (re) *v.t*, to evaporate; vent. **s'~**, to evaporate.

évaser (evase) *v.t*, to flare, bellmouth.

évasif, ive† (evazif, i¡v) *a*, evasive. **évasion** (zjɔ̃) *f*, escape, flight.

évêché (eveʃe) *m*, bishopric; see; bishop's house.

éveil (evɛ¡j) *m*, alert, guard; warning; awakening (*fig.*). **éveillé, e** (veje) *a*, wide-awake; perky. **éveiller** (je) *v.t*, to wake [up]. **s'~**, to awaken (*fig.*).

événement (evenmã) *m*, event, occurrence, incident; emergency; outcome, issue.

évent (evã) *m*, [open] air; vent; air hole; flaw; flatness (*liquor*). **éventail** (ta¡j) *m*, fan. **éventaire** (tɛ¡r) *m*, peddler's tray; street stand or stall. **éventé, e** (te) *p.a*, stale, flat, dead; giddy, flighty. **éventer** (te) *v.t*, to fan; air; turn over; flatten;

fill (*sail*); open; get wind of; let out.

éventrer (evãtre) *v.t*, to rip open, r. up; disembowel, eviscerate.

éventualité (evãtɥalite) *f*, eventuality, contingency. **éventuel**, le† (tɥɛl) *a*, contingent.

évêque (evɛːk) *m*, bishop.

évertuer (s') (evɛrtɥe) *v.pr*, to exert oneself, strive.

éviction (eviksjɔ̃) *f*, eviction.

évidence (evidãːs) *f*, evidence. *en* ~, in e., conspicuous. **évident**, e (dã, ã.;t) *a*, evident, obvious, plain. **évidemment** (damã) *ad*, evidently.

évider (evide) *v.t*, to hollow out; cut away; groove, flute.

évier (evje) *m*, sink (*kitchen*).

évincer (evɛ̃se) *v.t*, to evict; oust, turn out.

évitable (evitabl) *a*, avoidable. **évitage** (ta:ʒ) *m*, ou **évitée** (te) *f*, sea room; swinging. **évitement** (tmã) *m*, ou *voie d'*~ (*Rly.*), passing place, turnout, shunting loop. **éviter** (te) *v.t*, to avoid, shun; eschew; evade, dodge, steer clear of; help; (*v.i. & abs.*) to swing (*Naut.*). ~ *de la tête*, to duck.

évocation (evɔkasjɔ̃) *f*, evocation, calling up, raising.

évoluer (evɔlɥe) *v.i*, to perform evolutions, maneuver, evolve. **évolution** (lysjɔ̃) *f*, evolution.

évoquer (evɔke) *v.t*, to evoke, conjure up.

ex- (eks) *pr*, ex-; ex; late.

exacerber (ɛgzasɛrbe) *v.t*, to exacerbate.

exact, e† (ɛgzakt) *a*, exact, accurate, correct; punctual. **exaction** (ksjɔ̃) *f*, exaction. **exactitude** (tityd) *f*, exactness, exactitude, accuracy; punctuality.

exagération (ɛgzaʒerasjɔ̃) *f*, exaggeration. **exagérer** (re) *v.t. & abs*, to exaggerate; overstate; overdo.

exalter (ɛgzalte) *v.t*, to exalt; extol; excite.

examen (ɛgzamɛ̃) *m*, examination; scrutiny. **examinateur, trice** (minatœːr, tris) *n*, examiner. **examiner** (ne) *v.t*, to examine; overhaul; look into.

exaspérer (ɛgzaspere) *v.t*, to exasperate; aggravate (*Med.*).

exaucer (ɛgzose) *v.t*, to hear (*prayer*), grant.

excavateur (ɛkskavatœːr) *m*, excavator, digger, shovel, navvy. **excavation** (sjɔ̃) *f*, excavation; pothole.

excédant (ɛksedã) *a*, surplus; excessive; exasperating; overwhelming (*odor*). **excédent** *m*, excess, surplus. ~ *de bagages*, surplus baggage. **excéder** (de) *v.t*, to exceed; tire, weary; importune.

excellemment (ɛksɛlamã) *ad*, excellently. **excellence** (lãːs) *f*, excellence; choiceness. *par* ~, preeminently. *Son E*~, *f*, His Excellency. **excellent**, e (lã, ã.;t) *a*, excellent. **exceller** (le) *v.i*, to excel.

excentricité (ɛksãtrisite) *f*, eccentricity; throw; remoteness. **excentrique** (trik) *a*, eccentric; outlying. ¶ (*Mech.*) *m*, eccentric, cam.

excepté (ɛksɛpte) *pr*, except[ing], save, but, barring. **excepter** (te) *v.t*, to except. **exception** (sjɔ̃) *f*, exception; plea (*law*). ~ *péremptoire*, demurrer. **exceptionnel**, le† (ɔnɛl) *a*, exceptional.

excès (ɛksɛ) *m*, excess; abuse; violence. **excessif, ive**† (sɛsif, iːv) *a*, excessive; fulsome; undue.

excitant (ɛksitã) *m*, stimulant. **excitation** (tasjɔ̃) *f*, excitation; incitement; excitement. **exciter** (te) *v.t*, to excite; incite; stir up; urge; rouse; stimulate, fan.

exclamation (ɛksklamasjɔ̃) *f*, exclamation; ejaculation. **s'exclamer** (me) *v.pr*, to exclaim against.

exclure (ɛksklyːr) *v.t.ir*, to exclude; shut out, debar. **exclusif, ive**† (klyzif, iːv) *a*, exclusive; sole. **exclusion** (zjɔ̃) *f*, exclusion. **exclusivité** (zivite) *f*, exclusive (*or* sole) right(s); scoop (*journalism*). *en* ~, first-run (*movie*).

excommunier (ɛkskɔmynje) *v.t*, to excommunicate.

excrément (ɛkskremã) *m*, excrement; scum (*fig.*).

excroissance (ɛkskrwasãːs) *f*, excrescence.

excursion (ɛkskyrsjɔ̃) *f*, excursion, trip, tour, outing. ~ *à pied*, walking tour, hike. ~ *accompagnée*, conducted tour. **excursionniste** (ɔnist) *n*, excursionist.

excuse (ɛkskyːs) *f*, excuse; (*pl.*) apology. **excuser** (kyze) *v.t*, to excuse.

exeat (ɛgzeat) *m*, exeat; dismissal.

exécrable† (ɛgzekrabl) *a*, execrable. **exécrer** (kre) *v.t*, to execrate.

exécutable (ɛgzekytabl) *a*, workable, practicable. **exécutant, e** (tɑ̃, ɑ̃ːt) *n*, performer (*Mus.*). **exécuter** (te) *v.t*, to execute; carry out; perform; fulfil; enforce; expel; buy in against, sell out against (*Stk Ex.*); distrain upon, sell up. **s'~**, to pay up; yield. **exécuteur (trice) testamentaire**, executor, trix. **exécution** (sjɔ̃) *f*, execution, etc. **exécutoire** (twaːr) *a*, executory; enforceable.

exemplaire (ɛgzɑ̃plɛːr) *a*, exemplary. ¶ *m*, copy, specimen. ~ *du souffleur*, prompt book. **exemple** (zɑ̃ːpl) *m*, example; lead; illustration; instance; copy. *par* ~!, you don't say!, it can't be true!

exempt, e (ɛgzɑ̃, ɑ̃ːt) *a*, exempt, free. **exempter** (zɑ̃te) *v.t*, to exempt, free; excuse. **s'~** *de*, to abstain from, get out of. **exemption** (zɑ̃psjɔ̃) *f*, exemption; immunity; freedom.

exercer (ɛgzɛrse) *v.t*, to exercise; train; drill; practice; ply (*trade*); exert; wield (*power*); try (*patience*); inspect (*excise*). **exercice** (sis) *m*, exercise; drill[ing]; practice; office; tenure (*of office*); inspection; trading; [financial] year, [accounting] period. ~ *de doigté*, five-finger exercise. ~*s de tir*, musketry (*Mil.*).

exfolier (s') (ɛksfɔlje) *v.pr*, to exfoliate.

exhalaison (ɛgzalɛzɔ̃) *f*, exhalation (*mist*). **exhalation** (lasjɔ̃) *f*, exhalation (*act*). **exhaler** (le) *v.t*, to exhale; vent; reek with; reek of.

exhausser (ɛgzose) *v.t*, to raise.

exhiber (ɛgzibe) *v.t*, to exhibit, produce, show. **exhibition** (bisjɔ̃) *f*, exhibition.

exhorter (ɛgzɔrte) *v.t*, to exhort, urge.

exhumer (ɛgzyme) *v.t*, to exhume, disinter; rake up.

exigeant, e (ɛgziʒɑ̃, ɑ̃ːt) *a*, particular, exacting, hard to please. **exigence** (ʒɑ̃ːs) *f*, unreasonableness; requirement; exigence, -cy. **exiger** (ʒe) *v.t*, to exact, require, demand; call for. **exigibilité** (ʒibilite) *f*, [re]payability; demand; current liability. **exigible** (bl) *a*, [re]payable; claimable, exigible.

exigu, ë (ɛgzigy) *a*, exiguous, scanty, jejune, small, diminutive. **exiguïté** (gyite) *f*, exiguity.

exil (ɛgzil) *m*, exile. **exilé, e** (le) *n*, exile. **exiler** (le) *v.t*, to exile.

existence (ɛgzistɑ̃ːs) *f*, existence; life; stock (*Com.*). **exister** (te) *v.i*, to exist, be; be extant.

existentialisme (ɛgzistɑ̃sjalism) *m*, existentialism (*Philos.*).

ex-libris (ɛkslibriːs) *m*, bookplate, ex-libris.

exode (ɛgzɔd) *m*, exodus, flight. *l'E~*, Exodus (*Bible*).

exonérer (ɛgzonere) *v.t*, to exonerate, exempt.

exorbitamment (ɛgzɔrbitamɑ̃) *ad*, exorbitantly. **exorbitant, e** (tɑ̃, ɑ̃ːt) *a*, exorbitant, extravagant.

exorciser (ɛgzɔrsize) *v.t*, to exorcise.

exorde (ɛgzɔrd) *m*, exordium; beginning.

exotique (ɛgzɔtik) *a*, exotic; foreign.

expansif, ive (ɛkspɑ̃sif, iːv) *a*, expansive; effusive. **expansion** (sjɔ̃) *f*, expansion.

expatrier (ɛkspatrie) *v.t*, to expatriate.

expectant, e (ɛkspɛktɑ̃, ɑ̃ːt) *a*, expectant; wait-&-see. **expectative** (tatiːv) *f*, expectation, expectancy.

expectorer (ɛkspɛktɔre) *v.t*. & *abs*, to expectorate.

expédient, e (ɛkspedjɑ̃, ɑ̃ːt) *a*, expedient. ¶ *m*, expedient, resource, shift.

expédier (ɛkspedje) *v.t*, to expedite; dispose of; bolt (*food*); dispatch, send, forward, ship; copy & authenticate (*law*). ~

[en *douane*] to clear (*a ship*) [outwards]. **expéditeur, trice** (ditœɪr, tris) n, sender; (m.) shipper; consignor; forwarding agent. **expéditif, ive** (tif, iɪv) a, expeditious. **expédition** (sjɔ̃) f, expedition; disposal; dispatch, sending, forwarding; shipment, consignment; transit; adventure; clearance [outwards]; copy; (pl.) [ship's clearance] papers. **expéditionnaire** (ɔnɛɪr) a, expeditionary. ¶ m, sender; dispatch clerk; shipping clerk; copying clerk.

expérience (ɛksperjãɪs) f, experiment; experience. **expérimental, e†** (rimãtal) a, experimental. **expérimenter** (te) v.t, to try; (abs.) to experiment.

expert, e (ɛkspɛɪr, ɛrt) a, expert, skilled. ¶ m, expert; surveyor. **~-comptable**, professional accountant. **expertise** (pɛrtiɪz) f, survey; examination; report. **expertiser** (tize) v.t, to survey.

expier (ɛkspje) v.t, to expiate, atone for.

expiration (ɛkspirasjɔ̃) f, expiration; expiry. **expirer** (re) v.t. & i, to expire.

explétif, ive (ɛkspletif, iɪv) a, expletive.

explicatif, ive (ɛksplikatif, iɪv) a, explanatory. **explication** (sjɔ̃) f, explanation; construction, rendering. **explicite†** (sit) a, explicit. **expliquer** (ke) v.t, to explain; account for; construe, render.

exploit (ɛksplwa) m, exploit, achievement, feat; writ. **exploitable** (tabl) a, workable; payable. **exploitant** (tã) m, operator, owner or [his] agent (mine, etc.). **exploitation** (tasjɔ̃) f, work[ing], operation; mining; exploitation; workings; farming; trading. **~ agricole**, farm. **exploiter** (te) v.t, to work, run, operate; farm; mine; exploit. **exploiteur, euse** (tœɪr, øɪz) n, exploiter.

explorateur, trice (ɛksploratœɪr, tris) n, explorer. **explorer** (re) v.t, to explore.

exploser (ɛksploze) v.i, to explode. **explosif** (zif) m, explosive.

¶ a, explosive; sensational. **explosion** (zjɔ̃) f, explosion; [out]burst.

exportateur (ɛksportatœɪr) m, exporter. **exportation** (sjɔ̃) f, export[ation]. **exporter** (te) v.t, to export.

exposant, e (ɛkspozã, ãɪt) n, exhibitor; petitioner (law); (m.) exponent, index (Math.). **exposé** (ze) m, statement; account. **exposer** (ze) v.t. & abs, to expose; show, display, exhibit; open; expound; explain; state. **exposition** (zisjɔ̃) f, exposition; exposure; exhibition, show; aspect, frontage (of house).

exprès, esse (ɛksprɛ, ɛs) a, express. **exprès**, ad, on purpose, purposely. ¶ m, express messenger. [train] **express** (prɛs) m, express [train]. bateau express, fast boat. **expressément** (prɛsemã) ad, expressly.

expressif, ive (ɛkspresif, iɪv) a, expressive. **expression** (sjɔ̃) f, expression; phrase. **exprimer** (prime) v.t, to express; squeeze out; voice.

exproprier (ɛksproprie) v.t, to expropriate.

expulser (ɛkspylse) v.t, to expel, drive out, eject.

expurger (ɛkspyrʒe) v.t, to expurgate, bowdlerize.

exquis, e (ɛkski, iɪz) a, exquisite. ¶ m, exquisiteness. **exquisément** (kizemã) ad, exquisitely.

exsangue (ɛksãːg) a, bloodless, anemic; corpse-like.

exsuder (ɛksyde) v.i, to exude.

extase (ɛkstɑːz) f, ecstasy; trance. **s'extasier** (tazje) v.pr, to go into ecstasies. **extatique** (tatik) a, ecstatic, rapturous.

extenseur (ɛkstãsœːr) m, extensor (muscle); chest expander; trouser stretcher. **extensible** (sibl) a, extensible, expanding; open-ended (computers). **extension** (sjɔ̃) f, extension. par ~, in a wider sense.

exsuder (ɛksyde) v.i, to exude.

extase (ɛkstɑːz) f, ecstasy; trance. **s'extasier** (tɑzje) v.pr, to go into ecstasies. **extatique** (tatik) a, ecstatic, rapturous.

extenseur (ɛkstãsœːr) m, extensor (*muscle*); chest expander; trouser stretcher. **extension** (sjɔ̃) *f*, extension. *par ~*, in a wider sense.

exténuer (ɛkstenɥe) *v.t*, to tire out, wear out.

extérieur, e† (ɛksterjœːr) *a*, exterior, external, outer, outside; outward; foreign. ¶ *m*, exterior, outside; foreign countries, abroad.

exterminer (ɛkstɛrmine) *v.t*, to exterminate.

externat (ɛkstɛrna) *m*, day school. **externe** (tɛrn) *a*, external, exterior. *pour l'usage ~*, for outward application, not to be taken (*Med.*). ¶ *n*, day scholar; nonresident assistant to hospital surgeon.

exterritorialité (ɛkstɛritɔrjalite) *f*, extraterritoriality.

extincteur [d'incendie] (ɛkstɛ̃ktœːr) *m*, [fire] extinguisher. **extinction** (sjɔ̃) *f*, extinction; slaking; quenching; paying off; loss (*of voice*). *~ des feux*, lights out (*Mil.*).

extirper (ɛkstirpe) *v.t*, to extirpate, eradicate.

extorquer (ɛkstɔrke) *v.t*, to extort, wring. **extorsion** (sjɔ̃) *f*, extortion.

extra (ɛkstra) *ad. & m*, extra; top quality (*food, etc.*).

extraction (ɛkstraksjɔ̃) *f*, extraction; winning (*Min.*); quarrying; birth, parentage.

extrader (ɛkstrade) *v.t*, to extradite. **extradition** (disjɔ̃) *f*, extradition.

extraire (ɛkstrɛːr) *v.t.ir*, to extract, take out; excerpt; get, win; quarry. **extrait** (trɛ) *m*, extract; excerpt. *~s d'auteurs*, extracts (*or* selections) from [the writings *or* works of] authors. *~ de naissance*, birth certificate. *~ mortuaire*, death c.

extraordinaire† (ɛkstraɔrdinɛːr) *a. & m*, extraordinary; special; unusual.

extravagance (ɛkstravagɑ̃ːs) *f*, extravagance; exorbitance; folly. **extravagant, e** (gɑ̃, ɑ̃ːt) *a*, extravagant, wild. **extravaguer** (ge) *v.i*, to rave.

extrême (ɛkstrɛːm) *a. & m*, extreme (*a. & m.*); utmost; drastic; dire. *~onction*, *f*, extreme unction. *l'E~-Orient*, *m*, the Far East. **extrêmement** (trɛmmɑ̃) *ad*, extremely; exceedingly; intensely. **extrémiste** (tremist) *n*, extremist. **extrémité** (te) *f*, extremity; end; tip.

extrinsèque (ɛkstrɛ̃sɛk) *a*, extrinsic.

exubérance (ɛgzyberɑ̃ːs) *f*, exuberance; luxuriance. **exubérant, e** (rɑ̃, ɑ̃ːt) *a*, exuberant; luxuriant.

exulter (ɛgzylte) *v.i*, to exult.

F

fa (fa) *m*, F (Mus.).

fable (faːbl) *f*, fable; story; byword, laughing stock. **fablier** (fablie) *m*, fabulist; book of fables.

fabricant (fabrikɑ̃) *m*, manufacturer, maker. **fabricateur, trice** (katœːr, tris) *n*, fabricator; forger. *~ de fausse monnaie*, counterfeiter. **fabrication** (sjɔ̃) *f*, manufacture; make; work; fabrication. **fabrique** (brik) *f*, [manu]factory, works, mill; fabric (*edifice*); vestry, church council; invention (*fig.*). **fabriquer** (ke) *v.t*, to manufacture, make; fabricate, invent, trump up.

fabuleux, euse† (fabylø, øːz) *a*, fabulous, fabled. **fabuliste** (list) *m*, fabulist.

façade (fasad) *f*, front, frontage, façade, frontispiece (*Arch.*).

face (fas) *f*, face; front; frontage (*extent of front*); side (*record*); obverse, head (*coin*); aspect. *~ à* facing. *en ~*, to one's face. *en ~ de*, *pr*, opposite, facing. *faire ~ à*, to face; keep pace with; front; meet.

face-à-main (fasamɛ̃) *m*, lorgnette.

facétie (fasesi) *f*, joke, jest. **facétieux, euse** (sjø, øːz) *a*, facetious, waggish, jocular.

facette (fasɛt) *f*, facet. **facetter** (te) *v.t*, to facet.

fâché, e (faʃe) *p.a,* angry; sorry. **fâcher** (ʃe) *v.t,* to make angry, anger; grieve, pain. **se ~,** to get (*or* be) angry. **fâcherie** (ʃri) *f,* bad feeling; tiff. **fâcheux, euse†** (ʃø, øːz) *a,* unfortunate, tiresome, troublesome; sad. ¶ *m,* unfortunate part; bore, nuisance (*pers.*).

facial, e (fasjal) *a,* facial; face (*att.*). **facies** (sjɛːs) *m,* facies; cast of features.

facile† (fasil) *a,* easy; facile; ready; fluent. **facilité** (lite) *f,* easiness, ease; facility; fluency; aptitude. **faciliter** (te) *v.t,* to facilitate.

façon (fasɔ̃) *f,* make; workmanship; making; labor; manner, fashion, way, wise, style, pattern; (*pl.*) manners; (*pl.*) ceremony, fuss. *de ~ à,* so as to. *de toute ~,* in any case. *en aucune ~,* by no means. *de ~ que,* so that. *faire des ~s,* to stand on ceremony.

faconde (fakɔ̃d) *f,* flow of language.

façonné, e (fasɔne) *p.a,* figured (*textiles*). **façonner** (ne) *v.t,* to make; shape, fashion, form, mold; dress. **façonnier, ère** (nje, ɛːr) *a,* [over-]ceremonious, fussy.

fac-similé (faksimile) *m,* facsimile.

factage (faktaːʒ) *m,* parcels delivery; porterage. **facteur** (tœːr) *m,* maker (*instruments*); postman; porter (*Rly.*); salesman; agent; factor, element. *~ des télégraphes,* telegraph messenger, t. boy.

factice (faktis) *a,* imitation (*att.*), artificial; factitious; forced; meretricious.

factieux, euse (faksjø, øːz), *a,* factious.

faction (faksjɔ̃) *f,* sentry duty, guard; faction. **factionnaire** (ɔnɛːr) *m,* sentry.

factorerie (faktɔrri) *f,* [foreign *or* colonial] agency.

factotum (faktɔtɔm) *m,* factotum, man Friday.

factrice (faktris) *f,* postwoman.

factum (faktɔm) *m,* diatribe; statement of claim (*law*).

facture (faktyːr) *f,* invoice, bill; note; treatment (*music, art*); workmanship. *~ fictive,* pro forma invoice. *~ générale,* statement [of account]. **facturer** (tyre) *v.t,* to invoice.

facultatif, ive† (fakyltatif, iːv) *a,* optional. **faculté** (te) *f,* faculty; option; right; power; leave; liberty; property; branch [of study]; (*pl.*) means; (*pl.*) cargo, goods (*marine Insce.*).

fadaise[s] (fadɛːz) *f.[pl.],* twaddle, flummery, rubbish, stuff & nonsense.

fadasse (fadas) *a,* sickly, insipid. **fade†** (fad) *a,* insipid, tasteless, flat; mawkish; namby-pamby. **fadeur** (dœːr) *f,* insipidity.

faffe (faf) *m,* piece of paper; banknote. (*pl.*) **fafiots** (jo) identity papers (*slang*).

fagot (fago) *m,* fagot; bundle. **fagoter** (gɔte) *v.t,* to fagot; bundle; dress like a swell.

faiblard, e (fɛblaːr, ard) *a,* weakly. ¶ *n,* weakling. **faible†** (bl) *a,* weak; feeble; low; faint; shallow; slight; thin; light; small; scant[y]; slack; bare. ¶ *m,* weak point; weakness, partiality, sneaking fondness; foible; failing. *les ~s,* the weak. **faiblesse** (blɛs) *f,* weakness; swoon. **faiblir** (bliːr) *v.i,* to weaken; slacken; give way; flag, fail.

faïence (fajɑ̃ːs) *f,* earthenware, pottery, crockery, china. **faïencerie** (jãsri) *f,* pottery [works]; earthenware. **faïencier, ère** (sje, ɛːr) *n,* earthenware; manufacturer *or* dealer.

faille (faːj) *f,* faille (*fabric*); fault (*Geol.*). **failli** (faji) *m,* bankrupt, insolvent. **failliblité** (bilite) *f,* fallibility. **faillible** (bl) *a,* fallible. **faillir** (jiːr) *v.i.ir,* to fail; to nearly . . .; to err. **faillite** (jit) *f,* failure; bankruptcy; insolvency.

faim (fɛ̃) *f,* hunger; starvation. *avoir ~, grand-~,* to be hungry, very hungry.

faine (fɛn) *f,* beechnut; (*pl.*) beechmast.

fainéant, e (feneɑ̃, ɑ̃ːt) *a,* idle, do-nothing. ¶ *n,* idler, lazybones, loafer. **fainéanter** (ɑ̃te) *v.i,* to idle, loaf. **fainéantise** (ti͟z) *f*, idleness, etc.

faire (fɛːr) *m*, technique (*art, etc.*). ¶ *v.t. & i. ir*, to make; do; create; form; perform; effect; write; play; commit; go; run; be; matter; have; get; keep; mind; get ready; lay; put; offer; o. up; give; take; take in (*provisions, etc.*); deal (*cards*); cut (*teeth*); make up (*face, the cash*); make out (*pretend*); wage (*war*); pay; ejaculate, say; charge; quote; accustom; call; turn. *cela fait mon affaire*, that suits me. *faites attention*, be careful. ~ *savoir*, to inform. se ~, to be done; be made; happen, take place; be; be getting; become; grow; make oneself; get; gain; turn. *ne vous en faites pas*, don't worry. **fairepart** (fɛrpaːr) *m*, announcement of betrothal, wedding, birth, death. **faisable** (fəzabl) *a*, feasible, practicable.

faisan, e (fɛzɑ̃, an) *n*, pheasant. **faisandé, e** (zɑ̃de) *a*, high, gamy; tainted. **faisandeau** (do) *m*, young pheasant. se **faisander** (de) *v. pr*, to get high. **faisanderie** (dri) *f*, pheasantry.

faisceau (fɛso) *m*, bunch, bundle, cluster, sheaf, nest; beam (*Opt.*); pencil (*Opt.*); pile, stack (*arms*); (*pl.*) fasces (*Hist.*).

faiseur, euse (fəzœːr, øːz) *n*, maker; doer; -monger; bluffer.

fait (fɛ; *in liaison*, fɛt) *m*, act, deed; feat; fact; point; occurrence, happening. ~*s divers*, news items. ~*s & dits*, sayings & doings. ~*s & gestes*, doings, exploits. *dans* (or *par*) *le* ~ or *en* ~, as a matter of fact. *de* ~, de facto, actual. *prendre sur le* ~, to catch redhanded.

faite, e (fɛ, ɛt) *p.p. & p.a*: ~ *de boue & de crachat*, jerry-built. ~ *par tailleur*, tailormade. *un homme fait*, a full-grown man.

faitage (fɛtaʒ) *m*, roofing; ridge pole; ridge capping. **faîte** (fɛːt) *m*, top, apex, summit, zenith. **faîtière** (fɛtjɛːr) *a.f*, ridge (*att.*). ¶ *f*, ridge tile; ridge pole (*tent*).

fait-tout (fɛtu) *m*, stewpan.

faix (fɛ) *m*, burden, load, weight, incubus.

fakir (fakiːr) *m*, fakir.

falaise (falɛːz) *f*, cliff (*on seashore*).

falbalas (falbala) *m.pl*, furbelows.

fallacieux, euse† (falasjø, øːz) *a*, fallacious, misleading.

falloir (falwaːr) *v.imp.ir*, to be necessary, must, should, ought, shall, to have to, shall (*or will*) have to; to want; to require; to take. *s'en* ~, to be wanting; be far, fall short. *comme il faut*, proper (*behavior*). *il s'en faut de beaucoup*, far from it.

falot (falo) *m*, lantern.

falot, e (falo, ɔt) *a*, funny little (*pers.*).

falourde (falurd) *f*, bundle of firewood logs.

falsifier (falsifje) *v.t*, to adulterate; debase; falsify, tamper with; forge.

famé, e (fame) *a*, -famed.

famélique (famelik) *a*, starveling.

fameux, euse† (famø, øːz) *a*, famous; notorious; capital, firstrate, rare, champion (*att.*).

familial, e (familjal) *a*, family (*att.*). **familiariser** (ljarize) *v.t*, to familiarize, accustom. **familiarité** (te) *f*, familiarity; intimacy; (*pl.*) liberties. **familier, ère** (lje, ɛːr) *a*, familiar; intimate; habitual; colloquial; household (*gods*). ¶ *m*, familiar. **famille** (miːj) *f*, family; people. *en* ~, at home.

famine (famin) *f*, famine, starvation.

fanage (fanaʒ) *m*, tedding; fallen leaves.

fanal (fanal) *m*, light, lamp.

fanatique (fanatik) *a*, fanatic(al); obsessed. ¶ *n*, fanatic; devotee. **fanatiser** (ze) *v.t*, to fanaticize. **fanatisme** (tism) *m*, fanaticism.

fanchon (fɑ̃ʃɔ̃) *f*, kerchief.

fane (fan) *f*, fallen leaf; top (*turnip, etc.*).

faner (fane) *v.t*, to ted, toss (*hay*); fade. **faneur, euse** (nœːr, øːz) (*pers.*) *n. &* (*Mach.*) *f*, haymaker, tedder.

fanfare (fɑ̃faːr) f, flourish of trumpets, fanfare; brass band. **fanfaron, ne** (farɔ̃, ɔn) a, blustering, swaggering, hectoring, bragging. **fanfaronnade** (rɔnad) & **fanfaronnerie** (nri) f, bluster, swagger, brag.

fanfreluches (fɑ̃frəlyʃ) f.pl, fallals, frills & furbelows.

fange (fɑ̃ːʒ) f, mire, mud, filth, muck; gutter (fig.). **fangeux, euse** (fɑ̃ʒø, øːz) a, miry.

fanion (fanjɔ̃) m, flag, banner. (Mil.) pennon.

fanon (fanɔ̃) m, dewlap; whalebone; fetlock; (Eccl.) maniple.

fantaisie (fɑ̃tezi) f, fancy, notion, whim; fantasy; fantasia. [objet de] ~, fancy [article]. **fantaisiste** (zist) a, fantastic, whimsical. **fantasmagorie** (tasmagori) f, phantasmagoria; fabrication. **fantasque** (task) a, whimsical, odd; temperamental.

fantassin (fɑ̃tasɛ̃) m, infantryman. ~ de la flotte, marine.

fantastique (fɑ̃tastik) a. & m, fantastic, fanciful; weird, eerie, uncanny.

fantoche (fɑ̃tɔʃ) m, puppet (pers.).

fantomatique (fɑ̃tomatik) a, ghostly, unearthly. **fantôme** (toːm) m, phantom, ghost.

faon (fɑ̃) m, fawn. **faonner** (fane) v.i, to fawn (of deer).

faquin (fakɛ̃) m, scurvy fellow, cad. **faquinerie** (kinri) f, scurvy trick.

faroud, e (faro, oːd) n, fop, dandy.

farce (fars) f, stuffing, forcemeat; farce; foolery; joke; practical joke; antic. faire ses ~s, to sow one's wild oats. ~s et attrapes, practical jokes, tricks. **farceur, euse** (sœːr, øːz) n, joker; humorist; practical joker; comedian. **farcir** (siːr) v.t, to stuff; cram.

fard (faːr) m, paint, grease p., make-up; disguise, guile.

fardage (fardaːʒ) m, dunnage; top hamper; hamper.

fardeau (fardo) m, burden, load, weight, onus.

farder (farde) v.t, to paint, make up (face); gloss, varnish (fig.);

dunnage (ship); (v.i.) to weigh [heavy]; sink. se ~, to make up.

fardier (fardje) m, trolley.

farfadet (farfadɛ) m, goblin, sprite.

farfelu (farfely) a, strange, bizarre. ¶ m, someone who behaves strangely.

farfouiller (farfuje) v.i, to rummage [about], fumble.

faribole[s] (faribɔl) f.[pl.], twaddle.

farinacé, e (farinase) a, farinaceous. **farine** (rin) f, flour, meal, farina. ~ de lin, linseed meal. ~ de riz, ground rice. ~ lactée, malted milk. **farineux, euse** (nø, øːz) a, floury, mealy; farinaceous. **farinier, ère** (nje, ɛːr) n, flour dealer; miller.

farouch[e] (faruʃ) m, crimson clover.

farouche (faruʃ) a, wild, savage, fierce; grim; surly; unapproachable, shy, coy.

farrago (farago) m, mixture (fodder); farrago; hotchpotch.

fascicule (fasikyl) m, fascicle; number, part, instalment (publication).

fascinateur, trice (fasinatœːr, tris.) a, fascinating. **fascination** (sjɔ̃) f, fascination; witchery.

fascine (fasin) f, fascine; fagot.

fasciner (fasine) v.t, to fascinate.

fascisme (fasism) m, fascism. **fasciste** (sist) m, fascist.

faste (fast) m. no pl, pomp, pageantry; show, ostentation; (m.pl.) fasti; annals.

fastidieux, euse† (fastidjø, øːz) a, tedious, wearisome, irksome, dull.

fastueux, euse† (fastɥø, øːz) a, given to display; ostentatious, showy, gaudy.

fat (fat) a.m, foppish. ¶ m, fop, coxcomb, jackanapes.

fatal, e† (fatal) a, fatal; fateful; latest, final. **fatalisme** (lism) m, fatalism. **fataliste** (list) n, fatalist. **fatalité** (te) f, fate, fatality; mischance.

fatidique (fatidik) a, fatidical, prophetic.

fatigant, e (fatigɑ̃, ɑ̃ːt) a, fatiguing, tiring; tiresome; tedious.

fatique (tig) *f*, fatigue, tiredness, fag; stress, [over]strain. *de* ~, working (*clothes*). **fatiguer** (ge) *v.t*, to fatigue, tire; stress, [over]strain, task, wear out; (*v.i.*) to labor (*ship*).

fatras (fatrɑ) *m*, jumble, medley. **fatrasser** (trase) *v.i*, to potter.

fatuité (fatɥite) *f*, self-conceit.

fauber[t] (fobɛɹr) *m*, swab (*Naut.*).

faubourg (fobuːr) *m*, suburb; quarter (*town*). **faubourien, ne** (burjɛ̃, ɛn) *a*. & *n*, working-class suburban (dweller).

faucard (fokaːr) *m*, river weeding shear.

fauchage (foʃaːʒ) *m*, mowing. **faucher** (ʃe) *v.t*, to mow; m. down. **fauchet** (ʃɛ) *m*, hay rake. **faucheur** (ʃœːr) *m*, mower (*pers.*). ~ *ou* **faucheux** (ʃø) *m*, daddy longlegs. **faucheuse** (ʃøːz) *f*, mower (*Mach.*). **faucille** (siːj) *f*, sickle, reaping hook.

faucon (fokɔ̃) *m*, falcon, hawk. ~ *pèlerin*, peregrine [falcon]. **fauconnerie** (kɔnri) *f*, falconry; hawking. **fauconnet** (nje) *m*, falconer. **fauconnière** (jɛːr) *f*, saddle bag.

faufiler (fofile) *v.t*, to tack, baste (*Need.*); slip in, insinuate. **faufilure** (lyːr) *f*, tacking, basting.

faune (foːn) *m*, faun; (*f.*) fauna.

faussaire (fosɛːr) *n*, forger. **faussement** (smɑ̃) *ad*, falsely; wrongfully. **fausser** (se) *v.t*, to bend; buckle; warp; strain; upset; derange; foul; falsify, pervert. **fausset** (sɛ) *m*, falsetto (*voice*); spigot, vent peg. **fausseté** (ste) *f*, falseness, falsity; falsehood, untruth.

faute (foːt) *f*, fault; mistake, error; blame; foul (*Foot.*); want, lack. ~ *d'orthographe*, misspelling. ~ *d'impression*, printer's error, misprint. ~ *de copiste*, ~ *de plume*, clerical error. ~ *de*, failing, in default of, for want of. *sans* ~, without fail.

fauteuil (fotœːj) *m*, armchair, easy chair; chair; seat; orchestra seat (*Theat.*). ~ *à bascule*, rocking chair. ~ [*de la présidence*], chair (*at meeting*).

fautif, ive (fotif, iːv) *a*, faulty, at fault, offending.

fauve (foːv) *a*, fawn[-colored], fallow; fulvous, tawny; buff; lurid (*light*). ¶ *m*, fawn; buff (*color*); (*pl.*) deer; wild beasts (*big felines*).

fauvette (fovɛt) *f*, warbler (*bird*). ~ *à tête noire*, blackcap. ~ *des haies*, hedge sparrow.

faux (fo) *f*, scythe; falx.

faux, fausse (fo, oːs) *a*, false; wrong; untrue; base, counterfeit; forged; spurious; bogus; unjust (*weight*); improper (*navigation*); blank, blind (*window*); attempted (*suicide*). **faux**, *comps:* ~ *bourdon*, drone [bee]. ~ *brillant*, imitation [stone], paste; tinsel (*fig.*). ~ *col*, see *col*. ~ *coup de queue*, miscue. ~ *ébénier*, laburnum. ~ *frais*, incidental expenses; untaxed costs (*law*). ~*-fuyant*, m, evasion, shift. ~*-monnayeur*, m, counterfeiter. ~ *nom*, alias. ~ *numéro* [*d'appel*], wrong number (*Teleph.*). ~ *pas*, mistake, slip. ~ *témoinage*, false evidence, perjury. **fausse**, *comps:* ~ *boîte*, dummy [box]. ~ *couche*, miscarriage. ~ *déclaration*, misstatement, misrepresentation. ~ *équerre*, bevel [square]. ~ *honte*, false shame; bashfulness. ~ *manche*, sleeve protector. **faux**, *ad*, falsely, wrongly; out of tune. *à* ~, wrongly, unjustly. ¶ *m*, forgery. *le* ~, the false.

faveur (favœːr) *f*, favor; boon; goodwill. *billet de* ~, complimentary ticket. **favorable**† (vɔrabl) *a*, favorable. **favori, ite** (ri, it) *a*. & *n*, favorite; pet; minion; (*m.pl.*) [side] whiskers. **favoriser** (ze) *v.t*, to favor, befriend; foster, promote. **favoritisme** (tism) *m*, favoritism.

fébrile† (febril) *a*, febrile, feverish.

fécond, e (fekɔ̃, ɔ̃ːd) *a*, fruitful, fecund, fertile, prolific; life-giving; bountiful. **féconder** (kɔ̃de) *v.t*, to fertilize, fecundate, impregnate; milt; fructify. **fécondité** (dite) *f*, fecundity, fertility, fruitfulness.

fécule (fekyl) *f*, starch, farina.

féculent, e (lã, ã;t) *a*, starchy (*food*).

fédéral, e (federal) *a*, federal. **fédération** (sjɔ̃) *f*, federation, union. **fédérer** (re) *v.t*, to federate.

fée (fe) *f*, fairy, pixy, -xie. **féerie** (feri) *f*, fairyhood; Fairyland; fairy scene. **féerique** (ferik) *a*, fairylike.

feindre (fɛ̃;dr) *v.t. & abs. tr*, to feign, pretend, sham; feint. **feint, e** (fɛ̃, ɛ̃;t) *p.a*, feigned, sham; false, blind (*door, etc.*). ¶ feint, pretence, sham.

fêler (fεle) *v.t*, to crack.

félicitation (felisitasjɔ̃) *f*, congratulation. **félicité** (te) *f*, happiness, felicity. **féliciter** (te) *v.t*, to congratulate.

félidés (felide) *m.pl*, Felidae. **félin, e** (lɛ̃, in) *a. & m*, feline, cat (*att.*).

félon, ne (felɔ̃, ɔn) *a*, disloyal. **félonie** (lɔni) *f*, disloyalty.

fêlure (fɛly;r) *f*, crack, split.

femelle (fəmεl) *f. & a*, female, she; hen; cow (*elephant, etc.*). **féminin, e** (feminɛ̃, in) *a*, feminine; womanish (*voice*); female. ¶ *m*, feminine (*Gram.*). **féminiser** (nize) *v.t*, to feminize. **féminisme** (nism) *m*, feminism. **féministe** (nist) *a. & n*, feminist. **femme** (fam) *f*, woman; female; wife. ~-**caoutchouc, ~-serpent,** *f*, contortionist. ~ **de chambre,** lady's maid; housemaid; chambermaid; stewardess (*ship*). ~ **de journée,** cleaning woman. ~ **de ménage,** cleaning woman. **femmelette** (mlεt) *f*, silly little woman; effeminate [man].

fémur (femy;r) *m*, femur.

fenaison (fənεzɔ̃) *f*, haymaking.

fendant (fãdã) *m*, swaggerer.

fendiller (fãdije) *v.t*, to crack, fissure. **fendre** (fã;dr) *v.t*, to split, cleave; rend; rive; crack; slot, nick, slit; break (*heart*). ~ **un cheveu en quatre,** to split hairs. **fendu, e** (fãdy) *a*, split, cleft. **bien fendu,** longlegged (*man*).

fenêtrage (fənεtra;ʒ) *m*, windows (*col.*). **fenêtre** (nε;tr) *f*, window. ~ **à guillotine,** sash w. ~ **à tabatière,** skylight. ~ **en**

saillie, bay window. ~ [*ordinaire*], casement [window].

fenil (fəni) *m*, hayloft.

fenouil (fənu;j) *m*, fennel; f. seed.

fente (fã;t) *f*, crack, cleft, split, slit; fissure, crevice, cranny; slot; nick.

féodal, e (feodal) *a*, feudal. **féodalité** (lite) *f*, feudalism, feudality.

fer (fε;r) *m*, iron; bar; section; shoe; bit; head (*lance, etc.*); tag (*laces*); sword, weapon; (*pl.*) irons, chains, shackles; fetters, manacles; obstetrical forceps. ~ **à friser,** curling irons. ~ **à repasser,** [flat] iron. ~ **à souder,** soldering iron, soldering bit. ~[*s*] **cavalier[s],** horseshoe bars, h. iron, h. sections. ~ **de** (ou à) **cheval,** horseshoe. ~ **de fonte,** cast iron. ~ **de lance,** spear head. ~**s dorés,** gilt tooling (*Bookb.*). ~ **en barre[s],** bar iron. ~ **en lame,** sheet i. ~ [*forgé*], wrought i.

fer-blanc (fεrblã) *m*, tin [plate], tinned [sheet] iron. **ferblanterie** (blãtri) *f*, tin plate working *or* trade; tinware. **ferblantier** (tje) *m*, tinsmith.

férié (ferje) *a*, **jour** ~, holiday (*not a working day*).

férir (feri;r) *v.t*: **sans coup** ~, without striking a blow.

ferler (fεrle) *v.t*, to furl (*sail*).

fermage (fεrma;ʒ) *m*, rent (*farm, land*); tenant farming.

fermant, e (fεrmã, ã;t) *a*, lockup; closing.

ferme† (fεrm) *a*, firm, solid, steady, steadfast, staunch. ¶ *ad*, firmly, firm, fast, hard. ¶ *i*, steadyǃ ¶ *f*, lease; farm; farmhouse; homestead; truss, girder (*Build.*); set piece (*Theat.*).

ferment (fεrmã) *m*, ferment; leaven. **fermentation** (tasjɔ̃) *f*, fermentation; ferment (*fig.*). **fermenter** (te) *v.i*, to ferment; to [be at] work (*fig.*).

fermer (fεrme) *v.t. & i*, to shut, s. up, s. down, close, c. up, c. down; do up; turn off, shut off; switch off; stop up; enclose. ~ [à clef] *v.t. & i*, to lock [up]. ~ **la marche,** to bring up the rear.

fermeté (fɛrməte) *f*, firmness, steadfastness, steadiness, strength.

fermeture (fɛrməty:r) *f*, shutting; closing; fastening; fastener. ~ *éclair*, zipper. ~ *pression*, snap fastener.

fermier, ère (fɛrmje, ɛɪr) *n*, farmer; tenant (*farm*); lessee; tenant farmer; (*att.*) leasing.

fermoir (fɛrmwaɪr) *m*, clasp, fastener, snap; double-beveled chisel.

féroce (ferɔs) *a*, ferocious, fierce, savage, wild. **férocité** (site) *f*, ferocity.

ferrage (fɛraːʒ) *m*, shoeing; tiring; tagging. **ferraille** (rɑːj) *f*, old iron, scrap iron. **ferrailler** (rɑje) *v.i*, to slash about. **ferrailleur** (jœːr) *m*, dealer in old iron; sword rattler. **ferré, e** (re) *p.a*, ironshod; shod; hobnailed; versed, conversant. ~ *à glace*, roughshod, frost-nailed. **ferrement** (fɛrmɑ̃) *m*, ironwork; shoeing; putting in irons. **ferrer** (re) *v.t*, to bind, to mordant (*with any metal*); shoe; tire; tag; strike (*fish*). **ferret** (rɛ) *m*, tag (*lace*). **ferreux** (rø) *a.m*, ferrous. **ferronnerie** (rɔnri) *f*, ironworks; iron warehouse; ironmongery. **ferronnier, ère** (nje, ɛɪr) *n*, iron worker; ironmonger. **ferrugineux, euse** (ryʒinø, øːz) *a*, ferruginous, **ferrure** (ryːr) *f*, ironwork; binding; shoeing; fitting, mounting.

ferroutage (ferutaʒ) *m*, piggyback transportation of truck trailers. **ferrouter** (te) *v.t*, to transport truck trailers piggyback.

fertile (fɛrtil) *a*, fertile, fruitful; prolific; fat (*land*). **fertiliser** (lize) *v.t*, to fertilize. **fertilité** (te) *f*, fertility.

féru, e (fery) *a*, struck; smitten (*love*).

férule (feryl) *f*, ferula (*Bot.*); bondage; cane (*Sch.*); lash (*fig.*).

fervent, e (fɛrvɑ̃, ɑ̃ːt) *a*, fervent, earnest. ¶ *n*, enthusiast, devotee. **ferveur** (vœːr) *f*, fervor, earnestness.

fesse (fɛs) *f*, buttock. *serrer les* ~*s*, to be afraid. **fessée** (se) *f*, spanking. **fesse-mathieu** (matjø) *m*, miser. **fesser** (se) *v.t*, to spank; birch.

festin (fɛstɛ̃) *m*, feast, banquet. **festiner** (tine) *v.t. & abs*, to feast. **festival** (val) *m*, musical festival. **feston** (fɛstɔ̃) *m*, festoon; scallop (*edging*). **festonner** (tɔne) *v.t*, to festoon; scallop. ¶ *v.i*, to reel about (*drunk*).

festoyer (fɛstwaje) *v.t. & i*, to feast.

fête (fɛːt) *f*, feast, festivity; festival; fête; holiday; saint's day; birthday; entertainment, treat. *la* ~ *de* [*l'anniversaire de*] *l'Armistice*, Armistice Day. *la Fête-Dieu*, Corpus Christi. ~ *foraine*, fête (*at a fair*). ~ *légale*, legal holiday. **fêter** (fɛte) *v.t*, to keep [as a holiday], celebrate; fête, entertain.

fétiche (fetiʃ) *m*, fetish; mascot (*as on car*); charm. **fétichisme** (ʃism) *m*, fetishism.

fétide (fetid) *a*, fetid, foul. **fétidité** (dite) *f*, fetidness, foulness.

fétu (fety) *m*, straw; (*fig.*) straw, rush, rap, fig, pin.

feu, (fø) *m*, fire; flame; flare; flash; light; lamp; firing (*Mil.*); heat (*fig.*); home, hearth. ~ *à éclipses*, intermittent light (*Naut.*). ~ *concentré*, group firing (*Mil.*). ~ *d'artifice*, firework. ~ *de bengale*, Bengal light. ~ *de bivouac*, campfire. ~ *de cheminée*, chimney on fire. ~*x de circulation*, traffic lights, stop & go lights. ~ *de joie*, bonfire. ~ *de paille* (*fig.*), flash in the pan. ~ *de peloton*, volley firing (*Mil.*). ~ *follet*, ignis fatuus, will-o'-the-wisp. ~ *roulant*, running fire. ~*!* fire! (*Mil.*). *au* ~*!* (*house, etc, on*) fire! *faire long* ~, to hang fire. *ni* ~ *ni lieu*, neither house nor home. *avez-vous du* ~*?*, do you have a light? (*for cigarette*).

feu, e (fø) *a*, late, the late (*deceased*).

feuillage (fœjaːʒ) *m*, foliage, leafage, leaves. **feuillaison** (jɛzɔ̃) *f*, leafing, foliation. **feuillard** (jaːr) *m*, hoop wood. ~ *de fer*, hoop iron, strap iron, strip iron. **feuille** (fœːj) *f*, sheet; leaf; slip; list; roll (*pay*); [news]paper; blade; flake; foil. ~ *d'appel*, muster roll. ~ *de chou*, rag (*worthless newspaper*). ~*-document*, data sheet. ~ *de* garde, endpaper. ~s de placage, veneer. ~ de présence, time sheet, attendance s. ~ de rose, rose leaf (petal). ~ de route, waybill. ~ de tirée, proof (Typ.). ~ de transfert, transfer deed, [deed of] transfer. ~ de vigne, fig leaf (art). ~ mobile, looseleaf (book). ~ volante, loose sheet (paper). feuillé, e (fœje) a, leafy, foliate. ¶ f, greenwood, trees. feuillet (jɛ) m, leaf (book); thin sheet, t. plate; lamina. feuilleter (fœjte) v.t, to run through, thumb (book); roll out (pastry); flake. feuilleton (tɔ̃) m, serial [story]. feuillu, e (jy) a, leafy. feuillure (jy:r) f, rabbet, rebate, fillister.

feutre (fø:tr) m, felt. ~ mou, ~ souple, soft felt (hat). ~ velours, velours. feutrer (føtre) v.t, to felt, pad. à pas feutrés, stealthily.

fève (fɛ:v) f, bean. ~ de marais, broad bean. féverole (fɛvrɔl) f, horse bean.

février (fevrie) m, February.

fez (fɛ:z) m, fez.

fi (fi) i, ughl fiel ~ donc! for shame! faire ~ de, to pooh-pooh.

fiabilité (fjabilite) f, reliability. essai de ~, reliability test.

fiacre (fjakr) m, cab, four-wheeler.

fiançailles (fjɑ̃sɑ:j) f.pl, engagement, betrothal. fiancé, e (se) n, fiancé, e, betrothed. fiancer (se) v.t, to betroth, engage, affiance.

fiasco (fjasko) m, fiasco, failure, breakdown.

fibre (fibr) f, fiber; string (fig.). ~ de coco, coir. fibreux, euse (brø, ø:z) a, fibrous, stringy. fibrille (bril) f, fibril.

ficelé, e (fisle) p.a, dressed (badly). ficeler (sle) v.t, to [tie with] string, tie up. ficelle (sɛl) f, string, twine; packthread; dodge, trick, game.

fiche (fiʃ) f, hinge; peg, pin, stake; plug, key; slip (paper); card (loose index); ticket; ~ de consolation, booby prize; some slight consolation. ~ de tournage, dope sheet (TV, cinema). ficher (ʃe) v.t, to drive in, stick. se ~ de, to laugh at; not care about. fichier

(ʃje) m, card index; file (computers).

fichtre (fiʃtr) i, good gracious!

fichu (fiʃy) m, neckerchief, fichu. ¶ a, done for. mal ~, out of sorts.

fictif, ive† (fiktif, i:v) a, fictitious, sham. fiction (sjɔ̃) f, fiction, figment.

fidéicommis (fideikɔmi) m, trust (law).

fidèle† (fidɛl) a, faithful; loyal; true; reliable, trustworthy; fast; retentive. les ~s, m.pl, the faithful. fidélité (delite) f, fidelity, faithfulness; truthfulness; reliability; retentiveness.

fidibus (fidiby:s) m, spill, pipe light.

fiduciaire (fidysjɛ:r) a, fiduciary.

fief (fjɛf) m, fief, feud, fee (Hist.); preserve (fig.). fieffé, e (fe) a, arrant, downright, unmitigated, egregious, regular, outright, rank, out & out, of the deepest dye.

fiel (fjɛl) m, gall; rancor. fielleux, euse (lø, ø:z) a, rancorous.

fiente (fjɑ̃:t) f, dung, droppings.

fier (fje) v.t, to entrust. se ~, to trust, rely.

fier, ère† (fjɛ:r) a, proud, haughty; lofty; stately; lordly; rare, fine; arrant. fier-à-bras (fjɛrabra) m, swaggerer. fierté (fjɛrte) f, pride; boldness (touch).

fièvre (fjɛ:vr) f, fever; heat (fig.). ~ aphteuse (aftø:z), foot-&-mouth disease. ~ des foins, hay fever. ~ paludéenne, malaria, marsh fever; ague. fiévreux, euse† (evrø, ø:z) a, feverish. ¶ f, fever case (pers.).

fifre (fifr) m, fife; fifer.

figé, e (fiʒe) a, frozen (fig.); set. figer (ʒe) v.t. & se ~, to congeal, coagulate, set.

fignoler (fiɲɔle) v.t. & abs, to overelaborate.

figue (fig) f, fig. ~ de Barbarie, prickly pear. figuier (gje) m, fig tree.

figurant, e (figyrɑ̃, ɑ̃:t) n, supernumerary; one who takes no prominent part. figuratif, ive† (ratif, i:v) a, figurative; pictorial (plan, map); picture (writing);

figure (gy₁r) *f*, figure; form, shape; face (*of pers.*), countenance; show[ing]; (*pl.*) court cards. ~ *de cire*, waxwork. ~ *de mots*, ~ *de rhétorique*, figure of speech. ~ *de proue*, figurehead (*ship*). ~ *en lame de couteau*, hatchet face. **figuré, e** (gyre) *p.a*, pictorial (*plan, map*); figure (*dance, stone*); figurative (*sense*). ¶ *m*, figurative sense. **figurément** (mã) *ad*, figuratively (*sense*). **figurer** (re) *v.t*, to figure, represent, picture, show; (*v.i.*) to appear, figure, show. **se ~**, to imagine, fancy, picture to oneself. **figurine** (rin) *f*, figurine, statuette.

fil (fil) *m*, thread; yarn; wire; filament; string (*pearls, etc.*); [cutting] edge; grain (*wood, etc.*); flaw. ~ *à plomb*, plumb line. ~ *carcasse des fleuristes*, flower wire. ~ *de fer barbelé*, barb[ed] wire. ~*s de la Vierge*, gossamer. ~ *[de lin]*, linen [thread]. ~ *souple*, flex[ible wire] (*Elec.*). **filage** (la₁ʒ) *m*, spinning; pouring (*oil on waves*). **filament** (lamã) *m*, filament; thread. **filandres** (lã₁dr) *f.pl*, gossamer; strings. **filandreux, euse** (lãdrø, ø₁z) *a*, stringy; long-drawn (*screw*); diffuse. **filant, e** (lã, ã₁t) *a*, ropy (*liquid*); falling, shooting (*star*). **filasse** (las) *f*, tow (*flax, hemp*).

filateur, trice (filatœ₁r, tris) *n*, spinner (*pers.*); (*m.*) spinner (*owner*). **filature** (ty₁r) *f*, cotton mill; spinning; shadowing (*a pers.*).

file (fil) *f*, file, line. ~ *d'attente*, queue.

filé (file) *m*, thread. **filer** (le) *v.t*, to spin; draw (*into wire*); pay out (*cable*); pour (*oil on waves*); shadow (*a pers.*); handle (*fig.*); (*v.i.*) to run; be off; make off; file off; flare (*lamp*). ~ *à l'anglaise*, to take French leave. ~ *doux*, to obey without a word.

filet (file) *m*, thread; string; filament; fillet; undercut; loin (*mutton*); worm (*screw*); trickle, stream; dash (*admixture*); rule (*Typ.*); net; netting. ~ *à bagage*, luggage rack (*Rly.*). ~ *à provisions*, string bag, net b. ~*s de*

sole, filleted sole. **filetage** (lta₁ʒ) *m*, screw cutting. **fileter** (lte) *v.t*, to thread, screw, **fileur, euse** (lœ₁r, ø₁z) *n*, spinner, net maker; shadower (*detectives, etc.*).

filial, e† (filjal) *a*, filial. [société] **filiale,** *f*, subsidiary [company]. **filiation** (sjɔ̃) *f*, filiation; relationship.

filière (filjɛ₁r) *f*, draw plate; die [plate]; screw plate; [screw] stock; wire gauge; purlin; regular channel[s] (*fig.*). ~ *garnie*, stock & dies.

filigrane (filigran) *m*, filigree [work]; watermark (*paper*).

fille (fi₁j) *f*, girl; maid; maiden; daughter; whore (*familiar*). ~ *de ferme*, dairy maid, milkmaid. ~ *de service*, maidservant, housemaid. **fillette** (fijet) *f*, little girl. **filleul, e** (fijœl) *n*, godchild, godson, god-daughter; protégé.

film (film) *m*, film; movie. ~ *interdit*, banned movie. ~ *muet*, silent m. ~ *parlant*, sound m. ~*-annonce*, trailer. ~ *à recette*, box-office success. ~ *en relief*, 3-D movie. **grand** ~, main feature.

filon (filɔ̃) *m*, lode; mine (*fig.*).

filoselle (filɔzɛl) *f*, floss silk.

filou (filu) *m*, pickpocket; sharper; swindler. **filouter** (te) *v.t*, to rob, filch; cheat. **filouterie** (tri) *f*, robbery; swindle.

fils (fis) *m*, son; junior. ~ *de ses œuvres*, self-made man. ~ *de son père*, chip off the old block. ~ *à papa*, well-connected young man; playboy.

filtrage (filtra₁ʒ) *m*. **& filtration** (trasjɔ̃) *f*, filtration, straining; percolation. **filtre** (tr) *m*, filter; percolator (*coffee*). **filtrer** (tre) *v.t. & i*, to filter, strain; percolate, leach.

fin (fɛ̃) *f*, end, close, finish, last; finis; object, aim, purpose. ~ *d'alerte*, all clear (*Mil.*).

fin (fɛ̃) *m*, fine metal; fine linen. *or à tant de grammes de* ~, gold so many grams fine.

fin, e (fɛ̃, in) *a*, fine; delicate; choice; slender; small; keen, sharp; subtle; smart. *fin fond*, farthest end, very depths. *fin matois*, artful dodger. *le fin mot*, the last word; the long & the short of it, the upshot. *fine à l'eau,* brandy & soda. *fine champagne,* liqueur brandy. *fines herbes,* savory herbs.

final, e† (final) *a,* final; last; ultimate. ¶ *f,* final (*sport*). **final[e], *m,*** finale (*Mus.*). **finalité** (lite) *f,* finality.

finance (finɑ̃:s) *f,* finance; (*pl.*) finances, cash, money. **financer** (nɑ̃se) *v.i,* to find money, finance. **financier, ère†** (sje, ɛːr) *a,* financial. ¶ *m,* financier.

finasser (finase) *v.i,* to finesse. **finasserie** (sri) *f,* trickery; cunning; (*pl.*) wiles. **finassier, ère** (sje, ɛːr) *n,* trickster.

finaud, e (fino, oːd) *a,* sly, wily. ¶ *n,* artful dodger, slyboots. **finauderie** (odri) *f,* sly dodge.

fine (fin) *f,* liqueur brandy.

finement (finmɑ̃) *ad,* finely; shrewdly. **finesse** (nɛs) *f,* fineness.

fini, e (fini) *a,* finished; over; consummate; finite (*being*). ¶ *m,* finish; (the) finite. **finir** (niːr) *v.t. & abs. & i,* to finish, end. ~ *de parler,* to finish (*or* leave off) speaking. *en* ~, to finish.

Finlande (la) (fɛ̃lɑ̃:d), Finland. **finnois, e** (finwa, aːz) & **finlandais, e** (fɛ̃lɑ̃dɛ, ɛ̃:z) *a,* Finnish. **Finnois, e** & **Finlandais, e,** *n,* Finn, Finlander. *le finnois,* Finnish (*language*).

fiole (fjɔl) *f,* flask, phial.

floriture (fjɔrityːr) *f,* grace [note]; flourish.

firmament (firmamɑ̃) *m,* firmament.

firme (firm) *f,* firm (*industrial, commercial*).

fisc (fisk) *m,* Treasury; taxes; Internal Revenue Service. **fiscal, e** (kal) *a,* fiscal (*att.*). **fiscalité** (lite) *f,* fiscal system; piling up of taxation; methods of [tax] collection.

fissa (fisa) *ad,* quick, sharp.

fissure (fisyːr) *f,* fissure, crack, cleft; hiatus.

fiston (fistɔ̃) *m,* son; youngster.

fistule (fistyl) *f,* fistula.

fixage (fiksaːʒ) *m. &* **fixation** (asjɔ̃) *f,* fixing, fixation; fastening. **fixatif** (tif) *m,* fixing [solution] (*Phot.*). **fixet†** (fiks) *a,* fixed, fast, stationary; intent; set. ¶ *i,* eyes front! ¶ *m,* fixed salary.

~-cravate, *m,* tie clip. **fixer** (kse) *v.t,* to fix, fasten, secure; set; settle; rivet (*fig.*). ~ *dans la mémoire,* to commit to memory, memorize. **fixité** (ksite) *f,* fixity, steadiness.

flaccidité (flaksidite) *f,* flaccidity, flabbiness.

flacon (flakɔ̃) *m,* bottle, flask, flagon. ~ *à couvercle vissé,* screw-capped bottle. ~ *à odeur,* scent b., smelling b.

flageller (flaʒɛle) *v.t,* to scourge, flagellate.

flageoler (flaʒɔle) *v.i,* to tremble, shake. **flageolet** (lɛ) *m,* flageolet (*Mus. & bean*).

flagorner (flagɔrne) *v.t,* to fawn [up]on, toady to. **flagornerie** (nəri) *f,* toadyism, soft soap. **flagorneur, euse** (nœːr, øːz) *n,* toady.

flagrant, e (flagrɑ̃, ɑ̃:t) *a,* flagrant, glaring. *en flagrant délit,* in the [very] act, redhanded.

flair (flɛːr) *m,* scent, smell, nose; acumen; keenness. **flairer** (flɛre) *v.t. & abs,* to scent, smell, scent out, nose [out].

flamand, e (flamɑ̃, ɑ̃:d) *a. & (language) m,* Flemish. F~, *n,* Fleming (*pers.*).

flamant (flamɑ̃) *m,* flamingo.

flambant, e (flɑ̃bɑ̃, ɑ̃:t) *a,* flaming, blazing; smart. *tout flambant neuf, toute flambante neuve,* brand new. **flambeau** (bo) *m,* torch; candlestick. **flambé, e** (be) p.p, lost, gone; done for. **flambée** (be) *f,* blaze. ~ *des prix,* runaway inflation. **flamber** (be) *v.i,* to flame, blaze, flare; (v.t.) to flame (*needle, Surg.*); singe. **flamberge** (bɛrʒ) *f,* sword (*jocularly*). **flamboyer** (bwaje) *v.i,* to blaze; flame, flare, flash.

flamme (flɑːm) *f,* flame; blaze, flare, light; passion; pennant, pendant, pennon, streamer. ~ *de bengale,* Bengal light. **flammèche** (flamɛʃ) *f,* spark, flake (*ignited matter*).

flan (flɑ̃) *m,* flan; custard; blank (*metal*); mold (*Typ.*). *c'est du* ~, it's baloney.

flanc (flɑ̃) *m,* side, flank; womb.

flancher (flɑ̃ʃe) *v.i,* to flinch; give in; break down (*auto*).

Flandre (la) (flɑ̃:dr), Flanders.
flandrin (flɑ̃drɛ̃) *m*, lanky fellow.
flanelle (flanɛl) *f*, flannel. ~ *de coton*, flannelette.
flâner (flɑne) & **flânocher** (nɔʃe) *v.i*, to saunter; stroll; lounge, loaf. **flânerie** (nri) *f*, sauntering. **flâneur, euse** (nœːr, øːz) *n*, saunterer.
flanquer (flɑ̃ke) *v.t*, to flank; fling, throw, chuck; land (*blow*).
flaque (flak) *f*, puddle; pool, plash. **une flaquée d'eau** (ke) some water (*thrown*).
flasque (flask) *a*, flabby, limp, flaccid. ¶ *m*, cheek, side.
flatter (flate) *v.t. & abs*, to flatter; stroke; pat; humor; please. **flatterie** (tri) *f*, flattery. **flatteur, euse** (tœːr, øːz) *n*, flatterer. ¶ *a*, flattering.
flatulence (flatylɑ̃:s) *f*, flatulence, -cy. **flatuosité** (tɥozite) *f*, flatus, wind.
fléau (fleo) *m*, flail; scourge; plague, bane, curse; beam (*scale*); bar.
flèche (flɛʃ) *f*, arrow, shaft; spire; jib, boom (*crane*); beam (*plow*); trail (*gun carriage*); flitch (*bacon*); sag, dip. ~ *littorale* (*Phys. Geog.*). **fléchette** (fleʃɛt) *f*, dart.
fléchir (fleʃiːr) *v.t. & i*, to bend, bow, flex; sag; move; flag, yield; give way; relent. **fléchisseur** (ʃisœːr) *a.m. & m*, flexor.
flegmatique (flɛgmatik) *a*, phlegmatic; stolid. **flegme** (flɛgm) *m*, coolness, phlegm (*fig.*), stolidity.
flet (flɛ) *m*, flounder (*fish*). **flétan** (fletɑ̃) *m*, halibut.
flétrir (fletriːr) *v.t*, to fade, wither, wilt, blight; brand. **flétrissure** (trisyːr) *f*, fading, withering; blight; stigma.
fleur (flœːr) *f*, flower; blossom; bloom; pick; prime, heyday, blush, flush. ~ *de la Passion*, passion flower. ~*s des bois*, ~*s des champs*, ~*s des prés*, wild flowers. *la* ~ *des pois*, the pick of the bunch. *à* ~ *de*, level (*or* even) (*or* flush) with. **fleurer** (flœre) *v.i*, to smell.
fleuret (flœrɛ) *m*, foil (*Fenc.*); drill.

fleurette (flœrɛt) *f*, floweret. *conter* ~, to make love. **fleuri, e** (ri) *a*, in bloom; flowery; florid. **fleurir** (riːr) *v.i*, to flower, blossom, bloom; flourish; (*v.t.*) to deck with flowers. **fleuriste** (rist) *n*, florist; (*att.*) floral, flower. **fleuron** (rɔ̃) *m*, flower work; flower; floret; colophon.
fleuve (flœːv) *m*, river.
flexible (flɛksibl) *a*, flexible, pliant, pliable. **flexion** (ksjɔ̃) *f*, flection; deflection; inflection, ending (*Gram.*)
flibustier (flibystje) *m*, filibuster, freebooter; swindler.
flic (flik) *m*, cop.
flic flac (flikflak), crack, smack.
flingue (flɛ̃:g) *m*, piece (*firearm*), gun. **flinguer** (ge) *v.t*, to bump off, kill, shoot.
flirt (flœrt) *m*, flirtation. **flirter** (te) *v.i*, to flirt.
floc (flɔk) *m*, thud; slash.
flocon (flɔkɔ̃) *m*, flock, tuft; flake. **floconneux, euse** (kɔnø, øːz) *a*, fleecy; flaky.
flonflon (flɔ̃flɔ̃) *m*, blare.
floraison (flɔrɛzɔ̃) *f*, flowering, blossoming, blooming. **floral, e** (ral) *a*, floral, flower (*att.*). **flore** (flɔːr) *f*, flora.
florence (flɔrɑ̃:s) *m*, sarsenet; [silkworm] gut.
florès (flɔrɛs): *faire* ~, to make a stir.
Floride (la) (flɔrid), Florida.
florissant, e (flɔrisɑ̃, ɑ̃:t) *a*, flourishing, thriving.
flot (flo) *m. oft. pl*, wave, billow; surge; rush; stream, flood; flood tide. ~ *de la marée*, tidal wave. *à* ~, afloat. *à* ~*s*, in torrents. **flottage** (flɔtaːʒ) *m*, floating (*lumber*), rafting. **flottant, e** (tɑ̃, ɑ̃:t) *a*, floating; flowing, waving; baggy; wavering; evasive, elusive. **flotte** (flɔt) *f*, fleet; float; floater. **flottement** (tmɑ̃) *m*, swaying; wavering. **flotter** (te) *v.i*, to float; waft; wave; hang; waver, fluctuate. **flotteur** (tœːr) *m*, raftsman; float; floater; ball. **flotille** (tiːj) *f*, flotilla.
flou, e (flu) *a*, fuzzy; woolly; hazy, blurry. **flou, ad**, fuzzily. ¶ *m*, fuzziness.

flouer (flue) *v.t*, to swindle.

fluctuation (flyktцasjɔ̃) *f*, fluctuation.

fluet, te (flyɛ, ɛt) *a*, slender, thin.

fluide (flyid) *a*, fluid, flowing. ¶ *m*, fluid (*imponderable*). **fluidité** (dite) *f*, fluidity.

fluor (flyɔːr) *m*, fluorine. **fluorescent, e** (ɔresɑ̃, ɑ̃ːt) *a*, fluorescent.

flûte (flyt) *f*, flute; flute [glass]; baton (*bread*). ~ *de Pan*, Pan's pipes. **flûté, e** (te) *a*, fluty. **flûter** (te) *v.i*, to flute, pipe. **flûtiste** (tist) *n*, flutist.

fluvial, e (flyvjal) *a*, fluvial, river (*att*.). **fluviatile** (atil) *a*, fluviatile.

flux (fly) *m*, flux; flow; flood; flush (*cards*). *le ~ et le re~*, the ebb and flow. **fluxion** (ksjɔ̃) *f*, swelling (*face*).

foc (fok) *m*, jib (*sail*).

focal, e (fokal) *a*, focal.

fœtus (fetyːs) *m*, fetus.

foi (fwa) *f*, faith; troth; belief; reliance, trust; witness. *ajouter ~ à*, to credit, believe in. *ma ~ non!* O dear no!

foie (fwa) *m*, liver (*Anat*.). *avoir les ~s blancs*, to be afraid.

foin (fwɛ̃) *m*. *oft. pl*, hay.

foire (fwaːr) *f*, fair, market.

foirer (fware) *v.i*, to have diarrhea; fail (*slang*).

fois (fwa) *f*, time. *à la ~*, at a time; at the same t., both; together.

foison (fwazɔ̃) *f*, plenty. *à ~*, galore. **foisonner** (zɔne) *v.i*, to abound, be plentiful; swarm; increase.

fol, folle, *see* fou.

folâtre (folɑːtr) *a*, playful, skittish, sportive, wanton. **folâtrer** (latre) *v.i*, to play about, romp, frolic.

foliacé, e (foljase) *a*, foliaceous. **foliation** (sjɔ̃) *f*, foliation; leafing.

folichon, ne (folijɔ̃, ɔn) *a*, wanton, unchaste.

folie (foli) *f*, madness; folly, foolishness; mania, passion, hobby. *à la ~*, to distraction.

folio (foljo) *m*, folio. **foliole** (ɔl) *f*, leaflet (*Bot*.). **folioter** (ɔte) *v.t*, to folio.

folk-lore (folklɔːr) *m*, folklore.

follement (folmɑ̃) *ad*, madly; foolishly. **follet, te** (lɛ, ɛt) *a*, frolicsome; downy, fluffy (*hair*). [esprit] **follet**, *m*, sprite, [hob] goblin, puck. **follette**, *f*, playful creature.

folliculaire (folikylɛːr) *m*, scribbler, hack (*writer*). **follicule** (kyl) *m*, follicle; leaflet.

fomentation (fomɑ̃tasjɔ̃) *f*, fomentation (*Med. & fig.*). **fomenter** (te) *v.t*, to foment.

foncé, e (fɔ̃se) *a*, dark, deep (*color*). **foncer** (se) *v.t*, to bottom (*cask, etc.*); sink (*well, etc.*); (*v.i*.) to rush; charge.

fonceur (fɔ̃sœːr) *m*, dynamic capitalist; financial "whiz kid."

foncier, ère (fɔ̃sje, ɛːr) *a*, landed, land, ground, property (*att*.); deep-seated, fundamental. **foncièrement** (ɛrmɑ̃) *ad*, thoroughly.

fonction (fɔ̃ksjɔ̃) *f. oft. pl*, function, duty, office. *faire ~ de*, to act as. **fonctionnaire** (ɔnɛːr) *n*, official, officer, functionary. ~ *public, ique*, civil servant. **fonctionnarisme** (narism) *m*, officialdom; officialism. **fonctionnel, le** (nɛl) *a*, functional. **fonctionner** (ne) *v.i*, to function, run, work, act.

fond (fɔ̃) *m*, bottom; ground; substratum; crown (*hat*); depth; floor; back; head; groundwork; background; seat (*trousers, chair*); heart; substance; main issue (*law*); undertone; undercurrent; staying power, stamina. ~ *de cale*, bilge (*ship*). *à ~*, thoroughly; home. *au ~*, after all, in reality. *de ~ en comble*, from top to bottom. *faire ~ sur*, to rely on.

fondamental, e† (fɔ̃damɑ̃tal) *a*, fundamental, basic; foundation (*stone*).

fondant, e (fɔ̃dɑ̃, ɑ̃ːt) *a*, melting (*ice*); that melts in the mouth, luscious, juicy. ¶ *m*, flux; fondant.

fondateur, trice (fɔ̃datœːr, tris) *n*, founder, foundress; promoter. **fondation** (sjɔ̃) *f*, foundation; bed; establishment.

fondé de pouvoir(s) (fɔ̃de) *m*, attorney; proxy; duly authorized representative.

fondement (fɔ̃dmɑ̃) *m. oft. pl,* foundation, ground, base, basis; fundament. **fonder** (de) *v.t,* to found; base, ground. **se ~,** to take one's stand; be based.

fonderie (fɔ̃dri) *f,* foundry; [smelting] works; founding. **fondeur** (dœ:r) *m,* founder.

fondre (fɔ̃:dr) *v.t,* to melt, dissolve; smelt; fuse; cast, found; merge; blend; (*v.i.*) to melt, dissolve, fuse; blow, go (*fuse*). **~ sur,** to fall [up]on, pounce on, swoop down on. **fondu** (dy) *m,* fade-out (*TV & cinema*); shunt (*sound, TV, etc.*). **~ au noir,** fade to black. **~ enchaîné,** lap dissolve. **~ ouvert,** fade-in.

fondrière (fɔ̃driɛ:r) *f,* pit, hollow, hole (*in road*); quagmire, morass.

fonds (fɔ̃) *m. oft. pl,* fund; funds; money, cash; capital; stock; security. **~ d'amortissement,** sinking fund. **~ [de commerce],** goodwill, business. **~ de prévoyance,** contingency fund. **~ de roulement,** working capital. **~ [de terre],** estate, [piece of] land. **à ~ perdu,** with capital sunk (*as in an annuity*).

fongueux, euse (fɔ̃gø, ø:z) *a,* fungous. **fongus** (gy:s) *m,* fungus.

fontaine (fɔ̃tɛn) *f,* fountain, spring, well; cistern (*house*). **~ de Jouvence,** fountain of youth. **fontainier** (nje) *m,* maker of (*or* dealer in) domestic water appliances (*cisterns, filters, etc.*); plumber; turncock; well sinker.

fonte (fɔ̃t) *f,* melting; smelting; casting, founding; melt; font (*Typ.*); holster. **~ d'acier,** cast steel. **~ [de fer],** [cast] iron. **~ [en gueuses], ~ en saumons,** pig [iron].

fonts (fɔ̃) *m.pl,* font (*Eccl.*).

football (futbɔl) *m,* football (*game*). [**~**] **rugby,** Rugby [f.].

for (fɔ:r) *m:* **~ intérieur,** conscience.

forage (fɔra:ʒ) *m,* boring, drilling.

forain, e (fɔrɛ̃, ɛn) *a,* nonresident; traveling, itinerant. ¶ *m,* [traveling] showman. [*marchand*] *fo-*

rain, peddler or boothkeeper at a fair.

forban (fɔrbɑ̃) *m,* [sea] rover; pirate; shark (*fig.*).

forçage (fɔrsa:ʒ) *m,* forcing (*Hort.*); overweight (*coin*).

forçat (fɔrsa) *m,* convict.

force (fɔrs) *f,* force; power; strength; potency; might; press (*of sail*); many, plenty of; (*pl.*) shears. **~ d'âme,** fortitude. **~ d'inertie,** inertia. **~ de bras,** hand power. **~ de cheval, ~ en chevaux,** horsepower. **~ de l'âge,** prime of life. **~ de levier,** leverage. **~ des choses,** force of circumstances. **~ du pouls,** pulse rate. **~ du sang,** call of the blood (*fig.*). **~ majeure,** force majeure, cause beyond control. **à ~ de,** by dint of. **à toute ~,** at all costs.

forcé, e (fɔrse) *p.a,* forced, compulsory; farfetched; strained. **forcément** (mɑ̃) *ad,* perforce, necessarily.

forcené, e (fɔrsəne) *n,* madman; fury.

forceps (fɔrsɛps) *m,* obstetrical forceps.

forcer (fɔrse) *v.t,* to force; wrench open; compel; make; drive; obtrude; strain; constrain; overcome; overwork; crowd; run down (*Hunt.*). **forcerie** (səri) *f,* forcing bed (*Hort.*).

forclore (fɔrklɔ:r) *v.t.ir,* to debar by time (*law*). **forclusion** (klyzjɔ̃) *f,* debarment by time.

forer (fɔre) *v.t,* to bore, drill.

forestier, ère (fɔrɛstje, ɛ:r) *a,* forest (*att.*). ¶ *m,* forester.

foret (fɔrɛ) *m,* drill; bit. **~ hélicoïdal,** twist drill.

forêt (fɔrɛ) *f,* forest; shock (*hair*). **la F~-Noire,** the Black Forest.

foreur (fɔrœ:r) *m,* driller (*pers.*). **foreuse** (rø:z) *f,* boring machine, drilling m.

forfaire à (fɔrfɛːr) *v.ir,* to fail in (*duty*); forfeit (*honor*). **forfait** (fɛ) *m,* crime; contract; fixed price, agreed sum. **à ~ ou forfaitaire** (tɛːr) *a,* on contract, contractual, at an agreed price; through (*rate*); standard (*charge*). **forfaiture** (ty:r) *f,* breach of trust.

forfanterie (fɔrfɑ̃tri) *f*, boasting, bragging.

forge (fɔrʒ) *f*, forge; smithy; blacksmith's shop; ironworks. **forger** (ʒe) *v.t*, to forge; fabricate; coin (*word*). **se ~**, to conjure up. **forgeron** (ʒərɔ̃) *m*, [black]smith. **forgeur, euse** (ʒœːr, øːz), *n*, fabricator, inventor (*stories, lies*); (*m.*) forgeman.

formaliser (se) (fɔrmalize) *v.pr*, to take exception, t. offense, t. amiss. **formaliste** (list) *a*, formal, precise. **formalité** (te) *f*, formality.

format (fɔrma) *m*, size (*book*), format; gauge. **~ de l'image**, frame size. **formation** (sjɔ̃) *f*, formation; structure; training. **forme** (fɔrm) *f*, form, shape; block (*hat*); last (*shoe*); (*pl.*) manners; form (*Typ.*). **rester en ~**, to keep fit, keep in form. **formel, le†** (mɛl) *a*, formal; express; strict; flat. **former** (me) *v.t*, to form, shape, fashion; frame; make; train. **~ les faisceaux**, to stack arms (*Mil.*). **~ une liste de jurés**, **~ un tableau**, to impanel a jury.

formidable† (fɔrmidabl) *a*, formidable.

Formose (fɔrmoːz) *f*, Formosa.

formulaire (fɔrmylɛːr) *m*, formulary. **formule** (myl) *f*, formula; form; prescription (*Med.*). **formuler** (le) *v.t*, to draw up; write out; formulate.

fornication (fɔrnikasjɔ̃) *f*, fornication.

fort, e (fɔːr, ɔrt) *a*, strong; powerful; heavy; stout; stiff; fortified; steep; large; great, big; high; good; bad; full; loud; well up; overweight (*coin*); hard (*solder*). **~ se faire fort** (*fort* is inv.), to undertake. **fort**, *ad*, hard; loud[ly]; very. **~ avant dans la nuit**, far into the night. **¶** *m* (the) strong (*pers.*); market porter; strongest part; thick[est]; height; depth; strong point, forte; lair, fort, stronghold. **au plus ~ du combat**, in the thick of the fight. **forte** (fɔrte) *ad*, forte (*Mus.*). **fortement** (təmɑ̃) *ad*, strongly; highly; hard.

forteresse (fɔrtərɛs) *f*, fortress, stronghold.

fortification (fɔrtifikasjɔ̃) *f*, fortification. **fortifier** (fje) *v.t*, to strengthen, brace, invigorate; fortify.

fortin (fɔrtɛ̃) *m*, small fort.

fortuit, e† (fɔrtɥi, it) *a*, fortuitous, chance, casual, accidental.

fortune (fɔrtyn) *f*, fortune; luck, chance. **~ de mer**, perils of the sea. **dîner à la ~ du pot**, to take pot luck. **de ~**, makeshift; chance (*att.*). **fortuné, e** (ne) *a*, fortunate, lucky; well-to-do, moneyed.

forum (fɔrɔm) *m*, forum.

forure (fɔryːr) *f*, bore, hole; pipe (*key*).

fosse (foːs) *f*, pit, hole; den; grave; deep (*ocean*); fosse. **~ [d'aisances]**, cesspool. **~ septique**, septic tank.

fossé (fose) *m*, ditch, trench; moat; rift (*fig.*). **sauter le ~**, to take the plunge (*fig.*). **fossette** (fosɛt) *f*, dimple.

fossile (fɔsil) *a. & m*, fossil.

fossoyeur (foswajœːr) *m*, gravedigger.

fou, fol, folle (fu, fɔl) *a*, mad, insane; wild, frantic; foolish; passionately fond; uncontrollable; tremendous. **~ à lier**, raving mad, stark m. **folle de son corps**, wanton (*woman*). **fou, folle**, *n*, madman, -woman, lunatic; homosexual (*slang*); (*m.*) fool; jester (*court*); bishop (*chess*).

fouailler (fwaje) *v.t*, to whip; castigate (*fig.*).

foucade (fukad) *f*, fit; start.

foudre (fudr) *f*, lightning; thunder, [thunder]bolt; (*m.*) thunderbolt (*fig. & Myth.*); tun. **coup de ~**, love at first sight. **foudroyer** (drwaje) *v.t*, to strike with lightning, blast; (*in. p.p.*) thunderstruck; crushed.

fouet (fwɛ) *m*, whip; whipcord; whisk (*egg*); tip (*wing*). **le ~**, a flogging. **fouetter** (te) *v.t. & i*, to whip, flog, lash; beat; whisk; stir (*the blood*).

fougère (fuʒɛːr) *f*, fern. **~ [à l'aigle]**, bracken, brake. **~ arborescente**, tree fern.

fougue (fug) *f*, fire (*fig.*), spirit, mettle. **fougueux, euse†** (gø, ø;z) *a*, fiery, spirited, mettlesome.

fouille (fu;j) *f*, excavation, cut, trench, pit. **fouille-au-pot** (fujopo) *m*, cook's boy. **fouiller** (fuje) *v.t. & abs. & i*, to excavate; dig; mine; burrow in[to]; burrow; nuzzle; root; rummage, ransack; search, dive, peer into; fumble, grope; pry. **fouilleur** (jœ;r) *m*, searcher. **fouillis** (ji) *m*, jumble, muddle, litter.

fouine (fwin) *f*, beech marten (*Zool.*); pitchfork; fish spear, grains. **fouiner** (ne) *v.i*, to slink away; nose about.

foulage (fula;ʒ) *m*, fulling; pressing (*grapes*); impression (*Typ.*).

foulard (fula;r) *m*, foulard.

foule (ful) *f*, crowd, throng; mob.

fouler (fule) *v.t*, to press; full, mill (*cloth*); give an impression (*Typ.*); tread [on], trample [on]; harass; sprain, wrench; gall. ~ **aux pieds**, to tread underfoot; ride roughshod over. **foulon** (lɔ̃) *m*, fuller.

foulque (fulk) *f*, coot.

foulure (fuly;r) *f*, sprain, wrench.

four (fu;r) *m*, oven; kiln; furnace; failure, fiasco. ~ **crématoire** (krematwa;r), crematorium.

fourbe (furb) *a*, knavish. ¶ *m*, knave, cheat. ¶ *f*. & **fourberie** (bəri) *f*, knavery, cheating.

fourbi (furbi) *m*, kit (*Mil.*) *tout le* ~, the whole kit and caboodle.

fourbir (furbi;r) *v.t*, to furbish, rub up.

fourbu, e (furby) *a*, foundered (*Vet.*); tired out.

fourche (furʃ) *f*, fork; pitchfork. **fourcher** (ʃe) *v.i*, to fork; branch off. **fourchette** (ʃɛt) *f*, fork (*table*); trencherman; bracket (*Mil. & statistics*); wishbone. **fourchon** (ʃɔ̃) *m*, prong; fork (*tree*). **fourchu, e** (ʃy) *a*, forked; cleft; cloven.

fourgon (furgɔ̃) *m*, wagon; truck; van; poker, rake. ~ **de déménagements**, moving van. ~ **des bagages**, baggage car. **fourgonner** (gɔne) *v.i*, to poke [about].

fourmi (furmi) *f*, ant, emmet;

(*pl.*) pins & needles (*fig.*). **fourmilier** (milje) *m*, anteater. **fourmilière** (lje;r) *f*, ant's nest. **fourmi-lion** (ljɔ̃) *m*, ant lion. **fourmiller** (mije) *v.t*, to swarm; teem; abound; tingle.

fournaise (furnɛ;z) *f*, furnace, inferno. **fourneau** (no) *m*, stove; furnace; bowl (*pipe*). ~ **à gaz, à pétrole**, gas, oil, stove. **haut** ~, blast furnace. *philanthropique*, soup kitchen. **fournée** (ne) *f*, batch.

fourni, e (furni) *p.a*, stocked; thick, bushy.

fournier, ère (furnje, ɛ;r) *n*, baker (*for public*). **fournil** (ni) *m*, bakehouse.

fourniment (furnimɑ̃) *f*, equipment (*soldier's*). **fournir** (ni;r) *v.t. & abs*, to furnish, supply, provide; afford, adduce; give; find; lodge, deposit; produce; follow (*cards*); (*v.i.*) to provide, contribute. ~ **la carrière**, to stay the course. ~ [à] **la couleur demandée**, to follow suit. **fournissement** (nismɑ̃) *m*, contribution. **fournisseur, euse** (sœ;r, ø;z) *n*, supplier; dealer; contractor; tradesman. ~ **de l'armée**, army contractor. ~ **de navires**, ship chandler, marine store dealer. **fourniture** (ty;r) *f*, supply, store; requisite; (*pl.*) stationery; material; supplying; trimmings (*tailor's*); seasoning (*for salad, i.e, savory herbs*).

fourrage (fura;ʒ) *m*, fodder, provender, forage; fur lining. **fourrager** (raʒe) *v.i. & t*, to forage; rummage; ravage. **fourrageur** (ʒœ;r) *m*, forager.

fourré (fure) *m*, thicket, brake; cover (*game*); jungle. **fourré, e** (re) *p.a*, fur-lined; stuffed (*Cook.*); wooded; jungly.

fourreau (furo) *m*, scabbard, sheath; case; cover; sleeve, cylinder.

fourrer (fure) *v.t*, to thrust, poke, shove; stuff, cram; line [with fur]. **fourre-tout** (rtu) *m*, hold-all. **fourreur, euse** (rœ;r, ø;z) *n*, furrier.

fourrier (furje) *m*, quartermaster; harbinger.

fourrière (furjεɪr) *f*, pound (*dogs*, etc.). *mettre à la* ~, to impound.

fourrure (furyɪr) *f*, fur, skin; welt, strap.

fourvoyer (furvwaje) *v.t*, to lead astray; mislead.

foutre (futr) *m*, sexual discharge (*obscene*). ¶ *v.t*, to fuck (*archaic*). *fous le camp*, scram. *fous-moi la paix*, let me be (*obscene*). *se foutre*, not give a damn. *je m'en fous*, I don't give a damn (*obscene*).

foutu (futy) *a*, done for; lousy. *mal* ~, out of sorts, luck; badly dressed; badly put together.

fox-terrier (fɔkstεrje) *m*, fox terrier.

fox-trot (fɔkstrɔt) *m*, fox trot.

foyer (fwaje) *m*, hearth; furnace; fire box; stoker (*mechanical*); fireside; home; seat; hotbed; focus. ~ *d'étudiants*, hospice. ~ *des artistes*, greenroom. ~ [*du public*], foyer (*Theat.*). [*pierre de*] ~, hearthstone.

frac (frak) *m*, dress coat.

fracas (fraka) *m*, crash; roar; din, row, noise, bluster. **fracasser** (kase) *v.t*, to smash, shatter, shiver.

fraction (fraksjɔ̃) *f*, fraction; group (politics); breaking (*holy bread*). ~ *périodique*, recurring (*or* circulating) decimal. **fractionnaire** (ɔnεɪr) *a*, fractional. **fractionner** (ne) *v.t*, to split.

fracture (fraktyɪr) *f*, fracture, breaking. **fracturer** (tyre) *v.t*, to fracture, break.

fragile (fraʒil) *a*, fragile; brittle; frail; [on parcels] with care. **fragilité** (lite) *f*, fragility, etc.

fragment (fragmɑ̃) *m*, fragment, piece, scrap; snatch. **fragmentaire** (tεɪr) *a*, fragmentary. **fragmenter** (te) *v.t*, to break [up].

frai (frε) *m*, spawning; spawn.

fraîchement (frεʃmɑ̃) *ad*, in the cool; coolly; freshly, newly, lately. **fraîcheur** (ʃœɪr) *f*, freshness; cool[ness]; chill; bloom (*fig.*). **fraîchir** (ʃiɪr) *v.i*, to freshen. **frais, aîche** (frε, εʃ) *a*, fresh; cool; chilly; new (*bread*,

etc.); recent; new-laid; wet (*paint, ink, fish*). *frais & gaillard*, *frais & dispos*, hale & hearty, fit & fresh. **frais, aîche** (*with p.p.*) *ad*, fresh[ly], newly, e.g, *des roses fraîches cueillies*, fresh[ly] gathered roses. **frais,** *m*, cool. *au* ~ *ou à la fraîche*, in the cool.

frais (frε) *m.pl*, expenses; expense; charges; cost; costs (*law*); efforts, pains. ~ *d'école*, ~ *scolaires*, tuition fees. ~ *de constitution*, preliminary expenses (*company*). ~ *de contentieux*, legal charges. ~ *divers*, general (*or* sundry) expenses. ~ *généraux*, standing (*or* establishment) (*or* overhead) expenses (*or* charges). *faux* ~, incidental expenses. *se mettre en* ~, to go to some expense.

fraise (frεːz) *f*, strawberry; countersink [bit]; [milling] cutter; ruff (*Hist., dress*). ~ *des bois*, wild strawberry. **fraiser** (frεze) *v.t*, to crimp; countersink; mill. **fraisier** (zje) *m*, strawberry plant.

fraisil (frεzi) *m*, breeze (*cinders*).

framboise (frɑ̃bwaːz) *f*, raspberry. **framboisier** (bwazje) *m*, raspberry bush.

franc (frɑ̃) *m*, franc = 100 centimes. ~*s-or*, ~*s-argent*, ~*s-papier*, gold, silver, paper, francs. *le nouveau* ~, the franc since 1960, when it was substituted for 100 *anciens francs*.

franc, anche (frɑ̃, ɑ̃ːʃ) *a*, free; frank, candid, outspoken; open, open-hearted; aboveboard; clear (*complete, of days*); clean (*break, jump*); downright, out & out, regular, arrant; volunteer (*corps*); ungrafted (*tree*). *franc arbitre*, free will. *franc (anche) de port ou franc le port (inv.*), carriage free; post free. **franc,** *ad*, frankly, candidly.

français, e (frɑ̃sε, εːz) *a*, French. **F~,** *n*, Frenchman, -woman. *les Français*, the French. *le français,* French (*language*).

franc-bord (frɑ̃bɔɪr) *m*, free-board (*ship*); open space.

France (la) (frɑ̃ːs), France.

Francfort (frãkfɔːr) *m*, Frankfort.

franchement (frãʃmã) *ad*, frankly, candidly, openly; downright; heartily; boldly.

franchir (frãʃiːr) *v.t*, to jump over, leap o., pass o., get o.; pass through; clear; pass; cross; overstep; shoot (*rapids*); bridge; span; turn (*a certain age*); make (*hoop, croquet*).

franchise (frãʃiːz) *f*, exemption; franking (*Post*); frankness, outspokenness; plain dealing; freedom; immunity (*diplomatic*). ~ *de poids*, ~ *de bagages*, weight allowed free, free allowance of luggage.

francisation (frãsizasjɔ̃) *f*, Frenchification; registration (*ship*).

franciscain (frãsiskɛ̃) *m*, Franciscan, gray friar.

franciser (frãsize) *v.t*, to Frenchify, gallicize.

francité (frãsite) *f*, overall characteristics of French civilization.

franc-jeu (frãʒø) *m*, fair play.

franc-maçon (frãmasɔ̃) *m*, freemason. **franc-maçonnerie** (sɔnri) *f*, freemasonry.

franco (frãko) *ad*, free, f. of charge. ~ [*à*] *bord*, free on board. ~ *à quai*, free at wharf, ex wharf. ~ *de port*, carriage paid; post p. ~ *wagon*, ~ *gare*, free on rail, f. on truck.

francophile (frãkɔfil) *a. & n*, Francophile. **francophobe** (fɔb) *a. & n*, Francophobe.

franc-tireur (frãtirœːr) *m*, sniper; free-lance.

frange (frãːʒ) *f*, fringe. **franger** (frãʒe) *v.t*, to fringe.

franquette (à la bonne) frã-kɛt), simply, without ceremony.

frappant, e (frapã, ãːt) *a*, striking. **frappe** (frap) *f*, stamp; minting; set of matrices (*Typ.*). *Force de* ~, striking force. **frapper** (pe) *v.t. & abs. & v.i*, to strike; hit; smite; tap; knock; slap; stamp; mint; impose, levy; be secured on; ice, chill (*bottle, etc.*). ~ [*de glace*], to ice. ~ *de nullité*, to render void.

frasque (frask) *f*, escapade.

frater (fratɛːr) *m*, lay brother. **fraternel, le†** (tɛrnɛl) *a*, fraternal, brotherly. **fraterniser** (nize) *v.i*, to fraternize. **fraternité** (te) *f*, fraternity, brotherhood. **fratricide** (trisid) *m*, fratricide; (*att.*) fratricidal.

fraude (froːd) *f*, fraud; smuggling. *la* ~ *fiscale*, evasion of tax. **frauder** (frode) *v.t*, to defraud, cheat; evade [payment of]. **fraudeur, euse** (dœːr, øːz) *n*, defrauder; smuggler. ~ *des droits du fisc*, tax dodger. **frauduleux, euse†** (dylø, øːz) *a*, fraudulent.

frayer (frɛje) *v.t. & i*, to open up, clear, blaze; rub; spawn; rub shoulders, associate. se ~, to force (*a passage*); fight (*or* grope) (*one's way*).

frayeur (frɛjœːr) *f*, fright, fear, dread.

fredaine (frədɛn) *f*, prank.

fredonner (frədɔne) *v.i. & t*, to hum (*tune*).

frégate (fregat) *f*, frigate.

frein (frɛ̃) *m*, brake; curb, check (*fig.*); frenum (*Anat.*). ~ *à ruban*, ~ *à bandé*, band brake. ~ *à vide*, vacuum b. ~ *sur jantes*, rim b. ~ *sur les quatre roues*, four-wheel b. ~ *sur moyeux*, hub b. ~ *sur pneu*, spoon b. **freiner** (frɛne) *v.i*, *ou* serrer les freins, to [put on *or* apply] the brake.

frelater (frəlate) *v.t*, to adulterate, doctor.

frêle (frɛl) *a*, frail; weak.

frelon (frəlɔ̃) *m*, hornet.

freluche (frəlyʃ) *f*, tassel; tuft. **freluquet** (kɛ) *m*, whippersnapper, puppy (*man*); coxcomb.

frémir (fremiːr) *v.i*, to rustle, murmur; simmer; vibrate, quiver, shudder. **frémissement** (fremismã) *m*, quivering, shivering, shuddering, etc.

frêne (frɛn) *m*, ash [tree, timber].

frénésie (frenezi) *f*, frenzy. **frénétique†** (tik) *a*, frantic, frenzied.

fréquemment (frekamã) *ad*, frequently, repeatedly, often. **fréquence** (kãːs) *f*, frequency; prevalence. **fréquent, e** (kã, ãːt) *a*, frequent; rapid (*pulse, etc.*). **fréquentation** (kãtasjɔ̃) *f*, frequentation; (*pl.*) companionship. **fréquenté, e** (te) *p.p.*, crowded. **fréquenter** (te) *v.i.*, to frequent; resort to; associate with.

frère (frɛːr) *m*, brother; (*pl.*) brethren (*Eccl.*); friar; sister [ship]. ~ **de lait**, foster brother. **frérot** (frero) *m*, [dear] little brother.

fresaie (frɛzɛ) *f*, barn owl, screech owl.

fresque (frɛsk) *f*, fresco.

fressure (frɛsyːr) *f*, innards (*butchery*).

fret (frɛ) *m*, freight. **prendre à** ~, to charter. **fréter** (frete) *v.t.*, to freight; charter. **fréteur** (tœːr) *m*, [ship]owner.

frétiller (fretije) *v.i.*, to frisk; wriggle; fidget; itch. ~ **de la queue**, to wag its tail (*dog*).

fretin (frətɛ̃) *m*, fry (*fish*); small fry (*pers.*); rubbish.

frette (frɛt) *f*, hoop, collar, band, ring, ferrule; fret (*Arch., Her.*). **fretter** (te) *v.t.*, to hoop, bind.

freux (frø) *m*, rook (*bird*).

friable (friabl) *a*, friable, crumbly.

friand, e (friɑ̃, ɑ̃ːd) *a*, dainty. ~ **de**, fond of. **friandise** (ɑ̃diːz) *f*, dainty, delicacy, sweet.

Fribourg (fribuːr) *m*, Fribourg, Freiburg (*Switzerland*). **F~-en-Brisgau** (brizgo) *m*, Freiburg (*Baden*).

fric (frik) *m*, dough, bread, money (*slang*).

fricassée (frikase) *f*, fricassee. **fricasser** (se) *v.t.*, to fricassee; fritter away. **fricasseur, euse** (sœːr, øːz) *n*, bad cook; squanderer.

friche (friʃ) *f*, waste land, fallow [land]. **en** ~, fallow; undeveloped.

fricot (friko) *m*, stew. **fricoter** (kɔte) *v.i.*, to stew; cook badly; (*v.t.*) to squander. **fricoteur, euse** (tœːr, øːz) *n*, jobber; shirker.

friction (friksjɔ̃) *f*, friction; rubbing; dry shampoo; scalp massage. **frictionner** (ɔne) *v.t.*, to rub, chafe.

frigidité (friʒidite) *f*, frigidity, coldness. **frigorifier** (gɔrifje) *v.t.*, to refrigerate, freeze (*meat, etc.*). **frigorifique** (fik) *a*, refrigerating,

freezing, cold (*att.*). ¶ *m*, cold store.

frileux, euse (frilø, øːz) *a*, chilly (*pers.*).

frimas (frimɑ) *m*, icy mist, rime.

frime (frim) *f*, sham, pretense.

frimousse (frimus) *f*, phiz, little face.

fringale (frɛ̃gal) *f*, hunger; craving. **avoir la** ~, to be famishing.

fringant, e (frɛ̃gɑ̃, ɑ̃ːt) *a*, frisky, lively; smart. **fringuer** (ge) *v.i.*, to frisk, skip about.

friper (fripe) *v.t.*, to [c]rumple, crease. **friperie** (pri) *f*, cast-off clothes; second-hand furniture; frippery, trumpery; secondhand dealer's shop. **fripier, ère** (pje, ɛːr) *n*, secondhand dealer.

fripon, ne (fripɔ̃, ɔn) *n*, knave, rogue, rascal; hussy, minx; thief. ¶ *a*, knavish, roguish, rascally. **friponner** (pone) *v.t. & abs.*, to cheat out of; steal from; cheat. **friponnerie** (nri) *f*, knavery, roguery, rascality.

friquet (frikɛ) *m*, tree sparrow.

frire (friːr) *v.t. & i. ir*, to fry.

frise (friːz) *f*, frieze. **la F~**, Friesland.

friser (frize) *v.t. & i*, to curl, frizzle, frizz, crimp; graze; border on. **frison** (zɔ̃) *m*, curl.

frison, ne (frizɔ̃, ɔn) *a. & F~**, *n*, Frisian.

frisotter (frizɔte) *v.t.*, to frizz[le].

frisquet (friskɛ) *a.m. & a.f.*, chilly.

frisquette (friskɛt) *f*, frisket (*Typ.*).

frisson (frisɔ̃) *m*, shiver, shudder, quiver; thrill. **frissonner** (sone) *v.i.*, to shiver, etc.

frisure (frizyːr) *f*, curling; curliness; (*pl.*) curls.

frites (frit) *pl.f*, French fries.

friture (frityːr) *f*, frying; crackling (*Teleph.*); fry; frying oil, frying fat; fried fish.

frivole (frivɔl) *a*, frivolous, flighty; trivial, fiddling, trumpery; flimsy, frothy. **frivolité** (lite) *f*, frivolity, trifle; tatting.

froc (frɔk) *m*, cowl; frock (*monk's*); monkery, monkhood; trousers (*slang*). **baisser son** ~, to accept humiliation.

froid, e† (frwa, ad) *a*, cold; frigid; cool, chill[y]. *en* ~, to be on unfriendly terms. **à froid,** *ad,* cold, when cold; in cold blood. ¶ *m,* cold; c. weather; frost (*degrees of*); coldness; chill[iness]; coolness. **froideur** (dœːr) *f,* coldness; chilliness; coolness; frigidity. **froidure** (dyːr) *f,* coldness, cold.

froisser (frwase) *v.t,* to bruise; crush; [c]rumple; offend, hurt, wound.

frôler (frole) *v.t,* to graze, brush [against]; come very near to (*fig.*).

fromage (frɔmaːʒ) *m,* cheese; soft job, a snap. ~ *à la crème,* double-cream cheese. ~ *blanc,* cream cheese. ~ *de porc,* brawn. **fromager, ère** (maʒe, ɛːr) *n,* cheese maker; cheesemonger; (*att.*) cheese. **fromagerie** (ʒri) *f,* cheese dairy.

froment (frɔmɑ̃) *m,* wheat.

fronce (frɔ̃ːs) *f,* gather; pucker. ~*s smock* (smɔk), smocking. **froncer** (frɔ̃se) *v.t,* to wrinkle; purse, pucker (lips); gather (*Need.*). ~ *le[s] sourcil[s],* to frown, knit one's brows.

frondaison (frɔ̃dɛzɔ̃) *f,* foliation, leafing; foliage.

fronde (frɔ̃ːd) *f,* sling; catapult (*boy's*); frond (*Bot.*); obstruction (*fig.*). **fronder** (frɔ̃de) *v.i,* to catapult; obstruct; (*v.t.*) to find fault with. **frondeur** (dœːr) *m,* slinger; faultfinder; critic. ~, euse (øːz) *att,* fault-finding.

front (frɔ̃) *m,* front; front [line] (*Mil.*); forehead; brow; face; head; impudence; cheek. *de* ~, abreast; frontal; front. *faire* ~ *à,* to face.

frontière (frɔ̃tjɛːr) *f. & att,* frontier, border.

frontispice (frɔ̃tispis) *m,* frontispiece (*book*); title page. **fronton** (tɔ̃) *m,* fronton, pediment.

frottage (frɔtaːʒ) *m,* polishing (*floors*). **frottée** (te) *f,* drubbing, thrashing. **frottement** (tmɑ̃) *m,* rubbing; friction; contact, intercourse. **frotter** (te) *v.t. & i,* to rub; polish; scumble; drub, pommel; box (*ears*); strike (*match*). *se* ~ *à* (*fig.*), to rub shoulders with. *se* ~ *les mains,*

to rub one's hands. **frotteur** (tœːr) *m,* floor polisher (*pers.*). **frottis** (ti) *m,* scumble; rubbing (*copy*). **frottoir** (twaːr) *m,* rubber, polisher.

frou-frou (frufru) *m,* rustling, swish.

frousse (frus) *f,* fear, funk.

fructifier (fryktifje) *v.i,* to fructify. **fructueux, euse†** (tɥø, øːz) *a,* fruitful (*fig. & Poet.*), profitable.

frugal, e† (frygal) *a,* frugal. **frugalité** (lite) *f,* frugality.

fruit (frɥi) *m,* fruit; profit; benefit; batter (*Build.*). ~ *tombé,* windfall. **fruiterie** (tri) *f,* fruit shop; f. trade. **fruitier, ère** (tje, ɛːr) *n,* fruiterer; greengrocer; (*att.*) fruit.

frusques (frysk) *f.pl,* clothes.

frusquin (fryskɛ̃) *m,* worldly goods.

fruste (fryst) *a,* defaced, worn.

frustrer (frystre) *v.t,* to deprive; defraud; frustrate; balk.

fuchsia (fyksja) *m,* fuchsia.

fugace (fygas) *a,* fleeting; unretentive (*memory*). **fugitif, ive** (ʒitif, iːv) *a,* fugitive, fleeting, transitory, short-lived. ¶ *n,* fugitive, runaway.

fugue (fyg) *f,* fugue (*Mus.*); flight, bolt; elopement.

fuir (fɥiːr) *v.i.ir,* to flee, fly, flit, run away; escape; recede; vanish; leak; (*v.t.ir.*) to flee [from], run away from; shun; eschew. **fuite** (fɥit) *f,* flight; escape; leak[age].

fulguration (fylgyrasjɔ̃) *f,* heat (*or* summer) lightning.

fulmicoton (fylmikɔtɔ̃) *m,* guncotton.

fulminer (fylmine) *v.i. & t,* to fulminate, thunder, storm.

fumage (fymaːʒ) *m,* smoking (*meat, fish*); manuring. **fume-cigarette,** *m,* cigarette holder. **fumée** (me) *f. oft. pl,* smoke; fume; steam, vapor; reek; phantom, vanity; (*pl.*) dung. **fumer** (me) *v.i. & t,* to smoke; cure; steam; reek; fume; manure. *cheminée qui fume,* smoky chimney. **fumerie** (mri) *f,* opium den. **fumet** (me) *m,* smell; bouquet; scent. **fumeur, euse** (mœːr, øːz) *n,* smoker. **fumeux, euse** (mø, øːz) *a,* smoky;

heady; hazy. **fumier** (mje) *m*, litter (*straw & dung*), dung, manure; muck; dunghill; contemptible person.

fumigation (fymigasjɔ̃) *f*, fumigation.

fumiste (fymist) *m*, heating engineer; practical joker. **fumisterie** (tri) *f*, heating engineering; practical joke. **fumivore** (vɔɹr) *a*, smoke-consuming. ¶ *m*, s. consumer, s. preventer. **fumoir** (mwaɹr) *m*, smoke house; smoking room.

fumure (fymyɹr) *f*, manuring; manure.

funambule (fynɑ̃byl) *n*, funambulist; rope walker. **funambulesque** (lɛsk) *a*, funambulatory; fantastic.

funèbre (fynɛːbr) *a*, funeral; funereal; dead (*march*); ill-omened (*birds*). **funérailles** (neraɹj) *f.pl*, funeral. **funéraire** (rɛɹr) *a*, funeral.

funeste (fynɛst) *a*, deadly, baneful, baleful, fatal.

funiculaire (fynikylɛɹr) *a. & m*, funicular, cable railway.

fur (fyɹr) *m*: au ~ & à mesure, in proportion. au ~ & à mesure des besoins, as [& when] required. au ~ & à mesure que, as [& when].

furet (fyrɛ) *m*, ferret. **fureter** (rte) *v.i. & t*, to ferret, f. about, pry. **fureteur, euse** (rtœːr, øːz) *n*, ferreter, rummager; collector, hunter; nosybody.

fureur (fyrœːr) *f*, fury, rage, wrath; passion; distraction; craze; frenzy; furore. *faire* ~, to be the rage. **furibond, e** (ribɔ̃, ɔ̃ːd) *a*, furious. ¶ *n*, madman; fury. **furie** (ri) *f*, fury. **F~**, Fury (*Myth.*). **furieux, euse**† (rjø, øːz) *a*, furious, raging, mad, raving; tremendous. ¶ *n*, madman, -woman.

furoncle (fyrɔ̃ːkl) *m*, boil (*Med.*).

furtif, ive† (fyrtif, iːv) *a*, furtive, stealthy, sly.

fusain (fyzɛ̃) *m*, spindle tree; charcoal [pencil]; c. drawing.

fuseau (fyzo) *m*, spindle (*spinning*); pintle.

fusée (fyze) *f*, rocket, fuse; fusee (*Horol.*); (*axle*) journal;

[out]burst (*fig.*). ~ volante, sky rocket. ~ éclairante, de signalisation, flare. **fusée-sonde** (fyzeɔ̃ːd) probe, sounding rocket.

fuselage (fyzlaːʒ) *m*, fuselage. **fuselé, e** (zle) *a*, spindle-shaped; tapering; streamlined.

fuser (fyze) *v.i*, to spread, run (*colors*); fuse, melt; burn slowly.

fusible (fyzibl) *a*, fusible.

fusil (fyzi) *m*, gun, rifle; steel (*sharpener*). ~ à air comprimé, ~ à vent, air gun. ~ à deux coups, double-barrelled g. ~ mitrailleur, machine g. ~ pour le tir à plomb, shotgun. ~ se chargeant par la culasse, breech-loader. coup de ~, gunshot; an unexpectedly high bill. **fusilier** (zilje) *m*, ~ marin, marine. ~ mitrailleur, machine gunner. **fusillade** (zijad) *f*, fusillade. **fusiller** (je) *v.t*, to shoot (*spy, deserter*); bombard (*fig.*).

fusion (fyzjɔ̃) *f*, fusion, melting, smelting. **fusionner** (one) *v.t. & i*, to amalgamate, merge.

fustiger (fystiʒe) *v.t*, to flog; rebuke.

fût (fy) *m*, stock (*rifle, plane*); handle; shank; shaft (*of column*); post; cask; drum.

futaie (fytɛ) *f*, timber-tree forest. **futaille** (fytaːj) *f*, cask, barrel. **futaine** (fytɛn) *f*, fustian.

futé, e (fyte) *a*, crafty; sly; sharp.

futile (fytil) *a*, futile, nugatory; trifling, idle. **futilité** (lite) *f*, futility; (*pl.*) trifles; (*pl.*) trash (*worthless contents of book*).

futur, e (fytyːr) *a*, future. ¶ *n*, intended (*husband, wife*). ¶ *m*, future; futurity. ~ antérieur, future perfect (*Gram.*). ~ [simple], future [tense].

fuyant, e (fɥijɑ̃, ɑ̃ːt) *a*, receding, retreating; vanishing (*perspective*); shifty. **fuyard, e** (jaɹr, ard) *n*, fugitive, runaway.

G

gabardine (gabardin) *f*, gabardine; raincoat.

gabare (gabaɹr) *f*, lighter, barge; dragnet.

gabarit (gabari) *m*, gauge, templet; mold (*ship*).

gabegie (gabʒi) *f*, mismanagement & dishonesty.

gabier (gabje) *m*, top[s]man (*Naut.*).

gâche (gɑːʃ) *f*, staple (*lock, wall*). **gâcher** (gɑʃe) *v.t*, to temper (*mortar*); spoil, botch, mess up. **gâchis** (ʃi) *m*, (*wet*) mortar; slush, sludge; mess.

gâchette (gɑʃɛt) *f*, trigger; catch; pawl (*Mech.*).

gadoue (gadu) *f*, night soil, sewage.

gaffe (gaf) *f*, boat hook; gaff (*Fish.*); blunder, howler. **gaffer** (fe) *v.t*, to hook, gaff; (*v.i.*) to blunder.

gage (gaːʒ) *m*, pledge, pawn, security, gage; hostage; forfeit (*at play*); token, proof; (*pl.*) wages, pay; forfeits (*game*). à ~s, paid, hired. **gager** (gaʒe) *v.t*, to pay; bet. **gageure** (ʒyːr) *f*, wager. **gagiste** (ʒist) *m*, employee.

gagnage (gɑɲaːʒ) *m*, pasturage.

gagnant, e (gɑɲɑ̃, ɑ̃ːt) *n*, winner; (*att.*) winning. **gagne-pain** (ɲpɛ̃) *m*, livelihood; breadwinner. **gagne-petit** (ɲpəti) *m*, knife grinder; one who earns (*or* makes) very little. **gagner** (ɲe) *v.t. & abs. & i*, to gain; be the gainer; get; make; earn; win; gain over; reach, get to; overtake; spread. ~ à être connu, to improve on acquaintance. se ~, to be catching; spread.

gai, e† (ge) *a*, gay, merry; lively; blithe; bright, cheerful. **gai, i,** merrily!

gaieté (gete) *f*, gaiety; cheerfulness; liveliness; merriment, mirth, glee. de ~ de cœur, out of sheer wantonness. **gaillard, e†** (gajaːr, ard) *a*, jolly, merry; hearty; free, ribald. ¶ *m*, fellow, fine f., jolly f. ¶ *f*, strapping gay wench. **gaillardise** (jardiːz) *f*, gaiety, jollity; broad humor.

gailletin (gajtɛ̃) *m*. ou **gaillette** (jet) *f*, cobbles, nuts (*coal*).

gain (gɛ̃) *m*, gain, profit, lucre; earnings; winning; winnings. ~ de cause, decision in one's favor; right, justification. en ~, in pocket, to the good.

gaine (gɛn) *f*, sheath, case; girdle; pedestal.

gala (gala) *m*, gala.

galamment (galamɑ̃) *ad*, courteously, gallantly; skillfully. **galant, e** (lɑ̃, ɑ̃ːt) *a*, gallant (*to women*); amatory; stylish. galant homme, gentleman. ¶ *m*, gallant; spark; philanderer; lover; slippery gentleman. **galanterie** (lɑ̃tri) *f*, politeness, gallantry (*to women*); love affair.

galbe (galb) *m*, contour, outline.

gale (gal) *f*, itch; mange; scab.

galée (gale) *f*, composing galley.

galène (galɛn) *f*, galena.

galère (galɛːr) *f*, galley (*Hist.*).

galerie (galri) *f*, gallery; arcade; level, drive, drift, road[way] (*Min.*); (*pl, Theat.*) balcony. ~ à écho, whispering gallery. ~ à flanc de coteau, adit. faire ~, to sit out.

galérien (galerjɛ̃) *m*, galley slave.

galerne (galɛrn) *f*, northwester (*wind*).

galet (galɛ) *m*, pebble; (*pl. or s.*) shingle; roller, wheel, runner; castor, caster.

galetas (galta) *m*, garret, attic.

galette (galɛt) *f*, ship biscuit, hardtack; money, loot (*slang*).

galeux, euse (gal∅, ∅ːz) *a*, itchy; scabby; mangy; scurfy.

galhauban (galobɑ̃) *m*, backstay (*Naut.*).

galimafrée (galimafre) *f*, hash, hotchpotch.

galimatias (galimatja) *m*, balderdash, gibberish.

galion (galjɔ̃) *m*, galleon (*Hist.*).

galle (gal) *f*, gall [nut].

Galles (le pays de) (gal), Wales. la Galles du Nord, du Sud, North, South, Wales.

gallican, e (galikɑ̃, an) *a. & n*, Gallican. **gallicisme** (sism) *m*, gallicism.

gallois, e (galwa, aːz) *a*, Welsh. G~, *n*, Welshman, -woman. le gallois, Welsh (*language*).

gallophobe (galɔfɔb) *a. & n*, Gallophobe, anti-French.

galoche (galɔʃ) *f*, rubber, overshoe.

galon (galɔ̃) *m*, braid, galloon; gimp; stripe (*N.C.O.'s, & Navy*); band (*officer's*). **galonner** (lɔne) *v.t*, to braid, lace.

galop (galo) *m*, gallop; galop

(*dance*); hot haste; scolding. **galoper** (lɔpe) *v.i*, to gallop; run, career. **galopin** (pɛ̃) *m*, urchin.

galuchat (galyʃa) *m*, shagreen.

galvanique (galvanik) *a*, galvanic. **galvaniser** (ze) *v.t*, to galvanize. **galvanisme** (nism) *m*, galvanism.

galvauder (galvode) *v.t*, to misuse; botch; (*v.i.*) to loiter. se ~, to sully one's name.

gambade (gɑ̃bad) *f*, gambol, frisk; (*pl.*) antics, capers. **gambader** (de) *v.i*, to gambol, etc.

gamberger (gɑ̃bɛrʒe) *v.i. & t*, to imagine; understand; stroll.

Gambie (la) (gɑ̃bi), Gambia.

gambiller (gɑ̃bije) *v.i*, to skip about.

gambit (gɑ̃bi) *m*, gambit (*chess*).

gamelle (gamɛl) *f*, mess kit; mess (*Nav.*).

gamin, e (gamɛ̃, in) *n*, urchin; youngster; (*f.*) hoyden, romp. ~ *des rues*, street child, s. arab. ¶ *a*, saucy. **gaminer** (mine) *v.i*, to play about. **gaminerie** (nri) *f*, child's prank; [tom]foolery.

gamme (gam) *f*, scale; gamut; range; tone, tune (*fig.*). *haut de* ~, high quality, first class.

ganache (ganaʃ) *f*, lower jaw (*horse*); duffer, fogey.

Gand (gɑ̃) *m*, Ghent.

Gange (le) (gɑ̃ːʒ), the Ganges.

ganglion (gɑ̃gliɔ̃) *m*, ganglion.

gangrène (gɑ̃grɛn) *f*, gangrene. **gangrener** (grəne) *v.t*, to gangrene; corrupt, canker.

gangue (gɑ̃ːg) *f*, gangue, matrix.

ganse (gɑ̃ːs) *f*, cord (*braided*); gimp; loop.

gant (gɑ̃) *m*, glove; gauntlet (*fig.*); (*pl.*) credit. ~*s de peau glacée*, glacé kid gloves. ~*s de Suède*, suède g. ~ *de toilette*, washcloth in shape of glove or mitt. **gantelée** (tle) *f*, foxglove. **gantelet** (tlɛ) *m*, gauntlet. **ganter** (te) *v.t*, to glove. se ~, to put on one's gloves. **ganterie** (tri) *f*, glove trade. **gantier, ère** (tje, ɛːr) *n*, glover.

garage (gara:ʒ) *m*, shunting (*Rly.*); garage, parking (*motor*); shed (*cycle*); docking (*boat*); hangar (*Avn.*).

garance (garɑ̃ːs) *f*, madder.

garant, e (garɑ̃, ɑ̃ːt) *n*, guarantor, surety (*pers.*); (*m.*) authority; warrant; [tackle] fall (*Naut.*). **garantie** (rɑ̃ti) *f*, guarantee, guaranty, warranty; security, indemnity; safeguard; underwriting (*Fin.*). **garantir** (tiːr) *v.t*, to guarantee; warrant; secure; keep, protect, shield; vouch for; underwrite (*Fin.*).

garce (gars) *f*, bitchy woman.

garcette (garsɛt) *f*, gasket; rope end.

garçon (garsɔ̃) *m*, boy, lad; son; [young] man; fellow, chap; bachelor, single man. ~ *d'écurie*, stableboy. ~ *d'honneur*, best man. ~ *de bureau*, messenger, commissionaire. ~ *de cabine*, steward. ~ [*de café*], waiter. ~ *de course*, errand boy. ~ *manqué*, tomboy, hoyden, romp. **garçonne** (sɔn) *f*, bachelor girl. **garçonnet** (sɔnɛ) *m*, little boy. **garçonnier, ère** (nje, ɛːr) *a*, (*of girl*) mannish, masculine; fond of men's society. ¶ *f*, bachelor flat.

garde (gard) *f*, guardianship; guard; keeping, charge, [safe] custody; watch; heed, care; protection; notice; hilt; covering card; endpaper. ~ *blanche*, flyleaf. ~ *descendante*, old guard (*Mil.*). ~ *montante*, new guard.

garde (gard) *m*, guard (*pers.*); keeper; watchman; watcher (*Cust.*); warder; ranger. ~-*barrière, n*, gatekeeper (*level crossing*). ~-*boue, m*, fender (*auto*). ~-*cendre, m*, fender (*fireplace*). ~ *champêtre, m*, rural policeman. ~-*chasse, m*, gamekeeper. ~-*chiourme, m*, prison guard; slave driver; foreman. ~-*corps, m*, rail (*ship*). ~-*côte, m*, coastguard ship. ~-*crotte, m*, fender (*auto*). ~-*fou, m*, handrail, railing. ~-*frein, m*, brakesman. ~-*malades, n*, [sick] nurse. ~-*manger, m*, pantry, larder. ~-*meuble, m*, furniture warehouse. ~-*robe, f*, wardrobe; privy. ~-*vue, m*, eyeshade.

gardénia (gardenja) *m*, gardenia.

garder (garde) *v.t*, to keep; retain; harbor; tend; look after, mind; guard, protect. se ~ *de*, to take care not to; beware of; refrain from. **garderie** (dəri) *f*, day nursery. **gardeur, euse** (dœːr, ɸːz) *n*, keeper, -herd (*cow, swine*). **gardien, ne** (djɛ̃, ɛn) *n*, guardian; keeper, caretaker, custodian; attendant; warder, dress. ~ *de but*, goal keeper. ~ *de la paix*, policeman.

gardon (gardɔ̃) *m*, roach (*fish*).

gare (gaːr) *i*, look out! take care! mind. ¶ *f*, station (*Rly.*). ~ *d'embranchement*, ~ *de bifurcation*, junction. ~ *d'évitement*, sidings. *chef de* ~, stationmaster. ~ *maritime*, harbor station. *en* ~, ~ *restante*, [at railway station,] to be called for.

garenne (garɛn) *f*, [rabbit] warren.

garer (gare) *v.t*, to shunt, switch (*train*); garage (*car*). se~, to shunt; pull to one side; get out of the way, take cover; park a car.

gargariser (se) (gargarize) *v.pr. & abs*, to gargle; gloat on. **gargarisme** (rism) *m*, gargle.

gargote (gargɔt) *f*, beanery.

gargouille (garguːj) *f*, gargoyle; waterspout (*rain*). **gargouiller** (guje) *v.i*, to gurgle; rumble (*bowels*).

gargousse (gargus) *f*, cartridge (*cannon*).

garnement (garnəmɑ̃) *m*. ou *mauvais* ~, scapegrace, scamp.

garni (garni) *m*, furnished room. ¶ *a*, furnished, trimmed.

garnir (garniːr) *v.t. & abs*, to furnish; stock; fill; line; lag; stuff; trim; garnish; decorate. **garnison** (nizɔ̃) *f*, garrison. **garniture** (tyːr) *f*, fittings; furniture; trimmings; packing, lagging, gasket; lining; garnish; seasoning (*of salad, i.e,* (*savory herbs*)); set. ~ *de foyer*, fire irons. ~ *de table*, luncheon set.

garrot (garo) *m*, withers; tourniquet; garrote. **garrotter** (rɔte) *v.t*, to pinion; strangle.

gars (gɑ) *m*, lad, boy; fellow. *allez les* ~, let's go, boys.

gascon, ne (gaskɔ̃, ɔn) *n*, braggart, Gascon. **gasconnade** (kɔnad) *f*, boasting, gasconade.

gaspillage (gaspijaːʒ) *m*, waste, squandering. **gaspiller** (pije) *v.t*, to waste, squander; spoil.

gastéropode (gasterɔpɔd) *m*, gastropod. **gastrique** (trik) *a*, gastric. **gastrite** (trit) *f*, gastritis. **gastronome** (trɔnɔm) *m*, gastronome. **gastronomie** (mi) *f*, gastronomy. **gastronomique** (mik) *a*, gastronomic(al).

gâté, e (gɑte) *p.a*, spoiled; damaged, rotten.

gâteau (gɑto) *m*, cake; comb (*honey*); spoils. ~ *sec*, cookie. *c'est du* ~, it's easy. *papa* ~, sugar daddy.

gâte-métier (gɑtmetje) *m*, [price] cutter; rat. **gâter** (te) *v.t*, to spoil; mar; soil; corrupt; taint; indulge, pamper. **gâterie** (tri) *f*, overindulgence (*to pers.*), spoiling.

gauche (goːʃ) *a*, left; crooked; awkward, clumsy; tactless. *tenir à* ~, to keep left. ¶ *f*, left. ¶ *le* [poing] **gauche**, the left (*Box.*) **gauchement** (goʃmɑ̃) *ad*, awkwardly, clumsily. **gaucher, ère** (ʃe, ɛːr) *a*, left-handed. ¶ *n*, left-hander (*pers. or player*). **gaucherie** (ʃri) *f*, awkwardness. **gauchir** (ʃiːr) *v.i. & t*, to turn aside; shuffle; buckle, bend; warp, wind.

gaudriole (godriɔl) *f*, broad joke.

gaufre (goːfr) *f*, comb (*honey*); waffle; wafer. **gaufrer** (gofre) *v.t*, to goffer, crimp; emboss; figure; tool (*Bookb.*). **gaufrette** (frɛt) *f*, wafer [biscuit] (*flat*).

gaule (goːl) *f*, pole; fishing rod; switch (*stick*).

gaulois, e (golwa, aːz) *a*, Gallic, joyous, broad, free. G~, *n*, Gaul. **gauloiserie** (lwazri) *f*, broadness; broad humor.

gausser (se) de (gose), to poke fun at.

gavage (gavaːʒ) *m*, cramming; forcible feeding.

gave (gaːv) *m*, mountain torrent.

gaver (gave) *v.t*, to cram (*poultry, pupil for exam*); feed forcibly; stuff.

gavotte (gavɔt) *f*, gavotte.

gaz (gɑːz) *m*, gas; flatus, wind. ~ *lacrymogène* (lakrimɔʒɛn), tear gas. ~ *moutarde*, mustard g.

gaze (gɑːz) *f*, gauze.

gazéifier (gazeifje) *v.t*, to gasify; aerate.

gazelle (gazɛl) *f*, gazelle.

gazer (gɑze) *v.t,* to cover with gauze; veil, tone down; gas (*war*); to speed ahead.

gazette (gazɛt) *f,* gazette; newsmonger, gossip.

gazeux, euse (gɑzø, øːz) *a,* gaseous; gassy; aerated; effervescing. **gazier** (zje) *m,* gas worker; gas fitter. **gazogène** (zɔʒɛn) *m,* gazogene, seltzogene; [gas] producer. **gazomètre** (mɛtr) *m,* gasometer.

gazon (gɑzɔ̃) *m,* grass; turf, sod; lawn, [green]sward. **gazonner** (zɔne) *v.t,* to turf.

gazouiller (gazuje) *v.i,* to warble, chirp, twitter; purl, babble; prattle.

geai (ʒe) *m,* jay (*bird*).

géant, e (ʒeɑ̃, ɑ̃ːt) *n,* giant, ess; (*att.*) giant.

géhenne (ʒeɛn) *f,* Gehenna, hell.

geignard, e (ʒeɲaːr, ard) *a,* whining, fretful. **geindre** (ʒɛ̃ːdr) *v.i.ir,* to whine, fret.

gel (ʒɛl) *m,* frost, freezing; freeze (*in diplomatic relations*).

gélatine (ʒelatin) *f,* gelatin[e]. **gélatineux, euse** (nø, øːz) *a,* gelatinous.

gelé, e (ʒəle) *a,* frozen; frostbitten. **gelée** (le) *f,* frost; jelly. ~ *blanche,* hoar frost, white f. ~ *noire,* ~ *à glace,* black f. **geler** (le) *v.t. & i. & imp. &* se ~, to freeze.

gémir (ʒemiːr) *v.i,* to groan, moan; complain. **gémissement** (mismɑ̃) *m,* groan[ing].

gemme (ʒɛm) *f,* gem; bud; (*att.*) gem (*stone*); rock (*salt*).

gênant, e (ʒɛnɑ̃, ɑ̃ːt) *a,* in the way; awkward; troublesome.

gencive (ʒɑ̃siːv) *f,* gum (*Anat.*).

gendarme (ʒɑ̃darm) *m,* gendarme, policeman; Amazon; martinet; spark; flaw; red herring. se **gendarmer** (me) *v.pr,* to be up in arms, fire up. **gendarmerie** (məri) *f,* state police force; headquarters of state police.

gendre (ʒɑ̃ːdr) *m,* son-in-law.

gêne (ʒɛːn) *f,* discomfort; inconvenience; constraint; want; straits, straitened circumstances. sans ~, indifferent (*to other people's convenience*), unconcerned, cool; unconventional, free & easy.

généalogie (ʒenealɔʒi) *f,* genealogy; pedigree. **généalogique** (ʒik) *a,* genealogical, family (*tree*).

gêner (ʒene) *v.t,* to hinder, hamper, cramp; pinch (*shoes, etc.*); interfere with; inconvenience.

général, e† (ʒeneral) *a,* general; common; prevailing. le ~, the general (*fig.*). ~ *de corps d'armée,* lieutenant general. ~ *de division,* major general. ~ *en chef,* (*full*) general. ¶ *f,* general's wife; dress rehearsal; alarm call. **généralat** (la) *m,* generalship. **généraliser** (lize) *v.t. & abs,* to generalize. se ~, to become general. **généralissime** (sim) *m,* generalissimo, commander-in-chief. **généralité** (te) *f,* generality.

générateur, trice (ʒeneratœːr, tris) *a,* generating. ¶ *m,* generator. **génération** (sjɔ̃) *f,* generation. *les appareils de troisième* ~, technically advanced equipment (*electronics*).

généreux, euse† (ʒenerø, øːz) *a,* generous, bounteous, bountiful.

générique (ʒenerik) *a,* generic. ¶ *m,* credits (*cinema*).

générosité (ʒenerozite) *f,* generosity, bounteousness; (*pl.*) acts of generosity.

Gênes (ʒɛːn) *f,* Genoa.

genèse (ʒənɛːz) *f,* genesis. *la G*~, Genesis (*Bible*).

genet (ʒəne) *m,* jennet (*horse*).

genêt (ʒəne) *m,* broom (*Bot.*). ~ *épineux,* furze, gorse, whin.

genette (ʒənɛt) *f,* genet (*civet*).

gêneur (ʒɛnœːr) *m,* nuisance (*pers.*).

Genève (ʒənɛːv) *f,* Geneva.

genévrier (ʒənevrie) *m,* juniper (*genus*).

génial, e (ʒenjal) *a,* [full] of genius. **génie** (ni) *m,* genius; spirit; Muse; bent; engineering.

genièvre (ʒənjɛːvr) *m,* juniper tree, berry; gin.

génisse (ʒenis) *f,* heifer.

génital, e (ʒenital) *a,* genital.

génitif (ʒenitif) *m*, genitive [case].

génois, e (ʒenwa, aːz) *a.* & **G~,** *n*, Genoese.

genou (ʒenu) *m*, knee; (*pl.*) lap. *à ~x*, on one's knees, kneeling. **genouillère** (jɛːr) *f*, kneepad; knuckle [joint] (*Mech.*).

genre (ʒɑ̃ːr) *m*, kind; sort; line; type; description; genus; manner, way; style; fashion; genre (*real-life picture*); gender (*Gram.*). *le ~ humain*, mankind.

gens (ʒɑ̃) *m.pl.* & *f.pl*, people, folk, men; servants; *les ~ du commun*, *m.pl*, [the] common people. **gent** (ʒɑ̃) *f*, tribe, race, folk.

gentiane (ʒɑ̃sjan) *f*, gentian.

gentil (ʒɑ̃ti) *m.* & *a.m*, gentile.

gentil, le (ʒɑ̃ti, iːj) *a*, nice, pretty, sweet; kind, good. *~ à croquer*, perfectly sweet (*pers.*). **gentilhomme** (tijɔm) *m*, nobleman; gentleman. *~ campagnard*, gentleman farmer. **gentilhommerie** (mri) *f*, gentility; gentlemanliness. **gentilhommière** (mjɛːr) *f*, country seat.

gentilité (ʒɑ̃tilite) *f*, pagandom; paganism.

gentillâtre (ʒɑ̃tijɑːtr) *m*, obscure gentleman.

gentillesse (ʒɑ̃tijɛs) *f*, prettiness; gracefulness; (*pl.*) pretty speeches; (*pl.*) pretty tricks; nasty trick. **gentillet, te** (jɛ, ɛt) *a*, rather nice. **gentiment** (mɑ̃) *ad*, nicely, prettily.

gentleman (dʒɛntləman) *m*, gentleman; (*att.*) gentlemanly.

génuflexion (ʒenyflɛksjɔ̃) *f*, genuflexion.

géodésie (ʒeɔdezi) *f*, geodesy. **géognosie** (ɔgnozi) *f*, geognosy. **géographe** (graf) *m*, geographer. **géographie** (fi) *f*, geography. **géographique†** (fik) *a*, geographic(al).

geôle (ʒoːl) *f*, jail; jailer's lodge. **geôlier, ère** (ʒolje, ɛːr) *n*, jailer; wardress.

géologie (ʒeɔlɔʒi) *f*, geology. *~ sur le terrain*, field g. **géologique** (ʒik) *a*, geologic(al). **géologue** (lɔg) *m*, geologist.

géométral, e† (ʒeɔmetral) *a*, flat, plane. **géomètre** (mɛtr) *m*,

geometer, geometrician; surveyor. *~ du cadastre*, ordnance surveyor. **géométrie** (metri) *f*, geometry. **géométrique†** (trik) *a*, geometric(al); mathematical (*precise*).

Georgie (la) (ʒɔrʒi), Georgia (*U.S.A.*).

Géorgie (la) (ʒeɔrʒi), Georgia (*Asia*).

gérance (ʒerɑ̃ːs) *f*, management; board of directors.

géranium (ʒeranjɔm) *m*, geranium.

gérant, e (ʒerɑ̃, ɑ̃ːt) *n*, manager, ess; (*att.*) managing.

gerbe (ʒɛrb) *f*, sheaf; shower; spray (*flowers*). *~ d'eau*, spray of water; splash. **gerber** (be) *v.t*, to bind, sheaf, pile.

gerboise (ʒɛrbwaːs) *f*, jerboa.

gerce (ʒɛrs) *f*, crack; clothes moth. **gercer** (se) *v.t*, to chap; crack. **gerçure** (syːr) *f*, chap; crack; shake (*timber*).

gérer (ʒere) *v.t*, to manage. *mal ~*, to mismanage.

germain, e (ʒɛrmɛ̃, ɛn) *a*, germane, own, full (*brother, sister*). *cousin ~*, first cousin. *issu de ~*, second cousin.

germe (ʒɛrm) *m*, germ; eye (*potato*); tread (*egg*); sprout; bud (*fig.*); seed (*fig.*). **germer** (me) *v.i*, to germinate; shoot, sprout; spring up, germ. **germination** (minasjɔ̃) *f*, germination.

gérondif (ʒerɔ̃dif) *m*, gerund.

géronte (ʒerɔ̃ːt) *m*, old man (*in comedy*); old fool.

gésier (ʒezje) *m*, gizzard.

gésir (ʒeziːr) *v.i.ir*, to lie (*sick, dead*).

gesse (ʒɛs) *f*, vetch, pea.

gestation (ʒɛstasjɔ̃) *f*, gestation.

geste (ʒɛst) *m*, gesture; motion; movement; action; wave, flourish, lift (*of the hand*); (*f.*) epic. **gesticuler** (tikyle) *v.i*, to gesticulate.

gestion (ʒɛstjɔ̃) *f*, management; administration; care.

geyser (ʒezɛːr) *m*, geyser.

ghetto (ɡeto) *m*, ghetto.

gibecière (ʒipsjɛːr) *f*, game bag; pouch; satchel, knapsack. **gi-**

berne (bɛrn) f, pouch (cartridge); knapsack.

gibet (ʒibɛ) m, gibbet, gallows.

gibier (ʒibje) m, game (Hunt.). ~ à poil, ground g. ~ de potence, gallows bird.

giboulée (ʒibule) f, shower; hailstorm.

giboyer (ʒibwaje) v.i, to go shooting. **giboyeux, euse** (jø, øːz), a, full of game, gamy.

gicler (ʒikle) v.i, to spirt, squirt, splash. **gicleur** (klœːr) m, jet; nozzle.

gifle (ʒifl) f, slap, smack. **gifler** (fle) v.t, to slap, smack.

gigantesque (ʒigɑ̃tɛsk) a, gigantic.

gigot (ʒigo) m, leg (of lamb, etc.). **gigoter** (gɔte) v.t, to fidget; jerk about.

gigue (ʒig) f, jig (Mus., dance).

gilet (ʒilɛ) m, waistcoat, vest; cardigan; woolly coat. ~ de sauvetage, life vest.

Gille (ʒil) m, clown, fool.

gingembre (ʒɛ̃ʒɑ̃ːbr) m, ginger.

girafe (ʒiraf) f, giraffe; microphone boom (cinema).

girandole (ʒirɑ̃dɔl) f, girandole; epergne.

giration (ʒirasjɔ̃) f, gyration. **giratoire** (twaːr) a, gyratory; traffic circle.

girofle (ʒirɔfl) m, clove (spice). **giroflée** (fle) f, stock (Bot.). ~ jaune, wallflower. **giroflier** (flie) m, clove tree.

giron (ʒirɔ̃) m, lap (of pers.); bosom, pale (of the church); tread (of stair step).

girouette (ʒirwɛt) f, vane, weathercock (lit. & fig.).

gisant, e (ʒizɑ̃, ɑ̃ːt) a, lying. ¶ n, recumbent figure (statue). **gisement** (zmɑ̃) m, lie, bearing (Naut.); bed, seam, deposit, stratum (Geol.).

gitane (ʒitan) m, f, gypsy.

gite (ʒit) m, home, shelter, lodging; form (hare); bed, seam, deposit (Geol.); leg of beef. ~ rural, vacation lodging on a farm.

givre (ʒiːvr) m, hoarfrost rime.

glabre (glɑːbr) a, glabrous, hairless; cleanshaven.

glace (glas) f. sometimes pl. in sense of ice, ice; ice cream. (pl.) frost, chill (fig., of age); glass; [looking] glass, mirror; icing (sugar); flaw. ~ de vitrage, plate glass. ~[s] flottante[s], ice floe. **glacé, e** (se) p.a, frozen; icy; chill; iced; stony (look); glacé. **glacer** (se) v.t, to freeze, chill; ice; glaze; gloss; scumble. se ~, to freeze; glaze. **glaciaire** (sjɛːr) (Geol.) a, glacial, glacier, ice (att.). **glacial, e** (sjal) a, glacial, icy; frozen; frosty; frigid. **glacier** (sje) m, ice-cream vender; confectioner; glacier. **glacière** (sjɛːr) f, ice house; freezer, icebox. **glacis** (si) m, slope; glacis; glaze; scumble. **glaçon** (sɔ̃) m, floe; piece of ice; icicle; ice cube.

gladiateur (gladjatœːr) m, gladiator.

glaïeul (glajœl) m, gladiolus.

glaire (glɛːr) f, glair, white of egg.

glaise (glɛːz) f, clay; pug, puddle. **glaiser** (glɛze) v.t, to clay, pug, puddle. **glaisière** (zjɛːr) f, clay pit.

glaive (glɛːv) (Poet.) m, sword, brand.

glanage (glanaːʒ) m, gleaning.

gland (glɑ̃) m, acorn; (pl.) tassel.

glande (glɑ̃ːd) f, gland; tumor. des ~s au cou, swollen glands.

glandée (glɑ̃de) f, acorn crop.

glane (glan) f, gleaning; rope (of onions, etc.). **glaner** (ne) v.t. & abs, to glean. **glaneur, euse** (nœːr, øːz) n, gleaner. **glanure** (nyːr) f, gleanings.

glapir (glapiːr) v.i, to yelp, yap, bark.

glas (glɑ) m, knell, passing bell.

glauque (gloːk) a, glaucous.

glèbe (glɛːb) f, glebe, soil.

glème (glɛːn) f, socket (bone); coil (rope).

glissade (glisad) f, slide, sliding, slip; glissade. **glissant, e** (sɑ̃, ɑ̃ːt) a, slippery. **glissé** (se) m, glide (Danc.). **glissement** (smɑ̃) m, sliding, slide, slip[ping]; slump; glide; gliding. **glisser** (se) v.i. & t, to slide; skid; slip; glide; slur. **glisseur, euse** (sœːr, øːz) n, slider (pers.). ¶ m, hydroplane, speed boat; glider (Avn.). ~ de course, racing boat. ~ de croisière, fast cruiser (*speedboat*). **glissière** (sjɛːr) *f*, slide, guide (*Mach.*). **glissoire** (swaːr) *f*, slide (*track on ice*).

global, e† (glɔbal) *a*, total, inclusive, aggregate (*sum*); grand, sum (*total*). **globe** (glɔb) *m*, globe (ball; orb. **globulaire** (bylɛːr) & **globuleux, euse** (lØ, Øːz) *a*, globular. **globule** (byl) *m*, globule.

gloire (glwaːr) *f*, glory; fame; pride; boast. *se faire* ~ *de*, to glory in, pride oneself on. **glorieux, euse†** (glɔrjØ, Øːz) *a*, glorious; proud; conceited. **glorifier** (rifje) *v.t*, to glorify, praise. *se* ~ *de*, to glory in, boast of. **gloriole** (rjɔl) *f*, vainglory, vanity; kudos.

glose (gloːz) *f*, gloss, commentary; criticism. **gloser** (sur) (gloze) *v.t. & i*, to find fault with. **glossaire** (glosɛːr) *m*, glossary. **glossateur** (satœːr) *m*, commentator.

glotte (glɔt) *f*, glottis.

glouglou (gluglu) *m*, gurgle, bubbling. **glouglouter** (te) *v.i*, to gobble (*of turkey*).

glousser (gluse) *v.i*, to cluck; chuckle; giggle, titter.

glouton, ne† (glutɔ̃, ɔn) *a*, gluttonous. ¶ *n*, glutton. **gloutonnerie** (tɔnri) *f*, gluttony.

glu (gly) *f*, birdlime; glue (*marine*). **gluant, e** (ɑ̃, ɑ̃ːt) *a*, gluey, sticky. **gluau** (o) *m*, (*bird*) lime twig.

glucose (glykoːz) *f*, glucose.

glume (glym) *f*, glume; chaff.

gluten (glytɛn) *f*, gluten. **glutineux, euse** (tinØ, Øːz) *a*, glutinous.

glycérine (gliserin) *f*, glycerin[e].

glycine (glisin) *f*, wistaria.

gnangnan (nɑ̃nɑ̃) *n. & a*, lackadaisical (*person*).

gneiss (gnɛs) *m*, gneiss.

gnome (gnoːm) *m*, gnome.

gnostique (gnɔstik) *a*, gnostic.

go (tout de) (go) *ad*, straight off, there & then.

gobelet (gɔblɛ) *m*, goblet; tumbler. *joueur des* ~*s*, shell game swindler.

gobelin (gɔblɛ̃) *m*, [hob]goblin, imp.

gobe-mouches (gɔbmuʃ) *m*, flycatcher (*bird*); flytrap (*plant*);

simpleton, gaper. **gober** (be) *v.t*, to bolt, gulp down; swallow (*fig.*). **goberger (se)** (gɔbɛrʒe) *v.pr*, to do oneself well.

godailler (gɔdaje) *v.i*, to carouse.

godelureau (gɔdlyro) *m*, country bumpkin.

goder (gɔde) *v.i*, to pucker; bag (*trousers*); have an erection (*slang*). **godet** (dɛ) *m*, cup; noggin; bucket (*elevator*); saucer (*artist's*); pucker, ruck.

godiche (gɔdiʃ) *a. & n*, awkward (person), hobbledehoy.

godille (gɔdiːj) *f*, scull (*stern oar*). **godiller** (dije) *v.t*, to scull.

goéland (gɔelɑ̃) *m*, sea gull.

goélette (gɔelɛt) *f*, schooner.

goémon (gɔemɔ̃) *m*, seaweed, wrack.

gogo (gogo) *m*, simpleton, gull. *à* ~, in plenty; in clover.

goguenarder (gɔgnarde) *v.i*, to banter, crack jokes; jeer; sneer.

goguette (être en) (gɔgɛt), to be jolly (*in drink*).

goinfre (gwɛːfr) *m*, guzzler. **goinfrer** (gwɛfre) *v.i*, to guzzle, gorge.

goitre (gwaːtr) *m*, goiter, wen.

golf (gɔlf) *m*, golf; golf course, golf links. ~ *miniature*, ~ *réduit*, miniature golf.

golfe (gɔlf) *m*, gulf, bay, bight. ~ *Arabique*, Arabian Gulf. ~ *de Gascogne* (gaskɔɲ). Bay of Biscay. ~ *Persique* (pɛrsik), Persian Gulf.

gommage (gɔmaːʒ) *m*, gumming. **gomme** (gɔm) *f*, gum. ~ [*à effacer*], eraser. ~ *à mâcher*, chewing gum. ~ *arabique*, g. arabic, ~ [*élastique*], [india] rubber. **gommer** (me) *v.t*, to gum; erase; eliminate. **gommeux, euse** (mØ, Øːz) *a*, gummy. **gommier** (mje) *m*, gum tree.

gond (gɔ̃) *m*, (*gate*) hook. ~ & *penture*, hook & hinge.

gond (gɔ̃) *m*, hinge (*door, etc.*) *sortir de ses* ~*s*, to fly off the handle.

gondole (gɔ̃dɔl) *f*, gondola.

gondoler (gɔ̃dɔle) *v.i*, to swell; warp.

gondolier (gɔ̃dɔlje) *m*, gondolier.

gonfler (gɔ̃fle) *v.t. & i. & se* ~, to swell, inflate, pump up (*tire*). **gonfleur** (flœːr) *m*, pump (*air*).

gong (gɔ̃g) *m,* gong.

gonzesse (gɔ̃zɛs) *f,* woman, broad, wife (*familiar, tending to be pejorative*); cowardly or weak man (*slang*).

gord (gɔːr) *m,* weir (*Fish.*).

goret (gɔrɛ) *m,* piglet, porker; pig (*child*).

gorge (gɔrʒ) *f,* throat, gullet; bosom, bust; neck; mouth (*of tunnel*); gorge; groove; tumbler (*lock*). **gorgée** (ʒe) *f,* mouthful, gulp. **gorger** (ʒe) *v.t,* to gorge, cram, load.

gorille (gɔriːj) *m,* gorilla.

gosier (gozje) *m,* throat, gullet.

gosse (gɔs) *m, f,* kid, brat, youngster, etc.

gothique (gɔtik) *a,* Gothic; old-fashioned.

goton (gɔtɔ̃) *f,* slut.

gouache (gwaʃ) *f,* gouache (*art*).

gouailler (gwaje) *v.t. & i,* to chaff, banter.

goudron (gudrɔ̃) *m,* tar. **goudronner** (drɔne) *v.t,* to tar, spray with tar. *toile goudronnée,* tarpaulin.

gouffre (gufr) *m,* gulf, abyss, chasm; whirlpool.

gouge (guːʒ) *f,* gouge (*tool*).

gouine (gwin) *f,* lesbian. (*slang*).

goujat (guʒa) *m,* cad, blackguard. **goujaterie** (tri) *f,* dirty trick.

goujon (guʒɔ̃) *m,* gudgeon (*fish & Mech.*); dowel, joggle, stud. **goujonner** (ʒɔne) *v.t,* to dowel; joggle, stud.

goule (gul) *f,* ghoul.

goulée (gule) *f,* mouthful, gulp. **goulet** (lɛ) *m,* narrows, gut (*Naut.*). **goulot** (lo) *m,* neck (*bottle*). *~ d'étranglement,* bottleneck. **goulotte** (lɔt) *f,* spout. **goulu,** e (ly) *a,* greedy. **goulûment** (lymɑ̃) *ad,* greedily.

goupille (gupiːj) *f,* pin; bolt. *~ fendue,* split pin; cotter. **goupillon** (pijɔ̃) *m,* holy-water sprinkler; bottle brush; penis (*slang*).

gourbi (gurbi) *m,* hut; hovel; dugout.

gourd, e (guːr, urd) *a,* numb.

gourde (gurd) *f,* gourd; flask; fool.

gourdin (gurdɛ̃) *m,* cudgel.

gourmade (gurmad) *f,* punch, blow.

gourmand, e (gurmɑ̃, ɑ̃d) *a,* gourmand; greedy. *~ de,* very fond of. ¶ *n,* gourmand; glutton. **gourmander** (mɑ̃de) *v.t,* to scold, chide; lard (*Cook.*). **gourmandise** (diːz) *f,* gluttony.

gourme (gurm) *f,* strangles (*Vet.*); wild oats (*fig.*). *jeter sa ~,* to sow one's wild oats.

gourmé, e (gurme) *p.a,* stiff, formal. **gourmer** (me) *v.t,* to curb (*horse*); punch, pommel.

gourmet (gurmɛ) *m,* gourmet, epicure; connoisseur, judge.

gourmette (gurmɛt) *f,* curb (*harness*). *lâcher la gourmette à,* to give a free rein to (*horse, pers.*).

gousse (gus) *f,* pod, shell. *~ d'ail,* clove of garlic. *~ de plomb,* net sinker, n. weight.

gousset (gusɛ) *m,* pocket (*vest*); fob; gusset.

goût (gu) *m,* taste; relish; flavor; tang; liking, fondness; style. **goûter** (te) *m,* afternoon snack. ¶ *v.t,* to taste; try; relish; like.

goutte (gut) *f,* drop; drip; dram; sip; spot, splash; gout (*Med.*). **gouttelette** (tlɛt) *f,* tiny drop. **goutteux, euse** (tø, øːz) *a,* gouty. **gouttière** (tjɛːr) *f,* roof gutter; (*pl.*) caves.

gouvernail (guvɛrnaːj) *m,* rudder; helm (*fig.*).

gouvernante (guvɛrnɑ̃ːt) *f,* governess; housekeeper. **gouvernants** (nɑ̃) *m.pl,* government in power. **gouverne** (vɛrn) *f,* guidance; steering. **gouvernement** (nəmɑ̃) *m,* government; management; care. **gouverner** (ne) *v.t. & abs,* to steer (*Naut.*); govern, rule; look after. **gouverneur** (nœːr) *m,* governor.

goyave (gɔjaːv) *f,* guava. **goyavier** (javje) *m,* gauva [tree].

grabat (graba) *m,* pallet, mean bed. **grabataire** (tɛːr) *a. & n,* bedridden (person).

grabuge (grabyːʒ) *m,* row, brawl.

grâce (grɑːs) *f,* grace; gracefulness; favor; mercy; pardon; thanks; (*pl.*) grace (*after meal*). *les* [*trois*] *G~s,* the Graces. *de ~, ad,* pray, please, for goodness' sake. **gracier** (grasje) *v.t,* to pardon, reprieve. **gracieusement**

(sjøzmã) *ad*, graciously; gratuitously, free. **gracieuseté** (zte) *f*,
graciousness; kindness; gratuity.
gracieux, euse (søj, ø:z) *a*, graceful, pleasing; gracious. *à titre ~*,
free of charge.

gracile (grasil) *a*, slender, slim.
gracilité (lite) *f*, slenderness.

gradation (gradasjõ) *f*, gradation. *~ [ascendante]*, climax
(*Rhet.*). *~ descendante*, anticlimax. **grade** (grad) *m*, grade; rank;
rating; degree (*Univ.*). *prendre
ses ~s*, to graduate. *en prendre
pour son ~*, to get bawled out.
gradé (de) *m*, noncommissioned
officer. *~s & soldats*, rank & file.
gradin (dẽ) *m*, tier; step; stope
(*Min.*). **gradué, e** (dɥe) *n*, graduate (*Univ.*). **graduel, le†** (dɥel) *a*,
gradual. **graduer** (dɥe) *v.t*, to
graduate; grade.

graillon (graJõ) *m*, burning
(*smell, taste, of burned meat,
fat*). **graillonner** (Jone) *v.i*, to
catch fire (*Cook.*); hawk (*with
throat*).

grain (grẽ) *m*, grain; seed; berry,
bean; bead; speck; dash; spice;
modicum; squall (*Naut.*). *~ de
beauté*, beauty spot; mole (*on
skin*). *~ de grêle*, hailstone. *~
de plomb*, pellet. *~ de raisin*,
grape.

graine (grɛ:n) *f*, seed; silkworms'
eggs. *~ d'anis*, aniseed. *~ de lin*,
linseed. *~ des canaris*, canary
seed. **grainier, ère** (nje, ɛ:r) *n*,
seedsman.

graissage (grɛsa:ʒ) *m*, greasing,
lubrication, oiling. **graisse** (grɛ:s)
f, fat; grease; blubber; ropiness
(*wine*). *~ de rognon*, suet. *~
de rôti*, dripping. **graisser** (grɛse)
v.t, to grease, lubricate. *~ [à
l'huile]*, to oil. **graisseur** (sœ:r)
m, greaser; oiler; lubricator.
graisseux, euse (sø, ø:z) *a*, greasy,
oily; fatty; messy.

gramen (gramen) *m*, lawn grass.
une graminée (mine) *a* grass
(*plant*).

grammaire (grammɛːr) *f*, grammar. *contre la ~*, ungrammatical. **grammairien, ne**
(mɛrjẽ, ɛn) *n*, grammarian. **grammatical, e†** (matikal) *a*,
grammatical.

gramine (gram) *m*, gram =
15.432 grains.
gramophone (gramɔfɔn) *m*,
phonograph.
grand, e (grã, ã:d) *a*, great,
large, big; noble; major (*prophet,
etc.*); high; tall; grown-up; long;
broad; wide; open (*air*); deep
(*mourning*); full (*dress, orchestra*); high-class (*wine*); loud;
heavy (*rain*); grand; main; trunk
(*line*); general (*public*); much,
many. **grand, comps:** *~ canot,
launch, pinnace. ~ chemin*, highway, main road. *~ danois*, great
Dane (*dog*). *un ~ homme manqué*,
a might-have-been. *un homme
~*, a tall man. *au ~ jour*, in broad
daylight; publicly. *~ jour [de la
publicité]*, limelight. *~ livre*,
ledger; register (*share, stock*).
~ magasin [de nouveautés], big
stores, department store. *le ~
monde*, [high] society, high life,
the upper crust. *le ~ nettoyage*,
the spring cleaning. *~ rabbin*,
chief rabbi. **grande, comps:** *~s
eaux*, spate, freshet; fountains.
à ~s journées, by forced marches.
~ largeur, double width (*cloth*).
~ marée, spring tide. *~ multiplication*, high gear. *~ pêche*, deep-
sea fishing (*whale & cod*). *~ pédale*, loud pedal. *~ personne*,
grown-up. *à [la] ~ pluie*, at much
rain (*barometer*). *~ tenue & ~
toilette*, full dress. *~s vacances*,
summer holidays.

grand (grã) *m*, great man; adult,
grown-up. (*the*) *great*; (*pl.*) (*the*)
great ones (*of the earth*). *~ de
l'eau*, high-water mark. *~s &
petits*, old & young. *en ~*, on a
large scale; life-size.

grand-chose (grãʃoːz) *pn. usually with neg*, much.

grand-crosse (grãkrɔs) *f*, driver
(*golf club*).

Grande-Bretagne (la) (grãd-
bretaɲ), [Great] Britain.

grandelet, te (grãdlɛ, ɛt) *a*,
growing (*big*); rather tall. **grandement** (dmã) *ad*, grandly; nobly;
greatly; altogether; ample, amply.
grandeur (dœːr) *f*, size; magnitude; height; greatness; mightiness; nobility; grandeur. *~ na-*

turelle, life-size. *Votre Ḡ~*, your Grace; your Lordship.

grand-fer (grɑ̃fɛɪr) *m*, driving iron (*golf*).

grandiloquence (grɑ̃dilɔkɑ̃ɪs) *f*, grandiloquence. **grandiloquent**, **e** (kɑ̃, ɑ̃ɪt) *a*, grandiloquent.

grandiose (grɑ̃djoɪz) *a*, grandiose, imposing.

grandir (grɑ̃diɪr) *v.i*, to grow taller; grow up; grow; (*v.t.*) to make taller *or* bigger; magnify. **grandissime** (disim) *a*, very great.

grand-maman (grɑ̃mamɑ̃) *f*, grandmamma, granny. **grand-mère** (grɑ̃mɛɪr) *f*, grandmother.

grand-messe (grɑ̃mɛs) *f*, high mass.

grand-oncle (grɑ̃tɔ̃ːkl) *m*, great-uncle.

grand-père (grɑ̃pɛɪr) *m*, grandfather.

grand-route (grɑ̃rut) *ou* **grande route** (ɑ̃ːd) *f*, highway, main road.

grand-tante (grɑ̃tɑ̃ːt) *f*, great-aunt.

grand-voile (grɑ̃vwaɪl) *f*, mainsail.

grange (grɑ̃ːʒ) *f*, barn.

granit (grani[t]) *m*, granite.

granule (granyl) *m*, granule. **granuler** (le) *v.t*, to granulate.

graphique† (grafik) *a*, graphic. ¶ *m*, diagram, chart, graph.

graphite (grafit) *m*, graphite, plumbago, black lead.

grappe (grap) *f*, bunch, cluster. **grappiller** (pije) *v.i. & t*, to glean (*grapes*); pick up, scrape up.

grappin (grapɛ̃) *m*, grapnel; creeper (*well*).

gras, se (grɑ, ɑɪs) *a*, fat; fatty; oily; oil (*varnish*); ropy (*wine*); plump (*chicken*); fatted (*calf*); greasy; thick; rich (*food, etc.*); meat (*diet, day, etc.*); full-face, bold-faced (*type*); smutty, ribald, broad (*story*). **gras**, *m*, fat. ~ *de la jambe*, calf. ~ *du bras*, fleshy part of the arm. **grassement** (grasmɑ̃) *ad*, (*to live*) on the fat of the land; handsomely. **grasset, te** (sɛ, ɛt) *a*, fattish. **grasseyer** (sɛje) *v.i*, to burr (*speaking*). **grassouillet, te** (suje, ɛt) *a*, plump; chubby.

gratification (gratifikasjɔ̃) *f*, bonus, gratuity. **gratifier** (fje) *v.t*, to bestow, confer.

gratin· (gratɛ̃) *m*, brown crust (*in pot*); gratin. *le ~*, the 400. **gratiner** (tine) *v.t*, to gratinate (*Cook.*).

gratis (gratis) *ad*, gratis, free.

gratitude (gratityd) *f*, gratitude.

gratte (grat) *f*, scrapings (*savings*); pickings, graft. **gratte-ciel**, *m*, skyscraper. **gratte-cul**, *m*, hip (*Bot.*). **gratte-miettes**, *m*, crumb scoop. **gratte-papier**, *m*, pen-pusher. **gratter** (te) *v.t*, to scrape; scratch; s. out, erase. **grattoir** (twaɪr) *m*, knife eraser; scraper.

gratuit, e† (gratɥi, it) *a*, gratuitous, free; unpaid (*no salary*); wanton (*insult*). **gratuité** (te) *f*, gratuitousness.

grave (graɪv) *a*, grave; solemn; serious; weighty; severe; grievous; deep (*sound*); heavy. ¶ *m*, lower register (*Mus.*).

graveleux, euse (gravlø, øːz) *a*, gravelly, gritty; smutty, ribald. **gravelle** (vɛl) *f*, gravel (*Med.*). **gravelure** (vlyɪr) *f*, smuttiness, ribaldry.

gravement (gravmɑ̃) *ad*, gravely; seriously; rather slowly (*Mus.*).

graver (grave) *v.t*, to engrave; grave; cut; inscribe; impress (*on memory*). ~ *à l'eau-forte*, to etch. ~ *en relief*, to emboss. **graveur** (vœːr) *m*, engraver.

gravier (gravje) *m*, gravel, grit.

gravir (graviːr) *v.i. & t*, to climb, clamber.

gravitation (gravitasjɔ̃) *f*, gravitation. **gravité** (te) *f*, gravity; weight (*fig.*); depth (*sound*). **graviter** (te) *v.i*, to gravitate.

gravure (gravyːr) *f*, engraving; cut; print; illustration. ~ *à l'eau-forte*, etching. ~ *à la manière noire*, mezzotint. ~ *au trait*, line engraving. ~ *dans le texte*, illustration in text. ~ *de mode*, fashion plate. ~ *en creux*, die sinking. ~ *hors texte*, illustration outside text. ~ *sur bois*, wood engraving; woodcut.

gré (gre) *m*, will; free will; wish; pleasure; liking; taste. *au ~ de*, according to; at the mercy of. *bon ~, mal ~,* willynilly. *de ~ ou de force,* by fair means or foul. *de ~ à ~,* by negotiation; by private treaty. *savoir ~ de,* to be grateful for.

grèbe (grɛb) *m,* grebe.

grec, ecque (grɛk) *a,* Greek, Grecian. G~, *n,* Greek (*pers.*). **le grec,** Greek (*language*). **la Grèce** (grɛːs), Greece. **grecque,** *f,* Greek fret (*Arch.*).

gredin, e (grədɛ̃, in) *n,* villain, scoundrel, miscreant. **gredinerie** (dinri) *f,* villainy.

gréement (gremɑ̃) (*Naut.*) *m,* rigging; gear. **gréer** (gree) *v.t,* to rig.

greffe (grɛf) *m,* registry (*legal*); (*f.*) graft (*Hort. & Surg.*), scion; grafting. **greffer** (fe) *v.t,* to graft. **greffier** (fje) *m,* clerk (*of court*); registrar. **greffon** (fɔ̃) *m,* graft, scion.

grégaire (gregɛːr) *a,* gregarious, herd (*att.*).

grège (grɛːʒ) *a,* raw (*silk*).

grégorien, ne (gregɔrjɛ̃, ɛn) *a,* Gregorian.

grêle (grɛːl) *a,* slender, thin (*legs, voice*); small (*intestine*). ¶ *f,* hail, shower (*fig.*). **grêlé, e** (grɛle) *p.a,* pockmarked, pitted; most unfortunate. **grêler** (le) *v.imp,* to hail; (*v.t.*) to damage by hail.

grelin (grəlɛ̃) *m,* hawser.

grêlon (grɛlɔ̃) *m,* (*big*) hailstone.

grelot (grəlo) *m,* bell (*spherical with ball inside*). **grelotter** (lɔte) *v.i,* to shiver (*cold*).

grenade (grənad) *f,* pomegranate; grenade. G~, *f,* Granada (Spain). **la G~,** Grenada (*W. Indies*). **grenadier** (dje) *m,* pomegranate [tree]; grenadier; virago. **grenadille** (diːj) *f,* granadilla (*Bot.*). **grenadin** (dɛ̃) *m,* grenadine (*Cook.*). **grenadine** (din) *f,* grenadine (*cordial, fabric*).

grenaille (grənɑːj) *f,* tailings (*grain*); shot.

grenat (grəna) *m,* garnet. ~ *~ cabochon,* carbuncle.

greneler (grənle) *v.t,* to grain (*leather*). **grené** (ne) *m,* stipple (*art*). **grener** (ne) *v.i,* to seed;

(*v.t.*) to granulate; grain. **grènetis** (grɛnti) *m,* milling (*on coin*). **grenier** (grənje) *m,* granary; loft; garner; garret; attic. *en ~,* in bulk.

grenouille (grənuːj) *f,* frog; money box; funds (*club, society*). *manger, bouffer, la ~,* to make off with entrusted funds. **grenouillère** (nujɛːr) *f,* froggery; swamp

grenu, e (grəny) *a,* grainy, seedy; grained. ¶ *m,* graining (*on leather*).

grès (grɛ) *m,* sandstone; grit; stoneware. ~ *meulier* (mœlje), millstone grit.

grésil (grezi) *m,* (*tiny hard pellets of*) hail. **grésiller** (je) *v.imp,* to hail; (*v.t.*) to shrivel [up].

gresserie (grɛsri) *f,* sandstone quarry; sandstone (*work*); stoneware.

grève (grɛːv) *f,* beach, shore, (*Poet.*) strand; strike. ~ *patronale,* lockout. ~ *perlée,* slowdown. ~ *sur le tas,* sitdown strike. ~ *sauvage,* wildcat s. ~ *thrombose,* partial s. ~ *surprise,* lightning s. *se mettre en ~, faire ~,* to [go on] strike.

grever (grəve) *v.t,* to burden, weight, encumber, saddle. [put] on, [put] upon.

gréviste (grevist) *n,* striker; (*att.*) strike.

grianneau (griano) *m,* young grouse.

gribouiller (gribuje) *v.t. & abs,* to scrawl; daub.

grief (grief) *m,* grievance; complaint. **grièvement** (ɛvmɑ̃) *ad,* seriously (*injured*).

griffe (grif) *f,* claw, talon; clutch; clip; grip; jaw; dog; tendril; facsimile signature; autograph stamp; stamp. *coup de ~,* scratch. **griffer** (fe) *v.t,* to claw, scratch; blaze (*tree*). **griffon** (fɔ̃) *m,* griffin, griffon. **griffonner** (fɔne) *v.t. & abs,* to scrawl; scribble. **griffure** (fyːr) *f,* scratch.

grignon (grinɔ̃) *m,* crust[y] end (*bread*).

grignoter (grinɔte) *v.t. & abs,* to nibble; get a few pickings (*profit*).

grigou (grigu) *m*, miser, screw, hunks.

gril (gri) *m*, gridiron; grill; grating. *sur le* ~, on tenterhooks (*fig.*). **grillade** (grijad) *f*, grilling; broiling; grill (*meat*). **grillage** (ja:ʒ) *m*, roasting (*ore*); grating; [wire] netting; grillage. **grille** (gri:j) *f*, grating; grill[e], grid; screen; wire guard; grate; railing[s]. ~*pain* (grijpɛ̃) ˈm, toaster. **griller** (grije) *v.t. & i*, to grill; broil; toast; roast; scorch; burn; long, itch; grate, rail in.

grillon (grijɔ̃) *m*, cricket (*insect*).

grimace (grimas) *f*, grimace, wry face, grin; sham. **grimacer** (se) *v.i*, to grimace, make faces, grin; pucker, crease. **grimacier, ère** (sje, ɛɪr) *a*, grinning; mincing; sham.

grime (grim) *m*, dotard (*of comedy*). **se grimer** (me) *v.pr*, to make up (*Theat.*).

grimoire (grimwaɪr) *m*, gibberish; scrawl.

grimper (grɛ̃pe) *v.i*, to climb, clamber; creep.

grincer (grɛ̃se) *v.i*, to grind, grate, creak. ~ *des* (ou *les*) *dents*, to grind (*or* gnash) one's teeth.

grincheux, euse (grɛ̃ʃø, øːz) *a*, churlish, crabbed.

gringalet (grɛ̃galɛ) *m*, shrimp (*pers.*).

grippe (grip) *f*, influenza; dislike. *prendre en* ~, to take a dislike to. **gripper** (pe) *v.t*, to snatch (*steal*); (*v.i.*) to seize (*Mach.*). *être grippé, e*, to have influenza. se ~, to pucker. **grippe-sou**, *m*, money grubber.

gris, e (gri, iːz) *a*, gray; brown (*paper*); grizzly; dull; tipsy, fuddled. ¶ *m*, gray. **grisaille** (grizaːj) *f*, grisaille. **grisailler** (zaje) *v.t*, to [paint] gray. **grisâtre** (zɑːtr) *a*, grayish. **griser** (ze) *v.t*, to fuddle, muddle, intoxicate. **grisette** (zɛt) *f*, grisette (*girl*); white-throat (*bird*).

grisbi (grizbi) *m*, money, dough, bread (*slang*).

grisoller (grizɔle) *v.i*, to carol (*lark*).

grison, ne (grizɔ̃, ɔn) *a*, grayish,

grizzled (*hair*). ¶ *m*, graybeard; donkey. **grisonner** (zɔne) *v.i*, to gray.

grisou (grizu) *m*, firedamp.

grive (griːv) *f*, thrush. ~ *chanteuse*, song t., throstle.

grivois, e (grivwa, aːz) *a*, broad, ribald.

Groenland (le) (grɔɛlɑ̃[ːd]), Greenland.

grog (grɔg) *m*, grog.

grogner (grɔɲe) *v.i*, to grunt; grumble. **grognon** (ɲɔ̃) *m*, grumbler.

groin (grwɛ̃) *m*, snout (*pig*).

grommeler (grɔmle) *v.i*, to grumble at, g. about.

gronder (grɔ̃de) *v.i*, to growl, snarl; roar; rumble, mutter, peal; howl (*wind*); grumble; (*v.t.*) to scold.

groom (grum) *m*, groom; page boy.

gros, se (gro, oɪs) *a*, big; large; great; broad; stout; loud; strong; hearty; pregnant; fraught; swollen; coarse; gross; thick; deep; high; heavy; structural (*repairs*). **gros**, *comps*: ~ *bonnet*, bigwig. ~ *boulet*, heavy weight (*throwing*). ~ *galet*, boulder. ~ *morceau*, lump. ~ *mots*, bad language, foul words. ~ *murs*, main walls. ~ *œuvre*, main structure (*of a building*). ~ *plan*, close-up (*Phot.*). ~ *poisson*, heavy fish. **grosse**, *comps*: ~ *caisse*, bass drum, big drum. ~ *pièce*, heavy casting, heavy fish, etc. **gros**, *ad*, a great deal, much. ¶ *m*, bulk, body, mass; main part; large (*coal*). **en** ~, *ad*, roughly, broadly. [commerce de (*ou* en) ~, wholesale [trade].

gros-bec (grobɛk) *m*, hawfinch, grosbeak.

groseille (grozɛːj) *f*, currant (*red, white*). ~ *verte*, ~ *à maquereau*, gooseberry. **groseillier** (zɛje) *m*, currant bush. ~ *à maquereau*, gooseberry bush.

gros-porteur (groportœːr) *m*, jumbo jet.

grosse (groːs) *f*, large hand, text hand (*writing*); engrossment (*law*); gross (*144*). **grossesse** (grosɛs) *f*, pregnancy. **grosseur** (sœːr) *f*, size; swelling. ~ *de* *ceinture, de poitrine,* waist, chest, measurement.

grossier, ère† (grosje, εɪr) *a,* coarse; rough; gross; rude; rank, crass; glaring; unmannerly, boorish; ribald. **grossièreté** (εrte) *f,* coarseness, etc.

grossir (grosiːr) *v.t. & i,* to make bigger, enlarge; magnify; swell, inflate; exaggerate.

grossiste (grosist) *m,* wholesaler.

grosso-modo (grosomɔdo) *ad,* roughly.

grossoyer (grɔswaje) *v.t,* to engross (*law*).

grotesque (grɔtεsk) *a,* grotesque. ¶ *m,* grotesque[ness]; clown; (*f.*) grotesque (*art*).

grotte (grɔt) *f,* grotto.

grouiller (gruje) *v.i,* to swarm, be alive (*with vermin*); seethe; move.

groupe (grup) *m,* group, batch, knot, cluster; company; party; unit (*Mil.*); pool (*typists, etc.*). **groupement** (pmã) *m,* grouping; pool (*Fin.*). **grouper** (pe) *v.t,* to group. **groupiste** (pist) *m,* groupman (*technical*).

grouse (gruːz) *f,* grouse (bird).

gruau (gryo) *m,* meal; groats; gruel. ~ *d'avoine,* oatmeal.

grue (gry) *f,* crane (*bird & hoist*); whore. *faire le pied de* ~, to wait patiently.

gruger (gryʒe) *v.t,* to bleed (*fig.*).

grume (grym) *f,* bark (*left on felled tree*). en ~, in the log.

grumeau (grymo) *m,* clot, curd. *se grumeler* (mle) *v.pr,* to clot, curdle.

gruyère (gryjεɪr) *m,* gruyère [cheese].

guano (gwano) *m,* guano.

gué (ge) *m,* ford. **gréable** (abl) *a,* fordable. **guéer** (gee) *v.t,* to ford (*river*); water (*horse*); rinse (*linen*).

guelte (gεlt) *f,* commission (*on sales*).

guenille (gəniɪj) *f,* rag, tatter.

guenon (gɔnɔ̃) & **guenuche** (nyʃ) *f,* she-monkey; fright (*woman*).

guêpe (gεɪp) *f,* wasp. **guêpier** (gepje) *m,* wasps' nest; hornets' nest (*fig.*); bee eater.

guère (ne . . .) (ne . . . gεɪr) *ad,* hardly, h. any; barely; not much;

not many; but little; only; hardly ever.

guéret (gerε) *m,* plowed land; fallow land; (*poet.*) field.

guéridon (geridɔ̃) *m,* occasional table; coffee t., cocktail t.

guérilla (gerilla) *f,* guerrilla.

guérillero (gerijero) *m,* guerrilla (*Mil.*).

guérir (geriːr) *v.t. & abs. & i. & se* ~, to cure; heal; recover; get better. **guérison** (rizɔ̃) *f,* cure, healing, recovery. **guérisseur, euse** (sœːr, øːz) *n,* healer; quack doctor, medicine man.

guérite (gerit) *f,* sentry box; signal box; lookout; hooded wicker chair.

Guernesey (gεrnəzε) *f,* Guernsey.

guerre (gεɪr) *f,* war, warfare; strife; feud. ~ *d'usure,* war of attrition. ~ *de mouvement,* open warfare. ~ *de plume,* paper warfare. ~ *sociale,* class war. *de bonne* ~ (*fig.*), fair [play]. **guerrier, ère** (gεrje, εɪr) *a,* warlike, martial, war (*att.*). ¶ *n,* warrior. **guerroyer** (rwaje) *v.i,* to [wage] war.

guet (gε) *m,* watch. *faire le* ~, to be on the alert, lookout. **~-apens** (getapã) *m,* ambush; trap; trick.

guêtre (gεɪtr) *f,* gaiter. *~s de ville,* spats.

guetter (gεte) *v.t,* to watch. **guetteur** (tœːr) *m,* lookout [man].

gueule (gœl) *f,* mouth (*animal*); trap (*mouth*). *faire la* ~, sulk. *se casser la* ~, to suffer injury (*physical, social, etc.*). *ta* ~!, shut up! *~-de-loup,* snapdragon; exhaust muffler. **gueuler** (le) *v.i,* to shout.

gueuler (gœle) *v.i,* to yell, bawl, etc.

gueules (gœl) *m,* gules (*Her.*).

gueuse (gøːz) *f,* pig (*iron*); heavy weight.

gueuser (gøze) *v.i,* to beg. **gueuserie** (zri) *f,* beggary. **gueux, euse** (gø, øːz) *n,* beggar; rascal. ¶ *a,* beggarly.

gui (gi) *m,* mistletoe.

guichet (giʃe) *m,* wicket [gate]; shutter; counter (*cashier's*). ~

[*de distribution des billets*], ticket office; ticket window. *à ~ ouvert*, on demand. *~ automatique*, automatic teller machine (*banks*). **guichetier** (ʃtje) *m*, turnkey.

guide (gid) *m*, guide; conductor; guide [book]; (*f.*) [driving] rein. **~âne**, *m*, manual, handbook. **guider** (de) *v.t*, to guide, conduct; steer. **guiderope** (rɔp) *m*, guide rope, trail r. (*Avn.*). **guidon** (dɔ) *m*, pennant; handlebar (*cycle*); foresight (*gun*). *~ de renvoi*, reference [mark].

guigne (giɲ) *f*, black cherry; bad luck.

guigner (giɲe) *v.t. & abs*, to peep at; peep; have an eye to.

guignier (giɲje) *m*, black cherry [tree].

guignol (giɲɔl) *m*, Punch & Judy [show]; puppet.

guignon (giɲɔ̃) *m*, bad luck.

guillaume (gijoːm) *m*, rabbet plane.

guillemeter (gijmete) *v.t*, to put in quotes. **guillemets** (mɛ) *m.pl*, quotation marks, (*in Fr. printed thus* « »; *written thus* « » *or thus* " ").

guilleret, te (gijrɛ, ɛt) *a*, lively, gay; broad (*story*).

guilleri (gijri) *m*, chirp[ing] (*sparrow*).

guillochis (gijɔʃi) *m*, guilloche; engine turning; checkering.

guillotine (gijɔtin) *f*, guillotine. *fenêtre à ~*, sash window. **guillotiner** (ne) *v.t*, to guillotine.

guimauve (gimoːv) *f*, marshmallow (*Bot. & candy*); sentimental person, song, etc.

guimbarde (gɛ̃bard) *f*, covered wagon; rattletrap (*vehicle*); Jew's harp.

guimpe (gɛ̃ːp) *f*, wimple; blouse front.

guindé, e (gɛ̃de) *p.a*, strained, stiff; stilted. **guinder** (de) *v.t*, to hoist; strain, force (*fig.*).

guinée (gine) *f*, guinea (21/-). *la G~*, Guinea (*Geog.*).

guingan (gɛ̃gɑ̃) *m*, gingham (*fabric*).

guingois (gɛ̃gwa) *m*, crookedness, wryness. *de ~*, awry, askew.

guinguette (gɛ̃gɛt) *f*, tavern with gardens & dance hall.

guipure (gipyːr) *f*, guipure.

guirlande (girlɑ̃ːd) *f*, garland, wreath.

guise (giːz) *f*, way. *en ~ de*, by way of.

guitare (gitaːr) *f*, guitar; repetition, (*same*) old story. *~ hawaïenne*, ukulele.

Gulf-Stream (gylfstriːm) *m*, Gulf Stream.

gustation (gystasjɔ̃) *f*, tasting.

gutta-percha (gytapɛrka) *f*, gutta-percha.

guttural, e (gytyral) *a. & f*, guttural.

Guyane (la) (gɥijan) Guiana.

gymnase (ʒimnaːz) *m*, gymnasium. **gymnasiarque** (nazjark) & **gymnaste** (nast) *m*, gymnast. **gymnastique** (tik) *a*, gymnastic. ¶ *f*, gymnastics, drill (*Swedish*); gymnastic (*of mind, etc.*). **gymnique** (nik) *f*, gymnastics.

gymnote (ʒimnɔt) *m*, electric eel.

gynécologie (ʒinekɔlɔʒi) *f*, gynecology.

gypse (ʒips) *m*, gypsum; plaster of Paris. **gypseux, euse** (sø, øːz) *a*, gypseous.

gyroscope (ʒirɔskɔp) *m*, gyroscope.

H

The sign ' *denotes that the* h *is aspirate in the French sense, i.e, no liaison or elision.*

habile† (abil) *a*, able, clever, skillful, cunning, skilled. **habileté** (lte) *f*, ability, skill.

habilité (abilite) *f*, competency (*law*). **habiliter** (te) *v.t*, to enable, capacitate.

habillement (abijmɑ̃) *m*, clothing; dress, raiment, habiliments. **habiller** (je) *v.t*, to dress, clothe; suit; abuse. **habilleuse** (jøːz) *f*, dresser (*Theat.*). **habit** (bi) *m*, mostly *pl*, clothes, suit; garb; habit; (*men's evening*) dress; vestment. *~ d'arlequin*, motley. *~s de tous les jours*, everyday clothes. *~ de soirée*, dress coat; (*pl.*) dress [suit], dress clothes.

habitable (abitabl) *a*, [in]habit-able.

habitacle (abitakl) *m*, abode; binnacle.

habitant, e (abitã, ã:t) *n*, inhabitant, dweller; occupier; resident, occupant, inmate; denizen. **habitat** (ta) *m*, habitat. **habitation** (sjɔ̃) *f*, habitation, dwelling, residence, abode, house. **habiter** (te) *v.t*, to inhabit, occupy, live in, l. at; (*v.i.*) to live, dwell.

habitude (abityd) *f*, habit; use; practice; wont. **habitué, e** (tɥe) *n*, frequenter. **habituel, le†** (tɥɛl) *a*, habitual, usual, wonted. **habituer** (tɥe) *v.t*, to habituate, accustom, inure.

'hâblerie (ablɘri) *f*, brag. **'hâbleur, euse** (blœːr, øːz) *n*, braggart.

'hache (aʃ) *f*, axe. ~ *à main*, hatchet. ~ *coupe-gazon*, edging knife. ~ *d'armes*, battle-axe, pole-axe. **'hacher** (ʃe) *v.t*, to chop [up]; hack; cut to pieces; hash, mince; hatch (*engrave*). **'hachis** (ʃi) *m*, hash, mince. **'hachoir** (ʃwaːr) *m*, mincer; chopping board.

'hagard, e (agaːr, ard) *a*, haggard, wild; drawn (*face*).

'haie (ɛ) *f*, hedge[row]; hurdle; line, row (*people*); beam (*plow*). ~ *vive*, quickset hedge. *faire la* ~, to line up on both sides.

'haillon (ajɔ̃) *m*, rag, tatter.

'haine (ɛn) *f*, hatred; odium; dudgeon. **'haineux, euse** (ɛnø, øːz) *a*, full of hatred. **'haïr** (aiːr) *v.t*, to hate, loathe.

'haire (ɛːr) *f*, hair shirt.

'haïssable (aisabl) *a*, hateful.

Haïti (aiti) *f*, Haiti.

'halage ([h]alaːʒ) *m*, towing.

'halbran (albrã) *m*, young, wild duck.

'hâle (aːl) *m*, [heat of the] sun, sunburn. **'hâlé, e** (ale) *p.a*, sunburned, tanned, weather-beaten.

haleine (alɛn) *f*, breath; wind; training (*fig.*); suspense. *de longue* ~, (*work, etc.*) of time, requiring long persistent effort.

'haler ([h]ale) *v.t*, to tow, haul, pull, heave; set on (*dog*).

'hâler (ale) *v.t*, to burn, tan. *se* ~, to get sunburned.

'haletant, e (altã, ã:t) *a*, panting; breathless. **'haleter** (te) *v.i*, to pant, gasp [for breath].

'hall ([h]ol) *m*, hall; lounge (*hotel*).

'halle (al) *f*, [covered] market; shed (*goods*).

'hallebarde (albard) *f*, halberd (*Hist.*).

'hallier (alje) *m*, covert (*game*).

hallucination (alysinasjɔ̃) *f*, hallucination.

'halo (alo) *m*, halo (*Astr., Anat.*); halation (*Phot.*).

'halot (alo) *m*, rabbit hole.

'halte (alt) *f*, halt, stop. ¶ ([h]alt) & ~*là* *i*, halt! stop!

'halte-garderie (altgardɘri) *m*, babysitting facility in a supermarket.

'haltère (altɛːr) *m*, dumbbell.

'hamac (amak) *m*, hammock.

Hambourg (ãbuːr) *m*, Hamburg.

'hameau (amo) *m*, hamlet.

'hameçon (amsɔ̃) *m*, [fish] hook; bait (*fig.*).

'hampe (ãːp) *f*, staff, shaft, handle; scape (*Bot.*).

'hanche (ãːʃ) *f*, hip; haunch. *les poings sur les* ~*s*, arms akimbo.

'handicap (ãdikap) *m*, handicap (*sport*). **'handicaper** (pe) *v.t*, to handicap. **'handicapeur** (pœːr) *m*, handicapper.

'hangar (ãgaːr) *m*, shed, outhouse. ~ [*d'aviation*], hangar.

'hanneton (antɔ̃) *m*, cockchafer; scatterbrain. *pas piqué des* ~*s*, up to snuff, what it should be.

Hanovre (anɔːvr) *m*, Hanover (*town*). **le H**~, Hanover (*province*).

'hanter (ãte) *v.t*, to frequent, haunt; keep (*bad company*). **'hantise** (tiːz) *f*, haunting; obsession.

'happe (ap) *f*, cramp [iron]; cramp, clamp. **'happer** (pe) *v.t*, to snap up; catch.

'haquet (akɛ) *m*, dray.

'harangue (arãːg) *f*, harangue, speech. **'haranguer** (rãge) *v.t. & i*, to harangue.

'haras (arɑ) *m*, stud farm; stud.

'harasse (aras) *f*, crate.
'harasser (arase) *v.t*, to tire out, weary.
'harceler (arsǝle) *v.t*, to harass, harry, bait; worry, pepper; heckle.
'harde (ard) *f*, herd (*deer*); leash (*set of dogs*). 'harder (de) *v.t*, to leash.
'hardes (ard) *f.pl*, clothes (*worn*).
'hardi†, e (ardi) *a*, bold, daring; hardy; rash; forward, pert. 'hardiesse (djɛs) *f*, boldness, daring, hardihood; forwardness, pertness; liberty.
'hardware (ardwɛːr) *m*, hardware (*computers*).
'harem (arɛm) *m*, harem.
'hareng (arɑ̃) *m*, herring. ~ bouffi, bloater. ~ salé & fumé, kipper. ~ saur (soːr), red herring. 'harengaison (gɛz5) *f*, herring season; h. fishery. 'harengère (ʒɛːr) *f*, fishwife. 'harenguier (gje) *m*, herring boat.
'hargneux, euse (arɲ� ø, øːz) *a*, surly, peevish, ill-tempered, nagging, snappy, fractious; snarling.
'haricot (ariko) *m*, kidney bean, haricot. ~ d'Espagne, scarlet runner, runner bean. ~s secs, beans (*dried*). ~s verts, stringbeans. la fin des ~s, the end of everything.
'haridelle (aridɛl) *f*, jade (*horse*).
harmonica (armɔnika) *m*, harmonica; musical glasses. ~ à bouche, mouth organ. harmonie (ni) *f*, harmony; (*in*) keeping; band. harmonieux, euse† (njø, øːz) *a*, harmonious, tuneful. harmonique† (nik) *a. & m*, harmonic. harmoniser (ze) *v.t*, to harmonize; attune. s'~, to harmonize, tone. harmonium (njɔm) *m*, harmonium.
'harnachement (arnaʃmɑ̃) *m*, harnessing; harness; trappings, rig. 'harnacher (ʃe) *v.t*, to harness; rig out. 'harnais (nɛ) *m*, harness; gear, tackle. blanchir sous le harnois (nwa), to grow old in the service.
'haro (aro) *m*, hue & cry; outcry.
harpagon (arpag5) *m*, miser, skinflint.

'harpe (arp) *f*, harp; toothing (*Build.*).
'harpie (arpi) *f*, harpy; hellcat.
'harpiste (arpist) *n*, harpist.
'harpon (arp5) *m*, harpoon. 'harponner (pone) *v.t*, to harpoon.
'hart (aːr) *f*, withe, withy; halter; hanging.
'hasard (azaːr) *m*, chance, luck, risk, venture; hazard. au ~, at random. 'hasarder (zarde) *v.t*, to hazard, risk, venture. 'hasardeux, euse† (dø, øːz) *a*, venturesome; hazardous, risky.
'hase ([h]aːz) *f*, doe hare.
'hâte (ɑːt) *f*, haste, hurry. avoir ~, to be in a hurry. 'hâter (ɑte) *v.t*, to hasten, hurry; quicken; expedite; force (*Hort.*). se ~, to make haste, hurry. 'hâtif, ive† (tif, iːv) *a*, hasty, hurried; cursory; forward, early (*fruit, etc.*). 'hâtiveau (vo) *m*, early pear, apple, pea, etc.
'hauban (obɑ̃) *m*, shroud (*Naut.*) guy, stay.
'hausse (oːs) *f*, raise; flashboard; wedge (*to pack up to level*); elevator (*in shoe*); backsight (*gun*) leaf (*rifle*). à la ~, on the rise 'haussement d'épaules (osmɑ̃) *m*, shrug[ging] [of the shoulders]. 'hausser (se) *v.t*, to raise, lift shrug; (*v.i.*) to raise. 'haussier (sje) *m*, bull (*Stk Ex.*).
'haussière (osjɛːr) *f*, hawser.
'haut, e (o, oːt) *a*, high; tall; lofty; upper; top; up; high-class; loud; deep; remote (*antiquity*); big. le haut commerce, [the] big traders, the merchant class. haut enseignement, higher education. haut fait [d'armes], feat of arms. de hauts faits, doughty deeds. haut fourneau, blast furnace. haute mer, high seas, open sea. haute taille, tallness (*pers.*). 'haut, *ad*, high; h. up; loudly, aloud. ~ les mains! hands up! ¶ *m*, top, head; higher notes (*Mus.*); perch (*fig.*). ~ de casse, upper case (*Typ.*). ~ du pavé, wall (*side of pavement*). de ~, high, in height. des ~s & des bas or du ~ & du bas, ups & downs. en ~, [up] above; aloft; upstairs.

'hautain, e (otɛ̃, ɛn) *a*, haughty, lordly; lofty, proud.

'hautbois (obwa) *m*, oboe, hautboy. **'hautboïste** (bɔist) *m*, oboist.

'hautement (otmɑ̃) *ad*, boldly, openly. **'hauteur** (tœːr) *f*, height; elevation; tallness (*steeple, etc.*); loftiness; altitude; level; hill; depth; haughtiness. *être à la ~ de*, to be equal to. *~ de marche*, rise (*of step*). *~ [musicale]*, pitch (*of a sound*).

'haut-fond (ofɔ̃) *m*, shoal.

'haut-le-cœur (olkœːr) *m*, heave, retch, nausea.

'haut-le-corps (olkɔːr) *m*, start, jump.

'haut-parleur (oparlœːr) *m*, loudspeaker.

'havane (avan) *m*, Havana (*cigar*). ¶ *a*, brown, tan (*boots*). *la H~*, Havana (*Geog.*).

'hâve (ɑːv) *a*, wan, emaciated.

'havre (ɑːvr) *m*, haven. *le H~*, Havre (*Geog.*).

'havresac (avrəsak) *m*, knapsack.

Hawaï (avai) *m*, Hawaii. **hawaïen, ne** (iɛ̃, ɛn) *a. & H~*, *n*, Hawaiian.

'Haye (la) (ɛ), the Hague.

'hé (e) *i*, hi! hoy! hey! hallo[a]! *~ là-bas!* hallo[a] there!

hebdomadaire (ɛbdɔmadɛːr) *a*, weekly.

héberger (ebɛrʒe) *v.t*, to harbor; lodge, entertain, put up.

hébéter (ebete) *v.t*, to dull; stupefy, daze.

hébraïque (ebraik) *a*, Hebraic, Hebrew. **l'hébreu** (brø) *m*, Hebrew (*language*); Greek (*jargon*).

hécatombe (ekatɔ̃b) *f*, hecatomb.

hectare (ɛktaːr) *m*, hectare = 100 ares *or* 2.4711 acres.

hectique (ɛktik) *a*, hectic (*fever*).

hectogramme (ɛktɔgram) *m*, hectogram = 100 grams *or* 3.527 ozs avoirdupois. **hectolitre** (litr) *m*, hectoliter = 100 liters *or* 2.75 imperial bushels *or* 22.01 imperial gallons. **hectomètre** (mɛtr) *m*, hectometer = 100 meters *or* 109.36 yards.

hégémonie (eʒemɔni) *f*, hegemony.

'hein ([h]ɛ̃) *i*, eyl what [do you say]?

hélas (elɑːs) *i*, alas!

'héler ([h]ele) *v.t*, to hail, call; speak (*ship*).

hélianthe (eljɑ̃ːt) *m*, helianthus.

hélice (elis) *f*, helix, spiral; screw, propeller; spinner (*Fish.*). **en ~ & hélicoïdal, e** (kɔidal) *a*, spiral, helical, twist (*drill*). **hélicoptère** (kɔptɛːr) *m*, helicopter.

héligare (eliga:r) *f*, helicopter terminal. **héliport** (elipɔ:r) *m*, heliport.

héliotrope (eljɔtrɔp) *m*, heliotrope; cherry-pie; bloodstone.

hélium (eljɔm) *m*, helium.

hélix (eliks) *m*, helix (*ear*).

hellénisme (ɛlenism) *m*, Hellenism.

hémisphère (emisfɛːr) *m*, hemisphere.

hémorragie (emɔraʒi) *f*, hemorrhage. **hémorroïdes** (rɔid) *f.pl*, hemorrhoids, piles.

'henné (ɛnne) *m*, henna.

'hennir ([h]ɛniːr) *v.i*, to neigh, whinny.

'hep (hɛp) *i*, fore! (*golf*).

héraldique (eraldik) *a*, heraldic. ¶ *f*, heraldry. **'héraut** (ro) *m*, herald (*Hist.*).

herbacé, e (ɛrbase) *a*, herbaceous. **herbage** (baːʒ) *m*, grass, pasture (*uncut*); herbage; green vegetables, green stuff, greens. **herbe** (ɛrb) *f*, herb; plant; grass; weed; wort (*Bot.*); marijuana. *l'~*, grass court (*Ten.*). *fines ~s*, herbs (*seasoning*). *l'~ longue*, the rough (*golf*). *~ menue*, fine grass. *~s menues*, fine herbs (*fine in texture, as savory herbs*). *en ~*, green; unripe; budding (*fig.*); in embryo (*fig.*). **herbette** (bɛt) (*poet.*) *f*, [green]sward. **herbeux, euse** (bø, ø:z) *a*, grassy. **herbier** (bje) *m*, herbal, herbarium. **herbivore** (bivɔːr) *a. & m*, herbivorous (*animal*). **herboriser** (bɔrize) *v.i*, to botanize, herborize. **herboriste** (rist) *n*, herbalist. **herbu, e** (by) *a*, grassy.

hercule (ɛrkyl) *m*, Hercules,

strong man. **herculéen, ne** (leẽ, ɛn) *a*, Herculean.

'hère (ɛːr) *m*, wretch, wight; young stag.

héréditaire† (ereditɛːr) *a*, hereditary. **hérédité** (te) *f*, heirship, inheritance (*right*); heredity.

hérésie (erezi) *f*, heresy. **hérétique** (tik) *a*, heretical. ¶ *n*, heretic.

'hérissé, e (erise) *p.a*, bristly; prickly; on end (*hair*); bristling, beset. **'hérisser** (se) *v.i. &* se —, to bristle [up], stand on end; (*v.t.*) to bristle, erect; stud. **'hérisson** (s5) *m*, hedgehog; (*sea*) urchin; clod crusher; sprocket wheel.

héritage (erita:ʒ) *m*, inheritance; heritage. **hériter** (te) *v.i. & t*, to inherit. **héritier, ère** (tje, ɛ:r) *n*, heir, heiress.

hermaphrodite (ɛrmafrɔdit) *m*, hermaphrodite.

hermétique† (ɛrmetik) *a*, hermetic.

hermine (ɛrmin) *f*, ermine, stoat. **herminette** (ɛrminɛt) *f*, adze.

'hernie (ɛrni) *f*, hernia, rupture.

héroï-comique (erɔikɔmik) *a*, heroicomic, mock-heroic. **héroïne** (in) *f*, heroine. **héroïque†** (ik) *a*, heroic. **héroïsme** (ism) *m*, heroism.

'héron (er5) *m*, heron. **'héronnière** (rɔnjɛːr) *f*, heronry.

'héros (ero) *m*, hero.

herpès (ɛrpɛs) *m*, herpes.

'herse (ɛrs) *f*, harrow; portcullis. **'herser** (se) *v.t*, to harrow

hésitation (ezitasj5) *f*, hesitation. **hésiter** (te) *v.i*, to hesitate, waver; falter.

hétaïre (etaiːr) *f*, hetaera, courtesan.

hétéroclite (eterɔklit) *a*, freak[ish], odd, queer; heteroclite. **hétérodoxe** (dɔks) *a*, heterodox, unorthodox. **hétérodoxie** (ksi) *f*, heterodoxy. **hétérogène** (ʒɛn) *a*, heterogeneous; mixed.

'hêtre (ɛːtr) *m*, beech [tree, wood]. — *rouge*, copper beech.

heure (œːr) *f. oft. pl*, hour; time; moment; present; o'clock. *l'* — *du coucher*, bedtime. — *du lieu*, local

time. *l'* — *du repas*, meal t. —*s bureau*, —*s d'ouverture*, business hours. —*s de pointe*, —*s d'affluence*, peak h—s, rush h—s. —*s supplémentaires*, overtime. *à la bonne* —, well & good, all right. *de bonne* —, *ad*, early, betimes, in good time. *c'est l'*—, the time has come, is up. *à tout à l'*—, see you soon. *l'* — *H*, zero hour.

heureux, euse† (œrø, ø:z) *a*, happy; pleased; fortunate; prosperous; blissful; blessed; successful; lucky; safe (*arrival*).

'heurt (œːr) *m*, shock, knock, bump. **'heurté, e** (œrte) *a*, contrasty. **'heurter** (te) *v.t. & i*, to run (against); knock; shock. **'heurtoir** (twaːr) *m*, stop blocks (*Rly.*); buffer.

hexagone (ɛgzagɔn) *m*, hexagon. *le H*—, continental France. ¶ *a*, hexagonal. **hexamètre** (mɛtr) *m*, hexameter.

hiatus (jaty:s) *m*, hiatus (*Gram.*).

hiberner (ibɛrne) *v.t*, to hibernate.

'hibou (ibu) *m*, owl; recluse; unsociable person.

'hic (ik) *m*, rub (*difficulty*).

'hideur (idœːr) *f*, hideousness. **'hideux, euse†** (dø, ø:z) *a*, hideous.

'hie (i) *f*, beetle, rammer; pile driver.

hiémal, e (jemal) *a*, winter (*att.*).

hier (iɛːr) *ad*, yesterday. — *[au] soir*, last night.

'hiérarchie (jerarʃi) *f*, hierarchy.

hiéroglyphe (jerɔglif) *m*, hieroglyph.

hilare (ilaːr) *a*, hilarious, laughing. **hilarité** (larite) *f*, hilarity, merriment, laughter.

hindou, e (ẽdu) *a. &* H—, *n*, Hindu, -doo. **l'hindoustani** (stani) *m*, Hindustani.

hippique (ippik) *a*, horse (*show, etc.*), equine. **hippocampe** (ippɔkã:p) *m*, hippocampus, sea horse. **hippodrome** (drɔ:m) *m*, hippodrome, circus. **hippopotame** (pɔtam) *m*, hippopotamus.

hirondelle (ir5dɛl) *f*, swallow. — *de fenêtre*, [house] martin. — *de rivage*, sand martin.

hirsute (irsyt) a, hirsute, shaggy; rough; boorish.

hisser ([h]ise) v.t, to hoist; raise.

histoire (istwa:r) f, history; story, tale, yarn; fib; (pl.) fuss. le plus beau de l'~, the best of the story. faire des ~s, to make a fuss. s'attirer des ~s, to get into trouble. **historié**, e (tɔrje) p.a, illuminated, ornamental. **historien** (rjɛ̃) m, historian. **historier** (rje) v.t, to ornament. **historiette** (rjɛt) f, anecdote. **historique**† (rik) a, historical, historic. ¶ m, history, account. ~ du régiment, regimental records.

histrion (istriɔ̃) m, histrion.

hiver (ivɛ:r) m, winter. **hivernage** (vernaʒ) m, wintering. **hivernal, e** (nal) a, winter (att.), wintry. **hiverner** (ne) v.i. & t, to winter.

ho (ho) i, hil ~, du navire! ship ahoy!

hobereau (ɔbro) m, hobby (bird); petty country gentleman.

hoche (ɔʃ) f, notch, nick (on tally).

hochement (ɔʃmɑ̃) m, shake; toss (head). **hochepot** (ʃpo) m, hodgepodge. **hochequeue** (kø) m, wagtail. **hocher** (ʃe) v.t. & i, to shake; toss; notch, nick. **hochet** (ʃe) m, rattle, coral; bauble, plaything.

hockey (ɔkɛ) m, hockey. ~ sur glace, ice h.

hoir (wa:r) m, heir. **hoirie** (wari) f, inheritance.

holà ([h]ɔla) i, hallo[a]! Hallo! enough!

hollandais, e (ɔlɑ̃dɛ, ɛ:z) a, Dutch. **H~,** n, Dutchman, -woman. le h~, Dutch (language). **la Hollande** (lɑ̃:d), Holland.

holocauste (ɔlɔko:st) m, holocaust, burnt offering; sacrifice.

hom ([h]ɔm) i, hum! humph!

homard (ɔma:r) m, lobster.

homélie (ɔmeli) f, homily.

homéopathe (ɔmeɔpat) m, homoeopath[ist]. **homéopathie** (ti) f, homoeopathy. **homéopathique** (tik) a, homoeopathic.

homérique (ɔmerik) a, Homeric.

homicide (ɔmisid) a, homicidal. ¶ n, homicide (pers.); (m.) homicide (act). ~ excusable, justifiable h. ~ involontaire, manslaughter. ~ volontaire, willful murder.

hommage (ɔmaʒ) m, homage; (pl.) respects, compliments; token, tribute.

hommasse (ɔmas) a, mannish, masculine (woman). **homme** (ɔm) m, man; (pl.) mankind. ~ à bonnes fortunes, lady-killer. ~ à femmes, ~ galant, ladies' (or lady's) man. ~ à projets, schemer. ~ à tout faire, man of all work, jack of all trades, handyman. ~ calé, man of substance; well-informed man. ~ -caoutchouc, ~-serpent, contortionist. ~ d'affaires, business man; business agent; steward. ~ d'État, statesman. ~ d'exécution, man of deeds. ~ dans les affaires, business man. ~ de barre, helmsman, steersman. ~ de couleur, mulatto. ~ de foyer, family man. l'~ de la rue, the man in the street. ~ de lettres, man of letters, literary m. ~ de métier, craftsman. ~ de mer, seaman, seafaring man. ~ de paille, strawman. ~ de peine, [common] laborer. ~ de science, scientist. ~ l' ~ intérieur, the inner man. ~-orchestre, one-man band. ~-sandwich, sandwich man. ~ sans aveu, vagrant, outcast.

homogène (ɔmɔʒɛ:n) a, homogeneous.

homologuer (ɔmɔlɔge) v.t, to ratify; prove (will); accept (a sport record).

homonyme (ɔmɔnim) m, homonym, namesake.

hongre (ɔ̃:gr) a.m, gelded. ¶ m, gelding. **hongrer** (ɔ̃gre) v.t, to geld.

Hongrie (la) (ɔ̃gri) Hungary. **hongrois, e** (grwa, a:z) a. & **H~,** n, Hungarian. le hongrois, Hungarian (language).

honnête† (ɔnɛ:t) a, honest, honorable, upright; respectable, straight, decent; well-bred, civil, courteous; fair, reasonable. **honnêteté** (nɛtte) f, honesty; decen-

cy, propriety; courtesy; fairness,
reasonableness; recompense.

honneur (ɔnœːr) *m*, honor; mettle; justice (*as to a meal*); credit;
pleasure (*e.g., of seeing you*).
jouer pour l'~, to play for love.
faire ~ à (*Com.*), to honor,
meet.

'honnir (ɔniːr) *v.t*, to disgrace.

honorable† (ɔnɔrabl) *a*, honorable; reputable; respectable.
honoraire (rɛːr) *a*, honorary. **~s,**
m.pl, fee[s], honorarium. **honorariat** (rarja) *m*, honorary
membership. **honorer** (re) *v.t*,
to honor; respect; favor; grace;
dignify; do credit to. **honorifique** (rifik), *a*, honorary.

'honte (ɔ̃ːt) *f.*, shame, disgrace;
reproach, scandal. *avoir ~*, to be
ashamed. *faire ~ à*, to put to
shame, make ashamed. **'honteux,
euse** (ɔ̃tø, øːz) *a*, ashamed; bashful, shamefaced; sheepish;
shameful, disgraceful, inglorious;
uncomplaining (*poor*).

hôpital (ɔpital) *m*, hospital. *~ de
contagieux*, isolation h.

'hoquet (ɔkɛ) *m*, hiccup; gasp.

horaire (ɔrɛːr) *m*, timetable; person paid by the hour.

'horde (ɔrd) *f*, horde.

'horion (ɔrjɔ̃) *m*, thump, whack.

horizon (ɔrizɔ̃) *m*, horizon. **horizontal, e** (tal) *a*, horizontal.
horizontalement (lmɑ̃) *ad*, horizontally; across (*crossword
clues*).

horloge (ɔrlɔ:ʒ) *f*, clock (*big*). *~
à carillon*, chiming c., musical c.
~ à sonnerie, striking c. *~ de la
mort*, deathwatch [beetle]. *~ de
parquet*, grandfather's clock.
horloger (lɔʒe) *m*, clockmaker,
watchmaker. **horlogerie** (ʒri) *f*,
horology; clock & watch making;
clocks & watches.

hormis (ɔrmi) *pr*, except, but,
save.

horoscope (ɔrɔskɔp) *m*, horoscope, nativity; fortune.

horreur (ɔrrœːr) *f*, horror, fright;
object. **horrible†** (ɔrribl) *a*, horrible, frightful; horrid. **horripiler**
(ɔrripile) *v.t*, to exasperate.

horrifier (ɔrrifje) *v.t*, to horrify.

'hors (ɔːr) & *~ de*, *pr*, out; out
of; without; outside; over; be-

yond; beside; except; save. *~
bord*, *a*. & *ad*, outboard. *~ concours*, not competing [for prize].
~ courant, dead (*wire*). *~
-d'œuvre*, *m*, addition (*to a building*); hors-d'œuvre (*Cook.*); extra, digression. *hors d'œuvre*,
att, (*part*) added (*to a building*);
outside (*Meas.*); unmounted
(*stone*); extra, digressive. *~ de
combat*, out of action; disabled.
~ des limites, out of bounds. *~
ligne*, out of the common, exceptional. *~ texte*, outside text
(*plate, illustration, map, etc.*).
~-texte, *m*, plate [outside text].
~ tout, over all (*Meas.*).

hortensia (ɔrtɑ̃sja) *m*, hydrangea.

horticole (ɔrtikɔl) *a*, horticultural. **horticulteur** (kyltœːr) *m*,
horticulturist. **horticulture** (tyːr)
f, horticulture, gardening.

hosanna (ɔzanna) *m*, hosanna;
hurrah.

hospice (ɔspis) *m*, asylum, home;
almshouse; hostel; hospice. **hospitalier, ère** (talje, ɛːr) *a*, hospitable; hospital (*att.*). ¶ *f*, sister
of mercy, s. of charity. **hospitalisé, a** (lize) *n*, inmate; inpatient. **hospitalité** (te) *f*, hospitality.

hostie (ɔsti) *f*, host (*Eccl.*).

hostile† (ɔstil) *a*, hostile, unfriendly, inimical. **hostilité** (lite)
f, hostility.

hôte, esse (oːt, otɛs) *n*, host,
hostess; guest, visitor; inmate;
denizen.

hôtel [*pour voyageurs*] (otɛl) *m*,
hotel. *~* [*particulier*], mansion;
town house. *~ de la Monnaie*,
~ des Monnaies, mint. *~ de
ville*, town hall. *~ des postes*,
general post office. *~ des ventes*,
auction rooms. *~-Dieu*, hospital.
~ garni, rooming house. *~ meublé*, furnished apartments. **hôtelier, ère** (tǝlje, ɛːr) *n*, hotelkeeper. **hôtellerie** (tɛlri) *f*, fashionable restaurant; (*archaic*)
hostelry.

hotte (ɔt) *f*, basket, hod.

'houblon (ublɔ̃) *m*, hop [plant];
hops. **'houblonner** (blɔne) *v.t*,
to hop (*beer*). **'houblonnière**
(njɛːr) *f*, hop field.

'houe (u) *f*, hoe. 'houer (ue) *v.t*, to hoe.

'houille (u:j) *f*, coal. ~ *blanche*, water power. 'houiller, ère (uje, ɛ:r) *a*, coal (*att.*), carboniferous. ¶ *f*, coal mine. 'houilleur (jœ:r) *m*, coal miner.

'houle (ul) *f*, swell, surge. ~ *de fond*, ground swell. ~ *longue*, roller.

'houlette (ulɛt) *f*, shepherd's crook; trowel (*Hort.*).

'houleux, euse (ulø, ø:z) *a*, swelling (*sea*); surging tumultuous.

'houper (upe) *v.t*, to halloo, hollo (*Hunt.*).

'houppe (up) & 'houpette (pɛt) *f*, tuft, tassel; (*powder*) puff.

'hourder (urde) *v.t*, to roughcast; pug.

'hourra (hurra) *m*, hurrah, hurray.

'hourvari (urvari) *m*, hullabaloo.

'houspiller (uspije) *v.t*, to maul; mob; taunt, abuse.

'housse (us) *f*, horse cloth; hammer cloth; dust sheet; furniture cover; dust cover (*computers*). 'housser (se) *v.t*, to dust; put loose cover(s) on (*furniture*). 'houssine (sin) *f*, switch. 'houssiner (ne) *v.t*, to switch. 'houssoir (swa:r) *m*, whisk, flick; feather duster.

'houx (u) *m*, holly.

'hoyau (wajo) *m*, mattock.

'hublot (yblo) *m*, scuttle, port [hole].

'huche (yʃ) *f*, trough, bin.

'hue (hy) *i*, gee up! 'huée (ɥe) *f*, whoop; hoot[ing]. 'huer (ɥe) *v.t*, to whoop, halloo; hoot, boo, barrack.

'huette (ɥɛt) *f*, wood owl, tawny owl.

'huguenote (ygnɔt) *f*, pipkin, casserole.

huilage (ɥila:ʒ) *m*, oiling. huile (ɥil) *f*, oil. ~ *à mécanisme*, machine o. ~ *d'éclairage*, lamp o. ~ *de coude*, elbow grease (*fig.*). ~ *de foie de morue*, cod-liver oil. ~ *de table*, ~ *comestible*, salad o. *c'est une* ~, he's a big shot. huiler (le) *v.t*, to oil. huilerie (lri)

f, oil mill; oil shop. huileux, euse (lø, ø:z) *a*, oily. huilier (lje) *m*, cruet; oil can.

huis clos (à) (ɥi), in camera; behind closed doors. huissier (sje) *m*, usher; bailiff.

'huit (ɥit; *before a consonant*, ɥi) *a. & m*, eight; eighth. ~ [*jours*] ou 'huitaine [de jours] (tɛn) *f*, week (e.g, *Friday to Friday*). 'huitième† (tjɛm) *a. & n*, eighth.

huître (ɥi:tr) *f*, oyster; booby, fool. ~*s du pays*, natives. ~ *perlière* (pɛrlje:r), pearl oyster.

'hulotte (ylɔt) *f*, wood owl, tawny owl.

humain, e† (ymɛ̃, ɛn) *a*, human; humane. humaniser (manize) *v.t*, to humanize. humanitaire (tɛ:r) *a. & m*, humanitarian. humanité (te) *f*, humanity (all senses).

humble† (œ̃:bl) *a*, humble, lowly.

humecter (ymɛkte) *v.t*, to moisten, damp, wet.

'humer (yme) *v.t*, to suck in; sip; inhale.

humérus (ymery:s) *m*, humerus.

humeur (ymœ:r) *f*, humor, mood; temper; ill-humor, [ill-] temper, petulance.

humide† (ymid) *a*, damp, moist, humid; watery, wet. humidifier (difje) *v.t*, to damp. humidité (te) *f*, damp[ness].

humilier (ymilje) *v.t*, to humiliate, humble. humilité (lite) *f*, humility, lowliness.

humoriste (ymɔrist) *m*, humorist. ¶ ~ & humoristique (tik) *a*, humorous. humour (mu:r) *m*, humor.

humus (ymy:s) *m*, humus, mold.

'hune (yn) *f*, top (*Naut.*). ~ *de vigie*, crow's nest. 'hunier (nje) *m*, topsail.

'huppe (yp) *f*, hoopoe; crest. 'huppé, e (pe) *a*, crested, tufted; smart (*moving in high society*); clever.

'hure (y:r) *f*, head (*boar, etc.*); jowl (*fish*); brawn.

'hurler (yrle) *v.i*, to howl, yell.

hurluberlu (yrlybɛrly) *m*, harum-scarum.

'hutte (yt) *f*, hut, shanty.

hyacinthe (jasɛ̃:t) *f*, hyacinth, jacinth.

hybride (ibrid) *a. & m*, hybrid.

hydrate (idrat) *m*, hydrate.

hydraulique (idrolik) *a*, hydraulic, water (*att.*). ¶ *f*, hydraulics.

hydravion (idravjɔ̃) *m*, seaplane. ~ *à coque*, flying boat.

hydre (i:dr) *f*, hydra.

hydrobase (idrɔba:z) *f*, seaplane base.

hydrocarbure (idrɔkarby:r) *m*, hydrocarbon. **hydrogène** (ʒɛn) *m. & att*, hydrogen. **hydrophile** (fil) *a*, absorbent (*cotton wool*). **hydrophobie** (fɔbi) *f*, hydrophobia, rabies. **hydropique** (pik) *a*, dropsical. **hydropisie** (pizi) *f*, dropsy. **hydroscope** (skɔp) *m*, water-diviner, dowser. **hydroscopie** (pi) *f*, water-divining, dowsing. **hydrothérapie** (terapi) *f*, hydropathy. **hydrothérapique** (pik) *a*, hydropathic.

hydroglisseur (idrɔglisœ:r) *m*, hydroglider; hydroplane.

hydroptère (idrɔptɛ:r) *m*, hydrofoil.

hyène (jɛn) *f*, hyena.

hygiène (iʒjɛn) *f*, hygiene, hygienics, health, sanitation. **hygiénique†** (ʒjenik) *a*, hygienic, healthy, sanitary; toilet (*paper*).

hymen (imɛn) *ou* **hyménée** (mene) *m*, hymen; wedlock. **hyménoptères** (nɔptɛ:r) *m.pl*, hymenoptera.

hymne (imn) *m*, hymn, song, anthem (*national*). ¶ *f*, hymn (*in church*).

hyperbole (ipɛrbɔl) *f*, hyperbole; hyperbola.

hypermarché (ipɛrmarʃe) *m*, outsized supermarket (*generally in suburbs of big city*).

hypnotiser (ipnɔtize) *v.t*, to hypnotize. **hypnotisme** (tism) *m*, hypnotism.

hypocondriaque (ipɔkɔ̃driak) *a. & n*, hypochondriac. **hypocrisie** (krizi) *f*, hypocrisy, cant. **hypocrite†** (krit) *a*, hypocritical. ¶ *n*, hypocrite. **hypodermique** (dɛrmik) *a*, hypodermic. **hypothèque** (tɛk) *f*, mortgage. **hypothéquer** (ke) *v.t*, to mortgage. **hypothèse** (tɛ:z) *f*, hypothesis. **hypothétique†** (tetik) *a*, hypothetic(al).

hystérie (isteri) *f*, hysteria. **hystérique** (rik) *a*, hysteric(al).

I

ïambe (jɑ̃:b) *m. & **iambique** (jɑ̃bik) *a*, iambic.

ibis (ibis) *m*, ibis.

iceberg (isbɛrg) *m*, iceberg.

ichtyologie (iktjɔlɔʒi) *f*, ichthyology.

ici (isi) *ad*, here; this; now. ~*-bas*, here below. ~ *X.*, X. speaking (*Teleph.*). *d'*~ *là*, between now & then.

icône (iko:n) *f*, icon. **iconoclaste** (kɔnɔklast) *m*, iconoclast.

ictère (iktɛ:r) *m*, jaundice.

idéal, e† (ideal) *a. & m*, ideal. **idéaliste** (list) *n*, idealist. **idée** (de) *f*, idea, notion; thought; mind; impression; view. ~ *directrice*, guiding principle.

idem (idɛm) *ad*, idem, ditto.

identifier (idɑ̃tifje) *v.t*, to identify. **identique†** (tik) *a*, identical. **identité** (te) *f*, identity, sameness.

idiome (idjo:m) *m*, language, dialect.

idiosyncrasie (idjɔsɛ̃krazi) *f*, idiosyncrasy.

idiot, e (idjo, ɔt) *a*, idiotic. ¶ *n*, idiot; imbecile, natural. **idiotie** (ɔsi) *f*, idiocy. **idiotisme** (idjɔtism) *m*, idiom, locution.

idolâtre (idɔlɑ:tr) *a*, idolatrous. ¶ *n*, idolater, tress. **idolâtrer** (latre) *v.t*, to idolize. **idolâtrie** (tri) *f*, idolatry. **idolâtrique** (trik) *a*, idolatrous. **idole** (dɔl) *f*, idol.

idylle (idil) *f*, idyll; romance (*love*).

if (if) *m*, yew [tree].

igname (iɲam) *f*, yam.

ignare (iɲa:r) *a*, ignorant. ¶ *n*, ignoramus.

igné, e (igne) *a*, igneous. **ignifuge** (niɸy:ʒ) *a*, fireproof. **ignifuger** (fyʒe) *v.t*, to fireproof. **ignition** (nisjɔ̃) *f*, ignition.

ignoble† (iɲɔbl) *a*, ignoble, base; filthy.

ignominie (iɲɔmini) *f*, ignominy. **ignominieux, euse†** (njø, ø:z) *a*, ignominious, inglorious.

ignorance (iɲɔrɑ̃ːs) *f*, ignorance; blunder. **ignorant, e** (rɑ̃, ɑ̃ːt) *a*, ignorant; unacquainted. ¶ *n*, ignoramus, dunce. **ignoré, e** (re) *p.a*, unknown. **ignorer** (re) *v.t. & abs*, to be ignorant (*or* unaware) of, not to know.

iguane (igwan) *m*, iguana.

il (il) *pn*, he; it; she (*of ship*); there; (*pl.*) they.

île (iːl) *f*, island, isle. *les îles Britanniques, les îles du Vent, etc.* See under *britannique, vent, etc.*

illégal, e† (illegal) *a*, illegal, unlawful. **illégitime†** (ʒitim) *a*, illegitimate; unlawful; spurious. **illégitimité** (mite) *f*, illegitimacy. **illettré, e** (illɛtre) *a. & n*, illiterate.

illicite† (illisit) *a*, illicit, unlawful.

illico (illiko) *ad*, directly, at once.

illimité, e (illimite) *a*, unlimited, unbounded, boundless; indefinite (*leave*).

illisible† (illizibl) *a*, illegible; unreadable.

illogique (illɔʒik) *a*, illogical. **illogisme** (ʒism) *m*, illogicality.

illumination (illyminasjɔ̃) *f*, illumination; inspiration. ~ *par projection*, floodlighting. **illuminé** (ne) *m*, visionary, madman. **illuminer** (ne) *v.t*, to illuminate; light up.

illusion (illyzjɔ̃) *f*, illusion; phantasm; delusion. ~ *d'optique*, optical illusion. **illusionner** (illyzjɔne) *v.t*, to fool, trick, deceive. **illusoire** (zwaːr) *a*, illusory, illusive.

illustration (illystrasjɔ̃) *f*, luster (*fig.*); celebrity (*pers.*); illustration. **illustre** (tr) *a*, illustrious. **illustrer** (tre) *v.t*, to make illustrious; illustrate. **illustrissime** (trisim) *a*, most illustrious.

îlot (ilo) *m*, islet; island, block (*houses*).

îlote (ilɔt) *m*, helot. **îlotisme** (tism) *m*, helotry.

image (imaːʒ) *f*, image; reflection; picture; likeness; idea; (*pl.*) imagery. ~ *d'écran*, soft copy (*computers*). ~*s-par-seconde*, frames

per second (*cinema*). **imagé, e** (maʒe) *p.a*, picturesque, ornate. **imaginaire** (ʒinɛːr) *a*, imaginary, fancied, fictive. **imagination** (nasjɔ̃) *f*, imagination, fancy. **imaginer** (ne) *v.t*, to imagine; fancy; devise, invent. s'~, to imagine, think.

imbécile† (ɛbesil) *a*, silly, stupid, imbecile, fatuous. ¶ *n*, fool. **imbécillité** (silite) *f*, stupidity, fatuity.

imberbe (ɛbɛrb) *a*, beardless; raw, callow.

imbiber (ɛbibe) *v.t*, to soak, imbue, wet. s'~ (de), to imbibe, sink in.

imbriquer (ɛbrike) *v.t*, to imbricate, overlap; interleave (*computers*).

imbrisable (ɛbrizabl) *a*, unbreakable.

imbroglio (ɛbrɔljo) *m*, imbroglio.

imbu, e (ɛby) *a*, imbued.

imbuvable (ɛbyvabl) *a*, undrinkable.

imitateur, trice (imitatœːr, tris) *n*, imitator, mimic. ¶ *a*, imitative, mimic. **imitation** (sjɔ̃) *f*, imitation. **imiter** (te) *v.t*, to imitate; mimic; resemble, be like.

immaculé, e (immakyle) *a*, immaculate.

immanent, e (immanɑ̃, ɑ̃ːt) *a*, immanent.

immangeable (imm- *ou* ɛmɑ̃ʒabl) *a*, uneatable.

immanquable† (imm- *ou* ɛmɑ̃kabl) *a*, sure [to happen]; unmistakable.

immatériel, le† (immaterjɛl) *a*, immaterial.

immatriculer (immatrikyle) *v.t*, to register, enter, enroll.

immédiat, e† (immedja, at) *a*, immediate; proximate; direct.

immémorial, e (immemɔrjal) *a*, immemorial.

immense (immɑ̃ːs) *a*, immense, huge, vast; boundless. **immensément** (mɑ̃semɑ̃) *ad*, immensely. **immensité** (site) *f*, immensity; vastness; infinitude. **immensurable** (syrabl) *a*, immeasurable.

immerger (immɛrʒe) *v.t*, to immerse, plunge, dip.

immérité, e (immerite) *a*, unmerited, undeserved, unearned.

immersion (immɛrsjɔ̃) *f*, immersion.

immeuble (immœbl) *m*. *oft. pl*, real estate, realty; premises.

immigration (immigrasjɔ̃) *f*, immigration.

imminence (imminã:s) *f*, imminence. **imminent, e** (nã, ã:t) *a*, imminent, impending.

immiscer (s') (immise) *v.pr*, to meddle, interfere. **immixtion** (mikstjɔ̃) *f*, interference.

immobile (immɔbil) *a*, immobile, set, unmovable, motionless, still; unmoved. **immobilier, ère** (lje, ɛ:r) *a*, real (*estate—law*); property (*market*); estate (*agency*); building (*society*). **immobilisations** (lizasjɔ̃) *f.pl*, capital expenditure. **immobiliser** (ze) *v.t*, to immobilize; lock up, tie up; capitalize.

immodéré†, e (immɔdere) *a*, immoderate; excessive; unrestrained.

immodeste† (immɔdɛst) *a*, immodest.

immolation (immɔlasjɔ̃) *f*, immolation, sacrifice; holocaust. **immoler** (le) *v.t*, to immolate, sacrifice; slay.

immonde (immɔ̃:d) *a*, unclean, foul. **immondice** (mɔ̃dis) *f*, *oft. pl*, dirt, refuse, rubbish, litter.

immoral, e (immɔral) *a*, immoral. **immoralité** (lite) *f*, immorality.

immortaliser (immɔrtalize) *v.t*, to immortalize. **immortalité** (te) *f*, immortality. **immortel, le†** (tɛl) *a*, immortal; everlasting, undying. ¶ *m*, immortal.

immuable† (immyabl) *a*, immutable, unchangeable; hard-&-fast.

immunité (immynite) *f*, immunity.

impair, e (ɛ̃pɛ:r) *a*, uneven, odd (*number*). ¶ *m*, blunder.

impalpable (ɛ̃palpabl) *a*, impalpable.

impardonnable (ɛ̃pardɔnabl) *a*, unpardonable, unforgivable.

imparfait, e† (ɛ̃parfɛ, ɛt) *a*, unfinished; imperfect. ¶ *m*, imperfect [tense].

imparité (ɛ̃parite) *f*, unevenness, oddness.

impartial, e† (ɛ̃parsjal) *a*, impartial, unbiased.

impartir (ɛ̃parti:r) *v.t*, to impart, bestow.

impasse (ɛ̃pɑ:s) *f*, blind alley, dead end; deadlock, cleft stick.

impassible (ɛ̃pasibl) *a*, impassible; impassive.

impatiemment (ɛ̃pasjamã) *ad*, impatiently. **impatience** (sjã:s) *f*, impatience; (*pl.*) fidgets. **impatient, e** (ã, ã:t) *a*, impatient; agog. **impatientant, e** (ãtã, ã:t) *a*, provoking, tiresome. **impatienter** (te) *v.t*, to put out of patience, provoke. **s'~**, to grow impatient.

impatroniser (s') (ɛ̃patrɔnize) *v.pr*, to become master (*in a household*).

impayable (ɛ̃pɛjabl) *a*, impayable; invaluable, priceless; highly amusing. **impayé, e** (je) *a*, unpaid; dishonored (*bill*).

impeccable (ɛ̃pɛkabl) *a*, impeccable; infallible.

impedimenta (ɛ̃pedimɛta) *m*. *pl*, impedimenta.

impénétrable† (ɛ̃penetrabl) *a*, impenetrable; impervious; inscrutable.

impénitence (ɛ̃penitã:s) *f*, impenitence; obduracy. **impénitent, e** (tã, ã:t) *a*, impenitent; obdurate.

impératif, ive† (ɛ̃peratif, i:v) *a*. & *m*, imperative.

impératrice (ɛ̃peratris) *f*, empress.

imperceptible† (ɛ̃pɛrsɛptibl) *a*, imperceptible. **~** [*à l'ouïe*], inaudible.

imperfection (ɛ̃pɛrfɛksjɔ̃) *f*, imperfection; incompletion.

impérial, e (ɛ̃perjal) *a*, imperial. ¶ *f*, imperial (*beard*); top, upper deck, outside (*bus*). **impérialiste** (list) *m*, imperialist; (*att.*) imperialistic.

impérieux, euse† (ɛ̃perjø, ø:z) *a*, imperious.

impérissable (ɛ̃perisabl) *a*, imperishable, undying.

impéritie (ɛ̃perisi) *f*, incapacity.

imperméabiliser (ɛ̃pɛrmeabilize) *v.t*, to [water]proof. **imper-**

méable (bl) *a*, impermeable, impervious, -proof; -tight (*air, etc.*); waterproof. ¶ *m*, raincoat.

impersonnel, le† (ɛpɛrsɔnɛl) *a*, impersonal.

impertinemment (ɛpɛrtinamɑ̃) *ad*, impertinently, pertly. **impertinence** (nɑ̃:s) *f*, [piece of] impertinence, pertness. **impertinent, e** (nɑ̃, ɑ̃:t) *a*, impertinent, pert; irrelevant (*law*).

imperturbable† (ɛpɛrtyrbabl) *a*, imperturbable, unruffled.

impétrant, e (ɛpetrɑ̃, ɑ̃:t) *n*, grantee.

impétueux, euse† (ɛpetɥø, ø:z) *a*, impetuous; hot-headed; gusty (*wind*). **impétuosité** (tɥozite) *f*, impetuosity.

impie (ɛpi) *a*, impious, ungodly, godless; unholy. **impiété** (pjete) *f*, impiety.

impitoyable† (ɛpitwajabl) *a*, pitiless, merciless, ruthless, relentless.

implacable† (ɛplakabl) *a*, implacable.

implanter (ɛplɑ̃te) *v.t*, to implant.

implicite† (ɛplisit) *a*, implicit; implied. **impliquer** (ke) *v.t*, to implicate; involve; imply.

implorer (ɛplɔre) *v.t*, to implore, beseech, crave.

impoli, e (ɛpɔli) *a*, impolite. **impolitesse** (tɛs) *f*, impoliteness, rudeness.

impolitique (ɛpɔlitik) *a*, impolitic.

impondérable (ɛpɔ̃derabl) *a. & m*, imponderable.

impopulaire (ɛpɔpylɛ:r) *a*, unpopular.

importance (ɛpɔrtɑ̃:s) *f*, importance, moment; extent, magnitude. **d'~,** *ad*, soundly. **important, e** (tɑ̃, ɑ̃:t) *a*, important. *faire l'~*, to give oneself airs. ¶ *m*, main thing.

importateur (ɛpɔrtatœ:r) *m*, importer. **importation** (sjɔ̃) *f*, import[ation]. **importer** (te) *v.t*, to import; (*v.i.*) to matter, signify. *n'importe*, no matter. *n'importe où*, anywhere. *n'importe quoi*, no matter what. *qu'importe*, what's the difference.

importun, e (ɛpɔrtœ̃, yn) *a*, im-

portunate, tiresome, troublesome. ¶ *n*, intruder; nuisance. **importuner** (tyne) *v.t*, to importune, worry, molest, pester. **importunité** (nite) *f*, importunity, molestation.

imposable (ɛpozabl) *a*, taxable, assessable, dutiable. **imposant** (zɑ̃) *a*, imposing, commanding, dignified. **imposé, e** (ze) *n*, taxpayer. **imposer** (ze) *v.t. & abs*, to impose; enforce; lay [on]; thrust; tax, rate, assess; [over]awe. *en ~ à*, to impose [up]on, deceive. **imposition** (zisjɔ̃) *f*, imposition; tax; assessment.

impossibilité (ɛpɔsibilite) *f*, impossibility. **impossible** (bl) *a*, impossible. **l'~,** *m*, impossibilities; one's [very] utmost.

imposte (ɛpɔst) *f*, impost (*Arch.*).

imposteur (ɛpɔstœ:r) *m*, impostor, humbug. **imposture** (ty:r) *f*, imposture, imposition.

impôt (ɛpo) *m*, tax; duty; taxes; taxation. *~ du timbre*, stamp duty. *~ foncier*, land tax, property tax. *~ général (ou global) sur le revenu*, surtax. *~ sur le revenu* ou *~[s] cédulaire[s]* (sedyle:r), income tax.

impotent, e (ɛpotɑ̃, ɑ̃:t) *a*, helpless, crippled. ¶ *n*, cripple.

impraticable (ɛpratikabl) *a*, impracticable; impassable.

imprécation (ɛprekasjɔ̃) *f*, imprecation, curse.

imprécis, e (ɛpresi, i:z) *a*, vague. **imprécision** (sizjɔ̃) *f*, vagueness.

imprégner (ɛpreɲe) *v.t*, to impregnate.

imprenable (ɛprǝnabl) *a*, impregnable. *vue ~*, unspoilable view.

impresario (ɛprezarjo) *m*, impresario.

impression (ɛprɛsjɔ̃) *f*, impression; impress; printing, machining, striking off (*Typ.*); print; issue; priming (*paint*); sensation. *~ de mémoire*, core dump (*computers*). **impressionnant, e** (ɔnɑ̃, ɑ̃:t) *a*, impressive. **impressionner** (ne) *v.t*, to impress, affect. **impressionnisme** (nism) *m*, impressionism.

imprévisible (ɛprevizibl) *a*, unforeseeable; unpredictable.

imprévoyance (ẽprevwajã:s) *f*, shortsightedness, improvidence. **imprévu, e** (vy) *a*. & *m*, unforeseen; unexpected; contingency (*n*.).

imprimante (ẽprimã:t) *f*, printer (*computers*). ~ *à grande vitesse*, high-speed printer.

imprimé (ẽprime) *m*, printed book, p. form; p. paper; (*pl.*) p. matter, literature; handbill, leaflet. **imprimer** (me) *v.t*, to imprint; impress; print; prime (*paint*); impart. **imprimerie** (mri) *f*, printing (*art*); p. plant; p. works, p. office. **imprimeur** (mœ:r) *m*, printer.

improbable (ẽprɔbabl) *a*, improbable.

improbation (ẽprɔbasjɔ̃) *f*, disapproval.

improbe (ẽprɔb) *a*, dishonest.

improductif, ive (ẽprɔdyktif, i:v) *a*, unproductive.

impromptu (ẽprɔ̃[p]ty) *ad*, *a. inv.* & *m*, impromptu; extempore; offhand.

impropre† (ẽprɔpr) *a*, wrong; inappropriate; unsuitable; unfit. **impropriété** (ẽprɔpriete) *f*, impropriety, incorrectness.

improuver (ẽpruve) *v.t*, to disapprove [of].

improvisateur, trice (ẽprɔvizatœ:r, tris) *n*, improvisator. **improviser** (ze) *v.t*. & *abs*, to improvise, extemporize; vamp (*Mus.*). **à l'improviste** (vist) *ad*, unexpectedly, unawares.

imprudemment (ẽprydamã) *ad*, imprudently. **imprudence** (dã:s) *f*, imprudence. **imprudent, e** (dã, ã:t) *a*, imprudent, incautious.

impubliable (ẽpybliable) *a*, unprintable.

impudence (ẽpydã:s) *f*, shamelessness; impudence. **impudent, e** (dã, ã:t) *a*. & *n*, shameless, etc, (person). **impudemment** (damã) *ad*, impudently, etc.

impudeur (ẽpydœ:r) *f*, immodesty; indecency. **impudicité** (disite) *f*, impudicity, lewdness. **impudique†** (dik) *a*, unchaste, lewd.

impuissance (ẽpɥisã:s) *f*, powerlessness; inability; impotence,

-cy. **impuissant, e** (sã, ã:t) *a*, powerless; impotent.

impulsif, ive (ẽpylsif, i:v) *a*, impulsive. **impulsion** (sjɔ̃) *f*, impulse; impetus; impulsion; spur (*of the moment*).

impunément (ẽpynemã) *ad*, with impunity. **impuni, e** (ni) *a*, unpunished, scot-free. **impunité** (te) *f*, impunity.

impur, e† (ẽpy:r) *a*, impure; unclean. **impureté** (pyrte) *f*, impurity.

imputer (ẽpyte) *v.t*, to impute, ascribe; charge.

inabordable (inabɔrdabl) *a*, inaccessible.

inacceptable (inaksɛptabl) *a*, unacceptable.

inaccessible (inaksɛsibl) *a*, inaccessible.

inaccordable (inakɔrdabl) *a*, irreconcilable; inadmissible.

inaccoutumé, e (inakutyme) *a*, unaccustomed; unusual.

inachevé, e (inaʃve) *a*, unfinished.

inactif, ive (inaktif, i:v) *a*, inactive; dull, flat. **inaction** (sjɔ̃) *f*, inaction, drift. **inactivité** (tivite) *f*, inactivity, dullness.

inadapté (inadapte) *a*, maladjusted; misfitted. ¶ *n*, maladjusted person, misfit.

inadmissible (inadmisibl) *a*, inadmissible.

inadvertance (inadvɛrtã:s) *f*, inadvertence, oversight.

inaliénable (inaljenabl) *a*, inalienable.

inaltérable (inalterabl) *a*, unalterable.

inamical, e (inamikal) *a*, unfriendly.

inamovible (inamɔvibl) *a*, irremovable.

inanimé, e (inanime) *a*, inanimate, lifeless.

inanité (inanite) *f*, inanity, futility.

inanition (inanisjɔ̃) *f*, inanition, starvation.

inaperçu, e (inapɛrsy) *a*, unseen, unnoticed.

inappétence (inapetã:s) *f*, loss of appetite.

inapplicable (inaplikabl) *a*, in-

applicable. inappliqué, e (ke) *a*, inattentive; unapplied.

inappréciable (inapresjabl) *a*, inappreciable; inestimable, priceless.

inapte (inapt) *a*, inapt, unfit.

inarticulé, e (inartikyle) *a*, inarticulate.

inattaquable (inatakabl) *a*, unassailable.

inattendu, e (inatãdy) *a*, unexpected.

inattention (inatãsj5) *f*, inattention.

inaugurer (inogyre) *v.t*, to inaugurate; unveil, open; usher in (*fig.*).

incalculable (ẽkalkylabl) *a*, incalculable.

incandescence (ẽkãdɛsã:s) *f*, incandescence, glow, white heat. **incandescent, e (sã, ã:t)** *a*, incandescent, glowing, white-hot.

incantation (ẽkãtasj5) *f*, incantation.

incapable (ẽkapabl) *a*, incapable; unfit; unable, unequal; incompetent; inefficient. **les ~s,** *m.pl*, the unemployable. **incapacité (site)** *f*, incapacity, etc; disablement, disability.

incarcérer (ẽkarsere) *v.t*, to incarcerate.

incarnadin, e (ẽkarnadẽ, in) *a*, incarnadine. **incarnat, e (na, at)** *a*, rosy, pink, roseate. **incarnation (sj5)** *f*, incarnation, embodiment. **incarné, e (ne)** *p.a*, incarnate; ingrowing (*nail*).

incartade (ẽkartad) *f*, prank, indiscretion, lapse; outburst, tirade.

incassable (ẽkɑsabl) *a*, unbreakable.

incendiaire (ẽsãdjɛ:r) *a. & n*, incendiary. **incendie (di)** *m*, [outbreak of] fire. ~ *volontaire,* arson, incendiarism. **incendié, e (dje)** *n*, sufferer by a fire. **incendier (dje)** *v.t*, to [set on] fire, set f. tq.

incertain, e (ẽsɛrtẽ, ɛn) *a*, uncertain, unsettled. **incertitude (tityd)** *f*, uncertainty; suspense.

incessamment (ẽsesamã) *ad*, incessantly; forthwith. **incessant, e (sã, ã:t)** *a*, incessant, unceasing, ceaseless.

incessible (ẽsɛsibl) *a*, inalienable; not transferable.

inceste (ẽsɛst) *m*, incest. **incestueux, euse† (tɥø, ø:z)** *a*, incestuous.

incidemment (ẽsidamã) *ad*, incidentally. **incident, e (dã, ã:t)** *a*, incidental; incident (*ray*). ¶ *m*, incident; point of law; difficulty.

incinérateur (ẽsineratœ:r) *m*, incinerator, destructor. **incinérer (re)** *v.t*, to incinerate; cremate.

inconcis, e (ẽsirk5si, i:z) *a*, uncircumcised.

inciser (ẽsize) *v.t*, to incise, cut; lance. **incisif, ive (zif, i:v)** *a*, incisive. [dent.] **incisive** *f*, incisor. **incision (zj5)** *f*, incision; lancing.

incitation (ẽsitasj5) *f*, incitement. **inciter (te)** *v.t*, to incite, instigate.

incivil, e† (ẽsivil) *a*, uncivil. **incivilité (lite)** *f*, incivility.

inclément, e (ẽklemã, ã:t) *a*, inclement.

inclinaison (ẽwlinɛz5) *f*, inclination; gradient; slope; slant; cant; tilt; dip; pitch; rake. **inclination (nasj5)** *f*, inclination; leaning, bent; bow, nod; attachment, love, sweetheart. **incliner (ne)** *v.t. & i. & s'~,* to incline; lean; slope, slant; cant; tilt; dip; pitch; rake; bow [down]; nod; bank (*Avn.*).

inclure (ẽkly:r) *v.t.ir*, to enclose. **inclusivement (klyzivmã)** *ad*, inclusively; inclusive (*dates*).

incognito (ẽkɔɲito ou ẽkɔgnito) *ad. & m*, incognito.

incohérence (ẽkɔerã:s) *f*, incoherence. **incohérent, e (rã, ã:t)** *a*, incoherent; rambling.

incolore (ẽkɔlɔ:r) *a*, colorless.

incomber (ẽkɔbe) *v.i*, to be incumbent, devolve, rest.

incombustible (ẽkɔbystibl) *a*, incombustible, fireproof.

incommensurable (ẽkɔmãsyrabl) *a*, incommensurable.

incommode (ẽkɔmɔd) *a*, inconvenient; uncomfortable; tiresome. **incommodé, e (de)** *p.a*, poorly (*health*); crippled, disabled; embarrassed. **incommodément (demã)** *ad*, uncomfortably. **incommoder (de)** *v.t*, to inconvenience,

incommode. **incommodité** (dite)
f, inconvenience; nuisance (*law*);
(*ship in*) difficulties (*navigation*).
incomparable† (ĕkɔ̃parabl) *a*,
incomparable.
incompatible (ĕkɔ̃patibl) *a*, incompatible.
incompétent, e (ĕkɔ̃petã, ã:t)
a, incompetent.
incomplet, ète† (ĕkɔ̃plɛ, ɛt) *a*,
incomplete.
incompréhensible (ĕkɔ̃preãsibl) *a*, incomprehensible. **incompréhension** (sjɔ̃) *f*, obtuseness.
incompris, e (ĕkɔ̃pri, i:z) *a*, misunderstood; unappreciated.
inconcevable (ĕkɔ̃svabl) *a*, inconceivable.
inconciliable (ĕkɔ̃siljabl) *a*, irreconcilable.
inconduite (ĕkɔ̃dɥit) *f*, misconduct, misbehavior.
incongru, e (ĕkɔ̃gry) *a*, incongruous; uncouth. **incongruité**
(gryite) *f*, incongruity; malapropism; impropriety.
inconnu, e (ĕkɔny) *a*, unknown.
¶ *n*, unknown person; stranger;
nobody . **P~**, *m*, the unknown.
[**quantité**] **inconnue**, *f*, unknown
[quantity].
inconsciemment (ĕkɔ̃sjamã)
ad, unconsciously. **inconscience**
(sjã:s) *f*, unconsciousness. **inconscient, e** (ã, ã:t) *a*, unconscious; irresponsible.
inconséquent, e (ĕkɔ̃sekã, ã:t)
a, inconsistent; inconsequent[ial];
flighty.
inconsidéré†, **e** (ĕkɔ̃sidere) *a*,
inconsiderate; thoughtless.
inconsistant, e (ĕkɔ̃sistã, ã:t) *a*,
inconsistent.
inconsolable† (ĕkɔ̃sɔlabl) *a*, inconsolable. **inconsolé, e** (le) *a*,
unconsoled, forlorn.
inconstant, e (ĕkɔ̃stã, ã:t) *a*, inconstant; changeable; fickle.
inconstitutionnel, le† (ĕkɔ̃stitysjɔnel) *a*, unconstitutional.
incontestable† (ĕkɔ̃tɛstabl) *a*,
undeniable. **incontesté, e** (te) *a*,
undisputed.
incontinent, e (ĕkɔ̃tinã, ã:t) *a*,
incontinent, unchaste.
inconvenance (ĕkɔ̃vnã:s) *f*, impropriety. **inconvenant, e** (vnã,

ã:t) *a*, unbecoming, unseemly,
indecorous.
inconvénient (ĕkɔ̃venjã) *m*, inconvenience; drawback.
incorporer (ĕkɔrpore) *v.t*, to
incorporate; blend.
incorrect, e (ĕkɔrɛkt) *a*, incorrect; inaccurate; unbusinesslike.
incorrectment (təmã) *ad*, incorrectly, etc; ungrammatically. **incorrection** (ksjɔ̃) *f*, incorrectness,
etc.
incorrigible† (ĕkɔriʒibl) *a*, incorrigible, irreclaimable, hopeless.
incorruptible (ĕkɔryptibl) *a*,
incorruptible.
incrédibilité (ĕkredibilite) *f*,
incredibility. **incrédule** (dyl) *a*,
incredulous. ¶ *n*, unbeliever. **incrédulité** (lite) *f*, incredulity; unbelief.
incréé, e (ĕkree) *a*, uncreated.
incriminer (ĕkrimine) *v.t*, to incriminate; challenge.
incroyable† (ĕkrwajabl) *a*, incredible.
incrustation (ĕkrystasjɔ̃) *f*, incrustation; inlay, inlaid work;
scale. **incruster** (te) *v.t*, to incrust; inlay; scale.
incubation (ĕkybasjɔ̃) *f*, incubation.
inculpé, e (ĕkylpe) *n*, accused.
inculper (pe) *v.t*, to inculpate,
charge.
inculquer (ĕkylke) *v.t*, to inculcate, instill.
inculte (ĕkylt) *a*, uncultivated,
waste; wild; unkempt; uncultured, untutored.
incurable† (ĕkyrabl) *a. & n*, incurable.
incurie (ĕkyri) *f*, carelessness.
incursion (ĕkyrsjɔ̃) *f*, incursion,
raid, inroad, foray.
inde (ɛ̃:d) *m*. ou *bleu d'~*, indigo
blue. **l'I~**, *f*, India.
indébrouillable (ĕdebrujabl) *a*,
inextricable.
indécemment (ĕdesamã) *ad*, indecently. **indécence** (sã:s) *f*, indecency. **indécent, e** (sã, ã:t) *a*,
indecent.
indéchiffrable (ĕdeʃifrabl) *a*,
undecipherable; illegible; unintelligible.
indécis, e (ĕdesi, i:z) *a*, unde

cided; unsettled; drawn (*battle*, *game*). **indécision** (sisjɔ̃) *f*, indecision.

indécrottable (ɛ̃dekrɔtabl) *a*, uncleanable; incorrigible.

indéfendable (ɛ̃defɑ̃dabl) *a*, indefensible.

indéfinit, e (ɛ̃defini) *a*, indefinite; undefined. **indéfinissable** (sabl) *a*, indefinable; unaccountable; nondescript.

indéfrisable (ɛ̃defrizabl) *a*, that which will not uncurl (*hair, etc.*) ¶ *f*, permanent wave.

indélébile (ɛ̃delebil) *a*, indelible.

indélicat, e† (ɛ̃delika, at) *a*, indelicate; tactless; unscrupulous, sharp. **indélicatesse** (tɛs) *f*, indelicacy.

indémaillable (ɛ̃demajabl) *a*, (*stocking*) runproof.

indemne (ɛ̃demn) *a*, unscathed, scatheless, unhurt, scot-free. **indemniser** (nize) *v.t*, to indemnify, compensate. **indemnité** (te) *f*, indemnity, compensation; claim, loss (*Insce.*); allowance, remuneration, bonus. ~ *de chômage*, unemployment benefit. ~ *de vie chère*, cost-of-living bonus. ~ *de licenciement*, severance pay.

indéniable (ɛ̃denjabl) *a*, undeniable.

indépendamment (ɛ̃depɑ̃damɑ̃) *ad*, independently. ~ *de*, irrespective of. **indépendance** (dɑ̃:s) *f*, independence. **indépendant**, e (dɑ̃, ɑ̃:t) *a*, independent; free; self-contained.

indéracinable (ɛ̃derasinabl) *a*, ineradicable.

indéréglable (ɛ̃dereglabl) *a*, foolproof.

indescriptible (ɛ̃dɛskriptibl) *a*, indescribable.

indésirable (ɛ̃dezirabl) *a*, undesirable; objectionable. ¶ *n*, undesirable.

indestructible (ɛ̃dɛstryktibl) *a*, indestructible.

indéterminé, e (ɛ̃detɛrmine) *a*, undetermined; indeterminate.

indévot, e (ɛ̃devo, ɔt) *a*, irreligious.

index (ɛ̃dɛks) *m*, index; pointer; first finger, forefinger; blacklist. ~ [*expurgatoire*] (ɛkspyrgatwa:r), index [expurgatorius].

indicateur, **trice** (ɛ̃dikatœ:r, tris) *n*, informer; (*m.*) timetable, time book; guide [book] (*Rly.*, *street, post*); indicator, gauge. ~ *universel des P.T.T.* (= *Postes, Télégraphes & Téléphones*), post office guide. **indicatif**, **ive** (tif; i:v) *a*, indicative. [mode] indicatif, *m*, i. [mood]; area code (*phone*). **indication** (sjɔ̃) *f. oft. pl*, indication; clue; information; particular; instruction, stage directions. ~ *de nom & de lieu de résidence de l'imprimeur*, printer's imprint. ~ *de nom* (ou *de firme*) *de l'éditeur*, publisher's imprint. **indice** (dis) *m*, indication; sign; index; figure; number. ~ *du coût de la vie*, cost-of-living index. ~ *inférieur*, *superieur*, subscript; superscript. **indicible** (sibl) *a*, unspeakable, unutterable.

indien, **ne** (ɛ̃djɛ̃, ɛn) *a*. & **I~**, *n*, Indian. ¶ *f*, print[ed cotton fabric].

indifféremment (ɛ̃diferamɑ̃) *ad*, indifferently; indiscriminately. **indifférence** (rɑ̃:s) *f*, indifference; unconcern. **indifférent**, e (rɑ̃, ɑ̃:t) *a*, indifferent; unconcerned.

indigène (ɛ̃diʒɛ:n) *a*, native, indigenous. ¶ *n*, native.

indigent, e (ɛ̃diʒɑ̃, ɑ̃:t) *a*. & *n*, indigent, poor, pauper (*n.*). ~ *de passage*, casual.

indigeste (ɛ̃diʒɛst) *a*, indigestible; undigested (*fig.*); crude. **indigestion** (tjɔ̃) *f*, indigestion.

indignation (ɛ̃dinasjɔ̃) *f*, indignation. **indigne**† (diɲ) *a*, unworthy; undeserving; disqualified (*law*); outrageous. **indigné**, e (ɲe) *p.a*, indignant. **indigner** (ɲe) *v.t*, to exasperate. **indignité** (ɲite) *f*, unworthiness; indignity; outrage.

indigo (ɛ̃digo) *m*, indigo. **indigotier** (ɡɔtje) *m*, indigo plant.

indiquer (ɛ̃dike) *v.t*, to indicate, show, point out; mark; mention, state.

indirect, e† (ɛ̃dirɛkt) *a*, indirect; consequential (*damages*); crooked (*fig.*).

indiscipliné, e (ɛ̃disipline) *a*, unruly.

indiscret, **ète**† (ɛ̃diskrɛ, ɛt) *a*,

indiscreet; forward; prying. **indiscrétion** (krɛsjɔ̃) *f*, indiscretion.

indiscutable† (ɛ̃diskytabl) *a*, indisputable.

indispensable† (ɛ̃dispɑ̃sabl) *a*, indispensable.

indisponible (ɛ̃disponibl) *a*, inalienable; unavailable; not available.

indisposé, e (ɛ̃dispoze) *a*, indisposed, unwell, poorly, out of sorts. **indisposer** (ze) *v.t*, to upset; set against. **indisposition** (zisjɔ̃) *f*, indisposition.

indissoluble† (ɛ̃disɔlybl) *a*, indissoluble.

indistinct, e (ɛ̃distɛ̃ːkt) *a*, indistinct. **indistinctement** (tɛktəmɑ̃) *ad*, indistinctly; indiscriminately.

individu (ɛ̃dividy) *m*, individual; fellow. **son ~**, oneself, number one. **individualité** (dɥalite) *f*, individuality. **individuel, le**† (dɥɛl) *a*, individual; several (law).

indivis, e (ɛ̃divi, iːz) *a*, undivided; joint. **par indivis** *ou* **indivisément** (vizemɑ̃) *ad*, jointly. **indivisible**† (zibl) *a*, indivisible.

Indochine (l') (ɛ̃dɔʃin) *f*, Indo-China (*Cambodia, Laos, Vietnam*).

indocile (ɛ̃dɔsil) *a*, intractable.

indolemment (ɛ̃dɔlamɑ̃) *ad*, indolently; lazily. **indolence** (lɑ̃ːs) *f*, indolence, sloth; apathy, indifference. **indolent, e** (lɑ̃, ɑ̃ːt) *a*, indolent, slothful; apathetic, indifferent, lackadaisical.

indolore (ɛ̃dɔlɔːr) *a*, painless.

indomptable (ɛ̃dɔ̃tabl) *a*, untamable; indomitable; uncontrollable. **indompté, e** (te) *a*, untamed; unconquered; unsubdued.

indu, e (ɛ̃dy) *a*, untimely (*hour*).

indubitable† (ɛ̃dybitabl) *a*, indubitable, undoubted.

induction (ɛ̃dyksjɔ̃) *f*, induction; inference. **induire** (dɥiːr) *v.t.ir*, to lead; infer; induce. **~ en erreur**, to mislead. **induit** (dɥi) *m*, armature (*dynamo*).

indulgence (ɛ̃dylʒɑ̃ːs) *f*, indulgence; forbearance, leniency. **indulgent, e** (ʒɑ̃, ɑ̃ːt) *a*, indulgent, lenient.

indûment (ɛ̃dymɑ̃) *ad*, unduly.

industrialiser (ɛ̃dystrialize) *v.t*, to industrialize. **industrialisme** (lism) *m*, industrialism. **industrie** (tri) *f*, ingenuity; industry; manufacture, trade. **~-clef**, key industry. **~ d'art**, handicraft. **industriel, le**† (ɛl) *a*, industrial; manufacturing. ¶ *m*, manufacturer; millowner; industrialist. **industrieux, euse**† (ø, øːz) *a*, industrious, busy.

inébranlable† (inebrɑ̃labl) *a*, unshakable; immovable; unyielding; steadfast.

inédit, e (inedi, it) *a*, unpublished (*book*); unusual.

ineffable (inefabl) *a*, ineffable, unutterable.

ineffaçable (inefasabl) *a*, ineffaceable.

inefficace† (inefikas) *a*, inefficacious; ineffectual; ineffective, nugatory.

inégal, e† (inegal) *a*, unequal; uneven. **inégalité** (lite) *f*, inequality; unevenness.

inélégant, e (inelegɑ̃, ɑ̃ːt) *a*, inelegant.

inéligible (ineliʒibl) *a*, ineligible.

inemployable (inɑ̃plwajabl) *a*, unusable (*tool, etc.*). **inemployé, e** (je) *a*, unemployed (*resources, etc.*).

inénarrable (inenarabl) *a*, indescribable.

inepte† (inɛpt) *a*, inept, inane, silly. **ineptie** (si) *f*, ineptitude.

inépuisable† (inepɥizabl) *a*, inexhaustible.

inerte (inɛrt) *a*, inert, sluggish. **inertie** (si) *f*, inertia; listlessness.

inespéré†, **e** (inɛspere) *a*, unhoped for, unexpected.

inestimable (inɛstimabl) *a*, inestimable, priceless.

inévitable† (inevitabl) *a*, inevitable; unavoidable.

inexact, e† (inɛgzakt) *a*, inexact, inaccurate, incorrect; unpunctual. **inexactitude** (tityd) *f*, inexactitude.

inexcusable (inɛkskyzabl) *a*, inexcusable.

inexécutable (inɛgzekytabl) *a*, unworkable; inexecutable. **inexécution** (sjɔ̃) *f*, nonperformance.

inexercé, e (inɛgzɛrse) *a*, unskilled.

inexigible (inɛgziʒibl) *a*, not due, undue.

inexistant, e (inɛgzistɑ̃, ɑ̃;t) *a*, nonexistent. **inexistence** (tɑ̃;s) *f*, nonexistence.

inexorable† (inɛgzɔrabl) *a*, inexorable.

inexpérience (inɛksperjɑ̃;s) *f*, inexperience. **inexpérimenté, e** (rimɑ̃te) *a*, inexperienced, unskilled.

inexplicable (inɛksplikabl) *a*, inexplicable. **inexpliqué, e** (ke) *a*, unexplained.

inexploré, e (inɛksplɔre) *a*, unexplored.

inexprimable (inɛksprimabl) *a*, inexpressible.

inexpugnable (inɛkspygnabl) *a*, impregnable.

in extenso (inɛkstɛso) *ad*, in extenso, in full.

inextinguible (inɛkstɛ̃gɥibl) *a*, inextinguishable; unquenchable; irrepressible, uncontrollable.

inextricable (inɛkstrikabl) *a*, inextricable.

infaillible† (ɛ̃fajibl) *a*, infallible; unerring.

infaisable (ɛ̃fəzabl) *a*, unfeasible; impracticable.

infamant, e (ɛ̃famɑ̃, ɑ̃;t) *a*, defamatory; opprobrious; infamous (*law*). **infâme** (fɑ;m) *a*, infamous, foul. **infamie** (fami) *f*, infamy.

infanterie (ɛ̃fɑ̃tri) *f*, infantry. **infanticide** (ɛ̃fɑ̃tisid) (*act*) *m*. & (*pers*.) *n*, infanticide. **infantile** (til) *a*, infant[ile] (*Med*.).

infatigable† (ɛ̃fatigabl) *a*, indefatigable, tireless.

infatuation (ɛ̃fatɥasjɔ̃) *f*, infatuation. **s'infatuer** (tɥe) *v.pr*, to become infatuated.

infécond, e (ɛ̃fekɔ̃, ɔ̃;d) *a*, barren.

infect, e (ɛ̃fɛkt) *a*, stinking, foul. **infecter** (te) *v.t*, to infect, taint; (*v.i.*) to stink. **infectieux, euse** (sjø, ø;z) *a*, infectious (*Med*.). **infection** (sjɔ̃) *f*, infection; stench.

inférence (ɛ̃ferɑ̃;s) *f*, inference. **inférer** (re) *v.t*, to infer.

inférieur, e (ɛ̃ferjœ;r) *a*, lower, bottom, under, nether; inferior; less. ¶ *m*, inferior (*pers*.). **in-**

fériorité (rjɔrite) *f*, inferiority.

infernal, e (ɛ̃fɛrnal) *a*, infernal, hellish.

infertile (ɛ̃fɛrtil) *a*, infertile, barren.

infester (ɛ̃fɛste) *v.t*, to infest, overrun.

infidèle† (ɛ̃fidɛl) *a*, unfaithful; faithless; inaccurate; dishonest; infidel. ¶ *n*, unfaithful person; infidel. **infidélité** (delite) *f*, infidelity; unfaithfulness; dishonesty; breach of trust.

infiltrer (s') (ɛ̃filtre) *v.pr*, to infiltrate, percolate.

infime (ɛ̃fim) *a*, lowest; insignificant; tiny.

infini, e (ɛ̃fini) *a*, infinite. **l'infini**, *m*, the infinite; infinity (*Math., Phot*.). **à l'infini**, *ad*, ad infinitum. **infiniment** (mɑ̃) *ad*, infinitely. **infinité** (te) *f*, infinity, infinitude. **une ~ de**, no end of. **infinitésimal, e** (tezimal) *a*, infinitesimal. [**mode**] **infinitif** (tif) *m*, infinitive [mood].

infirme (ɛ̃firm) *a*, infirm, invalid. ¶ *n*, invalid. **infirmer** (me) *v.t*, to invalidate; quash; weaken. **infirmerie** (məri) *f*, infirmary, sick room (*Sch., etc*.). **infirmier, ère** (mje, ɛ;r) *n*, hospital attendant, h. orderly, h. nurse, male n., sick n. *infirmière en chef*, head nurse, matron. **infirmité** (mite) *f*, infirmity; frailty; weakness.

inflammable (ɛ̃flamabl) *a*, inflammable. **inflammation** (sjɔ̃) *f*, ignition; inflammation.

inflation (ɛ̃flasjɔ̃) *f*, inflation (*Fin*.).

infléchir (ɛ̃fleʃi;r) *v.t*, to inflect, bend. **inflexible†** (flɛksibl) *a*, inflexible. **inflexion** (ksjɔ̃) *f*, inflection.

infliger (ɛ̃fliʒe) *v.t*, to inflict.

influence (ɛ̃flyɑ̃;s) *f*, influence, sway. **influencer** (ɑ̃se) *v.t*, to influence, sway. **influent, e** (ɑ̃, ɑ̃;t) *a*, influential. **influer sur (e)**, to influence.

infographie (ɛ̃fɔgrafi) *f*, computer graphics.

in-folio (ɛ̃fɔljo) *a.m*. & *m*, folio (*book*).

informateur, trice (ɛ̃fɔrma-tœ;r, tris) *n*, informant. **informa-**

tion (sjɔ̃) *f. mostly pl*, inquiry; (*pl.*) newscast (*radio*).

informatique (ɛ̃fɔrmatik) *f*, data processing. ~ *absolue*, integrated d. p. ~ *commercial*, business d. p. *cours d'*~, computer training course. *reseau* ~, c. network. **informatiser** (tize) *v.t*, to computerize.

informe (ɛ̃fɔrm) *a*, shapeless, formless; informal (*law*).

informé (ɛ̃fɔrme) *m*, inquiry (*law*). **informer** (me) *v.t*, to inform, acquaint. **s'** ~, to inquire.

infortune (ɛ̃fɔrtyn) *f*, misfortune; adversity; mischance. **infortuné, e** (ne) *a. & n*, unfortunate.

infraction (ɛ̃fraksjɔ̃) *f*, infraction, infringement, breach; offense.

infranchissable (ɛ̃frɑ̃ʃisabl) *a*, impassable; insuperable.

infréquenté, e (ɛ̃frekɑ̃te) *a*, unfrequented.

infroissable (ɛ̃frwasabl) *a*, wrinkle-proof, uncrushable.

infructueux, euse† (ɛ̃fryktɥø̃ø̃:z) *a*, fruitless (fig.).

infus, e (ɛ̃fy, y:z) *a*, inborn, innate. **infuser** (fyze) *v.t*, infuse; instill. [s']~, to draw (*tea*). **infusible** (zibl) *a*, infusible. **infusion** (zjɔ̃) *f*, infusion; tea. **infusoires** (zwa:r) *m.pl*, infusoria.

ingambe (ɛ̃gɑ̃:b) *a*, nimble.

ingénier (s') (ɛ̃ʒenje) *v.pr*, to try, contrive.

ingénierie (ɛ̃ʒenjəri) *f*, project study & development; engineering.

ingénieur (ɛ̃ʒenjœ:r) *m*, engineer. ~-*conseil*, consulting e.

ingénieux, euse† (ɛ̃ʒenjø̃, ø̃:z) *a*, ingenious. **ingéniosité** (jozite) *f*, ingenuity.

ingénu†, e (ɛ̃ʒeny) *a*, ingenuous, artless; unsophisticated. ¶ *f*, ingénue (*Theat.*). **ingénuité** (nɥite) *f*, ingenuousness, etc.

ingérer (s') (ɛ̃ʒere) *v.pr*, to interfere, meddle.

ingouvernable (ɛ̃guvɛrnabl) *a*, ungovernable; uncontrollable.

ingrat, e (ɛ̃gra, at) *a*, ungrateful; thankless; unpromising; unpleasing. **ingratitude** (tityd) *f*, ingratitude.

ingrédient (ɛ̃gredjɑ̃) *m*, ingredient, constituent.

inguérissable (ɛ̃gerisabl) *a*, incurable; inconsolable.

ingurgiter (ɛ̃gyrʒite) *v.t*, 'to swallow, wolf down; be made to swallow.

inhabile† (inabil) *a*, incapable.

inhabitable (inabitabl) *a*, uninhabitable. **inhabité, e** (te) *a*, uninhabited, untenanted.

inhabitué (inabitye) *a*, unaccustomed.

inhaler (inale) *v.t*, to inhale.

inharmonieux, euse (inarmɔnjø̃, ø̃:z) *a*, inharmonious; unmusical.

inhérent, e (inerɑ̃, ɑ̃:t) *a*, inherent.

inhospitalier, ère (inɔspitalje, ɛ:r) *a*, inhospitable.

inhumain, e† (inymɛ̃, ɛn) *a*, inhuman. **inhumanité** (manite) *f*, inhumanity.

inhumer (inyme) *v.t*, to inter, bury.

inimaginable (inimaʒinabl) *a*, unimaginable.

inimitable (inimitabl) *a*, inimitable.

inimitié (inimitje) *f*, enmity, ill feeling.

ininflammable (inɛ̃flamabl) *a*, uninflammable.

inintelligent, e (inɛ̃teliʒɑ̃, ɑ̃:t) *a*, unintelligent. **inintelligible†** (ʒibl) *a*, unintelligible.

ininterrompu, e (inɛ̃tɛrɔ̃py) *a*, uninterrupted, unbroken.

inique† (inik) *a*, iniquitous, nefarious, unrighteous. **iniquité** (kite) *f*, iniquity, sin.

initial, e (inisjal) *a*, initial; opening. ¶ *f*, initial [letter]. **initiation** (sjɔ̃) *f*, initiation. **initiative** (ti:v) *f*, initiative; push, drive. **initié, e** (sje) *n*, initiate. **initier** (sje) *v.t*, to initiate.

injecté, e (ɛ̃ʒekte) *a*, bloodshot; flushed; impregnated (*wood*). **injecter** (te) *v.t*, to inject. **injecteur** (tœ:r) *m*, injector. **injection** (ksjɔ̃) *f*, injection.

injonction (ɛ̃ʒɔ̃ksjɔ̃) *f*, injunction.

injure (ɛ̃ʒy:r) *f*, injury, wrong; insult; (*pl.*) abuse; (*s. or pl.*) ravages. **injurier** (ʒyrje) *v.t*, abuse, insult, revile. **injurieux, euse†** (rjø, ø:z) *a*, abusive, insulting, offensive, opprobrious, injurious.

injuste† (ɛ̃ʒyst) *a. & m*, unjust; unrighteous; unfair; inequitable; wrong. **injustice** (tis) *f*, injustice; unrighteousness; unfairness; wrong. **injustifiable** (tifjabl) *a*, unjustifiable.

inlassable (ɛ̃lasabl) *a*, untiring, unflagging.

inné, e (inne) *a*, innate, inborn, inbred. **innéité** (ite) *f*, innateness.

innocemment (inɔsamɑ̃) *ad*, innocently. **innocent, e** (sɑ̃, ɑ̃:t) *a*, innocent; guiltless, not guilty; sinless, blameless; guileless, artless; harmless. ¶ *n*, innocent; simpleton. **innocence** (sɑ̃:s) *f*, innocence, etc. **innocenter** (sɑ̃te) *v.t*, to find not guilty.

innocuité (innɔkɥite) *f*, harmlessness.

innombrable (innɔ̃brabl) *a*, innumerable, numberless, countless, untold.

innommé, e (innɔme) *a*, unnamed. **innommable** (mabl) *a*, unnamable.

innovation (innɔvasjɔ̃) *f*, innovation, [new] departure.

inobservance (inɔpsɛrvɑ̃:s) & **inobservation** (vasjɔ̃) *f*, inobservance, disregard. **inobservé, e** (ve) *a*, not complied with (*rules*).

inoccupé, e (inɔkype) *a*, unoccupied, idle; vacant.

inoculation (inɔkylasjɔ̃) *f*, inoculation. **inoculer** (le) *v.t*, to inoculate.

inodore (inɔdɔ:r) *a*, odorless.

inoffensif, ive (inɔfɑ̃sif, i:v) *a*, innocuous; innoxious; inoffensive; harmless.

inondation (inɔ̃dasjɔ̃) *f*, inundation, flood. **inonder** (de) *v.t*, to inundate, flood, deluge.

inopérant, e (inɔperɑ̃, ɑ̃:t) *a*, inoperative.

inopiné†, e (inɔpine) *a*, unexpected, sudden.

inopportun, e (inɔpɔrtœ̃, yn) *a*, inopportune.

inorganique (inɔrganik) *a*, inorganic.

inoubliable (inubliabl) *a*, unforgettable.

inouï, e (inwi) *a*, unheard of.

inoxydable (inɔksidabl) *a*, stainless, rustless.

inquiet, ète (ɛ̃kjɛ, ɛt) *a*, uneasy; troubled; restless, fidgety. **inquiéter** (jete) *v.t*, to make uneasy; disquiet; disturb; trouble; molest. **inquiétude** (tyd) *f*, uneasiness, disquiet[ude]; restlessness.

inquisiteur, trice (ɛ̃kizitœ:r, tris) *a*, inquisitive. **inquisition** (sjɔ̃) *f*, inquisition.

insaisissable (ɛ̃sezisabl) *a*, not distrainable; difficult to catch, elusive; imperceptible.

insalubre (ɛ̃salybr) *a*, unhealthy; insanitary.

insanité (ɛ̃sanite) *f*, insanity (*folly*), nonsense.

insatiable† (ɛ̃sasjabl) *a*, insatiable.

insciemment (ɛ̃sjamɑ̃) *ad*, unknowingly.

inscription (ɛ̃skripsjɔ̃) *f*, inscription; writing; epitaph; registration, registry; entry; matriculation; quotation (*in Stk Ex. list*). ~ *de* (ou *en*) *faux*, pleading of forgery. *prendre des* (*ses*) ~s, to matriculate. **inscrire** (skri:r) *v.t.ir*, to inscribe; register; enter; write; quote. *s'inscrire en faux*, to plead forgery (*law*); deny the truth (*contre* = of). *s'*~, to register.

inscrutable (ɛ̃skrytabl) *a*, inscrutable.

insecte (ɛ̃sɛkt) *m*, insect. **insecticide** (tisid) *a. & m*, insecticide. **insectivore** (vɔ:r) *a*, insectivorous. ~s, *m.pl*, insectivora.

insécurité (ɛ̃sekyrite) *f*, insecurity.

insensé, e (ɛ̃sɑ̃se) *a*, insensate, mad; senseless. ¶ *n*, madman, -woman. **insensible†** (sibl) *a*, insensible; unfeeling, callous.

insensibiliser (ɛ̃sɑ̃sibilize) *v.t*, to anesthetize.

inséparable† (ɛ̃separabl) *a*, inseparable. ~s, *n.pl*, inseparables (*pers.*); love birds.

insérer (ɛ̃sere) *v.t*, to insert, put in. insert (sert) *m*, cut-in, insert, inlay (*cinema*). ~ *filmé*, film insert. **insertion** (sersjɔ̃) *f*, insertion.

insidieux, euse† (ɛ̃sidjø, ø:z) *a*, insidious.

insigne (ēsiɲ) a, signal conspicuous; distinguished; arrant,
rank, notorious. ¶ m, badge;
(pl.) insignia. ~s de la royauté,
regalia.

insignifiant, e (ēsiɲifjā, ɑ̃:t) a,
insignificant, trifling, trivial, vacuous.

insinuation (ēsinɥasjɔ̃) f, insinuation; innuendo. insinuer (nɥe)
v.t, to insinuate; hint at; introduce.

insipide (ēsipid) a, insipid;
tasteless, vapid.

insistance (ēsistɑ̃:s) f, insist-
ence. insister (te) v.i, to insist.

insociable (ēsɔsjabl) a, unsociable.

insolation (ēsɔlasjɔ̃) f, insolation; sun bathing; sunstroke.

insolemment (ēsɔlamɑ̃) ad, in-
solently. insolence (lɑ̃:s) f, insolence. insolent, e (lɑ̃, ɑ̃:t) a,
insolent; overbearing; extraordinary.

insolite (ēsɔlit) a, unusual, unwonted.

insoluble (ēsɔlybl) a, insoluble.

insolvabilité (ēsɔlvabilite) f, insolvency. insolvable (bl) a, insolvent.

insomnie (ēsɔmni) f. oft. pl, insomnia, sleeplessness.

insondable (ēsɔ̃dabl) a, unfathomable, fathomless.

insonore (ēsɔnɔ:r) a, sound-
proof.

insouciant, e (ēsusjɑ̃, ɑ̃:t) a,
careless, unconcerned; jaunty.
insoucieux, euse (sjø, øɪz) a,
heedless, regardless.

insoumis, e (ēsumi, i:z) a, unsubdued. ¶ m, absentee (Mil.).

insontenable (ēsutnabl) a, untenable, indefensible; insufferable.

inspecter (ēspɛkte) v.t, to inspect, examine. inspecteur, trice
(tœr, tris) n, inspector; examiner; floorwalker. ~ du travail,
factory inspector. inspection
(ksjɔ̃) f, inspection, examination; inspectorship.

inspiration (ēspirasjɔ̃) f, inspiration. inspirer (re) v.t, to inspire (air & fig.); prompt.

instabilité (ēstabilite) f, insta-

bility. instable (bl) a, unstable,
unsteady.

installation (ēstalasjɔ̃) f, installation; induction (Eccl.). installer (le) v.t, to install; induct;
settle.

instamment (ēstamɑ̃) ad, ear-
nestly; urgently. instance (stɑ̃:s)
f, (pl.) entreaties; (law) instance. instant, e (stɑ̃, ɑ̃:t) a,
urgent, instant. ¶ m, instant, moment. à l'~, a moment ago; at
once. instantané†, e (stɑ̃tane) a,
instantaneous. ¶ m, snapshot.

instar de (à l') (ēsta:r) pr, like,
as in.

instigation (ēstigasjɔ̃) f, instigation.

instiller (ēstille) v.t, to instill
(liquid).

instinct (ēstē) m, instinct. instinctif, ive† (stēktif, i:v) a, instinctive.

instituer (ēstitɥe) v.t, to institute; appoint. institut (ty) m, institute, institution. instituteur,
trice (tœ:r, tris) n, teacher; governess. institution (sjɔ̃) f, institution; school; hostel.

instructeur (ēstryktœ:r) m, instructor; drill sergeant. instructif, ive (tif, i:v) a, instructive.
instruction (sjɔ̃) f, instruction;
education; schooling; tuition;
training; lesson; pleading (law).
~ par écrit, pleadings (law).
sans ~, uneducated. instruire
(strɥi:r) v.t.ir, to instruct; teach;
educate; train; inform; plead
(law). s'~, to learn.

instrument (ēstrymɑ̃) m, instrument; implement; tool. instrumental, e (tal) a, instrumental. instrumentiste (tist) n, in-
strumentalist.

insu de (à l') (ēsy) pr, unknown to. à mon insu, without
my knowledge.

insubmersible (ēsybmɛrsibl) a,
unsinkable.

insubordonné, e (ēsybɔrdɔne)
a, insubordinate.

insuccès (ēsyksɛ) m, failure, miscarriage.

insuffisamment (ēsyfizamɑ̃)
ad, insufficiently. insuffisance
(zɑ̃:s) f, insufficiency, shortage.

~ *d'imposition,* underassessment.
insuffisant, e (zã, ã₁t) *a,* insufficient, inadequate; incompetent.
insulaire (ε̃sylε₁r) *a,* insular. ¶ *n,* islander.
Insulinde (ε̃sylε̃₁d) *f,* Indian Archipelago.
insulte (ε̃sylt) *f,* insult. **insulter** (te) *v.t,* to insult. ~ *à,* to jeer at; be an insult to.
insupportable† (ε̃syportabl) *a,* insupportable; unbearable; insufferable.
insurgé, e (ε̃syrʒe) *a. & n,* insurgent. **s'insurger** (ʒe) *v.pr,* to revolt.
insurmontable (ε̃syrmõtabl) *a,* insurmountable, insuperable.
insurrection (ε̃syrεksjõ) *f,* insurrection.
intact, e (ε̃takt) *a,* intact; whole; unblemished.
intaille (ε̃ta₁j) *f,* intaglio.
intangible (ε̃tãʒibl) *a,* intangible.
intarissable† (ε̃tarisabl) *a,* unfailing, perennial, inexhaustible. *il est* ~, he never stops talking.
intégral, e† (ε̃tegral) *a,* integral, whole, entire, [in] full; unexpurgated. **l'intégralité** (lite) *f,* the whole, the entirety.
intègre (ε̃tegr) *a,* upright; honest. **intégrité** (tegrite) *f,* integrity.
intégrer (ε̃tegre) *v.t,* to integrate, incorporate. **s'~,** to combine with, join with.
intellect (ε̃telεkt) *m,* intellect. **intellectuel, le†** (tɥεl) *a. & m,* intellectual; brain, *att.*
intelligemment (ε̃telizamã) *ad,* intelligently. **intelligence** (ʒã₁s) *f,* intelligence, intellect; understanding; knowledge; (*on good*) terms; (*pl.*) correspondence; (*pl.*) dealings. **intelligent, e** (ʒã, ã₁t) *a,* intelligent. **intelligible†** (ʒibl) *a,* intelligible; audible.
intempérance (ε̃tãperã₁s) *f,* intemperance; insobriety; excess. **intempérant, e** (rã, ã₁t) *a,* intemperate. **intempérie** (ri) *f. usually pl,* [inclemency of the] weather.
intempestif, ive† (ε̃tãpestif, i₁v) *a,* unseasonable, untimely, ill-timed.

intenable (ε̃tnabl) *a,* untenable.
intendance (ε̃tãdã₁s) *f,* stewardship. ~ *militaire,* commissariat. **intendant** (dã) *m,* steward, bailiff.
intense (ε̃tã₁s) *a,* intense; strenuous. **intensif, ive†** (tãsif, i₁v) *a,* intensive. **intensifier** (fje) *v.t,* to intensify. **intensité** (te) *f,* intensity; strength, depth (*color*). ~ *lumineuse en bougies,* candlepower.
intenter (ε̃tãte) *v.t,* to enter, bring, institute (*action at law*).
intention (ε̃tãsjõ) *f,* intention; intent, purpose; meaning; will. *à l'~ de,* for [the sake of]. **intentionné, e** (ɔne) *a,* -intentioned, -meaning, -disposed. **intentionnel, le†** (nεl) *a,* intentional.
inter (l') (ε̃tε₁r) *abb,* long distance (*Teleph.*).
intercaler (ε̃tεrkale) *v.t,* to intercalate.
intercéder (ε̃tεrsede) *v.i,* to intercede.
intercepter (ε̃tεrsεpte) *v.t,* to intercept.
intercesseur (ε̃tεrsεsœ₁r) *m,* intercessor. **intercession** (sjõ) *f,* intercession.
interchangeable (ε̃tεrʃãʒabl) *a,* interchangeable.
interclasser (ε̃tεrklase) *v.t,* to collate (*computers*). **interclassement** (mã) *m,* collation (*computers*). **interclasseuse** (ø₁z) *f,* collator (*computers*).
interdiction (ε̃tεrdiksjõ) *f,* interdiction; prohibition; ban; deprivation (*rights*). **interdire** (di₁r) *v.t.ir,* to interdict, prohibit; forbid; ban; taboo; inhibit; deprive (*Eccl.*); disconcert, nonplus. **interdit** (di) *m,* person under judicial interdiction; interdict (*Eccl.*). *sens ~,* no thoroughfare.
intéressé, e (ε̃terεse) *n,* interested party. ¶ *a,* selfish. **intéresser** (se) *v.t,* to interest; concern. **intérêt** (rε) *m,* interest; stake.
interférence (ε̃tεrferã₁s) *f,* interference (*Phys.*).
interfolier (ε̃tεrfolje) *v.t,* to interleave.
intérieur, e† (ε̃terjœ₁r) *a,* inte-

rior; internal; inner; inward; inside; inland; home, domestic. ¶ *m*, interior, inside; home; home life, private life.

intérim (ēterim) *m*, interim. *faire l'~*, to deputize. **intérimaire** (mɛir) *a*, interim; acting.

interjection (ēterzɛksjɔ̃) *f*, interjection; ejaculation; lodging (*appeal*). **interjeter** (ʒəte) *v.t*, to lodge (*appeal*).

interligne (ēterliɲ) *m*, space between lines; space (*Mus.*); (*f.*) lead (*Typ.*). **interligner** (ɲe) *v.t*, to lead. **interlinéaire** (lineɛir) *a*, interlinear.

interlocuteur, trice (ēterlɔkytœir, tris) *n*, interlocutor.

interlope (ēterlɔp) *a*, dubious, suspect.

interloquer (ēterlɔke) *v.t*, to take aback.

interlude (ēterlyd) *m*, interlude (*Mus., etc.*); voluntary (*organ*).

intermède (ētermɛd) *m*, intermezzo; interlude. **intermédiaire** (medjɛir) *a*, intermediate. ¶ *m*, intermission; intermediary, middleman, go-between; instrumentality, medium.

interminable (ēterminabl) *a*, interminable.

intermittent, e (ētermitɑ̃, ɑ̃it) *a*, intermittent.

internat (ēterna) *m*, boarding school; boarding-in, living-in; internship.

international, e (ēternasjɔnal) *a*, international; foreign (*postal system*). ¶ *f*, international (*association*); internationale (*hymn*). **internationaliste** (list) *n. & a*, internationalist.

interne (ētern) *a*, internal; inward. [**élève**] ~, *n*, boarder. ¶ *m*, intern. **interné, e** (ne) *n*, internee; inmate (*asylum*). **interner** (ne) *v.t*, to intern (*war, etc.*); place under restraint (*lunatic*).

interpeller (ēterpɛlle) *v.t*, to interpellate; to challenge, call upon, heckle, accost (*someone*).

interphone (ɛterfɔn) *m*, intercom.

interplanétaire (ēterplanetɛir) *a*, interplanetary.

interpoler (ēterpɔle) *v.t*, to interpolate.

interposer (ēterpoze) *v.t*, to interpose. *s'~*, to interpose, mediate.

interprétation (ēterpretasjɔ̃) *f*, interpretation; construction; rendering. **interprète** (prɛt) *n*, interpreter; exponent. **interpréter** (prete) *v.t*, to interpret; render.

interrègne (ēterrɛɲ) *m*, interregnum.

interrogateur, trice (ēterɔgatœir, tris) *n*, interrogator, questioner; examiner. **interrogatif, ive†** (tif, iːv) *a*, interrogative. **interrogation** (sjɔ̃) *f*, interrogation; question, query. **interrogatoire** (twaːr) *m*, interrogatory. **interroger** (ʒe) *v.t*, to interrogate.

interrompre (ēterɔ̃ːpr) *v.t*, to interrupt, break, stop. **interrupteur, trice** (ryptœir, tris) *n*, interrupter; (*m.*) switch; circuit breaker. **interruption** (sjɔ̃) *f*, interruption, break.

intersection (ētersɛksjɔ̃) *f*, intersection.

interstice (ēterstis) *m*, interstice.

interurbain, e (ēteryrbɛ̃, ɛn) *a*, interurban; long distance (*Teleph.*). Cf. *inter* (*l'*).

intervalle (ēterval) *m*, interval; space; gap; interlude.

intervenant (ētervənɑ̃) *m*, acceptor for honor (*Com.*). **intervenir** (vəniːr) *v.i.ir*, to intervene, interfere; happen. **intervention** (vɑ̃sjɔ̃) *f*, intervention.

interversion (ētervɛrsjɔ̃) *f*, inversion. **intervertir** (tiːr) *v.t*, to invert.

interview (ētervju) *f*, interview (*for news*). **interviewer** (vjuve) *v.t*, to interview.

intestat (ētɛsta) *a.inv*, intestate.

intestin, e (ētɛstɛ̃, in) *a*, intestine; internal. ¶ *m*, intestine, bowel, gut. **intestinal, e** (tinal) *a*, intestinal.

intime† (ētim) *a*, intimate; in-[ner]most; inward; close, near; private. ¶ *m*, intimate. **intimer** (me) *v.t*, to notify.

intimider (ētimide) *v.t*, to intimidate, cow, overawe.

intimité (ētimite) *f*, intimacy, closeness.

intitulé (ētityle) *m*, title, name; premises (*deed*). **intituler** (le) *v.t*, to entitle, call, name.

intolérable† (ētɔlerabl) *a*, intolerable, insufferable. **intolérance** (rãːs) *f*, intolerance. **intolérant, e** (rã, ãːt) *a*, intolerant.

intonation (ētɔnasjɔ̃) *f*, intonation.

intoxication (ētɔksikasjɔ̃) *f*, poisoning. **intoxiquer** (ke) *v.t*, to poison.

intraduisible (ētradɥizibl) *a*, untranslatable.

intraitable (ētrɛtabl) *a*, intractable; unreasonable.

intransigeant, e (ētrãziʒã, ãːt) *a*, intransigent, uncompromising. ¶ *n*, intransigent, die-hard.

intransitif, ive† (ētrãzitif, iːv) *a*, intransitive.

intrépide† (ētrepid) *a*, intrepid, fearless, dauntless. **intrépidité** (dite) *f*, intrepidity, etc.

intrigant, e (ētrigã, ãːt) *a*, intriguing, designing. ¶ *n*, intriguer, schemer, wirepuller. **intrigue** (trig) *f*, intrigue; plot. **intriguer** (ge) *v.t*, to rouse the interest (*or* curiosity) of, intrigue, puzzle; (*v.i.*) to intrigue, plot, scheme, pull the wires.

intrinsèque† (ētrɛ̃sɛk) *a*, intrinsic.

introducteur, trice (ētrɔdyktœːr, tris) *n*, introducer. **introduction** (ksjɔ̃) *f*, introduction; opening (*law case*). **introduire** (dɥiːr) *v.t.ir*, to introduce; show in, usher in. **s'~**, to get in, gain admittance; intrude.

introït (ētrɔit) *m*, introit.

introniser (ētronize) *v.t*, to enthrone.

introspection (ētrɔspɛksjɔ̃) *f*, introspection.

introuvable (ētruvabl) *a*, undiscoverable; peerless.

intrus, e (ɛtry, yːz) *n*, intruder, interloper; trespasser. (*law*). **intrusion** (tryzjɔ̃) *f*, intrusion; trespass.

intuitif, ive (ētɥitif, iːv) *a*, intuitive. **intuition** (sjɔ̃) *f*, intuition.

inusable (inyzable) *a*, hard-wearing; for hard wear. **inusité, e**

(zite) *a*, uncustomary; obsolete.

inutile† (inytil) *a*, useless; unprofitable; unnecessary, needless. **inutilisable** (lizabl) *a*, unusable; unserviceable. **inutilisé, e** (ze) *a. & p.p*, unutilized. **inutilité** (te) *f*, uselessness; (*pl.*) useless things.

invalide† (ēvalid) *a*, invalid; invalided. ¶ *m*, old *or* disabled soldier; pensioner. **invalider** (de) *v.t*, to invalidate; unseat. **invalidité** (dite) *f*, invalidity; disablement, disability.

invariable† (ēvarjabl) *a*, invariable, unchangeable.

invasion (ēvazjɔ̃) *f*, invasion; inrush; influx.

invective (ēvɛktiːv) *f*, invective. **invectiver** (tive) *v.i*, to inveigh, rail.

invendable (ēvãdabl) *a*, unsalable. **invendu, e** (dy) *a*, unsold.

inventaire (ēvãtɛːr) *m*, inventory; list; stock-taking; valuation; accounts, balance sheet & schedules. **inventer** (te) *v.t*, to invent; devise; trump up. **inventeur, trice** (tœːr, tris) *n*, inventor; discoverer; finder; author (*fig.*). **inventif, ive** (tif, iːv) *a*, inventive. **invention** (sjɔ̃) *f*, invention. **inventorier** (tɔrje) *v.t*, to inventory, list; take stock of; value.

inversable (ēvɛrsabl) *a*, uncapsizable (*boat*); unspillable (*ink bottle*).

inverse† (ēvɛrs) *a*, inverse; reciprocal; reverse; contrary; contra. ¶ *m*, inverse; reverse; reciprocal. **inverser** (se) *v.t*, to reverse. **inversion** (sjɔ̃) *f*, inversion; reversal.

invertébré, e (ēvɛrtebre) *a. & m*, invertebrate.

invertir (ēvɛrtiːr) *v.t*, to invert; reverse.

investigation (ēvɛstigasjɔ̃) *f*, investigation.

investir (ēvɛstiːr) *v.t*, to invest (*all Eng. senses*); vest; dignify; blockade. **investissement** (tismã) *m*, investment (*Mil.*). **investiture** (tyːr) *f*, investiture.

invétéré, e (ēvetere) *p.a*, inveterate, ingrained. **s'invétérer** (re) *v.pr*, to become inveterate.

invincible† (ɛ̃vɛ̃sibl) a, invincible; insurmountable.

inviolable† (ɛ̃vjɔlabl) a, inviolable. **inviolé, e (le)** a, inviolate.

invisible† (ɛ̃vizibl) a, invisible; never to be seen. *devenir ~,* to vanish.

invitation (ɛ̃vitasjɔ̃) f, invitation. **invite** (vit) f, call (*cards*). **invité, e (te)** n, guest. **inviter** (te) v.t, to invite, ask; court; request; tempt; call for (*trumps*).

invocation (ɛ̃vɔkasjɔ̃) f, invocation.

involontaire† (ɛ̃vɔlɔ̃tɛɪr) a, involuntary; unintentional.

invoquer (ɛ̃vɔke) v.t, to invoke, call upon.

invraisemblable† (ɛ̃vrɛsãblabl) a, unlikely; improbable. **invraisemblablement** (blǝmã) ad, unlikely, improbably. **invraisemblance** (blãːs) f, unlikelihood, improbability.

invulnérable (ɛ̃vylnerabl) a, invulnerable.

iode (jɔd) m, iodine.

ion (iɔ̃) m, ion.

ionien, ne (iɔnjɛ̃, ɛn), **ionique** (nik) a, Ionian, Ionic.

iota (jɔta) m, iota, jot, tittle, whit.

irascible (irasibl) a, irascible, testy.

iridium (iridjɔm) m, iridium.

iris (iris) m, iris; rainbow. *~ des marais,* yellow iris, flag. **irisation** (zasjɔ̃) f, iridescence. **irisé, e (ze)** a, iridescent.

irlandais, e (irlãdɛ, ɛːz) a, Irish. **I~,** n, Irishman, -woman. **l'Irlandais,** m, Irish (*language*). **l'Irlande** (lãːd) f, Ireland. *mer d'Irlande,* Irish Sea.

ironie (irɔni) f, irony. **ironique** (nik) a, ironic(al).

irrachetable (irraʃtabl) a, irredeemable (*Fin.*).

irradiation (irradjasjɔ̃) f, irradiation.

irraisonnable (irrɛzɔnabl) a, irrational, unreasoning. **irraisonnel, le** (irrasjɔnɛl) a, irrational.

irréalisable (irrealizabl) a, unrealizable.

irrecevable (irəsəvabl) a, inadmissible (*evidence*); unacceptable.

irréconciliable (irrekɔ̃siljabl) a, irreconcilable.

irrécouvrable (irrekuvrabl) a, irrecoverable.

irrécupérable (irrekypɛrabl) a, unrecoverable; irretrievable.

irrécusable (irrekyzabl) a, unimpeachable, unexceptionable.

irrédentisme (irredãtism) m, irredentism.

irréductible (irredyktibl) a, irreducible; indomitable (*will*).

irréel, le (irreɛl) a, unreal.

irréfléchi, e (irrefleʃi) a, unconsidered. **irréflexion** (fiɛksjɔ̃) f, thoughtlessness.

irréfutable† (irrefytabl) a, irrefutable. **irréfuté, e (te)** a, unrefuted.

irrégularité (irregylarite) f, irregularity. **irrégulier, ère†** (lje, ɛɪr) a, irregular; erratic.

irréligieux, euse† (irrelizjø, øːz) a, irreligious.

irrémédiable† (irremedjabl) a, irremediable.

irremplaçable (irrãplasabl) a, irreplaceable.

irréparable† (irreparabl) a, irreparable, irretrievable.

irréprochable† (irreprɔʃabl) a, irreproachable.

irrésistible† (irrezistibl) a, irresistible.

irrésolu, e (irrezɔly) a, irresolute.

irrespectueux, euse† (irrespektyø, øːz) a, disrespectful.

irrespirable (irrespirabl) a, unbreathable.

irresponsable (irrespɔ̃sabl) a, irresponsible.

irrétrécissable (irretresisabl) a, unshrinkable.

irrévérencieux, euse (irreverãsjø, øːz) a, disrespectful. **irrévérent, e** (rã, ãːt) a, irreverent.

irrévocable† (irrevɔkabl), a, irrevocable.

irrigateur (irrigatœɪr) m, irrigator; garden hose, etc. **irrigation** (sjɔ̃) f, irrigation. **irriguer** (ge) v.t, to irrigate.

irritable (irritabl) a, irritable, testy. **irritation** (sjɔ̃) f, irritation. **irriter** (te) v.t, to irritate; anger; excite. **s'~,** to grow angry; fret, chafe.

irruption (irrypsjɔ̃) *f*, irruption, inroad, inrush.
Islam (islam) *m*, Islam.
islandais, e (islɑ̃dɛ, ɛːz) *a*. & (*language*) *m*, Icelandic. **I~,** *n*, Icelander. **l'Islande** (lɑ̃ːd) *f*, Iceland.
isolateur (izɔlatœːr) *m*, insulator. **isolé, e** (le) *a*, isolated; detached; unattached (*Mil*.); lonely; alone; aloof. **isolement** (lmɑ̃) *m*, isolation; loneliness; insulation. **isolément** (lemɑ̃) *ad*, separately; singly. **isoler** (le) *v.t*, to isolate; insulate. **isoloir** (lwar) *m*, insulator; voting booth.
isoloir (lwar) *m*, insulator; voting booth.
israélien, ienne, (israeljɛ̃, ɛn) *a*. & *n*, Israeli.
israélite (iz- *ou* israelit) *n*, Israelite, Jew. ¶ *a*, Jewish.
issu, e (isy) *a*, descended, born, sprung. **issue** (sy) *f*, issue; end; solution; egress, exit, way out; outlet; outcome, upshot; (*pl*.) offal, garbage; by-products. **à l'~ de,** *ad*, at the end of, on leaving.
isthme (ism) *m*, isthmus.
Italie (l') (itali) *f*, Italy. **Italien, ne** (ljɛ̃, ɛn) *a*, & **I~,** *n*, Italian. **l'italien,** Italian (*language*).
italique (italik) *a*, italic. ¶ *m*, italics.
item (itɛm) *ad*, item, likewise; ditto.
itinéraire (itinerɛːr) *m*, itinerary, route.
ivoire (ivwaːr) *m*, ivory.
ivraie (ivrɛ) *f*, cockle, darnel; tares (*fig*.).
ivre (iːvr) *a*, drunk[en], intoxicated, inebriate[d], tipsy. **~ à pleurer,** maudlin. **~ mort,** dead drunk. **ivresse** (ivrɛs) *f*, drunkenness, intoxication; frenzy, rapture. **ivrogne** (vrɔɲ) *a*, drunken. ¶ *m*, drunkard, toper, inebriate, sot. **ivrognerie** (ɲri) *f*, drunkenness. **ivrognesse** (ɲɛs) *f*, drunkard, inebriate, sot.

J

jabot (ʒabo) *m*, crop (*bird*);
frill. **jaboter** (bɔte) & **jac.** (kase) *v.i*, to jabber, chatter.
jachère (ʒaʃɛːr) *f*, fallow [land]. **jachérer** (ʃere) *v.t*, to fallow.
jacinthe (ʒasɛ̃ːt) *f*, hyacinth (*Bot*.); jacinth (*Miner*.). **~ des bois,** wild hyacinth, bluebell.
jacobée (ʒakɔbe) *f*, ragwort.
jacobin (ʒakɔbɛ̃) *m*, jacobin.
jactance (ʒaktɑ̃ːs) *f*, boasting. **avoir de la ~,** to have the gift of gab.
jade (ʒad) *m*, jade (*Miner*.).
jadis (ʒadis) *ad*, formerly, once. **au temps ~,** in the olden time.
jaguar (ʒagwaːr) *m*, jaguar.
jaillir (ʒajiːr) *v.i*, to gush, spout, spurt, squirt, jet; fly; splash; spring; well; flash. **jaillissant** (sɑ) *a*, gushing, shouting. **jaillissement** (smɑ̃) *m*, gushing, spurt. **~ d'éloquence,** burst of eloquence.
jais (ʒɛ) *m*, jet (*lignite*).
jalon (ʒalɔ̃) *m*, peg, stake, picket; range pole; landmark (*fig*.). **jalonner** (lɔne) *v.t*, to peg, stake [out]; dot. **jalonneur** (nœːr) *m*, marker (*Mil*.).
jalouser (ʒaluze) *v.t*, to be jealous of. **jalousie** (zi) *f*, jealousy; Venetian blind; jalousie. **jaloux, ouse†** (lu, uːz) *a*, jealous; anxious.
Jamaïque (la) (ʒamaik), Jamaica.
jamais (ʒamɛ) *ad*, ever; never. **à ~ ou pour ~,** forever. **ne . . . ~,** never, ne'er (*Poet*.).
jambage (ʒɑ̃baːʒ) *m*, pier (*Build*.); jamb; down stroke; pothook. **jambe** (ʒɑ̃ːb) *f*, leg; shank. **~ de force,** strut. **~ deçà, ~ delà,** astride, astraddle. **jambière** (ʒɑ̃bjeːr) *f*, legging; shin guard; legwarmer. **jambon** (bɔ̃) *m*, ham (*hog, boar*).
jante (ʒɑ̃ːt) *f*, felloe, felly; rim. **jantille** (ʒɑ̃tiːj) *f*, paddle [board] (*waterwheel*).
janvier (ʒɑ̃vje) *m*, January.
Japon (ʒapɔ̃) *m*, Japanese porcelain; J. paper. **le ~,** Japan (*Geog*.) **japonais, e** (pɔnɛ, ɛːz) *a*. & **J~** (*pers*.) *n*, Japanese. **le japonais,** Japanese (*language*). **japonerie** (nri) *f*, Japanese curio, etc.

japper (ʒape) *v.i*, to yap, yelp.
jaquette (ʒakɛt) *f*, morning coat, tail c. (*man's*); short c. (*woman's*). *être de la ~*, to be a homosexual (*male*).
jard (ʒaːr) *m*, river gravel.
jardin (ʒardɛ̃) *m*, garden. *~ de rocaille*, *~ alpestre*, rock g. *~ anglais*, landscape g. *~ d'enfants*, kindergarten. *~ de fenêtre*, window box. *~ de l'église*, churchyard. *~ des plantes*, botanical gardens. *~ maraîcher*, market garden. *~ potager*, kitchen garden. **jardinage** (dina:ʒ) *m*, gardening; garden plots. **jardiner** (ne) *v.i*, to garden. **jardinet** (nɛ) *m*, small garden. **jardinier**, **ère** (nje, ɛːr) *n*, gardener; (*f.*) flower stand, jardinière.
jargon (ʒargɔ̃) *m*, jargon; lingo; slang, cant; jargoon (*Miner.*). **jargonner** (ɡɔne) *v.i. & t*, to jabber.
jarre (ʒaːr) *f*, jar (*pot*).
jarret (ʒarɛ) *m*, bend of the knee; ham (*in man*); hock, hough (*horse*); knuckle (*veal*); shin (*beef*). **jarretelles** (rtɛl) *f.pl*, [sock and stocking] suspenders. **jarretière** (rtjɛːr) *f*, garter; gunsling.
jars (ʒaːr) *m*, gander.
jas (ʒa) *m*, stock (*anchor*).
jaser (ʒaze) *v.i*, to chatter; blab. **jaserie** (zri) *f*, chatter. **jaseur**, **euse** (zœːr, øːz) *n*, chatterer.
jasmin (ʒasmɛ̃) *m*, jasmine.
jaspe (ʒasp) *m*, jasper. *~ sanguin*, bloodstone. **jasper** (pe) *v.t*, to marble; mottle. **jaspure** (pyːr) *f*, marbling.
jatte (ʒat) *f*, bowl.
jauge (ʒoːʒ) *f*, gauge; gauging rod; register[ed tonnage] (*ship*). *~ à huile*, dipstick. **jauger** (ʒoʒe) *v.t*, to gauge; measure (*ship*); size up (*pers.*).
jaunâtre (ʒonɑːtr) *a*, yellowish; sallow. **jaune** (ʒoːn) *a*, yellow; sallow; [light] brown (*boots*). *la mer Jaune*, the Yellow Sea. *rire ~*, to give a sickly smile. ¶ *m*, yellow; yolk (*egg*); strikebreaker; (*pl.*) yellow races. **jaunir** (ʒoniːr) *v.t. & i*, to yellow. **jaunisse** (nis) *f*, jaundice.

Java (ʒava) *m*, Java. **javanais**, **e** (nɛ, ɛːz) *a. & J~*, *n*, Javan[ese].
javelle (ʒavɛl) *f*, swath; chlorinated water; javel w. **javelliser** (lize) *v.t*, to chlorinate.
javelot (ʒavlo) *m*, javelin.
je, **j'** (ʒə, ʒ) *pn*, I.
jean-foutre (ʒɑ̃futr) *m*, good-for-nothing (*strong slang*).
jérémiade (ʒeremjad) *f*, jeremiad.
jersey (ʒɛrzɛ) *m*, stockinet; jersey. **J~**, *f*, Jersey (*Geog.*). **jersiais**, **e** (zjɛ, ɛːz) *a*, Jersey (*cattle*).
Jérusalem (ʒeryzalɛm) *f*, Jerusalem.
jésuite (ʒezɥit) *m*, Jesuit. **jésuitique** (tik) *a*, Jesuitical.
Jésus (ʒezy) *m*, Jesus. **Jésus-Christ** (kri) *m*, Jesus Christ.
jet (ʒɛ) *m*, throw[ing]; cast[ing]; toss[ing]; fling; pouring (*metal*); catch (*fish*); folds (*drapery*); flash (*light*); spurt; burst; jet (*aircraft*); stream; nozzle, spout; shoot, sprout; attempt, go. *~ [à la mer]*, jettison. *~ d'eau*, spray; ornamental fountain. *du premier ~*, at first try. **jeté** (ʒəte) *m*, over (*Knit.*). *~ de lit*, bedspread, overlay. **jetée** (te) *f*, jetty, pier; finger (*air terminal*). *~ promenade*, pier (*seaside*). **jeter** (te) *v.t. & abs*, to throw; cast; dash; fling; hurl; toss; pitch; splash; put; lay (*foundations*); shed (*light*); heave (*sigh*); utter (*cry*); run, discharge (*of abscess*); sprout; strike (*root*); pour, run (*metal*). *~ [à la mer]*, to jettison. *se ~*, to throw oneself; jump; fall, run. **jeton** (tɔ̃) *m*, counter; tally; token. *~s de présence*, directors' fees; fees. *avoir les ~s*, to be afraid. *faux ~*, hypocrite.
jeu (ʒø) *m*, play; game; sport; pastime; gaming; gambling; speculation; execution; acting, trick; play (*Mech.*); slack; clearance; lash; stroke (*piston, etc.*); blowing [out] (*fuse*); set, assortment; stop (*organ*); pack (*cards*); hand (*cards*); stake[s]. *~ d'adresse*, game of skill. *~ d'anneaux*, ship quoits, ring quoits. *~ d'esprit*, witticism. *~ de baquet*, tipping (*or* tilting) the

bucket. ~ *de boules*, [game of] bowls. ~ *de chat*, touch [last], tag. ~ *de fléchettes*, darts. ~ *de jambes*, foot work (*sport*). ~ [*bizarre*] *de la nature*, freak [of nature]. ~ *de la scie*, cat's-cradle. ~x *de main*, horseplay, rough & tumble. ~ *de mots*, play on words, pun. ~ *de patience*, jigsaw puzzle. ~ *de paume*, real tennis (*ancient game*). ~x *de physionomie*, play of features. ~x *de salon*, ~x *de société*, parlor games, indoor games. ~ *de scène*, stage trick. ~ *de tennis*, game of tennis; t. court. ~ *de volant*, badminton. ~ *du cochonnet*, [game of] bowls. ~x *innocents*, parlor games, forfeits. ~, *manche*, & *partie*, game-set-match (*Ten.*). ~ *muet*, dumb show. *pas du* (ou *de*) ~, not fair.

eudi (ʒødi) *m*, Thursday.

eun (à) (ʒœ̃) *ad*, fasting; on an empty stomach.

eune (ʒœn) *a*, young; youthful; juvenile; rising (*generation*); younger; minor. ~ *personne*, *f*, young lady; young person, juvenile. [le] ~, junior, the younger. ¶ *n*, young person.

eûne (ʒøːn) *m*, fast[ing]; abstinence. **jeûner** (ʒøne) *v.i*, to fast.

eunement (ʒœnmɑ̃) *ad*, youthfully. **jeunesse** (nɛs) *f*, youth; childhood; youthfulness; boyhood; girlhood; girl. **jennet**, **te** (nɛ, ɛt) *a*, [very] young.

iu-jitsu (ʒyʒitsy) *m*, ju-jutsu, ju-jitsu, judo.

oaillerie (ʒwajri) *f*, jewelry. **joaillier**, **ère** (je, ɛːr) *n*, jeweler.

obard, **e** (ʒɔbaːr, ard) *n*, simpleton, fool.

ockey (ʒɔkɛ) *m*, jockey (*turf*).

ocko (ʒɔko) *m*, orangutan.

ocrisse (ʒɔkris) *m*, simpleton.

oie (ʒwa) *f*, joy[fulness], glee; mirth, merriment, pleasure; gaiety.

oignant, **e** [à] (ʒwaɲɑ̃, ɑ̃ːt) *a*, adjoining. **joindre** (ʒwɛ̃ːdr) *v.t.* & *i. ir.* & *se* ~, to join; unite; fold (*hands*); combine; adjoin; attach; add; meet. **joint** (ʒwɛ̃) *n*, joint, join. **jointif**, **ive** (tif,

i;v) *a*, close. **jointoyer** (twaje) *v.t*, to point (*masonry*). **jointure** (ty;r) *f*, juncture; joint; knuckle.

joli, **e** (ʒɔli) *a*, pretty; good-looking; nice; fine. **joliment** (mɑ̃) *ad*, prettily; very well.

jonc (ʒ5) *m*, rush; bulrush; cane; hoop ring. **joncher** (ʃe) *v.t*, to strew, litter.

jonction (ʒ5ksj5) *f*, junction, meeting.

jongler (ʒ5gle) *v.i*, to juggle. **jonglerie** (gləri) *f*, juggling; juggle, trick. **jongleur** (glœ;r) *m*, juggler; trickster.

jonque (ʒ5;k) *f*, junk (*Chinese*).

jonquille (ʒ5ki;j) *f*, jonquil.

jouailler (ʒuaje) *v.i*, to play [for] low [stakes]; play a little (*music*).

joubarbe (ʒubarb) *f*, houseleek.

joue (ʒu) *f*, cheek; jowl; flange. *mettre* (ou *coucher*) *en* ~, to [take] aim at.

jouée (ʒwe) *f*, reveal (*Arch.*).

jouer (ʒwe) *v.i.* & *t.* & *abs*, to play; sport; toy; move (*chess, etc.*); gamble; be on the gamble; speculate; operate; work; perform; act (*Theat.*); trifle; trick, fool; stake; back (*horse*); feign; look like; blow [out] (*fuse*). ~ *sur le*(*s*) *mot*(*s*), to play on words, pun. *a qui à* ~? whose move is it? *se* ~ *de*, to make light of. **jouet** (ʒwɛ) *m*, toy; plaything; sport, butt. **joueur**, **euse** (ʒwœːr, øːz), *n*, player; performer; gambler; speculator; operator; (*good, bad*) loser; (*att.*) fond of play. ~ *un de plus*, odd player (*golf*).

jouffln, **e** (ʒufly) *a*, chubby.

joug (ʒu[g]) *m*, yoke.

jouir de (ʒwi;r) to enjoy; e. the company of; avail oneself of the services of; use; have. **jouissance** (ʒwisɑ̃;s) *f*, enjoyment; pleasure, delight; use; possession; tenure; fruition; due date of coupon, interest payable (*date*).

joujou (ʒuʒu) *m*, plaything, toy.

jour (ʒu;r) *m*, day; daytime; [day]light; opening, gap; day, surface, grass (*Min.*); (*pl.*) openwork (*Need.*). *le* ~ *de l'an*, New Year's Day. *son* ~ [*de réception*], her at-home day. le ~ des Cendres, Ash Wednesday. le ~ des morts, All Soul's Day. le ~ des propitiations, the day of atonement. ~ du terme, quarter day. ~ férié (ferje), [public] holiday; holy day. ~ gras, meat day (Eccl.). les ~s gras, Shrovetide. ~ maigre, fast day. à ~, open; openwork[ed]; through; up to date. à ce ~, to date. au ~ le ~, from day to day; from hand to mouth. à la ~, by the day. femme de ~, cleaning woman.

Jourdain (le) (ʒurdɛ̃), the Jordan.

journal (ʒurnal) m, journal; diary; log [book]; book; register; [news]paper; gazette. ~ parlé, weather & news (radio). ~ de bord, log book, flight log. ~ des transmissions, transmission log (computers). **journalier, ère** (lje, ɛːr) a, daily; inconstant; fickle. ¶ m, day laborer. **journalisme** (lism) m, journalism; press. **journaliste** (list) m, journalist, reporter, columnist.

journée (ʒurne) f, day; daytime; day's work; day's pay. ~ de chemin, day's journey. **journellement** (nɛlmɑ̃) ad, daily.

joute (ʒut) f, joust; tilt[ing]; contest; fight. ~ sur l'eau, water tournament. **jouter** (te) v.i, to joust.

jouvenceau, elle (ʒuvɑ̃so, ɛl) n, youth, damsel.

jovial, e† (ʒɔvjal) a, jovial, merry, jolly.

joyau (ʒwajo) m, jewel.

joyeux, euse† (ʒwajø, øːz) a, joyful, joyous, jolly, genial, convivial, merry, jocund. ¶ f.pl, testicles (slang).

jubilaire (ʒybilɛːr) a, jubilee, holy (year). **jubilation** (lasjɔ̃) f, jubilation, jollification, jollity. **jubilé** (le) m, jubilee.

jucher (ʒyʃe) v.i. & se ~, to roost, perch. **juchoir** (ʃwaːr) m, roost, perch.

judaïque† (ʒydaik) a, Judaic.

Judas (ʒyda) m, Judas (traitor). **j~**, spyhole, peephole, judas; window mirror.

judiciaire† (ʒydisjɛːr) a, judicial; legal.

judicieux, euse† (ʒydisjø, øːz) a, judicious, discerning.

juge (ʒyːʒ) m, judge; justice; magistrate; umpire. les Juges, Judges (Bible). ~ d'instruction, examining magistrate. **jugement** (ʒyʒmɑ̃) m, judgment; trial; estimation; discernment; sentence; decree. **juger** (ʒe) v.t. & abs, to judge; try (case); pass judgment; think, deem.

jugulaire (ʒygylɛːr) f, chin strap. [veine] ~, f, jugular [vein]. **juguler** (le) v.t, to strangle.

juif, ive (ʒɥif, iːv) n, Jew, Jewess. Juif errant, Wandering Jew. ¶ a, Jewish.

juillet (ʒɥijɛ) m, July.

juin (ʒɥɛ̃) m, June.

juiverie (ʒɥivri) f, ghetto.

jujube (ʒyʒyb) m, jujube. **jujubier** (bje) m, jujube [shrub].

julep (ʒylɛp) m, julep.

jules (ʒyl) m, husband; pimp; chamberpot. **julie** (li) f, wife, girl friend. faire sa ~, to be goody goody.

jumeau, elle (ʒymo, ɛl) a, twin; semidetached. ¶ n, twin; (f.) binocular [glass], glass[es]; upright, standard, housing. ~[s] de théâtre, opera glass[es]. **jumeler** (mle) v.t, to pair.

jument (ʒymɑ̃) f, mare.

jungle (ʒɔ̃ːgl) f, jungle.

jupe (ʒyp) f, skirt. ~-culotte, divided s. **jupier, ère** (pje, ɛːr) m, skirt maker. **jupon** (pɔ̃) m, petticoat.

juré, e (ʒyre) a, sworn. ¶ m, jury man, juror. **jurer** (re) v.t. & abs, to swear; s. by; blaspheme; vow; (v.i.) to clash, jar. **jureur** (rœːr) m, swearer.

juridiction (ʒyridiksjɔ̃) f, jurisdiction; province, line. **juridique†** (dik) a, juridical, law (att.). **jurisconsulte** (riskɔ̃sylt) m, jurist. **jurisprudence** (prydɑ̃ːs) f, jurisprudence, law. **juriste** (rist) m, jurist.

juron (ʒyrɔ̃) m, (profane) oath.

jury (ʒyri) m, jury; selection committee. ~ d'admission, hanging committee (art). ~ d'examen, board of examiners.

jus (ʒy) m, juice; gravy; coffee; electric current. c'est le même ~

it's the same thing. ~ de réglisse, licorice.

usant (ʒyzɑ̃) m, ebb.

usque & poet. jusques (ʒysk) pr, to; as (or so) far as; till, until; even; up to. jusqu'à ce que, till, until. jusqu'à concurrence de, up to, not exceeding. jusqu'à quand? till when? how long? jusqu'ici, so far, thus far; till now, hitherto. jusqu'où? how far? jusque-là, so far; till then. uste (ʒyst) a, just; right; fair; legitimate; correct; accurate; exact; proper; true; condign; upright; righteous; tight (fit). ~ milieu, happy medium, golden mean. à ~ titre, fairly, rightly. le ~, the right. les ~s, m.pl, the just, the righteous. ¶ ad, just; right; barely. justement (təmɑ̃) ad, justly; exactly, just. justesse (tɛs) f, accuracy; correctness. justice (tis) f, justice; equity; right; rights; righteousness; justness, fairness; judicature; court of law; law; law officers. Palais de J~, law courts. justiciable (sijabl) a, under the jurisdiction; amenable. justicier (sje) m, justiciary. justifiable (fjabl) a, justifiable, warrantable. justificatif, ive (fikatif, iːv) a, justificative; voucher (att.). justifier (fje) v.t, to justify; warrant; vindicate; prove.

ute (ʒyt) m, jute.

uter (ʒyte) v.i, to be juicy. juteux, euse (tø, øːz) a, juicy.

uvénile (ʒyvenil) a, juvenile, youthful.

uxtaposer (ʒykstapoze) v.t, to juxtapose.

K

xakatoès (kaktɔɛs) m, cockatoo.

xaki (kaki) a, khaki.

xaléidoscope (kaleidɔskɔp) m, kaleidoscope.

xangourou (kɑ̃guru) m, kangaroo.

xaolin (kaɔlɛ̃) m, kaolin, china clay.

Xénia (le) (kenja), Kenya.

xépi (kepi) m, cap (peaked).

xermesse (kɛrmɛs) f, kermis, fête, fair.

khédive (kediːv) m, Khedive.

kif (kif) m, dope (drug). ~-~, a, the same, likewise.

kilogramme (kilɔgram) m, kilogram = 1000 grams or 2.2046 (about 2⅕) lbs.

kilomètre (kilɔmɛtr) m, kilometer = 1000 meters or 0.62137 (about ⅝) mile. Kilometrique (metrik) a, kilometric(al).

kimono (kimɔno) m, kimono.

kiosque (kjɔsk) m, kiosk; stall; bookstall; conning tower (submarine). ~ à musique, bandstand. ~ de jardin, summer house.

klaxon (klaksɔn) m, horn (auto). klaxonner (ne) v.t & i, to honk a horn.

krach (krak) m, crash, smash (Fin.).

kyrielle (kirjɛl) f, string, rigmarole.

kyste (kist) m, cyst (Med.).

L

la (la) m, A (Mus.). donner le ~ (fig.), to set the fashion.

là (la) ad, there; then; that. ~-bas, [over] yonder, over there. ~-dedans, in there; within. ~-dehors, outside, without. ~-dessous, under there, underneath. ~-dessus, on that, thereon; thereupon. ~-haut, up there. de ~, away, off; out of there; from then. par ~, that way; through there, thereby. ¶ i, there [now]! oh ~ ~! wow!

labeur (labœːr) m, labor, toil; book work (Typ.).

labial, e (labjal) a. & f, labial.

laboratoire (labɔratwaːr) m, laboratory.

laborieux, euse† (labɔrjø, øːz) a, laborious, hard-working; working (class); arduous, toilsome, hard; labored.

labour (labuːr) m, plowing, tillage. labourable (burabl) a, arable, plow (land). labourage (raːʒ) m, plowing, tillage. labourer (re) v.t. & abs, to plow, till; plow up; drag (anchor); graze (sea bottom). laboureur (rœːr) m, plowman.

labyrinthe (labirɛ̃ːt) *m*, labyrinth, maze.

lac (lak) *m*, lake, mere. *Note.*— For named lakes, see under proper name, e.g, *le lac Léman*, under *Léman*. ~ *de cirque*, tarn. ~ *salé*, salt lake.

lacer (lase) *v.t*, to lace [up].

lacérer (lasere) *v.t*, to lacerate, tear.

lacet (lasɛ) *m*, lace (*shoe, etc.*); winding (*road*); nosing (*of locomotive*); snare, noose; (*pl.*) toils.

lâche† (lɑːʃ) *a*, loose; slack; lax; faint-hearted, cowardly, unmanly, dastardly, mean. **lâcher** (lɑʃe) *v.t*, to loose[n]; slacken; let out; relax; let fly; release; liberate; let go; let down; jilt; drop; [let] slip; blurt out; open, turn on (*tap*); utter; fire (*shot*). ~ *pied*, to give way. ~ *prise*, to let go. **lâcheté** (ʃte) *f*, cowardice; meanness.

lacis (lasi) *m*, network; plexus.

laconique† (lakɔnik) *a*, laconic.

lacrymal, e (lakrimal) *a*, lachrymal, tear (*att.*).

lacrymogène (lakrimɔʒɛn) *a*, tear-inducing. *gaz* ~, tear gas.

lacs (lɑ) *m*, toils (*fig.*). ~ *d'amour*, love knot, true-love[r's] knot.

lacté, e (lakte) *a*, lacteal; milk (*att.*); milky.

lacune (lakyn) *f*, lacuna; gap; hiatus; blank.

lacustre (lakystr) *a*, lacustrine, lake (*att.*).

lad (lad) *m*, stable boy (*turf*).

ladre (lɑːdr) *n*, miser, niggard, skinflint. ¶ *a*, stingy, mean, niggardly. **ladrerie** (lɑdrəri) *f*, stinginess.

lagune (lagyn) *f*, lagoon.

lai (lɛ) *a.m*, lay (*brother*). ¶ *m*, lay (*poem*).

laïc see **laïque**.

laiche (lɛʃ) *f*, sedge.

laid, e (lɛ, ɛd) *a*, ugly, plain, illfavored, unsightly; naughty. **laideron** (drɔ̃) *m*, plain girl. **laideur** (dœːr) *f*, ugliness.

laie (lɛ) *f*, wild sow.

lainage (lɛnaːʒ) *m*, woolen goods, woolens; teaseling. **laine** (lɛn) *f*, wool. ~ *peignée*, worsted.

lainer (lɛne) *v.t*, to teasel. **lainerie** (nri) *f*, woolen mill; w. trade, wool shop. **laineux, euse** (nø, øːz) *a*, woolly. **lainier, ère** (nje ɛːr) *a*, wool (*trade, etc.*) ¶ *m*, woolen manufacturer.

laïque (laik) *a. & m*, laic, lay (man); undenominational.

laisse (lɛs) *f*, leash, slip; sea ware; watermark (*tidal*).

laissé-pour-compte (lɛse) *m*, returned or rejected article.

laissées (lɛse) *f.pl*, droppings, dung.

laisser (lese) *v.t*, to leave; let; allow; let have. ~ *aller & ~ échapper*, to let go. ~ *courre* (kuːr), to slip (*hounds*). ~ *tomber*, to drop; let fall. *laissez donc*, leave off! **laisser-aller**, *m*, unconstraint; carelessness. **laisser-faire**, *m*, noninterference, drift. **laissez-passer**, *m*, pass; 500-franc note (*slang*).

lait (lɛ) *m*, milk. ~ *condensé*, ~ *concentré*, ~ *conservé*, condensed m. ~ *de beurre*, buttermilk. ~ *de chaux*, whitewash. **laitage** (taːʒ) *m*, milk food. **laitance** (tɑ̃ːs) *ou* **laite** (lɛt) *f*, soft roe, milt. **laité, e** (te) *a*, soft-roed. **laiterie** (tri) *f*, dairy. **laiteux, euse** (tø, øːz) *a*, milky.

laitier (lɛtje) *m*, slag, scoria[e].

laitier, ère (lɛtje, ɛːr) *m*, milkman, milkmaid, dairyman. ¶ *f*, milker (*cow*).

laiton (lɛtɔ̃) *m*, brass.

laitue (lɛty) *f*, lettuce. ~ *pommée*, cabbage l. ~ *romaine*, Romaine lettuce.

laize (lɛːz) *f*, width (*of cloth*).

lama (lama) *m*, lama (*pers.*); llama (*Zool.*).

lamaneur (lamanœːr) *m*, branch pilot.

lamantin (lamɑ̃tɛ̃) *m*, manatee, sea cow.

lambeau (lɑ̃bo) *m*, rag, tatter; shred; remnant.

lambin, e (lɑ̃bɛ̃, in) *n*, dawdler, slowcoach; (*att.*) dawdling, slow, dilatory, leisurely. **lambiner** (bine) *v.i*, to dawdle, lag.

lambourde (lɑ̃burd) *f*, joist; wall-plate.

lambris (lɑ̃bri) *m*, wainscot, paneling. ~ *d'appui*, dado. ~

dorés, gilded apartments. **lam-brisser** (se) v.t, to wainscot; panel; line.

lame (lam) f, [thin] sheet; plate; lamina; flake; blade; cutter; lath, slat (blind); spangle; wave, sea, billow; swordsman. **lamé**, e (lame) a. & m, lamé. **lamelle** (mɛl) f, lamina, flake.

lamentable† (lamɑ̃tabl) a, lamentable, deplorable, pitiful, pitiable; woeful. **lamentation** (sjɔ̃) f, lament[ation], wail[ing]. se **lamenter** (te) v.pr, to lament, wail. se ~ sur, to bewail, deplore.

laminer (lamine) v.t, to roll (metal); laminate. **laminoir** (nwaɪr) m, rolling mill.

lampadaire (lɑ̃padɛɪr) m, lamp standard.

lampas (lɑ̃pɑ) m, lampas (silk & Vet.).

lampe (lɑ̃ːp) f, lamp; radio tube. ~ à alcool, spirit lamp. ~ à pied, floor l. ~ de poche, ~ électrique, flashlight. ~ de travail, reading lamp. ~éclair, f, flashbulb.

lamper (lɑ̃pe) v.t, to toss off, swill, swig.

lampion (lɑ̃pjɔ̃) m, fairy light, f. lamp. ~ en papier, paper lantern. **lampiste** (pist) m, lampman. **lampisterie** (təri) f, lamp room.

lamproie (lɑ̃prwa) f, lamprey.

lampyre (lɑ̃piɪr) m, glowworm.

lance (lɑ̃ːs) f, spear; lance; (hose) branch. ~-flamme, m, flamethrower. ~-torpille, m, torpedo launcher. **lancement** (lɑ̃smɑ̃) m, throwing; launch[ing]; floating, promotion. ~ du javelot, du disque, du gros boulet, du marteau, throwing the javelin, the discus, the heavy weight, the hammer. ~ du poids, putting the shot. base de ~, f, launching base. **lancer** (se) m, release (pigeons); starting (Hunt.). ¶ v.t, to throw; cast; put (the shot); fling; hurl; shy; drop (bombs); dart; shoot; fire; toss; pitch; let off; ejaculate; initiate; launch; catapult (airplane); float; promote; issue; set (dog on, fashion); deliver (ball, Ten.); fly (kite); start (stag, game). **lancette** (sɛt) f, lancet. **lanceur** (sœɪr) m, pitcher (baseball); launcher,

launch vehicle. **lanciers** (sje) m.pl, lancers (Danc.). **lancinant**, e (sinɑ̃, ɑ̃ːt) a, shooting (pain).

landau (lɑ̃do) m, landau. ~ [pour enfant], baby carriage, perambulator. ~ pliant, folding carriage. **landaulet** (lɛ) m, landaulet.

lande (lɑ̃ːd) f, heath, moor[land]) links.

langage (lɑ̃gaɪʒ) m, language, speech, parlance. ~ de poissarde, ~ des halles, abusive language.

lange (lɑ̃ːʒ) m, diaper; (pl, lit. & fig.) swaddling clothes.

langoureux, euse† (lɑ̃gurø, øːz) a, languorous.

langouste (lɑ̃gust) f, spiny lobster, (sea) crayfish. **langoustine** (stin) f, prawn.

langue (lɑ̃ːg) f, tongue; language; speech. ~ verte, slang. ~ vulgaire, vernacular. mauvaise ~, backbiter. donner sa ~ au chat, to give up (riddle, etc.). **languette** (lɑ̃gɛt) f, tongue; pointer, feather (as on a board—Carp., & Mach.); strip; cleat.

langueur (lɑ̃gœɪr) f, languor; listlessness; languishment. **languir** (giɪr) v.i, to languish, pine [away]; mope; long, weary; droop, flag, drag. **languissant**, e (gisɑ̃, ɑ̃ːt) a, languishing; languid; lackadaisical; flat, dull.

lanière (lanjɛɪr) f, thong, lash; strip; lace (leather).

lanterne (lɑ̃tɛrn) f, lantern; lamp; (pl.) nonsense. ~ sourde, dark l. ~-tempête, hurricane lamp. ~ vénitienne, paper lantern. **lanterner** (ne) v.i, to shilly-shally; trifle; (v.t.) to humbug. **lanternier** (nje) m, lantern maker; lamplighter; shilly-shallier.

lapalissade (lapalisad) f, truism.

laper (lape) v.i. & t, to lap [up], lick up.

lapereau (lapro) m, young rabbit.

lapidaire (lapidɛɪr) a. & m, lapidary. **lapider** (de) v.t, to stone; throw stones at; pelt; set on (someone).

lapin, e (lapɛ̃, in) n, [buck, doe] rabbit, coney. ~ bélier, lop-ear[ed r.]. ~ domestique, ~ de *clapier*, ~ *de choux*, tame r. ~ *de garenne*, wild r. *chaud* ~, a skirt chaser. *poser un* ~ *à quelqu'un*, to stand somebody up. **lapinière** (pinjɛ:r) *f*, rabbitry.

lapis[-lazuli] (lapis[lazyli]) *m*, lapis lazuli.

lapon, one (lapɔ̃, ɔn) *a. & L~*, *n*, Lapp, Laplander (*n.*). **la Laponie** (pɔni), Lapland.

laps de temps (laps) *m*, lapse of time. **lapsus** (sy:s) *m*, lapsus, lapse, slip.

laquais (lakɛ) *m*, lackey, flunkey, menial.

laque (lak) *f*, lac; lake (*paint*). ~ *en écailles*, shellac. ¶ *m*, lacquer, l. work; japan. **laquer** (ke) *v.t*, to lacquer, japan, enamel.

larbin (larbɛ̃) *m*, flunkey.

larcin (larsɛ̃) *m*, larceny; crib, plagiarism.

lard (la:r) *m*, bacon; fat; blubber. *faire du* ~, to grow fat in idleness. *tête de* ~, pigheaded person. **larder** (larde) *v.t*, to lard (*Cook.*); [inter]lard; load; pierce. **lardon** (dɔ̃) *m*, lardoon, gibe; young child (*slang*).

lares (la:r) *m.pl*, home. [dieux] ~, Lares.

largage (larga:ʒ) *m*, parachute dropping of troops or materiel; release of bombs from plane.

large† (larʒ) *a*, broad; wide; large; loose; extensive; sweeping; free; liberal. ¶ *m*, room, space; open sea; offing. *au* ~, in the offing; out at sea; well off. *au* ~*!* keep off! *de* ~, wide, broad (*Meas.*). **largesse** (ʒɛs) *f*, liberality; bounty, largess[e]. **largeur** (ʒœ:r) *f*, breadth; width; beam (*ship*); gauge (*Rly. track*).

larguer (large) *v.t*, to let go, cast off, slip.

larix (lariks) *m*, larch [tree].

larme (larm) *f*, tear; drop (*of drink*). **larmier** (mje) *m*, drip[stone]. **larmoiement** (mwamɑ̃) *m*, watering of the eyes. **larmoyant, e** (jɑ̃, ɑ̃:t) *a*, weeping, in tears; tearful; maudlin. **larmoyer** (je) *v.i*, to water; weep, shed tears.

larron (larɔ̃) *m*, thief.

larve (larv) *f*, larva, grub.

laryngite (larɛ̃ʒit) *f*, laryngitis. **larynx** (rɛ̃:ks) *m*, larynx.

las, asse (lɑ, ɑ:s) *a*, tired, weary.

lascar (laska:r) *m*, fellow, guy. *drôle de* ~, funny, strange, guy.

lascif, ive† (lasif, i:v) *a*, lascivious, wanton.

lasser (lɑse) *v.t*, to tire; weary.

lasso (laso) *m*, lasso.

latent, e (latɑ̃, ɑ̃:t) *a*, latent, hidden.

latéral, e† (lateral) *a*, lateral, side (*att.*).

latex (latɛks) *m*, latex.

latin, e (latɛ̃, in) *a. & m*, Latin. ~ *de cuisine*, dog Latin.

latitude (latityd) *f*, latitude; scope.

latte (lat) *f*, lath. **latter** (te) *v.t*, to lath. **lattis** (ti) *m*, lathing.

laudanum (lodanɔm) *m*, laudanum.

laudatif, ive (lodatif, i:v) *a*, laudatory.

lauréat (lɔrea) *a.m*, laureate. ¶ *m*, prizeman; prize winner. **laurier** (rje) *m*, laurel, bay; (*pl, fig.*) laurels. ~*-rose*, *m*, oleander.

lavable (lavabl) *a*, washable. **lavabo** (bo) *m*, washstand; bathroom. **lavage** (va:ʒ) *m*, washing, w. out.

lavallière (lavaljɛ:r) *f*, Lavallière [neck]tie.

lavande (lavɑ̃:d) *f*, lavender.

lavasse (lavas) *f*, slops.

lave (la:v) *f*, lava.

lavement (lavmɑ̃) *m*, enema; washing (*hands, feet*).

laver (lave) *v.t*, to wash; w. out; scrub. ~ *la vaisselle*, to wash the dishes. **laverie** (vri) *f*, washhouse. **lavette** (vɛt) *f*, dish mop; dish cloth. **laveur, euse** (vœ:r, ø:z) *n*, washer. *laveuse de linge*, washerwoman. *laveuse mécanique*, washing machine. **lavis** (vi) *m*, wash (*art*); wash drawing. **lavoir** (vwa:r) *m*, washhouse, scullery; washer (*Mach.*).

lawn-tennis (lɔntɛnis) *m*, lawn tennis.

laxatif, ive (laksatif, i:v) *a. & m*, laxative, aperient, opening (medicine).

layetier (lɛjtje) *m*, box maker. ~ *emballeur*, packing-case maker. **layette** (jɛt) *f*, baby linen, layette.

lazaret (lazarɛ) *m*, lazaret[to].
lazzi (lazi) *m*, buffoonery.
le, l'; la, l'; les (lə, l; la, l; le) *art*, the; a, an (*weight, etc.*). Often untranslated, as in *le paradis*, paradise. *l'enfer*, hell. *le Japon*, Japan. *la nature*, nature. *l'histoire*, history. *la France*, France. *les enfers*, Hades.
le, l'; la, l'; les (lə, l; la, l; le) *pn*, him; her; it; them; he; she; they; so.
lé (le) *m*, width(*of cloth*).
leader (lidœːr) (*pers.*) *m*, leader (*political*).
lèche (lɛʃ) *f*, thin slice. ~-*botte*, ~-*cul*, bootlicker, flatterer. **lèche-frite** (frit) *f*, dripping pan. **lécher** (leʃe) *v.t*, to lick; overelaborate. ~ *les vitrines*, to go window-shopping.
lèche-vitrines (lɛʃvitrin) *m*, window shopping.
leçon (ləsɔ̃) *f*, lesson; lecture; reading (*text*); story. ~ *de choses*, object lesson.
lecteur, trice (lektœːr, tris) *n*, reader. ~ *optique*, optical character reader (*computers*). **lecture** (tyːr) *f*, reading; perusal.
ledit, ladite, lesdits, lesdites (lədi, ladit, ledi, ledit) *a*, the said (*law*).
légal, e† (legal) *a*, legal; statutory; lawful. **légaliser** (lize) *v.t*, to legalize.
légat (lega) *m*, legate. **légataire** (tɛːr) *n*, legatee. ~ *particulier*, specific l. ~ *universel*, residuary l. **légation** (sjɔ̃) *f*, legation.
lège (lɛːʒ) *a*, light (*Naut.*).
légendaire (leʒɑ̃dɛːr) *a*, legendary, fabled. **légende** (ʒɑ̃ːd) *f*, legend; characteristics, reference note, explanatory note, signs & symbols (*on map*).
léger, ère† (leʒe, ɛːr) *a*, light; flighty, frivolous; fast; slight; mild; weak (*tea, etc.*). ~ *à la course*, fleet of foot. *à la légère*, lightly, scantily; without due consideration. **légèreté** (ʒɛrte) *f*, lightness; levity.
légiférer (leʒifere) *v.i*, to legislate (*with* sur).
légion (leʒjɔ̃) *f*, legion. *ils s'appellent* ~, their name is legion.

législateur, trice (leʒislatœːr, tris) *n*, legislator, lawgiver. **législatif, ive** (tif, iːv) *a*, legislative; parliamentary (*election*). **législation** (sjɔ̃) *f*, legislation. **législature** (tyːr) *f*, legislature. **légiste** (ʒist) *m*, legist, lawyer. **légitime†** (ʒitim) *a*, legitimate; lawful; rightful. ~ *défense*, self-defense. **légitimer** (me) *v.t*, to legitimatize; legitimate; justify. **légitimité** (mite) *f*, legitimacy, lawfulness.
legs (lɛg *ou* lɛ) *m*, legacy, bequest. **léguer** (lege) *v.t*, to bequeath, will, devise, leave.
légume (legym) *m*, vegetable. *les grosses* ~*s*, bigshots. **légumier** (mje) *m*, vegetable dish. **légumineux, euse** (minø, øːz) *a*, leguminous. ¶ *f*, legume[n], pulse.
leitmotiv (laitmotif) *m*, leitmotiv, -if.
Léman (le lac) (lemɑ̃), the Lake of Geneva, Lake Leman.
lendemain (lɑ̃dmɛ̃) *m*, next day, day after, morrow; future. *sans* ~, short-lived.
Léningrad (leningrad) *m*, Leningrad.
lent, e† (lɑ̃, ɑ̃ːt) *a*, slow; dilatory; lingering; low (*fever, speed*). ¶ *f*, nit. **lenteur** (lɑ̃tœːr) *f*, slowness.
lenticulaire (lɑ̃tikylɛːr) *a*, lenticular. **lentille** (tiːj) *f*, lentil; lens; freckle; bob, ball. ~ *d'eau*, ~ *de marais*, duckweed.
lentisque (lɑ̃tisk) *m*, lentisk, mastic [tree].
léonin, e (leɔnɛ̃, in) *a*, leonine; one-sided.
léopard (leɔpaːr) *m*, leopard.
lépas (lepɑs) *m*, limpet.
lépidoptères (lepidɔptɛːr) *m.pl*, Lepidoptera.
lèpre (lɛpr) *f*, leprosy. **lépreux, euse** (leprø, øːz) *a*, leprous. ¶ *n*, leper. **léproserie** (prozri) *f*, leper hospital.
lequel, laquelle, lesquels, lesquelles (ləkɛl, lakɛl, lekɛl) *pn*, who; whom; which.
lèse-majesté (lɛzmaʒeste) *f*, [high] treason; lese-majesty. **léser** (leze) *v.t*, to injure; wrong.
lésiner (lezine) *v.i*, to be stingy, haggle. **lésinerie** (nri) *f*, stinginess, meanness.
lésion (lezjɔ̃) *f*, lesion, injury, hurt.

lessive (lɛsiːv) *f*, washing, wash; lye; detergent. **lessiver** (sive) *v.t*, to wash; scrub, swill; leach. *être lessivé*, to be exhausted (*slang*). **lessiveuse** (vøːz) *f*, wash boiler.

lest (lɛst) *m*, ballast.

leste† (lɛst) *a*, nimble; smart; flippant; free, indecorous.

lester (leste) *v.t*, to ballast. *se ~ l'estomac*, to line one's stomach.

léthargie (letarʒi) *f*, lethargy. **léthargique** (ʒik) *a*, lethargic. **Léthé** (lete) *m*, Lethe.

léthifère (letifɛːr) *a*, deadly, lethal.

letton, onne (lɛtɔ̃, ɔn) *a*. & **L~,** *n*, Lett; Latvian. **la Lettonie** (tɔni), Latvia.

lettrage (lɛtraːʒ) *m*, lettering. **lettre** (tr) *f*, letter; note. *~ avion*, airmail letter. *~ close* (*fig.*), sealed book. *~ d'un autre œil*, wrong font. *~ de change*, bill of exchange. *~ de crédit, ~ de créance*, letter of credit. *~s de créance*, credentials. *~ de [faire] part*, notice announcing a birth, marriage, or death. *~s de naturalisation*, naturalization papers. *~[s] de service*, commission (*officer's*). *~ de voiture*, consignment note. *~ missive*, letter missive. *~ moulée*, block letter. *~ recommandée*, registered letter. *en toutes ~*, in full, fully. **lettré, e** (tre) *a*. & *n*, lettered, literate, well-read (person). **lettrine** (trin) *f*, drop letter (*Typ.*); catchword (*at head of dictionary page*).

leur (lœːr) *a*, their. **le ~, la, ~ les ~s,** *pn*, theirs.

leurre (lœːr) *m*, lure; catch (*fig.*). **leurrer** (lœre) *v.t*, to lure. **se ~,** to delude oneself.

levain (ləvɛ̃) *m*, leaven, yeast, barm. *sans ~*, unleavened.

levant (ləvɑ̃) *a.m*, rising (*sun*). ¶ *m*, east. *du ~ au couchant*, from east to west. **L~,** *m*, Levant. **levantin, e** (tɛ̃, in) *a*. & **L~,** *n*, Levantine.

levé [de plans] (ləve) *m*, survey-[ing]. **levée** (ve) *f*, raising; lifting; lift; levy, removal; close (*sitting*); collection (*letters*); clearing (*letter box*); trick (*cards*); embankment; causeway. **lever**

(ve) *m*, rising, getting up (*from bed*); rise (*sun*). *~ [de plans]*, survey[ing]. *~ de rideau*, curtain raiser. ¶ *v.t*, to lift; hoist; raise; take up; remove; cut off; levy; clear (*letter box*); close (*sitting*); break up (*camp*); weigh (*anchor*); plot (*plan*); (*v.i.*) to rise; shoot (*plant*). *faire ~*, to raise, leaven (*dough*). **se~,** *v.pr*. & *abs*, to rise, get up; stand up.

léviathan (levjatɑ̃) *m*, leviathan.

levier (ləvje) *m*, lever; handspike.

lévite (levit) *m*, Levite; priest; satellite. **le Lévitique** (tik), Leviticus.

levraut (ləvro) *m*, leveret, young hare.

lèvre (lɛːvr) *f*, lip.

levrette (ləvrɛt) *f*, greyhound [bitch]. **lévrier** (levrie) *m*, greyhound. *~ de mer*, ocean greyhound (*fig.*). *~ russe*, borzoi.

levure (ləvyːr) *f*, yeast, barm.

lexicographe (lɛksikɔgraf) *m*, lexicographer. **lexique** (sik) *m*, lexicon.

Leyde (lɛd) *f*, Leyden.

lézard (lezaːr) *m*, lizard.

lézarde (lezard) *f*, crack, crevice, chink. **lézarder** (de) *v.i*, to sun oneself. *v.t*, to crack, split (*plaster*). **se ~,** to crack, split.

liais (ljɛ) *m*, kind of Portland stone.

liaison (ljɛzɔ̃) *f*, connection; bond; liaison; slur (*Mus.*); tie (*Mus.*); thickening (*Cook.*). **liaisonner** (zɔne) *v.t*, to bond (*masonry*).

liane (ljan) *f*, liana, liane.

liant, e (ljɑ̃, ɑ̃ːt) *a*, pliant; sociable, responsive. ¶ *m*, pliancy.

liard (ljaːr) *m*, farthing (*fig.*), rap. **liarder** (arde) *v.i*, to haggle.

lias (ljɑ) *m*, lias (*Geol.*). **liasique** (azik) *a*, liassic.

liasse (ljas) *f*, bundle; file.

libation (libasjɔ̃) *f*, libation; drinking.

libelle (libɛl) *m*, libel.

libellé (libɛlle) *m*, drawing [up]; wording; particulars. **libeller** (le) *v.t*, to draw [up], make; word.

libelliste (libɛllist) *m*, libeler.

libellule (libɛllyl) *f*, dragonfly.

libéral, e† (liberal) *a*, liberal, open-handed; learned (*profession*, in France such as médicin, avocat, notaire, not in the pay of the State, or under its control). ¶ *m*, liberal. **libéralisme** (lism) *m*, liberalism. **libéralité** (te) *f*, liberality.

libérateur, trice (liberatœːr, tris) *n*, liberator, deliverer. **libération** (sjɔ̃) *f*, liberation; discharge; release; paying up. **libérer** (re) *v.t*, to liberate. **liberté** (bɛrte) *f*, liberty, freedom. ~ [*de langage*], ~ *de parole*, outspokenness. ~ *de parler*, free-[dom of] speech.

libertin, e (libɛrtɛ̃, in) *a*, libertine, rakish; wayward. ¶ *m*, libertine, rake. **libertinage** (tinaːʒ) *m*, licentiousness; waywardness.

libraire (librɛːr) *m*, bookseller. ~*-éditeur*, b. & publisher. **librairie** (brɛri) *f*, book trade; bookstore; publishing house.

libre† (libr) *a*, free; at liberty, disengaged; available; vacant; spare; open; welcome; clear (*way*); unstamped (*paper*). ~ *arbitre*, *m*, free will. ~*-échange*, *m*, f. trade. ~*-échangiste* (eʃɑ̃ʒist) *m*, f. trader. ~ *parole*, f. speech. ~ *penseur*, freethinker. ~*-service*, self-service.

librettiste (librɛtist) *m*, librettist.

lice (lis) *f*, lists, arena; bitch hound; warp.

licence (lisɑ̃ːs) *f*, license; licentiate's degree; leave; licentiousness. **licencié, e** (sɑ̃sje) *n*, licentiate, bachelor (*laws*, *arts*); dismissed employee. **licencier** (sje) *v.t*, to disband (*troops*); dismiss, discharge. **licencieux, euse**† (sjø, øːz) *a*, licentious, ribald.

lichen (likɛn) *m*, lichen.

licher (liʃe) *v.t*, to lick; drink; tipple.

licite† (lisit) *a*, licit, lawful.

licorne (likɔrn) *f*, unicorn.

licou (liku) *or poet.*, *before vowel*, **licol** (kɔl) *m*, halter (*harness*).

licteur (liktœːr) *m*, lictor.

lie (li) *f*, lees, dregs; offscourings; scum. **faire chère lie**, to live well.

lié, e (lje) *p.a*, bound, tied; intimate, thick.

liège (ljɛːʒ) *m*, cork.

lien (ljɛ̃) *m*, bond; tie; link; binder; strap. **lier** (lje) *v.t*, to bind; tie

[up]; join; link; knit; connect; enter into; tie (*Mus.*); slur (*Mus.*); thicken (*sauce*).

lierre (ljɛːr) *m*, ivy. ~ *terrestre*, ground i.

lieu (ljø) *m*, place; stead; ground[s], occasion; (*s. & pl.*) spot; (*pl.*) premises. ~*x* [*d'aisance*] ou *petit* ~, watercloset, privy, latrine, john. ~*x communs*, commonplaces (*Rhet. & platitudes*). ~*x de pêche*, where to fish. *au* ~ *de*, instead of, in lieu of. *au* ~ *que*, whereas. *avoir* ~, to take place.

lieue (ljø) *f*, league (= 4 kilometers); mile(s) (*long way*). *d'une* ~, a mile off.

lieur (ljœːr) (*pers.*) *m. &* **lieuse** (øːz) (*Mach.*) *f*, binder (*sheaf*).

lieutenant (ljøtnɑ̃) *m*, lieutenant; mate (*ship*). ~*-colonel*, lieutenant colonel. ~ *de vaisseau*, [naval] lieutenant.

lièvre (ljɛːvr) *m*, hare.

ligament (ligamɑ̃) *m*, ligament. **ligature** (tyːr) *f*, ligature.

lige (liːʒ) *a. &* **vassal** ~, *m*, liege.

lignage (liɲaːʒ) *m*, lineage, descent; linage (*Typ.*).

ligne (liɲ) *f*, line; rank. ~ *d'autobus*, bus route. ~ *de but*, *de touche*, goal, touch, l. (*Foot.*). ~ *de départ*, starting l.; scratch l. ~ *de faîte*, watershed. ~ *de flottaison* (flɔtɛzɔ̃), water line (*ship*). ~ *de fond*, *de côté*, *de service*, *médiane de service*, base, side, service, center service, l. (*Ten.*). ~ *supplémentaire*, ledger l. (*Mus.*). *à la* ~, new paragraph. *en* ~, on line (*computers*).

lignée (liɲe) *f*, issue, line, stock.

ligneux, euse (liɲø, øːz) *a*, ligneous, woody. **lignite** (ɲit) *m*, lignite.

ligoter (ligɔte) *v.t*, to bind, lash.

ligue (lig) *f*, league. **liguer** (ge) *v.t*, to l.

lilas (lilɑ) *m. & att*, lilac.

lilliputien, ne (lilipysjɛ̃, ɛn) *a*, Lilliputian.

limace (limas) *f*, slug (*Mol.*); Archimedean screw. **limaçon** (sɔ̃) *m*, snail (*Mol.*). *en* ~, spiral, winding.

limaille (limaːj) *f*, filings, dust.

limande (limã:d) *f*, dab (*fish*).
limbe (lɛ̃:b) *m*, limb (*Math.*); (*pl.*) limbo.
lime (lim) *f*, file (*tool*). **limer** (me) *v.t*, to file; polish (*fig.*).
limier (limje) *m*, bloodhound; sleuth-hound.
liminaire (liminɛ:r) *a*, prefatory.
limitation (limitasjɔ̃) *f*, limitation. ~*des naissances*, birth control. **limite** (mit) *f*, limit; bound[ary]. ~ *des neiges éternelles*, snow line. **limiter** (te) *v.t*, to limit; bound; restrict. **limitrophe** (trɔf) *a*, bordering.
limoger (limɔʒe) *v.t*, to fire (*job*).
limon (limɔ̃) *m*, mud, slime, ooze, silt; clay (*fig.*); string (*stairs*); shaft, thill (*cart*); lime (*citrus*). **limonade** (mɔnad) *f*, lemonade. ~ *gazeuse*, carbonated lemonade. ~ *non gazeuse*, still lemonade. **limonadier, ère** (dje, ɛ:r) *n*, light refreshment caterer, café keeper. **limoneux, euse** (nø, ø:z) *a*, muddy, slimy. **limonier** (nje) *m*, lime [tree] (*citrus*).
limousine (limuzin) *f*, limousine.
limpide (lɛ̃pid) *a*, limpid, clear, pellucid.
limure (limy:r) *f*, filing; filings.
lin (lɛ̃) *m*, flax; linen.
linceul (lɛ̃sœl *ou* œ:j) *m*, shroud, winding sheet.
linéaire (lineɛ:r) *a*, linear; lineal. **linéament** (neamã) *m*, lineament, feature; outline.
linge (lɛ̃:ʒ) *m*, linen; cloth. ~ *à thé*, tea cloth. ~ *de table*, table linen. **linger, ère** (lɛ̃ʒe, ɛ:r) *n*, lingerie maker; fancy draper; (*f.*) wardrobe keeper. **lingerie** (ʒri) *f*, fancy drapery, lingerie; linen room.
lingot (lɛ̃go) *m*, ingot; slug (*bullet & Typ.*).
lingual, e (lɛ̃gwal) *a. & f*, lingual. **linguiste** (gɥist) *m*, linguist. **linguistique** (tik) *f*, linguistics.
linière (linjɛ:r) *a.f*, linen (*industry*). ¶ *f*, flax field.
liniment (linimã) *m*, liniment.
linoléum (linɔleɔm) *m*, linoleum. ~ *imprimé*, printed linoleum, oilcloth. ~ *incrusté*, inlaid linoleum.
linon (linɔ̃) *m*, linon; lawn (*fabric*).

linot (lino) *m*, ou **linotte** (nɔt) *f*, linnet.
linotype (linɔtip) *a. & f*, linotype.
linteau (lɛ̃to) *m*, lintel, transom.
lion (ljɔ̃) *m*, lion. ~ *marin*, sea l. **lionceau** (so) *m*, l. cub, l. whelp. **lionne** (ɔn) *f*, lioness; fury.
lippe (lip) *f*, thick underlip. *faire la* ~, to pout. **lippu, e** (py) *a*, thick-lipped.
liquéfaction (likefaksjɔ̃) *f*, liquefaction. **liquéfier** (fje) *v.t*, to liquefy. **liqueur** (kœ:r) *f*, liquor, drink; solution (*Chem.*). ~ *d'ammoniaque*, liquid ammonia, hartshorn. ~ [*de dessert*], liqueur. ~ *de ménage*, homemade wine. ~*s fortes*, strong drink. ~*s fraîches*, nonalcoholic drinks. ~ [*spiritueuse*], spirit.
liquidateur (likidatœ:r) *m*, liquidator. **liquidation** (sjɔ̃) *f*, liquidation, winding up; closing; settlement, account (*Stk Ex.*); [liquidation] sale, closing-down sale, selling off.
liquide (likid) *a*, liquid; wet (*goods*). *argent* ~, ready cash. ¶ *m*, liquid; fluid; liquor (*alcoholic*); (*f.*) liquid (*Gram.*).
liquider (likide) *v.t*, to liquidate, wind up; close; settle; pay off; sell off.
liquoreux, euse (likɔrø, ø:z) *a*, sweet (*wine*). **liquoriste** (rist) *n*, wine & spirit merchant.
lire (li:r) *v.t. & abs. ir*, to read; hear from.
lis (lis) *m*, lily. ~ *tigré*, tiger lily.
Lisbonne (lizbɔn) *f*, Lisbon.
liseré (lizere) *m*, piping (*braid*); border.
liseron (lizrɔ̃) *ou* **liset** (ze) *m*, bindweed.
liseur, euse (lizœ:r, ø:z) *m*, reader. ~ *de pensées*, mind r. ¶ *f*, reading stand; bed jacket. **lisible†** (zibl) *a*, legible; readable (*interesting*).
lisière (lizjɛ:r) *f*, selvedge, list; leading-strings; border, edge, skirt.
lisse (lis) *a*, smooth; sleek; plain; flush. ¶ *f*, warp; rail (*ship*). **lisser** (se) *v.t*, to smooth. **lissoir** (swa:r) *m*, smoother.
listage (lista:ʒ) *m*, listing (*com-*

liste (list) *f*, list, roll; panel (*jury*). ~ *des admis*, pass list (*exams*). ~ *électorale*, register of voters.

lit (li) *m*, bed; bedstead; layer; marriage; set (*of tide, etc.*). ~ *à colonnes*, four-poster. ~ *de douleur*, sick bed. *être exposé sur un* ~ *de parade*, to lie in state.

litanie (litani) *f*, rigmarole; (*pl.*) litany.

liteau (lito) *m*, stripe (*on cloth*); runner (*for shelf*); haunt (*wolves'*).

litée (lite) *f*, group (*collection of animals in the same den or lair*).

literie (litri) *f*, bedding.

litharge (litar3) *f*, litharge.

lithine (litin) *f*, lithia. **lithium** (tiom) *m*, lithium.

lithographe (litɔgraf) *m*, lithographer. **lithographie** (fi) *f*, lithography; lithograph. **lithographier** (fje) *v.t*, to lithograph. **lithographique** (fik) *a*, lithographic.

litière (litjɛːr) *f*, litter (*straw & dung; also palanquin*).

litige (litiː3) *m*, litigation; dispute. **litigieux, euse** (ti3jø, øːz) *a*, litigious; contentious.

litorne (litɔrn) *f*, fieldfare.

litre (litr) *m*, liter. = 1.75980 (about 1¾) pints; liter measure; liter bottle.

littéraire† (literɛːr) *a*, literary. **littéral, e†** (literal) *a*, literal. **littérateur** (literɑtœːr) *m*, literary man. **littérature** (tyːr) *f*, literature; learning; empty talk.

littoral, e (litɔral) *a*, littoral. ¶ *m*, littoral, seaboard.

Lit[h]uanie (la) (lituani), Lithuania.

liturgie (lityrʒi) *f*, liturgy.

liure (ljyːr) *f*, cart rope.

livide (livid) *a*, livid, ghastly.

Livourne (livurn) *f*, Leghorn.

livrable (livrabl) *a*, deliverable. ¶ (*Com.*) *m*, forward, terminal, [for] shipment; futures, options. **livraison** (vrɛzɔ̃) *f*, delivery; part, number (*publication*).

livre (liːvr) *f*, pound = ½ kilogram; franc. *Note*.—The word *livre* (meaning a present-day French franc) is still sometimes used, but almost exclusively in literature. ~ [*sterling*], pound [sterling]. *la* ~, sterling, the £.

livre (liːvr) *m*, book; journal; register; diary; day book. *grand* ~, ledger. ~ *à feuille[t]s mobiles*, looseleaf book. ~ *à succès*, ~ *à grand tirage*, bestseller. ~*s d'agrément*, light reading. ~ *d'exemples*, copybook. ~ *d'images*, picture b. ~ *d'office*, ~ *d'église*, ~ *de prières*, prayer b. ~ *de bord & ~ de loch*, log [b.]. ~ *de chevet*, favorite b. ~ *de lecture*, reader. ~ *de signatures*, autograph book. ~ *feint*, dummy book (*for bookshelf*). ~ *généalogique*, stud b.; herd b. ~ *de poche*, paperback book. *à* ~ *ouvert*, at sight. *faire un* ~, to make book (*betting*).

livrée (livre) *f*, livery; servants; badge.

livrer (livre) *v.t*, to deliver; d. up; surrender; consign; commit; confide; join, give (*battle*). ~ *par erreur*, to misdeliver.

livret (livrɛ) *m*, book (*small register*); handbook; libretto. ~ *militaire*, service record.

livreur, euse (livrœːr, øːz) *n*, delivery man *or* boy *or* girl.

lobe (lɔb) *m*, lobe.

lobélie (lɔbeli) *f*, lobelia.

local, e† (lɔkal) *a*, local. ¶ *m*. oft. *pl*, premises. **localiser** (lize) *v.t*, to place; localize. **localité** (te) *f*, locality, place. **locataire** (tɛːr) *n*, tenant, occupier; leaseholder; lodger; renter; hirer. **locatif, ive** (tif, iːv) *a*, tenant's (*repairs*); rental, letting (*value*). **location** (sjɔ̃) *f*, letting, renting, hire; reservation, booking; tenancy.

loch (lɔk) *m*, log (*float—ship's*).

loche (lɔʃ) *f*, loach (*fish*); slug (*Mol.*).

lock-out (lɔkaut) *m*, lockout.

locomobile (lɔkɔmɔbil) *f*, agricultural engine, traction e. **locomoteur, trice** (tœːr, tris) *a*, locomotive. **locomotion** (sjɔ̃) *f*, locomotion. **locomotive** (tiːv) *f*, locomotive, [railway] engine; a hit movie which a theater can acquire only if it also accepts less successful films; an influential person capa-

ble of drawing customers to res-
taurants, clubs, etc.

locuste (lɔkyst) *f*, locust; shrimp,
prawn.

locution (lɔkysjɔ̃) *f*, phrase.

lof (lɔf) *m*, windward side (*ship*);
luff. **lofer** (fe) *v.t*, to luff.

logarithme (lɔgaritm) *m*, logarithm.

loge (lɔːʒ) *f*, lodge (*porter's, freemasons'*); loggia; box (*Theat.*);
dressing room (*actor's*); cage
(*menagerie*); loculus. **logeable**
(lɔʒabl) *a*, tenantable, [in]habit-
able. **logement** (ʒmã) *m*, lodging, housing, billeting; accommodation, quarters. **loger** (ʒe) *v.i.
& t*, to lodge, live; stay; accommodate; house; billet; stable. **logeur, euse** (ʒœːr, øːz) *n*, landlord, -lady, lodging-house keeper.

logiciel (lɔʒisjɛl) *m*, software
(*computers*).

logicien (lɔʒisjɛ̃) *m*, logician.
logique† (ʒik) *a*, logical. ¶ *f*,
logic.

logis (lɔʒi) *m*, house, home.

loi (lwa) *f*, law; enactment; statute; act; standard (*of coin*). *hors
la ~*, outlaw.

loin (lwɛ̃) *ad*, far, f. away, f. off;
f. back; afar; afield; a long way.
~ de compte, out of one's reckoning, wide of the mark. **lointain, e** (tɛ̃, ɛn) *a*, remote, far off,
distant. ¶ *m*, distance.

loir (lwaːr) *m*, dormouse.

loisible (lwazibl) *a*, permissible.
loisir (ziːr) *m. oft. pl*, leisure,
[spare] time. *à ~, ad*, at leisure.

lolo (lolo) *m*, milk (*babytalk*). *les
~s*, women's breasts (*slang*).

lombaire (lɔ̃bɛːr) *a*, lumbar.

Lombardie (la) (lɔ̃bardi), Lombardy.

lombes (lɔ̃ːb) *m.pl*, loins.

londonien, ne (lɔ̃dɔnjɛ̃, ɛn) *a*,
London. **L~, n**, Londoner. **Londres** (lɔ̃ːdr) *m*, London.

long, ue (lɔ̃, ɔ̃ːg) *a*, long; lengthy;
slow, dilatory. *long échange*,
rally (*Ten.*). *à la longue*, in the
long run, in the end. ¶ *m*, length.
au ~, at length, at large. *au ~ &
au large*, far & wide. *de ~*, long
(*Meas.*). *de ~ en large*, to & fro,
up & down. *en ~*, lengthways. *le*

~ de, along; alongside. [*syllabe*]
longue, f, long [syllable].

longanimité (lɔ̃ganimite) *f*,
long-suffering, forbearance.

long-courrier (lɔ̃kurje) *m*,
ocean-going ship. **long cours**, *m*,
deep-sea navigation; ocean (*or
foreign*) voyage.

longe (lɔ̃ːʒ) *f*, lead rope (*attached
to halter*); leading rein; tether;
loin (*veal*).

longer (lɔ̃ʒe) *v.t*, to run along,
skirt.

longévité (lɔ̃ʒevite) *f*, longevity.

longitude (lɔ̃ʒityd) *f*, longitude.
longitudinal, e† (dinal) *a*, longitudinal.

longtemps (lɔ̃tã) *ad*, long; a
long while. **longuement** (lɔ̃gmã)
ad, long; lengthily. **longuet, te**
(gɛ, ɛt) *a*, longish. **longueur**
(gœːr) *f*, length; lengthiness; delay. *en ~*, lengthways; slowly.
longue-vue (lɔ̃gvy) *f*, telescope,
spyglass.

lopette (lɔpɛt) *m*, homosexual
(*slang*).

lopin (lɔpɛ̃) *m*, patch, plot (*of
ground*), allotment.

loquace (lɔkwas) *a*, loquacious,
talkative, garrulous. **loquacité**
(site) *f*, loquacity.

loque (lɔk) *f*, rag, tatter.

loquet (lɔkɛ) *m*, latch (*door*).
loqueteau (kto) *m*, catch (*window*).

loqueteux, euse (lɔktø, øːz) *a.
& n*, ragged (person).

lord (lɔːr) *m*, lord (*Eng.*).

lorgner (lɔrɲe) *v.t*, to quiz; eye;
ogle, leer at. **lorgnette[s] de spectacle** (ɲɛt) *f. [pl.]*, opera glass-
[es]. **lorgnon** (ɲɔ̃) *m*, eyeglasses,
pince-nez.

loriot (lɔrjo) *m*, [golden] oriole.

lors (lɔːr) *ad*, then. *~ de*, at the
time of. *~ même que*, even
though. **lorsque** (lɔrskə) *c*,
when.

losange (lɔzã:ʒ) (*Geom.*) *m*,
lozenge, rhomb[us], diamond.

lot (lo) *m*, lot; portion; prize (*lottery*); consignment; kit. *~ de réparation*, repair kit. *gros ~*, jack-
pot. **loterie** (lɔtri) *f*, lottery;
sweepstake[s]; raffle, draw; gamble.

lotion (losjɔ̃) *f*, lotion; washing.

lotir (lɔti:r) *v.t*, to allot, parcel out. *bien loti*, lucky. **lotissement** (tismɑ̃) *m*, allotment; development (*land*).

loto (lɔto) *m*, lotto (*game*).

lotus (lɔty:s) *ou* **lotos** (tɔs) *m*, lotus.

louable (lwabl) *a*, laudable, praiseworthy; deserving of praise.

louage (lwa:ʒ) *m*, letting, renting, hiring; hire.

louange (lwɑ̃:ʒ) *f*, praise; commendation. **louanger** (ɑ̃ʒe) *v.t*, to laud [to the skies].

louche (luʃ) *a*, cross-eyed, squint[ing]; cloudy; shady, suspicious. ¶ *f*, soup ladle. **loucher** (ʃe) *v.i*, to squint.

louer (lwe) *v.t*, to let [out], rent, hire; reserve, book; praise, laud. *à ~*, to [be] let; for hire. *se ~ de*, to be pleased with. **loueur** (euse) **de chaises** (lwœ:r, ø:z), chair attendant.

loufoque (lufɔk) *a*, screwball, loony. ¶ *m*, screwball, crackpot.

lougre (lu:gr) *m*, lugger (*Naut.*).

louis (lwi) *m*, louis (*old gold coin = 20 present-day francs*).

Louisiane (lwizjan) *f*, Louisiana.

loulou (lulu) *m*, Pomeranian [dog], pom.

loup (lu) *m*, wolf; waster. *loup-cervier* (sɛrvje) *m*, [common] lynx (*N. Europe*). *~ de mer* (*pers.*), hard-bitten sailor, old salt, [jack] tar.

loupe (lup) *f*, wen (*Med.*); bur[r] (*on tree*); lens, [magnifying] glass. **louper** (pe) *v.i*, to slack; (*v.t.*) to botch.

loup-garou (lugaru) *m*, werewolf; bugbear; bear (*pers.*).

lourd, e† (lu:r, urd) *a*, heavy; weighty; dull; sluggish; close (*weather*). **lourdaud, e** (lurdo, o:d) *n*, lubber, lout, bumpkin, dolt, fathead, oaf. **lourdeur** (dœ:r) *f*, heaviness.

loustic (lustik) *m*, wag, funny man.

loutre (lutr) *f*, otter.

louve (lu:v) *f*, [she-]wolf; lewis. **louveteau** (luvto) *m*, wolf cub (*Zool. & scouting*).

louvoyer (luvwaje) *v.i*, to tack [about].

lover (lɔve) *v.t*, to coil (*rope*).

loyal, e† (lwajal) *a*, honest, straight[forward]; fair; true, loyal. **loyalisme** (lism) *m*, loyalty, allegiance (*to sovereign*); loyalism. **loyaliste** (list) *a. & n*, loyalist. **loyauté** (jote) *f*, honesty, etc.

loyer (lwaje) *m*, rent; hire; price; wages.

lubie (lybi) *f*, whim, crotchet, vagary, fad, kink.

lubricité (lybrisite) *f*, lubricity, lewdness. **lubrifier** (fje) *v.t*, to lubricate, grease. **lubrique** (brik) *a*, lewd, wanton.

lucarne (lykarn) *f*, dormer [window].

lucide (lysid) *a*, lucid, clear. **lucidité** (dite) *f*, lucidity.

luciole (lysjɔl) *f*, firefly; glowworm.

Lucques (lyk) *f*, Lucca.

lucratif, ive (lykratif, i:v) *a*, lucrative. **lucre** (lykr) *m*, lucre, pelf, gain.

luette (lɥɛt) *f*, uvula.

lueur (lɥœ:r) *f*, glimmer; gleam; glimpse; spark.

luge (ly:ʒ) *f*, luge. **luger** (lyʒe) *v.i*, to luge.

lugubre† (lygy:br) *a*, lugubrious, doleful, gloomy.

lui, leur (lɥi, lœ:r) *pn*, [to] him, her, it, them; at him, etc.

lui, eux (lɥi, ø) *pn.m*, he, it, they; him, it, them. *lui-même, eux-mêmes*, himself, itself, themselves.

luire (lɥi:r) *v.i.ir*, to shine, gleam. **luisant, e** (lɥizɑ̃, ɑ̃:t) *a*, shining, gleaming; bright; glossy. ¶ *m*, shine, gloss, sheen.

lumbago (lɔ̃bago) *m*, lumbago.

lumière (lymjɛ:r) *f*, light; luminary (*pers.*); [port] hole; oil hole; spout hole; hole; vent; mouth; throat; (*pl.*) understanding, insight; (*pl.*) enlightenment. *~ éclair*, flash (*Phot.*). *~ magnésique* (maɲezik), magnesium light. **lumignon** (miɲɔ̃) *m*, snuff (*wick*); candle end; dim light. **luminaire** (nɛ:r) *m*, luminary; light; lights; lights. **lumineux,**

euseт (nø, ø:z) a, luminous; bright.

lunaire (lynɛːr) a, lunar. ¶ f, honesty (Bot.).

lunatique (lynatik) a. & n, whimsical (person).

lundi (lœ̃di) m, Monday.

lune (lyn) f, moon; arse (slang). ~ de miel, honeymoon; threshold (fig.). clair de ~, moonlight.

lunetier (lyntje) m, spectacle maker, optician. **lunette** (nɛt) f, (pl.) glasses, goggles; wishing bone; rim (watch). ~ [d'approche], [refracting] telescope. ~ de repère, finder. ~s en écaille, horn-rimmed spectacles. ~ arrière, rear window (auto).

lupin (lypɛ̃) m, lupin[e] (Bot.).

lupus (lypy:s) m, lupus.

lurette (lyrɛt) f: il y a belle ~ que, it is ages since.

luron (lyrɔ̃) m, jolly sturdy fellow. **luronne** (rɔn) f, jovial stout-hearted woman.

lusin (lyzɛ̃) m, marline.

lustre (lystr) m, luster; gloss; foil (fig.); chandelier. **lustrer** (tre) v.t, to luster; gloss; glaze.

lut (lyt) m, lute (cement). **luter** (te) v.t, to lute.

luth (lyt) m, lute (Mus.). **lutherie** (tri) f, musical instrument making.

luthérien, ne (lyterjɛ̃, ɛn) a. & n, Lutheran.

luthier (lytje) m, musical instrument maker.

lutin, e (lytɛ̃, in) a, roguish, impish. ¶ m, [hob]goblin, sprite, elf, imp. **lutiner** (tine) v.t. & i, to plague, tease.

lutrin (lytrɛ̃) m, lectern, reading desk.

lutte (lyt) f, wrestling; struggle; fight, contest, tussle, fray. ~ à la corde, tug of war. ~ libre, no holds barred. **lutter** (te) v.i, to wrestle; struggle, fight, contend; vie. **lutteur** (tœːr) m, wrestler.

luxation (lyksasjɔ̃) f, dislocation (Surg.).

luxe (lyks) m, luxury; sumptuousness; profusion.

Luxembourg (lyksɑ̃buːr) m, Luxemburg.

luxer (lykse) v.t, to dislocate.

luxueux, euse (lyksɥø, øːz) a, luxurious. **luxure** (ksyːr) f, lust. **luxuriant, e** (ksyrjɑ̃, ɑ̃:t) a, luxuriant, lush, rank. **luxurieux, euse** (rjø, øːz) a, lustful, lewd.

luzerne (lyzɛrn) f, alfalfa.

lycée (lise) m, secondary school. **lycéen, ne** (seɛ̃, ɛn) n, student (at a lycée), schoolboy, -girl.

lymphe (lɛ̃:f) f, lymph; sap.

lyncher (lɛ̃ʃe) v.t, to lynch.

lynx (lɛ̃:ks) m, lynx.

lyophiliser (ljofilize) v.t, to freeze-dry.

Lyon (ljɔ̃) m, Lyons.

lyre (li:r) f, lyre. & toute la ~, & all the rest of it. **lyrique** (lirik) a, lyric; lyrical; opera (house). ¶ m, lyric poet. **lyrisme** (rism) m, lyricism.

M

ma see mon.

maboul, e (mabul) a, nutty, cracked. ¶ n, loon, madman, idiot.

mac (mak) m, pimp (slang).

macab (makab) m, corpse (slang).

macabre (makɑ:br) a, macabre; grim, gruesome, ghastly.

macadam (makadam) m, macadam. **macadamiser** (mize) v.t, to macadamize.

macaque (makak) m, macaco, macaque.

macareux (makarø) m, puffin.

macaron (makarɔ̃) m, macaroon.

macaroni (makarɔni) m, macaroni.

macchabée (makabe) m, corpse (slang).

macédoine (masedwan) f, macédoine, salad (fruit); medley.

macérer (masere) v.t, to macerate.

mâchefer (maʃfɛ:r) m, clinker.

mâcher (maʃe) v.t, to chew; masticate; champ (bit). ne pas le ~, not to mince matters. **mâcheur, euse** (ʃœːr, øːz) n, chewer.

machiavélique (makjavelik) a, Machiavellian.

machin (maʃɛ̃) m, thing, gadget; what's-his-name.

machinal, e† (maʃinal) *a*, mechanical (*fig.*). **machination** (sjɔ̃) *f*, machination. **machine** (ʃin) *f*, machine; (*pl.*) machinery; engine; gadget. ~ *à coudre*, sewing machine. ~ *à écrire*, typewriter. ~ *à vapeur*, steam engine. ~-*outil*, *f*, machine tool. ~ *routière*, traction engine. **machiner** (ne) *v.t*, to scheme, plot. **machinerie** (nri) *f*, machinery; engine room, e. house. **machinisme** (nism) *m*, mechanization. **machiniste** (nist) *m*, scene shifter; engineer; bus driver; stagehand, grip, dolly man.

mâchoire (maʃwaːr) *f*, jaw.

mâchonner (maʃɔne) *v.t*, to chew; mumble.

mâchurer (maʃyre) *v.t*, to black, smudge.

macis (masi) *m*, mace (*spice*).

macle (makl) *f*, twin (*crystal*).

maçon (masɔ̃) *m*, mason; bricklayer. **maçonnage** (sɔnaːʒ) *m*, masonry; brickwork. **maçonner** (ne) *v.t*, to mason; brick up. **maçonnerie** (nri) *f*, masonry; stonework; brickwork. **maçonnique** (nik) *a*, masonic.

macule (makyl) *f*, spot, stain; sun spot, macula. **maculer** (le) *v.t. & i*, to stain; offset (*Typ.*).

madame, *oft.* **M~** (madam) *f*, madam; Mrs.; mistress; lady.

madeleine (madlɛn) *f*, sponge cake.

mademoiselle, *oft.* **M~** (madmwazɛl) *f*, Miss; lady; waitress‖

Madère (madɛːr) *f*, Madeira.

madone (madɔn) *f*, madonna.

madras (madrɑ[ːs]) *m*, madras (*fabric*).

madré, e (madre) *a*, speckled, spotted; bird's-eye (*maple*); crafty, deep.

madrépore (madrepɔːr) *m*, madrepore.

madrier (madrie) *m*, plank.

madrigal (madrigal) *m*, madrigal.

mafflu, e (mafly) *a*, heavy-cheeked.

magasin (magazɛ̃) *m*, shop; store[s]; warehouse; magazine. ~ *à prix unique*, one-price shop; five and ten. ~ *à succursales multiples*, chain store. ~ *général*, bonded warehouse. *en* ~, in stock. **magasinage** (zinaːʒ) *m*, warehousing, storage. **magasinier** (nje) *m*, storekeeper, warehouseman. **magazine** (zin) *m*, magazine (*periodical*).

mages (maːʒ) *m.pl*, Magi.

magicien, ne (maʒisjɛ̃, ɛn) *n*, magician; wizard; sorcerer. **magie** (ʒi) *f*, magic, wizardry; witchery. ~ *noire*, black magic, b. art. **magique** (ʒik) *a*, magic(al).

magister (maʒistɛːr) *m*, pedagogue. **magistère** (tɛːr) *m*, dictatorship. **magistral, e†** (tral) *a*, magisterial; masterly; masterful. **magistrat** (tra) *m*, magistrate; judge. **magistrature** (tyːr) *f*, magistracy. ~ *assise*, bench. ~ *debout*, body of public prosecutors.

magnanerie (maɲanri) *f*, silkworm nursery; s. breeding.

magnanime† (maɲanim) *a*, magnanimous. **magnanimité** (mite) *f*, magnanimity.

magnat (magna) *m*, magnate (*Fin., etc.*).

magnésie (maɲezi) *f*, magnesia. **magnésium** (zjɔm) *m*, magnesium.

magnétique (maɲetik) *a*, magnetic; mesmeric. **magnétisation** (zasjɔ̃) *f*, magnetization (*Phys.*). **magnétiser** (ze) *v.t*, to mesmerize, magnetize (*fig.*). **magnétiseur** (zœːr) *m*, mesmerizer. **magnétisme** (tism) *m*, magnetism (*Phys. & fig.*); magnetics; mesmerism. **magnéto** (to) *f*, magneto. ~-*électrique*, *a*, magneto-electric.

magnétophone (maɲetɔfɔn) *m*, tape recorder.

magnificat (magnifikat) *m*, magnificat.

magnificence (maɲifisɑ̃ːs) *f*, magnificence; grandeur; (*pl.*) lavishness; (*pl.*) fine things. **magnifier** (fje) *v.t*, to magnify (*the Lord*). **magnifique†** (fik) *a*, magnificent, splendid, grand, fine; munificent.

magnolia (magnɔlja) *m*, magnolia.

magot (mago) *m*, magot (*ape &*

Chinese *figure*); Barbary ape; fright (*pers.*); hoard.

mahométan, e (maɔmetɑ̃, an) *n, & att,* Mohammedan, Moslem, Muslim. **mahométisme** (tism) *m,* Mohammedanism.

mai (mɛ) *m,* May (*month*); maypole.

maigre (mɛːgr) *a,* lean; meager; scanty; thin; skinny; straggling (*beard*); poor; spare; meatless (*meal*); fast (*day*); vegetable (*soup*). ¶ *m,* lean. **maigrelet, te** (mɛgrəlɛ, ɛt) *a,* thinnish, slight. **maigrement** (grəmɑ̃) *ad,* meagerly, scantily. **maigreur** (grœːr) *f,* leanness. **maigrir** (griːr) *v.i,* to grow thin; (*v.t.*) to [make] thin.

maille (mɑːj) *f,* stitch (*Knit., crochet, etc.*); mesh; speckle; bud; (*pl.*) mail (*armor*). ~ échappée, ~ perdue, run (*stocking*); dropped stitch (*Knit.*). ~ glissée, slip stitch (*Knit.*).

maillechort (majʃɔːr) *m,* German silver.

maillet (majɛ) *m,* mallet. **mailloche** (jɔʃ) *f,* mallet, maul.

maillon (mɑjɔ̃) *m,* link (*chain*); shackle.

maillot (majo) *m,* swaddling clothes (*baby*); tights, *or* any close-fitting woven garment, as bathing suit, football jersey, leotard. *le ~ jaune,* yellow jersey worn by Tour de France leader.

main (mɛ̃) *f,* hand; hand[writing]; handle (*drawer*); scoop; tendril; quire (*in Fr. 25 sheets*); trick (*cards*); lead (*cards*); deal (*cards*). ~ courante, handrail. ~-d'œuvre, workmanship; labor. ~-forte, assistance (to police).

mainmise (mɛ̃miːz) *f,* hold (*influence*).

mainmorte (mɛ̃mɔrt) *f,* mortmain. *biens de ~,* property in mortmain.

maint, e (mɛ̃, ɛ̃ːt) *a,* many a, many.

maintenant (mɛ̃tnɑ̃) *ad,* now. **maintenir** (tniːr) *v.t.ir,* to maintain, keep; uphold. *se ~,* to keep; hold one's own. **maintien** (tjɛ̃) *m,* maintenance, keeping; deportment, bearing.

maïolique (maʒɔlik) *f,* majolica.

maire (mɛːr) *m,* mayor. **mairie** (mɛri) *f,* mayoralty; town hall, town clerk's office, registry [office].

mais (mɛ) *c. & ad,* but; why. ~ *non!* why no! not at all! ¶ *m,* but,. objection.

maïs (mais) *m,* maize, Indian corn.

maison (mɛzɔ̃) *f,* house; home; household; firm; friary; convent. ~ d'aliénés, mental institution. ~ d'arrêt, prison, jail; lockup; guardhouse. ~ d'éducation, educational establishment. ~ d'habitation, dwelling house. ~ de commerce, business house, firm. ~ de correction, reformatory. ~ de jeu, gaming house. ~ de plaisance, weekend cottage. ~ de rapport, revenue-earning house. ~ de retraite, home for the aged. ~ de santé, nursing home. ~ de ville, town hall. ~ des étudiants, hostel. ~ isolée, detached house. ~ jumelle, semidetached house. ~ pour fournitures (de sports, etc.), outfitter. à la ~, [at] home, indoors. **maisonnée** (zɔne) *f,* household, family. **maisonnette** (nɛt) *f,* bungalow.

maistrance (mɛstrɑ̃ːs) *f,* petty officers (*Nav.*). **maître** (mɛːtr) *m,.* master; teacher; Mr. (*courtesy title of lawyers*); petty officer. ~-autel, high altar. ~ chanteur,. blackmailer. ~-coq, cook (*ship's*). ~ d'armes, fencing master. ~ [d'équipage], boatswain; master of the hounds. ~ d'hôtel,. [house] steward; headwaiter,. superintendent (*restaurant*). ~ de chapelle, choirmaster. ~ de conférences, lecturer. ~ de forges, ironmaster. ~ de timonerie,. quartermaster (*Naut.*). ~ des cérémonies, Master of the Ceremonies. ~ drain, main drain. ~ homme, masterful man. ~ Jacques, Jack of all work *or* trades. ~ sot, champion idiot. **maîtresse** (mɛtrɛs) *f,* mistress; paramour. ~ de piano, piano teacher. ~ femme, masterful woman. ~ poutre, main beam. **maîtrise** (triːz) *f,* mastery; control; choir. **maîtriser** (trize) *v.t,* to [over]master; overpower; subdue; control.

majesté (maʒɛste) *f,* majesty; stateliness. *Sa M~,* His (*or* Her) Majesty. **majestueux, euse†** (tɥø, øːz) *a,* majestic; stately.

majeur, e (maʒœːr) *a,* major; greater. *être ~,* to come of [full] age (*law*). *le lac Majeur,* Lago Maggiore.

majolique (maʒɔlik) *f,* majolica.

major (maʒɔːr) (*Mil.*) *m,* adjutant; medical officer. *état-~,* staff. **majoration** (ʒɔrasjɔ̃) *f,* increase (*price*); overvaluation; overcharge. **majordome** (dɔm), majordomo; comptroller of the Royal Household. **majorer** (re) *v.t,* to increase (*price*); overvalue; overcharge for *or* in. **majorité** (rite) *f,* majority.

Majorque (maʒɔrk) *f,* Majorca.

majuscule (maʒyskyl) *a. & f,* capital (letter).

mal (mal) *m,* evil; ill; wrong; harm; hurt; mischief; difficulty; damage; pain; ache; sore; ailment; trouble; disease; illness; sickness. *j'ai ~ au doigt,* I have a sore finger. *~ aux yeux, ~ d'yeux,* eye trouble, sore eyes. *~ blanc,* gathering sore. *~ d'enfant,* labor [pains]. *~ de cœur,* sickness, qualms. *~ de dents, ~ aux dents,* toothache. *~ de gorge,* sore throat. *~ de mer,* seasickness. *avoir le ~ de mer,* to be seasick. *~ de tête,* headache. *~ du pays,* homesickness. ¶ *ad,* ill; badly; evil; wrong; amiss. *~ famé, e,* ill-famed. *~ gérer,* to mismanage. *~ réussir,* to fail, turn out badly. *mal venu, e,* stunted; ill-advised. *de ~ en pis,* from bad to worse. *~ ¶ a. inv,* bad.

malachite (malakit) *f,* malachite.

malade (malad) *a,* ill, sick, unwell; diseased; bad, sore; in a bad way. ¶ *n,* sick person; invalid; patient. *~ du dehors,* outpatient. *~ interné, e,* in-patient. *faire le ~ ou simuler la maladie,* to malinger. **maladie** (di) *f,* illness, sickness, complaint, disease, disorder; obsession. *~ de lan-*

gueur, decline. *~ [des chiens],* distemper. *~ du sommeil,* sleeping sickness. *~ professionnelle,* industrial disease. **maladif, ive** (dif, iːv) *a,* sickly; morbid.

maladresse (maladrɛs) *f,* awkwardness, clumsiness. **maladroit, e†** (drwa, at) *a. & n,* awkward, clumsy (person), maladroit.

malais, e (malɛ, ɛːz) *a. & M~, n,* Malay[an].

malaise (malɛːz) *m,* indisposition; uneasiness; straits. **malaisé, e** (leze) *a,* difficult; not easy; awkward. **malaisément** (mɑ̃) *ad,* with difficulty.

Malaisie (la) (malɛzi), Malaysia.

malandrin (malɑ̃drɛ̃) *m,* bandit.

malappris, e (malapri, iːz) *a. & n,* ill-bred (person).

malaria (malarja) *f,* malaria.

malart (malaːr) *m,* mallard.

malavisé, e (malavize) *a,* ill-advised; unwise.

malaxer (malakse) *v.t,* to mix; work up (*butter*).

malbâti, e (malbɑti) *a. & n,* misshapen (person).

malchance (malʃɑ̃ːs) *f,* ill luck; mischance. **malchanceux, euse** (ʃɑ̃sø, øːz) *a. & n,* unlucky (person).

maldonne (maldɔn) *f,* misdeal (*cards*); mistake, misunderstanding.

mâle (mɑːl) *m. & a,* male; he; cock; buck; bull; dog; man (*child*); masculine; manly, virile.

malédiction (malediksjɔ̃) *f,* malediction, curse.

maléfice (malefis) *m,* [evil] spell. **maléfique** (malefik) *a,* maleficent. *étoile ~,* unlucky star.

malencontreux, euse† (malɑ̃kɔ̃trø, øːz) *a,* untoward, unlucky, unfortunate.

mal-en-point (malɑ̃pwɛ̃) *ad,* in a bad way, in a sorry plight.

malentendu (malɑ̃tɑ̃dy) *m,* misunderstanding, misapprehension, misconception.

malfaçon (malfasɔ̃) *f,* bad workmanship.

malfaisant, e (malfəzɑ̃, ɑ̃ːt) *a,* malicious; injurious. **malfaiteur** (fɛtœːr) *m,* malefactor, evil-

doer. ~ *public*, public menace
(*pers.*).

malfamé, e (malfame) *a*, ill-
famed.

malformation (malformasjɔ̃) *f*,
malformation.

malgracieux, euse (malgrasjø,
ø:z) *a*, ungracious, rude.

malgré (malgre) *pr*, in spite of,
notwithstanding. ~ *tout*, for all
that.

malhabile† (malabil) *a*, unskillful; tactless.

malheur (malœ:r) *m*, misfortune; ill luck; unhappiness; evil
days; woe. **malheureux, euse†**
(lœrø, ø:z) *a*, unlucky; unfortunate; unhappy, miserable; woeful; sad; wretched; pitiful. ¶ *n*,
unfortunate [person]; wretch.

malhonnête† (malɔnɛːt) *a*, dishonest; rude, ill-mannered, unmannerly. **malhonnêteté** (nɛtte)
f, dishonesty; rudeness.

malice (malis) *f*, malice, spite;
artfulness; roguishness; practical
joke. **malicieux, euse†** (sjø, ø:z)
a, malicious, spiteful; roguish,
arch.

malignité (maliɲite) *f*, malig-
nity; maliciousness; mischievous-
ness (*playful*). **malin, igne†** (lɛ̃,
iɲ) *a. & n*, malicious; malignant;
evil (*spirit*); mischievous, wicked, roguish; artful (person). *le*
malin [*esprit*], the Evil One.

maline (malin) *f*, spring tide.

malines (malin) *f*, Mechlin [lace].

malingre (malɛ̃:gr) *a*, sickly,
puny.

malintentionné, e (malɛ̃tɑ̃s-
jone) *a. & n*, evil-disposed (person).

malitorne (malitɔrn) *m*, lout.

mal-jugé (malʒyʒe) *m*, miscarriage of justice.

malle (mal) *f*, trunk; mail (*post*);
mail steamer, m. boat, m. packet.
~*-armoire*, wardrobe trunk. ~ *de*
paquebot, ~ *de cabine*, cabin t.
~[*-poste*], mail [coach] (*stage*).
se faire la ~, to take off on the
sly.

malléable (malleabl) *a*, malleable.

malléole (malleɔl) *f*, ankle
[bone].

malletier (maltje) *m*, trunk &

bag manufacturer. **mallette** (lɛt)
f, suitcase; attaché c. ~ *garnie*,
dressing c., fitted c.

malmener (malməne) *v.t*, to
abuse; maul, handle roughly.

malotru, e (malɔtry) *n*, ill-bred
person.

malpeigné (malpɛɲe) *m*, unkempt fellow.

malpropre† (malprɔpr) *a*, dirty;
indecent. **malpropreté** (prəte) *f*,
dirtiness, etc.

malsain, e (malsɛ̃, ɛn) *a*, unhealthy; noisome; unwholesome;
insanitary, unsanitary.

malséant, e (malseɑ̃, ɑ̃:t) *a*, unbecoming, unseemly.

malsonnant, e (malsɔnɑ̃, ɑ̃:t)
a, offensive (*words*).

malt (malt) *m*, malt.

maltais, e (maltɛ, ɛːz) *a. & M~*,
n, Maltese. **Malte** (malt) *f*,
Malta.

malterie (maltəri) *f*, malting,
malt house.

maltôte (maltoːt) *f*, extortion
(*taxes*).

maltraiter (maltrɛte) *v.t*, to
maltreat, ill-treat, ill-use, misuse;
wrong.

malveillance (malvɛjɑ̃:s) *f*,
malevolence, ill will, spite. **malveillant, e** (jɑ̃, ɑ̃:t) *a. & n*, malevolent, ill-disposed (person).

malvenu, e (malvəny) *a*, stunted;
ill-advised.

malversation (malvɛrsasjɔ̃) *f*,
malpractice, embezzlement, pec-
ulation.

mamamouchi (mamamuʃi) *m*,
panjandrum.

maman (ma- *ou* mɑ̃mɑ̃) *f*, mama.

mamelle (mamɛl) *f*, breast; udder. **mamelon** (mlɔ̃) *m*, nipple,
teat; hummock, mamelon, pap.

mamel[o]uk (mamluk) *m*, Mam-
eluke (*Hist.*); henchman, myrmidon.

mamillaire (mamillɛːr) *a*, mamillary.

mammifère (mamifɛːr) *m*,
mammal, (*pl.*) mammalia.

mammouth (mamut) *m*, mammoth.

mamours (mamuːr) *m.pl*, caresses, billing & cooing.

manant (manɑ̃) *m*, boor, churl.

manche (mɑ̃:ʃ) *m*, handle, helve;

haft; stick (*umbrella*); neck (*violin*); knuckle [bone] (*mutton*). ~ *à balai*, broomstick. ¶ *f*, sleeve; hose (*pipe*); channel; game, hand (*cards*); set (*Ten.*). ~ *à air*, ~ *à vent*, ventilator (*ship*). ~ *de chemise*, shirt sleeve. la M~, the [English] Channel. **manchette** (mãʃɛt) *f*, cuff (*dress*); ruffle; headline (*news*). **manchon** (ʃɔ̃) *m*, muff (*ladies'*); coupling (*Mach.*); sleeve; socket; bush[ing]; mantle (*gas*). ~ *d'embrayage*, clutch.

manchot, e (mãʃo, ɔt) *a. & n*, one-handed *or* one-armed (*person*); (*m.*) penguin.

mandant (mãdã) *m*, principal, mandator.

mandarin (mãdarɛ̃) *m*, mandarin. **mandarine** (rin) *f*, mandarin[e] [orange], tangerine [orange].

mandat (mãda) *m*, mandate; order; instructions; trust; procuration, power [of attorney], proxy; order [to pay], money order, withdrawal notice; writ, warrant (*law*). ~[-*poste*], money order, postal o. **mandataire** (tɛːr) *m*, mandatary, -ory; agent; attorney; proxy. **mandater** (te) *v.t*, to authorize [the payment of]; commission.

mandement (mãdmã) *m*, charge, pastoral letter. **mander** (de) *v.t*, to tell; inform.

mandibule (mãdibyl) *f*, mandible; jaw.

mandoline (mãdɔlin) *f*, mandolin.

mandragore (mãdragɔːr) *f*, mandrake.

mandrill (mãdril) *m*, mandrill (*Zool.*).

mandrin (mãdrɛ̃) *m*, mandrel, -il; spindle; arbor; chuck (*lathe*); drift[pin].

manège (manɛːʒ) *m*, training (*horses*); horsemanship, riding; r. school; horse gear; trick. ~ *de chevaux de bois*, merry-go-round.

mânes (mɑːn) *m.pl*, manes, shades.

manette (manɛt) *f*, handle, lever.

manganèse (mãganɛːz) *m*, manganese.

mangeable (mãʒabl) *a*, eatable. **mangeaille** (ʒɑːj) *f*, food, feed. **mangeoire** (ʒwaːr) *f*, manger, crib. **manger** (ʒe) *v.t. & abs*, to eat; feed; have one's meals, mess; eat up; devour; squander; clip (*one's words*). ~ *le morceau*, to turn stoolpigeon. ¶ *m*, food. **mangetout** (mãʒtu) *m*, spendthrift; skinless pea *or* bean. **mangeur, euse** (ʒœːr, øːz) *n*, eater, feeder. **mangeure** (ʒyːr) *f*, bite (*place bitten by worm, mouse*).

manglier (mãglie) *m*, mangrove.

mangouste (mãgust) *f*, mongoose.

mangue (mãːg) *f*, mango. **manguier** (mãgje) *m*, mango [tree].

maniable (manjabl) *a*, supple; manageable; handy.

maniaque (manjak) *a*, maniac(al). ¶ *n*, maniac; faddist, crank. **manie** (ni) *f*, mania; craze; fad.

maniement (manimã) *m*, feeling; handling; management, conduct, care. ~ *des* (*ou d'*)*armes*, manual [exercise], rifle drill. **manier** (nje) *v.t*, to feel; handle; wield; work; ply; manage, conduct. *au* ~, by the feel.

manière (manjɛːr) *f*, manner, way, wise; sort, kind; mannerism; style; (*pl.*) manners (*bearing*). *par* ~ *d'acquit*, perfunctorily. ~ *noire*, mezzotint. **maniéré, e** (jere) *a*, affected, finical; mannered (*style, etc.*). **maniérisme** (rism) *m*, mannerism.

manieur (manjœːr) *m*, one who knows how to handle (*money, men*).

manifestant, e (manifɛstã, ãːt) *n*, demonstrator (*Pol., etc.*). **manifestation** (tasjɔ̃) *f*, manifestation; demonstration. **manifeste**† (fɛst) *a*, manifest, obvious, overt. ¶ *m*, manifesto; manifest (*Ship.*). **manifester** (te) *v.t*, to manifest, show; (*v.i.*) to demonstrate.

manigance (manigãːs) *f*, intrigue. **manigancer** (gãse). *v.t*, to concoct, plot.

manille (maniːj) *m*, Manila [cheroot]; (*f.*) shackle. M~, *f*, Manila (*Geog.*).

manioc (manjɔk) *m*, manioc.

manipuler (manipyle) *v.t*, to manipulate, handle.

manitou (manitu) *m*, big shot, boss (*slang*). être le ~ de l'affaire, to be in charge of the operation.

manivelle (manivεl) *f*, crank; handle, winch.

manne (man) *f*, manna; basket, hamper.

mannequin (mankē) *m*, lay figure, manikin; dress stand; display figure, d. model; dummy; mannequin, model; puppet; basket.

manœuvre (manœːvr) *f*, working, handling, manipulation; shunting (*Rly.*); seamanship; maneuver; move; (*pl.*) field day; rope (*Naut.*); (*pl.*) rigging (*Naut.*); (*pl.*) scheming. ~s électorales, electioneering. ~s frauduleuses, swindling (*law*). ¶ *m*, laborer; hack [writer, etc.]. **manœuvrer** (nœvre) *v.t. & i*, to work, handle, manipulate; shunt; steer (*Ship.*); maneuver. **manœuvrier** (vrie) *m*, (*skillful*) seaman; maneuverer; tactician.

manoir (manwaːr) *m*, manor [house], country seat.

manomètre (manɔmɛtr) *m*, [pressure] gauge, manometer.

manquant, e (mãkã, ãːt) *a*, missing; absent. ¶ *m*, deficiency, shortage. ~ à l'appel, A.W.O.L. (*Mil.*). **manque** (mãːk) *m*, want, lack, shortage, deficiency; breach; dropped stitch (*Knit.*); run. ~ de pose, underexposure (*Phot.*). **manqué, e** (mãke) *p.a*, missed; spoiled; misfit (*att.*); unsuccessful; abortive; wasted. un peintre, etc., manqué, a failure as a painter, etc. Cf. garçon ~ & grand homme ~. **manquer** (ke) *v.i*, to fail; miss; default; misfire, miss fire; be taken [away] (*die*); be wanting; be missing; be disrespectful; (*v.t.*) to miss; fail in. ~ de, to want, lack, run short (*or* out) of; be out of stock of; to nearly . . . ~ de parole, to break one's word.

mansarde (mãsard) *f*, dormer [window]; attic, garret.

mansuétude (mãsɥetyd) *f*, meekness; forbearance.

mante (mãːt) *f*, mantle. **manteau** (mãto) *m*, coat, cloak, mantle,

wrap. ~ de cheminée, mantelpiece. ~ de cour, court train. ~ de fourrure, fur coat. sous [le ~ de] la cheminée, sub rosa, under the rose. sous le ~ de la religion, under the cloak of religion. **mantelet** (tlε) *m*, tippet; mantelet; port lid (*Nav.*). **mantille** (tiːj) *f*, mantilla.

Mantoue (mãtu) *f*, Mantua.

manucure (manykyːr) *n*, manicurist (*pers.*); (*f.*) manicure (*treatment*); m. set.

manuel, let† (manɥεl) *a*, manual; hand (*as work*). ¶ *m*, manual, handbook; text book.

manufacture (manyfaktyːr) *f*, manufactory; staff. **manufacturier, ère** (tyrje, εːr) *a*, manufacturing. ¶ *m*, manufacturer.

manuscrit, e (manyskri, it) *a*, manuscript, written. ¶ *m*, manuscript.

manutention (manytãsjɔ̃) *f*, handling; commissary; post exchange; bakehouse (*Mil.*). ~ maritimes, stevedoring.

mappemonde (mapmɔ̃ːd) *f*, map of the world in hemispheres. ~ céleste, map of the heavens in hemispheres.

maquereau (makro) *m*, mackerel; pimp.

maquette (makεt) *f*, model (*of statuary*); dummy (*publishing*).

maquignon (makiɲɔ̃), *m*, horse dealer; jobber (*shady*). **maquignonnage** (ɲɔnaːʒ) *m*, horse dealing; jobbery. **maquignonner** (ne) *v.t*, to bishop (*horses*); manipulate (*bad sense*).

maquillage (makijaːʒ) *m*, making up; makeup. **maquiller** (je) *v.t*, to make up (*face*); camouflage. **maquilleur, euse** (œːr, øːz) *n*, makeup artist.

maquis (maki) *m*, scrub; resistance (*war*).

marabout (marabu) *m*, marabout; marabou.

maraîcher (marεʃe) *m*, truck gardener. **marais** (rε) *m*, marsh, swamp, bog, fen, morass. ~ salant, saltern.

marasme (marasm) *m*, marasmus; stagnation.

marasquin (maraskē) *m*, maraschino.

marâtre (mara:tr) *f*, [cruel] stepmother.

maraudage (maroda:ʒ) *m*. & **maraude** (ro:d) *f*, marauding, foray; pilfering; *en maraude*, cruising (*taxi*). **marauder** (rode) *v.i*, to maraud, raid; cruise (*taxi*). **maraudeur** (dœ:r) *m*, marauder; petty thief; cabdriver in search of fares.

marbre (marbr) *m*, marble; [marble] slab *or* top; [imposing] stone; bed (*printing press*); [engineer's] surface plate; overset, overmatter (*newspaper work*). ~ *de foyer*, hearthstone. **marbrer** (bre) *v.t*, to marble; mottle. **marbrerie** (brəri) *f*, marble work; m. works. **marbreur** (brœ:r) *m*, marbler. **marbrier** (brie) *m*, marble mason; monumental mason; marble merchant. **marbrière** (brie:r) *f*, marble quarry. **marbrure** (bry:r) *f*, marbling.

marc (ma:r) *m*, marc (*fruit refuse*); grounds (*coffee*); used leaves (*tea*). **au ~ le franc**, pro rata, proportionally, in proportion.

marcassin (markasɛ̃) *m*, young wild boar.

marcassite (markasit) *f*, marcasite.

marchand, e (marʃɑ̃, ɑ̃:d) *n*, dealer, trader, merchant; shopkeeper, tradesman, -woman, vender; (*att.*) merchant[able], mercantile, commercial, market-[able], salable, sale (*att.*) ~ *de journaux*, newsagent. ~ *de volaille*, poulterer. ~ *des quatre saisons*, fruit and vegetable peddler. ~ *en magasin*, warehouseman. **marchandage** (ʃɑ̃da:ʒ) *m*, bargaining, haggling. **marchander** (de) *v.t*. & *abs*, to haggle (over), bargain, palter; grudge; (*v.i.*) to hesitate. **marchandeur, euse** (dœ:r, ø:z) *n*, haggler, bargainer. **marchandise** (di:z) *f*. *oft. pl*, goods, merchandise, wares; commodity; cargo. ~*s d'occasion*, job lot.

marche (marʃ) *f*, walk, walking; march, marching; procession; sailing, steaming; running, run; working; speed; motion; movement, move; journey, course; way, path; progress; step, stair; treadle. ~ *à suivre*, procedure. ~-*pied*, running board.

marché (marʃe) *m*, market; contract; bargain; dealing. ~ *aux bestiaux*, cattle market. ~ *commercial*, produce m. ~ *des valeurs*, ~ *des titres*, share m., stock m. ~ *aux puces*, flea market, thieves' market. *par-dessus le* ~, into the bargain.

marchepied (marʃəpje) *m*, [pair of] steps, stepladder; steps; footboard; stepping stone (*fig.*).

marcher (marʃe) *v.i*, to walk; tread; step; travel; tramp; march; be on the march; be driven (*Mach.*); sail; proceed, move on, advance, progress, go, go on; run, ply; work. *faire* ~, to spoof, put one over on. **marcheur, euse** (ʃœ:r, ø:z) *n*, walker; (*m.*) (*good, bad, fast*) sailer (*ship*).

marcotte (markɔt) *f*, layer (*Hort.*). **marcotter** (te) *v.t*, to layer.

mardi (mardi) *m*, Tuesday. *M~ gras*, Shrove Tuesday.

mare (ma:r) *f*, pond, pool. **marécage** (mareka:ʒ) *m*, marsh, swamp, fen, bog. **marécageux, euse** (kaʒø, ø:z) ~a, marshy, swampy, boggy.

maréchal (mareʃal) *m:* ~ *de France* (*Fr.*), Field Marshal (*Eng.*). ~ *des logis*, sergeant (*mounted troops*). ~ *des logis chef*, s. major. **maréchalat** (la) *m*, marshalship. **maréchalerie** (lri) *f*, farriery. **maréchalferrant** (fɛrɑ̃) *m*, farrier, shoeing smith.

marée (mare) *f*, tide, water; saltwater fish (*caught & fresh*), fresh sea fish, wet fish. ~ *noire*, oil slick.

marelle (marɛl) *f*, hopscotch.

mareyeur, euse (marɛjœ:r, ø:z) *n*, fish merchant & salesman, -woman.

margarine (margarin) *f*, margarine.

marge (marʒ) *f*, margin. **marger** (ʒe) *v.t*, to lay on, feed (*Typ.*); set a margin (*typing*). **marginal, e** (ʒinal) *a*, marginal.

margelle (marʒɛl) *f*, curb (*street*); lip (*well*).

margotin (margɔtɛ) *m*, bundle of firewood.

margouillis (marguji) *m*, mess.

marguerite (margərit) *f*, (*petite*) daisy; (*grande*) marguerite, ox-eye daisy; print wheel (*typewriter, etc.*). ~ *de la Saint-Michel*, Michaelmas daisy.

mari (mari) *m*, husband. **mariable** (rjabl) *a*, marriageable. **mariage** (rjaːȝ) *m*, marriage, matrimony, wedlock; match; wedding. **marié, e** (rje) *n*, bridegroom, bride. **marier** (rje) *v.t. & se* ~, to marry, wed; get married; match, unite. **marieur, euse** (rjœːr, øːz) *n*, matchmaker.

Marianne (marjan) *f*, the French Republic (*equivalent of Uncle Sam*).

marie-couche-toi-là (marikuʃtwala) *f*, slut, easy lay.

marie-jeanne (mariȝan) *f*, marijuana (*slang*).

marie-salope (marisalɔp) *f*, slut; mud-dredger or barge; bloody Mary (*drink*).

marin, e (marɛ̃, in) *a*, marine; sea (*att.*); nautical (*mile*); sailor (*suit*). ¶ *m*, seaman, mariner, sailor; waterman, boatman. ~ *d'eau douce*, freshwater sailor, landlubber. **marine** (rin) *f*, marine, shipping, maritime navigation; seascape. ~ [*militaire*], ~ *de guerre*, navy. **mariné, e** (rine) *a*, sea-damaged. **mariner** (ne) *v.t*, to pickle; marinade.

maringouin (marɛ̃gwɛ̃) *m*, mosquito.

marinier (marinje) *m*, bargeman, bargee.

marionnette (marjɔnɛt) *f*, puppet, marionette.

marital, e† (marital) *a*, marital.

maritime (maritim) *a*, maritime, marine, sea (*att.*); shipping (*att.*); ship (*canal, broker, etc.*); naval.

maritorne (maritɔrn) *f*, slut, slattern.

marivauder (marivode) *v.i*, to bandy flirtatious remarks.

marjolaine (marʒɔlɛn) *f*, [sweet] marjoram.

marmaille (marmɑːj) *f.col*, children, brats.

Marmara (mer de) (marmara), Sea of Marmara.

marmelade (marməlad) *f*, preserve, marmalade. ~ *de pommes,*

de prunes, stewed apples, plums. *en* ~, reduced to a pulp (*as cooked meat*); to (*or* in) a jelly (*as face by blow*).

marmenteaux (marmɑ̃to) *m.pl*, ornamental trees.

marmitage (marmitaːȝ) *m*, shelling (*Artil.*). **marmite** (mit) *f*, boiler, pot; pot hole (*Geol.*); heavy shell (*Artil.*). ~ *autoclave* steamer, steam cooker. **marmiter** (te) *v.t*, to shell. **marmiteux, euse** (tø, øːz) *a. & n*, miserable (wretch). **marmiton** (tɔ̃) *m*, kitchen boy; scullion.

marmonner (marmɔne) *v.t*, to grumble about.

marmot, te (marmo, ɔt) *n*, youngster. (*f.*) marmot (*Zool.*); kerchief. **marmotter** (mɔte) *v.t*, to mutter, mumble.

marmouset (marmuzɛ) *m*, little fellow; firedog.

marne (marn) *f*, marl. **marner** (ne) *v.t*, to marl. **marneux, euse** (nø, øːz) *a*, marly. **marnière** (njɛːr) *f*, marl pit.

Maroc (le) (marɔk), Morocco. **marocain, e** (kɛ̃, ɛn) *a. & M~, n*, Moroccan.

maronner (marɔne) *v.i*, to grumble.

maroquin (marɔkɛ̃) *m*, morocco [leather]. **maroquinerie** (kinri) *f*, fancy leather goods; f. l. shop.

marotique (marɔtik) *a*, archaic, quaint.

marotte (marɔt) *f*, bauble (*Hist.*), cap & bells; milliner's dummy; hairdresser's dummy; pet theory, weakness, craze, [mono]mania.

marquant, e (markɑ̃, ɑ̃ːt) *p.a*, prominent, outstanding; of note, leading. **marque** (mark) *f*, mark; stamp; brand; pit (*smallpox*); score; bookmark; badge; token; tally. ~ *de commerce, de fabrique*, trademark. ~ *déposée*, registered t. m. ~ *typographique*, colophon. *de* ~, branded, by well-known (*or* leading) maker(s); high-class. **marqué, e** (ke) *p.a*, marked; decided. **marquer** (ke) *v.t*, to mark; stamp; brand; score; show; (*v.i.*) to stand out. ~ *le pas*, to mark time. ~ *un but*, to kick (*or* score) a goal (*Foot.*). **marqueter** (markəte) *v.t*, to speckle, spot; inlay. **marqueterie** (kɛtri) *f*, marquetry, inlaid work; mosaic; patchwork.

marqueur, euse (markœːr, øːz) (*pers.*) *n*, marker; scorer.

marquis (marki) *m*, marquis, -quess. **marquise** (kiːs) *f*, marchioness; marquise; canopy (*Arch.*); awning.

marraine (marɛn) *f*, godmother, sponsor.

marrant, e (marā, ãt) *a*, side-splitting, funny. *il n'est pas ~*, he's a dull tool.

marre (maːr) *ad, en avoir ~*, to be fed up (*with it*). **se marrer** (səmare) *v*, to have fun, a good laugh.

marron (marɔ̃) *m*, chestnut; maroon (*firework*); marron (*glacé*) (*att.*) maroon (*color*). *~ d'Inde,* horse chestnut.

marron, ne (marɔ̃, ɔn) *a*, [run] wild (*animal*); outside (*broker*); unlicensed; unqualified; pirate (*publisher*); chestnut-colored, maroon. *nègre marron, négresse marronne,* maroon. **marronnage** (rɔnaːʒ) *m*, running away (*slaves*).

marronnier (marɔnje) *m*, chestnut [tree]. *~ d'Inde,* horse chestnut [tree].

marrube (maryb) *m*, hoarhound.

mars (mars) *m*, March. **M~**, Mars, warfare.

marseillais, e (marsɛjɛ, ɛːz) *a. & M~, n*, (*att.*) Marseilles. *la Marseillaise,* the Marseillais (*anthem*). **Marseille** (sɛːj) *f*, Marseilles.

marsouin (marswɛ̃) *m*, porpoise; colonial infantryman.

marsupial (marsypjal) *m*, marsupial.

marteau (marto) *m*, hammer. *~ d'eau,* water h. *~ de porte,* door knocker. *~-pilon,* power hammer. *être un peu ~,* to be a little cracked, nutty. **martel en tête** (tɛl) *m*, uneasiness, worry. **martelé, e** (tole) (*fig.*) *p.a,* labored; strongly stressed. **marteler** (le) *v.t. & abs,* to hammer. *se ~ [le cerveau],* to make oneself uneasy, worry oneself.

martial, e (marsjal) *a*, martial, warlike.

martinet (martinɛ) *m*, swift (*bird*); tilt hammer; scourge (*whip*).

martingale (martɛ̃gal) *f*, martingale (*harness, betting*); betting system.

martin-pêcheur (martɛ̃pɛʃœːr) ou **martinet-pêcheur** (tinɛ) *m*, kingfisher.

martre (martr) *f*, marten. *~ zibeline,* sable (*Zool.*).

martyr, e (martiːr) *n*, martyr; victim. **martyre**, *m*, martyrdom; torment. **martyriser** (tirize) *v.t*, to martyr[ize]; torture. **martyrologe** (rɔlɔːʒ) *m*, martyrology (*list*).

mascarade (maskarad) *f*, masquerade.

mascaret (maskarɛ) *m*, [tidal] bore. *un ~ humain,* shoals of people.

mascaron (maskarɔ̃) *m*, mascaron, mask.

mascotte (maskɔt) *f*, mascot, charm.

masculin, e (maskylɛ̃, in) *a*, male; masculine. ¶ *m*, masculine [gender]. **masculinité** (linite) *f*, masculinity; male descent.

masque (mask) *m*, mask; blind; features; masker, -quer. *~ à gaz,* gas mask, respirator. ¶ *f*, hussy, minx. **masquer** (ke) *v.t*, to mask; cover, conceal. **se ~**, to masquerade.

massacrant, e (masakrã, ãːt) *a*, very bad (*temper*). **massacre** (kr) *m*, massacre, slaughter. **massacrer** (kre) *v.t*, to massacre, slaughter; smash; murder; botch. **massacreur, euse** (krœːr, øːz) *n*, slaughterer; smasher; botcher.

massage (masaːʒ) *m*, massage.

masse (mas) *f*, mass, lump; solid; body; bulk; aggregate; funds; fund; sledge [hammer]; mace (*ceremonial*). *~ [d'armes],* mace (*Hist.*). *~ d'eau,* reed mace, bulrush. *à la ~* (*Elec.*), grounded, connected to frame.

massepain (maspɛ̃) *m*, marzipan.

masser (mase) *v.t*, to mass; massage.

massette (masɛt) *f*, reed mace, bulrush.

masseur, euse (masœːr, øːz) *n*, masseur, euse.

massicot (masiko) *m*, lead ochre; guillotine (*for paper cutting*).

massier, ère (masje, εɪr) *n*, treasurer; (*m.*) mace bearer.

massif, ive† (masif, iːv) *a*, massive; bulky; heavy; solid. ¶ *m*, [solid] mass; block; body; clump; massif.

massue (masy) *f*, club, bludgeon.

mastic (mastik) *m*, mastic; putty.

mastication (mastikasjɔ̃) *f*, mastication. **mastiquer** (ke) *v.t*, to masticate; putty.

mastoc (mastɔk) *a.inv*, lumpish.

mastodonte (mastɔdɔ̃:t) *m*, mastodon; elephant[ine person].

mastoïde (mastɔid) *a*, mastoid.

masure (mazyːr) *f*, hovel, ruin.

mat₂ e (mat) *a*, mat (*color*), unpolished, lusterless, dead, flat, dull.

mat (mat) *a.m*, checkmated. *faire ~*, to [check]mate (*chess*).

mât (mɑ) *m*, mast; pole. *~ de charge*, derrick (*ship's*). *~ de cocagne* (kɔkaɲ), greasy pole. *~ de fortune*, jury mast. *~ de hune*, topmast. *~ de misaine*, foremast. *~ de pavillon*, flagstaff. *~ de pavoisement* (pavwazmɑ̃), Venetian mast. *~ de signaux*, signal post. *~ de tente*, tent pole.

matador (matadɔːr) *m*, matador (*pers. & games*); magnate (*Fin., etc.*).

matamore (matamɔːr) *m*, swaggerer.

match (matʃ) *m*, match (*boxing, wrestling, tennis, football, chess, etc.*). *~ aller*, first match. *~ nul*, draw[n game]. *~ retour*, return match.

matelas (matla) *m*, mattress. **matelasser** (lase) *v.t*, to stuff, pad. **matelassier, ère** (sje, εɪr) *n*, mattress maker.

matelot (matlo) *m*, sailor, seaman. *~ coq*, cook's mate. *~ de deuxième classe*, able[-bodied] seaman. *~ de pont*, deck hand. *~ de première classe*, seaman first-class. *~ de troisième classe*, ordinary s. [*vaisseau*] *~*, consort (*Navy*).

mater (mate) *v.t*, to [check]mate (*chess*); mortify; humble.

mâter (mɑte) *v.t*, to mast (*a ship*); toss (*oars*).

matérialiser (materjalize) *v.t*, to materialize. **matérialisme** (lism) *m*, materialism. **matérialiste** (list) *n*, materialist. ¶ *a*, materialistic. **matériaux** (rjo) *m.pl*, materials. **matériel, le†** (rjel) *a*, material, physical, bodily. ¶ *m*, plant, material, stock; hardware (*computers*). *~ roulant*, rolling stock.

maternel, le† (maternɛl) *a*, maternal, motherly; mother's (*side*); mother, native (*tongue*). *école ~*, nursery school. **maternité** (nite) *f*, maternity, motherhood; maternity hospital.

mathématicien, ne (matematisjɛ̃, ɛn) *n*, mathematician. **mathématique†** (tik) *a*, mathematical. *~s, f.pl*, mathematics. *~ spéciales*, higher mathematics.

matière (matjɛ:r) *f*, matter; material, stuff; type metal; subject; grounds; gravamen. *~ à réflexion*, food for thought. *~s d'or & d'argent*, bullion. *~ médicale*, materia medica. *~s premières*, raw material[s] (*used in trade*).

matin (matɛ̃) *m*, morning. *un de ces ~s*, one of these fine days. ¶ *ad*, early.

mâtin (mɑtɛ̃) *m*, mastiff; large watch dog; rascal.

matinal, e (matinal) *a*, [up] early, early riser (*être =* to be an); morning (*att.*).

mâtiné, e (mɑtine) *a*, mongrel, cross-bred; mixed.

matinée (matine) *f*, morning; forenoon; morning performance, matinée; dressing jacket. **matines** (tin) *f.pl*, matins. **matineux, euse** (nø, øːz) *a*, [up] early, early riser (*être =* to be an).

matir (matiːr) *v.t*, to mat, dull. **matité** (tite) *f*, dullness, deadness.

matois, e (matwa, aːz) *a. & n*, sly (person).

matou (matu) *m*, tom [cat]; lover (*slang*). *un vilain ~*, a nasty customer.

matraque (matrak) *f*, bludgeon, club, blackjack; repetition of "hit" song on radio.

matriarcat (matriarka) *m*, matriarchy. **matrice** (tris) *f*, womb; matrix; gangue; die; standard (*weight, measure*). ~ **du rôle des contributions**, assessment book (*taxes*). **matricule** (kyl) *f*, register, roll. [**numéro**] ~, *m*, army serial number. **matrimonial**, e (mɔnjal) *a*, matrimonial. **matrone** (trɔn) *f*, matron, dame.

maturation (matyrasjɔ̃) *f*, maturation, ripening.

mâture (maty:r) *f*, masts (*col.*); masting; mast[ing] house.

maturité (matyrite) *f*, maturity, ripeness.

maudire (modi:r) *v.t.ir*, to curse. **maudit**, e (di, it) *p.a*, [ac]-cursed, confounded.

maugréer (mogree) *v.i*, to fume, bluster, curse.

Maure (mo:r) *m*, Moor. **m~**, *a*, Moorish. **mauresque** (mɔrɛsk) *a*, Moresque. ¶ *f*, Morisco, morris [dance].

Maurice [(**l'île**)] (mɔris) *f*, Mauritius.

mausolée (mozɔle) *m*, mausoleum.

maussade (mosad) *a*, sullen, peevish, disgruntled; dull, flat. **maussaderie** (dri) *f*, sullenness; sulks.

mauvais, e (movɛ, ɛ:z) *a*, bad; ill; evil; nasty; wrong; faulty; broken (*English, French, etc.*). **mauvais**, *comps:* ~ **coucheur**, quarrelsome fellow. ~ **œil**, evil eye. ~ **pas**, tight corner; scrape, fix (*fig.*). ~ **plaisant**, practical joker. ~ **quart d'heure**, bad time [of it], trying time. ~ **service**, disservice. ~ **sujet**, ne'er-do-well, scapegrace; bad boy (*Sch.*). ~ **ton**, bad form. **mauvaise**, *comps:* ~ **action**, ill deed. ~ **gestion**, mismanagement, maladministration. ~ **herbe**, weed. ~ **honte**, false shame; bashfulness. ~ **langue**, scandalmonger. **mauvais**, *ad*. & *m*, bad.

mauve (mo:v) *f*, mallow. ¶ *m*. & *att*, mauve.

mauviette (movjɛt) *f*, lark (*bird*); puny creature. **mauvis** (vi) *m*, red wing (*thrush*).

maxi (maksi) *m* or *f*, "new look" length skirt or coat.

maxillaire (maksilɛ:r) *a*, maxillary, jaw (*bone*).

maxime (maksim) *m*, maxim.

maximum, **ma** (maksimɔm, ma) *a*. & *m*, maximum, peak, top (*att.*). ~ **de charge**, burden, burthen (*ship*).

Mayence (majɑ̃:s) Mayence, Mainz.

mayonnaise (majɔnɛ:z) *f*. & *att*, mayonnaise.

mazette (mazɛt) *f*, weakling; duffer, rabbit (*at a game*).

mazout (mazu) *m*, oil fuel.

me, m' (mə, m) *pn*, me; [to] me; myself. ~ **voici**, here I am.

méandre (meɑ̃:dr) *m*, meander, winding.

mécanicien (mekanisjɛ̃) *m*, mechanician, mechanist; mechanic; engineman; engine driver; engineer (*ship*); (*att.*) mechanical (engineer). **mécanique**† (nik) *a*, mechanical; power (*att.*); clockwork (*train, motor car, or other toy*). ¶ *f*, mechanics; mechanism; brake [gear] (*carriage*). **fait à la ~**, machinemade. **mécaniser** (ze) *v.t*, to mechanize, motorize. **mécanisme** (nism) *m*, mechanism, machinery, gear; works (*as of a watch*); technique.

mécanographie (mekanɔgrafi) *f*, data processing; multicopy business, service.

mécène (mesɛn) *m*, patron (*as of the arts*).

méchant, e (meʃɑ̃, ɑ̃:t) *a*, wicked; evil; ill-natured; unkind; spiteful; mischievous, naughty; wretched, paltry, poor, sorry; unpleasant. ~ **poète**, poetaster. ¶ *n*, wicked, etc. person. **méchamment** (ʃamɑ̃) *ad*, wickedly, etc. **méchanceté** (ʃɑ̃te) *f*, wickedness, etc.

mèche (mɛʃ) *f*, wick (*lamp*); tinder; fuse, match, cracker, snapper (*whip*); lock (*hair*); tassel; bit, drill; worm (*corkscrew*); tent (*Surg.*); secret, plot.

mécompte· (mekɔ̃t) *m*, miscalculation, disappointment.

méconnaissable (mekɔnɛsabl) *a*, unrecognizable. **méconnaître** (nɛ:tr) *v.t.ir*, to fail to recognize or diagnose, not to know; disown; disregard, ignore, misunderstand, slight.

mécontent, e (mekɔ̃tɑ̃, ɑ̃:t) *a*, discontent[ed], dissatisfied, disgruntled. ¶ *m*, malcontent. **mécontentement** (tɑ̃tmɑ̃) *m*, discontent[ment], dissatisfaction. **mécontenter** (te) *v.t*, to dissatisfy, displease.

Mecque (la) (mɛk), Mecca.

mécréant, e (mekreɑ̃, ɑ̃:t) *a*, unbelieving. ¶ *n*, unbeliever.

médaille (medɑ:j) *f*, medal; coin (*Greek, Roman*); badge (*porter's*). ~ *d'honneur*, prize medal. **médaillé, e** (daje) *a*, decorated (*Mil.*). ¶ *n*, medalist (*recipient*), prize winner. **médailler** (je) *v.t*, to award a medal (to). **médailleur** (jœ:r) *m*, medalist, medal maker. **médaillier** (je) *m*, coin (*or* medal) cabinet; collection of coins *or* medals. **médaillon** (jɔ̃) *m*, medallion; locket.

médecin (medsɛ̃) *m*, medical man, m. officer, physician, surgeon, doctor; (*of time*) healer. ~ *aliéniste* (aljenist), mental specialist. **médicine** (sin) *f*, medicine; surgery; physic. ~ *légale*, medical jurisprudence, forensic medicine.

médiateur, trice (medjatœ:r, tris) *n*, mediator. **médiation** (sjɔ̃) *f*, mediation.

médical, e (medikal) *a*, medical. **médicament** (mɑ̃) *m*, medicament, medicine. **médicamenter** (te) *v.t*, to doctor, physic, dose. **médicamenteux, euse** (tø, ø:z) *a*, medicinal, curative; medicated. **médicastre** (kastr) *m*, quack. **médication** (sjɔ̃) *f*, medication. **médicinal, e** (sinal) *a*, medicinal. **médico-légal, e** (kolegal) *a*, medico-judicial.

médiéval, e (medjeval) *a*, medieval. **médiéviste** (vist) *n*, medievalist.

médiocre (medjɔkr) *a*, mediocre, poor; middling, moderate. ¶ *m*, mediocrity (*pers. & quality*). **médiocrité** (krite) *f*, mediocrity (*quality*); moderate condition of life.

médire de (medi:r) *v.ir*, to speak ill of, slander. **médisance** (dizɑ̃:s) *f*, slander, backbiting, scan-

dal; scandalmongers. **médisant, e** (zɑ̃, ɑ̃:t) *a*, slanderous. ¶ *n*, slanderer, scandalmonger.

méditatif, ive (meditatif, i:v) *a*, meditative. **méditation** (sjɔ̃) *f*, meditation. **méditer** (te) *v.t. & abs*, to meditate ([up]on), ponder, muse, pore; think; contemplate; plan.

méditerrané, e (mediterrane) *a*, mediterranean, landlocked. *la* [*mer*] *Méditerranée*, the Mediterranean [sea]. **méditerranéen, ne** (neɛ̃, ɛn) *a*, Mediterranean.

médium (medjɔm) *m*, middle register (*Mus.*); medium (*spiritualism*).

médius (medjy:s) *m*, second finger, middle f.

médullaire (medyllɛ:r) *a*, medullary.

méduse (medy:z) *f*, medusa, jellyfish, sea nettle. *la tête de M~* (*fig.*), a terrible shock. **méduser** (dyze) *v.t*, to petrify (*fig.*).

meeting (mitiŋ) *m*, meeting (*Pol., sport, social*).

méfait (mefɛ) *m*, misdeed, malpractice.

méfiance (mefjɑ̃:s) *f*, mistrust, distrust. **méfiant, e** (jɑ̃, ɑ̃:t) *a*, mis- *or* distrustful. *se méfier de* (fje), to mis- *or* distrust; beware of.

mégalomanie (megalɔmani) *f*, megalomania.

mégarde (par) (megard) *ad*, inadvertently.

mégère (meʒɛ:r) *f*, termagant, virago, shrew.

mégie (meʒi) *& mégisserie** (sri) *f*, leather dressing, tawing.

mégot (mego) *m*, cigarette butt.

meilleur, e (mejœ:r) *a*, better. *à meilleur marché*, cheaper. *le ~, la ~*, the better, the best. ¶ *m*, best.

Mein (le) (mɛ̃), the Main (*river*).

mélancolie (melɑ̃kɔli) *f*, melancholia; melancholy. **mélancolique†** (lik) *a*, melancholy, melancholic.

Mélanésie (la) (melanezi), Melanesia.

mélange (melɑ̃:ʒ) *m*, mixture; blending; medley; mash; (*pl.*) miscellany (*literary*); miscellaneous works. **mélanger** (lãʒe) *v.t*, to mix, mingle, blend. *laine mélangée*, wool mixture.

mélasse (melas) *f*, molasses, treacle; misfortune; poverty. *être dans la* ~, to be down on one's luck.

mêlé, e (mele) *p.a*, mixed, miscellaneous, medley. ¶ *f*, fight, mêlée, scrimmage, scramble. **mêler** (le) *v.t*, to mix, mingle; medley; shuffle (*cards*); mash. **se** ~, to interfere, meddle.

mélèze (mele:z) *m*, larch [tree].

mélodie (melɔdi) *f*, melody. **mélodieux, euse†** (djø, ø:z) *a*, melodious, tuneful.

mélodramatique (melɔdramatik) *a*, melodramatic. **mélodrame** (dram) *m*, melodrama.

melon (məlɔ̃) *m*, melon. [chapeau] ~, derby (*hat*).

membrane (mãbran) *f*, membrane; web (*bird's foot*). ~ *du tympan*, eardrum.

membre (mã:br) *m*, member; limb; rib (*ship*). **membré, e** (mãbre) *a*, -limbed. **membrure** (bry:r) *f*, limbs; frame; ribs (*ship*).

mémé (meme), **mémère** (mɛ:r) *f*, granny, grandma; old woman.

même (mɛ:m) *a*, same; like; very; self; itself. ¶ *m*, same [thing]. ¶ *ad*, even, indeed. à ~ *de*, in a position to, able to. *de* ~, *ad*, the same, likewise. *de* ~ *que*, *c*, [just] as, like.

mémento (memẽto) *m*, memento, reminder, note; handbook.

mémoire (memwa:r) *f*, memory; recollection; fame; storage (*computers*). *de* ~, from memory, by heart. *de* ~ *d'homme*, within living memory. *pour* ~, as a memorandum, no[t] value[d] (*in account*). ~ *morte*, read only memory (*computers*). ~ *vive*, random access memory (*computers*). ~ *à ferrites*, core storage (*computers*). ¶ *m*, memorandum; paper (*learned*); bill, account; memoir. **mémorable** (mɔrabl) *a*, memorable. **mémorandum** (rãdɔm) *m*, memorandum; memorial (*State paper*). **mémorial** (rjal) *m*, memoirs.

menace (mənas) *f*, threat, menace. **menacer** (se) *v.t. & abs*, to threaten, menace.

ménade (menad) *f*, maenad.

ménage (mena:ʒ) *m*, housekeeping, housewifery; house[hold], establishment; household goods; home, family; housework. [petit] ~, miniature (*or* dolls') home set. ~ *à trois*, matrimonial triangle. *de* ~, household (*bread*); homespun; house *or* domestic (*as coal*); homemade (*as wine*). *faire des* ~*s*, to clean the house, do housekeeping work. *femme de* ~, cleaning woman. **ménagement** (naʒmã) *m*, *oft. pl*, care, stint; consideration, deference; tact. **ménager** (ʒe) *v.t*, to husband, manage, economize; save; take care of; look after; make the most of; keep; arrange; make; contrive; bring about; keep in with, humor; handle tactfully; spare. *sans* ~ *les termes*, without mincing one's words. **ménager, ère** (ʒe, ɛ:r) *a*, economical, thrifty; careful; sparing; domestic. ¶ *f*, housekeeper; housewife; cruet. **ménagerie** (ʒri) *f*, menagerie.

mendiant, e (mãdjã, ã:t) *n*, beggar; mendicant; (*att.*) mendicant; (*m.pl.*) dessert fruit & nuts. **mendicité** (disite) *f*, begging, mendicancy, mendicity; beggary. **mendier** (dje) *v.i. & t*, to beg; canvass.

meneau (məno) *m*, mullion; transom (*window*).

menée (məne) *f*, (*underhand*) intrigue; track (*Hunt.*). **mener** (ne) *v.t*, to lead, conduct; take, carry; drive; steer; partner (*lady at dance*). *mené par sa femme*, henpecked.

ménestrel (menɛstrɛl) *m*, minstrel (*Hist.*). **ménétrier** (netrie) *m*, (village) fiddler.

meneur, euse (mənœ:r, ø:z) *n*, leader; ringleader. ~ *de train*, pacemaker.

menhir (mɛni:r) *m*, menhir.

méninge (menẽ:ʒ) *f*, meninx (*Anat.*). *se creuser les* ~*s*, to rack one's brains. **méningite** (menẽʒit) *f*, meningitis.

menotte (mənɔt) *f*, small hand; (*pl.*) handcuffs, manacles.

mensonge (mãsɔ̃:ʒ) *m*, lie, false-hood, untruth; fiction; vanity. ~ *innocent*, fib, story. ~ *pieux*, *officieux*, white lie. **mensonger**, **ère†** (sɔ̃ʒe, ɛ:r) *a*, lying, menda-cious; untrue, false, deceitful.

mensualité (mãsɥalite) *f*, monthly payment, drawing, sal-ary, or like. **mensuel**, **le†** (sɥɛl) *a*, monthly (*a. & ad.*). ¶ *m*, em-ployee paid by month.

mensurable (mãsyrabl) *a*, meas-urable.

mensuration (mãsyrasjɔ̃) *f*, mensuration.

mental, **e†** (mãtal) *m*, mental. **mentalité** (lite) *f*, mentality.

menterie (mãtri) *f*, story, fib.

menteur, **euse** (tœ:r, ø:z) *n*, liar. ¶ *a*, lying; deceptive.

menthe (mã:t) *f*, mint. ~ *poivrée*, peppermint. *pastille de ~*, pep-permint [lozenge]. ~ *verte*, spearmint, garden mint. **menthol** (mãtɔl) *m*, menthol.

mention (mãsjɔ̃) *f*, mention, ref-erence. **mentionner** (ɔne) *v.t*, to mention, make reference to.

mentir (mãti:r) *v.i.ir*, to lie. *sans ~*, to tell the truth (*candidly*).

mentor (mɛ̃tɔ:r) *m*, mentor. (ou *en*) *galoche*, slipper chin. M~, Mentone (*Geog.*). **menton-net** (tɔnɛ) *m*, latch catch.

mentor (mɛ̃tɔ:r) *m*, mentor.

menu, **e** (mɜny) *a*, small; slight; petty; minor (*repairs*); minute; fine. *le menu peuple*, the hum-bler classes. *menu plomb*, bird-shot. *menue paille*, chaff. *me-nues herbes*, fine herbs (*fine in texture, as savory herbs*). *argent pour menus plaisirs*, pocket money. *menus propos*, small talk. **menu**, *ad*, small, fine. ¶ *m*, fare; menu, bill of fare. *par le ~*, in detail. **menuet** (nɥɛ) *m*, minuet. **menuiser** (nɥize) *v.i*, to carpenter. **menuiserie** (zri) *f*, joinery; cabinet making, c. work; woodwork. **menuisier** (zje) *m*, joiner; carpenter; cabinet maker; woodworker.

méphitique (mefitik) *a*, mephit-ic, noxious, dank.

méplat, **e** (mepla, at) *a. & m*, flat.

méprendre (se) (meprã:dr)

v.pr.ir, to be mistaken. *se ~ sur*, to mistake.

mépris (mepri) *m*, contempt, scorn. **méprisable** (zabl) *a*, con-temptible, despicable, scurvy; disregardable. **méprisant**, **e** (zã, ã:t) *a*, contemptuous, scornful. **méprise** (pri:z) *f*, mistake; over-sight. **mépriser** (prize) *v.t*, to despise, scorn; disregard, scoff at.

mer (mɛ:r) *f*, sea, ocean. ~ *du Nord*, North Sea. *Note.*—For other seas, see under proper name, e.g., *la mer Egée*, under *Egée*. *un homme à la ~!* [a] man overboard!

mercanti (mɛrkãti) *m*, profiteer. **mercantile** (til) *a*, mercantile, mercenary. **mercantilisme** (lism) *m*, mercantilism, commercialism.

mercenaire (mɛrsənɛ:r) *a*, mer-cenary. ¶ *m*, mercenary, hireling; [paid] worker.

mercerie (mɛrsri) *f*, notions shop. **mercerisé**, **e** (ze) *a*, mer-cerized.

merci (mɛrsi) *f*, mercy; (*m.*) thanks. ¶ *i*, thanks! thank you! no, thank you! *Dieu ~!* thank God!

mercier, **ère** (mɛrsje, ɛ:r) *n*, no-tions shopkeeper.

mercredi (mɛrkrədi) *m*, Wednes-day. *le ~ des Cendres*, Ash Wednesday.

mercure (mɛrky:r) *m*, mercury, quicksilver. **mercuriale** (kyrjal) *f*, mercury (*Bot.*); reprimand; official list (*grain, etc, prices*). **mercuriel**, **e** (rjɛl) *a*, mercurial, blue (*pill*).

merde (mɛrd) *f*, excrement; shit; hash (*drug*); break a leg! (*Theat.*). ~*!*, damn it! *il ne se prend pas pour de la ~*, he's got a pretty good opinion of himself.

mère (mɛ:r) *f*, mother; parent (*lit. & fig.*); dam. *notre ~ com-mune*, mother earth. ~ *abeille*, queen bee. ~ *branche*, bough, limb. *la ~ Gigogne* (ʒigɔɲ), the Old Woman who lived in a shoe. *une ~ Gigogne*, the mother of many children. ~ *patrie*, parent state. *l'idée ~*, the main idea (*of book*).

méridien, **ne** (meridjɛ̃, ɛn) *a*,

meridian. ¶ m, meridian (as of Greenwich); (f.) siesta; couch. **méridional**, e (djɔnal) a, meridional, southern, south. ¶ (pers.) n, meridional, southerner.

meringue (mərɛ̃:g) f, meringue.

mérinos (merinɔs) m, merino.

merise (məri:z) f, wild cherry, merry. **merisier** (rizje) m, wild cherry [tree].

méritant, e (meritɑ̃, ɑ̃:t) a, deserving, meritorious. **mérite** (rit) m, merit, desert, worth. **mériter** (te) v.t, to merit, deserve; be worth; earn; require. **méritoire** (twa:r) a, meritorious.

merlan (merlɑ̃) m, whiting (fish).

merle (merl) m, blackbird; ouzel, ousel. c'est le ~ blanc, he is a strange mixture (of qualities). je vous donnerai le (ou un) ~ blanc, I'll eat my hat (if you can do that). **merlette** (lɛt) f, [hen] blackbird.

merlin (merlɛ̃) m, cleaving axe (wood); pole axe.

merluche (merlyʃ) f, dried cod; dried hake. **merlus** (ly) m, hake.

merrain (merɛ̃) m, stave wood.

merveille (mɛrvɛ:j) f, marvel, wonder. à ~, excellently; wonderfully; capitally. **merveilleux, euse†** (vɛjø, ø:z) a, marvelous, wonderful. le ~, the marvelous; the wonderful part. ¶ (pers.) (Hist.) n, fop.

mes see **mon**.

mésalliance (mezaljɑ̃:s) f, misalliance. **mésallier** (lje) v.t, to misally. se ~, to make a misalliance.

mésange (mezɑ̃:ʒ) f, tit[mouse]. ~ charbonnière, tomtit.

mésaventure (mezavɑ̃ty:r) f, misadventure, mishap.

mésentente (mezɑ̃tɑ̃:t) f, misunderstanding, disagreement.

mésestime (mezɛstim) f, disrepute. **mésestimer** (me) v.t, to undervalue, underestimate, underrate.

mésintelligence (mezɛ̃tɛliʒɑ̃:s) f, variance; misunderstanding.

mesquin, e† (mɛskɛ̃, in) a, mean, shabby; poky; stingy, niggardly; paltry; scanty. **mesquinerie** (kinri) f, meanness, etc.

mess (mɛs) m, mess (officers').

message (mɛsa:ʒ) m, message; errand; TV commercial. **message**, ère (saʒe, ɛr) n, messenger; (m.) carrier; harbinger. **messagerie** (ʒri) f. oft. pl, parcels [service]; mail, passenger & parcels service.

messe (mɛs) f, mass (Eccl.). ~ basse, low m. ~ chantée, high m.

messeoir (mɛswa:r) v.i.ir, to be unbecoming.

Messie (mɛsi) m, Messiah.

messieurs, oft. M~ (mesjø) pl. of monsieur, messieurs, Messrs.

Messine (mɛsin) f, Messina.

mesurage (məzyra:ʒ) m, measurement. **mesure** (zy:r) f, measure; measurement; size; (pl.) mensuration; extent; meter (Poet.); time (Mus.); measure, (& commonly but wrongly) bar (Mus.); bounds; propriety. à ~, in proportion. à ~ que, [according] as. en ~ de, able to. sur ~, to measure, custom-made. **mesuré**, e (zyre) a; guarded (language). **mesurer** (re) v.t, to measure; weigh (fig.); proportion. se ~ avec, to cope with.

mésuser (mezyze) v.t, to misuse; abuse.

métairie (metɛri) f, farm worked on shares.

métal (metal) m, metal. ~ anglais, britannia m. **métallifère** (tallifɛ:r) a, metalliferous. **métallique** (tallik) a, metallic; iron &/or steel; wire (att.); spring (att.). **métallurgie** (tallyrʒi) f, metallurgy. **métallurgiste** (ʒist) m, metallurgist.

métallo (metal[l]o) m, metalworker.

métamorphose (metamɔrfo:z) f, metamorphosis. **métamorphoser** (foze) v.t, to metamorphose.

métaphore (metafɔ:r) f, metaphor. ~ incohérente, mixed m. **métaphorique†** (fɔrik) a, metaphorical.

métaphysicien (metafizisjɛ̃) m, metaphysician. **métaphysique** (zik) f, metaphysics. ¶ a, metaphysical.

métayage (meteja:ʒ) m, cultivation on shares.

météore (meteɔ:r) m, meteor.

météorique (ɔrik) *a*, meteoric. **météorologie** (rɔlɔʒi) *f*, meteorology. **météorologique** (ʒik) *a*, meteorologic(al); weather (*forecast, etc.*).

méthode (metɔd) *f*, method, way, system. **méthodique†** (dik) *a*, methodical. **méthodisme** (dism) *m*, methodism. **méthodiste** (dist) *n*, methodist.

méthyle (metil) *m*, methyl (*Chem.*).

méticuleux, euse† (metikylø, ø:z) *a*, meticulous, punctilious.

métier (metje) *m*, trade; craft; profession, business, calling, line; experience; loom; frame (*Need.*). ~ *à broder*, embroidery hoops; tambour frame. ~ *de tailleur*, tailoring. *sur le* ~ (*fig.*), in the works. *faire son* ~, to mind one's own business.

métis, se (metis) *a*, halfbred; crossbred; mongrel; hybrid (*Bot.*). ¶ *n*, halfbreed; cross; mongrel. **métissage** (tisa:ʒ) *m*, crossbreeding.

métonymie (metɔnimi) *f*, metonymy.

métrage (metra:ʒ) *m*, measurement, measuring; length (*in meters*); [quantity] surveying; footage (*cinema*). *court* ~, film short. *long* ~, feature film. **mètre** (mɛtr) *m*, meter (*verse*); meter = 39.370113 inches; meter measure *or* tape *or* stick (1 *meter long*). ~ *carré*, square meter = 10.7639 sq. feet. ~ *cube*, cubic meter = 35.3148 cub. feet. **métrer** (metre) *v.t*, to measure, survey. **métreur** (trœ:r) *m*, [quantity] surveyor. **métrique** (trik) *a*, metrical; metric. ¶ *f*, metrics, prosody.

métro (metro) *m*, subway.

métronome (metrɔnɔm) *m*, metronome.

métropole (metrɔpɔl) *f*, metropolis; mother country, home c. **métropolitaine, e** (litɛ̃, ɛn) *a*, metropolitan; mother (*church*); home, domestic.

mets (mɛ) *m*, dish, food, viand.

mettable (metabl) *a*, wearable. **metteur** (tœ:r) *m*: ~ *en œuvre*, stone (*gem*) setter; adapter (*pers., fig.*). ~ *en scène*, director (*cinema, TV*); producer (*Theat.*).

mettre (tr) *v.t.ir*, to put; place; lay; stake; set; poke; draw; make; bring; reduce; put on, wear; tear; take; throw. ~ *à l'encre*, to ink in. ~ *à la retraite*, to pension. ~ *au point*, to focus; adjust; tune up. ~ *bas*, to take off (*hat, etc.*); drop, foal, whelp. ~ *dedans*, to humbug, bamboozle. ~ *en accusation*, to arraign, commit for trial. ~ *en commun*, to pool. ~ *en état*, to enable. ~ *les pouces*, to knuckle under. **se** ~, to put oneself; sit [down]; lie [down]; begin; take to; dress; get; go; set. *se* ~ *en habit pour dîner*, to dress for dinner. *se* ~ *sur deux rangs*, to line up in twos.

meuble (mœbl) *a*, movable (*property*); light, loose, mellow (*earth*). ¶ *m*, piece of furniture; suite [of f.]; cabinet; (*pl.*) furniture; movables (*law*). ~*classeur*, filing cabinet. ~ *de famille*, heirloom. **meublé** (ble) *m*, lodgings. **meubler** (ble) *v.t*, to furnish; stock, store (*fig.*).

meugler (møgle) *v.i*, to bellow, low.

meule (mø:l) *f*, grindstone, millstone; (*circular*) stack *or* rick (*hay*); round, wheel (*of cheese*). ~ [*de moulin*], millstone. ~ *de dessous*, ~ *gisante*, bedstone. ~ *de dessus*, ~ *courante*, runner. ~ *en grès*, grindstone. **meulière** (møljɛ;r) *f*, millstone grit; m. g. quarry. **meulon** (lɔ̃) *m*, cock (*hay*).

meunerie (mønri) *f*, milling (*flour*). **meunier, ère** (nje, ɛ;r) *n*, miller; (*m.*) chub (*fish*).

meurt-de-faim (mœrdəfɛ̃) *m*, starveling.

meurtre (mœrtr) *m*, murder; sin, shame (*vandalism*). **meurtrier, ère** (trie, ɛ;r) *a*, murderous; internecine; deadly. ¶ *n*, murderer, ess; (*f.*) loophole.

meurtrir (mœrtri;r) *v.t*, to bruise. **meurtrissure** (trisy;r) *f*, bruise.

meute (mø;t) *f*, pack (*hounds, enemies*).

mévente (mevɑ̃;t) *f*, slump [in trade], negligible sales (*enabling publisher to close account with author*).

mexicain, e (mɛksikɛ̃, ɛn) *a. & M*~, *n*, Mexican. **Mexico** (ko)

m, Mexico [City]. **le Mexique** (sik), Mexico (*country*).

mezzo-soprano (mɛdzosɔprano) *m*, mezzo-soprano.

mi (mi) *m*, E (*Mus.*). ¶ *word inv*, half, mid. *mi-bas*, *m.pl*, socks. **la mi-carême**, mid-lent. *à mi-chemin*, midway, halfway. *à mi-corps*, to the waist, waist-high *or* deep. *à mi-hauteur*, halfway up [the hill]. *mi-fil*, *m*, union (*linen & cotton thread*). **la mi-juin**, mid-June. *mi-lourd*, light-heavy (*Box.*). *mi-moyen*, welter (*Box.*). *mi-parti, e*, equally divided; half ... & half ... **la mi-temps**, half time (*Foot.*).

miasmatique (mjasmatik) *a*, malarial. **miasme** (asm) *m*, miasma.

miauler (mjole) *v.i*, to miaow, mew.

mica (mika) *m*, mica.

miche (miʃ) *f*, round loaf (*bread*); *pl*, buttocks. ¶ *m*, john (*prostitute's client*). **micheton** (tɔ̃) *m*, john (*prostitute's client*); hick who can easily be defrauded.

micheline (miʃlin) *f*, electric railway car.

micmac (mikmak) *m*, dirty work (*fig.*).

micro (mikro) *f*, mike.

microbe (mikrɔb) *m*, microbe.

micromètre (mikrɔmɛtr) *m*, micrometer.

micro-mioche (mikromjoʃ) *n*, computer kid.

micro-onde (mikrɔ̃:d) *f*, microwave.

microphone (mikrɔfɔn) *m*, microphone.

microplaquette (mikrɔplakɛt) *f*, chip (*computers*).

microprogramme (mikrɔprogram) *m*, microprogram, **microprogrammer** (me) *v.t*, to microprogram.

microscope (mikrɔskɔp) *m*, microscope. **microscopique** (pik) *a*, microscopic(al).

microsillon (mikrɔsijɔ̃) *m*, microgroove; long-playing record.

midi (midi) *m*, noon, midday, noonday, twelve o'clock [in the day]; noontide; heyday (*of life*); south.

mie (mi) *f*, crumb (*bread*, opp. *crust*).

miel (mjɛl) *m*, honey. **mielleux, euse†** (lø, øːz) *a*, bland; mealy-mouthed; honeyed; mawkish.

mien, ne (*with* **le, la, les**) (mjɛ̃, ɛn) *pn. & m*, mine; my own.

miette (mjɛt) *f*, crumb (*broken bread, etc.*); bit, atom.

mieux (mjø) *ad. & a*, better; rather; more; best; better-looking. **le ~, m**, [the] best. **le ~, m**, [the] best. *à qui ~ ~*, in competition.

mièvre (mjɛːvr) *a*, [childishly] affected, finical.

mignard, e (miɲaːr, ard) *a*, mincing; girlish. **mignardise** (nardiːz) *f*, daintiness; affectation; (*pl.*) pretty ways; pink (*Bot.*). **mignon, ne** (ɲɔ̃, ɔn) *a*, dainty, petite; sweet; pet. ¶ *n*, pet, darling; (*m.*) minion. **mignonnette** (ɲɔnɛt) *f*, mignonette (*lace*); pink (*Bot.*); gimp nails; ground pepper; broken pebblestone.

migraine (migrɛn) *f*, migraine, bad headache.

migrateur, trice (migratœːr, tris) *a*, migratory; migrant. **migration** (sjɔ̃) *f*, migration.

mijaurée (miʒɔre) *f*, affected woman.

mijoter (miʒɔte) *v.t*, to [let] simmer; (*v.i.*) to simmer. **se ~**, to be brewing.

mil (mil) *m*, mil[le] (*1000*); millet; Indian club. ¶ *a*, thousand (*dates*).

milan (milɑ̃) *m*, kite (*bird*). **Milan** (milɑ̃) *m*, Milan. **milanais, e** (lanɛ, ɛːz) *a. & M~, n*, Milanese.

mildiou (mildju) *m*, mildew (*on vines*).

milice (milis) *f*, militia. **milicien** (sjɛ̃) *m*, militiaman.

milieu (miljø) *m*, middle, midst, center; mean; medium; circle, milieu; underworld. *au ~ de*, in the midst of, amidst, among. *au ~ du navire*, amidships. **le juste ~**, the golden mean.

militaire† (militɛːr) *a*, military. ¶ *m*, soldier, military man. **les ~s**, the military. **militant, e** (tɑ̃, ɑ̃:t) *a*, militant. ¶ *n*, fighter. **militariser** (tarize) *v.t*, to militarize. **militer** (te) *v.i*, to militate, tell.

mille (mil) *m. & a. inv*, (a *or* one) thousand; mile. *les M~ & une Nuits*, the Arabian nights. **millefeuille** *ou* **millefeuille** (fœːj) *f*, milfoil, yarrow; (*m.*) Genoese pastry, napoleon (*slang*). **millénaire** (millenɛːr) *a. & m*, millenary (*a. & n.*); millennium (*n.*). **mille-pieds** (pje) *ou* **mille-pattes** (pat) *m*, centipede. **millésime** (millezim) *m*, date, year.

millet (mijɛ) *m*, millet grass; millet. ~ *des oiseaux*, canary seed. **milliard** (miljaːr) *m*, billion, 1,000,000,000 francs. **milliardaire** (jardɛːr) *n. & a*, multimillionaire.

milliasse (miljas) *f*, swarm[s].

millième (miljɛm) *a. & m*, thousandth. **millier** (je) *m*, thousand [or so]. **milligramme** (milligram) *m*, milligram = 0.015 grain. **millimètre** (millimɛtr) *m*, millimeter = 0.03937 inch.

million (miljɔ̃) *m*, million; 1,000,000 francs. **millionième** (jɔnjɛm) *a. & m*, millionth. **millionnaire** (nɛːr) *n*, millionaire.

mime (mim) *m*, mime; mimic. **mimer** (me) *v.t. & abs*, to mime; mimic. **mimétisme** (metism) *m*, mimicry (*Zool.*), mimesis. **mimique** (mik) *a*, mimic. ¶ *f*, mimicry.

mimosa (mimoza) *m*, mimosa.

minable (minabl) *a*, pitiable; wretched. **minauder** (minode) *v.i*, to mince, simper, smirk. **minauderie** (dri) *f*, mincing, etc. **minaudier, ère** (dje, ɛːr) *a*, mincing, etc.

mince (mɛ̃ːs) *a*, thin, slender; slight. **minceur** (mɛ̃sœːr) *f*, thinness, etc.

mine (min) *f*, appearance, countenance, face, mien, look, looks. *de bonne ~*, good-looking.

mine (min) *f*, mine (*lit. & fig.*); mint (*fig.*); lead (*pencil*). ~ *de plomb*, black lead. **miner** (ne) *v.t*, to mine; undermine; sap; hollow; wear; prey [up]on (*mind*). **mineral** (nrɛ) *m*, ore. **minéral, e** (neral) *a. & m*, mineral; inorganic (*chemistry*). **minéralogie** (lɔʒi) *f*, mineralogy. **minéralogique** (ʒik) *a*, mineralogical. **minéralogiste** (ʒist) *m*, mineralogist.

minet, te (minɛ, ɛt) *n*, puss[y]; elegant young man or woman. *faire minette*, perform cunnilingus.

mineur (minœːr) *m*, miner; sapper (*Mil.*).

mineur, e (minœːr) *a*, minor; under age. ¶ *n*, minor (*pers.*), infant (*law*); (*m.*) minor (*Mus.*); (*f.*) minor premise (*Log.*).

miniature (minjatyːr) *f*, miniature. **miniaturiser** (tyrize) *v.t*, to miniaturize. **miniaturiste** (tyrist) *n*, miniaturist.

minidisque (minidisk) *m*, floppy disk (*computers*).

minier, ère (minje, ɛːr) *a*, mining (*att.*). ¶ *f*, gangue, matrix; surface mine, diggings.

minimarge (minimarʒ) *m*, discount store.

minime (minim) *a*, minute, trifling, trivial.

minimum, ma (minimɔm, ma) *a. & m*, minimum.

ministère (ministɛːr) *m*, department; ministry; office; secretaryship; board; agency, services, good offices, ministration. *M~ des Affaires étrangères*, State Department. *M~ des Finances*, Treasury Department. *M~ du Commerce*, Commerce Department. ~ *public*, public prosecutor. **ministériel, le** (terjɛl) *a*, ministerial; State nominated (*officer*); Government (*organ*). **ministre** (tr) *m*, minister; secretary [of state]; clergyman, vicar. ~ *de l'Intérieur*, Secretary of the Interior.

minium (minjɔm) *m*, minium; red lead.

minois (minwa) *m*, face, looks.

minon (minɔ̃) & **minou** (nu) *m*, puss[y].

minorité (minorite) *f*, minority; nonage; infancy (*law*).

Minorque (minɔrk) *f*, Minorca.

minoterie (minɔtri) *f*, [flour] milling; flour mill. **minotier** (tje) *m*, miller; flour merchant.

minuit (minɥi) *m*, midnight, twelve o'clock [at night].

minuscule (minyskyl) *a*, minute, tiny. ¶ *f*, small letter.

minute (minyt) *f*, minute; small

hand (*writing*); original; draft.
minuter (te) *v.t*, to minute, draw
[up], draft. **minuterie** (tri) *f*, time
switch.
minutie (minysi) *f*, trifle, (*pl.*)
minutiae; minuteness, great care.
minutieux, euse† (sjø, ø:z) *a*,
meticulous; minute, thorough.
mioche (mjɔʃ) *m*, youngster, kid,
tot.
mirabelle (mirabɛl) *f*, mirabelle
[plum].
miracle (mirɑ:kl) *m*, miracle;
marvel; miracle [play], mystery
[play]. *à ~*, admirably. **miraculeux**, euse† (rakylø, ø:z) *a*, miraculous; marvelous.
mirage (mira:ʒ) *m*, mirage; testing, candling (*eggs*). **mire** (mi:r)
f, sight (*gun*); aiming stake.
mirer (mire) *v.t. & abs*, to aim
at, take aim; test, candle (*eggs*).
se ~, to look at oneself; see oneself reflected.
mirettes (mirɛt) *f.pl*, eyes, peep-
ers (*slang*).
mirifique (mirifik) *a*, marvelous.
mirliflore (mirliflɔ:r) *m*, spark,
dandy.
mirliton (mirlitɔ̃) *m*, mirliton
(*musical toy pipe*).
mirobolant, e (mirɔbɔlɑ̃, ɑ̃:t) *a*,
wonderful.
miroir (mirwa:r) *m*, mirror, [look-
ing] glass. ~ *d'eau*, ornamental
lake. ~ *déformant*, distorting
mirror. **miroiter** (rwate) *v.i*, to
flash, gleam, glisten, glint, sparkle. **miroiterie** (tri) *f*, mirror
trade. **miroitier** (tje) *m*, mirror
manufacturer *or* dealer.
misaine (mizɛn) *f*, foremast.
misanthrope (mizɑ̃trɔp) *m*, misanthrope, -pist. ¶ ~ *& **misanthropique** (pik) *a*, misanthropic.
mise (mi:z) *f*, putting, etc, as
mettre; stake (*gaming*); bid (*auction*); get-up. ~ *à prix*, reserve
[price], upset p. ~ *à terre*, landing. ~ *au point*, focusing; adjustment; tuning (*motor*). ~ [*de
fonds*], putting up of money; investment; capital; stake. ~
[*de*]*hors*, disbursement. ~ *en accusation*, indictment. ~ *en
marche*, starting. ~ *en œuvre*, application. ~ *en pages*, making up;
page proof. ~ *en scène*, staging;

production; setting. ~ *en train*,
starting; making ready (*Typ.*);
practice (*sport*). *de ~*, in fashion;
current; admissible. *être de ~*, to
be appropriate. **miser** (mize) *v.t.
& i*, to stake, bid.
misérable† (mizerabl) *a*, miserable; wretched; unfortunate;
worthless. ¶ *n*, unfortunate, poor
wretch; villain, scoundrel. **misère**
(zɛ:r) *f*, misery, wretchedness,
distress, destitution; misfortune;
trifle; misère (*cards*). ~ *de santé*,
ailment. **miserere** (zerere) *m*,
miserere. **miséreux**, euse (zerø,
ø:z) *a. & n*, poverty-stricken
(person).
miséricorde (mizerikɔrd) *f*,
mercy; misericord. ¶ *i*, mercy on
us! good gracious! **miséricordieux**, euse† (djø, ø:z) *a*, merci-
ful.
misogyne (mizɔʒin) *a*, misogynic.
¶ *m*, misogynist, woman hater.
missel (misɛl) *m*, missal.
mission (misjɔ̃) *f*, mission. **missionnaire** (ɔnɛ:r) *m*, missionary.
missive (si;v) *f*, missive.
mistral (mistral) *m*, mistral
(*wind*).
mitaine (mitɛn) *f*, mitten.
mite (mit) *f*, mite (*insect*); moth.
miteux, euse (tø, ø:z) *a*, shabby.
mitiger (mitiʒe) *v.t*, to mitigate,
temper.
mitonner (mitɔne) *v.t. & i*, to
simmer.
mitoyen, ne (mitwajɛ̃, ɛn) *a*,
party (*wall, structure*). **mitoyen-
neté** (jɛnte) *f*, party rights.
mitraille (mitrɑ:j) *f*, grapeshot;
group firing. **mitrailleur** (trɑ-
jœ:r) *m*, machine gunner. **mitrailleuse** (jø:z) *f*, machine
gun.
mitre (mitr) *f*, miter; cowl
(*chimney*). **mitré**, e (tre) *a*, mi-
tered. **mitron** (trɔ̃) *m*, baker's
man.
mixage (miksaʒ) *m*, mixing (*cinema, TV*). ~ *son*, sound mixing.
~ *de pistes multiple*, multi-track
mixing.
mixeur (miksœ:r) *m*, mixer; swiz-
zlestick.
mixte (mikst) *a*, mixed; composite; joint; promiscuous. **mix-

tion (tjɔ̃) *f*, mixture (*medicinal*). **mixture** (ty:r) *f*, mixture; concoction.

mnémonique (mnemɔnik)· *a*, mnemonic. **la** ~, mnemonics.

mobile (mɔbil) *a*, movable; portable; mobile; changeable, fickle. ¶ *m*, moving body (*Mech.*); motive power; prime mover; motive, incentive. **mobilier**, **ère** (lje, ɛ:r) *a*, personal, movable (*law*); transferable (*securities*). ¶ *m*, furniture, suite [of f.]. **mobilisation** (lizasjɔ̃) *f*, mobilization. **mobiliser** (ze) *v.t. & abs*, to mobilize. **mobilité** (te) *f*, mobility; fickleness.

moche (mɔʃ) *a*, ugly; lousy; rotten, etc.

modalité (mɔdalite) *f*, modality; method. **mode** (mɔd) *f*, mode, way; fashion, vogue; (*pl.*) millinery. *à la* ~ *& de* ~, in the fashion, fashionable, modish, stylish. *à la* ~, *ad*, fashionably, modishly, stylishly. ¶ *m*, mode; method; mood (*Gram.*). ~ *d'emploi*, directions for use. ~ *de circulation*, rule of the road.

modelage (mɔdla:ʒ) *m*, modeling; pattern making (*foundry*). **modèle** (dɛl) *m*, model, pattern; specimen; paragon; (*att.*) model, exemplary. ~ *de broderie*, sampler. **modelé** (dle) *m*, modeling (*relief of forms*). **modeler** (dle) *v.t. & abs*, to model; pattern; mold, shape. **modeleur** (dlœ:r) *m*, modeler; patternmaker.

Modène (mɔdɛːn) *f*, Modena.

modération (mɔderasjɔ̃) *f*, moderation; mitigation. **modéré†**, **e** (re) *a*, moderate. **les modérés**, the moderates (*Pol.*). **modérer** (re) *v.t*, to moderate; check, curb; mitigate.

moderne (mɔdɛrn) *a*, modern; up to date; new. **les** ~**s**, *m.pl*, the moderns. **moderniser** (nize) *v.t*, to modernize.

modeste† (mɔdɛst) *a*, modest; quiet (*dress*). **modestie** (ti) *f*, modesty.

modicité (mɔdisite) *f*, moderateness; lowness.

modification (mɔdifikasjɔ̃) *f*, modification, alteration, varia-

tion. **modifier** (fje) *v.t*, to modify, alter, vary.

modique† (mɔdik) *a*, moderate (*price*); small (*sum, etc.*).

modiste (mɔdist) *f*, milliner, modiste.

modulation (mɔdylasjɔ̃) *f*, modulation. **module** (dyl) *m*, module; modulus. **moduler** (le) *v.i. & t*, to modulate.

moelle (mwal) *f*, marrow; pith. ~ *épinière*, spinal cord. **moelleux**, **euse†** (lø, ø:z) *a*, marrowy; pithy; mellow; soft. ¶ *m*, softness; mellowness.

moellon (mwalɔ̃) *m*, quarry stone, rubble. ~ *d'appareil*, ashlar.

mœurs (mœrs) *f.pl*, manners, habits; morals, morality. *les* ~, police vice squad.

mohair (mɔɛ:r) *m*, mohair.

moi (mwa) *pn*, me; [to] me, I. *à* ~*l au secours!* help, help! ¶ *m*, self; ego. ~**-même**, *pn*, myself.

moignon (mwaɲɔ̃) *m*, stump (*limb, tree*).

moindre (mwɛ̃:dr) *a*, less; lesser, lower; minor. **le**, **la**, ~, the least; the slightest. [ne . . .] *pas le* **moindrement** (mwɛ̃drəmɑ̃), not in the least.

moine (mwan) *m*, monk, friar; bed warmer. ~ *bourru*, bugaboo, bugbear, goblin, bog[e]y; bear, brute.

moineau (mwano) *m*, sparrow. ~ *franc*, English sparrow. *un drôle de* ~, a queer bird (*person*).

moinerie (mwanri) *f*, monkhood, monkery.

moins (mwɛ̃) *ad. & pr*, less; not so [much]; fewer; under; minus; to (*of the hour*). [signe] ~, *m*, minus [sign]. *à* ~ *de*, for less than; barring; unless; without. *à* ~ *que*, unless. *au* ~, at least; however, above all. *le* ~, the least. *pas le* ~ *du monde*, not in the least.

moins-value (mwɛ̃valy) *f*, depreciation; deficit.

moire (mwa:r) *f*, moire, watering. ~ *de soie* ou *soie moirée* (mware), watered silk, moiré, s. **moirer** (re) *v.t*, to water, moiré.

mois (mwa) *m*, month; month's pay, rent, or like.

moise (mɔiːz) *m*, wicker cradle.
moise (mwaːz) *f*, brace (*Carp.*); ledger (*Build.*). **moiser** (mwaze) *v.t*, to brace.
moisi, e (mwazi) *p.p*, moldy, mildewy; musty; frowsy. **moisir** (ziːr) *v.t. & i, & se ~*, to mildew, turn moldy. **moisissure** (zisyːr) *f. & moisi* (zi) *m*, mildew, mold, moldiness, mustiness.
moissine (mwasin) *f*, vine branch with grapes hanging (*as ceiling decoration*).
moisson (mwasɔ̃) *f*, harvest, reaping. **moissonner** (sɔne) *v.t. & abs*, to reap, harvest; cut off (*fig.*). **moissonneur, euse** (nœːr, øːz) *n*, reaper, harvester (*pers.*); (*f.*) reaping machine, reaper. *moissoneuse-batteuse*, combine harvester. *moissoneuse-lieuse*, reaper-binder.
moite (mwat) *a*, moist, damp; clammy. **moiteur** (tœːr) *f*, moistness; clamminess.
moitié (mwatje) *f*, half, moiety; better half (*wife*). ¶ *ad*, half, partly. *à ~*, half, by half; on half profits. *à ~ chemin*, halfway. *de ~*, by half. *être* (ou *se mettre*) *de ~ avec*, to go halves with.
Moka (mɔka) *m*, Mocha. *m~ ou café de M~*, mocha, M. coffee; coffee (*ordinary*).
mol *see* **mou**.
molaire (mɔlɛːr) *a. & f*, molar.
môle (moːl) *m*, mole, breakwater.
moléculaire (mɔlekylɛːr) *a*, molecular. **molécule** (kyl) *f*, molecule.
moleskine (mɔlɛskin) *f*, moleskin; oilcloth.
molester (mɔlɛste) *v.t*, to taunt.
moleter (mɔlte) *v.t*, to mill, knurl. **molette** (lɛt) *f*, rowel; muller; milled nut; knurl; milling tool; cutter wheel.
mollasse (mɔlas) *a*, flabby; flimsy; spineless (*fig.*). **mollement** (lmɑ̃) *ad*, softly; gracefully; feebly; voluptuously. **mollesse** (lɛs) *f*, softness; mildness; feebleness; flabbiness; overindulgence; voluptuousness. **mollet, te** (lɛ, ɛt) *a*, softish; soft-boiled (*eggs*); fancy (*roll*). ¶ *m*, calf (*leg*). **molletière** (ltjɛːr) *f*, legging. **molle-**

ton (ltɔ̃) *m*, swansdown (*cloth*).
mollir (liːr) *v.i. & t*, to soften; slacken; lull.
mollo (mɔlo) *ad*, gently, with care. *vas-y ~!*, take it easy!
mollusque (mɔlysk) *m*, mollusc.
Moluques (les) (mɔlyk) *f.pl*, the Moluccas.
môme (moːm) *n*, youngster.
moment (mɔmɑ̃) *m*, moment; time; momentum. **momentané†, e** (tane) *a*, momentary, temporary.
momerie (mɔmri) *f*, pose (*fig.*); mummery.
momie (mɔmi) *f*, mummy; sleepyhead. **momifier** (fje) *v.t*, to mummify.
mon, ma, mes (mɔ̃, ma, me) *a*, my. *oui, mon colonel, etc*, yes, sir (*in the army*).
monacal, e† (mɔnakal) *a*, monastic, monkish.
monarchie (mɔnarʃi) *f*, monarchy. **monarchique** (ʃik) *a*, monarchic(al). **monarchiste** (ʃist) *m. & att*, monarchist. **monarque** (nark) *m*, monarch.
monastère (mɔnastɛːr) *m*, monastery; convent. **monastique** (tik) *a*, monastic.
monceau (mɔ̃so) *m*, heap, pile.
mondain, e (mɔ̃dɛ̃, ɛn) *a*, worldly, mundane; (*att.*) society. ¶ *n*, society man, woman; worldling; police vice squad. **mondanité** (danite) *f*, worldliness; (*pl.*) social events (*news*). **monde** (mɔ̃ːd) *m*, world; people; company; set; crowd; servants. *le ~ inanimé*, inanimate nature. *tiers ~*, third world. *tout le ~*, everybody. *elle a du ~ au balcon*, she's got big breasts (*slang*).
monder (mɔ̃de) *v.t*, to hull.
mondial, e (mɔ̃djal) *a*, worldwide.
monétaire (mɔnetɛːr) *a*, monetary, money (*att.*).
mongol, e (mɔ̃gɔl) *a. & M~, n*, Mongol[ian]. **la Mongolie** (li), Mongolia.
moniteur (mɔnitœːr) *m*, adviser; coach; (*name of many French newspapers*).
monnaie (mɔnɛ) *f*, money; currency; coin; coinage; [small] change. *~ de papier*, [converti-

ble] paper money. *faire de la* ~, to make or get change. *payer en* ~ *de singe*, to defraud. la M~, the mint. **monnayer** (nɛje) *v.t*, to coin, mint; commercialize (*fig.*). **monnayeur** (jœːr) *m*, minter. *faux* ~, counterfeiter.

monochrome (mɔnɔkroːm) *a*, monochrome. **monocle** (kl) *m*, monocle, eyeglass. **monocorde** (kɔrd) *m*, single-string instrument; monochord; monotonist (*pers.*). **monogamie** (gami) *f*, monogamy. **monogramme** (gram) *m*, monogram. **monographie** (grafi) *f*, monograph. **monolithe** (lit) *a*, monolithic. ¶ *m*, monolith. **monologue** (lɔg) *m*, monologue. **monologuer** (ge) *v.i*, to monologize, soliloquize. **monomanie** (mani) *f*, monomania. **monoplan** (plɑ̃) *m*, monoplane. **monopole** (pɔl) *m*, monopoly. **monopoliser** (lize) *v.t*, to monopolize. **monosyllabe** (silab) *m*, monosyllable. ¶ ~ & **monosyllabique** (bik) *a*, monosyllabic. **monotone** (tɔn) *a*, monotonous; humdrum. **monotonie** (ni) *f*, monotony, sameness. **monotype** (tip) *f*, monotype.

mons (mɔ̃ːs) *m*, Master (*so-&-so*) (*jocularly*). **monseigneur**, *oft.* M~ (mɛ̃sɛɲœːr) *m*, His (*or* Your) Royal Highness; my lord, his (*or* your) lordship, his (*or* your) Grace; jimmy (*burglar's*). **monsieur**, *oft.* M~ (məsjø) *m*, gentleman; Mr.; Esq.; sir; my (*or* the) master; man. ~ *le juge*, your, his, Honor.

monstre (mɔ̃ːstr) *m. & att*, monster. **monstrueux, euse†** (mɔ̃stryø, øːz) *a*, monstrous; freakish. **monstruosité** (ozite) *f*, monstrosity; freak [of nature].

mont (mɔ̃) *m*, mount, mountain; (*pl.*) Alps. *le* ~ *Blanc, etc*. See under *blanc, etc. par* ~*s & par vaux*, up hill & down dale. ~*-de-piété*, pawnshop.

montage (mɔ̃taːʒ) *m*, raising; mounting; setting; erection; fit (*Mech.*); editing (*movie*). ~ *des mailles*, casting on (*Knit.*). ~*-son*, sound editing (*movie*).

montagnard, e (mɔ̃taɲaːr, ard) *a*, highland, mountain (*att.*). ¶ *n*,

highlander, mountaineer. *les Montagnards*, the wild men (*Pol.*). **montagne** (taɲ) *f*, mountain; mountains. ~*s russes*, scenic railway, switchback. **montagneux, euse** (nø, øːz) *a*, mountainous.

montant, e (mɔ̃tɑ̃, ɑ̃ːt) *a*, rising, ascending; incoming (*tide*); uphill; up (*train, etc.*); high; high-necked (*dress*); stand-up (*collar*). ¶ *m*, upright; post; stile; amount; total; tang. **monte** (mɔ̃ːt) *f*, covering (*of animals*); mount (*turf*); riding; jockey. **montecharge** (mɔ̃tʃarʒ) *m*, freight elevator, hoist. **montée** (mɔ̃te) *f*, ascent, rise, rising.

monténégrin, e (mɔ̃tenegrɛ̃, in) *a. & M~, n*, Montenegrin. le Monténégro (groY), Montenegro.

monter (mɔ̃te) *v.i. & t*, to go up, ascend; mount; climb; ride; command (*ship*); amount; raise, hoist, elevate; take up, carry up; set up, put up; erect; fit; set; string (*violin*); wind [up] (*spring*); turn up (*wick*); stage (*play*); cast on (*Knit.*); excite. ~ *en amazone*, to ride side-saddle. ~ *en graine*, to run to seed. ~ *en voiture*, to take one's seat in a carriage. ~ *sur un vaisseau, en avion*, to [go on] board a ship, a plane. se ~, to amount; equip oneself. **monteur** (tœːr) *m*, setter, mounter; fitter, erector.

monticule (mɔ̃tikyl) *m*, hillock, mound, knoll, hummock.

montjoie (mɔ̃ʒwa) *f*, cairn.

montoir (mɔ̃twaːr) *m*, horse block.

montrable (mɔ̃trabl) *a*, presentable. **montre** (mɔ̃ːtr) *f*, parade; show; display; [shop]-window (*display*); sample; watch. ~*-bracelet*, wristwatch. **montrer** (mɔ̃tre) *v.t*, to show; point [out]; teach. ~ *du doigt*, to point at. **montreur** (trœːr) *m*, showman; exhibitor.

montueux, euse (mɔ̃tɥø, øːz) *a*, hilly.

monture (mɔ̃tyːr) *f*, mount (*animal*); mount[ing]; setting; hook to gut (*Fish.*). ~ *de rideaux*, cornice pole. *sans* ~, rimless (*glasses*).

monument (mɔnymɑ̃) *m*, monument, memorial; building (*public or historic*). ~ *aux morts* [*de la guerre*], war memorial. ~ *historique*, national monument, building, etc, of historic interest. **monumental, e** (tal) *a*, monumental.

moquer (se) de (mɔke), to mock (at), deride, jeer at, laugh at, ridicule, make fun of. *s'en moquer*, not to care. **moquerie** (kri) *f*, mockery, jeer[s]. **moquette** (kɛt) *f*, moquette, velvet pile, saddle bag; Brussels carpet. **moqueur, euse** (kœːr, ǿːz) *n*, mocker, scoffer. ¶ *a*, mocking. [*oiseau*] *moqueur*, mocking bird.

moraillon (mɔrɑjɔ̃) *m*, hasp.

moraine (mɔrɛːn) *f*, moraine.

moral, e (mɔral) *a*, moral; mental. ¶ *m*, mind; moral[e]. **morale** (ral) *f*, morals (*ethics*); moral (*of story*). **moralement** (lmɑ̃) *ad*, morally. **moraliser** (lize) *v.i. & t*, to moralize; lecture. **moraliste** (list) *m*, moralist. **moralité** (te) *f*, morality (*principles, drama*); moral (*of fable*).

moratoire (mɔratwaːr) *a*, moratory; on overdue payments (*interest*); postponement of some social goals in favor of others. ¶ ~ *& moratorium* (tɔrjɔm) *m*, moratorium.

Moravie (la) (mɔravi), Moravia.

morbac (mɔrbak) *m*, crab (*body louse*); young child.

morbide (mɔrbid) *a*, morbid; unwholesome.

morceau (mɔrso) *m*, piece, bit; morsel; snack; lump, knob; scrap, fragment. ~*x choisis*, selections (*from writings*). ~ *d'ensemble*, part song, p. music. ~ *de concours*, test piece (*music, etc.*). *un ~ de femme*, a slip of a woman. ~ *honteux*, last piece (*left on dish*). *casser le ~ à quelqu'un*, to tell someone off. *casser un ~*, to have a bite to eat. *emporter le ~*, to win (*deal, argument, etc.*). **morceler** (sǝle) *v.t*, to parcel [out]; subdivide.

mordant, e (mɔrdɑ̃, ɑ̃ːt) *a*, mordant, biting; pungent. ¶ *m*, mordant; pungency; keenness; shrillness. **mordicus** (dikyːs) *ad*, dog-

gedly. **mordiller** (dije) *v.t*, to nibble.

mordoré, e (mɔrdɔre) *a*, reddish-brown; bronze (*shoes*).

mordre (mɔrdr) *v.t. & abs*, to bite, nip; nibble. *ça mord!* I have a bite! (*Fish.*). ~ *à*, to take to (*a study*). ~ *sur* (*fig.*), to find fault with. ~ *sur la latte*, to go over the mark (*Jump.*).

More (mɔːr) *m*, Moor. **m~, a**, Moorish.

morelle (mɔrɛl) *f*, nightshade.

moresque (mɔrɛsk) *a*, Moresque. ¶ *f*, Morisco, morris [dance].

morfil (mɔrfil) *m*, wire edge.

morfondre (mɔrfɔ̃ːdr) *v.t*, to chill. **se ~**, to be bored; to wait in vain, cool one's heels. **morfondu, e** (fɔ̃dy) *p.a*, [as if] frozen stiff.

morganatique† (mɔrganatik) *a*, morganatic.

morgeline (mɔrʒǝlin) *f*, chickweed; pimpernel.

morgue (mɔrg) *f*, haughtiness; morgue.

moribond, e (mɔribɔ̃, ɔ̃ːd) *a. & n*, moribund, dying (man, woman).

moricaud, e (mɔriko, oːd) *n*, blackamoor.

morigéner (mɔriʒene) *v.t*, to take to task.

morne (mɔrn) *a*, gloomy, dismal, dreary, bleak, cheerless.

morose (mɔroːz) *a*, morose, sullen, moody. **morosité** (rozite) *f*, moroseness, etc.

Morphée (mɔrfe) *m*, Morpheus.

morphine (fin) *f*, morphia, -phine. **morphinomane** (nɔman) *n*, morphinomaniac.

morphologie (mɔrfɔlɔʒi) *f*, morphology; accidence (*Gram.*).

mors (mɔːr) *m*, bit (*bridle*); jaw (*vise*).

morse (mɔrs) *m*, walrus, morse.

morsure (mɔrsyːr) *f*, bite; sting (*fig.*).

mort (mɔːr) *f*, death. *à ~*, to d.; to the d.; mortal (*strife*); mortally; deadly. ~ *& passion*, excruciating pains; agonies (*fig.*). **mort, e** (mɔːr, ɔrt) *a*, dead; still (*water, life*); spent (*shot*). *les morts*, the dead. *le jour des morts*, All Souls' Day. **mort**, *m*, dummy (*cards*).

mortaise (mɔrtɛːz) *f*, mortise, -ice; slot.

mortalité (mɔrtalite) *f*, mortality; death rate. **mort-aux-rats** (mɔrora) *f*, rat poison. **mort-bois** (mɔrbwɑ) *m*, underwood, brushwood. **morte-eau** (mɔrto) *f*, neap tide. **mortel, le†** (tɛl) *a*, mortal, deadly, lethal; fatal (*accident*). ¶ *n*, mortal. **morte-saison** (təsɛzɔ̃) *f*, dead season, off season.

mortier (mɔrtje) *m*, mortar (*plaster, vessel, Mil.*). ~ *de tranchée*, trench mortar.

mortifier (mɔrtifje) *v.t*, to mortify; make tender (*meat, game*). **morti-né, e** (mɔrne) *a*, stillborn. **mortuaire** (mɔrtɥɛːr) *a*, mortuary, [of] death; burial (*fees*). *le drap* ~, a pall.

morue (mɔry) *f*, cod[fish]. **morutier** (tje) *m*, cod fisher.

morve (mɔrv) *f*, mucus of the nose; glanders.

mosaïque (mozaik) *a*, Mosaic (*law*). ¶ *f*, mosaic, tessellated pavement.

Moscou (mɔsku) *m*, Moscow.

mosquée (mɔske) *f*, mosque.

mot (mo) *m*, word; saying; cell (*computers*); cue. ~ *à* ~ (motamo), ~ *pour* ~, word for word, verbatim. ~*s croisés* [-*énigmes*], crossword [puzzle]. ~ *d'ordre*, password; keynote. ~ *de l'énigme*, answer to the riddle. ~ *de passe*, password. ~ *de ralliement*, countersign (*Mil.*). Note.— In Fr., the ~ *de ralliement* is given in reply to the ~ *d'ordre*. ~ *en vedette*, word displayed in bold type, catchword. ~ *piquant*, quip. ~ *pour rire*, joke. ~ *de Cambronne*, shit (*reply of Napoleonic general to a demand for surrender*). ~ *de cinq lettres*, shit (*merde*). *gros* ~, swear word.

motard (mɔtaːr) *m*, motorcycle policeman.

moteur (mɔtœːr) *m*, engine, motor; mover. ~ *à essence*, gasoline engine. ~ *à gaz*, gas e. ~ *à pétrole*, oil e. ~*-fusée*, rocket e. **moteur, trice** (tœːr, tris) *att*, motive, driving. **motif** (tif) *m*, motive; reason; cause; (*pl.*) grounds; intentions (*matrimonial*); design, motif, traced article, (*pl.*) traced

goods; theme, motto (*Mus.*). **motion** (mosjɔ̃) *f*, motion (*proposal at meeting*). **motiver** (mɔtive) *v.t*, to state the reason for; justify.

motivation (mɔtivasjɔ̃) *f*, motivation. *études de* ~, motivational research.

motoculture (mɔtokyltyːr) *f*, tractor farming, mechanized f. **motocyclette** (siklɛt) *abb*. **moto** (mɔto) *f*, motor [bi]cycle. **motocycliste** (klist) *n*, motorcyclist.

motoriser (mɔtrize) *v.t*, to motorize.

motte (mɔt) *f*, clod; turf, sod; roll (*butter*); mound.

motu proprio (mɔty prɔprio), of one's own accord.

motus (mɔtyːs) *i*, mum['s the word]!

mou, mol, molle (mu, mɔl) *a*, soft; lax; slack; inelastic (*Phys.*); limp, flabby; languid; muggy; close; indolent. **mou**, *m*, lights (*animal lungs*).

mouchard (muʃaːr) *m*, spy; police spy. **moucharder** (ʃarde) *v.t*, to spy.

mouche (muʃ) *f*, fly; patch, beauty spot; spot (*Bil.*); tuft (*on chin*); police spy; bull's-eye (*target*); bull (*shot*). ~ *à feu*, firefly. ~ *à miel*, honeybee. ~ *à viande*, meat fly, blowfly. ~ *bleue*, bluebottle. ~ *commune*, housefly. ~ *de mai*, May fly. ~ *noyée*, wet fly (*Fish.*). *poids* ~, fly weight (*Box.*). *prendre la* ~, to take offense.

moucher (muʃe) *v.t*, to wipe (*child's*) nose; snuff (*candle*); snub; tell off; beat up. *se* ~, to blow one's nose.

moucherolle (muʃrɔl) *f*, flycatcher (*bird*). **moucheron** (ʃrɔ̃) *m*, midge, gnat; whippersnapper; snuff (*candle*).

moucheté, e (muʃte) *a*, spotted, speckled; tabby (*cat*).

mouchettes (muʃɛt) *f.pl*, snuffers.

moucheture (muʃtyːr) *f*, spot, speckle.

mouchoir (muʃwaːr) *m*, handkerchief. ~ *de cou*, silk scarf.

moudre (mudr) *v.t. & abs. ir*, to grind, mill. *en* ~, to pedal hard (*bicycle*); to practice prostitution.

moue (mu) *f*, pout[ing]. *faire la* ~, to pout.

mauette (mwɛt) *f*, [sea] gull, [sea] mew.

mouffette (mufɛt) *f*, skunk (*Zool.*).

moufle (mufl) *f*, pulley block, tackle b.; mitt[en]; (*m.*) pulley block, tackle b.; muffle (*Chem.*).

mouillage (muja:ʒ) *m*, wetting; watering (*wine, etc.*); mooring; moorings, anchorage, berth. **mouille-bouche** (mujbuʃ) *f*, bergamot (*pear*). **mouillée** (je) *p.a.f*, palat[al]ized (*consonant*). **mouiller** (je) *v.t. & abs*, to wet, moisten, damp; water; anchor, moor, berth. ~ *quelqu'un*, to compromise someone. *se* ~, to take a risk. **mouillette** (jɛt) *f*, sippet. **mouilloir** (jwa:r) *m*, damper (*stamps, labels*). **mouillure** (jy:r) *f*, wetting; damp mark (*in books*).

mouise (mwi:z) *f*, poverty. *être dans la* ~, to be broke.

moulage (mula:ʒ) *m*, molding (*act*); casting. **moule** (mul) *m*, mold, (*f.*) mussel. **mouler** (le) *v.t*, to mold, cast; shape; print (*handwriting*). **mouleur** (lœ:r) *m*, molder.

moulin (mulɛ̃) *m*, mill; moulin (*glacier*). ~ *à paroles*, chatterbox; windbag. ~ *à prières*, prayer wheel. ~ *à vent*, windmill. **mouliné, e** (line) *p.a. & p.p*, worm-eaten (*wood*); thrown (*silk*). **moulinet** (nɛ) *m*, winch; reel (*Fish.*); turnstile (X *on post*). *faire le* ~ *avec*, to whirl, twirl. **moulu, e** (ly) *p.a:* ~ *de fatigue*, dead beat. *tout* ~, aching all over.

moulure (muly:r) *f*, molding (*ornamental strip*).

mourant, e (murɑ̃, ɑ̃:t) *a*, dying, languishing (*eyes*); faint (*voice*). **les mourants**, *m.pl*, the dying. **mourir** (ri:r) *v.i.ir*, to die, be dying; die away; d. out; d. down. *faire* ~, to execute (*criminal*). *se* ~, to be dying; fade out, give out.

mouron (murɔ̃) *m*, pimpernel. ~ [*des oiseaux*], chickweed. *se faire du* ~, to get into a stew.

mousquet (muskɛ) *m*, musket. **mousquetaire** (kətɛ:r) *m*, musketeer; (*att.*) double (*cuffs*). **mous-**

queton (tɔ̃) *m*, carbine; snap hook.

mousse (mus) *m*, cabin boy; (*f.*) moss; froth; foam; lather; head (*on glass of beer*); mousse (*cream*).

mousseline (muslin) *f*, muslin; mousseline.

mousser (muse) *v.i*, to froth; foam; lather; effervesce, sparkle. *faire* ~ (*fig.*), to make much of; advertise; make angry. **mousseux, euse** (sø, ø:z) *a*, mossy; moss (*rose*); frothy; foamy; sparkling (*wine*). *non mousseux*, still (*wine*).

mousson (musɔ̃) *f*, monsoon.

moussu, e (musy) *a*, mossy, moss-grown; moss (*rose*).

moustache (mustaʃ) *f*, mustache; whiskers (*animal*). ~ *en brosse*, toothbrush m. ~ *en croc*, turned up m. **moustachu, e** (ʃy) *a*, mustached.

moustiquaire (mustikɛ:r) *f*, mosquito net. **moustique** (tik) *m*, mosquito.

moût (mu) *m*, must, stum; wort.

moutard (muta:r) *m*, youngster, urchin.

moutarde (mutard) *f. & att*, mustard. *de la* ~ *après dîner*, too late to be useful. *la* ~ *lui est montée au nez*, he lost his temper. **moutardier** (dje) *m*, mustard pot; m. maker.

mouton (mutɔ̃) *m*, sheep; wether; mutton; sheep[skin]; lamb (*pers.*); spy (*on prisoner*); monkey; ram tup (*pile driving*); yoke, stock (*of bell*); (*pl.*) sheep; (*pl.*) whitecaps (*waves*); (*pl.*) fluff (*under furniture*). **moutonner** (tɔne) *v.i*, to [break into] foam (*sea*). *nuages moutonnés, ciel moutonné*, fleecy clouds, sky fleeced with clouds. **moutonneux, euse** (nø, ø:z) *a*, foamy; crested (*waves*). **moutonnier, ère** (nje, ɛ:r) *a*, sheeplike (*pers.*).

mouture (muty:r) *f*, milling; maslin.

mouvant, e (muvɑ̃, ɑ̃:t) *a*, moving, shifting, unstable; quick (*sand*). **mouvement** (vmɑ̃) *m*, motion; movement; progress; impulse; action, bustle, stir, life; arrangement (*Art.*); conformation (*of ground*); change; changes (*staff*); appointments & promotions; move (*Mil.*); burst (*oratory*); attack (*fever*); fluctuation; traffic; circulation; turnover; statistics (*population*); transaction; works (*Horol.*). ~ des navires, shipping intelligence, s. news, movements of ships. ~ *populaire*, civil commotion. ~ *vissé*, clockwise movement. ~ *d'humeur*, bad-tempered gesture or mood. *dans le ~* (*fig.*), in the swim. *de son propre ~*, of one's own accord. **mouvementé, e** (te) *a*, lively, bustling, busy; eventful; stirring; broken (*ground*). **mouvoir** (vwa:r) *v.t.ir. & se ~*, to move; actuate; propel.

moyen, ne (mwajɛ̃, ɛn) *a*, middle; mean, average; medium; middling; intermediate (*course, Sch.*); doubtful (*virtue*). *d'âge moyen*, middle-aged (*pers.*). *le ~ âge*, the Middle Ages. *du ~ âge*, medieval. ~ *terme*, middle course (*conduct*). ~ [*terme*], middle [term] (*Log.*). **moyen**, *m*, means, way; help; (*pl.*) means (*pecuniary*); grounds (*law*). ~ *de fortune*, makeshift. **moyenâgeux, euse** (jɛnɑʒø, ø:z) *a*, medieval. **moyennant** (nɑ̃) *pr*, in consideration of; on; at; with the help of. **moyenne** (jɛn) *f*, average, mean. **moyennement** (nmɑ̃) *ad*, moderately, fairly.

moyeu (mwajø) *m*, nave; hub; boss. ~ *arrière à roue libre & frein contre-pédalage*, coaster hub.

mucilage (mysilaʒ) *m*, mucilage.

mucosité (mykozite) *f. & mucus* (ky:s) *m*, mucus, phlegm.

mue (my) *f*, molt[ing]; slough[ing]; mew; [hen] coop; breaking (*voice*). **muer** (mɥe) *v.i.*, to molt; slough; break; (*v.t.*) to change.

muet, te (mɥɛ, ɛt) *a. & n*, dumb (*person*); mute; speechless; silent. *à la muette*, without speaking.

muezzin (mɥɛzɛ̃) *m*, muezzin.

mufle (myfl) *m*, muzzle, muffle; cad. **muflier** (flie) *m*, antirrhinum, snapdragon.

muge (my:ʒ) *m*, gray mullet.

mugir (myʒi:r) *v.i*, to low; bellow; roar; whistle (*wind*).

muguet (mygɛ) *m*, lily of the valley.

mulâtre (mylɑ:tr) *a. & m*, **mulâtresse** (lɑtrɛs) *f*, mulatto. **mule** (myl) *f*, [she] mule; mule (*slipper*); slipper *or* toe (*of pope as kissed*). **mulet** (lɛ) *m*, [he] mule; mule (*pers.*); cross, hybrid, mule; gray mullet; test auto (*not mass produced*). **muletier** (ltje) *m*, muleteer; (*att.*) mule (*track*).

mulot (mylo) *m*, field mouse.

multicolore (myltikɔlɔ:r) *a*, multicolor[ed], many-colored.

multicopie (myltikɔpi) *f*, photocopy, Xerox, etc.

multiple (myltipl) *a*, multiple, manifold, multifarious. ¶ *m*, multiple. **multiplicande** (plikɑ̃:d) *m*, multiplicand. **multiplicateur** (katœ:r) *m*, multiplier. **multiplication** (sjɔ̃) *f*, multiplication; gear [ratio]. **multiplicité** (site) *f*, multiplicity. **multiplier** (plie) *v.t. & i. & se ~*, to multiply.

multiplet (myltiple) *m*, byte.

multitude (myltityd) *f*, multitude, crowd.

municipal, e (munisipal) *a*, municipal, town (*att.*). **municipalité** (lite) *f*, municipality; [municipal] corporation.

munificence (mynifisɑ̃:s) *f*, munificence, bounty.

munir (myni:r) *v.t*, to supply, provide, furnish; fortify. **munitions** (nisjɔ̃) *f.pl*, ammunition. ~ *de bouche*, provisions, food. ~ *de guerre*, war[like] stores, munitions.

muqueux, euse (mykø, ø:z) *a*, mucous. [**membrane**] **muqueuse**, *f*, m. membrane.

mur (my:r) *m*, wall.

mûr, e (my:r) *a*, ripe, mature; mellow; worn threadbare.

muraille (myrɑ:j) *f*, wall. **mural, e** (ral) *a*, mural, wall (*att.*).

mûre (my:r) *f*, mulberry. ~ *sauvage*, ~ *de ronce*, blackberry.

mûrement (myrmɑ̃) *ad*, closely, thoroughly.

murer (myre) *v.t*, to wall; w. up; screen (*fig*).

mûrier (myrje) *m*, mulberry [tree].

mûrir (myri:r) *v.i. & t*, to ripen, mature; mellow.

murmure (myrmy:r) *m*, murmur; grumbling; mutter; whisper; hum;

brawling; gurgle; soughing. **murmurer** (myre) *v.i.* & *t*, to murmur, etc.

mûron (myrɔ̃) *m*, blackberry; wild raspberry bush.

musaraigne (myzarɛɲ) *f*, shrew [mouse].

musarder (myzarde) *v.i*, to dawdle.

musc (mysk) *m*, musk; m. deer. [noix] **muscade** (kad) *f*, nutmeg. **muscadier** (dje) *m*, nutmeg [tree]. **muscat** (ka) *a.* & *m*, muscat (grape, wine).

muscle (myskl) *m*, muscle. **musclé, e** (kle) *a*, -muscled. **musculaire** (kylɛːr) & **musculeux, euse** (lø, øːz) *a*, muscular.

Muse (myːz) *f*, Muse.

museau (myzo) *m*, muzzle, snout.

musée (myze) *m*, museum.

museler (myzle) *v.t*, to muzzle. **muselière** (zəljɛːr) *f*, muzzle (dog).

muser (myze) *v.i*, to dawdle, moon [about].

musette (myzɛt) *f*, musette (*Mus.*); nosebag; haversack; bag.

muséum (myzeɔm) *m*, natural history museum.

musical, e† (myzikal) *a*, musical. music hall (myzik hɔl) *m*, music hall variety theater. **musicien, ne** (sjɛ̃, ɛn) *n*, musician; player; bandsman; (*att.*) musical. **musique** (zik) *f*, music; band; toy musical instrument; blackmail. *connaître la ~*, to have had the experience. *~ de chats*, caterwauling.

musoir (myzwaːr) *m*, pierhead.

musquer (myske) *v.t*, to [perfume with] musk.

musulman, e (myzylmɑ̃, an) *n.* & *att*, Mussulman.

mutabilité (mytabilite) *f*, mutability. **mutation** (sjɔ̃) *f*, mutation, change; transfer, conveyance (*law*). **muter** (te) *v.t*, to transfer (*official, soldier*).

mutilation (mytilasjɔ̃) *f*, mutilation, maiming; defacement. **mutilé de la guerre** (le) *m*, disabled soldier, disabled sailor. **mutiler** (le) *v.t*, to mutilate, etc.

mutin, e (mytɛ̃, in) *a.* & *n*, roguish (child); mischievous (child); mutinous; mutineer. **se mutiner**

(tine) *v.pr.* & **mutiner**, *v.abs*, to mutiny, rebel; be unruly. **mutinerie** (nri) *f*, mutiny; refractoriness; roguishness.

mutisme (mytism) *m*, dumbness, muteness.

mutualiste (mytɥalist) *n*, member of a mutual society *or* association. **mutualité** (te) *f*, mutuality; mutual association. *~ de crédit*, mutual loan association. **mutuel, le**† (tɥɛl) *a*, mutual.

mycélium (miseljɔm) *m*, mycelium, spawn.

myope (mjɔp) *a.* & *n*, shortsighted (person), nearsighted (person). **myopie** (pi) *f*, myopia.

myosotis (mjɔzɔtis) *m*, myosotis, forget-me-not.

myriade (mirjad) *f*, myriad. **myriagramme** (gram) *m*, myriagram = 10000 grams *or* 22.046 lbs. **myriapode** (pɔd) *m*, myriapod.

myrrhe (miːr) *f*, myrrh.

myrte (mirt) *m*, myrtle. **myrtille** (til) *f*, whortleberry, bilberry.

mystère (mistɛːr) *m*, mystery; m. [play], miracle [play]. *~ de la Passion*, passion play. **mystérieux, euse**† (terjø, øːz) *a*, mysterious. **mysticisme** (tisism) *m*, mysticism. **mysticité** (te) *f*, mysticalness. **mystificateur, trice** (fikatœːr, tris) *n*, hoaxer, humbug. **mystifier** (fje) *v.t*, to mystify; hoax, humbug. **mystique**† (tik) *a*, mystic(al). ¶ *n*, mystic (*pers.*); (*f.*) mystical theology; mysterious appeal (*as of the olden times*).

mythe (mit) *m*, myth. **mythique** (tik) *a*, mythic(al). **mythologie** (tɔlɔʒi) *f*, mythology. **mythologique** (ʒik) *a*, mythologic(al). **mythologue** (lɔg) *n*, mythologist.

N

nabab (nabab) *m*, nabob.

nabot, e (nabo, ɔt) (*pers.*) *n*, midget, shrimp, manikin.

nacelle (nasɛl) (*Avn.*) *f*, car, nacelle, gondola; cockpit; skiff, dinghy; pontoon boat.

nacre (nakr) *f*, mother of pearl. **nacré, e** (kre) *a*, pearly.

nadir (nadiːr) *m*, nadir.

nævus (nevy:s) *m*, birthmark, mole.

nage (na:ȝ) *f*, swimming; stroke. ~ [*d'aviron*], rowing. ~ *à la pagaie*, paddling. ~ *de côté*, sidestroke. ~ *en grenouille*, breaststroke. ~ *en couple*, sculling. *en* ~, bathed in perspiration. **nageoire** (naȝwa:r) *f*, fin (*fish*); flipper. **nager** (ȝe) *v.i*, to swim, float; welter, revel; row. ~ *debout*, to tread water; row standing up. ~ *en couple*, to scull. ~ *entre deux eaux*, to swim under water. **nageur, euse** (ȝœ:r, ø:z) *n*, swimmer; rower, oarsman.

naguère (nagɛ:r) *ad*, not long since.

naïade (najad) *f*, naiad, water nymph.

naïf, ïve (naif, i:v) *a*, artless, naïve, unaffected ingenuous; unsophisticated; simpleminded, green.

nain, e (nɛ̃, ɛn) *n. & att*, dwarf.

naissance (nɛsɑ̃:s) *f*, birth; descent; rise (*river*); spring[ing] (*Arch.*). ~*du jour*, dawn, break of day. **naissant, e** (sɑ̃, ɑ̃:t) *a*, dawning; budding; nascent. **naître** (nɛ:tr) *v.i.ir*, to be born; grow; bud; [a]rise, spring up. *à* ~, unborn.

naïvement (naivmɑ̃) *ad*, artlessly, etc. **naïveté** (vte) *f*, artlessness, etc.

nana (nana) *f*, woman (*slang*).

nankin (nɑ̃kɛ̃) *m*, nankeen.

nanti, e (nɑ̃ti) *p.p*: ~ *de* (*fig.*), secured by. *homme* ~, man who has made his pile. **nantir** (ti:r) *v.t*, to secure; provide; register (*mortgage*). **nantissement** (smɑ̃) *m*, hypothecation, collateral security.

napel (napɛl) *m*, wolfsbane.

naphtaline (naftalin) *f*, naphthalene. **naphte** (naft) *m*, naphtha.

napolitain, e (napɔlitɛ̃, ɛn) *a. & N~*, *n*, Neapolitan.

nappe (nap) *f*, tablecloth; cloth; sheet (*water, flame*). **napperon** (prɔ̃) *m*, cloth (*tea, tray*).

narcisse (narsis) *m*, narcissus. ~ *des prés*, daffodil.

narcotique (narkɔtik) *a. & m*, narcotic, opiate.

narguer (narge) *v.t*, to flout.

narguilé, -ghileh (nargile) *m*, hookah.

narine (narin) *f*, nostril.

narquois, e (narkwa, a:z) *a*, sly, cunning, bantering.

narrateur, trice (narratœ:r, tris) *n*, narrator, storyteller. **narratif, ive** (tif, i:v) *a*, narrative. **narration** (sjɔ̃) *f*, narrative, story; narration; essay (*Sch.*). **narrer** (re) *v.t*, to narrate, relate, tell.

narval (narval) *m*, narwhal.

nasal, e (nazal) *a. & f*, nasal. **nasarde** (zard) *f*, fillip; snub. **naseau** (zo) *m*, nostril (*horse*). **nasiller** (zije) *v.i*, to speak through the nose, snuffle, twang.

nasse (nas) *f*, eel pot; lobster pot; net; trap.

natal, e (natal) *a*, native; natal. **natalité** (lite) *f*, birthrate, natality.

natation (natasjɔ̃) *f*, swimming, natation.

natif, ive (natif, i:v) *a*, native, inborn. **les natifs**, *m. pl*, the natives.

nation (nasjɔ̃) *f*, nation; people. **national, e** (ɔnal) *a*, national. **nationalisme** (lism) *m*, nationalism. **nationaliste** (list) *n. & a*, nationalist. **nationalité** (te) *f*, nationality. **nationaux** (no) *m.pl*, nationals.

nativité (nativite) *f*, nativity.

natte (nat) *f*, mat, matting; plait. **natter** (te) *v.t*, to mat; plait. se ~, to plait one's hair. **nattier** (tje) *m*, mat maker.

naturalisation (natyralizasjɔ̃) *f*, naturalization. **naturaliser** (ze) *v.t*, to naturalize; stuff (*animal*); preserve (*plant*). **naturaliste** (list) *m*, naturalist. ~ [*fourreur*], taxidermist. **nature** (ty:r) *f*, nature; life (*art*); life size; plain [-boiled]. ~ *morte*, still life. *en* ~, in kind. **naturel, le†** (tyrɛl) *a*, natural; native; unaffected; illegitimate. ¶ *m*, naturalness; nature, disposition; native (*pers.*).

naufrage (nofra:ȝ) *m*, wreck, shipwreck. *faire* ~, to be [ship]wrecked. **naufragé, e** (fraȝe) *n*, shipwrecked person, castaway.

nauséabond, e (nozeabɔ̃, ɔ̃:d) *a*, nauseous, sickening, foul. **nau-**

sée (ze) *f*, nausea. **nauséeux, euse** (zeø, ø:z) *a*, neauseating.

nautile (notil) *ou* **nautilus** (ly:s) *m*, nautilus. **nautique** (tik) *a*, nautical; aquatic (*sports*). **nautonier, ère** (tɔnje, ɛ:r) (*Poet.*) *n*, mariner; ferryman.

naval, e (naval) *a*, naval, sea (*att.*); ship (*att.*).

navet (navɛ) *m*, turnip; bad painting; unsuccessful play. ~ *de Suède*, Swede turnip (*Agric.*).

navette (navɛt) *f*, rape (*oil seed plant*); incense box; shuttle. *faire la* ~, to go to & fro.

navigable (navigabl) *a*, navigable. **navigateur** (tœ:r) *m*, navigator; (*att.*) seafaring. **navigation** (sjɔ̃) *f*, navigation; sailing; shipping. **naviguer** (ge) *v.i*, to navigate, sail.

navire (navi:r) *m*, ship, vessel, boat, bottom. ~ *à vapeur*, steamship. ~*-citerne*, *m*, tank ship. ~ *de charge*, cargo boat. ~ *frère*, ~ *jumeau*, sister ship. ~ *de ligne* [*régulière*], liner. ~ *pose-mines*, mine layer.

navrant, e (navrã, ã:t) *a*, heartrending, heartbreaking, harrowing. **navrer** [**le cœur**] (vre) *v.t*, to break one's heart, harrow.

ne, n' (nə, n) *neg. particle, used mostly with the words* **pas** *or* **point**, not, n't. *n'importe!* no matter!

né, e (ne) *a*, born. *Je suis* ~, I was born.

néanmoins (neãmwɛ̃) *ad*, nevertheless, notwithstanding, yet, still.

néant (neã) *m*, nothing[ness], nought; nil, none.

nébuleux, euse (nebylø, ø:z) *a*, nebulous, cloudy; clouded. ¶ *f*, nebula (*Astr.*).

nécessaire† (nesesɛ:r) *a*, necessary, needful. ¶ *m*, necessary, -ries, needful; busybody; outfit, case. ~ *à ouvrage*, workbox, workbasket, needlework case. **nécessité** (site) *f*, necessity. **nécessiter** (te) *v.t*, to necessitate. **nécessiteux, euse** (tø, ø:z) *a*, necessitous, needy. *les* ~, *m.pl*, the needy, the destitute.

néorologe (nekrolɔ:ʒ) *m*, necrology, obituary (*roll, book*). **nécrologie** (lɔʒi) *f*, deaths, obitu-

ary, necrology (*notice*). **nécromancie** (mãsi) *f*, necromancy. **nécromancien, ne** (sjɛ̃, ɛn) *n*, necromancer. **nécropole** (pol) *f*, necropolis. **nécrose** (kro:z) *f*, necrosis.

nectaire (nɛktɛ:r) *m*, nectary. **nectar** (ta:r) *m*, nectar.

néerlandais, e (neerlãdɛ, ɛ:z) *a*, Netherlandish, Dutch. N~, *n*, Netherlander, Dutchman, -woman. **la Néerlande** (lã:d), the Netherlands.

nef (nɛf) *f*, nave (*church*); bark, ship (*Poet.*).

néfaste (nefast) *a*, luckless, illfated, ill-starred, disastrous.

nèfle (nɛfl) *f*, medlar. **néflier** (neflie) *m*, medlar [tree].

négatif, ive† (negatif, i:v) *a*, negative. ¶ *m*, negative (*Phot.*). **la négative**, the negative (*statement, etc.*). **négation** (sjɔ̃) *f*, negation; negative (*Gram.*).

négligé, e (negliʒe) *p.a*, neglected; unheeded; loose; slovenly; slipshod. ¶ *m*, undress, neglige; tea gown. **négligeable** (ʒabl) *a*, negligible. **négligemment** (ʒamã) *ad*, negligently, carelessly. **négligence** (ʒã:s) *f*, negligence, neglect, carelessness; default. **négligent, e** (ʒã, ã:t) *a*, negligent, careless, neglectful, remiss. **négliger** (ʒe) *v.t*, to neglect, slight. *se* ~, to neglect oneself; slack; be careless.

négoce (negɔs) *m*, trade; business. **négociable** (sjabl) *a*, negotiable; marketable. **négociant, e** (sjã, ã:t) *n*, trader, merchant. **négociateur, trice** (atœ:r, tris) *n*, negociàtor. **négociation** (sjɔ̃) *f*, negotiation; transaction; dealing; bargain. **négocier** (sje) *v.t*, to negotiate.

nègre (nɛ:gr) *a.m. & a.f.*, Negro. ¶ *m*, Negro; one who does the donkey work, underling (*vulg.*); ghost-writer, literary hack. **négresse** (negrɛs) *f*, Negress. **négrier** (grie) *m*, slaver, slave trader; s. driver (*hard employer*).

négritude (negrityd) *f*, overall cultural & spiritual values of people of black race.

neige (nɛ:ʒ) *f. oft. pl*, snow. *de la* ~ *fondue*, sleet; slush. *tomber* *de la* ~ *fondue,* to sleet. **neiger** (neʒe) *v.imp,* to snow. **neigeux, euse** (zø, ø:z) *a,* snowy.

Némésis (nemezi:s) *f,* Nemesis.

ne m'oubliez pas (nəmubliepɑ) *m,* forget-me-not.

nénuphar (nenyfa:r) *m,* water lily.

néologisme (neɔlɔʒism) *m,* neologism.

néon (ne5) *m,* neon.

néophyte (neɔfit) *n,* neophyte.

néo-zélandais, e (neɔzelɑ̃dɛ, ɛ:z) *a,* New Zealand (*att.*). **Néo-Zélandais, e,** *n,* New Zealander.

népotisme (nepɔtism) *m,* nepotism.

Néréide (nereid) *f,* Nereid, sea nymph.

nerf (nɛ:r & nɛrf) *m,* nerve; band (*Bookb.*); sinews (*of war*); (*pl.*) thews; (*pl.*) nerves, hysterics; (*pl.*) tantrums.

nerveux, euse† (nɛrvø, ø:z) *a,* nervous; highly strung; hysterical; fidgety. **nervosité** (vozite) *f,* irritability. **nervure** (vy:r) *f,* rib, nerve, nervure, vein (*Bot., etc.*).

net, te (nɛt) *a,* clean; flawless; clear; sharp; empty; free; net. *mettre au net,* to make a clean copy of net. **net,** *ad,* clean; plainly, flatly, outright. **nettement** (tmɑ̃) *ad,* clearly; frankly, plainly, flatly, downright. **netteté** (nɛtte) *f,* cleanness; clearness. **nettoiement** (nɛtwamɑ) & **nettoyage** (ja:ʒ) *m,* cleaning, cleansing. **nettoyer** (je) *v.t,* to clean, cleanse; clear. ~ *à sec,* to dryclean. **nettoyeur, euse** (jœ:r, ø:z) *n,* cleaner.

neuf (nœf & nœ & nœv) *a. & m,* nine; ninth. ~ *fois sur dix,* nine times out of ten.

neuf, euve (nœf, œ:v) *a,* new; inexperienced; raw.

neurasthénie (nørasteni) *f,* neurasthenia. **neurologiste** (rɔlɔʒist) *ou* **neurologue** (lɔg) *n,* nerve specialist, neurologist.

neutraliser (nøtralize) *v.t,* to neutralize. **neutralité** (te) *f,* neutrality. **neutre** (nø:tr) *a,* neutral; noncommittal; neuter; undenominational (*school*). ¶ *m,* neuter; neutral.

neuvième† (nœvjɛm) *a. & n,* ninth.

neveu (nəvø) *m,* nephew. *nos* ~*x,* posterity.

névralgie (nevralʒi) *f,* neuralgia. **névralgique** (ʒik) *a,* neuralgic; sore (*point*). **névrite** (vrit) *f,* neuritis. **névrose** (vro:z) *f,* neurosis. **névrosé, e** (vroze) *a,* neurotic.

nez (ne) *m,* nose; face; nosing (*stair*); scent (*dogs*). *à vue de* ~, at the first blush. *avoir un verre dans le* ~, to be tipsy. ~ *à* ~, face to face.

ni (ni) *c,* nor; or; neither. ~ *fleurs,* ~ *couronnes,* no flowers, by request. ~ *l'un* (*l'une*) *ni l'autre,* *pn. & a,* neither.

niable (njabl) *a,* deniable.

niais, e† (njɛ, ɛ:z) *a. & n,* silly. **niaiser** (ɛze) *v.i,* to play the fool. **niaiserie** (zri) *f,* silliness.

niche (niʃ) *f,* niche; trick, prank, practical joke. ~ *à chien,* dog kennel. **nichée** (ʃe) *f,* nest[ful]; brood. **nicher** (ʃe) *v.i,* to nest; (*v.t.*) to put, ensconce. **nichet** (ʃɛ) *m,* nestegg.

nichon (niʃ5) *m,* breast (*slang*). *faux* ~*s,* falsies, gay deceivers.

nickel (nikɛl) *m,* nickel. **nickeler** (kle) *v.t,* to nickle.

nicodème (nikɔdɛ:m) *m,* booby.

nicotine (nikɔtin) *f,* nicotine.

nid (ni) *m,* nest; den. ~ *d'hirondelle,* edible bird's nest. ~ *de pie,* crow's nest (*Naut.*). *il croit avoir trouvé la pie au* ~, he has found a mare's nest.

nièce (njɛs) *f,* niece.

nielle (njɛl) *f,* smut, blight (*Agric.*). ¶ *m,* niello.

nier (nje) *v.t,* to deny; repudiate; (*abs.*) to deny it. ~ *sa culpabilité,* to plead not guilty.

nigaud, e (nigo, o:d) *a,* silly. ¶ *n,* noodle, ninny, booby, nincompoop. **nigauder** (gode) *v.i,* to play the fool. **nigauderie** (dri) *f,* silliness.

nigelle de Damas (niʒɛl) *f,* love-in-a-mist.

nihiliste (niilist) *m,* nihilist.

Nil (le) (nil), the Nile.

nimbe (nɛ̃:b) *m,* nimbus, halo,

glory. nimbus (nēby:s) *m*, nimbus (*Meteor.*).

Ninive (nini:v) *f*, Nineveh.

nippes (nip) *f.pl*, old clothes; togs. **nipper** (pe) *v.t*, to rig out, outfit someone. *se ~ aux puces*, to buy one's clothes secondhand, at a flea market.

nitouche (**sainte**) (nituf) *f*, [prudish & demure] little hypocrite.

nitrate (nitrat) *m*, nitrate. **nitre** (tr) *m*, niter, saltpeter. **nitrique** (trik) *a*, nitric. **nitroglycérine** (trɔgliserin) *f*, nitroglycerin[e].

niveau (nivo) *m*, level. *~ à bulle d'air*, spirit l. *~ de vie*, standard of living. *de ~*, level, at grade. **niveler** (vle) *v.t*, to level. **niveleur** (vlœ:r) *m*, leveler. **niveleuse** (løz) *f*, grader (*Build.*). **nivellement** (velmã) *m*, leveling.

nobiliaire (nɔbilje:r) *a*, nobiliary. ¶ *m*, peerage (*book*). **noble**† (bl) *a*, noble. ¶ *n*, noble[man], noblewoman. **noblesse** (blɛs) *f*, nobility; nobleness; noblesse.

noce (nɔs) *f*, wedding festivities; wedding party; jollification; spree; (*pl.*) wedding, marriage, nuptials. *~s d'argent, d'or, de diamant*, silver, golden, diamond, wedding. **noceur, euse** (sœ:r, ø:z) *n*, reveler.

nocher (nɔʃe) (*Poet.*) *m*, boatman; ferryman.

nocif, ive (nɔsif, i:v) *a*, noxious.

noctambule (nɔktãby:l) *n*, sleepwalker. **nocturne** (tyrn) *a*, nocturnal, night (*att.*). ¶ *m*, nocturne.

Noël (nɔɛl) *m*, Christmas[tide], yule[tide]. *à la [fête de] ~, à ~*, at Christmas[tide], at yuletide. **n~**, [Christmas] carol.

nœud (nø) *m*, knot; node; cluster; crux; rub; tie, bond (*fig.*). *~ coulant*, slip knot, running k.; noose. *~ [de ruban]*, bow. *~ gordien* (gɔrdjɛ̃), Gordian knot. *~[-papillon]*, bow tie. *~ plat*, reef knot.

noir, e (nwa:r) *a*, black; dark; swarthy; brown (*bread*); black & blue (*bruised*); gloomy; drunk (*slang*). *noir sur blanc* [down] in black & white (*writing*). *la mer Noire*, the Black Sea. ¶ *m*,

black; b. mark (*bruise*); b. [man, boy], man of color; bull's eye (*target*). ¶ *f*, black [ball] (*gaming*); crotchet (*Mus.*). **noirâtre** (nwarɑ:tr) *a*, blackish; darkish. **noiraud, e** (ro, o:d) *a. & n*, swarthy (man, woman). **noirceur** (sœ:r) *f*, blackness; black spot; smudge, smut. **noircir** (si:r) *v.t. & i*, to blacken; black; blot (*paper with useless writing*). **noircissure** (sisy:r) *f*, smudge.

noise (nwa:z) *f*, quarrel.

noisetier (nwaztje) *m*, hazel (*bush*), nut tree. **noisette** (zɛt) *f*, hazelnut; nut; hazel (*color, eyes*); nut-brown. *les ~s*, testicles (*slang*).

noix (nwa) *f*, walnut; nut. *~ de coco*, coconut. *~ de galle*, nut gall. *~ vomique* (vɔmik), nux vomica.

nolis (nɔli) *m*, freight. **noliser** (ze) *v.t*, to freight, charter.

nom (nɔ̃) *m*, name; style; noun. *~ de baptême*, Christian name. *~ [de famille], ~ patronymique*, surname. *~ de plume*, assumed name, alias; stage n.; pen n. *~ de jeune fille*, maiden n. *~ de plume*, pen n. *~ de théâtre*, stage n. *~ & prénoms*, full n. *sous un ~ interposé*, in a nominee's n. *petit nom*, given n.

nomade (nɔmad) *a*, nomad(ic). ¶ *m*, nomad, wanderer.

nombre (nɔ̃:br) *m*, number. *les N~s* (*Bible*), Numbers. *~ des adhérents*, membership. *avoir du ~*, to be well-balanced (*phrase*). **nombrer** (nɔ̃bre) *v.t*, to number, count. **nombreux, euse** (brø, ø:z) *a*, numerous; well-balanced (*style, prose*).

nombril (nɔ̃bri) *m*, navel; eye (*fruit*). *se prendre pour le ~ du monde*, to think oneself very important. **nombrilisme** (lism) *m*, navel gazing.

nomenclature (nɔmãklaty:r) *f*, nomenclature. **nominal, e**† (minal) *a*, nominal; face (*value*). *appel ~*, roll call. **nominatif, ive** (tif, i:v) *a*, nominal, of [the] names; registered (*securities*). ¶ *m*, nominative [case]. **nomination** (sjɔ̃) *f*, nomination; appointment; commissioning (*officer*);

gift (*of an office*); award (*at a show*); **nominativement** (tivmã) *ad,* by name. **un nommé . . . (me),** a man called . . . , one . . . [by name]. **nommément** (memã) *ad,* namely, to wit, by name. **nommer** (me) *v.t,* to name; call; nominate; appoint; commission; return, elect. **se ~,** to give one's name; be called. *je me nomme Adam,* my name is Adam.

non (nõ) *neg. particle,* no; not. *ni moi ~ plus,* nor I either. ¶ *m,* no, nay.

non-activité (en) (nɔnaktivite) *f,* on the unemployed list (*Mil.*).

nonagénaire (nɔnaʒenɛɪr) *a. &' n,* nonagenarian.

non avenu, e (nɔnavny) *a,* void, non avenu.

nonce du Pape *ou* **nonce apostolique** (nõɪs) *m,* papal nuncio.

nonchalamment (nõʃalamã) *ad,* nonchalantly, listlessly. **nonchalance** (lãɪs) *f,* nonchalance, listlessness. **nonchalant, e** (lã, ãɪt) *a,* nonchalant, listless.

nonciature (nõsjatyɪr) *f,* nunciature.

non-combat (nõkõba) *m,* no contest (*Box.*). **non-combattant, e** (batã, ãɪt) *a. & m,* noncombatant (*Mil.*).

non-conformiste (nõkõformist) *n. & att,* nonconformist.

non-être (nɔnɛːtr) (*Philos.*) *m,* nonentity, nonexistence.

non-intervention (nɔnɛ̃tervãsjõ) (*Pol.*) *f,* nonintervention, noninterference.

non-lieu (nõljø) *m,* no case to answer (*law*).

nonne (nɔn) & **nonnain** (nɛ̃) *f,* nun.

nonobstant (nɔnɔpstã) *pr,* notwithstanding.

non-paiement (nõpɛmã) *m,* nonpayment; dishonor (*bill*).

non-sens (nõsãːs) *m,* nonsense. *un ~,* all nonsense, meaningless.

non-valeur (nõvalœːr) *f,* unproductiveness; worthless security; valueless stock; (*pl.*) irrecoverable arrears (*taxes*); bad debt; noneffective (*Mil.*); useless person.

nord (nɔɪr) *m,* north; (*att.*) north[ern]. *mer du N~,* North Sea. *perdre le ~,* to get confused. **nord-est** (nɔr[d]ɛst; *Naut.,* nɔre) *m,* northeast; northeast wind; (*att.*) northeast[ern]. **nordique** (dik) *a,* Nordic. **nord-ouest** (nɔr[d]wɛst; *Naut.,* nɔrwa) *m,* northwest, northwest wind; (*att.*) northwest[ern].

normal, e† (nɔrmal) *a,* normal; standard; ordinary. **normalien, ne** (ljẽ, ɛn) *n,* student [of a normal school].

normand, e (nɔrmã, ãɪd) *a,* Norman; noncommittal (*fig.*); evasive; feigned. *les îles Normandes,* the Channel Islands. *N~, n,* Norman. *un fin n~,* a shrewd crafty fellow. **la Normandie** (mãdi), Normandy.

norme (nɔrm) *f,* norm.

norois (l'ancien) (nɔrwa) *m,* Old Norse (*language*).

Norvège (la) (nɔrvɛɪʒ), Norway. **norvégien, ne** (veʒjẽ, ɛn) *a. & N~, n,* Norwegian, Norseman. *le norvégien,* Norwegian, Norse (*language*).

nos, our, *possessive adjective plural, see* **notre.**

nostalgie (nɔstalʒi) *f,* nostalgia, homesickness; pining. **nostalgique** (ʒik) *a,* nostalgic, homesick.

nota [bene] (nɔta bene) (*abb.* N.B.) *m,* note, nota bene, N.B. **notabilité** (notabilite) *f,* notability. **notable†** (bl) *a,* notable; especial; eminent, distinguished. ¶ *m,* person of distinction, notable.

notaire (notɛɪr) *m,* notary.

notamment (notmã) *ad,* especially, notably.

notation (notasjõ) *f,* notation.

note (nɔt) *f,* note, memorandum; mark (*Sch.*); record (*of service*); bill, account; tune (*fig.*). *~ d'agrément,* grace note (*Mus.*). *~ de passage,* passing note (*Mus.*). *~ naturelle,* natural [note] (*Mus.*). **noter** (te) *v.t,* to note; n. down; write down; mark (*pupil, etc.*). **notice** (tis) *f,* notice, account; review (*book*). **notifier** (tifje) *v.t,* to notify.

notion (nosjõ) *f,* notion, smattering.

notoire† (nɔtwaːr) *a*, well-known.
notoriété (tɔrjete) *f*, notoriety. ~ *publique*, common knowledge.

notre (nɔtr) *a*, our. *Notre-Dame*, Our Lady. *Notre-Seigneur*, our Lord. **le nôtre, la ~, les ~s** (noːtr) *pn*, ours; our own. *il est des nôtres*, he is one of us.

noue (nu) *f*, valley (*roof*); water meadow.

nouer (nwe) *v.t*, to tie; knot; knit (*fig.*); form. **noueux, euse** (nuø, øːz) *a*, knotty; gnarled.

nougat (nugɑ) *m*, nougat.

nouilles (nuːj) *f.pl*, vermicelli.

nounou (nunu) *f*, nanny, nursy.

nourrain (nurɛ̃) *m*, fry (*fish*).

nourri, e (nuri) *p.p. & p.a*, fed; (*fig.*) copious; full; steeped; prolonged (*applause*); brisk (*fire, Mil.*). *mal ~, pas ~*, underfed, ill-fed. **nourrice** (ris) *f*, [wet] nurse. *être la ~ de*, to nurse, suckle. *mère ~*, nursing mother. **nourrir** (riːr) *v.t*, to nourish; nurture, rear; suckle, nurse; feed; board, keep; foster, cherish, harbor, entertain. **nourrissage** (risaːʒ) *m*, rearing (*cattle*). **nourrissant, e** (sɑ̃, ɑ̃ːt) *a*, nourishing, nutritious. **nourrisseur** (sœːr) *m*, dairy farmer; feed-roll (*Mech.*). **nourrisson** (sɔ̃) *m*, nurseling; suckling; foster child. **nourriture** (tyːr) *f*, food, nourishment, nutriment; sustenance; board; feeding; nurture.

nous (nu) *pn*, we; us, to us, ourselves; each other. *chez ~*, at our house. *à ~!* help! *~-mêmes*, ourselves.

nouveau, el, le (nuvo, ɛl) *a. & ad*, new; newly; recent; novel; fresh; another, further. *le Nouveau-Brunswick* (brɔ̃zvik), New Brunswick. *nouveau marié, nouvelle mariée*, bridegroom, bride (*about to be married or on marriage day*). *nouveaux mariés*, [newly] married couple; bride & bridegroom. *nouveau-né, e, n. & att*, newborn (child). *nouveau riche*, upstart. *nouveau venu, nouvelle venue*, newcomer. *la Nouvelle-Écosse*, Nova Scotia. *la Nouvelle-Galles du Sud*, New South Wales. *la Nouvelle-Guinée*, New Guinea. *la Nouvelle-*

Orléans, New Orleans. *la Nouvelle-Zélande* (zelɑ̃ːd), New Zealand. *la Nouvelle-Zemble* (ʒɑ̃bl), Nova Zembla. *le nouveau, m*, the new, a novelty, something new. *le nouveau, la nouvelle*, the new boy, man, girl (*Sch., etc.*). *à nouveau*, anew, afresh; carried forward. *de nouveau*, again, afresh. **nouveauté (te)** *f*, newness; novelty; new thing, book, play, etc; innovation; (*pl.*) new styles, latest fashions; ladies' & children's wear; drapery.

nouvelle (nuvɛl) *f.*, *oft. pl. in sense of* news, [piece of] news; tidings, intelligence; tale, short story, novelette. *~s à la main* (*journalism*), today's gossip, looking at life.

nouvellement (nuvɛlmɑ̃) *ad*, newly, recently.

nouvelliste (nuvɛlist) *n*, newsmonger, intelligencer, quidnunc.

novateur, trice (nɔvatœːr, tris) *n*, innovator.

novembre (nɔvɑ̃ːbr) *m*, November.

novice (nɔvis) *n*, novice; probationer; tyro; apprentice (*Naut.*). ¶ *a*, inexperienced, raw, fresh, green. **noviciat** (sja) *m*, noviciate; apprenticeship.

noyade (nwajad) *f*, drowning (*fatality*); noyade (*Hist.*).

noyau (nwajo) *m*, stone (*fruit*); kernel, core, center; nucleus; newel.

noyer (nwaje) *m*, walnut [tree, wood].

noyer (nwaje) *v.t*, to drown; flood, deluge; sink; swamp; play (*fish*). *un noyé* (je), a drowned man; a drowning man. *les noyés*, the [apparently] drowned.

nu, e (ny) *a*, naked, nude; bare; barebacked (*horse*); plain. *à l'œil nu*, with the naked eye. *~ comme un ver*, stark naked. *nu-pieds, inv. ou pieds nus*, barefoot[ed]. *nu-tête, inv. ou tête nue*, bareheaded. ¶ *m*, nakedness, nudity; nude; bareness. *le nu*, the nude. *les nus*, the naked. *à nu*, bare, naked; bareback[ed] (*riding*).

nuage (nyaːʒ) *m*, cloud; volume (*of smoke, etc.*); haze, mist (*fig.*);

suspicion. **nuageux, euse** (aȝø, ø:z) a, cloudy; hazy.

nuance (nyɑ̃:s) f, shade; hue; tinge; nuance; (pl.) lights & shades; sign of expression (Mus.) **nuancer** (ɑ̃se) v.t, to shade; mark (or observe) the signs of expression; execute with feeling.

Nubie (la) (nybi), Nubia. **nubien, ne** (bjɛ̃, ɛn) a. & N~, n, Nubian.

nubile (nybil) a, nubile, marriageable.

nucléaire (nyklɛɛ:r) a, nuclear. *centrale* ~, nuclear power plant. *rayonnement* ~, nuclear radiation.

nudité (nydite) f, nudity, nakedness; bareness; nude (art).

nue (ny) (poetic) f, high clouds. *oft. pl,* cloud, sky. **nuée** (nye) f, storm cloud, thunder cloud; cloud (fig.), host, swarm; shower.

nuire (nqi:r) v.i.ir. & ~ à, to harm, hurt, injure, wrong, prejudice. **nuisible** (nqizibl) a, harmful, hurtful, injurious, noxious, noisome.

nuit (nqi) f, night; dark[ness]. *cette* ~, tonight; last night. *à [la]* ~ *close,* after dark. *à la* ~ *tombante,* at nightfall. ~ *américaine,* day-for-night shooting (cinema, TV). **nuitamment** (tamɑ̃) ad, by night, in the n.

nul, le (nyl) a, no; not any; null; nugatory; nil; of no account; drawn (game); dead (heat). *nul(le)* & *non avenu(e)* (avny), null & void. *nulle part,* ad, nowhere. **nul,** pn, no one, none. **nulle,** f, null (in cipher). **nullement** (lmɑ̃) ad, in no way, not at all, by no means, nowise. **nullité** (lite) f, nullity; emptiness; nonentity, cipher (pers.).

nûment (nymɑ̃) ad, openly, frankly, nakedly.

numéraire (nymerɛ:r) a, numerary. ¶ m, coin, cash, specie. **numéral, e** (ral) a, numeral. **numérateur** (tœ:r) m, numerator (Arith.). **numérique†** (rik) a, numerical; digital. **numéro** (ro) m, number; size; issue (periodical); turn (music hall). **numérotage** (rɔta:ȝ) m, numbering. **numéroter** (te) v.t, to number.

numismate (nymismat) m, numismatist. **numismatique** (tik) f, numismatics.

nuptial, e (nypsjal) a, nuptial, bridal, wedding (att.), marriage (att.).

nuque (nyk) f, nape (of neck).

nutritif, ive (nytritif, i:v) a, nutritive, nutritious. **nutrition** (sjɔ̃) f, nutrition.

nymphe (nɛ̃:f) f, nymph.

O

ô (o) i, O! oh!

oasis (oazis) f, oasis (lit. & fig.).

obédience (ɔbedjɑ̃:s) f, obedience (Eccl.). **obéir** (i:r) v.i, to obey. ~ à, to obey; submit to, yield to; comply with; respond to. **obéissance** (isɑ̃:s) f, obedience; allegiance; authority; compliance; submission. **obéissant, e** (sɑ̃, ɑ̃:t) a, obedient; dutiful; submissive.

obélisque (ɔbelisk) m, obelisk.

obérer (ɔbere) v.t, to encumber [with debts].

obèse (ɔbɛ:z) a, obese, fat. **obésité** (bezite) f, obesity, fatness.

obier (ɔbje) m, guelder rose.

objecter (ɔbȝɛkte) v.t, to object (que = that); o. to, o. against; allege. **objectif, ive†** (tif, i:v) a. & m, objective (Philos.). ¶ m, objective, aim. [verre] *objectif,* objective, object glass, lens. **objection** (ksjɔ̃) f, objection; demur. **objet** (ȝɛ) m, object; subject; article. ~ *d'art,* work of art.

objurgation (ɔbȝyrgasjɔ̃) f, objurgation.

oblation (ɔblasjɔ̃) f, oblation, offering (Lit.).

obligataire (ɔbligatɛ:r) m, bondholder, debenture h. **obligation** (sjɔ̃) f, obligation; bond; debenture: recognizance. **obligatoire** (twa:r) a, obligatory, compulsory, binding. *sens* ~, one-way street, road. **obligé, e** (ȝe) a, usual; obbligato (Mus.). ¶ n, debtor (for services). **obligeamment** (ȝamɑ̃) ad, obligingly, kindly. **obligeant, e** (ȝɑ̃, ɑ̃:t) a, obliging, kind[ly]; complimentary. **obliger** (ȝe) v.t, to oblige, bind, compel; obligate. s'~, to bind oneself; undertake.

oblique† (oblik) *a*, oblique, slanting, skew; side (*glance*); crooked (*fig.*), underhand. **obliquer** (ke) *v.i*, to slant. **obliquité** (kite) *f*, obliquity; crookedness.

oblitérer (oblitere) *v.t*, to obliterate; cancel.

oblong, ongue (obl5, 5:g) *a*, oblong.

obnubiler (obnybile) *v.t*, to cloud.

obole (obol) *f*, [brass] farthing, stiver; mite.

obscène (opsɛːn) *a*, obscene. **obscénité** (senite) *f*, obscenity.

obscur, e (opsky:r) *a*, dark; dim, murky; obscure. **obscurcir** (skyrsi:r) *v.t*, to darken; overcast, overshadow. **obscurément** (remã) *ad*, darkly, etc. **obscurité** (rite) *f*, dark[ness], etc.

obséder (opsede) *v.t*, to worry; obsess.

obsèques (opsɛk) *f.pl*, obsequies. **obséquieux, euse†** (sekjø, øːz) *a*, obsequious. **obséquiosité** (kjozite) *f*, obsequiousness.

observance (opsɛrvãːs) *f*, observance (*Theol.*). **observation, trice** (vatœːr, tris) *n*, observer; (*att.*) observant. **observation** (sjɔ̃) *f*, observance; observation; remark. **observatoire** (twaːr) *m*, observatory; observation post (*Mil.*). **observer** (ve) *v.t*, to observe; keep; watch; spot. s'~, to be careful, cautious.

obsession (opsɛsjɔ̃) *f*, obsession. **obstacle** (opstakl) *m*, obstacle. *faire ~ à*, to stand in the way of.

obstétrical, e (opstetrikal) *a*, obstetric(al). **obstétrique** (trik) *f*, obstetrics, midwifery.

obstination (opstinasjɔ̃) *f*, obstinacy, stubbornness, wilfulness; doggedness. **obstiné†, e** (ne) *a*, obstinate, etc. s'**obstiner** (ne) *v.pr*, to persist.

obstruction (opstryksjɔ̃) *f*, obstruction; stoppage; filibuster. **obstruer** (strye) *v.t*, to obstruct; block.

obtempérer à (optãpere), to obey, comply with.

obtenir (optəniːr) *v.t.ir*, to obtain, secure, get. *j'ai obtenu de*

. . ., I induced . . .; I managed to . . .

obturateur (optyratœːr) *m*, obturator, plug; shutter (*Phot.*). **obturer** (re) *v.t*, to stop [up].

obtus, e (opty, yːz) *a*, obtuse.

obus (obyːs) *m*, shell. ~ *à balles*, shrapnel. **obusier** (byzje) *m*, howitzer.

obvier à (obvje), to obviate, prevent.

ocarina (okarina) *m*, ocarina.

occasion (okazjɔ̃) *f*, opportunity; opening; occasion; bargain. *d'~*, second-hand, used; occasional (*occupation*). **occasionnel, le** (onɛl) *a*, causative; occasional (*Philos.*). **occasionnellement** (lmã) *ad*, occasionally, now & then. **occasionner** (ne) *v.t*, to occasion.

occident (oksidã) *m*, west. **occidental, e** (tal) *a*, west[ern].

occiput (oksipyt) *m*, occiput.

occire (oksiːr) *v.t*, to slay.

occulte (okylt) *a*, occult, hidden.

occupant (okypã) *m*, occupant (*law*). **occupation** (pasjɔ̃) *f*, occupation; pursuit. **occupé, e** (pe) *p.a*, busy. **occuper** (pe) *v.t*, to occupy; hold. s'~, to occupy (*or* busy) oneself, be engaged; be interested in (*with* de).

occurrence (okyrãːs) *f*, occurrence; emergency; juncture.

océan (oseã) *m*, ocean, sea. *l'~ Atlantique, Pacifique, Indien*, the Atlantic, Pacific, Indian, O. *l'~ Glacial arctique, antarctique*, the Arctic, Antarctic, O. **l'Océanie** (ani) *f*, Oceania.

ocre (okr) *f*, ocher.

octave (oktaːv) *f*, octave. **octavon, ne** (tavɔ̃, ɔn) *n*, octaroon. **octobre** (tobr) *m*, October. **octogénaire** (ʒenɛːr) *a. & n*, octogenarian. **octogone** (gɔn) *a*, octagonal. ¶ *m*, octagon.

octroi (oktrwa) *m*, octroi (*duty on goods entering town*). **octroyer** (trwaje) *v.t*, to grant.

oculaire (okylɛːr) *a*, ocular, eye (*att.*). *témoin* ~, eyewitness. [verre] ~, *m*, eyepiece, ocular. **oculiste** (list) *m*, oculist. *médecin* ~, eye doctor.

ode (od) *f*, ode.

odeur (odœɪr) *f*, odor, smell, scent.

odieux, euse† (ɔdjø, ø:z) *a*, odious, hateful, heinous, outrageous; obnoxious; invidious. ¶ *m*, odium.

odorant, e (ɔdɔrã, ã:t) & **odoriférant, e** (riferã, ã:t) *a*, fragrant, [sweet-]scented, odoriferous. **odorat** (ra) *m*, [sense of] smell.

odyssée (ɔdise) *f*, Odyssey (*fig.*).

oé (oe) *i*, wo!, whoa!

œil (œ:j) *m*, eye; look; loop; hole; face (*Typ.*); luster; gloss. ~-*de-bœuf*, bull's eye (*window*). ~-*de-chat*, cat's-eye (*jewel*). ~-*de-perdrix*, soft corn (*foot*). *à l'*~, free of charge. *se rincer l'*~, to watch a sexy show. *coup d'*~, a glance. *faire de l'*~, to ogle. **œillade** (œjad) *f*, glance (*loving*); ogle. **œillère** (jeːr) *f*, blinker; eye bath. [*dent*] ~, eyetooth. **œillet** (jɛ) *m*, eyelet; e. hole; pink (*Bot.*); [*des fleuristes*], carnation. ~ *de poète*, sweet-william. **œilleton** (jtɔ̃) *m*, sucker, offset (*Hort.*).

œsophage (ezɔfaːʒ) *m*, oesophagus.

œstre (ɛstr) *m*, oestrum, oestrus, gad-fly.

œuf (œf) *m*, egg; (*pl, de poisson*) hard roe, spawn. ~ *à la coque*, soft-boiled egg. ~ *dur*, hardboiled e. ~ *brouillé*, scrambled e. ~ *sur le plat*, fried e. ~*s coque*, very fresh eggs. ~*s au jambon*, ham & eggs. *tondre un* ~, to be miserly. **œuvé, e** (ve) *a*, hardroed.

œuvre (œːvr) *f*, work; setting (*jewel*); (*pl.*) charity; (*pl.*) work (*social*). ¶ *m*, carcass, carcase (*of a building*); works (*of an artist*).

offensant, e (ɔfãsã, ã:t) *a*, offensive, obnoxious, objectionable, insulting. **offense** (fãːs) *f*, offense; trespass (*Theol.*). ~ *à la cour*, contempt of court. **offensé, e** (fãse) *n*, aggrieved party. **offenser** (se) *v.t*, to offend; trespass against; injure. *s'*~, to take offense. **offenseur** (sœːr) *m*, offender. **offensif, ive†** (sif, iːv) *a. & f*, offensive (*attacking*).

offertoire (ɔfɛrtwaːr) *m*, offertory (*Lit.*); voluntary (*organ, between credo & sanctus*).

office (ɔfis) *m*, office; service; worship; department (*government*). ~ *des morts*, burial service. *d'*~, official[ly]; arbitrary (*assessment*); as a matter of course. ¶ *f*, pantry, servants' hall. **officiel, le†** (sjel) *a*, official. ¶ *m*, official (*sport, etc.*). **officier** (sje) *v.i*, to officiate (*Eccl.*). ¶ *m*, officer. ~ *à la suite*, supernumerary o. ~ *d'ordonnance*, orderly o. ~ *de l'état civil*, registrar (*births, etc.*). ~ *de marine*, naval officer. ~ *du génie*, engineer (*Mil.*). **officieux, euse†** (sjø, ø:z) *a*, officious (*diplomacy*), informal, semiofficial, unofficial; white (*lie*). **officine** (sin) *f*, dispensary; hotbed (*fig.*); shady office, thieves' kitchen.

offrande (ɔfrãːd) *f*, offering. **le plus offrant [& dernier enchérisseur]** (frã), the highest bidder. **offre** (fr) *f*, offer; tender. ~ *d'emploi*, help wanted. *l'*~ & *la demande*, supply & demand. **offrir** (friːr) *v.t.ir*, to offer, proffer, tender; bid; present; offer up. ~ *sa main*, to propose (*marriage to a man*). ~ *son nom*, to propose (*to a woman*).

offusquer (ɔfyske) *v.t*, to obfuscate, obscure; dazzle; offend.

ogive (ɔʒiːv) *f*, ogive, pointed arch.

ognon (ɔɲɔ̃) *m*, bulb (*Bot.*).

ogre, ogresse (ɔgr, grɛs) *n*, ogre, ogress.

oh (o) *i*, oh! O!

ohé (o[h]e) *i*, hi! hullo[a]!; ahoy!; wo! whoa!

oie (wa) *f*, goose.

oignon (ɔɲɔ̃) *m*, onion; bulb (*Bot.*); bunion. *personne qui se mêle des* ~*s des autres*, meddlesome person, meddler, officious person. **oignonière** (ɔɲɛːr) *f*, onion bed.

oindre (wẽːdr) *v.t.ir*, to anoint.

oiseau (wazo) *m*, bird, fowl; guy. ~ *de mauvais augure*, bird of ill omen. ~-*mouche, m*, humming bird. ~ *rare*, rare bird, rara avis. *à vol d'*~, as the crow flies. *vue à vol d'*~, bird's-eye

view. **oiselet** (zlɛ) *m*, small bird.
oiseleur (zlœːr) *m*, bird catcher,
fowler. **oiselier** (zəlje) *m*, bird
fancier. **oisellerie** (zɛlri) *f*, bird
fancying; aviary.
oiseux₂ euse (wazø. øːz) *a*, idle
(*words, etc.*). **oisif, ive**† (zif,
iːv) *a*, idle (*pers., money*).
oisillon (wazijɔ̃) *m*, fledgling.
oisiveté (wazivte) *f*, idleness.
oison (wazɔ̃) *m*, gosling. ~ *bridé*
(*fig.*), simpleton.
oléagineux, euse (ɔleaʒinø, øːz)
a, oleaginous, oily; oil (*seed*).
oléandre (ɔleɑ̃ːdr) *m*, oleander.
oléoduc (ɔleɔdyk) *m*, pipeline.
olfactif, ive (ɔlfaktif, iːv) *a*, olfactory.
olibrius (ɔlibriyːs) *m*, conceited
fool.
oligarchie (ɔligarʃi) *f*, oligarchy.
olivade (ɔlivad) *f*, olive harvest.
olivaie (vɛ) *f*, o. grove. **olivaison**
(vɛzɔ̃) *f*, o. season; o. harvest.
olivâtre (vaːtr) *a*, olive (*complexion*). **olive** (liːv) *f*, olive.
couleur [*d'*]~, olive[-green]. **olivier** (livje) *m*, o. [tree]; o. [wood].
olympe (ɔlɛ̃ːp) *m*, Olympus
(*fig.*). **olympique** (lɛ̃pik) *a*,
Olympic.
ombilic (ɔ̃bilik) *m*, umbilicus;
navel.
omble[-chevalier] (ɔ̃ːbl) *m*,
char (*fish*).
ombrage (ɔ̃braːʒ) *m*, [spread of]
foliage; shade; umbrage. **ombragé, e** (braʒe) *p.a*, shady. **ombrager** (ʒe) *v.t*, to shade, overshadow. **ombrageux, euse** (ʒø,
øːz) *a*, shy, skittish (*beast*);
touchy. **ombre** (ɔ̃ːbr) *f*, shade;
shadow; ghost. ~*s chinoises*,
shadow play. ~ *portée*, cast
shadow. ¶ *m*, grayling, umber
(*fish*). ~*-chevalier*, char (*fish*).
ombrelle (ɔ̃brɛl) *f*, sunshade,
parasol. **ombrer** (bre) *v.t*, to
shade (*art*). **ombreux, euse**
(brø, øːz) *a*, shady (*Poet.*).
oméga (ɔmega) *m*, omega.
omelette (ɔmlɛt) *f*, omelet[te].
~ *aux confitures*, jelly o. ~ *aux
fines herbes*, savory o.
omettre (ɔmɛtr) *v.t.ir*, to omit,
leave out. **omission** (misjɔ̃) *f*,
omission.
omnibus (ɔmnibyːs) *m*, [omni]-

bus; (*att.*) slow (*train, boat*).
omnipotence (ɔmnipotɑ̃ːs) *f*,
omnipotence. **omnipotent, e** (tɑ̃,
ɑ̃ːt) *a*, omnipotent.
omniscience (ɔmnisjɑ̃ːs) *f*, omniscience. **omniscient, e** (jɑ̃, ɑ̃ːt)
a, omniscient.
omnivore (ɔmnivɔːr) *a*, omnivorous.
omoplate (ɔmɔplat) *f*, shoulder
blade.
on (ɔ̃), *oft*. **l'on**, *pn*, one; a man,
woman, etc; we; you; they; peo-
ple; somebody; anybody. ~ *demande . . .*, wanted . . . (*advertisement*). ~ *dit*, it is said, they
say. ~**-dit** (ɔ̃di) *m*, hearsay, rumor. *on n'embauche pas*, no
help wanted. *on ne passe pas*,
no thoroughfare.
once (ɔ̃ːs) *f*, ounce (*Zool.*), snow
leopard; grain, particle (*fig.*).
oncle (ɔ̃ːkl) *m*, uncle.
onction (ɔ̃ksjɔ̃) *f*, unction; rubbing [with oil]. **onctueux, euse**†
(tɥø, øːz) *a*, unctuous; oily;
greasy.
onde (ɔ̃ːd) *f*, wave, billow; (*Poet.*)
sea, main; water; stream. *en* ~*s*,
wavy (*hair*). ~ *sonore*, sound
wave. **ondé, e** (ɔ̃de) *a*, waved,
wavy; grained (*wood*). **ondée**
(de) *f*, heavy shower. **ondoyer**
(dwaje) *v.i*, to undulate, wave;
billow; surge. **ondulation** (dy-
lasjɔ̃) *f*, undulation; wave. ~
permanente, permanent wave
(*hair*). **ondulé, e** (le) *a*, undulating, wavy; corrugated
(*iron*). **onduler** (le) *v.i*, to undulate; (*v.t.*) to wave (*hair*). *se
faire onduler* [*les cheveux*], to
have one's hair waved.
onéreux, euse (ɔnerø, øːz) *a*,
onerous, burdensome.
ongle (ɔ̃ːgl) *m*, nail; claw; hoof.
onglée (ɔ̃gle) *f*, numbness [of the
fingers]. **onglet** (gle) *m*, guard
(*Bookb.*); tab; miter (*Carp.*).
onglier (glie) *m*, manicure set.
~ [*en*] *écrin*, box m. s.
onguent (ɔ̃gɑ̃) *m*, ointment,
salve.
ongulé, e (ɔ̃gyle) *a*, hoofed.
onomatopée (ɔnɔmatɔpe) *f*, onomatopoeia.
onyx (ɔniks) *m*, onyx.

onze (ɔ̃z) *a. & m*, eleven; eleventh. **onzième†** (ɔ̃zjɛm) *a. & n*, eleventh. (*Note.—*Say le onze, le onzième, *not* l'onze, l'onzième.)

oolithe (ɔɔlit) *m*, oolite.

opacité (ɔpasite) *f*, opacity.

opale (ɔpal) *f*, opal. **opalin, e** (lɛ̃, in) *a*, opaline.

opaque (ɔpak) *a*, opaque.

opéra (ɔpera) *m*, opera; o. [house]. ~ *bouffe*, comic opera, musical comedy. ~*comique*, opera comique (*spoken dialogue*).

opérateur, trice (ɔperatœ:r, tris) *n*, operator; cameraman (*film*). **opération** (sjɔ̃) *f*, operation; stage; working; transaction, dealing. **opéré, e** (re) *n*, surgical case (*pers.*). **opérer** (re) *v.t. & abs*, to operate, work, effect; make; do; act; deal; operate on (*Surg.*).

opérette (ɔperɛt) *f*, operetta, light opera, musical play.

ophtalmie (ɔftalmi) *f*, ophthalmia. **ophtalmique** (mik) *a*, ophthalmic.

opiacé, e (ɔpjase) *a*, opiated.

opinant (ɔpinɑ̃) *m*, speaker (*in debate*). **opiner** (ne) *v.i*, to opine; vote. ~ *du bonnet*, to say nothing but ditto to everything. **opiniâtre†** (njɑ:tr) *a. & n*, [self-]opinionated; self-willed; obstinate, pertinacious, stubborn (person). **s'opiniâtrer** (ɑtre) *v.pr*, to persist. **opiniâtreté** (trəte) *f*, obstinacy, etc. **opinion** (njɔ̃) *f*, opinion; view; mind; vote.

opiomane (ɔpjɔman) *n*, opium addict. **opium** (jɔm) *m*, opium.

opossum (ɔpɔsɔm) *m*, opossum.

opportun, e (ɔpɔrtœ̃, yn) *a*, opportune, seasonable, timely, well-timed. **opportunément** (tynemɑ̃) *ad*, opportunely, etc. **opportunisme** (nism) *m*, opportunism. **opportuniste** (nist) *n*, opportunist, timeserver. **opportunité** (te) *f*, opportuneness; opportunity.

opposant, e (ɔpozɑ̃, ɑ̃:t) *n*, opponent; (*att.*) opposing; opponent. **opposé, e** (ze) *a*, opposed; opposite. ¶ *m*, opposite, reverse, contrary. **opposer** (ze) *v.t. &*

s'~ à, to oppose. ~ *une exception*, to demur (*law*). **à l'opposite** (pozit) *ad*, opposite, facing. **opposition** (sjɔ̃) *f*, opposition; contrast; contradistinction; stop; objection.

oppresser (ɔprese) *v.t*, to oppress (*Med. & fig.*). **oppresseur** (sœ:r) *m*, oppressor. **oppressif, ive** (sif, i:v) *a*, oppressive. **oppression** (sjɔ̃) *f*, oppression. **opprimer** (prime) *v.t*, to oppress.

opprobre (ɔprɔbr) *m*, disgrace, opprobrium.

opter (ɔpte) *v.i*, to choose.

opticien (ɔptisjɛ̃) *m*, optician.

optime (ɔptime) (*Latin word*), very well, all right. **optimisme** (mism) *m*, optimism. **optimiste** (mist) *a*, optimistic, hopeful, sanguine. ¶ *n*, optimist.

option (ɔpsjɔ̃) *f*, option.

optique (ɔptik) *a*, optic; optical. ¶ *f*, optics; perspective (*Theat.*).

opulence (ɔpylɑ̃:s) *f*, opulence, affluence, wealth; buxomness. **opulent, e** (lɑ̃, ɑ̃:t) *a*, opulent, etc.

opuscule (ɔpyskyl) *m*, short treatise, tract.

or (ɔ:r) *c*, now. ~ *çà*, now then.

or (ɔ:r) *m*, gold. ~ *laminé*, rolled g. ~ *moulu*, ormolu. *ni pour* ~ *ni pour argent*, for love or money. *d'~*, gold; golden.

oracle (ɔra:kl) *m*, oracle.

orage (ɔra:ʒ) *m*, thunderstorm; storm. **orageux, euse†** (raʒø, ø:z) *a*, stormy; thundery.

oraison (ɔrezɔ̃) *f*, prayer. ~ *dominicale*, Lord's prayer. ~ *funèbre*, funeral oration.

oral, e† (ɔral) *a*, oral, viva voce.

orange (ɔrɑ̃:ʒ) *f*, orange. ~ *amère*, Seville o. ~ *sanguine*, blood o. **orange**, *m. & a. &* **orangé, e** (rɑ̃ʒe) *a. & m*, orange (*color*). **orangeade** (ʒad) *f*, orangeade. **oranger** (ʒe) *m*, orange [tree]. **orangerie** (ʒri) *f*, orangery.

orang-outang (ɔrɑ̃utɑ̃) *m*, orangutan.

orateur (ɔratœ:r) *m*, orator, speaker. **oratoire** (twa:r) *a*, oratorical; rhetorical, declamatory. *l'art* ~, oratory. ¶ *m*, oratory (*chapel*). **oratorio** (tɔrjo) *m*, oratorio.

orbe (ɔrb) *m*, orb (*heavenly body*). **orbite** (bit) *f*, orbit; socket (*eye*).

Orcades (les) (ɔrkad) *f.pl*, the Orkneys.

orchestral, e (ɔrkɛstral) *a*, orchestral. **orchestre** (tr) *m*, orchestra, band; orchestra seats (*Theat.*). **orchestrer** (tre) *v.t*, to orchestrate, score.

orchidée (ɔrkide) *f*, orchid. **orchis** (kis) *m*, orchis.

ordalie (ɔrdali) *f*, ordeal (*Hist.*).

ordinaire† (ɔrdinɛːr) *a*, ordinary; common; customary; usual, everyday. ¶ *m*, wont; ordinary; [company] mess (*Mil.*).

ordinal (ɔrdinal) *a.m*, ordinal.

ordinateur (ɔrdinatœːr) *m*, computer, data processer. *~ domestique*, home computer. **ordinogramme** (ɔgram) *m*, process chart (*computers*).

ordination (ɔrdinasjɔ̃) *f*, ordination (*Eccl.*); data processing, computing.

ordonnance (ɔrdɔnɑ̃ːs) *f*, ordering (*arrangement*); organization; regulation (*police*); [treasury] warrant; prescription (*Med.*). ¶ *f. or m*, orderly. **ordonnancer** (nɑ̃se) *v.t*, to pass for payment; schedule (*computers*). **ordonnateur, trice** (natœːr, tris) *n*, director; master of ceremonies. **ordonné, e** (ne) *p.a*, tidy, orderly (*pers.*). **ordonner** (ne) *v.t. & abs*, to order; organize; prescribe; ordain. **ordre** (dr) *m*, order; rate. *~ d'exécution*, death warrant. *~ du jour*, agenda, business [before the meeting]; order of the day. *numéro d'~*, serial number. *~ public*, law & order, peace; public policy. *à l'~!* order!; chair!

ordure (ɔrdyːr) *f*, filth, dirt, muck; refuse, dust; ordure; smut. **ordurier, ère** (dyrje, ɛːr) *a*, filthy; scurrilous; smutty.

orée (ɔre) *f*, verge, skirt (*of a wood*).

oreille (ɔrɛːj) *f*, ear; lug; wing (*nut*). *avoir l'~ dure*, to be hard of hearing. *avoir l'~ juste*, to have a good ear (*for music*). *~-d'ours*, bear's-ear, auricula. *~-*

de-souris, forget-me-not. **oreiller** (rɛje) *m*, pillow. **oreillette** (jɛt) *f*, auricle (*heart*); ear (*Bot.*). **oreillon** (jɔ̃) *m*, ear flap; ear (*Bot.*); (*pl.*) mumps.

orémus (ɔremyːs) *m*, prayer.

Orénoque (l') (ɔrenɔk) *m*, the Orinoco.

ores (ɔːr) *ad*: *d'~ & déjà*, now & henceforth.

orfèvre (ɔrfɛːvr) *m*, goldsmith &/or silversmith. **orfèvrerie** (fɛvrəri) *f*, gold[smith's] &/or silver[smith's] work.

orfraie (ɔrfrɛ) *f*, osprey.

organdi (ɔrgɑ̃di) *m*, organdy; book muslin.

organe (ɔrgan) *m*, organ; spokesman; (*pl, Mach.*) parts, gear. **organique** (nik) *a*, organic. **organisateur, trice** (zatœːr, tris) *n*, organizer. **organisation** (zasjɔ̃) *f*, organization. **organiser** (ze) *v.t*, to organize. *une tête bien organisée, un cerveau organisé*, a level-headed person. **organisme** (nism) *m*, organism. **organiste** (nist) *n*, organist (*Mus.*).

orge (ɔrʒ) *f*, barley. *~ perlé*, *m*, pearl b. **orgeat** (ʒa) *m*, orgeat. **orgelet** (ʒəlɛ) *m*, stye (*eye*).

orgie (ɔrʒi) *f*, orgy; riot (*fig.*).

orgue (ɔrg) *m, the pl. is f*, organ; o. loft. *~ de Barbarie*, barrel organ.

orgueil (ɔrgœːj) *m*, pride. **orgueilleux, euse†** (gœjø, øːz) *a. & n*, proud (*person*).

orient (ɔrjɑ̃) *m*, orient, east. *l'O~* (*Geog.*), the Orient, the East. *~ moyen*, the Middle East. **orientable** (tabl) *a*, adjustable; revolving, swiveling. **oriental, e** (tal) *a*, oriental, eastern. O~, *n*, Oriental, Eastern. **orientation** (tasjɔ̃) *f*, orientation; bearings; direction; aspect; trend; trimming (*sails, yards*). **orienter** (te) *v.t*, to orient[ate]; direct; point; trim (*sails, yards*). *s'~*, to get one's bearings.

orifice (ɔrifis) *m*, mouth, aperture, port, orifice.

oriflamme (ɔriflaːm) *f*, oriflamme; banner.

originaire† (ɔriʒinɛːr) *a*, original. *être ~ de*, to come from, be a native of. **original, e†** (nal) *a,* original; first (*edition*); inventive; odd, queer. ¶ *m,* original; oddity. **originalité** (lite) *f,* originality. **origine** (ʒin) *f,* origin; beginning, outset. **originel, le†** (nɛl) *a,* original.

oripeaux (ɔripo) *m.pl,* tinsel; tawdry finery; rags.

Orléans (ɔrleɑ̃) *m. or f,* Orleans.

ormaie (ɔrmɛ) *ou* **ormoie** (mwa) *f,* elm grove. **orme** (ɔrm) & **ormeau** (mo) *m,* elm [tree]. *orme de montagne,* wych-elm. **ormille** (miːj) *f,* elm row.

orné, e (ɔrne) *p.a,* ornate. **ornemaniste** (nəmanist) *n,* ornamentalist. **ornement** (mɑ̃) *m,* ornament. *sans ~s,* unadorned. **ornemental, e** (tal) *a,* ornamental. **ornementation** (tasjɔ̃) *f,* ornamentation. **orner** (ne) *v.t,* to ornament, adorn; grace.

ornière (ɔrnjɛːr) *f,* rut; groove.

ornithogale (ɔrnitɔgal) *m,* star of Bethlehem. **ornithologie** (lɔʒi) *f,* ornithology. **ornithologiste** (ʒist) *ou* **ornithologue** (lɔg) *n,* ornithologist.

orpailleur (ɔrpɑjœːr) *m,* gold washer (*pers.*).

orphelin (ɔrfəlɛ̃, in) *n. & att,* orphan. *~ de père,* fatherless. **orphelinat** (lina) *m,* orphanage.

orphéon (ɔrfeɔ̃) *m,* choral society.

orphie (ɔrfi) *f,* garfish.

orpin (ɔrpɛ̃) *m,* stonecrop.

orque (ɔrk) *f,* orc, grampus.

orteil (ɔrtɛːj) *m,* toe. *gros ~,* big toe.

orthodoxe (ɔrtɔdɔks) *a,* orthodox. **orthodoxie** (ksi) *f,* orthodoxy. **orthographe** (graf) *f,* orthography, spelling. **orthographie** (fi) *f,* orthography (*Arch.*). **orthographier** (fje) *v.t. & abs,* to spell. *mal ~,* to misspell. **orthographique** (fik) *a,* orthographic; spelling (*att.*). **orthopédie** (pedi) *f,* orthopedics. **orthopédique** (dik) *a,* orthopedic.

ortie (ɔrti) *f,* nettle. *~ brûlante, ~ grièche* (griɛʃ), stinging nettle.

ortolan (ɔrtɔlɑ̃) *m,* ortolan.

orvet (ɔrvɛ) *m,* slowworm, blindworm.

orviétan (ɔrvjetɑ̃) *m: marchand d'~s,* quack.

os (ɔs, *pl.* o) *m,* bone. *~ à moelle,* marrow b. *tomber sur un ~,* to run into a problem.

osciller (ɔsile) *v.i,* to oscillate, swing, sway about; fluctuate; waver. **oscillation** (lasjɔ̃) *f,* oscillation, etc.

osé, e (oze) *p.a,* daring, bold.

oseille (ozɛːj) *f,* sorrel; money (*slang*). *la faire à l'~,* to pull a fast one.

oser (oze) *v.t,* to dare, d. to, venture, v. to.

oseraie (ozrɛ) *f,* osier bed.

oseur, euse (ozœːr, øːz) *n,* bold man, woman.

osier (ozje) *m,* osier, wicker.

osmium (ɔsmjɔm) *m,* osmium.

ossature (ɔsatyːr) *f,* frame[work]. **osselet** (slɛ) *m,* ossicle; (*pl.*) knuckle bones, dibs. **ossements** (smɑ̃) *m.pl,* bones (*dead*). **osseux, euse** (sø, øːz) *a,* bony, osseous. **ossifier** (sifje) *v.t,* to ossify. **ossu, e** (sy) *a,* big-boned, bony. **ossuaire** (sɥɛːr) *m,* ossuary.

Ostende (ɔstɑ̃ːd) *m,* Ostend.

ostensible† (ɔstɑ̃sibl) *a,* fit (*or* intended) to be shown; open. **ostensoir** (swaːr) *m,* ostensory, monstrance. **ostentateur, trice** (tatœːr, tris) & **ostentatoire** (twaːr) *a,* ostentatious, showy. **ostentation** (sjɔ̃) *f,* ostentation, show.

ostracisme (ɔstrasism) *m,* ostracism.

ostréiculture (ɔstreikyltyːr) *f,* oyster culture.

ostrogot[h], e (ɔstrɔgo, ɔt) (*fig.*) *n,* goth, barbarian.

otage (ɔtaːʒ) *m,* hostage.

otalgie (ɔtalʒi) *f,* earache.

otarie (ɔtari) *f,* otary, sea lion.

ôté (ote) *pr,* barring, except. **ôter** (te) *v.t,* to remove, take away; t. out; t. off, pull off; doff. *s'~,* to get out (*of way, etc.*).

ottoman, e (ɔtɔmɑ̃, an) *a. &* **O~,** *n,* Ottoman. **ottomane,** *f,* ottoman.

ou (u) *c,* or; either. *~ bien,* or [else].

où (u) *ad*, where, whither; whence; how far; which; what; when; in. *d'~*, whence, where from. *par ~*, [by] which way, through which.

ouailles (wɑːj) *f.pl*, flock (*Christians*).

ouate (wat) *f*, wadding, cotton wool. **ouater** (te) *v.t*, to wad, pad; quilt.

oubli (ubli) *m*, forgetfulness; oblivion; neglect; oversight, lapse. **oublie** (bli) *f*, cone, cornet, wafer (*ice cream*). **oublier** (blie) *v.t. & abs*, to forget; neglect; overlook. **oubliettes** (ɛt) *f.pl*, oubliette. **oublieux, euse** (ø, øːz) *a*, forgetful, oblivious.

Ouessant (wɛsɑ̃) *m*, Ushant.

ouest (wɛst) *m*, west; (*att.*) west, western.

ouf (uf) *i*, oh!, what a relief!

oui (wi) (*particle*), yes; ay; so. ¶ *m*, (*le ~, un ~*), yes; ay. *~-da, i*, [yes] indeed!

oui-dire (widiːr) *m*, hearsay. **ouïe** (wi) *f*, hearing; (*pl.*) sound holes (*Mus.*); (*pl.*) gills (*fish*).

ouiller (uje) *v.t*, to fill up (*ullaged cask*).

ouïr (wiːr) *v.t.ir*, to hear (*witness—law*).

ouragan (uragɑ̃) *m*, hurricane.

Oural (l') (ural) *m*, the Ural. *les monts Ourals*, the Ural Mountains.

ourdir (urdiːr) *v.t*, to warp (*yarn*); hatch (*fig.*); weave (*fig.*).

ourler (urle) *v.t*, to hem. *~ à jour*, to hemstitch. **ourlet** (lɛ) *m*, hem; rim. *~ à jour*, hemstitch. *~ piqué*, stitched hem.

ours (urs) *m*, bear. *~ blanc*, polar b. *~ grizzlé* (grizle), grizzly b. *~ [Martin]*, *~ de peluche*, teddy b. **ourse** (urs) *f*, [she-]bear; Bear (*Astr.*). **oursin** (sɛ̃) *m*, sea urchin; bearskin (*cap*). **ourson** (sɔ̃) *m*, bear's cub; bearskin (*cap*).

oust (ust) *i*, beat it! scram!

outarde (utard) *f*, bustard.

outil (uti) *m*, tool. **outillage** (tijaːʒ) *m*, tools; plant, machinery; equipment, outfit. *~ national*, national capital (*eco-*

nomics). **outiller** (je) *v.t*, to equip, fit out.

outrage (utraːʒ) *m*, outrage; insult; offense; ravages (*time*). **outrageant, e** (traʒɑ̃, ɑ̃ːt) *a*, insulting, scurrilous. **outrager** (ʒe) *v.t*, to insult; outrage. **outrageux, euse†** (ʒø, øːz) *a*, insulting, scurrilous.

outrance (utrɑ̃ːs) *f*, excess. *à ~*, to the death; mortal; internecine; desperately, to the bitter end; out & out. **outrancier, ère** (trɑ̃sje, ɛːr) *a*, extremist (*att.*), out & out.

outre (utr) *f*, leather bottle. **outre** (utr) *pr. & ad*, beyond; further. *d'~ en ~*, through [& through]. *nos voisins d'~-Manche*, our neighbors across the Channel. *en ~*, moreover, besides, further[more]. *passer ~*, to go on; ignore. *~-mer, ad. & d'~-mer, a*, oversea[s]. **outré, e** (utre) *a*, excessive, farfetched, overdone, fulsome, outré; carried away; disgusted.

outrecuidance (utrəkɥidɑ̃ːs) *f*, presumptuousness. **outrecuidant, e** (dɑ̃, ɑ̃ːt) *a*, overweening.

outremer (utrəmeːr) *m*, ultramarine (*pigment*).

outrepasser (utrəpase) *v.t*, to go beyond, overstep.

outrer (utre) *v.t*, to overdo; overstrain; provoke.

ouvert, e† (uvɛːr, ɛrt) *p.a*, open; free; frank. **ouverture** (vɛrtyːr) *f*, opening; aperture; orifice; hole; port; gap; spread; overture; openness.

ouvrable (uvrabl) *a*, workable; business (*day*). **ouvrage** (vraːʒ) *m*, work; doing (*fig.*). *~s d'agrément*, fancy work. *~s d'art*, permanent works, [p.] structures. *~s de dames*, fancy needlework, art n. *~s de ville*, job work (*Typ.*). **ouvragé, e** (vraʒe) *a*, [highly] worked, elaborated.

ouvre-boîte (uvrə) *m*, can opener. **ouvre-gants**, *m*, glove stretcher.

ouvrer (uvre) *v.t*, to work; (*v.t.*) to work; diaper.

ouvreur, euse (uvrœːr, øːz) *n*, opener; (*f.*) box attendant (*Theat.*).

ouvrier, ère (uvrie, ɛːr) *n*, workman; workwoman; worker; operative; factory hand; journeyman; laborer (*farm*). ~ *d'art*, handicraftsman. ¶ *a*, working, laboring (*class*); workmen's; labor (*troubles, etc.*).

ouvrir (uvriːr) *v.t. & abs. ir*, to open; unlock; disburden; open up; cut; propose; head (*as a list*); turn on, switch on; draw back (*curtains*); sharpen (*appetite*); (*v.i.ir.*) to open. *la maison reste ouverte pendant les travaux*, business as usual during alterations. *s'~*, to open; unburden oneself.

ouvroir (uvrwaːr) *m*, workroom (*convent*).

ovaire (ɔvɛːr) *m*, ovary.

ovale (ɔval) *a. & m*, oval. ~ [*de table*], doily.

ovation (ɔvasjɔ̃) *f*, ovation. **ovationner** (ne) *v.t*, to acclaim.

ovine (ɔvin) *a.f*, ovine.

ovipare (ɔvipaːr) *a*, oviparous.

oxhydrique (ɔksidrik) *a*, oxyhydrogen (*blowpipe, etc.*); lime (*light*).

oxyde (ɔksid) *m*, oxide. ~ *de carbone*, carbon monoxide. **oxyder** (de) *v.t*, to oxidize. **oxygène** (ʒɛn) *m*, oxygen.

ozone (ozɔn) *m*, ozone.

P

pacage (pakaːʒ) *m*, grazing; pasturage. **pacager** (kaʒe) *v.t*, to pasture, graze.

pachyderme (paʃidɛrm) *m*, pachyderm.

pacificateur, trice (pasifikatœːr, tris) *n*, peacemaker. ¶ *a*, pacifying. **pacifier** (fje) *v.t*, to pacify; appease. **pacifique†** (fik) *a*, pacific, peaceable; peaceful. **le P~**, the Pacific. **pacifiste** (fist) *n. & a*, pacificist, pacifist.

package (pakaʒ) *m*, software package.

pacotille (pakɔtiːj) *f*, barter goods; trash.

pacte (pakt) *m*, [com]pact, covenant. **pactiser avec** (tize), to compound with (*condone*); compound (*felony*).

Pactole (le) (paktɔl) (*fig.*), a gold mine.

Padoue (padu) *f*, Padua.

pæan (peã) *m*, paean.

paf (paf) *m*, penis (*obscene*). *beau comme un ~*, elegant (*ironic*). *tomber sur un ~*, to fail, suffer defeat.

pagaie (pagɛ) *f*, paddle (*canoe*).

pagaie, pagaille (pagaːj) *f*, clutter, mess, disorder, etc.

paganisme (paganism) *m*, paganism, heathenism.

pagayer (pagɛje) *v.t*, to paddle (*canoe*). **pagayeur, euse** (jœːr, øːz) *n*, paddler.

page (paːʒ) *f*, page (*book*); chapter (*of one's life*). *à la ~*, up to date. ¶ *m*, page (*noble youth*); bellhop.

pagel (paʒɛl) *m*, [sea] bream.

paginer (paʒine) *v.t*, to page, paginate.

pagode (pagɔd) *f*, pagoda; mandarin (*toy*).

paie (pɛ) *f*, pay, wages; (*good, bad*) payer. **paiement** (mɑ̃) *m*, payment.

païen, ne (pajɛ̃, ɛn) *a. & n*, pagan, heathen.

paillard, e (pajaːr, ard) *a. & n*, lewd (*person*). **paillasse** (jas) *f*, straw mattress; drainboard; whore (*slang*). ¶ *m*, clown (*pagliaccio*). **paillasson** (sɔ̃) *m*, doormat; matting (*Hort.*); servile person; slut, easy lay (*slang*). **paille** (paːj) *f*, straw; flaw; (*fig.*) mote (*in eye*). ~ *de bois*, wood shaving. ~ *de fer*, steel wool. *une ~!*, a trifle! (*ironic*). [*couleur*] ~, straw-color[ed]. **pailler** (paje) (*fig.*) *m*, dunghill. ¶ *v.t*, to mulch; rush (*chair*). **paillet** (jɛ) *a.m*, pale (*red wine*). **paillet d'abordage**, *m*, collision mat. **pailleté, e** (jte) *a*, spangled. **paillette** (jɛt) *f*, spangle; flake, scale; chaff, window (*radar*). **pailleux** (jø) *a.m*, strawy; flawy. **paillis** (ji) *m*, mulch. **paillon** (jɔ̃) *m*, straw casing (*bottle*); spangle; foil; grain (*solder*). **paillote** (pajɔt) *f*, straw hut (*native*).

pain (pɛ̃) *m*, bread; loaf (*bread, sugar*); biscuit (*dog*); cake (*soap, fish, etc.*); tablet; pat (*butter*).

à cacheter, signet wafer. ~ *à chanter*, wafer (*Eccl.*). ~ *d'épice*, gingerbread. ~ *de bougie*, taper (*coiled*). ~ *de munition*, ration bread. ~ *de régime*, diet b. ~ *grillé*, ~ *rôti, toast*. ~ *complet*, whole wheat bread. ~ *de mie*, sandwich b.

pair (pɛːr) *a.m*; **paire**, *Arith. only, a.f*, equal, like; even (*number*). ¶ *m*, peer; equal; par, equality; mate (*bird*). *au ~*, (*engagement*) on mutual terms; room and board (*no salary*). *marcher de ~ avec*, to keep pace with; rank with.

paire (pɛːr) *f*, pair; brace; yoke (*oxen, etc.*).

pairesse (pɛrɛs) (*Eng.*) *f*, peeress. **pairie** (ri) (*Fr. Hist. & Eng.*) *f*, peerage.

paisible† (pɛzibl) *a*, peaceable, peaceful.

paître (pɛːtr) *v.t. & i. ir*, to graze, pasture, browse; feed; tend.

paix (pɛ) *f*, peace; pax (*Eccl.*). ¶ *i*, hush! be quiet!

pal (pal) *m*, pale, stake.

palabre (palaːbr) *f. or m*, palaver. **palabrer** (labre) *v.i*, to palaver.

paladin (paladɛ̃) *m*, paladin; knight errant (*fig.*).

palais (palɛ) *m*, palace; [law] courts; court; law; palate; roof of the mouth. ~ *dur*, hard palate, bony p. ~ *mou*, soft p.

palan (palɑ̃) *m*, pulley block; tackle, purchase. **palanche** (lɑ̃ːʃ) *f*, yoke (*for pails*).

palanque (palɑ̃ːk) *f*, stockade.

palatal, e (palatal) *a*, palatal.

palatine (palatin) *f*, fur cape, tippet.

pale (pal) *f*, shut-off; sluice gate; blade (*oar, air propeller*).

pâle (pɑːl) *a*, pale, pallid, wan; (*fig.*) colorless.

palée (pale) *f*, sheet piling.

palefrenier (palfrənje) *m*, groom, [h]ostler. **palefroi** (frwa) (*Poet.*) *m*, palfrey.

palémon (palemɔ̃) *m*, prawn.

paléographie (paleɔgrafi) *f*, paleography. **paléontologie** (3tɔlɔʒi) *f*, paleontology.

Palerme (palɛrm) *f*, Palermo.

paleron (palrɔ̃) *m*, shoulder blade (*horse, ox*).

palet (palɛ) *m*, quoit; quoits; puck (*ice hockey*).

paletot (palto) *m*, overcoat; greatcoat.

palette (palɛt) *f*, battledore; bat; palette; pallet; paddle.

palétuvier (paletyvje) *m*, mangrove.

pâleur (palœːr) *f*, pallor, paleness.

palier (palje) *m*, landing (*stairs*); floor; bearings, plummer block; level.

palimpseste (palɛ̃psɛst) *m. & a*, palimpsest.

palinodie (palinɔdi) *f*, recantation.

pâlir (paliːr) *v.i. & t*, to pale, blanch; wane; fade.

palis (pali) *m*, pale, paling. **palissade** (sad) *f*, palisade, fence; stockade; hoarding (*street*). **palissader** (de) *v.t*, to palisade, fence.

palissandre (palisɑ̃ːdr) *m*, rosewood.

palladium (paladjɔm) *m*, palladium; safeguard.

palliatif, ive (palljatif, iːv) *a. & m*, palliative. **pallier** (pallje) *v.t*, to palliate.

palmarès (palmarɛːs) *m*, prize list, honors l. ~ *de la chanson*, hit parade (*popular song*).

palme (palm) *f*, palm [branch], p. [tree]. **palmé, e** (me) *a*, palmate[d]; webbed.

palmer (palmɛːr) *m*, micrometer.

palmeraie (palmɛrɛ) *f*, palm grove. **palmier** (mje) *m*, palm [tree]. **palmipède** (mipɛd) *a*, webfooted. **palmiste** (mist) *m*, cabbage tree.

palombe (palɔ̃ːb) *f*, ring dove, wood pigeon.

pâlot, te (palo, ɔt) *a*, palish, wan.

palourde (palurd) *f*, clam (*Mol.*).

palpable (palpabl) *a*, palpable. **palpe** (palp) *f. or m*, palp[us], feeler. **palper** (pe) *v.t*, to feel, finger. **palpitation** (pitasjɔ̃) *f*, palpitation, throbbing, fluttering. **palpiter** (te) *v.i*, to palpitate, etc; go pit-[a-]pat; thrill.

paltoquet (paltɔkɛ) *m*, churl.

paludéen, ne (palydeɛ̃, ɛn) *a*, marshy; malarial. **paludisme** (dism) *m*, malaria.

pâmer (pame) *v.i.* & se ~, to swoon, faint; die (*of laughing*, *etc.*).

pampas (pɑ̃pɑs) *f.pl*, pampas.

pamphlet (pɑ̃flɛ) *m*, lampoon. **pamphlétaire** (fletɛːr) *m*, lampooner.

pamplemousse (pɑ̃pləmus) *f*, grapefruit.

pampre (pɑ̃ːpr) *m*, vine branch.

pan (pɑ̃) *m*, skirt, flap; tail (*coat*); face, side; pane, slab; frame. *à 6 ~s*, hexagonal. *à 8 ~s*, octagonal.

pan (pɑ̃) *onomatopoeia*, bang! ~*l* ~*l* rat-tat[-tat]!

panacée (panase) *f*, panacea, nostrum.

panache (panaʃ) *m*, plume, tuft; mettle, go, dash. *faire* ~, to have a spill, turn right over. **panacher** (ʃe) *v.t*, to plume, tuft; streak, variegate, mix. *la bière panaché*, shandy.

panais (panɛ) *m*, parsnip.

panama (panama) *m*, panama, Panama hat.

Paname (panam) *m*, Paris (*slang*).

panaris (panari) *m*, whitlow.

pancarte (pɑ̃kart) *f*, placard, bill, show card.

pancréas (pɑ̃kreɑs) *m*, pancreas.

pandémonium (pɑ̃demɔnjɔm) *m*, pandemonium.

pandit (pɑ̃di) *m*, pundit.

pandour (pɑ̃dur) *m*, pandor, brute (*pers.*).

panégyrique (paneʒirik) *m*, panegyric, encomium.

paner (pane) *v.t*, to crumb (*Cook.*).

panerée (panre) *f*, basketful.

panetière (pantjɛːr) *f*, sideboard.

pangermanisme (pɑ̃ʒɛrmanism) *m*, pan-Germanism.

panier (panje) *m*, basket, hamper; pannier; straw hive; lobster basket; basketful. ~ *à ouvrage*, work basket. ~ *[à papiers]*,

wastepaper b. ~ *à pêche*, creel. ~ *à provisions*, shopping basket; luncheon b. ~ *roulant*, go-cart. ~ *à salade*, prison van, Black Maria.

panique (panik) *a.* & *f*, panic, scare.

panne (pan) *f*, lard; plush; purlin; pane (*hammer*); breakdown, failure. *avoir une* ~ *d'essence* ou *une* ~ *sèche*, to run out of gas. *laisser en* ~, to leave in the lurch. *mettre en* ~, to heave to (*Naut.*). *en* ~, out of order.

panneau (pano) *m*, panel; snare. ~*-réclame*, *m*, billboard.

panneton (pantɔ̃) *m*, bit, web (*key*).

panonceau (panɔ̃so) *m*, medallion, tablet, sign.

panoplie (panɔpli) *f*, panoply; trophy (*wall*).

panorama (panɔrama) *m*, panorama. **panoramique** (mik) *m*, pan shot (*cinema*, *TV*). ~ *rapide*, *filé*, whip pan, swish p. **panoramiquer** (mike) *v.i*, to pan, tilt.

panse (pɑ̃ːs) *f*, belly, paunch.

pansement (pɑ̃smɑ̃) *m*, dressing (*wound*). **panser** (se) *v.t*, to dress; groom (*horse*).

pansu, e (pɑ̃sy) *a*, corpulent.

pantagruélique (pɑ̃tagryelik) *a*, sumptuous (*fare*).

pantalon (pɑ̃talɔ̃) *m*, [pair of] trousers. **pantalonnade** (lɔnad) *f*, comic turn; clownery; [tom-]foolery; masquerade, sham.

pantelant, e (pɑ̃tlɑ̃, ɑ̃ːt) *a*, panting; twitching (*flesh*). **panteler** (le) *v.i*, to pant.

panthéisme (pɑ̃teism) *m*, pantheism.

panthéon (pɑ̃teɔ̃) *m*, pantheon.

panthère (pɑ̃tɛːr) *f*, panther.

pantin (pɑ̃tɛ̃) *m*, (*toy*) jumping jack; (*pers.*) monkey on a stick (*gesticulator*); shallow-brained & fickle person. *mener une vie de* ~, to run wild.

pantographe (pɑ̃tɔgraf) *m*, pantograph.

pantois, e (pɑ̃twa, aːz) *a*, flabbergasted.

pantomime (pɑ̃tɔmim) (*pers.*) *n*, pantomimist. ¶ *f*, pantomime, dumb show.

pantoufle (pãtufl) *f*, slipper. ~*s en tapisserie*, carpet s—s. *en ~s*, in a free & easy way; informal.

panure (pany;r) *f*, [grated] bread crumbs.

paon (pã) *m*, peacock; p. butter-fly. **paonne** (pan) *f*, peahen. **paon-neau** (pano) *m*, peachick.

papa (papa) *m*, papa, dad[dy]. *à la ~*, without hurrying, simply.

papal, e (papal) *a*, papal. **papauté** (pote) *f*, papacy. **pape** (pap) *m*, pope.

papegai (papgɛ) *m*, popinjay (*Hist.*); clay bird (*pigeon shoot-ing*).

papelard, e (papla;r, ard) *a. & n*, sanctimonious (person).

paperasse (papras) *f*, useless old paper. **paperterie** (pap[ɛ]tri) *f*, paper mill; p. making; p. trade; stationery store; stationery; s. case, writing case. **papetier, ère** (paptje, ɛ;r) *n*, paper maker; stationer. **papier** (pje) *m*, paper; bills (*Fin.*). ~ *à calquer*, /*-cal-que*, tracing paper. ~ *à lettres*, note p., letter p. ~ *autovireur* (otoviRœ;r), self-toning p. ~ *bu-vard*, /~broui*llard*, blotting p. ~ *carbone*, carbon [p.] (*duplicat-ing*). ~ *de Chine*, rice p. ~ *de journal*, newsprint. ~ *de soie*, tissue p. ~ *de verre*, sandpaper. ~ *hygiénique*, toilet p. ~ *im-perméable à la graisse*, ~ *sul-furisé*, grease-proof p. ~ *indien*, India p. ~ *machine*, typewriting p. ~ [*peint*]. ~*-tenture*, *m*, wall-paper. ~ *pelure*, tissue p. ~ *quadrillé* (kadrije), graph p., plot-ting p., section[al] p. ~ *tue-mouches*, fly p. ~ *timbré*, official (stamped) p. ~ *à en-tête*, letter-head p. ~ *de brouillon*, scrap p.

papillon (papijɔ̃) *m*, butterfly; wing nut; bow (*necktie*); slip (*paper*); parking ticket. ~*s noirs*, gloomy ideas. ~ [*de nuit*], moth; throttle (*auto*). **papillonner** (jɔne) *v.i*, to flit about.

papillote (papijɔt) *f*, curl paper; foiled chocolate. **papilloter** (te) *v.i*, to flicker; blink; dazzle; slur (*Typ.*).

papisme (papism) *m*, popery. **papiste** (pist) *n*, papist. ¶ *a*, popish.

papoter (papɔte) *v.i*, to gossip.
papule (papyl) *f*, pimple.
papyrus (papiry;s) *m*, papyrus.
pâque (pɑ;k) *f*, Passover. **Pâques** (pɑ;k) *m.s*, Easter. **Pâques fleuries**, *f.pl*, Palm Sunday.
paquebot (pakbo) *m*, passenger &/*or* mail boat, liner, packet [boat]. ~ *à vapeur*, passenger steamer. ~ *aérien*, airship.
pâquerette (pakRɛt) *f*, daisy.
paquet (pakɛ) *m*, packet, pack-age, bundle, pack; parcel, lot, block; clincher; (*att.*) plump. ~*un ~ de mer*, a [heavy] sea. **paque-tage** (kta;ʒ) *m*, pack (*soldier's*).
par (par) *pr*, by; through; across; via; out of; per; a; in; into; with; on; about; over; from; for; at; during. ~ *an*, per annum. ~*-ci*, ~*-là*, *ad*, here & there, hither & thither; at odd times. ~*-dessous*, ~*-dessus*. See *dessous, dessus*. ~ *ici*, this way, through here. ~ *là*, that way, through there; by that. *de ~ le monde*, somewhere in the world. ~ *les présentes*, hereby (*law*). ~ *où?* which way? ~ *trop*, far too, too much, unduly.
parabole (parabɔl) *f*, parable; parabola. **parabolique†** (lik) *a*, parabolic(al) (*Geom.*).
parachever (paraʃve) *v.t*, to finish [off], perfect.
parachute (paraʃyt) *m*, para-chute.
parade (parad) *f*, parade; show; parry[ing]; repartee. **parader** (de) *v.i*, to parade; show off.
paradis (paradi) *m*, paradise; top balcony (*Theat.*). le ~ [*ter-restre*], [the earthly] paradise, [the Garden of] Eden.
paradoxal, e (paradɔksal) *a*, paradoxical. **paradoxe** (dɔks) *m*, paradox.
parafe (paraf) *m*, initials; flourish; paraph. **parafer** (fe) *v.t*, to ini-tial.
paraffine (parafin) *f*, paraffin [wax].
parage (para;ʒ) *m*, lineage; (*pl.*) grounds (*fishing, cruising*), waters. *dans ces ~s*, in these parts, here-abouts.
paragraphe (paragraf) *m*, para-

graph; section mark (§).

paraître (parɛːtr) *v.i.ir*, to appear; show; be published, come out; seem, look. *vient de~*, just out, published. ¶ *m*, seeming. *l'être & le ~*, the seeming & the real.

Paralipomènes (paralipɔmɛn) *m. pl*, Chronicles (*Bible*).

parallaxe (paralaks) *f*, parallax. **parallèle**† (lɛl) *a*, parallel. ¶ *f*, parallel (*Geom., Mil.*). ¶ *m*, parallel (*of latitude; comparison*). **parallélipipède** (lelipiped) *m*, parallelepiped. **parallélogramme** (lɔgram) *m*, parallelogram.

paralyser (paralize) *v.t*, to paralyze; cripple (*fig.*). **paralysie** (zi) *f*, paralysis. *~ progressive*, creeping paralysis. **paralytique** (tik) *a*. & *n*, paralytic.

parangon (parɑ̃gɔ̃) *m*, paragon.

parapet (parapɛ) *m*, parapet.

paraphe (paraf) *m*, initials; flourish, paraph. **parapher** (fe) *v.t*, to initial.

paraphrase (parafrɑːz) *f*, paraphrase; circumlocution. **paraphraser** (frɑze) *v.t*. & *abs*, to paraphrase; amplify.

parapluie (paraplɥi) *m*, umbrella.

parasitaire (parazitɛːr) *a*, parasitic(al) (*Biol.*). **parasite** (zit) *m*, parasite; hanger-on; sponger. *~s atmosphériques*, static (*radio*). ¶ *a*, parasitical; redundant.

parasol (parasɔl) *m*, sunshade, umbrella (*garden, beach, held over potentate*); tent umbrella.

paratonnerre (paratɔnɛːr) *m*, lightning rod.

paravent (paravɑ̃) *m*, screen (*folding & fig.*).

paraverse (paravers) *m*, raincoat.

parbleu (parblø) *i*, why, of course! to be sure!

parc (park) *m*, park; enclosure; yard; paddock; pen, fold; range, run; bed (*oyster*); playpen. *~ à bestiaux* (cattle) & *~ à matières* (materials), stockyard. *~ à voitures*, car park. *~ d'agrément*, pleasure grounds. **parcage** (kaːჳ) *m*, parking; penning.

parcelle (parsɛl) *f*, particle, scrap; driblet; parcel, plot, patch.

parce que (pars[ə]kə) *c*, because.

parchemin (parʃəmɛ̃) *m*, parchment; (*fig.*) title; diploma.

parcimonie (parsimɔni) *f*, parsimony. **parcimonieux, euse**† (njø, øːz) *a*, parsimonious, penurious.

parcourir (parkuriːr) *v.t.ir*, to travel over, cover; perambulate; run through. **parcours** (kuːr) *m*, distance, stretch; run; haul; course. *~ de 18 trous*, 18-hole course (*golf*).

pardessus (pardəsy) *m*, overcoat.

pardi (pardi) *i*, of course!

pardon (pardɔ̃) *m*, pardon, forgiveness. **pardonnable** (dɔnabl) *a*, pardonable. **pardonner** (ne) *v.t*. & *~ à*, to pardon, forgive; excuse.

pare- (par) *prefix*: *~battage*, *m*, fender (*Naut.*). *~boue*, *m*, fender; *~brise*, *m*, windshield. *~chocs*, *m*, bumper. *~étincelles*, *m*, fireguard.

parégorique (paregɔrik) *a*, paregoric.

pareil, le (parɛːj) *a*, like, alike, similar, to match; equal; parallel; such. ¶ *n*, like, equal; parallel; match, fellow. *la ~*, the like (treatment). *sans pareil*, unequalled, matchless. **pareillement** (rɛjmɑ̃) *ad*, in like manner; also, likewise.

parement (parmɑ̃) *m*, facing; face; cuff (*coat*); cloth (*altar*); curbstone.

parent, e (parɑ̃, ɑ̃ːt) *n*, relative, kinsman, -woman; relation; (*m. pl.*) parents, kin. **parenté** (rɑ̃te) *f*, relationship, kinship; relations.

parenthèse (parɑ̃tɛːz) *f*, parenthesis; bracket (,). *par ~*, parenthetically.

parer (pare) *v.t*. & *i*, to adorn, deck; dress; ward [off], fend [off]; parry; guard.

paresse (parɛs) *f*, laziness, idleness, sloth; sluggishness. **paresser** (se) *v.i*, to idle; laze; loll, lounge. **paresseux, euse**† (sø, øːz) *a*. & *n*, idle, etc (person). ¶ *m*, sloth (*Zool.*).

parfaire (parfɛːr) *v.t.ir*, to finish [off]; make up. **parfait, e** (fɛ, ɛt) *a*, perfect; thorough; capital. ¶ *m*, perfect [tense]. **parfaitement** (tmɑ̃) *ad*, perfectly; thoroughly;

quite; quite so, exactly.

parfiler (parfile) *v.t*, to unravel.

parfois (parfwa) *ad*, sometimes, at times, now & again.

parfum (parfœ̃) *m*, perfume, fragrance; scent; flavor. *être au ~*, to be in on it (*trick, scheme*). **parfumer** (fyme) *v.t*, to scent; perfume; wise someone up. **parfumerie** (mri) *f*, perfumery. **parfumeur, euse** (mœːr, øːz) *n*, perfumer; (*m*.) perfume distiller.

pari (pari) *m*, bet, wager.

paria (parja) *m*, outcaste, untouchable; pariah, outcast.

parier (parje) *v.t*, to bet, wager, lay. *~ sur*, to back (*horse*). *il y a à ~ que . . .*, the odds are that *. . .* **parieur, euse** (jœːr, øːz) *n*, bettor, backer.

parisien, ne (parizjɛ̃, ɛn) *a.* & **P~**, *n*, Parisian.

parité (parite) *f*, parity, equality, likeness; equivalent.

parjure (parʒyːr) *m*, perjury; breach of oath. ¶ *n*, perjurer. ¶ *a*, perjured, forsworn. **se parjurer** (ʒyre) *v.pr*, to perjure (*or* forswear) oneself.

parking (parkiŋ) *m*, parking lot.

parlant, e (parlɑ̃, ɑ̃ːt) *a*, speaking, talking (*film, eyes*); lifelike; talkative. **parlé** (le) *m*, spoken part (*opera*); patter (*in song*).

parlement (parləmɑ̃) *m*, parliament. **parlementaire** (tɛːr) *a*, parliamentary; of truce (*flag*). ¶ *m*, member of parliament; bearer of a flag of truce. **parlementer** (te) *v.i*, to parley.

parler (parle) *v.i.* & *abs*. & *v.t*, to speak, talk; t. about; tell, mention, say. *~ du nez*, to speak through the nose. ¶ *m*, way of speaking; speech; dialect. **parleur, euse** (lœːr, øːz) *n*, talker; (*att*.) talking (*bird*). **parloir** (lwaːr) *m*, parlor (*convent, school*). **parlote** (lɔt) *f*, debating society; gossip.

Parme (parm) *f*, Parma.

parmi (parmi) *pr*, among[st], amid[st].

parodie (parɔdi) *f*, parody. **parodier** (dje) *v.t*, to parody. **parodiste** (dist) *m*, parodist.

paroi (parwa) *f*, wall (*partition, etc.*); side; coat[ing] (*stomach, etc.*).

paroisse (parwas) *f*, parish; p. church. **paroissial, e** (sjal) *a*, parish (*att*.), parochial. **paroissien, ne** (sjɛ, ɛn) *n*, parishioner. ¶ *m*, prayer book.

parole (parɔl) *f*, word; utterance; delivery; speaking; speech; parole. *~ d'Évangile*, gospel [truth]. *avoir la ~*, to have the floor.

paroxysme (parɔksism) *m*, paroxysm.

parpaillot, e (parpajo, ɔt) *n*, heretic.

Parque (park) *f*, Fate (*Myth*.).

parquer (parke) *v.t*, to pen, fold; park.

parquet (parkɛ) *m*, floor, parquet; well (*of court*); central floor of Fr. *Bourse* reserved for use of *agents de change*. **parqueter** (kəte) *v.t*, to floor, parquet.

parrain (parɛ̃) *m*, godfather, sponsor; proposer, recommender. **parrainage** (rɛnaːʒ) *m*, sponsorship; recommendation.

parricide (parisid) (*pers*.) *n.* & (*act*) *m*, parricide; (*att*.) parricidal.

parsemer (parsəme) *v.t*, to strew, intersperse.

parsi (parsi) *m.* & **parse** (pars) *m.* & *a*, Parsee.

part (paːr) (*law*) *m*, child, birth.

part (paːr) *f*, share; part; portion; hand, side. *~ du lion*, lion's share. *à ~*, apart; aside; except. *autre ~*, elsewhere, somewhere else. *d'autre ~*, on the other hand *or* side. *de la ~ de*, on the part of, on behalf of, from. *de ~ en ~*, right through. *faire ~*, to share; acquaint, inform. *à ~ entière*, completely (*un français à part entière*, a full-fledged French citizen).

partage (partaːʒ) *m*, division, sharing; share, lot. *~ [des voix]*, equality of votes. *~ de temps*, time-sharing (*computers*). **partagé, e** (taʒe) *p.a*, reciprocal, mutual (*love*); halved (*hole*) (*golf*). **partageable** (ʒabl) *a*, divisible. **partager** (ʒe) *v.t*, to divide, share, split.

partance (partɑ̃:s) *f*, sailing. *en ~*, about to sail, outward bound. **partant** (tɑ̃) *ad*, hence, therefore. ¶ *m*, starter (*horse, runner*).

partenaire (partənɛ:r) *n*, partner. *~ d'entraînement*, sparring partner.

parterre (partɛ:r) *m*, bed (*garden*), plot, parterre; orchestra pit (*Theat.*).

parti (parti) *m*, party, side; part; course; decision; match (*marriage*). *~ pris*, set purpose; prejudice, bias. *faire un mauvais ~ à*, to ill-treat. *prendre ~*, to take sides, to side. *tirer ~ de*, to make use of, turn to account.

partial, e† (parsjal) *a*, partial, biased, unfair. **partialité** (lite) *f*, partiality.

participation (partisipasjɔ̃) *f*, participation, sharing; partaking; share; joint [ad]venture, joint account. *~ aux bénéfices*, profit-sharing. **participe** (sip) *m*, participle (*Gram.*). **participer** (pe) *v.i*, to participate, share; partake.

particulariser (partikylarize) *v.t*, to particularize. **particularité** (te) *f*, particularity, peculiarity. **particule** (kyl) *f*, particle; speck. **particulier, ère†** (lje, ɛ:r) *a*, particular; peculiar; [e]special; private. ¶ n, [private] individual.

partie (parti) *f*, part; parcel, lot, block; match, round, game; excursion, trip; line (*of business*); party; client (*lawyer's*). *~ de trois*, threesome (*golf*). *~ double*, doubles game (*Ten.*); foursome (*golf*); double entry (*Bkkpg.*) *~ du discours*, part of speech. *~ civile*, plaintiff. *~ nulle* (*sports*). *prendre à ~*, to take to task.

partiel, le (parsjɛl) *a*, partial (*not entire*). **partiellement** (lmɑ̃) *ad*, partially, partly.

partir (parti:r) *v.i.ir*, to depart, set out, start, go; leave; sail; go off; emanate, proceed. *êtes-vous prêts? partez!* are you ready? go! *à ~ de*, from; on & after. *il est parti*, he is drunk.

partisan (partizɑ̃) *m*, partisan, henchman, follower, believer; supporter; guerrilla (*soldier*).

partitif, ive (partitif, i:v) *a*, partitive (*Gram.*). **partition** (sjɔ̃) *f*, score (*Mus.*).

partouse, partouze (partu:z) *f*, orgy (*slang*).

partout (partu) *ad*, everywhere. *2, 3, jeux ~*, 2, 3, all (*Ten.*). *~ où*, wherever.

parure (pary:r) *f*, adornment; ornament; dress, attire; dressing (*meat*); set (*jewels, underclothing*).

parution (parysjɔ̃) *f*, publication, appearance, issue (*book, magazine*).

parvenir (parvəni:r) *v.i. & abs. ir*, to arrive; succeed. *~ à*, to arrive at, reach; attain [to]; manage to; succeed in. **parvenu, e** (ny) *n*, upstart, parvenu.

parvis (parvi) *m*, parvis, square; court.

pas (pɑ) *m*, step; pace; stride; gait; walk; march; time (*Mil.*); dance, pas; progress; precedence (*in rank*); footfall; footprint; threshold; pass (*Phys. Geog.*); strait[s]; pitch, thread (*screw*). *~ accéléré*, quick march. *P~ de Calais*, Straits of Dover. *~ de clerc*, blunder. *~ de la porte*, doorstep. *à ~ de tortue*, at a snail's pace. *~ seul*, solo dance. *au ~*, drive slowly, dead slow (*traffic sign*). *au ~ gymnastique*, at the double (*Mil.*). *faux ~*, slip; misstep.

pas (pɑ) *neg. particle usually coupled with* ne, not; no. *~ libre*, [I am] sorry, the line is busy. (*Teleph.*). *~ possible!* you don't say so!

pascal, aux (paskal, ko) *a*, paschal; Easter.

pasquin (paskɛ̃) *m*, lampooner; lampoon. **pasquinade** (kinad) *f*, pasquinade, lampoon, squib.

passable† (pɑsabl) *a*, passable, tolerable, fair, pretty good. **passade** (sad) *f*, passing fancy (*liaison*); passade. **passage** (sa:ʒ) *m*, passage; passing; crossing; going; transit; transition; pass; passageway, gangway, way, thoroughfare; arcade; ferry; right of way; toll; run (*computers*). *~ à niveau*, grade crossing. *~ clouté*, studded crossing (*pedestrian crossing*). *~*

d'escalier, stairway. ~ *interdit [au public]*, no thoroughfare. ~ *souterraine*, underground passage.

passager, ère (pɑsaʒe, ɛːr) *a*, passing, fleeting, transient, fugitive, short-lived, momentary. ¶ *n*, passenger; visitor, sojourner. ~ *clandestin*, stowaway. ~ *d'entrepont*, steerage passenger. **passagèrement** (ʒɛrmɑ̃) *ad*, in passing, for a short time. **passant, e** (pɑsɑ̃, ɑ̃ːt) *n*, passerby.

passavant (pɑsavɑ̃) *m*, gangway (*on ship*); permit.

passe (pɑːs) *f*, pass; passage; plight; way; thrust; cut; fairway, channel; brim (*hat*); passkey; passport. *mauvaise* ~, bad fix. ~ *étroite*, narrow[s] (*Naut.*).

passé, e (pɑse) *p.a*, past, [by]gone, last; over; faded. *passé maître*, a past master. ¶ *m*, past; p. [tense]; satin stitch (*Emb.*). **passé**, *pr*, after.

passe-droit (pɑsdrwa) *m*, injustice, invidious distinction.

passe-lacet (pɑslase) *m*, bodkin. *raide comme un* ~, stone broke.

passement (pɑsmɑ̃) *m*, lace, braid; gimp. **passementerie** (tri) *f*, passementerie, trimmings.

passe-partout (pɑspartu) *m*, master key.

passe-passe (pɑspɑs) *m*, sleight-of-hand. *tour de* ~, conjuring trick.

passe-plats (pɑspla) *m*, service hatch.

passepoil (pɑspwal) *m*, piping (*braid*).

passeport (pɑspɔːr) *m*, passport; clearance (*ship*).

passer (pɑse) *v.i. & t*, to pass; p. on; p. by; p. away; go; cross; spend; call, look in; ferry over; slip on; exceed; rank; enter, post; enter into; give, place; file (*a return at a registry*). ~ *à tabac*, to beat brutally (*slang*). ~ *l'arme à gauche*, to cash in one's chips, die. se ~ de, to do without, dispense with.

passereau (pɑsro) *m*, sparrow.

passerelle (pɑsrɛl) *f*, footbridge; bridge (*ship's*); gangway; catwalk (*Theat., cinema*).

passerose (pɑsroːz) *f*, hollyhock.

passe-temps (pɑstɑ̃) *m*, pastime.

passeur (pɑsœːr) *m*, ferryman.

passible (pɑsibl) *a*, liable. ~ *de droits*, dutiable.

passif, ive (pɑsif, iːv) *a*, passive. ¶ *m*, passive [voice]; liabilities.

passiflore (pɑsiflɔːr) *f*, passion flower.

passion (pɑsjɔ̃) *f*, passion. **passionnant, e** (ɔnɑ̃, ɑ̃ːt) *a*, thrilling. **passionné†, e** (ne) *a*, passionate; impassioned. *il est* ~ *pour*, he is passionately fond of; his hobby is. **passionner** (ne) *v.t*, to impassion; enthral[l]. se ~, to become impassioned; become enamored.

passivement (pɑsivmɑ̃) *ad*, passively. **passiveté** (vite) *f*, passivity.

passoire (pɑswaːr) *f*, colander; strainer.

pastel (pɑstɛl) *m*, crayon; pastel; woad.

pastèque (pɑstɛk) *f*, watermelon.

pasteur (pɑstœːr) *m*, shepherd; pastor, minister.

pasteuriser (pɑstœrize) *v.t*, to pasteurize.

pastiche (pɑstiʃ) *m*, pastiche; imitation, copy.

pastille (pɑstiːj) *f*, lozenge, pastille, drop; patch (*tire*).

pastoral, e (pɑstɔral) *a*, pastoral. ¶ *f*, pastoral; pastorale.

pastoriser (pɑstɔrize) *v.t*, to pasteurize.

pat (pat) *m*, stalemate (*chess*); (*att.*) stalemated. *faire* ~, to stalemate.

patache (pataʃ) *f*, rattletrap (*vehicle*).

pataquès (patakɛːs) *m*, malaprop[ism].

patarafe (pataraf) *f*, scrawl.

patard (pataːr) *m*, coin of little value.

patate (patat) *f*, sweet potato; potato.

patatras (patatrɑ) *onomatopoeia*, crash!

pataud, e (pato, oːd) *a. & n*, clumsy (person). ¶ *m*, big-pawed puppy.

patauger (patoʒe) *v.i*, to flounder, squelch; wade.

pâte (pɑːt) *f*, paste; dough; pulp;

impasto; pie (*printers'*). **pâté** (pate) *m*, pie, pasty; pâté; mud pie; blot; block (*houses*); pie (*printers'*). **pâtée** (te) *f*, mash (*poultry*); dog food.

patelin, e (patlɛ̃, in) *a*, wheedling. ¶ *m*, village.

patelle (patɛl) *f*, limpet.

patène (patɛn) *f*, paten.

patent, e (patɑ̃, ɑ̃:t) *a*, patent (*obvious*). ¶ *f*, license. ~ *de santé*, bill of health.

Pater (patɛ:r) *m*, paternoster.

patère (patɛ:r) *f*, base, block (*on wall*); hat peg.

paterne (patɛrn) *a*, patronizing. **paternel, le†** (nɛl) *a*, paternal, fatherly; father's (*side*). **paternité** (nite) *f*, paternity, fatherhood; authorship.

pâteux, euse (patø, ø:z) *a*, pasty, clammy, thick.

pathétique† (patetik) *a*, pathetic. ¶ *m*, pathos.

pathologie (patɔlɔʒi) *f*, pathology. **pathologique** (ʒik) *a*, pathological. **pathologiste** (ʒist) *n*, pathologist.

pathos (patɔs) *m*, bathos.

patibulaire (patibylɛ:r) *a*, hangdog.

patiemment (pasjamɑ̃) *ad*, patiently. **patience** (sjɑ̃:s) *f*, patience; button stick (*Mil.*); patience (*cards*); dock (*Bot.*). **patient, e** (sjɑ̃, ɑ̃:t) *a*, patient, enduring. ¶ *n*, patient; sufferer. **patienter** (ɑ̃te) *v.i*, to have patience.

patin (patɛ̃) *m*, skate; runner; skid; shoe; flange. ~*s à glace*, (1) *à visser*, (2) *à griffes*, iceskates, (1) screw-on, (2) clamp-on. ~*s à roulettes*, roller skates. ~*s de course*, racing s. ~*s de figure*, figure s. ~*s de hockey*, hockey s. **patinage** (tina:ʒ) *m*, skating; skidding, slipping. **patine** (tin) *f*, patina. **patiné, e** (ne) *p.p*, patinated; fumed (*oak*). **patiner** (ne) *v.i*, to skate; skid, slip. **patinette** (net) *f*, scooter. **patineur, euse** (nœ:r, ø:z) *n*, skater. **patinoire** (wa:r) *f*, skating rink.

pâtir (pɑti:r) *v.i*, to suffer. **pâtiras** (tira) *m*, drudge.

pâtis (pɑti) *m*, grazing ground, pasture.

pâtisser (pɑtise) *v.i*, to make pastry. **pâtisserie** (sri) *f*, pastry; confectionery; bakery; tea shop. **pâtissier, ère** (sje, ɛ:r) *n*, pastrycook [*&/or* confectioner]. **pâtissoire** (swa:r) *f*, pastry board.

patois (patwa) *m*, dialect; jargon.

patouiller (patuje) *v.i*, to flounder.

patraque (patrak) *a*, out of sorts, slightly sick; worn out, not working well. ¶ *f*, watch (*slang*).

pâtre (pɑ:tr) *m*, herdsman.

patriarcal, e (patriarkal) *a*, patriarchal. **patriarche** (arʃ) *m*, patriarch.

patrice (patris) *m. & **patricien, ne** (sjɛ̃, ɛn) *a. & n*, patrician. **patrie** (tri) *f*, native land, [n.] country, fatherland; home. [*petite*] ~, birthplace. **patrimoine** (trimwan) *m*, patrimony; inheritance, heritage. **patriote** (ɔt) *n*, patriot. ¶ ~.& **patriotique** (tik) *a*, patriotic. **patriotisme** (tism) *m*, patriotism. **patron, ne** (trɔ̃, ɔn) *n*, patron, ess; patron saint; employer, principal; master, mistress; governor; skipper; coxswain. ¶ *m*, pattern (*for dress, etc.*); templet, template; stencil [plate]. *dès patron-minet*, at early dawn. **patronage** (trona:ʒ) *m*, patronage; advowson; benevolence; guild, club (*church*). **patronal,e** (nal) *a*, patronal, patron saint's (*day*); employer's, ers' (*att.*). **patronat** (na) *m*, employers (*col.*). Patronat (*Conseil National du Patronat Français—CNPF*), French employers' association. **patronner** (ne) *v.t*, to patronize; stencil. **dame patronnesse** (nɛs) *f*, patroness (*fête, etc.*). **nom patronymique** (nimik) *m*, patronymic; surname.

patrouille (patru:j) *f*, patrol. **patrouiller** (truje) *v.i*, to patrol.

patte (pat) *f*, paw; foot; leg; claw; tab; strap, clip; clamp, holdfast; fluke (*anchor*). *à quatre ~s,* on all fours. ~*d'oie*, [*f*, multiple fork, crowfoot [forking] (*of roads*); crow's-foot (*wrinkle*).

pâturage (pɑtyra:ʒ) *m*, pasturage. **pâture** (ty:r) *f*, pasture;

food (*fig.*). **pâturer** (tyre) *v.i*, to pasture, graze.

paturon (patyr5) *m*, pastern.

paume (po:m) *f*, palm (*hand*); real tennis (*ancient game*).

paumer (pome) *v.t*, to slap; swipe; lose. **se faire ~**, to be caught, nabbed.

paupérisme (poperism) *m*, pauperism.

paupière (popjɛːr) *f*, eyelid.

pause (poːz) *f*, pause, stop; rest (*Mus.*).

pauvre† (poːvr) *a. & m*, poor (man); pauper; penurious; scanty, meager. **pauvresse** (povrɛːs) *f*, beggar woman. **pauvret, te** (vrɛ, ɛt) *n*, poor little thing (*pers.*). **pauvreté** (vrəte) *f*, poverty; poorness; commonplace.

pavage (pavaːʒ) *m*, pavement; paving.

pavaner (se) (pavane) *v.pr*, to strut [about].

pavé (pave) *m*, paving stone, pavement; pavé; street(s) (*fig.*); 10,000 francs (*slang*). **sur le ~**, out of work. **pavement** (vmɑ̃) *m*, paving; pavement. **paver** (ve) *v.t*, to pave. **paveur** (vœːr) *m*, paver.

pavie (pavi) *f*, clingstone.

Pavie (pavi) *f*, Pavia (*Geog.*).

pavillon (pavij5) *m*, pavilion; lodge; box (*Hunt.*); summer house; house (*club*); flag, colors (*Naut. & Nav.*); flare; horn; earpiece. **~ de poupe**, ensign.

pavois (pavwa) *m*, bulwark (*ship's*); flags (*col.*). **pavoiser** (ze) *v.t*, to dress (*ship*); deck with flags; (*abs.*) to dress ship.

pavot (pavo) *m*, poppy. **~ somnifère**, opium poppy.

payable (pejabl) *a*, payable. **~ à la commande**, cash with order. **~ comptant**, pay cash. **payant, e** (jɑ̃, ɑ̃:t) *a*, paying. ¶ *n*, payer. **paye** (pɛːj) *f*, pay, wages; (*good, bad*) payer. **payement** (pɛ[j]mɑ̃) *m*, payment. **payer** (je) *v.t. & abs*, to pay; p. for; p. out; cash (*check*); stand (*drink*). **~ d'audace**, to brazen it out. **~ de sa personne**, to risk one's neck. **payeur, euse** (jœːr, øːz) *n*, payer; paymaster; drawee.

pays (pei) *m*, country, land; native

place. **~ de cocagne** (kɔkaɲ), land of milk & honey, l. of plenty. **les Pays-Bas**, the Netherlands. **mal du ~**, homesickness. **paysage** (zaːʒ) *m*, landscape; l. painting; description of scenery; (*pl.*) scenery. **paysagiste** (zaʒist) *m*, landscape painter; (*att.*) landscape (*gardener*).

paysan, ne (peizɑ̃, an) *n. & att*, peasant, rustic. **les paysans**, the peasantry. **paysannerie** (zanri) *f*, portrait of peasant life.

péage (peaːʒ) *m*, toll; t. house. **péager** (aʒe) *m*, toll collector.

péan (peɑ̃) *m*, paean.

peau (po) *f*, skin, fell, pelt; scruff (*neck*); slough; leather; rind, peel; shell (*nut*); case (*sausage*). **~ de tambour**, drumhead. **P~ Rouge**, *m*, redskin, red Indian. **peausserie** (sri) *f*, skin dressing; skins, peltry. **peaussier** (sje) *m*, skin dresser. **[médecin] peaussier** ou **[médecin] peaucier** (sje) *m*, skin specialist.

pécari (pekari) *m*, peccary.

peccadille (pɛkadiːj) *f*, peccadillo, slip.

pêche (pɛːʃ) *f*, peach (*fruit*); fishing (*act & right*); fishery; catch. **~ à la crevette**, shrimping. **~ à la ligne**, line fishing, rod f., angling. **~ à la mouche noyée**, wet fly f. **~ à la mouche sèche**, dry fly f. **~ à traîner**, trolling. **~ au bord de la mer**, shore fishing. **~ au lancer**, casting. **~ au large**, **~ hauturière** (otyrjɛːr), offshore fishing, deep-sea f. **~ au vif**, live-bait f. **~ chalutière** (ʃalytjeːr), trawling. **~ côtière**, **~ dans les eaux territoriales**, inshore fishing. **~ de fond**, ground angling, bottom fishing. **~ de grand sport**, big-game fishing. **~ de plage**, surf f., beach f. **~ en eaux douces**, **~ d'eau douce**, freshwater f. **~ de (ou, en) mer**, sea f., saltwater f.

péché (peʃe) *m*, sin. **~ d'habitude**, besetting s. **~ mignon**, pet vice, weak point. **pécher** (ʃe) *v.i*, to sin; err; offend.

pêcher (peʃe) *m*, peach [tree]. ¶ *v.t*, to fish for; fish; f. up; drag

(*pond*); pick up, get hold of. ~ *à la ligne*, to angle. ~ *à la traîne*, to troll. pêcherie (ʃri) *f*, fishery, fishing ground. pêcheur, euse ʃœːr, øːz) *n*, fisherman, angler.
pêcheur, eresse (peʃœːr, ʃrɛs) *n*, sinner.
péculat (pekyla) *m*, embezzlement (*public funds*). pécule (kyl) *m*, savings, nest egg; earnings (*of convict*); mustering-out money (*on discharge, Mil., Nav.*).
pécuniaire† (pekynjɛːr) *a*, pecuniary.
pédagogue (pedagɔg) *m*, pedagogue.
pédale (pedal) *f*, pedal; treadle; homosexual (*slang*). ~ *d'embrayage*, clutch (*auto*). ~ *forte*, loud p. ~ *sourde*, soft p. *lacher les* ~*s*, to renounce (*slang*). *perdre les* ~*s*, to lose one's head (*slang*). pédaler (le) *v.i*, to pedal; cycle. pédalier (lje) *m*, pedal [key]board; crank gear (*cycle*). pédalo (lo) *m*, pedal boats.
pédant, e (pedɑ̃, ɑ̃ːt) *n*, pedant; prig; wiseacre. ¶ ~ & pédantesque† (dɑ̃tɛsk) *a*, pedantic, priggish. pédanterie (tri) *f*. & pédantisme (tism) *m*, pedantry.
pédé (pede) *m*, homosexual (*slang*).
pédestre (pedɛstr) *a*, pedestrian (*statue*). pédestrement (trəmɑ̃) *ad*, on foot.
pédicure (pediky:r) *n*, chiropodist.
pedigree (pedigri) *m*, pedigree (*beast*).
Pégase (pegɑ:z) *m*, Pegasus (*fig.*).
pègre (pɛːgr) *f*, underworld.
peignage (pɛɲa:ʒ) *m*, combing, carding (*textiles*). peigne (pɛɲ) *m*, comb; card; pecten, scallop. ~ *à décrasser*, ~ *fin*, scurf comb, [small] tooth c. ~ *coiffeur*, hair c. peignée (ɲe) *f*, drubbing, thrashing. peigner (ɲe) *v.t*, to comb; card; chase (*screws*). peignier (nje) *m*, comb maker. peignoir (ɲwaːr) *m*, dressing gown. ~ *de bain*, bathrobe. ~ *éponge*, toweling beach coat. peignures (ɲyːr) *f.pl*, combings.
peinard (pɛnaːrd) *a*, easygoing. *père* ~, easygoing fellow. *se tenir*

~, to behave cautiously. ¶ *m*, toiler (*archaic*); one who takes it easy.
peindre (pɛ̃ːdr) *v.t. & abs. ir*, to paint; depict, portray.
peine (pɛn) *f*, punishment, penalty, pain; sorrow; infliction; anxiety; pains, trouble; difficulty. *à* ~, hardly, scarcely, barely. *être en* ~ *de*, to be at a loss to. *valoir la* ~, to be worthwhile. peiner (ne) *v.t*, to pain, grieve; (*v.i.*) to labor, [toil &] moil; be difficult. ~ *en lisant un livre*, to wade through a book.
peintre (pɛ̃ːtr) *m*, painter; portrayer. ~ *d'enseignes*, sign writer. ~ *en bâtiments*, house painter. ~ *verrier*, stained glass artist. peinture (pɛ̃tyːr) *f*, painting; picture; paint, color; portrayal. peinturlurer (tyrlyrer) *v.t*, to daub.
péjoratif, ive (peʒɔratif, iːv) *a*, pejorative, disparaging, depreciatory.
Pékin (pekɛ̃) *m*, Peking (*Geog.*). p~, *m*, pekin (*fabric*); civilian. *être en* ~, to be in civilian clothes. pékinois (kinwa) *m*, Pekinese, peke (*dog*).
pelage (pəla:ʒ) *m*, coat, wool, fur.
pélargonium (pelargɔnjɔm) *m*, pelargonium.
pelé, e (pəle) *p.a*, bare, bald. peler (le) *v.t. & i*, to strip, peel, skin.
pêle-mêle (pɛlmel) *ad. & m*, pellmell, helter-skelter.
pèlerin, e (pɛlrɛ̃, in) *n*, pilgrim; fox (*pers.*). ¶ *f*, cape, pelerine. pèlerinage (lrina:ʒ) *m*, pilgrimage; place of pilgrimage.
pélican (pelikɑ̃) *m*, pelican.
pelisse (pəlis) *f*, pelisse.
pelle (pɛl) *f*, shovel; scoop. ~ *à poussière*, dustpan. ~ *à sel*, salt spoon. ~ *à tarte*, pastry server. ~-*bêche*, entrenching tool. pelletée (lte) *f*, shoveful, spadeful.
pelleterie (pɛltri) *f*, furriery; peltry. pelletier, ère (ltje, ɛːr) *n*, furrier.
pellicule (pellikyl) *f*, pellicle, skin; film; (*pl.*) dandruff, scurf. ~ *en bobine*, roll film (*Phot.*). *la* ~ *blanche et noire*, black-and-white film. *la* ~ *en couleurs*, color f.

pelote (plɔt) *f*, ball (*wool, string*); pincushion; pile (*money*); pelota. **peloter** (te) *v.i*, to knock the balls about (*Ten.*). ~ *en attendant partie*, to fill in time; caress (*slang*). **peloton** (tɔ̃) *m*, ball; knot, cluster; squad, party, platoon (*Mil.*). ~ *d'exécution*, firing squad. **pelotonner** (tɔne) *v.t*, to ball, wind. se ~, to curl up, snuggle.

pelouse (pluːz) *f*, lawn, green; public enclosures (*turf.*). ~ *d'arrivée*, putting green (*golf*).

peluche (plyʃ) *f*, plush. **pelucher** (ʃe) *v.i*, to fluff up. **pelucheux, euse** (ʃø, øːz) *a*, fluffy.

pelure (plyːr) *f*, peel, skin, rind; onionskin paper.

pénal, e (penal) *a*, penal; criminal (*law*); penalty (*clause*). **pénalité** (lite) *f*, penalty.

pénates (penat) *m.pl*, home. *dieux* ~, Penates, household gods.

penaud, e (pəno, oːd), *a*, crestfallen; sheepish.

penchant, e (pɑ̃ʃɑ̃, ɑ̃ːt) *a*, leaning; tottering. ¶ *m*, slope; brink, verge; leaning, inclination, bent, propensity, proclivity, fondness. **penché, e** (ʃe) *p.a*, leaning (*tower*); drooping (*looks*). **penchement** (ʃmɑ̃) *m*, bend[ing]; stoop[ing]. **pencher** (ʃe) *v.t. & i. & se* ~, to bend, incline, tilt; lean; bank; stoop; verge. *faire* ~ *la balance*, to turn the scale. *se* ~ *sur*, to make a study of.

pendable (pɑ̃dabl) *a*, [deserving of] hanging; outrageous. **pendaison** (dezɔ̃) *f*, [death by] hanging. **pendant, e** (dɑ̃, ɑ̃ːt) *a*, hanging [down]; dangling; drooping; pendent, -ant; pending. ¶ *m*, drop (*ear*); frog (*sword*); counterpart, fellow, match. *les [deux]* ~*s*, the pair (*pictures, etc.*).

pendant (pɑ̃dɑ̃) *pr*, during, for. ~ *que*, while, whilst.

pendard, e (pɑ̃daːr, ard) (*jocular*) *n*, rascal; hussy; gallowsbird. **pendeloque** (pɑ̃dlɔk) *f*, drop (*ear, chandelier*). **pendentif** (dɑ̃tif) *m*, pendentive; pendant, -ent. **penderie** (dri) *f*, closet, wardrobe. **pendiller** (dije) *v.i*, to hang, dangle. **pendre** (dr) *v.t. & i*, to hang; h. up, h. out.

pendule (dyl) *m*, pendulum. ¶ ~ *& pendulette* (lɛt) *f*, timepiece, clock. *pendule à sonnerie & à carillon*, striking & chiming clock.

pêne (pɛːn) *m*, bolt (*lock*).

pénétrant, e (penetrɑ̃, ɑ̃ːt) *a*, penetrating, piercing, searching. **pénétration** (trasjɔ̃) *f*, penetration; insight. **pénétrer** (tre) *v.t. & i*, to penetrate, pierce; break into; permeate, pervade, sink in; fathom; see through; imbue.

pénible† (penibl) *a*, laborious, hard; painful.

péniche (peniʃ) *f*, barge, landing craft.

péninsulaire (penɛ̃syleːr) *a*, peninsular. **péninsule** (syl) *f*, peninsula.

pénitence (penitɑ̃ːs) *f*, penitence; penance; punishment; penalty, forfeit (*at play*). **pénitencier** (tɑ̃sje) *m*, penitentiary, reformatory; convict prison. **pénitent, e** (tɑ̃, ɑ̃ːt) *a. & n*, penitent. **pénitentiaire** (tɑ̃sjeːr) *a*, penitentiary.

penne (pɛn) *f*, quill [feather].

pénombre (penɔ̃ːbr) *f*, penumbra; twilight; background (*fig.*).

pensant, e (pɑ̃sɑ̃, ɑ̃ːt) *a*, thinking; -minded (*bien* = right), -disposed (*mal* = ill). **pense-bête** (pɑ̃sbɛt) *m*, memory jogger. **pensée** (se) *f*, thought; thinking; meditation; mind; idea; pansy, heartsease. *arrière-*~, ulterior motive. **penser** (se) *v.i. & t. & abs*, to think; mean. ¶ *m*, thought (*Poet.*). **penseur** (sœːr) *m*, thinker. **pensif, ive** (sif, iːv) *a*, pensive, thoughtful.

pension (pɑ̃sjɔ̃) *f*, room & board; boarding house; b. school; pension; annuity. ~ *alimentaire*, alimony. ~ *pour les chevaux*, livery stables. **pensionnaire** (ɔnɛːr) *n*, boarder; paying guest; inmate; pensioner. **pensionnat** (na) *m*, boarding school. **pensionner** (ne) *v.t*, to pension.

pensum (pɛ̃sɔm) *m*, extra work (*Sch.*).

Pen[n]sylvanie (la) (pɛ̃silvani), Pennsylvania.

Pentateuque (le) (pɛ̃tatøːk), the Pentateuch.

pente (pã:t) *f*, slope, incline, [downward] gradient; bent (*fig.*).

Pentecôte (la) (pãtko:t), Whitsun[tide]; Pentecost.

penture (pãty:r) *f*, hinge (*of hook & hinge*).

pénultième (penyltjɛm) *a*, penultimate.

pénurie (penyri) *f*, penury, scarcity, dearth, lack.

pépie (pepi) *f*, pip (*poultry*); thirst. **pépier** (pje) *v.i*, to peep, chirp.

pépin (pepɛ) *m*, pip (*fruit*); stone (*grape*); umbrella; accident; breakdown. *avoir le ~ pour quelqu'un*, to have the hots for someone. *avoir des ~s*, to be in trouble. *risquer le ~*, to risk trouble (*all slang*). pépinière (pinje:r) *f*, nursery (*Hort. & fig.*). [jardinier] pépiniériste (njerist) *m*, nurseryman.

pépite (pepit) *f*, nugget.

péplum (peplɔm) *m*, peplos, peplum (*ancient Greek costume*); historical movie epic.

perçant, e (pɛrsã, ã:t) *a*, piercing; keen, sharp; shrill. **mettre en perce** (pɛrs), to broach, tap (*cask*). **percée** (se) *f*, opening; cutting. **perce-neige**, *f*, snowdrop. **perce-oreille**, *m*, earwig.

percepteur (pɛrseptœ:r) *m*, collector (*tax*). **perceptible** (tibl) *a*, collectable, -ible; perceptible, discernible, noticeable. ~ *à l'ouïe*, audible. **perception** (sjɔ̃) *f*, collection; collectorship; collector's office; perception.

percer (pɛrse) *v.t. & i*, to pierce; bore; drill; lance; stab; spear; broach, tap; hole; drive; open; penetrate; break through; reveal itself; make one's way. **perceur** (sœ:r) *m*, driller (*pers.*). **perceuse** (sø:z) *f*, drill[ing machine].

percevoir (pɛrsəvwa:r) *v.t*, to collect; charge; perceive.

perche (pɛrʃ) *f*, pole; perch (*fish*). ~ *d'étendoir*, clothes prop. **percher** (ʃe) *v.i*, to perch, roost. **perchoir** (ʃwa:r) *m*, perch, roost.

perchiste, perchman (pɛrʃist, man) *m*, boom operator, perchist, perchman (*TV & cinema*).

perclus, e (pɛrkly, y:z) *a*, crippled.

percussion (pɛrkysjɔ̃) *f*, percussion, impact. **percutant, e** (tã, ã:t) *a*, percussive.

perdant, e (pɛrdã, ã:t) *n*, loser. ¶ *a*, losing. **perdition** (disjɔ̃) *f*, perdition. *en ~*, in a sinking condition (*ship*). **perdre** (dr) *v.t. & abs*, to lose; waste; ruin. **perdu** (dy) *a*, lost; ruined; spent (*bullet*).

perdreau (pɛrdro) *m*, young partridge. **perdrix** (dri) *f*, partridge. ~ *des neiges*, ptarmigan.

père (pɛr) *m*, father, parent; sire (*Poet. & beast*); senior. *le ~ Noël*, Santa Claus. *de ~ de famille* (*investment*). *en bon ~ de famille*, with due & proper care.

pérégrination (peregrinasjɔ̃) *f*, peregrination.

péremptoire† (perãptwa:r) *a*, peremptory.

péréquation (perekwasjɔ̃) *f*, equalization. ~ *des prix*, standardization of charges (*freight, taxes*).

perfection (pɛrfɛksjɔ̃) *f*, perfection. **perfectionner** (ɔne) *v.t*, to perfect; improve.

perfide† (pɛrfid) *a. & n*, treacherous, perfidious (person). **perfidie** (di) *f*, treachery, perfidy.

perforateur (pɛrfɔratœ:r) *m*, punch (*paper*). **perforatrice** (tris) *f*, drill (*rock, etc.*); card punch (*data processing*). **perforer** (re) *v.t*, to perforate; drill; punch.

perforeur, euse (pɛrfɔrœ:r, ø:z) *n*, card punch, key p.; card punch, key p. operator.

performance (pɛrfɔrmã:s) *f*, performance (*sport*). ~ *classée*, winning performance. **performant, e** (mã, ãt) *a*, capable of high performance; competitive.

pergola (pɛrgɔla) *f*, pergola.

péricliter (periklite) *v.i*, to be in danger.

péril (peril) *m*, peril. **périlleux, euse†** (rijø, ø:z) *a*, perilous.

périmé, e (perime) *p.p*, out of date (*ticket, etc.*); exploded (*theory*). **périmer** (me) *v.i*, to lapse, expire.

périmètre (perimɛtr) *m,* perimeter; limit.

période (perjɔd) *f,* period, stage;
spell; repetend; phrase (*Mus.*). ~
radioactive, radioactive halflife
(*Phys.*). ¶ *m,* pitch; stage. **pério-
dique†** (dik) *a,* periodic; periodical; recurrent, recurring. ¶ *m,* periodical.

péripétie (peripesi) *f,* sudden
change; vicissitude.

périphérie (periferi) *f,* periphery.

périphrase (perifrɑ:z) *f,* periphrasis.

périr (peri:r) *v.i,* to perish, be
lost; die; lapse.

périscope (periskɔp) *m,* periscope.

périssable (perisabl) *a,* perishable.

péristyle (peristil) *m,* peristyle.

péritonite (peritɔnit) *f,* peritonitis.

perle (pɛrl) *f,* pearl; bead; treasure (*fig.*). ~ *de culture,* cultured
pearl. **perlé, e** (le) *a,* pearly;
exquisitely done.

permanence (pɛrmanɑ̃:s) *f,* permanence. *en* ~, without interruption. **permanent, e** (nɑ̃, ɑ̃:t)
a, permanent, standing; continuous; abiding; perennial.

permanganate (pɛrmɑ̃ganat) *m,*
permanganate.

perméable (pɛrmeabl) *a,* permeable, pervious.

permettre (pɛrmɛtr) *v.t.ir,* to
permit, to allow; may. *se* ~, to
allow oneself, indulge in. *se* ~
de, to venture to. **permis** (mi)
m, permit, license, order. ~ [*de
circulation*], [free] pass (*Rly.*). ~
de conduire [*les automobiles*],
driver's license. **permission** (sjɔ̃)
f, permission; leave, pass (*Mil.*).
permissionnaire (ɔnɛ:r) *m. & a,*
(soldier) on leave.

permutation (pɛrmytasjɔ̃) *f,* exchange (*of posts*); permutation;
transposition.

pernicieux, euse† (pɛrnisj/ø,
ø:z) *a,* pernicious, baneful.

péroné (perɔne) *m,* fibula, splint
[bone].

péronnelle (perɔnɛl) *f,* pert
hussy.

péroraison (perɔrɛzɔ̃) *f,* peroration. **pérorer** (re) *v.i,* to hold
forth, speechify.

Pérou (le) (peru), Peru. *ce n'est
pas le* ~, it's not Eldorado, not a
lot of money.

Pérouse (peru:z) *f,* Perugia.

peroxyde (perɔksid) *m,* peroxide.

perpendiculaire† (pɛrpɑ̃diky-
lɛ:r) *a. & f,* perpendicular.

perpétrer (pɛrpetre) *v.t,* to perpetrate.

perpétuation (pɛrpetɥasjɔ̃) *f,*
perpetuation. **perpétuel, le†**
(tɥɛl) *a,* perpetual, permanent;
for life. **perpétuer** (tɥe) *v.t,* to
perpetuate. **perpétuité** (tɥite) *f,*
perpetuity. *à* ~, in perpetuity;
for life.

perplexe (pɛrplɛks) *a,* perplexed,
puzzled; perplexing. **perplexité**
(ksite) *f,* perplexity.

perquisition (pɛrkizisjɔ̃) *f,*
search (*law*).

perron (pɛrɔ̃) *m,* front steps, perron.

perroquet (pɛrɔkɛ) *m,* parrot;
topgallant. **perruche** (ryʃ) *f,*
parakeet; hen parrot; high-flown
random talker (*woman*).

perruque (pɛryk) *f,* wig; old fogy.
perruquier (kje) *m,* wigmaker.

pers, e (pɛ:r, ɛrs) *a,* greenish-blue.

persan (pɛrsɑ̃, an) *a. & P~,
n,* Persian (*modern*). *le persan,*
Persian (*language*). **la Perse**
(pɛrs), Persia. **perse,** *a. & P~,
n,* Persian (*ancient*). **perse,** *f,*
chintz.

persécuter (pɛrsekyte) *v.t,* to
persecute; bait; dun. **persécuteur, trice** (tœ:r, tris) *n,* persecutor. **persécution** (sjɔ̃) *f,* persecution.

persévérance (pɛrseverɑ̃:s) *f,*
perseverance. **persévérer** (re) *v.i.
& abs,* to persevere; persist.

persienne (pɛrsjɛn) *f,* shutter,
persienne, Persian blind.

persiflage (pɛrsiflɑ:ʒ) *m,* banter,
persiflage. **persifler** (fle) *v.t,* to
banter, chaff.

persil (pɛrsi) *m,* parsley. **persillé,
e** (sije) *a,* blue-moldy (*cheese*).

persistance (pɛrsistɑ̃:s) *f,* per-
sistence, -ency. **persistant, e** (tɑ̃,

ã:t) *a*, persistent. **persister** (te) *v.i*, to persist.

personnage (pɛrsɔna:ʒ) *m*, personage; character; (*pl.*) dramatis personae. ~ *de carton*, figurehead. *être un* ~, to be somebody. **personnalité** (nalite) *f*, personality; (*pl.*) [well-known] people. **personne** (sɔn) *f*, person; self; (*pl.*) people. ~ *à charge*, dependent person; hanger-on. ~ *collante*, burr, sticker. ~ *interposée*, nominee. ~ *morale*, ~ *juridique*, ~ *civile*, body corporate, legal entity. ¶ *pn.m*, anybody, anyone; nobody, no one, none. **personnel**, le† (nɛl) *a*, personal; private; selfish. ¶ *m*, staff, personnel. **personnifier** (nifje) *v.t*, to personify; impersonate.

perspective (pɛrspɛkti:v) *f*, perspective; outlook, view, prospect; vista. *en* ~, in view.

perspicace (pɛrspikas) *a*, perspicacious. **perspicacité** (site) *f*, perspicacity.

persuader (pɛrsɥade) *v.t. & abs*, to persuade; prevail. **persuasif**, **ive** (zif, i:v) *a*, persuasive. **persuasion** (zjɔ̃) *f*, persuasion; belief.

perte (pɛrt) *f*, loss; leak[age]; waste; casualty (*Mil.*); ruin; swallow (*river*); discount (opp. *premium*). ~ *sèche*, dead loss. *à* ~, at a loss. *à* ~ *de vue*, as far as the eye can reach. *en* ~, out of pocket, to the bad, a loser. *en pure* ~, to no purpose.

pertinent, e (pɛrtinã, ã:t) *a*, pertinent, apposite, relevant. **pertinemment** (namã) *ad*, pertinently, etc.

pertuis (pɛrtɥi) *m*, sluiceway; strait[s] (*Geog.*).

perturbateur, trice (pɛrtyrbatœ:r, tris) *n*, disturber. **perturbation** (sjɔ̃) *f*, disturbance, perturbation.

péruvien, ne (peryvjɛ̃, ɛn) *a. & P~*, *n*, Peruvian.

pervenche (pɛrvã:ʃ) *f*, periwinkle (*Bot.*).

pervers, e (pɛrvɛ:r, ɛrs) *a*, perverse. ¶ *m*, evil-doer, pervert. **perversion** (vɛrsjɔ̃) *f*, perversion.

perversité (site) *f*, perversity. **pervertir** (ti:r) *v.t*, to pervert.

pesade (pəzad) *f*, rearing (*horse*).

pesage (pəsa:ʒ) *m*, weighing; (*turf*) w. in; w. in room; paddock. **pesamment** (zamã) *ad*, heavily; ponderously. **pesant, e** (zã, ã:t) *a*, heavy, weighty; ponderous, unwieldy; ponderable. *son pesant d'or*, his, its, weight in gold. **pesant**, *ad*, in weight. **pesanteur** (zãtœ:r) *f*, heaviness, weight; gravity (*Phys.*); dullness [*spirit*]. **pesée** (ze) *f*, weighing; prize, -se; wrench. **pèse-lettre** (pɛzlɛtr) *m*, letter scales. **peser** (pəze) *v.t*, to weigh; ponder; (*v.i.*) to weigh; lie heavy; bear, press; dwell. **peseur** (zœ:r) *m*, weigher. **peson** (zɔ̃) *m*, balance (*spring, etc.*).

pessimisme (pɛsimism) *m*, pessimism. **pessimiste** (mist) *m*, pessimist. ¶ *a*, pessimistic.

peste (pɛst) *f*, plague, pestilence. ~ *bovine*, cattle plague, rinderpest. **pester** (te) *v.i*, to rail (*contre* = at). **pestiféré, e** (tifere) *a. & n* plague-stricken (person). **pestilentiel, le** (lãsjɛl) *a*, pestilential.

pet (pɛ) *m*, fart. *ne pas valoir un* ~ *de lapin*, to be worthless. **péter** (te) *v.i*, to fart. ~ *dans la soie*, to be very rich. ~ *plus haut que le cul*, to show off; bite off more than one can chew (*both slang*).

pétale (petal) *m*, petal.

pétarade (petarad) *f*, sp[l]utter; frisking. **pétarader** (de) *v.i*, to sp[l]utter. **pétard** (ta:r) *m*, shot, blast; detonator, fog signal; firecracker; scandal (*news*). **pétarder** (tarde) *v.t*, to blow up, blast.

pétaudière (petodjɛ:r) *f*, bedlam, bear garden.

pète-sec (pɛtsɛk) *m*, martinet.

pétiller (petije) *v.i*, to crackle; sparkle; fizz[le], bubble [over].

pétiole (pesjɔl) *m*, petiole, leaf stalk.

petiot, e (pətjo, ɔt), tiny, wee. ¶ *n*, dot, tot, chickabiddy. **petit, e** (ti, it) *a*, little, small; short; diminutive; young; junior; low, slow; lesser; minor; petty; slight;

light; mean; retail. **petit,** *comps*:
au ~ *bonheur*, I'll risk it, come
what may; hit or miss. *le P~
Chaperon rouge*, Little Red Riding Hood. ~ *chat*, kitten. ~
chien, pup[py]. ~ *comité*, select
party, informal gathering. *le ~
commerce*, [the] small traders,
tradespeople, the retail trade. ~
commis, office boy. *le ~ déjeuner*, coffee & rolls, early morning coffee. ~ *enfant*, little child,
infant. ~*s-enfants*, grandchildren.
~*fils*, grandson, -child. *au ~ galop*, at a canter. ~*s jeux*, parlor
games, forfeits. *le ~ jour*, daybreak. ~ *juif*, funny bone. ~*lait*,
whey. ~ *lieu*, ~ *endroit*, privy.
~*-maître*, fop, coxcomb. ~ *ménage*, miniature (*or* dolls') home
set. *le ~ monde*, little people; the
lower classes; the child world. *le
~Noël*, a Christmas present (*to
a child*). ~ *nom*, Christian name.
~ *nom d'amitié*, pet name. ~
pain, roll. *le ~ peuple*, [the] common people. ~*s pois*, green peas.
~ *salé*, pickled pork. ~ *salon*, sitting room, parlor. ~ *trot*, jogtrot.
petite, *comps*: ~ *chatte*, kitten. ~
correspondance, answers to correspondents. *la ~ épargne*, the small
investor. ~*fille*, grand-daughter,
grandchild. ~ *gorgée*, sip. ~
guerre, mimic war. *à ~s journées*,
by easy stages. ~ *largeur*, single
width (*cloth*). *à ~ mentalité*,
mentally deficient. ~ *multiplication*, low gear. ~ *noblesse*, gentry.
~ *pédale*, soft pedal. *une ~ santé*,
poor health. ~*s tables*, separate
tables (*meal*). ~ *vérole*, smallpox. ~ *vérole volante*, chicken
pox. *en ~ vitesse* (*Rly.*), by slow
train; by freight train. **petit, e, n,**
little boy, l. girl, l. one. **un petit,**
a young one, cub, pup, whelp.
les petits, the small, the little
(*people*); little things. **petitement**
(titmã) *ad*, meanly; pettily. **petitesse** (tɛs) *f*, littleness, small-
ness; shortness; pettiness.

pétition (petisjɔ̃) *f*, petition. ~
de principe, begging the question. *faire une ~ de principe*, to
beg the question. **pétitionnaire**
(sjɔnɛːr) *n*, petitioner. **pétition-**

ner (ne) *v.i*, to petition.
peton (pətɔ̃) *m*, tiny foot, tootsy
[-wootsy].
pétoncle (petɔ̃ːkl) *f*, scallop
(*Mol.*).
pétrel (petrɛl) *m*, storm[y] petrel.
pétrification (petrifikasjɔ̃) *f*,
petrifaction. **pétrifier** (fje) *v.t*,
to petrify.
pétrin (petrɛ̃) *m*, kneading
trough; fix, mess. **pétrir** (triːr)
v.t, to knead, work, make; shape;
steep. **pétrissage** (trisaːʒ) *m*,
kneading, etc.
pétrochimie (petrɔʃimi) *f*, petrochemistry. **pétrochimique** (mik) *a*,
petrochemical.
pétrole (petrɔl) *m*, petroleum,
oil. ~ *à brûler*. ~ *lampant* (lɑ̃pɑ̃),
paraffin [oil], kerosene. **pétrolier,
ère** (lje, ɛːr) *a*, petroleum, oil
(*att.*) [*navire*] *pétrolier*, tanker.
pétulant, e (petylɑ̃, ɑ̃ːt) *a*, lively,
impetuous.
pétunia (petynja) *m*, petunia.
peu (pø) *ad*, little, not much; few,
not many; not very. ¶ *m*, little;
bit; few; lack; little while. *à ~
[de chose] près*, about, nearly.
peulven (pølvɛn) *m*, menhir.
peuplade (pœplad) *f*, tribe. **peuple** (pl) *m*, people, nation; tribe.
¶ *a*, plebeian, common. **peupler**
ple) *v.t*, to people, populate;
stock, plant; fill; (*v.i.*) to multiply.
peuplier (pœplie) *m*, poplar.
peur (pœːr) *f*, fear, fright. *avoir ~*,
to be afraid. *faire ~*, to frighten.
de ~ que, lest. **peureux, euse**†
(pœrø, ø:z) *a*, timid, nervous.
peut-être (pœtɛːtr) *ad. & m*, perhaps, maybe, perchance, possibly.
phaéton (faetɔ̃) *m*, phaeton.
phalange (falɑ̃ːʒ) *f*, phalanx;
host.
phalène (falɛn) *f*, moth.
phantasme (fɑ̃tasm) *m*, phantasm.
pharaon (faraɔ̃) *m*, Pharaoh; faro
(*cards*).
phare (faːr) *m*, lighthouse; light;
beacon; headlight, headlamp. ~
anti-éblouissant, ~*-code*, antidazzle lamp *or* light. ~ *anti-
brouillard*, fog light. ~ *de croise-*

ment, courtesy l. ~ *de roulement*, taxi l.

pharisaïque (farizaik) *a*, Pharisaic(al). **pharisien** (zjɛ̃) *m*, Pharisee.

pharmaceutique (farmasøtik) *a*, pharmaceutical. **pharmacie** (si) *f*, pharmacy; dispensary; drug store; medicine chest. **pharmacien, ne** (sjɛ̃, ɛn) *n*, druggist; pharmacist.

pharyngite (farɛ̃ʒit) *f*, pharyngitis, relaxed throat. **pharynx** (rɛ̃;ks) *m*, pharynx.

phase (fɑ;z) *f*, phase; stage.

phébus (feby;s) *m*, bombast, fustian.

phénicien, ne (fenisjɛ̃, ɛn) *a*, Phoenician.

phénix (feniks) *m*, phoenix; paragon.

phénol (fenɔl) *ou* **acide phénique** (nik) *m*, phenol, carbolic acid.

phénoménal, e (fenɔmenal) *a*, phenomenal. **phénomène** (mɛn) *m*, phenomenon; freak [of nature].

Philadelphie (filadɛlfi) *f*, Philadelphia.

philanthrope (filɑ̃trɔp) *n*, philanthropist. **philanthropie** (pi) *f*, philanthropy. **philanthropique** (pik) *a*, philanthropic.

philatélisme (filatelism) *m*, philately. **philatéliste** (list) *n*, philatelist.

philharmonique (filarmɔnik) *a*, philharmonic.

philippique (filipik) *f*, philippic.

philistin (filistɛ̃) *m*, Philistine.

philologie (filɔlɔʒi) *f*, philology. **philologue** (lɔg) *m*, philologist.

philosophe (filɔzɔf) *n*, philosopher; student in philosophy. ¶ *a*, philosophic(al) (*calm*). **philosopher** (fe) *v.i*, to philosophize. **philosophie** (fi) *f*, philosophy. **philosophique†** (fik) *a*, philosophic(al).

philtre (filtr) *m*, philter, love potion.

phlébite (flebit) *f*, phlebitis.

phlox (flɔks) *m*, phlox.

phobie (fɔbi) *f*, morbid fear, dread.

phonétique (fɔnetik) *a*, pho-

netic. ¶ *f*, phonetics. **phonographe** (nɔgraf) *m*, phonograph. ~*coffret*, tabletop phonograph.

phoque (fɔk) *m*, seal (*Zool.*).

phosphate (fɔsfat) *m*, phosphate. **phosphore** (fɔ;r) *m*, phosphorus. **phosphorescence** (forɛsɑ̃;s) *f*, phosphorescence. **phosphorescent, e** (sɑ̃, ɑ̃;t) *a*, phosphorescent.

photographe (fɔtɔgraf) *n*, photographer. ~ *de plateau*, still photographer (*cinema*). **photographie** (fi) *f*, photography; photograph. **photographier** (fje) *v.t*, to photograph. **photographique** (fik) *a*, photographic. **photogravure** (vy;r) *f*, photogravure. **photojumelle**, *f*, binocular camera.

phrase (frɑ;s) *f*, sentence; phrase. ~*s à effet*, claptrap. **phraséologie** (frazeɔlɔʒi) *f*, phraseology. **phraser** (ze) *v.t. & i*, to phrase.

phrénologie (frenɔlɔʒi) *f*, phrenology. **phrénologiste** (ʒist) *m*, phrenologist.

phtisie (ftizi) *f*, phthisis, consumption. **phtisique** (zik) *a. & n*, consumptive.

physicien, ne (fizisjɛ̃, ɛn) *n*, physicist.

physiologie (fizjɔlɔʒi) *f*, physiology.

physionomie (fizjɔnɔmi) *f*, physiognomy, face, countenance; aspect; character.

physique† (fizik) *a*, physical; bodily. ¶ *f*, physics. ¶ *m*, physique.

piaffer (pjafe) *v.i*, to paw the ground; prance.

piailler (pjaje) *v.i*, to cheep; screech.

pianiste (pjanist) *n*, pianist. **piano** (no) *m*, piano[forte]. ~ *à demi-queue*, baby grand[piano]. ~ *à queue*, [concert] grand piano. ~ *droit*, upright piano. ~ *mécanique*, piano player, player piano; piano organ. ~ *oblique*, overstrung piano.

piaule (pjo;l) *f*, pad, digs, room, place (*where one lives*).

piauler (pjole) *v.i*, to cheep; whimper.

pic (pik) *m*, pick; peak; woodpecker. *à ~*, sheer, precipitous.

piccolo (pikɔlo) *m*, piccolo.

piohet (piʃɛ) *m*, pitcher; small jug.

pick-up (pikœp) *m*, phonograph.

picorer (pikɔre) *v.i*, to forage, peck.

picot (piko) *m*, splinter; barb; picot. **picoté de petite vérole** (kɔte), pockmarked. **picoter** (te) *v.t*, to prick; pit; peck; sting, make smart, make tingle; tease.

picotin (pikɔtɛ̃) *m*, peck.

piorate (pikrat) *m*, cheap wine (*slang*).

piotural, e (piktyral) *a*, pictorial.

pie (pi) *f*, magpie. ¶ *a*, piebald; charitable (*works*).

pièce (pjɛs) *f*, piece; bit; fragment; part; man (*chess*); head (*cattle*, *game*); joint (*meat*); document; paper; tip (*gratuity*); cask, barrel; puncheon; gun; room (*house*). [*la*] *~*, apiece, each. *~ à conviction*, exhibit (*criminal law*). *~ à succès*, hit. *~ à thèse*, problem play. *~ d'artifice*, firework. *~ d'eau*, ornamental lake. *~ [coulée]*, casting. *~ [de monnaie]*, coin. *~ de rechange*, spare [part]. *~ [de théâtre]*, [stage] play. *~ historique*, costume piece, c. play. *~ justificative*, *~ à l'appui*, exhibit (*civil law*); voucher (*Com.*). *~ moulée*, molding, cast.

pied (pje) *m*, foot; trotter; base, bottom; leg (*chair*); stalk; footing; foothold; stand; standard. *~-à-terre*, *m*, small apartment in town. *~ [à trois branches]*, tripod. *~-d'alouette*, larkspur, delphinium. *~-debiche*, claw [bar] forceps. *~-droit*, pier (*of arch*). *~-fumeur*, smoker's stand. *au ~ de la lettre*, literally. *avoir le ~ marin*, to have got one's sea legs. *mettre sur ~*, to establish. *sur ~*, on foot; standing (*crops*). *faire un ~ de nez*, to thumb one's nose. *prendre son ~*, to have an orgasm (*slang*). **piédestal** (pjedɛstal) *m*, pedestal.

pied-noir (pjɛnwaːr) *m* & *f*, Algerian-born French citizen (*generally one who has been repatriated*).

piège (pjɛːʒ) *m*, trap, snare, pit-

fall. **piéger** (e) *v.t*, to snare, entrap.

pie-grièche (pigrjɛʃ) *f*, shrike; shrew (*pers.*).

Piémont (le) (pjemɔ̃), Piedmont.

pierraille (pjɛrɑːj) *f*, small stones. **pierre** (pjɛːr) *f*, stone. *~ à aiguiser*, grindstone; hone. *~ [à briquet]* & *~ à fusil*, flint. *~ à chaux*, *~ calcaire*, limestone. *~ à gué*, stepping stone. *~ blanche*, hearthstone. *~ d'achoppement* (aʃɔpmɑ̃), stumbling block, snag. *~ d'aimant*, loadstone, lodestone. *~ de lune*, moonstone. *~ de taille*, freestone. *~ de touche*, touchstone (*lit. & fig.*); test. *~ philosophale* (filɔzɔfal), philosophers' stone. *~ précieuse*, precious stone, gem [stone]. *~ tombale* (tɔ̃bal), *~ tumulaire*

pierrot (pjɛro) *m*, pierrot, clown; sparrow.

piété (pjete) *f*, piety, godliness; devotion.

piétiner (pjetine) *v.t*, to trample on, stamp on; tread; (*v.i.*) to dance (*with rage*). *~ sur place*, to mark time (*fig.*). **piéton, ne** (tɔ̃, ɔn) *n*, pedestrian, foot passenger; walker.

piètre† (pjɛtr) *a*, wretched, poor, shabby.

pieu (pjø) *m*, stake, post; pile.

pieuvre (pjœːvr) *f*, octopus.

pieux, euse† (pjø, øːz) *a*, pious, godly; reverent.

pige (piːʒ) *f*, arbitrary measure; year (*of age, penal servitude*). **piger** (ʒe) *v.t*, to look at, admire; understand. *se faire ~*, to get caught.

pigeon, ne (piʒɔ̃, ɔn) *n*, pigeon, dove; greenhorn, gull. *~ artificiel*, clay bird. *~ grosse gorge*, pouter. *~ ramier*, wood pigeon, ring dove. *~ voyageur*, carrier pigeon, homing p. **pigeonneau** (ʒɔno) *m*, young pigeon, squab; gull, dupe. **pigeonnier** (nje) *m*, dovecote.

pigment (pigmɑ̃) *m*, pigment.

pignocher (piɲɔʃe) *v.i*, to pick at one's food.

pignon (piɲɔ̃) *m*, gable; pinion. *~ de chaîne*, sprocket wheel.

pilastre (pilastr) *m*, pilaster; newel.

pile (pil) *f*, pile, heap; stack (*of wood*); pier (*bridge*); battery, cell (*Elec.*); reverse (*coin*); reactor (*nuclear*). ~ *ou face?* heads or tails?

piler (pile) *v.t*, to pound, pestle, grind.

pilier (pilje) *m*, pillar, column, post.

pillage (pija:ʒ) *m*, pillage, looting; pilfering. **piller** (je) *v.t*, to pillage, plunder, loot, sack, ransack; pilfer; seize, worry (*of dog*).

pilon (pilɔ̃) *m*, pestle; stamp (*ore*); rammer; hammer (*power*); drumstick (*fowl*). **pilonner** (ne) *v.t*, to pound; pulp; flatten (*military target*).

pilori (pilɔri) *m*, pillory. **pilorier** (rje) *v.t*, to pillory, gibbet.

pilotage (pilɔta:ʒ) *m*, pile work; piloting; attitude control. *bloc de* ~, automatic pilot. **pilote** (lɔt) *m*, pilot. ~ *d'essai*, test pilot. *industrie* ~, key industry. **piloter** (te) *v.t*, to pile; pilot; guide. ~ *dans*, to show (*pers.*) round (*town*). **pilotis** (ti) *m*, pile (*stake*); piling.

pilou (pilu) *m*, flannelette.

pilule (pilyl) *f*, pill.

pimbêche (pɛ̃bɛʃ) *f*, conceited woman.

piment (pimɑ̃) *m*, pimento, capsicum, allspice. **pimenter** (te) *v.t*, to spice.

pimpant, e (pɛ̃pɑ̃, ɑ̃:t) *a*, smart, spruce, spick & span.

pin (pɛ̃) *m*, pine [tree], fir [tree]. ~ *du Chili*, Chili pine, monkey puzzle.

pinacle (pinakl) *m*, pinnacle.

pince (pɛ̃:s) *f*, grip, hold; (*oft. pl.*) pliers, nippers; forceps; tweezers; tongs; (*s.*) clip; clamp; crowbar; claw, nipper (*crab, etc.*); pleat; hand (*slang*). ~*s à épiler*, eyebrow tweezers. ~*monseigneur*, *f*, jimmy (*burglar's*). ~*nez*, *m*, eyeglasses. ~*sans-rire*, *m*, man of dry humor. **pincé, e** (pɛse) *a*, affected, prim; stiff; wry; pursed (*lips*).

pinceau (pɛso) *m*, paintbrush; brush; touch (*fig.*); pencil (*Opt.*). ~ *à barbe*, shaving brush.

pincée (pɛse) *f*, pinch (*snuff, etc.*). **pincer** (se) *v.t*, to pinch, nip, squeeze; purse (*lips*); pluck (*strings*); play (*harp, etc.*), twang; grip; catch. **pincettes** (sɛt) *f.pl*, tweezers; tongs (*fire*). **pinçon** (s5) *m*, mark, bruise (*left on the skin by a pinch*).

pine (pin) *f*, penis (*obscene*).

pineraie (pinrɛ) *f*, pine wood (*forest*).

pingouin (pɛ̃gwɛ̃) *m*, auk. ~ *royal*, king penguin.

pingre (pɛ̃:gr) *a*, stingy. ¶ *m*, skinflint.

pinnule (pinnyl) *f*, pinnule; sight [vane].

pinson (pɛ̃sɔ̃) *m*, finch; chaffinch.

pintade (pɛtad) *f*, guinea fowl.

pioche (pjɔʃ) *f*, pick; pickaxe; mattock. **piocher** (ʃe) *v.t. & i*, to pick up; work hard, grind.

piolet (pjɔlɛ) *m*, ice axe.

pion (pjɔ̃) *m*, pawn (*chess*); man (*checkers*).

pionnier (pjɔnje) *m*, pioneer.

pipe (pip) *f*, pipe (*cask, tobacco*); cigarette (*slang*). *se fendre la* ~, to split one's side laughing. **pipeau** (po) *m*, [reed] pipe; lime twig; bird call. **pipée** (pe) *f*, bird catching. **piper** (pe) *v.t*, to lure (*birds*); dupe; load (*dice*); mark (*card*).

pipi[t] (pipi[t]) *m*, pipit, titlark.

piplet (piplɛ) *m*, concierge (*slang*).

piquant, e (pikɑ̃, ɑ̃:t) *a*, prickly; stinging; cutting; pointed; pungent; racy; piquant. ¶ *m*, prickle; sting; quill (*porcupine*); spike; pungency; point, zest, pith. **pique** (pik) *f*, pike (*weapon*); pique, spite; tiff; (*m.*) spade[s] (*cards*). ~*-nique* (nik) *m*, picnic. ~*-notes*, *m*, bill file. ~*-assiette* (asʃɛt) *m. & f*, freeloader. **piqué, e** (ke) *a*, quilted; padded; staccato (*notes*); crazy. ~ *des mouches*, flyblown. ~ *des vers*, worm-eaten, motheaten. ¶ *m*, quilting. **piquer** (ke) *v.t*, to prick; sting; bite; spur; goad; prod; nettle; pique; puncture; pit; lard; stitch; quilt; nibble (*fish*); stick; scale (*boiler*). ~ *du nez*, to nose dive (*Avn.*). se ~, to pride oneself; take offense; turn sour (*wine*). **piquet** (kɛ) *m*, peg, stake; picket; piquet (*cards*). **piqueter** (te) *v.t*, to stake out (*claim*); picket. **piqueur** (kœːr) *m*, whipper-in, huntsman; stud groom. **piqueuse** (køːz) *f*, stitcher, sewer (*pers.*). **piqûre** (kyːr) *f*, injection; vaccination; prick; sting; bite; puncture; pit, hole; spot, speck; quilting.

pirate (pirat) *m*, pirate. **pirater** (te) *v.i*, to pirate. **piraterie** (tri) *f*, piracy.

pire (piːr) *a*, worse. le ~, the worst.

Pirée (le) (pire), Piraeus.

pirogue (pirɔg) *f*, canoe. ~ *de barre*, surf boat. ~ *en écorce*, birch-bark canoe.

pirouette (pirwɛt) *f*, whirling; pirouette. **pirouetter** (te) *v.i*, to pirouette, twirl.

pis (pi) *m*, udder, dug.

pis (pi) *ad*, worse. le ~, the worst. ~ *aller*, *m*, last resource; makeshift. *au* ~ *aller*, at the worst.

pisciculture (pisikyltyːr) *f*, pisciculture. **piscine** (sin) *f*, swimming pool.

Pise (piːz) *f*, Pisa.

pissenlit (pisɑ̃li) *m*, dandelion.

pistache (pistaʃ) *f*, pistachio [nut]. **pistachier** (ʃje) *m*, pistachio tree.

piste (pist) *f*, track (*running, racing*); run (*toboggan*); rink (*skating*); racecourse; runway (*Avn.*); track, trail, scent, clue; sound track (*cinema*). ~ *de cirque*, ring. ~ *en cendrée*, cinder track; dirt t. **pister** (te) *v.t*, to track; tail someone (*slang*).

pistil (pistil) *m*, pistil.

pistolet (pistɔlɛ) *m*, pistol.

piston (pistɔ) *m*, piston; cornet (*Mus.*); influence, pull (*slang*). **pistonner** (tɔne) *v.t*, to pull strings for someone.

pitchpin (pitʃpɛ̃) *m*, pitchpine.

piteux, euse† (pitø, øːz) *a*, piteous, woeful, pitiable; sorry. **pitié** (tje) *f*, pity, mercy.

piton (pitɔ̃) *m*, screw eye; peak (*mountain*).

pitoyable† (pitwajabl) *a*, pitiable, pitiful; wretched, paltry.

pitre (piːtr) *m*, clown; buffoon.

pittoresque† (pitɔresk) *a*, picturesque, beauty (*spot*); quaint; graphic; pictorial (*magazine*). ¶ *m*, picturesqueness.

pituite (pitɥit) *f*, phlegm, mucus.

pivoine (pivwan) *f*, peony.

pivot (pivo) *m*, pivot, pin; tap root; crux. **pivoter** (vɔte) *v.i*, to pivot, turn, hinge; slew; wheel (*Mil.*).

pix (pi) (*Geog.*) *m*, pap, mamelon.

placage (plakaːʒ) *m*, veneering; patchwork (*fig.*).

placard (plakaːr) *m*, wall cupboard; placard, poster, bill; galley [proof]. **placarder** (karde) *v.t*, to post (*bills*); placard.

place (plas) *f*, place; room; way; stead; seat; fare; berth; spot; patch; ground; town; market; square (*in town*); churchyard (*public square surrounding a church or cathedral*). ~ *aux dames!* ladies first! ~ *d'armes*, parade ground, drill g. ~ [*de voitures*], cabstand. ~*s debout seulement!* standing room only! ~ *dénudée d'herbes*, bare patch (*golf*). ~ *forte*, ~ *de guerre*, fortified place. **placement** (smɑ̃) *m*, placing; investment. *bureau de* ~, employment agency. **placer** (se) *v.t*, to place, put, set; dispose of; deposit; invest (*money*).

placer (plasɛːr) (*Min.*) *m*, placer, diggings.

placide† (plasid) *a*, placid. **placidité** (dite) *f*, placidity.

placier (plasje) *m*, canvasser, salesman.

plafond (plafɔ̃) *m*, ceiling; maximum, peak [figure]. **plafonner** (fɔne) *v.t*, to ceil. **plafonnier** (nje) *m*, ceiling fixture (*light*).

plage (plaːʒ) *f*, beach, shore; seaside resort; sands.

plagiaire (plaʒjɛːr) *m*, plagiarist. **plagiat** (ʒja) *m*, plagiarism. **plagier** (ʒje) *v.t*, to plagiarize.

plaid (plɛd) *m*, plaid; traveling rug.

plaider (plɛde) *v.i. & t*, to plead, argue. **plaideur, euse** (dœːr, ø:z) *n*, litigant; suitor. **plaidoirie** (dwari) *f*, pleading; counsel's speech. **plaidoyer** (dwaje) *m*, speech for the defense.

plaie (plɛ) *f*, wound, sore; evil; plague.

plaignant, e (plɛɲɑ̃, ɑ̃:t) *n*, plaintiff, prosecutor.

plain, e (plɛ̃, ɛn) *a*, plain; open. **plain-chant**, *m*, plainsong. **de plain-pied**, on one floor, on a level.

plaindre (plɛ̃:dr) *v.t.ir*, to pity, be sorry for. **se ~**, to complain; moan, groan.

plaine (plɛn) *f*, plain (*Phys. Geog.*).

plainte (plɛ̃:t) *f*, moan, groan; complaint; action (*law*). **plaintif, ive†** (plɛtif, i:v) *a*, plaintive, doleful; querulous.

plaire (plɛːr) *v.t.ir*, to please. *s'il vous plaît*, [if you] please. *plût au ciel que . . .*, would to heaven that . . . **~ à**, to please (*v.t.*). **se ~**, to be pleased; like; thrive. **plaisamment** (plɛzamɑ̃) *ad*, funnily; ludicrously. **de plaisance** (zɑ̃:s), pleasure (*boat*); weekend (*cottage*). **Plaisance**, *f*, Piacenza. **plaisant, e** (zɑ̃, ɑ̃:t) *a*, funny, droll, jocular; comical; ludicrous; pleasant. ¶ *m*, wag, joker, fool; comical side. **plaisanter** (zɑ̃te) *v.i*, to joke, jest, trifle; (*v.t.*) to chaff. **plaisanterie** (tri) *f*, joke, jest; fun. **plaisir** (zi:r) *m*, pleasure, delight; treat; convenience; will; sake; amusement, enjoyment; cone, cornet, wafer (*ice cream*). *à ~*, gratuitously.

plan, e (plɑ̃, an) *a*, plane, even, level, flat. ¶ *m*, plane, level; ground (*of painting*); plan; map; table; project, scheme; shot (*cinema, TV*). **~ américain**, medium close shot. **~ d'archives**, stock s. **~ cassé**, angle s. **~ d'essai**, test s. **~ moyen**, medium s. **~ séquence**, deep-focus s. **~ serré**, close-up s. **~ de situation**, establishing s. **gros ~**, close-up. **~ des support**, media planning.

planche (plɑ̃:ʃ) *f*, board; shelf; bed (*Hort.*); plate (*Typ.*). **~ de salut**, sheet anchor (*fig.*). *faire la ~*, to float (*Swim.*). **planchéier** (plɑ̃ʃeje) *v.t*, to board; floor. **plancher** (ʃe) *m*, floor. *le ~ des vaches*, terra firma. **planchette** (ʃɛt) *f*, slat; plane table (*Surv.*).

plancton (plɑ̃ktɔ̃) *m*, plankton.

plane (plan) *m*, plane [tree]; (*f.*) drawing knife.

planer (plane) *v.t*, to smooth; plane; planish; (*v.i.*) to soar; hover; look down; glide (*Avn.*) fly (*drugs*).

planétaire (planetɛ:r) *a*, planetary. ¶ *m*, planetarium, orrery. **planète** (nɛt) *f*, planet. *heureuse ~*, lucky star (*fig.*).

planeur (planœ:r) *m*, planisher (*pers.*); glider (*Avn.*).

planification (planifikasjɔ̃) *f*, planning (*computers*). **~ des naissances**, family planning. **planifier** (ifje) *v.i*, to plan (*political economy*).

plant (plɑ̃) *m*, sapling, set, slip; plantation. **plantage** (ta:ʒ) *m*, planting; plantation. **plantain** (tɛ̃) *m*, plantain (*Plantago*). **plantanier** (tanje) *m*, plantain (*banana*). **plantation** (sjɔ̃) *f*, planting; plantation. **plante** (plɑ̃:t) *f*, sole (*foot*); plant (*Bot.*). **~ annuelle**, annual. **~ marine**, seaweed. **~ potagère**, vegetable. **~ vivace**, perennial. **planter** (plɑ̃te) *v.t*, to plant, set. **planteur, euse** (tœ:r, ø:z) *n*, planter; grower. **plantoir** (twa:r) *m*, dibble. **planton** (tɔ̃) (*Mil.*) *m*, orderly; o. duty.

planque (plɑ̃:k) *f*, hiding place; sinecure (*slang*).

plantureux, euse† (plɑ̃tyrø, ø:z) *a*, copious; fleshy; fertile.

planure (plany:r) *f*, shaving[s].

plaque (plak) *f*, plate; sheet; slab; plaque; tablet; badge. **~ d'identité**, identity badge. **~ minéralogique**, car license-plate. **~ de gazon**, turf, sod. **~ tournante**, turntable (*Rly.*). **plaqué** (ke) *m*, electroplate. **plaquer** (ke) *v.t*, to plate; veneer; lay on; cake; lay down (*turf*); jilt, leave flat. **pla-**

quette (kɛt) f, thin slab or plate; disc; booklet.

plastique (plastik) a, plastic.

plastron (plastrɔ̃) m, breast-plate; front (*shirt*); butt (*pers., fig.*). **plastronner** (ne) v.i, to pose; put on the dog.

plat, e (pla, at) a, flat; level; lank, straight (*hair*); smooth (*sea*); dead (*calm*); dull, bald (*fig.*). à ~, flat. *à plat* [*ventre*], flat on one's face. ¶ m, flat; blade (*oar*); side, board (*book*); pan (*scale*); dish; mess; course (*dinner*). ~ *de quête*, collection plate. ~ *du jour*, special dish for the day.

platane (platan) m, plane [tree].

plat-bord (plabɔːr) m, gunwale, gunnel.

plate (plat) f, punt (*boat*).

plateau (plato) m, tray; salver; pan (*scale*); dish (*soap*); stage, platform (*Theat.*); plateau, table land; upland; plate, table; face plate, chuck (*lathe*). ~ *roulant*, service wagon.

plate-bande (platbɑ̃ːd) (*Hort.*) m, border; bed.

platée (plate) f, dishful.

plate-forme (platfɔrm) f, platform, stage; flat roof.

platement (platmɑ̃) ad, flatly; dully.

platine (platin) f, plate, platen; stage (*microscope*); lock (*firearm*). ¶ m, platinum.

platitude (platityd) f, flatness (*fig.*), dullness; platitude.

platonique (platɔnik) a, Platonic.

plâtre (plɑːtr) m, plaster; p. cast. ~ *de moulage*, p. of Paris. **plâtrer** (platre) v.t, to plaster. **plâtrier** (trie) m, plasterer. **plâtrière** (ɛːr) f, gypsum quarry.

plausible† (plozibl) a, plausible.

plébéien, ne (plebejɛ̃, ɛn) a, plebeian. **plébiscite** (bisit) m, plebiscite, referendum.

plein, e† (plɛ̃, ɛn) a, full; replete; fraught; whole; mid; high (*tide, seas*); solid; open; pregnant (*animals*). ~ *comme un œuf*, chock full. *en plein jour, en plein midi*, in broad daylight. *faire le* ~, fill it

up (*gas, water, etc.*). ¶ m, plenum; full; height; thick stroke, downstroke. **plénier, ère** (plenje, ɛːr) a, full; plenary. **plénipotentiaire** (nipɔtɑ̃sjɛːr) m. & att, plenipotentiary. **plénitude** (tyd) f, plenitude, fullness; repletion.

pléonasme (pleɔnasm) m, pleonasm.

pléthore (pletɔːr) f, plethora, glut.

pleur (plœːr) m. usually pl, tear. **pleurard, e** (plœraːr, ard) n, whimperer; (*att.*) whimpering; tearful; maudlin (*voice*). **pleurer** (re) v.i. & t, to weep; mourn; bewail; cry; water, run (*eyes*); drip; bleed.

pleurésie (plœrezi) f, pleurisy.

pleureur, euse (plœrœːr, ∅ːz) n, whimperer; mute, [hired] mourner; (*att.*) weeping. **pleurnicher** (niʃe) v.i, to whimper, whine, snivel.

pleutre (pl∅ːtr) m, cad.

pleuvoir (plœvwaːr) v.i.ir, to rain; pour, shower.

plèvre (plɛvr) f, pleura.

plexus (plɛksyːs) m, plexus.

pli (pli) m, fold; pleat; wrinkle, pucker, crease; bend; ply; cover, envelope. *mise en* ~, hairset, wave. *sous ce* ~, enclosed. **pliable** (abl) a, pliable. **pliant, e** (ɑ̃, ɑ̃ːt) a, pliant; folding. ¶ m, camp stool.

plie (pli) f, plaice.

plier (plie) v.t. & t, to fold; strike (*tent*); bend; bow. ~ *bagage*, to pack up; decamp; die.

plinthe (plɛ̃ːt) f, plinth; skirting [board].

plisser (plise) v.t. & i, to pleat; fold; kilt; crease, crumple, wrinkle, crinkle, pucker.

plomb (plɔ̃) m, lead; shot; came; plumb, plummet; plomb (*Cust.*); sink; ballast (*fig.*). ~ [*fusible*], fuse (*Elec.*). *faire sauter un* ~, to blow a fuse. *à* ~, upright. **plombage** (baːʒ) m, plumbing; filling (*teeth*). **plombagine** (baʒin) f, plumbago, graphite, black lead. **plomber** (be) v.t, to lead, plumb; plomb; fill (*tooth*). **plomberie** (bri) m, plumbing; lead works. **plombier** (bje) m, plumber.

plombe (plɔ̃be) *f*, hour (*slang*). *j'ai attendu trois ~s*, I waited three hours.

plongée (plɔ̃ʒe) *f*, high-angle shot (*cinema, TV*).

plongeoir (plɔ̃ʒwaːr) *m*, diving board. **plongeon** (ʒɔ̃) *m*, diver (*bird*); dive, plunge. **plonger** (ʒe) *v.i. & t*, to plunge; dive; submerge; dip; duck; immerse; thrust. **plongeur, euse** (ʒœːr, øːz) *n*, diver (*Swim.*); (*m.*) diver (*in diving dress*); dishwasher (*man*); plunger (*pump*).

plot (plo) *m*, stud (*Elec. contact*).

ployer (plwaje) *v.t. & i*, to bend, bow; wrap up; give way.

pluie (plɥi) *f*, rain; shower; wet. *~ d'or*, golden rain (*fireworks*).

plumage (plymaːʒ) *m*, plumage, feathers. **plumard** (aːr) *m*, feather duster; bed (*slang*). **plumasserie** (masri) *f*, feather trade. **plume** (plym) *f*, feather (*bird & Box.*); pen. *~* [*à écrire*], nib; bed. *~ d'oie*, quill [pen]. *sans ~s*, unfledged, callow. **plumeau** (mo) *m*, feather duster; eiderdown quilt. **plumée** (me) *f*, penful, dip (*ink*). **plumer** (me) *v.t*, to pluck; fleece (*fig.*); (*v.i.*) to feather (*rowing*). **plumet** (mɛ) *m*, plume. **plumeux, euse** (mø, øːz) *a*, feathery, plumose. **plumier** (mje) *m*, pen tray, pencilcase. **plumitif** (mitif) *m*, minute book; quill driver.

plupart (la) (plypaːr), most, the generality, the majority.

plural, e (plyral) *a*, plural (*vote*). **pluralité** (lite) *f*, plurality; majority. **pluriel, le** (rjɛl) *a. & m*, plural (*Gram.*).

plus (ply; *finally only* plys; *in liaison*, plyz) *ad*, more; -er (*suffix forming comparatives*); longer; any l., anymore. **le ~**, the most; -est (*suffix forming superlatives*). [*signe*] ~ (plys) *m*, plus [sign]. **plusieurs** (zjœːr) *a. & pn*, several. **plusque-parfait** (plyskəparfɛ) *m*, pluperfect. **plus-value** (plyvaly) *f*, appreciation; surplus; [unearned] increment.

plutôt (plyto) *ad*, rather, sooner, instead.

pluvial, e (plyvjal) *a*, rain (*water*); rainy.

pluvier (plyvje) *m*, plover.

pluvieux, euse (plyvjø, øːz) *a*, rainy; wet.

pneumatique (pnømatik) (*abb.* **pneu**) *m*, [pneumatic] tire. ¶ *a*, pneumatic, air (*att.*); express letter (*in Paris*).

pneumonie (pnømɔni) *f*, pneumonia.

Pô (le) (po), the Po (*river*).

pochade (pɔʃad) *f*, rapid sketch.

pochard (pɔʃaːr) *m*, drunkard. **pocharder (se)** (de) *v.t*, to make drunk. *se ~*, to get drunk.

poche (pɔʃ) *f*, pocket; sack; pouch; case; crop (*bird*); ladle; pucker. *~ rapportée*, patch pocket. **pocher** (ʃe) *v.t*, to poach (*eggs*); black (*eye*); dash off (*sketch*). **pochette** (ʃɛt) *f*, pocket; pocket case, packet. *~ en soie, de couleur*, silk colored handkerchief. **pochoir** (ʃwaːr) *m*, stencil [plate].

poêle (pwaːl) *f*, frying pan; pan. ¶ *m*, pall; canopy; stove, range. *~ à pétrole*, oil heater. **poêlier** (pwalje) *m*, stove & range maker. **poêlon** (lɔ̃) *m*, saucepan, pipkin.

poème (pɔɛːm) *m*, poem. **poésie** (ezi) *f*, poetry; poem, piece of poetry. *~ enfantine*, nursery rhyme. **poète** (ɛt) *m*, poet. **poétereau** (etro) *m*, poetaster. **poétesse** (tɛs) *f*, poetess. **poétique†** (tik) *a*, poetic; poetical.

pognon (pɔɲɔ̃) *m*, money, dough, bread (*slang*).

poids (pwa) *m*, weight; shot (*in sport of putting the shot*); heaviness; burden, brunt. *~ spécifique*, specific gravity. *~lourd*, heavy truck.

poignant, e (pwaɲɑ̃, ɑ̃ːt) *a*, poignant.

poignard (pwaɲaːr) *m*, dagger, dirk, poignard. **poignarder** (narde) *v.t*, to stab, knife. **poigne** (pwaɲ) *f*, grip; energy. **poignée** (ɲe) *f*, handful; handle, grip, hilt; hank. *~ de main*, handshake. **poignet** (ɲɛ) *m*, wrist; wristband, cuff (*soft*).

poil (pwal) *m*, hair (*on animal & body pers.*); fur, coat; pile, nap; bristle; down (*plant*); energy.

~ *de chèvre d'Angora*, mohair.
~*follet*, down (*chin, etc.*). *à* ~,
naked; bareback. *à* ~ *ras*, short-
haired, smooth-haired (*dog*). *au*
~ *rude*, rough-haired, wirehaired
(*dog*). **poilu, e** (ly) *a*, hairy,
shaggy. ¶ *m*, French soldier.

poinçon (pwēsɔ̃) *m*, punch
(*solid*); awl, point; stamp; puncheon. ~ *de contrôle*, hallmark.
poinçonner (sɔne) *v.t*, to punch;
stamp; hallmark.

poindre (pwɛ̃ːdr) *v.i.ir*, to dawn,
break; come up.

poing (pwɛ̃) *m*, fist, hand.

point (pwɛ̃) *m*, point; dot; speck;
mark; tick; score (*games*); [full]
stop, period; note; stitch; point
[lace]; degree, extent; verge (*fig.*);
focus. ~ *à terre*, landmark
(*Naut.*). ~ *arrière*, backstitch.
~ *coupé*, cut openwork stitch.
~ *croisé*, herringboning. ~ *d'appui*, fulcrum. ~ *d'appui de la
flotte*, naval station (*foreign*).
~ *d'éclair*, ~ *d'inflammabilité*,
flash[ing] point. ~ *d'interrogation*, note of interrogation, question mark. ~ *d'ourlet*, hemming.
~ *de chaînette*, chain stitch. ~
de côté, stitch in the side (*Med.*).
~ *de croix*, cross-stitch. ~ *de
fuite*, vanishing point. ~ *de languette*, ~ *de feston*, blanket stitch,
buttonhole s. (*Emb.*). ~*de marque*, marking stitch. ~*de mire*,
aim; cynosure (*fig.*). ~ *de piqûre*,
lockstitch. ~ *de repère*, reference
mark, datum point; bench mark;
landmark (*fig.*). ~ *de surjet*,
oversewing stitch, seam s. ~ *de
tige*, ~ *coulé*, crewel s. ~ *de vue*,
point of view, standpoint. ~ *devant*, running stitch. ~ *du jour*,
daybreak, dawn. ~ & *virgule* ou
~*virgule*, *m*, semicolon. ~ *mort*,
dead center; neutral (*auto*). ~
chaud, trouble spot. ~ *de non-re-
tour*, point of no return. ~ *noir*,
blackhead. *à* ~, [just] in time, to
a turn. *à* ~ *nommé*, in the nick of
time; at the right moment.

point (pwɛ̃) *ad*, no, not at all, [not]
any.

pointage (pwɛ̃taːʒ) *m*, ticking
[off], checking; timekeeping; timing; scoring; aiming, pointing,
laying, training (*gun*).

pointe (pwɛ̃ːt) *f*, point (*sharp
end*); tip; head; top; peak; toe
(*shoe, sock*); (*pl.*) toe dancing;
center (*lathe*); nail, brad; touch;
quip, quirk. ~ *de Paris*, wire nail,
French n., sprig. ~ *de terre*,
headland, foreland. ~ *du jour*,
daybreak, dawn. *sur la* ~ *du pied*,
on tiptoe. ~ *sèche*, drypoint (*engraving*).

pointeau (pwɛ̃to) *m*, center
punch.

pointer (pwɛ̃te) *v.t*, to tick [off],
check, tally; point, aim, level,
lay, train; thrust; (*v.i.*) to soar;
appear, sprout. *se* ~, to show up
at a rendezvous (*slang*). **pointeur**
(tœːr) *m*, checker; timekeeper;
marker, scorer; gun layer. **pointille** (tiːj) *f*, punctilio. **pointiller**
(tije) *v.t*, to dot; stipple; bait;
(*v.i.*) to cavil; split hairs. **pointillerie** (jri) *f*, captiousness, hairsplitting. **pointilleux, euse** (jø, ∅ːz)
a, captious, touchy; fastidious,
punctilious.

pointu, e (pwɛ̃ty) *a*, pointed;
sharp; shrill.

pointure (pwɛ̃tyːr) *f*, size (*of
shoes, gloves, etc.*).

poire (pwaːr) *f*, pear; bulb, ball;
dupe; face (*slang*). **poire** (pware)
m, perry.

poireau (pwaro) *m*, leek; wart;
simpleton (*slang*). **poireauter** (te)
v.i, to be kept waiting (*slang*).

poirier (pwarje) *m*, pear tree;
pear wood.

pois (pwa) *m*, pea; dot (*Emb.*);
spot (*as on tie*). ~ *cassés*, split
peas. ~ *chinois*, soy[a] bean. ~
de senteur, sweet pea. *petit* ~,
~*verts*, green peas.

poison (pwazɔ̃) *m*, poison.

poissard, e (pwasaːr, ard) *a*, vulgar. ¶ *f*, fishwife.

poisse (pwas) *f*, bad luck. ¶ *m*,
thief; pimp.

poisser (pwase) *v.t*, to pitch; wax
(*thread*); make sticky. **poisseux,
euse** (sø, ∅ːz) *a*, sticky.

poisson (pwasɔ̃) *m*, fish. *faire un
~ d'avril à*, to make an April fool
of. ~ *de grand sport*, big-game
fish. ~ *de mer*, salt-water fish,
sea fish. ~ *rouge*, goldfish. *faire
une queue de* ~, to cut sharply in

front of another driver. **poissonnaille** (sɔnɑːj) f, fry. **poissonnerie**
(nri) f, fish market; f. shop. **poissonneux, euse** (nø, øːz) a, full of
fish. **poissonnier, ère** (nje, ɛːr) n,
fishmonger. ¶ f, fish kettle
(*Cook.*).
poitrail (pwatrɑːj) m, breast
(*horse*). **poitrinaire** (trinɛːr) a. &
n, consumptive. **poitrine** (trin) f,
chest, breast; brisket.
poivre (pwaːvr) m, pepper. ~ *de
Cayenne* (kajen), ~ *rouge*, Cayenne p., red p. **poivré, e** (pwavre)
p.a, peppery; spicy (*tale*). **poivrer**
(vre) v.t, to pepper. **poivrier** (vrie)
m, pepper plant; p. box. **poivrière**
(vriɛːr) f, pepper box. **poivron**
(vrɔ̃) m, pimento.
poix (pwɑ) f, pitch; cobbler's wax.
polaire (pɔlɛːr) a, polar; pole
(*star*). **pôle** (poːl) m, pole (*Astr.,
Phys., etc.*).
polar (pɔlar) m, detective novel
(*slang*).
polémique (pɔlemik)ʼ a, po-
lemic(al). ¶ f, polemic; polemics.
poli, e (pɔli) p.a, polished, bright;
glossy, sleek; polite, mannerly,
refined. ¶ m, polish, gloss.
police (pɔlis) f, policing; police
regulations; police [force]; policy
(*Insce.*), ~ *de la circulation*,
traffic police. *faire la* ~, to keep
order. **policer** (se) v.t, to control,
organize,, civilize. **policier** (je) m,
policeman.
polichinelle (pɔliʃinel) m,
Punch; buffoon. *avoir un* ~ *dans
le tiroir*, to be pregnant (*slang*).
poliment (pɔlimɑ̃) ad, politely.
polir (liːr) v.t, to polish; buff;
smooth; refine. **polissoir** (swaːr) f,
buffer.
polisson, ne (pɔlisɔ̃, ɔn) a, street
child; rascal, scamp; immodest
person; (*att.*) naughty, precocious, indecent. **polissonner**
(sɔne) v.i, to run the streets
(*child*); be lewd.
politesse (pɔlites) f, politeness;
compliment.
politicien (pɔlitisjɛ̃) m, politician (*as a trade*). **politique†**
(tik) a, political; politic. ¶ m,
politician. ¶ f, policy; polity;
politics. **politiquer** (ke) v.i, to
talk politics.

polka (pɔlka) m, polka.
pollen (pɔllɛn) m, pollen.
polluer (pɔllɥe) v.t, to pollute,
defile; profane. **pollution** (pɔlly-
sjɔ̃) f, pollution.
polo (pɔlo) m, polo; polo cap.
Pologne (la) (pɔlɔɲ), Poland.
polonais, e (nɛ, ɛːz) a, Polish.
P~, n, Pole. **le polonais,** Polish
(*language*). **polonaise,** f, polonaise.
poltron, ne (pɔltrɔ̃, ɔn) a, cowardly. ¶ n, poltroon, coward.
poltronnerie (trɔnri) f, cowardice.
polycopier (pɔlikɔpje) v.t, to
mimeograph, etc.
polygame (pɔligam) n, polygamist. ¶ a, polygamous. **polygamie**
(mi) f, polygamy. **polyglotte** (glɔt)
a. & n, polyglot. **polygone** (gɔn)
m, polygon. **la Polynésie** (nezi),
Polynesia. **polype** (lip) m, polyp;
polypus. **polysyllabe** (silab) a,
polysyllabic. ¶ m, polysyllable.
polytechnique (tɛknik) a, polytechnic. **polytechnicien** (tɛknisjɛ̃)
m, student or graduate of the
École Polytechnique. **polythéisme**
(teism) m, polytheism.
pommade (pɔmad) f, pomade;
salve. *passer de la* ~, to butter
up, flatter. **pommader** (de) v.t, to
pomade.
pomme (pɔm) f, apple; cone (*fir,
pine*); knob; head (*stick, cabbage*); head (*person; slang*). *tomber dans les* ~s, to faint (*slang*).
~ *d'Adam* (adɑ̃), Adam's apple.
~ *de terre*, potato. ~s *de terre en
robe* [*de chambre*], jacket potatoes. ~ *sauvage*, crab [apple].
pommé, e (me) (*fig.*) p.a, downright. **pommeau** (mo) m, pommel.
pommelé, e (mle) p.a, dapple[d];
mackerel (*sky*). **pommeraie** (mrɛ)
f, apple orchard. **pommette** (met)
f, cheekbone. **pommier** (mje) m,
apple tree. ~ *sauvage*, crab
[apple tree].
pompe (pɔ̃ːp) f, pomp; pump.
~ *à incendie*, fire engine. ~ *aspirante*, suction pump. ~ *foulante*, force pump. ~ *funèbre*,
funeral; (*pl.*) undertaking.
Pompéi (pɔ̃pei) f, Pompeii.

pomper (pɔ̃pe) *v.t. & i,* to pump; suck up.

pompeux, euse† (pɔ̃pø, ø:z) *a,* pompous; stately.

pompier (pɔ̃pje) *m,* pump maker; fireman; conventionalist, formulist; (*att.*) conventional, formulistic. **pompiste** (pist) *m,* gas station attendant.

pompon (pɔ̃pɔ̃) *m,* pompon, tuft, tassel.

pomponner (pɔ̃pɔne) *v.t,* to smarten or dress up.

ponce (pɔ̃:s) *f,* pumice; pounce (*art*).

ponceau (pɔ̃so) *m,* culvert; poppy.

poncer (pɔ̃se) *v.t,* to pumice; sandpaper; pounce. **poncif** (sif) (*fig.*) *m,* conventionalism.

ponction (pɔ̃ksjɔ̃) (*Surg.*) *f,* puncture, tapping.

ponctualité (pɔ̃ktɥalite) *f,* punctuality.

ponctuation (pɔ̃ktɥasjɔ̃) *f,* punctuation.

ponctuel, le† (pɔ̃ktɥɛl) *a,* punctual.

ponctuer (pɔ̃ktɥe) *v.t. & abs,* to punctuate; emphasize.

pondérable (pɔ̃derabl) *a,* ponderable. **pondérer** (re) *v.t,* to balance.

pondre (pɔ̃:dr) *v.t. & abs,* to lay (*eggs*); be delivered of (*fig.*).

poney (pɔnɛ) *m,* pony.

pont (pɔ̃) *m,* bridge; platform; deck (*ship*). ~ *à bascule,* drawbridge. ~ *abri,* awning deck, hurricane d. ~ *de manœuvre,* hurricane deck. ~ *roulant,* traveling crane. ~ *suspendu,* suspension bridge. ~ *suspendu à chaînes,* chain bridge. ~ *tournant,* swing bridge. ~ *aérien,* airlift. *faire le* ~, to make a long holiday weekend. **pontage** (ta:ʒ) *m,* bridging; bridge building; bypass (*Surg.*).

ponte (pɔ̃:t) *f,* laying (*eggs*); (*m.*) punt[er] (*cards, etc.*).

ponté, e (pɔ̃te) *a,* decked. *non* ~, open (*boat*).

ponter (pɔ̃te) *v.i,* to punt (*cards, etc.*).

pontife (pɔ̃tif) *m,* pontiff; pundit. **pontifical, e†** (fikal) *a. & m,*

pontifical. **pontificat** (ka) *m,* pontificate.

pont-levis (pɔ̃ləvi) *m,* drawbridge (*castle*).

ponton (pɔ̃tɔ̃) *m,* pontoon; hulk; landing stage.

popeline (pɔplin) *f,* poplin.

popote (pɔpɔt) *f,* canteen, mess (*Mil.*). *faire la* ~, to cook (*slang*).

popotin (pɔpɔtɛ̃) *m,* buttock, backside (*slang*).

populace (pɔpylas) *f,* populace, rabble. **populacier, ère** (sje, ɛːr) *a,* vulgar. **populaire†** (lɛːr) *a,* popular. **popularité** (larite) *f,* popularity. **population** (sjɔ̃) *f,* population. **populeux, euse** (lø, ø:z) *a,* populous.

porc (pɔːr) *m,* pig, swine; pork. ~ [*châtré*], hog.

porcelaine (pɔrsəlɛn) *f,* porcelain, china[ware]; cowrie. ~ *de Saxe,* Dresden china. **porcelainier, ère** (nje, ɛːr) *n,* china manufacturer; china dealer.

porc-épic (pɔrkepik) *m,* porcupine.

porche (pɔrʃ) *m,* porch.

porcher, ère (pɔrʃe, ɛːr) *n,* swineherd. **porcherie** (ʃəri) *f,* pigsty. **porcine** (sin) *a.f,* porcine, pig (*att.*).

pore (pɔːr) *m,* pore. **poreux, euse** (pɔrø, ø:z) *a,* porous. **porosité** (rozite) *f,* porousness.

pornographe (pɔrnɔgraf) *m,* pornographer. **pornographie** (fi) *f,* pornography. **pornographique** (fik) *a,* pornographic.

porphyre (pɔrfiːr) *m.* porphyry.

port (pɔːr) *m,* port, harbor, haven; carrying; wearing; carriage; postage; bearing; burden (*ship*). ~ *d'armes,* gun license. ~ *d'armement,* home port. ~ *d'attache,* port of registry. ~ *de guerre,* ~ *militaire,* naval port, n. station, n. base. ~ *de toute marée,* deepwater harbor. *à bon* ~, safe[ly]; to a happy issue. **portable** (pɔrtabl) *a,* wearable.

portail (pɔrtaːj) *m,* portal.

portant, e (pɔrtɑ̃, ɑ̃:t) *a,* bearing. *à bout* ~, pointblank. *bien* ~, in good health. *mal* ~, in bad h. ¶ *m,* chest handle, lifting h.;

outrigger (*for rowlocks*). **portatif, ive** (tatif, i:v) *a*, portable; small (*arms*).

porte (pɔrt) *f*, door, doorway; gate, gateway; arch. ~ *brisée*, folding door. ~ *charretière*, carriage entrance. ~ *cochère* (kɔʃɛːr), built-over carriage entrance. ~ *de service*, back door, tradesmen's entrance. ~*fenêtre*, French window. ~ *matelassée*, baize door. ~ *à tambour*, revolving door. ~ *va-et-vient*, swing door.

porte- (pɔrt; *sometimes* portə *as noted*) *comps, all m*: ~ *à faux*, overhang. ~*avions*, aircraft carrier. ~*bagages*, luggage carrier. ~*bonheur*, charm. ~*bouquet*, flower holder. ~*bouteilles*, bottle rack; bin. ~*cartes* (təkart), card case; map case. ~*chapeaux*, hat & coat stand. ~*cigare*, cigar holder. ~*cigares*, c. case. ~*clefs* (təklə), turnkey; key ring. ~*couteau*, knife rest. ~ *crayon* (təkrɛjɔ̃), pencil case. ~*en-dehors*, outrigger (*for rowlocks*). ~*épée*, frog (*sword*). ~*étendard*, standard bearer. *feuille*, billfold. ~*jarretelles*, garter belt. ~*malheur*, bringer of ill luck; bird of ill omen, Jonah. ~*menu* (təmny), menu holder. ~*monnaie*, purse. ~*parapluies*, umbrella stand. ~*parole*, spokesman, mouthpiece (*pers.*). ~*potiche*, pedestal (*for vase*). ~*queue* (təkø), train bearer. ~*respect*, person of imposing appearance; weapon. ~*serviettes*, towel rod, ring. ~*trésor*, jewel case (*traveling*). ~*vêtements*, clothes hanger. ~*voix* (təvwa), megaphone.

porté, e (pɔrte) *p.a*, inclined, disposed, prone, apt; fond.

portée (pɔrte) *f*, bearing; litter (*of pups*); span; reach, range, radius, scope, compass, shot; significance, purport; stave, staff (*Mus.*). *à ~ de la voix*, within call.

portefaix (pɔrtəfɛ) *m*, porter (*street, etc.*); rough fellow.

portefeuille (pɔrtəfœ:j) *m*, portfolio; letter case, wallet; office

(*in ministry*). ~*titres*, investments, securities, share holdings, stocks & shares.

portemanteau (pɔrtmɑ̃to) *m*, hat & coat stand, portemanteau.

porter (pɔrte) *v.t. & i*, to bear; carry; take; bring; lay; wear, have on; shoulder (*arms*); drink (*health*); deal, strike (*blow*); enter, put, mark; post (*Bkkpg.*); prompt, lead, incline; raise; rest; tell (*shot, word*); turn (*discussion*). ~ *à faux*, to overhang; miss the point (*fig.*). se ~, to go; be; do; stand. **porteur, euse** (tœːr, øːz) *n*, porter; carrier; (*m.*) bearer; holder. *porteurs des cordons du poêle*, pall bearers.

portier, ère (pɔrtje, ɛːr) *n*, porter, doorkeeper, caretaker. ¶ *f*, door (*carriage, car*); door curtain.

portion (pɔrsjɔ̃) *f*, portion, share, part; helping (*food*).

portique (pɔrtik) *m*, portico, porch; gantry; gallows (*Gym.*).

Porto (pɔrto) *m*, Oporto. *ou vin de Porto*, *m*, port [wine].

portrait (pɔrtrɛ) *m*, portrait, likeness; image; description. ~ *en buste*, half-length portrait. ~ *en pied*, full-length portrait.

portugais, e (pɔrtygɛ, ɛːz) *a. & P~*, *n*, Portuguese. *le portugais*, Portuguese (*language*). **le Portugal** (gal), Portugal.

posage (poza:ʒ) *m*, laying, fixing. **pose** (po:z) *f*, laying; pose, posture; lie (*golf ball*); exposure (*Phot.*). ~*mètre*, exposure meter. **posé†, e** (poze) *p.a*, staid, sedate; steady. **poser** (ze) *v.i*, to rest, lie; pose, sit (*portrait*); (*v.t.*) to place, put; p. down; lay; l. down; set; hang (*bells*); pose; post (*sentry*); state; grant. ~ *ses clous*, to down tools. se ~, to settle, alight; set up; pose. **poseur, euse** (zœːr, øːz) *n*, layer; setter; hanger (*bells*); affected person. *poseur de mines*, minelayer. *poseur de voie*, platelayer.

positif, ive† (pozitif, i:v) *a*, positive, real; practical, matter-of-fact. ¶ *m*, real[ity].

position (pozisjɔ̃) *f*, position; situation; book (*Stk Ex.*); posture; stance.

posologie (pozɔlɔ3i) *f*, dosage (*drugs, etc.*).

possédé, e (pɔsede) *p.a*, possessed (*mad*). ¶ *n*, one possessed. **posséder** (de) *v.t*, to possess, own, have, hold; be master of. **possesseur** (sɛsœːr) *m*, possessor, owner. **possession** (sjɔ̃) *f*, possession; tenure.

possibilité (pɔsibilite) *f*, possibility. **possible** (bl) *a*. & *m*, possible.

postal, e (pɔstal) *a*, postal, post, mail (*att.*).

postdater (pɔstdate) *v.t*, to postdate.

poste (pɔst) *f*, mail; post [office]. ~ *restante*, general delivery, to be called for. *aller un train de ~*, to go posthaste. **postier, ère** (je, jɛːr) *n*, post-office employee.

poste (pɔst) *m*, post, station; guard room; berth; radio (*slang*); head[ing]; item; shift (*men*). ~ *central*, exchange (*Teleph.*). ~ *de l'équipage*, forecastle, foc's'le. ~ *de police*, police station. ~ *de secours*, first-aid station. ~ *supplémentaire*, extension [line] (*Teleph.*). ~ *éloigné*, remote terminal (*computers*). **poster** (te) *v.t*, to post, station.

postérieur, e† (pɔsterjœːr) *a*, posterior, subsequent, later; hind[er], back. ¶ *m*, posterior.

postérité (pɔsterite) *f*, posterity, issue.

posthume (pɔstym) *a*, posthumous.

postiche (pɔstiʃ) *a*, false, artificial; sham. *cheveux ~s*, wig.

postillon (pɔstijɔ̃) *m*, postillion.

post-scriptum (pɔstskriptɔm) (*abb.* P.-S.) *m*, postscript, P.S.

postulant, e (pɔstylɑ̃, ɑ̃ːt) *n*, candidate, applicant; postulant. **postuler** (le) *v.t*, to apply for; (*v.i.*) to act for (*client, law*).

posture (pɔstyːr) *f*, posture; position.

pot (po; *before à, au*, pɔt) *m*, pot, jug, ewer; tankard; can; jar. ~*-au-feu*, stock pot, soup p; beef and vegetables; (*att.*) stay-at-home (*pers.*). ~ *d'échappement*, muffler (*auto*). ~ *perdu*, no-de-

posit jar, bottle. *avoir du ~*, to be lucky. *manque de ~*, bad luck. *payer les ~s cassés*, to pay the damages. ~*-de-vin*, bribe. ~ *pourri*, hodgepodge; medley.

potable (pɔtabl) *a*, drinkable, drinking (*water*).

potache (pɔtaʃ) *m*, schoolboy (*slang*).

potage (pɔta:ȝ) *m*, soup. ~ *ou consommé?* thick or clear? (*at dinner*). *pour tout ~*, all told. **potager, ère** (taȝe, ɛːr) *a*, pot (*herb*); kitchen (*garden*). ¶ *m*, kitchen garden; dinner pail; kitchen stove, charcoal-fired cooker.

potasse (pɔtas) *f*, potash. **potassium** (sjɔm) *m*, potassium.

potasser (pɔtase) *v.t*, to study hard, cram (*slang*).

pote (pɔt) *m*, pal, buddy.

poteau (pɔto) *m*, post, pole. ~ [*d'arrivée*], [winning] post. ~ *de départ*, starting p. ~ *de signalisation* (siɲalizasjɔ̃), traffic sign. ~ *indicateur*, signpost.

potée (pɔte) *f*, potful, jugful; swarm. ~ *d'étain*, putty powder.

potelé, e (pɔtle) *a*, plump; chubby.

potelet (pɔtlɛ) *m*, stud (*scantling in wall*).

potence (pɔtɑ̃:s) *f*, gallows, gibbet; bracket.

potentat (pɔtɑ̃ta) *m*, potentate.

potentiel, le (pɔtɑ̃sjɛl) *a*. & *m*, potential.

poter (pɔte) *v.t*, to putt (*golf*).

poterie (pɔtri) *f*, pottery, earthenware; ware. ~ *de grès*, stoneware.

poterne (pɔtɛrn) *f*, postern.

poteur (pɔtœːr) *m*, putter (*golf club*).

potiche (pɔtiʃ) *f*, vase (*Chinese, or like*).

potier (pɔtje) *m*, potter. ~ *d'étain*, pewterer.

potin (pɔtɛ̃) *m*, gossip; row, fuss.

potion (posjɔ̃) *f*, potion, draft.

potiron (pɔtirɔ̃) *m*, pumpkin.

pou (pu) *m*, louse.

pouah (pwa) *i*, ugh!

poubelle (pubɛl) *f*, garbage can, trash c.

pouce (pu:s) *m*, thumb.

pouding (pudiɲ) *m*, pudding.

poudre (pu:dr) *f*, powder; dust. ~ *à canon*, gunpowder. ~ *à lever*, baking powder. ~ *d'or*, gold dust. ~ *de mine*, blasting powder. ~ *de riz*, face powder, toilet powder. **poudrer** (pudre) *v.t*, to powder. **poudrerie** (drəri) *f*, powder mill. **poudreux, euse** (drø, ø:z) *a*, dusty. **poudrier** (drie) *m*, powder box; salt sifter. **poudrière** (ɛ:r) *f*, powder magazine.

pouf (puf) *m*, overstuffed footstool. **pouffiase** (fjas) *f*, slut, slattern (*slang*).

pouffer [de rire] (pufe), to burst out laughing.

pouilleux, euse (pujø, ø:z), *a*, lousy.

poulailler (pulaje) *m*, hen house; poulterer; top balcony, cheap seats (*Theat.*).

poulain (pulɛ̃) *m*, colt, foal.

poulaine (pulɛn) *f*, bedroom slipper.

poularde (pulard) *f*, table fowl. **poule** (pul) *f*, hen, fowl; sweepstake[s]; round robin (*sports*); whore (*slang*). *chair de* ~, gooseflesh. ~ *d'eau*, moor hen. ~ *d'Inde*, turkey [hen]. ~ *faisane*, hen pheasant. ~ *mouillée*, milksop (*pers.*). **poulet** (lɛ) *m*, chicken, chick; policeman, cop (*slang*). **poulette** (lɛt) *f*, pullet; girl.

pouliche (puliʃ) *f*, filly, foal.

poulie (puli) *f*, pulley, block, sheave.

pouliner (puline) *v.i*, to foal. [jument] **poulinière** (njɛ:r) *f*, brood mare, breeder.

poulpe (pulp) *m*, octopus.

pouls (pu) *m*, pulse (*as in wrist*).

poumon (pumɔ̃) *m*, lung.

poupard, e (pupa:r, ard) *a*, chubby; baby (*face*). ¶ *m*, baby; baby doll.

poupe (pup) *f*, stern, poop.

poupée (pupe) *f*, doll; puppet; dummy; block. **poupin, e** (pɛ̃, in) *a*, doll-faced. **poupon, ne** (pɔ̃, ɔn) *n*, baby. **pouponner** (pɔne) *v.t*, to fondle, dandle, cuddle.

pouponnière (njɛ:r) *f*, day nursery.

pour (pu:r) *pr*, for; instead of; per; pro; as; on; to; (*money's*) worth. ~ *ainsi dire*, so to speak. ~ *cent*, percent. ~ *que*, in order that. *le* ~ *& le contre*, the pros & cons, for & against.

pourboire (purbwa:r) *m*, tip, gratuity.

pourceau (purso) *m*, hog, pig, swine.

pourcentage (pursɑ̃ta:ʒ) *m*, percentage, rate.

pourchasser (purʃase) *v.t*, to pursue; dun.

pourfendre (purfɑ̃:dr) *v.t*, to fend, cleave.

pourlécher (purleʃe) *v.t*, to lick all over. *se* ~ *les babines*, to lick one's chops.

pourparlers (purparle) *m.pl*, parley; negotiations.

pourpre (purpr) *f*, purple (*robe*); crimson (*color*); (*m.*) purple (*color*); (*att.*) crimson (*color*). **pourpré, e** (pre) *a*, purple (*red—color*).

pourquoi (purkwa) *ad. & c*, why, wherefore, what. ¶ *m*, why, why.

pourri, e (puri) *p.a*, rotten. **pourrir** (ri:r) *v.i. & t*, to rot, **pourriture** (rity:r) *f*, rotting; rot; rottenness.

poursuite (pursɥit) *f*, pursuit, chase; tracking (*spacecraft*); (*oft. pl.*) lawsuit, proceedings; prosecution. **poursuivant** (vɑ̃) *m*, plaintiff, prosecutor; suitor, wooer. **poursuivre** (vr) *v.t.ir*, to pursue, chase; haunt; follow up; prosecute, sue.

pourtant (purtɑ̃) *ad*, yet, nevertheless, however.

pourtour (purtu:r) *m*, circumference; surround; precincts, close; gangway.

pourvoi (purvwa) *m*, appeal; petition. **pourvoir** (vwa:r) *v.i. & t. ir*, to provide, supply, furnish. **pourvoyeur** (vwajœ:r) *m*, purveyor, provider, caterer. **pourvu que** (vy) *c*, provided [that].

poussah (pusa) *m*, tumbler (*toy*); tub[by man].

pousse (pus) *f*, growth; cutting (*teeth*); shoot, sprout. ~*-pousse,* *m*, ricksha[w]. **poussée** (se) *f*, push, shove; thrust; pressure; outburst; buoyancy. **pousser** (se) *v.t. & i*, to push, shove, thrust; drive; urge; utter, give; grow, shoot, spring up. ~ *à la perche*, ~ *du fond*, to punt (*boating*). ~ *au large*, to push off (*Naut.*).

poussette (puset) *f*, stroller; shopping cart.

poussier (pusje) *m*, dust (*coal*, *etc.*). **poussière** (sjɛːr) *f*, dust. ~ *d'eau*, spray. *des* ~*s*, small change left after paying bill (*often left for waiter*). **poussiéreux, euse** (sjerø, øːz) *a*, dusty.

poussif, ive (pusif, iːv) *a*, broken-winded; wheezy.

poussin (pusɛ̃) *m*, chick; spring chicken. **poussinière** (sinjɛːr) *f*, coop; incubator.

poussoir (puswaːr) *m*, push [button].

poutre (putr) *f*, beam; girder. **poutrelle** (trɛl) *f*, small beam; skid (*Artil.*).

pouvoir (puvwaːr) *m*, power; authority; power of attorney; proxy; (*pl.*) credentials. ¶ *v.i. & t. ir*, to be able; can; can do; may. *se* ~, to be possible. *cela se peut*, it may be.

prairie (prɛri) *f*, meadow; grassland; prairie.

praline (pralin) *f*, burnt almond, praline.

praticable (pratikabl) *a*, practicable, feasible; passable (*road*). **praticien** (sjɛ̃) *m*, practician; practitioner. **pratiquant** (pratikɑ̃) *a*, church-going. **pratique†** (tik) *a*, practical. ¶ *f*, practice; experience; observance; (*pl.*) dealings; pratique; custom; customer. **pratiquer** (ke) *v.t*, to practice; make; frequent. *se* ~, to be done; rule (*prices*).

pré (pre) *m*, meadow.

préalable† (prealabl) *a*, previous; preliminary. ¶ *m*, preliminary.

préambule (preɑ̃byl) *m*, preamble.

préau (preo) *m*, courtyard, quadrangle; playground (*covered*).

préavis (preavi) *m*, [previous] notice, warning. *avec* ~ *pour . . .*, person-to-person call for . . .

prébende (prebɑ̃ːd) *f*, prebend. **prébendier** (bɑ̃dje) *m*, prebendary.

précaire† (prekɛːr) *a*, precarious.

précaution (prekosjɔ̃) *f*, precaution; caution, wariness. **précautionner** (sjɔne) *v.t*, to caution, warn.

précédemment (presedamɑ̃) *ad*, previously. **précédent, e** (dɑ̃, ɑ̃ːt) *a*, preceding, previous, before. ¶ *m*, precedent. **précéder** (de) *v.t*, to precede.

précepte (presɛpt) *m*, precept. **précepteur** (tœːr) *m*, tutor, teacher, preceptor. **préceptorat** (tɔra) *m*, tutorship.

prêche (prɛʃ) *m*, sermon. **prêcher** (ʃe) *v.t. & abs*, to preach; extol; exhort; lecture. **prêcheur** (ʃœːr) *m*, sermonizer.

précieux, euse† (presjø, øːz) *a*, precious; valuable; affected.

précipice (presipis) *m*, precipice.

précipitamment (presipitamɑ̃) *a*, precipitately, headlong. **précipitation** (sjɔ̃) *f*, precipitancy, haste; precipitation. **précipité, e** (te) *a*, precipitate, hasty, hurried, headlong. ¶ *m*, precipitate. **précipiter** (te) *v.t*, to precipitate; hasten; plunge. *se* ~, to rush.

précis, e (presi, iːz) *a*, precise, exact; sharp (*hour*); definite. ¶ *m*, abstract, summary, précis. **précisément** (sizemɑ̃) *ad*, precisely, exactly. **préciser** (ze) *v.t*, to state precisely, specify. **précision** (zjɔ̃) *f*, precision, accuracy; (*pl.*) particulars.

précité, e (presite) *a*, aforesaid, above.

précoce (prekɔs) *a*, precocious; early, forward. **précocité** (site) *f*, precociousness, etc.

préconçu, e (prekɔ̃sy) *a*, preconceived.

préconiser (prekɔnize) *v.t*, to preconize; [re]commend, advocate.

précurseur (prekyrsœːr) *m*, precursor, forerunner; (*att.*) precursory, premonitory.

prédécès (predesɛ) *m*, predecease.

prédécesseur (predesɛsœːr) *m*, predecessor.

prédestination (predɛstinasjɔ̃) *f*, predestination.

prédicant (predikɑ̃) *m*, preacher.

prédicat (predika) *m*, predicate.

prédicateur (predikatœːr) *m*, preacher. **prédication** (sjɔ̃) *f*, preaching.

prédiction (prediksjɔ̃) *f*, prediction; forecast.

prédilection (predilɛksjɔ̃) *f*, predilection, partiality. *de ~*, favorite.

prédire (prediːr) *v.t.ir*, to predict, foretell.

prédisposer (predispoze) *v.t*, to predispose.

prédominer (predɔmine) *v.i*, to predominate, prevail.

prééminent, e (preeminɑ̃, ɑ̃ːt) *a*, preeminent.

préemption (preɑ̃psjɔ̃) *f*, preemption.

préfabriquer (prefabrike) *v.t*, to prefabricate.

préface (prefas) *f*, preface, foreword; preliminaries; forerunner.

préfecture (prefɛktyːr) *f*, prefecture; headquarters (*of police*).

préférable† (preferabl) *a*, preferable, better. **préférence** (rɑ̃ːs) *f*, preference. **préférer** (re) *v.t*, to prefer.

préfet (prefɛ) *m*, prefect. *~ de police*, police commissioner.

préfixe (prefiks) *m*, prefix. ¶ *a*, prefixed.

préhenseur (preɑ̃sœːr) *a.m*, prehensile.

préhistorique (preistɔrik) *a*, prehistoric.

préjudice (preʒydis) *m*, prejudice, detriment; injury. **préjudiciable** (sjabl) *a*, prejudicial, detrimental. **préjudicier** (sje) *v.i*, to be detrimental to. **préjugé** (ʒe) *m*, prejudice; presumption. **préjuger** (ʒe) *v.t*, to prejudge.

prélart (prelaːr) *m*, tarpaulin.

prélasser (se) (prelɑse) *v.pr*, to strut along; loll. **prélat** (la) *m*, prelate.

prélèvement (prelɛvmɑ̃) *m*, deduction, levy. *~ de sang*, blood

test. **prélever** (lve) *v.t*, to deduct, levy.

préliminaire (preliminɛːr) *a. & m*, preliminary.

prélude (prelyd) *m*, prelude; voluntary. **préluder** (de) *v.i*, to prelude (*Mus.*). *~ à*, to preface, lead up to.

prématuré†, e (prematyre) *a*, premature, untimely.

préméditation (premeditasjɔ̃) *f*, premeditation; malice aforethought, m. prepense. **préméditer** (te) *v.t*, to premeditate.

prémices (premis) *f.pl*, firstfruits; beginning.

premier, ère (prəmje, ɛːr) *a*, first; opening (*price*); leading: early; earliest; next; prime; primary; premier. **premier**, *comps*: *~ choix*, best quality, finest q. *~ garçon*, headwaiter. *~ ministre*, prime minister, premier. *~-né, m*, first-born. *de ~ order*, first-class, first-rate; gilt-edged (*securities*). *~ plan*, foreground; close-up (*Phot.*). *~ rôle*, leading part; l. man, l. lady. ¶ *m*, first. ¶ *f*, first; f. night; forewoman. *~ mondiale*, world premiere (*film*). *~s* [galeries], dress circle. **premièrement** (mjɛrmɑ̃) *ad*, first[ly].

prémisses (premis) *f.pl*, premis[s]es (*Log.*).

prémonitoire (premɔnitwaːr) *a*, premonitory.

prémunir (premyniːr) *v.t*, to forewarn. *se ~ contre*, to provide against.

prenable (prənabl) *a*, pregnable; corruptible. **prenant, e** (nɑ̃, ɑ̃ːt) *a*, taking; prehensile. **prendre** (prɑ̃ːdr) *v.t.ir*, to take; t. up; t. in; t. over; lay hold of; seize; clasp; catch; pick up; assume; acquire; come to; charge; put on; assume; wreak; (*v.i.ir*.) to set; congeal; curdle; freeze; catch; take root, strike; take, catch on; bear (*to right, left*).*~ le large*, to sail out to sea. *à tout ~*, all in all. se *~*, to catch; congeal; cling; clasp. s'en *~ à*, to blame. s'y *~*, to set about it. **preneur, euse** (prənœːr, øːz) *n*, taker; captor; buyer; lessee.

prénom (prenɔ̃) *m*, first name, Christian n.

préoccupation (preɔkypasjɔ̃) *f*, preoccupation. **préoccuper** (pe) *v.t*, to preoccupy.

préopinant (preɔpinɑ̃) *m*, previous speaker.

préparateur, trice (preparatœ:r, tris) *n*, tutor, coach; assistant. **préparatifs** (tif) *m.pl*, preparations. **préparation** (sjɔ̃) *f*, preparation. ~ *automatisée*, process automation (*data processing*). **préparatoire** (twa:r) *a*, preparatory. **préparer** (re) *v.t*, to prepare, make ready; lay (*fire*); coach (*pupil*); read for (*exam*). se ~, to prepare, get ready; brew (*storm*).

prépondérance (prepɔ̃derɑ̃:s) *f*, preponderance. **prépondérant, e** (rɑ̃, ɑ̃:t) *a*, preponderant; casting (*vote*).

préposé, e (prepoze) *n*, servant; officer; official; clerk. **préposer** (ze) *v.t*, to appoint.

préposition (prepɔzisjɔ̃) *f*, preposition.

prérogative (prerɔgati:v) *f*, prerogative; privilege.

près (prɛ) *ad. & pr*, near; by; close; to. *à* . . . ~, save on, save in, except for; to *a*; within. *à peu* ~, nearly, about, pretty much.

présage (preza:ʒ) *m*, presage, omen, portent, foreboding, premonition. **présager** (zaʒe) *v.t*, to presage, portend, [fore]bode; augur.

pré-salé (presale) *m*, salt-meadow sheep; salt-meadow mutton.

presbyte (prɛzbit) *n. & att*, far-sighted (person).

presbytère (prɛzbitɛ:r) *m*, presbytery; rectory, vicarage, parsonage. **presbytérien, ne** (terjɛ̃, ɛn) *n. & att*, Presbyterian.

prescience (presjɑ̃:s) *f*, prescience, foreknowledge.

prescription (prɛskripsjɔ̃) *f*, prescription; bar of the statute of limitations; directions. **prescrire** (skri:r) *v.t.ir*, to prescribe, ordain. se ~, to be statute barred.

préséance (preseɑ̃:s) *f*, precedence (*in rank*).

présence (prezɑ̃:s) *f*, presence; attendance; sight. **présent, e** (zɑ̃, ɑ̃:t) *a*, present; this (*letter, etc.*). ¶ *m*, present; gift. *à* ~, now. **présentable** (zɑ̃tabl) *a*, presentable. **présentation** (sjɔ̃) *f*, presentation; introduction. **présentement** (zɑ̃tmɑ̃) *ad*, at present, now; with immediate possession (*house*). **présenter** (te) *v.t*, to present; offer; pay (*respects*); produce, show; introduce. se ~, to sit for an exam, go for an interview, etc.

préservatif (prezɛrvatif) *m. & a*, preservative, preventive; contraceptive. **préservation** (sjɔ̃) *f*, preservation. **préserver** (ve) *v.t*, to preserve, keep.

présidence (prezidɑ̃:s) *f*, presidency; chairmanship. **président, e** (dɑ̃, ɑ̃:t) *n*, president; chairman; presiding judge. ~ *du conseil* [*des ministres*], premier. **présidentiel, le** (dɑ̃sjɛl) *a*, presidential. les **présidentielles**, *f.pl*, presidential elections. **présider** [à] (de) *v.t. & i*, to preside at, over; superintend.

présomptif, ive (prezɔ̃ptif, i:v) *a*, presumptive; (*heir*) apparent. **présomption** (sjɔ̃) *f*, presumption. **présomptueux, euse†** (tɥø, ø:z) *a*, presumptuous.

presque (prɛsk) *ad*, almost, nearly, all but; scarcely, hardly (*ever*). **presqu'île** (kil) *f*, peninsula.

pressant, e (presɑ̃, ɑ̃:t) *a*, pressing, urgent. **presse** (prɛs) *f*, press; clamp, cramp; squeezer; crowd, throng; pressure, congestion; hurry; newspapers, the press. *attaché de* ~, press agent. **presse-citron**, *m*, lemon squeezer. **presse-purée**, *m*, potato masher.

pressentiment (presɑ̃timɑ̃) *m*, presentiment, foreboding, misgiving. **pressentir** (ti:r) *v.t.ir*, to have a presentiment of; sound (*pers.*).

presse-papiers (prɛspapje) *m*, paperweight. **presser** (se) *v.t*, to press; squeeze; clasp; ply; hurry, push. se ~, to press, crowd, throng; hurry. **pression** (sjɔ̃) *f*, pressure. *bière à la* ~, draft beer. **pressoir** (swa:r) *m*, press (*wine, etc.*). **pressurer** (syre) *v.t*, to press (*grapes, etc.*); grind (*fig.*).

prestance (prɛstɑ̃ɪs) *f*, presence, bearing, portliness.

prestation (prɛstasjɔ̃) *f*, provision; taking (*oath*).

prestet (prɛst) *a*, quick, nimble. **prestesse** (tɛs) *f*, quickness.

prestidigitateur (prɛstidiʒitatœɪr) *m*, conjurer, juggler. **prestidigitation** (sjɔ̃) *f*, conjuring, sleight-of-hand, legerdemain.

prestige (prɛstiːʒ) *m*, marvel, magic, glamour; prestige. **prestigieux, euse** (tiʒjø, øːz) *a*, marvelous; influential.

présumer (prezyme) *v.t. & abs*, to presume, suppose.

présupposer (presypoze) *v.t*, to presuppose, take for granted.

présure (prezyɪr) *f*, rennet.

prêt, e (prɛ, ɛɪt) *a*, ready, prepared, game.

prêt (prɛ) *m*, loan; advance.

prêt-à-manger (prɛtamɑ̃ʒe) *m. & a*, fast food.

prêt-à-monter (prɛtamɔ̃te), *m*, do-it-yourself kit.

prêt-à-porter (prɛtapɔrte) *m*, ready-to-wear (*mass-produced garments*).

prêt-bail (prɛbaj) *m*, lend-lease.

prétendant, e (pretɑ̃dɑ̃, ɑ̃ːt) *n*, applicant; claimant; pretender; (*m.*) suitor, wooer. **prétendre** (tɑ̃ːdr) *v.t. & i*, to claim, require, pretend; assert; contend; aspire. **prétendu, e** (tɑ̃dy) *p.a*, alleged; would-be; so-called. ¶ *n*, intended (*in marriage*).

prête-nom (prɛtnɔ̃) *m*, dummy (*pers.*).

pretentaine (courir la) (pretɑ̃tɛn), to gad about.

prétentieux, euse (pretɑ̃sjø, øːz) *a*, pretentious. **prétention** (sjɔ̃) *f*, claim, pretension.

prêter (prɛte) *v.t*, to lend; give; take (*oath*); attribute. ~ *serment*, to take oath, swear.

prétérit (preterit) *m*, preterite.

prêteur, euse (prɛtœːr, øːz) *n*, lender. ~ *sur gages*, money lender; pawnbroker.

prétexte (pretɛkst) *m*, pretext, pretense, plea, excuse. **prétexter** (te) *v.t*, to plead.

prêtre (prɛːtr) *m*, priest. **prêtresse** (pretrɛs) *f*, priestess. **prêtrise** (triːz) *f*, priesthood, [holy] orders.

preuve (prœːv) *f*, proof; evidence; token. ~ *par l'absurde*, reductio ad absurdum. ~ *par présomption*, circumstantial evidence.

preux (prø) *a.m*, doughty, valiant.

prévaloir (prevalwaɪr) *v.i.ir*, to prevail. **se** ~ **de**, to presume [up]on.

prévaricateur, trice (prevarikatœɪr, tris) *n*, unjust judge; defaulter. **prévarication** (sjɔ̃) *f*, breach of trust, default. **prévariquer** (ke) *v.i*, to fail in one's duty; betray one's trust.

prévenance (prevnɑ̃ːs) *f*, [kind] attention. **prévenant, e** (vnɑ̃, ɑ̃ːt) *a*, attentive, kind, considerate, thoughtful; prepossessing. **prévenir** (vniːr) *v.t.ir*, to forestall, prevent; ward off; prepossess; prejudice, bias; [fore]warn, inform. **prévention** (vɑ̃sjɔ̃) *f*, prepossession, prejudice; imprisonment on suspicion, preventive arrest. **prévenu, e** (vny) *n*, accused, prisoner. **prévenu, a**, prejudiced; warned; accused.

prévision (previʒjɔ̃) *f*, prevision, forecast, expectation. **prévoir** (vwaɪr) *v.t. & abs. ir*, to foresee, forecast; provide for.

prévôt (prevo) *m*, provost.

prévoyance (prevwajɑ̃ːs) *f*, foresight, forethought; precaution. ~ *sociale*, state insurance. **prévoyant, e** (jɑ̃, ɑ̃ːt) *a*, provident; far-sighted.

prie-Dieu (pridjø), *m*, prayer stool. **prier** (e) *v.t*, to pray (to); beg, ask, request, beseech, entreat; invite. *je vous en prie*, you're welcome, don't mention it. **prière** (ɛɪr) *f*, prayer; request, entreaty. ~ *de . . .*, please . . . **prieur, e** (œːr) *n*, prior, ess. **prieuré** (œre) *m*, priory.

primage (primaːʒ) *m*, primage (*Ship.*).

primaire (primɛɪr) *a*, primary; elementary (*Sch.*).

primat (prima) *m*, primate. **primatie** (si) *f*, primacy. **primauté**

(mote) *f*, primacy; lead (*cards*, *etc.*).

prime (prim) *a*, first; earliest. ¶ *f*, premium; bounty, bonus; gift (*for coupons*); option (*Stk Ex.*). **primé, e** (me) *p.a*, bounty-fed; prize (*bull, etc.*). **primer** (me) *v.t*, to surpass; override; award a prize to; (*v.i.*) to excel; rank before.

primesautier, ère (primsotje, ɛɪr) *a*, impulsive.

primeur (primœɪr) *f*, freshness, newness; early vegetable, early fruit.

primevère (primvɛɪr) *f*, primrose. ~ *des champs*, cowslip.

primitif, ive† (primitif, iɪv) *a*, primitive, original; primeval; pristine; primary; crude.

primo (primo) *ad*, first[ly].

primogéniture (primɔʒenityɪr) *f*, primogeniture.

primordial, e† (primɔrdjal) *a*, primordial, primary; primeval.

prince (prɛ̃ːs) *m*, prince. *bon* ~, a good fellow.

princeps (prɛ̃sɛps) *a.inv*, first (*edition*).

princesse (prɛ̃sɛs) *f*, princess. **princier, ère** (sje, ɛɪr) *a*, princely.

principal, e† (prɛ̃sipal) *a*, principal, chief, head, main; staple (*product*); major (*planet*); senior. ¶ *m*, principal; chief; headmaster; main thing.

principauté (prɛ̃sipote) *f*, principality.

principe (prɛ̃sip) *m*, principle; beginning.

printanier, ère (prɛ̃tanje, ɛɪr) *a*, vernal, spring (*att.*). **printemps** (tɑ̃) *m*, spring[time].

priorité (priɔrite) *f*, priority, precedence.

pris, p.p, prendre.

prise (priːz) *f*, taking; catch; hold, purchase, grip; setting (*cement*); prize (*Naut.*); pinch (*snuff*); dose; electric plug. ~ *d'eau*, intake of water, tapping; hydrant. ~ *de bec*, altercation, set-to. ~ *de courant*, wall socket. ~ *de corps*, arrest. ~ *de sang*, blood test. ~ *de tête à terre*, nelson (*wrestling*). ~ *de vues*, filming, shooting (*cin-*

ema, TV). *être aux* ~*s avec*, to struggle with.

prisée (prize) *f*, valuation. **priser** (ze) *v.t*, to appraise, value; prize; snuff up; (*abs.*) to take snuff. **priseur** (zœɪr) *m*, appraiser; snuff taker.

prismatique (prismatik) *a*, prismatic. **prisme** (prism) *m*, prism.

prison (prizɔ̃) *m*, prison, jail; cells; imprisonment (*term*). **prisonnier, ère** (zɔnje, ɛɪr) *n*, prisoner.

privation (privasjɔ̃) *f*, deprivation, loss; privation, hardship.

privatisation (privatizasjɔ̃) *f*, denationalization (*industry, public utility, etc.*).

privauté (privote) *f*, familiarity, liberty.

privé†, e (prive) *a*, private. ¶ *m*, privy, water closet.

priver (prive) *v.t*, to deprive, bereave.

privilège (privilɛːʒ) *m*, privilege, prerogative; lien, charge. **privilégié, e** (leʒje) *p.a*, privileged; preferential. **privilégier** (ʒje) *v.t*, to privilege; charter.

prix (pri) *m*, price; value, worth, cost; consideration [money]; terms; rate; charge; fare; prize, stakes (*turf*). ~ *affiché*, posted price. ~ *courant*, market p. ~ *homologué*, established p. ~ *d'excellence*, class prize. ~ *de revient* (rəvje), ~ *coûtant* (kutɑ̃), cost [price]. ~ *de sagesse*, good-conduct prize.

probabilité (prɔbabilite) *f*, probability, likelihood. **probable†** (bl) *a*, probable, likely.

probant, e (prɔbɑ̃, ɑ̃ːt) *a*, convincing, cogent. **probation** (basjɔ̃) *f*, probation (*Eccl.*). **probe** (prɔb) *a*, honest, upright. **probité** (bite) *f*, probity, honesty.

problématique (prɔblematik) *a*, problematic(al). **problème** (blɛm) *m*, problem; puzzle; poser, teaser.

proboscide (prɔbɔsid) *f*, proboscis.

procédé (prɔsede) *m*, proceeding, dealing; behavior; process; tip

(*Bil. cue*). **procéder** (de) *v.i*, to proceed. ~ *à l'impression*, to go to press. **procédure** (dyɪr) *f*, procedure; proceedings. **procès** (sɛ) (*law*) *m*, proceedings, action, case. ~ *civil*, [law]suit. ~ *criminel*, [criminal] trial. **processif, ive** (sɛsif, iːv) *a*, litigious. **procession** (sjɔ̃) *f*, procession. **processus** (sy:s) *m*, process, course. **procès-verbal**, *m*, report; minutes.

prochain, e (prɔʃɛ̃, ɛn) *a*, nearest; next; near; proximate; forthcoming; coming; neighboring. ¶ *m*, neighbor, fellow creature. **prochainement** (ʃɛnmɑ̃) *a*, shortly, soon. **proche** (prɔʃ) *ad*, near, close. ¶ *a*, near, at hand. ~ *Orient*, Near East. ~*s* [*parents*] *m.pl*, near relations, next of kin.

proclamation (prɔklamasjɔ̃) *f*, proclamation. **proclamer** (me) *v.t*, to proclaim, publish; declare.

procrastination (prɔkrastinasjɔ̃) *f*, procrastination.

procréer (prɔkree) *v.t*, to procreate.

procuration (prɔkyrasjɔ̃) *f*, procuration, proxy, power of attorney. **procurer** (re) *v.t*, to procure, obtain, get. **procureur** (rœːr) *m*, proxy; attorney.

prodigalement (prɔdigalmɑ̃) *a*, lavishly. **prodigalité** (lite) *f*, prodigality, lavishness; wastefulness; (*pl.*) extravagance.

prodige (prɔdiːʒ) *m*, prodigy, wonder. **prodigieux, euse†** (diʒjø, øːz) *a*, prodigious, stupendous.

prodigue (prɔdig) *a*, prodigal, lavish, unsparing, profuse; wasteful. ¶ *n*, prodigal, spendthrift. **prodiguer** (ge) *v.t*, to lavish; squander.

prodrome (prɔdroːm) *m*, premonitory symptom.

producteur, trice (prɔdyktœːr, tris) *n*, producer. ¶ ~ & **productif, ive** (tif, iːv) *a*, producing, productive, bearing. **production** (sjɔ̃) *f*, production, output, yield; product. **produire** (dɥiːr) *v.t.ir*, to produce, bring forth, bear, yield; show. ~ *dans le monde*, to introduce into society, bring out. se ~, to occur, happen. **produit** (dɥi) *m*, product, produce, proceeds, yield; takings, receipts. ~ *pharmaceutique*, patent medicine.

proéminent, e (prɔeminɑ̃, ɑ̃ːt) *a*, prominent.

profanation (prɔfanasjɔ̃) *f*, profanation. **profane** (fan) *a*, profane; secular; unconsecrated (*ground*). ¶ *n*, layman; outsider; (the) profane. **profaner** (ne) *v.t*, to profane, desecrate.

proférer (prɔfere) *v.t*, to utter.

profès, esse (prɔfɛ, ɛs) *a*, professed. **professer** (se) *v.t*, to profess; teach. **professeur** (sœːr) *m*, professor; teacher; master, mistress; lecturer; instructor. **profession** (sjɔ̃) *f*, profession; occupation; calling, business, trade. **professionnel, le** (ɔnɛl) *a. & n*, professional. **professorat** (sɔra) *m*, professorship.

profil (prɔfil) *m*, profile, side face; contour, outline, section. ~ *de l'horizon*, skyline. **profiler** (le) *v.t*, to profile, streamline.

profit (prɔfi) *m*, profit, benefit. **profitable** (tabl) *a*, profitable. **profiter** (te) *v.i*, to benefit, profit; avail oneself (*de* = of); thrive. **profiteur, euse** (tœːr, øːz) *n*, profiteer.

profond, e (prɔfɔ̃, ɔ̃ːd) *a*, deep, profound; low (*bow*); sound (*sleep*). **profondément** (demɑ̃) *ad*, deeply, etc. **profondeur** (dœːr) *f*, depth; profundity.

profus, e (prɔfy, yːz) *a*, profuse (*perspiration*). **profusément** (fyzemɑ̃) *ad*, profusely, lavishly. **profusion** (zjɔ̃) *f*, profusion, lavishness.

progéniture (prɔʒenityr) *f*, progeny, offspring.

progiciel (prɔʒisjɛl) *m*, package (*computers*).

prognathe (prɔgnat) *a*, prognathous.

programmathèque (prɔgramatɛk) *f*, program library (*computers*).

programmation (prɔgramasjɔ̃) *f*, programming (*computers, data processing, cinemas*).

programme (prɔgram) *m*, program; syllabus; platform (*Pol.*). ~ *d'études*, curriculum. ~ *des courses*, race card. ~ *d'arrière-plan*, *de coulisse*, background program (*computers*). ~ *en boîte*, computer software program. *feuilles de* ~, computer instruction mànual. **programmer** (e) *v.i*, to program (*computers*). **programmeur, euse** (œːr, øz) *n*, programmer (*computers*).

progrès (prɔgrɛ) *m*, *oft. pl*, progress, [head]way. **progresser** (grɛse) *v.i*, to progress. **progressif, ive†** (sif, iːv) *a*, progressive, forward. **progression** (sjɔ̃) *f*, progression.

prohiber (prɔibe) *v.t*, to prohibit, forbid. **prohibitif, ive** (bitif, iːv) *a*, prohibitory; prohibitive. **prohibition** (sjɔ̃) *f*, prohibition. **prohibitionniste** (ɔnist) *m*, prohibitionist.

proie (prwa) *f*, prey; quarry.

projecteur (prɔʒɛktœːr) *m*, projector; searchlight; floodlight. ~ *orientable* (ɔrjɑ̃tabl), spotlight. **projectile** (til) *a. & m*, projectile, missile. **projection** (sjɔ̃) *f*, projection. **projet** (ʒɛ) *m*, project, scheme, plan; draft. ~ *de loi*, bill, measure. **projeter** (ʒte) *v.t*, to project, throw, cast; plan, contemplate.

prolétaire (prɔletɛːr) *m*, proletarian. **prolétariat** (tarja) *m*, proletariat. **prolétarien, ne** (rjɛ̃, ɛn) *a*, proletarian.

proliférer (prɔlifere) *v.t. & i*, to proliferate, spread.

prolifique (prɔlifik) *a*, prolific.

prolixe (prɔliks) *a*, prolix, long-winded.

prologue (prɔlɔg) *m*, prologue.

prolongation (prɔlɔ̃gasjɔ̃) *f. &* **prolongement** (lɔ̃gmɑ̃) *m*, prolongation; extension. **prolonge** (lɔ̃ːʒ) *f*, ammunition wagon. **prolonger** (lɔ̃ʒe) *v.t*, to prolong, protract, extend, lengthen.

promenade (prɔmnad) *f*, walking; walk, stroll; ride; drive; trip, outing, ramble; promenade. *sur la* ~ [*de la mer*], on the [sea] front. ~ *en bateau*, row; sail. ~ *militaire*, route march. **promener**

(mne) *v.t*, to take for a walk; pass, run, cast. ~ *par*, ~ *dans*, to show round. **se~**, to [go for a] walk, stroll. *allez vous ~!* be off with you! **promeneur, euse** (mnœːr, øːz) *n*, walker. **promenoir** (mnwaːr) *m*, promenade; walk; lounge.

promesse (prɔmɛs) *f*, promise. **prometteur, euse** (tœːr, øːz) *a*, promising. **promettre** (mɛtr) *v.t. & abs. ir*, to promise. *terre promise* (miːz), *terre de promission* (misjɔ̃), promised land, land of promise. **se** ~, to resolve.

promis (prɔmi) *a*, promised; intended. ¶ *m*, fiancé.

promiscuité (prɔmiskɥite) *f*, promiscuity.

promontoire (prɔmɔ̃twaːr) *m*, promontory.

promoteur, trice (prɔmɔtœːr, tris) *n*, promoter. **promotion** (sjɔ̃) *f*, promotion, preferment. ~ *des ventes*, sales promotion. **promotionel, le** (sjɔnɛl) *a*, relating to promotion. *vente* ~, special sale offer. **promouvoir** (muvwaːr) *v.t.ir*, to promote, prefer.

prompt e† (prɔ̃, ɔ̃ːt) *a*, prompt, ready, quick. **promptitude** (prɔ̃tityd) *f*, promptitude, dispatch.

promu, e (prɔmy) *a*, decorated, promoted. ¶ *n*, person who has been decorated or promoted.

promulguer (prɔmylge) *v.t*, to promulgate.

prône (proːn) *m*, sermon; homily. **prôner** (prone) *v.t*, to extoll; puff.

pronom (prɔnɔ̃) *m*, pronoun. **pronominal, e†** (nɔminal) *a*, pronominal.

prononcer (prɔnɔ̃se) *v.t. & abs*, to pronounce; utter; speak; mention; deliver (*speech*); pass (*sentence*). **se** ~, to declare oneself; be pronounced (*letter*, *syllable*). **prononciation** (sjasjɔ̃) *f*, delivery; passing; pronunciation.

pronostic (prɔnɔstik) *m*, prognostic[ation], forecast; selection (*betting*); omen. **pronostiquer** (ke) *v.t*, to prognosticate, forecast.

propagande (prɔpagɑ̃ːd) *f,* propaganda; advertising.

propager (prɔpaʒe) *v.t,* to propagate, spread.

propension (prɔpɑ̃sjɔ̃) *f,* propensity.

prophète, étesse (prɔfɛt, etɛs) *n,* prophet, ess, seer. **prophétie** (fesi) *f,* prophecy. **prophétique†** (tik) *a,* prophetic(al). **prophétiser** (ze) *v.t,* to prophesy.

propice (prɔpis) *a,* propitious, auspicious, lucky.

propitiation (prɔpisjasjɔ̃) *f,* propitiation. **propitiatoire** (twaːr) *m,* mercy seat.

proportion (prɔpɔrsjɔ̃) *f,* proportion, ratio, percentage. **proportionnel, le†** (ɔnɛl) *a,* proportional. **proportionner** (ɔne) *v.t,* to proportion.

propos (prɔpo) *m,* purpose; subject, matter; remark, (*pl.*) talk. ~ *de couloir, pl,* lobbying. à ~, *a. & ad,* to the point, apropos, opportune(ly); seasonable, -bly; apposite(ly); pertinent(ly); apt-(ly); by the way. à ~ *de, pr,* with regard to, about. *à tout* ~, at every turn. *de* ~ *délibéré,* deliberately, purposely. **proposer** (ze) *v.t,* to propose; move; propound; offer; put forward; recommend. se ~, to offer oneself; purpose, mean. **proposition** (zisjɔ̃) *f,* proposal, proposition; motion; clause (*Gram.*).

propre† (prɔpr) *a,* clean, neat; proper; peculiar; inherent; literal; own; appropriate, fit, suited. *un* ~ *à rien,* a good-for-nothing, a ne'er-do-well. *c'est du* ~, a nice thing, that is (*ironic*). ¶ *m,* characteristic, property; literal sense (*word*). **propret, te** (prɛ, ɛt) *a,* neat, tidy. **propreté** (prəte) *f,* cleanliness; neatness, tidiness.

propriétaire (prɔprietɛːr) *n,* proprietor, owner; landlord, -lady. **propriété** (te) *f,* ownership; property, estate, holding; rights; propriety. ~ [*littéraire*], copyright.

propulseur (prɔpylsœːr) *m,* propeller; engine, jet, thruster. ~ *auxiliaire,* booster (*rocket, spacecraft*). **propulsion** (sjɔ̃) *f,* propulsion.

prorata (prɔrata) *m: au* ~ *de, pr,* in proportion to, pro rata to.

proroger (prɔrɔʒe) *v.t,* to prorogue; extend.

prosaïque† (prɔzaik) *a,* prosaic.

prosateur (prɔzatœːr) *m,* prose writer.

proscrire (prɔskriːr) *v.t.ir,* to proscribe, outlaw, banish; do away with. **proscrit, e** (skri, it) *n,* outlaw.

prose (proːz) *f,* prose.

prosélyte (prɔzelit) *n,* proselyte.

prosodie (prɔzɔdi) *f,* prosody.

prospecter (prɔspɛkte) *v.t,* to prospect (*Min.*). **prospecteur** (tœːr) *m,* prospector. **prospection** (sjɔ̃) *f,* prospecting.

prospectus (prɔspɛktyːs) *m,* prospectus; handbill.

prospère (prɔspɛːr) *a,* prosperous, thriving; favorable, kind. **prospérer** (pere) *v.i,* to prosper, thrive. **prospérité** (rite) *f,* prosperity.

prostate (prɔstat) *f,* prostate [gland].

prosternation (prɔstɛrnasjɔ̃) *f,* prostration; (*pl.*) bowing & scraping. **prosterné, e** (ne) *p.a,* prostrate, prone. **prosterner** (ne) *v.t,* to prostrate. se ~, to bow down (*before, etc.*).

prostituer (prɔstitɥe) *v.t,* to prostitute.

prostration (prɔstrasjɔ̃) *f,* prostration, break down. **prostré, e** (tre) *a,* prostrate[d].

protagoniste (prɔtagɔnist) *m,* protagonist.

protecteur, trice (prɔtɛktœːr, tris) *n,* protector; patron, ess; (*m.*) protector, shield, guard. ¶ *a,* protective; patronizing. **protection** (sjɔ̃) *f,* protection; patronage. **protectionniste** (ɔnist) *m. & att,* protectionist. **protectorat** (tɔra) *m,* protectorate. **protégé, e** (teʒe) *n,* protégé, e. **protéger** (ʒe) *v.t,* to protect, shield, guard; patronize.

protestant, e (prɔtɛstɑ̃, ɑ̃ːt) *n. & a,* Protestant. **protestation** (tasjɔ̃) *f,* protest[ation]. **protester** (te) *v.t. & i,* to protest; vow. **protêt** (tɛ) *m,* protest (*bill of exchange*).

protocole (prɔtɔkɔl) *m*, protocol; etiquette.

prototype (prɔtɔtip) *m*, prototype.

protubérance (prɔtyberɑ̃ːs) *f*, protuberance.

prone (pru) *f*, prow; nose (*Avn.*).

prouesse (pruɛs) *f*, prowess, valor; feat.

prouver (pruve) *v.t*, to prove; show.

provenance (prɔvnɑ̃ːs) *f*, origin, provenance; (*s. & pl.*) produce.

provende (prɔvɑ̃ːd) *f*, provender, fodder.

provenir (prɔvniːr) *v.i.ir*, to proceed, come, arise.

proverbe (prɔvɛrb) *m*, proverb. **proverbial, e†** (bjal) *a*, proverbial.

providence (prɔvidɑ̃ːs) *f*, providence; godsend; good angel. **providentiel, le†** (dɑ̃sjɛl) *a*, providential.

province (prɔvɛ̃ːs) *f*, province; provinces, country. **provincial, e** (vɛ̃sjal) *a*, provincial, country (*att.*).

proviseur (prɔvizœːr) *m*, headmaster. **provision** (zjɔ̃) *f*, provision, store, stock, supply; deposit; funds; cover, margin (*Fin.*); consideration (*law*); retainer (*law*). ~s de bouche, provisions, food. ~s de guerre, munitions. **provisionnel, le** (ɔnɛl) *a*, provisional. **provisoire†** (zwaːr) *a*, provisional, interim, pro tem; nisi (*decree*). **provisorat** (zɔra) *m*, headmastership.

provoquer (prɔvɔke) *v.t*, to provoke; challenge; incite, instigate; induce. **provocateur** (katœːr) *m*, provoker; instigator; aggressor. agent ~, professional agitator. **provocation** (kasjɔ̃) *f*, provocation.

proxénète (prɔksenɛt) *n*, procurer, procuress.

proximité (prɔksimite) *f*, proximity, nearness, propinquity, vicinity. ~ du sang, near relationship.

prude (pryd) *a*, prudish. ¶ *f*, prude.

prudemment (prydamɑ̃) *ad*, prudently. **prudence** (dɑ̃ːs) *f*, prudence, discretion; wisdom. **prudent, e** (dɑ̃, ɑ̃ːt) *a*, prudent.

pruderie (prydri) *f*, prudery, prudishness.

prud'homme (prydɔm) *m*, man of experience and integrity; member of conciliation board. **prud'-hommesque** (mɛsk) *a*, pompous & sententiously dull.

prune (pryn) *f*, plum. **pruneau** (no) *m*, prune; bullet; bruise; black eye. **prunelaie** (nlɛ) *f*, plum orchard. **prunelle** (nɛl) *f*, sloe; pupil, apple (*eye*). [*liqueur de*] ~, sloe gin. **prunellier** (lje) *m*, blackthorn, sloe tree. **prunier** (nje) *m*, plum [tree]. ~ de damas, damson [tree].

prurit (pryrit) *m*, pruritus, itching.

Prusse (la) (prys), Prussia. **prussien, ne** (sjɛ̃, ɛn) *a. & P~, n*, Prussian. **prussique** (sik) *a*, prussic.

psalmiste (psalmist) *m*, psalmist. **psalmodie** (mɔdi) *f*, psalmody; singsong. **psalmodier** (dje) *v.i. & t*, to intone, chant; drone. **psaume** (psoːm) *m*, psalm. **psautier** (psotje) *m*, psalter.

pseudonyme (psødɔnim) *m*, pseudonym.

psychanalyse (psikanaliːz) *f*, psychoanalysis. **psyché** (ʃe) *f*, cheval glass, full-length mirror. **psychiatre** (kjaːtr) *m*, psychiatrist. **psychique** (ʃik) *a*, psychic (-al). **psychologie** (kɔlɔʒi) *f*, psychology. **psychologique** (ʒik) *a*, psychological. **psychologue** (lɔg) *m*, psychologist. **psychose** (koːz) *f*, psychosis. ~ traumatique (tromatik), shell shock.

ptomaïne (ptɔmain) *f*, ptomaine.

puant, e (pyɑ̃, ɑ̃ːt) *a*, stinking; foul. **puanteur** (ɑ̃tœːr) *f*, stink, stench.

puberté (pybɛrte) *f*, puberty.

public, ique† (pyblik) *a*, public; common; national (*debt*); civil (*service*). ¶ *m*, public. **publicain** (kɛ̃) *m*, publican (*Bible*); extortioner. **publication** (kasjɔ̃) *f*, publication; publishing; issue.

publiciste (sist) *m*, publicist; advertising man. **publicité** (te) *f*, publicity, advertising. **~sur les nuages**, sky writing. **publier** (e) *v.t*, to publish; proclaim; issue.

puce (pys) *f*, flea; chip (*computers*). secouer les ~s, to tell someone off. ¶ *a*, puce.

pucelle (pysɛl) *f*, maid[en], virgin.

puceron (pysrɔ̃) *m*, plant louse.

pudding (pudiŋ) *m*, pudding.

puddler (pydle) *v.t*, to puddle (*iron*).

pudeur (pydœːr) *f*, modesty, decency, shame. **pudibond, e** (dibɔ̃, ɔ̃:d) *a*, prudish. **pudique†** (dik) *a*, chaste, modest.

puer (pɥe) *v.i*, to stink, smell; (*v.t.*) to stink of, smell of.

puériculture (pɥerikyltyːr) *f*, rearing of children. **~ sociale**, child welfare. **puéril, e†** (ril) *a*, puerile, childish. **puérilité** (lite) *f*, puerility, childishness.

pugilat (pyʒila) *m*, pugilism; set-to. **pugiliste** (list) *m*, pugilist.

pugnace (pygnas) *a*, pugnacious.

puîné, e (pɥine) *a. & n*, younger (brother, sister).

puis (pɥi) *ad*, then, afterwards, next; besides.

puisard (pɥizaːr) *m*, sink, sump. **puisatier** (zatje) *m*, well-digger. **puiser** (ze) *v.t. & i*, to draw, derive.

puisque, puisqu' (pɥisk[ə]) *c*, since, as, seeing that.

puissamment (pɥisamɑ̃) *ad*, powerfully, mightily. **puissance** (sɑ̃:s) *f*, power; might; strength, force; authority, sway, **~ lumineuse en bougies**, candlepower. **puissant, e** (sɑ̃, ɑ̃:t) *a*, powerful; mighty; strong; potent; weighty. *les puissants*, the mighty ones.

puits (pɥi) *m*, well, hole; shaft (*Min.*); cockpit (*Avn.*); fount (*fig.*).

pull (pul) *m*, pullover, sweater. **pull-over** (ɔvœːr) *m*, pullover, sweater.

pulluler (pyllyle) *v.i*, to pullulate, swarm.

pulmonaire (pylmɔnɛːr) *a*, pulmonary.

pulpe (pylp) *f*, pulp. **pulper** (pe) *v.t*, to pulp.

pulsation (pylsasjɔ̃) *f*, pulsation, throb[bing].

pulvériser (pylverize) *v.t*, to pulverize, powder; spray. **pulvérulent, e** (rylɑ̃, ɑ̃:t) *a*, powdery.

puma (pyma) *m*, puma, cougar.

punais, e (pynɛ, ɛːz) *a*, foul-breathed.

punaise (pynɛːz) *f*, bug; thumbtack.

punch (pɔ̃:ʃ) *m*, punch (*drink*).

punir (pyniːr) *v.t*, to punish; avenge. **punissable** (nisabl) *a*, **punishable. punition** (sjɔ̃) *f*, punishment.

pupille (pypil) *n*, ward. ¶ *f*, pupil (*eye*).

pupitre (pypitr) *m*, desk; stand (*music*); console (*TV*, *computers*). **~ à clavier**, keyboard console. **~ de mélange**, mixing c, audio-mixer, switcher. **~ de régie**, control c. **pupitreur** (trœːr) *m*, console operator.

pur, e† (pyːr) *a*, pure; unalloyed; plain; mere; sheer; clear; neat (*unwatered*).

purée (pyre) *f*, mash; [thick] soup. **~ de pommes de terre, de navets**, mashed potatoes, turnips.

pureté (pyrte) *f*, purity; clearness (*sky*).

purgatif, ive (pyrgatif, iːv) *a. & m*, purgative. **purgation** (sjɔ̃) *f*, purging; purge. **purgatoire** (twaːr) *m*, purgatory. **purger** (ʒe) *v.t*, to purge, cleanse, clear; redeem (*mortgage*). **~ une peine**, to serve a prison sentence.

purifier (pyrifje) *v.t*, to purify, cleanse. **puriste** (rist) *n*, purist.

purin (pyrɛ̃) *m*, liquid manure.

puritain, e (pyritɛ̃, ɛn) *n*, Puritan. ¶ *a*, Puritan; puritanic(al).

purpurin, e (pyrpyrɛ̃, in) *a*, purplish.

purulent, e (pyrylɑ̃, ɑ̃:t) *a*, purulent, mattery. **pus** (py) *m*, pus, matter.

pusillanime (pyzillanim) *a*, pusillanimous.

pustule (pystyl) *f*, pustule, pimple.

putain (pytɛ̃) *f*, whore, prostitute; slut.

putatif, ive (pytatif, i:v) *a*, putative, reputed.

putois (pytwa) *m*, polecat.

putréfaction (pytrefaksjɔ̃) *f*, putrefaction. **putréfier** (fje) *v.t*, to putrefy. **putride** (trid) *a*, putrid.

puy (pɥi) *m*, mountain, peak.

pygmée (pigme) *m*, pygmy.

pyjama (piʒama) *m*, pajamas.

pylône (pilo:n) *m*, pylon, tower.

pyorrhée (pyɔre) *f*, pyorrhea.

pyramide (piramid) *f*, pyramid. **Pyrénées (les)** (pirene) *f.pl*, the Pyrenees.

pyrite (pirit) *f*, pyrites.

pyrogravure (pirɔgravy:r) *f*, poker work.

pyrotechnie (pirɔtɛkni) *f*, pyrotechnics.

python (pitɔ̃) *m*, python.

Q

quadrangulaire (kwadrɑ̃gylɛ:r) *a*, quadrangular.

quadrant (kwadrɑ̃) *m*, quadrant (*Math.*).

quadrupède (kwadrypɛd) *a*, quadruped(al), four-footed. ¶ *m*, quadruped.

quadruple (kwadrypl) *a. & m*, quadruple, fourfold. ~ **croche**, *f*, semi- *or* hemi-demisemiquaver.

quai (ke) *m*, quay, wharf; embankment (*river*); platform (*Rly*).

quaiche (kɛʃ) *f*, ketch.

qualifier (kalifje) *v.t*, to qualify, call, style; describe. **qualité** (te) *f*, quality; property; qualification, profession; capacity. ~ *d'amateur*, amateur status.

quand (kɑ̃) *c. & ad*, when; [al]though, even if. ~ *même*, all the same, notwithstanding, nevertheless.

quant à (kɑ̃ta) *pr*, as for, as to, as regards, for. **quant-à-moi**, **quant-à-soi**, *m*, dignity, reserve, stand-offishness.

quantième (kɑ̃tjɛm) *m*, day of the month, date.

quantité (kɑ̃tite) *f*, quantity; amount; lots, a lot. ~ *de pluie* [*tombée*], rainfall.

quantum (kwɑ̃tɔm) *m*, quantum.

quarantaine (karɑ̃tɛn) *f*, [about] forty; quarantine; Lent. *mettre en ~*, to quarantine (*ship*); send (*pers.*) to Coventry. **quarante** (rɑ̃:t) *a*, forty. ¶ *m*, forty; 40th. **quarantième** (rɑ̃tjɛm) *a. & n*, fortieth.

quart (ka:r) *m*, quarter, fourth [part]; ¼ liter; watch (*Naut.*). ~ *d'heure*, quarter of an hour. ~ *de cercle*, quadrant (*Surv. instrument*). ~ [*de vent*], point [of the compass]. **quarte** (kart) *f*, fourth (*Mus.*).

quarteron, ne (kartərɔ̃, ɔn) *n*, quadroon.

quartier (kartje) *m*, quarter; portion, lump; haunch (*meat*); gammon (*bacon*); ward, district; neighborhood; quarters. ~ *général*, headquarters.

quartz (kwarts) *m*, quartz.

quasi (kɑzi) *ad*, almost, quasi. ~ *aveugle*, almost blind, purblind. ~ *-délit*, *m*, quasi-delict, technical offense. **Quasimodo** (kazimɔdo) *f*, Low Sunday.

quassia (kwasja) *m*, quassia (*bark*). **quassier** (sje) *m*, quassia (*tree*).

quatorze (katɔrz) *a. & m*, fourteen; 14th. **quatorzième†** (zjɛm) *a. & n*, fourteenth.

quatrain (katrɛ̃) *m*, quatrain.

quatre (katr) *a. & m*, four; 4th. *lac des Q~Cantons*, Lake of Lucerne. ~ *jumeaux*, quadruplets. *à ~ pattes*, on all fours. **~-vingt-dix** (trəvɛ̃di[s]) *a. & m*, ninety. ~ *-vingt-onze* (vɛ̃:z), 91. **~-vingt-dixième** (zjɛm) *a. & n*, ninetieth. **~-vingtième** (tjɛm) *a. & n*, eightieth. *~-vingts & ~vingt*, *a. & m*, eighty. *~vingt-un* (vɛ̃œ̃), 81. **quatrième†** (triɛm) *a. & n*, fourth.

quatuor (kwatɥɔ:r) *m*, quartet.

que, qu' (kə, k) *c. & ad*, that; than; as; whether; how; but; only; lest; let, may. ¶ *pn*, whom; which; that; what. *qu'est-ce que?* (kɛskə) *& qu'est-ce qui* (ki)? what?

quel, le (kɛl) *a*, what; what a;

which; who. ~ *que*, whatever; whoever.

quelconque (kɛlkɔ̃:k) *a*, any; some; ordinary, mediocre.

quelque (kɛlk[ə]) *a*, some, any; a few, ~ *chose*, *m*, something; anything. ~*fois*, *ad*, sometimes. ~ *part*, *ad*, somewhere.

quelqu'un, quelqu'une (kɛl-kœ̃, kyn) *pn*, somebody, someone, one, anybody, anyone. *quelques-uns, unes* (kəzœ̃, yn) *pl*, some [people], a few.

quémander (kemɑ̃de) *v.i*, to beg; (*v.t.*) to beg for, solicit.

qu'en-dira-t-on (le) (kɑ̃dira-tɔ̃) *m*, what people may say.

quenouille (kənu:j) *f*, distaff; bedpost.

querelle (kərɛl) *f*, quarrel, row. ~ *d'ivrognes*, drunken brawl. **quereller** (le) *v.t*, to quarrel with; scold. se ~, to quarrel, wrangle. **querelleur, euse** (lœ:r, ø:z) *n*, quarreler, wrangler; (*att.*) quarrelsome.

question (kɛstjɔ̃) *f*, question; query; point, matter, issue. ~ *d'intérêt secondaire*, side issue. **questionnaire** (ɔnɛ:r) *m*, list of questions. **questionner** (ne) *v.t*, to question.

quête (kɛ:t) *f*, quest, search; collection, offertory. **quêter** (kɛte) *v.t*, to seek for; collect (*alms*).

queue (kø) *f*, tail; brush (*fox*); pigtail; stem; stalk; handle, shank; cue (*Bil.*); train; rear; queue, file; penis (*obscene*). ~ *d'aronde* (darɔ̃:d) *f*, dovetail. ~-*de-morue* (dmɔry) ou ~-*de-pie* (dpi) *f*, [swallow] tails (*dress coat*). en ~, in the rear. *faire* ~, to wait in line. *faire une* ~ *de poisson*, to cut in front of another automobile. *finir en* ~ *de poisson*, to end badly. **queuter** (køte) *v.i*, to push the ball (*Bil.*).

qui (ki) *pn*, who; whom; which; that. ~ *vive?* who goes there?

quiconque (kikɔ̃:k) *pn*, who[so]-ever.

quiétude (kɥietyd) *f*, quietude.

quignon (kiɲɔ̃) *m*, [c]hunk, hunch.

quille (ki:j) *f*, skittle, ninepin; keel. **quillier** (kije) *m*, skittle alley.

quincaillerie (kɛ̃kajri) *f*, hardware. **quincaillier** (je) *m*, hardware man.

quinconce (kɛ̃kɔ̃:s) *m*, staggered arrangement.

quinine (kinin) *f*, quinine.

quinquennal, e (kɥɛ̃kɛnnal) *a*, quinquennial; five-year (*plan*).

quinquina (kɛ̃kina) *m*, Peruvian bark.

quintal [métrique] (kɛ̃tal) *m*, [metric] quintal = 100 kilos.

quinte (kɛ̃:t) *f*, quint; fifth (*Mus.*); caprice, crotchet. ~ [*de toux*], fit of coughing.

quintessence (kɛ̃tesɑ̃:s) *f*, quintessence.

quintette (kɥɛ̃tɛt) *f*, quintet[te].

quinteux, euse (kɛ̃tø, ø:z) *a*, crotchety; fitful.

quintuple (kɛ̃typlə) *a*, quintuple, fivefold. ¶ *m*, fivefold.

quinzaine (kɛ̃zɛn) *f*, [about] fifteen; fortnight. **quinze** (kɛ̃:z) *a. & m*, fifteen; 15th. ~ *jours*, fortnight. **quinzième†** (kɛ̃zjɛm) *a. & n*, fifteenth.

quiproquo (kiprɔko) *m*, mistake, misunderstanding (*mistaking one for another*).

quittance (kitɑ̃:s) *f*, receipt. **quittancer** (tɑ̃se) *v.t*, to r. **quitte** (kit) *a*, quit, rid, free. ~ *à* ~, *ad*, quits. ~ *ou double*, double or quits. *nous sommes* ~*s*, we're even. **quitter** (te) *v.t. & i*, to leave, quit, vacate; give up; swerve from. *ne quittez pas!* hold on! hold the line! (*Teleph.*). **quitus** (kity:s) *m*, discharge.

qui-vive (kivi:v) *m*, challenge (*sentry's*); qui vive, look-out, alert.

quoi (kwa) *pn. & i*, what; which; that. ~ *qu'il en soit*, be that as it may. *de* ~, something; enough, the wherewithal.

quoique, quoiqu' (kwak[ə]) *c*, [al]though.

quolibet (kɔlibɛ) *m*, gibe; quibble.

quorum (kɔrɔm) *m*, quorum.

quota (kwɔta) *m*, quota. ~ *d'exploitation*, exhibitor's quota. *sondage par* ~, quota sampling.

quote-part (kɔtpaːr) *f*, share, quota.

quotidien, ne (kɔtidjɛ̃, ɛn) *a*, daily; everyday. [**journal**] **quotidien**, *m*, daily [paper]. **quotidiennement** (ɛnmɑ̃) *ad*, daily.

quotient (kɔsjɑ̃) *m*, quotient.

quotité (kɔtite) *f*, quota, share.

R

rabâchage (rabɑʃaːʒ) *m*, endless repetition. **rabâcher** (baʃe) *v.i*, to repeat over and over. *il rabâche toujours les mêmes choses*, he is always harping on the same string.

rabais (rabɛ) *m*, allowance, rebate. *adjudication au* ~, award to the lowest bidder. **rabaisser** (se) *v.t*, to lower; disparage, belittle.

rabat (raba) *m*, beating (for game). ~**-joie**, *m*, killjoy. **rabatteur, euse** (tœːr ɸːz) *n*, tout; (*m.*) beater. **rabattre** (tr) *v.t.ir*, to beat down, bring d., turn d., press d., lower; bate; take off; beat up (*hunting*). **se** ~, to turn off, change; come down.

rabbin (rabɛ̃) *m*, rabbi.

râble (rɑːbl) *m*, back; saddle (hare). **râblé** (ble) *a*, strong, sturdy, husky.

rabot (rabo) *m*, plane (*tool*). **raboter** (bote) *v.t*, to plane; polish (*fig.*). **roboteux, euse** (tɸ, ɸːz) *a*, rough, rugged; knotty.

rabougrir (rabugriːr) *v.t*, to stunt (*growth*).

rabouter (rabute) *ou* **raboutir** (tiːr) *v.t*, to join [up].

rabrouer (rabrue) *v.t*, to rebuff, snub; rebuke.

racaille (rakɑːj) *f*, rabble, riffraff.

raccommodage (rakɔmɔdaːʒ) *m*, mending, repairing. **raccommodement** (dmɑ̃) *m*, reconciliation. **raccommoder** (de) *v.t*, to mend, repair; reconcile. **se** ~, to make it up. **raccommodeur, euse** (dœːr, ɸːz) *n*, mender, repairer.

raccord (rakɔːr) *m*, join; joint; connection, union, coupling; continuity shot (*cinema*). **raccorder** (kɔrde) *v.t*, to join, connect, couple, patch (*computers*).

raccourci (rakursi) *m*, abridgement; epitome; shortcut; foreshortening; bypass (*computers*). **raccourcir** (siːr) *v.t*, to shorten; abridge; curtail; foreshorten. [**se**] ~, to draw in (*days*).

raccroc (rakro) *m*, fluke, lucky stroke. **raccrocher** (krɔʃe) *v.t*, to hook up, hang up, replace. **se** ~, to clutch, catch; cling.

race (ras) *f*, race, descent, ancestry; strain, blood, breed, stock, tribe, species. *de* ~, thoroughbred. **racé, e** (se) *a*, thoroughbred.

rachat (raʃa) *m*, repurchase; redemption; ransom; surrender (*Insce*). **racheter** (ʃte) *v.t*, to repurchase, buy back; redeem; surrender; ransom; atone for.

rachitisme (raʃitism) *m*, rachitis, rickets.

racine (rasin) *f*, root; root, fang (*of tooth*); [silkworm] gut (*Fish.*). ~ *d'iris*, orris root. ~ *pivotante*, taproot.

raclée (rɑkle) *f*, thrashing, hiding. **racler** (kle) *v.t*, to scrape; rake; rasp; strike (*measure*). **racloir** (klwaːr) *m*, scraper; squeegee. **racloire** (klwaːr) *f*, strickle, strike (*grain*). **raclure** (klyːr) *f*, scrapings.

racoler (rakɔle) *v.t*, to recruit; tout for.

racontar (rakɔ̃taːr) *m*, gossip, scandal. **raconter** (te) *v.t*, to relate, recount, narrate, tell; (*abs.*) to tell a story (*well, etc.*). **en** ~, to tell tall tales.

racornir (rakɔrniːr) *v.t*, to harden; shrivel.

rade (rad) *f*, roadstead, roads (*Naut.*).

radeau (rado) *m*, raft.

radial, e (radjal) *a*, radial. **radiateur** (tœːr) *m*, radiator; fire (*gas, Elec.*). **radiation** (sjɔ̃) *f*, striking out; s. off; radiation.

radical, e† (radikal) *a. & m*, radical; root.

radier (radje) *v.t*, to strike out; s. off.

radieux, euse (radjø, ø:z) *a*, radiant, beaming.

radin (radɛ̃) *a*, stingy. ¶ *m*, miser, stingy person.

radio (radjo) *f*, radio; cablegram; X-ray; radio operator.

radioactif, ive (radjoaktif, i:v) *a*, radioactive. **radiodiffuser** (ɔdifyze) *v.t*, to broadcast. **radiodiffusion** (zjɔ̃) *f*, broadcasting. **radiogramme** (gram) *m*, radiogram. **radiographie** (fi) *f*, radiography. **radiotélégraphie** (telegrafi) *f*, radiotelegraphy. **radiothérapie** (terapi) *f*, X-ray treatment, radiotherapy.

radis (radi) *m*, radish. *sans un ~*, without a cent.

radium (radjɔm) *m*, radium.

radius (radjy:s) *m*, radius (*Anat.*).

radoter (radɔte) *v.i*, to drivel (*talk*), dote. **radoteur, euse** (tœ:r, ø:z) *n*, dotard.

radouber (radube) *v.t*, to repair (*ship*).

radoucir (radusi:r) *v.t*, to soften; make milder.

rafale (rafal) *f*, squall, gust. *~ de pluie*, cloudburst.

raffermir (rafɛrmi:r) *v.t*, to harden; strengthen.

raffinage (rafina:ʒ) *m*, refining. **raffiné, e** (ne) *p.a*, refined; subtle. **raffinement** (nmɑ̃) *m*, refinement, subtlety. **raffiner** (ne) *v.t. & abs*, to refine. **raffinerie** (nri) *f*, refinery.

raffoler de (rafɔle), to be very fond of, dote on.

rafistoler (rafistɔle) *v.t*, to patch up.

rafle (rɑ:fl) *f*, stalk (*grape*); cob (*corn*); clean sweep; raid; round up; swag, loot. **rafler** (rɑfle) *v.t*, to carry off; round up. *~ le tout*, to sweep the board.

rafraîchir (rafrɛʃi:r) *v.t. & abs. & i*, to cool, refresh, freshen; revive; trim (*hair, grass*). **rafraîchissements** (ʃismɑ̃) *m.pl*, [light] refreshments.

ragaillardir (ragajardi:r) *v.t*, to cheer up.

rage (ra:ʒ) *f*, rage; rabies, madness; mania. *~ de dents*, raging

toothache. **rager** (raʒe) *v.i*, to rage. **rageur, euse†** (ʒœ:r, ø:z) *a. & n*, passionate (person), spitfire.

ragot (rago) *m*, gossip, scandal.

ragoût (ragu) *m*, stew. *~ de mouton*, lamb stew. **ragoûtant, e** (tɑ̃, ɑ̃:t) *a*, tempting.

ragréer (ragree) *v.t*, to clean up; do up (*repair house, etc.*).

rai (rɛ) *m*, ray; spoke.

raid (rɛd) *m*, raid; endurance test.

raide (rɛd) *a*, stiff; stark; tight; taut, tense; steep. *être ~*, to be broke. ¶ *m*, 10-franc note (*slang*). **raideur** (dœ:r) *f*, stiffness. **raidir** (di:r) *v.t*, to stiffen; tighten.

raie (rɛ) *f*, line, stroke; streak; stripe; ridge (*Agric.*); part (*hair*); ray, skate (*fish*).

raifort (rɛfɔ:r) *m*, horseradish.

rail (rɑ:j) *m*, rail (*Rly. metal or transport*). *~ de courant*, live rail.

railler (rɑje) *v.t. & abs*, to jeer at, laugh at; joke. **raillerie** (jri) *f*, raillery, banter, joke, jesting.

rainure (rɛny:r) *f*, groove, slot. *~ de clavette*, keyway.

raire (rɛ:r) *v.i.ir*, to troat, bell.

raisin (rɛzɛ̃) *m*, grape, grapes. *~s de Corinthe*, currants (*dried*). *~ de serres*, hothouse grapes. *~s de Smyrne*, sultanas. *~ de treille*, dessert grapes. *~ de vigne*, wine grapes. *~s secs*, raisins. *~s secs muscats*, muscatels.

raison (rɛzɔ̃) *f*, reason, motive, ground; sanity, senses; sense; satisfaction; ratio, rate. *~ [sociale]*, firm [name], trade name. *avoir ~*, to be right. *à ~ de*, at the rate of. **raisonnable†** (zɔnabl) *a*, reasonable; rational; fair, adequate. **raisonnement** (nmɑ̃) *m*, reasoning; argument. **raisonner** (ne) *v.i*, to reason, argue; (*v.t.*) to consider; reason with. **raisonneur, euse** (nœ:r, ø:z) *n*, reasoner, arguer; (*att.*) reasoning, argumentative.

rajeunir (raʒœni:r) *v.t*, to rejuvenate; make look younger; renovate.

rajouter (raʒute) *v.t*, to add more of something.

rajuster (raȝyste) *v.t*, to readjust; put straight; refit.

râle (rɑːl) *m*, rail (*bird*); rattle (*in throat*). **râler** (le) *v.i*, to rattle (*throat*); gasp one's last; grumble.

ralenti (ralɑ̃ti) *m*, slow motion (*cinema*). travail au ~, slowdown strike.

ralentir (ralɑ̃tiːr) *v.t*. & *i*, to slacken, slow down.

rallier (ralje) *v.t*, to rally; rejoin.

rallonge (ralɔ̃ːȝ) *f*, lengthening piece; leaf (*table*). **rallonger** (lɔ̃ȝe) *v.t*, to lengthen.

rallumer (ralyme) *v.t*, to relight, rekindle.

rallye (rali) *m*, race meeting, rally. ~-*paper* (pepœːr) *m*, paper chase, hare & hounds.

ramage (ramaːȝ) *m*, floral design; song (*of birds*).

ramas (ramɑ *m*, heap.

ramasse (ramɑs) *f*, sledge (*alpine*). ~-*couverts*, *m*, plate basket. ~-*miettes*, *m*, crumb tray. ~-*miettes automatique*, crumb sweeper. **ramassé**, e (se) *p.a*, thickset, stocky. **ramasser** (se) *v.t*, to gather, collect; pick up. **ramasseur, euse** (sœːr, ‿øːz) *n*, collector, gatherer. **ramassis** (si) *m*, heap; set.

rame (ram) *f*, stick (*Hort.*); oar; ream (*500 sheets*); train (*of cars, etc.*). ~ *directe*, through portion (*Rly.*).

rameau (ramo) *m*, branch; bough; palm (*Eccl.*). dimanche des ~x, Palm ‿Sunday. **ramée** (me) *f*, green‿wood, arbor.

ramener (ramne) *v.t*, to bring back; reduce; restore; reset.

ramer (rame) *v.t*, to stick (*Hort.*); (*v.i.*) to row, pull (*oar*). ~ *à rebours*, to back water. **rameur, euse** (mœːr, ‿øːz) *n*, rower, oarsman, -woman.

ramier (ramje) *m*, ring dove, wood pigeon.

ramification (ramifikasjɔ̃) *f*, ramification. **se ramifier** (fje) *v.pr*, to ramify. **ramilles** (miːj) *f.pl*, twigs.

ramolli, e (ramɔli) *p.a*, dull-witted. **ramollir** (liːr) *v.t*, to soften; enervate.

ramoner (ramɔne) *v.t*, to sweep (*chimney*). **ramoneur** (nœːr) *m*, chimney sweep[er].

rampant, e (rɑ̃pɑ̃, ‿ɑ̃ːt) *a*, rampant; creeping; crawling; reptile; groveling. **rampe** (rɑ̃p) *f*, rise, slope; upgrade; rack; banisters, handrail; footlights; ramp. ~ *de lancement*, launching ramp (*missiles*). **ramper** (rɑ̃pe) *v.i*, to creep, crawl; cringe, truckle, fawn, grovel.

ramure (ramyːr) *f*, branches; antlers.

rancart (mettre au) (rɑ̃kaːr), to cast aside.

rance (rɑ̃ːs) *a*, rancid, rank. **rancir** (rɑ̃siːr) *v.i*, to become rancid.

rancœur (rɑ̃kœːr) *f*, rancor, bitterness.

rançon (rɑ̃sɔ̃) *f*, ransom. **rançonner** (sɔne) *v.t*, to ransom; fleece.

rancune (rɑ̃kyn) *f*, rancor, spite; grudge. **rancunier, ère** (nje, ‿ɛːr) *a*, rancorous, spiteful.

randonnée (rɑ̃dɔne) *f*, circuit; trip, run.

rang (rɑ̃) *m*, row, line; tier; rank, station, place; rate, class. **rangé**, e (ȝe) *p.a*, tidy; steady (*man*); pitched (*battle*). **rangée** (ȝe) *f*, row, line; tier; array. **ranger** (ȝe) *v.t*, to arrange, marshal, array; tidy, put away; rank, range. *se* ~, to draw up; fall in, side; stand aside; sober down; veer. *rangés comme des harengs en caque*, packed like sardines (*people*).

ranimer (ranime) *v.t*, to revive; stir up; cheer.

rapace (rapas) *a*, rapacious.

rapatrier (rapatrie) *v.t*, to repatriate, send home.

râpe (rɑːp) *f*, rasp; grater (*nutmeg, etc.*) **râpé**, e (rɑpe) *p.a*, grated; threadbare, shabby. **râper** (pe) *v.t*, to rasp; grate; wear threadbare. **rapeux, euse** (pø, ‿øːz) *a*, grating, harsh (*wine*).

rapetasser (raptase) *v.t*, to patch, cobble.

rapetisser (raptise) *v.t*. & *i*, to shorten; dwarf.

rapide† (rapid) *a*, rapid, fast,

swift; speedy; cursory; steep. ¶ *m*, rapid (*river*); fast train, express.

rapiécer (rapjese) *v.t*, to piece, patch.

rapin (rapɛ̃) *m*, art student; dauber.

rapine (rapin) *f*, rapine. **rapiner** (ne) *v.t. & i*, to pillage.

rappareiller (raparɛje) & **rapparier** (rje) *v.t*, to match, pair.

rappel (rapɛl) *m*, recall; call[ing]; reminder; repeal. **rappeler** (ple) *v.t*, to recall; call (*to order, etc.*); summon; remind; r. of; remember; repeal. **se** ~, to recollect, remember.

rapport (rapɔːr) *m*, yield, return; report, account, statement; tale; relation, connection; regard; (*pl.*) terms; (*pl.*) intercourse; ratio. ~ *à*, because of. ~*s probables*, betting forecast. **rapporter** (pɔrte) *v.t. & abs*, to bring back; retrieve (*game*); yield; get; add; inset; report, state; tell tales; refer, ascribe; revoke. se ~, to agree, tally; refer, relate. **rapporteur, euse** (tœːr, øːz) *n*, talebearer; (*m.*) protractor.

rapprendre (raprɑ̃ːdr) *v.t.ir*, to learn again.

rapprocher (raprɔʃe) *v.t*, to bring nearer; b. together; reconcile; compare.

rapt (rapt) *m*, abduction; kidnapping.

raquette (rakɛt) *f*, racket; battledore. ~ *à neige*, snowshoe.

rare (rɑːr) *a*, rare; scarce; uncommon; unusual; sparse, thin. **raréfier** (rarefje) *v.t*, to rarefy. **rarement** (rarmɑ̃) *ad*, rarely, seldom. **rareté** (te) *f*, rarity; scarcity; curiosity.

ras, e (rɑ, ɑːz) *a*, close-cropped; c.-shaven; bare, naked, open. *à* (ou *au*) *ras de*, level with, flush with. ~ *du cou*, crew-necked. *en avoir* ~ *le bol*, to be weary of something, have "had it." *rase campagne*, open country. **rasade** (razad) *f*, bumper (*brimful glass*).

raser (raze) *v.t*, to shave; raze; graze, brush, skim. *se* ~, to be bored (*slang*). **rasoir** (zwaːr) *m*, razor; bore (*slang*).

rassasier (rasazje) *v.t*, to satisfy; satiate, sate, surfeit, cloy, glut.

rassembler (rasɑ̃ble) *v.t*, to reassemble; assemble, muster, collect.

rasseoir (raswaːr) *v.t.ir*, to reseat; settle. **se** ~, to sit down again.

rasséréner (se) (raserene) *v.pr*, to clear [up] (*weather*); calm.

rassis, e (rasi, iːz) *p.a*, settled, calm, staid, sedate, sane; stale (*bread*).

rassortir (rasɔrtiːr) *v.t*, to match; restock.

rassurer (rasyre) *v.t*, to reassure, cheer, hearten; strengthen.

rat, (ra) *m*, rat; ballet girl. *un* ~ *dans la tête*, a bee in one's bonnet. ~ *de bibliothèque* bookworm (*pers.*). ~ *de cave*, exciseman; taper (*coiled*). ~ *des champs*, field mouse. ~ *musqué*, muskrat, musquash.

ratatiné, e (ratatine) *p.a*, shriveled, shrunken; wizened.

rate (rat) *f*, spleen, milt (*Anat.*); she-rat.

raté (rate) *m*, misfire; failure; flop.

râteau (rɑto) *m*, rake. **râteler** (tle) *v.t*, to rake up. **râtelier** (təlje) *m*, rack; denture.

rater (rate) *v.i*, to misfire; miscarry, fail; (*v.t.*) to miss; fail in; fail to obtain.

ratier (ratje) *m*, ratter (*dog*). **ratière** (tjɛːr) *f*, rattrap.

ratifier (ratifje) *v.t*, to ratify, confirm.

ration (rasjɔ̃) *f*, ration, allowance.

rationalisme (rasjɔnalism) *m*, rationalism. **rationnel, le†** (nɛl) *a*, rational; pure (*mechanics*).

rationner (rasjɔne) *v.t*, to ration; stint.

ratisser (ratise) *v.t*, to rake; scrape.

raton (ratɔ̃) *m*, young rat; darling; Arab (*pejorative*). ~ *laveur*, raccoon. **ratonnade** (ad) *f*, brutal police raid.

rattacher (rataʃe) *v.t*, to refasten; bind; connect.

rattraper (ratrape) *v.t*, to recap-

ture; overtake, catch up; recover.
rature (raty:r) *f*, erasure. **raturer**
(tyre) *v.t*, to erase, scratch out.
rauque (ro:k) *a*, hoarse, raucous,
harsh.
ravage (rava:ʒ) *m. oft. pl*, ravage, havoc, devastation. **ravager**
(vaʒe) *v.t*, to ravage, devastate,
lay waste. *ravagé(e) [par les intempéries]*, weather-beaten.
ravaler (ravale) *v.t*, to swallow
again; eat (*one's words*); disparage; rough-cast (*wall*). se ~,
to lower oneself, stoop (*fig.*).
ravauder (ravode) *v.t. & abs*,
to mend; darn.
rave (ra:v) *f*, rape, coleseed.
Ravenne (ravɛn) *f*, Ravenna.
ravi (ravi) *a*, entranced.
ravigoter (ravigɔte) *v.t*, to revive, enliven.
ravilir (ravili:r) *v.t*, to degrade.
ravin (ravɛ̃) *m*, ravine. **ravine** (vin) *f*,
ravine, gully. **raviner** (vine) *v.t*,
to gully; furrow.
ravir (ravi:r) *v.t*, to ravish, carry
off; delight, enrapture.
raviser (se) (ravize) *v.pr*, to
change one's mind.
ravissant (ravisɑ̃) *a*, ravishing,
delightful; predatory; ravenous.
ravissement (mɑ̃) *m*, rapture; kidnapping; rape. **ravisseur** (œ:r)
m, ravisher; kidnapper.
ravitailler (ravitaje) *v.t*, to [re]-victual.
raviver (ravive) *v.t*, to revive.
ravoir (ravwa:r) *v.t*, to get
(*something*) back.
rayer (rɛje) *v.t*, to scratch, score;
rule; stripe, streak; rifle; strike
out, delete.
ray-grass (rɛgra:s) *m*, rye grass.
rayon (rɛjɔ̃) *m*, ray, beam; gleam;
radius; spoke; comb (*honey*);
drill, furrow, row; shelf; department; rayon, artificial silk. **rayonnant, e** (jɔnɑ̃, ɑ̃:t) *a*, radiant;
beaming. **rayonnement** (nmɑ̃)
m, radiation; radiance, effulgence.
rayonner (ne) *v.i*, to radiate,
beam, shine; (*v.t.*) to fit with
shelves.
rayure (rɛjy:r) *f*, scratch, etc., as
rayer.
raz de marée (ra) *m*, tide race,
bore; tidal wave.

razzia (razja) *f*, raid, foray. **razzier** (zje) *v.t*, to raid.
ré (re) *m*, D (*Mus.*).
réactif (reaktif) *m*, reagent
(*Chem.*). **réacteur** (tœ:r) *m*, jet engine; reactor; nuclear pile. ~ *à
fission*, fission reactor. ~ *producteur de matière fissile*, ~ *surrégénérateur*, breeder r. **réaction** (sjɔ̃)
f, reaction. *avion à* ~, jet plane.
réactionnaire (ɔnɛ:r) *a. & n*, reactionary. **réagir** (ʒi:r) *v.i*, to react.
réalisateur (realizatœ:r) *m*, director (*cinema*). **réalisation**
(zasjɔ̃) *f*, direction (*cinema*).
réaliser (realize) *v.t*, to realize;
make (*profit*); close (*bargain*).
réaliste (list) *a. & n*, realist. **réalité**
(te) *f*, reality.
réanimer (reanime) *v.t*, to revive, resuscitate.
réapparition (reaparisjɔ̃) *f*, reappearance.
réassurer (reasyre) *v.t*, to reinsure.
rébarbatif, ive (rebarbatif, i:v)
a, grim; surly.
rebâtir (rəbɑti:r) *v.t*, to rebuild;
reconstruct.
rebattre (rəbatr) *v.t.ir*, to beat
again; reshuffle (*cards*); repeat.
rebattu, e (ty) *p.a*, beaten (*track*);
hackneyed.
rébecca (rebɛka) *m. & f*, rumpus,
row. *faire du* ~, kick up a fuss.
rebelle (rəbɛl) *a*, rebellious; refractory. ¶ *n*, rebel. se **rebeller**
(le) *v.pr*, to rebel. **rébellion** (rebɛljɔ̃) *f*, rebellion.
rebiffer (se) (rəbife) *v.pr*, to
show temper.
rebondi, e (rəbɔ̃di) *a*, rounded,
plump. **rebondir** (di:r) *v.i*, to rebound, bounce; crop up again.
rebondissement (dismɑ̃) *m*, rebound; repercussion.
rebord (rəbɔ:r) *m*, edge, rim;
hem; ledge; flange.
rebours (rəbu:r) *m*, wrong way;
contrary, reverse. *à* ~, the wrong
way; backward. *prendre à* ~, to
misconstrue.
rebouteur, euse (rəbutœ:r, ø:z)
n, bonesetter.
rebrousse-poil (à) (rəbruspwal)
ad, against the nap, the wrong

way. **rebrousser** (se) *v.t*, to rub the wrong way. ~ [*chemin*], to retrace one's steps.

rebuffade (rəbyfad) *f*, rebuff.

rébus (reby:s) *m*, picture puzzle; riddle.

rebut (rəby) *m*, waste, refuse, rubbish; dead letter (*Post.*); scum (*fig.*). **rebutant, e** (tã, ã:t) *a*, disheartening; repellent. **rebuter** (te) *v.t*, to rebuff, repulse; dishearten.

récalcitrant, e (rekalsitrã, ã:t) *a. & n*, recalcitrant; refractory.

recaler (rəkale) *v.t*, to set (*someone*) on his feet again; flunk, fail (*someone*) in examination.

récapituler (rekapityle) *v.t*, to recapitulate.

receler (rəsle) *v.t*, to conceal; harbor (*criminal*); receive (*stolen goods*). **receleur, euse** (sloe:r, ø:z) *n*, receiver, fence.

récemment (resamã) *ad*, recently, lately.

recensement (rəsãsmã) *m*, census, return; counting (*votes*); stocktaking. **recenser** (se) *v.t*, to take the census of; count.

récent, e (resã, ã:t) *a*, recent, late; fresh.

receper (rəsəpe) *v.t*, to cut back (*Hort.*).

récépissé (resepise) *m*, receipt. **réceptacle** (sɛptakl) *m*, receptacle; repository. **récepteur** (tœ:r) *m*, receiver (*Teleph., etc.*). **réception** (sjɔ̃) *f*, receipt; reception; welcome; acceptance; party, at-home. **recette** (rəsɛt) *f*, receipts, takings; gate money; collectorship; recipe. **recevable** (səvabl) *a*, admissible. **receveur, euse** (vœ:r, ø:z) *n*, collector (*taxes, etc.*); conductor (*bus*); (*f.*) attendant (*Theat.*). ~ *des postes*, postmaster, -mistress. **recevoir** (vwa:r) *v.t. & abs*, to receive; admit; get; meet with; accept; welcome; take in (*boarders*); be at home (*to visitors*). *être reçu à*, to pass (*exam*).

récession (resɛjɔ̃) *f*, recession (*economic*).

rechange (rəʃã:ʒ) *m*, change, spare. *pièce de* ~, spare part.

réchapper (reʃape) *v.i*, to escape; recover.

recharger (rəʃarʒe) *v.t*, to recharge; reload.

réchaud (reʃo) *m*, stove; ring (*gas*); heater; hot plate. **réchauffer** (ʃofe) *v.t*, to reheat, warm up; revive.

rêche (rɛʃ) *a*, rough, harsh.

recherche (rəʃɛrʃ) *f*, search, quest, pursuit; research, inquiry; prospecting; studied elegance. **recherché, e** (ʃe) *p.a*, sought after, in request; choice; studied; elaborate. **rechercher** (ʃe) *v.t*, to search for, seek.

rechigner (rəʃiɲe) *v.i*, to look sour. *en rechignant* (ɲã), with a bad grace.

rechute (rəʃyt) *f*, relapse, backsliding.

récidiver (residive) *v.i*, to relapse into crime. **récidiviste** (vist) *n*, person with previous convictions; old offender.

récif (resif) *m*, reef (*of rocks*).

récipiendaire (resipjãdɛ:r) *n*, new member. **récipient** (pjã) *m*, receiver, vessel.

réciproque (resiprɔk) *a*, reciprocal, mutual; inverse; converse. **réciproquement** (kmã) *ad*, reciprocally, etc; vice versa.

récit (resi) *m*, recital, account, narration, narrative; solo (*Mus.*). **récital** (tal) *m*, recital (*Mus.*). **récitatif** (tatif) *m*, recitative (*Mus.*). **récitation** (sjɔ̃) *f*, recitation. **réciter** (te) *v.t*, to recite; say (*lessons*).

réclamant, e (reklamã, ã:t) *n*, claimant. **réclamation** (masjɔ̃) *f*, claim; complaint, protest. *bureau de* ~, complaint department. **réclame** (klam) *f*, advertisement, blurb. **réclamer** (me) *v.i*, to complain, protest, object; (*v.t.*) to claim; crave; call for. ~ *à grands cris*, to clamor for.

reclus, e (rəkly, y:z) *n*, recluse. **réclusion** (reklyzjɔ̃) *f*, reclusion, seclusion; solitary imprisonment.

recoin (rəkwɛ̃) *m*, nook, recess.

récolte (rekɔlt) *f*, harvest[ing]; crop; vintaging; vintage; collection. **récolter** (te) *v.t*, to harvest; collect.

recommander (rəkɔmɑ̃de) *v.t,* to [re]commend; register (*mail*).

recommencer (rəkɔmɑ̃se) *v.t. & i,* to recommence; begin again.

récompense (rekɔ̃pɑ̃:s) *f,* recompense, reward; retribution, requital. **récompenser** (pɑ̃se) *v.t,* to recompense.

réconcilier (rekɔ̃silje) *v.t,* to reconcile.

reconduire (rəkɔ̃dɥi:r) *v.t.ir,* to escort; see home; show out.

réconfort (rekɔ̃fɔ:r) *m,* comfort, consolation; stimulant. **réconforter** (fɔrte) *v.t,* to strengthen; comfort.

reconnaissable (rəkɔnɛsabl) *a,* recognizable. **reconnaissance** (sɑ̃:s) *f,* recognition; acknowledgment; gratitude, thankfulness; reconnaissance, exploration; pawn ticket. **reconnaissant, e** (sɑ̃, ɑ̃:t) *a,* grateful, thankful. **reconnaître** (nɛ:tr) *v.t.ir,* to recognize; tell; sight (*land*); acknowledge; be grateful for; reconnoiter, explore.

reconquérir (rəkɔ̃keri:r) *v.t.ir,* to reconquer; regain.

reconstituer (rəkɔ̃stitye) *v.t,* to reconstitute; reconstruct (*crime*); restore.

reconstitution (rəkɔ̃stitysjɔ̃) *f,* reconstruction (*fig.*).

reconstruction (rəkɔ̃stryksjɔ̃) *f,* rebuilding. **reconstruire** (strɥi:r) *v.t.ir,* to rebuild.

reconvention (rəkɔ̃vɑ̃sjɔ̃) *f,* counterclaim.

recopier (rəkɔpje) *v.t,* to recopy; revise; transcribe (*computers*).

record (rəkɔ:r) *m,* record (*sports*). **recorder** (kɔrde) *v.t,* to con, go over; restring. **recors** (kɔ:r) *m,* bailiff's man; minion (*of the law*).

recoupe (rəkup) *f,* middlings (*flour*); chips; clippings. **recoupement** (mɑ̃) *m,* cross-checking of information.

recourber (rəkurbe) *v.t,* to bend, crook.

recourir (rəkuri:r) *v.i.ir,* to run again; have recourse, resort. **recours** (ku:r) *m,* recourse, resort; appeal; remedy (*law*).

recouvrement (rəkuvrəmɑ̃) *m,*

recovery; cover[ing]; [over]lap; overlay (*computers*); (*pl.*) book debts. **recouvrer** (vre) *v.t,* to recover, regain.

recouvrir (rəkuvri:r) *v.t.ir,* to re-cover; cover.

récréation (rekreasjɔ̃) *f,* recreation; playtime.

récréer (rekree) *v.t,* to recreate, divert, entertain; enliven, refresh; re-create.

récrier (se) (rekrie) *v.pr,* to cry out, exclaim.

récrimination (rekriminasjɔ̃) *f,* recrimination. **récriminer** (ne) *v.i,* to recriminate; countercharge; retort.

récrire (rekri:r) *v.t.ir,* to re-write; write again; reply.

recroqueviller (se) (rəkrɔkvije) *v.pr,* to shrivel.

recrudescence (rəkrydɛsɑ̃:s) *f,* recrudescence.

recrue (rəcry) *f,* recruit. **recruter** (te) *v.t,* to recruit.

recta (rɛkta) *ad,* on the nail, punctually.

rectangle (rɛktɑ̃:gl) *a,* right-angled. ¶ *m,* rectangle. ~ [de table], doily. **rectangulaire** (tɑ̃gylɛ:r) *a,* rectangular.

recteur (rɛktœ:r) *m,* rector.

rectifier (rɛktifje) *v.t,* to rectify; amend; true, straighten.

rectiligne (rɛktiliɲ) *a,* rectilinear.

rectitude (rɛktityd) *f,* straightness; rectitude, soundness, sanity.

recto (rɛkto) *m,* recto, front, face.

rectum (rɛktɔm) *m,* rectum.

reçu (rəsy) *m,* receipt. *au ~ de,* on receipt of. ¶ *a,* received, accepted, customary. *être ~,* to pass (*examination*).

recueil (rəkœ:j) *m,* collection; book. ~ *factice,* miscellany. **recueillement** (kœjmɑ̃) *m,* self-communion. **recueillir** (ji:r) *v.t.ir,* to collect, gather; pick up; reap. **se ~,** to collect one's thoughts.

recuire (rəkɥi:r) *v.t.ir,* to re-bake; reheat; anneal.

recul (rəkyl) *m,* recoil, kick; setback. **reculade** (lad) *f,* backward movement; retreat. **reculé, e** (le) *p.a,* distant, remote. **reculer** (le) *v.i.* & *t,* to draw back; move back; recede; retreat; back; recoil; kick; postpone. **à reculons** (lɔ̃) *ad,* backward[s].

récupérer (rekypere) *v.t,* to recover, recoup.

récurer (rekyre) *v.t,* to scour, clean.

récuser (rekyze) *v.t,* to challenge, object to. **se ~,** to disclaim competence.

recyclage (rəsiklaːʒ) *m,* reprocessing; recycling; retraining. **recycler** (le) *v.t,* to reprocess; recycle; retrain.

rédacteur, trice (redaktœːr, tris) *n,* writer, drafter (*documents*). **~ en chef,** editor. **rédaction** (sjɔ̃) *f,* drafting, editing; editorial staff; newsroom.

reddition (reddisjɔ̃) *f,* surrender; rendering (*of accounts*).

redemander (rədmɑ̃de) *v.t,* to ask for again; ask for more; ask for back.

Rédempteur (redɑ̃[p]tœːr) *m,* Redeemer. **rédemption** ([p]sjɔ̃) *f,* redemption (*Theol.*).

redescendre (rədɛsɑ̃ːdr) *v.i,* to come down again; fall again (*barometer*); back (*wind*).

redevable (rədəvabl) *a,* indebted, beholden; liable. **¶** *n,* debtor. **redevance** (vɑ̃ːs) *f,* rent[al]; royalty. **redevoir** (vwaːr) *v.t,* to still owe.

rédiger (rediʒe) *v.t,* to draw up, draft; write; edit.

redingote (rədɛ̃gɔt) *f,* frock coat (*man's*); coat (*woman's*).

redire (rədiːr) *v.t.ir,* to say again; repeat. **trouver à ~ à,** to find fault with. **redite** (dit) *f,* repetition.

redondant, e (redɔ̃dɑ̃, ɑ̃ːt) *a,* redundant.

redonner (redɔne) *v.t,* to give again; restore; (*v.i.*) to fall again; charge again.

redoubler (rəduble) *v.t,* to redouble; repeat (*a class*); reline (*clothing*).

redoutable (rədutabl) *a,* redoubtable, formidable.

redoute (rədut) *f,* redoubt; gala night (*at dance hall*).

redouter (rədute) *v.t,* to dread, fear.

redresser (rədrɛse) *v.t,* to reerect; straighten; redress; right.

réduction (redyksjɔ̃) *f,* reduction; reducing; cut. **réduire** (dɥiːr) *v.t.ir,* to reduce; boil down. **réduit** (dɥi) *m,* retreat, nook; redoubt.

rééditer (reedite) *v.t,* to republish, reissue.

réel, le† (reɛl) *a,* real; actual. **¶** *m,* real[ity].

réélection (reelɛksjɔ̃) *f,* reelection. **rééligible** (liʒibl) *a,* reeligible. **réélire** (liːr) *v.t.ir,* to reelect.

réer (ree) *v.i,* to troat, bell.

réexporter (reɛkspɔrte) *v.t,* to reexport.

refaire (rəfɛːr) *v.t.ir,* to remake, do [over] again; do up, repair; recover. **refait** (fɛ) *m,* draw[n game]; new horns (*stag*). **réfection** (refɛksjɔ̃) *f,* restoration. **réfectoire** (twaːr) *m,* refectory.

refendre (rəfɑ̃ːdr) *v.t,* to split; rip.

référence (referɑ̃ːs) *f,* reference. **referendum** (referɛ̃dɔm) *m,* referendum. **référer** (fere) *v.t.* & *i.* & *se ~,* to refer; ascribe.

réfléchi, e (refleʃi) *p.a,* reflective; thoughtful; considered, deliberate; reflexive (*Gram.*). **réfléchir** (ʃiːr) *v.t.* & *i,* to reflect; think over, ponder, consider. **réflecteur** (flɛktœːr) *m,* reflector. **reflet** (rəflɛ) *m,* reflection; reflex; shimmer, glint. **~s irisés,** play of colors. **refléter** (flete) *v.t,* to reflect; mirror. **réflexe** (reflɛks) *a.* & *m,* reflex. **réflexion** (ksjɔ̃) *f,* reflection; thought. **~ après coup,** afterthought.

refluer (rəflye) *v.i,* to flow back, ebb; surge. **reflux** (fly) *m,* reflux, ebb.

refondre (rəfɔ̃ːdr) *v.t,* to recast, remodel. **refonte** (fɔ̃ːt) *f,* recasting; recoinage; reorganization; reconstruction.

réformateur, trice (reforma-

tœːr, tris) *n*, reformer. **réforma-**
tion (sjɔ̃) *f*, reformation. **ré-**
forme (fɔrm) *f*, reform[ation];
discharge, retirement (*Mil.*, *Nav.*).

reformer (rəfɔrme) *v.t*, to re-
form.

réformer (reforme) *v.t*, to re-
form, amend; discharge, retire;
reverse (*law*).

refouler (rəfule) *v.t*, to drive
back; stem; compress; ram
home; repress; (*v.i.*) to flow
back, ebb. **refouloir** (lwaːr) *m*,
rammer (*gun*).

réfractaire (refraktɛːr) *a*, refractory; fire[-proof]. ¶ *m*, draft-
dodger (*Mil.*).

réfracter (refrakte) *v.t*, to refract.

refrain (rəfrɛ̃) *m*, refrain; burden; theme. ~ *en chœur*, chorus.

refréner (rəfrene) *v.t*, to curb,
bridle.

réfrigération (refriʒerasjɔ̃) *f*,
refrigeration, cooling, chilling.

refrogner (se) (rəfrɔɲe) *v.pr*,
to frown, scowl, look sullen.

refroidir (rəfrwadiːr) *v.t*. & *i.*
& *se* ~, to cool, chill; damp
(*fig.*); get cold.

refuge (rəfyːʒ) *m*, refuge, shelter; [street] refuge. **réfugié, e**
(refyʒje) *n*, refugee. **se réfugier**
(ʒje) *v.pr*, to take refuge.

refus (rəfy) *m*, refusal. ~ *d'obéis-*
sance, insubordination; contempt
of court. **refuser** (ze) *v.t*, to refuse, decline; deny; reject; flunk,
fail (*exam*); disable (*computers*).
se ~, to object, refuse, decline.

réfuter (refyte) *v.t*, to refute,
confute, rebut, disprove.

regagner (rəgaɲe) *v.t*, to regain,
win back, recover; make up for;
get back to.

regain (rəgɛ̃) *m*, aftergrowth;
renewal; new lease (*of life*).

régal (regal) *m*, feast; treat. **ré-**
galer (le) *v.t*, to entertain, feast;
treat; regale.

regard (rəgaːr) *m*, look, gaze,
glance, eye(s); attention, notice;
peephole; manhole. ~ *appuyé*,
stare. ~ *polisson*, leer. *en* ~,
opposite, facing. **regardant, e**

(gardɑ̃, ɑ̃ːt) *a*, close-fisted, mean.

regarder (de) *v.t*. & *abs*, to look
(at, on), see, eye; consider, regard, mind, be one's business;
face, front. ~ *fixement*, to stare
at.

régate (regat) *f*, regatta. [*cravate*]
~, open-end tie.

régence (reʒɑ̃ːs) *f*, regency.

régénérer (reʒenere) *v.t*, to regenerate.

régent, e (reʒɑ̃, ɑ̃ːt) *n*. & *a*,
regent. **régenter** (ʒɑ̃te) *v.t*, to
dictate to; dominate; (*abs.*) to
domineer.

régicide (reʒisid) *m*, regicide;
(*att.*) regicidal.

régie (reʒi) *f*, administration (*of*
property); State (*control*); excise.

regimber (rəʒɛ̃be) *v.i*, to kick,
balk.

régime (reʒim) *m*, regime[n],
rules, system, conditions; diet;
object (*Gram.*); bunch, cluster
(*bananas*, etc.). ~ *de faveur*,
preference (*Cust.*).

régiment (reʒimɑ̃) *m*, regiment;
swarm. **régimentaire** (tɛːr) *a*,
regimental.

région (reʒjɔ̃) *f*, region, district.
régional, e (ɔnal) *a*, regional,
district (*att.*); toll (*att.*, *Teleph.*).

régir (reʒiːr) *v.t*, to govern, rule,
manage. **régisseur** (ʒisœːr) *m*,
manager, steward, bailiff (*farm*);
stage manager. ~ *d'extérieur*, location m. (*cinema*). ~ *de plateau*,
studio m. (*cinema*). ~ *général*,
casting director.

registre (rəʒistr) *m*, register,
book; record, note; damper
(*flue*). ~ *des délibérations*, minute book.

règle (rɛgl) *f*, rule; ruler; order.
~ *à calcul*, sliderule. *les* ~*s*,
menses. **réglé, e** (regle) *p.a*, regular, steady; set, stated; ruled
(*paper*). **règlement** (rɛgləmɑ̃)
m, settlement, adjustment; regulation, rule. **réglementaire** (tɛːr)
a, regulation (*att.*), prescribed.
réglementer (te) *v.t*, to regulate.
régler (regle) *v.t*, to rule; regulate; order; settle, adjust; set,
time.

réglisse (reglis) *f*, licorice.

règne (rɛɲ) *m*, reign; sway; kingdom (*Nat. Hist.*). **régner** (ɲe) *v.i*, to reign, rule; obtain; prevail, be prevalent; extend, run.

regorger (rəgɔrʒe) *v.i. & t*, to overflow, brim, abound, teem; burst.

regrattier, ère (rəgratje, ɛ:r) *n*, huckster.

régresser (regrese) *v.i*, to regress; diminish (*amount, intensity*).

regret (rəgrɛ) *m*, regret. *à* ~, reluctantly. **regrettable** (tabl) *a*, regrettable, unfortunate. **le** (**la**) **regretté, e** . . . (te), the [late] lamented . . . **regretter** (te) *v.t*, to regret, be sorry (for); miss.

régulariser (regylarize) *v.t*, to regularize. **régularité** (te) *f*, regularity. **régulateur** (tœ:r) *m*, regulator, governor. **régulier, ère†** (lje, ɛ:r) *a*, regular; orderly, businesslike.

réhabiliter (reabilite) *v.t*, to rehabilitate, reinstate; discharge (*bankrupt*).

rehausser (rəose) *v.t*, to raise; enhance; heighten. **rehauts** (o) *m.pl*, highlights (*art*).

réimporter (reɛpɔrte) *v.t*, to reimport.

réimposer (reɛpoze) *v.t*, to reimpose.

réimpression (reɛprɛsjɔ̃) *f*, reprint[ing]. **réimprimer** (prime) *v.t*, to reprint.

Reims (rɛ̃:s) *m*, Rheims.

rein (rɛ̃) *m*, kidney; (*pl.*) loins, back. *mal aux* ~*s*, backache.

reine (rɛn) *f*, queen (*pers. & chess*); belle (*of ball*). ~*claude* (klo:d), greengage. ~ *des abeilles*, queen bee. ~*des-prés*, meadow-sweet. ~*marguerite*, China aster.

reinette (rɛnɛt) *f*, pippin, rennet. ~ *grise*, russet (*apple*).

réinjection (reɛ̃ʒɛksjɔ̃) *f*, feedback (*computers*).

réintégrer (reɛ̃tegre) *v.t*, to reinstate.

réitérer (reitere) *v.t*, to reiterate, repeat.

rejaillir (rəʒaji:r) *v.i*, to gush out; reflect, redound.

rejet (rəʒɛ) *m*, throwing out; rejection; shoot (*Hort.*). **rejeter** (ʒ[ə]te) *v.t*, to throw back; t. out; t. up; reject, set aside; negate; dismiss; disallow. **rejeton** (ʒtɔ̃) *m*, shoot, cane (*raspberry*); scion, offspring.

rejoindre (rəʒwɛ̃:dr) *v.t. & abs. ir*, to re-join; rejoin (*one's regiment*).

rejouer (rəʒwe) *v.t. & i*, to replay; play again.

réjoui, e (reʒwi) *p.a*, jolly, joyous, jovial, merry. **réjouir** (ʒwi:r) *v.t. & se* ~, to rejoice, gladden; cheer; be glad; enjoy oneself. **réjouissance** (ʒwisɑ̃:s) *f*, rejoicing; makeweight (*butcher's*).

relâche (rəlɑ:ʃ) *m*, respite, intermission, breathing space, relaxation; no performance, closed (*Theat.*); (*f.*) call[ing] (*Naut.*); port of call. **relâcher** (lɑʃe) *v.t. & i*, to loosen, slacken; relax; release; call, put in (*Naut.*).

relais (rəlɛ) *m*, relay; shift; stage, relay station; sand flats.

relancer (rəlɑ̃se) *v.t*, to throw back; return (*ball, Ten.*); badger. **relanceur, euse** (sœ:r, ø:z) *n*, receiver (*Ten.*).

relaps, e (rəlaps) *n*, apostate, backslider.

rélargir (relarʒi:r) *v.t*, to widen; let out.

relater (rəlate) *v.t*, to relate, state. **relatif, ive†** (tif, i:v) *a*, relative, relating. **relation** (sjɔ̃) *f*, relation, connection, intercourse; acquaintance; narrative.

relaxer (rəlakse) *v.t*, to relax; release.

relayer (rəlɛje) *v.t*, to relay; change with; change horses. *se* ~, to take turns, shifts.

reléguer (rəlege) *v.t*, to relegate, consign; intern (*prisoner in Fr. colony*).

relent (rəlɑ̃) *m*, bad odor.

relevailles (rəlvɑ:j) *f.pl*, churching. **relève** (lɛ:v) *f*, relief (*from turn of duty*). **relevé, e** (lve) *p.a*, high, exalted, lofty; strong (*flavor*). ¶ *m*, statement, abstract,

return. ~ *de potage*, course after
soup. ¶ *f*, afternoon. **relever**
(lve) *v.t*, to raise, lift [up]; pick
up; turn up; take up; restore;
make out (*account*); take, read
(*meter*); point out, note; set off,
enhance, exalt; season; relieve;
release; plot (*ground*); (*v.i.*) to
depend, rest; recover. ~ *le men-
ton à*, to chuck under the
chin.

relief (rəljɛf) *m*, relief; (*pl.*)
leftovers.

relier (rəlje). *v.t*, to [re]tie; unite;
bind (*book*); [re]hoop (*cask*).
relieur, euse (jœːr, øːz) *n*, [book]-
binder.

religieux, euse† (rəliʒjø, øːz)
a, religious; sacred (*song, etc.*);
scrupulous. ¶ *m*, monk, friar.
¶ *f*, nun; cream puff. **religion**
(ʒjɔ̃) *f*, religion; vows; bounden
duty; sanctity (*oath*).

reliquaire (rəlikɛːr) *m*, reliquary, shrine.

reliquat (rəlika) *m*, balance,
residue.

relique (rəlik) *f*, relic.

reliure (rəljyːr) *f*, [book]bind-
ing. ~ *amateur*, extra binding.
~ *pleine*, full b., whole b.

relogement (rəlɔʒmɑ̃) *m*, rehousing.

relouer (rəlue) *v.t*, to relet; re-
rent; sublet.

reluire (rəlɥiːr) *v.i.ir*, to shine,
glitter; enjoy oneself; have an orgasm (*slang*). **reluisant, e** (lɥizɑ̃,
ɑ̃ːt) *a*, shining; creditable; brilliant.

reluquer (rəlyke) *v.t*, to ogle;
covet.

remâcher (rəmaʃe) *v.t*, to chew
again; ruminate on, brood over,
chew (*fig.*).

remanier (rəmanje) *v.t*, to rehandle; manipulate; relay; recast.

remarquable† (rəmarkabl) *a*,
remarkable; noteworthy; conspicuous. **remarque** (mark) *f*, remark, note. **remarquer** (ke) *v.t*,
to re-mark; remark, observe, notice, note, mark.

remballer (rɑ̃bale) *v.t*, to repack.

rembarquer (rɑ̃barke) *v.t. & i*,
to reembark, reship.

remblai (rɑ̃blɛ) *m*, filling up
(*with earth*); embankment. **remblayer** (je) *v.t*, to fill [up], [em]-
bank.

remboîter (rɑ̃bwate) *v.t*, to [re]-
set; recase.

rembourrer (rɑ̃bure) *v.t*, to
stuff, pad, upholster.

rembourser (rɑ̃burse) *v.t*, to
repay, pay off, return, refund;
redeem; reimburse.

rembrunir (rɑ̃bryniːr) *v.t*, to
darken, gloom.

rembucher (se) (rɑ̃byʃe) *v.pr*,
to return to cover[t].

remède (rəmɛd) *m*, remedy, cure.
~ *de charlatan*, nostrum. **remédier à** (medje), to remedy, cure,

remembrer (rəmɑ̃bre) *v.t*, to re-
group (*farmland*), reallocate. **re-
membrement** (brəmɑ̃), *m*, re-
grouping of farmland.

remémorer (se) (rəmemɔre)
v.pr, to remember.

remerciement (rəmɛrsimɑ̃) *m*,
oft. pl, thanks. **remercier** (sje)
v.t, to thank; dismiss, fire.

réméré (remere) *m*, repurchase.

remettre (rəmɛtr) *v.t. & abs. ir*,
to put back [again]; put on again;
restore; remit, send [in]; hand
[over], deliver; commend; put
off, postpone; pardon; entrust;
remember; calm; set (*bone*). ~ *à
blanc, à zéro*, to clear (*computers*). *remettez-vous!* get a grip on
yourself. se ~, to become well
again, start off again.

remeubler (rəmœble) *v.t*, to refurnish.

réminiscence (reminisɑ̃ːs) *f*, reminiscence.

remise (rəmiːz) *f*, putting back;
restoration; remittance; remission; delivery; postponement; allowance, discount; commission;
coach house; shed; cover (*game*).
~ [*sur marchandises*], [trade] discount. *une voiture de* ~ ou *un*
~, a hired carriage. **remiser**
(mize) *v.t*, to put up (*vehicle*).
remisier (zje) *m*, intermediate
broker.

rémission (remisjɔ̃) *f*, remission.

rem[m]aillage (rɑ̃majaːʒ) *m*,
grafting (*Knit.*).

remmancher (rãmãʃe) *v.t*, to rehandle; resume.

remmener (rãmne) *v.t*, to take back.

remontant (rəmɔ̃tã) *m*, stimulant, tonic, pick-me-up. **remonte** (mɔ̃:t) *f*, remount[ing] (*Mil.*). ~*-pentes*, *m*, ski lift. **remonter** (mɔ̃te) *v.i. & t*, to [re]ascend; remount; go back; raise; rise; wind [up] (*spring*); restock, replenish; restage; veer (*wind*). **remontoir** (twa:r) *m*, winder, key; keyless watch. ~ *à heures sautantes*, jumping-hour watch.

remontrance (rəmɔ̃trã:s) *f*, remonstrance, expostulation. **remontrer** (tre) *v.t. & abs*, to show again; point out; remonstrate.

remords (rəmɔ:r) *m*, remorse.

remorque (rəmɔrk) *f*, tow[ing]; trailer. **remorquer** (ke) *v.t*, to tow, haul. **remorqueur** (kœ:r) *m*, tug [boat].

rémouleur (remulœ:r) *m*, [knife] grinder.

remous (rəmu) *m*, eddy, [back]-wash, swirl.

rempart (rãpa:r) *m*, rampart; bulwark (*fig.*).

remplaçant, e (rãplasã, ã:t) *n*, substitute. **remplacer** (se) *v.t*, to replace; take the place of; supersede.

rempli (rãpli) *m*, tuck. **remplier** (e) *v.t*, to tuck; turn over (*paper wrapper—Bookb.*).

remplir (rãpli:r) *v.t*, to fill up, refill, replenish; fill; swamp (*boat*); fulfil, comply with; perform.

remplumer (se) (rãplyme) *v.pr*, to get new feathers; put on flesh again; pick up again.

remporter (rãporte) *v.t*, to take away; carry off, win, gain.

rempoter (rãpote) *v.t*, to repot.

remuant, e (rəmɥã, ã:t) *a*, restless. **remue-ménage** (mymena:ʒ) *m*, bustle, stir, upset. **remue-méninges** (menɛ̃:ʒ) *m*, brainstorming. **remuement** (mã) *m*, moving, removal; bustle, stir. **remuer** (mɥe) *v.t. & i*, to move; stir [up], rake up; shake, wag, swish; remove, shift.

rémunérateur, trice (remyneratœ:r, tris) *a*, remunerative, paying. ¶ *m*, rewarder. **rémunération** (sjɔ̃) *f*, remuneration, payment; consideration; return. **rémunérer** (re) *v.t*, to remunerate, pay for, reward.

renâcler (rənakle) *v.t*, to snort; hang back; refuse. ~ *à la besogne*, to shirk work.

renaissance (rənɛsã:s) *f*, rebirth; revival; renaissance. **renaître** (twa:tr) *v.i.ir*, to be born again; spring up again; revive.

renard (rəna:r) *m*, fox. ~ *argenté*, silver f. **renarde** (nard) *f*, vixen. **renardeau** (do) *m*, fox cub. **renardière** (djɛ:r) *f*, fox earth, fox's hole.

rencaisser (rãkese) *v.t*, to rebox; recash.

rencarder (rãkarde) *v.t*, to inform, wise up.

renchéri, e (rãʃeri) *n*, fastidious person. **renchérir** (ri:r) *v.i*, to get dearer, go up. ~ *sur*, to outbid, outdo, improve on.

rencogner (rãkɔɲe) *v.t*, to drive into a corner.

rencontre (rãkɔ̃:tr) *f*, meeting, encounter; occurrence; occasion; collision, clash; duel. ~ *de front*, head-on collision. **rencontrer** (kɔ̃tre) *v.t*, to meet, m. with, encounter, come across, strike; run into, collide with.

rendement (rãdmã) *m*, yield, return; output, capacity; efficiency. **rendez-vous** (devu) *m*, appointment; place of meeting; resort, haunt.

rendormir (rãdormi:r) *v.t*, to send to sleep again. **se** ~, to go to sleep again.

rendre (rã:dr) *v.t*, to give back, return; restore; give up; render; give; pay; dispense; repay; yield; deliver; surrender; vomit; make; drive (*one mad*). ~ *l'âme*, to die. **se** ~, to make oneself; go; surrender, yield. **rendu** (rãdy) *m*, rendering (*art*); return (*article, goods—Com.*).

rêne (rɛn) *f*, rein.

renégat, e (rənega, at) *n*, renegade, turncoat.

renfermé (rãfɛrme) *m*, musty smell. **renfermer** (me) *v.t*, to shut up; confine; comprise, contain; restrict.

renflement (rãfləmã) *m*, swell-[ing]; bulge, boss. **renfler** (fle) *v.i*, to swell.

renflouer (rãflue) *v.t*, to refloat (*ship*).

renfoncement (rãfõsmã) *m*, driving in; recess; inden[ta]tion (*Typ.*); punch (*blow*). **renfoncer** (se) *v.t*, to drive in; knock in; indent.

renforcé, e (rãforse) *p.a*, stout, strong; out & out; arrant. **renforcer** (se) *v.t*, to reinforce; strengthen; brace; intensify (*Phot.*). **renfort** (foːr) *m*, reinforcement (*Mil.*). *à grand ~ de*, with plenty of.

renfrogner (se) (rãfrɔɲe) *v.pr*, to frown, scowl, look sullen.

rengager (rãgaʒe) *v.t*, to re-engage; (*v.i.*) to reenlist.

rengaine (rãgɛːn) *f*, tag, story; catchword; hackneyed refrain.

rengainer (rãgɛne) *v.t*, to sheathe; suppress.

rengorger (se) (rãgɔrʒe) *v.pr*, to bridle [up]; strut, swagger.

reniement (rənimã) *m*, denial; disavowal.

renier (rənje) *v.t*, to disown, deny.

renifler (rənifle) *v.i. & t*, to sniff; snuffle; snort; tolerate. *je ne peux pas le ~* I can't bear him.

renne (rɛn) *m*, reindeer.

renom (rənõ) *m*, renown, fame; repute. **renommé, e** (nɔme) *p.a*, renowned, famed, noted. ¶ *f*, fame, renown; name; rumor, report. **renommer** (me) *v.t*, to re-appoint.

renonce (rənõːs) (*cards*) *f*, re-nounce; revoke. **renoncement** (nõsmã) *m*, renunciation, self-denial. **renoncer** (se) *v.i. & t. & ~ à*, to renounce, give up, forgo; disown, deny; revoke (*cards*). **renonciation** (sjasjõ) *f*, renunciation, disclaimer. ✔

renoncule (rənõkyl) *f*, ranun-culus, buttercup, crowfoot. *~ bulbeuse*, kingcup.

renouer (rənwe) *v.t*, to retie; re-new, resume.

renouveau (rənuvo) *m*, re-newal; return of spring. **re-nouveler** (vle) *v.t*, to renew, renovate; change; revive. **réno-ver** (renɔve) *v.t*, to renovate, restore.

renseignement (rãsɛɲmã) *m*. *oft. pl*, information, intelligence, particular; inquiry. **renseigner** (ɲe) *v.t*, to inform. *se ~*, to in-quire.

rente (rãːt) *f*, income; annuity; pension; interest; stock. *~ vi-agère*, life endowment, annuity. **renter** (rãte) *v.t*, to endow. **ren-tier, ère** (tje, ɛːr) *n*, stockholder, fundholder, investor; annuitant; person of independent means.

rentraire (rãtrɛːr) *v.t.ir*, to fine-draw.

rentrant, e (rãtrã, ãːt) *a*, re-entrant; sunk. **rentré, e** (tre) *p.a*, suppressed (*rage, etc.*). ¶ *f*, re-turn; reentry; reappearance; re-opening; ingathering; collection; receipt. **rentrer** (tre) *v.i*, to re-enter; return; reappear; reopen; (*v.t.*) to bring in, house; indent (*Typ.*). *~ dans*, to recover; re-enter; return to, rejoin. **rentrez!** all in! (*Sch.*).

renverse (à la) (rãvɛrs) *ad*, backwards, on one's back. **ren-verser** (se) *v.t*, to throw down, overthrow, upset; invert, reverse; astound. *se ~ sur sa chaise*, to lean (*or* lie) back (*or* recline) in one's chair.

renvoi (rãvwa) *m*, return; dis-missal; postponement; reference; caret; repeat (*Mus.*); alteration; eructation; countershaft. **ren-voyer** (je) *v.t*, to send back, re-turn; dismiss; put off, adjourn; refer. *~ à une autre audience*, to remand. *~ une page*, to page-out (*computers*).

réorganiser (reɔrganize) *v.t*, to reorganize.

réouverture (reuvɛrtyːr) *f*, re-opening.

repaire (rəpɛːr) *m*, den, lair; nest; haunt.

repaître (rəpɛːtr) *v.t*, to feed, feast.

répandre (repɑ̃:dr) *v.t*, to pour out, spill, shed; spread, diffuse, waft, scatter, sprinkle. **répandu, e** (pɑ̃dy) *p.a*, widespread; well-known.

réparable (reparabl) *a*, reparable, repairable.

reparaître (rəparɛ:tr) *v.i.ir*, to reappear.

réparateur, trice (reparatœ:r, tris) *n*, repairer, mender. **réparation** (sjɔ̃) *f*, repair; reparation; amends, atonement, redress. **réparer** (re) *v.t*, to repair, mend; retrieve; make amends for; make up for; redress; rectify.

repartie (rəparti) *f*, repartee, retort, rejoinder. **repartir** (ti:r) *v.i.ir*, to retort; set out again.

répartir (reparti:r) *v.t*, to distribute, apportion, allot; assess; spread. **répartiteur** (tœ:r) *m*, assessor (*taxes*); dispatcher (*transport*). **répartition** (tisjɔ̃) *f*, distribution, etc.

repas (rəpɑ) *m*, meal, repast, spread. ~ *de corps*, regimental dinner. ~ *de noce*, wedding breakfast, w. banquet.

repasser (rəpɑse) *v.i. & t*, to repass; recross; come again; reexamine, con, go over, think over; grind, sharpen; set; strop; iron (*linen*); rerun (*computers*). **repasseur** (sœ:r) *m*, grinder; strop (*razor*). **repasseuse** (sø:z) *f*, ironer, laundress.

repêcher (rəpeʃe) *v.t*, to fish up, f. out; give a second chance to (*exam*).

repentir (rəpɑ̃ti:r) *m*, repentance. se ~, *v.pr.ir*, to repent. se ~ de, to repent (*v.t.*), to rue, be sorry for.

repercer (rəpɛrse) *v.t*, to retap (*cask*); pierce (*metal*).

répercussion (reperkysjɔ̃) *f*, repercussion. **répercuter** (te) *v.t*, to reverberate.

repère (rəpɛ:r) *m*, reference mark; bench mark. *point de* ~, guidemark, landmark.

répertoire (repɛrtwa:r) *m*, index, list, register; directory; repertory; repository (*fig.*). ~ *à onglets*, thumb index. **répertorier** (tɔrje) *v.t*, to index.

répéter (repete) *v.t. & abs*, to repeat; rehearse; claim back (*law*). **répétiteur, trice** (titœ:r, tris) *n*, assistant teacher; tutor, coach. **répétition** (sjɔ̃) *f*, repetition, recurrence; reproduction, replica, duplicate; rehearsal; private lesson; claiming back. ~ *générale*, dress rehearsal.

repeupler (rəpœple) *v.t*, to repeople; restock; replant.

repiquer (rəpike) *v.t*, to prick again; restitch; plant out.

répit (repi) *m*, respite.

replacer (rəplase) *v.t*, to replace; reinvest.

replanter (rəplɑ̃te) *v.t*, to replant.

replâtrer (rəplɑtre) *v.t*, to replaster; patch up.

replet, ète (rəplɛ, ɛt) *a*, stout (*pers.*). **réplétion** (replesjɔ̃) *f*, repletion, corpulence.

repli (rəpli) *m*, fold, crease; coil (*snake*); recess (*heart*); falling back (*Mil.*). **replier** (plie) *v.t*, to fold up. se ~, to fold up; coil up; fall back.

réplique (replik) *f*, retort, rejoinder, answer; cue (*Theat.*); replica. **répliquer** (ke) *v.t*, to retort, rejoin, answer [back].

répondant, e (repɔ̃dɑ̃, ɑ̃:t) *n*, respondent; surety; sponsor; bail[sman]. **repondeur** (dœ:r) *m*, telephone answering machine. **répondre** (pɔ̃:dr) *v.t. & i*, to answer, reply, respond; say in reply; write back (*in reply*); correspond; agree; answer for, guarantee. **répons** (pɔ̃) *m*, response (*Lit.*). **réponse** (pɔ̃:s) *f*, answer, reply; response.

report (rəpɔ:r) *m*, carry forward; c. over. **reportage** (pɔrta:ʒ) *m*, reporting; report (*news*). **reporter** (te) *v.t*, to carry forward; bring forward; carry over (*Stk Ex.*). se ~, to refer; look back to. **reporter** (tœ:r) *m*, reporter (*news*).

repos (rəpo) *m*, rest, repose; quiet; ease; peace; pause (*Mus., Pros.*); half-cock (*gun*); resting place, seat; landing (*stairs*). *de tout* ~, safe, reliable. *valeur de tout* ~, gilt-edged security. **reposant, e** (rəzɑ̃, ɑ̃:t) *a*, restful. **reposé, e** (ze) *p.a*, refreshed; fresh. *à tête* ~, at leisure. ¶ *f*, lair. **reposer** (ze) *v.t*, to replace; re-lay; rest; refresh; order (*arms*); (*v.i.*) to lie; rest; sleep; be based. se ~, to rest, lie down, recline; rely.

repoussant, e (rəpusɑ̃, ɑ̃:t) *a*, repulsive, repellent. **repoussé, e** (se) *p.a*, embossed. **repoussement** (smɑ̃) *m*, rejection; recoil, kick. **repousser** (se) *v.t*, to push back; repel, repulse, reject; deny; spurn; (*v.i.*) to recoil; sprout again, grow again. **repoussoir** (swa:r) *m*, punch (*tool*); set-off, foil.

répréhensible (repreɑ̃sibl) *a*, reprehensible.

reprendre (rəprɑ̃:dr) *v.t. & i. ir*, to retake, recapture; take up [again]; take back; recover; resume; regain; pick up [again]; reprove, find fault with; reply; rejoin; take root again; set again; freeze again. ~ *de volée*, to volley (*Ten.*). ~ *sous œuvre*, to underpin; reconstruct (*fig.*).

représaille (rəprezɑ:j) *f. oft. pl*, reprisal, retaliation.

représentant, e (rəprezɑ̃tɑ̃, ɑ̃:t) *n*, representative; agent. **représentatif, ive** (tatif, i:v) *a*, representative. **représentation** (sjɔ̃) *f*, representation; production; [purchase] consideration; performance (*Theat.*). ~ *à bénéfice*, benefit performance. **représenter** (te) *v.t*, to present again; represent; produce, show; perform, act; personate; picture; (*abs.*) to bear oneself; (*abs.*) to entertain.

répression (represjɔ̃) *f*, repression.

réprimande (reprimɑ̃:d) *f*, reprimand, reproof, rebuke. **réprimander** (mɑ̃de) *v.t*, to reprimand, reprove, rebuke.

réprimer (reprime) *v.t*, to repress, curb; put down, quell.

repris de justice (rəpri) *m*, habitual criminal, old offender, jailbird. **reprisage** (za:ʒ) *m*, darning, mending (*stockings, etc.*). **reprise** (pri:z) *f*, retaking, recapture; recovery; rally; resumption; renewal; revival; repetition; occasion, time; round (*Box.*); bout (*Fenc.*); darn[ing]; repair; key

money (*for apartment*). ~ *perdue*, invisible mending. **repriser** (prize) *v.t*, to darn, mend.

réprobation (reprɔbasjɔ̃) *f*, reprobation.

reproche (rəprɔʃ) *m*, reproach, blame. **reprocher** (ʃe) *v.t*, to reproach, blame, upbraid; taunt, twit.

reproduction (rəprɔdyksjɔ̃) *f*, reproduction. **reproduire** (dɥi:r) *v.t.ir*, to reproduce. se ~, to recur; reproduce, breed.

reprographie (rəprɔgrafi) *f*, duplicating (*document, etc.*).

réprouvé, e (repruve) *n*, outcast; reprobate. **réprouver** (ve) *v.t*, to reprobate; reject, disapprove of, deprecate.

reptation (reptasjɔ̃) *f*, creeping, crawling. **reptile** (til) *m*, reptile.

repu (rəpy) *a*, satiated, glutted, full. ~ *de fatigue*, dog-tired.

républicain, e (repyblikɛ̃, ɛn) *a. & n*, republican. **république** (lik) *f*, republic; commonwealth; community.

répudier (repydje) *v.t*, to repudiate; renounce.

répugnance (repynɑ̃:s) *f*, repugnance; reluctance. **répugnant, e** (nɑ̃, ɑ̃:t) *a*, repugnant. **répugner** (ɲe) *v.i*, to feel repugnance, feel loath; be repugnant.

répulsif, ive (repylsif, i:v) *a*, repulsive, repellent. **répulsion** (sjɔ̃) *f*, repulsion.

réputation (repytasjɔ̃) *f*, reputation, repute; name; character. **réputé, e** (te) *p.a*, well-known; of repute. **réputer** (te) *v.t*, to repute, deem, hold.

requérant, e (rəkerɑ̃, ɑ̃:t) *n*, applicant, plaintiff. **requérir** (ri:r) *v.t.ir*, to require; summon. **requête** (kɛ:t) *f*, request, suit, petition.

requiem (rekɥiɛm) *m*, requiem.

requin (rəkɛ̃) *m*, shark (*fish & preying pers.*).

requinquer (se) (rəkɛ̃ke) *v.pr*, to smarten oneself up.

requis (rəki) *a*, required, requisite. ¶ *m*, labor conscript (*WW II*).

réquisition (rekizisjɔ̃) *f*, requisition, levy. **réquisitionner**

(ɔne) v.t, to requisition, commandeer, impress. **réquisitoire** (twa:r) m, charge, indictment.

rescapé, e (rɛskape) n, survivor, saved [person].

rescision (rɛssizjɔ̃) f, rescission.

rescousse (à la) (rɛskus) to the rescue.

rescrit (rɛskri) m, rescript.

réseau (rezo) m, netting; network; system; area; plexus; tracery. ~ *de fils de fer*, wire entanglement (*Mil.*). ~ *banalisé*, shared network (*computers*).

réséda (rezeda) m, reseda, mignonette.

réservation (rezɛrvasjɔ̃) f, reservation. **réserve** (zɛrv) f, reservation; booking (*seats*); reserve; store; exception, qualification; preserve (*Hunt.*); sanctuary (*animals*). *sous* ~ *de*, subject to. *sous* ~ *que*, on condition that. **réservé, e** (ve) a, reserved; cautious, guarded; shy; coy. **réserviste** (vist) m, reservist. **réservoir** (vwa:r) m, reservoir, tank, cistern, well.

résidence (rezidɑ̃:s) f, residence, dwelling, abode. **résident, e** (dɑ̃, ɑ̃:t) n. & a, resident (*diplomatic*); settler (*colony*). **résider** (de) v.i, to reside, dwell, live; lie, rest. **résidu** (dy) m, residue.

résignation (rezinasjɔ̃) f, resignation; submissiveness. **résigner** (ne) v.t, to resign.

résilier (rezilje) v.t, to cancel, annul.

résille (rezi:j) f, hairnet; cames.

résine (rezin) f, resin, rosin. **résineux, euse** (nø, ø:z) a, resinous.

résistance (rezistɑ̃:s) f, resistance; opposition; strength; toughness; endurance, stamina; underground army. **résistant, e** (tɑ̃, ɑ̃:t) a, resistant, strong, tough. **résister à** (te), to resist, withstand.

résolu†, e (rezɔly) p.a, resolute, determined. **résolution** (sjɔ̃) f, resolution; solution; cancelation; resolve.

résonance (rezɔnɑ̃:s) f, reso-

nance. **résonnant, e** (nɑ̃, ɑ̃:t) a, resonant. **résonner** (ne) v.i, to resound; ring; reecho; twang.

résorber (rezɔrbe) v.t, to reabsorb; absorb, imbibe.

résoudre (rezu:dr) v.t.ir, to resolve, solve; annul.

respect (rɛspɛ) m, respect, regard, deference. **respectable** (pɛktabl) a, respectable. **respecter** (te) v.t, to respect; spare. **respectif, ive†** (tif, i:v) a, respective, several. **respectueux, euse†** (tɥø, ø:z) a, respectful, dutiful. ~ *des lois*, law-abiding.

respiration (rɛspirasjɔ̃) f, respiration, breathing. **respirer** (re) v.i. & t, to breathe; respire; inhale; exhale.

resplendir (rɛsplɑ̃di:r) v.i, to be resplendent, shine, glitter. **resplendissant, e** (disɑ̃, ɑ̃:t) a, resplendent; aglow; glorious.

responsabilité (rɛspɔ̃sabilite) f, responsibility; liability; care. **responsable** (bl) a, responsible, answerable, liable. ¶ m, person in charge. **responsif, ive** (sif, i:v) a, in reply (*law*).

resquille (rɛski:j) f, [gate] crashing. **resquilleur, euse** (kijœ:r, ø:z) n, [gate] crasher.

ressac (rəsak) m, undertow; surf.

ressaisir (rəsɛzi:r) v.t, to recover.

ressasser (rəsase) v.t, to resift; repeat.

ressaut (rəso) m, projection, setoff.

ressemblance (rəsɑ̃blɑ̃:s) f, resemblance, likeness. **ressemblant, e** (blɑ̃, ɑ̃:t) a, [a]like. **ressembler à** (blə), to resemble, be like, look like.

ressemeler (rəsəmle) v.t, to resole.

ressentiment (rəsɑ̃timɑ̃) m, resentment. **ressentir** (ti:r) v.t, to feel; resent. **se ~**, to feel.

resserre (rəsɛ:r) f, storeroom. **resserrer** (sɛre) v.t, to tighten; close up; bind; put away [again]; contract, narrow, confine, restrict; condense.

ressort (rəsɔ:r) m, spring; elasticity; buoyancy; incentive; province; purview; resort, appeal. ~ à boudin, spiral spring. à ~, spring (scale, etc.). **ressortir** (sortiːr) v.i, to be under the jurisdiction of; (v.i.ir.) to go out again; stand out (in relief); result, appear.

ressource (rəsurs) f, resource; expedient, shift, resort.

ressouvenir (rəsuvniːr) m, remembrance, memory. **se ~**, v.pr. ir, to remember.

ressuer (rəsɥe) v.i, to sweat (walls).

ressusciter (resysite) v.t, to resuscitate, revive; raise (the dead.)

restant, e (rɛstɑ̃, ɑ̃ːt) a, remaining, left.

restaurant, e (rɛstɔrɑ̃, ɑ̃ːt) a, restorative. ¶ m, restorative; restaurant, eating house. **restaurateur, trice** (ratœːr, tris) n, restorer; restaurant keeper, caterer. **restauration** (sjɔ̃) f, restoration. **restaurer** (re) v.t, to restore, reestablish; refresh.

reste (rɛst) m, rest, remainder, remains; leavings, remnant. au, du ~, besides, moreover. ~s mortels, mortal remains. **rester** (te) v.i, to remain, be left; stay, stop, stand, sit, keep, stick; last; live.

restituer (rɛstitɥe) v.t, to restore, return. **restitution** (tysjɔ̃) f, restitution; restoration.

restoroute (rɛstɔrut) m, restaurant on turnpike, highway, etc.

restreindre (rɛstrɛ̃ːdr) v.t.ir, to restrict, limit. **restriction** (triksjɔ̃) f, restriction; reservation.

résultat (rezylta) m, result, outcome. **résulter** (te) v.i, to result, follow, ensue.

résumé (rezyme) m, summary, abstract. ~ des débats, summing up. **résumer** (me) v.t, to summarize; sum up.

résurrection (rezyrɛksjɔ̃) f, resurrection.

retable (rətabl) m, reredos, altar piece.

rétablir (retabliːr) v.t, to reestablish, restore; retrieve; reinstate.

retaille (rətɑːj) f, cutting, paring (snip, bit).

rétamer (retame) v.t, to replate, retin. **être rétamé**, to be drunk; exhausted; broke.

retaper (rətape) v.t, to do up; recast.

retard (rətaːr) m, delay. **en ~**, late, behind[hand]; overdue; in arrears; slow (clock). **retardataire** (tardatɛːr) a, late, in arrears; overstaying pass (Mil.). ¶ n, latecomer. **retarder** (de) v.t, to retard, delay; hinder; put off; put back (clock); (v.i.) be slow; lag.

retâter (rətate) v.t. & i, to touch again; try again.

retenir (rətniːr) v.t.ir, to keep back, retain, withhold, stop; keep; engage; reserve, book; detain; hold; h. back, check, restrain; remember; carry (Arith.). **se ~**, to refrain; catch hold. **rétention** (retɑ̃sjɔ̃) f, retention.

retentir (rətɑ̃tiːr) v.i, to [re]sound, echo, ring. **retentissant** (tisɑ̃) a, resounding, echoing; sonorous.

retenu, e (rətny) a, cautious, discreet. ¶ f, stoppage (on pay, etc.); carry (Arith.); reserve, discretion. **mettre en ~**, to keep in (Sch.).

réticence (retisɑ̃ːs) f, reticence; concealment.

réticule (retikyl) m, reticule; reticle.

rétif, ive (retif, iːv) a, restive; stubborn.

rétine (retin) f, retina.

retiré, e (rətire) p.a, solitary, secluded. **retirer** (re) v.t, to redraw; draw back; withdraw; retire (bill); take out; remove; extract; draw, get, derive; recall; reclaim (from vice). **se ~**, to retire, withdraw; stand down; recede; shrink.

retombée (rətɔ̃be) f, spring[ing] (arch); repercussions, consequences (bad); fallout (nuclear). **retomber** (be) v.i, to fall down [again]; relapse; fall [back], devolve; hang down.

rétorquer (retɔrke) v.t, to retort.

retors, e (rətɔːr, ɔrs) *a*, twisted; crafty.

retouche (rətuʃ) *f*, retouch[ing]; patch (*computers*). **retoucher** (ʃe) *v.t.* & ~ **à**, to retouch, touch up.

retour (rətuːr) *m*, turn; return; recurrence; reversion; reversal; decline (*life*), wane; ruse. ~ *de flamme*, backfire. ~ *de manivelle*, backfire [kick]. ~ *en arrière*, flashback (*TV*, *cinema*, *literature*, etc.). *être de* ~, to be back. **retourne** (turn) *f*, turn-up (*card*), trumps. **retournement** (nəmɑ̃) *m*, turning, reversal. ~ *de bras*, hammerlock (*wrestling*). **retourner** (ne) *v.i.* & *t.* to return; revert; turn (*coat, etc.*); t. over; t. up; mix (*salad*). ~ *un plan*, to retake a shot (*cinema*). se ~, to turn [round], veer (*opinion*).

retracer (rətrase) *v.t.* to retrace, recall. se ~, to recur.

rétracter (retrakte) *v.t.* to retract, recant.

retrait, e (rətrɛ, ɛt) *p.a*, shrunken. ¶ *m*, withdrawal; deprivation; shrinkage; recess. ¶ *f*, retreat; tattoo; withdrawal; retirement; superannuation; pension; retired pay; shelter; seclusion; shrinkage; offset (*Arch.*). ~ *aux flambeaux*, torchlight tattoo. *prendre sa* ~, to retire. **retraité, e** (te) *a*, pensioned off, superannuated. [*officier*] *retraité*, officer on the retired list.

retrancher (rətrɑ̃ʃe) *v.t.* to cut off; c. out; take away; deduct; subtract; entrench.

rétrécir (retresiːr) *v.t.* & *i*, to narrow; shrink. se ~, to shrink.

retremper (rətrɑ̃pe) *v.t.* to retemper; brace.

rétribuer (retribɥe) *v.t.* to remunerate, pay. **rétribution** (byɔsjɔ̃) *f*, remuneration, salary, reward.

rétro (retrɔ) *a*, harking back to or imitating the past. ¶ *m*, return to the past (*abbrev. of* "rétrograde").

rétroactif, ive (retroaktif, iːv) *a*, retroactive. **rétroaction** (aksjɔ̃) *f*, feedback (*computers*).

rétrocéder (retrɔsede) *v.i.* to retrocede; recede; go back. **rétrocession** (sɛsjɔ̃) *f*, retrocession; recession.

rétrograde (retrɔgrad) *a*, retrograde, backward. **rétrograder** (de) *v.i*, to go back[wards]; (*v.t.*) to reduce to lower rank (*Mil.*).

rétrospectif, ive† (retrɔspektif, iːv) *a*, retrospective. ¶ *f*, retrospect.

retrousser (rətruse) *v.t*, to turn up; tuck up; curl (*lip*).

retrouver (rətruve) *v.t*, to find [again], recover; recognize; retrieve (*computers*). se ~, to meet again.

rétroviseur (retrɔvizœːr) *m*, rearview mirror (*auto*).

rets (rɛ) *m*, net; (*pl.*) toils (*fig.*).

réunion (reynjɔ̃) *f*, [re]union; assembly, gathering, function, meeting. **réunir** (niːr) *v.t*, to [re]unite; join; combine; lump. se ~, to meet, foregather.

réussi, e (reysi) *p.a*, successful. **réussir** (siːr) *v.i*, to succeed; prosper. **réussite** (sit) *f*, success; solitaire (*cards*).

revaloir (rəvalwaːr) *v.t.ir*, to pay (*someone*) out, be even with (*someone*).

revanche (rəvɑ̃ʃ) *f*, revenge; return; requital, return match.

rêvasser (rɛvase) *v.i*, to have troubled dreams; muse. **rêve** (rɛːv) *m*, dream; day dream.

revêche (rəvɛʃ) *a*, cantankerous.

réveil (revɛj) *m*, waking, awakening; revival (*Relig.*); reveille; alarm clock. **réveille-matin** (vɛj) *m*, alarm clock; awakener. **réveiller** (vɛje) *v.t.* to awake[n], wake[n], call [a]rouse; revive. se ~, to wake [up]; revive. **réveillon** (jɔ̃) *m*, Christmas or New Year's Eve supper.

révélateur, trice (revelatœːr, tris) *n*, revealer; (*m.*) developer (*Phot.*). **révélation** (sjɔ̃) *f*, revelation; disclosure; eye-opener. **révéler** (le) *v.t*, to reveal, disclose; develop (*Phot.*).

revenant (rəvnɑ̃) *m*, ghost.

revenant-bon (rəvnɑ̃bɔ̃) *m*, perquisite.

revendeur, euse (rəvɑ̃dœːr, øːz) *n*, second-hand dealer; retailer; peddler.

revendication (rəvɑ̃dikasjɔ̃) *f*, demand; claim; claiming.

revendiquer (rəvãdike) *v.t*, to claim, assert.

revendre (rəvã:dr) *v.t*, to resell. *avoir à ~*, to have enough & to spare.

revenir (rəvni:r) *v.i.ir*, to come [back], return; come again, recur; revert; recover; cost; amount. *~ sur*, to retrace; go back on; reconsider; rake up (*past*). *je n'en reviens pas*, I can't believe it. *faire ~*, to sauté lightly.

revente (rəvã:t) *f*, resale.

revenu (rəvny) *m*, revenue, income. **revenue** (ny) *f*, new growth, young wood.

rêver (reve) *v.i. & t*, to dream; d. of; muse; ponder.

réverbère (revɛrbɛ:r) *m*, street lamp; reflector. **réverbérer** (bere) *v.t*, to reverberate.

reverdir (rəverdi:r) *v.i*, to grow green again; grow young again.

révérence (reverã:s) *f*, reverence; bow, curtsy. **révérenciel, le** (rãsjel) *a*, reverential. **révérencieux, euse†** (sjø, øːz) *a*, obsequious; over-polite. **révérend, e** (rã, ã:d) *a*, reverend. **révérendissime** (rãdisim) *a*, most reverend, right r. **révérer** (re) *v.t*, to revere, reverence.

rêverie (rɛvri) *f*, reverie, musing; idle fancy.

revers (rəvɛ:r) *m*, reverse; back; backhand [stroke, blow]; facing, lapel; turnover [top] (*stocking, etc.*).

reverser (rəverse) *v.t*, to pour out again; pour back; transfer.

réversible (reversibl) *a*, reversible; revertible. **réversion** (sjõ) *f*, reversion.

revêtement (rəvɛtmã) *m*, facing (*wall, etc.*); lining; revetment. **revêtir** (ti:r) *v.t*, to clothe, dress; don, put on; assume; provide; face, line; revet.

rêveur, euse (rɛvœ:r, øːz) *a*, dreaming; dreamy. ¶ *n*, dreamer.

revient (rəvjɛ̃) *m*, cost. *prix de ~*, cost price.

revigorer (rəvigɔre) *v.t*, to reinvigorate.

revirement (rəvirmã) *m*, change, turn; turnover; veering.

reviser (rəvize) *v.t*, to revise; review, reconsider; overhaul. **reviseur** (zœ:r) *m*, examiner; proof-reader. **revision** (jõ) *f*, revision; review; proofreading; medical examination (*recruits*); overhaul (*engine, etc.*). *conseil de ~*, draft board.

revivifier (rəvivifje) *v.t*, to revivify, revive. **revivre** (vi:vr) *v.i.ir*, to live again, come to life again; revive.

révocation (revɔkasjõ) *f*, revocation; repeal; dismissal, removal.

revoici (rəvwasi) *pr*, here . . . again. *le ~*, here he is again. **revoilà** (la) *pr*, there . . . again.

revoir (rəvwa:r) *v.t.ir*, to see again; meet again; revise; review. *au ~!* good-bye!

revoler (rəvɔle) *v.i*, to fly again; fly back.

révoltant, e (revɔltã, ã:t) *a*, revolting. **révolte** (vɔlt) *f*, revolt, rebellion, mutiny. **révolté, e** (te) *n*, rebel, insurgent, mutineer. **révolter** (te) *v.t*, to cause to revolt; shock. *se ~*, to revolt, rebel, mutiny.

révolu, e (revɔly) *a*, completed. **révolution** (sjõ) *f*, revolution; revulsion. **révolutionnaire** (ɔnɛ:r) *a. & n*, revolutionary. **révolutionner** (ne) *v.t*, to revolutionize; upset. **revolver** (revɔlvɛ:r) *m*, revolver (*gun*); capstan, turret (*lathe*). *~ à six coups*, six-shooter.

revomir (rəvɔmi:r) *v.t*, to vomit [up, again].

révoquer (revɔke) *v.t*, to revoke, repeal; dismiss; recall.

revue (rəvy) *f*, review, inspection; magazine; revue.

révulsion (revylsjõ) *f*, revulsion (*Med.*).

rez-de-chaussée (redʃose) *m*, ground floor.

rhabiller (rabije) *v.t*, to repair, mend, overhaul; dress again; reclothe.

rhapsodie (rapsɔdi) *f*, rhapsody (*all Eng. senses*).

rhénan, e (renã, an) *a*, Rhine (*att.*).

rhétorique (retɔrik) *f*, rhetoric. **Rhin (le)** (rɛ̃) the Rhine.

rhinocéros (rinɔserɔs) *m*, rhinoceros.

rhododendron (rɔdɔdẽdrɔ̃) *m*, rhododendron.

rhombe (rɔ̃;b) *m*, rhomb[us].

Rhône (le) (ro:n) the Rhone.

rhubarbe (rybarb) *f*, rhubarb.

rhum (rɔm) *m*, rum.

rhumatismal, e (rymatismal) *a*, rheumatic. **rhumatisme** (tism) *m*, rheumatism. **rhume** (*de cerveau, de poitrine*) (rym) *m*, cold (in the head, on the chest).

rhythme (ritm) *m*, rhythm. **rhythmique** (mik) *a*, rhythmic[al].

riant, e (riɑ̃, ɑ̃;t) *a*, smiling; cheerful.

ribambelle (ribɑ̃bɛl) *f*, string, swarm.

ribote (ribɔt) *f*, drunken bout.

ricaner (rikane) *v.i*, to snigger, sneer.

richard (riʃa;r) *m*, [rich] upstart. **riche†** (riʃ) *a*, rich, wealthy; copious; valuable; handsome. **richesse** (ʃɛs) *f*, wealth, riches; richness.

ricin (risẽ) *m*, castor oil plant.

ricocher (rikɔʃe) *v.i*, to ricochet. **ricochet** (ʃɛ) *m*, ricochet; (*pl.*) duck & drake.

rictus (rikty;s) *m*, grin.

ride (rid) *f*, wrinkle, line; puckering; ripple; lanyard. **rideau** (do) *m*, curtain; [drop] curtain; screen; veil (*fig.*). ~ *de fer*, safety curtain (*Theat.*); iron curtain. *lever de* ~, curtain raiser. **rider** (de) *v.t*, to wrinkle, line; shrivel; ripple, ruffle.

ridicule† (ridikyl) *a*, ridiculous. ¶ *m*, ridiculousness; ridicule. **ridiculiser** (lize) *v.t*, to ridicule.

rien (rjẽ) *pn.m*, anything; (*oft. with* ne) nothing. ~ *à* ~, love all (*Ten.*). *de* ~, don't mention it, you're welcome. ¶ *m*, trifle, mere nothing; (*pl.*) small talk.

rieur, euse (rjœ:r, ø:z) *n*, laugher; (*att.*) laughing.

riflard (rifla:r) *m*, jack plane; gamp.

rigide† (riʒid) *a*, rigid; stiff. **rigidité** (dite) *f*, rigidity, stiffness. ~ *cadavérique* (kadaverik), rigor mortis.

rigolade (rigɔlad) *f*, lark, nonsense; joke.

rigole (rigɔl) *f*, channel, ditch, trench.

rigoler (rigɔle) *v.i*, guffaw; furrow, channel. **rigolo (lo)** *a*, comic, funny.

rigoureux, euse† (rigurø, ø:z) *a*, rigorous, severe; strict. **rigueur** (gœ:r) *f*, rigor, severity; hardship; strictness. *à la* ~, if necessary. *de* ~, required.

rimailler (rimɑje) *v.i*, to write bad verse. **rimailleur** (jœ:r) *m*, rhym[est]er. **rime** (rim) *f*, rhyme. **rimer** (me) *v.t*, to versify; (*v.i.*) to rhyme. **rimeur** (mœ:r) *m*, rhym[est]er.

rincer (rɛ̃se) *v.t*, to rinse; r. out. **rinçure** (sy:r) *f*, rinsings, slops.

ringard (rɛ̃ga:r) *m*, poker, rake.

ripaille (ripɑ:j) *f*, feasting, carousal.

riper (ripe) *v.t. & i*, to scrape; slide; shift (*cargo*).

ripopée (ripɔpe) *f*, slops; mishmash.

riposte (ripɔst) *f*, riposte, counter[stroke]; retort. **riposter** (te) *v.t*, to riposte.

rire (ri:r) *m*, laughter; laugh. *fou* ~, uncontrolled laughter. ~ *moqueur*, sneer. ¶ *v.i.ir*, to laugh, smile; joke. ~ *en dedans*, ~ *en dessous*, to laugh inwardly, snigger.

ris (ri) *m*, reef (*sail*). ~ *de veau*, sweetbread.

risée (rize) *f*, jeer, mockery; laughing stock, butt. **risible†** (zibl) *a*, ludicrous, laughable.

risque (risk) *m*, risk. **risquer** (ke) *v.t*, to risk, chance. ~ *le paquet*, to chance it.

rissole (risɔl) *f*, rissole. **rissoler** (le) *v.t*, to brown (*Cook.*).

ristourne (risturn) *f*, return, refund; discount.

rite (rit) *m*, rite. **rituel, le** (tɥɛl) *a. & m*, ritual.

rivage (riva;ʒ) *m*, shore, foreshore, beach, strand; bank, side.

rival, e (rival) *n. & a*, rival. **rivaliser avec** (lize), to rival, vie with, emulate. **rivalité** (te) *f*, rivalry, emulation.

rive (riːv) *f*, bank, side, shore.

river (rive) *v.t*, to rivet, clinch.

riverain, e (rivrɛ̃, ɛn) *a*, riparian, riverside, waterside; wayside.

rivet (rive) *m*, rivet; pin, bolt.

rivière (rivjɛːr) *f*, river; rivière (*gems*); single openwork (*Need.*). ~ *à truites*, trout stream. *la R~ de Gênes*, the Riviera (*French & Italian*).

rixe (riks) *f*, scuffle, brawl, fight.

ris (ri) *m*, rice. **rizière** (zjɛːr) *f*, rice field.

rob (rɔb) *m*, rubber (*cards*).

robe (rɔb) *f*, dress, gown, frock; robe; robe (*legal dress*); cloth (*clerical dress*); coat (*animal's*); skin (*onion, bean, etc.*); wrapper (*cigar*); color (*wine*). ~ *de chambre*, dressing gown. ~ *de mariée*, wedding dress. **robin** (bɛ̃) *m*, lawyer.

robert (rɔbɛːr) *m*, breast (*vulgar*).

robinet (rɔbinɛ) *m*, cock, faucet. spigot.

robre (rɔbr) *m*, rubber (*cards*).

robuste† (rɔbyst) *a*, robust, lusty, sturdy, able-bodied; stout; hardy (*plant*). **robustesse** (tɛs) *f*, robustness, strength.

roc (rɔk) *m*, rock. **rocaille** (kaj) *f*, rockwork. **rocailleux, euse** (kajø, øːz) *a*, rocky, stony, rugged.

rocade (rɔkad) *m*, castling (*chess*). *ligne de* ~, castling base (*chess*). *voie de* ~, *chemin de fer de* ~, strategic road or railroad paralleling a military front.

rocambolesque (rɔkɑ̃bɔlɛsk) *a*, fantastic, incredible.

roche (rɔʃ) *f*, rock, stone, boulder. **rocher** (ʃe) *m*, rock, crag, cliff. ~ *artificiel*, rock garden. ~ *branlant*, rocking stone, logan [stone]. **rochet** (rɔʃɛ) *m*, ratchet; rochet (*surplice*).

rocheux, euse (rɔʃø, øːz) *a*, rocky.

rococo (rɔkɔko) *m. & att*, rococo.

roder (rɔde) *v.t*, to grind, lap; break in (*Motor.*).

rôder (rode) *v.i*, to prowl, hang about. **rôdeur** (dœːr) *m*, prowler. ~ *de grève*, beachcomber.

rodomontade (rɔdɔmɔ̃tad) *f*, bluster.

rogations (rɔgasjɔ̃) tions.

rogatons (rɔgatɔ̃) (*food*); odds & ends

Roger-Bontemps (happy-go-lucky fello

rogne (rɔɲ) *f*, itch, [bad] temper.

rogner (rɔɲe) *v.t*, to pare; cut down; cut book); (*v.i.*) to grum

rogneux, euse (rɔɲ mangy, scabby.

rognon (rɔɲɔ̃) *m*, ki mal); nodule.

rognonner (rɔɲɔne) grumble.

rognure (rɔɲyːr) *f*, clip ing (*bit*).

rogue (rɔg) *a*, arrogant,

roi (rwa) *m*, king; champ *des* ~s, Twelfth Night. ~ *de* nature, lord of creation.

roide (rɛd & rwad) *a*, roideur (dœːr) *f*, **roidir** (diːr) *v.t*. Same as *raide*, etc.

roitelet (rwatlɛ) *m*, kinglet; wren.

rôle (roːl) *m*, roll, list, roster, rot calendar (*prisoners for trial* part, rôle. ~ *travesti*, man's part acted by a woman. *à tour de* ~, in rotation, in turn.

romain, e (rɔmɛ̃, ɛn) *a. & R~ (pers.)* n, Roman. **romain**, *m*, roman (*Typ.*). **romaine**, *f*, romaine lettuce, cos l.; steelyard.

roman, e (rɔmɑ̃, an) *a. & m*, Romance (*language*); Romanesque (*Arch.*). ¶ *m*, novel; fiction; romance. ~ *à deux sous*, pulp novel. ~ *policier* (polisje), detective story. **romance** (mɑ̃ːs) *f*, song, ballad; sloppiness, maudlin[ism]. ~ *sans paroles*, song without words. ¶ *a*, sloppy, maudlin. **romancier, ère** (mɑ̃sje, ɛːr) *n*, novelist. **romand, e** (mɑ̃, ɑ̃ːd) *a*, French-speaking (*Switzerland* **romanesque†** (manɛsk) *a*, rom tic. **romanichel** (maniʃɛl) *m*, sy, romany. **romantique** (m *a*, romantic (*literature*).

romarin (rɔmarɛ̃) *m*, rose

rompre (rɔ̃ːpr) *v.t. & i*, to b. up; b. in; b. off; snap; disrupt; burst; interrupt upset; cancel. ~ *charg*

ship (*Rly.*). ~ *les chiens*, to call off the hounds; change the subject. *rompez!*, dismissed (*Mil.*). **rompu**, e (rɔ̃py) *p.a*, broken; b. in, used, inured. ~ [*de fatigue*], tired out. *à batons ~s*, by fits and starts.

omsteck (rɔmstɛk) *m*, rump steak.

once (rɔ̃:s) *f*, bramble; blackberry bush; barb[ed] wire; annoyance. ~ *de noyer*, walnut burr. ~-*framboise*, loganberry.

onchonner (rɔʃɔne) *v.i*, to grumble.

ond, e (rɔ̃, ɔ̃:d) *a*, round; rounded; rotund; even (*money*); drunk; broke (*money*). ¶ *m*, round; circle; ring. ~-*de-cuir*, pen-pusher, bureaucrat; air cushion. ~ *de serviette*, napkin ring. ¶ *f*, round; beat; roundelay; round hand; semibreve. **rondelet**, te (rɔ̃dlɛ, ɛt) *a*, roundish. **rondelle** (dɛl) *f*, washer; ring (*umbrella*); disc. **rondement** (dmɑ̃) *ad*, roundly, briskly, bluntly. **rondeur** (dœ:r) *f*, roundness, rotundity; fullness; frankness. **rondin** (dɛ̃) *m*, billet, log. **rond-point** (rɔ̃pwɛ̃), *m*, traffic circle.

ronflant, e (rɔ̃flɑ̃, ɑ̃:t) (*fig.*) *a*, sonorous, highsounding. **ronfler** (fle) *v.i*, to snore; boom, roar, hum, whir, buzz.

ronger (rɔ̃ʒe) *v.t*, to gnaw, nibble; pick (*bone*); eat [away, into], corrode; undermine; fret; prey. **rongeur**, **euse** (ʒœ:r, ø:z) *a*, rodent, gnawing; corroding. ¶ *m*, rodent.

ronron (rɔ̃rɔ̃) *m*, purr[ing]; hum; drone.

roquer (rɔke) *v.t*, to castle (*chess*); roquet (*croquet*).

roquet (rɔkɛ) *m*, pug [dog]; cur, mongrel.

roquette (rɔkɛt) *f*, rocket (*Bot.*).

rosace (rozas) *f*, rosette; rose; rose window. **rosacé**, e (se) rosaceous. ¶ *f.pl*, Rosaceae. **rosaire** (zɛ:r) *m*, rosary (*beads*).

rosbif (rɔzbif) *m*, roast beef; roast sirloin.

rose (ro:z) *f*, rose; rose window; rose diamond. ~ *des vents*, compass card. ~ *moussue*, moss rose. ~ *muscade*, musk r. ~ *thé*, tea r.

~ *trémière* (tremjɛ:r), hollyhock. ¶ *m*. & *a*, rose [color], pink. *le mont Rose*, Monte Rosa. **rosé**, e (roze), *a*, roseate, rosy.

roseau (rozo) *m*, reed; broken reed (*fig.*).

rosée (roze) *f*, dew.

roselet (rɔslɛ) *m*, ermine (*fur*).

roseraie (rozrɛ) *f*, rose garden, rosary, rosery. **rosette** (zɛt) *f*, rosette; bow (*ribbon*); red ink, r. chalk. **rosier** (zje) *m*, rose bush. ~ *grimpant*, rambler [rose]. **rosière** (jɛ:r) *f*, innocent girl.

rosse (rɔs) *f*, jade, sorry steed; nasty (*or* objectionable) person. **rosser** (se) *v.t*, to thrash, beat.

rossignol (rɔsiɲɔl) *m*, nightingale; picklock; whistle; unsalable article, white elephant.

rot (ro) *m*. belch.

rôt (ro) *m*, roast [meat]; roast meat course.

rotation (rɔtasjɔ̃) *f*, rotation. **rotatoire** (twa:r) *a*, rotary.

roter (rɔte) *v.i*, to belch.

rôti (roti) *m*, roast [meat]; r. m. course. ~ *de porc*, r. pork. **rôtie** (ti) *f*, [round of] roast. ~ *à l'anglaise*, ~ *au fromage*, Welsh rabbit, W. rarebit.

rotin (rɔtɛ̃) *m*, rattan; r. cane.

rôtir (roti:r) *v.t*. & *i*, to roast, broil; toast; scorch. **rôtisserie** (tisri) *f*, shop where one buys cooked meats. **rôtissoire** (tiswa:r) *f*, roaster, Dutch oven.

rotonde (rɔtɔ̃:d) *f*, rotunda; cloak. **rotondité** (tɔ̃dite) *f*, rotundity.

rotule (rɔtyl) *f*, knee cap, patella. ~ *sphérique*, ball & socket.

roture (rɔty:r) *f*, commonalty. **roturier**, **ère** (tyrje, ɛ:r) *n*, commoner.

rouage (rwa:ʒ) *m*, wheels, wheelwork, works; machinery (*fig.*).

rouan, **ne** (rwɑ̃, an) *a*. & *n*, roan (*animal*).

roucouler (rukule) *v.i*, to coo; bill & coo; (*v.t.*) to warble.

roue (ru) *f*, wheel. ~ *libre*, free w. *faire la ~*, to spread its tail (*peacock*); turn catherine wheels. ~ *de secours*, spare w. ~ *d'impression*, print w. **roué** (rwe) *m*, rake,

profligate. **rouelle** (rwɛl) *f*, round [slice]; fillet (*veal*).

rouennerie (rwanri) *f*, printed cotton goods.

rouer (rwe) *v.t*, to coil (*rope*); break upon the wheel. ~ *de coups*, to thrash. **rouerie** (ruri) *f*, trickery. **rouet** (rwɛ) *m*, spinning wheel; sheave.

rouflaquette (ruflakɛt) *f*, lovelock, earlock, cowlick.

rouge (ruː3) *m*, red (*color & pers. in Pol.*); rouge; red wine. ¶ *a*, red; red-hot; blushing; glowing. *mer R~*, Red Sea. ~ *gorge, m*, [robin] redbreast. ~ *à lèvres, m*, lipstick. **rougeâtre** (ru3aːtr) *a*, reddish. **rougeaud, e** (3o, oːd) *a*, red-faced, ruddy. **rougeole** (3ɔl) *f*, measles. **rouget** (3ɛ) *m*, red mullet. **rougeur** (3œːr) *f*, redness; blush, flush; red spot (*skin*). **rougir** (3iːr) *v.t., & i*, to redden; blush, flush.

rouille (ruːj) *f*, rust; mildew, blight (*Agric.*). **rouillé, e** (ruje) *a*, rusty; mildewed; out of practice. **rouiller** (je) *v.t*, to rust. **rouillure** (jyːr) *f*, rustiness.

roulade (rulad) *f*, roll (*downhill*); roulade, run (*Mus.*). **roulage** (laː3) *m*, haulage. **roulant, e** (lɑ̃, ɑ̃ːt) *a*, rolling; traveling; circulating (*capital*). **rouleau** (lo) *m*, roller; roll; spool (*film ~Phot.*); scroll; twist (*tobacco*); coil (*rope*). *~de pâtissier*, rolling pin. *au bout de son ~*, at the end of one's rope, at one's wits' end. **roulement** (lmɑ̃) *m*, roll[ing]; working, running; r. gear; rumbling (*traffic*); bearings; turnover (*capital*); rotation. ~ *à billes*, ball bearings. **rouler** (le) *v.t*, to roll; r. up; coil; haul (*v.i.*) to roll; run, work; turn, rotate; travel, drive, rove, roam; circulate freely; fluctuate; fleece, cheat. *faire ~ la presse*, to machine (*Typ.*). *~[sur le sol]*, to taxi (*Avn.*). **roulette** (lɛt) caster, -or; roller, wheel; tape [measure] (*coiled*); roulette. **roulier** (lje) *m*, carter, waggoner. **roulis** (li) *m*, rolling (*ship*). **roulotte** (lɔt) *f*, caravan (*house on wheels*); trailer.

roumain, e (rumɛ̃, ɛn) *a & R~, n. & le roumain* (*language*), R[o]umanian. **la Roumanie** (mani), R[o]umania.

roupiller (rupije) *v.i*, to snooze.

rouspéter (ruspete) *v.i*, to complain, protest; resist; gripe.

roussâtre (rusɑːtr) *a*, reddish. **rousseau** (so) *m. & att*, red-haired (person). **rousserolle** (srɔl) *f*, sedge warbler. **rousseur** (sœːr) *f*, redness. *tache de ~*, freckle. **roussi** (si) *m*, [smell of] burning. **roussir** (siːr) *v.t. & i*, to redden; brown (*meat*); scorch, singe.

route (rut) *f*, road, path, track; route, course, way; transit; journey. *grande ~, ~ nationale*, highway. ~ *départementale*, secondary road. ~ *déviée*, loopway. **routier, ère** (tje, ɛːr) *a*, road (*att.*). ¶ *m*, campaigner, stager. **routine** (tin) *f*, routine; rote; red tape.

rouvieux (ruvjø) *m*, mange; (*att.*) mangy.

rouvrir (ruvriːr) *v.t.ir*, to reopen.

roux, rousse (ru, rus) *a. & n*, russet; brown[ed]; red (*hair*); red-haired (person). ¶ *m*, russet (*color*); brown sauce.

royal, e† (rwajal) *a*, royal, regal, kingly. **royaliste** (list) *a. & n*, royalist. **royaume** (joːm) *m*, kingdom, realm. **royanté** (ɔte) *f*, royalty; kingship; dominance.

ruade (rɥad) *f*, lashing out; kick (*horse*).

ruban (rybɑ̃) *m*, ribbon; band; tape. ~ *perforé*, punched tape (*data processing*).

rubéole (rybeɔl) *f*, German measles.

rubicond, e (rybikɔ̃, ɔ̃d) *a*, rubicund, florid.

rubis (rybi) *m*, ruby; jewel (*Horol.*).

rubrique (rybrik) *f*, red chalk; rubric; heading, section; column (*special subject news*); publisher's imprint (*place of publication*).

ruche (ryʃ) *f*, [bee]hive; ruche. **rucher** (ʃe) *m*, apiary.

rude† (ryd) *a*, rough; rugged; harsh; hard; severe; gruff; stiff; steep. **rudesse** (dɛs) *f*, roughness, etc.

rudiment (rydimɑ̃) *m*, rudiment. **rudimentaire** (tɛːr) *a*, rudimentary.

rudoyer (rydwaje) *v.t*, to use roughly, brow-beat.

rue (ry) *f*, street; rue (*Bot.*). ~ *à sens unique*, one-way street. ~ *piétonne*, pedestrian mall.

ruée (rɥe) *f*, rush, onrush, onslaught.

ruelle (rɥɛl) *f*, lane, alley; ruelle (*bedside*).

ruer (rɥe) *v.t*, to lash out, kick (*horse*). *se* ~ *sur*, to hurl oneself at, rush at.

rugir (ryʒiːr) *v.i*, to roar. **rugissement** (ʒismɑ̃) *m*, roar, roaring; howling (*storm*).

rugosité (rygozite) *f*, ruggedness, roughness; corrugation.

rugueux, euse (ryg∅, ∅ːz) *a*, rough, rugged.

ruine (rɥin) *f*, ruin, [down]fall. **ruiner** (ne) *v.t*, to ruin. **ruineux, euse** (n∅, ∅ːz) *a*, ruinous.

ruisseau (rɥiso) *m*, stream[let], brook, rivulet, rill; gutter (*street & fig.*). **ruisseler** (sle) *v.i*, to stream, run down, trickle.

rumeur (rymœːr) *f*, hum (*voices, etc.*); uproar; rumor.

ruminant, e (ryminɑ̃, ɑ̃ːt) *a. & m*, ruminant. **ruminer** (ne) *v.t. & abs*, to ruminate; ponder.

rupture (ryptyːr) *f*, breaking; rupture; fracture; breaking off, breach.

rural, e (ryral) *a*, rural, country (*att.*).

ruse (ryːz) *f*, ruse, trick[ery], wile, dodge; stratagem. **rusé, e** (ryze) *a*, artful, crafty, wily. **ruser** (ze) *v.i*, to use cunning.

russe (rys) *a. & R~, n. & le russe* (*language*), Russian. **la Russie** (si), Russia.

rustaud, e (rysto, oːd) *a*, boorish, uncouth. ¶ *n*, boor. **rusticité** (ti-site) *f*, rusticity; boorishness. **rustique†** (tik) *a*, rustic; country (*att.*); hardy (*plant*); crazy (*pavement*). **rustre** (str) *m*, boor, churl.

rustine (rystin) *f*, inner-tube patch.

rut (ryt) *m*, rut, heat (*animals*).

rutabaga (rytabaga) *m*, rutabaga.

rutilant (rytilɑ̃) *a*, glowing, gleaming red.

rythme (ritm) *m*, rhythm. **rythmique** (mik) *a*, rhythmic(al).

S

sa *see* **son**.

sabbat (saba) *m*, sabbath (*Jewish, witches'*); row, racket.

sable (sɑːbl) *m*, sand; gravel (*Med.*); sable (*fur, Her.*). ~ *mouvant*, quicksand. **sabler** (sɑble) *v.t*, to sand, gravel (*path*); swig, toss off. **sablier** (blie) *m*, hourglass, sand g. **sablière** (ɛːr) *f*, sand pit, gravel pit; wall plate. **sablon** (blɔ̃) *m*, fine sand. **sablonneux, euse** (blɔn∅, ∅ːz) *a*, sandy. **sablonnière** (njɛːr) *f*, sand pit.

sabord (sabɔːr) *m*, port [hole]. **saborder** (borde) *v.t*, to scuttle (*ship*).

sabot (sabo) *m*, clog, sabot; shoe; skid; hoof; whipping top; tub (*bad ship*); rubbishy instrument or tool. **sabotage** (botaːʒ) *m*, sabotage, foul play. **saboter** (te) *v.t*, to botch; damage wilfully, wreck. **sabotière** (tjɛːr) *f*, clog dance.

sabouler (sabule) *v.t*, to jostle; rate, scold.

sabre (sɑːbr) *m*, saber, sword, broadsword, cutlass; swordfish. **sabrer** (sɑbre) *v.t. & abs*, to saber, slash; slash about; cut down, blue-pencil.

sac (sak) *m*, sack, bag, pouch, sac; sackcloth (*Theol.*); sacking, pillage; 100-franc note (*slang*). ~ *à main*, handbag. ~ *à ouvrage*, work b. ~ *à provisions*, shopping b. ~ *à terre*, sand b. ~ *d'ordonnance* (*Mil.*), knapsack. ~ *de couchage*, sleeping bag. ~ *de touriste*, ~ *de montagne*, ~ *d'alpinisme*, rucksack. *vider son* ~, to get something off one's chest.

saccade (sakad) *f*, jerk, start. **saccadé, e** (de) *p.a*, jerky; irregular; staccato (*voice*).

saccager (sakaʒe) *v.t*, to sack, pillage; ransack; upset.

saccharin, e (sakarɛ̃, in) *a*, saccharine, sugary; sugar (*att.*). ¶ *f*, saccharin.

sacerdoce (sasɛrdɔs) *m*, priesthood; ministry. **sacerdotal, e** (tal) *a*, sacerdotal, priestly.

sachée (saʃe) *f*, sackful, bagful. **sachet** (ʃɛ) *m*, bag. ~ *à parfums*, scent bag, sachet. **sacoche** (koʃ) *f*, saddlebag; courier's bag; tool b.

sacramental (sakramãtal) *m*, sacramental. **sacramentel, le†** (tɛl) *a*, sacramental, binding. **sacre** (kr) *m*, anointing, coronation; consecration (*bishop*). **sacré, e** (kre) *a*, holy, sacred, consecrated; damned, cursed. **sacrement** (krəmã) *m*, sacrament. **sacrer** (kre) *v.t*, to anoint, crown; consecrate; curse, swear. **sacrifice** (krifis) *m*, sacrifice; offering. **sacrifier** (fje) *v.t. & abs*, to sacrifice. **sacrilège** (lɛːʒ) *m*, sacrilege; (*att.*) sacrilegious.

sacripant (sakripã) *m*, rascal, bully.

sacristain (sakristɛ̃) *m*, sacristan. **sacristie** (ti) *f*, vestry, sacristy. **sacro-saint, e** (krɔsɛ̃, ɛ̃t) *a*, sacrosanct.

sadique (sadik) *a*, sadistic. ¶ *m*, sadist. **sadiste** (dist) *m*, sadist.

safran (safrã) *m*, saffron, crocus.

sagace (sagas) *a*, sagacious, shrewd. **sagacité** (site) *f*, sagacity, shrewdness.

sage† (saːʒ) *a*, wise, sage, sapient; judicious, prudent, sensible; well-behaved, good (*child*); chaste. ¶ *m*, sage, wise man. ~**-femme**, *f*, midwife. **sagesse** (ʒɛs) *f*, wisdom, etc; good conduct.

sagou (sagu) *m*, sago. **sagou[t]ier** ([t]je) *m*, sago palm.

sagouin (sagwɛ̃) *m*, saguin (*monkey*); sloven.

saignant, e (sɛɲã, ãːt) *a*, bleeding; raw; rare (*meat*). **saignée** (ɲe) *f*, bleeding, blood letting; bend of the arm; trench; holocaust. **saigner** (ɲe) *v.i. & t*, to bleed; stick (*pig*); tap (*tree, etc.*); drain; rankle.

saillant, e (sajã, ãːt) *a*, salient, projecting, prominent; striking, outstanding. **saillie** (ji) *f*, spurt, bound; projection; ledge; protrusion; sally; covering. **saillir** (jiːr) *v.i.ir*, to gush out; project; protrude; sally; (*v.t.ir.*) to service (*of animals*).

sain, e† (sɛ̃, ɛn) *a*, sound; wholesome; healthy, hale; sane. *sain & sauf*, safe & sound.

saindoux (sɛ̃du) *m*, lard.

saint, e (sɛ̃, ɛːt) *n*, saint, patron s. *le ~ des saints*, the holy of holies, sanctum. ¶ *a*, holy; sainted; saintly, godly; consecrated, hallowed. *saint-frusquin*, worldly goods. *Saint-Siège*, Holy See. *sainte table*, communion table. *la Sainte Vierge*, the Blessed Virgin. *Saint, comps*: *le ~-Esprit* (sɛ̃tɛspri), the Holy Ghost, the Holy Spirit. *la ~-Jean* (sɛ̃ʒã), Midsummer Day. *le ~-Laurent* (lɔrã), the St. Lawrence. *la ~-Martin* (martɛ̃), Martinmas. *la ~-Michel* (miʃɛl), Michaelmas. *la ~-Sylvestre* (silvɛstr), New Year's eve. **Sainte-Hélène** (sɛ̃tɛlɛn) *f*, St. Helena. **saintement** (tmã) *ad*, holily, in a godly manner, righteously. **sainteté** (tɛte) *f*, holiness, saintliness; sanctity.

saisie (sɛzi) *f*, seizure; distraint, execution; distress (*law*); foreclosure (*mortgage*). **saisir** (ziːr) *v.t*, to seize, lay hold of, grasp; catch; snatch; distrain, attach; foreclose; startle; lay before (*court*). **saisissant, e** (zisã, ãːt) *a*, piercing (*cold*); startling, striking; thrilling. **saisissement** (smã) *m*, shock; thrill.

saison (sɛzɔ̃) *f*, season, time (*of year*). *marchand des quatre-~s*, street vendor.

salade (salad) *f*, salad; jumble. *panier à ~*, Black Maria, police wagon. **saladier** (dje) *m*, salad bowl.

salage (salaːʒ) *m*, salting, curing.

salaire (salɛːr) *m*, wage[s], pay; hire; reward. ~ *de famine*, starvation wage.

salaison (salɛzɔ̃) *f*, salting, curing; (*pl.*) salt provisions.

salamalec (salamalɛk) *m*, salaam.
salamandre (salamɑ̃:dr) *f*, salamander. ~ *aquatique*, newt, eft.
Salamanque (salamɑ̃:k) *f*, Salamanca.
salant (salɑ̃) *a.m*, salt (*marsh*), saline.
salarié, e (salarje) *p.a*, wage-earning, paid. **salarier** (je) *v.t*, to pay a wage to.
salaud (salo) *m*, (*pers.*) skunk, bastard.
sale† (sal) *a*, dirty, unclean, filthy; foul; nasty; soiled (*linen*); messy.
salé, e (sale) *p.a*, salt, salted; corned (*beef*); briny; keen; broad (*story*); stiff (*price*). [*porc*] *salé*, *m*, salt pork. **saler** (le) *v.t*, to salt, pickle, cure, corn; overcharge (*someone*).
Salerne (salɛrn) *f*, Salerno.
saleté (salte) *f*, dirtiness; dirt, filth; mess; rubbish, trash[y goods].
salicole (salikɔl) *a*, salt (*industry*); saliferous. **salicoque** (kɔk) *f*, shrimp. **salière** (ljɛ:r) *f*, salt cellar; salt box. **salin, e** (lɛ̃, in) *a*, saline, briny, salt[y]. ¶ *f*, salt works; rock salt mine.
saligaud (saligo) *m*, bastard, swine (*person*).
salir (sali:r) *v.t*, to dirty, soil; foul; sully. **salissant** (lisɑ̃) *a*, dirtying; easily soiled. **salissure** (lisy:r) *f*, stain.
salive (sali:v) *f*, saliva, spittle. **saliver** (live) *v.i*, to salivate.
salle (sal) *f*, hall; room; ward (*hospital*); house (*Theat., etc.*); auditorium; office. ~ *à manger*, dining room; d. saloon (*ship*); coffee room (*hotel*); mess room (*Mil.*). ~ *de séjour*, living room. ~ *d'armes*, armory; fencing school. ~ *d'attente*, waiting room (*Rly.*). ~ *de bain*, bathroom. ~ *de classe*, schoolroom. ~ *de police*, guardroom (*Mil.*). ~ *des festins*, banqueting hall. ~ *des pas perdus*, waiting room (*Rly.*); lobby. ~ *de deuxième vision*, second-run movie theater. ~ *d'exclusivité*, first run m. t.
salmigondis (salmigɔ̃di) *m*, hodgepodge.

salon (salɔ̃) *m*, reception room; drawing room; parlor; saloon; room; salon, exhibition, show. ~ *d'exposition*, showroom. ~ *de l'automobile*, auto show. ~ *de l'aviation*, aircraft exhibition. ~ *de pose*, studio (*Phot.*).
Salonique (salɔnik) *f*, Salonica.
salope (salɔp) *f*, slattern, slut. **saloperie** (pri) *f*, filth, muck; trash. **salopette** (pɛt) *f*, overalls; dungarees, jeans.
salpêtre (salpɛ:tr) *m*, saltpeter, niter.
salsepareille (salsparɛj) *f*, sarsaparilla.
saltimbanque (saltɛ̃bɑ̃:k) *m*, showman, tumbler; mountebank.
salubre (salybr) *a*, salubrious, healthy; wholesome. **salubrité** (brite) *f*, salubrity; health (*public*).
saluer (salɥe) *v.t*, to salute, bow to; greet, hail.
salure (saly:r) *f*, saltness; tang.
salut (saly) *m*, safety; welfare; salvation; salutation, bow, greeting; salute; evening service (*Eccl.*). ¶ *i*, hail! greeting! **salutaire†** (tɛ:r) *a*, salutary, wholesome, beneficial. **salutation** (tasjɔ̃) *f*, salutation, greeting, bow.
salve (salv) *f*, salvo, salute; round (*applause*).
samedi (samdi) *m*, Saturday.
samovar (samɔva:r) *m*, urn (*for tea, coffee*).
sanatorium (sanatɔrjɔm) *m*, sanatorium.
sanctifier (sɑ̃ktifje) *v.t*, to sanctify, hallow. **sanction** (sjɔ̃) *f*, sanction, assent; penalty, punishment. **sanctionner** (ɔne) *v.t*, to sanction, approve. **sanctuaire** (tɥɛ:r) *m*, sanctuary; sanctum.
sandale (sɑ̃dal) *f*, sandal, shoe.
sandwich (sɑ̃dwitʃ) *m*, sandwich.
sang (sɑ̃) *m*, blood, gore; race, lineage, kinship. ~*-froid*, coolness, self-possession, nerve. [*homme de*] ~ *mêlé*, half-caste. *se faire des mauvais* ~, to worry, be uneasy. **sanglant, e** (glɑ̃, ɑ̃:t) *a*, bloody; sanguinary; deadly; cutting, scathing; outrageous.

ability, tact, gumption, know-how. ~-vivre, m, good manners.
savon (savɔ̃) m, soap. ~ à barbe en bâton, shaving stick. **savonner** (vɔne) v.t, to soap, wash; lather; reprimand severely (slang). **savonnerie** (nri) f, soap works; s. trade. **savonneux, euse** (nø, ø:z) a, soapy. **savonnier** (nje) m, soap maker.
savourer (savure) v.t, to taste; relish, enjoy. **savoureux, euse** (rø, ø:z) a, savory, tasty; enjoyable.
saxe (saks) m, Dresden china. **la Saxe**, Saxony.
saxhorn (saksɔrn) m, saxhorn.
saxon, ne (saksɔ̃, ɔn) a. & S~, n, Saxon.
saxophone (saksɔfɔn) m, saxophone.
saynète (sɛnɛt) f, playlet, sketch.
sbire (zb:r) m, sbirro; myrmidon.
scabieux, euse (skabjø, ø:z) a, scabious, scabby. ¶ f, scabious (Bot.).
scabreux, euse (skabrø, ø:z) a, rough; ticklish; scabrous, improper.
scalpel (skalpɛl) m, scalpel.
scalper (skalpe) v.t, to scalp.
scandale (skɑ̃dal) m, scandal, shame. **scandaleux, euse†** (lø, ø:z) a, scandalous, shameful. **scandaliser** (lize) v.t, to scandalize, shock.
scander (skɑ̃de) v.t, to scan (verse); stress (Mus.); syllabize (articulate by syllables).
scandinave (skɑ̃dina:v) a. & S~, n, Scandinavian. **la Scandinavie** (navi), Scandinavia.
scanner (skɑ̃ne) v.t, to scan. **scanneur** (nœ:r) m, scanner.
scansion (skɑ̃sjɔ̃) f, scansion, scanning.
scaphandre (skafɑ̃:dr) m, diving dress. **scaphandrier** (fɑ̃drie) m, diver (in diving dress).
scarabée (skarabe) m, beetle; scarab.
scarifier (skarifje) v.t, to scarify.
scarlatine (skarlatin) f, scarlatina, scarlet fever.
scarole (skarɔl) f, endive.
sceau (so) m, seal; stamp (fig.).

scélérat, e (selera, at) a, villainous, wicked. ¶ n, villain, scoundrel, miscreant. **scélératesse** (tɛs) f, villainy, wickedness.
scellé (sɛle) m, seal (official). **sceller** (le) v.t, to seal; s. up.
scénario (senarjo) m, scenario. **scène** (sɛn) f, stage; scene; action; local[e]; shindy. **scénique** (senik) a, scenic, theatrical, stage (att.).
scepticisme (sɛptisism) m, skepticism. **sceptique** (tik) a, skeptical. ¶ n, skeptic.
sceptre (sɛptr) m, scepter.
Schaffhouse (ʃafu:z) f, Schaffhausen.
schampooing (ʃɑ̃pwɛ̃) m, shampoo.
schéma (ʃema) ou **schème** (ʃɛm) m, diagram, plan.
schisme (ʃism) m, schism.
schiste (ʃist) m, shale, schist.
schlitte (ʃlit) f, lumber sledge.
schooner (ʃunɛ:r) m, schooner (Naut.).
sciage (sja:ʒ) m, sawing.
sciatique (sjatik) a, sciatic. ¶ f, sciatica.
scie (si) f, saw; bore, nuisance; joke; catchword; catch phrase, gag. ~ à chantourner, jig saw. ~ à métaux, hack s. ~ du jour, hit tune. jeu de la ~, cat's cradle. monter une ~, to play a practical joke. quelle ~!, what a nuisance!
sciemment (sjamɑ̃) ad, knowingly, wittingly. **science** (sjɑ̃:s) f, knowledge, learning, lore; science. ~ économique, economics. **scientifique†** (ɑ̃tifik) a, scientific. ¶ m, scientifically-oriented person. **scientiste chrétien** (tist) m, Christian Scientist.
scier (sje) v.t, to saw; saw off; reap; bore (weary); (v.i.) to back water. **scierie** (siri) f, saw mill. **scieur** (sjœ:r) m, sawyer.
scinder (sɛ̃de) v.t, to divide, split (fig.).
scintillation (sɛ̃tillasjɔ̃) f, scintillation; twinkling. **scintiller** (tije) v.i, to scintillate; twinkle.
scion (sjɔ̃) m, shoot, scion (Hort.); top [joint] (fishing rod).
scission (sisjɔ̃) f, scission, split, cleavage; secession.

sciure (sjyːr) *f*, sawdust.
sclérose (skleroːz) *f*, sclerosis.
scolaire (skɔlɛːr) *a*, school (*att.*); academic (*year*); educational. **scolastique** (lastik) *a*, scholastic.
scolopendre (skɔlɔpɑ̃ːdr) *f*, centipede.
sconse (skɔ̃ːs) *m*, skunk (*fur*).
scorbut (skɔrby) *m*, scurvy.
scorie (skɔri) *f*. oft. *pl*, slag, scoria; dross; scale.
scorpion (skɔrpjɔ̃) *m*, scorpion.
scotch (skɔtʃ) *m*, scotch whiskey; self-adhesive tape (*trademark used as generic term*).
scribe (skrib) *m*, scribe; copyist.
script (skript) *m*, scrip (*Fin.*); script (*TV & cinema*); continuity, script person (*cinema*).
scrofules (skrɔfyl) *f.pl*, scrofula. **scrofuleux, euse** (lø, øːz) *a*, scrofulous.
scrupule (skrypyl) *m*, scruple, qualm. **scrupuleux, euse†** (lø, øːz) *a*, scrupulous.
scrutateur (skrytatœːr) *m*, scrutinizer; poll watcher. **scruter** (te) *v.t*, to scrutinize, scan; peer into; search. **scrutin** (tɛ̃) *m*, poll, ballot, voting, vote.
sculpter (skylte) *v.t*, to sculpt; carve. **sculpteur** (tœːr) *m*, sculptor; carver. **sculpture** (tyːr) *f*, sculpture. ~ *sur bois*, wood carving.
se, s' (sə, s) *pn*, oneself; himself, herself, itself; themselves; each other, one another. *Note:* An English intransitive is often expressed in French by the pronominal form (se, s'); thus, to depreciate, *v.t*, déprécier, avilir; to depreciate, *v.i*, se déprécier, s'avilir. The pronominal form also serves to give to a transitive verb a passive meaning; as, lettre qui se prononce, letter which is pronounced.
séance (seɑ̃ːs) *f*, seat (*at a council*); sitting, session, meeting; performance. ~ *de spiritisme*, seance. ~ *tenante*, during the sitting; forthwith, there & then, on the spot. **séant, e** (ɑ̃, ɑ̃ːt) *p.a*, sitting (*à* = at), in session. ¶ *a*, becoming, seemly, proper. *sur son*

séant, in a sitting posture, sitting up.
seau (so) *m*, pail, bucket; pailful. ~ *à biscuits*, biscuit barrel. ~ *à charbon*, coal scuttle. ~ *à ordures*, trashbin. ~ *de toilette*, slop pail.
sébile (sebil) *f*, wooden bowl.
sec, sèche (sɛk, sɛʃ) *a*, dry; dried; spare, gaunt, lean; curt; bald (*style*). sec, *ad*, drily (*answer coldly*); hard (*drinking*); neat (*drinking*). à sec, *ad*, [when] dry; dried up; broke. sec, *m*, dry; dry place; dry land; dry fodder.
sécateur (sekatœːr) *m*, pruning shears.
sécession (sesesjɔ̃) *f*, secession.
sèchement (sɛʃmɑ̃) *ad*, drily, curtly; baldly. **sécher** (seʃe) *v.t. & i*, to dry; d. up; season (*wood*); wither, pine away. ~ *à un examen*, to flunk an exam. ~ *une classe*, to cut a class. **sécheresse** (ʃrɛs) *f*, dryness; drought; spareness, as *sec*. **séchoir** (ʃwaːr) *m*, drying room; drier; airer; towel bar.
second, e† (səgɔ̃, ɔ̃ːd) *a*, second; junior (*partner*). second plan, *m*, middle distance; background (*fig.*). seconde vue, *f*, second sight, clairvoyance. un second, une seconde, another (*like*). ¶ *m*, second (*pers., floor*); first mate (*Naut.*). ¶ *f*, second (*class*); second (*time*). ~ [*épreuve*], revise (*Typ.*). **secondaire†** (gɔ̃dɛːr) *a*, secondary; minor; side (*att.*). **seconder** (gɔ̃de) *v.t*, to second, support, back up, further.
secouer (səkwe) *v.t. & abs*, to shake; s. up; s. down; s. off; toss; buffet; jolt; rate, scold.
secourable (səkurabl) *a*, helpful, helping; relievable. secourir (riːr) *v.t.ir*, to succor, help, relieve. secours (kuːr) *m*, help, succor, relief, aid. *au* ~! help! *de* ~, (*att.*) emergency; breakdown, relief, spare; backup (*computers*). roue de ~, spare wheel.
secousse (səkus) *f*, shake, jerk, jolt, shock.
secret, ète† (səkrɛ, ɛt) *a*, secret. ¶ *m*, secret; s. spring; secrecy, privacy; solitary confinement.

secrétaire (kretɛːr) *m*, secretary, amanuensis; writing desk. ~ *de mairie*, town clerk. ~ *intime*, private s. secrétariat (tarja) *m*, secretaryship; secretariat. sécréter (sekrete) *v.t*, to secrete (*physiology*). sécrétion (sjɔ̃) *f*, secretion.

sectaire (sɛktɛːr) *m. & att*, secretarian. sectateur (tatœːr) *m*, follower, votary. secte (sɛkt) *f*, sect.

secteur (sɛktœːr) *m*, sector; quadrant; district. section (sjɔ̃) *f*, section; division; fare zone (*bus*); platoon.

séculaire (sekylɛːr) *a*, secular (*100*); time-honored. séculier, ère† (lje, ɛːr) *a*, secular (*clergy*, etc.); laic; worldly (*life*). ¶ *m*, layman; (*pl.*) laity.

sécurité (sekyrite) *f*, security, reliability; safety. ~ *d'abord*, safety first. *de* ~, backup (*computers*).

sédatif, ive (sedatif, iːv) *a. & m*, sedative.

sédentaire (sedɑ̃tɛːr) *a*, sedentary; fixed, stationary.

sédiment (sedimɑ̃) *m*, sediment, deposit.

séditieux, euse† (sedisjø, øːz) *a*, seditious; mutinous. sédition (sjɔ̃) *f*, sedition; revolt.

séducteur, trice (sedyktœːr, tris) *n*, tempter; seducer. séduire (dɥiːr) *v.t.ir*, to seduce, entice; [al]lure; bribe, suborn. séduisant, e (dɥizɑ̃, ɑ̃ːt) *a*, seductive, tempting; fascinating.

segment (sɛgmɑ̃) *m*, segment; ring (*piston*).

ségrégation (segregasjɔ̃) *f*, segregation.

seiche (sɛʃ) *f*, cuttle fish.

séide (seid) *m*, blind supporter, henchman.

seigle (sɛgl) *m*, rye.

seigneur (sɛɲœːr) *m*, lord; squire; noble[man]. *le Seigneur*, the Lord. seigneurie (ɲœri) *f*, lordship; manor.

seille (sɛːj) *f*, pail, bucket.

sein (sɛ̃) *m*, breast; bosom; lap (*luxury*); bowels (*earth*); members; womb.

seine (sɛn) *f*, seine (*net*).

seing (sɛ̃) *m*, signature, signing.

séisme (seism) *m*, earthquake. séismique (mik) *a*, seismic.

seize (sɛːz) *a. & m*, sixteen; 16th. seizième† (sɛzjɛm) *a. & n*, sixteenth.

séjour (seʒuːr) *m*, stay, sojourn; abode, regions; resort. ~ *linguistique*, a stay with family in foreign country (*to learn language*). séjourner (ʒurne) *v.i*, to stay, tarry, sojourn; lie.

sel (sɛl) *m*, salt; piquancy, wit. ~ *ammoniac* (amɔnjak), sal-ammoniac. ~ *fin*, table salt. ~ *gemme*, rock salt. ~*s pour bains*, bath salts. ~*s* [*volatils*] *anglais*, smelling salts.

sélection (selɛksjɔ̃) *f*, selection, choice. sélectionner (ɔne) *v.t*, to select.

selle (sɛl) *f*, saddle; seat; stool; motion (*Med.*). seller (le) *v.t*, to saddle. sellerie (lri) *f*, saddlery; harness room. sellette (lɛt) *f*, stool; pedestal (*vase*). tenir, mettre, quelqu'un sur la ~, to cross-examine someone. sellier (lje) *m*, saddler, harness maker.

selon (səlɔ̃) *pr*, [according] to. ~ *moi*, in my opinion. *c'est* ~, it all depends.

semailles (səmɑːj) *f.pl*, seed time; sowing.

semaine (səmɛn) *f*, week; week's work, pay. *la* ~ *seulement*, weekdays only.

sémaphore (semafɔːr) *m*, semaphore.

semblable† (sɑ̃blabl) *a*, [a]like, similar; such. ¶ *m*, fellow [man]; like. semblant (blɑ̃) *m*, semblance, appearance, show. [*faux*] ~, pretence, sham. *un* ~ *de* . . ., an apology (*bad specimen*) for a . . . sembler (ble) *v.i*, to seem, appear, look, strike.

semelle (səmɛl) *f*, sole (*shoe, etc.*); foot (*stocking*); sock (*cork, loofa*); tread (*tire*).

semence (səmɑ̃s) *f*, seed; brads. ~ *de perles*, seed pearls. semer (me) *v.t*, to sow; scatter, strew, spread; powder (*Emb.*); shake off (*somebody following*). ~ *la merde*, to create confusion (*vulgar*).

semestre (səmɛstr) *m*, semester,

term; half-year; 6 months' pay, duty, leave. **semestriel, le** (triɛl) *a*, half-yearly.

semeur, euse (səmœːr, øːz) *n*, sower; spreader.

semi- (səmi) *prefix*, semi-, half-.

sémillant, e (semijã, ãːt) *a*, sprightly, bright.

séminaire (seminɛːr) *m*, seminary, college.

semis (səmi) *m*, seed plot, seedlings; powdering (*Emb.*).

sémitique (semitik) *a*, Semitic.

semoir (səmwaːr) *m*, sowing machine, drill.

semonce (səmɔ̃ːs) *f*, call (*to a ship*); reprimand, scolding. **semoncer** (mɔ̃se) *v.t*, to call upon (*ship*); lecture, scold; summon.

semoule (səmul) *f*, semolina.

sénat (sena) *m*, senate. **sénateur** (tœːr) *m*, senator.

séné (sene) *m*, senna.

seneçon (sənsɔ̃) *m*, groundsel.

Sénégal (le) (senegal), Senegal.

sénestre (senɛstr) *a*, sinister (*Her.*).

sénevé (senve) *m*, mustard (*Bot.*); m. seed.

sénile (senil) *a*, senile. **sénilité** (lite) *f*, senility.

sens (sãːs, sã) *m*, sense; judgment, understanding; opinion; meaning, import; direction, way. ~ *commun* (sã), [common] sense, senses. ~ *dessus dessous* (sã), upside down; topsy-turvy. ~ *devant derrière* (sã), back to front. ~ *interdit*, no entry, one way street. ~ *unique*, entry only, one way street. **sensation** (sãsasjɔ̃) *f*, sensation; feel[ing], sense. *à* ~ *&* **sensationnel, le** (sjɔnɛl) *a*, sensational, thrilling, exciting. **sensé†, e** (se) *a*, sensible, judicious. **sensibilité** (sibilite) *f*, sensitiveness; feeling. **sensible** (sibl) *a*, sensitive, susceptible, responsive, sensible, alive; sentient; sensitized (*Phot.*); tender, sore; appreciable, palpable, perceptible. **sensiblement** (bləmã) *a*, appreciably; deeply. **sensiblerie** (ri) *f*, sentimentality. **sensitif, ive** (tif, iːv) *a*, sensitive; sensory.

sensoriel, ielle (sãsɔrjɛl) *a*, sensorial, sensory.

sensualiste (sãsɥalist) *n*, sensualist. **sensualité** (te) *f*, sensuality; voluptuousness. **sensuel, le†** (sɥɛl) *a*, sensual.

sente (sãːt) *f*, footpath.

sentence (sãtãːs) *f*, maxim; sentence (*law*); award. **sentencieux, euse†** (tãsjø, øːz) *a*, sententious.

senteur (sãtœːr) *f*, scent, odor, perfume. *pois de* ~, sweet pea (*Bot.*).

senti, e (sãti) *p.a*, well-expressed, strong. *bien* ~, heartfelt (*words*).

sentier (sãtje) *m*, footpath, path, track. ~ *pour cavaliers*, bridle path.

sentiment (sãtimã) *m*, feeling, sensation; sense; sentiment; opinion. **sentimental, e** (tal) *a*, sentimental. **sentimentalité** (lite) *f*, sentimentality, gush.

sentine (sãtin) *f*, well (*ship*); sink (*iniquity*).

sentinelle (sãtinɛl) *f*, sentry, sentinel; guard, watch.

sentir (sãtiːr) *v.t. & abs. tr*, to feel; be conscious of; smell; scent; taste of; smell of; smack of; be redolent of. *se* ~, to feel.

seoir (swaːr) *v.i.ir*, to sit; be situated.

seoir (swaːr) *v.i.ir*, to suit, become.

séparation (separasjɔ̃) *f*, separation, parting, severance; dispersal; partition (*wall*). ~ *de l'Église & de l'État*, disestablishment [of the Church]. **séparé†, e** (re) *p.a*, separate, distinct; apart. **séparer** (re) *v.t. & se* ~, to separate, part; sever; divide; disband. **séparez!** break! (*Box.*).

sépia (sepja) *f*, sepia; sepia [drawing].

sept (sɛ; *alone & in liaison*, sɛt) *a. & m*, seven; 7th.

septembre (sɛptãːbr) *m*, September.

septentrion (sɛptãtriɔ̃) *m*, north. **septentrional, e** (ɔnal) *a*, northern. ¶ *n*, northerner.

septième† (sɛtjɛm) *a. & n*, seventh.

septique (sɛptik) *a*, septic.

septuor (sɛptɥɔːr) *m*, septet.

sépulcral, e (sepylkral) *a*, sepulchral. **sépulcre** (kr) *m*, sepulcher. **sépulture** (tyːr) *f*, burial; burial place, resting place; tomb.

séquelle (sekɛl) *f*, crew, gang; string.

séquence (sekɑ̃ːs) *f*, sequence, run (*cards, etc.*); film sequence.

séquestre (sekɛstr) *m*, sequestration.

sérail (seraːj) *m*, seraglio.

séraphin (serafɛ̃) *m*, seraph. **séraphique** (fik) *a*, seraphic.

serbe (sɛrb) *a*. & S~, *n*, Serb[ian]. *le serbe*, Serb[ian] (*language*). *la Serbie* (bi), Serbia.

serein, e (sərɛ̃, ɛn) *a*, serene, calm; halcyon. ¶ *m*, evening dew, evening damp.

sérénade (serenad) *f*, serenade.

sérénité (serenite) *f*, serenity; equanimity.

serf, serve (sɛrf, sɛrv) *n*, serf, thrall.

serfouir (sɛrfwiːr) *v.t*, to hoe.

serge (sɛrʒ) *f*, serge.

sergent (sɛrʒɑ̃) *m*, sergeant; cramp (*tool*). ~ *de ville*, policeman. ~ *instructeur*, drill sergeant.

sériciculture (serisikyltyːr) *f*, silkworm breeding.

série (seri) *f*, series; range; set; chapter (*accidents*); break (*Bil.*). *en* ~, standardized; mass-produced.

sérieux, euse† (serjø, øːz) *a*, serious; grave; sober (*dress*); earnest, genuine, bona fide. ¶ *m*, seriousness, gravity.

serin, e (s[ə]rɛ̃, in) *n*, canary; silly, noodle. **seriner** (rine) *v.t*, to teach (*bird*); din it into (*pers.*); drum (*à* = into).

seringa (s[ə]rɛ̃ga) *m*, syringa, seringa.

seringue (s[ə]rɛ̃ːg) *f*, syringe, squirt. ~ [*à lavement*], enema. ~ *de Pravaz* (pravα), hypodermic syringe. **seringuer** (rẽge) *v.t*, to syringe, squirt, inject.

serment (sɛrmɑ̃) *m*, oath.

sermon (sɛrmɔ̃) *m*, sermon; lecture (*scolding*). **sermonner** (mɔne)

v.t. & *abs*, to sermonize, lecture.

serpe (sɛrp) *f*, bill hook.

serpent (sɛrpɑ̃) *m*, serpent, snake. ~ *à sonnettes*, rattlesnake. ~ *caché sous les fleurs*, snake in the grass. **serpentaire** (tɛːr) *m*, secretary bird. **serpenteau** (to) *m*, young snake; squib (*firework*). **serpenter** (te) *v.i*, to wind, meander. **serpentin, e** (tɛ̃, in) *a*, serpentine. ¶ *m*, worm (*still, etc.*); coil; [paper] streamer. ¶ *f*, serpentine (*rock*).

serpette (sɛrpɛt) *f*, pruning knife; bill hook.

serpillière (sɛrpijɛːr) *f*, sacking; apron.

serpolet (sɛrpɔlɛ) *m*, wild thyme.

serrage (sɛraːʒ) *m*, tightening, application (*brake*). **serre** (sɛːr) *f*, greenhouse, glasshouse, conservatory; grip; claw, talon. ~ *à palmiers*, palm house. ~ *à vignes*, vinery. ~ *chaude*, hothouse. **serré, e** (sɛre) *p.a*, tight, close, serried; clenched. **serre-frein** (sɛrfrɛ̃) *m*, brakesman. **serre-joint**, *m*, cramp, clamp (*tool*). **serre-livres**, *m*, bookends. **serrement** (rmɑ̃) *m*, pressure; squeeze, shake (*hand*). ~ *de cœur*, pang. **serrer** (re) *v.t*, to press, squeeze; clasp, hug, wring, grip; clench; shake (*hand*); tighten; put on (*brake*); put away, stow away; furl (*sail*). ~ *sous clef*, to lock up. **serre-tête**, *m*, headband. **serrure** (ryːr) *f*, lock. ~ *à demi-tour*, latch. *trou de* ~, keyhole. **serrurerie** (ryri) *f*, locksmithery; metal work, ironwork. **serrurier** (rje) *m*, locksmith; metal worker, ironworker.

sertir (sɛrtiːr) *v.t*, to set (gem); crease.

sérum (serɔm) *m*, serum.

servage (sɛrvaːʒ) *m*, serfdom, thraldom. **servant** (vɑ̃) *a.m*, lay (*brother*). ¶ *m*, gunner; server (*Ten.*). **servante** (vɑ̃ːt) *f*, [maid-]-servant; waitress; service table; dumbwaiter. **serviable** (vjabl) *a*, obliging. **service** (vis) *m*, service; serve (*Ten.*); running; booking; supply; department; duty; attendance, waiting (*hotel, etc.*); course (*meal*); set (*utensils*). ~ *de table & dessert*, dinner service. ~ *par en bas*, underhand service (*Ten.*). ~ *par en haut*, overhand s. ~ *compris*, s. included. ~ *militaire*, military s. *en* ~, in operation. *libre* ~, self-service. **serviette** (vjɛt) *f*, dispatch case, document c. ~ [*de table*], [table] napkin. ~ [*de toilette*], towel. ~ *éponge*, Turkish towel. ~ *hygiénique*, sanitary napkin.

serveur, euse (sɛrvœːr, øːz) *m*, barman, -woman; waiter, waitress; server (*Ten.*).

servile† (sɛrvil) *a*, servile, menial; slavish. **servilité** (lite) *f*, servility; slavishness.

servir (sɛrviːr) *v.i. & t. & abs. ir*, to serve; be of use; wait (on); attend; serve up. se ~ *chez*, to deal with (*tradesman*). se ~ *de*, to use. **serviteur** (vitœːr) *m*, servant. **servitude** (tyd) *f*, servitude, slavery; easement (*law*).

ses see **son.**

sésame (sezam) *m*, sesame (*Bot.*). *S~, ouvre-toi*, open sesame.

session (sɛsjɔ̃) *f*, session, sitting, term.

seuil (sœːj) *m*, threshold, sill.

seul, e (sœl) *a*, alone, by oneself, solo; lonely; only; one, single; sole; mere, bare, very. **seulement** (lmɑ̃) *ad*, only; solely, merely.

sève (sɛːv) *f*, sap (*plant*); vigor.

sévère† (sevɛːr) *a*, severe, stern; hard; strict. **sévérité** (verite) *f*, severity, etc.

sévices (sevis) *m.pl*, maltreatment, cruelty (*in law*).

Séville (sevil) *f*, Seville.

sévir (seviːr) *v.i*, to deal severely (*contre* = with); rage, be rife, be rampant.

sevrage (səvraːʒ) *m*, weaning. **sevrer** (vre) *v.t*, to wean; deprive.

sexe (sɛks) *m*, sex; genitals.

sextant (sɛkstɑ̃) *m*, sextant.

sextuor (sɛkstɥɔːr) *m*, sextet.

sexuel, le (sɛksɥɛl) *a*, sexual.

seyant, e (sɛjɑ̃, ɑ̃ːt) *a*, becoming.

shake-hand (ʃɛkɑ̃ːd) *m*, handshake.

si, s' (si, s) *c*, if, whether; how [much]; what if, suppose. ~ *le temps le permet*, weather permitting. *si, ad*, so; so much; such; however; yes. ~ *fait*, yes, indeed. ¶ *m*, if; B (*Mus.*).

Siam (le) (sjam), Siam. **siamois, e** (mwa, aːz) *a. & S~, n*, Siamese. **le siamois**, Siamese (*language*).

Sibérie (la) (siberi), Siberia. **sibérien, ne** (rjɛ̃, ɛn) *a. & S~, n*, Siberian.

sicaire (sikɛːr) *m*, hired assassin.

siccatif (sikatif) *m*, drier[s] (*painter's*).

Sicile (la) (sisil), Sicily. **sicilien, ne** (ljɛ̃, ɛn) *a. & S~, n*, Sicilian.

sicle (sikl) *m*, shekel (*Bible*).

sidéral, e (sideral) *a*, sidereal.

sidéré (sidere) *a*, thunderstruck, flabbergasted.

siècle (sjɛkl) *m*, century; age, times; world. *les ~s d'ignorance*, the dark ages.

siège (sjɛːʒ) *m*, seat; bench; box (*driver's*); bottom (*chair*); see (*Eccl.*); siege (*Mil.*). ~ *arrière*, back seat; pillion. ~ *social*, head office. *Saint-Siège*, Holy See. **siéger** (eʒe) *v.i*, to have its headquarters; sit; be seated.

sien, ne (with le, la, les) (sjɛ̃, ɛn) *pn. & m*, his, hers; one's own, his own, her own.

Sienne (sjɛn) *f*, Sienna.

sieste (sjɛst) *f*, siesta, nap.

sieur (sjœːr) *m*, Mr.

siffler (sifle) *v.i. & t*, to whistle; pipe; hiss; whirr, whizz; wheeze. **sifflet** (flɛ) *m*, whistle; pipe (*boatswain's*); hiss, catcall. [canard] **siffleur** (flœːr) *m*, widgeon. **siffloter** (flɔte) *v.i*, to whistle softly.

sigle (sigl) *m*, set of initials often used as word. i.e. O.N.U. (*Organisation des Nations Unies*), U.N. (*United Nations*).

signal (siɲal) *m*, signal. **signalé, e** (le) *p.a*, signal; conspicuous; well-known. **signalement** (lmɑ̃) *m*, description. **signaler** (le) *v.t*, to signalize, point out; signal; notify. **signaleur** (lœːr) *m*, signaler (*Mil.*); signalman (*Rly.*). **signalisation** (izasjɔ̃) *f*, signaling; road signs. ~ *routière internationale*, international road signs system.

signataire (siɲatɛːr) *n*, signatory, signer. **signature** (ty:r) *f*, signing, signature. **signe** (siɲ) *m*, sign, token, mark; motion, wave (*hand*). ~ *d'omission*, caret. ~ [*de tête*], nod. ~ *des yeux*, wink. **signer** (ɲe) *v.t*, to sign. ~ *à*, to witness. **se** ~, to cross oneself. **signet** (ɲɛ) *m*, bookmark, signet.

significatif, ive (siɲnifikatif, i:v) *a*, significant, meaning, of deep significance (*look*). **signification** (sjɔ̃) *f*, signification, meaning, sense, import; service (*writ*). **signifier** (fje) *v.t*, to signify, mean; notify, intimate; serve (*a notice*).

silence (silɑ̃:s) *m*, silence, stillness, hush; pause; rest (*Mus.*). **silencieux, euse†** (lɑ̃sjø, ø:z) *a*, silent, noiseless, still. ¶ *m*, silencer.

Silésie (la) (silezi), Silesia. **silésienne** (zjɛn) *f*, silesia (*fabric*). **silex** (silɛks) *m*, silex, flint.

silhouette (silwɛt) *f*, silhouette. **silicate** (silikat) *m*, silicate. **silice** (lis) *f*, silica.

sillage (sija:ʒ) *m*, wake, track; headway (*ship*). **sillet** (jɛ) *m*, nut (*violin*). **sillon** (jɔ̃) *m*, furrow; drill (*furrow*); (*pl., Poet.*) fields; wrinkle; track, trail; streak; groove. **sillonner** (ɔne) *v.t*, to furrow; plow (*seas*); wrinkle; streak, groove.

silo (silo) *m*, silo.

simagrée (simagre) *f. oft. pl*, pretence; affectation.

simiesque (simjɛsk) *a*, apelike, apish.

similaire (similɛ:r) *a*, similar, like. **simili-** (li) *prefix*, imitation (*att.*), artificial. **similigravure** (ligravy:r) *f*, process engraving, halftone e. **similitude** (tyd) *f*, similitude, similarity; simile.

simonie (simɔni) *f*, simony.

simple† (sɛ̃:pl) *a*, simple; single; ordinary; private (*soldier*); plain; homely; mere; simple[-minded]; half-witted. ¶ *m*, single (*Ten.*); half-wit; (*pl.*) medicinal herbs. **simplicité** (sɛ̃plisite) *f*, simplicity. **simplifier** (fje) *v.t*, to simplify.

simulacre (simylakr) *m*, simulacrum, image; dummy (*Mil.*); show. ~ *de combat*, sham fight, mock f. **simulé, e** (le) *p.a*, feigned; sham; bogus, fictitious. **simuler** (le) *v.t*, to simulate. ~ *la maladie*, to malinger.

simulie (simyli) *f*, sand fly.

simultané†, e (simyltane) *a*, simultaneous.

Sinaï (le mont) (sinai), Mount Sinai.

sinapisme (sinapism) *m*, mustard plaster.

sincère† (sɛ̃sɛ:r) *a*, sincere, candid, unfeigned, genuine. **sincérité** (serite) *f*, sincerity, candor.

sinécure (sineky:r) *f*, sinecure.

Singapour (sɛ̃gapu:r) *m*, Singapore.

singe (sɛ̃:ʒ) *m*, monkey, ape; copycat; winch; boss (*slang*). **singer** (sɛ̃ʒe) *v.t*, to ape, mock. **singerie** (ʒri) *f*, monkey house; grimace, grotesque imitation.

singulariser (sɛ̃gylarize) *v.t*, to make conspicuous. **singulier, ère†** (lje, ɛ:r) *a*, singular; peculiar; odd, queer, quaint; single (*combat*). ¶ *m*, singular (*Gram.*). **singularité** (larite) *f*, singularity, etc.

sinistre† (sinistr) *a*, sinister, ominous; grim; lurid, baleful. ¶ *m*, disaster, casualty; loss (*Insce.*). **sinistré** (tre) *m*, victim of a disaster (*fire, flood, bombing*). ¶ *a*, homeless, bombed-out, etc.

sinistrose (sinistro:z) *f*, conduct of person traumatized by accident, generally on the job.

sinon (sinɔ̃) *c*, otherwise, else; except, save.

sinueux, euse (sinɥø, ø:z) *a*, sinuous, winding. **sinuosité** (nɥozite) *f*, sinuosity, bend.

sinus (siny:s) *m*, sinus; sine.

sionisme (sjɔnism) *m*, Zionism.

siphon (sifɔ̃) *m*, siphon; trap (*drain*).

sire (si:r) *m*, sire (*to king*).

sirène (sirɛn) *f*, siren, mermaid; hooter.

sirop (siro) *m*, syrup. **siroter** (rɔte) *v.t*, to sip. **sirupeux, euse** (rypø, ø:z) *a*, syrupy.

sis, e (si, i:z) *p.p.* situated.

sismique (sismik) *a,* seismic. **sismographe** (mɔgraf) *m,* seismograph.

site (sit) *m,* site, location.

sitôt (sito) *ad,* as soon, so soon.

situation (situasjɔ̃) *f,* situation, position; condition, state; statement, report. **situé, e** (tɥe) *p.p. & p.a,* situated.

six (si; *in liaison,* siz; *at end of phrase,* sis)- *a. & m,* six; 6th. **sixième†** (sizjɛm) *a. & n,* sixth. **sixte** (sikst) *f,* sixth (*Mus.*).

ski (ski) *m,* ski. ~*s de saut,* jumping skis.

slave (sla:v) *a. & S~, n,* Slav.

slip (slip) *m,* underpants; trunks.

sloughi (slugi) *m,* saluki.

smic (smik) or **smig** (ig) *m,* guaranteed minimum wage (*salaire minimum interprofessionnel de croissance, garanti*). ~**ard,** ~**arde** (kar, kard) *n,* person covered by *smic.*

smilax (smilaks) *m,* smilax (*Bot.*).

smoking (smɔkiŋ) *m,* tuxedo.

Smyrne (smirn) *f,* Smyrna.

snob (snɔb) *a,* snobbish. **snobisme** (bism) *m,* snobbishness, snobbery.

sobre† (sɔbr) *a,* sober, temperate, abstemious; sparing, chary. **sobriété** (briete) *f,* sobriety.

sobriquet (sɔbrikɛ) *m,* nickname.

soc (sɔk) *m,* plowshare.

sociable† (sɔsjabl) *a,* sociable; companionable, genial. **social, e** (sjal) *a,* social; corporate; registered (*capital, offices*); of the firm; company's. **socialisme** (lism) *m,* socialism. **socialiste** (list) *n. & a,* socialist. **sociétaire** (sjetɛ:r) *n,* member; stockholder. **société** (te) *f,* society; community; companionship, fellowship; club; company; firm; partnership. ~ *anonyme,* corporation. *S~ des Nations,* League of Nations. ~ *immobilière,* building society. ~ *par actions,* joint-stock company. **sociologie** (sjɔlɔʒi) *f,* sociology.

socle (sɔkl) *m,* pedestal, stand.

socque (sɔk) *m,* clog, pattern. **socquettes** (kɛt) *f.pl,* ankle socks.

sodium (sɔdjɔm) *m,* sodium.

sœur (sœ:r) *f,* sister. *et ta ~?,* mind your own business. **sœurette** (sœret) *f,* [dear] little sister.

sofa (sofa) *m,* sofa.

soffite (sɔfit) *m,* soffit.

software (sɔftwɛ:r) *m,* software (*computers*).

soi (swa) & ~**même,** *pn,* oneself; himself, herself, itself. ~**disant** (dizɑ̃) *a.inv,* self-styled, would-be; so-called.

soie (swa) *f,* silk; bristle (*hog*); tang (*of tool*). ~ *floche* (flɔʃ), floss silk. **soierie** (ri) *f,* silk goods, silks; silk mill; silk trade.

soif (swaf) *f,* thirst; craving, hankering. *avoir ~,* to be thirsty, to thirst.

soigné, e (swaɲe) *p.a,* carefully done; trim, neat. **soigner** (ɲe) *v.t,* to take care of, look after, attend to; tend; nurse; manicure. **soigneur** (ɲœ:r) *m,* minder; second (*Box.*). **soigneux, euse†** (ɲø, ø:z) *a,* careful, painstaking; tidy. **soin** (swɛ̃) *m. oft. pl,* care, attention, pains; nursing. ~ *des mains,* manicure. ~ *des pieds,* chiropody. *aux* [*bons*] ~*s de,* care of, c/o. *premiers* ~*s,* first aid.

soir (swa:r) *m,* evening, night; afternoon. **soirée** (sware) *f,* evening; [evening] party. *de ~,* evening (*dress, etc.*).

soit (swa) *c,* either; or; whether; suppose, let. ~ *que,* whether. ~*!* (swat), so be it! agreed! *tant ~ peu,* ever so little.

soixantaine (swasɑ̃ten) *f,* sixty [or so]. **soixante** (sɑ̃:t) *a. & m,* sixty. ~**dix** (sɑ̃tdis) *a. & m,* seventy. ~ *& onze,* ~*douze,* 71, 72. ~**dixième** (zjɛm) *a. & n,* seventieth. **soixantième** (tjɛm) *a. & n,* sixtieth.

soja (sɔja) *m,* soybean.

sol (sɔl) *m,* ground, earth; soil; G (*Mus.*).

solaire (sɔlɛ:r) *a,* solar, sun (*att.*). *cadran ~,* sun dial.

soldat (sɔlda) *m,* soldier. ~ *de plomb,* tin soldier. *le S~ inconnu,* the Unknown Soldier. **soldatesque** (tɛsk) *f,* (*unruly*) soldiery.

solde (sɔld) *f,* pay (*Mil., Nav., etc.*). ¶ *m,* balance; settlement;

surplus stock, job lot; [clearance] sale. ~ *d'édition*, remainder (*books*). ~ *de dividende*, final dividend. *vente de ~s*, clearance sale. ~*s de dégriffés*, s. of clothes with labels removed. **solder** (de) *v.t*, to balance (*a/c*); pay off, settle; sell off, clear; remainder. **soldeuse** (dø:z) *f*, woman who buys everything at sales.

sole (sɔl) *f*, sole (*fish, hoof, bed plate*). ~ *limande*, lemon sole.

solécisme (sɔlesism) *m*, solecism.

soleil (sɔlɛj) *m*, sun; sunshine; sunflower; catherine wheel (*fireworks*). ~ *couchant*, setting sun, sunset. *coup de ~*, sunstroke.

solennel, le† (sɔlanɛl) *a*, solemn; formal; state (*att.*); impressive. **solenniser** (nize) *v.t*, to solemnize, celebrate. **solennité** (te) *f*, solemnity; celebration.

solfège (sɔlfɛ:ʒ) *m*, sol-fa, solfeggio. **solfier** (fje) *v.t. & abs*, to sol-fa.

solidaire† (sɔlidɛ:r) *a*, mutually responsible; interdependent; solidary. **solidariser** (lidarize) *v.t*, to make jointly responsible. se ~, to make common cause. **solide†** (lid) *a*, solid; strong; substantial; hefty; firm; fast (*color*); sound; sterling (*fig.*). ¶ *m*, solid; s. foundation, s. ground; main chance. **solidifier** (difje) *v.t*, to solidify. **solidité** (te) *f*, solidity; strength; soundness.

soliloque (sɔlilɔk) *m*, soliloquy.

soliste (sɔlist) *n*, soloist; solo (*violin*).

solitaire† (sɔlitɛ:r) *a*, solitary, lonely. ¶ *m*, hermit; solitaire (*gem & game*). **solitude** (tyd) *f*, solitude, loneliness; wilderness, wild.

solive (sɔli:v) *f*, joist, beam, girder.

solliciter (sɔllisite) *v.t*, to solicit, ask for, apply for; canvass; entreat; urge; attract. **sollicitude** (tyd) *f*, solicitude; anxiety.

solo (sɔlo) *m*, solo (*Mus.*).

solstice (sɔlstis) *m*, solstice.

soluble (sɔlybl) *a*, soluble; solvable. **solution** (sjɔ̃) *f*, solution; break; discharge (*law*).

solvabilité (sɔlvabilite) *f*, solvency (*Fin.*). **solvable** (bl) *a*, solvent.

sombre (sɔ̃:br) *a*, dark, somber, gloomy; dim.

sombrer (sɔ̃bre) *v.i*, to founder, sink, go down.

sommaire† (sɔmɛ:r) *a*, summary, compendious; scant. ¶ *m*, summary, synopsis.

sommation (sɔmasjɔ̃) *f*, summons, appeal.

somme (sɔm) *f*, sum, amount; burden. ~ *toute* ou *en ~*, [up] on the whole.

somme (sɔm) *m*, nap, snooze. **sommeil** (mɛj) *m*, sleep, slumber; sleepiness. **sommeiller** (mɛje) *v.i*, to slumber, doze, nod.

sommelier (sɔməlje) *m*, wine waiter.

sommer (sɔme) *v.t*, to summon, call on; sum up.

sommet (sɔmɛ) *m*, summit, top; vertex, apex; acme.

sommier (sɔmje) *m*, pack animal; transom, lintel; dossier; register; bed mattress, spring m.

sommité (sɔmmite) *f*, summit, top; leading man, (*pl.*) leading people.

somnambule (sɔmnɑ̃byl) *n*, somnambulist, sleepwalker. **somnambulisme** (lism) *m*, somnambulism. **somnolent, e** (nɔlɑ̃, ɑ̃:t) *a*, sleepy. **somnoler** (nɔle) *v.i*, to doze, drowse.

somnifère (sɔmnifɛ:r) *m*, opiate; narcotic; sleeping pill.

somptueux, euse† (sɔ̃ptɥø, ø:z) *a*, sumptuous. **somptuosité** (tɥozite) *f*, sumptuousness.

son, sa, ses (sɔ̃, sa, se) *a*, his, her, its, one's.

son (sɔ̃) *m*, sound; clang; tone; bran.

sonate (sɔnat) *f*, sonata.

sonde (sɔ̃:d) *f*, [sounding] lead, plummet; probe; spit; drill (*Min.*); taster (*cheese*). **sonder** (sɔ̃de) *v.t*, to sound; probe; fathom. **sondeur** (dœ:r) *m*, leadsman; driller.

songe (sɔ̃:ʒ) *m*, dream. ~-**creux**, *m*, dreamer, visionary. **songer** (sɔ̃ʒe) *v.i*, to dream, muse. ~ *à*, to think of, intend. **songeur, euse** (ʒœːr, øːz) *a*, dreamy; pensive.

sonnaille (sɔnɑːj) *f*, cowbell. **sonnailler** (naje) *m*, bellwether. ¶ *v.i*, to keep ringing [the bell]. **sonnant, e** (nɑ̃, ɑːt) *a*, [re]sounding; hard (*cash*). **sonné, e** (ne) *p.a*, past, struck (*hour*); turned (*a certain age*). **sonner** (ne) *v.i*. & *t*, to sound; ring; r. for; toll; strike. **sonnerie** (nri) *f*, ringing; bells; bell; call (*trumpet, bugle*). **sonnet** (nɛ) *m*, sonnet. **sonnette** (nɛt) *f*, bell; pile driver. **sonneur** (nœːr) *m*, bell ringer. **sonore** (nɔːr) *a*, sonorous; loud (*laugh, cheers*); sound (*att.*). **sonoriser** (nɔrize) *v.t*, to add sound track to film. **sonorité** (nɔrite) *f*, sonorousness, volume [of sound].

sophisme (sɔfism) *m*, sophism; fallacy. **sophistique** (tik) *f*, sophistry. **sophistiquer** (ke) *v.t*. & *i*, to sophisticate.

soporifique (sɔpɔrifik) *a*. & *m*, soporific.

soprano (sɔprano) *m*, soprano (*voice & pers.*).

sorbet (sɔrbɛ) *m*, ices (*flavored*). **sorbetière** (btjɛːr) *f*, ice-cream freezer.

sorbier (sɔrbje) *m*, service tree, sorb. ~ *des oiseaux*, mountain ash.

sorcellerie (sɔrsɛlri) *f*, sorcery, witchcraft. **sorcier, ère** (sje, ɛːr) *n*, sorcerer, ess, wizard, witch; hag. *sorcier guérisseur*, medicine man, witch doctor. *ce n'est pas sorcier*, it's not that difficult, complicated.

sordide† (sɔrdid) *a*, sordid; filthy, squalid.

sorgho (sɔrgo) *m*, sorghum.

Sorlingues (îles) (sɔrlɛ̃g) *f.pl*, Scilly Islands, Scilly Isles.

sornettes (sɔrnɛt) *f.pl*, nonsense.

sort (sɔːr) *m*, lot, fate; spell. **sortable** (sɔrtabl) *a*, suitable; eligible. **sortant** (tɑ̃) *a.m*, drawn, winning (*number*); retiring, outgoing (*pers.*).

sorte (sɔrt) *f*, sort, kind; manner, way. *en quelque* ~, in a way, as it were.

sortie (sɔrti) *f*, going out; coming out; exit; issue; sally, sortie; outlet; way out, egress. ~ *de bal*, ~ *de théâtre*, opera cloak, evening wrap.

sortilège (sɔrtilɛːʒ) *m*, witchcraft, spell.

sortir (sɔrtːr) *v.i.ir*, to go out; come out; leave; emerge, issue, spring; stand out; (*v.t.ir*.) to bring out; take out; pull out. *X. sort, exit X.* (*Theat.*). ~ *sur imprimante*, to print out (*computers*).

sosie (sɔzi) *m*, double (*pers.*).

sot, te† (so, ɔt) *a*, silly, foolish; sheepish. ¶ *n*, fool. **sot-l'y-laisse** (sɔliɛs) *m*, pope's nose. **sottise** (sɔtiːz) *f*, silliness, foolishness, folly; (*pl.*) nonsense; insult.

sou (su) *m*, sou = 5 centimes; penny (*in sense of very little money*).

soubassement (subɑsmɑ̃) *m*, basement; base.

soubresaut (subrəso) *m*, start, leap, jolt.

souche (suʃ) *f*, stump, stock, stub; founder (*family*); shaft, stack (*chimney*); counterfoil. *à la* ~, unissued (*stocks, shares*).

souci (susi) *m*, care, concern; worry; marigold. ~ *d'eau*, marsh marigold, kingcup. **se soucier de** (sje), to care for, mind. **soucieux, euse** (sjø, øːz) *a*, anxious.

soucoupe (sukup) *f*, saucer.

soudain, e† (sudɛ̃, ɛn) *a*, sudden. **soudain**, *ad*, suddenly. **soudaineté** (dɛnte) *f*, suddenness.

soude (sud) *f*, soda; saltwort.

souder (sude) *v.t*, to solder; weld.

soudoyer (sudwaje) *v.t*, to hire; bribe.

soudure (sudyːr) *f*, soldering; solder; welding; joint; weld.

souffle (sufl) *m*, breath; puff, waft, inspiration. *second* ~, second wind. **souffler** (fle) *v.i*. & *t*, to blow; b. up; b. out; pant; breathe; prompt, prime, whisper. **soufflerie** (fləri) *f*, bellows (*organ*). **soufflet** (flɛ) *m*, bellows; hood (*carriage*); box on the ear[s]; slap; snub. **souffleter** (flɛte) *v.t*, to box (*someone's*) ears, slap. **souffleur** (flœːr) *m*, blower; prompter. **soufflure** (fly:r) *f*, blowhole; flaw (*casting*).

souffrance (sufrã:s) *f*, sufferance (*law*); suffering, pain. en ~, in suspense, in abeyance, held over; unclaimed, on hand (*goods*); undeliverable (*parcel*). **souffrant**, e (frã, ã:t) *a*, suffering; ailing, unwell, poorly. **souffre-douleur** (frədulœ:r) *m*, butt; scapegoat. **souffreteux**, **euse** (tø, ø:z) *a*, sickly. **souffrir** (frir) *v.t. & i. ir*, to suffer; bear; endure, stand; undergo; allow.

soufre (sufr) *m*, sulfur, brimstone. **soufrière** (friɛ:r) *f*, sulfur mine.

souhait (swɛ) *m*, wish. ~s de bonne année, New Year's wishes, season's greetings. **souhaitable** (tabl) *a*, desirable. **souhaiter** (te) *v.t*, to wish; w. for. ~ la (ou une bonne) fête à quelqu'un, to wish someone many happy returns [of the day].

souille (su:j) *f*, wallow. **souiller** (suje) *v.t*, to soil, dirty; pollute; taint; stain, sully, besmirch. **souillon** (jõ) *n*, sloven; (*f.*) slut, slattern. **souillure** (jy:r) *f*, spot, stain; blot, blemish.

soûl, **e** (su, ul) *a*, drunk; gorged. ¶ *m*, fill. **soûlard**, e (la:r, ard) *n*, drunkard. **soûler** (le) *v.t*, to glut (*food, drink*); inebriate.

soulager (sulaʒe) *v.t*, to relieve, lighten, ease, alleviate; comfort. **souleur** (sulœ:r) *f*, shock (*startling emotion*).

soulèvement (sulɛvmã) *m*, rising; heaving; upheaval (*Geol.*); revolt. **soulever** (lve) *v.t*, to raise, lift; make heave; moot; rouse. se ~, to rise, heave; revolt. **soulier** (sulje) *m*, shoe; slipper. **souligner** (suliɲe) *v.t*, to underline; emphasize.

soulte (sult) *f*, balance (*in cash*). **soumettre** (sumɛtr) *v.t.ir*, to subdue; submit; subject. se ~, to submit, yield, give in. **soumis**, e (mi, i:z) *p.a*, submissive, dutiful; subject, amenable; liable. **soumission** (misjõ) *f*, submission; submissiveness; tender; bond. **soumissionner** (ɔne) *v.t*, to tender for.

soupape (supap) *f*, valve; plug (*bath, etc.*). ~ d'échappement, exhaust v. ~ de sécurité, safety v.

soupçon (supsõ) *m*, suspicion; surmise; dash; touch. **soupçonner** (sɔne) *v.t*, to suspect; surmise. **soupçonneux**, **euse** (nø, ø:z) *a*, suspicious, distrustful.

soupe (sup) *f*, soup; food; chow (*Mil.*).

soupente (supã:t) *f*, loft.

souper (supe) *m*, supper. ~ assis, sit-down supper. ~ debout, buffet (*at a ball*). ¶ *v.i*, to have supper, sup.

soupeser (supəze) *v.t*, to feel the weight of.

soupière (supjɛ:r) *f*, soup tureen.

soupir (supi:r) *m*, sigh; breath; crotchet rest (*Mus.*). **soupirail** (pira:j) *m*, airhole, vent. **soupirant** (rã) *m*, suitor, wooer. **soupirer** (re) *v.i*, to sigh; yearn.

souple (supl) *a*, supple, pliant, pliable; lithe[some], lissom[e]; limp (*binding*); versatile. feutre ~, soft felt (*hat*). **souplesse** (plɛs) *f*, suppleness.

source (surs) *f*, source, spring, fountainhead; well; rise; wellspring, fount. **sourcier**, **ère** (sje, ɛ:r) *n*, water diviner, dowser.

sourcil (sursi) *m*, eyebrow. **sourciller** (je) *v.i*, to frown; wince. **sourcilleux**, **euse** (jø, ø:z) *a*, beetling; frowning, anxious.

sourd, **e** (su:r, urd) *a*, deaf, dull; hollow (*voice*); mute[d]; muffled; underhand. ¶ *n*, deaf person. **sourdement** (surdəmã) *ad*, dully; secretly. **sourdine** (din) *f*, mute (*Mus.*); damper. en ~, on the sly. **sourd-muet**, **sourde-muette** (surmɥɛ, dmɥɛt) *a*, deaf & dumb. ¶ *n*, deaf-mute.

sourdre (surdr) *v.i*, to spring, well up.

souriant, **e** (surjã, ã:t) *a*, smiling.

souriceau (suriso) *m*, young mouse. **souricière** (sjɛ:r) *f*, mousetrap; trap (*police*).

sourire (suri:r) *m*, smile. ¶ *v.i.ir*, to smile. ~ à, to be attractive to, please.

souris (suri) *f*, mouse; knuckle end (*mutton*).

sournois, e† (surnwa, a:z) *a*, sly, underhand.

sous (su; *in liaison*, suz) *pr*, under[neath], beneath, below; in; by; with; within; on. sous, *comps*: ~-*affermer*, *v.t*, to sublet. ~-*bail*, *m*, sublease. ~-*cutané*, *e*, *a*, subcutaneous. ~-*entendre*, *v.t*, to understand, imply. ~-*entendu*, *m*, implication; double entendre. *sous-estimer*, *v.t*, to underestimate, undervalue, underrate. *sous-jacent*, *e* (suʒasã, ã:t) *a*, underlying. ~-*lieutenant*, *m*, second lieutenant. ~-*locataire*, *n*, subtenant. ~-*louer*, *v.t*, to sublet; rent (*as subtenant*). ~-*marin*, *e*, *a*. & *m*, submarine. en ~-*œuvre*, underpinned. ~-*officier*, *m*, noncommissioned officer. ~-*ordre*, *m*, subordinate, underling; sub-order. en ~-*ordre*, subordinate(ly). ~-*produit*, *m*, byproduct. ~-*secrétaire*, *m*, undersecretary. ~-*sol*, *m*, subsoil; basement. ~-*titre*, *m*, subtitle, caption. ~-*traitant* (tretã) *m*, subcontractor. ~-*traité*, *m*, subcontract. ~-*ventrière* (vãtriɛ:r) *f*, bellyband; [saddle] girth. ~-*vêtement*, *m*, undergarment; (*pl.*) underwear, underclothing.

souscripteur (suskriptœ:r) *m*, subscriber; applicant (*shares*); drawer (*bill*); underwriter (*Insce*). **souscription** (sjʃ5) *f*, execution, signing (*deed*); signature; subscription; application; underwriting. **souscrire** (skri:r) *v.t*. & *i*. ir, to execute, sign; subscribe; draw; apply for; underwrite.

sous-développement (sudevlɔpmã) *f*, underdevelopment (*economics*).

sous-prolétariat (suprɔletarja) *m*, unemployables leading a marginal social life. Equivalent of German *Lumpenprolatariat*.

soussigné, e (susiɲe) *a*. & *n*, undersigned.

soustraction (sustraksjɔ̃) *f*, abstraction; subtraction. **soustraire** (strɛ:r) *v.t.ir*, to abstract (*steal*), purloin; withdraw; screen; subtract (*Arith.*). se ~ à, to elude,

avoid. *se ~ à la justice*, to abscond.

soutache (sutaʃ) *f*, braid. **soutacher** (ʃe) *v.t*, to braid.

soutane (sutan) *f*, cassock; cloth (*clergy*).

soute (sut) *f*, storeroom (*Naut.*); magazine, bunker, locker; tank.

soutenable (sutnabl) *a*, bearable; tenable. **soutenir** (tni:r) *v.t.ir*, to sustain, support, hold up; uphold; keep, maintain; back [up]; stand, bear; afford. **soutenu**, e (tny) *p.a*, sustained; unremitting; lofty, rhetorical (*style*).

souterrain, e (sutɛrɛ̃, ɛn) *a*, underground, subterranean; underhand. ¶ *m*, tunnel; cavern.

soutien (sutjɛ̃) *m*, support; mainstay; upholder. ~ *de famille*, breadwinner. ~-*gorge*, *m*, brassière.

soutirer (sutire) *v.t*, to draw off, rack [off] (*wine*); extract (*money*).

souvenance (suvnã:s) *f*, memories. **souvenir** (vni:r) *m*, remembrance, recollection; memory; memento; keepsake. se ~, *v.pr. ir*, to remember, recollect.

souvent (suvã) *ad*, often.

souverain, e† (suvrɛ̃, ɛn) *a*, sovereign; supreme, superlative. ¶ *n*, sovereign. **souveraineté** (vrɛnte) *f*, sovereignty.

soviet (sɔvjɛt) *m*, soviet. **soviétique** (etik) *a*, soviet (*att.*).

soya (sɔja) *m*, soybean.

soyeux, **euse** (swajø, ø:z) *a*, silky.

spacieux, **euse**† (spasjø, ø:z) *a*, spacious, roomy, capacious.

spadassin (spadasɛ̃) *m*, ruffian.

sparadrap (sparadra) *m*, adhesive tape, court plaster.

sparte (spart) *m*, esparto [grass]. **spartiate** (sparsjat) *a*. & *n*, Spartan.

spasme (spasm) *m*, spasm. **spasmodique** (mɔdik) *a*, spasmodic (*Med.*).

spath (spat) *m*, spar.

spatial, aux (spasjal, o) *a*, relating to space; astounding (*slang*).

spatule (spatyl) *f*, spatula; spoonbill.

speaker (spikœ:r) *m*, announcer (*radio*); speaker.

spécial, e† (spesjal) *a*, special, particular. **se spécialiser dans** (lize), to specialize in. **spécialiste** (list) *n*, specialist. **spécialité** (te) *f*, specialty. ~ *pharmaceutique*, patent medicine.

spécieux, euse† (spesjø, ø:z) *a*, specious.

spécification (spesifikasjɔ̃) *f*, specification. **spécifier** (fje) *v.t*, to specify. **spécifique**† (fik) *a*. & *m*, specific.

spécimen (spesimɛn) *m*, specimen; free copy (*book*).

spectacle (spɛktakl) *m*, spectacle, sight, scene; play, entertainment, show. ~ *forain*, sideshow (*fair*). ~ *payant*, sideshow (*exhibition*). ~ *permanent*, continuous performance (*movies*). ~ *solo*, one-man show. **spectateur, trice** (tœ:r, tris) *n*, spectator, onlooker, bystander; (*m.pl.*) audience (*Theat.*).

spectral, e (spɛktral) *a*, spectral; ghostly, unearthly, eerie, -ry, weird. **spectre** (tr) *m*, specter, ghost; spectrum. **spectroscope** (trɔskop) *m*, spectroscope.

spéculateur, trice (spekylatœ:r, tris) *n*, speculator. **spéculatif, ive** (tif, i:v) *a*, speculative. **spéculation** (sjɔ̃) *f*, speculation. **spéculer** (le) *v.i*, to speculate.

spermatozoaire (spɛrmatɔzɔɛ:r) *m*, spermatozoon. **sperme** (spɛrm) *m*, sperm.

sphère (sfɛ:r) *f*, sphere, orb, globe. **sphérique** (sferik) *a*, spherical.

sphincter (sfɛ̃ktɛ:r) *m*, sphincter.

sphinx (sfɛ̃:ks) *m*, sphinx.

spinal, e (spinal) *a*, spinal.

spinelle (spinɛl) *m*. & *att*, spinel.

spiral, e (spiral) *a*, spiral. ¶ *m*, hairspring; (*f.*) spiral. **spire** (spi:r) *f*, turn, spire, whorl.

spirite (spirit) *n*, spiritualist (*psychics*). **spiritisme** (tism) *m*, spiritualism. **spiritualisme** (tɥalism) *m*, spiritualism (*Philos.*). **spiritualiste** (list) *n*, spiritualist. **spirituel, le**† (tɥɛl) *a*, spiritual; sacred (*concert*); witty. **spiri-**

tueux, euse (tɥø, ø:z) *a*, spirituous. ¶ *m.pl*, spirits.

Spitzberg (le) (spitsbɛrg), Spitzbergen.

spleen (splin) *m*, spleen, dumps, blues.

splendeur (splɑ̃dœ:r) *f*, splendor. **splendide**† (did) *a*, splendid, gorgeous.

spolier (spɔlje) *v.t*, to despoil, rob, rifle.

spongieux, euse (spɔ̃ʒjø, ø:z) *a*, spongy.

spontané†, e (spɔ̃tane) *a*, spontaneous; willing.

sporadique (spɔradik) *a*, sporadic.

spore (spɔ:r) *f*, spore.

sport (spɔ:r) *m*, sport, sports. **sportif, ive** (spɔrtif, i:v) *a*, fond of sport[s]; sporting; sports (*att.*); athletic (*meeting*); game .(*fish, fishing, etc.*). *un sportif*, a sportsman.

square (skwa:r) *m*, park, square.

squelette (skəlɛt) *m*, skeleton; scrag (*pers.*).

stabilité (stabilite) *f*, stability. **stabiliser** (ze) *v.t*, to stabilize (*Fin.*). **stable** (bl) *a*, stable; lasting.

stade (stad) *m*, stadium; stage (*Med.*).

stage (sta:ʒ) *m*, probation; course; stage, period. **stagiaire** (staʒjɛ:r) *n*, probationer.

stagnant, e (stagnɑ̃, ɑ̃:t) *a*, stagnant; standing (*water*). **stagnation** (nasjɔ̃) *f*, stagnation.

stalactite (stalaktit) *f*, stalactite.

stalagmite (stalagmit) *f*, stalagmite.

stalle (stal) *f*, seat (*Theat.*); box (*horse*); garage.

stance (stɑ̃:s) *f*, stanza.

stand (stɑ̃:d) *m*, stand (*racetrack, exhibition*); shooting gallery, rifle range.

standing (stɑ̃diŋ) *m*, elevated standard of living; status. *immeuble de grand* ~, luxury apartment house.

station (stasjɔ̃) *f*, station; halt; stop (*bus*); stand (*cab*); resort. ~ *balnéaire*, spa, seaside resort. ~ *climat[ér]ique*, health resort. **stationnaire** (ɔnɛ:r) *a*, stationary.

stationnement (nmɑ̃) *m*, stopping, standing, halt; parking. ~ *interdit*, no parking. **stationner** (ne) *v.i*, to stop; stand; station; park.

station-aval (stasjɔ̃-aval) *f*, downrange station.

statique (statik) *a*, static(al). ¶ *f*, statics.

statisticien (statistisjɛ̃) *m*, statistician. **statisque** (tik) *a*, statistic(al). ¶ *f*, statistics, return[s]. ~ *militaire*, intelligence department.

statuaire (statɥɛːr) *a*, statuary. ¶ *f*, [art of] statuary. ¶ *m*, statuary (*pers.*). **statue** (ty) *f*, statue; (*pl. col.*) statuary.

statuer (statɥe) *v.t*, to ordain. ~ *sur*, to decide, resolve on.

statuette (statɥɛt) *f*, statuette.

stature (statyːr) *f*, stature, height (*of pers.*).

statut (staty) *m*, statute; (*pl.*) memorandum & articles [of association]; status. **statutaire** (tɛːr) *a*, statutory.

stéarine (stearin) *f*, stearin. **stéatite** (tit) *f*, steatite.

steeple-chase (stiplətʃɛs) *m*, hurdle race.

stellaire (stɛllɛːr) *a*, stellar.

sténodactylographe (stenɔdaktilɔgraf) *n*, shorthand-typist. **sténographe** (graf) *n*, stenographer. **sténographie** (fi), *f*, shorthand, stenography. **sténographier** (fje) *v.t*, to take down [in shorthand].

stère (stɛːr) *m*, stere = 1 cub. meter (*firewood*).

stéréoscope (stereɔskɔp) *m*, stereoscope.

stéréotyper (stereɔtipe) *v.t*, to stereotype.

stérile† (steril) *a*, sterile, barren; effete; unfruitful; fruitless. **stériliser** (lize) *v.t*, to sterilize. **stérilité** (te) *f*, sterility, etc.

stérilet (sterile) *m*, I.U.D., coil, loop (*contraceptive device*).

sterling (stɛrliŋ) *a.inv*, sterling. **sterne** (stɛrn) *m*, tern (*bird*).

sternum (stɛrnɔm) *m*, sternum, breast bone.

stethoscope (stetɔskɔp) *m*, stethoscope.

stigmate (stigmat) *m*, stigma,

brand. **stigmatiser** (tize) *v.t*, to stigmatize, brand.

stimulant (stimylɑ̃) *m*, stimulant; whet; stimulus. **stimuler** (le) *v.t*, to stimulate, exhilarate, whet.

stimulateur (stimylatœːr) *m*, pacemaker (*Med.*).

stipendiaire (stipɑ̃djɛːr) *a*, mercenary.

stipuler (stipyle) *v.t*, to stipulate.

stock (stɔk) *m*, stock (*goods, gold*).

stockfisch (stɔkfiʃ) *m*, stockfish. **stockiste** (stɔkist) *m*, warehouseman (*trade goods*); accredited dealer.

stoïcien, ne (stɔisjɛ̃, ɛn) *a*. & *m*, Stoic. **stoïcisme** (sism) *m*, stoicism. **stoïque**† (ik) *a*, stoical.

stomacal, e (stɔmakal) *a*, stomachal; stomach (*pump*). **stomachique** (ʃik) *a*. & *m*, stomachic.

stop (stɔp) *i*, stop (*Naut., in telegrams*). **stoppage** (stɔpaːʒ) *m*, invisible mending. **stopper** (pe) *v.t*. & *i*, to stop (*ship*); reweave.

store (stɔːr) *m*, blind, shade, awning.

strangulation (strɑ̃gylasjɔ̃) *f*, strangulation.

strapontin (strapɔ̃tɛ̃) *m*, jumpseat.

Strasbourg (strazbuːr) *m*, Strasburg.

strasse (stras) *f*, floss silk.

stratagème (strataʒɛm) *m*, stratagem. **stratège** (tɛːʒ) *m*, strategist. **stratégie** (teʒi) *f*, strategy; generalship. **stratégique** (ʒik) *a*, strategic(al).

stratification (stratifikasjɔ̃) *f*, stratification.

strict, e† (strikt) *a*, strict. **strident, e** (stridɑ̃, ɑ̃ːt) *a*, strident, shrill, grating.

strie (stri) *f*, stria, score; ridge. **strié, e** (e) *a*, striate[d]; fluted. **striure** (yːr) *f*, striation.

strophe (strɔf) *f*, stanza, verse.

structure (stryktyːr) *f*, structure, make.

strychnine (striknin) *f*, strychnine.

stuc (styk) *m*, stucco.

studieux, euse† (stydjø, øːz) *a*, studious.

stupéfiant (stypefjã) *m*, narcotic, drug. **stupéfier** (fje) *v.t*, to stupefy; amaze. **stupeur** (pœːr) *f*, stupor; amazement. **stupide†** (pid) *a*, stupid. **stupidité** (dite) *f*, stupidity.

style (stil) *m*, style. **styler** (le) *v.t*, to train. **stylet** (lɛ) *m*, stiletto; stylet; probe.

stylo (stilɔ) *m*, fountain pen. ~ *à bille*, ball-point pen.

su (sy) *m*: *au* ~ *de*, to the knowledge of.

suaire (sɥɛːr) *m*, shroud, winding sheet.

suant, e (sɥã, ãːt) *a*, sweating; sweaty.

suave† (sɥaːv) *a*, sweet, soft; suave, bland. **suavité** (avite) *f*, sweetness, suavity.

subalterne (sybaltɛrn) *a*, subordinate, minor. ¶ *m*, underling; subaltern.

subconscience (sybkɔ̃sjãːs) *f*, subconsciousness. **subconscient, e** (sjã, ãːt) *a. & m*, subconscious.

subdiviser (sybdivize) *v.t*, to subdivide.

subir (sybiːr) *v.t*, to undergo, submit to, suffer; serve (*a sentence*).

subit, e† (sybi, it) *a*, sudden. **subito** (to) *ad*, all of a sudden.

subjectif, ive† (sybʒɛktif, iːv) *a. & m*, subjective.

subjonctif (sybʒɔ̃ktif) *m*, subjunctive [mood].

subjuguer (sybʒyge) *v.t*, to subjugate, subdue.

sublime† (syblim) *a. & m*, sublime. **sublimer** (me) *v.t*, to sublimate; refine. **sublimité** (mite) *f*, sublimity.

sublunaire (syblynɛːr) *a*, sublunar[y].

submerger (sybmɛrʒe) *v.t*, to submerge, flood, swamp. **submersion** (sjɔ̃) *f*, submersion; flooding; drowning (*of pers.*).

subodorer (sybɔdɔre) *v.t*, to scent [out], suspect.

subordonné, e (sybɔrdɔne) *a. & n*, subordinate. **subordonner** (ne) *v.t*, to subordinate.

suborner (sybɔrne) *v.t*, to suborn, tamper with.

subrécargue (sybrekarg) *m*, supercargo.

subreptice† (sybrɛptis) *a*, surreptitious.

subroger (sybrɔʒe) *v.t*, to subrogate.

subséquemment (sypsekamã) *ad*, subsequently. **subséquent, e** (kã, ãːt) *a*, subsequent, ensuing.

subside (sypsid) *m*, subsidy.

subsidiaire† (sypsidjɛːr) *a*, subsidiary.

subsistance (sypsistãːs) *f*, subsistence, sustenance; (*pl.*) provisions, supplies. **subsister** (te) *v.i*, to subsist.

substance (sybstãːs) *f*, substance; gist, kernel (*fig.*). **substantiel, le†** (stãsjɛl) *a*, substantial. **substantif** (tif) *a.m. & m*, substantive.

substituer (sybstitɥe) *v.t*, to substitute; entail (*law*). **substitut** (ty) *m*, deputy; surrogate.

substruction (sybstryksjɔ̃) *f*, substructure.

subterfuge (sybtɛrfyːʒ) *m*, subterfuge, shift.

subtil, e† (syptil) *a*, subtle; pervasive; keen; fine. **subtiliser** (lize) *v.t*, to filch; (*v.i.*) to subtilize. **subtilité** (te) *f*, subtlety.

suburbain, e (sybyrbɛ̃, ɛn) *a*, suburban.

subvenir à (sybvəniːr) *v.ir*, to come to the aid of; provide for. **subvention** (vãsjɔ̃) *f*, subsidy, subvention, grant. **subventionner** (ɔne) *v.t*, to subsidize.

subversif, ive (sybvɛrsif, iːv) *a*, subversive. **subversion** (sjɔ̃) *f*, subversion, overthrow.

suc (syk) *m*, juice; pith (*fig.*).

succédané (syksedane) *m*, substitute (*product*). **succéder à** (de), to succeed; s. to; follow; inherit. **succès** (sɛ) *m*, success; issue. ~ *fou*, smash hit. **successeur** (sɛsœːr) *m*, successor. **successif, ive** (sif, iːv) *a*, successive, running. **succession** (sjɔ̃) *f*, succession, sequence; inheritance, estate. **successivement** (sivmã) *ad*, successively; seriatim.

succinct, e† (syksɛ̃, ɛ̃ːkt) *a*, succinct; meager.

succion (syksjɔ̃) *f*, suction, suck-ing.

succomber (sykɔ̃be) *v.i,* to suc-cumb; sink; yield; die.

succulent, e (sykylɑ̃, ɑ̃ːt) *a*, suc-culent, juicy, luscious, toothsome.

succursale (sykyrsal) *f*, branch (*establishment*).

sucer (syse) *v.t*, to suck; imbibe. **sucette** (sɛt) *f*, lollipop; pacifier. **suçoir** (swaːr) *m*, sucker (*of in-sect*).

sucre (sykr) *m*, sugar. ~ *cristal-lisé*, granulated s. ~ *d'orge*, bar-ley s., ~ *en morceaux*, ~ *cassé*, lump s., cube s. ~ *en poudre*, powdered s. ~ *semoule*, granu-lated s. **sucré, e** (kre) *p.a*, sug-ared, sweet[ened]; sugary (*fig.*). *elle fait la sucrée*, butter wouldn't melt in her mouth. **sucrer** (kre) *v.t*, to sugar, sweeten; suppress or eliminate (*slang*). ~ *un texte*, to eliminate part of a text. *se faire* ~, to be arrested. **sucrerie** (krəri) *f*, sugar refinery; (*pl.*) candy. *aimer les* ~s, to have a sweet tooth. **sucrier, ère** (krie, ɛːr) *a*, sugar (*att.*). ¶ *m*, sugar refiner; sugar bowl.

sud (syd) *m*, south; (*att.*) south-[ern]. ~*-africain, e,* South Afri-can. ~*-américain, e,* South Amer-ican. ~*-est* (sydɛst; *Naut.*, syɛ) *m*, southeast. ~*-ouest* (sydwɛst; *Naut.*, syrwɛ) *m*, southwest. *le* S~*-Ouest africain*, South West Africa.

Suède (la) (sɥɛd), Sweden. **sué-dois, e** (edwa, aːz) *a.* & (*lan-guage*) *m*, Swedish. **S~,** *n*, Swede (*pers.*).

suée (sɥe) *f*, sweat (*state*). **suer** (e) *v.i.* & *t*, to sweat, perspire, ooze; reek of, with. ~ *à grosses gouttes*, to sweat profusely. ~ *d'ahan* (a[h]ɑ̃), to toil & moil. *faire* ~, to annoy, irritate. **sueur** (œːr) *f*, sweat, perspiration.

suffire (syfiːr) *v.i.ir,* to suffice, be enough, do. ~ *à*, to be equal to, satisfy, cope with. *suffit que*, suffice it to say that. **suffisam-ment** (fizamɑ̃) *ad*, sufficiently, enough, adequately. **suffisance** (zɑ̃ːs) *f*, sufficiency, adequacy, enough; self-importance, bump-tiousness. **suffisant, e** (zɑ̃, ɑ̃ːt) *a*, sufficient, etc.

suffixe (syfiks) *m*, suffix. ¶ *a*, suffixed.

suffocation (syfɔkasjɔ̃) *f*, suf-focation, choking. **suffoquer** (ke) *v.t.* & *i*, to suffocate, stifle, choke.

suffragant (syfragɑ̃) *a.m.* & *m*, suffragan.

suffrage (syfraːʒ) *m*, suffrage, vote.

suffusion (syfysjɔ̃) *f*, suffusion.

suggérer (syɡʒere) *v.t*, to sug-gest; prompt. **suggestion** (syɡʒɛs-tjɔ̃) *f*, suggestion, hint. **sugges-tionner** (ɔne) *v.t*, to affect by sug-gestion (*psychology*).

suicide (sɥisid) *m.* & **suicidé (de)** (*pers.*) *m*, suicide. *suicide du genre humain*, race suicide. **se suicider** (de) *v.pr*, to commit suicide.

suie (sɥi) *f*, soot.

suif (sɥif) *m*, tallow; (*mutton*) fat; candle grease; reprimand (*slang*). *chercher du* ~, to look for a quar-rel. **suiffer** (fe) *v.t*, to tallow, grease.

suint (sɥɛ̃) *m*, grease (*in wool*). **suinter** (te) *v.i*, to ooze, run; leak.

suisse (sɥis) *a*, Swiss. ¶ *m*, Swiss (*man*), Swiss guard; beadle. *en suisse, faire suisse*, to eat or drink without inviting others present. **la** S~, Switzerland. **Suissesse** (sɛs) *f*, Swiss (*woman*).

suite (sɥit) *f*, continuation; conse-quence, result, effect; sequence, series, succession, run; sequel; suite; attendants, retinue, train; set; coherence, consistency. *don-ner* ~ *a*, to deal with, carry out, decision or order. *la* ~ *au pro-chain numéro*, to be continued in our next. ~ *& fin*, concluded (*se-rial*). **suivant, e** (vɑ̃, ɑ̃ːt) *a*, next, following, ensuing. ¶ *n*, follower, attendant; (*f.*) lady's maid. **sui-vant,** *pr*, along; according to, pur-suant to. ~ *que*, according as. **suivi, e** (vi) *p.a*, coherent; consis-tent; steady; well-attended. **suivre** (sɥiːvr) *v.t.ir*, to follow; succeed; pursue; watch, observe; attend; practise. ~ *la balle*, to follow through. *à* ~, to be continued (*se-

rial). faire ~, to forward, readdress; run on (*Typ.*).

sujet, te (syʒɛ, ɛt) *a*, subject, amenable, liable, prone. ¶ *n*, subject (*of a State*). ¶ *m*, subject, topic, matter, theme; cause, grounds; stock (*Hort.*); fellow. **sujétion** (ʒesjɔ̃) *f*, subjection, subservience; constraint; sedulousness.

sulfate (sylfat) *m*, sulfate. **sulfite** (fit) *m*, sulfite. **sulfure** (fy:r) *m*, sulfide. **sulfuré, e** (fyre) *a*, sulfurreted. **sulfureux, euse** (rø, ø:z) *a*, sulfurous. **sulfurique** (rik) *a*, sulfuric.

sultan (syltã) *m*, sultan; silklined basket; sachet. **sultane** (tan) *f*, sultana (*pers.*).

sumac (symak) *m*, sumac. ~ *vénéneux*, poison ivy, oak, sumac.

superbe† (sypɛrb) *a*, superb, stately; vainglorious. ¶ *f*, vainglory.

supercherie (sypɛrʃəri) *f*, fraud, hoax.

superfétation (sypɛrfetasjɔ̃) *f*, redundancy.

superficie (sypɛrfisi) *f*, superficies, surface; area. **superficiel, le†** (sjel) *a*, superficial, shallow, skin-deep.

superfin, e (sypɛrfɛ̃) *a*, superfine.

superflu, e (sypɛrfly) *a*, superfluous. **superflu,** *m*. & **superfluité** (ite) *f*, superfluity.

supérieur, e (sypɛrjœ:r) *a*, superior; upper; higher. ¶ *n*, superior, chief; better (*pers.*). **supérieurement** (œrmã) *ad*, superlatively, in a masterly way. ~ *à*, better than. **supériorité** (rjɔrite) *f*, superiority.

superlatif, ive (sypɛrlatif, i:v) *a*, superlative (*Gram.*); consummate. ¶ (*Gram.*) *m*, superlative.

supermarché (sypɛrmarʃe) *m*, supermarket.

superposer (sypɛrpoze) *v.t*, to super[im]pose; overlay (*computers*).

superstitieux, euse† (sypɛrstisjø, ø:z) *a*, superstitious. **superstition** (sjɔ̃) *f*, superstition.

supplanter (syplãte) *v.t*, to supplant.

suppléance (sypleã:s) *f*, substitution; deputyship; temporary term. **suppléant, e** (ã, ã:t) *n*. & *a*, substitute, deputy. **suppléer** (ee) *v.t*, to supply, make up for; deputize for; eke out. ~ *à*, to make up for; fill (*vacancy*). **supplément** (mã) *m*, supplement, addition, excess, extra [charge, fare]. **supplémentaire** (tɛ:r) *a*, supplementary, additional, extra, further; relief (*train*).

suppliant, e (sypliã, ã:t) *a*. & *n*, suppliant. **supplication** (kasjɔ̃) *f*, supplication, entreaty. **supplice** (plis) *m*, punishment, torture, torment; (*extreme*) penalty; rack (*fig.*). **supplier** (plie) *v.t*, to beseech, entreat, implore, supplicate. **supplique** (plik) *f*, petition, prayer.

support (sypɔ:r) *m*, support, stay; rest, stand, holder. ~ *à chariot*, slide rest (*lathe*). **supportable** (portabl) *a*, supportable, bearable, endurable, tolerable. **supporter** (te) *v.t*, to support; endure, bear, suffer, stand. **supports-chaussettes,** *m.pl*, garters (*men's*).

supposé, e (sypoze) *p.a*, supposititious; fictitious. **supposé que**, supposing [that]. **supposer** (ze) *v.t*, to suppose; assume, infer, take; imply; put forward as genuine (*what is false—law*). **supposition** (zisjɔ̃) *f*, supposition, assumption. ~ *de personne*, impersonation (*law*).

suppôt (sypo) *m*, tool (*pers.*), myrmidon.

suppression (sypresjɔ̃) *f*, suppression; discontinuance (*train*); concealment. **supprimer** (prime) *v.t*, to suppress, do away with, cut out; discontinue; conceal.

suppurer (sypyre) *v.i*, to suppurate.

supputer (sypyte) *v.t*, to compute, reckon.

suprématie (sypremasi) *f*, supremacy. **suprême†** (prɛ:m) *a*, supreme; highest; crowning; paramount.

sur (syr) *pr*, on, upon; over, above; by; after; in; about; as to; to; towards; out of. ~ *ce*, thereupon.

sur, e (sy:r) *a*, sour, tart.

sûr, e (sy:r) *a*, sure, safe, secure; reliable; settled (*weather*).

surabondant, e (syrabɔ̃dɑ̃, ɑ̃:t) *a*, superabundant.

suraigu, uë (syregy) *a*, high-pitched, shrill.

suralimenter (syralmɑ̃te) *v.t*, to overfeed (*person*); supercharge (*engine*).

suranné, e (syrane) *a*, out-of-date, antiquated, superannuated.

surboum (syrbum) *f*, surprise party, dance, celebration.

surcharge (syrʃarʒ) *f*, overload; excess weight (*luggage*); weight handicap; surcharge; correction, overprint. **surcharger** (ʒe) *v.t*, to overload; overtax; surcharge; correct, alter (*write over*).

surchauffer (syrʃofe) *v.t*, to overheat; superheat.

surcroît (syrkrwa) *m*, increase. *par ~*, in addition, to boot.

surdité (syrdite) *f*, deafness.

sureau (syro) *m*, elder [tree].

surélever (syrelve) *v.t*, to heighten; raise; tee (*golf*).

sûrement (syrmɑ̃) *ad*, surely, as *sûr*.

surenchère (syrɑ̃ʃɛ:r) *f*, higher bid. **surenchérir sur** (ʃeri:r), to bid higher than, outbid.

surestaries (syrɛstari) *f.pl*, demurrage (*ship*).

surestimer (syrɛstime) *v.t*, to overestimate, overvalue, overrate.

sûreté (syrte) *f*, safety, security, safe keeping; sureness, reliability. *la S~ Nationale* (*Fr.*), equivalent of Federal Bureau of Investigation in the U.S.

surexciter (syrɛksite) *v.t*, to overexcite.

surface (syrfas) *f*, surface; area; standing, repute. *~ des étages*, floor space (*building*). *une grande ~*, supermarket, shopping center.

surfaire (syrfɛ:r) *v.t. & abs. ir*, to overcharge (for); overrate, overestimate.

surfin, e (syrfɛ̃, in) *a*, superfine.

surgelé (syrʒale) *a*, deep-frozen. *produits ~s*, frozen foods. **surgeler** *v.t*, to deep-freeze.

surgeon (syrʒɔ̃) *m*, sucker (*Hort.*).

surgir (syrʒi:r) *v.i*, to rise; arise, loom.

surhausser (syrose) *v.t*, to heighten, raise.

surhomme (syrɔm) *m*, superman.

surhumain, e (syrymɛ̃, ɛn) *a*, superhuman.

surimposer (syrɛ̃poze) *v.t*, to overtax, overassess.

surintendant, e (syrɛ̃tɑ̃dɑ̃, ɑ̃:t) *n*, superintendent, overseer, steward.

surjet (syrʒɛ) *m*, oversewing stitch, seam s.

sur-le-champ (syrləʃɑ̃) *ad*, there & then; out of hand, off-hand.

surlendemain (syrlɑ̃dmɛ̃) *m*, day after tomorrow.

surmener (syrməne) *v.t*, to overwork; overdrive, override (*horse*); jade.

surmonter (syrmɔ̃te) *v.t*, to surmount, [over]top; overcome.

surnager (syrnaʒe) *v.i*, to float [on the surface]; survive.

surnaturel, le† (syrnatyrɛl) *a. & m*, supernatural, preternatural.

surnom (syrnɔ̃) *m*, surname, family name; nickname. **surnommer** (nɔme) *v.t*, to [nick]name, call.

surnombre (syrnɔ̃:br) *m*, surplus.

surnuméraire (syrnymerɛ:r) *a. & m*, supernumerary.

suroît (syrwa) *m*, sou'wester (*wind, hat*).

surpasser (syrpase) *v.t*, to surpass, overtop, exceed, outdo; astonish.

surpayer (syrpɛje) *v.t*, to overpay.

surplis (syrpli) *m*, surplice.

surplomb (syrplɔ̃) *m*, overhang. **surplomber** (be) *v.i. & t*, to overhang.

surplus (syrply) *m*, surplus, excess; rest. *au ~*, moreover, besides.

surprenant, e (syrprənɑ̃, ɑ̃:t) *a*, surprising. **surprendre** (prɑ̃:dr) *v.i.ir*, to surprise; catch [unawares]; overtake; intercept; detect; deceive; obtain by fraud. **surprise** (pri:z) *f*, surprise.

surproduction (syrprɔdyksjɔ̃) *f*, overproduction.

surrégénérateur (syrreʒenratœr) *m*, breeder reactor.

surréservation (syrrezɛrvasjɔ̃), *f*, overbooking.

sursaut (syrso) *m*, start, jump; burst (*energy*). **sursauter** (te) *v.i*, to start. *faire* ~, to startle.

surseoir à (syrswa:r) (*law*) *v.ir*, to suspend, delay, stay. ~ *l'exécution de*, to reprieve. **sursis** (si) *m*, stay [of proceedings]; reprieve, respite, postponement, or exemption, in many senses, e.g, *condamné à un an de prison avec* ~, means sentenced to a year's imprisonment but with suspended sentence.

surtaxe (syrtaks) *f*, surtax; surcharge; overassessment; fee; duty. **surtaxer** (kse) *v.t*, to surtax; surcharge; overassess.

surtout (syrtu) *ad*, above all, especially. ¶ *m*, centerpiece, epergne; overcoat, surtout.

surveillance (syrvejɑ̃:s) *f*, supervision; watch. **surveillant, e** (jɑ̃, ɑ̃:t) *n*, supervisor, overseer. **surveiller** (je) *v.t.*, to supervise, superintend, watch [over], look after.

survenir (syrvəni:r) *v.i.ir*, to arrive unexpectedly; supervene; come upon one; befall.

survie (syrvi) *f*, survivorship; survival. **survivance** (vɑ̃:s) *f*, survival, outliving. ~ *du plus apte*, survival of the fittest. **survivant, e** (vɑ̃, ɑ̃:t) *n*, survivor. **survivre à** (vi:vr) *v.ir*, to survive, outlive. *se* **survivre**, to survive; live again.

survol (syrvɔl) *m*, overflight; panning (*cinema*).

sus (sy; *in liaison*, syz) *ad*, [up]on; come on! *en* ~, extra, to boot. *en* ~ *de*, over & above.

susceptibilité (sysɛptibilite) *f*, susceptibility; touchiness. **susceptible** (bl) *a*, susceptible; capable; apt; sensitive; touchy.

susciter (sysite) *v.t*, to raise up; give rise to; stir up.

suscription (syskripsjɔ̃) *f*, superscription.

susdit, e (sysdi, it) *a. & n*, aforesaid. **susmentionné, e** (mɑ̃sjone) *a*, above-mentioned. **susnommé, e** (nome) *a*, above-named.

suspect, e (syspɛkt) *a*, suspicious, questionable, doubtful, suspect. **suspecter** (te) *v.t*, to suspect, question.

suspendre (syspɑ̃:dr) *v.t*, to suspend, hang up; sling; stop; stay. *en* **suspens** (pɑ̃), in abeyance, outstanding. **suspension** (sjɔ̃) *f*, suspension, hanging; discontinuance. **suspensoir** (swa:r) *m*, suspensory bandage. **suspens** (syspɑ̃) *a*, suspended. ¶ *m*, suspense.

suspicion (syspisjɔ̃) *f*, suspicion. **sustenter** (systɑ̃te) *v.t*, to sustain, nourish.

susurrer (sysyre) *v.i. & t*, to murmur, whisper.

suture (syty:r) *f*, suture; join.

suzerain, e (syzrɛ̃, ɛn) *a*, paramount. ¶ *n*, suzerain. **suzeraineté** (rɛnte) *f*, suzerainty.

svastika (svastika) *m*, swastika.

svelte (svɛlt) *a*, slender, slim.

sybarite (sibarit) *m*, sybarite.

sycomore (sikɔmɔ:r) *m*, sycamore.

sycophante (sikɔfɑ̃:t) *m*, sycophant.

syllabaire (silabɛ:r) *m*, spelling book. **syllabe** (lab) *f*, syllable.

syllogisme (silɔʒism) *m*, syllogism.

sylphe (silf) *m*, **sylphide** (fid) *f*, sylph.

sylvestre (silvɛstr) *a*, woodland (*att*.). **sylviculture** (vikylty:r) *f*, forestry.

symbole (sɛ̃bɔl) *m*, symbol. *le* ~ [*des apôtres*], the [Apostles'] Creed. **symbolique** (lik) *a*, symbolic(al). **symboliser** (ze) *v.t*, to symbolize.

symétrie (simetri) *f*, symmetry. **symétrique†** (trik) *a*, symmetric(al).

sympa (sɛ̃pa) *a*, likable, attractive.

sympathie (sɛ̃pati) *f*, sympathy, fellow feeling; (*pl.*) (*one's*) likes.

sympathique (tik) *a*, sympathetic; congenial; likable; invisible (*ink*).
sympathiser (tize) *v.i*, to sympathize.
symphonie (sɛ̃fɔni) *f*, symphony.
symptôme (sɛ̃ptoːm) *m*, symptom.
synagogue (sinagɔg) *f*, synagogue.
synchrone (sɛ̃krɔn) *a*, synchronous.
syncope (sɛ̃kɔp) *f*, syncope; syncopation. **syncoper** (pe) *v.t*, to syncopate.
syndic (sɛ̃dik) *m*, syndic; trustee; assignee (*bankruptcy*); agent. **syndicaliste** (kalist) *m*, trade unionist. **syndicat** (ka) *m*, trusteeship; syndicate; association, federation; labor union. ~ *de placements*, pool (*Fin*.). ~ *d'initiative*, tourist information bureau. **syndicataire** (tɛːr) *m*, member of a syndicate; underwriter (*Fin*.). **syndiquer** (ke) *v.t*, to syndicate.
synode (sinɔd) *m*, synod.
synonyme (sinɔnim) *a*, synonymous. ¶ *m*, synonym.
syntaxe (sɛ̃taks) *f*, syntax.
synthèse (sɛ̃tɛːz) *f*, synthesis. **synthétique**† (tetik) *a*, synthetic(al).
Syrie (**la**) (siri), Syria. **syrien, ne** (rjɛ̃, ɛn) *a*. & S~, *n*, Syrian.
systématique† (sistematik) *a*, systematic; hidebound (*fig*.). **système** (tɛm) *m*, system; plan. *le ~ D* (*de la debrouillardise*), resourcefulness, ability to manage.

T

ta *see* ton.
tabac (taba) *m*, tobacco; tobacco shop. *passer à* ~, to beat up (*slang*). ~ *à priser*, snuff. **tabatière** (batjɛːr) *f*, snuffbox; skylight.
tabasser (tabase) *v.t*, to beat up (*slang*).
tabernacle (tabɛrnakl) *m*, tabernacle.
table (tabl) *f*, table; telephone switchboard; slab; tablet; list; index. ~ *à pied central*, pedestal table. ~ *à rallonge(s)*, leaf t. ~

alphabétique, alphabetical list; a. table; index (*book*). ~ *d'harmonie*, soundboard (*Mus*.). ~ *de jeu*, gaming table; card t. ~ *de nuit*, ~ *de chevet*, bedside t. ~ *des hors-texte*, list of plates. ~ *des matières*, contents (*book*). ~ *gigogne* (ʒigɔɲ), nested table, nest of 3 tables. ~ *rase*, tablet for inscription; open mind; clean sweep (*fig*.). *se mettre à* ~, to sit down to table; confess (*slang*). **tableau** (blo) *m*, board; picture; view; tableau; curtain!; scene; list, table; roll, rolls; panel; bag (*of game*). ~ *d'autel*, altarpiece. ~ *de bord*, dashboard. ~ *de commande, de connexions*, control panel (*computers*). ~ *de distribution*, switchboard. ~ *noir*, blackboard. **tablette** (blet) *f*, shelf; slab; cake, tablet, lozenge. ~ *de cheminée*, mantel-shelf. **tabletterie** (tri) *f*, fancy goods (*ivory, inlay*). **tablier** (blie) *m*, apron; board (*chess*); floor, deck (*of bridge*). ~ [*d'enfant*], pinafore.
tabou (tabu) *m*, taboo. *il est* ~, he, it, is taboo.
tabouret (taburɛ) *m*, stool; footstool; stocks (*Hist*.); shepherd's purse. ~ *de piano*, music stool, piano s.
tache (taʃ) *f*, stain, spot, speck, blot, blemish, stigma, taint. ~ *d'humidité*, damp mark (*in books*). ~ *de naissance*, birthmark. ~ *de rousseur*, freckle. ~ *de vin*, portwine mark, birthmark.
tâche (taːʃ) *f*, task; job. *à la* ~, piecework.
tacher (taʃe) *v.t*, to stain, spot; sully.
tâcher (taʃe) *v.i*, to try, endeavor; strive. **tâcheron** (ʃrɔ̃) *m*, jobber.
tacheter (taʃte) *v.t*, to spot, speckle.
tachymètre (takimɛtr) *m*, speedometer.
tacite† (tasit) *a*, tacit, implied.
taciturne (tasityrn) *a*, taciturn, silent.
tacot (tako) *m*, jalopy; has-been (*sports journalism*).
tact (takt) *m*, touch; tact.
tacticien (taktisjɛ̃) *m*, tactician.

tactile (taktil) *a*, tactile, tactual.

tactique (taktik) *a*, tactical. ¶ *f*, tactics.

tadorne (tadɔrn) *m*, sheldrake.

taffetas (taftɑ) *m*, taffeta. ~ *d'Angleterre*, ~ *gommée*, court plaster; adhesive tape.

tafia (tafja) *m*, tafia. ~ *de laurier*, bay rum.

Tage (le) (taːȝ), the Tagus.

taïaut (tajo) *i*, tally-ho!

taie (tɛ) *f*, case, slip (*pillow*); cover (*cushion*).

taillade (tajad) *f*, cut, slash, gash. **taillader** (de) *v.t*, to slash, slit, gash; whittle.

taillanderie (tajɑ̃dri) *f*, edge tools. **taillandier** (dje) *m*, toolmaker. **taillant** (jɑ̃) *m*, [cutting] edge. **taille** (tɑːj) *f*, cutting; cut; pruning; edge (*sword*); height, stature; size; shape; waist; tally [stick]. ~-*crayon*, *m*, pencil sharpener. ~-*douce*, *f*, copperplate [engraving]. ~ *hors série*, outsize. ~-*mer*, *m*, cutwater (*bow*). *il n'est pas de* ~, he's not up to it (*job*, *etc.*). **tailler** (tɑje) *v.t*, to cut; cut out; prune; trim; clip; dress; hew; carve; sharpen, point. ~ *une plume* or *une pipe*, to practice fellatio (*obscene*). se ~, to take off, beat it, escape. **tailleur** (tɑjœːr) *m*, cutter; hewer; tailor; tailored suit; (*att.*) tailormade, tailored. **taillis** (ji) *m*, copse, coppice; brushwood, underwood. **tailloir** (tajwaːr) *m*, trencher (*platter*).

tain (tɛ̃) *m*, silvering (*for mirror*), foil.

taire (tɛːr) *v.t.ir*, to say nothing about; not to mention; leave unsaid; conceal. *faire* ~, to silence, hush. se ~, to hold one's tongue, be silent.

talc (talk) *m*, talc; French chalk; talcum.

talent (talɑ̃) *m*, talent; faculty; gift.

talion (taljɔ̃) *m*, talion, retaliation, eye for eye.

talisman (talismɑ̃) *m*, talisman.

talle (tal) *f*, sucker (*Hort.*).

taloche (talɔʃ) *f*, cuff, clout.

talon (talɔ̃) *m*, heel; butt (*cue*);

counterfoil; (*pl. fig.*) footsteps. ~ *rouge* (*fig.*), aristocratic. **talonner** (lɔne) *v.t*, to follow on the heels of, dog; dun; spur on. **talonnette** (nɛt) *f*, heel piece; heel (*rubber*).

talus (taly) *m*, slope, batter; bank.

tamarin (tamarɛ̃) *m*, tamarind.

tambour (tɑ̃buːr) *m*, drum; drummer; barrel; tambour; frame. ~ *de basque*, tambourine. ~-*major*, drum major. **tambouriner** (burine) *v.i*, to drum; thrum; (*v.t.*) to cry (*news*); cry up.

tamis (tami) *m*, sieve; sifter; strainer; gauze.

Tamise (la) (tamiːz), the Thames.

tamiser (tamize) *v.t*, to sift; strain; subdue (*light*).

tampon (tɑ̃pɔ̃) *m*, plug; bung; tampion; rubber stamp; wad; pad; buffer. **tamponner** (pɔne) *v.t*, to plug; pad; dab; collide with.

tam-tam (tamtam) *m*, tomtom; gong.

tan (tɑ̃) *m*, tan, bark (*tanners'*).

tancer (tɑ̃se) *v.t*, to scold.

tandem (tɑ̃dɛm) *m*, tandem (*carriage, cycle*).

tandis que (tɑ̃di[s]) *c*, while, whilst; whereas.

tangage (tɑ̃gaːȝ) *m*, pitching (*ship*).

tangent, e (tɑ̃ȝɑ̃, ɑ̃ːt) *a*, tangent[ial]. ¶ *f*, tangent.

Tanger (tɑ̃ȝe) *m*, Tangier.

tangible (tɑ̃ȝibl) *a*, tangible.

tango (tɑ̃go) *m*, tango.

tanguer (tɑ̃ge) *v.i*, to pitch (*ship*).

tanière (tanjɛːr) *f*, den, lair; hole, earth.

tannin (tanɛ̃) *m*, tannin. **tanne** (tan) *f*, blackhead. **tanné, e** (ne) *p.a*, tanned; tan[-colored]. **tanner** (ne) *v.t*, to tan, cure; tire, bore. **tannerie** (nri) *f*, tannery, tan yard. **tanneur** (nœːr) *m*, tanner.

tant (tɑ̃) *ad*, so much; so many; such; so; as much; as well [as]; as long; as far. ~ *pis*, ~ *mieux*, so much the worse, so much the better. ~ *soit peu*, ever so little. ~ *s'en faut*, far from it.

tantale (tɑ̃tal) *m*, tantalum.

tante (tɑ̃:t) *f*, aunt; homosexual (*pejorative*). ma ~, pawnshop (*slang*).

tantième (tɑ̃tjɛm) *m*, percentage.

tantinet (tɑ̃tinɛ) *m*, tiny bit, little bit, dash.

tantôt (tɑ̃to) *ad*, soon, presently, anon, by & by; in the afternoon; just now; sometimes, now.

taon (tɑ̃) *m*, gadfly, horsefly.

tapage (tapa:ʒ) *m*, noise, uproar, disturbance, row; fuss, ado, stir. **tapageur, euse** (paʒœ:r, ø:z) *a*, noisy, rowdy, uproarious; loud, flash[y], showy, garish. ¶ *n*, roisterer, rowdy, brawler.

tape (tap) *f*, tap, rap, pat, slap. **tapé, e** (pe) *p.a*, dried (*apples, etc, in rings*); smart (*answer*). **tapecul** (pky) *m*, jigger (*sail*); rattletrap. **tapée** (pe) *f*, heaps, swarm. **taper** (pe) *v.t. & abs*, to tap, smack, slap; beat; pat; type-[write]; stamp (*foot*).

tapette (tapɛt) *f*, bat; carpet beater; homosexual (*slang*).

tapin (tapɛ̃) *m*, prostitute, whore (*slang*).

tapinois (en) (tapinwa) *ad*, stealthily.

tapioca (tapjɔka) *m*, tapioca.

tapir (tapi:r) *m*, tapir.

tapir (se) (tapi:r) *v.pr*, to squat, crouch, cower; nestle.

tapis (tapi) *m*, carpet; tapis; cloth; cover. ~-*brosse, m*, doormat. ~ *de gazon*, [green]sward. ~ *roulant*, assembly line. ~ *vert*, green baize; gaming table. **tapisser (se)** (se) *v.t*, to hang with tapestry; paper (*wall*); cover, line; carpet (*with flowers*). **tapisserie** (sri) *f*, tapestry, hangings, arras; tapestry work; rug work. *faire* ~, to be a wallflower (*dance*). **tapissier, ère** (sje, ɛ:r) *n*, tapestry maker; upholsterer. ¶ *f*, delivery truck.

tapon (tapɔ̃) *m*, knot, tangle.

tapoter (tapɔte) *v.t*, to tap; strum, thrum.

taquet (takɛ) *m*, stop, block; cleat (*rope*).

taquin, e (takɛ̃, in) *n*, tease. **taquiner** (kine) *v.t. & i*, to tease, torment; worry.

tarabiscoter (tarabiskɔte) *v.t*, to groove (*moldings, etc.*); over-decorate.

tarabuster (tarabyste) *v.t*, to pester, worry, plague.

taraud (taro) *m*, (*screw*) tap. **taraudage** (da:ʒ) *m*, screw cutting, tapping, threading. **tarauder** (de) *v.t*, to tap, screw, thread.

tard (ta:r) *ad*, late; later. *sur le* ~, late in the day; late in life. **tarder** (tarde) *v.i*, to delay, be long; loiter; (*v.imp*.) to long. **tardif, ive†** (dif, i:v) *a*, tardy, belated; late; slow, sluggish; backward. **tardiveté** (divte) *f*, lateness, backwardness.

tare (ta:r) *f*, defect; taint; tare (*Com.*).

taré, e (tare) *p.a*, damaged, tainted; defective (*child*); depraved.

tarentelle (tarɑ̃tɛl) *f*, tarantella. **tarentule** (tyl) *f*, tarantula.

tarer (tare) *v.t*, to spoil, damage; tare (*Com.*).

targette (tarʒɛt) *f*, bolt (*door*).

targuer (se) de (targe), to pride oneself on, plume oneself on.

tarière (tarjɛ:r) *f*, auger.

tarif (tarif) *m*, tariff, rate, rates, scale; price list; fare. **tarifer** (fe) *v.t*, to tariff, rate, price.

tarin (tarɛ̃) *m*, siskin.

tarir (tari:r) *v.t. & i*, to dry up; stop. **tarissable** (sabl) *a*, likely to run dry, out.

Tarragone (taragɔn) *f*, Tarragona.

tarse (tars) *m*, tarsus.

tartan (tartɑ̃) *m*, tartan (*cloth, garment*).

tarte (tart) *f*, tart, pie; slap, smack. **tartine** (tin) *f*, slice of bread & butter; bread & jam; rigmarole, screed.

tartre (tartr) *m*, tartar; scale, fur. **tartrique** (trik) *a*, tartaric.

tartufe (tartyf) *m*, sanctimonious hypocrite.

tas (tɑ) *m*, heap, pile; pack; cock (*hay*); shock, mow; stake [anvil].

Tasmanie (la) (tasmani), Tasmania.

tasse (tɑ:s) *f*, cup; mug. ~ *à café*,

coffee cup. ~ *de café*, cup of coffee.

tassé, e (tɑse) *p.a*, squat, dumpy.

tasseau (tɑso) *m*, strip, cleat.

tassement (tɑsmɑ̃) *m*, settling, sinking; setback. **tasser (se)** *v.t*, to press down; squeeze; (*v.i.*) to grow thick. **se ~**, to settle, sink; settle down; have a setback.

tâter (tɑte) *v.t*, to feel, touch; try; taste. *en ~*, to know how to go about it. **se ~**, to feel for a bruise, think it over.

tatillon, ne (tatijɔ̃, ɔn) *n*, fusser; busybody. **tatillonner** (jɔne) *v.i*, to fuss, meddle.

tâtonnement (tɑtɔnmɑ̃) *m*, groping; tentative effort; (*pl.*) trial & error. **tâtonner** (ne) *v.i*, to grope; fumble. **à tâtons** (tɔ̃) *ad*, gropingly; warily.

tatou (tatu) *m*, armadillo.

tatouage (tatwaːʒ) *m*, tattooing; tattoo (*on skin*). **tatouer** (twe) *v.t*, to tattoo.

taudis (todi) *m*, hovel; slum.

taule (toːl) *f*, prison, jail (*slang*).

taupe (toːp) *f*, mole (*Zool.*); moleskin. **taupière** (topjɛːr) *f*, mole trap. **taupinière** (pinjɛːr) *f*, molehill; mean dwelling, hovel.

taureau (tɔro) *m*, bull.

tauromachie (tɔrɔmaʃi) *f*, bullfighting.

tautologie (totɔlɔʒi) *f*, tautology.

taux (to) *m*, rate, price. ~ *officiel* [*d'escompte*], bank rate.

taverne (tavɛrn) *f*, tavern.

taxation (taksasjɔ̃) *f*, taxation, rating; assessment; charges. **taxe** (taks) *f*, tax rate, duty, due; charge, fee. ~ *de séjour*, visitors' tax. **taxer** (kse) *v.t*, to tax, rate, assess; charge with duty; charge [for]; fix the minimum price of; accuse.

taxi (taksi) *m*, taxi [cab].

tchécoslovaque (tʃekɔslɔvak) *a*. & T~, *n*, Czechoslovak. **Tchécoslovaquie** (ki) *f*, Czechoslovakia. **tchèque** (tʃɛk) *a*. & (*language*) *m*. & T~ (*pers.*) *n*, Czech.

te, t' (tə, t) *pn*, you, yourself, thee, thyself.

té (te) *m*, T, tee. ~ [*à dessin*], T square.

technique† (tɛknik) *a*, technical. ¶ *f*, technique. **technologie** (nɔlɔʒi) *f*, technology.

technocratie (tɛknɔkrasi) *f*, technocracy.

teck (tɛk) *m*, teak.

tégument (tegymɑ̃) *m*, tegument.

teigne (tɛɲ) *f*, moth; ringworm.

teindre (tɛ̃dr) *v.t.ir*, to dye; stain; tincture. **teint** (tɛ̃) *m*, dye, color; complexion. **teinte** (tɛ̃ːt) *f*, tint, shade, hue; tinge, touch, strain. **teinter** (tɛ̃te) *v.t*, to tint; tone (*paper*); fume (*wood*); tinge. **teinture** (tyːr) *f*, dyeing; dye; tinge; smattering; tincture. **teinturerie** (tyri) *f*, dyeing; dye works. **teinturier, ère** (tyrje, ɛːr) *n*, dyer [& cleaner].

tel, telle (tɛl) *a*, such; like; as; so. ¶ *pn*, such a one, some. *un tel, une telle*, so-&-so. *tel que*, such, as. ~ *quel*, as it is.

télécommande (telekɔmɑ̃ːd) *f*, remote control. *dispositif de ~*, remote control system. **télécommander** (de) *v.t*, to telecommand.

télédétection (teledetɛksjɔ̃) *f*, remote sensing.

télégramme (telegram) *m*, telegram, wire. **télégraphe** (graf) *m*, telegraph. **télégraphie** (fi) *f*, telegraphy. ~ *sans fils*, (*abb.* T.S.F.), wireless t., radio. **télégraphier** (fje) *v.t*. & *abs*, to telegraph, wire. **télégraphique†** (fik) *a*, telegraphic, telegraph (*att.*).

téléguider (telegide) *v.t*, to radio-control; operate by remote control.

téléimprimeur (teleɛ̃primœːr) *m*, teleprinter, teletypewriter.

téléinformatique (teleɛ̃formatik) *f*, data communication.

télémètre (telemɛtr) *m*, range finder.

téléobjectif (telebʒɛktif) *m*, telephoto lens, telelens.

télépathie (telepati) *f*, telepathy.

téléphone (telefɔn) *m*, telephone. ~ *rouge*, "hot line" between White House & Kremlin. **téléphoner** (ne) *v.t*. & *abs*, to telephone. **téléphonie** (ni) *f*, telephony. **téléphonique** (nik) a, telephonic, telephone (att.).

télescope (teleskɔp) m, [reflecting] telescope. se **télescoper** (pe) v.pr, to telescope (trains). **télescopique** (pik) a, telescopic; minor (planet).

téléspectateur (telespɛktatœːr) m, televiewer.

télétraitement (teletrɛtmɑ̃) m, teleprocessing. ~ par lots, remote batch processing (computers).

téléviser (televize) v.t, to televise. **téléviseur** (vizœr) m, television set. **télévision** (vizjɔ̃) f, television.

tellement (tɛlmɑ̃) ad, so, in such a way.

téméraire† (temerɛːr) a, rash, reckless, foolhardy. **témérité** (rite) f, temerity, rashness.

témoignage (temwaɲaːʒ) m, testimony, evidence, witness; mark, token. **témoigner** (ɲe) v.i. & t, to testify, bear witness, give evidence; evince, show, prove. **témoin** (mwɛ̃) m, witness; second (duel); telltale, pilot (lamp, etc.); baton (relay race). ~ à charge, witness for the prosecution. ~ à décharge, w. for the defense. ~ muet, circumstantial evidence.

tempe (tɑ̃ːp) m, temple (Anat.).

tempérament (tɑ̃peramɑ̃) m, temperament, constitution. à ~, installment buying.

tempérance (tɑ̃perɑ̃ːs) f, temperance. **tempérant, e** (rɑ̃, ɑ̃ːt) a, temperate.

température (tɑ̃peratyːr) f, temperature. **tempéré, e** (re) a, temperate; limited (monarchy). **tempérer** (re) v.t, to temper, moderate.

tempête (tɑ̃pɛːt) f, storm, tempest. à la ~, at stormy (barometer). **tempêter** (pɛte) v.i, to storm, fume. **tempétueux, euse** (petɥø, ø:z) a, tempestuous, stormy; boisterous.

temple (tɑ̃ːpl) m, temple; church.

temporaire† (tɑ̃pɔrɛːr) a, temporary. **temporel, le**† (rɛl) a, temporal. **temporiser** (rize) v.i, to temporize. **temps** (tɑ̃; in liaison, tɑ̃z) m, time; while; times, days,

age; season; weather; tense (Gram.); beat (Mus.); phase. quel ~ fait-il? what's the weather? au ~! as you were! en ~ & lieu, in due course. ~ mort, idle time (computers). ~ réel, real t. (computers). ~ de panne, down t. (computers). partage de ~, timesharing (computers).

tenable (tənabl) a, tenable; bearable.

tenace (tənas) a, tenacious; adhesive; tough, stiff; stubborn; retentive. **ténacité** (tenasite) f, tenacity.

tenaille (tənɑːj) f, tongs; (pl.) pincers. **tenailler** (naje) v.t, to be gnawed at, racked by (remorse, hunger).

tenancier, ère (tənɑ̃sje, ɛːr) n, keeper; lessee. **tenant** (nɑ̃) m, champion, supporter.

tendance (tɑ̃dɑ̃ːs) f, tendency, trend. **tendancieux, euse** (dɑ̃sjø, ø:z) a, tendentious; leading (question).

tender (tɑ̃dɛːr) m, tender (locomotive).

tendeur (tɑ̃dœːr) m, layer (carpets); setter (traps); strainer, stretcher, tightener.

tendon (tɑ̃dɔ̃) m, tendon, sinew.

tendre (tɑ̃ːdr) v.t, to stretch, tighten, strain; bend (bow); crane (neck); hold out (hand, etc.); pitch (tent); lay, spread, set; drape; (v.i.) to tend, lead, conduce.

tendre† (tɑ̃ːdr) a, tender, soft; sensitive; new (bread); early (youth); fond. **tendresse** (tɑ̃drɛs) f, tenderness, fondness, love; (pl.) caresses. **tendreté** (drəte) f, tenderness (meat). **tendron** (drɔ̃) m, tender shoot; gristle (veal); maiden.

tendu, e (tɑ̃dy) p.a, tense, taut, tight.

ténèbres (tenɛːbr) f.pl, dark[ness], gloom. **ténébreux, euse**† (nebrø, ø:z) a, dark, murky; gloomy; obscure.

teneur, euse (tənœːr, ø:z) n, holder. **teneur**, f, tenor, purport; terms; content[s], percentage; grade (ore).

ténia (tenja) *m*, tapeworm.

tenir (təni;r) *v.t.ir*, to hold; h. on; keep; have; contain; take; t. up (*space*); consider; (*v.i.ir*.) to hold; last; cling; border on; owe; partake, savor, be like; be owing to; rest, lie; be anxious; sit. ~ *tête à*, to resist. se ~, to keep; stand; sit; stick; contain oneself. *à quoi s'en tenir*, what to believe in.

tennis (tenis) *m*, [lawn] tennis; t. court.

tenon (tənɔ̃) *m*, tenon.

ténor (tenɔ;r) *m*, tenor (*voice, singer*).

tension (tɑ̃sjɔ̃) *f*, tension; tightness; strain; pressure; voltage. ~ *artérielle*, blood pressure.

tentacule (tɑ̃takyl) *m*, tentacle, feeler.

tentateur, trice (tɑ̃tatœ;r, tris) *n*, tempter, temptress. **tentation** (sjɔ̃) *f*, temptation.

tentative (tɑ̃tati;v) *f*, attempt, endeavor. ~ *d'assassinat*, attempted murder.

tente (tɑ̃;t) *f*, tent; awning. ~ *conique*, bell tent. ~ *de plage*, bathing t. ~*-pavillon*, *f*, marquee. *dresser une* ~, to pitch a t.

tenter (tɑ̃te) *v.t*, to attempt, try; tempt.

tenture (tɑ̃ty;r) *f*, hangings; wallpaper.

tenu, e (təny) *p.a*, (*well, ill*) kept; neat, trim; (*to be*) bound (*à* = to); firm (*price*). ¶ *m*, hold (*Box.*). ¶ *f*, holding; keeping; bearing, carriage, behavior; seat (*on horse*); dress, clothes, uniform, order; firmness. ~ *de ville*, street dress.

ténu, e (təny) *a*, thin, slender, tenuous, fine; watery (*fluid*). **ténuité** (nɥite) *f*, thinness.

tercet (tersɛ) *m*, tercet, triplet (*Pros., Mus.*).

térébenthine (terebɑ̃tin) *f*, turpentine.

tergiverser (tergiverse) *v.i*, to be shifty, beat around the bush.

terme (term) *m*, term, end; time; date; account, settlement (*Stk Ex.*); quarter (*year*), q.'s rent; installment. **terminaison** (minɛzɔ̃) *f*, termination, ending. **terminer**
(ne) *v.t*, to terminate, end, wind up. **terminus** (nyːs) *m*, terminus (*Rly.*).

termite (termit) *m*, termite, white ant.

terne (tern) *a*, dull, lusterless, drab. **ternir** (niːr) *v.t*, to tarnish, dull; dim; sully.

terrain (terɛ̃) *m*, ground, land; field; site; course, links (*golf*); court (*croquet*). ~ *d'aviation*, airfield.

terrasse (teras) *f*, terrace, bank; flat roof; [pavement] outside (*café*). **terrassement** (smɑ̃) *m*, earthwork. **terrasser** (se) *v.t*, to bank up; throw, floor. **terrassier** (sje) *m*, day laborer; earthwork contractor.

terre (tɛ;r) *f*, earth; ground; land; soil; estate; loam; clay; shore (*Naut.*); world. ~ *battue*, hard court (*Ten.*). ~ *cuite*, terra-cotta. ~ *d'ombre*, umber. *la T*~ *de Feu*, Tierra del Fuego. ~ *de Sienne brûlée*, burnt sienna. ~ *à* ~, commonplace. *la* ~ *ferme*, the continent, the mainland; terra firma. *T*~ *Sainte*, Holy Land. *ventre à* ~, at full speed. **terreau** (tɛro) *m*, [vegetable] mold. ~ *de feuilles*, leaf m. **Terre-Neuve**, *f*, Newfoundland. **terre-neuve**, *m*, N. [dog]. **terre-plein**, *m*, open space; roadbed (*Rly.*); terrace. **terrer** (tɛre) *v.t*, to earth up; (*v.i.*) to burrow. **se** ~, to burrow; entrench oneself. **terrestre** (restr) *a*, terrestrial; ground (*att.*); land (*att.*); earthy.

terreur (tɛrœ;r) *f*, terror, dread.

terreux, euse (tɛrø, ø;z) *a*, earthy; dull.

terrible† (teribl) *a*, terrible, terrific; dreadful.

terrien, ne (terjɛ̃, ɛn) *a. & n*, landed (proprietor); (*m.*) landsman. **terrier** (rje) *m*, burrow, hole; earth (*fox*); terrier (*dog*).

terrifier (terifje) *v.t*, to terrify.

terrine (terin) *f*, [earthenware] pot, pan; (*pl.*) potted meats. **terrinée** (ne) *f*, panful.

territoire (teritwaːr) *m*, territory. **territorial, e** (torjal) *a. & m*, territorial. **terroir** (rwaːr) *m*, soil.

terroriser (tɛrɔrize) *v.t,* to terror-ize.

tertre (tɛrtr) *m,* hillock, knoll, mound. *~ de départ,* teeing ground (*golf*).

tes *see* **ton.**

Tessin (le) (tɛsɛ̃), the Ticino.

tesson (tɛsɔ̃) *m,* piece of broken glass *or* earthenware, potsherd.

testament (tɛstamɑ̃) *m,* will, tes-tament. **testamentaire** (tɛ:r) *a,* testamentary. **testateur, trice** (tœ:r, tris) *n,* testator, trix. **tester** (te) *v.i,* to make one's will.

testicule (tɛstikyl) *m,* testicle.

tétanos (tetanɔs) *m,* tetanus, lock-jaw.

têtard (tɛta:r) *m,* tadpole; pollard. **tête** (tɛ:t) *f,* head; top; face; lead; brains; wits. *~-à-~, m,* pri-vate interview, p. conversation; 2-cup tea set; sofa. *~ de linotte,* feather-brained person. *~ forte, forte ~,* good head, strong-minded person. *faire la ~ à quel-qu'un,* to frown at someone. *faire une ~,* to look unhappy. *faire à sa ~,* to have one's own way.

téter (tete) *v.t. & abs,* to suck (*of child*).

têtière (tɛtjɛ:r) *f,* infant's cap; headstall; chair back.

tétin (tetɛ̃) *m,* nipple, pap, teat (*pers.*). **tétine** (tin) *f,* dug; nip-ple (*nursing bottle*). **téton** (tɔ̃) *m,* breast (*of woman*).

tétras (tetrɑ) *m,* grouse.

tette (tɛt) *f,* dug, teat (*animal*).

têtu, e (tety) *a,* stubborn, mulish.

teuton, ne (tøtɔ̃, ɔn) *& teutoni-que** (tɔnik) *a,* Teutonic.

texte (tɛkst) *m,* text. *~ [composé],* letterpress.

textile (tɛkstil) *a. & m,* textile.

textuel, le† (tɛkstɥɛl) *a,* textual.

texture (tɛksty:r) *f,* texture; ar-rangement.

thaumaturge (tomatyrʒ) *n,* mir-acle worker; magician.

thé (te) *m,* tea; t. plant; t. party. *~ complet,* tea, roll & butter. *~ de viande,* beef tea.

théâtral, e† (teatral) *a,* theatri-cal; dramatic. **théâtre** (ɑ:tr) *m,*

theater, playhouse; stage; drama; scene; seat (*as of war*).

théière (tejɛ:r) *f,* teapot.

théisme (teism) *m,* theism.

thème (tɛm) *m,* theme; topic; exercise, composition (*Sch.*); stem (*Gram.*).

théodolite (teɔdɔlit) *m,* theo-dolite.

théologie (teɔlɔʒi) *f,* theology. **théologien, ne** (ʒjɛ̃, ɛn) *n,* theo-logian, divine. **théologique†** (ʒik) *a,* theological.

théorème (teɔrɛm) *m,* theorem. **théoricien** (risjɛ̃) *m,* theorist. **théorie** (ri) *f,* theory; procession (*poetic*). **théorique†** (rik) *a,* the-oretic(al).

théosophie (teɔzɔfi) *f,* theosophy.

thérapeutique (terapøtik) *a,* therapeutic; apothecaries' (*meas-ure, weight*). ¶ *f,* therapeutics.

thermal, e (tɛrmal) *a,* thermal, hot. **thermes** (tɛrm) *m.pl,* ther-mal baths.

thermomètre (tɛrmɔmɛtr) *m,* thermometer. *~ médical,* clini-cal thermometer.

thésauriser (tezɔrize) *v.i,* to hoard.

thèse (tɛ:z) *f,* thesis, argument.

thon (tɔ̃) *m,* tuna.

thorax (tɔraks) *m,* thorax.

thune (tyn) *f,* 5-franc coin (*slang*).

thym (tɛ̃) *m,* thyme.

thyroïde (tiroid) *a,* thyroid.

tiare (tja:r) *f,* tiara.

tibia (tibja) *m,* tibia, shinbone; shin.

Tibre (le) (tibr), the Tiber.

tic (tik) *m,* tic; twitching; habit, mannerism, trick.

tic tac (tiktak) *m,* tick[-tack], pit-[a-]pat.

tiède† (tjɛd) *a,* tepid, lukewarm. **tiédeur** (tjedœ:r) *f,* tepidness, etc. **tiédir** (di:r) *v.i,* to become tepid.

tien, ne (*with* **le, la, les**) (tjɛ̃, ɛn) *pn. & m,* yours, thine, thy own.

tiens (tjɛ̃) *v. abs. imperative,* well! indeed!

tiercé (tjɛrse) *m,* three-horse bet.

tiers, tierce (tjɛ:r, ɛrs) *a,* third. ¶ *m,* third person, t. party. ¶ *f,* third. **tiers arbitre,** *m,* referee.

tige (ti:3) *f*, stem, stalk; trunk (*tree*); shaft; shank, leg (*boot, stocking*); rod.

tignasse (tiɲas) *f*, shock, mop (*hair*).

tigre, tigresse (tigr, grɛs) *n*, tiger, tigress. le Tigre, the Tigris. **tigré, e** (gre) *a*, striped, tabby.

tillac (tijak) *m*, deck (*ship*).

tille (ti:j) *f*, bast, bass. **tilleul** (tijœl) *m*, lime [tree], linden [tree]; lime blossom.

timbale (tɛbal) *f*, kettledrum; cup (*metal*).

timbrage (tɛbra:3) *m*, stamping. **timbre** (tɛ:br) *m*, stamp; bell; gong; timbre; postmark. ~ *humide*, pad stamp, rubber s. ~ [-*poste*], *m*, [postage] s. ~-*quittance*, *m*, receipt s. ~ *sec*, ~ *fixe*, embossed s., impressed s. **timbré, e** (tɛbre) *p.a*, stamped; cracked, nuts (*pers.*). **timbrer** (bre) *v.t*, to stamp; postmark.

timide† (timid) *a*, timid; nervous; shy, bashful, diffident. **timidité** (dite) *f*, timidity.

timon (timɔ̃) *m*, pole (*carriage*); helm (*fig.*). **timonier** (monje) *m*, helmsman; signalman (*Naut.*); quartermaster (*Naut.*).

timoré, e (timɔre) *a*, timorous.

tinctorial, e (tɛ̃ktɔrjal) *a*, dye (*stuffs, etc.*).

tine (tin) *f*, butt, cask; tub.

tintamarre (tɛ̃tama:r) *m*, din, racket, noise.

tinter (tɛ̃te) *v.i. & t*, to ring, toll; tinkle; jingle; clink; chink; tingle, buzz. **tintement** (tmɑ̃) *m*, ringing, etc; singing (*ears*).

tintouin (tɛ̃twɛ̃) *m*, trouble, worry.

tipule (tipyl) *f*, daddy-longlegs, crane fly.

tique (tik) *f*, tick (*insect*). **tiquer** (ke) *v.i*, to twitch; wince.

tiqueté, e (tikte) *a*, speckled, variegated.

tir (ti:r) *m*, shooting; musketry; gunnery; fire, firing; rifle range; shooting gallery. ~ *à l'arc*, archery. *à* ~ *d'aile*, at full speed.

tirade (tirad) *f*, tirade; long speech (*Theat.*).

tirage (tira:3) *m*, drawing; pull[ing]; draft; towing; tow[ing] path; extension (*camera*); printing; hard copy (*computers*); circulation (*news*). ~ *au sort*, drawing lots.

tiraillement (tirɑjmɑ̃) *m*, tugging; gnawing (*stomach*); wrangling. **tirailler** (je) *v.t*, to tug, pull; pester; (*v.i.*) to blaze away. **tirailleur** (jœ:r) *m*, skirmisher; sharpshooter, rifleman; freelance.

tirant (tirɑ̃) *m*, string, strap; tie; tag; stay; sinew (*meat*).

tire (tir) *comps, all m*: ~-*botte*, bootjack. ~-*bouchon*, corkscrew. ~-*bouton*, buttonhook. ~-*feu*, lanyard (*gun*). ~-*ligne*, drawing pen.

tiré, e (tire) *p.a*, drawn, pinched, haggard. ~ *à quatre épingles*, spick & span, dapper. ~ *par les cheveux*, farfetched.

tirelire (tirli:r) *f*, piggy bank.

tirer (tire) *v.t. & i*, to draw; pull; drag; tug; haul; get, derive; take; wreak; put out (*tongue*); raise; doff (*hat*); milk (*cow*); fire; shoot, let off; print, machine; incline; verge. ~ [*à pile ou face*], to toss a coin. se ~, to extricate oneself. *se* ~ *d'affaire*, to get over a difficulty. *s'en* ~, to make ends meet, get along.

tiret (tire) *m*, dash (*line*); hyphen.

tirette (tirɛt) *f*, curtain or blind cord; leaf (*table*).

tireur, euse (tirœ:r, ø:z) *n*, drawer; marksman, shot. ~ *d'armes*, fencer. ~ *de cartes*, fortune-teller. ~ *isolé*, sniper.

tiroir (tirwa:r) *m*, drawer (*table, etc.*); slide; slide valve. ~ *de caisse*, till.

tisane (tizan) *f*, infusion, (*herb*) tea.

tison (tizɔ̃) *m*, brand, firebrand. **tisonner** (zɔne) *v.t*, to meddle with the fire. **tisonnier** (nje) *m*, poker.

tissage (tisa:3) *m*, weaving. **tisser** (se) *v.t*, to weave. **tisserand** (srɑ̃) *m*, weaver. **tisseranderie** (dri) *f*, weaving [trade]. **tissu** (sy) *m*, texture, weave; textile, fabric, cloth, gauze; tissue. ~ *éponge*, toweling. **tissure** (sy:r) *f*, texture, tissue. **tistre** (tistr) *v.t.ir*, to weave.

titi (titi) *m*, street urchin.

titiller (titille) *v.t*, to titillate, tickle.

titre (titr) *m*, title; [title] deed, muniment, document; proof, evidence; status; title page; heading; certificate, scrip, warrant, bond, security, stock, share; holding; claim; fineness (*coins*); grade; strength (*solution*). à ~ d'office, ex officio. à ~ de, by right of, in virtue of, as. au ~, standard (*gold*). en ~, titular. **titré**, e (tre) *a*, titled; standard (*solution*). **titrer** (tre) *v.t*, to give a title to; titrate; assay.

tituber (titybe) *v.i*, to stagger, lurch.

titulaire (tityle:r) *a*, titular. ¶ *n*, holder; occupant; incumbent.

toast (tɔst) *m*, toast (*health*); buttered toast.

toboggan (tɔbɔgã) *m*, toboggan.

toc (tɔk) *m*, fake, sham goods.

tocsin (tɔksɛ̃) *m*, alarm bell; tocsin, hue & cry.

toge (tɔːʒ) *f*, toga; gown, robe.

tohu-bohu (tɔyboy) *m*, chaos; hurly-burly.

toi (twa) *pn*, you, thee, thou. ~-même, yourself, thyself.

toile (twal) *f*, linen; cloth; canvas; gauze; curtain (*Theat.*); sail (*Naut.*); (*pl.*) toils (*Hunt.*); 10,000 francs (*slang*). ~ à calquer, tracing cloth. ~ à matelas, tick[ing]. ~ à voiles, sailcloth, canvas. ~ cirée, oilcloth. ~ d'araignée, spider's web, cobweb. ~ de matelas, tick. ~ de ménage, homespun [linen]. ~ de sol, ground sheet. ~ écrue, ~ bise, unbleached linen. ~ huilée, vernie, oilskin. ~ ouvrée, huckaback. ~ peinte, print[ed fabric].

toilette (twalɛt) *f*, toilet, washing, dressing; dress; dressing table; washstand; lavatory.

toilier, ère (twalje, ɛ:r) *n*, linen draper.

toise (twa:z) *f*, height standard (*apparatus*); standard (*comparison*). **toiser** (twaze) *v.t*, to measure; look (*one*) up & down.

toison (twazɔ̃) *f*, fleece.

toit (twa) *m*, roof; housetop; shed. **toiture** (ty:r) *f*, roof[ing].

tôle (to:l) *f*, sheet; [sheet] iron; plate. ~ ondulée, corrugated iron. ~ de blindage, armor plate.

Tolède (tɔlɛd) *f*, Toledo.

tolérable (tɔlerabl) *a*, tolerable. **tolérance** (rã:s) *f*, tolerance; toleration; sufferance; margin, limit. maison de ~, licensed brothel. **tolérant** (rã, ã:t) *a*, tolerant. **tolérer** (re) *v.t*, to tolerate, bear, suffer.

toletière (tɔltjɛ:r) *f*, rowlock.

tollé (tɔlle) *m*, outcry, hue & cry.

tomate (tɔmat) *f*, tomato.

tombe (tɔ̃:b) *f*, tomb, grave; death (*fig.*). **tombeau** (tɔ̃bo) *m*, tomb, vault, monument; death.

tombée (tɔ̃be) *f*, fall. ~ de pluie, downpour; rainfall. **tomber** (be) *v.i*, to fall, tumble; drop; crash; flag; crumble; lapse; hang [down]; (*v.t.*) to throw (*wrestling*); damn (*a play*). ~ d'accord, to come to an agreement. ~ bien, ~ mal, to come at right, wrong, time. **tombereau** (bro) *m*, [tip] cart; cartload; tumbril. **tombola** (bɔla) *f*, raffle.

tombeur (tɔ̃bœ:r) *m*, professional wrestler; ladykiller.

Tombouctou (tɔ̃buktu) *m*, Timbuctoo.

tome (to:m) *m*, volume, tome.

ton, ta, tes (tɔ̃, ta, te) *a*, your, thy.

ton (tɔ̃) *m*, tone; tune (*fig.*); style; manners, breeding, form; [whole] tone (*in distinction from a semitone*); key (*Mus.*).

tondeur, euse (tɔ̃dœ:r, ø:z) *n*, shearer. ¶ *f*, shearing machine, shears; clippers; mower (*lawn*). **tondre** (tɔ̃:dr) *v.t*, to shear, clip, crop, mow; fleece (*pers.*).

tonique (tɔnik) *a*, tonic. ¶ *m*, tonic (*Med.*). ¶ *f*, tonic (*Mus.*), keynote.

tonitruer (tɔnitrye) *v.i*, to thunder.

tonnage (tɔna:ʒ) *m*, tonnage; burden (*ship*); shipping. **tonne** (tɔn) *f*, tun; ton. Fr. tonne = 1000 kilos. **tonneau** (no) *m*, cask, barrel, tun; butt, tub; bin; drum; governess car[t]; tonneau (*auto*); roll (*Avn.*); ton (*Ship.——Fr.*

tonneau = 1000 *kilos*). ~ *d'arrosage*, water[ing] cart. **tonnelet** (nlɛ) *m*, keg. **tonnelier** (nəlje) ʁ, cooper. **tonnelle** (nɛl) *f*, arbor, bower. **tonnellerie** (lri) *f*, cooperage.

tonner (tɔne) *v.i.* & *imp*, to thunder; boom; inveigh. **tonnerre** (nɛːr) *m*, thunder; thunderbolt; breech (*firearm*).

tonsure (tɔ̃syːr) *f*, tonsure. **tonsurer** (syre) *v.t*, to tonsure.

tonte (tɔ̃ːt) *f*, shearing; clipping; mowing.

tonton (tɔ̃tɔ̃) *m*, uncle (*children & slang*).

topaze (tɔpaːz) *f*, topaz.

toper (tɔpe) *v.t*, to agree, consent.

topinambour (tɔpinɑ̃buːr) *m*, Jerusalem artichoke.

topique (tɔpik) *a*, topical (*Med*.); local; to the point; in point.

topographie (tɔpɔgrafi) *f*, topography.

toquade (tɔkad) *f*, craze, fancy.

toque (tɔk) *f*, cap; toque.

toqué, e (tɔke) *p.a*, crazy, cracked.

torche (tɔrʃ) *f*, torch; mat, pad. **torcher** (ʃe) *v.t*, to wipe. **torchère** (ʃɛːr) *f*, cresset; floor lamp. **torchis** (ʃi) *m*, loam; cob (*Build*.). **torchon** (ʃɔ̃) *m*, dishcloth, swab, duster; twist of straw. *coup de* ~, short but violent battle; police raid.

torcol (tɔrkɔl) *m*, wryneck (*bird*).

tordant (tɔrdɑ̃) *a*, howlingly funny.

tordre (tɔrdr) *v.t*, to twist; distort; wring; wrest. **se** ~, to writhe; be convulsed (*laughing*).

toréador (tɔreadɔr) *m*, toreador.

tornade (tɔrnad) *f*, tornado.

toron (tɔrɔ̃) *m*, strand (*rope*).

torpeur (tɔrpœːr) *f*, torpor. **torpide** (pid) *a*, torpid.

torpille (tɔrpiːj) *f*, torpedo; mine (*war*). **torpiller** (pije) *v.t*, to torpedo; mine. **torpilleur** (jœːr) *m*, torpedo boat; **t. man.** *contre-*~, destroyer.

torréfier (tɔrrefje) *v.t*, to roast.

torrent (tɔrɑ̃) *m*, torrent; flood; flow; stream; rush. **torrentiel, le** (rɑ̃sjɛl), *a*, torrential.

torride (tɔrid) *a*, torrid.

tors, e (tɔːr, ɔrs) *a*, twisted; contorted; crooked; wry. **torsade** (tɔrsad) *f*, twist, coil; bullion (*fringe*). **torse** (trs) *m*, torso, trunk. **torsion** (sjɔ̃) *f*, torsion.

tort (tɔːr) *m*, wrong; fault; mistake; injury, harm. *à* ~, wrongly. *à* ~ & *à travers*, at random. *faire* ~ *à*, to wrong.

torticolis (tɔrtikɔli) *m*, crick, stiff neck.

tortillage (tɔrtijaːʒ) *m*, involved language. **tortiller** (je) *v.t*, to twist; twirl; twiddle; kink; (*v.i.*) to shuffle. **se** ~, to wriggle; writhe. **tortillon** (jɔ̃) *m*, twist; pad (*for carrier's head*); bun (*hair*).

tortionnaire (tɔrsjɔnɛːr) *a*, torturous. *appareil* ~, instrument of torture. ¶ *m*, torturer.

tortu, e (tɔrty) *a*, crooked; tortuous.

tortue (tɔrty) *f*, tortoise; tortoise shell butterfly. ~ *de mer*, turtle.

tortueux, euse† (tɔrtɥø, øːz) *a*, tortuous; winding; underhand, crooked.

torture (tɔrtyːr) *f*, torture; rack. **torturer** (tyre) *v.t*, to torture, strain. *se* ~ *l'esprit*, to rack, cudgel, one's brains.

toscan, e (tɔskɑ̃, an) *a*. & T~, *n*, Tuscan. **la Toscane**, Tuscany.

tôt (to) *ad*, soon; quickly; early, betimes. ~ *ou tard*, sooner or later. *le plus* ~ *possible*, as soon as possible.

total, e† (tɔtal) *a*. & *m*, total, whole; (*a.*) utter. **totalis[at]eur** (liz[at]œːr) *m*, totalizer; adding machine. **totalité** (te) *f*, whole, totality.

toton (tɔtɔ̃) *m*, teetotum.

toubib (tubib) *m*, doctor (*slang*).

toucan (tukɑ̃) *m*, toucan.

touchant, e (tuʃɑ̃, ɑ̃ːt) *a*, touching, moving, affecting. **touchant**, *pr*, touching, concerning, about. **touchau[d]** (ʃo) *m*, touch needle. **touche** (tuʃ) *f*, touch; hit; nibble (*fish*); key (*piano, typewriter, etc.*); finger board (*violin*); fret (*guitar, etc.*). **touche-à-tout**, *a*, meddlesome, officious. ¶ *m*, meddler, busybody, officious person.

toucher (ʃe) *m*, touch; feel. ¶ *v.t.* & *i*, to touch; feel; finger; tap; hit; strike; whip; move, affect; concern; play (*piano, etc.*); ink up (*Typ.*); draw, receive, cash; test; touch on, allude to; meddle; adjoin. **toucheur** (ʃœːr) *m*, drover.

touer (twe) *v.t*, to tow, warp (*Naut.*). **toueur** (twœːr) *m*, tug.

touffe (tuf) *f*, tuft; wisp; clump; bunch. ~ *de gazon*, divot (*golf*).

touffeur (tufœːr) *f*, stifling heat (*of room*).

touffu, e (tufy) *a*, bushy, thick; overloaded.

toujours (tuʒuːr) *ad*, always, ever; still; anyhow. ~ *vert*, evergreen. *essayez* ~, try anyway.

toupet (tupɛ) *m*, tuft of hair, forelock; cheek, impudence. *avoir du* ~, to be impudent.

toupie (tupi) *f*, [peg] top. ~ *d'Allemagne*, humming t. **toupiller** (je) *v.i*, to spin round.

tour (tuːr) *f*, tower; castle, rook (*chess*); derrick. ¶ *m*, turn; revolution; round; stroll, walk; trip, tour; spell; bout; row (*stitches*); circumference; size, measurement; lathe; wheel (*potter's*); trick; feat. ~ *de Babel* (babɛl), babel (*fig.*). ~ *de bâton*, perquisites, pickings. ~ *de cartes*, card trick. ~ *de col*, collar (*fur, etc.*). ~ *de cou*, necklet, wrap. ~ *de main*, knack; trick of the trade. *en un* ~ *de main*, in a jiffy, in a trice. ~ *de nage*, swim. ~ *de passepasse*, conjuring trick; juggle; clever trick. ~ [*de piste*], lap. ~ *de reins*, strain in the back. ~*s & retours*, twists & turns. ~ *de lancement*, launching rail. ~ *de montage*, servicing tower. *un trente-trois* ~*s*, an LP record.

tourbe (turb) *f*, peat; rabble, mob. **tourbeux, euse** (bø, øːz) *a*, peaty, boggy. **tourbière** (bjɛːr) *f*, peat bog, peatery.

tourbillon (turbijɔ̃) *m*, whirlwind; whirl, swirl; whirlpool; vortex; bustle. **tourbillonner** (jɔne) *v.i*, to whirl, swirl, eddy.

tourelle (turɛl) *f*, turret; capstan (*lathe*).

touret (turɛ) *m*, wheel; reel.

tourie (turi) *f*, carboy.

tourillon (turijɔ̃) *m*, axle, trunnion, gudgeon, journal, pin, pivot.

tourisme (turism) *m*, touring, travel for pleasure. **touriste** (rist) *n*, tourist.

tourment (turmɑ̃) *m*, torment, torture; pain; pang; worry; plague. **tourmentant, e** (tɑ̃, ɑ̃ːt) *a*, tormenting; troublesome. **tourmente** (mɑ̃ːt) *f*, storm, gale; turmoil. ~ *de neige*, blizzard. **tourmenté, e** (mɑ̃te) *p.a*, distorted; broken; labored. **tourmenter** (te) *v.t*, to torment, torture, rack; worry; plague; overelaborate.

tournage (turnaːʒ) *m*, turning (*lathe*); shooting (*cinema*).

tournailler (turnaje) *v.i*, to wander around. **tournant, e** (nɑ̃, ɑ̃ːt) *a*, turning, revolving; swing (*bridge*); winding. ¶ *m*, turning; t. space; t. point; bend; corner (*street*); eddy; shift. **tourné, e** (ne) *p.a*, turned; shaped; disposed; sour (*milk*). **tourne-à-gauche** (nagoːʃ) *m*, wrench; saw set. **tournebride** (nəbrid) *m*, roadhouse; roadside inn; somewhere to stay. **tournebroche** (nəbrɔʃ) *m*, turnspit. **tournée** (ne) *f*, round, tour; circuit. **tourner** (ne) *v.t. & i*, to turn; t. over; t. out; rotate; revolve; gyrate; swivel; hinge; swing; wind; belay; shoot (*film*); film. **tournesol** (nəsɔl) *m*, sunflower; litmus. **tourneur** (nœːr) *m*, turner. **tournevis** (nəvis) *m*, screwdriver. **tourniquet** (nikɛ) *m*, turnstile; swivel; tourniquet.

tourne-disque (turnədisk) *m*, record player; disk drive (*computers*).

tournoi (turnwa) *m*, tournament (*Hist., chess, etc.*); tourney. ~ *par élimination*, elimination tournament (*Ten.*). **tournoyer** (nwaje) *v.i*, to spin, whirl; wheel; swirl.

tournure (turnyːr) *f*, turn, course; cast; shape, figure; face.

tourte (turt) *f*, pie, tart. **tourteau** (to) *m*, oil cake.

tourtereau (turtəro) *m*, young

turtledove. **tourterelle** (tərɛl) *f*, turtledove.

tourtière (turtjɛːr) *f*, pie dish; baking tin.

Toussaint (la) (tusɛ̃), All Saints' day. *la veille de la* ~, Halloween.

tousser (tuse) *v.i*, to cough.

tout (tu) *pn*, all, everything. **le** ~, the whole, the lot. **tout**, e (tu, tut) *a.s*, **tous** (tu & tuːs) *a.m.pl*, all, the whole [of]; every; any; full; only, sole. *tout le monde*, everybody, everyone. *tout le monde descend!* everybody out! (*Rly.*). ¶ *ad*, quite; very; thoroughly; all; right; ready (*made*, *cooked*); wide; stark (*naked*); bolt (*upright*); just. ~ . . . *que*, however, [al]though. **tout**, *comps*: ~ *à coup*, suddenly, all at once. ~ *à fait*, quite; altogether; perfectly. ~ *à l'heure*, presently, by & by; just now. ~ *à vous*, yours very truly. ~ *d'un coup*, suddenly. ~ *de suite*, at once, directly. ~ *en parlant*, while speaking. **tout-à-l'égout**, *m*, main drainage. **toute-épice**, *f*, allspice. **toute-fois**, *ad*, yet, however, nevertheless, still. **toute-puissance**, *f*, omnipotence. **tout-puissant**, **toute-puissante**, *a*, almighty, omnipotent; all-powerful; overpowering. *le Tout-Puissant*, the Almighty, the Omnipotent.

toutou (tutu) *m*, bowwow, doggie.

toux (tu) *f*, cough[ing].

toxine (tɔksin) *f*, toxin. **toxique** (ksik) *a*, toxic, poisonous, poison (*gas*). ¶ *m*, poison.

trac (trak) *m*, fright; stage fright.

tracas (trakɑ) *m*, worry, bother. **tracasser** (kase) *v.t*, to worry. **tracasserie** (sri) *f*, wrangling.

trace (tras) *f*, trace; trail; track; spoor; scent; print; footprint; [foot]step; mark; weal. **tracé** (se) *m*, outline; graph; traced pattern. **tracer** (se) *v.t*, to trace; lay out; mark out; map out; draw, sketch, outline.

trachée-artère (traʃeartɛːr) *f*, trachea, windpipe.

tractation (traktasjɔ̃) *f*, dealing; bargaining.

tracteur (traktœːr) *m*, tractor. **traction** (ksjɔ̃) *f*, traction, haulage, draft; drive (*auto*). ~ *avant*, front wheel drive.

tradition (tradisjɔ̃) *f*, tradition; folklore; delivery (*law*). **traditionnel**, **le†** (sjɔnɛl) *a*, traditional.

traducteur, trice (tradyktœːr, tris) *n*, translator. **traduction** (ksjɔ̃) *f*, translation; pony, crib. **traduire** (dɥiːr) *v.t.ir*, to summon; translate; express, interpret. *se* ~, to show.

trafic (trafik) *m*, traffic; trading; trade. **trafiquant** (kɑ̃) *m*, trader, trafficker. **trafiquer** (ke) *v.i*, to traffic, trade, deal.

tragédie (traʒedi) *f*, tragedy. **tragédien**, **ne** (djɛ̃, ɛn) *n*, tragedian, tragedienne. **tragi-comédie** (ʒikɔmedi) *f*, tragicomedy. **tragicomique** (mik) *a*, tragicomic. **tragique†** (ʒik) *a*, tragic(al).

trahir (traiːr) *v.t*, to betray; reveal. **trahison** (izɔ̃) *f*, treachery; treason; betrayal.

train (trɛ̃) *m*, train, string; raft; set; suite; quarters (*horse*); pace, rate; progress; routine; mood. ~ *de paquebot*, boat train. *le* ~ [*des équipages*], the army service corps. ~ *militaire*, troop train. ~ *omnibus*, local t. ~*-poste*, *m*, mail t. ~ *d'atterrissage*, landing gear (*Avn.*); undercarriage. *en* ~ *de*, in the process of.

traînant, **e** (trɛnɑ̃, ɑ̃ːt) *a*, trailing; shambling; listless, languid; singsong. **traînard** (naːr) *m*, straggler, laggard; slowcoach. **traînasser** (nase) *v.t*, to draw out; drag out; (*v.i.*) to loiter; laze. **traîne** (trɛːn) *f*, train (*of dress*). *à la* ~, in tow. **traîneau** (trɛno) *m*, sledge, sleigh. **traînée** (ne) *f*, trail; train; ground line (*Fish.*); streetwalker. **traîner** (ne) *v.t. & i*, to drag, draw, haul; trail; draggle; drawl; lag; flag, droop; straggle; loiter; loaf. ~ *la jambe*, to shuffle along. *ça traîne les rue*, it's not rare, not hard to find.

train-train (trɛ̃trɛ̃) *m*, jogtrot, routine.

traire (trɛːr) *v.t.ir*, to milk; draw.

trait (trɛ) *m*, pull[ing]; draft;

stretch; trace (*harness*); leash; arrow, dart; shot; beam; thunderbolt; dash (*Teleg.*); stroke; streak; line; flash; sally; gulp; feature; trait; touch; reference, bearing. ~ *d'union*, hyphen. ~ *de balance*, turn of the scale. ~ *d'esprit*, witticism. *tout d'un* ~, suddenly. **traitable** (tabl) *a*, tractable, manageable. **traite** (tret) *f*, stretch; stage (*journey*); trade, traffic; transport; trading; draft, bill; milking. *la* ~ *des noirs, la* ~ *des nègres*, the slave trade. **traité** (te) *m*, treatise; treaty; agreement. **traitement** (tmã) *m*, treatment; usage; salary, pay, stipend; processing, computing; adaptation (*cinema*). ~ *automatique des données*, automatic data processing. ~ *de l'information*, d. p. ~ *par lots*, batch processing (*computers*). ~ *de texte*, word p. ~ *d'inactivité*, pension. **traiter** (te) *v.t. & i*, to treat, use; entertain; deal; negotiate. ~ *de*, to treat of; call, dub. **traiteur** (tœːr) *m*, caterer.

traître, traîtresse (trɛːtr, trɛtrɛs) *n*, traitor, traitress; betrayer; villain (*Theat.*). ¶ *a*, treacherous, traitorous. **traîtreusement** (trøzmã) *ad*, treacherously. **traîtrise** (triːz) *f*, treachery.

trajectoire (traʒɛktwaːr) *f*, trajectory; path (*storm, etc.*). **trajet** (ʒɛ) *m*, journey, passage, transit, trip, run, ride, course.

tramail (tramaːj) *m*, trammel [net].

trame (tram) *f*, woof, weft; web; thread (*of life*); half-tone screen; plot. **tramer** (me) *v.t*, to weave; hatch (*plot*).

tramway (tramwɛ) *m*, streetcar, trolley car.

tranchant, e (trãʃã, ãːt) *a*, cutting, sharp, keen; edge[d]; trenchant; peremptory; glaring. ¶ *m*, [cutting] edge. **tranche** (trãːʃ) *f*, slice, cut; steak; rasher; slab; block, portion, set; edge (*book, coin*). *doré sur* ~, gilt-edged. *~s rognées*, cut edges. **tranché, e** (trãʃe) *a*, well-marked; distinct. **tranchée** (ʃe) *f*, trench; drain; cutting; (*pl.*) colic, gripes.

tranchefile (ʃfil) *f*, headband (*Bookb.*). **trancher** (ʃe) *v.t*, to slice; cut; chop off; cut short; settle; contrast. **tranchoir** (ʃwaːr) *m*, trencher, cutting board.

tranquille† (trãkil) *a*, tranquil, quiet, calm, peaceful, still, undisturbed, easy. **tranquilliser** (lize) *v.t*, to calm, soothe. **tranquillité** (te) *f*, tranquillity, peace.

transaction (trãzaksjɔ̃) *f*, transaction, dealing; compromise.

transatlantique (trãzatlãtik) *a*, transatlantic. ¶ *m*, deckchair; liner.

transborder (trãsbɔrde) *v.t*, to tranship. **transbordeur** (dœːr) *m*, car ferry.

transcendant, e (trãsãdã, ãːt) *a*, transcendent.

transcription (trãskripsjɔ̃) *f*, transcript[ion]; copy; posting (*Bkkpg.*). **transcrire** (skriːr) *v.t*, *ir*, to transcribe; post.

transe (trãːs) *f*, fright, scare; trance.

transept (trãsɛpt) *m*, transept.

transférer (trãsfere) *v.t*, to transfer; translate (*bishop*); alter the date of (*function*). **transfert** (fɛːr) *m*, transfer.

transfiguration (trãsfigyrasjɔ̃) *f*, transfiguration. **transfigurer** (re) *v.t*, to transfigure.

transformateur (trãsfɔrmatœːr) *m*, transformer. **transformer** (me) *v.t*, to transform, change, convert.

transfuge (trãsfyːʒ) *m*, deserter (*to enemy*); turncoat, rat.

transfuser (trãsfyze) *v.t*, to transfuse.

transgresser (trãsgrɛse) *v.t*, to transgress.

transhumer (trãzyme) *v.t*, to move flock to new pasture; transplant.

transiger (trãziʒe) *v.i*, to compound, compromise.

transir (trãsiːr) *v.t*, to chill; paralyze (*fig.*).

transit (trãzit) *m*, transit (*Cust.*).

transitif, ive† (trãzitif, iːv) *a*, transitive.

transition (trãzisj5) *f*, transition. **transitoire** (twa:r) *a*, transitory, transient.

translation (trãslasj5) *f*, translation (*bishop*); transfer, conveyance; alteration of date (*function*).

translucide (trãslysid) *a*, translucent.

transmetteur (trãsmɛtœ:r) *m*, transmitter. **transmettre** (tr) *v.t. ir*, to transmit; pass on; hand down; transfer, convey. **transmission** (misj5) *f*, transmission; drive, driving, shaft[ing] (*Mech.*).

transmuer (trãsmɥe) *v.t*, to transmute.

transparence (trãsparɑ̃:s) *f*, transparency. **transparent, e** (rã, ɑ̃:t) *a*, transparent. ¶ *m*, transparency (*picture*); black lines.

transpercer (trãspɛrse) *v.t*, to transfix, pierce.

transpirer (trãspire) *v.i*, to perspire; transpire.

transplanter (trãsplãte) *v.t*, to transplant.

transport (trãspɔ:r) *m*, transport, conveyance, carriage; visit (*of experts, etc*; *law*); transfer (*law*); troopship; rapture. ~ *au cerveau*, light-headedness, delirium. **transportation** (pɔrtasj5) *f*, transportation. **transporter** (te) *v.t*, to transport, etc.

transposer (trãspoze) *v.t*, to transpose.

transsubstantiation (trãssypstãsjasj5) *f*, transubstantiation.

transvaser (trãsvɑze) *v.t*, to decant.

transversal, e† (trãsvɛrsal) *a*, transverse, cross (*att.*).

trapèze (trapɛ:z) *m*, trapeze.

trappe (trap) *f*, trap, pitfall; trapdoor. **trappeur** (pœ:r) *m*, trapper.

trapu, e (trapy) *a*, thickset, dumpy, squat, stocky.

traque (trak) *f*, beating (*game*). **traquenard** (kna:r) *m*, trap. **traquer** (ke) *v.t*, to beat (*game*); surround; track down. **traqueur** (kœ:r) *m*, beater.

traumatiser (tromatize) *v.t*, to traumatize.

travail (trava:j) *m. oft. pl*, work; working; labor, toil; piece of work, job; employment; stress (*Mech.*); childbirth; workmanship. ~ *d'artisan*, craftsmanship. *travaux forcés*, hard labor. ~ *en série*, mass production. **travaillé, e** (vaje) (*fig.*) *p.a*, labored, elaborate. **travailler** (je) *v.i*, to work, labor, toil; be in stress; (*v.t.*) to torment; work; w. up; elaborate. ~ *comme un pied*, *sabot*, to work badly. ~ *d'arrache-pied*, w. hard. **travailleur, euse** (jœ:r, ø:z) *n*, worker; workman; laborer; toiler. ¶ *f*, workstand (*lady's*).

travée (trave) *f*, bay (*Arch.*); span (*bridge, roof*).

travelling (travəliŋ) *m*, dolly (*cinema*); dolly shot.

travers (travɛ:r) *m*, breadth; beam (*ship*), broadside; fault. à ~, through. **de** ~, askew, awry, amiss, wrong; askance. **en** ~, *ad*, across, athwart, cross[wise]. **en** ~ **de**, *pr*, across, athwart. **traverse** (vɛrs) *f*, shortcut; crossbar; crossbeam; crossroad; transom; sill; tie (*rail track*); hitch, setback. **traversée** (se) *f*, crossing, passage. ~ *des piétons*, pedestrian crossing. **traverser** (se) *v.t*, to traverse, cross, go through; thwart. **traversin** (sɛ̃) *m*, bolster (*bed*).

travestir (travesti:r) *v.t*, to disguise; travesty, burlesque; misrepresent.

trayon (trɛj5) *m*, dug, teat (*cow, etc.*).

trébucher (trebyʃe) *v.i*, to stumble, trip. **trébuchet** (ʃɛ) *m*, trap; balance (*scales*).

tréfiler (trefile) *v.t*, to wiredraw (*metal*).

trèfle (trɛfl) *m*, trefoil; clover; clubs (*cards*).

tréfonds (tref5) *m*, subsoil.

treillage (trɛja:ʒ) *m*, trellis, lattice. **treillis** (ji) *m*, trellis, lattice; netting; sackcloth. **treillisser** (se) *v.t*, to trellis, lattice.

treize (trɛ:z) *a. & m*, thirteen; 13th. ~ *douze*, baker's dozen. **treizième†** (trɛzjɛm) *a. & n*, thirteenth.

tréma (trema) *m*, diaeresis.

tremblaie (trãblɛ) *f*, aspen plantation. **tremble** (trã:bl) *m*, asp[en].

tremblement (trãbləmã) *m*, trembling, trepidation, quavering, shaking; tremor. *~ de terre*, earthquake. **tremblé, e** (ble) *p.a*, wavy, waved; shaky. **trembler** (ble) *&* **trembloter** (blɔte) *v.i*, to tremble, shake, vibrate, quake, quiver, quaver, quail, shiver, flutter, flicker.

trémie (tremi)*f*, hopper (*Mach.*).

tremolo (tremolo) *m*, tremolo (*Mus.*).

trémousser (se) (tremuse) *v.pr*, to fidget; flounce about; bestir oneself. *trémousser de l'aile*, to flutter, flap its wings.

trempe (trã:p) *f*, damping; tempering, hardening; temper; stamp, kidney (*fig.*). **tremper** (trãpe) *v.t. & i*, to steep, soak, dip; drench; damp, wet; temper; imbrue.

tremplin (trãplɛ̃) *m*, spring board, diving b.; ski jump; jumping-off ground (*fig.*).

trentaine (trãtɛn) *f*, thirty [or so]. **trente** (trã:t) *a*, thirty. ¶ *m*, thirty; 30th. *~ et quarante*, rouge et noir. **T~**, *f*, Trent (*Italy*). **trentième** (trãtjɛm) *a. & n*, thirtieth. **le Trentin** (tɛ̃), the Trentino.

trépan (trepã) *m*, trepan; bit, chisel (*boring*). **trépaner** (pane) *v.t*, to trepan.

trépas (trepɑ) *m*, death, decease. **trépasser** (se) *v.i*, to die, pass away. **les trépassés** (se), the dead, the departed.

trépidation (trepidasjɔ̃) *f*, tremor; vibration (*of machinery, car, ship*).

trépied (trepje) *m*, tripod; trivet (*stove*).

trépigner (trepiɲe) *v.i*, to stamp (*rage*).

trépointe (trepwɛ̃t) *f*, welt (*shoe*).

très (trɛ; *in liaison*, trɛz) *ad*, very, most, [very] much.

trésor (trezɔ:r) *m*, treasure;

treasury. **trésorerie** (zɔrri) *f*, treasury; finances. **trésorier, ère** (zɔrje, ɛ:r) *n*, treasurer; paymaster.

tressaillir (tresaji:r) *v.i.ir*, to start; thrill; wince.

tressauter (tresote) *v.i*, to start, jump.

tresse (trɛs) *f*, plait, tress; braid; tape; gasket. **tresser** (se) *v.t*, to plait; braid; weave (*wicker, etc.*).

tréteau (treto) *m*, trestle, horse; (*pl.*) boards, stage.

treuil (trœ:j) *m*, winch, windlass, hoist.

trêve (trɛ:v) *f*, truce; respite.

Trèves (trɛ:v) *f*, Treves, Trier.

trévire (trevi:r) *f*, parbuckle.

tri (tri) *&* **triage** (a:ʒ) *m*, sorting.

triangle (triã:gl) *m*, triangle (*Geom. & Mus.*). **triangulaire** (ãgylɛ:r) *a*, triangular.

tribord (tribɔ:r) *m*, starboard.

tribu (triby) *f*, tribe.

tribulation (tribylasjɔ̃) *f*, tribulation, trial.

tribun (tribœ̃) (*pers.*) *m*, tribune (*Hist.*); demagogue. **tribunal** (bynal) *m*, tribunal; bench; court. **tribune** (byn) *f*, tribune; rostrum; platform; gallery; loft (*organ*); grandstand; discussion or debate (*TV*).

tribut (triby) *m*, tribute. **tributaire** (tɛ:r) *a. & m*, tributary (*pers., river*); dependent.

triceps (trisɛps) *a. & m*, triceps.

tricher (triʃe) *v.i. & t*, to cheat; trick; doctor. **tricherie** (ʃri) *f*, cheating; trickery. **tricheur, euse** (ʃœ:r), ø:z) *n*, cheat; trickster; sharper.

trichromie (trikrɔmi) *f*, three-color process.

tricot (triko) *m*, knitting (*art*); sweater; knitted garment; (*pl.*) knit[ted] wear. *~ à l'envers*, purl knitting. **tricotage** (kɔta:ʒ) *m*, knitting (*act*). **tricoter** (te) *v.t. & abs*, to knit. **tricoteur, euse** (tœ:r, ø:z) *n*, knitter.

trictrac (triktrak) *m*, backgammon; b. board.

tricycle (trisikl) *m*, tricycle.

trident (tridᾶ) *m*, trident; fish spear.

triennal, e (triɛnnal) *a*, triennial.

trier (trie) *v.t*, to sort; pick. **trieur, euse** (œ:r, ø:z) *n*, sorter; picker.

trigonométrie (trigonometri) *f*, trigonometry.

trille (tri:j) *m*, trill, shake (*Mus.*).

trillion (triljɔ̃) *m*, a million millions.

trimbaler (trɛbale) *v.t*, to drag about.

trimer (trime) *v.i*, to slave, drudge.

trimestre (trimɛstr) *m*, quarter, 3 months; term (*Sch.*); quarter's rent, salary, etc. **trimestriel, le** (triɛl) *a*, quarterly.

tringle (trɛ̃:gl) *f*, rod; curtain rod; chalk line (*mark*).

Trinité (la) (trinite), the Trinity; Trinidad.

trinquer (trɛ̃ke) *v.i*, to clink glasses; hobnob.

trio (trio) *m*, trio. **triolet** (ɔlɛ) *m*, triolet; triplet (*Mus.*).

triomphal, e† (triɔ̃fal) *a*, triumphal. **triomphe** (ɔ̃:f) *f*, triumph; exultation. **triompher** (ɔ̃fe) *v.i*, to triumph; exult; excel; gloat.

tripaille (tripɑ:j) *f*, garbage, offal.

tripe de velours (trip) *f*, velveteen.

triperie (tripri) *f*, tripe shop. **tripes** (trip) *f.pl*, tripe. **tripier, ère** (pje, ɛ:r) *n*, tripe dealer.

triplet† (tripl) *a. & m*, treble, triple, threefold, 3 times; triplicate. **~ croche**, *f*, demisemiquaver. **~ saut**, *m*, hop, step, & jump. **tripler** (ple) *v.t. & i*, to treble, triple. **triplicata** (plikata) *m*, triplicate.

tripoli (tripoli) *m*, tripoli.

tripot (tripo) *m*, bawdy house; gambling den. **tripoter** (pɔte) *v.t. & abs*, muddle up; plot; job, rig; handle; gamble; meddle with. **tripoteur** (pɔtœ:r) *m*, intriguer; shady speculator; mischiefmaker.

triptyque (triptik) *m*, triptych.

trique (trik) *f*, cudgel, bludgeon. *avoir la ~*, to have an erection (*obscene*).

triqueballe (trikbal) *m*, sling cart.

trisaïeul, e (trizajœl) *n*, greatgreat-grandfather, -mother.

triste† (trist) *a*, sad, sorrowful, woeful; dreary, gloomy, dismal; bleak, depressing; sorry, wretched. **tristesse** (tɛs) *f*, sadness.

triton (tritɔ̃) *m*, triton; merman; newt; eft.

triturer (trityre) *v.t*, to triturate, grind.

trivial, e† (trivjal) *a*, vulgar, coarse; not in decent use (*expression*); trite, hackneyed. **trivialité** (lite) *f*, vulgarity, etc; vulgarism.

troc (trɔk) *m*, truck, exchange, barter.

trochée (trɔʃe) *m*, head of shoots (*tree stump*).

troène (trɔɛn) *m*, privet (*Bot.*).

troglodyte (trɔglɔdit) *m*, troglodyte, cave dweller.

trognon (trɔɲɔ̃) *m*, core (*apple*); stump (*cabbage*).

trois (trwa; *in liaison*, trwaz) *a. & m*, three; third. *~ fois*, three times, thrice. *~ jumeaux*, triplets. *~-mâts*, *m*, three-master. **troisième†** (zjɛm) *a*, third. ¶ *m*, third (*number, pers., floor*). ¶ *f*, third (*class*). *~s* [*galeries*], gallery (*Theat.*).

trolley (trɔlɛ) *m*, troll[ey] (*grooved wheel*).

trombe (trɔ̃:b) *f*, waterspout. *~ d'eau*, cloudburst. *entrer en ~*, to burst in.

trombone (trɔ̃bɔn) *m*, trombone; paper clip.

trompe (trɔ̃:p) *f*, horn; hooter; trumpet; proboscis; trunk. *~ ~ d'Eustache* (østaʃ), Eustachian tube.

trompe-l'œil (trɔ̃plœ:j) *m*, stilllife deception; bluff, window dressing (*fig.*). **tromper** (pe) *v.t*, to deceive, delude; cheat; mislead; disappoint; outwit; beguile. *se ~*, to be mistaken, mistake. **tromperie** (pri) *f*, deceit, deception, imposture; illusion.

trompeter (trɔ̃pɛte) *v.t.* to trumpet (*secret*). **trompette** (pɛt) *f*, trumpet, trump (*last, of doom*); whelk. ¶ *m*, trumpeter.

trompeur, euse (trɔ̃pœːr, øːz) *n*, deceiver, cheat. ¶ *a*, deceitful; deceptive.

tronc (trɔ̃) *m*, trunk; parent stock; frustum. *~ des pauvres*, poor box. **tronçon** (sɔ̃) *m*, (*broken*) piece, stump; section; dock (*of tail*). **tronçonner** (sɔne) *v.t*, to cut up.

trône (troːn) *m*, throne. **trôner** (trone) *v.i*, to sit enthroned, sit in state.

tronquer (trɔ̃ke) *v.t*, to truncate; mutilate.

trop (tro; *in liaison*, trɔp) *ad. & m*, too; over-; too much, too many; too long; too well; excess. *~ cuit, e*, overdone. *être de ~*, to be in the way, be unwelcome; superfluous.

trope (trɔp) *m*, trope.

trophée (trɔfe) *m*, trophy.

tropical, e (trɔpikal) *a*, tropical. **tropique** (pik) *m*, tropic.

trop-plein (trɔplɛ̃) *m*, overflow.

troquer (trɔke) *v.t*, to barter, exchange.

trot (tro) *m*, trot. **trotte** (trɔt) *f*, distance, step. **trotter** (te) *v.i. & t*, to trot; run (*in one's head*). **trotteur, euse** (tœːr, øːz) *n*, trotter (*horse*). **trottin** (tɛ̃) *m*, errand girl. **trottiner** (tine) *v.i*, to trot; toddle. **trottinette** (nɛt) *f*, scooter. **trottoir** (twaːr) *m*, pavement, footway, footpath. *bordure du ~*, curb. *faire le ~*, to walk the streets (*prostitute*).

trou (tru) *m*, hole; eye; blank ~ *barré*, stimy, stymie (*golf*). ~ *d'air*, air pocket (*Avn.*); ~ [*d' arrivée*], hole (*golf*). ~ *d'homme*, manhole. ~ *de sonde*, bore hole.

troubadour (trubaduːr) *m*, troubadour.

trouble (trubl) *a*, troubled, turbid, muddy, cloudy; dim, blurred, misty; overcast; confused. ¶ *m*, disorder; disturbance; trouble. ~*-fête* (bləfɛːt) *m*, spoilsport, killjoy. **troubler** (ble) *v.t*, to dis-

turb; muddy; dim; mar; hamper; upset.

trouée (true) *f*, gap. **trouer** (e) *v.t*, to pierce with holes.

troufion (trufjɔ̃) *m*, soldier, private (*slang*).

trouille (truːj) *f*, fear (*slang*). *avoir la ~*, to be afraid.

troupe (trup) *f*, troop, band; host; set, gang; troop; troupe; flock. **troupeau** (po) *m*, herd, drove; flock. **troupier** (pje) *m*, soldier, campaigner.

trousse (trus) *f*, truss; bundle; case; kit; outfit; roll. ~ *manicure*, manicure set. *aux ~s de*, at the heels of. **trousseau** (so) *m*, bunch (*keys*); outfit, kit; trousseau. **trousser** (se) *v.t*, to tuck up; turn up; truss; dispatch; polish off. ~ *bagage*, to pack up; decamp; die. **troussis** (si) *m*, tuck.

trouvaille (truvaːj) *f*, [lucky] find. **trouver** (ve) *v.t*, to find; discover; get; think; like; spare (*the time*). *objets trouvés*, lost and found. *enfant trouvé*, foundling. *se ~*, to be; feel; happen.

truc (tryk) *m*, knack; trick, dodge; gadget; platform car (*Rly.*).

truca (tryka) *m*, optical printer (*cinema*).

trucage (trykaːʒ) *m*, faking; camouflage; trick photography; gerrymandering.

truchement (tryʃmɑ̃) *m*, interpreter, spokesman.

truculent, e (trykylɑ̃, ɑ̃ːt) *a*, truculent.

trudgeon (trydʒ5̃) *m*, trudgen (*Swim.*).

truelle (tryɛl) *f*, trowel. ~ *à poisson*, fish slice.

truffe (tryf) *f*, truffle.

truie (trɥi) *f*, sow.

truisme (tryism) *m*, truism.

truite (trɥit) *f*, trout. ~ *saumonée* (somone), salmon t. **truité, e** (te) *a*, speckled, mottled.

trumeau (trymo) *m*, pier (*Arch.*); pierglass; leg of beef.

truquage (trykaːʒ) *m*, fake; trick shot (*TV, cinema*). **truquer** (ke) *v.t*, to fake.

tu (ty) *pn*, you, thou.
tuant, e (tɥɑ̃, ɑ̃:t) *a*, killing; boring.
tuba (tyba) *m*, tuba.
tube (tyb) *m*, tube; telephone (*slang*); hit song (*slang*).
tubercule (tybɛrkyl) *m*, tuber; tubercle. **tuberculeux, euse** (lø, ø:z) *a*, tuberculous. ¶ *n*, consumptive. **tuberculose** (lo:z) *f*, tuberculosis.
tubéreuse (tyberø:z) *f*, tuberose.
tubulaire (tybylɛ:r) *a*, tubular.
tue-mouches (tymuʃ) *m*, flyswat[ter], flyflap. **tuer** (tɥe) *v.t*, to kill, slay; slaughter; swat (*fly*); bore. *tué à l'ennemi*, killed in action. *les tués*, the killed. *un tué, une tuée*, a fatality (*accident*). **tuerie** (tyri) *f*, slaughter, butchery, carnage. *à tue-tête*, at the top of one's voice. **tueur** (tɥœ:r) *m*, killer, slayer.
tuile (tɥil) *f*, tile; bad luck (*slang*). **tuilerie** (lri) *f*, tile works. **tuilier** (lje) *m*, tile maker.
tulipe (tylip) *f*, tulip. **tulipier** (pje) *m*, tulip tree.
tulle (tyl) *m*, tulle, net.
tumeur (tymœ:r) *f*, tumor.
tumulte (tymylt) *m*, tumult, uproar, turmoil; riot. **tumultueux, euse†** (tɥø, ø:z) *a*, tumultuous, riotous.
tumulus (tymyly:s) *m*, tumulus, barrow.
tungstène (tœ̃gstɛn) *m*, tungsten.
tunique (tynik) *f*, tunic; coat (*Anat., Bot.*).
Tunis (tynis) *m*, Tunis (*capital*). **la Tunisie** (zi), Tunis (*state*). **tunisien, ne** (zjɛ̃, ɛn) *a. &* T~, *n*, Tunisian.
tunnel (tynɛl) *m*, tunnel.
turban (tyrbɑ̃) *m*, turban.
turbin (tyrbɛ̃) *m*, work, grind (*slang*). *le ~ journalier*, the daily grind. **turbiner** (ne) *v.t*, to work hard; cram.
turbine (tyrbin) *f*, turbine.
turbot (tyrbo) *m*, turbot.
turbulence (tyrbylɑ̃:s) *f*, turbulence. **turbulent, e** (lɑ̃, ɑ̃:t) *a*, turbulent, unruly, restless; boisterous.

turc, turque (tyrk) *a*, Turkish. *être assis à la turque*, to sit crosslegged. T~, *n*, Turk. **le turc**, Turkish (*language*). **Turcoman** (kɔmɑ̃) (*pers.*) *m*, Turkoman.
turf (tyrf) *m*, racetrack, racecourse. *le ~*, the turf.
turgescent, e (tyrʒɛsɑ̃, ɑ̃:t) *a*, turgescent, turgid.
turlupin (tyrlypɛ̃) *m*, buffoon. **turlupiner** (pine) *v.i*, to play the fool. *v.t*, to bother, worry.
turpitude (tyrpityd) *f*, turpitude, baseness.
Turquie (tyrki) *f*, Turkey.
turquoise (tyrkwa:z) *f. & att*, turquoise.
tutélaire (tytelɛ:r) *a*, tutelar[y], guardian; (*m.*) prop (*Hort.*). **tutelage**, guardianship; protection. **tuteur, trice** (tœ:r, tris) *n*, guardian; (*m.*) prop (*Hort.*).
tutoyer (tytwaje) *v.t*, to address as "tu" and "toi." *se faire ~*, to be severely reprimanded.
tutu (tyty) *m*, ballet skirt.
tuyau (tɥijo) *m*, pipe; tube; hose; flue; stem; hint. *avoir des ~x*, to be in the know. *~ acoustique*, speaking tube. *~ d'arrosage*, garden hose. *~ d'échappement*, exhaust pipe. **tuyauter** (te) *v.t*, to flute, frill, plait; tip off. **tuyauterie** (tri) *f*, pipe system, p. factory.
tuyère (tɥiɛ:r) *f*, nozzle; pipe. *~ orientable*, swiveling nozzle.
tympan (tɛ̃pɑ̃) *m*, tympanum, ear drum; tympan. **tympanon** (panɔ̃) *m*, dulcimer.
type (tip) *m*, type (*model & Typ.*); standard; fellow, guy.
typhoïde (tifɔid) *a*, typhoid.
typhon (tifɔ̃) *m*, typhoon.
typhus (tify:s) *m*, typhus.
typique (tipik) *a*, typical.
typographie (tipɔgrafi) *f*, typography; printing works. **typographique** (fik) *a*, typographic(al).
tyran (tirɑ̃) *m*, tyrant. **tyrannie** (rani) *f*, tyranny. **tyrannique†** (nik) *a*, tyrannic(al); high-handed. **tyranniser** (nize) *v.t*, to tyrannize [over].
Tyrol (le) (tirɔl), the Tyrol.

tyrolien, ne (ljẽ, ɛn) *a. & T~, n,* Tyrolese.

tzigane (tsigan) *n. & a,* gipsy, zigane.

U

ubiquité (ybikɥite) *f,* ubiquity.

ulcération (ylserasjɔ̃) *f,* ulceration. **ulcère** (sɛːr) *m,* ulcer. **ulcérer** (sere) *v.t,* to ulcerate; embitter.

ultérieur, e (ylterjœːr) *a,* ulterior, later, subsequent. **ultérieurement** (œrmɑ̃) *ad,* later [on].

ultimatum (yltimatɔm) *m,* ultimatum. **ultime** (tim) *a,* final, ultimate.

ultra (yltra) *m,* ultraist, extremist. **~-violet, te,** *a,* ultraviolet.

ululer (ylyle) *v.i,* to hoot, ululate.

un (œ̃) *m,* one. **un, une** (œ̃, yn) *a,* one; a, an. ~ *à* ~, one by one; one after another. *l'*~, each (*price of articles*). *l'*~ *l'autre, les uns* (*les unes*) *les autres,* one another, each other. *l'*~ & *l'autre,* both. *l'*~ *ou l'autre,* either. *ni l'*~ *ni l'autre,* neither. *une fois,* once. *une fois, deux fois,* [*trois fois*]; *adjugé!* going, going; gone! *une fois pour toutes,* once for all. *en une* [*seule*] *fois,* in a lump sum, outright (*opp.* by installments). *il y avait (ou il était) une fois,* once upon a time. **la une,** *the front page.*

unanime† (ynanim) *a,* unanimous. **unanimité** (mite) *f,* unanimity, consensus. *à l'*~, unanimously.

uni, e (yni) *p.a,* united; even; level; smooth; plain; uniform.

unième† (ynjɛm) *a,* first (*only after* 20, 30, *etc, e.g, vingt & ~,* 21st; *cent ~,* 101st).

unifier (ynifje) *v.t,* to unify, consolidate; standardize. **uniforme** (fɔrm) *a,* uniform, even. ¶ *m,* uniform; regimentals. **uniformément** (memɑ̃) *ad,* uniformly, evenly. **uniformité** (mite) *f,* uniformity.

unilatéral, e (ynilateral) *a,* unilateral; one-sided.

uniment (ynimɑ̃) *ad,* smoothly, evenly; plainly; simply.

union (ynjɔ̃) *f,* union; unity. *U~ des Républiques soviétiques socialistes,* Union of Soviet Socialist Republics. *U~ Sud-Africaine,* Union of South Africa.

unique (ynik) *a,* only; sole; single; one; unique. *prix* ~, dime store. *sens* ~, one way. **uniquement** (kmɑ̃) *ad,* solely, uniquely, only.

unir (yniːr) *v.t,* to unite; join; level, smooth. **unisson** (nisɔ̃) *m,* unison. **unitaire** (tɛːr) *a,* unitary; unit (*att.*). **unité** (te) *f,* unit; unity; one; oneness. ~ *d'affichage,* display unit (*computers*).

univers (yniveːr) *m,* universe. **universalité** (versalite) *f,* universality. **universel, le†** (sel) *a,* universal; world[-wide]. **universitaire** (siteːr) *a,* university (*att.*). **université** (te) *f,* university.

Untel (œtɛl) *m, M.* ~, Mr. So-and-so.

uranium (yranjɔm) *m,* uranium.

urbain, e (yrbẽ, ɛn) *a,* urban. **urbanisme** (banism) *m,* town planning. **urbanité** (te) *f,* urbanity.

urée (yre) *f,* urea. **urémie** (mi) *f,* uremia.

urètre (yrɛːtr) *m,* urethra.

urgence (yrʒɑ̃ːs) *f,* urgency. *d'*~, urgently; emergency (*as a brake*). **urgent, e** (ʒɑ̃, ɑ̃ːt) *a,* urgent.

urinal (yrinal) *m,* urinal (*vessel*). **urine** (rin) *f,* urine. **uriner** (ne) *v.i,* to urinate; (*v.t.*) to pass. **urinoir** (nwaːr) *m,* urinal (*place*). **urique** (rik) *a,* uric.

urne (yrn) *f,* urn. ~ *électorale,* ballot box.

urticaire (yrtikɛːr) *f,* nettle rash.

us & coutumes (ys) *m.pl,* use & wont. **usage** (zaːʒ) *m,* use; purpose; wear; usage, custom, practice. ~ [*du monde*], ways of society. *article d'*~, serviceable article. *faire de l'*~, to wear well. *valeur d'*~, value as a going concern. **usagé, e** (zaʒe) *a,* used, secondhand. **usager** (ʒe) *m,* user. **usé, e** (ze) *a,* worn [out]; shabby. ~ [*jusqu'à la corde*], threadbare, hackneyed, stale. **user** (ze) *v.t,* to use; wear [out, away]; abrade. ~ *de,* to use, exercise.

s'~, to wear [away]. *être d'un bon user*, to wear well.

usine (yzin) *f*, works; factory; mill; (*power*) station. **usiner** (ne) *v.t*, to machine, tool; exploit. **usinier** (nje) *m*, mill owner.

usité, e (yzite) *a*, used, in use. *peu usité*, rare (*word*).

ustensile (ystãsil) *m*, utensil; implement, tool.

usuel, le† (yzɥɛl) *a*, usual, customary.

usufruit (yzyfrɥi) *m*, usufruct.

usuraire† (yzyrɛ:r) *a*, usurious. **usure** (zy:r) *f*, usury; interest; wear [& tear], wearing; attrition. *guerre d'~*, war of attrition. **usurier**, ère (zyrje, ɛ:r) *n*, usurer.

usurpateur, trice (yzyrpatœ:r, tris) *n*, usurper. **usurpation** (sjɔ̃) *f*, usurpation; encroachment. **usurper** (pe) *v.t*, to usurp; (*v.i.*) to encroach.

ut (yt) *m*, C (*Mus.*).

utérin, e (yterɛ̃, in) *a*, uterine. **utérus** (ry:s) *m*, uterus.

utile† (ytil) *a*, useful, serviceable; effective; due, good (*time*). **utiliser** (lize) *v.t*, to utilize. **utilitaire** (tɛ:r) *a. & n*, utilitarian. **utilité** (te) *f*, utility, use[fulness]; utility [man] (*Theat.*).

utopie (ytɔpi) *f*, utopia. **utopique** (pik) *a. & utopiste* (pist) *a. & n*, utopian.

uvule (yvyl) *f*, uvula.

V

va *see* aller.

vacance (vakɑ:s) *f*, vacancy; (*pl.*) holiday[s]; vacation, recess; opening. **vacant**, e (kã, ã:t) *a*, vacant, unoccupied.

vacarme (vakarm) *m*, uproar, din, row.

vacation (vakasjɔ̃) *f*, attendance, sitting (*experts*); (*pl.*) fees (*lawyer's*); (*pl.*) recess (*courts*).

vaccin (vaksɛ̃) *m*, vaccine, lymph. **vaccination** (sinasjɔ̃) *f*, vaccination. **vaccine** (sin) *f*, cowpox. **vacciner** (ne) *v.t*, to vaccinate.

vache (vaʃ) *f*, cow; cowhide. *~ à lait*, ~ *laitière*, milch cow; policeman (*pejorative*). *bouffer de la ~*

enragée, to endure a period of hard times. *mort aux ~s*, off the pigs. **vacher**, ère (ʃe, ɛ:r) *n*, cowherd, neatherd. **vacherie** (ʃri) *f*, cow house; dairy [farm].

vaciller (vasile) *v.i*, to be unsteady, wobble; vacillate, waver; flicker.

vacuité (vakɥite) *f*, vacuity, emptiness.

vadrouiller (vadruje) *v.i*, to roam the streets; knock about.

va-et-vient (vaevjɛ̃) *m*, come-&-go; to & fro; reciprocating motion; swing (*door*); ferry boat; two-way wiring (*Elec.*).

vagabond, e (vagabɔ̃, ɔ̃:d) *a*, vagabond, vagrant, roving; truant. ¶ *n*, vagabond, vagrant, tramp. **vagabondage** (bɔ̃da:ʒ) *m*, vagrancy; truancy. **vagabonder** (de) *v.i*, to rove, wander.

vagin (vaʒɛ̃) *m*, vagina. **vaginé** (ʒine) *a*, sheathed (*Anat.*). **vaginite** (ʒinit) *f*, vaginitis.

vagir (vaʒi:r) *v.i*, to wail, cry (*of baby*). **vagissement** (ʒismã) *m*, wailing (*infant*); squeaking (*hare*).

vague (va:g) *f*, wave, billow; surge.

vague† (va:g) *a*, vague; hazy; waste (*land*). ¶ *m*, vagueness; void. **vaguer** (vage) *v.i*, to wander [about].

vaguemestre (vagmɛtr) *m*, baggage master (*Mil.*); postman (*Mil.*).

vaillamment (vajamã) *ad*, valiantly, gallantly. **vaillance** (jã:s) *f*, gallantry, valor. **vaillant**, e (jã, ã:t) *a*, valiant, gallant. **vaillantise** (jãti:z) *f*, prowess.

vain, e† (vɛ̃, ɛn) *a*, vain; useless; conceited. *vaine pâture*, common [land]. *en vain*, in vain, fruitlessly.

vaincre (vɛ̃:kr) *v.t.ir*, to vanquish, conquer; beat; overcome. les **vaincus** (vɛ̃ky) *m.pl*, the vanquished. **vainqueur** (kœ:r) *m*, conqueror, victor; winner (*sport*).

vairon (vɛrɔ̃) *m*, minnow.

vaisseau (vɛso) *m*, vessel; ship; boat; body (*as nave of church*), main hall. ~ *amiral,* flagship. ~-*école,* training s. ~-*hôpital,* hospital s. ~ *rasé,* hulk. ~ *sanguin,* blood vessel. **vaisselier** (səlje) *m,* sideboard; dresser. **vaisselle** (sɛl) *f,* crockery, plates & dishes. *faire la* ~, to do the dishes.

val (val) *m,* vale, glen. *par monts & par vaux,* over hill & dale.

valable† (valabl) *a,* valid; good; available *(law).*

valence (valɑ̃:s) *f,* valence, -cy *(Chem.).*

Valence (valɑ̃:s) *f,* Valencia *(Spain).*

valet (valɛ) *m,* valet; man[servant]; groom *(stable);* stand; knave, jack *(cards).* ~ *de chambre,* valet. ~ *de charrue,* plowman. ~ *de ferme,* farmhand. ~ *de pied,* footman; flunkey. **valetaille** (ltɑ:j) *f,* menials, flunkeydom. **faire valeter** (lte) to make *(someone)* fetch & carry.

Valette (la) (valet), Valetta.

valétudinaire (valetydinɛ:r) *a. & n,* valetudinarian.

valeur (valœ:r) *f,* value; worth; valor, gallantry; value [date], as at *(Com.);* security *(Fin.);* stock; share; investment; holding; asset; bill; paper; money. ~ *déclarée: fr.* —, insured for: —francs. *avec* ~ *déclarée,* insured *(parcel). sans* ~ *déclarée,* uninsured. ~*s mobilières,* stocks & shares, transferable securities. [*objet de*] ~, valuable [article], a. of value. *mettre en* ~, to emphasize; enhance; develop *(property, etc.).* **valeureux, euse**† (lœrø, ø:z) *a,* valorous.

valide† (valid) *a,* valid; available; ablebodied, fit for service *(pers.).* **valider** (de) *v.t,* to validate; enable *(computers).* **validité** (dite) *f,* validity.

valise (vali:z) *f,* portmanteau; suitcase, grip.

vallée (vale) *f,* valley. **vallon** (l5) *m,* dale, vale, glen.

valoir (valwa:r) *v.i. & t. ir,* to be worth; win; gain. *cela vaut la peine,* it is worth while. *il vaut mieux,* it is better to. *autant vaut,* one might as well. *à* ~ *sur,* on account of. *faire* ~, to turn to account, make the best of; develop; enforce.

valse (vals) *f,* waltz. **valser** (se) *v.i,* to waltz. **valseur, euse** (sœ:r, ø:z) *n,* waltzer. *m.pl,* buttocks. *f.pl,* testicles *(slang).*

valve (valv) *f,* valve.

vampire (vɑ̃pi:r) *m,* vampire.

vandale (vɑ̃dal) *m,* vandal. **vandalisme** (lism) *m,* vandalism, wanton destruction.

vandoise (vɑ̃dwa:z) *f,* dace.

vanille (vani:j) *f,* vanilla.

vanité (vanite) *f,* vanity, conceit. **vaniteux, euse** (tø, ø:z) *a,* vain, conceited.

vannage (vana:ʒ) *m,* winnowing; gating. **vanne** (van) *f,* sluice gate, floodgate; gate; shutter; unkind comment *(slang).* **vanneau** (no) *m,* lapwing, pewit. *œufs de* ~, plovers' eggs *(Cook.).* **vanner** (ne) *v.t,* to winnow, fan *(grain).* **vannerie** (nri) *f,* basket making; b. work, wicker work. **vanneur, euse** (nœ:r, ø:z) *n,* winnower. **vannier** (nje) *m,* basket maker.

vantail (vɑ̃ta:j) *m,* leaf *(door, shutter).*

vantard, e (vɑ̃ta:r, ard) *a,* boastful. ¶ *n,* boaster, braggart. **vantardise** (tardi:z) & **vanterie** (tri) *f,* boast[ing], brag[ging]. **vanter** (te) *v.t,* to praise, extol, cry up, vaunt. **se** ~, to boast, vaunt, brag.

va-nu-pieds (vanypje) *n,* ragamuffin.

vapeur (vapœ:r) *f,* vapor; fume; mist; steam. *à* ~, steam *(engine, boat).* ¶ *m,* steamer, steamship, steamboat. ~-*citerne,* tank steamer. ~ *de charge,* cargo boat. ~ *de ligne* [*régulière*], liner. **vaporeux, euse** (porø, ø:z) *a,* vaporous, -ry; misty; hazy; filmy, gauzy. **vaporisateur** (rizatœ:r) *m,* spray[er], atomizer. **vaporiser** (ze) *v.t,* to vaporize; spray.

vaquer (vake) *v.i,* to be vacant *(employ);* not to sit *(court).* ~ *à,* to attend to.

varech (varɛk) *m,* seaweed, wrack.

varenne (varɛn) *f,* waste pasturage.

vareuse (varø:z) f, jumper (sailor's); blouse (Mil.); cardigan [jacket] (woman's).

variable (varjabl) a, variable, changeable, unsettled. au ~, at change (barometer). **variante** (rjã:t) f, variant. **variation** (rjasjɔ̃) f, variation, change.

varice (varis) f, varicose vein.

varicelle (varisɛl) f, chicken pox.

varier (varje) v.t. & i, to vary, change; variegate, diversify; differ. **variété** (rjete) f, variety, diversity; (pl.) miscellany.

variole (varjɔl) f, smallpox. **varioleux, euse** (lø, ø:z) n, smallpox case (pers.).

varlet (varlɛ) m, varlet (Hist.).

varlope (varlɔp) f, plane (Carp.).

Varsovie (varsɔvi) f, Warsaw.

vasculaire (vaskylɛ:r) a, vascular.

vase (vɑ:z) f, mud, silt, slime, ooze. ¶ m, vessel, vase. ~ à filtrations chaudes, beaker. ~ clos, retort. ~ de nuit, chamber pot.

vaseline (vazlin) f, vaseline.

vaseux, euse (vazø, ø:z) a, muddy, slimy.

vasistas (vazistɑ:s) m, transom; casement window.

vasque (vask) f, ornamental basin (fountain); bowl.

vassal, e (vasal) n, vassal (Hist.).

vaste (vast) a, vast, spacious, wide.

va-tout (vatu) m, (one's) all.

vaudeville (vodvil) m, vaudeville.

vaudoise (vodwa:z) f, dace.

vau-l'eau (à) (volo) ad, downstream; to rack & ruin.

vaurien, ne (vorjɛ̃, ɛn) n, blackguard; rascal.

vautour (votu:r) m, vulture.

vautre (votr) m, boar hound.

vautrer (se) (votre) v.pr, to wallow; sprawl.

veau (vo) m, calf; veal; calf[skin]. ~ d'or, golden calf. ~ gras, fatted c. ~ raciné (rasine), tree calf.

vécés (vese) m.pl, W.C., john, toilet.

vecteur (vɛktœ:r) m, vector.

vécu, e (veky) p.a, true to life (novel, etc.).

vedette (vədɛt) f, mounted sentry;

scout (warship); motor boat; leader; leading counter; star (Theat., film). en ~, prominent[ly], in the limelight; starred; displayed in bold type. **vedettariat** (tarja) m, stardom; overemphasis on "star" personalities.

végétal, e (veʒetal) a, plant (life); vegetable. ¶ m, plant. **végétarien, ne** (tarjɛ̃, ɛn) a. & n, vegetarian. **végétarisme** (rism) m, vegetarianism. **végétation** (sjɔ̃) f, vegetation; growth. ~s [adénoïdes], adenoids. **végéter** (te) v.i, to vegetate.

véhémence (veemɑ̃:s) f, vehemence. **véhément, e†** (mɑ̃, ɑ̃:t) a, vehement.

véhicule (veikyl) m, vehicle; medium. **véhiculer** (le) v.t, to cart; convey.

veille (vɛ:j) f, watch, vigil, staying up; lookout; wakeful night; eve; day before; brink; point. **veillée** (vɛje) f, evening; vigil; night nursing; wake. **veiller** (je) v.i. & t, to sit up, stay up, lie awake; watch. ~ à, to see that. ~ sur, to look after, take care of. **veilleur, euse** (jœ:r, ø:z) n, watchman; watcher; (f.) night-light. mettre en veilleuse, to douse lights, cut back production.

veinard (vɛna:r) a, lucky, fortunate.

veine (vɛn) f, vein; tricklet (water); luck. **veiner** (ne) v.t, to vein, grain.

vêler (vele) v.i, to calve.

vélin (velɛ̃) m, vellum.

velléité (vɛlleite) f, (irresolute) intention.

vélo (velo) m, bike. **vélocipède** (lɔsiped) m, velocipede; cycle. **vélocité** (te) f, swiftness. **vélodrome** (dro:m) m, cycle track.

velours (vəlu:r) m, velvet. ~ à [grosses] côtes, ~ côtelé, corduroy. ~ de coton, velveteen. **velouté, e** (lute) a, velvet[y].

velu, e (vəly) a, hairy (skin, caterpillar, leaf).

venaison (vənɛzɔ̃) f, venison.

vénal, e† (venal) a, venal; market[able], sale (value). **vénalité** (lite) f, venality.

venant (vənɑ̃) m, comer.

vendable (vãdabl) *a*, salable, marketable.

vendange (vãdãːʒ) *f*, grape gathering; vintage. **vendanger** (dãʒe) *v.t. & abs*, to gather. **vendangeur, euse** (ʒœːr, øːz) *n*, vintager.

vendetta (vɛ̃dɛtta) *f*, vendetta, feud.

vendeur, euse (vãdœːr, øːz) *n*, seller, vendor; salesman, -woman. **vendeur, eresse** (dœːr, drɛs) *n*, vendor (*law*). **vendre** (dr) *v.t*, to sell, sell at; sell for.

vendredi (vãdrədi) *m*, Friday. le ~ *saint*, Good Friday.

vénéneux, euse (venenø, øːz) *a*, poisonous, venomous (*plant, food*).

vénérable (venerabl) *a*, venerable. **vénération** (sjɔ̃) *f*, veneration. **vénérer** (re) *v.t*, to venerate; worship (*saints, relics*).

vénerie (venri) *f*, hunting (*science*).

vénérien, ne (venerjɛ̃, ɛn) *a*, venereal.

Vénétie (la) (venesi), Venetia.

veneur (vənœːr) *m*, huntsman.

vengeance (vãʒãːs) *f*, vengeance; revenge. **venger** (ʒe) *v.t*, to avenge, revenge. **vengeur, eresse** (ʒœːr, ʒrɛs) *n*, avenger. ¶ *a*, avenging, vengeful.

véniel, le† (venjɛl) *a*, venial.

venimeux, euse (vənimø, øːz) *a*, venomous, poisonous (*bite, animal, & fig.*). **venin** (nɛ̃) *m*, venom, poison.

venir (vəniːr) *v.i.ir*, to come; strike (*idea*); occur, happen; hail (*de* = from); grow. en ~ *aux mains*, to come to blows. *je viens de* . . ., I have just . . .

Venise (vəniːz) *f*, Venice. **vénitien, ne** (venisjɛ̃, ɛn) *a. & V~, n*, Venetian.

vent (vã) *m*, wind; air; blast; draft; scent (*hunting*); inkling; windage; flatus. ~ *coulis*, draft. en plein ~, in the open air. *îles du V~*, Windward Islands. *îles sous le V~*, Leeward Islands.

vente (vãːt) *f*, sale, selling. ~ à *tempérament*, ~ *par abonnement*, installment plan. ~ *aux*

enchères, auction sale. ~ *de blanc*, white sale. ~ *de charité*, [charity] bazaar.

venter (vãte) *v.imp*, to be windy, blow. **venteux, euse** (tø, øːz) *a*, windy; breezy. **ventilateur** (tilatœːr) *m*, fan, ventilator. **ventilation** (sjɔ̃) *f*, ventilation, airing; apportionment, analysis. **ventiler** (le) *v.t*, to ventilate, etc.

ventouse (vãtuːz) *f*, cupping glass; air hole; sucker (*of leech*); boring or leechlike person. *voiture* ~, car parked in same spot for long time. **ventouser** (tuze) *v.t*, to cup (*Surg.*).

ventral, e (vãtral) *a*, ventral. **ventre** (vãːtr) *m*, belly, abdomen; womb; bulge; bilge (*cask*). faire [le] ~, to bulge, belly. **ventrée** (vãtre) *f*, litter (*pups, etc.*).

ventricule (vãtrikyl) *m*, ventricle.

ventriloque (vãtrilɔk) *n*, ventriloquist. **ventriloquie** (ki) *f*, ventriloquism, -quy.

ventru, e (vãtry) *a*, paunchy.

venu, e (vəny) *n*, comer; (*f.*) coming; appearance; inrush; occurrence; growth. ¶ *a*, come. le premier ~, the first to come; anybody. mal ~, displeasing; unwelcome.

vêpres (vɛːpr) *f.pl*, vespers, evensong.

ver (vɛːr) *m*, worm; grub; maggot; moth. ~ à *soie*, silkworm. ~ *luisant*, glowworm. ~ *rongeur*, canker[worm]; remorse. ~ *solitaire*, tapeworm.

véracité (verasite) *f*, veracity, truthfulness.

véranda (verãda) *f*, veranda.

verbal, e† (verbal) *a*, verbal. **verbaliser** (lize) *v.i*, to take particulars; draw up a report. **verbe** (verb) *m*, verb; [tone of] voice. le *Verbe*, the Word (*Theol.*). **verbeux, euse** (bø, øːz) *a*, verbose, prosy; wordy. **verbiage** (bjaːʒ) *m*, verbiage. **verbosité** (bozite) *f*, verbosity, wordiness, prosiness.

verdal (verdal) *m*, pavement light.

verdâtre (verdɑːtr) *a*, greenish.

verdelet, te (dǝlɛ, ɛt) *a*, tartish (*wine*); hale. **verdet** (dɛ) *m*, verdigris. **verdeur** (dœːr) *f*, greenness; unripeness; tartness.

verdict (vɛrdikt) *m*, verdict.

verdier (vɛrdje) *m*, greenfinch. **verdir** (diːr) *v.t. & i*, to green. **verdoyant, e** (dwajɑ̃, ɑ̃ːt) *a*, verdant. **verdoyer** (je) *v.i*, to green. **verdure** (dyːr) *f*, verdure, greenery; greenness; greensward; greens.

véreux, euse (verø, øːz) *a*, wormy, maggoty, grubby; shady, bogus, fishy; bad (*debt*).

verge (vɛrʒ) *f*, rod; wand, verge; beam (*scales*); shank (*anchor*); (*vulgar*) penis; (*pl.*) birch [rod]. **vergé** (ʒe) *a*, laid (*paper*). **verger** (ʒe) *m*, orchard. **vergeture** (ʒǝtyːr) *f*, weal.

verglas (vɛrglɑ) *m*, glazed frost, silver thaw.

vergne (vɛrɲ) *m*, alder [tree].

vergogne (sans) (vɛrgɔɲ), shameless.

vergue (vɛrg) *f*, yard (*Naut.*).

véridique† (veridik) *a*, truthful, veracious. **vérificateur** (fikatœːr) *m*, examiner, inspector; gauge; calipers. ~ **comptable**, auditor. **vérification** (sjɔ̃) *f*, verification, inspection, examination, checking, vouching, audit[ing]. ~ *de testament*, probate. **vérifier** (fje) *v.t*, to verify.

vérin (verɛ̃) *m*, jack (*Mach.*); actuator, control (*Avn.*). ~ *d'escamotage*, retraction actuator.

véritable† (veritabl) *a*, true; real; veritable; regular. **vérité** (te) *f*, truth, verity; fact.

vermeil, le (vɛrmɛːj) *a*, vermillion; ruby, rosy. ¶ *m*, silver gilt.

vermicelle (vɛrmisɛl) *m*, vermicelli; *v.* soup.

vermillon (vɛrmijɔ̃) *m*, vermillion.

vermine (vɛrmin) *f*, vermin. **vermoulu, e** (muly) *a*, wormeaten. **vermoulure** (lyːr) *f*, wormhole; dust from wormholes.

vermouth (vɛrmut) *m*, vermouth.

vernal, e (vɛrnal) *a*, vernal, spring (*att.*).

verne (vɛrn) *m*, alder [tree].

verni, e (vɛrni) *a*, varnished, as *vernir*; patent (*leather*), patent leather (*shoes*). ¶ *m.pl*, patent leather shoes; dress shoes.

vernier (vɛrnje) *m*, vernier.

vernir (vɛrniːr) *v.t*, to varnish; japan; gloss over. **vernis** (ni) *m*, varnish; japan; glaze; veneer (*fig.*). ~ *à l'alcool*, spirit varnish. ~ *gras*, oil varnish. **vernissage** (nisaːʒ) *m*, varnishing, varnishing day, private viewing (*art exhibit*). **vernisser** (se) *v.t*, to glaze (*pottery*).

vérole (verɔl) *m*, syphilis. *petite* ~, smallpox. *quelle* ~, what a pain in the ass.

Vérone (verɔn) *f*, Verona.

véronique (verɔnik) *f*, speedwell, veronica.

verrat (vɛra) *m*, boar.

verre (vɛːr) *m*, glass. ~ *à vin*, wineglass. ~ *de vin*, glass of wine. ~ *soluble*, water glass. ~ *pilé*, ground g. ~ *perdu*, nondeposit bottle. **verrerie** (vɛrri) *f*, glass making; g. works; glass[ware]. **verrier** (rje) *m*, glass maker. **verrière** (rjɛːr) *f*, stained-glass window. **verroterie** (rɔtri) *f*, [small] glassware; [glass] beads.

verrou (vɛru) *m*, bolt. *sous les* ~*s*, under lock & key, locked up. **verrouiller** (ruje) *v.t*, to bolt; lock up (*prisoner*).

verrue (vɛry) *f*, wart. **verruqueux, euse** (kø, øːz) *a*, warty.

vers (vɛːr) *m*, verse, line (*poetry*). ~ *blancs*, blank verse. ¶ *pr*, towards; to; about.

versant (vɛrsɑ̃) *m*, side, slope (*hill*).

versatile (vɛrsatil) *a*, fickle. **versatilité** (lite) *f*, fickleness.

verse (vɛrs) *f*, laying, lodging (*corn*). *à* ~, fast, hard (*rain*). **versé(e) dans** (se), versed in, conversant with. **versement** (sǝmɑ̃) *m*, payment, paying in; p. up; remittance; installment; call; deposit (*savings bank*); pouring; spilling, etc. **verser (se)** *v.t. & i*, to pour [out]; shed, spill; tip;

overturn, upset, capsize; pay;
p. in, p. up; deposit; issue (*Mil.*).
verset (sɛ) *m*, verse (*Bible*); versicle (*Lit.*). **verseuse** (sø₁z) *f*,
coffeepot.

versificateur (vɛrsifikatœːr) *m*,
versifier. **versifier** (fje) *v.i.* & *t*, to
versify. **version** (sjɔ̃) *f*, version;
translation. ~ *originale*, film
shown in original language.

verso (vɛrso) *m*, verso, back. *au*
~, overleaf.

vert, e (vɛːr, ɛrt) *a*, green; verdant; unripe; unseasoned; callow;
raw; sour; sharp; fresh; hale;
smutty. *donner le feu* ~, to authorize. ¶ *m*, green; grass. **vert-de-
gris** (vɛrdəgri) *m*, verdigris.

vertébral, e (vɛrtebral) *a*, vertebral; spinal (*column*). **vertèbre**
(tɛːbr) *f*, vertebra. **vertébré, e**
(tebre) *a*. & *m*, vertebrate; (*m.
pl.*) Vertebrata.

vertement (vɛrtəmɑ̃) *ad*, sharply,
soundly.

vertical, e (vɛrtikal) *a*, vertical,
upright. ¶ *f*, vertical. **verticalement** (lmɑ̃) *ad*, vertically; down
(*crossword clues*).

verticille (vɛrtisil) *m*, verticil,
whorl.

vertige (vɛrtiːʒ) *m*, dizziness;
giddiness; vertigo. **vertigineux,
euse** (tiʒinø, øːz) *a*, dizzy, giddy.
vertigo (go) *m*, staggers (*Vet.*).

vertu (vɛrty) *f*, virtue. *en* ~ *de*,
in (*or* by) v. of; in pursuance of.
vertueux, euse† (tɥø, øːz) *a*, vir-
tuous; righteous.

verve (vɛrv) *f*, verve.

verveine (vɛrvɛn) *f*, verbena.

vesce (vɛs) *f*, vetch, tare.

vésicatoire (vezikatwaːr) *m*,
blister (*plaster*). **vésicule** (kyl) *f*,
vesicle, bladder. ~ *biliaire*, gall b.

vespasienne (vɛspazjɛn) *f*, urinal (*street*).

vessie (vɛsi) *f*, bladder. *prendre
des* ~*s pour des lanternes*, not to
know which end is up.

vestale (vɛstal) *f*, vestal [virgin].

veste (vɛst) *f*, jacket (*short, usually waiter's, etc.*). **vestiaire** (tjɛːr)
m, cloakroom; dressing room;
locker r.

vestibule (vɛstibyl) *m*, vestibule,
[entrance] hall, lobby.

vestige (vɛstiːʒ) *m*, footprint,
track, trace; (*pl.*) vestiges, remains.

veston (vɛstɔ̃) *m*, jacket (*man's*);
lounge coat. ~ *d'intérieur*, smoking jacket.

Vésuve (le) (vezyːv) Vesuvius.
vésuvien, ne (zyvjɛ̃, ɛn) *a*, Vesuvian.

vêtement (vɛtmɑ̃) *m*, garment;
vestment; (*pl.*) clothes, clothing.
~ *de dessous*, undergarment
(*woman's*); (*pl.*) underclothing,
underwear (*women's*).

vétéran (veterɑ̃) *m*, veteran;
long-service man (*Mil.*). **vétérance** (rɑ̃ːs) *f*, long service.

vétérinaire (veterinɛːr) *a*, veterinary. [*médecin*] ~, *m*, veterinary [surgeon].

vétille (vetiːj) *f*, trifle. **vétilleux,
euse** (tijø, øːz) *a*, finical, ticklish.

vêtir (vetiːr) *v.t.ir*, to clothe,
dress.

veto (veto) *m*, veto.

vêture (vɛtyːr) *f*, taking the habit,
taking the veil (*Eccl.*).

vétusté (vetyste) *f*, decay, [old]
age.

veuf, veuve (vœf, vœːv) *a*, wid-
owed; deprived, bereft. ¶ *m*,
widower. ¶ *f*, widow, relict.

veuillez *see* **vouloir.**

veule (vœːl) *a*, slack, flabby.

veuvage (vœvaːʒ) *m*, widower-
hood, widowhood.

vexatoire (vɛksatwaːr) *a*, vexatious. **vexer** (kse) *v.t*, to vex,
provoke.

viabilité (vjabilite) *f*, good condition (*of roads*); viability.
viable (bl) *a*, viable.

viaduc (vjadyk) *m*, viaduct.

viager, ère (vjaʒe, ɛːr) *a*, life
(*att.*), for life. *rente* ~*e*, life annuity.

viande (vjɑ̃ːd) *f*, meat. ~ *de
boucherie*, butcher's meat. ~ *de
cheval*, horseflesh.

viatique (vjatik) *m*, provision
for journey; viaticum.

vibration (vibrasjɔ̃) *f*, vibration
(*Phys.*). **vibrer** (bre) *v.i*, to vibrate (*Phys. & fig.*).

vicaire (vikɛːr) *m*, vicar; curate.
vicariat (karja) *m*, vicariate;
curacy.

vice (vis) *m*, vice; defect, fault, flaw.

vice (vis) *prefix*, vice: ~-*président*, *e*, *n*, vice- (*or* deputy) chairman *or* president. ~-*roi*, *m*, viceroy.

vicelard, **e** (visla:r, ard) *a*, vicious, cunning; depraved. ¶ *n*, depraved person.

Vicence (visɑ̃:s) *f*, Vicenza.

vicier (visje) *v.t*, to vitiate, foul. **vicieux**, **euse†** (sjø, ø:z) *a*, vicious; faulty; unsound. *locution vicieuse*), faulty expression (*Gram.*).

vicinal, **e** (visinal) *a*, parish, local (*road*).

vicissitude (visisityd) *f*, vicissitude.

vicomte (vikɔ̃:t) *m*, viscount. **vicomtesse** (vikɔ̃tɛs) *f*, viscountess.

victime (viktim) *f*, victim; casualty; sufferer.

victoire (viktwa:r) *f*, victory; win. **victoria** (tɔrja) *f*, victoria (*carriage*). **victorieux**, **euse†** (rjø, ø:z) *a*, victorious, triumphant.

victuailles (viktɥa:j) *f.pl*, victuals.

vidange (vidɑ̃:ʒ) *f*, emptying; clearing; ullage; (*pl.*) night soil. *en ~*, ullaged (*cask*). **vidanger** (dɔʒe) *v.t*, to empty. **vidangeur** (ʒœ:r) *m*, nightman. **vide** (vid) *a*, empty, void; idle. ¶ *m*, void; vacuum; space; gap; vacancy; empty (*case*). *à ~*, [when] empty. ~-*pomme*, *m*, apple corer. ~-*poche*, *m*, pin tray; glove compartment (*auto*). ~-*vite*, *m*, fuel jettison apparatus. **vider** (de) *v.t*, to empty, vacate (*les lieux* = the premises); settle (*dispute*); thresh out; bone (*cannon*); draw (*fowl*); gut (*fish*); stone (*fruit*); core (*apple*, *etc.*); dump (*computers*).

viduité (vidɥite) *f*, widowhood.

vie (vi) *f*, life; lifetime; living, livelihood. *la ~ à trois*, the eternal triangle. *à ~*, for life.

vieil, **vieille** *see* vieux.

vieillard (vjɛja:r) *m*, old man. *les ~s*, the aged (*either sex*). **vieilleries** (jri) *f.pl*, old things. **vieillesse** (jɛs) *f*, [old] age. **vieilli**, **e** (ji) *a*, antiquated; obsolete, archaic; aged. **vieillir** (ji:r) *v.i*, to grow old, age, become obsolete;

(*v.t.*) to age, make [look] old[er]. **vieillissant**, **e** (jisɑ̃, ɑ̃:t) *a*, aging; obsolescent. **vieillot**, **te** (jo, ɔt) *a*, oldish, quaint. ¶ *n*, little old man, little old woman.

Vienne (vjɛn) *f*, Vienna. **viennois**, **e** (nwa, a:z) *a*. & **V~**, *n*, Viennese.

vierge (vjɛrʒ) *f*, virgin, maid. ¶ *a*, virgin; blank (*page*); free; unexposed (*Phot.*).

vieux, **vieil**, **vieille** (vjø, vjɛj) *a*, old; stale; obsolete, archaic. *vieille fille*, old maid. **vieux**, **vieille**, *n*, old man, old woman. *le vieux*, the old (*opp.* the new). *les vieux*, the old (*either sex*).

vif, **vive** (vif, i:v) *a*, alive; live; living; quick; lively; sprightly; brisk; smart; sharp; vital; keen; crisp, tangy; hasty; spirited; vivid; bright; spring (*water*, *tide*). *de vive force*, by main (*or* sheer) force. *de vive voix*, by word of mouth, viva voce. **le vif**, the quick (*flesh*, *etc.*); the heart (*of a matter*); life (*art*). **vif-argent**, *m*, quicksilver.

vigie (viʒi) *f*, lookout; lookout [man]; vigia.

vigilance (viʒilɑ̃:s) *f*, vigilance, watchfulness. **vigilant**, **e** (lɑ̃, ɑ̃:t) *a*, vigilant, watchful. **vigile** (ʒil) *f*, vigil, eve (*Eccl.*).

vigne (viɲ) *f*, vine, vineyard. ~ *vierge*, Virginia creeper. **vigneron**, **ne** (nɔrɔ̃, ɔn) *n*, winegrower. **vignette** (nɛt) *f*, vignette; cut; ornamental border; revenue label; car license (*special auto tax*). **vignoble** (nɔbl) *m*, vineyard.

vigogne (vigɔɲ) *f*, vicugna, vicuña.

vigoureux, **euse†** (vigurø, ø:z) *a*, vigorous, strong, forceful; stout, sturdy, robust, lusty; plucky (*Phot.*). **vigueur** (gœ:r) *f*, vigor, strength. *mettre en ~*, to put in force, enforce.

vil, **e†** (vil) *a*, vile, base, mean. *à vil prix*, dirt-cheap. **vilain**, **e†** (lɛ̃, ɛn) *a*, ugly; wretched; nasty; scurvy; naughty. ¶ *n*, villain, villein (*Hist.*); naughty boy, girl, villain; scurvy fellow.

vilebrequin (vilbrəkɛ̃) *m*, brace, bit stock; wimble; crank shaft.

vilenie (vilni) *f*, meanness; dirty trick; abuse. **vileté** (lte) *f*, cheapness; worthlessness. **vilipender** (lipɑ̃de) *v.t*, to vilify.

villa (vila) *f*, villa. **village** (vila:ʒ) *m*, village. **villageois, e** (laʒwa, a:z) *n*, villager; (*att.*) rustic, country. **ville** (vil) *f*, town, city. ~ *d'eaux*, watering place, spa. *hôtel de* ~, town hall, city h. **villégiature** (leʒjaty:r) *f*, stay in the country; holiday.

vin (vɛ̃) *m*, wine. ~ *blanc du Rhin*, hock. ~ *ordinaire*, table wine. ~ *de liqueur*, sweet dessert wine. ~ *du cru*, wine of the country. ~ *en cercles*, wine in the wood. ~ *de marque*, vintage wine. ~ *mousseux*, sparkling wine. **vinage** (vina:ʒ) *m*, fortification (*of wine*). **vinaigre** (nɛgr) *m*, vinegar. **vinaigrer** (negre) *v.t*, to vinegar. **vinaigrette** (negrɛt) *f*, oil & vinegar dressing. **vinaigrerie** (grəri) *f*, vinegar works.

vindas (vɛ̃da:s) *m*, crab [capstan]; giant['s] stride.

vindicatif, ive (vɛ̃dikatif, i:v) *a*, vindictive, revengeful; avenging. **vindicte** (dikt) *f*, (*public*) prosecution (*of crime*).

vinée (vine) *f*, vintage (*crop*). **viner** (ne) *v.t*, to fortify (*wine*). **vineux, euse** (nø, ø:z) *a*, vinous; winy; full-bodied (*wine*); rich in vineyards; rich in wines.

vingt (vɛ̃) *a*, twenty. ¶ *m*, twenty; 20th. ~-*deux!* watch it! look out! **vingtaine** (tɛ:n) *f*, score, twenty [or so]. **vingtième** (tjɛm) *a*. & *n*, twentieth.

vinicole (vinikɔl) *a*, wine-growing. **vinosité** (nozite) *f*, vinosity.

viol (vjɔl) *m*, rape, ravishment.

violacé, e (vjɔlase) *a*, violaceous. **violacées**, *f.pl*, Violaceae.

violariacée (vjɔlarjase) *f*, viola (*Bot.*); (*pl.*) Viola (*genus*).

violateur, trice (vjɔlatœ:r, tris) *a*, violator; transgressor. **violation** (sjɔ̃) *f*, violation, transgression, breach; desecration.

violâtre (vjɔlɑ:tr) *a*, purplish.

viole (vjɔl) *f*, viol; jackscrew.

violemment (vjɔlamɑ̃) *ad*, violently. **violence** (lɑ̃:s) *f*, violence; duress; stress. **violent, e** (lɑ̃, ɑ̃:t) *a*, violent. **violenter** (lɑ̃te) *v.t*, to do violence to. **violer** (le) *v.t*, to violate, transgress, break; rape, ravish; desecrate.

violet, te (vjɔlɛ, ɛt) *a*, violet, purple. **violet, m**, violet (*color*). **violette**, *f*, violet (*Bot.*). ~ *de chien*, dog v. ~ *de Parme*, Parma v. ~ *odorante*, sweet v. **violier** (lje) *m*, stock. ~ *jaune*, wallflower.

violon (vjɔlɔ̃) *m*, violin, fiddle; lockup, clink. **violoncelle** (sɛl) *m*, violoncello, [']cello. **violoncelliste** (list) *n*, [violon]cellist. **violoniste** (lɔnist) *n*, violinist.

vipère (vipɛ:r) *f*, viper, adder.

virage (vira:ʒ) *m*, turning, slewing, swinging; tacking (*Naut.*); turn, bend, corner; toning (*Phot.*).

virago (virago) *f*, amazon (*forceful woman*).

virement (virmɑ̃) *m*, turning; tacking (*Naut.*); bank transfer; transfer (*Bkkpg.*). **virer** (re) *v.i*, to turn; bank (*Avn.*); heave (*Naut.*); (*v.t.*) to transfer; tone (*Phot.*). ~ *de bord*, to tack (*Naut.*).

vireux, euse (virø, ø:z) *a*, noxious.

virginal, e† (virʒinal) *a*, virginal, maiden[ly]. **virginie** (ni) *m*, Virginia [tobacco]. **la V~**, Virginia (*Geog.*). **virginité** (te) *f*, virginity, maidenhood.

virgule (virgyl) *f*, comma. ~ [*décimale*], decimal point. *Note:* — The decimal point is indicated in French by a comma.

viril, e (viril) *a*, virile, manly. **virilité** (lite) *f*, virility, manliness; manhood.

virole (virɔl) *f*, ferrule.

virtuel, le (virtɥɛl) *a*, virtual. **virtuellement** (lmɑ̃) *ad*, virtually, to all intents & purposes.

virtuose (virtɥo:z) *n*, virtuoso. **virtuosite** (ozite) *f*, virtuosity.

virulence (virylɑ̃:s) *f*, virulence. **virulent, e** (lɑ̃, ɑ̃:t) *a*, virulent. **virus** (ry:s) *m*, virus.

vis (vis) *f*, screw. ~ *ailée*, wing s. ~ *d'Archimède* (arʃimɛd), Archimedean s. ~ *sans fin*, worm.

visa (viza) *m*, visa; initials, signature.

visage (viza:ʒ) *m*, face, visage; aspect. *à ~ découvert*, barefacedly.

vis-à-vis (vizavi) & *~ de*, *pr. & ad*, opposite, o. to; face to face; facing; vis-à-vis; towards. ¶ *m*, person opposite; vis-à-vis.

viscères (vise:r) *m.pl*, viscera.

viscose (visko:z) *f*, viscose. **viscosité** (kozite) *f*, viscosity, stickiness.

visée (vize) *f*, sight[ing], observation, aim; (*pl.*) aims, designs, ambition. **viser** (ze) *v.t*, to aim at; sight; cater for; visa; initial, sign; refer to; have in view; certify. *~ à*, to aim at. **viseur** (zœ:r) *m*, [view]finder (*Phot.*); dial (*calculating mach.*). *~ redresseur*, collapsible viewfinder. **visibilité** (zibilite) *f*, visibility. **visible†** (bl) *a*, visible; obvious; at home. *pas ~*, engaged; not accessible. **visière** (zjɛ:r) *f*, peak (*cap*); eyeshade; visor (*Hist.*). **vision** (zjɔ̃) *f*, vision, sight; seeing; fantasy; hallucination. **visionnaire** (zjɔnɛ:r) *a. & n*, visionary.

visioconférence (vizjɔkɔ̃ferɑ̃:s) *f*, videoconference.

visitation (vizitasjɔ̃) *f*, visitation (*Eccl.*). **visite** (zit) *f*, visit, call; attendance; inspection, examination, survey. **visiter** (te) *v.t*, to visit. **visiteur, euse** (tœ:r, ø:z) *n*, visitor, caller; inspector, examiner.

vison (vizɔ̃) *m*, mink (*Zool. & fur*).

visqueux, euse (viskø, ø:z) *a*, viscous, sticky, tacky.

visser (vise) *v.t*, to screw [on, down, up].

Vistule (la) (vistyl), the Vistula.

visu (vizy) *f*, display device (*computers*).

visuel, le (vizɥɛl) *a*, visual, (*line, etc.*) of sight. ¶ *m*, display device (*computers*).

vital, e (vital) *a*, vital. **vitalité** (lite) *f*, vitality. **vitamine** (min) *f*, vitamin.

vite (vit) *a*, swift, quick, fast. ¶ *ad*, quick[ly], fast.

vitesse (vitɛs) *f*, speed, velocity, quickness. *première ~*, low gear.

viticole (vitikɔl) *a*, viticultural. **viticulteur** (kyltœr) *m*, viticultur[al]ist, winegrower. **viticulture** (ty:r) *f*, viticulture.

vitrage (vitra:ʒ) *m*, glazing; windows, glass work; glass door; curtain net, vitrage. **vitrail** (tra:j) *m*, leaded window. *vitraux peints*, stained glass. **vitre** (tr) *f*, [window] pane. **vitrer** (tre) *v.t*, to glaze (*window*). **vitrerie** (trəri) *f*, glaziery. **vitreux, euse** (trø, ø:z) *a*, vitreous, glassy; lackluster. **vitrier** (trie) *m*, glazier. **vitrifier** (fje) *v.t*, to vitrify. **vitrine** (trin) *f*, glass case, showcase; display cabinet, china cabinet; curio cabinet; shop window.

vitriol (vitriɔl) *m*, vitriol.

vitupération (vityperasjɔ̃) *f*, abuse. **vitupérer** (pere) *v.t*, to abuse. *v.i*, to protest against.

vivable (vivabl) *a*, livable.

vivace (vivas) *a*, long-lived; inveterate; perennial (*Bot.*). **vivacité** (site) *f*, vivacity, liveliness; heat; hastiness; petulance; vividness.

vivandier, ère (vivɑ̃dje, ɛːr) *n*, sutler, canteen-keeper.

vivant, e (vivɑ̃, ɑ̃:t) *a*, alive; living; lifelike; live; modern (*language*); lively; vivid. ¶ *m*, living being; lifetime; life. **vivat** (vat) *i. & m*, hurrah, -ray!; cheer. **vive-eau**, *f*, spring tide. **vivement** (vmɑ̃) *ad*, briskly; sharply; keenly; warmly. **viveur** (vœ:r) *m*, gay man, fast liver, rake. **vivier** (vje) *m*, fish pond. **vivifier** (vifje) *v.t*, to vivify, quicken; vitalize; invigorate, brace. **vivipare** (pa:r) *a*, viviparous. **vivisection** (sɛksjɔ̃) *f*, vivisection. **vivoter** (vivote) *v.i*, to scrape by; live from hand to mouth. **vivre** (vi:vr) *v.i. & t. ir*, to live; be alive; subsist; endure; behave. ¶ *m*, living; food; (*pl.*) provisions, victuals; rations. *le ~ & le couvert*, room & board.

vizir (vizi:r) *m*, vizier.

vocable (vɔkabl) *m*, vocable. **vocabulaire** (bylɛ:r) *m*, vocabulary. **vocal, e** (kal) *a*, vocal. **vocaliser**

(lize) *v.t*, to vocalize. **vocatif** (katif) *m*, vocative [case]. **vocation** (sjɔ̃) *f*, vocation, calling; call (*divine*).

vociférer (vɔsifere) *v.i*, to vociferate, shout, bawl, yell.

vœu (vø) *m*, vow; wish; prayer.

vogue (vɔg) *f*, fashion, vogue; request; run. *vogue la galère!*, come what may! **voguer** (ge) *v.i*, to row; sail.

voici (vwasi) *pr*, here is, here are; here; this is. *me ~!* here I am.

voie (vwa) *f*, way; road; route; track; line; duct; scent; means; course; process. *~ de départ*, aircraft runway. *~ d'eau*, leak; waterway. *~s de fait*, assault [& battery]; blows, violence, force. *~ de garage*, siding. *~ ferrée*, railway. *~ lactée*, Milky Way, galaxy. *~ navigable*, waterway. *~ publique*, public thoroughfare, highway. *~ à double sens*, two-way street.

voilà (vwala) *pr*, there is, there are; that is.

voile (vwal) *f*, sail, canvas. ¶ *m*, veil; velum; cloth; voile; mist; fog; mask; blind. **voiler** (le) *v.t*, to veil; cloak; muffle; fog; [en]shroud; buckle. **voilerie** (lri) *f*, sail loft; s. making. **voilier** (lje) *m*, sail maker; sailing ship; (*good, bad*) sailer (*ship*). **voilure** (lyːr) *f*, sails (*col.*); buckling.

voir (vwaːr) *v.t. & abs. ir*, to see; look [at, on]; behold; sight; understand; examine; visit. *faire ~*, to show.

voire (vwaːr) *ad*, nay; even. *~ même, & even*, indeed.

voirie (vwari) *f*, highways committee; refuse dump.

voisin, e (vwazɛ̃, in) *a*, neighboring; akin; next. ¶ *n*, neighbor. **voisinage** (zinaːʒ) *m*, neighborhood; vicinity. **voisiner** (ne) *v.i*, to border on, be near.

voiture (vwatyːr) *f*, conveyance; carriage; coach; car; wagon; cart; van. *en ~!* all aboard! *~ cellulaire*, patrol wagon. *~ d'enfant*, baby carriage. *~ de course*, racing car. *~ d'occasion*, second hand c. *~ hors série*, custom-built

c. **voiturer** (tyre) *v.t*, to convey, carry, cart. **voiturette** (rɛt) *f*, trap; light car, runabout. **voiturier** (rje) *m*, carter; carrier.

voix (vwa) *f*, voice; register; speech; word; dictate[s]; opinion; say; vote. *~ de stentor* (stɑ̃tɔːr), stentorian voice. *de vive ~*, by word of mouth.

vol (vɔl) *m*, flying, flight; wing; flock (*birds*). *~ à voile*, gliding (*Avn.*). *à ~ d'oiseau*, as the crow flies. *~ piqué*, dive (*Avn.*).

vol (vɔl) *m*, theft, stealing, robbery. *~ à l'américaine*, confidence trick. *~ à l'étalage*, shoplifting. *~ à la tire*, pocket, picking; bag snatching. *~ à main armée*, armed robbery. *~ de grand chemin*, highway robbery. *~ [de nuit avec effraction]*, burglary.

volage (vɔlaːʒ) *a*, fickle, inconstant.

volaille (vɔlaːj) *f*, poultry, fowls; police (*pejorative*).

volant, e (vɔlɑ̃, ɑ̃ːt) *a*, flying; loose; portable. *soucoupe ~e*, flying saucer. ¶ *m*, shuttlecock; leaf (*opp*. counterfoil); flywheel; sail (*windmill*); flounce. [*jeu de*] *~*, battledore & shuttlecock. *feuille ~e*, looseleaf. *~ au filet*, badminton. *~ de direction*, steering wheel.

volatil, e (vɔlatil) *a*, volatile. **volatile** (til) *m*, winged creature. **volatiliser** (lize) *v.t*, to volatilize. *se~*, to volatilize; vanish.

volcan (vɔlkɑ̃) *m*, volcano. **volcanique** (kanik) *a*, volcanic.

volée (vɔle) *f*, flight; wing; flock; volley; peal (*bells*); rank (*class*); splinter bar, swingle-tree; chase (*gun*). *~ de coups*, drubbing. *à la ~*, in the air; on the wing; promptly; broadcast; at random. **voler** (le) *v.i*, to fly; (*v.t.*) to chase, fly at (*hawking*); steal, rob. **volerie** (lri) *f*, hawking (*falconry*); thieving.

volet (vɔlɛ) *m*, shutter; volet; sorting board; flap (*Avn.*); wipe (*cinema*).

voleter (vɔlte) *v.i*, to flutter; flit; skip.

voleur, euse (vɔlœːr, øːz) *n*,

thief, robber; *(att.)* thievish *(pers.)*. ~ *à la tire*, pickpocket; bag snatcher. ~ *de grand chemin*, highwayman.

volière (vɔljɛːr) *f*, aviary; run *(pheasants, etc.)*.

volige (vɔliːʒ) *f*, batten; lath.

volition (vɔlisjɔ̃) *f*, volition.

volontaire† (vɔlɔ̃tɛːr) *a*, voluntary; wilful, wayward. ¶ *m*, volunteer *(Mil.)*. **volonté** (te) *f*, will; *(pl.)* whims. *dernières ~s*, last will & testament. **volontiers** (tje) *ad*, willingly, gladly; fain; apt, rather.

volt (vɔlt) *m*, volt. **voltage** (taːʒ) *m*, voltage. **voltaïque** (taik) *a*, voltaic.

volte-face (vɔltəfas) *f*, about-face; change of front.

voltige (vɔltiːʒ) *f*, trick riding & similar circus gymnastics. **voltiger** (tiʒe) *v.i*, to fly about, flit, hover; flutter, flap; perform on horseback; perform on the slack rope.

voltmètre (vɔltmɛtr) *m*, voltmeter.

volubile (vɔlybil) *a*, twining *(Bot.)*; voluble, glib *(speaker)*. **volubilis** (lis) *m*, convolvulus. **volubilité** (lite) *f*, volubility, glibness.

volume (vɔlym) *m*, volume; tome; bulk; measurement. **volumineux, euse** (minø, øːz) *a*, voluminous, bulky.

volupté (vɔlypte) *f*, voluptuousness, pleasure, delight. **voluptueux, euse**† (tɥø, øːz) *a*, voluptuous. ¶ *n*, voluptuary.

volute (vɔlyt) *f*, volute, scroll.

vomir (vɔmiːr) *v.t. & abs*, to vomit, spew, belch out. **vomissement** (mismã) *m*, vomiting; vomit. **vomitif** (mitif) *m*, emetic, vomitory.

vorace† (vɔras) *a*, voracious. **voracité** (site) *f*, voracity.

vos *see* **votre**.

votant (vɔtã) *m*, voter. **votation** (tasjɔ̃) *f*, voting. **vote** (vɔt) *m*, vote, poll. **voter** (te) *v.i. & t*, to vote; pass, carry. ~ *à main levée*, to vote by a show of hands. **votif, ive** (tif, iːv) *a*, votive.

votre, *pl*. **vos** (vɔtr, vo) *a*, your.

~ *affectionné, e*, yours affectionately. **vôtre** (voːtr) *a*, yours. *le vôtre, la vôtre, les vôtres*, yours, your own.

vouer (vwe) *v.t*, to vow; dedicate; devote.

vouloir (vulwaːr) *m*, will. ¶ *v.t.ir*, to will; want, wish; like; [be] please[d to]; mean; intend; require, need. *en ~ à*, to bear ill will. *s'en ~ de*, to be angry with oneself for. *veuillez agréer*, please accept. **voulu, e** (ly) *p.a*, required, requisite; deliberate, intentional; studied. *en temps ~*, in due time.

vous (vu) *pn*, you; ye; to you; yourself, yourselves; each other. *~-même*, *~-mêmes*, yourself, yourselves.

voussoir (vuswaːr) *m*, voussoir, arch stone. **voûte** (vut) *f*, vault; arch; dome; canopy. ~ *palatine*, ~ *du palais*, roof of the mouth. **voûté, e** (te) *p.a*, vaulted; arched; stooping, bent, round-shouldered. **voûter** (te) *v.t*, to vault, arch; bow.

voyage (vwajaːʒ) *m*, journey, voyage, trip, tour. **voyager** (jaʒe) *v.i*, to travel; journey; migrate. **voyageur, euse** (ʒœːr, øːz) *n*, traveler; passenger; fare.

voyant, e (vwajã, ãːt) *a*, seeing; gaudy, garish; showy; conspicuous. ¶ *n*, clairvoyant.

voyelle (vwajɛl) *f*, vowel.

voyer (vwaje) *m*, surveyor *(roads)*.

voyou (vwaju) *m*, guttersnipe; hooligan.

vrac (en) (vrak), in bulk; loose.

vrai, e (vrɛ) *a*, true, truthful; real, genuine; right; downright, thorough, arrant. **vrai & vraiment** (mã) *ad*, truly, really; indeed. **vrai**, *m*, truth. **vraisemblable**† (sãblabl) *a*, probable, likely. **vraisemblance** (blãːs) *f*, probability, likelihood, verisimilitude.

vrille (vriːj) *f*, tendril; gimlet; tailspin *(Avn.)*. **vriller** (vrije) *v.t*, to bore; *(v.i.)* to kink, corkscrew. **vrillette** (jɛt) *f*, deathwatch [beetle].

vrombir (vrɔ̃biːr) *v.i*, to buzz; throb; purr; whirr; hum. **vrom-**

bissement (bismã) *m*, buzzing, hum, etc.

vu (vy) *m*, sight, inspection. ¶ *pr*, considering, seeing. ~ *que*, seeing that; whereas.

vue (vy) *f*, [eye]sight; eyes, eye; view; sight; prospect, outlook; slide; window, light. ~ *cavalière*, ~ *à vol d'oiseau*, bird's-eye view. ~*s fondantes*, dissolving views. *à* ~ *d'œil*, at a rough estimate; visibly. *à* ~ *de nez*, a rough guess. *prise de* ~*s*, shooting (*cinema*, *TV*). ~ *en coupe*, sectional drawing.

vulcain (vylkɛ̃) *m*, red admiral (*butterfly*).

vulcaniser (vylkanize) *v.t*, to vulcanize.

vulgaire† (vylgɛ:r) *a*, vulgar; common; low; everyday; vernacular. le ~, the common people, the vulgar [herd]. **vulgariser** (garize) *v.t*, to popularize; vulgarize. **vulgarité** (te) *f*, vulgarity. **la Vulgate** (gat), the Vulgate.

vulnérable (vylnerabl) *a*, vulnerable.

---

phobic. ¶ *m*, xenophobe. **xénophobie** (fɔbi) *f*, xenophobia.

xérès (kerɛs) *m*, sherry.

xylophone (ksilɔfɔn) *m*, xylophone.

Y

y (i) *ad*, there; here; at home. ¶ *pn*, of it, him, etc; to it; about it; at it; by it; in it; it. *ça* ~ *est!* it's done! that's it! *il* ~ *a*, there is, there are. *je n'* ~ *suis pour rien*, I had nothing to do with it. ~ *compris*, including.

yacht (jɔt) *m*, yacht. *Note.—le* yacht, *not* l'yacht.

yaourt (jaurt) *m*, yogurt.

yeuse (jø:z) *f*, ilex, holm oak.

yeux *see* œil.

yole (jɔl) *f*, gig, skiff, yawl, *Note:* —la yole.

yougoslave (jugɔsla;v) *a. & Y~*, *n*, Yugoslav. **la Yougoslavie** (slavi) Yugoslavia.

youpin, e (jupɛ̃, in) *n*, Jew, Jewess (*pejorative*).

ypérite (iperit) *f*, mustard gas.

W

wagon (vagɔ̃) (*Rly.*) *m*, carriage, coach, car; wagon, truck. ~*-lit*, sleeping car. ~ *de marchandise*, freight car. ~*-poste*, mail car. ~*-restaurant*, restaurant car, dining car. ~*-salon*, observation car, parlor c. ~*-citerne*, tank c.

wagonnet (vagɔnɛ) *m*, dump truck.

warrant (warã;t) *m*, warrant (*dock, warehouse*).

waters (watɛ;r) *pl.m*, toilet, lavatory, john.

watt (wat) *m*, watt.

Westphalie (la) (vɛstfali), Westphalia.

whisky (wiski) *m*, whiskey.

whist (wist) *m*, whist (*cards*). ~ *à trois avec un mort*, dummy w. ~ *de Gand*, solo w.

X

xénophobe (ksenɔfɔb) *a*, xeno-

Z

zazou (zazu) *m*, zoot-suiter; snappy dresser (*WW II*).

zèbre (zɛbr) *m*, zebra; individual, type, guy. *faire le* ~, to play the fool. *un drôle de* ~, a peculiar fellow. **zébré, e** (zebre) *a*, striped.

zélateur, trice (zelatœ;r, tris) *n*, zealot. **zèle** (zɛ;l) *m*, zeal. *faire du* ~, to be unnecessarily zealous. **zélé, e** (zele) *a*, zealous.

zénith (zenit) *m*, zenith.

zéphyr (zefi;r) *m*, zephyr.

zeppelin (zɛplɛ̃) *m*, zeppelin.

zéro (zero) *m*, cipher, nought, 0; love (*Ten.*); zero (See *centigrade* Fr-Eng.); nobody. ~ *partout*, love-all (*Ten.*).

zeste (zɛst) *m*, woody partitions (*walnut*); peel (*orange, lemon*); straw (*fig.*). ~ *confit*, candied peel.

zézayer (zezɛje) *v.i*, to lisp.

zibeline (ziblin) *f*, sable (*Zool., fur*).

zigzag (zigzag) *m*, zigzag. *disposé en ~*, staggered.

zizi (zizi) *m*, penis (*children's slang*).

zinc (zɛ̃:g) *m*, zinc, spelter; bar, counter. **zincogravure** (zɛ̃kɔgravy:r) *f*, zincography. **zingueur** (gœ:r) *m*, zinc worker.

zircon (zirkɔ̃) *m*, zircon.

zizanie (zizani) *f*, discord.

zob (zɔb) *m*, penis (*slang*).

zodiaque (zɔdjak) *m*, zodiac.

zone (zo:n) *f*, zone; belt; area. *~ des calmes*, doldrums. *~ bleue*, limited parking area. *~ crépusculaire*, gray area (*statistics*). *citoyen de seconde ~*, second-class citizen. *la Z~*, slum, shantytown; city outskirts.

zoologie (zɔɔlɔʒi) *f*, zoology. **zoologique** (ʒik) *a*, zoological. **zoologiste** (ʒist) *n*, zoologist.

zoulou (zulu) *a*. & *Z~*, *n*, Zulu.

zozo (zozo) *m*, idiot, clod, fool.

zozoter (zozote) *v.i*, to lisp (*slang*).

zut (zyt) *i*, darn it! go to the devil!

Zuyderzée (le) (zɥidɛrze), the Zuyder Zee.

Order of tenses & parts:

(1) = Indicative Present
(2) =   "   Imperfect
(3) =   "   Preterit
(4) =   "   Future
(5) = Conditional Present
(6) = Imperative
(7) = Subjunctive Present
(8) =   "   Imperfect
(9) = Participle Present
(10) =   "   Past

Prefixed verbs not included in the list, such as **abattre, sourire, désapprendre, satisfaire,** follow the second or last element (**battre, rire, prendre, faire**).

absoudre.—(1) j'absous, tu absous, il absout, nous absolvons, vous absolvez, ils absolvent. (2) j'absolvais. (4) j'absoudrai. (5) j'absoudrais. (6) absous, absolvons, absolvez. (7) que j'absolve. (9) absolvant. (10) absous, oute.

abstraire.—*like* **traire,** *but only in* (1) (2) *and compound tenses.*

accroître.—*like* **croître,** *but* (10) accru, *no circumflex accent.*

acquérir.—(1) j'acquiers, tu acquiers, il acquiert, nous acquérons, vous acquérez, ils acquièrent. (2) j'acquérais. (3) j'acquis. (4) j'acquerrai. (5) j'acquerrais. (6) acquiers, acquérons, acquérez. (7) que j'acquière. (8) que j'acquisse. (9) acquérant. (10) acquis, e.

aller.—(1) je vais, tu vas, il va, nous allons, vous allez, ils vont. (2) j'allais. (3) j'allai. (4) j'irai. (5) j'irais. (6) va (*but* vas-y), allons, allez. (7) que j'aille. (8) que j'allasse. (9) allant. (10) allé, e.

s'en aller.—*like* **aller.** *The auxiliary* être *is used in the compound tenses and is placed between* en *and* allé; *thus,* je m'en suis allé. (6) va-t-en, allons-nous-en, allez-vous-en.

apparaître.—*like* **connaître.**

assaillir.—(1) j'assaille, tu assailles, il assaille, nous assaillons, vous assaillez, ils assaillent. (2) j'assaillais. (3) j'assaillis. (4) j'assaillirai. (5) j'assaillirais. (6) assaille, assaillons, assaillez. (7) que j'assaille. (8) que j'assaillisse. (9) assaillant. (10) assailli, e.

asseoir.—(1) j'assieds, tu assieds, il assied, nous asseyons, vous asseyez, ils asseyent. (2) j'asseyais. (3) j'assis. (4) j'assiérai *ou* j'asseyerai. (5) j'assiérais *ou* j'asseyerais. (6) assieds, asseyons, asseyez. (7) que j'asseye. (8) que j'assisse. (9) asseyant. (10) assis, e. *This verb is sometimes conjugated in maintaining throughout the* oi *of the radical; thus,* (1) j'assois, nous assoyons. (2) j'assoyais, etc.

astreindre.—*like* **atteindre.**

atteindre.—(1) j'atteins, tu atteins, il atteint, nous atteignons, vous atteignez, ils atteignent. (2) j'atteignais. (3) j'atteignis. (4) j'atteindrai. (5) j'atteindrais. (6) atteins, atteignons, atteignez. (7) que j'atteigne. (8) que j'atteignisse. (9) atteignant. (10) atteint, e.

avoir.—(1) j'ai, tu as, il a, nous avons, vous avez, ils ont. (2) j'avais. (3) j'eus. (4) j'aurai. (5) j'aurais. (6) aie, ayons, ayez. (7) que j'aie. (8) que j'eusse. (9) ayant. (10) eu, e.

battre.—(1) je bats, tu bats, il bat, nous battons, vous battez, ils battent. (2) je battais. (3) je battis. (4) je battrai. (5) je battrais. (6) bats, battons, battez. (7) que je batte. (8) que je battisse. (9) battant. (10) battu, e.

boire.—(1) je bois, tu bois, il boit, nous buvons, vous buvez, ils boivent. (2) je buvais. (3) je bus. (4) je boirai. (5) je boirais. (6) bois, buvons, buvez. (7) que je boive. (8) que je busse. (9) buvant. (10) bu, e.

bouillir.—(1) je bous, tu bous, il bout, nous bouillons, vous bouillez, ils bouillent. (2) je bouillais. (3) je bouillis. (4) je bouillirai. (5) je bouillirais. (6) bous, bouillons, bouillez. (7) que je bouille. (8) que je bouillisse. (9) bouillant. (10) bouilli, e.

braire.—*like* **traire** *but seldom used except in infinitive & in 3rd persons of* (1) (4) & (5).

bruire.—*Seldom used except in infinitive and in 3rd person s.* of (1) il bruit, *and in 3rd persons* of (2) il bruissait, ils bruissaient.

ceindre.—*like* **atteindre.**

choir.—(10) chu, e. *Others not used.*

circoncire.—*like* **confire,** *but* (10) circoncis, e.

circonscrire.—*like* **écrire.**

clore.—(1) je clos, tu clos, il clôt. (4) je clorai, etc. (6) clos. (7) que je close, etc. (10) clos e. *Other forms not, or very seldom, used.*

comparaître.—*like* **connaître,** *but* (10) comparu (*inv.*).

conclure.—(1) je conclus, tu conclus, il conclut, nous concluons, vous concluez, ils concluent. (2) je concluais. (3) je conclus. (4) je conclurai. (5) je conclurais. (6) conclus, concluons, concluez. (7) que je conclue. (8) que je conclusse. (9) concluant. (10) conclu, e.

conduire.—(1) je conduis, tu conduis, il conduit, nous conduisons, vous conduisez, ils conduisent. (2) je conduisais. (3) je conduisis. (4) je conduirai. (5) je conduirais. (6) conduis, conduisons, conduisez. (7) que je conduise. (8) que je conduisisse. (9) conduisant. (10) conduit, e.

confire.—(1) je confis, tu confis, il confit, nous confisons, vous confisez, ils confisent. (2) je confisais. (3) je confis. (4) je confirai. (5) je confirais. (6) confis, confisons, confisez. (7) que je confise. (8) que je confisse. (9) confisant. (10) confit, e.

connaître.—(1) je connais, tu connais, il connaît, nous connaissons, vous connaissez, ils connaissent. (2) je connaissais. (3) je connus. (4) je connaîtrai. (5) je connaîtrais. (6) connais, connaissons, connaissez. (7) que je connaisse. (8) que je connusse. (9) connaissant. (10) connu, e.

conquérir.—*like* **acquérir.**

construire.—*like* **conduire.**

contraindre.—*like* **craindre.**

contredire.—*like* **dire,** *except* (1) vous contredisez. (6) contredisez.

coudre.—(1) je couds, tu couds, il coud, nous cousons, vous cousez, ils cousent. (2) je cousais. (3) je cousis. (4) je coudrai. (5) je coudrais. (6) couds, cousons, cousez. (7) que je couse. (8) que je cousisse. (9) cousant. (10) cousu, e.

courir.—(1) je cours, tu cours, il court, nous courons, vous courez, ils courent. (2) je courais. (3) je courus. (4) je courrai. (5) je courrais. (6) cours, courons, courez. (7) que je coure. (8) que je courusse. (9) courant. (10) couru, e.

couvrir.—*like* **ouvrir.**

craindre.—(1) je crains, tu crains, il craint, nous craignons, vous craignez, ils craignent. (2) je craignais. (3) je craignis. (4) je craindrai. (5) je craindrais. (6) crains, craignons, craignez. (7) que je craigne. (8) que je craignisse. (9) craignant. (10) craint, e.

croire.—(1) je crois, tu crois, il croit, nous croyons, vous croyez, ils croient. (2) je croyais. (3) je crus. (4) je croirai. (5) je croirais. (6) crois, croyons, croyez. (7) que je croie. (8) que je crusse. (9) croyant. (10) cru, e.

croître.—(1) je croîs, tu croîs, il croît, nous croissons, vous croissez, ils croissent. (2) je croissais. (3) je crûs. (4) je croîtrai. (5) je croîtrais. (6) croîs, croissons, croissez. (7) que je croisse. (8) que je crûsse. (9) croissant. (10) crû, crue (*pl.* crus, crues).

cueillir.—(1) je cueille, tu cueilles, il cueille, nous cueillons, vous cueillez, ils cueillent. (2) je cueillais. (3) je cueillis. (4) je cueillerai. (5) je cueillerais. (6) cueille, cueillons, cueillez. (7) que je cueille. (8) que je cueillisse. (9) cueillant. (10) cueilli, e.

cuire.—*like* **conduire.**

déchoir.—(1) je déchois, tu déchois, il déchoit. (3) je déchus. (4) je décherrai. (7) que je déchoie. (8) que je déchusse. (10) déchu, e.

déconfire.—(10) déconfit, e.

découvrir.—*like* ouvrir.

décrire.—*like* écrire.

décroître.—*like* croître, *except* (10) décru, e.

dédire.—*like* dire, *except* (1) vous dédisez. (6) dédisez.

déduire.—*like* conduire.

défaillir.—(1) nous défaillons, vous défaillez, ils défaillent. (2) je défaillais, etc. (3) je défaillis, etc. (9) défaillant. *Other forms seldom used.*

démentir.—*like* sentir.

dépeindre.—*like* atteindre.

dépourvoir.—(10) dépourvu, e.

déteindre.—*like* atteindre.

détruire.—*like* conduire.

devoir.—(1) je dois, tu dois, il doit, nous devons, vous devez, ils doivent. (2) je devais. (3) je dus. (4) je devrai. (5) je devrais. (6) dois, devons, devez. (7) que je doive. (8) que je dusse. (9) devant. (10) dû, due (*pl.* dus, dues).

dire.—(1) je dis, tu dis, il dit, nous disons, vous dites, ils disent. (2) je disais. (3) je dis. (4) je dirai. (5) je dirais. (6) dis, disons, dites. (7) que je dise. (8) que je disse. (9) disant. (10) dit, e.

disparaître.—*like* connaître.

dissoudre.—*like* absoudre.

dormir.—(1) je dors, tu dors, il dort, nous dormons, vous dormez, ils dorment. (2) je dormais. (3) je dormis. (4) je dormirai. (5) je dormirais. (6) dors, dormons, dormez. (7) que je dorme. (8) que je dormisse. (9) dormant. (10) dormi (*inv.*).

échoir.—(1) il échoit *ou* il échet. (4) il écherra. (9) échéant. (10) échu, e. *Other forms hardly ever used.*

éclore.—(1) il éclôt, ils éclosent. (4) il éclora. (5) il éclorait. (7) qu'il éclose. (10) éclos, e.

écrire.—(1) j'écris, tu écris, il écrit, nous écrivons, vous écrivez, ils écrivent. (2) j'écrivais. (3) j'écrivis. (4) j'écrirai. (5) j'écrirais. (6) écris, écrivons, écrivez.

(7) que j'écrive. (8) que j'écrivisse. (9) écrivant. (10) écrit, e.

élire.—*like* lire.

embatre.—*like* battre, *but with one t only.*

empreindre.—*like* atteindre.

enceindre.—*like* atteindre.

enduire.—*like* conduire.

enfreindre.—*like* atteindre.

enquérir.—*like* acquérir.

épreindre.—*like* atteindre.

éteindre.—*like* atteindre.

être.—(1) je suis, tu es, il est, nous sommes, vous êtes, ils sont. (2) j'étais. (3) je fus. (4) je serai. (5) je serais. (6) sois, soyons, soyez. (7) que je sois. (8) que je fusse. (9) étant. (10) été (*inv.*).

étreindre.—*like* atteindre.

exclure.—*like* conclure.

faillir.—(1) il faut (*in* s'en faut). (3) je faillis, etc. (10) failli, e. *Seldom used in other forms.*

faire.—(1) je fais, tu fais, il fait, nous faisons, vous faites, ils font. (2) je faisais. (3) je fis. (4) je ferai. (5) je ferais. (6) fais, faisons, faites. (7) que je fasse. (8) que je fisse. (9) faisant. (10) fait, e.

falloir.—(1) il faut. (2) il fallait. (3) il fallut. (4) il faudra. (5) il faudrait. (7) qu'il faille. (8) qu'il fallût. (10) fallu (*inv.*).

feindre.—*like* atteindre.

forclore.—(10) forclos, e.

frire.—(1) je fris, tu fris, il frit, nous faisons frire, vous faites frire, ils font frire. (2) je faisais frire. (4) je frirai. (5) je frirais. (6) fris. (10) frit, e.

fuir.—(1) je fuis, tu fuis, il fuit, nous fuyons, vous fuyez, ils fuient. (2) je fuyais. (3) je fuis. (4) je fuirai. (5) je fuirais. (6) fuis, fuyons, fuyez. (7) que je fuie. (8) que je fuisse. (9) fuyant. (10) fui, e.

geindre.—*like* atteindre.

gésir.—(1) je gis, tu gis, il gît, nous gisons, vous gisez, ils gisent. (2) je gisais, etc. (9) gisant. *Other forms not used.*

inclure.—*like* conclure.

induire.—*like* conduire.

inscrire.—*like* écrire.

instruire.—*like* **conduire.**

interdire.—*like* **dire,** *except* (1) vous interdisez. (6) interdisez.

introduire.—*like* **conduire.**

joindre.—(1) je joins, tu joins, il joint, nous joignons, vous joignez, ils joignent. (2) je joignais. (3) je joignis. (4) je joindrai. (5) je joindrais. (6) joins, joignons, joignez. (7) que je joigne. (8) que je joignisse. (9) joignant. (10) joint, e.

lire.—(1) je lis, tu lis, il lit, nous lisions, vous lisez, ils lisent. (2) je lisais. (3) je lus. (4) je lirai. (5) je lirais. (6) lis, lisons, lisez. (7) que je lise. (8) que je lusse. (9) lisant. (10) lu, e.

luire.—*like* **conduire,** *except* (10) lui. (*inv.*) & *no* (3) *or* (8).

maudire.—(1) je maudis, tu maudis, il maudit, nous maudissons, vous maudissez, ils maudissent. (2) je maudissais. (3) je maudis. (4) je maudirai. (5) je maudirais. (6) maudis, maudissons, maudissez. (7) que je maudisse. (8) que je maudisse. (9) maudissant. (10) maudit, e.

méconnaître.—*like* **paraître.**

médire.—*like* **dire,** *except* (1) vous médisez. (6) médisez.

mentir.—*like* **sentir.**

messeoir.—*like* **seoir,** *in sense to suit.*

mettre.—(1) je mets, tu mets, il met, nous mettons, vous mettez, ils mettent. (2) je mettais. (3) je mis. (4) je mettrai. (5) je mettrais. (6) mets, mettons, mettez. (7) que je mette. (8) que je misse. (9) mettant. (10) mis, e.

moudre.—(1) je mouds, tu mouds, il moud, nous moulons, vous moulez, ils moulent. (2) je moulais. (3) je moulus. (4) je moudrai. (5) je moudrais. (6) mouds, moulons, moulez. (7) que je moule. (8) que je moulusse. (9) moulant. (10) moulu, e.

mourir.—(1) je meurs, tu meurs, il meurt, nous mourons, vous mourez, ils meurent. (2) je mourais. (3) je mourus. (4) je mourrai. (5) je mourrais. (6) meurs,

mourons, mourez. (7) que je meure. (8) que je mourusse. (9) mourant. (10) mort, e.

mouvoir.—(1) je meus, tu meus, il meut, nous mouvons, vous mouvez, ils meuvent. (2) je mouvais. (3) je mus. (4) je mouvrai. (5) je mouvrais. (6) meus, mouvons, mouvez. (7) que je meuve. (8) que je musse. (9) mouvant. (10) mû, mue (*pl.* mus, mues).

naître.—(1) je nais, tu nais, il naît, nous naissons, vous naissez, ils naissent. (2) je naissais. (3) je naquis. (4) je naîtrai. (5) je naîtrais. (6) nais, naissons, naissez. (7) que je naisse. (8) que je naquisse. (9) naissant. (10) né, e.

nuire.—*like* **conduire,** *except* (10) nui (*inv.*).

offrir.—*like* **ouvrir.**

oindre.—*like* **joindre.**

ouïr.—(10) ouï, ïe.

ouvrir.—(1) j'ouvre, tu ouvres, il ouvre, nous ouvrons, vous ouvrez, ils ouvrent. (2) j'ouvrais. (3) j'ouvris. (4) j'ouvrirai. (5) j'ouvrirais. (6) ouvre, ouvrons, ouvrez. (7) que j'ouvre. (8) que j'ouvrisse. (9) ouvrant. (10) ouvert, e.

paître.—(1) je pais, tu pais, il paît, nous paissons, vous paissez, ils paissent. (2) je paissais. (4) je paîtrai. (5) je paîtrais. (6) pais, paissons, paissez. (7) que je paisse. (9) paissant.

paraître.—*like* **connaître,** *but* (10) paru (*inv.*).

partir.—(1) je pars, tu pars, il part, nous partons, vous partez, ils partent. (2) je partais. (3) je partis. (4) je partirai. (5) je partirais. (6) pars, partons, partez. (7) que je parte. (8) que je partisse. (9) partant. (10) parti, e.

peindre.—*like* **atteindre.**

plaindre.—*like* **craindre.**

plaire.—(1) je plais, tu plais, il plaît, nous plaisons, vous plaisez, ils plaisent. (2) je plaisais. (3) je plus. (4) je plairai. (5) je plairais. (6) plais, plaisons, plaisez. (7) que je plaise. (8)

que je plusse. (9) plaisant. (10) plu (*inv.*).

pleuvoir.—(1) il pleut. (2) il pleuvait. (3) il plut. (4) il pleuvra. (5) il pleuvrait. (7) qu'il pleuve. (8) qu'il plût. (9) pleuvant. (10) plu (*inv.*).

poindre.—*like* joindre, *but seldom used except in infinitive &* (4).

pourvoir.—(1) je pourvois, tu pourvois, il pourvoit, nous pourvoyons, vous pourvoyez, ils pourvoient. (2) je pourvoyais. (3) je pourvus. (4) je pourvoirai. (5) je pourvoirais. (6) pourvois, pourvoyons, pourvoyez. (7) que je pourvoie. (8) que je pourvusse. (9) pourvoyant. (10) pourvu, e.

pouvoir.—(1) je peux *ou* je puis, tu peux, il peut, nous pouvons, vous pouvez, ils peuvent. (2) je pouvais. (3) je pus. (4) je pourrai. (5) je pourrais. (7) que je puisse. (8) que je pusse. (9) pouvant. (10) pu (*inv.*).

prédire.—*like* dire, *except* (1) vous prédisez. (6) prédisez.

prendre.—(1) je prends, tu prends, il prend, nous prenons, vous prenez, ils prennent. (2) je prenais. (3) je pris. (4) je prendrai. (5) je prendrais. (6) prends, prenons, prenez. (7) que je prenne. (8) que je prisse. (9) prenant. (10) pris, e.

proscrire.—*like* écrire.

prévaloir.—*like* valoir, *but* (7) que je prévale.

prévoir.—*like* voir, *except* (4) je prévoirai. (5) je prévoirais.

produire.—*like* conduire.

promouvoir.—*like* mouvoir, *but seldom used except in infinitive &* (10) promu, e (*no circumflex accent*).

proscrire.—*like* écrire.

raire.—*like* traire, *but the only forms in common use are* (1) il rait, ils raient.

reclure.—(10) reclus, e.

reconquérir.—*like* acquérir.

reconstruire.—*like* conduire.

recouvrir.—*like* ouvrir.

récrire.—*like* écrire.

recuire.—*like* conduire.

réduire.—*like* conduire.

réélire.—*like* lire.

reluire.—*like* luire.

renaître.—*like* naître, *but no* (10) *or compound tenses.*

reparaître.—*like* paraître.

repentir (se).—*like* sentir.

reproduire.—*like* conduire.

requérir.—*like* acquérir.

résoudre.—(1) je résous, tu résous, il résout, nous résolvons, vous résolvez, ils résolvent. (2) je résolvais. (3) je résolus. (4) je résoudrai. (5) je résoudrais. (6) résous, résolvons, résolvez. (7) que je résolve. (8) que je résolusse. (9) résolvant. (10) résolu, e.

restreindre.—*like* atteindre.

rire.—(1) je ris, tu ris, il rit, nous rions, vous riez, ils rient. (2) je riais. (3) je ris. (4) je rirai. (5) je rirais. (6) ris, rions, riez. (7) que je rie. (8) que je risse. (9) riant. (10) ri (*inv.*).

rouvrir.—*like* ouvrir.

saillir.—*like* assaillir.

savoir.—(1) je sais, tu sais, il sait, nous savons, vous savez, ils savent. (2) je savais. (3) je sus. (4) je saurai. (5) je saurais. (6) sache, sachons, sachez. (7) que je sache. (8) que je susse. (9) sachant. (10) su, e.

séduire.—*like* conduire.

sentir.—(1) je sens, tu sens, il sent, nous sentons, vous sentez, ils sentent. (2) je sentais. (3) je sentis. (4) je sentirai. (5) je sentirais. (6) sens, sentons, sentez. (7) que je sente. (8) que je sentisse. (9) sentant. (10) senti, e.

seoir.—*In sense to sit,* (9) séant. (10) sis, e. *In sense to suit,* (1) il sied, ils siéent. (2) il seyait, ils seyaient. (4) il siéra, ils siéront. (7) qu'il siée, qu'ils siéent. (9) séant *ou* seyant. *No other forms.*

servir.—(1) je sers, tu sers, il sert, nous servons, vous servez, ils servent. (2) je servais. (3) je servis. (4) je servirai. (5) je servirais. (6) sers, servons, servez. (7) que je serve. (8) que je servisse. (9) servant. (10) servi, e.

sortir.—(1) je sors, tu sors, il sort, nous sortons, vous sortez, ils sortent. (2) je sortais. (3) je sortis. (4) je sortirai. (5) je sortirais. (6) sors, sortons, sortez. (7) que je sorte. (8) que je sortisse. (9) sortant. (10) sorti, e.

souffrir.—*like* **ouvrir.**

souscrire.—*like* **écrire.**

suffire.—*like* **confire.**

suivre.—(1) je suis, tu suis, il suit, nous suivons, vous suivez, ils suivent. (2) je suivais. (3) je suivis. (4) je suivrai. (5) je suivrais. (6) suis, suivons, suivez. (7) que je suive. (8) que je suivisse. (9) suivant. (10) suivi, e.

surseoir.—(1) je sursois, tu sursois, il sursoit, nous sursoyons, vous sursoyez, ils sursoient. (2) je sursoyais. (3) je sursis. (4) je surseoirai. (5) je surseoirais. (6) sursois, sursoyons, sursoyez. (7) que je sursoie. (8) que je sursisse. (9) sursoyant. (10) sursis, e.

taire.—*like* **plaire,** *except* (1) il tait (*no circumflex*) & (10) tu, e.

teindre.—*like* **atteindre.**

tenir.—(1) je tiens, tu tiens, il tient, nous tenons, vous tenez, ils tiennent. (2) je tenais. (3) je tins. (4) je tiendrai. (5) je tiendrais. (6) tiens, tenons, tenez. (7) que je tienne. (8) que je tinsse. (9) tenant. (10) tenu, e.

tistre.—*Used only in* (10) tissu, e, *and compound tenses.*

traduire.—*like* **conduire.**

traire.—(1) je trais, tu trais, il trait, nous trayons, vous trayez, ils traient. (2) je trayais. (4) je trairai. (5) je trairais. (6) trais, trayons, trayez. (7) que je traie. (9) trayant. (10) trait, e.

transcrire.—*like* **écrire.**

tressaillir.—*like* **assaillir.**

vaincre.—(1) je vaincs, tu vaincs, il vainc, nous vainquons, vous vainquez, ils vainquent. (2) je vainquais. (3) je vainquis. (4)

je vaincrai. (5) je vaincrais. (6) vaincs, vainquons, vainquez. (7) que je vainque. (8) que je vainquisse. (9) vainquant. (10) vaincu, e.

valoir.—(1) je vaux, tu vaux, il vaut, nous valons, vous valez, ils valent. (2) je valais. (3) je valus. (4) je vaudrai. (5) je vaudrais. (6) vaux, valons, valez. (7) que je vaille. (8) que je valusse. (9) valant. (10) valu, e.

venir.—(1) je viens, tu viens, il vient, nous venons, vous venez, ils viennent. (2) je venais. (3) je vins. (4) je viendrai. (5) je viendrais. (6) viens, venons, venez. (7) que je vienne. (8) que je vinsse. (9) venant. (10) venu, e.

vêtir.—(1) je vêts, tu vêts, il vêt, nous vêtons, vous vêtez, ils vêtent. (2) je vêtais. (3) je vêtis. (4) je vêtirai. (5) je vêtirais. (6) vêts, vêtons, vêtez. (7) que je vête. (8) que je vêtisse. (9) vêtant. (10) vêtu, e.

vivre.—(1) je vis, tu vis, il vit, nous vivons, vous vivez, ils vivent. (2) je vivais. (3) je vécus. (4) je vivrai. (5) je vivrais. (6) vis, vivons, vivez. (7) que je vive. (8) que je vécusse. (9) vivant. (10) vécu (*inv.*).

voir.—(1) je vois, tu vois, il voit, nous voyons, vous voyez, ils voient. (2) je voyais. (3) je vis. (4) je verrai. (5) je verrais. (6) vois, voyons, voyez. (7) que je voie. (8) que je visse. (9) voyant. (10) vu, e.

vouloir.—(1) je veux, tu veux, il veut, nous voulons, vous voulez, ils veulent. (2) je voulais. (3) je voulus. (4) je voudrai. (5) je voudrais. (6) veuille & veux, veuillons & voulons, veuillez & voulez. (7) que je veuille. (8) que je voulusse. (9) voulant. (10) voulu, e.

In French, words are divided into syllables according to the following rules.

(1) *A consonant between two vowels begins a new syllable:*
ca-pi-tal, ca-pi-ta-li-ser, ca-pi-ta-lis-me, ca-pi-ta-lis-te, li-bé-ra-toi-re, dé-sa-bon-ne-ment, a-rith-mé-ti-que, pri-vi-lè-ge, su-bor-don-né, é-ti-que-ta-ge, e-xa-men, e-xer-ci-ce, i-ne-xac-te-ment, to-xi-que, i-nu-ti-le, u-ne, u-na-ni-me-ment, vi-gueur, vi-gou-reux, vi-gou-reu-se, paie-ment, em-pla-ce-ment, vé-hi-cu-le, pa-ral-lé-li-pi-pè-de. *Note:*—In order not to misrepresent the pronunciation of certain prefixes, there are a few exceptions to this rule, and collaterally to rule 3 also; such as sur-é-le-ver, sur-en-ché-rir, and the like; in-ter-o-cé-a-ni-que, in-ter-ur-bain, and the like.

(2) *Two adjoining consonants (except Rule 4 digraphs) between two vowels separate into two syllables:*
ac-com-mo-der, at-ter-ris-sage, bail-le-res-se, chan-geant, chan-gean-te, cor-res-pon-dan-ce, des-cen-dre, di-a-phrag-me, ex-cep-ti-on-nel-le-ment, ex-pé-di-ti-on-nai-re, in-nom-ma-ble, em-bar-ras-sant, in-ter-val-le, ir-res-pon-sa-bi-li-té, os-cil-ler, fais-ceau, ras-seoir, re-con-nais-san-ce, res-ti-tu-er, sub-di-vi-ser, sur-taux, veil-le, el-les, mal-heur, in-hé-rent, ex-hi-ber, mo-les-ki-ne.

(3) *A vowel can only begin a syllable, other than an initial syllable, when preceded by another vowel:*
ac-cue-il-lir, a-é-ro-pla-ne; po-è-me, a-gré-er, an-ci-en, ar-ri-è-re, bé-né-fi-ci-ai-re, ca-mi-on, ca-out-chouc, co-as-so-ci-é, co-ef-fi-ci-ent, coïn-ci-der, dé-pou-il-le-ment, ex-tra-or-di-nai-re, feu-il-le, li-er, mi-eux, na-ti-on, ou-est, ré-u-ni-on, vic-tu-

ail-les, vi-e-il-lir, ré-é-li-re, voi-li-er, pay-a-ble, ba-lay-u-res, en-voy-er, voy-a-ge, roy-au-me, en-nuy-eux.

(4) *The following digraph consonants are inseparable:*
bl, cl, fl, gl, pl: a-bla-taf, pu-bli-que, (*Exception:* sub-lu-nai-re); é-clec-tis-me, ex-clu-sif; ré-fle-xe, ré-fle-xi-on; é-glan-ti-ne, rè-gle-ment; é-plu-cher.

br, cr, dr, fr, gr, pr, tr, vr: a-bri-cot, su-bré-car-gue, (*Exception:* sub-ro-ger & *derivatives*); é-cri-tu-re, ma-nus-crit, pres-cri-re, sous-cri-re, des-crip-ti-ve; a-dres-ser; re-frain; a-gri-co-le; a-près; a-tro-ce; a-vril, ou-vri-er.

ch, dh, ph, rh: é-choir, re-cher-che; ré-dhi-bi-toi-re; té-lé-pho-ne, pho-no-gra-phe; en-rhu-mer; ar-rhes.

gn: en-sei-gne-ment, si-gnal, es-pa-gnol, i-gna-re (*but* mag-nat, mag-no-li-a, di-ag-nos-ti-que, ig-né, *because here* gn *is not palatalized; in other words, the* g *is hard*).

ng: ving-ti-è-me (*but* sin-gu-li-er, *because here* ng *is not digraph, i.e., expressing one sound*).

pt: lé-pi-do-pte-res.

(5) (a) *ns, bs, and rs are separable if followed by a vowel:*
con-sa-crer, con-seil-ler, con-si-dé-rer, in-sé-rer, in-sol-va-ble, in-suf-fi-sant, tran-sac-ti-on, tran-sat-lan-ti-que, tran-si-tif; ab-sor-ber, ob-ser-ver; per-su-a-der.

(b) *ns, bs, and rs are inseparable if followed by a consonant:*
cons-pi-rer, cons-ta-ter, cons-ti-tu-er, ins-pec-ter, ins-tal-ler, trans-cen-dant, trans-fè-re-ment, trans-port; no-nobs-tant, obs-ta-cles, subs-tan-ce; in-ters-ti-ce, pers-pec-ti-ve.

(c) *ns and bs are inseparable if followed by a consonant coupled with* r:
cons-trui-re, ins-cri-re, trans-cri-

re, trans-gres-ser; abs-trac-ti-
on, obs-truc-ti-on.

(*d*) ns *and* bs *are separable
before* ci:
con-sci-en-ci-eux, in-sci-em-ment;
ab-scis-se.

(6) (*a*) mp *and* nc *followed by* t
are inseparable:
a-comp-te, comp-ta-ble, es-comp-
ter, pré-emp-ti-on; fonc-ti-on,
sanc-ti-on.

(*b*) *In all other combinations*
mp *and* nc *are separable:*
em-ploy-er, em-prun-ter, im-por-
tant; a-van-cer, fran-çais, franche, fran-co.

(7) *In writing or in print no syllable is separable which does
not include a vowel; thus,* tri-
graph *consonants are inseparable initially:* scru-tin, *but may
be separable medially:* ins-cru-
ta-ble.

ENGLISH-FRENCH
DICTIONARY

A

A, *letter*, (*Mus.*) la, *m*; (*house number*) bis, **a**, *indefinite art.* or *a*, un, une. *what ~ ... !*, quel! quelle! *such ~ ...*, tel, telle. *2 or 3 times ~ day*, 2 ou 3 fois par jour.

aback, *ad*: *taken ~*, interloqué, déconcerté.

abacus, *n*, abaque, *m*.

abaft, *ad*, vers l'arrière. ¶ *pr*, sur l'arrière de.

abandon, *v.t*, abandonner, délaisser. ~**ment**, *n*, abandon, délaissement, *m*.

abase, *v.t*, abaisser, humilier.

abash, *v.t*, décontenancer, confondre.

abate, *v.t*, diminuer, rabattre; (*v.i.*) [se] calmer; (*weather, etc.*) s'apaiser. **abatement**, *n*, diminution, *f*; rabais, *m*.

abbess, *n*, abbesse, *f*. **abbey**, *n*, abbaye, *f*. **abbot**, *n*, abbé, *m*.

abbreviate, *v.t*, abréger. **abbreviation**, *n*, abréviation, *f*.

A B C, *n*, A b c, abécédaire, alphabet, *m*; enfance, *f*.

abdicate, *v.t. & i*, abdiquer. **abdication**, *n*, abdication, *f*.

abdomen, *n*, abdomen, ventre, *m*. *lower part of the ~*, bas-ventre, *m*. **abdominal**, *a*, abdominal. ~ *belt*, ceinture ventrière, *f*.

abduct, *v.t*, détourner, enlever.

abeam, *ad*, par le travers.

abed, *ad*, au lit, couché.

aberration, *n*, aberration, *f*, égarement, *m*.

abet, *v.t*, soutenir, encourager, exciter.

abeyance, (*law*) *n*, vacance, *f*. *in ~*, en suspens, en souffrance.

abhor, *v.t*, abhorrer, haïr, avoir en horreur. **abhorrence**, *n*, horreur, haine, *f*. **abhorrent**, *a*, répugnant.

abide, *v.i. & t. ir*, demeurer, rester; souffrir, supporter. *to ~ by* (*laws*), s'en tenir à. **abiding**, *a*, durable, permanent.

ability, *n*, capacité, habileté, *f*, talent, savoir-faire, *m*.

abject, *a*, abject. ~**ion**, *n*, abjection, *f*.

abjure, *v.t*, abjurer, renoncer.

ablative [**case**], *n*, ablatif, *m*.

ablaze, *ad*, en feu, en flammes.

able, *a*, capable, habile; efficace. ~*-bodied*, robuste, valide. ~ [*-bodied*] *seaman*, matelot de deuxième classe, *m*. *to be ~ to*, pouvoir, savoir, être en mesure (*ou* à même) de, suffire a. **ably**, *ad*, habilement, bravement.

abnegation, *n*, abnégation, *f*.

abnormal†, *a*, anormal. ~**ity**, *n*, anormal, *m*.

aboard, *ad*, à bord. ¶ *pr*, à bord de.

abode, *n*, domicile, *m*, demeure, habitation, *f*; séjour, *m*.

abolish, *v.t*, abolir, supprimer.

abominable†, *a*, abominable. **abominate**, *v.t*, abominer. **abomination**, *n*, abomination, *f*.

aboriginal, *a. & n*, aborigène, *a. & m*. **aborigines**, *n.pl*, aborigènes, *m.pl*.

abortion, *n*, avortement; (*creature*) avorton, *m*. **abortive**, *a*, abortif; (*fig.*) avorté, manqué.

abound, *v.i*, abonder, foisonner, fourmiller, affluer.

about, *pr*, autour de; auprès de; pour; dans; en; par; vers; sur; à propos de, touchant. ¶ *ad*, autour, çà & là; environ, à peu [de chose] près. *to be ~ to*, être sur le point de, aller. *what is it all ~?* de quoi s'agit-il?

above, *pr*, au-dessus de; sur; plus de; en amont de; en contre-haut. ¶ *ad*, en haut; là-haut; au-dessus; ci-dessus. *from ~*, d'en haut. *~ all*, surtout, avant tout. ~*board*, franc, cartes sur table. ~*-mentioned*, susmentionné, ci-dessus. ~*-named*, susnommé.

abrade, *v.t*, user; (*skin*) écorcher. **abrasion**, *n*, (*Phys.*) attrition; (*skin*) écorchure, *f*.

abreast, *ad*, de front; (*Naut.*) par le travers. *~ of*, à la hauteur de.

abridge, *v.t*, abréger, raccourcir. **abridgment**, *n*, abrégé, raccourci, *m*.

abroad, *ad*, à l'étranger, à l'extérieur; au large. *from ~*, de l'étranger, de l'extérieur. *there is* *a rumor ~ that . . .*, le bruit court que . . .

abrogate, *v.t*, abroger. **abrogation**, *n*, abrogation, *f*.

abrupt, *a*, abrupt; brusque. *to treat ~ly*, brusquer. *~ly*, *ad*, brusquement. *~ness*, *n*, brusquerie, *f*.

abscess, *n*, abcès, *m*.

abscond, *v.i*, s'enfuir, se soustraire à la justice.

absence, *n*, absence, *f*, éloignement; défaut, *m*. *~ of mind*, absence [d'esprit], distraction, *f*. *leave of ~*, permission, *f*; congé, *m*. **absent**, *a*, absent, manquant. *~minded*, distrait. ¶ *~ oneself*, s'absenter. **absentee**, *n*, absent; (*Mil.*) insoumis, *m*. **absently**, *ad*, distraitement.

absinthe, *n*, absinthe, *f*.

absolute, *a*, absolu. *~ly*, *ad*, absolument.

absolution, *n*, absolution, *f*. **absolve**, *v.t*, absoudre.

absorb, *v.t*, absorber. **absorbent, absorbing**, *a*, absorbant; (*cotton wool*) hydrophile. **absorption**, *n*, absorption, *f*.

abstain, *v.i*, s'abstenir. *~er*, *n*, abstème, *m.f*. **abstemious**, *a*, abstème, sobre. **abstention**, *n*, abstention, *f*. **abstinence**, *n*, abstinence, *f*.

abstract, *a*, abstrait. ¶ *n*, extrait, relevé, résumé, *m*. *the ~* (opp. *concrete*), l'abstrait, *m*. ¶ *v.t*, abstraire; relever; (*steal*) distraire, soustraire, détourner. **abstraction**, *n*, abstraction; distraction, soustraction, *f*, détournement, *m*.

abstruse, *a*, abstrus.

absurd†, *a*, absurde. *the ~, an absurdity*, l'absurde, *m*, une absurdité.

abundance, *n*, abondance, *f*. **abundant**, *a*, abondant. *~ly*, *ad*, abondamment.

abuse, *n*, abus; excès, *m*; injures, insultes, *f.pl*. ¶ *v.t*, abuser de; injurier, malmener, maltraiter. **abusive†**, *a*, abusif; injurieux.

abutment (*Arch.*) *n*, culée, butée, *f*.

abyss, *n*, abîme, abysse, gouffre, *m*.

Abyssinia, *n*, l'Abyssinie, *f*. **Abyssinian**, *a*, abyssinien, abyssin. ¶ *n*, Abyssinien, ne, Abyssin, e.

acacia, *n*, acacia, *m*.

academic(al), *a*, académique; (*year*) scolaire. **academician**, *n*,

académicien, ne. **academy**, *n*, académie, *f*.

accede, *v.i*, accéder.

accelerate, *v.t*, accélérer. **accelerator**, *n*, accélérateur, *m*.

accent, *n*, accent, *m*. **accent & accentuate**, *v.t*, accentuer.

accept, *v.t*, accepter, agréer; (*a sport record*) homologuer. *~able*, *a*, acceptable; de mise; agréable. *~ance*, *n*, acceptation; réception, *f*. *~ation*, *n*, acception, *f*. *~ed term*, terme consacré, *m*. *~or*, *n*, accepteur, *m*. *~ for honor* (*Com.*), intervenant, *m*.

access, *n*, accès, abord, entrée, *f*. (*computers*) *direct ~*, accès direct; *serial ~*, accès séquentiel, *m*. *~ible*, *a*, accessible, abordable. *~ion*, *n*, accession, *f*, avènement, *m*.

accessory†, *a*, accessoire. ¶ *n*, accessoire, *m*; (*law*) complice, *m.f*.

accidence (*Gram.*) *n*, morphologie, *f*.

accident, *n*, accident; sinistre, *m*. [*personal*] *~ insurance*, assurance contre les accidents [corporels] *f*. **accidental†**, *a*, accidentel, fortuit. ¶ (*Mus.*) *n*, accident, *m*.

acclaim, *v.t*, acclamer. **acclamation**, *n*, acclamation, *f*.

acclimatisation, *n*, acclimatation, *f*, acclimatement, *m*. **acclimatize**, *v.t*, acclimater.

acclivity, *n*, montée, *f*.

accommodate, *v.i*, arranger; contenir; loger. *~ oneself to*, s'accommoder à. **accommodating**, *p.a*, accommodant, complaisant, coulant, débonnaire. **accommodation**, *n*, accommodation, *f*; aménagement; logement, *m*. *~ paper*, billet de complaisance, *m*.

accompaniment, *n*, accompagnement, *m*. **accompanist**, *n*, accompagnateur, trice. **accompany**, *v.t*, accompagner.

accomplice, *n*, complice, *m.f*.

accomplish, *v.t*, accomplir. *~ed*, *a*, accompli, achevé, émérite. *~ment*, *n*, accomplissement, *m*; (*pl.*) arts d'agrément, *m.pl*.

accord, *n*, accord, *m*. *of one's own ~*, de son propre mouvement, de son plein gré, d'office. *with one ~*, d'un commun accord. ¶ *v.t*, accorder; (*v.i.*) s'a. *~ance*, *n*, conformité, *f*. **according as**, à mesure que, selon que, suivant que. **according to**, selon, suivant; conforme à, conformément à; conséquemment à; d'après; à. **accordingly**, *ad*, par conséquent; en conséquence: conséquemment.

accordion, *n*, accordéon, *m*.

accost, *v.t*, accoster, aborder.

account, *n*, compte, *m*; (*pl*.) écritures [comptables] *f.pl*; (*pl*.) comptabilité, *f*; (*pl*.) inventaire; exercice; état, exposé, mémoire, *m*, note, *f*; récit, *m*, relation, notice, *f*, historique; (*Stk Ex*.) terme, *m*, liquidation, *f*. *of no ~*, nul. *on ~* (*Com*.), à compte, à valoir. *on ~ of*, à cause de; (*Com*.) pour le compte de, à l'acquit de. *on no ~*, en aucune manière, aucunement. *~ book*, livre de comptabilité, *m*. ¶ *~ for*, rendre compte de; expliquer. ~**able**, *a*, comptable; responsable. ~**ancy**, *n*, comptabilité, *f*. ~**ant**, *n*, comptable, *m,f*, agent comptable, *m*. ~**ing**, *n*, comptabilité, *f*. *~ machine*, machine comptable, *f*. *~ period*, exercice, *m*.

accoutre, *v.t*, équiper; harnacher. ~**ment**, *n*, équipement, *m*.

accredit, *v.t*, accréditer. ~**ed**, *p.a*, accrédité, attitré. *~ dealer*, stockiste, *m*.

accrue, *v.i*, courir, accroître, s'acquérir. *~d interest*, intérêt couru, *m*, intérêts accrus, *m.pl*. *accruing interest*, intérêts à échoir.

accumulate, *v.t*, accumuler, amonceler; (*v.i*.) s'accumuler, s'amonceler. **accumulation**, *n*, accumulation, *f*, amoncellement, *m*. **accumulator**, *n*, accumulateur, *m*.

accuracy, *n*, exactitude, justesse, *f*. **accurate†**, *a*, exact, juste.

accursed, *a*, maudit.

accusation, *n*, accusation, *f*. **accusative [case]**, accusatif, *m*. **accuse**, *v.t*, accuser; taxer. *the ~d*, l'accusé, e, l'inculpé, e. **accuser**, *n*, accusateur, trice. **accusing**, *a*, accusateur.

accustom, *v.t*, accoutumer, habituer, familiariser, faire. *~ed*, *a*, accoutumé, coutumier, habituel. *to get ~ to*, s'accoutumer à.

ace, *n*, as, *m*. *within an ~ of*, à deux doigts de.

acerbity, *n*, âpreté, aigreur, *f*.

acetate, *n*, acétate, *m*. **acetic**, *a*, acétique.

acetylene, *n*, acétylène, *m*. *~ lamp*, lampe à acétylène, *f*.

ache, *n*, mal, *m*, douleur, *f*. ¶ *v.i*, faire mal; souffrir. *my head aches*, j'ai mal à la tête.

achieve, *v.t*, accomplir, exécuter. ~**ment**, *n*, accomplissement, exploit, *m*.

aching, *a*, endolori. *~ all over*, tout moulu.

acid, *a. & n*, acide, *a. & m*. ~**ity**, *n*, acidité *f*. **acidulate**, *v.t*, aciduler.

acknowledge, *v.t*, reconnaître, avouer, s'accuser de, confesser. *~ receipt of*, accuser réception de. **acknowledgment**, *n*, reconnaissance, *f*; accusé de réception; reçu, *m*; (*pl*.) remerciements, *m.pl*.

acme, *n*, apogée, comble, sommet, *m*.

acne, *n*, acné, couperose, *f*.

acolyte, *n*, acolyte, *m*.

acorn, *n*, gland, *m*. *~ crop*, glandée, *f*.

acoustic, *a*, acoustique. *~s*, *n.pl*, acoustique, *f*.

acquaint, *v.t*, faire connaître, faire savoir, faire part, informer. *to get ~ed with*, faire la connaissance de. ~**ance**, *n*, connaissance, relation, *f*.

acquiesce, *v.i*, acquiescer. **acquiescence**, *n*, acquiescement, *m*.

acquire, *v.t*, acquérir; prendre. ~**ments**, *n.pl*, acquis, *m.s. & m.pl*, connaissances, *f.pl*. **acquisition**, *n*, acquisition, *f*.

acquit, *v.t*, acquitter. **acquittal**, *n*, acquittement, *m*.

acre, *n*, acre, arpent, *m*.

acrid, *a*, âcre. ~**ity**, *n*, âcreté, *f*.

acrimonious, *a*, acrimonieux. **acrimony**, *n*, acrimonie, *f*.

acrobat, *n*, acrobate, *m,f*. **acrobatic**, *a*, acrobatique. *~s*, *n.pl*, acrobatie, *f*.

across, *ad*, en travers; (*crossword clues*) horizontalement. ¶ *pr*, en travers de, par. *our neighbors ~ the Channel*, nos voisins d'outre-Manche.

acrostic, *n*, acrostiche, *m*.

act, *n*, acte, *m*, action, *f*, fait, *m*. *~ [of the legislature]*, loi [votée] *f*. *in the [very] ~*, sur le fait; en flagrant délit. ¶ *v.t*, jouer, représenter; faire; (*v.i*.) agir; fonctionner; opérer. *~ as*, faire fonction de. *~ for* (*client, law*), postuler. **acting** (*Theat*.) *n*, jeu, *m*.

~*manager*, directeur intérimaire, *m*. ~ *partner*, commandité, *m*.
action, *n*, action, *f*; effet; mouvement; geste, *m*; scène, *f*; combat; procès, *m*, plainte, *f*.
active†, *a*, actif, agissant, agile, allant, énergique. *in* ~ *service*, en activité [de service]. ~ *voice*, voix active, *f*, actif, *m*. **activity**, *n*, activité, agilité, *f*, allant, *m*.
actor, tress, *n*, acteur, trice, comédien, ne.
actual, *a*, actuel, réel, effectif, véritable; de fait. ~**ity**, *n*, actualité, réalité, *f*. ~**ly**, *ad*, réellement, *a.m. & m*.
actuary, *n*, actuaire, *m*.
actuate, *v.t*, actionner, animer, mouvoir.
acumen, *n*, flair, *m*.
acute, *a*, aigu; vif, poignant. ~*-angled*, acutangle. ~**ly**, *ad*, vivement. ~**ness**, *n*, acuité; finesse, subtilité; vivacité, *f*.
A.D. (*Anno Domini*), ap. J.C.
adage, *n*, adage, *m*.
adamant (to be), être inflexible.
Adam's apple, pomme d'Adam, *f*.
adapt, *v.t*, adapter, accommoder, approprier. ~**ation**, *n*, adaptation, *f*. ~**er**, *n*, (*Phot*.) adapteur; (*pers. fig*.) metteur en œuvre, *m*.
add, *v.t*, ajouter; joindre; additionner. (*part*) **added** (*to a building*), hors-d'œuvre, *e.g. an added room*, un cabinet hors-d'œuvre.
adder, *n*, vipère, *f*.
addict, *n*, toxicomane, camé, *m*.
addict oneself to (to), s'adonner à, se livrer à.
addition, *n*, addition, *f*; supplément; (*to a building*) hors-d'œuvre, *m*. ~**al**, *a*, additionnel, supplémentaire.
addled, *a*, couvi; pourri. **addleheaded**, *a*, écervelé.
address, *n*, adresse; allocution, *f*. ¶ *v.t*, adresser; s'adresser à. ~**ee**, *n*, destinataire, *m,f*.
adduce, *v.t*, alléguer, fournir.
adenoids, *n.pl*, végétations [adénoïdes] *f.pl*.
adept, *a*, habile, versé, expérimenté. ¶ *n*, adepte, *m,f*.
adequate, *a*, suffisant; efficace; raisonnable. ~**ly**, *ad*, suffisamment, raisonnablement; dignement.
adhere, *v.i*, adhérer, s'en tenir. **adherence**, *n*, adhésion, *n*, adhésiveness, *n*, adhérence, adhésion, ténacité, *f*. **adhesive**, *a*, ad-

hésif, tenace. ~ *stamp*, timbre mobile, *m*. ~ *tape*, bande gommée, *f*; sparadrap, *m*.
adieu, *i*. & *n*, adieu, *i*. & *m*.
adipose, *a*, adipeux.
adit, *n*, galerie à flanc de coteau, *f*.
adjacent, *a*, adjacent, contigu.
adjectival, *a*. & **adjective**, *n*, adjectif, *a.m. & m*.
adjoin, *v.t*, joindre, être contigu à, toucher. ~**ing**, *a*, contigu, attenant, adjacent, joignant [à].
adjourn, *v.t*, ajourner, renvoyer, remettre. ~**ment**, *n*, ajournement, renvoi, *m*, remise, *f*.
adjudge, adjudicate, *v.t*, adjuger. **adjudication**, *n*, adjudication, *f*.
adjunct, *n*, accessoire, *m*.
adjure, *v.t*, adjurer.
adjust, *v.t*, ajuster, régler, mettre au point. ~*able wrench*, clef à molette, *f*. ~**ment**, *n*, ajustement, règlement, réglage, *m*, mise au point, *f*.
adjutant, *n*, adjudant major, major, *m*.
administer, *v.t*, administrer, gérer; (*oath*) déférer. **administration**, *n*, administration, gestion; régie, *f*. **administrative**, *a*, administratif. **administrator, trix**, *n*, administrateur, trice; curateur, trice; cadre, *m*.
admirable†, *a*, admirable.
admiral, *n*, amiral, *m*. ~ *of the fleet*, a. commandant d'escadre. **Admiralty**, *n*, (*Eng*.) Amirauté, *f*; (*Fr*.) Conseil supérieur de la Marine, *m*. ~ [*Office*], Ministère de la Marine, *m*.
admiration, *n*, admiration, *f*. **admire**, *v.t*, admirer. **admirer**, *n*, admirateur, trice. **admiringly**, *ad*, avec admiration.
admissible, *a*, admissible; recevable. **admission**, *n*, admission, entrée, *f*; aveu, *m*. **admit**, *v.t*, admettre, reconnaître; (*as member*) recevoir, agréger. ~ *bearer*, laissez passer. **admittance**, *n*, admission, entrée, *f*.
admixture, *n*, dosage, *m*.
admonish, *v.t*, admonester. **admonition**, *n*, admonition, admonestation, *f*.
ado, *n*, façons, *f.pl*, cérémonie, *f*; aria, bruit, tapage, *m*.
adolescence, *n*, adolescence, *f*. **adolescent**, *a*. & *n*, adolescent, *m*.
Adonis, *n*, adonis, beau, *m*.

adopt, *v.t.* adopter; prendre. **adopted, adoptive** (*of pers.*) *a,* adoptif. **adoption,** *n,* adoption; prise, *f.*

adorable, *a,* adorable. **adoration,** *n,* adoration, *f.* **adore,** *v.t,* adorer. **adorer,** *n,* adorateur, trice.

adorn, *v.t,* parer, orner, agrémenter, empanacher; (*of pers.*) faire l'ornement de. *to ~ oneself,* se parer. **~ment,** *n,* parure, *f,* ornement, *m.*

Adriatic, *a. & n,* Adriatique, *a. & f.*

adrift, *ad,* en (*ou* à la) dérive.

adroit†, *a,* adroit. **~ness,** *n,* dextérité, *f.*

adulate, *v.t,* aduler. **adulation,** *n,* adulation, *f.* **adulatory,** *a,* adulateur.

adult, *a. & n,* adulte, *a. & m.f.*

adulterate, *v.t,* falsifier, frelater, sophistiquer, altérer. **adulteration,** *n,* falsification, *f,* frelatage, *m,* sophistication, altération, *f.*

adulterer, **ess,** *n,* adultère, *m.f.* **adulterous,** *a,* adultère. **adultery,** *n,* adultère, *m.*

advance, *n,* avance; anticipation; hausse, *f;* prêt, *m.* *in ~,* en avance, d'a., par a., à l'a. ¶ *v.t,* avancer; hausser; (*v.i.*) [s']avancer, cheminer. **~ment,** *n,* avancement, *m.*

advantage, *n,* avantage, bénéfice, *m.* *~* [*game*] (*Ten.*), avantage [de jeu]. *~ in,* a. dedans, a. au servant. **~ous†,** *a,* avantageux.

advent, *n,* venue, apparition, *f;* (*of Christ*) avènement; (*Eccl.*) l'avent, *m.*

adventure, *n,* aventure, expédition, *f.* ¶ *v.t,* aventurer. **adventurer,** *n,* aventurier, chercheur d'aventures, chevalier d'industrie, *m.* **adventuress,** *n,* aventurière, *f.* **adventurous,** *a,* aventureux.

adverb, *n,* adverbe, *m.* *~ of number,* a. de quantité. **adverbial†,** *a,* adverbial.

adversary, *n,* adversaire, *m.* **adverse,** *a,* adverse; contraire; déficitaire. **adversity,** *n,* adversité, infortune, *f.*

advert, *v.i,* faire allusion.

advertise, *v.t,* annoncer, publier; afficher; (*v.i.*) faire une annonce (des annonces), faire de la publicité. *~ for,* demander par voie d'annonces. **~ment,** *n,* annonce; réclame, *f.* *~ billboard,*

panneau-réclame, *m.* **advertiser,** *n,* annonceur, *m.* **advertising,** *n,* publicité, réclame, *f.* *~ agency,* agence de publicité, *f.*

advice, *n,* avis, conseil, *m.* **advisable,** *a,* à conseiller, expédient, convenable. **advise,** *v.t,* conseiller; engager; aviser. **advisedly,** *ad,* de propos délibéré, en connaissance de cause. **adviser,** *n,* conseiller, ère, moniteur, *m.* **advisory,** *a,* consultatif.

advocate, *n,* avocat, défenseur; partisan, *m.* ¶ *v.t,* préconiser.

adze, *n,* herminette, *f.*

Aegean Sea (the), la mer Égée.

aegis, *n,* égide, *f.*

Aeolian, *a,* éolien.

aerate, *v.t,* aérer; gazéifier. *~d water,* eau gazeuse, *f.* **aeration,** *n,* aération, *f.*

aerial, *a,* aérien. ¶ (*radio*) *n,* antenne, *f.*

aerie, *n,* aire, *f.*

aerodynamic, *a. & ~s,* *n,* aérodynamique, *a. & f.*

aerolite, *n,* aérolithe, météorite, *m.*

aeronaut, *n,* aéronaute, *m.f.* **~ic(al),** *a,* aéronautique. **~ics,** *n,* aéronautique, *f.*

aerospatial, *a,* aérospatial.

afar, *ad,* loin, au loin. *from ~,* de loin.

affability, *n,* affabilité, *f.* **affable,** *a,* affable. **affably,** *ad,* avec affabilité.

affair, *n,* affaire, *f.*

affect, *v.t,* affecter, concerner, atteindre, impressionner; toucher, émouvoir, attendrir. **~ation,** *n,* affectation, afféterie, *f,* apprêt, *m.* **~ed,** *a,* affecté, affété, précieux, apprêté, maniéré, pincé. **~edly,** *ad,* avec affectation. **~ing,** *p.a,* touchant. **affection,** *n,* affection, *f.* **~ate†,** *a,* affectueux, aimant, affectionné.

affiance, *n,* confiance, foi, *f;* fiançailles, *f.pl.* ¶ *v.t,* fiancer.

affidavit, *n,* déclaration sous serment, *f.*

affiliate, *v.t,* affilier. ¶ *n,* compagnie associée, *f.*

affinity, *n,* affinité, *f.*

affirm, *v.t,* affirmer, assurer. **~ation,** *n,* affirmation, *f.* **~ative†,** *a,* affirmative, *f.*

affix, *n,* affixe, *m.* ¶ *v.t,* apposer. **~ture,** *n,* apposition, *f.*

afflict, *v.t,* affliger, chagriner. **~ion,** *n,* affliction, *f,* chagrin, *m.*

affluence, *n,* affluence; opulence, aisance, *f.* **affluent,** *a,* affluent, tributaire; opulent, aisé. ¶ *n,* affluent, *m.*

afford, *v.t,* donner, fournir, accorder. **can ~ to,** avoir les moyens de, pouvoir.

afforest, *v.t,* boiser. **~ation,** *n,* boisement, *m.*

affray, *n,* échauffourée, rixe, *f.*

affront, *n,* affront, *m,* avanie, *f.* ¶ *v.t,* offenser.

Afghan, *a,* afghan. ¶ *n,* Afghan, e.

afield, *ad:* **far ~,** très loin.

afire, *ad,* en feu, embrasé, brûlant.

afloat, *ad. & a,* à flot, sous voile, flottant; (*fig.*) sur pied, en circulation.

afoot, *ad,* à pied; sur pied; en cours; en route.

aforesaid, *a,* susdit, précité. ¶ *n,* susdit, e.

afraid, *a,* craintif. **to be ~ of,** avoir peur de, craindre.

afresh, *ad,* de nouveau, à nouveau.

Africa, *n,* l'Afrique, *f,* **African,** *a,* africain. ¶ *n,* Africain, e.

aft, *a,* arrière. ¶ *ad,* sur l'arrière, derrière.

after, *ad,* après; suivant; passé; à l'issue de. ¶ *c,* après que. ¶ *pr,* après, passé; d'après; à; sur. **~ all,** après tout, au bout de compte. **~ the event,** après coup.

aftermath, *n,* regain, *m;* répercussions, conséquences.

afternoon, *n,* après-midi, *m.*

aftertaste (*nasty*) *n,* arrièregoût, déboire, *m.*

afterthought, *n,* réflexion après coup, *f.*

afterwards, *ad,* après, ensuite, puis, plus tard.

again, *ad,* encore, de nouveau. **~ & ~,** mille [& mille] fois. **never ~,** jamais plus. **now and ~,** de temps à autre. **again** *after a verb is often expressed by the prefix* **re-** *as,* **to set out again,** repartir.

against, *pr,* contre, contraire à; sauf. **~ the grain,** à contre-fil, à rebours. **~ the light,** à contrejour.

agate, *n,* agate, *f.*

age, *n,* âge; siècle; temps, *m;* époque; (*old age*) vieillesse; (*decay*) vétusté, *f.* **10 years of ~** or **~d 10,** agé de 10 ans. **he is not of** (or **is under**) **~,** il n'est pas en âge. **to come of** [*full*] **~,**

être majeur, e. **it is ~s since,** il y a belle lurette que. ¶ *v.i,* vieillir.

aged (*of an advanced age*) *a,* âgé. **he has ~ considerably,** il a bien vieilli. **the ~** (either sex), les vieillards, *m.pl.*

agency, *n,* action; entremise, *f,* ministère, *m;* (*Com.*) agence, *f,* bureau; comptoir, *m;* factorerie; représentation, *f.*

agenda, *n,* ordre du jour, agenda, *m.*

agent, *n,* agent, commissionnaire, *m;* représentant, e; stockiste, *m;* mandataire, *m,f;* régisseur, *m.*

agglomerate, *v.t,* agglomérer.

agglutinate, *v.t,* agglutiner.

aggravate, *v.t,* aggraver. **aggravation,** *n,* aggravation, *f.*

aggregate, *a,* global, d'ensemble. ¶ *n,* total global; ensemble, *m,* masse, *f.* **aggregation,** *n,* agrégation, *f.*

aggression, *n,* agression, *f.* **aggressive,** *a,* agressif. **aggressor,** *n,* agresseur, *m.*

aggrieve, *v.i,* chagriner; léser. **aggrieved party,** offensé, e.

aghast, *a,* épouvanté, ébahi.

agile†, *a,* agile. **agility,** *n,* agilité, *f.*

agitate, *v.t,* agiter, remuer. **agitation,** *n,* agitation, *f.* **agitator,** *n,* agitateur, *m.*

aglow, *a,* resplendissant.

ago, *ad. & a,* passé, écoulé. **many years ~,** il y a de nombreuses années.

agog, *a,* en branle-bas; animé; impatient.

agonizing, *a,* déchirant, cuisant.

agony, *n,* douleur déchirante, d. cuisante, (*pl.*) mort & passion; (*death pangs*) agonie, *f.*

agrarian, *a,* agraire.

agree, *v.t,* faire accorder, faire concorder, faire cadrer, apurer; (*v.i.*) s'accorder, s'arranger, s'entendre, cadrer, concorder, convenir. **~ to,** consentir à, souscrire à, s'engager à. **quite ~ with,** abonder dans le sens de. **meat does not ~ with me,** je ne digère pas la viande. **~able†,** *a,* agréable, amène; conforme. **~d price,** prix convenu, [prix à] forfait, *m.* **~ment,** *n,* accord, *m,* entente, convention, concordance, conformité, *f;* acte, contrat, marché, traité, *m.* **to be in ~,** être d'accord.

agricultural, *a,* agricole, aratoire. **~ implements,** instruments aratoires, *m.pl.* ~ *show*, concours (*ou* comice) agricole, *m.*

agricultur[al]ist, *n*, agriculteur, cultivateur, *m.* **agriculture**, *n*, agriculture, *f.*

agronomist, *n*, agronome, *m.* **agronomy**, *n*, agronomie, *f.*

aground, *ad. & a,* échoué. **to run ~,** *v.i. & t,* [s']échouer.

ague, *n,* fièvre paludéenne, *f.*

ahead, *ad,* en avant, devant. *go ~!* en avant!

ahoy, *i,* ho!, ohé! *ship ~!* ho! du navire.

aid, *n,* aide, assistance, *f,* secours, *m.* ¶ *v.t,* aider, assister, secourir.

aide-de-camp, *n,* aide de camp, *m.*

ail, *v.t. & i,* avoir, souffrir. ~**ing**, *a,* maladif, souffrant. ~**ment**, *n,* mal, malaise, *m.*

aim, *n,* point de mire, *m,* visée, *f;* but, objectif, *m,* fin, *f.* ¶ *v.t,* pointer, coucher en joue. ~ *at,* viser [à], ajuster, coucher (*ou* metter) en joue. ~**less**, *a,* ~**lessly**, *ad,* sans but.

air, *n,* air; vent; ciel, *m. to give oneself ~s,* faire l'important, e. ~*craft carrier,* porte-avions, *m.* ~ *craft exhibition,* salon de l'aviation. *m.* ~ *current,* courant d'air, *m.* ~ *cushion,* coussin à air, *m.* ~*field,* terrain d'aviation, *m.* ~ *gun,* fusil à air comprimé, f., à vent, *m.* ~*hole,* aspirail, soupirail, évent, *m;* souffture, *f.* ~*line,* ligne aérienne, ligne d'avion, *f.* ~ *liner,* avion de ligne régulière. *m.* ~*lock,* bouchon de vapeur, *m.* ~*mail,* poste aérienne, posteavion, *f. by ~mail,* par avion. ~*man,* aviateur, *m.* ~ *mechanic,* mécanicien d'avions, *m.* ~ *minded,* tourné vers l'aviation. ~ *parcel,* colis-avion, *m.* ~*plane,* avion, *m.* ~ *pocket,* trou d'air, *m.* ~*port,* aéroport, *m.* ~ *pump,* pompe à air, *f;* (*Phys.*) machine pneumatique, *f.* ~ *race,* course d'avions, *f.* ~ *raid,* raid aérien, *m.* ~*shaft* (Min.), puits d'aérage, *m.* ~*ship,* dirigeable, paquebot aérien, *m.* ~*-tight,* [à fermeture] hermétique, imperméable à l'air. ~*way* (Min.) galerie d'aérage. ¶ *v.t,* aérer, ventiler; donner de l'air à; éventer; chauffer, sécher; étaler. ~**ing**, *n,* aérage, *m,* aération, ventilation, *f.* ~**less**, *a,* sans

air, privé d'air. ~**y**, *a,* ventilé, aéré; en l'air; vain.

air-condition, *v.t,* climatiser. ~**ed**, *a,* climatisé. ~**er**, *n,* climatiseur, *m.*

aisle, *n,* aile, *f,* bas-côté, *m.*

ajar, *a,* entrebâillé, entrouvert. *be ~,* bâiller.

akimbo, *ad: to set one's arms ~,* faire le pot à deux anses. *with arms ~,* les mains sur les hanches.

akin, *a,* apparenté, voisin.

alabaster, *n,* albâtre, *m.*

alacrity, *n,* empressement, *m.*

alarm, *n,* alarme, alerte, *f;* avertisseur, *m.* ~ *clock,* réveillematin, réveil, *m.* ¶ *v.t.* alarmer. ~**ing**, *a,* alarmant.

alas, *i,* hélas!

alb, *n,* aube, *f.*

albatross, *n,* albatros, *m.*

albino, *n,* albinos, *m,f.*

album, *n,* album, *m.*

albumen, *n,* albumen, *m.* **albumin**, *n,* albumine, *f.*

alchemist, *n,* alchimiste, *m.* **alchemy**, *n,* alchimie, *f.*

alcohol, *n,* alcool, *m.* ~**ic**, *a. & n,* alcoolique, *a. & m,f.*

alcove, *n,* alcôve, *f.*

alder, *n,* aune, ver[g]ne, *m.*

ale, *n,* bière, ale, *f.*

alert, *a,* alerte. *on the ~,* alerte, en éveil, sur le qui-vive.

Alexandria, *n,* Alexandrie, *f.* **Alexandrian & Alexandrine**, *a,* alexandrin.

alfresco, *a. & ad,* en plein air.

algebra, *n,* algèbre, *m.*

Algeria, *n,* l'Algérie, *f.* **Algerian**, *a,* algérien. ¶ *n,* Algérien, ne. **Algiers**, *n,* Alger, *m.*

alias, *ad,* alias, autrement dit. ¶ *n,* faux nom; nom de guerre, *m.*

alibi, *n,* alibi, *m.*

alien, *a,* étranger. ¶ *n,* étranger, ère.

alienate, *v.t,* aliéner. (Theat.) *alienation effect,* distanciation, *f.*

alight, *a,* allumé. ¶ *v.i,* descendre, débarquer; atterrir; se poser. ~ [*on the water*] (seaplane), amerrir.

align, *v.t,* aligner. ~**ment**, *n,* alignement, *m.*

alike, *a,* semblable, pareil; ressemblant. ¶ *ad,* également; à la fois. *to be ~,* se ressembler.

alimentary, *a,* alimentaire. **alimony**, *n,* pension alimentaire, *f.*

alive, *a*, en vie, vivant, vif, au monde, animé; sensible; éveillé, dégourdi. *to be ~ with vermin*, grouiller de vermine.

alkali, *n*, alcali, *m*. alkaline, *a*, alcalin.

all, *a*, tout. *~ the year* [round], [pendant] toute l'année. *~* [those] *who*, tous ceux qui, toutes celles qui. *at ~ hours*, à toute heure. *on ~ occasions*, en toute occasion. ¶ *ad*, tout; entièrement. *~ at once*, tout à coup. *~ but*, presque, à peu près. *~ right!* très bien! c'est bien! à la bonne heure! *~ the better*, tant mieux. *~ the same*, tout de même, quand même. ¶ *n*, tous, *m.pl.*; tout; avoir, *m*. *~ of us*, nous tous. *that is ~*, c'est tout, voilà tout. *that is not ~*, il s'en faut de beaucoup. *is that ~?* est-ce là tout? n'est-ce que cela? *one's ~*, tout son avoir, son tout, son va-tout. *~ clear* (Mil.), fin d'alerte. *~ in*, fatigué. *~ told* or *in ~*, tout compte fait, pour tout potage.

allay, *v.t*, calmer, apaiser, adoucir.

allegation, *n*, allégation, *f*. allege, *v.t*, alléguer, prétendre, objecter.

allegiance, *n*, fidélité, obéissance, *f*, loyalisme, *m*.

allegoric(al†), *a*, allégorique. allegory, *n*, allégorie, *f*.

allergy, *n*, allergie, *f*.

alleviate, *v.t*, alléger, soulager, adoucir. alleviation, *n*, allégement, soulagement, adoucissement, *m*.

alley, *n*, ruelle, *f*, passage, *m*. *blind ~*, impasse, *f*.

All Fools' Day, le jour des poissons d'avril.

alliance, *n*, alliance, *f*.

allied, *a*, allié; parent.

alligator, *n*, alligator, *m*.

all-important, *ad*, de toute importance.

allocate, *v.t*, allouer. allocation, *n*, allocation, *f*.

allot, *v.t*, attribuer, répartir; destiner. *~ment*, *n*, attribution, répartition, distribution, *f*; lopin de terre, allotissement, *m*. allotee, *n*, attributaire, *m.f*.

allow, *v.t*, permettre, autoriser; admettre; souffrir; laisser; allouer, accorder, faire, bonifier. *~ance*, *n*, allouance, allocation; ration; pension; tolérance; boni-

fication, remise, déduction, *f*, rabais, décompte, *m*, ristourne, indemnité, *f*.

alloy, *n*, alliage, *m*. ¶ *v.t*, allier.

all-powerful, *a*, tout-puissant.

all-round, *a*, complet.

All Saints' Day, la Toussaint.

All Souls' Day, le jour des morts.

allspice, *n*, toute-épice, *f*, piment, *m*.

allude to (to), toucher.

allure, *v.t*, amorcer, allécher, affrioler, affriander, appâter. *~ment*, *n*, amorce, *f*, allèchement, appât, *m*. *~ing*, *a*, séduisant.

allusion, *n*, allusion, *f*.

alluvion, alluvium, *n*, alluvion, *f*.

ally, *n*, allié, e. ¶ *v.t*, allier, apparenter.

almanac, *n*, almanach, *m*.

almighty, *a*, tout-puissant. *the Almighty*, le Tout-Puissant.

almond, *n*, amande, *f*. *~ eyes*, des yeux en amande, des yeux bridés, *m.pl*. *~* [tree], amandier, *m*.

almost, *ad*, presque.

alms, *n.s. & pl*, aumône, l'aumône, charité, *f*. *~giving*, distribution des aumônes, charité, *f*.

aloe, *n*, aloès; (*pl*.) [suc d']aloès, *m*.

aloft, *ad*, en haut; dans la mâture.

alone, *a*, seul; isolé. *to let* (or *leave*) *~*, laisser tranquille. ¶ *ad*, seulement.

along, *pr. & ad*, le long de; suivant. *~side of* (pers.), côte à côte avec. *~side* [the ship], le long [du bord]. *to come ~side*, accoster. *come ~!* venez donc! *all ~*, tout du long; tout le temps.

aloof, *ad*, à l'écart, en dehors, isolé (*from* = de). ¶ *a*, distant.

aloud, *ad*, à haute voix, tout haut.

alpaca, *n*, alpaga, *m*.

alpha, *n*, alpha, *m*. alphabet, *n*, alphabet, *m*. *~ical†*, *a*, alphabétique.

Alpine, *a*, alpin; alpestre. *the Alps*, les Alpes, *f.pl*, les monts, *m.pl*.

already, *ad*, déjà.

Alsace, *n*, l'Alsace, *f*. Alsatian, *a*, alsacien. ¶ *n*, (pers.) Alsacien, ne; (dog) chien-loup, *m*.

also, *ad*, aussi, également, pareillement.

altar, *n*, autel, *m*. *~ cloth*, nappe

d'a., *f.* ~ *piece*, tableau d'a.;
retable, *m.*

alter, *v.t*, changer, modifier; surcharger; (*v.i.*) [se] changer. ~
the date of (function, etc.),
transférer. ~**ation,** *n,* changement, *m,* modification; surcharge, *f,* renvoi [en marge], *m.*

altercation, *n,* altercation, prise
de bec, *f.*

alternate†, *a,* alternatif. ~
months (newspaper appearing),
bimensuel. ¶ *v.i.* & *t,* alterner.
alternating, *p.a,* alternatif. **al-**
ternative, *a,* alternatif. ¶ *n,* alternative, *f.*

although, *c,* quoique, bien que,
encore que, quand, tout . . . que.

altitude, *n,* altitude, élévation,
hauteur, *f.*

alto, *n.* & ~ *saxhorn*, alto, *m.* ~
clef, clef d'ut, *f.*

altogether, *ad,* tout à fait; en
tout; grandement.

altruist, *n.* & ~**ic,** *a,* altruiste,
m,f. & *a.*

alum, *n,* alun, *m.*

aluminum, *n,* aluminium, *m.*

always, *ad,* toujours.

amalgam, *n,* amalgame, *m.*
~**ate,** *v.t,* amalgamer, fusionner.

amanuensis, *n,* secrétaire, *m.*

amass, *v.t,* amasser.

amateur, *n,* amateur; dilettante,
m. ~ *status,* qualité d'amateur,
f, statut d'a., *m.* **amatory,** *a,*
galant, érotique.

amaze, *v.t,* étonner, stupéfier.
~**ment,** *n,* étonnement, *m,* stupeur, *f.*

Amazon, *n,* amazone; virago,
f. **the** ~ (*river*), l'Amazone, *m,*
le fleuve des Amazones.

ambassador, dress, *n,* ambassadeur, drice.

amber, *n,* ambre, *m.* ~**gris,** *n,*
ambre gris, *m.*

ambiguity, *n,* ambiguïté, équivoque, *f.* **ambiguous†,** *a,* ambigu,
équivoque.

ambition, *n,* ambition, *f.* **am-**
bitious†, *a,* ambitieux.

amble along (to), aller son
petit train.

ambrosia, *n,* ambroisie, *f.*

ambulance, *n,* ambulance, *f.*

ambuscade, ambush, *n,* embuscade, *f,* guetapens, *m.* **to**
place in ~, embusquer. **ambush,**
v.i, s'embusquer.

ameliorate, *v.t,* améliorer. **ame-**
lioration, *n,* amélioration, *f.*

amen, *i.* & *n,* amen, *i.* & *m.*

amenable, *a,* sujet, soumis; susceptible; justiciable; docile.

amend, *v.t,* amender; réformer;
rectifier; changer. ~**s,** *n,* réparation, *f. make* ~ *for,* réparer, corriger, racheter.

amenity, *n,* aménité, *f;* agrément,
m.

America, *n,* l'Amérique, *f.*
American, *a,* américain. ¶ *n,*
Américain, e.

amethyst, *n,* améthyste, *f.*

amiability, *n,* amabilité, *f.* **ami-**
able, *a,* aimable, accort. **amia-**
bly, *ad,* avec amabilité.

amicable†, *a,* amical, amiable.

amid, amidst, *pr,* au milieu de,
parmi. **amidships,** *ad,* au milieu
du navire.

amiss, *ad.* & *a,* de travers; mal,
en mal, en mauvaise part. *to
take* ~, prendre mal.

ammonia, *n,* ammoniaque, *f.*

ammunition, *n,* munitions, *f.pl.*
~ *wagon,* prolonge, *f.*

amnesia, *n,* amnésie, *f.*

amnesty, *n,* amnistie, *f.*

among, amongst, *pr,* parmi,
entre, dans; au milieu de; au
nombre de; chez. ~ *strangers,*
dépaysé.

amorous†, *a,* amoureux.

amorphous, *a,* amorphe.

amortisation, *n,* amortissement,
m. **amortize,** *v.t,* amortir.

amount, *n,* montant, *m,* somme,
f, chiffre, *m,* quantité, *f.* ¶ *v.i,*
monter, se chiffrer, s'élever; revenir. ~*ing to,* à concurrence de.

ampere, *n,* ampère, *m.*

amphibian, *n,* amphibie, *m.* **am-**
phibious, *a,* amphibie.

amphitheater, *n,* amphithéâtre,
m.

ample†, *a,* ample. ~**ness,** *n,* ampleur, *f.* **amplifier** (*radio*) *n,*
amplificateur, *m.* **amplify,** *v.t.* &
i, amplifier; développer; paraphraser. **amplitude,** *n,* amplitude, *f.*

amputate, *v.t,* amputer.

amulet, *n,* amulette, *f.*

amuse, *v.t,* amuser, divertir, distraire. ~**ment,** *n,* amusement, *m,*
plaisir, divertissement, *m,* distraction, *f.*

amusing, *a,* amusant.

an, *indefinite art.* or *a,* un, une.

anachronism, *n,* anachronisme,
m.

anagram, *n,* anagramme, *f.*

analogous, *a*, analogue. **analogy**, *n*, analogie, *f*.

analyze, *v.t*, analyser; (*Bkkpg.*) dépouiller, ventiler. **analysis**, *n*, analyse; ventilation, *f*. **analyst**, *n*, analyste, *m*. **analytic(al†)**, *a*, analytique.

anarchic(al), *a*, anarchique. **anarchist**, *n*, anarchiste, *m,f*. **anarchy**, *n*, anarchie, *f*.

anatomical†, *a*, anatomique. **anatomy**, *n*, anatomie, *f*.

ancestor, *n*, ancêtre, *m*. **ancestral**, *a*, ancestral. **ancestry**, *n*, race, *f*, ascendants, *m.pl*.

anchor (*all senses*) *n*, ancre, *f*. ¶ (*Naut.*) *v.t*. & *i*, mouiller; (*Build.* & *fig.*) *v.t*, ancrer. ~**age** (*Naut.*) *n*, mouillage, *m*.

anchoret, anchorite, *n*, anachorète, *m*.

anchovy, *n*, anchois, *m*. ~ *paste*, beurre d'anchois, *m*.

ancient†, *a*, ancien; antique. ¶ *n*, ancien, *m*. ~**ness**, *n*, ancienneté, antiquité, *f*.

and, *c*. (*abb.* &), et, &. ~ *even*, voire même. ~ *so on* or ~ *so forth*, et ainsi de suite. ~ *so on*, ~ *so forth*, et patati, et patata. *go* ~ *see*, allez voir. *more* ~ *more*, de plus en plus. *two* ~ *two*, deux à deux. *steak* ~ *potatoes*, bifteck aux pommes.

andiron, *n*, chenet, *m*.

anecdote, *n*, anecdote, historiette, *f*.

anemia, *n*, anémie, *f*. **anemic**, *a*, anémique.

anemone, *n*, anémone, *f*.

aneroid [*barometer*], baromètre anéroïde, *m*.

anesthetic, *a*. & *n*, anesthetique, *a*. & *m*. ¶ *v.t*, **anesthetize**, insensibiliser.

anew, *ad*, à nouveau, de nouveau.

angel, *n*, ange, *m*. ~**ic(al†)**, *a*, angélique. **angelus** [*bell*], Angélus, *m*.

anger, *n*, colère, *f*, courroux, *m*. ¶ *v.t*, mettre en colère, fâcher, courroucer, irriter.

angina, *n*, angine, *f*. ~ *pectoris*, angine de poitrine.

angle, *n*, angle, *m*. ~ [*iron*], fer cornière, *m*, cornière, *f*.

angle, *v.i*, pêcher à la ligne. **angler**, *n*, pêcheur à la ligne, *m*.

Anglicism, *n*, anglicisme, *m*.

angling, *n*, pêche à la ligne, *f*. ~ *at set pitches*, pêche au coup.

Anglomania, *n*, anglomanie, *f*. **Anglophil[e]**, *a*. & *n*, anglophile,

a. & *m,f*. **Anglophobe**, *a*. & *n*, anglophobe, *a*. & *m,f*. **Anglo-Saxon**, *a*, anglo-saxon. ¶ *n*, Anglo-Saxon, ne.

angrily, *ad*, avec colère. **angry**, *a*, en colère, fâché, irrité. *to get* (or *be*) ~, se fâcher. *to be* ~ *with oneself for*, s'en vouloir de.

anguish, *n*, angoisse, *f*. ¶ *v.i*, angoisser.

angular, *a*, angulaire.

aniline, *n*, aniline, *f*. ~ *dye*, teinture d'aniline, *f*.

animal, *a*, animal. ¶ *n*, animal, *m*.

animate, *a*, animé, doué de vie. ¶ *v.t*, animer. **animation**, *n*, animation, *f*.

animosity, animus, *n*, animosité, *f*.

aniseed, *n*, anis, *m*, graine d'anis, *f*.

ankle, *n*, cheville [du pied], malléole, *f*.

annals, *n.pl*, annales, *f.pl*, fastes, *m.pl*.

anneal, *v.t*, recuire. ~**ing**, *n*, recuit, *m*, recuite, *f*.

annex, *v.t*, annexer. ~**ation**, *n*, annexion, *f*. **annex[e]**, *n*, annexe, dépendance, *f*.

annihilate, *v.t*, anéantir, annihiler. **annihilation**, *n*, anéantissement, *m*, annihilation, *f*.

anniversary, *a*. & *n*, anniversaire, *a*. & *m*.

annotate, *v.t*, annoter.

announce, *v.t*, annoncer. ~**ment**, *n*, annonce, *f*. **announcer** (*radio*) *n*, speaker; annoncier, *m*.

annoy, *v.t*, agacer, tracasser, contrarier, ennuyer. *to be* ~*ed with*, savoir mauvais gré à. ~**ance**, *n*, agacement, *m*, tracasserie, contrariété; fâcherie, *f*. ~**ing**, *a*, agaçant, contrariant.

annual†, *a*, annuel. ¶ *n*, plante annuelle, *f*; (*book*) annuaire, *m*. **annuitant**, *n*, rentier, ère. **annuity**, *n*, annuité, rente [à terme], *f*.

annul, *v.t*, annuler, annihiler.

annular, *a*, annulaire.

annum, *n*: *per* ~, par an.

Annunciation (the), l'Annonciation, *f*.

anode, *n*, anode, *f*.

anodyne, *a*, anodin. ¶ *n*, anodin, *m*.

anoint, *v.t*, oindre, sacrer. ~**ed**, *a*. & *n*, oint, *a.m*. & *m*.

anomalous, *a*, anomal. **anomaly**, *n*, anomalie, *f*.

anon, *ad*, tantôt, tout à l'heure.

anonymous, a, anonyme.

another, n, un (une) autre; autre; encore un, encore une; nouveau; un (une) second, e.

answer, n, réponse; réplique, f. ~s to correspondents, petite correspondance, f. ~ to the riddle, mot de l'énigme, m. ¶ v.t, répondre à. ~ [back], répliquer. ~ for, répondre pour, de. ~able, a, responsable.

ant, n, fourmi, f. ~eater, fourmilier, m. ~hill, fourmilière, f.

antagonism, n, antagonisme, m. **antagonist,** n, antagoniste, m. **antagonize,** v.t, rendre hostile.

antarctic, a, antarctique. the A~ Ocean, l'océan Glacial antarctique, m.

antecedent, a. & n, antécédent, a. & m.

antechamber, n, antichambre, f.

antedate, v.t, antidater.

antediluvian, a, antédiluvien.

antelope, n, antilope, f.

ante meridiem (abb. a.m.), avant midi; du matin.

antenna, n, antenne, f.

anterior†, a, antérieur.

anteroom, n, antichambre, f.

anthem, n, antienne, f; (national) hymne, m.

anther, n, anthère, f.

anthology, n, anthologie, f.

anthracite, n, anthracite, m.

anthrax (Med.) n, anthrax, m.

antiaircraft, a, anti-aérien, contre-avions.

antibiotic, n, antibiotique, m.

antibody, n, anticorp, m.

anti-British, a, anglophobe.

antic, n, (pl.) gambades, f.pl.

antichrist, n, antéchrist, m. the A~, l'A.

anticipate, v.t, anticiper, prévenir, escompter. **anticipation,** n, anticipation, prévision, f.

anticlimax, n, gradation descendante, f.

anticyclone, n, anticyclone, m.

antidote, n, antidote, contre-poison, m.

antifreeze, n, antigel, m.

anti-French, a, gallophobe.

antiglare, a, anti-aveuglant.

antimony, n, antimoine, m.

antipathetic, a, antipathique. antipathy, n, antipathie, f.

antipodes, n.pl, antipodes, m.pl.

antiquary, antiquarian, n, antiquaire, m.f. **antiquated,** a, suranné, vieilli. **antique,** a, antique. ¶ n, (style) antique, m;

(relic) antique, f. **antiquity,** n, antiquité; ancienneté, f.

antiseptic, a. & n, antiseptique, a. & m.

antithesis, n, antithèse, f.

antler, n, andouiller, m, (pl.) bois, m.pl.

Antwerp, n, Anvers, m.

anus, n, anus, m.

anvil, n, enclume, f.

anxiety, n, anxiété, inquiétude; sollicitude, f. **anxious,** a, anxieux, inquiet; soucieux; désireux, jaloux. ~ly, ad, avec anxiété.

any, a, ad. & pn, quelque; quelconque; de; du, de la, des; aucun; tout; plus; quelqu'un. has he ~? en a-t-il? I don't have ~, je n'en ai pas. ~ farther, ~ further, plus loin. ~ more, encore; (neg.) plus. ~way, n'importe comment; en tout cas.

anybody, anyone, n. & pn, quelqu'un; on; personne; aucun; tout le monde; le premier venu.

anyhow, ad, de toute façon; en tout cas, toujours; n'importe comment; à l'abandon, à la débandade.

anything, pn. & n, quelque chose, m; (neg.) rien, m; quoi que ce soit; n'importe quoi.

anywhere, ad, n'importe où; quelque part; (neg.) nulle part.

aorta, n, aorte, f.

apace, ad, à grands pas.

apart, ad, à part; de côté; séparément. ~ from, abstraction faite de. to move ~, se séparer, s'écarter. to tell ~, distinguer.

apartment, n, appartement, logement, m, salle, pièce, f. ~ house, maison de rapport, f.

apathetic, a, apathique, indolent. **apathy,** n, apathie, indolence, f.

ape, n, singe (sans queue), m. ¶ v.t, singer.

aperture, n, ouverture, f, orifice, m.

apex, n, sommet, faîte, m.

aphorism, n, aphorisme, m.

apiary, n, rucher, m.

apiece, ad, [la] pièce.

apish, a, simiesque.

apogee, n, apogée, m.

apologetic, a, apologétique. **apologize,** v.i, faire ses excuses. **apology,** n, apologie, f; excuses, f.pl; semblant, m.

apoplectic, a. & n, apoplectique, a. & m. ~ fit, attaque d'apo-

plexie, *f*, coup de sang, *m*. apoplexy, *n*, apoplexie, *f*.
apostasy, *n*, apostasie, *f*. **apostate**, *n*. & *a*, apostat, *m*. & *att*,
relaps, e.
apostle, *n*, apôtre, *m. the* [*A~s'*]
Creed, le symbole [des apôtres].
apostolate, apostleship, *n*, apostolat, *m*. **apostolic**(al†), *a*, apostolique.
apostrophe, *n*, apostrophe, *f*.
apostrophize, *v.t*, apostropher.
apothecaries' measure, mesure pharmaceutique, *f*.
apotheosis, *n*, apothéose, *f*.
appall, *v.t*, épouvanter. **appalling**,
a, épouvantable.
apparatus, *n*, appareil, attirail,
m.
apparel, *n*, habillement, *m*, vêtements, *m.pl*.
apparent, *a*, apparent; (*heir*)
présomptif. **~ly**, *ad*, apparemment.
apparition, *n*, apparition, *f*.
appeal, *n*, appel; pourvoi; recours; attrait, *m*. ¶ *v.i*, en appeler; faire appel; appeler.
appear, *v.i*, paraître, sembler; apparaître; figurer, ressortir; comparaître. **~ance**, *n*, apparition;
apparence, venue, *f*, semblant,
aspect, *m*; mine; comparution, *f*;
(*pl.*) apparences, *f.pl*, dehors,
m.pl.
appease, *v.t*, apaiser, adoucir;
pacifier. **~ment**, *n*, apaisement,
m, conciliation, *f*.
appellation, *n*, surnom, *m*;
désignation, *f*.
append, *v.t*, apposer. **~age**, appendix, *n*, appendice, *m*. **appendicitis**, *n*, appendicite, *f*.
appertain, *v.i*, appartenir.
appetite, *n*, appétit, *m*. **appetizer**, *n*, apéritif, *m*. **appetizing**,
a, appétissant.
applaud, *v.t*, applaudir [à]. **applause**, *n*, applaudissement[s] *m*.
[*pl.*].
apple, *n*, pomme; (*eye*) prunelle,
f. ~ *corer*, vide-pomme, *m*. ~
orchard, pommeraie, *f*. ~ *pie*,
tourte aux pommes, *f*. ~ *tree*,
pommier, *m*.
appliance, *n*, engin, appareil;
(*pl.*) attirail, *m*.
applicant, *n*, demandeur, euse;
postulant, e; souscripteur, *m*. **application**, *n*, application; contention; affectation; demande, réclamation; souscription; mise en
œuvre, *f*; (*brake*) serrage, *m*. on

~, sur demande. **applied** (*of
sciences*) *a*, appliqué. **appliqué**
lace, [dentelle d']application, *f*.
appliqué [work] (*metal*), applique, *f*. **appliqué** (*or applied*)
work (*Emb.*), broderie-applica-
tion, *f*. **apply**, *v.t*, appliquer, affecter; (*brake*) serrer. ~ *for*,
solliciter, postuler, demander, réclamer; souscrire. ~ *to*, s'a-
dresser à.
appoint, *v.t*, nommer, instituer,
constituer, désigner, préposer.
~ment, *n*, nomination, désignation, constitution, *f*; rendezvous;
(*pl.*) aménagement, emménagement, *m*.
apportion, *v.t*, répartir, ventiler.
apposite, *a*, à propos, pertinent.
apposition, *n*, apposition, *f*.
appraise, *v.t*, priser. **~ment**, *n*,
prisée, *f*. **appraiser**, *n*, priseur, *m*.
appreciable, *a*, appréciable, sensible. **appreciably**, *ad*, sensiblement. **appreciate**, *v.t*, apprécier;
améliorer; (*v.i.*) s'améliorer. **appreciation**, *n*, appréciation; amélioration, plus-value, *f*.
apprehend, *v.t*, appréhender; redouter; saisir. **apprehension**, *n*,
appréhension, *f*. **apprehensive**,
a, inquiet.
apprentice, *n*, apprenti, e;
(*Naut.*) novice, *m*. ¶ *v.t*, mettre
en apprentissage. **~ship**, *n*, apprentissage; noviciat, *m*.
apprise, *v.t*, prévenir, informer.
approach, *n*, approche, *f*; accès,
abord, *m*. ¶ *v.t*, [s']approcher de,
aborder; (*v.i.*) [s']approcher.
~able, *a*, abordable, accessible.
approbation, *n*, approbation, *f*.
appropriate†, *a*, propre, convenable, approprié. *to be* ~, être
de mise. ¶ *v.t*, s'approprier; consacrer, distraire, affecter. **appropriation**, *n*, somme affectée, destination, *f*.
approval, *n*, approbation, *f*,
agrément, *m*, sanction, *f*. on ~,
à condition. **approve**, *v.t*, approuver, agréer, sanctionner.
approximate†, *a*, approximatif.
¶ *v.t*, rapprocher, approcher. **approximation**, *n*, approximation,
f.
apricot, *n*, abricot, *m*. ~ *tree*,
abricotier, *m*.
April, *n*, avril, *m*. *to make an* ~
fool of, donner un poisson d'avril
à.
apron, *n*, tablier, *m*.
apropos, *ad*, à propos.

apse, *n*, abside, *f.*

apt, *a*, enclin, sujet, disposé, porté; à propos; apte. ~ly, *ad*, à propos. ~ness, *n*, àpropos, *m*. aptitude, *n*, aptitude, facilité, *f*, dispositions, *f.pl.*

aqua-fortis, eau-forte, *f*. aquamarine, *n*, aigue-marine, *f*. aquaregis, eau régale, *f*.

aquarium, *n*, aquarium, *m*.

aquatic, *a*, (*plant*) aquatique; (*sport*) nautique.

aqueduct, *n*, aqueduc, *m*.

aqueous, *a*, aqueux.

aquiline, *a*, aquilin.

Arab, *a*, arabe. ¶ *n*, Arabe, *m,f*. arabesque, *n*, arabesque, *f*. Arabia, *n*, l'Arabie, *f*. Arabian, *a*, arabe. the ~ Nights, les Mille & une Nuits. ¶ *n*, Arabe, *m,f*. Arabic (*language*) *n*, l'arabe, *m*. Arabic numerals, chiffres arabes, *m.pl.*

arable, *a*, arable, labourable.

arbiter, *n*, arbitre, *m*. arbitrage & arbitrament, *n*, arbitrage, *m*. arbitrary†, *a*, arbitraire; conventionnel; d'office. arbitrate, *v.t*, arbitrer. arbitration, *n*, arbitrage, *m*. ~ clause, clause compromissoire, *f*. arbitrator, *n*, arbitre; (*law*) amiable compositeur, *m*.

arbor, *n*, arbre, mandrin, *m*, broche, *f*.

arbor, *n*, tonnelle, *f*, verger, *m*.

arc, *n*, arc, *m*. ~ lamp, lampe à arc, *f*.

arcade, *n*, arcades, *f.pl*, galerie, *f*, passage, bazar, *m*.

arch, *a*, espiègle, malicieux. ¶ *n*, voûte, *f*, arceau, *m*, arcade, *f*, arche; porte, *f*; arc, cintre, *m*. ~ support (for foot in shoe), cambrure-support, *f*. ¶ *v.t*, cintrer, arquer, cambrer, voûter.

archaeologic(al), *a*, archéologique. archaeologist, *n*, archéologue, *m*. archaeology, *n*, archéologie, *f*.

archaic, *a*, archaïque, vieux, vieilli.

archangel, *n*, archange, *m*.

archbishop, *n*, archevêque, *m*. archbishopric, *n*, archevêché, *m*.

archdeacon, *n*, archidiacre, *m*.

archer, *n*, archer, *m*. ~y, *n*, tir à l'arc, *m*.

Archimedean screw, vis d'Archimède, limace, *f*.

archipelago, *n*, archipel, *m*.

architect, *n*, architecte; (*fig.*) artisan, *m*. architectural, *a*, ar-

chitectural. architecture, *n*, architecture, *f*.

archives, *n.pl*, archives, *f.pl.*

archly, *ad*, malicieusement. archness, *n*, espièglerie, *f*.

archway, *n*, arcade, *f*, passage voûté; portail, *m*.

arctic, *a*, arctique. the A~ Ocean, l'océan Glacial arctique, *m*.

ardent, *a*, ardent. ~ly, *ad*, ardemment. ardor, *n*, ardeur, *f*, zèle, *m*.

arduous, *a*, ardu, pénible, laborieux.

are see be.

area, *n*, aire, superficie, surface; zone, étendue, *f*; réseau, *m*.

arena, *n*, arène, *f*.

argentine, *a*, argentin. A~ (*Geog.*) *a*, argentin. ¶ *n* (*pers.*), Argentin, e. the ~, l'Argentine, *f*.

argue, *v.i. & t*, argumenter, raisonner, discuter, débattre, prétendre, plaider. argument, *n*, argument, raisonnement, *m*, thèse, *f*. ~ation, arguing, *n*, argumentation, *f*. ~ative, *a*, raisonneur.

aria (*Mus.*) *n*, air, *m*.

arid, *a*, aride. ~ity, *n*, aridité, *f*.

aright, *ad*, bien, justement.

arise, *v.i.ir*, s'élever, surgir, naître, survenir.

aristocracy, *n*, aristocratie, *f*. aristocrat, *n*, aristocrate, *m,f*. aristocratic(al†), *a*, aristocratique.

arithmetic, *n*, arithmétique, *f*, calcul, *m*. ~al†, *a*, arithmétique. ~ian, *n*, arithméticien, ne.

ark, *n*, arche, *f*. the A~ of the Covenant, l'arche d'alliance, *f*.

arm, *n*, (*limb*) bras; (*of cross*) croisillon, *m*; (*weapon*) arme, *f*; (*pl., Her.*) armes, armoiries, *f.pl*, blason, *m*; (*rest*) bras, accotoir, accoudoir, *m*. ~ in ~, bras dessus, bras dessous. to be up in ~s, se gendarmer. ~chair, fauteuil, *m*. ~hole, emmanchure, *f*. ~pit, aisselle, *f*. ~s race, course aux armements, *f*. ¶ *v.t*, armer; (*v.i.*) [s']armer.

armadillo, *n*, tatou, *m*.

armament, *n*, armement, *m*.

armature, *n*, (*Phys.*) armature, armure, *f*; (*dynamo*) induit, *m*.

Armenia, *n*, l'Arménie, *f*. Armenian, *a*, arménien. ¶ *n*, Arménien, ne.

armful, *n*, brassée, *f*.

armistice, n, armistice, m. A~ Day, la fête [de l'anniversaire] de l'Armistice, le jour anniversaire de l'Armistice.

armlet, n, brassard, m.

armor, n, armure; (sheathing) armature, cuirasse, f. ~ plate, plaque de blindage, f. ~ plating, blindage, m. ~ed, a, armé; blindé, cuirassé, protégé. ~ car, automobile blindée, f. ~er, n, armurier, m. ~y, n, salle d'armes, f. **armorial**, a. & n. armorial, a. & m. ~ bearings, armoiries, armes, f.pl, blason, m.

army, n, armée, f. ~ contractor, fournisseur de l'armée, m.

arnica, n, arnica, f.

aroma, n, arôme; bouquet, m. **aromatic**, a, aromatique.

around, ad, autour, alentour. ¶ pr, autour de.

arouse, v.t, réveiller; provoquer.

arpeggio, n, arpège, m.

arraign, v.t, accuser; traduire en justice. ~ment, n, mise en accusation, f.

arrange, v.t, arranger, disposer, agencer, ménager; distribuer; accommoder; débattre, arbitrer. ~ment, n, arrangement, m, disposition, f, agencement, mouvement, m; économie; distribution, f; accommodement; dispositif, m.

arrant, a, franc, insigne, fieffé, achevé, fier.

arras, n, tapisserie, f.

array, n, ordre; appareil, m; série, rangée, f. ¶ v.t, ranger; ajuster; revêtir.

arrears, n.pl, arrérages, m. in arrear[s], en arrière, arriéré en retard, retardataire; en demeure.

arrest, n, arrestation, prise de corps, f; arrêt, m. under ~, (civil) en état d'arrestation; (Mil.) aux arrêts. ¶ v.t, arrêter; appréhender. ~er (Elec., etc.) n, déchargeur, m.

arrival, n, arrivée, f; arrivage, m. **arrive**, v.i, arriver; parvenir. ~ unexpectedly, survenir.

arrogance, n, arrogance, f. **arrogant**, a, arrogant, rogue. ~ly, ad, arrogamment. **to arrogate** [to oneself], s'arroger.

arrow, n, flèche, f, trait, m.

arsenal, n, arsenal, m.

arsenic, n, arsenic, m. ~al, a, arsenical.

arson, n, incendie volontaire, m.

art, n, art; artifice, m. ~ school, école des beaux-arts, f.

arterial (Anat.) a, artériel. ~ road (Eng.), route nationale de grand itinéraire, f. (= in Fr. a widened main road). **artery**, n, artère, f.

artesian, a, artésien. ~ well, puits artésien, m.

artful†, a, artificieux, astucieux, rusé. ~ dodger, fin matois, finaud, m. ~ness, n, artifice, art, m, astuce, finauderie, finasserie, ruse, malice, f.

arthritis, n, arthrite, f.

artichoke, n, artichaut, m. Jerusalem ~, topinambour, m.

article, n, article, objet, envoi; (pl.) stage, apprentissage; (pl.) contrat; (pl.—ship's) rôle d'équipage, rôle d'armement, m. ~s [of association], statuts, m.pl. (newspaper) lead ~, article de fond, m.

articulate, v.t, articuler; (v.i.) [s']articuler. **articulation**, n, articulation, f.

artifice, n, artifice, art, m.

artificer, n, [mécanicien] adjusteur, serrurier mécanicien; (fig.) artisan, m.

artificial†, a, artificiel, factice, simili-, postiche.

artillery, n, artillerie, f. ~man, n, artilleur, m.

artisan, n, artisan, e.

artist, & **artiste**, n, artiste, m,f. **artistic**, a, artistique; artiste. ~ novelties, articles de Paris, m.pl. ~ally, ad, artistiquement, avec art.

artless†, a, sans art, naturel; innocent; naïf, ingénu.

Aryan, a, aryen.

as, ad. & c, comme; ainsi que; de même que; parce que; puisque, aussi; que; à titre de; pour. ~ also, ainsi que. ~ [& when], au fur & à mesure que. ~ [& when] required, au fur & à mesure des besoins. ~ before, comme par le passé. ~ for, ~ to, ~ regards, quant à. ~ if, comme si. ~ in (like, equal to), à l'instar de. ~ it were, en quelque sorte. ~ per, suivant, dont. ~ well, aussi bien que, en même temps que. ~ you were! au temps!

asbestos, n, asbeste, m.

ascend, v.t. & i, [re]monter, faire l'ascension de. ~ancy, ~ency, & ~ant, ~ent, n, ascendant, m. **ascension**, n, ascension, f. A~

Day, l'Ascension. **ascent**, *n*, ascension; montée, *f*.

ascertain, *v.t*, constater, reconnaître, se rendre compte de.

ascetic, *a*, ascétique. ¶ *n*, ascète, *m,f*.

ascribe, *v.t*, attribuer, imputer, rapporter.

ash, *n. oft. pl*, cendre, *f. oft. pl*. ~ *blonde* (color), blond cendré *m*. ~ *pit*, fosse aux cendres, *f*. ~*tray*, cendrier [de fumeur] *m*. ~ [*tree*], frêne, *m*. A~ *Wednesday*, le mercredi (*ou* le jour) des Cendres.

ashamed, *a* honteux. *to be* ~, avoir honte, rougir.

ashen, **ashy** (*ash-colored*) *a*, cendré.

ashlar, *n*, moellon d'appareil, *m*.

ashore, *ad*, à terre.

Asia, *n*, l'Asie, *f*. ~ *Minor*, l'Asie Mineure. **Asiatic**, *a*, asiatique. ¶ *n*, Asiatique, *m,f*.

aside, *ad*, de côté; à part; à l'écart; en aparté. ¶ *n*, aparté, *m*.

ask, *v.t*, demander, prier, inviter, interroger, solliciter; poser; s'enquérir. ~ *not to come* (guests), désinviter, décommander.

askance, *ad*, de travers, de biais.

askew, *ad*, en biais, de travers, de guingois.

aslant, *ad*, en biais, obliquement.

asleep, *a*, endormi. *to fall* ~, s'endormir.

asp, *n*, (*serpent*) aspic; (*tree*) tremble, *m*.

asparagus, *n*, asperge, *f*; asperges, *f.pl*. ~ *tongs*, pince à asperges, *f*.

aspect, *n*, aspect, *m*; face, *f*, visage, *m*; exposition, orientation, *f*.

aspen, *n*, tremble, *m*. ~ *plantation*, tremblaie, *f*.

asperity, *n*, aspérité, âpreté, *f*.

asperse, *v.t*, asperger; diffamer, calomnier, noircir. **aspersion**, *n*, aspersion; diffamation, calomnie, *f*.

asphalt, *n*, asphalte, bitume, *m*. ¶ *v.t*, bitumer.

asphyxia, *n*, asphyxie, *f*. **asphyxiate**, *v.t*, asphyxier.

aspirant, *n*, aspirant, e. **aspirate**, *v.t*, aspirer. **aspiration**, *n*, aspiration, *f*. *to* **aspire** *to*, aspirer à, prétendre à, affecter, ambitionner, briguer.

aspirin, *n*, aspirine, *f*.

ass, *n*, âne, *m*, (*she*) ânesse, *f*. *ass's foal*, ânon. *m*. *ass's* (or

asses') *milk*, lait d'ânesse, *m*.

assail, *v.t*, assaillir. ~**ant**, *n*, assaillant, *m*.

assassin, *n*, assassin, e. ~**ate**, *v.t*, assassiner. ~**ation**, *n*, assassinat, *m*.

assault, *n*, assaut; attentat, *m*, (*law*) agression, *f*. ~ [*& battery*], voies de fait, *f.pl*. ¶ *v.t*, assaillir, attaquer.

assay, *n*, essai, *m*. ~ *bureau de garantie* (government), bureau de garantie, *m*. ¶ *v.t*, essayer; (*v.i.*) titrer. ~**er**, *n*, essayeur, *m*.

assemblage, *n*, assemblage, *m*. **assemble**, *v.t*, [r]assembler, réunir. **assembly**, *n*, assemblée, réunion, *f*.

assent, *n*, assentiment; consentement, *m*, sanction, *f*. *to* ~ *to*, donner son assentiment à.

assert, *v.t*, soutenir; affirmer; prétendre; revendiquer. **assertion**, *n*, assertion, *f*; dire, *m*.

assess, *v.t*, coter, imposer. évaluer, taxer. ~**ment**, *n*, cote, cotisation, imposition, répartition, taxation, *f*.

asset, *n*, valeur [active] *f*; (*pl.*) actif, *m*, capitaux, *m.pl*. ~*s nil*, carence, *f*. ~*s transferred* or *taken over*, apport[s] *m.[pl.]*.

assiduity, *n*, assiduité, *f*. **assiduous**, *a*, assidu. ~**ly**, *ad*, assidûment.

assign, *v.t*, assigner; céder; apporter; affecter, destiner. ~**ation**, *n*, assignation, *f*. ~**ment**, *n*, assignation; cession, *f*; apport, *m*; (*Sch.*) devoir, *m*.

assimilate, *v.t*, assimiler.

assist, *v.t*, assister, aider, secourir. ~**ance**, *n*, assistance, aide, *f*, secours; concours, *m*; (*to police*) main-forte, *f*. ~**ant**, *n*, aide, *m,f*, adjoint, e, assistant, auxiliaire, *m*.

assize, *n*, **assizes**, *n.pl*, assises, *f. pl*.

associate, *n*, associé, e. ¶ *v.t*, associer, adjoindre; (*v.i.*) s'associer, frayer. **association**, *n*, association, société, *f*; syndicat, *m*; caisse, *f*.

assort, *v.t*, assortir. ~**ment**, *n*, assortiment, classement, *m*.

assuage, *v.t*, apaiser, adoucir.

assume, *v.t*, prendre, affecter, revêtir; assumer; s'arroger; supposer; (*name*) emprunter. **assuming**, *a*, prétentieux, arrogant.

assumption, *n*, supposition; arrogance, *f*. A~ (*Eccl.*) *n*, assomption, *f*.

assurance, *n*, assurance, *f*. **assure**, *v.t*, assurer. **assuredly**, *ad*, assurément, à coup sûr.

Assyria, *n*, l'Assyrie, *f*. **Assyrian**, *a*, assyrien. ¶ *n*, Assyrien, ne.

aster, *n*, aster, *m*.

asterisk, *n*, astérisque, *m*, étoile, *f*.

astern, *ad*, derrière, en arrière, à (*ou* sur) l'arrière.

asteroid, *n*, astéroïde, *m*.

asthma, *n*, asthme, *m*. **asthmatic**, *a*, asthmatique.

astigmatic, *a*, astigmate.

astir, *ad. & a*, en mouvement, en branle-bas; agité, en émoi.

astonish, *v.t*, étonner, émerveiller, surprendre. **~ingly**, *ad*, étonnamment. **~ment**, *n*, étonnement, *m*, surprise, *f*.

astound, *v.t*, ébahir.

astray, *ad. & a*, hors du [bon] chemin; égaré. *to go ~*, s'égarer.

astride, **astraddle**, *ad. & a*, à califourchon, à cheval, affourché; jambe deçà, jambe delà.

astringent, *a. & n*, astringent, *a. & m*.

astrologer, *n*, astrologue, *m*. **astrology**, *n*, astrologie, *f*.

astronaut, *n*, astronaute, *m*.

astronomer, *n*, astronome, *m*. astronomic(al†), *a*, astronomique. astronomy, *n*, astronomie, *f*.

astute, *a*, fin, rusé; astucieux.

asunder, *ad*, en deux; éloigné l'un de l'autre.

asylum, *n*, asile, hospice, *m*.

at, *pr*, à; en; dans; de; par; contre; chez; moyennant. *~ a loss, profit*, à perte, profit. *~ all*, du tout. *~ first*, d'abord. *~ hand*, à portée [de la main]. *~ home*, chez soi, chez moi, chez lui, chez nous, chez vous, etc; à la maison; au logis; visible; en famille; à son aise. *~ last, ~ length*, enfin. *~ least*, au moins. *~ once*, tout de suite; à la fois, incessamment. *~ sea*, en mer. *~ the same time*, en même temps. *~ war*, en guerre.

Athanasian Creed (the), le symbole attribué à saint Athanase.

atheism, *n*, athéisme, *m*. **atheist**, *n*, athée, *m*. **atheistic**, *a*, athée. **Athenian**, *a*, athénien. ¶ *n*, Athénien, ne. **Athens**, *n*, Athènes, *f*.

athirst, *ad*, altéré; avide.

athlete, *n*, athlète, *m*. **athletic**, *a*, athlétique. **athletics**, *n.pl*, athlétisme, *m*.

at-home, *n*, réception, *f*. *her ~ day*, son jour [de réception].

athwart, *ad*, en travers. ¶ *pr*, en travers de.

Atlantic, *a*, atlantique. *~ liner*, [paquebot] transatlantique, *m*. *the A~* [*Ocean*], l'[océan] Atlantique, *m*.

atlas, *n*, atlas, *m*.

atmosphere, *n*, atmosphère, *f*. **atmospheric(al)**, *a*, atmosphérique.

atoll, *n*, atoll, *m*.

atom, *n*, atome, *m*; miette, *f*. *~*ic(al), *a*, atomique. *~*ize, *v.t*, atomiser, pulvériser. *~*izer, *n*, vaporisateur, *m*.

atone for (to), expier, racheter. **atonement**, *n*, expiation, réparation, satisfaction, *f*.

atrocious†, *a*, atroce. **atrocity**, *n*, atrocité, *f*.

atrophy, *n*, atrophie, *f*. ¶ *v.i*, atrophier.

attach, *v.t*, attacher; atteler; annexer, joindre; (*law*) saisir. **attaché**, *n*, attaché, *m*. *~ case*, mallette, *f*. **attachment**, *n*, attachement, *m*, inclination; attache, *f*; attelage; appareil, *m*; (*law*) saisie, *f*.

attack, *n*, attaque, *f*; accès, *m*, crise, *f*. ¶ *v.t*, attaquer, s'attaquer à.

attain, *v.t*, atteindre, parvenir à. *~*der, *n*, condamnation, *f*. *~*ment, *n*, atteinte, *f*; (*pl*.) acquis, *m.s. & pl*, connaissances, *f.pl*.

attar, *n*, essence de roses, *f*.

attempt, *n*, tentative, *f*, essai, coup, jet; (*criminal*) attentat, *m*. *to make an ~ on*, attenter à. ¶ *v.t*, tenter, essayer, tâcher. *~ed murder*, tentative d'assassinat, *f*. *~ed suicide*, faux suicide, *m*.

attend, *v.t*, accompagner; assister à, suivre; soigner; visiter. *~ to*, faire attention à, écouter; s'occuper de; soigner, servir. *~*ance, *n*, présence; assistance; visite, *f*; service, *m*. *~*ant, *n*, suivant, e; (*pl*.) suite, *f*; gardien, ne; (*Theat.*) receveuse; (*Theat. box*) ouvreuse, *f*. **attention**, *n*, attention, *f*; soin; regard, *m*; prévenance, *f*. *to pay ~*, faire attention. *~!* (*Mil.*), garde-à-vous! **attentive†**, *a*, attentif, empressé; prévenant.

attenuate, *v.t*, atténuer.

attest, *v.t,* attester, constater. **~ation,** *n,* attestation, constatation, *f.*

Attic, *a,* attique.

attic, *n,* mansarde, *f,* grenier, *m.*

attire, *n,* vêtement, costume, *m;* parure, *f.* ¶ *v.t,* vêtir; parer.

attitude, *n,* attitude, posture, pose, *f.*

attorney, *n,* avoué, *m,* mandataire, *m,f;* procureur, *m.* ~ *general,* procureur de la République, *m.*

attract, *v.t,* attirer; solliciter. **attraction,** *n,* attraction; attirance, *f;* (*pl.*) attraits, appas, charmes, *m.pl.* **attractive,** *a,* attrayant, attirant; (*Phys.*) attractif.

attributable, *a,* attribuable. **attribute,** *n,* attribut, emblème, *m.* ¶ *v.t,* attribuer; prêter. **attribution,** *n,* attribution, *f.* **attributive adjective,** adjectif épithète, *m.* **attributively** (*Gram.*) *ad,* adjectivement; en apposition.

attrition, *n,* attrition; usure, *f.*

attune, *v.t,* accorder, harmoniser.

auburn hair, cheveux blond ardent, *m.pl.*

auction, *n,* enchère[s] *f.[pl.].* ~ *bridge,* bridge aux enchères, *m.* ~ *mart,* ~ *rooms,* hôtel des ventes, *m.* ¶ *v.t,* vendre aux enchères. **~eer,** *n,* commissaire priseur, *m.*

audacious†, *a,* audacieux. **audacity,** *n,* audace, *f.*

audible, *a,* perceptible à l'ouïe, intelligible.

audience, *n,* (*hearing*) audience; (*pers.*) assistance, *f;* spectateurs, *m.pl.*

audit, *v.t.* vérifier. **~[ing],** *n,* vérification [comptable] *f.* **audition,** *n,* audition, *f.* **auditor,** *n,* vérificateur comptable, censeur; auditeur, *m.* **auditorium,** *n,* salle, *f.*

auger, *n,* tarière, *f,* laceret, *m.*

aught, *n,* quelque chose, rien, *m.*

augment, *v.t,* augmenter.

augur, *n,* augure, *m.* ¶ *v.t,* augurer. **~y,** *n,* augure, présage, *m.*

august, *a,* auguste. **A~,** *n,* août, *m.*

auk, *n,* pingouin, *m.*

aunt, *n,* tante, *f.*

aureole, *n,* auréole, *f.*

auricle (*heart*) *n,* oreillette, *f.* **auricula,** *n,* oreille-d'ours, *f.* **auricular,** *a,* auriculaire.

auriferous, *a,* aurifère.

aurora, *n,* aurore, *f.* ~ *borealis,* a. boréale.

auspice, *n,* (*usually pl.*) auspice, *m. under the* ~*s of,* sous les auspices de. **auspicious,** *a,* propice, favorable, de bon augure.

austere†, *a,* austère, sévère. **austerity,** *n,* austérité, *f.*

austral, *a,* austral. **Australasia,** *n,* l'Australasie, *f.* **Australia,** *n,* l'Australie, *f.* **Australian,** *a,* australien. ¶ *n,* Australien, ne.

Austria, *n,* l'Autriche, *f.* **Austrian,** *a,* autrichien. ¶ *n,* Autrichien, ne.

authentic, *a,* authentique. **~ity,** *n,* authenticité, *f.*

author, *n,* (*lit. & fig.*) auteur; (*fig. only*) artisan, inventeur, *m.*

authoritative, *a,* autoritaire; d'autorité. **~ly,** *ad,* avec autorité, en maître. **authority,** *n,* autorité, puissance; source, *f. to be regarded as an* ~, faire autorité. *the authorities,* les autorités, *f.pl,* l'administration, *f.*

authorization, *n,* autorisation, *f.* **authorize,** *v.t,* autoriser, mandater.

authorship, *n,* métier d'auteur, *m;* paternité, *f.*

autobiography, *n,* autobiographie, *f.*

autocracy, *n,* autocratie, *f.* **autocrat,** *n,* autocrate, trice. **autocratic**(**al**), *a,* autocratique.

autogenous, *a,* autogène.

autograph, *n. & a.* autographe, *m. & a.* ~ *book,* livre de signatures, *m.*

auto, automobile, *n,* auto, automobile, *f.*

automatic(**al**)**†,** *a,* automatique. **automaton,** *n,* automate, *m.*

autonomous, *a,* autonome. **autonomy,** *n,* autonomie, *f.*

autopsy, *n,* autopsie, *f.*

autumn, *n,* automne, *f.* **~al,** *a,* automnal.

auxiliary, *a. & n,* auxiliaire, *a. & m.*

avail, *n,* effet, *m.* **to ~ oneself of,** profiter de. *to ~ oneself of the services of,* jouir de. **~able,** *a,* disponible; libre.

avalanche, *n,* avalanche, *f.*

avarice, *n,* avarice, *f.* **avaricious†,** *a,* avare, avaricieux.

avenge, *v.t,* venger, punir. **avenger,** *n,* vengeur, eresse. **avenging,** *a,* vengeur.

avenue, *n,* avenue, *f,* boulevard, cours, *m.*

aver, *v.t,* soutenir, affirmer.

average, *a,* moyen; commun.

¶ *n*, moyenne, *f*; (*marine law*) avarie[s] *f.*[*pl.*]. ¶ *v.t*, établir la moyenne de.

averse to, ennemi de. *I am ~*, il me répugne de. **aversion**, *n*, aversion, répugnance, *f*, dégoût, *m*.

avert, *v.t*, détourner; écarter.

aviary, *n*, volière, oisellerie, *f*.

aviation, *n*, aviation, *f*. **aviator**, *n*, aviateur, trice.

avid†, *a*, avide. **~ity**, *n*, avidité, *f*.

avocations, *n.pl*, occupations, *f.pl*, travaux, *m.pl*.

avoid, *v.t*, éviter, se soustraire à, fuir. **~able**, *a*, évitable.

avow, *v.t*, avouer, s'accuser de. **~al**, *n*, aveu, *m*.

await, *v.t*, attendre.

awake, *a*, réveillé; vigilant. ¶ *v.t.ir*, réveiller; (*v.i.*) se réveiller. **awaken**, *v.t*, réveiller. **~ing**, *n*, [r]éveil, *m*.

award, *n*, décision, sentence; (*at a show*) nomination, *f*. ¶ *v.t*, décerner; adjuger. *~ a medal to*, médailler. *~ a prize to*, couronner; primer. *~ the contract for*, adjuger.

aware, *a*: *to be ~ of*, savoir, connaître, ne pas ignorer. *not to be ~ of*, ignorer.

away, *ad*, d'ici; de là. *~* [*from home*], absent. *right ~*, tout de suite. *to go ~*, s'en aller. *to keep ~*, se tenir à l'écart. *~ with you!* allez-vous-en!

awe, *n*, crainte, *f*. **~struck**, saisi de crainte. ¶ *v.t*, imposer à. **awful**†, *a*, effroyable, terrible; redoutable; solennel.

awhile, *ad*, un instant, un peu.

awkward, *a*, incommode, embarrassant, malaisé; gauche, maladroit, **emprunté.** *~ age*, l'âge **ingrat**, *m*. *~ incident*, contretemps, *m*.

awl, *n*, alène, *f*, poinçon, *m*.

awn, *n*, barbe, arête, *f*.

awning, *n*, tente, banne, *f*, tendelet, *m*. *~ deck*, pont abri, *m*.

awry, *ad. & a*, de travers, de guingois.

axe, *n*, hache, cognée, *f*.

axiom, *n*, axiome, *m*.

axis, *n*, axe, *m*.

axle, *n*, arbre, essieu, *m*. **axletree**, *n*, essieu, *m*.

ay, *i. & n*, oui, *particle & m*.

azalea, *n*, azalée, *f*.

azimuth, *n*, azimut, *m*.

Azores (the), les Açores, *f.pl*.

azure, *a*, azur. ¶ *n*, azur, *m*.

B

B (*Mus.*) letter, si, *m*.

baa, *v.i*, bêler. **baa[ing]**, *n*, bêlement, *m*.

babble, *n*, babil, *m*. ¶ *v.i*, babiller; (*stream*) gazouiller; (*of hound*) clabauder.

babel (*fig.*) *n*, tour de Babel, *f*.

baboon, *n*, babouin, *m*.

baby, *n*, bébé, enfant, petit, *m*. *~ carriage*, landau [pour enfant] *m*. *~ face*, physionomie pouparde, *f*. *~ grand*, piano à demi-queue, crapaud, *m*. **~hood**, *n*, première enfance, *f*. **~ish**, *a*, enfantin.

Babylonian, *a*, babylonien.

babysitter, *n*, gardienne d'enfant, *f*. **babysitting**, *n*, garde d'enfants, *m*. (*supermarket*, *dept. store*) *~ facility*, *n*, halte-garderie, *m*.

Bacchanalia, *n.pl*, bacchanales, *f.pl*. **Bacchic**, *a*, bachique.

bachelor, *n*, célibataire, garçon, *m*; (*science*, *etc.*) bachelier, ère, licencié, e. *~ flat*, garçonnière, *f*. *~ girl*, garçonne, *f*.

back, *ad*, en arrière; en retour. *Note:—After a verb* **back** *is sometimes expressed by* re- *as*, *to come back*, revenir. ¶ *n*, dos; derrière; arrière; revers; envers; dossier; fond; verso; dessus, *m*; reins, *m.pl*; (*book*) dos, *m*. *~ to front*, sens devant derrière. *to ~ up*, faire marche arrière. *with one's ~ to the light*, à contrejour. ¶ *v.t*, [faire] reculer; adosser; épauler; appuyer, soutenir, seconder; (*betting*) parier sur, jouer; (*v.i.*) reculer; (*of wind*) redescendre.

backache, *n*, mal de reins, *m*.

backbite, *v.i*, clabauder. **backbiting**, *n*, médisance, *f*, cancans, *m.pl*.

backbone, *n*, épine dorsale, échine; énergie, *f*.

back door, porte de derrière, p. de service, *f*.

backer, *n*, partisan; (*betting*) parieur, *m.* *financial ~*, bailleur de fonds, *m*.

backfire, retour de flamme, *m*. *backfire* [*kick*], retour de manivelle, *m*.

backgammon, *n. & ~ board*, trictrac, *m*.

background, *n*, arrière-plan,

fond, enfoncement, second plan, m; pénombre, f.

backhand, n, arrière-main, revers, m.

back number (*news*), vieux numéro, a.

back-pedal, v.i, contre-pédaler.

backsight (*gun*) n, hausse, f.

backslider n, relaps, e. **backsliding**, n, rechute, f.

backstay (*Naut.*) n, galhauban, m.

backstitch, n, point arrière, arrière-point, m.

back tooth, dent du fond, f.

backup, n, (*computers*) de secours, m, de sécurité, f.

backward, a, peu avancé, tardif; rétrograde; (*child*) arriéré. ¶ ~, ~s, ad, en arrière; à reculons; à la renverse; à rebours. ~ness, n, tardiveté; répugnance, f.

backwash, n, remous, m.

backwater (**to**), v, scier, ramer à rebours. ¶ n, eau arrêtée, f, ressac, m.

bacon, n, lard, bacon, m.

bacteria, n.pl, bactéries, f.pl.

bad, a, mauvais; mal, malade; grave; fort; irrégulier; véreux. to go ~ (meat), s'avarier. ~ language, gros mots, m.pl. ~ time [of it], mauvais quart d'heure, m. in a ~ way, mal-en-point, malade. ~ workmanship, malfaçon, f. too ~! tant pis! ¶ n, mauvais, m. from ~ to worse, de mal en pis. to the ~ (out of pocket), en perte.

badge, n, insigne, m, marque; plaque, médaille, f; brassard; symbole, m; livrée, f.

badger, n, blaireau, m. ¶ v.t, harceler, relancer.

badly, ad, mal; gravement.

badminton, n, badminton, volant au filet, m.

badness, n, mauvais état, m; méchanceté, f.

baffle, v.t, déjouer, déconcerter, frustrer; défier; échapper à. ~ [plate] n, chicane, f.

bag, n, sac, m; bourse; valise, f; (*of game*) tableau, m. ~snatcher, voleur à la tire, m. ¶ v.t, ensacher; empocher, chiper; (v.i, *trousers*) goder. ~ful, n, sachée, f.

bagatelle, n, (*trifle*) bagatelle, f. ~ (game) ~ board, billard japonais, m.

baggage, n, bagage; attirail, m.

~ car, fourgon, m. ~ check, bulletin de bagages, m.

baggy, a, avachi, flottant.

bagpipe[s], n, cornemuse, f.

bail, n, caution, f, cautionnement, m. bail[sman], n, caution, f, répondant, e. ¶ v.t, cautionner. ~ [out] (*boat*) v.t, écoper, vider. ~er, n, écope, épuisette, f.

bailiff, n, huissier; intendant, régisseur, m.

bait, n, amorce, f, appât; hameçon (*fig.*) m. ¶ v.t, amorcer, appâter; (*pers.*) harceler, pointiller, persécuter.

baize, n, bayette, f, tapis, drap, m. ~ door, porte matelassée, f.

bake, v.t, cuire [au four]; (v.i.) cuire. ~house, n, fournil, m; (*Mil.*) manutention, f. baker, n, boulanger, ère. ~y, n, boulangerie, f. baking, n, cuisson; cuite; boulangerie, f. ~ powder, poudre à lever, f. ~ pan, tourtière, f.

balance, n, balance, f; peson; équilibre; solde, reliquat, surplus, m; soulte, f. ~ of power (*Pol.*), équilibre, m. ~ sheet, bilan, m. ~ sheet & schedules, inventaire, m. ~ weight, contrepoids, m. ~ wheel (*Horol.*), balancier, m. ¶ v.t. & i, balancer, équilibrer, pondérer; solder. ~d lever, bascule, f. balancing, n, balancement, m. ~ pole (tightrope), balancier, m.

balcony, n, balcon, m.

bald, a, chauve; nu, pelé; (*style*) plat, sec, décharné.

balderdash, n, galimatias, m.

baldness, n, calvitie; nudité, f.

bale, n, balle, f, ballot, m. ¶ v.t, emballer.

baleful, a, sinistre, funeste.

balk, n, tronc d'arbre équarri, m, poutre, f. ¶ v.t, frustrer; (*horse*) se dérober.

Balkan, a, balkanique; (*states, peninsula*) des Balkans. the ~s, les Balkans, m.pl.

ball, n, balle; bille; boule, f; boulet; ballon; (*eye, lightning*) globe, m; (*thumb*) éminence; (*pendulum*) lentille; (*wool, string*) pelote, f, peloton, m; (*Danc.*) bal, m. ~ & socket, rotule sphérique, f. ~ bearings, roulement à billes, m. ~ cartridge, cartouche à balle, f. ~ cock, robinet à flotteur, m. ~ frame, boulier, m. (*pen*) ~ point, bic, *m.* ~ *room*, salle de bal, *f.* ¶ *v.t*, pelotonner; mettre en boule.

ballad, *n*, (*poem*) ballade; (*song*) chanson, romance, complainte, *f*.

ballast, *n*, (*road*, *Rly.*) ballast, *m*; (*Build.*) blocaille, *f*; (*Naut.*, *Avn.*) lest; (*fig.*) plomb, *m*. ¶ *v.t*, lester.

ballet, *n*, ballet, *m*. ~ *dancer*, danseur, euse, figurant, e, ballerine, *f*. ~ *skirt*, tutu, *m*.

ballistics, *n*, balistique, *f*.

balloon, *n*, ballon; aérostat, *m*. ~ *fabric*, toile d'avion, *f*. ~ed (*dress*) *p.a*, ballonné. ~ing, *n*, aérostation, *f*. ~ist, *n*, aérostier, *m*.

ballot, *n*, [tour de] scrutin, *m*. ~ *box*, urne électorale, *f*. ~ *paper*, bulletin de vote, *m*. ¶ *v.i*, voter au scrutin.

balm, *n*, baume, *m*. ~y, *a*, embaumé, balsamique.

balsam, *n*, baume, *m*; (*garden plant*) balsamine, *f*. ~ [*tree*], baumier, balsamier, *m*. ~ic, *a*, balsamique.

Baltic [**sea**] (**the**), la [mer] Baltique.

baluster, *n*, balustre, *m*. **balustrade**, *n*, balustrade, *f*.

bamboo, *n*, bambou, *m*.

bamboozle, *v.t*, enjôler, mettre dedans.

ban, *n*, ban, *m*; interdiction, *f*. ¶ *v.t*, interdire.

banana, *n*, banane, *f*. ~ [*plant or tree*], bananier, *m*.

band, *n*, bande; frette; courroie, *f*; ruban; (*Bookb.*) nerf, *m*; musique, *f*, orchestre, *m*. harmonie, *f*. ~box, carton de modiste, *m*. ~ brake, frein à ruban, *f*. à bande, *m*. ~ saw, scie à ruban, *f*. ~master, chef de musique, *m*. (*CB radio*) citizen's ~, canal banalisé, *m*. ¶ *v.t*, lier, fretter; (*v.i.*) se liguer.

bandage, *n*, bandage, bandeau, *m*, bande, *f*. ¶ *v.t*, bander. **bandeau**, *n*, bandeau, *m*.

bandit, *n*, bandit, *m*.

bandoleer, *n*, bandoulière, *f*.

bandy, *v.t*, ballotter, se renvoyer. ~ *words with*, faire assaut de paroles avec. ~[-*legged*], *a*, bancal.

bane (*fig.*) *n*, fléau, *m*. ~ful, *a*, pernicieux, funeste.

bang, *n*, battement, *m*; détonation, *f*. ¶ *i*, pan! ¶ *v.t. & i*, frapper, faire battre; battre, cogner.

bangle, *n*, bracelet; porte-bonheur, *m*.

banish, *v.t*, bannir.

banishment, *n*, exile, *m*.

banister, *n*, balustre, *m*; (*pl.*) rampe, *f*.

bank, *n*, rive, berge, *f*, bord; talus; banc, *m*; (*Fin.*) banque, caisse, *f*, crédit, *m*. ~ *note*, billet de banque, *m*. ~ [*pass*] *book*, carnet de banque, c. de compte, *m*. ~ *rate*, taux officiel [d'escompte] *m*. ~ *transfer*, virement, *m*. ¶ *v.t*, terrasser, remblayer; verser à la banque; (*v.i.*) virer, pencher. ~ *on*, compter sur. ~er, *n*, banquier, *m*. ~ing, *n*, banque, *f*.

bankrupt, *n*, banqueroutier, ère; failli, *m*. *to go* ~, faire banqueroute; faire faillite. ~cy, *n*, banqueroute; faillite, *f*.

banner, *n*, bannière, *f*; pavillon, *m*; oriflamme, *f*.

banns, *n.pl*, bans de mariage, *m.pl*.

banquet, *n*, banquet, festin, *m*. ~ing hall, salle des festins, *f*.

bantam weight (*Box.*), poids coq, *m*.

banter, *n*, badinage, *m*. ¶ *v.t*, badiner.

baptism, *n*, baptême, *m*. ~al, *a*, baptismal. **baptist**[e]ry, *n*, baptistère, *m*. **baptize**, *v.t*, baptiser.

bar, *n*, barre, *f*, barreau, *m*, barrette; bille, brique; barrière, *f*; fer, *m*; (*Mus.*, *vertical line*) barre; (*commonly but incorrectly*, *portion between two bar lines*) mesure, *f*; (*window*) croisillon; (*counter*) comptoir, *m*, buvette, *f*, bar, *m*. ~ *bell*, barre à sphères, *f*. ~ *iron*, fer en barre, *m*. ¶ *v.t*, barrer.

barb, *n*, barbe, *f*; picot, *m*. ~[ed] wire, fil de fer barbelé, *m*, ronce, *f*. ¶ *v.t*, barbeller; barder.

Barbados, *n*, la Barbade.

barbarian, *a. & n*, barbare, *a. & m*. **barbaric**, **barbarous**, *a*, barbare. **barbarism**, *n*, barbarie, *f*; (*Gram.*) barbarisme, *m*. **barbarity**, *n*, barbarie, *f*.

Barbary ape, magot, *m*.

barbecue, *n*, (*grill*) barbecue, *m*.

barber, *n*, barbier, *m*.

Barcelona, *n*, Barcelone, *f*.

bard, *n*, (*poet*) barde; chantre, *m*.

the Bard of Avon, le chantre d'Avon.

bare, *a*, nu; à nu; chenu; découvert; pelé; simple, seul; (*majority*) faible. ~**back**[ed] (*riding*), à nu, à poil, à cru. ~**back horse**, cheval nu, *m*. ~**faced**, éhonté, effronté. ~**facedly**, à visage découvert. ~**foot**[ed], nu-pieds, pieds nus, déchaussé. ~**headed**, nu-tête, tête nue. ¶ *v.t*, mettre à nu, dénuder, dépouiller, découvrir, déchausser. ~**ly**, *ad*, à peine, juste, tout au plus; ne . . . guère. ~**ness**, *n*, nudité, *f*.

bargain, *n*, marché, *m*, négociation, affaire; occasion; emplette, *f*. *into the* ~, pardessus le marché. ¶ *v.i*, marchander. ~**er**, *n*, marchandeur, euse.

barge, *n*, chaland, *m*, gabare, allège, péniche, *f*. **bargee**, **bargeman**, *n*, batelier, marinier, *m*.

baritone, *n. & ~ saxhorn*, baryton, *m*.

bark, *n*, (*tree*) écorce; (*left on felled tree*) grume, *f*; (*dog*) aboiement, *m*; (*boat*) barque, *f*; (*Poet.*) nef, *f*. ¶ *v.t*, écorcer, décortiquer, peler; (*v.i.*) aboyer. ~**ing**, *n*, (*tree*) décortication, *f*; (*dog*) aboiement, *m*.

barley, *n*, orge, *f*. ~ *sugar*, sucre d'orge, *m*. ~ *water*, eau d'orge, *f*.

barm, *n*, levure, *f*, levain, *m*.

barman, *n*, barman, serveur, *m*.

barn, *n*, grange, *f*. ~ *owl*, effraie, fresaie, *f*. ~**yard**, basse-cour, *f*.

barnacle, *n*, (*Crust.*) bernacle, *f*, cravan, *m*.

barometer, *n*, baromètre, *m*. **barometric**(*al*), *a*, barométrique.

baron, **ess**, *n*, baron, ne.

barque, *n*, barque, *f*.

barrack, *n. oft. pl*, caserne, *f*. ~ *room*, chambrée [militaire], *f*. ¶ *v.t*, caserner.

barrage, *n*, barrage, *m*.

barrel, *n*, baril, fût, *m*, futaille, pièce, *f*, tonneau, *m*, caque, *f*; corps, cylindre, tambour, canon, *m*. ~ *organ*, orgue de Barbarie, *m*. ¶ *v.t*, mettre en baril, entonner, [en]caquer.

barren, *a*, stérile, aride. ~**ness**, *n*, stérilité, aridité, *f*.

barricade, *n*, barricade, *f*. ¶ *v.t*, barricader.

barrier, *n*, barrière, *f*; barrage, *m*; digue, *f*.

barring, *pr*, ôté, sauf, à part, hormis, excepté, à moins de.

barrow, *n*, brouette; (*peddler's*) baladeuse, *f*; (*mound*) tumulus, *m*.

barter, *n*, échange, troc, *m*. ~ *goods*, pacotille, *f*. ¶ *v.t*, échanger, troquer.

basal, *a*, basique.

basalt, *n*, basalte, *m*.

bascule bridge, pont à bascule, *m*.

base, *a*, bas, vil, ignoble, ~ *metal*, bas métal, métal vil, m. pauvre, *m*. ¶ *n*, base, assiette, *f*, fondement[s] *m*.[*pl*.]; soubassement; culot, *m*. *launching* ~, base de lancement, *f*. ¶ *v.t*, asseoir, fonder. ~**less**, *a*, sans fondement, ~**ly**, *ad*, bassement, lâchement. ~**ment**, *n*, soubassement, sous-sol, *m*. ~**ness**, *n*, bassesse, *f*.

bashful, *a*, timide. ~**ness**, *n*, timidité, fausse honte, mauvaise honte, *f*.

basic, *a*, fondamental; (*Chem.*) basique.

basil, *n*, (Bot.) basilic, *m*; (*hide*) basane, *f*.

basilica, *n*, basilique, *f*.

basilisk, *n*, basilic, *m*.

basin, *n*, bassin; bol, *m*; cuvette, *f*.

basis, *n*, base, assiette, *f*, fondement[s] *m*.[*pl*.].

bask, *v.i*, se chauffer.

basket, *n*, panier, *m*, corbeille; manne; benne; bourriche, *f*. ~*ball*, basket-ball, ballon au panier, *m*. ~ *maker*, vannier, *m*. ~ *making*, ~ *work*, vannerie, *f*. ~**ful**, *n*, panier, *m*, panerée, *f*.

bas-relief, *n*, bas-relief, *m*.

bass, *n*, (*fish*) bar, *m*. ~ [voice, singer, string, tuba], basse, *f*. ~ *clef*, clef de fa, *f*. ~ *drum*, grosse caisse, *f*.

bassinet, *n*, bercelonnette, *f*.

bassoon, *n*, basson, *m*.

bast, *n*, tille, *f*.

bastard, *a*, bâtard. ¶ *n*, bâtard, e. ~**y**, *n*, bâtardise, *f*.

baste, *v.t*, (*Need.*) bâtir, baguer, faufiler; (*meat*) arroser; (*beat*) bâtonner.

bat, *n*, bat, *m*; batte; palette, *f*; (*Zool.*) chauve-souris, *f*.

batch, *n*, fournée, *f*; groupe, *m*.

bate, *v.t*, rabattre.

bath, *n*, bain, *m*; (*tub*) baignoire, *f*. ~ *attendant*, baigneur, euse. B~ *chair*, fauteuil roulant, *m*.

~ *robe*, peignoir de bain, *m.*
~man, baigneur, *m.* ~mat, tapis de bain, *m.* ~room, salle de bain, *f.* ~ *salts*, sel pour bain, *m.* ~tub, baignoire, *m.* **bathe**, *v.t*, baigner; (*v.i.*) baigner, se b.; s'abreuver. **bather**, *n*, baigneur, euse. **bathing**, *n*, bains, *m.pl*; bain, *m.* ~ *cap*, bonnet de bain, *m.* ~ *suit*, maillot (*ou* costume) de bain, *m.* ~ *place*, baignade, *f.* ~ *resort*, station balnéaire, *f.*

bathos, *n*, pathos, *m.*

baton, *n*, bâton; (*relay race*) témoin, *m.*

battalion, *n*, bataillon, *m.*

batten, *n*, [latte] volige, *f.* ~ *down* (*Naut.*), condamner. ~ *on*, s'engraisser de.

batter, pâte, *f.* ¶ *v.t*, battre, bossuer, bosseler, cabosser. ~ing-ram, *n*, bélier, *m.* ~y, *n*, batterie; pile, *f.*

battle, *n*, bataille, *f*, combat, *m.* ~-axe, hache d'armes, *f.* ~ *cruiser*, croiseur cuirassé de combat, *m.* ~field, champ de bataille, *m.* ~ship, [navire] cuirassé, *m.* ¶ *v.i*, lutter; batailler.

battledore, *n*, palette, raquette, *f*, battoir, *m.* ~ *& shuttlecock*, [jeu de] volant, *m.*

battlement, *n*, créneau, *m.* ~ed, *a*, crénelé.

bauble, *n*, babiole, *f*, brimborion, *m*; (*fool's*) marotte, *f.*

Bavaria, *n*, la Bavière. **Bavarian**, *a*, bavarois. ¶ *n*, Bavarois, e.

bawl, *v.i*, brailler, beugler.

bawl out, *v.t*, engueuler. *to be* ~ed *out*, se faire engueuler.

bay, *a*, bai. ¶ *n*, (*horse*) bai, *m*; (*Geog.*) baie, *f*; golfe, *m*; (*Arch.*) travée, *f. B~ of Biscay*, golfe de Gascogne, *m.* ~ *rum*, tafia de laurier, *m.* ~[*tree*], laurier, *m.* ~ *window*, fenêtre baie, *f. at* ~, aux abois. ¶ *v.i*, aboyer. ~ing, *n*, aboiement, *m.*

bayonet, *n*, baïonnette, *f.*

bazaar, *n*, bazar, *m*; vente de charité, *f.*

B.C. (*before Christ*), av. J.C.

be, *v.i.ir*, être; exister; avoir; faire; se faire; aller, se trouver, se porter; y avoir. ~ *that as it may*, quoi qu'il en soit. *it is* . . . *since*, il y a . . . que. *there is* (*are*) *some*, il y en a. *there is none left*, il n'y en a plus. *I am leaving*, je vais partir, je pars. *a man to be feared*, un homme à crain-

dre. *not to be confused with* . . ., à ne pas confondre avec . . . **to be off**, s'en aller, filer, se sauver. *be off with you!* allez vous promener!

beach, *n*, plage, grève, *f*, rivage, *m.* ~comber, rôdeur de grève, *m.* ~ *fishing*, pêche de plage, *f.* ~head, tête de pont, *f.* ¶ *v.t. & i*, échouer; tirer à sec.

beacon, *n*, balise, *f*; phare, *m.* ¶ *v.t*, baliser.

bead, *n*, perle, *f*, grain, *m*; goutte; (*Arch.*) baguette, *f.* [*glass*] ~s, verroterie, *f.* [*string of*] ~s, chapelet, *m.*

beadle, *n*, apparateur; bedeau, suisse, *m.*

beak, *n*, bec, *m.* ~er, *n*, buire, *f*; vase à filtrations chaudes, *m.*

beam, *n*, (*timber*) poutre; (*plow*) flèche, haie, *f*, timon; (*Mach.*) balancier; (*scale*) fléau, *m*, verge, *f*; (*ship's timber*) bau, *m*; (*ship's breadth*) largeur, *f*, travers; (*ray*) rayon, trait; (*rays*) faisceau, *m.* ~ *radio* ~, signal par radio. ¶ *v.i*, rayonner.

bean, *n*, fève, *f*; haricot; (*coffee*) grain, *m.*

bear, *n*, ours, e; (B~, *Astr.*) ourse, *f*; (*pers.*) bourru, dogue, *m*; (*Mach.*) poinçonneuse, *f*; (*Stk Ex.*) baissier, *m.* ~ *garden* (fig.), pétaudière, *f.* ~s *cub*, ourson, *m.* ~skin (*cap*), oursin, ourson, *m.* ¶ *v.t. & i. ir*, porter; supporter, souffrir, tolérer, endurer, compatir; appuyer, peser; produire, rapporter; enfanter; (*to right, left*) prendre. *to* ~ *out*, confirmer. *to* ~ *up*, résister. ~able, *a*, supportable, tenable.

beard, *n*, barbe; (*Bot.*) barbe, arête, *f.* ~ed, *a*, barbu, à barbe, chevelu. ~less, *a*, imberbe.

bearer, *n*, porteur, euse; (*Fin.*) porteur, *m.* ~ *of a flag of truce*, parlementaire, *m. stretcher*~, brancardier, *m.* **bearing**, *n*, portée, *f*; rapport, trait; aspect; (*Naut.*) gisement, *m*; (*pl. fig.*) orientation, *f*; (*gait*) port, *m*, mine, tenue, démarche, contenance, *f*, maintien, *m*; conduite, *f*; (*Mech., oft. pl.*) coussinet, *m*, *oft. pl*; palier; dé; roulement, *m*; chape, *f*; (*pl. Her.*) armes, armoiries, *f.pl.* ~ *rein*, fausse rêne, *f.* ~ *surface*, surface portante, s. de portée, *f.*

beast, *n*, bête, *f*; animal; abruti,

m. ~ of burden, bête de somme.
~ly, a, bestial; dégoûtant.

beat, n, battement; coup; temps,
m; tournée, ronde; (Hunt.) battue, f. ¶ v.t. & i. ir, battre; taper;
assommer, bâtonner, brosser;
fourrer; fouetter; (Hunt.) rabattre, traquer; vaincre; l'emporter
sur, enchérir sur. ~ back, ~ off,
repousser. ~en path, chemin
[re]battu, c. frayé, m. ~er, n,
batteur, battoir, m, batte, f;
(Hunt.) rabatteur, traqueur, m.

beatify, v.t, béatifier.

beating, n, battement, battage,
m; batterie; brossée; défaite, f;
(Hunt.) rabattage, m, traque, f.
~ rain, pluie battante, f.

beau, n, amoureux, galant, m.

beautiful, a, beau; magnifique.
¶ n, beau, m. **beautify**, v.t, embellir. **beauty**, n, beauté; belle, f.
B~ & the Beast, la Belle & la
Bête. ~ parlor, institut de beauté,
m. ~ spot, site pittoresque, m;
(patch on face) mouche, f;
(mole) grain de beauté, m.

beaver, n, castor, m.

becalmed, a, encalminé, pris par
le calme.

because, c, parce que; car. ~ of,
à cause de.

beck, n, signe, m; ordres, m.pl.
beckon, v.i, faire signe.

become, v.i.ir, devenir. With p.p,
often rendered by pronominal
form of verb, as, to become accustomed, s'accoutumer; (v.t.ir.)
convenir à. **becoming**, a, convenable; [bien]séant, seyant; assortissant, décent.

bed, n, lit, m, couche, f; coucher,
m; assise, assiette, fondation,
plate-forme, f; banc, gisement,
gîte; (oyster) parc; (Hort.)
carré, m, plate-bande, planche, f,
parterre, m. to go to ~, [aller]
se coucher. ~bug, punaise, f.
~clothes, draps & couvertures.
~fellow, camarade de lit. ~pan,
bassin [de garde-robe], b. pour
malade, b. de lit, m. ~post, quenouille, f. ~ridden, alité, grabataire. ~room, chambre [à
coucher] f. ~side, chevet, m.
~side carpet, descente de lit, f. a
good ~side manner, une bonne
manière professionnelle. ~side
table, table de chevet, t. de nuit,
f. ~spread, couvrelit, dessus de
lit, jeté de l., m. ~stead, bois de
lit; lit, m. ~time, l'heure du

coucher, f. ¶ v.t, coucher; asseoir; [faire] précipiter. **bedding**,
n, coucher, m, literie, garniture
de lit; stratification, f.

bedeck, v.t, parer, chamarrer.

bedew, v.t, arroser, humecter.

bedizen, v.t, attifer, chamarrer.

bedlam, n, maison de fous; (fig.)
pétaudière, f.

bedraggle, v.t, traîner dans la
boue.

bee, n, abeille, f. ~ eater, guêpier,
m. ~hive, ruche, f. ~ keeping,
apiculture, f. a ~ in one's bonnet,
un rat dans la tête.

beech [tree], n, hêtre, m. ~ marten, fouine, f. ~mast, faînes, f.pl.
~nut, faîne, f.

beef, n, bœuf, m. ~ steak, bifteck,
m. ~ tea, thé de viande, bouillon
de bœuf, m. corned ~, bœuf
salé, m.

beer, n, bière, f. ~pump, pompe
à b., f.

beet, n, bette; betterave, f. ~
sugar, sucre de betterave, m.
beetroot, n, betterave, f.

beetle, n, coléoptère, scarabée;
escarbot, m; (rammer) dame,
demoiselle, hie, f, pilon, m. ¶ v.t,
pilonner. **beetling** brows, sourcils fournis, m.pl. **beetling** crag,
rocher qui surplombe, m.

befall, v.i.ir, arriver, advenir, survenir.

befit, v.t, convenir à. **befitting**, a,
convenable.

before, ad, devant; avant; auparavant; en avant; déjà; jusqu'ici; précédent. ¶ c, avant que.
¶ pr, devant; avant; pardevant;
avant [que] de. ~ you could say
Jack Robinson, crac! ~hand, ad,
à l'avance, d'a., en a., par a.

befriend, v.t, favoriser; secourir.

beg, v.t. & i, mendier, quémander,
chercher, gueuser; demander,
prier; (Com.) avoir l'honneur
de; (dog) faire le beau. I ~
your pardon, je vous demande
pardon. ~ for, solliciter, quémander. ~ the question, faire
une pétition de principe.

beget, v.t.ir, engendrer; faire naître.

beggar, n, mendiant, m. ¶ v.t,
appauvrir, ruiner. ~ly, a, gueux;
misérable. ~y, n, mendicité,
gueuserie, misère, f. reduced to
~, réduit à la besace.

begin, v.t. & i. ir, commencer;
débuter; entamer, amorcer; ou-

vrir; se mettre. ~ *again*, recommencer. **beginner**, *n*, commençant, e, débutant, e. **beginning**, *n*, commencement, début, *m*; amorce; ouverture; origine, *f*; prémices, *f.pl*.

begone, *i*, va-t-en! allez-vous-en!

begonia, *n*, bégonia, *m*.

begrudge, *v.t*, envier.

beguile, *v.t*, tromper; séduire; charmer, amuser.

behalf of (on), de la part de; à l'acquit de; pour le compte de.

behave, *v.i. & reflexive*, se comporter, se conduire, vivre. ~ [*properly*]! (to child), tiens-toi bien! **behavior**, *n*, conduite, *f*, manières, *f.pl*, tenue, *f*, procédé, *m*.

behead, *v.t*, décapiter. ~**ing**, *n*, décapitation, *f*.

behest, *n*, commandement, ordre, *m*.

behind, *ad*, derrière, en arrière. ¶ *pr*, derrière, en arrière de. ~**hand**, *ad*, en arrière, arriéré, en retard.

behold, *v.t. & i. ir*, voir. ¶ *i*, voyez! ~*en to*, à charge à, redevable à. ~**er**, *n*, spectateur, trice.

behoof, *n*, profit, *m*. **behove**, *v.t.imp*, incomber, convenir à.

being, *n*, être, *m*; existence, *f*. *for the time* ~, actuel; actuellement.

belabor, *v.t*, charger de coups, bourrer, rosser, échiner.

belated, *a*, attardé; tardif.

belay, *v.t*, tourner, amarrer.

belch[ing], *n*, rot, *m*; crudité, éructation, *f*. **belch**, *v.i*, roter; éructer (*v.t, fig*.) vomir.

beldam[e], *n*, vieille sorcière, *f*.

beleaguer, *v.t*, assiéger.

belfry, *n*, beffroi, clocher, *m*.

Belgian, *a*, belge. ¶ *n*, Belge, *m.f*. **Belgium**, *n*, la Belgique, *f*.

belie, *v.t*, démentir.

belief, *n*, croyance, foi; persuasion, *f*. **believable**, *a*, croyable. **believe**, *v.t. & i*, croire. *to make . . .* ~, faire [ac]croire à . . . **believer**, *n*, croyant, e; partisan, *m*.

belittle, *v.t*, décrier, rabaisser, déprécier.

bell, *n*, cloche; clochette, sonnette, sonnerie, *f*, timbre; (*globular*) grelot, *m*. ~*boy*, groom d'hôtel, *m*. ~ [*flower*], campanule, clochette, *f*. ~ *glass & ~ jar*, cloche, *f*. ~ *push*, bouton de sonnette,

m. ~ *ringer*, sonneur, carillonneur, *m*. ~ *tent*, tente conique, *f*. ~ *tower*, campanile, *m*. ~ *turret*, clocheton, *m*. ~*wether*, sonnailler, *m*. ¶ *v.i*, bramer, raire, réer.

belladonna, *n*, belladone, *f*.

belle, *n*, beauté, reine, *f*.

bellicose, *a*, belliqueux. **belligerent**, *a. & n*, belligérant, e.

bellow, *v.i*, beugler, mugir. ¶ *n*, mugissement, *m*.

bellows, *n.pl*, soufflet, *m*; soufflerie, *f*.

belly, *n*, ventre, *m*, panse, *f*; bombement, *m*. ~ *band*, sous-ventrière; sangle, *f*. ¶ *v.i*, faire [le] ventre, bomber.

belong, *v.i*, appartenir, dépendre, être. ~**ings**, *n.pl*, effets, *m.pl*.

beloved, *a. & n*, bien-aimé, e, chéri, e.

below, *ad*, en bas; au-dessous; dessous; ci-dessous; ci-après; là-bas; en contrebas. ¶ *pr*, sous; au-dessous de; en aval de.

belt, *n*, ceinture, *f*; ceinturon, *m*; (*Mech*.) courroie; bande; (*Geog*.) zone, *f. fan* ~, courroie de ventilateur, *f. safety* ~, ceinture de sécurité, *f*. ¶ *v.t*, ceindre. ~**ing**, *n*, courroies [de transmission] *f.pl*.

belvedere, *n*, belvédère, *m*.

bemoan, *v.t*, déplorer; pleurer.

bench, *n*, banc, *m*; banquette, *f*; établi; siège, *m*; cour; magistrature, assise, *f*, tribunal, *m*. ~ *mark*, [point de] repère, *m*.

bend, *n*, coude, *m*; courbe, courbure, *f*; pli, *m*; inflexion, *f*; tournant, virage; (*knot*) nœud, *m*. ~ *of the arm*, saignée, *f*. ~ *of the knee*, jarret, *m*. ¶ *v.t. & i. ir*, courber, se c., couder; bander; tendre; cintrer; fléchir, plier, ployer; fausser; se f., gauchir. *on* ~*ed knees*, à genoux.

beneath, *ad*, dessous; par-dessous; en bas. ¶ *pr*, au-dessous de, sous.

benediction, *n*, bénédiction, *f*.

benefaction, *n*, bienfait, *m*. **benefactor, tress**, *n*, bienfaiteur, trice.

benefice, *n*, bénéfice, *m*.

beneficence, *n*, bienfaisance, *f*. **beneficent**, *a*, bienfaisant.

beneficial, *a*, avantageux, profitable, salutaire. **beneficiary**, *n*, bénéficiaire, *m.f*. **benefit**, *n*, bénéfice, bienfait, avantage, fruit, profit; secours, *m*; (*Theat.*) représentation à bénéfice, *f.* ~ *society*, société de secours mutuels, *f.* ¶ *v.t,* faire du bien à, avantager; (*v.i.*) profiter, bénéficier.

benevolence, *n,* bienfaisance, *f;* patronage, *m.* **benevolent,** *a,* bienfaisant.

Bengal, *n,* le Bengale. ~ *light,* feu de bengale, *m,* flamme de b., *f.* **Bengali, -lee,** *a,* bengali, *inv.* ¶ *n,* (*pers.*) Bengali, (*bird*) bengali, *m.*

benighted, *a,* (*fig.*) ignorant; plongé dans les ténèbres.

benign, benignant, *a,* bénin. **benignly, benignantly,** *ad,* bénignement.

bent, *a,* courbé, coudé; faussé, gauchi. ~ *lever,* levier coudé, *m.* ~*wood furniture,* meubles en bois courbé, *m.pl.* ¶ *n,* penchant, *m,* pente, *f,* biais, génie, attrait, *m.* ¶ *to be ~ on,* s'aheurter à, se buter à, s'acharner à.

benumb, *v.t,* engourdir, morfondre.

benzine, benzoline, *n,* benzine, *f.*

benzoin, *n,* benjoin, *m.*

benzol[e], benzene, *n,* benzol, *m.*

bequeath, *v.t,* léguer. **bequest,** *n,* legs, *m.*

bereave, *v.t.ir,* priver; enlever, ravir. ~**ment,** *n,* deuil, *m.*

beret, *n,* béret [basque] *m.*

bergamot, *n,* (*orange, pear*) bergamote; (*pear*) mouille-bouche, *f.* ~ *oil,* essence de bergamote, *f.* ~ [*tree*] (orange), bergamotier, *m.*

Bermudas (the), les Bermudes, *f.pl.*

berry, *n,* baie, *f;* (*coffee*) grain, *m.*

berth, *n,* poste de mouillage, mouillage, emplacement, poste, *m,* place; couchette, *f.*

beryl, *n,* béryl, *m.*

beseech, *v.t.ir,* supplier, adjurer, implorer.

beset, *v.t.ir,* entourer, assiéger. *besetting sin,* péché d'habitude, *m.*

beside, *pr,* à côté de; auprès de; hors de; excepté. ~ *oneself,* hors de soi. **besides,** *ad. & pr,* d'ailleurs, du reste, de plus, d'autre part, en outre, puis.

besiege, *v.t,* assiéger. **besieger,** *n,* assiégeant, *m.*

besmear, *v.t,* barbouiller.

besmirch, *v.t,* souiller.

besom, *n,* balai [de bouleau] *m.*

besotted, *a,* abruti.

bespangle, *v.t,* pailleter; parsemer.

bespatter, *v.t,* éclabousser, crotter.

bespeak, *v.t.ir,* retenir; commander; stipuler.

besprinkle, *v.t,* arroser.

best, *a,* [le] meilleur; le mieux; le plus beau *ou* grand *ou* fort. ~ *man* (wedding), garçon d'honneur, *m.* ~ *quality,* premier choix, *m.* ~*seller,* livre à succès, l. à grand tirage, *m.* ¶ *ad,* mieux, le mieux; plus. ¶ *the* ~, le mieux. *the* ~ *of it,* le meilleur de l'affaire; le plus beau de l'histoire; le dessus. *in one's* [*Sunday*] ~, endimanché. *do the* ~ *you can!* arrangez-vous!

bestial†, *a,* bestial.

bestir oneself (to), se remuer, s'empresser.

bestow, *v.t,* accorder, gratifier, déférer; impartir, donner.

bestride, *v.t.ir,* enjamber, enfourcher.

bet, *n,* pari, *m.* ¶ *v.t,* parier; gager.

betake oneself (to), *v.reflexive ir,* se livrer, recourir; se rendre.

bethink oneself (to), *v.reflexive ir,* s'aviser.

betide, *v.t,* arriver à. *whate'er* ~, arrive (*ou* advienne) que pourra.

betimes, *ad,* de bonne heure, tôt.

betoken, *v.t,* présager; désigner; dénoter; annoncer.

betray, *v.t,* trahir; tromper; révéler, accuser. ~ *one's trust,* prévariquer. ~**al,** *n,* trahison, *f.* ~**er,** *n,* traître, traîtresse.

betroth, *v.t,* fiancer. ~**al,** *n,* fiançailles, *f.pl.* ~**ed,** *n. & a,* fiancé, e.

better, *a,* meilleur; préférable. *my* ~ *half* (wife), ma [chère] moitié. ~*-looking,* mieux. *to be* ~ (health), se porter (*ou* aller) mieux. *it is* ~ *to,* il vaut mieux. ¶ *ad,* mieux. *so much the* ~, tant mieux. ¶ (*pers.*) *n,* supérieur, e. ¶ *v.t,* améliorer. ~**ment,** *n,* amélioration, *f.*

better, bettor, *n,* parieur, euse. **betting,** *n,* pari, *m;* (*odds*) cote, *f.* ~ *system,* martingale, *f.* ~ *with bookmakers,* pari à la cote.

between, *pr,* entre; de; à. ~ *now & then,* d'ici là. ~ *this & ..., d'ici à ... . ~* [*times*], dans l'intervalle. **~decks**, n, entrepont, m.

bevel, n, biseau, m. ~ [square], fausse équerre, sauterelle, f. ~ gear, roue d'angle, f. ¶ v.t, biseauter.

beverage, n, breuvage, m, boisson, f.

bevy, n, compagnie; volée; troupe, f.

bewail, v.t, pleurer, déplorer, se lamenter sur.

beware, v.i, se garder, se méfier, se défier, prendre garde. ~ of pickpockets! méfiez-vous des voleurs!

bewilder, v.t, égarer, désorienter; ahurir. **~ment**, n, affolement, m.

bewitch, v.t, ensorceler, envoûter, enchanter. **~ing**, a, ensorcelant, enchanteur. **~ingly**, ad, à ravir.

beyond, ad, au-delà, plus loin. ¶ pr, au-delà de, par-delà, delà; hors; au-dessus de; sans; outre. the ~ (future life), l'au-delà, m.

bezel, n, chaton, m.

bias, n, biais; (fig.) penchant, parti pris, m, partialité, f. ¶ v.t, influencer, détourner; biaiser. **biased**, p.a, partial.

bib, n, bavoir, m, bavette, f.

Bible, n, Bible, f. ~ Society, Société biblique, f. **biblical**, a, biblique.

bibliography, n, bibliographie, f. **bibliophile**, n, bibliophile, m.

bibulous, a, absorbant; adonné à la boisson.

biceps, n, biceps, m.

bicker, v.i, disputailler, se chamailler.

bicycle, n, bicyclette, f; bicycle, m. **bicyclist**, n, cycliste, m,f.

bid, n, (Stk Ex.) demande; (auction) enchère, mise, f. to make a ~ for, vouloir capter. ¶ v.t & i. ir, commander, ordonner; (adieu) dire; offrir; enchérir, miser; (Stk Ex.) demander. ~ higher than, surenchérir sur. **bidder**, n, enchérisseur, m.

bide one's time (to), attendre son heure, se réserver.

biennial, a, biennal, bisannuel.

bier, n, civière, f.

bifurcation, n, bifurcation, f.

big, a, gros; grand; fort; considérable; haut; (pregnant) grosse, enceinte, (animals) pleine. **~-boned**, ossu. to talk ~, le prendre de haut.

bigamist, n, bigame, m,f. **bigamous**, a, bigame. **bigamy**, n, bigamie, f.

bight, n, golfe, enfoncement; (rope) double, m.

bigness, n, grosseur; grandeur, f.

bigot, n. & **~ed**, a, bigot, e. **~ry**, n, bigoterie, f.

bigshot, n, grosse légume, f.

bigwig, n, gros bonnet, m.

bike, n, vélo, m.

bilberry, n, airelle, myrtille, f.

bile, n, bile, f.

bilge, n, (ship) fond de cale; (cask) bouge, ventre, m. ~ water, eau de cale, f.

bilious, a, bilieux.

bilk, v.t, frustrer; flouer.

bill, n, (bird) bec, m; (notice) affiche, pancarte, f, placard; écriteau; prospectus; programme; (legislative) projet de loi, m; (account) note, f, mémoire, m; addition; facture, f; (Fin.) effet, billet, mandat, m, échéance, traite, remise, lettre, valeur, f; (pl.) portefeuille[-effets], papier, m. ~ file, pique-notes, m. to settle a ~, régler une note. ~ head[ing], en-tête de facture, m. **~-hook**, croissant, m, serpe, serpette, f. ~ of exchange, lettre de change, traite, f. ~ of fare, carte de restaurant; carte du jour, f, menu, m. ~ of health, patente de santé, f. ~ of lading, connaissement, m. ~ payable, receivable, effet à payer, à recevoir, m. **~poster, ~sticker**, afficheur, colleur, m. ¶ v.t, afficher, placarder; facturer; (v.i.) se becqueter. ~ & coo, faire des mamours, roucouler.

billet, n, (Mil.) billet de logement; (pl.) cantonnement, m; (log) bûche, f, rondin, m. ¶ v.t, cantonner; (on householder) loger.

billiard: ~ ball, bille [de billard] f. ~ room, salle de billard, f. billard, m. ~ table, table de billard, f, billard, m. ~s, n, pl, billard, m.

billingsgate, n, langage de poissarde, l. des halles, m.

billion, n, milliard, m.

billow, n, vague, lame, onde, f, flot, m. ¶ v.i, ondoyer. **~y**, a, houleux.

billy goat, bouc, m.

bimonthly, a, (in alternate months) bimestriel; (½ monthly) semi-mensuel.

bin, *n*, huche, *f*; tonneau, tonnelet, *m*; trémie, case, *f*, casier, caisson, coffre; porte-bouteilles, *m*.

binary, *a*, binaire.

bind, *v.t.ir*, lier, attacher, ligoter; (*sheaf*) [en]gerber; bander; assujettir; serrer; enchaîner; astreindre; border; engager, obliger; (*books*) relier; (*paper covers*) brocher; (*with metal*) ferrer; (*Med.*) resserrer, constiper. I'll be bound, j'en réponds. ~**er**, *n*, (*sheaf, pers.*) lieur, *m*; (*Mach.*) lieuse, *f*; (*book*) relieur, euse; brocheur, euse; (*tie*) lien, *m*, attache, *f*; (*papers*) biblorhapte, *m*. ~**ing**, *a*, obligatoire. ¶ *n*, reliure, *f*; brochage, *m*, brochure; bordure, *f*, galon, *m*, tresse, *f*.

bindweed, *n*, liseron, liset, *m*.

bine, *n*, sarment, *m*.

binnacle, *n*, habitacle, *m*.

binocular, *n*, jumelle, *f*.

biographer, *n*, biographe, *m*. **biography**, *n*, biographie, *f*.

biologist, *n*, biologiste, biologue, *m*. **biology**, *n*, biologie, *f*.

biped, *n*, bipède, *m*. ~[**al**], *a*, bipède.

biplane, *n*, biplan, *m*.

birch, *n*, (*tree*) bouleau, *m*; (*rod*) verges, *f.pl.* ~**bark** [*canoe*], pirogue en écorce, *f*. ~ **broom**, balai de bouleau, *m*. ¶ *v.t*, frapper de verges. ~**ing**, *n*, (des) coups de verges, *m.pl.*

bird, *n*, oiseau, (*small*) oiselet, *m*. ~ **call**, appeau, pipeau, *m*. ~ **catcher**, oiseleur, *m*. ~**lime**, *n*, glu, *f*; (*v.t.*) engluer. ~ **of ill omen**, oiseau de mauvais augure; porte-malheur, *m*. ~ **of paradise**, oiseau de paradis. ~**'s-eye view**, vue à vol d'oiseau, *f*. ~ **shot**, menu plomb, *m*, dragée, *f*.

birth, *n*, naissance; extraction, *f*; enfantement, *m*; (*childbed*) couches, *f.pl.* ~ **certificate**, acte de naissance, *m*. ~ **control**, limitation des naissances, *f*. ~**day**, jour de naissance, anniversaire de ma (de sa, etc.) naissance, *m*, fête, *f*. ~**mark**, tache de naissance, envie, *f*, nævus, *m*. ~**place**, lieu de naissance, *m*, [petite] patrie, *f*. ~ **rate**, natalité, *f*, pourcentage des naissances, *m*. ~**right**, droit d'aînesse; droit du sang, *m*.

biscuit, *n*, biscuit, *m*.

bisect, *v.t*, diviser en deux parties

égales. **bisection**, *n*, bissection, *f*.

bishop, *n*, évêque, *m*; (*chess*) fou, *m*. ~**'s house** & **bishopric**, *n*, évêché, *m*.

bismuth, *n*, bismuth, *m*.

bison, *n*, bison, *m*.

bit, *n*, morceau, fragment, *m*, pièce, miette, *f*; bout, brin; peu; (*bridle*) mors, frein; (*borer*) foret, *m*, mèche, *f*; (*key*) panneton; (*iron of plane, etc.*) fer, *m*; (*computers*) bit, *m*.

bitch, *n*, chienne; (*woman*) garce, *f*. ~ **fox**, renarde, *f*. ~ **wolf**, louve, *f*.

bite, *n*, morsure, *f*, coup de dents; mordant, *m*; (*sting*) piqûre; (*to eat*) bouchée; (*place bitten by worm, mouse*) mangeure, *f*. I have a ~! (*Fish.*), ça mord! ¶ *v.t.* & *i. ir*, mordre; piquer.

biting, *a*, mordant, piquant; (*cold*) cuisant.

bitter, *a*, amer; aigre; cuisant; cruel; acharné. ~ **pill** (*fig.*), couleuvre, *f*. ~**-sweet**, *a*, aigredoux; (*n. Bot.*) douce-amère, *f*. ~**ly**, *ad*, amèrement; aigrement; (*cold*) extrêmement. **cry** ~, pleurer à chaudes larmes. ~**ness**, *n*, amertume, *f*, amer, fiel, *m*. ~**s**, *n*, amers, *m.pl.*

bittern, *n*, butor, *m*.

bitumen, *n*, bitume, *m*. **bituminous**, *a*, bitumineux.

bivalve, *a*. & *n*, bivalve, *a*. & *m*.

bivouac, *n*, bivouac, *m*. ¶ *v.i*, bivouaquer.

blab, *v.t*, divulguer; (*v.i.*) bavarder, jaser.

black, *a*, noir. ~ & **blue**, meurtri, noir. [*down*] **in** ~ & **white**, noir sur blanc. ~**ball** (*voting*), boule noire, *f*. ~**beetle**, blatte, *f*, cafard, *m*. ~**berry**, mûre sauvage, *m*. de ronce, *f*. ~**berry bush**, ronce, *f*. ~**bird**, merle, *m*, (*hen*) merlette, *f*. ~**board**, tableau [noir] *m*. ~**-bordered envelope**, enveloppe deuil, *f*. ~ **currant(s)** & ~ **currant bush** & ~ **currant cordial**, cassis, *m*. ~ **eye**, œil poché, pochon, *m*. **to give someone a** ~ **eye**, pocher l'œil à quelqu'un. B~ **Forest**, Forêt-Noire, *f*. ~**guard**, canaille, *f*, goujat, *m*. ~**head**, point noir, *m*, tanne, *f*. ~**jack**, assommoir, *m*, matraque, *f*. ~ **lead**, mine de plomb, plombagine, *f*, graphite, *m*. ~**list**, *n*, index, *m*; (*v.t.*)

mettre à l'i. ~ *magic*, ~ *art*, magie noire, *f*. ~*mail*, *n*, chantage, *m*; (*v.t.*) faire chanter. ~*mailer*, maître chanteur, *m*. ~ *mark* (bruise), noir, *m*. ~ *market*, marché noir, *m*. ~ *out*, black-out, *m*. B~ *Sea*, mer Noire, *f*. ~ *sheep* (fig.), brebis galeuse, *f*. ~*smith*, forgeron, *m*. ~*thorn*, épine noire, *f*, prunellier, *m*. ¶ *n*, (*color, man*) noir, *m*; (*ball—gaming*) noire, *f*. ¶ *v.t*, noircir; charbonner; mâchurer; (*boots*) cirer.

blackamoor, *n*, moricaud, e; noir, e.

blacken, *v.t*, noircir. **blacking**, *n*, noircissement; (*boots*) cirage; cirage pour chaussures, *m*. ~ *brush*, brosse à cirer, b. à étendre, *f*. **blackish**, *a*, noirâtre. **blackness**, *n*, noirceur, *f*.

bladder, *n*, vessie; (*Bot.*) vésicule, *f*.

blade, *n*, (*grass*) brin, *m*; (*knife*) lame, feuille; (*vane*) aile, aube; (*propeller*) palette; (*oar*) pale, *f*, plat, *m*.

blame, *n*, blâme, reproche, *m*, faute, *f*. ¶ *v.t*, blâmer, reprocher, accuser, s'en prendre à. ~*less*, *a*, innocent. ~*worthy*, *a*, digne de blâme.

blanch, *v.t. & i*, blanchir, faire pâlir, pâlir.

bland, *a*, doux, suave, doucereux, mielleux. ~*ishment*, *n*, flatterie, chatterie, *f*.

blank, *a*, blanc, vierge. ~ *cartridge*, cartouche à blanc, *f*. ~ *verse*, vers blancs, *m.pl*. ¶ *n*, blanc, *m*; lacune, *f*, trou, *m*; (*lottery*) billet perdant; (*for coin*) flan, *m*.

blanket, *n*, couverture [en laine], couverte, *f*. ~ *stitch* (*Emb.*), point de languette, p. de feston, *m*.

blare, *n*, flonflon, *m*. ¶ *v.i*, retentir.

blarney, *n*, blague, *f*.

blaspheme, *v.i. & t*, blasphémer, jurer. **blasphemer**, *n*, blasphémateur, trice. **blasphemous**, *a*, blasphématoire. **blasphemy**, *n*, blasphème, *m*.

blast, *n*, vent, coup de vent, courant d'air, souffle, *m*, chasse d'air, *f*; coup; coup [de mine], pétard, *m*, mine, *f*. ~ *furnace*, haut fourneau, *m*. ¶ *v.t*, faire sauter; pétarder; foudroyer; (*blight*) brouir, flétrir. ~*ing*, *n*, travail

aux explosifs (*ou* à la poudre), *m*. ~ *powder*, poudre de mine, *f*.

blatant, *a*, bruyant, criard.

blaze, *n*, flambée, *f*; éclat, *m*. in a ~, en flammes. ¶ *v.i*, flamber; flamboyer; (*v.t, tree*) griffer. ~ *a trail*, frayer un chemin. **blazing**, *a*, flambant, flamboyant, ardent, d'enfer; éclatant.

blazon, *v.t*, blasonner, armorier, proclamer. ~*ry*, *n*, blason, *m*.

bleach, *v.t*, blanchir. ~*er*, *n*, blanchisseur, euse, buandier, ère; (*pl.*) (*seats*) gradins, *m.pl*. ~*ery*, *n*, blanchisserie, *f*. ~*ing*, *n*, blanchiment, *m*.

bleak, *a*, morne, triste.

blear-eyed, *a*, chassieux.

bleat, *v.i*, bêler; (*goat & fig.*) chevroter. **bleat[ing]**, *n*, bêlement, *m*.

bleed, *v.t. & i. ir*, saigner; pleurer. ~*ing*, *n*, saignement, *m*; saignée, *f*.

blemish, *n*, tache, tare, défectuosité, *f*, défaut, *m*. ¶ *v.t*, tacher; ternir.

blench, *v.i*, reculer; fuir; broncher.

blend, *n*, assortiment, *m*. ¶ *v.t.ir*, assortir; fondre; confondre; incorporer; (*wines*) mélanger, couper; (*v.i.ir.*) [s']assortir, se confondre, s'apparenter. ~*ing* (*wines*) *n*, mélange, coupage, *m*.

bless, *v.t*, bénir; (*bell, etc.*) baptiser; favoriser. **blessed**, **blest**, *a*, béni; heureux; bienheureux. *the Blessed Virgin* [*Mary*], la Sainte Vierge. *to be ~ with*, avoir le bonheur d'avoir, de posséder; jouir de. **blessedness**, *n*, béatitude; félicité, *f*. **blessing**, *n*, bénédiction, *f*; bonheur; (*grace*) bénédicité, *m*.

blight, *n*, brouissure, nielle, rouille, *f*. ¶ *v.t*, brouir, nieller, rouiller; flétrir.

blind, *a*, aveugle; borgne. ~ *alley*, impasse, *f*, cul-de-sac, *m*. ~ *man*, *woman*, aveugle, *m,f*. *the* ~, les aveugles, *m.pl*. ~ *man's buff*, colin-maillard, *m*. ~*-worm*, orvet, *m*. ¶ *n*, store, *m*; jalousie; (*shop*) banne, *f*; (*fig.*) voile, masque, faux-semblant, *m*. ¶ *v.t*, aveugler. ~*fold*, *v.t*, bander [les yeux à, de]. ~*ly*, *ad*, aveuglément, à l'aveuglette. ~*ness*, *n*, cécité, *f*; (*fig.*) aveuglement, *m*.

blink, n, clign[ot]ement, m. ¶ v.i,
clign[ot]er, ciller; vaciller, papilloter; (v.t.) se cacher. ~er, n,
œillère, f.

bliss, n, béatitude, félicité, f.
~ful, a, heureux; bienheureux;
béat.

blister, n, ampoule, bulle, cloque,
f; (plaster) vésicatoire, m. ¶ v.t,
faire venir des ampoules à. I ~
easily, il me vient facilement des
ampoules.

blithe, a, gai, joyeux.

blizzard, n, tourmente de neige,
f.

bloat, v.t, bouffir. **bloater,** n. or
bloated herring, hareng bouffi,
m.

block, n, bloc, massif, m; motte,
f; paquet, m; partie, tranche, f,
ensemble; (chopping) billot, m;
(shape) forme, poupée, f;
(houses) pâté, îlot, m; (pulley)
moufle, poulie, f; (stoppage) embarras, encombrement, embouteillage, m. ~ letters (e.g. child's
writing), lettres moulées, f.pl.
in ~ letters (as on coupon), en
caractères d'imprimerie. ~ writing, la lettre moulée. ¶ v.t, obstruer, encombrer; embouteiller;
bloquer; (Bookb.) dorer. ~ up
(door), condamner.

blockade, n, blocus, m. ¶ v.t,
bloquer.

blockhead, n, bûche, f, imbécile,
m,f.

blockhouse, n, blockhaus, m.

blond, as applied to a woman
blonde, a, blond (blonde, f.).
¶ n, (color) blond, m; (pers.)
blond, e.

blood, n, sang, m; race, f; (dandy)
petit-maître, élégant, m. ~ heat,
température du sang, f. ~hound,
limier, m. ~ letting, saignée, f.
~ orange, orange sanguine, f. ~
poisoning, empoisonnement du
sang, m. ~ pressure, tension artérielle, f. ~ red, rouge sang, m.
~ relationship, consanguinité, f.
~shed, effusion de sang, f; carnage, m. ~shot, injecté [de
sang], éraillé. ~stone, jaspe sanguin, héliotrope, m, sanguine, f.
~sucker, sangsue, f. ~ test, prise
de sang, f, prélèvement de s., m.
~thirsty, altéré de sang, sanguinaire. ~ vessel, vaisseau sanguin, m. ~y Mary, marie-salope,
f. ~less, a, exsangue; non sanglant. ~y, a, ensanglanté, sanglant, en sang; sanguinaire.

bloom, n, fleur; fraîcheur, f. ¶ v.i,
fleurir. ~ing, a, fleurissant; (fig.)
florissant. ¶ n, floraison, f.

blossom, n, fleur, f. ¶ v.i, fleurir.
~ing, n, floraison, f.

blot, n, pâté, m, tache, f. ¶ v.t,
faire un pâté sur, tacher; (paper
with useless writing) noircir;
(with blotting paper) éponger.
~ out, effacer.

blotch, n, pustule; tache, f. ¶ v.t,
tacher.

blotting: ~ case, ~ pad, **blotter,**
n, buvard, sous-main, m. ~
paper, papier buvard, papier
brouillard, m.

blouse, n, chemisette, blouse, f.
~ front, guimpe, f.

blow, n, coup, m; bourrade; atteinte, f; (pl.) voies de fait, f.pl;
échec, m. ~fly, mouche à viande,
f. ~ gun, ~pipe, ~ tube, (dart
tube), sarbacane, f. ~[hole]
soufflure, f, bouillon, m. ~out,
crevaison, f. ~pipe, chalumeau,
m. ¶ v.t.ir, souffler; (wind instrument) souffler dans, emboucher;
(to puff, to wind) essouffler;
(v.i.ir.) souffler; venter; (flower)
s'épanouir; (fuse) fondre, jouer.
~ a horn, corner. ~ one's brains
out, se brûler la cervelle. ~ one's
nose, se moucher. ~ out, souffler. ~ up, v.t, souffler; faire
sauter, pétarder; (v.i.) sauter.
~er, n, souffleur, m.

blubber, n, graisse, f, lard, m.
¶ v.i, sangloter.

bludgeon, n, assommoir, gourdin, m, trique, f, massue, f.

blue, a, bleu. Bluebeard, Barbe-
Bleue, m. ~bell, jacinthe des
bois, f. ~bottle, mouche bleue,
f. ~eyed, aux yeux bleus.
~jacket, marin de l'État, m. ~
mark (bruise), bleu, m. ~
moldy (cheese), persillé. ~pen-
cil, v.t, marquer au crayon bleu;
sabrer, barrer. ~ peter, pavillon de partance, m. ~print, bleu,
m. ~stocking, bas-bleu, m. out
of the ~, soudainement. to feel
~, avoir le cafard. ¶ n, bleu;
(pl.) spleen, m. ¶ v.t, bleuir.

blueberry, n, airelle, f.

bluff, a, brusque; franc; escarpé.
¶ n, cap à pic; trompe-l'œil, m.
¶ v.t, leurrer, ~er, n, faiseur, m.

bluish, a, bleuâtre.

blunder, n, bévue, bourde, ignorance, f, impair, m ¶ v.i, faire

des bévues, gaffer. ~er, n, gaffeur, maladroit, m.

blunt, a, émoussé; contondant; brusque, cru. ¶ v.t, émousser, épointer. ~ly, ad, brusquement, crûment, rondement. ~ness, n, état émoussé; sans-façon, m; brusquerie, f.

blur, n, tache, f; embrouillement, m. ¶ v.t, tacher, barbouiller; [em]brouiller.

blurb, n, réclame, publicité, f.

blurred, p.a, trouble, **blurry,** a, flou.

blurt out, v.t, lâcher, laisser échapper.

blush, n, rougeur; fleur, f. at the first ~, à vue de nez. ¶ v.i, rougir. ~ing, p.a, rougissant, rouge.

bluster, n, fracas, m; fanfaronnade, rodomontade, f. ¶ v.i, tempêter; maugréer. ~er, n, fanfaron, m.

boa (wrap) n, boa, m. ~ constrictor, boa constrictor, m.

boar, n, verrat; (wild) sanglier; (young wild) marcassin, m. ~ hound, vautre, m. ~ hunting, chasse au sanglier, m. ~'s head, hure de sanglier, f. ~ spear, épieu, m.

board, n, planche, f, ais; plat; tableau; tablier; (notice) écriteau, m, enseigne, f; (Naut.) bord, m; bordée, f. on ~, à bord. room & ~, pension complète. ~ [of directors], conseil [d'administration] m, administration, f. ~ of examiners, jury d'examen, m. ¶ v.t, planchéier; (ship) monter sur, aborder; (train, car) monter dans; (feed) nourrir. ~ up (window), condamner. ~er, n, pensionnaire; [élève] interne, m,f. ~ing, n, planchéiage, m. ~house, pension, f. ~-in, internat, m. ~ school, pensionnat, internat, m, pension, f.

boast, n, vanterie; gloire, f. ¶ v.t, vanter; (v.i.) se vanter. ~er, n, vantard, e, fanfaron, ne. ~ful, a, vantard.

boat, n, bateau, canot, m, embarcation, barque, f; navire, bâtiment, vaisseau, m. ~ deck, pont des embarcations, m. ~ fishing, pêche en bateau, f. ~ hook, gaffe [pour l'amarrage des bateaux] f, croc [de batelier] m. ~house,

garage [des bateaux] m. ~load, batelée, f. ~man, marin, canotier, m. ~ train, train de paquebot, m. ¶ v.i, canoter. ~ing, m, canotage, m. **boatswain,** n, maître [d'équipage] m.

bob, n, secousse, f; révérence, f; lentille, poire, f; plomb; poids, m. ¶ v.i, balloter; branler. bob[bed hair], coiffure à la Ninon, coiffure à la Jeanne d'Arc, f.

bobbin, n, bobine, canette, f.

bobsleigh, n, traîneau, bobsleigh, m.

bobtail, n, queue écourtée, f.

bode, v.t, présager.

bodice, n, corps, corsage, m.

bodily, a, corporel; physique; matériel; (fear) pour sa personne. ¶ ad, corporellement; en masse.

bodkin, n, passe-lacet, m, aiguille à passer, f.

body, n, corps, m; carcasse, f; vaisseau; massif, m; masse, f; gros, m; (water) masse, (vehicle) carrosserie, f. ~ belt, gaine, f. ~ corporate, personne morale, p. juridique, p. civile, f.

bog, n, marais, marécage, m, fondrière, f. ¶ v.t, embourber.

bogey [man], n, croque-mitaine, m.

boggle, v.i, reculer, hésiter.

boggy, a, marécageux, tourbeux.

bogus, a, faux, simulé; véreux.

Bohemia (fig.) n, la bohème, f. **Bohemian** (fig.) n. & a, bohème, m,f. & a.

boil (Path.) n, furoncle, clou, m.

boil, v.t, faire bouillir; cuire [à l'eau]; (v.i.) bouillir; bouillonner. ~ down, condenser, réduire. ~ed, p.a: ~ beef, bœuf bouilli, m. ~ egg, œuf à la coque, m. ~ potatoes, pommes de terre à l'eau, p—s de t. nature, p—s de t. vapeur, f.pl. ~er, n, (steam) chaudière, f; (pot) marmite, f. ~ maker, chaudronnier, m. ~ making & ~ works, [grosse] chaudronnerie, f. ~ plate, tôle de chaudière, f. ~ room, chambre de chauffe, chaufferie, f. double ~, bain-marie, m. ~ing, n, ébullition, f; bouillonnement, m. ~ point, point d'ébullition, m. (212° F. or 100° C.).

boisterous†, *a*, bruyant, turbulent.

bold, *a*, hardi, osé, audacieux, téméraire, assuré; net. ~*-faced* (type), gras. *displayed in* ~ *type*, en vedette. ~*ly*, *ad*, hardiment, audacieusement; hautement, franchement. ~*ness*, *n*, hardiesse, audace; fierté (*de touche*) *f*.

Bolivia, *n*, la Bolivie. **Bolivian**, *a*, bolivien. ¶ *n*, Bolivien, ne.

bollard, *n*, canon d'amarrage, poteau d'a., *m*.

Bologna, *n*, Bologne, *f*.

bolster, *n*, traversin, chevet; coussin, *m*. ~ *up*, *v.t*, (*doctrine*) étayer; (*pers.*) soutenir.

bolt, *n*, boulon, *m*, cheville, *f*; (*door*) verrou; (*lock*) pêne, *m*; (*thunder*) foudre; (*flight*) fugue, *f*. ¶ *v.t*, boulonner; cheviller; verrouiller; (*sift*) bluter; (*food*) expédier, gober; (*v.i.*) (*horse*) s'emporter, s'emballer; (*pers.*) prendre la poudre d'escampette.

bolt upright, tout droit.

bolus, *n*, bol, *m*.

bomb, *n*, bombe, *f*. ~*proof*, à l'épreuve des b—s. ~*shell* (*fig.*), bombe, *f*. ~*thrower*, lance-bombe, *m*. ¶ *v.t*, (*Avn.*) bombarder; (*Mil.*) lancer des bombes à. **bombard**, *v.t*, bombarder, canonner; fusiller (*fig.*). ~*ier*, *n*, bombardier, *m*. ~*ment*, *n*, bombardement, *m*.

bombast, *n*, emphase, *f*, phébus, *m*. ~*ic*, *a*, emphatique, ampoulé, boursouflé, bouffi.

bomber, *n*, (*Avn.*) bombardier; (*pers.*) grenadier, *m*.

bond, *n*, lien, *m*, attache, *f*; nœud, *m*; liaison; chaîne, *f*; agglutinant; (*Fin.*) bon, *m*; obligation, *f*; titre, *m*, valeur, *f*; (*law*) acte, contrat; cautionnement; compromis, *m*; soumission, *f*. *bond[ed warehouse]*, entrepôt [légal *ou* de douane] *m*. *in bond[ed warehouse]*, en (*ou* à l')entrepôt. **bond**, *v.t*, entreposer; (*masonry*) liaisonner. **bondage**, *n*, captivité, servitude, *f*, esclavage, *m*.

bone, *n*, os, *m*; (*fish*) arête, *f*; (*pl*, *dead*) ossements, *m.pl*; (*castanets*) cliquettes, *f.pl*. ~ *of contention*, pomme de discorde, *f*. ~*setter*, rebouteur, euse. ¶ *v.t*, désosser; ôter les arêtes de.

bonfire, *n*, feu de joie, bûcher, *m*.

bonnet, *n*, chapeau; (*auto*) capot, *m*, capote, *f*.

bonny, *a*, joli; bien portant; gai.

bonus, *n*, gratification, prime, indemnité, *f*. ~ *shares*, actions gratuites, *f.pl*.

bony, *a*, osseux; (*big-boned*) ossu. ~ *palate*, palais dur, *m*.

boo, *v.t*, huer, conspuer.

booby, *n*, nigaud, e, benêt, dadais, *m*, huître, *f*. ~ *prize*, fiche de consolation, *f*. ~ *trap*, attrape-nigaud, *m*.

book, *n*, livre; livret; carnet; registre; journal; cahier; recueil; album; (*old & of little value*) bouquin, *m*. ~*binder*, relieur, euse. ~*binding*, reliure, *f*. ~*case*, bibliothèque, *f*. ~*ends*, serre-livres, *m*. ~*keeper*, teneur de livres, *m*, comptable, *m,f*. ~*keeping*, tenue de[s] livres, comptabilité, *f*. ~ *lover*, bibliophile, *m*. ~*maker*, bookmaker, *m*. ~*mark[er]*, signet, *m*, marque, *f*. ~*matches*, allumettes en carnet, *f.pl*. ~*muslin*, organdi, *m*. ~ *plate*, ex-libris, *m*. ~ *rest*, pupitre, *m*. ~*seller*, libraire, *m*. ~*seller & publisher*, libraire-éditeur, *m*. ~*[seller's] shop*, librairie, *f*. ~*shelf*, rayon, *m*. ~*stall*, bibliothèque, *f*; kiosque, *m*. ~ *value*, valeur comptable, *f*. ~*worm* (*pers.*), rat de bibliothèque, *m*. ~ *work* (*Typ.*), labeur, *m*. ¶ *v.t*, enregistrer; engager, retenir; louer; réserver; demander; (*v.i.*) prendre un billet, des billets. **booking**, *n*, enregistrement; engagement, *m*, location; réserve, *f*; transport, voyage, service, *m*. **booklet**, *n*, brochure, *f*, livret. *m*.

Boolean, *a*, booléen, ne. ~ *algebra*, algèbre booléenne. ~ *operation*, opération booléenne.

boom, *n*, (*harbor*) estacade; (*crane*) flèche, *f*; (*prices*) emballement [à la hausse]; (*noise*) grondement, *m*. (*cinema*) ~ *operator*, perchiste, *m*. ¶ *v.i*, gronder, bourdonner, ronfler, tonner.

boon, *a*, gai, joyeux. ~ *companion*, bon compagnon; camarade de bouteille, *m*. ¶ *n*, bienfait, *m*, faveur, *f*.

boor, *n*, rustre, manant, *m*, rustaud, e. ~*ish*, *a*, rustaud, grossier. ~*ishness*, *n*, rusticité, grossièreté, *f*.

boost, n, poussée; augmentation, f. ~**er**, n, (*rocket, spacecraft*) propulseur auxiliaire, m. ¶ v.t, pousser; augmenter; (*Elec.*) doper.

boot, n, chaussure [montante]; bottine, botte, f; brodequin. ~ & *shoe repairer*, cordonnier, m. ~ & *shoe trade*, cordonnerie, f. ~*black*, cireur de bottes, m. ~*jack*, tire-botte, m. ~*lace*, lacet de chaussure, m. ~*maker*, bottier, m. ~*tree*, embouchoir, embauchoir, m. ¶ v.t, chausser; botter. ~**ee**, n, chausson, m.

booth, n, baraque, boutique, échoppe, f.

bootless, a, inutile, vain, futile.

booty, n, butin, m.

booze, v.i, riboter, godailler.

boracic, a, borique. **borax**, n, borax, m.

border, n, bord, m, bordure; frontière; lisière, f; cordon, m; (*garden*) plate-bande, f. ~ *land*, pays limitrophe, m. ¶ v.t, border. ~ [*up*]*on*, avoisiner, côtoyer, friser.

bore, n, alésage, calibre; (*Min.*) sondage, forage, m; (*tidal*) barre d'eau, f, mascaret, m; (*nuisance*) scie, f; (*pers.*) raseur, euse, endormeur, casse-pieds, m, scie, f, crampon, m. ~ *core*, témoin, m, carotte, f. ~*hole*, trou de sonde, m. ¶ v.t, percer, forer; vriller; aléser, vider; (*fig.*) ennuyer, embêter, scier, assommer, tuer, assassiner, ~**dom**, n, ennui, m.

boric, a, borique.

born, p.p. & a, né; issu; de naissance. ~ *blind*, aveugle de naissance, aveugle-né. *to be* ~, naître.

borough, n, bourg, m.

borrow, v.t, emprunter. ~**er**, n, emprunteur, euse. ~**ing**, n, emprunt, m. oft. pl.

borzoi, n, lévrier russe, m.

bosom, n, sein, m; gorge, f; (*church*) sein, giron, m. ~ *friend*, ami de cœur, m.

Bosphorus (the), le Bosphore.

boss, n, bosse, f; moyeu; (*pers.*) patron, chef, m.

botanic(al), a, botanique. ~ *gardens*, jardin des plantes, m. **botanist**, n, botaniste, m. **botanize**, v.i, herboriser. **botany**, n, botanique, f.

botch, n, bousillage, m. ¶ v.t, bousiller, gâcher, massacrer.

both, a. & ad, tous [les] deux, deux; l'un(e) & l'autre; (*at the same time*) à la fois ... et ...

bother, n, tracas, aria, m. ¶ v.t, tracasser.

bottle, n, bouteille; canette, f; flacon; bocal, m; burette, f. ~ *brush*, rince-bouteille, m. ~ *neck*, embouteillage, goulot d'étranglement, m. ¶ v.t, mettre en bouteille(s), embouteiller. ~ *up* (block), embouteiller.

bottom, n, fond, bas, m, base, f, pied, bout; dessous; derrière, cul; (*of chair*) siège; (*lowland*) bas-fond; (*ship*) navire, m; (*of ship*) carène, f. ¶ a, inférieur; de fond; de dessous; le plus bas. ~*less*, a, sans fond.

bough, n, mère branche, f; rameau, m.

boulder, n, roche, f, gros galet, caillou, m.

bounce, n, bond, m; vanterie, blague, f. ¶ v.i, bondir; se vanter, faire le fanfaron.

bound, n, borne, limite, f; bond, saut, rebond, m. *to exceed all* ~*s*, dépasser la mesure. ¶ v.t, borner, limiter; (*v.i.*) bondir, sauter. ~ *for* (ship), à destination de. *to be* ~ *to*, être tenu(e) de (*ou* à), être obligé(e) de. **boundary**, n, limite, borne, f. **boundless**, a, illimité, sans bornes, immense.

bounteous†, a, généreux. **bountiful†**, a, généreux, libéral, bienfaisant; fécond. **bounty**, n, générosité, munificence, largesse; prime, f.

bouquet, n, bouquet; (*wine*) bouquet, fumet, m.

bourn, n, ruisseau, m.

bout, n, tour, assaut, m, partie, reprise, f.

bovine, a, bovin.

bow, n, (*knot*) nœud, nœud de ruban; (*necktie*) nœud[-papillon]; (*curve*) arc; (*fiddle*) archet; (*saddle*) arçon, m; (*padlock*) anse, f. ~ *compasses*, compas à balustre. ~ *window*, bowwindow, m.

bow, n, salut, coup de chapeau, m, inclination, révérence, f; (*ship*) avant, m. ¶ v.t. & i, courber, incliner, fléchir, plier. ~ &

scrape, faire des courbettes. ~ *to*, saluer; s'incliner devant.

bowdlerize, *v.t*, expurger.

bowels, *n.pl*, entrailles, *f.pl*, intestins, *m.pl*; tripes, *f.pl*.

bower, *n*, tonnelle, *f*, berceau, cabinet de verdure, *m*.

bowing & scraping, prosternations, *f.pl*.

bowl, *n*, bol, bassin, *m*, écuelle, coupe, cuvette, jatte, sébile *f*; plateau; (*pipe*) fourneau, *m*; (*game*) boule, *f*. [*game of*] ~*s*, boules, *f.pl*, jeu de boules, *m*. ~*ful*, *n*, écuellée, *f*.

bowlegged, *a*, bancal.

bowler [hat], *n*, [chapeau] melon; (*player*) joueur, *m*.

bowling: ~ *alley*, jeu de boules couvert, *m*. ~ *green*, jeu de boules découvert.

bowman, *n*, archer; (*boat*) brigadier, *m*.

bowsprit, *n*, beaupré, *m*.

bow-wow, *n*, toutou, *m*.

box, *n*, boîte; caisse, *f*; coffre; coffret; tronc; boîtier; (*cardboard*) carton; (*driver's*) siège, *m*; (*jury*) banc, *m*; (*Theat.*) loge, *f*. ~ *office*, bureau [de location], contrôle, *m*. ~ *on the ear*[*s*], soufflet, *m*. ~*-spring mattress*, sommier élastique, *m*. ~ [*tree*] & ~*wood*, buis, *m*. ¶*v.t*, encaisser; (*someone's ears*) souffleter, frotter; (*fight*) boxer; (*v.i.*) boxer. ~*er*, *n*, boxeur, *m*. ~*ing*, *n*, boxe, *f*. ~ *match*, combat de b., assaut de b., match de b., *m*.

boy, *n*, garçon, garçonnet, enfant, gars, *m*. ~ *scout*, boy-scout, éclaireur, scout, *m*. ~*hood*, *n*, jeunesse, *f*. ~*ish*, *a*, enfantin, puéril.

boycott, *n*, boycottage, *m*. ¶*v.t*, boycotter.

brace, *n*, (*strut*, *stay*) entretoise, *f*, étrésillon; arc-boutant, *m*, contre-fiche, bielle, *f*; tirant, *m*; moise, *f*; (*tool*) vilebrequin; cliquet; (*pair*) couple, paire. ¶ *v.t*, renforcer, armer; moiser; fortifier, retremper; bander; accolader.

bracelet, *n*, bracelet, *m*.

bracing, *a*, fortifiant, vivifiant.

bracken, *n*, fougère [à l'aigle] *f*.

bracket, *n*, console, potence, applique, *f*; (*Typ.*) [,], crochet, *m*;

(,), parenthèse; {, }, accolade, *f*. ¶ *v.t*, accoler.

brackish, *a*, saumâtre.

brad, *n*, pointe, *f*. ~*awl*, *n*, poinçon, *m*.

brag, *n*, vanterie, hâblerie, blague, fanfaronnade, *f*. ¶ *v.i*, se vanter. **braggart**, *n*, vantard, e, hâbleur, euse, fanfaron, ne.

brahmin, *n*, brahmane, *m*.

braid, *n*, tresse, soutache, *f*, bordé, galon; passement, *m*. ¶ *v.t*, tresser, soutacher, galonner, passementer.

brain, *n*. & ~*s*, *pl*, cerveau, *m*, cervelle, tête, *f*; (*pl. Cook.*) cervelle[s]. ~ *fatigue*, fatigue cérébrale, *f*. ~ *fever*, fièvre cérébrale, *f*. ~*storming*, remue-méninges, *m*. *to rack one's* ~*s*, se creuser les méninges. ~*less*, *a*, sans cervelle.

braise, *v.t*, braiser.

brake, *n*, (*on wheel*) frein; (*waggonette*) break, *m*; (*bracken*) fougère [à l'aigle] *f*; (*thicket*) fourré, *m*. ~ [*gear*], timonerie des freins; (*carriage*) mécanique, *f*. ¶ *v.t*, enrayer. *to put on* (*or apply*) *the* ~*s*, freiner, serrer les freins. **brakeman**, *n*, serre-frein, garde-frein, *m*.

bramble, *n*, ronce, *f*.

bran, *n*, son, *m*.

branch, *n*, branche, *f*; rameau; embranchement; (*Elec.*) branchement, *m*. ~ [*line*] (*Rly*), ligne (*ou* voie) secondaire, *f*. ~ [*office*], succursale, *f*; comptoir, *m*. ¶ *v.t*, brancher; (*v.i.*) se ramifier. ~ *off*, *v.t*, embrancher; (*v.i.*) fourcher.

brand, *n*, (*fire*) tison, brandon, *m*; (*fig.*) flétrissure, *f*, stigmate; (*Poet.*) glaive, *m*; (*Com. & hot iron*) marque, *f*. **brand new**, battant (*ou* tout flambant) neuf. ¶ *v.t*, marquer [à chaud]; flétrir, stigmatiser. **brandish**, *v.t*, brandir.

brandy, *n*, eau-de-vie, *f*, cognac, *m*. ~ *& soda*, fine à l'eau, *f*.

brass, *n*, laiton, cuivre [jaune]; (*Poet.*) airain; (*bearing*) coussinet, *m*; (*cheek*) effronterie, *f*, toupet, *m*. *the* ~*es* (*Mus.*), les cuivres. ~ *band*, fanfare, *f*. ~ *foundry*, fonderie de cuivre, robinetterie, *f*. ~*wares*, dinanderie, *f*.

brassière, *n,* soutien-gorge, *m.*

brassy, *a,* cuivré.

brat, *n,* gamin, e, marmot, *m,* gosse, *m,f,* (*pl, col.*) marmaille, *f.*

bravado, *n,* bravade, *f.* **bravet,** *a,* brave. ~ **man,** [homme] brave, *m.* ¶ *v.t,* braver, affronter, défier. ~ry, *n,* bravoure, *f.* **bravo,** *i,* bravo!

brawl, *a,* mêlée, bagarre, rixe, querelle, *f;* tapage, *m.* ¶ *v.i,* se chamailler; (*stream*) murmurer. ~er, *n,* tapageur, euse, casseur d'assiettes, *m.*

brawn, *n,* hure, *f,* fromage de porc, *m;* (*fig.*) force musculaire, *f.* ~y, *a,* charnu, musculeux.

bray, *v.i,* braire. ~[ing], *n,* braiment, *m.*

braze, *v.t,* braser. **braze** (*joint*) & **brazing,** *n,* brasure, *f.*

brazen, *a,* d'airain. ~[-*faced*], effronté. **to ~ it out,** crâner, faire le crâne.

brazier, *n,* (*pers.*) chaudronnier; dinandier; (*pan*) brasero, *m.*

Brazil, *n,* le Brésil. **Brazilian,** *a,* brésilien. ¶ *n,* Brésilien, ne.

breach, *n,* brèche; infraction, violation, contravention, *f.* ~ **of faith,** manque de foi, *m.* ~ **of promise,** violation de promesse de mariage, *f.* ~ **of trust,** infidélité, prévarication, forfaiture, *f,* abus de confiance, *m.*

bread, *n,* pain, *m;* (*money*) pognon, *m.* ~ **crumbs** (*Cook.*), panure, chapelure, *f.* ~ **knife,** couteau à pain, *m.* ~ **winner,** soutien de famille, *m.* **sandwich** ~, pain de mie. **whole wheat** ~, pain complet.

breadth, *n,* largeur; envergure, *f;* travers, *m;* (*of stuffs*) largeur, *f,* lé, *m.*

break, *n,* rupture, cassure, brisure; solution; (*gap*) trouée, *f;* (*day*) point, *m;* (*voice*) mue; (*prices*) dérobade, *f;* (*Bil.*) série, *f.* ¶ *v.t.ir,* casser; briser; fracturer; fragmenter; rompre; crever; fendre; concasser; enfreindre, violer; (*the bank, gaming*) faire sauter; (*a set*) dépareiller; (*news*) faire part de; (See also *broken*); (*v.i.ir.*) [se] casser, se briser, etc; (*voice*) muer; (*dawn*) poindre; (*waves*) déferler. ¶ (*Box.*), séparez! ~ **cover** (*Hunt.*), débucher. ~ **down,** *v.t,*

abattre; (*v.i.*) avoir une panne. ~ **into,** envahir; pénétrer; entamer. ~ **loose,** se déchaîner. ~ **of the habit,** déshabituer, désaccoutumer. ~ **one's arm,** se casser le bras. ~ **one's back,** s'échiner. ~ **one's word,** manquer de parole. ~ **open,** enfoncer. ~ **out,** (*fire*) éclater, se déclarer; (*fig.*) déborder, se débonder. ~ **their engagement** (marriage), se désaccorder. ~ **through,** percer. ~ **upon the wheel,** rouer. **breakable,** *a,* fragile. **breakage,** *n,* casse, rupture, *f,* bris, *m.* **breakaway,** *n,* dislocation; dérive, *f.* **breakdown,** *n,* (*failure*) fiasco, *m;* (*car, etc.*) panne; (*health*) prostration, *f.* **breaker,** *n,* (*pers.*) casseur; démolisseur; (*wave*) brisant, *m.* **breakfast,** *n,* déjeuner [du matin] *m.* ¶ *v.i,* déjeuner. **breaking,** *n,* rupture, fracture, *f,* brisement, *m;* (*holy bread*) fraction; (*voice*) mue, *f.* **breakneck,** *n,* casse-cou, *m.* **breakwater,** *n,* brise-lames, brisant, môle, *m.*

bream, *n,* brème, *f;* (*sea*) pagel, *m.*

breast, *n,* sein, *m;* poitrine, *f;* (*horse*) poitrail; (*fowl*) blanc, *m.* **at the** ~, à la mamelle. ~**bone,** sternum, *m.* ~**high,** à hauteur d'appui. ~**stroke** (*Swim.*), brasse, nage en grenouille, *f.*

breath, *n,* haleine, *f;* souffle; soupir, *m.* **breathe,** *v.i. & t,* respirer; souffler; soupirer. **breathing,** *n,* respiration, *f.* ~ **space,** temps de respirer, relâche, *m.* **breathless,** *a,* inanimé; haletant, essoufflé, à bout de souffle.

breech, *n,* derrière, *m;* (*gun*) culasse, *f,* tonnerre, *m.* ~**loading,** se chargeant par la culasse. **breeches,** *n.pl,* culotte, *f.*

breed, *n,* race, *f.* ¶ *v.t.ir,* élever; engendrer; (*v.i.ir.*) multiplier, se reproduire. ~**er** (*stock*) *n,* éleveur, *m.* ~**ing,** *n,* (*animals*) élevage, *m;* (*pers.*) éducation, *f,* ton, *m.*

breeze, *n,* (*wind*) brise, *f.* **breezy,** *a,* venteux; frais.

Bremen, *n,* Brême, *f.*

brethren, *n.pl,* frères, *m.pl.*

breviary, *n,* bréviaire, *m.*

brevity, *n,* concision; brièveté, *f.*

brew, *v.t,* brasser; (*tea*) faire in-

fuser; (*v.i.*) faire de la bière;
(*storm*) couver, se préparer;
(*fig.*) couver, se tramer, se mijoter. ~er, *n*, brasseur, *m*. ~ery,
n, brasserie, *f*. ~ing, *n*, brassage,
m.

briar, *n*, églantier, *m*; (*pipe wood*)
bruyère, *f*.

bribe, *n*, pot-de-vin, *m*. ¶ *v.t*, corrompre, séduire, soudoyer. ~ry,
n, corruption, *f*.

brick, *n*, brique, *f*. ~ kiln, four
à briques, *m*. ~layer, maçon, *m*.
~maker, briquetier, *m*. ~ paving, carrelage en briques, *m*.
~work, briquetage, *m*. ~yard,
briqueterie, *f*.

bridal, *a*, nuptial; de mariée.
bride, *n*, nouvelle mariée; (*about
to be married* or *on marriage
day*) mariée, *f*. ~ & ~groom,
nouveaux mariés, *m.pl*. ~groom,
nouveau marié; marié, *m*. **bridesmaid**, demoiselle d'honneur, *f*.

bridge, *n*, pont, *m*; (*foot &
ship's*) passerelle, *f*; (*violin*) chevalet; (*nose*) dos; (*cards*) bridge,
m. ~head, tête de pont, *f*. ¶ *v.t*,
jeter un pont sur; franchir.

bridle, *n*, bride, *f*. ~ path, sentier
pour cavaliers, *m*, piste cavalière,
f. ¶ *v.t*, brider; refréner; (*v.i.*)
se rengorger.

brief, *a*, bref, concis; de courte
durée. ¶ *n*, cause, *f*, dossier, *m*.
~case, serviette, *f*. ¶ *v.t*, confier
une cause à, constituer. ~ly, *ad*,
brièvement, bref, en abrégé.

brier, églantier, *m*; (*pipe wood*)
bruyère, *f*.

brig, *n*, brick, *m*.

brigade, *n*, brigade, *f*; corps, *m*.
¶ *v.t*, embrigader.

brigand, *n*, brigand, *m*. ~age, *n*,
brigandage, *m*.

bright, *a*, brillant, éclatant, luisant; vif; beau; gai; poli; lumineux, clair; encourageant; intelligent. ~ interval (*Meteor.*),
éclaircie, *f*. ~en, *v.t*, faire briller; polir; éclaircir; aviver, animer. ~ly, *ad*, brillamment,
clairement. ~ness, *n*, brillant,
éclat, *m*; bonne orientation, *f*.

brill, *n*, barbue, *f*.

brilliance, *n*, éclat, brillant, *m*.
brilliant, *a*, brillant, éclatant.
¶ *n*, brillant, *m*. ~ine, *n*, brillantine, *f*. ~ly, *ad*, brillamment.

brim, *n*, bord, *m*. ¶ ~ over, déborder. ~ful, *a*, plein jusqu'aux
bords, à pleins bords.

brimstone, *n*, soufre, *m*.

brindled, *a*, tacheté.

brine, *n*, saumure; (*Poet.*) onde
amère, *f*; larmes, *f.pl*.

bring, *v.t.ir*, apporter; amener;
conduire; faire; mettre; porter.
~ *about*, déterminer; ménager.
~ *an action against*, intenter une
action à, actionner, attaquer en
justice. ~ *back*, rapporter; ramener. ~ *forth*, mettre au
monde; produire. ~ *forward*
(*Bkkpg*), reporter. ~ *in* (house),
rentrer. ~ *up*, élever, bercer,
nourrir; (*food*) rendre. ~ *up the
rear*, fermer la marche. ~ing up,
éducation, *f*.

brink, *n*, bord; penchant, *m*;
veille, *f*.

briny, *a*, saumâtre; (*Poet.*) amer.

briquet[te], *n*, briquette, *f*, aggloméré, *m*.

brisk†, *a*, vif, actif, animé, allègre. ~ *fire* (Mil.), feu nourri,
m.

brisket, *n*, poitrine, *f*.

briskness, *n*, vivacité; activité, *f*.

bristle, *n*, soie, *f*; poil, *m*. ¶ *v.t*,
hérisser; (*v.i.*) [se] hérisser.
bristling, *p.a*. & **bristly**, *a*, hérissé.

Bristol Channel (the), le
canal de Bristol.

Britain, *n*, la Grande-Bretagne.
Britannia metal, métal anglais,
m. **British**, *a*, britannique; anglais. ~ *ambassador*, ambassadeur d'Angleterre, *m*. ~ *consul*,
consul britannique, *m*. ~ *Isles*,
îles Britanniques, *f.pl*.

Brittany, *n*, la Bretagne.

brittle, *a*, cassant, fragile. ~ness,
n, fragilité, *f*.

broach, *n*, (*spit*) broche, *f*;
(*Mech.*) alésoir, *m*. ¶ *v.t*, (*cask*)
percer; (*bore*) aléser; (*fig.*) entamer, aborder.

broad, *a*, grand; gros; ample;
plein; (*accent*) prononcé; (*ribald*)
libre, cru, gras; (*hint*) peu voilé,
assez clair. ~ *bean*, fève de marais, *f*. ~-brimmed hat, chapeau à
grands bords, *m*. *in* ~ daylight,
au grand jour, en plein jour, en
plein midi. ~-minded, à l'esprit
large. ~-shouldered, large d'é-
paules. ~side, (Naut.) flanc, travers, côté, *m*; (*guns, fire*) bordée,
f; (*fig.*) jeu de massacre, *m*.
~sword, sabre, *m*. ~en, *v.t*, élargir. ~ly, *ad*, largement, ouverte-

ment; en gros. ~ness, *n*, largeur; grossièreté, *f*; accent prononcé, *m*.

broadcast, *v.t.* (*radio & TV*) diffuser, émettre. ¶ *n*, émission, radio-diffusion, *f*. *live* ~, émission en direct. *pre-recorded* ~, é. en differée. *pre-enregistrée*, *f*. *broadcasting station*, station émettrice, *f*.

brocade, *n*, brocart, *m*.

broil, *n*, bagarre, *f*; tumulte, *m*. ¶ *v.t*, brasiller, griller. ~er, *n*, gril, *m*. **broiling**, *a*, brûlant.

broke (*hard up*), *a*, aux abois, fauché; raide.

broken, *a*, (*country*) tourmenté, accidenté, mouvementé; (*health*) délabrée, caduque, *f*; (*speech, sleep, etc.*) entrecoupé; (*English, French*) mauvais. *to be* ~*down* (car), être (*ou* rester) en panne. *to be* ~*hearted*, avoir le cœur navré (*ou* serré de douleur). ~*winded*, poussif.

broker, *n*, courtier, ère; agent; banquier, *m*. ~**age**, *n*, courtage, *m*. ~ *fees*, commissions de courtier, *f.pl*.

bromide, *n*, bromure, *m*.

bronchia, *n.pl*, bronches, *f.pl*. **bronchitis**, *n*, bronchite, *f*.

bronze, *n*, bronze, *m*. ~ *shoes*, souliers mordorés, *m.pl*. ¶ *v.t*, bronzer.

brooch, *n*, broche; (*bar shaped*) barrette, *f*.

brood, *n*, couvée; nichée, engeance, *f*. ~ *hen*, couveuse, *f*. ~ *mare*, [jument] poulinière, *f*. ¶ *v.i*, couver; ruminer. ~**ing time**, couvaison, *f*.

brook, *n*, ruisseau, *m*. ¶ *v.t*, digérer, tolérer. ~**let**, *n*, ruisselet, *m*.

broom, *n*, balai; (*Bot.*) genêt, *m*. ~**stick**, manche à balai, *m*.

broth, *n*, bouillon; potage, *m*.

brothel, *n*, bordel, *m*.

brother, *n*, frère; confrère, *m*. ~*in-law*, beau-frère. ~**hood**, fraternité, confrérie; confraternité, *f*. ~**ly**, *a*, fraternel.

brow, *n*, sourcil; (*forehead & cliff*) front; (*hill*) sommet, *m*. ~**beat**, *v.t*, rudoyer.

brown, *a*, brun; (*bread—light*) bis; (*bread—dark*) noir; (*sunburnt*) bruni. ~ *crust* (in pot), gratin, *m*. ~ *hair*, cheveux châtains, *m.pl*. ~ *owl*, chat-huant,

m. ~ *study*, rêverie, *f*. ~ *sugar*, cassonade, *f*. ¶ *n*, brun, *m*. ¶ *v.t*, brunir; (*meat*) roussir, rissoler. ~**ish**, *a*, brunâtre.

brownie, *n*, elfe, *m*.

browse, *n*, brout, *m*. ¶ *v.i. & t*, brouter, paître.

bruise, *n*, contusion, meurtrissure, *f*, pinçon, *m*; (*dent*) bosse, *f*. ¶ *v.t*, contusionner, meurtrir, froisser; bossuer, bosseler. ~**d**, *p.a*, meurtri, contus.

brunette, *a*, brun, brunet. ¶ *n*, femme brune, *f*.

brunt, *n*, poids; choc, *m*.

brush, *n*, brosse, *f*; pinceau; coup de brosse; (*Elec.*) balai, *m*; (*fox*) queue; (*affray*) échauffourée, *f*. ~ *maker*, brossier, ère. ~**making**, brosserie, *f*. ~**wood**, broussailles, *f.pl*, [bois] taillis, mortbois, *m*. ¶ *v.t*, brosser; (*mud off*) décrotter; (*graze*) raser, effleurer, frôler. ~ *one's hair, teeth*, se brosser la tête, les dents. ~ *up* (fig.), repolir, dérouiller. ~ *aside*, écarter.

brusque, *a*, brusque.

Brussels, *n*, Bruxelles, *f*. ~ *carpet*, tapis de moquette, *m*, moquette, *f*. ~ *sprout*, chou de Bruxelles, *m*.

brutal†, *a*, brutal. ~**ity**, *n*, brutalité, *f*. ~**ize**, *v.t*, abrutir. **brute**, *n*, brute, *f*, animal, *m*. ~ *beast*, bête brute, *f*. *the* ~ *creation*, l'espèce animale, *f*. ~ *force*, force brute, *f*. **brutish**†, *a*, brutal, abruti.

bubble, *n*, bulle, *f*; bouillon; projet en l'air, *m*. ¶ *v.i*, bouillonner; pétiller. **bubbly**, *a*, mousseux, pétillant.

buccaneer, *n*, boucanier, *m*.

buck, *n*, (*deer*) daim; (*jump*) saut de mouton; (*pers.*) luron, gaillard, *m*. ~ *rabbit*, lapin mâle, bouquin, *m*. ~**skin**, peau de daim, *f*, daim, *m*; (*pl.*) culotte de peau, *f*. ~**shot**, chevrotine, *f*. ¶ *v.i*, ruer.

bucket, *n*, seau, *m*, seille, *f*; godet, *m*, auge, *f*, auget; baquet, *m*; benne, *f*. ~ *shop*, maison de contrepartie, *f*. ~**ful**, *n*, seau, *m*; augée, *f*.

buckle, *n*, boucle, *f*. ¶ *v.t*, boucler. (*v.i.*) se boucler; se corder. ~ *down to*, s'appliquer à.

buckram, *n*, bougran, *m*.

buckthorn, *n*, nerprun, *m*.

buckwheat, n, [blé-]sarrasin, blé noir, m.

bucolic, a, bucolique.

bud, n, bourgeon, bouton, m, gemme, f; (*fig.*) germe, m. ¶ v.i, bourgeonner; naître.

buddhist, a, bouddhique. ¶ n, bouddhiste, m.

budding (*fig.*) a, naissant; en herbe.

buddy, n, copain, m.

budge, v.i, bouger.

budget, n, budget, m. ~ **for,** porter au b.

buff (*color*) a. & n, fauve, a. & m. ~ [*leather*], buffle, m, peau de buffle, f. ¶ v.t, polir. **buffalo,** n, buffle, m.

buffer, n, tampon [de choc], heurtoir, butoir, m. ~ **state,** état tampon, m.

buffet, n, (*blow*) soufflet; (*sideboard*) buffet; (*at a ball*) souper debout, m. ~ **car,** wagon-restaurant, m. ¶ v.t, secouer.

buffoon, n, bouffon, ne, pitre, m. ~**ery,** n, bouffonnerie, f.

bug, n, punaise, f. ~**bear,** n, loup-garou, croque-mitaine, épouvantail, cauchemar, m.

bugle, n, clairon, m; (*Bot.*) bugle, f. ~ **call,** sonnerie, f. **bugler,** n, clairon, m.

build, n, construction, f. *of sturdy* ~ *or well built* (man), bien charpenté. ¶ v.t.ir, bâtir, construire. ~ **up,** édifier, échafauder. ~**er,** n, constructeur, entrepreneur [de bâtiments], m. ~**ing,** n, construction, f, bâtiment, édifice; monument, m. ~ **materials,** matériaux de construction, m.pl. ~ **site,** terrain à bâtir, m.

bulb, n, (*Bot.*) bulbe, f, o[i]gnon, m; (*Anat.*) bulbe, m; (*lamp, thermometer*) ampoule, f; (*Chem.*) ballon, m; (*rubber*) poire, f. ~**ous,** a, bulbeux.

Bulgaria, n, la Bulgarie. **Bulgarian,** a, bulgare. ¶ n, Bulgare, m,f.

bulge, n, bombement, ventre, m. ¶ v.i. & t, bomber, boucler, bouffer, faire [le] ventre.

bulk, n, volume; gros, m; masse, f. *in* ~ (*Ship.*), en vrac, en grenier. ~**head,** cloison, f. ~**y,** a, volumineux, massif; encombrant.

bull, n, taureau, m; (*Pope's*) bulle, f; (*incongruity*) prudhommerie,

f, contresens, m; (*Stk Ex.*) haussier, m. ~ **calf,** veau mâle, taurillon, m. ~**dog,** bouledogue, m. ~**fight,** course de taureaux, f. ~**'s-eye** (*target*) noir, m, mouche, f; (*window*) œil-de-bœuf, m. ~**'s-eye** [*lantern*], lanterne avec projecteur à lentille faisant saillie, f.

bulldozer, n, bouteur, m.

bullet, n, balle, f.

bulletin, n, bulletin, m.

bullfinch, n, bouvreuil, m.

bullion, n, or en barres, m.

bullock, n, bœuf, m.

bully, n, bravache, brutal, m. ¶ v.t, malmener, brutaliser.

bulrush, n, jonc, m; (*reed mace*) massette, masse d'eau, f.

bulwark, n, rempart; boulevard; (*ship's*) pavois, m.

bum, n, vagabond, m.

bumblebee, n, bourdon, m.

bump, n, bosse, f; cahot, heurt, m. ¶ v.t. & i, cogner, heurter, se heurter; cahoter.

bumper, n, (*brimful glass*) rasade, f, rouge bord; (*auto*) pare-chocs, m.

bumpkin, n, rustre, lourdaud, m.

bumptious, a, suffisant. ~**ness,** n, suffisance, f.

bun (*hair*) n, torpillon, m.

bunch, n, bouquet, m; botte, f; (*keys*) trousseau, m; (*grapes*) grappe, f; (*bananas, etc.*) régime, m. ¶ v.t, botteler.

bundle, n, paquet; faisceau, m; botte, f; fagot, m; liasse, f. ¶ v.t, empaqueter; botteler; fagoter; mettre en liasse.

bung, n, bondon, m, bonde, f, bouchon, tampon, m. ~[*hole*], bonde, f. ¶ v.t, bondonner, boucher.

bungalow, n, maisonnette, f.

bungle, n, bousillage, m, mauvaise besogne, f. ¶ v.t, bousiller, barbouiller, massacrer. **bungler,** n, bousilleur, euse, fagoteur, m.

bunion, n, oignon, m.

bunk, n, couchette, f.

bunker, n, soute, f; caisson, m; (*golf*) banquette, f. ~ **coal,** charbon de soute, m.

bunkum, n, blague, f.

bunt, v.t, pousser, encorner.

bunting, n, (*stuff*) étamine à pavillon, f; (*flags*) draperie, f; (*bird*) bruant, m.

buoy, n, bouée, f. ¶ v.t, baliser.

~ *up*, soutenir. ~**ancy**, *n*, flottabilité; poussée, *f*; (*fig.*) ressort, *m*. ~**ant**, *a*, flottant; élastique; vif, animé.

burden, *n*, fardeau, *m*, charge, *f*, poids, faix; (*ship*) port, maximum de charge, tonnage; (*song*) refrain, *m*. ¶ *v.t*, charger; grever. ~**some**, *a*, onéreux.

burdock, *n*, bardane, *f*.

bureau, *n*, bureau; cabinet, *m*. *weather* ~, office de météorologie, *m*.

bureaucracy, *n*, bureaucratie, *f*. **bureaucrat**, *n*, bureaucrate, *m*.

burglar, *n*, cambrioleur, *m*. ~ *alarm*, appareil avertisseur contre le vol, *m*. ~**y**, *n*, cambriolage, vol [de nuit avec effraction] *m*. ~ *insurance*, assurance contre le vol, *f*. **Burgle**, *v.t*, cambrioler.

burgundy, *n*, bourgogne, vin de B., *m*.

burial, *n*, enterrement, *m*. ~ *ground*, cimetière, *m*. ~ *place*, lieu de sépulture, *m*. ~ *service*, office des morts, *m*.

burlap, *n*, serpillière, *f*.

burlesque, *a*. & *n*, burlesque, *a*. & *m*. ¶ *v.t*, travestir.

burly, *a*, solidement bâti; corpulent.

Burma, *n*, la Birmanie. **Burmese**, *a*, birman. ¶ *n*, Birman, e.

burn, *n*, brûlure, *f*. ¶ *v.t*. & *i.ir*, brûler; incendier; calciner; (*of sun*) hâler. *I have burned my arm*, je me suis brûlé le bras. *to burn one's fingers* (*fig.*), s'échauder. ~**er**, *n*, brûleur, bec, *m*. ~**ing**, *a*, brûlant, en feu; enflammé; ardent; cuisant. ¶ *n*, combustion; ignition; cuisson, cuite, *f*; (*smell*) brûlé, roussi, graillon, *m*.

burnish, *v.t*, (*metal, etc.*) brunir; (*paper, etc.*) satiner. ~**ing**, *n*, brunissage; satinage, *m*.

burnout, *n*, (*nuclear*) arrêt par épuisement, *m*.

burnt, *p.a*: ~ *almond*, praline, *f*. ~ *offering*, holocauste, *m*. ~ *Sienna*, terre de Sienne brûlée, *f*.

burnup, *n*, (*nuclear*) combustion, *f*.

burr, *n*, barbes, *f.pl*; (*speech*) grasseyement, *m*. ¶ (*speaking*) *v.i*, grasseyer.

burrow, *n*, terrier, clapier, *m*. ¶ *v.i*, terrer; se terrer; fouiller.

bursar, *n*, économe, *m*, dépensier,

ère. ~*'s office* & ~**ship**, *n*, économat, *m*.

burst, *n*, éclat, jet; (*light*) coup; (*speed*) emballement; (*eloquence*) mouvement; (*passion, etc.*) transport, élan, *m*. ¶ *v.t.ir*, faire éclater, [faire] crever; rompre; (*v.i.ir*) éclater; crever; se précipiter. ~**ing**, *n*, éclatement, *m*, crevaison, *f*.

bury, *v.t*, enterrer, ensevelir.

bus, *n*, autobus, bus, *m*.

bush, *n*, buisson, arbuste, *m*; (*scrub*) brousse; (*Mach.*) coquille, bague, *f*, manchon, *m*.

bushel, *n*, boisseau, *m*.

bushy, *a*, touffu, fourni; embroussaillé, buissonneux.

busily, *ad*, activement.

business, *n*, affaires, *f.pl*, commerce, négoce, *m*; affaire, entreprise, *f*; fonds [de commerce] *m*; qualité, *f*, métier, *m*; délibérations, questions [à délibérer] *f.pl*, ordre du jour; (*right*) droit; (*fuss*) aria, *m*. ~ *as usual during alterations*, la maison reste ouverte pendant les travaux. ~ *card*, bristol, *m*, carte d'adresse, *f*. ~ *day*, jour non férié, *m*. ~ *hours*, heures d'affaires, heures d'ouverture, *f.pl*. ~**like**, régulier; pratique, entendu. ~**man**, homme d' (*ou* dans les) affaires, *m*. ~ *premises*, locaux commerciaux, *m.pl*; immeuble commercial, *m*. ~ *quarter*, quartier commerçant, *m*. ~ *world*, monde des affaires, *m*.

buskin, *n*, brodequin; cothurne, *m*.

bust, *n*, buste, *m*; gorge, *f*, corsage, *m*. ~ *measurement*, [con]tour de poitrine, *m*.

bustard, *n*, outarde, *f*.

bustle, *n*, mouvement; remue-ménage, *m*; animation, *f*, tourbillon, *m*. ¶ *v.i*, se remuer.

busy, *a*, occupé, affairé, embesogné; industrieux; mouvementé; actif; empressé; diligent. ~ *bee*, abeille industrieuse, *f*. ~ *man*, *woman*, affairé, e. ~*body*, touche-à-tout, *m*, commère, *f*, tatillon, ne, nécessaire, *m*.

but, *c*, mais; que; or. ~ *for*, sans. ¶ *ad*. & *pr*, hormis, excepté, seulement; ne ... que. ¶ *n*, mais, *m*.

butcher, *n*, boucher, *m*. ~*'s shop*, boucherie, *f*. ¶ *v.t*, massacrer. ~**y**, *n*, carnage, *m*.

butler, *n*, sommelier; maître d'hôtel, *m*.

butt, (*cask*) tonneau, *m*; (*pl., behind target*) butte; (*cigarette*) mégot, *m*; (*rifle*) crosse, *f*; (*cue*) talon; (*pers.*) plastron, bouffon, *m*, cible, risée, *f*, souffre-douleur; (*ram, etc.*) coup de corne, coup de tête, *m*. ¶ *v.i.* & *t*, cosser; heurter de la tête; buter.

butter, *n*, beurre, *m*. ~ *dish*, beurrier, *m*. ~*milk*, lait de beurre, babeurre, *m*. ¶ *v.t*, beurrer. ~*ed toast*, rôties au beurre, *f.pl*, toast, *m*.

buttercup, *n*, bassinet, bouton d'or, *m*.

butterfly, *n*, papillon [diurne] *m*.

buttock, *n*, fesse, *f*; (*beef*) cimier, *m*.

button, *n*, bouton, *m*. ~*hole*, boutonnière, *f*. ~*hole stitch* (*Emb.*), point de languette, p. de feston, *m*. ~*hole* (detain), cueillir. ~*hook*, tire-bouton, *m*. ¶ *v.t*, boutonner. ~ *oneself up*, se b.

buttress, *n*, contrefort, éperon; (*flying*) arc-boutant, *m*. ¶ *v.t*, arc-bouter; soutenir.

buxom, *a*, opulent, plantureux, rondelet & de bonne mine. ~*ness*, *n*, opulence, *f*.

buy, *v.t.ir*, acheter, acquérir. ~ *back*, racheter. ~ *out*, désintéresser. ~ *up*, enlever, accaparer. ~*er*, *n*, acheteur, euse, acquéreur, preneur, *m*. ~*ing*, *n*, achat, *m*, acquisition, *f*.

buzz, *v.i*, bourdonner, ronfler, tinter.

buzzard, *n*, buse, *f*.

by, *pr*, par; à; sur; sous; en; près. ¶ *ad*, près, à part. ~ & ~, tantôt. ~ *the* ~, ~ *the way*, à propos, en passant.

bylaw, *n*, règlement, *m*.

by-election, *n*, élection de remplacement, *f*.

bygone, *a*, passé, ancien, d'autrefois.

bypass, *n*, route d'évitement; (*gas*) veilleuse, *f*; (*computers*) raccourci, *m*; (*Surg.*) pontage, *m*.

bypath, *n*, chemin écarté, sentier détourné, *m*.

by-product, *n*, sous-produit, *m*.

bystander, *n*, assistant, e, spectateur, trice, curieux, *m*.

byte, *n*, (*computers*) multiplet, *m*.

byway, *n*, chemin détourné, *m*.

byword, *n*, dicton, *m*; risée, fable, *f*.

C

C (*Mus.*) letter, ut, do, *m*. ~ *clef*, clef d'ut, *f*.

cab, *n*, taxi, fiacre, *m*, voiture [de place], *f*; (*locomotive*) abri, *m*. ~*man*, cocher, chauffeur, *m*. ~*stand*, station de taxis, *f*.

cabal, *n*, cabale, *f*.

cabaret [**show**], *n*, attractions, *f.pl*.

cabbage, *n*, chou, *m*. ~ *lettuce*, laitue pommée, *f*. ~ *tree*, palmiste, *m*.

cabin, *n*, cabine, chambre; cabane, case; guérite, *f*. ~ *boy*, mousse, *m*. ~ *passenger*, passager (ère) de cabine. ~ *trunk*, malle de paquebot, malle de cabine, *f*.

cabinet, *n*, cabinet, *m*; armoire, *f*, meuble, *m*. ~ *council*, Conseil des ministres, C. de Cabinet, *m*. ~*maker*, menuisier, ébéniste, *m*. ~*making* & ~*work*, menuiserie, ébénisterie, *f*. ~ *minister*, ministre d'État, *m*.

cable, *n*, câble, *m*. ~ *railway*, [chemin de fer] funiculaire, *m*. *feeder* ~, coaxial, *m*. ¶ (*Teleg.*) *v.t*, câbler.

cacao, *n*, cacao, *m*. ~ [*tree*], cacaoyer, cacaotier, *m*.

cachet, *n*, cachet, *m*.

cachou, *n*, cachou, *m*.

cackle, *n*, caquet, *m*. ¶ *v.i*, caqueter.

cactus, *n*, cactus, *m*.

cad, *n*, canaille, *f*, goujat, pleutre, mufle, *m*.

caddie (*golf*) *n*, cadet, te.

caddy, *n*, boîte [à thé] *f*.

cadence, *n*, cadence, *f*.

cadet, *n*, cadet; élève (*de l'école navale*), *m*.

cadge, *v.t*, écornifler. **cadger**, *n*, écornifleur, euse.

Cadiz, *n*, Cadix, *m*.

cafeteria, *n*, restaurant de libre service, *m*.

cage, *n*, cage; cabine; loge, *f*. ~ *bird*, oiseau de volière, *m*. ¶ *v.t*, encager.

cairn, *n*, montjoie, *f*.

Cairo, *n*, le Caire.

caisson, *n*, caisson; (*dock*) bateau-porte, *m*.

cajole, *v.t*, cajoler, amadouer. ~ry, *n*, cajolerie, *f*.

cake, *n*, gâteau; (*soap*) pain; (*oilseed*) tourteau, *m*. ¶ *v.i*, se cailler, faire croûte.

calabash, *n*, calebasse, *f*.

calamitous, *a*, calamiteux. **calamity**, *n*, calamité, *f*.

calcareous, *a*, calcaire.

calcine, *v.t*, calciner.

calcium, *n*, calcium, *m*.

calculate, *v.t*, calculer; (*v.i.*) compter. ~d to, propre à, de nature à. **calculating machine**, machine à calculer, *f*. **calculation** & **calculus** (*Med.*) *n*, calcul, *m*. **calculator**, *n*, (*small*) calculateur, *m*, (*large*) calculatrice, *f*.

caldron, *n*, chaudron, *m*.

calendar, *n*, calendrier; (*prisoners for trial*) rôle, *m*. ~ *year*, année civile, *f*.

calender, *n*, calandre, *f*. ¶ *v.t*, calandrer, cylindrer.

calf, *n*, veau; (*leg*) mollet, gras de la jambe, *m*. ~[*skin*], peau de veau, *f*, [cuir de] veau, *m*.

caliber, *n*, calibre, *m*. **calibrate**, *v.t*, calibrer.

calico, *n*, calicot, *m*.

California, *n*, la Californie. **Californian**, *a*, californien. ¶ *n*, Californien, ne.

caliper, *n*, calibre; (*pl.*) compas [de calibre] *m*. ¶ *v.t*, calibrer.

caliph, *n*, calife, *m*.

call, *n*, appel; rappel; *m*; demande; (*trumpet, bugle*) sonnerie; visite; communication; (*Relig.*) vocation; (*to a ship*) semonce; (*of a ship*) escale; relâche, *f*; (*Fin.*) appel [de fonds], versement; terme, *m*; option, faculté; (*cards*) invite, *f*. ~ *of the blood* (*fig.*), force du sang, *f*. ~ *to arms*, appel aux armes. ¶ *v.t*. & *i*, appeler; héler; rappeler; convoquer; faire venir; prendre; réveiller; qualifier; traiter de; nommer; surnommer; intituler; passer; s'arrêter; faire; (*ship*) faire escale; relâcher. ~ *back*, rappeler. ~ *for*, demander, réclamer; (*trumps*) inviter; exiger. ~ *off*, contremander, décommander; (*hounds*) rompre. ~ *out*, appeler, crier. ~ [*up*]*on*, sommer, invoquer. **caller**, *n*, visiteur, euse. **calling**, *n*, appel, *m*; convocation; vocation, profession, *f*, métier, *m*.

callosity & **callus**, *n*, callosité,

f, cal, durillon, *m*. **callous**, *a*, endurci, insensible; (*skin*) calleux.

callow, *a*, sans plumes. ~ *youth*, la verte jeunesse; jeune homme imberbe, blanc-bec, *m*.

calm, *a*, calme. ¶ *v.t*, calmer. ~ly, *ad*, tranquillement. ~[ness], *n*, calme, *m*, tranquillité, *f*.

calorie, *n*, calorie, *f*.

calumniate, *v.t*, calomnier. **calumny**, *n*, calomnie, *f*.

Calvary (*place*) *n*, Calvaire, *m*. **calvary** (*representation*) *n*, calvaire, *m*.

calve, *v.i*, vêler.

calyx, *n*, calice, *m*.

cam, *n*, came, *f*, excentrique, *m*.

camber, *n*, bombement, *m*, cambrure, *f*.

cambric, *n*, batiste, *f*.

came, *n*, plomb, *m*, (*pl.*) résille, *f*.

camel, *n*, chameau, *m*. ~ *driver*, chamelier, *m*.

camellia, *n*, camélia, *m*.

cameo, *n*, camée, *m*.

camera, *n*, appareil photographique, *m*. ~*man* (*cinema*) cadreur, *m*. ~ *obscura* (*Opt.*), chambre noire, c. obscure, *f*. *in* ~, à huis clos.

camisole, *n*, cache-corset, *m*.

camomile, *n*, camomille, *f*.

camouflage, *n*, camouflage, *m*. ¶ *v.t*, camoufler, maquiller.

camp, *n*, camp, *m*. ~ *bed*, lit de camp, *m*. ~ *stool*, [siège] pliant, *m*. ¶ *v.i*. & *t*, camper. ~ *out*, bivouaquer.

campaign, *n*, campagne, *f*. ~er, *n*, routier, troupier, *m*.

campanula, *n*, campanule, *f*.

camper, *n*, (*mobile home*) autocaravane, *f*.

camphor, *n*, camphre, *m*. ~ate, *v.t*, camphrer.

camping, *n*, camping, *m*. *to go* ~, faire le camping.

can, *n*, bidon, *m*; burette; boîte, *f*; pot, *m*. ~ *opener*, ouvre-boîtes, *m*. ¶ *v.t*, mettre en boîte(s), *m*. en conserve. *canned salmon*, saumon en boîte(s), *m*.

can, *v.aux.ir*, pouvoir; savoir.

Canada, *n*, le Canada. **Canadian**, *a*, canadien. ¶ *n*, Canadien, ne.

canal, *n*, canal, *m*. ~ize, *v.t*, canaliser.

canary, *n*, serin, e, canari, *m*. ~ *seed*, graine des canaris, *f*, millet des oiseaux, *m*. *the C*~

Islands, the Canaries, les [îles] Canaries, *f.pl.*

cancel, *n,* (*Typ.*) carton; (*Mus.*) bécarre, *m.* ¶ *v.t,* biffer, effacer; oblitérer; annuler, résilier, rompre; décommander.

cancer (*Med.*) *n,* cancer, *m.* ~ous, *a,* cancéreux.

candelabrum, *n,* candélabre, *m.*

candid†, *a,* sincère, franc, désintéressé.

candidacy, *n,* candidature, *f.* **candidate,** *n,* candidat, e, postulant, e, aspirant, e, prétendant, e.

candied peel, zeste confit, *m.*

candle, *n,* chandelle, bougie, *f;* cierge, *m.* ~ *grease,* suif, *m.* ~ *power,* puissance (*ou* intensité) lumineuse en bougies, *f. a 60 c.p. lamp,* une lampe de 60 bougies. ~*stick,* bougeoir; chandelier; flambeau, *m.* ¶ (*eggs*) *v.t,* mirer. **candling,** *n,* mirage, *m.*

candor, *n,* sincérité, franchise, *f.*

candy, *v.i,* se candir. ¶ *n,* bonbon, candi, *m.* ~ *shop,* confiserie, *f.*

cane, *n,* canne; badine; (*Sch.*) férule, *f;* jonc, *m.* ~ *sugar,* sucre de canne, *m.* ¶ *v.t,* donner de la férule à; (*chair*) canner.

canine, *a,* canin.

canister, *n,* boîte [métallique] *f.*

canker, *n,* (*lit. & fig.*) chancre, *m.* ~*worm,* ver rongeur, *m.* ¶ *v.t,* gangrener.

canned goods, conserves [en boîtes] *f.pl.*

cannibal, *n. & a,* cannibale, *m,* anthropophage, *m. & a.*

cannon, *n,* canon; (*Bil.*) carambolage, *m.* ~ *ball,* boulet, *m.* ~ *shot,* coup de canon, *m.* ~ade, *x,* cannonade, *f.* ¶ *v.t,* canonner.

canny, *a,* fin, sagace; avisé; rusé.

canoe, *n,* canoë, *m;* périssoire; (*dugout*) pirogue, *f.*

canon, *n,* (*Eccl. rule*) canon; (*pl, taste*) code; (*pers.*) chanoine, *m.* ~ *law,* droit canon, *m.* **canonicate, canonry,** *n,* canonicat, *m.* **canonize,** *v.t,* canoniser.

canopy, *n,* dais; baldaquin; ciel, *m;* voûte, calotte, *f,* dôme, *m;* (*Arch.*) marquise, *f.*

cant, *n,* argot; jargon, *m;* hypocrisie, *f;* (*slope*) devers, *m,* inclinaison, *f.* ¶ *v.t,* incliner.

cantaloupe, *n,* melon cantaloup, *m.*

cantankerous, *a,* revêche, hargneux. ~ *fellow,* mauvais coucheur, *m.*

cantata, *n,* cantate, *f.*

canteen, *n,* cantine, *f;* (*bottle*) bidon, *m.* ~ *keeper,* cantinier, ère.

canter, *n,* petit galop, *m;* (*pers.*) cafard, e, tartufe, *m.*

Canterbury bell, campanule à grandes fleurs, *f.*

canticle, *n,* cantique, *m.*

cantilever, *n,* encorbellement, *m.*

canto, *n,* chant, *m.* **cantor,** *n,* chantre, *m.*

canvas, *n,* canevas, *m,* toile; toile à voiles; voile, *f.* ~ *shoe with hempen sole,* espadrille, *f.*

canvass, *v.t,* débattre; solliciter; solliciter des suffrages; s. des commandes; faire (*the town* = la place). ~er, *n,* solliciteur, euse; placier, démarcheur, *m.*

canyon, cañon, *n,* canon, *m.*

cap, *n,* bonnet, chapeau, *m;* (*peaked*) casquette, *f,* képi, *m;* toque; calotte, *f;* culot, *m;* chape; coiffe, *f;* couvercle; chapiteau, bouchon; bout; (*bullet*) détonateur, *m,* capsule, amorce, *f.* ~ *& bells* (*Hist.*), marotte, *f.* ~ *case* (*Typ.*), haut de casse, *m.* ¶ *v.t,* coiffer; couronner.

capability, *n,* capacité, *f.* **capable,** *a,* capable; apte, susceptible. **capacious,** *a,* spacieux. **capacitate,** *v.t,* rendre capable; (*law*) habiliter. **capacity,** *n,* capacité, *f;* rendement, débit, *m;* qualité; habilité, *f.*

caparison, *v.t,* caparaçonner.

cape, *n,* (*Phys. Geog.*) cap, *m;* (*dress*) pèlerine, *f.* C~ *Colony,* la colonie du Cap. *the* C~ *of Good Hope,* le cap de Bonne-Espérance. C~ *Verde,* le cap Vert.

caper, *n,* cabriole, gambade, *f,* entrechat, *m;* (*Bot.*) câpre, *f.* ¶ *v.i,* cabrioler.

capillary, *a,* capillaire.

capital†, *a,* capital; admirable, fameux, parfait, chic; ¶ *n,* (*country, province*) [ville] capitale, *f;* (*county, department*) chef-lieu, *m;* (*letter*) [lettre] majuscule, [lettre] capitale, *f;* (*Arch.*) chapiteau, *m;* (*Fin.*) capital, *m,* capitaux, *m.pl;* fonds, *m.s. & pl,* mise [de fonds] *f;* (*brought in*) apport, *m.* C~ *& Labor,* le capital & le travail. ~ *expenditure,* immobilisations, *f.pl*, établissement, *m*. ~ **stock** & ~ **sum**, capital, *m*. ~ **value**, valeur en capital, *f*. ~**ist**, *n*, capitaliste, *m.f*; (*financial "whiz"*) fonceur, *m*. ~**ize**, *v.t*, capitaliser; immobiliser; écrire avec une majuscule.

capitulate, *v.i*, capituler.

capon, *n*, chapon, *m*.

caprice, *n*, caprice, *m*. **capricious**, *a*, capricieux.

capsicum, *n*, piment, *m*.

capsize, *v.t*, [faire] chavirer; (*v.i.*) chavirer, capoter, faire capot. *f*.

capstan, *n*, cabestan, *m*; (*lathe*) revolver, *m*, tourelle, *f*.

capsule, *n*, capsule, *f*.

captain, *n*, (*Mil., Naut., sport*) capitaine; (*Nav.*) capitaine de vaisseau, *m*. ~ **of merchant ship**, capitaine marchand.

caption, *n*, sous-titre, *m*; légende, *f*.

captious, *a*, captieux, difficultueux.

captivate, *v.t*, captiver. **captive**, *a*, captif. ¶ *n*, captif, ive. **captivity**, *n*, captivité, *f*. **capture**, *n*, capture, prise, *f*. ¶ *v.t*, capturer.

Capuchin friar, nun, capucin, e.

car, *n*, voiture, auto, *f*; wagon; char, chariot, *m*. ~ **park**, parking, *m*. **custom-built** ~, voiture hors serie, *f*. **dining** ~, wagon-restaurant, *m*. **racing** ~, voiture de course, *f*. **second-hand** ~, v. d'occasion, *f*.

caramel, *n*, caramel, *m*.

carapace, *n*, carapace, *f*.

carat, *n*, carat, *m*.

caravan, *n*, caravane; (*house on wheels*) roulotte, *f*. **caravanserai**, *n*, caravansérail, *m*.

caraway, *n*, carvi, *m*. ~ **seed**, graine de c., *f*.

carbide, *n*, carbure, *m*.

carbine, *n*, carabine, *f*, mousqueton, *m*.

carbolic acid, acide phénique, phénol, *m*.

carbon, *n*, (*Chem.*) carbone; (*Elec.*) charbon, *m*. ~ [*copy*], double, *m*. ~ **monoxide**, oxyde de carbone, *m*. ~ [*paper*] (duplicating), papier-carbone, *m*. **carbonate**, *n*, carbonate, *m*. **carbonic**, *a*, carbonique. **carboniferous**, *a*, carbonifère, houiller. **carbonize**, *v.t*, carboniser; (*v.i.*) [se] charbonner.

carboy, *n*, tourie, *f*.

carbuncle, *n*, (*jewel*) grenat cabochon; (*Med.*) charbon, anthrax, *m*.

carburetor, *n*, carburateur, *m*.

carcass, *n*, carcasse, *f*, cadavre, *m*; (*ship*) carcasse; (*building*) bâtisse, *f*, œuvre, *m*.

card, *n*, carte, *f*; (*loose index*) fiche, *f*; (*textiles*) peigne, *m*. ~**board**, carton, *m*. ~ **case**, porte-cartes, *m*. ~ **index** & ~ **index** [*cabinet*], fichier, *m*. ~ **sharper**, bonneteur, *m*. ~ **table**, table de jeu, *f*. ~ **trick**, tour de cartes, *m*. **punched** ~, carte perforée, *f*. (*car*) **registration** ~, carte grise, *f*. ¶ *v.t*, peigner.

cardigan [**jacket**], *n*, vareuse, *f*, gilet, *m*.

cardinal, *a*, cardinal. ¶ *n*, cardinal, *m*.

cardiogram, *n*, cardiogramme, *m*. **cardiographer**, *n*, cardiograph. *m*. **cardiologist**, *n*, cardiologue, *m*.

care, *n*, soin, *m*. oft. *pl*, attention; précaution; garde, *f*; souci, *m*; responsabilité; charge; tenue; conservation, *f*; maniement, *m*, manutention, gestion, *f*, gouvernement, *m*. **with due & proper** ~, en bon père de famille. ~ **of**, c/o, chez, aux [bons] soins de. ~**taker**, gardien, ne, portier. ère. ~**worn**, miné (*ou* rongé) par les soucis. **to take** ~ **of**, avoir soin de. ¶ *v.i*, se soucier, s'inquiéter.

careen, *v.t*, caréner.

career, *n*, carrière; profession; course, *f*. ¶ *v.i*, galoper.

careful, *a*, soigneux, attentif; ménager. ~**ness**, *n*, soin, *m*, attention, *f*. **careless**, *a*, insouciant; négligent. ~**ly**, *ad*, négligemment. ~**ness**, *n*, négligence, inattention, incurie, *f*, laisseraller, *m*.

caress, *n*, caresse, *f*; (*pl.*) mamours, *f.pl. only*. ¶ *v.t*, caresser.

caret, *n*, signe d'omission, renvoi, *m*.

cargo, *n*, cargaison, *f*, chargement, *m*, charge, *f*; marchandises, (*Insce.*) facultés, *f.pl*. ~ **boat, steamer**, cargo; navire, vapeur, de charge, *m*.

Caribbean Sea (the), la mer des Antilles.

caricature, *n*, caricature, charge, *f*. ¶ *v.t*, caricaturer, charger.

carload, *n*, chargement d'un wagon, *m*.

Carmelite, *n*, (*friar*) carme, *m*; (*nun*) carmélite, *f*.

carmine, *n*, carmin, *m*.

carnage, *n*, carnage, *m*.

carnal†, *a*, charnel.

carnation (*Bot.*) *n*, œillet [des fleuristes] *m*.

carnelian, *n*, cornaline, *f*.

carnival, *n*, carnaval, *m*.

carnivorous, *a*. & **carnivore**, *n*, carnassier, carnivore, *a*. & *m*.

carob [bean], *n*, caroube, *f*.

carol, *n*, chant, chanson, cantique, *m*. [*Christmas*] ~, noël, *m*. ¶ *v.i*, chanter; (*lark*) grisoller.

carousal, *n*, orgie, débauche, ripaille, *f*. **carouse**, *v.i*, faire [la] débauche.

carp (*fish*) *n*, carpe, *f*. ~ **at**, chicaner.

Carpathians (the), les Carpathes, *m.pl*.

carpenter, *n*, charpentier, menuisier, *m*. ¶ *v.t*, charpenter; (*v.i.*) menuiser. **carpentry**, *n*, charpenterie, *f*.

carpet, *n*, tapis, *m*. ~ *slippers*, pantoufles en tapisserie, *f.pl*. ~ *sweeper*, balai, *m*, (*ou* balayeuse, *f*.) mécanique. ¶ *v.t*, recouvrir d'un tapis; (*with flowers, etc.*) tapisser.

carriage, *n*, voiture, *f*; wagon; équipage; (*gun*) affût; (*Mach.*) chariot, *m*; démarche, allure, tenue, *f*; transport, port; prix du transport (*ou* de la voiture) *m*. ~ *entrance*, porte charretière, *f*. *baby* ~, voiture d'enfant, *f*.

carrier, *n*, porteur; messager, voiturier, transporteur, entrepreneur de transports (*ou* de roulage); (*Mach.*) chariot, *m*; porte-, *e.g*, *luggage* ~, porte-bagage, *m*. ~ *pigeon*, pigeon voyageur, *m. airplane* ~, porte-avions, *m*.

carrion, *n*, charogne, *f*.

carrot, *n*, carotte, *f*. ~*y hair*, des cheveux [rouge] carotte, *m.pl*.

carry (*Arith.*) *n*, retenue, *f*. ¶ *v.t*, porter; emporter; transporter; véhiculer; mener, conduire; charrier, voiturier; (*Arith.*) retenir; adopter, prendre; voter. ~ *away*, enlever, emporter, entraîner; emballer, enthousiasmer. ~ *forward* (*Bkkpg*) reporter. ~ *on*,

poursuivre, opérer. ~ *out*, exécuter, effectuer; suivre.

cart, *n*, charrette; voiture; carriole, *f*; tombereau, *m*. ~ *horse*, cheval de charrette, *m*. ~*load*, charretée, *f*; tombereau, *m*. ¶ *v.t*, charrier, charroyer, voiturer, camionner. ~*age*, *n*, charroi, roulage; camionnage; factage; prix du transport, *m*. ~*er*, *n*, charretier, voiturier, camionneur, *m*.

Carthusian [monk], *n*, chartreux, *m*. ~ *monastery*, chartreuse, *f*.

cartilage, *n*, cartilage, *m*.

carton, *n*, carton, *m*.

cartoon, *n*, carton; dessin, *m*; caricature, *f. animated* ~, dessin, *m*. ~*ist*, *n*, dessinateur, trice; caricaturiste, *m.f*; (*cinema*) animateur, trice, *m.f*.

cartouche, *n*, cartouche, *m*. **cartridge**, *n*, cartouche, *f*; (*cannon*) gargousse, *f*. ~ *belt*, ceinture cartouchière, *f*. ~ *pouch*, sac à cartouches, *m*, cartouchière, *f*.

carve, *v.t*, sculpter; tailler; (*meat*) découper. **carver** (*pers.*) *n*, sculpteur, *m*; découpeur, euse. **carving**, *n*, sculpture, *f*; découpage, *m*. ~ *knife*, couteau à découper, *m*. ~ *tool*, outil de sculpteur, *m*.

cascade, *n*, cascade, cascatelle, *f*.

case, *n*, cas; état, *m*; question, *f*; exemple, *m*; cause, affaire, *f*, procès, *m*; caisse, boîte; mallette, *f*; sac; étui; écrin, *m*; gaine, *f*; trousse; pochette, poche, cassette, *f*, nécessaire; fourreau; boîtier; portefeuille, *m*; douille; chemise; enveloppe; (*for firework*) cartouche; (*sausage*) peau; (*precision balance*) cage, *f*; (*piano*) coffre, *m*; (*Typ.*) casse, *f*. ~ *opener*, ciseau à déballer, *m*. *in any* ~ , en tout cas. ¶ *v.t*, encaisser, envelopper, [en]gainer; (*Min.*) cuveler.

caseharden, *v.t*, aciérer, cémenter. ~*ed* (*fig.*) *p.a*, bronzé, cuirassé.

casemate, *n*, casemate, *f*.

casement, *n*, châssis de fenêtre. ~ [window], fenêtre [ordinaire], croisée, *f*. ~ *stay*, entrebâilleur de fenêtre, *m*.

cash, *n*, espèces, *f.pl*, numéraire, argent, *m*, finances, *f.pl*; comptant, *m*; caisse, encaisse, *f*, fonds, *m.pl*. ~*book*, livre de caisse, *m*. ~ *box*, coffret à monnaie, *m*; caisse, *f*. ~ *discount*, escompte de caisse (*ou* au comptant) *m*. ~ *down* or *in* ~ & *for* ~, [au] comptant. ~ *in hand*, [en]caisse, fonds (*ou* espèces) en caisse. ~ *on delivery*, envoi contre remboursement, *m*. ~ *register*, caisse enregistreuse (*ou* contrôleuse). ~ *with order*, payable à la commande. ¶ *v.t.* encaisser; (*check*) toucher; escompter, payer. **~ier**, *n*, caissier, ère. ¶ *v.t.* destituer, casser.

cashmere, *n*, cachemire, *m*.

casing, *n*, enveloppe, *f*; bâti, dormant, *m*.

cask, *n*, tonneau, *m*, barrique, *f*, baril, fût, *m*, futaille, pièce, *f*.

casket, *n*, cassette, *f*, écrin; (*coffin*) cercueil, *m*.

Caspian Sea (the), la mer Caspienne.

casserole, *n*, casserole, *f*.

cassette, *n*, (*magnetic tape*) cassette, *f*.

cassia, *n*, casse, *f*. ~ *tree*, cassier, *m*.

cassock, *n*, soutane, *f*.

cast, *n*, jet, *m*, coulée; pièce moulée, *f*; coup de filet, *m*; addition; (*Theat.*) distribution, *f*. ~ *of features*, physionomie, *f*, facies, *m*. ~ *of mind*, tournure d'esprit, mentalité, *f*. ¶ *v.t.ir*, jeter, lancer; promener; fondre, couler, mouler; additionner; distribuer. *to* ~ *lots*, tirer au sort. ~ *iron*, fonte [de fer] *f*, fer de fonte, *m*; (*att.*, *fig.*) rigide. ~ *its skin*, se dépouiller. ~ *net*, épervier, *m*. ~ *off*, (*Typ.*) évaluer; (*Knit.*) faire une chaîne de mailles. ~*off clothing*, défroque, *f*. ~ *on* (*Knit.*), monter. ~ *out*, chasser, rejeter. ~ *steel*, acier coulé, *m*, fonte d'acier, *f* [*crucible*] ~ *steel*, acier fondu [au creuset], *m*. *to have a* ~ *in the eye*, loucher.

castanet, *n*, castagnette, *f*.

castaway, *n*, réprouvé, e; naufragé, e.

caste, *n*, caste, *f*.

castellated, *a*, crénelé.

castigate, *v.t.*, châtier. **castigation**, *n*, châtiment, *m*.

casting, *n*, jet, *m*; coulée, fonte; pièce [coulée], *f*, moulage, coulé, *m*; pêche au lancer, *f*. ~ *off*, (*Typ.*) évaluation, *f*; (*Knit.*) chaîne de mailles, *f*. ~ *on* (*Knit.*), montage des mailles, *m*. ~ *rod*, canne à lancer, *f*. *to give*

the ~ *vote*, départager les voix.

castle, *n*, château, *m*; (*chess*) tour, *f*. ¶ (*chess*) *v.i.* roquer.

castor, *n*, (*bottle*) saupoudroir, *m*; (*roller*) roulette, *f*, galet [pivotant] *m*; (*beaver*) castor, *m*. **castor oil**, huile de ricin, *f*. **castor oil plant**, ricin, *m*.

castrate, *v.t.* châtrer. **castration**, *n*, castration, *f*.

casual†, *a*, casuel, accidentel, fortuit; sans cérémonie; (*remark*) en passant. ¶ *n*, indigent(e) de passage. **~ty**, *n*, sinistre, *m*; (*pers.*) victime; (*Mil.*) perte, *f*.

casuistry, *n*, casuistique, *f*.

cat, *n*, chat, te. ~ *burglar*, cambrioleur chat, *m*. ~*call*, sifflet, *m*. ~*calling*, sifflerie, aubade, *f*. ~'*s cradle*, jeu de la scie, *m*. ~'*s eye* (jewel), oeil-de-chat, *m*. ~'*s paw* (fig.), patte du chat, *f*. *to be someone's* ~'*s paw*, tirer les marrons du feu pour quelqu'un.

cataclysm, *n*, cataclysme, *m*.

catacomb, *n*, catacombe, *f*.

catafalque, *n*, catafalque, *m*.

catalog, *n*, catalogue, *m*. ¶ *v.t.* cataloguer.

catapult, *n*, (*Hist.* & *Avn.*) catapulte; (*boy's*) fronde, *f*. ¶ *v.t.* & *abs*, fronder; (*Avn.*) lancer.

cataract (*falls* & *Med.*) *n*, cataracte, *f*.

catarrh, *n*, catarrhe, *m*.

catastrophe, *n*, catastrophe, *f*.

catch, *n*, prise; (*fish*) prise, pêche, *f*, coup de filet, jet, *m*; (*trick*) attrape, *f*, leurre; (*Mech.*) arrêt, mentonnet, cran; (*window*) loqueteau, *m*. ~ *phrase*, scie, *f*. ~*word*, rengaine, scie, *f*. ¶ *v.t.* & *i. ir*, attraper; saisir; accrocher; s'engager; gagner; capturer; capter; happer; prendre; se p.; surprendre; frapper. ~ *up with*, rattraper. ~*[as~~]can*, lutte libre, *f*. ~ *fire*, prendre feu, s'enflammer; (*Cook.*) graillonner. ~ *on*, prendre; comprendre. ~*er*, *n*, preneur, chasseur, *m*. ~*ing*, *a*, contagieux; séduisant.

catechism, *n*, catéchisme, *m*. **catechize**, *v.t.* catéchiser.

categorical†, *a*, catégorique. **category**, *n*, catégorie, *f*.

cater, *v.i.* donner à manger. ~ *for*, pourvoir à; s'adresser à, viser. **caterer**, *n*, restaurateur, trice, cafetier, ère, traiteur; pourvoyeur, *m*.

caterpillar, n, chenille, f; tracteur, m.

caterwaul, v.i, miauler. **~ing,** n, miaulement, m, musique de chats, f.

catgut, n, corde à boyau, f.

cathead, n, bossoir, m.

cathedral, n, cathédrale, f.

catherine wheel, soleil, m. to turn ~ ~s, faire la roue.

cathode, n, cathode, f.

catholic, a. & n, catholique, a. & m.f. **~ism,** n, catholicisme, m.

cattle, n, bétail, m, bestiaux, m.pl. ~ market, marché aux bestiaux, m. ~show, concours (ou comice) agricole, m.

catwalk, n, (Theat. & cinema) passerelle, f.

Caucasian, a, caucasien. ¶ n, Caucasien, ne. the Caucasus, le Caucase.

caucus, n, cabale, f.

cauldron, n, chaudron, m.

cauliflower, n, chou-fleur, m.

caulk, v.t, calfater.

causative, a, occasionnel; (Gram.) causal. **cause,** n, cause, raison, f, sujet, motif; cas, m. ¶ v.t, causer, occasionner, provoquer, entraîner; faire, e.g. to ~ to vary, faire varier.

causeway, n, chaussée, levée, f.

caustic, a. & n, caustique, a. & m. **canterize,** v.t, cautériser. **cautery,** n, cautère, m.

caution, n, prudence, précaution, f; avertissement, m. ¶ v.t, prémunir, précautionner, avertir. **cautious,** a, prudent, réservé, retenu, sur ses gardes, en garde. **~ly,** ad, avec circonspection. **~ness,** n, prudence, f.

cavalcade, n, cavalcade, f.

cavalier†, a, cavalier. ¶ n, cavalier, m.

cavalry, n, cavalerie, f.

cave, n, caverne, f, antre, m. ~ dweller, troglodyte, m. ~ in, v.i, s'effondrer, ébouler; céder.

cavern, n, caverne, f, souterrain, m. **~ous,** a, caverneux.

caviar, n, caviar, m.

cavil, n, chicane, argutie, f. ¶ v.i, chicaner, ergoter.

cavity, n, cavité, f, creux, m.

caw, v.i, croasser.

Cayenne pepper, poivre de Cayenne, m.

cease, v.i. & t, cesser. without ~, sans cesse. **~less,** a, incessant. **~lessness,** n, continuité, f.

cedar, n, cèdre, m. ~ of Lebanon, cèdre du Liban.

cede, v.t, céder.

ceil, v.t, plafonner. **~ing,** n, plafond, m.

celebrate, v.t. & i, célébrer; solenniser; fêter. **~d,** p.a, célèbre, fameux, renommé. **celebrity,** n, célébrité; illustration, f.

celery, n, céleri, m.

celestial, a, céleste.

celibacy, n, célibat, m. **celibate,** n, célibataire, m.f.

cell, n, cellule, f; cachot, m; pile électrique, f. ~ jar, bac d'éléments, m.

cellar, n, cave, f, caveau, m. ¶ v.t, encaver. **~er,** n, cellérier, m.

cellist, n, violoncelliste, m. [°] **cello,** n, basse, f, violoncelle, m.

cellular, a, cellulaire. **celluloid,** n, celluloïd, m. **cellulose,** n, cellulose, f.

Celt, n, Celte, m.f. **Celtic,** a. & (language) n, celtique, a. & m.

cement, n, ciment, m. ¶ v.t, cimenter; (metal) cémenter. reinforced ~, ciment armé, m.

cemetery, n, cimetière, m.

cenotaph, n, cénotaphe, m.

cense, v.t, encenser. **censer,** n, encensoir, m.

censor, n, censeur, m. **~ious,** a, critique. **~ship & [vote of] censure,** n, & [board of] censors, censure, f. **censure,** v.t, censurer.

census, n, recensement, dénombrement, m.

cent, n, (1/100 of a dollar) sou, m. without a ~, sans un sou.

centaur, n, centaure, m.

centenarian, n, centenaire, m.f. **centenary,** n, centenaire, m.

centigrade, a, centigrade. (See note in French-English section.)

centipede, n, scolopendre, f.

center, n, centre, milieu; noyau; (Arch.) cintre, m; (lathe) pointe, f. ¶ v.t, centrer; (fig.) concentrer. **central,** a, central. C~ America, l'Amérique Centrale, f. ~ heating, chauffage central, m. **~ize,** v.t, centraliser; canaliser. **centrifugal,** a, centrifuge. **centripetal,** a, centripète.

century, n, siècle, m.

ceramics, n, céramique, f.

cereal, a. & n, céréale, a.f. & f.

ceremonial, n, cérémonial, m.

¶ *a*, de cérémonie. ceremonious†, *a*, cérémonieux, façonnier. ceremony, *n*, cérémonie; façon, *f*. oft. pl.

certain†, *a*, certain. ~ty, *n*, certitude, *f*. for a ~, à coup sûr.

certificate, *n*, certificat; diplôme; brevet; acte, *m*; attestation; déclaration, *f*; extrait; titre, *m*. ~d, *p.a*, diplômé. certify, *v.t*, certifier; viser; attester; déclarer.

certitude, *n*, certitude, assurance, *f*.

cessation, *n*, arrêt, *m*, suspension, *f*.

cesspool, *n*, fosse [d'aisances] *f*; cloaque, *m*.

Ceylon, *n*, Ceylan, *m*.

chafe, *v.t*, frictionner; écorcher; (*v.i*.) s'écorcher; s'irriter.

chaff, *n*, balle; glume; menue paille, *f*; badinage, *m*. ¶ *v.t*, plaisanter, gouailler, berner.

chaffinch, *n*, pinson, *m*.

chafing dish, chauffe-plats, *m*,

chagrin, *n*, chagrin, *m*. ¶ *v.t*, chagriner.

chain, *n*, chaîne; chaînette, *f*. ~ bridge, pont suspendu à chaînes, *m*. ~ stitch, point de chaînette, *m*. ~ store, magasin à succursales multiples, *m*. ¶ ~ & ~ up, *v.t*, enchaîner.

chair, *n*, chaise; (*Univ*.) chaire, *f*; (at meeting) fauteuil [de la présidence], *m*.

chairman, *n*, président, e. ~ship, *n*, présidence, *f*.

chalcedony, *n*, calcédoine, *f*.

chalice, *n*, calice, *m*, coupe, *f*.

chalk, *n*, craie, *f*; (Bil.) blanc, *m*. ~ pit, carrière de craie, *f*. French ~, talc, *m*. ¶ *v.t*, marquer à la craie. ~y, *a*, crayeux.

challenge, *n*, défi, cartel, *m*, provocation, *f*; (auditing) sondage; (Mil.) qui-vive; (sport) challenge, *m*. ~ cup, coupe challenge, *f*; challenge, *m*. ~ match, match défi, *m*. ¶ *v.t*, défier, provoquer, contester; récuser; incriminer.

chamber, *n*, chambre, *f*; (pl.) cabinet, *m*, étude, *f*. ~maid, femme de chambre, *f*. ~ music, musique de chambre, *f*. ~ [pot], vase de nuit, *m*. air ~, chambre à air, *f*.

chameleon, *n*, caméléon, *m*.

chamois, *n*, chamois, *m*. ~

[leather], peau de chamois, *f*, chamois, *m*.

champ, *v.t*, ronger, mâcher.

champagne, *n*, champagne, vin de Champagne, *m*. ~ glass, coupe à c., *f*.

champion, *n*, champion, *m*. ¶ *v.t*, défendre, protéger. ~ship, *n*, championnat, *m*.

chance, *a*, de hasard; de fortune; d'occasion, fortuit, aléatoire. ¶ *n*, chance; fortune, *f*; hasard, aléa, *m*. to ~ it, risquer le paquet, brusquer l'aventure.

chancel, *n*, chœur, *m*.

chancellery, *n*, chancellerie, *f*. chancellor, *n*, chancelier, *m*.

chancre, *n*, chancre, *m*.

chandelier, *n*, lustre, *m*.

chandler, *n*, chandelier, *m*; épicier, ère.

change, *n*, changement; mouvement, *m*; altération; mutation; variation, *f*; revirement, *m*; saute; vicissitude; (money) monnaie, *f*, appoint, *m*; (exchange) bourse, *f*. at ~ (barometer), au variable. make or give ~, faire de la monnaie. ~ of clothes, vêtements de rechange, *m.pl*. ¶ *v.t*. & *i*, changer; c. de; se c., convertir; altérer; sauter. ~ here for . . ., on change de train pour . . . ~ one's mind, one's linen, changer d'avis, de linge. ~ the subject, quitter le sujet, rompre les chiens. ~able, *a*, changeant; mobile; variable, inconstant.

channel, *n*, chenal, *m*, passe, *f*; canal, *m*, rigole; manche; cannelure; (fig.) voie, entremise; (television) chaîne, *f*. the [English] C~, la Manche. the C~ Islands, les îles [Anglo-]Normandes, *f.pl*. ¶ *v.t*, raviner, canneler. channeling, *n*, cannelure, *f*.

chant, *n*, chant, *m*. ¶ *v.i*. & *t*, chanter, psalmodier. chanty, *n*, chanson [de bord] *f*.

chaos, *n*, chaos, *m*. chaotic, *a*, chaotique.

chap, *n*, garçon; gaillard, *m*; (pl.) (on the skin) crevasses, gerçures, *f.pl*; (animal) babines, bajoues; (vice) mâchoires, *f.pl*. ¶ *v.t*. & *i*, crevasser, gercer, se gercer.

chapel, *n*, chapelle, *f*. ~ of ease, [église] succursale, *f*.

chaperon, *n*, chaperon, *m*. ¶ *v.t*, chaperonner.

chaplain, n, aumônier; chapelain, m.

chaplet, n, guirlande, f; (beads) chapelet, m.

chapter, n, chapitre, m; (fig.) page; série, f.

char (fish) n, omble[-chevalier], ombre-chevalier, m. ¶ v.t, carboniser; (v.i.) [se] charbonner.

character, n, caractère, m; nature, allure; réputation; cote, f; rôle; personnage; certificat, m. **characteristic,** a, caractéristique. ¶ n, caractéristique, f, caractère propre, m; (pl, of map) légende, f. **characterize,** v.t, caractériser.

charade, n, charade, f.

charcoal, n, charbon [de bois] m. ~ burner (pers.), charbonnier, m. ~ drawing, [dessin au] fusain, m. ~ [pencil], fusain, charbon à dessin, m.

charge, n, charge, f; soin, m, garde; accusation, inculpation, f; privilège, m; affectation; assignation; imputation, f; (bishop's) mandement; prix, m, taxe, f, frais, m.pl, dépense; redevance, f. ~ account, compte dans un magasin. ¶ v.t, charger; foncer sur; demander; prendre; mettre à [la] charge; taxer; percevoir; imputer; inculper; affecter, appliquer; accuser. ~able, a, à la charge; imputable; affectable; applicable.

charger (horse) n, cheval de bataille; (Poet.) coursier, m.

charily, ad, prudemment; chichement.

chariot, n, char, m.

charitable†, a, charitable, bienfaisant. **charity,** n, charité; bienfaisance, assistance, f, œuvres [pies] f.pl, aumône, l'aumône, f.

charlatan, n, charlatan, banquiste, m.

charm, n, charme, enchantement, agrément, m; (pl.) appas, attraits, m.pl; (trinket) breloque, amulette; mascotte, f, fétiche, m. ¶ v.t, charmer, enchanter. ~er, n, charmeur, euse, enchanteur, teresse.

charnel house, charnier, ossuaire, m.

chart, n, carte, f; graphique, diagramme, m. ¶ v.t, porter sur la carte, le graphique, etc.

charter, n, charte, f. ¶ v.t, [af]-fréter, prendre à fret; privilégier.

~er, n, affréteur, m. ~ing, n, affrètement, m.

chary, a, prudent; avare, chiche, sobre.

chase, n, chasse, poursuite; (gun) volée, f; (Typ.) châssis, m. ¶ v.t, chasser, poursuivre; (hawking) voler; (metals) ciseler; (screws) peigner. **chaser** (Nav.) n, chasseur, m.

chasm, n, abîme, gouffre, m.

chassé, n, chassé, m. ¶ v.t, chasser.

chassis, n, châssis, m.

chaste†, a, chaste, pudique.

chasten & chastise, v.t, châtier. **chastisement,** n, châtiment, m.

chastity, n, chasteté, pudicité, f.

chasuble, n, chasuble, f.

chat, n, causerie, causette, f. ¶ v.i, causer, deviser.

chattel, n, chose, f; (pl.) biens, effets, m.pl.

chatter, n, babil, m, jaserie, f. ¶ v.i, babiller, jaser; jacasser; (teeth) claquer; (tool) brouter. ~box, moulin à paroles, m, babillard, e.

chauffeur, n, chauffeur, m.

cheap, a, (article, etc.) [à] bon marché; (ticket, etc.) à prix réduit; (price) bas. ~ edition, édition à bon marché, f. ~er, a, [à] meilleur marché, moins cher. ~[ly], ad, à bon marché, à peu de frais. ~ness, n, bon marché, m, vileté, f.

cheat (pers.) n, fourbe, m, f; tricheur, euse. ¶ v.i. & i, tromper; frauder; friponner, tricher, filouter. ~[ing], n, fourberie; tromperie; tricherie, f.

check, n, échec, m; bride, f, frein; contrôle, pointage; chèque bancaire; bulletin; (design) dessin à carreaux, m; (fabric) étoffe à carreaux, é. en damier; (restaurant) addition, f; (att.) de contrôle, contradictoire, témoin. ~book, carnet de chèques, m. ~erboard, damier, m. ¶ v.t, brider, enrayer, modérer; contrôler, vérifier; pointer. ¶ (chess) i, échec! ~mate, n, échec & mat, m; (v.t.) mater, faire [échec &] mat; (fig.) faire échec à.

Cheddar [cheese], n, chester, m.

cheek, n, joue; impudence, f, front, toupet, sans-gêne, m. ~bone, pommette, f. ~y, a, impudent, hardi, effronté.

cheep, v.i, piailler, piauler.

cheer, *n*, (*food*) chère; consolation, *f*; applaudissement, vivat, hourra, bravo, *m*. ¶ *v.t*, réjouir, égayer, rassurer, consoler; applaudir. ~ *up*, ragaillardir. ~ *up!* [du] courage! ~fult, *a*, gai, joyeux, riant, allègre. ~fulness, *n*, gaieté, allégresse, *f*. ~less, *a*, triste, morne.

cheese, *n*, fromage, *m*. ~ *knife*, couteau à dessert, *m*.

cheetah, *n*, guépard, *m*.

chemical†, *a*, chimique. ¶ *n*, produit chimique, *m*.

chemise, *n*, chemise de jour, *f*.

chemist, *n*, chimiste, *m,f*. ~ry, *n*, chimie, *f*.

cherish, *v.t*, chérir, bercer, caresser, nourrir, choyer.

cherry, *n*, cerise, *f*. ~ *orchard*, cerisaie, *f*. ~red, *a*. & *n*, cerise, *a*. & *m*. ~ *stone*, noyau de cerise, *m*. ~ [*tree*], cerisier; (*wild*) merisier, *m*.

cherub, *n*, chérubin, *m*.

chervil, *n*, cerfeuil, *m*.

chess, *n*, échecs, *m.pl*. ~board, échiquier, *m*. ~men, pièces, *f.pl*, échecs, *m.pl*.

chest, *n*, (*Anat.*)poitrine, *f*; (*box*) coffre, *m*, caisse, boîte, *f*; bahut, *m*. ~ *measurement*, grosseur de poitrine, *f*. ~ *of drawers*, commode, *f*.

chesterfield, *n*, (*overcoat*) pardessus chesterfield; (*couch*) canapé-divan, *m*.

chestnut, *n*, châtaigne, *f*, marron, *m*. ~-brown, châtain. ~ [*tree*], châtaignier, marronnier, *m*.

cheval dressing table, coiffeuse psyché, *f*. **cheval glass**, psyché, *f*.

chew, *v.t*. & *i*, mâcher; (*tobacco*) chiquer; (*fig.*) remâcher. ~ *the cud*, ruminer. ~ing, *n*, mastication, *f*. ~ *gum*, gomme à mâcher, *f*.

chiaroscuro, *n*, clair-obscur, *m*.

chicane, *v.t*. & *i*, chicaner. ~ry, *n*, chicane[rie] *f*.

chick, *n*, poussin, poulet, *m*. **chick-pea**, *n*, pois chiche, *m*. **chicken**, *n*, poulet, te. ~ *heart* (*pers.*) poule mouillée, *f*, poltron, ne. ~-hearted, poltron. ~ *pox*, varicelle, *f*.

chickweed, *n*, mouron [des oiseaux] *m*, morgeline, *f*.

chicory, *n*, chicorée; endive, *f*.

chide, *v.t*. & *i.ir*, gronder.

chief, *a*, premier, principal; en chef. ~ *attraction*, clou de la fête, *m*. *to be* ~ *mourner*, conduire (*ou* mener) le deuil. ¶ *n*, chef; supérieur, *m*. ~ly, *ad*, principalement, surtout. **chieftain**, *n*, chef, *m*.

chiffon, *n*, chiffon, *m*. **chiffonier**, *n*, chiffonnier, *m*.

chilblain, *n*, engelure, *f*.

child, *n*, enfant, *m,f. from a* ~, dès l'enfance. *with* ~, enceinte. ~bed, couches, *f.pl*. ~birth, travail [d'enfant], accouchement, *m*. ~'s play, un jeu d'enfant, jeu d'e., *m*. ~hood, *n*, enfance, *f*. ~ish, *a*, enfantin; puéril. ~ishly, *ad*, puérilement. ~ishness, *n*, enfantillage, *m*, puérilité, *f*. ~less, *a*, sans enfant. ~like, *a*, comme un enfant, en enfant. **children**, *n.pl*, enfants, *m.pl*.

Chile, *n*, le Chili. **Chilean**, -lian, *a*, chilien. ¶ *n*, Chilien, ne.

chill, *a*, froid, glacé. ¶ *n*, froid, frisson, aigre, *m*, fraîcheur, *f*; coup d'air, c. de froid; *m*; (*fig., of age*) glaces, *f.pl*. *to take the* ~ *off* (*water*) faire dégourdir; (*wine*) chambrer. ¶ *v.t*, refroidir, glacer, transir, morfondre. **chilliness**, *n*, froideur, *f*, froid, *m*. **chilly**, *a*, froid; frisquet; (*pers.*) frileux.

chime[s], *n*.[*pl*.], carillon, *m*. ¶ *v.i*, carillonner. ~ *in*, placer son mot. *chiming clock*, pendule à carillon, *f*.

chimera, *n*, chimère, *f*. **chimerical**, *a*, chimérique.

chimney, *n*. & ~ *piece*, cheminée, *f*. ~ *corner*, coin du feu, *m*. ~ *pot*, cheminée, *f*. ~ *sweep[er]*, ramoneur, *m*.

chimpanzee, *n*, chimpanzé, *m*.

chin, *n*, menton, *m*. ~ *strap*, jugulaire, *f*.

china & ~ware, *n*, porcelaine, faïence [fine] *f*. ~ *cabinet*, vitrine, armoire vitrée, *f*. ~ *clay*, terre à porcelaine, *f*, kaolin, *m*. ~ *manufacturer* & ~ *dealer*, porcelainier, ère. ~ *shop*, magasin de porcelaines, *m*.

China (*Geog.*) *n*, la Chine. ~ aster, reinemarguerite, *f*.

chine, *n*, échine; (*Cook.*) échinée, *f*.

Chinese, *a*, chinois. ~ *curio*, chinoiserie, *f*. ~ *lantern*, lanterne vénitienne, *f*, lampion [en papier] *m*. ~ *puzzle* (*fig.*), casse-tête chinois, *m.* ¶ *n*, (*language*) chinois, *m*; (*pers.*) Chinois, e.

chink, *n*, lézarde, fente, crevasse, *f.* ¶ *v.t*, fendiller.

chintz, *n*, perse, *f.*

chip, *n*, copeau, éclat, *m*, écaille, écornure, *f*; (*computers*) micro-plaquette, pastille, "puce," *f.* ~ *off the old block*, fils de son père, *m.* ¶ *v.t*, tailler par éclats; buriner; écorner; ébrécher; (*v.i.*) s'écorner.

chipmunk, *n*, tamia, *m.*

chiropodist, *n*, pedicure, *m.f.* **chiropody,** *n*, soin des pieds, *m.*

chiropractic, *n*, chiropraxie, *f.* **chiropractor,** *n*, chiropracteur, *m*, chiropracticien, ne.

chirp, *n*, pépiement, guilleri; (*insect*) cri, cricri, *m.* ¶ *v.i*, pépier; crier.

chisel, *n*, ciseau, burin, *m.* ¶ *v.t*, ciseler, buriner.

chit, *n*, marmot, te; [petit] bout, *m.* ~ *of a girl*, petite fille, *f.*

chitchat, *n*, causerie, *f*; commérage, *m.*

chivalrous, *a*, chevaleresque. **chivalry,** *n*, chevalerie, *f.*

chive, *n*, cive[tte], ciboulette, *f.*

chivy, *v.t*, chasser.

chlorate, *n*, chlorate, *m.* **chloride,** *n*, chlorure, *m.* ~ *of lime*, c. de chaux. **chlorinate,** *v.t*, javelliser. **chlorine,** *n*, chlore, *m.* **chloroform,** *n*, chloroforme, *m.* ¶ *v.t*, chloroformer.

chocolate, *n*, chocolat, *m*; (*pl.*) bonbons au c., *m.pl.* ~ *box*, bonbonnière, *f.* ~ *cream*, crème chocolatée, *f.* ~ *creams*, chocolats fourrés à la crème, *m.pl.* ~ *éclair*, éclair au chocolat, *m.* ~ *manufacturer* or *seller*, chocolatier, ère. ~ *pot*, chocolatière, *f.*

choice, *a*, choisi, de [grand] choix; fin; recherché. ¶ *n*, choix, *m*; élite, fleur, *f.* ~**ness,** *n*, excellence, *f.*

choir, *n*, chœur, *m.* ~ *boy*, enfant de chœur, *m.* ~ *master*, maître de chapelle, *m.*

choke, *v.t*, suffoquer, étouffer, étrangler; engorger, bourrer. ¶ *n*, (*auto*), obturateur, *m.*

cholera, *n*, choléra, *m.*

choose, *v.t.ir*, choisir; élire; (*v.i.ir.*) opter.

chop, *n*, coup, *m*; côtelette, *f*; (*pl.*) babines, bajoues, *f.pl.* ¶ *v.t*, (*meat*) hacher; (*firewood*) débiter. ~ *off*, couper, trancher. **chopper,** *n*, couperet, *m.* **chopping block,** hachoir, billot, *m.* **chopping board,** hachoir, *m.* **choppy** (*sea*) *a*, clapoteuse.

chopstick, *n*, bâtonnet, *m.*

choral, *a*, choral. ~ *society*, [société] chorale, *f*, orphéon, *m.*

chord, *n*, corde, *f*; (*Mus.*) accord, *m.*

chore, *n*, besogne, *f.*

choreography, *n*, chorégraphie, *f.*

chorister, *n*, choriste, *m.f*; enfant de chœur, *m.* **chorus,** *n*, chœur; refrain en c.; concert, *m.* ~ *singer* (opera), choriste, *m.f.* *to* [*repeat in*] ~, faire chorus. *to join in the* ~, faire chœur au refrain.

Christ, *n*, le Christ. **christen,** *v.t*, baptiser. **Christendom,** *n*, chrétienté, *f.* **christening,** *n*, baptême, *m.* **Christian,** *a*, chrétien, ~ *name*, nom de baptême, petit nom, prénom, *m.* ~ *Science*, le culte des scientistes chrétiens. ¶ *n*, chrétien, ne. **Christianity,** *n*, christianisme, *m.* **christianize,** *v.t*, christianiser. **christianly,** *ad*, chrétiennement.

Christmas & ~tide (*abb.* Xmas) *n*, Noël, *m.* *at* ~, à la [fête de] Noël, à Noël. ~ *present. In Fr.*, *presents are given on or about Jan. 1 and called* étrennes, *f.pl.* *a* ~ *present* (to child), le petit Noël. ~ *eve*, nuit de Noël, *f.* ~ *pudding*, pudding de Noël, plum-pudding, *m.*

chromate, *n*, chromate, *m.*

chromatic, *a*, chromatique.

chrome, *n*, chrome, *m*; (*att., steel, leather*) chromé; (*yellow*) de chrome. **chromium,** *n*, chrome, *m*; (*att., steel*) chromé. ~**-plated,** chromé.

chronic, *a*, chronique.

chronicle, *n*, chronique, *f.* *C~s* (*Bible*) *pl*, Paralipomènes, *m.pl.* ¶ *v.t*, enregistrer, consigner. **chronicler,** *n*, chroniqueur, *m.*

chronological†, *a*, chronologique. **chronology,** *n*, chronologie, *f.*

chronometer, *n*, chronomètre, *m.*

chrysalis, *n*, chrysalide, *f.*

chrysanthemum, *n,* chrysan-thème, *m.*

chub (*fish*) *n,* chabot, meunier, *m.*

chubby, *a,* joufflu, potelé.

chuck (*lathe*) *n,* mandrin, pla-teau, *m.* ¶ (*throw*), *v.t,* flanquer. ~ *out,* flanquer à la porte. ~ *under the chin,* relever le men-ton à.

chuckle, *v.i,* glousser, rire sous cape.

chum, *n,* camarade, *m,f,* copain, *m.*

chump, *n,* bûche, *f;* lourdaud, *m.*

chunk, *n,* quignon, chanteau, *m.*

church, *n,* église, *f;* temple, *m.* *the* C~ *of England,* l'Église anglicane. ~ *service,* office divin, *m.* ~*warden,* marguillier, *m.* ~*yard,* cour de l'église, *f;* jardin de l'église; champ du repos, cimetière, *m;* (*public square sur-rounding a church*) place, *f, e.g,* la Place de la Madeleine.

churl, *n,* manant, bourru, rustre, *m.* ~**ish,** *a,* bourru, aigre.

churn, *n,* baratte, *f.* ~ *dash[er],* batte à beurre, *f;* babeurre, *m.* ¶ *v.t,* baratter, battre.

chute, *n,* glissière, *f. garbage* ~, vide-ordures, *m.*

cider, *n,* cidre, *m.*

cigar, *n,* cigare, *m.* ~ *case,* porte-cigares, *m.* ~ *cutter,* coupe-ci-gares, *m.* ~ *holder,* porte-cigare, fume-cigare, *m.*

cigarette, *n,* cigarette, *f.* ~ *box,* coffret à c~s, *m.* ~ *case,* étui à c~s, *m.* ~ *holder,* porte-ciga-rette, fume-cigarette, *m.*

cinch, *n,* sangle, *f.* ¶ *v.t,* sangler.

cinder[s], *n.[pl.],* escarbille[s], *f.[pl.],* fraisil, *m,* braise, *f;* scorie[s], *f.[pl.];* cendrée, *f. burnt to a* ~ (*meat*), en charbon. ~ *sifter,* tamis à escarbilles, *m.* ~ *track,* piste en cendrée, *f.*

Cinderella, *n,* Cendrillon, *f.*

cinema, *n,* cinéma, cinémato-graphe, *m.*

cinerary, *a,* cinéraire.

Cingalese, *a,* cingalais. ¶ *n,* Cingalais, e.

cinnabar, *n,* cinabre, *m.*

cinnamon, *n,* cannelle, *f.*

cipher†, *n,* chiffre; zéro, *m;* nullité, *f,* comparse, *m. word in* ~, mot en chiffre, *m.* ¶ *v.t. & i,* chiffrer.

circle, *n,* cercle; milieu, *m.* ¶ *v.t,* ceindre, cerner. **circlet,** *n,* cou-ronne, *f.* **circuit,** *n,* circuit, tour,

m; tournée, *f.* ~**ous,** *a,* détourné. **circular†,** *a. & n,* circulaire, *a. & f.* **circulate,** *v.t,* faire circuler, ré-pandre; (*v.i.*) circuler, rouler. **circulating,** *a,* circulant; roulant. ~ *decimal,* fraction périodique, *f.* ~ *library,* bibliothèque circu-lante, *f.* **circulation,** *n,* circula-tion, *f;* mouvement, *m;* (*news-paper*) tirage, *m.*

circumcise, *v.t,* circoncire.

circumference, *n,* circonférence, *f,* tour, *m.*

circumflex, *a. & n,* circonflexe, *a. & m.*

circumlocution, *n,* circonlocu-tion, *f,* circuit de paroles, *m,* paraphrase, *f.*

circumscribe, *v.t,* circonscrire.

circumspect, *a,* circonspect, mesuré, avisé. ~**ly,** *ad,* avec cir-conspection.

circumstance, *n,* circonstance, *f;* état; cas, *m;* cérémonie, *f. in easy* ~*s,* à son aise. *in straitened* (*or reduced*) ~*s,* dans la gêne. ~*s permitting,* sauf imprévu. *under no* ~*s,* en aucun cas. **circum-stantial,** *a:* ~ *account,* relation circonstanciée, *f.* ~ *evidence,* témoin muet, *m,* preuve par pré-somption, *f.*

circumvent, *v.t,* circonvenir.

circus, *n,* cirque; hippodrome, *f.*

cirrhosis, *n,* cirrhose, *f.*

cirrus (*Meteor.*), *n,* cirrus, *m.*

cistern, *n,* fontaine, *f;* réservoir, *m;* citerne; (*barometer*) cuvette, *f.*

citadel, *n,* citadelle, *f.*

citation, *n,* citation; mention, *f.*

cite, *v.t,* citer, alléguer; assigner.

citizen, *n,* citoyen, ne, citadin, e. ~**ship,** *n,* droit de cité, *m.*

citric, *a,* citrique. **citron,** *n,* cédrat, citron, *m.*

city, *n,* ville; cité, *f.* ¶ *a,* urbain; municipal. ~ *hall,* la mairie, *f.*

civet [*cat*], *n,* civette, *f.*

civic, *a,* civique.

civil†, *a,* civil; honnête. ~ *engi-neering,* génie civil, *m.* ~ *ser-vant,* employé(e) d'administra-tion, fonctionnaire public, *m,* fonctionnaire publique, *f.* ~ *service,* administration publique, *f.* ~**ian,** *n,* civil, *m.* ~**ity,** *n,* civilité, *f.*

civilization, *n,* civilisation, *f.* **civilize,** *v.t,* civiliser. **civilizing,** *a,* civilisateur.

clack, n. claquement; caquet, m.
~ [*valve*], clapet, m.

claim, n. réclamation, revendication, f. recours; titre, m, prétention, exigence, demande, demande d'indemnité; indemnité, f.
¶ v.t. réclamer, revendiquer, prétendre [à], demander, s'attribuer. ~ant, n, réclamant, e, prétendant, e.

clairvoyance, n, seconde vue, f. **clairvoyant,** n, voyant, e.

clam (*Mol.*) n, palourde, peigne, f.

clamber [up], v.i. & t, gravir, grimper.

clamminess, n, moiteur, f. **clammy,** a, moite, pâteux.

clamorous, a, bruyant, criard. ~ly, ad, à cor & à cri. **clamor,** n, clameur, f. ¶ v.i, crier, vociférer. ~ for, réclamer à grands cris.

clamp, n, bride [de serrage], presse, happe, f, serre-joint[s], crampon, m; pince, f. ¶ v.t, brider, cramponner, bloquer.

clan, n, clan, m.

clandestine†, a, clandestin.

clang, n, son, m. ¶ v.i, retentir.

clank, n, cliquetis, m. ¶ v.t, cliqueter.

clap, n, coup; battement, m. ~trap, phrases à effet, f.pl, boniment, m. ¶ v.t, & i, claquer; battre. **clapper,** n, claquet, claquoir, m, claquette, f; (*bell*) battant, m. **clapping,** n, battement [de mains] m.

claret, n, bordeaux [rouge], vin de Bordeaux, m.

clarify, v.t, clarifier.

clarion, n, clairon, m. **clarinet,** n, clarinette, f.

clarity, n, clarté, lumière, f.

clash, n, choc, m, rencontre, collision, f; fracas; cliquetis; conflit, m. ¶ v.i, s'entrechoquer; être en conflit; jurer.

clasp, n, agrafe, f, fermoir, m; étreinte, f, serrement, m. ~ knife, couteau à virole, c. à cran d'arrêt, m. ¶ v.t, agrafer; prendre, se prendre; presser, étreindre, serrer.

class, n, classe; catégorie; cote, f; cours, m. ~consciousness, l'esprit de caste, m. ~mate, camarade de classe, c. de promotion, m,f. ~room, [salle de] classe, f. ~ war, guerre sociale,

f. ¶ v.t, classer; coter. **classic** & **classical†,** a, classique. **classic,** n, classique, m. **classification,** n, classification, f. **classify,** v.t, classer. **classing,** n, classement, f.

clatter, n, fracas, tapage, m. ¶ v.i, claquer, carillonner.

clause, n, clause, f, article, m; (*Gram.*) proposition, f.

claustral, a, claustral.

claw, n, griffe, serre, patte, f, ongle, m; pince, f, pied-de-biche, m. ¶ v.t, griffer, s'agriffer à; égratigner.

clay, n, argile; glaise; terre, f. ~ pigeon, pigeon artificiel, papegai, m. ~ pipe, pipe en terre, f. ~ pit, carrière d'argile, glaisière, f. **clayey,** a, argileux.

clean, a, propre; blanc; net; pur; sain; sans réserves; (*Typ. proof*) peu chargée. ~-shaven, glabre, entièrement rasé. ~ slate (*fig.*), coup d'éponge, m. ~ sweep (*fig.*), table rase; rafle, f. ¶ v.t, nettoyer; blanchir; dégraisser; débourber. ~er, n, nettoyeur, euse; femme de ménage, femme de journée, f. ~ing, n, nettoyage; dégraissage; curage, f. **cleanliness,** n, propreté, netteté, f. **cleanse,** v.t, assainir, purger; [é]curer.

clear, a, clair; limpide; pur; net; distinct; libre; franc. ~ soup, consommé, m. ~-sighted, clairvoyant. ¶ v.t, éclaircir; débarrasser; dégager; franchir; évacuer; déblayer; défricher; purger; (*table*) desservir; (*computers*) remettre à blanc, à zéro; (*letter box*) [re]lever; (*check*) compenser; (*shop goods*) solder; (*Cust.—goods*) dédouaner; (*a ship inwards*) faire l'entrée [en douane]; (*a ship outwards*) expédier [en douane]. ~ up, v.t, éclaircir, tirer au clair, mettre au net, débrouiller; (v.i.) s'éclaircir, se rasséréner. ~ance, n, (*Mech.*) jeu, m, chasse, f; (*goods through Cust.*) dédouanement, m; (*ship through Cust.*) expédition, f; (*foreign ship leaving French port*) passeport; (*French ship leaving French port*) congé, m. ~ papers (ship's), expéditions, f.pl. ~ sale, solde, m. ~ing (*glade*) n, éclaircie, clairière, f. ~ house (*bank-*

ing), chambre de compensation, *f.* ~**ly**, *ad,* clair[ement], nettement, bien. ~**ness**, *n,* clarté, netteté; pureté, *f.*

cleat, *n,* tasseau, *m,* languette, *f;* taquet, *m.*

cleavage, *n,* fendage; (*Miner.*) clivage, *m;* (*fig.*) scission, *f.* **cleave**, *v.t.ir,* fendre, refendre; cliver; (*v.i.ir.*) se fendre; se cliver; se coller, s'attacher. **cleaver**, *n,* fendoir, couperet, *m.*

clef, *n,* clef, clé, *f.*

cleft, *n,* fente, fissure, *f.* ~ *stick,* piquet fourchu, *m.*

clematis, *n,* clématite, *f.*

clemency, *n,* clémence, *f.* **clement**, *clément.*

clench, *v.t,* crisper; serrer.

clergy, *n,* clergé, *m,* gens d'Église, *m.pl.* ~**man**, *n,* ecclésiastique; ministre, *m.* **cleric**, *n,* ecclésiastique, *m.* ~**al**, *a,* d'employé, de commis; (*of clergy*) ecclésiastique, clérical. ~ *error,* erreur (*ou* faute) de plume (*ou* de copiste) *f;* (*law*) vice (*ou* pas) de clerc, *m.* ¶ *n,* clérical, *m.* **clerk**, *n,* employé, e, commis [de bureau], *m,* préposé, e; (*law & Eccl.*) clerc; (*court*) greffier, *m.*

clever, *a,* habile; adroit. ~ *move,* adresse, *f.* ~**ness**, *n,* dextérité, habileté, *f.*

clew, *n,* fil, *m.*

cliché, *n,* banalité, *f,* cliché, *m.*

click, *n,* cliquetis, tic tac; (*Mech.*) cliquet, déclic, *m,* détente, *f.* ¶ *v.i,* cliqueter, faire tic tac. ~ *heels,* claquer talons.

client, *n,* client, e; partie, *f.* **clientele**, *n,* clientèle, *f.*

cliff, *n,* (*coast*) falaise, *f;* (*inland*) rocher [en escarpement] *m.*

climacteric, *a,* critique, climatérique.

climate, *n,* climat; ciel, *m.* **climatic**, *a,* climatérique, climatique.

climax, *n,* (*Rhet.*) gradation [ascendante] *f;* point culminant; bouquet, *m.*

climb, *n,* ascension, montée, *f.* ¶ *v.t. & i,* gravir, monter, faire l'ascension de, grimper. ~ *over,* escalader. ~**er**, *n,* grimpeur, alpiniste, *m;* plante grimpante, *f.* ~**ing boots,** bottines d'escalade, *f.pl.*

clime (*Poet.*) *n,* terre, *f;* ciel, *m.*

clinch (*Box.*) *n,* corps à corps, *m.* ¶ *v.t,* river; (*fig.*) conclure.

cling, *v.i.ir,* se cramponner, s'attacher, s'agriffer, se coller, s'aheurter, tenir.

clinic, *n,* clinique, *f.* ~**al**, *a,* clinique; (*thermometer*) médical. ~**ian**, *n,* clinicien, *m.*

clink, *n,* (*glasses*) choc; (*jail*) violon, *m.* ¶ *v.t,* choquer, trinquer; (*v.i.*) tinter.

clinker, *n,* mâchefer, *m.*

clip, *n,* pince, serre, griffe, attache, patte [d'attache], *f;* (*paper*) trombone, *m.* ¶ *v.t,* cisailler; tailler; tondre; rogner; (*ticket*) poinçonner; (*words*) estropier, manger. **clippers**, *n.pl,* ciseaux, *m.pl,* tondeuse, *f.* **clippings**, *n.pl,* rognures; (*newspaper*) coupures de journal, *f.pl.*

clique, *n,* clique, coterie, *f.*

cloak (*lit. & fig.*) *n,* manteau, *m.* ~ *room,* vestiaire, *m.* ¶ *v.t,* voiler, masquer.

clock, *n,* (*big*) horloge; (*small*) pendule, pendulette, *f;* (*on stocking*) baguette, *f.* ~ *& watch maker,* horloger, *m.* ~**work** [*movement*] mouvement d'horlogerie, *m.* alarm ~, réveillematin, *m.*

clod, *n,* motte, *f.* ~[*hopper*] rustre, rustaud, lourdaud, *m.*

clog, *n,* sabot, socque, *m,* galoche, *f;* (*fig.*) entrave[s] *f.[pl.].* ~ *dance,* sabotière, *f.* ¶ *v.t,* encrasser; engorger; charger; entraver.

cloister, *n,* cloître, *m.* ¶ *v.t,* cloîtrer. **cloistral**, *a,* claustral.

close, *a,* clos; fermé; étroit; serré; dense; [r]enfermé; lourd, mou; minutieux; vif; intime; près, proche; appliqué; jointif; soutenu. ~*-fitting garment,* vêtement collant; (*woven*) maillot, *m.* ~ *season,* temps prohibé, *m,* période d'interdiction, *f.* ~*-shaven,* rasé de près, ras. ¶ *ad,* près, de près; auprès. ~*-up,* premier plan, gros plan, *m.* ¶ *n,* fin; clôture; levée, *f.* the ~ *of day,* la chute du jour. ¶ *v.t,* fermer; clore; arrêter; régler; lever; liquider, réaliser; serrer; barrer, boucher; (*v.i.*) fermer, se *f;* clore; chômer. ~**d** (*Theat.*), relâche. ~**ly**, *ad,* de près; attentivement; strictement; étroitement. ~**ness**, *n*, compacité; intimité; proximité, *f*; manque d'air, *m*; lourdeur, *f*. **closet**, *n*, cabinet, *m*. ¶ *v.t*, chambrer, claquemurer.

closing, *n*, fermeture, clôture, *f*; liquidation. *f*. ~ *date*, date de clôture, *f*. ~ *price*, dernier cours, c. de clôture, *m*. **closure**, *n*, clôture, *f*.

clot, *n*, caillot, grumeau, *m*. ¶ *v.i*, se cailler, se grumeler.

cloth, *n*, drap, *m*; toile; étoffe, *f*; voile; tissu; linge; tapis, *m*; nappe, *f*; parement, *m*; couverture, *f*; napperon; torchon, *m*; robe, soutane, *f*. ~ *trade*, draperie, *f*. **clothe**, *v.t.ir*, habiller, vêtir; revêtir. **clothes**, *n.pl*, habits, vêtements, *m.pl*, tenue, *f*, entretien, *m*; (*worn*) hardes, *f.pl*. ~ *brush*, brosse à habits, *f*. ~ *hanger*, porte-vêtements, cintre, *m*. ~ *line*, étendoir, *m*, corde à linge, *f*, (*pl*.) étendage, *m*. ~ *pin*, pince à linge, *f*. **clothier**, *n*, drapier, *m*; confectionneur, euse. **clothing**, *n*, habillement, vêtement, *m*. *ready-to-wear* ~, prêt-à-porter, *m*.

cloud, *n*, nuage, *m*; (*fig.*) nuée; (*Poet.*) nue, *f*. ~ *burst*, trombe d'eau, rafale de pluie, *f*. *in the* ~*s* (*fig.*), dans le bleu. ¶ *v.t*, couvrir de nuages; obscurcir, voiler, obnubiler; assombrir. ~*less*, *a*, sans nuage. ~*y*, *a*, nuageux, nébuleux, couvert, chargé; bas; terne, trouble, louche.

clout, *n*, torchon; chiffon, *m*; (*blow*) gifle, *f*.

clove, *n*, [clou de] girofle, *m*. ~ *of garlic*, gousse d'ail, *f*.

cloven hoof, pied fourchu, *m*.

clover, *n*, trèfle, *m*. *in* ~ (*fig.*), dans l'abondance.

clown, *n*, paillasse, pierrot, clown, Gille, pitre, cercle, baladin, bouffon, *m*. ¶ *v.i*, faire le clown. ~*ery*, *n*, bouffonnerie, clownerie, pantalonnade, *f*. ~*ish*, *a*, bouffon.

cloy, *v.t*, rassasier (*with* = de).

club, *n*, massue, casse-tête, *f*, gourdin, *m*; (*golf*) crosse, *f*, club, *m*. (Clubs such as brassie, mashie, niblick are named the same in French and are *m*.); (*people*) club, cercle, *m*, société, *f*; (*church*) patronage; (*cards*, *s.* & *pl.*) trèfle, *m*. ~ *foot*, pied

bot, *m*. ~ *together*, se cotiser. ¶ *v.t*, frapper, assommer.

cluck, *n*, gloussement, *m*. ¶ *v.i*, glousser.

clue, *n*, indication; clef, piste, *f*.

clump, *n*, masse; motte; botte; touffe, *f*, massif, bouquet, *m*.

clumsiness, *n*, gaucherie, maladresse, *f*. **clumsy**, *a*, gauche, maladroit, empoté, pataud; incommode. ~ *fellow*, maladroit, pataud, *m*.

cluster, *n*, faisceau, nœud, bouquet, peloton, groupe, *m*, grappe, *f*, régime, *m*. ¶ *v.i*, se grouper.

clutch, *n*, griffe; (*eggs*) couvée, *f*; (*Mech.*) [manchon d']embrayage, *m*. ¶ *v.t. & i*, empoigner, [a]gripper; se raccrocher. *to let out the* ~, débrayer.

clutter, *n*, désordre, *m*; confusion, *f*. ¶ *v.t*, mettre en désordre.

coach, *n*, voiture, *f*, wagon; carrosse, coche; (*tutor*) répétiteur, préparateur; (*sport*) entraîneur, instructeur; (*boating*) capitaine d'entraînement, *m*. ~ *horse*, carrossier, *m*. ~ *house*, remise, *f*. ~*man*, cocher, *m*. ¶ *v.t*, préparer; entraîner; endoctriner.

coagulate, *v.t*, coaguler; (*v.i.*) se coaguler.

coal, *n*, charbon [de terre] *m*, houille, *f*; (*pl*.) charbon[s]. ~ *mine*, mine de charbon (*ou* de houille), houillère, *f*. ~ *miner*, houilleur, mineur de houille, *m*. ~ *scuttle*, seau à charbon, *m*. ~ *tar*, goudron de houille, coaltar, *m*. ~ *yard*, chantier (*ou* parc) à charbon, *m*, charbonnerie, *f*. ¶ *v.i*, faire du charbon.

coalesce, *v.i*, se confondre. **coalition**, *n*, coalition, *f*, bloc, cartel, *m*.

coarse†, *a*, grossier, gros; rude; brutal. ~*ness*, *n*, grossièreté, rudesse, *f*.

coast, *n*, côte[s] *f.[pl.]*, littoral, *m*, bord[s] *m.[pl.]*. ¶ *v.i*, côtoyer; (*auto & fig.*) débrayer.

coat, *n*, habit, *m*; (*man's*) pardessus; manteau; (*woman's*) redingote, *f*; (*long*) manteau, *m*; (*short*) jaquette, *f*; (*woolly*) gilet, *m*; (*Mil.*) tunique; (*animal's*) robe, *f*, poil, pelage, *m*; (*Anat.*) paroi; tunique; (*layer*) couche, *f*, enduit, *m*. ~ *hanger*, porte-manteau, *m*. ~ *of arms*, armes, armoiries, *f.pl*, blason, *m*. ~ *of mail*, cotte de mailles, *f*. ¶ *v.t*, enduire, revêtir.

coax, *v.t*, enjôler, amadouer.

cob, *n*, (*horse*) bidet; (*corn*) épi, *m*, rafle, *f*. ~[*nut*], grosse noisette, aveline, *f*.

cobalt, *n*, cobalt, *m*.

cobble [stone], *n*, galet, pavé, *m*. ¶ *v.t*, saveter, rapetasser. **cobbler**, *n*, savetier, *m*. ~'s wax, poix, *f*.

cobra, *n*, cobra, *m*.

cobweb, *n*, toile d'araignée, *f*.

cocaïne, *n*, cocaïne, *f*.

cochineal, *n*, cochenille, *f*.

cock, *n*, coq; (*tap*) robinet; (*hay*) meulon; (*of gun*) chien, *m*. ~-*a-doodle-doo*, coquerico, cocorico, *m*. ~-*&-bull story*, coqà-l'âne, *m*, contes en l'air, *m.pl*. ~*crow*[*ing*], chant du coq, *m*. ~ *of the walk*, coq du village, *m*. ~ *pheasant*, [coq] faisan, *m*. *safety* ~, cran d'arrêt, *m*. ¶ *v.t*, relever, [re]dresser; (*gun*) armer. ~*ed hat*, chapeau à cornes, *m*.

cockade, *n*, cocarde, *f*.

cockatoo, *n*, cacatoès, *m*.

cockchafer, *n*, hanneton, *m*.

cockerel, *n*, cochet, *m*.

cockle, *n*, (*Mol.*) clovisse, coque; (*Bot.*) ivraie, *f*.

cockpit, *n*, arène, *f*; (*Avn.*) nacelle, *f*.

cockroach, *n*, cafard, cancrelat, *m*, blatte, *f*.

cockscomb, *n*, crête de coq; (*Bot.*) crête-de-coq, *f*.

cocktail (*drink*) *n*, cocktail, *m*. ~ *bar*, bar-cocktail, *m*. ~ *shaker*, shaker, *m*. ~ *snack*, amusegueules, *m.pl*.

cocky, *a*, impertinent, insolent.

cocoa, *n*, cacao, *m*.

coco[**nut**], *n*, coco, *m*, noix de c., *f*. ~ *palm*, cocotier, *m*.

cocoon, *n*, cocon, *m*.

cod[**fish**], *n*, morue, *f*, cabillaud, *m*; (*dried*) merluche, *f*. ~ *fisher*, morutier, *m*. ~ *liver oil*, huile de foie de morue, *f*.

coddle, *v.t*, dorloter, câliner, choyer.

code, *n*, code, *m*. ~ *word*, mot convenu, *m*. ¶ *v.t*, chiffrer, codicil, *n*, codicille, *m*; avenant, *m*. **codify**, *v.t*, codifier.

coefficient, *n*, coefficient, *m*.

coerce, *v.t*, contraindre.

coffee, *n*, café; moka, *m*. ~ *cup*,

tasse à café, *f*. ~ *pot*, cafetière, *f*. ~ *spoon*, cuiller à café, c. à moka, *f*. ~ *table*, guéridon, *m*. ~ *tree* & ~ *planter*, caféier, *m*.

coffer, *n*, coffre, *m*, caisse, *f*.

coffin, *n*, cercueil, *m*, bière, *f*.

cog, *n*, dent, *f*; alluchon, *m*. ~*wheel*, roue dentée, *f*. ¶ *v.t*, [en]denter.

cogency, *n*, force, *f*. **cogent**, *a*, convaincant, probant.

cogitate, *v.i*, méditer, réfléchir.

cognate, *a*, de même origine.

cognizance, *n*, connaissance, *f*. *cognizant of*, instruit de.

cognomen, *n*, surnom, *m*.

cohabit, *v.i*, cohabiter.

cohere, *v.i*, adhérer. **coherence**, *n*, cohérence; suite, *f*. **coherent**, *a*, cohérent; suivi. ~*ly*, *ad*, avec cohérence. **cohesion**, *n*, cohésion, *f*. **cohesive**, *a*, cohérent.

cohort, *n*, cohorte, *f*.

coil, *n*, rouleau, (*contraceptive device*) stérilet, *m*; (*Elec.*) bobine, *f*. ¶ *v.t*, lover.

coin, *n*, pièce, [pièce de] monnaie, *f*; numéraire, *m*, espèces [monnayées] *f.pl*; (*ancient*) médaille, *f*. ~ *machine*, appareil à sous, *m*. ¶ *v.t*, monnayer, frapper, battre; (*fig.*) forger, inventer; fabriquer. ~*age*, *n*, monnayage, *m*, frappe, *f*; monnaie[s] *f.[pl.]*, numéraire, *m*.

coincide, *v.i*, coïncider. **coincidence**, *n*, coïncidence, *f*.

coir, *n*, fibre de coco, *f*.

coke, *n*, coke, *m*.

colander, *n*, passoire, *f*.

cold†, *a*, froid; à froid. *in* ~ *blood* or ~-*blooded*, de sang-froid, à froid. ~-*blooded* (animal), à sang froid. ~ *chisel*, burin (*ou* ciseau) à froid, *m*. ~ *snap*, coup de froid, *m*. ~ *steel*, arme blanche, *f*. ¶ *n*, froid, *m*, froidure, *f*; (*Path.*) rhume, coup d'air, *m*. ~ *on the chest*, *in the head*, rhume de poitrine, de cerveau.

coleopter[**an**], *n*, coléoptère, *m*. **coleopterous**, *a*, coléoptère.

colic, *n*, colique, *f*, tranchées, *f.pl*.

collaborate, *v.i*, collaborer. **collaborator**, *n*, collaborateur, trice.

collapse, *n*, effondrement, écroulement; affaissement; *m*; chute, débâcle, *f*. ¶ *v.i*, s'effondrer, crouler, s'écrouler, s'affaisser. **collapsible**, *a*, pliant.

collar, n, collier, collet; col; frette, bague, f. [*shirt*] ~ (detached), faux col, m. *attached* ~ (to shirt), col tenant. ~ *bone*, clavicule, f. ~ *size*, n, encolure, f. ~ *button*, bouton de col, m. ¶ v.t, colleter.

collate, v.t, collationner; (*computers*) interclasser. **collation**, n, (*computers*) interclassement, m. **collator**, n, (*computers*) interclasseuse, f.

collateral, a, collatéral. ~ *security*, nantissement, m.

collation, n, collationnement, m; (*snack*) collation, f.

colleague, n, collègue, m.

collect, n, collecte, f. ¶ v.t, recueillir, rassembler, réunir; retirer, enlever; [re]lever; capter; collectionner; recouvrer, récupérer; percevoir; encaisser; quêter. ~ed, p.a, recueilli, calme. ~ion, n, rassemblement, recueil, m; réunion, f; captage; recouvrement, m; récupération; perception, rentrée; levée, f; relevage; encaissement; enlèvement, apport, m; quête, collecte, f; cabinet, m. ~ *of coins or medals*, médaillier, m. ~ive†, a, collectif. ~or, n, collecteur, receveur, percepteur; collectionneur, fureteur, curieux, ramasseur, euse.

college, n, collège, m; faculté, académie, f. **collegian**, n, collégien, ne. **collegiate**, a, collégial.

collide, v.i, s'aborder, se rencontrer, se tamponner. ~ *with*, aborder, rencontrer, tamponner.

collier, n, (*pers.*) houilleur; (*ship*) charbonnier, m. ~y, n, houillière, f; (*col. pl.*) charbonnage, m.

collision, n, abordage, m, collision, rencontre, f, tamponnement, m. ~ *mat*, paillet d'abordage, m.

colloquial†, a, de la conversation; (*words, phrases*) familier. ~ism, n, expression familière, f.

colloquy, n, colloque, m.

collusion, n, collusion, f.

Colombia, n, la Colombie.

colon, n, deux-points; (*Anat.*) côlon, m.

colonel, n, colonel, m.

colonial, a, colonial. **colonist**, n, colon, m. **colonize**, v.t, coloniser.

colonnade, n, colonnade, f.

colony, n, colonie, f.

colophon, n, marque (typographique) f, chiffre, fleuron, m.

color, n, couleur, f; teint; coloris, m; peinture, f; (*pl.*) couleurs, f.pl, drapeaux, m.pl; pavillon, m. *under* ~ *of* (*fig.*), sous couleur de. ~ *bar*, distinction sociale (*ou* légale) entre la race blanche & la race noire, f. ~-*blind*, daltonien. ~ *blindness*, cécité pour les c—s, f. ¶ v.t, colorer, colorier; enluminer. ~ed, p.a. & p.p: ~ *dress*, robe de couleur, f. ~ *sketch*, croquis en couleurs, m. ~ing, n, coloris, m. ~less, a, sans couleur, incolore, fade.

colossal†, a, colossal. **colossus**, n, colosse, m.

colt, n, poulain, m. **coltsfoot** (*Bot.*) n, pas-d'âne, tussilage, m.

columbine (*Bot.*) n, ancolie, f.

column, n, colonne, f; pillier, m; (*news on special subject*) rubrique, f. ~ist, n, journaliste, m.

coma, n, (*Med.*) coma, m; (*Bot. & comet*) chevelure, f. **comatose**, a, comateux.

comb, n, peigne, m; (*crest*) crête, f; (*honey*) rayon, gâteau, m, gaufre, f. ¶ v.t, peigner. ~ *out* (*fig.*), éliminer.

combat, n, combat, m. ¶ v.t, combattre. ~ant, n, combattant, m. ~ive, a, batailleur. ~iveness, n, combativité, f.

combination, n, combinaison, f. **combine**, n, coalition; combine; (*Agric.*) batteuse, f. ¶ v.t, combiner, réunir; joindre; (v.i.) se combiner; se coaliser.

combings, n.pl, peignures, f.pl.

combustible, a, combustible. **combustion**, n, combustion, f. ~ *chamber* (motor), chambre d'explosion, f.

come, v.i.ir, venir; provenir; arriver; se présenter; se faire; entrer; être. ~ *along!*, ~ *on!* allons!, venez!, marchons! ~ *about*, se faire. ~ *across*, rencontrer. ~ *back*, revenir. ~ *down*, descendre. ~ *for*, venir chercher. ~ *from* (be a native of), être originaire de. ~ *home*, rentrer; revenir; porter coup. ~ *in!* entrez! ~ *now!* enfin!, ah! çà. ~ *off*, se détacher; (*ink*) décharger. ~ *off on* (dye), déteindre sur. ~ *out*, sortir; débuter; (*book, etc.*) paraître. ~ *to*, se monter à; revenir à; (*decision*) prendre.

~ *to an agreement*, tomber d'accord. ~ *to blows*, en venir aux mains. ~ *to light*, se découvrir. ~ *to pass*, arriver, advenir. ~ *to terms*, s'arranger. ~ *undone*, se défaire. ~ *up* (sprout), poindre. ~ *upon*, tomber sur. ~ *what may*, arrive (*ou* advienne) que pourra, au petit bonheur.

comedian, *n*, comédien, ne; farceur, *m*. **comedy**, *n*, comédie, *f*, comique, *m*.

comeliness, *n*, beauté, grâce, bonne mine, *f*. **comely**, *a*, beau, gracieux, avenant.

comer, *n*, venant, *m*; venu, e. ~**s** & **goers**, allants & venants, *m.pl*.

comet, *n*, comète, *f*.

comfort, *n*, consolation, satisfaction, aise, *f*, [ré]confort, *m*. ¶ *v.t*, consoler, réconforter, soulager. ~**able**†, *a*, aisé, confortable. ~**er**, *n*, consolateur, trice; (*blanket*) couvre-pied, *m*.

comic & **comical**, *a*, comique; humoristique, cocasse; plaisant, bouffon, bouffe, burlesque. ~ *actor*, comique, *m*. ~ *opera*, opéra bouffe, *m*. ~ *song*, chanson burlesque, chansonnette, *f*. ~ *turn*, pantalonnade, *f*.

coming, *p.a*, à venir; d'avenir; futur. ¶ *n*, venue, arrivée, *f*; (*of Christ*) avènement, *m*. [*I am*] ~*l* j'y vais! on y va! voilà! ~ & *going*, allées & venues, *f.pl*. ~ *out* (in society), début, *m*, entrée dans le monde, *f*.

comma, *n*, virgule, *f*. *Note:*— Sets of three figures, separated in Eng. by commas, are separated in Fr. either by points or by spaces.

command, *n*, commandement, *m*; ordre[s] *m.[pl.]*; empire, *m*; facilité, *f*. (*computers*) ~ *key*, touche de commande, *f*. ¶ *v.t*, commander; monter; ordonner; avoir à sa disposition; (*a view of*) donner sur. ~**ant**, *n*, commandant, chef, *m*.

commandeer, *v.t*, réquisitionner.

commander, *n*, commandant, chef; (*Nav.*) capitaine de frégate, *m*. *commanding officer*, commandant, chef, *m*.

commandment, *n*, commandement, *m*.

commemorate, *v.t*, commémorer.

commence, *v.t*. & *i*, commencer, entamer. ~**ment**, *n*, commencement, début, *m*.

commend, *v.t*, recommander; applaudir à, préconiser; remettre. ~**able**, *a*, recommandable, louange; recommandation, *f*.

commensurate, *a*, proportionné.

comment & **commentary**, *n*, commentaire, *m*, glose, *f*. **to comment on**, commenter [sur]. **commentator**, *n*, commentateur.

commerce, *n*, commerce, négoce, *m*. **commercial**, *a*, commercial, commerçant, marchand, de commerce, d'affaires. ~**ism**, *n*, mercantillisme, *m*. ~**ize**, *v.t*, achalander, monnayer. ~**ly**, *ad*, commercialement.

commiserate, *v.t*, plaindre.

commissariat, *n*, intendance militaire, *f*.

commission, *n*, commission, remise, *f*; courtage, *m*; (*shop*) guelte, *f*; (*officer's*) lettre[s] de service, *f.[pl.]*. ~ *agent*, commissionaire, *m*. ¶ *v.t*, commissioner, mandater; (*officer*) nommer; (*ship*) armer. ~**ed** *work*, ouvrage de commande, *m*. **commissioner**, *n*, commissaire, *m*.

commit, *v.t*, commettre, faire; livrer; confier; renvoyer. ~ *for trial*, mettre en accusation. ~ *oneself*, s'engager; se compromettre. ~ *to prison*, ordonner l'incarcération de. ~ *to writing*, coucher (*ou* mettre) par écrit. ~**ment** (*Com.*) *n*, engagement, *m*.

committee, *n*, comité; bureau, *m*.

commode, *n*, chaise [percée] *f*.

commodious, *a*, commode. ~**ly**, *ad*, commodément. ~**ness**, *n*, commodité, *f*.

commodity, *n*, produit, *m*, denrée, marchandise, matière [première] *f*, article, *m*; ressource, *f*.

commodore, *n*, chef d'escadre, *m*.

common, *a*, commun; général; coutumier; ordinaire; vulgaire; peuple; banal; simple; type; public. ~ [*land*], communal, *m*, champs communs, *m.pl*, vaine pâture, *f*. ~ *law*, droit coutumier, *m*. [*the*] ~ *people*, les gens du commun, *m.pl*, le petit peuple, le vulgaire. ~ *sense*, sens commun, bon sens, *m.* the ~ *weal*, la chose publique. *in, out of the*, ~, en, hors du, commun. **~ly**, *ad*, communément, couramment. **~ness**, *n*, fréquence, *f.* **~place**, *a*, banal, commun; (*n.*) banalité; pauvreté, *f.* (*pl.*) lieux communs, *m.pl.* **~wealth**, *n*, république; communauté, *f.*

commonalty, *n*, roture, *f.* **commoner**, *n*, roturier, ère.

commotion, *n*, commotion, *f*, mouvement, *m.*

communal, *a*, communal. **commune**, *v.i*, converser. **communicant**, *n*, communiant, e. **communicate**, *v.t. & i*, communiquer; correspondre; (*Eccl.*) communier. **communication**, *n*, communication, *f.* ~ *cord*, corde de signal d'alarme, *f.* ~ *trench*, branche de tranchée, *f*, boyau de t., *m.* **communicative**, *a*, communicatif. **communion**, *n*, communion, *f.* ~ *cup*, calice, *m.* ~ *service*, office du saint sacrement, *m.* ~ *table*, sainte table, *f.* **communism**, *n*, communisme, *m.* **communist**, *n*, communiste, *m.f.* **community**, *n*, communauté; société, république, *f.* ~ *singing*, chansons en chœur, *f.pl. bedroom* ~, cité-dortoire, *f.*

commutation, *n*, commutation; substitution, *f*; replacement; échange, *m.* ~ *ticket*, carte d'abonnement au chemin de fer, *f.*

commutator, *n*, commutateur, *m.*

commute, *v.t*, commuer. **~r**, *n*, abonné des chemins de fer, *m.*

Como (**Lake**), le lac de Côme.

compact, *a*, compact. ¶ *n*, pacte, *m*; (*powder*) poudrier, *m*; (*auto*) voiture compact, *f.* **~ness**, *n*, compacité, *f.*

companion, *n*, compagnon, *m*, compagne, *f*, camarade, *m,f*; (*thing*) pendant, *m.* [*lady*] ~, dame, demoiselle, de compagnie. **~able**, *a*, sociable. **~ship**, *n*, compagnie, société, *f*, fréquentations, *f.pl.*

company, *n*, compagnie; société; bande; troupe, *f*; groupe; équipage; monde, *m.*

comparable, *a*, comparable. **comparative†**, *a*, comparatif; (*sciences*) comparé. ¶ (*Gram.*)

n, comparatif, *m.* **compare**, *v.t*, comparer, assimiler; rapprocher, collationner; conférer. **comparison**, *n*, comparaison, *f*, rapprochement, *m.*

compartment, *n*, compartiment, *m*; case, *f.*

compass, *n*, cadre, *m*, étendue, portée; (*magnetic*) boussole, *f*; compas; (*voice*) diapason; (*musical*) clavier, *m.* ~ *card*, rose des vents, *f.* **compass[es]**, *n.[pl.]*, compas, *m.* *compasses with pen point*, *with pencil point*, compas à tire-ligne, à porte-crayon. **compass**, *v.t*, cerner, ceindre.

compassion, *n*, compassion, *f.* **~ate**, *a*, compatissant.

compatible, *a*, compatible. **compatriot**, *n*, compatriote, *m,f.* **compeer**, *n*, égal, e, pair, *m.* **compel**, *v.t*, contraindre, astreindre, obliger, forcer.

compendious, *a*, sommaire. **compendium**, *n*, compendium, *m.*

compensate, *v.t*, compenser, indemniser, dédommager. **compensation**, *n*, compensation, indemnité, *f*, dédommagement, *m.*

compete for, concourir pour, à. ~ *with*, faire concurrence à.

competence, **-cy**, *n*, aisance; compétence; aptitude, *f.* **competent**, *a*, compétent, apte.

competition, *n*, concurrence; compétition, *f*; concours, *m.* **competitor**, *n*, concurrent, e, compétiteur, trice.

compile, *v.t*, compiler.

complacency, *n*, contentement, *m.* **complacent**, *a*, content de soi. **~ly**, *ad*, avec un air suffisant.

complain, *v.i*, se plaindre; réclamer, gémir. ~ *of* (*medically*), accuser. **~ant**, *n*, plaignant, e. **complaint**, *n*, plainte, doléance, réclamation, *f*, grief; gémissement, *m*; (*Med.*) affection, maladie, *f.* ~ *department*, bureau de reclamation, *m.*

complaisance, *n*, complaisance, *f.* **complaisant**, *a*, complaisant.

complement, *n*, complément, effectif, *m.* **~ary**, *a*, complémentaire.

complete†, *a*, complet, au complet. ¶ *v.t*, compléter. **~d** (*time, age*) *p.p*, révolus. **completion**, *n*, complètement, achèvement, *m.*

complex, *a. & n*, complexe, *a. & m.*

complexion, *n,* (*of face*) teint; (*fig.*) caractère, aspect, *m.*

complexity, *n,* complexité, *f.*

compliance, *n,* conformité, *f.* **compliant,** *a,* facile, complaisant.

complicate, *v.t,* compliquer. **complication,** *n,* complication, *f.*

complicity, *n,* complicité, *f.*

compliment, *n,* compliment, *m*; (*pl.*) compliments, *m.pl*, civilités, politesses, *f.pl*, hommages, *m.pl*, choses, *f.pl*. ~*s of the season,* souhaits de bonne année, *m.pl.* ¶ *v.t,* complimenter. ~**ary,** *a,* flatteur; (*free*) gratis.

comply, *v.i.abs,* se soumettre. ~ *with,* se conformer à, condescendre à, observer, obéir à, remplir, respecter. *not complied with* (rule), inobservée.

component, *a,* constituant; composant. ¶ *n,* composant, *m.* ~ [*part*], pièce détachée, *f.*

compose, *v.t,* composer. *to be* ~*d of,* se c. de. ~ *oneself,* se calmer. ~**d,** *p.p,* composé, calme. **composer** (*Mus.*) *n,* compositeur, trice, auteur, *m.* *composing stick* (*Typ.*), composteur, *m.* **composite,** *a,* composé, mixte. **composition,** *n,* composition; constitution, *f*; thème, *m.* **compositor** (*Typ.*) *n,* compositeur, trice.

composure, *n,* calme, sang-froid, *m.*

compound, *a,* composé; (*steam*) compound. ~ *interest,* intérêt[s] composé[s] *m.[pl.].* ¶ *n,* composé; combiné, corps composé, *m.* ¶ *v.t,* composer; pactiser avec (*a felony* = un crime); (*v.i.*) transiger; pactiser.

comprehend, *v.t,* comprendre. **comprehension,** *n,* compréhension, *f.* **comprehensive,** *a,* compréhensif.

compress, *n,* compresse, *f.* ¶ *v.t,* comprimer, refouler. ~**ion,** *n,* compression, *f.* ~**or,** *n,* compresseur, *m.*

comprise, *v.t,* comprendre, renfermer, contenir.

compromise, *n,* compromis, accommodement, *m.,* transaction, *f.* ¶ *v.t. & i,* compromettre, transiger; capituler. ~ *oneself,* se compromettre.

comptroller, *n,* contrôleur, *m.*

compulsion, *n,* contrainte, *f.* **compulsorily,** *ad,* forcément. **compulsory,** *a,* forcé, obligatoire.

compunction, *n,* componction, *f.*

computation, *n,* supputation, *f.* **compute,** *v.t,* supputer, computer.

computer, *n,* ordinateur, *m.* ~ *kid,* micro-mioche, *m. & f.* ~ *network,* réseau informatique, *m.* ~ *process chart,* ordinogramme, *m.* ~ *training course,* cours d'informatique, *m.* *home* ~, ordinateur domestique, *m.* ~**ize,** *v.t,* informatiser.

comrade, *n,* camarade, *m,f.* ~**ship,** *n,* camaraderie, *f.*

concatenation, *n,* caténation, *f.*

concave, *a,* concave. **concavity,** *n,* concavité, *f.*

conceal, *v.t,* cacher; celer; dérober; dissimuler; supprimer; taire; receler. ~**ment,** *n,* réticence; dissimulation; suppression, *f*; recèlement, *m.*

concede, *v.t,* accorder, concéder.

conceit, *n,* vanité, suffisance, *f.* ~**ed,** *a,* vain, vaniteux, suffisant.

conceivable, *a,* concevable. **conceive,** *v.t. & i,* concevoir.

concentrate, *v.t,* concentrer; canaliser. **concentration,** *n,* concentration, *f.*

concentric, *a,* concentrique.

concept, *n,* concept, *m*; idée, *f.* ~**ion,** *n,* conception, *f.*

concern, *n,* affaire, *f*; souci, *m,* sollicitude, inquiétude; entreprise, exploitation; boutique, *f.* ¶ *v.t,* concerner, intéresser, regarder, toucher, appartenir. ~**ing,** *pr,* concernant, touchant, à l'égard de.

concert, *n,* concert, *m*; audition, *f.* ~ *grand* [*piano*], piano à queue, *m.* ¶ *v.t,* concerter. **concerto,** *n,* concerto, *m.*

concession, *n,* concession, *f.* **concessionaire,** *n,* concessionnaire, *m,f.*

conch, *n,* conque, *f*; coquillage, *m.* ~**ology,** *n,* conchyliogie, *f.*

conciliate, *v.t,* concilier. **conciliation,** *n,* conciliation, *f.* ~ *board,* conseil de prud'hommes, *m.*

concise, *a,* concis; (*edition*) compacte. ~**ness,** *n,* concision, *f.*

conclave, *n,* conclave, *m*; assemblée, *f.*

conclude, *v.t. & i,* conclure; arrêter, clore. **conclusion,** *n,* conclusion; décision, *f.* **conclusive,** *a,* démonstratif; concluant; décisif.

concoct, *v.t.* confectionner; *(fig.)* cuisiner, machiner, tramer. **concoction**, *n,* mixture; machination, *f.*

concomitant, *n,* accompagnement, *m.*

concord, *n,* concorde, *f*; accord, *m*; concordance, *f.* ~**ance**, *n,* concordance, *f.*

concourse, *n,* concours, *m,* affluence, *f.*

concrete, *a,* concret. the concrete (opp. *abstract*), le concret. ¶ *n,* béton, *m.*

concubine, *n,* concubine, *f.*

concupiscence, *n,* concupiscence, *f.*

concur, *v.i.* concourir. **concurrence**, *n,* concours, *m.*

concussion, *n,* ébranlement, *m.* ~ *of the brain*, commotion au cerveau, *f.*

condemn, *v.t.* condamner. ~**ed** *man, woman,* condamné(e) à mort. **condemnation**, *n,* condamnation, *f.*

condensation, *n,* condensation, *f.* **condense**, *v.t.* condenser; resserrer. ~**d** *milk,* lait condensé, l. concentré, l. conservé, *m.* **condenser**, *n, (Phys., Elec., Opt.)* condensateur; *(steam)* condenseur, *m.*

condescend, *v.i.* condescendre. **condescension**, *n,* condescendance, *f.*

condiment, *n,* condiment, assaisonnement, *m.*

condition, *n,* condition, *f*; état, *m. on* ~ *that,* à condition que, à [la] charge de, sous réserve que. ¶ *v.t.* conditionner. ~**al†**, *a,* conditionnel.

condole with, exprimer ses condoléances à. **condolence**, *n,* condoléance, *f.*

condone, *v.t.* passer sur, fermer les yeux sur.

conduce, *v.t.* contribuer, conduire, tendre.

conduct, *n,* conduite, *f*; maniement, *m.* ¶ *v.t.* conduire, guider, gérer, manier, mener. ~**ed** *tour,* excursion accompagnée, *f.* **conductor, tress,** *n,* conducteur, trice; guide, *m*; receveur, euse, chef d'orchestre, *m.*

conduit, *n,* conduit; caniveau, *m.*

cone, *n, (Geom.)* cône, *m*; *(fir, pine)* pomme, *f*; *(ice cream)* cornet de glace, *m.*

confectioner, *n,* confiseur, euse; pâtissier, ère, glacier, *m.* ~**'s** *shop,* confiserie, pâtisserie, *f.* ~**y**, *n,* confiserie, *f,* bonbons, *m.pl,* sucreries, *f.pl*; pâtisserie, *f.*

confederacy, *n,* confédération, *f.* **confederate**, *n,* compère, *m,* complice, *m,f, (pl.)* consorts, *m.pl.* ¶ *v.i,* se confédérer. **confederation**, *n,* confédération, *f.*

confer, *v.t.* conférer; accorder; *(v.i.)* conférer. ~**ence**, *n,* conférence, *f.*

confess, *v.t,* confesser, avouer, s'accuser de; *(v.i.)* se confesser. ~**edly**, *ad,* de son propre aveu. **confession**, *n,* confession, *f,* aveu, *m*; confesse, *f.* ~**al**, *n,* confessional, *m.* **confessor**, *n,* confesseur, *m.*

confidant, e, *n,* confident, e. **confide**, *v.t,* confier, livrer; *(v.i.)* se confier. **confidence**, *n,* confiance; assurance; *(secret)* confidence, *f.* ~ *trick,* vol à l'américaine, *m.* ~ *man,* escroc, *m.* **confident**, *a,* confiant, assuré. **confidential**, *a, (of things)* confidentiel; *(of pers.—in good sense)* de confiance; *(bad sense)* affidé. ~**ly**, *ad,* confidentiellement, confidemment. **confiding**, *p.a,* confiant.

confine, *v.t,* confiner, borner; chambrer, enfermer, renfermer, resserrer; retenir, faire garder. ~ *oneself to, within,* se borner à, dans, se cantonner dans. ~ *[to barracks],* consigner. *to be* ~**d** (woman), accoucher, faire ses couches. ~**ment**, *n,* détention, *f; (woman)* couches, *f.pl,* accouchement, *m.* ~ *to barracks,* consigne, *f.* **confines,** *n.pl,* confins, *m.pl.*

confirm, *v.t,* confirmer; ratifier, approuver, adopter. ~**ation**, *n,* confirmation; ratification, approbation, adoption, *f.* ~**ed**, *p.a,* invétéré, acharné, fieffé, émérite. ~ *invalid,* incurable, *m,f.*

confiscate, *v.t,* confisquer. **confiscation**, *n,* confiscation, *f.*

conflagration, *n,* embrasement, *m*; conflagration, *f.*

conflict, *n,* conflit, *m.* ¶ *v.i. & abs,* se contredire. ~**ing**, *p.a,* en conflit; contradictoire.

confluence, *n,* confluent; concours, *m.*

conform, *v.t,* conformer; *(v.i.)*

se c. ~able, a, conforme. ~ably, ad, conformément. ~ation, n, conformation, f. ~ity, n, conformité, f.

confound, v.t, confondre. ~ed, p.a, maudit.

confraternity, n, confraternité; (pers.) confrérie, f.

confront, v.t, affronter; confronter; faire face à.

confuse, v.t, confondre, mêler; embrouiller. **confused**, a, confus. ~ly, ad, confusément. **confusion**, n, confusion, f, désarroi, m.

confute, v.t, réfuter.

congeal, v.t, congeler, geler, figer; (v.i.) se congeler; prendre, se prendre.

congenial, a, sympathique; agréable.

congenital, a, congénital.

conger [eel], n, congre, m.

congest (Med.) v.t, congestionner, engorger. ~ion, n, (Med.) congestion, f, engorgement; (traffic, etc.) encombrement, m, presse, f. ~ of the blood, of the brain, of the lungs, congestion sanguine, cérébrale, pulmonaire. ~ of the liver, engorgement au foie.

conglomerate, n, conglomérat, m.

congratulate, v.t, féliciter, complimenter. ~ oneself, se féliciter, s'applaudir. **congratulation**, n, félicitation, f, compliment, m.

congregate, v.t, rassembler; (v.i.) se r., s'assembler. **congregation**, n, assemblage, m; (of pers.) assemblée, f.

congress, n, congrès, m. member of the (or a) ~, congressiste, m,f.

congruity, n, convenance, f. **congruous**, a, congru. ~ly, ad, congrûment.

conic(al), a, conique.

conifer, n, conifère, m. ~ous, a, conifère.

conjectural†, a, conjectural. **conjecture**, n, conjecture, f. ¶ v.i, conjecturer.

conjoin, v.t, conjoindre. **conjoint†**, a, conjoint.

conjugal†, a, conjugal.

conjugate, v.t, conjuguer. **conjugation**, n, conjugaison, f.

conjunction, n, conjonction, f. **conjuncture**, n, conjoncture, f.

conjure, v.t, (adjure) conjurer; (enchant) ensorceler; (v.i.) escamoter. ~ away, escamoter. ~ [up], évoquer, se forger. **conjurer, -or**, n, escamoteur, prestidigitateur, m. **conjuring**, n, escamotage, m, prestidigitation, f. ~ trick, tour de passe-passe, m.

connect, v.t, relier, raccorder, joindre, réunir; lier; (Elec.) [ac]coupler. ~ed, p.a, suivi; apparenté. connecting rod, bielle, f. **connection**, n, connexion; liaison; relation, f; raccord; contact; rapport, m; correspondance, f; parent, e; clientèle, f, achalandage, m. travel ~, liaison, correspondance, f.

conning tower, blockhaus; (submarine) kiosque, m.

connivance, n, connivence, f. **connive at**, être de connivence pour.

connoisseur, n, connaisseur, euse; gourmet, m.

connubial, a, conjugal, matrimonial.

conquer, v.t, vaincre, conquérir. **conqueror, conqueress**, n, vainqueur, m, conquérant, e. William the Conqueror, Guillaume le Conquérant. **conquest**, n, conquête, f.

consanguinity, n, consanguinité, f.

conscience, n, conscience, f, for intérieur, m. ~ money, restitution anonyme, f. to be ~-stricken, avoir une conscience bourrelée de remords. **conscientious†**, a, consciencieux. ~ness, n, conscience, f.

conscious, a: to be ~, avoir sa connaissance. to be ~ of, avoir conscience de, être conscient de, sentir. ~ly, ad, sciemment. ~ness, n, connaissance; conscience, f.

conscript, n, conscrit, m. ~ion, n, conscription, f.

consecrate, v.t, consacrer; bénir; sacrer. ~d, p.a, bénit; sacré; saint. **consecration**, n, consécration; bénédiction, f; sacre, m.

consecutive†, a, consécutif.

consensus, n, unanimité, f.

consent, n, consentement, accord, agrément, aveu, m. ¶ v.i, consentir, accéder, entendre (to = à).

consequence, n, conséquence, suite; importance, f. **consequent**, a, conséquent. consequential *damages,* dommages indirects, *m.pl.* **consequently,** *ad,* conséquemment, par conséquent, aussi.

conservation, *n,* conservation, préservation, *f.*

conservative, *a,* conservateur. ¶ *n.* & **conservator,** *n,* conservateur, trice. **conservatory,** *n,* serre, *f.*

consider, *v.t,* considérer, regarder; délibérer sur; (*v.i.* & *abs.*) songer, réfléchir. ~**able!** *a,* considérable. ~**ate,** *a,* prévenant. ~**ation,** *n,* considération, *f;* égard, *m;* délibération, *f;* ménagements, *m.pl;* (*law*) provision, cause, *f. in* ~ *of* (value received), moyennant. (matter) *under* ~, sur le bureau. *without due* ~, à la légère. ~**ing,** *pr,* attendu, vu, eu égard à.

consign, *v.t,* livrer; confier; remettre, expédier; reléguer; (*goods*) consigner. ~**ee,** *n,* consignataire, destinataire, réceptionnaire, *m.* ~**ment,** *n,* consignation; expédition, *f;* envoi, chargement, *m.* (goods) *on* ~, en consignation. ~**or,** *n,* consignateur, *m.*

consist, *v.i,* consister, se composer. ~**ence,** ~**cy,** *n,* consistance; suite, *f.* ~**ent,** *a,* conséquent, compatible; qui ne se dément point; suivi. ~*ently with,* conséquemment à. ~**ory,** *n,* consistoire, *m.*

consolation, *n,* consolation, *f.* ~ *prize,* prix de c., *m.* **console,** *v.t,* consoler. ¶ *n,* console, *f;* (*computers & TV*) pupitre, *m.* ~ *operator,* pupitreur, *m.* keyboard ~, pupitre à clavier, *m. control* ~, p. de régie, *m. mixing* ~, p. de mélange, *m.*

consolidate, *v.t,* consolider; unifier. **consolidation,** *n,* consolidation; unification, *f.*

consonance, *n,* consonance, *f.* **consonant,** *a,* (*Mus., words*) consonant. ~ *with,* en rapport avec. ¶ *n,* consonne, *f.*

consort, *n,* époux, ouse; (*Naut.*) conserve, *f,* navire d'escort; (*prince*) consort, *m.* ¶ *v.i,* s'associer.

conspicuous, *a,* voyant, en évidence; insigne, signalé, remarquable. *to make oneself* ~, se faire remarquer, se singulariser.

conspiracy, *n,* conspiration, conjuration, *f.* **conspirator,** *n,* conspirateur, trice, conjuré, *m.* **conspire,** *v.i.* & *t,* conspirer, conjurer.

constancy, *n,* constance, *f.* **constant,** *a,* constant. ¶ *n,* constante, *f.* ~**ly,** *ad,* constamment.

constellation, *n,* constellation, *f.*

consternation, *n,* consternation, *f.*

constipate, *v.t,* constiper. **constipation,** *n,* constipation, *f.*

constituency, *n,* circonscription électorale, *f,* collège électoral, *m;* électeurs, *m.pl.* **constituent,** *a,* constituant, composant. ¶ *n,* composant; ingrédient, *m;* (*pl.*) électeurs, commettants, *m.pl.* **constitute,** *v.t,* constituer. **constitution,** *n,* constitution, *f;* tempérament, *m.* ~**al†,** *a,* constitutionnel.

constrain, *v.t,* contraindre, gêner, forcer. **constraint,** *n,* contrainte, gêne, sujétion, *f.*

construct, *v.t,* construire, établir. ~**ion,** *n,* construction; interprétation; explication, *f.* ~**ional,** *a,* de construction. ~**ive,** *a,* constructif. ~**or,** *n,* constructeur, *m.*

construe, *v.t,* construire; expliquer.

consul, *n,* consul, *m.* ~**ar,** *a,* consulaire. ~**ate** & ~**ship,** *n,* consulat, *m.*

consult, *v.t,* consulter. ~**ation,** *n,* consultation, *f.* **consulting,** *p.a:* ~ *engineer,* ingénieur-conseil, *m.* ~ *physician,* médecin consultant, *m.* ~ *room,* cabinet de consultation, salon de c., *m.*

consume, *v.t,* consumer, dévorer; (*use*) consommer. **consumer,** *n,* consommateur, *m.*

consummate, *a,* consommé, fini, superlatif. ¶ *v.t,* consommer. **consummation,** *n,* consommation, *f.*

consumption, *n,* (*destruction*) consomption; (*Med.*) consomption, phtisie; (*use*) consommation, dépense, *f.* **consumptive,** *a.* & *n,* tuberculeux, euse, poitrinaire, phtisique, *a.* & *m.f.*

contact, *n,* contact; attouchement; frottement, *m.* ¶ *v.t,* être en relations avec, être en contact avec.

contagion, *n,* contagion, *f.* **contagious,** *a,* contagieux. ~**ness,** *n,* contagion, *f.*

contain, *v.t,* contenir, tenir, renfermer. ~er, n, conténant; recipient; container ou conteneur, m. ~ization, n, conteneurisation, f. ~ize, v.t, conteneuriser.

contaminate, v.t, contaminer, souiller. **contamination,** n, contamination, souillure, f.

contemplate, v.t, contempler; méditer; projeter; envisager; (v.i.) méditer. **contemplation,** n, contemplation, f. in ~, en vue. **contemplative,** a, contemplatif.

contemporaneous & contemporary, a, contemporain. **contemporary,** n, contemporain, e.

contempt, n, mépris, m. oft. pl, dédain, m. ~ of court, offense à la cour, f; refus d'obéissance, m. ~ible, a, méprisable. **contemptuous,** a, méprisant, dédaigneux.

contend, v.t. & i: ~ that, prétendre que. ~ with, combattre; lutter contre; disputer.

content, a, content. ¶ n, contentement, m; (holding) contenance; teneur, f, titre; (pl.) contenu, m; table des matières, f. ¶ v.t, contenter. ~ed with, satisfait de. ~edly, ad, content.

contention, n, démêlé, m; dispute, discorde, f. my ~ is that . . ., ce que je prétends, c'est que . . . **contentious,** a, litigieux; contentieux.

contentment, n, contentement, m.

contest, n, lutte, f, combat; concours, m, joute, dispute, f. ¶ v.t, contester; disputer.

context, n, contexte, m.

contexture, n, contexture, f.

contiguity, n, contiguïté, f. **contiguous,** a, contigu.

continence, n, continence, f. **continent,** a, continent. ¶ n, continent, m; terre ferme, f. the C~ (Europe), le continent. ~al, a, continental.

contingency, n, contingence, éventualité, f, imprévu, m. ~ fund, fonds de prévoyance, m. **contingent,** a, contingent, aléatoire, éventuel. ¶ n, contingent; évènement fortuit, m.

continual†, a, continuel. **continuance,** n, continuation, f. **continuation,** n, continuation, suite, f. **continue,** v.t. & i, continuer; prolonger. to be ~d (serial), à suivre,

la suite au prochaine numéro. **continuity,** n, continuité, f. (cinema), ~ shot, raccord, m. **continuous,** a, continu. (movies) ~ performance, spectacle permanent, m. ~ly, ad, continûment.

contort, v.t, contourner. ~ed, p.a, tors. **contortion,** n, contorsion, f. ~ist, n, homme-caoutchouc, homme-serpent, m; femme-caoutchouc, femme-serpent, f.

contour, n, contour; profil, tracé, galbe, m. ~ line, courbe de niveau, f. ~ map, carte en courbes de niveau, f.

contraband, n, contrebande, f; (att.) de c.

contrabass, n, contrebasse, f.

contraceptive, a, contraceptif. ¶ n, préservatif, (slang) capote anglaise, f.

contract, n, contrat, m, convention, f, acte, traité, m. on ~ or by ~, à l'enterprise, à forfait, forfaitaire; par contrat. ~ bridge, bridge plafond, b. contrat, m. ¶ v.t, (shrink) contracter, [r]étrécir, resserrer; (law) contracter; [entre]prendre; (v.i. or abs.) contracter, s'étrécir, se rétrécir, se resserrer; (law) contracter. ~ant (pers.) n, contractant, e. ~ing, a, contractant. ~ion, n, contraction, f, [r]étrécissement, resserrement, m; abréviation, f. ~or, n, entrepreneur, euse; fournisseur, euse; adjudicataire, m.f. **contractual,** a, contractuel, forfaitaire.

contradict, v.t, contredire, démentir. ~ion, n, contredit, démenti, m. ~ory, a, contradictoire.

contradistinction, n, opposition, f.

contralto, n, contralto, m.

contrariety, n, contrariété, f. **contrarily & contrary,** ad, contrairement. **contrary,** a, contraire; opposé; inverse. ¶ n, contraire, opposé, rebours; contre-pied, m; contrepartie, f. on the ~, au contraire.

contrast, n, contraste, m, opposition, f. ¶ v.t. & i, mettre en contraste; contraster, trancher. ~y, a, heurté.

contravene, v.t, contrevenir à, enfreindre. **contravention,** n, contravention, infraction, f.

contribute, v.t, contribuer; (v.i.) contribuer à, collaborer à. ~ to (journal), collaborer à. **contribution**, n, contribution, f; apport, fournissement, m, cote, cotisation, f. to lay under ~, mettre à contribution. **contributor** (to journal) n, collaborateur, trice.

contrite, a, contrit. **contrition**, n, contrition, f, brisement de cœur, m.

contrivance, n, combinaison, f, dispositif; artifice, m. **contrive**, v.t, combiner; ménager. ~ to, faire en sorte que, s'ingénier à.

control, n, contrôle, m; commande, f; empire, m, maîtrise, f. ¶ v.t, contrôler, contenir, maîtriser; policer. **controller**, n, contrôleur, m.

controversial, a, de controverse. **controversy**, n, controverse, f. **controvert**, v.t, discuter.

contumacy, n, contumace, f.

contumely, n, outrage; opprobre, m.

contuse, v.t, contusionner. **contusion**, n, contusion, f.

conundrum, n, devinette, énigme, f.

convalesce, v.i, entrer en convalescence. **convalescence**, n, convalescence, f. **convalescent**, a. & n, convalescent, e.

convene, v.t, convoquer.

convenience, n, commodité, convenance; aise, f; (toilet) commodités, f.pl. **convenient**, a, commode, convenable. ~ly, ad, commodément.

convent, n, couvent, m. ~ school, couvent, m.

convention, n, convention, f. ~al, a, conventionnel, de convention; pompier. ~alism, n, poncif, m, le style pompier. ~alist, n, pompier, m.

converge, v.i, converger. **convergent**, a, convergent.

conversant, a, versé, ferré.

conversation, n, conversation, f; colloque, m. ~al, a, de, de la, conversation. ~[al]ist, n, causeur, euse.

converse, a. & n, contraire, a. & m; converse, a.f. & f, réciproque, a. & f. ¶ v.i, converser, causer.

conversion, n, conversion, f, convertissement (Fin.) m; transformation, f. **convert**, n, converti, e. ¶ v.t, convertir, transformer.

~ed goal, but de transformation, m. to become ~ed (Relig.), se convertir. ~er, n, convertisseur, m; adapteur, m. ~ible, a, convertible; (stocks) convertissable. ¶ n, (auto) décapotable, m.

convex, a, convexe. ~ity, n, convexité, f.

convey, v.t, [trans]porter, véhiculer, conduire, charrier, voiturer; (law, etc.) transmettre; communiquer, exprimer. ~ance, n, transport, charriage, m; voiture; (law) translation, transmission, mutation, f; (deed) acte de transmission, acte translatif de propriété, m.

convict, n, condamné, e, forçat, m. ~ prison, bagne, m. ¶ v.t, convaincre; condamner. ~ion, n, conviction, f; condamnation, f. person with previous ~s, récidiviste, m.f.

convince, v.t, convaincre. **convincing**, p.a, convaincant.

convivial, a: ~ gathering, joyeuse compagnie, f. ~ person, joyeux convive, bon c., m.

convocation, n, convocation, f. **convoke**, v.t, convoquer.

convolvulus, n, convolvulus, volubilis, m, belle-de-jour, f.

convoy, n, convoi, m; escorte, f. ¶ v.t, convoyer, escorter.

convulse, v.t, bouleverser. to be ~d (laughing), se tordre. **convulsion**, n, convulsion, f, bouleversement, m. **convulsive†**, a, convulsif.

cony, n, lapin, m.

coo, n, roucoulement, m. ¶ v.i, roucouler.

cook, n, cuisinier, ère; (ship's) [maître-]cook, m. ~book, livre de cuisine, m. ~'s mate, matelot coq, m. ¶ v.t, [faire] cuire; (fig.) cuisiner, falsifier; (v.i.) cuisiner. **cookery**, n, cuisine, f. **cookie**, n, petit gateau, biscuit, m. **cooking**, n, cuisine; cuisson, f. ~ apples, pommes à cuire, f.pl.

cool†, a, frais; froid; calme; hardi, sans gêne. ~-headed, à l'esprit calme. ¶ n, frais, m, fraîcheur, f. ¶ v.t, attiédir; rafraîchir; refroidir; (v.i.) s'attiédir, se refroidir. ~ down, se calmer, caler [la voile]. ~ one's heels, se morfondre. ~er, n, rafraîchisseur; refroidisseur, m; prison, f. ~ness, *n*, fraîcheur; froideur, *f*, froid; calme, sang-froid, flegme; sans-gêne, *m*.

coop, *n*, cage [à poulets], mue, *f*, poulailler, *m*. ~[up], *v.t*, claque-murer.

cooper, *n*, tonnelier, *m*. ~age, *n*, tonnellerie, *f*.

cooperate, *v.i*, coopérer. **co-operation**, *n*, coopération, *f*. **cooperative**, *a*, coopératif. ~ *society*, [société] coopérative, *f*.

coordinate, *v.t*, coordonner. ¶ *a*, coordonné.

coot, *n*, foulque, *f*.

cope, *n*, chape, *f*. ¶ *v.i*, lutter. ~ *with*, tenir tête à, suffire à.

Copenhagen, *n*, Copenhague, *f*.

coping, *n*, chaperon, couronne-ment, *m*.

copious†, *a*, copieux, riche, plan-tureux; nourri.

copper, *n*, cuivre [rouge] *m*. ~ [*coin*], cuivre, *m*, monnaie de cuivre, *f*, billion, *m*. ~ *beech*, hêtre rouge, *m*. ~*colored*, cuivré. ~*plate*, planche de cuivre, *f*, cuivre, *m*. ~*plate* [*engraving*], gravure sur cuivre, taille-douce, *f*. ~*smith*, chaudronnier, *m*. ¶ *v.t*, cuivrer.

copperas, *n*, couperose, *f*.

coppice, copse, *n*, taillis, *m*.

copulation, *n*, copulation, *f*.

copy, *n*, copie; transcription, *f*; calque, exemplaire; exemple, *m*. ~*book*, cahier d'écriture, livre d'exemples, *m*. ~*cat*, singe, *m*. ¶ *v.t*, copier; transcrire; calquer.

copying, *n*, transcription, *f*.

copyist, *n*, copiste, *m.f*.

copyright, *n*, droit d'auteur, *m*, propriété [littéraire] *f*. ~ *by so-&-so*, tous droits de reproduc-tion, de traduction, d'adaptation & d'exécution réservés pour tous pays.

coquet, *v.i*, coqueter. ~*ry*, *n*, coquetterie, *f*. **coquettish**, *a*, coquet.

coral, *n*, corail, *m*. ~ *fisher*, co-railleur, *m*. ~ *reef*, banc coral-lifère, *m*.

corbel, *n*, corbeau, *m*.

cord, *n*, corde; cordelette, *f*; cor-don; câble, *m*; (*braided*) ganse, *f*, spinal ~, moelle épinière, *f*. ¶ *v.t*, corder. ~*age*, *n*, cordages, *m.pl*.

cordial†, *a*, cordial, chaleureux. ¶ *n*, cordial, *m*. ~*ity*, *n*, cordia-lité, *f*.

corduroy, *n*, velours côtelé, *m*.

core, *n*, cœur, trognon; noyau, *m*; âme, *f*. (*computers*) ~ *storage*, mémoire à ferrites, m. à tores (magnétiques), *f*. ¶ *v.t*, vider (*une pomme, etc.*).

co-respondent, *n*, complice en adultère, *m.f*.

Corinth, *n*, Corinthe, *f*. **Corin-thian**, *a*, corinthien. ¶ *n*, Corin-thien, ne.

cork, *n*, liège; bouchon [en liège] *m*. ~ *jacket*, brassière de sauve-tage, *f*. ~*screw*, tire-bouchon, *m*. ~*screw curl*, boudin, *m*. ~*screw*, *v.i*, vriller. ~*tipped* (*cigarettes*), à bouts de liège. ~ *tree*, chêne-liège, *m*. ¶ *v.t*, boucher. ~*y*, *a*, liégeux. ~ *taste*, goût de bouchon, *m*.

cormorant, *n*, cormoran, *m*.

corn, *n*, maïs; (*on feet*) cor, *f*, (*soft*) œil-de-perdrix, *m*. ~ *cob*, épi de maïs, *m*, rafle, *f*. ~*flower*, bleuet, *m*.

corned beef, bœuf salé, *m*.

corner, *n*, coin, angle; tournant, virage, *m*; encoignure, *f*; recoin; (*Com.*) accaparement, *m*; (*att.*) cornier, d'angle; d'encoignure, de coin, du coin. ~ *cupboard*, encoignure, *f*. ~*stone*, pierre angulaire, *f*. ¶ *v.t*, acculer, ren-cogner; (*monopolize*) accaparer.

cornet, *n*, (*cone*) cornet; (*Mus.*) cornet à pistons, piston; (*ice cream wafer*) plaisir, *m*, oublie, *f*.

cornice, *n*, corniche, *f*.

Cornish, *a*, de Cornouailles.

cornucopia, *n*, corne d'abon-dance, *f*.

Cornwall, *n*, la Cornouailles.

corolla, *n*, corolle, *f*.

corollary, *n*, corollaire, *m*.

corona, *n*, couronne, *f*. **corona-tion**, *n*, couronnement, sacre, *m*, **coronet**, *n*, couronne, *f*.

coroner, *n*, coroner, *m*.

corporal† & corporeal†, *a*, corporel. **corporal**, *n*, caporal; (*cavalry*) brigadier, *m*. ~*ate*, *a*, social. ¶ *v.i*, faire corps. **corporation**, *n*, société, corpora-tion, *f*.

corps, *n*, corps, *m*.

corpse, *n*, cadavre, corps [mort] *m*. ~*like*, cadavéreux.

corpulence, -ency, *n*, cor-pulence, *f*, embonpoint, *m*, ré-plétion, *f*. **corpulent**, *a*, corpu-lent, ventru.

Corpus Christi, la Fête-Dieu.
corpuscle, *n*, corpuscule, *m*.
corral, *n*, enclos, *m*. ¶ *v.t*, enfermer dans un enclos.
correct†, *a*, correct; exact, juste. ¶ *v.t*, corriger; rectifier, redresser; surcharger. ~**ed copy**, corrigé, *m*. ~**ion**, *n*, correction; rectification, *f*, redressement, *m*; surcharge, *f*. ~**ional†**, *a*, correctionnel. ~**ive**, *n*, correctif, *m*. ~**ness**, *n*, correction, exactitude, justesse, *f*. ~**or**, *n*, correcteur, trice.
correlate, *v.t*, (*statistics*) corréler; relier, mettre en relation. **correlation**, *n*, corrélation, *f*. **correlative**, *a*, correlatif, ive.
correspond, *v.i*, correspondre; répondre. ~**ence**, *n*, correspondance, *f*; intelligences, *f.pl*. ~**ent**, *n*, correspondant, e. ~**ing**, *p.a*, correspondant.
corridor, *n*, couloir, corridor, *m*.
corroborate, *v.t*, corroborer.
corrode, *v.t*, corroder; ronger; miner. **corrosion**, *n*, corrosion, *f*. **corrosive**, *a*. & *n*, corrosif, *a*. & *m*.
corrugate, *v.t*, canneler, strier; onduler. ~**d** [*sheet*] **iron** & ~**d iron sheet**, tôle ondulée, *f*.
corrupt, *v.t*, corrompre, débaucher, vicier, gâter, gangrener. ~**ible**, *a*, corruptible; prenable. ~**ion**, *n*, corruption, *f*.
corsair, *n*, corsaire, *m*.
corset, *n*, corset, *m*. ~ **maker**, corsetier, ère. ¶ *v.t*, corseter.
Corsica, *n*, la Corse. **Corsican**, *a*, corse. ¶ *n*, Corse, *m,f*.
corundum, *n*, corindon, *m*.
coruscate, *v.i*, scintiller.
cos, *n*. or **Cos lettuce**, [laitue] romaine, *f*.
cosily, *ad*, à son aise, confortablement.
cosmetic, *a*. & *n*, cosmétique, *a*. & *m*.
cosmic(al), *a*, cosmique.
cosmopolitan & **cosmopolite**, *a*. & *n*, cosmopolite, *a*. & *m*.
cost, *n*, coût, prix, *m*; frais, *m.pl*, dépense, *f*. **at all** ~**s**, coûte que coûte, à toute force. ~ **of living bonus**, indemnité de vie chère, *f*. ~ **of living figure**, indice du coût de la vie, *m*. ~ [*price*], prix de revient, p. coûtant, p. d'acquisition, *m*. ¶ *v.i.ir*, coûter; revenir.
costive, *a*, constipé. ~**ness**, *n*, constipation, *f*.

costliness, *n*, cherté; somptuosité, *f*. **costly**, *a*, coûteux, dispendieux; somptueux.
costume, *n*, costume, *m*. ~ **piece**, ~ **play**, pièce historique, *f*. **costum[i]er**, *n*, couturier, *m*.
cot, *n*, lit d'enfant; lit pliant, lit de camp, *m*.
coterie, *n*, coterie, chapelle, *f*. ~ **of wits**, bureau d'esprit, *m*.
cottage, *n*, chaumière; habitation ouvrière, *f*; cottage, chalet; (*fig*.) chaume, *m*.
cotter, *n*, clavette, *f*. ~ **pin**, goupille, *f*.
cotton, *n*, coton, *m*; (*thread*) fil à coudre, *m*. ~ [*cloth*], cotonnade, toile de coton, *f*. **absorbent** ~, coton hydrophile, *m*. ~ **goods**, cotonnade, *f*. ~ **mill**, filature de coton, *f*. ~ **plant**, cotonnier, *m*. ~ **waste**, bourre de coton, *f*. ~ **wool**, ouate [de coton] *f*, coton [en laine] *m*. ~**y**, *a* cotonneux.
couch, *n*, couche; chaise longue, *f*; canapé, *m*. ¶ *v.i*, se coucher; se tapir, se blottir. ~**ed in these terms**, ainsi conçu. ~ [*grass*] *n*, chiendent, *m*.
cough, *n*, toux, *f*. ~ **mixture**, sirop, *m*, (*ou* potion, *f*.) pour la toux. ~ **drop**, pastille pour la t., *f*. **whooping** ~, coqueluche, *f*. ¶ *v.i*, tousser, ~ **up**, expectorer.
council, *n*, conseil; (*Eccl*.) concile, *m*. **councillor**, *n*, conseiller, ère.
counsel, *n*, conseil, *m*; délibération, *f*; (*pers*.) avocat, conseil, défenseur, *m*. ¶ *v.t*, conseiller. **counselor**, *n*, conseiller, ère.
count, *n*, compte, (*pers*.) comte, *m*. ~ **down**, compte à rebours, *m*. ~ **of indictment**, chef d'accusation, *m*. ¶ *v.t*. & *i*, compter; nombrer; (*votes*) recenser, dépouiller.
countenance, *n*, contenance; physionomie, figure, mine, *f*. ¶ *v.t*, approuver; encourager.
counter, *n*, riposte, *f*; (*play*) jeton, *m*, fiche, *f*; (*shop*) comptoir, *m*; (*cashier's*) caisse, *f*, guichet, *m*. ¶ *v.t*, riposter. **to run** ~ **to**, aller à l'encontre de.
counteract, *v.t*, contrecarrer.
counterattack, *n*, contre-attaque, *f*.
counterbalance, *n*, contrepoids, *m*. ¶ *v.t*, contrebalancer, équilibrer.

counterclaim, *n*, reconvention, *f*.

counterfeit, *a*, contrefait, faux. ¶ *n*, contrefaçon, *f*. ¶ *v.t*, contrefaire. ~er, *n*, contrefacteur, faux monnayeur, *m*.

counterfoil, *n*, souche, *f*, talon, *m*.

counter instructions, contrordre, *m*.

countermand, *v.t*, contremander; (*Com.*) décommander. ¶ *n*, contrordre, *m*.

counterpane, *n*, couverture [de lit] *f*.

counterpart, *n*, contrepartie, *f*; (*pers.*) pendant; (*deed*) double, *m*.

counterpoint, *n*, contrepoint, *m*.

counterpoise, *n*, contrepoids, *m*. ¶ *v.t*, contrebalancer, équilibrer.

countershaft, *n*, arbre secondaire, a. de renvoi, *m*.

countersign, (*Mil.*) *n*, mot de ralliement, *m*. ¶ *v.t*, contresigner.

countersink, *n*, fraisure, *f*. ~ [*bit*], fraise, *f*. ¶ *v.t*, fraiser.

counterstroke, *n*, riposte, *f*.

counterweight, *n*, contrepoids, *m*.

countess, *n*, comtesse, *f*.

counting, *n*, compte; recensement, *m*. **countless**, *a*, innombrable.

country, *n*, pays, *m*; contrée; campagne; province; patrie, *f*; corps électoral, *m*. ~ *club*, country-club, *m*. ~ *house*, maison de campagne, *f*. ~ *life*, vie champêtre, v. rurale, *f*. ~*man*, -*woman*, campagnard, e. [*fellow*] ~*man* -*woman*, compatriote, *m,f.*, campagne, campagne, *f*. ~ *town*, ville de province, *f*. *open* ~, rase campagne, *f*.

county, *n*, comté, *m*. ~ *seat*, chef-lieu, *m*.

couple, *n*, (*things*) couple, *f*; (*pers.*, *Mech.*) couple, *m*. ¶ *v.t*, coupler, accoupler; atteler. **couplet**, *n*, distique, *m*. **coupling**, *n*, accouplement; manchon; attelage, *m*.

coupon, *n*, coupon, *m*.

courage, *n*, courage, *m*. ~**ous†**, *a*, courageux.

courier, *n*, courrier, *m*.

course, *n*, cours; courant, *m*; carrière; route; direction, *f*; chenal; trajet, *m*; marche, *f*; processus; parti; stage; (*meal*) service, plat, *m*; (*Build.*) assise; couche, *f*; (*ground*) champ; terrain; parcours, *m*. *in due* ~, en temps & lieu. *of* ~, naturellement, bien entendu, certainement. *why, of* ~*!* parbleu! ¶ *v.t*. & *i*, chasser, courir. **courser** (*Poet.*) *n*, coursier, *m*. **coursing**, *n*, chasse au lévrier, *f*.

court, *n*, cour, *f*; tribunal; conseil, *m*; chambre; audience, *f*; (*Ten.*) court, jeu; tennis; (*croquet*) terrain, *m*. ~ *house*, palais de justice, *m*. ~ *martial*, conseil de guerre, *m*. ~ *plaster*, taffetas d'Angleterre, *m*. ~*yard*, cour, *f*; préau, *m*. ¶ *v.t*, faire sa cour à, courtiser; (*favor*) briguer; (*disaster*) inviter.

courteous†, *a*, courtois, honnête. **courtesan**, *n*, courtisane, hétaïre, *f*. **courtesy**, *n*, courtoisie, honnêteté, *f*. **courtier**, *n*, courtisan, *m*; (*pl.*) gens de cour, *m.pl*. **courtly**, *a*, courtois. **courtship**, *n*, cour, *f*.

cousin, *n*, cousin, e. *first* ~, cousin germain, *m*.

cove (*bay*) *n*, anse, *f*, accul, *m*.

covenant, *n*, convention, *f*, pacte, *m*. ¶ *v.i*, s'engager.

Coventry (*to send to*) (*fig.*), mettre en quarantaine.

cover, *n*, couverture; enveloppe, *f*; tapis; pli, *m*; gaine, *f*; couvercle; capot, *m*; chape, *f*, chapeau; plateau, *m*; chemise, *f*; étui; fourreau; couvert; abri; fourré, *m*, remise, *f*; masque, voile, *m*; provision, marge, *f*, acompte, *m*; prévision, *f*. ¶ *v.t*, couvrir, recouvrir, envelopper, revêtir, tapisser; masquer; parcourir. ~*ed walk*, allée en berceau, *f*. ~*ing*, *n*, couverture, *f*; vêtement, *m*. ~*let*, *n*, couverture pour berceau, *f*.

covert, *a*, voilé, indirect.

covet, *v.t*, convoiter, reluquer. ~**ous**, *a*, convoiteux, cupide. ~**ousness**, *n*, convoitise, *f*.

covey, *n*, compagnie, *f*.

cow, *n*, vache, *f*; (*att.*, *of elephants, etc.*) femelle. ~ *bell*, clarine, sonnaille, *f*. ~*herd*, vacher, ère. ~ *hide*, [peau de] vache, *f*, cuir de v., *m*. ~ *shed*, étable à vaches, vacherie, *f*. ~*lick* (hair), épi, *m*. ~*pox*, vaccine, *f*. ¶ *v.t*, intimider.

coward, *n*, poltron, ne, lâche,

couard, *m.* ~ice, *n*, poltronnerie, lâcheté, couardise, *f.* ~ly, *a*, poltron, lâche, couard.

cower, *v.i*, se blottir, se tapir, s'accroupir.

cowl, *n*, capuchon, *m*, capote, *f*, champignon, *m*, mitre, *f.*

cowrie, *n*, porcelaine, *f.*

cowslip, *n*, coucou, *m*, primevère des champs, *f.*

coxcomb, *n*, fat, freluquet, *m.*

coxswain (*abb.* cox) *n*, barreur, patron, *m.*

coy, *a*, réservé, farouche. ~ness, *n*, réserve, *f.*

cozen, *v.t*, duper; séduire.

cozy, *a*, confortable; douillet.

crab, *n*, (*Crust.*) crabe, cancre; (*hoisting*) treuil, *m.* ~ [*apple*], pomme sauvage, *f.* ~ [*apple tree*], pommier sauvage, *m.* ~ [*louse*], morpion, *m.* crabbed, *a*, acariâtre, revêche, grincheux, bourru. ~ handwriting, écriture de pattes de mouche, *f.*

crack, *n*, fente, fissure, crevasse, fêlure; craquelure, *f*; (*noise*) craquement; claquement; coup sec, crac, *m*, cric crac, flic flac. ~ of doom, dernier jugement, *m.* ¶ *v.t*, fendre; fêler; fendiller; gercer; crever; (*nuts*) casser; (*open a bottle*) décoiffer. ~ed (*daft*) *p.a*, timbré, toqué.

cracker, *n*, (*food*) craquelin, (*petroleum*) craqueur, *m.*

crackle, *v.i*, craque[te]r, crépiter; pétiller. crackling, *n*, friton, gratton, *m.*

Cracow, *n*, Cracovie, *f.*

cradle, *n*, berceau, moïse; (*Surg.*) arceau, cerceau, *m.* ¶ *v.t*, bercer.

craft, *n*, adresse, *f*; artifice, *m*; astuce, *f*; métier, *m*; (*Naut.*) embarcation, allège, *f.* craftily, *ad*, artificieusement. craftsman, *n*, homme de métier, artisan, *m.* ~ship, *n*, travail d'artisan, *m.* crafty, *a*, artificieux, rusé, futé, cauteleux, retors.

crag, *n*, rocher, *m.* craggy, *a*, anfractueux.

cram, *v.t*, bonder, bourrer, fourrer; farcir; (*poultry*) gaver; (*exam*) potasser, gaver, chauffer.

cramp, *n*, crampe, colique, *f.* ¶ *v.t*, resserrer, entraver, gêner; cramponner.

cranberry, *n*, canneberge, *f.*

crane, *n*, (*bird & hoist*) grue, *f.* ¶ *v.t*, tendre le cou.

cranium, *n*, crâne, *m.*

crank, *n*, (*Mach.*) manivelle, *f*, coude; (*pers.*) excentrique, original, *m*, maniaque, *m,f*; (*whim*) marotte, *f.* ~ gear (cycle), pédalier, *m.* ~ pin, bouton de manivelle, *m.* ~ shaft, arbre à manivelle, arbre coudé, vilebrequin, *m.* ~ tool, [outil à] crochet, *m.* ¶ *v.t*, couder.

cranny, *n*, fente, crevasse, *f.*

crash, *n*, fracas, écrasement; krach, *m*, débâcle, chute, *f.* ¶ *i*, patatras! ¶ *v.i*, s'abattre; tomber, s'écraser (*sur le sol, la chaussée, etc.*).

crass, *a*, crasse (*a.f.*), grossier.

crate, *n*, caisse à claire-voie, harasse, *f.*

crater, *n*, cratère; (*mine, Mil.*) entonnoir, *m.*

crave, *v.t*, implorer. ~ for, appéter.

craven, *a*, poltron, lâche.

craving, *n*, ardent désir, *m*, soif, appétence, fringale, *f.*

crawl, *n*, (*Swim.*) crawl, *m.* ¶ *v.i*, ramper, se traîner.

crayfish, *n*, (*river*) écrevisse; (*sea*) langouste, *f.*

crayon, *n*, [crayon] pastel, *m.*

craze, *n*, folie, fureur, toquade, marotte, manie, *f*, crazy, *a*, délabré; dément, détraqué, toqué, piqué. to drive someone ~, rompre la cervelle à quelqu'un.

creak, *v.i*, grincer, crier, craquer. ¶ *n*, grincement, crissement, *m.*

cream, *n*, crème, *f*; (*of story*) bon, *m.* ¶ *v.t*, écrémer, battre en crème. ~ cheese, fromage blanc, *m.* ~colored, couleur crème. ~ jug, crémier, *m.* ~ery, *n*, crémerie, *f.* ~y, *a*, crémeux.

crease, *n*, pli, faux pli, godet, *m.* ¶ *v.t*, plisser; (*v.i.*) [se] plisser. ~less, *a*, infroissable.

create, *v.t*, créer; faire, produire; provoquer. creation, *n*, création, *f.* creative, *a*, créateur. creator, *n*, créateur, trice. creature, *n*, créature, *f*, être; animal, *m*, bête, *f.* ~ comforts, aises, *f.pl.*

credence, *n*, créance, *f.* credentials, *n.pl*, lettres de créance; l—s d'introduction, *f.pl*; pouvoirs, *m.pl.* credibility, *n*, crédibilité, *f.* credible, *a*, croyable; digne de foi. credibly, *ad*, de bonne source.

credit, *n*, croyance, foi, créance, consistance, *f*; honneur; crédit, avoir, *m. do ~ to*, honorer. *~ bal-ance*, solde créditeur, *m.* ¶ *v.t*, ajouter foi à; créditer, bonifier. *~able, a.* reluisant. *~s, n, (cin-ema)* générique, *m. ~or, n,* créancier, ère. créditeur, *m.*

credo, *n,* credo, symbole, *m.*

credulity, *n,* crédulité, bonho-mie, *f.* **credulous,** *a,* crédule.

creed, *n,* credo, symbole; culte, *m,* croyance, *f.*

creek, *n,* crique, *f.*

creel, *n,* panier à pêche, *m.*

creep, *v.i.ir,* ramper; cheminer. *it makes one's flesh ~,* cela fait venir la chair de poule. *~er, n,* plante grimpante, *f; (grapnel)* grappin, *m. ~ing paralysis,* para-lysie progressive, *f.*

cremate, *v.t,* incinérer. **crema-tion,** *n,* crémation, incinération, *f.* **crematorium,** *n,* four créma-toire, *m.*

Cremona, *n,* Crémone, *f.*

creole, *n. & a,* créole, *m,f. & a.*

creosote, *n,* créosote, *f.*

crepitate, *v.i,* crépiter.

crescendo, *ad. & n,* crescendo, *ad. & m.*

crescent, *n,* croissant, *m; (of buildings)* demilune, *f.*

cresset, *n,* torchère, *f.*

crest, *n,* crête; huppe, *f;* cimier, *m. ~fallen,* penaud. *~ed, a,* crêté, huppé, aigretté; *(sea)* moutonneuse.

Crete, *n,* la Crète.

cretonne, *n,* cretonne, *f.*

crevasse, *n,* crevasse [glaciaire] *f.* **crevice,** *n,* crevasse, fente, lézarde, *f.*

crew, *n, (ship)* équipage, *m; (boat)* équipe, *f; (set, gang)* bande, *f.*

crewel stitch *(Emb.),* point de tige, point coulé, *m.*

crib, *n,* crèche, mangeoire; ca-bane; couchette, *f;* larcin, *m.* ¶ *v.t,* chiper.

cribbage, *n,* cribbage, *m.*

crick *(in neck) n,* torticolis, *m.*

cricket, *n,* grillon, criquet, cricri; *(game)* cricket, *m.*

crier, *n,* crieur, *m.*

crime, *n,* crime, forfait, *m.*

Crimea (the), la Crimée.

criminal†, *a,* criminel. *~ law,* droit pénal, *m.* ¶ *n,* criminel, le. **criminate,** *v.t,* incriminer, charger.

crimp, *v.t,* friser, crêper; fraiser, gaufrer.

crimson, *a,* cramoisi, pourpre. *~ clover,* trèfle incarnat, farouch[e] *m.* ¶ *n,* cramoisi, *m,* pourpre, *f.* ¶ *v.t,* empourprer.

cringe, *v.i,* faire le chien cou-chant. **cringing,** *p.a,* servile.

crinkle, *n,* plissement, *m.* ¶ *v.t. & i,* plisser.

cripple, *n,* impotent, e, estropié, e. ¶ *v.t,* estropier; *(fig.)* para-lyser. *~d, a,* impotent, estropié, éclopé, perclus; *(ship)* incom-modé.

crisis, *n,* crise, *f.*

crisp, *a,* cassant, croquant; *(air)* vivifiant, vif; *(hair)* frisé; *(style)* concis. ¶ *v.t,* crêper.

crisscross, *v.i,* s'entrecroiser.

criterion, *n,* critère, critérium, *m.*

critic, *n,* critique; censeur; fron-deur, *m. ~al, a,* critique; décisif. **criticism,** *n,* critique, glose, *f.* **criticizable,** *a,* critiquable. **criti-cize,** *v.t,* critiquer; censurer.

croak, *v.i, (raven)* croasser; *(frog)* coasser.

crochet, *n, & ~ hook,* crochet, *m.*

crockery, *n,* faïence, vaisselle, *f.*

crocodile, *n,* crocodile, *m. ~ tears,* larmes de crocodile, *f.pl.*

crocus, *n,* crocus, safran, *m.*

Croesus, *n,* Crésus, *m.*

crone, *n,* vieille femme momifiée, *f.*

crony, *n,* compère, *m.*

crook, *n,* crochet, *m;* houlette, crosse, *f; (pers.)* escroc, *m.* ¶ *v.t,* recourber. *~ed, a,* crochu, tortu, tors; gauche; de travers; *(legs)* cagneux; *(fig.)* tortueux, oblique, indirect. *~edly, ad,* de travers; tortueusement. *~edness, n,* guin-gois, *m.*

crop, *n,* récolte; cueillette, *f; (bird)* jabot, *m,* poche; *(whip)* cra-vache, *f.* ¶ *v.t,* tondre, bretau-der; *(ears)* essoriller, écourter. *~ up,* surgir. *~ up again,* re-bondir.

croquet, *n,* croquet, *m. ~ court,* terrain de croquet, *m.* ¶ *v.t,* croquer.

crosier, *n,* crosse, *f.*

cross, *a,* de méchante humeur. ¶ *comps: ~bar, ~beam,* tra-verse, *f. ~belt,* bandoulière, *f;* baudrier, *m. ~bred,* métis, mâ-tiné. *~breed,* race croisée, *f,* métis, se. *~breeding,* croise-ment, métissage, *m. (informa-*

tion) ~-checking, recoupement, m. ~-country running, race, cross-country, m. ~-examine someone, faire subir à quelqu'un un interrogatoire; tenir qqn sur la sellette. ~-eyed, louche. ~piece, entretoise, f. to be at ~-purposes, se contrecarrer. ~ reference, référence croisée, f. ~-road, chemin de traverse, m. traverse, f; (pl.) carrefour, m. ~ section, coupe en travers, f, profil transversal, m. ~-stitch, point de croix, m. ~word [puzzle], mots croisés [-énigmes], m.pl. ¶ n, croix; (fig.) croix, f, calvaire; croisement; croisillon, m; (on a letter t) barre, f. ¶ v.t, croiser; traverser, couper, passer, franchir; (a "t") barrer; contrarier, contrecarrer. ~ oneself, se signer. ~ out, rayer, radier, biffer, barrer.

crossing, n, croisement, m; traversée, f, passage, m.

crotchet, n, (Mus.) noire, f; (whim) boutade, lubie, quinte, f. ~ rest (Mus.), soupir, m. ~y, a, quinteux.

crouch, v.i, se tapir, se blottir, s'accroupir.

croup (Med.) n, croup, m.

croup (rump) n, croupe, f.

crow, n, corbeau, m, corneille, f; (cock's) chant, m. ~[bar], pince [à levier] f. ~foot (Bot.), renoncule, f. ~'s-foot (wrinkle), patte-d'oie, f. ~'s-nest (Naut.), nid de pie, m; 'hune de vigie, f. as the ~ flies, à vol d'oiseau. ¶ v.i.ir, chanter. ~ over, chanter victoire par.

crowd, n, foule, presse, f, rassemblement, monde, m, cohue, f. ~ round, se presser autour de, assiéger. ~ed, p.a, fréquenté, comble.

crown, n, couronne, f; (head, arch) sommet; (hat) fond, m. ¶ v.t, couronner; (checkers) damer. ~ing, n, couronnement, m. ¶ a, suprême.

crucial, a, décisif, critique.

crucible, n, creuset, pot, m.

crucifix, n, crucifix, christ, m. ~ion, n, crucifiement, m, crucifixion, f. crucify, v.t, crucifier.

crude, a, cru, brut; informe; indigeste; primitif. ~ly, ad, crûment. ~ness, n, crudité, f.

cruel†, a, cruel. ~ty, n, cruauté, f; (in law) sévices, m.pl.

cruet, n, ménagère, f, huilier, m; (Eccl.) burette, f.

cruise, n, croisière; campagne, f. ¶ v.i, croiser; (for sexual partner) draguer. cruiser, n, croiseur, m. cruising: ~ fleet & ~ ground, croisière, f. ~ taxicab, taxi en maraude, m.

crumb, n, miette; (opp. crust) mie, f. ¶ (Cook.) v.t, paner.

crumble, v.t, émietter; (v.i.) s'émietter; crouler, tomber. crumbly, a, friable.

crumple, v.t, chiffonner; (v.i.) se c. ~ up, s'écraser.

crunch, v.t. & i, croquer, craquer. ¶ i, crocl

crupper, n, croupe; (harness) croupière, f.

crusade, n, croisade, f. ¶ v.i, entreprendre une croisade. crusader, n, croisé, m.

crush, (crowd) n, cohue, f. ¶ v.t, écraser; froisser; broyer, concasser. ~er, n, broyeur, concasseur, m.

crust, n, croûte; croustille; (earth's) écorce, croûte, f; morceau de pain, m. crustacean, a. & n, crustacé, a. & m. crusted, a, encroûté. crusty, a, (bread) croustillant; (fig.) irritable, bourru. crust[y] end (bread), croûton, grignon, m.

crutch, n, béquille, f.

crux, n, pivot, nœud, m.

cry, n, cri, m. ~ baby, pleurnicheur, m. to be in full ~, aboyer. ¶ v.i, crier, s'écrier; pleurer; (v.t.) crier, chanter; tambouriner. ~ out, crier; s'écrier. ¶ n, cri[s] m.[pl.].

crypt, n, crypte, f.

crystal, n, cristal, m. ¶ a, de cristal. ~ gazing, cristallomancie, f. ~ [glass], cristal, m. ~ glass[ware] making or works, cristallerie, f. crystalline, a, cristallin. ~ lens (eye), cristallin, m. crystalize, v.t, cristalliser; (v.i.) [se] cristalliser. crystalized fruits, fruits candis, m.pl.

cub, n, petit, m.

Cuban, a, cubain. ¶ n, Cubain, e.

cube, n, cube, m. ~ root, racine cubique, r. cube, f. ~ sugar, sucre en morceaux, s. cassé, m. ¶ v.t, cuber. cubic, a, cube; cubique. ~ foot, pied cube, m. = 0.028317 cubic meter. ~ inch, pouce cube, *m.* = 16.387 cubic centimeters. ~ *yard*, yard cube, *m.* = 0.764553 cubic meter. ~al, *a*, cubique.

cubicle, *n*, alcôve de dortoir, *f.*

cubism, *n*, cubisme, *m.* **cubist**, *n*, cubiste, *m.f.*

cuckoo, *n*, coucou, *m.* ~ *clock*, pendule à coucou, *f*, coucou, *m.*

cucumber, *n*, concombre, *m.*

cud, *n*, aliment ruminé, *m.*

cuddle, *v.t*, câliner, pouponner, serrer dans ses bras. ~ *up*, se pelotonner, se blottir.

cudgel, *n*, bâton, gourdin, *m*, trique, *f.* ¶ *v.t*, bâtonner; (*one's brains*) torturer. **cudgeling**, *n*, bastonnade, *f.*

cue, *n*, (*Theat.*) réplique; (*Bil.*) queue, *f.*

cuff, *n*, (*blow*) calotte, taloche, *f*; (*shirt*) manchette, *f*; poignet; (*coat*) parement, *m.* ~ *links*, boutons de manchettes, *m.pl.* ¶ *v.t*, calotter.

cuirass, *n*, cuirasse, *f.* ~ier, *n*, cuirassier, *m.*

culinary, *a*, culinaire.

cull, *v.t*, cueillir; recueillir.

culminate, *v.i*, atteindre sa plus grande hauteur; aboutir; (*Astr.*) culminer. **culminating**, *a*, culminant.

culpability, *n*, culpabilité, *f.* **culpable**, *a*, coupable. **culprit**, *n*, coupable, *m.f.*

cultivate, *v.t*, cultiver. **cultivation**, *n*, culture, *f.* **cultivator**, *n*, cultivateur, trice. **culture**, *n*, culture, *f.* ~d (*pers., pearl*) *p.a*, de culture.

culvert, *n*, ponceau, *m.*

cumber, *v.t*, embarrasser, encombrer. ~some, **cumbrous**, *a*, embarrassant, encombrant.

cumulative, *a*, cumulatif.

cumulus, *n*, cumulus, *m.*

cuneiform, *a*, cunéiforme.

cunning, *a*, rusé, artificieux; habile. ¶ *n*, finesse, finasserie, ruse, *f.*

cup, *n*, tasse; coupe; timbale, *f*; calice, bol, *m.* ~ *bearer*, échanson, *m.* ~board, armoire, *f*; buffet; (*wall*) placard, *m.* ¶ (*Surg.*) *v.t*, ventouser.

cupel, *n*, coupelle, *f.* ¶ *v.t*, coupeller.

Cupid, *n*, Cupidon, *m.*

cupidity, *n*, cupidité, *f.*

cupola, *n*, coupole, *f.*

cupping glass, ventouse, *f.*

cur, *n*. roquet, *m.*

curable, *a*, curable.

curacy, *n*, vicariat, *m.* **curate**, *n*, vicaire, *m.*

curative, *a*, curatif, médicamenteux.

curator, *n*, conservateur, trice.

curb, *n*, (*harness*) gourmette; (*street*) bordure, margelle, *f*; (*fig.*) bride, *f*, frein, *m.* ¶ *v.t*, (*horse*) gourmer; (*street*) border; (*fig.*) brider, modérer.

curd[s], *n.[pl.]*, caillé, *m*, caillebotte, *f.* **curdle**, *v.t*, cailler; (*fig.*) glacer.

cure, *n*, guérison; cure, *f*; remède, *m*; (*souls*) charge, *f.* ¶ *v.t*, guérir; remédier à; (*salt*) saler; (*smoke*) fumer; (*herrings*) caquer.

curfew, *n*, couvre-feu, *m.*

curiosity & curio, *n*, curiosité, rareté, *f*, bibelot, *m. curio cabinet*, vitrine, table vitrée, *f.* **curious**, *a*, curieux. *the ~ part or thing*, le curieux. ~ *person*, curieux, euse.

curl, *n*, boucle, *f*, frison, *m.* (*pl.*) frisure; spirale, *f.* ¶ *v.t*, friser, boucler, bichonner; (*lip*) retrousser. ~ *up*, se mettre en boule, se pelotonner. **curler** (*hair*) *n*, épingle [à friser] *f*; (*leather*) bigoudi [à friser] *m.*

curlew, *n*, courlis, courlieu, *m.*

curliness, *n*, frisure, *f.* **curling**, *n*, frisure, *f.* ~ *tongs*, fer à friser, *m.* **curly**, *a*, frisé, bouclé.

curmudgeon, *n*, bourru; ladre, pingre, *m.*

currant, *n*, (*red, white*) groseille [à grappes] *f*; (*black*) cassis; (*dried*) raisin de Corinthe, *m.* ~ *bush*, groseillier [à grappes]; cassis, *m.*

currency, *n*, cours, *m*, circulation; monnaie, *f.* [*foreign*] ~, devise [étrangère], monnaie étrangère, *f.* **current**, *a*, courant, en cours; de mise. ~ *events*, actualités, *f.pl.* ~ *liabilities*, exigibilités, *f.pl.* ¶ *n*, courant, *m. peak* ~, courant de pointe, *m.*

curriculum, *n*, programme d'études, *m.*

curry (*Cook.*) *n*, cari, kari, *m.* ¶ *v.t*, (*leather*) corroyer; (*horse*) étriller. ~ *favor with*, se faufiler dans les bonnes grâces de. ~comb, étrille, *f.* ~ing, *n*, corroi; étrillage, *m.*

curse, n, malédiction, imprécation, f; fléau, m. ¶ v.t, maudire; affliger; (v.i.) blasphémer, jurer. **cursed**, a, maudit.

cursor, n, (computers) curseur, m.

cursory, a, hâtif, rapide.

curt, a, bref, sec, cassant, brusque.

curtail, v.t, raccourcir, écourter; (output) contingenter.

curtain, n, rideau; brise-bise, m; toile, f; tableau! ~ holder, embrasse, f. ~ net, vitrage, m. ~ raiser, lever de rideau, m. ~ rod, tringle de rideau; tringle de brise-bise, f.

curtly, ad, brusquement.

curtsy, n, révérence, f.

curvature, n, courbure, f. ~ of the spine, déviation de la colonne vertébrale, f.

curve, n, courbe, f. ¶ v.t, courber, cintrer. **curvet**, n, courbette, f. ¶ v.i, faire des courbettes. **curvilinear**, a, curviligne.

cushion, n, coussin; coussinet; bourrelet; carreau, m; (Bil.) bande, f. ¶ v.t, amortir. ~ cover, dessus de coussin, m, taie de coussin, f.

custard, n, flan, m; crème, f.

custodian, n, gardien, ne. **custody**, n, garde, charge; arrestation, f.

custom, n, usage, m, coutume; pratique, f; achalandage, m. ~ary, a, usuel, d'usage, ordinaire; coutumier. ~er, n, client, e; chaland, e; (at café) consommateur, m; (at bank) déposant, e.

customization, adaptation à l'usager, f.

customs, n.pl, douane[s] f.[pl.]. ~ or custom house, douane, f. ~ [duty], douane, f, droit[s] de douane, m.[pl.]. ~ agent, agent en douane, m. ~ officer, agent de la douane, douanier, m.

cut, n, coupure, coupe, entaille, saignée; fouille, f, déblai, m; taille, passe; taillade, balafre, f; coup, m, atteinte, f, affront; morceau, m, tranche; réduction, compression, f; dégrèvement, m; vignette; gravure, f. short~, raccourci, m. ¶ v.t.ir, couper; tailler; entailler; entamer; découper; trancher; rogner; fendre; cingler; (teeth) faire; graver. have one's hair ~, se faire couper les che-

veux. ~ a class, sécher une classe. ~ & dried or dry, tout taillé, tout fait. ~ back (Hort.) receper. ~ [crystal] glass, cristal taillé, m. ~ down, abattre; moissonner; rogner; sabrer. ~ off, couper; retrancher; amputer; intercepter; isoler; moissonner. ~ out, découper, couper, tailler; retrancher; supprimer. ~ short, écourter; trancher. ~throat, coupe-jarret, escarpe, m. ~ up, découper, dépecer; débiter; tronçonner.

cutaneous, a, cutané.

cute, a, attirant; fin, rusé.

cuticle, n, cuticule, f.

cutlass, n, sabre, m.

cutler, n, coutelier, ère. **cutlery**, n, coutellerie, f.

cutlet, n, côtelette, f.

cutter, n, (clothes, etc.) coupeur, euse; (gems, stone, files) tailleur; (price) gâte-métier, m; (tool) lame, f, couteau, m; fraise; molette, f; (boat) cotre; canot, m. ~ wheel, molette, f. **cutting**, p.a, coupant, tranchant; piquant, caustique, acéré. ~ board, tranchoir, m. ~ edge, tranchant, coupant, fil, m. ¶ n, taille; coupe; (teeth) pousse; (newspaper) coupure; tranchée, f, déblai, m; percée, f; copeau, m; rognure, f; (snip of cloth) chanteau, m, retaille; (plant) bouture, f. ~ out (clothes), coupe, f.

cuttle fish, seiche, f.

cutwater, n, (bow) taille-mer, f; (bridge) bec, m.

cyanide, n, cyanure, m.

cyclamen, n, cyclamen, m.

cycle, n, cycle, m; bicyclette, f; vélocipède, m. ~ track, vélodrome, m. ¶ v.i, aller à bicyclette, pédaler. **cycling**, n, cyclisme, m. **cyclist**, n, [bi]cycliste, m,f.

cyclone, n, cyclone, m.

cygnet, n, jeune cygne, m.

cylinder, n, cylindre; corps; barillet; fourreau, m. **cylindrical**, a, cylindrique.

cymbals, n.pl, cymbales, f.pl.

cynic, n, cynique, m. ¶ ~ & **cynical†**, a, cynique. **cynicism**, n, cynisme, m.

cynosure (fig.) n, pointe de mire, m.

cypress, n, cyprès. m.

Cyprus, n, Chypre, f.

cyst (*Med.*) *n*, kyste, *m*.

Czech, *a.* & (*language*) *n*, tchèque, *a.* & *m*. ¶ (*pers.*) *n*, Tchèque, *m.f.* **Czechoslovak**, *n*, Tchécoslovaque, *m.f.* **Czechoslovakia**, *n*, Tchécoslovaquie, *f.*

D

D (*Mus.*) letter, ré, *m*.

dab, *n*, coup de tampon, d'éponge, de mouchoir, etc; petit tas mou, *m*; (*fish*) limande, *f.* ¶ *v.t*, tamponner; éponger. **dabber**, *n*, tampon, *m*.

dabble, *v.i*, barboter, patauger. ~ *on the stock exchange*, boursicoter.

dace, *n*, vandoise, vaudoise, *f*, dard, *m*.

dachshund, *n*, basset allemand, *m*.

dad[dy], *n*, papa, *m*.

daddy longlegs, *n*, tipule, *f.*

dado, *n*, lambris d'appui, *m*.

daffodil, *n*, narcisse des prés, *m*.

daft, *a*, timbré.

dagger, *n*, poignard, *m*; (*Typ.*) croix, *f. at ~s drawn*, à couteaux tirés.

dahlia, *n*, dahlia, *m*.

daily, *a*, quotidien, journalier. ~ [*paper*], [journal] quotidien, *m*. ¶ *ad*, journellement, quotidiennement.

dainties, *n.pl*, friandises, chatteries, douceurs, *f.pl*. **daintily**, *ad*, délicatement. **daintiness**, *n*, délicatesse, chatterie, *f*. **dainty**, *a*, friand, délicat; mignon.

dairy, *n*, laiterie, crémerie, *f.* ~ [*farm*], vacherie, *f*. ~*maid*, fille de ferme, *f*. ~*man*, laitier, crémier, *m*.

dais, *n*, estrade, *f*.

daisy, *n*, marguerite, pâquerette, *f.*

dale, *n*, vallon, val, *m*, combe, *f*.

dally, *v.i*, s'amuser, batifoler; tarder.

Dalmatia, *n*, la Dalmatie. **Dalmatian**, *a*, dalmate.

dam, *n*, barrage, *m*, digue; (*animal*) mère, *f*. ¶ *v.t*, barrer, endiguer.

damage, *n*, dommage, dégât, *m*, avarie, *f*, mal, *m*; (*pl., law*) dommages-intérêts, *m.pl.* ¶ *v.t*, endommager, avarier. ~ *wilfully*, saboter.

damascene, *v.t*, damasquiner.

Damascus, *n*, Damas, *m*. **damask**, *n*, damas, *m*.

damn, *v.t*, damner; (*a play*) tomber. ~*able*, *a*, damnable, maudit. ~*ation*, *n*, damnation, *f*. ~*ed*, *a*, damné, maudit; sacré. *the* ~, les damnés. ~*ing*, *p.a*, accablant, écrasant.

damp, *a*, humide; moite. ~ *mark* (*in books*), tache d'humidité, mouillure, *f*. ¶ *n*, humidité, *f.* ¶ *v.t*, humecter, mouiller, tremper; (*fig.*) refroidir; (*shock*) amortir. ~*er*, *n*, (*piano*) étouffoir; (*furnace*) registre; (*radio*) amortisseur, *m*, sourdine, *f*; (*stamps, labels*) mouilloir, *m*. ~*ness*, *n*, humidité, *f*.

damsel, *n*, demoiselle, jeune fille, *f.*

damson, *n*, damas, *m*. ~ [*tree*], prunier de damas, *m*.

dance, *n*, danse, *f*; bal; pas, *m*. ~ *hall*, salle de bal, *f*, bal, *m*. *D~ of Death*, *D~ Macabre*, Danse macabre. ¶ *v.i.* & *t*, danser; faire danser. ~ *attendance* (*on*), s'empresser (auprès de); faire le pied de grue. **dancer**, *n*, danseur, euse. **dancing**, *n*, la danse. ~ *master*, maître de danse, *m*.

dandelion, *n*, pissenlit, *m*.

dandle, *v.t*, bercer, dodeliner, pouponner.

dandruff, *n*, pellicules, *f.pl.*

dandy, *n*, dandy, gandin, élégant, *m*.

Dane, *n*, Danois, e.

danger, *n*, danger, *m*. *this patient is out of* ~, ce malade est hors d'affaire. ~*ous*†, *a*, dangereux.

dangle, *v.i*, pendiller, brimballer; (*v.t.*) brandiller.

Danish, *a*, danois. ¶ (*language*) *n*, le danois.

dank, *a*, méphitique.

dapper, *a*, tiré à quatre épingles; bellot.

dappled, *p.a*, pommelé.

dare, *v.i.ir*, oser, s'aviser; (*v.t.ir*) défier, braver, oser. ¶ *i*, *I* ~ *you!* chiche! ~*devil*, casse-cou, *m*.

daring†, *a*, audacieux, osé, hardi. ¶ *n*, audace, hardiesse, *f*.

dark, *a*, obscur; sombre; noir; ténébreux; foncé; brun; sourd. *the* ~ *ages*, les siècles d'ignorance, *m.pl.* ~ *horse*, outsider, *m*. ~ *man*, ~ *boy*, brunet, *m*. ~ *room* (*Phot.*), chambre noire, *f*. ~ *woman*, ~ *girl*, brunette, *f*.

¶ *n*, obscurité, nuit, *f*, ténèbres, *f.pl. after* ~, à [la] nuit close. *in the* ~ (*fig.*), à l'aveuglette. ~**en**, *v.t*, obscurcir; assombrir, embrumer, rembrunir. ~**ish**, *a*, noirâtre. ~**ly**, *ad*, obscurément; sourdement. ~**ness**, *n*, obscurité, nuit, *f*, ténèbres, *f.pl*; teinte foncée, *f*.

darling, *a*, chéri, bien-aimé, favori. ¶ *n*, chéri, e, bien-aimé, e, bijou, *m*, mignon, ne, câlin, e, chou[chou]; coco, *m*, cocotte, *f*, Benjamin, *m*; favori, ite, coqueluche, *f*.

darn, *n*, reprise, *f*. ¶ *v.t*, repriser. ~**ing**, *n*, reprisage, *m*, reprise, *f*. ~ *needle*, aiguille à repriser, *f*.

dart, *n*, élan; dard, trait, *m*; fléchette, *f*; (*pl.*) jeu de fléchettes, *m*. ¶ *v.t*, darder, lancer; (*v.i.*) s'élancer.

dash, *n*, élan, *m*, fougue, *f*, panache, entrain; grain, tantinet, filet, soupçon; (*Teleg.*) trait; (*Typ.*) tiret, *m. to make a* ~ *at*, *for*, s'élancer sur, vers. ~ *board*, tableau de bord, *m*. ¶ *v.t*, heurter, jeter; briser, abattre; confondre. ~**ing**, *a*, fougueux; pimpant.

dastard, *n*, lâche. *m*. ~**ly**, *a*, lâche.

data, *n.pl*, données, *f.pl.* ~ *bank*, banque de données. *f*. ~ *communication*, téléinformatique, *f*. ~ *processing*, informatique, ordination, *f*. ~ *safety*, sauvegarde des données, *m*. ~ *set*, ensemble de données, *m*. ~ *sheet*, feuille-document, *f. automatic* ~ *processing*, traitement automatique des données, *m*.

date, *n*, date, *f*; échéance; époque; (*with pers.*) rendez-vous; (*fruit*) datte, *f. to* ~, à ce jour. *up to* ~, à jour. ~ *palm*, dattier, *m*. ~ *stamp*, timbre à date, *m*. ¶ *v.t*, dater.

dative [*case*], *n*, datif, *m*.

datum, *n*, donnée, *f*; repère, *m*.

daub, *n*, barbouillage, *m*; (*painting*) croûte, *f*; (*for walls*) bousillage, *m*. ¶ *v.t*, barbouiller, peinturlurer; bousiller.

daughter, *n*, fille, *f*. ~-*in-law*, belle-fille, *f*.

daunt, *v.t*, intimider, décourager. ~**less**, *a*, intrépide.

davit, *n*, bossoir, *m*.

dawdle, *v.i*, flâner, muser, lambiner.

dawn, *n*, aube, *f*, point du jour, *m*, naissance du jour, (*of day & fig.*) aurore, *f*. ¶ *v.i*, poindre; naître. ~**ing**, *a*, naissant.

day, *n*, jour, *m*; journée, *f. the* ~ *after*, le lendemain. *the* ~ *after the morrow*, le surlendemain. *the* ~ *after tomorrow*, après-demain. *the* ~ *before*, la veille. *the* ~ *before yesterday*, avanthier. *one of these fine* ~*s*, un de ces matins. ~ *boarder*, demi-pensionnaire, *m.f.* ~*break*, point du jour, *m*, pointe du j., *f*, le petit jour. ~*dream*, rêve, *m*. ~ *laborer*, journalier, *m*. ~*light*, jour, *m*. ~ *nursery*, crèche, garderie, pouponnière, *f*. ~ *of atonement*, jour des propitiations. ~*'s journey*, journée de chemin, *f*. ~*'s pay & ~'s work*, journée, *f*. ~*time*, heures de jour, *f.pl*, jour, *m*, journée, *f*.

daze, *v.t*, ahurir, hébéter; étourdir. ¶ *n*, étourdissement, *m*; confusion, *f*.

dazzle, *n*, éblouissement, *m*. ¶ *v.t*, éblouir, offusquer; (*v.i.*) papilloter. **dazzling**, *a*, éblouissant.

deacon, *n*, diacre, *m*.

dead, *a. & ad*, mort; terne; éteint (*fire*). ~ *beat*, ~ *tired*, éreinté, fourbu, moulu de fatigue, flapi. ~ *calm*, calme plat, *m*. ~ *center*, point mort, *m*. ~ *drunk*, ivre mort. ~ *end*, impasse, rue borgne, *f*. ~*fall*, assommoir, *m*. ~ *heat*, épreuve nulle, course nulle, c. à égalité, *f*. ~ *letter*, (*post*) rebut, *m*; (*fig.*) lettre morte, *f*. ~-*letter office*, bureau des rebuts, *m*. ~*lock*, impasse, *f*. ~ *loss*, perte sèche, *f*. ~ *reckoning* (*Naut.*), estime, estimation, *f*. *D*~ *Sea*, mer Morte, *f*. ~ *season*, morte-saison, *f*. ~ *wire*, fil hors courant, *m*. *the* ~, les morts, les trépassés, *m.pl*. ~**en**, *v.t*, amortir; étourdir. ~**ly**, *a*, mortel, à mort; léthifère; funeste, meurtrier. ~ *nightshade*, belladone, *f*. ~ *sins*, péchés capitaux, *m.pl*.

deaf, *a*, sourd. ~ *& dumb*, sourd-muet. ~-*mute*, sourd-muet, *m*, sourde-muette, *f*. ~**en**, *v.t*, assourdir. ~**ening**, *a*, assourdissant. ~**ness**, *n*, surdité, *f*.

deal, *n*, (*cards*) donne, main, *f*; [bois de] sapin, *m. a great* ~, *a good* ~, beaucoup, bien. ¶ *v.t.ir*, (*cards*) donner, faire; (*blow*) porter, assener; (*v.i.ir*) traiter; faire les cartes. ~ *out*, distribuer. ~ *with* (shop), se servir chez. ~er, *n*, marchand, e, débitant, e, fournisseur, *m*; (*cards*) donneur, euse. ~ing, *n*, affaire, opération, négociation, *f*; procédé; (*pl.*) commerce, *m*, pratique, *f*, intelligences, accointances, *f.pl.*

dean, *n*, doyen, ne. ~ery, *n*, (*office*) doyenné, décanat; (*house*) doyenné, *m*.

dear, *a.* & *ad*, cher. *my* ~, ma chère. *my* ~ *fellow*, mon cher. *O* ~*!*aïe!, oh là [là]! *O dear no!* ma foi non! ~*est* (*pers.*), mon chéri, ma chérie. ~ly, *ad*, chèrement, cher. ~ness (*price*) *n*, cherté, *f*.

dearth, *n*, disette, *f*.

death, *n*, mort, *f*; décès, trépas, *m*; (*pl.*, *obituary*) nécrologie, *f*. ~*bed*, lit de mort, *m*. ~ *blow*, coup mortel, *m*. ~ *certificate*, extrait mortuaire, *m*. ~ *knell*, glas funèbre, *m*. ~ *rate*, mortalité, *f*, taux de la m., *m*. ~ *trap*, casse-cou, *m*. ~ *warrant*, ordre d'exécution; (*fig.*) arrêt de mort, *m*. ~*watch* [*beetle*], horloge de la mort, vrillette, *f*. ~*less*, *a*, immortel.

debar, *v.t*, exclure, priver. ~ *by time* (*law*), forclore. ~*ment by time*, forclusion, *f*.

debase, *v.t*, avilir; altérer, falsifier.

debatable, *a*, discutable, contestable, en litige. **debate,** *n*, débat, *m*, discussion, *f*. ¶ *v.t*, débattre, discuter, agiter.

debauch, *v.t*, débaucher. ~*ee*, *n*, débauché, e. ~[*ery*], *n*, débauche, crapule, *f*.

debenture, *n*, obligation, *f*. ~ *holder*, obligataire, *m,f*.

debilitate, *v.t*, débiliter, déprimer. **debility,** *n*, débilité, *f*.

debit, *n*, débit, doit, *m*. ¶ *v.t*, débiter. **debt** [**due by the trader**] *n*, dette [passive] *f*. **debt** [**due to the trader**] *n*, créance, dette [active] *f*. *debt collector*, agent de recouvrements, *m*. *in debt*, endetté. *involve in debt*, endetter. *run into debt*, s'endetter. **debtor,** *n*, débiteur, trice; redevable, *m,f*; obligé, e. ~ [*side*], débit, doit, *m*.

debug, *v.t*, (*computers*) épurer.

decade, *n*, décade, decennie, *f*.

decadence, *n*, décadence, *f*. **decadent,** *a*, décadent.

decaffeinate, *v.t*, décaféiner. ~d, *a*, décaféiné.

decagon, *n*, décagone, *m*.

decamp, *v.i*, décamper, plier bagage.

decant, *v.t*, décanter, transvaser. ~er, *n*, carafe, *f*, (*small*) carafon, *m*.

decapitate, *v.t*, décapiter.

decay, *n*, décadence; carie, *f*. ¶ *v.i*, dépérir; se carier.

decease, *n*, décès, trépas, *m*. ¶ *v.i*, décéder. ~d, *n*, défunt, e.

deceit, *n*, tromperie, *f*. ~ful, *a*, trompeur, mensonger. **deceive,** *v.t*, tromper, décevoir, abuser. **deceiver,** *n*, trompeur, euse.

decelerate, *v.t*, ralentir.

December, *n*, décembre, *m*.

decency, *n*, décence, *f*.

decennial, *a*, décennal.

decent, *a*, décent; honnête. ~ly, *ad*, décemment; honnêtement.

decentralize, *v.t*, décentraliser.

deception, *n*, tromperie, *f*. **deceptive,** *a*, trompeur, décevant, menteur.

decibel (*Phys.*) *n*, décibel, *m*.

decide, *v.t*, décider; statuer sur; (*v.i.*) [se] décider. **decided,** *a*, décidé, arrêté, marqué. ~ly, *ad*, décidément.

deciduous, *a*, décidu.

decimal, *a*, décimal. ~ *point*, virgule [décimale] *f*. *Note:*—The decimal point is indicated in French by a comma. ¶ *n*, décimale, *f*.

decimate, *v.t*, décimer.

decipher, *v.t*, déchiffrer.

decision, *n*, décision; délibération, *f*; parti, *m*. ~ *in one's favor*, gain de cause, *m*. **decisive**†, *a*, décisif.

deck, *n*, pont, tillac; (*of bridge*) tablier, *m*. ~ *cabin, chair*, cabine, chaise, de pont, *f*. ~ *hand*, matelot de p., *m*. ~ *tennis*, decktennis, *m*. *flight* ~, pont d'envol, *m*. ¶ *v.t*, parer, orner; (*ship*) ponter. ~ *with flags*, pavoiser. ~ *with flowers*, fleurir.

declaim, *v.i*, déclamer. **declamatory,** *a*, (*bad sense*) déclamatoire; (*good sense*) oratoire.

declaration, *n*, déclaration, *f*. **declare,** *v.t*, déclarer, constater; proclamer, dénoncer.

declension (*Gram.*) *n*, déclinaison, *f*.

decline, *n*, déclin; retour, *m*;
maladie de langueur; baisse, *f*.
¶ *v.i.* & *t*, décliner; pencher;
baisser; refuser.

declivity, *n*, déclivité, pente, *f*.

decoction, *n*, décoction, *f*.

decode, *v.t*, déchiffrer.

decompose, *v.t*, décomposer.

decorate, *v.t*, décorer; garnir;
orner. **decoration**, *n*, décoration,
f; décor, *m*. **decorative**, *a*, décoratif. **decorator**, *n*, décorateur, *m*.

decorous†, *a*, convenable, bienséant. **decorum**, *n*, décorum, *m*.

decoy, *n*, (*bait*) leurre, *m*; (*place*)
canardière, *f*; (*pers.*) mouton,
m. ~ *bird*, appelant, *m*. ¶ *v.t*,
leurrer.

decrease, *n*, décroissement, *m*,
décroissance, *f*. ¶ *v.i*, décroître.

decree, *n*, décret, arrêt; jugement,
m. ¶ *v.t*, décréter; édicter.

decrepit, *a*, décrépit, caduc. **decrepitude**, *n*, décrépitude, caducité, *f*.

decry, *v.t*, décrier.

dedicate, *v.t*, dédier, [dé]vouer;
consacrer. **dedication**, *n*, consécration, dédicace, *f*; envoi, *m*.

deduce, *v.t*, déduire.

deduct, *v.t*, déduire, retrancher,
défalquer, rabattre. ~**ion**, déduction, défalcation, *f*.

deed, *n*, action, *f*; acte; fait; exploit; contrat; titre, *m*.

deem, *v.t*, juger, estimer, considérer. ~**ed**, *p.p*, censé, réputé.

deep, *a*, profond; creux; (*in depth*)
de (*ou* en) profondeur; (*colors*)
foncé, gros; (*mourning*) grand;
(*sound*) grave. ~*sea fishing*,
pêche au large, p. hauturière;
(*whale & cod*) grande pêche, *f*.
~*sea navigation* & ~*sea voyage*,
long cours, *m*. ~*seated*, profond, foncier. ~*water harbor*,
port de toute marée, *m*. ¶ *n*, profondeur; fosse, *f*. ~**en**, *v.t*, approfondir, creuser. ~[**ly**] *ad*,
profondément, avant; sensiblement, fortement.

deer, *n*, daim; cerf, *m*; (*col.*) bêtes
fauves, *f.pl*, fauves, *m.pl*. ~*skin*,
peau de daim, *f*. ~ *stalking*,
chasse au cerf à l'affût, *f*.

deface, *v.t*, défigurer, mutiler.
~**d**, *p.a*, fruste.

defalcate, *v.i*, commettre des dé-

tournements. **defalcation**, *n*, détournement de fonds, *m*.

defamation, *n*, diffamation, *f*.
defamatory, *a*, diffamatoire,
diffamant, infamant. **defame**,
v.t, diffamer.

default, *n*, défaut, *m*, défaillance,
négligence, *f*. *in ~ of*, à défaut
de, faute de. ¶ *v.i*, manquer.
~**er**, *n*, défaillant; délinquant, *m*.

defeat, *n*, défaite, *f*. ¶ *v.t*, défaire; frustrer.

defecate, *v.t.* & *i*, déféquer.

defect, *n*, défaut, *m*, défectuosité,
f, vice, *m*, tare, *f*. ~**ion**, *n*, défection; apostasie, *f*. ~**ive†**, *a*,
défecteux; (*Gram.*) défectif.

defense, *n*, défense, *f*. *self-~*, légitime défense, *f*. ~*less*, *a*, sans
défense. **defend**, *v.t*, défendre.
~**ant**, *n*, défendeur, eresse. ~**er**,
n, défenseur, *m*. **defensible**, *a*, défendable. **defensive**, *a*, défensif.
¶ *n*, défensive, *f*.

defer, *v.t*, & *i*, différer, remettre,
arriérer, éloigner; (*submit*) déférer. ~**ence**, *n*, déférence, *f*,
respect, *m*, ménagements, *m. pl*.
deferential, *a*, déférent.

defiance, *n*, défi, *m*. **defiant**, *a*,
de défi.

deficiency, *n*, défaut, *m*, insuffisance, *f*; déficit, manquant, *m*.
deficient, *a*, défectueux; insuffisant. *to be ~ in*, manquer de.
deficit, *n*, déficit, *m*, moins-value,
f.

defile, *n*, défilé, *m*. ¶ *v.i*, défiler;
(*v.t.*) souiller. ~**ment**, *n*, souillure, *f*.

definable, *a*, définissable. **define**,
v.t, définir. **definite**, *a*, défini;
déterminé; précis. ~**ly**, *ad*, décidément. **definition**, *n*, définition, *f*. **definitive†**, *a*, définitif.

deflate, *v.t*, dégonfler, désenfler.
deflation, *n*, dégonflement, *m*;
(*Fin.*) déflation, *f*.

deflect, *v.t*, défléchir, détourner,
dévier. **deflection**, *n*, déviation;
flexion, *f*.

defloration, *n*, (*ravishment*) défloration; (*stripping of flowers*)
défloraison, *f*. **deflower**, *v.t*,
(*ravish*) déflorer; (*strip of
flowers*) défleurir, déflorer.

deforest, *v.t*, déboiser.

deform, *v.t*, déformer, contrefaire. ~**ed**, *a*, difforme, contrefait. ~**ity**, *n*, difformité, *f*.

defraud, *v.t*, frauder, frustrer.

defray, *v.t*, défrayer.

defrost, *v.t*, dégivrer. ~*ing device*, dégivreur, *m*.

deft†, *a*, adroit. ~**ness**, *n*, adresse, *f*.

defunct, *a*, défunt. ¶ *n*, défunt, e.

defy, *v.t*, défier; braver.

degeneracy & degeneration, *n*, dégénérescence, dégénération, *f*, abâtardissement, *m*. **degenerate**, *v.i*, dégénérer, s'abâtardir. ¶ *n*, dégénéré, *m*. ¶ *a*, dégénéré.

degradation, *n*, dégradation, *f*; avilissement, *m*. **degrade**, *v.t*, dégrader; déclasser; [r]avilir.

degree, *n*, degré; point; (*Univ.*) diplôme, grade, *m*.

dehydrate, *v.t*, déshydrater.

deify, *v.t*, déifier, diviniser.

deign to (to), daigner, condescendre à.

deity, *n*, divinité, déité, *f*.

dejected, *a*, abattu, découragé. **dejection**, *n*, abattement, accablement, *m*.

delay, *n*, retard, délai, sursis, *m*. ¶ *v.t*, différer, retarder, atermoyer; (*v.i.*) tarder.

delectation, *n*, délices, *f.pl*.

delegate, *n*, délégué, e, député, *m*. ¶ *v.t*, déléguer. **delegation**, *n*, délégation, *f*.

delete, *v.t*, effacer, biffer, rayer.

deleterious, *v.t*, délétère.

deliberate, *a*, réfléchi; délibéré; lent. ¶ *v.i*, délibérer. ~**ly**, *ad*, délibérément. **deliberation**, *n*, délibération, *f*.

delicacy, *n*, délicatesse; friandise, chatterie, *f*. **delicate†**, *a*, délicat; fin.

delicious†, *a*, délicieux. **delight**, *n*, délice, enchantement, *m*; jouissance; volupté, *f*. ¶ *v.t*, délecter, charmer, enchanter, ravir.

delimit[ate], *v.t*, délimiter.

delineate, *v.t*, tracer; [dé]peindre. **delineation**, *n*, délinéation; peinture, *f*.

delinquency, *n*, faute; négligence, *f*, méfait, *m*. **delinquent**, *n*, délinquant, e.

deliquescence, *n*, déliquescence, *f*.

delirious, *a*, délirant. *to be* ~, délirer. **delirium**, *n*, délire, *m*.

deliver, *v.t*, délivrer; livrer; remettre; rendre; distribuer; (*Med.*) accoucher; (*ball, Ten., etc.*) lancer; (*speech, etc.*) pro-

noncer; (*pump*) refouler. *to be* ~*ed of*, accoucher de; (*fig.*) pondre. ~**ance**, *n*, délivrance, *f*. ~**er**, *n*, libérateur, trice. ~**y**, *n*, délivrance; livraison; remise; distribution; tradition, *f*; accouchement, *m*; prononciation, déclamation, diction, parole, *f*, débit; refoulement, *m*. ~ *man*, ~ *boy*, ~ *girl*, livreur, euse. ~ *truck*, voiture de livraison, *f*.

dell, *n*, vallon, *m*.

delouse, *v.t*, épouiller.

delphinium, *n*, pied-d'alouette, *m*.

delta, *n*, delta, *m*.

delude, *v.t*, tromper, abuser.

deluge, *n*, déluge. *m*. ¶ *v.t*, inonder, noyer.

delusion, *n*, illusion, *f*. **delusive†**, *a*, illusoire.

delve, *v.t*, fouir, sonder.

demagogue, *n*, démagogue, *m*.

demand, *n*, demande, *f*; débit, *m*; exigence, *f*. *on* ~, sur demande, à vue, à bureau ouvert, à guichet ouvert, à présentation. ¶ *v.t*, demander; exiger. ~**ing**, *a*, exigeant.

demarcation, *n*, démarcation, *f*.

demean oneself (to) (*behave*), se comporter; (*misbehave*) s'abaisser. **demeanor**, *n*, allure, *f*, maintien, *m*.

demented, *p.p*, dément. **dementia**, *n*, démence, *f*.

demerit, *n*, démérite, *m*.

demesne, *n*, domaine, *m*.

demigod, *n*, demi-dieu, *m*.

demijohn, *n*, dame-jeanne, *f*.

demise, *n*, mutation, *f*; décès, *m*. ¶ *v.t*, transmettre; léguer.

demisemiquaver, *n*, triple croche, *f*.

demobilize, *v.t*, démobiliser.

democracy, *n*, démocratie, *f*. **democrat**, *n*, démocrate, *m*. ~**ic**, *a*, démocratique.

demolish, *v.t*, démolir. **demolition**, *n*, démolition, *f*; (*pl.*) démolitions, *f.pl*, abattis, *m*, abats, décombres, *m.pl*.

demon, *n*, démon, *m*.

demonetize, *v.t*, démonétiser.

demoniac, *n*, démoniaque, *m.f*. ~(**al**), *a*, démoniaque.

demonstrate, *v.t*, démontrer; (*v.i.*) manifester. **demonstration**, *n*, démonstration; (*political, etc.*) manifestation, *f*. **demonstrative**, *a*, démonstratif. **demon-**

strator, *n*, manifestant, e; (*Sch.*) démonstrateur, *m*.

demoralize, *v.t*, démoraliser.

demur, *n*, objection, *f*. ¶ *v.i*, opposer des objections; (*law*) opposer une exception.

demure, *a*, composé; (*look*) de sainte nitouche; (*woman*) qui fait la sucrée.

demurrage, *n*, surestaries, *f.pl*.

demurrer, *n*, exception péremptoire, *f*.

demy, *n*, carré, *m*; coquille, *f*.

den, *n*, antre, repaire, *m*, tanière, caverne, *f*; bouge; nid; cabinet, *m*.

denationalization, *n*, privatisation, *f*.

denature, *v.t*, dénaturer.

denial, *n*, dénégation, *f*, démenti; refus; reniement, *m*.

denizen, *n*, habitant, hôte, *m*.

Denmark, *n*, le Danemark.

denominate, *v.t*, dénommer. **denomination**, *n*, dénomination; (*sect*) communion; (*unit*) coupure, *f*. **~al**, *a*, confessionnel. **denominator**, *n*, dénominateur, *m*.

denote, *v.t*, dénoter.

denounce, *v.t*, dénoncer.

dense†, *a*, dense, compact, épais. **density**, *n*, densité, épaisseur, *f*.

dent, *n*, bosse, *f*. ¶ *v.t*, bossuer, bosseler, cabosser.

dental, *a*, (*Anat.*) dentaire, dental; (*Gram.*) dental. ~ *surgeon*, chirurgien dentiste, *m*. ¶ (*Gram.*) *n*, dentale, *f*. **dentate**, *a*, denté. **dentist**, *n*, dentiste, *m*. ~**ry**, *n*, l'art dentaire, *m*. **dentition**, *n*, dentition, *f*. **denture**, *n*, dentier, *m. permanent* ~, dentier définitif, *m. removable* ~, d. amovible, *m*.

denude, *v.t*, dénuder, mettre à nu.

denunciation, *n*, dénonciation, *f*.

deny, *v.t*, nier, dénier, se défendre de; renier; refuser. *to* ~ *it*, nier.

deodorize, *v.t*, désodoriser, désinfecter.

depart, *v.i*, partir; s'éloigner. ~ *this life*, quitter la vie, q. ce monde, trépasser. ~**ed**, *a*, défunt, e, trépassé, e.

department, *n*, département, *m*; division, *f*; service; rayon; office, *m*. ~ *store*, grand magasin, *m*. ~**al**, *a*, départemental.

departure, *n*, départ, *m*, sortie, *f*;

(*lapse*) manquement, *m*; innovation, *f*.

depend, *v.i*, dépendre, s'appuyer, compter. ~**ant**, ~**ent**, *n*, personne à charge, *f*. ~**ence**, *n*, dépendance; confiance, *f*. ~**ency**, *n*, dépendance; (*country*) annexe, *f*. ~**ent**, *a*, dépendant. *to be* ~ *on*, être à la charge de; être tributaire de.

depict, *v.t*, dépeindre, peindre.

depilate, *v.t*, épiler. **depilatory**, *a*, dépilatoire. ¶ *n*, dépilatoire, *m*.

deplete, *v.t*, amoindrir; épuiser.

deplorable†, *a*, déplorable, lamentable. **deplore**, *v.t*, déplorer, se lamenter sur.

deploy, *v.t*, déployer. ~**ment**, *n*, déploiement, *m*.

depoliticization, *n*, dépolitisation, *f*. **depoliticize**, *v.t*, dépolitiser.

deponent (*pers.*) *n*, déposant, e.

depopulate, *v.t*, dépeupler. **depopulation**, *n*, (*action*) dépeuplement, *m*; (*state*) dépopulation, *f*.

deport, *v.t*, déporter. ~**ation**, *n*, déportation, *f*.

deportment, *n*, maintien, *m*, tenue, *f*, manières, *f.pl*.

depose, *v.t*, déposer.

deposit, *n*, dépôt, *m*; consignation, *f*; (*bottles, etc.*) consigne, *f*. versement; cautionnement, *m*; provision [de garantie] *f*; arrhes, *f.pl*, (*Geol.*) dépôt, gîte, gisement, *m. non*~ *bottle, jar*, verre, pot, perdu, *m*. ¶ *v.t*, déposer; consigner; verser; placer; mettre; fournir. ~**ary**, *n*, dépositaire, *m,f*. ~**ion**, *n*, déposition, *f*; dépôt, *m*. ~**or**, *n*, déposant, e. ~**ory**, *n*, dépôt, *m*; (*fig.*) répertoire, *m*. **depot**, *n*, dépôt, *m*; gare, *f*.

depravation & depravity, *n*, dépravation, *f*. **deprave**, *v.t*, dépraver. ~**d**, *p.a*, dépravé, taré, vicélard. ~ *person*, viélard, e.

deprecate, *v.t*, réprouver.

depreciate, *v.t*, déprécier, avilir; amortir. **depreciation**, *n*, dépréciation, moins-value, *f*, avilissement; amortissement, *m*. **depreciatory**, *a*, péjoratif.

depredation, *n*, déprédation, *f*.

depress, *v.t*, déprimer. ~**ing**, *p.a*, décourageant; triste. ~**ion**, *n*, dépression, *f*; enfoncement, *m*; (*economic*) crise, *f*.

deprivation, *n*, privation, interdiction, *f*, retrait, *m*. **deprive**, *v.t*, priver, dépourvoir, sevrer; (*Eccl.*) interdire.

depth, *n*, profondeur; hauteur, *f*; fond; (*winter*) cœur, fort, *m*; (*color*) intensité; (*sound*) gravité, *f*. ~ *charge*, grenade sous-marine, *f*.

deputation, *n*, députation, délégation, *f*. **depute**, *v.t*, députer, déléguer. **deputize for**, suppléer, faire l'intérim de. **deputy**, *n*, député, *m*; délégué, e; suppléant, e, substitut, *m*. ~ *chairman*, vice-président, e. ~ *governor*, sous-gouverneur, *m*.

derail, *v.i*, dérailler. ~**ment**, *n*, déraillement, *m*.

derange, *v.t*, déranger, fausser; aliéner, détraquer.

derelict, *a*, abandonné. ¶ *n*, navire abandonné, *m*, épave, *f*; (*pers.*) clochard, *m*. ~**ion**, *n*, abandon; manquement, *m*.

deride, *v.t*, se moquer de. **derision**, *n*, dérision, *f*. **derisive**, *a*, de dérision. **derisory**, *a*, dérisoire.

derivation, *n*, dérivation, *f*. **derivative**, *n*, dérivé, *m*. **derive**, *v.t*, tirer, retirer, puiser. *to be* ~*d from*, dériver de.

dermatology, *n*, dermatologie, *f*.

derogate, *v.t*, déroger. **derogatory** (*disparaging*) *a*, dénigrant.

derrick, *n*, grue, *f*, derrick, *m*; (*ship's*) mât de charge, *m*.

dervish, *n*, derviche, dervis, *m*.

descant, *v.i*, disserter, discourir, s'étendre.

descend, *v.i. & t*, descendre. ~**ed** *from*, issu de. ~**ant**, *n*, descendant, e. **descent**, *n*, descente; (*lineage*) descendance, naissance, race, *f*.

describe, *v.t*, décrire, définir, qualifier. **description**, *n*, description, *f*, libellé[s], *m.*[*pl.*]; signalement, *m*; qualités, *f.pl*, profession; espèce, *f*, genre, *m*. **descriptive**, *a*, descriptif; (*catalog*) raisonné.

descry, *v.t*, découvrir, apercevoir.

desecrate, *v.t*, profaner, violer.

desert, *a*, désert, désertique. ¶ *n*, désert; mérite, *m*. ¶ *v.t. & i*, déserter; abandonner, délaisser.

~**ed**, *a*, abandonné, désert, ~**er**, *n*, déserteur, *m*. ~**ion**, *n*, désertion, *f*; abandon, délaissement, *m*.

deserve, *v.t*, mériter. **deservedly**, *ad*, à juste titre. **deserving**, *a*, méritant; digne (*of* = de). ~ *of praise*, louable.

desiccate, *v.t*, dessécher. **desiccation**, *n*, dessèchement, *m*, dessiccation, *f*.

desideratum, *n*, desideratum, *m*.

design, *n*, dessein; modèle; dessin; motif, *m*. ¶ *v.t*, destiner, affecter; projeter, se proposer; dessiner.

designate, *v.t*, désigner. **designation**, *n*, désignation, *f*.

designedly, *ad*, à dessein. **designer**, *n*, dessinateur, trice; auteur, *m*. **designing**, *a*, intrigant.

desirable, *a*, désirable, à désirer, souhaitable. **desire**, *n*, désir; appétit, *m*; envie; demande; prière, *f*. ¶ *v.t*, désirer. **desirous**, *a*, désireux. *to be* ~ *of*, désirer.

desist, *v.i*, se départir.

desk, *n*, pupitre; bureau, *m*; chaire, *f*.

desolate, *a*, désert; désolé. ¶ *v.t*, désoler. **desolation**, *n*, désolation, *f*.

despair, *n*, désespoir, *m*. *to drive to* ~ *&* ~, *v.i*, désespérer.

desperado, *n*, apache, escarpe, *m*. **desperate**, *a*, désespéré; acharné; éperdu. ~**ly**, *ad*, désespérément; à outrance; éperdument. **desperation**, *n*, désespoir; acharnement, *m*.

despicable, *a*, méprisable, lâche. **despise**, *v.t*, mépriser, dédaigner.

despite, *n*, dépit, *m*.

despoil, *v.t*, dépouiller, spolier.

despond, *v.i*, perdre courage, se décourager. ~**ency**, *n*, abattement, découragement, *m*. ~**ent**, *a*, abattu, découragé.

despot, *n*, despote, *m*. ~**ic**†, *a*, despotique. ~**ism**, *n*, despotisme, *m*.

dessert, *n*, dessert, *m*. ~ *fruit & nuts*, mendiants, *m.pl*. ~ *spoon*, cuiller à dessert, c. à entremets, *f*.

destination, *n*, destination, *f*. **destine**, *v.t*, destiner. **destiny**, *n*, destin, *m*, destinée, *f*.

destitute, *a*, dans le dénuement; dépourvu, dénué (*of* = de). *the* ~, les nécessiteux, *m.pl*. **destitution**, *n*, dénuement, délaissement, *m*, misère, *f*.

destroy, *v.t,* détruire. ~**er,** *n,* destructeur, trice; (*ship*) contre-torpilleur, destroyer, *m.* **destruction,** *n,* destruction, *f;* ravages, *m.pl.* **destructive,** *a,* destructif, destructeur. ~ *person,* brise-tout, *m.* **destructor,** *n,* incinérateur, *m.*

desultorily, *ad,* à bâtons rompus. **desultory,** *a,* décousu.

detach, *v.t,* détacher; isoler. ~**able,** *a,* amovible, rapporté. ~**ed house,** maison isolée, *f.* ~**ment,** *n,* détachement, *m.*

detail, *n,* détail, *m.* ¶ *v.t,* détailler; circonstancier; (*Mil.*) détacher.

detain, *v.t,* détenir, retenir, empêcher de partir; arrêter.

detect, *v.t,* découvrir; surprendre. ~**ion,** *n,* découverte, *f.* ~**ive,** *n,* détective, *m.* ~ *story,* roman policier, polar, *m.* ~**or,** *n,* détecteur, *m.*

detent, *n,* détente, *f,* chien, *m.* ~**ion,** *n,* détention, *f;* arrêt, *m;* (*Sch.*) retenue, colle, *f,* arrêt, *m.*

deter, *v.t,* détourner; décourager.

detergent, *n,* détersif, *m.*

deteriorate, *v.t,* se détériorer.

determinate, *a,* déterminé. **determination,** *n,* détermination; résolution, *f.* **determine,** *v.t,* déterminer, décider, définir, résoudre. ~**d,** *a,* déterminé, résolu.

deterrent, *n,* déterrent, *m. military* ~, arme de dissuasion, *f.*

detest, *v.t,* détester, abhorrer. ~**able,** *a,* détestable.

dethrone, *v.t,* détrôner.

detonate, *v.i,* détoner; (*v.t.*) faire détoner. **detonation,** *n,* détonation, *f.* **detonator,** *n,* détonateur, pétard, *m.*

detour, *v.i,* prendre un détour. ¶ *n,* détour, *m.*

detoxicate, *v.t,* désintoxiquer.

detract from, rabaisser, dénigrer. **detractor,** *n,* détracteur, *m.*

detrain, *v.i,* débarquer.

detriment, *n,* détriment, préjudice, *m.* ~**al,** *a,* préjudiciable. *be* ~ *to,* préjudicier.

detritus, *n,* détritus, *m.*

deuce, *n,* diantre, diable; (*cards, dice*) deux, *m.*

Deuteronomy, *n,* Deutéronome, *m.*

devaluation, *n,* dévaluation, *f.*

devastate, *v.t,* dévaster, ravager.

devastator, *n,* dévastateur, trice.

develop, *v.t,* développer; faire valoir; (*Min.*) tracer. ~**er** (*Phot.*) *n,* révélateur, *m.* ~**ing bath,** bain de développement, bain révélateur, *m.* ~**ment,** *n,* développement; traçage, *m.*

deviate, *v.i,* dévier; s'écarter. **deviation,** *n,* déviation, *f;* écart, *m.*

device, *n,* moyen, expédient; dispositif, *m;* (*emblem*) devise, *f.*

devil, *n,* diable, démon, *m. the* ~*!* diable! ~**ish,** *a,* diabolique, diable de, satané. ~**ment,** *n,* malice; verve endiablée; diablerie, *f.* ~**ry,** *n,* diablerie, *f.*

devious, *a,* détourné.

devise, *v.t,* combiner, inventer, imaginer; (*law*) léguer.

devoid, *a,* dépourvu, dénué.

devolve, *v.t,* échoir, incomber, retomber.

devote, *v.t,* dévouer, consacrer, dédier, vouer; livrer. **devotee,** *n,* dévot, e, fervent, e, fanatique, *m,f.* **devotion,** *n,* (*Relig.*) dévotion; piété, *f;* (*zeal*) dévouement, attachement, *m.* ~**al,** *a,* dévot, de dévotion, de piété.

devour, *v.t,* dévorer, avaler, manger.

devout†, *a,* dévot; sincère. ~**ness,** *n,* dévotion, *f.*

dew, *n,* rosée, *f.* ~**drop,** goutte de r., *f.*

dewlap, *n,* fanon, *m.*

dewy, *a,* couvert de rosée.

dexterity, *n,* dextérité, adresse, *f.* **dextrous†,** **dexterous†,** *a,* adroit.

dextrin, *n,* dextrine, *f.*

diabetes, *n,* diabète, *m.*

diabolic(al)†, *a,* diabolique.

diacritical, *a,* diacritique.

diadem, *n,* diadème, *m.*

diaeresis, *n,* tréma, *m.*

diagnose, *v.t,* diagnostiquer. **diagnosis,** *n,* diagnostic, *m.*

diagonal†, *a,* diagonal. ¶ *n,* diagonale, *f.*

diagram, *n,* diagramme; graphique; abaque; schéma, *m;* épure, *f.*

dial, *n,* (*plate*) cadran; (*calculating mach.*) viseur; (*Teleph.*) disque [d'appel] *m;* (*compass*) boussole, *f.* ¶ *v.t,* composer un numéro.

dialect, *n,* dialecte, parler, idiome, patois, *m.*

dialectics, *n,* dialectique, *f.*

dialogue, *n,* dialogue, *m.*

diameter, *n,* diamètre, *m.* **diametric†,** *a,* diamétral.

diamond, *n,* diamant; *(Geom.)* losange, rhombe; *(pl., cards)* carreau, *m. baseball ~,* terrain de base-ball, *m. ~ wedding,* noces de diamant, *f.pl.*

diaper, *n,* étoffe diaprée *f;* linge ouvré, *m; (infant)* couche, *f.*

diaphanous, *a,* diaphane.

diaphragm, *n,* diaphragme, *m.*

diarrhea, *n,* diarrhée, courante, *f.*

diary, *n,* agenda; livre; *(of one's life)* journal, *m.*

diatonic, *a,* diatonique.

diatribe, *n,* diatribe, *f,* factum, *m.*

dibble, *n,* plantoir, *m.*

dice, *n.pl,* dés, *m.pl. ~ box,* cornet [à dés] *m.*

dicker, *v.i,* marchander.

dictate, *v.t. & abs,* dicter. *~ to,* régenter. *~[s], n.[pl.],* voix, *f.* **dictation,** *n,* dictée, *f.* **dictator,** *n,* dictateur, *m. ~ial,* a, dictatorial. *~ship,* *n,* dictature, *f;* magistère, *m.*

diction, *n,* diction, *f. ~ary,* *n,* dictionnaire, *m.*

dictum, *n,* dicton, *m.*

didactic, *a,* didactique.

die, *n,* dé [à jouer]; *(Mech.)* dé, *m;* filière, *f;* coussinet, *m;* lunette; matrice, *f. ~ sinker,* graveur en creux, *m.*

die, *v.i.ir,* mourir, trépasser, succomber; périr; s'éteindre; *(animals)* crever; *(of laughing, etc.)* mourir, [se] pâmer. *~ away, ~ down,* mourir, s'assoupir. *~hard,* intransigeant, *m.*

diet, *n,* diète, *f,* régime [alimentaire] *m.* ¶ *v.t,* mettre à la diète; *(v.i.)* suivre un régime. *~ary,* *n,* régime diététique, *m. ~ bread,* pain de régime, *m.*

differ, *v.i,* différer, varier, s'éloigner. *~ence,* *n,* différence, *f,* écart; différend, *m. ~ent,* a, différent. **differential,** a, différentiel. **differentiate,** *v.t,* différencier. **differently,** *ad,* différemment, autrement.

difficult, *a,* difficile, malaisé *~ to catch,* insaisissable. *~y,* *n,* difficulté; peine, *f;* embarras, mal, *m. with ~,* difficilement, malaisément. *(ship in)* **difficulties** *(Nav.),* incommodité, *f.*

diffidence, *n,* défiance de soi-même; timidité, *f.* **diffident†,** *a,* timide.

diffuse, *v.t,* diffuser; répandre. ¶ *a,* diffus, filandreux. *~d,* a, diffus. **diffusion,** *n,* diffusion, *f.*

dig, *n,* coup; *(fig.)* coup de patte, *m.* ¶ *v.t. & i. ir,* creuser; bêcher; fouiller. *~ up,* déterrer; arracher.

digest, *v.t. & i,* digérer. ¶ *n,* compilation, *f.* digeste, *m. ~ible,* a, digestible. *~ion,* *n,* digestion, *f. ~ive,* a. & *n,* digestif, a. & *m.*

digit, *n,* doigt, *m. a ~* (0-9), un [seul] chiffre. **digitalis** *(Phar.)* *n,* digitale, *f.*

dignified, *a,* digne. **dignify,** *v.t,* ennoblir; investir; honorer, décorer. **dignitary,** *n,* dignitaire, *m.* **dignity,** *n,* dignité, *f.*

digress, *v.i,* divaguer. *~ion,* *n,* digression, divagation, *f,* écart, hors-d'œuvre, *m.* **digressive,** a, hors d'œuvre.

dike, *n,* digue, *f; (Geol. & Min.)* filon d'injection, *m.* ¶ *v.t,* endiguer.

dilapidate, *v.t,* dégrader; délabrer, détériorer. *~d state* (building), caducité, *f.*

dilate, *v.t,* dilater; *(v.i.)* se d.; s'étendre.

dilatoriness, *n,* lenteur, *f.* **dilatory,** *a,* lent, dilatoire.

dilemma, *n,* dilemme, *m.*

dilettante, *n,* dilettante, *m.*

diligence, *n,* diligence, *f.* **diligent,** a, diligent. *~ly,* ad, diligemment.

dilly-dally, *v.i,* lanterner, barguigner.

dilute, *v.t,* étendre, diluer, détremper; délayer, couper, *(wine)* baptiser. **dilution,** *n,* dilution, *f.*

diluvial, *a,* diluvien.

dim, *a,* obscur, sombre; indistinct; vague; trouble. ¶ *v.t,* obscurcir; ternir; offusquer; *(auto lights)* mettre en code. **dimmed lights,** éclairage code, *m.*

dimension, *n,* dimension, *f;* échantillon, *m.*

dime store, *n,* prix unique, Prisunic, Monoprix, *m.*

diminish, *v.t. & i,* diminuer. **diminution,** *n,* diminution, *f.* **diminutive,** a, exigu; fort petit; *(Gram.)* diminutif. ¶ *(Gram.)* *n,* diminutif, *m.*

dimness, *n,* obscurcissement, *m;* obscurité, *f.*

dimple, *n,* fossette, *f.* ~d, *a,* à fossettes.

din, *n,* bruit, tintamarre, *m.* ¶ *v.t,* assourdir.

dine, *v.i,* dîner. ~ *out,* dîner en ville. **diner,** *n,* dîneur, euse.

dinghy, *n,* canot, youyou, *m.*

dingy, *a,* terne; sale; borgne.

dining: ~ *car,* wagon-restaurant, *m.* ~ *room,* salle à manger, *f.* ~ *table,* table de salle à manger, *f.* **dinner,** *n,* dîner, *m.* at ~, à table. ~ *jacket,* smoking, *m.* give a ~ [*party*], donner à dîner. ~ *plate,* assiette plate, *f.* ~ *service,* service de table & dessert, *m.* ~ *time,* heure du dîner, *f.*

dint, *n,* bosse, *f.* by ~ of, à force de.

diocesan, *a,* diocésain. **diocese,** *n,* diocèse, *m.*

diopter, *n,* dioptrie, *f.* **dioptric,** *a,* dioptrique.

dip, *n,* plongement, *m,* plongée; baignade, *f*; pendage, *m,* inclinaison; flèche; (*ink*) plumée, *f. dipper switch,* basculeur de phares, *m.* ¶ *v.t,* plonger, tremper, immerger; (*auto headlights*) faire basculer; (*v.i.*) plonger; s'incliner.

diphtheria, *n,* diphtérie, *f.*

diphthong, *n,* diphtongue, *f.*

diploma, *n,* diplôme, *f;* (*fig.*) parchemin, *m.*

diplomacy, *n,* diplomatie, *f;* doigté, *m.* **diplomatic,** *a,* diplomatique. **diplomat[ist],** *n,* diplomate, *m.*

dipper, *n,* écope, *f.*

dipstick, *n,* jauge à huile, *f.*

dire, *a,* (*distress*) dernière, extrême; (*necessity*) dure.

direct, *a,* direct; immédiat. ~ *current* (*Elec.*), courant continu, *m.* ~ *trade,* commerce direct, *m.* ¶ *ad,* directement. ¶ *v.t,* diriger; administrer; conduire; charger; adresser; acheminer; orienter. *to* ~ *me to . . . ,* m'indiquer le chemin pour aller à . . . ~ion, *n,* direction; administration; conduite; orientation; (*Theat. & Cinema*) réalisation, *f;* sens, côté, *m;* adresse, *f;* (*pl.*) instructions, *f.pl,* charge, prescription, *f.* ~s *for use,* mode d'emploi, *m.* **directly,**

ad, directement; immédiatement, à l'instant, aussitôt.

director, *n,* (*of company*) administrateur, trice; (*manager*) directeur, trice; ordonnateur, trice; (*Theat. & cinema*) metteur en scène, réalisateur, *m. casting* ~, régisseur général, *m.* ~ate, *n,* administration, *f.*

directory, *n,* (*Teleph.*) annuaire; répertoire, *m.*

direful, *a,* terrible; sinistre.

dirge, *n,* chant, funèbre, chant de mort, *m.*

dirigible, *a. & n,* dirigeable, *a. & m.*

dirk, *n,* dague, *f,* poignard, *m.*

dirt, *n,* saleté, crasse, ordure, immondice, crotte, boue; terre, *f.* ~-*cheap,* à vil prix. ~ *track,* piste en cendrée, *f.* **dirtily,** *ad,* salement. **dirtiness,** *n,* saleté, *f.* **dirty,** *a,* sale, malpropre, crasseux; crotté, boueux. ~ *pig,* cochon, *m.* ~ *trick,* vilain tour, croc-en-jambe, *m,* vilenie, goujaterie, saleté, *f.* ~ *work* (*fig.*), sale besogne, *f,* micmac, *m.* ¶ *v.t,* salir; souiller; crotter, barbouiller.

disable, *v.t,* rendre incapable; rendre hors de combat; (*ship*) désemparer. ~d *soldier,* ~d *sailor,* mutilé de la guerre, *m.* ~ment & **disability,** *n,* incapacité, invalidité, *f.*

disabuse, *v.t,* désabuser.

disadvantage, *n,* désavantage, *m. place at a* ~, désavantager. ~ous†, *a,* désavantageux.

disaffection, *n,* désaffection, *f.*

disagree, *v.i,* n'être pas d'accord, être en désaccord; ne pas convenir. ~able†, *a,* désagréable. ~ment, *n,* désaccord, *m,* discordance, *f;* dissentiment, *m.*

disallow, *v.t,* rejeter.

disappear, *v.i,* disparaître. ~ance, *n,* disparition, *f.*

disappoint, *v.t,* désappointer; tromper, décevoir. *don't* ~ *me,* ne manquez pas à votre parole, à v. promesse. ~ment, *n,* désappointement, *m,* déception, *f,* mécompte, démenti, déboire, *m.* ~ *in love,* déception, *f,* (*ou* chagrin, *m.*) d'amour.

disapprobation & disapproval, *n,* désapprobation, improbation, *f.* **disapprove,** *v.t & *

~ *of*, désapprouver, réprouver, improuver.

disarm, *v.t.* désarmer. **disarmament**, *n*, désarmement, *m*.

disarrange, *v.t*, déranger, désajuster. ~ (*someone's hair*) décoiffer.

disarray, *n*, désarroi, *m*.

disaster, *n*, désastre, sinistre; cataclysme, *m*. **disastrous**, *a*, désastreux, néfaste.

disavow, *v.t*, désavouer. ~**al**, *n*, désaveu, *m*.

disband, *v.t*, licencier; (*v.i.*) se séparer.

disbelief, *n*, manque de foi, *m*. **disbelieve**, *v.t*, ne pas croire.

disbud, *v.t*, ébourgeonner, éborgner.

disburden, *v.t*, décharger.

disburse, *v.t*, débourser. ~**ment**, *n*, déboursement, débours, déboursé, *m*, mise [de]hors, *f*.

disc, *n*, disque, plateau, *m*; rondelle, *f*. ~ *jockey*, animateur, *m*.

discard, *v.t*, laisser de côté; (*cards*) écarter.

discern, *v.t*, discerner. ~**ible**, *a*, perceptible. ~**ing**, *a*, judicieux. ~**ment**, *n*, discernement, jugement, *m*.

discharge, *n*, décharge, *f*; déversement, *m*, évacuation, *f*; débit; (*Med.*) écoulement, *m*, suppuration, *f*; libération, *f*, acquit[tement] *m*, quittance, *f*, quitus; renvoi, congé, *m*; (*Mil. Navy*) réforme; (*bankrupt*) réhabilitation, *f*. ¶ *v.t. & i.* décharger; déverser; débiter; (*wound*) suppurer; débarquer; libérer, [ac]quitter; liquider; renvoyer, congédier; réformer; réhabiliter. *to get* (*obligation*) *discharged*, apurer.

disciple, *n*, disciple, *m*. **disciplinarian**, *n*, disciplinaire, *m*. **disciplinary**, *a*, disciplinaire; de discipline. **discipline**, *n*, discipline, *f*. ¶ *v.t*, discipliner.

disclaim, *v.t*, désavouer; dénier. ~**er**, *n*, dénégation, *f*; désaveu, *m*; renonciation, *f*.

disclose, *v.t*, révéler, divulguer, dévoiler. **disclosure**, *n*, révélation, divulgation, *f*.

discoloration, *n*, décoloration, *f*. **discolor**, *v.t*, décolorer.

discomfit, *v.t*, confondre. ~**ure**, *n*, déconvenue, *f*.

discomfort, *n*, incommodité, *f*, malaise, *m*, gêne, *f*.

discompose, *v.t*, troubler. **discomposure**, *n*, trouble, *m*.

disconcert, *v.t*, déconcerter, interdire, désorienter.

disconnect, *v.t*, désassembler; (*Mech.*) débrayer; (*Elec.*) rompre. ~**ed**, *a*, détaché; isolé, incohérent.

disconsolate, *a*, désolé.

discontent[ed], *a*, *p.p.* mécontent. **discontent[ment]**, *n*, mécontentement, *m*.

discontinuance, *n*, cessation, suspension; suppression, *f*. **discontinue**, *v.t*, discontinuer; (*a train*) supprimer. ~ *one's subscription*, se désabonner.

discord, *n*, discorde, *f*; (*Mus.*) désaccord, *m*, dissonance, *f*. ~**ance**, *n*, discordance, *f*. ~**ant**, *a*, discordant, dissonant.

discount, *n*, escompte, *m*; remise, *f*; rabais, *m*; (opp. *premium*) perte, *f*. ¶ *v.t*, escompter.

discountenance, *v.t*, s'opposer à.

discounter, *n*, escompteur, *m*. **discounting**, *n*, escompte, *m*.

discourage, *v.t*, décourager. ~**ment**, *n*, découragement, *m*.

discourse, *n*, discours, *m*. ¶ *v.i*, discourir.

discourteous, *a*, discourtois. **discourtesy**, *n*, discourtoisie, *f*.

discover, *v.t*, découvrir. ~**er**, *n*, inventeur, *m*. ~**y**, *n*, découverte, *f*.

discredit, *n*, discrédit, *m*. ¶ *v.t*, discréditer, déconsidérer, démonétiser. ~**able**, *a*, déshonorant.

discreet†, *a*, discret, retenu.

discrepancy, *n*, contradiction, *f*.

discrete, *a*, discret.

discretion, *n*, discrétion, retenue, prudence, *f*. ~**ary**, *a*, discrétionnaire. *full ~ power*, carte blanche, *f*.

discriminate, *v.t*, distinguer, discerner, faire le départ. **discrimination**, *n*, discernement, *m*, discrimination, *f*.

discursive, *a*, discursif.

discus, *n*, disque, *m*.

discuss, *v.t*, discuter, débattre, agiter. ~**ion**, *n*, discussion, *f*, débat, *m*.

disdain, *n*, dédain, *m*. ¶ *v.t*, dédaigner. ~**ful†**, *a*, dédaigneux.

disease, *n*, maladie, *f*; mal, *m*. ~**d**, *a*, malade; (*meat*) provenant d'animaux malades.

disembark, *v.t. & i*, débarquer. ~**ation**, *n*, débarquement, *m*.

disembody, *v.t*, désincorporer.

disembowel, *v.t*, éventrer.

disenchant, *v.t*, désenchanter.

disencumber, *v.t*, désencombrer; (*Fin.*) dégrever.

disengage, *v.t*, dégager; (*Mech.*) débrayer. ~**d**, *a*, libre.

disentangle, *v.t*, démêler, débrouiller.

disestablishment [of the Church] *n*, séparation de l'Église & de l'État, *f*.

disfavor, *n*, défaveur, *f*.

disfigure, *v.t*, défigurer, enlaidir. ~**ment**, *n*, enlaidissement, *m*.

disforest, *v.t*, déboiser.

disgorge, *v.t*, dégorger.

disgrace, *n*, disgrâce; honte, *f*; déshonneur, opprobre, *m*. ¶ *v.t*, disgracier; déshonorer. ~**ful†**, *a*, honteux, ignominieux.

disgruntled, *a*, maussade, mécontent.

disguise, *n*, déguisement, *m*; dissimulation, *f*. ¶ *v.t*, déguiser, camoufler; travestir; contrefaire.

disgust, *n*, dégoût, *m*, ¶ *v.t*, dégoûter; (*slang*) débecter, débecqueter. ~**ing**, *a*, dégoûtant.

dish, *n*, plat, *m*; (*food*) mets, *m*. ~**es**, vaisselle, *f*. ~**cloth**, torchon [de cuisine] *m*, lavette, *f*. ~ *warmer*, chauffe-plats, *m*. ~ *washer*, laveur de vaisselle, plongeur, *m*. ~ *up*, *v.t*, dresser, servir. ~**ed**, *a*, à cuvette. ~**ful**, *n*, platée, *f*.

dishabille, *n*, déshabillé, *m*.

dishearten, *v.t*, décourager, rebuter.

disheveled, *a*, échevelé, ébouriffé.

dishonest†, *a*, malhonnête, infidèle, déloyal. ~**y**, *n*, malhonnêteté, infidélité, *f*.

dishonor, *n*, déshonneur, *m*. ¶ *v.t*, déshonorer. ~**able**, *a*, peu honnête, déshonorant.

disillusion, *n*, désillusion, *f*. ¶ *v.t*, désillusionner, dégriser, désenchanter.

disinclination, *n*, éloignement, *m*. **disincline**, *v.t*, éloigner.

disinfect, *v.t*, désinfecter. ~**ant**, *n*, désinfectant, *m*. ~**ion**, *n*, désinfection, *f*.

disingenuous, *a*, peu sincère.

disinherit, *v.t*, déshériter.

disintegrate, *v.t*, désagréger, effriter.

disinter, *v.t*, déterrer, exhumer.

disinterested, *a*, désintéressé. ~**ness**, *n*, désintéressement, *m*.

disinterment, *n*, exhumation, *f*.

disjoin, *v.t*, disjoindre.

disjoint, *v.t*, désassembler. ~**ed**, *a*, décousu.

disk, *n*, disque, plateau, *m*; rondelle, *f*. (*computers*) ~ *drive*, tourne-disque, *m*. (*computers*) *floppy* ~, minidisque, *m*, disquette, *f*.

diskette, *n*, disquette, *f*, minidisque, *m*.

dislike, *n*, dégoût, éloignement, *m*, aversion, antipathie, grippe, *f*. ¶ *v.t*, ne pas aimer, avoir en aversion, avoir de l'aversion pour (*ou* contre), prendre en grippe.

dislocate, *v.t*, disloquer, luxer, démettre, déboîter, démancher.

dislocation, *n*, dislocation, luxation, *f*.

dislodge, *v.t*, déchausser, débusquer, disloquer.

disloyal†, *a*, déloyal, infidèle. ~**y**, *n*, déloyauté, infidélité, *f*.

dismal†, *a*, lugubre, morne, sombre.

dismantle, *v.t*, démanteler, dégarnir.

dismast, *v.t*, démâter.

dismay, *n*, consternation, *f*. ¶ *v.t*, consterner.

dismember, *v.t*, démembrer.

dismiss, *v.t*, renvoyer, congédier, remercier, destituer; chasser; rejeter. ~**al**, *n*, renvoi, congé, *m*, destitution, *f*.

dismount, *v.i*, descendre; (*v.t.*) démonter.

disobedience, *n*, désobéissance, *f*. **disobedient**, *a*, désobéissant. **disobey**, *v.t*, désobéir à; (*v.i.*) désobéir.

disoblige, *v.t*, désobliger. **disobliging**, *a*, désobligeant. ~**ness**, *n*, désobligeance, *f*.

disorder, *n*, désordre; trouble, *m*; maladie, *f*. ¶ *v.t*, dérégler. ~**ly**, *a*, désordonné.

disorganize, *v.t*, désorganiser.

disorient, *v.t*, désorienter, déphaser.

disown, *v.t*, désavouer, renier, méconnaître.

disown, v.t, désavouer, renier, méconnaître.

disparage, v.t, dénigrer, rabaisser, déprécier, ravaler. **~ment**, n, dénigrement, m. **disparaging**, a, dénigrant; péjoratif.

disparate, a, disparate. **disparity**, n, disparité, f.

dispassionate, a. & **~ly**, ad, sans passion; sans parti pris.

dispatch, n, expédition, f, envoi, acheminement, m; diligence, célérité, promptitude, rapidité; (message) dépêche, f. ~ case, serviette, f. ¶ v.t, expédier, envoyer, acheminer; dépêcher, brasser. **~er**, n, (transport) répartiteur, m.

dispel, v.t, dissiper, chasser.

dispensary, n, officine, pharmacie, f; (charitable) dispensaire, m. **dispensation**, n, (of Providence) disposition; (exemption) dispense, f. **dispense**, v.t, dispenser; départir; rendre; (Med.) préparer [& débiter]. ~ with, se passer de; supprimer. **dispenser**, n, dispensateur, trice; (Med.) pharmacien, ne.

dispersal & **dispersion**, n, dispersion, séparation, f. **disperse**, v.t, disperser; dissiper.

dispirit, v.t, décourager, déprimer.

displace, v.t, déplacer; (from office) destituer; (securities, Fin.) déclasser. **~ment**, n, déplacement, m; destitution, f; déclassement, m.

display, n, montre, parade, f; étalage, m. ~ cabinet, vitrine, armoire vitrée, f. ~ model, mannequin, m. (computers) ~ unit, unité d'affichage, f. ¶ v.t, exposer, étaler; faire preuve de. ~ed in bold type, en vedette.

displease, v.t, déplaire à; mécontenter. **displeasure**, n, déplaisir, mécontentement, m.

disposable, a, disponible. **disposal**, n, disposition; expédition, f. **dispose**, v.t, disposer. ~ of, disposer de; placer; expédier. well, ill, ~d towards, bien, mal, disposé pour, envers. **disposition**, n, disposition, f; naturel, m.

dispossess, v.t, déposséder.

disproof, n, réfutation, f.

disproportion, n, disproportion, f. **~ate**, a, disproportionné.

disprove, v.t, réfuter.

dispute, n, dispute, contestation, f, litige, m. ¶ v.t. & i, disputer, contester. ~ every inch of the ground (Mil.), chicaner le terrain.

disqualification, n, disqualification, f. **disqualified** (law) p.p. & p.a, indigne. **disqualify**, v.t, disqualifier; (law) frapper d'incapacité.

disquiet, v.t, inquiéter. **~[ude]**, n, inquiétude, f.

disquisition, n, dissertation, f.

disrate, v.t, déclasser.

disregard, n, indifférence, f; dédain, m. ¶ v.t, négliger; mépriser.

disrelish, n, dégoût, m.

disreputable, a, peu honorable; de mauvaise réputation. **disrepute**, n, discrédit, décri, m.

disrespect, n, manque de respect, m, irrévérence, f. **~ful†**, a, irrespectueux, irrévérencieux.

disrobe, v.t, déshabiller.

disrupt, v.t, rompre.

dissatisfaction, n, mécontentement, m. **dissatisfied**, p.a, mécontent.

dissect, v.t, disséquer. **~ion**, n, dissection, f.

dissemble, v.t. & i, dissimuler. **dissembler**, n, dissimulateur, trice.

disseminate, v.t, disséminer.

dissension, n, dissension, f. **dissent**, n, dissentiment, m; dissidence, f. ¶ v.i, s'opposer. **~er** & **dissentient**, n, dissident, e. **~ing** & **dissentient**, a, dissident.

dissertation, n, dissertation, f.

disservice, n, mauvais service, m.

dissidence, n, dissidence, f. **dissident**, a, dissident.

dissimilar, a, dissemblable, dissimilaire. **~ity**, n, dissemblance, f.

dissimulate, v.t. & i, dissimuler. **dissimulation**, n, dissimulation, f, duplicité, f.

dissipate, v.t, dissiper. **dissipation**, n, dissipation, f.

dissociate, v.t, dissocier.

dissolute, a, dissolu. **~ness**, n, dissolution, f.

dissolution, n, dissolution, f. **dissolve**, v.t, dissoudre, fondre. **dissolvent**, a. & n, dissolvant, a. & m. dissolving views, vues fondantes, f.pl.

dissonance, n, dissonance, f. **dissonant**, a, dissonant.

dissuade, *v.t*, dissuader, déconseiller.

dissyllable, *n*, dissyllabe, *m*.

distaff, *n*, quenouille, *f*.

distance, *n*, distance, *f*; éloignement; écart; lointain, *m*; trotte, *f*. keep one's ~ garder ses distances. ~ apart or between, écartement, *m*. ¶ *v.t*, éloigner; distancer. **distant**, *a*, éloigné, reculé, lointain; distant.

distaste, *n*, dégoût, *m*. ~ful, *a*, désagréable au goût.

distemper, *n*, maladie [des chiens]; (*paint*) détrempe, *f*, badigeon, *m*. ¶ *v.t*, peindre à la détrempe, badigeonner.

distend, *v.t*, distendre, ballonner. **distension**, *n*, distension, *f*, ballonnement, *m*.

distil, *v.t*, distiller. **distillate** & **distillation**, *n*, distillation, *f*. **distiller**, *n*, distillateur, *m*. ~y, *n*, distillerie, *f*.

distinct†, *a*, distinct; tranché. ~ion, *n*, distinction, *f*. ~ive, *a*, distinctif. **distinctness**, *n*, netteté, *f*. **distinguish**, *v.t*, distinguer. to be ~able from, se distinguer de. ~ed, *a*, distingué, de distinction, éminent, notable, insigne.

distort, *v.t*, déformer; défigurer, dénaturer, tordre. ~ing mirror, miroir déformant, *m*. ~ion, *n*, déformation; distorsion, *f*; (*fig.*) travestissement, *m*.

distract, *v.t*, distraire, détourner; déchirer. ~ed†, *p.a*, éperdu, affolé. ~ion, *n*, distraction, *f*; affolement, *m*; folie, fureur, *f*.

distrain upon, (*pers.*) exécuter, contraindre par saisie de biens; (*goods*) saisir. ~able, *a*, saisissable. not ~, insaisissable. **distraint**, *n*, saisie, exécution, *f*.

distress, *n*, détresse; misère; (*law*) saisie, *f*. ¶ *v.t*, affliger, désoler, angoisser. ~ing, *a*, affligeant, désolant, angoissant.

distribute, *v.t*, distribuer, répartir. **distribution**, *n*, distribution, répartition, *f*.

district, *n*, district, *m*; région, *f*; quartier, *m*.

distrust, *n*, défiance; méfiance, *f*. ¶ *v.t*, se défier de; se méfier de. ~ful, *a*, défiant; méfiant, soupçonneux.

disturb, *v.t*, troubler, déranger; remuer; inquiéter. ~ance, *n*, dérangement, trouble, *m*; perturbation, *f*; tapage, *m*; émeute, *f*.

disunion, *n*, désunion, *f*. **disunite**, *v.t*, désunir.

disuse, *n*, désuétude, *f*. ~d, *p.a*, hors d'usage.

ditch, *n*, fossé; canal, *m*; rigole; douve, *f*.

ditto, *n*, dito, idem (*ad.*). to say nothing but ~ to everything, opiner du bonnet.

ditty, *n*, chanson, chansonnette, *f*.

divan, *n*, divan, *m*.

dive, *n*, plongeon; (*Avn.*) vol piqué, *m*; (*seamy café*) caboulot, *m*. ¶ *v.i*, plonger; fouiller; (*Avn.*) piquer. **diver**, *n*, (*Swim.*) plongeur, euse; (*in diving dress*) plongeur, scaphandrier; (*bird*) plongeon, *m*.

diverge, *v.i*, diverger. **divergence**, *n*, divergence, *f*. **divergent**, *a*, divergent.

diverse†, *a*, divers, varié. **diversify**, *v.t*, diversifier, varier. **diversion**, *n*, diversion, *f*; divertissement, *m*. **diversity**, *n*, diversité, variété, *f*. **divert**, *v.t*, détourner, dériver, écarter; (*amuse*) divertir.

Dives, *n*, riche; (*Bible*) le mauvais riche, *m*.

divest, *v.t*, dépouiller.

divide, *v.t*, diviser; scinder; partager; répartir. ~d skirt, jupe-culotte, *f*. **dividend**, *n*, dividende, *m*; répartition, *f*. **dividers**, *n.pl*, (*instrument*) compas à pointes sèches, *m*.

divination, *n*, divination, *f*. **divine**†, *a*, divin. ¶ *n*, théologien, *m*. ¶ *v.t*, deviner. **diviner**, *n*, devin, *m*, devineresse, *f*.

diving: ~ bell, cloche à plongeur, *f*. ~ board, plongeoir, tremplin, *m*. ~ suit, scaphandre, *m*.

divining rod, baguette divinatoire, *f*.

divinity, *n*, divinité; (*science*) théologie, *f*.

divisible, *a*, divisible; partageable. **division**, *n*, division, *f*; partage, *m*; section; coupe; séparation; case, *f*. **divisor**, *n*, diviseur, *m*.

divorce, *n*, divorce, *m*. ¶ *v.t*, divorcer d'avec.

divot (*golf*) *n*, touffe de gazon, *f*.

divulge, *v.t*, divulguer.

dizziness, *n*, vertige, *m*. **dizzy**, *a*, vertigineux.

do, *v.t.ir*, faire; opérer; (*v.i.ir.*) faire; agir; s'acquitter; aller; se trouver, se porter; convenir, faire l'affaire; suffire. ~ *away with*, supprimer, abolir. ~*-it-your-selfer*, bricoleur, *m.* [*please*] *do not touch*, défense de toucher. ~-*nothing*, *a*, fainéant. ~ *odd jobs*, bricoler. ~ *one's hair*, se coiffer. ~ *one's utmost to*, s'efforcer de. ~ *over again*, refaire. ~ *without*, se passer de. *I have done*, j'ai fini. *that will* ~, cela suffit. *well-to-*~, aisé, cossu.

docile†, *a*, docile. **docility**, *n*, docilité, *f.*

dock, *n*, (*tail*) tronçon, *m*; (*Bot.*) patience, *f*; (*court*) banc des prévenus; (*Naut.*) bassin, dock, *m*; forme, cale, *f. dry* ~, cale sèche, *f.* ~ *company*, compagnie des docks, *f.* ~ *strike*, grève des travailleurs des docks, *f.* ~ *ware-house*, dock[-entrepôt] *m. naval* ~*yard*, arsenal maritime, *m.* ¶ *v.t*, (*wages*) diminuer; rogner; faire entrer en bassin; (*v.i.*) entrer en bassin. ~**er**, *n*, docker, déchargeur, débardeur, *m.*

docket, *n*, étiquette, *f.* ¶ *v.t*, étiqueter.

docking, *n*, accostage, amarrage, *m.*

doctor, *n*, médecin, docteur, *m*; (*slang*) toubib, *m.* ¶ *v.t*, médicamenter; soigner; (*falsify*) frelater; (*patch up*) tricher. ~**ate**, *n*, doctorat, *m.*

doctrinaire, *n. & a*, doctrinaire, *m. & a.* **doctrine**, *n*, doctrine, *f.*

document, *n*, document, écrit, *m*, pièce, *f*; acte, titre, *m.* ~ *cabinet*, cartonnier, *m.* ~ *case*, serviette, *f.* ¶ *v.t*, documenter. ~**ary**, *a*, documentaire.

dodder (*Bot.*) *n*, cuscute, *f.* ¶ *v.i*, brandiller [de] la tête.

dodge, *n*, biais; détour; truc; *m*; ruse, *f.* ¶ *v.t*, esquiver, éviter; (*v.i.*) biaiser. **dodger**, *n*, biaiseur, euse. *artful* ~, finassier, rusé compère, *m.*

doe, *n*, (*deer*) daine; (*hare*) hase; (*rabbit*) lapine, *f.* ~**skin**, *n*, peau de daim, *f*, daim, *m.*

doer, *n*, faiseur, euse.

doff, *v.t*, ôter, tirer.

dog, *n*, chien; (*fire*) chenet, *m.* ~ *biscuit*, pain de chien, *m.* ~ *cart*, charrette anglaise, *f.* ~ *days*, canicule, *f.* ~ *fish*, chien

de mer, *m.* ~ *Latin*, latin de cuisine, *m.* ~ *racing* or *dogs*, courses de lévriers, *f.pl.* ~ *rose*, rose de chien, églantine, *f*; (*bush*) églantier, rosier sauvage, *m.* ~[*'s*] *ear*, *n*, corne, *f*; (*v.t.*) [é]corner. ~ *show*, exposition canine, *f.* ~ *violet*, violette de chien, *f.* ¶ *v.t*, talonner. **dogged**, *a*, tenace. ~**ly**, *ad*, mordicus. ~**ness**, *n*, obstination, *f.*

doggerel, *n*, méchants vers, *m.pl.*

doggy or **doggie**, *n*, toutou, *m.*

dogma, *n*, dogme, *m.* **dogmatic-(al)**†, *a*, dogmatique. **dogmatize**, *v.i*, dogmatiser.

doily, *n*, rond, ovale, rectangle [de table] *m.*

doings, *n.pl*, faits & gestes; (*underhand*) agissements, *m.pl.* *your doing* (*fig.*), votre ouvrage.

do-it-yourselfer, *n*, bricoleur, *m.*

doldrums (*Naut.*) *n.pl*, calmes, *m.pl*, zone des calmes, *f. to be in the* ~ (*fig.*), broyer du noir.

dole, *n*, charité; indemnité de chômage, *f.* ~ *out*, distribuer parcimonieusement. ~**ful**†, *a*, plaintif, dolent.

doll, *n*, poupée, *f.* ~*-faced*, poupin. ~*'s house*, maison de poupée, *f.*

dollar, *n*, dollar, *m.*

dolly, *n*, chariot, diabolo, *m.* ~ *shot*, travelling, *m.*

dolphin, *n*, (*porpoise*) dauphin, *m*; (*dorado*) dorade, *f*; (*mooring*) corps mort, *m.*

dolt, *n*, lourdaud, e.

domain, *n*, domaine, *m.*

dome, *n*, dôme, *m*, coupole, voûte, *f.*

domestic, *a*, domestique; (*coal, or like*) de ménage; (*trade*) intérieur, métropolitain. ¶ *n*, domestique, *m,f.* **domesticate**, *v.t*, domestiquer. **domesticated**, (*pers.*) *a*, d'intérieur. **domestically**, *n*, domesticité, *f.*

domicile, *n*, domicile, *m.* ¶ *v.t*, domicilier.

dominant, *a*, dominant. **dominate**, *v.t. & i*, dominer, régenter. **domination**, *n*, domination, *f.* **domineer**, *v.t*, dominer; (*v.i.*) régenter. ~**ing**, *a*, dominateur.

Dominican, *n*, dominicain, e.

dominion, *n*, domination, *f*, empire, *m.* *D*~ *of Canada, of New*

Zealand, Dominion du Canada, de la Nouvelle-Zélande, *m.*

domino, *n,* domino, *m.*

don, *v.t,* mettre, endosser, revêtir.

donate, *v.i. & t,* donner, accorder. **donation,** *n,* don, *m,* donation; (*pl.*) bienfaisance, *f.*

done, *p.p,* fait; (*Cook.*) cuit.

donee, *n,* donataire, *m,f.*

donkey, *n,* âne, baudet, grison, *m,* bourrique, *f.* ~ *driver,* ânier, ère. ~ *engine,* petit cheval, *m.* ~ *pump,* pompe alimentaire, *f.*

donor, *n,* donneur, euse; (*law*) donateur, *m,* donatrice, *f.*

doom, *n,* destin; jugement, *m.* ¶ *v.t,* condamner. **doomsday,** *n,* jour du jugement [dernier] *m.*

door, *n,* porte; fermeture; (*carriage, car*) portière, *f;* (*peephole*) regard, *m.* ~ *curtain,* portière, *f.* ~*keeper,* concierge, *m, f,* portier, ère, gardien, ne. ~*mat,* essuie-pieds, *m.* ~*step,* pas de la porte, *m.* ~*way,* [baie de] porte, *f.*

dope, *n,* stupéfiant, *m.* ¶ *v.t,* droguer; doper.

Doric, *a. & n,* dorique, *a. & m.*

dormant, *a,* dormant, endorml. **dormer** [**window**], *n,* mansarde, lucarne, *f.* **dormitory,** *n,* dortoir, *m.* **dormouse,** *n,* loir, *m.*

dosage, *n,* posologie, *f.* **dose,** *n,* dose, prise, *f.* ¶ *v.t,* médicamenter; doser.

dot, *n,* point; (*Emb.*) pois, *m.* ¶ *v.t,* marquer d'un point, mettre un p. sur; (*Mus.*) pointer; pointiller; jalonner, parsemer. *dotted line,* ligne pointillée, *f.*

dotage, *n,* enfance, *f;* radotage, *m.* **dotard,** *n,* radoteur, euse; (*of comedy*) grime, *m.* **dote** *or* **doat,** *v.i,* radoter. ~ *on,* être fou, folle, de, raffoler de.

double, *a,* double. ~*acting,* à double effet. ~*barreled gun,* fusil à deux coups, *m.* ~ *bass,* contrebasse, *f.* ~ *bed,* lit à deux places, *m.* ~[*bedded*] *room,* chambre à deux lits, *f.* ~*breasted,* croisé. ~*dealing,* duplicité, *f;* (*a.*) double. ~*entry bookkeeping,* tenue des livres en partie double, *f.* ~*faced,* à double face. ~*fronted* (house), à deux façades. ~ *meaning or* ~ *entendre,* mot à double entente, *m,* phrase à d. e., *f.* ~ *width* (cloth), grande largeur, *f.*

¶ *ad,* double. ¶ *n,* double; (*person*) sosie, *m.* ~ *or nothing,* quitte ou double. *the* ~ (*Mil.*), au pas gymnastique. ~*s game* (*Ten.*), partie double, *f.* ¶ *v.t. & i,* doubler. **doubly,** *ad,* doublement.

doubt, *n,* doute, *m.* ¶ *v.i,* douter; (*v.t.*) douter de. ~*fult,* *a,* douteux; suspect; (*virtue*) moyenne. ~*less,* *a,* sans doute.

dough, *n,* pâte, *f.*

doughty, *a,* preux. ~ *deeds,* hauts faits, *m.pl,* prouesses, *f.pl.*

dour, *a,* froid & sévère; peu démonstratif.

douse, *v.t,* éteindre; tremper.

dove, *n,* colombe, *f;* pigeon, *m.* ~*cot*[*e*], colombier, pigeonnier, *m.* ~*tail,* queue d'aronde, *f.*

dowager, *n,* douairière, *f.*

dowdy, *a,* [mal] fagoté.

dowel, *n,* goujon, *m.* ¶ *v.t,* goujonner.

dower, dowry, *n,* dot, *f;* don, *m.* ¶ *v.t,* doter.

down, *a,* descendant. ~*grade,* pente, *f.*

down, *ad,* en bas; à bas; bas; à terre; par terre; en aval; (*prices*) en baisse; (*sun, moon*) couché, e; (*crossword clues*) verticalement. *to walk with the head* ~, *the hands* ~, marcher la tête basse, les mains basses. ~ *at heel,* en savates. ~ *there,* ~ *below,* là-bas. ~ *to,* jusqu'à, jusque.

down, *comps:* ~*cast,* *a,* baissé; abattu. ~*fall,* *n,* chute, *f,* effondrement, *m,* ruine, *f.* ~*hearted,* *a,* découragé, abattu. ~*hill,* *a,* en pente; (*ad.*) en descendant. ~*pour,* *n,* tombée de pluie, *f,* déluge, *m.* ~*right,* *a,* franc, fieffé, pommé, vrai; (*ad.*), franchement, nettement. ~*stairs,* *ad,* en bas. ~*stream,* *ad,* en aval, à vau-l'eau. ~*stroke,* *n,* (*piston*) course descendante, *f;* (*writing*) jambage, plein, *m.* ~*trodden,* *a,* foulé [aux pieds]. ~*ward,* *a,* descendant; de baisse; à la baisse. ~*ward*[*s*], *ad,* en bas, en contrebas.

down, *i,* à bas! ~ *with* . . , à bas . . .! conspuez . . .!

down, *n,* duvet, poil follet; poil, *m;* bourre, *f;* coton, *m;* (*sand hill*) dune, *f.* ~ *quilt,* couvre-pied, *m.*

down, pr, en bas de, au bas de; en aval de.

down, v.t, abattre; baisser; renverser.

downy, a, duveté, douillet, follet, cotonneux, bourru.

dowral, a, dotal. **dowry,** n, dot, f.

dowser, n, sourcier, ère, hydroscope, m. **dowsing,** n, hydroscopie, f. ~ **rod,** baguette divinatoire, f.

doze, v.i, sommeiller, s'assoupir. to have a ~, faire un somme.

dozen, n, douzaine, f. by the ~, à la d.

drab, a, gris brun; terne.

drachm, n, (apothecaries' measure) = 3.552 milliliters; (a—s' weight) = 3.888 grams.

drachma, n, drachme, f.

draft, n, vent, courant d'air; vent coulis; appel d'air; aérage; tirage; tirant d'eau; trait, coup; breuvage, m; potion, f; coup de filet, m, pêche, prise, f; tracé, plan, m, (outline) projet, ébauche, f; (Mil.) conscription, f. ~ animal, animal de trait, m. ~ beer, bière au tonneau; b. à la pompe, f. ~ board, conseil de revision, m. ¶ v.t, ébaucher, tracer; (writings) minuter. **draftsman,** n, dessinateur, traceur; (writings) rédacteur, m. **drafty,** a, exposé aux courants d'air.

draftee, n, conscrit, m.

drag, n, drague, f; sabot [d'enrayage]; tirage, m; résistance, f. ~net, traîneau, m, drague, f. ¶ v.t, traîner; arracher; (wheel) enrayer; (pond) draguer, pêcher; (anchor) chasser; (v.i.) se traîner; languir; chasser. ~ about, v.t, trimbaler.

draggle, v.t, & i, traîner.

dragon, n, dragon, m. ~fly, libellule, demoiselle, f. ~'s blood, sang-[de-]dragon, m.

dragoon, n, dragon, m. ¶ ~ into, forcer à embrasser.

drain, n, drain, m; tranchée, f; égout; (demand) drainage, m. ~pipe, tuyau de drainage; drain, m. ¶ v.t, drainer, assécher, dessécher, saigner, épuiser, [faire] égoutter, faire écouler; purger. ~ [away], s'écouler; s'égoutter. ~age, n, drainage, assèchement, dessèchement, épuisement, écoulement, m; purge, f; (surplus water) égout, m. ~er, n. & ~ing rack, égouttoir, m.

drake, n, canard, m.

dram, n, (avoirdupois) = 1.772 grams; (draft) goutte, f.

drama, n, drame, m. the ~, le théâtre. **dramatic†,** a, dramatique; théâtral. dramatis personae, personnages, m.pl, rôle scénique, m, **dramatist,** dramaturge, n, auteur dramatique, dramatiste, m, dramaturge, m,f. **dramatize,** v.t, dramatiser.

drape, v.t, draper; tendre. **draper,** n, (cloth) drapier; (general) marchand de nouveautés, m. ~y, n, draperie, f; nouveautés, f.pl.

drastic, a, drastique, extrême.

draw, n, tirage, m; loterie, f; attrait, m, attraction, f; appât, m; (game) partie nulle, f, match nul, refait, m.

draw, v.t.ir, tirer; retirer; attirer; traîner; entraîner; remorquer; (Min.) remonter; (metal) étirer; arracher; extraire; puiser; aspirer; (so much water—ship) caler; dessiner; tracer; (wages) toucher; (fowl) vider; (v.i.ir.) tirer; (tea) [s']infuser. ~ [a game], faire match nul, f. partie nulle. ~ aside, tirer à l'écart. ~ back, reculer; (curtains) ouvrir. ~ down, faire descendre, baisser. ~ in (days), [se] raccourcir. ~ near, approcher. ~ off, tirer; soutirer. ~ on, mettre à contribution. ~ out (days), croître. ~ up, (writing) dresser, rédiger, formuler; (carriage) s'arrêter.

drawback, n, désavantage, inconvénient, m.

drawbridge, n, pont levant; pont à bascule; (Hist.) pont-levis, m.

drawee, n, tiré, payeur, m.

drawer, n, tireur, euse; (of bill, check) tireur, souscripteur, m; (receptacle) tiroir; carton, m; (pl., chest) commode, f; (pl., dress) caleçon, m.

drawing, n, dessin; (lottery) tirage, m. ~ board, planche à dessin, f. ~ knife, plane, f. ~ pen, tire-ligne, m. ~ room, [grand] salon, m.

drawl, v.t, traîner.

drawn: ~ battle, bataille indécise, f. ~ face, visage tiré, v. hagard, m. ~ game, partie nulle, p. indécise, p. remise, f. ~ number, numéro sortant, m. with ~ sword, sabre au clair.

dray, n, haquet, m. ~horse, cheval de h., m.

dread, *a,* redouté. ¶ *n,* terreur, crainte; phobie, *f.* ¶ *v.t,* redouter, craindre. ~**ful†,** *a,* terrible, épouvantable, affreux. **dread-nought** (*Nav.*) *n,* dreadnought, *m*; (*cloth*) ratine, *f.*

dream, *n,* rêve, songe, *m*; **rêverie,** *f.* ¶ *v.i. & t.* ir, rêver, songer. ~ *of,* rêver. ~**er,** *n,* rêveur, euse; songe-creux, *m.* ~**y,** *a,* rêveur, songeur.

drear[y], *a,* triste, morne. **dreari-ness,** *n,* tristesse, *f,* aspect morne, *m.*

dredge, *n,* drague, *f.* ¶ *v.t,* dra-guer; (*sprinkle*) saupoudrer. **dredger,** *n,* dragueur; saupou-droir, *m.* mud~, marie-salope, *f.* **dredging,** *n,* dragage, *m.*

dregs, *n.pl,* lie, *f.*

drench, *v.t,* tremper; · saucer; abreuver. ~**ing rain,** pluie bat-tante, *f.*

Dresden, *n,* Dresde, *f.* ~ **china,** porcelaine de Saxe, *f,* saxe, *m.*

dress, *n,* habillement; entretien; costume, *m*; robe; mise; toilette; tenue; parure, *f*; chiffons, *m.pl.* ~ *circle,* premières [galeries] *f.pl,* [premier] balcon, *m.* ~ *coat,* habit de soirée, *m.* ~*maker,* cou-turière; entrepreneuse de confec-tion, *f.* ~*making,* confections pour dames, *f.pl.* ~ *rehearsal,* avant-première, répétition géné-rale, *f.* ~ *shirt,* chemise de soirée, *f.* ¶ *v.t,* habiller, [re]vêtir; (*in fancy dress*) costumer; orner, parer; (*ship with flags*) pavoiser; (*wound*) panser; (*food*) apprê-ter; (*salad*) assaisonner; (*mate-rials*) dresser, tailler, corroyer; (*Mil.*) aligner. ~ [*oneself*], s'habiller, se mettre, se vêtir. ~ *for dinner,* se mettre en habit pour dîner. ~ *the window*(*s*), faire l'étalage. **dressing,** *n,* habil-lement, *m*; toilette, *f*; (*of wound*) pansement; (*on wound*) appareil; (*food*) apprêt, *m*; (*meat*) parure, *f*; (*salad*) assaisonnement, *m.* ~*gown,* robe de chambre, *f,* pei-gnoir, saut de lit, *m.* ~ *room,* cabinet de toilette, *m.* (*Theat.*) loge, *f.* ~ *table,* [table de] toi-lette, coiffeuse, *f.*

dribble, *n,* goutte; (*slaver*) bave, *f.* ¶ *v.i,* dégoutter; baver; (*v.t,* *Foot.*) dribbler. **dribbling** (*Foot.*) *n,* dribbling, *m.* **in driblets,** par parcelles.

dried, *p.a,* séché; (*raisins, fruits,*

fish, etc.) sec; (*apples, etc., in rings*) tapé. **drier,** *n,* séchoir; (*s. or pl, for paint*) siccatif, *m.*

drift, *n,* poussée, tendance, portée, *f*; laisser-faire, *m,* inaction; dé-viation, *f*; (*snow*) amas, *m*; (*Naut. & fig.*) dérive; (*Min.*) galerie, *f*; (*Geol.*) apport[s] *m.* [*pl.*]. ~*wood,* bois flotté, *m.* ¶ *v.t,* charrier, entraîner, apporter; chasser; amonceler; (*Mech.*) bro-cher; (*v.i.*) chasser; (*Naut.*) dé-river, aller en dérive; s'amon-celer. ~**er** (*boat*) *n,* cordier, *m.*

drill, *n,* foret, *m,* mèche; (*Min. etc.*) perforatrice, foreuse, per-ceuse, sonde, *f*; (*furrow*) sillon; (*Agric. mach.*) semoir; (*Mil.*) exercice, *m,* école, *f*; (*fabric*) coutil, *m.* ~ *ground,* champ de manœuvres, *m,* place d'armes, *f.* ~[*holder*], porte-foret, porte-mèche, *m.* ~ *sergeant,* [sergent] instructeur, *m.* ¶ *v.t,* percer, forer, perforer; (*Mil.*) exercer, faire faire l'exercice à; (*v.i.*) faire l'exercice. **drilling,** *n,* perçage, percement, *m,* perforation, *f*; forage, sondage; (*Mil.*) exercice, *m.* ~ *machine,* machine à percer, perceuse; foreuse, *f.*

drink, *n,* boisson; consommation, *f*; breuvage, *m*; liqueur, *f.* to *have a* ~, boire un coup. ¶ *v.t. & i.* ir, boire; consommer. ~**able,** *a,* buvable, potable. ~**er,** *n,* buveur, euse. ~**ing,** att: ~ *fountain,* fon-taine publique, *f.* ~ *song,* chan-son à boire, c. bachique, *f*; air à boire, *m.* ~ *straw,* chalumeau, *m.* ~ *trough,* abreuvoir, *m.* ~ *water,* eau potable, *f.*

drip, *n,* goutte, *f.* ~[*stone*], lar-mier, *m.* ¶ *v.i,* [dé]goutter, dé-couler, pleurer, ruisseler. **drip-ping,** *n,* graisse de rôti, *f.* ~ *pan,* lèchefrite, *f.* ~ *wet,* tout trempé, saucé.

drive, *n,* promenade; avenue; allée; initiative; (*Hunt.*) battue; (*Mach.*) commande, transmis-sion; (*golf*) crossée, *f*; (*Ten.*) drive, *m*; (*Min.*) galerie, *f. front-wheel* ~, traction avant, *f.* ¶ *v.t.ir,* chasser, pousser, forcer; (*horse, car*) conduire, mener; (*golf*) driver; (*Ten.*) chasser; (*Mach.*) actionner, commander; (*Min.*) chasser, percer [en direc-tion]; (*nail*) enfoncer; forcer, con-traindre; faire; (*one mad*) rendre;

(*v.i.ir.*) aller (*ou* se promener) en voiture, rouler. ~ *ashore* (ship), dériver à la côte. ~ *away*, chasser. ~ *back*, refouler. ~ *into a corner*, acculer, rencogner. ~ *out*, ~ *off*, chasser, débusquer. ~ *slowly* (traffic sign), au pas. *what are you ~ing at?* où voulez-vous en venir?

drivel, *n*, bave, *f*. ¶ *v.i*, baver; (*fig.*) radoter.

driver, *n*, conducteur; cocher; chauffeur; (*Rly*) mécanicien, *m*; (*golf*) grand-crosse, *f*. ~'*s license*, permis de conduire [les automobiles] *m*. **driving,** *n*, conduite; commande, transmission, *f*; serrage; percement; (*nails, piles*) enfoncement; (*piles*) battage, *m*. ~ *iron* (*golf*), grand-fer, *m*. ~ *rain*, pluie battante, *f*. ~ *shaft*, arbre moteur, arbre de couche, *m*.

drizzle, *n*, bruine, *f*. ¶ *v.imp*, bruiner.

droll, *a*, drôle, cocasse, plaisant. ~*ery*, *n*, drôlerie, *f*. **drolly,** *ad*, drôlement.

dromedary, *n*, dromadaire, *m*.

drone, *n*, ronron; (*Mus.*) bourdon, *m*. ~ [*bee*], [faux] bourdon, *m*. ¶ *v.i*, ronronner, bourdonner; (*v.t.*) psalmodier.

droop, *v.i*, pendre, traîner; (*wilt*) s'étioler. ~*ing*, *p.a*, pendant, tombant. ~ *looks*, airs penchés, *m.pl.* ~ *spirits*, forces défaillantes, *f.pl.*

drop, *n*, goutte; larme; chute; baisse; pastille, *f*; pendant, *m*; pendeloque, *f*. ~ *curtain*, rideau, *m*. ~*forged*, estampé. ¶ *v.t*, laisser tomber goutte à goutte; laisser tomber, lâcher; lancer; (*letter in mail*) jeter; (*a line*) envoyer; (*a stitch*) sauter; (*her young*) mettre bas; (*v.i.*) tomber. *dropped stitch* (*Knit.*), manque, *m*, maille échappée, *m*. perdue, *f*. **dropper,** *n*, compte-gouttes, *m*. **droppings** (*dung*) *n.pl*, fiente, crotte, *f*.

dropsical, *a*, hydropique. **dropsy,** *n*, hydropisie, *f*.

dross, *n*, écume, crasse, scorie, chiasse, *f*.

drought, *n*, sécheresse; disette d'eau, *f*.

drove, *n*, troupeau, *m*. **drover,** *n*, conducteur [de bestiaux], toucheur, *m*.

drown, *v.t*, noyer; (*sounds*) couvrir; (*v.i.*) boire. ~ *oneself*, se noyer. ~*ing*, *n*, submersion; (*fatality*) noyade, *f*. *a ~ man*, un noyé.

drowse, *v.i*, sommeiller; somnoler.

drowsiness, *n*, assoupissement, *m*. **drowsy,** *a*, endormi, ensommeillé. *to make ~*, assoupir.

drub, *v.t*, [b]rosser, frotter, etriller. **drubbing,** *n*, [b]rossée, frottée, peignée, volée de coups, *f*.

drudge, *n*, souffre-douleur, cheval de bât, pâtiras, *m*. ¶ *v.i*, trimer. ~*ry*, *n*, besognes fastidieuses, *f.pl*, corvée, *f*, collier de misère, *m*.

drug, *n*, drogue, *f*; stupéfiant, narcotique, *m*. ~ *addict*, toxicomane, *m. & f*. ~ *traffic*, trafic des stupéfiants, *m*. ~ *store*, pharmacie, *f*. ¶ *v.t*, narcotiser.

drugget, *n*, droguet, *m*.

druggist, *n*, pharmacien; (*wholesale*) droguiste, *m*.

Druid, *n*, druide, *m*.

drum, *n*, tambour, *m*, caisse, *f*; (*ear*) tympan; cylindre, barillet; tonneau, fût, *m*. ~*s & bugles* (*Mil. band*), clique, *f*. ~*head*, peau de tambour, *f*. ~*head court-martial*, cour martiale, *f*. ~ *major*, tambour-major, *m*. ~*stick*, baguette de tambour, *f*; (*fowl*) pilon, *m*. ¶ *v.i*, tambouriner. ~ *into*, seriner à. **drummer,** *n*, tambour, *m*.

drunk, *a*, ivre, soûl. *to get ~*, s'enivrer. ~*ard*, *n*, ivrogne, *m*. ~*en*, *a*, ivrogne. ~ *bout*, débauche de boisson, ribote, *f*. ~ *brawl*, querelle d'ivrognes, *f*. ~*enness*, *n*, ébriété ivresse; (*habitual*) ivrognerie, *f*.

dry, *a*, sec; à sec; desséché; tari. ~*clean*, nettoyer à sec. ~ *dock*, cale sèche, *f*, bassin [à] sec, *m*, forme de radoub, *f*. ~ *fly fishing*, pêche à la mouche sèche, *f*. ~ *measure*, mesure de capacité pour les matières sèches, *f*. ~ *nurse*, nourrice sèche, *f*. ~ *rot*, carie sèche, *f*. ¶ *v.t. & i*, sécher; assécher. ~ *up*, tarir, dessécher.

dryad, *n*, dryade, *f*.

drying, *n*, séchage; assèchement, *m*. ~ *room*, séchoir, *m*. **dryly,** *ad*, (*answer coldly*) sèchement, sec. **dryness,** *n*, sécheresse, aridité, *f*.

drymounting, *n*, (*Phot.*) collage à sec, *m*.

dual, *a,* double. **~ity,** *n,* dualité, *f.*

dub, *v.t,* (*knight*) armer; (*nickname*) baptiser; (*movies*) doubler.

dubious†, *a,* douteux, incertain; équivoque; interlope.

ducal, *a,* ducal. **duchess,** *n,* duchesse, *f.* **duchy,** *n,* duché, *m.*

duck, *n,* canard, *m,* cane, *f,* barboteur; (*dip*) plongeon; (*cloth*) coutil, *m.* **~ & drake** (game), ricochets, *m.pl.* **~ decoy & ~ pond,** canardière, *f.* **~'s egg,** œuf de cane, *m.* **~weed,** lentille d'eau, l. de marais, *f.* ¶ *v.t,* plonger; (*v.i.*) faire le plongeon, éviter de la tête, faire une courbette. **~ling,** *n,* canneton, *m,* canette, *f.*

duct, *n,* canal, conduit, *m,* voie, *f.*

ductile, *a,* (*metals*) ductile; (*pers.*) docile, souple.

dudgeon (**in**), en haine.

due, *a,* dû; échu; régulier; requis, voulu, utile. *the train is ~ at . . .,* le train arrive (*ou* doit arriver) à . . . *in ~ course,* en temps & lieu. **~ date,** échéance, *f.* ¶ *ad,* droit; directement. ¶ *n,* dû, *m;* (*duty*) droit, *m;* taxe, *f.*

duel, *n,* duel, *m,* rencontre, *f.* **duelist,** *n,* duelliste, *m.*

duenna, *n,* duègne, *f.*

duet, *n,* duo, *m.*

duffer, *n,* cancre, *m,* ganache, *f,* imbécile, *m,f;* (*at a game*) mazette, *f.*

dug, *n,* trayon, pis, *m,* tétine, *f.*

dugout, *n,* pirogue; cagna, *f;* abri [de bombardement] *m.*

duke, *n,* duc, *m.* **~dom,** *n,* duché, *m.*

dulcet, *a,* doux.

dulcimer, *n,* tympanon, *m.*

dull, *a,* lourd; obtus; assoupissant, assommant, fastidieux; fade; maussade; inactif; atone; plat; terne; mat; sombre; gris; sourd; émoussé. ¶ *v.t,* ternir; émousser; hébéter. **~ard,** *n,* lourdaud, e. **~ness,** *n,* pesanteur, *f,* appesantissement, ennui, *m;* inactivité, atonie; platitude; ternissure; matité, *f.*

duly, *ad,* dûment; régulièrement; bien. *~ authorized representative,* fondé de pouvoir(s) *m.*

dumb†, *a,* muet. *~ animals,* animaux, *m. pl.* **~bell,** haltère, *m.* **~ show,** jeu muet, *m,* pantomime, *f.*

dumbfound, *v.t,* ébahir, atterrer.

dumbness, *n,* mutisme, *m.*

dumbwaiter, *n,* monte-plat, *m.*

dummy, *a,* feint; faux. **~ book** (for bookshelf), livre feint, *m.* ¶ *n,* prête-nom; mannequin, *m;* poupée; fausse boîte; (*publisher's blank book*) maquette, *f;* (*Mil.*) simulacre; (*cards*) mort, *m.*

dump, *n,* chantier de dépôt, *m.* *core ~,* impression de mémoire, *f. to be in the ~s,* avoir le spleen. ¶ *v.t,* culbuter, chavirer; (*computers*) vider. **~ing** (*economy*) *n,* dumping, *m.* **~y,** *a,* trapu, boulot, courtaud.

dun, *a,* fauve gris. ¶ *n,* fauve gris; créancier importun; agent de recouvrements, *m.* ¶ *v.t,* importuner, pourchasser, assiéger, persécuter.

dunce, *n,* ignorant, e, cancre, âne, *m.* *~ cap,* bonnet d'âne, *m.*

dunderhead, *n,* imbécile, *m.*

dune, *n,* dune, *f.*

dung, *n,* fiente, *f;* crottin, *m;* bouse, crotte, *f.* *~ beetle,* escarbot, *m.* *~hill,* fumier; (*fig.*) pailler, *m.* ¶ *v.t,* fumer.

dungeon, *n,* cachot, *m.*

dunk, *v.t,* tremper.

Dunkirk, *n,* Dunkerque, *m.*

dunnage, *n,* fardage, grenier, chantier [d'arrimage] *m.*

dupe, *n,* dupe, *f.* ¶ *v.t,* duper, blouser, piper. **~ry,** *n,* duperie, *f.*

duplicate, *a,* double; (*tools, parts*) de rechange. ¶ *n,* double, duplicata, *m,* ampliation; pièce de rechange; répétition, *f.* ¶ *v.t,* faire le double de; (*train*) dédoubler. **duplication,** *n,* double emploi, *m.* **duplicity,** *n,* duplicité, *f.*

durable, *a,* durable. **duration,** *n,* durée, *f.*

duress, *n,* violence, *f.*

during, *pr,* pendant, durant, par, dans.

dusk, *n,* la brune. *at ~,* sur (*ou* à) la brune, entre chien & loup. **~y,** *a,* brun.

dust, *n,* poussière, *f;* poussier, *m;* poudre, *f;* cendres; ordures, *f.pl.* **~coat,** cache-poussière, *m.* **~ cover** (*furniture*) housse, *f.* **~ jacket** (*book*) couvre-livre, *m.* **~pan,** pelle à poussière, *f. saw ~,* sciure, *f.* ¶ *v.t,* épousseter; hous-

ser; (*sprinkle*) saupoudrer. ~er,
n, essuie-meuble, *m*. ~y, *a*, poussiéreux, poudreux.

Dutch, *a*, hollandais, de Hollande,
néerlandais. ~ *cheese*, fromage
de Hollande, *m*. ~ *courage*,
courage arrosé, *m*. ~*man*, -*woman*, Hollandais, e, Néerlandais,
e. ~ *oven*, rôtissoire, *f*. ¶ (*language*) *n*, le hollandais.

dutiable, *a*, passible de droits,
sujet à des droits, imposable.

dutiful† & **duteous**†, *a*, obéissant,
soumis, respectueux. **duty**, *n*, devoir, *m*; charge, fonction, *f*, office; service; droit, *m*, taxe, *f*,
impôt, *m*, surtaxe, *f*. *on* ~, de
service, de garde. ~-*free*, *a*, ex-
empte d'impôt.

dwarf, *n*. & *a*, nain, e. ¶ *v.t*, rapetisser.

dwell, *v.i.ir*, habiter, demeurer;
insister, peser. ~er, *n*, habitant,
e. ~ing, *n*, habitation, demeure,
f, logis, *m*. ~ *house*, maison
d'habitation, *f*.

dwindle, *v.i*, dépérir. **dwindling**,
n. dépérissement, *m*.

dye, *n*, teinture, *f*. ~ *stuffs*, matières tinctoriales, *f.pl*. *of the
deepest* ~ (*fig.*), de la plus belle
eau, fieffé. ¶ *v.t*, teindre. ~ing,
n, teinture; teinturerie, *f*. **dyer**
[& **cleaner**], *n*, teinturier, ère.

dying, *a*, mourant; à l'agonie,
agonisant; moribond. *the* ~, les
mourants, *m.pl*. *to be* ~, [*se*]
mourir. ~ *words*, dernières paroles, *f.pl*.

dynamic(al), *a*, dynamique. **dynamics**, *n*, dynamique, *f*.

dynamite, *n*, dynamite, *f*.

dynamo, *n*, dynamo, *f*.

dynasty, *n*, dynastie, *f*.

dysentery, *n*, dysenterie, *f*.

dyspepsia, *n*, dyspepsie, *f*.

E

E (*Mus.*) *letter*, mi, *m*.

each, *a*. & *pn*, chaque; chacun, e;
l'un, l'une, [la] pièce. ~ *one*,
chacun, e. ~ *other*, l'un (l'une)
l'autre, les uns (les unes) les
autres; se, nous, vous.

eager, *a*, ardent, assoiffé, acharné,
avide, empressé. *to be* ~ *for*,
ambitionner. ~ly, *ad*, ardemment, avidement. ~ness, *n*,

ardeur, avidité, *f*, empressement,
m.

eagle, *n*, (*bird*) aigle, *m,f*; (*standard*) aigle, *f*. **eaglet**, *n*, aiglon, ne.

ear, *n*, oreille, *f*. ~ache, douleur
d'oreille, otalgie, *f*. ~drum,
membrane du tympan, *f*, tympan,
m. ~ *flap*, oreillon, *m*. ~mark,
affecter. ~-phones, casque, *m*.
~ring, boucle [d'oreille] *f*. ~
trumpet, cornet acoustique, *m*.

earliness, *n*, heure peu avancée;
précocité, *f*. **early**, *a*, peu avancé;
prématuré; avancé; précoce; hâ-
tif; premier; (*youth*) tendre; ancien. ~ *fruits*, ~ *vegetables*,
primeurs, *f.pl*. *to be* [*up*] ~, *to
be an* ~ *riser*, être matinal, être
matineux. ¶ *ad*, de bonne heure,
tôt, matin.

earn, *v.t*, gagner, acquérir; mériter.

earnest, *a*, sérieux; ardent, fervent. ¶ *n*, gage; (*fig.*) avant-goût,
m. ~ly, *ad*, sérieusement; ardemment; instamment. ~ness, *n*,
ardeur, ferveur, instance, *f*.

earning, *n*, acquisition, *f*; (*pl.*)
gain[s] *m.[pl.]*.

earth, *n*, terre, *f*; sol; (*of fox*) terrier, *m*, tanière, *f*. ~quake, tremblement de t., *m*. ~work, terrassement, *m*. ¶ *v.t*, (*Hort.*)
butter, chausser, terrer. ~en, *a*,
de terre. ~enware, *n*, poterie
[de terre], faïence, *f*. ~ly, *a*, terrestre. ~y, *a*, terreux.

earthquake, *n*, tremblement de
terre, séisme, *m*.

earwig, *n*, perce-oreille, *m*.

ease, *n*, aise, aisance; facilité, *f*;
repos; soulagement, *m*. ¶ *v.t*,
adoucir; soulager; décharger;
(*v.i.*) mollir.

easel, *n*, chevalet, *m*.

easement, *n*, soulagement, *m*.

easily, *ad*, aisément, facilement;
doucement. *not* ~, malaisément.

east, *n*, est; (le) levant; orient, *m*.
from ~ *to west*, du levant au
couchant. *the* E~ (*Geog.*), l'
Orient. ¶ *a*, d'est, de l'est; oriental. *Near* ~, Proche-Orient.
Far ~, Extrême-Orient.

Easter, *n*, Pâques, *m.s*. ~ *egg*,
œuf de P., *m*.

easterly, *a*, d'est. **eastern**, *a*, de
l'est; oriental; (*question, etc.*)
d'Orient.

easy, *a*, facile, aisé; doux; commode; coulant; tranquille; désin-

volte. ~ *chair*, fauteuil, *m*. ~-
going person, personne commode, *f*, sans-souci, *m.f. by ~
stages*, à petites journées. ~ *to
get on with (pers.)*, d'un commerce agréable. *it's ~*, c'est du
gâteau (*slang*).

eat, *v.t. & i. ir*, manger. ~ *away*,
~ *into*, ronger. ~ *up*, dévorer.
~able, *a*, mangeable. **~ables**,
n.pl, comestibles, *m.pl*. **~er**, *n*,
mangeur, euse. **~ing**: ~ *apples*,
pommes à couteau, *f.pl*.

eaves, *n.pl*, avant-toit, *m*. **eavesdrop**, *v.i*, écouter aux portes.
eavesdropper, *n*, écouteur (euse)
aux portes.

ebb, *n*, jusant, reflux, *m*. ~ *tide*,
courant de jusant, *m. the ~ and
flow*, le flux et le reflux. ¶ *v.i*, refluer, refouler.

ebonite, *n*, ébonite, vulcanite, *f*.
ebony *n*, ébène, *f*; (*tree*) ébénier,
m.

ebullition, *n*, ébullition, *f*.

eccentric, *a. & (Mech.) n*, excentrique, *a. & m*. **~ity**, *n*, excentricité, *f*.

Ecclesiastes, *n*, l'Ecclésiaste, *m*.
ecclesiastic, *n. & ~al†, a*, ecclésiastique, *m. & a*. **Ecclesiasticus**,
n, l'Ecclésiastique, *m*.

echo, *n*, écho, *m*. ¶ *v.i*, faire écho,
retentir; (*v.t*.) se faire l'écho de.

eclectic, *a*, éclectique. **eclecticism**, *n*, éclectisme, *m*.

eclipse, *n*, éclipse; défaillance, *f*.
¶ *v.t*, éclipser. *to become ~d*,
s'éclipser. **ecliptic**, *a. & n*, écliptique, *a. & f*.

ecological, *a*, écologique. **ecology**, *n*, écologie, *f*.

economic, *a*, économique.
~(al)†, *a*, économique; économe, ménager. **~s**, *n.pl*, science
économique, *f*. **economist**, *n*,
économiste, *m*. **economize**, *v.t. &
i*, économiser, ménager. **economy**, *n*, économie, *f. planned ~*,
dirigisme économique.

ecstasy, *n*, extase, *f. to go into
ecstasies*, s'extasier. **ecstatic**, *a*,
extatique.

Ecuador, *n*, l'Équateur, *m*.

eczema, *n*, eczéma, *m*.

eddy, *n*, remous, tournant, *m*. ¶
v.i, tourbillonner.

edelweiss, *n*, édelweiss, *m*.

Eden (*fig.*) *n*, éden, *m*. [*the Gar-

den of*] ~, l'Eden, le paradis [ter-
restre].

edge, *n*, bord, rebord, *m*, bordure;
lisière; arête, *f*; tranche, *f*; tranchant, coupant, taillant, *m*. **~-
ways**, **~wise**, *ad. or on ~*, de
chant. ¶ *v.t*, border, edging, *n*,
bordure, *f*, bord, *m*. ~ *knife*,
hache coupe-gazon, *f*.

edible, *a*, comestible.

edict, *n*. édit, *m*.

edifice, *n*, édifice, *m*. **edify**, *v.t*,
édifier.

Edinburgh, *n*, Édimbourg, *m*.

edit, *v.t*, éditer, rédiger. **~ion**, *n*,
édition, *f*. **editor**, *n*, rédacteur
(trice) en chef. **editorial**, *a*, de la
rédaction; (*n.*) article, *m*, (ou
note, *f.*) [émanant] de la rédaction. ~ *staff*, rédaction, *f*.

educate, *v.t*, élever, instruire,
éduquer. **education**, *n*, éducation, *f*; enseignement, *m*; instruction, *f*. **~al**, *a*, d'éducation; scolaire; (*book*) classique. ~ *establishment*, maison d'éducation, *f*.
educator, *n*, éducateur, trice.

educe, *v.t*, tirer; dégager.

eel, *n*, anguille, *f*. ~ *pot*, nasse, *f*.

eerie, **-y**, *a*, fantastique.

efface, *v.t*, effacer. **~able**, *a*, effa-
çable.

effect, *n*, effet, *m*; suite; action,
f; (*pl.*) effets, *m.pl*. ¶ *v.t*, effectuer, faire, opérer; contracter.
~ive†, *a*, effectif; utile. ¶ *n*, effectif, *m*.

effectual†, *a*, efficace.

effeminacy, *n*, caractère efféminé, *m*. **effeminate**, *a*, efféminé.
to [make] ~, efféminer. ~ *[man]*,
n, efféminé, *m*, femmelette, *f*.

effervesce, *v.t*, être en effervescence; faire e.; mousser. **effervescence**, **-ency**, *n*, effervescence,
f. **effervescent**, *a*, effervescent.
effervescing (*drink*) *p.a*, gazeux.

effete, *a*, épuisé.

efficacious†, *a*, efficace.

efficiency, *n*, efficacité, *f*; rendement, *m*. **efficient†**, *a*, efficace;
capable.

effigy, *n*, effigie, *f*.

effloresce, *v.i*, [s']effleurir. **efflorescence**, *n*, efflorescence, *f*.

effluence, *n*, émanation, *f*.

effluvium, *n*, effluve, *m*.

efflux, *n*, dépense; émanation, *f*.

effort, *n*, effort, *m*.

effrontery, *n*, effronterie, *f*.

effulgence, *n*, rayonnement, *m*.

effusion, *n,* effusion, *f,* épanchement, *m.* **effusive,** *a,* expansif. ~**ness,** *n,* effusion, *f.*

eft, *n,* triton, *m,* salamandre aquatique, *f.*

egg, *n,* œuf, *m*; (*pl., silkworm*) graine, *f.* ~ *cup,* coquetier, *m.* ~*plant,* aubergine, *f.* ~*shell,* coquille d'œuf, *f. boiled* ~, œuf à la coque. *fried* ~, œuf sur le plat. *scrambled* ~*s,* œufs brouillés. ~ **on,** *v.t,* pousser.

eglantine, *n,* églantine odorante, *f.*

ego, *n,* moi, *m.* **egoism,** *n,* égoïsme, *m.* **egoist,** *n,* égoïste, *m,f.* **egoistic(al),** *a,* égoïste. **egotism,** *n,* égotisme, *m.* **egotist,** *n,* égotiste, *m,f.* **egotistic(al),** *a,* égotiste.

egregious, *a,* insigne, énorme, grossier, lourd; fieffé.

egress, *n,* sortie, issue, *f.*

egret (*bird & tuft*) *n,* aigrette, *f.*

Egypt, *n,* l'Égypte, *f.* **Egyptian,** *a,* égyptien. ¶ *n,* Égyptien, ne. **Egyptologist,** *n,* égyptologue, *m.* **Egyptology,** *n,* égyptologie, *f.*

eh, *i,* eh! hein!

eider [**duck**]*, n,* eider, *m.* ~**down,** édredon, *m.*

eight, *a. & n,* huit, *a. & m.* **eighteen,** *a. & n,* dix-huit, *a. & m.* 18-*hole course,* parcours (*ou* golf) de 18 trous, *m.* **eighteenth,** *a. & n,* dix-huitième, *a. & m,f*; dix-huit, *m.* **eighth,** *a. & n,* huitième, *a. & m,f*; huit, *m.* ~**ly,** *ad,* huitièmement. **eightieth,** *a. & n,* quatre-vingtième, *a. & m,f.* **eighty,** *a. & n,* quatre-vingts, quatre-vingt, *a. & m.* 81, *etc,* quatre-vingt-un, etc.

either, *pn,* l'un (l'une) ou l'autre; l'un d'eux, l'une d'elles; un, une; chaque. ¶ *c,* ou; soit. ¶ *ad,* non plus. *nor I* ~, ni moi n. p.

ejaculate, *v.t. & abs,* lancer, faire; (*fluid*) éjaculer. **ejaculation,** *n,* interjection, exclamation; (*fluid*) éjaculation, *f.*

eject, *v.t,* expulser. ~**ion,** *n,* expulsion, *f.*

eke out, *v.t,* allonger; suppléer.

elaborate, *a,* travaillé; étudié; recherché. ¶ *v.t,* élaborer; travailler.

elapse, *v.i,* s'écouler, [se] passer.

elastic, *a,* élastique. ¶ *n,* élastique, caoutchouc, *m.* ~ *band,* bande

en caoutchouc, *f.* ~**ity,** *n,* élasticité, *f,* ressort, *m.*

elate, *v.t,* enivrer; enorgueillir.

Elba (**the Island of**), l'île d'Elbe, *f.*

Elbe (**the**) (*river*), l'Elbe, *m.*

elbow, *n,* coude, *m.* **to rest on one's** ~(*s*), s'accouder. ~ *grease* (*fig.*), huile de coude, *f.* ~ *room,* coudées franches, *f.pl.* ¶ *v.t,* coudoyer. **to** ~ **one's way,** jouer des coudes.

elder, *a,* aîné, plus âgé. ¶ *n,* aîné, e; (*Eccl.*) ancien; (*Bot.*) sureau, *m. our* ~*s,* nos aînés. ~ *berry,* baie de sureau, *f.* ~**ly,** *a,* d'un certain âge. **eldest,** *n. & a,* aîné, e.

El Dorado, *n,* eldorado, *m.*

elect, *v.t,* élire, nommer. *the* ~ (*Relig.*), les élus, *m.pl.* ~*ed member,* élu, e. **election,** *n,* élection, *f.* **electioneering,** *n,* manœuvres électorales, *f.pl.* **elector,** *n,* électeur, trice. ~**ate,** *n,* corps électoral, *m.*

electric, *a,* électrique. ~ *eel,* gymnote, *m.* ~ *sign,* enseigne (*ou* affiche) lumineuse, *f.* ~**al,** *a,* électrique. ~ *engineer,* ingénieur électricien, *m.* ~**ally,** *ad,* par l'électricité. ~**ian,** *n,* électricien, *m.* ~**ity,** *n,* électricité, *f.* **electrify,** *v.t,* électriser; (*Rly, etc.*) électrifier. **electrocute,** *v.t,* électrocuter. **electrode,** *n,* électrode, *f.* **electrolysis,** *n,* électrolyse, *f.* **electromagnet,** *n,* électroaimant, *m.* **electron,** *n,* électron, *m.* **electroplate,** *v.t,* plaqué, *m.* ¶ *v.t,* argenter. **electrotype** (*printing*) *n,* galvano, *m.*

elegance, *n,* élégance, *f.* **elegant,** *a,* élégant. ~**ly,** *ad,* élégamment.

elegy, *n,* élégie, *f.*

element, *n,* élément; facteur; (*Chem.*) corps simple; (*voltaic*) couple, *m.* ~**ary,** *a,* élémentaire; (*Sch.*) primaire.

elephant, *n,* éléphant, *m.* ~[*ine person*], mastodonte, *m.*

elevate, *v.t,* élever; [re]monter. **elevation,** *n,* élévation; altitude, hauteur, *f.* **elevator,** *n,* ascenseur; (*Surg.*) élévatoire, *m*; (*in shoe*) hausse, *f.*

eleven, *a. & n,* onze, *a. & m.* **eleventh**†, *a. & n,* onzième, *a. & m,f*; onze, *m.*

elf, *n,* elfe, lutin, *m.* **elfin,** *a,* des elfes. **elfish,** *a,* des elfes; lutin, espiègle.

elicit, *v.t*, tirer, soutirer.

elide, *v.t*, élider.

eligible, *a*, éligible; sortable.

eliminate, *v.t*, éliminer. **elimination**, *n*, élimination, *f*.

elision, *n*, élision, *f*.

elixir, *n*, élixir, *m*.

elk, *n*, élan, *m*.

ellipse & ellipsis, *n*, ellipse, *f*. **elliptic(al)**†, *a*, elliptique.

elm [tree], *n*, orme, ormeau, *m*. ~ *grove*, ormaie, ormoie, *f*. ~ *row*, ormille, *f*.

elocution, *n*, élocution; déclamation, *f*.

elongate, *v.t*, allonger.

elope, *v.i*, se faire enlever (*with* = par); s'enfuir. ~**ment**, *n*, enlèvement, *m*, fugue, *f*.

eloquence, *n*, éloquence, *f*. **eloquent**, *a*, éloquent. ~**ly**, *ad*, éloquemment.

else, *ad*, autre; autrement, sinon, encore. *everything* ~, tout le reste. ~**where**, *ad*, autre part, ailleurs.

Elsinore, *n*, Elseneur, *f*.

elucidate, *v.t*, élucider, dégager.

elude, *v.t*, éluder, se soustraire à, se dérober à. **elusive**, *a*, insaisissable; flottant.

Elysian, *a*, élyséen. **Elysium**, *n*, élysée; (*Myth.*) Élysée, *m*.

emaciated, *p.p*, émacié, décharné, étique, hâve.

emanate, *v.i*, émaner.

emancipate, *v.t*, émanciper, affranchir.

emasculate, *v.t*, émasculer.

embalm, *v.t*, embaumer.

embank, *v.t*, remblayer, terrasser, encaisser. ~**ment**, *n*, remblai, encaissement; quai, *m*; levée, *f*.

embargo, *n*, embargo, *m*.

embark, *v.t*, embarquer. ~**ation**, *n*, embarquement, *m*.

embarrass, *v.t*, embarrasser. ~**ment**, *n*, embarras, *m*.

embassy, *n*, ambassade, *f*.

embattle, *v.t*, ranger en bataille; (*Arch.*) créneler.

embed, *v.t*, encastrer.

embellish, *v.t*, embellir.

ember days, Quatre-Temps, *m. pl*.

embers, *n.pl*, braise, *f*, charbon, *m*; cendre[s] *f.[pl.]*.

embezzle, *v.t*, détourner. ~**ment**, *n*, détournement, *m*, malversation, *f*; péculat, *m*.

embitter, *v.t*, envenimer, enfieller, aigrir.

emblazon, *v.t*, blasonner.

emblem, *n*, emblème, *m*. ~**atic(al)**, *a*, emblématique.

embodiment, *n*, incarnation, *f*. **embody**, *v.t*, incarner; englober.

embolden, *v.t*, enhardir.

embolism, *n*, embolie, *f*.

emboss, *v.t*, graver en relief; estamper, gaufrer; bosseler. ~**ed** *stamp*, timbre sec, timbre fixe, *m*.

embrace, *n*, embrassement, *m*, étreinte, *f*. ¶ *v.t*, embrasser.

embrasure, *n*, embrasure, *f*.

embrocation, *n*, embrocation, *f*.

embroider, *v.t*, broder. ~**er**, ~**ess**, *n*, brodeur, euse. ~**y**, *n*, broderie, *f*. ~ *cotton*, coton à broder, *m*. ~ *hoops*, métier à broder, *m*.

embroil, *v.t*, [em]brouiller.

embryo, *n*, embryon, *m*. *in* ~ (*fig.*), en e., en herbe. **embryonic**, *a*, embryonnaire.

emend, *v.t*, corriger. ~**ation**, *n*, correction, *f*.

emerald, *n*, émeraude, *f*.

emerge, *v.i*, émerger, déboucher. **emergence**, *n*, émergence, *f*.

emergency, *n*, urgence, *f*; événement [inattendu] *m*, occurrence, *f*. ~ *brake*, frein d'urgence, *m*. ~ *exit*, sortie de secours, *f*.

emeritus, *a*, émérite.

emery, *n*, émeri, *m*. ~ *cloth*, toile d'é., *f*.

emetic, *a. & n*, émétique, *a. & m*.

emigrant, *n*, émigrant, e. **emigrate**, *v.i*, émigrer. **emigration**, *n*, émigration, *f*. ~ *officer*, commissaire d'émigration, *m*.

eminence, *n*, éminence, *f*. *His E*~ (*cardinal*), son Éminence, *f*. **eminent**, *a*, éminent; notable, considérable. ~**ly**, *ad*, éminemment.

emir, *n*, émir, *m*.

emissary, *n*, émissaire, *m*. **emission**, *n*, émission, *f*. **emit**, *v.t*, émettre; dégager.

emollient, *a. & n*, émollient, *a. & m*.

emoluments, *n.pl*, émoluments, *m.pl*.

emotion, *n*, émotion, *f*, émoi, *m*. ~**al**, *a*, facile à émouvoir.

empanel a jury, former une liste de jurés, former un tableau.

emperor, *n*, empereur, *m*.

emphasis, *n*, emphase; énergie, *f*. *to lay* ~ *upon* or **emphasize**, *v.t*, appuyer sur, souligner, accentuer, ponctuer. **emphatic†**, *a*, emphatique; énergique.

empire, *n*, empire, *m*.

empiric(al)†, *a*, empirique. **empiricism**, *n*, empirisme, *m*. **empiric[ist]**, *n*, empirique, *m*.

employ, *v.t*, employer; se servir de. *he is in my ~*, je l'emploie. *~ee*, *n*, employé, e. *~er*, *n*, patron, ne, employeur, euse. *~ment*, *n*, emploi, travail, *m*. *~ agency*, bureau de placement, *m*.

emporium, *n*, entrepôt; grand magasin, *m*.

empower, *v.t*, autoriser, investir du pouvoir.

empress, *n*, impératrice, *f*.

emptiness, *n*, vacuité, *f*; vide, *m*; nullité, *f*. **empty**, *a*, vide; à vide; à blanc; net; désert; creux; vain; en l'air. *~-handed*, les mains vides. *to be ~-headed*, avoir la tête vide. *on an ~ stomach*, à jeun. ¶ (*case, etc.*) *n*, vide, *m*. ¶ *v.t*, vider, vidanger, épuiser, décharger.

empyrean, *n*, empyrée, *m*.

emulate, *v.t*, rivaliser avec. **emulation**, *n*, émulation, rivalité, *f*. **emulator**, *n*, émule, *m*.

emulsion, *n*, émulsion, *f*.

enable, *v.t.* mettre à même; permettre; (*law*) habiliter; (*computers*) valider.

enact, *v.t*, décréter, édicter. *~ment*, *n*, loi, *f*, décret, *m*.

enamel, *n. & ~ ware*, émail, *m*. ¶ *v.t*, émailler, laquer. **enameling**, *n*, émaillage, *m*.

enamored, *p.p*, épris, amoureux.

encage, *v.t*, encager.

encamp, *v.i. & t*, camper. *~ment*, *n*, campement, *m*.

encase, *v.t*, encaisser, enrober.

encash, *v.t*, encaisser.

encaustic, *a. & n*, encaustique, *a. & f*.

enchain, *v.t*, enchaîner.

enchant, *v.t*, enchanter. *~er*, *~ress*, *n*, enchanteur, eresse. *~ing*, *p.a*, enchanteur. *~ment*, *n*, enchantement, *m*.

encircle, *v.t*, encercler, ceindre, cerner.

enclave, *n*, enclave, *f*.

enclose, *v.t*, enfermer; [en]clore, enceindre; (*in letter*) inclure, joindre. *~d*, *p.p*, ci-inclus, ci-joint. **enclosure**, *n*, enceinte, clôture, *f*, [en]clos, parc, *m*; (*in letter*) [pièce] annexe, pièce jointe, *f*.

encode, *v.t*, encoder. *~r*, *n*, (*computers, etc.*) encodeur, *m*. **encoding**, *n*, encodage, *m*.

encomium, *n*, panégyrique, éloge, *m*.

encompass, *v.t*, entourer, ceindre.

encore, *i. & n*, bis, *ad. & m*. ¶ *v.t*, bisser.

encounter, *n*, rencontre, *f*. ¶ *v.t*, rencontrer.

encourage, *v.t*, encourager.

encroach on (to), empiéter sur; envahir; anticiper sur. *~ment*, *n*, empiètement, envahissement, *m*.

encumber, *v.t*, embarrasser, encombrer; grever, obérer. **encumbrance**, *n*, embarras, *m*; charge, *f*.

encyclic(al), *a. & n*, encyclique, *a. & f*.

encyclopedia, *n*, encyclopédie, *f*.

end, *n*, fin, *f*, terme, *m*; extrémité; issue, *f*; bout; but, *m*. *no ~ of*, une infinité de. *on ~*, debout; (*hair*) hérissés; (*fig.*) d'arraché-pied. *~ paper*, [feuille de] garde, *f*. ¶ *v.t*, finir, achever, terminer; (*v.i.*) finir, prendre fin; aboutir.

endanger, *v.t*, mettre en danger.

endear, *v.t*, rendre cher. *~ment*, *n*, caresse, *f*.

endeavor, *n*, effort, *m*, tentative, *f*. ¶ *v.i*, s'efforcer, tâcher, travailler.

ending, *n*, fin, *f*; dénouement, *m*; (*Gram.*) terminaison, désinence, *f*.

endive, *n*, scarole, endive, *f*.

endless, *a. & ~ly*, *ad*, sans fin.

endorse, *v.t*, endosser; (*fig.*) souscrire à. *~ment*, *n*, (*bill, check, etc.*) endos, endossement; (*Insce*) avenant, *m*. **endorser**, *n*, endosseur, *m*.

endow, *v.t*, renter, doter; douer; avantager. *~ment*, *n*, dotation, *f*.

endue, *v.t*, revêtir; douer.

endurable, *a*, supportable. **endurance**, *n*, endurance; résistance, *f*. *~ test*, épreuve d'endurance, *f*, raid, *m*. **endure**, *v.t*, endurer, supporter; (*v.i.*) vivre.

enema, *n*, (*instrument*) irrigateur, *m*; (*action*) lavement, *m*.

enemy, *n. & a*, ennemi, e.

energetic†, *a*, énergique. *~s* (*Phys.*) *n.pl*, énergétique, *f*. en-

ergize, *v.t*, infuser de l'ardeur dans; (*Elec.*) amorcer. **energy**, *n*, énergie; poigne, *f*; travail, *m*.

enervate, *v.t*, énerver, [r]amollir.

enfeeble, *v.t*, affaiblir.

enfilade, *n*, enfilade, *f*. ¶ *v.t*, enfiler.

enfold, *v.t*, envelopper; étreindre.

enforce, *v.t*, imposer; faire valoir; mettre en vigueur, exécuter. **~able**, *a*, exécutoire. **~ment**, *n*, contrainte; exécution, *f*.

enfranchise, *v.t*, affranchir; accorder le droit de vote à.

engage, *v.t*, engager, retenir; embaucher; arrêter; prendre; (*Mech.*) engrener; embrayer; (*v.i.*) s'engager, se mettre; engager le combat. **~ment**, *n*, engagement; (*Mech.*) engrenage, *f*; fiançailles, *f.pl*. **~ ring**, bague de fiançailles, *f*. **engaging**, *p.a*, engageant, attrayant, attachant.

engender, *v.t*, engendrer.

engine, *n*, machine, *f*, moteur, *m*; (*Rly*) locomotive, *f*; (*of war*) engin, *m*; (*jet*) réacteur, *m*. ~ *driver*, ~*man*, mécanicien, *m*. **engineer**, *n*, ingénieur; (*maker*) ingénieur constructeur; (*ship*) mécanicien; (*Mil.*) officier du génie; soldat du génie, *m*. ¶ *v.t*, provoquer. **engineering**, *n*, l'art (*m*.) (ou la science) de l'ingénieur; construction, *f*; génie, *m*. **engineless**, *a*, sans moteur.

England, *n*, l'Angleterre, *f*. **English**, *a*, anglais. *the ~ Channel*, la Manche. **~man**, **~woman**, Anglais, e. ¶ (*language*) *n*, l'anglais, *m*.

engrave, *v.t*, graver; buriner. **engraver**, *n*, graveur, *m*. **engraving**, *n*, gravure, estampe, *f*.

engross, *v.t*, absorber; s'emparer de; (*law*) grossoyer. **~ment** (*law*) *n*, grosse, *f*.

engulf, *v.t*, engouffrer, engloutir.

enhance, *v.t*, rehausser; augmenter.

enigma, *n*, énigme, *f*. **enigmatic(al)**†, *a*, énigmatique.

enjoin, *v.t*, enjoindre.

enjoy, *v.t*, jouir de, savourer, goûter. ~ *oneself*, s'amuser, se réjouir. **~able**, *a*, agréable, savoureux. **~ment**, *n*, jouissance, *f*; plaisir, *m*.

enlarge, *v.t*, agrandir, augmenter, élargir. ~ *upon*, s'étendre sur.

~ment, *n*, agrandissement, *m*. **enlarger** (*Phot.*) *n*, agrandisseur, *m*.

enlighten, *v.t*, éclairer, édifier.

enlist, *v.t*, enrôler, engager. **~ment**, *n*, enrôlement, engagement, *m*.

enliven, *v.t*, [r]animer, vivifier, égayer.

enmity, *n*, inimitié, *f*.

ennoble, *v.t*, anoblir; (*fig.*) ennoblir.

enormity, *n*, énormité, *f*. **enormous**, *a*, énorme. **~ly**, *ad*, énormément. **~ness**, *n*, énormité, *f*.

enough, *a*, assez de; assez; suffisant. ¶ *ad*, assez; suffisamment. ¶ *n*, suffisance, *f*, assez, de quoi. *to have ~ & to spare*, avoir à revendre.

enquire, *etc.* Same as *inquire*, etc.

enrage, *v.t*, rendre furieux, faire enrager.

enrapture, *v.t*, enchanter, ravir, enthousiasmer.

enrich, *v.t*, enrichir.

enroll, *v.t*, enrôler, immatriculer, embrigader, enrégimenter. **enrollment**, *n*, enrôlement, *m*.

ensconce, *v.t*, camper, nicher.

enshrine, *v.t*, enchâsser.

enshroud, *v.t*, envelopper; voiler.

ensign, *n*, (*banner*, *flag*) enseigne, *f*; (*Naut.*) pavillon de poupe; (*pers.*) enseigne, *m*.

enslave, *v.t*, asservir, enchaîner.

ensnare, *v.t*, attraper.

ensue, *v.i*, s'ensuivre, résulter. **ensuing**, *p.a*, suivant, subséquent.

ensure, *v.t*, assurer.

entablature, *n*, entablement, *m*.

entail, *v.t*, entraîner; (*law*) substituer.

entangle, *v.t*, empêtrer, emmêler, embarrasser.

enter, *v.t*, entrer dans; pénétrer; engager; (*names, etc.*) inscrire, enregistrer; (*v.i.*) entrer; pénétrer; s'engager. ~ *into* (bargain, contract), faire, passer, souscrire, contracter, intervenir dans. ~ *X*. (*Theat.*), X. entre [en scène].

enterprise, *n*, entreprise, *f*; esprit entreprenant, *m*. **enterprising**, *a*, entreprenant.

entertain, *v.t*, recevoir, héberger; régaler, fêter; (*abs.*) traiter; représenter; amuser, divertir, défrayer; (*idea*) concevoir, nourrir; accueillir favorablement. **~ment**, **n**, amusement, divertissement;

spectacle, *m*. ~ *tax*, taxe sur les spectacles, *f*.

enthrall, *v.t*, captiver, enchaîner; passionner.

enthrone, *v.t*, introniser. ~**ment**, *n*, intronisation, *f*.

enthusiasm, *n*, enthousiasme, *m*. **enthusiast**, *n*, enthousiaste, *m,f*, fervent, e. ~**ic**, *a*, enthousiaste. ~**ically**, *ad*, avec enthousiasme.

entice, *v.t*, allécher; séduire. ~**ment**, *n*, allèchement, *m*, séduction, *f*. **enticing**, *p.a*, alléchant, acquinant, séduisant.

entire†, *a*, entier, intégral. ~**ty**, *n*, entier, *m*; intégralité, *f*.

entitle, *v.t*, intituler; donner droit à.

entity, *n*, entité, *f*.

entomb, *v.t*, ensevelir.

entomologist, *n*, entomologiste, *m*. **entomology**, *n*, entomologie, *f*.

entr'acte (*Theat.*) *n*, entracte, *m*.

entrails, *n.pl*, entrailles, *f.pl*.

entrain, *v.t*, embarquer.

entrance, *n*, entrée; porte, *f*. ~ [*fee*], cotisation d'admission, *f*; droit d'entrée, *m*.

entrance, *v.t*, jeter en extase; ravir.

entrap, *v.t*, attraper.

entreat, *v.t*, supplier, prier instamment. ~**y**, *n*, supplication, prière, *f,(pl.)* instances, *f.pl*.

entrench, *v.t*, retrancher. ~**ing tool**, pellebêche, *f*.

entrust, *v.t*, confier, charger, remettre.

entry, *n*, entrée, *f*; engagement, *m*; inscription, *f*, enregistrement, *m*.

entwine, *v.t*, enlacer, entortiller.

enumerate, *v.t*, énumérer.

enunciate, *v.t*, énoncer.

envelope, *n*, enveloppe, *f*, pli, *m*. ¶ *v.t*, envelopper.

envenom, *v.t*, envenimer.

enviable, *a*, enviable. **envious**, *a*, envieux.

environ, *v.t*, environner. ~**ment**, *n*, entourage, milieu, *m*, ambiance, *f*. **environs**, *n.pl*, environs, entours, *m.pl*.

envisage, *v.t*, envisager.

envoy, *n*, envoyé, *m*.

envy, *n*, envie, *f*. ¶ *v.t*, envier.

epaulet, *n*, épaulette, *f*.

epergne, *n*, surtout [de table] *m*, girandole, *f*.

ephemeral, *a*, éphémère.

epic, *a*, épique. ¶ *n*, épopée, *f*.

epicure, *n*, gourmet, *m*, friand, e. **epicurean**, *a*. & *n*, épicurien, *a*. & *m*.

epidemic, *n*, épidémie, *f*. ~(**al**), *a*, épidémique.

epidermis, *n*, épiderme, *m*.

epiglottis, *n*, épiglotte, *f*.

epigram, *n*, épigramme, *f*.

epigraph, *n*, (*prefixed to book or chapter*) épigraphe; (*on stone*) inscription, *f*.

epilepsy, *n*, épilepsie, *f*. **epileptic**, *a*. & *n*, épileptique. *a*. & *m,f*.

epilogue, *n*, épilogue, *f*.

Epiphany, *n*, Épiphanie, *f*.

episcopal, *a*, épiscopal. **episcopate & episcopacy**, *n*, épiscopat, *m*.

episode, *n*, épisode, *m*.

epistle, *n*, épître, *f*. **epistolary**, *a*, épistolaire.

epitaph, *n*, épitaphe, *f*.

epithet, *n*, épithète, *f*.

epitome, *n*, épitomé, abrégé, raccourci, *m*. **epitomize**, *v.t*, abréger; personnifier.

epoch, *n*, époque, ère, *f*.

epsom salt[s], sel d'Epsom, *m*.

equable†, *a*, égal. **equal†**, *a*, égal, pareil; pair. ~ *to* (task), à la hauteur de. ¶ *n*, égal, e, pareil, le, pair, *m*. ¶ *v.t*, égaler. ~**ity**, *n*, égalité, *f*, pair, *m*; (*rights*) concurrence, *f*, concours; (*votes*) partage, *m*. ~**ize**, *v.t*, égaliser, égaler.

equanimity, *n*, sérénité, *f*.

equation, *n*, équation, *f*.

equator, *n*, équateur, *m*. ~**ial**, *a*, équatorial.

equerry, *n*, écuyer, *m*.

equestrian, *a*, équestre. ¶ *n*, cavalier, ère; écuyer, ère [de cirque].

equilibrate, *v.t*, équilibrer. **equilibrium**, *n*, équilibre, *m*.

equine, *a*, chevalin, hippique.

equinoctial, *a*, équinoxial. **equinox**, *n*, équinoxe, *m*.

equip, *v.t*, équiper, armer, outiller. ~**age**, *n*, équipage, *m*. ~**ment**, *n*, équipement, armement, outillage; fourniment, *m*.

equipoise, *n*, équilibre, *m*.

equitable†, *a*, équitable. **equity**, *n*, équité, *f*.

equivalent, *a*. & *n*, équivalent, *a*. & *m*; parité, *f*. *to be* ~, équivaloir.

equivocal, *a*, équivoque. **equivocate**, *v.i*, équivoquer. **equivocation**, *n*, équivoques, *f.pl.*

era, *n*, ère, époque, *f*.

eradicate, *v.t*, déraciner, extirper.

erase, *v.t*, raturer, gratter, effacer. **eraser**, *n*, (*knife*) grattoir, *m*; (*rubber*) gomme [à effacer] *f*. **erasure**, *n*, rature, *f*, grattage, *m*, effaçure, *f*.

ere, *c*, avant que. ~ *long*, sous peu.

Erebus, *n*, l'Érèbe, *m*.

erect, *a*, droit; debout, *ad*; dressé. ¶ *v.t*, ériger; construire; élever; monter; dresser; hérisser. ~**ion**, *n*, érection; construction, *f*; montage; dressage, *m*. *to have an* ~, bander (*obscene*).

Erie (Lake), le lac Érié.

ermine, *n*, hermine, *f*.

erode, *v.t*, éroder. **erosion**, *n*, érosion, *f*.

erotic, *a*, érotique.

err, *v.i*, errer, pécher.

errand, *n*, commission, ambassade, course, *f*, message, *m*. ~ *boy*, garçon de course, (*law office*) saute-ruisseau, *m*.

errant, *a*, errant.

erratic, *a*, irrégulier; (*Geol., Med.*) erratique.

erratum, *n*, erratum, *m*. **erroneous**, *a*, erroné, faux. ~**ly**, *ad*, par erreur. **error**, *n*, erreur, faute, *f*, mécompte; écart, *m*.

eructation, *n*, éructation, *f*.

erudite, *a*, érudit. **erudition**, *n*, érudition, *f*.

eruption, *n*, éruption, *f*.

escalation, *n*, (*Mil.*) escalade, *f*. **escalator**, *n*, escalier roulant, *m*.

escallop, *n*, pétoncle, *m*.

escapade, *n*, escapade; équipée, frasque, *f*.

escape, *n*, fuite; évasion, *f*; échappement, *m*; issue, *f*. *fire*~, échelle de sauvetage, *f*. ¶ *v.i*, s'échapper; échapper; fuir; s'enfuir; se sauver; s'évader; se débonder; (*v.t.*) échapper à; échapper de; échapper. *escaped prisoner*, évadé, *m*. ~**ment**, *n*, échappement, *m*.

escarpment, *n*, escarpement, *m*.

escheat, *n*, déshérence, *f*. ¶ *v.i*, tomber en déshérence; (*v.t.*) confisquer.

eschew, *v.t*, éviter, fuir.

escort, *n*, escorte, *f*; cavalier, *m*. ¶ *v.t*, escorter, reconduire, accompagner.

escutcheon, *n*, écusson, *m*.

espagnolette, *n*, espagnolette, crémone, *f*.

espalier, *n*, espalier, *m*.

especial, *a*, notable, digne d'être signalé, qui mérite une mention particulière; particulier; tout spécial. ~**ly**, *ad*, surtout; notamment; particulièrement. ~ *as*, d'autant que.

espionage, *n*, espionnage, *m*.

esplanade, *n*, esplanade, *f*.

espousal, *n*, adoption, adhésion, *f*. **espouse**, *v.t*, épouser; embrasser.

espy, *v.t*, apercevoir, aviser, découvrir.

esquire, (*Hist.*) *n*, écuyer, *m*. **Esquire**, *n*. (*abb*. Esq.), Monsieur, *m*. (*Note.—As a form of address on envelope or in letter*, Monsieur *should not be abbreviated*.)

essay, *n*, essai, *m*, composition, dissertation, narration, *f*. ¶ *v.t*, essayer. ~**ist**, *n*, essayiste, *m,f*.

essence, *n*, essence, *f*. **essential**†, *a*, essentiel; capital. ¶ *n*, essentiel, *m*.

establish, *v.t*, établir; créer; asseoir; constater. *the* ~*ed Church*, l'Église d'État, *f*. ~**ment**, *n*, établissement, *m*; création; fondation; constatation, *f*; ménage, *m*.

estate, *n*, bien[s] *m*.[*pl.*], propriété[s] *f*.[*pl.*]; domaine, fonds, *m*, terre; succession, *f*. *real* ~ *agency*, agence immobilière, *f*.

esteem, *n*, estime, *f*. ¶ *v.t*, estimer; considérer (*ou* regarder) comme.

Esthonia, *n*, l'Estonie, *f*.

estimate, *n*, estimation, appréciation, évaluation, prisée, *f*; état (*ou* devis) estimatif; (*pl.*) budget, *m*. ¶ *v.t*, estimer, apprécier, évaluer, priser. ~**d**, *p.a*, estimatif. **estimation**, *n*, jugement, *m*, estime, *f*.

estrange, *v.t*, éloigner, aliéner.

estuary, *n*, estuaire, *m*.

etch, *v.t*, graver à l'eau-forte. ~**er**, *n*, graveur à l'eau-forte, aquafortiste, *m*. ~**ing**, *n*, [gravure à l']eau-forte, *f*.

eternal†, *a*, éternel. *the* ~ *triangle*, la vie à trois. **etern[al]ize**, *v.t*, éterniser. **eternity**, *n*, éternité, *f*.

ether, *n,* éther, *m.* **ethereal,** *a,* éthéré.

ethical, *a,* éthique. **ethics,** *n.pl,* éthique, *f.*

Ethiopia, *n,* l'Éthiopie, *f.* **Ethiopian,** *a,* éthiopien. ¶ *n,* Éthiopien, ne.

ethnic, *a,* ethnique.

ethnography, *n,* ethnographie, *f.* **ethnologic(al),** *a,* ethnologique. **ethnologist,** *n,* ethnologue, *m.* **ethnology,** *n,* ethnologie, *f.*

ethyl, *n,* éthyle, *m.*

etiolate, *v.t,* étioler.

etiquette, *n,* étiquette, *f,* décorum, protocole, *m.*

etymologic(al), *a,* étymologique. **etymology,** *n,* étymologie, *f.*

eucalyptus, *n,* eucalyptus, *m.*

Eucharist, *n,* Eucharistie, *f.*

eugenic, *a,* eugénique. ~s, *n.pl,* eugénie, *f.*

eulogist†, *a,* élogieux. **eulogize,** *v.t,* faire l'éloge de. **eulogy,** *n,* éloge, *m.*

eunuch, *n,* eunuque, *m.*

euphemism, *n,* euphémisme, *m.* **euphemistic,** *a,* euphémique.

euphonic & euphonious, *a,* euphonique. **euphony,** *n,* euphonie, *f.*

Euphrates (the), l'Euphrate, *m.*

Europe, *n,* l'Europe, *f.* **European,** *a,* européen. ¶ *n,* Européen, ne.

eustachian tube, trompe d'Eustache, *f.*

euthanasia, *n,* euthanasie, *f.*

evacuate, *v.t,* évacuer.

evade, *v.t,* éviter, éluder, esquiver; frauder.

evaluate, *v.t,* évaluer.

evanescent, *a,* évanescent.

evangelic(al)†, *a,* évangélique. **evangelist,** *n,* évangéliste, *m.*

evaporate, *v.t,* [faire] évaporer; (*v.i.*) s'évaporer. **evaporation,** *n,* évaporation, *f.*

evasion, *n,* échappatoire, *f,* fauxfuyant, subterfuge, *m,* défaite, *f,* atermoiement, *m.* ~ *of tax,* la fraude fiscale. **evasive†,** *a,* évasif; flottant; normand.

eve, *n,* veille, *f.* **even** (*Poet.*) *n,* soir, *m.* ~**song,** vêpres, *f.pl.* ~**tide,** chute du jour, *f.*

even, *a,* uni; plan; égal; uniforme; pair; (*games*) but à but. ~ *money,* compte rond, *m.* ~ *number,* nombre pair, *m.* *to be* ~ *with* (someone), revaloir. ¶ *ad,* même; jusque. ~ *if,* ~ *though,*

même si, quand, lors même que. ¶ *v.t,* égaliser; aplanir.

evening, *n,* soir, *m*; soirée; veillée, *f*; (*fig.*) déclin, *m.* ~ *dew,* ~ *damp,* serein, *m.* ~ *dress,* (man) tenue de soirée; (*woman*) toilette de s., *f.* ~ *gown,* robe du soir, *f.*

evenly, *ad,* uniment; uniformément. **evenness,** *n,* égalité; uniformité, *f.*

event, *n,* événement; cas, *m*; (*sport*) épreuve, *f.* ~**ful,** *a,* plein d'événements; mouvementé, accidenté.

eventual†, *a,* éventuel. ~**ity,** *n,* éventualité, *f.* **eventuate,** *v.i,* aboutir.

ever, *ad,* jamais; toujours. *for* ~, à (*ou* pour) jamais (*ou* toujours). ~ *so little,* tant soit peu. *hardly* ~, presque jamais. *if* ~, si jamais.

evergreen, *n,* arbre toujours vert, *m.*

everlasting†, *a,* éternel; immortel.

evermore, *ad,* toujours. *for* ~, à tout jamais.

every, *a,* chaque; tout, e; tous (toutes) les. ~*body,* **everyone,** *every one* (every person), tout le monde, chacun, *m.* *only.* ~*day,* *a,* quotidien; vulgaire; ordinaire. ~*day clothes,* vêtements ordinaires, habits de tous les jours, *m.pl.* ~ *one* (each), chacun, e. ~*thing,* *n,* tout, *pn.* ~*where,* *ad,* partout.

evict, *v.t,* évincer, expulser. ~**ion,** *n,* éviction, *f.*

evidence, *n,* évidence; preuve, *f*; témoignage, *m*; déposition, *f*; titre, *m.* *to give* ~, témoigner. ¶ *v.t,* constater. **evident,** *a,* évident. ~**ly,** *ad,* évidemment.

evil, *a,* mauvais; méchant; malin, malfaisant. ~*-minded* (*person*), *a.* & *n,* malintentionné, e. ~ *doer,* malfaiteur, *m.* ~ *eye,* mauvais œil, *m.* *the E*~ *One,* le malin [esprit], l'esprit malin, *m.* ~ *speaking,* médisance, *f.* ~ *spirit,* esprit malin, malin esprit, *m.* ¶ *ad,* mal. ¶ *n,* mal, *m,* plaie, *f.*

evince, *v.t,* manifester, témoigner.

eviscerate, *v.t,* éventrer.

evocation, *n,* évocation, *f.* **evoke,** *v.t,* évoquer.

evolution, *n,* déroulement; *m*; (*Biol.*, etc.) évolution, *f*; (*Geom.*)

développement; (*Chem.*) dégagement, *m.* **evolve**, *v.t.* élaborer; dégager; (*v.i.*) évoluer.

ewe, *n*, brebis, *f.* ~ **lamb**, agneau femelle, *m.*

ewer, *n*, pot à eau, broc de toilette, *m*; aiguière, *f.*

ex-, *prefix*: ~*professor*, ex-professeur, ancien professeur, *m.* ~*serviceman*, ancien combattant, *m.*

exacerbate, *v.t.* exacerber.

exact, *a*, exact, précis. ¶ *v.t.* exiger. ~**ing**, *p.a.* exigeant. ~**ion**, **x**, exaction, *f.* ~**ly**, *ad*, exactement, au juste, précisément, parfaitement. ~**ness**, **exactitude**, *n*, exactitude, *f.*

exaggerate, *v.t. & abs*, exagérer, grossir.

exaggeration, *n*, exagération, *f.*

exalt, *v.t*, exalter, relever.

examination, *n*, examen, *m*; inspection; visite, *f*; concours; interrogatoire, *m*; instruction; expertise, *f.* **examine**, *v.t*, examiner; interroger; inspecter; visiter; (*documents*) compulser. **examinee**, *n*, candidat, e. **examiner**, *n*, examinateur, trice; interrogateur, trice; inspecteur, trice; visiteur; vérificateur; contrôleur, *m.*

example, *n*, exemple, *m.*

exasperate, *v.t*, exaspérer, énerver, indigner.

excavate, *v.t*, creuser, fouiller. **excavation**, *n*, excavation, fouille, *f*, déblai, *m.* **excavator** (*Mach.*) *n*, excavateur, *m.*

exceed, *v.t*, excéder, [dé]passer, outrepasser. ~**ingly**, *ad*, excessivement, extrêmement.

excel, *v.i*, exceller, primer; (*v.t.*) surpasser. **excellence**, *n*, excellence, *f.* **His Excellency**, Son Excellence, *f.* **excellent**, *a*, excellent. ~**ly**, *ad*, excellemment, à merveille.

except, *c*, sinon. ~ & ~**ing**, *pr*, excepté, à l'exception de, hors, hormis, sauf, ôté, à part. ¶ *v.t*, excepter. ~**ion**, *n*, exception; réserve, *f. to take* ~ *to*, se formaliser de. ~**ionable**, *a*, récusable, critiquable. ~**ional**†, *a*, exceptionnel, hors ligne.

excerpt, *n*, extrait, *m*, bribe, *f.* ¶ *v.t*, extraire.

excess, *n*, excès; excédent; surplus, trop, *m*; outrance, *f*; débordement, *m*; intempérance, *f.*

~ *profits*, surplus des bénéfices. ~ *weight*, excédent de poids, *m*, surcharge, *f.* ~**ive**†, *a*, excessif, immodéré, outré.

exchange, *n*, échange; change; troc, *m*; permutation, *f*; (*Teleph.*) bureau [central], poste central, *m.* ~ *rates*, cote des changes, *f.* ~ *stock* ~, Bourse, *f.* ¶ *v.t*, échanger; changer; troquer.

exchequer, *n*, trésor, *m*, trésorerie, *f*; (*Eng.*) échiquier, *m*; (*of pers.*) finances, *f.pl.*

excise, *n*, (*Fr.*) régie; (*Eng.*) accise, *f.*

excite, *v.t*, exciter, provoquer; irriter, exalter; agacer. ~**ment**, *n*, excitation; exaltation; émotion, *f.*

exclaim, *v.i*, s'écrier, se récrier, s'exclamer. ~ *against*, *abs*, s'exclamer. **exclamation**, *n*, exclamation, *f.*

exclude, *v.t*, exclure. **exclusion**, *n*, exclusion, *f.* **exclusive**†, *a*, exclusif. ~ *right(s)*, droit[s] exclusif[s] *m.[pl.]*, exclusiveté, *f.*

excommunicate, *v.t*, excommunier.

excoriate, *v.t*, écorcher.

excrement, *n*, excrément, *m.*

excrescence, *n*, excroissance, *f.*

excruciating†, *p.a*, atroce.

exculpate, *v.t*, disculper.

excursion, *n*, excursion; partie; promenade, *f.* ~ *ticket*, billet d'excursion, *m.* ~**ist**, *n*, excursionniste, *m.f.*

excusable, *a*, excusable.

excuse, *n*, excuse, *f*, prétexte, *m.* ¶ *v.t*, excuser, pardonner; exempter, dispenser de; faire remise de. ~ *me*, excusez-moi; pardon!

execrable†, *a*, exécrable. **execrate**, *v.t*, exécrer.

execute, *v.t*, exécuter; effectuer; (*document*) souscrire; exécuter [à mort], faire mourir. **execution**, *n*, exécution, *f*; jeu, *m*; souscription; saisie[-exécution] *f.* ~**er**, *n*, bourreau, *m.* **executive**, *n*, bureau; État-major, *m.* **executor**, **-trix**, *n*, exécuteur (trice) testamentaire. **executory**, *a*, exécutoire.

exemplary, *a*, exemplaire, modèle. **exemplify**, *v.t*, éclaircir par un exemple, des exemples.

exempt, *a*, exempt. ¶ *v.t*, exempter. ~**ion**, *n*, exemption, franchise, *f.*

exercise, *n*, exercice; (*Sch.*) devoir; thème, *m*. ~ *book*, cahier, *m*. ¶ *v.t*, exercer, user de; (*Stk Ex. option*) consolider; lever; (*v.i.*) prendre de l'exercice.

exert, *v.t*, exercer. ~ *oneself*, s'évertuer, faire un effort. ~**ion**, *n*, effort, *m*.

exfoliate, *v.i*, s'exfolier.

exhalation, *n*, (*act*) exhalation; (*mist*) exhalaison, *f*. **exhale**, *v.t*, exhaler, respirer.

exhaust, *n*, échappement, *m*. ¶ *v.t*, épuiser; aspirer. ~**ion**, *n*, épuisement, *m*; aspiration, *f*. ~**ive**, *a*, approfondi. ~**ively**, *ad*, à fond, mûrement.

exhibit, *n*, objet exposé, produit [à présenter] *m*; (*law, civil*) pièce justificative, p. à l'appui; (*criminal*) p. à conviction. ¶ *v.t*, exposer; exhiber. ~**ion**, *n*, exposition, *f*; salon, *m*; exhibition. **exhibitor**, *n*, exposant, e; montreur, *m*.

exhilarate, *v.t*, émoustiller, égayer, stimuler.

exhort, *v.t*, exhorter, prêcher [à].

exhume, *v.t*, exhumer, déterrer.

exigence, -**cy**, *n*, exigence, *f*.

exile, *n*, exil, *m*; (*pers.*) exilé, e. ¶ *v.t*, exiler.

exist, *v.i*, exister. ~**ence**, *n*, existence, *f*.

exit, *n*, sortie, issue, *f*, dégagement, *m*. ~ X. (*Theat.*), X. sort.

exodus, *n*, exode, *m*. E~ (*Bible*), l'Exode.

exonerate, *v.t*, exonérer.

exorbitance, *n*, extravagance, *f*. **exorbitant**, *a*, exorbitant. ~**ly**, *ad*, exorbitamment.

exorcise, *v.t*, exorciser.

exotic, *a*, exotique. ¶ *n*, plante exotique, *f*.

expand, *v.t*, étendre; déployer; dilater. **expanse**, *n*, étendue; envergure, *f*. **expansion**, *n*, expansion; dilatation; détente, *f*. **expansive**, *a*, expansif.

expatiate, *v.i*, s'étendre.

expatriate, *v.t*, expatrier.

expect, *v.t*, attendre, s'attendre à; espérer. ~**ancy**, *n*, expectative, *f*. ~**ant**, *a*, expectant. ~ *mother*, femme enceinte, *f*. ~**ation**, *n*, attente, expectative; espérance, prévision, *f*.

expectorate, *v.t. & abs*, expectorer.

expedience, -**cy**, *n*, convenance, *f*. **expedient**, *a*, expédient, con-

venable. ¶ *n*, expédient, *m*, ressource, *f*. **expedite**, *v.t*, expédier; hâter. **expedition**, *n*, expédition, *f*. ~**ary**, *a*, expéditionnaire. **expeditious**, *a*, expéditif, diligent.

expel, *v.t*, expulser, chasser, bannir.

expend, *v.t*, dépenser. **expenditure**, *n*, dépense[s] *f.*[*pl.*]. **expense**, *n*, frais, *m.pl*, dépense, charge, *f*, dépens, *m.pl*. *at the ~ of*, aux frais (*ou* dépens) (*ou* crochets) de; à la charge de. *incidental ~s*, faux frais. **expensive**†, *a*, cher, coûteux, dispendieux.

experience, *n*, expérience, pratique, *f*, métier, *m*, acquis, *m.s. & pl.* ~**d**, *a*, expérimenté, expert. ¶ *v.t*, éprouver, faire l'expérience de. **experiment**, *n*, expérience, *f*. ¶ *v.i*, expérimenter. ~ *on*, faire des expériences sur. ~**al**†, *a*, expérimental.

expert, *a. & n*, expert. *a. & m*. ~**ness**, *n*, habileté, *f*.

expiate, *v.t*, expier.

expiration, *n*, expiration, échéance, déchéance, *f*. **expire**, *v.t & abs*, expirer; (*v.i.*) expirer, échoir, périmer.

explain, *v.t*, expliquer, exposer. ~**able**, *a*, explicable. **explanation**, *n*, explication, *f*. **explanatory**, *a*, explicatif.

expletive (*Gram.*) *a*, explétif. ¶ *n*, mot explétif, *m*, (*in verse*) cheville, *f*; (*oath*) gros mot, juron, *m*.

explicit†, *a*, explicite; clair.

explode, *v.t*, faire exploser, *f*. éclater; *f*. sauter; (*fig.*) démolir; (*v.i.*) exploser, éclater, faire explosion. ~**d** *theory*, théorie périmée, *f*.

exploit, *n*, exploit, *m*. ¶ *v.t*, exploiter. ~**ation**, *n*, exploitation, *f*.

explore, *v.t*, explorer, reconnaître. **explorer**, *n*, explorateur, trice.

explosion, *n*, explosion, *f*. **explosive**, *n*, explosif, *m*.

exponent, *n*, exposant; interprète, *m*; (*Math.*) exposant, *m*.

export, *v.t*, exporter. ~[**ation**] *n*, exportation, *f*. ~**er**, *n*, exportateur, *m*.

expose, *v.t*, exposer, mettre à nu; (*Phot.*) [ex]poser. **exposition**, *n*, exposition, *f*.

expostulate, *v.i,* faire des remontrances. **expostulation,** *n,* remontrance, *f.*

exposure, *n,* exposition, mise à nu; (*Phot.*) pose, exposition, *f.*

expound, *v.t,* exposer.

express, *a,* exprès, formel. ¶ (*Post, etc.*) *n,* exprès, *m.* ~ [*train*], [train] express, *m.* ¶ *v.t,* exprimer; énoncer; traduire. ~ion, *n,* expression, *f.* ~ive, *a,* expressif. **expressly,** *ad,* expressément.

expropriate, *v.t,* exproprier.

expulsion, *n,* expulsion, *f.*

expunge, *v.t,* rayer, effacer.

expurgate, *v.t,* expurger.

exquisite, *a,* exquis; vif. ~ly, *ad,* exquisément. ~ness, *n,* exquis, *m.*

extant (to be) exister.

extempore, *a,* improvisé, impromptu. ¶ *ad,* d'abondance, impromptu. **extemporize,** *v.t. & i,* improviser.

extend, *v.t,* étendre; prolonger. **extension,** *n,* extension, *f,* prolongement, *m;* prolongation, *f;* (*Teleph.*) poste supplémentaire, *m.* ~ *ladder,* échelle à coulisse, *f.* ~ *tripod,* trépied extensible, *m.* **extensive,** *a,* étendu, large. ~ly, *ad,* largement. **extensor** (*muscle*)*n,* extenseur, *m.* **extent,** *n,* étendue; importance; *f;* degré, point, *m,* mesure, *f.*

extenuate, *v.t,* atténuer.

exterior†, *a,* extérieur, externe. ¶ *n,* extérieur; dehors, *m;* enveloppe (*fig.*) *f.*

exterminate, *v.t,* exterminer.

external, *a,* externe, extérieur. ~ly, *ad,* extérieurement.

extinct, *a,* éteint. ~ion, *n,* extinction, *f.* **extinguish,** *v.t,* éteindre. ~er, *n,* (*light*) éteignoir; (*fire*) extincteur, *m.*

extirpate, *v.t,* extirper.

extol, *v.t,* exalter; vanter; prôner.

extort, *v.t,* extorquer, arracher. ~ion, *n,* extorsion; maltôte, *f.* ~ionate, *a,* exorbitant. ~ioner, *n,* écorcheur, euse, *m.*

extra, *a,* supplémentaire, supplément de, en sus, hors d'œuvre. ~ *fare,* supplément [de taxe] *m.* ¶ *ad,* extra. ¶ *n,* extra, supplément, *m,* plus-value, *f;* hors-d'œuvre, *m;* (*movies*) figurant,

m; (*newspaper*) édition spéciale, *f.*

extract, *n,* extrait, *m.* ¶ *v.t,* extraire; arracher; [sou]tirer, retirer. ~ion, *n,* extraction, *f.*

extradite, *v.t,* extrader. **extradition,** *n,* extradition, *f.*

extraneous, *a,* étranger.

extraordinary†, *a,* extraordinaire; insolent. ¶ *n,* extraordinaire, *m.*

extraterritoriality, *n,* exterritorialité, *f.*

extravagance, *n,* extravagance, *f;* dévergondage (*fig.*) *m;* (*money*) folles dépenses, *f.pl,* dissipation [s] *f.*[*pl.*], prodigalités, *f.pl.* **extravagant,** *a,* extravagant; (*of pers.*) dépensier; (*price*) exorbitant. ~ly, *ad,* follement.

extreme†, *a. & n,* extrême, *a. & m.* ~ *penalty,* dernier supplice, *m.* ~ *unction,* extrême-onction, *f.* **extremist,** *n,* extrémiste, *m,f,* ultra, *m;* (*att.*) outrancier. **extremity,** *n,* extrémité, *f,* bout, *m.*

extricate, *v.t,* dégager, débarrasser, débarbouiller, dépêtrer, tirer.

extrinsic, *a,* extrinsèque.

exuberance, *n,* exubérance, *f.* **exuberant,** *a,* exubérant.

exude, *v.i,* exsuder; (*v.t.*) distiller.

exult, *v.i,* exulter, triompher. ~ation, *n,* exaltation, *f.*

eye, *n,* œil, *m;* paupière; vue, *f;* (*needle, etc.*) œil, chas, trou; (*fruit*) nombril; (*potato*) germe, *m;* boucle, *f;* regard, *m;* porte, *f.* ~*ball,* globe de l'œil, *m;* prunelle, *f.* ~ *bath,* œillière, *f.* ~*brow,* sourcil, *m.* ~*brow pencil,* crayon pour les yeux, *m.* ~*brow tweezers,* pinces à épiler, *f.pl.* ~ *doctor,* médecin oculiste, *m.* ~*s front!* (*Mil.*), fixe! ~*glass,* monocle, *m;* (*pl.*) binocle, lorgnon, pince-nez, *m.* ~*lash,* cil, *m.* ~*lid,* paupière, *f.* ~ *opener,* révélation, *f.* ~*piece,* [verre] oculaire. *m.* ~*shade,* visière, *f,* garde-vue, *m.* ~*sight,* vue, *f.* ~*sore,* objet qui choque la vue, *m.* ~*tooth,* [dent] œillère, *f.* ~*trouble,* mal aux (*ou* d') yeux, *m.* ~*witness,* témoin oculaire, *m.* to keep an ~ on, ne pas perdre de vue. to make ~s at, faire les yeux doux à. ¶ *v.t,* regarder; lorgner. **eyelet,** *n,* œillet, *m.*

eyrie, *n,* aire (*de l'aigle*) *f.*

F

F (*Mus.*) letter, fa, *m.* ~ **clef**, clef de fa, *f.*

fable, *n,* fable, *f.* ~**d,** *p.p,* légendaire, fabuleux.

fabric, *n,* tissu, *m,* étoffe, *f.* ~**ate,** *v.t,* fabriquer. ~**ation,** *n,* fabrication; fantasmagorie, *f.* ~**ator,** *n,* fabricateur, trice.

fabulist, *n,* fabuliste, *m.* **fabulous†,** *a,* fabuleux.

façade, *n,* façade, *f.*

face, *n,* face, *f;* visage, *m,* figure, *f;* mine; grimace; tournure, *f;* parement; pan; recto; (*cloth*) endroit; (*cards*) dessous; (*of type*) œil, *m.* ~ *lifting,* chirurgie esthétique du visage, *f.* ~ *massage,* massage facial, *m.* ~ *powder,* poudre de riz, *f.* ~ *to* ~, vis-à-vis. ~ *value* (*Fin.*), valeur nominale, *f.* to about ~, faire demi-tour. *to lose* ~, perdre contenance. ¶ *v.t,* faire face à; affronter; braver; donner sur; être exposé à; dresser. ~**d with** (silk), à revers de.

facet, *n,* facette, *f.* ¶ *v.t,* facetter.

facetious, *a,* facétieux.

facial, *a,* facial.

facile, *a,* facile. **facilitate,** *v.t,* faciliter. **facility,** *n,* facilité, *f.*

facing, *n,* revers; parement; revêtement, *m.* ¶ *ad. & pr,* en face (de), face à, vis-à-vis (de), à l'opposite (de).

facsimile, *n,* fac-similé, *m.*

fact, *n,* fait, *m;* vérité; chose, *f.*

faction, *n,* faction, brigue, *f.* **factious,** *a,* factieux. **factitious,** *a,* factice.

factor, *n,* facteur; (*pers.*) commissionnaire, *m.*

factoring, *n,* (*Fin.*) affacturage, *m.*

factory, *n,* manufacture, fabrique, usine, *f.* ~ *hand,* ouvrier (ère) [de fabrique]. ~ *inspector,* inspecteur du travail, *m.*

factotum, *n,* factotum, *m.*

faculty, *n,* faculté; aptitude, *f,* talent, *m.*

fad, *n,* dada, *m,* marotte, lubie, vogue, manie, *f.* **faddist,** *n,* maniaque, *m,f.*

fade, *v.i,* se faner, se défraîchir, déteindre, se flétrir, pâlir. ~ *away,* s'évanouir. ~ *out,* se mourir. ~**d,** *p.a,* fané, défraîchi, passé. **fading,** *n,* (*radio, sound, etc.*) évanouissement, *m,*

fade-in, *n,* (*TV & cinema*) fondu ouvert, *m.*

fadeout, *n,* (*TV & cinema*) fondu, *m.*

fagot, *n,* fagot, cotret, *m.* ¶ *v.t,* fagoter.

Fahrenheit, *a,* Fahrenheit. See note under *centigrade* in French-English section.

fail, *v.i,* manquer, faire défaut, défaillir, échouer, mal réussir, rater, chavirer; faiblir; (*Com.*) faire faillite; (*v.t.*) manquer à. ~ *in one's duty,* manquer à son devoir, prévariquer. *without* ~, sans faute. ~**ing,** *n,* faible, *m;* défaillance, *f.* ¶ *pr,* à défaut de, faute de. ~**ure,** *n,* défaut, insuccès, échec, *m,* chute, *f,* coup manqué; four, fiasco, *m;* (*Elec.*) panne; (*Com.*) faillite, *f.*

fain, *a. & ad:* to be ~ *to,* être amené par nécessité à, être réduit à. *I would* ~ *be* . . ., je serais volontiers . . . *I would* ~ *have* . . ., j'aurais bien voulu . . .

faint, *a,* faible; mourant; défaillant. ~**-hearted,** lâche. ¶ *v.i,* s'évanouir, défaillir, [se] pâmer. ~**ing** [fit], évanouissement, *m,* défaillance, *f.*

fair, *a,* beau; (*skin*) blanche; (*hair*) blonds; juste, équitable, loyal, honnête; raisonnable; passable. *at* ~ (barometer), au beau. ~**-haired,** aux cheveux blonds. ~**-haired person,** blond, e. *by* ~ *means or foul,* de gré ou de force. ~ *play,* franc jeu, *m,* de bonne guerre; traitement honnête, *m.* *not* ~, pas du (*ou* de) jeu. ~ *sex,* beau sexe, *m.* ~**-spoken,** bien-disant. ~**way,** chenal, *m,* passe, *f.* ¶ *n,* foire, *f.* ~**ly,** *ad,* à juste titre; bel & bien; loyalement; assez; moyennement. ~**ness,** *n,* beauté, *f;* teint blond, *m;* équité; loyauté, honnêteté, *f.*

fairy, *n,* fée, *f.* **Fairyland,** féerie, *f.* ~**like,** féerique. ~ *ring,* cercle des fées, *m.* ~ *tale,* conte de fées, conte bleu, *m.*

faith, *n,* foi; confiance; croyance, communion, *f.* ~**ful†,** *a,* fidèle. *the* ~, les fidèles, les croyants, *m.pl.* **fulness,** *n,* fidélité, *f.* ~**less,**

a, sans foi, infidèle. **~lessness**, *n*, infidélité, *f*.

fake, *n*, truquage, *m*. ¶ *v.t*, truquer.

fakir, *n*, fakir, *m*.

falcon, *n*, faucon, *m*. **~er**, *n*, fauconnier, *m*. **falconry**, *n*, fauconnerie, *f*.

fall, *n*, chute; tombée; descente; (*prices*) baisse, *f*; abaissement, *m*; culbute; ruine, *f*; éboulement; éboulis, *m*; cascade, *f,m*; (*pl.*) chute, *f*; automne, *m* (*government*) renversement, *m*. ¶ *v.i.ir*, tomber; descendre; baisser; s'abaisser. ~ *back*, se replier. ~ *down*, tomber [par terre]. ~ *due*, échoir. ~ *in* (*cave in*) ébouler; (*Mil.*) se mettre en rangs; à vos rangs! ~ *in love*, s'enamourer, s'éprendre. ~ *in with* (opinion), se ranger à. ~ *off*, tomber [à bas] de; *business, etc.*) ralentir. ~ *out with*, ~ *foul of*, se brouiller avec. ~ *through* (fail), échouer.

fallacious, *a*, fallacieux. **fallacy**, *n*, erreur, *f*; (*Log.*) sophisme, *m*.

fallen angel, ange déchu, *m*. **fallen leaves**, feuilles tombées, fanes, *f.pl*, fanage, *m*.

fallibility, *n*, faillibilité, *f*. **fallible**, *a*, faillible.

falling star, étoile tombante, é. filante, *f*.

fallout, *n*, (*nuclear*) retombée, *f*. *nuclear* ~, les retombées radioactives.

fallow, *a*, (*color of deer*) fauve; (*land*) en jachère, en friche. ~ *deer*, daim, *m*. to lie ~, rester en friche, chômer. ¶ *v.t*, jachérer.

false, *a*, faux; mensonger; postiche; feint. ~ *bottom*, double fond, faux f., *m*. ~ *shame*, fausse honte, mauvaise h., *f*. ¶ *ad*, faux. **~hood**, *n*, mensonge, *m*. **~ly**, *ad*, faussement. **~ness**, *n*, fausseté, *f*. **falsetto**, *n*, fausset, *m*. **falsify**, *v.t*, falsifier, fausser. **falsity**, *n*, fausseté, *f*.

falter, *v.i*, chanceler, défaillir; hésiter; (*speech*) ânonner, bégayer.

fame, *n*, renommée, *f*, renom, *m*, gloire, mémoire, *f*. **~d**, *a*, renommé.

familiar†, *a*, familier. ~ *face*, figure de connaissance, *f*. ¶ *n*, familier, *m*. **~ity**, *n*, familiarité, privauté, *f*. **~ize**, *v.t*, familiariser.

family, *n*, famille, *f*; ménage, *m*; maisonnée, *f*. ~ *likeness*, air de famille, *m*. ~ *life*, vie de f., v. familiale, *f*. ~ *man*, père de famille; homme de foyer, *m*. ~ *tree*, arbre généalogique, *m*.

famine, *n*, famine, *f*. **famish**, *v.t*, affamer. *to be ~ing*, avoir la fringale.

famous†, *a*, fameux, célèbre, renommé. ~ *case* (*law*), cause célèbre, *f*.

fan, *n*, éventail; ventilateur, *m*. ~ *light*, vasistas, *m*. ~ *tail*, pigeon paon, *m*. ¶ *v.t*, éventer; (*grain*) vanner; (*fire, & fig.*) souffler; exciter, attiser.

fanatic, *n*, fanatique, *m,f*. **~(al)**, *a*, fanatique. **fanaticism**, *n*, fanatisme, *m*. **fanaticize**, *v.t*, fanatiser.

fancied, *p.a*, imaginaire. **fancier**, *n*, grand amateur (de . . .) *m*. **fanciful**, *a*, de fantaisie; fantastique, chimérique. **fancy**, *n*, fantaisie; envie; toquade; boutade, *f*, caprice, *m*; imagination; idée, *f*. ~ *dress*, déguisement, *m*. **~-dress ball**, bal costumé, b. travesti, *m*. ~ *leather goods or shop*, maroquinerie, *f*. ~ *needlework*, ouvrages de dames, *m.pl*. ~ *work*, ouvrages d'agrément, *m.pl*. ¶ *v.t*, imaginer; s'imaginer; se figurer. ~ *oneself*, se complaire.

fang, *n*, croc, *m*.

fantasia, *n*, fantaisie, *f*. **fantastic**, *a*, fantastique; *fantaisiste*. **fantasy**, *n*, vision; fantaisie, *f*.

far, *ad*, loin, au loin; avant; beaucoup; bien. *from ~*, de loin. *how ~ is it to . . .?* combien y a-t-il d'ici à . . .? ~ *& wide*, au long & au large. *as ~ as*, jusqu'à; autant que. *as ~ as the eye can reach*, à perte de vue. *by ~*, de beaucoup. **~-fetched**, tiré par les cheveux, forcé, outre. ~ *into the night*, fort avant dans la nuit. ~ *off*, lointain. **~-reaching**, étendu. **~sighted**, prévoyant. ~ *too*, par trop. ¶ *a*, éloigné. *the F~ East*, l'Extrême-Orient, *m*.

farce, *n*, farce, *f*. **farcical**, *a*, burlesque, bouffon.

fare, *n*, prix [de la place], prix de passage, tarif, *m*, place; course, *f*; voyageur, euse; chère, *f*, menu, *m*. ¶ *v.i*, aller. *to ~* (feed) *well*, faire bonne chère. **~well**, *i. & n*, adieu, *i. & m*.

farina, n, farine; fécule, f. **farinaceous,** a, farineux, farinacé.

farm, n, ferme, f. ~ **hand,** valet de ferme, m. ~**house,** ferme, f. ~ **products,** produits agricoles, m.pl. ~**yard,** cour de f., basse-cour, f. ¶ v.t, exploiter; cultiver; (lease) affermer. ~ **out,** amodier. ~**er,** n, fermier, ère, cultivateur, trice, agriculteur, m. ~**ing,** n, exploitation [d'une ferme], agriculture, culture, f; (att.) aratoire.

faro (cards) n, pharaon, m.

farrago, n, farrago, salmigondis, m.

farrow, n, cochonnée, f. ¶ v.t, cochonner.

fart, n, pet, m.

farther, ad, plus loin, [plus] en delà. **farthest,** a, le plus éloigné. ¶ ad, le plus loin.

farthing, n, farthing, m. = ¼ penny; (fig.) liard, m, obole, f.

fasces (Hist.) n.pl, faisceaux, m.pl.

fascinate, v.t, fasciner. **fascinating,** a, fascinateur. **fascination,** n, fascination, f.

fascine, n, fascine, f.

fascism, n, fascisme, m. **fascist,** n, fasciste, m.

fashion, n, façon; mode, f. genre, m. after a ~, tant bien que mal. ~ **plate,** gravure de mode, f. ¶ v.t, façonner. ~**able,** a, à la mode, élégant. ~ **society,** le beau monde. ~**ably,** ad, à la mode.

fast, a, fixe; fidèle; (dissipated) léger; rapide, vite; express, de grande vitesse; (of clock) en avance. ~ **asleep,** profondément endormi. ~ **color,** bon teint, t. solide, m. ~ **cruiser** (speedboat) glisseur de croisière, m. ¶ ad, ferme; bien; vite; (rain) à verse. to hold ~, tenir bon. to make ~, amarrer. ¶ n, jeûne, m; (Naut.) amarre, f. ¶ v.i, jeûner. ~**ing,** ad, à jeun. ~[ing] day, jour de jeûne, j. maigre, m.

fasten, v.t, fixer; assujettir; attacher; agrafer. ~ **off** (Need.), arrêter. ~**er** & ~**ing,** n, attache; armature; fermeture; agrafe, f.

fastidious (to be), être pointilleux, faire le (of woman, la) dégoûté(e), f. le difficile, f. le délicat, f. le (la) renchéri(e).

fat, a, gras; obèse; (land) fertile. ~**head,** lourdaud, e; couillon, m. ~ **profits,** profits substantiels,

m.pl. ¶ n, gras, m; graisse, f; lard; suif, m. to live on the ~ of the land, vivre grassement.

fatal†, a, fatal, funeste; mortel. ~**ism,** n, fatalisme, m. ~**ist,** n, fataliste, m.f. ~**ity,** n, fatalité, f; accident mortel, m; tué, e.

fate, n, destin, sort, m, fatalité, f. the Fates (Myth.), les Parques, f.pl. to be ~d to, être destiné à. ~**ful,** a, fatal.

father, n, père, m. ~**-in-law,** beau-père, m. ~**land,** patrie, f. ~'s side (family), côté paternel, m. ~**hood,** n, paternité, f. ~**less,** a, sans père, orphelin de père. ~**ly,** a, paternel, de père. ¶ v.t, patronner. ~ **upon,** attribuer à.

fathom, n, brasse, f. (Eng. fathom = 6 feet; Fr. brasse marine = 1 meter 62). ¶ v.t, sonder, pénétrer. ~**less,** a, insondable.

fatigue, n, fatigue; (Mil.) corvée, f. ¶ v.t, fatiguer. **fatiguing,** a, fatigant.

fatness, n, obésité; fertilité, f. fatted calf, veau gras, m. **fatten,** v.t, engraisser. **fattish,** a, grasset. **fatty,** a, gras, graisseux, adipeux.

fatuity, n, imbécillité, f. **fatuous,** a, imbécile.

fauces, n.pl, arrière-bouche, f.

faucet, n, robinet, fausset, m; douille, f.

fault, n, faute, f; tort; défaut, vice; dérangement, m; (Geol.) faille, f. to find ~ with, trouver à redire à, reprendre, mordre sur, censurer, fronder, gloser [sur]. ~ **finder,** critiqueur, frondeur, m. ~**less,** a, sans faute; sans défaut; irréprochable. ~**y,** a, fautif, vicieux, défectueux, mauvais.

faun, n, faune, m. **fauna,** n, faune, f.

favor, n, faveur, grâce, f; plaisir, m. ¶ v.t, favoriser, avantager, honorer. **favorable†,** a, favorable; prospère. **favorite,** a, favori. ~ **author,** auteur de prédilection, m. ~ **book,** livre de chevet, m. ¶ n, favori, ite. the ~, le [cheval] favori. **favoritism,** n, favoritisme, m, cote d'amour, f.

fawn, n, faon, chevrotin; (color) fauve, m. ~ [-colored], fauve. ¶ (of deer) v.i, faonner. ~ [up] on, flagorner, courtiser, ramper devant. ~**ing,** n, servilité, flatterie, f.

fear, n, crainte, peur, frayeur, f; danger, m. ¶ v.t. & i, craindre, redouter. ~ful†, a, affreux, épouvantable; craintif. ~less, a, sans peur, intrépide. ~lessness, n, intrépidité, f.

feasibility, n, praticabilité, f. **feasible,** a, faisable, praticable.

feast, n, fête, f; festin, régal, m. ¶ v.i. & t, festiner, festoyer, régaler; (fig.) repaître. ~ing, n, bombance, f.

feat, n, fait, exploit; tour, m, prouesse, f.

feather, n, plume, f; (pl.) plumage, m; penne; (Carp. & Mach.) languette, f. ~ bed, lit de plume, m. ~brained person, tête de linotte, f, évaporé, e. ~ duster, plumeau, houssoir, m. ~ stitch, point de plume, f; (Box.), poids plume, m. ¶ (rowing) v.i, plumer. to ~ one's nest, s'enrichir. ~ed, p.a: ~ game, gibier à plume, m. ~ hat, chapeau orné de plumes, m. ~y, a, plumeux.

feature, n, trait, linéament, m; caractéristique, f. ¶ v.i, mettre en vedette.

February, n, février, m.

fecund, a, fécond. ~ate, v.t, féconder. ~ity, n, fécondité, f.

federal, a, fédéral. **federate,** v.t, fédérer. **federation,** n, fédération, f; syndicat, m.

fee, n. oft. pl, honoraires, m.pl; frais, m.pl; cotisation, f; droit, m; taxe; surtaxe, f. admission ~, droit d'entrée, m.

feeble†, a, faible, débile.

feed, n, nourriture; mangeaille; pâture, f; (of oats) picotin, m; alimentation, f; (Mach.) avancement, entraînement, m. ~ pump, pompe alimentaire, f. ¶ v.t.ir, nourrir; [re]paître; alimenter; (v.i.ir.) manger. ~ forcibly, gaver. ~er, n, mangeur, euse; appareil d'alimentation, m; (stream, Rly) affluent, m; (Elec.) artère, f. ~ing bottle, biberon, m.

feedback, n, (computers) rétroaction, réinjection, f.

feel, n, manier, toucher, tact, m. ¶ v.t. & i. ir, tâter, palper, manier; toucher; sentir, se s., ressentir, se r., éprouver; se trouver. to ~ one's way, avancer à tâtons. to ~ like, avoir envie de. ~er, n,

antenne, f, palpe, f. or m; (fig.) ballon d'essai, m. **feeling,** a, sensible, touchant, tendre. ¶ n, maniement, m; sensation; sensibilité, f; (pl.) cœur; sentiment; esprit, m. ~ly, ad, avec émotion.

feign, v.t, feindre, simuler, jouer. **feint,** n, feinte, f. ¶ v.i, feindre.

felicitous, a, heureux, à propos. **felicity,** n, félicité, f.

feline, a. & n, félin, a. & m.

fell, n, peau, f; abat[tis] m. ¶ v.t, abattre; assommer. ~er, n, abatteur, m. ~ing, n, abattage, m.

fellow, n, compagnon, m, camarade, m,f, pareil, pendant; garçon, gaillard, individu, sujet, m. ~ boarder, commensal, e. ~ citizen, concitoyen, ne. ~ countryman, -woman, compatriote, m.f. ~ creature, ~ man, semblable, prochain, m. ~ feeling, sympathie, f. ~ passenger, ~ traveler, compagnon de voyage, m, compagne de voyage, f. ~ student, camarade de collège, m, f, condisciple, m. ~ sufferer, camarade de malheur, compagnon de malheur, compagne de malheur, f. good ~, chic type, m. ~ship, n, société; camaraderie, f; situation universitaire, f.

felon, n, criminel, le. ~ious, a, criminel. ~y, n, crime, m.

felt, n, feutre, m. ~ [hat], [chapeau de] feutre, m. ¶ v.t, feutrer.

female, a, femelle; de femme; (pers.) féminin. ¶ n, (animal) femelle; (pers.) femme, f. **feminine,** a, & n, féminin, a. & m. **feminism,** n, féminisme, m. **feminist,** a. & n, féministe, a. & m.f. **feminize,** v.t, féminiser.

femur, n, fémur, m.

fen, n, marais, marécage, m.

fence, n, clôture, barrière, palissade, f; (Mach.) guide, m; (pers.) receleur, euse. to be on the ~, être indécis. ¶ v.t, palissader; (v.i.) faire (ou tirer) des armes. ~ in, enclore. ~ off, barrer. **fencer,** n, tireur d'armes, m. **fencing,** n, clôture, enceinte; (foils) escrime, f. ~ master, maître d'armes, m. ~ school, salle d'armes, s. d'escrime, f.

fend [off], v.t, parer. ~ for oneself, se suffire. ~er, n, gardecendre; (*Naut.*) parebattage; (auto) pare-boue, *m.*

fennel, *n,* & ~ *seed,* fenouil, *m.*

ferment, *n,* ferment, *m*; (*fig.*) fermentation, effervescence, *f.* ¶ *v.i,* fermenter; (*v.t.*) faire f. **~ation,** *n,* fermentation, *f.*

fern, *n,* fougère, *f.*

ferocious, *a,* féroce. **ferocity,** *n,* férocité, *f.*

ferret, *n,* furet, *m.* ¶ *v.i.* & *t,* fureter. ~ *about,* fureter. ~ *out,* dénicher.

ferrous, *a,* ferreux.

ferrule, *n,* virole, bague, frette, *f,* [em]bout, *m.* ¶ *v.t,* mettre une virole, etc., à.

ferry, *n,* passage, *m.* ~[*boat*], bateau de passage, bac, *m.* ~**man,** passeur, *m.* car ~, transbordeur, *m.* ~ *over,* passer [l'eau].

fertile, *a,* fertile, fécond, plantureux. **fertility,** *n,* fertilité, fécondité, *f.* **fertilize,** *v.t,* fertiliser. **fertilizer,** *n,* engrais fertilisant, *m.*

fervent & **fervid,** *a,* fervent, ardent. **fervently** & **fervidly,** *ad,* avec ferveur, ardemment. **fervor** & **fervency,** *n,* ferveur, ardeur, *f.*

fester, *v.i,* s'ulcérer. ¶ *n,* ulcère, *m*; suppuration, *f.*

festival, *n,* fête, *f*; (*musical*) festival, *m.* **festive,** *a,* de fête. **festivity,** *n,* fête, *f.*

festoon, *n,* feston, *m.* ¶ *v.t,* festonner.

fetch, *v.t,* apporter; aller chercher. ~ *it!* (to dog), apporte! ~ *over,* passer [l'eau].

fete, *n,* fête; kermesse; (*at a fair*) fête foraine, *f.* ¶ *v.t,* fêter.

fetid, *a,* fétide. **~ness,** *n,* fétidité, *f.*

fetish, *n,* fétiche, *m.* **fetishism,** *n,* fétichisme, *m.*

fetlock, *n,* fanon, *m.*

fetter, *n. oft. pl,* entrave, *f,* fer, *m,* chaîne, *f.* ¶ *v.t,* entraver, enchaîner.

fettle, *n,* état, *m,* forme, *f.*

fetus, *n,* fœtus, *m.*

feud, *n,* guerre, vendetta, *f*; (*Hist.*) fief, *m.* **~al,** *a,* féodal. **~alism** & **~ality,** *n,* féodalité, *f.*

fever, *n,* fièvre, *f.* ~ *case* (*pers.*), fiévreux, euse. *scarlet* ~, scarlatine, *f.* **~ish†,** *a,* fiévreux; fébrile.

few, *a.* & *n,* peu de; peu, *m*; quelques; quelques-uns, -unes. ~ & *far between,* clairsemé. **~er,** *a,* moins; moins de.

fez, *n,* fez, *m.*

fiasco, *n,* fiasco, four, *m.*

fiat, *n,* décret, *m.*

fib, *n,* mensonge innocent, *m,* menterie, *f.* ¶ *v.i,* débiter des bourdes. **fibber,** *n,* menteur, *m.*

fiber, *n,* fibre, *f*; crin, *m.* **fibril,** *n,* fibrille, *f.* **fibrous,** *a,* fibreux.

fickle, *a,* volage, changeant, mobile, versatile, inconstant. **~ness,** *n,* inconstance, mobilité, versatilité, *f.*

fiction, *n,* fiction, *f,* mensonge, *m*; (*prose*) le roman, les romans. **fictitious†,** *a,* fictif, supposé. **fictive,** *a,* imaginaire.

fiddle, *n,* violon, crincrin, *m.* ~ *stick,* archet, *m*; (*pl., i.*) chansons, chansons! ¶ *v.i,* jouer du violon; (*fig.*) baguenauder. **fiddler,** *n,* ménétrier, *m.*

fidelity, *n,* fidélité, *f.*

fidget, *v.i,* remuer, frétiller, se trémousser. **~s,** *n.pl,* impatiences, crispations, *f.pl.* **~y,** *a,* inquiet, nerveux.

fiduciary, *a,* fiduciaire.

fie, *i,* fi!

fief (*Hist.*) *n,* fief, *m.*

field, *n,* champ, *m*; (*pl.*) campagne, *f*; (*pl., poet.*) sillons, *m.pl*; terrain, *m*; (*Mil.*) campagne, *f*; (*Her.*) champ, *m,* table d'attente. *f.* ~ *artillery,* artillerie de campagne, *f.* ~ *day,* manœuvres, *f.pl*; (*fig.*) grand jour; débat important, *m.* ~ *geology,* géologie sur le terrain, *f.* ~ *glass*[es], jumelle de campagne, *f.* ~ *mouse,* rat des champs, mulot, *m.* ~ *sports,* la chasse, la pêche, & sports analogues. (*TV & cinema*) depth of ~, profondeur de champ, *m.* landing ~, terrain d'atterrissage, *m.*

fiend, *n,* démon, *m*; enragé, e. **~ish,** *a,* diabolique.

fierce, *a,* féroce, farouche, acharné. **~ly,** *ad,* avec férocité. **~ness,** *n,* férocité, *f.*

fiery, *a,* de feu; ardent, bouillant, fougueux.

fife & **fifer,** *n,* fifre, *m.*

fifteen, *a.* & *n,* quinze, *a.* & *m.* **~th†,** *a.* & *n,* quinzième, *a.* & *m.f*; quinze, *m.* **fifth†,** *a,* cinquième. ¶ *n,* cinquième, *m.f*; cinq, *m*; (*Mus.*) quinte, *f.* **fiftieth,** *a.* & *n,* cinquantième, *a.* & *m.f.* ~ *anniversary,* cinquantenaire, *m.* **fifty,**

fig 523 **fine**

a. & n, cinquante, *a. & m*. ~ [*or so*], une cinquantaine.

fig, *n*, figue, *f*; (*fig.*) fétu, *m*. ~ *leaf*, feuille de figuier; (*Art*) feuille de vigne, *f*. ~ *tree*, figuier, *m*.

fight, *n*, combat, *m*; lutte, joute, bataille, mêlée, batterie, *f*. *air* ~, combat aérien, *m*. *hand-to-hand* ~, corps-à-corps, *m*. ¶ *v.i.ir*, se battre, combattre, lutter, batailler; (*v.t.ir.*) se battre avec, combattre, lutter contre; (*a battle*) livrer; (*one's way*) se frayer. ~*er*, *n*, combattant; batailleur; militant, avion de combat, *m*.

figment, *n*, fiction, *f*.

figurative, *a*, figuratif. ~ *sense*, [sens] figuré, *m*. ~*ly*, *ad*, figurativement; (*sense*) figurément, au figuré. **figure**, *n*, figure; (*bodily shape*) taille, tournure, *f*; (*Arith.*) chiffre, *m*. ~ *dance*, danse figurée, *f*. ~*head*, (*ship*) figure de proue, *f*; personnage de carton, *m*. ~ *of speech*, figure de mots, figure de rhétorique. ~ *skates*, patins de figure, *m.pl*. ¶ *v.t. & i*, chiffrer; gaufrer; figurer; (*Mus.*) chiffrer.

filament, *n*, filament; fil; filet, *m*.

filbert, *n*, aveline, *f*. ~ [*tree*], avelinier, *m*.

filch, *v.t*, escamoter, subtiliser, filouter.

file, *n*, (*rank*) file; (*of people*) file, queue, *f*; (*for letters*) classeur, *m*; (*bundle*) liasse; collection; (*tool*) lime, *f*; (*computers*) fichier, *m*. ~ *card*, fiche, *f*. ¶ *v.t*, classer; déposer, passer, enregistrer; limer. ~ *past*, défiler.

filial†, *a*, filial. **filiation**, *n*, filiation, *f*.

filigree [**work**], *n*, filigrane, *m*. ~**d**, *a*, façonné en filigrane.

filing, *n*, classement; dépôt; limage, *m*; (*pl.*) limaille, *f*. ~ *cabinet*, [meuble-]classeur, *m*.

fill, *n*, suffisance, *f*, content, soûl, *m*. ¶ *v.t*, [r]emplir; combler; charger; peupler; suppléer à; (*tooth*) plomber. ~ *in*, inserer, remplir. ~ *in time*, peloter en attendant partie. (*gas, water*) *to* ~ *it up*, faire le pleine. ~ *up*, remplir.

fillet, *n*, filet; (*Arch.*) congé, *m*. ~ *of veal*, rouelle de veau, *f*. ~*ed sole*, filets de sole, *m.pl*.

filling, *n*, remplissage, chargement; (*tooth*) plombage, *m*. ¶ *a*, (*food*) bourratif.

fillip, *n*, chiquenaude, *f*; (*fig.*) coup de fouet, *m*.

fillister, *n*, feuillure, *f*.

filly, *n*, pouliche, *f*.

film, *n*, pellicule, *f*; film, *m*; (*movies*) bande, *f*; (*fig.*) voile, *m*. ~ *library*, cinémathèque, *f*. ~*maker*, cinéaste, *m*. ~ *pack*, bloc-film, *m*. ~ *projector*, ciné-projecteur, *m*. ~ *rights*, droits d'adaption au cinématographe, *m.pl*. ~ *serial*, ciné-roman, *m*. ~ *short*, court métrage, *m*. ~ *star*, vedette de l'écran, v. de cinéma, *f*. *feature* ~, long métrage, *m*. *silent* ~, film muet, *m*. ¶ *v.t*, mettre à l'écran, tourner. ~*y*, *a*, vaporeux.

filter, *n*, filtre; (*Phot.*) écran, *m*. ¶ *v.t. & i*, filtrer.

filth, *n*, immondice, fange, ordure, crasse, saleté, *f*. **filthiness**, *n*, saleté, *f*. **filthy**†, *a*, sale, crasseux; crapuleux, ignoble.

fin, *n*, nageoire, *f*, (*Avn.*) aileron, *m*.

final†, *a*, final, dernier, fatal. ~ [*heat*], [épreuve] finale, *f*. **finale** (*Mus.*) *n*, final[e] *m*. **finality**, *n*, finalité, *f*.

finance, *n*, finance; commandite, *f*; (*pl.*) finances, *f.pl*, trésorerie, *f*. ¶ *v.i*, financer; (*v.t.*) commanditer. **financial**†, *a*, financier. **financier**, *n*, financier, *m*.

finch, *n*, pinson, *m*.

find, *n*, trouvaille, découverte, *f*. ¶ *v.t.ir*, trouver, retrouver; découvrir; rechercher; s'apercevoir; reconnaître; procurer, se procurer; fournir. ~ *out*, découvrir, se rendre compte. ~*er*, *n*, inventeur; (*camera*) viseur, *m*; (*telescope*) lunette de repère, *f*. ~*ing* (*jury*) *n*, déclaration, *f*.

fine, *a*, beau; fin; délicat; bon; menu; ténu; joli; magnifique. ~ *arts*, beaux-arts, *m.pl*. *one of these* ~ *days*, un de ces matins, un beau matin. ~ *speaking*, bien-dire, *m*. ~ *things*, objets magnifiques, *m.pl*, magnificences, *f.pl*. ¶ *n*, amende, *f*. ¶ *v.t*, mettre (*ou* condamner) à l'amende; (*wine*) coller, clarifier. ~*ly*, *ad*, finement; joliment. ~*ness*, *n*, finesse; ténuité, *f*; (*gold*, *etc.*) titre, *m.* **finery**, *n*, chiffons, colifichets, affiquets, atours, *m.pl.* **finesse**, *n*, finesse, *f.* ¶ *v.t*, finasser. *finest quality*, premier choix, *m.*

finger, *n*, doigt, *m.* ~ *board*, touche, *f.* ~ *bowl*, bol rince-doigts, *m.* ~ *print*, empreinte digitale, *f. middle* ~, médius, *m. ring* ~, annulaire, *m.* ¶ *v.t*, toucher, palper; (*Mus.*) doigter. ~*ing* (*Mus.*) *n*, doigté, *m.*

finical, *a*, dégoûté, difficile, maniéré, vétilleux, mièvre.

finis, *n*, fin, *f.* **finish**, *n*, fini, *m;* (*end*) fin, *f*, bout, *m.* ¶ *v.t. & abs. & i*, finir; en finir; achever; parachever, parfaire. *to* ~ *speaking*, finir de parler. ~*ing stroke*, coup de grâce, *m.* ~*ing touches*, dernière main, *f.*

finite, *a*, fini; (*Gram.*) défini.

Finland, *n*, la Finlande. **Finn**, **Finlander**, *n*, Finnois, e, Finlandais, e. **Finnish**, *a*, finnois, finlandais. ¶ (*language*) *n*, le finnois.

fir [**tree**], *n*, sapin, pin, *m.* ~ *plantation*, sapinière, *f.*

fire, *n*, feu; incendie; tir, *m;* fougue, *f.* (*house, etc, on*) ~*!* au feu! ~ *alarm*, avertisseur d'incendie, *m.* ~*arms*, armes à feu, *f.pl.* ~*box*, foyer, *m;* boîte à feu, *f.* ~*brand*, tison, brandon, boute-feu, *m.* ~*brick*, brique réfractaire, *f.* ~ *brigade*, sapeurs-pompiers, *m.pl.* ~*clay*, argile réfractaire, *f.* ~*damp*, grisou, *m.* ~ *dog*, chenet, *m.* ~ *engine*, pompe à incendie, *f.* ~ *escape*, échelle de sauvetage, *f.* ~ *extinguisher*, extincteur d'incendie, *m.* ~*fly*, mouche à feu, luciole, *f.* ~*guard*, garde-feu, pare-étincelles, *m.* ~ *hydrant*, ~ *plug*, bouche d'incendie, *f.* ~ *insurance*, assurance contre l'incendie, *f.* ~ *irons*, garniture de foyer, *f.* ~ *lighter*, allume-feu, *m.* ~*man*, pompier, sapeur-pompier; (*stoker*) chauffeur, *m.* ~*place*, cheminée, *f*, âtre, *m.* ~*proof*, *a*, ignifuge, incombustible, à l'épreuve du feu; (*v.t.*) ignifuger. ~*side*, coin du feu, foyer, *m.* ~*side chair*, chauffeuse, *f.* ~ *station*, poste d'incendie, p. de pompiers, *m.* ~*wood*, bois à brûler, b. de chauffage, *m.* ~ *work*, feu d'artifice, *m*, pièce d'a., *f.* ¶ *v.t*, enflammer, embraser, mettre le feu à; incen-

dier; allumer; chauffer; (*shot*) tirer, lâcher, lancer; (*v.i.*) prendre feu; (*gun*) tirer, faire feu. ~*!* (*Mil.*), feu! **firing**, *n*, chauffage, *m*, chauffe, *f;* combustible; (*Mil.*) feu, tir, *m.*

firm†, *a*, ferme; solide; consistant; tenu. ¶ *n*, maison [de commerce]; société [en nom collectif] *f.* ~ [*name*], raison [sociale] *f.* ~'*s capital*, capital social, *m.*

firmament, *n*, firmament, *m.*

firmness, *n*, fermeté, assiette, solidité; consistance; tenue, *f.*

first, *a*, premier; (*after 20, 30, etc.*) unième; (*cousins*) germain. ~ *aid*, premiers soins, *m.pl.* ~ *appearance & ~ work*, début, *m. to make one's* ~ *appearance*, débuter. ~ *attempt*, coup d'essai, *m.* ~ *born*, premier-né, *m. 1st class*, 1ʳᵉ classe, *f. the* ~ *comer*, le premier venu, la première venue. ~ *edition*, édition originale, é. princeps, *f.* ~ *finger*, index, *m.* ~ [*floor*], premier [étage] *m.* ~ *fruits*, prémices, *f.pl.* ~*rate*, de premier ordre; fameux. (*movie*) ~*run*, en exclusivité. ¶ *ad*, premièrement, primo. ~, *at* ~, *of all*, [tout] d'abord, de premier abord, de prime abord. ~ *& foremost*, en premier. *the first*, le premier, la première. *the 1st January*, le 1ᵉʳ janvier, primo. ~*ly*, *ad*, premièrement, primo.

firth, *n*, estuaire, *m.*

fiscal, *a*, fiscal. ~ *system*, fiscalité, *f.* ~ *year*, année budgétaire, *f.*

fish, *n*, poisson, *m.* ~*bone*, arête, *f.* ~*bowl*, bocal, *m.* ~ *glue*, colle de poisson, *f.* ~*hook*, hameçon, *m.* ~ *kettle*, poissonnière, *f.* ~ *market*, halle aux poissons, poissonnerie, *f.* [*wet*] ~*monger*, poissonnier, ère. ~ *out of water* (*pers.*), déraciné, e. ~ *pond*, vivier, *m.* ~*pond*, poissonnerie, *f.* ~ *slice*, truelle à poisson, *f.* ~ *spear*, fouine, *f*, trident, *m.* ~*wife*, poissarde, harengère, *f.* ¶ *v.i. & t.* ~ *for*, pêcher. ~ *out*, ~ *up*, [re]pêcher. ~[*plate*], *v.t*, éclisser. ~*erman*, *n*, pêcheur, euse. ~*ery*, *n*, pêche; (*ground*) pêcherie, *f.* ~*ing* (*act or right*) *n*, pêche, *f.* ~ *boat*, bateau de pêche, *m.* ~ *ground*, parage de

pêche, *m*, pêcherie, *f*. ~ *rod*,
canne à pêche, gaule, *f*. ~ *tackle*,
engins de pêche, *m.pl*, harnais
de p., *m*. ~y, *a*, sauvagin; (*fig.*)
véreux.
fission, *n*, fission, *f*.
fissure, *n*, fissure, fente, *f*. ¶ *v.t*,
fendiller.
fist, *n*, poing, *m*. **fisticuffs**, *n.pl*,
coup[s] de poing, *m.[pl.]*.
fistula, *n*, fistule, *f*.
fit, *a*, propre, bon, apte, convenable, approprié, à propos; capable; dispos, frais. ~ *for service*,
valide. ¶ *n*, accès, *m*, attaque,
crise, boutade, bouffée, *f*; (*Mech.*)
montage, *m*. ~ *of coughing*,
quinte [de toux] *f*. *by* ~*s &
starts*, par sauts & par bonds, par
boutades, à bâtons rompus. ¶
v.t, ajuster, adapter, agencer;
aménager, cadrer; monter, épouser [la forme de]; chausser; botter; coiffer; (*v.i.*) s'ajuster; aller.
~ *in*, emboîter, enclaver. ~ *out*,
équiper, armer, outiller. ~ *tightly*, coller. **fitful**, *a*, changeant;
agité; saccadé; quinteux. **fitly**,
ad, convenablement. **fitness**, *n*,
convenance, aptitude, *f*. **fitter**, *n*,
ajusteur, monteur, appareilleur,
m; (*clothes*) essayeur, euse. **fit-
ting†**, *a*, convenable. ~**s**, *n.pl*,
armature, *f*; garnitures; ferrures,
f.pl; appareillage, *m*. ~ [*& fixtures*], agencement, *m*.
five, *a. & n*, cinq, *a. & m*. ~-*finger
exercise*, exercice de doigté, *m*.
~ *year plan*, plan quinquennal, *m*.
fix, *n*, impasse, *f*, embarras, pétrin,
m. ¶ *v.t*, fixer, assujettir, asseoir;
ancrer; arrêter. ~**ed†**, *a*, fixe; à
demeure. ~ *salary*, fixe, *m*. ~**ing**,
n, fixage, *m*, fixation, pose, *f*. ~
& toning bath, bain de virage-
fixage, *m*. ~ [*solution*] (*Phot.*),
fixateur, *m*. **fixture**, *n*, pièce fixe,
p. à demeure, *f*; engagement, *m*.
~**s & fittings**, agencement, *m*.
fizz[le], *v.i*, pétiller. *fizzle out*,
n'aboutir à rien.
flabbergast, *v.t*, atterrer, ébahir.
flabbiness & flaccidity, *n*, flaccidité, mollesse, *f*. **flabby & flaccid**, *a*, flasque, mollasse, avachi,
mou, veule.
flag, *n*, drapeau, pavillon; (*pl.*) pavois; (*Bot.*) iris des marais, *m*. ~
at half-mast, drapeau en berne,
m. ~ *of truce*, (*Mil.*) drapeau parlementaire; (*Nav.*) pavillon p.

~*ship*, [vaisseau] amiral, *m*. ~
staff, mât de pavillon, *m*.
~[*stone*], dalle, *f*. ¶ *v.t*, daller;
pavoiser; faire des signaux; (*v.i.*)
fléchir; faiblir, languir, tomber,
traîner.
flagellate, *v.t*, flageller.
flageolet, *n*, flageolet, *m*.
flagitious, *a*, scélérat, infâme.
flagon, *n*, flacon, *m*, bouteille [len-
ticulaire] (pour le vin) *f*.
flagrant, *a*, flagrant.
flail, *n*, fléau, *m*.
flair, *n*, aptitude, *f*, dispositions,
f.pl.
flake, *n*, (*snow*) flocon, *m*; écaille;
lame; lamelle; feuille; paillette;
fiammèche, *f*. ¶ *v.i*, floconner;
s'écailler. **flaky**, *a*, floconneux;
écailleux; feuilleté; laminé.
flame, *n*, flamme, *f*, feu, *m*. ~
thrower, lance-flamme, *m*. ¶ *v.i*,
flamber, flamboyer; s'enflammer;
(*v.t.*) flamber.
flamingo, *n*, flamant, *m*.
Flanders, *n*, la Flandre.
flange, *n*, bride, *f*; boudin; rebord;
bourrelet; patin, *m*; aile, *f*. ¶ *v.t*,
border.
flank, *n*, flanc, *m*. ¶ *v.t*, flanquer.
flannel, *n*, flanelle, *f*. ~**ette**, *n*,
flanelle de coton, *f*, pilou, *m*.
flap, *n*, coup; clapet; bord; pan;
abattant, *m*; trappe; patte; oreille,
f. ¶ *v.t. & i*, battre, voltiger.
flare, *n*, feu, *m*, flamme, *f*; évase-
ment, pavillon, *m*. ¶ *v.i*, flamber,
flamboyer; (*lamp*) filer; (*bellmouth*) s'évaser. *to* ~ *up*, (*anger*) s'emporter.
flash, *a*, tapageur. ¶ *n*, éclair;
éclat; feu; trait, *m*; saillie, *f*.
~*back*, retour en arrière, *m*. ~ *in
the pan* (*fig.*), feu de paille. ~
light, lampe de poche. ~ *of light
& ~ of lightning*, éclair, *m*.
~[*ing*] *point*, point d'éclair, p.
d'inflammabilité, *m*. ¶ *v.i*, étinceler; miroiter; éclater; jaillir; flamboyer. ~**y**, *a*, voyant, tapageux.
flask, *n*, bouteille; gourde, *f*; flacon, *m*; ballon, *m*; fiole, *f*.
flat, *a*, plat; méplat; aplati; (*nose*)
épaté; à plat; plan; géométral;
couché; net, formel, catégorique,
direct; fade, éventé; maussade,
inactif; mat; (*Mus.*) bémol. ~
iron, fer à repasser, *m*. ~*roof*,
toit en terrasse, *m*, terrasse, plate-
forme, *f*. ¶ *ad*, à plat. ~ *on one's*

face, à plat [ventre]. *to sing* ~, détonner. ¶ *n*, plat; méplat; (*rooms*) appartement; (*plain, shoal*) bas-fond, haut-fond, *m*, basse, *f*; (*Theat.*) châssis; (*Mus.*) bémol, *m*. ~**ly**, *ad*, platement; nettement, [tout] net, carrément. ~**ness**, *n*, aplatissement; (*liquor*) évent, *m*; fadeur, platitude, *f*. **flatten**, *v.t*, aplatir; éventer; affadir.

flatter, *v.t*, flatter, caresser. ~**er**, *n*, flatteur, euse. ~**ing**, *a*, flatteur. ~**y**, *n*, flatterie, *f*.

flatulence, -**cy**, *n*, flatulence, *f*. **flatus**, *n*, flatuosité, *f*, gaz, vent, *m*.

flaunt, *v.t*, étaler, faire parade de.

flautist, *n*, flûtiste, *m,f*.

flavor, *n*, saveur, *f*, goût, *m*. ¶ *v.t*, assaisonner. ~**ing**, *n*, assaisonnement, *m*. ~**less**, *a*, insipide, fade.

flaw, *n*, paille, *f*, défaut, *m*, défectuosité; glace, *f*, crapaud; vice, *m*. ¶ *v.t*, rendre défectueux. ~**less**, *a*, sans défaut, net. ~**y**, *a*, pailleux.

flax, *n*, lin, *m*. ~ *field*, linière, *f*. ~**en**, *a*. & *n*, blond, *a*. & *m*.

flay, *v.t*, écorcher.

flea, *n*, puce, *f*. ~ *bite*, piqûre de puce, *f*.

fleck, *n*, tache, moucheture, *f*.

fledged (to be), avoir sa plume. **fledgling**, *n*, oisillon, *m*.

flee, *v.i*. & *t. ir*, fuir, s'enfuir.

fleece, *n*, toison, *f*. ¶ *v.t*, tondre, plumer, écorcher, étriller. **fleecy**, *a*, floconneux. ~ *clouds*, *sky fleeced with clouds*, nuages moutonnés, *m.pl*, ciel moutonné, *m*.

fleet, *n*, flotte, *f*. ~ *of foot*, léger (ère) à la course. ~**ing**, *a*, passager, fugitif, fugace.

Fleming, *n*, Flamand, e. **Flemish**, *a*. & (*language*) *n*, flamand, *a*. & *m*.

flesh, *n*, chair, *f*; chairs *f.pl*; charnure, *f*; (*meat*) viande, *f*; embonpoint, *m*. ¶ ~**y**, *a*, charnu; plantureux. ~ *part of the arm*, gras du bras, *m*.

flexible, *a*, flexible, souple. *to make* ~, assouplir. **flexor**, *a*. & *n*, fléchisseur, a.m. & *m*.

flick, *n*, chiquenaude, *f*; (*sound*) flic flac, *m*.

flicker, *v.i*, papilloter, trembler, vaciller.

flier, *n*, aviateur, *m*.

flight, *n*, fuite, *f*; vol, envol, *m*, volée; envolée, *f*, essor; élan;

exode, *m*; bande, *f*; écart, *m*. ~ *of stairs*, volée d'escalier, *f*. ~**y**, *a*, volage, léger, étourdi, frivole.

flimsy, *a*, sans consistance, mollasse; frivole. ¶ *n*, (*tissue*) papier pelure, *m*.

flinch, *v.i*, défaillir, broncher.

fling, *n*, coup; trait, *m*. ¶ *v.t.ir*, jeter, lancer, darder. ~ *away* & ~ *off*, rejeter.

flint, *n*, silex; caillou, *m*; pierre à fusil; pierre [à briquet] *f*. ~ & *steel*, briquet, *m*. ~ *glass*, flintglass, *m*. ~**y**, *a*, siliceux; caillouteux; de pierre.

flip, *v.t*, voleter.

flippant, *a*, léger, désinvolte.

flipper, *n*, nageoire, *f*.

flirt (*pers.*) *n*, coquet, te. ¶ *v.t*, coqueter, flirter. ~**ation**, *n*, coquetterie, *f*, flirt, *m*.

flit, *v.i*, voleter, voltiger; fuir. ~ *about*, papillonner.

float & ~**er**, *n*, flotte, *f*; flotteur; bouchon, *m*. ~**[board]**, aube, palette, *f*, aileron, *m*. ~**plane**, hydravion à flotteurs, *m*. ¶ *v.t*, faire flotter; mettre à flot, renflouer; (*Fin.*) lancer; (*v.i.*) flotter; [sur]nager; (*Swim.*) faire la planche. ~**ation**, (*Fin.*) *n*, lancement, *m*. ~**ing**, *a*, flottant.

flock, *n*, troupeau; vol. *m*, bande, troupe, *f*; ouailles, *f.pl*; (*wool*, *etc.*) flocon; *m*; bourre, *f*. ¶ *v.i*, s'assembler [en troupe]; affluer.

floe, *n*, banquise, *f*; glaçon, *m*.

flog, *v.t*, fouetter, fustiger, cravacher. *a flogging*, le fouet.

flood, *n*, inondation, *f*, déluge; flot; torrent, *m*; crue, *f*; (*of the tide*) flux, *m*. ~ *gate*, vanne; (*fig.*) écluse, *f*. ~ *lighting*, éclairage par projection, *m*, illumination par p., *f*. ~ *tide*, marée de flot, *f*, flot, *m*. ¶ *v.t*, inonder, noyer, submerger.

floor, *n*, plancher; parquet; carreau; carré, *m*; aire, *f*; plateau; chantier; tablier; (*story*) étage, palier, *m*. *on one* ~ (*rooms*), de plain-pied. *to take the* ~, prendre la parole. ~ *lamp*, lampe à pied, torchère, *f*. ~ *polisher* (*pers.*) frotteur, *m*; (*Mach.*) cireuse, *f*. ~ *space*, surface des étages, *f*; encombrement, *m*. ¶ *v.t*, planchéier; parqueter; jeter par terre; terrasser, désarçonner.

flora, *n*, flore, *f*. **floral**, *a*, floral;

fleuriste. ~ *design*, ramage, *m.*
florid, *a,* fleuri; rubicond. **Flor-ida**, *n,* la Floride. **florist**, *n,* fleuriste, *m,f.*

floss, *n,* bourre, *f.* ~ *silk*, soie floche, filoselle, strasse, *f.*

flotation (*Fin.*) *n,* lancement, *m.*

flotilla, *n,* flottille, escadrille, *f.*

flotsam, *n,* épaves [flottantes] *f.pl.*

flounce, *n,* volant, *m.* ¶ *v.t,* garnir de volants. ~ *about,* se trémous-ser.

flounder, (*fish*) *n,* flet, *m.* ¶ *v.i,* se débattre; barboter, patauger, patouiller.

flour, *n,* farine, *f.* ~ *mill,* moulin à farine, *m,* minoterie, *f.*

flourish, *n,* floriture, *f;* parafe, *m;* fanfare, *f;* (*of hand*) geste; (*with stick*) moulinet, *m.* ¶ *v.t,* brandir; (*v.i.*) fleurir; faire le moulinet. ~*ing, a,* florissant.

floury, *a,* farineux.

flout, *v.t,* narguer. ~ *at,* se railler de.

flow, *n,* écoulement; cours, *m;* coulée, *f;* débit; flux; torrent, *m.* ~ *of words,* flux de paroles, *m,* faconde, *f.* ¶ *v.i,* couler, s'écou-ler, affluer.

flower, *n,* fleur, *f.* ~ *garden,* jardin fleuriste, *m.* ~ *girl,* bou-quetière, *f.* ~ *holder,* porte-bou-quet, *m.* ~ *market,* marché aux fleurs, *m.* ~ *pot,* pot à fleurs, *m.* ~ *show,* exposition de fleurs, e. florale, *f.* ~ *stand,* jardinière, *f.* ~ *wire,* fil carcasse des fleuristes, *m.* ¶ *v.i,* fleurir. ~*et, n,* fleurette, *f.* ~*ing, a,* à fleurs. ¶ *n,* florai-son, *f.* ~*y, a,* fleuri.

flowing, *a,* coulant, fluide; flot-tant, tombant.

flu, *n,* grippe, *f.*

fluctuate, *v.i,* osciller; flotter. **fluctuation**, *n,* fluctuation, oscil-lation, *f,* mouvement, *m.*

flue, *n,* tuyau; carneau; aspirail, *m.*

fluency, *n,* facilité, *f.* **fluent**, *a,* facile, disert. ~*ly, ad,* couram-ment.

fluff, *n,* bourre, *f;* coton, *m;* (*un-der furniture*) moutons; (*hair*) cheveux follets, *m.pl.* **to** ~ **up,** pelucher. ~*y, a,* duveté; follet; cotonneux; pelucheux.

fluid, *a,* fluide. ¶ *n,* (*impondera-ble*) fluide; (*ponderable*) liquide, *m.* ~*ity, n,* fluidité, *f.*

fluke, *n,* (*anchor*) patte, *f;* coup de hasard, raccroc, *m.*

flummery, *n,* fadaises, *f.pl.*

flunk, *v.t,* échouer; être recalé.

flunkey, *n,* laquais, valet de pied, larbin, *m.* ~*dom, n,* valetaille, *f.*

fluorescent, *a,* fluorescent. **fluor-orine**, *n,* fluor, *m.* **fluorspar,** spath fluor, *m.*

flurry, *n,* ahurissement; coup de vent, *m.* ¶ *v.t,* ahurir.

flush, *a,* à fleur, au ras, de niveau; noyé; lisse; bien pourvu. ¶ *n,* accès, transport; flot de sang, *m;* bouffée; rougeur; fleur; chasse [d'eau] *f;* (*cards*) flux, *m.* ¶ *v.t,* affleurer; laver à grande eau; (*hunting*) faire lever; (*v.i.*) rougir. ~*ed face,* face injectée, *f.*

Flushing, *n,* Flessingue, *f.*

fluster, *v.t,* ahurir, troubler; (*with drink*) griser.

flute, *n,* flûte; (*groove*) cannelure, *f.* ~ [*glass*], flûte, *f.* **flutist**, *n,* flûtiste, *m,f.*

flutter, *n,* battement; émoi, *m.* ¶ *v.i. & t,* voleter; voltiger; pal-piter.

fluty, *a,* flûté.

fluvial, fluviatile, *a,* fluvial, fluviatile.

flux, *n,* flux; (*Chem. & Metall.*) fondant, *m.*

fly, *n,* mouche; (*trouser*) bra-guette, *f.* ~*blown,* piqué des mouches. ~*catcher* (bird), gobe-mouches, *m,* moucherolle, *f.* ~ *fishing,* pêche à la mouche, *f.* ~*leaf,* garde blanche, *f.* ~*paper,* papier tue-mouches, *m.* ~*speck,* chiure, *f.* ~ *swat*[*ter*], tue-mou-ches, *m.* ~*trap* (plant), gobe-mouches, *m.* ~*weight* (*Box.*), poids mouche, *m.* ~ *wheel,* vo-lant, *m.* ~ *whisk,* chasse-mou-ches, émouchoir, *m.* ¶ *v.i,ir,* vol-er, s'envoler; [s'en]fuir; déni-cher; éclater; sauter; jaillir; (*v.t.ir.*) fuir; (*flag*) battre; (*kite*) lancer. ~ *about,* voltiger. ~ *at,* s'élancer sur; sauter à; s. sur; apostropher; voler. ~ *open,* s'ouvrir en coup de vent. ~*ing, n,* vol, *m;* aviation, *f.* ~ *ace,* as de l'aviation, *m.* ~ *buttress,* arc-boutant, *m.* ~ *field,* champ d' aviation, *m.* ~ *fish,* poisson vol-ant, *m.* ~ *squad,* brigade (*de police*) mobile, *f.* ~ *start,* départ lancé, *m.* ~ *visit,* camp volant, *m.*

foal, *n,* poulain, *m,* pouliche, *f;* (*ass's*) ânon, *m.* ¶ *v.i,* pouliner; mettre bas.

foam, *n,* écume, mousse, *f.* ¶ *v.i,*

écumer, mousser; (sea) moutonner. ~y, a, écumeux, mousseux; (sea) moutonneuse.

focal, a, focal. **focus,** n, foyer, m.
¶ v.t, mettre au point; canaliser
(fig.).

fodder, n, fourrage, m, provende,
f.

foe, n, ennemi, e, adversaire, m.

fog, n, brouillard, m, brume, f;
(Phot.) voile, m. ~ dispersal, dénébulation, f. ~-dispersal device,
dénébulateur, m. ~ horn, trompe
de brume, f. ~ light, phare anti-
brouillard, m. ¶ v.t, embrumer;
(Phot.) voiler. **foggy,** a, brumeux.

fog[e]y, n, or old ~, croûton, m,
[vieille] ganache, [vieille] perruque, f. **fogyish,** a, encroûté.

foible, n, faible, m.

foil, n, (tinsel) feuille, f, clinquant; paillon; tain; (Fenc.)
fleuret; (fig.) repoussoir, lustre,
m. ¶ v.t, déjouer; dépister.

foist, v.t, glisser; colloquer; attribuer.

fold, n, pli, repli; parc, m, bergerie, f; (Relig.) bercail, m. ¶
v.t, plier; (arms) [se] croiser;
(hands) joindre; (sheep) parquer. ~ up, v.t, [re]plier; (v.i.)
se replier. ~er, n, plieur, euse;
chemise [pour dossier] f; (publicity) dépliant, m. ~ing, p.a:
~ door, porte brisée, f. ~ machine,
machine à plier, plieuse, f. ~
stool, pliant, m.

foliaceous, a, foliacé. **foliage,** n,
feuillage, m, frondaison, f, ombrage, m, chevelure, f. **foliate,** a,
feuillé. **foliation,** n, foliation,
feuillaison, frondaison, f.

folio, n, folio, m; (book) n. & a,
in-folio, m. & a. ¶ v.t, folioter.

folklore, n, folk-lore, m, tradition, f.

folks, n.pl, gens, m.pl. & f.pl.

follicle, n, follicule, m, crypte, f.

follow, v.t, suivre; (cards) fournir
de; (v.i.) s'ensuivre, résulter. ~
suit, (cards) fournir [à] la couleur demandée; (fig.) faire de
même. ~ through, suivre la balle.
~ up, [pour]suivre. ~ [shot]
(Bil.) n, coulé, m. ~er, n, suivant, e; disciple, partisan, sectateur, m; suite [de lettre] f. ~ing
(day, etc.) a, suivant. in the ~
manner, & voici comment. the
~ [persons], les personnes dont

les noms suivent. the ~ story,
l'histoire que voici. ¶ n, parti-
sans, m.pl.

folly, n, folie; sottise, bêtise, f.

foment, v.t, fomenter; étuver. ~
ation, n, fomentation, f.

fond†, a, tendre, affectueux. to be
~ of, aimer; affectionner; être
friand de, ê. gourmand de; ê.
porté pour; ê. amateur de.

fondle, v.t, caresser, câliner, pouponner.

fondness, n, affection, tendresse,
f; penchant, goût, m.

font, n, (Eccl.) fonts, m.pl; (Typ.)
fonte, f.

food, n, nourriture, f, aliment, m,
vivres, m.pl; mangeaille, f, mets,
m; table, cuisine; pâture, f. ~ &
drink, le boire & le manger. ~ for
thought, matière à réflexion, f. ~
stuff, matière d'alimentation,
denrée alimentaire, f. fast ~,
prêt-à-manger, m.

fool, n, sot, te; bête, f; imbécile,
m,f, idiot, e; plaisant, m; (Hist.,
court) fou, m. to play the ~, faire
l'imbécile, nigauder, niaiser. ~
hardiness, témérité, f. ~hardy,
téméraire. ¶ v.t, duper; jouer,
amuser. ~ [about], v.i, baguenauder. ~ery, n, farce, f, vains
propos, m.pl, pantalonnade, f,
calembredaines, f.pl, bouffonnerie, f; badinage, m, gaminerie,
f. ~ish†, a, sot bête, benêt. ~ish-
ness, n, folie, sottise, f. ~proof,
a, indéréglable.

foot, n, pied, m; patte; semelle;
base, f; bas, m; (Meas.) pied =
0.30480 meter. ~ mouth disease, fièvre aphteuse, f. ~ball,
ballon de football; (game) football, m. ~ bath, bain de pieds, m.
~bridge, passerelle, f. ~fall, pas,
m. ~ fault (Ten.), faute de pied,
f. ~hold, assiette pour le pied,
f, pied, m. ~lights, rampe, f.
~man, valet de pied, laquais, m.
~note, apostille, f. ~path, sentier, m, sente, f; (street) trottoir,
m. ~print, empreinte de pas, e.
du pied, f, pas, vestige, m; trace,
f. ~ race, course à pied, f. ~sore,
éclopé. ~step, pas, m. ~stool,
tabouret [de pied] m. ~ warmer,
chauffepieds, m, chaufferette,
bouillotte, f. ~wear, chaussures,
f.pl. ~ work, jeu de jambes, m.

on ~, à pied. **~ing**, *n*, pied, *m*; assiette pour le pied, *f*.

fop, *n*, fat, *m*. **foppish**, *a*, fat.

for, *pr*, pour; par; à; de; à cause de; pendant; il y a; depuis; malgré. ~ *all that*, malgré cela, malgré tout. ~ *& against*, le pour & le contre. ¶ *c*, car.

forage, *n*, fourrage, *m*. ¶ *v.i*, fourrager; (*bird*) picorer. **forager**, *n*, fourrageur, *m*.

forasmuch, *c*, étant donné.

foray, *n*, incursion, maraude, *f*.

forbear, *v.i.ir*, s'abstenir, s'empêcher. **~ance**, *n*, indulgence, longanimité, mansuétude, *f*.

forbid, *v.t.ir*, défendre, interdire. *God ~!* à Dieu ne plaise! **forbidden**, *a*, interdit. **forbidding**, *a*, rebutant, repoussant.

force, *n*, force, *f*; effort; effectif, *m*; armée, *f*. ~ *of circumstances*, force des choses. *by* ~, à main armée. *in* ~, en vigueur. ~ *pump*, pompe foulante, *f*. ¶ *v.t*, forcer; hâter; se frayer. **forced**, *p.a*, forcé; factice. *by* ~ *marches*, à grandes journées. **forcedly**, *ad*, forcément. **forceful**†, *a*, vigoureux. **forcemeat**, *n*, farce, *f*.

forceps, *n.s. & pl*, (*Surg.*) pince, *f*; (*dental*) davier; (*obstetrical*) forceps, *m*, fers, *m.pl*.

forcible, *a*, énergique, corsé. ~ *feeding*, gavage, *m*. **forcibly**, *ad*, énergiquement; de force.

ford, *n*, gué, *m*. ¶ *v.t*, guéer. **~able**, *a*, guéable.

fore, *a*, de devant, *e.g*, ~*paw*, patte de devant, *f*; (*Naut.*) de l'avant. ¶ *ad*, à l'avant. ~ *& aft*, de l'avant à l'arrière. ¶ (*golf*) *i*, attention!, hep!, balle! ¶ *n*, devant; (*Naut.*) avant, *m*.

forearm, *n*, avant-bras, *m*. ¶ *v.t*, prémunir.

forebode, *v.t*, présager. **foreboding**, *n*, présage, pressentiment, *m*.

forecast, *n*, prévision, *f*, pronostic, *m*. *weather* ~, prévision météorologique, *f*. ¶ *v.t*, pronostiquer, prédire.

forecastle *or* **foc's'le**, *n*, gaillard d'avant; poste de l'équipage, *m*.

foreclose, *v.t*, saisir. **foreclosure**, *n*, saisie, *f*.

forecourt, *n*, (*house*) cour de devant; (*castle*, *palace*), avant-cour, *f*.

forefathers, *n.pl*, aïeux, *m.pl*.

forefinger, *n*, index, *m*.

foregoing, *p.a*, précédent. *the* ~, ce qui précède. *foregone conclusion*, décision prise d'avance, *f*.

foreground, *n*, premier plan, *m*, devants, *m.pl*.

forehand [stroke] (*Ten.*) *n*, [coup d']avant-main, *m*.

forehead, *n*, front, *m*.

foreign, *a*, étranger; extérieur; exotique. ~ *exchange rates* (table), cote des changes, *f*. ~ *service*, service diplomatique, *m*. **~er**, *n*, étranger, ère.

foreknowledge, *n*, prescience, *f*.

foreland, *n*, cap, *m*, pointe [de terre] *f*.

forelock (*hair*) *n*, toupet, *m*.

foreman, *n*, contremaître, chef d'équipe, chef, *m*. ~ *of the jury*, chef du jury.

foremast, *n*, mât de misaine, *m*.

foremost (**the**), le plus avancé; le tout premier.

forenoon, *n*, matinée, *f*.

forensic, *a*, de palais; (*medicine*) légale.

forerunner, *n*, avant-coureur, précurseur, *m*, préface, *f*.

foresee, *v.t.ir*, prévoir.

foreshadow, *v.t*, annoncer.

foreshore, *n*, rivage, *m*.

foreshorten, *v.t*, raccourcir.

foresight, *n*, prévoyance, *f*.

forest, *n*, forêt, *f*; (*att.*) forestier.

forestall, *v.t*, anticiper; prévenir; devancer.

forester, *n*, (*officer*) forestier; habitant de la forêt, *m*. **forestry**, *n*, sylviculture, *f*.

foretaste, *n*, avant-goût, *m*.

foretell, *v.t.ir*, prédire, annoncer.

forethought, *n*, prévoyance; préméditation, *f*.

forewarn, *v.t*, prévenir, prémunir, avertir.

forewoman, *n*, première, *f*.

foreword, *n*, avant-propos, *m*, préface, *f*.

forfeit, *n*, dédit, *m*, pénalité, *f*; (*at play*) gage, *m*, pénitence, *f*; (*pl.*) gages, jeux innocents, petits jeux, *m.pl*. ¶ *v.t*, déchoir de; (*honor*) forfaire à. ~**ure**, *n*, perte; (*rights*) déchéance; forfaiture, *f*.

forgather, *v.i*, se réunir.

forge, *n*, forge, *f*. ¶ *v.t*, (*metal & fig.*) forger; falsifier, contrefaire. **~d**, *p.a*, faux. **forgeman**, *n*, forgeur, *m.* **forger,** *n,* faussaire, *m,f.* fabricateur, trice. **forgery,** *n,* faux; crime de faux, *m;* contrefaçon, *f.*

forget, *v.t.ir,* oublier. ~-me-not, ne m'oubliez pas, myosotis, *m,* oreille-de-souris, *f.* ~ oneself, s'échapper, s'émanciper. ~ful, *a,* oublieux. ~fulness, *n,* oubli, *m.*

forgive, *v.t.ir,* pardonner; (*pers.*) pardonner à; faire grâce à, remettre. ~ness, *n,* pardon, *m;* rémission; remise, *f.*

forgo, *v.t.ir,* s'abstenir de; renoncer à.

fork, *n,* fourche; (*table, etc.*) fourchette, *f;* (*tree*) fourchon, *m;* (*road, etc.*) bifurcation, *f.* tuning ~, diapason, *m.* ¶ *v.i,* fourcher, bifurquer. ~ed, *a,* fourchu. ~ lightning, éclair ramifié, *m.*

forlorn, *a,* délaissé; désolé, inconsolé. ~ hope, vague espoir, *m.*

form, *n,* forme, *f,* ton, *m;* (*paper*) formule, *f,* bulletin, *m;* (*seat*) banc; (*hare*) gîte, *m.* ¶ *v.t,* former; façonner; constituer; nouer; faire; se faire, se former. ~ single file, dédoubler les rangs. ~al†, *a,* formel; de forme; dans les formes; cérémonieux; solennel; formaliste. ~ality, *n,* formalité, *f.* ~ation, *n,* formation; constitution, *f.* **form** (*Typ.*) *n,* forme, *f.*

former, *a,* ancien; passé; précédent. the ~, celui-là. ~ly, *ad,* autrefois, jadis, anciennement, ci-devant.

formidable†, *a,* formidable.

Formosa, *n,* Formose, *f.*

formula, *n,* formule, *f.* ~ry, *n,* formulaire, *m.* **formulate,** *v.t,* formuler. **formulism,** *n,* le style pompier. **formulist,** *n. & ~ic,* *a,* pompier, *m. & att.*

fornication, *n,* fornication, *f.*

forsake, *v.t.ir,* délaisser, abandonner.

forsooth, *ad,* en vérité, ma foi.

forswear, *v.t.ir,* abjurer. ~ oneself, se parjurer.

fort, *n,* fort, (*small*) fortin, *m.* **forte** (*Mus.*) *ad,* forte. ¶ (*strong point*) *n,* fort, *m.*

forth, *ad,* en avant. ~coming, *a,* [prêt] à paraître; à venir; prochain. ~with, *ad,* incessamment, sur-le-champ, séance tenante.

fortieth, *a. & n,* quarantième, *a. & m,f.*

fortification, *n,* fortification, *f.* (*wine*) vinage, *m.* **fortify,** *v.t,* fortifier; munir; corser; viner. *fortified place,* place forte, p. de guerre, *f.* **fortitude,** *n,* force d'âme, *f,* courage, *m.*

fortnight, *n,* quinze jours, *m.pl,* quinzaine, *f.* ~ly, *ad,* tous les quinze jours.

fortress, *n,* forteresse, *f.*

fortuitous†, *a,* fortuit.

fortunate, *a,* heureux, fortuné. ~ly, *ad,* heureusement, par bonheur. **fortune,** *n,* fortune, *f;* horoscope, *m.* to tell ~s, dire la bonne aventure. ~teller, diseur (euse) de bonne aventure; tireur (euse) de cartes, cartomancien, ne.

forty, *a. & n,* quarante, *a. & m.*

forum, *n,* forum, *m.*

forward, *a,* avancé; d'avance; avant; progressif; précoce, hâtif; hardi, indiscret; (*Com.*) à terme, à livrer. ~[s], *ad,* [en] avant. ¶ *n,* (*Foot.*) avant, *m.* ¶ *v.t,* avancer; hâter; expédier; acheminer; faire suivre, transmettre. ~ing agent, commissionnaire de transport[s], expéditeur, *m.* ~ness, *n,* précocité; hardiesse, *f.*

fossil, *a. & n,* fossile, *a. & m.*

foster, *v.t,* encourager; favoriser; nourrir. ¶ *a,* adoptif. ~ brother, frère de lait, *m.* ~ child, nourrisson, *m.*

foul, *a,* sale; crasseux; immonde; mauvais, vilain; infect; vicié; fétide; puant; infâme; (*words*) gros. ~mouthed, mal embouché. ~ play, vilain tour; sabotage, *m.* ¶ *n,* faute, *f;* coup déloyal, *m.* ¶ *v.t,* salir, souiller, encrasser; vicier; fausser; (*Naut., rope, etc.*) engager; (*ship*) entrer en collision; (*sports*) violer la règle. ~ness, *n,* fétidité; noirceur, *f.*

found, *v.t,* fonder, créer; (*metal*) fondre, mouler. **foundation,** *n,* fondation, *f;* fondement; établissement, *m;* assiette; assise, *f.* ~ stone, pierre fondamentale, première p., *f.* **founder,** *n,* fondateur, créateur; (*race*) auteur, *m;* (*family*) souche, *f;* (*metal*) fondeur, *m.* ¶ *v.i,* sombrer, couler, c. à fond, c. à pic, c. bas.

foundling, *n,* enfant trouvé, *m.*

foundress, *n,* fondatrice, créatrice, *f.*

foundry, *n,* fonderie, *f.*

fount, *n,* fontaine, *f;* puits; *m;*

(*Typ.*) fonte, *f.* **fountain,** *n,* fontaine, source, *f;* jet d'eau, *m;* (*pl.*) [grandes] eaux, *f.pl.* ~**head,** source, *f.* ~ *of youth,* fontaine de Jouvence. ~ *pen,* stylographe, porte-plume [à] réservoir, *m.*

four, *a.* & *n,* quatre, *a.* & *m.* ~**fold,** quadruple. ~**footed,** quadrupède. ~**poster,** lit à colonnes, *m.* ~**score,** *a.* & *n,* quatre-vingts, quatre-vingt, *a.* & *m.* ~**some** (*golf*), partie double, *f.* ~**wheeled,** à quatre roues. *on all* ~**s,** à quatre pattes. **fourteen,** *a.* & *n,* quatorze, *a.* & *m.* ~**th†,** *a.* & *n,* quatorzième, *a.* & *m,f;* quatorze, *m.* **fourth†,** *a,* quatrième. ~ *finger,* petit doigt, [doigt] auriculaire, *m.* ¶ *n,* quatrième, *m,f;* quatre, *m;* (*part*) quart, *m;* (*Mus.*) quatre, *f.*

fowl, *n,* oiseau; o. de basse-cour, *m;* volaille; poule; poularde, *f.* ~**er,** *n,* oiseleur, *m.* ~**ing,** *n,* chasse aux oiseaux, *f.* ~ *piece,* canardière, *f.*

fox, *n,* renard, *m.* ~ *cub,* renardeau, *m.* ~*'s hole,* renardière, *f.* ~**glove,** gantelée, digitale, *f.* ~**hound,** foxhound, *m.* ~ *hunting,* chasse au renard, *f.* ~ *terrier,* fox-terrier, *m.* ~*-trot,* fox-trot, *m.* ~**y** (*fig.*) *a,* rusé.

foyer, *n,* foyer [du public] *m.*

fraction, *n,* fraction, *f.* ~**al,** *a,* fractionnaire.

fractious, *a,* hargneux.

fracture, *n,* fracture; cassure, rupture, *f.* ¶ *v.t,* fracturer.

fragile, *a,* fragile. **fragility,** *n,* fragilité, *f.*

fragment, *n,* fragment, morceau, éclat, *m.* ~**ary,** *a,* fragmentaire.

fragrance, *n,* bonne odeur, *f,* parfum, *m.* **fragrant,** *a,* odoriférant, odorant.

frail, *a,* frêle; fragile; caduc. ¶ *n,* cabas, *m;* bourriche, *f.* ~**ty,** *n,* fragilité; infirmité, *f.*

frame & ~**work,** *n,* cadre; bâti; châssis, *m;* charpente; membrure; ossature; carcasse; armature; monture; châsse, *f;* pan, *m;* case, *f;* (*Need.*) métier, *m.* ~ *of mind,* état d'esprit, *m,* disposition, *f.* ¶ *v.t,* former; charpenter; (*picture, etc.*) encadrer; (*cinema*) cadrer. **framing** (*act*) *n,* encadrement, *m;* (*cinema*) cadrage, *m.*

France, *n,* la France.

franchise, *n,* droit électoral, électorat, *m.*

Franciscan, *n,* franciscain, *m.*

Francophil[e], *a.* & *n,* francophile, *a.* & *m,f.* **Francophobe,** *a.* & *n,* francophobe, *a.* & *m,f.*

frank†, *a,* franc, ouvert, en dehors. ~**ness,** *n,* franchise, rondeur, *f.*

Frankfort, *n,* Francfort, *m.*

frankfurter, *n,* saucisse, *f.*

frankincense, *n,* encens mâle, *m.*

frantic†, *a,* frénétique; effréné, fou.

fraternal†, *a,* fraternel. **fraternity,** *n,* fraternité, *f.* **fraternize,** *v.i,* fraterniser. **fratricide,** *n,* & **fratricidal,** *a,* fratricide, *m.* & *a.*

fraud, *n,* fraude; supercherie, *f.* **fraudulent†,** *a,* frauduleux.

fraught with, plein de, gros de.

fray, *n,* lutte, rixe, bagarre; bataille, *f.*

fray, *v.t,* érailler, effranger, effilocher.

freak, *n,* caprice, *m.* ~ [*of nature*], monstruosité, *f,* jeu [bizarre] de la nature, phénomène, *m.* ~**ish†,** *a,* capricieux; bizarre; hétéroclite; monstrueux.

freckle, *n,* tache de rousseur, lentille, éphélide, *f.* ¶ *v.t,* tacheter de rousseurs.

free, *a,* libre; ouvert; large; débarrassé; dépourvu; exempt; privé; gratuit; net; indépendant; quitte; dégagé, désinvolte. ~ *allowance of luggage* or *weight allowed* ~, franchise de bagages, *f.* de poids, *f.* ~ *& easy,* sans gêne, bohème, cavalier. ~ *& easy manner,* désinvolture, *f.* ~ *hand* (*fig.*), carte blanche, *f.* ~*hand drawing,* dessin à main levée, *m.* ~ *lance,* franc-tireur, tirailleur, *m.* ~*mason,* franc-maçon, *m.* ~ *pass,* billet de faveur; (*Rly*) permis de circulation, *m.* ~*stone,* pierre franche, *f.* ~*thinker,* libre penseur, esprit fort, *m.* ~*thinking,* ~ *thought,* libre pensée, *f.* ~ *trade,* libre-échange, *m.* ~*trader,* abolitioniste, *m.* ~ *verse,* vers libres, *m.pl.* ~ *wheel,* roue libre, *f.* ~ *will,* [plein] gré, *f.* (*Philos.*) libre (*ou* franc) arbitre, *m.* ¶ *ad,* gratis; gracieusement; franco; en franchise. ¶ *v.t,* libérer, affranchir; dégager; exempter. **freedom**, *n*, liberté; exemption; franchise; aisance, *f*. *free[dom of] speech*, libre parole, liberté de parler, *f*. **freely**, *ad*, librement; franchement; largement.

freeway, *n*, autoroute, *f*.

freeze, *v.t.ir*, geler, glacer, congeler, réfrigérer; (*v.i.ir*.) geler; se g., [se] glacer, prendre. ¶ *n*, (*diplomacy*) gel, *m*; (*price &/or wage*) blocage, *m*. **freezer**, *n*, glacière; sorbetière, *f*. *freezing point*, température de congélation, *f*. (*thermometer*) *at freezing*, à glace.

freeze-dry, *v.t*, lyophiliser.

Freiburg (*Baden*) *n*, Fribourg-en-Brisgau, *m*.

freight, *n*, fret, *m*. ~ *train*, train de marchandises, *m*. ¶ *v.t*, fréter.

French, *a*, français. ~ *ambassador*, *consul*, ambassadeur, consul, de France, *m*. ~ *chalk*, talc, *m*. ~ *fries*, frites, *f.pl*. ~ *horn*, cor d'harmonie, *m*. *to take ~ leave*, filer à l'anglaise. ~ *lesson*, *master*, leçon, *f*, professeur, *m*, de français. ~ *man*, ~ *woman*, Français, e. ~ *polish*, *n*, vernis au tampon, *m*; (*v.t.*) vernir au t. ~ *speaking Switzerland*, la Suisse romande. ~ *window*, porte-fenêtre, *f*. ¶ (*language*) *n*, le français. the ~, *pl*, les Français, *m.pl*. **Frenchify**, *v.t*, franciser.

frenzied, *p.p*, frénétique; délirant. **frenzy**, *n*, frénésie, fureur, ivresse, *f*.

frequency, *n*, fréquence, *f*. **frequent**, *a*, fréquent. ¶ *v.t*, fréquenter, pratiquer, hanter, courir. ~**er**, *n*, habitué, e, coureur, euse. ~**ly**, *ad*, fréquemment.

fresco, *n*, fresque, *f*.

fresh, *a*, frais; récent; vert; reposé; nouveau; novice. ~ *from the wash*, blanc de lessive. ~ *water*, eau fraîche; (*not salt*) e. douce, *f*. ~ *water fishing*, pêche en eaux douces, p. d'eau douce, *f*. ~**en**, *v.t. & i*, rafraîchir; (*Naut*.) fraîchir. ~**et**, *n*, crue, *f*, grandes eaux, *f.pl*. ~**ly** & ~, *ad*, fraîchement; (*with p.p.*) frais, aîche, *e.g. fresh[ly] gathered roses*, des roses fraîches cueillies. ~**ness**, *n*, fraîcheur; nouveauté; primeur, *f*.

fret, *n*, (*on guitar*) touche; (*Arch*., *Her*.) frette, *f*. ~ *saw*, *n*, scie à découper, *f*; (*v.t. & i.*) découper. ~ *work*, découpure, *f*. ¶ *v.i*, s'irriter, se chagriner, geindre; (*v.t.*) ronger; chagriner, tracasser. ~**ful**, *a*, chagrin, geignard.

friable, *a*, friable.

friar, *n*, moine, frère, religieux, *m*.

friction, *n*, friction, *f*, frottement, *m*.

Friday, *n*, vendredi, *m*. *Good ~*, vendredi saint.

fried fish, poisson frit, *m*, friture, *f*.

friend, *n*, ami, e; cousin, e. ~**less**, *a*, sans ami. ~**liness**, *n*, bienveillance, *f*. ~**ly**, *a*, ami, amical, amiable. ~**ship**, *n*, amitié, camaraderie, *f*.

Friesland, *n*, la Frise.

frieze, *n*, frise, *f*.

frigate, *n*, frégate, *f*.

fright, *n*, frayeur, épouvante, peur, *f*, effroi, *m*, transe, *f*; (*pers*.) horreur, *f*, magot, *m*. ~**en**, *v.t*, effrayer, épouvanter. ~**ful**, *a*, effrayant, épouvantable, affreux.

frigid†, *a*, glacial, froid. ~**ity**, *n*, frigidité, froideur, *f*.

frill, *n*, ruche, *f*; jabot, *m*. ~**s** & *furbelows*, fanfreluches, *f.pl*. ¶ *v.t*, rucher.

fringe, *n*, frange, crépine, *f*, effilé; bord, *m*. ¶ *v.t*, franger; border.

frippery, *n*, friperie, *f*, falbalas, colifichets, *m.pl*.

Frisian, *a*, frison. ¶ *n*, Frison, ne.

frisk, *n*, gambade, *f*. ¶ *v.i*, gambader, fringuer, frétiller; (*search*) palper.

frisky, *a*, frétillant, fringant.

fritter (*Cook*.) *n*, beignet, *m*. ~ *away*, éparpiller, dissiper, fricasser.

frivolity, *n*, frivolité, *f*. **frivolous**, *a*, frivole, léger.

frizzle, *v.t*, crêper, friser. **frizzle** (*bacon, etc.*) *v.t*, faire se recoquiller.

frock, *n*, robe, *f*, costume, *m*; (*smock*) blouse, *f*; (*monk's*) froc, *m*. ~ *coat*, redingote, *f*.

frog, *n*, grenouille; (*horse*) fourchette, *f*; (*Rly*) croisement; (*sword*) porte-épée, pendant, *m*.

frolic, *v.i*, folâtrer. ~**some**, *a*, follet.

from, *pr*, de; d'avec; de chez; depuis; dès; à; d'après; à partir de;

à dater de; de la part de; par. ~ *that point of view*, à ce point de vue. ~ *what you do*, d'après ce que vous faites. ~ *the beginning*, dès le commencement. *the train ~ Paris*, le train de Paris.

frond, *n*, fronde, *f*.

front, *a*, de devant; d'avant; de front; de tête; de face; premier. ~ *[line]* (*Mil.*), front, *m*, première ligne, *f*. ¶ *n*, devant; avant, *m*, tête; devanture; face; façade, *f*; front; recto, *m*; (*shirt*) plastron, *m*. *in ~ & in ~ of*, devant. *on the [sea] ~*, en bordure de la mer; sur la promenade [de la mer]; (*hotel*) sur la mer. ¶ *v.t*, affronter, faire face à; donner sur; ~**age**, *n*, devant, *m*; (*extent*) face; façade; exposition, *f*. ~**al**, *a*, de front; (*Anat.*) frontal.

frontier, *n. & att*, frontière, *f. & att*.

frontispiece, *n*, (*book*) frontispice, *m*; (*Arch.*) façade, *f*.

frost, *n*, gelée, *f*; (*degrees of*) froid, *m*; (*fig., of age*) glaces, *f.pl*. ~**bite**, congélation, *f*. ~**bitten**, gelé. ~**ed glass**, verre dépoli, *m*. ~**y**, *a*, glacial, de glace.

froth, *n*, écume; mousse, *f*. ¶ *v.i*, écumer; mousser. ~**y**, *a*, écumant; mousseux; frivole.

frown, *n*, froncement des sourcils, *m*. ¶ *v.i*, froncer le[s] sourcil[s], sourciller, se re[n]frogner. ~ *[up]on*, regarder d'un mauvais œil, désapprouver.

frowzy, *a*, moisi; borgne.

frozen, *p.a*, gelé, glacé; glacial; (*meat, etc.*) frigorifié; (*credit*) gelé. *[as if] ~ stiff*, morfondu.

fructify, *v.i*, fructifier; (*v.t.*) féconder.

frugal†, *a*, frugal. ~**ity**, *n*, frugalité, *f*.

fruit, *n*, fruit, *m*. ~ *bowl*, coupe à fruits, *f*, compotier, *m*. ~ *salad*, macédoine de fruits, salade de f—s, *f*. ~ *store*, fruiterie, *f*. ~ *tree*, arbre fruitier, a. à fruit, *m*. **fruitful†**, *a*, fertile, fécond; fructueux (*fig. & poet.*). ~**ness**, *n*, fertilité, fécondité, *f*. **fruition**, *n*, jouissance; réalisation, *f*. **fruitless**, *a*, sans fruit; (*fig.*) infructueux; vain. ~**ly**, *ad*, en vain.

frump, *n*, femme mal fagotée, *f*.

frustrate, *v.t*, frustrer, déjouer. **frustration**, *n*, insuccès, renversement, *m*.

frustum, *n*, tronc, *m*.

fry, *n*, (*fish*) fretin, frai, alevin, nourrain, *m*, poissonnaille, blanchaille; (*Cook.*) friture, *f*. *French fries*, pommes frites, *f.pl*. ¶ *v.t*, [faire] frire; (*v.i.*) frire. ~**ing**, *n*, & ~ *oil* or *fat*, friture, *f*. ~ *pan*, poêle [à frire] *f*.

fuchsia, *n*, fuchsia, *m*.

fuddle, *v.t*, griser. ~**d**, *p.a*, gris.

fuel, *n*, combustible, *f*; (*fig.*) aliment, *m*. ~ *oil*, pétrole combustible, *m*. ¶ *v.t*, alimenter; chauffer.

fugitive, *a*, fugitif, passager. ¶ *n*, fugitif, ive, fuyard, e.

fugleman, *n*, chef de file; meneur; porteparole, *m*.

fugue, *n*, fugue, *f*.

fulcrum, *n*, [point d']appui, *m*.

fulfil, *v.t*, remplir, accomplir; satisfaire à, exécuter. ~**ment**, *f*, accomplissement, *m*, exécution, *f*.

full, *a*, plein; comble; rempli; complet; au complet; entier; plénier; tout; copieux; nourri; intégral; germain. ~**blooded**, sanguin. ~**bodied** (*wine*), vineux, corsé. ~ *dress*, grande tenue, tenue de cérémonie; grande toilette, *f*. ~**grown**, fait. ~**length mirror**, psyché, *f*. ~**length portrait**, portrait en pied, *m*. ~ *name*, (*pers.*) nom & prénoms; (*stock, etc.*) désignation détaillée, *f*. ~ *of fish* (*river, lake*), poissonneux. ~ *orchestra*, grand orchestre, *m*. ~**page illustration**, gravure en pleine page, *f*. ~ *size*, grandeur naturelle, *f*. *I am ~*, je suis rassasié. *in ~*, in extenso. *Also = fully*. ¶ *n*, plein, *m*.

full, *v.t*, fouler. ~**er**, *n*, foulon, *m*. ~**'s earth**, terre à foulon, *f*.

fully, *ad*, pleinement; complètement; entièrement; intégralement; bien; en toutes lettres.

fulminate, *v.i. & t*, fulminer.

fullness, *n*, plénitude; ampleur; rondeur, abondance, *f*. **fulsome**, *a*, outré, excessif, exagéré, écœurant.

fumble, *v.i*, [far]fouiller, tâtonner.

fume, *n*, fumée, vapeur, bouffée, buée; colère, *f*. ¶ *v.i. & t*, fumer; enrager, maugréer. ~**d** (*oak*), a, patiné, teinté.

fumigate, *v.t*, faire des fumigations dans.

fun, *n*, amusement, *m*; plaisanterie, drôlerie, *f*. *in ~*, pour rire. *to make ~ of*, se moquer de, se divertir aux dépens de.

function, *n,* fonction, *f,* office, *m;* réunion, *f.* ¶ *v.i,* fonctionner; opérer. ~**al,** *a,* fonctionnel. ~**ary,** *n,* fonctionnaire, *m,f.*

fund, *n,* fonds, *m,* caisse, masse *f;* (*pl.*) fonds, deniers, *m.pl,* fonds, *m,* masse, provision, *f.* **sinking** ~, caisse d'amortissement, *f.* ¶ *v.t.,* consolider.

fundament, *n,* fondement, *m.* —**al**†, *a,* fondamental, foncier.

funeral, *n,* enterrement, *m;* (*elaborate*) funérailles, *f. pl;* convoi, *m,* pompe funèbre, *f.* ¶ *a,* funéraire; funèbre. ~ *oration,* oraison funèbre, *f.* **funereal,** *a,* funèbre, d'enterrement.

fungous, *a,* fongueux; transitoire.

fungus, *n,* fongus; champignon [vénéneux] *m.*

funicular, *a. & n,* funiculaire, *a. & m.*

funnel, *n,* entonnoir, *m;* (*Naut.*) cheminée, *f.*

funny, *a,* comique, drôle, plaisant. ~ *bone,* petit juif, *m.* ~ *little* (*pers.*), falot, *a.* ~ *man,* comique de la troupe, loustic, *m.* a ~ (*queer*) *man,* un drôle. *the* ~ *part,* le comique.

fur, *n,* fourrure, *f,* poil; pelage; dépôt, tartre, *m,* incrustation, *f.* ~ *coat,* manteau de fourrure, *m.* ~**-lined,** fourré. ~ *lining,* fourrage, *m.* ~ *trade,* pelleterie, *f.*

furbelows, *n.pl,* falbalas, *m.pl.*

furbish, *v.t,* fourbir.

furious†, *a,* furieux, acharné.

furl, *v.t,* serrer, ferler.

furlong, *n,* furlong, *m.* = ⅛ mile or 201.168 meters.

furlough, *n,* (*Mil.*) permission, *f.*

furnace, *n,* four; fourneau; foyer, *m;* fournaise, *f. blast* ~, haut fourneau, *m.*

furnish, *v.t,* fournir; pourvoir; garnir; meubler. ~*ed apartments* or *rooms,* [appartement] meublé, hôtel meublé, *m.* **furniture,** *n,* meubles, *m.pl;* ameublement, mobilier, *m;* garniture, *f,* accessoires, *m.pl.* ~ *polish,* encaustique pour meubles, *f.* ~ *warehouse,* garde-meuble, *m.*

furore, *n,* fureur, *f.*

furred (*tongue*) *p.a,* chargée.

furier, *n,* fourreur, pelletier, *m.* ~**y,** *n,* pelleterie, *f.*

furrow, *n,* sillon, *m.* ¶ *v.t,* sillonner; raviner.

furry, *a,* à fourrure; (*tongue*) chargée.

further, *a,* supplémentaire, nouveau; plus éloigné. ¶ *ad,* plus loin; au-delà; [plus] en delà; [en] outre, de plus; encore, davantage. ¶ *v.t,* avancer, seconder. ~**ance,** *n,* avancement, *m.* ~**more,** *ad,* de plus, d'ailleurs, en outre. **furthest,** *a,* le plus éloigné. ¶ *ad,* le plus loin.

furtive†, *a,* furtif.

fury, *n,* furie, fureur, *f,* acharnement, *m;* (*pers.*) furie, forcenée, *f.* **F~** (*Myth.*), Furie, *f.*

furze, *n,* ajonc, genêt épineux, *m.*

fuse, *n,* fusée; mèche; étoupille, *f;* (*Elec.*) plomb [fusible] *m. to blow a* ~, faire sauter un plomb. ¶ *v.t. & i,* fondre.

fusee (*Horol.*) *n,* fusée, *f.*

fuselage, *n,* fuselage, *m.*

fusible, *a,* fusible.

fusillade, *n,* fusillade, *f.*

fusion, *n,* fusion, *f.*

fuss, *n,* bruit, tapage, *m,* cérémonies, façons, histoires, *f. pl.* ¶ *v.i,* tatillonner, faire des histoires. ~**y,** *a,* façonnier, difficultueux.

fustian, *n,* futaine; (*fig.*) emphase, *f,* phébus, *m.*

fusty, *a,* qui sent le renfermé; moisi.

futile, *a,* futile. **futility,** *n,* futilité, *f.*

future, *a,* futur; d'avenir; à venir; (*Com.*) à terme. ¶ *n,* avenir, futur; (*pl., Com.*) livrable, *m.* ~ [*tense*], futur [simple] *m.* ~ *perfect,* futur antérieur. **futurity,** *n,* futur, *m.*

fuzzy, *a,* (*hair*) crépu; (*image*) flou.

G

G (*Mus.*) letter, sol, *m.* ~ *clef,* clef de sol, *f.*

gabble, *v.t,* débiter trop vite; (*v.i.*) caqueter, babiller.

gable, *n,* pignon, *m.* ~ *roof,* comble sur pignon(s), *m.*

gad about, courir çà & là, c. la pretentaine. **gadabout,** *n,* coureur, euse.

gadfly, *n,* œstre, taon, *m.*

gadget, *n,* machine, *f,* truc, bidule, gadget, *m.*

gaff, *n,* (*spear*) gaffe; (*spar*) corne, *f.*

gag, *n,* bâillon, *m; (actor's)* scie, cascade, *f,* ¶ *v.t,* bâillonner.

gage, *n,* gage, *m;* assurance, *f.* See also *gauge.*

gaiety, *n,* gaieté, joie; gaillardise, *f.* **gaily,** *ad,* gaiement.

gain, *n,* gain, *m.* ¶ *v.t,* gagner; remporter; valoir; *(v.i.)* profiter; *(clock)* avancer. ~ *admittance,* s'introduire. *to be the gainer (by),* gagner *(à).*

gainsay, *v.t,* contredire, disconvenir de.

gait, *n,* démarche, allure, *f,* pas, *m.*

gaiter, *n,* guêtre, *f.*

gala, *n,* gala, *m; (att., day, night, dress, performance)* de gala. ~ *night,* soirée de gala, *f.*

galaxy, *n,* (Astr.) voie lactée; *(fig.)* constellation, *f.*

gale, *n,* coup de vent, *m.*

gall, *n,* fiel; amer, *m;* écorchure, *f.* ~*bladder,* vésicule biliaire, *f.* ~ *[nut],* [noix de] galle, *f.* ¶ *v.t,* écorcher, blesser.

gallant, *a,* vaillant, brave; *(to women)* galant. ¶ *n,* galant, *m.* ~**ly,** *ad,* vaillamment; galamment. ~**ry,** *n,* vaillance; galanterie, *f.*

galleon *(Hist.) n,* galion, *m.*

gallery, *n,* galerie; tribune, *f;* *(Theat.)* troisièmes [galeries], dernières galeries, *f.pl,* poulailler, paradis, *m.*

galley, *n, (boat)* galère; *(cook's)* cuisine; *(Typ.)* galée, *f.* ~ *[proof],* épreuve en placard, *f.* ~ *slave,* galérien, *m.*

Gallic, *a,* gaulois. **Gallican,** *a.* & *n,* gallican, e. **gallicism,** *n,* gallicisme, *m.* **gallicize,** *v.t,* franciser.

gallipot, *n,* pot de faïence, *m.*

gallon, *n,* gallon, *m.*

gallop, *n,* galop, *m.* ¶ *v.i,* galoper. ~*ing consumption,* phtisie galopante, *f.*

Gallophile, *a.* & *n,* francophile, *a.* & *m,f.* **Gallophobe,** *a.* & *n,* gallophobe, *a.* & *m,f.*

gallows, *n.pl.* & *s,* potence, *f,* gibet. ~ *bird,* gibier de potence, *m,* pendard, e.

galop *(dance) n,* galop, *m.*

galore, *ad,* à foison.

galosh, *n,* caoutchouc, *m.*

galvanic, *a,* galvanique. **galvanism,** *n,* galvanisme, *m.* **galvanize,** *v.t,* galvaniser.

Gambia, *n,* la Gambie.

gambit, *n,* gambit, *m.*

gamble, *n,* spéculation de hasard, *f.* ¶ *v.i,* jouer, agioter. ~ *away,* perdre au jeu. **gambler,** *n,* joueur, euse; agioteur, m. **gambling,** *n,* jeu[x], *m.[pl.];* agiotage, *m.* ~ *den,* tripot, *m.*

gamboge, *n,* gomme-gutte, *f.*

gambol, *n,* gambade, *f.* ¶ *v.i,* gambader.

game, *n,* jeu, *m;* partie; *(dodge)* ficelle, *f;* *(Hunt.)* gibier, *m.* ~ *bag,* carnassière, *f,* carnier, *m,* gibecière, *f.* ~ *cock,* coq de combat, *m.* ~*keeper,* garde-chasse, *m.* ~ *of skill,* jeu d'adresse, *m.* ¶ *a,* courageux; prêt; sportif. ~ *fishing,* pêche sportive, *f.* *to have a* ~ *leg,* être estropié de la jambe. ¶ *v.i,* jouer. ~*ster, n,* joueur, euse. **gaming,** *n,* jeu. *m.* ~ *house,* maison de j., *f.* ~ *table,* table de j., *f,* tapis vert, *m.*

gamut, *n,* gamme, *f.*

gamy, *a,* giboyeux; *(Cook.)* faisandé.

gander, *n,* jars, *m.*

gang, *n,* bande; brigade, équipe, *f.*

Ganges (the), le Gange.

ganglion, *n,* ganglion, *m.*

gangrene, *n,* gangrène, *f.* ¶ *v.t,* gangrener.

gangster, *n,* bandit, gangster, *m.*

gangue, *n,* gangue, matrice, *f.*

gangway, *n,* passage; pourtour; *(on ship)* passavant, *m;* *(to shore)* passerelle, *f.*

gannet, *n,* fou [de Bassan] *m.*

gantry, *n,* portique; beffroi, *m.*

gap, *n,* brèche, trouée, ouverture, *f,* intervalle, vide, *m,* lacune, *f.*

gape, *v.i,* bâiller. ~ *[at the moon],* bayer aux corneilles. **gaper,** *n,* gobe-mouches, *m,* badaud, e.

garage, *n,* garage, *m.* ~ *space,* box, *m.* ¶ *v.t,* garer.

garb, *n,* costume, habit, accoutrement, *m.*

garbage, *n,* rebuts, *m.pl;* ordures, *f.pl.* ~ *can,* poubelle, *f.*

garble, *v.t,* altérer, tronquer.

garden, *n,* jardin; *(small)* jardinet, *m.* ~ *flower,* fleur de jardin, *f.* ~ *hose,* tuyau d'arrosage, *m.* ~ *mint,* menthe verte, *f.* *the G*~ *of Eden,* Éden, *m,* le paradis [terrestre]. ~ *party,* garden-party, *f.* ~ *plant,* plante jardinière, *f.* ~ *plots,* jardinage, *m.* ~ *tools,* outils de jardinage, *m.* ¶ *v.i,* jardiner. ~**er,** *n,* jardinier, ère.

gardenia, *n,* gardénia, *m.*

gardening, n, jardinage, m, horticulture, f.

garfish, n, orphie, f.

gargle, n, gargarisme, m. ¶ v.i, se gargariser.

gargoyle, n, gargouille, f.

garish, a, éblouissant; voyant, tapageur, cru.

garland, n, guirlande, f.

garlic, n, ail, m.

garment, n, vêtement, m.

garner, n, grenier, m. ¶ v.t, engranger; rassembler.

garnet, n, grenat, m.

garnish, n, garniture, f. ¶ v.t, garnir

garret, n, mansarde, f.

garrison, n, garnison, f. ~artillery, artillerie de place, f.

garrulous, a, bavard, loquace.

garter, n, jarretière, f. ~ belt, porte-jarretelles, m.

gas, n, gaz, m; (gasoline) essence, f. ~ burner, bec de gaz, m. ~ lighting, éclairage au gaz, m. ~ man, employé du gaz, m. ~ mask, (war) masque à g.; (fire) casque respiratoire, m. ~ meter, compteur à gaz, m. ~ pipe, tuyau de g., m. ~ shell, obus à g., m. ~ station attendant, pompiste, m. ~ works, usine à gaz, f. tear ~, gaz lacrymogène, m. ¶ v.t, asphyxier; (war) gazer. ~eous, a, gazeux.

gash, n, balafre, estafilade, f. ¶ v.t, balafrer.

gasket, n, garcette, f, raban, m; tresse; garniture, f.

gasogene, n, gazogène, m. **gasometer,** n, gazomètre, m.

gasoline, n, essence, f.

gasp, n, halètement; souffle coupé; hoquet, m. to ~ for breath, haleter.

gassy, a, gazeux; verbeux.

gastropod, n, gastéropode, m. **gastric,** a, gastrique. **gastritis,** n, gastrite, f. **gastronome,** m. **gastronomic(al),** a, gastronomique. **gastronomy,** n, gastronomie, f.

gate, n, porte; barrière; (sluice) vanne, f. ~-crasher, resquilleur, euse. ~-crashing, resquille, f. ~-keeper, portier, ère; (level crossing) garde-barrière, m,f. ~-money, recette, f. ~way, porte, f.

gather, n, fronce, f. ¶ v.t, [r]assembler; [r]amasser; [re]cueillir;

récolter; vendanger; inférer; (Need.) froncer. ~er, n, ramasseur, euse. ~ing, n, rassemblement, m; accumulation; cueillette; réunion, f; (Med.) mal blanc, abcès, m.

gating (Hyd.) n, vannage, m.

gaudy, a, fastueux, voyant, tapageur.

gauge, n, calibre, m; jauge, f; gabarit; (Rly. track) écartement, m, voie, largeur, f; manomètre; indicateur, m. ¶ v.t, calibrer; jauger; cuber.

gaunt, a, décharné, sec.

gauntlet, n, gantelet, f; (fig.) gant, m.

gauze, n, gaze; toile, f, tissu, tamis, m. **gauzy,** a, vaporeux.

gavotte, n, gavotte, f.

gawky, a, dégingandé.

gay, a, gai.

gaze, n, regard, m. to ~ at, contempler, couver des yeux.

gazelle, n, gazelle, f.

gazette, n, gazette, f, journal, m; journal officiel; moniteur, m.

gazetteer, n, dictionnaire géographique, m.

gear, n, appareil[s] m.[pl.]; engins; organes; agrès, m.pl; mécanisme; dispositif; harnais, m; armature, f; gréement, m; (toothed) engrenage[s] m.[pl.]; (ratio) multiplication, f; (bicycle) développement, m. ~ box, boîte à engrenages; boîte de changement de vitesse, f. ~ case, carter; couvre-engrenages, m. ~ ratio, multiplication, f. ~-shift, changement de vitesse, m. ~ wheel, roue d'engrenage, f. ¶ v.t, engrener.

gee-gee, n, dada, m. **gee up,** i, hue!

gehenna, n, géhenne, f.

gelatin, n, gélatine, f. **gelatinous,** a, gélatineux.

geld, v.t, châtrer, hongrer. ~ing, n, castration, f; [cheval] hongre, m.

gem, n, pierre précieuse, [pierre] gemme, f; bijou, m; (pl.) pierreries, f.pl.

gender, n, genre, m.

genealogical, a, généalogique. **genealogy,** n, généalogie, f.

general, a, général, d'ensemble; commun; collectif. ~ effect, ensemble, m. ~ expenses, frais divers, m.pl. ~ post office, hôtel des postes, *m. the ~ public*, le grand public. *to become ~*, se généraliser. ¶ *n*, général en chef, chef, *m.* ~*ity*, *n*, généralité; plupart, *f.* ~*ize*, *v.t.* & *i*, généraliser. ~*ly*, *ad*, généralement; communément. ~*ship*, *n*, généralat, *m*; stratégie, *f.*

generate, *v.t*, engendrer; produire. **generating**, *p.a*, générateur. **generation**, *n*, génération, *f.* **generator**, *n*, générateur, *m.*

generic, *a*, générique.

generosity, *n*, générosité, *f.* **generous**†, *a*, généreux, donnant.

genesis, *n*, genèse, *f.* **G~** (*Bible*), la Genèse.

genet (*civet*) *n*, genette, *f.*

geneva (*gin*) *n*, genièvre, *m.* **G~** (*Geog.*), Genève, *f. Lake of G~*, lac de Genève, lac Léman, *m.*

genial, *a*, bienfaisant; chaleureux; joyeux; sociable. ~*ity*, *n*, bonhomie, *f.*

genital, *a*, génital.

genitive [**case**], *n*, génitif, *m.*

genius, *n*, génie; démon, *m.*

Genoa, *n*, Gênes, *f.* **Genoese**, *a*, génois. ¶ *n*, Génois, e.

genteel, *a*, distingué, de bon ton.

gentian, *n*, gentiane, *f.*

gentile, *n*, gentil, *m.*

gentle, *a*, doux. *of ~ birth*, de qualité. ~*folk*[*s*], gens de qualité, *m.pl.* ~*man*, monsieur; galant homme; homme de qualité, gentilhomme, gentleman; cavalier, *m.* ~*man farmer*, gentilhomme campagnard, *m.* ~*manliness*, savoir-vivre, *m*, gentilhommerie, *f.* ~*manly*, comme il faut; distingué; gentleman. ~*woman*, femme de qualité, *f.* ~*ness*, *n*, douceur, *f.* **gently**, *ad*, doucement, bellement. **gentry**, *n*, petite noblesse, *f.*

genuflexion, *n*, génuflexion, *f.*

genuine, *a*, vrai; authentique; sincère; sérieux. ~*ness*, *n*, authenticité; sincérité, *f.*

genus, *n*, genre, *m.*

geodesy, *n*, géodésie, *f.* **geognosy**, *n*, géognosie, *f.* **geographer**, *n*, géographe, *m.* **geographic(al)**†, *a*, géographique. **geography**, *n*, géographie, *f.* **geologic**(*al*), *a*, géologique. **geologist**, *n*, géologue, *m.* **geology**, *n*, géologie, *f.* **geometer** & **geometrician**, *n*, géomètre, *m.* **geometric(al)**†, *a*,

géométrique. **geometry**, *n*, géométrie, *f.*

Georgia, *n*, (*U.S.A.*) la Georgie; (*Asia*) la Géorgie.

geranium, *n*, géranium, *m.*

germ, *n*, germe, *m.*

german, *a*, germain.

German, *a*, allemand; d'Allemagne. *~ measles*, rubéole, *f.* ¶ *n*, (*pers.*) Allemand, e; (*language*) l'allemand, *m.*

germander (*Bot.*) *n*, germandrée, *f.*

germane to, se rapportant à.

Germany, *n*, l'Allemagne, *f.*

germinate, *v.i*, germer. **germination**, *n*, germination, *f.*

gerund, *n*, gérondif, *m.*

gestation, *n*, gestation, *f.*

gesticulate, *v.i*, gesticuler.

gesture, *n*, geste, *m.*

get, *v.t.ir*, obtenir; gagner; acquérir; procurer; se p.; se faire; se mettre; tirer; recevoir; retirer; trouver; avoir; (*v.i.ir.*) aller; arriver; parvenir; devenir; se faire; se trouver. *Often rendered by se, e.g. ~ an opinion into one's head*, se chausser d'une opinion. *~ away*, s'échapper; se sauver. *~ back*, *v.t*, ravoir; (*v.i.*) revenir. *~ down*, descendre. *~ hold of*, s'emparer de; saisir. *~ in*, entrer; s'introduire; (*grain*) engranger. *~ married*, se marier. *~ on*, s'arranger; s'entendre; réussir. *~ out*, sortir. *~ out of the way*, s'ôter, de là, se garer. *~ over*, franchir, surmonter. *~ ready*, préparer; se préparer. *~ rid of*, se débarrasser de. *~ round* (someone), entortiller. *~ up*, se lever. *~ up steam*, chauffer.

getup, *n*, mise, *f*; affiquets, *m.pl.*

gewgaw, *n*, colifichet, *m.*

geyser, *n*, (*spring*) geyser, *m.*

ghastly, *a*, de spectre, de déterré; macabre; blême, livide; affreux.

Ghent, *n*, Gand, *m.*

gherkin, *n*, cornichon, *m.*

ghetto, *n*, ghetto, *m*; juiverie, *f.*

ghost, *n*, esprit, *m*; fantôme, spectre, revenant, *m*, ombre, *f.* *~ story*, histoire de revenants, *f.* *~ writer*, nègre, *m.* ~*ly*, *a*, spectral, fantomatique.

ghoul, *n*, goule, *f.*

giant, *a*, géant. **giant**, **ess**, *n*, géant, e, colosse, *m.* **giant**[*'s*] *stride*, pas de géant, vindas, *m.*

gibber, *v.i*, baragouiner. ~*ish*, *n*, baragouin, galimatias, *m.*

gibbet, *n,* gibet, *m,* potence, *f.*
¶ *(fig.) v.t,* pilorier.

gibe, *n,* brocard, quolibet, lardon,
m. ¶ *v.i,* lancer des brocards *ou*
des lardons *(at =* à).

giblets, *n.pl,* abattis, *m.* & *m.pl.*

giddiness, *n,* vertige, étourdissement, *m.* **giddy,** *a,* *(height)* vertigineux; *(flighty)* écervelé. **it
makes me feel ~,** cela me donne
le vertige.

gift, *n,* don; cadeau, *m;* donation;
(for coupons) prime; *(of an
office)* nomination, *f;* talent, *m.*
the ~ of the gab, du bagou. **~ed,**
a, doué, de talent.

gig, *n,* cabriolet, *m;* *(boat)* yole, *f.*

gigantic, *a,* gigantesque.

giggle, *v.i,* rire bêtement, glousser.

gild, *v.t.ir,* dorer. **~er,** *n,* doreur,
euse. **~ing,** *n,* dorure, *f.*

gill, *n.* *(fish)* ouïe, branchie, *f.*

gilt, *n,* dorure, *f.* ¶ *p.a,* doré.
~-edged, *(book, bill of exchange)*
doré sur tranche; *(investment, security)* de premier ordre. **~tool-
ing,** fers dorés, *m.pl.* **~ top,** tête
dorée, *f.*

gimcrack, *n,* bibelot, *m;* pacotille,
patraque, *f.* ¶ *a,* de camelote;
délabré.

gimlet, *n,* vrille, *f.*

gimp, *n,* ganse, *f,* galon, bordé,
passement, *m.*

gin, *n,* *(snare)* trébuchet, *m;*
(hoist) chèvre, *f;* treuil, *m;* *(cotton)* égreneuse, *f;* *(spirit)* gin, *m.*
¶ *v.t,* égrener.

ginger, *n,* gingembre, *m.* **~ bread,**
pain d'épice, *m.* **~ nut,** non-
nette, *f.* **~ly,** *ad,* en tâtonnant.

gingham, *(fabric)* *n,* guingan,
m.

giraffe, *n,* girafe, *f.*

girandole, *n,* girandole, *f.*

girasol[e] *(opal)* *n,* girasol, *m.*

gird, *v.t.ir,* [en]ceindre. **~er,** *n,*
poutre; solive; ferme, *f.* **~le,** *n,*
ceinture, *f.* ¶ *v.t,* ceindre.

girl, *n,* fille, jeune fille, fillette, enfant, demoiselle, *f.* **~ friend,**
amie, copine, *f.* **~hood,** *n,* jeunesse, *f.* **~ish,** *a,* de jeune fille;
mignard.

girth, *n,* sangle; sous-ventrière,
circonférence, *f.*

gist, *n,* substance, *f.*

give, *v.t.* & *i. ir,* donner; accorder;
prêter; apporter; passer; rendre;
fournir; *(cry)* pousser. **~ & take,**
donnant donnant. **~ back,** ren-

dre. **~ one's name,** décliner son
nom, se nommer. **~ in,** céder.
~ oneself away, s'enferrer soi-
même. *(lamp, etc.)* se mourir. **~
someone a piece of one's mind,**
dire son fait à quelqu'un. **~ up,**
renoncer à; livrer; abandonner,
quitter; céder; *(patient)* condamner. **~ way,** céder; fléchir;
s'effondrer. **given to,** adonné à;
enclin à. **giver,** *n,* donneur, euse.

gizzard, *n,* gésier, *m.*

glacé kid gloves, gants de peau
glacée, *m.pl.*

glacial, *a,* glacial; *(Geol.)* glaciaire. **glacier,** *n,* glacier, *m.*

glad, *a,* [bien] aise; content;
heureux; joyeux. **gladden,** *v.t,* réjouir.

glade, *n,* clairière, *f.*

gladiator, *n,* gladiateur, *m.*

gladiolus, *n,* glaïeul, *m.*

gladly, *ad,* volontiers. **gladness,**
n, joie, *f.*

glamour, *n,* enchantement; éclat;
prestige, *m.*

glance, *n,* coup d'œil, regard, *m;*
(loving) œillade, *f.* ¶ *v.i,* effleurer.
~ at, jeter un coup d'œil sur.

gland, *n,* glande, *f.*

glanders, *n.pl,* morve, *f.*

glare, *n,* éclat; éblouissement; regard perçant, r. furieux, *m.*
¶ *v.i,* éblouir. **~ at** *(pers.)* lancer
un regard furieux à. **glaring,** *a,*
éclatant, éblouissant; grossier; flagrant; criant; tranchant.

glass, *n,* verre, *m;* vitre, *f;* miroir,
m; lunette, *f;* *(pl.)* lunettes, *f.pl;*
jumelle, *f.* **~[with care],** fragile.
~ beads, verroterie, *f.* **~ case,** vitrine, *f.* **~ cutter,** diamant de
vitrier; *(wheel)* coupe-verre à
molette, *m.* **~ door,** porte vitrée,
f, vitrage, *m.* **~maker,** verrier,
m. **~ making** & **~works,** verrerie, *f.* **~ of beer,** bock, *m,*
chope, *f.* **~[ware],** verrerie;
(small) verroterie, *f.* **field~,** jumelles, *f.pl.* **magnifying ~,** loupe,
f. **shatterproof ~,** verre incassable, *m.* **~y,** *a,* vitreux.

glaucous, *a,* glauque.

glaze, *n,* émail, vernis, *m,* couverte, *f;* lustre, *m.* ¶ *v.t,* *(window)*
vitrer; émailler, vernir, vernisser;
lustrer; satiner; glacer; dorer;
(v.i.) se glacer. **~d frost,** verglas,
m. **glazier,** *n,* vitrier, *m.* **~y,** *n,*
vitrerie, *f.*

gleam, *n,* lueur, *f,* rayon, *m.* ¶ *v.i,*
luire, miroiter.

glean, v.t, glaner; (*grapes*) grappiller. **~er,** n, glaneur, euse. **~ing,** n, glanage, m, glane; (*pl.*) glanure, f.

glebe, n, glèbe; terre d'église, f.

glee, n, joie, gaieté; chanson à plusieurs voix, f.

gleet, n, écoulement, m.

glen, n, vallon, val, m.

glib, a, (*pers.*) volubile; (*tongue*) déliée.

glide, n, glissement; (*Danc.*) glissé, m. ¶ v.i, glisser; couler. **glider** (*Avn.*) n, planeur, m. **gliding** (*Avn.*) n, vol à voile, m.

glimmer, n, lueur, f. ¶ v.i, jeter une faible lueur.

glimpse, n, lueur, f; coup d'œil, m; échappée [de vue] f. *catch a ~ of,* entrevoir.

glint, n, reflet, m. ¶ v.i, étinceler, miroiter.

glisten, glitter, v.i, briller, reluire, miroiter. **glitter,** n, brillant, m.

gloaming, n, crépuscule, m, brune, f.

gloat over, triompher de; couver des yeux.

globe, n, globe, m, sphère, f; (*fish bowl*) bocal, m. **globular,** a, globulaire, globuleux. **globule,** n, globule, m.

gloom, v.t, rembrunir. **~[iness],** n, obscurité, f, ténèbres, f.pl; air sombre, m, tristesse, f. **~y,** a, sombre, ténébreux, triste, morne, noir, lugubre.

glorify, v.t, glorifier. **glorious†,** a, glorieux; resplendissant. **glory,** n, gloire, f; nimbe, m. **~ in,** se glorifier de, se faire gloire de.

gloss, n, luisant, lustre, poli, œil, m; (*comment*) glose, f. ¶ v.t, lustrer; glacer; (*text*) gloser. **~ [over],** vernir, farder. **~ary,** n, glossaire, m. **~y,** a, luisant; lustré; brillant.

glottis, n, glotte, f.

glove, n, gant, m. *~ trade,* ganterie, f. ¶ v.t, ganter. *to put on one's ~s,* se ganter. **glover,** n, gantier, ère.

glow, n, incandescence, f; embrasement, m; chaleur, f; élan, m; (*pleasant, in the body*) moiteur, f. **~worm,** ver luisant, lampyre, m, luciole, f. ¶ v.i, briller d'un vif éclat. *~ing with health,* rouge de santé.

glower at, regarder d'un air féroce.

glucose, n, glucose, f.

glue, n, colle forte; colle; (*marine*) glu, f. *~ pot,* pot à colle, m. ¶ v.t, coller. **~y,** a, gluant.

glum, a, morose, chagrin.

glut, n, pléthore, f; encombrement, m. ¶ v.t, gorger, rassasier; encombrer.

gluten, n, gluten, m. **glutinous,** a, glutineux.

glutton, n, glouton, ne, gourmand, e. **~ous†,** a, glouton, gourmand. **~y,** n, gloutonnerie, gourmandise, f.

glycerin[e], n, glycérine, f.

gnarl, n, broussin, m. **~ed,** a, noueux.

gnash one's teeth, grincer des (*ou* les) dents.

gnat, n, moucheron, m.

gnaw, v.i, ronger. **~ing,** n, rongement; tiraillement, m.

gnome, n, gnome, m.

gnostic, n, gnostique, m.

go, n, entrain, allant, panache, m; mode, vogue, f; jet, m. ¶ v.i. & t. ir, aller; se rendre, se porter; se mettre; marcher; passer; partir; s'en aller; faire; tourner; devenir. *are you ready? go!* êtes-vous prêts? partez! *who goes there? qui vive?* ~ *astray,* s'égarer; se dévoyer. ~ *away,* s'en aller; partir. ~ *back,* retourner. *~between* intermédiaire, m; entremetteur, euse. ~ *by,* passer. *~cart,* chariot, panier roulant, m. ~ *down,* descendre; baisser; (*sun, moon*) se coucher; (*ship*) sombrer, couler; (*swelling*) désenfler. ~ *for,* aller chercher; a. faire; a. prendre. ~ *in,* entrer; monter. ~ *off,* partir. *~on,* aller; avancer; continuer. ~ *on!* allons donc! ~ *on board a ship, an airplane,* monter sur un navire, en avion. ~ *out,* sortir; (*light*) s'éteindre. ~ *over,* passer sur; traverser; parcourir; (*Jump.*) dépasser, mordre sur (*the mark =* la latte). ~ *through,* passer par, traverser, parcourir; dépouiller. ~ *to press,* procéder à l'impression. ~ *to sleep,* s'endormir. ~ *up,* monter; remonter; renchérir. ~ *with,* accompagner. ~ *without,* se passer de.

goad, n, aiguillon, m. ¶ v.t, aiguillonner, piquer.

goal, n, but, m. ~ *keeper, kick, post,* gardien, coup [de pied], poteau, de b., m.

goat, *n,* chèvre, *f;* (*he*) bouc, *m.*
~**herd,** chevrier, ère. ~**ee,** *n,*
barbe de bouc, barbiche, *f.*

gobble, *v.t,* manger goulûment;
(*v.i, of turkey*) glouglouter.

goblet, *n,* gobelet, *m;* coupe, *f.*

goblin, *n,* lutin, follet, farfadet,
gobelin, *m.*

God, *n,* Dieu, *m.* ~**child,** filleul, e.
~**daughter,** filleule, *f.* ~**father,**
parrain, *m.* ~**head,** divinité, *f.*
~**mother,** marraine, *f.* ~**send,**
providence, aubaine, chapechute,
f. ~**son,** filleul, *m.* **goddess,** *n,*
déesse, *f.* **godless,** *a,* sans Dieu;
impie. **godlike,** *a,* divin. **godliness,** *n,* piété, *f.* **godly,** *a,* pieux,
saint, de Dieu.

goffer, *n,* tuyau, *m.* ¶ *v.t,* gaufrer,
tuyauter.

goggles, *n,pl,* lunettes, *f.pl.*

going, *n,* aller, *m.* ~ *& coming,*
allées *&* venues, *f.pl.* ~ *back to
school,* rentrée des classes, *f.* ~
concern, affaire roulante, *f.* ~ *value
as a* ~ *concern,* valeur d'usage, *f.*
~, ~, *gone!* une fois, deux fois,
[trois fois]; adjugé! ~*s-on,* procédés! agissements, *m.pl.*

goiter, *n,* goitre, *m.*

gold, *n,* or, *m.* ~*beater's skin,*
baudruche, *f. the* G~ *Coast,* la
Côte de l'Or, *f.* ~*digger,* chercheur
d'or, *m.* ~*field,* champ aurifère,
m. ~*finch,* chardonneret, *m.*
~*fish,* poisson rouge, *m,* dorade,
f. ~ *mine,* mine d'or, *f.* ~*smith*
&/or silversmith, orfèvre, *m.*
~[*smith's*] *&/or silver*[*smith's*]
work, orfèvrerie, *f.* ~ *standard,*
étalon d'or, *m.* ¶ *a,* d'or, en or. ~
francs, francs-or, *m.pl.* ~*en, a,*
d'or; doré; (*hair*) blond doré. ~
calf, veau d'or, *m.* ~ *mean,* juste
milieu, *m.* ~ *rain,* pluie d'or, *f.* ~
wedding, noces d'or, *f.pl,* cinquantaine, *f.*

golf, *n,* golf, *m.* ~ *club* (*pers. &
stick*) club de g, *m.* ~ *course,*
~ *links,* [terrain de] golf, *m.* ~*er,*
n, joueur (euse) de golf.

golosh, *n,* caoutchouc, *m.*

gondola, *n,* gondole, *f;* (*Avn.*) nacelle, *f.* **gondolier,** *n,* gondolier,
m.

gong, *n,* gong, tam-tam; timbre, *m.*

good, *a,* bon; beau; de bien; brave;
(*of a child*) sage; avantageux;
valable; utile. ~ *angel,* bon ange,
m; providence, *f.* ~ *breeding,*

politesse, *f,* savoir-vivre, *m.* ~*bye,*
i. & n, adieu, *i. & m;* au revoir!
a ~ *ear* (for music), l'oreille juste.
~ *evening!* ~ *night!* bonsoir!
bonne nuit! (*a*) ~*for-nothing,*
n. & a, (un) propre à rien. G~
Friday, le vendredi saint. ~
gracious! miséricorde! ~*looking,*
joli, de bonne mine. *my* ~ *man,*
mon brave. ~ *morning!* ~ *afternoon!* ~ *day!* bonjour! ~ *nature,*
bonhomie, *f,* bon naturel, *m.*
~*natured,* (*pers.*) bon enfant;
(*laugh*) jovial. ~ *offices,* ministère, *m. the* ~ *old days,* le bon
vieux temps. ~*will,* bienveillance,
bonne volonté, faveur, *f;* fonds
[de commerce] *m,* clientèle, *f.* ¶
i, bon!, bien! ¶ *n,* bien, *m.* *for*
~, pour de bon. *it's no* ~ . . .,
inutile de . . . *to the* ~, en gain.

goodies, *n.pl,* [du] nanan, *m.*

goodness, *n,* bonté, *f.* *for* ~
sake, de grâce.

goods, *n.pl,* marchandises, *f.pl;*
biens; effets, *m.pl.*

goose, *n,* oie, *f.* ~*flesh* (*fig.*), chair
de poule, *f.* ~ *step,* pas de l'oie,
m.

gooseberry, *n,* groseille verte, g.
à maquereau, *f.* ~ *bush,* grosei-
lier à maquereau, *m.*

Gordian knot, nœud gordien,
m.

gore, *n,* sang [caillé] *m.* ¶ *v.t,* percer de coups de corne.

gorge, *n,* gorge, *f.* ¶ *v.t,* gorger.

gorgeous†, *a,* magnifique, splendide.

gorilla, *n,* gorille, *m.*

gormandize, *v.i,* goinfrer, bâfrer.

gorse, *n,* ajonc, genêt épineux, *m.*

gory, *a,* sanglant, ensanglanté.

goshawk, *n,* autour, *m.*

gosling, *n,* oison, *m.*

gospel, *n,* Évangile; credo, *m.* ~
[*truth*], parole d'Évangile, *f.*

gossamer, *n,* fils de la Vierge,
m.pl, filandres, *f.pl.*

gossip, *n,* commérage, bavardage
de commères, racontar, *m;*
(*pers.*) commère, *f.* ~ *columnist,*
échotier, *m.* ¶ *v.i,* commérer, bavarder.

goth (*fig.*) *n,* ostrogot[h], e.
Gothic, *a,* gothique.

gouache (*Art*) *n,* gouache, *f.*

gouge, *n,* gouge, *f.*

gourd, *n,* courge, calebasse, *f.*

gourmand, *a. & n,* gourmand, e.

gourmet, *n,* gourmet, *m.*

gout, *n*, goutte, *f*. ~**y**, *a*, goutteux.

govern, *v.t*, gouverner, régir; (*Gram.*) régir. ~**ess**, *n*, gouvernante, *f*. ~**ment**, *n*, gouvernement; État, *m*. ~ *in power*, gouvernants, *m.pl*. ~ *organ*, journal ministériel, *m*. ~**or**, *n*, gouverneur; (*Mach.*) régulateur, *m*.

gown, *n*, robe, *f*. *dressing* ~, peignoir, *m*. *night*~, chemise de nuit, *f*.

grab, *v.t*, empoigner, agripper.

grace, *n*, grâce, *f*; (*before meal*) le bénédicité; (*after*) les grâces, *f.pl*. ~ *note*, note d'agrément, *f*. *the G*~*s*, les [trois] Grâces. *his G*~, monseigneur, *m*. *your G*~, Votre Grandeur, *f*. ¶ *v.t*, orner; honorer. ~**ful**†, *a*, gracieux.

gracious†, *a*, gracieux. ~**ness**, *n*, gracieuseté, *f*.

gradation, *n*, gradation, *f*. **grade**, *n*, grade, degré, *m*; teneur, *f*; titre, *m*. ¶ *v.t*, classer; graduer; régulariser. **gradient**, *n*, (*up*) rampe; (*down*) pente; (*up or down*) inclinaison, *f*. **gradual**†, *a*, graduel. **graduate**, *v.t*, graduer; (*v.i.*) prendre ses grades. ¶ *n*, gradué, e. **graduation**, *n*, graduation; gradation; (*Univ.*) licence, grade, *f*.

graft, *n*, (*Hort.*) greffe, ente; (*Surg.*) greffe; (*spoils*) gratte, *f*. ¶ *v.t*, greffer; enter. ~**ing** (*Knit.*) *n*, remmaillage, *m*.

grain, *n*, (*wheat, etc.*) céréales, *f.pl*; grain, *m*; (*wood*) fil; (*weight*) grain, *m*; (*pl*. *brewer's*) drèche, drague, *f*. *against the* ~, à rebours. ¶ *v.t*, grener, greneler; veiner. ~**ed**, *p.a*, (*leather*) grenu; (*wood*) ondé. ~**ing**, *n*, grenu, *m*.

gram, *n*, gramme, *m*.

grammar, *n*, grammaire, *f*. ~**ian**, *n*, grammairien, ne. **grammatical**†, *a*, grammatical.

grampus, *n*, épaulard, *m*, orque, *f*.

Granada (*Spain*) *n*, Grenade, *f*.

granary, *n*, grenier, *m*.

grand†, *a*, grand; magnifique. ~**child**, ~**son**, ~**daughter**, petit-fils, *m*, petite-fille, *f*. ~**children**, petits-enfants, *m.pl*. ~**father**, grand-père, aïeul, *m*. ~**father's clock**, horloge de parquet, *f*. ~**mamma**, grand-maman, bonne maman, *f*. ~**mother**, grand-mère, aïeule, *f*. ~ *piano*, piano à queue, *m*. ~ *staircase*, escalier d'honneur, *m*. ~ *stand*, tribune, *f*. ~

total, somme toute, *f*. **grandee**, *n*, grand, *m*. **grandeur**, *n*, grandeur, majesté; splendeur, *f*.

grandiloquence, *n*, grandiloquence, *f*. **grandiloquent**, *a*, grandiloquent, doctoral.

grandiose, *a*, grandiose.

granite, *n*, granit, *m*.

granny, *n*, grand-maman, bonne maman, *f*.

grant, *n*, concession; allocation; subvention, *f*. ¶ *v.t*, accorder; concéder; octroyer; admettre; poser. *to take for* ~*ed*, présupposer. ~**ee**, *n*, concessionnaire, *m,f*; impétrant, e. ~**or**, *n*, cédant, e.

granulate, *v.t*, grener; granuler. ~*d sugar*, sucre semoule, *m*. **granule**, *n*, granule, *m*.

grape, *n*, grain de raisin, *m*; (*pl.*) raisin[s] *m.[pl.]*. ~*fruit*, pamplemousse, *f*. ~*shot*, mitraille, *f*.

graph, *n*, graphique, tracé, *m*. ~**ic**†, *a*, graphique; pittoresque. ~**ics**, *n*, graphie; (*computers*) infographie, *f*. ¶ *v.t*, tracer un graphique, faire un diagramme.

graphite, *n*, graphite, *m*, plombagine, *f*.

grapnel, *n*, grappin, *m*. **grapple**, *v.t*, accrocher. ~ *with*, s'attaquer à; colleter.

grasp, *n*, prise; étreinte; poigne; poignée; portée, *f*. ¶ *v.t*, saisir, empoigner; serrer. ~ *round the body*, ceinturer. ~**ing**†, *p.a*, avide, cupide, âpre [au gain].

grass, *n*, herbe, *f*, herbage; gazon, *m*; verdure, *f*; vert, *m*. ~*hopper*, sauterelle; cigale, *f*. ~*land*, pré, prairie, *f*. ~ *snake*, couleuvre à collier, *f*. ~ *widow*, veuve à titre temporaire, *f*. ~**y**, *a*, herbeux, herbu.

grate, *n*, grille, *f*. ¶ *v.t*, griller; râper; (*teeth*) grincer [de]; (*ears*) écorcher, blesser. ~*d bread crumbs*, panure, chapelure, *f*.

grateful†, *a*, reconnaissant; agréable. *to be* ~ *to*, savoir [bon] gré à. ~**ness**, *n*, reconnaissance, *f*.

grater, *n*, râpe, *f*.

gratification, *n*, satisfaction, *f*, plaisir, *m*. **gratify**, *v.t*, satisfaire, contenter.

gratin, *n*, gratin, *m*. ~**ate**, *v.t*, gratiner.

grating, *n*, grille, *f*; grillage; gril, *m*; claire-voie; crapaudine, *f*. ¶ *p.a*, strident.

gratis, *ad,* gratis, gratuitement.
gratitude, *n,* reconnaissance, gratitude, *f.*
gratuitous†, *a,* gratuit, gracieux; sans motif. **~ness,** *n,* gratuité, *f.* **gratuity,** *n,* gratification, *f,* pourboire, *m.*
gravamen, *n,* matière, *f.*
grave†, *a,* grave, sérieux. ¶ *n,* fosse; tombe, *f,* tombeau, *m.* **~digger,** fossoyeur, *m.* **~stone,** pierre tombale, tombe, *f.* **~yard,** cimetière, *m.* ¶ *v.t,* (*ship*) radouber.
gravel, *n,* gravier[s] *m.[pl.];* (*Med.*) graviers, *m.pl,* gravelle, *f,* sable, *m.* **~ path, ~ walk,** allée sablée, *f.* **~ pit,** gravière, *f.* **~ly,** *a,* graveleux.
graver, *n,* burin, ciselet, *m.*
graving dock, forme de radoub, *f.*
gravitate, *v.i,* graviter. **gravitation,** *n,* gravitation, *f.* **gravity,** *n,* (*Phys.*) gravité, pesanteur, *f,* poids, *m;* (*fig.*) gravité, *f;* sérieux, *m.*
gravy, *n,* jus, *m.* **~ boat,** saucière, *f.* **~ spoon,** cuiller à ragoût, *f.*
gray, *a,* gris. ¶ *v.t,* grisailler. **~ish,** *a,* grisâtre. **~ness,** *n,* couleur grise, *f.*
graze, *n,* écorchure, *f.* ¶ *v.t. & i,* effleurer, raser, friser, frôler; écorcher; (*sea bottom*) labourer; (*cattle*) paître, pâturer, pacager. **grazier,** *n,* éleveur, *m.*
grease, *n,* graisse, *f;* (*in wool*) suint, *m.* **~ box,** boîte à graisse, *f.* **~ paint,** fard, *m.* **~-proof paper,** papier imperméable à la graisse, p. sulfurisé, *m.* ¶ *v.t,* graisser; suiffer. **greasiness,** *n,* onctuosité, *f.* **greasy,** *a,* graisseux, gras, onctueux. **~ pole,** mât de cocagne, *m.*
great, *a,* grand; gros; fort. **~ aunt,** grand-tante, *f.* **~ bell,** bourdon, *m.* **G~ Britain,** la Grande-Bretagne. **~coat,** pardessus, *m;* (*Mil.*) capote, *f.* **~ Dane,** grand danois, *m.* **a ~ deal, a ~ many,** beaucoup. **~grandchildren,** arrière-petits-enfants, *m.pl.* **~granddaughter,** **-son,** arrière-petite-fille, *f,* a.-petit-fils, *m.* **~grandfather,** **-mother,** arrière-grand-père, *m,* a.-grand-mère, *f,* bisaïeul, e. **~~-grandfather,** **-mother,** trisaïeul, e. **~ toe,** gros doit du pied, orteil, *m.* **~ uncle,**

grand-oncle, *m.* **the ~** (*fig.*), le grand. **the ~ ones,** les grands (*de la terre*). **~ly,** *ad,* grandement; fort. **~ness,** *n,* grandeur, *f.*
grebe, *n,* grèbe, *m.*
Grecian, *a,* grec. **Greece,** *n,* la Grèce.
greed[iness], *n,* avidité, âpreté; gourmandise, *f.* **greedy†,** *a,* avide; gourmand, goulu.
Greek, *a,* grec. **~ fret** (*Arch.*), grecque, *f.* ¶ *n,* (*pers.*) Grec, ecque; (*language*) le grec; (*fig.*) du grec, de l'hébreu (*to me =* pour moi).
green, *a,* vert; en herbe; novice; naïf. **~ baize,** tapis vert, drap v., *m.* **~finch,** verdier, *m.* **~fly,** puceron, *m.* **~gage,** [prune de] reine-claude, *f.* **~horn,** novice, conscrit, pigeon, *m.* **~house,** serre, *f.* **~ peas,** petits pois, pois verts, *m.pl.* **greens,** *n.pl,* herbages, légumes verts, *m.pl,* verdure, *f.* **~sward,** tapis de gazon, *m,* herbette, verdure, *f;* (*roadside*) accotement, *m.* **~wood,** feuillée, ramée, *f.* ¶ *n,* vert, *m;* (*grass plot & golf*) pelouse, *f. through the ~* (*golf*), à travers le parcours. ¶ *v.t. & i,* verdir, verdoyer. **~ery,** *n,* verdure, *f.* **~ish,** *a,* verdâtre.
Greenland, *n,* le Groenland.
greenness, *n,* verdure; verdeur; naïveté, *f.*
greet, *v.t,* saluer; accueillir. **~ing,** *n,* salutation, *f,* salut, *m.*
gregarious, *a,* grégaire.
Gregorian, *a,* grégorien.
Grenada (*W. Indies*) *n,* la Grenade. **grenade,** *n,* grenade, *f.* **grenadine,** *n,* (*cordial, fabric*) grenadine, *f;* (*Cook.*) grenadin, *m.*
greyhound, *n,* lévrier, *m,* levrette, *f.* **~ racing,** courses de lévriers, *f.pl.*
grid, *n,* grille, *f.* **~iron,** gril; (*sports*) terrain de football, *m.*
griddle, *n,* gril, *m.*
grief, *n,* chagrin, *m,* douleur, peine, affliction, *f.* **grievance,** *n,* grief, *m.* **grieve,** *v.t,* chagriner, affliger, peiner, fâcher. **grievous†,** *a,* grave; cruel.
griffin, griffon, *n,* griffon, *m.*
grill, *n,* gril, *m;* (*meat*) grillade, *f.* ¶ *v.t,* [faire] griller.
grille, *n,* (*grating*) grille, *f.*
grim, *a,* farouche, rébarbatif; macabre.

grimace, *n*, grimace, *f*, rictus, *m*. ¶ *v.i*, grimacer.

grime, *n*, crasse, *f*. ¶ *v.t*, encrasser, noircir. **grimy**, *a*, crasseux, noir.

grin, *n*, grimace, *f*. ¶ *v.i*, grimacer.

grind, *v.t.ir*, moudre; broyer; (*knife*) aiguiser, affûter, repasser; roder; grincer [de]; pressurer, opprimer; jouer. ~ *at*, piocher. ~*stone*, meule en grès, *f*. ~**ery**, *n*, crépins, *m.pl*. ~**ing** (*grain*) *n*, mouture, *f*.

grip, *n*, prise, pince, serre; poigne; étreinte; poignée; griffe, *f*. ¶ *v.t*, saisir, empoigner, serrer, étreindre; pincer, agripper.

gripes, *n.pl*, tranchées, *f.pl*; colique, *f*.

grippe, *n*, grippe, *f*.

grisly, *a*, effrayant, horrible, affreux.

grist, *n*, blé à moudre, *m*.

gristle, *n*, cartilage, *m*. **gristly**, *a*, cartilagineux.

grit, *n*, graviers, *m.pl*, sable; grès, *m*; (*fig.*) courage, *m*. **gritty**, *a*, graveleux; pierreux.

grizzled, *a*, grison. *grizzly bear*, ours grizzly, ours grizzlé, *m*.

groan, *n*, gémissement, *m*. ¶ *v.i*, gémir.

groats, *n.pl*, gruau; gruau d'avoine, *m*.

grocer, *n*, épicier, ère. ~*'s shop* & **grocery**, *n*, épicerie, *f*.

grog, *n*, grog, *m*. **groggy**, *a*, ivre; aviné; chancelant.

groin, *n*, aine; (*Arch.*) arête, *f*.

groom, *n*, palefrenier, *m*. ¶ *v.t*, panser.

groove, *n*, rainure; cannelure, *f*; sillon, *m*; gorge; ornière, *f*. ¶ *v.t*, canneler; sillonner.

grope, *v.t. & i*, fouiller, tâtonner. *to ~ for*, chercher à tâtons.

grosbeak, *n*, gros-bec, *m*.

gross†, *a*, grossier; gros; (*Com.*) brut. ¶ (*144*) *n*, grosse, *f*. ~**ness**, *n*, grossièreté, *f*.

grotesque†, *a. & ~[ness]* *n*, grotesque. *a. & m*. ¶ (*Art*), *n*, grotesque, *f*.

grotto, *n*, grotte, *f*.

grouch, *n*, ronchon, *m*. ¶ *v.i*, ronchonner.

ground, *n*, terre, *f*; sol; terrain; champ, *m*; place, *f*; fond; plan; sujet, lieu, *m*, raison, (*pl.*) cause, *f*, lieu, *m*, matière, *f*; (*pl*, *law*) motifs, moyens, *m.pl*; (*pl*, *dregs*)

marc, *m*; effondrilles, *f.pl*; sédiment, *m*; (*of mansion*) dehors, *m.pl*, parc, *m*; (*fishing, cruising*) parages, *m.pl*. ~ *floor*, rez-de-chaussée, *m*. ~ *game*, gibier à poil, *m*. ~ *ivy*, lierre terrestre, *m*. ~ *line* (*Fish.*), ligne de fond, traînée, *f*. ~*nut*, arachide, cacahuète, *f*. ~ *rent*, redevance foncière, *f*. ~*sheet*, toile de sol, *f*. ~ *swell*, houle de fond, *f*. ~*work*, base, *f*; canevas, *m*. *stand one's* ~, tenir bon. ¶ *p.p*, en poudre; moulu; (*rice, etc.*) farine de . . .; (*glass*) dépoli. ¶ *v.t. & i*, mettre à terre; (*Elec.*) m. à la terre; fonder; (*ship*) échouer, engraver. ~**less**, *a*. & ~**lessly**, *ad*, sans fondement; en l'air.

groundsel, *n*, seneçon, *m*.

group, *n*, groupe, *m*. ~ *firing* (*Artil.*), feu concentré, *m*, mitraille, *f*. ¶ *v.t*, grouper.

grouse, *n*, petit coq de bruyère, tétras, *m*, grouse, *f*, (*young*) grianneau, *m*. ¶ *v.i*, grogner.

grout[ing] (*Build.*) *n*, coulis, *m*.

grove, *n*, bocage, bosquet, *m*.

grovel, *v.i*, ramper.

grow, *v.i.ir*, croître; pousser; venir; grandir; [s']accroître; devenir, se faire; *often expressed by* se, *e.g.*, ~ *cold*, se refroidir; (*v.t.ir*) cultiver. ~ *green again* & ~ *young again*, reverdir. ~**er**, *n*, cultivateur, trice, planteur, euse. ~**ing** *crops*, récoltes sur pied, *f.pl*.

growl, *n*, grondement, *m*. ¶ *v.i*, gronder.

grown-up, grand. **grown-up**, *a*. & *n*, adulte, *a*. & *m,f*, grande personne, *f*. **growth**, *n*, croissance; venue; pousse; végétation, *f*; (*vintage*) cru; développement, *m*.

grub, *n*, larve, *f*, ver, *m*. **grubby**, *a*, (*wormy*) véreux; (*dirty*) crasseux.

grudge, *n*, rancune, *f*. ¶ *v.t*, marchander, reprocher à.

gruel, *n*, gruau, *m*, bouillie, *f*.

gruesome, *a*, macabre.

gruff, *a*, rude, brusque, bourru.

grumble, *v.i*, murmurer, gronder, grogner; ~ *at*, ~ *about*, grommeler, marmonner. **grumpy**, *a*, bourru.

grunt, *n*, grognement, *m*. ¶ *v.i*, grogner.

guano, *n*, guano, *m*.

guarantee, -ty, *n*, garantie; caution, *f*; aval, *m*. ¶ *v.t*, garantir;

cautionner; avaliser. **guarantor,** n, garant, e, caution, f.

guard, n, garde; sentinelle, f; protecteur, m; (pers.) garde; (Bookb.) onglet. m. on ~, en faction; sur le qui-vive. ~**house,** ~**room,** corps de garde, poste, m, salle de police, f. ¶ v.t. & i, [se] garder; se prémunir; parer. ~**ed,** p.a, mesuré; réservé. **guardian,** n, gardien, ne; curateur, trice, tuteur, trice, correspondant, e; (att.) gardien, tutélaire. ~**ship,** n, garde; (law) tutelle, curatelle, f.

guava, n, goyave, f; (tree) goyavier, m.

gudgeon, n, goujon; tourillon, m.

guelder rose, boule de neige, f, obier, m.

guerrilla, n, guérilla, f, partisan, guérillero, m. ~ war[fare], guerre de guérillas, g. de partisan, f.

Guernsey, n, Guernesey, f.

guess, n, conjecture, f. ¶ v.t. & i, deviner, conjecturer.

guest, n, convive, m,f, convié, e; hôte, muse, invité, e. ~ room, chambre d'ami, f. ~ of honor, invité(e) d'honneur.

guffaw, v.i, rigoler.

Guiana, n, la Guyane.

guidance, n, direction; gouverne, f. **guide,** n, guide; cicerone, m. ~ [book], guide; indicateur, m. ~ post, poteau indicateur, m. ~ rope, câble-guide; (Avn.) guiderope, m. ¶ v.t, guider, conduire. guiding principle, idée directrice, f.

guild, n, corps de métier, m, corporation; association, f; (church) patronage, m.

guile, n, ruse, astuce, f, artifice, m. ~**less,** a, innocent, candide; naïf.

guillotine, n, guillotine, f. ¶ v.t, guillotiner.

guilt, n, culpabilité, f. ~**less,** a, innocent, ne. ~**y,** a, coupable, criminel.

guinea (21/-) n, guinée, f. ~ fowl, pintade, f. ~ pig, cochon, d'Inde, cobaye, m. G~ (Geog.), la Guinée.

guise, n, apparence, f.

guitar, n, guitare, f.

gules (Her.), n, gueules, m.

gulf, n, golfe; gouffre, abîme, m. G~ Stream, Gulf-Stream, m.

gull, n, (sea) mouette, f, goéland, m; (pers.) dupe, f. ¶ v.t, duper.

gullet, n, gosier, m, gorge, f.

gullible, a, crédule.

gully, n, ravine, f, ravin; (gutter) caniveau, m.

gulp, n, goulée, gorgée, f, trait, m. to ~ down, gober.

gum, n, gomme; (Anat.) gencive, f. ~ arabic, gomme arabique. ~**boil,** abcès aux gencives, m. ~ tree, gommier, m. ¶ v.t, gommer. **gummy,** a, gommeux.

gumption, n, entregent, savoir-faire, m.

gun, n, fusil; canon, m, pièce, f. ~**boat,** [chaloupe] canonnière, f. ~ carriage, affût, m. ~**cotton,** coton-poudre, fulmicoton, m. ~ license, port d'armes, m. ~ metal, bronze [industriel] m. ~**powder,** poudre à canon, f. ~**shot,** coup de fusil, c. de canon, m. ~**shot wound,** blessure d'arme à feu, f. ~**smith,** armurier, m. **gunner,** n, artilleur, canonnier, m. ~**y,** n, tir, m, artillerie, f, canonnage, m.

gunwale, gunnel, n, plat-bord, m.

gurgle, n, glouglou, m. ¶ v.i, faire glouglou; gargouiller.

gurnard, n, trigle, grondin, rouget, m.

gush, n, jaillissement, bouillon, m; sentimentalité, f. ¶ v.i, jaillir.

gusset, n, gousset, m.

gust, n, coup, m, bourrasque, rafale, bouffée, f.

gusto, n, entrain, m.

gusty, a, (wind) impétueux; (day) de grand vent.

gut, n, boyau; intestin; (Fish.) crin, florence, m, racine, f; (Naut.) goulet, m. he has ~s, il a du cran. ¶ v.t, vider, étriper.

gutta-percha, n, gutta-percha, f.

gutter, n, (roof) gouttière, f, chéneau; (street) ruisseau; (conduit) caniveau; chenal, m; rigole, f; (book) blancs de petit fond, m.pl.; (fig.) ruisseau; carrefour, m, crasse, fange, crotte, f. ~ language, langage de carrefour, m. ~**snipe,** voyou, m. ¶ v.i, couler.

guttural, a, guttural. ¶ n, gutturale, f.

guy, n, (rope) hauban, m; (pers.) type, m. hefty ~, costaud, m. laid-back ~, type décontracté, m.

guzzle, v.i, bâfrer, goinfrer.

gymnasium, n, gymnase, m. **gymnast,** n, gymnaste, gymnasiarque, m. ~ic, a. & n, gymnastique, a. & f. ~ics, n.pl, gymnastique, gymnique, f.

gynecology, n, gynécologie, f.

gypseous, a, gypseux. **gypsum,** n, gypse, m. ~ **quarry,** plâtrière, f.

gypsy, n, gitan, e.

gyrate, v.i, tourner. **gyration,** n, giration, f. **gyratory,** a, giratoire. **gyroscope,** n, gyroscope, m.

H

haberdasher, n, chemisier, mercier, m. ~y, n, mercerie, chemiserie, f.

habiliment, n, attirail; (pl.) habillement, m.

habit, n, habitude, coutume, f; (pl.) mœurs, f.pl; tic; (dress) habit, m. to be in the ~ of doing so, être coutumier (ère) du fait. ~able, a, habitable. **habitat,** n, habitat, m. **habitation,** n, habitation, f. **habitual†,** a, habituel, familier. ~ criminal, repris de justice, m. **habituate,** v.t, habituer.

hack, n, entaille, f; cheval de louage; c. de selle, m; (jade) rosse, f. ~ saw, scie à métaux, f. ~ [writer], écrivailleur, m. ¶ v.t, écharper, hacher, charcuter.

hackneyed, p.p, banal, rebattu, usé jusqu'à la corde. ~ phrase, cliché, m. ~ refrain, rengaine, f.

haddock, n, aigrefin, m.

Hades, n, les enfers, m.pl.

haft, n, manche, m, poignée, f.

hag, n, sorcière, f.

haggard, a, hagard, tiré.

haggle, v.i, marchander, barguigner, chipoter.

Hague (the), la Haye.

hail, n, grêle, f, grésil, m. to damage by ~, grêler. ~stone, grain de grêle, (big) grêlon, m. ~ storm, orage [accompagné] de grêle, m, giboulée, f. ¶ i, salut! ~ fellow well met, de pair à compagnon. H~ Mary, Ave Maria. ¶ v.i.imp, grêler, grésiller; (v.t.) faire pleuvoir; saluer; héler; acclamer. ~ from, venir de. within ~, à portée de la voix.

hair, n, (un) cheveu, m; (des)

cheveux, m.pl; chevelure, f; poil; crin, m; soie; bourre, f. ~brush, brosse à cheveux, b. à tête, f. ~ comb, peigne coiffeur, m. ~ curler, bigoudi, m. ~cut, coupe de cheveux, f. ~dresser, coiffeur, euse. ~ drier, appareil à douche d'air, m. ~ mattress, matelas de crin, m. ~ net, filet à cheveux, m, résille, f. ~ oil, huile pour les cheveux, f. ~pin, épingle à cheveux, f. ~pin bend, virage en é. à c., m. ~ shirt, haire, f. ~splitting, pointillerie, argutie, f. ~less, a, sans poils; glabre. ~y, a, velu; poilu; chevelu.

Haiti, n, Haïti, m.

hake, n, merlus, m; (dried) merluche, f.

halation (Phot.) n, halo, m.

halberd (Hist.) n, hallebarde, f.

halcyon days, jours alcyoniens; (fig.) jours sereins, m.pl.

hale, a, sain, vert, verdelet, frais. ~ & hearty, frais & gaillard, frais & dispos.

half, n, moitié; demie, f; demi; (Rly ticket) coupon. by ~, à moitié; de moitié. to go halves with, être (ou se mettre) de moitié avec. No 29½ (house), Nº 29 bis. ¶ a, demi-. ¶ ad, moitié; à moitié; à mi-; à demi. ~ a cup, la moitié d'une tasse, une demi-tasse. ~ an hour, une demi-heure. ~back (Foot.), demi, m. ~breed, métis, métisse. ~brother, demi-frère, m. ~caste, [homme de] sang mêlé, m. ~ fare, ~ price, demi-place, f. ~ holiday, demi-congé, m. ~ light, demi-jour, m. at ~mast (flag), en berne. ~open, a, entrouvert, entrebâillé; (v.t.) entrouvrir. ~ past twelve, midi & demi; minuit & demi. ~ past two, deux heures & demie. on ~ pay, en demi-solde. ~sister, demi-sœur, f. ~ time (Foot.), la mi-temps. ~title, faux titre, m. ~way, à mi-chemin, à moitié chemin. ~witted, simple. ~yearly, a, semestriel; (ad.) par semestre.

halibut, n, flétan, m.

hall, n, vestibule; hall, m; salle; enceinte, f; château, m. ~mark, n, [poinçon de] contrôle, m; (v.t.) contrôler, poinçonner. ~ porter, concierge, m. town ~, hôtel de ville, m.

hallelujah, n, Alléluia, m.

hallo[a], *i*, holà!, hé! ~ *there!* hé là-bas! **halloo**, *n*, cri [d'appel] *m*. ¶ *v.i*, crier, huer; (*v.t*, *dogs*) houper, encourager. ~ *to*, appeler à grands cris.

hallow, *v.t*, sanctifier, consacrer. ~ed, *p.a*, saint. *Hallowe'en*, vigile de la Toussaint, *f*.

hallucination, *n*, hallucination, vision, *f*.

halo, *n*, halo, *m*, auréole, *f*, nimbe, *m*.

halt, *n*, halte, station, *f*; stationnement, *m*. ¶ *i*, halte[-là]! ¶ *v.i*, faire halte; stationner; (*waver*) balancer; (*limp*) boiter.

halter, *n*, (*harness*) licou, *m*; (*hanging*) corde, *f*.

halting, *a*, boiteux.

halve, *v.t*, partager en deux, p. par la moitié.

halyard, *n*, drisse, *f*.

ham, *n*, (*in man*) jarret; (*hog*, *boar*) jambon, *m*. ~ & *eggs*, œufs au jambon, *m.pl*.

Hamburg, *n*, Hambourg, *m*.

hames, *n.pl*, attelles, *f.pl*.

hamlet, *n*, hameau, *m*.

hammer, *n*, marteau; (*power*) pilon; (*gun*) chien, *m*. ~*lock* (*wrestling*), retournement de bras, *m*. ¶ *v.t*, marteler, battre.

hammock, *n*, hamac, *m*.

hamper, *n*, [gros] panier, *m*, manne; malle en osier, *f*; (*impedimenta*) bataclan. ¶ *v.t*, empêtrer; troubler.

hand, *n*, main, *f*; poing, *m*; (*pointer*) aiguille; écriture; signature, *f*; (*side*) côté, *m*, part; (*cards*) main, *f*, jeu, *m*; (*horse*) = 4 inches *or* 10.16 centimeters; (*pl*, *men*) bras, hommes, *m.pl*; (*att.*) à main, à bras; à la main; manuel. *on the other* ~, de l'autre côté, d'autre part. ~*bag* (*lady's*, *etc.*), sac à main, *m*. ~*bill*, prospectus, imprimé; (*political*, *etc.*) tract, *m*. ~*book*, manuel, livret, aide-mémoire, guide-âne, mémento, *m*. ~*cuff*, *v.t*, mettre les menottes à; (*n.pl.*) menottes, *f.pl*. ~*kerchief*, mouchoir, *m*; (*silk*) pochette, *f*. ~*s off!* bas les mains! ~*rail*, main courante, rampe, *f*, garde-fou, *m*. ~*shake*, poignée de main, *f*; *shake-hand*, *m*. ~ *to* ~ (*fight*), corps à corps. *from* ~ *to mouth*, au jour le jour. ~*s up!* haut les mains! ~*writing*, écriture, *f*. *get the upper* ~, prendre le dessus.

¶ *v.t*, passer. ~ *down* (*fig.*) transmettre. ~ *in*, déposer. ~ [*over*], remettre, délivrer. ~ *over* (to justice), remettre, déférer. ~*ful*, *n*, poignée, *f*.

handicap, *n*, (*sport*) handicap; (*fig.*) désavantage, *m*. ¶ *v.t*, handicaper; désavantager. **handicapper**, *n*, handicapeur, *m*.

handicraft, *n*, industrie d'art, *f*. *handicraftsman*, ouvrier d'art, *m*.

handle, *n*, manche, *m*; poignée; (*umbrella*) poignée; main; manivelle; manette, *f*; bras; fût, *m*; (*basket*) anse; queue; branche; boucle, *f*; (*door*) bouton, *m*. ~*bar* (cycle), guidon, *m*. *to fly off the* ~, sortir de ses gonds. ¶ *v.t*, manier; manipuler; traiter; filer; emmancher. *one who knows how to* ~ (*money*, *men*), manieur, *m*. *to* ~ *roughly*, malmener. **handling**, *n*, manutention, *f*, maniement, *m*, manipulation, *f*. **hand-made**, *a*, fait à la main.

handsome, *a*, beau; riche. ~*ly*, *ad*, joliment, généreusement, grassement. ~*ness*, *n*, beauté, *f*.

handy, *a*, sous la main; commode; maniable; adroit; (*man*) à tout faire.

hang, *v.t. & i.ir*, pendre; suspendre; [r]accrocher; tomber; tapisser; tendre; poser. ~ *about*, rôder. ~ *back*, hésiter. ~ *heavy* (time), durer. ~ *out* (washing), étendre. ~*dog*, *a*, patibulaire. ~*man*, bourreau, *m*. ~ *nail*, envie, *f*.

hangar, *n*, hangar, *m*.

hanger, *n*, crochet, *m*. ~*on*, personne à charge, *f*; parasite, *m*. **hanging**, *p.a*, suspendu. ~ *committee* (Art), jury d'admission, *m*. ~ *garden*, jardin suspendu, *m*. ~ *lamp*, baladeuse, *f*. ~ *matter*, cas pendable, *m*. [*death by*] ~, pendaison, mort par suspension, *f*. **hangings**, *n.pl*, tapisserie, *f*.

hank, *n*, écheveau, *m*, poignée, *f*.

hanker after, soupirer après, avoir soif de.

Hanover, *n*, Hanovre, *m*; (*province*) le H.

haphazard, *ad*, au hasard, à l'aventure.

hapless, *a*, infortuné.

happen, *v.i*, arriver; advenir, venir, se passer, se trouver. ~*ing*, *n*, événement, *m*.

happiness, *n*, bonheur, *m*; félicité, *f*. **happy†**, *a*, heureux. ~*-go-lucky person*, sans-souci, *m,f*. *to a* ~ *issue*, à bon port. ~ *medium*, juste milieu, *m*. *a* ~ *New Year*, la bonne année.

harangue, *n*, harangue, *f*. ¶ *v.t. & i*, haranguer.

harass, *v.t*, harceler, fouler.

harbinger, *n*, avant-coureur, messager, fourrier, *m*.

harbor, *n*, port; refuge, *m*. ~ *master*, capitaine de port, *m*. ¶ *v.t*, héberger; nourrir; garder; (*criminal*) receler.

hard, *a*, dur; rude; rigoureux; ardu, laborieux, pénible; (*water*) crue. ~ *& fast*, absolu, immuable. ~*-bitten sailor*, loup de mer, *m*. ~*-boiled* (egg), dur. ~ *cash*, espèces sonnantes, *f.pl*. ~ *court* (*Ten.*) terre battue, *f*. ~ *labor*, travail disciplinaire, *m*. ~ *luck*, mauvais sort, *m*. ~ *palate*, palais dur, *m*. ~ *roe*, œufs, *m.pl*. ~ *tack*, biscuit de mer, *m*. ~ *to please*, exigeant. ~*ware*, quincaillerie; (*computers*) 'hardware, *m*. (*builder's*) serrurerie, *f*. ~*wearing & for* ~ *wear*, inusable. ~*-working*, laborieux. ¶ *ad*, dur; durement; fort; fortement; (*drink*) sec; (*look*) fixement; (*raining*) à verse. ~ *up*, à sec, aux abois. **harden**, *v.t*, durcir, endurcir; (*to temper metal*) tremper. **hardihood**, *n*, hardiesse, *f*. **hardly**, *ad*, durement; à peine; ne . . . guère; presque. **hardness**, *n*, dureté; rigueur; (*water*) crudité, *f*. ~ *of hearing*, dureté d'oreille. **hardship**, *n*, privation; rigueur, *f*. **hardy**, *a*, hardi; (*plant*) robuste, rustique.

hard copy, *n*, (*computers*) tirage, *m*.

hare, *n*, lièvre, (*young*) levraut, *m*. ~ *& hounds*, rallye-paper, *m*. ~*bell*, campanule, clochette, *f*. ~*brained*, écervelé. ~*lip*, bec-delièvre, *m*.

harem, *n*, harem, *m*.

haricot beans (*dried*), haricots secs, *m.pl*.

hark, *i*, écoute! écoutez!

harlequin, *n*, arlequin, *m*. ~*ade*, *n*, arlequinade, *f*.

harlot, *n*, prostituée, *f*.

harm, *n*, mal; tort, *m*. ¶ *v.t*, faire

du mal à; nuire à. ~*ful*, *a*, nuisible, pernicieux. ~*less*, *a*, inoffensif, innocent, anodin. ~*lessness*, *n*, innocuité; innocence, *f*.

harmonic†, *a. & n*, harmonique, *a. & m*. **harmonica**, *n*, harmonica, *m*. **harmonioust**, *a*, harmonieux. **harmonium**, *n*, harmonium, *m*. **harmonize**, *v.t*, harmoniser. **harmony**, *n*, harmonie, *f*; ensemble, *m*.

harness, *n*, harnais; harnachement, *m*. *die in* ~, mourir debout. ~ *maker*, bourrelier; sellier, *m*. ¶ *v.t*, harnacher; (*waterfall*) aménager.

harp, *n*, harpe, *f*. *to be always* ~*ing on the same string*, chanter toujours la même antienne, rabâcher toujours les mêmes choses. ~*ist*, *n*, harpiste, *m,f*.

harpoon, *n*, harpon, *m*. ¶ *v.t*, harponner.

harpsichord, *n*, clavecin, *m*.

harpy, *n*, harpie, *f*.

harrow, *n*, herse, *f*. ¶ *v.t*, herser; (*fig.*) déchirer, navrer. ~*ing*, *a*, déchirant.

harry, *v.t*, harceler; dévaster.

harsh†, *a*, dur; rude; âpre; aigre. ~*ness*, *n*, dureté; rudesse; âpreté; aigreur, *f*.

hart, *n*, cerf, *m*. **hartshorn**, *n*, liqueur d'ammoniaque, *f*.

harum-scarum, *n*, hurluberlu, *m*.

harvest, *n*, moisson; récolte, *f*. ~ *festival*, fête de la moisson, *f*. ~*man* (insect), faucheur, faucheux, *m*. ¶ *v.t*, moissonner; récolter. ~*er*, *n*, moissonneur, euse; (*Mach.*) moissonneuse, *f*.

hash, *n*, hachis, *m*, capilotade, *f*. ¶ *v.t*, hacher.

hasp, *n*, moraillon, *m*.

hassock, *n*, agenouilloir; carreau, coussin, *m*.

haste, *n*, hâte; précipitation, *f*. *to* [make]~ *& hasten*, *v.i*, se dépêcher, se hâter, s'empresser. **hasten**, *v.t*, hâter, presser, précipiter. **hasty†**, *a*, hâtif, à la hâte, précipité; vif, emporté.

hat, *n*, chapeau, *m*. ~ *& coat stand*, portechapeaux, portemanteau, *m*. ~*box*, boîte à chapeau(x), *f*. ~ *peg*, patère, *f*. ~ *shop & ~ trade*, chapellerie, *f*. ~*s off!*, chapeaux bas! (*In student circles* *the cry "chapeau!" warns of-fender to remove his/her hat.*).

hatch (*brood*) *n*, couvée, *f.* ~[way], *n*, panneau, *m*, écoutille, *f.* ¶ *v.i.* (*eggs*) éclore; (*v.t.*) faire éclore; (*fig.*) couver, ourdir, tramer; (*engrave*) hacher.

hatchet, *n*, hache à main, *f.* ~ *face*, figure en lame de couteau, *f.*

hatching, *n*, éclosion; (*engraving*) hachure, *f.*

hatchment, *n*, écusson; blason funèbre, *m*.

hate, *n*, haine, *f.* ¶ *v.t.* haïr; détester. ~ful†, *a*, haïssable; odieux. **hatred**, *n*, haine, *f.* *full of* ~, haineux.

hatter, *n*, chapelier, *m*.

haughtily, *ad*, avec hauteur, d'une manière hautaine. **haughtiness**, *n*, hauteur, morgue, *f.* **haughty**, *a*, hautain, altier, arrogant.

haul, *n*, coup de filet; parcours, trajet, *m*; acquisition, *f.* ¶ *v.t*, haler; traîner, tirer, remorquer; transporter.

haunch, *n*, hanche, *f*; (*meat*) quartier, cuissot, cimier; (*Arch.*) rein, *m*.

haunt, *n*, rendez-vous, lieu fréquenté (*of* = par); repaire, *m*, caverne, *f*, liteau, *m*. ¶ *v.t*, hanter, fréquenter; poursuivre.

hautboy (*Mus.*), *n*, hautbois, *m*.

Havana, *n*, la Havane. ~ [*cigar*], cigare de la Havane, havane, *m*.

have, *v.t.ir*, avoir; posséder; jouir de; tenir; prendre; faire. ~ *on* (*wear*), porter, avoir. *I* ~ *come*, je suis venu. *I* ~ *been had*, on m'a eu.

haven, *n*, havre, port; (*fig.*) asile, *m*.

haversack, *n*, musette, *f*, sac, *m*.

havoc, *n*, ravage[s] *m*.[*pl*.], dégâts, *m.pl.*

Havre, *n*, le Havre.

haw (*Bot.*) *n*, cenelle, *f.* ~*finch*, gros-bec, *m*. ¶ *v.i*, ânonner.

Hawaii, *n*, Hawaï, *m*. ~*an*, *a*, hawaïen.

hawk, *n*, faucon, *m*. ¶ *v.i*, chasser au faucon; (*throat*) graillonner; (*v.t.*) colporter. ~*er*, *n*, colporteur, *m*; crieur, euse; camelot, *m*. ~*ing* (*falconry*) *n*, volerie, *f*.

hawser, *n*, haussière, amarre, *f*, grelin, *m*.

hawthorn, *n*, aubépine, *f*.

hay, *n*, foin, *m*. oft. pl. ~*cock*, tas de foin, *m*. ~ *fever*, fièvre des foins, *f*. ~*loft*, fenil, *m*. ~*maker*, faneur, euse. ~*making*, fenaison, *f*. ~*stack*, meule de foin, *f*.

hazard, *n*, hasard, *m*; (*golf*) hasard, accident, *m*. ¶ *v.t*, hasarder. ~*ous†*, *a*, hasardeux, chanceux.

haze, *n*, brume, *f*, brouillard; nuage, *m*.

hazel, *n*, noisetier, coudrier, *m*; (*att., color, eyes*) [de] noisette. ~*nut*, noisette, *f*.

hazy, *a*, brumeux; nuageux; vaporeux; vague; flou.

he, *pn*, il; lui; celui; ce, c'. ¶ *n. & att*, mâle, *m*. *it is* ~, c'est lui. *there* ~ *is*, le voilà.

head, *n*, tête, *f*; cerveau, *m*; [*of hair*] chevelure, *f*; chef; titre; haut; fond; chapeau; cap, *m*; pointe; pomme; rubrique, *f*, poste, chapitre; en-tête; (*bed*) chevet, *m*; (*on glass of beer*) mousse; (*coin*) face; (*book page*) tête, tranche supérieure, *f*; (*deer*) bois, *m*; (*game*) pièce; (*boar, etc.*) hure, *f*; (*lathe*) poupée, *f*; (*spear*) fer, *m*. ~*s or tails?* pile ou face? ~*ache*, mal de tête, *m*. ~*band*, bandeau, serre-tête, *m*; (*Bookb.*) tranchefile, comète, *f*. ~ *cook*, chef [de cuisine] *m*. ~*dress*, ~*gear*, coiffure, coiffe, *f*, couvre-chef, *m*. ~*land*, pointe de terre, *f*, cap, *m*. ~*light*, feu d'avant, fanal de tête; (*auto*) phare, *m*. ~*line*, (*book*) titre courant, *m*; (*news*) manchette, *f*. ~*long*, *a*, précipité; (*ad.*) précipitamment. ~*master*, directeur; principal; proviseur, *m*. ~*mistress*, directrice, *f*. ~ *office*, siège [principal], siège social, *m*. ~*on collision*, rencontre de front, *f*. ~*phones*, casque, *m*. ~*quarters*, quartier général; (*staff*) Etat-major; chef-lieu, *m*; préfecture, *f*. ~*room*, échappée, *f*. ~*sman*, bourreau, *m*. ~*stone*, pierre tombale, tombe, *f*. ~*strong*, entêté, entier. ~*waiter*, maître d'hôtel, premier garçon, chef de salle, *m*. ~ *waters*, amont, *m*. ~*way*, chemin, progrès, *m*; (*Naut.*) erre, *f*. ~*wind*, vent debout, *m*. ¶ *v.t*, être (*ou* se mettre) à la tête de. ~ *the procession*, ouvrir la marche. ~*ed* (*paper*) *p.a*, à en tête. ~*ing*, *n*, titre; en-tête, *m*. ~*y* (*liquor*) *a*, capiteux.

heal, *v.t*, guérir; (*v.i.*) [se] g. ~*er*,

n, guérisseur, euse; (*of time*) médecin, *m.* ~**ing**, *n*, guérison, *f.*

health, *n*, santé; salubrité; hygiène, *f.* ~**y**, *a*, sain; salubre; hygiénique.

heap, *n*, tas, amas, monceau, *m.* ¶ *v.t*, entasser, amonceler, amasser.

hear, *v.t. & i. ir*, entendre; écouter; (*witness—law*) ouïr; (*learn*) apprendre; (*prayer*) exaucer. ~ *from*, lire. ~**er**, *n*, auditeur, trice. ~**ing**, *n*, ouïe; oreille; audition; **audience**, *f*; débats, *m.pl. to be hard of* ~, avoir l'ouïe (*ou* l'oreille) dure. ~**say**, on-dit, ouï-dire, *m.*

hearse, *n*, corbillard, char [funèbre], char de deuil, *m.*

heart, *n*, cœur, *m*; âme, *f*; entrailles, *f.pl*; fond, vif, *m. by* ~, par cœur, de mémoire. ~ *attack*, crise cardiaque, *f.* ~ *& soul* (*fig.*), tout son cœur. ~*beat*, battement de cœur, *m.* ~*break*, brisement de cœur, *m.* ~*breaking*, ~*rending*, désespérant, navrant, déchirant. ~*burn*, ardeur d'estomac, *f.* ~ *case* (pers.), cardiaque, *m.f.* ~ *disease*, maladie de cœur, *f. in one's* ~ *of* ~*s*, au fond du cœur. ~**en**, *v.t*, encourager, rassurer. ~**felt**, *a*, bien senti. *to be* ~**less**, n'avoir point de cœur. ~*less person*, sans-cœur, *m.f.* **heartsease** (*Bot.*) *n*, pensée, *f.*

hearth, *n*, âtre; foyer; feu; (*smith's*) bâti, *m.* ~ *brush*, balai d'âtre, *m.* ~ *rug*, tapis de foyer, t. de cheminée, *m.* ~*stone*, pierre de foyer, *f*, [marbre de] foyer, *m*; (*whitening*) pierre blanche, *f.*

heartily, *ad*, cordialement; franchement. **hearty**, *a*, cordial; (*fit*) dispos; (*laugh*) gros; (*meal*) solide, copieux.

heat, *n*, chaleur, *f*; calorique, *m*; température; chauffe; fièvre; vivacité, ardeur, *f*, feu, *m*; (*sport*) épreuve, *f*; (*animals*) rut, *m.* ~ *lightning*, éclair[s] de chaleur, *m.*[*pl.*], fulguration, *f.* ~*stroke*, coup de chaleur, *m.* ~ *wave*, vague de c., *f.* ¶ *v.t*, chauffer, échauffer. ~**er**, *n*, calorifère; radiateur; réchaud, *m.*

heath, *n*, (*land*) bruyère, brande, lande, *f*; (*shrub*) bruyère, brande, *f.* ~*cock*, coq de bruyère, *m.*

heathen, *n*, païen, ne. ~[**ish**], *a*, païen. ~**ism**, *n*, paganisme, *m.*

heather, *n*, bruyère, brande, *f.*

heating, *n*, chauffage; échauffement, *m.* ~ *engineer*, fumiste, *m.* ~ *surface*, surface de chauffe, *f.*

heave, *v.t.ir*, soulever; pousser; jeter; lancer; haler; virer; (*v.i.ir.*) palpiter; (*retch*) faire des haut-le-cœur. ~ *to* (*Naut.*), mettre en panne.

heaven, *n*, ciel, *m*, cieux, *m.pl.* ~**ly**, *a*, céleste. **heavily**, *ad*, lourdement, pesamment. **heaviness**, *n*, pesanteur, *f*, poids, *m*; lourdeur, *f.* **heavy**, *a*, lourd; pesant; massif; fort; chargé; grave; gros; grand. ~ *shell* (*Artil.*), marmite, *f.* ~ *weight*, (*for lifting*) gueuse [d'athlétisme] *f*; (*for throwing*) gros boulet; (*Box.*) poids lourd, *m.*

Hebraic & Hebrew, *a*, hébraïque. **Hebrew** (*language*) *n*, l'hébreu, *m.*

hecatomb, *n*, hécatombe, *f.*

heckle, *v.t*, harceler [de questions].

hectic (*fever*) *a*, hectique.

hector, *n*, bravache, fanfaron, *m.*

hedge, *n*, haie, *f.* ~*hog*, hérisson, *m.* ~*row*, haie, *f.* ~ *sparrow*, fauvette des haies, *f*, mouchet, *m.* ¶ *v.t*, entourer d'une haie. (*v.i.*) chercher des échappatoires; (*Fin.*) faire un arbitrage, se couvrir. ~ *in*, []renfermer.

heed, *n*, attention; garde, *f.* ¶ *v.t*, faire attention à. ~**less**, *a*, insoucieux.

heel, *n*, talon, *m*; (*rubber*) talonnette; (*Naut.*) bande, *f. at the* ~*s of*, aux trousses de. *down at the* ~*s*, dans la dèche.

hefty, *a*, solide.

hegemony, *n*, hégémonie, *f.*

heifer, *n*, génisse, *f.*

height, *n*, hauteur, élévation, altitude, *f*; comble, plein, apogée, *m*; (*stature*) taille, *f*; (*of summer*) cœur, fort, *m.* ~**en**, *v.t*, rehausser, surélever.

heinous†, *a*, odieux; atroce.

heir, ess, *n*, héritier, ère, hoir, *m.* ~*loom*, bijou de famille, meuble de famille, *m.* ~*ship*, *n*, hérédité, *f.*

helical, *a*, en hélice, hélicoïdal.

helicopter, *n*, hélicoptère, *m.* **heliport**, *n*, héliport, *m.* ~ *terminal*, héligare, *f.*

heliotrope, n, héliotrope, m.
helium, n, hélium, m.
helix, n, hélice, f; (ear) hélix, m.
hell, n, enfer, m; géhenne, f. ~cat, harpie, f.
Hellenism, n, hellénisme, m.
hellish, a, infernal.
hello (Teleph.) i, allô!
helm, n, barre, f; (fig.) gouvernail, timon, m, helmsman, timonier, homme de barre, m.
helmet, n, casque, m.
helot, n, ilote, m. ~ism, n, ilotisme, m.
help, n, aide, assistance, f, moyen, secours; remède, m. ¶ v.t. & i, aider, assister, secourir. I can't ~ saying, je ne peux m'empêcher de dire. ~ one another, s'entraider. ~ yourself, servez-vous. ~! au secours! à l'aide! à moi! à nous! ~er, n, aide, m.f. ~ful & ~ing, a, utile; serviable. ~ing (food) n, portion, f. ~less, a, impuissant; impotent.
helter-skelter, ad. & n, pêle-mêle, ad. & m.
helve, n, manche, m.
hem, n, ourlet, m; [re]bord, m, bordure, f. ¶ v.t, ourler; border; (v.i.) ânonner. ~ in, cerner.
hematite, n, hématite, f.
hemidemisemiquaver, n, quadruple croche, f.
hemisphere, n, hémisphère, m.
hemlock, n, ciguë, f.
hemorrhage, n, hémorragie, f. **hemorrhoids,** n.pl, hémorroïdes, f.pl.
hemming, n, point d'ourlet, m.
hemp, n, chanvre, m. ~ seed, chènevis, m. ~[en], a, de chanvre.
hemstitch, n, ourlet à jour, m. ¶ v.t, ourler à jour.
hen, n, poule, f. ~ coop, cage à poulets, mue, f. ~ house, poulailler, m. ~ partridge, perdrix femelle, f. ~pecked, mené par sa femme. ~ pheasant, [poule] faisane, f. ~ roost, juchoir, m.
hence, ad, d'ici; de là; dans; partant; donc. ~forth, ~forward, ad, désormais, dorénavant, dès maintenant.
henchman, n, partisan, satellite, séide. mamel[o]uk, m.
henna, n, henné m.
her, pr, elle; la; lui; son, sa, ses.
herald, n, (Hist.) héraut m; (fig.) avant-coureur, m. ¶ v.t, annon-

cer. ~ic, a, héraldique. ~ry, n, blason, m. héraldique, f.
herb, n, herbe, f. ~aceous, a, herbacé. ~age, n, herbage, m. ~al, n, herbier, m. ~alist, n, herboriste, m.f. ~arium, n, herbier, m. ~ivorous, a. & ~ animal, herbivore, a. & m. herborize, v.i, herboriser.
Herculean, a, herculéen. a Hercules, un hercule.
herd, n, troupeau, m; (deer) harde, f. the [common] ~, le vulgaire. the ~ instinct, le sentiment grégaire. ~ together, vivre en troupe. ~ed together, empilé. herdsman, n, bouvier, pâtre, m.
here, ad, ici; que voici; y; présent! ~ a little & there a little, de bric & de broc. ~ & there, ici & là; [de]çà & [de]là; par-ci, par-là. ~ below, ici-bas. ~ I am, me voici. ~ is, ~ are, voici. ~ lies (grave), ci-gît, ici repose. [look] ~! tenez!
hereabout[s], ad, ici près, dans ces parages. hereafter, ad, désormais, à l'avenir; dans la vie future. hereby (law) ad, par les présentes.
hereditary†, a, héréditaire. heredity, n, hérédité, f.
herein (law) ad, dans les présentes. hereinafter, ad, ci-après.
heresy, n, hérésie, f. heretic, n, hérétique, m.f. ~al, a, hérétique.
hereunder, ad, ci-dessous; de ce chef. hereupon, ad, sur ces entrefaites. herewith, ad, ci-joint, ci-inclus.
heritage, n, héritage, patrimoine, m.
hermaphrodite, n, hermaphrodite, m.
hermetic†, a, hermétique.
hermit, n, ermite, solitaire, m. ~ crab, bernard-l'ermite, m. ~age, n, ermitage, m.
hernia, n, hernie, f.
hero, n, héros, m. ~ worship, culte des héros, m. ~ic†, a, héroïque. ~icomic, a, héroï-comique. ~ine, n, héroïne, f. ~ism, n, héroïsme, m.
heron, n, héron, m. ~ry, n, héronnière, f.
herpes, n, herpès, m.
herring, n, hareng, m. ~ boat, harenguier, m. ~boning (Need.) point croisé, m. ~ fishery & ~ season, harengaison, f. red ~, hareng saur, m.

hers, *pn,* le sien, la sienne, les siens, les siennes; ses; à elle. **herself,** *pn,* elle même; elle; soi, soi-même; se.

hesitate, *v.i,* hésiter, balancer, marchander. **hesitation,** *n,* hésitation, *f.*

heterodox, *a,* hétérodoxe. **~y,** *n,* hétérodoxie, *f.*

heterogeneous, *a,* hétérogène.

hew, *v.t.ir,* (*tree*) abattre, couper; (*stone*) tailler.

hexagon, *n,* hexagone, *m.* **~al,** *a,* hexagone. **~ nut,** écrou à 6 pans, *m.* **hexameter,** *n,* hexamètre, *m.*

heyday of life, fleur de l'âge, *f.*

hi, *i,* ohé!

hiatus, *n,* fissure; lacune, *f*; (*Gram.*) hiatus, *m.*

hibernate (*Zool.*) *v.i,* hiberner.

hiccup, *n,* hoquet, *m.* ¶ *v.i,* avoir le h.

hickory, *n,* (*tree, wood*) noyer d'Amérique, *m.*

hidden, *p.p,* caché; dérobé; occulte; latent. **hide,** *v.t.ir,* cacher. **~** [*oneself*], se cacher. **~-&-seek,** cache-cache, *m.*

hide, *n,* peau, *f,* cuir, *m.* *a,* **~ bound,** à l'esprit étroit.

hideous†, *a,* hideux.

hiding (*thrashing*) *n,* raclée, *f.*

hiding place, cache[tte] *f,* affût, *m.*

hierarchy, *n,* hiérarchie, *f.*

hieroglyph, *n,* hiéroglyphe, *m.*

higgledy-piggledy, *ad,* pêle-mêle.

high, *a,* haut; plein; élevé; grand; gros; fort; (*dear*) cher; (*meat*) avancé; (*game*) faisandé; (*in height*) de haut, haut de. **~** *altar,* maître-autel, grand autel, *m.* **~** **&** *dry* (*Naut.*), échoué à sec. **~born,** de haute naissance. **~class,** de marque; (*wine*) grand; haut; perfectionné. **~** *collar,* faux col montant, *m.* **~** *dive,* plongeon d'une grande hauteur, *m.* **~flown,** ampoulé. **~handed,** arbitraire; tyrannique. **~** *hat,* chapeau haut de forme, *m.* **~** *jump,* saut en hauteur, *m.* **~lights** (*Art*), rehauts, *m.pl.* **~** *mass,* grand-messe, messe chantée, *f.* **~-necked dress,** robe montante, *f.* **~** *priest,* grand prêtre, *m.* **~** *society,* **~** *life,* le grand monde. **~** *tide,* marée haute, pleine mer, *f.* *to be* **~-waisted** (*dress*), avoir la taille haute. **~**

water mark, grand de l'eau, *m,* laisse de haute mer, *f*; (*fig.*) apogée, *m.* **~way,** grand chemin, *m,* grand-route, grande route; voie publique, *f.* **~way code,** code de la route, *m.* **~wayman,** voleur de grand chemin, *m.* **~way robbery,** vol de grand chemin, brigandage, *m.* ¶ *ad,* haut. **~er,** *a,* plus haut; supérieur. **~** *bid,* surenchère, *f.* **~** *education,* haut enseignement, *m.* **~** *mathematics,* mathématiques spéciales, *f.pl.* **~** *notes* (*Mus.*), haut, *m.* *the* **~est** *bidder,* le plus offrant [& dernier enchérisseur]. **~ly,** *ad,* hautement; fortement, éminemment. **~** *amusing,* désopilant, impayable. **~** *paid,* très bien payé. **~strung,** nerveux. **~ness,** *n,* hauteur; (*title*) altesse, *f.*

hiker, *n,* excursionniste à pied, *m,f.*

hilarious, *a,* hilare. **hilarity,** *n,* hilarité, *f.*

hill, *n,* colline, *f,* coteau, *m,* côte, hauteur, *f.* **~side,** flanc de coteau. **~top,** cime, *f.* **~ up** **~** **&** *down dale,* par monts & par vaux. ¶ (*Hort.*) *v.t,* butter, chausser. **hillock,** *n,* monticule, tertre, *m,* butte, *f.* **hilly,** *a,* montueux; accidenté.

hilt, *n,* poignée; garde, *f.*

him, *pn,* le; lui. **himself,** *pn,* lui-même; lui; soi, soi-même; se.

hind (*deer*) *n,* biche, *f.*

hind, *a,* de derrière; [d']arrière.

hinder, *v.t,* empêcher, gêner, entraver.

hindmost, *a,* dernier.

hindrance, *n,* empêchement, *m.* *without* **~,** sans encombre.

Hindu, -doo, *a,* hindou. ¶ *n,* Hindou, e. **Hindustani,** *n,* l'hindoustani, *m.*

hinge, *n,* charnière; fiche; penture, *f*; gond, *m.* (*fig.*) pivot, *m.* ¶ *v.i,* tourner, pivoter. **~d,** *p.a,* à charnière(s).

hinny, *n,* petit mulet, bardot, *m.*

hint, *n,* allusion; suggestion, *f*; mot [couvert] *m.* ¶ *v.t,* laisser entendre. **~** *at,* insinuer.

hip, *n,* hanche, *f.* (*Arch.*) arête, croupe, *f.* **~** *bath,* bain de siège, *m.* **~** *bone,* os iliaque, *m.* **~** *measurement,* [con]tour de hanches, *m.*

hippodrome, *n,* hippodrome, *m.*

hippopotamus, *n,* hippopotame, *m.*

hire, *n*, louage, *m*, location, *f*;
loyer, *m*. ¶ *v.t*, louer; (*assassin*,
etc.) soudoyer. ~d, *p.p*, de louage;
à gages; mercenaire. ~ling,
n, mercenaire, *m.f*. **hirer**, *n*, loueur, euse.

hirsute, *a*, hirsute.

his, *pn*, le sien, la sienne, les siens,
les siennes; son, sa, ses; à lui; de
lui.

hiss, *v.t*. & *i*, siffler; chuter.
~[ing,] *n*, sifflement; sifflet, *m*.

historian, *n*, historien, *m*. **historic** & ~al†, *a*, historique; d'histoire. **history**, *n*, histoire, *f*; historique, *m*.

histrion, *n*, histrion, *m*. ~ic, *a*,
du théâtre.

hit, *n*, coup, *m*; pièce à succès;
touche; balle au but, balle mise, *f*,
coup au but, *m*. ~ & run driver,
chauffard, *m*. ~ or miss, au petit
bonheur. (*slang*) ~ song, tube, *m*.
smash ~, succès fou. ¶ *v.t.i.ir*,
frapper; toucher; atteindre; attraper.

hitch, *n*, accroc, contretemps, *m*.
¶ *v.t*, accrocher. ~hiking, autostop, *m*.

hither *ad*, ici, y. ~ & thither, çà
& là; par-ci, par-là. ~to, *ad*,
jusqu'à présent, jusqu'ici.

hive, *n*, ruche, *f*.

hives, *n*, urticaire, *m*.

hoard, *n*, amas; magot, *m*. ¶ *v.t*,
amasser; (*v.i.*) thésauriser.

hoarding, *n*, clôture en planches,
f, palissade, *f*.

hoarfrost, gelée blanche, *f*, givre,
m.

hoarhound, *n*, marrube, *m*.

hoarse, *a*, enroué, éraillé; rauque.
~ness, *n*, enrouement, *m*.

hoary, *a*, blanc; blanchi.

hoax, *n*, mystification; attrape, *f*;
canard, *m*; supercherie, *f*. ¶ *v.t*,
mystifier; attraper. ~er, *n*, mystificateur, trice.

hob, *n*, plaque de cheminée, *f*; dessus [de fourneau] *m*.

hobble, *v.i*, clocher, clopiner, boiter; (*v.t.*) entraver. **hobbledehoy**, *n*, [garçon] godiche, *m*. **hobbling along**, clopin-clopant.

hobby, *n*, (*bird*) hobereau, *m*.
(*an art, collecting, gardening*) **is**
his ~, il est [grand] amateur de
. . ., . . . est sa folie, . . . est sa
distraction. (*a sport*) **is his** ~,

il est passionné pour le . . . ~
horse, cheval de bois; dada, *m*.

hobgoblin, *n*, esprit follet, *m*.

hobnail, *n*, caboche, *f*, gros clou,
m. ~ed, *p.a*, ferré.

hobnob with, être à tu & à toi
avec; trinquer avec.

hobo, *n*, clochard, *m*.

Hobson's choice (**it is**), c'est à
prendre ou à laisser.

hock, *n*, vin blanc du Rhin; (*horse*)
jarret, *m*.

hockey, *n*, hockey, *m*. ~ skates,
patins de h., *m.pl*. ~ stick, crosse
de h., canne de h., *f*, bâton de
h., *m*.

hocus, *v.t*, mystifier, attraper. ~
pocus, *n*, tour de passe-passe, *m*.

hod, *n*, oiseau [de maçon], *m*.

hodgepodge, *n*, méli-mélo, *m*.

hoe, *n*, houe; binette, *f*; sarcloir, *m*.
¶ *v.t*, houer; biner; serfouir.

hog, *n*, cochon; pourceau, porc
[châtré] *m*. ~backed, en dos
d'âne. **hoggish**, *a*, bestial.

hogshead, *n*, barrique, *f*, boucaut, *m*.

hoist, *n*, treuil; monte-charge, *m*.
¶ *v.t*, [re]monter; lever; hisser;
guinder; (*flag*) arborer.

hold, *n*, prise, pince; emprise,
mainmise, *f*; (*Box.*) tenu; empire,
m; (*ship*) cale, *f*. ¶ *v.t.ir*, tenir;
retenir; détenir; occuper; contenir; posséder, avoir; réputer;
célébrer. ~ back, ~ in, retenir.
~fast, crampon, *m*; patte, *f*; valet, *m*. ~ forth, pérorer. ~ on,
tenir [bon], t. sa position. ~ on!
~ the line! (*Teleph.*), ne quittez
pas! ~ one's own, se maintenir.
~ one's nose, se boucher le nez.
~ one's tongue, se taire. ~ out,
tendre; présenter; durer. ~ up,
soutenir. ~er, *n*, support, *m*;
porte- *always m, e.g, tool* ~,
porte-outil, *m*; douille, *f*; (*pers.*)
détenteur, trice; titulaire, *m.f*;
porteur, *m*. ~ing, *n*, tenue; détention; possession; propriété, *f*;
avoir, *m*; valeur, *f*; portefeuille,
m.

hole, *n*, trou; orifice, *m*; ouverture,
(*fox's*) tanière; fosse, *f*, puits;
œil, *m*; lumière, *f*; creux, *m*; piqûre, *f*; (*golf*) trou [d'arrivée], *m*.
¶ *v.t*, trouer, percer; (*golf*) jouer
dans le trou.

holiday, *n*, jour de fête; jour férié, *m*; fête, *f*; vacances, *n*, *f.pl*;
[jour de] congé, *m*.

holily, ad, saintement. **holiness,**
n, sainteté, f.
Holland (Geog.) n, la Hollande.
h~, n, toile écrue, toile bise, f.
hollo, v.t, houper. See hallo.
hollow, a, creux; cave; caverneux; (voice) sourde. to beat
~, battre à plate couture. ¶ n,
creux; enfoncement; entonnoir;
m; cavité, f. ~ [out], v.t, creuser;
évider; caver.
holly, n, houx, m. ~ berry, cenelle, f.
hollyhock, n, rose trémière, passerose, f.
holocaust, n, holocauste, m; (fig.)
immolation saignée, f.
holster, n, (pistol) etui, m, (saddle) fonte, f.
holy, a, saint; sacré; (bread,
water) bénit, e; (day) férié. Holy
Ghost, Saint-Esprit, m. H~
Land, Terre Sainte, f. ~ orders,
ordres sacrés, m.pl, prêtrise, f.
H~ See, Saint-Siège, m. ~-water
basin, bénitier, m. ~-water sprinkler, aspersoir, goupillon, m. H~
Writ, l'Ecriture sainte, f. ~ year,
année jubilaire, f.
homage, n, hommage[s] m.[pl.].
home, n, foyer familial, foyer
[domestique]; chez-moi; chez-
soi; intérieur; logis, m; maison, f;
gîte, m; ménage, m; pays, m; patrie, f; asile; hospice, m. ~ for the
aged, maison de retraite. at ~.
See under at. ¶ ad, chez soi; à la
maison; juste; à fond; à bloc. ¶ a,
domestique; de famille; indigène;
intérieur; métropolitain. ~-land,
terre natale, f. ~ life, vie d'intérieur, f. ~sick, nostalgique. ~sick-
ness, mal du pays, m, nostalgie,
f. ~ truths, vérités bien senties,
bonnes vérités, f.pl. ~work,
(Sch.) devoirs [à faire à la maison]
m.pl. ~less, a, sans foyer, sans
asile. **homeliness,** n, sans façon,
m. **homely,** a, simple, sans façon,
bourgeois.
homeopath[ist], n, homéopathe,
m. **homeopathic,** a, homéopathique. **homeopathy,** n, homéopathie, f.
Homeric, a, homérique.
homespun, n, toile de ménage, f.
homestead, n, ferme, f, manoir,
m. **homeward,** a. & ad, de retour;
en r. ~ bound, en retour, ef-

fectuant son voyage de retour.
~s, ad, en retour.
homicidal, a, homicide. **homicide,** n, (pers.) homicide, m,f;
(act) homicide, m.
homily, n, homélie, f, prône, m.
homing pigeon, pigeon voyageur, m.
homogeneous, a, homogène.
homonym, n, homonyme, m.
homosexual, n, (slang) folle, f,
pédé, m.
hone, n, pierre à aiguiser, f. ¶ v.t,
(razor) repasser; affiler.
honest†, a, honnête, probe, droit,
intègre; brave, de bien. ~y, n,
honnêteté, probité, intégrité.
honey, n, miel; (pers.) chou[chou]
m. ¶ v.t, sucrer. ~ bee, mouche
à miel, f. ~comb, n, gâteau de
miel; rayon de m., m. ~moon,
lune de miel, f, ~suckle, chèvrefeuille, m. ~ed, a, [em]miellé;
mielleux.
honk, n, coup de klaxon, m. ¶ v.i,
klaxoner.
honor, n, honneur, m. ¶ v.t, honorer; faire honneur à, accueillir.
~able†, a, honorable. ~ed, p.a,
honoré; respecté.
honorarium, n, honoraires, m.pl.
honorary, a, honoraire; honorifique; sans rétribution. ~ membership, honorariat, m.
hood, n, capuchon; chapeau;
(auto) capot, m; capote; cape;
capeline, f; dais; soufflet, m;
hotte, f. ~wink, éberluer.
hoof, n, sabot, m. ~ed, a, ongulé.
hook, n, crochet; croc; gond, m;
agrafe, f; (Fish.) hameçon;
(Box.) crochet, m. ~ & eye,
agrafe & porte. ~ & hinge, gond
& penture. by ~ or by crook, de
façon ou d'autre. ¶ v.t, accrocher; agrafer. ~[ed] (nose) a,
aquilin.
hooky [to play] v.i, faire l'école
buissonnière.
hookah, n, narghileh, m.
hooligan, n, apache, voyou, m.
hoop, n, cercle; cerceau, m; frette,
f; arceau, m. ~ iron, feuillard de
fer, m. ~ ring, jonc, m. ¶ v.t,
[en]cercler; relier; fretter.
hoopoe, n, huppe, f.
hoot, v.t, huer, conspuer; (v.i.)
(owl) chuinter. ~[ing] (boo[ing])
n, huée[s] f.[pl.].
hop, n, saut; (pl.) houblon, m. ~

[*plant*], houblon, *m.* ~ *field*, houblonnière, *f.* ~*scotch*, marelle, *f.* ~, *step*, & *jump*, triple saut, *m.* ¶ *v.i,* houblonner; (*v.i.*)sauter à cloche-pied; (*like a sparrow*) sautiller. ~ *about*, s'ébattre.

hope, *n*, espérance, *f*; espoir, *m.* ¶ *v.t.* & *i,* espérer. ~**ful**, *a,* plein d'espoir; encourageant; confiant; optimiste; (*lad*) de grandes espérances. ~**less**, *a,* sans espoir, désespéré; incorrigible. ~**lessness,** *n,* désespérance, *f.*

hopper, *n,* (*insect*) sauteur, *m*; (*Mach.*) trémie, *f.*

horde, *n,* horde, *f.*

horehound, *n,* marrube, *m.*

horizon, *n,* horizon, *m.* **horizontal†,** *a,* horizontal.

hormonal, *a,* hormonal, aux. **hormone,** *n,* hormone, *f.*

horn, *n,* corne, *f*; (*pl, deer*) bois, *m.pl*; (*insect*) antenne, *f*; cor; cornet, *m*; trompe, *f.* ~ *of plenty,* corne d'abondance, *f.* ~*rimmed spectacles,* lunettes en écaille, *f.pl.* **horned cattle,** bêtes à cornes, bêtes cornues, *f.pl.*

hornet, *n,* frelon, *m.* ~*'s nest* (*fig.*), guêpier, *m.*

horny, *a,* corné; (*hands*) calleuses.

horology, *n,* horlogerie, *f.*

horoscope, *n,* horoscope, *m.*

horrible† & **horrid†,** *a,* horrible. **horror,** *n,* horreur, *f.* **horrify,** *v.t,* horrifier.

horse, *n,* cheval, *m*; (*pl.*) cavalerie, *f*; (*trestle*) chevalet, *m,* chèvre, *f.* on ~*back,* à cheval. ~ *bean,* féverole, *f.* ~ *box,* wagon-écurie, *m.* ~-*chestnut,* marron d'Inde; (*tree*) marronnier d'I., *m.* ~ *dealer,* marchand de chevaux, maquignon, *m,* ~*fly,* taon, *m.* ~*hair,* crin, *m.* ~*man,* cavalier, écuyer, *m.* ~*manship,* équitation, *f,* manège, *m.* ~ *play,* jeux de main, *m.pl.* ~*pond,* abreuvoir, *m.* ~ *power,* cheval [vapeur] *m,* force de cheval, *f.* en chevaux, *f.* *a 10* ~ [*power*] *car,* une [automobile de] 10 chevaux. ~ *race,* course de chevaux, *f.* ~ *racing,* les courses, *f.pl.* ~*radish,* raifort, *m.* ~*shoe,* fer à cheval, *m.* ~ *show,* concours hippique, *m.* ~*tail plume,* crinière, *f.* ~*whip,* *n,* cravache, *f*; (*v.t.*) cravacher. ~*woman,* cavalière, écu-

yère, amazone, *f.* ~*y, a,* de cheval, chevalin.

horticultural, *a,* horticole. **horticulture,** *n,* horticulture, *f.* **horticulturist,** *n,* horticulteur, *m.*

hosanna, *n,* hosanna, *m.*

hose, *n,* (*dress, col. as pl.*) bas, *m.pl*; (*pipe*) tuyau, boyau, *m,* manche, *f.* **hosier,** *n,* chemisier, bonnetier, *m.* ~*y, n,* chemiserie, bonneterie, *f.*

hospitable, *a,* hospitalier. **hospital,** *n,* hôpital, *m.* ~ *attendant,* ~ *nurse,* infirmier, ère. ~ *ship,* vaisseau-hôpital, *m.* **hospitality,** *n,* hospitalité, *f.* **hospitalize,** *v.t,* hospitaliser.

host, *n,* (*pers.*) hôte, *m*; armée, *f,* bataillon, *m,* troupe, nuée, phalange; (*Eccl.*) hostie, *f.* ~**ess,** *n,* hôtesse, *f.*

hostage, *n,* otage, *f*; (*fig.*) gage, *m.*

hostel, *n,* auberge, *f,* foyer d'étudiants, *m,* maison des étudiants, auberge de jeunesse, *f*; hospice, *m,* institution, *f.* ~**ry** (*archaic*) *n,* hôtellerie, *f.*

hostile†, *a,* hostile. **hostility,** *n,* hostilité, *f.*

hostler, *n,* garçon d'écurie, palefrenier, *m.*

hot, *a,* chaud; à chaud; ardent; brûlant. *to get* ~ chauffer. ~*bed,* (*Hort.*) couche [de fumier] *f*; (*fig.*) foyer, *m.* *in* ~ *haste,* en toute hâte, au [grand] galop. ~*head,* cerveau brûlé, *m,* échauffé, e. ~*headed,* bouillant, impétueux. ~*house,* serre chaude, *f.* ~*house grapes,* raisin de serres, *m.* ~ *plate,* réchaud, *m.* ~ *spring,* source thermale, *f.* ~ *water bottle,* boule d'eau chaude, *f.*

hotchpotch, *n,* (*Cook.*) hochepot, (*Cook. & fig.*) salmigondis, pot pourri, *m.*

hotel, *n,* hôtel, *m.* ~ *keeper,* hôtelier, ère.

hot line, *n,* téléphone rouge, *m,* ligne r., *f.*

hotly, *ad,* chaleureusement.

hound, *n,* chien courant, c. de chasse, chien, *m*; (*bitch*) lice, *f.* ~ *out,* chasser.

hour, *n,* heure, *f.* ~*glass,* sablier, *m.* ~ *hand,* petite aiguille, *f.* *office* ~*s,* heures de bureau, *f.pl.* ~*ly, a,* par heure; (*ad.*) d'heure en heure.

house, *n*, maison, *f*; logis, *m*; habitation, *f*; hôtel; pavillon, *m*; bâtiment; ménage, *m*; (*Theat.*) salle, *f*. *neither ~ nor home*, ni feu ni lieu. *~ boat*, bateau d'habitation, *m*. *~breaking*, effraction, *f*, cambriolage, *m*. *~ fly*, mouche commune, *f*. *~ full* (*Theat.*) complet. *~hold*, ménage, *m*; (*staff*) maison, domesticité, *f*. *~hold gods*, dieux familiers, dieux pénates, *m.pl*. *~hold goods*, ménage, *m*. *~hold linen*, linge de maison, *m*. *~keeper*, femme de charge; ménagère, *f*. *~keeping*, ménage, *m*; économie domestique, *f*. *~maid*, fille de service, servante, *f*. *~ martin*, hirondelle de fenêtre, *f*. *~ number*, numéro d'habitation, *m*. *~ painter*, peintre en bâtiments, *m*. *~ top*, toit, *m*. *to give a ~warming*, pendre la crémaillère. *~wife*, maîtresse de maison; ménagère, *f*. *~wifery*, ménage, *m*. *~work*, ménage, *m*. ¶ *v.t*, loger; mettre à l'abri; (*carp.*, *etc.*) encastrer, emboîter; (*harvest*) rentrer, engranger. **housing**, *n*, logement, *m*. *~ problem*, crise du logement, *f*.

hovel, *n*, taudis, bouge, *m*, baraque, *f*.

hover, *v.i*, planer, voltiger; se balancer.

hovercraft, *n*, aéroglisseur, *m*.

how, *ad*, comment; comme; que. *any~*, de toute façon. *~ are you?*, ça va? *~ long?* combien de temps? *~ much? ~ many?* combien?

however, *ad*, de quelque manière que; quelque . . . que, si . . . que; tout . . . que; pourtant.

howitzer, *n*, obusier, *m*.

howl, *n*, hurlement, *m*. ¶ *v.i*, hurler; (*wind*) gronder. *~er*, *n*, bévue, gaffe, *f*.

hoyden, *n*, gamine bruyante, *f*, garçon manqué, *m*.

hub, *n*, moyeu; (*fig.*) centre, *m*.

hubbub, *n*, brouhaha, charivari, *m*.

hubcap, *n*, enjoliveur, *m*.

huckaback, *n*, toile ouvrée, *f*. *~ towel*, serviette nid d'abeilles, *f*.

huckster, *n*, agent de publicité, marchande des quatre-saisons, colporteur, *m*. ¶ *v.t*, colporter; marchander.

huddle, *v.t*, entasser; (*v.i.*) se blottir.

hue, *n*, teinte; nuance, *f*.

hue & cry, haro, tocsin, tollé, *m*.

huff, *v.i*, souffler; (*anger*) s'emporter; malmener. *he is in a ~*, il a pris la mouche.

hug, *n*, étreinte, *f*, embrassement, *m*, accolade, *f*. ¶ *v.t*, serrer, étreindre, embrasser; (*the wind*, *Naut.*) pincer le vent; (*the shore*) côtoyer; (*an error*) chérir.

huge, *a*, énorme, immense, démesuré. *~ly*, *ad*, énormément, immensément, démesurément.

hulk, *n*, vaisseau rasé; ponton, *m*. *~ing*, *a*, balourd.

hull, *n*, (*husk*) cosse; (*ship*) coque, *f*, corps, *m*. ¶ *v.t*, monder.

hullabaloo, *n*, hourvari, *m*.

hullo[a], *i*, hé! ohé! tiens!

hum, *v.i. & t*, (*bee, etc.*) bourdonner; (*top*) ronfler; (*tune*) fredonner, chantonner. ¶ *n*, fredon, *m*. ¶ *i*, hem! hom!

human†, *a*, humain. **humane†**, *a*, humain. **humanitarian**, *a. & n*, humanitaire. *a. & m*. **humanity**, *n*, humanité, *f*. **humanize**, *v.t*, humaniser.

humble†, *a*, humble. ¶ *v.t*, humilier, abaisser, mater. *~ness*, *n*, humilité; (*birth*) bassesse, *f*. *the humbler classes*, le menu peuple.

humbug, *n*, blague; mystification, *f*; (*pers.*) blagueur, euse; mystificateur, trice; imposteur, *m*. ¶ *i*, chansons! chansons! ¶ *v.t*, mystifier; lanterner, enjôler; mettre dedans.

humdrum, *a*, monotone; banal; assoupissant.

humerus, *n*, humérus, *m*.

humid, *a*, humide. *~ity*, *n*, humidité, *f*.

humiliate, *v.t*, humilier. **humiliation**, *n*, humiliation, *f*. **humility**, *n*, humilité, *f*.

humming bird, oiseau-mouche, colibri, *m*.

humming top, toupie d'Allemagne, *f*.

hummock, *n*, mamelon; monticule, *m*.

humorist, *n*, humoriste, *m*; farceur, euse. **humorous**, *a*, humoriste; humoristique; drôle, drolatique. *~ly*, *ad*, avec humour; par facétie. **humor**, *n*, (*mood*) humeur, disposition, *f*; (*jocosity*) humour, *m*. ¶ *v.t*, complaire à, flatter; ménager.

hump, *n*, bosse, *f*. *~back*, *n*. & *~backed*, *a*, bossu, e.

humph, i, hem!, hom!

hunch, n, bosse, f; (*chunk*) chanteau, m; (*feeling*) pressentiment, m. ~ back, n. & ~backed, a, bossu, e.

hundred, a. & n, cent, a. & m. ~ [*or so*], centaine, f. ~fold, n, centuple, m. ~th, a. & n, centième, a. & m.

Hungarian, a, hongrois. ¶ n, Hongrois, e; (*language*) le hongrois. **Hungary,** n, la Hongrie.

hunger, n, faim, fringale, f. ~ strike, grève de la faim, f. ~ striker, gréviste de la faim, m,f. ~ after, être affamé de, avoir une fringale de. **hungrily,** ad, d'un œil affamé; avidement. **hungry,** a, affamé. to be ~, very ~, avoir faim, grand-faim.

hunk, n, chanteau, (*bread*) guignon, m.

hunt, n, chasse; (*riding to hounds*) chasse à courre; (*équipage de chasse,* m. ¶ v.t. & i, chasser, courir. ~ for, chercher. ~er, n, chasseur; cheval de chasse; (*curios*) dénicheur, m. **hunting,** n, chasse; c. à courre; (*science*) vénerie, f. **huntress,** n, chasseuse, f. **huntsman,** n, chasseur; (*man in charge*) veneur, piqueur, m.

hurdle, n, claie; haie, f. ~ fence, échalier, m. ~ race, course de haies, f; steeple-chase, m.

hurl, v.t, lancer, darder, projeter.

hurly-burly, n, tohu-bohu, m.

hurrah, ~ray, n, hourra, hosanna, m. ¶ i, bravo! vivat!

hurricane, n, ouragan, m. ~ deck, pont de manœuvre; pont abri, m. ~lamp, lanterne-tempête, f.

hurry, n, précipitation, hâte; presse, f. ¶ v.t, presser, hâter, précipiter; (v.i.) se hâter. ~ up, se dépêcher. be in a ~, avoir 'hâte.

hurt, n, mal, m; blessure, lésion, f; tort, m. ¶ v.t.ir, faire [du] mal à; blesser; nuire à.

husband, n, mari, époux, m. ¶ v.t, ménager.

husbandman, n, cultivateur, m. **husbandry,** n, économie rurale, agronomie, f.

hush, n, silence, m. ~ money, prix du silence, m. ¶ i, silence!; chut!; motus!; paix! ¶ v.t, faire taire. ~ up, étouffer.

husk, n, cosse, f; (*walnut*) brou,

m; (*grain*) balle, f. ¶ v.t, (*corn*) éplucher; (*barley*) monder; écosser. ~y, (*hoarse*) a, enroué, éraillé.

hussy, ~zzy, n, coquine, friponne, drôlesse, masque, f.

hustle, v.t, bousculer.

hut, n, hutte, cabane, baraque, f.

hutch, n, cabane, f, clapier, m.

hyacinth, n, jacinthe, hyacinthe, f.

hybrid, a, hybride, métis. ¶ n, hybride, mulet, m.

hydra, n, hydre, f.

hydrangea, n, hortensia, m.

hydrant, n, bouche [d'eau], prise d'eau, f.

hydrate, n, hydrate, m.

hydraulic, a. & ~s, n.pl, hydraulique, a. & f.

hydrocarbon, n, hydrocarbure, m. **hydrochloric,** a, chlorhydrique. **hydrofoil,** n, hydroptère, m. **hydrogen,** n, hydrogène, m. **hydropathic,** a, hydrothérapique. ¶ n, établissement hydrothérapique, m. **hydropathy,** n, hydrothérapie, f. **hydrophobia,** n, hydrophobie, f. **hydroplane,** n, hydravion, hydroglisseur, m.

hyena, n, hyène, f.

hygiene & hygienics, n, hygiène, f. **hygienic(al)**†, a, hygiénique.

hymen, n, hymen, hyménée, m.

hymenoptera, n.pl, hymenoptères, m.pl.

hymn, n, hymne, m; (*in church*) hymne, f, cantique, m. ~ book, recueil d'hymnes, m.

hyperbola & hyperbole, n, hyperbole, f.

hyphen, n, trait d'union, tiret, m; (*end of line*) division, f.

hypnotism, n, hypnotisme, m. **hypnotize,** v.t, hypnotiser.

hypochondriac, a. & n, hypochondriaque, a. & n. **hypocrisy,** n, hypocrisie, f. **hypocrite,** n, hypocrite, m.f. **hypocritical**†, a, hypocrite. **hypodermic,** a, hypodermique. ~ syringe, seringue de Pravaz, f. **hypothecation,** n, nantissement, m. **hypothesis,** n, hypothèse, f. **hypothetic(al)**†, a, hypothétique.

hysteria, n, hystérie, f. **hysteric(al)**, a, hystérique; nerveux. **hysterics,** n.pl, crise de nerfs, f, nerfs, m.pl.

I

I, *pn*, je; moi.
iambic, *a*, ïambique. ¶ *n*, ïambe, *m*.
ibex, *n*, bouquetin, *m*.
ibis, *n*, ibis, m.
ice, *n*, glace, *f*. oft. pl. ~ age, période glaciaire, *f*. ~ *berg*, iceberg, *m*. ~*bucket*, sceau à glace, *m*. ~ *cream*, glace, *f*. ~ *cream freezer*, sorbetière, *f*. ~ *cream pop*, esquimau, *m*. ~ *cream vender*, glacier, *m*. ~ *cube*, glaçon, *m*. ~ *hockey*, hockey sur glace, *m*. ~ *pack*, banquise, *f*. ~*pick*, piolet, *m*. ~ *skates*, patins à glace, *m.pl.* ¶ *v.t.* glacer; (*wine*) frapper [de glace].
Iceland, *n*, l'Islande, *f*. ~**er**, *n*, Islandais, e. ~**ic**, *a*. & (*language*) *n*, islandais, *a*. & *m*.
ichthyology, *n*, ichtyologie, *f*.
icicle, *n*, glaçon, *m*. **icing**, (*sugar*) *n*, glace, *f*.
icon, *n*, icône, *f*. **iconoclast**, *n*, iconoclaste, démolisseur, *m*.
icy, *a*, glacé, glacial.
idea, *n*, idée, pensée; image, *f*. ~ *man*, concepteur, *m*. **ideal**†, *a*. & *n*, idéal, *a*. & *m*. ~**ism**, *n*, idéalisme, *m*. ~**ist**, *n*, idéaliste, *m,f*.
identical†, *a*, identique. **identification**, *n*, identification, *f*. **identify**, *v.t*, identifier. **identity**, *n*, identité, *f*.
idiocy, *n*, idiotie, *f*.
idiom, *n*, (*dialect*) idiome; (*phrase*) idiotisme, *m*.
idiosyncrasy, *n*, idiosyncrasie, *f*.
idiot, *n*. & ~**ic**, *a*, idiot, e.
idle, *a*, oisif; paresseux; fainéant; inoccupé; désœuvré; de loisir; sans affaires; futile; oiseux, en l'air. ~ *fancy*, rêverie, *f*. ¶ *v.i*, paresser, fainéanter; (*motor*) tourner au ralenti. ~**ness**, *n*, oisiveté; paresse, *f*; chômage, *m*. **idler**, *n*, oisif, ive, paresseux, euse, fainéant, e; badaud, e. **idly**, *ad*, dans l'oisiveté.
idol, *n*, idole, *f*; amour, *m*. **idolater**, **tress**, *n*, idolâtre, *m.f*. **idolatrous**, *a*, idolâtre, idolâtrique. **idolatry**, *n*, idolâtrie, *f*. **idolize**, *v.t*, idolâtrer.
idyll, *n*, idylle, *f*. **idyllic**, *a*, idyllique.

if, *c*, si, s'. ~ *not*, sinon.
igneous, *a*, igné. **ignis fatuus**, *n*, feu follet, *m*. **ignite**, *v.t*, enflammer; allumer. **ignition**, *n*, ignition; inflammation, *f*; allumage, *m*. ~ *key*, clef de contact, *m*. ~ *lock*, antivol, *m*. *to switch off the* ~, couper l'allumage.
ignoble†, *a*, ignoble.
ignominious†, *a*, ignominieux. **ignominy**, *n*, ignominie, *f*.
ignoramus, *n*, ignorant, e, ignare, *m,f*. **ignorance**, *n*, ignorance, *f*. **ignorant**, *a*, ignorant, ignare. *to be* ~ *of*, ignorer.
ignore, *v.t*, méconnaître; ne faire aucune attention à.
iguana, *n*, iguane, *m*.
ill, *n*, mal, *m*. *speak* ~ *of*, médire de. ¶ *a*, malade; souffrant; mauvais; méchant. ¶ *ad*, mal; peu. ~-*advised*, malavisé; malvenu, mal venu. ~-*assorted*, disparate. ~-*bred*, mal élevé, malappris, sans éducation. ~-*famed*, malfamé, mal famé. ~-*fated*, ~-*starred*, néfaste. ~ *feeling*, inimitié, *f*. ~-*gotten gains*, biens mal acquis, *m.pl.* ~ *humor*, humeur, *f*. ~ *luck*, mauvaise chance, malchance, *f*, malheur, *m*. ~-*mannered*, malhonnête. ~-*natured* (*person*), méchant, e. ~-*omened*, de mauvis augure, funèbre. ~-*temper*, humeur [chagrine] *f*. ~-*tempered*, d'h. c., revêche, hargneux. ~-*timed*, intempestif; déplacé. ~-*use*, maltraiter, faire un mauvais parti à. ~ *will*, malveillance, *f*. *to bear* ~ *will*, en vouloir à.
illegal†, *a*, illégal.
illegible†, *a*, illisible.
illegitimacy, *n*, illégitimité, *f*. **illegitimate**†, *a*, illégitime.
illicit†, *a*, illicite.
illiterate, *a*, illettré.
illness, *n*, maladie, *f*, mal, *m*.
illogical, *a*, illogique. ~**ity**, *n*, illogisme, *m*.
illuminate, *v.t*, éclairer; (*festively*) illuminer, embraser; (*MS.*) enluminer, historier. **illumination**, *n*, éclairage, *m*; illumination, *f*, embrasement *m*; enluminure, *f*. **illumine**, *v.t*, éclairer.
illusion, *n*, illusion, tromperie, *f*. **illusive**, **illusory**, *a*, illusoire.
illustrate, *v.t*, illustrer. ~*d price*

list, tarif-album, *m.* **illustration**, *n*, illustration; gravure, *f;* exemple, *m.* **illustrious**, *a*, illustre. *to make ~*, illustrer.

image, *n*, image, *f.* **~ry**, *n*, images, *f.pl.* **imaginary**, *a*, imaginaire.

imagination. *n*, imagination, *f.*

imagine, *v.t. & i*, imaginer; s'imaginer; se figurer.

imbecile, *a*, imbécile. ¶ *n*, idiot, e.

imbibe, *v.t*, absorber; s'imbiber de; boire, sucer.

imbricate, *v.t*, imbriquer.

imbroglio, *n*, imbroglio, *m.*

imbrue, *v.t*, tremper.

imbue, *v.t*, impregner, (*fig.*) pénétrer. *~d*, *p.p*, imbu, inspiré.

imitate, *v.t*, imiter; contrefaire. **imitation**, *n*, imitation; contrefaçon, *f;* (*att.*) [d']imitation, simili-; faux. **imitator**, *n*, imitateur, trice.

immaculate, *a*, immaculé. *the I~ Conception*, l'Immaculée Conception, *f.*

immanent, *a*, immanent.

immaterial, *a*, immatériel; sans importance.

immature, *a*, prématuré; . pas mûr.

immeasurable, *a*, immensurable.

immediate†, *a*, immédiat.

immemorial, *a*, immémorial.

immense, *a*, immense. **~ly**, *ad*, immensément. **immensity**, *n*, immensité, *f.*

immerse, *v.t*, immerger, plonger. **immersion**, *n*, immersion, *f.*

immigrant, *n*, immigrant, *m.* **immigrate**, *v.i*, immigrer.

imminence, *n*, imminence, *f.* **imminent**, *a*, imminent.

immobile, *a*, immobile. **immobility**, *n*, immobilité, *f.* **immobilization**, *n*, immobilisation, *f.* **immobilize**, *v.t*, immobiliser.

immoderate†, *a*, immodéré.

immodest†, *a*, immodeste.

immolate, *v.t*, immoler.

immoral, *a*, immoral. **~ity**, *n*, immoralité, *f.*

immortal†, *a. & n*, immortel, *a. & m.* **~ity**, *n*, immortalité, *f.* **~ize**, *v.t*, immortaliser. **immortelle**, *n*, immortelle, *f.*

immovable†, *a*, inébranlable, immobile; (*feelings*) insensible.

immunity, *n*, immunité; exemption; franchise, *f.*

immunize, *v.t*, immuniser.

immure, *v.t*, claquemurer, cloîtrer.

immutable†, *a*, immuable.

imp, *n*, diablotin, lutin, démon, *m.*

impact, *n*, choc, *m;* percussion,

impair, *v.t*, détériorer; endommager; altérer; compromettre.

impale, *v.t*, embrocher; (*Hist.*) empaler.

impalpable, *a*, impalpable.

impanel a jury, former une liste de jurés, former un tableau.

impart, *v.t*, impartir; imprimer; faire part de.

impartial†, *a*, impartial. **~ity**, *n*, impartialité, *f.*

impassable, *a*, impraticable, infranchissable.

impassible & impassive, *a*, impassible.

impassioned, *p.p*, passionné.

impasto, *n*, empâtement de couleurs, *m.*

impatience, *n*, impatience, *f.* **impatient**, *a*, impatient. *to grow ~*, s'impatienter. **~ly**, *ad*, impatiemment.

impeach, *v.t*, accuser. **~ment**, *n*, accusation, *f.*

impecunious, *a*, besogneux.

impede, *v.t*, entraver, empêcher. **impediment**, *n*, empêchement, obstacle, *m. ~ of speech, ~ in one's speech*, empêchement (*ou* embarras) de la langue, *m.* **impedimenta**, *n.pl*, impedimenta, *m.pl.*

impel, *v.t*, pousser, animer.

impending, *p.a*, imminent.

impenetrable, *a*, impénétrable.

impenitence, *n*, impénitence, *f.* **impenitent**, *a*, impénitent.

imperative†, *a. & n*, impératif, *a. & m.*

imperceptible†, *a*, imperceptible, insaisissable.

imperfect†, *a. & ~ [tense]*, *n*, imparfait, *a. & m.* **~ion**, *n*, imperfection, *f.*

imperial, *a*, impérial; (*weights & measures*) *anglais*. ¶ (*beard*) impériale, *f.* **~ist**, *n. & ~istic**, *a*, impérialiste, *m. & a.*

imperil, *v.t*, mettre en danger.

imperious†, *a*, impérieux.

imperishable, *a*, impérissable.

impermeable, *a*, imperméable.

impersonal†, *a*, impersonnel.

impersonate, v.t, personnifier.
impersonation, n, personnification; (Theat.) création; (law) supposition de personne, f.
impertinence, n, impertinence, f. **impertinent**, a, impertinent. ~ly, ad, impertinemment.
imperturbable†, a, imperturbable.
impervious, a, imperméable, impénétrable.
impetuous†, a, impétueux.
impetus, n, impulsion, f, élan, branle, m.
impiety, n, impiété, f.
impinge [up]on, venir en contact avec; empieter sur.
impious, a, impie.
impish, a, lutin, espiègle.
implacable†, a, implacable.
implant, v.t, implanter.
implement, n, instrument, ustensile, m. ¶ v.t, rendre effectif; ajouter.
implicate, v.t, impliquer. not ~d, désintéressé. **implication**, n, implication, f; sous-entendu, m. **implicit†**, a. & **implied**, p.a, implicite, tacite.
implore, v.t, implorer, supplier.
imply, v.t, impliquer; insinuer; sous-entendre.
impolite†, a, impoli. ~ness, n, impolitesse, f.
impolitic, a, impolitique.
imponderable, a. & n, impondérable, a. & m.
import, n, (meaning) portée, signification, f, sens, m; (Com., etc.) importation, f. ~ duty, droit d'entrée, m, entrée, f. ¶ v.t, signifier; (Com., etc.) importer.
importance, n, importance, f. **important**, a, important.
importation, n, importation, f. **importer**, n, importateur, m.
importunate, a, importun. **importune**, v.t, importuner. **importunity**, n, importunité, f.
impose, v.t, imposer; (fine) frapper. ~ [up]on someone, en faire accroire à (ou en imposer à) quelqu'un. person of imposing appearance, porte-respect, m. **imposition**, n, imposition; imposture, f.
impossibility, n, impossibilité, f, l'impossible, m. **impossible**, a, impossible.
impost (Arch.) n, imposte, f.

impostor, n, imposteur, m. **imposture**, n, imposture, f.
impotence, ~cy, n, impotence; (sexual) impuissance, f. **impotent**, a, impotent; (sexual) impuissant.
impound, v.t, mettre à la fourrière; enfermer; confisquer.
impoverish, v.t, appauvrir.
impracticable, a, infaisable, impraticable.
imprecation, n, imprécation, f.
impregnable, a, imprenable, inexpugnable.
impregnate, v.t, imprégner; féconder. ~d (wood) p.a, injecté.
impresario, n, impresario, m.
impress, n, empreinte, impression, f. ¶ v.t, imprimer, empreindre; graver; impressionner; réquisitionner. ~ion, n, impression; empreinte, f; (Typ.) foulage, m. to be under the ~, avoir dans l'idée. ~ionism, n, impressionnisme, m. **impressive**, a, impressionnant; solennel.
imprint, n, empreinte; marque de l'éditeur, m. ¶ v.t, imprimer, empreindre.
imprison, v.t, emprisonner. ~ment, n, emprisonnement, m; prison, f.
improbability, n, improbabilité, invraisemblance, f. **improbable**, a, improbable, invraisemblable. **improbably**, ad, invraisemblablement.
impromptu, ad. a. & n, impromptu, ad. a.inv. & m.
improper, a, impropre, abusif; inconvenant, incongru; vice de . . .; faux. ~ly, ad, improprement; abusivement. **impropriety**, n, inconvenance, incongruité; impropriété, f.
improve, v.t, améliorer; perfectionner; bonifier; amender. ~ on, renchérir sur. ~ on acquaintance, gagner à être connu. ~ment, n, amélioration, f; perfectionnement, m; bonification, f; embellissement, m.
improvidence, n, imprévoyance, f. **improvident**, a, imprévoyant.
improvise, v.t, improviser.
imprudence, n, imprudence, f. **imprudent**, a, imprudent. ~ly, ad, imprudemment.
impudence, n, impudence, f, toupet, m. **impudent**, a, impu-

dent. **~ly**, *ad*, impudemment.
impudicity, *n*, impudicité, *f*.
impugn, *v.t*, attaquer.
impulse & impulsion, *n*, impulsion, *f*; mouvement; branle, *m*. **impulsive**, *a*, impulsif; primesautier.
impunity, *n*, impunité, *f*. *with ~*, impunément.
impure†, *a*, impur. **impurity**, *n*, impureté, *f*.
imputation, *n*, imputation, *f*. **impute**, *v.t*, imputer.
in, *pr*, dans; en; à; au; entre; chez; auprès de; sur; sous; par; de; pour; à la. ¶ *ad*, dedans; chez, y; arrivé. **~** *between*, entre deux. **~** *demand*, demandé. **~** *fashion*, à la mode, de mode, de mise. **~** *print*, imprimé, disponible. **~** *there*, là-dedans. **ins & outs**, détours; êtres, *m.pl*.
inability, *n*, incapacité, *f*.
inaccessible, *a*, inaccessible, inabordable.
inaccuracy, *n*, inexactitude, infidélité, *f*. **inaccurate†**, *a*, inexact, infidèle.
inaction, *n*, inaction, *f*. **inactive**, *a*, inactif.
inadequate, *a*, insuffisant. **~ly**, *ad*, insuffisamment.
inadmissible, *a*, inadmissible.
inadvertently, *ad*, par inadvertance, par mégarde.
inalienable, *a*, inaliénable, incessible.
inane, *a*, inepte, absurde.
inanimate, *a*, inanimé. **~** *nature*, le monde inanimé. **inanition**, *n*, inanition, *f*.
inanity, *n*, inanité, ineptie, *f*.
inapplicable, *a*, inapplicable.
inapposite, *a*, hors de propos.
inappreciable, *a*, inappréciable.
inappropriate†, *a*, impropre, qui ne convient pas, peu en situation.
inapt, *a*, inapte. **inaptitude**, *n*, inaptitude, *f*.
inarticulate, *a*, inarticulé.
inasmuch, *ad*, étant donné. **~** *as*, vu que.
inattentive, *a*, inattentif.
inaudible†, *a*, imperceptible [à l'ouïe].
inaugurate, *v.t*, inaugurer.
inauspicious, *a*, défavorable.
inborn & inbred, *a*, inné, infus, naturel, natif.
incalculable, *a*, incalculable.
incandescence, *n*, incandes-

cence, *f*. **incandescent**, *a*, incandescent; (*lamp, etc.*) à incandescence.
incantation, *n*, incantation, *f*.
incapable, *a*, incapable; inhabile; non-susceptible. **incapably**, *ad*, inhabilement. **incapacitate**, *v.t*, rendre incapable. **incapacity**, *n*, incapacité; impéritie, *f*.
incarcerate, *v.t*, incarcérer.
incarnate, *a*, incarné. **incarnation**, *n*, incarnation, *f*.
incautious, *a*, imprudent.
incendiarism, *n*, incendie volontaire, *m*. **incendiary**, *a. & n*, incendiaire, *a. & m.f*.
incense, *n*, encens, *m*. **~** *burner*, brûle-parfum, *m*. ¶ *v.t*, (*perfume*) encenser; (*enrage*) courroucer.
incentive, *n*, aiguillon; mobile, ressort, *m*.
inception, *n*, commencement, *m*.
incessant, *a*, incessant. **~ly**, *ad*, incessamment.
incest, *n*, inceste, *m*. **incestuous**, *a*, incestueux.
inch, *n*, pouce, *m* = 2.54 (about 2½) centimètres.
incidence, *n*, incidence, *f*. **incident**, *n*, incident, événement, *m*. ¶ *a*, incident. **~al**, *a*, incident. **~** *expenses*, faux frais, *m.pl*. **~ally**, *ad*, incidemment.
incinerate, *v.t*, incinérer. **incinerator**, *n*, incinérateur, *m*.
incipient, *a*, naissant.
incise, *v.t*, inciser. **incision**, *n*, incision, *f*. **incisive**, *a*, incisif. **incisor**, *n*, [dent] incisive, *f*.
incite, *v.t*, inciter, provoquer; exciter. **~ment**, *n*, incitation; excitation, *f*.
incivility, *n*, incivilité, *f*.
inclemency, *n*, inclémence, *f*. **inclement**, *a*, inclément.
inclination, *n*, inclination, *f*; penchant; attrait, *m*; inclinaison, *f*. **incline**, *n*, plan incliné, *m*; (*down*) pente; (*up*) rampe, *f*. ¶ *v.t. & i*, incliner; pencher; porter; (*color*) tirer. **inclined**, *p.a* & *p.p*, (*plane*) incliné; (*fig.*) enclin, porté.
include, *v.t*, comprendre, englober, renfermer. *the tip is ~d*, le service est compris. **including**, *participle*, y compris. *not ~*, non compris. **inclusive**, *a*, tout compris; (*sum*) globale; (*dates*) inclusivement. **~** *of*, y compris. **~ly**, *ad*, inclusivement.

incognito, *ad.* & *n,* incognito, *ad.* & *m.*

incoherence, *n,* incohérence, *f.* **incoherent,** *a,* incohérent.

incombustible, *a,* incombustible.

income, *n,* revenu, *m. oft. pl;* rapport, *m;* rente, *f. oft. pl.* ~ *tax,* impôt sur le revenu, *m,* impôt[s] cédulaire[s], *m.[pl.].* ~ *tax return,* déclaration de revenu, *f.*

incoming, *a,* à l'arrivée; d'arrivée; d'entrée; à échoir; (*tide*) montante.

incommensurable, *a,* incommensurable. **incommensurate with,** hors de proportion avec.

incommode, *v.t.* incommoder.

incomparable†, *a,* incomparable.

incompatibility, *n,* incompatibilité, *f.* ~ *of temper,* incompatibilité d'humeurs. **incompatible,** *a,* incompatible.

incompetence, -cy, *n,* incompétence, incapacité, *f.* **incompetent,** *a,* incompétent, incapable, insuffisant.

incomplete†, *a,* incomplet. **incompletion,** *n,* imperfection, *f.*

incomprehensible, *a,* incompréhensible.

inconceivable, *a,* inconcevable.

inconclusive, *a,* non concluant.

incongruity, *n,* incongruité, disparate, *f.* **incongruous,** *a,* incongru, disparate. ~**ly,** *ad,* incongrûment.

inconsequent[ial], *a,* inconséquent.

inconsiderable, *a,* sans importance.

inconsiderate†, *a,* inconsidéré.

inconsistency, *n,* inconséquence; inconsistance, *f.* **inconsistent,** *a,* inconséquent; inconsistant.

inconsolable†, *a,* inconsolable, inguérissable.

inconspicuous, *a,* peu (*ou* pas) en évidence.

inconstancy, *n,* inconstance, *f.* **inconstant,** *a,* inconstant, volage, journalier.

incontinent, *a,* incontinent.

incontrovertible, *a,* incontestable.

inconvenience, *n,* incommodité, *f;* inconvénient, *m.* ¶ *v.t,* incommoder. **inconvenient,** *a,* incommode.

incorporate, *v.t,* incorporer; encadrer; enchâsser; (*a company*) s'incorporer, former une société.

incorrect†, *a,* incorrect; inexact. ~**ness,** *n,* incorrection; inexactitude, *f.*

incorrigible†, *a,* incorrigible, indécrottable.

incorruptible, *a,* incorruptible.

increase, *n,* augmentation, *f,* accroissement, *m,* majoration, *f.* ¶ *v.t,* augmenter, accroître; aggraver, majorer. **increasing,** *p.a.,* croissant. ~**ly,** *ad,* de plus en plus.

incredibility, *n,* incrédibilité, *f.* **incredible†,** *a,* incroyable. **incredulity,** *n,* incrédulité, *f.* **incredulous,** *a,* incrédule.

increment, *n,* accroissement, *m;* plus-value, *f.*

incriminate, *v.t,* incriminer, charger.

incrust, *v.t,* incruster.

incubate, *v.t.* & *i,* couver. **incubation,** *n,* incubation, *f.* **incubator,** *n,* couveuse artificielle, poussinière, *f.*

incubus, *n,* cauchemar; faix, *m.*

inculcate, *v.t,* inculquer.

inculpate, *v.t,* inculper.

incumbent, *n,* bénéficier, titulaire, *m. to be* ~ *on,* incomber à.

incur, *v.t,* encourir; courir; s'attirer.

incurable†, *a.* & *n,* incurable, *a.* & *m,f.*

incursion, *n,* incursion, *f.*

indebted, *a,* redevable. ~**ness,** *n,* dette; créance, *f;* dettes & créances, *f.pl.*

indecency, *n,* indécence, malpropreté, *f.* **indecent,** *a,* indécent, malpropre. ~**ly,** *ad,* indécemment, malproprement.

indecision, *n,* indécision, *f.*

indecorous, *a,* inconvenant.

indeed, *ad,* vraiment, en effet; certes; bien, voire même, même. ¶ *i,* vraiment!, tiens!

indefatigable†, *a,* infatigable.

indefensible, *a,* indéfendable.

indefinable, *a,* indéfinissable. **indefinite†,** *a,* indéfini; (*leave*) illimité.

indelible, *a,* indélébile.

indelicacy, *n,* indélicatesse, *f.* **indelicate†,** *a,* indélicat.

indemnify, *v.t,* indemniser, dédommager. **indemnity,** *n,* indemnité; caution, *f.*

indent, *v.t,* denteler, échancrer; (*Typ.*) renfoncer, [faire] rentrer. **indentation,** *n,* dentelure, échancrure, *f;* (*Typ.*) renfoncement, *m.* **indention,** *n,* renfoncement, *m.* **indenture,** *n,* acte, contrat; (*pl.*) brevet, *m.*

independence, *n,* indépendance, *f.* **independent,** *a,* indépendant. *to be* ~, (*financially*) avoir une fortune indépendante. *person of* ~ *means,* rentier, ère. ~**ly,** *ad,* indépendamment.

indescribable, *a,* indescriptible, indicible.

indestructible, *a,* indestructible.

indeterminate, *a,* indéterminé.

index, *n,* indice, *m;* table; table alphabétique, *f;* index; répertoire, *m.* ~ *expurgatorius,* index expurgatoire. ¶ *v.t,* dresser la table [alphabétique] de, répertorier.

India, *n,* l'Inde, *f.* ~ *paper,* papier indien, *m.* **Indian,** *a,* indien. ~ *Archipelago,* archipel Indien, *m,* Insulinde, *f.* ~ *club,* massue en bois, *f,* mil, *m.* ~ *corn,* blé de Turquie, maïs, *m.* ~ *ink,* encre de Chine, *f.* ~ *Ocean,* océan Indien, *m,* mer des Indes, *f.* ¶ *n,* Indien, ne.

indicate, *v.t,* indiquer, désigner. **indication,** *n,* indication, *f;* indice, *m.* **indicative,** *a,* indicatif. ~ [*mood*], *n,* [mode] indicatif, *m.* **indicator,** *n,* indicateur, *m.*

indict, *v.t,* accuser. ~**ment,** *n,* acte d'accusation, réquisitoire, *m.*

Indies (the) *n.pl,* les Indes, *f.pl.*

indifference, *n,* indifférence; indolence, *f.* **indifferent,** *a,* indifférent; indolent; sans gêne. ~**ly,** *ad,* indifféremment.

indigence, *n,* indigence, *f.*

indigenous, *a,* indigène.

indigent, *a,* indigent.

indigestible, *a,* indigeste, cru [à l'estomac]. **indigestion,** *n,* indigestion, *f.*

indignant, *a,* indigné. ~**ly,** *ad,* avec indignation. **indignation,** *n,* indignation, *f.* **indignity,** *n,* indignité, *f.*

indigo, *n,* indigo, *m.* ~ *blue,* [bleu d']inde, *m.* ~ *plant,* indigotier, *m.*

indirect†, *a,* indirect.

indiscreet†, *a,* indiscret. **indiscretion,** *n,* indiscrétion; imprudence, *f.*

indiscriminate, *a,* sans aucun

discernement; confus. ~**ly,** *ad,* indistinctement, sans distinction.

indispensable†, *a,* indispensable.

indisposed, *p.p,* indisposé. **indisposition,** *n,* indisposition, *f,* malaise, *m;* disposition peu favorable, *f.*

indisputable†, *a,* indiscutable.

indissoluble†, *a,* indissoluble.

indistinct†, *a,* indistinct.

indite, *v.t,* rédiger; composer.

individual†, *a,* individuel. ¶ *n,* individu; particulier, *m.* ~**ity,** *n,* individualité, *f.*

indivisible†, *a,* indivisible.

Indochina, *n,* l'Indochine, *f.*

indoctrinate, *v.t,* endoctriner.

indolence, *n,* indolence, *f.* **indolent,** *a,* indolent, mou. ~**ly,** *ad,* indolemment.

indomitable, *a,* indomptable; (*will*) irréductible.

indoor, *a,* d'intérieur; de cabinet; (*games*) de société. ~**s,** *ad,* à la maison; à l'abri.

indorse, *v.t,* endosser; adopter; confirmer; garantir. ~**ment,** *m,* endossement, endos, *m;* souscription; adhésion; garantie, *f.*

indubitable†, *a,* indubitable.

induce, *v.t,* porter; décider; engager; induire; provoquer. ~**ment,** *n,* mobile, motif, *m;* tentation, *f.*

induct, *v.t,* installer; introduire. ~**ion,** *n,* induction; (*Eccl.*) installation, *f.*

indulge, *v.t,* gâter; caresser. ~ *in,* se permettre. **indulgence,** *n,* indulgence, *f.* **indulgent,** *a,* indulgent.

indurate, *v.t,* [en]durcir.

industrial†, *a,* industriel. ~ *disease,* maladie professionnelle, *f.* ~**ism,** *n,* industrialisme, *m.* ~**ist,** *n,* industriel, *m.* ~**ize,** *v.t,* industrialiser. **industrious,** *a,* industrieux, diligent, travailleur, assidu. **industriously,** *ad,* industrieusement, diligemment. **industry,** *n,* industrie; diligence, *f.*

inebriate, *a,* ivre. ¶ *n,* ivrogne, *m,* ivrognesse, *f.* ¶ *v.t,* enivrer.

ineffable, *a,* ineffable.

ineffaceable, *a,* ineffaçable.

ineffective† & **ineffectual†** & **inefficacious†,** *a,* inefficace.

inefficient, *a,* incapable.

inelastic, *a,* sans élasticité; sans souplesse.

inelegant, *a,* inélégant.
ineligible, *a,* inéligible.
inept, *a,* inepte. **ineptitude,** *n.* ineptie, *f.*
inequality, *n,* inégalité, *f.*
inequitable†, *a,* injuste.
ineradicable, *a,* indéracinable.
inert, *a,* inerte. **inertia,** *n,* inertie, *f.*
inestimable, *a,* inestimable.
inevitable†, *a,* inévitable.
inexact†, *a,* inexact. **inexactitude,** *n,* inexactitude, *f.*
inexcusable, *a,* inexcusable.
inexecutable, *a,* inexécutable.
inexhaustible†, *a,* inépuisable, intarissable.
inexorable†, *a,* inexorable.
inexpedient, *a,* pas expédient.
inexpensive, *a,* peu coûteux.
inexperience, *n,* inexpérience, *f.* **~d,** *a,* inexpérimenté, novice, neuf.
inexplicable, *a,* inexplicable.
inexplicit, *a,* pas explicite.
inexpressible, *a,* inexprimable.
inextinguishable, *a,* inextinguible.
inextricable, *a,* inextricable.
infallible†, *a,* infaillible, impeccable.
infamous, *a,* infâme; (*law*) infamant. **infamy,** *n,* infamie, *f.*
infancy, *n,* enfance, *f;* bas âge, *m;* (*law*) minorité, *f.* **infant,** *n,* [petit, e] enfant, *m,f;* (*law*) mineur, e. **~ mortality,** mortalité infantile, *f.* **~ prodigy,** enfant prodige. **infanticide,** *n,* infanticide (*act*) *m;* (*pers.*) *m,f.* **infantile,** *a,* enfantin; (*Med.*) infantile.
infantry, *n,* infanterie, *f.* **~man,** fantassin, *m.*
infarct, *n,* infarctus, *m.*
infatuate, *v.t,* affoler, embéguiner. *to become* **~d,** s'infatuer, s'engouer. **infatuation,** *n,* infatuation, *f,* engouement, *m.*
infect, *v.t,* infecter, empester. **~ion,** *n,* infection, *f.* **~ious,** *a,* infectieux; contagieux.
infer, *v.t,* inférer, conclure, supposer, déduire. **~ence,** *n,* inférence, conclusion, déduction, *f.* **inferential,** *a,* déductif. **~ly,** *ad,* par déduction.
inferior†, *a. & n,* inférieur, *a. & m.* **~ity,** *n,* infériorité, *f.* **~ complex,** complexe d'i., *m.*

infernal, *a,* infernal. **inferno,** *n,* enfer, *m.*
infertile, *a,* infertile.
infest, *v.t,* infester.
infidel, *a. & n,* infidèle, *a. & m,f.* **~ity,** *n,* infidélité, *f.*
infighting (*Box.*) *n,* combat de près, *m.*
infiltrate, *v.i,* s'infiltrer.
infinite†, *a,* infini. **the ~,** l'infini, *m.* **infinitesimal,** *a,* infinitésimal. **infinitive** [**mood**], *n,* [mode] infinitif, *m.* **infinitude & infinity,** *n,* infinité; immensité, *f.* **infinity** (*Math., Phot.*) *n,* l'infini, *m.*
infirm, *a,* infirme. **~ary,** *n,* infirmerie, *f.* **~ity,** *n,* infirmité, *f.*
inflame, *v.t,* enflammer; exalter. **inflammable,** *a,* inflammable. **inflammation,** *n,* inflammation, *f.*
inflate, *v.t,* gonfler; (*fig.*) enfler; grossir; charger. **~d** (*fig.*) *p.p,* enflé, ampoulé, boursouflé. **inflation,** *n,* gonflement, *m;* enflure; (*Fin.*) inflation, *f.* **runaway ~,** flambée des prix, *f.*
inflect, *v.t,* infléchir. **~tion,** *n,* inflexion; flexion, *f.* **inflexible†,** *a,* inflexible.
inflict, *v.t,* infliger. **~ion,** *n,* infliction, *f;* châtiment, *m;* peine, *f.*
influence, *n,* influence, *f;* crédit, *m;* cote d'amour, *f.* ¶ *v.t,* influer sur; influencer. **influential,** *a,* influent, prestigieux.
influenza, *n,* grippe, *f.*
influx, *n,* venue; invasion, *f.*
inform, *v.t,* informer, instruire, renseigner, faire part, mander, prévenir. **~al,** *a,* sans cérémonie; officieux; (*law*) informe. **~ality,** *n,* vice de forme, *m.* **~ant,** *n,* informateur, trice, auteur, *m.* **~ation,** *n,* renseignement[s], *m.* [*pl.*], indication[s] *f.*[*pl.*]; (*law*) dénonciation, *f.* **~er,** *n,* délateur, trice, indicateur, trice.
infraction, *n,* infraction, *f.*
infrequent, *a,* peu fréquent, rare.
infringe, *v.t,* enfreindre, contrevenir à; contrefaire. **~ment,** *n,* infraction, contravention; contrefaçon, *f.* **~ of copyright,** contrefaçon littéraire, c. de librairie.
infuriate, *v.t,* faire enrager.
infuse, *v.t,* infuser. **infusible,** *a,* infusible. **infusion,** *n,* infusion; tisane, *f.*
ingenious†, *a,* ingénieux. **ingenuity,** *n,* ingéniosité, industrie, *f.*

ingenuous†, *a*, ingénu, naïf, candide.

inglenook, coin du feu, *m*.

inglorious†, *a*, honteux, ignominieux; obscur.

ingoing, *a*, entrant.

ingot, *n*, lingot, saumon, *m*.

ingrained, *a*, enraciné, invétéré.

ingratiate oneself with, s'insinuer dans les bonnes grâces de.

ingratitude, *n*, ingratitude, *f*.

ingredient, *n*, ingrédient, *m*.

ingress, *n*, entrée, *f*.

ingrowing (*nail*) *a*, incarné.

inhabit, *v.t*, habiter. ~**able**, *a*, habitable. ~**ant**, *n*, habitant, *e*.

inhale, *v.t*, inhaler, aspirer, respirer, humer.

inherent, *a*, inhérent; propre.

inherit, *v.t. & abs*, hériter, succéder à. ~**ance**, *n*, héritage, patrimoine, *m*, succession; (*right*) hérédité, *f*.

inhibit, *v.t*, interdire, réprimer. ~**ed**, *a*, (*psychologically*) refoulé. ~**ion**, *n*, interdiction, inhibition, *f*.

inhospitable, *a*, inhospitalier.

inhuman†, *a*, inhumain. ~**ity**, *n*, inhumanité, *f*.

inimical, *a*, ennemi, hostile.

inimitable, *a*, inimitable.

iniquitous†, *a*, inique. **iniquity**, *n*, iniquité, *f*.

initial, *a*, initial. ¶ *n*, initiale, *f*; (*pl.*) parafe, *m*, initiales, *f.pl*. ¶ *v.t*, parafer, viser.

initiate, *n*, initié, *e*. ¶ *v.t*, prendre l'initiative de; (*pers.*) initier; entamer, lancer. **initiation**, *n*, initiation, *f*. **initiative**, *n*, initiative, *f*.

inject, *v.t*, injecter; seringuer. ~**ion**, *n*, injection, *f*. ~**or**, *n*, injecteur, *m*.

injudicious, *a*, peu judicieux.

injunction, *n*, injonction, *f*.

injure, *v.t*, léser; nuire à; offenser; endommager; blesser. ~ *fatally*, blesser à mort. **injurious†**, *a*, nuisible; malfaisant; préjudiciable; injurieux. **injury**, *n*, injure, *f*; préjudice, tort, *m*; lésion, blessure, *f*.

injustice, *n*, injustice, *f*; passe-droit, *m*.

ink, *n*, encre, *f*. ~ *eraser*, gomme pour l'encre, *f*. ~*well*, encrier, *m*. ¶ *v.t*, encrer; tacher d'encre. ~ *in*, mettre à l'encre. ~ *up* (*Typ.*), toucher.

inkling, *n*, indication, idée, *f*.

inlaid, *p.a*: ~ *linoleum*, linoléum incrusté, *m*. ~ *work*, incrustation; marqueterie, *f*.

inland, *a*, intérieur. ¶ *ad*, dans l'intérieur [du pays].

inlay, *v.t.ir*, incruster; marqueter.

inlet, *n*, crique; entrée; arrivée, *f*.

inmate, *n*, habitant, *e*; hôte, esse; (*paying*) pensionnaire, *m,f*; (*asylum*) interné, *e*; hospitalisé, *e*.

inmost, *a*, le plus intime.

inn, *n*, auberge, *f*. ~*keeper*, aubergiste, *m,f*.

innate, *a*, inné, infus. ~**ness**, *n*, innéité, *f*.

inner, *a*, intérieur, interne. ~ *harbor*, arrière-port, *m*. the ~ *man*, l'homme intérieur. ~ *tube* (tire), chambre à air, *f*.

innermost, *a*, le plus intime.

innings, *n*, tour, *m*.

innocence, *n*, innocence, *f*. **innocent**, *a. & n*, innocent, *a. & m*. ~**ly**, *ad*, innocemment.

innocuous, *a*, inoffensif.

innovation, *n*, innovation, nouveauté, *f*. **innovator**, *n*, novateur, trice.

innuendo, *n*, insinuation, allusion, *f*.

innumerable, *a*, innombrable.

inobservance, *n*, inobservance, inobservation, *f*.

inoculate, *v.t*, inoculer. **inoculation**, *n*, inoculation, *f*.

inodorous, *a*, inodore.

inoffensive, *a*, inoffensif.

inoperative, *a*, inopérant.

inopportune, *a*, inopportun. ~**ly**, *ad*, mal à propos, à contretemps.

inordinate†, *a*, démesuré.

inorganic, *a*, (*matter*) inorganique; (*body*) brut; (*chemistry*) minérale.

inpatient, *n*, malade interné, *e*, hospitalisé, *e*.

input-output, *n*, (*computers*) entrée-sortie, *f*.

inquest, *n*, enquête, *f*.

inquire, *v.t. & i*, demander; s'informer (de); s'enquérir (de); se renseigner; s'adresser; enquêter. **inquirer**, *n*, chercheur, euse; demandeur de renseignements. *inquiring mind*, [esprit] chercheur, *m*. **inquiry**, *n*, demande, *f*; renseignements, *m.pl*; informations, *f.pl*; recherche; enquête, *f*;

informé, *m*. ~ *office*, bureau de renseignements, *m*.

inquisition, *n*, inquisition, *f*.
inquisitive, *a*, inquisiteur; curieux.

inroad & **inrush,** *n*, incursion; irruption, venue, *f*.

insane, *a*, fou; insensé. **insanity,** *n*, démence, aliénation d'esprit; (*folly*) insanité, *f*.

insanitary, *a*, insalubre, malsain.

insatiable†, *a*, insatiable.

inscribe, *v.t*, inscrire; graver; dédier. **inscription,** *n*, inscription; dédicace, *f*.

inscrutable, *a*, inscrutable, impénétrable.

insect, *n*, insecte, *m*. ~ *powder*, poudre insecticide, *f*. **insectivora,** *n.pl*, insectivores, *m.pl*. **insectivorous,** *a*, insectivore.

insecure, *a*, mal assuré. **insecurity,** *n*, insécurité, *f*.

insensate, *a*, insensé. **insensible†,** *a*, insensible; sans connaissance. **insensitive,** *a*, insensible.

inseparable†, *a*. & *n*, inséparable, *a*. & *m,f*.

insert (*Bookb.*) *n*, encart, *m*. ¶ *v.t*, insérer; (*Bookb.*) encarter. **~ion,** *n*, insertion, *f*; intercolage; ajout, *m*.

inset, *n*, pièce rapportée, *f*. ¶ *v.t.ir*, rapporter, encarter.

inshore, *a*, côtier. ~ *fishing*, pêche côtière, pêche dans les eaux territoriales, *f*.

inside, *n*, dedans; intérieur, *m*. ¶ *a*, intérieur; d'i. ¶ *ad*, [en] dedans, à l'intérieur; (*Meas.*) dans œuvre. ~ *out*, à l'envers.

insidious†, *a*, insidieux.

insight, *n*, pénétration, *f*. aperçu, *m*.

insignia, *n.pl*, insignes, *m.pl*.

insignificant, *a*, insignifiant, infime.

insincere, *a*, qui n'est pas sincère; faux; dissimulé. **insincerity,** *n*, absence de sincérité, dissimulation *f*.

insinuate, *v.t*, insinuer, faufiler.

insipid, *a*, insipide, fade, fadasse.

insist, *v.i*, insister. **~ence,** *n*, insistance, *f*.

insobriety, *n*, intempérance, *f*.

insolation, *n*, insolation, *f*.

insolence, *n*, insolence, *f*. **insolent,** *a*, insolent. **~ly,** *ad*, insolemment.

insoluble, *a*, insoluble.

insolvency, *n*, insolvabilité, carence, faillite; déconfiture, *f*. **insolvent,** *a*, insolvable. ¶ *n*, failli, *m*.

insomnia, *n*, insomnie[s] *f*.[*pl*.].

inspect, *v.t*, inspecter, visiter; contrôler; (*excise*) exercer. **~ion,** *n*, inspection, visite, *f*, contrôle; exercice, *m*; revue, *f*. ~ *committee*, comité de surveillance, *m*. **~or,** *n*, inspecteur, trice; visiteur; contrôleur; (*weights*) vérificateur, *m*. **~orship,** *n*, inspection, *f*.

inspiration, *n*, inspiration; aspiration; illumination, *f*, souffle, *m*. **inspire,** *v.t*, inspirer; aspirer.

inspirit, *v.t*, animer. **~ing,** *a*, entraînant.

instability, *n*, instabilité, *f*.

install, *v.t*, installer, emménager. **~ation,** *n*, installation, *f*.

installment, *n*, acompte, paiement à compte; versement; terme; fascicule, *m*. ~ *plan*, vente à tempérament, *f*; facilités de paiement, *f.pl*.

instance, *n*, cas, *m*; demande; (*law*) instance, *f*. *for* ~, par exemple. ¶ *v.t*, citer. **instant,** *a*, instant; (*month*) courant. ¶ *n*, instant, *m*. **instantaneous,** *a*, instantané. **~ly,** *ad*, instantanément.

instead, *ad*, plutôt. ~ *of*, au lieu de, à la place de, pour.

instep, *n*, cou-de-pied, *m*.

instigate, *v.t*, provoquer, inciter. **instigation,** *n*, instigation, *f*.

instill, *v.t*, instiller; (*fig.*) inculquer, infuser, faire pénétrer.

instinct, *n*, instinct, *m*. ¶ *a*, doué, animé. **~ive†,** *a*, instinctif.

institute, *n*, institut, *m*. ¶ *v.t*, instituer; intenter. **institution,** *n*, institution, *f*; institut, établissement, *m*.

instruct, *v.t*, instruire; charger; (*counsel*) constituer. **~ion,** *n*, instruction, *f*; (*pl.*) instructions, indications, *f.pl*, charge, *f*, mandat, *m*. **~ive,** *a*, instructif. **instructor,** *n*, professeur; (*Mil.*) instructeur; (*Mil. gym.*) moniteur, *m*. **instructress,** *n*, professeur, *m*.

instrument, *n*, instrument; (*law*) instrument, acte, *m*. ~ *board*, tableau de bord, *m*. **~al,** *a*, instrumental. **~alist,** *n*, instrumentiste, *m,f*. **~ality,** *n*, intermédiaire, *m*.

insubordinate, *a*, insubordonné.

insufferable†, *a,* insupportable.
insufficiency, *n,* insuffisance, *f.* **insufficient,** *a,* insuffisant. **~ly,** *ad,* insuffisamment.
insular, *a,* insulaire. **~ity,** *n,* insularité, *f.*
insulate, *v.t,* isoler. **insulation,** *n,* isolement, *m.* **insulator,** *n,* isolateur, *m.*
insult, *n,* insulte, injure, *f,* outrage, *m.* ¶ *v.t,* insulter, outrager. **~ing†,** *a,* injurieux, offensant, outrageant, outrageux.
insuperable, *a,* insurmontable.
insupportable†, *a,* insupportable.
insurance, *n,* assurance, *f;* (*mail*) chargement, *m.* **~ company,** compagnie d'assurance[s] *f.* **insure,** *v.t,* assurer, faire a.; (*mail*) charger; (*v.i.*) s'assurer, se faire assurer. **~d** (*pers.*) *n,* assuré, e. **~d package,** colis avec valeur déclarée, colis chargé, *m.* **insurer,** *n,* assureur, *m.*
insurgent, *n. & a,* insurgé, e, révolté, e.
insurmountable, *a,* insurmontable.
insurrection, *n,* insurrection, *f.*
intact, *a,* intact.
intaglio, *n,* intaille, *f.*
intake, *n,* prise, admission, *f,* appel, *m.*
intangible, *a,* intangible.
integer, *n,* [nombre] entier, *m.* **integral†,** *a,* intégral. **integrate,** *v.t,* intégrer. **integrity,** *n,* intégrité, *f.*
intellect, *n,* intellect, *m,* intelligence, *f,* cerveau, *m.* **intellectual†,** *a. & n,* intellectuel, *a. & m.*
intelligence, *n,* intelligence, *f,* entendement, *m;* nouvelles, *f.pl;* chronique, *f,* courrier, *m.* **~ department,** service des renseignements, *m,* statistique militaire, *f.* **intelligent,** *a,* intelligent. **~ly,** *ad,* intelligemment. **intelligible†,** *a,* intelligible.
intemperance, *n,* intempérance, *f.* **intemperate,** *a,* intempérant.
intend, *v.t,* se proposer, avoir l'intention, compter; vouloir; destiner. **~ed,** *n,* prétendu, e, futur, e.
intense, *a,* intense. **~ly,** *ad,* extrêmement. **intensifier** (*Phot.*) *n,* renforçateur, *m.* **intensify,** *v.t,* intensifier; (*Phot.*) renforcer. **intensity,** *n,* intensité, *f.*

intent, *a,* fixe. **~ on,** tout entier à. ¶ *n,* intention, *f,* but, *m.* **to all ~s & purposes,** virtuellement. **~ion,** *n,* intention, *f,* but; motif *m.* **~ional†,** *a,* intentionnel, voulu. **-intentioned,** *a,* intentionné. **intentness,** *n,* contention, *f.*
inter, *v.t,* enterrer, inhumer.
intercalate, *v.t,* intercaler.
intercede, *v.i,* intercéder.
intercept, *v.t,* intercepter, surprendre.
intercession, *n,* intercession, *f.* **intercessor,** *n,* intercesseur, *m.*
interchange, *n,* communication, *f,* échange, *m.* **~able,** *a,* interchangeable.
intercom, *n,* interphone, *m.*
intercourse, *n,* commerce, *m;* relations, *f.pl;* rapports, *m.pl.*
interdict, *n,* interdit, *m.* ¶ *v.t,* interdire. **~ion,** *n,* interdiction, *f.*
interest, *n,* intérêt, *m;* intérêts, *m.pl;* arrérages, *m.pl;* usure; commandite, *f.* **to take no further ~,** se désintéresser de. **~ on overdue payments,** intérêts moratoires. **~ payable** (date) jouissance. ¶ *v.t,* intéresser. **~ed,** *p.a,* intéressé; curieux. **~ party,** intéressé, e. **~ing,** *p.a,* intéressant; attachant. **in an ~ condition** (pregnant), dans une situation intéressante.
interfere, *v.i,* intervenir, s'immiscer, s'ingérer. **~ with** (hinder), contrarier, gêner. **interference,** *n,* intervention, immixtion, ingérence; (*Phys.*) interférence, *f;* (*radio*) brouillage, *m.*
interim, *n,* intérim, *m.* **~ dividend,** acompte de dividende, dividende intérimaire, dividende provisoire, *m.*
interior†, *a, & n,* intérieur, *a. & m.*
interject, *v.t,* placer. **~ion,** *n,* interjection, *f.*
interlace, *v.t,* entrelacer.
interlard, *v.t,* entrelarder.
interleave, *v.t,* interfolier.
interline, *v.t,* écrire dans l' (*ou* en) interligne. **interlinear,** *a,* interlinéaire. **interlineation,** *n,* entre-ligne, *m.*
interlock, *v.i,* s'engrener, s'entrelacer.

interlocutor, tress or trix, *n*, interlocuteur, trice.

interloper, *n*, intrus, e.

interlude, *n*, intervalle, intermède; (*Mus.*) interlude, *m.*

intermarriage, *n*, mariage entre individus de tribus diverses (*ou* de races différentes), *m*, alliance, *f.* **intermarry**, *v.i*, se marier entre eux, s'allier.

intermeddle, *v.i*, se mêler, s'immiscer.

intermediary, *n.* & *a*, intermédiaire, *m.* & *a.* **intermediate**, *a*, intermédiaire. ~ *course*, (*Sch.*), cours moyen, *m.*

interment, *n*, enterrement, *m*, inhumation, *f.*

intermezzo, *n*, intermède, *m.*

interminable, *a*, interminable.

intermingle, *v.t*, entremêler.

intermission, *n*, (*Theat.*) entracte; relâche, intermédiaire, *m.* **intermittent**, *a*, intermittent.

intermix, *v.t*, entremêler.

intern, *v.t*, interner. ¶ *n*, interne, *m.*

internal, *a*, interne; intérieur; intestin. ~**ly**, *ad*, intérieurement.

international, *a*, international. ~**ist**, *n.* & *a*, internationaliste, *m,f.* & *a.*

internecine, *a*, meurtrier, à outrance.

internment, *n*, internement, *m.* ~ *camp*, (*civil*) camp de concentration; (*Mil.*) camp de prisonniers, *m.*

interplanetary, *a*, interplanétaire.

interpolate, *v.t*, interpoler.

interpose, *v.t*, interposer; (*v.i.*) s'interposer.

interpret, *v.t*, interpréter; traduire. ~**ation**, *n*, interprétation, *f.* ~**er**, *n*, interprète, *m,f.*

interregnum, *n*, interrègne, *m.*

interrogate, *v.t*, interroger. **interrogation**, *n*, interrogation, *f.* **interrogative**†, *a*, interrogatif. **interrogatory**, *n*, interrogatoire, *m.*

interrupt, *v.t*, interrompre; couper. ~**er**, *n*, (*pers.*) interrupteur, trice; (*Elec.*) rupteur, *m.* **interruption**, *n*, interruption, *f.*

intersect, *v.t*, couper; entrecouper. ~**ion**, *n*, intersection, *f.*

intersperse, *v.t*, entremêler; émailler.

interstice, *n*, interstice, *m.*

intertwine, *v.t*, entrelacer.

interval, *n*, intervalle, entretemps, *m.*

intervene, *v.i*, intervenir. **intervention**, *n*, intervention, *f.*

interview, *n*, entretien, *m*, entrevue, *f*; (*for news*) interview, *m.* ¶ *v.t*, interviewer.

interweave, *v.t.ir*, entrelacer. *interwoven pattern* (fabrics), brochure, *f.*

intestate, *a*, intestat (*inv.*).

intestinal, *a*, intestinal. **intestine**, *a.* & *n*, intestin. *a.* & *m.*

intimacy, *n*, intimité, familiarité, *f.* **intimate**†, *a.* & *n*, intime, *a.* & *m*, lié, *a*, familier, *a.* & *m.* ¶ *v.t*, faire entendre, signifier. **intimation**, *n*; indication, premonition, *f.*

intimidate, *v.t*, intimider.

into, *pr*, dans; en; à; entre; par; par-dessus.

intolerable†, *a*, intolérable. **intolerance**, *n*, intolérance, *f.* **intolerant**, *a*, intolérant.

intonation, *n*, intonation, *f.* **intonate**, **intone**, *v.t*, entonner.

intoxicate, *v.t*, enivrer. ~**d**, *a*, ivre, enivré. **intoxication**, *n*, ivresse, *f.*

intractable, *a*, intraitable, indocile.

intransitive†, *a*, intransitif.

intrench, *v.t*, retrancher.

intrepid†, *a*, intrépide. ~**ity**, *n*, intrépidité, *f.*

intricacy, *n*, complication; *f*; embrouillement, *m.* **intricate**, *a*, compliqué, embrouillé.

intrigue, *n*, intrigue, brigue, *f.* ¶ *v.i*, intriguer, briguer, cabaler; (*v.t.*) intriguer. **intriguer**, *n.* & **intriguing**, *a*, intrigant, e.

intrinsic†, *a*, intrinsèque.

introduce, *v.t*, introduire; insinuer; présenter. ~ *into society*, produire dans le monde. ~ *oneself*, se présenter, se faire connaître. **introducer**, *n*, introducteur, trice. **introduction**, *n*, introduction; présentation, *f.*

introit, *n*, introït, *m.*

introspection, *n*, introspection, *f.*

intrude, *v.i*, s'introduire [contre le droit *ou* la forme], se faufiler. **intruder**, *n*, intrus, e, importun, e. **intrusion**, *n*, intrusion, *f.*

intuition, *n*, intuition, *f.* **intuitive**, *a*, intuitif. ~**ly**, *ad*, par intuition.

inundate, v.t, inonder. **inundation**, n, inondation, f.

inure, v.t, aguerrir, accoutumer; habituer.

invade, v.t, envahir. **invader**, n, envahisseur, m.

invalid, a, malade, infirme, invalide; (law) invalide; non valable. ¶ n, malade, infirme, m,f, invalide, m. ¶ v.t, réformer. ~ate, v.t, invalider, casser. **invalided**, p.a, invalide, réformé. **invalidity**, n, invalidité, f.

invaluable, a, inestimable, impayable.

invariable†, a, invariable.

invasion, n, invasion, f, envahissement, m.

invective, n, invective, f. **inveigh**, v.i, invectiver, tonner.

inveigle, v.t, enjôler.

invent, v.t, inventer, imaginer. ~**ion**, n, invention, f. ~**ive**, a, inventif, original. **inventor, tress**, n, inventeur, trice, m.

inventory, n, inventaire, m, description, f. ¶ v.t, inventorier.

inverse†, a, inverse, réciproque. **inversion**, n, inversion, f; renversement, m. **invert**, v.t, renverser; invertir.

invertebrate, a. & n, invertébré, a. & m.

invest, v.t, revêtir; investir; cerner; (money) placer, investir.

investigate, v.t, rechercher, examiner. **investigation**, n, investigation, enquête, f. **investigator**, n, investigateur, trice.

investiture, n, investiture, f.

investment, n, placement, m; valeur, f; portefeuille, m; mise [de fonds] f; (Mil.) investissement, m. **investor**, n, personne qui place ses fonds, f.

inveterate, a, invétéré, acharné, vivace.

invidious, a, méchant; odieux. ~ distinction, distinction contre le droit & l'usage ordinaire, f, passe-droit, m.

invigorate, v.t, fortifier, vivifier.

invincible†, a, invincible.

inviolable†, a, inviolable. **inviolate**, a, inviolé.

invisible†, a, invisible. ~ mending, reprise perdue, f, stoppage, m.

invitation, n, invitation, f; appel, m. **invite**, v.t, inviter, prier;

convier; appeler, faire appel à. **inviting**, p.a, engageant.

invocation, n, invocation, f.

invoice, n, facture, f. ¶ v.t, facturer.

invoke, v.t, invoquer.

involuntary†, a, involontaire.

involve, v.t, envelopper; entraîner; impliquer; empêtrer. ~**d**, p.a, compliqué, embrouillé. ~ language, tortillage, m.

invulnerable, a, invulnérable.

inward, a, intérieur; interne; intime; d'entrée. ~ bound, en retour; effectuant son voyage de retour. ~[s] & ~ly, ad, intérieurement, en dedans. ~s, n.pl, entrailles, f.pl.

iodine, n, iode, m.

ion, n, ion, m.

Ionian, Ionic, a, ionien, ionique.

iota, n, iota, m.

ipecac, n, ipéca, m.

irascible, a, irascible. **irate**, a, irrité, en colère. **ire**, n, courroux, m.

Iraq, n, Irak, m.

Iraqi, n, Irakien, enne.

Ireland, n, l'Irlande, f.

iridescence, n, irisation, f. **iridescent**, a, irisé, chatoyant.

iridium, n, iridium, m.

iris, n, iris, m.

Irish, a, irlandais. ~man, ~woman, Irlandais, e. ~ Sea, mer d'Irlande, f. ¶ (language) n, l'irlandais, m.

irksome, a, ennuyeux, fastidieux.

iron, n, (metal for linen, golf, etc.) fer, m; (cast, pig) fonte; (sheet) tôle, f. ¶ a, en fer, de fer; en (ou de) fonte. ~ [& steel] constructional work, charpenterie métallique, f. ~ [or steel] bridge, pont métallique, m. ~ & steel shares, valeurs sidérurgiques, v—s du groupe forges & fonderies, f.pl. ~clad, [navire] cuirassé, m. ~ constitution, santé de fer, f. ~master, maître de forges, m. ~monger, (small) quincaillier; (big) ferronnier; (builders') serrurier, m. ~mongery, quincaillerie; ferronnerie; serrurerie, f. scrap ~, ferraille, f. ~-shod, ferré. ~work, ferrement, m; ferrure; serrurerie; (girders, etc.) charpente en fer, f. ~worker, ferronnier; serrurier; charpentier en fer, *m.* ~*works,* ferronnerie, *f;* forge[s] *f.*[*pl.*]; usine sidérurgique, *f.* wrought ~, fer forgé, *m.* ¶ *v.t,* ferrer; (*linen*) repasser. ~*out,* défroncer, déplisser. ~*er,* *n,* repasseuse, *f.* ~*ing,* *n,* repassage, *m.*

ironic(al)†, *a,* ironique. **irony,** *n,* ironie, *f.*

irradiation, *n,* irradiation, *f.*

irrational, *a,* irrationnel, irraisonnable.

irreclaimable†, *a,* (*pers.*) incorrigible; (*land*) indéfrichable.

irreconcilable, *a,* irréconciliable; inconciliable.

irrecoverable, *a,* irrécouvrable. ~ *arrears* (taxes), non-valeurs, *f.pl.*

irredeemable†, *a,* irrachetable.

irredentism, *n,* irrédentisme, *m.*

irreducible, *a,* irréductible.

irrefutable†, *a,* irréfutable.

irregular†, *a,* irrégulier; saccadé. ~*ity,* *n,* irrégularité, *f;* déréglement, *m.*

irrelevant, *a,* hors de propos, non pertinent, étranger; (*law*) impertinent.

irreligious†, *a,* irréligieux, indévot.

irremediable†, *a,* irrémédiable.

irremovable, *a,* inamovible: immuable.

irreparable†, *a,* irréparable.

irrepressible, *a,* irrépressible; (*laughter*) inextinguible.

irreproachable†, *a,* irréprochable.

irresistible†, *a,* irrésistible.

irresolute, *a,* irrésolu.

irrespective of, indépendamment de, sans égard à.

irresponsible, *a,* irresponsable, inconscient.

irretrievable†, *a,* irréparable.

irreverent, *a,* irrévérent.

irrevocable†, *a,* irrévocable.

irrigate, *v.t,* irriguer. **irrigation,** *n,* irrigation, *f.* **irrigator,** *n,* irrigateur, *m.*

irritable, *a,* irritable. **irritate,** *v.t,* irriter; agacer. **irritation,** *n,* irritation, *f;* agacement, *m.*

irruption, *n,* irruption, *f.*

isinglass, *n,* colle de poisson, *f.*

Islam›, *n,* Islam, *m.*

island, *n,* île, *f;* (*houses*) îlot, *m.* ~*er,* *n,* insulaire, *m.f.* **isle,** *n,* île, *f.* **islet,** *n,* îlot, *f.*

isolate, *v.t,* isoler. **isolation,** *n,* isolement, *m.* ~ *hospital,* hôpital de contagieux, *m.*

Israeli, *a.* & *n,* Israélien, ienne. **Israelite,** *n,* israélite, *m.f.*

issue, *n,* issue, *f;* événement, *m;* distribution; délivrance; sortie, *f;* succès, *m;* (*money*) émission; impression; publication, *f;* (*newspaper*) numéro, *m;* lignée, postérité; (*law*) question, *f.* ¶ *v.i,* sortir; découler; émaner; (*v.t.*) lancer; émettre; publier; distribuer; délivrer.

isthmus, *n,* isthme, *m.*

it, *pn,* il, elle; le, la; lui, elle, elle; ce, c', ç'; cela; y. ~ *is said that . . .,* on dit que . . . *about* ~, en; y. *at* ~, y. *by* ~, y; en. *for* ~, en. *from* ~, en. *of* ~, en; y. *to* ~, y; lui. *pour* cela.

Italian, *a,* italien. ¶ *n,* (*pers.*) Italien, ne; (*language*) l'italien, *m.*

italic, *a.* & ~*s,* *n.pl,* italique, *a.* & *m.*

Italy, *n,* l'Italie, *f.*

itch, *v.i,* démanger. *my arm itches,* le bras me démange. *I am* ~*ing to,* j'ai grande envie de. ~[*ing*], *n,* démangeaison, *f,* prurit, *m,* gale, *f.* ~*y,* *a,* galeux.

item, *n,* article, poste, chapitre, *m.* ¶ *ad,* item.

itinerant, *a,* ambulant. **itinerary,** *n,* itinéraire, *m.*

its, *pn,* son, sa, ses; en.

itself, *pn,* lui[-même], elle[-même], soi[-même]; même; se.

ivory, *n,* ivoire, *m.* *the I~ Coast,* la Côte d'Ivoire.

ivy, *n,* lierre, *m.* *poison* ~, sumac vénéneux, *m.*

J

jab, *v.t,* piquer. ¶ *n,* (*Box.*) coup sec; coup de canif, *m.*

jabber, *v.i.* & *t,* jaboter, bredouiller, jargonner.

jacinth, *n,* jacinthe, *f.*

jack, *n,* (*Mach.*) vérin; (*auto*) cric, *m;* chèvre, *f;* (*spit*) tournebroche; (*fish*) brochet; (*cards*) valet, *m.* ~*ass,* âne, baudet, *m.* ~*boots,* bottes à genouillère, *f.pl.* ~*daw,* choucas, *m.* ~*-in-the-box,* boîte à surprise, *f.* ~ *knife,* couteau à virole, c. à cran d'arrêt, *m. J~ of all trades* or *work*, homme à tout faire, maître Jacques, *m. before you could say J~ Robinson*, crac!; en moins d'un instant.

jackal, *n*, chacal, *m*.

jackanapes, *n*, fat, *m*.

jackass, *n*. (*animal*) âne; (*person*) sot, *m*.

jacket, *n*, (*lounge*) veston, *m*; (*short*) veste, *f*; (*cardigan*) gilet; (*book*) couvre-livre, *m*; (*steam, water*) chemise, *f*.

Jacobin, *n*, jacobin, *m*.

jade, *n*, (*horse*) rosse, haridelle; (*woman*) coquine, *f*; (*Miner.*) jade, *m*. ~d, *p.p.*, surmené.

jag, *v.t*, ébrécher, denteler, déchiqueter. **jagged**, *a*, dentelé.

jaguar, *n*, jaguar, *m*.

jail, *n*, prison, geôle, *f*. ~bird, cheval de retour, *m*. ~er, *n*, geôlier, *m*.

jalopy, *n*, bagnole, *f*, tacot, *m*.

jam, *n*, (*fruit*) confiture, *f*. oft. *pl*; (*squeeze*) coincement; (*traffic*) embouteillage; (*radio*) brouillage, *m*. ~ *pot*, pot à confitures, *m*. ¶ *v.t*, coincer. ~mer, *n*, (*radio*) brouilleur, *m*.

Jamaica, *n*, la Jamaïque.

jamb, *n*, jambage, *m*.

jangle, *n*, ébranlement, *m*. ¶ *v.t*, ébranler.

janitor, *n*, concierge, *m*.

January, *n*, janvier, *m*.

japan, *n*, laque [de Chine], vernis [japonais] *m*. ¶ *v.t*, laquer, vernir. **Japan**, *n*, le Japon. **Japanese**, *a*, japonais. ~ *curio*, japonerie, *f*. ~ *paper* & ~ *porcelain*, Japon, *m*. ¶ *n*, (*pers.*) Japonais, e; (*language*) le japonais.

jar, *n*, secousse, *f*, battement; pot, *m*, jarre, bouteille, *f*, bocal, *m*. ¶ *v.i*, détoner, jurer; (*shake*) secouer. ~ *upon*, agacer.

jardinière, *n*, (*stand*) jardinière, *f*; (*pot*) cachepot, *m*.

jargon, *n*, jargon, baragouin, patois, *m*.

jarring, *a*, discordant.

jasmine, *n*, jasmin, *m*.

jasper, *n*, jaspe, *m*.

jaundice, *n*, jaunisse, *f*, ictère, *m*.

jaunt, *n*, course, promenade, *f*. ~y†, *a*, insoucieux, crâne.

Java, *n*, Java, *m*. **Javanese**, *a*, javanais. ¶ *n*, Javanais, e.

javelin, *n*, javelot, *m*.

jaw, *n*, mâchoire; mandibule, *f*; mors, bec, *m*; (*pl, of death*) bras, *m.pl*. ~ *bone*, [os] maxillaire, *m*.

jay (*bird*) *n*, geai, *m*.

jealous† , *a*, jaloux. ~y, *n*, jalousie, *f*.

jeer, *n*, risée, moquerie, *f*. ¶ *v.i*, goguenarder. ~ *at*, insulter à, se moquer de; (*pers.*) railler, se moquer de, dauber [sur].

jejune, *a*, maigre; exigu.

jelly, *n*, gelée, *f*. *to* (or *in*) *a* ~ (as face by blow), en marmelade, en compote. ~*fish*, méduse, *f*.

jeopardize, *v.t*, mettre en danger. **jeopardy**, *n*, danger, *m*.

jerboa, *n*, gerboise, *f*.

jeremiad, *n*, jérémiade, *f*.

jerk, *n*, à-coup, *m*, saccade, secousse, *f*. ¶ *v.t*, donner un à-coup, des secousses, à. ~y, *a*, saccadé.

jerry-build, *v.t*, bousiller. ~er, *n*, bousilleur, *m*. ~ing, *n*, bâtisse, *f*. **jerry-built**, *a*, de carton, fait de boue & de crachat. **jerrywork**, *n*, bousillage, *m*.

jersey, *n*, maillot, *m*; jersey, *m*. **Jersey** (*Geog.*), *n*, Jersey, *f*. *J~ cow*, vache jersiaise, *f*.

Jerusalem, *n*, Jérusalem, *f*.

jest, *n*, plaisanterie, *f*. ¶ *v.i*, plaisanter, badiner. ~er, *n*, plaisant, *m*, bouffon, ne; (*court*) fou, *m*.

Jesuit, *n*, jésuite, *m*. ~ical, *a*, jésuitique.

Jesus, *n*, Jésus, *m*. *Jesus Christ*, Jésus-Christ, *m*.

jet, *n*, jet; bec; (*lignite*) jais; avion à réaction, *m*. ~[-*black*], noir comme [du] jais. ~ *stream*, courant-jet, *m*. ¶ *v.t*, jeter.

jetsam, *n*, épaves [rejetées] *f.pl*. **jettison**, *n*, jet [à la mer] *m*. ¶ *v.t*, jeter [à la mer].

jetty, *n*, jetée, estacade, *f*.

Jew, *n*, juif, israélite, *m*; (*woman*) juive, *f*. ~'s *harp*, guimbarde, *f*. ~ish, *a*, juif, israélite.

jewel, *n*, bijou, joyau; (*Horol.*) rubis, *m*. ~ *case*, ecrin [à bijoux] *m*. **jeweler**, *n*, bijoutier, ère, joaillier, ère. **jewelry**, *n*, bijouterie, joaillerie, *f*.

jib, *n*, (*sail*) foc, *m*; (*crane*) volée, flèche, *f*. ¶ *v.i*, regimber, se cabrer, s'acculer.

jiffy, *n*, tour de main, instant, *m*.

jig, *n*, (*Mus., dance*) gigue, *f*. ~*saw*, sauteuse, scie à chantourner, *f.* ~*saw puzzle*, jeu de patience, *m.*

jiggle, *v.t. & i*, sautiller, gigoter.

jilt, *v.t*, délaisser, lâcher.

jingle, *n*, tintement; cliquetis, *m.* ¶*v.i. & t*, tinter.

jingoism, *n*, chauvinisme, *m.*

job, *n*, tâche; besogne; *f*; travail; emploi, *m*; affaire, *f.* ~ *lot*, marchandises d'occasion, *f.pl*, solde, *m.*

jockey (*turf*) *n*, jockey, *m.* J~ *Club*, Jockey-Club, *m.*

jocose, *a*, badin.

jocular, *a*, enjoué, facétieux, plaisant. ~*ly*, *ad*, en plaisantant.

jocund, *a*, joyeux.

jog, *v.t*, secouer, pousser. ~ *along*, aller son chemin. ~ *on*, aller cahin-caha. ~ *trot*, petit trot; (*fig.*) train-train, *m.*

joggle, *n*, secousse, *f*; (*Carp.*) embrèvement; goujon, *m.* ¶*v.t*, embrever.

John Dory, *n*, dorée, *f.*

join, *v.t*, joindre; assembler; [ré]unir; raccorder; rabouter, raboutir; relier; rejoindre. ~ *in*, faire chorus. ~*er*, *n*, menuisier, *m.* **joint**, *n*, joint, *m*; jointure; articulation, *f*; assemblage; (*fishing rod*) brin, *m*; (*meat*) pièce, *f. to put out of* ~, démettre, disloquer. ~ *owners*, *tenants*, copropriétaires, *m.pl.* ¶*v.t*, articuler; assembler. ¶†, *a*, conjoint; indivis; co-; (*commission*) mixte. ~ *manager*, codirecteur, cogérant, *m.* ~*stock company*, société par actions, *f.*

joist, *n*, solive, *f*; soliveau, *m*, poutrelle; lambourde, *f.*

joke, *n*, plaisanterie, facétie, *f*, mot pour rire, *m*; (le) comique de l'histoire. ¶*v.i*, plaisanter, rire, railler. **joker**, *n*, farceur, euse, plaisant, *m.*

jollification & jollity, *n*, jubilation, noce, gaillardise, gaieté, *f.* **jolly**†, *a*, gaillard, jovial, gai.

jolt, *n*, cahot, *m.* ¶*v.i. & t*, cahoter.

Jonah (*fig.*) *n*, porte-malheur, *m.*

jonquil, *n*, jonquille, *f.*

Jordan (*river*) *n*, le Jourdain, *m*; (*country*) la Jordanie, *f.*

jostle, *v.t*, coudoyer, bousculer.

jot, *n*, iota, *m.* ~ *down*, tenir note (*ou* registre) de.

journal, *n*, journal; livre; (*shaft*) tourillon, *m*; (*axle*) fusée, *f.* ~*ism*, *n*, journalisme, *m.* ~*ist*, *n*, journaliste, *m.*

journey, *n*, voyage, *m*; marche; route, *f*; trajet; parcours, *m. on the* ~, en route. *to take a* ~, faire un voyage.

joust, *n*, joute, *f.* ¶*v.i*, jouter.

jovial†, *a*, jovial, réjoui. ~*ity*, *n*, jovialité, *f.*

jowl, *n*, joue; (*fish*) hure, *f.*

joy, *n*, joie, *f.* ~*ful*† & ~*ous*†, *a*, joyeux. ~*fulness*, *n*, allégresse, *f.*

jubilation, *n*, jubilation, *f.* **jubilee**, *n*, jubilé, *m.* ~ *year*, année jubilaire, *f.*

Judaic, *a*, judaïque.

judo, *n*, judo, *m.*

judge, *n*, juge; magistrat; arbitre, *m.* ¶*v.t. & i*, juger. **judgment**, *n*, jugement; arrêt; avis; sens; coup d'œil, *m.* **Judges** (*Bible*) *n.pl*, les Juges, *m.pl.*

judicature, *n*, justice, *f.* **judicial**†, *a*, judiciaire.

judicious†, *a*, judicieux, sage, sensé.

jug, *n*, cruche, *f*, broc, pot, *m*; carafe, *f.* ~*ful*, *n*, potée, *f.*

juggle, *v.i*, jongler; escamoter. ¶~ & ~*ry*, *n*, tour de passepasse, *m*, jonglerie, *f*; escamotage, *m.* **juggler**, *n*, jongleur; escamoteur, *m.*

jugular [**vein**], *n*, [veine] jugulaire, *f.*

juice, *n*, jus; suc, *m.* **juicy**, *a*, juteux; succulent; fondant.

ju-jitsu, *n*, jiu-jitsu, *m.*

jujube, *n*, jujube, *m*; pastille, *f.* ~ [*shrub*], jujubier, *m.*

julep, *n*, julep, *m.*

July, *n*, juillet, *m.*

jumble, *n*, pêle-mêle, fouillis, fatras, *m*, salade, *f.* ~ *sale*, vente au déballage, *f.* ~ *shop*, capharnaüm, *m.* ¶*v.t*, brouiller; jeter pêle-mêle.

jump, *n*, saut; sursaut; haut-le-corps, *m.* ¶*v.i. & t*, sauter; se jeter. ~ *over*, sauter, franchir. ~*er*, *n*, (*pers.*) sauteur, euse; (*sailor's*) vareuse; (*woman's*) casaque, *f.* ~*ing*: ~ *jack*, pantin, *m.* ~*off ground* (*fig.*), tremplin, *m.* ~ *skis*, skis de saut, *m.pl.*

junction, *n*, jonction; (*Rly line*, *etc.*) bifurcation, *f*, embranchement, *m*; (*Rly station*) gare de bifurcation, gare d'embranche-

ment, *f.* **juncture,** *n,* jonction;
occurrence, *f.*
June, *a,* juin, *m.*
jungle, *n,* jungle, *f.*
junior, *a,* cadet; (*partner*) second,
dernier; (*clerk*) petit. ¶ *n,* cadet,
te; [le] jeune; (*son*) fils; (*sports*)
junior, *m.* ~ *event,* épreuve pour
juniors, *f.*
juniper, *n,* (*genus*) genévrier;
(*common*) genièvre, *m.*
junk, *n,* (*Chinese*) jonque; (*tow*)
étoupe, *f;* (*refuse*) rebut, *m.* ¶ *v.t,*
mettre au rebut.
junket, *v.i,* faire bombance.
juridical†, *a,* juridique. **jurisdiction,** *n,* juridiction; compétence,
f. **jurist,** *n,* juriste, jurisconsulte,
m.
juror, juryman, *n,* juré, *m.*
jury, *n,* jury, *m.*
just, *a,* juste; équitable. ¶ *ad,*
juste; justement; ne . . . que; tout.
~ *as,* de même que. ~ *out,* vient
de paraître. *I have* ~ . . ., je
viens de . . . ~**ice,** *n,* justice, *f;*
(*as to a meal*) honneur; (*pers.*)
juge, *m.*
justifiable, *a,* justifiable; (*homicide*) excusable. **justification,** *n,*
justification, *f;* gain de cause, *m.*
justify, *v.t,* justifier; motiver.
justly, *ad,* justement, équitable-
ment. **justness,** *n,* justice, *f.*
jut [out], *v.i,* faire saillie, [s']
avancer.
jute, *n,* jute, *m.*
juvenile, *a,* juvénile; jeune;
(*books*) pour la jeunesse. ¶ *n,*
jeune personne, *f.*
juxtapose, *v.t,* juxtaposer.

K

kale, *n,* chou frisé, *m.*
kaleidoscope, *n,* kaléidoscope,
m.
kangaroo, *n,* kangourou, *m.*
kedge [anchor], *n,* ancre à jet, *f.*
keel, *n,* quille, *f.* **keelson,** *n,* carlingue, *f.*
keen, *a,* acéré; tranchant; vif; fin;
mordant; (*sportsman, etc.*) ardent, déterminé. *a* ~ *disappointment,* un crève-cœur. ~*ly, ad,*
vivement. ~**ness,** *n,* acuité; finesse, *f;* mordant; flair, *m.*

keep, *n,* entretien; (*castle*) donjon,
m. ¶ *v.t.ir,* tenir; maintenir; garder; retenir; ménager; entretenir;

hanter; nourrir; conserver; garantir; préserver; avoir; faire; observer; (*v.i.ir.*) se tenir; se
conserver; rester. ~ *a saint's
day,* chômer une fête. ~ *away,*
s'absenter. ~ *back,* retenir. ~
from, s'abstenir de; empêcher de.
~ *in* (*Sch.*) mettre en retenue.
~ *off,* s'éloigner; au large[
please] ~ *off the grass,* ne mar-
chez pas sur les pelouses, défense de circuler sur l'herbe.
~ [*on*], continuer. ~ *one's hand
in,* s'entretenir la main. ~ *oneself to,* se cantonner dans. ~**er,**
n, garde, *m;* gardien, ne; concierge, *m,f;* conservateur, *m.*
~**ing,** *n,* garde; conservation;
tenue, *f. in* ~ *with,* en harmonie
avec, à l'avenant de.
keepsake, *n,* souvenir, *m.*
keg, *n,* caque, *f;* baril[let]; tonnelet, *m.*
ken, *n,* connaissance, *f.*
kennel, *n,* niche, cabane, *f;*
(*hounds*) chenil, *m.*
Kenya, *n,* Kénia, *m.*
kerchief, *n,* fichu, carré, foulard,
m.
kernel, *n,* (*of nut, stone-fruit,
seed*) amande, *f;* (*nucleus*) noyau, *m;* (*gist*) substance, *f.*
kerosene, *n,* pétrole à brûler, p.
lampant, *m,* huile de pétrole, *f.*
kestrel, *n,* crécerelle, *f,* émouchet,
m.
ketch, *n,* quaiche, *f.*
kettle, *n,* bouilloire, bouillotte, *f,*
coquemar, *m.* ~*drum,* timbale,
f. ~*drummer,* timbalier, *m.*
key, *n,* clef, clé, *f;* (*winder*) remontoir, *m;* (*piano*) touche, *f;* (*to
school book*) corrigé; (*Mus.*) ton,
m; (*Mech.*) clavette; cale, *f;* coin,
m. ~*board,* clavier, *m.* ~ *chain,*
châtelaine, *f.* ~*hole,* trou de serrure, *m.* ~*hole saw,* scie à guichet, *f.* ~ *industry,* industrie-clef,
f. ~ *money,* denier à Dieu, *m;* reprise, *f.* ~ *note,* [note] tonique, *f;*
(*fig.*) mot d'ordre, *m.* ~ *ring,* [an-
neau] porte-clefs, *m.* ~ *signature*
(*Mus.*), armature, *f.* ~*stone,* clef
de voûte, *f.* ¶ *v.t,* caler; coincer;
harmoniser. ~**ed,** *p.a,* à clef.
khaki, *n,* kaki, *m.*
Khedive, *n,* khédive, *m.*
kick, *n,* coup de pied, *m;* (*horse*)
ruade, *f;* (*gun*) recul, *m.* ~*off*

(*Foot.*), coup [de pied] d'envoi, *m.* ¶ *v.t.* donner un coup (des coups) de pied à; (*a goal*) marquer; (*v.i.*) (*horse*) ruer, regimber; (*gun*) reculer. ~ *about*, gigoter. ~ *at* (*fig.*), regimber contre. ~er, *n*, rueur, euse.

kid, *n*, chevreau, *m*, chevrette, *f*; cabri; (*child*) gosse, *m*. ~ *gloves*, gants de [peau de] chevreau, g—s de chevrotin, *m.pl.*

kidnap, *v.t*, enlever, kidnapper. **kidnapper,** *n*, kidnappeur, *m*. **kidnapping,** *n*, rapt, kidnapping, *m*.

kidney, *n*, (*Anat.*) rein; (*meat*) rognon; (*fig.*) acabit, *m*, trempe, *f*. ~ *bean*, haricot, *m*.

kill, *v.t*, chasse, *f*; abattis, *m*. ¶ *v.t*, tuer, assassiner; abattre. *to nearly* ~, assommer. *killed in action*, tué à l'ennemi. *the killed*, les tués, *m.pl.* ~*joy*, rabat-joie, trouble-fête, *m*. ~**ing,** *n*, tuerie, *f*; abattage, *m*. ¶ *a*, tuant, assommant.

kiln, *n*, four, *m*. ~*dry*, sécher au four.

kilogram, *n*, kilogramme, *m*.

kilometric(al), *a*, kilométrique.

kilowatt, *n*, kilowatt, *m*.

kilt, *v.t*, plisser.

kimono, *n*, kimono, saut de lit, *m*.

kin, *n*, parents, *m.pl*; parenté, *f*.

kind, *a*, bon; aimable; gentil; bienveillant, obligeant; prospère. ~ *regards*, amitiés, *f.pl*; compliments, *m.pl.* ¶ *n*, genre, *m*; espèce; sorte; manière; (*of wood*) essence, *f*. *in* ~, en nature.

kindergarten, *n*, jardin d'enfants, *m*.

kindle, *v.t*, allumer.

kindliness, *n*, bienveillance; bénignité, *f*. **kindly,** *a*, bienveillant, obligeant; ami. ¶ *ad*, aimablement. **kindness,** *n*, bonté; amabilité; attention, *f*.

kindred, *n*, parenté, *f*. ¶ *a*, de la même famille.

kinescope, *n*, cinégramme, cinéscope, *m*.

king, *n*, roi, *m*; (*checkers*) dame, *f*. ~*bolt*, cheville ouvrière, *f*. ~*post*, poinçon, *m*. ~*fisher*, martin-pêcheur, martinet-pêcheur, *m*. *oil, steel,* ~, roi des pétroles, de l'acier. ~**dom,** *n*, royaume; (*Nat. Hist.*) règne, *m*. ~**ly,** *a*, royal.

kink, *v.t*, tortiller; (*v.i.*) vriller. ~*y, a,* noué; crépu.

kinship, *n*, parenté, *f*, sang, *m*. **kinsman,** -**woman,** *n*, parent, e.

kiosk, *n*, kiosque; édicule, *m*.

kipper, *n*, hareng salé & fumé, *m*. ¶ *v.t*, saler & fumer, saurer.

kiss, *n*, baiser, *m*. ¶ *v.t*, embrasser; baiser (*see note under this word*). ~ & *cuddle*, baisoter.

kit, *n*, équipement; trousseau, *m*; trousse; (*Mil.*) musette, fourbi, *f*. *mess* ~, cantine, *f*. ~ & *caboodle*, tout le fourbi. *do-it-yourself* ~, prêt-à-monter, *m*. *repair* ~, lot de réparation, *m*. *survival* ~, équipement de survie, *m*.

kitchen, *n*, cuisine, *f*. ~ *garden*, [jardin] potager, *m*. ~ *maid*, fille de cuisine, *f*.

kite, *n*, (*bird*) milan; (*toy*) cerf-volant, *m*.

kith & kin, amis & parents, *m.pl.*

kitten, *n*, chaton, petit chat, *m*, petite chatte, *f*.

kleptomania, *n*, cleptomanie, *f*. **kleptomaniac,** *n*, cleptomane, *m,f*.

knack, *n*, don, coup; truc, tour de main, *m*. *to have a* ~ *for*, avoir la bosse de.

knapsack, *n*, sac; havresac, *m*.

knave, *n*, fripon, coquin, fourbe; (*cards*) valet, *m*. ~*ry, n*, friponnerie, coquinerie, fourberie, fourbe, *f*. **knavish,** *a*, fourbe.

knead, *v.t*, pétrir.

knee, *n*, genou, *m*. ~ *breeches*, culotte, *f*, ~*cap*, (*Anat.*) rotule; (*pad*) genouillère, *f*. ~*hole desk*, bureau ministre, *m*.

kneel [**down**], *v.i.ir*, [s']agenouiller.

knell, *n*, glas, *m*.

knickerbockers & knickers, *n.pl*, culotte, *f*.

knick-knack, *n*, colifichet, brimborion, *m*.

knife, *n*, couteau, *m*. ~*edge*, couteau, *m*. ~, *fork, & spoon,* couvert, *m*. ~ *grinder*, rémouleur, *m*. ~ *rest*, porte-couteau, *m*. *pocket* ~, canif, *m*. ¶ *v.t*, poignarder.

knight, *n*, chevalier; (*chess*) cavalier, *m*. ~*errant*, chevalier errant; (*fig.*) paladin, *m*. ~*errantry*, chevalerie errante, *f*. ~*hood*, *n*, chevalerie, *f*. ~*ly, a*, chevaleresque.

knit, *v.t. & i. ir*, tricoter; (*brow*)

froncer; (*fig.*) lier, nouer. **knitted** (*vest, etc.*) *p.a,* de tricot. ~ *garment,* tricot, *m.* **knitter,** *n,* tricoteur, euse. **knitting,** *n,* tricotage; tricot. *m.* ~ *needle,* aiguille à tricoter, *f.* **knitwear,** *n,* tricots, *m.pl.*

knob, *n,* bouton, *m;* pomme, *f.*

knock, *n,* coup; (*at the door*) coup de marteau, *m,* ¶ *v.t. & i,* frapper; heurter; cogner; taper. *to ~ about,* vadrouiller. ~ *down,* assommer; terrasser; abattre; (*auction*) adjuger. ~*-kneed,* cagneux. ~**er** (*door*), *n,* marteau, *m.*

knoll, *n,* monticule, tertre, *m,* butte, *f.*

knot, *n,* nœud; (*cluster*) peloton; (*tangle*) tapon. *m.* ¶ *v.t,* nouer. **knotty,** *a,* noueux, raboteux; (*fig.*) épineux.

know, *v.t. & i. ir,* connaître; savoir. ~ *how to,* savoir. *let me ~,* faites-moi savoir. *not to ~,* ignorer. ~**ing,** *a,* savant. ~**ingly,** *ad,* savamment, sciemment, à bon escient. **knowledge,** *n,* connaissance; intelligence; science, *f;* savoir, *m;* notoriété, *f. to my ~,* à mon su. *without my ~,* à mon insu. **known,** *n,* connu, *m.*

knuckle, *n,* jointure, articulation, *f;* (*veal*) jarret, *m.* ~ *fighting,* boxe à poings nus, *f.* ~ [*joint*] (Mech.), genouillère, *f. knuckle under* or *down,* mettre les pouces, caler [la voile].

knurl, *n,* molette, *f.* ¶ *v.t,* moleter.

kohlrabi, *n,* chou-rave, *m.*

Koran, *n,* Coran, *m.*

Korea, *n,* la Corée.

kosher, *a,* kascher.

kudos, *n,* gloriole, *f.*

L

label, *n,* étiquette, *f.* ¶ *v.t,* étiqueter.

labial, *a,* labial. ¶ *n,* labiale, *f.*

laboratory, *n,* laboratoire, *m.*

labor, *n,* main-d'œuvre, *f;* travail; labeur, *m;* peine; façon, *f.* ~ *market,* marché du travail. *m.* ~ [*pains*], mal d'enfant, *m.* ~*saving, a,* économisant la main-d'œuvre. ~ *troubles,* troubles ouvriers, *m.pl.* ¶ *v.i. & t,* travailler, peiner; (*ship*) fatiguer. ~**ed** (*fig.*) *p.a,* travaillé, martelé,

tourmenté, laborieux. ~**er,** *n,* manœuvre, homme de peine; ouvrier, *m.* **laborious†,** *a,* pénible; laborieux.

laburnum, *n,* faux ébénier, cytise, *m.*

labyrinth, *n,* labyrinthe, dédale, *m.*

lace, *n,* dentelle, *f;* point; passement; (*shoe*) lacet, cordon, *m;* (*leather*) lanière, *f.* ~ *boots,* bottines (*or if high,* bottes) à lacets (*ou* à lacer), *f.pl,* brodequins, *m.pl.* ~ *insertion,* entretoile, *f.* ¶ *v.t,* galonner; (*fasten*) lacer.

lacerate, *v.t,* déchirer, lacérer.

lack, *n,* manque, défaut, *m,* pénurie, disette, *f,* peu, *m.* ¶ *v.t,* manquer de. ~*ing in,* destitué de. ~*luster, a,* atone; vitreux.

lackadaisical, *a,* languissant; indolent, apathique, gnangnan.

lackey, *n,* laquais, *m.*

laconic†, *a,* laconique.

lacquer, *n. & ~ work,* laque, *m.* ¶ *v.t,* laquer.

lacrosse, *n,* la crosse canadienne.

lacteal, *a,* lacté.

lacuna, *n,* lacune, *f.*

lacustrine, *a,* lacustre.

lad, *n,* garçon; enfant, gars, *m.*

ladder, *n,* échelle, *f.*

laden, *a,* chargé.

ladle, *n,* louche, *f.* ~**ful,** *n,* cuillerée, *f.*

lady, *n,* dame; madame; mademoiselle, *f. Ladies & Gentlemen!* Mesdames, Messieurs! *ladies first!* place aux dames! ~*bird,* coccinelle, bête à bon Dieu, *f.* *L~ chapel,* chapelle de la Vierge, *f. L~ Day,* fête de l'Annonciation, *f;* le 25 mars. ~*-killer,* bourreau des cœurs, homme à bonnes fortunes, *m. his (my)* ~*-love,* la dame de ses (de mes) pensées. ~ *of the manor,* châtelaine, *f.* ~*'s maid,* femme de chambre, *f.* ~*'s* (*or ladies'*) *man,* homme galant, h. à femmes. *m.* ~*-like,* de dame, comme il faut.

lag, *v.i,* traîner; lambiner; (*v.t.*) garnir. ¶*n,* décalage, *m.*

lager [*beer*], *n,* bière, *f.*

lagoon, *n,* lagune, *f.*

laic, *n. & laic(al), a,* laïque, séculier, *m. & a.*

laid paper, papier vergé, *m.* **laid up** (*in bed*) alité; (*ship*) désarmé.

lair, *n,* tanière, *f,* repaire, antre, *m.*

laity, *n,* laïques, *m.pl.*

lake, *n,* lac, *m.* ~ *dwelling,* habitation lacustre, *f.*

lama, *n,* lama, *m.*

lamb, *n,* agneau; (*pers.*) agneau, mouton, *m.* ¶ *v.i,* agneler. ~**kin**, *n,* agnelet, *m.*

lambent, *a,* [doucement] radieux, lumineux.

lame, *a,* boiteux, éclopé, estropié; (*fig.*) qui cloche. ¶ *v.t,* estropier.

lamé, *a.* & *n,* lamé, *a.* & *m.*

lameness, *n,* claudication; boiterie, *f.*

lament, *n,* lamentation, *f;* chant funèbre, *m.* ¶ *v.i,* se lamenter. ~**able**†, *a,* lamentable. ~**ation**, *n,* lamentation; *f.* **the** [late] ~**ed** . . ., le (la) regretté, e . . .

lamina, *n,* lamelle, lame, *f,* feuillet, *m.* **laminate,** *v.t,* laminer.

lamp, *n,* lampe; lanterne, *f;* fanal; feu; (*street*) réverbère, *m.* ~ *black,* noir de fumée, *m.* ~*man,* lampiste, *m.* ~ *oil,* huile d'éclairage, h. de lampe, *f.* ~ *post,* poteau de réverbère; lampadaire, *m.* ~ *shade,* abat-jour, *m.* **kerosene** ~, lampe à pétrole, *f.*

lampoon, *n,* satire, *f,* libelle, pasquin, pamphlet, *m.* ¶ *v.t,* chansonner, écrire une satire contre. ~**er**, *n,* faiseur de pasquinades, pamphlétaire, *m.*

lamprey, *n,* lamproie, *f.*

lance, *n,* lance, *f.* ¶ (*Surg.*) *v.t,* inciser, percer, ouvrir. **lancers** (*Danc.*) *n.pl,* lanciers, *m.pl.* **lancet,** *n,* lancette, *f.*

land, *n,* terre, *f;* terrain; pays, *m.* ~*locked property,* enclave, *f.* ~*lord,* ~*lady,* propriétaire, *m,f;* logeur, euse; aubergiste, *m,f.* ~*lubber,* marin d'eau douce, *m.* ~*mark,* borne, *f;* point à terre, amer; point de repère, *m.* ~ *of milk & honey,* ~ *of plenty,* pays de cocagne. ~*owner,* propriétaire foncier, *m,f,* terrien, ne. ~*scape* & ~*scape painting,* paysage, *m.* ~*scape garden,* jardin anglais, *m.* ~*scape gardener,* dessinateur de jardins, architecte (*ou* jardinier) paysagiste, *m.* ~*scape painter,* [peintre] paysagiste, *m.* ~*slide,* éboulement de terres, *m.* ~*slide* (*Pol.*) débâcle, *f.* ¶ *v.t,* mettre à terre, débarquer; (*blow*) flanquer; (*v.i.*) débarquer;

aborder; (*Avn.*) atterrir; (*on moon*) alunir.

landed property, propriété foncière, *f,* biensfonds, *m.pl.*

landing, *n,* mise à terre, *f,* débarquement; atterrissage; (*stairs*) palier, repos, *m.* (*Avn.*) ~ *gear,* train d'atterrissage, *m.* ~ *place,* embarcadère, débarcadère, ponton, *m.* ~ *ticket,* carton de débarquement, *m.*

lane, *n,* chemin, *m;* allée; ruelle; clairière, *f;* (*running*) couloir, *m.*

language, *n,* langage, *m;* langue, *f.*

languid, *a,* mou; languissant; traînant. **languish,** *v.i,* languir. ~**ing**, *a,* languissant, mourant. **langor,** *n,* langueur, *f.* ~**ous**, *a,* langoureux.

lank, *a,* efflanqué; (*hair*) plats. ~**y**, *a,* efflanqué.

lantern, *n,* lanterne, *f;* falot, *m.* ~*jawed,* aux joues en lanterne.

lanyard, *n,* (*Naut.*) ride, *f;* (*gun*) tire-feu, *m.*

lap, *n,* (*of pers.*) giron, *m,* genoux, *m.pl;* (*of luxury*) sein; (*of dress*) pan; (*overlap*) recouvrement, *m;* (*layer*) couche, *f;* (*sport*) tour [de piste]. ~*dog,* chien de salon, *m,* bichon, ne. ~ *scorer,* contrôleur des tours, *m.* ¶ *v.t,* envelopper; (*grind*) roder. ~ *over,* *v.i.* chevaucher, croiser. ~ [*up*], *v.t,* laper.

lapel, *n,* revers, *m.*

lapidary, *a.* & *n,* lapidaire, *a.* & *m.*

lapis lazuli, *n,* lapis[-lazuli] *m.*

Lapland, *n,* la Laponie. **Lapp,** *a,* lapon. **Lapp, Laplander,** *n,* Lapon, ne.

lapse, *n,* lapsus; oubli, *m;* (*moral*) défaillance, incartade; (*expiration*) déchéance, *f;* (*time*) laps, *m.* ¶ *v.i,* périmer, périr, devenir caduc; (*time*) s'écouler; tomber.

lapwing, *n,* vanneau, *m.*

larceny, *n,* larcin, *m.*

larch, *n,* mélèze, larix, *m.*

lard, *n,* saindoux, *m.* ¶ *v.t,* (*Cook.*) larder, piquer; (*fig.*) larder, chamarrer. ~**er**, *n,* garde-manger, *m.*

large, *a,* gros; grand; fort; considérable; large. *at* ~, en liberté; [tout] au long; en général. ~**ly**, *ad,* grandement; en grande partie. ~**ness**, *n,* grandeur, *f.*

largess[e], *n,* largesse, *f.*

lark, *n,* (*bird*) alouette; mauviette;

(*frolic*) équipée, escapade, *f.*
~*spur*, pied-d'alouette, *m.*

larva, *n,* larve, *f.*

laryngitis, *n,* laryngite, *f.* **larynx,**
n, larynx, *m.*

lascivious†, *a,* lascif.

lash, *n,* (*of whip*) lanière; (*cut
with a whip*) coup de fouet;
(*eye*) cil; (*Mech.*) jeu, *m;* (*fig.*)
férule, *f.* ¶ *v.t,* cingler, sangler,
fouetter; ligoter; (*Naut.*) amarrer.
~ *out,* ruer.

lass[ie], *n,* [jeune] fille, fillette, *f.*

lassitude, *n,* lassitude, *f.*

lasso, *n,* lasso, *m.* ¶ *v.t,* prendre
au lasso.

last, *a,* dernier; final; (*honors*)
suprêmes. ~ *but one, a. & n,*
avant-dernier, ère. ~ *night,* cette
nuit; hier [au] soir. ~ *piece* (left
on dish), morceau honteux, *m.* ~ *resort,* pis aller, *m.* ~ *straw,*
comble [de nos maux] *m.* ~ *week,* la semaine dernière, la s.
passée. ~ *will & testament,* acte
de dernière volonté, *m. the ~ word,* le dernier [mot], le fin mot.
the ~ word in (as elegance), le
nec plus ultra de. ¶ *ad,* pour la
dernière fois; en dernier lieu.
¶ *n,* dernier, ère; fin; (*shoe*)
forme, *f. at ~,* enfin. ¶ *v.i,*
durer, tenir. ~*ing, a,* durable,
stable. ~*ly, ad,* en dernier lieu,
enfin.

latch, *n,* (*gate*) loquet, *m;* (*door*)
serrure à demi-tour, *f.* ~ *key,*
clef de maison, *f.*

late, *a,* tardif; en retard, retardataire; avancé; récent; dernier;
ancien, ex-; (*deceased*) feu;
défunt. ~*comer,* retardataire,
m,f. ~ *season,* arrière-saison, *f.*
¶ *ad,* tard; en retard. ~ *in the
day & ~ in life,* sur le tard. ~*ly,
ad,* dernièrement; récemment.
~*ness, n,* tardiveté, *f. the ~ of
the hour,* l'heure tardive, *f.*

latent, *a,* latent; caché.

later, *a,* postérieur, ultérieur. ~
[on], *ad,* plus tard, ultérieurement.

lateral†, *a,* latéral.

latest, *a,* dernier; fatal. ~ *style*
(in dress), dernière mode;
[haute] nouveauté, *f.* ~ [*thing
out*], dernier cri, *m.*

latex, *n,* latex, *m.*

lath, *n,* latte, *f;* volige; (*blind*) lame,
f. ¶ *v.t,* latter; voliger.

lathe, *n,* tour, *m.*

lather, *n,* mousse; écume, *f.* ¶ *v.i,*
mousser; (*v.t.*) savonner.

lathing, *n,* lattis, *m.*

Latin, *a. & n,* latin, *a. & m.*

latitude, *n,* latitude, *f.* .

latrine, *n,* lieux [d'aisance] *m.pl.*

latter (the), *ce* dernier, cette
dernière; celui-ci, celle-ci, ceux-
ci, celles-ci. ~*ly, ad,* dernièrement.

lattice, *n,* treillis, treillage, *m.*
¶ *v.t,* treillisser.

Latvia, *n,* la Lettonie. **Latvian,**
a, letton. ¶ *n,* Letton, ne.

laud, *v.t,* louer. ~ [*to the skies*],
louanger. ~**able,** *a,* louable.
laudatory, *a,* laudatif.

laugh, *n,* rire, *m.* ¶ *v.i,* rire; se r.,
se moquer. ~ *derisively,* ricaner.
~ *heartily,* rire aux éclats.
~**able†,** *a,* risible; dérisoire. *it is
no ~ing matter,* il n'y a pas [là]
de quoi rire. ~*ing stock,* risée, *f.*
laughter, *n,* rire[s] *m.* [*pl.*], hilarité, *f.*

launch, *n,* chaloupe, *f;* grand
canot, *m.* ¶ *v.t,* lancer; (*Mil.*) déclencher. ~[*ing*], *n,* lancement,
m. ~ *pad,* aire de lancement, *f.* ~
ramp, rampe de l., *f.*

launder, *v.t,* blanchir. **laundress,**
n, blanchisseuse [de fin], repasseuse [de linge fin] *f.* **laundry,**
n, blanchisserie; buanderie, *f.*

laureate, *a,* lauréat, *a.m.*

laurel, *n,* laurier, *m;* (*pl, fig.*)
lauriers, *m.pl.*

lava, *n,* lave, *f.*

lavatory, *n,* lavabo, *m.*

lavender, *n,* lavande, *f.*

lavish, *a,* prodigue. ¶ *v.t,* prodiguer. ~**ly,** *ad,* prodigalement.
~**ness,** *n,* prodigalité, magnificences, *f.pl.*

law, *n,* loi, *f;* droit, *m;* justice; jurisprudence; *f;* palais, *m.* ~*abiding,* respectueux des lois. ~ &
order, ordre public, *m.* ~ *case,*
affaire contentieuse, *f.* ~ *costs,*
frais de justice, dépens, *m.pl.* ~
courts, cours de justice, *f.pl,* tri-
bunaux, *m.pl;* palais [de justice]
m. ~ *department,* [service du]
contentieux, *m.* ~*giver,* législateur, *m.* ~ *suit,* procès civil, *m,*
affair, *f. commercial* ~, droit
commercial, *m.* ~**ful†,** *a,* légale;
légitime; licite. ~**fulness,** *n,* léga-

lité, légitimité, *f.* ~less, *a*, sans loi; déréglé.

lawn, *n*, pelouse, *f*, gazon, boulingrin; (*linen*) linon, *m*. ~ *mower*, tondeuse, *f*. ~ *tennis*, le [lawn-] tennis.

lawyer, *n*, homme de loi; avoué; légiste, juriste, jurisconsulte, *m*.

lax†, *a*, lâche; relâché; mou. ~ative, *a*. & *n*, laxatif, *a*. & *m*. ~ity, *n*, relâchement, *m*.

lay, *a:* ~ *brother*, frère lai, f. convers, f. servant, frater, *m*. ~*man*, laïque, séculier; profane, *m*. ~ *sister*, sœur converse, *f*. ¶ *n*, chanson, f; chant, *m*; complainte; (*of ground*) configuration, *f*. ¶ *v.t.ir*, mettre; poser; dresser; porter; déposer; abattre; coucher; imposer; [é]tendre; (*fire*) préparer; (*gun*) pointer; (*eggs*) pondre; (*a wager*) faire; (*to bet*) parier. ~ *bare*, mettre à nu, déshabiller. ~ *before* (court), saisir. ~ *down*, [dé]poser; plaquer. ~ *hold of* (a thing), saisir, s'agriffer à, agripper. ~ *in* [*a stock of*], s'approvisionner de. ~ *out*, disposer; aménager; ajuster; tracer; débourser. ~ *waste*, dévaster.

lay day (*Ship.*) *n*, jour de planche, *m*.

layer, *n*, (*stratum, bed*) couche, *f*, lit, *m*; (*Hort.*) marcotte, *f*.

laying, *n*, mise; pose; (*eggs*) ponte, *f*.

layout, *n*, disposition, *f*; tracé, *m*.

laze, *v.i*, paresser, traînasser. **lazily**, *ad*, paresseusement; indolemment. **laziness**, *n*, paresse, *f*. **lazy**, *a*, paresseux. ~*bones*, paresseux, euse, fainéant, e, cagnard, e.

lea (*Poet.*) *n*, pré, *m*, prairie, *f*.

leach, *v.t*. & *i*, lessiver; filtrer.

lead, *n*, plomb, *m*; (*for pencils*) mine [de plomb]; (*Typ.*) interligne, *f*; (*Naut.*) plomb [de sonde] *m*, sonde, *f*. ~ *poisoning*, intoxication par le plomb, *f*, saturnisme, *m*. ¶ *v.t*, plomber; (*Typ.*) interligner.

lead, *n*, direction, conduite; avance; tête, *f*; exemple, *m*; (*cards*) main, primauté, *f*; (*Elec.*) conducteur principal; (*Elec. service*) branchement, *m*; (*leash*) laisse, *f*. ~ *rope* (attached to halter), longe, *f*. ¶ *v.t. & i. ir*, mener; conduire; diriger; amener; aboutir; induire; porter;

tendre; (*cards*) débuter. ~ *astray*, égarer, dérouter, fourvoyer; débaucher. ~ *back*, reconduire. ~ *up to* (fig.), amener, préluder à.

leaden, *a*, de plomb; (*sky*) de plomb, plombé.

leader, *n*, directeur; meneur; chef de file, *m*, vedette, *f*; (*political*) leader; (*violin, chorus*) chef d'attaque; (*horse*) cheval de volée; (*Anat.*) tendon, *m*; (*Typ.*) points conducteurs, *m.pl*; (*tape, etc.*) amorce, *f*. ~*ship*, *n*, direction; autorité, *f*. **leading**, *n*, principal; premier; marquant. ~ *lady* (*Theat.*) premier rôle, *m*; vedette, *f*. ~ *man*, premier rôle, *m*. ~ *part* (*Theat.*), premier rôle, *m*. ~ *question*, question tendancieuse, *f*.

leadsman, *n*, sondeur, *m*.

leaf, *n*, feuille, *f*; feuillet; volant; (*door*) battant, vantail, *m*; (*table*) rallonge, *f*. ~ *mold*, terreau de feuilles, *m*. ~ *stalk*, pétiole, *m*. ~ *table*, table à rallonge(s) *f*. ~*age*, *n*, feuillage, *m*. ~less, *a*, dénudé. ~*let*, *n*, dépliant, imprimé, tract, *m*. ~y, *a*, feuillu, feuillé.

league, *n*, ligue; (*of Nations*) société; (*Meas.*) lieue, *f*. ¶ *v.t*, liguer.

leak & ~**age**, *n*, fuite, perte, *f*, échappement, coulage, *m*; voie d'eau, *f*. ¶ *v.i*, fuir, perdre, s'échapper, couler, faire eau. ~y, *a*, qui perd, qui fuit; qui fait eau.

lean, *a*, maigre; sec. ¶ *n*, maigre, *m*. ¶ *v.t.ir*, appuyer, accoter, adosser; (*v.i.ir*) (*rest*) s'appuyer; (*slope*) pencher. ~ *back in*, se renverser sur. ~ *on one's elbow(s)*, s'accouder. ~*ing* (fig.) *n*, penchant, *m*. ~ *tower* (Pisa) tour penchée, *f*. ~*ness*, *n*, maigreur, *f*. ~*to*, *n*, appentis, *m*.

leap, *n*, saut, bond; soubresaut, *m*. *by* ~*s & bounds*, par sauts & par bonds. ¶ *v.t. & i. ir*, sauter, bondir. ~*frog*, saute-mouton, saut de mouton, *m*. ~ *year*, année bissextile, *f*. **leaper**, *n*, sauteur, euse.

learn, *v.t. & i.ir*, apprendre. ~*ed*, *a*, savant, érudit, docte, instruit; (*profession*) libérale. ~*edly*, *ad*, savamment, doctement. ~*er*, *n*, apprenti, e; commençant, e. ~*ing*, *n*, érudition, connaissances, *f.pl*, savoir, *m*, science, *f*.

lease, *n*, bail, *m*; ferme, *f*. ¶ *v.t.* (*grant*) donner à bail, affermer, arrenter; (*take*) prendre à bail; amodier. ~*holder*, locataire, *m,f*. **leasing**, *n*, (*land, fishing rights, etc.*) amodiation, *f*.

leash, *n*, laisse, [ac]couple, attache, *f*, trait, *m*; (*set of dogs*) harde, *f*. ¶ *v.t*, harder.

least (the), *a*, le moindre; le plus petit. ¶ *ad. & n*, le moins. *at ~*, au moins; du moins. *not in the ~*, pas le moins du monde; [ne . . .] pas le moindrement.

leather, *n*, cuir, *m*, peau, *f*. ~ *dressing*, mégie, mégisserie, *f*. ~**ette**, *n*, similicuir, *m*. ~**y**, *a*, coriacé.

leave, *n*, permission; autorisation; faculté, liberté, *f*; congé, *m*. *by your ~l* attention! *on ~*, en permission, permissionnaire. *sick ~*, congé de convalescence, *m*. ¶ *v.t. ir*, laisser, abandonner; partir de, sortir de, quitter; léguer; (*v.i.ir.*) partir; déloger. ~ *off*, cesser; laissez donc! ~ *out*, omettre. *on leaving*, à l'issue de.

leaven, *n*, levain; ferment, *m*. ¶ *v.t*, faire lever; (*fig.*) assaisonner.

leavings, *n.pl*, restes, *m.pl*, bribes, *f.pl*.

lecherous†, *a*, débauché, lascif.

lectern, *n*, lutrin, pupitre, *m*.

lecture, *n*, leçon; conférence; (*scolding*) semonce, mercuriale, *f*, sermon, *m*. ¶ *v.t*, sermonner, chapitrer, moraliser. ~ *on*, faire une leçon, une conférence, sur. **lecturer**, *n*, professeur, *m*; conférencier, ère, maître de conférences, *m*.

ledge, *n*, rebord; appui, *m*; saillie, *f*.

ledger, *n*, grand livre, *m*; (*Build.*) moise, *f*. ~ *line* (*Mus.*), ligne supplémentaire, *f*.

lee [side], *n*, côté sous le vent, *m*.

leech, *n*, sangsue, *f*.

leek, *n*, poireau, *m*.

leer, *n*, regard polisson, *m*. *to ~ at*, lorgner.

lees, *n.pl*, lie, *f*.

leeward, *a*, sous le vent. *L~ Islands*, îles sous le Vent, *f.pl*. **leeway**, *n*, dérive, *f*.

left, *a. & n*, gauche, *a. & f. the ~* (*Box.*), le [poing] gauche. ¶ *ad*, à gauche. ~*handed*, *a*. (pers. or player) *n*, gaucher, ère.

left (to be), rester. *left-overs*, *n.pl*, (*food, etc.*) restes, *m.pl*; bribes, *f.pl*.

leg, *n*, jambe; (*birds, insects, etc.*) patte; (*fowl*) cuisse, *f*; (*mutton*) gigot; (*table, etc.*) pied, *m*; (*compass, etc.*) branche; (*boot, stocking*) tige, *f*. ~ *lock* (*wrestling*), croc-en-jambe, *m*. *on one ~*, à cloche-pied.

legacy, *n*, legs, *m*.

legal†, *a*, légal; judiciaire. ~ *aid*, assistance judiciaire, *f*. ~ *charges*, frais de contentieux, *m.pl*. ~ *entity*, personne morale, p. juridique, p. civile, *f*. ~ *maxim*, adage de droit, *m*. ~ *tender* [*currency*], (*value*) pouvoir libératoire, *m*; (*money*) monnaie légale, *f*. ~**ize**, *v.t*, légaliser.

legate, *n*, légat, *m*. **legatee**, *n*, légataire, *m,f*. **legation**, *n*, légation, *f*.

legend, *n*, légende, *f*. ~**ary**, *a*, légendaire.

legerdemain, *n*, prestidigitation, *f*.

leggings, *n.pl*, molletières; jambières, *f.pl*.

Leghorn, *n*, Livourne, *f*.

legible†, *a*, lisible.

legion, *n*, légion, *f*. *their name is ~*, ils s'appellent légion.

legislate, *v.i*, faire les lois; légiférer. **legislation**, *n*, législation, *f*. **legislator**, *n*, législateur, *m*. **legislature**, *n*, législature, *f*. **legist**, *n*, légiste, *m*.

legitimacy, *n*, légitimité, *f*. **legitimate**†, *a*, légitime. **legitim[at]ize**, *v.t*, légitimer.

legwarmer, *n*, jambière, *f*.

leisure, *n*, loisir[s] *m.pl*. *at ~*, à loisir. *a ~ly man*, un homme lambin. [*in a*] ~*ly* [*way*], *ad*, sans se presser, sans hâte, avec lenteur.

leitmotiv, -if, *n*, leitmotiv, *m*.

lemon, *n*, citron, *m*. ~ *squash*, citron pressé, *m*. ~ *squeezer*, presse-citron, *m*. ~ *tree*, citronnier, *m*. ~**ade**, *n*, limonade, citronnade, *f*.

lend, *v.t.ir*, prêter. ~**er**, *n*, prêteur, euse. ~**ing**, *n*, prêt, *m*, prestation, *f*. ~ *library*, bibliothèque de prêt, *f*, cabinet de lecture, *m*.

lend-lease, *n*, prêt-bail, *m*.

length, *n*, longueur, *f*, long, *m*; étendue; durée; (*piece of a stuff*) coupe, *f*. *at* ~, au long; à la fin. ~en, *v.t*, [r]allonger; prolonger. ~*ening piece*, [r]allonge, *f*. ~ways, ~wise, *ad*, en long. ~y, *a*, long.

lenient, *a*, indulgent, clément; de douceur.

Leningrad, *n*, Léningrad, *m*.

lens, *n*, lentille; loupe, *f*; (*camera, microscope, etc.*) objectif, *m*. *telephoto* ~, télé-objectif, *m*.

Lent, *n*, carême, *m*. ~en, *a*, de carême.

lenticular, *a*, lenticulaire.

lentil, *n*, lentille, *f*.

leonine, *a*, léonin.

leopard, *n*, léopard, *m*. ~ess, *n*, l. femelle, *m*.

leper, *n*, lépreux, euse. ~ *hospital*, léproserie, *f*.

leprosy, *n*, lèpre, *f*. **leprous**, *a*, lépreux.

lesbian, *n*, lesbienne, (*slang*) gouine, *f*.

lesion, *n*, lésion, *f*.

less, *a*, moindre; inférieur. ~, *suffix*, sans; in-. ¶ *ad*, moins, *m*. de. ¶ *n*, moins, *m*. ~en, *v.t. & i*, diminuer, amoindrir.

lessee, *n*, preneur, euse; fermier, ère; tenancier, ère.

lesser, *a*, plus petit; moindre; petit.

lesson, *n*, leçon, *f*.

lessor, *n*, bailleur, eresse.

lest, *c*, de peur que . . . [ne].

let, *v.t. & aux*. *ir*, laisser; permettre; faire; louer. *to* [*be*] ~, à louer. ~ *down*, [a]baisser; (*fail pers. at need*) lâcher, laisser en panne. ~ *go* (hold), lâcher prise, démordre; larguer. ~ *have*, céder. ~ *loose*, déchaîner. ~ *in*, faire entrer. ~ *off*, faire grâce à; (*gun*) tirer; (*epigram*) décocher. ~ *out*, laisser sortir; l. échapper, lâcher; (*clothes*) [r]élargir.

lethal, *a*, léthifère, mortel. ~ *chamber*, chambre de [mise à] mort, *f*. ~ *weapon*, assommoir, *m*.

lethargic, *a*, léthargique. **lethargy**, *n*, léthargie, *f*. **Lethe**, *n*, Léthé, *m*.

letter, *n*, lettre; épître; cote, *f*. ~ *box*, boîte aux lettres, *f*. ~ *head*,

en-tête, *m*. ~ *opener*, ouvre-lettre[s] *m*. ~ *paper*, papier à lettres, *m*. ~*press*, texte [composé] *m*. ~*press printing*, impression typographique, *f*. ~ *scales*, pèse-lettre, *m*. ~ *writer*, (*pers.*) épistolier, ère, *m*. ~*ing*, *n*, lettrage, *m*.

lettuce, *n*, laitue, *f*.

letup, *n*, détente, *f*.

Levant, *n*, Levant, *m*. **Levantine**, *a*, levantin; (*ports*) du Levant. ¶ *n*, Levantin, e.

level, *a*, de niveau; en palier; plat; plan; uni; égal. *a* ~*-headed person*, une tête bien organisée, un cerveau organisé. ~ *with*, à fleur de, à ras de. ¶ *n*, niveau; plan, *m*; hauteur, *f*; palier, *m*; (*Min.*) galerie, *f*. ¶ *v.t*, niveler; aplanir; égaliser; unir; (*gun, etc.*) pointer. **leveling**, *n*, nivellement, *m*.

lever, *n*, levier, *m*; manette, *f*. ~ [*up*] *v.t*, soulever au moyen d'un levier. ~*age*, *n*, force de levier, *f*; (*fig.*) avantage, *m*.

leveret, *n*, levraut, *m*.

leviathan, *n*, léviathan, *m*.

Levite, *n*, lévite, *m*. **Leviticus**, *n*, le Lévitique.

levity, *n*, légèreté, *f*.

levy, *n*, levée, réquisition, *f*; prélèvement, *m*. ¶ *v.t*, [pré]lever, imposer, frapper.

lewd†, *a*, impudique, crapuleux. ~*ness*, *n*, impudicité, *f*.

lewis, *n*, louve, *f*.

lexicographer, *n*, lexicographe, *m*.

lexicon, *n*, lexique, *m*.

Leyden, *n*, Leyde, *f*.

liability, *n*, obligation, *f*; engagement, *m*; responsabilité, *f*; (*pl*, *Fin.*) passif, *m*. **liable**, *a*, tenu; soumis; sujet; passible; responsable; solidaire.

liaison officer, agent de liaison, *m*.

liar, *n*, menteur, euse.

lias, *n*, lias, *m*. **liassic**, *a*, liasique.

libation, *n*, libation, *f*.

libel, *n*, libelle, *m*; diffamation, *f*. ~ *action*, action en diffamation, *f*. ¶ *v.t*, diffamer. ~*ous*, *a*, diffamatoire.

liberal†, *a*, libéral; large. ¶ *n*, libéral, *m*. ~*ism*, *n*, libéralisme, *m*. ~*ity*, *n*, libéralité, *f*.

liberate, *v.t*, libérer; affranchir; lâcher; (*from complexes*) défouler.

libertine, a. & n, libertin, a. & m.

liberty, n, liberté; faculté; privauté, f. at ~, libre.

librarian, n, bibliothécaire, m,f. **library,** n, bibliothèque, f.

librettist, n, librettiste, m. **libretto,** n, livret, m.

license, n, licence, f; permis, m; dispense, f; brevet; bon; acte, m; concession, f. ~ plate, plaque matricule, de contrôle, f. ~ to sell, droit de vendre; (tobacco, spirits) débit, m. driver's ~, permis de conduire, m. license, v.t, accorder un permis à; breveter. **licentious†,** a, licencieux, dévergondé, décolleté. ~ness, n, licence, f, dévergondage, m.

lichen, n, lichen, m.

licit†, a, licite.

lick, v.t, lécher. ~ one's chops, se pourlecher les babines. ~ up, laper.

licorice, n, réglisse, f; jus de réglisse, m.

lictor, n, licteur, m.

lid, n, couvercle, m; (eye) paupière, f.

lie, n, mensonge; démenti, m. give the ~ to, démentir. ¶ v.i, mentir.

lie, n, (of ground) disposition, configuration; (Naut.) gisement, m. ¶ v.i.ir, coucher, reposer; gésir; séjourner, stationner; résider, tenir. ~ dormant, dormir. ~ down, se coucher. ~ idle, chômer. ~ in wait, se tenir en embuscade, s'embusquer.

liege, a, lige. ¶ n, vassal lige, m.

lien, n, privilège; droit de rétention, d. de gage, m. ~or, n, créancier gagiste, m.

lieu of (in), au lieu de.

lieutenant, n, lieutenant; (naval) l. de vaisseau, m. ~ colonel, lieutenant-colonel, m. ~ commander, capitaine de corvette, m. ~ general, général de corps d'armée, m.

life, n, vie; existence, f; vivant, m; durée, f; mouvement, m. for ~, à vie, viager; perpétuel, à perpétuité. from ~ (Art), d'après nature, au vif, sur le vif. to the ~, au naturel. 2 lives lost, 2 personnes ont péri. ~ & property (law), corps & biens. ~ [& soul] (of the party), boute-entrain, m. ~ annuity, rente viagère, f, viager, m. ~ belt, ceinture de sauve-

tage, f. ~ boat, bateau de s., m. ~ buoy, bouée de s., f. ~-giving, fécond. ~ insurance, assurance sur la vie, f. ~ jacket, brassière de sauvetage, f, gilet de s., m. ~-saving, sauvetage, m. ~ size, en grand, grandeur naturelle, nature, f. ~-time, vivant, m. ~-less, a, sans vie; inanimé. ~like, a, vivant; parlant. ~long, a, de toute la vie.

lift, n, coup d'épaule; (of the hand) geste, m. ¶ v.t, lever; soulever; élever; enlever; relever.

liftoff, n, (aircraft, etc.) décollage, m. ¶ v.i, (aircraft) décoller.

ligament, n, ligament, m. **ligature,** n, ligature, f.

light, a, léger; faible; petit; (ship unladen) lège; (Rly engine) haut le pied; (color) clair; (earth) meuble. ~-headed, délirant. ~-headedness, transport, m. ~ lager, bière blanche, b. blonde, f. ~ meal, collation, f. ~ opera, opérette, f. ~ reading, livres d'agrément, m.pl. ~ refreshments, rafraîchissements, m.pl. ~weight (Box.), poids léger, m. ¶ n, lumière, f; jour; éclairage, m; vue; clarté, f, clair; feu, fanal, phare, m; flamme, f. against the ~, à contre-jour. ~s out (Mil.), extinction des feux, f, couvre-feu, m. ~ & shade, (Art) clair-obscur, m. ~house, phare, m. ~ meter, cellule, f. ~ship, bateau-feu, m. do you have a ~? avez-vous du feu? ¶ v.t.ir, allumer; éclairer. ~ up, illuminer. ~ [up]on, tomber sur.

lighten, v.t, alléger; soulager; éclairer; (v.imp.) éclairer, faire des éclairs.

lighter, a, plus léger.

lighter, n, (pers.) allumeur; (pipe, etc.) briquet, m; (boat) allège, gabare, f, chaland, m. **lighting,** n, éclairage, m.

lightly, ad, légèrement; à la légère. **lightness,** n, légèreté, f.

lightning, n, éclair, m. oft. pl, foudre, f. ~ rod, paratonnerre, m.

lights (animal lungs) n.pl, mou, m.

ligneous, a, ligneux. **lignite,** n, lignite, m. **lignum vitae,** [bois de] gaïac, m.

likable, a, sympathique. **like,** a,

pareil; pair; semblable; analogue; approchant; ressemblant; même; tel; à l'égal de. *to be ~*, ressembler, approcher de, imiter. *to look ~*, avoir l'air de, ressembler. ¶ *n*, pareil, le; semblable, *m*. ~*s & dislikes*, sympathies & antipathies, *f.pl.* ¶ *pr*, *ad*, comme; de même que; tel que; à l'instar de; en. ¶ *v.t. & i*, aimer; affectionner; vouloir; se plaire à; trouver; goûter.

likelihood, *n*, probabilité; apparence; vraisemblance, *f.* **likely**, *a*, probable, vraisemblable. *very ~*, vraisemblablement.

liken, *v.t*, comparer, assimiler.

likeness, *n*, ressemblance; parité, *f*; air, *m*; image, *f*; portrait, *m*.

likewise, *ad*, pareillement, également, aussi, de même.

liking, *n*, goût; gré, *m*; affection, *f.*

lilac, *n. & a*, lilas, *m. & att*.

Lilliputian, *a*, lilliputien.

lily, *n*, lis, *m. ~ of the valley*, muguet, *m*.

limb, *n*, membre, *m*; (*tree*) mère branche, *f*; (*Math., etc.*) limbe, *m*. **-limbed**, *a*, membré.

limber, *a*, souple. ¶ *n*, avant-train, *m. ~ up*, mettre l'avant-train.

limbo, *n*, les limbes, *m.pl.*

lime, *n*, chaux, *f*; (*citrus*) limon, *m. ~ burner*, chaufournier, *m. ~ juice*, jus de limon, *m. ~ kiln*, four à chaux, chaufour, *m. ~ light*, lumière oxhydrique, *f. to be in the ~light*, être sous les feux de la rampe; (*fig.*) être en vedette. ~*stone*, pierre à chaux, p. calcaire, *f*, calcaire, *m. ~ [tree]*, (*citrus*) limonier; (*linden*) tilleul, *m. ~ twig*, gluau, pipeau, *m.* ¶ *v.t*, (*Agric.*) chauler; (*twig*) engluer.

limit, *n*, limite, borne, *f*; périmètre, *m.* ¶ *v.t*, limiter, borner. **~ation**, *n*, limitation, *f.* **limited**, *p.p. & p.a*, limité, borné, étroit; (*monarchy*) tempérée; (*edition*) à tirage restreint. ~ *partnership*, [société en] commandite, *f.*

limousine, *n*, limousine, *f.*

limp, *a*, flasque, mou; (*binding*) souple. ¶ *n*, claudication, *f*, boitement, clochement, *m.* ¶ *v.i*, boiter, clocher.

limpet, *n*, lépas, *m*, patelle, *f.*

limpid, *a*, limpide. **~ity**, *n*, limpidité, *f.*

linchpin, *n*, clavette d'essieu, esse, *f.*

linden, *n*, tilleul, *m.*

line, *n*, ligne; file; haie; voie, *f*; trait, *m*; raie; ride; (*Teleph.*) ligne, *f*, poste; (*Poet.*) vers; câble, *m*; corde, *f*; cordeau, *m*; amarre, *f*; genre; métier; emploi; département; ressort, *m*; partie; juridiction, *f. ~ cut*, cliché, *m. ~ engraving*, taille-douce; gravure au trait, *f. plumb ~*, fil à plomb, *m. wait in ~*, faire queue. ¶ *v.t*, (*clothes*) doubler; tapisser; garnir; revêtir; rider, sillonner; border. ~ *one's stomach*, se lester l'estomac. **lineage**, *n*, descendance, *f*, parage, *m.* **lineal**, *a*, linéaire; (*pers.*) en ligne directe. **lineament**, *n*, linéament, trait, *m.* **linear**, *a*, linéaire.

linen, *n*, toile [de lin] *f*; [tissu de lin]; linge, *m. ~ [thread]*, fil [de lin] *m. ~ trade*, industrie linière, toilerie, *f.*

liner, *n*, (*ship*) transatlantique, paquebot; (*aircraft*) avion de transport, *m.*

ling, *n*, (*fish*) grande morue barbue; (*Bot.*) bruyère, brande, *f.*

linger, *v.i*, s'attarder; traîner. ~*ing death*, mort lente, *f.*

lingerie, *n*, lingerie [fine] *f.*

lingo, *n*, jargon, baragouin, *m.*

lingual, *a*, lingual. ¶ *n*, linguale, *f.* **linguist**, *n*, linguiste, *m.* ~**ics**, *n*, linguistique, *f.*

liniment, *n*, liniment, *m.*

lining, *n*, doublure; garniture; chemise; (*hat*) coiffe, *f*; revêtement, *m.*

link, *n*, chaînon, maillon, anneau, *m*; (*Mach.*) coulisse, *f*; (*fig.*) lien, *m.* ¶ *v.t*, articuler; enchaîner. ~ *up*, raccorder.

links, *n.pl. & s*, lande, *f*; (*golf*) terrain, *m.*

linnet, *n*, linotte, *f*, linot, *m.*

linoleum, *n*, linoléum, *m.*

linotype, *n. & att*, linotype, *f. & a.*

linseed, *n*, graine de lin, *f. ~ oil*, huile de [graine de] lin, *f.*

lint, *n*, charpie, *f.*

lintel, *n*, linteau, sommier, *m*, traverse, *f.*

lion, ess, *n*, lion, ne. ~ *cub*, ~ *whelp*, lionceau, *m. ~'s share*, part du lion, *f.*

lip, *n*, lèvre; babine, *f*; bec, *m*. ~*stick*, rouge à lèvres, *m*.

liquefaction, *n*, liquéfaction, *f*. **liquefy**, *v.t*, liquéfier.

liqueur, *n*, liqueur [de dessert] *f*. ~ *brandy*, fine champagne, *f*.

liquid, *a*, liquide; (*Com., Fin.*) liquide, disponible; (*fig.*) coulant, doux. ~ *ammonia*, liqueur d'ammoniaque, *f*. ~ *assets*, disponibilités, *f.pl.* ¶ *n*, liquide, *m*; (*phonetics*) liquide, *f*.

liquidate, *v.t*, liquider. **liquidation**, *n*, liquidation, *f*. **liquidator**, *n*, liquidateur, *m*.

liquor, *n*, liquide, *m*, boisson; liqueur, *f*.

Lisbon, *n*, Lisbonne, *f*.

lisp, *v.i*, zézayer. ¶ *n*, zézeiements, *m*.

lissom[e], *a*, souple.

list, *n*, liste, *f*; bordereau, *m*; feuille, *f*; rôle; tableau, *m*; table, *f*; inventaire; bulletin; catalogue, *m*; cote, *f*; (*Naut.*) bande; (*selvage*) lisière, *f*; (*pl.*) lice, arène, barrière, *f*. ~ *of plates*, table des hors-texte. ¶ *v.t*, cataloguer; inventorier; (*door*) calfeutrer; (*computers*) lister. (*v.i, Naut.*) donner [de] la bande. ~*ing*, *n*, (*computers*) listage, *m*.

listen, *v.i. & ~ in* (*radio*), écouter. ~*er*, *n*, (*hearer & radio*) auditeur, *m*; (*spy*) écouteur, euse.

listless†, *a*, nonchalant, distrait, traînant.

litany, *n*, litanies, *f.pl*.

literal†, *a*, littéral. ~ [*error*], coquille, *f*. ~ *sense*, (*passage*) sens littéral; (*word*) [sens] propre, *m*.

literary, *a*, littéraire. ~ *man*, homme de lettres, littérateur, *m*. **literate**, *a*, qui sait lire; lettré. **literature**, *n*, littérature, *f*.

litharge, *n*, litharge, *f*.

lithe, *a*, souple, agile.

lithia, *n*, lithine, *f*. **lithium**, *n*, lithium, *m*.

lithograph & ~*y*, *n*, lithographie, *f*. ¶ *v.t*, lithographier. ~*er*, *n*, lithographe, *m*. ~*ic*, *a*, lithographique.

Lithuania, *n*, la Lit[h]uanie.

litigant, *n*, plaideur, euse. **litigation**, *n*, litige, *m*. **litigious**, *a*, litigieux, processif.

litmus, *n*, tournesol, *m*. ~ *paper*, papier tournesol, *m*.

litter, *n*, (*palanquin*) litière, civière, *f*, brancard, *m*; (*straw & dung*) litière, *f*, fumier, *m*; (*young*) portée, ventrée; (*pigs*) cochonnée, *f*; encombrement, fouillis, *m*; immondices, *f.pl*, détritus, débris, *m.pl.* ¶ *v.t*, encombrer; joncher.

little, *a*, petit. ~ *devil*, diablotin, *m*. ~ *finger*, petit doigt, [doigt] auriculaire, *m*. ~ *ones*, petits enfants; (*cubs*) petits, *m.pl*. *L~ Red Riding Hood*, le Petit Chaperon Rouge. *a ~* [*while*] *longer*, un peu. ¶ *ad*, peu; ne . . . guère. ¶ *n*, peu, *m*. ~*ness*, *n*, petitesse *f*.

livable, *a*, vivable; supportable; habitable.

live, *a*, vif; vivant; (*coal*) ardent; (*axle*) tournant; (*Elec.*) en charge; (*shell*) chargé. ~*bait fishing*, pêche au vif, *f*. ~*stock*, animaux vivants, *m.pl.* ~ *rail*, rail conducteur, *m*.

live, *v.i. & t*, vivre; durer; se nourrir (*on milk, etc. =* de); demeurer, habiter.

livelihood, *n*, subsistance, *f*, gagne-pain, *m*.

liveliness, *n*, vivacité, animation, *f*, entrain, *m*. **lively**, *a*, vif, vivant, animé, mouvementé; allègre, fringant, émerillonné.

liver (*Anat.*) *n*, foie, *m*.

livery, *n*, livrée, *f*. ~ *stables*, pension pour les chevaux, *f*.

livid, *a*, livide. ~*ity*, *n*, lividité, *f*.

living, *a*, vivant; en vie; (*force*) vive. ~ *being*, vivant, *m*. ~ *wage*, minimum vital, *m*. *within* ~ *memory*, de mémoire d'homme. ¶ *n*, vie, *f*, vivre, *m*; (*fare*) chère, *f*; (*Eccl.*) bénéfice, *m*. ~ *expenses*, dépense de bouche, *f*. ~-*in*, internat, *m*. ~ *room*, salon, *m*; salle de séjour, *f*. *the* ~, les vivants, *m.pl. to earn a* ~, gagner sa vie.

lizard, *n*, lézard, *m*.

llama, *n*, lama, *m*.

loach, *n*, loche, *f*.

load, *n*, charge, *f*; fardeau, *m*. ~ [*water*] *line*, ligne de [flottaison en] charge, *f*. ¶ *v.t*, charger; combler; couvrir; (*dice*) piper; (*v.i.*) prendre charge. ~*ed*, *p.p*, chargé. ~*er*, *n*, chargeur, *m*. ~*ing*, *n*, charge, *f*; chargement, *m*. [*now*] ~ (*ship*), en charge.

loaf, *n.* & ~ *of bread,* pain, *m;* (*round loaf*) miche, *f.*

loaf, *v.i,* fainéanter, battre le pavé. ~**er,** *n,* fainéant, batteur de pavé, *m.*

loam, *n,* terre grasse; terre, *f.*

loan, *n,* prêt; emprunt, *m.* ~*shark,* usurier, *m.*

loath (to be), ne vouloir pas, répugner. **loathe,** *v.t,* haïr, abhorrer. **loathing,** *n,* dégoût, *m.* **loathsome,** *a,* dégoûtant.

lob (*Ten.*) *n,* chandelle, *f.*

lobby, *n,* vestibule; couloir, *m.* ¶ *v.i,* faire les couloirs. ~**ing,** *n,* propos de couloir, *m.pl.*

lobe, *n,* lobe, *m.*

lobelia, *n,* lobélie, *f.*

lobster, *n,* homard, *m.* ~ *pot,* ~ *basket,* nasse, *f,* panier, *m.*

local, *a,* local; topique; de clocher; (*custom*) de place, des lieux. ~[e], *n,* scène, *f.* ~**ity,** *n,* localité, *f.* ~**ize,** *v.t,* localiser. ~**ly,** *ad,* localement; sur place.

locate, *v.t,* fixer [l'emplacement de]; repérer; rechercher.

lock, *n,* serrure; (*canal*) écluse; (*hair*) boucle, mèche; (*pl.*) chevelure; (*gun*) platine, *f.* ~ *under* ~ & *key,* sous clef. ~**jaw,** tétanos, *m.* ~**nut,** contre-écrou, *m.* ~**out,** lockout, *m,* grève patronale, *f.* ~**smith,** serrurier, *m.* ~ *stitch,* point de piqûre, *m.* ~**up,** (*police*) violon; (*att.*) fermant à clef. ¶ *v.t,* fermer [à clef]; bloquer. ~ *out,* fermer la porte à clef sur; (*workmen*) renvoyer en masse. ~ *up,* fermer à clef; mettre (*ou* serrer) sous clef; verrouiller, enfermer, coffrer, boucler; (*Fin.*) immobiliser, bloquer.

locker, *n,* case, *f;* caisson, *m;* soute, *f.*

locket, *n,* médaillon, *m.*

locksmith, *n,* serrurier, *m.*

locomotion, *n,* locomotion, *f.* **locomotive,** *a,* locomoteur. ¶ *n,* locomotive, *f. locomotor ataxy,* ataxie locomotrice, *f.*

loculus, *n,* loge, *f.*

locust, *n,* sauterelle, locuste, *f,* criquet, *m.* ~ [*bean*], caroube, *f.*

locution, *n,* façon de s'exprimer, *f,* tour de langage, idiotisme, *m.*

lode, *n,* filon, *m.* ~*star,* étoile polaire, *f.* ~*stone,* pierre d'aimant, *f.*

lodge, *n,* loge, *f;* pavillon, *m.*

¶ *v.t,* loger; déposer, [re]mettre; fournir; (*appeal*) interjeter; (*v.i.*) [se] loger, camper. **lodger,** *n,* locataire, *m,f.* **lodging,** *n,* logement, *m,* chambre, *f,* le couvert; (*pl.*) meublé *m.*

loft, *n,* grenier, *m;* soupente; (*organ*) tribune, *f.* ¶ (*golf*) *v.t,* enlever. **loftiness,** *n,* élévation, hauteur, *f.* **lofty,** *a,* élevé; relevé; fier; hautain, altier; (*style*) soutenu.

log, *n,* bûche, *f;* (*Naut.*) loch, *m.* (*computers*) transmission ~, journal des transmissions, *m.* ~ [*book*], livre de loch; journal de bord, *m.* ~ *cabin,* ~ *hut,* cabane de bois, *f.* ~*wood,* [bois de] campêche, *m.*

loganberry, *n,* ronce-framboise, *f.*

logarithm, *n,* logarithme, *m.*

loggerheads (at), en bisbille.

logic, *n,* logique, *f.* ~**al**†, *a,* logique. ~**ian,** *n,* logicien, *m.*

loin, *n,* (*veal*) longe, *f;* (*mutton*) filet, *m;* (*pl.*) reins, lombes, *m.pl.* ~ *chop,* côtelette de filet, *f.* ~ *cloth,* pagne, *m.*

loiter, *v.i,* s'attarder, traîner, s'amuser. ~**er,** *n,* traînard, *m.*

loll, *v.i,* se prélasser; (*tongue*) pendre.

lollipop, *n,* sucette, *f.*

Lombardy, *n,* la Lombardie.

London, *n,* Londres, *m;* (*att.*) londonien. ~**er,** *n,* Londonien, ne.

loneliness, *n,* solitude, *f,* isolement, *m.* **lonely** & **lone[some]**, *a,* solitaire, isolé, esseulé. *lone cottage,* chartreuse, *f.*

long, *a,* long; grand; allongé; (*Meas.*) de long. ~*boat,* chaloupe, *f.* ~*distance racé,* course de fond, *f.* ~*drawn,* filandreux. ~*haired,* chevelu. ~*legged* (man), bien fendu. ~*lived,* vivace. ~ *service,* vétérance, *f.* ~*shoreman,* débardeur, *m.* ~ *a* ~ *while,* un long temps, longtemps, *ad.* ~*winded,* prolixe, diffus. ¶ *ad,* longtemps; le long de. ~ *ago,* il y a longtemps. *not* ~ *since,* naguère. ~*suffering,* longanimité, *f.* ¶ *n: the* ~ & *the short of it,* le fin mot. ¶ *v.i: I* ~ *to,* il me tarde de, je brûle de, je grille de. ~ *for,* languir pour, soupirer après. *to be* ~ (delay), tarder.

longest way round, chemin des écoliers, *m.*

longevity, *n*, longévité, *f*.

longing, *n*, [grande] envie, démangeaison, *f*.

longitude, *n*, longitude, *f*. **longitudinal†**, *a*, longitudinal.

look, *n*, regard; coup d'œil; œil; air, *m*; mine; apparence, *f*, aspect, *m*. ~*out*, veille, vigie, *f*, qui-vive, *m*; (*post*) guérite, *f*; (*man*) guetteur, *m*; affaire, *f*. ¶ *v.i*, regarder; avoir l'air; sembler; paraître. ~ *after*, veiller à, soigner, ménager, gouverner. ~ *at*, regarder. ~ *down* (from on high), planer. ~ *down* [*up*]*on*, mépriser. ~ *for*, chercher; s'attendre à. ~ *into*, examiner. ~ *like*, ressembler à, jouer. ~ *on*, regarder; envisager; (*front*) donner sur. ~ *out!* attention!, gare!, alerte!, vingt-deux! ~ *out for*, chercher; s'attendre à. ~ *out of the window*, regarder par la fenêtre. ~ *over*, parcourir; repasser. ~ *up a word in the dictionary*, chercher un mot dans le dictionnaire. *to translate by looking up every other word in the dictionary*, traduire à coups de dictionnaire. ~**ing glass**, glace, *f*, miroir, *m*.

loom, *n*, métier [à tisser] *m.*

loom, *v.i*, se dessiner, émerger, surgir.

loop, *n*, boucle; coque, *f*; œil, *m*; ganse, *f*. ~*hole*, meurtrière, *f*, créneau, *m*; (*fig.*) échappatoire, *f*. ¶ *v.t*, boucler. ~ *the* ~, boucler la boucle.

loose, *a*, mobile; volant; branlant; flottant; coulant; large; lâche; (*pulley*) folle; libre; négligé; desserré; décousu; (*in bulk*) en vrac. *at a* ~ *end*, désœuvré. **loose**[**n**], *v.t*, [re]lâcher; délier; desserrer.

loot, *n*, butin, *m*. ¶ *v.t. & i*, piller.

lop, *v.t*, élaguer, ébrancher. ~*ear* [*ed rabbit*], lapin bélier, *m.* ~*sided*, de guingois; (*boat*) bordier.

loquacious, *a*, loquace. **loquacity**, *n*, loquacité, *f*.

lord, *n*, seigneur; (*Eng.*) lord, *m.* ~ *of creation*, roi de la nature, *m.* ~ *of the manor*, châtelain, *m.* *the Lord* (God), le Seigneur. *Lord's Prayer*, oraison dominicale, *f*. *Lord's Supper*, communion, Cène, *f*. ~ *it over*, faire le maître avec. ~**ly**, *a*, hautain,

altier, fier. ~**ship**, *n*, seigneurie, *f*. *Your L~*, Votre grandeur, *f*.

lore, *n*, science, *f*.

lorgnette, *n*, face à main, *f*.

lose, *v.t. & i. ir*, perdre; (*train*) manquer; (*clock*) retarder. ~ *heart*, se décourager. **loser**, *n*, perdant, e; (*good, bad*) joueur, euse. **loss**, *n*, perte; déperdition, *f*; déchet[s] *m.*[pl.]; sinistre, *m.* ~ *of appetite*, inappétence, *f*. ~ *of voice*, extinction de voix, *f*. *at a* ~, à perte; (*fig.*) empêché. *dead* ~, perte seche. **lost**, *p.p. & p.a*, perdu; égaré; dépaysé; (*in thought*) absorbé, abîmé; (*motion*) rejetée. ~ *& found office*, bureau des objets trouvés, *m.*

lot, *n*, lot, *m*; partie, *f*; paquet; partage; sort, destin, *m*, destinée, *f*. *the* ~, le tout. *to draw* ~*s*, tirer au sort.

lotion, *n*, lotion, *f*.

lottery, *n*, loterie, *f*.

lotto, *n*, loto, *m*.

lotus, *n*, lotus, lotos, *m*.

loud, *a*, haut; fort; grand; gros; sonore; bruyant; tapageur. ~ *cheers*, vivats sonores, *m.pl.* ~ *pedal*, grande pédale, p. forte, *f*. ~*speaker*, haut-parleur, *m.* ~[**ly**], *ad*, [tout] haut; fort.

Louisiana, *n*, la Louisiane.

lounge, *n*, (*hotel, etc.*) hall; (*music hall, etc.*) promenoir; canapé, *m.* ¶ *v.i*, flâner, paresser. **lounger**, *n*, flâneur, batteur de pavé, *m.*

louse, *n*, pou, *m.* **lousy** *a*, pouilleux.

lout, *n. & ~ish*, *a*, rustre, rustaud, *m. & a.*

lovable, *a*, aimable. **love**, *n*, amour, *m*; inclination; tendresse, *f*; chéri, e, bijou, *m*. *for* ~ *or money*, ni pour or ni pour argent. *in* ~, amoureux, épris. *fall in* ~, s'enamourer, s'éprendre. *make* ~ *to*, faire la cour à. *play for* ~, jouer pour l'honneur. ~ *all* (*Ten.*), zéro partout, égalité à rien, rien à rien. ~ *at first sight*, coup de foudre, *m.* ~ *bird*, inséparable, *m. ou f.* ~ *knot*, lacs d'amour, *m.* ~ *letter*, billet doux, *m.* ~*lock* (as worn by a man) rouflaquette, *f*; (by a woman) accrochecœur, *m.* ~ *match*, mariage d'amour, mariage d'inclination, *m.*

~ *potion*, philtre, *m*. ~*-sick*, qui languit d'amour. ~ *story*, roman d'amour, *m*. ¶ *v.t. & i*, aimer; chérir. ~ *one another*, s'entr'aimer.

loveliness, *n*, beauté, *f*. **lovely**, *a*, beau; adorable; du nanan.

lover, *n*, amant, *m*; amoureux, euse; galant; ami, e; amateur, *m*. ~ *of old books*, bouquineur, *m*. **loving†**, *a*, affectueux, aimant.

low, *a*, bas; petit; faible; (*fever, speed*) lente; (*bow*) profonde; vulgaire. L~ *Countries*, Pays-Bas, *m.pl*. ~ *gear*, première vitesse, *f*. ~ *mass*, messe basse, petite m., *f*. ~ *relief*, bas-relief, *m*. L~ *Sunday*, Quasimodo, *f*. ~*-water mark*, (*sea*) laisse de basse mer, *f*; (*river*) étiage, *m*. ¶ *ad*, bas; profondément. ~*-necked* (*dress*), décolleté, *a*. & *m*. ~*-spirited*, abattu. *to be* ~*-waisted* (dress), avoir la taille basse.

low, *v.i*, mugir, beugler.

lower, *a*, plus bas; inférieur; bas; moindre. ~ *register* (*Mus.*), grave, *m*. ~ *tooth*, dent de dessous, *f*. ¶ *v.t*, [a]baisser; rabattre; descendre, avaler. ~ *oneself* (*fig.*), se ravaler. *award, etc., to the lowest tenderer*, adjudication, *etc.*, au rabais, *f*.

lowlands, *n.pl*, basses terres, *f.pl*.

lowliness, *n*, humilité, *f*. **lowly**, *a*, humble.

lowness, *n*, peu de hauteur, *m*; (*price, etc.*) modicité; (*vileness*) bassesse, *f*.

lox, *n*, saumon fumé, *m*.

loyal†, *a*, loyal, fidèle. ~*ism*, *n*, loyalisme, *m*. ~*ist*, *n*. & *att*, loyaliste, *m.f. & a*. ~*ty*, *n*, loyauté, *f*; (*to sovereign*) loyalisme, *m*.

lozenge, *n*, pastille, tablette, *f*; (*Geom.*) losange, *m*.

lubber, *n*, lourdaud, mastoc, *m*.

lubricate, *v.t*, graisser, lubrifier. *lubricating oil*, huile à graisser, *f*. **lubricator**, *n*, graisseur, *m*.

Lucca, *n*, Lucques, *f*.

Lucerne (*Lake of*), lac des Quatre-Cantons, *m*.

lucid, *a*, lucide. ~*ity*, *n*, lucidité, *f*.

luck, *n*, chance, *f*, hasard, *m*; veine; fortune, *f*; bonheur, *m*. ~*less*, *a*, malheureux, néfaste. ~*y†*, *a*, heureux, chanceux, for-

tuné, bien loti; propice. ~ *star*, bonne étoile, *f*.

lucrative, *a*, lucratif. **lucre**, *n*, lucre, gain, *m*.

lucubration, *n*, élucubration, *f*.

ludicrous†, *a*, risible, comique; plaisant.

luff, *n*, lof, *m*. ¶ *v.t*, lofer.

lug, *n*, oreille, *f*, ergot, *m*. ¶ *v.t*, traîner.

luggage, *n*, bagage[s] *m.[pl.]*. ~ *carrier*, porte-bagages, *m*.

lugger, *n*, lougre, *m*.

lugubrious†, *a*, lugubre.

lukewarm, *a*, tiède. ~*ness*, *n*, tiédeur, *f*.

lull, *n*, accalmie, embellie, *f*. ¶ *v.t*, bercer; mollir; assoupir. **lullaby**, *n*, berceuse, *f*.

lumbago, *n*, lumbago, *m*. **lumbar**, *a*, lombaire.

lumber, *n*, bois [de charpente] *m*. ~*man*, bûcheron, *m*.

luminary, *n*, luminaire, astre, *m*; (*pers.*) lumière, *f*. **luminous†**, *a*, lumineux. ~ *dial* (watch), cadran lumineux, *m*.

lump, *n*, [gros] morceau, *m*, masse, *f*, bloc, *m*, motte, *f*. ~ *sugar*, sucre en morceaux, *s*. cassé, *m*. ~ *sum*, somme grosse, *f*. *in a* ~ *sum* (opp. *by installments*), en une [seule] fois. ¶ *v.t*, bloquer, réunir. ~*ish*, *a*, balourd, mastoc (*inv.*).

lunacy, *n*, aliénation d'esprit, aliénation mentale, démence, *f*.

lunar, *a*, lunaire.

lunatic, *n*, aliéné, e. ~ *asylum*, hospice (*ou* asile) d'aliénés, *m*.

lunch & **luncheon**, *n*, déjeuner [de midi], lunch, *m*. *lunch[eon] basket*, panier-repas, *m*. **lunch**, *v.i*, déjeuner.

lung, *n*, poumon, *m*.

lunge, *n*, (*fencing*) botte, *f*; coup porté, *m*. ¶ *v.i*, (*fencing*) porter une botte; allonger un coup [à].

lupus (*Med.*) *n*, lupus, *m*.

lurch, *n*, embardée, *f*. *leave in the* ~, camper là, planter là, laisser en panne. ¶ *v.i*, tituber.

lure, *n*, leurre, *m*. ¶ *v.t*, leurrer; (*birds*) piper.

lurid, *a*, blafard; cuivré, fauve; sinistre.

lurk, *v.i*, se cacher; se dissimuler.

luscious, *a*, succulent; fondant.

lush, *a*, luxuriant.

lust, *n*, luxure, convoitise, *f*. ~

after, convoiter. ~**ful**, *a*, luxurieux.

luster, *n*, lustre, éclat, *m*. ¶ *v.t*, lustrer. ~**less**, *a*, terne.

lusty†, *a*, vigoureux, robuste.

lute, *n*, (*Mus.*) luth; (*cement*) lut, *m*. ¶ *v.t*, luter.

Lutheran, *a.* & *n*, luthérien, ne.

Luxembourg, *n*, Luxembourg, *m.*

luxuriance, *n*, exubérance, *f*. **luxuriant**, *a*, luxuriant, exubérant. **luxurious**, *a*, luxueux; voluptueux. **luxury**, *n*, luxe; délice, *m*.

lye, *n*, lessive, *f*.

lying, *a*, mensonger, menteur. ¶ *n*, mensonge, *m*.

lymph, *n*, lymphe, *f*.

lynch, *v.t*, lyncher.

lynx, *n*, lynx; (*common*) loup-cervier, *m*.

Lyons, *n*, Lyon, *m*.

lyre, *n*, lyre, *f*. ~**bird**, oiseau-lyre, *m*.

lyric & ~**al**, *a*, lyrique. **lyricism**, *n*, lyrisme, *m*.

M

macadam, *n*, macadam, *m*. ~**ize**, *v.t*, macadamiser.

macaque, *n*, macaque, *m*.

macaroni, *n*, macaroni, *m*.

macaroon, *n*, macaron, *m*.

macaw, *n*, ara, *m*.

mace, *n*, masse, *f*; (*spice*) macis, *m*. ~ *bearer*, massier, *m*.

macerate, *v.t*, macérer.

Machiavellian, *a*, machiavélique.

machination, *n*, machination, *f*.

machine, *n*, machine, *f*. ~**-cut**, taillé à la machine. ~ *gun*, fusil mitrailleur, *m*, mitrailleuse, *f*. ~ *gunner*, [fusilier] mitrailleur, *m*. ~**-made**, fait à la mécanique. ~ *oil*, huile pour machine, *f*. ~ *tool*, machine-outil, *f*. ¶ *v.t*, usiner, façonner. **machinery**, *n*, machinerie, *f*, machines, *f.pl*, outillage; (*fig.*) rouage, *m*. **machinist**, *n*, machiniste, mécanicien, *m.*

mackerel, *n*, maquereau, *m*. ~ *sky*, ciel pommelé, *m*.

mackintosh, *n*, imperméable, caoutchouc, *m*.

mad, *a*, fou; insensé; furieux (*pers. & bull*); enragé (*pers. & dog*). ~*cap*, écervelé; e, cerveau brûlé, *m*. ~*man*, *-woman*, fou, *m*, folle,

f, insensé, e, forcené, e, désespéré, e, enragé, e.

madam, *n*, madame, *f*.

madden, *v.t*, rendre fou; affoler; faire enrager. ~**ing**, *p.a*, enrageant.

madder, *n*, garance, *f*.

Madeira, *n*, Madère, *f*.

madly, *ad*, follement, en fou. **madness**, *n*, folie; démence; (*dog's*) rage, *f*.

madonna, *n*, madone, *f*.

madras (*fabric*) *n*, madras, *m*.

madrepore, *n*, madrépore, *f*.

madrigal, *n*, madrigal, *m*.

magazine, *n*, magasin, *m*; (*warehouse*) soute; (*periodical*) revue, *f*, magazine, *m*.

Maggiore (Lago), le lac Majeur.

maggot, *n*, ver; asticot, *m*. ~**y**, *a*, véreux.

Magi, *n.pl*, mages, *m.pl*.

magic, *a*, magique. ¶ *n*, magie, *f*; enchantement; prestige, *m*. ~**al**, *a*, magique. ~**ally**, *ad*, d'une façon magique. ~**ian**, *n*, magicien, ne.

magisterial, *a*, de magistrat; (*fig.*) magistral. ~**ly**, *ad*, en magistrat; magistralement. **magistracy**, *n*, magistrature, *f*. **magistrate**, *n*, magistrat; juge, *m*.

magnanimity, *n*, magnanimité, *f*. **magnanimous**†, *a*, magnanime.

magnate, *n*, magnat, gros bonnet, *m*.

magnesia, *n*, magnésie, *f*. **magnesium**, *n*, magnésium, *m*. ~ *light*, lumière magnésique, *f*.

magnet, *n*, aimant, *m*. ~**ic**, *a*, magnétique; (*bar, needle*) aimanté, e; (*fig.*) attirant. ~**ics**, *n*. & ~**ism**, *n*, magnétisme, *m*. ~**ize**, *v.t*, aimanter; (*fig.*) magnétiser. **magneto**, *n*, magnéto, *f*. ~**electric**, *a*, magnéto-électrique.

magnificat, *n*, magnificat, *m*.

magnificence, *n*, magnificence, *f*. **magnificent**†, *a*, magnifique.

magnify, *v.t*, grossir, grandir; (*the Lord*) magnifier. *magnifying glass*, loupe, *f*.

magniloquence, *n*, emphase, *f*. **magniloquent**, *a*, emphatique.

magnitude, *n*, grandeur; importance, *f*.

magnolia, *n*, magnolia, *m*.

magot (*Chinese figure & ape*), *n*, magot, *m*.

magpie, *n*, pie, *f*.

mahogany, *n,* acajou, *m.*

mahout, *n,* cornac, *m.*

maid, *n,* fille; vierge, pucelle, *f.* ~[*servant*], fille [de service], bonne, domestique, servante, *f.* *maid of all work,* bonne à tout faire. *maid of honor,* demoiselle d'honneur, *f. maid's room,* chambre de domestique, *f.*

maiden, *n,* vierge, fille; pucelle, *f.* ~ [*lady*], demoiselle, *f.* ¶ *a,* virginal; (*speech*) de début, premier; (*trip*) premier. ~*hair* [*fern*], capillaire, *m.* ~ *name,* nom de jeune fille, *m.* ~*hood,* *n,* virginité, *f.* ~*ly, a,* de jeune fille, virginal.

mail, *n,* (*armor*) mailles, *f.pl;* (*post*) poste, *f,* courrier, *m. air* ~, poste aérienne, *f.* ~ *bag,* sac à dépêches, *m.* ~ *boat,* ~ *steamer,* paquebot-poste, *m.* ~ *box,* boîte aux lettres, *f.* ~ *man,* facteur, *m.* ~ *order business,* affaires par correspondance, *f.pl.* ~ [*train*], train-poste, *m.*

maim, *v.t,* estropier, mutiler.

main, *a,* principal; grand; maître, esse. *n* [*portion of*] *building,* corps de logis, c. de bâtiment, *m.* ~ *deck,* pont principal, *m.* ~ *drain,* maître drain, d. collecteur, *m. by* ~ *force,* de vive force. ~ *hall* (body of building), vaisseau, *m. the* ~ *idea* (of a book), l'idée mère. ~ *issue* (*law*), fond, *m.* ~*land,* continent, *m,* terre ferme, *f.* ~ *line* (*Rly*), ligne principale, grande l., *f.* ~*mast,* grand mât, *m. the* ~ *point,* le point principal, l'essentiel, *m.* ~ *road,* grand chemin, *m,* grand-route, *f.* ~*sail,* grand-voile, *f.* ~*spring,* grand ressort, *m;* (*fig.*) cheville ouvrière, *f,* mobile, *m.* ~*stay* (*fig.*), âme, *f;* soutien, *m. the* ~ *thing,* le principal, l'important, *m.* ~ *walls,* gros murs, *m.pl.* ¶ *n,* (*pipe*) conduite [maîtresse]; (*pl.*) canalisation, *f;* (*Elec.*) conducteur principal, *m;* (*sea, Poet.*) onde, *f. in the* ~, en général. *the* M~ (river), le Mein. ~*ly, ad,* principalement.

maintain, *v.t,* maintenir, soutenir; entretenir. **maintenance,** *n,* maintien, soutien; entretien, *m.*

Mainz, *n,* Mayence, *f.*

maize, *n,* maïs, *m.*

majestic†, *a,* majestueux. **majesty,** *n,* majesté, *f. His, Her,* M~, Sa Majesté.

majolica, *n,* majolique, maïolique, *f.*

major, *a,* majeur; (*prophet, etc.*) grand; (*pers.*) aîné. ~ *planet,* planète principale, *f.* ~ *road,* route de priorité, *f.* ¶ (*Mil.*) *n,* commandant, chef de bataillon, *m.* ~ *general,* général de division, *m.*

Majorca, *n,* Majorque, *f.*

majority, *n,* majorité; pluralité, (la) plupart, *f.*

make, *n,* façon; fabrication, *f.* ~*-believe,* feinte, frime, *f.* ~*shift,* moyen de fortune, pis aller, *m.* ~*up,* maquillage, fard, *m.* ~*weight,* complément de poids, *m;* (*butcher's*) réjouissance, *f;* (*fig.*) remplissage, *m.* ¶ *v.t.ir,* faire; dresser; pratiquer; fabriquer; confectionner; créer; rendre; forcer; réaliser; mettre; (*inquiries*) prendre; (*v.i.ir.*) se diriger [vers]; contribuer [à]; faire [comme si]. ~ *away with,* se défaire de; détourner. ~ *faces,* grimacer. ~ *hay,* faire les foins. ~ *it up,* se raccommoder. ~ *light of,* faire peu de cas de. ~ *money,* s'enrichir. ~ *much of,* faire mousser. ~ *off,* filer, décamper. ~ *one's will,* tester. ~ *out,* distinguer; déchiffrer; comprendre; dresser. ~ *the most of,* ménager. ~ *up,* (*quarrel*) se réconcilier; confectionner; (*face*) se farder, se maquiller; (*Theat.*) se grimer; (*Typ.*) mettre en pages. ~ *up for,* suppléer [à]. ~ *up one's mind,* se décider, se déterminer. **maker,** *n,* créateur, trice; faiseur, euse; fabricant; constructeur, *m.* **making,** *n,* création; fabrication; construction; confection, *f.*

malachite, *n,* malachite, *f.*

maladjusted, *a,* mal ajusté; inadapté. ¶ *n,* (*person*) inadapté, e.

maladministration, *n,* mauvaise gestion, *f.*

maladroit†, *a,* maladroit.

malady, *n,* maladie, *f.*

Malagasy, *a,* malgache. ¶ *n,* Malgache, *m,f.*

malaprop[ism], *n,* incongruité, *f,* pataquès, *m.*

malaria, *n,* paludisme, *m,* malaria, *f.* **malarial,** *a,* paludéen; miasmatique.

Malay[an], *a,* malais. ¶ *n,* (*pers.*) Malais, e; (*language*) le malais.

Malaysia, *n,* la Malaisie; Malaysia.

malcontent, *a. & n,* mécontent, *a. & m.*

male, *n,* mâle, *m.* ¶ *a,* mâle; masculin. ~ *descent,* masculinité, *f.* ~ *nurse,* infirmier, *m.*

malediction, *n,* malédiction, *f.*

malefactor, *n,* malfaiteur, *m.*

malevolent, *a,* malveillant.

malformation, *n,* malformation, *f,* vice de conformation, *m.*

malice, *n,* malice, rancune, *f.* ~ *aforethought,* préméditation, *f.* **malicious†,** *a,* malicieux.

malign, *v.t,* diffamer, calomnier. **malign†, malignant†,** *a,* malin.

malinger, *v.i,* faire le malade, simuler la maladie.

mallard, *n,* malart, *m.*

malleable, *a,* malléable.

mallet, *n,* maillet, *m,* mailloche, batte, *f.*

mallow, *n,* mauve, *f.*

malnutrition, *m,* sous-alimentation, *f.*

malpractice, *n,* incurie; malfaçon, *f.*

malt, *n,* malt, *m.* ¶ *v.t,* convertir en malt. ~**ing,** *n,* malterie, *f.* ~**ster,** *n,* malteur, *m.*

Malta, *n,* Malte, *f.* **Maltese,** *a,* maltais. ~ *cross,* croix de Malte, *f.* ~ [*dog, bitch*], chien(ne) de Malte, bichon, ne. ¶ *n, (pers.)* Maltais, e; *(language)* le maltais.

maltreat, *v.t,* maltraiter, brutaliser. ~**ment,** *n,* mauvais traitements; sévices, *m.pl.*

mamillary, *a,* mamillaire.

mama, *n,* maman, *f.*

mammal, *n,* mammifère, *m.* **mammalia,** *n.pl,* mammifères, *m.pl.*

mammoth, *n,* mammouth, *m.*

man, *n,* homme; monsieur; cavalier; employé; ouvrier; valet, *m;* (*checkers*) pion, *m.* (*chess*) pièce, *f.* ~ & *wife,* mari & femme. ~ *child,* enfant mâle, *m.* ~*-eater,* mangeur d'hommes, *m.* ~ *Friday,* factotum, *m.* ~**hole,** (*Mach.*) trou d'homme; (*sewer, etc.*) regard, *m.* the ~ in the street, l'homme de la rue. ~ of all work, homme à tout faire. ~ of fashion, élégant, *m.* ~ of substance, homme, calé. ~*-of-war,* bâtiment de guerre, *m.* ~'s estate, l'âge viril, *m.* ~[*servant*], domestique, valet, *m.* ~**slaughter,**

homicide involontaire, *m.* ¶ *v.t,* (*boat, etc.*) armer; équiper. ~**hood,** ~**kind,** ~**ly,** *etc.* See below.

manacle, *v.t,* mettre des menottes à; (*fig.*) enchaîner. ~**s,** *n.pl,* menottes, *f.pl,* fers, *m.pl.*

manage, *v.t,* diriger, administrer; gérer; conduire; manier; ménager; (*v.i.*) s'arranger; (*slang*) démerder. ~ *to,* parvenir à; obtenir de. ~**ment,** *n,* direction, administration; gérance, gestion; conduite; économie, *f;* maniement, *m.* joint ~, cogestion, *f.* **manager,** ess, *n,* directeur, trice, gérant, e; chef; (*ship's*) armateur, *m.* (*cinema*) location ~, régisseur d'exterieur, *m.* managing director, administrateur délégué, a. directeur, a. gérant, *m.*

manatee, *n,* lamantin, *m.*

Manchuria, *n,* la Mandchourie. **Manchu[rian],** *a,* mandchou. ¶ *n,* Mandchou, e.

mandarin, *n,* mandarin, *m.*

mandatory, *n,* mandataire, *m.* **mandate,** *n,* mandat, *m.* ~*d territory,* pays sous mandat, **mandator,** *n,* mandant, *m.*

mandible, *n,* mandibule, *f.*

mandolin[e], *n,* mandoline, *f.*

mandrake, *n,* mandragore, *f.*

mandrel, -il (*lathe*) *n,* mandrin, arbre, *m.*

mandrill (*baboon*) *n,* mandrill, *m.*

mane, *n,* crinière, *f,* crins, *m.pl.*

manege, -ège, *n,* manège, *m.*

manes, *n.pl,* mânes, *m.*

maneuver, *n,* manœuvre, *f.* ¶ *v.t. & t,* manœuvrer, évoluer.

manfully, *ad,* en homme, courageusement.

manganese, *n,* manganèse, *m.*

mange, *n,* gale, rogne, *f,* rouvieux, *m.*

mangel[-wurzel] *or* **mangold** [-wurzel], *n,* betterave fourragère, *f.*

manger, *n,* mangeoire, crèche, *f.*

mangle, *n,* calandre, *f.* ¶ *v.t,* mutiler; (*linen*) calandrer.

mango, *n,* mangue, *f.* ~ [*tree*], manguier, *m.*

mangrove, *n,* manglier, palétuvier, *m.*

mangy, *a,* galeux, rogneux, rouvieux.

manhandle, *v.t,* malmener.

manhood, *n,* virilité, *f;* âge viril, *m.*

mania, *n,* manie; folie; rage; marotte, *f.* **maniac,** *n.* & ~(**al**), *a,* maniaque, *m,f.* & *a.*

manicure, *n,* soin des mains, *m,* manucure, *f.* ~ *set,* onglier, *m,* manucure, *f.* ~ *the hands,* soigner les mains, faire de la manucure. **manicurist,** *n,* manucure, *f,m.*

manifest†, *a,* manifeste. ¶ (*ship.*) *n,* manifeste, *m.* ¶ *v.t,* manifester.

manifesto, *n,* manifeste, *m.*

manifold, *a,* multiple. ~ *book,* carnet genre manifold, cahier de copie, *dit* manifold, *m.*

manikin, *n,* [petit] bout d' homme; mannequin, *m.*

Manila, *n,* (*Geog.*) Manille, *f;* (*cheroot*) manille, *m.*

manioc, *n,* manioc, *m.*

manipulate, *v.t,* manœuvrer, manipuler; (*pers.*) empaumer.

mankind, *n,* le genre humain, l'espèce humaine; les hommes. **manliness,** *n,* virilité, *f.* **manly,** *a,* mâle, viril; (*woman*) hommasse.

manna, *n,* manne, *f.*

mannequin, *n,* mannequin, *m.*

manner, *n,* manière; façon, *f;* air; genre, *m;* (*pl.*) manières, formes, mœurs, *f.pl,* ton, *m.* he has no ~s, il n'a pas de savoir-vivre. ~**ed** (*style, etc.*) *a,* maniéré. ~**ism,** *n,* maniérisme, *m,* manière, *f,* tic, *m.* ~**ly,** *a,* poli.

mannish, *a,* garçonnier, hommasse.

manometer, *n,* manomètre, *m.*

manor, *n,* manoir, château, *m,* seigneurie, *f.*

mansard roof, comble brisé, *m.*

mansion, *n,* hôtel [particulier]; château; (*pl.*) immeuble à appartements, *m.*

manslaughter, *n,* homicide involontaire, *m.*

mantelpiece, *n,* manteau de cheminée, *m,* cheminée, *f.* **mantelshelf,** *n,* tablette de cheminée, *f.*

mantilla, *n,* mantille, *f.*

mantle, *n,* manteau; (*gas*) manchon, *m.* ~ *maker,* couturier, *m.* ¶ *v.t,* couvrir.

Mantua, *n,* Mantoue, *f.*

manual†, *a,* manuel, à bras. ~ [*exercise*] (*Mil.*), maniement des

(*ou* d') armes, *m.* ¶ *n,* manuel, guide-âne; (*organ*) clavier, *m.*

manufacture, *n,* fabrication, industrie, *f.* **manufacturer,** *n,* industriel, fabricant, manufacturier, *m.* ~'s *price,* prix de fabrique, *m.* **manufacturing,** *p.a,* manufacturier.

manure, *n,* fumier; engrais, *m.* ¶ *v.t,* engraisser; fumer.

manuscript, *n.* & *a,* manuscrit, *m.* & *a.*

Manx, *a,* de l'île de Man.

many, *a,* beaucoup; bien des; force; grand; maint, divers. ~ *a,* plus d'un, maint. *how* ~? combien? ~-*colored,* multicolore. ~-*sided,* complexe. *a great* ~, un grand nombre (de). *as* ~, autant. *so* ~, tant. *the* ~, la multitude. *too* ~, trop.

map, *n,* carte, *f;* plan, *m.* ~ *case,* porte-cartes, *m.* ~ *of the heavens.* carte céleste, *f.* ~ *of the world in hemispheres,* mappemonde, *f.* ~ *producer,* cartographe, *m.* road ~, carte routière, *f.* ¶ *v.t,* dresser (*ou* faire) la carte de. ~ *out,* tracer.

maple, *n,* érable, *m.*

mar, *v.t,* gâter; troubler.

marabou & **marabout,** *n,* marabout, *m.*

maraschino, *n,* marasquin, *m.*

marasmus, *n,* marasme, *m.*

marathon [*race*], *n,* course de Marathon, *f.*

maraud, *v.t,* marauder. ~**er,** *n,* maraudeur, *m.* ~**ing,** *n,* maraudage, *m,* maraude, *f.*

marble, *n,* marbre, *m;* (*games*) bille, *f.* ~ *mason* & ~ *merchant,* marbrier, *m.* ~ *quarry,* marbrière, *f.* ~ *work* & ~ *works,* marbrerie, *f.* ¶ *v.t,* marbrer. **marbler,** *n,* marbreur, *m.* **marbling,** *n,* marbrure, *f.*

marc (*fruit refuse*) *n,* marc, *m.*

marcasite, *n,* marcassite, *f.*

March, *n,* mars, *m.*

march, *n,* marche, *f;* pas, *m.* ¶ *v.i,* marcher. ~ *in,* entrer. ~ *off,* se mettre en marche. ~ *out,* sortir. ~ *past,* défiler. ~**ing,** *n,* marche, *f.* ~ *song,* chanson de route, *f.*

marchioness, *n,* marquise, *f.*

mare, *n,* jument, *f.* he has found *a* ~'s nest, il croit avoir trouvé la pie au nid.

margarine, *n,* margarine, *f.*

margin, *n,* marge; (*book page*) marge, *f,* blanc; bord, *m;* provision; tolérance, *f.* ~**al,** *a,* marginal.

marguerite, *n,* grande marguerite, *f.*

marigold, *n,* souci, *m.*

marine, *a,* maritime; marin. ~ **glue,** glu marine, *f.* ~ **stores,** fournitures pour navires, f—s maritimes, *f.pl.* ¶ *n,* (*shipping*) marine, *f;* (*pers.*) soldat d'infanterie de marine, fantassin de la flotte, fusillier marin, *m.* **mariner,** *n,* marin, *m.* ~**'s compass,** boussole marine, *f.*

marionette, *n,* marionnette, *f.*

marital, *a,* marital.

maritime, *a,* maritime.

marjoram, *n,* marjolaine, *f.*

mark, *n,* marque, *f;* point; signe; repère, *m;* trace, *f;* but, *m;* estampille; cote, *f;* témoignage; (*Sch.*) point, *m,* note, *f.* ~ *of origin,* estampille, *f.* *question* ~, point d' interrogation, *m.* ¶ *v.t,* marquer; indiquer; porter [la mention]; noter; estampiller; coter; remarquer; faire attention à; (*card*) piper. ~ *out,* tracer; borner. ~ *time,* marquer le pas; piétiner sur place. ~ *my words,* écoutez-moi bien. ~**ed,** *p.a,* marqué, prononcé, sensible; (*man*) noté; (*cards*) biseautées. ~**er,** *n,* pointeur; repère; indicateur, *m.*

market, *n,* marché, *m;* place; bourse; (*covered*) halle, *f;* débouché; débit, *m.* ~ *town,* ville à marché, *f,* bourg, *m.* ~ *value,* valeur marchande, v. vénale, *f.* ¶ *v.t,* mettre en vente. ~**able,** *a,* marchand; de vente; vénal; négociable. ~**ing,** *n,* mise en vente, *f.*

marking, *n,* marquage, *m;* cote, *f.* ~ *ink,* encre à marquer le linge, *f.*

marksman, *n,* [bon] tireur, *m.*

marl, *n,* marne, *f.* ~ *pit,* marnière, *f.* ¶ *v.t,* marner.

marline, *n,* lusin, *m.* ~ *spike,* marlinspike, épissoir, *m.*

marly, *a,* marneux.

marmalade, *n,* confitures (*d'oranges*) *f.pl;* marmelade, *f.*

Marmora (Sea of), mer de Marmara, *f.*

marmot (*Zool.*) *n,* marmotte, *f.*

maroon, *a,* marron. ¶ *n,* couleur marron, *f;* (*pers.*) nègre marron, *m,* négresse marronne, *f.*

marquee, *n,* tente-pavillon, *f.*

marquetry, *n,* marqueterie, *f.*

marquis, -quess, *n,* marquis, *m.*

marriage, *n,* mariage, *m;* noces, *f.pl.* ~ *license,* dispense de bans, *f.* ~ *of convenience,* mariage de raison, m. de convenance. ~ *portion,* dot, *f.* ~ *settlement,* constitution de dot, *f.* ~ *tie,* lien conjugal, *m.* *cousin by* ~, cousin par alliance. ~**able,** *a,* mariable; nubile. ~ *daughter,* fille à marier, *f.* **married,** *p.a,* marié. [*newly*] ~ *couple,* nouveaux mariés, *m.pl.* ~ *life,* vie conjugale, *f.* *get* ~, se marier.

marrow, *n,* moelle; (*vegetable*) courge à la moelle, *f.* ~*bone,* os à moelle, *m.* ~*fats,* pois carrés, *m.pl.* ~*y,* *a,* moelleux.

marry, *v.t,* marier; épouser; (*v.i.*) se marier; s'allier. ~ *a second, a third, time,* convoler en secondes, en troisièmes, noces. ~ *again,* se remarier, convoler. ~ *into,* s'apparenter à.

Marseilles, *n,* Marseille, *f.* *the Marseillaise* (*anthem*), la Marseillaise.

marsh, *n,* marais, marécage, *m.* ~ *marigold,* souci d'eau, *m.*

marshal, *n,* (*Mil.*) maréchal. ¶ *v.t,* classer; ranger; trier. ~ *ship,* *n,* maréchalat, *m.*

marshmallow, *n,* guimauve, *f.*

marshy, *a,* marécageux, paludéen.

marsupial, *n,* marsupial, *m.*

mart, *n,* centre des affaires; marché, *m.*

marten, *n,* martre; fouine, *f.*

martial, *a,* martial; (*pers.*) guerrier. ~ *law* (in a town), état de siège, *m.*

martin, *n,* hirondelle de fenêtre, *f.*

martinet, *n,* gendarme, pète-sec, *m.*

martingale, (*harness, betting*) *n,* martingale, *f.*

Martinmas, *n,* la Saint-Martin.

martyr, *n,* martyr, e. ~**dom,** *n,* martyre, *m.* ~**[ize],** *v.t,* martyriser. ~**ology** (*list*) *n,* martyrologe, *m.*

marvel, *n,* merveille, *f;* prestige, miracle, *m.* ¶ *v.i,* s'émerveiller, s'étonner. **marvelous**†, *a,* merveilleux, prestigieux.

marzipan, *n,* massepain, *m.*

mascot, *n,* mascotte, *f,* porte-bonheur, fétiche, *m.*

masculine, *a,* masculin, mâle; (*woman*) hommasse, garçonnier. ~ [*gender*], [genre] masculin, *m.* **masculinity,** *n,* masculinité, *f.*

mash, *n,* mélange; (*cattle*) barbotage, *m;* (*poultry*) pâtée; (*Cook.*) purée, *f.* ¶ *v.t,* mélanger, brasser; réduire en purée. ~*ed potatoes, turnips,* purée de pommes de terre, de navets, *f.*

mask, *n,* masque; (*Arch.*) mascaron, *m;* (*Phot.*) cache, *f.* ¶ *v.t,* masquer, cacher. ~*ed ball,* bal masqué, *m.* **masker, -quer** (*pers.*) *n,* masque *m.*

maslin, *n,* mouture, *f.*

mason, *n,* maçon, *m.* ¶ *v.t,* maçonner. ~**ic,** *a,* maçonnique. ~**ry,** *n,* maçonnerie, *f;* maçonnage, *m.*

masquerade, *n,* mascarade; (*fig.*) mascarade, pantalonnade, *f.* ¶ *v.i,* se masquer, se déguiser.

mass, *n,* masse, *f;* amas, *m;* (*Relig.*) messe, *f.* ~ *production,* production en masse, fabrication en série, *f.* ¶ *v.t,* masser.

massacre, *n,* massacre, *m.* ¶ *v.t,* massacrer.

massage, *n,* massage, *m.* ¶ *v.t,* masser. **masseur, euse,** *n,* masseur, euse.

massive†, *a,* massif; en-amas; en masses.

mast, *n,* mât, *m;* (*pl.*) mâture, *f;* (*beech*) faînes, *f.pl;* (*oak*) glands, *m.pl,* glandée, *f.* ¶ *v.t,* mâter.

master, *n,* maître; professeur; directeur; chef; patron; capitaine, *m. be ~ of,* posséder. *be one's own* ~, s'appartenir. ~ *key,* passepartout, *m.* ~ *mind,* cheville ouvrière, *f.* ~ *of the hounds,* maître d'équipage. ~*piece,* chef-d'œuvre, *m.* ~ *stroke,* coup de maître, *m.* ¶ *v.t,* maîtriser. ~**ful,** *a,* (*tone*) magistral. ~ *man,* ~ *woman,* maître homme, maîtresse femme. ~**ly,** *a,* de maître, magistral. *in a* ~ *way,* magistralement. ~**y,** *n,* maîtrise, *f,* empire; dessus, *m.*

mastic, *n,* mastic, *m.* ~ [*tree*], lentisque, *m.*

masticate, *v.t,* mâcher, mastiquer. **mastication,** *n,* mastication, *f.*

mastiff, *n,* mâtin, *m.*

mastodon, *n,* mastodonte, *m.*

mastoid, *a,* mastoïde.

mat, *a,* mat. ¶ *n,* natte, *f;* paillasson; tapis; (*plate*) dessous, *m.* ~ *maker,* nattier, *m.* ¶ *v.t,* natter. *matted hair,* cheveux embroussaillés, *m.pl.*

matador, *n,* matador, *m.*

match, *n,* (*light*) allumette; alliance, *f,* parti, *m;* assortiment; pendant; (*pers.*) pareil, le; (*Ten., etc.*) partie, *f,* match; (*Box., wrestling*) combat, match, *m.* ~*board,* planche bouvetée, *f.* ~*box,* boîte à allumettes, *f.* ~*maker,* marieur, euse. ~ *play* (*golf*), concours par trous, *m.* ¶ *v.t,* allier; marier; égaler; assortir; (*r*)appareiller; (*r*)apparier. *to* ~, pareil. ~**less,** *a,* sans pareil.

mate, *n,* camarade, *m,f,* compagnon, *m,* compagne, *f;* aide, *m,f;* (*bird*) pair; (*Naut.*) second, lieutenant; (*chess*) mat, *m.* ¶ *v.t,* appareiller, accoupler; (*chess*) faire mat, mater.

material†, *a,* matériel; essentiel. ¶ *n,* matière, *f;* matériel, *m;* étoffe, *f;* (*pl.*) matières, *f.pl;* matériaux, *m.pl;* fournitures, *f.pl;* articles, *m.pl. raw* ~, matière première, *f.* ~**ism,** *n,* matérialisme, *m.* ~**ist,** *n.* & ~**istic,** *a,* matérialiste. ~**ize,** *v.t,* matérialiser; (*v.i.*) se m.; aboutir.

maternal†, *a,* maternel. **maternity,** *n.* & ~ *hospital,* maternité, *f.* ~ *doctor,* accoucheur, *m.*

mathematical†, *a,* mathématique; (*precise*) géométrique; (*instruments*) de mathématiques. **mathematician,** *n,* mathématicien, ne. **mathematics,** *n.pl,* mathématiques, *f.pl.*

matinée, *n,* matinée, *f.* **matins,** *n.pl,* matines, *f.pl.*

matriarchy, *n,* matriarcat, *m.*

matriculate, *v.i,* prendre des (ses) inscriptions. **matriculation,** *n,* inscription, *f.*

matrimonial†, *a,* conjugal; (*law, agent, etc.*) matrimonial. ~ *triangle,* ménage à trois, *m.* **matrimony,** *n,* mariage, *m,* vie conjugale, *f.*

matrix, *n,* matrice; gangue, *f.*

matron, *n,* matrone; (*hospital, etc.*) infirmière en chef, *f.* ~**ly,** *a,* de matrone.

matter, *n,* matière; affaire; chose; question, *f;* propos; cas; sujet; article; chapitre; (*Med.*) pus, *m.*

as a ~ of course, comme une chose toute naturelle *ou* qui va de soi. *as a ~ of fact,* dans (*ou* par) le fait, en fait. *~-of-fact,* positif. *~ of history,* fait historique, *m. what's the ~?* qu'avez-vous? ¶ *v.i,* importer, faire. *no ~!* n'importe!

Matterhorn (the), le mont Cervin.

mattery, *a,* purulent.

matting, *n,* natte[s] *f.[pl.],* paillasson; abrivent, *m.*

mattins, *n.pl,* matines, *f.pl.*

mattock, *n,* pioche-hache, *f;* hoyau, *m.*

mattress, *n,* matelas; sommier, *m.. ~ maker,* matelassier, ère.

mature†, *a,* mûr. ¶ *v.i. & t,* mûrir; (*Com.*) échoir. **maturity,** *n,* maturité; échéance, *f.*

maudlin, *a,* bêtement sentimental; ivre à pleurer; pleurard, larmoyant. *~[ism],* *n,* romance, *f.*

maul, *v.t,* malmener. *~stick,* appui-main, *m.*

Mauritius, *n,* [l'île] Maurice, *f.*

mausoleum, *n,* mausolée, *m.*

mauve, *n. & a,* mauve, *m. & att.*

mawkish†, *a,* mielleux, doucereux, fade.

maxim, *n,* maxime, sentence, *f;* adage, *m.*

maximum, *n,* maximum; plafond, *m.* ¶ *a,* maximum.

May (*month*) *n,* mai, *m. May Day,* le premier mai. *May fly,* mouche de mai, *f,* éphémère, *m. maypole,* mai, *m.*

may (*Bot.*) *n,* fleurs d'aubépine, *f.pl. ~* [*bush*], aubépine, épine blanche, *f.*

may, *v. aux. ir,* pouvoir; permettre; que. *it ~ be,* cela se peut. *~be, ad,* peut-être.

mayonnaise, *n. & att,* mayonnaise, *f. & att.*

mayor, *n,* maire, *m. ~alty,* *n,* mairie, *f.*

maze, *n,* labyrinthe, dédale, *m.*

mazurka, *n,* mazurka, *f.*

me, *pn,* me; moi.

meadow & (*Poet.*) **mead,** *n,* pré, *m,* prairie, *f. meadowsweet,* reine des prés, *f.*

meager†, *a,* maigre, pauvre. *~ness,* *n,* maigreur, pauvreté, *f.*

meal, *n,* repas, *m;* (*grain*) farine, *f. ~ time,* l'heure du repas, *f. at ~ times,* aux heures de repas. *~y, a,* farineux. *~mouthed,* mielleux, doucereux.

mean†, *a,* bas; vil; abject; chétif; mesquin; ladre; chiche; petit; (*average*) moyen. *in the ~ time* (*or while*) or *~time,* *~while,* *ad,* en attendant; entretemps, cependant. ¶ *n,* milieu, *m;* (*Math.*) **moyenne,** *f;* (*pl.*) moyen, *m;* moyens, *m.pl,* facultés, *f.pl. by no ~s,* nullement. *private ~s,* fortune personnelle, *f.* ¶ *v.t. & i. ir,* se proposer; avoir l'intention de; vouloir; compter; penser; vouloir dire; signifier; entendre; destiner; faire exprès. *~ well,* avoir de bonnes intentions.

meander, *n,* méandre, *m.* ¶ *v.i,* cheminer, serpenter.

meaning, *n,* signification, *f,* sens, *m;* intention, *f. ~meaning, a,* intentionné. *~less, a,* sans aucun sens, un non-sens.

meanness, *n,* bassesse, abjection, ladrerie, vilenie, *f.*

measles, *n.pl,* rougeole, *f.*

measurable, *a,* mesurable, appréciable. **measure,** *n,* mesure; dose; démarche; (*tape*) mesure, *f;* mètre; centimètre, *m;* (*bill*) projet de loi, *m;* (*pl, Geol.*) étage, *m,* série, *f,* terrain, *m. to ~* (*clothes*), sur mesure. ¶ *v.t. & i,* mesurer; métrer; arpenter; jauger; cuber; toiser; (*the body*) mensurer; (*for fitting*) prendre mesure à; avoir. *~ out,* doser. *~d, a,* mesuré, modéré. *~ment,* *n,* mesurage, *m;* mesure; grosseur, *f;* volume; arpentage; jaugeage, *m.*

meat, *n,* viande; chair, *f. ~ breakfast,* déjeuner à la fourchette, *m. ~ day* (*Eccl.*), jour gras, *m. ~y, a,* charnu; (*food*) carné.

Mecca, *n,* la Mecque.

mechanic, *n,* [ouvrier] mécanicien, mécanique, *m. ~al†,* *a,* mécanique; (*fig.*) machinal. *~ dentistry,* prothèse dentaire, *f. ~ drawing,* dessin industriel, *m. ~ engineer,* ingénieur mécanicien, *m. ~ engineering,* l'art de la mécanique, *m;* construction mécanique, *f.* **mechanician** & **mechanist,** *n,* mécanicien, *m.* **mechanics,** *n.pl,* mécanique, *f.* **mechanism,** *n,* mécanisme, *m,* mécanique, *f,* organes, *m.pl.* **mechanization,** *n,* machinisme, *m.* **mechanize,** *v.t,* mécaniser.

Mechlin [*lace*], *n,* malines, *f.*

medal, *n,* médaille, *f. ~ cabinet & collection of ~s,* médaillier, *m.* ~ *maker* or **medalist,** *n,* médailleur, *m. award a ~ to,* médailler. **medaled,** *a,* médaillé. **medallion,** *n,* médaillon, *m.* **medalist** (*recipient*) *n,* médaillé, e.

meddle, *v.i,* se mêler, s'immiscer, s'ingérer; toucher. **meddler,** *n,* or **meddlesome person,** touche-à-tout, *n,* personne qui se mêle des oignons des autres, *f.* **meddling,** *n,* immixtion, ingérence, *f.*

median, *a,* médian; moyen.

mediate, *v.i,* s'interposer. **mediation,** *n,* médiation, *f.* **mediator, trix,** *n,* médiateur, trice.

medical, *a,* médical; (*school, etc.*) de médecine; (*student*) en médecine. ~ *examination* (recruits), revision, *f.* ~ *jurisprudence,* médecine légale, *f.* ~ *man,* ~ *officer,* médecin, *m.* **medicament,** *n,* médicament, *m.* **medicated,** *p.a,* médicamenteux. **medicinal,** *a,* médicinal; médicamenteux. **medicine,** *n,* médecine, *f;* médicament, *m.* ~ *cabinet,* ~ *chest,* pharmacie; caisse à médicaments, *f.* ~ *man,* [sorcier] guérisseur, *m.* **medico-judicial,** *a,* médico-légal.

medieval, *a,* médiéval, moyenâgeux.

mediocre, *a,* médiocre. **mediocrity,** *n,* (*quality*) médiocrité, *f,* médiocre, *m;* (*pers.*) médiocre, *m.*

meditate ([up]on), *v.t. & i,* méditer (sur), contempler. **meditation,** *n,* méditation, *f,* pensées, *f.pl.* **meditative,** *a,* méditatif.

mediterranean, *a,* méditerrané. M~, *a,* méditerranéen. **the M~** [Sea], la [mer] Méditerranée.

medium, *a,* moyen. ¶ *n,* milieu; agent; véhicule, *m;* (*ether*) atmosphère; (*agency*) entremise, *f,* intermédiaire; (*spiritualism*) médium, *m.*

medlar, *n,* nèfle, *f.* ~ [*tree*], néflier, *m.*

medley, *n,* mélange, bariolage, (*Mus.*) pot pourri, *m.* ¶ *a,* mêlé. ¶ *v.t,* mêler; bigarrer.

medullary, *a,* médullaire.

medusa (*jelly fish*) *n,* méduse, *f.*

meek, *a,* doux; débonnaire. ~**ly,** *ad,* avec douceur. ~**ness,** *n,* douceur, mansuétude, *f.*

meerschaum, *n,* écume de mer, *f.*

meet (*Hunt.*) *n,* assemblée, *f.* ¶ *v.t.ir,* rencontrer; trouver; faire face à; accueillir; honorer;

(*v.i.ir.*) se rencontrer; confluer; s'assembler; se réunir. ~ *with,* éprouver, essuyer. ~*ing,* *n,* rencontre; jonction, *f;* confluent, *m;* entrevue; assemblée; réunion, *f;* meeting; concours, *m;* séance; (*of engagements, bills of exchange*) bonne fin, *f.*

megaphone, *n,* porte-voix, *m.*

melancholia & melancholy, *n,* mélancolie, *f.* **melancholic & melancholy,** *a,* mélancolique.

Melanesia, *n,* la Mélanésie.

mellow, *a,* mûr; moelleux; (*earth*) meuble. ¶ *v.t,* mûrir.

melodious†, *a,* mélodieux. **melody,** *n,* mélodie, *f,* chant, *m.*

melon, *n,* melon, *m.*

melt, *v.t. & i. ir,* fondre; attendrir; s'*a. that ~s in the mouth* (as a pear), fondant. ~**er,** *n,* fondeur, *m.* ~**ing,** *n,* fonte, fusion, *f.* ~ *point,* point de fusion, *m.* ~ *pot,* creuset, pot, *m.*

member, *n,* membre, *m,* adhérent, e, associé, e; représentant, *m.* ~ *of a conciliation board,* prud'homme, *m.* ~ *of a* (or *the*) *congress,* congressiste, *m.f.* ~ *of legislature,* représentant à la Chambre, *m.* ~**ship,** *n,* qualité [de membre]; adhésion; charge; (*legislature*) députation, *f;* nombre des adhérents, *m.*

membrane, *n,* membrane, *f.*

memento, *n,* mémento; souvenir, *m.*

memoir, *n,* mémoire, *m;* (*pl, book*) mémorial, *m.*

memorable, *a,* mémorable. **memorandum,** *n,* mémorandum, *m,* note, *f,* mémoire, *m. as a ~,* pour mémoire. ~ *book,* carnet, calepin, *m.* **memorial,** *n,* mémorial, monument, *m.* **memorize,** *v.t,* apprendre par cœur. **memory,** *n,* mémoire, *f;* souvenir, *m;* (*pl.*) souvenances, *f.pl. from ~,* de mémoire. (*computers*) *read only ~,* mémoire morte, *f. random access ~,* m. vive, *f.*

menace, *n,* menace, *f. public ~* (*pers.*), malfaiteur public, *m.* ¶ *v.t,* menacer.

menagerie, *n,* ménagerie, *f.*

mend, *v.t,* raccommoder, réparer; repriser; améliorer; réformer. ~ *one's ways,* changer de conduite.

mendacious, *a,* mensonger. **men-**

dacity, *n*, l'habitude du mensonge, *f*.

mender, *n*, raccommodeur, euse, réparateur, trice.

mendicancy & mendicity, *n*, mendicité, *f*. **mendicant**, *a.* & *n*, mendiant, e.

mending, *n*, raccommodage, *m*, réparation; reprise, *f*.

menhir, *n*, menhir, peulven, *m*.

menial, *a*, servile. ¶ *n*, laquais, *m*.

meningitis, *n*, méningite, *f*.

menopause, *n*, ménopause, *f*. menses, *n*, règles, *f.pl*.

mensuration, *n*, mesure, *f*; (*science*) mesures, *f.pl*; (*of the body*) mensuration†, *f*.

mental, *a*, mental; moral. ~ *arithmetic*, calcul mental, *m*. ~ *institution*, maison d'aliénés, *f*, asile d'a—s, *m*. ~ *patient*, aliéné, e. ~ *reservation*, restriction mentale, arrière-pensée, *f*. ~ity, *n*, mentalité, *f*. ~ly, *ad*, mentalement. ~ *deficient*, à petite mentalité.

menthol, *n*, menthol, *m*.

mention, *n*, mention; constatation, *f*. ~ *in dispatches*, citation à l'ordre de l'armée, *f*. ¶ *v.t*, mentionner, parler de, prononcer; indiquer; citer; constater. *don't* ~ *it!* il n'y a pas de quoi, du tout!

Mentone, *n*, Menton, *m*.

menu, *n*, menu, *m*; carte du jour, *f*. ~ *holder*, porte-menu, *m*.

meow, *n*, miaulement. *m*. ¶ *v.i*, miauler.

mercantile, *a*, marchand, commercial, de commerce; (*mercenary*) mercantile.

Mercator's projection, projection de Mercator, *f*.

mercenary, *a*, mercenaire, stipendiaire, vénal, mercantile. ¶ *n*, mercenaire, *m*.

mercer, *n*, marchand de soieries, *m*. ~ized, *a*, mercerisé.

merchandise, *n*, marchandise, *f*. *oft. pl.* **merchant**, *n*, négociant, e, commerçant, e; marchand, e. ~ *marine*, marine marchande, *f*.

merciful†, *a*, miséricordieux, clément. **merciless†**, *a*, impitoyable.

mercurial, *a*, (*Chem.*) mercuriel; (*barometer, etc.*) à mercure; (*fig.*) vif. **mercury**, *n*,

(*metal*) mercure, *m*; (*Bot.*) mercuriale, *f*.

mercy, *n*, miséricorde, merci, clémence, grâce, *f*, bienfait, bien, *m*; pitié, *f*. *at the* ~ *of*, à la merci de; au gré de. ~ *on us!* miséricorde!

meret†, *a*, simple, pur, seul. *a* ~ *nothing*, un rien. ¶ *n*, lac, *m*.

meretricious, *a*, de courtisane; factice.

merge, *v.t*, fusionner; se fondre; s'amalgamer.

meridian, *n.* & *a*, méridien, *m*. & *a.* **meridional**, *a.* & *n*, méridional, e.

meringue, *n*, meringue, *f*.

merino, *n*, mérinos, *m*.

merit, *n*, mérite, *m*. ¶ *v.t*, mériter. **meritorious**, *a*, méritoire; (*of pers.*) méritant.

merlin (*bird*) *n*, émerillon, *m*.

mermaid, *n*, sirène, *f*. **merman**, *n*, triton, *m*.

merrily, *ad*, gaiement, joyeusement. **merriment**, *n*, gaieté, joie, hilarité, *f*. **merry**, *a*, gai, joyeux; jovial. *a* ~ *Christmas!* joyeux Noël! make ~, se réjouir, s'égayer. *make* ~ *over*, se divertir [aux dépens] de. ~-*go-round*, manège de chevaux de bois, carrousel, *m*. ~*making*, réjouissances, *f.pl*.

mesh, *n*, maille, *f*. *in* ~ (*Mech.*), en prise. ¶ *v.t*, s'engrener.

mesmeric, *a*, magnétique. **mesmerism**, *n*, magnétisme, *m*. **mesmerist**, *n*, magnétiseur, *m*. **mesmerize**, *v.t*, magnétiser.

mess, *n*, (*Mil., Nav.*) popote, gamelle, *f*; ordinaire; plat; (*fig.*) gâchis, margouillis, pétrin, *m*; saleté, *f*. ~ *kit*, gamelle, *f*. ~*mate*, camarade de plat, *m,f*, commensal, e. ¶ *v.t*, salir; (*v.i.*) manger. ~ *about*, tripoter. ~ *up*, gâcher.

message, *n*, message, *m*; dépêche, *f*. **messenger**, *n*, messager, ère; envoyé, e; courrier; commissionnaire; porteur; chasseur; garçon de bureau, *m*.

Messiah, *n*, Messie, *m*.

Messina, *n*, Messine, *f*.

messy, *a*, sale, graisseux.

metal, *n*, métal, *m*. ~ *saw*, scie à métaux, *f*. **metallic**, *a*, métallique; (*voice*) cuivrée. **metalliferous**, *a*, métallifère. **metallurgist**, *n*, métallurgiste, *m*. **metallurgy**, *n*, métallurgie, *f*.

metamorphose, *v.t,* métamorphoser. **metamorphosis,** *n,* métamorphose, *f.*

metaphor, *n,* métaphore, *f.* **~ical†,** *a,* métaphorique.

metaphysical, *a,* métaphysique. **metaphysician,** *n,* métaphysicien, *m.* **metaphysics,** *n.pl,* métaphysique, *f.*

mete [out], *v.t,* mesurer, doser.

meteor, *n,* météore, *m.* **~ic,** *a,* météorique. **~ite,** *n,* aérolithe, *m.* **~ologic(al),** *a,* météorologique. **~ology,** *n,* météorologie, *f.*

meter, *n,* (*Meas.*) mètre; (*Poet.*) mesure, mètre; (*gasoline*) jaugeur; compteur, *m.*

method, *n,* méthode, *f,* mode, *m,* modalité, *f.* **~ical†,** *a,* méthodique. **~ism,** *n,* méthodisme, *m.* **~ist,** *n,* méthodiste, *m,f.*

methyl (*Chem.*), *n,* méthyle, *m.* **~ated** *spirit,* alcool dénaturé, alcool à brûler, *m.*

meticulous†, *a,* méticuleux.

metric & metrical, *a,* métrique. **metrics** (*Poet.*) *n,* métrique, *f.*

metronome, *n,* métronome, *m.*

metropolis, *n,* capitale; métropole, *f.* **metropolitan,** *a,* de la capitale; métropolitain.

mettle, *n,* fougue, *f,* panache, cran; honneur, *m.* **~some,** *a,* fougueux.

mew, *n,* (*sea gull*) mouette; (*cage for hawks*) mue, *f.* ¶ *v.i,* miauler. **~[ing],** *n,* miaulement, *m.* **mews,** *n,* écuries, *f.pl.*

Mexican, *a,* mexicain. ¶ *n,* Mexicain, e. **Mexico** (*country*) *n,* le Mexique. **~** [*City*], Mexico, *m.*

mezzanine [floor], *n,* entresol, *m.* **mezzo-relievo,** *n,* demi-relief, *m.* **mezzo-soprano,** *n,* mezzosoprano, *m.* **mezzotint,** *n,* manière noire; gravure à la m. n., *f.*

miasma, *n,* miasme, *m.*

mica, *n,* mica, *m.*

Michaelmas, *n,* la Saint-Michel. **~** *daisy,* marguerite de la Saint-Michel, *f.*

microbe, *n,* microbe, *m.*

microgroove, *n,* microsillon, *m.* **micrometer,** *n,* micromètre, palmer, *m.* **microphone,** *n,* microphone, *m.* **microprocessing,** *m,* microtraitement, *m,* micro-informatique, *f.* **microprocessor,** *n,* microprocesseur, *m.* **microscope,** *n,* microscope, *m.*

microprogram, *v.t,* micropro-

grammer. ¶ *n,* microprogramme, *m.*

microwave, *n,* micro-onde, *f.*

mid, *a*: *in* **~** *air, Channel,* au milieu de l'air, de la Manche. **~day,** midi, *m.* **~iron** (*golf*), fer moyen, *m.* **~** *lent,* la micarême. **~night,** minuit, *m.* **~shipman,** aspirant [de marine] *m.* **~summer,** milieu de l'été. **Midsummer Day,** la Saint-Jean; le 24 juin. **~way,** *ad,* à moitié chemin, à mi-chemin. **~wife,** sage-femme, *f. in* **~** *winter,* en plein hiver.

middle, *a,* du milieu; moyen. **~-aged** d'âge moyen, entre deux âges. **M~ Ages,** moyen âge, *m.* **~** *class[es],* classe moyenne, bourgeoisie, *f.* **~-class** *house,* maison bourgeoise, *f.* **~-class** *man, woman,* bourgeois, e. **~** *course* (*conduct*), moyen terme, *m.* **~** *distance,* second plan, *m.* *the* **M~** *East,* Moyen-Orient, *m.* **~** *finger,* doigt du milieu, médius, *m.* **~man,** intermédiaire, *m.* **~** *register* (*Mus.*), médium, *m.* **~** *[term]* (*Log.*), moyen [terme] *m.* **~weight** (*Box.*), poids moyen, *m.* ¶ *n,* milieu; centre, *m*; (*waist*) ceinture, *f.*

middling†, *a,* moyen; médiocre. ¶ *ad,* assez bien, entre deux, comme ci, comme ça, cahin-caha. **~s** (*flour*) *n.pl.,* recoupe, *f.*

midge (*age*), *n,* moucheron, cousin, *m.*

midget, *n,* nabot, e, [petit] bout d'homme, *m.*

midnight, midshipman, *etc.* See under **mid.**

midst, *n,* milieu, sein, *m.*

mien, *n,* mine, *f,* air, *m.*

might, *n,* puissance; force, *f.* **~** *with* **~** *& main,* de toutes ses forces. *one* **~** *as well,* autant vaut. *a* **~-have-been,** un grand homme manqué. **mightiness,** *n*; puissance; grandeur, *f.* **mighty†,** *a,* puissant. *the* **~** *ones,* les puissants, *m.pl.*

mignonette, *n,* (*Bot.*) réséda, *m*; (*lace*) mignonnette, *f.*

migrant, *a,* migrateur. **migrate,** *v.i,* émigrer. **migration,** *n,* migration *f.* **migratory,** *a,* migrateur, voyageur, de passage.

Milan, *n,* Milan, *m.* **~ese,** *a,* milanais. ¶ *n,* Milanais, e.

milch *cow,* vache à lait, vache laitière; (*fig.*) vache à lait, *f.*

mild†, *a,* doux; bénin; anodin.

mildew, *n*, moisi, *m*, moisissure; (*blight on plants*) rouille, *f*; (*on vines*) mildiou, *m*. ¶ *v.t*, moisir; (*v.i.*) [se] moisir.

mildness, *n*, douceur, *f*.

mile, *n*, mille [anglais] *m*. = 1.6093 kilometers (*Note:—To convert miles to kilometers, approximately, multiply miles by 8 and divide by 5*); (*long way*) lieue, *f. a ~ off*, d'une lieue. **~stone**, pierre milliaire, *m*. (*Fr.*) borne kilométrique, *f*.

militant, *a. & n*, militant, *a. & m*. **militarize**, *v.t*, militariser. **military**†, *a. & ~ man*, militaire, *a. & m. the ~*, les militaires, *m.pl*. *~ pageant*, scène militaire à grand spectacle, *f*. **militate**, *v.i*, militer. **militia**, *n*, milice, *f*. **~ man**, milicien, *m*.

milk, *n*, lait, *m*. *~ chocolate*, chocolat lacté, c. au lait, *m. ~ diet*, régime lacté, *m*, diète lactée, *f. ~ fever*, fièvre de lait, *f. ~ food*, laitage, *m*. **~maid**, fille de ferme, *f*. **~man, ~woman**, laitier, ère. **~sop** (*pers.*), poule mouillée, *f. ~ tooth*, dent de lait, *f. ~ train*, wagon-laitière, *m*. ¶ *v.t*, traire, tirer. **~er**, *n*, trayeur, euse; (*cow*) laitière, *f*. **~ing**, *n*, traite, mulsion, *f*. **milky**, *a*, laiteux. *M~ Way*, voie lactée, *f*.

mill, *n*, moulin, *m*; fabrique; usine, *f*; atelier, *m*. **~board**, carton [épais] *m*. **~hand**, ouvrier (ère) d'usine. **~owner**, industriel, usinier, *m*. **~stone**, meule de moulin, *f. ~stone grit & ~stone grit quarry*, meulière, *f. textile ~*, usine de textiles, *f*. ¶ *v.t*, moudre; (*ore, etc.*) bocarder, broyer; (*cloth*) fouler; (*to knurl*) moleter, (*to slot*) fraiser; (*a coin*) créneler. **~ed edge**, cordon[net], crénelage, *f*.

millenary, *a. & n*, millénaire, *a. & m*. **millennium**, *n*, millénaire; (*fig.*) bonheur sans mélange, paradis terrestre, *m*.

millepede, *n*, mille-pieds, mille-pattes, *m*.

miller, *n*, meunier, ère, minotier, *m*; farinier, ère.

millet, *n*, millet, mil, *m. ~ grass*, millet, *m*.

milliner, *n*, modiste, *f*; marchand(e) de modes; chapelier, *m*. **~'s head**, marotte, *f*. **~y**, *n*, modes, *f.pl*, articles de modes, *m. pl*; chapeaux, *m.pl*.

milling, *n*, (*flour*) meunerie, minoterie, *f*; (*ore*) broyage; (*cloth*) foulage; (*metal*) fraisage; (*coins*) crénelage, grènetis, *m*. fraise, *f. ~ machine*, machine à fraiser, *f*.

million, *n*, million, *m. the ~s*, la multitude, la masse du peuple. **millionaire**, *n*, millionnaire, *m,f*. **millionth**, *a. & n*, millionième, *a. & m*.

milt, *n*, (*in mammals*) rate; (*in fish*) laitance, laite, *f*. ¶ *v.t*, féconder.

mime, *n*, mime, *m*. ¶ *v.i*, mimer. **mimic**, *a*, mimique, imitateur. ¶ *n*, mime, *m*, imitateur, trice. ¶ *v.t*, mimer, imiter, contrefaire. **mimicry**, *n*, mimique, *f*. **mimicry or mimesis** (*Zool.*) *n*, mimétisme, *m*.

mimosa, *n*, mimosa, *m*.

mince, *n*, hachis, *m*. **~meat**, hachis, *m*. ¶ *v.t*, (*meat*) hacher [menu]; (*v.i.*) minauder. *~ one's words*, ménager les termes; parler avec affectation. *not to ~ matters*, ne pas le mâcher. **mincer**, *n*, hachoir, *m*. **mincing** (*fig.*) *n*, minauderie, *f*. ¶ *a*, minaudier, mignard, affété, grimacier.

mind, *n*, esprit, *m*; âme, *f*; moral; cerveau, *m*, cervelle, *f*; envie; idée, pensée, *f*; avis, *m*, opinion, *f. go out of one's ~*, perdre la raison. ¶ *v.t*, faire attention à; se soucier de; regarder à; garder. *I don't ~*, cela m'est égal. *bear in ~*, tenir compte de. *make up one's ~*, se décider. *~ your own business!* mêlez-vous de vos affaires! **~ed**, *a*, disposé, porté, pensant, enclin. **~ful**, *a*, attentif.

mine, *pn*, le mien, la mienne, les miens, les miennes; à moi. *a friend of ~*, un de mes amis, un ami à moi.

mine, *n*, mine; (*fig.*) mine, *f*, filon, *m*; (*war*) mine, torpille, *f. ~ crater*, entonnoir, *m. ~ layer*, poseur de mines, *m. ~ sweeper*, dragueur de mines, *m*. ¶ *v.t. & i*, exploiter; abattre; fouiller; miner; caver; torpiller. **miner**, *n*, mineur, *m*. **mineral**, *a. & n*, minéral, *a. & m. ~ water*, eau minérale [naturelle] *f. ~* [*water*], eau minérale [artificielle] *f*. **mineralogical**, *a*, minéralogique. **mineralogist**, *n*, minéralogiste, *m*. **mineralogy**, *n*, minéralogie, *f*.

mingle, *v.t*, mélanger, mêler, confondre.

miniature, n, miniature, f; diminutif, m. ~ *golf*, golf miniature, m. **miniaturist**, n, miniaturiste, m.f. **miniaturize**, v.t, miniaturiser.

minimize, v.t, atténuer. **minimum**, n. & a, minimum, m. & a.

mining, n, exploitation [de mines] f; (att.) minier. ~ *engineer*, ingénieur [civil] des mines, m.

minion, n, mignon, favori, m. ~s *of the law*, recors de la justice, m.pl.

minister, n, ministre; pasteur, m. ~ *to*, pourvoir à; servir; (Eccl.) desservir. ~ial, a, ministériel. ~*ing angel*, ange de bonté, m.; sœur de charité, f. **ministration**, n, ministère, m. **ministry**, n, ministère; département; sacerdoce, m.

miniver, n, petit-gris, m.

mink (Zool. & fur) n, vison, m.

minnow, n, vairon, m.

minor, a, petit; secondaire, subalterne; moindre; peu important; peu grave; mineur; (repairs) menues; (planet) télescopique; (pers.) jeune, cadet; (poet) de second ordre. ¶ n, (pers.) mineur, e; (Mus.) mineur, m.

Minorca, n, Minorque, f.

minority, n, minorité, f.

minster, n, église de monastère, é. abbatiale; cathédrale, f.

minstrel, n, (Hist.) ménestrel; chanteur, musicien; acteur comique, m.

mint, n, Monnaie, f, hôtel de la Monnaie, h. des Monnaies, m; (fig.) mine; (Bot.) menthe, f. a ~ *of money*, un argent fou. ¶ v.t, monnayer, frapper. ~er, n, monnayeur, m.

minuet, n, menuet, m.

minus, pr, moins. ~ *quantity*, déficit, m. ~ [*sign*], n, [signe] moins, m.

minute, a, menu, minime, minuscule; minutieux. ¶ n, minute, f, (pl.) procès-verbaux, m. ~ *book*, registre des délibérations, r. des procès-verbaux, plumitif, m. ~ *hand*, aiguille des minutes, f. ¶ v.t, minuter; constater par procès-verbal. ~ly, ad, minutieusement. ~ness & **minutia**, n, minutie, f.

minx, n, coquine, friponne, masque, f.

miracle, n, miracle, m. ~ [*play*],

miracle, mystère, m. **miraculous**†, a, miraculeux.

mirage, n, mirage, m.

mire, n, fange, boue, f. ¶ v.t, embourber.

mirror, n, miroir, m, glace, f. *rearview* ~, rétroviseur, m. ¶ v.t, refléter.

mirth, n, joie, gaieté, f. ~ful†, a, joyeux, gai.

miry, a, fangeux, boueux.

misadventure, n, mésaventure, f.

misalliance, n, mésalliance, f. *make a* ~, se mésallier. **misally**, v.t, mésallier.

misanthrope, -pist, n, misanthrope, m. **misanthropic(al)**, a, misanthropique, misanthrope.

misapply, v.t, mal appliquer; détourner.

misapprehend, v.t, mal comprendre. **misapprehension**, n, malentendu, m.

misappropriate, v.t, détourner, dilapider.

misbehave [oneself], se comporter mal. **misbehavior**, n, mauvaise conduite, inconduite, f.

miscalculate, v.i, se tromper. **miscalculation**, n, erreur de calcul, f, mécompte, m.

miscarriage, n, (letter, etc.) égarement, m; (Med.) fausse couche, f; (failure) avortement, insuccès, m. ~ *of justice*, erreur judiciaire, f. **miscarry**, v.i, s'égarer; (Med.) faire une fausse couche; (fail) avorter, échouer, rater.

miscellaneous, a, divers; mêlé. ~ *works* or **miscellany** or **miscellanea**, n, mélanges, m.pl, variétés, f.pl, recueil factice, m.

mischance, n, infortune, fatalité, f.

mischief, n, mal; (playful) espièglerie, f. ~ *maker*, boutefeu, m. **mischievous**†, a, méchant; espiègle.

misconceive, v.i, mal concevoir. **misconception**, n, malentendu, m.

misconduct, n, déportements, m.pl., inconduite, f. ~ *oneself*, se conduire mal.

misconstruction, n, contresens, m. **misconstrue**, v.t, prendre à rebours.

miscreant, n, gredin, scélérat, m.

miscue, n, faux coup de queue, m.

misdeal (cards) n, maldonne, f.

misdeed, n, méfait, m.

misdeliver, v.t, livrer par erreur.

misdemeanant, n, délinquant, e. **misdemeanor**, n, délit, m.

misdirect, v.t, mal diriger; (a letter) se tromper d'adresse sur.

miser, n, avare, m.f, harpagon, m.

miserable†, a, misérable, malheureux; chétif.

miserere, n, miserere, m.

misericord, n, miséricorde, f.

miserly, a, avare.

misery, n, misère, f; souffrances, f.pl.

misfire, n, raté [d'allumage] m. ¶ v.i, rater, manquer.

misfit, n, vêtement mal ajusté, v. manqué, m; chaussure manquée, f.

misfortune, n, malheur, m, infortune, adversité, disgrâce, misère, f.

misgiving, n, doute; pressentiment, m.

misgovern, v.t, mal gouverner. ~ment, n, mauvais gouvernement, m.

misguide, v.t, égarer; abuser. **misguided**, p.p, mal dirigé, dévoyé.

mishap, n, contretemps, m, mésaventure, f.

misinform, v.t, mal renseigner.

misinterpretation, n, contresens, m.

misjudge, v.t, mal juger.

mislay, v.t, égarer.

mislead, v.t, égarer, fourvoyer, abuser; induire en erreur; tromper. ~ing, p.a, décevant, fallacieux.

mismanage, v.t, mal faire, mal gérer. ~ment, n, mauvaise gestion, f.

misnamed, p.p, mal nommé.

misnomer, n, erreur de nom, f.

misogynist, n, misogyne, m.

misplace, v.t, mal placer.

misprint, n, faute d'impression, erreur typographique, coquille, f.

mispronounce, v.t, mal prononcer. **mispronunciation**, n, vice de prononciation, m.

misquotation, n, citation inexacte, f. **misquote**, v.t, citer à faux.

misrepresent, v.t, représenter mal, travestir, dénaturer. ~ation, n, travestissement, m; déclaration inexacte, f.

misrule, n, mauvaise administration, f.

miss, n, manque [à toucher] m; demoiselle, f. M~, mademoiselle; Mademoiselle, f. ¶ v.t. & i, manquer; rater; regretter; sauter. ~ fire, rater, manquer. ~ the point, porter à faux.

missal, n, missel, m.

misshapen, a, contrefait, biscornu, difforme, malbâti.

missile, n, projectile, m.

missing, a, manquant; (ship) [perdu] sans nouvelles. ~ link, chaînon manquant, m. the ~ (Mil.), les disparus, m.pl. be ~, manquer.

mission, n, mission, f. ~ary, n, missionnaire, m. **missive**, n, missive, f.

misspell, v.t, mal orthographier. ~ing, n, faute d'orthographe, f.

misstatement, n, déclaration inexacte, f.

mist, n, brouillard, m, brume; brouillasse; vapeur, f, nuage, voile, m.

mistake, n, erreur, faute, bévue; méprise, f, quiproquo, tort, m. ¶ v.t.ir, se méprendre sur, se tromper de, confondre. **mistaken**, a, erroné. ~ identity, erreur de (ou sur la) personne, f. ~ kindness, indulgence mal comprise, f. be ~, se tromper.

mister, n, monsieur, m.

mistletoe, n, gui, m.

mistranslation, n, contresens, m.

mistreat, v.t, maltraiter.

mistress, n, maîtresse; patronne; institutrice, f; professeur, m; madame, f. be one's own ~, s'appartenir.

mistrust, n, méfiance, défiance, f. ¶ v.t, se méfier de, se défier de. ~ful, a, méfiant, défiant.

misty, a, brumeux; vaporeux; trouble.

misunderstand, v.t.ir, mal comprendre, méconnaître. ~ing, n, malentendu, m; mésintelligence, brouille, f; quiproquo, m. **misunderstood** (pers.) p.a, incompris.

misuse, n, abus, m. ¶ v.t, abuser de; maltraiter; mésuser.

mite, n, (farthing) obole, f, denier, m; (child) petit, e; (insect) mite, f, acare, ciron, m.

miter, n, (bishop's) mitre, f; (Carp.) onglet, m. ~ed, a, mitré; (Carp.) à onglet.

mitigate, *v.t*, atténuer; mitiger, modérer.

mitt[en], *n*, moufle, mitaine, *f*.

mix, *v.t*, mêler, mélanger, malaxer; (*salad*) retourner. **mixed**, *a*, mêlé; mixte; hétérogène. ~ *bathing*, bain mixte, *m*. ~ *double* (*Ten.*), double mixte, *m*. ~ *metaphor*, métaphore incohérente, *f*. **mixing** (*TV & cinema*) mixage, *m*. **mixture**, *n*, mélange, *m*; mixture, *f*; ambigu, *m*; (*Med.*) mixtion, *f*; (*fodder*) farrago; (*cloth*) drap mélangé, *m*. *wool* ~, laine mélangée, *f*.

miz[z]en [sail], *n*. & **miz[z]en mast**, artimon, *m*.

mizzle, *n*, bruine, *f*. ¶ *v.imp*, bruiner.

mnemonic, *a*, mnémonique. **~s**, *n.pl*, la mnémonique.

moan, *n*, gémissement, *m*, plainte, *f*. ¶ *v.i*, gémir, se plaindre.

moat, *n*, fossé, *m*, douve, *f*.

mob, *n*, foule; canaille, populace, *f*. ~ *law*, la loi de la populace, *f*. ¶ *v.t*, houspiller.

mobile, *a*, mobile. **mobility**, *n*, mobilité, *f*.

mobilization, *n*, mobilisation, *f*. **mobilize**, *v.t*, mobiliser.

mocha, *n*, moka, *m*. **mocha coffee** or *mocha*, *n*, café de Moka, moka, *m*.

mock, *v.t*, se moquer de; singer. ¶ *a*, faux, imité. ~ *fight*, simulacre de combat, *m*. **~-heroic**, héroï-comique. **~er**, *n*, moqueur, euse. **~ery**, *n*, moquerie, *f*. **~ing bird**, [oiseau] moqueur, *m*.

mode, *n*, (*way, fashion*) mode, *f*; (*form, method*) mode, *m*.

model, *n*, modèle, *m*; maquette, *f*; mannequin, *m*; (*att.*) modèle. ¶ *v.t*, modeler. **~er**, *n*, modeleur, *m*. **~ing**, *n*, modelage; modelé, *m*.

moderate, *a*, modéré; (*price*) modique. ¶ *v.t*, modérer, tempérer. **~ly**, *ad*, modérément, moyennement. **~ness**, *n*, modicité, *f*. **moderation**, *n*, modération, *f*.

modern, *a*. & *n*, moderne. *a*. & *m*. ~ *language*, langue vivante, *f*. **~ize**, *v.t*, moderniser.

modest†, *a*, modeste. **~y**, *n*, modestie, *f*.

modicum, *n*, petite quantité; légère dose, *f*, grain, *m*.

modification, *n*, modification, *f*. **modify**, *v.t*, modifier.

modish, *a*, à la mode, de mode. **~ly**, *ad*, à la mode.

modulate, *v.t*, moduler. **modulation**, *n*, modulation, *f*. **module** & **modulus**, *n*, module, *m*.

mohair, *n*, poil de chèvre d'Angora, mohair, *m*.

Mohammedan, *n*. & *a*, mahométan, e. **~ism**, *n*, mahométisme, *m*.

moiety, *n*, moitié, *f*.

moil, *v.i*, peiner.

moire, *n*, moire, *f*. **moiré**, *v.t*, moirer. ~ *silk*, moire de soie, soie moirée, *f*.

moist, *a*, humide; moite. **~en**, *v.t*, humecter; mouiller. **~ness** & **~ure**, *n*, humidité; moiteur; buée, *f*.

molar, *a*. & *n*, molaire, *a*. & *f*.

molasses, *n*, mélasse, *f*.

mold, *n*, moule, creux, *m*; (*Typ.*) empreinte, *f*, flan; (*vegetable*) terreau, humus; (*ship*) gabarit; (*decay*) moisi, *m*, moisissure, *f*. ¶ *v.t*, mouler; modeler; (*fig.*) prendre l'empreinte de. **~er**, *n*, mouleur, *m*. **~er [away]**, *v.i*, tomber en poussière. **moldiness**, *n*, moisissure, *f*, moisi, *m*. **molding**, *n*, (*act*) moulage, *m*; (*ornamental strip*) moulure, *f*. **moldy**, *a*, moisi. *turn* ~, [se] moisir.

mole, *n*, nævus, *m*, couenne, *f*, grain de beauté; (*jetty*) môle, *m*; (*Zool.*) taupe, *f*. **~hill**, taupinière, *f*. **~skin**, [fourrure de] taupe; moleskine, *f*. ~ *trap*, taupière, *f*.

molecular, *a*, moléculaire. **molecule**, *n*, molécule, *f*.

molest, *v.t*, tourmenter, inquiéter, importuner. **~ation**, *n*, importunité, *f*.

mollify, *v.t*, amollir; adoucir.

mollusk, *n*, mollusque, *m*.

molt, *v.i*, se déplumer.

molten, *p.p*, fondu, en fusion, en bain.

Moluccas (the), les Moluques, *f.pl*.

moment, *n*, moment; instant, *m*; importance, *f*. *a* ~ *ago*, à l'instant. **~ary†**, *a*, momentané, passager. **~ous**, *a*, de la dernière importance. **momentum**, *n*, (*Mech.*) moment; (*impetus*) élan, *m*.

monarch, *n*, monarque, *m*. **~ic(al)**, *a*, monarchique. **~ist**, *n*, monarchiste, *m.* ~y, *n*, monarchie, *f.*

monastery, *n*, monastère, couvent, *m.* **monastic**, *a*, monastique, monacal. **monastically**, *ad*, monacalement.

Monday, *n*, lundi, *m.*

monetary, *a*, monétaire. **monetize**, *v.t*, transformer en monnaie. **money**, *n*, argent, *m*; monnaie, *f*; numéraire, *m*; fonds, *m.pl*; capital, *m*, capitaux, *m.pl*; valeurs; finances, *f.pl*; deniers, *m.pl.* ~ *changer*, changeur, *m.* ~ *box*, tirelire; cassette, grenouillère, *f.* ~ *grubber* grippesou, *m.* ~*lender*, bailleur de fonds, *m.* ~ *order*, mandat [de poste] *m.* ~**ed**, *a*, fortuné.

Mongolia, *n*, la Mongolie. **Mongol[ian]**, *a*, mongol. ¶ *n*, Mongol, e.

mongoose, *n*, mangouste, *f.*

mongrel, *a*, métis, bâtard, mâtiné. ¶ *n*, métis, se, bâtard, e; (*cur*) roquet, *m.*

monk, *n*, moine, religieux, *m.* ~*'s-hood* (*Bot.*), aconit, napel, *m.* ~**ery** & ~**hood**, *n*, moinerie, *f.* ~**ish**, *a*, monacal.

monkey, *n*, singe, *m*, (*she*) guenon, guenuche, *f*; (*pile driving*) mouton, *m.* ~ *house*, singerie, *f.* ~ *trick*, singerie, *f.* ~ *wrench*, clef anglaise, *f.*

monochord, *n*, monocorde, *m.* **monochrome**, *a*, monochrome. **monocle**, *n*, monocle, *m.* **monogamy**, *n*, monogamie, *f.* **monogram**, *n*, monogramme, chiffre, *m.* **monograph**, *n*, monographie, *f.* **monolith**, *n.* & ~**ic**, *a*, monolithe, *m.* & *a.* **monologize**, *v.i*, monologuer. **monologue**, *n*, monologue, *m.* **monomania**, *n*, monomanie, *f.* **monoplane**, *n*, monoplan, *m.* **monopolist**, *n*, accapareur, euse. **monopolize**, *v.t*, monopoliser, accaparer, s'emparer de. **monopoly**, *n*, monopole, *m.* **monosyllabic**, *a*, monosyllabique, monosyllabe. **monosyllable**, *n*, monosyllabe, *m.* **monotonist** (*pers.*) *n*, monocorde, *m.* **monotonous**, *a*, monotone. **monotony**, *n*, monotonie, *f.* **monotype**, *n*, monotype, *f.*

monster, *n.* & *a*, monstre, *m.* & *att.*

monstrance, *n*, ostensoir, *m.*

monstrosity, *n*, monstruosité, *f.* **monstrous†**, *a*, monstrueux.

Mont Blanc, le mont Blanc. **Montenegrin**, *a*, monténégrin. ¶ *n*, Monténégrin, e. **Montenegro**, *n*, le Monténégro. **Monte Rosa**, le mont Rose.

month, *n*, mois, *m.* ~*'s pay, rent, or like*, mois, *m.* ~**ly**, *a*, mensuel; au mois. ¶ ~ *payment, drawing, salary, or like*, mensualité, *f.* ~ *statement* (*Com.*), relevé de fin de mois, *m.* ¶ *ad*, mensuellement, par mois. ¶ *n*, revue mensuelle, *f.*

monument, *n*, monument; (*tombstone*) tombeau, *m.* ~**al**, *a*, monumental.

moo, *v.i*, beugler. ¶ *n*, beuglement, *m.*

mood, *n*, humeur, *f*, train; (*Gram.*) mode, *m.* ~**y**, *a*, morose, chagrin.

moon, *n*, lune, *f.* ~*beam*, rayon de l., *m.* ~*light*, clair de l., *m.* ~*lit*, éclairé par la l. ~*shine*, contes en l'air, *m.pl.* ~*stone*, pierre de lune, *f.* ~*struck*, toqué. ~ [*about*], muser.

moor & ~*land*, *n*, lande, brande, bruyère, *f.* ~*cock*, coq de bruyère *m.* ~*hen*, poule d'eau, *f.*

Moor (*pers.*) *n.* More, Maure, *m.*

moor, *v.t*, amarrer, mouiller. ~**ing**, *n*, amarrage, mouillage; (*pl.*) mouillage, *m.*

Moorish, *a*, more, maure.

moose, *n*, élan, *m.*

moot, *a*, discutable, contestable. ¶ *v.t*, soulever.

mop, *n*, balai à laver; (*Naut.*) écouvillon, *m*; (*of hair*) tignasse, *f.* ¶ *v.t*, éponger. ~ *up*, essuyer, éponger.

mope, *v.i*, languir.

moraine, *n*, moraine, *f.*

moral†, *a*, moral. ¶ *n*, (*of story, of fable*) morale, moralité, *f*; (*pl, manners*) mœurs, *f.pl*; (*pl, ethics*) morale, *f.* ~[*e*], *n*, moral, *m.* ~**ist**, *n*, moraliste, *m.* ~**ity**, *n*, moralité, *f*; [bonnes] mœurs, *f.pl.* ~**ize**, *v.i.* & *t*, moraliser.

morass, *n*, fondrière, *f*, marais, marécage, *m.*

moratorium, *n*, moratorium, moratoire, *m.*

Moravia, *n*, la Moravie.

morbid, *a*, morbide, maladif. ~**ness**, *n*, état maladif, *m.*

mordant, *a.* & *n*, mordant, *a.* & *m.*

more, *a*, plus de; plus. ¶ *ad*, plus; davantage; encore; de plus. *all the* ~, d'autant plus. *never* ~, jamais plus. ~ *and* ~, de plus en plus. ~*over*, *ad*, d'ailleurs, aussi bien, en outre, du reste, encore.

moresque, *a*, moresque, mauresque.

morganatic†, *a*, morganatique.

moribund, *a*, moribond.

morning & (*Poet.*) **morn**, *n*, matin, *m*; matinée; aurore, *f*. ~ *star*, étoile du matin, é. matinière, *f*.

Moroccan, *a*, marocain. ¶ *n*, Marocain, e. **Morocco**, *n*, le Maroc. *morocco* [*leather*], maroquin, *m*.

morose, *a*, morose. ~**ness**, *n*, morosité, *f*.

Morpheus, *n*, Morphée. *m*. **morphia, -phine**, *n*, morphine, *f*.

morrow (**the**) & **on the** ~, le lendemain.

morsel, *n*, morceau, *m*.

mortal†, *a*, mortel; (*strife*) à mort, à outrance. ¶ *n*, mortel, le. ~**ity**, *n*, mortalité, *f*.

mortar (*plaster, vessel, Mil.*) *n*, mortier, *m*.

mortgage, *n*, hypothèque, *f*. ¶ *v.t*, hypothéquer; engager. **mortgagee**, *n*, créancier hypothécaire, *m*. **mortgagor**, *n*, débiteur h., *m*.

mortification, *n*, mortification, *f*. **mortify**, *v.t*, mortifier, affliger, mater.

mortise, *n*, mortaise, *f*. ¶ *v.t*, emmortaiser.

mortmain, *n*, mainmorte, *f*. *property in* ~, biens de mainmorte, *m.pl*.

mortuary, *a*, mortuaire. ¶ *n*, institut médico-légal; établissement de pompes funèbres, *m*.

Mosaic (*of Moses*) *a*, mosaïque.

mosaic, *n*, mosaïque, marqueterie, *f*.

Moscow, *n*, Moscou, *m*.

Moslem, *n*. & *a*, mahométan, e.

mosque, *n*, mosquée, *f*.

mosquito, *n*, moustique; maringouin, *m*. ~ *net*, ~ *curtain*, moustiquaire, *f*.

moss, *n*, mousse, *f*. ~**y**, *a*, mousseux; moussu.

most, *a*, le plus de; la plupart de. ~ *eminent*, éminentissime. ~ *illustrious*, illustrissime. ~ *reverend*, révérendissime. ¶ *ad*, le plus; très. ~**ly**, *ad*, pour la plupart.

mote, *n*, (*dust*) atome, *m*; (*in eye, fig.*) paille, *f*.

moth, *n*, papillon [de nuit] *m*; teigne, gerce, *f*, artison; ver, *m*, mite, *f*. ~*ball*, boule de naphtaline, *f*. ~*-eaten*, mangé aux mites, artisonné.

mother, *n*, mère, *f*. ~ *church*, église métropolitaine, *f*. ~ *earth*, notre mère commune. ~*hood*, maternité, *f*. ~*-in-law*, belle-mère, *f*. ~*-of-pearl*, nacre, *f*. ~*'s side* (*family*), côté maternel, *m*. ~ *superior*, mère supérieure, *f*. ~ *tongue*, (*native*) langue maternelle; (*original*) l. mère, *f*. ~ *wit*, esprit naturel, *m*. ¶ *v.t*, servir de mère à; (*fig.*) couver. ~**less**, *a*, sans mère. ~**ly**, *a*, maternel, de mère.

motif, *n*, (*art, Need.*) motif, *m*; (*literary*) donnée, *f*. **motion**, *n*, mouvement, *m*, marche, *f*; signe, *m*; (*proposal*) motion; proposition, *f*. ¶ *v.i*, faire signe. ~**less**, *a*, sans mouvement, immobile. **motive**, *a*, moteur. ~ *power*, force motrice, *f*, mobile, *m*. ¶ *n*, raison, *f*; motif; mobile, *m*.

motley, *a*, bariolé, bigarré; mêlé. ¶ *n*, bariolage; habit d'arlequin, *m*.

motor, *n*, moteur, *m*. ~ [*bi*]*cycle*, motocyclette, moto, *f*; cyclomoteur, *m*. ~ *boat*, canot automobile, *m*. vedette, *f*. ~ *bus*, autobus, *m*. ~ [*car*], automobile, auto, *f*. ~ *coach*, autocar, *m*. ~ *cyclist*, motocycliste, *m.f*. ~*man*, machiniste, *m*. ~ *road*, autoroute, *f*. ~ *show*, salon de l'automobile, *m*. ¶ *v.i*, aller en auto. ~**ing**, *n*, automobilisme, *m*. ~**ist**, *n*, automobiliste, *m.f*. ~**ize**, *v.t*, mécaniser; motoriser.

mottled, *a*, marbré.

motto, *n*, devise; (*prefixed to book or chapter*) épigraphe, *f*.

mound, *n*, monticule, *m*, butte, *f*, tertre, *m*, bosse, motte, *f*.

mount, *n*, (*as Etna*) le mont; carton [pour montage photographique] *m*; (*horse, etc.*) monture; (*horse racing*) monte, *f*. ¶ *v.i. & t*, monter.

mountain, *n*, montagne, *f*. ~ *ash*, sorbier des oiseaux, *m*. ~ *sickness*, mal de montagne, *m*. ~*eer*, *n*, (*dweller*) montagnard, e; (*climber*) alpiniste, ascensionniste, *m.f*. ~*eering*, *n*, l'alpinisme,

m. ~ous, *a,* montagneux; énorme.
mountebank, *n,* saltimbanque; baladin, *m.*
mounted, *p.a,* à cheval; monté.
mounter, *n,* monteur, *m.* **mounting,** *n,* montage, *m;* monture; ferrure, *f.*
mourn, *v.t. & i,* pleurer. **the ~ers,** le deuil. **[hired]** ~er, pleureur, euse. ~ful†, *a,* douloureux. ~ing, *n,* deuil, *m.* ~ band, brassard de d., *m.*
mouse, *n,* souris, *f;* (*young*) souriceau, *m.* ~trap, souricière, *f.*
moustache, *n,* moustache, *f.* ~d, *a,* moustachu.
mouth, *n,* bouche; embouchure; (*vulgar*) gueule, *f;* bec; (*pers.*) trou, *m;* entrée, *f.* ~ organ, harmonica à bouche, *m.* ~piece, embouchure, *f;* bec; (*pers.*) organe, porte-parole, *m.* ~wash, eau dentifrice, *f.* ~ful, *n,* bouchée, goulée, gorgée, *f.*
movable, *a,* mobile; (*law*) meuble, mobilier, **move,** *n,* mouvement, *m;* manœuvre, *f;* (*chess, etc.*) coup, *m. whose ~ is it?* à qui à jouer? ¶ *v.t,* [faire] mouvoir; remuer; déplacer; jouer; affecter; toucher, émouvoir, attendrir; proposer; (*v.i.*) se mouvoir; bouger; déloger. ~ *along,* cheminer. ~ *back,* reculer. ~ *in* (house), emménager. ~ *off,* s'éloigner, s'ébranler. ~ *on!* circulez! ~ *[out]* (house), déménager. ~ment, *n,* mouvement, *m,* marche, *f;* geste, *m.* **moving,** *a,* mouvant; touchant.
movie, *n,* cinéma, film, *m.* ~ *camera,* camera, *m.*
mow, *v.t.tr,* faucher; tondre. ~ *down,* faucher. ~er, *n,* (*pers.*) faucheur, *m;* (*Mach.*) faucheuse; (*lawn*) tondeuse, *f.*
Mr, Monsieur, M.; (*partner in firm*) sieur; (*courtesy title of lawyers*) maître, *m.* **Mrs,** Madame, Mme; (*law*) la dame.
much, *a. & ad,* beaucoup (de); grand-chose (*usually with neg.*); bien (de); très; cher. *as ~,* autant (de). *as ~ as,* autant que. *how ~?* combien? *so ~,* [au]tant (de). *too ~,* trop. *very ~,* beaucoup.
mucilage, *n,* mucilage, *m.*
muck, *n,* fumier, *m;* fange; cochonnerie; saloperie, *f.*
mucous, *a,* muqueux. ~ *membrane,* [membrane] muqueuse, *f.*

mucus, *n,* mucosité, *f,* mucus, *m,* pituite, morve, *f.*
mud, *n,* boue, *f.* oft. pl, crotte, bourbe, fange; (*river*) vase, *f,* limon, *m.* ~ *bath,* brain de boue [s minérales] *m.* ~guard, garde-boue, *m.* ~lark, barboteur, *m.* ~ *pie,* pâté, *m.* ~ *spring,* source boueuse, *f.*
muddle, *n,* [em]brouillamini; fouillis, *m.* ¶ *v.t,* [em]brouiller, emmêler; (*with drink*) griser. ~ *up,* tripoter. **muddler,** *n,* barboteur, euse, fatrassier, ère, brouillon, ne.
muddy, *a,* boueux, crotté, bourbeux, fangeux; vaseux, limoneux; trouble. ¶ *v.t,* embouer.
muezzin, *n,* muezzin, *m.*
muff, *n,* manchon; (*pers.*) serin, *m,* jobard, e, huître, *f.* **muffle** (*Chem.*) *n,* moufle, *m.* ¶ *v.t,* assourdir; (*drum*) voiler. ~ *up,* embéguiner, emmitoufler. ~d *p.a.* sourd. **muffler,** *n,* cache-nez; (*auto*) amortisseur de son; pot d'échappement, *m.*
mufti (**in**), en civil, en bourgeois.
mug, *n,* timbale, tasse, *f,* pot, *m.*
muggy, *a,* mou.
mulatto, *n,* mulâtre, *m,* mulâtresse, *f.* ¶ *a,* mulâtre.
mulberry, *n,* mûre, *f.* ~ [*tree*], mûrier, *m.*
mulch, *n,* paillis, *m.* ¶ *v.t,* pailler.
mulct, *v.t,* frapper d'une amende.
mule, *n,* (*he & pers.*) mulet, *m,* (*she*) mule, *f;* (*pl, slippers*) mules, babouches, *f.pl.* ~ *track,* piste muletière, *f.* **muleteer,** *n,* muletier, *m.* **mulish,** *a,* têtu.
mulled wine, vin brûlé, *m.*
muller (*grinding*), *n,* molette, *f.*
mullet, *n,* (*gray*) mulet, muge; (*red*) rouget, *m.*
mullion, *n,* meneau, *m.*
multicolor[ed], *a,* multicolore.
multifarious, *a,* multiple.
multimillionaire, *n. & a,* milliardaire, *m,f. & a.*
multiple, *n. & a,* multiple, *m. & a.* **multiplicand,** *n,* multiplicande, *m.* **multiplication,** *n,* multiplication, *f.* **multiplicity,** *n,* multiplicité, *f.* **multiplier,** *n,* multiplicateur, *m.* **multiply,** *v.t,* multiplier; (*v.i.*) [se] m.; peupler.
multitude, *n,* multitude, *f.*
mum['s the word], motus!, bouche close!

mumble, *v.i,* marmotter, balbutier, barboter.

mummer, *n,* cabotin, e. ~**y,** *n,* momerie, *f.*

mummify, *v.t,* momifier. **mummy,** *n,* momie; (*mother*) maman, *f.*

mumps, *n,* (*Med.*) oreillons, *m.pl.*

munch, *v.i,* croquer.

mundane, *a,* du monde, de ce m.; mondain.

municipal, *a,* municipal. ~**ity,** *n,* municipalité, *f.*

munificence, *n,* munificence, *f.* **munificent,** *a,* magnifique.

muniment, *n,* acte, titre, *m.*

munitions, *n.pl,* provisions de guerre, munitions de guerre, *f.pl.*

mural, *a,* mural.

murder, *n,* meurtre, assassinat, *m.* ~! à l'assassin! ¶ *v.t,* assassiner; (*fig.*) massacrer; (*language*) estropier, écorcher. ~**er,** ~**ess,** *n,* meurtrier, ère, assassin, e. ~**ous,** *a,* meurtrier.

murky, *a,* sombre, obscur, ténébreux.

murmur, *n,* murmure, *m.* ¶ *v.i. & t,* murmurer; bruire.

murrain, *n,* peste, *f.*

muscat [grape, wine], [raisin, vin] muscat, *m.* **muscatels,** *n.pl,* raisins secs muscats, *m.pl.*

muscle, *n,* muscle, *m.* -**muscled,** *a,* musclé. **muscular,** *a,* (*force*) musculaire; (*pers.*) musculeux.

Muse, *n,* Muse, *f;* génie, *m.*

muse, *v.i,* méditer; rêver, rêvasser.

museum, *n,* musée; (*natural history*) muséum, *m.*

mush, *n,* bouillie, *f.*

mushroom, *n,* champignon [comestible] *m;* (*att.*) éphémère, d'un jour. ~ *bed,* champignonnière, *f.*

music, *n,* musique, *f.* ~ *case,* porte-musique, *m.* ~ *hall,* music-hall, *m.* ~ *master,* professeur de musique, *m.* ~ *stand,* pupitre à m., *m.* **musical,** *a,* musical; chantant; (*pers.*) musicien. ~ *box,* boîte à musique, *f.* ~ *chairs,* chaises musicales, *f.pl.* ~ *clock,* horloge à carillon, *f.* ~ *comedy,* opéra bouffe, *f.* ~ *director,* directeur musical, chef de théâtre, *m.* ~ *ear,* oreille pour la musique, *f.* ~ *instrument,* instrument de musique, *m;* (*toy*) musique, *f.* ~ *instrument maker,* luthier, *m.* ~ *interlude,* entracte de musique, *m.* ~ *play,* opérette, *f.* ~**e,** soirée

musicale, *f.* **musician,** *n,* musicien, ne.

musing, *n,* rêverie, *f.*

musk, *n,* musc, *m.* ~ *deer,* [porte-] musc, chevrotin, *m.* ~**rat;** rat musqué, *m.* ~ *rose,* rose muscade, *f.* to [*perfume with*] ~, musquer.

musket, *n,* mousquet, *m.* ~**eer** (*Hist.*) *n,* mousquetaire, *m.* ~**ry** (*Mil.*) *n,* tir, *m,* exercices de tir, *m.pl.*

Muslim, *n. & a,* mahométan, e.

muslin, *n,* mousseline, *f.*

musquash, *n,* rat musqué; (*fur*) castor du Canada, *m.*

muss, *v.t,* déranger.

mussel, *n,* moule, *f.*

Mussulman, *n. & a,* musulman, e, *m,f. & att.*

must, *v.aux.ir,* falloir; devoir.

must, *n,* (*grapes*) moût, *m.*

mustard, *n,* moutarde; (*Bot.*) moutarde, *f,* sénevé, *m.* ~ *gas,* gaz moutarde, *m,* ypérite, *f.* ~ *maker & ~ pot,* moutardier, *m.* ~ *plaster,* sinapisme, *m.* ~ *sauce,* sauce moutarde, *f.* ~ *seed,* graine de m., *f,* sénevé, *m.* ~ *spoon,* cuiller à m., pelle à m., *f.*

muster, *n,* appel [nominal] *m.* ~ *roll,* feuille d'appel, *f.* ¶ *v.t,* faire l'appel de; rassembler. ~ *out,* démobiliser.

musty, *a,* moisi; (*smell*) de renfermé.

mutability, *n,* mutabilité, *f.* **mutation,** *n,* mutation, *f.*

mute, *a,* muet; sourd. ¶ *n,* muet, te; (*Mus.*) sourdine, *f.* ~**d,** *p.a,* sourd; en sourdine. ~**ly,** *ad,* en silence.

mutilate, *v.t,* mutiler. **mutilation,** *n,* mutilation, *f.*

mutineer, *n,* mutin, révolté, *m.* **mutinous,** *a,* mutin. **mutiny,** *n,* mutinerie, révolte, *f.* ¶ *v.i,* [se] mutiner, se révolter.

mutter, *v.i,* murmurer [entre ses dents], marmotter; (*of thunder*) gronder.

mutton, *n,* mouton, *m.* ~ *chop,* côtelette de mouton, *f.*

mutual†, *a,* mutuel; réciproque, partagé. ~ *association,* mutualité, *f.* ~ *loan association,* mutualité de crédit. *on* ~ *terms* (engagement), au pair. ~**ity,** *n,* mutualité; réciprocité, *f.*

muzzle, *n,* (*animal*) museau, *m;* (*gun*) bouche, gueule; (*for dog*) muselière, *f.* ~*-loading*, se chargeant par la bouche. ¶ *v.t*, museler.

my, *a*, mon, ma, mes.

myopia, *n*, myopie, *f.* **myopic,** *a*, myope.

myriad, *n*, myriade, *f.* e, *m.*

myriapod, *n*, myriapode, *m.*

myrmidon, *n*, suppôt, *m.*

myrrh, *n*, myrrhe, *f.*

myrtle, *n*, myrte, *m.* ~ *berry*, baie de m., *f.*

myself, *pn*, moi-même; moi; me.

mysterious†, *a*, mystérieux. **mystery,** *n*, mystère, *m.* ~ [*play*], mystère, miracle, *m.* **mystic** (*pers.*) *n*, mystique, *m,f.* ~(al)†, *a*, mystique. **mysticalness,** *n*, mysticité, *f.* **mysticism,** *n*, mysticisme, *m.* **mystify,** *v.t*, mystifier.

myth, *n*, mythe, *m.* ~**ic(al),** *a*, mythique. ~**ologic(al),** *a*, mythologique. ~**ologist,** *n*, mythologue, *m,f.* ~**ology,** *n*, mythologie, *f.*

N

nab, *v.t*, saisir, arrêter. *to be nabbed*, se faire paumer.

nabob, *n*, nabab, *m.*

nadir, *n*, nadir, *m.*

nag, *n*, bidet, *m.* ~ (*at*), *v.t. & i*, criailler (après), quereller. **nagging,** *p.a*, hargneux.

naiad, *n*, naïade, *f.*

nail, *n*, (*finger, toe*) ongle; (*metal*) clou, *m*; pointe, *f. hit the* ~ *on the head*, tomber juste. ~ *brush*, brosse à ongles, *f.* ~ *extractor*, arrache-clou, *m.* ~ *file*, lime à ongles, *f.* ~ *maker*, cloutier, *m.* ~ *scissors*, ciseaux à ongles, *m. pl.* ~ [*up*], *v.t*, clouer.

naïve†, *a*, naïf. **naïvety,** *n*, naïveté, *f.*

naked, *a*, nu; à nu; ras. *with the* ~ *eye*, à l'œil nu. ~**ly** (*fig.*) *ad*, nûment. ~**ness,** *n*, nudité, *f.*

namby-pamby, *a*, fade.

name, *n*, nom, *m*; dénomination; raison, *f*; intitulé, *m*; renommée; réputation, *f. by* ~, (*to mention*) nommément; (*be called on*) nominativement. *Christian* ~, nom de baptême, *m. my* ~ *is Adam*, je m'appelle Adam, je me nomme A. *given* ~, petit nom, *m.* ~ *plate*, plaque de porte, *f.* ~*sake*,

homonyme, *m.* **nick**~, sobriquet, *m.* ¶ *v.t*, nommer; dénommer; intituler. ~**less,** *a*, sans nom. ~**ly,** *ad*, [à] savoir; (*of pers.*) nommément.

nankeen, *n*, nankin, *m.*

nanny, *n*, (*nursemaid*) nounou, *f.* ~ [*goat*], chèvre, bique, *f.*

nap, *n*, (*sleep*) somme, *m*, sieste, *f*; (*pile*) poil; duvet, *m. to catch napping*, prendre au dépourvu. ¶ *v.i*, sommeiller.

nape [*of the neck*], *n*, nuque, *f.*

naphtha, *n*, naphte, *m.* **naphthalene,** *n*, naphtaline, *f.*

napkin, *n*, serviette [de table]. ~ *ring*, rond de serviette, *m.*

narcissus, *n*, narcisse, *m.*

narcotic, *a*, narcotique. ¶ *n*, narcotique, stupéfiant, *m.*

narrate, *v.t*, narrer, raconter. **narration** & **narrative,** *n*, narration, *f*, récit, *m.* **narrative,** *a*, narratif. **narrator,** *n*, narrateur, trice, conteur, euse.

narrow†, *a*, étroit, resserré. *to have a* ~ *escape*, l'échapper belle. ~*-gauge railway*, chemin de fer à voie étroite, *m.* ~*-minded*, à l'esprit étroit. ¶ *n*, (*Naut.*) (*pl.*) détroit, *m.* ¶ *v.t*, [r]étrécir, resserrer, étrangler. ~**ness,** *n*, étroitesse, *f.*

nasal, *a*, nasal. ¶ (*Gram.*) *n*, nasale, *f.*

nascent, *a*, naissant.

nastiness, *n*, saleté; méchanceté, *f.*

nasturtium, *n*, capucine, *f.*

nasty†, *a*, sale; désagréable; vilain; rosse. *be in a* ~ *situation*, être dans les beaux draps.

natal, *a*, natal.

natation, *n*, natation, *f.*

nation, *n*, nation, *f*, peuple, *m.* ~**al,** *a*, national; public. ~ *capital* (*economics*), outillage national, *m.* ~ *monument*, monument historique, *m.* ~**alism,** *n*, nationalisme; étatisme, *m.* ~**alist,** *n. & att*, nationaliste, *m, f.* & *a.* ~**ality,** *n*, nationalité, *f.* ~**alize,** *v.t*, nationaliser. ~**als,** *n.pl*, nationaux, *m.pl.*

native, *a*, naturel; natif; natal; originaire; indigène; maternel. ~ *land*, ~ *country*, patrie, *f.* ¶ *n*, natif, ive; indigène, *m,f*; naturel, *m.* **nativity,** *n*, nativité; naissance, *f.*

natty, *a,* chic, coquet, propret.

natural†, *a,* naturel. ¶ *n,* idiot, e; (*Mus.*) (*note*) note naturelle, *f*; (*cancel sign*) bécarre, *m.* ~ *history museum,* muséum [d'histoire naturelle] *m.* ~**ist,** *n,* naturaliste, *m.* ~**ization,** *n,* naturalisation, *f.* ~ *papers,* lettres de n., *f.pl.* ~**ize,** *v.t,* naturaliser. ~**ness,** *n,* naturel, *m.* **nature,** *n,* nature, *f*; naturel, caractère, acabit, *m.* -**natured,** *a,* d'un (*bon, mauvais*) naturel.

naught, *n,* rien; (*Arith.*) zéro, *m.*

naughtiness, *n,* méchanceté, *f.* **naughty†,** *a,* méchant, vilain, laid; (*indecent*) polisson, croustilleux, graveleux, gras.

nausea, *n,* nausée, *f.* **nauseate,** *v.t,* écœurer. **nauseating,** *a,* nauséeux. **nauseous,** *a,* nauséabond.

nautical, *a,* (*science, almanac*) nautique; (*mile*) marin.

nautilus, *n,* nautile, nautilus, *m.*

naval, *a,* naval; maritime; de marine; de la m. ~ *cadet,* élève de l'école navale, *m.* ~ *dockyard,* arsenal maritime, *m.* ~ *officer,* officier de marine, *m.* ~ *station,* port de guerre, p. militaire; point d'appui de la flotte, *m.*

nave, *n,* (*wheel*) moyeu, *m*; (*church*) nef, *f.*

navel, *n,* nombril, *m.*

navigable, *a,* navigable. **navigate,** *v.i,* naviguer; (*v.t.*) naviguer sur, faire naviguer. **navigation,** *n,* navigation, *f.* **navigator,** *n,* navigateur, *m.*

navy, *n,* marine [militaire], *m.* de guerre, *f.* ~ *blue,* bleu marine, *m.*

nay, *neg. particle,* & qui plus est, voire. ¶ *n,* non, *m.*

Neapolitan, *a,* napolitain. ¶ *n,* Napolitain, e.

neap tide, morte-eau, *f.*

near, *a,* proche; près de; rapproché; intime. *the N~ East,* le Proche Orient. ~ *relations,* proches [parents] *m.pl.* ~ *relationship,* proximité du sang, *f.* ~*sighted* (*person*), myope, *a.* & *m,f.* ¶ *ad,* près; proche; auprès; de près. ¶ *pr,* près de; auprès de. ¶ *v.i,* s'approcher de. ~*ly,* *ad,* de près; à peu [de chose] près; presque. *he* ~ *fell,* il a manqué de tomber. *I* ~ *missed the train,* j'ai failli manquer le train. ~**ness,** *n,* proximité, *f.*

neat†, *a,* propre; soigné; bien tenu; (*drink*) pur, sec; adroit. ~*herd,*

bouvier, ère, vacher, ère, pâtre, *m.* ~*'s foot oil,* huile de pied de bœuf, *f.* ~**ness,** *n,* propreté, *f.*

nebula (*Astr.*) *n,* nébuleuse, *f.* **nebulous,** *a,* nébuleux.

necessarily, *ad,* nécessairement, forcément. **necessary,** *a,* nécessaire. *if* ~, s'il est n.; au besoin. ¶ *n.* & **necessaries,** *n.pl,* le nécessaire. **necessitate,** *v.t,* nécessiter. **necessitous,** *a,* nécessiteux. **necessity,** *n,* nécessité, *f.*

neck, *n,* cou, *m*; gorge; encolure, *f*; col; collet; goulot; (*violin*) manche, *m.* ~*band,* bande de col, brisure, *f.* ~*lace,* collier, *m.* ~ *measurement,* ~ *size,* encolure, *f.* ~*tie,* cravate, *f.* *stiff* ~, torticolis, *m. to win by a* ~, gagner par une encolure. **neckerchief,** *n,* fichu, *m.*

necrology, *n,* (*notice*) nécrologie, *f*; (*roll, book*) nécrologe, *m.* **necromancer,** *n,* nécromancien, ne. **necromancy,** *n,* nécromancie, *f.* **necropolis,** *n,* nécropole, *f.* **necrosis,** *n,* nécrose, *f.*

nectar, *n,* nectar, *m.* ~**ine,** *n,* brugnon, *m.* ~**y,** *n,* nectaire, *m.*

need, *n,* besoin, *m.* ¶ *v.i.* & *t,* avoir b. (de); vouloir. ~*ful,* *a.* & *n,* nécessaire, *a.* & *m.* ~*iness,* *n,* besoin, *m,* gêne, indigence, *f.*

needle, *n,* aiguille, *f.* ~*point lace,* dentelle au point à l'aiguille, *f.* ~*woman,* couturière, *f.* ~*work,* travail à l'aiguille, *m,* couture, *f. to do* ~*work,* travailler à l'a., chiffonner. ~*ful,* *n,* aiguillée, *f.*

needless†, *a,* inutile. **needs,** *ad,* nécessairement. **needy,** *a,* nécessiteux, besogneux.

ne'er (*Poet.*) *ad,* ne . . . jamais. *a* ~*do-well* (*m*) un mauvais sujet, un propre à rien.

nefarious†, *a,* inique, abominable.

negation, *n,* négation, *f.* **negative†,** *a,* négatif. ¶ *n,* la négative; (*Gram.*) négation, *f*; (*Phot.*) cliché, négatif, *m.*

neglect, *v.t,* négliger, oublier. **neglect** & **negligence,** *n,* négligence, *f,* oubli *m.* **neglectful†** & **negligent†,** *a,* négligent. **negligible,** *a,* négligeable.

negotiable, *a,* négociable. ~ *instrument,* effet de commerce, *m.* **negotiate,** *v.t.* & *i,* négocier, traiter, trafiquer. **negotiation,** *n,* négociation, *f*; (*pl.*) pourparlers, *m.pl.* by ~, de gré à gré. **negotiator, tress** *or* **trix,** *n,* négociateur, trice.

Negro, *n,* nègre, *m;* (*woman*) nègresse *f.* ¶ *a,* nègre, *a.m.,* & *a.f.*

neigh, *v.i,* hennir. ~[**ing**], *n,* hennissement, *m.*

neighbor, *n,* voisin, e; prochain, *m.* ~**hood,** *n,* voisinage, *m,* environs, *m.pl;* quartier, *m.* ~**ing,** *a,* voisin, avoisinant, prochain. *in a* ~*ly way,* en bon voisin.

neither, *pn.* & *a,* ni l'un (l'une) ni l'autre. ¶ *c,* ni; ne . . . pas non plus. ¶ *ad,* non plus.

nelson (*wrestling*) *n,* prise de tête à terre, *f.*

Nemesis, *n,* Némésis, *f.*

neologism, *n,* néologisme, *m.*

neon, *n,* néon, *m.* ~ *light,* lumière néon, *f.*

neophyte, *n,* néophyte, *m,f.*

nephew, *n,* neveu, *m.*

nepotism, *n,* népotisme, *m.*

Nereid, *n,* néréide, *f.*

nerve, *n,* nerf, *m;* (*Bot.*) nervure, *f;* (*fig.*) audace, *f,* courage, sangfroid, *m.* ~ *specialist,* neurologiste, neurologue, *m,f.* **nervous**†, *a,* nerveux; peureux, timide. ~ *breakdown,* prostration nerveuse, *f.* ~**ness,** *n,* timidité, *f.*

nest, *n,* nid; faisceau; (*fig.*) repaire, *m.* ~ *egg,* nichet; (*savings*) pécule, *m.* ~ *of drawers,* casier, *m.* ~ *of* (*insect's*) *eggs,* couvain, *m.* ¶ *v.i,* nicher. ~**ed** *table or* ~ *of 3 tables,* table gigogne, *f.* ~[**ful**], *n,* nichée, *f.* **nestle,** *v.i,* se blottir, se tapir. **nestling,** *n,* petit oiseau au nid, *m.*

net, *n,* filet; rets; tulle, *m;* résille; *f.* ~ *maker,* fileur, euse. ~ *sinker,* ~ *weight* (*Fish.*), gousse de plomb, *f.* ~**work,** réseau; lacis, *m.* ¶ (*Com.*) *a,* net. ¶ (*catch*) *v.t,* prendre au filet.

nether, *a,* inférieur, bas. ~ *regions,* enfers, *m.pl.* **Netherlander,** *n,* Néerlandais, e. **Netherlandish,** *a,* néerlandais. **the Netherlands,** les Pays-Bas, *m.pl,* la Néerlande. **nethermost,** *a,* (le) plus bas.

netting, *n,* filet, *m,* filoche, *f;* (*wire*) treillis, treillage, grillage, réseau, *m.*

nettle, *n,* ortie, *f.* ~ *rash,* urticaire, *f.* ¶ *v.t,* piquer.

network, *n,* lacis; réseau, *m*

(*computers*) *shared* ~, réseau banalisé.

neuralgia, *n,* névralgie, *f.* **neuralgic,** *a,* névralgique. **neurasthenia,** *n,* neurasthénie, *f.* **neuritis,** *n,* névrite, *f.* **neurologist,** *n,* neurologiste, -logue, *m,f.* **neurosis,** *n,* névrose, *f.* **neurotic,** *a,* névrosé.

neuter, *a.* & *n,* neutre, *a.* & *m.* **neutral,** *a.* & *n,* neutre, *a.* & *m.* ~**ity,** *n,* neutralité, *f.* ~**ize,** *v.t,* neutraliser.

never, *ad,* jamais; ne . . . jamais; ne . . . pas. ~*ending,* éternel. ~ *mind,* cela ne fait rien. ~*more,* jamais plus. **nevertheless,** *ad.* & *c,* néanmoins; cependant; toutefois; pourtant, quand même.

new, *a,* neuf; nouveau; récent; frais, tendre. ~*born* (*child*), nouveau-né, e. ~*comer,* nouveau venu, *m,* nouvelle venue, *f.* *Newfoundland* [*dog*], terre-neuve, *m.* ~ *growth* (*forestry*), revenue, *f.* ~*laid,* frais [pondu]. ~ *lease on life,* regain de vie, *m.* ~ *member* (*of a society*), récipiendaire, *m,f.* ~ *par*[*agraph*], alinéa, *m.* N~ *Testament,* Nouveau Testament, *m.* N~*Year's day,* le jour de l'an. N~*Year's eve,* veille de j. de l'a., *f,* la Saint-Sylvestre. N~*Year's wishes,* souhaits (*ou* vœux) de bonne année, *m.pl.*

New (*Geog.*) *a:* ~ *Brunswick,* le Nouveau-Brunswick. ~*foundland,* Terre-Neuve, *f.* ~ *Guinea,* la Nouvelle-Guinée. ~ *Orleans,* la Nouvelle-Orléans. ~ *South Wales,* la Nouvelle-Galles du Sud. ~ *York,* New York, *m.* ~ *Zealand,* la Nouvelle-Zélande; (*att.*) néo-zélandais. ~ *Zealander,* Néo-Zélandais, e.

newel, *n,* noyau; pilastre, *m.*

newly, *ad,* nouvellement, fraîchement. **newness,** *n,* nouveauté; primeur, *f.*

news, *n,* nouvelle, *f.* oft. pl; courrier; bruit, *m;* (*reel*) actualités, *f.pl.* ~ *agency,* agence, d'information, presse, *f.* ~ *boy,* vendeur de journaux, *m.* ~ [*bulletin*] (*radio*), informations, *f.pl.* ~*paper,* journal, *m.*

newt, *n,* triton, *m,* salamandre aquatique, *f.*

next, *a,* voisin; d'à côté; prochain; plus prochain; suivant; (*world*) autre. *the ~ day*, le lendemain. *the ~ day but one*, le surlendemain. *~ door to*, à côté de. ¶ *ad*, après; ensuite; puis. *~ to*, [au]près de; à côté de; presque. ¶ *~ of kin*, plus proche parent, e, proches [parents] *m.pl.*

nib, *n*, plume [à écrire], *f*, bec, *m*.

nibble (*Fish.*) *n*, touche, *f*. ¶ *v.t.* & *i*, grignoter, chipoter, mordiller; (*grass*) brouter; (*fish*) piquer, mordre.

nice, *a*, bon; agréable; friand; délicat; beau; joli; gentil. *~ly*, *ad*, bien; joliment; gentiment.

Nicene Creed (**the**), le symbole de Nicée.

nicety, *n*, précision; subtilité, *f*. *to a ~*, à point.

niche, *n*, niche, *f*.

nick, *n*, [en]coche, hoche, entaille, *f*, cran, *m*, saignée, fente, *f*. *in the ~ of time*, à point nommé. ¶ *v.t*, encocher, entailler, hocher, fendre.

nickel, *n*, nickel, *m*. ¶ *v.t*, nickeler.

nickname, *n*, sobriquet, surnom, *m*. ¶ *v.t*, baptiser; surnommer.

nicotine, *n*, nicotine, *f*.

niece, *n*, nièce, *f*.

niggard, *n*, ladre, *m.f*. *~ly*, *a*, ladre, mesquin, chiche.

nigh, *a*, proche. ¶ *ad*, près; presque.

night, *n*, nuit, *f*; soir, *m*. *at ~*, la nuit, le soir; (*hour*) du soir. *by ~*, de nuit, nuitamment. *the ~ before last*, avant-hier soir. *~club*, boîte de n., *f*. *~gown*, chemise de nuit, *f*. *~fall*, la tombée de la nuit, la chute du jour. *at ~fall*, à la nuit tombante. *~ lamp* & *~light*, veilleuse, *f*. *~mare*, cauchemar, *m*. *~ nurse*, veilleuse de nuit, *f*. *~ nursing*, veillée, *f*. *~shade*, morelle, *f*. *~shirt*, chemise de nuit, *f*. *~ soil*, vidanges, *f.pl*, gadoue, *f*.

nightingale, *n*, rossignol, *m*.

nightly, *a*, de nuit. ¶ *ad*, toutes les nuits; tous les soirs.

nihilist, *n*, nihiliste, *m*.

nil, *n*, rien, néant, *m*, nul, *a*.

Nile (**the**), le Nil.

nimble†, *a*, agile, leste, preste, ingambe. *~ness*, *n*, agilité, prestesse, *f*.

nimbus, *n*, nimbe; (*Meteor.*) nimbus, *m*.

nincompoop, *n*, nigaud, e.

nine, *a. & n*, neuf, *a. & m*. *9-hole course*, parcours (*ou* golf) de 9 trous, *m*. *~pins*, quilles, *f.pl*. *~ times out of ten*, neuf fois sur dix. **nineteen**, *a. & n*, dix-neuf, *a. & m*. **nineteenth**, *a. & n*, dix-neuvième, *a. & m,f*; dix-neuf, *m*. **ninetieth**, *a. & m,f*, quatre-vingt-dixième, *a. & m,f*. **ninety**, *a. & n*, quatre-vingt-dix, *a. & m*. *91, 92, etc.*, quatre-vingt-onze, -douze, *etc*.

Nineveh, *n*, Ninive, *f*.

ninny, *n*, nigaud, e, dadais, *m*.

ninth, *a. & n*, neuvième, *a. & m,f*; neuf, *m*. *~ly*, *ad*, neuvièmement.

nip, *n*, (*liquor*) doigt, *m*; (*bite*) morsure, *f*. ¶ *v.t*, pincer; serrer; mordre; brûler. **nipper**, *n*, (*boy*) gamin, *m*; (*of crustacean*) pince, *f*; (*pl.*) pinces [de serrage], tenailles, *f. pl*.

nipple, *n*, mamelon, bout du sein, *m*; (*nursing bottle*) tétine, *f*.

nit, *n*, lente, *f*.

nitrate, *n*, nitrate, azotate, *m*. **niter**, *n*, nitre, salpêtre, *m*. **nitric**, *a*, azotique, nitrique. **nitrogen**, *n*, azote, *m*. **nitroglycerin[e]**, *n*, nitroglycérine, *f*. **nitrous**, *a*, azoteux.

no, *ad*, non; pas. ¶ *n*, non, *m*. ¶ *a*, aucun; nul; ne ... pas de; pas de; pas moyen de. *~ admittance* [*except on business*], entrée interdite, défense d'entrer [sans autorisation]. *~ contest* (*Box.*), noncombat. *~ doubt*, sans doute. *~ entry*, [*one way street*], sens interdit. *~ flowers, by request*, ni fleurs, ni couronnes. *~ matter!* n'importe! *~ occupation*, sans profession. *~ one*, personne, *m*, aucun, e. *~ parking*, stationnement interdit. *~ performance*, relâche. *~ smoking*, défense de fumer. *~ thoroughfare*, défense de passer, passage interdit [au public].

Noah's ark, l'arche de Noé, *f*.

nobility, *n*, noblesse; grandeur, *f*.
noble†, *a*, noble; grand. *~[man]*, noble, seigneur, gentilhomme, *m*. *~woman*, noble, *f*. *~ness*, *n*, noblesse, *f*.

nobody, *n*, personne, *pn.m*. *a ~*, un zéro; un (une) inconnu, e.

nocturnal, *a. & nocturne*, *n*, nocturne, *a. & m*.

nod, *n*, signe [de tête] *m*, inclination de t., *f.* ¶ *v.i*, s'incliner; s'assoupir.

node, *n*, nœud, *m.* **nodule,** *n*, rognon, *m.*

noggin, *n*, godet, *m*; (*Meas.*) ½ pint.

noise, *n*, bruit; fracas, tapage, vacarme; (*in ears*) tintement; (*fig.*) éclat, retentissement, *m.* ~*abroad*, ʋ.*t*, ébruiter, carillonner, claironner. ~*less†*, *a*, silencieux.

noisome, *a*, nuisible; malsain.

noisy†, *a*, bruyant; tapageur.

nomad, *n.* & ~(**ic**), *a*, nomade, *m.* & *a.*

nomenclature, *n*, nomenclature, *f.*

nominal†, *a*, nominal; (*of* [*the*] *names, area*) (*a list*) nominatif. **nominate,** *v.t*, nommer, désigner. **nomination,** *n*, nomination, désignation, *f.* **nominative** [*case*], nominatif, *m.* **nominee,** *n*, personne nommée; personne interposée, *f. in a* ~'*s name*, sous un nom interposé.

non, *prefix:* ~*alcoholic drinks*, liqueurs fraîches, *f.pl.* ~*combatant*, *n.* & *att*, noncombattant; civil, *m.* & *a.* ~*commissioned officer*, sous-officier, gradé, *m.* ~*committal*, qui n'engage à rien, normand. *to be* ~*committal*, rester neutre. ~*existence*, inexistence, *f*; (*Philos.*) non-être, *m.* ~*existent*, inexistant. ~*interference*, ~*intervention*, non-intervention, *f*, laissez-faire, *m.* ~*payment*, nonpaiement, *m.* ~*performance*, inexécution, *f.* ~*skid*, *a*, antidérapant. ~*stop*, *a*, sans arrêt, *s.* escale. ~*vintage wine*, vin sans année, v. non-millésimé, *m.*

nonage, *n*, minorité, *f.*

nonagenarian, *a.* & *n*, nonagénaire. *a.* & *m,f.*

nonce, *n*, circonstance, *f*; (*att.*) de c.

nonchalance, *n*, nonchalance, *f.* **nonchalant,** *a*, nonchalant. ~*ly*, *ad*, nonchalamment.

nonconformist, *n.* & *att*, nonconformiste, *m,f.* & *att.*

nondescript, *a*, indéfinissable.

none, *a.* & *pn*, aucun; nul; pas un; pas; personne, *pn.m.*

nonentity, *n*, (*Philos.*) non-être, *m*; (*pers.*) nullité *f*, homme nul, *m.*

nonplus, *n*, embarras, *m.* ¶ *v.t*, embarrasser, dérouter, démonter.

nonsense, *n*, non-sens, *m*, absurdité, insanité, *f*, sottises, bêtises,

lanternes, sornettes; chinoiseries, *f.pl. all* ~, un non-sens. ¶ *i*, allons donc!; chansons, chansons!

nonsuit, *v.t*, débouter.

noodle, *n*, (*food*) nouille, *f.* nigaud, e, bêta, *m.*

nook, *n*, recoin, réduit, *m.*

noon & **noonday** & **noontide,** *n*, midi, *m.*

noose, *n*, nœud coulant; lacet, *m.*

nor, *c*, ni; ne . . . pas non plus.

Nordic, *a*, nordique.

norm, *n*, norme, *f.* **normal†**, *a*, normal.

Norman, *a*, normand. ¶ *n*, Normand, e. **Normandy,** *n*, la Normandie.

Norse, *a.* & *n.* & ~*man*, *n*, norvégien, *a.* & *m. Old Norse* (language), l'ancien norois, *m.* **north,** *n*, nord; septentrion, *m.* ¶ *ad*, au nord. ¶ *a*, [du] nord; septentrional. N~ *Africa*, l'Afrique septentrionale, *f.* N~ *America*, l'Amérique du Nord, *f.* ~*east*, *n*, nord-est, *m.* N~ *pole*, pôle nord, *m.* N~ *Sea*, mer du Nord, *f.* N~ *Star*, étoile polaire, *f.* ~*west*, *n*, nord-ouest, *m.* ~*wester* (wind) *n*, galerne, *f.* **northerly,** *a*, du nord. **northern,** *a*, [du] nord, boréal. ~ *lights*, aurore boréale, *f.* **northerner,** *n*, septentrional, e. **northward[s],** *ad*, vers le nord.

Norway, *n*, la Norvège. **Norwegian,** *a*, norvégien. ¶ *n*, (*pers.*) Norvégien, ne; (*language*) le norvégien.

nose, *n*, nez; (*beast*) museau; (*tool*) bec; (*scent*) flair, *m. to blow one's* ~, se moucher. ~ *cone*, coiffe, *f.* ~*dive*, *v.i*, piquer du nez. ~*gay*, bouquet, *m.* ~*about*, fouiner. ~ [*out*], *v.t*, flairer. **nosing,** *n*, (*of step*) nez; (*of locomotive*) lacet, *m.*

nostalgia, *n*, nostalgie, *f.* **nostalgic,** *a*, nostalgique.

nostril, *n*, narine, *f*; (*horse*) naseau, *m.*

nostrum, *n*, remède de charlatan, *m*, drogue; panacée, *f.*

not, *n*'**t**, *ad*, ne . . . pas, ne . . . point, ne, n'; non; pas; non pas. ~ *at all*, pas du tout, point du tout, nullement, mais non, aucunement. ~ *at home*, absent. *not competing* [*for prize*], hors concours. ~ *exceeding*, jusqu'à concurrence de, ne dépassant pas.

~ *guilty*, innocent. *to find* ~
guilty, innocenter. ~ *negotiable*
(*check*), non négociable. ~ *to
be confused with* . . ., à ne pas
confondre avec . . .
notability, *n,* notabilité, *f.* **nota-
ble†,** *a,* notable.

notary, *n,* notaire, *m.*

notation, *n,* notation, *f.*

notch, *n,* [en]coche, entaille, hoche, *f,* cran, *m.* ¶ *v.t,* [en]cocher,
entailler, hocher.

note, *n,* note, *f,* mémento, *m;* remarque, *f;* billet, *m;* lettre, *f;*
bulletin; bordereau, *m;* facture,
f; bon; permis, *m;* (*Mus.*) note,
f; (*please observe*) nota [bene].
(pers.) *of* ~, de marque. ~*book,*
carnet, calepin, *m.* ~ *of hand,*
billet à ordre. ~ *paper,* papier
à lettres, *m.* ~*worthy,* digne de
remarque, remarquable. ¶ *v.t,*
noter; relever; constater; remarquer. **noted,** *p.p,* renommé, célèbre.

nothing, *n,* rien; rien de; néant;
zéro, *m.* ~ *at all,* rien du tout.
~*ness,* *n,* néant, *m.*

notice, *n,* observation, *f;* regard,
m; attention, garde, *f;* avis,
m; préavis; avertissement, *m;* notice, *f;* écriteau, *m. at short* ~, à
bref délai; (*loan*) à court terme.
until further ~, jusqu'à nouvel
avis. ~ *of meeting,* avis de convocation, *m,* convocation d'assemblée, *f.* ~ [*to quit*], congé, *m.*
¶ *v.t,* observer, remarquer, faire
attention à. ~**able,** *a,* digne d'attention; perceptible. *to become
more* ~, s'accentuer, *v.i. to* **notify,**
v.t, notifier, avertir, signaler,
aviser, intimer.

notion, *n,* notion, idée, *f.*

notoriety, *n,* notoriété, *f.* **notori-
ous†,** *a,* notoire; insigne, fameux.

notwithstanding, *pr,* malgré,
nonobstant. ¶ *ad,* néanmoins,
quand même.

noun, *n,* nom, substantif, *m.*

nourish, *v.t,* nourrir. ~**ing,** *a,*
nourrissant. ~**ment,** *n,* nourriture, *f.*

nous, *n,* esprit, *m;* savoir-faire, *m.*

Nova Scotia, la Nouvelle-Écosse.

novel, *a,* nouveau, inédit. ¶ *n,*
roman, *m.* ~**ette,** *n,* nouvelle, *f.*
~**ist,** *n,* romancier, ère. ~**ty,** *n,*
nouveauté, *f.*

November, *n,* novembre, *m.*

novice, *n,* novice, *m,f,* apprenti, e.
noviciate, *n,* noviciat, *m.*

now, *ad,* maintenant, à présent,
actuellement; tantôt. ¶ *c,* or.
¶ *n,* [moment] présent, *m.* ¶ *i,*
voyons! ~ *then!* eh bien!, ah! çà,
or çà! ~ & *again,* de temps à
autre, à diverses reprises, parfois,
occasionnellement. ~ & *henceforth,* d'ores & déjà. *between* ~
& *then,* d'ici là. [*every*] ~ &
then, de temps en temps. *from*
~, d'ici. *from* ~ *onward,* dorénavant. *right* ~, tout de suite.
nowadays, *ad,* de nos jours, aujourd'hui; par le temps qui court.

nowhere, *ad,* nulle part, en aucun lieu. **nowise,** *ad,* nullement,
aucunement.

noxious, *a,* nocif, malsain, nuisible. ~**ness,** *n,* nocivité, *f.*

nozzle, *n,* ajutage, bec, jet, *m;*
tuyère, buse, *f.*

Nubia, *n,* la Nubie. **Nubian,** *a,* nubien. ¶ *n,* Nubien, ne.

nubile, *a,* nubile.

nuclear, *a,* nucléaire. ~ *fission,*
fission n., *f.* ~ *power plant,* centrale n., *m.* ~ *radiation,* rayonnement n., *m.*

nucleus, *n,* noyau, *m.*

nude, *a. & n,* nu, *m. & m.*

nudge, *n,* coup de coude, *m.* ¶ *v.t,*
donner un coup de coude à,
pousser du coude.

nudity, *n,* nudité, *f;* nu, *m.*

nugatory, *a,* futile; inefficace;
nul.

nugget, *n,* pépite, *f.*

nuisance, *n,* ennui, embêtement,
m, contrariété, scie; (*law, etc.*)
incommodité, *f;* (pers.) gêneur,
m, importun, e, brebis galeuse, *f;*
(*child*) tourment, *m.*

null, *a,* nul. ~ & *void,* nul(le) &
non avenu(e). ¶ *n,* nulle, *f.* **nullify,** *v.t,* annuler. **nullity,** *n,* nullité, caducité, *f.*

numb, *a,* engourdi, gourd, transi.
¶ *v.t,* engourdir, transir. ~**ness,**
n, engourdissement, *m.*

number, *n,* nombre; numéro,
chiffre, *m,* cote, *f;* (*publication*)
livraison, *f.* N~**s** (*Bible*), lès
Nombres. ¶ *v.t,* compter; nombrer; numéroter, chiffrer; coter.
~**ing,** *n,* numérotage, *m.* ~**less,**
a, innombrable.

numeral, *a,* numéral. ¶ *n,* chiffre,
m. **numerary,** *a,* numéraire. **nu-**

merator (*Arith.*) *n*, numérateur, *m*. **numerical**, *a*, numérique. **numerous**, *a*, nombreux.

numismatics, *n*, numismatique, *f*. **numismatist**, *n*, numismate, *m*.

numskull, *n*, lourdaud, e.

nun, *n*, religieuse, nonne, *f*.

nunciature, *n*, nonciature, *f*. **nuncio**, *n*, nonce, *m*.

nunnery, *n*, couvent, *m*.

nuptial, *a*, nuptial. ~s, *n.pl*, noces, *f.pl*.

nurse, *n*, nourrice, *f*; infirmier, ère; gardemalades, *m.f.* ~[*maid*], bonne [d'enfant] *f*. ¶ *v.t*, nourrir, allaiter; soigner; dorloter. **nursery**, *n*, nursery, chambre d'enfants; (*Hort. & fig.*) pépinière, *f*. ~ *language*, langage enfantin, *m*. ~*man*, [jardinier] pépiniériste, *m*. ~ *rhyme*, poésie enfantine, *f*; conte rimé, *m*. ~ *school*, école maternelle, *f*. ~ *tale*, conte de nourrice, conte de fées, *m*. **nursing**, *n*, allaitement, *m*; soins, *m.pl*. ~ *home*, maison de santé, clinique, *f*. ~ *mother*, mère nourrice, *f*. **nursling**, *n*, nourrisson, *m*.

nurture, *n*, éducation; nourriture, *f*. ¶ *v.t*, nourrir.

nut, *n*, noix; noisette, *f*; (*violin, etc.*) sillet; (*for bolt*) écrou, *m*; (*pl, coal*) gaillette, *f*, gailletin, *m*. *chest*~, châtaigne, *f*. ~*-brown*, noisette. ~*crackers*, casse-noisettes, casse-noix, *m*. ~*shell*, coquille de noix, *f*. ~*tree*, noisetier, *m*.

nutmeg, *n*, [noix] muscade, *f*. ~ [*tree*], muscadier, *m*.

nutriment, *n*, aliment, *m*. **nutrition**, *n*, nutrition, *f*. **nutritious** & **nutritive**, *a*, nourrissant, nutritif.

nutty, *a*, (*taste, smell*) qui sent la noisette.

nuzzle, *v.i. & t*, fouiller; se blottir.

nylon, *n*, Nylon, *m*. ~s, (*stockings*) des nylons.

nymph, *n*, nymphe; bergère, *f*.

O

O, *i*, ô! (*of pain*), aïe!

oaf, *n*, enfant disgracié par la nature; lourdaud, *m*,

oak [*tree*], *n*, chêne, *m*. ~ [*wood or timber*] [bois de] chêne, *m*. ~

apple, pomme de chêne, *f*. ¶ *att*. & ~*en*, *a*, de chêne.

oakum, *n*, étoupe, *f*.

oar, *n*, rame, *f*, aviron, *m*. ~ *lock*, porte-rame, *m*. **oarsman**, *n*, rameur, nageur, canotier, *m*. **oarswoman**, *n*, rameuse, *f*.

oasis (*lit. & fig.*) *n*, oasis, *f*.

oat, *n*, (*pl.*) avoine, *f*. ~*meal*, farine d'avoine, *f*, gruau d'avoine, *m. sow one's wild* ~s, jeter sa gourme.

oath, *n*, serment; (*profane*) juron, *m*.

obdurate *a*, endurci; impénitent.

obedience, *n*, obéissance, soumission; (*Eccl.*) obédience, *f*. **obedient**, *a*, obéissant, soumis. ~*ly*, *ad*, avec obéissance, avec soumission. **obeisance**, *n*, révérence, *f*.

obelisk, *n*, obélisque, *m*; (*Typ.*) croix, *f*.

obese, *a*, obèse. **obesity**, *n*, obésité, *f*.

obey, *v.t*, obéir à; (*v.i.*) obéir.

obfuscate, *v.t*, offusquer, obscurcir.

obituary, *n*, nécrologie, *f*.

object, *n*, objet; but, *m*; (*Gram.*) régime, *m*. ~ *lesson* leçon de choses; (*fig.*) application pratique, *f*. ¶ *v.t*. & *i* objecter; réclamer. **objection**, *n*, objection, *f*; mais, *m*; opposition, *f*. ~*able*, *a*, susceptible d'objections; indésirable; offensant, rosse. **objective†**, *a*, objectif. ¶ (*aim, Opt.*) *n*, objectif, *m*. ~ [*case*], régime direct, *m*. *the* ~ (*Philos.*), l'objectif, *m*.

objurgation, *n*, objurgation, *f*.

oblation, *n*, oblation, offrande, *f*.

obligate, *v.t*, obliger. **obligation**, *n*, obligation, *f*. **obligatory**, *a*, obligatoire. **oblige**, *v.t*, obliger. **obliging**, *a*, obligeant, serviable, arrangeant. ~*ly*, *ad*, obligeamment.

oblique, *a*, oblique. ~*ly*, *ad*, en biais. **obliquity**, *n*, obliquité, *f*.

obliterate, *v.t*, oblitérer, effacer.

oblivion, *n*, oubli, *m*; (*Pol.*) amnistie, *f*. **oblivious**, *a*, oublieux.

oblong, *a*, oblong. ¶ *n*, figure oblongue, *f*, carré long, *m*.

obloquy, *n*, reproche; dénigrement, *m*.

obnoxious, *a*, offensant, odieux.

oboe, *n*, hautbois, *m*. **oboist**, *n*, hautboïste, *m*.

obscene, *a*, obscène. **obscenity**, *n*, obscénité, *f*.

obscure, *a*, obscur, ténébreux, fumeux. ¶ *v.t*, obscurcir, offusquer. ~**ly**, *ad*, obscurément. **obscurity**, *n*, obscurité, *f*.

obsequies, *n.pl*, obsèques, *f.pl*. **obsequious**†, *a*, obséquieux. ~**ness**, *n*, obséquiosité, *f*.

observance, *n*, observation; (*Theol.*) observance; (*religious*) pratique, *f*. **observant**, *a*, observateur. **observation**, *n*, observation, *f*. ~ *post* (*Mil.*) & **observatory**, *n*, observatoire, *m*. **observe**, *v.t*, observer; remarquer; suivre. **observer**, *n*, observateur, trice.

obsess, *v.t*, obséder. *to be* ~*ed by*, *with*, être obsédé par, être fanatique de, s'aheurter à. ~**ion**, *n*, obsession, aheurtement, dada, *m*, hantise, *f*.

obsolescent, *a*, vieillissant. **obsolete**, *a*, vieux, vielli, inusité, désuet.

obstacle, *n*, obstacle, *m*. ~ *race*, course d'obstacles, *f*.

obstetric(al), *a*, obstétrical. **obstetrics**, *n.pl*, obstétrique, *f*.

obstinacy, *n*, obstination, opiniâtreté, *f*, entêtement; acharnement, *m*. **obstinate**, *a*, obstiné, opiniâtre, entêté; acharné; rebelle. ~**ly**, *ad*, obstinément, opiniâtrement.

obstreperous, *a*, turbulent.

obstruct, *v.t*, obstruer, boucher; (*v.i.*) fronder. ~**ion**, *n*, obstruction; (*fig.*) obstruction, *f*.

obtain, *v.t*, obtenir, procurer; (*v.i.*) régner, prévaloir, avoir cours.

obtrude, *v.t*, forcer, imposer; (*v.i.*) s'introduire de force; être importun.

obtuse, *a*, obtus.

obverse (*coin*) *n*, avers, *m*, face, *f*.

obviate, *v.t*, obvier à.

obvious†, *a*, évident, manifeste, visible.

ocarina, *n*, ocarina, *m*.

occasion, *n*, occasion; circonstance; cause, raison, *f*; sujet, *m*. ¶ *v.t*, occasionner, donner lieu à; causer. ~**al**, *a*, par occasion; (*occupation*) d'occasion; de circonstance; de temps en temps; (*cause*, *Philos.*) occasionnelle.

~**ally**, *ad*, occasionnellement, parfois.

occidental, *a*. & *n*, occidental.

occiput, *n*, occiput, *m*.

occult, *a*, occulte. ~**ism**, *n*, occultisme, *m*.

occupant, *n*, habitant, e; occupant, *m*; titulaire, *m,f*. **occupation**, *n*, occupation; profession, *f*, état, *m*, qualités, *f.pl*. **occupy**, *v.t*, occuper; habiter.

occur, *v.i*, [sur]venir, se présenter, s'offrir; arriver, advenir. **occurrence**, *n*, occurrence, venue, *f*, fait, événement, *m*.

ocean, *n*, océan, *m*, mer, *f*. ~[-*going*], *a*, au long cours. **Oceania**, *n*, l'Océanie, *f*.

ocher, *n*, ocre, *f*.

o'clock, heure(s).

octagon, *n*. & ~**al**, *a*, octogone, *m*. & *a*. ~**al** *nut*, écrou à 8 pans, *m*. **octave**, *n*, octave, *f*. **octavo**, *a*. & *n*. (*abb*. 8vo), in-octavo, in-8°, *a.m.* & *m*. **October**, *n*, octobre, *m*. **octogenarian**, *a*. & *n*, octogénaire, *a*. & *m,f*. **octopus**, *n*, poulpe, *m*, pieuvre, *f*. **octoroon**, *n*, octavon, ne.

ocular, *a*. & *n*, oculaire, *a*. & *m*. **oculist**, *n*, oculiste, *m*.

odd, *a*, (*number*) impair; & quelques; & quelque chose; (*pair or set*) dépareillé; singulier, étrange, bizarre, baroque, original, drôle. ~ *jobs*, bricoles, *f.pl*. *at* ~ *times*, par-ci, par-là. ~**ity**, *n*, singularité, bizarrerie, *f*; (*pers.*) original, drôle de corps, *m*. ~**ly**, *ad*, étrangement, bizarrement. ~**ments**, *n.pl*, articles dépareillés, *m.pl*. ~**ness**, *n*, imparité; singularité, *f*. **odds**, *n.pl*, chances; forces supérieures, *f.pl*; avantage, *m*; différence; (*turf*) cote, *f*. *to lay* ~ *of 3 to 1*, parier 3 contre 1. *the* ~ *are that* . . ., il y a à parier que . . . ~ & *ends*, bribes, *f.pl*, rogatons, *m.pl*.

ode, *n*, ode, *f*.

odious†, *a*, odieux. **odium**, *n*, haine, *f*; odieux, *m*.

odoriferous, *a*, odoriférant, odorant. **odor**, *n*, odeur, *f*. ~**less**, *a*, inodore. ~**ous**, *a*, odorant.

Odyssey (*fig.*) *n*, odyssée, *f*.

of, *pr*, de; en; parmi; entre; d'entre; à; chez.

off, *pr*, éloigne de; au large de; de dessus; de là. ~ *and on*, de temps à autre ~*hand*, *a*. & *ad*, im-

promptu; sur-le-champ; sans cérémonie; cavalier; brusque. ~-
handedness, sans-gêne, *m.* ~-
peak hours, heures creuses. ~
season, morte-saison, *f.* ~*shore
fishing*, pêche au large, p. hauturière, *f.* ¶ *ad*, de distance; d'ici.
to be ~, s'en aller; partir.

offal, *n*, issues, *f.pl*, tripaille, *f.*

offend, *v.t*, offenser, blesser, choquer, offusquer; (*v.i.*) pécher.
~**er**, *n*, offenseur, *m*; coupable,
m,f; délinquant, e. **offense**, *n*,
offense, blessure, *f*, outrage; délit; crime, *m*; infraction, contravention, *f*. *to take* ~, s'offenser,
se formaliser. **offensive**, *a*, offensant, blessant, choquant; malsonnant; (*attacking*) offensif.

offer, *n*, offre, *f*. ¶ *v.t*, offrir; proposer; présenter. ~ *up*, offrir.
~**ing**, *n*, offrande; oblation, *f*;
sacrifice, *m*. ~**tory**, *n*, (*Lit.*) offertoire, *m*; (*collection*) quête, *f.*

office, *n*, charge, *f*, office, exercice, *m*, fonction, *f*. *oft. pl*, place,
f, ministère; portefeuille; bureau;
cabinet, *m*, étude; salle, *f*; siège;
comptoir, *m*; caisse, recette, *f*. ~
boy, petit commis, *m*. *main* ~,
siège social, *m*. **officer**, *n*, officier,
m; fonctionnaire, *m,f*; agent, *m*,
préposé, e. ¶ *v.t*, encadrer. **official**, *a*, officiel; d'office. ~ *statement* (to press), communiqué,
m. ¶ *n*, fonctionnaire, *m,f*, préposé, e; (*sport*, *etc.*) officiel, *m*.
~**dom** & ~**ism**, *n*, fonctionnarisme, *m*. **officiate**, *v.i*, (*Eccl.*)
officier; exercer les fonctions (*as
=* de). **officious**, *a*, touche-à-
tout; (*diplomacy*) officieux. ~
person, touche-à-tout, *m*, personne qui se mêle des oignons
des autres, *f.*

offing, *n*, large, *m*. *in the* ~, au
l., dehors.

off-line, *a*, (*computers*) autonome.

offscourings, (*fig.*) *n.pl*, lie, *f*,
bas-fonds, *m.pl*.

offset, *n*, compensation, *f*; (*Hort.*)
rejeton, œilleton; (*Arch.*) ressaut, *m*. ~ *process*, offset, *m.*

offshoot, *n*, rejeton, *m.*

offspring, *n*, rejeton, *m*; progéniture, *f.*

often & (*Poet.*) **oft**, *ad*, souvent.
how often? combien de fois?

ogee, *n*, doucine, *f*. **ogive**, *n*,
ogive, *f.*

ogle, *n*, œillade, *f*. ¶ *v.t*, lorgner,
reluquer.

ogre, **ogress**, *n*, ogre, *m*, ogresse,
f.

oh, *i*, oh!; ô!; ah!

oil, *n*, huile, *f*; pétrole, *m*; essence,
f. ~ *can*, (*storage*) bidon à huile,
m; (*nozzled*) burette à h., *f.*
~*cloth*, (*table*, *etc.*) toile cirée,
moleskine, *f*; (*floor*) linoléum,
m. ~ *color*, ~ *paint*, couleur à
l'huile, *f*. ~ *engine*, moteur à pétrole, *m*. ~ *field*, champ de pétrole, *m*. ~ *fuel*, mazout, pétrole
combustible, *m*. ~ *heater*, poêle
à pétrole, *m*. ~ *hole*, trou de
graissage, *m*, lumière, *f*. ~ *painting*, peinture à l'huile, *f*. ~
shares, valeurs de pétrole, *f.pl*. ~
skin, toile huile, *f*; (*garment*) ciré,
m. ~ *slick*, marée noire, *f*. ~
stone, pierre à huile, *f*. ~ *stove*,
fourneau à pétrole, *m*. ~ *varnish*,
vernis gras, *m*. ~ *well*, puits de pétrole, *m*. ¶ *v.t*, graisser [à l'huile],
huiler. ~**y**, *a*, huileux; onctueux;
oléagineux.

ointment, *n*, onguent, *m.*

okay, **o.k.**, *i*, d'accord, d'ac, dac;
très bien.

old, *a*, vieux; ancien. *how* ~ *is
he*? *he is 10 years* ~, quel âge
a-t-il? il a 10 ans. *the* ~, (*opp.
new*) le vieux; (*people*) les vieux,
m.pl. ~ & *young*, grands & petits.
of ~, jadis, anciennement. ~ *age*,
la vieillesse; (*decay*) vétusté, *f*.
~ *age pension fund*, caisse de retraites pour la vieillesse, *f*. ~
clothes, vieilles hardes, nippes, *f*.
pl. ~*established*, fort ancien. ~-
fashioned, à l'ancienne mode;
passé de mode, démodé; arriéré;
gothique. ~ *gold*, vieil or, *m*. ~
guard (*Mil.*), garde descendante,
f. ~ *maid*, vieille fille, *f*. ~ *man*,
vieillard, vieux; (*in comedy*) géronte, *m*. ~ *master* (*art*), ancien
maître, *m*. ~ *offender*, récidiviste,
m,f, repris de justice, cheval de
retour, *m*. ~ *salt* (sailor), loup
de mer, *m*. *the same* ~ *story*, la
même histoire, la même guitare.
O~ Testament, Ancien Testament, *m*. ~ *things*, vieilleries,
f.pl. *the good* ~ *times*, le bon
vieux temps. ~ *woman*, vieille

[femme] *f. the O~ Woman who lived in a shoe*, la mère Gigogne. **in the ~en time**, au temps jadis. **~ish**, *a*, vieillot.

oleaginous, *a*, oléagineux.

oleander, *n*, laurier-rose, oléandre, *m*.

olfactory, *a*, olfactif.

oligarchy, *n*, oligarchie, *f*.

olive, *n*, olive, *f.~ [tree, wood]*, olivier, *m. ~* (complexion) *a, olivâtre. ~[-green]*, vert olive, couleur [d']olive. *~ grove*, olivaie, *f. ~ oil*, huile d'olive, *f*.

Olympic games, jeux olympiques, *m.pl*. **Olympus** (fig.) *n*, olympe, *m*.

omega, *n*, oméga, *m*.

omelet, *n*, omelette, *f*.

omen, *n*, augure, présage, auspice, pronostic, *m*. **ominous**, *a*, de mauvais augure; sinistre; menaçant.

omission, *n*, omission, *f*. **omit**, *v.t*, omettre.

omnibus, *n*, omnibus, *m*.

omnipotence, *n*, omnipotence, toute-puissance, *f*. **omnipotent**, *a*, omnipotent, tout-puissant. *the Omnipotent*, le Tout-Puissant. **omniscience**, *n*, omniscience, *f*. **omniscient**, *a*, omniscient.

omnivorous, *a*, omnivore.

on, *pr*, sur; à; de; en; après; par; pour; sous. *~ & after*, à partir de, à dater de. *~ hand*, (orders) en carnet, en portefeuille; (cash) en caisse, disponible. *~ leave*, en congé. ¶ *ad*, dessus; en avant. *~ that*, là-dessus.

once, *ad*, une fois; une seule fois. *at ~*, tout de suite; à la fois. *~ again*, *~ more*, encore une fois, encore un coup. *~ for all*, une fois pour toutes. *~ upon a time*, il y avait (*ou* il était) une fois, autrefois.

one, *a*, un; seul; unique. *~-act play*, pièce en un acte, *f*, acte, *m*, *~-armed & ~-handed* (person), manchot, ote. *~-eyed*, borgne. *~-man band*, homme-orchestre, *m*. *~-price shop*, magasin à prix unique, *m*. *~-self*, soi, soi-même. *~-sided*, unilatéral; (fig.) léonin. *~-way street*, rue à sens unique, *f*. *~-way traffic*, circulation à s. u., *f*. ¶ *n*, un, *m*; unité, *f*. ¶ *pn*, celui, celle; quelqu'un, e; on; un(e) nommé(e), un(e) certain(e). *~ & all*, tous sans ex-

ception. *~ another*, l'un(e) l'autre; les uns (les unes) les autres; se. *~ by ~ or ~ after another*, un à un, une à une. *he is ~ of us*, il est des nôtres. *~ness*, *n*, unité, *f*.

onerous, *a*, onéreux.

one's, *pn*, son, sa, ses. **oneself**, *pn*, soi-même; soi; se; son individu.

onion, *n*, oignon, *m. ~ bed*, oignonière, *f. ~ sauce*, sauce à l'oignon, *f. ~ skin*, *~ peel*, pelure d'oignon, *f*.

on-line, *a*, (computers) en direct, en ligne, connecté.

onlooker, *n*, assistant, e, spectateur, trice, curieux, *m*.

only, *a*, seul, unique, tout. ¶ *ad*, seulement, rien que, ne . . . guère; uniquement.

onomatopoeia, *n*, onomatopée, *f*.

onset, **onrush**, **onslaught**, *n*, attaque, ruée, *f*, assaut, choc, *m*.

onus, *n*, charge, *f. ~ of proof*, charge de la preuve.

onward, *a*, progressif. *~[s]*, *ad*, en avant; plus loin.

onyx, *n*, onyx, *m*.

ooze, *n*, vase, *f*, limon; suintement, *m*. ¶ *v.i*, suinter, suer. *~ out*, transpirer.

opacity, *n*, opacité, *f*.

opal, *n*, opale, *f. ~ine*, *a*, opalin.

opaque, *a*, opaque. *~ness*, *n*, opacité, *f*.

open, *v.t*, ouvrir; percer; entamer; écarter; découvrir; exposer; inaugurer; (bottle) déboucher; (oysters) écailler; (Med.) débonder; (v.i.) ouvrir; s'o.; (flowers) s'épanouir. *~ sesame*, Sésame, ouvre-toi. ¶ *a*, ouvert; découvert, à découvert; exposé; ostensible; libre; franc; (boat) non ponté. *in the ~* [air], en plein air, au grand air, à ciel ouvert. *the ~* [country], la pleine campagne, la rase c. *in the open* (publicly), au grand jour. *~-handed*, libéral. *~-hearted*, franc. *~ house*, table ouverte, *f. ~-mouthed*, bouche béante, b. bée. *in the ~ sea*, en pleine (*ou* haute) mer, au large. *~ space*, terre-plein, franc-bord, *m. ~ warfare*, guerre de mouvement, *f. ~[work]*, *att*, à jour, ajouré, à claire-voie. *~work* (Need.) *n*, (les) jours, *m.pl. ~er*, *n*, ouvreur, euse. **~ing**, *n*, ouverture; percée; éclaircie; (*neck*) échancrure; introduction, *f*; débouché, *m*; occasion, *f*. ¶ *a*, initial; d'ouverture; de début; préliminaire; premier. **~ly**, *ad*, ouvertement; ostensiblement; hautement; franchement. **~ness**, *n*, franchise, candeur, *f*.

opera, *n*. & **~ house**, opéra, *m*. **~ cloak**, sortie de bal, *s*. de théâtre, *f*. **~ glass[es]**, jumelle[s] de théâtre, lorgnette[s] de spectacle, *f*.[*pl*.]. **~ hat**, [chapeau] claque, *m*.

operate, *v.t*, opérer; exploiter; (*v.i*.) opérer, agir; jouer. **~ on** (*Surg*.), opérer.

operatic, *a*, d'opéra; lyrique.

operating room *or* **theater**, salle d'opération, *f*. **operation**, *n*, opération; exploitation, *f*. **operative**, *n*, ouvrier, ère, artisan, e. ¶ *a*, actif, efficace. **operator**, *n*, opérateur, trice.

operetta, *n*, opérette, *f*.

ophthalmia, *n*, ophtalmie, *f*. **ophthalmic**, *a*, ophtalmique.

opiate, *n*, narcotique, *m*. **~d**, *a*, opiacé.

opine, *v.i*, opiner. **opinion**, *n*, opinion, voix, *f*; sentiment, avis, sens, *m*; (*legal*) consultation, *f*. **~ated**, *a*, opiniâtre.

opium, *n*, opium, *m*. **~ addict**, opiomane, *m.f*. **~ den**, fumerie, *f*. **~ poppy**, pavot somnifère, *m*.

opossum, *n*, opossum, *m*; sarigue, *m.f*.

opponent, *n*, opposant, e, adversaire, antagoniste, *m*. ¶ *a*, opposant.

opportune, *a*, opportun, à propos. **~ly**, *ad*, opportunément, à propos. **~ness**, *n*, opportunité, *f*, à-propos, *m*. **opportunism**, *n*, opportunisme, *m*. **opportunist**, *n*, opportuniste, *m.f*. **opportunity**, *n*, occasion; opportunité, *f*.

oppose, *v.t*, opposer, s'opposer à; combattre. **~d**, *p.p*, opposé, contraire. **opposing**, *p.a*, opposant, adverse. **opposite**, *n*, opposé, contraire, contre-pied, *m*. **~ (to)**, *a*, *pr*, *ad*, opposé; en face (de), vis-à-vis (de), en regard (de), contraire (à); (*sex*) opposé. **opposition**, *n*, opposition; résistance, *f*.

oppress, *v.t*, opprimer; oppresser (*Med*. & *fig*.). **~ion**, *n*, oppression, *f*. **~ive**, *a*, oppressif, assommant. **~or**, *n*, oppresseur, *m*.

opprobrious, *a*, infamant, injurieux. **opprobrium**, *n*, opprobre, *m*.

optic, *a*, optique. **~al**, *a*, optique; (*glass*, *instruments*, *illusion*), d'optique. **optician**, *n*, opticien; lunetier, *m*. **optics**, *n*, optique, *f*.

optimism, *n*, optimisme, *m*. **optimist**, *n*. & **~(ic)**, *a*, optimiste, *m,f*. & *a*.

option, *n*, option; alternative, *f*, choix, *m*; (*Stk Ex*.) prime, *f*. **~al†**, *a*, facultatif.

opulence, *n*, opulence, *f*. **opulent**, *a*, opulent.

or, *c*, ou; soit; (*neg*.) ni. **~ else**, ou bien, autrement. *2 ~ 3 times a day*, de 2 à 3 fois par jour.

oracle, *n*, oracle, *m*.

oral†, *a*, oral. **~ examination**, examen oral, *m*.

orange, *n*, orange, *f*; (*color*) orange, *m*, orangé, *m*. ¶ *a*, orange, orangé. **~ [tree]**, oranger, *m*. **~ blossom**, fleurs d'oranger, *f.pl*. **~ marmalade**, confitures d'oranges, *f.pl*. **~ peel**, pelure d'orange, écorce d'o., *f*. **~ade**, *n*, orangeade, *f*. **~ry**, *n*, orangerie, *f*.

orangutan, *n*, orang-outang, *m*.

oration, *n*, discours, *m*; (*funeral*) oraison, *f*. **orator**, *n*, orateur, *m*. **~ical**, *a*, oratoire. **oratorio**, *n*, oratorio, *m*. **oratory**, *n*, l'art oratoire, *m*, éloquence, *f*; (*chapel*) oratoire, *m*.

orb, *n*, globe, *m*, sphère, *f*, orbe, *m*. **orbit**, *n*, orbite, *f*.

ore, *n*, orque, *f*, épaulard, *m*.

orchard, *n*, verger, *m*.

orchestra, *n*, orchestre, *m*. **~ seat**, fauteuil d'orchestre, *m*. **orchestral**, *a*, orchestral. **orchestrate**, *v.t*, orchestrer.

orchid, *n*, orchidée, *f*.

ordain, *v.t*, ordonner; décréter; prescrire.

ordeal, *n*, épreuve; (*Hist*.) ordalie, *f*.

order, *n*, ordre, *m*; règle, *f*; état, *m*; classe, *f*; classement, *m*; commande, *f*; mandat, bon, permis; arrêté, *m*; décoration; (*pl*, *Mil*.) ordres, *m.pl*, consigne, *f*. **~! à l'ordre!** *in ~ that*, afin que, pour que. *in ~ to*, afin de. **~ book**, livre (*ou* carnet) de commandes, *m*. **~ form**, bon (*ou* bulletin) de commande, *m.* out of ~, (*Mach.*) en panne. ¶ *v.t,* ordonner; statuer; régler; charger; (*goods*) commander; (*arms*, *Mil.*) reposer. ~ing, *n,* ordonnance, disposition, *f.* ~ly, *a,* ordonné, rangé, régulier. ¶ *n,* (*Mil.*) ordonnance, *f.* or *m,* planton, *m;* (*hospital*) infirmier, *m.* on ~ *duty,* de planton. ~ *officer,* officier d'ordonnance, *m.* ~ *room,* salle du rapport, *f.*

ordinal [number], *n,* nombre ordinal, *m.*

ordinance, *n,* décret, *m;* (*law*) ordonnance, *f.*

ordinary†, *a,* ordinaire; commun; normal. ~ *seaman,* simple matelot, matelot de troisième classe, *m.*

ordination, *n,* ordination, *f.*

ordnance, *n,* artillerie, *f;* matériel de guerre, *m.* ~ [*survey*] *map,* carte d'État-major, *f.*

ore, *n,* mineral, *m.*

organ, *n,* organe; (*Mus.*) orgue, *m.* ~ *grinder,* joueur d'orgue de Barbarie, *m.* ~ *loft,* tribune d'orgues, *f.* ~ *pipe,* tuyau d'orgue, *m.*

organdie, *n,* organdi, *m.*

organic, *a,* organique. **organism,** *n,* organisme, *m.* **organization,** *n,* organisation; (*fête*) ordonnance, *f.* **organize,** *v.t,* organiser; ordonner; policer. **organizer,** *n,* organisateur, trice; ordonnateur, trice.

orgy, *n,* orgie, *f.*

orient, *n,* orient, *m.* the O~ (*Geog.*), l'O. ~al, *a,* oriental. O~, *n,* Oriental, e. ~[ate], *v.t,* orienter.

orifice, *n,* orifice, *m,* ouverture, *f.*

oriflamme, *n,* oriflamme, *f.*

origin, *n,* origine; provenance, *f.* ~al†, *a,* (*not copied*) original; (*primitive*) originaire, originel. ¶ *n,* original, *m.* ~ality, *n,* originalité, *f.* ~ate, *v.t,* prendre l'initiative de; (*v.i.*) tirer son origine, dériver. **originator,** *n,* auteur, *m.*

oriole (*bird*) *n,* loriot, *m.*

Orleans, *n,* Orléans, *m.* or *f.*

ormolu, *n,* or moulu, *m.*

ornament, *n,* ornement, *m;* parure, *f.* ¶ *v.t,* orner, agrémenter. ~al, *a,* ornemental; d'ornement; d'agrément. **ornamentation,** *n,* ornementation, *f.* **ornate,** *a,* orné; imagé.

ornithologist, *n,* ornithologiste,

ornithologue, *m.f.* **ornithology,** *n,* ornithologie, *f.*

orphan, *n.* & *a,* orphelin, e. ~age (*asylum*) *n,* orphelinat, *m.*

orrery, *n,* planétaire, *m.*

orris root, racine d'iris, *f.*

orthodox, *a,* orthodoxe; catholique. ~y, *n,* orthodoxie, *f.* **orthography,** *n,* orthographe, *f.* **orthopedic,** *a,* orthopédique. **orthopedy,** *n,* orthopédie, *f.*

ortolan, *n,* ortolan, *m.*

oscillate, *v.i,* osciller; (*v.t.*) faire osciller. **oscillation,** *n,* oscillation, *f.*

osier, *n,* osier, *m.* ~ *bed,* oseraie, *f.*

osmium, *n,* osmium, *m.*

osprey, *n,* orfraie, *f.*

osseous, *a,* osseux. **ossicle,** *n,* osselet, *m.* **ossify,** *v.t,* ossifier. **ossuary,** *n,* ossuaire, charnier, *m.*

Ostend, *n,* Ostende, *m.*

ostensible, *a,* avoué. **ostensibly,** *ad,* en apparence, sous prétexte.

ostensory, *n,* ostensoir, *m.* **ostentation,** *n,* ostentation, *f,* faste, *m.* **ostentatious,** *a,* ostentateur, ostentatoire, fastueux.

ostracism, *n,* ostracisme, *m.* **ostracize,** *v.t,* frapper d'ostracisme.

ostrich, *n,* autruche, *f.* ~ *feather,* plume d'autruche, *f.*

other, *a.* & *pn,* autre. every ~ *day,* tous les deux jours. the ~ *side* (opinion, pers.), la contrepartie. on the ~ *side* or *hand,* de l'autre côté. ~s, ~ *people,* les autres, d'autres, autrui. ~wise, *ad,* autrement, sinon, sans quoi, sans cela.

otter, *n,* loutre, *f.*

Ottoman, *a,* ottoman. ¶ *n,* Ottoman, e. o~, *n,* ottomane, *f.*

oubliette, *n,* oubliettes, *f.pl.*

ought, *v.aux.ir,* devoir; falloir.

ounce, *n,* (*Zool.*) once; (*Meas.*) once, *f:* (*avoirdupois*) = 28.350 grams; (*troy* & *apothecaries' weight*) = 31.1035 grams; (*apothecaries' measure*) = 2.84123 centiliters.

our, *a,* notre, nos, *pl.* Our Lady, Notre-Dame, *f.* Our Lord, Notre-Seigneur, *m.* ~s, *pn,* le nôtre, la nôtre, les nôtres; nos; à nous; de nous. **ourselves,** *pn,* nous-mêmes; nous.

oust, *v.t,* débusquer, dégommer; évincer, déposséder.

out, *ad.* & *pr.* dehors; hors; sorti,

absent, en course; en fleur; paru; éteint. ~ & *out*, franc, fieffé, achevé, renforcé, à tous crins, à outrance, outrancier. ~ *loud*, tout haut. ~[, *see copy*] (*Typ.*), bourdon, *m.* ~ *there*, là-dehors. **out of**, *comps*: ~ *action*, hors de combat. ~ *bounds*, hors des limites. ~ *breath*, à bout de souffle. ~ *date*, suranné, démodé; (*ticket, etc.*) périmé. ~ *doors*, dehors, au grand air. ~ *fashion*, passé de mode, démodé. ~ *hand*, sur-le-champ; échappé à tout contrôle. ~ *one's element*, hors de son élément, dépaysé. ~ *one's reckoning*, loin de compte. ~ *order*, (*Mech.*) en panne. ~ *place* (*fig.*), déplacé, hors de propos. ~ *pocket*, en perte. ~ *practice*, rouillé. ~ *print*, épuisé. ~ *shape*, avachi. ~ *sight*, hors de vue. ~ *sorts*, indisposé, dolent. *to be* ~ *stock of*, être à court de, manquer de. ~ *the common*, hors ligne. *out-of-the-way*, *a*, écarté, retiré, reculé. ~ *tune*, faux. *to be out* [*of work*], être sans travail, chômer. **out**, *i*, dehors! hors d'ici! (*Box.*) dehors! ~ *with him!* à la porte! ~ *with it!* achevez donc!

outbid, *v.t.ir*, [r]enchérir sur, surenchérir sur.

outboard, *ad*, hors bord. ~ *motor*, propulseur amovible, *m*.

outbreak, *n*, début, *m*; (*riot*) émeute; (*disease*) épidémie, *f*. ~ *of fire*, incendie, *m*. *at the* ~ *of war*, quand la guerre éclata.

outbuilding, *n*, dépendance, *f*.

outburst, *n*, débordement, emportement, déchaînement, élan, accès, *m*, poussée, explosion; incartade, *f*.

outcast, *n*, déclassé, e, réprouvé, e, paria, homme sans aveu, *m*.

outcaste, *n*, paria, *m*.

outcome, *n*, conséquence, issue, *f*, résultat, *m*.

outcry, *n*, cri, *m*, clameur, *f*.

outdistance, *v.t*, distancer.

outdo, *v.t.ir*, surpasser; l'emporter sur; devancer.

outdoor, *a*, en plein air, au grand air, de plein air.

outer, *a*, extérieur. ~ *harbor*, avant-port, *m*.

outfall, *n*, décharge, *f*; (*mouth*) débouché, *m*.

outfit, *n*, équipement, équipage, nécessaire, trousseau, *m*, trousse,

f. **outfitter**, *n*, maison pour fournitures (*de sports, etc.*) *f*; confectionneur, euse.

outflank, *v.t*, déborder.

outflow, *n*, écoulement, *m*, décharge, *f*.

outgoing, *a*, sortant, de sortie, de départ, au départ; (*tide*) descendante. ~**s**, *n.pl*, débours, déboursés, *m.pl*.

outgrow, *v.t.ir*, devenir trop grand pour; se guérir de.

outhouse, *n*, dépendance, *f*; appentis, *m*.

outing, *n*, course, excursion, promenade, *f*.

outlandish, *a*, bizarre.

outlast, *v.t*, durer plus longtemps que.

outlaw, *n*, proscrit, e. ¶ *v.t*, proscrire, mettre hors la loi. ~**ry**, *n*, proscription, *f*.

outlay, *n*, débours, déboursés, *m.pl*.

outlet, *n*, issue, sortie, *f*; débouché, *m*.

outline, *n*, contour, tracé, crayon, galbe, canevas, aperçu, *m*, esquisse, ébauche, *f*. ~ *drawing*, dessin au trait, *m*. ¶ *v.t*, établir les grandes lignes de, tracer, dessiner, crayonner, esquisser.

outlive, *v.t*, survivre à, enterrer.

outlook, *n*, perspective, vue, *f*; avenir, *m*.

outlying, *a*, éloigné; avancé; excentrique.

outmaneuver, *v.t*, déjouer.

outnumber, *v.t*, surpasser en nombre.

outpatient, *n*, malade du dehors, *m.f*.

outpost, *n*, avant-poste, *m*.

outpouring, *n*, épanchement, *m*, effusion, *f*.

output, *n*, rendement, *m*, production, *f*.

outrage, *n*, outrage, *m*, indignité, *f*; attentat, *m*. ¶ *v.t*, outrager, faire outrage à; violer. ~**ous**†, *a*, indigne; odieux; pendable; sanglant; énorme.

outrider, *n*, piqueur, *m*.

outrigger, *n*, (*boat*) outrigger; (*for rowlocks*) porte-en-dehors, *m*.

outright, *a*, fieffé. ¶ *ad*, net, carrément; (*opp. by installments*) en une [seule] fois.

outrival, *v.t*, devancer.

outrun, *v.t*, dépasser à la course.

outset, *n*, début, *m*, origine, *f*.

outshine, *v.t.ir*, éclipser.

outside, *a*, extérieur. ¶ *ad*, [en] dehors, là-dehors, à l'extérieur. ¶ *n*, extérieur, dehors, *m*; (*café*) terrasse, *f*. at the ~, tout au plus. **outsider**, *n*, (*pers.*) profane, *m,f*; (*horse*) outsider, *m*.

outsize, *n*, taille hors série, *f*.

outskirts, *n.pl*, environs, entours, *m.pl*; banlieue, *f*.

outspoken, *a*, franc. ~**ness**, *n*, franchise, liberté [de langage], liberté de parole, *f*.

outspread, *a*, étendu.

outstanding, *a*, (*Fin.*) à payer; arriéré; en suspens; marquant, saillant.

outstretched, *a*, étendu.

outstrip, *v.t*, devancer.

outward, *a*, extérieur; d'aller; de sortie. ~ *bound*, en partance; effectuant son voyage d'aller. ~[s], *ad*, en dehors.

outwit, *v.t*, déjouer, circonvenir, tromper.

oval, *a. & n*, ovale, *a. & m*.

ovary, *n*, ovaire, *m*.

ovation, *n*, ovation, *f*.

oven, *n*, four, *m*; (*fig.*) étuve, *f*.

over, *ad*, dessus; par-dessus; au-dessus; davantage, en sus; trop; fini; passé. ~ *again*, de nouveau, encore une fois. ~ & *above*, en sus de. ~ *there*, là-bas. ¶ *pr*, sur; par-dessus; au-dessus de; plus de; en sus de; de l'autre côté de; par. ~ *all* (*Meas.*), hors tout.

overact, *v.t*, charger.

overalls, *n*, salopette, *f*.

overarm stroke, coupe, *f*.

overassess, *v.t*, surimposer, surtaxer. **overassessment**, *n*, surimposition, surtaxe, *f*.

overawe, *v.t*, intimider.

overbalance, *v.i*, perdre l'équilibre.

overbearing, *a*, insolent, arrogant, excédent.

overboard (*Naut.*) *ad*, par-dessus bord. [*a*] *man* ~! un homme à la mer!

overbooking, *n*, (*hotel, airline*) surréservation, *f*.

overburden, (*Min.*) *n*, terrains de couverture, *m.pl*. ¶ *v.t*, surcharger.

overcast, *a*, couvert, chargé, trouble. ¶ *v.t.ir*, obscurcir. ¶ (*Emb.*) *n*, cordonnet, *m*.

overcautious, *a*, prudent à l'excès.

overcharge, *n*, majoration, *f*. ¶ *v.t. & i*, surcharger; faire payer trop cher, écorcher; (*weapon*) charger trop.

overcoat, *n*, pardessus, *m*; (*Mil.*) capote, *f*.

overcome, *v.t.ir*, surmonter, vaincre; accabler.

overcrowd, *v.t*, encombrer.

overdo, *v.t.ir*, outrer, charger. **overdone**, *a*, exagéré, outré; (*Cook.*) trop cuit.

overdose, *n*, trop forte dose, *f*.

overdraft, *n*, découvert, *m*, avance à découvert, *f*. **overdraw**, *v.t.ir*, mettre à découvert; tirer un chèque sans provisions.

overdrive, *v.t.ir*, surmener.

overdue, *a*, arriéré, en retard.

overelaborate, *v.t*, tourmenter, fignoler, lécher.

overestimate, *v.t*, surestimer, surfaire, majorer.

overexcite, *v.t*, surexciter.

overexposure (*Phot.*) *n*, surexposition, *f*.

overfeed, *v.t.ir*, trop nourrir; suralimenter.

overflow, *n*, débordement; trop-plein, *m*. ¶ *v.i*, [se] déborder; surabonder.

overgrow, *v.t.ir*, envahir. **overgrown**, *p.a*, couvert, encombré; trop grand. **overgrowth**, *n*, surcroissance, *f*.

overhang, *n*, surplomb, porte à faux, *m*. ¶ *v.i. & t.ir*, surplomber.

overhaul, *n*, (*engine, etc.*) revision, *f*. ¶ *v.t*, reviser; visiter; examiner; remettre à point.

overhead, *a*, aérien; de plafond; au-dessus; en haut. ~*charges*, frais généraux, *m.pl*. ¶ *ad*, au-dessus de la tête; en haut, en l'air, au ciel.

overhear, *v.t.ir*, entendre par hasard.

overheat, *v.t*, surchauffer.

overindulgence, *n*, excès d'indulgence, *m*, mollesse; gâterie, *f*.

overjoyed, *p.p*, comblé de joie, ravi.

overladen, *p.p*, surchargé.

overland, *ad. & a*, par terre, de terre.

overlap, *v.t. & i*, chevaucher, recouvrir, déborder, imbriquer.

overleaf, *ad*, au verso.

overload, *v.t*, surcharger.

overlook, *v.t*, donner sur; dominer; laisser échapper; oublier, négliger.

overmantel, n, étagère de cheminée, f.

overmatter (*newspaper work*) n, marbre, m.

overmuch, ad, [par] trop, à l'excès.

overnight, ad, pendant la nuit; la veille au soir.

overpay, v.t.ir, surpayer, trop payer.

over-polite, a, révérencieux.

overpower, v.t, maîtriser; accabler. ~ing, a, accablant; tout-puissant.

overprint, v.t, surimprimer, surcharger. ¶ n, surimpression, surcharge, f.

overproduction, n, surproduction, f.

overrate, v.t, surestimer, surfaire.

overreach, v.t, dépasser; circonvenir.

override, v.t.ir, surmener; primer.

overripe, a, trop mûr, blet.

overrule, v.t, écarter; l'emporter sur; gouverner.

overrun, v.t.ir, envahir; infester; (*Typ.*) remanier.

oversea[s], a, d'outre-mer. ¶ ad, outre-mer.

overseer, n, surveillant, inspecteur, m.

oversewing stitch, [point de] surjet, m.

overshadow, v.t, ombrager; obscurcir, éclipser.

overshoe, n, caoutchouc, m.

overshoot, v.t.ir, dépasser.

oversight, n, inadvertance, f, oubli, m, méprise; surveillance, f.

overspread, v.t.ir, se répandre sur.

overstate, v.t, exagérer.

overstaying pass (*Mil.*), retardataire, a.

overstep, v.t, outrepasser, franchir.

overstock, v.t, encombrer [de].

overstrain, v.t, outrer; surmener.

overtraining, n, surentraînement, m.

overt₁, a, manifeste.

overtake, v.t.ir, rattraper, surprendre, atteindre, gagner; (*auto*) doubler.

overtax, v.t, surtaxer, surimposer; surcharger.

overthrow, v.t.ir, renverser, bouleverser, subvertir.

overtime, n, heures supplémentaires, f.pl.

overtop, v.t, surpasser, surmonter.

overture, n, ouverture, f.

overturn, v.t, [ren]verser, [faire] chavirer; (*auto*) capoter.

overvalue, v.t, surestimer, surfaire, majorer.

overweening, a, outrecuidant.

overweight, n, poids fort, excédent de poids, m.

overwhelm, v.t, accabler, atterrer, assommer; combler.

overwork, v.t, surmener, forcer.

ovine, a, ovine, a.f.

oviparous, a, ovipare.

owe, v.t, devoir, être redevable de. **owing**, a, dû, échu; arriéré.

owl, n, hibou, m, chouette, f.

own, a, propre; (*brother, sister*) germain, e. *not my* ~, pas à moi, pas le mien. *one's* ~, son [propre]; à soi. ¶ v.t, posséder; reconnaître; avouer. **owner**, n, propriétaire, m,f; possesseur; (*ship's manager*) armateur; (*ship's proprietor*) propriétaire, m. ~*-driver*, propriétaire-conducteur, m. ~ship, n, propriété, f.

ox, n, bœuf, m. ~*eye daisy*, grande marguerite, f. **oxford**, n, (*shoe*) richelieu, m.

oxide, n, oxyde, m. **oxidize**, v.t, oxyder. **oxygen**, n, oxygène, m. **oxyhydrogen** (*blowpipe, etc.*) att, oxhydrique.

oyster, n, huître, f. ~ *bed*, banc d'h—s; parc à h—s, m. ~ *culture*, ostréiculture, f. ~*man*, ~*woman*, écailler, ère.

ozone, n, ozone, m.

P

pace, n, pas, m; allure, f; train, m. *to keep* ~ *with*, marcher du même pas que; (*fig.*) marcher de pair avec. ~*maker*, meneur de train, entraîneur, m. ¶ v.t, arpenter; entraîner.

pachyderm, n, pachyderme, m.

pacific, a, pacifique. P~ [Ocean], [océan] Pacifique, m. **pacificist**, **pacifist**, n. & att, pacifiste, m,f. & a. **pacify**, v.t, pacifier. **pacifying**, p.a, pacificateur.

pack, n, ballot, m, paquet; (*soldier's*) paquetage, m; bande, f, tas, m; (*hounds*) meute, f; (*cards*) jeu, *m*; (*ice*) banquise, *f*. ~**horse**, cheval de bât, *m*. ~**saddle**, bât, *m*. ~**thread**, ficelle, *f*. ¶ *v.t*, emballer, empaqueter; (*hounds*) ameuter. ~ [*up*], plier (*ou* trousser) bagage, faire ses malles. ~**age**, *n*, colis; envoi; (*computers*) progiciel, *m*. ~**ed**, *p.a*, ~ *like sardines* (*people*), rangés comme des harengs en caque. ~**er**, *n*, emballeur, *m*. ~**et**, *n*, paquet; envoi, *m*; pochette, *f*. ~ [*boat*], paquebot, *m*. ~**ing**, *n*, emballage, *m*; garniture, *f*. ~ *case*, caisse d'emballage, *f*.

pact, *n*, pacte; contrat, *m*; convention, *f*.

pad, *n*, coussinet, bourrelet; (*for carrier's head*) tortillon; (*stamp*) tampon; (*blotting*) sous-main; (*writing*) bloc-notes, bloc de correspondance, *m*. ¶ *v.t*, [rem]bourrer, matelasser, feutrer, ouater; tamponner; (*verses*) cheviller. *padded cell*, cabanon, *m*. **padding**, *n*, [rem]bourrage, *m*; bourre, *f*.

paddle (*canoe*) *n*, pagaie, *f*. ~ *wheel*, roue à aubes, *f*. ¶ *v.i*, pagayer; (*splash about*) barboter.

paddock, *n*, enclos, paddock, *m*; (*turf*) enceinte du pesage, *f*, pesage, *m*.

padlock, *n*, cadenas, *m*. ¶ *v.t*, cadenasser.

Padua, *n*, Padoue, *f*.

paean, *n*, péan, pæan, *m*.

pagan, *a. & n*, païen, ne. ~**ism &** ~**dom**, *n*, paganisme, *m*.

page, *n*, (*book*) page, *f*; (*Hist.*, *noble youth*) page, *m*. ~ [*boy*], chasseur, *m*. ~ *proof*, mise en pages, *f*. *the front* ~, la Une. ¶ *v.t*, paginer; (*have called*) envoyer chercher par un chasseur.

pageant, *n*, scène à grand spectacle, *f*; cortège [à spectacle] *m*, cavalcade, *f*. ~**ry**, *n*, faste, *m*.

paid, *p.p*, payé; versé; [pour] acquit; salarié, à gages. ~ *up*, (*capital*) versé, effectif, réel; (*shares*) libérées.

pail, *n*, seau, *m*. ~[**ful**], *n*, seau, *m*.

pain, *n*, douleur, souffrance, *f*, mal, *m*; peine, *f. in* ~, souffrant. *to take* ~ *s*, se donner du mal. ~ *killer*, antalgique, *m*. ¶ *v.t*, faire mal à; angoisser, peiner, fâcher.

~**ful†**, *a*, douloureux; dolent; pénible; cruel. ~**less**, *a*, sans douleur, indolent, indolore. **pains**, *n.pl*, peine, *f*, soin, *m*, frais, *m.pl*. ~**taking**, *a*, soigneux.

paint, *n*, peinture, couleur, *f*; (*face*) fard, *m*. ~**brush**, brosse à peindre, pinceau, *m*. ¶ *v.t*, peindre; (*face*) farder. *to* ~ *the town red*, faire la bombe. ~**er**, *n*, peintre, *m*; (*boat*) bosse, *f*. ~**ing**, *n*, peinture, *f*.

pair, *n*, paire, *f*; couple, *m*. ~ *of scissors*, ciseaux, *m.pl*. ~ *of trousers*, pantalon, *m*. *the* ~ (*pictures, etc.*), les [deux] pendants, *m.pl*. ¶ *v.t*, apparier, appareiller, accoupler, jumeler.

pajamas, *n.pl*, pyjama, *m*.

pal, *n*, copain, *m*.

palace, *n*, palais, *m*.

paladin, *n*, paladin, *m*.

palatable, *a*, agréable [au goût], bon. **palatal**, *a*, palatal. **palate**, *n*, palais, *m*.

palatial, *a*, vaste & somptueux.

palaver, *n*, palabre, *f. or m*. ¶ *v.i*, palabrer.

pale, *a*, pâle; blafard, blême; clairet, paillet. ¶ *n*, palis; pal, *m*. ¶ *v.i*, pâlir, blêmir. ~**ness**, *n*, pâleur, *f*.

paleography, *n*, paléographie, *f*.

paleontology, *n*, paléontologie, *f*.

Palermo, *n*, Palerme, *f*.

palette, *n*, palette, *f*. ~ *knife*, couteau à palette, *m*.

paling, *n*, palis, *m*; clôture à claire-voie, *f*.

palisade, *n*, palissade, *f*. ¶ *v.t*, palissader.

palish, *a*, pâlot.

pall, *n*, poêle, drap mortuaire, *m*. ~ *bearers*, porteurs des cordons du poêle, *m.pl*. ¶ *v.t. & i*, s'affadir; rendre insipide.

pallet, *n*, palette, *f*; (*bed*) grabat, *m*.

palliasse, *n*, paillasse, *f*.

palliate, *v.t*, pallier. **palliative**, *a. & n*, palliatif, *a. & m*.

pallid, *a*, pâle, blafard, blême. **pallor**, *n*, pâleur, *f*.

palm (*hand*) *n*, paume, *f*. ~ [*branch*], palme, *f*. ~ [*tree*], palmier, *m*, palme, *f*. ~ *grove*, palmeraie, *f*. ~ *oil*, huile de palme, *f*. *P*~ *Sunday*, dimanche des Rameaux, *m*. ~ *off*, faire passer. ~**ist**, *n*, chiromancien, ne.

~istry, *n*, chiromancie, *f*. ~y
days, beaux jours, *m.pl.*

palpable, *a*, palpable, sensible.
palpitate, *v.i*, palpiter. **palpitation**, *n*, palpitation, *f*.

palter, *v.i*, tergiverser; marchander; se jouer. **paltry**, *a*, mesquin,
méchant, chétif, pitoyable.

pampas, *n.pl*, pampas, *f.pl.*

pamper, *v.t*, gâter; dorloter.

pamphlet, *n*, brochure, *f*, pamphlet, *m*.

pan, *n*, poêle; terrine; casserole;
bassine, *f*; (scale) bassin, plateau,
plat, *m*; cuvette, *f*. (cinema) ~
shot, panoramique, survol, *m*.

panacea, *n*, panacée, *f*.

panama, *n*. or Panama hat, panama, *m*.

pancake, *n*, crêpe, *f*.

pancreas, *n*, pancréas, *m*.

pandemonium, *n*, pandémonium; tumulte, *m*.

pander to, se faire le ministre
complaisant de.

Pandora's box, la boîte de Pandore.

pane, *n*, (glass) carreau, *m*, vitre,
f; (side or face) pan, *m*.

panegyric, *n*, panégyrique, *m*.

panel, *n*, panneau; (wall) lambris;
tableau, *m*, liste, *f*. (computers)
control ~, tableau de commande,
m. jury ~, liste des jurés, *f*, jury,
m. ¶ *v.t*, lambrisser.

pang, *n*, serrement de cœur, tourment, *m*, angoisse, *f*; (pl.)affres,
f.pl.

panic, *n*, [terreur] panique, *f*. ¶ *a*,
de panique.

panjandrum, *n*, mamamouchi,
m.

pannier, *n*, panier; *m*; (on back)
hotte, *f*.

pannikin, *n*, petit pot, *m*.

panoply, *n*, panoplie, *f*.

panorama, *n*, panorama, *m*.

pansy, *n*, pensée, *f*.

pant, *v.i*, haleter, panteler. ~**ing**,
p.a, haletant, pantelant.

pantheism, *n*, panthéisme, *m*.

pantheon, *n*, panthéon, *m*.

panther, *n*, panthère, *f*.

pantograph, *n*, pantographe, *m*.

pantomime (dumb show), *n*,
pantomime, *f*. **pantomimist**, *n*,
pantomime, *m,f.*

pantry, *n*, office, *f*, garde-manger,
m.

pants, *n,pl*, pantalon, *m*.

pantyhose, *n*, collant, *m*.

pap, *n*, bouillie; pulpe,*f*; mamelon,
m.

papa, *n*, papa, *m*.

papacy, *n*, papauté, *f*. **papal**, *a*,
papal. ~ nuncio, nonce du Pape,
n. apostolique, *m*.

paper, *n*, papier, *m*; pièce, *f*;
bulletin; (news) journal, *m*,
feuille, *f*; (learned) mémoire, *m*;
(Sch.) composition, copie, *f*. ~
back book, livre de poche, *m*. ~
clip, ~ fastener, attache [de
bureau] *f*. ~hanger, colleur, *m*.
~ knife, coupe-papier, *m*. ~ lantern (Chinese, Japanese), lampion en papier, *m*, lanterne vénitienne, *f*. ~ maker, papetier, ère.
~ making & ~ trade, papeterie, *f*.
~ money, (convertible) monnaie
de papier, *f*; (inconvertible) papier-monnaie, *m*. ~ streamer, serpentin, *m*. ~ weight, presse-papiers, *m*. ¶ *v.t*, tapisser.

papist, *n*, papiste, *m,f.*

papyrus, *n*, papyrus, *m*.

par, *n*, pair, *m*. ~ value, valeur
au pair, *f*.

parable & parabola, *n*, parabole, *f*. **parabolic(al)**†, *a*, en
paraboles; (Geom.) parabolique.

parachute, *n*, parachute. *m*. ~
drop, largage, *m*.

parade, *n*, parade, *f*; défilé; cortège, *m*. ~ ground, place
d'armes, *f*, champ de manœuvres,
m.

paradise, *n*, paradis, *m*; (Eden)
le paradis [terrestre].

paradox, *n*, paradoxe, *m*. ~ical,
a, paradoxal.

paraffin [oil], *n*, huile de pétrole,
f, pétrole à brûler, pétrole lampant, *m*. ~ [wax], *n*, paraffine, *f*.

paragon, *n*, parangon, modèle,
phénix, *m*.

paragraph (abb. par) *n*, paragraphe; alinéa; entrefilet, *m*. new
~, à la ligne.

parallax, *n*, parallaxe, *f*.

parallel†, *a*, parallèle; (drill
shank, etc.) cylindrique; (fig.)
pareil. ~ bars, barres parallèles,
f.pl. ~ ruler, règle à tracer des
parallèles, *f*. ¶ *n*, (Geom., Mil.)
parallèle, *f*; (of latitude) parallèle, *m*; (comparison) parallèle,
pareil, *m*. **parallelepiped**, *n*,
parallélipipède, *m*. **parallelogram**, *n*, parallélogramme, *m*.

paralyze, *v.t,* paralyser; transir. **paralysis,** *n,* paralysie, *f.* **paralytic,** *a.* & *n,* paralytique, *a.* & *m, f.* ~ *stroke,* attaque de paralysie, *f.*

paramount, *a,* suprême; suzerain.

paramour, *n,* amant, *m,* maîtresse, *f.*

parapet, *n,* parapet, *m.*

paraphernalia, *n.pl,* attirail, bataclan, *m.*

paraphrase, *n,* paraphrase, *f.* ¶ *v.t.* & *i,* paraphraser.

parasite, *n,* parasite, *m.* **parasitic(al),** *a,* parasite; parasitaire.

parasol, *n,* ombrelle, *f.*

parboil, *v.t,* faire bouillir à demi.

parbuckle, *n,* trévire, *f.* ¶ *v.t,* trévirer.

parcel, *n,* colis; envoi; *m*; paquet, *m,* parcelle, *f.* ~ *post,* service des colis postaux, *m. by* ~ *post,* par colis postal. ~ [out], *v.t,* morceler, lotir.

parch, *v.t,* brûler; dessécher.

parchment, *n,* parchemin, *m.*

pardon, *n,* pardon, *m*; grâce, *f.* ¶ *v.t,* pardonner, pardonner à; gracier. ~able, *a,* pardonnable, excusable.

pare, *v.t,* rogner; éplucher; peler.

paregoric, *a,* parégorique.

parent, *n,* père, *m*; mère; (*fig.*) mère, *f*; (*pl.*) parents, *m.pl*; (*att.*) mère. ~age, *n,* extraction, *f.* ~al, *a,* de père, de mère, des parents.

parenthesis, *n,* parenthèse, *f.* **parenthetic(al),** *a,* entre parenthèses. **parenthetically,** *ad,* par parenthèse.

pariah, *n,* paria, *m.*

paring, *n,* rognure; retaille; épluchure, *f.*

parish, *n,* (*civil*) commune; (*Eccl.*) paroisse, *f*; (*att.*) communal; paroissial. ~ *church,* église paroissiale, paroisse, *f.* **parishioner,** *n,* habitant (e) de la commune; paroissien, ne.

Parisian, *a,* parisien. ¶ *n,* Parisien, ne.

parity, *n,* parité, *f.*

park, *n,* parc; bois, *m.* ¶ *v.t,* parquer; garer; (*v.i.*) stationner. ~ing, *n,* stationnement, parcage, *m. no* ~, défense de stationner. *squeeze into a* ~ *space,* faire un créneau. ~ *lot,* parking, *m.*

parlance, *n,* langage, *m,* termes, *m.pl.*

parley, *n,* pourparlers, *m.pl.* ¶ *v.i,* parlementer.

parliament, *n,* parlement, *m.* ~ary, *a,* (*government*) parlementaire; (*election*) législative; (*candidate*) à la députation.

parlor, *n,* [petit] salon; (*convent, school*) parloir, *m. beauty* ~, salon de coiffure, *m.* ~ *games,* jeux de salon; jeux innocents, petits jeux, *m.pl.* ~maid, femme de chambre (*servant à table*) *f.*

Parma, *n,* Parme, *f.* ~ *violet,* violette de Parme, *f.*

parochial, *a,* (*civil*) communal; (*Eccl.*) paroissial; (*fig.*) de clocher.

parodist, *n,* parodiste, *m.* **parody,** *n,* parodie, *f.* ¶ *v.t,* parodier.

parole, *n,* parole, *f.* ¶ *v.t,* libérer sur parole.

paroxysm, *n,* paroxysme, *m.*

parquet, *n,* parquet, *m.* ¶ *v.t,* parqueter.

parrakeet, *n,* perruche, *f.*

parricidal, *a,* parricide. **parricide,** *n,* (*pers.*) parricide, *m,f*; (*act*) parricide, *m.*

parrot, *n,* perroquet, *m,* (*hen*) perruche, *f.*

parry, *v.t,* parer; esquiver. ¶ *n,* parade, *f.*

parse, *v.t,* analyser.

parsimonious†, *a,* parcimonieux. **parsimony,** *n,* parcimonie, *f.*

parsing, *n,* analyse grammaticale, *f.*

parsley, *n,* persil, *m.*

parsnip, *n,* panais, *m.*

parson, *n,* curé; ecclésiastique, *m.* ~'s nose, croupion, as de pique, sot-l'y-laisse, *m.* ~age, *n,* presbytère, *m.*

part, *n,* partie, part, portion; (*hair*) raie, *f*; endroit, parage, *m*; pièce, *f,* organe; (*Theat.*) rôle, emploi; (*book*) fascicule, *m,* livraison, *f.* ~ *time,* mi-temps, *f. spare* ~s, pièces de rechange, *f.pl.* ¶ *v.t,* diviser; séparer; (*metals*) départir; (*v.i.*) se séparer; se décoller. ~ *with,* se défaire de; céder.

partake, *v.i.ir,* participer.

partial†, *a,* (*biased*) partial; (*not entire*) partiel. *to be* ~ *to,* avoir un faible pour. ~ity, *n,* partialité; prédilection, *f,* faible, *m.*

participate, v.i, participer.
participial adjective, (*present*) adjectif verbal; (*past*) participe passé employé (*ou* pris) adjectivement, m. **participle,** n, participe, m.
particle, n, particule, parcelle; (*Gram.*) particule, f.
particolored, a, bigarré, bariolé.
particular†, a, particulier; spécial; exigeant; méticuleux. ¶ n, particularité, f, point, détail, m; (*pl.*) détails, m.pl, indications, f.pl, libellé, m, renseignements, m.pl, précisions, f.pl. ~ity, f, particularité, f. ~ize, v.t, particulariser.
parting, n, séparation, f; décollement; entredeux, m; adieu, m.
partisan, n, partisan, m.
partition, n, séparation; cloison, f. ~ off, cloisonner. **partitive** (*Gram.*) a, partitif.
partly, ad, [en] partie; moitié; partiellement.
partner, n, (*Com.*) associé, e; (*sports, games, Danc., & husband*) partenaire, m,f; (*wife*) compagne, f; (*Danc.*) danseur, euse, cavalier, m, dame, f. ¶ (*a lady, Danc.*) v.t, mener. ~ship, n, société, association, f. to enter into ~ with, s'associer avec.
partridge, n, perdrix, f, (*young*) perdreau, m.
party, n, (*body united in cause*) parti, m; (*united in pleasure*) partie, (*young people's*) sauborum, f; complice (*to* = de); groupe, m; réception; soirée, f. to give a ~, recevoir du monde, donner une soirée.
paschal, a, pascal.
pass, n, passage, m; passe, f; col, pas; laissez-passer, sauf-conduit; permis, m; (*Mil.*) permission, f. ~ book, carnet de compte, c. de banque, m. ~word, mot de passe, m. (*Mil.*) mot d'ordre, m. ¶ v.i. & t, passer; admettre, être reçu à; prononcer; faire; adopter, prendre, approuver; voter; dépasser, franchir; croiser; (*auto*) doubler. ~ by, passer. ~ for payment, ordonnancer. ~ on, transmettre; passer [son chemin]; p. outre. ~ out, (*faint*) s'évanouir. ~able†, a, passable; (*road, etc.*) praticable. ~age, n, passage, m; traversée, f; trajet; canal; couloir,

corridor, m. ~ money, prix de passage, p. de voyage, m.
passenger, n, (*land, sea, or air*) voyageur, euse; (*sea or air*) passager, ère. ~ elevator, ascenseur, m. ~ ship, paquebot, m. ~ train, train de voyageurs, m, grande vitesse, f.
passerby, n, passant, e, (*pl.*) allants & venants, m.pl. **passing,** n, passage, m; adoption, f, in ~, en passant, passagèrement. ~ events, actualités, f.pl. ~ fancy, caprice, m; (*liaison*) passade, f. ~ note (*Mus.*), note de passage, f.
passion, n, passion; flamme; fureur; colère, f. ~ flower, fleur de la Passion, passiflore, f. ~ play, mystère de la Passion, m. ~ate, a, emporté, rageur; passionné, ardent. ~ately, ad, rageusement; passionnément, ardemment, à la folie. ~ fond of, fou de.
passive†, a, passif. ~ [voice], n, passif, m. **passivity,** n, passivité, f.
Passover, n, la Pâque.
passport, n, passeport, m.
past, n, passé, m. ¶ a. & p.p, passé. a ~ master, passé maître, m. ~ [tense], [temps] passé, m. it is ~ ten, il est dix heures sonnées.
paste, n, pâte; colle [de pâte]; pierre d'imitation, p. factice, f, faux brillant, m. ~board, carton [de collage] m. ¶ v.t, coller.
pastel, n, pastel, m. ~ist, n, pastelliste, m,f.
pasteurize, v.t, pasteuriser, pastoriser.
pastil[le], n, pastille, f.
pastime, n, passe-temps, jeu, m.
pastor, n, pasteur, m. ~al, a, pastoral. ~al & ~ale, n, pastorale, f.
pastry, n, pâtisserie, f. ~ board, pâtissoire, f. ~cook [& confectioner], pâtissier, ère.
pasturage, n, pâturage, pacage, gagnage, m. **pasture,** n, pâture, f, pâtis; (*uncut*) herbage, m. ¶ v.t, faire paître, pacager.
pasty, a, pâteux. ¶ n, pâté, m, bouchée, f.
pat, a. & ad, à propos, tout juste. ¶ n, tape, f; (*butter*) rond de beurre, m. ¶ v.t, taper, tapoter; (*an animal*) flatter, caresser. ~

oneself on the back, se complaire.

patch, *n,* (*ground*) lopin, coin; (*cabbages, etc.*) caré, *m;* (*face*) mouche; (*tire*) pastille, (*inner-tube*) rustine, *f;* (*computers*) retouche, *f.* ~ *pocket,* poche rapportée, *f.* ~-*work,* rapiéçage, *m;* marqueterie, *f,* placage, *m.* ¶ *v.t,* rapiécer; (*computers*) raccorder. ~ *up,* replâtrer, rafistoler.

pate, *n,* caboche, *f.*

paten, *n,* patène, *f.*

patent, *a,* breveté; (*obvious*) patent. ~ *leather,* cuir verni, *m;* (*att.*) verni. ~ *medicine,* spécialité pharmaceutique, *f.* ¶ *n,* brevet [d'invention] *m.* ¶ *v.t,* [faire] breveter.

paternal†, *a,* paternel. **paternity,** *n,* paternité, *f.* **paternoster,** *n,* Pater, *m.*

path, *n,* sentier, chemin, *m;* allée; (*storm, etc.*) trajectoire, *f.*

pathetic†, *a,* pathétique.

pathological, *a,* pathologique. **pathologist,** *n,* pathologiste, *m,f.* **pathology,** *n,* pathologie, *f.*

pathos, *n,* pathétique, *m.*

patience, *n,* patience; constance; (*cards*) réussite, patience, *f.* to *put out of* ~, impatienter. **patient†,** *a,* patient, endurant. ¶ *n,* malade, *m,f,* patient, e, client, e.

patina, *n,* patine, *f.* **patinated,** *a,* patiné.

patriarch, *n,* patriarche. *m.* ~**al,** *a,* patriarcal.

patrician, *a. & n,* patricien, ne.

patrimony, *n,* patrimoine, *m.*

patriot, *n,* patriote, *m,f.* ~**ic,** *a,* patriotique; patriote. ~**ism,** *n,* patriotisme, *m.*

patrol, *n,* patrouille, *f.* ¶ *v.i,* patrouiller; (*v.t.*) patrouiller sur.

patron, *n,* patron, protecteur, mécène, *m;* (*shop*) chaland, e, client, *m.* ~ [*saint*], patron, ne, saint, e. ~ *saint's day,* fête patronale, *f.* ~**age,** *n,* patronage, *m,* protection, *f;* (*shop*) achalandage, *m.* ~**ess,** *n,* patronne, protectrice; (*fête, etc.*) dame patronnesse, *f.* **patronize,** *v.t,* patronner, protéger. ~**d** (*shop*) *p.p,* achalandé. **patronizing,** *a,* paterne, protecteur.

patronymic, *n,* nom patronymique, *m.*

patten, *n,* socque, patin, *m.*

patter, *n,* bruit [des pas, des sabots]; (*in song*) parlé; (*showman's*) boniment, *m.* ¶ *v.i,* trottiner; (*rain*) crépiter. *a* ~*ing of feet,* un bruit de pas précipités.

pattern, *n,* modèle; échantillon; calibre, gabarit; patron; dessin, *m.* ~ *maker* (*foundry*), modeleur, *m.* ~ *making,* modelage, *m.* ¶ *v.t,* modeler.

patty, *n,* bouchée, *f.*

paunch, *n,* panse, *f.*

pauper, *n,* indigent, e, pauvre, *m.* ~**ism,** *n,* paupérisme, *m.*

pause, *n,* pause, *f;* silence; repos, *m.* ¶ *v.i,* faire une pause.

pave, *v.t,* paver; (*fig.*) frayer. ~**ment,** *n,* pavage, pavement; pavé; dallage; trottoir, *m;* (*outside café*) terrasse, *f.* ~ *light,* ~ *glass,* verdal, *m.* **paver, pavior,** *n,* paveur, *m.*

Pavia, *n,* Pavie, *f.*

pavilion, *n,* pavillon, *m.*

paving, *n,* pavage, pavement, *m.* ~ *stone,* pavé; grès à paver, *m.*

paw, *n,* patte, *f. to* ~ *the ground,* piaffer.

pawl, *n,* cliquet, chien, *m.*

pawn, *n,* gage, *m;* pension (*Fin.*) *f;* (*chess*) pion, *m.* ~**broker,** prêteur sur gages, *m.* ~**shop,** mont-de-piété, *m.* ¶ *v.t,* engager.

pay, *n,* paie, paye, *f,* salaire, traitement, *m,* gages, *m.pl;* solde, *f.* (*computers*) ~**load,** charge utile, *f.* ~**master,** payeur, trésorier; commissaire, *m.* ~ *roll,* état de paiements, *m. severance* ~, indemnité de licenciement, *f.* ¶ *v.t.* & *i. ir,* payer; verser; solder, gager; rémunérer; rapporter; (*visit*) faire; (*respects*) présenter; (*homage*) rendre. ~ *back,* rembourser, rendre. ~ *for,* payer, rémunérer. ~ *in,* verser. ~ *off,* solder; désintéresser; casser aux gages, congédier; (*mortgage*) purger. ~ *out,* payer, verser; (*cable*) filer. ~ *up,* (*v.t.*) libérer; (*v.i.*) se libérer, s'exécuter. ~**able,** *a,* payable; exigible; à payer; à la charge; exploitable. ~**ee,** *n,* bénéficiaire, *m, f.* ~**er,** *n,* payeur, euse, payant, e; (*good, bad*) paie, paye, *f.* ~**ing,** *a,* payant, rémunérateur. ~ *guest,* pensionnaire, *m,f.* ~**ment,** *n,* paiement, payement; versement, *m*; rémunéra-tion, *f. advance ~*, à valoir, *m*.

pea, *n*, pois, *m. green ~s*, petits pois, *m.pl. ~chick*, paonneau, *m*. *~cock*, paon, *m. ~hen*, paonne, *f. ~nut*, cacahuète, *f. ~ shooter*, sarbacane, *f. ~ soup*, purée de pois, *f*.

peace, *n*, paix; tranquillité, *f*, repos; ordre public, *m. ~maker*, pacificateur, trice. *~able†* & *~-ful†*, *a*, paisible, pacifique; tran-quille.

peach, *n*, pêche, *f. ~ [tree]*, pêcher, *m*.

peak, *n*, cime, *f*, sommet; piton, pic, *m*, dent; (*cap*) visière; pointe, *f*, maximum, plafond, *m. ~ hours*, heures de pointe, *f.pl. ~load*, charge de pointe, *f*.

peal, *n*, carillon, *m*, volée, *f*; (*laughter*) éclat; coup, *m*.

pear, *n*, poire, *f. ~ tree* & *~ wood*, poirier, *m*.

pearl, *n*, perle, *f. mother-of-~*, nacre, *f. ~ button*, bouton de nacre, *m. ~ barley*, orge perlé, *m. ~ oyster*, huître perlière, *f. ~y*, *a*, de perle, perlé; nacré.

peasant, *n*. & *att*, paysan, ne. *~ry*, *n*, les paysans, *m.pl*.

peat, *n*, tourbe, *f. ~ bog*, *~ery*, *n*, tourbière, *f. ~y*, *a*, tourbeux.

pebble, *n*, caillou; galet, *m*.

peccadillo, *n*, peccadille, *f*.

peccavi, *n*, meâ-culpâ, *m*.

peck, *n*, coup de bec, *m. ¶ v.t*, becqueter, picoter; (*v.i.*) picorer. *to be ~ish*, (*hunger*) avoir la fringale.

peculate, *v.t*, détourner. **pecula-tion,** *n*, détournement, *m*, malver-sation, *f*.

peculiar†, *a*, particulier; propre; singulier, bizarre. *~ity*, *n*, parti-cularité, singularité, *f*.

pecuniary†, *a*, pécuniaire.

pedagogue, *n*, pédagogue, ma-gister, *m*.

pedal, *n*, pédale, *f. ~ [key]board*, pédalier, *m. ¶ v.i*, pédaler.

pedant, *n*, pédant, e. *~ic†*, *a*, pédant; pédantesque. *~ry*, *n*, pédanterie, *f*, pédantisme, *m*.

peddle, *v.i*. & *t*, baguenauder; détailler; colporter. **peddler,** *n*, colporteur, *m*.

pedestal, *n*, piédestal, pied, socle, *m*, gaine; sellette, *f*, porte-potiche, *m. ~ desk*, bureau-

ministre, *m. ~ table*, table à pied central, *f*.

pedestrian, *n*, piéton, *m. ~ crossing*, traversée des piétons, *f. ~ mall*, rue piétonne, *f. ¶ a*, à pied; (*statue*) pédestre.

pedigree, *n*, généalogie, *f*; pedi-gree, *m*.

pediment, *n*, fronton, *m*.

pedometer, *n*, podomètre, compte-pas, *m*.

peel, *n*, peau, pelure, écorce, *f*; zeste, *m. ¶ v.t*, peler, éplucher, écorcer, décortiquer. *~ [off]*, (*v.i*) se peler, s'écailler. *~ings*, *n.pl*, épluchures, *f.pl*.

peep, *n*, regard [furtif] *m*; échap-pée [de vue] *f. ~hole*, regard, judas, *m. ¶ v.i*, regarder; regarder sans faire semblant, guigner; émerger; (*chirp*) pépier. *~ at*, guigner.

peer, *n*, pair, *m. ~ into*, scruter; fouiller. *~age*, *n*, pairie, *f*; (*book*) nobiliaire, *m. ~ess*, *n*, pairesse, *f. ~less*, *a*, sans pair, introuvable.

peevish, *a*, maussade.

peewit, *n*, vanneau, *m*.

peg, *n*, cheville; fiche, *f*; jalon; (*degree*) cran, *m. ¶ v.t*, cheviller; jalonner. *~ [away]*, persister.

Pegasus (*fig*.) *n*, Pégase, *m*.

pekin (*fabric*) *n*, pékin, *m*. **Peki-nese** or **peke** (*dog*) *n*, pékinois, *m*. **Peking** (*Geog*.) *n*, Pékin, *m*.

pelf, *n*, lucre, gain, *m*.

pelican, *n*, pélican, *m*.

pelisse, *n*, pelisse, *f*.

pellet, *n*, boulette, *f*; grain de plomb, *m*.

pellicle, *n*, pellicule, *f*.

pell-mell, *ad*. & *n*, pêle-mêle, *ad*. & *m*.

pellucid, *a*, limpide.

pelt, *n*, peau, *f. ¶ v.t*, lapider; assaillir à coups (*with =* de). *~ing rain*, pluie battante, *f. ~ry*, *n*, peausserie; pelleterie, *f*.

pelvis, *n*, bassin, *m*.

pen, *n*, plume, *f*; parc; (*cattle*, *etc*.) enclos, *m. ballpoint ~*, pointe-bille, *f. ~ & ink drawing*, dessin à la plume, *m. ~holder*, porte-plume, *m. ~knife*, canif, *m. ~manship*, calligraphie, *f. ~ name*, nom de plume, n. de guerre, pseudonyme, *m. ¶ v.t*, écrire, composer; parquer.

penal, *a*, pénal. *~ty*, *n*, pénalité, peine, sanction; pénitence, *f*, dédit, m. ~ *area* (*Foot.*), surface de réparation, *f.* ~ *clause,* clause pénale, *f.* ~ *kick,* coup de réparation, c. de pénalité, *m.* **penance,** *n,* pénitence, *f.*

pencil, *n,* crayon; pinceau, *m.* ~ *case,* porte-crayon. ~ *sharpener,* taille-crayon, *m.* ¶ *v.t,* crayonner.

pendant, *n,* pendentif, *m;* (*Nav.*) flamme, *f.* **pendant,** *a,* pendant. **pendentive** (*Arch.*) *n,* pendentif, *m.* **pending,** *a,* pendant. ¶ *pr,* en attendant. **pendulum,** *n,* pendule; (*Horol.*) balancier, *m.*

penetrate, *v.t. & i,* pénétrer; percer.

penguin, *n,* manchot, *m.*

peninsula, *n,* péninsule, presqu'île, *f.* **peninsular,** *a,* péninsulaire.

penis, *n,* pénis, *m;* (*slang*) bite, queue, *f,* zob, *m.*

penitence, *n,* pénitence, *f.* **penitent,** *a. & n,* pénitent, e. **penitentiary,** *a,* pénitentiaire. ¶ *n,* pénitencier, *m,* maison de correction, *f.*

pennant, *n,* flamme, *f;* guidon, *m.*

penniless, *a,* sans le sou.

pennon, *n,* flamme, *f.*

Pennsylvania, *n,* la Pen[n]sylvanie.

penny, *n,* penny, = ¹⁄₁₀₀ of a dollar; (*very little money*) sou, *m.* ~*royal,* pouliot, *m.* ~*weight,* *Meas.* = 1.5552 grams.

pension, *n,* pension, rente, *f.* ¶ *v.t,* pensionner. ~ *off,* retraiter. ~er, *n,* pensionnaire, *m,f;* (*Mil.*) invalide, *m.*

pensive, *a,* pensif, songeur.

pentagon, *n,* pentagone, *m.*

Pentateuch (the), le Pentateuque.

Pentecost, *n,* la Pentecôte.

penthouse, *n,* appentis, auvent, *m.*

penultimate, *a,* pénultième.

penumbra, *n,* pénombre, *f.*

penurious†, *a,* pauvre. **penury,** *n,* pénurie, disette d'argent, *f.*

peony, *n,* pivoine, *f.*

people, *n,* peuple, *m;* nation, *f;* gens, *m.pl. & f.pl;* personnes; personnalités, *f.pl;* population, *f;* monde, *m;* famille, *f.* ~ *say,* on dit. ¶ *v.t,* peupler.

pepper, *n,* poivre, *m.* ~*corn,* grain de poivre, *m.* ~*mint,* menthe poivrée, *f.* ~*mint* [*lozenge*], pastille de menthe, *f.* ~*shaker,*

poivrière, *f.* ~ *plant,* poivrier, *m.* ¶*v.t,* poivrer; (*shot*) canarder; (*questions*) harceler. ~**y,** *a,* poivré; irascible, colérique.

per, *pr,* par; pour. ~ *annum,* par an, l'an. ~ *cent,* pour cent. ~ *contra,* en contrepartie, porté ci-contre.

perambulate, *v.t,* parcourir. **perambulator,** *n,* voiture d'enfant, *f,* landau [pour e.] *m.*

perceive, *v.t,* apercevoir; s'apercevoir de; (*Philos.*) percevoir.

percentage, *n,* pourcentage, tant pour cent, *m;* proportion, *f.*

perceptible, *a,* perceptible. **perception,** *n,* perception, *f.*

perch, *n,* (*bird's*) perchoir, bâton; (*fig.*) haut, *m;* (*fish*) perches, *f;* *Meas.* = 25.293 sq. meters. ¶ *v.i,* percher, jucher, brancher.

perchance, *ad,* peut-être.

percolate, *v.i. & t,* filtrer.

percussion, *n,* percussion, *f.* ~ *cap,* capsule, amorce, *f.* ~ *instruments,* instruments de percussion, *m. pl,* batterie, *f.* **percussive,** *a,* percutant.

perdition, *n,* perdition, *f.*

peregrination, *n,* pérégrination, *f.* **peregrine** [*falcon*], *n,* faucon pèlerin, *m.*

peremptory†, *a,* péremptoire; tranchant, absolu.

perennial, *a,* permanent, intarissable; vivace. ¶ *n,* plante vivace, *f.*

perfect†, *a,* parfait; achevé; vrai. ¶ *v.t,* [par]achever; perfectionner. ~**ion,** *n,* perfection, *f.* ~*ly sweet* (*pers.*), gentil à croquer.

perfidious†, *a,* perfide. **perfidy,** *n,* perfidie, *f.*

perforate, *v.t,* perforer.

perforce, *ad,* forcément.

perform, *v.t. & i,* faire; exécuter; accomplir; jouer, donner, représenter. ~*ance,* *n,* exécution, *f,* accomplissement, *m;* (*sport*) performance; (*Theat.*) représentation; (*movies, etc.*) séance, *f.* ~er, *n,* exécutant, e; joueur, euse; concertant, e; artiste, *m,f.* ~*ing dog,* chien savant, *m.*

perfume, *n,* parfum, *m.* ~ *distiller,* parfumeur, *m.* ¶ *v.t,* parfumer; embaumer. **perfumer,** *n,* parfumeur, euse. ~**y,** *n,* parfumerie, *f.*

perfunctory, *a,* fait par manière d'acquit.

pergola, *n*, pergola, *f*.

perhaps, *ad*, peut-être.

peril, *n*, péril, *m*. ~**ous†**, *a*, périlleux.

perimeter, *n*, périmètre, *m*.

period, *n*, période; époque, *f*; terme; exercice; (*punctuation*) point, *m*; (*menses*) les règles, *f.pl.* to have one's ~, avoir ses règles. ~**ic** & ~**ical†**, *a*, périodique. ~**ical**, *n*, périodique, *m*.

periphery, *n*, périphérie, *f*.

periphrasis, *n*, périphrase, *f*.

periscope, *n*, périscope, *m*.

perish, *v.i*, périr. ~**able**, *a*, périssable.

peristyle, *n*, péristyle, *m*.

peritonitis, *n*, péritonite, *f*.

periwinkle, *n*, (*Mol.*) bigorneau, *m*; (*Bot.*) pervenche, *f*.

perjure oneself, se parjurer. ~**d**, *p.a*, parjure. **perjurer**, *n*, parjure, *m,f*; (*law*) faux témoin, *m*. **perjury**, *n*, faux témoignage; parjure, *m*.

perky, *a*, éveillé; dégagé.

permanence, *n*, permanence, *f*. **permanent**, *a*, permanent; perpétuel. ~ *wave*, indéfrisable, *f*. ~**ly**, *ad*, de façon permanente.

permanganate, *n*, permanganate, *m*.

permeable, *a*, perméable. **permeate**, *v.t*, pénétrer; saturer.

permissible, *a*, loisible. **permission**, *n*, permission, *f*. **permit**, *n*, permis, *m*. ¶ *v.t*, permettre.

pernicious†, *a*, pernicieux.

peroration, *n*, péroraison, *f*.

peroxide, *n*, peroxyde, *m*.

perpendicular†, *a*. & *n*, perpendiculaire, *a*. & *f*.

perpetrate, *v.t*, perpétrer, commettre; faire. **perpetrator** (*crime*) *n*, auteur, *m*.

perpetual†, *a*, perpétuel. **perpetuate**, *v.t*, perpétuer. **perpetuity**, *n*, perpétuité, *f*.

perplex, *v.t*, embarrasser. ~**ed** & ~**ing**, *a*, perplexe. ~**ity**, *n*, perplexité, *f*, embarras, *m*.

perquisite, *n*, revenant-bon, *m*, (*pl.*) casuel, *m*.

persecute, *v.t*, persécuter. **persecution**, *n*, persécution, *f*. **persecutor**, *n*, persécuteur, trice.

perseverance, *n*, persévérance, constance, *f*. **persevere**, *v.i*, persévérer.

Persia (*Iran*), *n*, la Perse. **Persian** (*modern*) *a*, persan. ~ *carpet*, tapis de Perse, *m*. ~ *cat*, chat persan, [c.] angora, *m*. ~ *Gulf*, golfe Persique, *m*. ¶ *n*, (*pers.*) Persan, e; (*language*) le persan. **Persian** (*ancient*) *a*, perse. ¶ *n*, Perse, *m.f*.

persist, *v.i*, persister, s'obstiner, s'opiniâtrer; persévérer. ~**ence**, ~**ency**, *n*, persistance, constance, *f*. ~**ent**, *a*, persistant.

person, *n*, personne, *f*. ~ *of independent means*, rentier, ère. ~ *opposite*, vis-à-vis, *m*. ~**age**, *n*, personnage, *m*. ~**al†**, *a*, personnel; mobilier, meuble. ~**ality**, *n*, personnalité, *f*. ~**alty**, *n*, biens meubles, *m.pl.* **personify**, *v.t*, personnifier.

perspective, *n*, perspective; (*Theat.*) optique, *f*.

perspicacious, *a*, perspicace. **perspicacity**, *n*, perspicacité, *f*. **perspicuous†**, *a*, clair, net.

perspiration, *n*, transpiration, sueur, *f*. *bathed in* ~, en nage. **perspire**, *v.i*, transpirer, suer.

persuade, *v.t*, persuader; décider. **persuasion**, *n*, persuasion; croyance, communion, *f*. **persuasive**, *a*, persuasif.

pert†, *a*, insolent; hardi; impertinent.

pertain, *v.i*, appartenir; avoir rapport.

pertinacious†, *a*, opiniâtre. **pertinacity**, *n*, opiniâtreté, *f*.

pertinent, *a*, pertinent, à propos. ~**ly**, *ad*, à propos.

pertness, *n*, hardiesse; impertinence, *f*.

perturb, *v.t*, troubler, agiter. ~**ation**, *n*, perturbation, agitation, *f*.

Peru, *n*, le Pérou.

Perugia, *n*, Pérouse, *f*.

perusal, *n*, lecture, *f*. **peruse**, *v.t*, lire attentivement.

Peruvian, *a*, péruvien. ~ *bark*, quinquina, *m*. ¶ *n*, Péruvien, ne.

pervade, *v.t*, pénétrer. **pervasive**, *a*, pénétrant, subtil.

perverse, *a*, pervers. **perversion**, *n*, perversion, *f*, perversity, *n*, perversité, *f*. **pervert** *n*, pervers, vicieux, *m*. ¶ *v.t*, pervertir; dénaturer; fausser.

pervious, *a*, perméable.

pessimism, *n*, pessimisme, *m*. **pessimist**, *n*. & ~**ic**, *a*, pessimiste, *m*. & *a*.

pest, *n*, peste, *f*.
pester, *v.t*, tourmenter, importuner.
pestilence, *n*, peste, *f*. **pestilential,** *a*, pestilentiel.
pestle, *n*, pilon, *m*. ¶ *v.t*, piler.
pet, *n*, accès de mauvaise humeur; animal favori, *m*; favori, ite, mignon, ne, chéri, e, chouchou, *m*. ~ *argument*, cheval de bataille, *m*. ~ *aversion*, bête noire, *f*. ~ *dog*, chien favori, *m*. ~ *name*, petit nom d'amitié, *m*. ~ *scheme*, plan favori, *m*. ~ *subject*, sujet favori, dada, *m*. ~ *theory*, marotte, *f*. ~ *vice*, péché mignon, *m*. ¶ *v.t*, câliner, choyer
petal, *n*, pétale, *m*.
petiole, *n*, pétiole, *m*.
petition, *n*, pétition, supplique; requête, *f*. ¶ *v.t*, adresser une requête à; (*v.i*.) pétitionner. ~**er,** *n*, pétitionnaire, *m,f*; requérant, e, demandeur, euse.
petrel, *n*, pétrel, *m*.
petrifaction, *n*, pétrification, *f*. **petrify,** *v.t*, pétrifier; méduser.
petroleum, *n*, pétrole, *m*. **petrochemical,** *a*, pétrochimique. **petrochemistry,** *n*; pétrochimie.*f*.
petticoat, *n*, jupon, cotillon, *m*, cotte, *f*.
pettifoggery, *n*, avocasserie; chicane[rie] *f*.
pettiness, *n*, petitesse, *f*.
pettish, *a*, maussade.
petty, *a*, petit; menu. ~ *officer*, maître, *m*; (*pl*, *col*.) maistrance, *f*. ~ *cash*, argent pour menus frais, *m*.
petulance, *n*, vivacité [de caractère], humeur, *f*.
petunia, *n*, pétunia, *m*.
pew, *n*, banc [d'église] *m*.
pewit, *n*, vanneau, *m*.
pewter, *m*, étain, *m*. ~**er,** *n*, potier d'é., *m*.
phaeton, *n*, phaéton, *m*.
phalanx, *n*, phalange, *f*.
phantasm, *n*, phantasme, *m*, illusion, *f*. **phantasy,** *n*, vision, *f*. **phantasmagoria,** *n*, fantasmagorie, *f*. **phantom,** *n*, fantôme, *m*.
Pharaoh, *n*, pharaon, *m*.
Pharisaic(al), *a*, pharisaïque. **Pharisee,** *n*, pharisien, *m*.
pharmaceutical, *a*, pharmaceutique. **pharmacy,** *n*, pharmacie, *f*.
pharyngitis, *n*, pharyngite, *f*. **pharynx,** *n*, pharynx, *m*.

phase, *n*, phase, *f*; temps, *m*. ~ *displacement*, déphasage, *m*. (*engine*) *out of* ~, décalé.
pheasant, *n*, faisan, e, (*young*) faisandeau, *m*. ~**ry,** *n*, faisanderie, *f*.
phenomenal, *a*, phénoménal. **phenomenon,** *n*, phénomène, *m*.
phial, *n*, fiole; ampoule, *f*.
Philadelphia, *n*, Philadelphie, *f*.
philander, *v.i*, faire le galant. ~**er,** *n*, galant, *m*.
philanthropic, *a*, philanthropique. **philanthropist,** *n*, philanthrope, *m,f*. **philanthropy,** *n*, philanthropie, *f*.
philatelist, *n*, philatéliste, *m,f*. **philately,** *n*, philatélisme, *m*.
philharmonic, *a*, philharmonique.
philippic, *n*, philippique, *f*.
Philistine, *n*, philistin, *m*.
philologist, *n*, philologue, *m*. **philology,** *n*, philologie, *f*.
philosopher, *n*, philosophe, *m*. ~*s' stone*, pierre philosophale, *f*. **philosophic(al)**†, *a*, philosophique; (*calm*) philosophe. **philosophize,** *v.i*, philosopher. **philosophy,** *n*, philosophie, *f*.
philter, *n*, philtre, *m*.
phlebitis, *n*, phlébite, *f*.
phlegm, *n*, mucosité, pituite, *f*; (*fig*.) flegme. *m*. ~**atic,** *a*, flegmatique.
phlox, *n*, phlox, *m*.
phoenix, *n*, phénix, *m*.
phonetic, *a*, phonétique. ~**s,** *n.pl*, phonétique, *f*.
phonograph, *n*, phonographe, *m*. ~ *needle*, saphir, *m*. ~ *record*, disque, *m*. ~*-record dealer*, disquaire, *m*.
phosphate, *n*, phosphate, *m*. **phosphorescence,** *n*, phosphorescence, *f*. **phosphorescent,** *a*, phosphorescent. **phosphorus,** *n*, phosphore, *m*.
photocopy, *n*, multicopie, *f*.
photograph, *n*, photographie, *f*. ~ *frame*, porte-photographie, *m*. ¶ *v.t*, photographier. ~**er,** *n*, photographe, *m,f*. *still* ~, photographe de plateau, *m*. ~**ic,** *a*, photographique. ~**y,** *n*, photographie, *f*. **photogravure,** *n*, photogravure, *f*.
phrase, *n*, locution, expression,

phrase; (*Mus.*) phrase, période, *f.*
¶ *v.t,* phraser. **phraseology**, *n,*
phraséologie, *f.*

phrenologist, *n,* phrénologiste,
m. **phrenology**, *n,* phrénologie, *f.*

phthisis, *n,* phtisie, *f.*

physic, *v.t,* médicamenter. ~**al**†,
a, physique; matériel. ~**ian**, *n,*
médecin, *m.* ~**ist**, *n,* physicien,
ne. ~**s**, *n.pl,* physique, *f.*

physiognomy, *n,* physionomie,
f.

physiology, *n,* physiologie, *f.*

physique, *n,* physique, *m.*

Piacenza, *n,* Plaisance, *f.*

pianist, *n,* pianiste, *m,f.* **piano-**
[forte], *n,* piano, *m.* ~ **stool**,
tabouret de piano, *m.* ~ **wire**,
corde à piano, *f.*

piccolo, *n,* piccolo, *m.*

pick, *n,* pic, *m,* pioche, *f;* choix,
m; élite, fleur, *f;* (*of the basket*)
dessus, *m.* ~**axe**, pioche, *f.* ~
lock, crochet [de serrurier], rossignol, *m.* ~**-me-up**, remontant,
m. the ~ *of the bunch*, la fleur des
pois. ~**pocket**, voleur à la tire,
pickpocket, *m.* ¶ *v.t,* cueillir;
trier; choisir; (*bone*) ronger;
(*lock*) crocheter; (*teeth*) curer;
(*quarrel*) chercher; (*peck*) becqueter. ~ *at one's food*, pignocher. ~ *up*, relever; ramasser;
(*passengers*) prendre; (*news*) écumer.

picked, *p.a,* choisi, de choix;
d'élite. **picker**, *n,* cueilleur, euse;
trieur, euse.

picket, *n,* piquet; jalon, *m.* ¶ *v.t,*
piqueter.

picking, *n,* cueillette, *f;* triage,
m; (*pl. pilferings*) gratte, *f,* tour
de bâton, *m.*

pickle, *n,* (*brine*) saumure, *f;*
(*plight*) arroi, *m;* (*pl.*) conserves
au vinaigre, *f.pl.* ¶ *v.t,* mariner,
saler; conserver [au vinaigre].
~**d**, *a,* (*vegetables*) au vinaigre;
(*meat*) salé. ~ *cucumbers*, cor-
nichons, *m.pl.*

picnic, *n,* pique-nique, *m,* partie
de plaisir, *f.* ~ *basket*, panier
pique-nique, *m.* ¶ *v.i,* pique-
niquer.

pictorial, *a,* pictural; en images;
(*journal*) illustré, pittoresque;
(*plan, map*) figuratif, figuré. **pic-**
ture, *n,* tableau, *m,* peinture;
image, *f.* ~ *book*, livre d'images,
album d'images pour enfants, *m.*

~ *gallery*, galerie de tableaux, *f.*
~ *postcard*, carte postale illustrée, *f.* ~ *writing*, écriture figurative, *f.* ¶ *v.t,* dépeindre, figurer,
représenter. ~ *to oneself*, se figurer. **picturesque**†, *a,* pittoresque, imagé. ~**ness**, *n,* pittoresque, *m.*

pie, *n,* (*meat*) pâté, *m;* (*fruit*)
tourte, *f;* (*printers'*) pâté, *m,*
pâte, *f.* ~ *dish*, tourtière, *f.*

piebald, *a,* pie.

piece, *n,* morceau; fragment; tronçon, *m;* pièce, *f.* ~ *of business*,
affaire, *f.* ~ *of furniture*, meuble,
m. ~ *of ice*, glaçon, *m.* ~
of impertinence, impertinence, *f.*
~ *of news*, nouvelle, *f.* ~ *of ord-*
nance, bouche à feu, *f.* ~ *of*
poetry, poésie, *f.* ~ *of work*,
travail, *m;* besogne, *f.* ~**work**,
travail à la tâche, *m.* ¶ *v.t,* rapiécer. ~ *together* (*fig.*), coudre
ensemble. **piecemeal**, *ad,* en
morceaux; par degrés.

pied, *a,* bigarré, bariolé.

Piedmont, *n,* le Piémont.

pier, *n,* jetée; jetée promenade;
pile, *f;* pied-droit; jambage, trumeau, *m.* ~**head**, musoir, *m.*

pierce, *v.t. & i,* percer; repercer;
pénétrer. **piercing**, *p.a,* perçant;
(*cold*) saisissant.

piety, *n,* piété, *f.*

pig, *n,* cochon, porc, pourceau;
(*child*) goret, *m.* (*metal*) gueuse,
f, saumon, *m.* ~ *breeding*, l'industrie porcine, *f.* ~**headed**,
têtu comme un mulet. ~ [*iron*],
fonte en gueuses, f. en saumons,
[gueuse de] fonte, *f.* ~ *meat*,
charcuterie, *f.* ~**skin**, peau de
porc, *f,* cuir de p., *m.* ~**sty** or
piggery, *n,* étable à pourceaux,
m, porcherie, *f.* ~**tail** (hair),
queue, *f.*

pigeon, *n,* pigeon, ne; (*young*)
pigeonneau, *m.* ~**hole**, boulin,
m; (*in desk*) case, *f.* [*set of*] ~
holes, casier, *m.* ~**ry**, *n,* pigeonnier, *m.*

piglet, *n,* goret, *m.*

pigment, *n,* pigment, *m.*

pigmy, *n,* pygmée, *f.*

pike, *n,* pique, *f;* (*fish*) brochet,
m.

pilaster, *n,* pilastre, *m.*

pilchard, *n,* sardine, *f.*

pile, *n,* pile, *f,* monceau, amas,
tas, *m;* pelote, *f;* (*mass of build-*

ings) amas; (*wood*) bûcher; (*arms*) faisceau; (*stake*) pieu, pilotis; (*nap*) poil, *m*; (*Elec.*) pile, *f*. *man who has made his* ~, homme nanti, *m*. ~ [up], *v.t*, empiler, entasser, amonceler, amasser.

piles (*Med.*) *n.pl*, hémorroïdes, *f.pl*.

pilfer, *v.t*, piller.

pilgrim, *n*, pèlerin, e. ~age, *n. & place of pilgrimage*, pèlerinage, *m*.

piling (*pile work*) *n*, pilotis, *m*.

pill, *n*, pilule, *f*.

pillage, *n*, pillage, *m*. ¶ *v.t*, piller.

pillar, *n*, pilier, *m*, colonne, *f*.

pillory, *n*, pilori, *m*. ¶ *v.t*, pilorier, draper.

pillow, *n*, oreiller; chevet; coussin, *m*. ~ *case*, taie d'oreiller, *f*. ~ *lace*, dentelle aux fuseaux, *f*.

pilot, *n*, pilote, *m. automatic* ~, bloc de pilotage, *m*. ~ *boat*, bateau-pilote, *m*. ~ *lamp*, lampe témoin, *f*. ¶ *v.t*, piloter.

pimpernel, *n*, mouron, *m*, morgeline, *f*.

pimple, *n*, bouton, bourgeon, *m*, pustule, *f*. *to break out in* ~s, boutonner, bourgeonner.

pin, *n*, épingle; (*peg*) cheville, *f*, boulon, *m*; goupille; clavette; broche; fiche, *f*; (*fig.*) épingle, *f*, fétu, *m*. ~s & *needles* (fig.), fourmis, *f.pl*. ~*cushion*, pelote [à épingles] *f*. ~ *money*, argent de poche, *m*. ~ *prick*, piqûre d'épingle, *f*, coup d'é., *m*. ¶ *v.t*, épingler; cheviller; clouer.

pinafore, *n*, tablier [d'enfant] *m*.

pincers, *n.pl*, tenailles; (*smith's*) tricoises, *f.pl*.

pinch, *n*, (*of salt*) pincée; (*snuff*) pincée, prise, *f*; pincement, *m*. *in a* ~, au besoin. ¶ *v.t*, pincer; blesser, brider, gêner. ~ed, *p.a*, tiré.

pine, *v.t*, languir; dépérir, sécher. ¶ *n*, pin, *m*.

pineapple, *n*, ananas, *m*.

ping-pong, *n*, ping-pong, tennis de table, *m*. ~ *set*, jeu de p.-p., jeu de t. de t., *m*.

pining, *n*, dépérissement, *m*; nostalgie, *f*.

pinion, *n*, aileron; (*Mech.*) pignon, *m*. ¶ *v.t*, couper les ailes à; (*pers.*) garrotter.

pink, *a*, rose, incarnat. ¶ *n*, rose; (*Bot.*) œillet, *m*, mignardise, *f*.

pinnace, *n*, grand canot, *m*.

pinnacle, *n*, pinacle, *m*.

pioneer, *n*, pionnier, *m*.

pious†, *a*, pieux.

pip, *n*, (*seed*) pépin; (*dominoes*) point, *m*; (*disease*) pépie, *f*.

pipe, *n*, tuyau, conduit, *m*, conduite, *f*; canal; (*key*) canon, *m*, forure; (*tobacco*) pipe, *f*; (*flute*) pipeau, chalumeau; (*boatswain's*) sifflet, *m*. ~ *clay*, terre de pipe, *f*; blanc de terre à pipe, *m*. ~ *line*, canalisation, *f*. ¶ *v.i. & t*, siffler. **piping** (*braid*) *n*, passepoil, liséré, *m*. ~ *hot*, bouillant.

pipkin, *n*, poêlon, *m*, huguenote, *f*.

pippin, *n*, reinette, *f*.

piquancy, *n*, goût piquant; (*fig.*) piquant, sel, *m*. **piquant**, *a*, piquant. **pique**, *n*, pique, *f*. ¶ *v.t*, piquer. **piquet**, *n*, piquet, *m*.

piracy, *n*, piraterie; contrefaçon, *f*. **pirate**, *n*, pirate; forban, *m*. ~ *publisher*, éditeur marron, *m*. ¶ *v.t*, contrefaire; (*v.i*) pirater.

Piraeus, *n*, le Pirée.

pirouette, *n*, pirouette, *f*. ¶ *v.i*, pirouetter.

Pisa, *n*, Pise, *f*.

pisciculture, *n*, pisciculture, *f*.

pistachio, *n*, (*nut*) pistache, *f*; (*tree*) pistachier, *m*.

pistil, *n*, pistil, dard, *m*.

pistol, *n*, pistolet, *m*. *a* ~ [*held*] *at one's head* (*fig.*), un couteau à la gorge.

piston, *n*, piston, *m*. ~ *rod*, tige, *f*.

pit, *n*, fosse, fouille, *f*, creux, puits, *m*; carrière; (*in metal*) piqûre; (*pock*) marque, couture, *f*. ~*fall*, trappe, *f*. piège; (*fig.*) écueil, *m*. ~ *saw*, scie de long, *f*. ¶ *v.t*, marquer; couturer; piquer; mettre aux prises; (*fruit*) denoyauter.

pit-[a-]pat (to go), faire tic tac, palpiter.

pitch, *n*, poix, *f*; brai, bitume; point, degré, *m*, période; inclinaison, pente, *f*; (*Mus.*) diapason, *m*, hauter [musicale] *f*; (*Mech.*) pas; (*Naut.*) coup de tangage; (*angler's*) coup, *m*. ~ *dark*, noir comme poix. ~*fork*, fourche à faner, fouine, *f*. ~*fork someone into an office*, bombarder quelqu'un à une place. ~*pine*, pitchpin, *m*. ~ *pipe*, diapason à bouche, *m.* ¶ *v.t*, poisser; jeter, lancer; dresser, tendre, asseoir; (*v.i.*) plonger; (*ship*) tanguer, canarder. ~*ed battle*, bataille rangée, *f.*

pitcher, *n,* cruche, *f,* broc; (*baseball*) lanceur, *m.*

piteous†, *a,* piteux, pitoyable.

pith, *n,* moelle; (*palm tree*) cervelle; (*fig.*) moelle, *f,* suc; (*of a story*) piquant, *m.* ~ *helmet,* casque en moelle, *m.* ~**y,** *a,* moelleux; (*fig.*) plein de moelle.

pitiable† & pitiful†, *a,* piteux, à faire pitié, pitoyable, lamentable. **pitiless†,** *a,* impitoyable, sans pitié.

pittance, *n,* maigre revenu, revenu dérisoire, *m*; faible portion, *f.*

pity, *n,* pitié, *f*; (*regret*) dommage, *m.* *to move to* ~, apitoyer. ¶ *v.t,* plaindre, avoir pitié de.

pivot, *n,* pivot, *m.* ¶ *v.i,* pivoter.

pixie, *n,* elfe, lutin, *m*; fée, *f.*

placard, *n,* placard, *m,* affiche, pancarte, *f.* ¶ *v.t,* placarder, afficher.

place, *n,* place, *f*; endroit; lieu, *m*; localité, *f.* *hiding* ~, cachette, *f.* *to take* ~, avoir lieu, se passer. ¶ *v.t,* placer; mettre; déposer; poser.

placer (*Min.*) *n,* placer, *m.*

placid†, *a,* placide. ~**ity,** *n,* placidité, *f.*

plagiarism, *n,* plagiat, larcin, *m.* **plagiarist,** *n,* plagiaire, *m.* **plagiarize,** *v.t,* plagier.

plague, *n,* peste; plaie, *f*; fléau; tourment, *m,* brebis galeuse, *f.* ~-*stricken* (*person*), pestiféré, e, *a. & n.* ¶ (*fig.*) *v.t,* tourmenter, assassiner; (*tease*) lutiner.

plaice, *n,* plie, *f,* carrelet, *m.*

plaid, *n,* plaid, tissu écossais, *m.*

plain, *a,* uni; lisse; plat; simple; (*cigarettes*) ordinaires; clair, évident; distinct; nu; au naturel; laid. ~ *cooking,* cuisine bourgeoise, *f.* ~ *dealing,* franchise, *f. in* ~ *figures,* en chiffres connus. ~ *girl,* jeune fille laide, *f,* laideron, *m.* ~ *language* (*Teleg.*), [langage] clair, *m.* ~*song,* plainchant, *m.* ¶ *n,* plaine, *f.* ~**ly,** *ad,* simplement; clairement; distinctement; nettement, net, bonnement. ~**ness,** *n,* simplicité; clarté; netteté; laideur, *f.*

plaintiff, *n,* demandeur, eresse,

plaignant, e. **plaintive†,** *a,* plaintif.

plait, *n,* natte, tresse, *f.* ¶ *v.t,* natter, tresser. *to* ~ *one's hair,* se natter.

plan, *n,* plan; projet, dessein, *m,* batterie, *f.* ¶ *v.t,* dresser le plan de; projeter, méditer, concerter; (*political economy*) planifier. ~**ing,** *n,* (*computers*) planification. *f. family* ~, planification des naissances.

plane, *a,* plan. ¶ *n,* plan, *m,* surface plane, *f*; (*tool*) rabot; avion, aéroplane, *m.* ~ [*tree*], platane, plane, *m.* ¶ *v.t,* raboter; planer.

planet, *n,* planète, *f.* **planetarium,** *n,* planétaire, *m.* **planetary,** *a,* planétaire.

plank, *n,* planche, *f,* madrier, *m.*

plankton, *n,* plancton, *m.*

plant, *n,* plante, herbe, *f,* végétal; (*factory*) usine, *f*; matériel, outillage, appareil, *m.* ~ *life,* vie végétale, *f.* ¶ *v.t,* planter; poser.

plantain, *n,* plantain; (*banana*) plantanier, *m.*

plantation, *n,* plantation, *f,* plantage, plant, *m.* **planter,** *n,* planteur, euse.

plaque, *n,* plaque, *f.*

plasma, *n,* plasma, *m.*

plaster, *n,* platre; (*Med.*) emplâtre, *m.* ~ *cast,* plâtre, *m.* ~ *of paris,* plâtre de moulage, gypse, *m.* ¶ *v.t,* plâtrer. ~**er,** *n,* plâtrier, *m.*

plastic, *a,* plastique. ~**ity,** *n,* plasticité, *f.*

plate, *n,* (*eating*) assiette, *f*; (*collection*) plat, bassin, *m*; (*Phot.*) plaque; (*book*) planche, *f,* horstexte, *m*; (*turf*) coupe; (*metal*) plaque, *f.* ~*s & dishes,* vaisselle, *f.* ~ *glass,* glace de vitrage, *f.* ~ *glass insurance,* assurance contre le bris de glaces, *f.* ~ *holder* (*Phot.*), châssis négatif, c. porteplaque(s) *m.* ¶ *v.t,* plaquer; argenter; (*ship*) border. ~[**ful**], *n,* assiettée, assiette, *f.*

plateau, *n,* plateau, *m.*

platen (*Typ.*) *n,* platine, *f.*

platform, *n,* plate-forme; estrade; tribune, *f*; pont; (*Rly.*) quai, débarcadère, embarcadère; (*Pol.*) programme, *m.* ~ *scales,* bascule romaine, *f.* ~ *ticket,* billet de quai, *m.*

platinotype, *n,* platinotypie, *f.*

platinum, *n*, platine, *m*. ~ *blonde* (color), blond platine, *m*.
platitude, *n*, platitude, *f*.
Platonic, *a*, platonique.
platoon, *n*, peloton, *m*.
plaudit, *n*, applaudissement, *m*.
plausible†, *a*, plausible.
play, *n*, jeu, *m*; récréation, *f*; essor, *m*, carrière; pièce [de théâtre] *f*; spectacle; (*Mech.*) jeu, *m*, chasse, *f*. ~*fellow*, ~*mate*, camarade de jeu, *m,f*. ~*goer*, coureur (euse) de spectacles. ~*ground*, cour de récréation, *f*, (*covered*) préau, *m*. ~ *of colors*, reflets irisés, *m.pl*. ~ *of features*, jeux de physionomie, *m.pl*. ~ *of light*, jeu de lumière, chatoiement, *m*. ~ *on words*, jeu de mots, *m*. ~ *pen*, parc d'enfant, *m*. ~*thing*, jouet, joujou, *m*, amusette, babiole, *f*. ~*time*, récréation, *f*. ~*wright*, auteur dramatique, dramatiste, *m*, dramaturge, *m,f*. ¶ *v.i*, jouer; (*v.t.*) jouer; j. de; faire; (*harp, etc.*) pincer; (*a fish*) noyer. ~*er*, *n*, joueur, euse; musicien, ne; acteur, trice, comédien, ne. ~ *piano*, piano mécanique, *m*. ~*ful*, *a*, folâtre, enjoué, badin. ~*fulness*, *n*, enjouement, *m. playing cards*, cartes à jouer, *f.pl*.
plea, *n*, prétexte, *m*; (*law*) défenses, *f.pl*; exception, *f*; (*pl.*) conclusions, *f.pl*. **plead**, *v.t. & i*, plaider, alléguer, prétexter. ~ *guilty*, s'avouer coupable, s'accuser soi-même. ~ *not guilty*, nier sa culpabilité. ~*ing* (*law*) *n*, (*oral advocacy*) plaidoirie; (*preparatory formalities*) instruction; (*pl, statement*) instruction par écrit, *f*.
pleasant†, *a*, agréable, aimable; commode. ~*ness*, *n*, agrément, *m*. ~*ry*, *n*, plaisanterie, *f*. **please**, *v.t*, plaire à, agréer à; sourire à; flatter; accommoder; (*abs.*) plaire. ¶ *imperative*, s'il vous plaît; veuillez; prière de . . .; de grâce! ~*d*, *p.a*, content, heureux, aise. **pleasing†**, *a*, agréable, amène; gracieux. **pleasurable†**, *a*, agréable. **pleasure**, *n*, plaisir; agrément, *m*; douceur; jouissance; volupté, *f*; honneur; gré, *m*. ~ *boat*, bateau de plaisance, *m*. ~ *trip*, voyage d'agrément, *m*.

pleat, *n*, pli, *m*, pince, *f*. ¶ *v.t*, plisser.
pledge, *n*, gage, engagement, *m*, plébiscite, *n*, plébiscite, *m*.
pledge, *n*, gage, engagement, *m*, assurance, *f*. ¶ *v.t*, engager; boire à la santé de.
plenary, *a*, plénier. **plenipotentiary**, *a. & n*, plénipotentiaire, *a. & m*. **plenitude**, *n*, plénitude, *f*. **plenteous†** & **plentiful†**, *a*, abondant. *to be plentiful*, foisonner. **plenty**, *n*, abondance; foison, *f*. ~ *of*, force. *with* ~ *of*, à grand renfort de. **plenum**, *n*, plein, *m*.
pleonasm, *n*, pléonasme, *m*.
plethora, *n*, pléthore, *f*.
pleura, *n*, plèvre, *f*. **pleurisy**, *n*, pleurésie, *f*.
plexus, *n*, plexus, réseau, lacis, *m*.
pliable, *a*, pliable, pliant, flexible, souple. **pliancy**, *n*, flexibilité, souplesse, *f*.
pliers, *n.pl*, pince, *f*, pinces, *f.pl*. *flat-nosed* ~, bec-de-cane, *m*.
plight, *n*, état, *m*, passe, *f*, arroi, *m*. ¶ *v.t*, engager.
plinth, *n*, plinthe, *f*.
plod on, along, *v.i*, avancer péniblement. **plodder**, *n*, bûcheur, euse.
plot, *n*, parcelle, *f*, lopin, coin; complot, *m*, conspiration, trame, intrigue; (*novel, play*) intrigue, *f*. ¶ *v.t. & i*, (*curve, etc.*) tracer; comploter, conspirer, machiner. **plotter**, *n*, conspirateur, trice.
plow, *n*, charrue, *f*. ~ *land*, terre labourable, *f*. ~*man*, laboureur, valet de charrue, *m*. ~*share*, soc, *m*. ¶ *v.t. & i*, labourer; (*fig.*) sillonner. ~*ing*, *n*, labourage, labour, *m*.
pluck, *n*, courage, estomac, cran, *m*; (*butchery*) fressure, *f*. ¶ *v.t*, arracher; [dé]plumer, dépiler; cueillir; (*Mus. strings*) pincer. ~*y†*, *a*, courageux, crâne.
plug, *n*, tampon, bouchon, obturateur, *m*; (*Elec.*) prise de courant, *f*; (*twist of tobacco*) carotte, *f*. ¶ *v.t*, tamponner, boucher. ~ *in*, brancher.
plum, *n*, prune, *f*; (*dried*) pruneau, *m*. ~ *orchard*, prunelaie, *f*. ~ *pudding*, plum-pudding, *m*. ~ [*tree*], prunier, *m*.
plumage, *n*, plumage, *m*.
plumb, *a*, droit, vertical. ¶ *ad*, à plomb, d'aplomb. ¶ *n*, plomb, *m*.

~ *line*, fil à plomb, *m*. ¶ *v.t*, plomber. **plumbago**, *n*, plombagine, *f*, graphite, *m*. **plumber**, *n*, plombier, fontainier, *m*. **plumbing**, *n*, plombage, *m*; plomberie, *f*.

plume, *n*, plumet, panache, *m*, aigrette, *f*. ¶ *v.t*, empanacher. ~ *its feathers*, s'éplucher. ~ *oneself on*, se piquer de, se targuer de.

plummet, *n*, plomb; fil à plomb, *m*; sonde, *f*.

plump, *a*, rebondi, dodu, potelé, en chair, paquet; (*chicken*) gras. ~**ness**, *n*, embonpoint, *m*.

plunder, *n*, pillage; butin, *m*. ¶ *v.t*, piller, butiner. ~**er**, *n*, pillard, e.

plunge, *n*, plongeon; (*Swim.*) plongeon sans élan, *m*. *to take the* ~ (*fig.*), faire le saut périlleux, sauter le fossé. ¶ *v.t*, plonger, immerger; ensevelir; (*v.i.*) [se] plonger. **plunger**, *n*, plongeur, *m*.

pluperfect, *n*, plus-que-parfait, *m*.

plural, *a*, plural; (*Gram.*) pluriel. ¶ *n*, pluriel, *m*. ~**ity**, *n*, pluralité, *f*; (*of offices*) cumul, *m*.

plus, *pr*, plus. *he is 10, 12*, ~, il a 10, 12, ans révolus. ~*fours*, culotte pour le golf, *f*. ~ [*sign*], [signe] plus, *m*.

plush, *n*, peluche, *f*.

ply, *n*, pli, *m*, épaisseur, *f*. ~*wood*, [bois] contreplaqué, *m*. ¶ *v.t*, (*tool*) manier; (*questions*) presser (*with* = de); (*trade*) exercer; (*v.i.*) faire le service, marcher.

pneumatic, *a*, pneumatique; à air comprimé. ~ [*tire*], [bandage] pneumatique, pneu, *m*.

pneumonia, *n*, pneumonie, *f*.

Po (the), le Pô.

poach, *v.t*, pocher; (*v.i.*) braconner. ~**er**, *n*, braconnier, *m*.

pocket, *n*, poche, *f*; (*vest*) gousset, *m*; (*Bil.*) blouse, *f*. *air* ~, trou d'air, *m*. ~ *money*, argent de poche, *m*. *in one's* ~ (*fig.*), en poche. ¶ *v.t*, empocher. ~*ful*, *n*, pleine poche, *f*.

pocketbook, *n*, sac à main; (*publishing*) livre de poche; (*wallet*) portefeuille; (*small purse*) portemonnaie, *m*.

pocketknife, *n*, canif, *m*.

pockmarked, *a*, marqué (*ou* picoté) de petite vérole, grêlé.

pod, *n*, cosse, gousse. *f*.

poem, *n*, poème, *m*, poésie, *f*. **poet**, *n*, poète, *m*. ~*aster*, *n*, poétereau, *m*. ~*ess*, *n*, poétesse, femme poète, *f*. ~*ic*, ~*ical†*, *a*, poétique. ~*ry*, *n*, poésie, *f*.

poignant, *a*, poignant, empoignant.

point, *n*, point; fait, *m*; pointe, *f*; poinçon; bec, *m*; (*Rly.*) aiguille, *f*; piquant, *m*; température; question, *f*. ~*blank*, *ad*, de but en blanc, à bout portant, à brûlepourpoint. ~ *lace*, point, *m*. ~ *of the compass*, aire de vent, *f*, quart de v., *m*. *6, 8*, ~ [*size*] (*Typ.*), corps 6, 8; corps de 6, de 8, points, *m*. *to the* ~, à propos. ¶ *v.t*, pointer; appointer, épointer, tailler [en pointe]; (*masonry*) jointoyer; (*v.t. & abs.*, *of dog*) arrêter. ~ *at*, montrer du doigt. ~ *out*, signaler, indiquer, désigner. ~*ed*, *a*, pointu; piquant; peu voilé, peu équivoque. ~*er*, *n*, (*rod*) baguette, *f*; index; chien d'arrêt, *m*.

poise, *n*, balance, *f*, équilibre, *m*. ¶ *v.t*, balancer, équilibrer.

poison, *n*, poison, toxique, *m*. ~ *gas*, gaz toxique, *m*. ¶ *v.t*, empoisonner, intoxiquer. ~*er*, *n*, empoisonneur, euse. ~*ing*, *n*, empoisonnement, *m*, intoxication, *f*. ~*ous*, *a*, toxique; vénéneux; venimeux. *substance which is* ~, substance qui empoisonne.

poke, *n*, coup, *m*. ¶ *v.t*, fourrer; mettre; (*fire*) attiser, fourgonner. ~ *about*, fourgonner. **poker**, *n*, tisonnier, *m*; (*cards*) poker, *m*. **poky**, *a*, resserré, étroit, mesquin.

Poland, *n*, la Pologne.

polar, *a*, polaire. ~ *bear*, ours blanc, *m*. **pole**, *n*, poteau, *m*, perche, gaule, *f*, mât; bâton; (*carriage*) timon; (*Astr., Phys.*, etc.) pôle, *m*; Meas. = 25.293 sq. meters. **P**~, *n*, Polonais, e. ~*axe*, merlin, assommoir, *m*; (*Hist.*) hache d'armes, *f*. ~*cat*, putois, *m*. ~ *jump*, saut à la perche, *m*. ~ *star*, étoile polaire, *f*. ¶ *v.t*, échalasser.

polarization, *n*, polarisation, *f*. **polarize**, *v.t*, polariser.

polemic(al), *a*, polémique. polemic, *n. & ~s*, *n.pl*, polémique, *f*.

police, *n*, police, *f*. ~ *court*, tribunal de simple police, *m*. ~ *department*, préfecture de police, *f*. ~ *headquarters*, commissariat, *m*. ~*man*, agent de police, gardien de la paix, sergent de ville, *m*. ~ *records*, casier judiciaire, *m*. ~ *station*, bureau de police, poste de p, *m*. ~ *wagon*, panier à salade, *m*. *motorcycle* ~*man*, motard, *m*.

policy, *n*, politique, *f*; (*public*) ordre, *m*; (*Insce*) police, *f*.

Polish, *a*, polonais. ¶ *n*, le polonais.

polish, *n*, poli; vernis, *m*; pâte à polir, *f*. ¶ *v.t*, polir; vernir; cirer; faire reluire; frotter; encaustiquer. ~*ing brush* (*shoes*), brosse à reluire, *f*.

polite, *a*, poli. **politely,** *ad*, poliment. ~**ness,** *n*, politesse; (*to women*) galanterie, *f*.

politic & ~**al†**, *a*, politique. ~**ian,** *n*, [homme] politique; (*as a trade*) politicien, *m*. ~**s,** *n.pl*. & **polity,** *n*, politique, *f*. *to talk politics,* politiquer.

polka, *n*, polka, *f*.

poll, *n*, scrutin, vote, *m*. ~ *tax*, capitation, *f*. ~*ing station,* bureau de scrutin, *m*.

pollard, *n*, têtard, *m*. ¶ *v.t*, étêter.

pollen, *n*, pollen, *m*.

pollute, *v.t*, polluer, souiller.

polo, *n*. & ~ *cap*, polo, *m*.

polonaise, *n*, polonaise, *f*.

poltroon, *n*, poltron, ne.

polyanthus, *n*, primevère des jardins, *f*. **polygamist,** *n*. & **polygamous,** *a*, polygame, *m,f*. & *a*. **polygamy,** *n*, polygamie, *f*. **polyglot,** *a*. & *n*, polyglotte, *a*. & *m,f*. **polygon,** *n*, polygone, *m*. **Polynesia,** *n*, la Polynésie. **polyp** & **polypus,** *n*, polype, *m*. **polysyllabic,** *a*. & **polysyllable,** *n*, polysyllabe, *a*. & *m*. **polytechnic,** *a*, polytechnique. **polytheism,** *n*, polythéisme, *m*.

pomade, *n*, pommade, *f*. ¶ *v.t*, pommader.

pomegranate, *n*, grenade, *f*. ~ [*tree*], grenadier, *m*.

Pomeranian [dog], *n*. or **pom,** *abb*, loulou [de Poméranie] *m*.

pommel, *n*, pommeau, *m*. ¶ *v.t*, rosser, frotter, gourmer.

pomp, *n*, pompe, *f*, faste, apparat, attirail, *m*.

Pompeii, *n*, Pompéi, *f*.

pomposity, *n*, emphase, *f*. **pompous†,** *a*, pompeux; emphatique; doctoral.

pond, *n*, étang, *m*, mare, *f*; (*of canal*) bief, *m*.

ponder, *v.i*, réfléchir, méditer, rêver; (*v.t.*) peser, ruminer. ~**able,** *a*, pondérable, pesant. ~**ous†,** *a*, pesant.

pontiff, *n*, pontife, *m*. **pontifical†,** *a*. & *n*, pontifical, *a*. & *m*. **pontificate,** *n*, pontificat, *m*.

pontoon, *n*, ponton, caisson, *m*. ~ *bridge,* pont de bateaux, *m*.

pony, *n*, poney, *m*.

poodle, *n*, caniche, *m,f*.

pooh, *i*, bah!, baste! **pooh-pooh,** *v.t*, faire fi de, repousser avec mépris.

pool, *n*, (*swimming*) piscine; mare, *f*, étang, *m*; (*cards*) poule, cagnotte, *f*; (*fencing, shooting, ice hockey*) poule, *f*; (*Com.*) pool; (*Fin.*) syndicat de placement, groupement, *m*; *betting,* pari mutuel, *m*. ¶ *v.t*, mettre en commun.

poop, *n*. & ~ *deck,* dunette, *f*.

poor, *a*, pauvre; indigent; maigre; méchant. ~ *box,* tronc des pauvres, *m*. ~ *health,* une santé médiocre, une petite santé. ~ *house,* hospice, *m*. ~ *little thing* (*pers.*), pauvret, te. *the* ~, les pauvres, les indigents, *m.pl*. ~**ly,** *ad*, pauvrement. ¶ *a*, indisposé, incommodé, souffrant. ~**ness,** *n*, pauvreté, *f*.

pope, *n*, pape, *m*. ~**ry,** *n*, papisme, *m*.

popinjay (*Hist.*) *n*, papegai, *m*.

popish, *a*, papiste.

poplar, *n*, peuplier, *m*.

poplin, *n*, popeline, *f*.

poppy, *n*, pavot; coquelicot, ponceau, *m*.

populace, *n*, populace, *f*. **popular†,** *a*, populaire; (*treatise*) de vulgarisation. ~**ity,** *n*, popularité, *f*. ~**ize,** *v.t*, vulgariser. **populate,** *v.t*, peupler. **population,** *n*, population, *f*. **populous,** *a*, populeux.

porcelain, *n*, porcelaine, *f*.

porch, *n*, porche, portique, *m*.

porcupine, *n*, porc-épic, *m*.

pore, *n*, pore, *m*. ~ *over,* s'ab-

sorber dans la lecture de; méditer
sur.

pork, n, porc, m; charcuterie, f.
~ *butcher,* charcutier, m. ~**er,** n,
cochon; goret, m.

pornographer, n, pornographe.
m. **pornographic,** a, pornographique, porno. **pornography,** n,
pornographie, porno, f.

porosity, n, porosité, f. **porous,**
a, poreux.

porphyry, n, porphyre, m.

porpoise, n, marsouin, m.

porridge, n, bouillie, f. **porringer,** n, écuelle, f.

port, n, port; (*side*) bâbord, m.
free ~, port franc, m. ~ [*hole*],
hublot, m. ~ *of call,* escale; relâche, f. ~ *of registry,* port
d'attache. ~ [*wine*], porto, vin de
Porto, m.

portable, a, portatif, mobile.

portage, n, portage, m.

portal, n, portail, m.

portcullis, n, herse, f.

portend, v.t, présager. **portent,**
n, présage, m. **portentous,** a, de
mauvais présage; prodigieux.

porter, n, concierge, portier; porteur; portefaix; commissionaire;
facteur, m. ~**age,** n, portage,
factage, m.

portfolio, n, portefeuille, m,
serviette, f.

portico, n, portique, m.

portion, n, portion, part, f, quartier, m; (*of Rly. train*) rame;
(*marriage*) dot, f. ¶ v.t, partager,
doter.

portland cement, chaux-limite,
f.

portliness, n, corpulence; prestance, f. **portly,** a, corpulent,
gros; d'un port noble.

portmanteau, n, valise, f.

portrait & ~**ure,** n, portrait, m.
portray, v.t, [dé]peindre. **portrayal,** n, peinture, f.

portress, n, concierge, portière, f.

Portugal, n, le Portugal. **Portuguese,** a, portugais. ¶ n, (*pers.*)
Portugais, e; (*language*) le portugais.

pose, n, pose; affectation, f. ¶ v.i.
& t, poser. **poser,** n, problème,
m. **position,** n, position, situation; posture; condition, f; emplacement; classement, m. ¶ v.t,
classer.

positive†, a, positif; absolu.

posse, n, brigade, f.

possess, v.t, posséder. ~**ed,** p.p,
possédé; *as if* ~, endiablé. *one*
~, possédé, e. ~**ion,** n, possession; jouissance, f; (*pl.*) possessions, f.pl, avoir, bien, m. *with
immediate* ~, présentement. ~**-
ive,** a, possessif. ~**or,** n, possesseur, m.

possibility, n, possibilité, f. **possible,** a. & n, possible, a. & m. *to
be* ~, se pouvoir. **possibly,** ad,
peut-être. *he cannot* ~ . . ., il est
impossible qu'il . . .

post, n, (*upright*) poteau; (*door*)
montant; pieu; étai, m; (*bed*)
colonne, f; (*place*) poste, m;
(*P.O.*) poste, f; (*letters*) courrier,
m. ~**card,** carte postale, f. *to go*
~**haste,** accourir dare-dare. ~**-
man,** facteur [des postes] m. ~**-
mark,** n, timbre, m; (*v.t.*) timbrer. ~**master, mistress,** maître
(maîtresse) de poste, receveur
(euse) des postes. ~**master general,** directeur général des postes,
télégraphes & téléphones, m. ~
office, bureau de poste, m, poste,
f. ~ *office guide,* indicateur universel des P.T.T., m. ~ *office
order,* mandat[-poste] m. ¶ v.t,
mettre à la poste: afficher, placarder; mettre au courant;
(*Bkkpg.*) [re]porter; (*men*)
[a]poster, poser. ~**age,** n, port,
m. ~ *stamp,* timbre-poste, m.
~**al,** a, postal. ~ *order,* mandat
[-poste] m. **postpaid,** ad, affranchi, post payé.

postdate, n, postdate, f. ¶ v.t,
postdater.

poster, n, affiche, f, placard, m.

posterior†, a. & n, postérieur, a.
& m.

posterity, n, postérité, f.

postern, n, poterne, f.

posthumous, a, posthume.

postillion, n, postillon, m.

posting, n, mise à la poste, f; affichage; (*Bkkpg.*) report, m; (*sentry*) pose, f.

post meridiem (*abb.* p.m.),
après midi; de l'après-midi, du
soir.

post mortem, n, autopsie, f.

postpone, v.t, remettre, renvoyer,
différer, ajourner.

postscript (*abb.* P.S.) n, post-
scriptum, P.-S., m.

postulant, n, postulant, e.

posture, *n*, posture, pose, attitude, *f*; état, *m*.

postwar, *a*, d'après-guerre.

posy, *n*, fleur, *f*.

pot, *n*, pot, *m*; marmite, *f*; chaudron, *m*; terrine, *f*; creuset, *m*; (*cards*) cagnotte, *f*. ~ *bellied*, ventru. ~ *boiler*, besogne alimentaire, *f*. ~ *herb*, herbe potagère, *f*. ~*hole*, excavation, marmite, *f*. ~*holder*, attrape-plats, *m*. ~*hook*, crémaillère, *f*; (*writing*) jambage, *m*. to take ~ *luck*, dîner à la fortune du pot. ¶ *v.t*, empoter. ~*ful*, *n*, potée, *f*.

potable, *a*, potable.

potash, *n*, potasse, *f*. **potassium**, *n*, potassium, *m*.

potato, *n*, pomme de terre, *f*. *sweet* ~, patate, *f*.

potency, *n*, force, *f*. **potent**†, *a*, puissant; fort. **potentate**, *n*, potentat, *m*. **potential**, *a*. & *n*, potentiel, *a*. & *m*.

potion, *n*, potion, *f*.

potted, *p.a*, en pot, en terrine.

potter, *n*, potier, *m*. ~'s *wheel*, tour de potier, *m*. ~**y**, *n*, poterie; faïence; faïencerie, *f*.

pouch, *n*, poche, *f*, sac, *m*, bourse; (*cartridge*) cartouchière, giberne; gibecière; (*tobacco*) blague, *f*.

pouf, *n*, pouf, *m*.

poulterer, *n*, marchand de volaille, *m*.

poultice, *n*, cataplasme, *m*.

poultry, *n*, volaille, *f*. ~ *farming*, aviculture, *f*. ~ *yard*, basse-cour, *f*.

pounce, *n*, ponce, *f*. ¶ *v.t*, poncer. ~ *on*, fondre sur.

pound, *n*, (*for cattle*) fourrière; (£) livre; (*avoirdupois weight*) livre [poids] *f*. = 0.45359243 kilogram. ¶ *v.t*, piler.

pour, *v.t*, verser; couler; jeter; répandre; épancher; (*oil on waves*) filer. *it is* ~*ing*, il pleut à verse. ~*ing rain*, pluie battante, *f*.

pout, *v.i*, faire la moue, faire la lippe. ~**er**, *n*, pigeon grosse gorge, *m*.

poverty, *n*, pauvreté, *f*. ~-*stricken* (*person*), miséreux, euse.

powder, *n*, poudre, *f*. ~ *box*, boîte à poudre, *f*, poudrier, *m*. ~ *magazine*, poudrière, *f*. ~ *puff*, houppe à poudrer, *f*. ¶ *v.t*, pulvériser; poudrer; saupoudrer. ~**y**, *a*, poudreux, pulvérulent.

power, *n*, puissance, *f*; pouvoir, *m*; énergie; force; faculté; autorité, *f*; (*att.*) mécanique; marchant au moteur. ~ *hammer*, marteau-pilon, *m*. ~ *house*, ~ *station*, usine de force motrice, *f*. ~**ful**†, *a*, puissant; fort; énergique. ~**less**, *a*, impuissant.

practicable, *a*, praticable, faisable, exécutable. **practical**†, *a*, pratique; (*pers.*) positif. ~ *joke*, farce, fumisterie; brimade, *f*. ~ *joker*, farceur, euse, fumiste, *m*. **practice**, *n*, pratique; habitude, *f*; usage, *m*; coutume, *f*; exercice; tir, *m*; (*sport*) mise en train, *f*; quelques coups d'essai, quelques échanges, *m.pl*; clientèle; charge; étude, *f*, cabinet, *m*. **practician**, *n*, praticien, *m*. **practice**, *v.t*, pratiquer; exercer; suivre; s'exercer à; user de. **practitioner**, *n*, praticien, *m*.

prairie, *n*, prairie, *f*.

praise, *n*, louange, *f*; éloge, *m*. ¶ *v.t*, louer; glorifier; prôner; vanter. ~*worthy*, digne d'éloges, louable.

prance, *v.i*, piaffer.

prank, *n*, escapade, espièglerie, *f*.

prate, *v.i*, bavarder.

pratique, *n*, [libre] pratique, *f*.

prattle, *n*, babil, gazouillement, *m*. ¶ *v.i*, babiller, gazouiller.

prawn, *n*, crevette rouge, *f*.

pray, *v.t. & i*, prier. ¶ (*form of address*) je vous prie, veuillez; de grâce; je vous le demande. **prayer**, *n*, prière; supplique, *f*, oremus, *m*. ~ *book*, livre d'église, l. de prières, l. d'office, paroissien, *m*. ~ *wheel*, moulin à prières, *m*.

preach, *v.t. & i*, prêcher. ~**er**, *n*, prédicateur; (*protestant*) prédicant, *m*. ~**ing**, *n*, prédication, *f*.

preamble, *n*, préambule, *m*.

prearranged, *p.a*, arrangé d'avance.

prebend, *n*, prébende, *f*. ~**ary**, *n*, prébendier, *m*.

precarious†, *a*, précaire.

precast, *a*, préfabriqué; précontraint.

precaution, *n*, précaution, prévoyance, *f*. ~**ary**, *a*, de précaution, de prévoyance.

precede, *v.t*, précéder; devancer. **precedence**, *n*, priorité; préséance, *f*, pas, *m*. **precedent**, *n*. & **preceding**, *a*, précédent, *m*. & *a*.

precentor, *n,* grand chantre, *m.*
precept, *n,* précepte, *m.* **~or,** *n,* précepteur, *m.*
precinct, *n,* enceinte, *f;* (*pl.*) pourtour, *m.*
precious†, *a,* précieux.
precipice, *n,* précipice, *m.* **precipitancy & precipitation,** *n,* précipitation, *f.* **precipitate,** *v.t. & i,* précipiter; brusquer. ¶ *a. & n,* précipité, *a. & m.* **~ly,** *ad,* précipitamment. **precipitous,** *a,* escarpé, à pic.
precise, *a,* précis; formaliste. **~ly,** *ad,* précisément. **to state ~,** préciser. **precision,** *n,* précision, *f.*
preclude, *v.t,* empêcher de.
precocious, *a,* précoce; (*too knowing*) savant; (*in vice*) polisson. **~ness,** *n,* précocité, *f.*
preconceived, preconcerted, *a,* préconçu, arrêté.
precursor, *n. &* **~y,** *a,* précurseur, *m. & a.m.*
predatory, *a,* rapace; de proie.
predecease, *n,* prédécès, *m.* ¶ *v.i,* prédécéder.
predecessor, *n,* prédécesseur, *m,* devancier, ère.
predestination, *n,* prédestination, *f.*
predicament, *n,* [mauvaise] passe, situation difficile; (*Log.*) catégorie, *f.*
predicate (*Log. & Gram.*) *n,* attribut, prédicat, *m.* ¶ *v.t,* attribuer; affirmer (*ou* énoncer) un rapport (*of* = entre). **predicative adjective,** adjectif attribut, *m.*
predict, *v.t,* prédire. **~ion,** *n,* prédiction, *f.*
predilection, *n,* prédilection, *f.*
predispose, *v.t,* prédisposer.
predominance, *n,* prédominance, *f.* **predominate,** *v.i,* prédominer.
preeminent, *a,* prééminent. **~ly,** *ad,* par excellence.
preemption, *n,* préemption, *f.*
preen, *v.t,* éplucher. **~ *its feathers,*** s'éplucher.
prefab, *a,* préfabriqué. **prefabrication,** *n,* préfabrication, *f.*
preface, *n,* préface, *f,* avant-propos, *m.* ¶ *v.t,* préluder à. **prefatory,** *a,* liminaire; à titre de préface.
prefect, *n,* préfet, *m.* **~ure,** *n,* préfecture, *f.*

prefer, *v.t,* préférer, aimer mieux; promouvoir; (*charges*) déposer. **~able†,** *a,* préférable. **~ence,** *n,* préférence, *f;* (*Cust.*) régime de faveur, *m,* préférence, *f.* **preferred stock,** actions de priorité, a—s privilégiées, *f.pl.* **preferential,** *a,* de préférence, privilégié. **preferment,** *n,* promotion, *f.*
prefix, *n,* préfixe, *m.* ¶ *v.t,* joindre à titre de préface; joindre comme préfixe. **~ed** (*Gram.*) *p.a,* préfixe.
pregnable, *a,* prenable.
pregnancy, *n,* grossesse, *f.* **pregnant,** *a,* enceinte, grosse; (*animal*) pleine; (*fig.*) gros, plein. **to become ~,** engrossir. **to make ~,** engrosser.
prehensile, *a,* préhenseur, *a.m.* **~ tail,** queue prenante, *f.*
prehistoric, *a,* préhistorique.
prejudge, *v.t,* préjuger. **prejudice,** *n,* préjudice, détriment; préjugé, *m,* prévention, *f,* parti pris, *m. without ~ to,* sans préjudice de. ¶ *v.t,* prévenir; nuire à. **prejudicial,** *a,* préjudiciable; attentatoire.
prelacy, *n,* prélature, *f.* **prelate,** *n,* prélat, *m.*
preliminary, *a,* préliminaire, préalable. **~ *expenses*** (company), frais de constitution, *m. pl.* **preliminaries,** *n.pl,* préliminaires, *m.pl,* préface, *f;* (*book, abb.* **prelims**) pièces liminaires, *f.pl.*
prelude, *n,* prélude, *m.* ¶ *v.i,* préluder.
premature†, *a,* prématuré; (*childbirth*) avant terme.
premeditate, *v.t,* préméditer. **premeditation,** *n,* préméditation, *f.*
premier, *a,* premier. ¶ *n,* président du conseil [des ministres], premier ministre, *m.* **~ship,** *n,* présidence du conseil.
premise, *v.t,* faire remarquer d'avance. **~s,** *n.pl,* immeuble, *m,* locaux, lieux, *m.pl;* (*deed*) intitulé, *m.* **premises** (*Log.*) *n.pl,* prémisses, *f.pl.*
premium, *n,* prime; récompense, *f.*
premonition, *n,* présage, *m.* **premonitory,** *a,* prémonitoire, avant-coureur, précurseur. **~ *symptom,*** prodrome, *m.*

preoccupation, *n*, préoccupation, *f*. **preoccupy**, *v.t*, préoccuper.

preparation, *n*, préparation; (*Sch.*) étude, *f*; (*pl.*) préparatifs, apprêts, *m.pl*. **preparatory**, *a*, préparatoire. ~ *work* (*Min.*), dispositifs de mines, *m.pl*. **prepare**, *v.t*, préparer; apprêter. **~d** (*ready*) *p.a*, prêt.

prepay, *v.t*, payer d'avance; affranchir.

preponderance, *n*, prépondérance, *f*. **to preponderate over**, l'emporter sur.

preposition, *n*, préposition, *f*.

prepossess, *v.t*, prévenir. **~ing**, *a*, prévenant, avenant. **~ion**, *n*, prévention, *f*.

preposterous†, *a*, déraisonnable, absurde, saugrenu.

prerequisite, *a*, requis. ¶ *n*, nécessité préalable, *f*.

prerogative, *n*, prérogative, *f*, privilège, *m*.

presage, *n*, présage, *m*. ¶ *v.t*, présager.

Presbyterian, *n*. & *a*, presbytérien, ne.

prescience, *n*, prescience, *f*.

prescribe, *v.t*, prescrire; (*Med.*) ordonner. **prescription**, *n*, prescription; (*Med.*) ordonnance, prescription, formule, *f*.

presence, *n*, présence; prestance, *f*. ~ *of mind*, présence d'esprit, *f*. **present**, *a*, présent; actuel; courant. ¶ *n*, (*gift*) cadeau, présent, *m*. *at* ~, présentement. ¶ *v.t*, présenter; offrir. **~able**, *a*, présentable; montrable. **presentation**, *n*, présentation, *f*. ~ *copy*, exemplaire en hommage, *m*.

presentiment, *n*, pressentiment, *m*. *to have a* ~ *of*, pressentir.

presently, *ad*, tantôt, tout à l'heure.

preservation, *n*, conservation; préservation, *f*. **preservative**, *n*. & *a*, préservatif; (*for food*) antiseptique, *m*. & *a*. **preserve**, *n*, conserve, *f*, confiture, *f*. *oft. pl*, marmelade; réserve, (*pl.*) chasse gardée, c. réservée, *f*; (*fig.*) fief, *m*; (*pl.*) conserves, *f.pl*. ¶ *v.t*, préserver; conserver; confire; (*plant*) naturaliser.

preside, *v.i*, présider. ~ *at*, *over*, présider [à]. **presidency**, *n*, présidence, *f*. **president**, *n*, président, e.

press, *n*, presse, *f*; pressoir, *m*; armoire, *f*; journalisme, *m*; (*of sail*) force, *f*. *the* ~ (*newspapers*), la presse. *in the* ~, sous presse. ~ *agency*, agence d'information, *f*. (*book*) exemplaire de presse, e. de publicité, *m*. ~ *cutting*, coupure de journal, *f*. ~*man*, (*Typ.*) pressier, *m*. ¶ *v.t*. & *i*, presser; serrer; pressurer; fouler; activer; appuyer; peser. **~ing**, *a*, pressant, pressé, urgent; (*debt*) criarde. **pressure**, *n*, pression, *f*; serrement, *m*; presse, *f*; accablement, *m*; (*Mech.*) poussée; tension, *f*. *blood* ~, tension artérielle, *f*. ~ *cooker*, autocuiseur, *m*, cocotte-minute, *f*. ~ *gauge*, manomètre, *m*.

prestige, *n*, prestige, *m*.

presume, *v.t*. & *i*, présumer. ~ [*up*]*on*, se prévaloir de. **presumption**, *n*, présomption, *f*; préjugé, *m*. **presumptuous**, *a*, présomptueux. **~ness**, *n*, outrecuidance, *f*.

presuppose, *v.t*, présupposer.

pretence, *n*, [faux] semblant, *m*, feinte, *f*; prétexte, *m*. **pretend**, *v.t*. & *i*, faire semblant; prétexter; feindre; prétendre. **~er**, *n*, prétendant, e. **pretension**, *n*, prétention, *f*. **pretentious**, *a*, prétentieux.

preterite, *n*, prétérit, *m*.

preternatural†, *a*, surnaturel.

pretext, *n*, prétexte, *m*.

prettiness, *n*, gentillesse, *f*. **pretty†**, *a*, joli, gentil, bellot. ¶ *ad*, assez. ~ *good*, passable, passablement bon. ~ *much*, à peu près. ~ *well*, assez bien.

prevail over, prévaloir sur, l'emporter sur. *prevail* [*up*]*on*, décider, persuader à. **prevailing**, *p.a*, dominant, régnant; général. **prevalence**, *n*, fréquence, prédominance, *f*. **prevalent**, *a*, régnant, prédominant. *to be* ~, régner.

prevaricate, *v.i*, tergiverser, équivoquer. **prevarication**, *n*, tergiversation, équivoque, *f*.

prevent, *v.t*, empêcher, obvier à, prévenir. **~ion**, *n*, empêchement, *m*; défense préventive, *f*. *society for the* ~ *of cruelty to animals*, société protectrice des animaux, *f*. **~ive**, *n*, préservatif, *m*.

previous†, *a*, précédent, antérieur, préalable. ~ *speaker*, préopinant, *m*.

prevision, *n*, prévision, *f*.

prewar, *a*, d'avant-guerre.

prey, *n*, proie, *f*. ~ [*up*]*on*, faire sa proie de; (*the mind*) miner, ronger.

price, *n*, prix; cours; taux; *m*; cote, *f*. *all at the same* ~, au choix. ~ *list*, prix courant, tarif, *m*. ¶ *v.t*, tarifer. ~**less**, *a*, sans prix, inappréciable, inestimable, impayable.

prick, *n*, piqûre, *f*; coup; (*conscience*) reproche, *m*. ¶ *v.t*, piquer; (*conscience*) bourreler. ~ *up* (ears), dresser. **prickle**, *n*, aiguillon, piquant, *m*. **prickly**, *a*, épineux, piquant, *s*. ~ *pear*, figue de Barbarie, *f*.

pride, *n*, orgueil, *m*, fierté, gloire, *f*; amour-propre, *m*; (*collection of animals*) troupe, *f*. ~ *oneself* [*up*]*on*, s'enorgueillir de, se faire gloire de, se piquer de, se targuer de.

priest, *n*, prêtre, *m*. ~**ess**, *n*, prêtresse, *f*. ~**hood**, *n*, prêtrise, *f*, sacerdoce; clergé, *m*. ~**ly**, *a*, sacerdotal.

prig, *n*, pédant, e. **priggish**, *a*, pédant.

prim, *a*, pincé, affecté, collet monté.

primacy, *n*, primatie, primauté, *f*.

primary†, *a*, primitif; premier; primordial; primaire. **primate**, *n*, primat, *m*. **prime**, *a*, premier; primordial; de première qualité. ~ *minister*, président du conseil [des ministres], premier ministre, *m*. ~ *mover*, mobile, *m*; cheville ouvrière, *f*. ~ *of life*, fleur de l'âge, force de l'âge, *f*. ¶ *v.t*, (*pump, blasting*) amorcer; (*with paint*) imprimer; (*pers.*) souffler. **primer**, *n*, premier livre de lecture, alphabet, A b c, abécédaire, *m*. **primeval**, *a*, primitif. **priming**, *n*, amorce; (*paint*) impression, *f*. **primitive†**, *a*, primitif; primordial. **primogeniture**, *n*, primogéniture, *f*. **primordial**, *a*, primordial. **primrose**, *n*, primevère, *f*.

prince, *n*, prince, *m*. ~**ly**, *a*, princier. **princess**, *n*, princesse, *f*.

principal†, *a*, principal; capital. ¶ *n*, principal; chef, *m*; directeur, trice; proviseur; patron, ne; mandant, commettant, donneur d'ordre; (*of debt*) capital, principal, *m*. ~**ity**, *n*, principauté, *f*.

principle, *n*, principe, *m*.

prink, *v.t*, éplucher.

print, *n*, empreinte; impression; (*Phot.*) épreuve [positive]; gravure; estampe, *f*; (*type*) caractères, *m.pl. out of* ~, épuisé. ¶ *v.t*, imprimer; tirer; (*with pen*) mouler. ~**er**, *n*, imprimeur, *m*; (*computers*) imprimante, *f*. ~*'s error*, faute d'impression, erreur typographique, *f*. ~*'s imprint*, indication de nom & de lieu de résidence de l'imprimeur, *f*. *high-speed* ~, imprimante à grande vitesse, *f*. *optical* ~, truca, *m*. ~**ing**, *n*, impression, *f*; tirage, *m*; (*art*) imprimerie, *f*. ~ *frame* (*Phot.*), châssis-presse, *m*. ~ *ink*, encre d'imprimerie, *f*. ~ *plant*, imprimerie, typographie, *f*. ~*-out paper* (*Phot.*), papier à image directe, papier à noircissement direct, *m*.

printout, *n*, (*computers*) copie en clair, *f*. ¶ *v.i*, (*computers*)· sortir sur imprimante.

prior, *a*, antérieur. ¶ *n*, prieur, *m*. ~**ess**, *n*, prieure, *f*. ~**ity**, *n*, priorité, antériorité, *f*. **priory**, *n*, prieuré, *m*.

prism, *n*, prisme, *m*. ~**atic**, *a*, prismatique.

prison, *n*, prison, *f*. ~ *breaking*, bris de p., *m*. ~**er**, *n*, prisonnier, ère; détenu, e, prévenu, e. ~*'s base*, jeu de barres, *m*, barres, *f.pl*.

pristine, *a*, primitif.

privacy, *n*, secret, *m*. **private**, *a*, privé; particulier; personnel; intime; bourgeois; simple; (*on door*) défense d'entrer. ~ [*soldier*], [simple] soldat, *m*. *by* ~ *treaty*, à l'amiable, de gré à gré. *in* ~, en particulier. ~ *means*, fortune personnelle, *f*. ~ *view* (*art*), avant-première, *f*. **privateer**, *n*, corsaire, *m*. **privateering**, *n*, course, *f*. **privately**, *ad*, en particulier; dans le privé; privément.

privation, *n*, privation, *f*. **privative** (*Gram.*) *a*. & *n*, privatif, *a*. & *m*.

privet, *n*, troène, *m*.

privilege, *n*, privilège, *m*; prérogative, *f*. ¶ *v.t*, privilégier.

privily, *ad*, en secret. **privy**, *a*, privé. ~ *to*, instruit de. ¶ *n*, privé, *m*, lieux [d'aisance] *m.pl*.

prize, *n*, prix, *m*; (*Nav.*) prise, *f*; (*lottery*) lot, *m*; (*leverage*) levier, *m*, pesée, *f*. ~ *bull*, taureau primé, *m*. ~ *fight*[*ing*], combat de boxe professionnel, *m*. ~ *fighter*, boxeur professionnel, professionnel de la boxe, *m*. ~ *giving*, distribution de prix, *f*. ~ *medal*, médaille d'honneur, *f*. ~ *winner*, médaillé, e, lauréat, *m*. ¶ *v.t*, (*value*) estimer, priser; (*lever*) forcer.

pro, *pr*, pour. *the* ~*s & cons*, le pour & le contre.

probability, *n*, probabilité, vraisemblance, *f*. **probable†**, *a*, probable, vraisemblable.

probate, *n*, vérification de testament, *f*.

probation, *n*, stage, *m*; (*Eccl.*) probation, *f*. ~**er**, *n*, stagiaire, novice, *m,f*.

probe, *n*, (*instrument*) sonde, *f*, stylet, *m*. ¶ *v.t*, sonder.

probity, *n*, probité, *f*.

problem, *n*, problème, *m*. ~ *play*, pièce à thèse, *f*, ~**atic(al)**, *a*, problématique.

proboscis, *n*, trompe; proboscide, *f*.

procedure, *n*, marche à suivre; (*law*) procédure, *f*. **proceed**, *v.i*, procéder; provenir; découler; partir; cheminer; s'acheminer; se rendre; marcher; continuer. ~ *against*, (*law*) poursuivre. ~**ing**, *n*, procédé, *m*; (*pl.*) actes, *m.pl*; démarches; délibérations, *f.pl*; débats, *m.pl*; procédure, *f*; poursuites, *f.pl*. **proceeds**, *n.pl*, produit, *m*.

process, *n*, cours; procédé; processus, *m*. *in the* ~ *of*, en train de.

procession, *n*, procession, *f*, défilé, *m*, marche, *f*, cortège, convoi, *m*.

processor, *n*, (*computers*) processeur, *m*. *word* ~, machine de traitement de texte, *f*. **processing**, *n*, traitement, *m*. *data* ~, traitement de l'information, *m*. *word* ~, t. de texte, *m*.

proclaim, *v.t*, proclamer; publier; annoncer; déclarer; dénoncer;

afficher. **proclamation**, *n*, proclamation; déclaration, *f*.

proclivity, *n*, penchant, *m*.

procrastinate, *v.i*, aller de délai en délai, atermoyer. **procrastination**, *n*, procrastination, *f*, atermoiement, *m*.

procreate, *v.t*, procréer.

proctor (*Univ.*) *n*, censeur, *m*.

procuration, *n*, procuration, *f*, mandat, *m*. **procure**, *v.t*, procurer. ~**ment**, *n*, obtention, *f*; approvisionnement, *m*.

procurer, *n*, proxénète, *m*. **procuress**, *n*, entremetteuse, *f*.

prod, *v.t*, piquer.

prodigal, *a*. & *n*, prodigue, *a*. & *m,f*. ~ *son*, enfant p., *m*. ~**ity**, *n*, prodigalité, *f*.

prodigious†, *a*, prodigieux. **prodigy**, *n*, prodige, *m*.

produce, *n*, produit[s] *m.[pl.]*; provenances, denrées, *f.pl*. ¶ *v.t*, produire; rapporter, fournir; exhiber, [re]présenter, communiquer. **producer**, *n*, producteur, trice; (*movies*) metteur en scène, *m*. **product**, *n*, produit, *m*, production, *f*. ~**ion**, *n*, production; exhibition; (*Theat.*) [re]présentation; mise en scène, *f*. ~**ive**, *a*, productif.

profanation, *n*, profanation, *f*. **profane**, *a*, profane; blasphémateur. ¶ *v.t*, profaner. **profanity**, *n*, irrévérence, *f*; blasphème, *m*.

profess, *v.t*, professer. ~**ed**, *a*, profès, déclaré. ~**ion**, *n*, profession, *f*; état, métier, *m*. ~**ional**, *a*. & *n*, professionnel, le. ~ *jealousy*, jalousie de métier, *f*. ~**or**, *n*, professeur, *m*. ~**orship**, *n*, professorat, *m*, chaire, *f*.

proficient, *a*, versé, expert.

profile, *n*, profil, *m*. ¶ *v.t*, profiler.

profit, *n*, profit, bénéfice, gain, *m*. ~*sharing*, participation aux bénéfices, *f*. ¶ *v.i*, profiter, bénéficier. ~**able**, *a*, rémunérateur, profitable, fructueux. ~**ably**, *ad*, fructueusement, ~**eer**, *n*, profiteur, mercanti, *m*.

profligacy, *n*, dérèglement, *m*. **profligate**, *a*, dissolu, débauché. ¶ *n*, dévergondé, e.

profound, *a*, profond, approfondi. ~**ly**, *ad*, profondément. **profundity**, *n*, profondeur, *f*.

profuse, *a*, abondant; prodigue; profus. ~**ly**, *ad*, abondamment;

profusément. **profusion**, *n*, profusion, *f*, luxe, *m*.
progenitor, *n*, auteur, *m*. *our* ~*s*, les auteurs de nos jours.
progeny, *n*, descendants, *m.pl*; progéniture, couvée, *f*.
prognathous, *a*, prognathe.
prognosticate, *v.t*, pronostiquer. **prognostic[ation]**, *n*, pronostic, *m*.
program, *n*, programme, *m*. ~ *library*, programmathèque, *f*. ¶ *v.t*, (*computers*) programmer. ~*ed instruction*, enseignement programmé, *m*. ~*mer*, *n*, programmeur, *m*. ~*ming*, *n*, (*computers*, *cinema*) programmation, *f*.
progress, *n*, progrès, *m*. *oft. pl* essor, *m*, marche, *f*, mouvement, train, *m*. *in* ~, en cours. ¶ *v.i*, s'avancer, progresser, faire des progrès. ~*ion*, *n*, progression, *f*. ~*ive†*, *a*, progressif.
prohibit, *v.t*, défendre, interdire, prohiber. ~*ion*, *n*, défense, interdiction, prohibition, *f*. ~*ionist*, *n*, prohibitionniste, *m*. ~*ive* & ~*ory*, *a*, prohibitif.
project, *n*, projet, plan, dessein, *m*. ¶ *v.t*, projeter; (*v.i.*) se p., faire saillie, saillir, avancer. ~*ile*, *n*. & *a*, projectile, *m*. & *a*. ~*ing*, *p.a*, en saillie, saillant, avancé. ~*ion*, *n*, projection, *f*, (*protruding*) saillie, avance, *f*; ressaut, *m*. *film* ~, projection cinématographique, *f*. ~*or* (*Opt.*) *n*, projecteur, *m*.
proletarian, *a*, prolétarien. ¶ *n*, prolétaire, *m*. **proletariat**, *n*, prolétariat, *m*.
proliferate, *v.t*. & *i*, proliférer.
prolific, *a*, prolifique; fécond, fertile.
prolix, *a*, prolixe. ~*ity*, *n*, prolixité, *f*.
prologue, *n*, prologue, *m*.
prolong, *v.t*, prolonger. ~*ation*, *n*, prolongation, *f*; prolongement, *m*. *prolonged applause*, applaudissements nourris, *m.pl*.
promenade, *n*, promenade, *f*; promenoir, *m*. ~ *deck*, pontpromenade, *m*.
prominence, *n*, proéminence; saillie, *f*. **prominent**, *a*, proéminent; saillant; éminent; en vedette.
promiscuity, *n*, promiscuité, *f*. **promiscuous**, *a*, confus; débauché. ~*ly*, *ad*, pêle-mêle.

promise, *n*, promesse, *f*; espérances, *f.pl*, avenir, *m*. ¶ *v.t*. & *i*, promettre; s'engager. ~*d land*, terre promise, t. de promission, *f*. **promising**, *a*, prometteur. *promissory note*, billet à ordre, *m*. *that's promising*, ça s'annonce bien.
promontory, *n*, promontoire, *m*.
promote, *v.t*, encourager, favoriser; avancer, promouvoir; lancer. **promoter**, *n*, promoteur, trice; lanceur, *m*, fondateur, trice. **promotion**, *n*, promotion, *f*; avancement; (*of a public company*, *pers.*) lancement, *m*; (*sales*) promotion des ventes.
prompt†, *a*, prompt. ~ *cash*, [argent] comptant, *m*. ¶ *v.t*, porter; suggérer, inspirer; (*Theat.*) souffler. ~ *book*, exemplaire du souffleur, *m*. ~*er*, *n*, souffleur, *m*. ~*itude*, *n*, promptitude, *f*.
promulgate, *v.t*, promulguer.
prone, *a*, couché sur le ventre; prosterné; sujet, enclin, porté. ~*ness*, *n*, inclination, *f*, penchant, *m*.
prong, *n*, dent, branche, *f*, fourchon, *m*.
pronominal†, *a*, pronominal. **pronoun**, *n*, pronom, *m*.
pronounce, *v.t*. & *i*, prononcer. **pronunciation**, *n*, prononciation, *f*; accent, *m*.
proof, *n*, preuve, *f*; titre; gage, *m*; épreuve, *f*. *in* ~ *of which*, à telles enseignes que. ~ *against*, à l'épreuve de; cuirassé contre. ~*reader*, correcteur d'imprimerie, réviseur, *m*. ~*reading*, correction des épreuves, revision, *f*. *water*~, *a*, imperméable.
prop, *n*, étai, *m*; chandelle, *f*; échalas; tuteur, *m*. ¶ *v.t*, étayer; échalasser.
propaganda, *n*, propagande, *f*.
propagate, *v.t*, propager.
propel, *v.t*, donner l'impulsion à, mouvoir. **propellant**, *n*, ergol, *m*. **propeller**, *n*, propulseur, *m*.
propensity, *n*, propension, *f*, penchant, *m*.
proper†, *a*, propre; bon; bien; convenable; [bien]séant, décent; (*behavior*) comme il faut. ~*ty*, *n*, propriété, *f*, bien, *m*. *oft. pl* avoir; domaine, *m*; chose; faculté, qualité, *f*, caractère,

propre, *m*; (*pl. Theat.*) accessoires, *m.pl.* (*Theat.*) ~ man, accessoiriste, *m.* ~ *tax*, impôt foncier, *m.*

prophecy, *n*, prophétie, *f.* **prophesy**, v.t. & i, prophétiser.
prophet, *n*, prophète; augure, *m.*
~ess, *n*, prophétesse, *f.* ~ic(al)†,
a, prophétique.

propinquity, *n*, proximité, *f.*

propitiate, *v.t*, rendre propice.
propitious, *a*, propice.

proportion, *n*, proportion, *f. out
of* ~, disproportionné. ¶ *v.t*, proportionner, mesurer. ~al†, *a*,
proportionnel.

proposal, *n*, proposition; demande, *f.* **propose**, v.t. & i, proposer; (*toast*) porter; (*marriage
to woman*) offrir son nom, (*to
man*) offrir sa main. **proposer**,
n, parrain, *m.* **proposition**, *n*,
proposition, affaire, *f.*

propound, *v.t*, proposer.

proprietary, *a*, (*rights*) de propriété. **proprietor, tress**, *n*, propriétaire, *m,f.* **propriety**, *n*, décence, bienséance, convenance,
mesure; correction, propriété, *f.*

propulsion, *n*, propulsion, *f.*

prorogue, *v.t*, proroger.

prosaic†, *a*, prosaïque.

proscenium, *n*, avant-scène, *f.*

proscribe, *v.t*, proscrire.

prose, *n*, prose, *f.* ~ *writer*, prosateur, *m.*

prosecute, *v.t*, poursuivre. **prosecution**, *n*, poursuites, *f.pl*, vindicte, *f.* **prosecutor, trix**, *n*, poursuivant, e, plaignant, e.

proselyte, *n*, prosélyte, *m,f.*

prosiness, *n*, verbosité, *f.*

prosody, *n*, prosodie, *f.*

prospect, *n*, vue; perspective, *f*,
avenir, *m.* ¶ *v.t*, prospecter.
~ing, *n*, prospection, *f*, recher-
ches, *f.pl.* ~ive, *a*, en perspective. ~or, *n*, prospecteur, *m.*

prospectus, *n*, prospectus, *m.*

prosper, *v.i*, prospérer, réussir.
~ity, *n*, prospérité, *f.* ~ous, *a*,
prospère, fortuné, florissant,
heureux.

prostate [gland], *n*, prostate, *f.*

prostitute, *v.t*, prostituer. ¶ *n*,
prostituée, putain, *f.*

prostrate, *a*, prosterné; prostré,
anéanti. ¶ *v.t*, prosterner; anéantir. ~ *oneself*, se prosterner.

prostration, *n*, prosternation;
(*Med.*) prostration, *f.*

prosy, *a*, verbeux, ennuyeux.

protagonist, *n*, protagoniste, *m.*

protect, *v.t*, protéger, garder, défendre, préserver. ~ion, *n*, protection, garde, défense, préservation, sauvegarde, *f.* ~ionist, *n.
& att*, protectionniste, *m. & att.*
~ive, *a*, protecteur. **protector,
tress**, *n*, protecteur, trice. ~ate,
n, protectorat, *m.*

protein, *n*, protéine, *f.*

protest, *n*, protestation, réclamation, *f.* ¶ *v.t. & i*, protester; crier.
~ant, *n. & a*, protestant, e.

protocol, *n*, protocole, *m.*

prototype, *n*, prototype, *m.*

protoplasm, *n*, protoplasme, *m.*

protract, *v.t*, prolonger. ~or, *n*,
rapporteur, *m.*

protrude, *v.i*, faire saillie.

protuberance, *n*, protubérance,
f.

proud†, *a*, fier; orgueilleux; glorieux. ~ *flesh*, chairs baveuses, *f.
pl.*

prove, *v.t*, prouver, faire la preuve
de, vérifier, justifier [de]; démontrer; constater; éprouver; (*will*)
homologuer.

provender, *n*, fourrage, *m*, provende, *f.*

proverb, *n*, proverbe, *m.* ~ial†,
a, proverbial.

provide, *v.t*, pourvoir, fournir,
munir; prescrire, stipuler, prévoir. ~ *against*, se prémunir
contre. ~d [*that*], pourvu que.
providence, *n*, prévoyance; providence; (*God*) Providence, *f.*
provident, *a*, prévoyant. ~ial†,
a, providentiel. **provider**, *n*,
pourvoyeur, *m.*

province, *n*, province; (*pl.*) province; (*sphere*) compétence, *f*,
ressort, domaine, département,
m, juridiction, *f.* **provincial**, *a*,
provincial; de province.

provision, *n*, provision; prestation; disposition; (*pl.*) provisions de bouche, munitions de b.
f.pl, vivres, comestibles, *m.pl*,
substances, *f.pl.* ¶ *v.t*, approvisionner. ~al†, *a*, provisoire;
provisionnel.

proviso, *n*, clause provisionnelle,
f.

provocation, *n*, provocation;
agacerie, *f.* **provoke**, *v.t*, provo-

quer, agacer, contrarier, vexer, impatienter.

provost, *n*, prévôt; recteur, *m*.

prow, *n*, proue, *f*.

prowess, *n*, prouesse, vaillantise, *f*.

prowl, *v.i*, rôder. ~**er**, *n*, rôdeur, *m*.

proximate†, *a*, prochain; immédiat. **proximity**, *n*, proximité, *f*.

proxy, *n*, procuration, *f*; mandataire, *m*, fondé de pouvoir(s), *m*. **by** ~, par procuration.

prude, *n*, prude, *f*.

prudence, *n*, prudence, sagesse, *f*. **prudent**†, *a*, prudent, sage, avisé. ~**ial**, *a*, de prudence.

prudery, *n*, pruderie, bégueulerie, *f*. **prudish**, *a*, prude, pudibond, bégueule.

prune, *n*, pruneau, *m*. ¶ *v.t*, tailler, émonder, élaguer. **pruning**, *n*, taille, *f*, émondage, élagage, *m*; (*pl.*) élagage, *m*, émondes, *f.pl.* ~ **hook**, serpe, *f*, croissant, *m*. ~ **knife**, serpette, *f*. ~ **shears**, sécateur, *m*.

pruriency, *n*, sensualité, *f*. **prurient**, *a*, sensuel, lascif.

Prussia, *n*, la Prusse. **Prussian**, *a*, prussien. ~ **blue**, bleu de Prusse, *m*. ¶ *n*, Prussien, ne. **prussic**, *a*, prussique.

pry, *v.i*, fureter, fouiller; soulever avec un levier. ~**ing**, *a*, indiscret, curieux.

psalm, *n*, psaume, *m*. ~**ist**, *n*, psalmiste, *m*. **psalter**, *n*, psautier, *m*.

pseudonym, *n*, pseudonyme, *m*.

psychiatrist, *n*, psychiatre, *m*. **psychic(al)**, *a*, psychique. **psychoanalysis**, *n*, psychanalyse, *f*. **psychological**, *a*, psychologique. **psychologist**, *n*, psychologue, *m*. **psychology**, *n*, psychologie, *f*. **psychosis**, *n*, psychose, *f*. **psychosomatic**, *a*, psychosomatique.

ptarmigan, *n*, perdrix des neiges, *f*.

ptomaine, *n*, ptomaïne, *f*. ~ *poisoning*, empoisonnement par les ptomaïnes, *m*.

puberty, *n*, puberté, *f*.

public†, *a*, public. ~ **spirited**, dévoué au bien public. ¶ *n*, public, *m*; clientèle, *f*. ~**an**, *n*, (*Bible*) publicain, *m*. ~**ation**, *n*, publication, *f*. ~**ist**, *n*, publiciste, *m*. ~**ity**, *n*, publicité, *f*. **publish**, *v.t*,

publier; éditer; faire paraître; proclamer. **to be** ~**ed** (book), vient de paraître. ~**er**, *n*, éditeur, *m*. ~'**s imprint**, indication de nom (*ou* de firme) de l'éditeur; (*place only*) rubrique, *f*. ~**ing**, *n*, publication, édition, *f*. ~ **house**, maison d'édition, librairie, *f*.

puce, *a*, puce.

puck, *n*, lutin, [esprit] follet; (*ice hockey*) palet, puck, *m*.

pucker, *n*, poche, fronce, *f*, godet, pli, *m*. ¶ *v.t*, froncer, plisser; (*v.i.*) goder, [se] plisser.

pudding, *n*, pudding, pouding, *m*.

puddle, *n*, flaque, *f*. ¶ *v.t*, (*clay*) corroyer; (*Metall.*) puddler.

puerile†, *a*, puéril.

puff, *n*, souffle, *m*; bouffée, réclame, *f*; (*powder*) houppe, *f*. ¶ *v.t*. & *i*, souffler; bouffer; époumoner; prôner. ~ **one's goods**, faire l'article.

puffin, *n*, macareux, *m*.

puffy, *a*, bouffi, soufflé.

pug (*clay*) *n*, corroi, *m*. ~ [*dog*], carlin, roquet, *m*. ~ **nose**, nez camus, *m*. ¶ *v.t*, corroyer; hourder.

pugilism, *n*, pugilat, *m*. **pugilist**, *n*, pugiliste, *m*. **pugnacious**, *a*, pugnace, batailleur.

pule, *v.i*, piauler.

pull, *n*, traction, *f*; effort [de traction] *m*; (*drink*) lampée; (*Typ.*) feuille de tirée, *f*; (*bell*) cordon; (*fig.*) avantage, *m*. ~ **over**, pullover, *m*. ¶ *v.t*. & *i*, tirer; arracher; (*trigger*) presser. ~ **down**, démolir. ~ **wires for** (*fig.*), intriguer pour; pistonner. ~ **to one side** (traffic), se garer. ~ **to pieces**, mettre en pièces; (*fig.*) éreinter.

pullet, *n*, poulette, *f*.

pulley, *n*, poulie, *f*. ~ **block**, moufle, *f*. *or m*.

Pullman [**car**], *n*, voiture Pullman, *f*.

pullover, *n*, pull-over, pull, *m*.

pullulate, *v.i*, pulluler.

pulmonary, *a*, pulmonaire.

pulp, *n*, pulpe; chair; (*paper making*) pâte; bouillie, *f*. ¶ *v.t*, pulper.

pulpit, *n*, chaire [du prédicateur] *f*.

pulsate, *v.i*, battre. **pulsation**, *n*, pulsation, *f*, battement, *m*. **pulse**, *n*, (*Anat.*) pouls, *m*; légumineuse, *f.* ~ *rate*, force du pouls, *f.*

pulverize, *v.t,* pulvériser.

puma, *n,* puma, couguar, *m.*

pumice [stone], *n,* [pierre] ponce, *f.* ¶ *v.t,* poncer.

pump, *n,* pompe, *f; (dress shoe)* escarpin, *m. gasoline* ~, pompe à essence, *f.* ~ *handle*, levier de pompe, *m,* brimbale, *f.* ~ *room* (at spa), buvette, *f.* ¶ *v.t. & i,* pomper; *(fig.)* sonder, cuisiner. ~ *up (tire),* gonfler.

pumpkin, *n,* citrouille, courge, *f,* potiron, *m.*

pun, *n,* calembour, jeu de mots, *m.* ¶ *v.i,* faire des calembours, jouer sur le(s) mot(s).

punch, *n,* coup de poing, renfoncement, *m,* gourmade, *f; (tool)* poinçon; emporte-pièce; *(drink)* punch, *m.* ~ *bowl,* bol à punch, *m.* P~, *n,* polichinelle, *m.* ~ *& Judy [show],* guignol, *m.* ¶ *v.t,* poinçonner; découper; *(hit)* battre; *(Rly. ticket)* composter. [*Note: this must be done before boarding train.*]

puncheon, *n,* poinçon, *m;* pièce, *f.*

punching bag, ballon de boxe, *m.*

punctilio, *n,* pointille, *f.* **punctilious**, *a,* pointilleux, méticuleux.

punctual†, *a,* ponctuel, exact. ~**ity**, *n,* ponctualité, exactitude, *f.*

punctuate, *v.t. & abs,* ponctuer.

punctuation, *n,* ponctuation, *f.*

puncture, *n,* piqûre; *(Surg.)* ponction; *(tire)* crevaison, *f.* ¶ *v.t. & i,* piquer; ponctionner; crever.

pundit, *n,* pandit, pontife, *m.*

pungency, *n,* piquant, *m;* âcreté, *f;* mordant, *m.* **pungent**, *a,* piquant; âcre; mordant.

punish, *v.t,* punir. ~**able**, *a,* punissable. ~**ment**, *n,* punition; peine, sanction, pénitence, *f;* supplice, *m.*

punster, *n,* faiseur de calembours, *m.*

punt, *(boat) n,* bachot, *m,* plate, *f.* ¶ *v.i, (cards)* ponter; *(boating)* pousser du fond; *(v.t.)* pousser *(un bateau)* à la perche.

puny, *a,* chétif, malingre.

pup, *n,* petit chien, *m.* ¶ *v.i,* mettre bas.

pupa, *n,* chrysalide, *f.*

pupil, *n, (eye)* pupille, prunelle, *f; (scholar)* élève, *m,f,* écolier, ère; pupille, *m,f.*

puppet, *n,* marionnette, poupée, *f,* mannequin, fantoche, *m.*

puppy, *n,* chiot; *(pers.)* freluquet, *m.*

purblind, *a,* quasi aveugle.

purchase, *n,* achat, *m,* acquisition; *(shopping)* emplette; *(hold)* prise, *f; (tackle)* palan, *m.* ¶ *v.t,* acheter, acquérir. **purchaser**, *n,* acheteur, euse, acquéreur, *m.*

pure†, *a,* pur. ~ *mechanics,* mécanique rationnelle, *f.* ~**ness**, *n,* pureté, *f.*

purgative, *a. & n,* purgatif, *a. & m.* **purgatory**, *n,* purgatoire, *m.* **purge**, *v.t,* purger. **purge, purging**, *n,* purge, purgation, *f.*

purify, *v.t,* purifier; épurer. **purist**, *n,* puriste, *m,f.* **Puritan**, *n. & a. & puritanic(al),* *a,* puritain, e. **purity**, *n,* pureté, *f.*

purl, *v.i,* murmurer, gazouiller. ~ *knitting,* tricot à l'envers, *m.*

purlieus, *n.pl,* environs, entours, *m.pl.*

purloin, *v.t,* soustraire.

purple, *n,* pourpre, *m; (robe)* pourpre, *f.* ¶ *a,* violet. ~ *red,* rouge pourpré, *m.* **purplish**, *a,* purpurin, violâtre.

purport, *n,* teneur, portée, *f.* ¶ *v.t,* signifier, vouloir dire; sembler, paraître.

purpose, *n,* but, *m,* fin; intention, *f;* propos; dessein; effet; usage, *m. to no* ~, en pure perte. ¶ *v.t,* se proposer. ~**ly**, *ad,* à dessein, exprès.

purr, *n,* ronron, *m.* ¶ *v.i,* faire ronron.

purse, *n,* porte-monnaie, *m,* bourse, *f.* ¶ *(lips) v.t,* pincer. **purser**, *n,* commissaire [de la marine marchande] *m.*

pursuant to, in pursuance of, en vertu de, suivant. **pursue**, *v.t,* [pour]suivre, chasser. **pursuit**, *n,* poursuite, chasse; recherche; occupation, *f.* ~ *plane,* avion de chasse, *m.*

purulent, *a,* purulent.

purvey, *v.t,* pourvoir. ~**or**, *n,* pourvoyeur, *m.*

purview, *n,* ressort; *(law)* dispositif, *m.*

pus, *n,* pus, *m.*

push, *n,* poussée; initiative, *f.* ~ *[button],* poussoir, *m.* ¶ *v.t,* pousser; presser; avancer. ~ *about*, bousculer. ~ *aside*, écarter. ~ *back*, repousser, reculer. ~ *off* (*Naut.*), pousser au large. ~ing, *a*, entreprenant.

pusillanimous, *a*, pusillanime.

puss[y], *n*, minet, te, minon, minou, *m. Puss in Boots*, le Chat botté.

pustule, *n*, pustule, *f*.

put, *v.t.ir*, mettre; placer; porter; poser; apposer; appliquer; faire. ~ (*things*) *away*, ranger, serrer. ~ *down*, réprimer; baisser. ~ *forward*, avancer; proposer. ~ *in*, insérer; (*Naut.*) relâcher. ~ *off*, remettre; différer. ~ *on*, mettre; revêtir; prendre; avancer; (*brake*) serrer. ~ *out*, éteindre; (*tongue*) tirer. ~ *out of joint*, démettre, disloquer. ~ *out of order*, dérégler, déranger. ~ *out of tune*, désaccorder. ~ *up*, (*money*) faire mise de; (*money at cards*) caver [de]; (*at hotel*) descendre. ~*up job*, coup monté, *m*. ~ *up with*, supporter.

putt, (*golf.*) *n*, coup [roulé] *m*. ¶ *v.t*, poter.

putrefaction, *n*, putréfaction, *f*. **putrefy,** *v.t*, putréfier; (*v.i.*) se p. **putrid,** *a*, putride.

puttee, *n*, bande molletière, *f*.

putter (*club*) *n*, poteur, *m*. ¶ *v.i*, bricoler. **putting green,** pelouse d'arrivée, *f*. **putting the shot,** lancement du poids, *m*.

putty, *n*, mastic, *m*. ~ *powder*, potée d'étain, *f*. ¶ *v.t*, mastiquer.

puzzle, *n*, casse-tête; problème, *m*; énigme, *f*. *crossword* ~, mots croisés, *m.pl*. ¶ *v.t*, intriguer, alambiquer. ~**d**, *p.a*, perplexe; empêché.

pygmy, *n*, pygmée, *m*.

pylon, *n*, pylône, *m*.

pyorrhoea, *n*, pyorrhée, *f*.

pyramid, *n*, pyramide, *f*.

pyre, *n*, bûcher, *m*.

Pyrenees (the), les Pyrénées, *f.pl*.

pyrethrum, *n*, pyrèthre, *m*.

pyrites, *n*, pyrite, *f*.

pyrotechnics, *n.pl*, pyrotechnie, *f*. **pyrotechnist,** *n*, artificier, *m*.

python, *n*, python, *m*.

Q

quack [doctor], *n*, charlatan, médicastre, *m*, guérisseur, euse. ~**ery,** *n*, charlatanisme, *m*.

quadrangle, *n*, figure quadrangulaire, *f*; préau, *m*; cour d'honneur, *f*.

quadrant, *n*, quadrant; quart de cercle; secteur, *m*.

quadroon, *n*, quarteron, ne.

quadruped, *n. & a*, quadrupède, *m. & a*.

quadruple, *a. & n*, quadruple, *a. & m*. **quadruplets,** *n.pl*, quatre jumeaux, *m.pl*.

quaff, *v.t*, boire.

quagmire, *n*, fondrière, *f*, bourbier, *m*.

quail, *n*, caille, *f*. ¶ *v.i*, trembler.

quaint, *a*, vieillot; pittoresque; baroque; étrange; curieux. ~**ness,** *n*, étrangeté; curiosité, *f*.

quake, *v.i*, trembler. ¶ *n*, tremblement, *m*.

qualification, *n*, qualité; capacité, aptitude, *f*. **qualified,** *p.a*, qualifié; capable, apte; sous réserve. **qualify,** *v.t*, qualifier; adoucir. **qualitative,** *a*, qualitatif, ive. **quality,** *n*, qualité, *f*; choix; aloi, *m*.

qualms, *n.pl*, mal de cœur, *m*; scrupules, *m.pl*.

quandary, *n*, embarras, *m*.

quantity, *n*, quantité, *f*.

quantum, *n*, quantum, *m*.

quarantine, *n*, quarantaine, *f*; (*station*) la santé. ¶ *v.t*, mettre en quarantaine.

quarrel, *n*, querelle, *f*. ¶ *v.i*, quereller. ~**some,** *a*, querelleur.

quarry, *n*, (*marble, etc.*) carrière; proie, *f*. ¶ *v.t*, extraire.

quarter, *n*, quartier; (¼ *th*) quart; (*3 months*) trimestre; terme, *m*; (*28 lbs*) = 12.70 kilos; (*8 bushels*) = 2.909 hectoliters; (*pl.*) logement; cantonnement, *m*; quartiers, *m.pl*; (*horse*) train, *m. a* ~ *of an hour*, un quart d'heure. ~ *deck*, gaillard d'arrière, *m*. ~*master*, (*Mil.*) fourrier; (*Naut.*) maître de timonerie, *m*. ~ *past*, un quart, et quart. ¶ *v.t*, diviser en quatre parties; écarteler; loger; cantonner. ~**ly,** *a*, trimestriel; (*ad.*) par trimestre.

quartet[te], *n*, quatuor, *m*.

quartz, *n*, quartz, *m*.

quash, *v.t*, casser, annuler, infirmer.

quasi, *c. & quasi-,** *prefix*, quasi (*ad.*), quasi-.

quassia, *n*, (*tree*) quassier; (*bark*) quassia, *m*.

quatrain, n, quatrain, m.
quaver (*Mus.*) n, croche, f. ¶ v.i, chevroter, trembler.
quay, n, quai, m.
queen, n, reine; (*cards, chess*) dame, reine, f. ~ *bee,* reine des abeilles, mère abeille, f. ¶ (*chess*) v.t, damer. ~ly, a, de reine.
queer†, a, étrange, bizarre, singulier, original, drôle; indisposé. a ~ *fellow,* un drôle de corps.
quell, v.t, réprimer, étouffer, apaiser.
quench, v.t, éteindre; (*thirst*) étancher, apaiser.
querulous†, a, *plaintif.*
query, n, question, interrogation, f. ¶ v.t, quête, recherche, f.
question, n, question; demande; interrogation, f. ~ *mark,* point d'interrogation, m. ¶ v.t, questionner, interroger; contester, mettre en question, suspecter. **questionable,** a, contestable; suspect, équivoque. **questionnaire,** n, questionnaire, m.
queue, n, file, f. v.i, faire la queue.
quibble, n, chicane, argutie, f. ¶ v.i, chicaner, ergoter.
quick, a, vif; rapide; prompt; preste. ~*change artist,* acteur à transformations, m. ~*lime,* chaux vive, f. ~*sand,* sable mouvant, m. ~*silver,* mercure, m. ~*step,* pas accéléré, m; en avant marche! ~*tempered,* emporté, vif. ¶ ad, vite, prestement. be ~! vite!; dépêchez-vous! ¶ n, vif, m. ~en, v.t, vivifier, animer; accélérer, activer. ~ly, ad, vite, tôt, promptement. ~ness, n, promptitude, prestesse, f.
quid (*tobacco*) n, chique, f.
quiescent, a, en repos. **quiet†,** a, tranquille; calme; doux; modeste. ¶ v.t, calmer, apaiser. ~[ness], n, tranquillité, f, repos, calme, m, quiétude, f.
quietus, n, (*Jur.*) quitus, m; (*death*) mort, f; coup de grâce, m.
quill, n, (*porcupine*) piquant, m; (*bird*) plume, f. ~ *driver,* gratte-papier, rond-de-cuir, plumitif, m. ~ [*feather*], penne, f. ~ [*pen*], plume d'oie, f.
quilt, n, couvre-pied, m. ¶ v.t, ouater, piquer, capitonner.
quince, n, coing, m. ~[*tree*], cognassier, m.
quinine, n, quinine, f.
quinquennial, a, quinquennal.

quinsy, n, angine, f.
quintessence, n, quintessence, f.
quintet[te], n, quintette, m.
quintuple, a, quintuple. ¶ n, quintuple, m. **quintuplet,** n, quintuplet, m.
quip, n, pointe, f, mot piquant, m.
quire, n, main, f. (*in Fr. 25 sheets*).
quirk, n (*quip*), pointe, f; caprice; (*Join.*) carré, m.
quit, a, quitte. ¶ v.t, renoncer à; cesser de; quitter.
quite, ad, tout à fait; tout, e; bien; complètement; parfaitement.
quits, a, quitte à quitte; quittes.
quiver (*for arrows*) n, carquois, m. ¶ v.i, trembler, frémir; frissonner. ~[ing], n, tremblement, frisson[nement] m.
Quixote, n, Don Quichotte, m. **quixotic,** a, de D. Q. ~ally, ad, en D. Q.
quiz, v.t, interroger; (*mock*) berner. ¶ n, examen, m. **quizzical,** a, (*mocking*) narquois.
quoin, n, coin; (*Typ.*) bois de corps, m.
quoit, n. & ~s, n.pl, palet, m.
quondam, a, ancien.
quorum, n, quorum, m.
quota, n, quote-part, quotité, cote, cotisation, f, contingent, quota, m. ~ *sampling,* sondage par quota, m.
quotation, n, citation; épigraphe; (*Com., Fin.*) cote, f, cours, prix, m; (*in Stk Ex. list*) inscription, f. ~ *marks,* guillemets, m.pl. **quote,** v.t, citer; alléguer; guillemeter; coter, faire; inscrire.
quotient, n, quotient, m.

R

rabbet, n, feuillure, f. ~ *plane,* guillaume, m.
rabbi, n, rabbin, m.
rabbit, n, lapin, e, (*young*) lapereau, m; (*pers. at game*) mazette, f. ~ *burrow,* ~ *hole,* terrier de lapin, clapier, m. ~ *hutch,* clapier, m.
rabble, n, canaille, populace, f.
rabid, a, acharné; enragé. **rabies,** n, la rage, hydrophobie, f.
racoon, n, raton laveur, m.
race, n, (*tribe*) race, f; sang, m; (*contest*) course, f; (*sea*) raz, m. ~*horse,* cheval de course, m. ~ *suicide,* suicide du genre hu-

main, *m.* ~*track*, champ de courses, *m*, piste, *f.* ~*[way]*, bief, canal, chenal, *m.* ¶ *v.i*, courir; (*v.t.*) (*horses*) faire courir.

racer, *n*, coureur, euse; cheval de course, *m*; bicyclette de course, *f.* **racial**, *a*, de race. **racing**, *f.pl.* courses; (*horse*) les courses, *f.pl.* ~ *calendar*, calendrier des courses, *m.* ~ *cyclist*, coureur cycliste, *m.*

rack, *n*, râtelier, *m*; rampe, *f*; caster, *m*; (*luggage, Rly.*) filet; supplice, *m*, torture, *f. hat* ~, porte-chapeau, *m. to* ~ *& ruin*, à vau-l'eau. *to* ~ *one's brains*, se torturer l'esprit, se casser la tête, se creuser le cerveau.

racket, *n*, tapage; bacchanal, *m*; raquette, *f.* ~ *press*, presse à raquette, *f.*

racy (*fig.*) *a*, piquant.

radial, *a*, radial. **radiance & radiation**, *n*, rayonnement, *m*. **radiancy**, *n*, éclat, *m*. **radiant**, *a*, rayonnant; radieux. **radiate**, *v.i*, rayonner. **radiator**, *n*, radiateur, *m.* ~ *cap*, bouchon de r., *m.*

radical†, *a. & n*, radical, *a. & m.*

radio†, *n*, radio, T.S.F., *f.* ~ *broadcast*, radiodiffusion, *f.* ¶ *v.t. & i*, émettre, radiodiffuser. **radioactive**, *a*, radioactif. **radiogram**, *n*, radiogramme, *m.* **radiography**, *n*, radiographie, *f.* **radiology**, *n*, radiologie, *f.* **radiotelegraphy**, *n*, radiotélégraphie, *f.* **radiotherapy**, *n*, radiothérapie, *f.*

radish, *n*, radis, *m.*

radium, *n*, radium, *m.*

radius, *n*, rayon, *m*; portée, *f*; (*Anat.*) radius, *m.*

raffle, *n*, loterie, tombola, *f.* ¶ *v.t*, mettre en loterie.

raft, *n*, radeau, *m*, drome, *f*; train [de bois] *m.*

rafter, *n*, chevron, *m.*

rag, *n*, chiffon; lambeau; haillon, *m*, loque, guenille, *f*; (*pl, for paper making*) drille; (*newspaper*) feuille de chou, *f*, canard; (*Sch.*) chahut, *m.* ~*picker*, ~ *[& bone] man*, chiffonnier, ère. ~*tag [& bobtail]*, canaille, *f.* ~*wort*, jacobée, *f.*

ragamuffin, *n*, petit va-nu-pieds, *m.*

rage, *n*, rage, fureur; colère, *f*, courroux, *m.* ¶ *v.i*, faire rage; (*of war*) sévir. *to be the* ~, être du dernier cri; faire fureur.

ragged, *a*, déguenillé, loqueteux.

raging, *a*, furieux. ~ *fever*, fièvre ardente, *f.* ~ *toothache*, rage de dents, *f.*

raid, *n*, incursion, descente, razzia, *f*, raid, *m*; rafle; attaque, *f. air* ~, raid aérien, *m.* ¶ *v.t*, razzier; marauder; faire une descente dans.

rail, *n*, barre, *f*; barreau, *m*; traverse; rampe, *f*, garde-fou, accoudoir, *m*; (*ship's*) lisse, *f*, garde-corps; (*Rly.*) rail; (*bird*) râle, *m.* ¶ *v.t*, barrer. ~ *at*, invectiver contre, pester contre. ~*ing*, *n*, grille, balustrade, *f*, balustre, garde-fou, *m.*

raillery, *n*, raillerie, *f.*

railway & railroad, *n*, chemin de fer, *m*, voie ferrée, *f.* ~*man*, employé de chemin de fer, cheminot, *m.* ~ *station*, gare, *f.* ~ *strike*, grève d'agents de chemins de fer, *f.*

raiment, *n*, vêtement, habillement, *m.*

rain, *n*, pluie, eau, *f.* ~*bow*, arc-en-ciel; (*halo*) iris, *m.* ~ *coat*, imperméable, *m.* ~*fall*, quantité de pluie [tombée] *f.* ~*water*, eau de pluie, *f*, eaux pluviales, *f.pl.* ¶ *v.i*, pleuvoir; (*v.t.*) faire pleuvoir. ~*y*, *a*, pluvieux, pluvial; (*day*) de pluie.

raise, *v.t*, lever; soulever; relever; remonter; [sur]élever; hausser; exhausser; augmenter; porter; (*hat*) tirer; (*flag*) arborer; cultiver; faire naître; produire; (*money for some purpose*) procurer; (*money for oneself*) se procurer; (*the dead*) ressusciter. ¶ *n*, hausse, augmentation, *f.* **raised**, *p.a*, en relief; saillant.

raisin, *n*, raisin sec, *m.*

rake, *n*, râteau, *f*; (*fire*) fourgon, ringard, *m*; inclinaison, *f*; libertin, débauché, roué, coureur, *m.* ¶ *v.t*, ratisser, râteler; enfiler. ~ *up*, remuer; revenir sur. *raking fire*, feu d'enfilade, *m. raking shore*, arc-boutant, *m*, contre-fiche, *f.* **rakish**, *a*, libertin.

rally, *n*, ralliement, *m*; reprise, *f*; (*Ten.*) long échange; (*race meeting*) rallye, *m.* ¶ *v.t*, rallier; (*v.i.*) se rallier; [se] reprendre.

ram, *n*, bélier; (*pile driving*) mouton, pilon; piston; (*battleship*) éperon, *m.* ¶ *v.t*, damer, battre; bourrer; refouler.

ramble, n, excursion, promenade, f. ¶v.i, errer; (rave) divaguer.
rambler, n, rosier grimpant, m.
rambling, a, errant; (discourse) décousu, incohérent.

ramification, n, ramification, f.
ramify, v.i, se ramifier.

rampant (Her.) a, rampant. to be ~, sévir, courir.

rampart, n, rempart, m.

ramrod, n, baguette, f.

ramshackle, a, délabré.

ranch, n, ranch, m.

rancid, a, rance. ~ness, n, rancidité, f.

rancorous, a, rancunier, fielleux.
rancor, n, rancune, rancœur, f, fiel, m.

random, a. & at ~, au hasard, à l'aventure, à l'abandon, à la volée, à coup perdu.

range, n, étendue; portée; distance, f; champ, m; série; gamme, f; (voice) diapason; (musical) clavier, m; (hills) chaîne, f; fourneau; parc, m. gas ~, fourneau à gaz, m. within ~, à portée de. ~ finder, télémètre, m. ¶v.t, étager; aligner; parcourir; ranger; (v.i.) s'aligner; varier. **ranger**, n, conservateur; garde, m.

Rangoon, n, Rangoun, Rangoon, m.

rank, n, rang; grade, m; dignité; (cab) station, place, f. ~ & file, les hommes de troupe, gradés & soldats. ¶v.t, ranger; (v.i.) prendre rang; marcher de pair. ¶a, luxuriant; rance; grossier; insigne, fieffé.

rankle, v.i, saigner.

ransack, v.t, saccager, piller; fouiller.

ransom, n, rançon, f, rachat, m. ¶v.t, rançonner, racheter.

rant, n, divagation, f. ¶v.i, déclamer.

ranunculus, n, renoncule, f.

rap, n, coup, m, tape, f. ¶v.t. & i, taper, frapper, donner de petits coups secs. I don't give a ~, je m'en moque.

rapacious, a, rapace. rape, n, (sexual) viol; (kidnapping) enlèvement, m; (oil seed plant) navette; (colerape) rave, f.

rapid†, a, rapide; (pulse) fréquent. ¶n, rapide, m. ~ity, n, rapidité, f.

rapier, n, rapière, f.

rapine, n, rapine, f.

rapt, a, ravi, en extase. **rapture**, n, ravissement, enthousiasme, m, ivresse, f. **rapturous**, a, extatique.

rare†, a, rare; (word) peu usité; fameux; (meat) saignante. **rarefy**, v.t, raréfier. **rareness**, n, rareté, f.

rascal, n, coquin, e, fripon, ne; canaille, f. ~ity, n, coquinerie, friponnerie, f. ~ly, a, canaille.

rash†, a, téméraire, hardi. ¶n, éruption, f. ~ness, n, témérité, f.

rasher, n, tranche, f.

rasp, n, râpe, f. ¶v.t, râper; racler. ~ing, a, rugueux.

raspberry, n, framboise, f. ~ bush, framboisier, m.

rat, n, rat, e, (young) raton; (pers.) gâtemétier; (Pol.) transfuge, m. ~ catcher, preneur de rats, m. ~ poison, mort aux rats, f. ~ trap, ratière, f. ¶v.i, tuer des rats; (Pol.) tourner casaque.

rate, n, taux; pourcentage; cours; prix; tarif; ordre, rang, m, classe; raison, f; train, m; taxe, contribution, f, impôt, m. at any ~, quoi qu'il en soit. ¶v.t, évaluer; tarifer; imposer; taxer.

rather, ad, un peu; assez; plutôt; mieux. ~ nice, gentillet. ~ slowly (Mus.), gravement. ~ than, plutôt que.

ratification, n, ratification, f. **ratify**, v.t, ratifier.

rating, n, classement; (Naut.) grade, m.

ratio, n, rapport, m, raison, proportion, f.

ration, n, ration, f, (pl.) vivres, m.pl. ¶v.t, rationner. ~al†, a, rationnel, raisonnable; conséquent; raisonné. **rationalism**, n, rationalisme, m. **rationalization**, n, organisation rationnelle, f. **rationing**, n, rationnement, m.

rattan, n. & ~ cane, rotin, m.

rat-tat[-tat], n, pan! pan!

ratter, n, [chien] ratier, m.

rattle, n, crécelle, f; (baby's) hochet; ballottement, claquement; (throat) râle, m. ~snake, serpent à sonnettes, m. ~trap, patraque, f; (vehicle) guimbarde, patache, f, tapecul, m. ¶v.i, & t, ballotter; cliqueter.

raucous, a, rauque.

ravage, v.t, ravager. ~s, n.pl, ravages, m.pl; (of time) injure[s], f.[pl.], outrage, m.

rave, *v.i*, être en délire; extravaguer.

raven, *n*, corbeau, *m*.

Ravenna, *n*, Ravenne, *f*.

ravenous†, *a*, vorace; dévorant.

ravine, *n*, ravin, *m*, ravine, *f*.

raving, *n*, délire, *m*. ~ *mad*, fou à lier.

ravish, *v.t*, ravir; violer. **ravishing**, *a*, ravissant. **ravishingly**, *ad*, à ravir.

raw, *a*, cru; brut; (*silk*) grège; (*meat*, *wound*) saignante; (*Sienna*) naturelle; (*material*) première; (*fig.*) vert; novice; imberbe; (*weather*) humide & froid. ~**ness**, *n*, crudité, *f*.

ray, *n*, rayon, *m*; (*fish*) raie, *f*.

rayon, *n*, rayon, *m*, soie artificielle, *f*.

raze, *v.t*, raser. **razor**, *n*, rasoir, *m*.

reach, *n*, portée; atteinte; étendue, *f*. *within* ~ *of*, à portée de. ¶ *v.t*, atteindre [à]; arriver à, parvenir à; s'élever à. ~ [*out*], étendre.

react, *v.i*, réagir. ~**ion**, *n*, réaction, *f*; contrecoup, *m*. ~**ionary**, *a*. & *n*, réactionnaire, *a*. & *m.f*.

reactor, *n*, (*nuclear*) réacteur, *m*. *breeder* ~, r. producteur de matière fissile, surrégénérateur, *m*. *fission* ~, r. à fission, *m*.

read, *v.t. & i. ir*, lire; (*report*) donner lecture de; (*meter*) relever. ~ *over*, collationner. ~**able**†, *a*, lisible.

reader, *n*, lecteur, trice; liseur, euse; livre de lecture, *m*.

readiness, *n*, promptitude, *f*; empressement, *m*; facilité, *f*.

reading, *n*, lecture; leçon; cote, *f*. ~ *desk*, pupitre, *m*; (*church*) lutrin, *m*. ~ *glass*, loupe à lire, *f*. ~ *stand*, liseuse, *f*. ~ *lamp*, lampe de travail, *f*. ~ *room*, salle de lecture, *f*; cabinet de l., *m*.

readjust, *v.t. & i*, rajuster. ~**ment**, *n*, rajustement, *m*.

ready†, *a*, prêt; prompt; facile. ~*made*, tout fait (*f*. toute faite), confectionné. ~*-to-wear*, prêt-à-porter. ~ *money*, [argent] comptant, *m*.

reagent, *n*, réactif, *m*.

real†, *a*, réel; positif; véritable; vrai; effectif; (*law*) immeuble, immobilier. ~ *estate*, propriété immobilière, *f*. ~**ist**, *n*. & *a*, réaliste, *m.f*. & *a*. ~**ity**, *n*, réalité, *f*, le réel; positif, *m*. ~**ize**, *v.t*, réaliser.

realm, *n*, royaume, *m*.

realty, *n*, biens immeubles, *m.pl*.

ream, *n*, rame, *f*. (*In Fr. 500 sheets.*) ¶ *v.t*, aléser. ~**er**, *n*, alésoir, *m*.

reanimate, *v.t*, réanimer. **reanimation**, *n*, réanimation, *f*.

reap, *v.t*, moissonner, recueillir (*fig.*). **reaper**, *n*, moissonneur, *m*; (*machine*) moissonneuse, *f*. ~ *& binder*, moissonneuse-lieuse, *f*. **reaping**, *n*, moisson, *f*.

reappear, *v.i*, reparaître, réapparaître. ~**ance**, *n*, réapparition, *f*.

reappoint, *v.t*, renommer.

rear, *n*, arrière, *m*; queue, *f*. ~ *admiral*, contre-amiral, *m*. ~ *guard*, arrière-garde, *f*. ~ *rank*, dernier rang, *m*. ¶ *v.t*, élever, nourrir; (*v.i.*) se cabrer, se dresser. ~*ing of children*, puériculture, *f*.

reason, *n*, raison; cause, *f*; motif, *m*. *to state the* ~ *for*, motiver. ¶ *v.i*, raisonner. ~ *with*, raisonner, catéchiser. ~**able**†, *a*, raisonnable; honnête. ~**er**, *n*, raisonneur, euse. ~**ing**, *n*, raisonnement, *m*.

reassure, *v.t*, rassurer.

rebate, *n*, rabais, *m*, ristourne; (*Join.*) feuillure, *f*.

rebel, *n*, rebelle, *m.f*, révolté, e. ¶ *v.i*, se rebeller, se révolter. **rebellion**, *n*, rébellion, révolte, *f*. **rebellious**, *a*, rebelle.

rebind, *v.t.ir*, relier de nouveau.

rebirth, *n*, renaissance, *f*.

rebound, *n*, [second] bond; contrecoup, *m*. ¶ *v.i*, rebondir.

rebuff, *n*, rebuffade, *f*. ¶ *v.t*, rebuter.

rebuild, *v.t.ir*, rebâtir, reconstruire.

rebuke, *n*, réprimande, *f*. ¶ *v.t*, réprimander.

rebut, *v.t*, réfuter.

recalcitrant, *a*. & *n*, récalcitrant, e.

recall, *n*, rappel, *m*. ¶ *v.t*, rappeler; retracer; révoquer; (*recollect*) se rappeler.

recant, *v.t*, rétracter. ~**ation**, *n*, rétractation, palinodie, *f*.

recapitulate, *v.t*, récapituler.

recapture, *n*, reprise, *f*. ¶ *v.t*, reprendre.

recast, *v.t.ir*, refondre; remanier.

recede, *v.i*, reculer; se retirer; fuir.

receding (*forehead, chin*) p.a, fuyant.

receipt, n, réception, f; reçu, m; quittance, f, acquit, m; récépissé, m; (pl.) recette, f. oft. pl. ¶ v.t, acquitter, quittancer. **receive,** v.t, recevoir; accueillir; (*money*) toucher; (*stolen goods*) receler. **receiver,** n, destinataire, m,f; receleur, euse; (*Teleph.*) écouteur; (*vessel*) récipient, m.

recent†, a, récent, nouveau, frais. **receptacle,** n, réceptacle, m. **reception,** n, réception, f; accueil, m. ~ *room*, salon, m.

recess, n, [r]enfoncement, retrait, m, retraite, enclave; embrasure; (*Sch.*) récréation, f; (*pl. heart*) replis, m.pl. ¶ v.t, défoncer; suspendre les séances.

recession, n, (*economic*) récession, f.

recipe, n, recette; (*Phar.*) formule, f.

recipient, n, destinataire, m,f.

reciprocal†, a, réciproque; inverse; partagé. **reciprocate,** v.t, payer de retour. **reciprocating,** p.a, alternatif, de va-et-vient. **reciprocity,** n, réciprocité, f.

recital, n, récit, m; énumération, f; (*Mus.*) récital, m; audition, f. **recitation,** n, récitation, f. **recitative,** n, récitatif, m. **recite,** v.t, réciter, déclamer; énumérer.

reckless, a, téméraire; insouciant. ~ *driver*, chauffard, m. ~**ly,** ad, témérairement; à corps perdu.

reckon, v.t. & i, compter, calculer, chiffrer; estimer. ~**ing,** n, compte, calcul, m; carte à payer; addition, f, écot, m.

reclaim, v.t, ramener dans la bonne voie; (*from vice*) retirer; (*uncultivated land*) défricher; (*submerged land*) aménager.

recline, v.i, se renverser, se reposer.

recluse, n, reclus, e. **reclusion,** n, réclusion, f.

recognition, n, reconnaissance, f. **recognizable,** a, reconnaissable. **recognizance,** n, obligation, f. **recognize,** v.t, reconnaître.

recoil, n, recul, m, repoussement. m. ¶ v.i, reculer, repousser.

recoin, v.t, refondre, refrapper.

recollect, v.t, se rappeler. ~**ion,** n, souvenir, m, mémoire, f.

recommence, v.t. & i, recommencer.

recommend, v.t, recommander; préconiser; proposer. ~**ation,** n, recommandation; proposition, f; (*for election*) parrainage, m. ~**er,** n, parrain, m.

recompense, n, récompense, f. ¶ v.t, récompenser.

reconcile, v.t, réconcilier; [r]accommoder; concilier. **reconciliation,** n, réconciliation; résignation, f.

recondite, a, abstrus, obscure.

reconnoiter, v.t, reconnaître.

reconsider, v.t, revenir sur, reviser.

reconstitute, v.t, reconstituer.

reconstruct, v.t, reconstruire; (*fig.*) constituer de nouveau, reprendre sous œuvre. ~**ion,** n, reconstruction; (*fig.*) reconstitution, f.

record, n, registre, m; note, f; dossier, m; (pl.) archives, f.pl; (pl.) historique; (*sport*) record; (*phonograph*) disque, m. off the ~, à titre confidentiel. ~ *player*, pick-up, tourne-disque, m. ¶ v.t, enregistrer; consigner; constater. ~**er,** n, enregistreur; compteur de sport, m. *flight* ~, enregistreur de vol.

re-count, v.t, recompter.

recount, v.t, raconter.

recoup, v.t, récupérer; dédommager.

recourse, n, recours, m.

re-cover, v.t, recouvrir.

recover, v.t, recouvrer; rattraper; (v.i.) se rétablir; [se] reprendre, se relever. ~**y,** n, recouvrement, m; reprise, f.

recreant, a. & n, lâche; apostat, a. & m.

re-create, v.t, recréer.

recreate, v.t, récréer. **recreation,** n, récréation, f, délassement, m.

recrimination, n, récrimination, f.

recrudescence, n, recrudescence, f.

recruit, n, recrue, f. ¶ v.t, recruter, racoler; (v.i.) se rétablir. ~**ing sergeant,** sergent recruteur, m.

rectangle, n, rectangle, carré long, m. **rectangular,** a, rectangulaire.

rectify, v.t, rectifier; redresser.

rectilinear, a, rectiligne.

rectitude, *n*, rectitude; droiture, *f*.

rector, *n*, recteur; curé, *m*. **~ship,** *n*, cure, *f*. **~y,** *n*, presbytère, *m*, cure, *f*.

rectum, *n*, rectum, *m*.

recumbent, *a*, couché. **~ figure** (statue), gisant, *m*.

recuperate, *v.i*, se récupérer.

recur, *v.i*, revenir, se reproduire, se retracer. **recurrence,** *n*, retour, *m*, répétition, *f*.

recycle, *v.t*, recycler. **recycling,** *n*, recyclage, *m*.

red, *a. & n*, rouge, *a. & m*; (*hair*) roux, *a*. the **~s** (Pol.), les rouges, *m.pl*. **~breast,** rouge-gorge, *m*. the *R~ Cross*, la Croix Rouge. **~-faced** (*person*), rougeaud, *e*. **~-haired** (*person*), roux, rousse, rousseau, *m. & att*. **~-handed,** sur le fait, en flagrant délit. **~-herring,** hareng saur, *m*. **~-hot,** (chauffé au) rouge; tout chaud. **~ Indian** or **~skin,** Peau Rouge, *m*. **~ lead,** minium, *m*. to be a **~-letter day,** faire époque. **~ mullet,** rouget, *m*. **~ pepper,** poivre rouge, *p*. de Cayenne, *m*. *R~ Sea*, mer Rouge, *f*. **~ tape,** chinoiseries, *f.pl*, routine, *f*. **~wood,** sequoia, *m*. **redden,** *v.t. & i*, rougir; roussir. **reddish,** *a*, rougeâtre; roussâtre; blond hasardé.

redeem, *v.t*, racheter; rembourser; amortir; dégager; purger; s'acquitter de. **Redeemer,** *n*, Rédempteur, *m*. **redemption,** *n*, rachat; remboursement; amortissement; dégagement, *m*; (*mortgage*) purge, *f*; (*Relig.*) rachat, *m*, rédemption, *f*.

redness, *n*, rougeur; rousseur, *f*.

redolent of, qui sent le, la.

redouble, *v.t*, redoubler.

redoubt, *n*, redoute, *f*, réduit, *m*.

redoubtable, *a*, redoutable.

redound, *v.i*, rejaillir.

redress, *n*, redressement, *m*, réparation, *f*. ¶ *v.t*, redresser, réparer.

reduce, *v.t*, réduire; diminuer; ramener; affaiblir. **~ to lower rank** (Mil.), rétrograder. **~ to the ranks,** casser, réduire à la condition de simple soldat. **reduction,** *n*, réduction; diminution, *f*; (*tax*) dégrèvement, *m*. **~ to the absurd** or *reductio ad absurdum*, démonstration (*ou* preuve) par l'absurde, *f*. **~ to the ranks,** cassation, *f*.

redundant, *a*, redondant.

reecho, *v.i*, résonner.

reed, *n*, roseau; (*pipe*) chalumeau, *m*; (*Mus.*) anche; (*Arch.*) baguette, *f*.

reef, *n*, récif, écueil, banc, brisant; (*in sail*) ris, *m*.

reek, *n*, odeur fétide; exhalaison pestilentielle, *f*. **~ with,** *of*, exhaler; suer. **~ing with,** fumant de.

reel, *n*, dévidoir, *m*, bobine, *f*; touret; (*Fish.*) moulinet, *m*. ¶ *v.t*, dévider, bobiner; (*v.i.*) chanceler; (*when drunk*) festonner.

reelect, *v.t*, réélire. **~ion,** *n*, réélection, *f*. **reeligible,** *a*, rééligible.

reembark, *v.t*, rembarquer; (*v.i.*) [se] r.

reengage, *v.t*, rengager.

reenlist, *v.i*, [se] rengager.

reenter, *v.i*, rentrer; (*v.t.*) rentrer dans. **reentrant,** *a*, rentrant. **reentry,** *n*, rentrée, *f*.

reestablish, *v.t*, rétablir, restaurer.

reeve (*Naut.*) *v.t.ir*, passer.

reexamine, *v.t*, repasser, revoir.

reexport, *v.t*, réexporter.

refectory, *n*, réfectoire, *m*.

refer, *v.t*, référer; renvoyer; déférer. **~ to,** se référer à, se reporter à; renvoyer à, consulter. **~ee,** *n*, arbitre; tiers arbitre; (*Box.*) [arbitre] directeur de combat, *m*. ¶ *v.t*, arbitrer. **reference,** *n*, renvoi, *m*; référence; mention, *f*; trait, *m*. **~ library,** bibliothèque où les livres se consultent sur place; b. d'ouvrages à consulter, *f*. **~ [mark],** [guidon de] renvoi, *m*. **~ point,** point de repère, *m*. **with ~ to,** à l'égard de. **referendum,** *n*, referendum, plébiscite, *m*.

refill, *v.t. & i*, remplir; réapprovisionner.

refine, *v.t*, affiner; raffiner; épurer; polir; (*v.i.*) raffiner. **~d,** *p.a*, raffiné, distingué; poli; délicat. **~ment** (*fig.*) *n*, raffinement, *m*. **refiner,** *n*, affineur; raffineur, *m*. **refinery,** *n*, raffinerie, *f*.

reflect, *v.t. & i*, réfléchir; refléter; rejaillir. **~ion,** *n*, réflexion; image, *f*; reflet, *m*; atteinte, *f*.

~ive, *a*, réfléchi. ~or, *n*, réflecteur, *m*. reflex, *a*, réflexe. ¶ *n*, reflet; réflexe, *m*. reflexive (*Gram.*) *a*, réfléchi.

refloat (*ship*) *v.t*, renflouer.

reflux, *n*, reflux, *m*.

re-form, *v.t*, reformer.

reform, *n*, réforme, *f*. ¶ *v.t*, réformer. ~ation, *n*, réformation; réforme, *f*. ~atory, *n*, maison de correction, *f*, pénitencier, *m*. ~er, *n*, réformateur, trice.

refract, *v.t*, réfracter. ~ing telescope, lunette [d'approche] *f*. refractoriness, *n*, mutinerie, *f*. refractory, *a*, réfractaire.

refrain, *n*, refrain, *m*. ¶ *v.i*, se retenir; s'abstenir.

refresh, *n*, rafraîchir; restaurer; délasser, reposer, récréer. refreshment, *n*, rafraîchissement, *m*. ~ bar, ~ room, buvette, *f*, buffet, *m*.

refrigerate, *v.t*, frigorifier. refrigeration, *n*, réfrigération, *f*. refrigerator, *n*, réfrigérateur, *m*.

refuge, *n*, refuge, *m*. to take ~, se réfugier. refugee, *n*, réfugié, e, émigré, e.

refulgent, *a*, éclatant.

refund, *v.t*, rembourser.

refurnish, *v.t*, remeubler.

refusal, *n*, refus, *m*. refuse, *n*, rebut, déchet, *m. oft. pl*; immondices, *f.pl*, ordure, *f*. ~ dump, dépotoir, *m*. ¶ *v.t. & i*, refuser, se r. ~ admittance, consigner à la porte.

refutation, *n*, réfutation, *f*. refute, *v.t*, réfuter.

regain, *v.t*, regagner; reconquérir.

regal†, *a*, royal.

regale, *v.t*, régaler.

regalia, *n*, insignes de la royauté; décors, *m. pl*.

regard, *n*, égard, *m*; considération, *f*; respect; rapport, *m. with ~ to, ~ing*, à l'égard de, à propos de, quant à, à l'endroit de. ¶ *v.t*, regarder; considérer. ~less, *a*, insoucieux, sans se soucier.

regatta, *n*, régate, *f. oft. pl*.

regency, *n*, régence, *f*.

regenerate, *v.t*, régénérer. regeneration, *n*, régénération, *f*.

regent, *n. & a*, régent, e.

regicidal, *a. &* regicide, *n*, régicide, *a. & m*.

regild, *v.t.ir*, redorer.

regime, *n*, régime, *m*. regimental, *n*, régiment, *m*. regimental, *a*,

regimentaire. ~ records, historique du régiment, *m*.

region, *n*, région, contrée, *f*. ~al, *a*, régional.

register, *n*, registre, livre, journal; grand livre; répertoire, *m*; matricule; voix, *f*; (*book mark*) signet, *m*. ~ of voters, liste électorale, *f*. ¶ *v.t*, enregistrer, inscrire, immatriculer; (*design, etc.*) déposer; recommander. registrar, *n*, greffier; archiviste, *m*. registration, *n*, inscription, immatriculation; recommandation, *f*. registry [office], *n*, (*marriage*) mairie, *f*; (*servants*) bureau de placement, *m*.

regress, *v.i*, régresser.

regret, *n*, regret, *m*. to send ~s, envoyer des excuses. ¶ *v.t*, regretter.

regular†, *a*, régulier; réglé; assidu; véritable; franc, fieffé. ~ channel[s] (*fig.*), filière, *f*. ~ity, *n*, régularité, *f*. ~ize, *v.t*, régulariser. regulate, *v.t*, régler; réglementer. regulation, *n*, réglementation, *f*; règlement, *m*, ordonnance, *f*; (*att.*) réglementaire. regulator, *n*, régulateur, *m*.

rehabilitate, *v.t*, réhabiliter.

rehandle, *v.t*, remmancher.

rehearsal, *n*, répétition, *f*. rehearse, *v.t*, répéter; énumérer.

rehousing, *n*, relogement, *m*.

reign, *n*, règne, *m*. ¶ *v.i*, régner. ~ing, *a*, régnant.

reimburse, *v.t*, rembourser.

reimport, *v.t*, réimporter.

reimpose, *v.t*, réimposer.

rein, *n*, rêne, guide, bride, *f*. ¶ *v.t*, guider, refréner.

reindeer, *n*, renne, *m*.

reinforce, *v.t*, renforcer; (*concrete*) armer. ~ment, *n*, renforcement, *m*; armature, *f*; (*men*) renfort, *m*.

reinstate, *v.t*, réintégrer, rétablir, réhabiliter.

reinsure, *v.t*, réassurer.

reinvest (*Fin.*) *v.t*, replacer.

reinvigorate, *v.t*, redonner de la vigueur à, revigorer.

reissue (*book*) *v.t*, réédition, *f*.

reiterate, *v.t*, réitérer.

reject, *v.t*, rejeter; repousser; refuser. ~ion, *n*, rejet; repoussement, *m*.

rejoice, *v.t*, réjouir; (*v.i.*) se r. rejoicing, *n*, réjouissance, *f*.

re-join, *v.t*, rejoindre.

rejoin, *v.t*, répliquer; (*one's regiment*) rejoindre, rallier. **rejoinder**, *n*, réplique, repartie, *f*.

rejuvenate, *v.t*, rajeunir.

rekindle, *v.t*, rallumer.

relapse, *n*, (*Med.*) rechute, *f*; (*Fin.*) recul, *m*; (*crime*) récidive, *f*. **¶** *v.i*, retomber; reculer. ~ *into crime*, récidiver.

relate, *v.t*, raconter, narrer, relater; (*v.i.*) se rapporter, avoir rapport. ~*d to*, parent avec, apparenté à. **relation**, *n*, relation, *f*; rapport, *m*; parent, e; allié, e; (*pl.*) parenté, *f*. **~ship**, *n*, parenté; filiation, *f*. **relative†**, *a*, relatif. **¶** *n* parent, e. **relativism**, *n*, relativisme, *m*. **relativity**, *n*, relativité, *f*.

relax, *v.t*, relâcher; détendre, débander; délasser; (*Med.*) [re]lâcher. ~**ation**, *n*, relâchement; relâche, délassement, *m*.

re-lay, *v.t.ir*, reposer.

relay, *n*, relais, *m*. ~ *race*, course de (*ou* à) relais, *f*. **¶** *v.t*, relayer.

release, *n*, relaxation, *f*, élargissement; (*pigeons*) lancer, *m*; libération; délivrance, *f*; (*Mech.*) déclic; (*Phot.*) déclencheur, *m*. **¶** *v.t*, relaxer, élargir; lancer; libérer; lâcher; délivrer; délier.

relegate, *v.t*, reléguer.

relent, *v.i*, fléchir. ~**less†**, *a*, impitoyable, acharné.

relet, *v.t.ir*, relouer. **reletting**, *n*, relocation, *f*.

relevant, *a*, pertinent; qui se rapporte à.

reliability, *n*, sûreté, sécurité; fidélité; (*test*) fiabilité, *f*. **reliable†**, *a*, sûr; de tout repos; de confiance. **reliance**, *n*, confiance, foi, *f*.

relic, *n*, relique, *f*; reste, *m*.

relief, *n*, soulagement; secours, *m*, assistance, *f*; (*tax*) dégrèvement; (*for dependants*, *Inc. tax*) abattement; (*art*) relief, *m*; (*Mil.*) relève, *f*. ~ *fund*, caisse de secours, *f*. ~ *train*, train supplémentaire, *m*. **relieve**, *v.t*, soulager, secourir, assister; relever; débarrasser.

relight, *v.t*, rallumer.

religion, *n*, religion, *f*. **religious†**, *a*, religieux; (*book*) dévot, de dévotion. ~**ness**, *n*, religiosité, *f*.

relinquish, *v.t*, abandonner.

reliquary, *n*, reliquaire, *f*.

relish, *n*, goût, *m*; saveur, *f*; assaisonnement, *m*. **¶** *v.t*, goûter; savourer.

reluctance, *n*, répugnance, *f*. *I am reluctant to*, il me répugne de, je me fais conscience de. **reluctantly**, *ad*, à contrecœur, à regret.

rely, *v.i*, compter, se reposer, faire fond.

remain, *v.i*, rester; demeurer. **remainder**, *n*, reste, restant; solde d'édition, *m*. ~ *sale*, soldes, *m.pl*. **¶** *v.t*, solder. **remains**, *n.pl*, restes, vestiges, débris, *m.pl*; dépouille, *f*.

remake, *v.t.ir*, refaire.

remand, *v.t*, renvoyer à une autre audience.

remark, *n*, remarque, observation, *f*, propos, *m*. **remark &** **remark**, *v.t*, remarquer. ~**able†**, *a*, remarquable.

remarriage, *n*, remariage, *m*. **remarry**, *v.t*, remarier.

remedy, *n*, remède; (*law*) recours, *m*. **¶** *v.t*, remédier à.

remember, *v.t*, se [res]souvenir de; se rappeler, retenir. **remembrance**, *n*, [res]souvenir, *m*; mémoire, *f*.

remind of, faire penser à, rappeler à. *you* ~ *me of someone*, vous me rappelez quelqu'un. ~**er**, *n*, mémento; rappel, *m*.

reminiscence, *n*, réminiscence, *f*.

remiss†, *a*, négligent. ~**ion**, *n*, rémission; remise, *f*. **remit**, *v.t*, remettre; envoyer. **remittance**, *n*, remise, *f*; envoi, *m*.

remnant, *n*, reste; coupon; lambeau, *m*; épave, *f*.

remodel, *v.t*, remodeler; refondre.

remonstrance, *n*, remontrance, *f*. **remonstrate**, *v.i*, faire des remontrances, [en] remontrer (*with* = à).

remorse, *n*, remords, *m*. ~**less**, *a*, & ~**lessly**, *ad*, sans remords.

remote, *a*, éloigné, écarté; (*antiquity*) reculée, haute. ~ *control*, télécommande, *f*. ~**ness**, *n*, éloignement, *m*.

remount, *n*, remonte, *f*. **¶** *v.t*, remonter.

removable, *a*, amovible. **removal**, *n*, déplacement; éloignement; déménagement; enlèvement, *m*; (*of officer*) destitution, *f*. **remove**, *v.t*, déplacer; éloigner; enlever; lever; destituer.

remunerate, v.t, rémunérer, rétribuer. **remuneration,** n, rémunération, rétribution, f.

renaissance, n, renaissance, f.

rename, v.t, débaptiser.

rend, v.t.ir, déchirer; (the air)
fendre.

render, v.t, rendre; expliquer; interpréter; (plaster) enduire. ~
void, frapper de nullité. ~ing, n,
(accounts) reddition, f; (art)
rendu, m; explication; interprétation, f; (plaster) enduit, m.

renegade, n, renégat, e.

renew, v.t, renouveler. ~al, n, re-
nouvellement, m; rénovation;
reprise, f.

rennet, n, présure; (apple) reinette, f.

renounce, v.t, renoncer à, répudier, abjurer.

renovate, v.t, renouveler, rénover, rajeunir.

renown, n, renommée, f, renom,
m. ~ed, a, renommé.

rent, n, (tear) déchirure, f; accroc; (periodical payment) loyer; fermage, m; redevance, f. ¶
v.t, louer; sous-louer. ~al, n,
prix de location, m; redevance;
valeur locative, f. ~er, n, locataire, m,f.

renunciation, n, renonciation,
répudiation, f, renoncement, m.

reopen, v.t, rouvrir; (v.i.) se r.;
rentrer. ~ing, n, réouverture;
rentrée, f.

reorganize, v.t, réorganiser.

repack, v.t, remballer.

repair, n, état, m; réparation, f.
beyond ~, irréparable. under ~,
en réparation. ¶ v.t, réparer; raccommoder; (v.i.) se rendre. ~
able & reparable, a, réparable.
reparation, n, réparation, f.

repartee, n, repartie, f.

repast, n, repas, m.

repatriate, v.t, rapatrier.

repay, v.t.ir, rembourser; rendre.
~ment, n, remboursement, m.

repeal, n, rappel, m, révocation, f.
¶ v.t, rappeler, révoquer.

repeat (Mus.) ad, bis. ¶ (Mus.)
n, renvoi, m. ¶ v.t, répéter, redire. ~edly, ad, fréquemment, à
plusieurs reprises. ~ing (rifle,
watch) p.a, à répétition.

repel, v.t, repousser. **repellent,** a,
rebutant, repoussant; (Phys.) répulsif.

repent, v.i, se repentir; (v.t.) se

repentir de. ~ance, n, repentir,
m.

repeople, v.t, repeupler.

repercussion, n, répercussion, f.

repertory, n, répertoire, m.

repetend, n, période, f. **repetition,** n, répétition; redite; reprise,
f.

repine, v.i, se chagriner.

replace, v.t, replacer; reposer;
remplacer. ~ment, n, remplacement, m.

replant, v.t, replanter.

replate, v.t, rétamer.

replay, v.t, rejouer.

replenish, v.t, remplir; remonter. **replete,** a, plein. **repletion,** n,
plénitude; réplétion, f.

replica, n, reproduction, f, fac-
similé, m.

reply, n, réponse, f. ~ paid, avec
réponse payée. in ~ (law), responsif. ¶ v.t. & i, répondre.

report, n, rapport; reportage; bulletin; compte rendu; procès-
verbal, m; expertise, f; bruit, m,
renommée; détonation, f. ¶ v.t,
rendre compte de, rapporter. ~
er (news) n, reporter, chroniqueur, journaliste d'information,
m. ~ing, n, reportage, m.

repose, n, repos, m. ¶ v.i. se reposer.

repository, n, dépôt, magasin;
réceptacle; (fig.) répertoire, m.

repot, v.t, rempoter.

repoussé work, travail de repoussé, m.

reprehend, v.t, reprendre, censurer. **reprehensible,** a, répréhensible.

represent, v.t., représenter. ~
ation, n, représentation, f. ~ative,
a, représentatif. ¶ n, représentant, e.

repress, v.t, réprimer, refouler,
comprimer. ~ion, n, répression,
compression, f.

reprieve, n, sursis, m. ¶ v.t, surseoir à l'exécution de, gracier.

reprimand, n, réprimande, semonce, mercuriale, f; blâme, m.
¶ v.t, réprimander, chapitrer; blâmer.

reprint, n, réimpression, f. ¶ v.t,
réimprimer.

reprisal, n, représaille, f.

reproach, n, reproche, m; honte,
f. ¶ v.t, faire des reproches à;
reprocher. ~ful, a, de reproche.
~fully, ad, d'un ton de reproche.

reprobate, *n*, réprouvé, *m*. ¶ *v.t*, réprouver. **reprobation,** *n*, réprobation, *f*.

reproduce, *v.t*, reproduire. **reproduction,** *n*, reproduction; répétition, *f*.

reproof, *n*, réprimande, *f*. **reprove,** *v.t*, reprendre.

reptile, *n*, reptile, *m*.

republic, *n*, république, *f*. ~**an,** *a. & n*, républicain, e.

republish, *v.t*, publier de nouveau.

repudiate, *v.t*, répudier, [re]nier.

repugnance, *n*, répugnance, *f*. **repugnant,** *a*, répugnant. *to be* ~ *to*, répugner à.

repulse, *n*, échec, *m*. ¶ *v.t*, repousser, rebuter. **repulsion,** *n*, répulsion, *f*. **repulsive,** *a*, repoussant; (*Phys.*) répulsif.

repurchase, *n*, rachat, *m*. ¶ *v.t*, racheter.

reputable, *a*, honorable. **reputation & repute,** *n*, réputation, renommée, *f*, renom, crédit, *m. of repute*, réputé. **reputed,** *p.p*, réputé; censé; putatif.

request, *n*, demande, prière, requête, instance, *f. by* ~, *on* ~, sur demande. ¶ *v.t*, demander, prier, inviter.

requiem, *n*, requiem, *m*.

require, *v.t*, exiger; requérir; demander; réclamer; vouloir; avoir besoin de; falloir. ~**ment,** *n*, exigence, *f*; besoin, *m*. **requisite,** *a*, requis, voulu. ¶ *n*, article, *m*; fourniture, *f*. **requisition,** *n*, réquisition, *f*. ¶ *v.t*, réquisitionner.

requital, *n*, récompense; revanche, *f*. **requite,** *v.t*, récompenser.

reredos, *n*, retable, *m*.

rerun, *v.t*, (*computers*) repasser.

resale, *n*, revente, *f*.

rescind, *v.t*, annuler. **rescission,** *n*, rescision, *f*.

rescript, *n*, rescrit, *m*.

rescue, *n*, délivrance, *f*; sauvetage, *m. to the* ~, à la rescousse. ¶ *v.t*, délivrer; sauver.

research, *n*, recherche, *f*. ~ *worker*, chercheur, euse. *motivational* ~, études de motivation, *f.pl*.

reseat, *v.t*, rasseoir; remettre un fond à.

resemblance, *n*, ressemblance, *f*. **resemble,** *v.t*, ressembler à, approcher de, imiter.

resent, *v.t*, s'indigner contre, ressentir. ~**ment,** *n*, ressentiment, *m*.

reservation, *n*, réserve, réservation; (*mental*) restriction, arrière-pensée; (*seats*) location, *f*.

reserve, *n*, réserve, provision; retenue, *f*. ¶ *v.t*, réserver; retenir, louer. ~*d seat ticket*, billet garde-place, billet de location de place, *m*. **reservist,** *n*, réserviste, *m*.

reservoir, *n*, réservoir, *m*.

reset, *v.t.ir*, remonter; remettre; (*Typ.*) recomposer. **resetting** (*Typ.*) *n*, recomposition, *f*.

reship, *v.t*, rembarquer.

reshuffle, *v.t*, rebattre.

reside, *v.i*, résider, demeurer. **residence,** *n*, résidence, *f*; séjour, *m*; demeure, *f*, domicile, *m*, habitation, *f*. **resident,** *n*, habitant, e; (*diplomatic*) résident, *m*.

residuary legatee, légataire universel, *m*. **residue,** *n*, résidu; reliquat, *m*.

resign, *v.t*, résigner, se démettre de; (*v.i.*) démissionner. **resignation,** *n*, résignation, démission; (*submission*) résignation, *f*.

resilient, *a*, élastique.

resin, *n*, résine; (*for violin*) colophane, *f*. ~**ous,** *a*, résineux.

resist, *v.t*, résister à; (*v.i.*) résister. ~**ance,** *n*, résistance, *f*.

resole, *v.t*, ressemeler.

resolute†, *a*, résolu, déterminé. **resolution,** *n*, résolution; détermination; délibération; décision; proposition, *f*. **resolve,** *n*, détermination, *f*. ¶ *v.t*, résoudre, déterminer. ~ *on*, statuer sur, décider.

resonance, *n*, résonance, *f*. **resonant,** *a*, resonnant.

resort, *n*, recours; ressort, *m*, ressource, *f*; rendez-vous; séjour, *m*; station, *f*, centre, *m. as a last* ~, en dernier ressort. *seaside* ~, station balnéaire, *f*. ~ *to*, recourir à; se rendre à; fréquenter.

resound, *v.i*, resonner, retentir.

resource, *n*, ressource, *f*; expédient, *m*. ~**ful,** *a*, de ressources; débrouillard. ¶ *n*, (*person*), débrouillard, *m*.

respect, *n*, respect; rapport, égard, *m*; acception, *f. in all* ~*s*, à tous égards. ¶ *v.t*, respecter. ~**able,** *a*, respectable, honorable, honnête. ~**ably,** *ad*, honorablement. ~**ful†,** *a*, respectueux.

~ing, *pr*, concernant. ~ive†, *a*, respectif.

respiration, *n*, respiration, *f*. respiratory, *a*, respiratoire.

respite, *n*, répit, relâche, *m*, trêve, *f*; sursis, *m*.

resplendent, *a*, resplendissant.

respond, *v.i*, répondre; obéir. ~ent, *n*, répondant, e; (*law*) défendeur, eresse. **response**, *n*, réponse, *f*; (*Eccl.*) répons, *m*. **responsibility**, *n*, responsabilité, *f*. **responsible**, *a*, responsable; solidaire. **responsive**, *a*, sensible, liant.

rest, *n*, repos; (*Mus.*) silence, *m*, pause, *f*; support; appui; (*Bil.*, etc.) chevalet; (*remainder*) reste, *m*. & all the ~ of it, & toute la lyre. ¶ *v.i*, se reposer; reposer; poser; s'appuyer; porter; tenir; résider; incomber; (*v.t.*) reposer, appuyer.

restage, *v.t*, remonter.

restaurant, *n*, restaurant, *m*. ~keeper, restaurateur, trice.

restful, *a*, reposant. **resting place**, repos, *m*; sépulture, *f*.

restitch, *v.t*, repiquer.

restitution, *n*, restitution, *f*.

restive, *a*, rétif.

restless, *a*, inquiet; agité; remuant; turbulent.

restoration, *n*, restauration; réfection, *f*; rétablissement, *m*; restitution, *f*. **restorative**, *a*. & *n*, restaurant, *a*. & *m*. **restore**, *v.t*, restaurer; rénover; rétablir; ramener; rendre; restituer. **restorer**, *n*, restaurateur, trice.

restrain, *v.t*, retenir, contenir, comprimer, contraindre. **restraint**, *n*, contrainte, *f*. to place (lunatic) under ~, interner.

restrict, *v.t*, restreindre, borner, renfermer. ~ion, *n*, restriction, *f*.

restring, *v.t.ir*, recorder.

result, *n*, résultat, *m*; suite, *f*. ¶ *v.i*, résulter.

resume, *v.t*, reprendre; renouer. **resumption**, *n*, reprise, *f*.

resurrection, *n*, résurrection, *f*.

resurvey, *n*, contre-expertise, *f*.

resuscitate, *v.t*, resusciter.

retail, *n*, [commerce de] détail; petit commerce, *m*. ¶ *v.t*, détailler, débiter. ~er, *n*, détaillant, e.

retain, *v.t*, retenir; arrêter. ~er, *n*, (*fee*) provision, *f*; (*pl.*) gens, *m.pl*.

retake, *v.t.ir*, reprendre.

retaliate, *v.i*, user de représailles (*upon* = envers). **retaliation**, *n*, représailles, *f.pl*, talion, *m*. **retaliatory**, *a*, de représailles.

retard, *v.t*, retarder.

retch, *v.i*, avoir des haut-le-cœur, vomir.

retention, *n*, rétention, *f*. **retentive**, *a*, tenace, fidèle.

reticence, *n*, réticence, *f*. to be reticent, se taire à dessein.

reticle & **reticule**, *n*, réticule, *m*.

retina, *n*, rétine, *f*.

retinue, *n*, suite, *f*, cortège, *m*.

retire, *v.t*, retirer; mettre à la retraite, prendre sa retraite; (*officer*) réformer; (*v.i.*) se retirer. ~d, *p.p*, retiré; en retraite. ~ment, *n*, retraite, *f*. **retiring**, *p.a*, (*pers.*) retiré en lui-même, qui fuit la société; (*manners*) effacées; (*director*) sortant; (*pension*) de retraite.

retort, *n*, réplique, riposte; (*Chem.*) cornue, *f*, vase clos, *m*. ¶ *v.t*. & *i*, rétorquer, répliquer, riposter.

retouch, *v.t*, retoucher, retoucher à. ~[ing], *n*, retouche, *f*.

retrace, *v.t*, retracer; revenir sur, rebrousser. ~ one's steps, rebrousser chemin.

retract, *v.t*, rétracter; (*v.i.*) se rétracter.

retreat, *n*, retraite; reculade; (*glacier*) décrue, *f*. ¶ *v.i*, se retirer, reculer.

retrench, *v.t*, retrancher, restreindre. ~ment, *n*, retranchement, *m*.

retribution, *n*, récompense, *f*.

retrieve, *v.t*, rétablir, réparer; (*game*) rapporter; (*computers*), retrouver. **retriever** (*dog*) *n*, retriever, *m*. *a good* ~, un chien qui rapporte bien.

retroactive, *a*, rétroactif.

retrograde, *a*, rétrograde.

retrospect, *n*, revue rétrospective, *f*. ~ive†, *a*, rétrospectif; (*effect of a law*) rétroactif.

return, *n*, retour, *m*; rentrée; restitution; revanche, *f*; remboursement; renvoi; rendu; état, relevé, *m*; déclaration; statistique; rémunération, *f*; rapport, rendement; (*pl.—books, newspapers*) bouillon, *m*. ~ address, adresse de l'expéditeur, *f.* ~ **match**, revanche, *f*, match retour, *m*. **by ~ mail**, par retour du courrier. ¶ *v.t*, rendre; restituer; renvoyer; retourner; rembourser; déclarer; élire, nommer; (*Ten.*) relever (*le service*); (*v.i.*) retourner; revenir; rentrer. ~**able**, *a*, restituable. ~**ed letter**, lettre renvoyée, *f*.

reunion, *n*, réunion, *f*. **reunite**, *v.t*, réunir.

reveal (*Arch.*) *n*, jouée, *f*. ¶ *v.t*, révéler.

reveille, *n*, réveil, *m*, diane, *f*.

revel, *n*. *oft. pl*, réjouissance, *f*. *oft. pl*; ripaille, *f*. ¶ *v.i*, ripailler, faire bombance. ~ **in**, nager dans.

revelation, *n*, révélation, *f*. *R~* (Bible), Apocalypse, *f*.

reveler, *n*, noceur, euse. **revelry**, *n*, ripaille, *f*.

revenge, *n*, vengeance; revanche, *f*. ~ **oneself**, se venger. ~**ful**, *a*, vindicatif.

revenue, *n*, revenu; rapport; fisc, *m*. ~ **stamp**, timbre fiscal, *m*. (*law*) réformer.

reverberate, *v.t*. & *i*, réverbérer. **reverberation**, *n*, réverbération, *f*.

revere, *v.t*, révérer. **reverence**, *n*, révérence, *f*. ¶ *v.t*, révérer. **reverend**, *a*, révérend. **reverent**, *a*, pieux. **reverential**, *a*, révérenciel. **reverentially**, *ad*, avec révérence.

reverie, *n*, rêverie, *f*.

reversal, *n*, retournement; retour, *m*, inversion, *f*. **reverse**, *n*, revers; envers; inverse; contraire, opposé; rebours; (*of coin, of medal*) revers, *m*, pile, *f*. ¶ *v.t*, renverser; inverser, invertir; (*law*) réformer. **reversible**, *a*, réversible. **reversion**, *n*, réversion, *f*; retour, *m*. **revert**, *v.i*, revenir, retourner.

revet, *v.t*, revêtir. ~**ment**, *n*, revêtement, *m*.

revictual, *v.t*, ravitailler.

review, *n*, revue; revision; (*book*) compte rendu, *m*, notice, critique [littéraire] *f*. ¶ *v.t*, revoir, reviser; (*Mil.*) passer en revue; (*book*) faire le compte rendu de. ~**er**, *n*, critique [littéraire] *m*.

revile, *v.t*, injurier.

revise (*Typ.*) *n*, seconde [épreuve] *f*. ¶ *v.t*, revoir, reviser. **revision**, *n*, revision, *f*.

revival, *n*, reprise; renaissance, *f*; rétablissement; (*Relig.*) réveil, *m*. **revive**, *v.t*, ranimer; raviver; réveiller.

revive, *v.t*, (*reanimate*) réanimer; (*film, play*) reprendre.

revoke, *v.t*, révoquer; (*v.i*, *cards*) renoncer.

revolt, *n*, révolte, *f*, soulèvement, *m*. ¶ *v.i*, se révolter, se soulever. ~**ing**, *a*, révoltant.

revolution, *n*, révolution, *f*; tour, *m*. ~**ary**, *a*. & *n*, révolutionnaire, *a*. & *m,f*. ~**ize**, *v.t*, révolutionner; modifier entièrement. **revolve**, *v.t*. & *i*, tourner.

revolver, *n*, révolver, *m*.

revue, *n*, revue, *f*.

revulsion, *n*, révolution; (*Med.*) révulsion, *f*.

reward, *n*, récompense, *f*. ¶ *v.t*, récompenser; couronner.

rewrite, *v.t.ir*, récrire.

rhapsody, *n*, rhapsodie, *f*.

Rheims, *n*, Reims, *m*.

rhetoric, *n*, rhétorique, *f*. ~**al**, *a*, oratoire soutenu.

rheumatic, *a*, rhumatismal. **rheumatism**, *n*, rhumatisme, *m*.

Rhine (**the**), le Rhin. ¶ *att*, rhénan; (*wine*) du Rhin. **the ~land**, les pays rhénans.

rhinoceros, *n*, rhinocéros, *m*.

rhododendron, *n*, rhododendron, *m*.

rhomb[us], *n*, rhombe, losange, *m*.

Rhone (**the**) le Rhône.

rhubarb, *n*, rhubarbe, *f*.

rhyme, *n*, rime, *f*. ¶ *v.i*, rimer. **rhym[est]er**, *n*, rim[aill]eur, *m*. **rhythm**, *n*, rythme, *m*, cadence, *f*. ~**ic(al)**, *a*, rythmique, cadencé.

rib, *n*, côte; nervure; (*ship*) côte, *f*, membre, *m*; (*umbrella*) baleine, *f*. ~ **steak**, entrecôte, *f*.

ribald, *a*, gaillard, égrillard, licencieux.

ribbed, *a*, côtelé, à côtes; à nervure(s).

ribbon or **riband**, *n*, ruban; cordon, *m*. ~ **maker**, rubanier, ère. ~ **trade**, rubanerie, *f*.

rice, *n*, riz, *m*. ~ **field**, rizière, *f*. ~ **paper**, papier de Chine, *m*.

rich†, *a*, riche; (*food*) gras. **the ~**, les riches, *m.pl*. **riches**, *n.pl*, richesse, *f*. *oft. pl*. **richness**, *n*, richesse, *f*.

rick, *n*, (*hay*) meule, *f*; (*strain*) effort, *m*.

rickets, *n,* rachitisme, *m.* **rickety,** *a,* rachitique; boiteux, bancal.

ricksha[w], *n,* pousse-pousse, *m.*

ricochet, *n,* ricochet, *m.* ¶ *v.i,* ricocher.

rid, *v.t.ir,* débarrasser. **riddance,** *n,* débarras, *m.*

riddle, *n,* énigme, devinette, *f,* rébus; (*sieve*) crible, *m.* ¶ *v.t,* cribler.

ride, *n,* promenade; chevauchée; cavalcade, *f;* trajet, *m.* ¶ *v.t. & i. ir,* monter; chevaucher; aller. ~ *sidesaddle,* monter en amazone. ~ *to death* (*fig.*), enfourcher, revenir sans cesse à. **rider,** *n,* cavalier, ère; écuyer, ère; (*document*) codicille; (*Com.*) allonge, *m.*

ridge, *n,* arête; strie; (*roof*) crête; (*hill*) croupe; (*Agric.*) raie, *f;* (*left by plow*) billon, *m.* ~ *pole,* faîtage, *m;* (*tent*) faîtière, *f.* ¶ (*Agric.*) *v.t,* butter.

ridicule, *n,* ridicule, *m.* ¶ *v.t,* ridiculiser. **ridiculous†,** *a,* ridicule. ~**ness,** *n,* ridicule, *m.*

riding, *n,* équitation, *f;* manège; chevauchement; *m;* (*turf*) monte, *f.* ~ *boots,* bottes à l'écuyère, *f.pl.* ~ *breeches,* culotte de cheval, *f.* ~ *habit,* amazone, *f.* ~ *school,* école d'équitation, *f,* manège, *m.* ~ *whip,* cravache, *f.*

rife (to be), courir, sévir.

riffraff, *n,* canaille, racaille, *f.*

rifle, *n,* fusil, *m;* carabine, *f.* ~ *drill,* maniement des (*ou* d') armes, *m.* ~**man,** fusilier, carabinier, *m.* ~ *range,* [champ de] tir; (*gallery*) tir, stand, *m.* ¶ *v.t,* (*rob*) dévaliser, spolier; (*groove*) rayer, canneler.

rift, *n,* crevasse; éclaircie, *f;* (*fig.*) fossé, *m.*

rig, *v.t,* équiper; accoutrer, harnacher; (*ship*) gréer. **rigging,** *n,* gréement, *m,* agrès, *m.pl.* ~ *the market,* tripotage de bourse, *m.*

right, *a,* droit; bon; bien; juste; vrai; qu'il faut. ~**-angled,** rectangle. ~**-handed** *person* or *player,* droitier, ère. ~**-minded,** bien pensant. *at the* ~ *moment,* à point nommé. ~ *side* (fabric), endroit, dessus, *m. to be* ~, avoir raison. ¶ *ad,* tout droit; bien; tout. *all* ~, très bien, ça va. ~ *away,* tout de suite. ~ *& left, ad,* à droite & à gauche. ~

through, de part en part; en entier. ¶ *n,* droit, *m;* faculté; raison, *f;* chef; gain de cause, *m;* (*side*) droite; (*pl.*) justice, *f.* ~ *of way,* [droit de] passage, *m. by* ~*s,* en toute justice. ¶ *v.t,* redresser.

righteous, *a,* vertueux; juste. ~**ly,** *ad,* droitement. ~**ness,** *n,* justice, *f.*

rightful†, *a,* légitime. **rightly,** *ad,* justement, bien; à juste titre.

rigid†, *a,* rigide. ~**ity,** *n,* rigidité, *f.*

rigmarole, *n,* litanie, kyrielle, tartine, *f.*

rigorous†, *a,* rigoureux. **rigor,** *n,* rigueur, *f.*

rill, *n,* ruisseau, *m.*

rim, *n,* [re]bord, *m,* bordure, *f,* ourlet, *m;* (*wheel*) jante; (*watch*) lunette, *f.* ~ *brake,* frein sur jantes, *m.* ¶ *v.t,* border. ~**less** (*glasses*) *a,* sans monture.

rime, *n,* givre, frimas, *m.*

rind, *n,* écorce, peau; (*cheese*) pelure, croûte; (*bacon*) couenne, *f.*

rinderpest, *n,* peste bovine, *f.*

ring, *n,* cercle; anneau, *m;* bague; boucle; frette, *f;* rond; segment; collier; cerne, *m;* couche; enceinte; arène; piste de cirque; coalition; bande, *f;* coup de sonnette; coup de téléphone, *m.* ~ *bolt,* boucle d'amarrage, *f.* ~ *finger,* [doigt] annulaire, *m.* ~**leader,** meneur; chef d'émeute, *m.* ~*s under the eyes,* les yeux cernés. ~**worm,** teigne, *f.* ¶ *v.t. & i. ir,* sonner; corner; tinter; résonner; retentir; cerner; (*bull*) boucler. ~ *a peal,* carillonner. ~ *for,* sonner.

ringlet, *n,* boucle, *f.*

rink, *n,* patinoir, *f.*

rinse & ~ *out, v.t,* rincer. **rinsings,** *n.pl,* rinçure, *f.*

riot, *n,* émeute, *f;* tumulte, *m;* (*fig.*) orgie, débauche, *f.* ¶ *v.i,* prendre part à une émeute; ripailler. ~**er,** *n,* émeutier, *m.* ~**ous†,** *a,* tumultueux.

rip, *n,* déchirure, *f.* ¶ *v.t,* fendre, déchirer; refendre; découdre; éventrer. ~ *off,* arracher. ~ *saw,* scie à refendre, *f.*

riparian, *a,* riverain.

ripe, *a,* mûr. **ripen,** *v.t. & i,* mûrir. **ripeness,** *n,* maturité, *f.* **ripening,** *n,* maturation, *f.*

ripple, *n*, ride, *f*. ¶ *v.t*, rider; (*v.i.*) se r.

riposte, *n*, riposte, *f*. ¶ *v.t*, riposter.

rise, *n*, élévation; montée; rampe, *f*; lever, *m*; crue; naissance; source; hausse; augmentation; (*of a step*) hauteur de marche, *f*. ¶ *v.i.ir*, se lever; se relever; se soulever; s'élever; monter; naître; croître; augmenter; hausser; (*dead*) ressusciter. **rising**, *n*, lever, *m*; ascension, *f*; soulèvement, *m*. ¶ *p.a*: ~ *generation*, jeune génération, *f*. ~ *sun*, soleil levant, *m*. ~ *tide*, marée montante, *f*.

risk, *n*, risque; hasard, *m*. ¶ *v.t*, risquer; hasarder. *I'll* ~ *it*, au petit bonheur. ~**y**, *a*, hasardeux, chanceux.

rite, *n*, rite, *m*. **ritual**, *a. & n*, rituel, *a. & m*.

rival, *a*, rival. ¶ *n*, rival, e, émule, *m,f*. ¶ *v.t*, rivaliser avec. ~**ry**, *n*, rivalité, *f*.

rive, *v.t.ir*, fendre; (*v.i.ir*) se fendre.

river, *n*, rivière, *f*; fleuve, *m*; (*att.*) de rivière, fluvial. ~*side*, bord de l'eau, *m*; (*att.*) riverain.

rivet, *n*, rivet, *m*. ¶ *v.t*, river; enchaîner, attacher. ~**ing**, *n*, rivure, *f*; rivetage, *m*.

Riviera (the), la Rivière de Gênes, la Côte d'Azur.

rivulet, *n*, ruisseau, *m*.

roach (*fish*) *n*, gardon, *m*.

road, *n*, route; voie, *f*; chemin, *m*. ~ *mender*, cantonnier, *m*. ~ *map*, carte routière, *f*. ~ *race*, course sur route, *f*. ~*side*, bord de la route, *m*; (*att.*) sur le b. de la r. ~ *stones*, cailloutis, *m*. *winding* ~, route en lacets, *f*.

roam, *v.i*, rouler, errer.

roan, *a*, (*animal*) rouan; (*shoes*) rouges. ¶ *n*, (*animal*) rouan, e; (*sheepskin*) basane, *f*.

roar, *v.i. & t*, rugir; mugir; gronder; ronfler; éclater. ¶ *n*, rugissement, *m*.

roast, *v.t. & i*, rôtir; cuire [au four]; brûler; griller; torréfier. ~ *beef*, bœuf rôti, rosbif, *m*. ~ [*meat*], rôti, *m*.

rob, *v.t*, voler, dérober, dévaliser, filouter. **robber**, *n*, voleur, euse, brigand, *m*. ~**y**, *n*, vol, *m*; filouterie, *f*. *armed* ~, vol à main armée.

robe, *n*, robe; toge, *f*. *lap* ~, plaid, *m*.

robin [**redbreast**], *n*, rouge-gorge, *m*.

robust, *a*, robuste, vigoureux.

rock, *n*, rocher; roc, *m*; roche, *f*. ~ *crystal*, cristal de roche, *m*. ~ *garden*, jardin de rocaille, jardin alpestre, *m*. ~ *salt*, sel gemme, *m*. ~*work*, rocaille, *f*. ¶ *v.t*, balancer; bercer. ~**er**, *n*, bascule; (*pers.*) berceuse, *f*. ~**ery**, *n*, rocher artificiel, *m*. ~**et**, *n*, fusée; (*Bot.*) roquette, *f*. ~ *engine*, moteur-fusée, *m*. ~**ing**, *n*, balancement; bercement, *m*. ~ *chair*, fauteuil à bascule, *m*, berceuse, *f*. ~ *horse*, cheval à bascule, *m*. ~ *stone*, rocher branlant, *m*. ~**y**, *a*, rocailleux; rocheux. *R*~ *Mountains*, montagnes Rocheuses, *f.pl*.

rococo, *n. & a*, rococo, *m. & att*.

rod, *n*, baguette, verge; barre; tige; (*curtain*) tringle; (*piston*) bielle; (*fishing*) canne, *f*.

rodent, *n. & a*, rongeur, *m. & a*.

roe, *n* (*fish*) œufs de poisson, *m.pl*. ~*buck*, chevreuil, *m*. ~*doe*, chevrette, *f*.

rogations, *n.pl*, rogations, *f.pl*.

rogue, *n*, coquin, e, fripon, ne; espiègle, *m,f*. **roguish**, *a*, fripon; espiègle, mutin, malicieux. **roguishness & roguery**, *n*, friponnerie; espièglerie, malice, *f*.

roisterer, *n*, tapageur, euse.

roll, *n*, rouleau; cylindre; (*downhill*) roulade; (*package*) trousse; (*butter*) motte, *f*; petit pain; rôle, *m*; matricule, *f*, tableau; (*pl.*) tableau, *m*. ~ *call*, appel [nominal] *m*. ~ *of the drum*, batterie de tambour, *f*. ¶ *v.t. & i*, rouler; cylindrer; laminer. ~*top desk*, bureau américain, b. à rideau, *m*. ~ *up*, rouler. ~*ed gold*, or laminé, *m*, doublé or. **roller**, *n*, rouleau; cylindre, *m*; roulette, *f*; galet; *m*; (*Mech.*) tambour, *m*. ~ *skates*, patins à roulettes, *m.pl*. ~ *skating*, patinage à r—s, *m*. ~ *towel*, essuie-main à rouleau, *m*.

rollick, *v.i*, faire la fête. ~**ing**, *a*, bruyant.

rolling, *n*, roulement; laminage; (*ship*) roulis, *m*. ~ *mill*, laminoir, *m*. ~ *pin*, rouleau de pâtissier, *m*. ~ *stock*, matériel roulant, *m*.

Roman, a, romain; (*nose*) aquilin.
~ *candle,* chandelle romaine, f.
~ *Catholic,* a. & n, catholique,
a. & m.f. ~ *Catholicism,* catholicisme, m. ¶ n, (*pers.*) Romain,
e; (*Typ.*) romain, m.

Romania, n, la Roumanie. **Romanian,** a, roumain. ¶ n, (*pers.*)
Roumain e; (*language*) le roumain.

romance, n, roman, m; romance,
idylle, f. R~, a. & n, roman,
a. & m. ¶ v.i, en raconter.

Romanesque, a, roman.

romantic, a, romanesque; (*literature*) romantique.

romp, n, jeu bruyant, m; gamine
bruyante, f, garçon manqué, m.
¶ v.i, folâtrer, batifoler. ~ers
(*child's*) n.pl, barboteuse, combinaison, f.

rood, n, croix, f.

roof, n, toit; comble, m; voûte, f.
~ *garden,* jardin sur le toit, m.
~ *of the mouth,* voûte palatine,
voûte du palais, f, palais, m.
¶ v.t, couvrir. ~ing, n, toiture,
couverture, f, faîtage, m.

rook, n, freux, m, corneille; (*chess*)
tour, f. ~ery, n, colonie de
freux; c. de miséreux, f.

room, n, pièce; chambre, f; cabinet; (*pl.*) appartement; salon, m;
salle; soute; place, f; large, espace, m. ~mate, compagnon de
chambre, m. ~ful, n, chambrée,
f. ~y, a, spacieux.

roost, n, juchoir, perchoir, m. ¶
v.i, [se] jucher, percher. ~er, n,
coq, m.

root, n, racine, f; radical, m. ¶ v.i,
s'enraciner; fouiller. ~ out, déraciner, extirper, dénicher.

rope, n, corde, f, cordage; câble,
m; manœuvre, f; chapelet, m,
glane, f. ~ *dancer,* danseur
(euse) de corde. ~ *end,* garcette, f. ~ *maker,* cordier, m.
~ *making & ~ works,* corderie,
f. ~ *walker,* funambule, m.f. ¶
v.t, corder. **ropiness** (*wine*) n,
graisse, f. **ropy,** a, (*liquid*) filant;
(*wine*) gras.

roquet (*croquet*) v.t, roquer.

rosary, n, rosaire, m; (*rose garden*) roseraie, f. **rose,** n, rose, f;
(*color*) rose, m; (*ceiling*) rosace;
(*can*) pomme; (*pipe*) crépine, f.
~ *bud,* bouton de rose, m.
~*bush,* rosier, m. ~ *grower,* ro-

siériste, m. ~ *window,* rose,
rosace, f. ~*wood,* palissandre,
m. **roseate,** a, rosé, incarnat.
rosemary, n, romarin, m. **rosery,**
n, roseraie, f. **rosette,** n, rosette;
cocarde; (*Arch.*) rosace, f.

rosin, n, résine, f; (*for violin*) colophane, f.

roster, n, contrôle, rôle, m.

rostrum, n, tribune, f.

rosy, a, [de] rose, rosé, incarnat,
vermeil.

rot, n, pourriture; carie, f. ¶ (*v.i.*)
pourrir; se carier; (*v.t.*) faire
pourrir; carier.

rota, n, rôle, m. **rotary,** a, rotatoire, tournant. **rotate,** v.t. & i,
tourner; rouler. **rotation,** n, rotation, f; (*in office*) roulement;
(*crops*) assolement, m. **in** ~, à
tour de rôle, par roulement.

rote, n, routine, f. **by** ~, par cœur.

rotten, a, pourri; carié; (*egg, etc.*)
gâté. ~ness, n, pourriture; carie,
f.

rotund, a, rond, arrondi; pompeux. **rotunda,** n, rotonde, f.
rotundity, n, rondeur, rotondité,
f.

rouge, n, rouge, m. ~ *et noir,*
trente et quarante. ¶ v.i, mettre
du rouge.

rough†, a, grossier; brut; rude;
brutal; bourru; raboteux; rugueux; âpre; (*sea*) agitée. **in a**
~ & *ready fashion,* à coups de
hache, à la serpe, à coups de
serpe. ~*cast* (walls) n, crépi,
m; (*v.t*) crépir, hourder, ravaler.
~ *draft,* brouillon, m. ~ *estimate,* aperçu, m. *at* (or *on*) *a* ~
estimate, à vue d'œil, par aperçu.
~*rider,* casse-cou, m. ~*shod*
(horse), ferré à glace. *to ride*
~*shod over,* fouler aux pieds,
traiter avec rudesse. ~ *grass,*
m. *the* ~ (*golf*), l'herbe longue,
f. ¶ ~, ~ *down,* ~ *out,* ~*hew,*
v.t, dégrossir, ébaucher. ~ness,
n, aspérité; rudesse; grossièreté;
âpreté, f.

round, a, rond. ~*shouldered,*
voûté. ~ *trip,* aller & retour.
¶ n, rond, m; (*slice*) rouelle, f;
(*rung*) échelon, m; (*tour*) ronde,
tournée; (*applause*) salve, f;
(*lap*) circuit, m; (*sport*) partie;
(*Box.*) round, m. ~ [*of ammunition*], cartouche, f. ¶ ad, autour.
~ *about,* alentour. ¶ pr, autour

de, alentour de. ¶ *v.t*, arrondir. ~ *up*, rafler. **roundabout**, *a*, détourné. **roundelay**, *n*, ronde, *f*. **roundish**, *a*, rondelet. **roundly**, *ad*, rondement. **roundness**, *n*, rondeur, *f*. **roundsman**, *n*, livreur, *m*.

rouse, *v.t*, [r]éveiller; exciter.

rout, *n*, déroute, débandade, *f*. ¶ *v.t*, mettre en déroute, défaire.

route, *n*, route, voie, *f*. ~ *march*, promenade militaire, *f*. ¶ *v.t*, acheminer.

routine, *n*, routine, *f*, train, *m*.

rove, *v.i*, rouler, errer, vagabonder; (*v.t.,*) écumer. **rover**, *n*, coureur; (*sea*) forban; (*croquet*) corsaire, *m*. **roving**, *a*, vagabond.

row, *n*, rang, *m*, rangée, *f*; (*of stitches*, *Knit.*, *etc.*) tour, *m*; haie, *f*; cordon; bruit; tapage, fracas, potin, *m*; promenade en bateau, *f*. *a* ~ *of houses*, une rangée de maisons, des maisons en enfilade, *f.pl*. ¶ *v.i*, ramer, aller à la rame, canoter, nager, voguer. ~[*ing*] *boat*, bateau à rames; bateau de promenade, *m*.

rowdy, *n. & a*, tapageur, *m. & a*.

rowel, *n*, molette, *f*.

rower, *n*, rameur, euse, nageur, canotier, *m*. **rowing**, *n*, canotage, *m*, nage [d'aviron] *f*, l'aviron, *m*.

royal†, *a*, royal. *His, Your, R~ Highness*, monseigneur, son, votre, altesse royale. ~**ist**, *n. & att*, royaliste, *m,f. & a*. ~**ty**, *n*, royauté, *f*; (*rent*) redevance, *f*; (*author's*) droit d'auteur, *m*.

rub, *n*, (*with a cloth*) coup de chiffon; (*fig.*) hic, nœud, *m*, enclouure, *f*. ~ *of the green* (*golf*), risque de jeu, *m*. ¶ *v.t. & i*, frotter; frictionner; (*inscription*) estamper. ~ *down* (*horse*), épousseter, bouchonner. ~ *one's hands*, se frotter les mains. ~ *out*, effacer. ~ *shoulders with*, se frotter à, frayer avec. **rubber**, *n*, frottoir; (*cards*) rob[re] *m*; (*3rd game*) belle, *f*; caoutchouc, *m*; gomme [élastique] *f*. ~ *stamp*, timbre en c., t. humide, *m*. **rubbing**, *n*, frottement, *m*; friction, *f. oft. pl*; (*with oil*) onction, *f*; (*copy*) frottis, *m*.

rubbish, *n*, décombres, *m.pl*, détritus, *m*; (*dirt*) immondice; (*trash*) camelote, saleté; (*nonsense*) blague, *f*, fadaises, *f.pl*.

rubble[**stone**], *n*, blocaille, *f*, moellon, *m*.

rubicund, *a*, rubicond.

rubric, *n*, rubrique, *f*.

ruby, *n*, rubis, *m*. ¶ (*lips*) *a*, vermeilles.

ruck, *n*, pli, godet, *m*.

rucksack, *n*, sac de touriste, s. de montagne, s. d'alpinisme, *m*.

rudder, *n*, gouvernail, *m*.

ruddy, *a*, coloré, rougeaud, rubicond.

rude†, *a*, grossier, malhonnête, malgracieux; rude. ~**ness**, *n*, grossièreté, rudesse, *f*.

rudiment, *n*, rudiment, *m*; (*pl, of a science, an art*) éléments, *m.pl*. ~**ary**, *a*, rudimentaire.

rue (*Bot.*) *n*, rue, *f*. ¶ *v.t*, se repentir de. ~**ful**†, *a*, triste.

ruff (*Hist., dress*) *n*, fraise, *f*.

ruffian, *n*, bandit, *m*. ~**ly**, *a*, de brigand.

ruffle, *n*, ruche, *f*. ¶ *v.t*, rider; froisser, chiffonner; (*hair*) ébouriffer.

rug, *n*, tapis de pied, *m*; carpette; descente de lit; (*traveling*) couverture, *f*, plaid, *m*. ~ *work*, tapisserie, *f*.

rugged, *a*, raboteux; rugueux; rocailleux; rude. ~**ness**, *n*, âpreté; rudesse, *f*.

ruin, *n*, ruine, perte, *f*. ¶ *v.t*, ruiner, perdre, abîmer. ~**ous**, *a*, ruineux.

rule, *n*, règle; domination, *f*; empire; (*Typ.*) filet, *m. as a* ~, ordinairement. ~ *of thumb*, procédé empirique, *m*; (*att.*) empirique. *by* ~ *of thumb*, empiriquement. ¶ *v.t*, régler; rayer; gouverner; régir; (*v.i.*) gouverner; régner; (*prices*) se pratiquer. **ruler**, *n*, gouvernant; dominateur, *m*; (*for lines*) règle, *f*. **ruling**, *p.a*, dominant; (*price*) pratiqué. ~ *passion*, passion dominante, *f*. ¶ *n*, réglage, *m*, réglure; décision; (*law*) sentence, *f*.

rum, *n*, rhum, *m*.

rumble, *v.i*, gronder; rouler; (*bowels*) gargouiller. ¶ *n*, grondement, grouillement, *m*.

ruminant, *n. & a*, ruminant, *m. & a*. **ruminate**, *v.i. & t*, ruminer.

rummage, *v.t. & i*, fouiller, farfouiller.

rumor, *n*, rumeur, renommée, *f*,

bruit, on-dit, *m. it is ~ed that,*
le bruit court que.

rump, *n,* croupe, *f; (bird)* croupion, *m; (beef)* culotte. *f.*
~steak, romsteck, *m.*

rumple, *v.t,* chiffonner, froisser.

rumpus, *n,* potin, chahut, *m; rébecca. *m. & f. to create a ~,* faire
du rébecca.

run, *n,* course; marche; campagne,
f; cours; parcours, trajet, *m;*
roulade; coulée; suite; séquence;
(stocking) maille, *f;* commun,
m; descente, ruée; volière, *f;*
parc, *m. in the long ~,* à la
longue. *~off (from dead heat),*
course de barrage, *f. ~[-up]*
(Jump.), course d'élan, *f,* élan,
m. ¶ *v.i.ir,* courir; accourir;
affluer; fonctionner; marcher;
(stockings) se démailler; circuler; trotter; couler; pleurer, suinter; tourner; rouler; aller; être;
(v.t.ir.) faire; faire courir; faire
marcher; actionner; conduire;
[en]courir. *~ about,* faire des
allées & venues. *~ against,*
heurter. *~ aground,* échouer. *~
along,* longer, border, côtoyer.
~ away, s'enfuir, se sauver. *~
into,* rencontrer. *~ out of
(stock),* manquer de, être à court
de. *~ out of gas,* avoir une
panne d'essence *ou* une p. sèche.
~ over, parcourir; déborder. *to
be ~ over,* être écrasé. *~
through,* parcourir; feuilleter;
transpercer, enferrer, embrocher.
~ to earth, dépister. *~ up against*
(pers.), coudoyer. **runabout,** *n,*
coureur, euse; voiturette, *f.* **runaway,** *n. & a,* fugitif, ive, fuyard,
e, échappé, e. **rundown,** *a,*
épuisé.

rung, *n,* échelon; barreau, *m.*

runner, *n,* coureur, euse; courrier; agent de transmission, *m;*
(Hort., Bot.) coulant; *(slider of
sledge)* patin, *m.* **running,** *n,*
courses, *f.pl;* marche, *f;* roulement; service, *m.* ¶ *p.a,* courant;
coulant; cursif; successif, de
suite. *~ dive,* plongeon avec
élan, *m. ~ water,* eau courante,
f.

runt, *n,* nabot, *m.*

runway, *n,* piste, *f.*

rupee, *n,* roupie, *f.*

rupture, *n,* rupture; *(Med.)* hernie, *f.* ¶ *v.t,* rompre. *to be ~d,*
avoir une hernie.

rural, *a,* rural, champêtre.

ruse, *n,* ruse, *f.*

rush, *n,* jonc, *m;* élan, *m;* ruée;
bousculade; presse; chasse, *f;*
flot, torrent. *m. ~ chair,* chaise
paillée, *f. ~ hours,* heures d'affluence, *f.pl. (TV & cinema) ~es,*
épreuves de tournage, *f.pl.* ¶ *v.t,*
brusquer; *(v.i.)* se précipiter, se
ruer, accourir, foncer.

rusk, *n,* biscotte, *f.*

russet, *a,* roux. ¶ *n,* roux, *m;*
(apple) reinette grise, *f.*

Russia, *n,* la Russie. ¶ *n (pers.)* Russe, *m,f;*
(language) le russe.

rust, *n,* rouille, *f. to rub off the
~ from,* dérouiller. ¶ *v.t,* rouiller;
(v.i.) se r. **rustiness,** *n,* rouillure,
f. **rustproof,** *a,* inoxydable.

rustic, *a,* rustique, agreste, paysan. ¶ *n,* rustre, paysan, *m.*
rusticate, *v.i,* être en villégiature.

rustle, *v.i,* frémir, bruire; *(dress)*
faire frou-frou.

rusty, *a,* rouillé.

rut, *n, (groove)* ornière, *f; (of
animals)* rut, *m.*

ruthless, *a,* impitoyable, acharné,
âpre.

rye, *n,* seigle. *m. ~ bread,* pain de
seigle, *m.*

S

S, *n. & S hook,* esse, *f,* S, *m.*

sabbath, *n,* sabbat; dimanche, *m.*

sable, *n, (Zool.) [martre]* zibeline;
(fur) zibeline, *f,* sable; *(Her.)*
sable, *m.*

saber, *n,* sabre, *m.* ¶ *v.t,* sabrer.

sabotage, *n,* sabotage. *m.* ¶ *v.t,*
saboter. **saboteur,** *n,* saboteur,
euse.

saccharin, *n,* saccharine, *f.*

sacerdotal, *a,* sacerdotal.

sachet, *n,* sachet à parfums, sultan, *m.*

sack, *n,* sac, *m. ~cloth, sacking,*
toile à sacs, *f,* treillis, *m,* serpillière, *f; (Theol.)* sac, *m. in
~cloth & ashes,* sous le sac & la
cendre. *~ race,* course en sacs,
f. ¶ *v.t,* ensacher; saccager;
mettre à sac. *~ful, n,* sachée, *f.*

sacrament, *n,* sacrement, *m,*
communion, *f. ~al†, a,* sacramentel. *~al, n,* sacramental, *m.*
sacred, *a,* sacré; saint; inviolable;

(*song*) religieux; (*concert*) spirituel; (*to the memory of*) consacré. **sacrifice,** *n*, sacrifice, *m*. ¶ *v.t.* & *i*, sacrifier, immoler. **sacrificial,** *a*, du sacrifice. **sacrilege,** *n*. & **sacrilegious,** *a*, sacrilège, *m*. & *a*. **sacristy,** *n*, sacristie, *f*. **sacrosanct,** *a*, sacro-saint.

sad, *a*, triste, douloureux, fâcheux. **sadden,** *v.t*, attrister, contrister.

saddle, *n*, selle; (*lathe*) cuirasse, *f*; (*mountain*) col, *m*. ~*backed*, ensellé. ~*bag*, sacoche, *f*. ~*bow*, arçon, *m*. ~ *horse*, cheval de selle, *m*. ¶ *v.t*, seller; (*pack animal*) embâter; (*fig.*) grever, charger. **saddler,** *n*, sellier, *m*. **saddlery,** *n*, sellerie, *f*.

sadism, *n*, sadisme, *m*. **sadist,** *n*, sadique, *m*. & *f*. **sadistic,** *a*, sadique. **sadomasochism,** *n*, sadomasochisme, *m*. **sadomasochist,** *a*. & *n*, sadomasochiste, *m*. & *f*.

sadly, *ad*, tristement; cruellement. **sadness,** *n*, tristesse, *f*.

safe, *a*, sauf; sûr; sans danger; assuré; de sécurité; (*investment*) sûr, de tout repos, de père de famille; (*arrival*) bonne, heureuse. ~ & *sound*, sain & sauf, bagues sauves. ~ *conduct*, sauf-conduit, *m*. sauvegarde, *f*. ~ *custody*, garde [en dépôt] *f*. ~ *keeping*, sûreté, *f*. ¶ *n*, coffrefort, *m*. ~ *deposit box*, coffre, *m*. ~*guard*, *n*, sauvegarde, garantie, *f*, palladium, *m*; (*v.t.*) garantir. ~*ly*, *ad*, en sûreté; sûrement; sans danger; sans accident; (*arrival*) à bon port. ~*ty*, *n*, sûreté; sécurité; *f*; salut, *m*. ~ *catch*, cran d'arrêt, *m*. ~ *first*, sécurité d'abord. ~ *pin*, épingle de sûreté, é. de nourrice, anglaise, *f*. ~ *razor*, rasoir de sûreté, *m*. ~ *valve* (*lit. & fig.*), soupape de sûreté, *f*.

saffron, *n*, safran, *m*.

sag, *n*, fléchissement, *m*. ¶ *v.i*, fléchir, donner.

sagacious, *a*, sagace. **sagacity,** *n*, sagacité, *f*.

sage, *n*, (*pers.*) sage, *m*; (*herb*) sauge, *f*. ¶ *a*, sage.

sago, *n*, sagou, *m*. ~ *palm*, sagou[t]ier, *m*.

said (the) (*law*) *p.a*, ledit.

sail, *n*, voile, toile, (*pl.*) voilure, *f*; (*windmill*) volant, *m*; promenade en bateau, *f*. ~*boat*, voilier, *m*. ~ *cloth*, toile à voiles, *f*. ~ *maker*, voilier, *m*. ¶ *v.i*, faire voile; naviguer; voguer; marcher, courir; partir; (*v.t.*) faire naviguer; naviguer sur. ~*er*, *n*, voilier, marcheur, *m*. ~*ing*, *n*, navigation [à voile] *f*; départ, *m*; partance; marche, *f*. ~ *ship*, navire à voiles, voilier, *m*. ~*or*, *n*, marin; matelot, *m*. ~ *suit*, costume marin, *m*.

saint, *a*, saint. ¶ *n*, saint, e. ~'s *day*, fête, *f*. *St. Bernard dog*, chien de Saint-Bernard, *m*. *Saint Helena*, Sainte-Hélène, *f*. *Saint Lawrence*, Saint-Laurent, *m*. *St. Vitus's dance*, danse de Saint-Guy, chorée, *f*. ¶ *v.t*, canoniser. ~*ed*, *p.p*, saint, canonisé. **saintliness,** *n*, sainteté, *f*. **saintly,** *a*, saint.

sake, *n*, cause, *f*; amour; plaisir; égard, *m*. *for God's* ~, pour l'amour de Dieu.

sal, *n*, sel, *m*. ~ *ammoniac*, sel ammoniac. ~ *volatile*, alcool ammon aromatique, spiritus aromaticus, *m*.

salaam, *n*, salamalec, *m*.

salable, *a*, vendable, de vente; marchand, vénal.

salacious, *a*, lascif, lubrique.

salad, *n*, salade, *f*. ~ *bowl*, saladier, *m*. ~ *oil*, huile de table, h. comestible, *f*.

Salamanca, *n*, Salamanque, *f*.

salamander, *n*, salamandre, *f*.

salaried, *p.a*, appointé. **salary,** *n*, appointements, *m.pl*, traitement; cachet, *m*; indemnité, *f*. *to put on a* ~ *basis*, appointer.

sale, *n*, vente, *f*; débit; solde, *m*; liquidation; enchère, *f*. *for* ~, à vendre. *on* ~, en vente.

Salerno, *n*, Salerne, *f*.

salesman, -woman, *n*, vendeur, euse; (*market*) facteur (de la halle) *m*. ~*ship*, l'art de vendre, *m*.

Salic law, loi salique, *f*.

salient, *a*. & *n*, saillant, *a*. & *m*.

saline, *a*, salin.

saliva, *n*, salive, *f*. **salivate,** *v.i*, saliver.

sallow, *a*, jaunâtre.

sally, *n*, (*Mil.*) sortie, saillie; (*wit*) saillie, *f*, trait d'esprit, *m*, boutade, *f*.

salmon, *n*, saumon, (*young*) saumoneau, *m.* ~ *pink,* rose saumon, *m.* ~ *trout,* truite saumonée, *f.*

Salonica, *n,* Salonique, *f.*

saloon, *n,* bar, estaminet, *m.*

salt, *n,* sel, *m.* ~*cellar,* salière, *f.* ~ *lake,* lac salé, *m.* ~ *pork,* [porc] salé, *m.* ~ *provisions,* salaisons, *f.pl.* ~ *spoon,* pelle à sel, *f.* ~ *water,* eau salée, *e.* saline, *f.* ~*water fish,* poisson de mer, *m;* (*caught & fresh*) marée, *f.* (*caught & fresh*) pêche en mer, *f. smelling* ~*s,* sels volatiles, *m.pl.* ¶ *v.t,* saler. ~*ing,* *n,* salage, *m; salaison, f. saltern, n,* marais salant, *m.* **saltpeter,** *n,* salpêtre, nitre, *m.* **salty,** *a,* salé.

salubrious, *a,* salubre.

salutary†, *a,* salutaire. **salutation,** *n,* salutation, *f,* salut, *m.* **salute,** *n,* salut; (*guns*) salut, *m,* salve, *f.* ¶ *v.t,* saluer.

salvage, *n,* sauvetage, *m.* ¶ *v.t,* sauver. **salvation,** *n,* salut, *m.* S~ *Army,* Armée du Salut, *f.* **salve,** *n,* onguent, *m;* pommade, *f.* ¶ (*fig.*) *v.t,* calmer.

salver, *n,* plateau, *m.*

salvo, *n,* salve, *f.*

Salzburg, *n,* Salzbourg, *m.*

same, *a,* même. *it's all the* ~ *to me,* cela m'est égal. ~*ness,* *n,* identité; monotonie, *f.*

sample, *n,* échantillon, *m.* ¶ *v.t,* échantillonner; (*taste wines*) déguster. **sampler,** *n,* modèle de broderie, *m.*

sanatorium, *n,* sanatorium, *m.*

sanctify, *v.t,* sanctifier. **sanctimonious†,** *a,* béat, cagot, papelard. **sanction,** *n,* sanction; consécration, *f.* ¶ *v.t,* sanctionner; consacrer. **sanctity,** *n,* sainteté; religion, *f.* **sanctuary,** *n,* sanctuaire; asile, *m;* réserve, *f.* **sanctum,** *n,* le saint des saints; sanctuaire, *m.*

sand, *n,* sable; sablon; *m;* (*pl.*) plage, *f.* ~ *bag,* sac à terre, *m.* ~ *bank,* banc de sable, ensablement, *m.* ~ *blast,* jet de sable, *m.* ~ *flats,* relais, *m.* ~ *fly,* simulie, *f.* ~ *glass,* sablier, *m,* horloge de sable, *f.* ~ *hill,* dune, *f.* ~*paper, n,* papier de verre, *m;* (*v.t.*) poncer. ~*piper,* bécasseau, *m.* ~ *pit,* sablière; sablonnière, *f.* ~*stone,* grès, *m.* ~*stone quarry,* gresserie, *f.* ¶ *v.t,* sabler.

sandal, *n,* sandale, *f.* ~ [*wood*], [bois de] santal, *m.*

sandwich, *n,* sandwich, *m.* ~ *man,* homme-sandwich, *m.*

sandy, *a,* sablonneux. ~ *hair,* chevelure blond roux, *f.*

sane, *a,* sain, rassis.

sanguinary, *a,* sanguinaire. **sanguine,** *a,* optimiste; plein d'espérance; (*full-blooded, Hist.*) sanguin.

sanitary, *a,* sanitaire; hygiénique. ~ *inspector,* inspecteur sanitaire, *m.* ~ *napkin,* serviette hygiénique, *f.* **sanitate,** *v.t,* assainir. **sanitation,** *n,* assainissement, *m;* hygiène, *f.*

sanity, *n,* raison, *f;* bon sens, *m;* rectitude, *f.*

sanserif, *a,* sans empattement.

Santa Claus, le père Noël, le bonhomme Noël.

sap, *n,* sève; lymphe; (*Mil.*) sape, *f.* ~*wood,* aubier, *m.* ¶ *v.t,* saper.

sapling, *n,* plant, *m.* **sapper,** *n,* [sapeur] mineur, *m.*

sapphire, *n,* saphir, *m.*

sappy, *a,* plein de sève.

Saragossa, *n,* Saragosse, *f.*

Saratoga [**trunk**], *n,* [malle] chapelière, *f.*

sarcasm, *n,* sarcasme, *m.* **sarcastic,** *a,* sarcastique.

sarcophagus, *n,* sarcophage, *m.*

sardine, *n,* sardine, *f.*

Sardinia, *n,* la Sardaigne. **Sardinian,** *a,* sarde. ¶ *n,* Sarde, *m,f.*

sardonic, *a,* sardonique.

sarsaparilla, *n,* salsepareille, *f.*

sarsenet, *n,* florence, *m.*

sash, *n,* ceinture; écharpe, *f;* (*window*) châssis, *m.* ~ *window,* fenêtre à guillotine, *f.*

Satan, *n,* Satan, *m.* ~**ic,** *a,* satanique.

satchel, *n,* cartable, *m;* gibecière, sacoche, *f.*

sate, *v.t,* rassasier.

sateen, *n,* satinette, *f.*

satellite, *n,* satellite, *m.*

satiate, *v.t,* rassasier. **satiety,** *n,* satiété, *f.*

satin, *n,* satin, *m.* ~ *stitch* (*Emb.*), passé, *m.* ~ *wood,* bois de satin, *m.* ~**y,** *a,* satiné.

satire, *n,* satire, *f.* **satiric & ~al,** *a,* satirique. **satirist,** *n,* satirique, *m.* **satirize,** *v.t,* satiriser.

satisfaction, *n,* satisfaction; raison, *f.* **satisfactorily,** *ad,* d'une

manière satisfaisante. **satisfactory,** a, satisfaisant. **satisfy,** v.t, satisfaire, satisfaire à; contenter.
saturate, v.t, saturer.
Saturday, n, samedi, m.
saturnalia, n.pl, saturnales, f.pl.
saturnine, a, sombre; (Chem.) saturnin.
satyr, n, satyre, m.
sauce, n, sauce, f. ~ boat, saucière, f. ~ ladle, cuiller à sauce, f. ~pan, casserole, f; poêlon, m.
saucer, n, soucoupe, f. flying ~, s. volante, f. **saucy,** a, gamin; impertinent.
sauerkraut, n, choucroute, f.
saunter, v.i, flâner. ~ing, n, flânerie, f.
sausage, n, (fresh) saucisse, f; (smoked) saucisson, m. ~ skin, ~ case, peau à saucisses, f.
savage†, a, sauvage; féroce, farouche. ¶ n, sauvage, m,f, sauvagesse, f, cannibale, m. ~ry, n, sauvagerie; férocité, f.
savant, n, savant, m.
save, v.t, sauver; épargner; ménager; économiser; gagner; capter; (v.i.) économiser. ¶ pr, sauf sinon, hormis, près. **saving,** n, épargne; économie, f. ~s bank, caisse d'épargne, f. **the Saviour,** le Sauveur.
savory (Bot.) n, sarriette, f.
savor, n, saveur, f. to ~ of, tenir de, sentir le, la. **savory,** a, savoureux. ~ herbs, fines herbes, f.pl. ~ omelet, omelette aux fines herbes, f.
Savoy, n, la Savoie. s~, chou de Milan, m.
saw, n, scie, f; dicton, adage, m. hand~, égoïne, f. ~ power~, scie mécanique, f. ~dust, sciure, f. ~mill, scierie, f. ¶ v.t.ir, scier; débiter. ~ off, scier. ~ing, n, sciage, m.
saxhorn, n, saxhorn, m.
saxifrage, n, saxifrage, f.
Saxon, a, saxon. ¶ n, Saxon, ne. **Saxony,** n, la Saxe.
saxophone, n, saxophone, m.
say, n, mot, m; voix, f. ¶ v.t. & i. ir, dire; réciter; parler. as they ~, comme on dit. you don't ~ sol pas possible! **saying,** n, mot, dire; dicton, adage, m. ~s & doings, faits & dits, m.pl.
scab, n, croûte, (Vet.) gale, f. (Hort.) rogne, f.
scabbard, n, fourreau, m.

scabby, a, scabieux, galeux, rogneux.
scaffold, n, échafaud, m. ~ing, n, échafaudage, m.
scald, n, brûlure, f. ¶ v.t, échauder, ébouillanter; blanchir.
scale, n, échelle; (Mus.) gamme, f; barême; tarif; (pan) plateau, bassin, m; (pl, lancet) châsse; écaille, paillette; incrustation; (s. or pl.) balance; bascule, f. ~ maker, balancier, m. ¶ v.t, (wall) escalader; (boiler) piquer; (v.i.) s'écailler. **scaly,** a, écailleux.
scallion, n, ciboule, f.
scallop, n, (Mol.) pétoncle; coquillage, (edging) feston, m. ¶ v.t, festonner.
scalp, n, cuir chevelu, m; (trophy) chevelure, f. ~ massage, friction, f. ¶ v.t, scalper.
scalpel, n, scalpel, m.
scamp, n, chenapan, vaurien, polisson, [mauvais] garnement, m. ¶ v.t, brocher, bâcler.
scamper away, s'enfuir en courant, détaler.
scan, v.t, scruter, éplucher; (verse) scander; scanner. ~ner, n, scanneur, m.
scandal, n, scandale, éclat, m; honte; médisance, f, cancan, racontar; pétard, m. ~monger, médisant, e; mauvaise langue, f. ~ize, v.t, scandaliser. ~ous†, a, scandaleux.
Scandinavia, n, la Scandinavie. **Scandinavian,** a, scandinave. ¶ n, Scandinave, m,f.
scansion, n, scansion, f.
scant[y], a, exigu; étriqué; maigre; faible; pauvre; mesquin; (attire) sommaire.
scape (Bot.) n, hampe, f. ~goat, bouc émissaire, souffre-douleur, m. ~grace, [mauvais] garnement, mauvais sujet, m.
scar, n, cicatrice, couture, balafre, f. ¶ v.t, cicatriser, couturer, balafrer.
scarab, n, scarabée, m.
scarce, a, rare; (time) cher. ~ly, ad, à peine; presque. **scarcity,** n, rareté; disette, f.
scare, n, panique, transe, f. ¶ v.t, épouvanter, effrayer, effarer. ~crow, n, épouvantail, m.
scarf, n, écharpe, f, cache-nez, m.
scarify, v.t, scarifier.
scarlatina, n. or scarlet fever,

[fièvre] scarlatine, *f.* **scarlet**, *n.* & *a*, écarlate, *f.* & *a.*

scarp, *n*, escarpe, *f.*

scatheless, *a*, indemne. **scathing**, *a*, cinglant, sanglant. ~ *attack* (fig.), jeu de massacre, *m.*

scatter, *v.t.* disperser, éparpiller; semer. ~**brained**, *a*, écervelé.

scavenge, *v.t.* balayer. **scavenger**, *n*, boueux, balayeur; animal qui se nourrit de charogne, *m.*

scenario, *n*, scénario, *m.* **scene**, *n*, scène, *f*; spectacle; tableau; théâtre, *m. behind the* ~*s*, dans la coulisse. ~ *painter*, peintre de décors, décorateur, *m.* ~ *shifter*, machiniste, *m.* ~ *shifting*, changement de décor[ation] *m.* **scenery**, *n*, paysages, *m.pl*; (Theat.) décors, *m.pl*, décoration, *f.* **scenic**, *a*, scénique. ~ *railway*, montagnes russes, *f.pl.*

scent, *n*, parfum, *m*; odeur; senteur, *f*; flair, fumet, nez; vent, *m*, piste, voie, *f.* ~ *bottle*, flacon à odeur, *m. to throw off the* ~, dépister. ¶ *v.t*, parfumer, embaumer; flairer, subodorer. ~**ed**, *a*, parfumé, odorant.

scepter, *n*, sceptre, *m.*

Schaffhausen, *n*, Schaffhouse, *f.*

schedule, *n*, horaire; (work) plan, (price) tarif, *m*; annexe, *f*; bordereau, *m.*

scheme, *n*, projet, plan; cadre, *m*, combinaison, *f.* ¶ *v.t*, projeter; machiner; (v.i.) former des projets; intriguer. **schemer**, *n*, homme à projets, *m*; intrigant, e. **scheming**, *n*, manœuvres, *f.pl.*

schism, *n*, schisme, *m.*

schist, *n*, schiste, *m.* ~**ose**, *a*, schisteux.

scholar, *n*, écolier, ère; savant, érudit, *m.* ~**ly**, *a*, savant, érudit. ~**ship**, *n*, savoir, *m*, érudition; bourse, *f.* **scholastic**, *a*, scolastique. **school**, *n*, école; classe, *f*; collège; conservatoire; (of fish) banc, *m. boarding* ~, pensionnat, *m.* ~ *book*, livre de classe, l. classique, l. scolaire, *m.* ~*boy*, ~*girl*, écolier, ère, lycéen, ne, collégien, ne. ~*fellow*, camarade d'école, *m,f*, condisciple, *m.* ~*master*, ~*mistress*, instituteur, trice. ~ *room*, [salle de] classe, *f.* **schooling**, *n*, instruction, *f.*

schooner, *n*, schooner, *m*, goélette, *f.*

sciatic, *a.* & **sciatica**, *n*, sciatique, *a.* & *f.*

science, *n.* science, *f.* **scientific†**, *a*, scientifique; (instruments) de précision. **scientist**, *n*, savant, homme de science, *m.*

Scilly Islands or **Isles**, îles Scilly, îles Sorlingues, *f.pl.*

scimitar, *n*, cimeterre, *m.*

scintillate, *v.i*, scintiller.

scion, *n*, (Hort.) scion; (pers.) rejeton, *m.*

scissors, *n.pl*, ciseaux, *m.pl. with* ~ & *paste* (fig.), à coups de ciseaux.

sclerosis, *n*, sclérose, *f.*

scoff at, se railler de; mépriser. **scoffer**, *n*, moqueur, euse, railleur, euse. **scoffing**, *n*, moquerie, *f.*

scold, *n*, grondeuse, mégère, *f.* ¶ *v.t*, gronder, tancer, semoncer, quereller; (v.i.) criailler.

scoop, *n*, pelle; main; cuiller; casse; écope, *f*; (journalism) article en exclusivité, *m.* ~ *out*, caver, vider; écoper.

scope, *n*, étendue, *f*, champ, *m*; latitude, *f*; cadre, *m*, portée; carrière, *f*; essor, *m.*

scorch, *v.t*, brûler, rôtir, roussir.

score, *n*, coche; strie, *f*; écot; point, *m*, marque, *f*; compte des points; c. des coups, *m*; (Mus.) partition; vingtaine, *f.* ¶ *v.t*, cocher; rayer; (game) marquer; (Mus.) orchestrer. **scorer**, *n*, marqueur, euse; pointeur, *m.*

scoria, *n*, scorie, *f.*

scoring, *n*, pointage, *m*; orchestration, *f.*

scorn, *n*, mépris, dédain, *m.* ¶ *v.t*, mépriser, dédaigner. ~**er**, *n*, contempteur, trice. ~**ful†**, *a*, dédaigneux.

scorpion, *n*, scorpion, *m.*

Scotch, *a*, écossais; d'Ecosse. ~*man*, *-woman*, Ecossais, e. *the* ~, les Ecossais, *m.pl.* ~ *mist*, brouillasse, *f.*

scot-free, *a*, indemne; impuni.

Scotland, *n*, l'Ecosse, *f.* **Scottish**, *a*, écossais.

scoundrel, *n*, scélérat, e, gredin, e.

scour, *n*, chasse [d'eau] *f.* ¶ *v.t*, donner une chasse à; dégraisser, décaper; (seas) écumer; (country) battre.

scourge, *n,* (*whip*) martinet; (*plague*) fléau, *m.* ¶ *v.t,* flageller.

scout, *n,* éclaireur; (*boy*) scout, *m*; (*warship*) vedette, *f.* ~ *master,* chef éclaireur, c. scout, *m.* ~ *mistress,* cheftaine, *f.* ¶ *v.i,* aller à la découverte; (*v.t.*) repousser avec mépris.

scowl, *v.i,* froncer le sourcil. ¶ *n,* froncement de sourcils, *m.*

scrag, *n,* (*mutton*) collet; (*pers.*) squelette, *m.* ~ *end,* bout saigneux, *m.* **scraggy,** *a,* décharné.

scramble, *n,* mêlée; (*for place, etc.*) curée, *f.* ~*d eggs,* œufs brouillés, *m.pl.* **scrambler,** *n,* (*code*) brouilleur, *m.*

scrap, *n,* bout, morceau; chiffon, *m*; (*metal*) déchets, débris, *m.pl*; (*pl.*) restes, *m.pl*; bribes, *f.pl.* ~*book,* album, *m.* ~ *iron,* ferraille, *f.* ¶ *v.t,* mettre au rebut; se débarrasser de.

scrape, *v.t,* gratter; racler; décrotter; (*golf*) érafler. ¶ *n,* embarras, *m.* **scraper,** *n,* grattoir; racloir, *m*; curette, *f*; (*mat*) décrottoir, *m.* **scrapings,** *n.pl,* raclure; (*savings*) gratte, *f.*

scratch, *n,* égratignure, *f*; coup de griffe, *m*; rayure, *f*; (*sport*) scratch, *m.* ¶ *v.t,* gratter; rayer; effleurer; (*sport*) rayer de l'épreuve. ~ *out,* gratter; raturer.

scrawl, *n,* griffonnage, *m,* patarafe, *f.* ¶ *v.t,* & *i,* griffonner.

scream & screech, *n,* cri, *m.* ¶ *v.i.* & *t,* crier. *screech owl,* chat-huant, *m.*

screed, *n,* tartine, *f.*

screen, *n,* écran; paravent; rideau; (*choir*) clôture; grille, *f*; crible, *m,* claie, *f.* ~ *door,* contreporte, *f.* ~*writer,* dialogiste, *m.* on ~, dans le champs. ¶ *v.t,* abriter; murer; soustraire; cribler; (*movies*) présenter à l'écran.

screw, *n,* vis; hélice. ~*-capped bottle,* flacon à couvercle vissé, *m.* ~*driver,* tournevis, *m.* ~ *eye,* piton, *m.* ¶ *v.t,* visser.

screwball, *n,* loufoque, *m.* ¶ *a,* loufoque, maboul, e.

scribble, *n,* griffonnage, *m.* ¶ *v.t,* griffonner; (*v.i,* *of author*) écrivailler. **scribbler,** *n,* griffonneur, euse; écrivassier, ère, folliculaire, *m.* **scribe,** *n,* scribe, *m.*

scrimmage, *n,* mêlée; bousculade, *f.*

scrip, *n,* titre provisoire; titre, *m.*

script, *n,* scénario, *m.* *shooting* ~, découpage, *m.* ~*writer,* *n,* scénariste, *m.*

Scripture, *n. oft. pl,* l'Écriture, *f. oft. pl.*

scrofula, *n,* scrofules, *f.pl.* **scrofulous,** *a,* scrofuleux.

scroll, *n,* rouleau, *m*; volute, *f.*

scrub (*bush*) *n,* broussailles, *f.pl.* ¶ *v.t,* brosser; laver, lessiver. *scrubbing brush,* brosse à laver, *f.*

scruff of the neck, peau du cou, *f,* collet, *m.*

scrunch, *v.t,* croquer. ¶ *i,* croc!

scrummage, *n,* mêlée; bousculade, *f.*

scruple, *n,* scrupule, *m.* ~ *to,* se faire scrupule de. **scrupulous†,** *a,* scrupuleux, religieux.

scrutineer, *n,* scrutateur, *m.* **scrutinize,** *v.t,* scruter. **scrutiny,** *n,* examen, *m.*

scuffle, *n,* rixe, bagarre, batterie, *f.* ¶ *v.i,* se bousculer; se battre.

scull, *n,* aviron de couple, *m*; (*stern oar*) godille, *f.* ¶ *v.i,* godiller; (*v.i.*) ramer en couple, nager en couple. ~*er,* *n,* rameur de couple, *m.*

scullery, *n,* lavoir [de cuisine] *m.*

scullion, *n,* marmiton fouille-au-pot, *m.*

sculptor, *n,* sculpteur, *m.* **sculptress,** *n,* femme sculpteur, *f.* **sculpture,** *n,* sculpture, *f.* ¶ *v.t,* sculpter.

scum, *n,* écume, crasse; (*fig.*) écume, lie, *f.*

scumble, *n,* frottis, glacis, *m.* ¶ *v.t,* frotter, glacer.

scupper, *n,* dalot, *m.*

scurrilous, *a,* outrageant, ordurier.

scurvy, *n,* scorbut, *m.* ¶ *a,* vilain; méprisable.

scutcheon, *n,* écusson, *m.*

scuttle, *n,* (*coal*) seau; (*Naut.*) hublot, *m.* ¶ *v.t,* saborder.

scythe, *n,* faux, *f.*

sea, *n,* mer, *f. on the high* ~s, sur la haute mer. *open* ~, pleine mer. ~*board,* littoral, *m.* ~*coast,* côte de la mer, *f.* ~ *cow,* lamantin, *m.* ~*farer,* homme de mer, *m.* ~*faring people,* peuple navigateur, *m.*

~ *fishing*, pêche en mer, *f.* ~*going* (ship), de mer. ~ *gull*, mouette, *f.*, goéland, *m.* ~ *horse*, cheval marin, hippocampe, *m. to have got one's* ~ *legs*, avoir le pied marin. ~ *level*, niveau de la mer, *m.* ~ *lion*, lion marin, *m.* otarie, *f.* ~*man*, marin, homme de mer, matelot; (skilful) manœuvrier, *m. in a* ~*manlike manner*, en bon marin. ~ *nymph*, nymphe de la mer, Néréide, *f.* ~ *plane*, hydravion, *m.* ~ *scape*, marine, *f.* ~*shore*, rivage de la mer, *m.* ~*sickness*, mal de mer, *m. to be* ~*sick*, avoir le m. de m. ~*side*, bord de la mer, *m.* ~*side resort*, plage, station balnéaire, *f.* ~ *urchin*, oursin, hérisson de mer, *m.* ~ *wall*, digue, *f.* ~*weed*, plante marine, algue, *f.*, varech, goémon, *m.* ~*worthy*, en [bon] état de navigabilité.

seal, *n*, sceau; cachet; *m*; (bottle) capsule, *f*; (Zool.) phoque, *m.* ~*skin*, peau de phoque, *f.* ¶ *v.t*, sceller; cacheter; boucher. ~*ed book* (fig.), lettre close, *f.* ~*ing wax*, cire à cacheter, *f.*

seam, *n*, couture; (Geol.) couche, *f*, gisement, *m.* ~ *stitch* (Need.), [point de] surjet, *m.* ¶ *v.t*, couturer. ~*less*, *a*, sans couture. **seamstress**, *n*, couturière, *f.* **seamy side** (lit. & fig.), envers, *m.*

seance, *n*, séance de spiritisme, *f.*

seaplane, *n*, hydravion, *m.* ~ *base*, hydrobase, *f.*

sear, *a*, desséché, fané. ¶ *v.t*, brûler; cautériser.

search, *n*, recherche, *f.* oft. *pl*; (law) perquisition, *f.* ~*light*, projecteur, *m*; lampe de poche, *f.* ~ *warrant*, mandat de perquisition, *m.* ¶ *v.t*, scruter. ~ *for*, [re]chercher. ~*er*, *n*, chercheur, euse, fouilleur, *m.* ~*ing*, *a*, pénétrant; scrutateur.

season, *n*, saison, *f*, temps, *m.* ~ *ticket*, carte d'abonnement, *f.* *slack* ~, saison creuse, *f.* ¶ *v.t*, assaisonner; relever; (wood) sécher; (fig.) aguerrir. ~*able*, *a*, de saison; opportun. ~*ably*, *ad*, à propos. ~*ing*, *n*, assaisonnement; *m*; (of a salad) garniture, fourniture, *f.*

seat, *n*, siège, *m*; place; place assise; stalle, *f*; chef-lieu; *m*; charge; séance, *f*; office; foyer;

château; banc, *m*; banquette; chaise, *f*; repos; (trousers chair) fond, *m*; assiette; (on horse) tenue, *f.* ¶ *v.t*, asseoir.

secede, *v.i*, faire scission, faire sécession.

secluded, *p.a*, retiré. **seclusion**, *n*, retraite; réclusion, *f.*

second†, *a*, second; deuxième; deux; (cousin) issu(e) de germain. ~ *finger*, doigt du milieu, médius, *m.* ~*hand*, d'occasion; de seconde main. ~*hand bookseller*, bouquiniste, *m.* ~*hand dealer*, revendeur, euse, brocanteur, euse. ~ *lieutenant*, sous-lieutenant, *m. one's* ~ *self*, un autre soi-même. *on* ~ *thoughts*, réflexion faite. [on] *the* ~ *of September*, le deux septembre. ¶ *n*, second, *m*; deuxième, *m,f*; (Box.) second, soigneur, (duel) témoin, *m*; (time) seconde, *f.* ~ *hand*, aiguille des secondes, *f.* ¶ *v.t*, seconder; appuyer. ~*ary*, *a*, secondaire. ~ *school*, école secondaire, *f*, lycée, *m.*

secrecy, *n*, secret, *m*; discrétion, *f.* **secret**, *a*, secret; caché; dérobé. ¶ *n*, secret, *m.* **secretary**, *n*, secrétaire, *m.* ~ *bird*, serpentaire, secrétaire, *m.* ~*ship & secretariat*, *n*, secrétariat; ministère, *m.* **secrete**, *v.t*, cacher; (physiology) sécréter. **secretion**, *n*, sécrétion, *f.* **secretive**, *a*, dissimulé, cachottier. **secretly**, *ad*, secrètement, en cachette; sourdement.

sect, *n*, secte, *f.* ~*arian*, *n. & a*, sectaire, *m. & att.*

section, *n*, section; coupe, *f*; profil; fer; tronçon; article, *m*, rubrique, *f.* ~*al*, *a*, démontable; (iron) profilé; (view) en coupe. **sector**, *n*, secteur, *m.*

secular†, *a*, séculier; profane; (100) séculaire.

secure†, *a*, sûr; à l'abri. ¶ *v.t*, mettre à l'abri; assurer; garantir; asseoir; fixer; obtenir. **security**, *n*, sécurité; sûreté; assiette; garantie; assurance; caution, *f*; cautionnement; titre, *m*; valeur, *f.*

sedan, *n*, (auto) berlin; (chair) chaise à porteurs, *f.*

sedate†, *a*, posé, rassis. **sedative**, *n. & a*, sédatif, calmant, *m. & a.* **sedentary**, *a*, sédentaire.

sedge, *n*, laîche, *f.*

sediment, *n*, sédiment, dépôt, *m.*

sedition, *n*, sédition, *f*. **seditious†**, *a*, séditieux.

seduce, *v.t*, séduire. ~ *from duty*, débaucher. **seducer**, *n*, séducteur, trice. **seduction**, *n*, séduction, *f*. **seductive**, *a*, séduisant.

sedulous, *a*, assidu. ~**ly**, *ad*, assidûment.

see, *n*, siège [épiscopal] *m*, chaire, *f*, évêché, *m*.

see, *v.t. & i. ir*, voir; regarder; reconduire; s'occuper; veiller. ~ *about*, s'occuper de. ~ *home*, reconduire. ~ *through*, pénétrer. ¶ (*vide*) *v.imperative*, voir, voyez.

seed, *n*, semence; graine, *f*; grain; (*fig.*) germe, *m*. ~ *pearls*, semence de perles. ~ *time*, semailles, *f.pl*. ¶ *v.i*, grener, s'égrener. ~ *the players* (Ten.), sélectionner les têtes de séries. ~**ling**, *n*, jeune plant, sauvageon, (*pl*.) semis, *m*. **seedsman**, *n*, grainier, ère.

seeing, *n*, vision, *f*. ~ *that*, vu que, attendu que, puisque.

seek, *v.t. & i. ir*, chercher, rechercher. ~**er**, *n*, chercheur, euse.

seem, *v.i*, sembler, paraître. **seeming**, *n*, paraître, *m*. *the* ~ *& the real*, l'être & le paraître. ¶ *p.a*, apparent. **seemingly**, *ad*, en apparence. **seemly**, *a*, [bien]séant.

seer, *n*, prophète, *m*.

seep, *v.i*, suinter; filtrer.

seesaw, *n*, bascule, balançoire, *f*. ¶ *v.i*, basculer, se balancer.

seethe, *v.i*, bouillonner; grouiller.

segment, *n*, segment, *m*.

segregate, *v.t*, séparer. **segregation**, *n*, ségrégation, *f*.

seine (*net*) *n*, seine, *f*.

seismic, *a*, sismique. **seismograph**, *n*, sismographe, *m*.

seize, *v.t*, saisir, arrêter, prendre, s'emparer de; (*v.i, Mach.*) gripper. **seizure**, *n*, saisie, *f*; arrêt, *m*; attaque de paralysie, *f*.

seldom, *ad*, rarement.

select, *a*, choisi; bien composé. ~ *party*, petit comité, *m*. ¶ *v.t*, choisir; (*sport*) sélectionner. ~**ion**, *n*, choix, *m*; sélection, *f*; recueil, *m*; (*pl, from writings*) morceaux choisis, *m.pl*.

self, *n*, personne, *f*; moi-même; moi, *m*; -même. ~*-centered*, égocentriste. ~*-contained*, indépendant. ~*-control*, empire sur soi-même, *m*, maîtrise de soi, *f*. ~*-*

defense, légitime défense, *f*. ~*-denial*, abnégation, *f*, renoncement, *m*. ~*-esteem*, amour-propre, *m*. ~*-government*, autonomie, *f*. ~*-importance*, suffisance, *f*. ~*-made man*, fils de ses œuvres, *m*. ~*-possession*, sang-froid, aplomb, *m*. ~*-reliance*, confiance en soi, *f*. ~*-respect*, amour-propre, *m*. ~*-sacrifice*, dévouement, *m*. ~*-satisfied*, béat. ~*-service*, libre service, *m*. ~*-styled*, soi-disant, *a.inv*. ~*-taught*, autodidacte. ~*-willed*, entier, opiniâtre, volontaire.

selfish†, *a*, égoïste, intéressé, personnel. ~**ness**, *n*, égoïsme, *m*.

sell, *v.t.ir*, vendre; débiter; (*v.i.ir*.) se vendre, s'écouler. ~ *off*, liquider, solder. **seller**, *n*, vendeur, euse.

seltzer, *n*, eau de Seltz, *f*.

selvage, **-edge**, *n*, lisière, *f*.

semaphore, *n*, sémaphore, *m*.

semblance, *n*, semblant, *m*, apparence, *f*.

semi, *prefix*: ~*breve*, ronde, *f*. ~*circle*, demi-cercle, *m*. ~*colon*, point & virgule, point-virgule, *m*. ~*demisemiquaver*, quadruple croche, *f*. ~*detached*, jumelle. ~*final*, demi-finale, *f*. ~*official*, semi-officielle, officieux. ~*quaver*, double croche, *f*. ~*tone*, demi-ton, *m*. ~*weekly*, *a*, bihebdomadaire.

seminary, *n*, séminaire, *m*.

Semitic, *a*, sémitique.

semolina, *n*, semoule, *f*.

senate, *n*, sénat, *m*. **senator**, *n*, sénateur, *m*.

send, *v.t. & i. ir*, envoyer; expédier; remettre. ~ *away* & ~ *back*, renvoyer. ~ *for*, envoyer chercher, faire appeler. ~ *to sleep*, endormir. ~**er**, *n*, envoyeur, euse, expéditeur, trice.

Senegal, *m*, le Sénégal.

senile, *n*, sénile. ~ *decay*, décrépitude, caducité, *f*. **senility**, *n*, sénilité, *f*.

senior, *a*, aîné; ancien; principal; chef. ¶ *n*, aîné, e; père, *m*; doyen, ne; (*sports*) senior, *m*. ~**ity**, *n*, aînesse, ancienneté, *f*.

senna, *n*, séné, *m*.

sensation, *n*, sensation; impression, *f*. ~**al**, *a*, sensationnel. ~ *affairs*, drame, *m*. **sense**, *n*, sens;

sentiment, *m*; sensation, *f*; esprit, *m*; raison, *f*; bons sens, sens commun, *m*; acception, part, *f*. ¶ *v.t*, entrevoir. ~less, *a*, insensé; sans connaissance. **sensibility**, *n*, sensibilité, *f*. **sensible**, *a*, sensé, sage; sensible. **sensibly**, *ad*, sensément. **sensitive**, *a*, sensible; sensitif; tendre; susceptible: chatouilleux. **sensitivity**, *n*, sensibilité, *f*. **sensitized** (*Phot.*) *a*, sensible.

sensory, *a*, sensoriel, ielle.

sensual†, *a*, sensuel, charnel. ~ist, *n*, sensualiste, *m.f.* ~ity, *n*, sensualité, *f*.

sentence, *n*, sentence, *f*, jugement, *m*; (*Gram.*) phrase, *f. death* ~, peine capitale, *f*. ¶ *v.t*, condamner. **sententious†**, *a*, sentencieux.

sentient, *a*, sensible; conscient. **sentiment**, *n*, sentiment. *m*. ~al†, *a*, sentimental. ~ality, *n*, sentimentalité, sensiblerie, *f*.

sentinel, *n*, sentinelle, *f*. **sentry**, *n*, sentinelle, *f*, factionnaire, *m*; (*mounted*) vedette, *f*. ~ *box*, guérite, *f*. ~ *duty*, faction, *f*.

separate†, *a*, séparé; distinct; à part. ~ *cell system*, emprisonnement cellulaire, *m*. *at* ~ *tables* (meal), par petites tables. ¶ *v.t*, séparer. **separation**, *n*, séparation, *f*. **separatism**, *n*, séparatisme, *m*. **separatist** *a*, séparatiste, *m. & f*.

sepia, *n*, sépia, *f*.

September, *n*, septembre, *m*.

septet[te], *n*, septuor, *m*.

septic, *a*, septique. ~ *tank*, fosse s., *f*.

septum, *n*, cloison, *f*.

sepulchral, *a*, sépulcral. **sepulcher**, *n*, sépulcre, *m*.

sequel, *n*, suite; conséquence, *f*. **sequence**, *n*, suite, succession; (*cards*) séquence, *f*. **sequestered**, *p.p*, retiré, écarté. **sequestration** (*law*) *n*, séquestre, *m*.

seraglio, *n*, sérail, *m*.

seraph, *n*, séraphin, *m*. ~ic, *a*, séraphique.

Serbia, *n*, la Serbie. **Serb[ian]**, *a*, serbe. ¶ *n*. (*pers.*) Serbe, *m.f*; (*language*) le serbe. **Serbo-Croatian**, *n*, (*language*) serbo-croate, *m*.

sere, *a*, desséché, fané.

serenade, *n*, sérénade, *f*. ¶ *v.t*, donner une sérénade à.

serene, *a*, serein. **serenity**, *n*, sérénité, *f*.

serf, *n*, serf, *m*, serve, *f*. ~dom, *n*, servage, *m*.

serge, *n*, serge, *f*.

sergeant, *n*, sergent; (*cavalry*) maréchal des logis; (*police*) brigadier, *m*. ~ *major*, adjudant; maréchal des logis chef, *m*.

serial, *a*, en série. ~ *rights*, droits de reproduction dans les journaux & périodiques, *m.pl*. ~ [*story*], [roman] feuilleton, *m*. ~ *number*, numéro matricule, *m*. **seriatim**, *ad*, successivement. **series**, *n*, série, suite, *f*.

serif, *n*, empattement, *m*.

seringa, *n*, seringa, *m*.

serious†, *a*, sérieux; grave. ~ness, *n*, sérieux, *m*; gravité, *f*.

sermon, *n*, sermon; prône; prêche, *m*. ~ize, *v.t*, sermonner. ~izer, *n*, prêcheur, *m*.

serpent, *n*, serpent, *m*. **serpentine**, *a*, serpentin. ¶ *n*, serpentine, *f*.

serration, *n*, denteleure; dent, *f*. **serrate[d]**, *a*, denté en scie, dentelé, en dents de scie.

serried, *a*, serré.

serum, *n*, sérum, *m*.

servant, *n*, employé, e; serviteur, *m*; domestique, *m.f*; bonne; (*pl.*) domesticité, livrée, *f*, gens, *m.pl*. ~ *girl*, fille de service, *f*. **serve** *v.t*. & *i*, servir; desservir; (*a sentence*) subir; (*a notice*) signifier; faire le service militaire; suffire. ~ *up*, servir. ¶ (*Ten.*) *n*, service, *m*. **server** (*Ten.*) *n*, servant, *m*. **service**, *n*, service, *m*; desserte; démarche, *f*, ministère; office, *m*; (*domestic*) domesticité, condition, *f*; (*china, etc.*) service, *m*; (*of writ*) signification, *f*. *to grow old in the* ~, blanchir sous le harnois. ~ *hatch*, passe-plats, *m*. ~ *station*, poste d'essence, *f*. ~ *tree*, sorbier, *m*. ~able, *a*, d'usage; utile. **servicing**, *n*, entretien, *m*; reparation, *f*.

servile†, *a*, servile. **servility**, *n*, servilité, *f*. **servitude**, *n*, servitude, *f*.

sesame, *n*, sésame, *m*.

session, *n*, session; séance; bourse, *f*.

set, *n*, série, *f*; jeu; assortiment; train, *m*; batterie; suite; garniture; trousse; (*Math.*) tranche;

parure, *f*; ensemble; service, *m*; (*fixity*) assiette; (*of saw*) voie, chasse, *f*; (*Theat.*) décor, *m*; (*Ten.*) manche, *f*, set, *m.* ~ *of* (*artificial*) *teeth*, dentier, *m.* ~ *back*, recul, tassement; décalage, *m*, traverse, *f.* ~*off*, compensation, *f*; (*foil*) repoussoir; (*Arch.*) ressaut, *m*; (*Typ.*) maculature; (*law*) reconvention, *f.* ~*to*, prise de bec; bagarre, *f*; pugilat, *m.* ¶ *v.t.ir*, mettre; poser; placer; aposter; fixer; planter; asseoir; assurer; (*bone*) remettre, remboîter; (*dog on, fashion, etc.*) lancer; (*gem*) sertir, enchâsser, monter; (*hen*) mettre couver; (*a sail*) établir; (*saw*) donner la voie à; (*seal*) apposer; (*shutter* —*Phot.*) armer; (*task, example*) donner; (*tools*) affiler, repasser; (*trap*) tendre, dresser; (*type*) composer; (*watch*) régler; (*v.i. ir.*) se figer, prendre; (*sun*) se coucher. ~ *about it*, s'y prendre ~ *down in writing*, coucher par écrit. ~ *off*, (*figure*) dégager. ~ *on* (*pers.*), lapider. ~ *out*, partir. ~ *up*, monter; ériger; établir. ¶ *p.a*: ~ *purpose*, parti pris, *m.* ~ *smile*, sourire figé, *m.* ~ *speech*, discours d'apparat, *m.*

settee, *n*, divan, *m*, causeuse, *f.*

setter, *n*, poseur, euse; tendeur; monteur, metteur; compositeur; chien couchant, *m.* **setting**, *n*, entourage, encadrement, *m*; (*cement*) prise; (*gem*) enchâssure, œuvre, *f*, chaton; (*sun*) coucher, *m*; (*type*) composition, *f.* ~ *aside*, abstraction faite de. ~ *sun*, soleil couchant, *m.*

settle, *n*, banc, *m.* ¶ *v.t*, régler; arranger; accommoder; trancher; liquider; établir, installer; emménager; (*property*) constituer; (*v.i.*) se fixer; s'établir; (*alight*) se poser; (*matter*) se déposer; (*ground*) [se] tasser. ~**d**, *p.a*, décidé, arrêté; (*weather*) sûr. ~**ment**, *n*, règlement, *m*; constitution, *f*; (*Stk Ex.*) terme, *m*, liquidation; colonie, colonie de peuplement, *f.* **settler**, *n*, colon, *m*, résident, e.

seven, *a. & n*, sept, *a. & m.* **seventeen**, *a. & n*, dix-sept, *a. & m.* **seventeenth**, *a. & n*, dix-septième, *a. & m,f*; dix-sept, *m.* ~**ly**, *ad*, en dix-septième lieu. **seventh**, *a. & n*, septième, *a. & m,f*; sept, *m.*

~**ly**, *ad*, septièmement. **seventieth**, *a. & n*, soixante-dixième, *a. & m,f.* **seventy**, *a. & n*, soixante-dix, *a. & m.* 71, 72, soixante et onze, soixante-douze.

sever, *v.t*, séparer. ~**al†**, *a*, divers, plusieurs; respectif; individuel. ~**ance**, *n*, séparation; distraction, *f.*

severe†, *a*, sévère; rigoureux; rude; grave. **severity**, *n*, sévérité; rigueur; gravité, *f.*

Seville, *n*, Séville, *f.* ~ *orange*, bigarade, orange amère, *f.*

sew, *v.t.ir*, coudre. ~**er**, *n*, couseur, euse, piqueuse, *f.* ~**ing**, *n*, couture, *f.* ~ *machine*, machine à coudre, *f.*

sewer, *n*, égout, *m.* **sew[er]age**, *n*, eaux d'égout, eaux-vannes, *f.pl.*

sex, *n*, sexe, *m.* ~ *appeal*, sex-appeal, *m.*

sextant, *n*, sextant, *m.*

sextet[te], *n*, sextuor, *m.*

sexton, *n*, sacristain, *m.*

sexual, *a*, sexuel. ~**ity**, *n*, sexualité, *f.*

shabby, *a*, usé, râpé, miteux; mesquin.

shack, *n*, hutte, cabane, *f.*

shackle, *n*, boucle; manille, *f*; maillon, *m*; (*fig.*) entrave, *f.* ¶ *v.t*, entraver.

shade, *n*, ombre, *f*; ombrage, *m*; (*pl*, *spirits*) mânes, *m.pl*; nuance, *f*; (*lamp*) abat-jour; écran; globe protecteur, *m.* ¶ *v.t*, ombrager; (*art*) ombrer; (*v.i.*) passer. ~ *off*, dégrader. **shadow**, *n*, ombre, *f.* ~ *boxing*, boxe contre son ombre, *f.* ¶ *v.t*, filer, suivre. **shady**, *a*, ombragé; (*Poet.*) ombreux; (*disreputable*) louche, véreux. *to be on the* ~ *side of 40*, avoir dépassé la quarantaine.

shaft, *n*, flèche, *f*, trait, *m*; (*spear*) hampe; (*of chimney*) souche, *f*; (*cart*) limon, brancard; (*Arch.*) fût, *m*, tige, *f*; (*Mech.*) arbre, *m*, transmission, *f*; (*Min.*) puits, *m*; (*elevator*) cage, *f.* ~ *horse*, brancardier, timonier, *m.*

shaggy, *a*, poilu, hirsute.

shagreen, *n*, chagrin, *m.*

shah, *n*, shah, chah, *m.*

shake, *n*, secousse, *f*; (*head*) hochement; (*hand*) serrement, *m*, poignée; (*timber*) gerçure, *f*, éclat; (*Mus.*) trille, *m.* ¶ *v.t.ir*, secouer; agiter; [é]branler; hocher; serrer; (v.i.ir.) trembler; s'ébranler; ballotter; flageoler, chevroter. **shaky**, a, branlant; chancelant; chevrotant; tremblé.

shale, n, schiste, m. ~ *oil*, huile de s., f.

shall, v.aux.ir, is expressed in Fr. by future tense. Also by falloir.

shallot, n, échalot, f.

shallow, a, peu profond, bas; faible; creux; frivole; superficiel. ~s, n.pl, bas-fond, m.

sham, n, feinte, f, [faux-]semblant, m. ¶ a, feint; simulé; fictif. ~ *fight*, simulacre de combat, m. ¶ v.t. & i, feindre, simuler.

shambles, n, décombres, m.pl, ruines, f.pl.

shambling, p.a, traînant.

shame, n, honte; pudeur, f; scandale, m. *for* ~l fi donc! ¶ v.t, faire honte à. ~*faced*, a, honteux, penaud. ~*ful†*, a, honteux; scandaleux. ~*less*, a, éhonté, dévergondé, impudent. ~*lessly*, ad, sans vergogne, impudemment.

shampoo, n, (wet) schampooing, m; (dry) friction, f. ¶ v.t, faire un schampooing à; faire une friction à.

shamrock, n, trèfle, m.

shank, n, jambe; queue; tige, f.

shanty, n, baraque, bicoque, f. ~*town*, bidonville, m.

shape, n, forme; figure; taille; tournure; carcasse, f; profil, m. ¶ v.t, former; façonner; mouler; modeler; pétrir. ~*less*, a, informe. ~*ly*, bien tourné.

share, n, part; quote-part, quotité, f; écot, m; (Fin.) action, valeur, f; titre; (plow) soc, m. ~*holder*, actionnaire; sociétaire, m,f. ¶ v.t. & i, partager, participer (à).

shark (fish & rapacious pers.) n, requin, m.

sharp, a, tranchant; aigu; acéré; fin; net; vif; perçant; (acid) aigre; (rebuke) verte. ~ *practices*, procédés indélicats, m.pl. ~*shooter*, tirailleur, m. ¶ ad. (hour), précise. *look* ~l dépêchez-vous! vitel ¶ (Mus.) n, dièse, m. ~*en*, v.t, aiguiser; affûter; repasser; tailler [en pointe]; (wits) déniaiser. ~*ly*, ad, vivement; nettement. ~*ness*, n, acuité; finesse; âcreté; netteté, f.

shatter, v.t, briser, fracasser.

shave, v.t, raser; (v.i.) se raser, se faire la barbe. *to have a close* ~, l'échapper belle. **shaving**, n, la barbe; (chip) copeau, m; rognure, planure, f. ~ *brush*, pinceau à barbe, blaireau, m. ~ *soap*, savon à barbe, m.

shawl, n, châle, m.

she, pn, elle; celle; ce, c', ç'; (of ship) il. ¶ n, femelle, f. ~*ass*, ânesse, bourrique, f. ~*bear*, ourse, f. ~*camel*, chamelle, f. ~*devil*, diablesse, f. ~*goat*, chèvre, chevrette, f. ~*monkey*, guenon, guenuche, f. ~*wolf*, louve, f.

sheaf, n, gerbe, f; faisceau, m. ¶ v.t, [en]gerber.

shear, v.t.ir, tondre; cisailler. ~*er*, n, tondeur, euse. ~*ing*, n, tonte, f. ~ *machine*, tondeuse, f. **shears**. n. pl, cisailles, forces, f.pl; ciseaux, m.pl, tondeuse, f.

sheath, n, gaine, f; fourreau, m. **sheathe**, v.t, [r]engainer; recouvrir.

sheave, n, poulie, f, rouet, m.

shed, n, hangar; garage, m; baraque; remise; étable, f. ¶ v.t.ir, verser, répandre; se dépouiller de. **shedding** (blood) n, effusion, f.

sheen, n, éclat; lustre, m.

sheep, n, mouton, m; brebis, f. *black* ~, brebis galeuse, f. ~ *dog*, chien de berger, m. ~*fold*, bergerie, f. ~*like* (pers.), moutonnier. ~*[skin]*, peau de mouton, f, basane, f. ~*ish*, a, penaud, sot, honteux.

sheer, a, pur; (force) vive; abrupt; à pic.

sheet, n, feuille; lame; nappe; couche; bâche; tôle, plaque; (Naut.) écoute, f; (bed) drap, m. ~ *anchor*, ancre de veille; (fig.) a. de salut, planche de s., f. ~ *glass*, verre à vitres, m. ~ *iron*, tôle [de fer] f. ~ *lead*, plomb en feuilles, m. ~ *lightning*, éclair diffus, é. en nappes, m.

sheik[h], n, cheik, m.

shekel (Bible) n, sicle, m.

sheldrake, n, tadorne, m.

shelf, n, planche, tablette, f; rayon; (Naut.) écueil, m. [set of] *shelves*, étagère, f.

shell, n, coquille; coque; carapace; cosse; écale; peau, f; coquillage, m; écaille; chape, f;

(*Artil.*) obus, *m.* ~*fish*, coquillage, *m.* ~ *hole*, entonnoir, *m.* ~ *shock*, commotion, psychose traumatique, *f.* ¶ *v.t*, écaler, écosser, égrener, cerner; bombarder, canonner, battre.

shellac, *n*, laque en écailles, gomme laque, *f.*

shelter, *n*, abri, *m*, le couvert, asile, refuge; édicule, *m.* ¶ *v.t*, abriter.

shelve, *v.i*, aller en pente; (*v.t.*) mettre de côté.

shepherd, *n*, berger; pasteur, *m.* ~*'s crook*, houlette, *f.* ~*'s-purse*, bourse à pasteur, *f*, tabouret, *m.* ~*ess*, *n*, bergère, *f.*

sherbet, *n*, sorbet, *m.*

sheriff, *n*, shérif, *m.*

sherry, *n*, xérès, vin de Xérès, *m.*

shield, *n*, bouclier; protecteur; (*armor*) bouclier, écu; (*Her.*) écusson, *m*; blindage, *m.* (*atomic physics*) *heat* ~, bouclier thermique, *m.* ¶ *v.t*, abriter; défendre; protéger; garantir.

shift, *n*, déplacement; changement, *m*; (*Naut., of wind*) saute; équipe, *f*, poste; expédient, tournant, *m*, ressource, *f*; subterfuge, biais, *m. gear* ~, changement de vitesse, *m.* ¶ *v.t. & i*, déplacer; se d.; changer; changer de place; sauter; (*cargo*) riper; biaiser. ~*ing*, *p.a*, changeant; (*sand*) mouvant. ~*y*, *a*, fuyant.

shilling (⅟₂₀ of a £) *n*, shilling, *m.* (In Fr. pronounced ʃəlē).

shilly-shally, *v.i*, lanterner, barguigner.

shimmer, *v.i*, chatoyer.

shin, *n*, tibia; (*beef*) jarret, *m.* ~ *bone*, tibia, *m.*

shindy, *n*, chahut, tapage, *m*; (*dance*) sauterie, *f.*

shine, *n*, brillant; luisant, *m.* ¶ *v.i.ir*, luire; briller; rayonner, reluire.

shingle, *n*, galets, *m.pl*, galet; (*Build.*) bardeau, *m.* (*pl.*) (*Med.*) zona, *m.* ¶ (*Metall.*) *v.t*, cingler. ~[*d hair*], nuque rasée, *f.*

shining & shiny, *a*, [re]luisant; brillant.

ship, *n*, navire; vaisseau; bâtiment, bateau; bord, *m.* ~*building*, construction navale, *f.* ~*mate*, camarade de bord, *m.* ~*owner*, armateur, *m.* ~*shape*, à sa place. ~*wreck*, naufrage, *m. to be*

~*wrecked*, faire naufrage. ~*wright*, constructeur de navires; charpentier de vaisseau, *m.* ~*yard*, chantier naval, *m.* ¶ *v.t*, charger; embarquer; expédier; (*oars*) border. **shipment**, *n*, chargement; embarquement, *m*; expédition, *f.* **shipper**, *n*, chargeur, expéditeur, *m.* **shipping**, *n*, navigation, *f*; transport maritime, *m*; marine, *f*; tonnage; armement, *m.* ~ *agent*, agent maritime, commissionaire chargeur, *m.* ~ *charges*, frais d'expédition, *m.pl.* ~ *clerk*, expéditionnaire, *m.*

shirk, *v.t*, éluder, se soustraire à; (*v.i.*) s'embusquer. ~[*er*], *n*, embusqué, fricoteur, *m.*

shirt, *n*, chemise, *f.* ~ *collar*, col de chemise; faux col, *m.* ~ *maker*, chemisier, ère. ~*ing*, *n*, toile à chemises, *f*, shirting, *m.*

shiver, *v.t*, briser, fracasser; (*v.i.*) frissonner, grelotter.

shoal, *n*, (*sand, fish*) banc; (*shallow*) haut-fond, *m.* ~*s of people*, un mascaret humain.

shock, *n*, choc; coup; saisissement, ébranlement, à-coup, *m*, secousse; (*hair*) tignasse, forêt, *f*; (*corn*) tas, *m.* ~ *absorber*, amortisseur, *m.* ¶ *v.t*, heurter, choquer; (*fig.*) choquer, scandaliser, révolter, blesser. **shoddy**, *a*, de camelote.

shoe, *n*, soulier, *m*, chaussure, *f*; chausson; (*horse*) fer; sabot; patin, *m.* ~ *brush*, brosse à souliers, *f.* ~ *horn*, chausse-pied, *m.* ~*lace*, lacet de soulier, *m.* ~ *maker*, cordonnier, *m.* ~ *polish*, cirage, *m*, crème à chaussure, *f.* ¶ *v.t.ir*, chausser; ferrer; saboter. **shoeing**, *n*, ferrage, *m.*

shoot, *n*, chasse, *f*, tiré, *m*; rejeton; couloir, *m.* ¶ *v.t.ir*, tirer; lancer; darder; chasser; blesser [d'un coup de fusil, d'une flèche]; tuer [d'un coup de fusil, *etc.*]; (*spy, deserter*) fusiller; (*tip*) culbuter; (*rapids*) franchir; (*v.i.ir.*) tirer; chasser [au fusil]; (*grow*) pousser, germer; (*Foot.*) shooter; (*pain*) élancer. ~ *a movie*, tourner un film. **shooting**, *n*, tir, (*TV & cinema*) tournage, *m*; chasse [au tir] *f.* ~ *gallery*, tir, stand, *m.* ~ *pains*, douleur lancinante, *f*,

élancement, *m.pl.* ~ *star*, étoile
filante, *f.*

shop, *n*, magasin, *m*, boutique, *f*;
débit; atelier, *m.* ~ *foreman*, chef
d'atelier, *m.* ~*front*, devanture de
magasin, *f.* ~*keeper*, marchand,
e, boutiquier, ère. ~*lifting*, vol à
l'étalage, *m.* ~*walker*, inspecteur, *m.* ~ *window*, vitrine,
montre, *f.* ~*worn*, défraîchi;
duty-free ~, boutique franche, *f.*
¶ *v.i*, faire des emplettes. shopping, *n*, achat, *m.* to go ~, aller
faire des courses. ~ *basket*, panier à provisions. ~ *cart*, pousette,
f.

shore, *n*, rivage, bord; étai; ac-
core, *m.* ~ *fishing*, pêche au
bord de la mer, *f. on* ~, à terre.
¶ *v.t*, étayer; chevaler; accorer.

short, *a*, court; petit; bref; déficitaire; cassant. ~ *circuit*,
court-circuit, *m.* ~*coming*, manquement, *m.* ~*cut*, raccourci, *m.*
~-*haired* (dog), à poil ras.
~*hand*, sténographie, *f.* ~*hand-
typist*, sténodactylographe, *m,f.*
~*hand writer*, sténographe, *m,f.*
~-*lived*, passager, fugitif, sans
lendemain. . . . *are* ~-*lived*, . . .
ne vivent pas longtemps. ~-
sighted, myope; à courtes vues;
imprévoyant. ~ *story*, conte, *m*,
nouvelle, *f.* ~ [*syllable*], [syllabe]
brève, *f.* ¶ *n.pl*, ~s, caleçon;
short, *m.* ¶ *ad*, [tout] court. *in*
~, bref, enfin. ~*age*, *n*, manque;
déficit, *m*, crise, *f.* ~*en*, *v.t*,
[r]accourcir. ~*ly*, *ad*, bientôt,
prochainement, sous peu; peu de
temps (*avant*, *après*); brièvement. ~*ness*, *n*, brièveté; courte
durée; petitesse, *f.* ~ *of breath*,
courte haleine, *f.*

shot, *n*, coup de feu; coup; trait;
boulet, *m*; balle, *f*; plomb, *m*;
grenaille, *f*; (*putting the shot*)
poids, *m*; portée, *f*; tireur, *m*; (*TV
& cinema*) plan, champ, *m*, prise
de vues, *f.* ~ *gun*, fusil de chasse,
m. close-up ~, plan serré, *m.
continuity* ~, raccord, *m. high-
angle* ~, plongée, *f. low-angle* ~,
contre-plongée, *f. stock* ~, plan
d'archives, *m. trick* ~, trucage,
truquage, *m.*

shot (*fabrics*) *p.p*, changeant,
chatoyant.

should, *v.aux*, is expressed in Fr.

by conditional mood. *Also by*
devoir, falloir.

shoulder, *n*, épaule, *f*; (*Carp.*)
épaulement, *m.* ~ *blade*, plat de
l'épaule, *m*, omoplate, *f*; (*horse,
ox*) paleron, *m.* ~ *strap*, bretelle;
épaulette, *f.* ¶ *v.t*, pousser de
l'épaule; prendre sur ses épaules;
(*arms*) porter; (*fig.*) endosser.

shout, *n*, cri; éclat, *m.* ¶ *v.t. & i*,
crier; vociférer.

shove, *n*, poussée, *f.* ¶ *v.t. & i*,
pousser. ~ *off*, pousser au large.

shovel, *n*, pelle, *f.* ¶ *v.t*, remuer
à la pelle. ~*ful*, *n*, pelletée, *f.*

show, *n*, semblant, simulacre;
étalage; déballage, *m*; parade;
représentation, *f*, spectacle, *m*;
exposition, *f*, concours, salon, *m.*
~ *case*, vitrine, *f.* ~*down*,
épreuve de force, *f.* ~*man*, forain; montreur, *m.* ~ *room*, salon
d'exposition, *m.* ¶ *v.t.ir*, montrer;
manifester; enseigner; accuser;
[re]présenter; constater; prouver;
(*v.i.ir.*) se montrer; paraître. ~ *in*,
faire entrer, introduire. ~ *off*,
faire parade (de); (*abs.*) parader.
~ *out*, reconduire. ~ *round*, piloter dans, promener par, promener
dans. ~ *the white feather*, caner.
~ *up*, démasquer, afficher.

shower, *n*, ondée; averse; giboulée; pluie; grêle; nuée;
avalanche, *f.* ~ *bath*, douche [en
pluie] *f.* ¶ *v.t*, faire pleuvoir;
combler.

showy, *a*, ostentateur, ostentatoire, fastueux, voyant.

shrapnel, *n*, obus à balles, *m.*

shred, *n*, lambeau, *m*; (*pl.*)
charpie, *f.* ¶ *v.t*, déchiqueter.

shrew, *n*, mégère, *f.* ~ [*mouse*]
musaraigne, *f.*

shrewd, *a*, sagace, clairvoyant;
adroit. ~*ness*, *n*, sagacité, clairvoyance; adresse, *f.*

shriek, *n*, cri, *m.* ¶ *v.i*, crier.

shrike, *n*, pie-grièche, *f.*

shrill, *a*, aigu, perçant, strident.
~*ness*, *n*, acuité, *f*; (*voice*) mordant, *m.*

shrimp, *n*, crevette, *f*; (*pers.*)
gringalet, *m.* ~*ing*, *n*, pêche à
la crevette, *f.*

shrine, *n*, châsse, *f*, reliquaire;
sanctuaire, *m.*

shrink, *v.i.ir*, [se] rétrécir; se retirer; (*v.t.ir.*) rétrécir. ~*age*, *n*,

rétrécissement; retrait, *m*, retraite, *f*.

shrivel, *v.t*, rider, grésiller, ratatiner, racornir.

shroud, *n*, linceul, suaire; (*Naut*.) hauban, *m*. ¶ *v.t*, envelopper; embrumer.

Shrovetide, *n*, les jours gras, *m.pl. Shrove Tuesday*, mardi gras, *m*.

shrub, *n*, arbrisseau, *m*. **shrubbery**, *n*, plantation d'arbrisseaux, *f*; bosquet, *m*.

shrug, *n*, haussement d'épaules, *m*. ¶ *v.t*, hausser.

shudder, *v.i*, frissonner, frémir.

shuffle, *v.t*, (*cards*) battre; (*v.i*.) biaiser, tortiller, tergiverser. ~ *along*, traîner la jambe. ¶ (*excuse*) *n*, défaite, *f*. **shuffling gait**, pas traînant, *m*.

shun, *v.t*, éviter, fuir.

shunt (*Elec*.) *n*, dérivation, *f*; (*Surg*.) pontage, *m*. ¶ *v.t*, (*Rly*.) garer, manœuvrer; (*Elec*.) dériver.

shut, *v.t.ir*, fermer; (*v.i*.) [se] f. ~ *in*, enfermer. ~ *out*, fermer la porte à; exclure. ~ *up*, fermer; enfermer; clouer la bouche à. **shutter**, *n*, volet; contrevent; (*Phot*.) obturateur, *m*.

shutdown, *n*, arrêt, *m*. **emergency ~**, arrêt d'urgence.

shuttle, *n*, navette, *f*. ~**cock**, volant, *m*.

shy†, *a*, timide, sauvage, réservé, farouche, ombrageux. ¶ *v.i*, faire un écart; (*v.t*.) lancer. ~**ness**, *n*, timidité, sauvagerie, *f*.

Siam, *n*, le Siam. **Siamese**, *a*, siamois. ~ *cat*, chat de Siam, *m*. ¶ *n*, (*pers*.) Siamois, e; (*language*) le siamois.

Siberia, *n*, la Sibérie. **Siberian**, *a*, sibérien. ¶ *n*, Sibérien, ne.

Sicilian, *a*, sicilien. ¶ *n*, Sicilien, ne. **Sicily**, *n*, la Sicile.

sick, *a*, malade; dégoûté. *to be ~*, être malade; (*stomach*) avoir mal au cœur. *the ~*, les malades, *m,f.pl.* ~ *& tired*, excédé. ~ *bed*, lit de douleur, *m*. ~ *headache*, mal de tête accompagné de nausées, *m*. ~ *leave*, congé de maladie, c. de convalescence, *m*. ~ *list*, état des malades, *m*. ~ *room*, chambre de malade; (*Sch., etc.*) infirmerie, *f*. ~**en**,

v.i, tomber malade; (*v.t*.) écœurer.

sickle, *n*, faucille, *f*.

sickly, *a*, maladif, souffreteux, malingre; chétif; doucereux, fadasse. **sickness**, *n*, maladie, *f*; (*stomach*) mal de cœur, *m*.

side, *n*, côté; flanc; bord, *m*, rive, *f*; versant; plat, *m*; face; part, *f*; parti; camp, *m*. ~ *by* ~, côte à côte. ~*board*, buffet, dressoir, *m*, panetière, crédence, *f*. ~ *car*, side-car, *m*. ~ *dish*, entremets, *m*. ~ *door*, porte latérale, *f*. ~ *glance*, regard oblique, *m*. ~ *issue*, question d'intérêt secondaire, *f*. ~*long*, de côté; (*glance*) en coulisse, *f*. ~ *saddle*, selle de dame, *f*. ~ *show*, spectacle payant; (*fair*) spectacle forain, *m*. ~*slip*, déraper. ~*step*, faire un écart. ~ *stroke*, nage de côté, *f*. ~*walk*, trottoir, *m*. ~*ways*, de côté. ~*whiskers*, favoris, *m.pl.* ~ *with*, se ranger du côté de.

sidereal, *a*, sidéral.

siding, *n*, voie de garage, *f*; (*private*) embranchement, *m*.

sidle in, entrer de guingois.

siege, *n*, siège, *m*.

Sienna, *n*, Sienne, *f*.

siesta, *n*, sieste, méridienne, *f*.

sieve, *n*, tamis, sas, crible, *m*. **sift**, *v.t*, tamiser, sasser, cribler; bluter; (*question*) éplucher. **siftings**, *n.pl*, criblure, *f*.

sigh, *n*, soupir, *m*. ¶ *v.i*, soupirer.

sight, *n*, vue; vision, *f*; aspect, *m*; présence; (*Surv*.) visée, *f*, coup [de lunette] *m*; (*gun*) mire, *f*; spectacle, *m*; curiosité; caricature, *f*. *at* ~, à première vue; (*reading*) à livre ouvert; (*Com*.) à vue. *by* ~, de vue. ¶ *v.t*, viser; voir; (*land*) reconnaître.

sign, *n*, signe, *m*. ~[*board*], enseigne, *f*; panonceau, *m*. ~ *of expression* (*Mus*.), nuance, *f*. ~ *post*, poteau indicateur, *m*. ¶ *v.t. & i*, signer; (*in the margin*) émarger; faire signe. ~ [*on*], engager.

signal *n*, signal, *m*. ~ *box*, cabine à signaux, *f*. ~*man* (*Rly*), signaleur, *m*. ¶ *a*, signalé, insigne. ~*ize & ~ize*, *v.t*, signaler. **signaler**, *n*, (*Mil*.) signaleur; (*Naut*.) timonier, *m*. **signatory** *or* **signer**, *n*, signataire, *m,f*. **signature**, *n*, signature; souscription; (*Mus*.) armature; (*Typ*.)

signature, *f.* **signet,** *n,* cachet, *m.*
~ *ring,* [bague à la] chevalière, *f.*
significance, *n,* portée, *f.* *look of
deep* ~, regard [fort] significatif,
r. d'intelligence, *m.* **significant,**
a, significatif. **signify,** *v.t.* & *i,*
signifier; importer.

silence, *n,* silence, *m.* ¶ *v.t,* faire
taire; (*enemy's fire*) éteindre.
silencer, *n,* silencieux; amortisseur de bruit, *m.* **silent,** *a,* silencieux, taciturne; (*Gram.*) muet.
~ *partner,* commanditaire, *m. to
be* ~, se taire.

Silesia, *n,* la Silésie. **s~,** *n,* silésienne, *f.*

silhouette, *n,* silhouette, *f.*

silica, *n,* silice, *f.* **silicate,** *n,* silicate, *m.* **silicon,** *n,* silicone, *m.*

silk, *n,* soie, *f.* ~ *goods* or *silks,*
soierie, *f.* ~ *hat,* chapeau de
soie, *m.* **silkworm,** *n,* ver à soie,
m. ~ *breeding,* magnanerie, sériciculture, *f.* ~'*s eggs,* graine, *f.*
silky, *a,* soyeux.

sill, *n,* (*door*) seuil; (*window*) rebord, *m.*

silliness, *n,* niaiserie, bêtise, *f.*
silly, *a,* niais, sot, bête.

silo, *n,* silo, *m.* ¶ *v.t,* ensiler.

silt, *n,* vase, *f,* limon, *m.* ~ *up,*
s'envaser.

silver, *n,* argent, *m.* ~ *birch,*
bouleau blanc, *m.* ~ *fox,* renard
argenté, *m.* ~*-gilt,* vermeil, *m.*
gent doré. ~ *mine,* mine d'ar-
gent, *f.* ~ *plate,* *n,* argenterie, *f;*
(*v.t.*) argenter. ~ *side,* gîte à
la noix, *m.* ~**smith,** orfèvre, *m.*
~[*smith's*] *work,* orfèvrerie, *f.*
~ *wedding,* noces d'argent, *f.pl.*
¶ *v.t,* argenter; (*mirror*) étamer.
~**ing** (*for mirror*) *n,* tain, *m.* ~**y,**
a, argenté; argentin.

simian, *a,* qui appartient au singe.

similar, *a,* semblable, pareil, similaire. ~**ity** & **similitude,** *n,* similitude, *f.* ~**ly,** *ad,* semblablement.
simile, *n,* comparaison, similitude, *f.*

simmer, *v.i.* & *t,* mijoter, cuire à
petit feu.

simony, *n,* simonie, *f.*

simoom, simoon, *n,* simoun, *m.*

simper, *n,* sourire affecté, *m.* ¶ *v.i,*
minauder.

simple†, *a.* & *n,* simple, *a.* & *m.*
~*-minded,* simple, naïf. **simpleton,** *n,* niais, e, gogo, *m.* innocent,
e. **simplicity,** *n,* simplicité; bon-

homie, *f.* **simplify,** *v.t,* simplifier.

simulacrum, *n,* simulacre, *m.*
simulate, *v.t,* simuler, feindre.

simultaneous†, *a,* simultané.

sin, *n,* péché, *m;* iniquité, *f.* ¶ *v.i,*
pécher.

Sinai (Mount), le mont Sinaï.

since, *ad.* & *pr,* depuis. ¶ *c,* depuis
que; que; puisque, comme.

sincere†, *a,* sincère. **sincerity,** *n,*
sincérité, *f.*

sine, *n,* sinus, *m.*

sinecure, *n,* sinécure, *f.*

sinew, *n,* tendon; (*in meat*) tirant;
(*pl. of war*) nerf, *m.*

sinful, *a,* coupable.

sing, *v.t.* & *i. ir,* chanter. ~ *to
sleep,* endormir en chantant.

Singapore, *n,* Singapour, *m.*

singe, *v.t,* flamber, brûler; roussir.

singer, *n,* chanteur, euse; cantatrice, *f.* **singing,** *n,* chant; (*ears*)
tintement, *m;* (*att.*) de chant;
(*kettle*) à sifflet.

single, *a,* unique; seul; simple.
~ *bed,* lit à une place, *m.* ~
blessedness, le bonheur du célibat. ~*-breasted,* droit. ~ *combat,* combat singulier, *m.* ~*-
handed,* tout seul, à moi seul.
a ~ *life,* le célibat. ~ *man,* célibataire, garçon, *m.* ~ *out,* distinguer. **singly,** *ad,* isolément;
un(e) à un(e).

singsong, *a,* chantant, traînant.
¶ *n,* psalmodie, *f.*

singular†, *a.* & *n,* singulier, *a.* &
m.

sinister, *a,* sinistre; (*Her.*) sénestre.

sink, *n,* évier; plomb; puisard;
(*fig.*) cloaque, *m,* sentine, *f.*
¶ *v.i.ir,* [s']enfoncer; s'affaisser;
se tasser; crouler; s'abaisser;
baisser; descendre; succomber;
(*ship*) couler [à fond], c. bas;
(*v.t.ir.*) enfoncer; noyer; foncer,
creuser; couler; (*die*) graver en
creux; (*money, a fortune*) enterrer (*in* = en); (*loan, national
debt*) amortir. ~ *in*[*to*], pénétrer; s'imbiber. *in a sinking condition* (ship), en perdition.
sinking fund, fonds d'amortissement, *m,* caisse d'amortissement,
f. ~**er,** *n,* plomb de ligne, *m.*

sinless, *a,* innocent. **sinner,** *n,*
pécheur, *m,* pécheresse, *f.*

sinuous, *a,* sinueux.

sinus, *n,* sinus, *m.*

sip, *n*, petite gorgée; goutte, *f.*
¶ *v.t. & i*, siroter, humer, buvoter.

siphon, *n*, siphon, *m.*

sir, *n*, monsieur, *m*; (*title*) sir. *no*,
~, (*army*) non, mon colonel, etc.;
(*navy*) non, amiral, etc.; (*but to
any officer in command of a
ship*) non, commandant. **sire**, *n*,
père; (*to kings*) sire, *m.* ¶ *v.t*,
engendrer.

siren (*Myth. & hooter*) *n*, sirène, *f.*

sirloin, *n*, aloyau, *m. a roast* ~,
un rosbif.

sister, *n*, sœur, *f.* ~-*in-law*, belle-
sœur, *f.* ~ [*ship*], [navire] frère,
n. jumeau, *m.* ~*hood*, confrérie;
communauté, *f.* ~*ly*, *a*, de sœur.

sit, *v.i.ir*, s'asseoir; rester; [se]
tenir; (*portrait*) poser; (*court*)
siéger; (*hen*) couver. ~ *down*,
s'asseoir. ~ *for* (portrait), poser
pour. ~ *enthroned &* ~ *in state*,
trôner. ~ *on* (eggs), couver. ~
out, faire galerie. ~ *out a dance*,
causer une danse. ~ *up*, se tenir
droit; veiller.

site, *n*, emplacement; terrain; site,
m; assiette, *f.*

sitting, *n*, séance; audience; pose,
f. ~ *hen*, couveuse, *f.* ~ *posture*,
séant, *m.* ~ *room*, petit salon,
m. ~ *time*, couvaison, *f.*

situated, *a*, situé; sis; placé; dans
une position. **situation**, *n*, situation, assiette, position; place, *f.*
~ *wanted*, demande d'emploi, *f.*

sitz bath, bain de siège, *m.*

six, *a. & n*, six, *a. & m.* **sixteen**, *a.
& n*, seize, *a. & m.* **sixteenth**†, *a.
& n*, seizième, *a. & m.f*; seize, *m.*
sixth†, *a. & n*, sixième, *a. & m.f*;
six, *m*; (*Mus.*) sixte, *f.* **sixtieth**, *a.
& n*, soixantième, *a. & m.f*, **sixty**,
a. & n, soixante, *a. & m.*

size, *n*, dimension, *f.* *oft. pl*; grandeur; grosseur; mesure; taille;
pointure, *f*; numéro; format; calibre, *m*; (*glue, etc.*) colle, *f*, encollage, *m.* ¶ *v.t*, classer en grosseur; [en]coller. ~ *up* (*pers.*),
jauger.

skate, *n*, patin, *m*; (*fish*) raie, *f.*
¶ *v.i*, patiner. **skater**, *n*, patineur,
euse. *skating rink*, patinoire, *f.*

skedaddle, *v.i*, prendre la poudre
d'escampette.

skein, *n*, écheveau, *m.*

skeleton, *n*, squelette, *m*; carcasse, *f*; canevas, *m.* ~ *in the*

cupboard, secret de la famille,
m. ~ *key*, crochet [de serrurier]
m.

skeptic, *n*, sceptique, *m, f.* ¶ *a*,
sceptique. ~*al*, *a*, sceptique.
skepticism, *n*, scepticisme, *m.*

sketch, *n*, esquisse, *f*, croquis, dessin, crayon, canevas, *m*; (*playlet*)
saynète, *f.* ~ *book*, album de
dessin, cahier de dessin, *m.* ¶ *v.t*,
esquisser, croquer, crayonner,
dessiner, tracer.

skew, *a*, biais, oblique. ¶ *n*, biais,
m.

skewer, *n*, brochette, *f.*

ski, *n*, ski, *m.* ~ *pole*, bâton de ski,
m. ¶ *v.i*, faire du ski. **skiing**, *n*,
courses en ski, *f.pl.*

skid, *n*, enrayure, *f*, sabot; (*Avn.*)
patin; (*slip*) dérapage, *m.* ¶ *v.t*,
enrayer; (*v.i.*) patiner; déraper.

skiff, *n*, skiff, esquif, *m*, yole, *f.*

skill, *n*, habileté, adresse, *f.* ~*ed*,
a, expérimenté, expert. ~*ful*†, *a*,
habile, adroit.

skim, *v.t*, écumer, dégraisser, écrémer; effleurer, raser. ~ *milk*,
lait écrémé, *m.* **skimmer**, *n*,
écumoire; écrémoire, *f.* **skimmings**, *n.pl*, écume, *f.*

skimp, *v.t*, étriquer.

skin, *n*, peau; (*pl.*) peausserie;
fourrure; dépouille, *f*; cuir, *m*;
pelure; écorce; enveloppe, *f.*
~-*deep*, superficiel. ~ *disease*,
maladie cutanée, *f.* ~ *dresser*,
peaussier, *m.* ~ *specialist*, spécialiste des maladies de peau,
[médecin] peaussier, [médecin]
peaucier, *m.* ¶ *v.t*, écorcher; dépouiller; peler. ~-*flint*, *n*, grippe-
sou, *m,f*, pingre, *m.* ~-*less pea
or bean*, mange-tout, *m.* **skinny**,
a, décharné, maigre.

skip, *n*, saut, *m.* ¶ *v.t. & i*, sauter;
voleter. ~ *about*, gambiller, fringuer. **skipper**, *n*, patron; capitaine, *f.* *skipping rope*, corde à
sauter, *f.*

skirmish, *n*, escarmouche, *f.*
¶ *v.i*, escarmoucher. ~*er*, *n*, tirailleur, *m.*

skirt, *n*, jupe; basque, *f*; (*of a
wood*) lisière, orée, *f.* ¶ *v.t*,
longer.

skit, *n*, sketch comique, *m.* **skittish**, *a*, (*horse*) ombrageux,
écouteux; folâtre; coquet.

skittle, *n*, quille, *f.* ~ *alley*, quillier, *m.*

skulk, *v.i,* se dissimuler.

skull, *n,* crâne, *m.* ~ *cap,* calotte, *f.*

skunk, *n,* mouffette, *f;* (*fur*) sconse; (*pers.*) ladre, *m.*

sky, *n,* ciel, *m;* (*pl, Poet.*) nues, *f.pl.* ~ *blue,* bleu de ciel, b. céleste, *m.* ~*lark,* alouette des champs, *f.* ~*light,* [fenêtre à] tabatière, *f.* ~ *line,* profil de l'horizon, *m.* ~ *rocket,* fusée volante, *f.* ~*scraper,* gratte-ciel, *m.* ~ *writing,* publicité sur les nuages, *f.*

slab, *n,* dalle, plaque, table, tranche, *f,* pan, *m;* tablette, *f;* (*Typ.*) marbre, *m.*

slack†, *a,* lâche; mou; faible. ~ *season,* morte saison, *f.* ~ *water* (*Naut.*), mer étale, *f,* l'étale de la marée, *m.* ¶ ~ & ~**en,** *v.t.* & *i,* détendre; se d.; relâcher; se r.; ralentir.

slag, *n,* scorie, *f,* laitier, *m.*

slake, *v.t,* éteindre.

slam (*cards*) *n,* chelem, *m.* ¶ (*bang*) *v.i.* & *t,* claquer.

slander, *v.t,* médire de, calomnier; diffamer. ~**ous,** *a,* médisant.

slang, *n,* argot, *m.*

slant, *n,* inclinaison, *f.* ¶ *v.i.* & *t,* incliner.

slap, *n,* gifle, tape, claque, *f,* soufflet, *m.* ¶ *v.t,* frapper, taper, claquer, souffleter, gifler.

slash, *v.t,* taillader; balafrer. ~ *about,* ferrailler.

slat, *n,* latte; planchette; (*blind*) lame, *f.*

slate, *n,* ardoise, *f.* ~*colored* ardoisé. ~ *pencil,* crayon d'ardoise, *m.* ~ *quarry,* ardoisière, *f.* ¶ *v.t,* couvrir d'ardoises.

slattern, *n,* souillon, salope, maritorne, *f.*

slaughter, *n,* tuerie, *f,* massacre, carnage, *m.* ~ *house,* abattoir, *m.* ~ *man,* abatteur, *m.* ¶ *v.t,* massacrer, égorger; (*cattle*) abattre.

Slav, *a,* slave. ¶ *n,* Slave, *m,f.*

slave, *n,* esclave, *m,f.* ~ *bangle,* bracelet esclave, *m.* ~ *driver* & ~ *trader,* négrier, *m.* ~ *trade,* traite des noirs, *f.* **slave,** *v.i,* s'échiner, trimer.

slaver, *n,* bave, *f.* ¶ *v.i,* baver.

slavery, *n,* esclavage, *m.* **slavish†,** *a,* servile. ~**ness,** *n,* servilité, *f.*

slay, *v.t.ir,* immoler. ~**er,** *n,* tueur, *m.*

sleazy, *a,* mal soigné, mal tenu.

sledge, *n,* traîneau, *m;* (*misguided, in the Alps*) ramasse, *f.* ~[*hammer*], masse, *f.* **sledging,** *n,* traînage, *m.*

sleek, *a,* lisse, poli.

sleep, *n,* sommeil, *m.* ~*walker,* somnambule, *m.f.* ¶ *v.i.* & *t. ir,* dormir; reposer; coucher. ~ *like a log,* dormir comme une souche. ~ *out,* découcher. ~**er,** *n,* dormeur, euse; (*Rly. track*) traverse, *f;* wagon-lit, *m.* **sleepiness,** *n,* envie de dormir, somnolence, *f,* sommeil, *m.* **sleeping,** *p.a,* endormi. ~ *bag,* sac de couchage, *m.* **the S**~ *Beauty,* la Belle au bois dormant. ~ *car,* wagon-lit, *m.* ~ *pill,* soporifique, *f.* ~ *sickness,* maladie du sommeil, *f.* **sleepless,** *a,* sans dormir. ~**ness,** *n,* insomnie, *f.* **sleepy,** *a,* ensommeillé, somnolent.

sleet, *n,* grésil. ¶ *v.i,* grésiller.

sleeve, *n,* manche, *f;* (*Mach.*) manchon, *m.* *to laugh up one's* ~, rire sous cape. ~**less,** *a,* sans manches.

sleigh, *n,* traîneau, *m.* ~**ing,** *n,* traînage, *m.*

sleight-of-hand, *n,* prestidigitation, *f.*

slender, *a,* mince; délié; fluet; grêle; gracile, svelte; faible.

sleuth hound, (*dog* & *fig.*) limier, *m.*

slew, *v.t,* faire pivoter.

slice, *n,* tranche; tartine, *f.* ~ *of bread* & *butter,* beurrée, tartine, *f.* ¶ *v.t,* trancher; (*ball*) couper.

slide, *n,* glissade; glissoire; débâcle; coulisse, *f;* tiroir; coulant; curseur; (*microscope*) porteobjet, *m;* (*Phot.*) diapositive, *f.* ~ *changer,* diapositif passe-vues, *m.* ~ *rule,* règle à calcul, *f.* ~ *valve,* tiroir, *m.* ¶ *v.i.ir,* glisser; couler. **sliding,** *p.a:* ~ *roof,* toit découvrable, *m.* ~ *scale,* échelle mobile, *f.*

slight†, *a,* léger; mince; faible; petit; menu, maigrelet. ¶ *n,* affront, *m.* ¶ *v.t,* négliger; faire un affront à. *the* ~**est,** le moindre, la moindre.

slim, *a,* svelte, gracile, élancé.

slime, n, bave; vase, f, limon, m, boue, f. **slimy**, a, baveux; visqueux; vaseux.

sling, n, fronde; écharpe; bretelle; élingue, f. ¶ v.t.ir, (throw) lancer; suspendre. slung [over the shoulders], en bandoulière.

slink away, v.i.ir, se dérober.

slip, n, glissement, m, glissade, f; faux pas; lapsus, m, erreur; peccadille; bande; fiche; feuille, f; papillon, m, (woman's) combinaison, f; (Hort.) plant, m, bouture; (Naut.) cale, f. ~cover, housse, f. ~ knot, nœud coulant. m. ~shod, en savates; négligé. ~ stitch, maille glissé, f. ¶ v.i. & t, glisser; couler; patiner; échapper; (rope) larguer. ~ in, v.t, faufiler. ~ on (garment), v.t, passer. **slipper**, n, pantoufle, f; chausson, m; mule, f. **slippery**, a, glissant.

slit, n, fente, f. ¶ (dress) p.a, taillade. ¶ v.t.ir, fendre.

slither, v.i, se glisser.

slobber, n, bave, f. ¶ v.i, baver.

sloe, n, prunelle, f. ~ gin, [liqueur de] prunelle, f. ~ [tree], prunellier, m.

slogan, n, devise publicitaire, f.

sloop, n, sloop, m.

slop [over], v.i, déborder. slop pail, seau de toilette, m.

slope, n, pente; rampe, f; talus, m. ¶ v.i, s'incliner, aller en pente.

sloppiness, n, état détrempé, m.

sloppy, a, débraillé, mal ajusté. **slops**, n.pl, rinçure, f; eaux ménagères, f.pl; (thin soup) lavasse, f; (liquid diet) bouillon, m.

slot, n, mortaise, rainure; (of a slot machine) fente, f. ~ machine, appareil à jetons, m.

sloth, n, paresse, indolence, f; (Zool.) paresseux, m. ~ful, a, paresseux, indolent.

slouch, v.i, donner un air disloqué à sa taille, à son attitude, à sa marche. ~ hat, chapeau rabattu, m.

slough, n, bourbier, m; (snake) dépouille, peau, mue; (Med.) escarre, f. ¶ v.i, se dépouiller, muer.

sloven, n, sagouin, e, souillon, m,f. ~ly, a, négligé.

slow†, a, lent; tardif; lambin; (train) omnibus, de petite vitesse; (clock) en retard. to be

~ (tedious), manquer d'entrain. ~motion picture, cinéma au ralenti, m. ¶ ad, lentement. ~ down, ralentir. **slowness**, n, lenteur, f.

slow-worm, n, orvet, m.

sludge, n, (mud) boue; (snow) neige fondue, f; (oil) cambouis, m.

slug, n, limace, loche, f; (bullet & Typ.) lingot, m.

sluggard, n, paresseux, euse. **sluggish†**, a, paresseux; inerte; tardif.

sluice, n, canal, m. ~ gate, vanne, f.

slum, n, taudis, m. ~ area, zône des taudis, f.

slumber, n, sommeil, m. ¶ v.i, sommeiller.

slump, n, (in prices) effondrement, m, dégringolade; (in trade) mévente; crise, f. ¶ v.i, s'effondrer.

slur, n, atteinte; (Mus.) liaison, f. ¶ v.t, (Mus.) lier. ~ over, glisser sur.

slush, n, de la neige fondue, f.

slut, n, garce, souillon, salope, f.

sly, a, sournois; rusé. ~boots, cachottier, ère, finaud, e. on the ~, à la dérobée.

smack, n, claque; (boat) barque, f, bateau, m. ¶ v.t, claquer, taper; (tongue) clapper. to ~ of, sentir le, la. to ~ one's lips, se lécher les babines.

small, a, petit; faible; modique; menu; fin; (intestine) grêle; (arms, Mil.) portatives. ~ fry (fig.), fretin, m. ~pox, petite vérole, variole, f. ~pox case (pers.), varioleux, euse. ~ stones, pierraille, f. ~ talk, menus propos, m.pl, conversation banale, f, choses indifférentes, f.pl, (dire) des riens, f. ¶ ~ of the back, chute des reins, f. ~ness, n, petitesse, f, peu d'importance, m.

smart, n, cuisson, f. ¶ v.i, picoter, cuire. ¶† a, vif; fin; beau, chic, pimpant, coquet; huppé. the ~ set, les gens huppés. ~en oneself up, se requinquer. ~ing, n, cuisson, f. ¶ p.a, cuisant. ~ness, n, finesse, f; chic, m.

smash, n, accident; (Fin.) krach; (Ten.) smash, m. to go ~ (bank), sauter. ¶ v.t, briser, fracasser, massacrer; (atom) désintégrer.

smattering, n, teinture, f.

smear, v.t, enduire; barbouiller.

smell, n, odorat, m; odeur, f. ¶ v.t. & i. ir, sentir, fleurer; flairer; puer; *smelling bottle*, flacon à odeur, m. *smelling salts*, sels [volatils] anglais, m.pl.

smelt, n, éperlan, m.

smelt, v.t, fondre. ~*ing works*, fonderie, f.

smilax, n, smilax, m.

smile, n, sourire, m. ¶ v.i, sourire. **smiling**, a, [sou]riant.

smirch, v.t, salir.

smirk, n, sourire affecté, m. ¶ v.i, minauder.

smite, v.t.ir, frapper. (Cf. *smitten*.)

smith, n, forgeron, m. ~'s hearth, bâti de forge, m. ~y, n, forge, f.

smitten, p.p, (*remorse*) pris; (*love*) épris, féru.

smock [**frock**], n, blouse, f, sarrau, m. **smocking**, n, fronces smock, f.pl.

smoke, n, fumée, f. ~ *screen*, écran de fumée, m. ~*stack*, cheminée, f. ¶ v.i. & t, fumer; enfumer; (*lamp*) charbonner. ~*d sausage*, saucisson, m. ~*less*, a, sans fumée. **smoker**, n, fumeur, euse. **smoking**, n, l'habitude de fumer, f. ~ *compartment*, compartiment pour fumeurs, m. ~ *room*, fumoir, m. ~ *strictly prohibited*, défense expresse de fumer. **smoky**, a, fumeux.

smolder, v.i, couver.

smooth, a, lisse; uni; doux; (*sea*) unie, plate. ~*bore*, à canon lisse. ~*haired* (dog), à poil ras. ~*tongued*, mielleux, doucereux. ¶ v.t, lisser; polir; unir; planer; aplanir; adoucir; défroncer. ~*ly*, ad, uniment; doucement. ~*ness*, n, égalité; douceur, f.

smother, v.t, étouffer.

smudge, n, noirceur, f. ¶ v.t, barbouiller, mâchurer.

smug†, a, béat.

smuggle, v.t, passer en contrebande; (v.i) faire la contrebande. ~ *in*, v.t, entrer en fraude. **smuggler**, n, contrebandier, ère.

smut, n, noirceur; (*Agric.*) nielle, f. **smutty**, a, noirci; niellé; (*obscene*) graveleux.

Smyrna, n, Smyrne, f.

snack, n, morceau [sur le pouce], cassecroûte, m, collation, f. *to have a* ~, collationner.

snag, n, (*stump*) chicot; (*fig.*) accroc, m.

snail, n, [co]limaçon; (*edible*) escargot, m. *at a* ~'s pace, à pas de tortue.

snake, n, serpent, (*young*) serpenteau, m. *there is a* ~ *in the grass*, le serpent est caché sous les fleurs.

snap, n, crac; cric crac!; coup sec, m; (*fastening*) agrafe, f, fermoir, m. ~*dragon*, muflier, m, gueule-de-loup, f. ~ *fastener*, fermeture pression, f. ~ [*shot*], instantané, m. ¶ v.t, casser, rompre; faire claquer. ~ *at*, bourrer. ~ *up*, happer; enlever. **snappy**, (*surly*) a, hargneux.

snare, n, piège; (*drum*) timbre, m. ~ *drum*, caisse claire, f. ¶ v.t, attraper.

snarl, v.i, gronder. (v.t.) s'enchevêtrer. ~*ing*, p.a, hargneux.

snatch (*scrap*) n, fragment, m, bribe, f. ¶ v.t, empoigner; enlever; arracher; dérober; (*kiss*) cueillir.

sneak, n, sournois, e; (*Sch.*) capon, ne. ~ *away*, s'en aller à la dérobée. *a* ~*ing fondness for*, du (*ou* un) faible pour.

sneakers, pl.n, chaussures de tennis, f.pl, baskets, m.pl.

sneer, n, rire moqueur, m. ¶ v.i, goguenarder. ~ *at*, railler.

sneeze, v.i, éternuer; (*animals*) s'ébrouer.

sniff, v.i. & t, renifler.

snigger, v.i, rire en dedans, rire en dessous.

snip, n, coup de ciseaux; bout, m. ¶ v.t, cisailler.

snipe, n, bécassine, f. ¶ v.t, canarder. **sniper**, n, tireur isolé, franc-tireur, m.

snivel, v.i, pleurnicher.

snob, n, snob, m. ~*ishness**, n, snobisme, m.

snooze, n, somme, m. ¶ v.i, roupiller, pioncer.

snore, v.i, ronfler.

snort, v.i, renifler, renâcler, s'ébrouer.

snout, n, museau; (*pig*) groin; (*boar*) boutoir, m.

snow, n, neige, f. oft. pl. ~*ball*, boule de neige, f. ~ *blindness*, cécité des neiges, f. ~ *boots*, chaussures pour la n., f.pl. ~*capped*, chenu. ~ *drift*, congère, *f.* ~*drop*, perce-neige, clochette d'hiver, *f.* ~*flake*, flocon de n, *m.* ~ *line*, limite des neiges éternelles, *f.* ~*man*, bonhomme de n., *m.* ~ *plow*, chasse-neige, *m.* ~ *shoes*, raquettes à n., *f.pl.* ~ *squall*, chasse-neige, *m.* ~ *storm*, tempête de n., *f.* ~*suit*, esquimau, *m.* ¶ *v.i.* neiger. ~y, *a,* neigeux.

snub, *n,* affront, soufflet, *m,* nasarde, *f.* ~*nosed*, camus, camard. ¶ *v.t,* rabrouer, mépriser.

snuff, *n,* tabac à priser, *m. to take* ~, prendre du tabac, priser. ~*box*, tabatière, *f.* ~ *taker*, priseur, euse. ¶ *v.t,* moucher.

snuffle, *v.i,* renifler, nasiller. ~s, *n.pl,* enchifrènement, *m.*

snug, *a,* confortable.

snuggle, *v.i,* se pelotonner, se blottir.

so, *ad. c. & pn,* ainsi; aussi; donc; si; oui; tellement; tel, telle; tant; le. ~*-&*~, un tel, une telle. ~ *called*, soi-disant, *a.inv.* prétendu. ~ *as to,* de manière à; afin de. ~ ~, comme ci, comme ça; couci-couça. ~ *that,* de sorte que; afin que. ~ *to speak*, pour ainsi dire.

soak, *v.t,* imbiber, [dé]tremper; (*dirty linen*) essanger. ~ **up**, absorber.

so-and-so, *n,* Untel, *m.* Mr. ~, M. Untel.

soap, *n,* savon, *m.* ~ *dish*, plateau à s., *m.* ~ *maker*, savonnier, *m.* ~ *opera*, mélo radiodiffusé, *m.* ~*stone*, pierre de savon, *f.* ~ *suds*, eau de s., *f.* ¶ *v.t,* savonner, ~y, *a,* savonneux.

soar, *v.i,* pointer, planer, prendre son essor.

sob, *n,* sanglot, *m.* ~ *story*, drame pleureur, *m.* ¶ *v.i,* sangloter.

sober†, *a,* sobre; sérieux; pas en état d'ébriété. *he is never* ~, il ne désenivre point, il ne dessoûle jamais. ¶ *v.t,* désenivrer, dégriser. ~**ness**, *n,* sobriété, *f.*

soccer, *n,* football, *m.*

sociable†, *a,* sociable, liant. **social**, *a,* social. ~ *events* (news), mondanités, *f.pl.* ~**ism**, *n,* socialisme, *m.* ~**ist**, *n. & a,* socialiste, *m.f. & a.* **society**, *n,* société, association; (*fashionable world*) société, *f,* le monde, le grand

monde; (*att.*) mondain. ~ *man*, *woman*, mondain, e. **sociology**, *n,* sociologie, *f.*

sock, *n,* chaussette, *f.* ¶ *v.t,* frapper.

socket, *n,* douille, *f,* manchon, *m;* (*eye*) orbite, *f;* (*tooth*) alvéole, *m;* (*lamp*) bec, *m;* (*bone*) glène, *f.* ¶ *v.t,* emboîter.

sod, *n,* gazon, *m;* plaque de gazon, motte, *f.*

soda, *n,* soude, *f;* (*washing*) cristaux de soude, *m.pl.* ~ [*water*], soda, *m,* eau de Seltz, *f. baking* ~, bicarbonate de soude, *m.*

sodden, *a,* détrempé.

sodium, *n,* sodium, *m.*

sofa, *n,* canapé, sofa, *m.*

soffit, *n,* soffite; intrados, *m.*

soft†, *a,* mou; doux; tendre; moelleux; (*fruit*) blet. ~*boiled* (eggs), mollet. ~ *collar*, col souple, *m.* ~ *corn*, œil-de-perdrix, *m.* ~ *felt* (hat), feutre souple, feutre mou, *m. a* ~ *job*, un fromage. ~ *palate*, palais mou, *m.* ~ *pedal*, petite pédale, p. sourde, *f.* ~ *soap* (fig.), flagornerie, *f;* (*v.t.*) amadouer. ~ *solder*, soudure tendre, *f.* ~**en**, *v.t,* [r]amollir; adoucir; attendrir. ~*ening of the brain*, ramollissement du cerveau, *m.* ~**ish**, *a,* mollet. ~**ness**, *n,* mollesse, *f;* moelleux, *m;* douceur; tendresse, *f.*

soft copy, *n,* (*computers*) image d'écran, *f.*

software, *n,* (*computers*) logiciel, *m.*

soil, *n,* sol, *m,* terre, *f,* terroir, *m,* glèbe, *f.* ¶ *v.t,* salir, souiller. ~**ed**, *p.a,* (*linen*) sale; (*shop goods*) défraîchi.

sojourn, *n,* séjour, *m.* ¶ *v.i,* séjourner.

solace, *n,* consolation, *f.* ¶ *v.t,* consoler.

solar, *a,* solaire. ~ *plexus*, plexus s., *m.*

solder & ~ing, *n,* soudure, *f.* ¶ *v.t,* souder. ~*ing iron*, fer à souder, *m.*

soldier, *n,* soldat, militaire, troupier, *m.* ~**y**, *n,* militaires, *m.pl;* (*unruly*) soldatesque, *f.*

sole†, *a,* seul; unique; tout; exclusif. ¶ *n,* (*foot*) plante; (*shoe*) semelle; (*hoof, plate, fish*) sole, *f.* ¶ (*shoes*) *v.t,* ressemeler.

solecism, *n,* solécisme, *m.*

solemn†, *a,* solennel; grave. **~ity,** *n,* solennité; gravité, *f.* **~ize,** *v.t,* solenniser; *(wedding, etc.)* célébrer.

solicit, *v.t,* solliciter, quémander; briguer. **~ous,** *a,* désireux; inquiet; jaloux. **~ude,** *n,* sollicitude, *f.*

solid†, *a,* solide; ferme; *(gold)* massif; plein. **~ rock,** roc vif, *m.* ¶ *n,* solide, *m.* **~ify,** *v.t,* solidifier. **~ity,** *n,* solidité, *f.*

soliloquize, *v.i,* monologuer. **soliloquy,** *n,* soliloque, *m.*

soling, *n,* ressemelage, *m.*

solitaire *(gem, game) n,* solitaire, *m.* **solitary†,** *a,* solitaire; retiré. **~ confinement,** secret, *m.* **~ imprisonment,** réclusion, *f.* **solitude,** *n,* solitude, *f.*

solo, *n,* solo; récit, *m.* **~ dance,** pas seul, *m.* **~ist,** *n,* soliste, *m,f.*

solstice, *n,* solstice, *m.*

soluble, *a,* soluble. **solution,** *n,* solution; résolution; issue; dissolution, liqueur, *f.* **solve,** *v.t,* résoudre. **solvency,** *n,* solvabilité, *f.* **solvent,** *a,* dissolvant; *(Com.)* solvable. ¶ *n,* dissolvant, *m.*

somber, *a,* sombre.

some, *a,* quelque, quelques; du, de la, des; certain. ¶ *pn,* quelques-uns, -unes; certains, certaines; les uns, les unes; en. **somebody & someone,** *n,* quelqu'un, *m;* on, *pn.* **~ else,** quelqu'un d'autre. **to be somebody,** être un personnage. **somehow** [or **other**], *ad,* d'une manière ou d'une autre; tant bien que mal.

somersault, *n,* culbute, *f,* (le) saut périlleux.

something, *n,* quelque chose, *m;* q. c. de; de quoi. **~ in the wind,** quelque anguille sous roche. **sometimes,** *ad,* quelquefois; parfois; tantôt. **somewhat,** *ad,* quelque peu, un peu, tant soit peu. **somewhere,** *ad,* quelque part. **~ else,** ailleurs, autre part. **~ in the world,** de par le monde. **~ to stay,** pied-à-terre, tourne-bride, *m.*

somnambulism, *n,* somnambulisme, *m.* **somnambulist,** *n,* somnambule, *m,f.* **somnolent,** *a,* somnolent.

son, *n,* fils; garçon, *m.* **~-in-law,** gendre, *m.* **step~,** beau-fils, *m.*

sonata, *n,* sonate, *f.*

song, *n,* chant, *m;* chanson; romance, *f;* air; cantique; *(of birds)* chant, ramage; *(mere trifle)* morceau de pain, *m.* **~bird,** oiseau chanteur, *m.* **~ book,** chansonnier, *m.* **~ thrush,** grive chanteuse, *f.* **~ without words,** romance sans paroles. **~ writer,** chansonnier, ère.

sonnet, *n,* sonnet, *m.*

sonorous, *a,* sonore; ronflant.

soon, *ad,* bientôt; tôt. **as ~ as,** [aus]sitôt que, dès que. **as ~ as possible,** le plus tôt possible. **see you soon,** à tout à l'heure. **~er,** *ad,* plus tôt; *(rather)* plutôt. **~ or later,** tôt ou tard. **no ~ said than done,** aussitôt dit, aussitôt fait.

soot, *n,* suie, *f.* **~y,** *a,* noir de suie.

soothe, *v.t,* adoucir, calmer. **soothing,** *a,* calmant.

soothsayer, *n,* devin, *m,* devineresse, *f.*

sop, *n,* trempette, *f;* *(fig.)* os à ronger, *m.* **sopping wet,** être trempé comme une soupe.

sophism, *n,* sophisme, *m.* **sophisticate,** *v.t,* sophistiquer. **~d,** *p.a,* savant. **sophistry,** *n,* sophistique, *f.*

soporific, *a. & n,* soporifique, *a. & m.*

soprano *(voice & pers.) n,* soprano, *m.*

sorcerer, ess, *n,* sorcier, ère, magicien, ne. **sorcery,** *n,* sorcellerie, *f.*

sordid†, *a,* sordide. **~ness,** *n,* vilenie, *f.*

sore†, *a,* douloureux, meurtri; malade; sensible; endolori; affligé; cruel. **I have a ~ finger,** j'ai mal au doigt. **~ eyes,** mal aux (ou d') yeux. **~ point,** endroit sensible, *m.* **~ throat,** mal à la gorge. ¶ *n,* plaie, *f.*

sorrel, *n,* oseille, *f.* ¶ *a,* saure.

sorrily, *ad,* tristement. **sorrow,** *n,* chagrin, *m,* douleur, peine, *f.* ¶ *v.i,* s'affliger. **~ful,** *a,* chagrin; triste. **~fully,** *ad,* tristement. **sorry,** *a,* fâché; triste; méchant, mauvais, pauvre, piteux. **I am ~,** je regrette. **to be ~ for,** être fâché de; plaindre; se repentir de. **in a ~ plight,** mal-en-point. **~! pardon!**

sort, *n,* sorte, *f,* genre, *m,* espèce, nature; manière, *f;* *(pl, Typ.)* assortiment, *m. all* ~s *of,* of toute sorte de. *of the same* ~, de même acabit. ¶ *v.t,* trier; classer. ~er, *n,* trieur, euse.

sortie, *n,* sortie, *f.*

sot, *n,* ivrogne, *m,* ivrognesse, *f.* **sottish,** *a,* abruti.

sough, *v.i,* bruire, murmurer.

sought after, recherché.

soul, *n,* âme, *f.* ~less, *a,* sans âme.

sound†, *a,* sain; bon; solide; (*sleep*) profond. ¶ *n,* son; (*Geog.*) bras de mer, détroit, *m;* (*probe*) sonde, *f.* ~[*ing*] board, abat-voix, *m;* (*Mus.*) table d'harmonie, *f.* ~ *effects man,* bruiteur, *m.* (*TV & cinema*) ~ *track,* piste sonore, *f.* ~*proof, a,* insonore. ¶ *v.t,* faire sonner; sonner; sonder; pressentir; (*Med.*) ausculter; (*v.i.*) sonner, résonner. ~ness, *n,* solidité; rectitude, *f.*

soup, *n,* potage, bouillon, *m;* soupe, purée, *f.* ~ *kitchen,* fourneau philanthropique, *m.* ~ *ladle,* cuiller à potage, louche, *f.* ~ *plate,* assiette creuse, *f.* ~ *tureen,* soupière, *f.*

sour, *a,* aigre, sur, acide, vert; (*milk, etc.*) tourné. ¶ *v.t,* aigrir, enfieller; (*v.i.*) a, aigrelet, suret. ~ly, *ad,* aigrement. ~ness, *n,* aigreur, acidité, *f.*

source, *n,* source, *f.*

south, *n,* sud; midi, *m.* ¶ *ad,* au sud. ¶ *a,* du sud; méridional; austral. S~ *Africa,* l'Afrique du Sud *ou* australe *ou* méridionale, *f.* S~ *African,* sud-africain. S~ *America,* l'Amérique du Sud, *f.* S~ *American,* sud-américain. ~*east,* sud-est, *m.* S~ *Pole,* pôle sud, *m.* S~ *Sea Islands,* îles du Pacifique, *f.pl.* ~*west,* sud-ouest, *m.* S~ *West Africa,* le Sud-Ouest africain, *m.* ~ **southern,** *a,* [du] sud; méridionale; austral. ~*er, n,* méridional, e. **southward[s],** *ad,* vers le sud.

souvenir, *n,* souvenir, *m.*

sou'wester (*wind, hat*) *n,* suroît, *m.*

sovereign, *a. &* (*pers.*) *n,* souverain, e; (£) souverain, *m.* ~ty, *n,* souveraineté, *f.*

soviet, *n,* soviet, *m;* (*att.*) soviétique.

sow, *n,* truie, coche; (*wild*) laie, *f.*

sow, *v.t. & i. ir,* semer; ensemencer.

~er, *n,* semeur, euse. **sowing,** *n,* ensemencement, *m,* semailles, *f.pl.* ~ *machine,* semoir, *m,* semeuse, *f.* ~ *time,* temps des semailles, *m,* semailles, *f.pl.*

soy[a] bean, soya, soja, pois chinois, *m.*

spa, *n,* ville d'eaux, *f,* eaux, *f.pl,* bains, *m.pl.*

space, *n,* espace; intervalle; entredeux; vide, creux; (*Mus.*) interligne, *m;* (*on printed form*) case; (*Typ.*) espace, *f.* ~ *between lines,* interligne, *m.* outer ~, espace cosmique, extra-atmospherique, *m.* ¶ *v.t,* espacer. **spacious,** *a,* spacieux.

spacecraft, *n,* astronef, *m.*

spade, *n,* bêche, *f;* (*pl, cards*) pique, *m.* ¶ *v.t,* bêcher. ~ful, *n,* pelletée, *f.*

Spain, *n,* l'Espagne, *f.*

span, *n,* (*wings*) envergure; portée, travée, ouverture, *f.* ¶ *v.t,* franchir, chevaucher.

spandrel, *n,* tympan, *m.*

spangle, *n,* paillette, *f.* ~d, *p.p,* pailleté.

Spaniard, *n,* Espagnol, e. **spaniel,** *n,* épagneul, e. **Spanish,** *a,* espagnol; d'Espagne. ~ *fly,* cantharide, *f.* ~ *onion,* oignon doux d'Espagne, *m.* ¶ *n,* l'espagnol, *m.*

spank, *v.t,* fesser. ~ing, *n,* fessée, *f.*

spar, *n,* (*Naut.*) espar; (*Miner.*) spath, *m.* ¶ *v.i,* boxer; s'entraîner à la boxe.

spare, *a,* maigre, sec; disponible; libre; de rechange. ~ [*bed*]*room,* chambre d'ami, *f.* ~ [*part*], pièce de rechange, *f.* ~ *time,* loisir, *m. oft. pl,* heures dérobées, *f.pl.* ~ *tire,* pneu de secours, *m.* ¶ *v.t,* épargner; ménager; accorder; se passer de; respecter; faire grâce de; trouver. *to have enough & to* ~, avoir à revendre. **sparing,** *p.a,* économe, ménager; chiche, avare.

spark, *n,* étincelle; flammèche, *f;* brandon; gendarme, *m;* lueur, *f;* (*pers.*) mirliflore, galant, *m.* ~ *plug,* bougie d'allumage, *f.* **sparkle,** *v.i,* étinceler, briller, miroiter; pétiller; mousser. **sparkling,** *a,* étincelant; émerillonné; (*wine*) mousseux.

sparring, *n,* entraînement, *m.* ~ *match,* assaut de démonstration, *m.* ~ *partner,* partenaire d'entraînement, *m.*

sparrow, *n,* moineau, passereau, pierrot, *m.* ~ *hawk,* épervier, *m.*

sparse, *a,* peu dense, clairsemé, rare.

Spartan, *a. & n,* spartiate, *a. & m,f.*

spasm, *n,* spasme, *m.* **spasmodic,** *a,* saccadé; (*Med.*) spasmodique. ~**ally,** *ad,* par saccades, par sauts & par bonds.

spate, *n,* grandes eaux, *f.pl,* crue, *f.*

spats, *n. pl,* guêtres de ville, *f.pl.*

spatter, *v.t,* éclabousser.

spatula, *n,* spatule, *f.*

spawn, *n,* (*fish*) frai; (*mushroom*) blanc, mycélium, *m.* ¶ *v.i,* frayer.

speak, *v.i. & t. ir,* parler; dire; prononcer; prendre la parole; (*ship*) héler. ~ *one's mind,* se déboutonner. ~**er,** *n,* opinant, orateur, *m.* loud~, haut-parleur, *m.* **speaking,** *n,* parole, *f;* parler, *m. X.* ~ (*Teleph.*), ici X. *without* ~, à la muette. *we are not on* ~ *terms,* nous ne nous parlons pas.

spear, *n,* lance, *f.* ~ *head,* fer de lance, *m.* ~*mint,* menthe verte, *f.* ¶ *v.t,* percer; darder.

special†, *a,* spécial; particulier; extraordinaire. ~ *correspondent,* envoyé spécial, *m.* ~ *dish for the day,* plat du jour, *m.* ~*ist,* *n,* spécialiste, *m,f.* ~**ity,** *n,* spécialité, *f.* ~*ize in,* se spécialiser dans.

specie, *n,* espèces, *f.pl,* numéraire, *m.*

species, *n,* espèce, *f.*

specific†, *a,* spécifique; déterminé. ~ *gravity,* poids spécifique, *m.* ¶ *n,* spécifique, *m.* ~**ation,** *n,* spécification; énonciation, *f;* devis; cahier des charges, *m.* **specify,** *v.t,* spécifier; énoncer; préciser. **specimen,** *n,* spécimen; échantillon; modèle; exemplaire, *m.* **specious†,** *a,* spécieux.

speck, *n,* point, *m;* petite tache, *f;* grain, *m,* particule; piqûre, *f.* ~**le,** *v.t,* tacheter, moucheter.

spectacle, *n,* spectacle, *m;* (*pl.*) lunettes, *f.pl.* ~ *case,* étui à 1-s, *m.* **spectacular,** *a,* à [grand] spectacle. **spectator,** *n,* spectateur, trice.

spectral, *a,* spectral. **specter,** *n,* spectre, *m.* **spectroscope,** *n,* spectroscope, *m.* **spectrum,** *n,* spectre, *m.*

speculate, *v.i,* spéculer; jouer, agioter. **speculation,** *n,* spéculation, *f;* jeu, *m.* **speculative,** *a,* spéculatif; de spéculation. **speculator,** *n,* spéculateur, trice; agioteur, *m,* joueur, euse.

speech, *n,* parole, *f;* langage, *m;* langue, *f;* parler; discours, *m,* allocution, harangue, *f.* ~**ify,** *v.i,* pérorer. ~**less,** *a,* sans voix, muet.

speed, *n,* vitesse; célérité; rapidité, *f. at full* ~, à toute allure. ~ *way,* autostrade, *f.* ¶ *v.i.ir,* se hâter, faire de la vitesse. ~ *up,* activer. **speedometer,** *n,* compteur de vitesse, *m.* **speedwell** (*Bot.*) *n,* véronique, *f.* **speedy,** *a,* rapide.

spell, *n,* charme, enchantement; sort; maléfice; tour, *m;* période, échappée, *f.* ~*bound,* fasciné. ¶ *v.t. & i. ir,* épeler; orthographier. **spelling,** *n,* orthographe; épellation, *f.* ~ *bee,* concours orthographique, *m.* ~ *book,* abécédaire, syllabaire, *m.*

spelter, *n,* zinc, *m.*

spend, *v.t. & i. ir,* dépenser; passer. ~*thrift,* *n. & att,* dépensier, ère, prodigue, *m,f. & a. spent bullet,* balle morte, *f.*

sperm, *n,* sperme, *m.* ~ *oil,* huile de spermaceti, *f.* ~ *whale,* cachalot, *m.* **spermaceti,** *n,* blanc de baleine, *m.* **spermatozoon,** *n,* spermatozoaire, *m.*

spew, *v.t. & i,* vomir.

sphere, *n,* sphère, *f.* **spherical,** *a,* sphérique.

sphincter, *n,* sphincter, *m.*

sphinx, *n,* sphinx, *m.*

spice, *n,* épice, *f;* (*fig.*) grain, *m.*

spick & span, tiré à quatre épingles, pimpant.

spicy, *a,* épicé, poivré.

spider, *n,* araignée, *f.* ~['*s*] *web,* toile d'a., *f.*

spigot, *n,* fausset, *m.*

spike, *n,* broche; cheville, *f,* crampon; (*pl. on wall*) chardon, artichaut; piquant; (*of flower*) épi, *m.* ¶ *v.t,* (*gun*) enclouer.

spill (*pipe light*) *n,* fidibus, *m. to have a* ~, faire panache. ¶ *v.t.ir,* répandre, renverser; verser.

spin, *n,* tournoiement; (*ball*) effet, *m;* (*Avn.*) vrille, *f.* ¶ *v.t.ir,* filer; (*top*) faire tourner, faire aller; (*v.i.*) tournoyer, toupiller. ~ *out,* délayer. ~ *yarns*, débiter des histoires.

spinach, *n*, épinard, *m*; (*Cook.*) épinards, *m.pl.*

spinal, *a*, spinal; (*column*) vertébrale. ~ *cord*, moelle épinière, *f.*

spindle, *n*, fuseau, *m*; broche, *f*; mandrin; arbre, *m.* ~ *tree*, fusain, *m.*

spindrift, *n*, embrun, *m.*

spine, *n*, (*Bot.*) épine; (*Anat.*) é. dorsale, *f*; (*of book*) dos, *m.* ~**less** (*fig.*) *a*, mollasse.

spinel, *n. & att*, spinelle, *m. & a.*

spinner, *n*, fileur, euse, filateur, trice; (*owner*) filateur, *m*; (*Fish.*) hélice, *f.*

spinney, *n*, bosquet, *m.*

spinning, *n*, filature; pêche à la [ligne] volante, *f.* ~ *mill*, filature, *f.* ~ *wheel*, rouet, *m.*

spinster, *n*, vieille fille, *f.*

spiny, *a*, épineux. ~ *lobster*, langouste, *f.*

spiral, *a*, spiral; hélicoïdal; (*spring*) à boudin; (*stairs*) tournant. ¶ *n*, spirale, *f.*

spire, *n*, flèche; (*whorl*) spire, *f.*

spirit, *n*, esprit, *m*; âme, *f*; génie; entrain, *m*; fougue; essence, *f*; alcool, *m*; liqueur [spiritueuse] *f*, (*pl.*) spiritueux, *m.pl.* ~ *lamp*, lampe à alcool, *f.* ~ *level*, niveau à bulle d'air, *m.* ~ *away*, faire disparaître comme par enchantement, escamoter. ~**ed**, *a*, vif, animé; ardent, fougueux; courageux. ~**less**, *a*, sans courage.

spiritual†, *a*, spirituel. **spiritualism**, *n*, (*psychics*) spiritisme; (*Philos.*) spiritualisme, *m.* **spiritualist**, *n*, (*psychics*) spirite; (*Philos.*) spiritualiste, *m.f.* **spirituous**, *a*, spiritueux.

spirt, *n*, jet, *m.* ¶ *v.i*, jaillir, gicler.

spit, *n*, (*roasting*) broche; (*Geog.*) flèche littorale, *m.* ¶ *v.t*, embrocher; sonder.

spit, *v.i. & t. ir*, cracher. ¶ *n*, crachat, *m.*

spite, *n*, dépit, *m*, malveillance, rancune, pique, *f.* in ~ *of*, en dépit de, malgré. ¶ *v.t*, dépiter. ~**ful†**, *a*, malicieux, malveillant, rancunier, méchant.

spitfire, *n*, rageur, euse.

spittle, *n*, salive, *f.* **spittoon**, *n*, crachoir, *m.*

Spitzbergen, *n*, le Spitzberg.

splash, *n*, (*of water*) gerbe d'eau,

f; (*into water*) floc, *m*; (*mud*) éclaboussure; (*color*) goutte, *f.* ¶ *v.t*, faire jaillir; éclabousser; (*v.i.*) gicler; (*tap*) cracher. ~ *about*, s'agiter.

splay, *v.t*, couper en sifflet, ébraser; (*dislocate*) épauler.

spleen, *n*, (*Anat.*) rate, *f*; (*dumps*) spleen; (*spite*) dépit, *m.*

splendid†, *a*, splendide, magnifique; brillant. **splendor**, *n*, splendeur, magnificence, *f.*

splice, *n*, épissure, *f.* ¶ *v.t*, épisser.

splicer, *n*, (*film*) colleuse, *f.* **splicing**, *n*, (*film*) collage, *m.*

splint, *n*, éclisse, attelle, *f.* ~ [*bone*], péroné, *m.*

splinter, *n*, éclat, *m*, écharde; (*bone*) esquille, *f.* ¶ *v.t*, faire éclater; (*v.i.*) éclater.

split, *n*, fente; fêlure; (*fig.*) scission, *f.* to do the ~, faire le grand écart. ¶ *v.t.ir*, fendre; refendre; fractionner; (*ears with noise*) déchirer; (*v.i.*) se fendre, éclater; crever. ~ *hairs*, fendre un cheveu en quatre, pointiller. ~ *peas*, pois cassés, *m.pl.* ~ *the atom*, désintégrer l'atome. *splitting headache*, mal de tête affreux, *m.*

splutter, *n*, pétarade, *f.* ¶ *v.i*, pétarader; bredouiller.

spoil, *n*, dépouille, *f*, butin, gâteau, *m.* ¶ *v.t*, gâter, gâcher, abîmer; corrompre. ~**sport**, trouble-fête, *m.*

spoke, *n*, rayon, *m.* ¶ *v.t*, enrayer.

spokesman, *n*, porte-parole, *m.*

spoliation, *n*, spoliation, *f.*

sponge, *n*, éponge, *f.* ~ *cake*, biscuit de Savoie, *m.* ~ *cloth*, tissu éponge, *m.* ¶ *v.t*, éponger.

sponger, *n*, pique-assiette, *m.*

spongy, *a*, spongieux.

sponsor, *n*, répondant, e; (*Eccl.*) parrain, *m*, marraine, *f.*

spontaneous†, *a*, spontané.

spook, *n*, fantôme, spectre, *m.*

spool, *n*, bobine, *f*; rouleau, *m.* ¶ *v.t*, bobiner.

spoon, *n*, cuiller, cuillère, *f.* ~**bill**, spatule, *f.* ~**ful**, cuillerée, *f.*

spoonerism, *n*, contre-petterie, *f.*

spoor, *n*, trace, *f*, erres, *f.pl.*

sporadic, *a*, sporadique.

spore, *n*, spore, *f.*

sport, *n*, jeu; (*s. & pl.*) sport, *m.* ~*s editor*, rédacteur sportif, *m.* ~*s ground*, terrain de jeux, *m.*

sportsman, *n,* sportif, amateur de sports, *m.*

spot, *n,* tache; macule; piqûre, *f;* goutte; place, *f,* endroit, site, lieu, *m,* lieux, *m.pl;* (*Bil.*) mouche, *f;* (*Com.*) disponible; comptant, *m. on the* ~, sur [la] place; séance tenante. ~*light,* projecteur orientable, *m. weak* ~, point faible, *m.* ¶ *v.t,* tacher; observer, repérer. **spotted,** *p.p,* tacheté, moucheté. **spotless,** *a,* sans tache.

spouse, *n,* époux, *m,* épouse, *f.*

spout, *n,* goulotte, *f;* bec; jet, *m.* ¶ *v.i. & t,* jaillir; déclamer, dégoiser.

sprain, *n,* entorse, foulure, *f. to* ~ *one's* . . ., se fouler le, la . . .

sprat, *n,* sprat, *m.*

sprawl, *v.i,* s'étaler, se vautrer.

spray, *n,* poussière [d'eau], gerbe [d'eau] *f;* (*sea*) embrun; (*jewels*) épi, *m;* (*flowers*) gerbe, chute; (*Need.*) chute, *f;* (*squirt*) vaporisateur, *m.* ¶ *v.t,* pulvériser, vaporiser. ~*er, n,* vaporisateur, *m,* arroseuse, *f.*

spread, *n,* développement, *m;* envergure; ouverture; propagation, *f;* (*food*) repas, *m.* ¶ *v.t.ir,* [é]tendre; déployer; répandre, semer; propager; échelonner, répartir, étager.

spree, *n,* noce, bamboche, *f.*

sprig, *n,* brin, *m,* brindille; pointe, *f.*

sprightly, *a,* vif, sémillant, éveillé; gai.

spring, *n,* élan, bond; ressort, *m;* élasticité; source, fontaine; (*arch*) naissance, retombée, *f;* (*season*) printemps, *m;* (*att.*) printanier. ~*board,* tremplin, *m.* ~ *cleaning,* grand nettoyage, *m.* ~ *tide,* grande marée, vive-eau, maline, *f.* ¶ *v.i.ir,* s'élancer, bondir; sourdre; dériver. ~ *up,* naître. ~*y, a,* élastique.

sprinkle, *v.t,* répandre; arroser; asperger; saupoudrer; (*book edges*) jasper. **sprinkler,** *n,* arrosoir, *m.*

sprint, *n,* course de vitesse, *f.* ~*er, n,* coureur de vitesse, *m.*

sprite, *n,* [esprit] follet, farfadet, *m.*

sprocket wheel, pignon de chaîne, *m.*

sprout, *n,* pousse, *f,* germe, *m.*

Brussels ~*s,* choux de Bruxelles, *m.pl.* ¶ *v.i,* pointer, germer.

spruce, *a,* pimpant, bien mis. ¶ *n,* sapin, *m.*

sprue, *n,* jet [de coulée] *m.*

sprung (*provided with springs*) *p.a,* à ressorts.

spur, *n,* éperon; (*bird*) ergot; (*mountain*) contrefort; (*Build.*) arc-boutant; (*fig.*) aiguillon, *m. on the* ~ *of the moment,* sous l'impulsion du moment. *railway* ~, embranchement, *m.* ¶ *v.t,* éperonner, talonner, piquer; aiguillonner.

spurious, *a,* faux, falsifié, contrefait, illégitime.

spurn, *v.t,* repousser, repousser du pied.

spurt, *v.i,* jaillir, gicler; (*price*) bondir, sauter. ¶ *n,* jet; bond, saut; (*running*) emballage; (*rowing*) enlevage, *m.*

sputter, *n,* pétarade, *f.* ¶ *v.i,* pétarader; bredouiller.

spy, *n,* espion, ne; (*police*) mouchard, *m.* ~*glass,* longue-vue, *f.* ¶ *v.t. & i,* espionner; moucharder; épier.

squab, *n,* pigeonneau, *m.*

squabble, *n,* querelle, *f.* ¶ *v.i,* se chamailler.

squad, *n,* escouade; brigade, *f;* peloton, *m.* **squadron,** *n,* (*cavalry*) escadron, *m;* (*navy*) escadre; (*air*) escadrille, *f.*

squalid, *a,* crasseux, sordide.

squall, *n,* grain, *m,* rafale, bourrasque, *f.* ¶ *v.i,* brailler. ~*y,* à grains, à rafales.

squalor, *n,* crasse, *f.*

squander, *v.t,* prodiguer, gaspiller, manger.

square, *a,* carré. ~ *foot,* pied carré, *m.* ~ *inch,* pouce carré, *m.* ~ *meal,* ample repas, *m.* ~ *measure,* mesure de surface, *f.* ~ *mile,* mille carré, *m.* ~ *root,* racine carrée, *f.* ~*shouldered,* carré des épaules. ~ *yard,* yard carré, *m.* ¶ *n,* carré, *m;* (*instrument & at right angles*) équerre; (*town*) place, *f;* (*parvis*) parvis, *m;* (*chessboard*) case, *f.* ¶ *v.t,* carrer; équarrir; régler. ~[*ly*] *ad,* carrément.

squash, *v.t,* écraser, écarbouiller; aplatir. ¶ *n,* courge, courgette, *f.*

squat, *v.i,* s'accroupir; se blottir, se tapir. ¶ *a,* ragot, boulot, tassé, écrasé.

squatter, n, squatter, m.

squawk, n, cri rauque, m.

squeak, n, cri, m. ¶ v.i, crier, piailler.

squeal, n, cri [perçant] m. ¶ v.i, crier, piailler.

squeamish, a, dégoûté.

squeegee, n, racloir, m.

squeeze, n, compression, f; serrement, m. ¶ v.t, presser; serrer; pincer. ~ out, exprimer; (fig.) arracher de.

squelch, v.i, déconcerter; (revolt) étouffer.

squib, n, serpenteau, m; (fig.) pasquinade, f.

squid, n, calmar, m.

squint, v.i, loucher.

squirm, v.i, se tortiller.

squirrel, n, écureuil, m.

squirt, n, seringue, f. ¶ v.t, seringuer; (v.i.) jaillir.

stab, n, coup (de poignard) m. ¶ v.t, percer; poignarder.

stability, n, stabilité; consistance, f. **stabilize**, v.t, rendre stable; (Fin.) stabiliser. **stable**, a, stable. ¶ n, écurie; cavalerie, f. ¶ v.t, loger; établer.

staccato, a, (note) piquée; (voice) saccadée.

stack, n, (Agric.) meule; (heap) pile, f; (arms) faisceau, m; (chimney) souche, f. ¶ v.t, empiler; mettre en meule.

stadium, n, stade, m.

staff, n, bâton, m; (pilgrim's) bourdon, m; (Mus.) portée, f; personnel; atelier; (Mil.) État-major, m. ~ officer, officier d'É.-m., m.

stag, n, cerf, (young) hère, m. ~ beetle, cerf-volant, m.

stage, n, estrade, f; échafaud, m; scène, f; théâtre, m; tréteaux, m.pl; platine, f; degré; stade, m, période, f. & m; phase; opération, f; relais, m; étape, traite, section, f. ~ door, entrée des artistes, f. ~ effect, effet scénique, artifice de théâtre, m. ~ fright, trac, m. ~hand, machiniste, m. ~ manager, régisseur, m. ~ name, nom de théâtre, m. ~ trick, jeu de scène, coup de théâtre, m. ~ whisper, aparté, m. ¶ v.t, mettre en scène, monter.

stagger, v.i, chanceler, tituber; (v.t.) consterner, ébouriffer; décaler.

stagnant, a, stagnant; (foul) croupissant. **stagnation**, n, stagnation, f, marasme, m.

staid, a, posé, rassis.

stain, n, tache; macule; souillure; couleur, f. ¶ v.t, tacher, souiller; colorer; mettre en couleur, teindre. stained glass, verre coloré, m; (church) vitraux peints, m. pl. stained-glass artist, peintre verrier, m. stained-glass window, verrière, f. **stainless**, a, sans tache; (steel) inoxydable.

stair, n, marche, f, degré, m. ~ carpet, tapis d'escalier, m. ~case & ~[s], escalier, m. ~ rail, rampe d'e., f.

stake, n, pieu, poteau, piquet, jalon; bûcher; intérêt; enjeu, m; mise, f; (pl, turf) prix, m. ¶ v.t, (bet) parier; garnir de pieux; (measure) jalonner. ~ one's reputation, jouer sa réputation.

stalactite, n, stalactite, f.

stalagmite, n, stalagmite, f.

stale, a, (bread) rassis; défraîchi; (liquor) éventé; vieilli.

stalemate (chess) n, pat, m. ¶ v.t, faire pat. ~d, p.a, pat.

stalk, n, tige, queue, f; pied, m. ¶ v.t, chasser à l'affût.

stall, n, stalle; chaise, f; kiosque; étalage, étal, m, échope, boutique, f. ¶ v.t, établer; (motor) caler.

stallion, n, étalon, m.

stalwart, a, robuste, vigoureux.

stamina, n, résistance, f, fond, m.

stammer, v.i. & t, bégayer. ~er, n, bègue, m.

stamp, n, poinçon; coin; pilon; bocard, m; marque; estampille, f; (postage, etc.) timbre, m; griffe; trempe, empreinte, f, cachet, sceau, m. rubber ~, timbre en caoutchouc, m. ¶ v.t. & i, frapper; piétiner, taper, trépigner; poinçonner; bocarder; marquer; étamper; estamper; estampiller; timbrer; affranchir. ~ed addressed envelope, enveloppe affranchie pour la réponse, f.

stampede, n, sauve-qui-peut, m.

stance, n, positition, f.

stanch, v.t, étancher.

stanchion, n, étançon, m; (ship) épontille, f.

stand, n, place, station, f; support; établi; pied; socle; affût; (music) lutrin; (exhibition) stand, _m; (stall)_ étalage, _m. (cinema)_ ~-_in_, doublure, _f._ ~_point_, point de vue, _m._ ~_still_, arrêt, _m._ ¶ _v.i.ir_, se tenir; se tenir debout; rester debout; se soutenir; stationner; se placer; se mettre; s'arrêter; se porter; tenir; durer; rester; reposer; (_v.t.ir._) supporter, soutenir; subir; résister à; souffrir; (_drink_) payer. ~ _aside_, se ranger. ~ _back!_ rangez-vous! ~ _fast_, tenir bon. ~ _in the way of_, faire obstacle à. ~ _on end_ (hair), [se] hérisser. ~ _out_, [res]sortir, se détacher, marquer. ~ _up_, se tenir debout; se lever; se dresser.

standard, _n_, étendard; (_values_) étalon, _m_; (_weight, measure_) matrice, _f_; (_gold_) titre, _m_; (_of coin_) loi, _f_; critère, criterium; niveau, _m_; toise; classe, _f_; pied; arbre de plein vent; (_vaulting_) sautoir, _m._ ~ _bearer_, porte-étendard, _m._ ¶ _att_, étalon; type; classique; (_gauge_) normale; (_edition_) définitive; (_charge_) forfaitaire; (_gold_) au titre; (_solution_) titrée. ~_ize_, _v.t_, standardiser; unifier; (_Chem._) titrer.

standing, _n_, place, pose, _f_, rang, _m._ _of long_ ~, de longue date, ancien. ¶ _a_, debout; (_crops_) sur pied; (_Naut._) dormant; (_water_) stagnante; (_orders_) permanent, e; (_expenses_) généraux; (_jump, dive_) sans élan; (_start_) arrêté. ~ _room only!_ places debout seulement! ~ _type_, conservation, _f_.

standoffish, _a_, distant, réservé. ~ness, _n_, quant-à-moi, quant-à-soi, _m_.

stanza, _n_, stance, strophe, _f_.

staple, _n_, (_wall_) crampon; (_wire_) cavalier, _m_; (_lock_) gâche; (_to fasten papers_) agrafe, _f_. ~ [_product_], produit principal, _m_, production principale, _f_. ~s, articles de première nécessité, _m.pl._ **stapler**, _n_, agrafeuse, _f_.

star, _n_, étoile, _f_; astre, _m_; (_lucky_) étoile, planète; (_Theat._) vedette, _f_; (_Typ._) astérisque, _m._ ~_fish_, étoile de mer, _f._ ~_gaze_, bayer aux corneilles. _shooting_ ~, étoile filante, _f_.

starboard, _n_, tribord, _m_.

starch, _n_, amidon, _m_; fécule, _f_; (_paste_) empois, _m._ ¶ _v.t_, empeser, amidonner. ~**y** (_food_) _a_, féculent.

stare, _n_, regard appuyé, _m._ ¶ _v.i_, écarquiller les yeux. ~ _at_, regarder fixement, dévisager.

stark, _a_, raide. ~ _mad_, fou à lier. ~ _naked_, tout nu, nu comme un ver.

starling (_bird_) _n_, sansonnet, étourneau, _m_.

starry, _a_, étoilé.

start, _n_, tressaillement, sursaut, soubresaut, haut-le-corps; commencement, début; départ, _m_; avance, _f._ ¶ _v.i_, tressaillir; partir; commencer, débuter; démarrer; (_v.t._) commencer; amorcer; mettre en marche; lancer; (_quarry_) lancer, débûcher. ~ _out_, se mettre en route. ~er, _n_, (_auto_) démarreur; (_signal giver_) starter; (_horse, runner_) partant, _m._ ~_ing line_, ligne de départ, _f._ ~_ing point_, point de d. ~_ing post_, poteau de d. _m_, barrière, _f_.

startle, _v.t_, faire tressaillir, effrayer, effaroucher, alarmer. **startling**, _p.a_, alarmant; saisissant.

starvation, _n_, inanition, faim, famine, _f._ ~ _diet_, diète absolue, _f._ ~ _wage_, salaire de famine, _m._ **starve**, _v.t_, priver de nourriture, affamer; (_v.i._) mourir de faim. ~_ling_, _n_, affamé, e, meurt-de-faim, _m._ **starving**, _p.a_, affamé.

state, _n_, état, _m_; disposition, _f_; apparat; (_stage of engraved or etched plate_) état, _m._ _to lie in_ ~ (of body), être exposé sur un lit de parade. ~ _controlled_, _managed_, en régie. ~_room_, cabine, _f._ S~ _socialism_, étatisme, _m._ ¶ _v.t_, énoncer; déclarer; relater; annoncer; poser. ~**liness**, _n_, majesté, _f._ ~**ly**, _a_, majestueux, pompeux, superbe; fier. ~**ment**, _n_, énoncé, _m_, déclaration, _f_; relevé, état, exposé; bordereau, _m_. **statesman**, _n_, homme d'État, _m_.

static(al), _a. & statics_, _n_, statique, _a. & f._ _radio static_, perturbation atmosphérique, _f_.

station, _n_, station, _f_, poste, _m_; gare, _f_; rang, _m._ _filling_ ~, poste d'essence, _m._ _police_ ~, poste de police, _m._ ~s _of the Cross_, chemin de la croix, _m._ ~ _master_, chef de gare, _m._ ¶ _v.t_, [a]poster. ~**ary**, _a_, stationnaire; fixe, à demeure.

stationer, _n_, papetier, ère, ~**y**,

n, papeterie, *f*; papier à lettres, *m*.

stationwagon, *n*, break, *m*.

statistic(al), *a*, statistique. **statistician**, *n*, statisticien, *m*. **statistics**, *n*, statistique, *f*; mouvement, *m*.

statuary, *a*, statuaire. ¶ *n*, statues, *f.pl*; (*art*) statuaire, *f*; (*pers.*) statuaire, *m*. **statue**, *n*, statue, *f*. **statuette**, *n*, statuette, figurine, *f*.

stature, *n*, stature, taille, *f*.

status, *n*, statut, titre, état, *m*, qualité, *f*, standing, *m*. (*For example, "un immeuble de grand standing" = a luxury apartment house*.)

statute, *n*, loi, *f*; statut, *m*. ~ **book**, code, *m*. **statutory**, *a*, légal.

staunch, *a*, étanche; ferme; dévoué.

stave, *n*, douve; (*Mus.*) portée, *f*. ~ **in**, *v.t.ir*, enfoncer, défoncer. ~ **off**, parer.

stay, *n*, séjour; support; étai; tirant; hauban; (*pl.*) corset; (*law*) sursis, *m*. ~ **in the country**, villégiature, *f*. ¶ *v.i*, rester; demeurer; séjourner; attendre; s'arrêter; (*v.t.*) suspendre; (*law*) surseoir à; étayer. ~**at-home**, *a. & n*, casanier, ère, pot-au-feu, *a*. ~ **away**, s'absenter. ~ **up**, veiller.

stead, *n*, lieu, *m*, place, *f*.

steadfast, *a*, constant, ferme. ~**ly**, *ad*, avec constance. ~**ness**, *n*, constance, *f*.

steady, *a*, ferme; stable; rangé; posé; réglé; suivi. ¶ *i*, ferm! ¶ *v.t*, fixer, affermir.

steak, *n*, tranche, *f*; (*beef*) bifteck, *m*, entrecôte, *f*.

steal, *v.t. & i. ir*, voler, dérober. ~ **away**, se dérober. ~ **in**, se glisser dans. ~**ing**, *n*, vol, *m*. **by stealth**, à la dérobée. **stealthy†**, *a*, furtif.

steam, *n*, vapeur; fumée; buée, *f*; (*att.*) à vapeur. ~ **engine**, machine à vapeur, *f*. ~ **room** (bath), étuve humide, *f*. ¶ *v.t*, (*Cook.*) mettre à l'étuvée; (*v.i.*) marcher [à la vapeur]; fumer. ~**er** or ~**boat** or ~**ship**, *n*, vapeur, *m*, bateau à v., navire à v., steamer, *m*. ~**ing** (*Cook.*) *n*, étuvée, étouffée, estouffade, *f*.

steed, *n*, coursier, *m*.

steel, *n*, acier; (*of tinder box*) briquet; (*sharpener*) fusil, *m*; (*corset*) baleine, *f*; (*att.*) d'acier, en acier; métallique. ~ **wool**, paille de fer, *f*. ~ **works**, aciérie, *f*. ¶ *v.t*, acérer; aciérer; (*fig.*) cuirasser.

steep, *a*, raide, escarpé, ardu, fort, rapide. ¶ *v.t*, tremper, baigner. ~**ed** in (*fig.*), pétri de. **steeple**, *n*, clocher [pointu] *m*. ~**chase**, course d'obstacles, *f*. **steepness**, *n*, raideur, *f*, escarpement, *m*.

steer, *n*, bouvillon, *m*. ¶ *v.t. & i*, diriger, conduire, guider; gouverner. ~ **clear of**, éviter. **steerage**, *n*, avant, *m*. ~ **passenger**, passager de l'a., p. d'entrepont, *m*. **steering**, *n*, direction; (*Naut.*) gouverne, *f*. ~ **compass**, compas de route, *m*. ~ **wheel** (auto) volant, *m*.

stellar, *a*, stellaire.

stem, *n*, tige; queue, *f*; (*ship*) étrave, *f*; (*Gram.*) thème, *m*. ~ **stitch**, point de tige, p. coulé, *m*. ¶ *v.t*, arrêter, refouler.

stench, *n*, puanteur, infection, *f*.

stencil, *n*, patron, pochoir; caractère à jour; (*typing*) stencil, *m*. ¶ *v.t*, patronner.

stenographer, *n*, sténographe, *m*,*f*. **stenography**, *n*, sténographie, *f*.

stentorian, *a*, de stentor.

step, *n*, pas, *m*; trotte; marche, *f*, degré; gradin; échelon, *m*; démarche; mesure; cadence, *f*; acheminement; (*pl.*) marchepied, *m*, échelle double, *f*. ~**brother**, demi-frère, *m*. ~**daughter**, belle-fille, *f*. ~**father**, beau-père, *m*. ~**ladder**, échelle double, *f*. ~**mother**, belle-mère; (*cruel*) marâtre, *f*. ~**sister**, demi-sœur, *f*. ~**son**, beau-fils, *m*. **to take** ~**s**, prendre des mesures. ¶ *v.i*, faire un pas; marcher; aller; venir; monter. ~ **in**, entrer. **stepping stone**, pierre à gué, *f*; (*fig.*) marchepied, échelon, *m*.

stereoscope, *n*, stéréoscope, *m*.

stereotype, *n*, cliché, *m*. ¶ *v.t*, clicher, stéréotyper.

sterile, *a*, stérile. **sterility**, *n*, stérilité, *f*. **sterilize**, *v.t*, stériliser.

sterling, *a*, (*Eng. money*) sterling, *a.inv*; (*fig.*) de bon aloi; solide. ¶ *n*, la livre.

stern†, *a*, sévère; austère. ¶ *n*, arrière, *m*; poupe, *f*. ~*post*, étambot, *m*. **sternness**, *n*, sévérité; austérité, *f*.

sternum, *n*, sternum, *m*.

stet (*Typ.*), bon. ¶ *v.t*, donner son bon à.

stethoscope, *n*, stéthoscope, *m*.

stevedore, *n*, déchargeur, débardeur, arrimeur, *m*.

stew, *n*, ragoût. *m*. ~*pan*, casserole, braisière, *f*, fait-tout, *m*. ¶ *v.t*, étuver; (*abs.*) fricoter. *stewed fruit*, compote de fruits, *f*.

steward, *n*, maître d'hôtel; intendant; régisseur; commissaire; économe; garçon de cabine; commis aux vivres; délégué, *m*. ~'*s mate* (ship), cambusier, *m*. ~'*s room*, dépense; (*ship*) cambuse, *f*.

stick, *n*, bâton, *m*; canne, *f*; (*umbrella*) manche, *m*; baguette, *f*; cotret, *m*, (*pl.*) du bois. ¶ *v.t.ir*, piquer; ficher; coller; (*Hort.*) ramer; (*pig*) saigner; (*v.i.ir.*) s'attacher; [se] coller, adhérer; rester, tenir. ~ *in the mud*, s'embourber. **stickiness**, *n*, viscosité, *f*.

stickleback, *n*, épinoche, *f*.

sticky, *a*, collant, gluant, visqueux.

stiff, *a*, raide; fort; rigide; tenace; (*strained*) empesé, guindé; (*price*) salé. ~ *collar*, faux col rigide, *m*. ~ *neck*, torticolis, *m*. ~*en*, *v.t*, raidir. ~*ness*, *n*, raideur; (*in the joints of the body*) courbature, *f*.

stifle, *v.t*, étouffer, suffoquer.

stigma, *n*, stigmate, *m*, flétrissure, tache, *f*. **stigmatize**, *v.t*, stigmatiser.

stile, *n*, échalier; (*door*) montant, *m*.

stiletto, *n*, stylet, *m*.

still, *a*, calme, tranquille; silencieux; immobile, en repos; (*water*) dormante, morte; (*wine*) non mousseux; (*lemonade*) non gazeuse. ~*born*, mort-né. ~ *life* (*art*), nature morte, *f*. ¶ *ad*, encore, toujours; cependant, néanmoins, toutefois. ¶ *n*, calme; alambic, *m*, cornue, *f*. ¶ *v.t*, calmer, apaiser, tranquilliser. ~*ness*, *n*, calme, *m*, tranquillité, *f*, silence, *m*.

stilt, *n*, échasse, *f*. ~*ed*, *a*, guindé.

stimulant, *n*, stimulant, remontant, réconfort, *m*. **stimulate**, *v.t*,

stimuler. **stimulus**, *n*, stimulant, aiguillon, *m*.

sting, *n*, aiguillon, dard, *m*, piqûre; (*fig.*) morsure, *f*. ¶ *v.t.* & *i. ir*, piquer; (*of conscience*) bourreler. **stinging**, *p.a*, piquant. ~ *nettle*, ortie brûlante, ortie grièche, *f*.

stingy, *a*, avare, pingre, mesquin, chiche.

stink, *n*, puanteur, *f*. ¶ *v.i.ir*, puer.

stint, *v.t*, épargner; rationner. ~ *oneself*, se priver; se rationner. *without* ~, sans réserve.

stipend, *n*, traitement, *m*.

stipple, *n*, pointillé, grené, *m*. ¶ *v.t*, pointiller.

stipulate, *v.t*, stipuler.

stir, *n*, remue-ménage, tapage; mouvement, *m*. *make a* ~, faire florès. ¶ *v.t*, remuer; agiter; (*fire*) attiser; (*the blood*) fouetter; (*v.i.*) remuer, bouger. ~ *up*, exciter, susciter, émouvoir. **stirring**, *p.a*, émouvant; vibrant.

stirrup, *n*, étrier, *m*. ~ *cup*, coup de l'étrier, *m*. ~ *leather*, étrivière, *f*.

stitch, *n*, point [de couture] *m*; (*Knit., crochet*) maille, *f*. ~ *in the side* (*Med.*), point de côté. ¶ *v.t*, coudre; (*leather*) piquer; (*books*) brocher. ~ *together*, appointer. ~*ed hem*, ourlet piqué, *m*. ~*er*, *n*, piqueuse, *f*. ~*ing*, *n*, point piqué, *m*.

stoat, *n*, hermine, *f*.

stock, *n*, (*descent*) race, lignée; (*tree, etc.*) souche, *f*, estoc; (*rifle, plane*) fût, bois, *m*; (*Hort.*) sujet, porte-greffe, (*wild*) sauvageon; (*vine*) cep, *m*; (*flower*) girofiée, *f*, violier, *m*; (*Com.*) stock, *m*, provision; approvisionnement; matériel, *m*; (*Fin.*) valeur, *f*. *oft. pl*, titre, *m. oft. pl*; effets, fonds, *m.pl*; actions, *f.pl*; (*Cook.*) consommé, *m*; (*pl, Naut.*) chantier, *m*, cale [de construction] *f*; (*pl, Hist.*) ceps, *m.pl*, tabouret, *m*. *in* ~, en magasin. ~*s & shares*, valeurs mobilières, *f.pl*. ~*broker*, agent de change; banquier en valeurs, *m*. ~ *exchange*, bourse [des valeurs] *f*. ~*fish*, stockfisch, *m*. ~*holder*, détenteur de titres, *m*; actionnaire, sociétaire, *m,f*, rentier, ère. ~ *in trade*, existence en magasin. ~ *phrase*, cliché, *m*. ~ *pot*, pot-au-feu, *m*. ~ *solution*

(*Phot.*), solution fondamentale, *f.* ~*still*, sans mouvement. ~ *taking*, inventaire; recensement, *m.* ~ *yard*, (*cattle*) parc à bestiaux; (*materials*) parc à matières, *m.* ¶ *v.t*, approvisionner; assortir; tenir; peupler; meubler; empoissonner.

stockade, *n*, palissade, palanque, *f.*

stocking, *n*, bas, *m.*

stocky, *a*, trapu, ramassé, étoffé.

Stoic, *n. & att*, stoïcien, *m. & a.* stoical†, *a*, stoïque. **stoicism**, *n*, stoïcisme, *m.*

stoke, *v.t*, chauffer. ~*hole*, ~*hold*, chaufferie, chambre de chauffe, *f.* **stoker**, *n*, chauffeur; (*mechanical*) chargeur, *m.*

stole, *n*, étole; écharpe, *f.*

stolid, *a*, flegmatique. ~*ity*, *n*, flegme, *m.*

stomach, *n*, estomac; (*fig.*) cœur, *m.* ~ *ache*, mal d'estomac, *m.* ~ *pump*, pompe stomacale, *f.* ¶ *v.t*, digérer, avaler.

stone, *n*, pierre; roche, *f*; caillou; (*fruit*) noyau; (*grape*) pépin; (*building*) moellon, *m.* grind~, meule, *f.* ~ *dead*, raide mort. ~ (*gem*) *setter*, metteur en œuvre, *m.* ~'*s throw*, jet de pierre, *m.* ~*ware*, poterie de grès, *f.* grès, *m*, gresserie, *f.* ~*work*, maçonnerie, *f.* ¶ *v.t*, (*to death*) lapider. **stony**, *a*, pierreux; caillouteux; (*heart*) de pierre, de roche[r]; (*look*) glacé.

stool, *n*, tabouret; escabeau, *m*; sellette; (*Med.*) selle, *f.* folding ~, pliant, *m.*

stoop, *v.i*, se pencher; s'abaisser.

stop, *n*, arrêt, *m*; halte; station; pause; opposition, *f*; (*buffer*) butoir, *m*; (*Mech.*) butée, *f*; (*organ*) jeu; (*Phot.*) diaphragme; (*Typ.*) point, *m.* *to put a* ~ *to*, faire cesser. ~*cock*, robinet [d'arrêt] *m.* ~*gap*, bouche-trou, *m.* ~*watch*, chronographe; compteur de sport, *m.* ¶ *v.t*, arrêter; (*Naut.*) stopper; interrompre; suspendre; mettre opposition sur; cesser; (*wages*) retenir; (*leak*) boucher, aveugler; (*v.i.*) s'arrêter; stationner; rester; cesser. ~ *up*, boucher. ¶ *i*, halte[-là]! (*Naut.*, *in telegrams*) stop.

stope (*Min.*) *n*, gradin, *m.*

stoppage, *n*, arrêt; chômage, *m*; retenue; obstruction, *f.* **stopper**, *n*, bouchon, *m.* ¶ *v.t*, boucher.

storage, *n*, [em]magasinage, *m.* **store**, *n*, approvisionnement, *m*, provision, fourniture; réserve; resserre, boutique, *f*, magasin, *m*; dépôt; entrepôt; économat, *m.* *department* ~, magasin de nouveautés, bazar, *m.* ~*keeper*, boutiquier, *m.* ¶ *v.t*, approvisionner; (*fig.*) meubler; emmagasiner; mettre en dépôt. ~ *up*, accumuler.

stork, *n*, cigogne, *f.*

storm, *n*, orage, *m*; tempête, tourmente, *f.* ~ *cloud*, nuée, *f.* ~ *of abuse*, algarade, *f.* ¶ *v.t*, donner l'assaut à; (*v.i.*) tempêter. **stormy**, *a*, orageux, tempétueux. *at* ~ (*barometer*), à la tempête.

story, *n*, histoire, *f*; conte, *m*; narration; fable; menterie, *f*; (*floor*) étage, *m.* ~ *book*, livre de contes, *m.* ~ *teller*, conteur, euse; narrateur, trice.

stout†, *a*, fort, vigoureux; robuste; renforcé; brave; gros, corpulent, replet. ¶ (*beer*) *n*, stout, *m.* ~*ness* (*of body*) *n*, embonpoint, *m.*

stove, *n*, poêle; fourneau; réchaud, *m*; étuve, *f.*

stow (*Naut.*) *v.t*, arrimer. ~ *away*, *v.t*, serrer; (*v.i.*) s'embarquer clandestinement. ~*away*, *n*, passager (ère) clandestin(e), *m.*

straddle, *v.t. & i*, chevaucher.

strafe, *v.t*, mitrailler.

straggle, *v.i*, traîner. **straggler**, *n*, traînard, *m.* **straggling**, *a*, (*houses*) éparses; (*village*) aux maisons éparses; (*beard*) maigre.

straight, *a*, droit; (*hair*) plats; (*respectable*) honnête. *go* ~ *ahead*, allez tout droit. ¶ *ad*, [tout] droit; directement. ~ *n*, ligne droite, *f.* ~*en*, *v.t*, [re]dresser, rectifier. **straightforward**, *a*, droit. **straightforwardly**, *ad*, sans détour; carrément. **straightforwardness**, *n*, droiture, *f*; sans-façon, *m.* **straightness**, *n*, rectitude, *f.*

strain, *n*, (*molecular*) tension; (*Mech.*) déformation; (*overstrain*) fatigue, *f*; (*Med.*) effort; (*Vet.*) écart, *m*; (*descent*) race; (*dash*) teinte, *f*; (*pl.*) accents, *m.pl.* ~ *in the back*, tour de reins, *m.* ¶ *v.t*, tendre; déformer; fatiguer; torturer; (*Med.*) fouler;

(*filter*) passer, filtrer, tamiser. ~ed (*fig.*) *p.a,* guindé. ~er, *n,* passoire, couloire, *f,* tamis, *m;* crépine, *f.*

strait, *n,* (*s. & pl.*) détroit, pertuis, *m;* (*pl.*) gêne, détresse, *f,* malaise, embarras, *m. S~s of Dover,* [détroit du] Pas de Calais, *m. S~s of Gibraltar,* détroit de Gibraltar. **straitjacket,** *n,* camisole de force, *f.* **straitlaced,** *a,* collet monté, bégueule. **in straitened circumstances,** dans la gêne.

strand, *n,* rivage; (*rope*) cordon, toron, brin, *m.* ¶ *v.t. & i,* échouer; jeter à la côte.

strange†, *a,* étrange; étranger; bizarre. **stranger,** *n,* étranger, ère; inconnu, e. **strangeness,** *n,* étrangeté; bizarrerie, *f.*

strangle, *v.t.,* étrangler, juguler. ~s (*V et.*) *n.pl,* gourme, *f.* **strangulation,** *n,* etranglement, *m,* strangulation, *f.*

strap, *n,* courroie; sangle; bande, *f;* bracelet; tirant; lien, *m.* ¶ *v.t,* sangler.

stratagem, *n,* stratagème, *m,* ruse, *f.* **strategic(al)†,** *a,* stratégique. **strategist,** *n,* stratège, *m.* **strategy,** *n,* stratégie, *f.*

stratified, *p.p,* stratifié. **stratum,** *n,* couche, *f,* gisement, *m.*

stratosphere, *n,* stratosphère, *f.*

straw, *n,* paille, *f;* fétu, *m.* (*drinking*) chalumeau; (*fig.*) fétu, *m. the last* ~, le comble [de nos maux]. ~board, carton-paille, *m.* ~ hat, chapeau de paille, *m.* ~ hut (*native*), paillote, *f.* ~ mattress, paillasse, *f.*

strawberry, *n,* fraise, *f.* ~ plant, fraisier, *m.*

stray, *v.i,* errer; s'écarter. ¶ *a,* égaré; errant; épave. ~ cat, chat de gouttières, *m.* ¶ *n,* épave, *f.*

streak, *n,* trait, sillon, *m,* raie, bande, *f.* ¶ *v.t,* rayer, sillonner. ~y (*meat*) *a,* entrelardée.

stream, *n,* cours d'eau; ruisseau; flot; jet; filet; cours; torrent, *m.* ~lined, profilé, fuselé, aérodynamique. ~lining, aérodynamisme, *m.* ¶ *v.i,* ruisseler. ~er, *n,* flamme, *f;* (*paper*) serpentin, *m.*

street, *n,* rue, *f;* (*s. & pl. fig.*) pavé, *m. back* ~, rue détournée, *f. main* ~, artère principale, *f.* ~ *lamp,* réverbère, *m.* ~ *musician,* musicien de carrefour, *m.*

streetcar, *n,* tramway, *m.*

streetcleaner, *n,* éboueur, *m.*

strength, *n,* force; puissance; résistance; robustesse; intensité, *f;* (*of a solution*) titre; (*men*) effectif, *m.* ~en, *v.t,* renforcer; consolider; fortifier.

strenuous†, *a,* énergique; (*life*) intense.

streptomycin, *n,* streptomycine, *f.*

stress, *n,* effort; travail, *m;* charge; fatigue; (*weather*) violence, *f;* accent, appui, *m. to be in* ~ (*Mech.*), travailler. ¶ *v.t,* charger; fatiguer; appuyer sur; accentuer; (*Mus.*) scander.

stretch, *n,* trait, *m;* étendue, traite; (*of person's arms*) envergure, *f;* parcours; (*Mech.*) allongement, *m.* ¶ *v.t,* étendre, étirer; allonger; tendre. ~ *oneself,* s'étirer. **stretcher,** *n,* brancard, *m;* civière, *f;* raidisseur; (*for painter's canvas*) châssis, *m.* ~ *bearer,* brancardier, *m.*

strew, *v.t.ir,* répandre; joncher; [par]semer.

stria, *n,* strie, *f.* **striate[d]** *a,* strié. striation, *n,* striure, *f.*

strickle, *n,* racloire, *f.*

strict†, *a,* strict; formel; rigoureux; sévère; exact. ~ness, *n,* rigueur; sévérité, *f.* ~ure, *n,* critique, *f;* (*Med.*) rétrécissement, *m.*

stride, *n,* enjambée, *f,* pas, *m;* (*pl.*) essor, *m.* ~ *along,* *v.i.ir,* marcher à grands pas.

strident, *a,* strident.

strife, *n,* guerre, *f;* conflit, *m.*

strike, *n,* (*coin*) frappe; (*labor*) grève. *f. wildcat* ~, grève sauvage, *f.* ¶ *v.t.ir,* frapper; assener, porter; choquer; (*match*) frotter; rencontrer; atteindre; battre; (*clock*) sonner; (*root, v.t. & abs.*) jeter, prendre; (*tent*) plier; (*sail*) caler; (*colors*) amener; (*a balance*) établier, faire; (*fish*) ferrer; (*v.i.ir.*) frapper; sonner; (*labor*) se mettre en grève. *it* ~s *me,* il me semble, il me vient l'idée. *without striking a blow,* sans coup férir. ~ *down,* abattre. ~ *out,* effacer, rayer, radier, biffer. ~ *up* (*tune*), entonner. **striker,** *n,* gréviste, *m,f.* **striking,** *p.a,* frappant, saisissant; marquant; saillant;

(*labor*) en grève. ~ *clock*, pendule à sonnerie, *f.*

string, *n*, ficelle; corde; cordelette, *f*; cordon; tirant; filet, *m*; fibre; filandre, *f*; chapelet; attirail; train, *m*; enfilade, *f*; (*Bil.*) boulier, *m. the* ~s (*Mus.*), les cordes. ~ *band*, orchestre à cordes, *m.* ¶ *v.t.ir*, corder; enfiler; (*violin*) monter. ~ed, *p.a*, à cordes.

stringbean, *n*, haricot vert, *m.*

stringent, *a*, rigoureux.

stringy, *a*, fibreux; filandreux.

strip, *n*, bande, *f*; ruban, *m.* ¶ *v.t*, dépouiller; dégarnir; (*v.i.*) se déshabiller.

stripe, *n*, raie, barre, *f*, liteau; (*N.C.O.'s Navy*) galon, *m.* ~d, *a*, rayé, à raies; tigré, zébré.

strive, *v.i.ir*, s'efforcer, tâcher; combattre.

stroke, *n*, coup, *m*; atteinte, *f*; battement, *m*; course, *f*; trait, *m*; raie, barre; attaque, *f*, coup de sang, *m*; (*Swim.*) nage; brassée; brasse, *f*; (*rowing*) chef de nage, *m. sun* ~, coup de soleil, *m.* ¶ *v.t*, caresser.

stroll, *n*, tour, *m*, promenade, *f.* ¶ *v.i*, se promener; errer; flâner. **stroller** *n*, flaneur; *m*; (*baby carriage*) pousette, *f.* **strolling**, *p.a*, ambulant.

strong†, *a*, fort; puissant; vigoureux; énergique; renforcé; résistant; solide; (*flavor*) relevé; (*wind*) carabiné; (*language*) corsé; (*well up in*) calé. ~ *box*, coffre-fort, *m.* ~ *drink*, liqueurs fortes, *f.pl.* ~*hold*, forteresse, citadelle, *f*, fort, *m.* ~ *man* (*professional*), hercule, *m.* ~-*minded person*, tête forte, forte tête, *f.* ~ *point*, fort, *m.* ~ *room*, cave forte; (*ship*) chambre des valeurs, *f.*

strop, *n*, cuir [à rasoir], affiloir; (*safety blade*) repasseur, *m.* ¶ *v.t*, repasser [sur le cuir, etc.].

structural, -*a*, (*steel*, *etc.*) de construction; (*repairs*) grosses. **structure**, *n*, structure; construction; formation, *f*; édifice; ouvrage d'art; (*fig.*) échafaudage, *m.*

struggle, *n*, lutte, *f.* ¶ *v.i*, lutter, bataille.

strum, *v.t*, tapoter.

strut, *n*, entretoise; contre-fiche; bielle, *f.* ¶ *v.i*, se pavaner, se rengorger, se carrer.

strychnine, *n*, strychnine, *f.*

stub, *n*, souche, *f*, chicot; bout; (*check*) talon, *m.*

stubble, *n*, chaume, *m*, éteule, *f.*

stubborn†, *a*, obstiné, entêté, têtu; tenace. ~*ness*, *n*, obstination, opiniâtreté; ténacité, *f.*

stucco, *n*, stuc, *m.* ¶ *v.t*, enduire de stuc.

stuck-up, *a*, fier.

stud, *n*, clou; crampon, *m*; pointe, *f*; goujon; bouton; plot [de contact]; (*scantling in wall*) potelet, *m*; (*horses*) écurie, *f*; (*breeding*) haras, *m.* ~ *book*, livre généalogique, stud-book, *m.* ~ *farm*, haras, *m.* ~ *horse*, étalon, *m.* ¶ *v.t*, clouter; parsemer, émailler; hérisser. *studded crossing* (*pedestrian*), passage clouté, *m*, les clous, *m.pl.*

student, *n*, élève, *m,f*; étudiant, e; normalien, ne. **studied**, *p.p*, étudié; recherché; (*deliberate*) voulu. ~ *elegance*, recherche, *f.* **studio**, *n*, atelier; théâtre; studio; salon de pose, *m.* **studious**†, *a*, studieux, appliqué. **study**, *n*, étude, *f*; cabinet de travail, *m.* ¶ *v.t. & i*, étudier.

stuff, *n*, matière; étoffe, *f*; (*fig.*) bois, *m.* ~ & *nonsense*, fadaises, *f.pl.* ¶ *v.t*, rembourrer; fourrer; bourrer; (*dead animal*) empailler; (*Cook.*) farcir. ~*ing*, *n*, bourre; (*Cook.*) farce, *f.* ~*y*, *a*, étouffant.

stultify, *v.t*, neutraliser.

stumble, *v.i*, broncher, trébucher, [s']achopper. *stumbling block*, pierre d'achoppement, *f.*

stump, *n*, tronçon; moignon; chicot, *m*; souche, *f*; trognon; bout, *m*; (*art*) estompe, *f.* ~ *orator*, déclamateur, *m.* ¶ *v.t*, faire une campagne électorale, marcher en clopinant.

stun, *v.t*, étourdir. *stunning blow*, coup de massue, *m.*

stunt, *n*, acrobatie, *f*, tour de force, *m.* ~*man*, cascadeur, *m.* ¶ *v.t*, rabougrir.

stunted, *p.p*, rabougri, avorté, malvenu, chétif.

stupefy, *v.t*, hébéter; (*narcotize*) stupéfier.

stupendous†, *a*, prodigieux.

stupid†, *a*, stupide; bête. ~*ity*, *n*, stupidité; bêtise, *f.* **stupor**, *n*, stupeur, *f.*

sturdy†, *a*, vigoureux, robuste.

sturgeon, *n,* esturgeon, *m.*

stutter, *v.i. & t,* bégayer ~er, *n,* bègue, *m,f.*

sty, *n,* étable à porcs; porcherie, *f.*

sty[e] (*on the eye*) *n,* orgelet, compère-loriot, *m.*

style, *n,* style, *m;* manière, *f,* genre, goût; chic; nom, *m;* (*firm name*) raison [sociale] *f.* ~ *of hairdressing,* coiffure, *f.* ¶ *v.t,* qualifier; donner le titre de.

stymie (*golf*) *n,* trou barré, *m.*

stylish†, *a,* élégant, galant, à la mode; chic; coquet.

suave†, *a,* suave. **suavity,** *n,* suavité, *f.*

sub-acid, *a,* aigre-doux.

subaltern, *n,* [officier] subalterne, *m.*

subcommittee, *n,* sous-comité, *m.*

subconscious, *a. & n,* subconscient, *a. & m.* ~ness, *n,* subconscience, *f.*

subcontract, *n,* sous-traité, *m.* ~or, *n,* sous-traitant, *m.*

subcutaneous, *a,* sous-cutané.

subdivide, *v.t,* subdiviser, morceler.

subdue, *v.t,* subjuguer, soumettre, assujettir; maîtriser; adoucir; (*light*) adoucir, tamiser.

subject, *n,* sujet; propos, *m;* (*pers.*) sujet, te. ~ *catalog,* catalogue par ordre de matières, *m.* ¶ *v.t,* soumettre, assujettir. ¶ ~ *to,* sujet(te) à; soumis(e) à; sous [le] bénéfice de; sous réserve de; sauf à. ~ion, *n,* sujétion, *f,* assujettissement, *m;* dépendance, *f.* ~ive†, *a. & n,* subjectif, *a. & m.*

subjoined, *p.p,* ci-joint.

subjugate, *v.t,* subjuguer.

subjunctive [**mood**], *n,* subjonctif, *m.*

sublet, *v.t.ir,* sous-louer, relouer.

sublimate, *v.t,* sublimer.

sublime†, *a. & n,* sublime, *a. & m.* sublimity, *n,* sublimité, *f.*

sublunar[y], *a,* sublunaire.

submachine gun, *n,* mitraillette, *f.*

submarine, *a. & n,* sous-marin, *a. & m.*

submerge, *v.t,* submerger; (*v.i.*) plonger.

submission, *n,* soumission, *f.* **submissive,** *a,* soumis, obéissant. ~ness, *n,* soumission, résignation, *f.* **submit,** *v.t,* soumettre. ~ *to,* se soumettre à, obéir à, subir.

suborder, *n,* sous-ordre, *m.*

subordinate, *a,* subordonné, subalterne, en sous-ordre. ¶ *n,* subordonné, e, sous-ordre, *m.* ¶ *v.t,* subordonner.

suborn, *v.t,* suborner, séduire. ~er, *n,* suborneur, euse.

subpoena, *n,* citation, assignation, *f.* ¶ *v.t,* citer, assigner, ajourner.

subscribe, *v.t. & i,* souscrire; s'abonner; se cotiser. **subscriber,** *n,* souscripteur, *m;* abonné, e. **subscription,** *n,* souscription, cotisation, *f;* abonnement, *m.*

subscript, *n,* indice inférieur, *m.*

subsection, *n,* alinéa, *m.*

subsequent†, *a,* subséquent, postérieur.

subservience, *n,* sujétion, *f.* **subservient,** *a,* auxiliaire, subalterne; servile.

subside, *v.i,* baisser; s'affaisser; [se] calmer. **subsidence,** *n,* baisse, *f;* affaissement, effondrement, *m.*

subsidiary†, *a,* subsidiaire; auxiliaire. ~ [*company*], [société] filiale, *f.*

subsidize, *v.t,* subventionner. **subsidy,** *n,* subvention, *f;* subside, *m.*

subsist, *v.i,* subsister; vivre. ~ence, *n,* subsistance, *f.*

subsoil, *n,* sous-sol; (*law*) tréfonds, *m.*

substance, *n,* substance, *f;* fond; corps; bien, *m.* **substantial,** *a,* substantiel; solide; (*lunch*) dînatoire. ~ly, *ad,* substantiellement, en substance. **substantiate,** *v.t,* établir.

substantive, *a. & n,* substantif, *a. & m.*

substitute, *n,* succédané, *m;* (*pers.*) remplaçant, e; suppléant, e. ¶ *v.t,* substituer.

substratum, *n,* fond, *m.*

substructure, *n,* substruction, *f.*

subtenant, *n,* sous-locataire, *m,f.*

subterfuge, *n,* subterfuge, *m.*

subterranean, *a,* souterrain.

subtitle, *n,* sous-titre, *m.*

subtle†, *a,* subtil, raffiné, fin. ~ty, *n,* subtilité, *f,* raffinement, *m.*

subtract, *v.t,* soustraire, retrancher. ~ion, *n,* soustraction, *f.*

suburb, *n,* faubourg, *m,* (*pl.*) banlieue, *f.* ~an, *a,* suburbain; de banlieue.

subvention, *n,* subvention, *f.*

subversive, *a*, subversif. **subvert**, *v.t*, renverser.

subway, *n*, passage souterrain; (*train*) métropolitain, métro, *m*.

succeed, *v.t*, succéder à; suivre; (*v.i.*) succéder; (*prosper*) réussir, succéder, arriver; parvenir. **~ing**, *p.a*, suivant. **success**, *n*, succès, *m*, réussite, *f*. **~ful†**, *a*, heureux; réussi. **succession**, *n*, succession; suite, *f*. **successive†**, *a*, successif. **successor**, *n*, successeur, *m*.

succinct†, *a*, succinct. **~ness**, *n*, concision, *f*.

succor, *n*, secours, *m*. ¶ *v.t*, secourir.

succulent, *a*, succulent.

succumb, *v.i*, succomber.

such, *a*, tel; pareil; semblable. **~ as**, tel que; comme.

suck, *v.t. & i*, sucer; téter; aspirer. **~ in**, humer. **~ up**, pomper. **~er**, *n*; (*of insect*) suçoir, *m*; (*of leech*) ventouse, *f*; (*Hort.*) drageon, surgeon, *m*, talle, *f*, œilleton, *m*; branche gourmande, *f*; (*fig.*) poire, *f*. **~le**, *v.t*, allaiter, nourrir. **~ling**, *n*, enfant à la mamelle; nourrisson, *m*. **suction**, *n*, succion; aspiration, *f*. **~ pump**, pompe aspirante, *f*.

sudden†, *a*, soudain, subit; brusque. **~ turn** (road), crochet, *m*. **all of a ~**, tout à coup. **~ness**, *n*, soudaineté, *f*.

suds, *n.pl*, eau de savon, *f*.

sue, *v.t*, (*legal*) traduire en justice, poursuivre, actionner.

suede, *n*, suède, daim, *m*.

suet, *n*, graisse de rognon de bœuf, de mouton, *f*.

suffer, *v.t*, supporter; subir; éprouver; tolérer; (*v.i.*) souffrir; pâtir. **~able†**, *a*, supportable. **~ance**, *n*, souffrance; tolérance, *f*. **~er**, *n*, victime, *f*; patient, e. **~ing**, *n*, souffrance, *f*. **~ing**, *p.a*, souffrant.

suffice, *v.i*, suffire. **~ it to say that**, suffit que. **sufficiency**, *n*, suffisance; aisance, *f*. **sufficient†**, *a*, suffisant.

suffix, *n*, suffixe, *m*. **~ed**, *p.a*, suffixe.

suffocate, *v.t*, suffoquer; asphyxier. **suffocation**, *n*, suffocation; asphyxie, *f*.

suffragan, *a. & n*, suffragant, *a.m. & m*.

suffrage, *n*, suffrage, *m*. **suffragette**, *n*, suffragette, *f*.

suffuse, *v.t*, se répandre sur; baigner. **suffusion**, *n*, suffusion, *f*.

sugar, *n*, sucre, *m*. **~ almond**, dragée, *f*. **~ bowl**, sucrier, bol à sucre, *m*. **~ beet**, betterave à s., *f*. **~ candy**, sucre candi, *m*. **~ cane**, canne à s., *f*. **~ refinery**, sucrerie, *f*. **~ sifter**, saupoudroir à sucre, *m*. **~ tongs**, pinces à s., *f.pl*. **granulated ~**, sucre semoule, *m*. **lump ~**, s. en morceaux, *m*. **maple ~**, s. d'érable, *m*. ¶ *v.t*, sucrer. **~y**, *a*, sucré; saccharin.

suggest, *v.t*, suggérer, dicter. **~ion**, *n*, suggestion, *f*. **~ive**, *a*, suggestif.

suicide, *n*, suicide, *m*; (*pers.*) suicidé, *m*. **to commit ~**, se suicider.

suit, *n*, procès civil; complet; habit; costume, (*slang*) costard, *m*; (*cards*) couleur, *f*. **~case**, valise, *m*. **~ of armor**, armure complète, *f*. **~ of clothes**, complet. **~ to measure**, complet sur mesure. ¶ *v.t*, adapter; approprier; assortir; aller à; convenir à; accommoder; (*v.i.*) cadrer; convenir. **~ability**, *n*, convenance; adaptation, *f*. **~able†**, *a. & ~ed*, *p.p*, convenable, sortable, adapté, approprié, assortissant; propre.

suite, *n*, suite, *f*, train, *m*; enfilade, *f*. **~ [of furniture]**, ameublement; mobilier, *m*. **~ [of rooms]**, appartement, *m*, chambres en enfilade, *f.pl*.

suitor, *n*, (*law*) plaideur; (*wooer*) aspirant, prétendant, soupirant, poursuivant, *m*.

sulfate, *n*, sulfate, *m*. **sulfide**, *n*, sulfure, *m*. **sulfite**, *n*, sulfite, *m*. **~ pulp**, pâte au bisulfite, *f*. **sulfur**, *n*, soufre, *m*. **~ bath**, bain sulfureux, *m*. **~ mine**, soufrière, *f*.

sulk, *v.i*, bouder; (*slang*) faire la gueule. **~y**, *a*, boudeur.

sullen, *a*, renfrogné, maussade, morose. **~ness**, *n*, maussaderie, *f*.

sully, *v.t*, souiller, tacher, ternir.

sultan, *n*, sultan, *m*. **sultana**, *n*, sultane, *f*.

sultry, *a*, étouffant, lourd, caniculaire.

sum, *n*, somme, *f*; calcul; comble,

m. ~ *total*, somme totale, *f*, montant global, *m.* ~ **up**, résumer; résumer les débats. **summarize**, *v.t*, résumer. **summary†**, *a*, sommaire. ¶ *n*, sommaire, résumé, *m.*

summer, *n*, été, *m.* ~ *house*, pavillon [de jardin], kiosque de j., *m.* ~ *lightning*, éclair[s] de chaleur, *m.*[pl.]. ~ *resort*, station estivale, *f.* ~ *vacation*, grandes vacances, *f.pl. Indian* ~, été de la Saint-Martin, *m.* ¶ *v.i*, passer l'été; (*v.t.*) estiver.

summing up, résumé des débats, *m.*

summit, *n*, sommet, *m*, cime, *f*, faîte, comble, *m.*

summon, *v.t*, citer, assigner; sommer; convoquer. ~ *back* & ~ *up*, rappeler. **summons**, *n*, sommation; citation, *f.* ¶ *v.t*, citer.

sump, *n*, puisard, *m.*

sumptuous†, *a*, somptueux; (*fare*) pantagruélique. ~**ness**, *n*, somptuosité, *f*, luxe, *m.*

sun, *n*, soleil, *m.* ~**bath**, bain de s., *m.* ~**bathing**, bains de s., *m.pl.* ~**beam**, rayon de s., *m.* ~**burn**, hâle, *m. to get* ~**burnt**, se hâler. ~**dial**, cadran solaire, *m.* ~**flower**, soleil, tournesol, *m.* ~**light**, lumière du s., *f.* ~**lit**, ensoleillé. ~**rise**, lever du s., *m.* ~**set**, coucher du s., s. couchant, *m. at* ~**set** *or at* ~**down**, au coucher du s. ~**shine**, soleil, *m.* ~**shiny day**, jour de s., *m.* ~**spot**, tache du s., t. solaire, macule, *f.* ~**stroke**, insolation, *f*, coup de s., *m.* ¶ *v.t*, ensoleiller. ~ *oneself*, se chauffer au soleil, lézarder.

Sunday, *n*, dimanche, *m. to put on one's* ~ *best*, s'endimancher.

sunder, *v.t*, séparer.

sundries, *n.pl*, [articles] divers, *m.pl*, **sundry**, *a*, divers.

sunken, *p.a*, creux; cave; noyé.

sunless, *a*, sans soleil. **sunny**, *a*, ensoleillé.

sup, *v.i*, souper.

superabundant†, *a*, surabondant.

superannuated, *p.p*, suranné.

superb†, *a*, superbe.

supercargo, *n*, subrécargue, *m.*

supercilious†, *a*, dédaigneux, hautain.

superficial†, *a*, superficiel. **superficies**, *n*, superficie, *f.*

superfine, *a*, superfin, surfin.

superfluity, *n*, superfluité, *f*, superflu, embarras, *m.* **superfluous**, *a*, superflu.

superheat, *v.t*, surchauffer.

superhuman, *a*, surhumain.

superimpose, *v.t*, superposer.

superintend, *v.t*, surveiller; présider à. ~**ence**, *n*, surveillance, *f.* ~**ent**, *n*, surveillant, e; surintendant, e; chef; (*police*) commissaire; (*restaurant*) maître d'hôtel, *m.*

superior†, *a.* & *n*, supérieur, e. ~**ity**, *n*, supériorité, *f.*

superlative†, *a*, souverain; (*Gram.*) superlatif. ¶ *n*, superlatif, *m.*

superman, *n*, surhomme, *m.*

supermarket, *n*, supermarché, (*outsized*) hypermarché, *m.*

supernatural†, *a.* & *n*, surnaturel, *a.* & *m.*

supernumerary, *a.* & *n*, surnuméraire, *a.* & *m.* ¶ (*Theat.*) *n*, figurant, e, comparse, *m.f.*

superscript, *n*, indice supérieur, *m.*

superscription, *n*, suscription, *f.*

supersede, *v.t*, remplacer.

supersonic, *a*, supersonique.

superstition, *n*, superstition, *f.* **superstitious†**, *a*, superstitieux.

superstructure, *n*, superstructure, *f.*

supervene, *v.i*, survenir.

supervise, *v.t*, surveiller, contrôler. **supervision**, *n*, surveillance, *f*, contrôle, *m.* **supervisor**, *n*, surveillant, e, contrôleur, *m.*

supine, *a*, couché sur le dos; indolent; léthargique.

supper, *n*, souper, *m. to have* ~, souper. ~ *time*, heure du s., *f.* ~*less*, *a*, sans s.

supplant, *v.t*, supplanter.

supple, *a*, souple. *to make* ~, assouplir.

supplement, *n*, supplément, *m.* ¶ *v.t*, augmenter. ~**ary**, *a*, supplémentaire.

suppleness, *n*, souplesse, *f.*

suppliant, *a.* & *n*, suppliant, e. **supplicate**, *v.t*, supplier. **supplication**, *n*, supplication, *f.*

supplier, *n*, fournisseur, euse. **supply**, *n*, provision, fourniture, *f*, approvisionnement, *m*; (*pl, food*) vivres, *m.pl.* ~ & *demand*, l'offre & la demande. ¶ *v.t*, fournir, approvisionner; pourvoir; assortir de; alimenter; suppléer.

support, *n*, support; soutien; appui; entretien, *m*. ¶ *v.t*, supporter; soutenir; appuyer; entretenir. **~er**, *n*, partisan, tenant, *m*, adhérent, e.

suppose, *v.t*, supposer; présumer. *supposing* [*that*], supposé que. **supposition**, *n*, supposition, *f*. **supposititious**, *a*, supposé.

suppository, *n*, supositoire, *m*.

suppress, *v.t*, supprimer. **~ed** *rage*, rage rentrée, *f*. **~ion**, *n*, suppression, *f*.

suppurate, *v.i*, suppurer.

supremacy, *n*, suprématie, *f*. **supreme†**, *a*, suprême; souverain.

surcharge, *v.t*, surcharger, surtaxer.

sure†, *a*, sûr; certain; assuré, immanquable. *to make ~ of*, s'assurer de. **~ness**, *n*, sûreté, *f*. **~ty**, *n*, sûreté; caution, *f*.

surf, *n*, ressac, *m*, brisants, *m.pl*. **~board**, aquaplane, *m*. *~ boat*, pirogue de barre, *f*. *~ fishing*, pêche de plage, *f*. *~riding*, sport de l'aquaplane, *m*.

surface, *n*, surface; superficie, *f*. *~ plate*, marbre, *m*. ¶ *v.t*, aplanir; (*Naut.*) remonter à la surface.

surfeit, *n*, satiété, *f*. ¶ *v.t*, rassasier; blaser.

surge, *n*, houle, *f*. ¶ *v.i*, refluer, ondoyer.

surgeon, *n*, chirurgien; médecin, *m*. **surgery**, *n*, chirurgie; médecine, *f*; cabinet de consultation, *m*, clinique, *f*. **surgical**, *a*, chirurgical. *~ case* (*pers.*), opéré, e.

surging, *p.a*, houleux.

surly, *a*, rébarbatif, bourru, maussade.

surmise, *n*, conjecture, supposition, *f*. ¶ *v.t*, soupçonner.

surmount, *v.t*, surmonter.

surname, *n*, nom [de famille] *m*.

surpass, *v.t*, surpasser. **~ing**, *a*, supérieur; suprême.

surplice, *n*, surplis, *m*.

surplus, *n*, surplus, excédent, *m*.

surprise, *n*, surprise, *f*; étonnement, *m*. *~ attack*, attaque faite à l'improviste, *f*, coup de main, *m*. ¶ *v.t*, surprendre; étonner. **surprising**, *a*, surprenant, étonnant. **~ly**, *ad*, étonnamment.

surrender, *n*, reddition, *f*; abandon; (*Insce.*) rachat, *m*. ¶ *v.t*, rendre; livrer; abandonner, ab-

diquer, céder; (*insurance policy*) racheter; (*v.i.*) se rendre.

surreptitious†, *a*, subreptice.

surrogate, *n*, substitut, *m*.

surround, *v.t*, entourer, enceindre, encadrer. ¶ *n*, pourtour, *m*. **~ing**, *p.a*, environnant; ambiant. **~ings**, *n.pl*, alentours, *m.pl*.

surtax, *n*, surtaxe, *f*; impôt général (*ou* global) sur le revenu, *m*. ¶ *v.t*, surtaxer.

survey, *n*, étude; visite; expertise, *f*; levé [de plans]; arpentage; cadastre; métrage, *m*. ¶ *v.t*, étudier; expertiser; (*land*) arpenter; cadastrer; métrer. **~or**, *n*, inspecteur; expert; (*land*) arpenteur, géomètre; (*quantity*) métreur; (*roads*) [agent] voyer, *m*.

survival, *n*, survivance, survie, *f*. *~ of the fittest*, survivance du plus apte. **survive**, *v.t*, survivre à; (*v.i.*) se survivre. **survivor**, *n*, survivant, e; rescapé, e. **~ship**, *n*, survie, *f*.

susceptible, *a*, susceptible, sensible.

suspect, *a*, suspect, interlope. ¶ *n*, suspect, *m*. ¶ *v.t*, suspecter; se douter de.

suspend, *v.t*, suspendre. **~er**, *n*, bretelle, *f*. **suspense**, *n*, incertitude, *f*. *in ~*, en suspens, en souffrance. **suspension**, *n*, suspension, *f*. *~ bridge*, pont suspendu, *m*.

suspicion, *n*, soupçon, *m*; (*law*) suspicion, *f*. **suspicious†**, *a*, soupçonneux; suspect; louche.

sustain, *v.t*, soutenir; sustenter; éprouver. **~ing**, *p.a*, (*power*) soutenant; (*food*) qui soutient. **sustenance**, *n*, subsistance, nourriture, *f*.

sutler, *n*, vivandier, ère.

suture, *n*, suture, *f*.

suzerain, *n*, suzerain, e. **~ty**, *n*, suzeraineté, *f*.

swab, *n*, torchon; (*Naut.*) faubert; (*Med.*) écouvillon, *m*.

swaddling clothes (*lit. & fig.*), langes, *m.pl*.

swage, *n*, étampe, *f*. ¶ *v.t*, étamper.

swagger, *v.i*, se rengorger, se carrer; faire le fanfaron. **~er**, *n*, fanfaron, bravache, *m*.

swain, *n*, galant, *m*.

swallow, *n*, hirondelle, *f*; gorgée, *f*; (*river*) perte, *f*. *~tail* (coat), queue-de-morue, queue-de-pie, *f*.

¶ *v.t*, avaler; engloutir; ingurgiter.

swamp, *n*, marais, marécage, *m*, grenouillère, *f*. ¶ *v.t*, remplir d'eau, submerger; engloutir, noyer. *be* ~*ed* (*work*), débordé de travail. ~*y*, *a*, marécageux.

swan, *n*, cygne, *m*. ~'s-*down*, duvet de cygne; (*cloth*) molleton, *m*. ~ *song*, chant du cygne, *m*.

sward, *n*, [tapis de] gazon, *m*, herbette, *f*.

swarm, *n*, (*bees*) essaim; (*multitude*) essaim, *m*, nuée, milliasse, potée, *f*. ¶ *v.i*, (*bees*) essaimer; pulluler, fourmiller, foisonner.

swarthy, *a*, noir; noiraud, basané.

swash, *v.i*, clapoter.

swastika, *n*, svastika, *m*.

swat (*fly*) *v.t*, tuer.

swath, *n*, javelle, *f*; (*path cut*) andain, *m*.

sway, *n*, balancement; empire, *m*; domination, puissance, *f*. ¶ *v.t*, balancer; influencer.

swear, *v.i. & t. ir*, jurer; prêter serment; (*witness*) assermenter. ~ *at*, maudire.

sweat, *n*, sueur; suée, *f*. ¶ *v.i. & t*, suer; ressuer; exploiter. ~ *profusely*, suer à grosses gouttes. ~*y*, *a*, suant.

sweater, *n*, pull-over, pull, chandail, *m*.

Swede, *n*. Suédois, e. s~, *n*, navet de Suède, rutabaga, *m*. **Sweden,** *n*, la Suède. **Swedish,** *a*, suédois. ¶ *n*, le suédois.

sweep, *n*, coup de balai; coup, mouvement; (*pers.*) ramoneur, *m*; boucle, courbe; étendue, *f*. ¶ *v.t. & i. ir*, balayer; (*chimney*) ramoner; (*Naut.*) draguer. ~ *away*, enlever. ~ *the board*, raffler le tout. ~*er*, *n*, balayeur, euse; (*Mach.*) balayeuse, *f*. ~*ing gesture*, geste large, *m*. ~*ings*, *n.pl*, balayures, *f.pl*. ~**stake**[s], *n*, sweepstake, *m*, loterie, *f*.

sweet†, *a*, doux; sucré; (*wine*) liquoreux; suave; charmant; gentil, mignon. ~*bread*, ris de veau, *m*. ~*briar*, églantine odorante, *f*; (*bush*) églantier odorant, *m*. ~*heart*, amoureux, euse, *f*. ~ *herbs*, herbes fines, *f.pl*. ~*meat*, sucrerie, *f*, bonbon, *m*. ~ *pea*, pois de senteur, *m*. ~ *potato*, patate, *f*. ~[-*scented*], odorant, odoriférant. *to have a* ~ *tooth,*

aimer les sucreries. ~-*william*, œillet de poète, *m*. **the** ~ (*opp. the bitter*), le doux. ~**en**, *v.t*, sucrer; adoucir. ~*ish*, *a*, douceâtre. ~*ness*, *n*, douceur; suavité, *f*; charme, *m*.

sweet-talk, *v.i. & t*, baratiner. ¶ *n*, baratin, *m*.

swell, *n*, bombement; renflement, *m*; (*sea*) houle, *f*; (*pers.*) élégant, e. ¶ *a*, chic. ¶ *v.i. & i. ir*, enfler; (*s'e.*) gonfler; se g.; renfler; grossir; dilater; bouffer, gondoler. **swelling**, *n*, enflure, grosseur, fluxion, *f*; gonflement; renflement, *m*.

swelter, *v.i*, étouffer de chaleur.

swerve, *n*, crochet, *m*, embardée, *f*. ¶ *v.i*, faire une embardée; s'écarter, se départir.

swift†, *a*, rapide, vite. ~-*footed*, au pied léger. ¶ *n*, martinet, *m*. ~*ness*, *n*, rapidité, célérité, vélocité, *f*.

swig, *v.t*, lamper, sabler.

swill, *v.t*, laver à grande eau, lessiver; (*drink*) siffler; (*v.i.*) (*food & drink*) boustifailler.

swim, *n*, tour de nage, *m. in the* ~, dans le mouvement. ¶ *v.i. & t. ir*, nager. ~ *across*, passer à la nage. ~ *under water*, nager entre deux eaux. **swimming**, *n*, natation, *f*. ~ *pool*, piscine, *f*. *swimsuit*, maillot de bain, *m*.

swindle, *n*, escroquerie, *f*. ¶ *v.t*, escroquer. **swindler**, *n*, escroc, filou, *m*.

swine, *n*, pourceau, porc, cochon, *m*. ~*herd*, porcher, ère.

swing, *n*, oscillation, *f*, balancement; branle, *m*; (*playground*) balançoire, escarpolette, *f*. *in full* ~, en pleine activité. ~ *bridge*, pont tournant, *m*. ~ *door*, porte va-et-vient, *f*. ¶ *v.t. & i. ir*, balancer; se b.; osciller; branler; basculer; tourner.

swingletree, *n*, volée, *f*.

swirl, *n*, tourbillon; remous, *m*. ¶ *v.i*, tourbillonner, tournoyer.

swish, *n*, sifflement; frou-frou, *m*. ¶ *v.t*, cingler; (*whip*) faire siffler; susurrer; remuer.

Swiss, *a*, suisse. ~ *guard*, suisse, *m*. ¶ *n*, Suisse, *m*, Suissesse, *f*.

switch, *n*, badine, houssine; (*Rly.*) aiguille, *f*; (*Elec.*) interrupteur, *m*. ~*back*, montagnes russes, *f.pl*. ~ *board*, tableau de distribution;

(*Tele.*) standard, *m.* ¶ *v.t,* (*whip*) houssiner. ~ *off,* couper, mettre hors circuit; (*light*) éteindre. ~ *on,* mettre en circuit; (*light*) allumer.

Switzerland, *n,* la Suisse.

swivel, *n,* émerillon; tourniquet, *m.* ¶ *v.i,* pivoter, tourner.

swollen glands, des glandes au cou, *f.pl.*

swoon, *n,* évanouissement, *m,* défaillance, *f.* ¶ *v.i,* s'évanouir, [se] pâmer.

swoop down on, fondre sur.

sword, *n,* épée, *f;* sabre; (*Poet.*) glaive, *m;* (*in fun*) flamberge, *f.* ~ *belt,* ceinturon, *m.* ~*fish,* espadon, *m.* ~ *rattler,* ferrailleur, *m.* **swordsman,** *n,* lame, *f.* **swordsmanship,** *n,* escrime, *f.*

Sybarite, *n,* sybarite, *m.*

sycamore, *n,* sycomore, *m.*

sycophant, *n,* sycophante, *m.*

syllabize, *v.t,* scander. **syllable,** *n,* syllabe, *f.*

syllabus, *n,* programme; (*Eccl.*) syllabus, *m.*

syllogism, *n,* syllogisme, *m.*

sylph, *n,* sylphe, *m,* sylphide, *f.*

sylvan, *a,* champêtre, bocager.

symbol, *n,* symbole, *m.* ~**ic(al),** *a,* symbolique. ~**ize,** *v.t,* symboliser.

symmetric(al)†, *a,* symétrique. **symmetry,** *n,* symétrie, *f.*

sympathetic, *a,* sympathique. **sympathize,** *v.i,* sympathiser, compatir. **sympathy,** *n,* sympathie, *f.*

symphony, *n,* symphonie, *f.*

symptom, *n,* symptôme, *m.* ~**atic,** *a,* symptomatique.

synagogue, *n,* synagogue, *f.*

synchronize, *v.t,* synchroniser.

synchronous, *a,* synchrone.

syncopate, *v.t,* syncoper. **syncopation & syncope,** *n,* syncope, *f.*

syndicate, *n,* syndicat, *m.* ¶ *v.t,* syndiquer.

synod, *n,* synode, *m.* ~**ic(al),** *a,* synodique.

synonym, *n.* & **synonymous,** *a,* synonyme, *m.* & *a.*

synopsis, *n,* argument, sommaire, *m.*

syntax, *n,* syntaxe, *f.*

synthesis, *n,* synthèse, *f.* **synthetic(al)†,** *a,* synthétique.

syphilis, *n,* vérole, *m.*

Syria, *n,* la Syrie, *f.* **Syrian,** *a,* syrien. ¶ *n,* Syrien, ne.

syringe, *n,* seringue, *f.* ¶ *v.t,* seringuer.

syrup, *n,* sirop, *m.* ~**y,** *a,* sirupeux.

system, *n,* système; régime; réseau, *m. communications* ~, réseau de transmissions, *m.* (*computers*) *dedicated* ~, ensemble spécialisé, *m.* ~**atic†,** *a,* systématique. ~**atize,** *v.t,* systématiser.

T

T, *n,* **T,** té, *m.* ~ *square,* té [à dessin] *m. to a* ~, tout craché.

tab, *n,* étiquette, *f;* (*index*) onglet, *m. to keep* ~*s on,* ne pas perdre de vue.

tabby cat, chat moucheté, chat tigré, *m.*

tabernacle, *n,* tabernacle, *m.*

table, *n,* table; tablette, *f;* bureau; plateau; tableau; plan; décompte, *m. card* ~, table à jeu, *f.* ~ *cloth,* nappe [de t.] *f.* ~ *companion,* convive, *m,f.* ~ *napkin,* serviette de t., *f.* ~ *salt,* sel fin, *m.* ~*spoon,* cuiller à bouche, c. à soupe, *f.* ~*spoonful,* cuillerée à bouche, *f.* ~ *talk,* propos de t., *m.pl.* ¶ *v.t,* déposer sur le bureau. **tableau,** *n.* & *i,* tableau, *m.* & *i.* **tablet,** *n,* table, tablette, plaque, *f;* pain, *m.*

taboo, *n,* tabou, *m. he, it, is* ~, il est tabou. ¶ *v.t,* déclarer tabou.

tabular, *a,* en forme de tableau.

tabulate, *v.t,* dresser en forme de tableau.

tachometer, *n,* tachymètre, compte-tours, *m.*

tacit†, *a,* tacite. **taciturn,** *a,* taciturne. ~**ity,** *n,* taciturnité, *f.*

tack, *n,* (*s.* & *pl.*) broquette, (*pl.*) semence; (*Naut.*) bordée, *f,* bord, *m;* (*of sail*) amure, *f.* ¶ *v.t,* clouer avec de la broquette, de la semence; (*Need.*) bâtir; (*fig.*) coudre; (*v.i.*) virer de bord, louvoyer.

tackle, *n,* engin, *m.* oft. *pl;* appareil, *m.* oft. *pl;* harnais, *m;* agrès, *m.pl;* treuil; palan; (*Foot.*) arrêt, *m.* ~ *block,* moufle, *f.* or *m. fishing* ~, articles de pêche, *m. pl.* ¶ *v.t,* s'attaquer à; (*Foot.*) plaquer; (*pers., fig.*) entreprendre.

tacky, *a*, collant, visqueux.

tact, *n*, tact, doigté, savoir-faire, *m*, ménagements, *m.pl*. ~**ful**, *a*, [plein] de tact. ~**less**, *a*, dépourvu de tact, malhabile.

tactical, *a*, tactique. **tactician**, *n*, tacticien, manœuvrier, *m*. **tactics**, *n.pl*, tactique, *f*.

tactile, *a*, tactile.

tadpole, *n*, têtard, *m*.

taffeta, *n*, taffetas, *m*.

taffrail, *n*, couronnement, *m*.

tag, *n*, ferret, *m*; (*stock phrase*) cliché, *m*; (*label*) étiquette, *f*; [jeu du] chat, *m*. ¶ *v.t*, (*label*) marquer, attacher une fiche; ferrer.

Tagus (the), le Tage.

Tahiti, *n*, Taïti, Tahiti, *m*.

tail, *n*, queue, *f*; arrière; aval; derrière; (*coat*) pan, *m*, basque; (*coin*) pile; (*book page*) queue, tranche inférieure, *f*. ~ *coat* or **tails**, (*evening*) queue-de-morue, queue-de-pie, (*morning*) jaquette, *f*. ~**piece**, cul-de-lampe, *m*. ~ **spin**, vrille, *f*. ~ **stock** (*lathe*), contre-pointe, *f*.

tailor, *n*, tailleur, *m*. ~-**made** or ~**ed**, [fait par] tailleur. ~**ing**, *n*, métier de tailleur, *m*.

taint, *n*, infection; tache, tare, *f*. ¶ *v.t*, corrompre, infecter; souiller. ~**ed** (*meat*) *p.a*, gâté, faisandé.

take, *v.t.ir*, prendre; porter; conduire, mener; faire; mettre; relever; tirer; tenir; supposer; falloir; (*v.i.*) prendre. ~ *away*, emmener; ôter; [r]emporter. ~ *back*, ramener; reprendre. ~ *cover*, se garer. ~ *down*, descendre; décrocher; démonter. ~ *down* [*in shorthand*], sténographier. ~ *in*, prendre; recevoir; faire; embrasser; attraper. ~ *off*, ôter, rabattre; (*a pers.*) contrefaire; (*Avn.*) décoller, prendre son vol. ~ *on* (*workers*), embaucher. ~ *out*, ôter; retirer; arracher; sortir; (*Insce policy*) contracter. ~ *over*, prendre. ~ *shape*, se dessiner. ~ *to*, s'appliquer à; s'adonner à, mordre à. ~ *to pieces*, désassembler, démonter. ~ *to task*, prendre à partie, morigéner. ~ *up*, relever; lever; monter; s'occuper de; occuper, tenir; prendre; (*option*) lever, consolider. ~ *your seats!* (in carriage), en voiture! **taker**, *n*, preneur, euse. **taking**, *a*,

séduisant, avenant. ¶ *n*, prise, *f*; (*pl.*) recette, *f. oft. pl*, produit, *m*. ~ *off* (*Avn.*), décollage, envol, *m*.

talc, *n*, talc, *m*.

tale, *n*, conte, *m*, histoire, nouvelle, *f*. ~-*bearer*, rapporteur, euse. *tall* ~, canular, *m*.

talent, *n*, talent, *m*. ~**ed**, *a*, de talent.

talisman, *n*, talisman, *m*.

talk, *n*, conversation, causerie, *f*, entretien; discours, *m*; propos, *m.pl*; bavardage, *m*. ¶ *v.i. & t*, parler; causer; converser; bavarder. ~ *into*, persuader de. ~ *out of*, dissuader de. ~**ative**, *a*, parlant, causeur, loquace. ~**er**, *n*, parleur, euse; causeur, euse; bavard, e. ~**ing**, *a*, parlant.

tall, *a*, grand; haut. ~**ness**, *n*, (*pers.*) haute taille; (*steeple*) hauteur, *f*. *how ~ are you?* quelle taille avez-vous?

tallow, *n*, suif, *m*. ¶ *v.t*, suifer.

tally, *n*, (*stick*) taille; marque, *f*; (*check*) pointage, *m*; (*label*) étiquette, *f*. ¶ *v.i*, concorder, correspondre, cadrer, se rapporter. ~-**ho**, *i*, taïaut!

talon, *n*, serre, *f*; (*counterfoil*) talon, *m*.

talus, *n*, talus, *m*.

tamarind, *n*, tamarin, *m*.

tambour, *n*, tambour, métier [à broder] *m*. ~**ine**, *n*, tambour de basque, *m*.

tame, *a*, apprivoisé; (*fig.*) anodin. ¶ *v.t*, apprivoiser, dompter. **tamer**, *n*, dompteur, euse.

tam-o'-shanter, *n*, béret écossais, *m*.

tamp, *v.t*, bourrer; damer, pilonner.

tamper with, falsifier; (*witness*) suborner.

tampion, *n*, tampon, *m*.

tan, *n*, tan; (*sunburn*) hâle, *m*. ¶ *v.t*, tanner; brunir, hâler, basaner. ¶ *a*, jaune-brun, hâlé.

tandem, *n*, tandem, *m*. ¶ *a. & ad*, en tandem.

tang, *n*, goût; montant, *m*; salure; (*shank*) queue, *f*. *there is a ~ in the air*, l'air est vif.

tangent, *n*, tangente, *f*. ~[**ial**], *a*, tangent.

tangerine, *n*, mandarine, *f*.

tangible, *a*, tangible, palpable.

Tangier, *n*, Tanger, *m*.

tangle, *n*, enchevêtrement, *m*. ¶ *v.t*, enchevêtrer, emmêler.

tango, *n*, tango, *m*.

tank, *n*, réservoir, *m*, citerne; bâche; cuve; caisse à eau, soute, *f*; (*Mil.*) char d'assaut, tank, *m*. *gasoline* ~, réservoir à essence, *m*. tanker, *n*, bateau-citerne, *m*, (*oil*) pétrolier, *m*.

tankard, *n*, pot (*d'étain*) *m*.

tanner, *n*, tanneur, *m*. ~**y,** *n*, tannerie, *f*. **tannin,** *n*, tanin, tannin, *m*.

tantalize, *v.t*, mettre au supplice. **tantalum,** *n*, tantale, *m*.

tantamount to (to be), équivaloir à.

tantrums, *n.pl*, nerfs, *m.pl*, bourrasques, *f.pl*.

tap, *n*, tape, *f*, coup; (*water*) robinet; (*screw*) taraud, *m*. ~ *dance,* claquettes, *f.pl*. ~*root,* racine pivotante, *f*, pivot, *m*. ¶ *v.t. & i,* taper; toucher; frapper; (*screw*) tarauder; (*cask*) mettre en perce; (*tree*) saigner; (*Surg.*) faire une ponction à.

tape, *n*, ruban, (*adhesive*) scotch, *m*; tresse; bande, *f. insulating* ~, chatterton, *m. punched* ~, ruban perforé, *m. red* ~, bolduc, *m*. ~ *measure,* mesure à ruban, *f*; mètre à r.; centimètre, *m*; roulette, *f*. ~ *recorder,* magnétophone, *m*. ~*worm,* ver solitaire, ténia, *m*.

taper, *n*, bougie filée; (*coiled*) bougie de poche, *f*, pain de bougie, rat de cave; (*church*) cierge; cône, *m*. ¶ *v.t*, diminuer, fuseler; (*v.i.*) aller en diminuant; se terminer en pointe. ~[**ing**] *a*, conique, fuselé.

tapestry, *n. & ~ work,* tapisserie, *f*.

tapioca, *n*, tapioca, *m*.

tapir, *n*, tapir, *m*.

tar, *n*, goudron; brai; (*pers.*) loup de mer, *m*. ~*paper,* carton goudronné, *m*. ¶ *v.t*, goudronner. ~ *& feather,* emplumer.

tarantella, *n*, tarentelle, *f*. **tarantula,** *n*, tarentule, *f*.

tardy†, *a*, tardif.

tare, *n*, vesce; (*pl, fig.*) ivraie; (*Com.*) tare, *f*.

target, *n*, cible, *f*, but *m*. ~ *practice,* tir à la cible, *m*.

tariff, *n*, tarif, *m*. ¶ *v.t*, tarifer.

tarnish, *v.t*, ternir; (*v.i.*) se ternir.

tarpaulin, *n*, bâche goudronnée, *f*, prélart, *m*.

tarragon, *n*, estragon, *m*.

Tarragona, *n*, Tarragone, *f*.

tarry, *v.i*, séjourner; tarder; attendre.

tarsus, *n*, tarse, *m*.

tart†, *a*, aigre, âcre, acide. ¶ *n*, (*open*) tarte; (*covered*) tourte; (*woman*) grue, *f*.

tartan, *n*, tartan, *m*.

tartar, *n*, tartre, *m*. ~**ic,** *a*, tartrique.

tartness, *n*, aigreur, âcreté, acidité, *f*.

task, *n*, tâche; besogne, *f*; devoir, *m. to take to* ~, prendre à partie, morigéner. ¶ *v.t*, mettre à l'épreuve; fatiguer.

tassel, *n*, gland, *m*, houppe, *f*.

taste, *n*, goût; gré; échantillon, *m*. ¶ *v.t. & i,* goûter; g. de; (*tea, wine*) déguster. ~ *of,* sentir le, la, les. ~**ful,** *a*, de bon goût. ~**less,** *a*, sans goût, fade, insipide. **taster,** *n*, dégustateur, *m*; (*device*) sonde, *f*. **tasting,** *n*, gustation; dégustation, *f*. **tasty,** *a*, savoureux.

tatter, *n*, haillon, lambeau, *m*. ~**ed,** *a*, déguenillé; en lambeaux.

tatting, *n*, frivolité, *f*.

tattle, *n*, babil[lage] *m*. ¶ *v.i*, babiller. **tattler,** *n. & tattling,** *a*, babillard, e.

tattoo, *n*, tatouage; *m*; (*Mil.*) retraite, *f*. ¶ *v.t*, tatouer; (*v.i.*) tambouriner.

taunt, *n*, sarcasme, *m*. ¶ *v.t*, houspiller, molester. ~ *with,* reprocher à.

taut, *a*, raide, tendu. ~**en,** *v.t*, raidir.

tautologic(al), *a*, tautologique. **tautology,** *n*, tautologie, *f*.

tavern, *n*, taverne, *f*, cabaret, *m*. ~ *with gardens & dance hall,* guinguette, *f*.

tawdriness, *n*, faux éclat, *m*. **tawdry,** *a*, qui a un faux éclat. ~ *finery,* oripeaux, *m.pl*.

tawny, *a*, fauve; basané. ~ *owl,* chat-huant, *m*, hulotte, *f*.

tax, *n*, impôt, *m*, taxe, contribution, imposition, *f. excise* ~, droit de régie, *m. income* ~, impôt sur le revenu, *m*. ~ *collector,* percepteur, collecteur d'impôts, *m*. ~ *dodger,* fraudeur (euse) des droits du fisc. ~ *free,* net d'impôts. ~*payer,* contribuable, *m,f*. ¶ *v.t*, imposer; taxer.

~**able**, *a*, imposable. ~**ation**, *n*, taxation, *f*, impôts, *m.pl.*

taxi (*Avn.*) *v.i*, rouler [sur le sol]. ~ [*cab*], taxi, *m*. ~ *driver*, chauffeur de taxi, conducteur de taxi, *m*. ~*meter*, compteur, *m*.

taxidermist, *n*, naturaliste [fourreur] *m*, empailleur, euse. **taxidermy**, *n*, empaillage, empaillement, *m*.

tea, *n*, thé, *m*; infusion, tisane, *f*. ~ *cosy*, couvre-théière, *m*. ~ *cup*, tasse à thé, *f*. ~ *party*, thé, *m*. ~*pot*, théière, *f*. ~, *roll, & butter*, thé complet. ~ *room(s)*, ~ *shop*, salon de thé, *m*. pâtisserie, *f*. ~ *rose*, rose thé, *f*. ~*spoon*, cuiller à thé, *f*. ~ *time*, l'heure du thé, *f*.

teach, *v.t. & i. ir*, enseigner, instruire; apprendre; professer; montrer à; (*bird*) seriner. ~ *someone a lesson*, donner une leçon à quelqu'un. ~ *someone manners*, donner à quelqu'un une leçon de politesse. ~**er**, *n*, instituteur, trice; professeur; précepteur, *m*; maître, esse. ~**ing**, *n*, enseignement, *m*; instruction, *f*.

teak, *n*, teck, tek, *m*.

teal, *n*, sarcelle, *f*.

team, *n*, attelage, *m*; équipe, *f*. ~ *spirit*, esprit de corps, *m*. ~**work**, travail d'équipe, *m*.

tear, *n*, déchirure, *f*; accroc, *m*. ¶ *v.t.ir*, déchirer; arracher. ~ *one another to pieces*, s'entre-déchirer.

tear, *n*, larme, *f*, pleur, *m*. ~ *gas*, gaz lacrymogène, *m*. ~**ful**, *a*, éploré, larmoyant.

tease, *v.t*, taquiner, lutiner; tourmenter. ¶ (*pers.*) *n*, taquin, e.

teaser, *n*, (*pers.*) taquin, e; problème, casse-tête, *m*. **teasing**, *n*, taquinerie, *f*.

teat, *n*, bout du sein, mamelon, tétin, *m*.

technical†, *a*, technique; d'ordre t. ~ *offense*, quasi-délit, *m*. ~ *school*, école pratique, *f*. **technique**, *n*, technique, *f*, faire, mécanisme, *m*. **technocracy**, *n*, technocratie, *f*. **technology**, *n*, technologie, *f*.

Teddy bear, ours [martin], o. de peluche, *m*.

tedious†, *a*, ennuyeux, fastidieux, fatigant. ~**ness** & **tedium**, *n*, ennui, *m*.

tee, *n*, té, T; (golf) dé, *m. to a* ~, tout craché. ¶ (*golf*) *v.t*, surélever. ~*ing ground* (*golf*), tertre de départ, *m*.

teem with, fourmiller de, regorger de.

teenager, *n*, adolescent, e.

teethe, *v.i*, faire ses dents. **teething**, *n*, dentition, *f*.

teetotal, *a*, antialcoolique. ~**ism**, *n*, antialcoolisme, *m*. **teetotaller**, *n*, abstinent, *n*.

teetotum, *n*, toton, *m*.

tegument, *n*, tégument, *m*.

telegram, *n*, télégramme, *m*, dépêche, *f*. **telegraph**, *n*, télégraphe, *m*. ~ *office*, [bureau du] télégraphe, *m*. ¶ *v.t. & i*, télégraphier. ~**ese**, *n*, style télégraphique, *m*. ~**ic†**, *a*, télégraphique. ~**y**, *n*, télégraphie, *f*.

telepathy, *n*, télépathie, *f*.

telephone, *n*, téléphone, *m*. ¶ *v.t. & i*, téléphoner. ¶ *att. & telephonic*, *a*, téléphonique. ~ *answering machine*, répondeur, *m*. ~ *booth*, cabine téléphonique, *f*. ~ *number*, numéro de téléphone, *m*. *person-to-person* ~ *call for*, avec préavis pour.

teleprinter, *n*, téléimprimeur, *m*.

teleprocessing, *n*, télétraitement, *m*.

telescope, *n*, (*reflecting*) télescope, *m*; (*refracting*) lunette; (*spy-glass*) longue-vue, *f*. ¶ *v.i*, se télescoper. **telescopic**, *a*, télescopique; (*sliding*) à coulisse.

televiewer, *n*, téléspectateur, *m*.

televise, *v.t*, téléviser. **television**, *n*, télévision, *f*. ~ *set*, téléviseur, *m*.

tell, *v.t. & i. ir*, dire; [ra]conter; narrer; apprendre; savoir; reconnaître; (*of remark*) porter; (*in one's favor*) militer. ~**er**, *n*, (*voting*) scrutateur; (*bank*) caissier, *m*. (*banks*) *automatic* ~ *machine*, guichet automatique, *m*. ~**ing**, *a*, qui porte. ~**tale**, *n*, (*pers.*) rapporteur, euse.

temerity, *n*, témérité, *f*.

temper, *n*, caractère, *m*; humeur; trempe; colère, *f*. *to lose one's* ~, s'emporter. ¶ *v.t*, (*metal*) tremper; (*mortar*) gâcher; (*fig.*) tempérer, mitiger. **temperament**, *n*, tempérament, *m*. ~**al**, *a*, constitutionnel; capricieux, fantasque. **temperance**, *n*, tempérance, *f*. **temperate**, *a*, tempérant, sobre; (*climate, speech*) tempéré. **temperature**, *n*, température, *f*. ~ **chart**, feuille de température, *f*.

tempest, *n*, tempête, *f*. **tempestuous**, *a*, tempétueux.

template, -plet, *n*, gabarit, calibre, *m*.

temple, *n*, temple, *m*; (*Anat.*) tempe, *f*.

temporal†, *a*, (*secular*) temporel. **temporary†**, *a*, temporaire, momentané. **temporize**, *v.i*, temporiser.

tempt, *v.t*, tenter; inviter; affriander. ~**ation**, *n*, tentation, *f*. **tempter, tress**, *n*, tentateur, trice, séducteur, trice. **tempting**, *a*, tentant, séduisant; (*food*) appétissant, ragoûtant.

ten, *a*, dix. ¶ *n*, dix, *m*; dizaine, *f*. ~**fold**, *a*. & *n*, décuple, *a* & *m*. *to increase* ~, décupler.

tenable, *a*, tenable; soutenable. **tenacious**, *a*, tenace. ~**ly**, *ad*, avec ténacité.

tenancy, *n*, location, *f*. **tenant**, *n*, locataire, *m,f*; (*farm*) fermier, ère. ~ *farmer*, fermier, ère. ~**able**, *a*, logeable.

tench, *n*, tanche, *f*.

tend, *v.t*, garder; soigner; (*v.i.*) tendre; conspirer. ~**ency**, *n*, tendance; disposition, *f*. **tendentious**, *a*, tendancieux. **tender**, *n*, soumission; offre; (*boat*) annexe, *f*; (*Naut.*) transbordeur, *m*. (*Rly.*) tender, *m*. ¶ *v.t*, offrir; donner. ~ *for*, soumissionner.

tender†, *a*, tendre; sensible; délicat. ~**ness**, *n*, tendresse; délicatesse; (*eatables*) tendreté, *f*.

tendon, *n*, tendon, *m*.

tendril, *n*, vrille, main, *f*.

tenement, *n*, habitation, *f*, logement, *m*, maison de rapport, *f*.

tenet, *n*, dogme, *m*, doctrine, *f*.

tennis, *n*, tennis, *m*. ~ *court*, jeu de tennis, [court de] tennis, *m*.

tenon, *n*, tenon, *m*. ~ *saw*, scie à t., *f*.

tenor, *n*, teneur; (*bill*) échéance, *f*; (*voice, singer*) ténor, *m*. ~ *clef*, clef d'ut, *f*.

tense, *a*, tendu, raide. ¶ *n*, temps, *m*. **tension**, *n*, tension, *f*.

tent, *n*, tente; (*Surg.*) mèche, *f*. ~ *pole*, mât de t., *m*.

tentacle, *n*, tentacule, *m*.

tentative [effort], tâtonnement, *m*.

tenterhook, *n*, crochet [du fabricant de drap]; clou à crochet, *m*. *on* ~*s*, sur des charbons [ardents], sur le gril, au supplice.

tenth†, *a*, dixième. ¶ *n*, dixième, *m,f*; dix, *m*.

tenuity, *n*, ténuité, *f*. **tenuous**, *a*, ténu.

tenure, *n*, possession; jouissance, *f*; mode de possession; exercice, *m*. *during his* ~ *of office*, pendant l'exercice de ses fonctions.

tepid†, *a*, tiède. ~**ness**, *n*, tiédeur, *f*.

term, *n*, terme, *m*; clause; durée; session, *f*; trimestre, *m*; (*pl.*) conditions, *f.pl*; prix, *m*; (*pl, opp.* [*for*] *cash*) à crédit; (*pl.*) rapports, *m.pl*, intelligence; teneur, *f*; accommodement, *m*. *to come to* ~*s*, conclure un arrangement. (*loan, etc.*) *short* ~, à courte échéance. ¶ *v.t*, appeler.

termagant, *n*, mégère, *f*, dragon, *m*.

terminable, *a*, résoluble. **terminal**, *a*, terminal; de tête de ligne. ¶ *n*, borne; extrémité, *f*; (*computers*) terminal, *m. remote* ~, poste éloigné, *m*. **terminate**, *v.t*, terminer; resoudre. **termination**, *n*, terminaison; fin, *f*. **terminus**, *n*, terminus, *m*.

termite, *n*, termite, *m*, fourmi blanche, *f*.

tern, *n*, sterne, *m*.

terrace, *n*, terrasse, *f*. ¶ *v.t*, étager.

terracotta, *n*, terre cuite, *f*.

terrain, *n*, terrain, *m*.

terrestrial, *a*, terrestre.

terrible†, *a*, terrible.

terrier, *n*, [chien] terrier, *m*.

terrific†, *a*, terrible. **terrify**, *v.t*, terrifier.

territorial, *a*. & *n*, territorial, *a*. & *m*. **territory**, *n*, territoire, *m*.

terror, *n*, terreur, *f*. ~**ism**, *n*, terrorisme, *m*. ~**ist**, *n*, terroriste, *m*. & *f*. ~**ize**, *v.t*, terroriser.

terse, *a*, concis. ~**ness**, *n*, concision, *f*.

tessellated pavement, mosaïque, *f*.

test, *n*, épreuve, *f*, essai, *m*; pierre

de touche, *f*. *blood* ~, prise de sang, *f*. ~ *tube*, éprouvette, *f*. ¶ *v.t*, essayer, éprouver; expérimenter; contrôler.

testament, *n*, testament, *m*. ~ary, *a*, testamentaire. **testator, trix**, *n*, testateur, trice. **testify**, *v.t*, & *i*, témoigner. **testimonial**, *n*, attestation, *f*; certificat, *m*. **testimony**, *n*, témoignage, *m*.

testicle, *n*, testicule, *m*.

testy, *a*, irritable, irascible.

tetanus, *n*, tétanos, *m*.

tether, *n*, longe, *f*. *at the end of one's* ~, au bout de son rouleau. ¶ *v.t*, mettre au piquet.

Teutonic, *a*, teutonique, teuton.

text, *n*, texte, *m*. ~**book**, manuel, *m*.

textile, *n*, textile, tissu, *m*. ¶ *a*, textile.

textual†, *a*, textuel; (*error*) de texte.

texture, *n*, texture, tissure, *f*, tissu, *m*, contexture, *f*.

Thames (**the**), la Tamise.

than, *c*. & *pr*, que; de.

thank, *v.t*, remercier; bénir. ~ *God!* Dieu merci! ~ *Heaven!* grâce au ciel! ~ *you!* & *no* ~ *you!* merci! ~**ful**, *a*, reconnaissant. ~**fully**, *ad*, avec reconnaissance. ~**fulness**, *n*, reconnaissance, gratitude, *f*. ~**less**, *a*, ingrat. **thanks**, *n.pl*, remerciements, *m.pl*. ¶ *i*, merci! ~ *to*, grâce à. **thanksgiving**, *n*, action[s] de grâce, *f.*[*pl.*].

that, *a*. & *pn*, ce, cet, cette; ce . . ., etc., -là, celui, celle; cela, ça; ce, c', ç'; qui; que; là. ~ *is all*, c'est tout; voilà tout. ~ *is to say*, c'est-à-dire. ~ *will do*, cela suffit. ¶ *c*, que; afin que; pour que.

thatch, *n*, chaume, *m*. ¶ *v.t*, couvrir en c. ~*ed cottage*, chaumière, *f*. ~**er**, *n*, couvreur en chaume, *m*.

thaw, *n*, dégel, *m*. ¶ *v.t*, & *i*, dégeler; se d.; (*fig*.) dégeler; se dégeler, se déraidir.

the, *art*, le, l', *m*, la, l', *f*, les, *m,f.pl*. *from* ~, *of* ~, du, de l', de la, des. *to* ~, *at* ~, au, à l', à la, aux.

theater, *n*, théâtre, *m*. **theatrical†**, *a*, de théâtre, du théâtre; théâtral, scénique. **theatricals**, *n.pl*, comédie, *f*.

thee, *pn*, te; toi.

theft, *n*, vol, *m*.

their, *a*, leur, leurs (*pl*.). **theirs**,

pn, le leur, la leur, les leurs; à eux, à elles.

theism, *n*, théisme, *m*. **theistic(al)**, *a*, théiste.

them, *pn*, eux, elles; les; leur; ceux, celles. ~*selves*, eux[-mêmes], elles[-mêmes]; se.

theme, *n*, thème; sujet; (*Mus*.) motif, *m*. ~ *song*, leitmotif, leitmotiv, *m*.

then, *ad*, alors; ensuite, puis; donc; lors. **thence**, *ad*, de là. **thenceforth**, **thenceforward**, *ad*, dès lors.

theodolite, *n*, théodolite, *m*.

theologian, *n*, théologien, *m*. **theological†**, *a*, théologique. **theology**, *n*, théologie, *f*.

theorem, *n*, théorème, *m*. **theoretic(al†)**, *a*, théorique. **theorist**, *n*, théoricien, *m*. **theory**, *n*, théorie, *f*.

theosophy, *n*, théosophie, *f*.

therapeutic, *a*. & ~*s*, *n.pl*, thérapeutique, *a*. & *f*.

there, *ad*, là; y; là-bas; il. ~ & *back*, aller & retour. ~ & *then*, séance tenante, sur-le-champ, tout de go. ~ *is*, ~ *are*, il y a. ~*about*, ~*abouts*, près de là; environ. ~*by*, de ce fait. ~*fore*, c'est pourquoi; donc, aussi, par conséquent. ~*on*, là-dessus. ~*upon*, sur ce, là-dessus.

thermal, *a*, thermal. **thermometer**, *n*, thermomètre, *m*.

thermonuclear, *a*, thermonucléaire.

thermostat, *n*, thermostat, *m*.

these, *pn*, ces; ces . . . -ci; ceux-ci, celles-ci.

thesis, *n*, thèse, *f*.

thews, *n.pl*, nerfs, *m.pl*.

they, *pn*, ils, elles; eux, elles; ceux, celles; il; ce, c'; on.

thick, *a*, épais; dense; puissant; gros; gras; dru; fourni; touffu; (*with someone*) lié. ~ *or clear* (soup)? potage ou consommé? ~*-lipped*, lippu. ~*-set*, trapu, ramassé; dru. ~*[ly]*, *ad*, épais; dru. *in the* ~ *of*, au fort de. *through* ~ & *thin*, envers & contre tous. ~*en*, *v.t*, épaissir; (*sauce*) lier. ~*ening*, *n*, épaississement *m*; (*for sauce*) liaison, *f*. ~*et*, *n*, fourré; bosquet, *m*. ~*ness*, *n*, épaisseur; puissance, *f*.

thief, *n*, voleur, euse, larron, *m*. **thieve**, *v.t*, voler. **thievish**, *a*, de voleur; (*pers*.) voleur.

thigh, n, cuisse, f. ~ *bone*, os de la c., m. ~ *boots*, bottes cuissardes, f.pl.

thill, n, limon, brancard, m.

thimble, n, dé [à coudre] m; (Naut.) cosse, f. ~*rigger*, joueur de gobelets, m. ~**ful,** n, doigt, m.

thin, a, mince; maigre; délié, ténu; faible; clair; (hair, grass) rare; (legs, voice) grêle. *to be* ~-*skinned* (fig.), avoir l'épiderme sensible. ~ *slice*, mince tranche, lèche, f. ¶ v.t, amincir, amenuiser; éclaircir; amaigrir.

thine, pn, le tien, la tienne, les tiens, les tiennes; à toi.

thing, n, chose; affaire, f; (pers.) être, m; (pl.) effets, m.pl. *the* ~ (*in fashion*), de mise.

think, v.t. & i. ir, penser; songer; juger; réfléchir; croire; trouver; s'imaginer. ~**er,** n, penseur, m. **thinking,** a, pensant. ¶ n, pensée; réflexion, f; avis, m.

thinly, ad, clair. ~ *sown*, semé clair, clairsemé. **thinness,** n, minceur, ténuité; maigreur; rareté, f. **thinnish,** a, maigrelet.

third†, a, troisième; tiers. ~ *finger*, [doigt] annulaire, m. ~ *person*, tiers, m, tierce personne, f; (Gram.) troisième personne, f. *T~ World*, tiers monde, m. ¶ n, tiers, m; tierce, f; troisième, m,f; trois, m.

thirst, n, soif, f. ~-*creating*, altérant. ~ *for*, avoir soif de. **thirsty,** a, altéré; (country) de la soif. *to be* ~, avoir soif.

thirteen, a. & n, treize, a & m. ~**th**†, a. & n, treizième, a. & m,f; treize, m.

thirtieth, a. & n, trentième, a. & m,f; trente, m. **thirty,** a. & n, trente, a. & m.

this, a. & pn, ce, cet, cette; ce . . ., -ci; celui-ci, celle-ci; ceci; présent. ~ *way!* par ici! ~ *way & that,* çà & là.

thistle, n, chardon, m. ~*down,* duvet du chardon, m.

thong, n, lanière, f.

thorax, n, thorax, m.

thorn, & ~ [*bush*] n, épine, f. ~**y,** a, épineux.

thorough, a, achevé; accompli; approfondi; minutieux; parfait. ~*bred* [*horse*], cheval pur sang, c. de race, c. racé, m. ~*fare,*

voie, f, passage, m; rue [passante]; artère, f. ~**ly,** ad, à fond, foncièrement; mûrement; complètement; parfaitement.

those, pn, ces; ces . . . -là; ceux, celles; ceux-là, celles-là; ce.

thou, pn, tu; toi. ¶ v.t, tutoyer.

though, c, quoique, bien que, quand; cependant, tout . . . que. *as* ~, comme si.

thought, n, pensée; réflexion; idée, f. ~*ful,* a, pensif, réfléchi. ~*less*†, a, étourdi; irréfléchi. ~*lessness,* n, étourderie; irréflexion, f.

thousand, a, mille; mil. ¶ n, mille; millier, m. ~**th,** a. & n, millième, a. & m.

thraldom, n, servage; esclavage, m. **thrall,** n, serf, m, serve, f; esclave, m,f.

thrash, v.t, battre, rosser. ~**ing,** n, peignée, f.

thread, n, fil, m; corde, f; filament, filé; (screw) filet; (of life) trame, f. ~*bare,* usé jusqu'à la corde, râpé; usé. ¶ v.t, enfiler; (screw) fileter.

threat, n, menace, f. ~**en,** v.t, menacer.

three, a. & n, trois, a. & m. ~-*color process,* trichromie, f. ~-*master,* trois-mâts, m. ~-*ply* [*wood*], contreplaqué en trois, bois plaqué triplé, m. ~*some,* partie de trois, f. ~-*speed gear,* dispositif à 3 vitesses, m. ~*fold,* a, triple.

thresh, v.t, battre, dépiquer. ~ *out,* vider. ~**er** (pers.) n, batteur en grange, m. ~**ing machine,** batteuse, f.

threshold, n, seuil, pas, m.

thrice, ad, trois fois.

thrift, n, économie, épargne, f. ~*less,* a, prodigue, dépensier. ~**y,** a, économe, ménager.

thrill, n, tressaillement, saisissement, frisson, m, vive émotion, f. ¶ v.t, électriser; empoigner; (v.i.) tressaillir, palpiter. ~**ing,** a, passionnant, palpitant, empoignant.

thrive, v.i.ir, prospérer; (plant) se plaire. *not to* ~, se déplaire. **thriving,** a, florissant, prospère.

throat, n, gorge, f; gosier, m.

throb, v.i, battre, palpiter; (Med.) élancer.

throe, n, douleur, f; (pl.) affres, f.pl.

throne, n, trône, m; (bishop's) chaire, f.

throng, n, foule, presse, f. ¶ v.t, accourir en foule à; assiéger; (v.i.) se presser.

throstle, n, grive chanteuse, f.

throttle, n, gosier; régulateur; (Mech.) étrangleur, m. ¶ v.t, étrangler.

through, pr, à travers; au t. de; par; à cause de. ~ thick & thin, envers & contre tous. ¶ ad, à travers; au t.; de part en part, à jour; jusqu'au bout; d'un bout à l'autre; directement. ¶ a, direct; à forfait, forfaitaire. ~ ticket, (to final destination) billet direct; (sea-land-sea) billet global, m. ~out, pr, par tout; pendant tout; (ad.) complète ment, jusqu'au bout.

throw, n, jet, m; (Mech.) excentricité, f. ¶ v.t.ir, jeter; lancer; démonter; terrasser; tomber; mettre. ~ away, jeter. ~ back, rejeter. ~ down, ~ over, renverser. ~ open, ouvrir. ~ out, chasser; rejeter. ~ up, jeter en l'air; vomir. ~ing, n, lancement, m.

thrum, v.t, tapoter (on = sur); (v.i.) tambouriner.

thrush, n, grive; (Med.) aphte, f.

thrust, n, coup, m; (Fenc.) botte, estocade; (Mech.) poussée, butée, f. ¶ v.t.ir, pousser; plonger; (sword) pointer; (Fenc.) estocader; imposer. ~ aside, repousser. ~ at (Fenc.), porter une botte à.

thud, n, coup sourd, son mat, floc, m.

thug, n, étrangleur, m.

thumb, n, pouce, m. ~ index, répertoire à onglets, m. ~screw, écrou à oreilles, papillon, m. ~tack, punaise, f. ¶ v.t, feuilleter. ~ one's nose, faire un pied de nez.

thump, n, coup sourd, m; bourrade, f, horion, m. ¶ v.t, cogner; sonner lourdement.

thunder, n, tonnerre, m, foudre, f. ~bolt, foudre, f, coup de foudre, tonnerre, m; (pl, Jove's) foudres, traits, m.pl. ~clap, coup de tonnerre, m. ~cloud, nuée, f. ~storm, orage, m. ~struck, foudroyé. ¶ v.i. & t, tonner; fulminer. ~y, a, orageux.

Thursday, n, jeudi, m.

thus, ad, ainsi, de cette façon. ~ far, jusqu'ici.

thwack, n, coup, m. ¶ v.t, frapper.

thwart, n, banc [de nage] m. ¶ v.t, croiser, contrecarrer, traverser.

thy, a, ton, ta, tes.

thyme, n, thym; (wild) serpolet, m.

thyroid, a, thyroïde.

thyself, pn, toi-même; toi; te.

tiara, n, tiare, f.

Tiber (the), le Tibre.

tibia, n, tibia, m.

tic, n, tic, m.

Ticino (the), le Tessin.

tick, n, coutil, m, (ticking) toile à matelas; (insect) tique, f, acare; tic tac; point, m; seconde, f. ~tack, tic tac, m. ¶ v.i, battre; (v.i.t.) pointer.

ticket, n, billet; bulletin; cachet, m; entrée; carte; étiquette; (auto) contravention, f. ~ collector, contrôleur, m. ~ window, guichet [de distribution des billets] m. ¶ v.t, étiqueter.

tickle, v.t. & i, chatouiller. **ticklish,** a, chatouilleux; critique, délicat, scabreux.

tidal, a: ~ basin, bassin de marée, m. ~ water, eaux à m., f.pl. ~ wave, flot de la marée, raz de m., m, barre de flot, f. **tide,** n, marée, f; courant, m. ebb ~, marée descendante, f. flood ~, marée montante, f. to ~ over a difficulty, se tirer d'affaire.

tidiness, n, propreté, f, bon ordre, m.

tidings, n.pl, nouvelles, f.pl.

tidy, a, bien tenu, rangé; (pers.) ordonné. ¶ v.t, ranger. ~ oneself up, s'ajuster, faire un bout de toilette.

tie, n, lien, m; attache, f; tirant, m; cravate, f; nœud, m; (Mus.) liaison; (voting) égalité de voix; (sport) égalité de points, f. ~ clip, fixe-cravate, m. ~ pin, épingle de cravate, f. ¶ v.t.ir, lier; attacher; clouer; (knot) faire; (v.i.) (sport) arriver à égalité; (exams) être [classé] ex æquo. ~ down, lier; astreindre. ~ up, lier; bander; mettre à l'attache.

tier, n, rangée, f, rang, étage, gradin, m.

tierce, n, tierce, f.

Tierra del Fuego, la Terre de Feu.

tiff, *n,* fâcherie, pique, difficulté, *f.*

tiger, *n,* tigre, *m.* ~ *cat,* chat-tigre, *m.* ~ *lily,* lis tigré, *m.*

tight, *a,* serré; tendu; raide; étroit, juste; collant; étanche. ~ *corner,* coin étranglé; mauvais pas, *m.* ~*wad,* grippe-sou, *m.* ~**en,** *v.t,* [res]serrer, tendre, raidir. ~**[ly],** *ad,* serré; étroitement. ~**ness,** *n,* tension, raideur; étroitesse; étanchéité, *f.*

tigress, *n,* tigresse, *f.*

Tigris (the), le Tigre.

tile, *n,* tuile, *f;* carreau, *m; (pl, roof)* gouttières, *f.pl.* ~ *floor-*[*ing*], carrelage, *m.* ~ *maker,* tuilier, *m.* ~ *works,* tuilerie, *f.* ¶ *v.t,* couvrir de tuiles; carreler.

till, *n,* caisse, *f,* tiroir de c., *m.* ¶ *v.t,* labourer. ¶ *pr,* jusqu'à; jusque; avant; à. ¶ *c,* jusqu'à ce que; en attendant que. **tillage,** *n,* labourage, *m.* **tiller,** *n,* laboureur, *m;* barre [du gouvernail] *f.*

tilt, *n,* bâche; joute; inclinaison, *f.* ¶ *v.t,* incliner; culbuter; *(v.i.)* s'incliner; jouter. **tilting** (*Hist.*) *n,* joute, *f.*

timber, *n,* bois [de charpente]; *(ship)* couple, *m.* ~ *tree,* arbre de haute futaie, *m.* ~*tree forest,* futaie, *f.* ~*work,* charpente [en bois] *f.* ¶ *v.t,* boiser; charpenter.

timbre, *n,* timbre, *m.*

Timbuctoo, *n,* Tombouctou, *m.*

time, *n,* temps; moment, *m;* époque; saison, *f;* siècle, *m;* heure; fois, reprise, *f;* terme, *m;* mesure; cadence, *f;* pas, *m. at* ~*s,* parfois. [*just*] *in* ~, à point. ~ *fuse,* fusée à temps, *f.* ~*-hon-ored,* séculaire. ~*keeper* (*pers.*), pointeur, contrôleur; (*sport*) chronométreur, *m.* ~*-piece,* pendule, *f.* ~*server,* opportuniste, *m,f,* caméléon, *m,* complaisant, e. (*computers*) ~*-sharing,* partage de temps, *m.* ~ *sheet,* feuille de présence, *f.* ~*table,* (*book*) indicateur; (*placard & scheme of work*) horaire, *m. at any* ~, n'importe quand. (*computers*) *down* ~, temps de panne, *m. from* ~ *to* ~, de temps en temps. (*computers*) *idle* ~, temps mort, *m. next* ~, la prochaine fois. ¶ *v.t,* (*watch*) régler; (*sport*) chronomé-

trer. ~*ing,* *n,* pointage, *m.* **timeli-ness,** *n,* opportunité, *f.* **timely,** *a,* opportun.

timid†, *a,* timide, peureux. ~**ity,** *n,* timidité, *f.* **timorous,** *a,* timoré.

tin, *n,* étain; (*can*) bidon, *m;* boîte [métallique] *f.* ~ *foil,* feuille d'étain, *f.* ~ [*plate*], fer-blanc, *m.* ~ *soldier,* soldat de plomb, *m.* ~*smith,* ferblantier, *m.* ~*ware,* ferblanterie, *f.* ¶ *v.t,* étamer; mettre en boîte(s), *m.* en conserve.

tincture, *n,* teinture, *f.* ¶ *v.t,* teindre.

tinder, *n,* amadou, *m.* ~ *box,* briquet, *m.*

tine, *n,* dent, branche, *f;* (*deer*) andouiller, *m.*

tinge, *n,* teinte, nuance, *f.* ¶ *v.t,* teinter.

tingle, *v.i,* picoter; fourmiller; (*ears*) tinter.

tinker, *n,* chaudronnier ambulant, *m.*

tinkle, *v.i,* tinter. ¶ *n,* tintement, *m.* ~*l* ~*l* drelin-drelin!

tinsel, *n,* clinquant, *m,* oripeaux, *m.pl;* (*fig.*) faux brillant, *m.*

tint, *n,* teinte, *f,* ton, *m.* ¶ *v.t,* teinter.

tiny, *a,* minuscule, petiot, infime. ~ *bit,* tantinet, tout petit peu, *m.* ~ *drop,* gouttelette, *f.*

tip, *n,* bout; bec, *m;* pointe; extrémité, *f;* (*wing*) fouet; (*Bil. cue*) procédé; (*gratuity*) pourboire, *m,* pièce, *f;* (*information*) tuyau, *m.* ¶ *v.t,* embouter; basculer; culbuter; verser; donner un pourboire à; donner un tuyau à. ~*cart,* tombereau, *m.*

tippet, *n,* palatine, *f,* mantelet, *m.*

tipple, *v.i,* buvoter, chopiner. **tippler,** *n,* biberon, ne.

tipster, *n,* donneur de tuyaux, *m.*

tipsy, *a,* ivre. *a* ~ *walk,* une démarche avinée.

tiptoe(on), sur la pointe du pied.

tiptop, *n,* comble, *m.* ¶ *a,* excellent, parfait.

tirade, *n,* tirade, incartade, *f.*

tire, *n,* bandage; pneu[matique], caoutchouc, *m. flat* ~, pneu crevé, *m. nonskid* ~, p. antidérapant, *m. snow* ~, p. neige, *m. spare* ~, p. de rechange, *m.*

tire, *v.t,* fatiguer, lasser, excéder; (*v.i.*) se fatiguer, se lasser. ~*out,* rompu [de fatigue]. ~**less,**

a, infatigable. **~some**, *a*, fatigant; ennuyeux, fâcheux.

tissue, *n*, tissu, *m*; tissure, *f*. **~ paper**, papier de soie, *m*.

tit (*bird*) *n*, mésange, *f*. **~ for tat**, donnant donnant; un prêté [pour un] rendu.

titbit, *n*, bonne bouche, *f*.

tithe, *n*, dîme, *f*. **not a ~**, pas un dixième.

titillate, *v.t*, titiller, chatouiller.

titivate, *v.t*, bichonner.

title, *n*, titre; intitulé; parchemin, *m*. **~ [deed]**, titre, *m*. **~ page**, page du titre, *f*, titre, frontispice, *m*. **~d**, *a*, titré.

titmouse, *n*, mésange, *f*.

titter, *v.i*, rire bêtement, glousser.

tittle, *n*, iota, *m*.

titular, *a*, titulaire, en titre.

to, *pr*, à; de; pour; afin de; en; dans; envers; vers; jusqu'à; chez; auprès de, près; sur; contre; (*of the hour*) moins. **~ go to & fro**, aller de long en large, aller deçà, delà; aller & venir, faire la navette. **~ be called for**, bureau restant, poste restante; télégraphe restant; gare restante, en gare. **~ be kept cool, dry** or **in a cool, dry, place**, craint la chaleur, l'humidité. **~ be taken after meals**, à prendre après les repas. **~ boot**, en sus, par surcroît, avec ça. **~ match**, pareil. **~ measure**, sur mesure. **~ wit**, savoir; (*of pers.*) nommément.

toad, *n*, crapaud, *m*. **~ hole**, crapaudière, *f*. **~stone**, crapaudine, *f*. **~stool**, champignon [vénéneux] *m*. **toady**, *n*, flagorneur, euse, chien couchant, *m*. **~ to**, flagorner. **~ism**, *n*, flagornerie, *f*.

toast, *n*, pain grillé, *m*, rôtie, *f*; (*buttered*) toast; (*health*) toast, *m*. **¶***v.t*, griller, rôtir; (*health*) porter un toast à. **~er**, *n*, grille-pain, *m*. **~ing fork**, fourchette à griller le pain, *f*.

tobacco, *n*, tabac, *m*. **~ pouch**, blague à t., *f*. **tobacconist**, *n*, débitant de t., *m*. **~'s shop**, débit de t., bureau de t., *m*.

toboggan, *n*, toboggan, *m*. **~ run**, piste de toboggan, *f*.

today, *ad. & n*, aujourd'hui, *ad. & m*. **~'s gossip**, nouvelles à la main, *f.pl*.

toddle, *v.i*, trottiner.

to-do, *n*, cérémonies, *f.pl*; aria, *m*.

toe, *n*, doigt [de pied], orteil, *m*;

(*shoe, sock*) pointe, *f*. **~ dancing**, pointes, *f.pl*. **~ nail**, ongle d'orteil, *m*.

toga, *n*, toge, *f*.

together, *ad*, ensemble; à la fois. **~ with**, avec, en compagnie de, ainsi que.

toil, *n*, travail, labeur, *m*; (*pl.*) lacets, lacs, rets, *m.pl*, toiles, *f.pl*. **¶***v.i*, peiner. **~ & moil**, suer d'ahan, peiner. **~er**, *n*, travailleur, euse.

toilet, *n*, toilette, *f*. **~ paper**, papier hygiénique, *m*.

toilsome, *a*, pénible, laborieux.

token, *n*, signe, témoignage, *m*, preuve, marque, *f*; gage, hommage; jeton, *m*.

Toledo, *n*, Tolède, *f*.

tolerable, *a*, tolérable; passable. **tolerably**, *ad*, passablement. **tolerance & toleration**, *n*, tolérance, *f*. **tolerate**, *v.t*, tolérer.

toll, *n*, péage, passage, *m*. **~ call** (*Teleph.*), communication régionale, *f*. **~ bridge**, pont payant, *m*. **~ gate**, barrière de péage, *f*. **¶***v.t. & i*, tinter, sonner. **~ing**, *n*, tintement funèbre, *m*.

tom: **~boy**, garçon manqué, *m*. **~ [cat]**, matou, chat, *m*. **~foolery**, farce, pantalonnade, gaminerie, *f*. **~tit**, mésange charbonnière, *f*.

tomato, *n*, tomate, *f*. **~ sauce**, sauce t., *f*.

tomb, *n*, tombe, *f*, tombeau, *m*, sépulture, *f*. **~stone**, pierre tombale, *f*.

tome, *n*, tome, volume, *m*.

tomorrow, *ad. & n*, demain, *ad. & m*. **~ morning**, demain matin. **~ night**, **~ evening**, demain soir.

tomtom, *n*, tam-tam, *m*.

ton, *n*, tonne, *f*; tonneau, *m*.

tone, *n*, ton; son; accent, *m*; gamme, *f*; dispositions, *f.pl*. **¶** (*v.t, Phot.*) virer; (*v.i.*) s'harmoniser. **~ down**, adoucir, assourdir, estomper.

tongs, *n.pl*, pince, tenaille, *f*, pincettes, *f.pl*.

tongue, *n*, langue; (*strip, slip*) languette, *f*. **~tied**, la langue liée.

Tonkin, le Tonkin.

tonic, *a*, tonique; remontant. **~ sol-fa**, tonic-sol-fa, *m*. **¶** *n*, (*Med. & drink*) tonique, remontant, *m*; (*Mus.*) tonique, *f*.

tonight, *ad. & n*, ce soir, cette nuit.

toning (*Phot.*) *n*, virage, *m*.

tonnage, *n*, tonnage, *m*; jauge, *f*.

tonsil, *n*, amygdale, *f*. **tonsilitis**, *n*, amygdalite, *f*.

tonsure, *n*, tonsure, couronne, *f*. ¶ *v.t*, tonsurer.

too, *ad*, trop; aussi; également; de même; encore. ~ *long*, (*length*) trop long; (*time*) trop [long-temps]. ~ *much*, ~ *many* & ~ *well*, trop.

tool, *n*, outil; instrument; ustensile; (*pers.*) suppôt, *m*, âme damnée, *f*. ~ *box*, boîte à outils, *f*. ~ *maker*, fabricant d'outils, taillandier, *m*. ¶ *v.t*, (*Mach.*) travailler; (*Bookb.*) gaufrer.

tooth, *n*, dent; *f*. ~*ache*, mal de dents, *m*, (*violent*) rage de dents, *f*. ~ *brush*, brosse à dents, *f*. ~ *brush moustache*, moustache en brosse, *f*. ~*paste*, pâte dentifrice, *f*, dentifrice, *m*. ~*pick*, cure-dents, *m*. ~ *powder*, poudre dentifrice, *f*, dentifrice, *m*. ¶ *v.t*, [en]denter, créneler. ~*some*, *a*, succulent.

top, *n*, haut; sommet, *m*; cime, *f*; faîte; comble; dessus, *m*; tête, pointe, *f*; (*bus*) impériale; (*Naut.*) hune; (*turnip*, *etc.*) fane; (*book page*) tête, tranche supérieure; (*toys*) toupie, *f*, sabot, *m*. *at the* ~ *of one's voice*, à tue-tête. *on* ~ *of*, par-dessus, sur. ~ *boots*, bottes à revers, *f.pl.* ~*coat*, pardessus, *m*. ~ *figure*, chiffre maximum, *m*. ~*gallant*, perroquet, *m*. ~ *hat*, chapeau haut de forme, *m*. ~*heavy*, trop lourd du haut. ~*mast*, mât de hune, *m*. ~*sail*, hunier, *m*. ¶ *v.t*, couronner; surpasser; dépasser; être à la tête de; (*tree*) étêter.

topaz, *n*, topaze, *f*.

topic, *n*, sujet, thème, *m*. ~*al song*, chanson de circonstance, *f*.

topographic(al), *a*, topographique. **topography**, *n*, topographie, *f*.

topple, *v.i*, dégringoler. ~ *over*, faire culbuter, renverser.

topsyturvy, *ad*, sens dessus dessous.

torch, *n*, flambeau, *m*, torche, *f*. ~ *bearer*, porte-flambeau, *m*. ~*by* ~*light*, à la lueur des flambeaux, aux flambeaux.

toreador, *n*, toréador, *m*.

torment, *n*, tourment, supplice, *m*. ¶ *v.t*, tourmenter; travailler; taquiner. **tormentor**, *n*, bourreau, *m*.

tornado, *n*, tornade, *f*.

torpedo, *n*, torpille, *f*. ~ *boat*, [bateau] torpilleur, *m*. ~ *launcher*, lance-torpille, *f*. ¶ *v.t*, torpiller.

torpid, *a*, torpide. **torpor**, *n*, torpeur, *f*.

torrent, *n*, torrent, *m*. *in* ~*s*, à torrents, à flots. ~*ial*, *a*, torrentiel, diluvien.

torrid, *a*, torride.

torsion, *n*, torsion, *f*.

torso, *n*, torse, *m*.

tort (*law*) *n*, acte dommageable, *m*.

tortoise, *n*, tortue, *f*. ~*shell*, écaille [de t.] *f*. ~*shell butterfly*, tortue, *f*. ~*shell cat*, chat d'Espagne, *m*.

tortuous†, *a*, tortueux, tortu.

torture, *n*, torture, *f*, tourment, supplice, *m*. *instrument of* ~, instrument de torture, appareil tortionnaire, *m*. ¶ *v.t*, torturer, tourmenter. **torturer**, *n*, tortionnaire, bourreau, *m*. **torturous**, *a*, tortionnaire.

toss, *v.t. & i*, jeter; ballotter; cahoter; secouer; (*head*) hocher; (*oars*) mâter. ~ *off* (drink), lamper, sabler. ~ [*up*] (coin), tirer [à pile ou face].

tot, *n*, (*child*) petiot, e; (*rum*, *etc.*) boujaron, *m*.

total†, *a*, total; global; complet. ¶ *n*, total; montant, *m*. **totalitarian**, *a*, totalitaire. **totalizer**, **totalizator**, *n*, totaliseur, totalisateur, *m*.

totter, *v.i*, chanceler; s'ébranler.

toucan, *n*, toucan, *m*.

touch, *n*, toucher; tact, *m*; touche, *f*; contact, *m*; communication, *f*; coup; (*art*) pinceau; soupçon, *m*; pointe, *f*. ~*stone*, pierre de touche, *f*. ~*wood*, amadou, *m*. ¶ *v.t. & i*, toucher; t. à; se t.; tâter; effleurer. *to keep in* ~, garder le contact. ~ *up*, retoucher; chatouiller. ~*ed* (*crazy*), *p.p*, toqué, timbré. ~*iness*, *f*, susceptibilité, *f*. ~*ing*, *a. & pr*, touchant. ~*y*, *a*, susceptible, chatouilleux.

tough†, *a*, dur; résistant; tenace; coriace. ¶ *n*, voyou, dur. ~*en*, *v.t*, durcir. ~*ness*, *n*, dureté; ténacité, résistance, *f*.

tour, *n,* tour, voyage, *m,* tournée, *f.* ~**ing,** *n,* tourisme. *m.* ~**ist,** *n,* touriste, *m,f.* ~ *agency,* agence de tourisme, *f.*

tournament, *n,* tournoi; concours, *m.*

tourniquet, *n,* tourniquet, garrot, *m.*

tousle, *v.t,* ébouriffer.

tow, *n,* filasse, étoupe, *f;* (*boat*) remorqué, *m.* in ~, à la remorque, à la traîne. ¶ *v.t,* remorquer; haler, touer. ~[**ing**] *path,* chemin de halage, tirage, *m.*

toward[s], *pr,* vers; envers; vis-à-vis de, à l'endroit de; sur.

towel, *n,* serviette [de toilette] *f,* essuie-mains, *m.* **toweling,** *n,* tissu éponge, *m.*

tower, *n,* tour, *f;* pylône, *m.* ~ *above,* dominer. ~*ing rage,* colère bleue, *f.*

town, *n,* ville; place, *f.* ~ *clerk,* secrétaire de mairie, *m.* ~ *crier,* crieur public, *m.* ~ *hall,* hôtel de ville, *m,* maison de ville, mairie, *f.* ~ *house,* hôtel, *m.* ~ *planning,* urbanisme, *m.* **townsman,** *n,* citadin, *m.*

toxic, *a,* toxique. **toxin,** *n,* toxine, *f.*

toy, *n,* jouet, joujou, *m,* babiole, *f.* ~ *balloon,* ballon d'enfant, *m.* ¶ *v.i,* jouer, badiner.

trace, *n,* trace, *f;* (*harness*) trait, *m;* (*Fish.*) bas de ligne avec émerillons, *m.* ~ *horse,* [cheval] côtier, cheval de renfort, *m.* ¶ *v.t,* tracer; calquer; suivre la trace de; suivre à la trace. ~ *back,* faire remonter. ~*d pattern,* tracé, *m.* ~**ry,** *n,* réseau, *m,* dentelle, *f.*

trachea, *n,* trachée-artère, *f.*

tracing, *n,* calque, *m.* ~ *paper,* papier calque, *m.*

track, *n,* trace; piste; voie, *f;* chemin, sentier, *m;* route, *f;* sillage; sillon, *m.* ~ *race,* course sur piste, *f.* ¶ *v.t,* suivre à la piste. ~ *down,* (*game*) dépister; (*criminal*) traquer.

tract, *n,* étendue, *f;* (*leaflet*) opuscule, *m.* ~**able,** *a,* traitable. **traction,** *n,* traction, *f.* ~ *engine,* machine routière; locomobile, *f.* **tractor,** *n,* tracteur, *m.*

trade, *n,* commerce; négoce; trafic, *m,* traite, *f;* métier, *m;* industrie, *f.* ~ *discount,* remise [sur marchandises] *f.* ~*mark,* marque de commerce, m. de fabrique, appellation, *f.* ~ *union,* syndicat ouvrier, *m.* ~ *unionist,* syndicaliste, syndiqué, *m.* ~ *winds,* vents alizés, *m.pl.* ¶ *v.i,* trafiquer (*in* = en), faire [le] commerce (*in* = de). **trader,** *n,* commerçant, e; trafiquant, *m;* (*col. pl.*) le commerce. **trading,** *n,* commerce, *m;* traite, *f;* exercice, *m.* ~ *account,* compte d'exploitation, *m.* **tradesman,** *n,* marchand; boutiquier; fournisseur, *m. tradesmen's entrance,* porte de service, *f.*

tradition, *n,* tradition, *f.* ~**al†,** *a,* traditionnel.

traduce, *v.t,* calomnier. ~**er,** *n,* diffamateur, *m.*

traffic, *n,* trafic, *m,* traite, *f;* mouvement, *m;* circulation, *f.* ~ *jam,* embouteillage, *m.* ~ *lights,* signaux lumineux de circulation, feux de c., *m.pl.* ~ *police,* police de la circulation, *f.* ~ *circle,* rond-point, *m.* ~ *sign,* poteau de signalisation, *m.* **trafficker,** *n,* trafiquant, *m.*

tragedian, *n,* [auteur] tragique, *m.* ~, *tragedienne,* tragédien, ne. **tragedy,** *n,* tragédie, *f;* drame, *m.* **tragic(al†),** *a,* tragique. **tragicomedy,** *n,* tragi-comédie, *f.* **tragicomic,** *a,* tragi-comique.

trail, *n,* piste, trace; traînée, *f,* sillon, *m;* (*gun carriage*) flèche, *f.* ~ *rope* (*Avn.*), guiderope, *m.* ¶ *v.t,* suivre à la piste; traîner. ~**er,** *n,* remorque; roulotte, *f;* (*cinema*) film-annonce, *m.*

train, *n,* train; convoi; *m;* suite, *f;* cortège, *m;* (*dress*) traîne, queue; (*comet*) queue; (*powder*) traînée, *f;* (*events*) enchaînement, *m.* ~ *ferry,* bac transbordeur, *m.* ¶ *v.t,* former, styler; instruire; dresser, éduquer; entraîner; (*gun*) diriger, pointer. ~**er,** *n,* dresseur; entraîneur, *m.* **training,** *n,* éducation; école; instruction, *f;* enseignement; dressage, manège; entraînement, *m,* haleine, *f.* ~ *ship,* vaisseau-école, *m.*

trait, *n,* trait, *m.*

traitor, tress, *n,* traître, *m,* traîtresse, *f.* ~**ous,** *a,* traître. ~**ously,** *ad,* en traître.

trajectory, *n,* trajectoire, *f.*

trammel, *n,* (*net*) tramail; *m;*

(*pl.*) entraves, *f.pl.* ¶*v.t*, entraver.

tramp, *n*, bruit de pas, *m*; (*horses*) battue; promenade [à pied] *f*; (*pers.*) chemineau, *m*, vagabond, e. ¶*v.i*, marcher pesamment; cheminer; marcher; (*v.t.*) arpenter. ~ *up & down*, courir.

trample [**on**] [**down**], *v.t*, fouler, piétiner.

trance, *n*, extase; (*hypnotic*) transe, *f*.

tranquil†, *a*, tranquille. **tranquility,** *n*, tranquillité, *f*.

transact, *v.t*, traiter, faire; délibérer sur. **~ion,** *n*, négociation; affaire, transaction; délibération, *f*; (*pl.*) actes, *m.pl.*

transatlantic, *a*, transatlantique.

transcend, *v.t*, dépasser; surpasser. **~ent,** *a*, transcendant.

transcribe, *v.t*, transcrire. **transcript & transcription,** *n*, transcription, *f*.

transept, *n*, transept, *m*.

transfer, *n*, transmission; cession, *f*; apport; (*law*) transfert; transport; virement, *m*; (*for china & as toy*) décalcomanie; (*bus*) billet de correspondance, *m*. ~ [*deed*], transfert, *m*, feuille de t., *f*. ¶*v.t*, transmettre; céder; apporter; transférer; transporter; virer; décalquer. **~able,** *a*, cessible; mobilier.

transfiguration, *n*, transfiguration, *f*.

transfix, *v.t*, transpercer.

transform, *v.t*, transformer. **~ation,** *n*, transformation, *f*. **~er,** *n*, transformateur, *m*.

transfuse, *v.t*, transfuser. **transfusion,** *n*, transfusion, *f*.

transgress, *v.t*, transgresser, contrevenir à. **~or,** *n*, violateur, trice; pécheur, eresse.

transient†, *a*, transitoire, passager.

transit, *n*, transit; passage; transport, *m*. *in* ~, en transit; en cours de route. **~ion,** *n*, transition, *f*, passage, *m*. **~ive†,** *a*, transitif. **~ory†,** *a*, transitoire.

translate, *v.t*, traduire; (*bishop*) transférer. **translation,** *n*, traduction; version; (*bishop*) translation, *f*. **translator,** *n*, traducteur, trice.

translucent, *a*, translucide.

transmigration, *n*, transmigration, *f*.

transmission, *n*, transmission; (*auto*) boîte de vitesse; (*radio*) émission, *f*.

transmit, *v.t*, transmettre; émettre. **transmitter,** *n*, transmetteur; (*radio*) émetteur, *m*.

transmute, *v.t*, transmuer.

transom, *n*, vasistas, *m*; traverse, *f*.

transparency, *n*, transparence, *f*; transparent, *m*; diapositive, *f*. **transparent,** *a*, transparent.

transpire, *v.i*, transpirer.

transplant, *v.t*, transplanter, dépiquer.

transport, *n*, transport, *m*. ¶*v.t*, transporter. **~ation,** *n*, transportation, *f*. *piggyback* ~, ferroutage, *m*.

transpose, *v.t*, transposer.

transubstantiation, *n*, transubstantiation, *f*.

transverse†, *a*, transversal.

trap, *n*, trappe, *f*, traquenard, piège; guetapens, *m*. *mouse* ~, souricière, *f*. **~door,** trappe, *f*. ¶*v.t*, prendre au piège, attraper.

trapeze, *n*, trapèze, *m*.

trapper, *n*, trappeur, *m*.

trappings, *n.pl*, harnachement, *m*; (*fig.*) parure, *f*.

trash, *n*, camelote, pacotille, saloperie, saleté, *f*; (*worthless contents of book*) futilités, *f.pl.*

traumatic, *a*, traumatique. **traumatism,** *n*, traumatisme, *m*. **traumatize,** *v.t*, traumatiser.

travel, *n*, voyage, *m*. ¶*v.i*, voyager; marcher; rouler. ~ *over*, parcourir. **traveler,** *n*, voyageur, euse; placier, *m*. **traveling,** *p.a*, ambulant.

traverse, *v.t*, traverser.

travesty, *n*, travestissement, *m*. ¶*v.t*, travestir.

trawl [**net**], *n*, chalut, *m*, traille, *f*. ¶*v.i*, pêcher au chalut, p. à la traille. **~er,** *n*, [bateau] chalutier, *m*. **~ing,** *n*, pêche chalutière, *f*.

tray, *n*, plateau, *m*.

treacherous†, *a*, perfide, traître. **treachery,** *n*, traîtrise, perfidie, trahison, *f*.

treacle, *n*, mélasse, *f*.

tread, *n*, pas; (*of stair step*) giron, *m*. ¶*v.i.ir*, marcher; (*v.t. ir.*) fouler. ~ *water*, nager debout. **~le,** *n*, marche, pédale, *f*.

treason, *n*, trahison, *f*, crime d'État, *m*.

treasure, *n. & ~ trove*, trésor, *m*.

¶ *v.t*, garder précieusement. **treasurer**, *n*, trésorier, ère. **treasury**, *n*, trésor, *m*; trésorerie, caisse, *f*; fisc, *m*.

treat, *n*, régal; plaisir, *m*; débauche, *f*. ¶ *v.t. & i*, traiter; régaler. **treatise**, *n*, traité, *m*. **treatment**, *n*, traitement, *m*; (*music, art*) facture, *f*. **treaty**, *n*, traité, *m*. *by private* ~, à l'amiable.

treble†, *a*, triple. ¶ *n*, triple; (*Mus*.) dessus, *m*; (*crochet*) bride, *f*. ~ *clef*, clef de sol, *f*. ¶ *v.t*, tripler.

tree, *n*, arbre, *m*. ~*top*, cime d'un arbre, *f*. ~*less*, *a*, sans arbre.

trefoil, *n*, trèfle, *m*.

trellis, *n*, treillis, treillage, *m*. ¶ *v.t*, treillisser.

tremble, *v.i*, trembler. **trembling**, *n*, tremblement, *m*.

tremendous, *a*, énorme, formidable, effroyable, furieux, tout.

tremolo, *n*, tremolo, *m*. **tremor**, *n*, tremblement, *m*, trépidation, *f*. **tremulous**, *a*, tremblant.

trench, *n*, tranchée, *f*, fossé, *m*. ~ *coat*, trench-coat, *m*. ~ *mortar*, mortier de tranchée, *m*. ~ *warfare*, guerre de tranchées, g. de position, *f*. ¶ *v.t*, creuser; (*Mil*.) faire des tranchées. ~*ant*, *a*, tranchant, à l'emporte-pièce. **trencher**, *n*, tranchoir, tailloir, *m*. **trencherman**, *n*, mangeur, *m*.

trend, *n*, direction; tendance, *f*. ¶ *v.i*, se diriger.

Trent, *n*, Trente, *f*. *the Trentino*, le Trentin.

trepan, *n*, trépan, *m*. ¶ *v.t*, trépaner.

trepidation, *n*, tremblement, *m*.

trespass, *n*, intrusion; offense, *f*. ¶ ~ *against*, offenser. ~ *on*, s'introduire sans droit dans; (*fig*.) empiéter sur, abuser de. ~*er*, *n*, intrus, e. ~*s will be prosecuted*, défense d'entrer sous peine d'amende.

tress, *n*, tresse, *f*.

trestle, *n*, tréteau, chevalet, *m*.

Treves, *n*, Trèves, *f*.

trial, *n*, essai, *m*, épreuve; tribulation, *f*, procès; jugement, *m*; débats, *m.pl. to bring to* ~, mettre en jugement. ~ *& error*, tâtonnements, *m.pl.* ~ *balance*, balance de vérification, b. d'ordre, *f*. ~ *trip*, voyage d'essai, *m*.

triangle (*Geom. & Mus*.) *n*, triangle, *m*. **triangular**, *a*, triangulaire.

tribe, *n*, tribu; race, *f*.

tribulation, *n*, tribulation, *f*.

tribunal, *n*, tribunal, *m*. **tribune**, *n*, tribune, *f*; (*Hist. pers*.) tribun, *m*.

tributary, *a*, tributaire. ¶ *n*, tributaire; affluent, *m*. **tribute**, *n*, tribut; hommage, *m*.

trice, *n*, clin d'œil, *m*.

triceps, *a. & n*, triceps, *a. & m*.

trick, *n*, tour, jeu, *m*; ruse; ficelle; jonglerie, *f*; truc, *m*; (*cards*) levée, *f*; (*habit*) tic, *m*. ~ *riding*, voltige, *f*. ¶ *v.t*, tricher, duper. ~*ery*, *n*, tricherie, finasserie, *f*.

trickle, *n*, filet, *m*. ¶ *v.i*, [dé]couler, ruisseler.

trickster, *n*, tricheur, euse, finassier, ère, jongleur, *m*. **tricky**, *a*, adroit à s'évader; délicat.

tricycle, *n*, tricycle, *m*.

trident, *n*, trident, *m*.

triennial, *n*, triennal.

trifle, *a*, bagatelle, vétille, *f*, rien, *m*; misère; futilité, *f*. ¶ *v.i*, s'amuser à des riens; baguenauder. ~ *with*, se jouer de. **trifler**, *n*, baguenaudier, homme futile, *m*. **trifling**, *a*, insignifiant, minime; futile.

triforium, *n*, triforium, *m*.

trigger, *n*, détente, *f*; déclic, *m*.

trigonometry, *n*, trigonométrie, *f*.

trill, *n*, trille, *m*. ¶ *v.t*, orner de trilles.

trillion, *n*, billion, *m*.

trim, *a*, soigné, bien tenu; coquet. ¶ *n*, ornement, *m*; assiette, allure, *f*; arrimage, *m*. ¶ *v.t*, tailler; parer; agrémenter; garnir; (*edges*) rogner; (*book edges*) ébarber; (*hair*) tailler, rafraîchir; (*wood*) dresser; (*ship*) arrimer; (*sails*) orienter. **trimmings**, *n.pl*, passementerie; garniture, *f*, fourniture, *f. oft. pl*; (*Cook*.) garniture, *f*.

trimonthly, *a*, trimestriel.

Trinidad, *n. & the Trinity*, la Trinité.

trinket, *n*, colifichet, bibelot, *m*.

trio, *n*, trio, *m*.

trip, *n*, (*fall*) croc-en-jambe; tour, voyage, *m*, excursion, *f*. ~ [*up*], *v.t*, faire trébucher, donner un croc-en-jambe à; (*Mech*.) déclencher; (*anchor*) déraper; (*v.i.*) trébucher. ~ *along*, sautiller.

tripe, *n*, tripes, *f.pl.*

triplet†, *a*, triple. ¶ *v.t. & i*, tripler. **triplet**, *n*, triolet, tercet; *m*; (*pl.*) trois jumeaux, *m.pl.* **triplicate**, *n*, triplicata, triple, *m*.

tripod, *n*, trépied, *m*.

tripoli, *n*, tripoli, *m*.

triptych, *n*, triptyque, *m*.

trite†, *a*, banal. ~**ness**, *n*, banalité, *f*.

triton, *n*, triton, *m*.

triumph, *n*, triomphe, *m*. ¶ *v.i.* triompher. ~**al**, *a*, triomphal, de triomphe. ~**ant**, *a*, triomphant, victorieux. ~**antly**, *ad*, triomphalement.

trivet, *n*, trépied, *m*, chevrette, *f*.

trivial, *a*, insignifiant, minime; frivole.

troglodyte, *n*, troglodyte, *m*.

Trojan, *a*, troyen; (*war*) de Troie.

troll (*Fish.*) *v.i.* pêcher à la traîne.

trolley, *n*, tramway, trolley, *m*. ~ *bus*, autobus à trolley, *m*.

trolling, *n*, pêche à traîner, *f*.

trombone, *n*, trombone, *m*.

troop, *n*, troupe; bande, *f*. ~ *ship*, transport, *m*. ~ *train*, train militaire, *m*. ~**er**, *n*, cavalier, *m*.

trope, *n*, trope, *m*.

trophy, *n*, trophée, *m*; panoplie, *f*.

tropic, *n*, tropique, *m*. ~ *of Cancer, of Capricorn*, tropique du Cancer, du Capricorne. ~**al**, *a*, tropical.

trot, *n*, trot, *m*. ¶ *v.i. & t*, trotter.

troth, *n*, foi, *f*.

trotter, *n*, trotteur, euse; (*pl.*) (*pigs' feet*) pieds, *m.pl.*

troubadour, *n*, troubadour, *m*.

trouble, *n*, peine, *f*; chagrin; ennui; mal; trouble, *m. engine* ~, panne de moteur, *f*. ~*shooter*, dépanneur, *m*. ~ *spot*, point chaud, *m*. ¶ *v.t*, inquiéter, tourmenter, chagriner; déranger. ~**d**, *p.a*, agité, inquiet. ~ *waters* (*fig.*), eau trouble, *f*. ~**some**, *a*, fâcheux; difficultueux; gênant; (*child*) tourmentant.

trough, *n*, bac, baquet, *m*, auge; huche, *f*; (*of wave*) creux; (*sea*) entre-deux, *m*.

trounce, *v.t*, rosser, étriller.

troupe, *n*, troupe, *f*.

trouser, *n*, (*pl.*) pantalon, *m*.

trousseau, *n*, trousseau, *m*.

trout, *n*, truite, *f*. ~ *fishing*,

pêche à la t., *f*. ~ *stream*, rivière à truites, *f*.

trowel, *n*, truelle; (*Hort.*) houlette, *f*, déplantoir, *m*.

truancy, *n*, vagabondage, *m*. **truant**, *a*, vagabond. *to play* ~, faire l'école buissonnière.

truce, *n*, trêve, *f*.

truck, *n*, (*Rly.*) wagon; chariot, camion; (*hand*) diable; (*engine*) bogie, *m*. ~ *load*, wagon complet. *dump* ~, camion à benne basculante, *m. tow* ~, dépanneuse, *f*. ¶ *v.t*, rouler.

truckle, *v.i*, ramper.

truculent, *a*, truculent.

trudge, *v.i*, cheminer, clopiner.

true, *a*, vrai; véritable; loyal; fidèle; juste; conforme; rectiligne. *in one's* ~ *colors*, en déshabillé. [*certified*] *a* ~ *copy*, pour copie conforme, pour ampliation. ~*-love[r's] knot*, lacs d'amour, *m*. ~ *to life*, vécu. ¶ *v.t*, dégauchir, rectifier; [re]-dresser.

truffle, *n*, truffe, *f*.

truism, *n*, truisme, *m*. **truly**, *ad*, vraiment, véritablement; fidèlement.

trump, *n*, trompette, *f*. ~[*card*], *n. &* ~*s*, *n.pl*, atout, *m*, retourne, *f*. ~ *up*, fabriquer, inventer.

trumpery, *n*, friperie; camelote; blague, *f*. ¶ *a*, de pacotille; frivole.

trumpet, *n*, trompette, *f*. ~ *call*, sonnerie de t., *f*. ¶ *v.t. & i*, (*fig.*) trompeter, corner; (*elephant*) barrir; (*Mus.*) sonner de la trompette. ~**er**, *n*, trompette, *m*.

truncate, *v.t*, tronquer.

truncheon, *n*, bâton, *m*.

trundle, *n*, roulette, *f*. ¶ *v.t*, rouler.

trunk, *n*, tronc, *m*; tige, *f*; torse, *m*; (*elephant*) trompe; malle, *f*, coffre; bahut, *m*; (*pl.*) caleçon court, *m*. (*pl, Teleph.*) l'inter, *m*. ~ *call*, communication interurbaine, *f*. ~ *line*, grande artère, *f*.

trunnion, *n*, tourillon, *m*.

truss, *n*, trousse, botte, *f*; bandage [herniaire], brayer, *m*; (*Build.*) ferme, *f*. ¶ *v.t*, (*fowl*) trousser; (*hay*) botteler; (*Build.*) armer.

trust, *n*, confiance; créance, foi,

f, credit, *m*; charge, *f*; mandat; (*oil, steel*) trust, *m*. ~ **deed**, acte de fidéicommis, *m*. ¶ *v.t.* & *i*, se fier à; croire; faire crédit à; espérer. ~**ed**, *p.a*, de confiance. ~**ee**, *n*, curateur, trice; dépositaire, *m,f*, consignataire; syndic, *m*. **board of** ~**s**, conseil d'administration, *m*. ~**ful**, *a*, confiant. ~**worthy**, *a*, digne de confiance; croyable, fidèle. ~**y**, *a*, loyal, fidèle, sûr.

truth, *n*, vérité, *f*, vrai, *m*. ~**ful**, *a*, vrai, véridique. ~**fulness**, *n*. véracité, *f*.

try, *n*, essai, coup, *m*. ¶ *v.t.* & *i*, essayer; éprouver; expérimenter; goûter; tenter; tâter; chercher; (*law case*) juger; (*patience*) exercer. ~ **on**, essayer. ~**ing**, *a*, difficile; contrariant. ~ **time**, mauvais quart d'heure, *m*.

tub, *n*, cuve, *f*, baquet, tub; tonneau, *m*; caisse, *f*; (*bad ship*) sabot, *m*. *tub*[*by man*], poussah, *m*.

tuba, *n*, tuba, *m*.

tube, *n*, tube; (*anatomy*) conduit, *m*; (*radio*) lampe, *f*.

tuber & **tubercle**, *n*, tubercule, *m*. **tuberculosis**, tuberculose, *f*. **tuberculous**, *a*, tuberculeux. **tuberous**, *n*, tubéreuse, *m*.

tubular, *a*, tubulaire. ~ [*tire*], boyau, *m*.

tuck, *n*, rempli, troussis, *m*. ¶ *v.t*, remplier. ~ **in**, border. ~ **up**, [re]trousser.

Tuesday, *n*, mardi, *m*.

tuft, *n*, touffe, *f*; bouquet; panache, *m*; huppe; houppe; (*on chin*) mouche, *f*. ~**ed**, *a*, touffu; aigretté, huppé, houppé.

tug, *n*, tiraillement; coup de collier; (*boat*) remorqueur, toueur, *m*. ~ **of war**, lutte à la corde, *f*; (*fig.*) effort suprême, *m*. ¶ *v.t*, tirer.

tuition, *n*, (*fees*) droit d'inscriptions, *m.pl*; enseignement, *m*.

tulip, *n*, tulipe, *f*.

tulle, *n*, tulle, *m*.

tumble, *n*, chute, dégringolade, culbute, *f*. *take a* ~, ramasser une bûche. ~ **down**, tomber, dégringoler, culbuter, débouler. ~**down**, *a*, délabré. **tumbler**, *n*, (*pers.*) acrobate; (*pigeon*) culbutant; (*toy*) poussah; (*glass*) [verre] gobelet, *m*. **tumbrel**, -**il**, *n*, tombereau, *m*.

tumor, *n*, tumeur, glande, *f*.

tumult, *n*, tumulte, *m*. **tumultuous†**, *a*, tumultueux, houleux.

tumulus, *n*, tumulus, *m*.

tun, *n*, tonneau, foudre, *m*.

tuna, *n*, thon, *m*.

tune, *n*, air; accord, *m*; (*fig.*) cadence; (*fig.*) note, *f*, ton, *m*, gamme, *f*. ¶ *v.t*, accorder, mettre d'accord. **tuner**, *n*, accordeur, *m*. **tuneful†**, *a*, harmonieux, mélodieux.

tungsten, *n*, tungstène, *m*.

tunic, *n*, tunique, *f*.

tuning, *n*, accordage, *m*; (*motor*) mise au point, *f*. ~ **fork**, diapason à branches, *m*.

Tunis, *n*, Tunis, *m*. **Tunisia**, *n*, la Tunisie. **Tunisian**, *a*, tunisien.

tunnel, *n*, tunnel, souterrain, *m*. ¶ *v.t*, percer un tunnel sous.

turban, *n*, turban, *m*.

turbid, *a*, trouble.

turbine, *n*, turbine, *f*.

turbot, *n*, turbot, (*young*) turbotin, *m*.

turbulence, *n*, turbulence, *f*. **turbulent**, *a*, turbulent.

tureen, *n*, soupière, *f*.

turf, *n*, gazon, *m*; plaque de g., motte, *f*. *the* ~ (*racing*), le turf. ¶ *v.t*, gazonner.

turgid, *a*, turgescent, boursouflé.

Turk, *n*, Turc, *m*, Turque, *f*. **Turkey**, *n*, la Turquie. *t*~ [*cock*], dindon, coq d'Inde, *m*. *t*~[*hen*], dinde, poule d'Inde, *f*. **turkish**, *a*, turc. ~ **bath**, bain turc, *m*. ~ **carpet**, tapis de Turquie, *m*. ~ **towel**, serviette-éponge, *f*. ¶ (*language*) *n*, le turc.

turmeric, *n*, safran des Indes, *m*.

turmoil, *n*, ébullition, tourmente, *f*, tumulte, *m*.

turn, *n*, tour; retour; détour; *m*; tournure, *f*; revirement; (*tide*) changement, renversement, *m*. ~ **of the scale**, trait de balance, *m*. *at every* ~, à tout propos. *in* ~, tour à tour, à la ronde. *to a* ~, à point. ¶ *v.t.* & *i*, tourner; se t.; retourner; se r.; virer; pivoter; transformer; convertir; changer; (*discussion*) porter (*on* = sur). ~ **aside**, écarter; détourner; se d. ~ **back**, rebrousser chemin. ~ **off**, (*tap*) fermer; (*water*) couper; (*light*) éteindre. ~ **on**, (*tap*) ouvrir, lâcher; (*water*) faire couler, ouvrir le robi-

net de; (*light*) allumer. ~ *out
& ~ over,* [re]tourner. ~ *out
badly,* mal réussir. ~ *right over,*
faire panache. ~ *round,* se retourner. ~ *the scale,* faire
pencher la balance. ~ *up,*
[re]tourner; [re]trousser. *~ed-up
moustache,* moustache en croc, *f.
take ~s,* se relayer.

turncoat, *n,* transfuge, rénégat,
m.

turncock, *n,* fontainier, *m.*

turned (*a certain age*) *p.p,* dépassé, franchi, (*tant d'ans*)
sonnés.

turnip, *n,* navet, *m.* ~ *tops,* fanes
de navets, *f.pl.*

turnkey, *n,* porte-clefs, guichetier, *m.*

turnout (*Rly.*) *n,* branchement,
m.

turnover, *n,* revirement; (*Fin.*)
chiffre d'affaires, roulement;
(*Cook.*) chausson; (*stocking,
etc.*) revers, *m.*

turnpike, *n,* autoroute, *f.* ~ *toll-
gate,* pont à péage, *m,* barrière à
p., *f.*

turnstile, *n,* (X *on post*) moulinet; (*admission*) tourniquet
[-compteur] *m.*

turntable, *n,* plaque tournante,
f; (*phonograph*) plateau, *m.*

turpentine, *n,* térébenthine, *f.*

turpitude, *n,* turpitude, *f.*

turquoise, *n. & att,* turquoise, *f.
& att.*

turret, *n,* tourelle, *f.* ~ *lathe,* tour
à revolver, *m.* ~ *ship,* navire à
tourelles, *m.*

turtle, *n,* tortue de mer, *f.* ~
dove, tourterelle, *f.* (*young*) tour-
terau, *m.* ~*neck,* col roulé, *m.*

Tuscan, *a,* toscan. ~*y, n,* la Toscane.

tusk, *n,* défense, *f;* croc, *m.*

tussle, *n,* lutte, *f.*

tutelage, *n,* tutelle, *f.* **tutelar[y],**
a, tutélaire. **tutor,** *n,* précepteur,
répétiteur, préparateur, *m.* ¶ *v.t,*
instruire. **tutorship,** *n,* préceptorat, *m.*

tuxedo, *n,* smoking, *m.*

twaddle, *n,* balivernes, *f.pl,* babil,
m.

twang, *n,* nasillement; son aigre,
m. ¶ *v.i,* nasiller; résonner. ~
[*on*] (*stringed instrument*), pincer de.

tweak, *v.t,* pincer, tirer.

tweed, *n,* tweed, *m.*

'**tween-decks,** *n,* entrepont, *m.*

tweezers, *n.pl,* brucelles, pincettes, pinces, *f.pl.*

twelfth†, *a. & n,* douzième, *a. &
m,f;* douze, *m.* T~ *Night,* soir de
l'Epiphanie, *m.* **twelve,** *a. & n,*
douze, *a. & m.* ~ *o'clock* [*in the
day*] midi; [*at night*] minuit, *m.*

twentieth, *a. & n,* vingtième, *a.
& m,f;* vingt, *m.* **twenty,** *a. & n,*
vingt, *a. & m.*

twice, *ad,* deux fois. ~ *as much,*
deux fois autant.

twiddle, *v.t,* tourner, tortiller.

twig, *n,* brindille, *f,* (*pl.*) ramilles,
broutilles, *f.pl.*

twilight, *n,* crépuscule, *m,* pénombre, *f,* demi-jour, *m.* ~ *sleep,*
anesthésie à la reine, *f.*

twill, *n,* croisé, *m.* ¶ *v.t,* croiser.

twin, *a,* jumeau; conjugué. ¶ *n,* jumeau, elle; (*pl.*) deux jumeaux,
deux jumelles; (*crystal*) macle, *f.*
~ *beds,* lits jumeaux, *m.pl.*

twine, *n,* ficelle, *f.* ¶ *v.t,* enlacer;
cordonner.

twinge, *n,* élancement, *m.*

twining (*Bot.*) *p.a,* volubile.

twinkle, *v.i,* scintiller, clignoter.
in the twinkling of an eye, en un
clin d'œil. ¶ *n,* scintillement,
clignement, *m.*

twirl, *v.t,* faire tournoyer; (*stick*)
faire le moulinet avec; (*mous-
tache*) tortiller; (*v.i.*) pirouetter.

twist, *n,* torsade, *f,* tortillon, *m;*
torsion, *f,* cordon, *m;* contorsion, *f;* (*of straw*) torchon, *m;*
(*tobacco*) carotte, *f,* rouleau, *m.*
~*s & turns,* tours & retours, *m.pl.*
¶ *v.t,* tordre; [en]tortiller; cordonner. ~*ed, p.p. & p.a,* tordu;
[re]tors.

twit, *v.t,* reprocher.

twitch, *v.i,* avoir un tic, tiquer;
palpiter; (*v.t.*) arracher, crisper.
~*ing, p.a,* pantelant. ~*ing, n,*
tic, *m.*

twitter, *v.i,* gazouiller.

two, *a. & n,* deux, *a. & m.* ~ *days
before,* l'avant-veille, *f.* ~*-footed,*
~*-legged,* bipède. ~*-piece set,*
ensemble deux pièces, *m.* ~*-way
switch,* commutateur va-et-vient,
m. ~*fold, a,* double.

tympan & tympanum, *n,* tympan, *m.*

type, *n,* type; genre; (*Typ.*) caractère [d'imprimerie], type, *m.* ~
founder, fondeur en caractères,

m. ~ *metal,* matière, *f.* ~ *setting,* composition, *f.* ~[**write**], *v.t,* écrire à la machine, taper [à la m.]. ~*writer,* machine à écrire, *f.* ~*writing,* écriture à la machine, dactylographie, *f.* ~*written,* [écrit] à la machine.
typhoid [**fever**], *n,* fièvre typhoïde, *f.*
typhoon, *n,* typhon, *m.*
typhus, *n,* typhus, *m.*
typical, *a,* typique.
typist, *n,* dactylographe, *m.f.*
typographic(al), *a,* typographique. **typography,** *n,* typographie, *f.*
tyrannic(al†), *a,* tyrannique. **tyrannize** [**over**], tyranniser. **tyranny,** *n,* tyrannie, *f.* **tyrant,** *n,* tyran, *m.*
tyro, *n,* novice, *m.f.*
Tyrol (the), le Tyrol. **Tyrolese,** *a,* tyrolien. ¶ *n,* Tyrolien, ne.

U

ubiquity, *n,* ubiquité, *f.*
udder, *n,* mamelle, *f,* pis, *m.*
ugh, *i,* pouah! fi!
ugliness, *n,* laideur, *f.* **ugly,** *a,* laid; vilain. [*as*] ~ *as sin,* laid comme un crapaud.
ulcer, *n,* ulcère, *m.* ~**ate,** *v.i,* s'ulcérer.
ulterior†, *a,* ultérieur. ~ *motive,* arrière-pensée, *f.*
ultimate†, *a,* final; définitif. **ultimatum,** *n,* ultimatum, *m.*
ultramarine, *n,* outremer, *m.*
ultraviolet, *a,* ultra-violet.
umber, *n,* terre d'ombre, *f.*
umbrage, *n,* ombrage, *m.*
umbrella, *n,* parapluie; (*garden, beach, held over potentate*) parasol, *m.* ~ *ring,* rondelle de parapluie, *f.* ~ *stand,* porte-parapluies, *m.* ~*-sunshade,* en-[tout-]cas, *m.*
umpire, *n,* arbitre, *m.* ¶ *v.t,* arbitrer.
unabated, *a,* sans diminution.
unable, *a,* incapable. *to be* ~ *to,* ne pouvoir [pas].
unabridged, *a,* complet.
unacceptable, *a,* inacceptable.
unaccompanied, *a,* non accompagné.
unaccountable, *a,* inexplicable.
unaccustomed, *a,* peu habitué; inaccoutumé.

unacknowledged, *a,* non reconnu; sans réponse.
unacquainted with (to be) être ignorant de; ne pas connaître.
unadorned, *a,* sans ornements.
unadulterated, *a,* non falsifié; sans mélange.
unaffected, *a,* naturel, naïf; inaltérable (*by* = à).
unafraid, *a,* sans peur.
unalloyed, *a,* sans alliage.
unalterable, *a,* inaltérable.
unambiguous, *a,* non équivoque, précis.
unambitious, *a,* sans ambition; sans prétentions.
unanimous, *a,* unanime. ~**ly,** *ad,* à l'unanimité, unanimement.
unanswerable, *a,* sans réplique.
unappreciated, *a,* inapprécié, incompris.
unapproachable, *a,* inabordable.
unarmed, *a,* sans armes, désarmé.
unasked, *a,* sans être invité.
unassailable, *a,* inattaquable, hors d'atteinte.
unassuming, *a,* sans prétentions.
unattached (*Mil.*) *a,* en disponibilité.
unattainable, *a,* impossible à atteindre.
unattended, *a,* sans suite; sans garde.
unattractive, *a,* peu attrayant; peu séduisant.
unavailable, *a,* indisponible. **unavailing,** *a,* inutile, vain.
unavoidable†, *a,* inévitable.
unaware of (*to be*), ignorer. **unawares,** *ad,* à l'improviste, au dépourvu; par mégarde.
unbalanced, *a,* déséquilibré; (*Mech.*) non compensé.
unballast, *v.t,* délester.
unbandage, *v.t,* débander.
unbearable†, *a,* insupportable.
unbecoming, *a,* inconvenant, malséant; qui ne va pas. *to be* ~, messeoir.
unbelief, *n,* incrédulité, *f.* **unbeliever,** *n,* incrédule, *m.f.*
unbend, *v.t.ir,* détendre; débander. ~**ing,** *a,* inflexible.
unbiased, *a,* sans prévention; impartial.
unbind, *v.t.ir,* délier, détacher.
unbleached, *a,* écru.
unblemished, *a,* sans tache, intact.

unblock, *v.t.* (*passage, finances, etc.*) débloquer.

unblushing, *a*, éhonté.

unbolt, *v.t.*, déverrouiller.

unborn, *a*, à naître.

unbosom oneself, s'ouvrir.

unbound (*book*) *a*, non relié.

unbounded, *a*, sans bornes, illimité.

unbreakable, *a*, incassable.

unbridled, *a*, débridé; effréné.

unbroken, *a*, intact; ininterrompu; (*horse*) non dressé.

unbuckle, *v.t*, déboucler.

unbuilt on, non bâti, non construit.

unburden oneself, s'ouvrir.

unburied, *a*, sans sépulture.

unbusinesslike, *a*, incorrect.

unbutton, *v.t*, déboutonner.

uncalled for remark, observation déplacée, *f*.

uncanny, *a*, fantastique.

uncap, *v.t*, décalotter.

uncapsizable, *a*, inversable.

uncared for, à l'abandon.

unceasing, *a*, incessant. **~ly**, *ad*, incessamment, sans cesse.

unceremoniously, *ad*, sans cérémonie.

uncertain, *a*, incertain. **~ty**, *n*, incertitude, *f*.

unchain, *v.t*, déchaîner.

unchangeable†, *a*, immuable, invariable.

uncharitable, *a*, peu charitable; critique.

unchaste†, *a*, impudique, incontinent.

unchecked, *a*, sans frein.

uncircumcised, *a*, incirconcis.

uncivil†, *a*, incivil. **~ized**, *a*, sauvage.

unclad, *a*, nu.

unclaimed, *a*, non réclamé; en souffrance.

unclassified, *a*, non classé.

uncle, *n*, oncle, (*children's slang*) tonton, *m*.

unclean, *a*, sale; impur, immonde.

unclothed, *a*, nu.

unclouded, *a*, sans nuages.

uncock (*gun*) *v.t*, désarmer.

uncoil, *v.t*, dérouler.

uncomely, *a*, peu avenant.

uncomfortable, *a*, incommode; (*of pers.*) mal à son aise.

uncommon†, *a*, rare; singulier.

uncommunicative, *a*, taciturne.

uncomplaining, *a*, résigné. *the*

~ *poor*, les pauvres honteux, *m. pl.*

uncompleted, *a*, inachevé.

uncompromising, *a*, intransigeant.

unconcerned, *a*, indifférent, insouciant.

unconditional, *a. & ~ly*, *ad*, sans condition.

unconfirmed, *a*, non confirmé.

unconnected (*desultory*) *a*, décousu.

unconquerable†, *a*, invincible.

unconscious†, *a*, inconscient; (*dead faint*) sans connaissance. **~ness**, *n*, inconscience, *f*; une perte de connaissance.

unconsecrated ground, terre profane, *f*.

unconstitutional†, *a*, inconstitutionnel.

unconstrained, *a*, dégagé. **unconstraint**, *n*, désinvolture, *f*, abandon, laisser-aller, *m*.

uncontested, *a*, incontesté.

uncontrollable, *a*, ingouvernable; indomptable; inextinguible.

unconventional, *a*, sans gêne, original; affranchi, libre.

unconvincing, *a*, peu vraisemblable.

uncork, *v.t*, déboucher.

uncorrected, *a*, non corrigé.

uncouple, *v.t*, découpler.

uncouth, *a*, grossier, rude, rustaud.

uncover, *v.t*, découvrir; (*v.i.*) se découvrir.

uncreated, *a*, incréé.

unction, *n*, onction, *f*. **unctuous†**, *a*, onctueux.

uncultivated & uncultured, *a*, inculte.

uncurbed, *a*, indompté.

uncurl, *v.t*, défriser; dérouler.

uncustomary, *a*, inusité.

uncut, *a*, (*gem*) brut; (*cake*) non entamé. ~ *edges* (book), tranches non rognées, *f.pl.*

undamaged, *a*, non endommagé; non avarié.

undated, *a*, sans date, non daté.

undaunted, *a*, intrépide.

undeceive, *v.t*, détromper, désillusionner.

undecided, *a*, indécis; incertain.

undecipherable, *a*, indéchiffrable.

undefended, *a*, sans défense; sans défenseur; (*law case*) non contestée; (*heard ex parte*) jugée par défaut.

undefiled, *a*, sans souillure.

undefined, *a*, indéfini.

undeliverable, *a*, en souffrance. undelivered, *a*, non livré; non distribué.

undeniable, *a*, indéniable, incontestable.

undenominational, *a*, laïque, neutre.

under, *pr*, sous; dessous; au-dessous de; en; à; sauf. ~ *there*, là-dessous. ~ *water*, entre deux eaux. ¶ *ad*, dessous; au-dessous.

underassessment, *n*, insuffisance d'imposition, *f*.

underclothing, *n*, (*women's*) [vêtements de] dessous; (*men's*) sous-vêtements, *m.pl*.

undercurrent, *n*, courant de fond; courant sous-marin; (*in air*) courant inférieur; (*fig.*) courant secret, fond, *m*.

undercut (*meat*) *n*, filet, *m*.

underdeveloped, *a*, sous-développé. underdevelopment, *n*, sous-développement, *f*.

underdone, *a*, pas [assez] cuit; peu cuit, saignant.

underestimate, *v.t*, sous-estimer, mésestimer.

underexposure (*Phot.*) *n*, manque de pose, *m*.

underfed, *a*, sous-alimenté.

undergarment, *n*, (*men's*) sous-vêtement; (*women's*) vêtement de dessous, *m*.

undergo, *v.t.ir*, subir, souffrir.

underground, *a*, souterrain. ¶ *n*, (*war*) Résistance, *f*. ¶ *ad*, en souterrain.

undergrowth, *n*, broussailles, *f.pl*.

underhand, *a*, clandestin, souterrain, sournois, sourd; (*Ten. service*) par en bas. ¶ *ad*, sous main, clandestinement.

underline, *v.t*, souligner.

underling, *n*, employé subalterne, *m*.

underlying, *a*, sous-jacent.

undermentioned, *a*, ci-dessous.

undermine, *v.t*, miner, affouiller, caver.

undermost, *a*, le plus bas.

underneath, *ad*, dessous; au-dessous. ¶ *pr*, sous.

underpay, *v.t.ir*, payer trop peu.

underpin, *v.t*, reprendre en sous-œuvre.

underrate, *v.t*, mésestimer, déprécier.

underscore, *v.t*, souligner.

undersea, *a*, sous-marin.

undersecretary, *n*, sous-secrétaire, *m*.

undersell, *v.t.ir*, vendre moins cher que.

undershirt, *n*, maillot, *m*; chemisette, *f*.

underside, *n*, dessous, *m*.

undersigned, *a*. & *n*, soussigné, e.

understand, *v.t*. & *i. ir*, comprendre, voir; entendre; s'e. à; apprendre; sous-entendre. ~ing, *n*, intelligence, *f*; entendement, sens, *m*; compréhension; entente, *f*.

understudy, *n*, doublure, *f*. ¶ *v.t*, doubler.

undertake, *v.t.ir*, entreprendre; se charger de; s'engager, se faire fort. undertaker, *n*, entrepreneur de pompes funèbres, *m*. undertaking, *n*, engagement, *m*; entreprise, *f*; pompes funèbres, *f.pl*.

undertone (**in an**) *n*, à demi-voix.

undertow, *n*, ressac, *m*.

undervalue, *v.t*, mésestimer, déprécier.

underwear, *n*. See *underclothing*.

underwood, *n*, [bois] taillis, mort-bois, *m*, broussailles, *f.pl*.

underworld, *n*, pègre, *f*; enfers; bas-fonds de la société, *m.pl*; milieu, *m*.

underwrite, *v.t.ir*, (*Insce.*) souscrire, s. pour; (*Fin.*) garantir. underwriter, *n*, souscripteur, assureur; (*Fin.*) syndicataire, *m*. underwriting, *n*, souscription; garantie, *f*.

undeserved, *a*, immérité. undeserving, *a*, peu méritant; indigne (*of* = de).

undesirable, *a*. & *n*, indésirable, *a*. & *m.f*.

undetermined, *a*, indéterminé.

undeveloped, *a*, en friche.

undigested, *a*, non digéré; (*fig.*) indigeste.

undignified, *a*, sans dignité.

undisciplined, *a*, indiscipliné.

undiscoverable, *a*, introuvable. undiscovered, *a*, non découvert.

undiscriminating, *a*, sans discernement.

undismayed, *a*, sans être découragé.

undisputed, *a*, incontesté.

undisturbed, *a*, tranquille.

undo, *v.t.ir*, défaire, détacher; (*knitting*) démailler. ~**ing**, *n*, ruine, *f. come undone*, se défaire.

undoubted†, *a*, indubitable.

undress, *n*, déshabillé, négligé, *m*; (*Mil., Nav.*) petite tenue, *f.* ¶ *v.t*, déshabiller; (*v.i.*) se déshabiller.

undrinkable, *a*, imbuvable.

undue, *a*, exagéré, excessif; inexigible.

undulate, *v.i*, onduler, ondoyer. **undulating**, *a*, ondulé. **undulation**, *n*, ondulation, *f*.

unduly, *ad*, indûment; par trop.

undutiful, *a*, qui manque à ses devoirs.

undying, *a*, impérissable, immortel.

unearned, *a*, non acquis; immérité. ~ *increment*, plus-value, *f*.

unearth, *v.t*, déterrer. ~**ly**, *a*, spectral, fantomatique.

uneasiness, *n*, malaise, *m*, inquiétude, *f*, martel en tête, *m*. **uneasy†**, *a*, inquiet.

uneatable, *a*, immangeable.

uneducated, *a*, sans instruction.

unemployable (**the**), les incapables, *m.pl*. **unemployed**, *a*, inemployé; (*pers.*) sans travail, en chômage. *the* ~, les sans-travail, les chômeurs, *m.pl*. **unemployment**, *n*, manque de travail; chômage [involontaire] *m*. ~ *benefit*, indemnité de chômage, *f*. ~ *insurance*, assurance contre le chômage, *f*.

unending, *a*, sans fin.

unenterprising, *a*, sans initiative.

unenviable, *a*, peu enviable.

unequal†, *a*, inégal. ~ *to* (task), pas à la hauteur de; incapable de.

unequaled, *a*, sans égal, sans pareil.

unequivocal, *a*, non équivoque.

unerring†, *a*, infaillible; sûr.

uneven†, *a*, inégal; (*number*) impair. ~**ness**, *n*, inégalité; (*number*) imparité, *f*.

unexceptionable, *a*, irrécusable.

unexpected, *a*, inattendu; inespéré.

unexpired, *a*, non expiré; non couru; non échu; non périmé.

unexplained, *a*, inexpliqué.

unexplored, *a*, inexploré.

unexpurgated, *a*, intégral.

unfailing, *a*, infaillible; (*spring*) intarissable.

unfair†, *a*, injuste; déloyal; partial. ~**ness**, *n*, injustice; déloyauté; partialité, *f*.

unfaithful†, *a*, infidèle. ~**ness**, *n*, infidélité, *f*.

unfamiliar, *a*, étranger.

unfasten, *v.t*, dégrafer, défaire.

unfathomable, *a*, insondable, abyssal.

unfavorable†, *a*, défavorable, contraire. ~ *light*, contre-jour, *m*.

unfeasible, *a*, irréalisable, impraticable, infaisable.

unfeeling, *a*, insensible.

unfeigned†, *a*, sincère.

unfenced, *a*, sans clôture.

unfettered, *a*, sans entraves.

unfinished, *a*, inachevé, imparfait.

unfit, *a*, impropre; hors d'état; inapte; incapable. *the* ~, les inaptes, *m.pl*. ~**ness**, *n*, inaptitude; incapacité, *f*. **unfitting**, *a*, inconvenant.

unflagging, *a*, soutenu.

unfledged, *a*, sans plumes.

unflinching, *a*, à toute épreuve.

unfold, *v.t*, déployer; dérouler.

unforeseen, *a*, imprévu.

unforgettable, *a*, inoubliable.

unforgivable, *a*, impardonnable. **unforgiving**, *a*, implacable.

unfortified, *a*, non fortifié; (*town*) ouverte.

unfortunate†, *a*, malheureux, infortuné; regrettable. *the* ~, les malheureux, les infortunés, *m.pl*.

unfounded, *a*, sans fondement.

unfrequented, *a*, infréquenté.

unfriendly, *a*, inamical; hostile.

unfrock, *v.t*, défroquer.

unfruitful, *a*, stérile. ~**ness**, *n*, stérilité, *f*.

unfulfilled, *a*, non accompli.

unfurl, *v.t*, déferler, déployer.

unfurnished, *a*, non meublé.

ungainly, *a*, dégingandé.

ungathered, *a*, non cueilli.

ungenerous, *a,* peu généreux.

ungodliness, *n,* impiété, *f.* **ungodly,** *a,* impie.

ungovernable, *a,* ingouvernable; indomptable.

ungraceful, *a,* disgracieux.

ungracious, *a,* malgracieux, disgracieux.

ungrafted, *a,* franc.

ungrammatical, *a,* contre la grammaire. **~ly,** *ad,* incorrectement.

ungrateful, *a,* ingrat. **~ness,** *n,* ingratitude, *f.*

ungrudgingly, *ad,* de bon cœur.

unguarded, *a,* sans défense; indiscret.

unhair (*skins*) *v.t,* dépiler, débourrer.

unhallowed, *a,* profane.

unhappiness, *n,* malheur, *m.* **unhappy†,** *a,* malheureux.

unharmed, *a,* indemne.

unharness, *v.t,* déharnacher.

unhatched, *a,* non éclos.

unhealthiness, *n,* insalubrité, *f.* **unhealthy,** *a,* insalubre; malsain.

unheard of, inouï.

unheeded, *a,* négligé.

unhesitatingly, *ad,* sans hésitation.

unhewn, *a,* non taillé.

unhindered, *a,* sans empêchement.

unhinge, *v.t,* démonter; troubler, aliéner.

unholiness, *n,* impiété, *f.* **unholy,** *a,* impie.

unhonored, *p.a,* méconnu.

unhook, *v.t,* décrocher.

unhoped for, inespéré.

unhorse, *v.t,* démonter, désarçonner.

unhurt, *a,* indemne, sauf.

unicorn, *n,* licorne, *f.*

uniform, *a,* uniforme; uni. ¶ *n,* uniforme, *m,* tenue, *f.* **~ity,** *n,* uniformité, *f.* **~ly,** *ad,* uniformément. **unify,** *v.t,* unifier.

unilateral, *a,* unilatéral.

unimaginable, *a,* inimaginable.

unimpeachable, *a,* irrécusable.

unimpeded, *a,* sans entraves.

unimportant, *a,* insignifiant.

uninflammable, *a,* ininflammable.

uninhabitable, *a,* inhabitable. **uninhabited,** *a,* inhabité.

uninhibited, *a,* (*psychology*) défoulé.

uninitiated person, profane, *m,f.*

uninjured, *a,* indemne.

uninstructed, *a,* ignorant.

uninsured, *a,* non assuré; (*mail*) sans valeur déclarée, non chargé.

unintelligent, *a,* inintelligent. **unintelligible,** *a,* inintelligible.

unintentional†, *a,* involontaire.

uninterested, *a,* indifférent. **uninteresting,** *a,* sans intérêt.

uninterrupted, *a,* ininterrompu. **~ly,** *ad,* sans interruption.

uninvited, *a,* sans invitation. **uninviting,** *a,* peu attrayant; peu appétissant.

union, *n,* (*labor*) syndicat, *m*; union; alliance, *f*; (*Mech.*) raccord; (*pipe*) mi-fil, *m.* **U~ of South Africa,** Union Sud-Africaine. **U~ of Soviet Socialist Republics,** Union des Républiques soviétiques socialistes.

unique, *a,* unique.

unison, *n,* unisson, *m.*

unissued (*stocks, shares*) *a,* à la souche.

unit, *n,* unité, *f*; élément, *m.* **~ bookcase,** bibliothèque transformable, *f.* **~ price,** prix unitaire, *m.* **unite,** *v.t,* unir; joindre; réunir; allier; marier. **united,** *a,* uni; joint; réuni. **U~ Kingdom** [*of Great Britain and Northern Ireland*], Royaume-Uni [de Grande-Bretagne et Irlande du Nord] *m.* **U~ States** [*of America*], États-Unis [d'Amérique] *m.pl.* **unity,** *n,* unité; union, *f*; ensemble, *m.*

universal†, *a,* universel. **~ity,** *n,* universalité, *f.* **universe,** *n,* univers, *m.* **university,** *n,* université, *f*; (*att.*) universitaire.

unjust†, *a,* injuste. **~ judge,** [juge] prévaricateur, *m.* **unjustifiable,** *a,* injustifiable.

unkempt, *a,* mal peigné, inculte.

unkind, *a,* désobligeant; méchant. **~ness,** *n,* désobligeance; méchanceté, *f.*

unknown, *a,* inconnu; ignoré. **~ person,** inconnu, e. **~ [quantity],** [quantité] inconnue, *f.* **~ to,** à l'insu de. **the ~,** l'inconnu, *m.* **the U~ Soldier,** le Soldat inconnu.

unlace, *v.t,* délacer.

unlawful†, *a,* illégal, illicite. **~ assembly,** attroupement, *m.* **~ness,** *n,* illégalité, *f.*

unlearn, *v.t,* désapprendre. ~ed, *a,* illettré.

unleavened, *a,* sans levain; (*Bible*) azyme.

unless, *c,* à moins que . . .[ne]; à moins de; si . . . ne . . . pas; sauf.

unlettered, *a,* illettré.

unlicensed, *a,* marron.

unlicked cub, ours mal léché, *m.*

unlike, *a,* dissemblable. ¶ *pr,* dissemblable à. **unlikelihood,** *n,* invraisemblance; improbabilité, *f.* **unlikely,** *a,* invraisemblable; improbable.

unlimber, *v.i,* décrocher l'avant-train.

unlimited, *a,* illimité.

unlined, *a,* non doublé.

unload, *v.t,* décharger; (*Fin.*) se défaire de.

unlock, *v.t,* ouvrir; (*Typ.*) desserrer.

unlooked for, *a,* inattendu.

unloose, *v.t,* lâcher.

unlovely, *a,* disgracieux.

unlucky†, *a,* malheureux, malchanceux, malencontreux.

unmake, *v.t.ir,* défaire.

unman, *v.t,* ôter tout courage de.

unmanageable, *a,* intraitable; impossible à conduire.

unmanly, *a,* lâche; efféminé.

unmannerly, *a,* grossier.

unmanufactured, *a,* brut.

unmarketable, *a,* invendable.

unmarried, *a,* non marié; célibataire. **unmarry,** *v.t,* démarier.

unmask, *v.t,* démasquer.

unmentionable, *a,* dont on ne parle pas.

unmerciful†, *a,* impitoyable.

unmerited, *a,* immérité.

unmethodical, *a,* non méthodique, incorrect.

unmindful, *a,* inattentif, oublieux.

unmingled, *a,* sans mélange, pur.

unmistakable†, *a,* évident, manifeste; immanquable.

unmitigated, *a,* fieffé, insigne; non adouci.

unmixed, *a,* sans mélange, pur.

unmolested, *a,* en paix.

unmoor, *v.t,* démarrer.

unmounted, *a,* non monté; (*gem*) hors d'œuvre; (*pers.*) à pied.

unmoved, *a,* immobile; impassible.

unmusical, *a,* inharmonieux.

unmuzzle, *v.t,* démuseler.

unnamable, *a,* innommable. **unnamed,** *a,* innomé; anonyme.

unnatural, *a,* dénaturé; contre nature.

unnavigable, *a,* non navigable, impropre à la navigation.

unnecessary†, *a,* inutile.

unneighborly way (in an), en mauvais voisin.

unnerve, *v.t,* ôter tout courage de.

unnoticed, unobserved, *a,* inaperçu. **unobservant,** *a,* inattentif.

unobstructed, *a,* non obstrué; (*view*) dégagée.

unobtainable, *a,* impossible à se procurer.

unobtrusive, *a,* effacé; discret. ~ly, *ad,* discrètement.

unoccupied, *a,* inoccupé; libre, disponible.

unoffending, *a,* inoffensif.

unofficial, *a,* non officiel; (*information*) officieux.

unopened, *a,* non ouvert.

unopposed, *a,* sans opposition.

unorganized, *a,* non organisé.

unorthodox, *a,* hétérodoxe.

unostentatious, *a.* & ~ly, *ad,* sans ostentation.

unpack, *v.t,* dépaqueter, déballer, décaisser. ~ed, *a,* à découvert.

unpaid, *a,* (*bill*) impayé; (*capital*) non verse; (*letters*) non affranchi; (*no salary*) gratuit.

unpalatable, *a,* désagréable au goût.

unparalleled, *a,* sans pareil.

unpardonable, *a,* impardonnable.

unparliamentary, *a,* peu parlementaire.

unpatriotic, *a,* antipatriotique.

unperceived, *a,* inaperçu.

unphilosophical, *a,* peu philosophique.

unpin, *v.t,* enlever les épingles de.

unpleasant†, *a,* désagréable, méchant. ~ness, *n,* désagrément, *m.*

unpleasing, *a,* déplaisant, ingrat.

unpoetic(al), *a,* peu poétique.

unpolished, *a,* non poli; mat; brut; rude.

unpolluted, *a,* non souillé.

unpopular, *a,* impopulaire. ~ity, *n,* impopularité, *f.*

unpractical, *a,* peu pratique.

unpractised, *a,* inexercé; novice.

unprecedented, *a,* sans précédent(s).

unprejudiced, *a,* sans préjugés, impartial.

unpremeditated, *a,* sans préméditation.

unprepared, *a,* sans être préparé, au dépourvu.

unprepossessing, *a,* peu engageant.

unpretentious, *a,* sans prétentions; modeste, discret.

unprincipled, *a,* sans principes.

unprintable, *a,* impubliable.

unprocurable, *a,* impossible à se procurer.

unproductive, *a,* improductif.

unprofessional, *a,* contraire aux usages de sa profession.

unprofitable, *a,* peu lucratif; inutile; ingrat. **unprofitably,** *ad,* sans profit; inutilement.

unpromising, *a,* qui ne promet guère; ingrat.

unpronounceable, *a,* non prononçable. **~ name,** nom à coucher dehors, *m.*

unpropitious, *a,* peu propice.

unprotected, *a,* découvert, à découvert.

unprovided, *a,* dépourvu (*with* = de).

unprovoked, *a,* sans provocation, gratuit.

unpublished (*book*) *a,* inédit.

unpunctual†, *a,* inexact. **~ity,** *n,* inexactitude, *f.*

unpunished, *a,* impuni.

unqualified, *a,* sans les qualités requises; marron; formel; sans réserve.

unquenchable, *a,* inextinguible.

unquestionable†, *a,* indiscutable.

unravel, *v.t,* démêler, débrouiller, parfiler; dénouer.

unread, *a,* illettré; sans être lu. **~able** (*writing, insupportable book*) *a,* illisible.

unreal, *a,* irréel. **~ity,** *n,* irréalité, *f.*

unrealizable, *a,* irréalisable.

unreasonable†, *a,* déraisonnable, intraitable. **~ness,** *n,* déraison, *f.* **unreasoning,** *a,* irraisonnable.

unrecognizable, *a,* méconnaissable.

unredeemable, *a,* irrachetable. **unredeemed,** *a,* (*stock*) non amorti; (*pledge*) non dégagé.

unrefined, *a,* non épuré; brut; grossier.

unrefuted, *a,* irréfuté.

unregistered, *a,* non enregistré; (*mail*) non recommandé; (*trademark*) non déposée.

unrelenting†, *a,* inexorable, implacable, acharné.

unreliable, *a,* peu sûr; inexact; sujet à caution.

unremitting†, *a,* incessant, soutenu.

unremunerative, *a,* peu lucratif.

unrepealed, *a,* non abrogé.

unrepentant, *a,* impénitent.

unreservedly, *ad,* sans réserve.

unresponsive, *a,* froid, difficile à émouvoir.

unrest, *a,* agitation, effervescence, *f.*

unrestrained, *a,* immodéré; effréné.

unrestricted, *a,* sans restriction.

unretentive (*memory*) *a,* fugace.

unrewarded, *a,* sans récompense.

unrighteous†, *a,* injuste. **~ness,** *n,* injustice, *f.*

unripe, *a,* verte; en herbe. **~ness,** *n,* verdeur, *f.*

unrivaled, *a,* sans rival.

unrivet, *v.t,* dériver.

unroll, *v.t,* dérouler.

unruffled, *a,* imperturbable; calme, tranquille.

unruly, *a,* indiscipliné; turbulent.

unsaddle, *v.t,* desseller; (*pack animal*) débâter.

unsafe, *a,* peu sûr, mal assuré.

unsalable, *a,* invendable.

unsalaried, *a,* sans rétribution.

unsalted, *a,* non salé.

unsanitary, *a,* malsain, insalubre.

unsatisfactorily, *ad,* d'une manière peu satisfaisante. **unsatisfactory,** *a,* peu satisfaisant; défectueux.

unsavory, *a,* peu savoureux.

unsay, *v.t.ir,* se dédire de. **to leave unsaid,** taire.

unscathed, *a,* indemne, sauf.

unscientific, *a,* peu scientifique.

unscrew, *v.t,* dévisser. **to come ~ed,** se d.

unscrupulous, *a,* peu scrupuleux, indélicat. **~ly,** *ad,* sans scrupule.

unseal, *v.t,* desceller; (*letter*) décacheter.

unseasonable, *a,* hors de saison; hors de propos, inopportun. **unseasonably,** *ad,* mal à propos, inopportunément. **unseasoned** (*wood*) *a*, vert.

unseat, *v.t*, invalider; (*rider*) désarçonner.

unseaworthy, *a*, en mauvais état de navigabilité.

unseemly, *a*, malséant, inconvenant, folichon.

unseen, *a*, inaperçu, invisible; occulte.

unselfish, *a*, désintéressé. ~**ness**, *n*, désintéressement, *m*.

unserviceable, *a*, inutilisable.

unsettle, *v.t*, déranger; (*pers.*) bouleverser. ~**d**, *a*, (*weather*) incertain, variable; (*question*) indécise.

unshakable†, *a*, inébranlable.

unshapely, *a*, difforme.

unshaven, *a*, non rasé.

unsheathe, *v.t*, dégainer.

unsheltered, *a*, sans abri; non protégé.

unship, *v.t*, débarquer; (*oars*) déborder.

unshoe (*horse*) *v.t.ir*, déferrer.

unshrinkable, *a*, irrétrécissable.

unsightliness, *n*, laideur, *f*. **unsightly**, *a*, laid.

unsigned, *a*, non signé.

unsinkable, *a*, insubmersible.

unskillful, *a*, malhabile, maladroit. ~**ness**, *n*, maladresse, *f*. **unskilled**, *a*, inexpérimenté.

unslaked lime, chaux vive, *f*.

unsociable, *a*, insociable.

unsocial, *a*, antisocial.

unsold, *a*, invendu.

unsolicited, *a*, non sollicité, spontané.

unsolved, *a*, non résolu.

unsophisticated, *a*, non frelaté; naïf, ingénu.

unsought, *a*, sans qu'on le cherche.

unsound, *a*, vicieux; défectueux. *of ~ mind*, ne . . . pas sain d'esprit.

unsparing, *a*, prodigue; impitoyable.

unspeakable, *a*, indicible; ineffable.

unspent, *a*, non dépensé; non épuisé.

unspotted, *a*, sans tache.

unstable, *a*, instable; mouvant.

unstained, *a*, non teint; sans tache.

unstamped, *a*, non timbré; (*paper with no revenue stamps*

on) libre; (*letter*) non affranchie.

unsteadiness, *n*, instabilité; vacillation, *f*. **unsteady**, *a*, instable; chancelant; vacillant.

unstinting, *a*, prodigue.

unstitch, *v.t*, découdre.

unstop, *v.t*, déboucher.

unstressed (*Gram.*) *a*, atone.

unstudied, *a*, naturel.

unsubdued, *a*, insoumis, indompté.

unsubstantial, *a*, sans substance; immatériel.

unsuccessful, *a*, sans succès; manqué; infructueux. ~**ly**, *ad*, sans succès.

unsuitable†, *a*, impropre. **unsuited**, *a*, mal adapté; peu fait.

unsullied, *a*, sans tache.

unsupported, *a*, en porte à faux; sans appui.

unsurpassed, *a*, non surpassé.

unsuspected &, *a*, non soupçonné. **unsuspecting** & **unsuspicious**, *a*, peu soupçonneux; exempt de soupçon. **unsuspectingly**, *ad*, sans défiance.

unsweetened, *a*, non sucré; (*wine*) brut.

unswerving, *a*, inébranlable.

unsymmetrical, *a*, dissymétrique.

untack (*Need.*) *v.t*, débâtir.

untainted, *a*, non corrompu, non gâté; sans tache.

untamable, *a*, indomptable. **untamed**, *a*, indompté.

untarnished, *a*, non terni.

untaught, *a*, ignorant; inculte.

untenable, *a*, (*position, etc.*) intenable; (*assertion, etc.*) insoutenable.

untenanted, *a*, inhabité.

unthinkable, *a*, inimaginable. **unthinking**, *a*, irréfléchi.

unthread, *v.t*, désenfiler.

untidiness, *n*, désordre, *m*. **untidy†**, *a*, malpropre, désordonné, mal tenu.

untie, *v.t*, délier, détacher; dénouer.

until, *pr*, jusqu'à; jusque; avant à. ¶ *c*, jusqu'à ce que; en attendant que. *not ~*, ne . . . pas avant de, ne . . . pas avant que.

untimely, *a*, intempestif, prématuré; (*hour*) indue.

untiring†, *a,* infatigable, inlassable.

untold, *a,* indicible; inimaginable;
innombrable.

untouchable, *n,* paria, *m.* un-
touched, *a,* intact; sans y toucher;
non ému.

untoward, *a,* malencontreux,
fâcheux.

untrained, *a,* inexpérimenté;
(*animal*) non dressé.

untranslatable, *a,* intraduisible.

untraveled, *a,* (*country*) non
parcouru; (*pers.*) qui n'a jamais
voyagé.

untried, *a,* non essayé, non
éprouvé.

untrimmed, *a,* sans garniture;
non rogné.

untrodden, *a,* non frayé, non
battu.

untroubled, *a,* calme, paisible,
tranquille.

untrue, *a,* faux; mensonger; infidèle. untruly, *ad,* faussement.

untrustworthy, *a,* indigne de
confiance.

untruth, *n,* contrevérité; fausseté, *f,* mensonge, *m.* ~ful, *a,*
peu véridique, menteur.

untutored, *a,* inculte.

untwist, *v.t,* détordre, détortiller.

unused, *a,* non employé; non
utilisé; peu habitué. unusual, *a,*
peu commun, inaccoutumé, insolite, rare. ~ly, *ad,* extraor-
dinairement.

unutterable, *a,* indicible, ineffable.

unvarnished, *a,* non verni; pur
& simple.

unvarying, *a,* uniforme, invariable.

unveil, *v.t,* dévoiler; inaugurer.

unventilated, *a,* non aéré; mal
aéré.

unversed in, peu versé dans.

unwarily, *ad,* sans précaution.

unwarlike, *a,* peu belliqueux.

unwarrantable, *a,* inexcusable,
injustifiable.

unwary, *a,* peu circonspect.

unwashed, *a,* non lavé; crasseux.

unwavering, *a,* inébranlable.

unweaned, *a,* non sevré.

unwearied, *a,* infatigable.

unwelcome, *a,* importun; de
trop; désagréable.

unwell, *a,* indisposé, souffrant.

unwholesome, *a,* malsain; morbide.

unwieldy, *a,* lourd, pesant; incommode.

unwilling, *a,* peu disposé, mal
disposé. ~ly, *ad,* à contre-cœur.
~ness, *n,* mauvaise volonté; répugnance, *f.*

unwind, *v.t.ir,* dévider, dérouler.

unwisdom, *n,* manque de sagesse,
m. unwise, *a,* peu sage, malavisé.
~ly, *ad,* follement.

unwittingly, *ad,* sans y penser.

unwonted, *a,* inaccoutumé, insolite.

unworkable, *a,* inexécutable,
impraticable. unworked, *a,* in-
exploité. in an unworkmanlike
manner, en mauvais ouvrier.

unworn, *a,* non usé.

unworthiness, *n,* indignité, *f.*
unworthy, *a,* indigne.

unwounded, *a,* non blessé.

unwrap, *v.t,* développer; découvrir.

unwrinkled, *a,* sans rides.

unwritten, *a,* non écrit. ~ *law,*
droit coutumier, *m.*

unwrought, *a,* non travaillé,
non ouvré.

unyielding, *a,* inflexible, inébranlable.

unyoke, *v.t,* dételer.

up, *a,* montant. ~grade, montée,
côte, *f.* ¶ *ad,* en haut; au haut;
haut; en amont; debout; sur
pied; fini; (*prices*) en hausse;
(*risen*) levé, e. ~ & *down,* en
haut & en bas; de long en large.
~stairs, en haut. ~stream, *ad,*
en amont. ~ *there,* là-haut. ~
to, jusqu'à [concurrence de]. ~
to date, à la page; (*Fin.*) à jour;
(*att.*) moderne. well ~ *in* (subject), fort en, calé en. ¶ *ups &
downs,* hauts & bas, *m.pl.* ¶ *up!*
debout! alerte! levez-vous!

upbraid, *v.t,* reprocher.

upheaval, *n,* (*Geol.*) soulèvement; (*fig.*) bouleversement, *m,*
convulsion, *f.*

uphill, *a,* montant; ardu. ¶ *ad,*
en montant.

uphold, *v.t.ir,* soutenir, maintenir.
~er, *n,* soutien, *m.*

upholster, *v.t,* tapisser, rembourrer. ~er, *n,* tapissier, ère. ~y,
n, tapisserie, *f.*

upkeep, *n,* entretien, *m.*

upland, *n,* [haut] plateau, *m.*

uplift, *v.t,* ennoblir.

upon, *pr,* sur; dessus.

upper, *a,* supérieur; haut; de dessus. ~ *case* (*Typ.*), haut de casse, *m.* the ~ *classes,* les hautes classes, *f.pl.* ~ *deck,* pont supérieur, *m;* (*bus*) impériale, *f.* the ~ *hand* (*fig.*), le dessus; l'avantage, *m.* ~ *register* (*Mus.*), aigu, *m.* ~ *tooth,* dent de dessus, *f.* ~most, *a,* le plus haut, le plus élevé; le plus fort.

upright, *a. & ad,* droit; debout; vertical; d'aplomb; intègre, honnête. ~ *piano,* piano droit, *m.* ~ness, *n,* perpendicularité; droiture, intégrité, *f.*

uprising, *n,* soulèvement, *m.*

uproar, *n,* tumulte, vacarme, tapage, bacchanal, *m.* ~ious†, *a,* bruyant, tapageur.

uproot, *v.t,* déraciner, arracher.

upset, *n,* remue-ménage, *m.* ¶ *v.t,* renverser; verser; chavirer; déranger; bouleverser, rompre.

upshot, *n,* issue, *f,* fin mot; dénouement, *m.*

upside down, *ad,* sens dessus dessous.

upstart, *n,* parvenu, e.

upstroke, *n,* (*piston*) course montante, *f;* (*writing*) délié, *m.*

up-to-date, *a,* à la page; (*records*) mis à jour.

upward, *a,* ascendant; ascensionnel; jeté vers le haut. ~[s], *ad,* en haut, en contre-haut; en montant; au-dessus. ~s *of,* plus de.

Ural (the), l'Oural, *m.* the ~ *Mountains,* les monts Ourals, *m.pl.*

uranium, *n,* uranium, *m.*

urban, *a,* urbain. ~ *planner,* aménageur, *m.* **urbane,** *a,* courtois, poli. ~ly, *ad,* avec urbanité.

urchin, *a,* gamin, galopin, moutard, *m.*

urethra, *n,* urètre, *m.*

urge, *n,* démangeaison, *f.* ¶ *v.t,* pousser, presser, solliciter; exhorter; alléguer. **urgency,** *n,* urgence, *f.* **urgent,** *a,* urgent, pressant, instant. ~ly, *ad,* instamment.

uric, *a,* urique. **urinal,** *n,* urinoir, *m,* vespasienne, *f;* (*vessel*) urinal, *m.* **urinate,** *v.i,* uriner. **urine,** *n,* urine, *f.*

urn, *n,* urne, *f;* (*tea*) samovar, *m.*

us, *pn,* nous.

usage, *n,* usage; traitement, *m.* **usance,** *n,* usance, *f.* **use,** *n,* usage; emploi; emprunt, *m;* jouissance; utilité; habitude; consommation, *f.* to be of ~, servir. to make ~ of, se servir de. ¶ *v.t,* se servir de, employer, emprunter; consommer; user de; traiter. to get ~d to, s'habituer. ~ no hooks, ne pas se servir de crochets. ~d, *p.a,* usité; accoutumé, rompu; ayant déjà servi; usagé, d'occasion. ~ *car,* voiture d'occasion, *f.* ~ful†, *a,* utile. ~fulness, *n,* utilité, *f.* ~less†, *a,* inutile; vain. ~ *person,* non-valeur, *f.* ~ *things,* inutilités, *f.pl.* ~lessness, *n,* inutilité, *f.* **user,** *n,* usager, *m.*

Ushant, *n,* Ouessant, *m.*

usher, *n,* (*court*) huissier, (*Theat.*) ouvreur, euse. ~in, introduire, annoncer; (*fig.*) inaugurer.

usual†, *a,* usuel; habituel; obligé; ordinaire.

usufruct, *n,* usufruit, *m.*

usurer, *n,* usurier, ère, fesse-mathieu, *m.* **usurious†,** *a,* usuraire.

usurp, *v.t,* usurper. ~ation, *n,* usurpation, *f.* ~er, *n,* usurpateur, trice.

usury, *n,* usure, *f.*

utensil, *n,* ustensile; vase, *m.*

uterine, *a,* utérin. **uterus,** *n,* utérus, *m.*

utilitarian, *a.& n,* utilitaire, *a. & m,f.*

utility, *n,* utilité, *f.* **utilize,** *v.t,* utiliser.

utmost, *a,* extrême, dernier. one's [very] ~, [tout] son possible, l'impossible, *m.* to the ~, à outrance.

utopia, *n,* utopie, *f.* **utopian,** *a,* utopique, utopiste. ¶ *n,* utopiste, *m,f.*

utter†, *a,* complet; total; extrême; grand. ¶ *v.t,* proférer, prononcer, dire, débiter; (*cry*) pousser; (*money*) passer. ~ance, *n,* articulation; parole, *f;* débit, *m.* ~most, *a,* extrême; le plus reculé.

uvula, *n,* luette, uvule, *f.*

V

vacancy, *n,* vacance, *f;* vide, *m.* **vacant,** *a,* vacant; libre, inoc-

cupé; distrait. **vacate**, *v.t.* (*office*) quitter; (*premises*) vider. **vacation**, *n*, vacances, *f.pl.*

vaccinate, *v.t.*, vacciner. **vaccination**, *n*, vaccination, *f*. **vaccine**, *n*, vaccin, *m*.

vacillate, *v.i*, vaciller. **vacillation**, *n*, vacillation, *f*.

vacuity, *n*, vacuité, *f*. **vacuous**, *a*, insignifiant. **vacuum**, *n*, vide, *m*. ~ *cleaner*, aspirateur [de poussières] *m*.

vagabond, *n*. & *a*, vagabond, e.

vagary, *n*, caprice, *m*, lubie, *f*.

vagina, *n*, vagin; (*slang*) abricot, *m*, chatte, *f*.

vagrancy, *n*, vagabondage, *m*. **vagrant**, *n*, vagabond, e, clochard, e. ¶ *a*, vagabond,

vague†, *a*, vague, imprécis. ~**ness**, *n*, vague, *m*, imprécision, *f*.

vain†, *a*, vain, vaniteux. ~**glorious**, *a*, vaniteux, glorieux, superbe. ~**glory**, *n*, gloriole, superbe, *f*.

valance, *n*, pente, *f*.

vale, *n*, vallon, val, *m*.

valedictory, *a*, d'adieu.

valence (*Chem.*) *n*, valence, *f*.

Valencia, *n*, Valence, *f*.

valet, *n*, valet [de chambre] *m*. ¶ *v.t*, faire office de valet à.

valetudinarian, *a*. & *n*, valétudinaire, *a*. & *m.f*.

valiant†, *a*, vaillant, brave.

valid†, *a*, valide; (*ticket*) valable. ~**ate**, *v.t*, valider. ~**ity**, *n*, validité, *f*.

valise, *n*, valise, *f*.

valley, *n*, vallée; (*of roof*) noue, *f*.

valorous†, *a*, valeureux. **valor**, *n*, valeur, vaillance, bravoure, *f*.

valuable, *a*, de valeur, de prix, riche; précieux. ~**s**, *n.pl*, valeurs, *f.pl*, objets de valeur, *m.pl*. **valuation**, *n*, évaluation, *f*. **value**, *n*, valeur, *f*; prix, *m. food* ~, valeur nutritive, *f. market* ~, v. marchande, *f*. ¶ *v.t*, évaluer; apprécier; faire cas de. ~**less**, *a*, sans valeur.

valve, *n*, soupape; valve, *f. exhaust* ~, soupape d'échappement, *f. safety* ~, s. de sécurité, *f*.

vamp (*shoe*), *n*, empeigne, *f*. ¶ *v.t*. & *i*, improviser.

vampire, *n*, vampire, *m*.

van, *n*, voiture; tapissière, *f*; wagon; fourgon, *m*. ~[*guard*], avant-garde, *f*.

vanadium, *n*, vanadium, *m*.

vandal, *n*, vandale, *m*. ¶ *a*, de vandale. ~**ism**, *n*, vandalisme, *m*.

vane, *n*, girouette; (*turbine*) aube; aile; (*technical*) pinnule, *f*.

vanilla, *n*, vanille, *f*.

vanish, *v.i*, s'évanouir, disparaître, devenir invisible; s'éclipser, se volatiliser, fuir. ~**ing point**, point de fuite, *m*.

vanity, *n*, vanité, *f*.

vanquish, *v.t*, vaincre. *the* ~*ed*, les vaincus, *m.pl*.

vantage, *n*, avantage, *m*.

vapid, *a*, insipide, fade, plat.

vaporize, *v.t*, vaporiser. **vaporizer**, *n*, vaporisateur, *m*. **vaporous**, -**ry**, *a*, vaporeux. **vapor**, *n*, vapeur, *f*.

variable, *a*, variable; changeant. *at variance*, en désaccord, en mésintelligence. **variant**, *n*, variante, *f*. **variation**, *n*, variation, *f*; changement, *m*; modification, *f*.

varicose vein, varice, *f*.

variegate, *v.t*, varier, bigarrer, panacher, diaprer. **variety**, *n*, variété, diversité; variation, *f*.

various†, *a*, différent, divers.

varlet (*Hist.*) *n*, varlet, *m*.

varnish, *n*, vernis, *m*. ¶ *v.t*, vernir. ~**ing**, *n*, vernissage, *m*.

vary, *v.t*. & *i*, varier; diversifier; modifier.

vascular, *a*, vasculaire.

vase, *n*, vase, *m*.

vaseline, *n*, vaseline, *f*.

vassal (*Hist.*) *n*, vassal, e.

vast, *a*, vaste, immense. ~**ly**, *ad*, grandement. ~**ness**, *n*, immensité, *f*.

vat, *n*, cuve, *f*, bac, *m*. ¶ *v.t*, encuver.

vaudeville, *n*, vaudeville, *m*.

vault, *n*, voûte; cave, *f*; caveau; tombeau; (*leap*) saut, *m*; chambre forte, *f*. ¶ *v.t*, voûter; (*v.i.*) sauter. ~**ing horse**, cheval de bois, *m*.

vaunt, *n*, vanterie, *f*. ¶ *v.t*, vanter; (*v.i.*) se vanter.

veal, *n*, veau, *m*. ~ *cutlet*, côtelette de v., *f*.

vector, *n*, vecteur, *m*.

veer, *v.i*, (*wind*) se ranger, remonter; (*opinion*) se retourner. ¶ *n*, virage, *f*. ~**ing** (*opinion*) *n*, revirement, *m*.

vegetable, *n*, légume, *m*, plante potagère, *f*. ¶ *a*, végétal. ~ *dish*, légumier. *m*. ~ *marrow*, courge à la moelle, *f*. **vegetarian,** *a*. & *n*, végétarien, ne. **vegetarianism,** *n*, végétarisme. *m*. **vegetate,** *v.i*, végéter. **vegetation,** *n*, végétation, *f*.

vehemence, *n*, véhémence, *f*. **vehement†,** *a*, véhément.

vehicle, *n*, (*carriage*) véhicule, *m*, voiture, *f*; (*medium*) véhicule, *m*. *vehicular traffic*, circulation des voitures, *f*.

veil, *n*, voile, *m*; voilette, *f*; (*fig.*) voile, rideau, bandeau, *m*. ¶ *v.t*, voiler.

vein, *n*, veine; (*leaf*) nervure, *f*. ¶ *v.t*. veiner.

vellum, *n*, vélin, *m*.

velocipede, *n*, vélocipède, *m*.

velocity, *n*, vitesse, *f*.

velour, *n*, feutre velours, *m*.

velum (*Anat.*) *n*, voile, *m*.

velvet, *n*, velours, *m*. ~ *pile*, moquette, *f*. **velveteen,** *n*, velours de coton, *m*, tripe de velours, *f*. **velvet[y],** *a*, velouté.

venal†, *a*, vénal. ~**ity,** *n*, vénalité, *f*.

vendor, *n*, vendeur, euse; marchand, e; (*law*) vendeur, eresse; (*law*) apporteur, *m*. ~'*s assets*, valeurs d'apport, *f.pl*.

veneer, *n*, bois de placage, *m*, feuilles de p., *f.pl*; (*fig.*) vernis, *m*. ¶ *v.t*, plaquer; (*fig.*) donner du vernis à.

venerable, *a*, vénérable. **venerate,** *v.t*, vénérer. **veneration,** *n*, vénération, *f*.

venereal, *a*, vénérien.

Venetia, *n*, la Vénétie. **Venetian,** *a*, vénitien. ~ *blind*, jalousie, *f*. ¶ *n*, Vénitien, ne.

vengeance, *n*, vengeance, *f*. **vengeful,** *a*, vengeur.

venial†, *a*, véniel.

Venice, *n*, Venise, *f*.

venison, *n*, venaison, *f*.

venom, *n*, venin, *m*. ~**ous,** *a*, venimeux; vénéneux.

vent, *n*, évent, aspirail, soupirail, *m*; lumière; cheminée, *f*; libre cours, *m*, carrière, *f*. ¶ *v.t*, exhaler; donner libre cours à, évaporer. **ventilate,** *v.t*, aérer, donner de l'air à, ventiler. **ventilation,** *n*, aérage, *m*, aération, ventilation, *f*. **ventilator,** *n*, ventilateur; *m*; (*ship*) manche à air, manche à vent, *f*.

ventral, *a*, ventral.

ventricle, *n*, ventricule, *m*.

ventriloquism, -quy, *n*, ventriloquie, *f*. **ventriloquist,** *n*, ventriloque, *m,f*.

venture, *n*, aventure, entreprise, spéculation, *f*; hasard, *m*. ~ *capital*, capital-risque. *m*. ¶ *v.t*, aventurer, hasarder. ~ *to*, oser, se permettre de. ~**some,** *a*, aventureux; hasardeux.

veracious†, *a*, véridique. **veracity,** *n*, véracité, *f*.

veranda[h], *n*, véranda, *f*.

verb, *n*, verbe, *m*. **verbal†,** *a*, verbal. **verbatim,** *ad*. & *a*, mot à mot, *m*. pour *m*. **verbiage,** *n*, verbiage, *m*. **verbose,** *a*, verbeux. **verbosity,** *n*, verbosité, *f*.

verdant, *a*, verdoyant; naïf.

verdict, *n*, verdict, *m*.

verdigris, *n*, vert-de-gris, verdet, *m*.

verdure, *n*, verdure, *f*.

verge, *n*, bord, *m*; orée, *f*; (*road*) accotement; (*fig.*) penchant, point, *m*; (*rod*) verge, *f*. ¶ ~ *on*, tirer à; pencher vers.

verification, *n*, vérification, *f*. **verify,** *v.t*, vérifier. **verisimilitude,** *n*, vraisemblance, *f*. **veritable†,** *a*, véritable. **verity,** *n*, vérité, *f*.

vermicelli, *n*, vermicelle, *m*, nouilles, *f.pl*.

vermilion, *n*, vermillon, *m*. ¶ *a*, vermeil.

vermin, *n*, vermine, *f*; animaux nuisibles, *m.pl*. ~**ous,** *a*, couvert de vermine.

vermouth, *n*, vermouth, *m*.

vernacular, *a*, vulgaire. ¶ *n*, langue vulgaire, *f*.

vernal, *a*, printanier; (*equinox*) de printemps.

vernier, *n*, vernier, *m*.

Verona, *n*, Vérone, *f*.

veronica, *n*, véronique, *f*.

versatile, *a*, souple. **versatility,** *n*, souplesse d'esprit, *f*.

verse, *n*, vers, *m*; vers, *m.pl*; verset; couplet, *m*, strophe, *f*. **versed in,** versé dans, ferré en. **versicle** (*Lit.*) *n*, verset, *m*. **versifier,** *n*, versificateur, *m*. **versify,** *v.t*, versifier, rimer. **version,** *n*, version, *f*. **verso,** *n*, verso, *m*.

versus, *pr*, contre.

vertebra, *n*, vertèbre, *f*. **vertebral,** *a*, vertébral. **vertebrate,** *a*. & *n*, vertébré, *a*. & *m*.

vertex, n, sommet, m. **vertical**, a, vertical. ¶ n, verticale, f. ~**ity**, n, verticalité, f. ~**ly**, ad, verticalement. ~ **strung piano**, piano à cordes droites, m.

vertiginous, a, vertigineux. **vertigo**, n, vertige, m.

verve, n, verve, f.

very, a, même; seul. ¶ ad, très; fort; bien; tout. ~ **much**, beaucoup.

vesicle, n, vésicule, f.

vespers, n.pl, vêpres, f.pl.

vessel, n, vase, récipient; (blood) vaisseau; (ship) vaisseau, bâtiment, navire, m.

vest, n, (man's) gilet, m; (woman's) chemise, camisole; f. ¶ v.t, investir; confier. ~**ed rights**, droits acquis, m.pl.

vesta, n, allumette, f.

vestal [virgin], n, vestale, f.

vestibule, n, vestibule, m.

vestige, n, vestige, m, trace, f.

vestment, n, vêtement, m.

vestry, n, sacristie; (council) fabrique, f.

Vesuvian, n, vésuvien. **Vesuvius**, n, le Vésuve.

veteran, n, vétéran; ancien combattant, m. ¶ a, qui a vieilli dans sa profession; de longue date; depuis longtemps sous les drapeaux.

veterinary, a, vétérinaire. ~ [surgeon], [médecin] vétérinaire, m.

veto, n, veto, m. ¶ v.t, mettre le (son) v. à.

vex, v.t, contrarier, chagriner, vexer. ~**ation**, n, contrariété, f; désagrément, m; vexation, f. **vexatious**, a, contrariant, vexatoire. **vexed** (question) p.a, controversée, longuement débattue.

via, pr, par la voie [de], par.

viability, n, viabilité, f. **viable**, a, viable.

viaduct, n, viaduc, m.

vial, n, fiole, f.

viand, n, mets, m.

vibrate, v.i, (Phys. & fig.) vibrer; (machinery, car) trembler. **vibration**, n, vibration; trépidation, f.

vicar, n, vicaire; curé; ministre, m. ~**age**, n, cure, f; presbytère, m. ~**ship**, n, cure, f.

vice, n, (depravity) vice, m.

vice-, prefix, vice-. ~-**chairman**, ~-**president**, vice-president, e. ~-**principal** (college), censeur,

m. ~-**reine**, vice-reine, f. ~-**roy**, vice-roi, m.

Vicenza, n, Vicence, f.

vice versa, ad, vice versa, réciproquement.

vicinity, n, voisinage, m, proximité, f.

vicious†, a, vicieux. ~ **circle**, cercle vicieux, m. ~**ness**, n, nature vicieuse, f.

vicissitude, n, vicissitude, péripétie, f, cahot, m.

victim, n, victime, f. ~**ize**, v.t, rendre victime.

victor, n, vainqueur, m. **victorious†**, a, victorieux. **victory**, n, victoire, f.

victual, v.t, ravitailler. ~**s**, n.pl, vivres, m.pl, victuailles, f.pl.

vicuña, n, vigogne, f.

video, a, vidéo. ¶ n, vidéo, m. ~ **tape**, bande ~, f. ~ **conference**, visioconférence, f.

vie, v.i, rivaliser; lutter; faire assaut.

Vienna, n, Vienne, f. **Viennese**, a, viennois. ¶ n, Viennois, e.

view, n, vue; perspective, f, coup d'œil; tableau, m; idée, opinion, f. **to have in ~**, viser. ~-**finder**, viseur, m. ¶ v.t, contempler; envisager.

vigil, n, veille; veillée; (Eccl.) vigile, f. ~**ance**, n, vigilance, f. ~**ant**, a, vigilant. ~**antly**, ad, avec vigilance.

vignette, n, vignette, f. ¶ v.t, dégrader. **vignetter**, n, dégradateur, m.

vigor, n, vigueur; sève, f. **vigorous†**, a, vigoureux.

vile, a, vil; abject. ~**ness**, n, bassesse; abjection, f. **vilify**, v.t, vilipender.

villa, n, villa, f. **village**, n, village, m; bourgade, f; (att.) villageois, de village, de clocher. **villager**, n, villageois, e.

villain, n, scélérat, e, misérable, m,f; bandit; (Theat.) traître, m; (Hist.) vilain, e. ~**ous**, a, scélérat. ~**y**, n, scélératesse, f. **villein**, n, vilain, e.

vindicate, v.t, justifier. **vindication**, n, justification, f.

vindictive, a, vindicatif.

vine, n, vigne, f. ~ **shoot**, sarment, m. **vinegar**, n, vinaigre, m. ~ **works**, vinaigrerie, f. ¶ v.t, vinaigrer. **vinery**, n, serre à vignes, f. **vineyard**, n, vigne, f; vignoble, m.

vinosity, *n*, vinosité, *f*. **vinous**, *a*, vineux. **vintage**, *n*, (*growth*) cru, *m*, cuvée; (*season*) vendange; (*crop*) récolte, vinée, *f*. ~ *wine*, vin millésimé, *m*. ~ *year*, année à millésime, *f*. **vintager**, *n*, vendangeur, euse.

viola, *n*, (*Mus.*) alto, *m*; (*Bot.*) violariacée, *f*. **violaceous**, *a*, violacé.

violate, *v.t*, violer. **violation**, *n*, violation, *f*; (*rape*) viol, *m*. **violator**, *n*, violateur, trice. **violence**, *n*, violence, *f*. *do* ~ *to*, violenter. **violent†**, *a*, violent.

violet, *n*, (*Bot.*) violette, *f*; (*color*) violet, *m*. ¶ *a*, violet.

violin, *n*, violon, *m*. ~**ist**, *n*, violoniste, *m,f*. **violoncellist**, *n*, violoncelliste, *m,f*. **violoncello**, *n*, violoncelle, *m*.

viper, *n*, vipère, *f*.

virago, *n*, dragon, *m*, mégère, *f*.

virgin, *n*, vierge; pucelle, *f*. ¶ *a*, vierge. ~**alt**, *a*, virginal. **Virginia** (*Geog.*) *n*, la Virginie, *f*. ~ *creeper*, vigne vierge, *f*. ~ [*tobacco*], virginie, *m*. **virginity**, *n*, virginité, *f*.

virile, *a*, viril, mâle. **virility**, *n*, virilité, *f*.

virtual†, *a*, virtuel. **virtue**, *n*, vertu, *f*. **virtuosity**, *n*, virtuosité, *f*. **virtuoso**, *n*, virtuose, *m,f*. **virtuous†**, *a*, vertueux.

virulence, *n*, virulence, *f*. **virulent**, *a*, virulent. **virus**, *n*, virus, *m*.

visa, *n*, visa, *m*. ¶ *v.t*, viser.

visage, *n*, visage, *m*, figure, *f*.

viscera, *n,pl*, viscères, *m,pl*.

viscid & **viscous**, *a*, visqueux. **viscose**, *n*, viscose, *f*. **viscosity**, *n*, viscosité, *f*.

viscount, *n*, vicomte, *m*. ~**ess**, *n*, vicomtesse, *f*.

vise, *n*, étau, *m*.

visibility, *n*, visibilité, *f*. **visible**, *a*, visible. **visibly**, *ad*, visiblement; à vue d'œil.

vision, *n*, vision, *f*. ~**ary**, *a*, visionnaire; chimérique. ¶ *n*, visionnaire, *m,f*; illuminé, *m*.

visit, *n*, visite, *f*. ¶ *v.t*, visiter; voir; (*Cust.*) arraisonner. ~**ation**, *n*, visite; (*Eccl.*) visitation, *f*. ~**ing card**, carte de visite, *f*. ~**or**, *n*, visiteur, euse; hôte, esse; passager, ère. ~**s' tax**, taxe de séjour, *f*.

visor, *n*, visière, *f*.

vista, *n*, échappée [de vue]; perspective, *f*.

Vistula (the), la Vistule.

visual, *a*, visuel. ~**ize**, *v.t*, se représenter.

vital, *a*, vital; (*fig.*) vif. ~**ity**, *n*, vitalité, *f*. ~**ize**, *v.t*, vivifier. ~**s**, *n,pl*, parties vitales, *f,pl*. **vitamin**, *n*, vitamine, *f*.

vitiate, *v.t*, vicier. **vitiation**, *n*, viciation, *f*.

viticultural, *a*, viticole. **viticultur[al]ist**, *n*, viticulteur, *m*. **viticulture**, *n*, viticulture, *f*.

vitreous, *a*, vitreux; (*humor*) vitrée. **vitrify**, *v.t*, vitrifier. **vitriol**, *n*, vitriol, *m*. ~**ic**, *a*, vitriolique.

vituperate, *v.t*, injurier, vilipender. **vituperation**, *n*, injures, *f,pl*.

vivacious, *a*, enjoué. *to be* ~, avoir de la vivacité. ~**ly**, *ad*, avec vivacité. **viva voce**, *de* vive voix. ¶ *a*, oral. ¶ *n*, examen oral, *m*. **vivid**, *a*, vif, vivant. **vividness**, *n*, vivacité, *f*. **vivify**, *a*, vivifier. **viviparous**, *a*, vivipare. **vivisection**, *n*, vivisection, *f*.

vixen, *n*, renarde; (*woman*) mégère, *f*.

viz, *ad. abb*, c'est-à-dire, [à] savoir.

vizier, *n*, vizir, *m*.

vocable, *n*, vocable, *m*. **vocabulary**, *n*, vocabulaire, *m*. **vocal**, *a*, vocal. ~**ist**, *n*, chanteur, euse, cantatrice, *f*. ~**ize**, *v.t*, vocaliser. **vocation**, *n*, vocation, *f*. **vocative** [*case*], *n*, vocatif, *m*.

vociferate, *v.i*, vociférer. **vociferous**, *a*, bruyant. ~**ly**, *ad*, bruyamment.

vogue, *n*, vogue, mode, *f*.

voice, *n*, voix, *f*. ¶ *v.t*, exprimer. ~**less**, *a*, aphone.

void, *a*, vide; nul. ¶ *n*, vide; vague, *m*. ¶ *v.t*, évacuer; annuler.

voile (*textile*) *n*, voile, *m*.

volatile, *a*, volatil. **volatilize**, *v.t*, volatiliser.

volcanic, *a*, volcanique. **volcano**, *n*, volcan, *m*.

volition, *n*, volition, *f*.

volley, *n*, volée; décharge, *f*. ~*ball*, volleyball, *m*. ~ *firing*, feu de peloton, *m*. ¶ (*Ten.*) *v.t*, [re]prendre à la (*ou* de) volée; (*abs.*) jouer à la (*ou* de) volée.

volplane, *n*, vol plané, *m*. ¶ *v.i*, descendre en vol plané, planer.

volt, *n*, volt, *m*. ~**age**, *n*, voltage, *m*, tension, *f*. *high* ~, haute tension, *f.* **voltaic,** *a,* voltaïque. **voltmeter,** *n,* voltmètre, *m.*

volubility, *n,* volubilité, *f.* **voluble,** *a,* volubile, fécond en paroles.

volume, *n,* volume; tome; *(of smoke, etc.)* nuage, *m.* **voluminous,** *a,* volumineux.

voluntary†, *a,* volontaire; bénévole. ¶ *(organ) n,* *(before service)* prélude; *(during)* interlude, *m*; *(after)* sortie, *f*; *(between credo & sanctus)* offertoire, *m.* **volunteer,** *n,* volontaire, *m.*

voluptuary, *n,* voluptueux, euse. **voluptuous†,** *a,* voluptueux. ~**ness,** *n,* volupté, sensualité, mollesse, *f.*

volute, *n,* volute, *f.*

vomit, *n,* vomissement, *m.* ¶ *v.t, & i,* vomir, revomir.

voracious, *a,* vorace. ~**ly,** *ad,* avec voracité. ~**ness, voracity,** *n,* voracité, *f.*

vortex, *n,* tourbillon, *m.*

votary, *n,* adorateur, trice; sectateur, *m.* **vote,** *n,* vote, scrutin, suffrage, *m,* voix, opinion, *f.* ¶ *v.t. & i,* voter, donner sa voix, opiner. ~ *by a show of hands,* voter à main levée. **voter,** *n,* votant, *m.* **voting,** *n,* votation, *f.* ~ *paper,* bulletin de vote, *m.* **votive,** *a,* votif.

vouch, *v.t,* attester; vérifier. ~ *for,* répondre de, garantir. ~**er,** *n,* pièce justificative, *f*; bon, bulletin, *m.* ~**safe,** *v.t,* accorder; daigner.

vow, *n,* vœu, *m.* ¶ *v.t,* vouer; *(v.i.)* faire vœu; jurer.

vowel, *n,* voyelle, *f.*

voyage, *n,* voyage, *m.* ¶ *v.i,* voyager.

vulcanite, *n,* caoutchouc vulcanisé, *m,* ébonite, *f.* **vulcanize,** *v.t,* vulcaniser.

vulgar†, *a,* vulgaire; populacier; trivial, commun, bas. *the* ~ *[herd],* le vulgaire. ~**ism,** *n,* expression vulgaire, trivialité, *f.* ~**ity,** *n,* vulgarité, trivialité, *f.* ~**ize,** *v.t,* vulgariser; banaliser. *the Vulgate,* la Vulgate.

vulnerable, *a,* vulnérable.

vulture, *n,* vautour, *m.*

W

wad, *n,* bourre, *f*; tampon, *m*; *(banknotes)* liasse, *f.* ¶ *v.t,* ouater. **wadding,** *n,* ouate, *f.*

waddle, *n,* dandinement, déhanchement, *m.* ¶ *v.i.* marcher comme une cane, se dandiner.

wade, *v.i,* se mettre à l'eau sans nager; patauger, barboter. ~ *through* (ford), passer à gué. ~ *through a book,* peiner en lisant un livre. **wader,** *n,* *(bird)* échassier, *m*; *(pl.)* bottes cuissardes, *f.pl.*

wafer, *n,* *(flat biscuit)* gaufrette; *(cornet biscuit)* oublie, *f,* plaisir; *(Eccl.)* hostie, *f.*

waffle, *n,* gaufre, *f.* ~ *irons,* gaufrier, *m.*

waft, *n,* souffle, *m.* ¶ *v.t,* flotter, transporter; *(v.i.)* flotter dans l'air, sur l'eau.

wag, *n,* plaisant, loustic, farceur, *m.* ¶ *v.t,* *(tail)* agiter, frétiller de; *(head)* branler, dodeliner de *(la tête).*

wage, *n, oft. pl,* salaire, *m,* paie, *f,* gages, loyers, *m.pl.* ~ *earner,* salarié, e. *minimum* ~, smig or smic (salaire minimum interprofessionnel garanti, de croissance), *m. to* ~ *war,* faire la guerre, guerroyer.

wager, *n,* pari, *m,* gageure, *f.* ¶ *v.t,* parier.

wagon, *n,* voiture, *f,* fourgon, chariot, *m.* ~**load,** charretée, *f.*

waggish, *a,* facétieux, badin.

waggle, *v.t. & i,* branler.

wagtail, *n,* hochequeue, *m,* bergeronnette, *f.*

waif, *n,* enfant abandonné, e, *m,f.*

wail, *n,* lamentation, *f.* ¶ *v.i,* se lamenter; *(of baby)* vagir.

wain, *n,* chariot, *m.*

wainscot, *n,* lambris, *m.* ¶ *v.t,* lambrisser.

waist, *n,* ceinture, taille, *f.* ~**band,** ceinture, *f.* ~**coat,** gilet, *m.* ~ *measurement,* tour de taille, *m,* grosseur de ceinture, *f.*

wait, *n,* attente, *f. to lie in* ~, se tenir en embuscade, s'embusquer. ¶ *v.t. & i,* attendre. ~-*&-see,* expectant. ~ *[up]on,* servir; se présenter chez. **waiter,** *n,* garçon, *m.* ~! garçon! **waiting,** *n,* attente, *f.* ~ *room,* salon d'attente, *m*; *(Rly)* salle d'a., *f.* **waitress,** *n,* servante, bonne, serveuse, *f.* ~! mademoiselle!

waive, *v.t,* renoncer à, se désister de.

wake, *n,* sillage, *m,* eaux, *f.pl*; *(fu-*

neral) veillée mortuaire, *f*. *follow in the ~ of* (*Naut. & fig.*), marcher dans les eaux de. ¶ *v.t.ir. & waken*, *v.t*, [r]éveiller; (*v.i.*) s'éveiller. **~ful**, *a*, privé de sommeil; vigilant. **~fulness**, *n*, insomnie, *f*.

Wales, *n*, le pays de Galles.

walk, *n*, marche; promenade [à pied] *f*, tour; pas, *m*; allure, démarche; allée, *f*; promenoir, *m*. *~ of life*, carrière, profession, *f*. *~ over*, (*sport*) walk-over, *m*; (*fig.*) victoire facile, *f*. ¶ *v.t. & i*, marcher; cheminer; aller à pied; aller au pas. *~ about*, se promener. *~ in*, entrer. *~ off*, s'en aller. *~ out*, sortir. **walker**, *n*, marcheur, euse; piéton, ne; promeneur, euse. **walking**, *n*, marche; promenade [à pied] *f*. ¶ *p.a. or att*, ambulant; (*boots*) de marche. *~ stick*, canne, *f*. *~ tour*, excursion à pied, *f*.

wall, *n*, mur, *m*, muraille; paroi, *f*; haut du pavé, *m*. *~ cupboard*, placard, *m*. *to be a ~flower*, faire tapisserie. *~ map*, carte murale, *f*. *~ paper*, papier peint, papier-tenture, *m*, tenture, *f*.

wallet, *n*, sacoche, *f*; portefeuille, *m*.

wallow, *n*, souille, *f*. ¶ *v.i*, se vautrer; croupir.

walnut, *n*, noix, *f*; (*tree, wood*) noyer, *m*.

walrus, *n*, morse, *m*.

waltz, *n*, valsé, *f*. ¶ *v.i*, valser. **~er**, *n*, valseur, euse.

wan, *a*, blême, blafard; (*face*) hâve.

wand, *n*, baguette, *f*.

wander, *v.i*, errer, vagabonder, vaguer; s'écarter; divaguer. *~ around*, tournailler. **~er**, *n*, coureur, nomade, *m*. *the Wandering Jew*, le Juif errant.

wane, *n*, déclin, retour, *m*. ¶ *v.i*, décroître; décliner.

want, *n*, besoin; manque, défaut, *m*, gêne, *f*. ¶ *v.t*, avoir besoin de; manquer de; désirer; falloir; vouloir. **~ed** (*Advt*), on demande.

wanton, *a*, folâtre; folichon; licencieux; lascif; gratuit, sans motif. *~ destruction*, vandalisme, *m*. *out of sheer ~ness*, de gaieté de cœur.

war, *n*, guerre, *f*; (*elements*) combat, *m*. *~ dance*, danse guerrière, *f*. *~ horse*, cheval de bataille, *m*. *W~ loan*, emprunt de la

Défense nationale, *m*. *~ memorial*, monument aux morts [de la guerre] *m*. *~ of attrition*, guerre d'usure. *~ship*, vaisseau de guerre, *m*. ¶ *v.i*, faire la guerre, guerroyer.

warble, *v.i*, gazouiller; (*v.t.*) roucouler. **warbler** (*bird*) *n*, fauvette, *f*.

ward, *n*, pupille, *m,f*; (*prison*) quartier; arrondissement, *m*; (*hospital*) salle; (*lock*) garde, *f*. *~room*, carré des officiers, *m*. *~ [off]*, *v.t*, parer. **~en**, *n*, gardien; gouverneur, *m*. **wardrobe**, *n*, armoire; garde-robe, *f*; vêtements, *m.pl*. *~ trunk*, malle-armoire, *f*.

warehouse, *n*, magasin; dépôt; entrepôt; dock, *m*. *~ keeper* (*bonded*), entreposeur, *m*. *~man*, magasinier; marchand en magasin, stockiste, *m*. ¶ *v.t*, emmagasiner; entreposer.

wares, *n.pl*, marchandise, *f*, articles, *m.pl*.

warily, *ad*, avec circonspection, à tâtons. **wariness**, *n*, précaution, *f*.

warlike, *a*, guerrier, belliqueux; martial.

warm†, *a*, chaud; (*fig.*) chaleureux. *it is ~*, il fait chaud. *I am ~*, j'ai chaud. ¶ *v.t*, chauffer; réchauffer; échauffer. **~ing pan**, bassinoire, *f*, chauffe-lit, *m*. **~th**, *n*, chaleur, *f*.

warn, *v.t*, avertir, prévenir, **~ing**, *n*, avertissement; préavis, *m*.

warp, *n*, chaîne, lice, lisse, *f*. ¶ *v.t*, déjeter; (*yarn*) ourdir; (*Naut.*) touer; (*v.i.*) se déjeter, gauchir, gondoler.

warrant, *n*, autorisation; ordonnance, *f*; garant; mandat; warrant, bulletin de gage; titre, *m*. ¶ *v.t*, garantir; justifier. **~able**, *a*, justifiable. **~y**, *n*, garantie, *f*.

warren, *n*, garenne, *f*.

warrior, *n*, guerrier, ère.

Warsaw, *n*, Varsovie, *f*.

wart, *n*, verrue, *f*, poireau, *m*. **~y**, *a*, verruqueux.

wary, *a*, circonspect; défiant.

wash, *n*, (*linen*) lessive, *f*; (*art*) lavis, *m*; (*mouth*) eau, *f*; (*ship*) remous, *m*; (*slops*) lavasse, *f*. *~basin*, cuvette, *f*. *~cloth*, gant de toilette, *m*. *~ drawing*, [dessin

au] lavis, *m.* ~*house*, lavoir, *m,*
laverie, buanderie, *f.* ~*stand*, lavabo, *m.* ~*tub*, cuvier, *m.* ¶ *v.t.*
& *i*, laver; se l.; blanchir; baigner.
~ *away*, emporter, entraîner; affouiller. ~ *the dishes*, laver la
vaisselle. ~**able,** *a,* lavable.
washed overboard, enlevé par la
mer. **washer,** *n,* (*pers.*) laveur,
euse; (*ring*) rondelle, *f.* ~*woman*,
laveuse de linge, blanchisseuse, *f.*
washing, *n,* lavage; blanchissage,
m; lessive; toilette; ablution; lotion, *f.* ~ *machine*, machine à
laver. *f.*
wasp, *n,* guêpe, *f.* ~*s' nest*, guêpier, *m.*
waste, *a,* (*land*) inculte, vague;
(*gas, heat*) perdu; (*matter*) de
rebut. *to lay* ~, dévaster, ravager.
¶ *n,* gaspillage, *m;* perte, *f;* déchet;
rebut, *m.* ¶ *comps:* ~ *paper,*
papier de rebut, *m;* papiers inu-
tiles, *m.pl.* ~ *paper basket,* corbeille à papiers, *f.* ~ *pipe,* trop-
plein, *m.* ~ *water,* eaux-vannes,
f.pl. ¶ *v.t,* gaspiller; perdre; consumer. ~ *away,* se consumer;
s'atrophier. ~*d life,* vie manquée,
f. **wasteful,** *a,* dissipateur, prodigue. **wastefulness,** *n,* prodigalité, *f.*
watch, *n,* veille; garde, sentinelle,
f; (*Naut.*) quart, *m,* bordée, *f.*
(*Horo.*) montre, *f.* *on the* ~,
aux aguets, à l'affût. ~ *chain,*
chaîne de montre, *f.* ~*dog,* chien
de garde, *m.* ~ *fire,* feu de bivouac, *m.* ~*maker,* horloger, *m.*
~*man,* veilleur, garde, *m.* *wrist*~,
montre-bracelet, *f.* ¶ *v.t.* & *i,* veiller; surveiller; observer; guetter;
suivre. ~**er,** *n,* veilleur, euse.
~**ful†,** *a,* vigilant. ~**fulness,** *n,*
vigilance, *f.*
water, *n,* eau, *f;* eaux, *f.pl;* (*tide*)
marée, *f,* eaux, *f.pl;* (*pl.*) eaux,
f.pl, parages, *m.pl. fresh* ~, eau
douce, *f.* ~ *closet,* cabinets,
m.pl, cabinet [d'aisance] *m.*
~*color,* aquarelle, *f.* ~*cress,*
cresson [de fontaine] *m.* ~*fall,*
chute d'eau; cascade, *f.* ~*fowl,*
oiseau aquatique, *m.* ~*glass,*
verre soluble, *m.* ~ *hazard* (*golf*),
douve, *f.* ~ *jug,* pot à eau, *m.* ~
jump (*turf*), douve, *f.* ~ *level,* niveau d'eau, *m.* ~ *lily,* nénuphar,
m. ~ *line,* ligne de flottaison, *f.*

~*logged,* imbibé d'eau; (*boat*) engagé. ~*mark,* (*tidal*) laisse, *f;*
(*paper*) filigrane, *m.* ~*melon,*
melon d'eau, *m,* pastèque, *f.* ~
meter, compteur à eau, *m.* ~ *mill,*
moulin à eau, *m.* ~ *nymph,*
naïade, *f.* ~ *on the brain,* hydro-
céphalie, *f.* ~ *on the knee,*
épanchement de synovie, *m.* ~
pipe, tuyau d'eau, *m.* conduite
d'eau, *f.* ~*power,* force hydraulique, houille blanche, *f.* ~*proof,*
a, imperméable [à l'eau]; (*v.t.*)
imperméabiliser. ~ *polo,* water-
polo, *m.* ~ *rat,* rat d'eau, *m.*
~*shed,* ligne de faîte, *f.* ~*side,*
bord de l'eau, *m;* (*att.*) riverain.
~*spout,* (*rain*) gargouille; (*Meteor.*) trombe, *f.* ~*tight,* étanche
[à l'eau]. ~ *tower,* château d'eau,
m. ~*way,* voie navigable, v.
d'eau, *f;* (*bridge*) débouché, *m.*
~*wheel,* roue hydraulique, *f.* ~
works, usine hydraulique, *f.* ¶ *v.t,*
(*garden*) arroser; (*horse*) abreuver; (*drink*) couper, baptiser;
(*stock, Fin.*) diluer; (*silk*) moirer;
(*v.i.*) (*eyes*) pleurer, larmoyer;
(*take in water*) faire de l'eau. *it
makes one's mouth* ~, cela fait
venir l'eau à la bouche. ~*ed silk,*
moire de soie, soie moirée, *f.*
~**ing,** *n,* arrosement; arrosage;
abreuvage, *m;* moire, *f.* ~ *place,*
abreuvoir, *m;* ville d'eaux, *f,*
eaux, *f.pl;* bains, *m.pl,* station
balnéaire, *f.* ~**less,** *a,* dépourvu
d'eau. ~**y,** *a,* aqueux; humide;
(*fluid*) ténu.
watt, *n,* watt, *m.*
wattle, *n,* (*rods & twigs*) claie;
(*bird*) barbe, caroncule, *f,* fanon,
m; (*fish*) barbe, *f.* ¶ *v.t,* clayon-
ner.

wave, *n,* vague, *f;* flot, *m;* lame, *f;*
coup de mer, *m;* onde; ondula-
tion, *f;* (*hand*) signe, geste;
(*wand*) coup, *m.* ~*length,* longueur d'onde, *f.* ~ *cold, heat* ~,
vague de chaleur, de froid, *f. permanent* ~, indéfrisable, *f.* ~ *shock*
~, onde de choc, *f. short* ~,
ondes courtes, *f.pl.* ¶ *v.i,* flotter;
ondoyer; (*v.t.*) agiter; faire signe
de; onduler. *to have one's hair*
~*d,* se faire onduler [les che-
veux]. **waver,** *v.i,* hésiter, va-

ciller, flotter, chanceler. **wavy,** *a*, onduleux, ondé, en ondes; *(line)* tremblée.

wax, *n*, cire; *(cobbler's)* poix, *f.* ~works, figures de cire, *f.pl.* ¶ *v.t*, cirer; *(v.i.)* croître; devenir. ~ed thread, fil poissé, *m*. ~y, *a*, comme cire.

way, *n*, chemin, *m*, route; voie; distance, *f*; passage, *m*; place, *f*; progrès, *m*; marche; direction, *f*; côté; sens, *m*; manière, façon, sorte, *f*; genre; moyen, *m*; allure, *f*, air; usage, *m*; guise, *f*; cours, *m*; passe; *(Naut.)* erre, *f. by the* ~, *(fig.)* à propos. *half~*, à mi-chemin. *in the* ~, encombrant, gênant. *to lose one's* ~, s'égarer. ~bill, feuille de route, *f*. ~farer, voyageur, euse. ~ in, entrée, *f*. ~lay, tendre une embûche à. ~ out, sortie; issue, *f*. ~side, bord de la route, *m*; *(att.)* sur le b. de la r.; riverain; *(Rly station)* de passage, d'escale.

wayward†, *a*, capricieux, volontaire, libertin. ~ness, *n*, libertinage, *m*.

we, *pn*, nous; on.

weak†, *a*, faible; débile; *(tea)* léger. ~ spot (fig. of pers.), côté faible, *m*. ~en, *v.t*, affaiblir; atténuer; *(v.i.)* faiblir. ~ling, *n*, faiblard, e. ~ly, *a*, débile, faiblard. ~ness, *n*, faiblesse, *f*; faible, *m*.

weal, *n*, bien, *m*. (Cf. *the common* ~); vergeture, trace d'un coup, *f*.

wealth, *n*, richesses, *f.pl*, opulence, *f*, biens, *m.pl*. ~y, *a*, riche, opulent.

wean, *v.t*, sevrer. ~ing, *n*, sevrage, *m*.

weapon, *n*, arme, *f*; porte-respect, *m*. ~less, *a*, sans armes.

wear, *n*, usage, *m*; usure, *f. the worse for* ~, patraque. ¶ *v.t.* & *i. ir*, user; s'u.; miner; porter; mettre. ~ out, user; épuiser, exténuer. ~ well, être d'un bon user. ~able, *a*, mettable, portable.

weariness, *n*, fatigue, lassitude, *f*.

wearing, *n*, usure, *f*; port, *m*.

wearisome, *a*, endormant, assommant; fastidieux. ~ness, *n*, ennui, *m*. **weary,** *a*, fatigué, las. ¶ *v.t*, fatiguer, lasser; ennuyer. ~ for, languir après.

weasel, *n*, belette, *f*.

weather, *n*, temps, *m*; intempéries, *f.pl*. ~-beaten, ravagé [par les intempéries]; hâlé. ~cock, girouette, *f*, coq, *m*; *(fig.)* girouette, *f*, sauteur, arlequin, *m*. ~ forecast, bulletin météorologique, *m*. ~ permitting, si le temps le permet. ~stripping, *n*, calfeutage, *m*. ¶ *v.t*, résister à; *(Geol.)* altérer, désagréger.

weave, *n*, tissu, *m*. ¶ *v.t.ir*, tisser; *(basket)* tresser; *(fig.)* ourdir, tramer. **weaver,** *n*, tisserand, *m*. **weaving,** *n*, tissage, *m*; tisseranderie, *f*.

web, *n*, toile; *(bird's foot)* membrane; *(girder)* âme, *f*; *(key)* panneton, *m*; *(of life)* trame, *f. spider's* ~, toile d'araignée, *f*. ~-footed, palmipède. **webbed,** *a*, palmé. **webbing,** *n*, sangle, *f*.

wed, *v.t*, épouser; marier; *(v.i.)* se m. **wedded,** *a*, conjugal; *(to opinion)* attaché. **wedding,** *n*, noces, *f.pl*, mariage, *m*. ~ breakfast, repas de noce, *m*. ~ cake, gâteau de noce, *m*. ~ day, jour de mariage, *m*. ~ dress, robe de mariée, *f*. ~ festivities & party, noce, *f*. ~ march, marche nuptiale, *f*. ~ present, cadeau de noce, *m*; *(bridegroom's)* corbeille [de mariage] *f*. ~ ring, alliance, *f*, anneau nuptial, *m*.

wedge, *n*, coin, *m*; cale; hausse, *f*. ¶ *v.t*, coincer; caler.

wedlock, *n*, mariage, *m*.

Wednesday, *n*, mercredi, *m*.

wee, *a*, petiot, tout petit.

weed, *n*, mauvaise herbe, *f*. ¶ *v.t*, sarcler. ~ out, éliminer, épurer. ~er, *n*, *(pers.)* sarcleur, euse; *(hoe)* sarcloir, *m*.

week, *n*, semaine; *(e.g, Friday to Friday)* semaine, huitaine, *f*, huit jours, *m.pl*. ~ day, jour de semaine, *m*. ~ days only, la semaine seulement. ~end, weekend, *m*. *long* ~end, weekend prolongé, *m*. ~ly, *a*, hebdomadaire.

weep, *v.i.* & *t. ir.* & ~ for, pleurer. ~er, *n*, pleureur, euse. **weeping,** *n*, pleurs, *m.pl*, larmes, *f.pl*. ¶ *a*, qui pleure, éploré; *(tree)* pleureur.

weevil, *n*, charançon, *m*. ~y, *a*, charançonné.

weft, *n*, trame, *f*.

weigh, *v.t*, peser; mesurer; *(an-*

chor) lever; (*v.i.*) peser; farder. ~ *down*, appesantir, affaisser. *to get under* ~, appareiller. **~er**, *n*, peseur, *m*. **weighing**, *n*, pesage, *m*; pesée, *f*. ~ *in* & ~ *in room*, pesage, *m*. ~ *machine*, [balance à] bascule, *f*. **weight**, *n*, poids, *m*; pesanteur; gravité; importance, *f*. *net* ~, poids net, *m*. ~ *allowed free*, franchise de poids, *f*. de bagages, *f*. *his*, *its*, ~ *in gold*, son pesant d'or. **~y†**, *a*, pesant; puissant; grave.

weir, *n*, barrage; déversoir; (*Fish.*) gord, *m*.

weird, *a*, fantastique.

welcome, *a*, bienvenu; libre. *you're* ~, de rien. ¶ *n*, bienvenue, *f*, [bon] accueil, *m*, réception, *f*. ¶ *v.t*, bien accueillir, recevoir.

weld, *n*, soudure, *f*. ¶ *v.t*, souder; corroyer.

welfare, *n*, bien-être, bonheur; (*public*) salut, *m*, chose, *f*.

well, *n*, puits, *m*; source, fontaine, *f*; réservoir, *m*; (*of ship*) sentine, *f*; (*of court*) parquet, *m*. ~ *sinker*, puisatier, fontainier, *m*. **~spring**, source, *f*. ¶ *v.i*, sourdre, jaillir.

well, *a*, bien; dispos, bien portant, en bonne santé. *he is* ~, il va bien. ¶ *ad*, bien. **~-advised**, bien conseillé. ~ & *good*, à la bonne heure. **~-attended**, suivi. **~-balanced**, bien équilibré. (*style*, *prose*) nombreux. *to be* ~ *balanced* (phrase), avoir du nombre. **~-behaved**, sage. **~-being**, bien-être, *m*. **~-beloved**, *a*. & *n*, bien-aimé, e, bienaimé, e. **~-bred**, bien élevé, bien appris, de bonne compagnie, honnête. **~-built**, **~-knit**, bien charpenté. **~-disposed** & **~-meaning**, bien intentionné. **~-done** (*Cook.*), bien cuit. ~ *done!* bravo! **~-informed**, calé. **~-known**, bien connu, réputé, signalé, répandu. ~ *off* & **~-to-do**, à son aise, aisé, au large, fortuné, calé, cossu. **~-read**, instruit, lettré. **~-spoken**, bien-disant. **~-timed**, opportun.

Wellingtons, *n.pl*, bottes montant aux genoux, *f.pl*.

Welsh, *a*, gallois; du pays de Galles. ¶ *n*, le gallois. **~man**, **~woman**, Gallois, e. ~ *rabbit*, ~ *rarebit*, rôtie à l'anglaise, r. au fromage, *f*.

welt, *n*, (*shoe*) trépoint, *f*; (*strap*) couvre-joint, *m*, fourrure, *f*. *wide* ~ (shoe), semelle débordante, *f*.

welter, *v.i*, nager, se baigner, s'abîmer. ~ *weight* (*Box.*), poids mi-moyen, *m*.

wen, *n*, loupe, *f*, goitre, *m*.

wench, *n*, donzelle, *f*.

wend, *v.i*, poursuivre.

werewolf, *n*, loup-garou, *m*.

west, *n*, ouest; (le) couchant; occident, *m*. ¶ *a*, de l'ouest, d'ouest, occidental. *W~ Africa*, l'Afrique occidentale, *f*. *the W~ Indies*, les Indes occidentales, les Antilles, *f.pl*. **westerly**, *a*, d'ouest. **western**, *a*, de l'ouest; occidental; d'Occident.

Westphalia, *n*, la Westphalie.

wet, *a*, mouillé; humide; pluvieux; (*goods*) liquide; (*paint*, *ink*) fraîche. ~ *blanket*, rabat-joie, *m*. ~ *fly fishing*, pêche à la mouche noyée, *f*. ~ *nurse*, nourrice, *f*. ~ *through*, trempé. **wet** & **~ness**, *n*, humidité, *f*. *out in the* ~, dans la pluie. ¶ *v.t*, mouiller; imbiber; humecter; arroser.

whack, *n*, coup, *m*. ¶ *v.t*, battre.

whale, *n*, baleine, *f*. **~boat**, baleinière, *f*. **~bone**, fanon de baleine, *m*, baleine, *f*. ~ *calf*, baleineau, *m*. **whaler**, *n*, baleinier, *m*.

wharf, *n*, quai, appontement, débarcadère, embarcadère, *m*. **wharfinger**, *n*, propriétaire de quai, *m*.

what, *pn*, *a*, & *ad*, quoi; qu'est-ce qui; qu'est-ce que; que; quel, quelle; ce qui; ce que; tant; comment. ~ *a*, quel, quelle. ~ *a relief!* ouf! ~ *for?* pourquoi? ~ *people may say*, le qu'en-dira-t-on. **whatever**, *pn*. & *a*, tout ce qui; tout ce que; quelque . . . qui; quelque . . . que; quelconque; quoi que; quel(le) que.

whatnot, *n*, étagère, *f*.

wheat, *n*, froment, blé, *m*. **~en**, *a*, de froment.

wheedle, *v.t*, cajoler, enjôler.

wheel, *n*, roue, *f*; volant; disque; galet, *m*; roulette; (*emery*, *etc.*) meule; (*helm*) barre; (*Mil.*) conversion, *f*. (*typewriter*, *etc.*) front ~, marguerite, *f*. *spare* ~, roue de rechange, *f*. **~barrow**, brouette, *f*. **~base**, écartment des

essieux, empattement, *m*.
~*chair*, fauteuil roulant, *m*. ¶ *v.t*,
rouler; (*v.i.*) (*birds*) tournoyer. ~-
wheeled, *a*, à . . . roues.

wheeze, *v.i*, siffler. **wheezy**, *a*,
sifflant; (*pers.*) poussif.

whelk, *n*, buccin, *m*.

when, *ad*, quand, lorsque; alors
que, après que. **whence**, *ad*, d'où.
whenever, *ad*, toutes les fois que.

where, *ad*, où; là où; à l'endroit
où. **whereabouts**, *ad*, où. *one's*
~, où on est. **whereas**, *ad*, tandis que, au lieu que; attendu que,
vu que. **whereat**, *ad*, sur quoi.
whereby, *ad*, par où, par lequel.
wherefore, *ad*, pourquoi. **where-
in**, *ad*, en quoi. **whereof**, *ad*,
dont. **where[up]on**, *ad*, sur quoi.
wherever, *ad*, partout où, où
que. *the wherewithal*, de quoi,
les moyens, *m.pl*.

wherry, *n*, bachot, *m*. ~**man**, ba-
choteur, *m*.

whet, *n*, stimulant, *m*. ¶ *v.t*, (*tools*)
repasser, aiguiser; (*appetite*) aiguiser, stimuler. ~**stone**, pierre
à aiguiser, *f*.

whether, *c*, soit; soit que; que; si.

whey, *n*, petit-lait, *m*.

which, *pn*. & *a*, qui; que; lequel;
laquelle; ce qui; ce que; ce dont;
quel, quelle. ~ *way*? par où?
whichever, *pn*, n'importe quel,
n'importe quelle.

whiff, *n*, bouffée, *f*.

while, *n*, temps, *m*. *it is worth* ~,
cela vaut la peine. **while** &
whilst, *c*, tandis que, pendant
que; [tout] en. *while away*,
(faire) passer; charmer, tromper.

whim, *n*, caprice, *m*, fantaisie;
boutade, *f*; (*Mach.*) treuil, cabestan, *m*.

whimper, *v.i*, pleurnicher, piauler, geindre. ~**er**, *n*, pleureur,
euse, pleurard, e.

whimsical†, *a*, capricieux, fantasque, lunatique.

whin, *n*, ajonc, genêt épineux, *m*.

whine, *v.i*, pleurnicher, piauler,
geindre.

whinny, *n*, hennissement, *m*. ¶
v.i, hennir.

whip, *n*, fouet, *m*. ~**cord**, [fil de]
fouet, *m*. ~ *hand* (*fig.*), dessus,
m. ¶ *v.t*. & *i*, fouetter; toucher.
whipper-in, *n*, piqueur, *m*.
whipper-snapper, *n*, moucheron,
freluquet, *m*. **whipping**, *n*, fusti-

gation, *f*, le fouet; (*Need.*)
point roulé, *m*. ~ *top*, sabot, *m*.

whir, *v.i*, siffler, ronfler.

whirl, *n*, ébullition, *f*; tourbillon,
m. ¶ *v.i*, tournoyer, tourbillonner. ~**pool**, tourbillon, *m*. ~
wind, tourbillon, *m*. **whirligig**,
n, pirouette, *f*; carrousel, *m*.

whisk, *n*, (*brush, broom*) balayette, *f*, houssoir, *m*; (*egg*)
fouet, *m*. ¶ *v.t*, (*dust*) épousseter;
(*eggs*) fouetter.

whiskers, *n.pl*, favoris, *m.pl*;
(*cat*) moustache, *f*.

whiskey, *n*, whisky, *m*.

whisper, *n*, chuchotement; murmure, *m*. ¶ *v.i*. & *t*, chuchoter;
murmurer. ~**er**, *n*, chuchoteur,
euse. ~**ing**, *n*, chuchoterie, *f*. ~
gallery, galerie à écho, *f*.

whist (*cards*) *n*, whist, *m*.

whistle, *n*, sifflet; coup de sifflet,
m. ¶ *v.t*. & *i*, siffler; (*wind*) mugir. **whistler**, *n*, siffleur, euse.

whit, *n*, iota, *m*.

white, *a*, blanc. ~ *ant*, fourmi
blanche, *f*, termite, *m*. ~*bait*,
blanchaille, *f*. ~*caps*, moutons,
m.pl. ~ *heat*, incandescence, *f*.
~-*hot*, chauffé à blanc, incandescent. ~ *lead*, blanc de céruse,
m, céruse, *f*. ~ *lie*, mensonge
pieux, *m*. officieux, *m*. ~*wash*,
n, blanc de chaux, *m*; (*v.t.*)
blanchir à la chaux; (*fig.*) blanchir. ¶ *n*, (*color, man*) blanc,
m; (*ball, woman*) blanche, *f*. ~
of egg, blanc d'œuf, *m*, glaire,
f. ~ *sale*, vente de blanc, *f*.
white[n], *v.t*, blanchir. **whiteness**, *n*, blancheur, *f*.

whither, *ad*, où.

whiting, *n*, blanc de craie; (*fish*)
merlan, *m*.

whitish, *a*, blanchâtre.

Whitsuntide, *n*, la Pentecôte.
Whit Sunday, dimanche de la
Pentecôte, *m*.

whittle, *v.t*, taillader.

whiz, *n*, sifflement, *m*. ¶ *v.i*, siffler.

who, *pn*, qui. ~ *goes there?* qui
vive?

whoa, *i*, oé!, ohé!

whoever, *pn*, quiconque.

whole, *a*, tout; entier; intégral; intact; complet; total; plein. ¶ *n*,
tout, *m*, totalité, intégralité, *f*.
[*up*]*on the* ~, à tout prendre,
en somme. **wholesale**, *a*, en
masse. ~ [*trade*], [commerce de
(*ou* en)] gros; (*small*) demi-

gros, *m.* **wholesome†**, *a*, sain; salubre; salutaire. **wholly**, *ad*, entièrement; intégralement; complètement; en totalité.

whom, *pn*, que; qui; lequel, laquelle, lesquels, lesquelles. **whomsoever**, *pn*, quiconque.

whoop, *n*, huée, *f*, cri, *m*. ¶ *v.i.* huer, crier. **~ing cough**, coqueluche, *f*.

whore, *n*, prostituée, *f*.

whorl, *n*, verticille, *m*, spire, *f*.

whortleberry, *n*, airelle, myrtille, *f*.

whose, *pn*, dont; de qui; à qui? **whosoever**, *pn*, quiconque.

why, *ad. & n*, pourquoi, *ad, c, & m*. ¶ *i*, mais!, comment!

wick, *n*, mèche, *f*.

wicked†, *a*, méchant, mauvais. **~ness**, *n*, méchanceté, *f*.

wicker, *n*, osier, *m*. **~ cradle**, moïse, *m*. **~work**, vannerie, *f*. ¶ *v.t*, clisser.

wicket, *n*, guichet; (*croquet*) arceau, *m*.

wide, *a*, large; vaste; grand; ample; étendu; (*Meas.*) large de, de largeur. **to be ~ awake**, être tout(e) éveillé(e). **~-awake**, éveillé, dégourdi, déluré, en éveil. **~ of the mark**, loin de compte. **~spread**, [largement] répandu. **~ly**, *ad*, largement. **widen**, *v.t*, [r]élargir; étendre. **in a wider sense**, par extension.

widgeon, *n*, [canard] siffleur, *m*.

widow, *n*, veuve, *f*. *the* **~'s mite**, le denier de la v. **~'s weeds**, deuil de v., *m*. **~ed**, *p.p*, veuf. **~er**, *n*, veuf, *m*. **~hood**, *n*, veuvage, *m*, viduité, *f*.

width, *n*, largeur, *f*; (*cloth*) largeur, laize, *f*, lé, *m*.

wield, *v.t*, manier; (*power*) exercer.

wife, *n*, femme; épouse, *f*.

wig, *n*, perruque, *f*. **~ maker**, perruquier, *m*.

wight, *n*, hère, *m*.

wild, *a*, sauvage; farouche; inculte; fou; endiablé; égaré, hagard. **~ beast**, bête féroce, b. sauvage, *f*, (*pl.*) bêtes fauves, *f.pl*, fauves, *m.pl*. **~ boar**, sanglier, (*young*) marcassin, *m*. **~ cherry**, merise, *f*; (*tree*) merisier, *m*. **~ flowers**, fleurs des bois, f—s des champs, f—s des prés, f—s sauvages, *f.pl*. **~ goose chase**, folle entreprise, *f*. *to sow one's*

~ oats, jeter sa gourme, faire ses farces. **~ rabbit**, lapin de garenne, *m*. **~ rose**, églantine, rose de chien, *f*; (*bush*) rosier sauvage, églantier, *m*. **wild & wilderness**, *n*, lieu sauvage, *m*, solitude, *f*, désert, *m*. **~ly**, *ad*, d'un air effaré; follement. **~ness**, *n*, état sauvage; égarement, *m*.

wile & wiliness, *n*, ruse, astuce, (*pl.*) finasserie, *f*.

wilful, *a*, volontaire, intentionnel. **~ misrepresentation**, dol, *m*. **~ murder**, homicide volontaire, assassinat, *m*. **~ly**, *ad*, volontairement; avec préméditation. **~ness**, *n*, obstination, *f*.

will, *n*, volonté; intention, *f*; vouloir; gré; plaisir; testament, *m*. ¶ *v.t. regular & ir*, vouloir; léguer par [son] testament; *v.aux, is expressed in Fr. by future tense. Also by* vouloir. **willing**, *a*, volontaire, spontané; (*hands*) de volontaires; complaisant. *to be* **~**, vouloir [bien]. **~ly**, *ad*, volontiers. **~ness**, *n*, bonne volonté, complaisance, *f*.

will-o'-the-wisp, *n*, feu follet, ardent, *m*.

willow, *n*, saule, *m*. **~ plantation**, saulaie, saussaie, *f*.

willynilly, *ad*, bon gré, mal gré.

wilt, *v.t*, flétrir; (*v.i.*) se f., se faner, s'étioler.

wily, *a*, rusé, finaud, astucieux.

wimple, *n*, guimpe, *f*.

win, *n*, victoire, *f*. ¶ *v.t.ir*, gagner; concilier; acquérir; (*prize*) remporter; valoir.

wince, *v.i*, sourciller; cligner; tiquer; tressaillir.

winch, *n*, moulinet; treuil, *m*; manivelle, *f*.

wind, *n*, vent, *m*; haleine; flatuosité, *f*. **~bag**, moulin à paroles, *m*. **~fall**, fruit tombé, *m*; [bonne] aubaine, chapechute, *f*. **~mill**, moulin à vent, *m*. **~pipe**, trachée-artère, *f*. **~row**, andain, *m*. **~shield**, pare-brise, *m*. **~shield wiper**, essuie-glace, *m*. *to get* **~** *of*, éventer. *second* **~**, second souffle, *m*. ¶ *v.t*, essouffler.

wind, *v.t.ir*, enrouler, dévider, bobiner, pelotonner; (*Min.*) [re]monter; (*v.i.*) serpenter, tourner. **~ up**, [re]monter; terminer; liquider. **~ing**, *a*, tournant; sinueux, anfractueux, tortueux.

¶ *n*, détour, *m*, sinuosité, *f*, lacet, méandre, *m*. ~ *sheet*, linceul, suaire, *m*. **windlass**, *n*, treuil, *m*.

window, *n*, fenêtre, *f*; (*pl, col.*) fenêtrage, vitrage, *m*; (*casement*) croisée, *f*; (*leaded*) vitrail, *m*; (*carriage*) glace; (*shop*) vitrine, devanture, montre, *f*, étalage, *m*. ~ *box*, jardin de fenêtre, *m*. ~ *dresser*, étalagiste, *m,f*. ~ *enve-lope*, enveloppe à fenêtre, e. à panneau, *f*. ~ *glass*, verre à vitres, *m*. ~*pane*, vitre, *f*. ~*shop-ping*, lèche-vitrines, *m*. ~*sill*, appui de fenêtre, *m*. rear ~, lu-nette arrière, *f*.

windward, *n*, coté du vent, *m*; (*a.*) au vent. W~ *Islands*, îles du Vent, *f.pl*. **windy,** *a*, venteux; (*day*) de grand vent. to be ~, ven-ter.

wine, *n*, vin, *m*; liqueur, *f*. ~ *glass*, verre à vin, *m*. ~ *grapes*, raisin de vigne, *m*. ~ *grower*, vig-neron, ne, viticulteur, *m*. ~ *growing*, *a*, vinicole, viticole. ~ *list*, carte des vins, *f*. ~ *of the country*, vin du cru, *m*. ~ *waiter*, sommelier, *m*. table ~, vin ordi-naire, *m*.

wing, *n*, aile, *f*; vol, essor, *m*; (*pl, Theat.*) coulisses, *f.pl*. ~ *collar*, faux col cassé, *m*. ~ *nut*, écrou à oreilles, [é.] papillon, *m*. ~ *spread*, ~ *span*, envergure, *f*. ~**ed**, *a*, ailé. ~ *creature*, volatile, *m*.

wink, *n*, clin d'œil, signe des yeux, clignement, *m*. ¶ *v.i*, cligner.

winkle (*Crust.*) *n*, bigorneau, *m*.

winner, *n*, gagnant, e; vainqueur, *m*. **winning,** *a*, gagnant; (*num-ber*) sortant; attrayant, attachant.

winnow, *v.t*, vanner. ~**ing,** *n*, vannage, *m*.

winsome, *a*, agréable.

winter, *n*, hiver, *m*. ¶ *v.i. & t*, hi-verner. ¶ ~, *att*. & **wintry,** *a*, d' hiver, hivernal, hiémal.

wipe, *n*, coup de chiffon, de mou-choir; (*cinema*) volet, *m*. ~ [up], *v.t*, essuyer; torcher; (*joint*) ébar-ber. ~ *off* (debt), apurer. ~ *out*, effacer.

wire, *n*, fil; câble, *m*; dépêche [té-légraphique] *f*. ~ *cutter*, bec-de-corbeau, *m*. ~ *entanglement*, ré-seau de fils de fer, *m*. ~ *fence*,

clôture en fil de fer, *f*. ~*haired* (dog), au poil rude. ~ *netting*, treillis métallique, grillage, *m*. ~ *puller*, intrigant, *m*. ~ *rope*, câble métallique, *m*. ¶ *v.t*, (*house, Elec.*) poser des fils dans; télégra-phier.

wisdom, *n*, sagesse; prudence, *f*. ~ *tooth*, dent de sagesse, *f*. **wise**†, *a*, sage. ~*acre*, sot qui se donne un air de sage, *m*. the Three W~ Men, les trois rois mages.

wish, *n*, désir; gré; souhait; vœu, *m*. ¶ *v.t. & i*, désirer; vouloir; souhaiter. ~ *someone many hap-py returns* [*of the day*], souhaiter la [*ou* une bonne] fête à quel-qu'un. ~**ful,** *a*, désireux. ~**bone,** lunette, fourchette, *f*. ~**ing cap,** bonnet magique, *m*.

wisp, *n*, bouchon, *m*, touffe, *f*.

wistaria, *n*, glycine, *f*.

wistful, *a*, désenchanté, pensif, de regret. ~**ly,** *ad*, avec envie.

wit, *n*, esprit; sel; (*pers.*) bel esprit, diseur de bons mots, *m*; (*pl.*) in-telligence, *f*, esprit, *m*; tête, *f*. at one's ~*s' end*, au bout de son rouleau, aux abois. to lose one's ~*s*, perdre la tête. ~*less*, *a*, sans esprit.

witch, *n*, sorcière, *f*. ~*craft*, sor-cellerie, *f*, sortilège, *m*. ~ *doctor*, sorcier guérisseur, *m*. ~ *hazel*, hamamélis, *m*. ~*hunt*, chasse aux sorcières, *f*. ~*ery*, *n*, magie, fascination, *f*.

with, *pr*, avec; à coups de; à; par; de; en; dans; sous; auprès de.

withdraw, *v.t.ir*, retirer; se désis-ter de; (*v.i.*) se retirer; se can-tonner; (*candidature*) se désister. ~*al*, *n*, retrait, *m*; retraite, *f*; dé-sistement, *m*.

wither, *v.t*, dessécher; (*v.i.*) se dessécher, dépérir. ~*ing* (*look*) *a*, foudroyant.

withers, *n.pl*, garrot, *m*.

withhold, *v.t.ir*, retenir.

within, *pr*, dans; en; en dedans de; là-dedans; à; sous. ~ *call*, à portée de la voix. from ~, de dedans.

without, *pr*, sans; sans que; en dehors de; là-dehors. from ~, de dehors. to do ~, se passer de.

withstand, *v.t.ir*, résister à.

witness, *n*, témoin; témoignage, *m*; foi, *f*. ~*box*, barre des té-moins, *f*. ~ *for the defense*, témoin à décharge. ~ *for the prosecution*, t. à charge. ¶ *v.t*, être témoin de; assister à; attester; signer à; certifier.

witticism, *n*, trait d'esprit, jeu d'esprit, *m*.

wittingly, *ad*, sciemment, à bon escient.

witty†, *a*, plein d'esprit; spirituel.

wizard, *n*, sorcier, magicien, *m*. ~**ry**, *n*, magie, *f*.

wizened, *a*, ratatiné.

wo, *i*, oé! ohé!

wobble, *v.i*, brimbaler; vaciller.

woe, *n*, douleur, *f*; malheur, *m*. ~**begone** & ~**ful†**, *a*, triste; malheureux; lamentable.

wolf, *n*, loup, *m*, louve, *f*. ~ *cub* (Zool.) louveteau, *m*. ~*sbane*, napel, *m*.

wolfram, *n*, wolfram, *m*.

woman, *n*, femme, *f*. ~ *doctor*, femme médecin, f. docteur, *f*. ~ *driver*, chauffeuse, *f*. ~ *hater*, misogyne, *m*. ~ *of fashion*, élégante, *f*. ~**ish**, *a*, efféminé; (*voice*) féminine. ~**ly**, *a*, de femme.

womb, *n*, ventre, sein, flanc, *m*.

wonder, *n*, étonnement, *m*; merveille, *f*; prodige, *m*. ¶ *v.i*, s'étonner (*at* = de); se demander (*why* = pourquoi). ~**ful†**, *a*, étonnant; merveilleux; admirable.

wont, *n*, coutume, *f*, ordinaire, *m*. ~**ed**, *a*, habituel.

woo, *v.t*, faire la cour à.

wood, *n*, bois, *m*. *in the* ~ (*wine*), en cercles. ~*bine*, chèvrefeuille, *m*. ~*carver*, sculpteur sur bois, *m*. ~*cock*, bécasse, *f*. ~*cut*, gravure sur bois, *f*. ~*land*, pays de bois, *m*; (*att.*) des bois; sylvestre. ~ *louse*, cloporte, *m*. ~*man*, bûcheron, *m*. ~ *nymph*, nymphe bocagère, *f*. ~ *owl*, chat-huant, *m*, hulotte, *f*. ~*pecker*, pic, *m*. ~ *pigeon*, [pigeon] ramier, *m*, palombe, *f*. ~*shed*, bûcher, *m*. *the* ~[*winds*], les bois, *m.pl*. ~*work*, menuiserie; boiserie, *f*. ~*worker*, artisan en bois, *m*. ~**ed**, *a*, boisé, fourré. ~**en**, *a*, de bois, en b. ~**y**, *a*, ligneux.

wooer, *n*, prétendant, soupirant, poursuivant, *m*.

woof, *n*, trame, *f*.

wool, *n*, laine, *f*; (*animal's coat*) pelage, *m*. **woolen**, *a*, de laine; lainier. ~ *goods* or ~*s*, *n.pl*, lainage, *m. oft. pl*. ~ *manufacturer*,

lainier, *m*. ~ *mill*, lainerie, *f*. ~ *trade*, industrie lainière, lainerie, *f*. **woolly**, *a*, laineux; (*fruit, style*) cotonneux; (*hair*) crépus; (*outline, sound*) flou.

word, *n*, mot, *m*; parole, *f*; terme, *m. by* ~ *of mouth*, de vive voix. *the Word* (*Theol.*), le Verbe. ~ *processing*, traitement de text, *m*. ¶ *v.t*, libeller, concevoir. **wordiness**, *n*, verbosité, *f*. **wording**, *n*, libellé, *m*, termes, *m.pl*. **wordy**, *a*, verbeux.

work, *n*, travail, *m*, *oft. pl*; fonctionnement; ouvrage, *m*; besogne; œuvre, *f*; (*social*) œuvres, *f.pl*; (*of art*) œuvre, *f*, objet; (*col. pl*, *of an artist*) œuvre, *m*; (*pl.*) rouage, *m. oft. pl*, mécanisme, mouvement, *m*; (*pl. & s.*) usine, fabrique, *f*; atelier, *m*. ~ *bag*, sac à ouvrage, *m*. ~ *box*, nécessaire à o., *m*. ~*man*, *-woman*, ouvrier, ère. ~*manlike*, en bon ouvrier. ~*manship*, main-d'œuvre, façon, facture, *f*, travail, *m*. ~*men's compensation insurance*, assurance contre les accidents du travail, *f*. ~*room*, atelier; (*convent*) ouvroir, *m*. ~*shop*, atelier, *m*. ¶ *v.t*, travailler; faire t.; manœuvrer; opérer; actionner; exploiter; ouvrer; faire; se f.; (*v.i.*) travailler; fonctionner; jouer; marcher; aller; rouler; agir; fermenter. ~ *hard*, travailler à force, piocher. ~ *loose*, prendre du jeu. ~ *out*, *v.t*, élaborer; épuiser; décompter; (*v.i.*) se chiffrer. ~ *up*, travailler; malaxer. ~*able*, *a*, exécutable; exploitable. ~*er*, *n*, travailleur, euse; ouvrier, ère. *blue-collar* ~, col-bleu, *m. white-collar* ~, col-blanc, *m*. ~ *bee*, abeille ouvrière, *f*. ~*ing*, *n*, travail, *m*; exploitation, *f*; fonctionnement, *m*; manœuvre; marche, *f*; jeu, *m*. ~ *capital*, capital de roulement, fonds de r., *m*. ~ *class*, classe ouvrière, c. laborieuse, *f*. ~ *clothes*, habits de fatigue, *m.pl*. ~ *day*, jour ouvrable, *m*; journée de travail, *f*. ~ *hours*, heures de travail, *f.pl*.

world, *n*, monde; siècle, *m*. ~ [*-wide*] *a*, mondial, universel. *Third W~*, tiers monde, *m*. **worldliness**, *n*, mondanité, *f*. **worldling**, *n*. &

worldly, *a*, mondain, e. *all one's worldly goods*, tout son [saint-] frusquin.

worm, *n*, ver; (*screw*) filet, *m*; (*corkscrew*) mèche; (*Mach.*) vis sans fin, *f*; (*still*) serpentin, *m*. ~-**eaten**, rongé des vers, vermoulu. ~ *fishing*, pêche au ver, *f*. ¶ *v.i*, (*secret*) soutirer; se faufiler; se tortiller. ~**y**, *a*, véreux.

worry, *n*, ennui, tourment, tracas, souci, *m*. ¶ *v.t*, ennuyer, tourmenter, tracasser, harceler; (*of dog*) piller.

worse, *a*, pire; plus mauvais; plus mal. (*machine*) *the* ~ *for wear*, patraque, *f*. & *a*. ¶ *ad*, pis. *grow* ~, s'empirer. *make* ~, empirer.

worship, *n*, culte, *m*; adoration, *f*; office, *m*. ¶ *v.t*. & *i*, (*God*, *gods*) adorer; (*saints, relics*) vénérer. **worshipper**, *n*, adorateur, trice.

worst, *a*, pire, plus mauvais. ¶ *ad*, pis. ¶ *n*, pis, pire, *m*. *at the* ~, au pis aller. ¶ *v.t*, vaincre.

worsted, *n*, laine peignée, estame, *f*.

wort, *n*, (*of beer*) moût, *m*; (*plant*) herbe, *f*.

worth, *n*, valeur, *f*; prix, *m*; mérite, *m*; (*money's*) pour. ¶ *a*, qui mérite; digne de. *to be* ~, valoir; mériter. ~**less**, *a*, sans valeur; misérable; (*check*) sans provision. ~**lessness**, *n*, vileté, *f*. ~**y**† , *a*, digne.

would, *v.aux*, is expressed in Fr. by conditional mood. *Also by* vouloir. ~ *to heaven that . . .*, plût au ciel que . . ., ~-**be**, *a*, soidisant, *inv*, prétendu, e.

wound, *n*, blessure; plaie, *f*. ¶ *v.t*, blesser. *the* ~**ed**, les blessés, *m.pl*.

wrangle, *n*, querelle, *f*. ¶ *v.i*, se quereller, se disputer. **wrangling**, *n*, tiraillement, *m*.

wrap, *n*, manteau; châle, *m*. ~ [up], *v.t*, envelopper; enrouler; entortiller; ployer. ~[oneself] *up*, s'empaqueter, se couvrir. **wrapper**, *n*, enveloppe; chemise; toilette; (*newspaper*) bande; (*cigar*) robe, *f*. *wrapping paper*, papier d'emballage, *m*.

wrath, *n*, courroux, *m*, fureur, *f*. ~**ful**, *a*, courroucé.

wreak, *v.t*, tirer, prendre (*vengeance*).

wreath, *n*, guirlande, couronne; couronne mortuaire, *f*; (*smoke*) panache, *m*. **wreathe**, *v.t*, enguirlander; ceindre.

wreck, *n*, naufrage; sinistre; délabrement, *m*. ~[age], *n*, débris, *m.pl*, épave, *f*, bris, *m*. **wreck**, *v.t*, causer le naufrage de; saboter; bouleverser. *to be* ~**ed**, faire naufrage.

wren, *n*, roitelet, *m*.

wrench, *n*, (*Med.*) entorse, foulure; (*twist*) pesée; (*tool*) clef, *f*, tourne-à-gauche; (*fig.*) crève-cœur, *m*. ¶ *v.t*, fouler, bistourner. ~ *open*, forcer.

wrest, *v.t*, tordre; arracher.

wrestle, *v.i*, lutter. **wrestler**, *n*, lutteur, catcheur, *m*. **wrestling**, *n*, lutte, *f*. ~ *match*, match de lutte, *m*.

wretch, *n*, malheureux, euse, misérable, *m.f*, hère, *m*. ~**ed**, *a*, malheureux, misérable; pitoyable, méchant, piètre. ~**edness**, *n*, misère, *f*.

wriggle, *v.i*, s'agiter, frétiller, se débattre.

wring, *v.t.ir*, tordre; étreindre; serrer; arracher; extorquer; (*linen*) essorer. ~**er**, *n*, essoreuse, *f*. ~**ing wet**, mouillé à tordre.

wrinkle, *n*, ride, *f*, pli, sillon; (*tip*) tuyau, *m*. ¶ *v.t*, rider, sillonner, plisser. ~**proof**, *a*, infroissable.

wrist, *n*, poignet, *m*. ~**band**, poignet, *m*, brisure, *f*. ~ *strap*, bracelet de force, *m*. ~**watch**, montre-bracelet, *f*.

writ, *n*, exploit; mandat, *m*; assignation, *f*.

write, *v.t*. & *i. ir*, écrire; inscrire; rédiger. ~ *back*, répondre; (*Bkkpg*) contrepasser. ~ *for* (*journal*) écrire dans, collaborer à. ~ *off*, amortir. ~ *out*, tracer; rédiger; formuler. **writer**, *n*, écrivain; auteur, *m*.

writhe, *v.i*, se tordre, se tortiller.

writing, *n*, écriture, *f*; écrit, *m*; inscription, *f*. *in* ~, par écrit. ~ *materials*, de quoi écrire. ~ *pad*, bloc-notes, bloc de correspondance, *m*. **written**, *p.p*, par écrit, manuscrit.

wrong, *a*, faux; mauvais; mal; erroné; inexact. ~ *font*, lettre d'un autre œil, *f*. ~ *side* (*fabric*), envers, dessous, *m*. ~ *side up*,

sens dessus dessous. *the ~ way,*
ad, à rebours; à contresens; à
contre-poil, à rebrousse-poil. *they*
are ~, ils ont tort. ¶ *ad,* mal; de
travers. ¶ *n,* mal; tort, préjudice,
m. ¶ *v.t,* faire [du] tort à, léser,
maltraiter, nuire à. ~ful†, *a,* injuste. ~ly, *ad,* à tort; à faux.
wrought iron, fer [forgé] *m.*
wry, *a, (neck)* tors; *(smile)* pincé.
~ *face,* grimace, *f.* ~*neck* (bird),
torcol, *m.* ~*ness, n,* guingois, *m.*

X

xenophobia, *n,* xénophobie, *f.*
Xmas, *abb.* See *Christmas.*
Xrays, *n.pl,* rayons X, *m.pl.* **to**
x-ray, radiographier.
xylonite, *n,* celluloïd, *m.*
xylophone, *n,* xylophone, *m.*

Y

yacht, *n,* yacht, *m.* ~**ing,** *n,* promenade en yacht, *f.*
yam, *n,* igname, *f.*
yap, *v.i,* glapir, japper.
yard, *n,* cour, *f;* parc, chantier,
m; (*Naut.*) vergue, *f;* yard, *f;*
Meas. = 0.914399 meter. ~ *arm,*
bout de vergue, *m.*
yarn, *n,* (*thread*) fil, *m;* (*tale*) histoire, *f.*
yaw, *n,* embardée, *f.* ¶ *v.i,* faire
une e.; (*Avn.*) gouverner.
yawl, *n,* yole, *f.*
yawn, *v.i,* bâiller. ~**ing,** *a,* béant.
ye, *pn,* vous.
year, *n,* année, *f;* an; (*Fin.*) exercice, *m.* ~*book,* annuaire, *m.* ~*s*
of discretion, l'âge de raison, *m.*
leap ~, année bissextile, *f.* ~*ly,*
a, annuel; (*ad.*) annuellement.
yearn for, soupirer après. **yearn-**
ing, *n,* aspiration, *f;* élancements,
m.pl.
yeast, *n,* levure, *f,* levain, *m.*
yell, *n,* hurlement, *m.* ¶ *v.i,* hurler.
yellow, *a. & n,* jaune, *a. & m. Y~*
Sea, mer Jaune, *f.* ¶ *v.t. & i,*
jaunir. ~*ish, a,* jaunâtre.
yelp, *v.i,* glapir, japper.
yeoman, *n,* (*Naut.*) commis aux
écritures.
yes, *particle,* oui; si. ¶ *n,* oui, *m.*
yesterday, *n,* hier, *m.* **yester-**
year, antan, *m.*

yet, *c,* cependant, toutefois, pourtant. ¶ *ad,* encore.
yew (tree), *n,* if, *m.*
yield, *n,* rendement, rapport, *m.*
¶ *v.t,* rendre, rapporter; (*v.i.*)
céder; obéir; succomber.
yodel, *v.i,* iouler, yodler. ¶ *n,*
ioulement, *m.* **yodler,** *n,* iouleur,
m.
yoga, *n,* yoga, *m.* **yogi,** *n,* yogi, *m.*
yogurt, *n,* yaourt, *m.*
yoke, *n,* joug, *m;* paire, couple, *f,*
attelage, *m;* (*for pail*) palanche, *f;*
(*dress*) empiècement, *m,* épaulette, *f.* ~ *elm,* charme, *m.* ¶ *v.t,*
atteler.
yokel, *n,* rustre, *m.*
yolk, *n,* jaune (d'œuf) *m.*
yonder, *a,* ce . . . -là. ¶ *ad,* là-bas.
yore (of), d'autrefois, jadis.
you, *pn,* vous, tu; on.
young, *a,* jeune; petit. ~ *lady,*
demoiselle, jeune personne, *f.* ~
one, petit, e. ¶ (*animals*) *n,*
petits, *m.pl.* ~*er, a,* [plus] jeune,
cadet. ~ *brother, sister,* puîné,
e. *to make look ~,* rajeunir.
~*ster, n,* gamin, moutard, *m,*
môme, *m,f.*
your, *a,* votre, vos; ton, ta, tes.
yours, *pn.* & *your own,* le vôtre,
la vôtre, les vôtres; à vous; de
vous. ~ *affectionately,* votre
affectionné, e. ~ *truly,* agréez
(*ou* recevez) monsieur, mes
salutations empressées. **yourself,**
yourselves, *pn,* vous-même, vous-
mêmes; vous.
youth, *n,* jeunesse; adolescence, *f;*
jeune homme adolescent, *m.*
~*ful†, a,* jeune; juvénile; de
jeunesse.
Yugoslav, *n,* Yougoslave, *m.* & *f.*
Yugoslavia, *n,* la Yougoslavie.
yule[tide], *n,* Noël, *m,* la [fête de]
Noël. **yule log,** bûche de Noël, *f.*

Z

zeal, *n,* zèle, *m.* **zealot,** *n,* zélateur,
trice. **zealous,** *a,* zélé, empressé.
~*ly, ad,* avec zèle.
zebra, *n,* zèbre, *m.*
zenith, *n,* zénith; (*fig.*) zénith,
faîte, apogée, *m.*
zephyr, *n,* zéphyr, *m.*
zeppelin, *n,* zeppelin, *m.*
zero, *n,* zéro, *m.* ~ *hour,* heure
H, *f.*

zest, *n*, piquant, *m*; ardeur, *f*.

zigzag, *n*, zigzag, *m*. ¶ *v.i*, aller en zigzag.

zinc, *n*, zinc, *m*. ~ *worker*, zingueur, *m*. **zincography**, *n*, zincogravure, *f*.

Zion, *n*, Sion, *f*. ~ism, *n*, sionism *m*. ~ist, *a*. & *n*, sioniste.

zipper, *n*, fermeture éclair, *f*.

zircon, *n*, zircon, *m*.

zither, *n*, cithare, *f*.

zodiac, *n*, zodiaque, *m*. ~al, *a*, zodiacal.

zone, *n*, zone, *f*.

zoo, *n*, zoo, jardin zoologique, *m*.

zoological, *a*, zoologique. **zoologist**, *n*, zoologiste, *m,f*. **zoology**, *n*, zoologie, *f*.

zoom, *v.i*, bourdonner, vrombir.

Zulu, *a*, zoulou. ¶ *n*, Zoulou, *m,f*.

Zuyder Zee (the), le Zuyderzée.

APPENDICES

TREACHEROUS LOOK-ALIKES

The list of words given below is intended to flag some of the pitfalls that can cause trouble for anyone who assumes too close a relation between English and French. Many of the words are cognates, but some are not, and so we have preferred to call them all "look-alikes." Occasionally, an English word will have the same meaning as its French cognate, but only in a restricted sense. For example, the French *une audience* is best translated by "a hearing," but it can be translated by "an audience" if by that we mean "a hearing."

In the lefthand column the French word is given in italics and its most usual translation listed below in roman. In the righthand column its English look-alike is given and below it, in italics, its most usual French translation. Needless to say, not all possible translations are covered.

French / English	English / French	French / English	English / French
abuser to deceive to misguide to misuse	to abuse *injurier* *dénigrer*	*audience* hearing	audience (people) *auditoire* *assistance*
actuel present existent	actual (real) *véritable* *réel*	*auditeur* listener hearer	auditor *vérificateur de comptes*
advertisement warning	advertisement *réclame* *announce*	*bail* lease	bail *caution*
affronter to confront	to affront *insulter*	*banquette* bench	banquet *banquet*
alienation insanity transfer	alienation *brouille* *éloignement*	*baraque* shack booth	barrack *caserne*
aliéné lunatic	alien *étranger*	*blesser* to wound	to bless *bénir*
annonceur advertiser	announcer *speaker*	*blindé* armored	blinded *aveuglé*
apparat pomp show	apparatus *appareil*	*blouse* smock overall	blouse *chemisier*
appareil apparatus	apparel *vêtements*	*bosse* bump hump	boss *patron*
appointer to put on salary to sharpen to a point	to appoint *nommer*	*bribe* morsel	bribe *un pot de vin*
arguer to indicate to infer	to argue *argumenter*	*cake* fruitcake	cake *gâteau*
		caméra movie camera	camera *appareil*
asparagus asparagus-fern	asparagus *asperge*	*candeur* credulousness naïveté	candor *franchise*
attendre to await to expect	to attend *assister à*	*cantine* PX or post exchange	canteen *bidon de soldat*

French English	English French	French English	English French
capon coward tattletale	capon *chapon*	*défendeur* defendant	defender *défenseur*
car intercity bus	car *voiture auto*	*défiance* distrust	defiance *défi*
cargo cargo ship	cargo *cargaison*	*déjection* evacuation (bowels)	dejection *abattement*
caution guarantee bail	caution *précaution*	*délayer* to dilute to drag out (speech)	to delay *tarder retarder*
chance luck	chance *hasard sort*	*demander* to request to ask	to demand *exiger*
chandelier candlestick candlemaker	chandelier *lustre*	*dépression* dejection	depression (economic) *krach récession*
chipie bad-tempered woman	chippy *femme de mœurs faciles*	*déranger* to disturb	to derange (make insane) *détraquer*
clairvoyant perspicacious	clairvoyant *voyant*	*dérider* to smoothe to unwrinkle	to deride *railler se moquer de*
combine scheme racket	combine *corporation trust*	*destitué* removed from office	destitute *misérable dépourvu*
complainte ballad, lay	complaint *plainte*	*déterrer* to dig up to unearth	to deter *décourager*
concussion misappropriation extortion	concussion *commotion cérébrale*	*détonner* to sing or play out of tune	to detonate *détoner*
contrôler to check to supervise	to control *maîtriser*	*dilapider* to waste	to become dilapidated *détérior*
corsage blouse	corsage *garniture de costume*	*dissemblance* dissimilarity	dissemblance *dissimulation*
crucial crosslike	crucial *critique*	*droguerie* housewares store	drugstore *pharmacie*
cure treatment	cure *guérison remède*	*drugstore* variety store	drugstore *pharmacie*
débonnaire meek easy-going	debonair *gai élégant*	*écrou* bolt nut	screw *vis*
déception disappointment	deception (trickery) *tromperie*	*éditeur* publisher	editor *rédacteur*

French English	English *French*	*French* English	English *French*
éduquer to bring up (children)	to educate (formally) *instruire*	*impotent* crippled helpless	impotent (sexual) *impuissant*
engin device	engine *moteur* locomotive	*improuver* to disapprove of	to improve *améliorer*
engrosser to make pregnant	to engross *absorber* *accaparer*	*incontrôlé* not verified	uncontrolled *effréné* *independant*
estampe print	stamp *timbre* *trépignement*	*ingénuité* ingenuousness	ingenuity *ingéniosité*
exténuer to exhaust to tire	to extenuate *atténuer* *diminuer*	*inhabité* uninhabited	inhabited *habité*
extravagant strange excessive	extravagant (money) *dépensier* *exorbitant*	*injurier* to insult to abuse to revile	to injure *blesser* *nuire à* *leser*
fabrique factory	fabric (cloth) *étoffe*	*journée* day day's pay	journey *voyage*
fade insipid	faded *fané*	*labourer* to plow	to labor *travailler* *peiner*
fastidieux tiresome	fastidious *difficile*	*laboureur* plowman	laborer *travailleur*
forgerie smithy	forgery *contrefaçon*	*large* broad generous	large *grand* *gros*
génial ingenious full of genius	genial *jovial* *cordial*	*librairie* bookstore	library *bibliothèque*
gentil nice	gentle *doux*	*licencier* to fire to disband	to license *autoriser* *breveter*
gourmander to scold	to gormandize *faire le glouton*	*location* renting hiring	location *emplacement* *situation*
grâcier to pardon	to grace *honorer* *embellir*	*luxure* lust	luxury *luxe*
gratification tip (money)	gratification *satisfaction*	*luxurieux* lustful sensual	luxurious *luxueux*
grossesse pregnancy	grossness *grossièreté*	*machin* thingamajig	machine *machine*
idiome language	idiom *idiotisme*	*magasin* store powder magazine	magazine *revue* *magazine*
idiotisme idiomatic expression	idiocy *idiotie*	*malicieux* mischievous naughty	malicious *malveillant* *méchant*
ignorer not to know	to ignore *faire semblant de ne pas voir*		

French English	English French	French English	English French
manéger	to manage	*prêtendre*	to pretend
to train	*administer*	to claim	(simulate)
(horse)	*s'en tirer*	to intend	*feindre*
			faire semblant de
marin	marine		
sailor	*soldat de la*	*prévention*	prevention
	marine	prejudice	*empêchement*
ménagère	manager	*procureur*	procurer
housekeeper	*directeur*	proxy	*entremetteur*
		attorney	
meurtrir	to murder		
to bruise	*assassiner*	*propreté*	property
		cleanliness	*biens*
muser	to muse		*propriété*
to dawdle	*rêvasser*		
to loiter		*provençal*	provincial
		from Provence	*provincial*
négociant	negotiator		*de province*
merchant	*négociateur*		
		prune	prune
nouvelle	novel	plum	*pruneau sec*
short story	*roman*		
		rafle	raffle
office	office	raid (police)	*tombola*
pantry	*bureau*	clean sweep	*loterie*
(le) pair	pair	*raisin*	raisin
peer	*(la) paire*	grape	*raisin sec*
equal			
		récipient	recipient
pamphlet	pamphlet	receptacle	*celui qui*
lampoon	*brochure*	vessel	*reçoit*
	opuscule		
		rente	rent
parents	parents	income	*loyer*
relatives—	*le père et la mère*		
including		*repli*	reply
mother &		fold	*réponse*
father		recess	
passer un	to pass an exam	*reporter*	to report
examen	*être reçu*	to carry back	*rapporter*
to undergo			*rendre compte*
(have) an			*de*
examination			
		retenue	retinue
pétulant	petulant	reserve	*suite*
lively	*grincheux*	discretion	
phrase	phrase	*retraiter*	to retreat
sentence	*locution*	to pension off	*se retirer*
physicien	physician	*rude*	rude (behavior)
physicist	*médecin*	rough	*impoli*
		hard	
piler	to pile		
to pound	*empiler*	*saucière*	saucer
to grind	*entasser*	gravy boat	*soucoupe*
plain	plain	*sentence*	sentence
level	*simple*	sentence	(grammar)
flat	*sans charme*	(judicial)	*phrase*
portemanteau	portmanteau	*sot*	sot
hat & coat	*valise*	fool	*ivrogne*
stand		dolt	

French English	English French	French English	English French
stoppage darning mending	stoppage *arrêt* *obstruction*	*vicieux* depraved defective	vicious *méchant* *haineux*
translation transfer removal	translation (language) *traduction*	*vilain* bondsman serf	villain *scélérat*
trépasser to die	to trespass *empiéter sur* *s'introduire* *sans droit*	*zeste* peel (orange, lemon)	zest *piquant* *saveur* *verve*

FRENCH ALPHABET SOUP: ABBREVIATIONS IN THE NEWS

A.C., Action Catholique.

A.C.F., Automobile Club de France.

A.C.P.G., Anciens Combattants et Prisoniers de Guerre (veterans association).

A.D.A.C., avion à décollage et atterissage courts (STOL: short takeoff and landing aircraft).

A.D.A.V., avion à décollage et atterissage verticaux (VTOL: vertical takeoff and landing aircraft).

A.d.S., Académie des Sciences.

A.E.L.E., Association Européenne de Libre-Échange (E.F.T.A.: European Free Trade Association).

A.F., allocations familiales (government family subsidy).

A.F.N.O.R., Association Française de Normalisation (French equivalent of A.N.S.I.: American National Standards Institute).

A.F.P., Agence France-Presse (news service, equivalent of Associated Press).

A.I.E.A., Agence Internationale de l'Énergie Atomique (I.A.E.A.: International Atomic Energy Association).

A.M., Arts et Métiers (university training for engineers).

A.P., Assistance Publique (government welfare administration).

A.S.L.V., assurance sur la vie (life insurance).

A.T., assurance contre les accidents du travail (workmen's compensation insurance).

B.D., bande dessinée (comic strip).

B.F., Banque de France (Bank of France).

B.N., Bibliothèque Nationale.

B.N.P., Banque Nationale de Paris.

B.Rh., Bas-Rhin.

Bx-A., Beaux-Arts.

c.-à-d., c'est-à-dire (that is to say).

C.A.P., certificat d'aptitude professionnelle (training certificate).

C.C.P., compte courant (chèque) postal (postal checking account).

C.-du-N., Côtes-du-Nord.

C.E.E., Communauté Économique Européenne (E.E.C.: European Economic Community).

C.E.N., Centre d'Études Nucléeaires (Center for Nuclear Studies).

C.E.P., Certificat d'Études Primaires (elementary school certificate).

C.G.T., Confédération Générale du Travail (France's largest labor confederation, Communist in orientation).

C.F.D.T., Confédération Française Démocratique du Travail (major rival of the C.G.T., it is Socialist in orientation).

C.N.P.F., Conseil National du Patronat Français (French employers' association known as the *Patronat*).

C.N.R.S., Centre National de la Recherche Scientifique.

C.R.F., Croix Rouge Française (French Red Cross).

C.R.S., Compagnies Républicaines de Sécurité (special riot police responsible for security).

D.C.A., défense contre avions (anti-aircraft defense).

D.E.U.G., Diplôme d'Études Universitaires Générales (certificate of study given after two years).

D.M., Docteur en Médecine (M.D.: Doctor of Medicine).

D.P., Défense Passive (C.D.: Civil Defense).

E.C.G., électrocardiogramme (EKG: electrocardiogram).

E.D.F., Électricité de France (nationalized in 1946).

E.N.A., École Nationale d'Administration (trains government civil service administrators; graduates known as *énarques*).

E.N.S., École Normale Supérieure (one of the Grandes Écoles; its graduates—*normaliens*—have dominated the intellectual life of France).

E.-U., États-Unis (U.S.: United States).

F.O., Force Ouvrière (a major labor union, reformist in orientation).

F.S.M, Fédération Syndical Internationale (W.F.T.U.: World Federation of Trade Unions).

F.M.I., Fonds Monétaire Internationale (I.M.F.: International Monetary Fund).

F.T.A., forces terrestre antiaériennes (anti-aircraft defense forces).

Gar., Garonne.

G.B., Grande Bretagne (G.B.: Great Britain).

G.D.F., Gaz de France (state-owned gas company).

G.E.P.A.N., Groupe d'Études des Phénomènes Aérospatiaux (Study Group for Aerospatial Phenomena).

Gir., Gironde.

H.-G., Haute-Garonne.

H.-L., Haute-Loire.

H.L.M., habitation à loyer modéré (subsidized low-cost government housing).

H.-M., Haute-Marne.

H.-P., Hautes-Pyrénées.

H.Q., [ouvriers] hautement qualifiés (highly trained workers, generally at foreman's level).

H.-Rh., Haut-Rhin.

H.S., hors de service (unfit for or out of service).

H.T., haute tension (high voltage).

H.V., Haute-Vienne.

I.D.H.E.C., Institut des Hautes Études Cinématographiques.

I.-et-L., Indre-et-Loire.

I.-et-V., Ille-et-Vilaine.

I.F.O.P., Institute Français d'Opinion Publique (French Institute of Public Opinion; surveys questions of public interest).

I.G.F., impôts sur les grandes fortunes (tax on private wealth, instituted by the controversial law of May 10, 1981).

I.N.S.E.A.D., Institut National des Sciences Économiques et de l'Administration (important business administration school at Fontainebleau).

I.R.C.A.M., Institut de Recherche et de Co-ordination Acoustique/Musique (research center for modern music set up in 1977 under Pierre Boulez).

J.O., *Journal Officiel* (reports on new laws and government regulations; issues publications similar to those of the Government Printing Office in the United States).

L.-et-C., Loire-et-Cher.

L.-et-G., Lot-et-Garonne.

M.-et-L., Maine-et-Loire.

M.-et-M., Meurthe-et-Moselle.

M.G., médecin de médecine générale (G.P.: general practitioner).

Mgr, Monseigneur (Mgr.: Monsignor).

M.L.F., Mouvement pour la Libération des Femmes (Women's Liberation Movement).

M.R.P., Mouvement Républicain Populaire (political party).

M.S.B.S., mer-sol-balistique-stratégique (underwater-to-land ballistic missile).

N.D.E., note de l'éditeur (publisher's note).

N.D.L.R., note de la rédaction (editor's note).

N.F., nouveau franc (the "new franc" was introduced in 1960, when it was substituted for 100 *anciens francs*; many older people still tend to give the prices of real estate, housing, etc., in *anciens francs*, which can be disconcerting).

N.R.F., *Nouvelle Revue Française* (along with *Les Temps Modernes*, for many years one of France's most important intellectual periodicals; the initials are also used as a logo for Gallimard, a prestigious publishing house).

O.A.A., Organisation pour l'Alimentation et l'Agriculture (F.A.O.: Food and Agriculture Organization).

O.C.D.E., Organisation de Coopération et de Développement Économique (O.E.C.D.: Organization for Economic Cooperation and Development).

O.E.A., Organisation des États Américains (O.A.S.: Organization of American States).

O.E.C.E., Organisation Européenne de Coopération Économique (O.E.E.C.: Organization for European Economic Cooperation).

O.I.P.C., Organisation Internationale de Police Criminelle (Interpol).

O.I.R., Organisation Internationale pour les Réfugiés (I.R.O.: International Refugee Organization).

O.I.T., Organisation Internationale du Travail (I.L.O.: International Labor Organization).

O.M.S., Organisation Mondiale de la Santé (W.H.O.: World Health Organization).

O.N.U., Organisation des Nations Unies (U.N.: United Nations).

O.P., ouvriers professionnels (workers having a C.A.P., *q.v.*).

O.R.T.F., Office de la Radiodiffusion et Télévision Françaises (government bureau controlling broadcasting, which is subject to control of party in power).

O.S., ouvriers spécialisés (semi-skilled workers).

O.T.A.N., Organisation du Traité de l'Atlantique Nord (NATO: North Atlantic Treaty Organization).

O.T.A.S.E., Organisation du Traité de l'Asie du Sud-Est (S.E.A.T.O.: South-East Asia Treaty Organization).

O.V.N.I., objet volant non identifié (U.F.O.: unidentified flying object).

P.-B., Pays-Bas (The Netherlands).

P.C.E.M., premier cycle d'études médicales.

P.C.F., Parti Communiste Français (French Communist Party; as often as not referred to simply as P.C.).

P.C.V., paiement contre vérification (collect phone call).

P.D.G., président directeur général (chairman, sometimes given as *pédégé*).

P.-de-C., Pas-de-Calais.

P.-de-D., Puy-de-Dôme.

P. et C., Ponts et Chausées (government department responsible for bridges and highways).

P.G., prisonnier de guerre (P.O.W.: prisoner of war).

P.J., Police Judiciaire (C.I.D.: Criminal Investigation Division).

P.-O., Pyrénées-Orientales.

P.S.U., Parti Socialiste Unifié.

P.T.T., Poste, Télégraphes et Téléphones (government post office, which also controls telephone and telegraph communications).

R.A.T.P., Régie Autonome des Transports Parisiens (Paris' equivalent of New York's M.T.A.).

R.A.U., République Arabe Unie (U.A.R.: United Arab Republic).

R.D.A., République Démocratique Allemande (G.D.R.: German Democratic Republic—East Germany).

R.E.R., Réseau Express Régional (suburban extension of the Paris Métro system).

R.F., République Française (French Republic).

R.F.A., République Fédérale Allemande (F.R.G.: Federal Republic of Germany—West Germany).

R.P.F., Rassemblement du Peuple Français (Reunion—or Rally—of the French People; political party founded by Charles de Gaulle in 1947).

r.g., rive gauche (left bank of Paris).

R.N.P., Rassemblement National Populaire (political party).

R.P., Révérend Père (Reverend Father).

S.A., société anonyme (Inc.).

S.-et-L., Saône-et-Loire.

S.-et-M., Seine-et-Marne.

S.-et-O., Seine-et-Oise.

S.M.I.C., or S.M.I.G., salaire minimum interprofessionnel de croissance, garanti (guaranteed minimum wage; those who come under its provisions are known as *smicards*).

S.N.C.F., Société Nationale des Chemins de Fer Français (French National Railways).

S.A.F.E.R.s., Sociétés d'Aménagements Foncier et d'Établissement Rural (regional societies empowered to acquire available farmland, improve and resell it).

S.I.C.A.s., Sociétés d'Intérêt Collectif Agricole (state-assisted farmers' marketing groups).

S.I.D.A., Syndrome d'Immunodéficience Acquise (AIDS: Acquired Immunity Deficiency Syndrome).

S.N.I.A.S., Société Nationale Industrielle Aérospatiale.

S.P.A., Société Protectrice des Animaux (French equivalent of the A.S.P.C.A.).

T.C.F., Touring Club de France.

T.E.P. Théâtre de l'Est Parisien (theater group founded by Guy Rétoré in Ménilmontant suburb to bring "serious"—and generally leftist —theater to popular audiences).

T.G.V., train à grande vitesse ("bullet train" destined to link Paris and Marseilles; first section went into operation in 1981; capable of speeds of up to 185 m.p.h.).

T.-et-G., Tarn-et-Garonne.

T.M.G., temps moyen de Greenwich (G.M.T.: Greenwich Mean Time).

T.N.P., Théâtre National Populaire (subsidized theater founded by Jean Vilar in 1951).

T.V.A., taxe sur la valeur ajoutée (value-added tax; in shops this is always included in the marked price).

U.R.S.S., Union des Républiques Socialistes Soviétiques (U.S.S.R.: Union of Soviet Socialist Republics).

FRENCH/AMERICAN CLOTHING SIZE EQUIVALENTS*

WOMEN

Dresses, suits, coats							
F.	38	40	42	44	46	48	50
USA	8	10	12	14	16	18	20

Knitwear, blouses						
F.	38	40	42	44	46	48
USA	32'	34	36	38	40	42

Stockings						
F.	0	1	2	3	4	5
USA	8	8½	9	9½	10	10½

Shoes						
F.	36	36½	37	37½	38	39
USA	4½	5	5½	6	6½	7½

MEN

Suits							
F.	34	36	38	40	42	44	46	48
USA	34	35	36	37	38	39	40	42

Sweaters			
F.	36–38	40–42	44–46	48–50
USA	S	M	L	XL

Shirts							
F.	36	37	38	39	40	41	42	43
USA	14	14½	15	15½	16	16½	17	17½

Shoes							
F.	39	40	41	42	43	44	45	46
USA	6½–7	7½	8	8½	9–9½	10–10½	11–11½	12–12½

* Because sizing, especially in women's clothing, is not really standardized either in the United States, or, to a lesser degree, in France, these equivalencies are only approximate.